God Girl Bible

· • ·

This Bible Is Presented To

_____

By

_____

On

_____

· • ·

Abide in me, and I in you.

John 15:4

God Girl Bible

ENGLISH STANDARD VERSION

CROSSWAY

WHEATON, ILLINOIS

WWW.ESVBIBLE.ORG

RRDS		22	21	20	19	18	17	16	15	14	13
13	12	11	10	9	8	7	6	5	4	3	2	1

Contents

THE BOOKS OF THE
Old and New Testaments
NUMERICAL AND ALPHABETICAL ORDER

Italics indicate New Testament books.

Abbreviations
OF BIBLE BOOKS

Genesis	Gen.	Nahum	Nah.
Exodus	Ex.	Habakkuk	Hab.
Leviticus	Lev.	Zephaniah	Zeph.
Numbers	Num.	Haggai	Hag.
Deuteronomy	Deut.	Zechariah	Zech.
Joshua	Josh.	Malachi	Mal.
Judges	Judg.	Matthew	Matt.
Ruth	Ruth	Mark	Mark
1 Samuel	1 Sam.	Luke	Luke
2 Samuel	2 Sam.	John	John
1 Kings	1 Kings	Acts	Acts
2 Kings	2 Kings	Romans	Rom.
1 Chronicles	1 Chron.	1 Corinthians	1 Cor.
2 Chronicles	2 Chron.	2 Corinthians	2 Cor.
Ezra	Ezra	Galatians	Gal.
Nehemiah	Neh.	Ephesians	Eph.
Esther	Est.	Philippians	Phil.
Job	Job	Colossians	Col.
Psalms	Ps.	1 Thessalonians	1 Thess.
Proverbs	Prov.	2 Thessalonians	2 Thess.
Ecclesiastes	Eccles.	1 Timothy	1 Tim.
Song of Solomon	Song	2 Timothy	2 Tim.
Isaiah	Isa.	Titus	Titus
Jeremiah	Jer.	Philemon	Philem.
Lamentations	Lam.	Hebrews	Heb.
Ezekiel	Ezek.	James	James
Daniel	Dan.	1 Peter	1 Pet.
Hosea	Hos.	2 Peter	2 Pet.
Joel	Joel	1 John	1 John
Amos	Amos	2 John	2 John
Obadiah	Obad.	3 John	3 John
Jonah	Jonah	Jude	Jude
Micah	Mic.	Revelation	Rev.

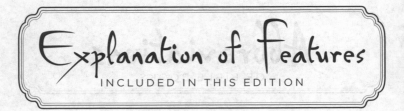

Explanation of Features
INCLUDED IN THIS EDITION

The *God Girl Bible: ESV Edition* includes a number of valuable features to encourage the reading and study of the Bible. A brief description is provided below explaining the purpose and use of these features.

Section Headings

Section headings have been included throughout the text of the *God Girl Bible: ESV Edition*. While the headings are not part of the Bible text itself, they have been provided to help identify and locate important themes and topics throughout the Bible.

Textual Footnotes

Several kinds of footnotes related to the ESV text are provided throughout the ESV Bible to assist the reader. These footnotes appear at the bottom of the page and are indicated in the ESV text by a superscript number that follows the word or phrase to which the footnote applies (e.g., "Isaac[2]"). Superscript letters that precede a word indicate cross-references (see explanation of cross-references).

The footnotes included in the ESV Bible are an integral part of the text and provide important information concerning the understanding and translation of the text.

In addition to the numeric (textual) notes, the New Testament portion of this edition of the ESV Bible includes two kinds of cross-reference notes. These are identified alphabetically and follow the numeric notes at the bottom of each page. These include (1) direct quotations from the Old Testament (indirect quotations and allusions are not included), and (2) parallel passages in the four Gospels. These cross-references are included to help the reader understand the relationship of the New Testament to the Old Testament, and the harmony of the Gospels in the New Testament.

Dear

God Girl,

In John 15:4, Jesus tells us that for a branch to produce any fruit, it has to stay connected to the vine. This idea of connectedness is the inspiration for the *God Girl Bible*. I am so excited about this Bible because of what it's going to mean to your life in Christ. Because it uses the *English Standard Version* translation, this Bible is accurate and clear, and not only that, but with the addition of all the helps and devotionals from us at Hungry Planet, it should be a journey into Scripture like you've never had before. In the Getting Started section I'll tell you a little bit about all the stuff we've added to help you apply God's Word to your life, but right now I just want to tell you that this is going to be an incredible Bible experience.

Have you ever opened up the Bible and not known where to start? Have you had some major questions in your life that you knew the Bible could help you out with but didn't know where to look? Let me say that I totally understand. But I also know that the Word of God really does address the whole of your life from top to bottom, and if you're ready to really study it so that it becomes a part of your everyday living, you will be blown away. So dig in and see if the *God Girl Bible* doesn't change the way you learn about, talk to, serve, and love your God.

Your sister in Christ,

Hayley DiMarco

Abide in me, and I in you.

As the branch
cannot bear
fruit by itself,

unless it

abides

in the vine,

neither can you,
unless you

abide in me.

John 15:4

Getting Started

The God Girl wants what every other girl wants: to love and to be loved. She wants acceptance and laughter. She wants hope and peace. But her life, like everyone else's, isn't perfect. It's messy and lonely, it's stressful and hard. But one thing sets her apart, one thing makes her life amazingly different from the lives of others, and that's her heart. Her heart is set on something above, something greater than she, that gives her strength and hope. She has found the truth, and the truth is that God loves her tremendously and accepts her wholeheartedly. He has adopted her, and she now calls him Father; she calls him God, and she calls him her salvation.

Because of that, the God Girl wants more than anything else to hear from God. She wants God's words to ring in her ears. She wants his answers and not the world's. And because of that she knows that God's Word, the Bible, can never be far from her mind.

As a God Girl, you cannot live without God's Word. This is God's great message of redemption in Jesus. You cannot know who you are or what your purpose is on this earth without opening up the pages of God's book and getting to know his thoughts, his ways, and his voice. The Bible calms your deepest fears. Without it you are making life up on your own, winging it—and even playing God. Most importantly, without God's written Word you will not know the grace of God in the gospel. The Word of God is God's declaration to you: "I love you! You are mine. Walk with me."

Sometimes reading the Bible can be overwhelming. Where do you start? What does it mean? How do you find the answers you need? Some of this is mystery. But mystery is beautiful, and it sure beats boredom. The mystery of God is something you will continue to unveil throughout your whole life, so don't worry that you don't get it all right now. You aren't alone in this struggle, but that doesn't mean you'll never get what you need or find the answers that you can't live without. It only means that, like all good things in life, reading the Bible takes work. But the work you put into reading and understanding God's Word is the best work you will ever do, with the best payoff—not only for your spirit but also for your emotions and your day-to-day life.

So Where Do You Start?

What do you do, now that you have this Bible in your hands? The answer is different for each person, and that means there's no one set way to read the Bible, no perfect plan, no rules or regulations. But sometimes it may seem as if it would be easier if there were a plan—a how-to guide that told you exactly what to do and when to do it. You won't get that here, but I do want to give you some motivation and some ideas on how to make God's Word your own, and how to dive into it so that you don't run into a wall and start telling yourself, "I just don't know where to start."

The truth is, there are hundreds of thousands of places to start and lots of ways to study. I'm not going to give you all of them, but I'll give you a few starters to get you going, because the best way to get something so big done is one step at a time. These are not laws, just hints and suggestions for kick-starting your study time.

Throughout the *God Girl Bible* you're going to find help: notes, ideas, directions that will help you to dive in deeper and to better understand how Scripture applies to your everyday life—because it really does! We'll go over all those elements so you understand what you've got in front of you, and later on we'll suggest some other ways to get started reading so you will get what you need for today. Ready to get started?

The God Girl Bible

This *God Girl Bible* is designed to help you read God's Word and make it a part of your life. Here's a quick overview of all the stuff you'll find in here so you know what to look for and why it's there:

Introductions—Each book of the Bible has an introduction. These devotional-style pieces give you a little background on the book. They help you to take a main theme of that book of the Bible and apply it to your life.

Along with the introduction, each book has a little background info like who wrote it, when they wrote it, and where they wrote it. This stuff will help you to get the gist of the book and give you a quick overview so you can know what you're about to read. It can also be a handy reference after you've read it.

The background info covers all this kind of stuff:

Author: Who wrote the book or experienced it. This might also be who edited it or compiled it, which means that they didn't experience it themselves but wrote down what the person who lived it told them, or put all their writings together for them.

Time: Approximately when the book was written. For a lot of them we don't know exact dates, but we can make an educated guess.

Place: Where the books were written isn't always certain either, so a lot of these places are probable but not definite.

Written to: A lot of authors say who they are writing to, but some of them never say. So some of this info will be specific and some will be much more general.

The gist: This is kind of a summary of the book. It gives you the theme and helps you understand what's happening in the text.

Things to look for: This section is to help you know where to start studying the book. It has some things to look for and some places to start looking, but not all of them—it's just a hint and a place to dive in. Use this section to help you get into the book and get more out of it.

Must-Know Facts, Terms, and Verses—This is a short list of verses that are important in each book, along with some basic facts and terms that should make it easier for you to study and understand the book. These verses would be good to know and to memorize to help you keep God's Word in your heart for just when you need it.

"Know This" Devotionals—These are sprinkled throughout the Bible. They are meant to help you know how to apply what you read to your life. In the back of this Bible you can look up specific devotionals by topic in the section called Quick Relief.

Prayers—These centuries-old prayers are very special to me. I came across them a while ago and have been reading them ever since. Most of them are based on Puritan prayers, many of which you can find online and in books, but I have rewritten them so that you don't get bogged down in all the old-timey language. These prayers are amazing in how they seem to take God's Word and put it into prayer. They are all based on Scripture, so you're not just praying how you feel at the time, but praying God's truth. As you read these prayers, make them real to yourself. Speak them out loud to God. Agree with them and learn from them. Use them as a kickoff to reading and studying the Bible. They are a great way to start off your morning time with God.

Ask Yourself—These sections are short and to the point. They are just questions to get you thinking about the Bible and how it fits into your life. This is your chance to get honest with yourself and to dig deeper into your spiritual life than maybe you ever have before. If you aren't sure of some of the answers, that's okay. Just dig into the Bible and find out what you believe so that you can find the answers to the questions that define you.

God Girl Stories—Throughout the Bible you'll find stories of amazing girls and women who loved God. These profiles are written like devotionals to give you a little bit of background on each girl but also some inspiration from them. You can read these as a way to begin your devotional time or as a way to dig in deeper to study and research.

God Girl Glossary—In the back of this Bible is a small glossary of some of the basic terms that will come up as you read. For deeper study I suggest you get a full Bible dictionary as well, but this is a great place to start with those hard words that you want to know more about.

Quick Relief: Where to Find Things in the Bible—The Quick Relief section is kind of a subject index or concordance for the *God Girl Bible*. You can look up topics (such as failure, hope, or fear) and see where you can find verses that relate to each topic. You won't find as many verses here as in a full concordance, but this will get you started with some key verses you need to know for your life right now.

Spiritual Self-Check—You can look at this list to see if there is anything in your life that needs some changing, then go to the Quick Relief guide and find answers in the Bible.

Bible Reading Plans—These plans will help you know what to read and when to read it. Choose from several plans and know exactly what you're going to read today and tomorrow. A lot of people like to read through the whole Bible in a year. I don't think that you have to do that every year, but I do think you should read through the whole Bible several times throughout your life. These plans will help you find a place to start and a path to follow, so check them out.

Subject Index—This topical index will lead you to all the helps—devotions, God Girl stories, Ask Yourself sidebars, and Prayers—that deal with important topics and themes.

Obedience and Grace

> I do not nullify the grace of God, for if righteousness were
> through the law, then Christ died for no purpose.
>
> Galatians 2:21

When it comes to God's Word, there are two popular lines of thought. One is that your salvation depends on doing all that it says. This is called legalism, and it's wrong. Salvation doesn't come from anything other than faith in Jesus Christ, who died and was raised for our salvation. When you turn your life over to him and trust him to forgive you, embracing him as your Lord, then you are saved. Period. The end.

The other line of thinking when it comes to God's Word is that, because of his grace— his great kindness—we are free to break the rules because he'll forgive us for it all, so why worry about it? This crazy kind of thinking goes like this: "I really want to do this sinful thing, and since it's too hard to say no, I'm just gonna do it and then ask for forgiveness later." This way of thinking is just as bad as legalism, and it becomes a way of life that is contradictory to God's Word. God's grace isn't cheap, and it's not meant to be abused or used as a loophole to sin.

The truth about God's grace and our salvation is that his grace saves us from both the penalty of sin and also the power of sin. Grace forgives us, but it also changes us. You don't need to keep any rules to be saved or to keep yourself saved, but you love him because of what he's done for you. And out of that love flows your obedience to his Word. Only God himself gives you the power to keep his law. People who try to keep it on their own are going to fail; it's just too hard. But through the help of the Holy Spirit, you can be faithful.

The law is powerless to save you and powerless to change you, but as you fall more and more in love with God, you will find yourself changing more and more into the image of Christ. That's because of his Holy Spirit who lives within you (see John 14:15–17). As you become more like Christ, you will naturally be pulled into an intense relationship with God's Word. You will want more and more of its life-giving message. You will want to know more about the heavenly Father you love, so that he may be the only one you serve. You will find following his law becoming your delight and not a chore.

As you read God's Word, remind yourself of the gospel message. Speak it to yourself. The gospel of grace is the central message of the entire Bible, Old Testament and New. Remember the life of Christ, his death, his burial, and his resurrection. And know that only this unmatched sacrifice can save you. Your life is a miracle. Your mind being opened to the life of Christ in you is a miracle. Your God has reached down and touched you, and because of that you are different. If you don't feel different or believe you are different, then take some time to read God's Word. Get to know him and his unfathomable kindness in that, while you were dead because of your failure, he made you alive together with Christ (see Eph. 2:5).

Nothing can keep you from this salvation but your own hard-heartedness. But if you sense within yourself a stirring to know God more, or to know the Bible, or to honor Christ, then you can rest in confidence that this is God himself at work within you. God promises to save you—all you have to do is believe it.

If the light hasn't come on for you yet and you aren't sure if you are saved or not, stop by www.GodGirl.com and do some digging and ask some questions. Then you can start to answer the question of your salvation. Don't put it off. Start today to realize the amazing grace of God and how freely he offers it to you.

> And you were dead in the trespasses and sins in which you once walked, following the course of this world, following the prince of the power of the air, the spirit that is now at work in the sons of disobedience—among whom we all once lived in the passions of our flesh, carrying out the desires of the body and the mind, and were by nature children of wrath, like the rest of mankind. But God, being rich in mercy, because of the great love with which he loved us, even when we were dead in our trespasses, made us alive together with Christ—by grace you have been saved—and raised us up with him and seated us with him in the heavenly places in Christ Jesus, so that in the coming ages he might show the immeasurable riches of his grace in kindness toward us in Christ Jesus. For by grace you have been saved through faith. And this is not your own doing; it is the gift of God, not a result of works, so that no one may boast. For we are his workmanship, created in Christ

Jesus for good works, which God prepared beforehand, that we should walk in them.

Ephesians 2:1–10

Notes on Devotion

The *God Girl Bible* is a devotional Bible. Its emphasis is on devoting your time and your mind to God. You cannot know God or hear from him unless you spend time with him. The more time you spend, the more you'll feel his presence in your life. In fact, if you feel lost, out of sorts, depressed, like God isn't there, or like you aren't good enough, then try spending more time in his presence. Comfort, peace, and yes, even answers for your deepest problems can be found in spending time with him.

With that in mind, I want to share with you something that changed my devotional life. It's called the "morning watch." A lot of people call it quiet time or devotionals, but I call it the morning watch because every morning I get up to watch for God, to see what he's going to do and say. I consider it my duty and privilege to get up early to give my best energy and time to him. I guarantee that if you are willing to take the challenge, **the morning watch will change your life.**

Here is an excerpt from an old book called *The School of Obedience*, by Andrew Murray. It's a great explanation of the morning watch, and I'll bet that, after reading it, you'll be more excited than ever to spend time with God and to find out what he has in store for your life:

> You tell me there are many Christians who are content with ten minutes or a quarter of an hour. There are, but you will certainly not as a rule find them strong Christians. . . . Christ asked great sacrifices of His disciples; He has perhaps asked little of you as yet. But now He allows, He invites, He longs for you to make some. Sacrifices make strong men. Sacrifices help wonderfully to wrench us away from earth and self-pleasing, and lift us heavenward. Do not try to pare down the time limit of the morning watch to less than the half-hour. There can be no question about the possibility of finding the time. Ten minutes from sleep, ten from company or amusement, ten from lessons. How easy where the heart is right, hungering to know God and His will perfectly! . . .

> The very fact of setting apart such a period helps to awaken the feeling: I have a great work to do, and I need time for it. It strengthens in your heart the conviction: I must have time to get near to God. It will give your Bible study new point, as you find time, between the reading, to be still and bow in humility for the Holy Spirit's hidden working, and wait till you get some real apprehension of God's will for you, through the Word. And, by the grace of God, it may help you to begin that habit of specific and definite intercession of which the Church so surely stands in need.

> Students! you know not whether in your future life your time may be more limited, your circumstances more unfavorable, your Christian earnestness feebler. Now is the accepted time. Today, as the Holy Ghost saith. Listen to the invitation of your brethren in all lands, and fear not to form an undiscourageable resolution to spend at least half an hour each morning with God alone.

God Girl, I encourage you to consider the benefit of practicing the morning watch. If your relationship with God is less than you want it to be, then start here. Wake up with him in mind, meet with him, center your day on him, and hear from him. Use this Bible to help you do that. Read a devotional, look up verses, follow his voice, and find out what he has for you today. If you are willing to deny your flesh and walk humbly with God, you will find him filling your life with truth and hope. It is the best thing you can do with your time, I promise you!

Great Bible Study Tools

When you are ready to dig into God's Word and discover his thoughts on life, you are ready to study. Hundreds of resources are out there for you to use to create your own studies, and I highly recommend using them to help you to make more of your Bible study time. Look for these tools in your local bookstore, in your church library, or online. They might seem overwhelming right now, but give them a try and see if you don't find one or two that really open up a whole new world to you.

GodGirl.com—Because we don't want you to do this thing all alone, we at Hungry Planet have created a place where we can all get together. GodGirl.com is a site where you can come to be mentored by me and other God Girls. As a part of the God Girl Academy, you can sign up to walk through a mentoring plan that will take you through the trials and challenges of your everyday life and into some deep study of the foundation of faith—God's Word—and how it applies to you. On the website you are going to find tons of studies you can do, resources, music, and even free books you can read to grow in your faith.

So as you work through this Bible, come by GodGirl.com and get started in a mentoring relationship today. I'd love to see you there and to hear how things are going. If you really want to challenge yourself and make God's Word come alive, then let's get together and study. I'm looking forward to the chance to speak into your life.

You can also find us at HungryPlanet.net.

Concordance—This is a kind of book that no God Girl should be without. A concordance is a list of words (like redemption, hope, justification, salvation) and verse references where you can find what God's Word says about those topics. So let's say you have a Q about dating and you have no idea where to start. You could look up words such as love or marriage. Each reference will take you to verses that might just give you the answers you were looking for or at least shine a bit of light in your direction. As you add them up, the truth becomes more and more clear.

Bible dictionary—Having a good Bible dictionary or two on hand is essential for understanding God's Word. Sometimes when I look up a word in a concordance it takes me on all kinds of rabbit trails and teaches me so much more than I would have gotten out of just reading the verse and kind of understanding it but not really getting the detail. Don't be afraid to say, "I don't know what that word means." Pick up a Bible dictionary and get into dissecting verses so you can understand it all and get the most possible out of it.

Commentary—A Bible commentary is a book that explains Scripture. Some go into a ton of detail about each verse and the history behind it all, and others give you just enough to kick-start your understanding of what is being said. There are literally hundreds of Bible commentaries out there, so finding the right one for you can be hard, but it's well worth it. The best thing to do is to check out a few of them and compare their answers. See which make the most sense to you and which speak your language. Commentaries are good to go to when you get stuck and you just don't understand what's going on in a particular verse or section. They aren't the Bible, they aren't perfect, but they are a good place to get started and can help you dig in a little deeper to find out what God's Word means.

Verse lists—We love verse lists here at Hungry Planet. These are nothing you buy or download but things you make yourself. You pick a topic that you want to know God's Word on, like how to deal with mean girls, and then you write down all the verses you find that relate to that topic. Since you won't find "mean girls" as a topic in a concordance, you create your own verse list custom-made for your own areas of study. I have things like stress, worry, fear, counseling others, and resting in my verse list. You'll see a lot of them in the Quick Relief section. Keep yours in a notebook or in a file on your computer, and add to them every time you read something that fits that topic. Pretty soon you'll have a reference list of your own, with all your favorite verses relating to all the topics you have collected. This is a great way to quickly find key verses for your life and for the lives of the people around you. It helps you to memorize Scripture and to keep truth at your fingertips.

Reading Methods

I know that the Bible can be an overwhelming book. It can make you say, "I just don't know where to start." There's so much in it, so what do you need to read today? To help you see how to apply the Bible to your life, we have compiled some reading methods that might help you choose a path and stick to it. So take a look at these and see if any of them sound like a good way for you to start your next study of God's Word.

Book by Book

One way to start reading the Bible is just by picking a book and reading it all the way through. This is especially good if you have never read the book before. Before you dive into picking certain sections and bits, it's best to get the entire story into you. So pick a book and read it, and then read it again. The more times you read it, the more you will know it. You might even decide to read one book over and over again for a whole week or a whole month. You'll really know your way around that book after that!

As you read each book, you don't have to hurry. In fact, you might want to read each one like this:

1. Read the entire book in one sitting. (If you can't, then do as much as you can, but don't take more than a few days.)

2. Read the entire book again, and this time write down all the important stories, parables, etc., that you can memorize and learn to repeat.

3. Create a verse list for the book by underlining all the important verses and writing the best ones down in a notebook you've set aside to collect all your notes, book by book.

4. Create memory cards. Pick out a few verses that you want to memorize and write them on cards you can carry around with you. The more you memorize, the quicker you'll have the answers for your life questions.

5. Reread the book, and this time underline or highlight all the commands in a different color and all the promises in yet another color. You might want to make a list of commands and promises in your journal as well.

6. Summarize the book. You can use the introduction and background info at the front of each book of the Bible to help you write a paragraph that summarizes the book. This will help you to learn the book and also to have a quick reference to go back to when you want to review your studies.

When you're done, start over with another book and do the same thing. Just in case you don't know which book to start with, here are some helpful hints to get you going.

If you are *new to the faith* and want to understand who your God is, what life is all about, and what's most important for you to know right now, then here are some ideas for your reading:

Your Question	Book to Read
Who is Jesus?	Matthew, Mark, Luke, and John
What is the meaning of life?	Romans
What is freedom in Christ?	Galatians
What about God's grace or kindness?	Ephesians
What is the history of our faith?	Genesis, Exodus

If you're *older in the faith*, you might have different questions:

Your Question	Book to Read
How do I do what's right?	1 John
Why does God let bad things happen?	Psalms
Where do I find wisdom?	Proverbs
How do I handle suffering?	Lamentations, Job, Philippians
What's faith?	Hebrews
What's the difference between faith and works?	James, 1 John
What does it mean to love?	1 Corinthians, Matthew

The Whole Thing

Another way to read the Bible is to start at the beginning and read the whole thing. But this can get you bogged down a bit with all the Old Testament chapters that take a lot of understanding and study. If you are new to the faith, you might want to mix things up more and read a couple Old Testament chapters, then a couple New Testament chapters, and keep going back and forth. Or you might just want to dive into Matthew, the first book of the New Testament, and read through to Revelation before tackling the Old Testament. Sometimes this is the best way for a new God Girl to get started.

Topical Study

This is a great way to study, if you like to stay focused on one thing at a time. What you do is pick a topic that you want to study. You might just have questions about that topic or want more info on it. You could study topics that come up in conversations with your friends. For example, if someone tells you something you don't agree with or understand, get into God's Word to find out what he has to say about it.

To get started you pick a topic, like obedience or sin, and you get out your concordance and look up all the verses on that topic. If you read a verse that makes you think of something else on the same topic but with a different spin, you look up that word in your dictionary or concordance and go down that path.

Here's a path you might take: you look up *love*, and as you read you see the word *humility*, so you do a study on humility and see how that relates to love. As you do you see the word *pride*, so you study up on that, and pretty soon you're all over the Bible collecting all kinds of good stuff that will teach you what God wants you to know about love.

This is a fun way to study because it's like solving a mystery. It takes work and time, but it's exciting and challenging, and it ends with good results.

Inductive Study

The inductive method of study involves looking at Scripture using observation, interpretation, and application. It helps you to understand the Bible by moving from specifics to the general application of those specifics. In this method it is important that you observe all of the facts in each section of Scripture you read—not the things you imagine were happening or what you think the people were feeling, just the facts. It's a great way to dig deeper and really pull everything out of a verse that you can.

Here's how to do a simple inductive study:

1. Pick a short section of Scripture, maybe three to ten verses.

2. Check out the passage. Ask yourself these Qs about it:
   Who? (Who is writing?)
   What? (What is it about?)
   When? (When did they write it?)
   Where? (Where does it take place?)
   Why? (Why are they writing?)

3. Then ask yourself these Qs:
   What are the commands in this section?
   What are the promises?
   What are the repeated words and ideas?
   What do I learn about God, Jesus, the Holy Spirit, humanity, and myself?

4. After you've asked all those Qs, the one big one left is, "What does it all mean?" At this step you could try to paraphrase what you've read and write a small devotional on it. When you learn something, it's always good to try to write it in your own words to help make it a part of you.

5. Do it. Now you have to decide, by the grace of God, how this is going to change your life. How are you going to apply what you've read and, in reliance on the Spirit, make it a part of who you are? If there is something specific you can do—like serving someone today or telling someone you love them—write it down and plan on doing it.

Paraphrase It

This is a great way to understand the Bible and to teach others about it too. Read a section, about three to ten verses, and then get out a piece of paper and write a paraphrase of what you have read—put it into your own words. Sometimes you can even try writing a devotional on the topic. As you do this, you learn the subject better and you become more able to talk about it and explain it not only to yourself but to other people.

Bible Reading Plans

You can use a simple Bible reading plan that lays out exactly what verses you should read each day. You can do the whole Bible in a year or do a study of the life of Jesus or the ministry of Paul. Just follow the plans you can find at the end of this Bible or online to know what you're reading and where you are going each day. But don't just read to get it done—read to learn. Underline, take notes, and memorize as you go, and you'll make God's Word a part of your everyday life.

Hearing from God is more than just haphazardly glancing through the pages of the Bible. It's about deliberately searching out the truth and answers to all the questions you might have about your life on this earth and God's role in it. I've given you just a few ways to get started, listening for the voice of God in your life and understanding what he wants of you. There are more ways of looking at Scripture. The thing is that you have to find a way that makes you want to do the work. So ask around, research, and find a way to study that gets you up in the morning and makes you want to **dig in for more!**

THE

Old Testament

INTRODUCTION TO
Genesis

Author: Moses

Time: Around the fifteenth century B.C.

Place: The wilderness of Sinai

Written to: The children of God

The gist

The purpose of Genesis is to tell the story of God's people. It teaches us about God's nature, omnipotence, and omnipresence and shows us how he first formed his covenant with Abraham. It lays out the history of the children of God and proves God's faithfulness to his people.

Things to look for

- The story of creation and the first sin (see Genesis 1–3)

- The account of Noah (see Gen. 6:9–9:29)

- The story of Abraham's life (see Gen. 11:27–25:11)

- The creation of the twelve tribes of Israel (see Gen. 29:32–30:24; 35:18; 48:1–20)

- The covenants of God (see Gen. 8:20–9:17; 12:1–3; 15:1–20; 17:1–22; 22:15–18; 26:2–5; 28:13–15; 50:24)

Know the Beginning

> In the beginning, God created the heavens and the earth.
>
> Genesis 1:1

In the beginning, God. In the middle, God. And in the end, God. As you read the Bible you will see that the real story is God: all that he is, all that he does, and all that he loves. In the beginning God created heaven and everything that lives in them. His character is so generous and so loving that he gave humans and animals all that they needed to have life and love. And though the first man and woman made a mess of things in the garden, God still didn't stop loving them.

Genesis reads like a great adventure novel. Those who lived in the beginning of time have gone down in history. As you read Genesis, notice how many times God saves his people from their sins. See that he is a just God who can't tolerate evil but oftentimes uses people's sins to lead them to salvation. Read about the covenants God made with his people, promises that he never broke and never will.

Knowing this history is very important for the life of the God Girl. Some people say that if you don't know the history of your people, then you are sure to repeat their mistakes in your own life. So take the words from Genesis and read them as the history of your people, the people of faith. Learn about their lives and more importantly about God and how he interacts with his people. Take your time as you go through the stories. Know that they are not fairy tales but truth, and learn more about the God who calls you his own.

Genesis is the foundation of all of Scripture; it sets the scene for the rest of the Bible. The covenant between God and his people that begins in Genesis has been fulfilled in the new covenant with the life, death, and resurrection of Jesus, and we now look at the Old Testament through the viewpoint of the New Testament. But all of Scripture is valuable and important, even today. Look at it in light of Jesus, and the Old Testament will come to life and mean more to you than you ever thought it could.

Must-Know Terms and Verses

Covenant

A formal agreement made between two people or groups of people where both parties have an obligation to fulfill in relationship to each other.

The Noahic Covenant

God's covenant made with Noah whereby God promised never to flood the earth again (see Gen. 9:11–17).

The Abrahamic Covenant

The covenant made between God and Abraham whereby God promised to give Abraham many descendants and to make them his people (see Gen. 12:1–3; 15:18; 22:15–18). The sign of this covenant is circumcision (see Gen. 17:11–12).

Offering

That which is sacrificed to God as an act of worship. It can be food, an animal, or money.

Sacrifice

Giving back to God what God has given; a gift offered to God on the altar, either as a symbol of worship or as atonement for sin. Sacrifice often refers to an offering involving the shedding of blood.

Sin

Anything you do that goes against the things God has commanded in the Bible. Sin is also known as disobedience.

In the beginning, God created the heavens and the earth. *Genesis 1:1*

Then the LORD God said, "It is not good that the man should be alone; I will make him a helper fit for him." *Genesis 2:18*

And God said, "This is the sign of the covenant that I make between me and you and every living creature that is with you, for all future generations: I have set my bow in the cloud, and it shall be a sign of the covenant between me and the earth." *Genesis 9:12–13*

Genesis

The Creation of the World

1 In the beginning, God created the heavens and the earth. [2] The earth was without form and void, and darkness was over the face of the deep. And the Spirit of God was hovering over the face of the waters.

[3] And God said, "Let there be light," and there was light. [4] And God saw that the light was good. And God separated the light from the darkness. [5] God called the light Day, and the darkness he called Night. And there was evening and there was morning, the first day.

[6] And God said, "Let there be an expanse[1] in the midst of the waters, and let it separate the waters from the waters." [7] And God made[2] the expanse and separated the waters that were under the expanse from the waters that were above the expanse. And it was so. [8] And God called the expanse Heaven.[3] And there was evening and there was morning, the second day.

[9] And God said, "Let the waters under the heavens be gathered together into one place, and let the dry land appear." And it was so. [10] God called the dry land Earth,[4] and the waters that were gathered together he called Seas. And God saw that it was good.

[11] And God said, "Let the earth sprout vegetation, plants[5] yielding seed, and fruit trees bearing fruit in which is their seed, each according to its kind, on the earth." And it was so. [12] The earth brought forth vegetation, plants yielding seed according to their own kinds, and trees bearing fruit in which is their seed, each according to its kind. And God saw that it was good. [13] And there was evening and there was morning, the third day.

[14] And God said, "Let there be lights in the expanse of the heavens to separate the day from the night. And let them be for signs and for seasons,[6] and for days and years, [15] and let them be lights in the expanse of the heavens to give light upon the earth." And it was so. [16] And God made the two great lights—the greater light to rule the day and the lesser light to rule the night—and the stars. [17] And God set them in the expanse of the heavens to give light on the earth, [18] to rule over the day and over the night, and to separate the light from the darkness. And God saw that it was good. [19] And there was evening and there was morning, the fourth day.

[20] And God said, "Let the waters swarm with swarms of living creatures, and let birds[7] fly above the earth across the expanse of the heavens." [21] So God created the great sea creatures and every living creature that moves, with which the waters swarm, according to their kinds, and every winged bird according to its kind. And God saw that it was good. [22] And God blessed them, saying, "Be fruitful and multiply and fill the waters in the seas, and let birds multiply on the earth." [23] And there was evening and there was morning, the fifth day.

[24] And God said, "Let the earth bring forth living creatures according to their kinds—livestock and creeping things and beasts of the earth according to their kinds." And it was so. [25] And God made the beasts of the earth according to their kinds and the livestock according to their kinds, and everything that creeps on the ground according to its kind. And God saw that it was good.

[26] Then God said, "Let us make man[8] in our image, after our likeness. And let them have dominion over the fish of the sea and over the birds of the heavens and over the livestock and over all the earth and over every creeping thing that creeps on the earth."

[1] Or *a canopy*; also verses 7, 8, 14, 15, 17, 20 [2] Or *fashioned*; also verse 16 [3] Or *Sky*; also verses 9, 14, 15, 17, 20, 26, 28, 30; 2:1 [4] Or *Land*; also verses 11, 12, 22, 24, 25, 26, 28, 30; 2:1 [5] Or *small plants*; also verses 12, 29 [6] Or *appointed times* [7] Or *flying things*; see Leviticus 11:19–20 [8] The Hebrew word for *man* (*adam*) is the generic term for mankind and becomes the proper name *Adam*

27 So God created man in his own
        image,
     in the image of God he created
        him;
     male and female he created them.

28 And God blessed them. And God said to them, "Be fruitful and multiply and fill the earth and subdue it, and have dominion over the fish of the sea and over the birds of the heavens and over every living thing that moves on the earth." 29 And God said, "Behold, I have given you every plant yielding seed that is on the face of all the earth, and every tree with seed in its fruit. You shall have them for food. 30 And to every beast of the earth and to every bird of the heavens and to everything that creeps on the earth, everything that has the breath of life, I have given every green plant for food." And it was so. 31 And God saw everything that he had made, and behold, it was very good. And there was evening and there was morning, the sixth day.

The Seventh Day, God Rests

2 Thus the heavens and the earth were finished, and all the host of them. 2 And on the seventh day God finished his work that he had done, and he rested on the seventh day from all his work that he had done. 3 So God blessed the seventh day and made it holy, because on it God rested from all his work that he had done in creation.

The Creation of Man and Woman

4   These are the generations
       of the heavens and the earth when
          they were created,
       in the day that the LORD God made
          the earth and the heavens.

5 When no bush of the field[1] was yet in the land[2] and no small plant of the field had yet sprung up—for the LORD God had not caused it to rain on the land, and there was no man to work the ground, 6 and a mist[3] was going up from the land and was watering the whole face of the ground— 7 then the LORD God formed the man of dust from the ground and breathed into his nostrils the breath of life, and the man became a living creature. 8 And the LORD God planted a garden in Eden, in the east, and there he put the man whom he had formed. 9 And

out of the ground the LORD God made to spring up every tree that is pleasant to the sight and good for food. The tree of life was in the midst of the garden, and the tree of the knowledge of good and evil.

10 A river flowed out of Eden to water the garden, and there it divided and became four rivers. 11 The name of the first is the Pishon. It is the one that flowed around the whole land of Havilah, where there is gold. 12 And the gold of that land is good; bdellium and onyx stone are there. 13 The name of the second river is the Gihon. It is the one that flowed around the whole land of Cush. 14 And the name of the third river is the Tigris, which flows east of Assyria. And the fourth river is the Euphrates.

15 The LORD God took the man and put him in the garden of Eden to work it and keep it. 16 And the LORD God commanded the man, saying, "You may surely eat of every tree of the garden, 17 but of the tree of the knowledge of good and evil you shall not eat, for in the day that you eat[4] of it you shall surely die."

18 Then the LORD God said, "It is not good that the man should be alone; I will make him a helper fit for[5] him." 19 Now out of the ground the LORD God had formed[6] every beast of the field and every bird of the heavens and brought them to the man to see what he would call them. And whatever the man called every living creature, that was its name. 20 The man gave names to all livestock and to the birds of the heavens and to every beast of the field. But for Adam[7] there was not found a helper fit for him. 21 So the LORD God caused a deep sleep to fall upon the man, and while he slept took one of his ribs and closed up its place with flesh. 22 And the rib that the LORD God had taken from the man he made[8] into a woman and brought her to the man. 23 Then the man said,

"This at last is bone of my bones
     and flesh of my flesh;
  she shall be called Woman,
     because she was taken out of Man."[9]

24 Therefore a man shall leave his father and his mother and hold fast to his wife, and they shall become one flesh. 25 And the man and his wife were both naked and were not ashamed.

[1] Or open country [2] Or earth; also verse 6 [3] Or spring [4] Or when you eat [5] Or corresponding to; also verse 20 [6] Or And out of the ground the LORD God formed [7] Or the man [8] Hebrew built [9] The Hebrew words for woman (ishshah) and man (ish) sound alike

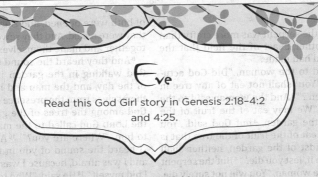

Eve

Read this God Girl story in Genesis 2:18–4:2
and 4:25.

For the LORD God is a sun and shield;
    the LORD bestows favor and honor.
No good thing does he withhold
    from those who walk uprightly.

Psalm 84:11

Have you ever thought that God is holding something back from you? Some great gift that you want or deserve? When you envy the lives of the people around you or complain about your own life, you accuse God of holding out on you. Your subconscious makes an assessment of your life and gives it a thumbs down, as if God has given you a raw deal. And you, like the first woman who existed, are tempted to throw it all away and take a bite of the fruit just to see what he's holding back.

When your life isn't all it "ought to be," it's easy to go from follower to leader. Instead of waiting for God to give you exactly what you need, when you need it, you make a list of all the things you think you need and do all you can to go after them. But have you ever considered that those things that God withholds from you, he withholds for your own good? Maybe if you got them they would destroy you emotionally, physically, or even spiritually.

When you think God isn't being good or is keeping you from what you want, it's easy to reject his rule in your life and start thinking his command-ments are a waste of time. Did you know that sin gets its strength when you are resentful? Resentment starts trying to convince you that nothing is more important than getting what you want, and it pretends that the punishment for sin can't compare with the amazing sensation of actually getting what you want. In these moments of deception you slide backward. You get off track. You forget the character of your God, and you fall.

Eve didn't know God's character well enough to trust him. And she's not alone—you can fall victim to your own ignorance when you don't study God's Word. As a God Girl, you can't let ignorance be an excuse. You have to go after knowledge and work on having the faith to trust God no matter what the temptation. Contentment is a good thing—no, it's an amazing thing! When you learn that God's nature is to give you exactly what you need, when you need it, you'll be set free from your harsh thoughts and fears. He will provide. In Jesus, he has already provided what you most need—forgiveness. And as soon as you see that all he gives is for your good, you'll be set free to live life to the fullest.

The Fall

3 Now the serpent was more crafty than any other beast of the field that the LORD God had made.

He said to the woman, "Did God actually say, 'You[1] shall not eat of any tree in the garden'?" [2] And the woman said to the serpent, "We may eat of the fruit of the trees in the garden, [3] but God said, 'You shall not eat of the fruit of the tree that is in the midst of the garden, neither shall you touch it, lest you die.' " [4] But the serpent said to the woman, "You will not surely die. [5] For God knows that when you eat of it your eyes will be opened, and you will be like God, knowing good and evil." [6] So when the woman saw that the tree was good for food, and that it was a delight to the eyes, and that the tree was to be desired to make one wise,[2] she took of its fruit and ate, and she also gave some to her husband who was with her, and he ate. [7] Then the eyes of both were opened, and they knew that they were naked. And they sewed fig leaves together and made themselves loincloths.

[8] And they heard the sound of the LORD God walking in the garden in the cool[3] of the day, and the man and his wife hid themselves from the presence of the LORD God among the trees of the garden. [9] But the LORD God called to the man and said to him, "Where are you?"[4] [10] And he said, "I heard the sound of you in the garden, and I was afraid, because I was naked, and I hid myself." [11] He said, "Who told you that you were naked? Have you eaten of the tree of which I commanded you not to eat?" [12] The man said, "The woman whom you gave to be with me, she gave me fruit of the tree, and I ate." [13] Then the LORD God said to the woman, "What is this that you have done?" The woman said, "The serpent deceived me, and I ate."

[14] The LORD God said to the serpent,

[1] In Hebrew *you* is plural in verses 1–5   [2] Or *to give insight*   [3] Hebrew *wind*   [4] In Hebrew *you* is singular in verses 9 and 11

Know Yourself

verses to read
Genesis 3:1–13

When someone makes you mad, who is more to blame, that person or you? After all, if they hadn't done what they did, then you wouldn't have to get all mad. Or if someone tempts you to do something you know you're not supposed to do and you do it, whose fault is it? Where does the blame lie? The truth is that at the first sign of trouble, the human mind tends to look for someone to blame. The mind is like a super detective: always getting to the bottom of things, always searching to figure out who started it and who is responsible for the mess we're in.

So it's not surprising that blame was the first response to the first spiritual mess people got into. Adam and Eve both blamed someone else instead of taking responsibility. Was it the snake's fault? Would they have taken a bite without him? It's hard to say. But either way, both Adam and Eve pointed the finger at someone else.

When you blame others for your mess-ups or misery, you miss out on the one thing that can help you—taking responsibility. Taking responsibility for the things you say, do, and think is the first step in the life of faith. When you confess your sin and accept Christ, you are taking responsibility, and suddenly something amazing happens: he takes responsibility for you as well. And voila! You have found all you wanted by doing the very thing you didn't want to do—accepting responsibility for your own life. If Adam and Eve hadn't tried to shift the focus off themselves, would life have been different for them? We'll never know, but what we do know is that blaming others makes it difficult for us to receive the gospel, because the gospel is only for people who know that they themselves have failed.

"Because you have done this,
　　cursed are you above all livestock
　　and above all beasts of the field;
on your belly you shall go,
　　and dust you shall eat
　　all the days of your life.
15 I will put enmity between you and
　　　the woman,
　　and between your offspring[1] and
　　　her offspring;
he shall bruise your head,
　　and you shall bruise his heel."

16 To the woman he said,

"I will surely multiply your pain in
　　childbearing;
　in pain you shall bring forth chil-
　　dren.
Your desire shall be for[2] your hus-
　　band,
　　and he shall rule over you."

17 And to Adam he said,

"Because you have listened to the
　　voice of your wife
　　and have eaten of the tree
of which I commanded you,
　　'You shall not eat of it,'
cursed is the ground because of you;
　in pain you shall eat of it all the
　　　days of your life;
18 thorns and thistles it shall bring
　　　forth for you;
　　and you shall eat the plants of the
　　　field.
19 By the sweat of your face
　　you shall eat bread,
till you return to the ground,
　　for out of it you were taken;
for you are dust,
　　and to dust you shall return."

20 The man called his wife's name Eve, because she was the mother of all living.[3] 21 And the LORD God made for Adam and for his wife garments of skins and clothed them.

[1] Hebrew *seed*; so throughout Genesis [2] Or *against* [3] *Eve* sounds like the Hebrew for *life-giver* and resembles the word for *living*

Know Yourself

verses to read
Genesis 3

The world might tell you that you are a victim. You were hurt, abused, rejected, and abandoned, and that's why you have issues, addictions, and drama in your life. But when you believe that your messed-up life is because of something beyond your control, you give away the power over your own life that you so desperately want. As long as you are busy blaming someone else for your life, you'll never be free. You'll never have control, and you'll never take responsibility for yourself.

Part of becoming a God Girl is choosing to stop running away from God's Word and being honest about your role in your own messed-up life, no matter who started it. It's called confession, and confession is good stuff. It purifies the soul because it gets to the bottom of what's going on in yourself without worrying about what someone else did or didn't do. Confession agrees with God and his Word about sin and says to him, "You are holy, and I want to be holy too." It says, "No matter what others do or have done, I'm going to be more concerned with my own failures than anyone else's—and receive God's love and forgiveness joyfully." And when you do that, you'll have all the protection and hope you need. Don't accept the pattern of avoiding honest confession like the first people did or like the world around you does. Confession might hurt, and it will probably feel totally uncomfortable and even dangerous, but the truth is, it's the safest and healthiest thing you could do. Confessing is good for the soul, and it proves that you don't belong to yourself but to God.

²² Then the LORD God said, "Behold, the man has become like one of us in knowing good and evil. Now, lest he reach out his hand and take also of the tree of life and eat, and live forever—" ²³ therefore the LORD God sent him out from the garden of Eden to work the ground from which he was taken. ²⁴ He drove out the man, and at the east of the garden of Eden he placed the cherubim and a flaming sword that turned every way to guard the way to the tree of life.

Cain and Abel

4 Now Adam knew Eve his wife, and she conceived and bore Cain, saying, "I have gotten[1] a man with the help of the LORD." ² And again, she bore his brother Abel. Now Abel was a keeper of sheep, and Cain a worker of the ground. ³ In the course of time Cain brought to the LORD an offering of the fruit of the ground, ⁴ and Abel also brought of the firstborn of his flock and of their fat portions. And the LORD had regard for Abel and his offering, ⁵ but for Cain and his offering he had no regard. So Cain was very angry, and his face fell. ⁶ The LORD said to Cain, "Why are you angry, and why has your face fallen? ⁷ If you do well, will you not be accepted?[2] And if you do not do well, sin is crouching at the door. Its desire is for[3] you, but you must rule over it."

⁸ Cain spoke to Abel his brother.[4] And when they were in the field, Cain rose up against his brother Abel and killed him. ⁹ Then the LORD said to Cain, "Where is Abel your brother?" He said, "I do not know; am I my brother's keeper?" ¹⁰ And the LORD said, "What have you done? The voice of your brother's blood is crying to me from the ground. ¹¹ And now you are cursed from the ground, which has opened its mouth to receive your brother's blood from your hand. ¹² When you work the ground, it shall no longer yield to you its strength. You shall be a fugitive and a wanderer on the earth." ¹³ Cain said to the LORD, "My punishment is greater than I can bear.[5] ¹⁴ Behold, you have driven me today away from the ground, and from your face I shall be hidden. I shall be a fugitive and a wanderer on the earth, and

whoever finds me will kill me." ¹⁵ Then the LORD said to him, "Not so! If anyone kills Cain, vengeance shall be taken on him sevenfold." And the LORD put a mark on Cain, lest any who found him should attack him. ¹⁶ Then Cain went away from the presence of the LORD and settled in the land of Nod,[6] east of Eden.

¹⁷ Cain knew his wife, and she conceived and bore Enoch. When he built a city, he called the name of the city after the name of his son, Enoch. ¹⁸ To Enoch was born Irad, and Irad fathered Mehujael, and Mehujael fathered Methushael, and Methushael fathered Lamech. ¹⁹ And Lamech took two wives. The name of the one was Adah, and the name of the other Zillah. ²⁰ Adah bore Jabal; he was the father of those who dwell in tents and have livestock. ²¹ His brother's name was Jubal; he was the father of all those who play the lyre and pipe. ²² Zillah also bore Tubal-cain; he was the forger of all instruments of bronze and iron. The sister of Tubal-cain was Naamah.

²³ Lamech said to his wives:

> "Adah and Zillah, hear my voice;
> you wives of Lamech, listen to
> what I say:
> I have killed a man for wounding
> me,
> a young man for striking me.
> ²⁴   If Cain's revenge is sevenfold,
> then Lamech's is seventy-seven-
> fold."

²⁵ And Adam knew his wife again, and she bore a son and called his name Seth, for she said, "God has appointed[7] for me another offspring instead of Abel, for Cain killed him." ²⁶ To Seth also a son was born, and he called his name Enosh. At that time people began to call upon the name of the LORD.

Adam's Descendants to Noah

5 This is the book of the generations of Adam. When God created man, he made him in the likeness of God. ² Male and female he created them, and he blessed them and named them Man[8] when they were created. ³ When Adam had lived 130 years, he fathered a son in his own likeness, after his image, and named him Seth.

---

[1] Cain sounds like the Hebrew for gotten [2] Hebrew will there not be a lifting up [of your face]? [3] Or against [4] Hebrew; Samaritan, Septuagint, Syriac, Vulgate add Let us go out to the field [5] Or My guilt is too great to bear [6] Nod means wandering [7] Seth sounds like the Hebrew for he appointed [8] Hebrew adam

⁴The days of Adam after he fathered Seth were 800 years; and he had other sons and daughters. ⁵Thus all the days that Adam lived were 930 years, and he died.

⁶When Seth had lived 105 years, he fathered Enosh. ⁷Seth lived after he fathered Enosh 807 years and had other sons and daughters. ⁸Thus all the days of Seth were 912 years, and he died.

⁹When Enosh had lived 90 years, he fathered Kenan. ¹⁰Enosh lived after he fathered Kenan 815 years and had other sons and daughters. ¹¹Thus all the days of Enosh were 905 years, and he died.

¹²When Kenan had lived 70 years, he fathered Mahalalel. ¹³Kenan lived after he fathered Mahalalel 840 years and had other sons and daughters. ¹⁴Thus all the days of Kenan were 910 years, and he died.

¹⁵When Mahalalel had lived 65 years, he fathered Jared. ¹⁶Mahalalel lived after he fathered Jared 830 years and had other sons and daughters. ¹⁷Thus all the days of Mahalalel were 895 years, and he died.

¹⁸When Jared had lived 162 years he fathered Enoch. ¹⁹Jared lived after he fathered Enoch 800 years and had other sons and daughters. ²⁰Thus all the days of Jared were 962 years, and he died.

²¹When Enoch had lived 65 years, he fathered Methuselah. ²²Enoch walked with God[1] after he fathered Methuselah 300 years and had other sons and daughters. ²³Thus all the days of Enoch were 365 years. ²⁴Enoch walked with God, and he was not,[2] for God took him.

²⁵When Methuselah had lived 187 years, he fathered Lamech. ²⁶Methuselah lived after he fathered Lamech 782 years and had other sons and daughters. ²⁷Thus all the days of Methuselah were 969 years, and he died.

²⁸When Lamech had lived 182 years, he fathered a son ²⁹and called his name Noah, saying, "Out of the ground that the LORD has cursed, this one shall bring us relief[3] from our work and from the painful toil of our hands." ³⁰Lamech lived after he fathered Noah 595 years and had other sons and daughters. ³¹Thus all the days of Lamech were 777 years, and he died.

³²After Noah was 500 years old, Noah fathered Shem, Ham, and Japheth.

Increasing Corruption on Earth

6 When man began to multiply on the face of the land and daughters were born to them, ²the sons of God saw that the daughters of man were attractive. And they took as their wives any they chose. ³Then the LORD said, "My Spirit shall not abide in[4] man forever, for he is flesh: his days shall be 120 years." ⁴The Nephilim[5] were on the earth in those days, and also afterward, when the sons of God came in to the daughters of man and they bore children to them. These were the mighty men who were of old, the men of renown.

⁵The LORD saw that the wickedness of man was great in the earth, and that every intention of the thoughts of his heart was only evil continually. ⁶And the LORD regretted that he had made man on the earth, and it grieved him to his heart. ⁷So the LORD said, "I will blot out man whom I have created from the face of the land, man and animals and creeping things and birds of the heavens, for I am sorry that I have made them." ⁸But Noah found favor in the eyes of the LORD.

Noah and the Flood

⁹These are the generations of Noah. Noah was a righteous man, blameless in his generation. Noah walked with God. ¹⁰And Noah had three sons, Shem, Ham, and Japheth.

¹¹Now the earth was corrupt in God's sight, and the earth was filled with violence. ¹²And God saw the earth, and behold, it was corrupt, for all flesh had corrupted their way on the earth. ¹³And God said to Noah, "I have determined to make an end of all flesh,[6] for the earth is filled with violence through them. Behold, I will destroy them with the earth. ¹⁴Make yourself an ark of gopher wood.[7] Make rooms in the ark, and cover it inside and out with pitch. ¹⁵This is how you are to make it: the length of the ark 300 cubits,[8] its breadth 50 cubits, and its height 30 cubits. ¹⁶Make a roof[9] for the ark, and finish it to a cubit above, and set the door of the ark in its side. Make it with lower, second, and third decks. ¹⁷For behold, I will bring a flood of waters upon the earth to destroy all flesh in which is the breath of life under heaven. Everything

---

[1] Septuagint *pleased God* [2] Septuagint *was not found* [3] *Noah* sounds like the Hebrew for *rest* [4] Or *My Spirit shall not contend with* [5] Or *giants* [6] Hebrew *The end of all flesh has come before me* [7] An unknown kind of tree; transliterated from Hebrew [8] A *cubit* was about 18 inches or 45 centimeters [9] Or *skylight*

that is on the earth shall die. ¹⁸But I will establish my covenant with you, and you shall come into the ark, you, your sons, your wife, and your sons' wives with you. ¹⁹And of every living thing of all flesh, you shall bring two of every sort into the ark to keep them alive with you. They shall be male and female. ²⁰Of the birds according to their kinds, and of the animals according to their kinds, of every creeping thing of the ground, according to its kind, two of every sort shall come in to you to keep them alive. ²¹Also take with you every sort of food that is eaten, and store it up. It shall serve as food for you and for them." ²²Noah did this; he did all that God commanded him.

7 Then the Lord said to Noah, "Go into the ark, you and all your household, for I have seen that you are righteous before me in this generation. ²Take with you seven pairs of all clean animals,¹ the male and his mate, and a pair of the animals that are not clean, the male and his mate, ³and seven pairs² of the birds of the heavens also, male and female, to keep their offspring alive on the face of all the earth. ⁴For in seven days I will send rain on the earth forty days and forty nights, and every living thing³ that I have made I will blot out from the face of the ground." ⁵And Noah did all that the Lord had commanded him.

⁶Noah was six hundred years old when the flood of waters came upon the earth. ⁷And Noah and his sons and his wife and his sons' wives with him went into the ark to escape the waters of the flood. ⁸Of clean animals, and of animals that are not clean, and of birds, and of everything that creeps on the ground, ⁹two and two, male and female, went into the ark with Noah, as God had commanded Noah. ¹⁰And after seven days the waters of the flood came upon the earth.

---

¹Or seven of each kind of clean animal ²Or seven of each kind ³Hebrew all existence; also verse 23

Know God

verses to read
Genesis 6

God's commands don't always make sense. They may sound unrealistic, unsafe, and crazy at times. Build an ark in the middle of town? Spend your money on the poor? Turn the other cheek when bad people hurt you? Pray for people who persecute you? Sometimes the things God asks you to do are going to hurt, and they might even make you look crazy. But you have to decide now, before that time comes, if you're going to do what he says no matter how it looks or how crazy it seems—or if you're going to run everything through your "common sense" filter.

You get it all backwards when you use common sense or the world's ideas of right and wrong as the final say on what you're going to do or think. Relying on your own smarts is rejecting the mind of God and saying your own mind deserves more respect and worship. As a God Girl, your final filter should always be God's Word, not the world's ideas. You have to ask yourself, "Is what I'm being asked to do consistent with God's Word? Is it crazy-sounding but biblical?" If so, then the question is, "Am I willing to do it anyway?"

It couldn't have made any sense to Noah and his family to build an ark where there was no body of water, but it was all part of God's plan. Faith can mean you have to do some things the world thinks are crazy. Take the pack of gum back to the clerk who forgot to charge you for it. Tell the truth when all of those around you are telling lies. Pray when others panic. Faith doesn't always make sense, but what does make sense is God's dependability. No matter what he wants you to do, you can be sure that it is for the best.

[11] In the six hundredth year of Noah's life, in the second month, on the seventeenth day of the month, on that day all the fountains of the great deep burst forth, and the windows of the heavens were opened. [12] And rain fell upon the earth forty days and forty nights. [13] On the very same day Noah and his sons, Shem and Ham and Japheth, and Noah's wife and the three wives of his sons with them entered the ark, [14] they and every beast, according to its kind, and all the livestock according to their kinds, and every creeping thing that creeps on the earth, according to its kind, and every bird, according to its kind, every winged creature. [15] They went into the ark with Noah, two and two of all flesh in which there was the breath of life. [16] And those that entered, male and female of all flesh, went in as God had commanded him. And the LORD shut him in.

[17] The flood continued forty days on the earth. The waters increased and bore up the ark, and it rose high above the earth. [18] The waters prevailed and increased greatly on the earth, and the ark floated on the face of the waters. [19] And the waters prevailed so mightily on the earth that all the high mountains under the whole heaven were covered. [20] The waters prevailed above the mountains, covering them fifteen cubits[1] deep. [21] And all flesh died that moved on the earth, birds, livestock, beasts, all swarming creatures that swarm on the earth, and all mankind. [22] Everything on the dry land in whose nostrils was the breath of life died. [23] He blotted out every living thing that was on the face of the ground, man and animals and creeping things and birds of the heavens. They were blotted out from the earth. Only Noah was left, and those who were with him in the ark. [24] And the waters prevailed on the earth 150 days.

The Flood Subsides

8 But God remembered Noah and all the beasts and all the livestock that were with him in the ark. And God made a wind blow over the earth, and the waters subsided. [2] The fountains of the deep and the windows of the heavens were closed, the rain from the heavens was restrained, [3] and the waters receded from the earth continually. At the end of 150 days the waters

had abated, [4] and in the seventh month, on the seventeenth day of the month, the ark came to rest on the mountains of Ararat. [5] And the waters continued to abate until the tenth month; in the tenth month, on the first day of the month, the tops of the mountains were seen.

[6] At the end of forty days Noah opened the window of the ark that he had made [7] and sent forth a raven. It went to and fro until the waters were dried up from the earth. [8] Then he sent forth a dove from him, to see if the waters had subsided from the face of the ground. [9] But the dove found no place to set her foot, and she returned to him to the ark, for the waters were still on the face of the whole earth. So he put out his hand and took her and brought her into the ark with him. [10] He waited another seven days, and again he sent forth the dove out of the ark. [11] And the dove came back to him in the evening, and behold, in her mouth was a freshly plucked olive leaf. So Noah knew that the waters had subsided from the earth. [12] Then he waited another seven days and sent forth the dove, and she did not return to him anymore.

[13] In the six hundred and first year, in the first month, the first day of the month, the waters were dried from off the earth. And Noah removed the covering of the ark and looked, and behold, the face of the ground was dry. [14] In the second month, on the twenty-seventh day of the month, the earth had dried out. [15] Then God said to Noah, [16] "Go out from the ark, you and your wife, and your sons and your sons' wives with you. [17] Bring out with you every living thing that is with you of all flesh—birds and animals and every creeping thing that creeps on the earth—that they may swarm on the earth, and be fruitful and multiply on the earth." [18] So Noah went out, and his sons and his wife and his sons' wives with him. [19] Every beast, every creeping thing, and every bird, everything that moves on the earth, went out by families from the ark.

God's Covenant with Noah

[20] Then Noah built an altar to the LORD and took some of every clean animal and some of every clean bird and offered burnt offerings on the altar. [21] And when the LORD smelled the pleasing aroma, the LORD said in his heart, "I will never again curse[2] the

---

[1] A *cubit* was about 18 inches or 45 centimeters   [2] Or *dishonor*

ground because of man, for the intention of man's heart is evil from his youth. Neither will I ever again strike down every living creature as I have done. ²²While the earth remains, seedtime and harvest, cold and heat, summer and winter, day and night, shall not cease."

9 And God blessed Noah and his sons and said to them, "Be fruitful and multiply and fill the earth. ²The fear of you and the dread of you shall be upon every beast of the earth and upon every bird of the heavens, upon everything that creeps on the ground and all the fish of the sea. Into your hand they are delivered. ³Every moving thing that lives shall be food for you. And as I gave you the green plants, I give you everything. ⁴But you shall not eat flesh with its life, that is, its blood. ⁵And for your lifeblood I will require a reckoning: from every beast I will require it and from man. From his fellow man I will require a reckoning for the life of man.

⁶ "Whoever sheds the blood of man,
    by man shall his blood be shed,
for God made man in his own image.

⁷And you,¹ be fruitful and multiply, increase greatly on the earth and multiply in it."

⁸Then God said to Noah and to his sons with him, ⁹"Behold, I establish my covenant with you and your offspring after you, ¹⁰and with every living creature that is with you, the birds, the livestock, and every beast of the earth with you, as many as came out of the ark; it is for every beast of the earth. ¹¹I establish my covenant with you, that never again shall all flesh be cut off by the waters of the flood, and never again shall there be a flood to destroy the earth." ¹²And God said, "This is the sign of the covenant that I make between me and you and every living creature that is with you, for all future generations: ¹³I have set my bow in the cloud, and it shall be a sign of the covenant between me and the earth. ¹⁴When I bring clouds over the earth and the bow is seen in the clouds, ¹⁵I will remember my covenant that is between me and you and every living creature of all flesh. And the waters shall never again become a flood to destroy all flesh. ¹⁶When the bow is in the clouds, I will see it and remember the everlasting covenant

between God and every living creature o all flesh that is on the earth." ¹⁷God said to Noah, "This is the sign of the covenant that I have established between me and all flesh that is on the earth."

> ## Ask Yourself . . .
> ### ABOUT GOD'S CALL
> - Have I heard God's call to do something?
> - Is there something his Word commands that I haven't done?
> - Am I willing to do whatever his Word asks?
> - Is there something that I have said I'll never do?
> - Whom do I let control my direction in life?
> - If given the choice between fame *without* God or an ordinary life *with* him, which would I choose?
> - What scares me about what God could ask me to do?
> - What are three things I know God wants me to do but I haven't done?
> - Why haven't I done them?

Noah's Descendants

¹⁸The sons of Noah who went forth from the ark were Shem, Ham, and Japheth. (Ham was the father of Canaan.) ¹⁹These three were the sons of Noah, and from these the people of the whole earth were dispersed.² ²⁰Noah began to be a man of the soil, and he planted a vineyard.³ ²¹He drank of the wine and became drunk and lay uncovered in his tent. ²²And Ham, the father of Canaan, saw the nakedness of his father and told his two brothers outside. ²³Then Shem and Japheth took a garment, laid it on both their shoulders, and walked backward and covered the nakedness of their father. Their faces were turned backward,

¹In Hebrew *you* is plural ²Or *from these the whole earth was populated* ³Or *Noah, a man of the soil, was the first to plant a vineyard*

and they did not see their father's naked-ness. 24 When Noah awoke from his wine and knew what his youngest son had done to him, 25 he said,

"Cursed be Canaan;
    a servant of servants shall he be to
        his brothers."

26 He also said,

"Blessed be the LORD, the God of Shem;
    and let Canaan be his servant.
27   May God enlarge Japheth,[1]
        and let him dwell in the tents of
            Shem,
        and let Canaan be his servant."

28 After the flood Noah lived 350 years. 29 All the days of Noah were 950 years, and he died.

Nations Descended from Noah

10 These are the generations of the sons of Noah, Shem, Ham, and Japheth. Sons were born to them after the flood.

2 The sons of Japheth: Gomer, Magog, Madai, Javan, Tubal, Meshech, and Tiras. 3 The sons of Gomer: Ashkenaz, Riphath, and Togarmah. 4 The sons of Javan: Elishah, Tarshish, Kittim, and Dodanim. 5 From these the coastland peoples spread in their lands, each with his own language, by their clans, in their nations.

6 The sons of Ham: Cush, Egypt, Put, and Canaan. 7 The sons of Cush: Seba, Havilah, Sabtah, Raamah, and Sabteca. The sons of Raamah: Sheba and Dedan. 8 Cush fathered Nimrod; he was the first on earth to be a mighty man.[2] 9 He was a mighty hunter before the LORD. Therefore it is said, "Like Nimrod a mighty hunter before the LORD." 10 The beginning of his kingdom was Babel, Erech, Accad, and Calneh, in the land of Shinar. 11 From that land he went into Assyria and built Nineveh, Rehoboth-Ir, Calah, and 12 Resen between Nineveh and Calah; that is the great city. 13 Egypt fathered Ludim, Anamim, Lehabim, Naphtuhim, 14 Pathrusim, Casluhim (from whom[3] the Philistines came), and Caphtorim.

15 Canaan fathered Sidon his firstborn and Heth, 16 and the Jebusites, the Amorites, the Girgashites, 17 the Hivites, the Arkites, the Sinites, 18 the Arvadites, the Zemarites, and the Hamathites. Afterward the clans of the Canaanites dispersed. 19 And the territory of the Canaanites extended from Sidon in the direction of Gerar as far as Gaza, and in the direction of Sodom, Gomorrah, Admah, and Zeboiim, as far as Lasha. 20 These are the sons of Ham, by their clans, their languages, their lands, and their nations.

21 To Shem also, the father of all the children of Eber, the elder brother of Japheth, children were born. 22 The sons of Shem: Elam, Asshur, Arpachshad, Lud, and Aram. 23 The sons of Aram: Uz, Hul, Gether, and Mash. 24 Arpachshad fathered Shelah; and Shelah fathered Eber. 25 To Eber were born two sons: the name of the one was Peleg,[4] for in his days the earth was divided, and his brother's name was Joktan. 26 Joktan fathered Almodad, Sheleph, Hazarmaveth, Jerah, 27 Hadoram, Uzal, Diklah, 28 Obal, Abimael, Sheba, 29 Ophir, Havilah, and Jobab; all these were the sons of Joktan. 30 The territory in which they lived extended from Mesha in the direction of Sephar to the hill country of the east. 31 These are the sons of Shem, by their clans, their languages, their lands, and their nations.

32 These are the clans of the sons of Noah, according to their genealogies, in their nations, and from these the nations spread abroad on the earth after the flood.

The Tower of Babel

11 Now the whole earth had one language and the same words. 2 And as people migrated from the east, they found a plain in the land of Shinar and settled there. 3 And they said to one another, "Come, let us make bricks, and burn them thoroughly." And they had brick for stone, and bitumen for mortar. 4 Then they said, "Come, let us build ourselves a city and a tower with its top in the heavens, and let us make a name for ourselves, lest we be dispersed over the face of the whole earth." 5 And the LORD came down to see the city and the tower, which the children of man had built. 6 And the LORD said, "Behold, they are one people, and they have all one language, and this is only the beginning of what they will do. And nothing that they propose to do will now be impossible for them. 7 Come, let us go down and there

[1] Japheth sounds like the Hebrew for enlarge [2] Or he began to be a mighty man on the earth [3] Or from where [4] Peleg means division

confuse their language, so that they may not understand one another's speech." [8] So the LORD dispersed them from there over the face of all the earth, and they left off building the city. [9] Therefore its name was called Babel, because there the LORD confused[1] the language of all the earth. And from there the LORD dispersed them over the face of all the earth.

Shem's Descendants

[10] These are the generations of Shem. When Shem was 100 years old, he fathered Arpachshad two years after the flood. [11] And Shem lived after he fathered Arpachshad 500 years and had other sons and daughters.

[12] When Arpachshad had lived 35 years, he fathered Shelah. [13] And Arpachshad lived after he fathered Shelah 403 years and had other sons and daughters.

[14] When Shelah had lived 30 years, he fathered Eber. [15] And Shelah lived after he fathered Eber 403 years and had other sons and daughters.

[16] When Eber had lived 34 years, he fathered Peleg. [17] And Eber lived after he fathered Peleg 430 years and had other sons and daughters.

[18] When Peleg had lived 30 years, he fathered Reu. [19] And Peleg lived after he fathered Reu 209 years and had other sons and daughters.

[20] When Reu had lived 32 years, he fathered Serug. [21] And Reu lived after he fathered Serug 207 years and had other sons and daughters.

[22] When Serug had lived 30 years, he fathered Nahor. [23] And Serug lived after he fathered Nahor 200 years and had other sons and daughters.

[24] When Nahor had lived 29 years, he fathered Terah. [25] And Nahor lived after he fathered Terah 119 years and had other sons and daughters.

[26] When Terah had lived 70 years, he fathered Abram, Nahor, and Haran.

Terah's Descendants

[27] Now these are the generations of Terah. Terah fathered Abram, Nahor, and Haran; and Haran fathered Lot. [28] Haran died in the presence of his father Terah in the land of his kindred, in Ur of the Chaldeans. [29] And Abram and Nahor took wives. The name of Abram's wife was Sarai, and the name of Nahor's wife, Milcah, the daughter of Haran the father of Milcah and Iscah. [30] Now Sarai was barren; she had no child.

[31] Terah took Abram his son and Lot the son of Haran, his grandson, and Sarai his daughter-in-law, his son Abram's wife, and they went forth together from Ur of the Chaldeans to go into the land of Canaan, but when they came to Haran, they settled there. [32] The days of Terah were 205 years, and Terah died in Haran.

Ask Yourself . . .

ABOUT YOUR FAITH

Common sense and book knowledge will get you only so far. What you believe ultimately has to be tested so that it can become real to you. You have to live through some trials in order to prove to yourself and to God that Christ will always be your first thought and not an afterthought. Ask yourself:

- Do I rely most often on God by faith, or on common sense?

- Has my faith been tested and proven to be a part of my very core?

- Am I afraid to have my faith tested, or am I ready to stand strong in the knowledge that God is who he says he is, no matter what's going on around me?

The Call of Abram

12 Now the LORD said[2] to Abram, "Go from your country[3] and your kindred and your father's house to the land that I will show you. [2] And I will make of you a great nation, and I will bless you and make your name great, so that you will be a blessing. [3] I will bless those who bless you, and him who dishonors you I will curse, and in you all the families of the earth shall be blessed."[4]

---

[1] *Babel* sounds like the Hebrew for *confused* [2] Or *had said* [3] Or *land* [4] Or *by you all the families of the earth shall bless themselves*

Sarah

Read this God Girl story in Genesis 11:27–12:20;
16; 18:1–15; 21:1–13; and 1 Peter 3:5–6.

Sarah obeyed Abraham, calling him lord. And you are her children,
if you do good and do not fear anything that is frightening.

1 Peter 3:6

What makes you afraid to do good? Is there something you are afraid of that keeps you from doing what you need to do? Call it fear, call it shyness, call it doubt—whatever the reason, you are afraid of the outcome, and so you don't do the good you should. But God makes it clear that God Girls don't let fear stop them from being obedient. After all, fear is really being afraid of the judgment of others. But what can others do to you? Of course you don't live to please people; you want to please God. And he is already wonderfully pleased with you, because you are adopted into his family! So take heart, stand strong, and step out to become a daughter of Sarah—maybe sometimes in fear, but determined to take courage and to trust that if God commanded it, he's going to help you do it.

Obeying authority can be one of the hardest things you'll ever do, but that doesn't make it any less of a requirement. Telling nonbelievers about Jesus can strike fear into the hearts of most girls, but that doesn't mean you shouldn't do it. The thing to always tell yourself when you're afraid to obey God is that whatever you fear can't kill you. It's a big old lie of the Enemy to convince you that what you fear is the worst thing that could ever happen to you. But the real question is, does God promise you destruction when you do the things he commands, or does he promise blessing? The answer is always blessing. Even if it comes in the midst of suffering, the result will always be blessing.

Feelings can never be a motive for disobedience. Nor are they an excuse for sin. How the God Girl feels about doing what God commands is really irrelevant to her, because she doesn't live for herself but for God. In order to demonstrate that you are a daughter of Sarah, you must fearlessly do the good that God wants of you, and then you can be sure that your life will be blessed.

[4] So Abram went, as the LORD had told him, and Lot went with him. Abram was seventy-five years old when he departed from Haran. [5] And Abram took Sarai his wife, and Lot his brother's son, and all their possessions that they had gathered, and the people that they had acquired in Haran, and they set out to go to the land of Canaan. When they came to the land of Canaan, [6] Abram passed through the land to the place at Shechem, to the oak[1] of Moreh. At that time the Canaanites were in the land. [7] Then the LORD appeared to Abram and said, "To your offspring I will give this land." So he built there an altar to the LORD, who had appeared to him. [8] From there he moved to the hill country on the east of Bethel and pitched his tent, with Bethel on the west and Ai on the east. And there he built an altar to the LORD and called upon the name of the LORD. [9] And Abram journeyed on, still going toward the Negeb.

Abram and Sarai in Egypt

[10] Now there was a famine in the land. So Abram went down to Egypt to sojourn there, for the famine was severe in the land. [11] When he was about to enter Egypt, he said to Sarai his wife, "I know that you are a woman beautiful in appearance, [12] and when the Egyptians see you, they will say, 'This is his wife.' Then they will kill me, but they will let you live. [13] Say you are my sister, that it may go well with me because of you, and that my life may be spared for your sake." [14] When Abram entered Egypt, the Egyptians saw that the woman was very beautiful. [15] And when the princes of Pharaoh saw her, they praised her to Pharaoh. And the woman was taken into Pharaoh's house. [16] And for her sake he dealt well with Abram; and he had sheep, oxen, male donkeys, male servants, female servants, female donkeys, and camels.

[17] But the LORD afflicted Pharaoh and his house with great plagues because of Sarai, Abram's wife. [18] So Pharaoh called Abram and said, "What is this you have done to me? Why did you not tell me that she was your wife? [19] Why did you say, 'She is my sister,' so that I took her for my wife? Now then, here is your wife; take her, and go." [20] And Pharaoh gave men orders concerning him, and they sent him away with his wife and all that he had.

Abram and Lot Separate

13 So Abram went up from Egypt, he and his wife and all that he had, and Lot with him, into the Negeb.

[2] Now Abram was very rich in livestock, in silver, and in gold. [3] And he journeyed on from the Negeb as far as Bethel to the place where his tent had been at the beginning, between Bethel and Ai, [4] to the place where he had made an altar at the first. And there Abram called upon the name of the LORD. [5] And Lot, who went with Abram, also had flocks and herds and tents, [6] so that the land could not support both of them dwelling together; for their possessions were so great that they could not dwell together, [7] and there was strife between the herdsmen of Abram's livestock and the herdsmen of Lot's livestock. At that time the Canaanites and the Perizzites were dwelling in the land.

[8] Then Abram said to Lot, "Let there be no strife between you and me, and between your herdsmen and my herdsmen, for we are kinsmen.[2] [9] Is not the whole land before you? Separate yourself from me. If you take the left hand, then I will go to the right, or if you take the right hand, then I will go to the left." [10] And Lot lifted up his eyes and saw that the Jordan Valley was well watered everywhere like the garden of the LORD, like the land of Egypt, in the direction of Zoar. (This was before the LORD destroyed Sodom and Gomorrah.) [11] So Lot chose for himself all the Jordan Valley, and Lot journeyed east. Thus they separated from each other. [12] Abram settled in the land of Canaan, while Lot settled among the cities of the valley and moved his tent as far as Sodom. [13] Now the men of Sodom were wicked, great sinners against the LORD.

[14] The LORD said to Abram, after Lot had separated from him, "Lift up your eyes and look from the place where you are, northward and southward and eastward and westward, [15] for all the land that you see I will give to you and to your offspring forever. [16] I will make your offspring as the dust of the earth, so that if one can count the dust of the earth, your offspring also can be counted. [17] Arise, walk through the length and the breadth of the land, for I will give it to you." [18] So Abram moved his

[1] Or terebinth [2] Hebrew we are men, brothers

ent and came and settled by the oaks[1] of Mamre, which are at Hebron, and there he built an altar to the LORD.

Abram Rescues Lot

14 In the days of Amraphel king of Shinar, Arioch king of Ellasar, Chedorlaomer king of Elam, and Tidal king of Goiim, [2] these kings made war with Bera king of Sodom, Birsha king of Gomorrah, Shinab king of Admah, Shemeber king of Zeboiim, and the king of Bela (that is, Zoar). [3] And all these joined forces in the Valley of Siddim (that is, the Salt Sea). [4] Twelve years they had served Chedorlaomer, but in the thirteenth year they rebelled. [5] In the fourteenth year Chedorlaomer and the kings who were with him came and defeated the Rephaim in Ashteroth-karnaim, the Zuzim in Ham, the Emim in Shaveh-kiriathaim, and the Horites in their hill country of Seir as far as El-paran on the border of the wilderness. [7] Then they turned back and came to En-mishpat (that is, Kadesh) and defeated all the country of the Amalekites, and also the Amorites who were dwelling in Hazazon-tamar.

[8] Then the king of Sodom, the king of Gomorrah, the king of Admah, the king of Zeboiim, and the king of Bela (that is, Zoar) went out, and they joined battle in the Valley of Siddim [9] with Chedorlaomer king of Elam, Tidal king of Goiim, Amraphel king of Shinar, and Arioch king of Ellasar, four kings against five. [10] Now the Valley of Siddim was full of bitumen pits, and as the kings of Sodom and Gomorrah fled, some fell into them, and the rest fled to the hill country. [11] So the enemy took all the possessions of Sodom and Gomorrah, and all their provisions, and went their way. [12] They also took Lot, the son of Abram's brother, who was dwelling in Sodom, and his possessions, and went their way.

[13] Then one who had escaped came and told Abram the Hebrew, who was living by the oaks[2] of Mamre the Amorite, brother of Eshcol and of Aner. These were allies of Abram. [14] When Abram heard that his kinsman had been taken captive, he led forth his trained men, born in his house, 318 of them, and went in pursuit as far as Dan. [15] And he divided his forces against them by night, he and his servants, and defeated them and pursued them to Hobah, north of Damascus. [16] Then he brought back all the possessions, and also brought back his kinsman Lot with his possessions, and the women and the people.

Abram Blessed by Melchizedek

[17] After his return from the defeat of Chedorlaomer and the kings who were with him, the king of Sodom went out to meet him at the Valley of Shaveh (that is, the King's Valley). [18] And Melchizedek king of Salem brought out bread and wine. (He was priest of God Most High.) [19] And he blessed him and said,

> "Blessed be Abram by God Most High,
>   Possessor[3] of heaven and earth;
> [20]   and blessed be God Most High,
>   who has delivered your enemies
>   into your hand!"

And Abram gave him a tenth of everything. [21] And the king of Sodom said to Abram, "Give me the persons, but take the goods for yourself." [22] But Abram said to the king of Sodom, "I have lifted my hand[4] to the LORD, God Most High, Possessor of heaven and earth, [23] that I would not take a thread or a sandal strap or anything that is yours, lest you should say, 'I have made Abram rich.' [24] I will take nothing but what the young men have eaten, and the share of the men who went with me. Let Aner, Eshcol, and Mamre take their share."

God's Covenant with Abram

15 After these things the word of the LORD came to Abram in a vision: "Fear not, Abram, I am your shield; your reward shall be very great." [2] But Abram said, "O Lord GOD, what will you give me, for I continue[5] childless, and the heir of my house is Eliezer of Damascus?" [3] And Abram said, "Behold, you have given me no offspring, and a member of my household will be my heir." [4] And behold, the word of the LORD came to him: "This man shall not be your heir; your very own son[6] shall be your heir." [5] And he brought him outside and said, "Look toward heaven, and number the stars, if you are able to number them." Then he said to him, "So shall your offspring be." [6] And he believed the LORD, and he counted it to him as righteousness.

---

[1]Or terebinths [2]Or terebinths [3]Or Creator; also verse 22 [4]Or I have taken a solemn oath [5]Or I shall die [6]Hebrew what will come out of your own loins

⁷And he said to him, "I am the LORD who brought you out from Ur of the Chaldeans to give you this land to possess." ⁸But he said, "O Lord GOD, how am I to know that I shall possess it?" ⁹He said to him, "Bring me a heifer three years old, a female goat three years old, a ram three years old, a turtledove, and a young pigeon." ¹⁰And he brought him all these, cut them in half, and laid each half over against the other. But he did not cut the birds in half. ¹¹And when birds of prey came down on the carcasses, Abram drove them away.

¹²As the sun was going down, a deep sleep fell on Abram. And behold, dreadful and great darkness fell upon him. ¹³Then the LORD said to Abram, "Know for certain that your offspring will be sojourners in a land that is not theirs and will be servants there, and they will be afflicted for four hundred years. ¹⁴But I will bring judgment on the nation that they serve, and afterward they shall come out with great possessions. ¹⁵As for you, you shall go to your fathers in peace; you shall be buried in a good old age. ¹⁶And they shall come back here in the fourth generation, for the iniquity of the Amorites is not yet complete."

¹⁷When the sun had gone down and it was dark, behold, a smoking fire pot and a flaming torch passed between these pieces. ¹⁸On that day the LORD made a covenant with Abram, saying, "To your offspring I give¹ this land, from the river of Egypt to the great river, the river Euphrates, ¹⁹the land of the Kenites, the Kenizzites, the Kadmonites, ²⁰the Hittites, the Perizzites, the Rephaim, ²¹the Amorites, the Canaanites, the Girgashites and the Jebusites."

¹Or have given

Know True Happiness

verses to read
Genesis 15:1–6

The only way to become right with God is to believe in him. It was faith that made Abram (who was later called Abraham) righteous in God's sight. It was his faith that made him do what God told him to do. And it's faith that will give you the power of God on your side.

People who don't believe don't get the gifts of God. Belief—not doubt, not suspicion, not fear, but belief—is your willingness to allow God to work in your life. Your sinful nature urges you not to believe and not to take the gifts of God into your life. You can choose not to hear from him, not to serve him, and not to love him. In fact, apart from God's powerful help, you can't choose otherwise. But by God's grace, you can choose to believe, like Abram did, and get more of what you need from the God who knows everything you need. Abram could have doubted God's promises—after all, they seemed preposterous!—but he chose to believe them anyway. And thousands of years later, Abraham is known for his faith.

During the time Jesus walked on this earth, he healed and forgave everyone who came to him with faith. If they hadn't believed him, they wouldn't have found what they were looking for. As a God Girl, your faith defines you and sets your limits. Want to move mountains? Then you have to know God more so that you are able to believe him, trust him, and wait upon him for the things he promises. You have to believe that God's Word is true, relevant, and practical for your daily life before you can grow in your faith. So think about what you believe: is it consistent with what God says? Don't let the world tell you a lie that sounds godly but is really just sin dressed up as righteousness. Go after the truth as if your life depended on it, and you'll be rewarded for your faith.

Sarai and Hagar

16 Now Sarai, Abram's wife, had borne him no children. She had a female Egyptian servant whose name was Hagar. ² And Sarai said to Abram, "Behold now, the LORD has prevented me from bearing children. Go in to my servant; it may be that I shall obtain children[1] by her." And Abram listened to the voice of Sarai. ³ So, after Abram had lived ten years in the land of Canaan, Sarai, Abram's wife, took Hagar the Egyptian, her servant, and gave her to Abram her husband as a wife. ⁴ And he went in to Hagar, and she conceived. And when she saw that she had conceived, she looked with contempt on her mistress.[2] ⁵ And Sarai said to Abram, "May the wrong done to me be on you! I gave my servant to your embrace, and when she saw that she had conceived, she looked on me with contempt. May the LORD judge between you and me!" ⁶ But Abram said to Sarai, "Behold, your servant is in your power; do to her as you please." Then Sarai dealt harshly with her, and she fled from her.

⁷ The angel of the LORD found her by a spring of water in the wilderness, the spring on the way to Shur. ⁸ And he said, "Hagar, servant of Sarai, where have you come from and where are you going?" She said, "I am fleeing from my mistress Sarai." ⁹ The angel of the LORD said to her, "Return to your mistress and submit to her." ¹⁰ The angel of the LORD also said to her, "I will surely multiply your offspring so that they cannot be numbered for multitude." ¹¹ And the angel of the LORD said to her,

"Behold, you are pregnant
    and shall bear a son.
You shall call his name Ishmael,[3]
    because the LORD has listened to
        your affliction.
¹² He shall be a wild donkey of a man,
    his hand against everyone
        and everyone's hand against him,
    and he shall dwell over against all his
        kinsmen."

¹³ So she called the name of the LORD who spoke to her, "You are a God of seeing,"[4] for she said, "Truly here I have seen him who looks after me."[5] ¹⁴ Therefore the well was called Beer-lahai-roi;[6] it lies between Kadesh and Bered.

¹⁵ And Hagar bore Abram a son, and Abram called the name of his son, whom Hagar bore, Ishmael. ¹⁶ Abram was eighty-six years old when Hagar bore Ishmael to Abram.

Abraham and the Covenant of Circumcision

17 When Abram was ninety-nine years old the LORD appeared to Abram and said to him, "I am God Almighty;[7] walk before me, and be blameless, ² that I may make my covenant between me and you, and may multiply you greatly." ³ Then Abram fell on his face. And God said to him, ⁴ "Behold, my covenant is with you, and you shall be the father of a multitude of nations. ⁵ No longer shall your name be called Abram,[8] but your name shall be Abraham,[9] for I have made you the father of a multitude of nations. ⁶ I will make you exceedingly fruitful, and I will make you into nations, and kings shall come from you. ⁷ And I will establish my covenant between me and you and your offspring after you throughout their generations for an everlasting covenant, to be God to you and to your offspring after you. ⁸ And I will give to you and to your offspring after you the land of your sojournings, all the land of Canaan, for an everlasting possession, and I will be their God.

⁹ And God said to Abraham, "As for you, you shall keep my covenant, you and your offspring after you throughout their generations. ¹⁰ This is my covenant, which you shall keep, between me and you and your offspring after you: Every male among you shall be circumcised. ¹¹ You shall be circumcised in the flesh of your foreskins, and it shall be a sign of the covenant between me and you. ¹² He who is eight days old among you shall be circumcised. Every male throughout your generations, whether born in your house or bought with your money from any foreigner who is not of your offspring, ¹³ both he who is born in your house and he who is bought with your money, shall surely be circumcised. So shall my covenant be in your flesh an everlasting covenant. ¹⁴ Any uncircumcised male

---

[1] Hebrew *be built up*, which sounds like the Hebrew for *children* [2] Hebrew *her mistress was dishonorable in her eyes*; similarly in verse 5 [3] *Ishmael* means *God hears* [4] Or *You are a God who sees me* [5] Hebrew *Have I really seen him here who sees me?* or *Would I have looked here for the one who sees me?* [6] *Beer-lahai-roi* means *the well of the Living One who sees me* [7] Hebrew *El Shaddai* [8] *Abram* means *exalted father* [9] *Abraham* means *father of a multitude*

who is not circumcised in the flesh of his foreskin shall be cut off from his people; he has broken my covenant."

Isaac's Birth Promised

¹⁵ And God said to Abraham, "As for Sarai your wife, you shall not call her name Sarai, but Sarah[1] shall be her name. ¹⁶ I will bless her, and moreover, I will give[2] you a son by her. I will bless her, and she shall become nations; kings of peoples shall come from her." ¹⁷ Then Abraham fell on his face and laughed and said to himself, "Shall a child be born to a man who is a hundred years old? Shall Sarah, who is ninety years old, bear a child?" ¹⁸ And Abraham said to God, "Oh that Ishmael might live before you!" ¹⁹ God said, "No, but Sarah your wife shall bear you a son, and you shall call his name Isaac.[3] I will establish my covenant with him as an everlasting covenant for his offspring after him. ²⁰ As for Ishmael, I have heard you; behold, I have blessed him and will make him fruitful and multiply him greatly. He shall father twelve princes, and I will make him into a great nation. ²¹ But I will establish my covenant with Isaac, whom Sarah shall bear to you at this time next year."

²² When he had finished talking with him, God went up from Abraham. ²³ Then Abraham took Ishmael his son and all those born in his house or bought with his money, every male among the men of Abraham's house, and he circumcised the flesh of their foreskins that very day, as God had said to him. ²⁴ Abraham was ninety-nine years old when he was circumcised in the flesh of his foreskin. ²⁵ And Ishmael his son was thirteen years old when he was circumcised in the flesh of his foreskin. ²⁶ That very day Abraham and his son Ishmael were circumcised. ²⁷ And all the men of his house, those born in the house and those bought with money from a foreigner, were circumcised with him.

18 And the LORD appeared to him by the oaks[4] of Mamre, as he sat at the door of his tent in the heat of the day. ² He lifted up his eyes and looked, and behold, three men were standing in front of him. When he saw them, he ran from the tent door to meet them and bowed himself to the earth ³ and said, "O Lord,[5] if I have found favor in your sight, do not pass by your servant. ⁴ Let a little water be brought, and wash your feet, and rest yourselves under the tree, ⁵ while I bring a morsel of bread, that you may refresh yourselves, and after that you may pass on— since you have come to your servant." So they said, "Do as you have said." ⁶ And Abraham went quickly into the tent to Sarah and said, "Quick! Three seahs[6] of fine flour! Knead it, and make cakes." ⁷ And Abraham ran to the herd and took a calf, tender and good, and gave it to a young man, who prepared it quickly. ⁸ Then he took curds and milk and the calf that he had prepared, and set it before them. And he stood by them under the tree while they ate.

⁹ They said to him, "Where is Sarah your wife?" And he said, "She is in the tent." ¹⁰ The LORD said, "I will surely return to you about this time next year, and Sarah your wife shall have a son." And Sarah was listening at the tent door behind him. ¹¹ Now Abraham and Sarah were old, advanced in years. The way of women had ceased to be with Sarah. ¹² So Sarah laughed to herself, saying, "After I am worn out, and my lord is old, shall I have pleasure?" ¹³ The LORD said to Abraham, "Why did Sarah laugh and say, 'Shall I indeed bear a child, now that I am old?' ¹⁴ Is anything too hard[7] for the LORD? At the appointed time I will return to you, about this time next year, and Sarah shall have a son." ¹⁵ But Sarah denied it,[8] saying, "I did not laugh," for she was afraid. He said, "No, but you did laugh."

¹⁶ Then the men set out from there, and they looked down toward Sodom. And Abraham went with them to set them on their way. ¹⁷ The LORD said, "Shall I hide from Abraham what I am about to do, ¹⁸ seeing that Abraham shall surely become a great and mighty nation, and all the nations of the earth shall be blessed in him? ¹⁹ For I have chosen[9] him, that he may command his children and his household after him to keep the way of the LORD by doing righteousness and justice, so that the LORD may bring to Abraham what he has promised him." ²⁰ Then the LORD said, "Because the outcry against Sodom and Gomorrah is great and their sin is very grave, ²¹ I will go down to see whether they have done altogether[10] according to the

---

[1] *Sarai* and *Sarah* mean *princess* [2] Hebrew *have given* [3] *Isaac* means *he laughs* [4] Or *terebinths* [5] Or *My lord* [6] A *seah* was about 7 quarts or 7.3 liters [7] Or *wonderful* [8] Or *acted falsely* [9] Hebrew *known* [10] Or *they deserve destruction*; Hebrew *they have made a complete end*

outcry that has come to me. And if not, I will know."

Abraham Intercedes for Sodom

²² So the men turned from there and went toward Sodom, but Abraham still stood before the LORD. ²³ Then Abraham drew near and said, "Will you indeed sweep away the righteous with the wicked? ²⁴ Suppose there are fifty righteous within the city. Will you then sweep away the place and not spare it for the fifty righteous who are in it? ²⁵ Far be it from you to do such a thing, to put the righteous to death with the wicked, so that the righteous fare as the wicked! Far be that from you! Shall not the Judge of all the earth do what is just?" ²⁶ And the LORD said, "If I find at Sodom fifty righteous in the city, I will spare the whole place for their sake."

²⁷ Abraham answered and said, "Behold, I have undertaken to speak to the Lord, I who am but dust and ashes. ²⁸ Suppose five of the fifty righteous are lacking. Will you destroy the whole city for lack of five?" And he said, "I will not destroy it if I find forty-five there." ²⁹ Again he spoke to him and said, "Suppose forty are found there." He answered, "For the sake of forty I will not do it." ³⁰ Then he said, "Oh let not the Lord be angry, and I will speak. Suppose thirty are found there." He answered, "I will not do it, if I find thirty there." ³¹ He said, "Behold, I have undertaken to speak to the Lord. Suppose twenty are found there." He answered, "For the sake of twenty I will not destroy it." ³² Then he said, "Oh let not the Lord be angry, and I will speak again but this once. Suppose ten are found there." He answered, "For the sake of ten I will not destroy it." ³³ And the LORD went his way, when he had finished speaking to Abraham, and Abraham returned to his place.

verses to read
Genesis 18:16–33

Prayer is direct contact with God. It isn't mindless contemplation but a conversation, a back-and-forth with the God who has the power to do all you could ask. Our prayers can get repetitive and boring. But the prayers you see in the Bible are totally different. When these men and women of God pray, they are relentless, not passive. They beg, plead, and ask over and over again. Abraham wouldn't give up asking for God to save the town of Sodom from destruction (see Gen. 18:20–33). Moses pleaded with God (see Ex. 32:11). Hannah poured out her heart to the Lord so much that people watching her thought she was drunk (see 1 Sam. 1:13–15). King Hezekiah and the prophet Isaiah called to heaven (see 2 Chron. 32:20). Paul fell to his knees in God's presence (see Eph. 3:14).

Prayer is where you plead with the one who can do anything to do what he wills. Prayer is free access to the Creator of the universe, available to all who make Jesus the Lord of their lives. And the Word of God says you can be sure that he hears your prayers and that he will answer according to his will (see 1 John 5:14–15). He listens to your pleadings. In fact, he expects them. When Jesus told the parable of the widow and the judge, he taught us that we should "cry to him day and night" (see Luke 18:2–8).

So make your prayers active. Be fearless about asking for what you need, knowing that God answers prayers and that, no matter what answer you get, you can be sure it's the best thing for you. Just don't neglect to pray. That's where the power lies. Be persistent. Be vocal. Talk to God as the only one who can help you and change you. And you'll find that he truly will.

God Rescues Lot

19 The two angels came to Sodom in the evening, and Lot was sitting in the gate of Sodom. When Lot saw them, he rose to meet them and bowed himself with his face to the earth ²and said, "My lords, please turn aside to your servant's house and spend the night and wash your feet. Then you may rise up early and go on your way." They said, "No; we will spend the night in the town square." ³But he pressed them strongly; so they turned aside to him and entered his house. And he made them a feast and baked unleavened bread, and they ate.

⁴But before they lay down, the men of the city, the men of Sodom, both young and old, all the people to the last man, surrounded the house. ⁵And they called to Lot, "Where are the men who came to you tonight? Bring them out to us, that we may know them." ⁶Lot went out to the men at the entrance, shut the door after him, ⁷and said, "I beg you, my brothers, do not act so wickedly. ⁸Behold, I have two daughters who have not known any man. Let me bring them out to you, and do to them as you please. Only do nothing to these men, for they have come under the shelter of my roof." ⁹But they said, "Stand back!" And they said, "This fellow came to sojourn, and he has become the judge! Now we will deal worse with you than with them." Then they pressed hard against the man Lot, and drew near to break the door down. ¹⁰But the men reached out their hands and brought Lot into the house with them and shut the door. ¹¹And they struck with blindness the men who were at the entrance of the house, both small and great, so that they wore themselves out groping for the door.

¹²Then the men said to Lot, "Have you anyone else here? Sons-in-law, sons, daughters, or anyone you have in the city, bring them out of the place. ¹³For we are about to destroy this place, because the outcry against its people has become great before the LORD, and the LORD has sent us to destroy it." ¹⁴So Lot went out and said to his sons-in-law, who were to marry his daughters, "Up! Get out of this place, for the LORD is about to destroy the city." But he seemed to his sons-in-law to be jesting.

¹⁵As morning dawned, the angels urged Lot, saying, "Up! Take your wife and your two daughters who are here, lest you be swept away in the punishment of the city." ¹⁶But he lingered. So the men seized him and his wife and his two daughters by the hand, the LORD being merciful to him, and they brought him out and set him outside the city. ¹⁷And as they brought them out, one said, "Escape for your life. Do not look back or stop anywhere in the valley. Escape to the hills, lest you be swept away." ¹⁸And Lot said to them, "Oh, no, my lords. ¹⁹Behold, your servant has found favor in your sight, and you have shown me great kindness in saving my life. But I cannot escape to the hills, lest the disaster overtake me and I die. ²⁰Behold, this city is near enough to flee to, and it is a little one. Let me escape there—is it not a little one?—and my life will be saved!" ²¹He said to him, "Behold, I grant you this favor also, that I will not overthrow the city of which you have spoken. ²²Escape there quickly, for I can do nothing till you arrive there." Therefore the name of the city was called Zoar.[1]

God Destroys Sodom

²³The sun had risen on the earth when Lot came to Zoar. ²⁴Then the LORD rained on Sodom and Gomorrah sulfur and fire from the LORD out of heaven. ²⁵And he overthrew those cities, and all the valley, and all the inhabitants of the cities, and what grew on the ground. ²⁶But Lot's wife, behind him, looked back, and she became a pillar of salt.

²⁷And Abraham went early in the morning to the place where he had stood before the LORD. ²⁸And he looked down toward Sodom and Gomorrah and toward all the land of the valley, and he looked and, behold, the smoke of the land went up like the smoke of a furnace.

²⁹So it was that, when God destroyed the cities of the valley, God remembered Abraham and sent Lot out of the midst of the overthrow when he overthrew the cities in which Lot had lived.

Lot and His Daughters

³⁰Now Lot went up out of Zoar and lived in the hills with his two daughters, for he was afraid to live in Zoar. So he lived in

---

[1] *Zoar* means *little*

a cave with his two daughters. ³¹And the firstborn said to the younger, "Our father is old, and there is not a man on earth to come in to us after the manner of all the earth. ³²Come, let us make our father drink wine, and we will lie with him, that we may preserve offspring from our father." ³³So they made their father drink wine that night. And the firstborn went in and lay with her father. He did not know when she lay down or when she arose.

³⁴The next day, the firstborn said to the younger, "Behold, I lay last night with my father. Let us make him drink wine tonight also. Then you go in and lie with him, that we may preserve offspring from our father." ³⁵So they made their father drink wine that night also. And the younger arose and lay with him, and he did not know when she lay down or when she arose. ³⁶Thus both the daughters of Lot became pregnant by their father. ³⁷The firstborn bore a son and called his name Moab.¹ He is the father of the Moabites to this day. ³⁸The younger also bore a son and called his name Ben-ammi.² He is the father of the Ammonites to this day.

Abraham and Abimelech

20 From there Abraham journeyed toward the territory of the Negeb and lived between Kadesh and Shur; and he sojourned in Gerar. ²And Abraham said of Sarah his wife, "She is my sister." And Abimelech king of Gerar sent and took Sarah. ³But God came to Abimelech in a dream by night and said to him, "Behold, you are a dead man because of the woman whom you have taken, for she is a man's wife." ⁴Now Abimelech had not approached her. So he said, "Lord, will you kill an innocent people? ⁵Did he not himself say to me, 'She is my sister'? And she herself said, 'He is my brother.' In the integrity of my heart and the innocence of my hands I have done this." ⁶Then God said to him in the dream, "Yes, I know that you have done this in the integrity of your heart, and it was I who kept you from sinning against me. Therefore I did not let you touch her. ⁷Now then, return the man's wife, for he is a prophet, so that he will pray for you, and you shall live. But if you do not return her,

know that you shall surely die, you and all who are yours."

⁸So Abimelech rose early in the morning and called all his servants and told them all these things. And the men were very much afraid. ⁹Then Abimelech called Abraham and said to him, "What have you done to us? And how have I sinned against you, that you have brought on me and my kingdom a great sin? You have done to me things that ought not to be done." ¹⁰And Abimelech said to Abraham, "What did you see, that you did this thing?" ¹¹Abraham said, "I did it because I thought, 'There is no fear of God at all in this place, and they will kill me because of my wife.' ¹²Besides, she is indeed my sister, the daughter of my father though not the daughter of my mother, and she became my wife. ¹³And when God caused me to wander from my father's house, I said to her, 'This is the kindness you must do me: at every place to which we come, say of me, "He is my brother."'"

¹⁴Then Abimelech took sheep and oxen, and male servants and female servants, and gave them to Abraham, and returned Sarah his wife to him. ¹⁵And Abimelech said, "Behold, my land is before you; dwell where it pleases you." ¹⁶To Sarah he said, "Behold, I have given your brother a thousand pieces of silver. It is a sign of your innocence in the eyes of all³ who are with you, and before everyone you are vindicated." ¹⁷Then Abraham prayed to God, and God healed Abimelech, and also healed his wife and female slaves so that they bore children. ¹⁸For the LORD had closed all the wombs of the house of Abimelech because of Sarah, Abraham's wife.

The Birth of Isaac

21 The LORD visited Sarah as he had said, and the LORD did to Sarah as he had promised. ²And Sarah conceived and bore Abraham a son in his old age at the time of which God had spoken to him. ³Abraham called the name of his son who was born to him, whom Sarah bore him, Isaac.⁴ ⁴And Abraham circumcised his son Isaac when he was eight days old, as God had commanded him. ⁵Abraham was a hundred years old when his son Isaac was born to him. ⁶And Sarah said, "God has made laughter for me; everyone who hears

¹ Moab sounds like the Hebrew for *from father* ² Ben-ammi means *son of my people* ³ Hebrew *It is a covering of eyes for all* ⁴ Isaac means *he laughs*

will laugh over me." ⁷ And she said, "Who would have said to Abraham that Sarah would nurse children? Yet I have borne him a son in his old age."

God Protects Hagar and Ishmael

⁸ And the child grew and was weaned. And Abraham made a great feast on the day that Isaac was weaned. ⁹ But Sarah saw the son of Hagar the Egyptian, whom she had borne to Abraham, laughing.¹ ¹⁰ So she said to Abraham, "Cast out this slave woman with her son, for the son of this slave woman shall not be heir with my son Isaac." ¹¹ And the thing was very displeasing to Abraham on account of his son. ¹² But God said to Abraham, "Be not displeased because of the boy and because of your slave woman. Whatever Sarah says to you, do as she tells you, for through Isaac shall your offspring be named. ¹³ And I will make a nation of the son of the slave woman also, because he is your offspring." ¹⁴ So Abraham rose early in the morning and took bread and a skin of water and gave it to Hagar, putting it on her shoulder, along with the child, and sent her away. And she departed and wandered in the wilderness of Beersheba.

¹⁵ When the water in the skin was gone, she put the child under one of the bushes. ¹⁶ Then she went and sat down opposite him a good way off, about the distance of a bowshot, for she said, "Let me not look on the death of the child." And as she sat opposite him, she lifted up her voice and wept. ¹⁷ And God heard the voice of the boy, and the angel of God called to Hagar from heaven and said to her, "What troubles you, Hagar? Fear not, for God has heard the voice of the boy where he is. ¹⁸ Up! Lift up the boy, and hold him fast with your hand, for I will make him into a great nation." ¹⁹ Then God opened her eyes, and she saw a well of water. And she went and filled the skin with water and gave the boy a drink. ²⁰ And God was with the boy, and he grew up. He lived in the wilderness and became an expert with the bow. ²¹ He lived in the wilderness of Paran, and his mother took a wife for him from the land of Egypt.

A Treaty with Abimelech

²² At that time Abimelech and Phicol the commander of his army said to Abraham,

"God is with you in all that you do. ²³ Now therefore swear to me here by God that you will not deal falsely with me or with my descendants or with my posterity, but as I have dealt kindly with you, so you will deal with me and with the land where you have sojourned." ²⁴ And Abraham said, "I will swear."

²⁵ When Abraham reproved Abimelech about a well of water that Abimelech's servants had seized, ²⁶ Abimelech said, "I do not know who has done this thing; you did not tell me, and I have not heard of it until today." ²⁷ So Abraham took sheep and oxen and gave them to Abimelech, and the two men made a covenant. ²⁸ Abraham set seven ewe lambs of the flock apart. ²⁹ And Abimelech said to Abraham, "What is the meaning of these seven ewe lambs that you have set apart?" ³⁰ He said, "These seven ewe lambs you will take from my hand, that this² may be a witness for me that I dug this well." ³¹ Therefore that place was called Beersheba,³ because there both of them swore an oath. ³² So they made a covenant at Beersheba. Then Abimelech and Phicol the commander of his army rose up and returned to the land of the Philistines. ³³ Abraham planted a tamarisk tree in Beersheba and called there on the name of the LORD, the Everlasting God. ³⁴ And Abraham sojourned many days in the land of the Philistines.

The Sacrifice of Isaac

22 After these things God tested Abraham and said to him, "Abraham!" And he said, "Here I am." ² He said, "Take your son, your only son Isaac, whom you love, and go to the land of Moriah, and offer him there as a burnt offering on one of the mountains of which I shall tell you." ³ So Abraham rose early in the morning, saddled his donkey, and took two of his young men with him, and his son Isaac. And he cut the wood for the burnt offering and arose and went to the place of which God had told him. ⁴ On the third day Abraham lifted up his eyes and saw the place from afar. ⁵ Then Abraham said to his young men, "Stay here with the donkey; I and the boy⁴ will go over there and worship and come again to you." ⁶ And Abraham took the wood of the burnt offering and laid it on Isaac his son. And he took in his

¹ Possibly *laughing in mockery* ² Or *you* ³ *Beersheba* means *well of seven* or *well of the oath* ⁴ Or *young man*; also verse 12

hand the fire and the knife. So they went both of them together. ⁷And Isaac said to his father Abraham, "My father!" And he said, "Here I am, my son." He said, "Behold, the fire and the wood, but where is the lamb for a burnt offering?" ⁸Abraham said, "God will provide for himself the lamb for a burnt offering, my son." So they went both of them together.

⁹When they came to the place of which God had told him, Abraham built the altar there and laid the wood in order and bound Isaac his son and laid him on the altar, on top of the wood. ¹⁰Then Abraham reached out his hand and took the knife to slaughter his son. ¹¹But the angel of the LORD called to him from heaven and said, "Abraham, Abraham!" And he said, "Here I am." ¹²He said, "Do not lay your

hand on the boy or do anything to him, for now I know that you fear God, seeing you have not withheld your son, your only son, from me." ¹³And Abraham lifted up his eyes and looked, and behold, behind him was a ram, caught in a thicket by his horns. And Abraham went and took the ram and offered it up as a burnt offering instead of his son. ¹⁴So Abraham called the name of that place, "The LORD will provide";¹ as it is said to this day, "On the mount of the LORD it shall be provided."²

¹⁵And the angel of the LORD called to Abraham a second time from heaven ¹⁶and said, "By myself I have sworn, declares the LORD, because you have done this and have not withheld your son, your only son, ¹⁷I will surely bless you, and I will surely multiply your offspring as the

¹Or will see ²Or he will be seen

Know Yourself

verses to read
Genesis 22:1–14

God is the giver of every good and perfect thing, but what happens when that thing he's given you is so good that you start to think it's more important than anything else, even him? We humans have a tendency to give the gift the worship and honor meant for the Giver.

Abraham never expected to have a kid. So when God gave him Isaac, it would have been easy for Abraham to fall deeply and even obsessively in love with his kid. And when God seemed to demand that Abraham sacrifice the child he adored, how easy it would have been to say, "No way, José!" But Abraham proved his faith in God when he refused to give in to his desire to protect the boy he loved so much and instead did what God asked him to do. Not many have had to experience such an agonizing call to obedience. But in the end that obedience would bring more glory than any agony could ever steal.

Obedience isn't always comfortable. In fact, true obedience demands something from us. It demands complete reliance on the wisdom, power, and love of the one who knows what is best, and it demands a ruthless determination to do whatever has to be done.

If God isn't demanding something of you, then you're not listening, God Girl. What could you do right now out of obedience that would lead you closer to God and deeper into the life of faith? To listen, turn the pages of his Word. Study his character and make his kindness part of your very essence. Love the unlovable, give to the needy, obey authority, offer forgiveness, turn the other cheek, humble yourself, and he will lift you up. Obey him today and find a reward far greater than you ever imagined could be yours. Nothing gives more to the life of a God Girl than obeying her Lord.

stars of heaven and as the sand that is on the seashore. And your offspring shall possess the gate of his[1] enemies, [18] and in your offspring shall all the nations of the earth be blessed, because you have obeyed my voice." [19] So Abraham returned to his young men, and they arose and went together to Beersheba. And Abraham lived at Beersheba.

[20] Now after these things it was told to Abraham, "Behold, Milcah also has borne children to your brother Nahor: [21] Uz his firstborn, Buz his brother, Kemuel the father of Aram, [22] Chesed, Hazo, Pildash, Jidlaph, and Bethuel." [23] (Bethuel fathered Rebekah.) These eight Milcah bore to Nahor, Abraham's brother. [24] Moreover, his concubine, whose name was Reumah, bore Tebah, Gaham, Tahash, and Maacah.

Sarah's Death and Burial

23 Sarah lived 127 years; these were the years of the life of Sarah. [2] And Sarah died at Kiriath-arba (that is, Hebron) in the land of Canaan, and Abraham went in to mourn for Sarah and to weep for her. [3] And Abraham rose up from before his dead and said to the Hittites,[2] [4] "I am a sojourner and foreigner among you; give me property among you for a burying place, that I may bury my dead out of my sight." [5] The Hittites answered Abraham, [6] "Hear us, my lord; you are a prince of God[3] among us. Bury your dead in the choicest of our tombs. None of us will withhold from you his tomb to hinder you from burying your dead." [7] Abraham rose and bowed to the Hittites, the people of the land. [8] And he said to them, "If you are willing that I should bury my dead out of my sight, hear me and entreat for me Ephron the son of Zohar, [9] that he may give me the cave of Machpelah, which he owns; it is at the end of his field. For the full price let him give it to me in your presence as property for a burying place."

[10] Now Ephron was sitting among the Hittites, and Ephron the Hittite answered Abraham in the hearing of the Hittites, of all who went in at the gate of his city, [11] "No, my lord, hear me: I give you the field, and I give you the cave that is in it. In the sight of the sons of my people I give it to you. Bury your dead." [12] Then Abraham bowed down before the people

of the land. [13] And he said to Ephron in the hearing of the people of the land, "But if you will, hear me: I give the price of the field. Accept it from me, that I may bury my dead there." [14] Ephron answered Abraham, [15] "My lord, listen to me: a piece of land worth four hundred shekels[4] of silver, what is that between me and you? Bury your dead." [16] Abraham listened to Ephron, and Abraham weighed out for Ephron the silver that he had named in the hearing of the Hittites, four hundred shekels of silver, according to the weights current among the merchants.

[17] So the field of Ephron in Machpelah, which was to the east of Mamre, the field with the cave that was in it and all the trees that were in the field, throughout its whole area, was made over [18] to Abraham as a possession in the presence of the Hittites, before all who went in at the gate of his city. [19] After this, Abraham buried Sarah his wife in the cave of the field of Machpelah east of Mamre (that is, Hebron) in the land of Canaan. [20] The field and the cave that is in it were made over to Abraham as property for a burying place by the Hittites.

Isaac and Rebekah

24 Now Abraham was old, well advanced in years. And the LORD had blessed Abraham in all things. [2] And Abraham said to his servant, the oldest of his household, who had charge of all that he had, "Put your hand under my thigh, [3] that I may make you swear by the LORD, the God of heaven and God of the earth, that you will not take a wife for my son from the daughters of the Canaanites, among whom I dwell, [4] but will go to my country and to my kindred, and take a wife for my son Isaac." [5] The servant said to him, "Perhaps the woman may not be willing to follow me to this land. Must I then take your son back to the land from which you came?" [6] Abraham said to him, "See to it that you do not take my son back there. [7] The LORD, the God of heaven, who took me from my father's house and from the land of my kindred, and who spoke to me and swore to me, 'To your offspring I will give this land,' he will send his angel before you, and you shall take a wife for my son from there. [8] But if the woman is not willing to follow you, then you will be free

[1] Or *their* [2] Hebrew *sons of Heth*; also verses 5, 7, 10, 16, 18, 20 [3] Or *a mighty prince* [4] A shekel was about 2/5 ounce or 11 grams

from this oath of mine; only you must not take my son back there." ⁹So the servant put his hand under the thigh of Abraham his master and swore to him concerning this matter.

¹⁰Then the servant took ten of his master's camels and departed, taking all sorts of choice gifts from his master; and he arose and went to Mesopotamia¹ to the city of Nahor. ¹¹And he made the camels kneel down outside the city by the well of water at the time of evening, the time when women go out to draw water. ¹²And he said, "O Lord, God of my master Abraham, please grant me success today and show steadfast love to my master Abraham. ¹³Behold, I am standing by the spring of water, and the daughters of the men of the city are coming out to draw water. ¹⁴Let the young woman to whom I shall say, 'Please let down your jar that I may drink,' and who shall say, 'Drink, and I will water your camels'— let her be the one whom you have appointed for your servant Isaac. By this² I shall know that you have shown steadfast love to my master."

¹⁵Before he had finished speaking, behold, Rebekah, who was born to Bethuel the son of Milcah, the wife of Nahor, Abraham's brother, came out with her water jar on her shoulder. ¹⁶The young woman was very attractive in appearance, a maiden³ whom no man had known. She went down to the spring and filled her jar and came up. ¹⁷Then the servant ran to meet her and said, "Please give me a little water to drink from your jar." ¹⁸She said, "Drink, my lord." And she quickly let down her jar upon her hand and gave him a drink. ¹⁹When she had finished giving him a drink, she said, "I will draw water for your camels also, until they have finished drinking." ²⁰So she quickly emptied her jar into the trough and ran again to the well to draw water, and she drew for all his camels. ²¹The man gazed at her in silence to learn whether the Lord had prospered his journey or not.

²²When the camels had finished drinking, the man took a gold ring weighing a half shekel,⁴ and two bracelets for her arms weighing ten gold shekels, ²³and said, "Please tell me whose daughter you are. Is there room in your father's house for us to spend the night?" ²⁴She said to him, "I am

the daughter of Bethuel the son of Milcah, whom she bore to Nahor." ²⁵She added, "We have plenty of both straw and fodder, and room to spend the night." ²⁶The man bowed his head and worshiped the Lord ²⁷and said, "Blessed be the Lord, the God of my master Abraham, who has not forsaken his steadfast love and his faithfulness toward my master. As for me, the Lord has led me in the way to the house of my master's kinsmen." ²⁸Then the young woman ran and told her mother's household about these things.

²⁹Rebekah had a brother whose name was Laban. Laban ran out toward the man, to the spring. ³⁰As soon as he saw the ring and the bracelets on his sister's arms, and heard the words of Rebekah his sister, "Thus the man spoke to me," he went to the man. And behold, he was standing by the camels at the spring. ³¹He said, "Come in, O blessed of the Lord. Why do you stand outside? For I have prepared the house and a place for the camels." ³²So the man came to the house and unharnessed the camels, and gave straw and fodder to the camels, and there was water to wash his feet and the feet of the men who were with him. ³³Then food was set before him to eat. But he said, "I will not eat until I have said what I have to say." He said, "Speak on."

³⁴So he said, "I am Abraham's servant. ³⁵The Lord has greatly blessed my master, and he has become great. He has given him flocks and herds, silver and gold, male servants and female servants, camels and donkeys. ³⁶And Sarah my master's wife bore a son to my master when she was old, and to him he has given all that he has. ³⁷My master made me swear, saying, 'You shall not take a wife for my son from the daughters of the Canaanites, in whose land I dwell, ³⁸but you shall go to my father's house and to my clan and take a wife for my son.' ³⁹I said to my master, 'Perhaps the woman will not follow me.' ⁴⁰But he said to me, 'The Lord, before whom I have walked, will send his angel with you and prosper your way. You shall take a wife for my son from my clan and from my father's house. ⁴¹Then you will be free from my oath, when you come to my clan. And if they will not give her to you, you will be free from my oath.'

¹Hebrew *Aram-naharaim* ²Or *By her* ³Or *a woman of marriageable age* ⁴A *shekel* was about 2/5 ounce or 11 grams

Rebekah

Read this God Girl story in Genesis 24:11–67; 25:19–28;
26:6–11; 26:34–27:46; and Romans 9:9–12.

> In him we have obtained an inheritance, having been predestined
> according to the purpose of him who works all things according
> to the counsel of his will.
>
> Ephesians 1:11

In the life of a God Girl there is no such thing as a coincidence or dumb luck. There are no accidental happenings, no haphazard events that seem to have a connection but are just the luck of the draw. God is continually working in the life of his children, so they can know that nothing happens unless he allows it. God's all-powerful hand is always on your life, preparing you and arranging for you. When you are willing to just wait for him and to trust that his will is the best will for you, you can be sure that he will give you just what you need.

When Abraham's servant asked God to bring him a young woman who would not only give him a drink of water from the well but would water his camels too, it was no coincidence that a second later Rebekah came up and did all that the servant had prayed for. The answer to his prayer was obvious, and this was the woman who would marry Isaac. Rebekah wasn't expecting to find the love of her life when she went to the well that day. She wasn't planning how to get his attention. She was just being the kind and generous woman that she was, and God blessed her with a man who would love her for the rest of her life.

You have no way to know how tomorrow might turn out, let alone the rest of your life, but one thing is for sure: if you'll remember that everything you do is for God, you can be sure that he will send you only what is best, and always at the right time—you are his daughter! Rebekah wasn't engineering her life but was living it in step with the Father. Think about her example and live your life today by walking quietly with God, trusting him to give you the desires of your heart.

42 "I came today to the spring and said, 'O Lord, the God of my master Abraham, if now you are prospering the way that I go, 43 behold, I am standing by the spring of water. Let the virgin who comes out to draw water, to whom I shall say, "Please give me a little water from your jar to drink," 44 and who will say to me, "Drink, and I will draw for your camels also," let her be the woman whom the Lord has appointed for my master's son.'

45 "Before I had finished speaking in my heart, behold, Rebekah came out with her water jar on her shoulder, and she went down to the spring and drew water. I said to her, 'Please let me drink.' 46 She quickly let down her jar from her shoulder and said, 'Drink, and I will give your camels drink also.' So I drank, and she gave the camels drink also. 47 Then I asked her, 'Whose daughter are you?' She said, 'The daughter of Bethuel, Nahor's son, whom Milcah bore to him.' So I put the ring on her nose and the bracelets on her arms. 48 Then I bowed my head and worshiped the Lord and blessed the Lord, the God of my master Abraham, who had led me by the right way[1] to take the daughter of my master's kinsman for his son. 49 Now then, if you are going to show steadfast love and faithfulness to my master, tell me; and if not, tell me, that I may turn to the right hand or to the left."

50 Then Laban and Bethuel answered and said, "The thing has come from the Lord; we cannot speak to you bad or good. 51 Behold, Rebekah is before you; take her and go, and let her be the wife of your master's son, as the Lord has spoken."

52 When Abraham's servant heard their words, he bowed himself to the earth before the Lord. 53 And the servant brought out jewelry of silver and of gold, and garments, and gave them to Rebekah. He also gave to her brother and to her mother costly ornaments. 54 And he and the men who were with him ate and drank, and they spent the night there. When they arose in the morning, he said, "Send me away to my master." 55 Her brother and her mother said, "Let the young woman remain with us a while, at least ten days; after that she may go." 56 But he said to them, "Do not delay me, since the Lord has prospered my way. Send me away that I may go to

my master." 57 They said, "Let us call the young woman and ask her." 58 And they called Rebekah and said to her, "Will you go with this man?" She said, "I will go." 59 So they sent away Rebekah their sister and her nurse, and Abraham's servant and his men. 60 And they blessed Rebekah and said to her,

"Our sister, may you become
    thousands of ten thousands,
and may your offspring possess
    the gate of those who hate him!"[2]

61 Then Rebekah and her young women arose and rode on the camels and followed the man. Thus the servant took Rebekah and went his way.

62 Now Isaac had returned from Beer-lahai-roi and was dwelling in the Negeb. 63 And Isaac went out to meditate in the field toward evening. And he lifted up his eyes and saw, and behold, there were camels coming. 64 And Rebekah lifted up her eyes, and when she saw Isaac, she dismounted from the camel 65 and said to the servant, "Who is that man, walking in the field to meet us?" The servant said, "It is my master." So she took her veil and covered herself. 66 And the servant told Isaac all the things that he had done. 67 Then Isaac brought her into the tent of Sarah his mother and took Rebekah, and she became his wife, and he loved her. So Isaac was comforted after his mother's death.

Abraham's Death and His Descendants

25 Abraham took another wife, whose name was Keturah. 2 She bore him Zimran, Jokshan, Medan, Midian, Ishbak, and Shuah. 3 Jokshan fathered Sheba and Dedan. The sons of Dedan were Asshurim, Letushim, and Leummim. 4 The sons of Midian were Ephah, Epher, Hanoch, Abida, and Eldaah. All these were the children of Keturah. 5 Abraham gave all he had to Isaac. 6 But to the sons of his concubines Abraham gave gifts, and while he was still living he sent them away from his son Isaac, eastward to the east country.

7 These are the days of the years of Abraham's life, 175 years. 8 Abraham breathed his last and died in a good old age, an old man and full of years, and was gathered to his people. 9 Isaac and Ishmael his sons buried him in the cave of

Machpelah, in the field of Ephron the son of Zohar the Hittite, east of Mamre, [10] the field that Abraham purchased from the Hittites. There Abraham was buried, with Sarah his wife. [11] After the death of Abraham, God blessed Isaac his son. And Isaac settled at Beer-lahai-roi.

[12] These are the generations of Ishmael, Abraham's son, whom Hagar the Egyptian, Sarah's servant, bore to Abraham. [13] These are the names of the sons of Ishmael, named in the order of their birth: Nebaioth, the firstborn of Ishmael; and Kedar, Adbeel, Mibsam, [14] Mishma, Dumah, Massa, [15] Hadad, Tema, Jetur, Naphish, and Kedemah. [16] These are the sons of Ishmael and these are their names, by their villages and by their encampments, twelve princes according to their tribes. [17] (These are the years of the life of Ishmael: 137 years. He breathed his last and died, and was gathered to his people.) [18] They settled from Havilah to Shur, which is opposite Egypt in the direction of Assyria. He settled[1] over against all his kinsmen.

The Birth of Esau and Jacob

[19] These are the generations of Isaac, Abraham's son: Abraham fathered Isaac, [20] and Isaac was forty years old when he took Rebekah, the daughter of Bethuel the Aramean of Paddan-aram, the sister of Laban the Aramean, to be his wife. [21] And Isaac prayed to the LORD for his wife, because she was barren. And the LORD granted his prayer, and Rebekah his wife conceived. [22] The children struggled together within her, and she said, "If it is thus, why is this happening to me?"[2] So she went to inquire of the LORD. [23] And the LORD said to her,

"Two nations are in your womb,
    and two peoples from within you[3]
       shall be divided;
the one shall be stronger than the
      other,
    the older shall serve the younger."

[24] When her days to give birth were completed, behold, there were twins in her womb. [25] The first came out red, all his body like a hairy cloak, so they called his name Esau. [26] Afterward his brother came out with his hand holding Esau's heel, so his name was called Jacob.[4] Isaac was sixty years old when she bore them.

[27] When the boys grew up, Esau was a skillful hunter, a man of the field, while Jacob was a quiet man, dwelling in tents. [28] Isaac loved Esau because he ate of his game, but Rebekah loved Jacob.

Esau Sells His Birthright

[29] Once when Jacob was cooking stew, Esau came in from the field, and he was exhausted. [30] And Esau said to Jacob, "Let me eat some of that red stew, for I am exhausted!" (Therefore his name was called Edom.[5]) [31] Jacob said, "Sell me your birthright now." [32] Esau said, "I am about to die; of what use is a birthright to me?" [33] Jacob said, "Swear to me now." So he swore to him and sold his birthright to Jacob. [34] Then Jacob gave Esau bread and lentil stew, and he ate and drank and rose and went his way. Thus Esau despised his birthright.

God's Promise to Isaac

26 Now there was a famine in the land, besides the former famine that was in the days of Abraham. And Isaac went to Gerar to Abimelech king of the Philistines. [2] And the LORD appeared to him and said, "Do not go down to Egypt; dwell in the land of which I shall tell you. [3] Sojourn in this land, and I will be with you and will bless you, for to you and to your offspring I will give all these lands, and I will establish the oath that I swore to Abraham your father. [4] I will multiply your offspring as the stars of heaven and will give to your offspring all these lands. And in your offspring all the nations of the earth shall be blessed, [5] because Abraham obeyed my voice and kept my charge, my commandments, my statutes, and my laws."

Isaac and Abimelech

[6] So Isaac settled in Gerar. [7] When the men of the place asked him about his wife, he said, "She is my sister," for he feared to say, "My wife," thinking, "lest the men of the place should kill me because of Rebekah," because she was attractive in appearance. [8] When he had been there a long time, Abimelech king of the Philistines looked out of a window and saw Isaac laughing with[6] Rebekah his

---

[1] Hebrew *fell* [2] Or *why do I live?* [3] Or *from birth* [4] *Jacob* means *He takes by the heel*, or *He cheats* [5] *Edom* sounds like the Hebrew for *red* [6] Hebrew may suggest an intimate relationship

wife. [9] So Abimelech called Isaac and said, "Behold, she is your wife. How then could you say, 'She is my sister'?" Isaac said to him, "Because I thought, 'Lest I die because of her.'" [10] Abimelech said, "What is this you have done to us? One of the people might easily have lain with your wife, and you would have brought guilt upon us." [11] So Abimelech warned all the people, saying, "Whoever touches this man or his wife shall surely be put to death."

[12] And Isaac sowed in that land and reaped in the same year a hundredfold. The LORD blessed him, [13] and the man became rich, and gained more and more until he became very wealthy. [14] He had possessions of flocks and herds and many servants, so that the Philistines envied him. [15] (Now the Philistines had stopped and filled with earth all the wells that his father's servants had dug in the days of Abraham his father.) [16] And Abimelech said to Isaac, "Go away from us, for you are much mightier than we."

[17] So Isaac departed from there and encamped in the Valley of Gerar and settled there. [18] And Isaac dug again the wells of water that had been dug in the days of Abraham his father, which the Philistines had stopped after the death of Abraham. And he gave them the names that his father had given them. [19] But when Isaac's servants dug in the valley and found there a well of spring water, [20] the herdsmen of Gerar quarreled with Isaac's herdsmen, saying, "The water is ours." So he called the name of the well Esek,[1] because they contended with him. [21] Then they dug another well, and they quarreled over that also, so he called its name Sitnah.[2] [22] And he moved from there and dug another well, and they did not quarrel over it. So he called its name Rehoboth,[3] saying, "For now the LORD has made room for us, and we shall be fruitful in the land."

[23] From there he went up to Beersheba. [24] And the LORD appeared to him the same night and said, "I am the God of Abraham your father. Fear not, for I am with you and will bless you and multiply your offspring for my servant Abraham's sake." [25] So he built an altar there and called upon the name of the LORD and pitched his tent there. And there Isaac's servants dug a well.

[26] When Abimelech went to him from Gerar with Ahuzzath his adviser and Phicol the commander of his army, [27] Isaac said to them, "Why have you come to me, seeing that you hate me and have sent me away from you?" [28] They said, "We see plainly that the LORD has been with you. So we said, let there be a sworn pact between us, between you and us, and let us make a covenant with you, [29] that you will do us no harm, just as we have not touched you and have done to you nothing but good and have sent you away in peace. You are now the blessed of the LORD." [30] So he made them a feast, and they ate and drank. [31] In the morning they rose early and exchanged oaths. And Isaac sent them on their way, and they departed from him in peace. [32] That same day Isaac's servants came and told him about the well that they had dug and said to him, "We have found water." [33] He called it Shibah;[4] therefore the name of the city is Beersheba to this day.

[34] When Esau was forty years old, he took Judith the daughter of Beeri the Hittite to be his wife, and Basemath the daughter of Elon the Hittite, [35] and they made life bitter[5] for Isaac and Rebekah.

Isaac Blesses Jacob

27 When Isaac was old and his eyes were dim so that he could not see, he called Esau his older son and said to him, "My son"; and he answered, "Here I am." [2] He said, "Behold, I am old; I do not know the day of my death. [3] Now then, take your weapons, your quiver and your bow, and go out to the field and hunt game for me, [4] and prepare for me delicious food, such as I love, and bring it to me so that I may eat, that my soul may bless you before I die."

[5] Now Rebekah was listening when Isaac spoke to his son Esau. So when Esau went to the field to hunt for game and bring it, [6] Rebekah said to her son Jacob, "I heard your father speak to your brother Esau, [7] 'Bring me game and prepare for me delicious food, that I may eat it and bless you before the LORD before I die.' [8] Now therefore, my son, obey my voice as I command you. [9] Go to the flock and bring me two

---

[1] *Esek* means *contention* [2] *Sitnah* means *enmity* [3] *Rehoboth* means *broad places*, or *room* [4] *Shibah* sounds like the Hebrew for *oath*
[5] Hebrew *they were bitterness of spirit*

good young goats, so that I may prepare from them delicious food for your father, such as he loves. ¹⁰ And you shall bring it to your father to eat, so that he may bless you before he dies." ¹¹ But Jacob said to Rebekah his mother, "Behold, my brother Esau is a hairy man, and I am a smooth man. ¹² Perhaps my father will feel me, and I shall seem to be mocking him and bring a curse upon myself and not a blessing." ¹³ His mother said to him, "Let your curse be on me, my son; only obey my voice, and go, bring them to me."

¹⁴ So he went and took them and brought them to his mother, and his mother prepared delicious food, such as his father loved. ¹⁵ Then Rebekah took the best garments of Esau her older son, which were with her in the house, and put them on Jacob her younger son. ¹⁶ And the skins of the young goats she put on his hands and on the smooth part of his neck. ¹⁷ And she put the delicious food and the bread, which she had prepared, into the hand of her son Jacob.

¹⁸ So he went in to his father and said, "My father." And he said, "Here I am. Who are you, my son?" ¹⁹ Jacob said to his father, "I am Esau your firstborn. I have done as you told me; now sit up and eat of my game, that your soul may bless me." ²⁰ But Isaac said to his son, "How is it that you have found it so quickly, my son?" He answered, "Because the LORD your God granted me success." ²¹ Then Isaac said to Jacob, "Please come near, that I may feel you, my son, to know whether you are really my son Esau or not." ²² So Jacob went near to Isaac his father, who felt him and said, "The voice is Jacob's voice, but the hands are the hands of Esau." ²³ And he did not recognize him, because his hands were hairy like his brother Esau's hands. So he blessed him. ²⁴ He said, "Are you really my son Esau?" He answered, "I am." ²⁵ Then he said, "Bring it near to me, that I may eat of my son's game and bless you." So he brought it near to him, and he ate; and he brought him wine, and he drank.

²⁶ Then his father Isaac said to him, "Come near and kiss me, my son." ²⁷ So he came near and kissed him. And Isaac smelled the smell of his garments and blessed him and said,

"See, the smell of my son
    is as the smell of a field that the
    LORD has blessed!
²⁸ May God give you of the dew of
        heaven
    and of the fatness of the earth
    and plenty of grain and wine.
²⁹ Let peoples serve you,
    and nations bow down to you.
Be lord over your brothers,
    and may your mother's sons bow
        down to you.
Cursed be everyone who curses you,
    and blessed be everyone who
        blesses you!"

³⁰ As soon as Isaac had finished blessing Jacob, when Jacob had scarcely gone out from the presence of Isaac his father, Esau his brother came in from his hunting. ³¹ He also prepared delicious food and brought it to his father. And he said to his father, "Let my father arise and eat of his son's game, that you may bless me." ³² His father Isaac said to him, "Who are you?" He answered, "I am your son, your firstborn, Esau." ³³ Then Isaac trembled very violently and said, "Who was it then that hunted game and brought it to me, and I ate it all before you came, and I have blessed him? Yes, and he shall be blessed." ³⁴ As soon as Esau heard the words of his father, he cried out with an exceedingly great and bitter cry and said to his father, "Bless me, even me also, O my father!" ³⁵ But he said, "Your brother came deceitfully, and he has taken away your blessing." ³⁶ Esau said, "Is he not rightly named Jacob?[1] For he has cheated me these two times. He took away my birthright, and behold, now he has taken away my blessing." Then he said, "Have you not reserved a blessing for me?" ³⁷ Isaac answered and said to Esau, "Behold, I have made him lord over you, and all his brothers I have given to him for servants, and with grain and wine I have sustained him. What then can I do for you, my son?" ³⁸ Esau said to his father, "Have you but one blessing, my father? Bless me, even me also, O my father." And Esau lifted up his voice and wept.

³⁹ Then Isaac his father answered and said to him:

---

[1] *Jacob* means *He takes by the heel*, or *He cheats*

"Behold, away from[1] the fatness of the
    earth shall your dwelling be,
    and away from[2] the dew of heaven
        on high.
[40]   By your sword you shall live,
    and you shall serve your brother;
    but when you grow restless
    you shall break his yoke from your
        neck."

[41] Now Esau hated Jacob because of the
blessing with which his father had blessed
him, and Esau said to himself, "The days of
mourning for my father are approaching;
then I will kill my brother Jacob." [42] But
the words of Esau her older son were told
to Rebekah. So she sent and called Jacob
her younger son and said to him, "Behold,
your brother Esau comforts himself about
you by planning to kill you. [43] Now therefore, my son, obey my voice. Arise, flee
to Laban my brother in Haran [44] and stay
with him a while, until your brother's fury
turns away— [45] until your brother's anger
turns away from you, and he forgets what
you have done to him. Then I will send
and bring you from there. Why should I be
bereft of you both in one day?"

[46] Then Rebekah said to Isaac, "I loathe
my life because of the Hittite women.[3] If
Jacob marries one of the Hittite women like
these, one of the women of the land, what
good will my life be to me?"

Jacob Sent to Laban

28 Then Isaac called Jacob and blessed
him and directed him, "You must not
take a wife from the Canaanite women.
[2] Arise, go to Paddan-aram to the house
of Bethuel your mother's father, and take
as your wife from there one of the daughters of Laban your mother's brother. [3] God
Almighty[4] bless you and make you fruitful
and multiply you, that you may become
a company of peoples. [4] May he give the
blessing of Abraham to you and to your
offspring with you, that you may take possession of the land of your sojournings that
God gave to Abraham!" [5] Thus Isaac sent
Jacob away. And he went to Paddan-aram,
to Laban, the son of Bethuel the Aramean,
the brother of Rebekah, Jacob's and Esau's
mother.

Esau Marries an Ishmaelite

[6] Now Esau saw that Isaac had blessed
Jacob and sent him away to Paddan-aram
to take a wife from there, and that as he
blessed him he directed him, "You must
not take a wife from the Canaanite women,"
[7] and that Jacob had obeyed his father and
his mother and gone to Paddan-aram. [8] So
when Esau saw that the Canaanite women
did not please Isaac his father, [9] Esau went
to Ishmael and took as his wife, besides
the wives he had, Mahalath the daughter
of Ishmael, Abraham's son, the sister of
Nebaioth.

Jacob's Dream

[10] Jacob left Beersheba and went toward
Haran. [11] And he came to a certain place
and stayed there that night, because the
sun had set. Taking one of the stones of
the place, he put it under his head and
lay down in that place to sleep. [12] And he
dreamed, and behold, there was a lad-
der[5] set up on the earth, and the top of it
reached to heaven. And behold, the angels
of God were ascending and descending on
it! [13] And behold, the LORD stood above
it[6] and said, "I am the LORD, the God of
Abraham your father and the God of Isaac.
The land on which you lie I will give to you
and to your offspring. [14] Your offspring shall
be like the dust of the earth, and you shall
spread abroad to the west and to the east
and to the north and to the south, and in
you and your offspring shall all the families of the earth be blessed. [15] Behold, I am
with you and will keep you wherever you
go, and will bring you back to this land.
For I will not leave you until I have done
what I have promised you." [16] Then Jacob
awoke from his sleep and said, "Surely the
LORD is in this place, and I did not know
it." [17] And he was afraid and said, "How
awesome is this place! This is none other
than the house of God, and this is the gate
of heaven."

[18] So early in the morning Jacob took the
stone that he had put under his head and
set it up for a pillar and poured oil on the
top of it. [19] He called the name of that place
Bethel,[7] but the name of the city was Luz
at the first. [20] Then Jacob made a vow, saying, "If God will be with me and will keep
me in this way that I go, and will give me

[1] Or Behold, of [2] Or and of [3] Hebrew *daughters of Heth* [4] Hebrew *El Shaddai* [5] Or *a flight of steps* [6] Or *beside him* [7] *Bethel* means *the house of God*

bread to eat and clothing to wear, [21] so that I come again to my father's house in peace, then the LORD shall be my God, [22] and this stone, which I have set up for a pillar, shall be God's house. And of all that you give me I will give a full tenth to you."

Jacob Marries Leah and Rachel

29 Then Jacob went on his journey and came to the land of the people of the east. [2] As he looked, he saw a well in the field, and behold, three flocks of sheep lying beside it, for out of that well the flocks were watered. The stone on the well's mouth was large, [3] and when all the flocks were gathered there, the shepherds would roll the stone from the mouth of the well and water the sheep, and put the stone back in its place over the mouth of the well. [4] Jacob said to them, "My brothers, where do you come from?" They said, "We are from Haran." [5] He said to them, "Do you know Laban the son of Nahor?" They said, "We know him." [6] He said to them, "Is it well with him?" They said, "It is well; and see, Rachel his daughter is coming with the sheep!" [7] He said, "Behold, it is still high day; it is not time for the livestock to be gathered together. Water the sheep and go, pasture them." [8] But they said, "We cannot until all the flocks are gathered together and the stone is rolled from the mouth of the well; then we water the sheep."

[9] While he was still speaking with them, Rachel came with her father's sheep, for she was a shepherdess. [10] Now as soon as Jacob saw Rachel the daughter of Laban his mother's brother, and the sheep of Laban his mother's brother, Jacob came near and rolled the stone from the well's mouth and watered the flock of Laban his mother's brother. [11] Then Jacob kissed Rachel and wept aloud. [12] And Jacob told Rachel that he was her father's kinsman, and that he was Rebekah's son, and she ran and told her father.

[13] As soon as Laban heard the news about Jacob, his sister's son, he ran to meet him and embraced him and kissed him and brought him to his house. Jacob told Laban all these things, [14] and Laban said to him, "Surely you are my bone and my flesh!" And he stayed with him a month.

[15] Then Laban said to Jacob, "Because you are my kinsman, should you therefore serve me for nothing? Tell me, what shall your wages be?" [16] Now Laban had two daughters. The name of the older was Leah, and the name of the younger was Rachel. [17] Leah's eyes were weak,[1] but Rachel was beautiful in form and appearance. [18] Jacob loved Rachel. And he said, "I will serve you seven years for your younger daughter Rachel." [19] Laban said, "It is better that I give her to you than that I should give her to any other man; stay with me." [20] So Jacob served seven years for Rachel, and they seemed to him but a few days because of the love he had for her.

[21] Then Jacob said to Laban, "Give me my wife that I may go in to her, for my time is completed." [22] So Laban gathered together all the people of the place and made a feast. [23] But in the evening he took his daughter Leah and brought her to Jacob, and he went in to her. [24] (Laban gave[2] his female servant Zilpah to his daughter Leah to be her servant.) [25] And in the morning, behold, it was Leah! And Jacob said to Laban, "What is this you have done to me? Did I not serve with you for Rachel? Why then have you deceived me?" [26] Laban said, "It is not so done in our country, to give the younger before the firstborn. [27] Complete the week of this one, and we will give you the other also in return for serving me another seven years." [28] Jacob did so, and completed her week. Then Laban gave him his daughter Rachel to be his wife. [29] (Laban gave his female servant Bilhah to his daughter Rachel to be her servant.) [30] So Jacob went in to Rachel also, and he loved Rachel more than Leah, and served Laban for another seven years.

Jacob's Children

[31] When the LORD saw that Leah was hated, he opened her womb, but Rachel was barren. [32] And Leah conceived and bore a son, and she called his name Reuben,[3] for she said, "Because the LORD has looked upon my affliction; for now my husband will love me." [33] She conceived again and bore a son, and said, "Because the LORD has heard that I am hated, he has given me this son also." And she called his name Simeon.[4] [34] Again she conceived and bore a son, and said, "Now this time my husband will be attached to me, because I have borne him three sons." Therefore his name was called

---

[1] Or soft   [2] Or had given; also verse 29   [3] Reuben means See, a son   [4] Simeon sounds like the Hebrew for heard

Levi.[1] [35] And she conceived again and bore a son, and said, "This time I will praise the LORD." Therefore she called his name Judah.[2] Then she ceased bearing.

30 When Rachel saw that she bore Jacob no children, she envied her sister. She said to Jacob, "Give me children, or I shall die!" [2] Jacob's anger was kindled against Rachel, and he said, "Am I in the place of God, who has withheld from you the fruit of the womb?" [3] Then she said, "Here is my servant Bilhah; go in to her, so that she may give birth on my behalf,[3] that even I may have children[4] through her." [4] So she gave him her servant Bilhah as a wife, and Jacob went in to her. [5] And Bilhah conceived and bore Jacob a son. [6] Then Rachel said, "God has judged me, and has also heard my voice and given me a son." Therefore she called his name Dan.[5] [7] Rachel's servant Bilhah conceived again and bore Jacob a second son. [8] Then Rachel said, "With mighty wrestlings[6] I have wrestled with my sister and have prevailed." So she called his name Naphtali.[7]

[9] When Leah saw that she had ceased bearing children, she took her servant Zilpah and gave her to Jacob as a wife. [10] Then Leah's servant Zilpah bore Jacob a son. [11] And Leah said, "Good fortune has come!" so she called his name Gad.[8] [12] Leah's servant Zilpah bore Jacob a second son. [13] And Leah said, "Happy am I! For women have called me happy." So she called his name Asher.[9]

[14] In the days of wheat harvest Reuben went and found mandrakes in the field and brought them to his mother Leah. Then Rachel said to Leah, "Please give me some of your son's mandrakes." [15] But she said to her, "Is it a small matter that you have taken away my husband? Would you take away my son's mandrakes also?" Rachel said, "Then he may lie with you tonight in exchange for your son's mandrakes." [16] When Jacob came from the field in the evening, Leah went out to meet him and said, "You must come in to me, for I have hired you with my son's mandrakes." So he lay with her that night. [17] And God listened to Leah, and she conceived and bore Jacob

a fifth son. [18] Leah said, "God has given me my wages because I gave my servant to my husband." So she called his name Issachar.[10]

[19] And Leah conceived again, and she bore Jacob a sixth son. [20] Then Leah said, "God has endowed me with a good endowment; now my husband will honor me, because I have borne him six sons." So she called his name Zebulun.[11] [21] Afterward she bore a daughter and called her name Dinah.

[22] Then God remembered Rachel, and God listened to her and opened her womb. [23] She conceived and bore a son and said, "God has taken away my reproach." [24] And she called his name Joseph,[12] saying, "May the LORD add to me another son!"

Jacob's Prosperity

[25] As soon as Rachel had borne Joseph, Jacob said to Laban, "Send me away, that I may go to my own home and country. [26] Give me my wives and my children for whom I have served you, that I may go, for you know the service that I have given you." [27] But Laban said to him, "If I have found favor in your sight, I have learned by divination that[13] the LORD has blessed me because of you. [28] Name your wages, and I will give it." [29] Jacob said to him, "You yourself know how I have served you, and how your livestock has fared with me. [30] For you had little before I came, and it has increased abundantly, and the LORD has blessed you wherever I turned. But now when shall I provide for my own household also?" [31] He said, "What shall I give you?" Jacob said, "You shall not give me anything. If you will do this for me, I will again pasture your flock and keep it: [32] let me pass through all your flock today, removing from it every speckled and spotted sheep and every black lamb, and the spotted and speckled among the goats, and they shall be my wages. [33] So my honesty will answer for me later, when you come to look into my wages with you. Every one that is not speckled and spotted among the goats and black among the lambs, if found with me, shall be counted stolen." [34] Laban said, "Good! Let it be as you have said." [35] But that day Laban removed the male goats that were striped and spotted,

---

[1] *Levi* sounds like the Hebrew for *attached* [2] *Judah* sounds like the Hebrew for *praise* [3] Hebrew *on my knees* [4] Hebrew *be built up*, which sounds like the Hebrew for *children* [5] *Dan* sounds like the Hebrew for *judged* [6] Hebrew *With wrestlings of God* [7] *Naphtali* sounds like the Hebrew for *wrestling* [8] *Gad* sounds like the Hebrew for *good fortune* [9] *Asher* sounds like the Hebrew for *happy* [10] *Issachar* sounds like the Hebrew for *wages*, or *hire* [11] *Zebulun* sounds like the Hebrew for *honor* [12] *Joseph* means *May he add*, and sounds like the Hebrew for *taken away* [13] Or *have become rich and*

and all the female goats that were speckled and spotted, every one that had white on it, and every lamb that was black, and put them in the charge of his sons. ³⁶ And he set a distance of three days' journey between himself and Jacob, and Jacob pastured the rest of Laban's flock.

³⁷ Then Jacob took fresh sticks of poplar and almond and plane trees, and peeled white streaks in them, exposing the white of the sticks. ³⁸ He set the sticks that he had peeled in front of the flocks in the troughs, that is, the watering places, where the flocks came to drink. And since they bred when they came to drink, ³⁹ the flocks bred in front of the sticks and so the flocks brought forth striped, speckled, and spotted. ⁴⁰ And Jacob separated the lambs and set the faces of the flocks toward the striped and all the black in the flock of Laban. He put his own droves apart and did not put them with Laban's flock. ⁴¹ Whenever the stronger of the flock were breeding, Jacob would lay the sticks in the troughs before the eyes of the flock, that they might breed among the sticks, ⁴² but for the feebler of the flock he would not lay them there. So the feebler would be Laban's, and the stronger Jacob's. ⁴³ Thus the man increased greatly and had large flocks, female servants and male servants, and camels and donkeys.

Jacob Flees from Laban

31 Now Jacob heard that the sons of Laban were saying, "Jacob has taken all that was our father's, and from what was our father's he has gained all this wealth." ² And Jacob saw that Laban did not regard him with favor as before. ³ Then the LORD said to Jacob, "Return to the land of your fathers and to your kindred, and I will be with you."

⁴ So Jacob sent and called Rachel and Leah into the field where his flock was ⁵ and said to them, "I see that your father does not regard me with favor as he did before. But the God of my father has been with me. ⁶ You know that I have served your father with all my strength, ⁷ yet your father has cheated me and changed my wages ten times. But God did not permit him to harm me. ⁸ If he said, 'The spotted shall be your wages,' then all the flock bore spotted; and if he said, 'The striped shall be your wages,'

then all the flock bore striped. ⁹ Thus God has taken away the livestock of your father and given them to me. ¹⁰ In the breeding season of the flock I lifted up my eyes and saw in a dream that the goats that mated with the flock were striped, spotted, and mottled. ¹¹ Then the angel of God said to me in the dream, 'Jacob,' and I said, 'Here I am!' ¹² And he said, 'Lift up your eyes and see, all the goats that mate with the flock are striped, spotted, and mottled, for I have seen all that Laban is doing to you. ¹³ I am the God of Bethel, where you anointed a pillar and made a vow to me. Now arise, go out from this land and return to the land of your kindred.'" ¹⁴ Then Rachel and Leah answered and said to him, "Is there any portion or inheritance left to us in our father's house? ¹⁵ Are we not regarded by him as foreigners? For he has sold us, and he has indeed devoured our money. ¹⁶ All the wealth that God has taken away from our father belongs to us and to our children. Now then, whatever God has said to you, do."

¹⁷ So Jacob arose and set his sons and his wives on camels. ¹⁸ He drove away all his livestock, all his property that he had gained, the livestock in his possession that he had acquired in Paddan-aram, to go to the land of Canaan to his father Isaac. ¹⁹ Laban had gone to shear his sheep, and Rachel stole her father's household gods. ²⁰ And Jacob tricked¹ Laban the Aramean, by not telling him that he intended to flee. ²¹ He fled with all that he had and arose and crossed the Euphrates,² and set his face toward the hill country of Gilead.

²² When it was told Laban on the third day that Jacob had fled, ²³ he took his kinsmen with him and pursued him for seven days and followed close after him into the hill country of Gilead. ²⁴ But God came to Laban the Aramean in a dream by night and said to him, "Be careful not to say anything to Jacob, either good or bad."

²⁵ And Laban overtook Jacob. Now Jacob had pitched his tent in the hill country, and Laban with his kinsmen pitched tents in the hill country of Gilead. ²⁶ And Laban said to Jacob, "What have you done, that you have tricked me and driven away my daughters like captives of the sword? ²⁷ Why did you flee secretly and trick me, and did not tell me, so that I might have

¹ Hebrew *stole the heart of*; also verses 26, 27 ² Hebrew *the River*

sent you away with mirth and songs, with tambourine and lyre? 28 And why did you not permit me to kiss my sons and my daughters farewell? Now you have done foolishly. 29 It is in my power to do you harm. But the God of your[1] father spoke to me last night, saying, 'Be careful not to say anything to Jacob, either good or bad.' 30 And now you have gone away because you longed greatly for your father's house, but why did you steal my gods?" 31 Jacob answered and said to Laban, "Because I was afraid, for I thought that you would take your daughters from me by force. 32 Anyone with whom you find your gods shall not live. In the presence of our kinsmen point out what I have that is yours, and take it." Now Jacob did not know that Rachel had stolen them.

33 So Laban went into Jacob's tent and into Leah's tent and into the tent of the two female servants, but he did not find them. And he went out of Leah's tent and entered Rachel's. 34 Now Rachel had taken the household gods and put them in the camel's saddle and sat on them. Laban felt all about the tent, but did not find them. 35 And she said to her father, "Let not my lord be angry that I cannot rise before you, for the way of women is upon me." So he searched but did not find the household gods.

36 Then Jacob became angry and berated Laban. Jacob said to Laban, "What is my offense? What is my sin, that you have hotly pursued me? 37 For you have felt through all my goods; what have you found of all your household goods? Set it here before my kinsmen and your kinsmen, that they may decide between us two. 38 These twenty years I have been with you. Your ewes and your female goats have not miscarried, and I have not eaten the rams of your flocks. 39 What was torn by wild beasts I did not bring to you. I bore the loss of it myself. From my hand you required it, whether stolen by day or stolen by night. 40 There I was: by day the heat consumed me, and the cold by night, and my sleep fled from my eyes. 41 These twenty years I have been in your house. I served you fourteen years for your two daughters, and six years for your flock, and you have changed my wages ten times. 42 If the God of my father,

the God of Abraham and the Fear of Isaac, had not been on my side, surely now you would have sent me away empty-handed. God saw my affliction and the labor of my hands and rebuked you last night."

43 Then Laban answered and said to Jacob, "The daughters are my daughters, the children are my children, the flocks are my flocks, and all that you see is mine. But what can I do this day for these my daughters or for their children whom they have borne? 44 Come now, let us make a covenant, you and I. And let it be a witness between you and me." 45 So Jacob took a stone and set it up as a pillar. 46 And Jacob said to his kinsmen, "Gather stones." And they took stones and made a heap, and they ate there by the heap. 47 Laban called it Jegar-sahadutha,[2] but Jacob called it Galeed.[3] 48 Laban said, "This heap is a witness between you and me today." Therefore he named it Galeed, 49 and Mizpah,[4] for he said, "The LORD watch between you and me, when we are out of one another's sight. 50 If you oppress my daughters, or if you take wives besides my daughters, although no one is with us, see, God is witness between you and me."

51 Then Laban said to Jacob, "See this heap and the pillar, which I have set between you and me. 52 This heap is a witness, and the pillar is a witness, that I will not pass over this heap to you, and you will not pass over this heap and this pillar to me, to do harm. 53 The God of Abraham and the God of Nahor, the God of their father, judge between us." So Jacob swore by the Fear of his father Isaac, 54 and Jacob offered a sacrifice in the hill country and called his kinsmen to eat bread. They ate bread and spent the night in the hill country.

55 [5] Early in the morning Laban arose and kissed his grandchildren and his daughters and blessed them. Then Laban departed and returned home.

Jacob Fears Esau

32 Jacob went on his way, and the angels of God met him. 2 And when Jacob saw them he said, "This is God's camp!" So he called the name of that place Mahanaim.[6]

3 And Jacob sent[7] messengers before him to Esau his brother in the land of Seir, the

---

[1] The Hebrew for *your* is plural here [2] Aramaic *the heap of witness* [3] Hebrew *the heap of witness* [4] *Mizpah* means *watchpost* [5] Ch 32:1 in Hebrew [6] *Mahanaim* means *two camps* [7] Or *had sent*

country of Edom, ⁴instructing them, "Thus you shall say to my lord Esau: Thus says your servant Jacob, 'I have sojourned with Laban and stayed until now. ⁵I have oxen, donkeys, flocks, male servants, and female servants. I have sent to tell my lord, in order that I may find favor in your sight.'"

⁶And the messengers returned to Jacob, saying, "We came to your brother Esau, and he is coming to meet you, and there are four hundred men with him." ⁷Then Jacob was greatly afraid and distressed. He divided the people who were with him, and the flocks and herds and camels, into two camps, ⁸thinking, "If Esau comes to the one camp and attacks it, then the camp that is left will escape."

⁹And Jacob said, "O God of my father Abraham and God of my father Isaac, O LORD who said to me, 'Return to your country and to your kindred, that I may do you good,' ¹⁰I am not worthy of the least of all the deeds of steadfast love and all the faithfulness that you have shown to your servant, for with only my staff I crossed

this Jordan, and now I have become two camps. ¹¹Please deliver me from the hand of my brother, from the hand of Esau, for I fear him, that he may come and attack me, the mothers with the children. ¹²But you said, 'I will surely do you good, and make your offspring as the sand of the sea, which cannot be numbered for multitude.'"

¹³So he stayed there that night, and from what he had with him he took a present for his brother Esau, ¹⁴two hundred female goats and twenty male goats, two hundred ewes and twenty rams, ¹⁵thirty milking camels and their calves, forty cows and ten bulls, twenty female donkeys and ten male donkeys. ¹⁶These he handed over to his servants, every drove by itself, and said to his servants, "Pass on ahead of me and put a space between drove and drove." ¹⁷He instructed the first, "When Esau my brother meets you and asks you, 'To whom do you belong? Where are you going? And whose are these ahead of you?' ¹⁸then you shall say, 'They belong to your servant Jacob. They are a present sent to my

Know God

verses to read
Genesis 32:9–12

If you want more faith, then you're going to need more prayer. As you pray, you learn to trust the God who answers prayer. It is like exercise. The more weight you lift, the stronger your body gets, and the more you pray, the stronger your faith gets. Neglecting God's call to prayer leads to spiritual weakness and failure. If you want more trust, if you want more hope, more faith, and more strength, then you need more prayer. You can't let prayer take a backseat in your life. It has to be the most important part of your day. It sets the tone for your life. Without it your faith is useless and weak.

When you love someone, you want to spend time with them and talk with them. And when you need something from someone, you have to communicate—you have to ask them for what you need. Prayer is your communication with God. It's the way you connect, the way you come into his presence and learn his character. It's the way your life comes to really mean something, because through praying for others you can change their lives. And as those lives change, your trust in God deepens and their lives improve. It's a win-win.

Prayer is a powerful thing in the hands of a God Girl. Don't ever underestimate its strength and its ability to change not only your life but the lives of the people you pray for. Jacob's willingness to go to God for his needs brought divine help for his entire family. And your prayers may just serve to help not only you but the people around you as well.

lord Esau. And moreover, he is behind us.'"
[19] He likewise instructed the second and the third and all who followed the droves, "You shall say the same thing to Esau when you find him, [20] and you shall say, 'Moreover, your servant Jacob is behind us.'" For he thought, "I may appease him[1] with the present that goes ahead of me, and afterward I shall see his face. Perhaps he will accept me."[2] [21] So the present passed on ahead of him, and he himself stayed that night in the camp.

Jacob Wrestles with God

[22] The same night he arose and took his two wives, his two female servants, and his eleven children,[3] and crossed the ford of the Jabbok. [23] He took them and sent them across the stream, and everything else that he had. [24] And Jacob was left alone. And a man wrestled with him until the breaking of the day. [25] When the man saw that he did not prevail against Jacob, he touched his hip socket, and Jacob's hip was put out of joint as he wrestled with him. [26] Then he said, "Let me go, for the day has broken." But Jacob said, "I will not let you go unless you bless me." [27] And he said to him, "What is your name?" And he said, "Jacob." [28] Then he said, "Your name shall no longer be called Jacob, but Israel,[4] for you have striven with God and with men, and have prevailed." [29] Then Jacob asked him, "Please tell me your name." But he said, "Why is it that you ask my name?" And there he blessed him. [30] So Jacob called the name of the place Peniel,[5] saying, "For I have seen God face to face, and yet my life has been delivered." [31] The sun rose upon him as he passed Penuel, limping because of his hip. [32] Therefore to this day the people of Israel do not eat the sinew of the thigh that is on the hip socket, because he touched the socket of Jacob's hip on the sinew of the thigh.

Jacob Meets Esau

33 And Jacob lifted up his eyes and looked, and behold, Esau was coming, and four hundred men with him. So he divided the children among Leah and Rachel and the two female servants. [2] And he put the servants with their children in front, then Leah with her children, and Rachel and Joseph last of all. [3] He himself went on before them, bowing himself to the ground seven times, until he came near to his brother.

[4] But Esau ran to meet him and embraced him and fell on his neck and kissed him, and they wept. [5] And when Esau lifted up his eyes and saw the women and children, he said, "Who are these with you?" Jacob said, "The children whom God has graciously given your servant." [6] Then the servants drew near, they and their children, and bowed down. [7] Leah likewise and her children drew near and bowed down. And last Joseph and Rachel drew near, and they bowed down. [8] Esau said, "What do you mean by all this company[6] that I met?" Jacob answered, "To find favor in the sight of my lord." [9] But Esau said, "I have enough, my brother; keep what you have for yourself." [10] Jacob said, "No, please, if I have found favor in your sight, then accept my present from my hand. For I have seen your face, which is like seeing the face of God, and you have accepted me. [11] Please accept my blessing that is brought to you, because God has dealt graciously with me, and because I have enough." Thus he urged him, and he took it.

[12] Then Esau said, "Let us journey on our way, and I will go ahead of[7] you." [13] But Jacob said to him, "My lord knows that the children are frail, and that the nursing flocks and herds are a care to me. If they are driven hard for one day, all the flocks will die. [14] Let my lord pass on ahead of his servant, and I will lead on slowly, at the pace of the livestock that are ahead of me and at the pace of the children, until I come to my lord in Seir."

[15] So Esau said, "Let me leave with you some of the people who are with me." But he said, "What need is there? Let me find favor in the sight of my lord." [16] So Esau returned that day on his way to Seir. [17] But Jacob journeyed to Succoth, and built himself a house and made booths for his livestock. Therefore the name of the place is called Succoth.[8]

[18] And Jacob came safely[9] to the city of Shechem, which is in the land of Canaan, on his way from Paddan-aram, and he camped before the city. [19] And from the sons of Hamor, Shechem's father, he bought

[1] Hebrew *appease his face* [2] Hebrew *he will lift my face* [3] Or *sons* [4] *Israel* means *He strives with God*, or *God strives* [5] *Peniel* means *the face of God* [6] Hebrew *camp* [7] Or *along with* [8] *Succoth* means *booths* [9] Or *peacefully*

for a hundred pieces of money[1] the piece of land on which he had pitched his tent. [20] There he erected an altar and called it El-Elohe-Israel.[2]

The Defiling of Dinah

34 Now Dinah the daughter of Leah, whom she had borne to Jacob, went out to see the women of the land. [2] And when Shechem the son of Hamor the Hivite, the prince of the land, saw her, he seized her and lay with her and humiliated her. [3] And his soul was drawn to Dinah the daughter of Jacob. He loved the young woman and spoke tenderly to her. [4] So Shechem spoke to his father Hamor, saying, "Get me this girl for my wife."

[5] Now Jacob heard that he had defiled his daughter Dinah. But his sons were with his livestock in the field, so Jacob held his peace until they came. [6] And Hamor the father of Shechem went out to Jacob to speak with him. [7] The sons of Jacob had come in from the field as soon as they heard of it, and the men were indignant and very angry, because he had done an outrageous thing in Israel by lying with Jacob's daughter, for such a thing must not be done.

[8] But Hamor spoke with them, saying, "The soul of my son Shechem longs for your[3] daughter. Please give her to him to be his wife. [9] Make marriages with us. Give your daughters to us, and take our daughters for yourselves. [10] You shall dwell with us, and the land shall be open to you. Dwell and trade in it, and get property in it." [11] Shechem also said to her father and to her brothers, "Let me find favor in your eyes, and whatever you say to me I will give. [12] Ask me for as great a bride price[4] and gift as you will, and I will give whatever you say to me. Only give me the young woman to be my wife."

[13] The sons of Jacob answered Shechem and his father Hamor deceitfully, because he had defiled their sister Dinah. [14] They said to them, "We cannot do this thing, to give our sister to one who is uncircumcised, for that would be a disgrace to us. [15] Only on this condition will we agree with you—that you will become as we are by every male among you being circumcised. [16] Then we will give our daughters to you, and we will take your daughters to ourselves, and we will dwell with you and become one people. [17] But if you will not listen to us and be circumcised, then we will take our daughter, and we will be gone."

[18] Their words pleased Hamor and Hamor's son Shechem. [19] And the young man did not delay to do the thing, because he delighted in Jacob's daughter. Now he was the most honored of all his father's house. [20] So Hamor and his son Shechem came to the gate of their city and spoke to the men of their city, saying, [21] "These men are at peace with us; let them dwell in the land and trade in it, for behold, the land is large enough for them. Let us take their daughters as wives, and let us give them our daughters. [22] Only on this condition will the men agree to dwell with us to become one people—when every male among us is circumcised as they are circumcised. [23] Will not their livestock, their property and all their beasts be ours? Only let us agree with them, and they will dwell with us." [24] And all who went out of the gate of his city listened to Hamor and his son Shechem, and every male was circumcised, all who went out of the gate of his city.

[25] On the third day, when they were sore, two of the sons of Jacob, Simeon and Levi, Dinah's brothers, took their swords and came against the city while it felt secure and killed all the males. [26] They killed Hamor and his son Shechem with the sword and took Dinah out of Shechem's house and went away. [27] The sons of Jacob came upon the slain and plundered the city, because they had defiled their sister. [28] They took their flocks and their herds, their donkeys, and whatever was in the city and in the field. [29] All their wealth, all their little ones and their wives, all that was in the houses, they captured and plundered.

[30] Then Jacob said to Simeon and Levi, "You have brought trouble on me by making me stink to the inhabitants of the land, the Canaanites and the Perizzites. My numbers are few, and if they gather themselves against me and attack me, I shall be destroyed, both I and my household." [31] But they said, "Should he treat our sister like a prostitute?"

[1] Hebrew *a hundred qesitah*; a unit of money of unknown value [2] *El-Elohe-Israel* means *God, the God of Israel* [3] The Hebrew for *your* is plural here [4] Or *engagement present*

God Blesses and Renames Jacob

35 God said to Jacob, "Arise, go up to Bethel and dwell there. Make an altar there to the God who appeared to you when you fled from your brother Esau." ² So Jacob said to his household and to all who were with him, "Put away the foreign gods that are among you and purify yourselves and change your garments. ³ Then let us arise and go up to Bethel, so that I may make there an altar to the God who answers me in the day of my distress and has been with me wherever I have gone." ⁴ So they gave to Jacob all the foreign gods that they had, and the rings that were in their ears. Jacob hid them under the terebinth tree that was near Shechem.

⁵ And as they journeyed, a terror from God fell upon the cities that were around them, so that they did not pursue the sons of Jacob. ⁶ And Jacob came to Luz (that is, Bethel), which is in the land of Canaan, he and all the people who were with him, ⁷ and there he built an altar and called the place El-bethel,[1] because there God had revealed himself to him when he fled from his brother. ⁸ And Deborah, Rebekah's nurse, died, and she was buried under an oak below Bethel. So he called its name Allon-bacuth.[2]

⁹ God appeared[3] to Jacob again, when he came from Paddan-aram, and blessed him. ¹⁰ And God said to him, "Your name is Jacob; no longer shall your name be called Jacob, but Israel shall be your name." So he called his name Israel. ¹¹ And God said to him, "I am God Almighty:[4] be fruitful and multiply. A nation and a company of nations shall come from you, and kings shall come from your own body.[5] ¹² The land that I gave to Abraham and Isaac I will give to you, and I will give the land to your offspring after you." ¹³ Then God went up from him in the place where he had spoken with him. ¹⁴ And Jacob set up a pillar in the place where he had spoken with him, a pillar of stone. He poured out a drink offering on it and poured oil on it. ¹⁵ So Jacob called the name of the place where God had spoken with him Bethel.

The Deaths of Rachel and Isaac

¹⁶ Then they journeyed from Bethel. When they were still some distance[6] from Ephrath, Rachel went into labor, and she had hard labor. ¹⁷ And when her labor was at its hardest, the midwife said to her, "Do not fear, for you have another son." ¹⁸ And as her soul was departing (for she was dying), she called his name Ben-oni;[7] but his father called him Benjamin.[8] ¹⁹ So Rachel died, and she was buried on the way to Ephrath (that is, Bethlehem), ²⁰ and Jacob set up a pillar over her tomb. It is the pillar of Rachel's tomb, which is there to this day. ²¹ Israel journeyed on and pitched his tent beyond the tower of Eder.

²² While Israel lived in that land, Reuben went and lay with Bilhah his father's concubine. And Israel heard of it.

Now the sons of Jacob were twelve. ²³ The sons of Leah: Reuben (Jacob's firstborn), Simeon, Levi, Judah, Issachar, and Zebulun. ²⁴ The sons of Rachel: Joseph and Benjamin. ²⁵ The sons of Bilhah, Rachel's servant: Dan and Naphtali. ²⁶ The sons of Zilpah, Leah's servant: Gad and Asher. These were the sons of Jacob who were born to him in Paddan-aram.

²⁷ And Jacob came to his father Isaac at Mamre, or Kiriath-arba (that is, Hebron), where Abraham and Isaac had sojourned. ²⁸ Now the days of Isaac were 180 years. ²⁹ And Isaac breathed his last, and he died and was gathered to his people, old and full of days. And his sons Esau and Jacob buried him.

Esau's Descendants

36 These are the generations of Esau (that is, Edom). ² Esau took his wives from the Canaanites: Adah the daughter of Elon the Hittite, Oholibamah the daughter of Anah the daughter[9] of Zibeon the Hivite, ³ and Basemath, Ishmael's daughter, the sister of Nebaioth. ⁴ And Adah bore to Esau, Eliphaz; Basemath bore Reuel; ⁵ and Oholibamah bore Jeush, Jalam, and Korah. These are the sons of Esau who were born to him in the land of Canaan.

⁶ Then Esau took his wives, his sons, his daughters, and all the members of his household, his livestock, all his beasts, and all his property that he had acquired in the land of Canaan. He went into a land away from his brother Jacob. ⁷ For their possessions were too great for them to

---

[1] El-bethel means God of Bethel [2] Allon-bacuth means oak of weeping [3] Or had appeared [4] Hebrew El Shaddai [5] Hebrew from your loins
[6] Or about two hours' distance [7] Ben-oni could mean son of my sorrow, or son of my strength [8] Benjamin means son of the right hand
[9] Hebrew; Samaritan, Septuagint, Syriac son; also verse 14

dwell together. The land of their sojournings could not support them because of their livestock. ⁸So Esau settled in the hill country of Seir. (Esau is Edom.)

⁹These are the generations of Esau the father of the Edomites in the hill country of Seir. ¹⁰These are the names of Esau's sons: Eliphaz the son of Adah the wife of Esau, Reuel the son of Basemath the wife of Esau. ¹¹The sons of Eliphaz were Teman, Omar, Zepho, Gatam, and Kenaz. ¹²(Timna was a concubine of Eliphaz, Esau's son; she bore Amalek to Eliphaz.) These are the sons of Adah, Esau's wife. ¹³These are the sons of Reuel: Nahath, Zerah, Shammah, and Mizzah. These are the sons of Basemath, Esau's wife. ¹⁴These are the sons of Oholibamah the daughter of Anah the daughter of Zibeon, Esau's wife: she bore to Esau Jeush, Jalam, and Korah.

¹⁵These are the chiefs of the sons of Esau. The sons of Eliphaz the firstborn of Esau: the chiefs Teman, Omar, Zepho, Kenaz, ¹⁶Korah, Gatam, and Amalek; these are the chiefs of Eliphaz in the land of Edom; these are the sons of Adah. ¹⁷These are the sons of Reuel, Esau's son: the chiefs Nahath, Zerah, Shammah, and Mizzah; these are the chiefs of Reuel in the land of Edom; these are the sons of Basemath, Esau's wife. ¹⁸These are the sons of Oholibamah, Esau's wife: the chiefs Jeush, Jalam, and Korah; these are the chiefs born of Oholibamah the daughter of Anah, Esau's wife. ¹⁹These are the sons of Esau (that is, Edom), and these are their chiefs.

²⁰These are the sons of Seir the Horite, the inhabitants of the land: Lotan, Shobal, Zibeon, Anah, ²¹Dishon, Ezer, and Dishan; these are the chiefs of the Horites, the sons of Seir in the land of Edom. ²²The sons of Lotan were Hori and Hemam; and Lotan's sister was Timna. ²³These are the sons of Shobal: Alvan, Manahath, Ebal, Shepho, and Onam. ²⁴These are the sons of Zibeon: Aiah and Anah; he is the Anah who found the hot springs in the wilderness, as he pastured the donkeys of Zibeon his father. ²⁵These are the children of Anah: Dishon and Oholibamah the daughter of Anah. ²⁶These are the sons of Dishon: Hemdan, Eshban, Ithran, and Cheran. ²⁷These are the sons of Ezer: Bilhan, Zaavan, and Akan. ²⁸These are the sons of Dishan: Uz and Aran. ²⁹These are the chiefs of the Horites: the chiefs Lotan, Shobal, Zibeon, Anah, ³⁰Dishon, Ezer, and Dishan; these are the chiefs of the Horites, chief by chief in the land of Seir.

³¹These are the kings who reigned in the land of Edom, before any king reigned over the Israelites. ³²Bela the son of Beor reigned in Edom, the name of his city being Dinhabah. ³³Bela died, and Jobab the son of Zerah of Bozrah reigned in his place. ³⁴Jobab died, and Husham of the land of the Temanites reigned in his place. ³⁵Husham died, and Hadad the son of Bedad, who defeated Midian in the country of Moab, reigned in his place, the name of his city being Avith. ³⁶Hadad died, and Samlah of Masrekah reigned in his place. ³⁷Samlah died, and Shaul of Rehoboth on the Euphrates¹ reigned in his place. ³⁸Shaul died, and Baal-hanan the son of Achbor reigned in his place. ³⁹Baal-hanan the son of Achbor died, and Hadar reigned in his place, the name of his city being Pau; his wife's name was Mehetabel, the daughter of Matred, daughter of Mezahab.

⁴⁰These are the names of the chiefs of Esau, according to their clans and their dwelling places, by their names: the chiefs Timna, Alvah, Jetheth, ⁴¹Oholibamah, Elah, Pinon, ⁴²Kenaz, Teman, Mibzar, ⁴³Magdiel, and Iram; these are the chiefs of Edom (that is, Esau, the father of Edom), according to their dwelling places in the land of their possession.

Joseph's Dreams

37 Jacob lived in the land of his father's sojournings, in the land of Canaan. ²These are the generations of Jacob.

Joseph, being seventeen years old, was pasturing the flock with his brothers. He was a boy with the sons of Bilhah and Zilpah, his father's wives. And Joseph brought a bad report of them to their father. ³Now Israel loved Joseph more than any other of his sons, because he was the son of his old age. And he made him a robe of many colors.² ⁴But when his brothers saw that their father loved him more than all his brothers, they hated him and could not speak peacefully to him.

⁵Now Joseph had a dream, and when he told it to his brothers they hated him even

¹Hebrew *the River* ²See Septuagint, Vulgate; or (with Syriac) *a robe with long sleeves*. The meaning of the Hebrew is uncertain; also verses 23, 32

more. [6]He said to them, "Hear this dream that I have dreamed: [7]Behold, we were binding sheaves in the field, and behold, my sheaf arose and stood upright. And behold, your sheaves gathered around it and bowed down to my sheaf." [8]His brothers said to him, "Are you indeed to reign over us? Or are you indeed to rule over us?" So they hated him even more for his dreams and for his words.

[9]Then he dreamed another dream and told it to his brothers and said, "Behold, I have dreamed another dream. Behold, the sun, the moon, and eleven stars were bowing down to me." [10]But when he told it to his father and to his brothers, his father rebuked him and said to him, "What is this dream that you have dreamed? Shall I and your mother and your brothers indeed come to bow ourselves to the ground before you?" [11]And his brothers were jealous of him, but his father kept the saying in mind.

Joseph Sold by His Brothers

[12]Now his brothers went to pasture their father's flock near Shechem. [13]And Israel said to Joseph, "Are not your brothers

Know God

verses to read
Genesis 37

If you feel depression coming on, you can stop it before it digs in and takes over, and all it takes is a God-reliant decision: decide not to think about it. Impossible, you say? No, no, no. By God's grace, it can be done.

In order to avoid depressing thoughts, as soon as you feel them coming on, think about something else. When you pray, don't agonize over your misery; just talk to God and say, "Your will be done," and then get on with something else. Sometimes prayer can just be an excuse to wallow in your pain and agony, and that's not right. Don't pretend to be praying when what you're really doing is worrying. Let your prayer remind you who God is, not what your problems are. What seems bigger, the thing that is closest to you or the thing that's off in the distance? The closer the bigger, so bring God closer by agreeing with him, adoring him, and praising him, and put your worries in the distance by refusing to stare at them, even in prayer. Know that God knows your situation, and then ask him to show himself to you so that you can find truth instead of the lie of depression.

The depressed mind is not trusting God to be who he says he is or to do what he says he'll do. You can kick the most common depressions of life on earth, but you have to know the one who is truth and trust that truth. God's Word confirms that faith should override feelings. Hebrews 11:1 says that faith means being certain of "things not seen"—in other words, not being controlled by what we feel. It might feel like all is lost, but for a true believer all is lost only when we have lost faith in God. And the truth is that nothing—not angels or rulers, not devils or evil people, not trials or suffering—can take us away from him (see Rom. 8:38–39). Nothing will destroy you. It's all meant for good and can all be used for good if you, like Joseph, are just willing to trust that God wouldn't let it happen if he wasn't going to make something amazing out of it.

Even if it all looks like darkness now, take the life of Joseph as your example. There certainly can be chemical causes for your depression, but the beginning of all efforts to lift your thought life up out of darkness should be to place your mind on God. Remember that Jesus came to set you free, not just from the wages of sin but from its chains as well.

pasturing the flock at Shechem? Come, I will send you to them." And he said to him, "Here I am." ¹⁴So he said to him, "Go now, see if it is well with your brothers and with the flock, and bring me word." So he sent him from the Valley of Hebron, and he came to Shechem. ¹⁵And a man found him wandering in the fields. And the man asked him, "What are you seeking?" ¹⁶"I am seeking my brothers," he said. "Tell me, please, where they are pasturing the flock." ¹⁷And the man said, "They have gone away, for I heard them say, 'Let us go to Dothan.'" So Joseph went after his brothers and found them at Dothan.

¹⁸They saw him from afar, and before he came near to them they conspired against him to kill him. ¹⁹They said to one another, "Here comes this dreamer. ²⁰Come now, let us kill him and throw him into one of the pits.¹ Then we will say that a fierce animal has devoured him, and we will see what will become of his dreams." ²¹But when Reuben heard it, he rescued him out of their hands, saying, "Let us not take his life." ²²And Reuben said to them, "Shed no blood; throw him into this pit here in the wilderness, but do not lay a hand on him"—that he might rescue him out of their hand to restore him to his father. ²³So when Joseph came to his brothers, they stripped him of his robe, the robe of many colors that he wore. ²⁴And they took him and threw him into a pit. The pit was empty; there was no water in it.

²⁵Then they sat down to eat. And looking up they saw a caravan of Ishmaelites coming from Gilead, with their camels bearing gum, balm, and myrrh, on their way to carry it down to Egypt. ²⁶Then Judah said to his brothers, "What profit is it if we kill our brother and conceal his blood? ²⁷Come, let us sell him to the Ishmaelites, and let not our hand be upon him, for he is our brother, our own flesh." And his brothers listened to him. ²⁸Then Midianite traders passed by. And they drew Joseph up and lifted him out of the pit, and sold him to the Ishmaelites for twenty shekels² of silver. They took Joseph to Egypt.

²⁹When Reuben returned to the pit and saw that Joseph was not in the pit, he tore his clothes ³⁰and returned to his brothers and said, "The boy is gone, and I, where shall I go?" ³¹Then they took Joseph's robe and slaughtered a goat and dipped the robe in the blood. ³²And they sent the robe of many colors and brought it to their father and said, "This we have found; please identify whether it is your son's robe or not." ³³And he identified it and said, "It is my son's robe. A fierce animal has devoured him. Joseph is without doubt torn to pieces." ³⁴Then Jacob tore his garments and put sackcloth on his loins and mourned for his son many days. ³⁵All his sons and all his daughters rose up to comfort him, but he refused to be comforted and said, "No, I shall go down to Sheol to my son, mourning." Thus his father wept for him. ³⁶Meanwhile the Midianites had sold him in Egypt to Potiphar, an officer of Pharaoh, the captain of the guard.

Judah and Tamar

38 It happened at that time that Judah went down from his brothers and turned aside to a certain Adullamite, whose name was Hirah. ²There Judah saw the daughter of a certain Canaanite whose name was Shua. He took her and went in to her, ³and she conceived and bore a son, and he called his name Er. ⁴She conceived again and bore a son, and she called his name Onan. ⁵Yet again she bore a son, and she called his name Shelah. Judah³ was in Chezib when she bore him.

⁶And Judah took a wife for Er his firstborn, and her name was Tamar. ⁷But Er, Judah's firstborn, was wicked in the sight of the LORD, and the LORD put him to death. ⁸Then Judah said to Onan, "Go in to your brother's wife and perform the duty of a brother-in-law to her, and raise up offspring for your brother." ⁹But Onan knew that the offspring would not be his. So whenever he went in to his brother's wife he would waste the semen on the ground, so as not to give offspring to his brother. ¹⁰And what he did was wicked in the sight of the LORD, and he put him to death also. ¹¹Then Judah said to Tamar his daughter-in-law, "Remain a widow in your father's house, till Shelah my son grows up"—for he feared that he would die, like his brothers. So Tamar went and remained in her father's house.

¹²In the course of time the wife of Judah, Shua's daughter, died. When Judah was comforted, he went up to Timnah to his

¹Or cisterns; also verses 22, 24 ²A shekel was about 2/5 ounce or 11 grams ³Hebrew He

sheepshearers, he and his friend Hirah the Adullamite. [13] And when Tamar was told, "Your father-in-law is going up to Timnah to shear his sheep," [14] she took off her widow's garments and covered herself with a veil, wrapping herself up, and sat at the entrance to Enaim, which is on the road to Timnah. For she saw that Shelah was grown up, and she had not been given to him in marriage. [15] When Judah saw her, he thought she was a prostitute, for she had covered her face. [16] He turned to her at the roadside and said, "Come, let me come in to you," for he did not know that she was his daughter-in-law. She said, "What will you give me, that you may come in to me?" [17] He answered, "I will send you a young goat from the flock." And she said, "If you give me a pledge, until you send it—" [18] He said, "What pledge shall I give you?" She replied, "Your signet and your cord and your staff that is in your hand." So he gave them to her and went in to her, and she conceived by him. [19] Then she arose and went away, and taking off her veil she put on the garments of her widowhood.

[20] When Judah sent the young goat by his friend the Adullamite to take back the pledge from the woman's hand, he did not find her. [21] And he asked the men of the place, "Where is the cult prostitute[1] who was at Enaim at the roadside?" And they said, "No cult prostitute has been here." [22] So he returned to Judah and said, "I have not found her. Also, the men of the place said, 'No cult prostitute has been here.'" [23] And Judah replied, "Let her keep the things as her own, or we shall be laughed at. You see, I sent this young goat, and you did not find her."

[24] About three months later Judah was told, "Tamar your daughter-in-law has been immoral.[2] Moreover, she is pregnant by immorality."[3] And Judah said, "Bring her out, and let her be burned." [25] As she was being brought out, she sent word to her father-in-law, "By the man to whom these belong, I am pregnant." And she said, "Please identify whose these are, the signet and the cord and the staff." [26] Then Judah identified them and said, "She is more righteous than I, since I did not give her to my son Shelah." And he did not know her again.

[27] When the time of her labor came, there were twins in her womb. [28] And when she was in labor, one put out a hand, and the midwife took and tied a scarlet thread on his hand, saying, "This one came out first." [29] But as he drew back his hand, behold, his brother came out. And she said, "What a breach you have made for yourself!" Therefore his name was called Perez.[4] [30] Afterward his brother came out with the scarlet thread on his hand, and his name was called Zerah.

Joseph and Potiphar's Wife

39 Now Joseph had been brought down to Egypt, and Potiphar, an officer of Pharaoh, the captain of the guard, an Egyptian, had bought him from the Ishmaelites who had brought him down there. [2] The LORD was with Joseph, and he became a successful man, and he was in the house of his Egyptian master. [3] His master saw that the LORD was with him and that the LORD caused all that he did to succeed in his hands. [4] So Joseph found favor in his sight and attended him, and he made him overseer of his house and put him in charge of all that he had. [5] From the time that he made him overseer in his house and over all that he had, the LORD blessed the Egyptian's house for Joseph's sake; the blessing of the LORD was on all that he had, in house and field. [6] So he left all that he had in Joseph's charge, and because of him he had no concern about anything but the food he ate.

Now Joseph was handsome in form and appearance. [7] And after a time his master's wife cast her eyes on Joseph and said, "Lie with me." [8] But he refused and said to his master's wife, "Behold, because of me my master has no concern about anything in the house, and he has put everything that he has in my charge. [9] He is not greater in this house than I am, nor has he kept back anything from me except you, because you are his wife. How then can I do this great wickedness and sin against God?" [10] And as she spoke to Joseph day after day, he would not listen to her, to lie beside her or to be with her.

[11] But one day, when he went into the house to do his work and none of the men of the house was there in the house, [12] she

---

[1] Hebrew *sacred woman*; a woman who served a pagan deity by prostitution; also verse 22   [2] Or *has committed prostitution*   [3] Or *by prostitution*   [4] *Perez* means *a breach*

caught him by his garment, saying, "Lie with me." But he left his garment in her hand and fled and got out of the house. [13] And as soon as she saw that he had left his garment in her hand and had fled out of the house, [14] she called to the men of her household and said to them, "See, he has brought among us a Hebrew to laugh at us. He came in to me to lie with me, and I cried out with a loud voice. [15] And as soon as he heard that I lifted up my voice and cried out, he left his garment beside me and fled and got out of the house." [16] Then she laid up his garment by her until his master came home, [17] and she told him the same story, saying, "The Hebrew servant, whom you have brought among us, came in to me to laugh at me. [18] But as soon as I lifted up my voice and cried, he left his garment beside me and fled out of the house."

[19] As soon as his master heard the words that his wife spoke to him, "This is the way your servant treated me," his anger was kindled. [20] And Joseph's master took him and put him into the prison, the place where the king's prisoners were confined, and he was there in prison. [21] But the LORD was with Joseph and showed him steadfast love and gave him favor in the sight of the keeper of the prison. [22] And the keeper of the prison put Joseph in charge of all the prisoners who were in the prison. Whatever was done there, he was the one who did it. [23] The keeper of the prison paid no attention to anything that was in Joseph's charge, because the LORD was with him. And whatever he did, the LORD made it succeed.

Joseph Interprets Two Prisoners' Dreams

40 Some time after this, the cupbearer of the king of Egypt and his baker committed an offense against their lord the king of Egypt. [2] And Pharaoh was angry with his two officers, the chief cupbearer and the chief baker, [3] and he put them in custody in the house of the captain of the guard, in the prison where Joseph was confined. [4] The captain of the guard appointed Joseph to be with them, and he attended them. They continued for some time in custody.

[5] And one night they both dreamed—the cupbearer and the baker of the king of Egypt, who were confined in the prison— each his own dream, and each dream with its own interpretation. [6] When Joseph came to them in the morning, he saw that they were troubled. [7] So he asked Pharaoh's officers who were with him in custody in his master's house, "Why are your faces downcast today?" [8] They said to him, "We have had dreams, and there is no one to interpret them." And Joseph said to them, "Do not interpretations belong to God? Please tell them to me."

[9] So the chief cupbearer told his dream to Joseph and said to him, "In my dream there was a vine before me, [10] and on the vine there were three branches. As soon as it budded, its blossoms shot forth, and the clusters ripened into grapes. [11] Pharaoh's cup was in my hand, and I took the grapes and pressed them into Pharaoh's cup and placed the cup in Pharaoh's hand." [12] Then Joseph said to him, "This is its interpretation: the three branches are three days. [13] In three days Pharaoh will lift up your head and restore you to your office, and you shall place Pharaoh's cup in his hand as formerly, when you were his cupbearer. [14] Only remember me, when it is well with you, and please do me the kindness to mention me to Pharaoh, and so get me out of this house. [15] For I was indeed stolen out of the land of the Hebrews, and here also I have done nothing that they should put me into the pit."

[16] When the chief baker saw that the interpretation was favorable, he said to Joseph, "I also had a dream: there were three cake baskets on my head, [17] and in the uppermost basket there were all sorts of baked food for Pharaoh, but the birds were eating it out of the basket on my head." [18] And Joseph answered and said, "This is its interpretation: the three baskets are three days. [19] In three days Pharaoh will lift up your head—from you!—and hang you on a tree. And the birds will eat the flesh from you."

[20] On the third day, which was Pharaoh's birthday, he made a feast for all his servants and lifted up the head of the chief cupbearer and the head of the chief baker among his servants. [21] He restored the chief cupbearer to his position, and he placed the cup in Pharaoh's hand. [22] But he hanged the chief baker, as Joseph had interpreted to them. [23] Yet the chief cupbearer did not remember Joseph, but forgot him.

Joseph Interprets Pharaoh's Dreams

41 After two whole years, Pharaoh dreamed that he was standing by the Nile, [2] and behold, there came up out of the Nile seven cows attractive and plump, and they fed in the reed grass. [3] And behold, seven other cows, ugly and thin, came up out of the Nile after them, and stood by the other cows on the bank of the Nile. [4] And the ugly, thin cows ate up the seven attractive, plump cows. And Pharaoh awoke. [5] And he fell asleep and dreamed a second time. And behold, seven ears of grain, plump and good, were growing on one stalk. [6] And behold, after them sprouted seven ears, thin and blighted by the east wind. [7] And the thin ears swallowed up the seven plump, full ears. And Pharaoh awoke, and behold, it was a dream. [8] So in the morning his spirit was troubled, and he sent and called for all the magicians of Egypt and all its wise men. Pharaoh told them his dreams, but there was none who could interpret them to Pharaoh.

[9] Then the chief cupbearer said to Pharaoh, "I remember my offenses today. [10] When Pharaoh was angry with his servants and put me and the chief baker in custody in the house of the captain of the guard, [11] we dreamed on the same night, he and I, each having a dream with its own interpretation. [12] A young Hebrew was there with us, a servant of the captain of the guard. When we told him, he interpreted our dreams to us, giving an interpretation to each man according to his dream. [13] And as he interpreted to us, so it came about. I was restored to my office, and the baker was hanged."

[14] Then Pharaoh sent and called Joseph, and they quickly brought him out of the pit. And when he had shaved himself and changed his clothes, he came in before Pharaoh. [15] And Pharaoh said to Joseph, "I have had a dream, and there is no one who can interpret it. I have heard it said of you that when you hear a dream you can interpret it." [16] Joseph answered Pharaoh, "It is not in me; God will give Pharaoh a favorable answer."[1] [17] Then Pharaoh said to Joseph, "Behold, in my dream I was standing on the banks of the Nile. [18] Seven cows, plump and attractive, came up out of the Nile and fed in the reed grass. [19] Seven other cows came up after them, poor and very ugly and thin, such as I had never seen in all the land of Egypt. [20] And the thin, ugly cows ate up the first seven plump cows, [21] but when they had eaten them no one would have known that they had eaten them, for they were still as ugly as at the beginning. Then I awoke. [22] I also saw in my dream seven ears growing on one stalk, full and good. [23] Seven ears, withered, thin, and blighted by the east wind, sprouted after them, [24] and the thin ears swallowed up the seven good ears. And I told it to the magicians, but there was no one who could explain it to me."

[25] Then Joseph said to Pharaoh, "The dreams of Pharaoh are one; God has revealed to Pharaoh what he is about to do. [26] The seven good cows are seven years, and the seven good ears are seven years; the dreams are one. [27] The seven lean and ugly cows that came up after them are seven years, and the seven empty ears blighted by the east wind are also seven years of famine. [28] It is as I told Pharaoh; God has shown to Pharaoh what he is about to do. [29] There will come seven years of great plenty throughout all the land of Egypt, [30] but after them there will arise seven years of famine, and all the plenty will be forgotten in the land of Egypt. The famine will consume the land, [31] and the plenty will be unknown in the land by reason of the famine that will follow, for it will be very severe. [32] And the doubling of Pharaoh's dream means that the thing is fixed by God, and God will shortly bring it about. [33] Now therefore let Pharaoh select a discerning and wise man, and set him over the land of Egypt. [34] Let Pharaoh proceed to appoint overseers over the land and take one-fifth of the produce of the land[2] of Egypt during the seven plentiful years. [35] And let them gather all the food of these good years that are coming and store up grain under the authority of Pharaoh for food in the cities, and let them keep it. [36] That food shall be a reserve for the land against the seven years of famine that are to occur in the land of Egypt, so that the land may not perish through the famine."

Joseph Rises to Power

[37] This proposal pleased Pharaoh and all his servants. [38] And Pharaoh said to

---

[1] Or (compare Samaritan, Septuagint) *Without God it is not possible to give Pharaoh an answer about his welfare* [2] Or *over the land and organize the land*

his servants, "Can we find a man like this, in whom is the Spirit of God?"[1] **39** Then Pharaoh said to Joseph, "Since God has shown you all this, there is none so discerning and wise as you are. **40** You shall be over my house, and all my people shall order themselves as you command.[2] Only as regards the throne will I be greater than you." **41** And Pharaoh said to Joseph, "See, I have set you over all the land of Egypt." **42** Then Pharaoh took his signet ring from his hand and put it on Joseph's hand, and clothed him in garments of fine linen and put a gold chain about his neck. **43** And he made him ride in his second chariot. And they called out before him, "Bow the knee!"[3] Thus he set him over all the land of Egypt. **44** Moreover, Pharaoh said to Joseph, "I am Pharaoh, and without your consent no one shall lift up hand or foot in all the land of Egypt." **45** And Pharaoh called Joseph's name Zaphenath-paneah. And he gave him in marriage Asenath, the daughter of Potiphera priest of On. So Joseph went out over the land of Egypt.

46 Joseph was thirty years old when he entered the service of Pharaoh king of Egypt. And Joseph went out from the presence of Pharaoh and went through all the land of Egypt. **47** During the seven plentiful years the earth produced abundantly, **48** and he gathered up all the food of these seven years, which occurred in the land of Egypt, and put the food in the cities. He put in every city the food from the fields around it. **49** And Joseph stored up grain in great abundance, like the sand of the sea, until he ceased to measure it, for it could not be measured.

50 Before the year of famine came, two sons were born to Joseph. Asenath, the daughter of Potiphera priest of On, bore them to him. **51** Joseph called the name of the firstborn Manasseh. "For," he said, "God has made me forget all my hardship and all my father's house."[4] **52** The name of the second he called Ephraim, "For God has made me fruitful in the land of my affliction."[5]

53 The seven years of plenty that occurred in the land of Egypt came to an end, **54** and the seven years of famine began to come, as Joseph had said. There was famine in all lands, but in all the land of Egypt there was bread. **55** When all the land of Egypt was famished, the people cried to Pharaoh for bread. Pharaoh said to all the Egyptians, "Go to Joseph. What he says to you, do."

[1] Or *of the gods* [2] Hebrew *and according to your command all my people shall kiss the ground* [3] *Abrek*, probably an Egyptian word, similar in sound to the Hebrew word meaning *to kneel* [4] *Manasseh* sounds like the Hebrew for *making to forget* [5] *Ephraim* sounds like the Hebrew for *making fruitful*

Know God

verses to read
Genesis 41:38–57

One of the hardest things you'll ever do is stay connected to God in the *good* times. Bad times tend to drive you to your knees. You need so much help and protection when times get tough that you run full speed to God. But look out for the good times: they can soften your faith and drive you off into a different direction.

Whenever you have a win, enjoy the chance to give God the credit and the thanks, and then to move on. You shouldn't concentrate on your wins, any more than you should concentrate on your failures. But spend your energy on God, and you'll find your faith on the increase. And when the bad times come, just think about them as a blessing in disguise—because the bad times remind you of the one who works everything out for the good of those who love him (see Rom. 8:28). They remind you that you can do nothing in this world without him. So be thankful and happy in the bad times, knowing always that this too shall pass as you rest under the graceful hand of the Savior.

⁵⁶ So when the famine had spread over all the land, Joseph opened all the storehouses[1] and sold to the Egyptians, for the famine was severe in the land of Egypt. ⁵⁷ Moreover, all the earth came to Egypt to Joseph to buy grain, because the famine was severe over all the earth.

Joseph's Brothers Go to Egypt

42 When Jacob learned that there was grain for sale in Egypt, he said to his sons, "Why do you look at one another?" ² And he said, "Behold, I have heard that there is grain for sale in Egypt. Go down and buy grain for us there, that we may live and not die." ³ So ten of Joseph's brothers went down to buy grain in Egypt. ⁴ But Jacob did not send Benjamin, Joseph's brother, with his brothers, for he feared that harm might happen to him. ⁵ Thus the sons of Israel came to buy among the others who came, for the famine was in the land of Canaan.

⁶ Now Joseph was governor over the land. He was the one who sold to all the people of the land. And Joseph's brothers came and bowed themselves before him with their faces to the ground. ⁷ Joseph saw his brothers and recognized them, but he treated them like strangers and spoke roughly to them. "Where do you come from?" he said. They said, "From the land of Canaan, to buy food." ⁸ And Joseph recognized his brothers, but they did not recognize him. ⁹ And Joseph remembered the dreams that he had dreamed of them. And he said to them, "You are spies; you have come to see the nakedness of the land." ¹⁰ They said to him, "No, my lord, your servants have come to buy food. ¹¹ We are all sons of one man. We are honest men. Your servants have never been spies."

¹² He said to them, "No, it is the nakedness of the land that you have come to see." ¹³ And they said, "We, your servants, are twelve brothers, the sons of one man in the land of Canaan, and behold, the youngest is this day with our father, and one is no more." ¹⁴ But Joseph said to them, "It is as I said to you. You are spies. ¹⁵ By this you shall be tested: by the life of Pharaoh, you shall not go from this place unless your youngest brother comes here. ¹⁶ Send one of you, and let him bring your brother, while you remain confined, that

your words may be tested, whether there is truth in you. Or else, by the life of Pharaoh, surely you are spies." ¹⁷ And he put them all together in custody for three days.

¹⁸ On the third day Joseph said to them, "Do this and you will live, for I fear God: ¹⁹ if you are honest men, let one of your brothers remain confined where you are in custody, and let the rest go and carry grain for the famine of your households, ²⁰ and bring your youngest brother to me. So your words will be verified, and you shall not die." And they did so. ²¹ Then they said to one another, "In truth we are guilty concerning our brother, in that we saw the distress of his soul, when he begged us and we did not listen. That is why this distress has come upon us." ²² And Reuben answered them, "Did I not tell you not to sin against the boy? But you did not listen. So now there comes a reckoning for his blood." ²³ They did not know that Joseph understood them, for there was an interpreter between them. ²⁴ Then he turned away from them and wept. And he returned to them and spoke to them. And he took Simeon from them and bound him before their eyes. ²⁵ And Joseph gave orders to fill their bags with grain, and to replace every man's money in his sack, and to give them provisions for the journey. This was done for them.

²⁶ Then they loaded their donkeys with their grain and departed. ²⁷ And as one of them opened his sack to give his donkey fodder at the lodging place, he saw his money in the mouth of his sack. ²⁸ He said to his brothers, "My money has been put back; here it is in the mouth of my sack!" At this their hearts failed them, and they turned trembling to one another, saying, "What is this that God has done to us?"

²⁹ When they came to Jacob their father in the land of Canaan, they told him all that had happened to them, saying, ³⁰ "The man, the lord of the land, spoke roughly to us and took us to be spies of the land. ³¹ But we said to him, 'We are honest men; we have never been spies. ³² We are twelve brothers, sons of our father. One is no more, and the youngest is this day with our father in the land of Canaan.' ³³ Then the man, the lord of the land, said to us, 'By this I shall know that you are honest men: leave one of your brothers with me, and take grain

[1] Hebrew *all that was in them*

for the famine of your households, and go your way. [34] Bring your youngest brother to me. Then I shall know that you are not spies but honest men, and I will deliver your brother to you, and you shall trade in the land.'"

[35] As they emptied their sacks, behold, every man's bundle of money was in his sack. And when they and their father saw their bundles of money, they were afraid. [36] And Jacob their father said to them, "You have bereaved me of my children: Joseph is no more, and Simeon is no more, and now you would take Benjamin. All this has come against me." [37] Then Reuben said to his father, "Kill my two sons if I do not bring him back to you. Put him in my hands, and I will bring him back to you." [38] But he said, "My son shall not go down with you, for his brother is dead, and he is the only one left. If harm should happen to him on the journey that you are to make, you would bring down my gray hairs with sorrow to Sheol."

Ask Yourself . . .

ABOUT STRUGGLES

Ask yourself when life gets rough:

- Who is in control of my life—other people or God?
- What am I willing to put up with in order to respond in love to God, in light of how deeply he has loved me, giving his own Son for me?
- Do I believe that God is still God even when things all around me tell me differently?
- How can I act today, when things are bad, in order to make the most of this trial?

Joseph's Brothers Return to Egypt

43 Now the famine was severe in the land. [2] And when they had eaten the grain that they had brought from Egypt, their father said to them, "Go again, buy us a little food." [3] But Judah said to him, "The man solemnly warned us, saying, 'You shall not see my face unless your brother is with you.' [4] If you will send our brother with us, we will go down and buy you food. [5] But if you will not send him, we will not go down, for the man said to us, 'You shall not see my face, unless your brother is with you.'" [6] Israel said, "Why did you treat me so badly as to tell the man that you had another brother?" [7] They replied, "The man questioned us carefully about ourselves and our kindred, saying, 'Is your father still alive? Do you have another brother?' What we told him was in answer to these questions. Could we in any way know that he would say, 'Bring your brother down'?" [8] And Judah said to Israel his father, "Send the boy with me, and we will arise and go, that we may live and not die, both we and you and also our little ones. [9] I will be a pledge of his safety. From my hand you shall require him. If I do not bring him back to you and set him before you, then let me bear the blame forever. [10] If we had not delayed, we would now have returned twice."

[11] Then their father Israel said to them, "If it must be so, then do this: take some of the choice fruits of the land in your bags, and carry a present down to the man, a little balm and a little honey, gum, myrrh, pistachio nuts, and almonds. [12] Take double the money with you. Carry back with you the money that was returned in the mouth of your sacks. Perhaps it was an oversight. [13] Take also your brother, and arise, go again to the man. [14] May God Almighty[1] grant you mercy before the man, and may he send back your other brother and Benjamin. And as for me, if I am bereaved of my children, I am bereaved."

[15] So the men took this present, and they took double the money with them, and Benjamin. They arose and went down to Egypt and stood before Joseph.

[16] When Joseph saw Benjamin with them, he said to the steward of his house, "Bring the men into the house, and slaughter an animal and make ready, for the men are to dine with me at noon." [17] The man did as Joseph told him and brought the men to Joseph's house. [18] And the men were afraid because they were brought to Joseph's house, and they said, "It is because of the money, which was replaced in our sacks

[1] Hebrew El Shaddai

the first time, that we are brought in, so that he may assault us and fall upon us to make us servants and seize our donkeys." ¹⁹ So they went up to the steward of Joseph's house and spoke with him at the door of the house, ²⁰ and said, "Oh, my lord, we came down the first time to buy food. ²¹ And when we came to the lodging place we opened our sacks, and there was each man's money in the mouth of his sack, our money in full weight. So we have brought it again with us, ²² and we have brought other money down with us to buy food. We do not know who put our money in our sacks." ²³ He replied, "Peace to you, do not be afraid. Your God and the God of your father has put treasure in your sacks for you. I received your money." Then he brought Simeon out to them. ²⁴ And when the man had brought the men into Joseph's house and given them water, and they had washed their feet, and when he had given their donkeys fodder, ²⁵ they prepared the present for Joseph's coming at noon, for they heard that they should eat bread there.

²⁶ When Joseph came home, they brought into the house to him the present that they had with them and bowed down to him to the ground. ²⁷ And he inquired about their welfare and said, "Is your father well, the old man of whom you spoke? Is he still alive?" ²⁸ They said, "Your servant our father is well; he is still alive." And they bowed their heads and prostrated themselves. ²⁹ And he lifted up his eyes and saw his brother Benjamin, his mother's son, and said, "Is this your youngest brother, of whom you spoke to me? God be gracious to you, my son!" ³⁰ Then Joseph hurried out, for his compassion grew warm for his brother, and he sought a place to weep. And he entered his chamber and wept there. ³¹ Then he washed his face and came out. And controlling himself he said, "Serve the food." ³² They served him by himself, and them by themselves, and the Egyptians who ate with him by themselves, because the Egyptians could not eat with the Hebrews, for that is an abomination to the Egyptians. ³³ And they sat before him, the firstborn according to his birthright and the youngest according to his youth. And the men looked at one another in amazement. ³⁴ Portions were taken to them from Joseph's table, but Benjamin's portion was five times as much as any of theirs. And they drank and were merry¹ with him.

Joseph Tests His Brothers

44 Then he commanded the steward of his house, "Fill the men's sacks with food, as much as they can carry, and put each man's money in the mouth of his sack, ² and put my cup, the silver cup, in the mouth of the sack of the youngest, with his money for the grain." And he did as Joseph told him.

³ As soon as the morning was light, the men were sent away with their donkeys. ⁴ They had gone only a short distance from the city. Now Joseph said to his steward, "Up, follow after the men, and when you overtake them, say to them, 'Why have you repaid evil for good?² ⁵ Is it not from this that my lord drinks, and by this that he practices divination? You have done evil in doing this.' "

⁶ When he overtook them, he spoke to them these words. ⁷ They said to him, "Why does my lord speak such words as these? Far be it from your servants to do such a thing! ⁸ Behold, the money that we found in the mouths of our sacks we brought back to you from the land of Canaan. How then could we steal silver or gold from your lord's house? ⁹ Whichever of your servants is found with it shall die, and we also will be my lord's servants." ¹⁰ He said, "Let it be as you say: he who is found with it shall be my servant, and the rest of you shall be innocent." ¹¹ Then each man quickly lowered his sack to the ground, and each man opened his sack. ¹² And he searched, beginning with the eldest and ending with the youngest. And the cup was found in Benjamin's sack. ¹³ Then they tore their clothes, and every man loaded his donkey, and they returned to the city.

¹⁴ When Judah and his brothers came to Joseph's house, he was still there. They fell before him to the ground. ¹⁵ Joseph said to them, "What deed is this that you have done? Do you not know that a man like me can indeed practice divination?" ¹⁶ And Judah said, "What shall we say to my lord? What shall we speak? Or how can we clear ourselves? God has found out the guilt of your servants; behold, we are my lord's servants, both we and he also in whose

¹ Hebrew *and became intoxicated* ² Septuagint (compare Vulgate) adds *Why have you stolen my silver cup?*

hand the cup has been found." **¹⁷**But he said, "Far be it from me that I should do so! Only the man in whose hand the cup was found shall be my servant. But as for you, go up in peace to your father."

¹⁸Then Judah went up to him and said, "Oh, my lord, please let your servant speak a word in my lord's ears, and let not your anger burn against your servant, for you are like Pharaoh himself. **¹⁹**My lord asked his servants, saying, 'Have you a father, or a brother?' **²⁰**And we said to my lord, 'We have a father, an old man, and a young brother, the child of his old age. His brother is dead, and he alone is left of his mother's children, and his father loves him.' **²¹**Then you said to your servants, 'Bring him down to me, that I may set my eyes on him.' **²²**We said to my lord, 'The boy cannot leave his father, for if he should leave his father, his father would die.' **²³**Then you said to your servants, 'Unless your youngest brother comes down with you, you shall not see my face again.'

²⁴"When we went back to your servant my father, we told him the words of my lord. **²⁵**And when our father said, 'Go again, buy us a little food,' **²⁶**we said, 'We cannot go down. If our youngest brother goes with us, then we will go down. For we cannot see the man's face unless our youngest brother is with us.' **²⁷**Then your servant my father said to us, 'You know that my wife bore me two sons. **²⁸**One left me, and I said, "Surely he has been torn to pieces," and I have never seen him since. **²⁹**If you take this one also from me, and harm happens to him, you will bring down my gray hairs in evil to Sheol.'

³⁰"Now therefore, as soon as I come to your servant my father, and the boy is not with us, then, as his life is bound up in the boy's life, **³¹**as soon as he sees that the boy is not with us, he will die, and your servants will bring down the gray hairs of your servant our father with sorrow to Sheol. **³²**For your servant became a pledge of safety for the boy to my father, saying, 'If I do not bring him back to you, then I shall bear the blame before my father all my life.' **³³**Now therefore, please let your servant remain instead of the boy as a servant to my lord, and let the boy go back with his brothers. **³⁴**For how can I go back to my father if the boy is not with me? I fear to see the evil that would find my father."

Joseph Provides for His Brothers and Family

45 Then Joseph could not control himself before all those who stood by him. He cried, "Make everyone go out from me." So no one stayed with him when Joseph made himself known to his brothers. **²**And he wept aloud, so that the Egyptians heard it, and the household of Pharaoh heard it. **³**And Joseph said to his brothers, "I am Joseph! Is my father still alive?" But his brothers could not answer him, for they were dismayed at his presence.

⁴So Joseph said to his brothers, "Come near to me, please." And they came near. And he said, "I am your brother, Joseph, whom you sold into Egypt. **⁵**And now do not be distressed or angry with yourselves because you sold me here, for God sent me before you to preserve life. **⁶**For the famine has been in the land these two years, and there are yet five years in which there will be neither plowing nor harvest. **⁷**And God sent me before you to preserve for you a remnant on earth, and to keep alive for you many survivors. **⁸**So it was not you who sent me here, but God. He has made me a father to Pharaoh, and lord of all his house and ruler over all the land of Egypt. **⁹**Hurry and go up to my father and say to him, 'Thus says your son Joseph, God has made me lord of all Egypt. Come down to me; do not tarry. **¹⁰**You shall dwell in the land of Goshen, and you shall be near me, you and your children and your children's children, and your flocks, your herds, and all that you have. **¹¹**There I will provide for you, for there are yet five years of famine to come, so that you and your household, and all that you have, do not come to poverty.' **¹²**And now your eyes see, and the eyes of my brother Benjamin see, that it is my mouth that speaks to you. **¹³**You must tell my father of all my honor in Egypt, and of all that you have seen. Hurry and bring my father down here." **¹⁴**Then he fell upon his brother Benjamin's neck and wept, and Benjamin wept upon his neck. **¹⁵**And he kissed all his brothers and wept upon them. After that his brothers talked with him.

¹⁶When the report was heard in Pharaoh's house, "Joseph's brothers have come," it pleased Pharaoh and his servants. **¹⁷**And Pharaoh said to Joseph, "Say to your brothers, 'Do this: load your beasts and go back to the land of Canaan, [18]and take your father and your households, and come to me, and I will give you the best of the land of Egypt, and you shall eat the fat of the land.' [19]And you, Joseph, are commanded to say, 'Do this: take wagons from the land of Egypt for your little ones and for your wives, and bring your father, and come. [20]Have no concern for[1] your goods, for the best of all the land of Egypt is yours.'"

[21]The sons of Israel did so: and Joseph gave them wagons, according to the command of Pharaoh, and gave them provisions for the journey. [22]To each and all of them he gave a change of clothes, but to Benjamin he gave three hundred shekels[2] of silver and five changes of clothes. [23]To his father he sent as follows: ten donkeys loaded with the good things of Egypt, and ten female donkeys loaded with grain, bread, and provision for his father on the journey. [24]Then he sent his brothers away, and as they departed, he said to them, "Do not quarrel on the way."

[25]So they went up out of Egypt and came to the land of Canaan to their father Jacob. [26]And they told him, "Joseph is still alive, and he is ruler over all the land of Egypt." And his heart became numb, for he did not believe them. [27]But when they told him all the words of Joseph, which he had said to them, and when he saw the wagons that Joseph had sent to carry him, the spirit of their father Jacob revived. [28]And Israel said, "It is enough; Joseph my son is still alive. I will go and see him before I die."

Joseph Brings His Family to Egypt

46 So Israel took his journey with all that he had and came to Beersheba, and offered sacrifices to the God of his father Isaac. [2]And God spoke to Israel in visions of the night and said, "Jacob, Jacob." And he said, "Here I am." [3]Then he said, "I am God, the God of your father. Do not be afraid to go down to Egypt, for there I will make you into a great nation. [4]I myself will go down with you to Egypt, and I will also

[1]Hebrew *Let your eye not pity*　[2]A *shekel* was about 2/5 ounce or 11 grams

---

Know Love

verses to read
Genesis 45:1–8

When people try to destroy you, God Girl, don't worry. You can't look at life from the world's perspective anymore; you have to look at it from God's perspective. Why would he let something bad happen unless it was for your good? Just look at the life of Joseph, whose brothers hated him and sold him into slavery, who was sent to jail unfairly, but who never stopped trusting God. God's plans aren't always like ours. They might seem totally off track from ours and even dangerous, but they're always the best. No one should go looking for their own destruction, but when it looks like the world is bent on yours, don't freak out. Trust God and go to him for comfort. Have faith and know that he works all things together for the good of those who love him (see Rom. 8:28).

When life throws you a curve ball, don't worry, God's got your back. You've got to know that, like Joseph, you can rise above mean people and overcome through faith in the one who sets the moon and the stars in place. You, child of the living God, are protected no matter how tragic your situation. No matter what they do to you, you will continue to go in the right direction if you trust that God works it all out in the end. When the world attacks, remember Joseph. All those things had to happen to him—even slavery and imprisonment—in order for him to get to the position of power where he needed to be in order to save his family. Suffering isn't something to worry about. Instead, it can be something to take hold of when your desire is only that God's will be done.

bring you up again, and Joseph's hand shall close your eyes."

⁵ Then Jacob set out from Beersheba. The sons of Israel carried Jacob their father, their little ones, and their wives, in the wagons that Pharaoh had sent to carry him. ⁶ They also took their livestock and their goods, which they had gained in the land of Canaan, and came into Egypt, Jacob and all his offspring with him, ⁷ his sons, and his sons' sons with him, his daughters, and his sons' daughters. All his offspring he brought with him into Egypt.

⁸ Now these are the names of the descendants of Israel, who came into Egypt, Jacob and his sons. Reuben, Jacob's firstborn, ⁹ and the sons of Reuben: Hanoch, Pallu, Hezron, and Carmi. ¹⁰ The sons of Simeon: Jemuel, Jamin, Ohad, Jachin, Zohar, and Shaul, the son of a Canaanite woman. ¹¹ The sons of Levi: Gershon, Kohath, and Merari. ¹² The sons of Judah: Er, Onan, Shelah, Perez, and Zerah (but Er and Onan died in the land of Canaan); and the sons of Perez were Hezron and Hamul. ¹³ The sons of Issachar: Tola, Puvah, Yob, and Shimron. ¹⁴ The sons of Zebulun: Sered, Elon, and Jahleel. ¹⁵ These are the sons of Leah, whom she bore to Jacob in Paddanaram, together with his daughter Dinah; altogether his sons and his daughters numbered thirty-three.

¹⁶ The sons of Gad: Ziphion, Haggi, Shuni, Ezbon, Eri, Arodi, and Areli. ¹⁷ The sons of Asher: Imnah, Ishvah, Ishvi, Beriah, with Serah their sister. And the sons of Beriah: Heber and Malchiel. ¹⁸ These are the sons of Zilpah, whom Laban gave to Leah his daughter; and these she bore to Jacob— sixteen persons.

¹⁹ The sons of Rachel, Jacob's wife: Joseph and Benjamin. ²⁰ And to Joseph in the land of Egypt were born Manasseh and Ephraim, whom Asenath, the daughter of Potiphera the priest of On, bore to him. ²¹ And the sons of Benjamin: Bela, Becher, Ashbel, Gera, Naaman, Ehi, Rosh, Muppim, Huppim, and Ard. ²² These are the sons of Rachel, who were born to Jacob—fourteen persons in all.

²³ The son¹ of Dan: Hushim. ²⁴ The sons of Naphtali: Jahzeel, Guni, Jezer, and Shillem. ²⁵ These are the sons of Bilhah, whom Laban gave to Rachel his daughter, and these she bore to Jacob—seven persons in all.

²⁶ All the persons belonging to Jacob who came into Egypt, who were his own descendants, not including Jacob's sons' wives, were sixty-six persons in all. ²⁷ And the sons of Joseph, who were born to him in Egypt, were two. All the persons of the house of Jacob who came into Egypt were seventy.

Jacob and Joseph Reunited

²⁸ He had sent Judah ahead of him to Joseph to show the way before him in Goshen, and they came into the land of Goshen. ²⁹ Then Joseph prepared his chariot and went up to meet Israel his father in Goshen. He presented himself to him and fell on his neck and wept on his neck a good while. ³⁰ Israel said to Joseph, "Now let me die, since I have seen your face and know that you are still alive." ³¹ Joseph said to his brothers and to his father's household, "I will go up and tell Pharaoh and will say to him, 'My brothers and my father's household, who were in the land of Canaan, have come to me. ³² And the men are shepherds, for they have been keepers of livestock, and they have brought their flocks and their herds and all that they have.' ³³ When Pharaoh calls you and says, 'What is your occupation?' ³⁴ you shall say, 'Your servants have been keepers of livestock from our youth even until now, both we and our fathers,' in order that you may dwell in the land of Goshen, for every shepherd is an abomination to the Egyptians."

Jacob's Family Settles in Goshen

47 So Joseph went in and told Pharaoh, "My father and my brothers, with their flocks and herds and all that they possess, have come from the land of Canaan. They are now in the land of Goshen." ² And from among his brothers he took five men and presented them to Pharaoh. ³ Pharaoh said to his brothers, "What is your occupation?" And they said to Pharaoh, "Your servants are shepherds, as our fathers were." ⁴ They said to Pharaoh, "We have come to sojourn in the land, for there is no pasture for your servants' flocks, for the famine is severe in the land of Canaan. And now,

¹ Hebrew sons

please let your servants dwell in the land of Goshen." [5] Then Pharaoh said to Joseph, "Your father and your brothers have come to you. [6] The land of Egypt is before you. Settle your father and your brothers in the best of the land. Let them settle in the land of Goshen, and if you know any able men among them, put them in charge of my livestock."

[7] Then Joseph brought in Jacob his father and stood him before Pharaoh, and Jacob blessed Pharaoh. [8] And Pharaoh said to Jacob, "How many are the days of the years of your life?" [9] And Jacob said to Pharaoh, "The days of the years of my sojourning are 130 years. Few and evil have been the days of the years of my life, and they have not attained to the days of the years of the life of my fathers in the days of their sojourning." [10] And Jacob blessed Pharaoh and went out from the presence of Pharaoh. [11] Then Joseph settled his father and his brothers and gave them a possession in the land of Egypt, in the best of the land, in the land of Rameses, as Pharaoh had commanded. [12] And Joseph provided his father, his brothers, and all his father's household with food, according to the number of their dependents.

Joseph and the Famine

[13] Now there was no food in all the land, for the famine was very severe, so that the land of Egypt and the land of Canaan languished by reason of the famine. [14] And Joseph gathered up all the money that was found in the land of Egypt and in the land of Canaan, in exchange for the grain that they bought. And Joseph brought the money into Pharaoh's house. [15] And when the money was all spent in the land of Egypt and in the land of Canaan, all the Egyptians came to Joseph and said, "Give us food. Why should we die before your eyes? For our money is gone." [16] And Joseph answered, "Give your livestock, and I will give you food in exchange for your livestock, if your money is gone." [17] So they brought their livestock to Joseph, and Joseph gave them food in exchange for the horses, the flocks, the herds, and the donkeys. He supplied them with food in exchange for all their livestock that year. [18] And when that year was ended, they came to him the following year and said to him, "We will not hide from my lord that our money is all spent. The herds of livestock are my lord's. There is nothing left in the sight of my lord but our bodies and our land. [19] Why should we die before your eyes, both we and our land? Buy us and our land for food, and we with our land will be servants to Pharaoh. And give us seed that we may live and not die, and that the land may not be desolate."

[20] So Joseph bought all the land of Egypt for Pharaoh, for all the Egyptians sold their fields, because the famine was severe on them. The land became Pharaoh's. [21] As for the people, he made servants of them[1] from one end of Egypt to the other. [22] Only the land of the priests he did not buy, for the priests had a fixed allowance from Pharaoh and lived on the allowance that Pharaoh gave them; therefore they did not sell their land.

[23] Then Joseph said to the people, "Behold, I have this day bought you and your land for Pharaoh. Now here is seed for you, and you shall sow the land. [24] And at the harvests you shall give a fifth to Pharaoh, and four fifths shall be your own, as seed for the field and as food for yourselves and your households, and as food for your little ones." [25] And they said, "You have saved our lives; may it please my lord, we will be servants to Pharaoh." [26] So Joseph made it a statute concerning the land of Egypt, and it stands to this day, that Pharaoh should have the fifth; the land of the priests alone did not become Pharaoh's.

[27] Thus Israel settled in the land of Egypt, in the land of Goshen. And they gained possessions in it, and were fruitful and multiplied greatly. [28] And Jacob lived in the land of Egypt seventeen years. So the days of Jacob, the years of his life, were 147 years.

[29] And when the time drew near that Israel must die, he called his son Joseph and said to him, "If now I have found favor in your sight, put your hand under my thigh and promise to deal kindly and truly with me. Do not bury me in Egypt, [30] but let me lie with my fathers. Carry me out of Egypt and bury me in their burying place." He answered, "I will do as you have said." [31] And he said, "Swear to me"; and he swore

---

[1] Samaritan, Septuagint, Vulgate; Hebrew *he removed them to the cities*

to him. Then Israel bowed himself upon the head of his bed.[1]

Jacob Blesses Ephraim and Manasseh

48 After this, Joseph was told, "Behold, your father is ill." So he took with him his two sons, Manasseh and Ephraim. [2] And it was told to Jacob, "Your son Joseph has come to you." Then Israel summoned his strength and sat up in bed. [3] And Jacob said to Joseph, "God Almighty[2] appeared to me at Luz in the land of Canaan and blessed me, [4] and said to me, 'Behold, I will make you fruitful and multiply you, and I will make of you a company of peoples and will give this land to your offspring after you for an everlasting possession.' [5] And now your two sons, who were born to you in the land of Egypt before I came to you in Egypt, are mine; Ephraim and Manasseh shall be mine, as Reuben and Simeon are. [6] And the children that you fathered after them shall be yours. They shall be called by the name of their brothers in their inheritance. [7] As for me, when I came from Paddan, to my sorrow Rachel died in the land of Canaan on the way, when there was still some distance[3] to go to Ephrath, and I buried her there on the way to Ephrath (that is, Bethlehem)."

[8] When Israel saw Joseph's sons, he said, "Who are these?" [9] Joseph said to his father, "They are my sons, whom God has given me here." And he said, "Bring them to me, please, that I may bless them." [10] Now the eyes of Israel were dim with age, so that he could not see. So Joseph brought them near him, and he kissed them and embraced them. [11] And Israel said to Joseph, "I never expected to see your face; and behold, God has let me see your offspring also." [12] Then Joseph removed them from his knees, and he bowed himself with his face to the earth. [13] And Joseph took them both, Ephraim in his right hand toward Israel's left hand, and Manasseh in his left hand toward Israel's right hand, and brought them near him. [14] And Israel stretched out his right hand and laid it on the head of Ephraim, who was the younger, and his left hand on the head of Manasseh, crossing his hands (for Manasseh was the firstborn). [15] And he blessed Joseph and said,

> "The God before whom my fathers
>   Abraham and Isaac walked,
> the God who has been my shep-
>   herd all my life long to this
>   day,
> [16] the angel who has redeemed me
>   from all evil, bless the boys;
> and in them let my name be car-
>   ried on, and the name of my
>   fathers Abraham and Isaac;
> and let them grow into a multi-
>   tude[4] in the midst of the earth."

[17] When Joseph saw that his father laid his right hand on the head of Ephraim, it displeased him, and he took his father's hand to move it from Ephraim's head to Manasseh's head. [18] And Joseph said to his father, "Not this way, my father; since this one is the firstborn, put your right hand on his head." [19] But his father refused and said, "I know, my son, I know. He also shall become a people, and he also shall be great. Nevertheless, his younger brother shall be greater than he, and his offspring shall become a multitude[5] of nations." [20] So he blessed them that day, saying,

> "By you Israel will pronounce bless-
>   ings, saying,
> 'God make you as Ephraim and as
>   Manasseh.' "

Thus he put Ephraim before Manasseh. [21] Then Israel said to Joseph, "Behold, I am about to die, but God will be with you and will bring you again to the land of your fathers. [22] Moreover, I have given to you rather than to your brothers one mountain slope[6] that I took from the hand of the Amorites with my sword and with my bow."

Jacob Blesses His Sons

49 Then Jacob called his sons and said, "Gather yourselves together, that I may tell you what shall happen to you in days to come.

[2]   "Assemble and listen, O sons of Jacob,
>   listen to Israel your father.

[3]   "Reuben, you are my firstborn,
>   my might, and the firstfruits of my
>   strength,
>   preeminent in dignity and preemi-
>   nent in power.

[1] Hebrew; Septuagint *staff* [2] Hebrew *El Shaddai* [3] Or *about two hours' distance* [4] Or *let them be like fish for multitude* [5] Hebrew *fullness*
[6] Or *one portion of the land*; Hebrew *shekem*, which sounds like the town and district called *Shechem*

4 Unstable as water, you shall not have
       preeminence,
     because you went up to your
         father's bed;
     then you defiled it—he went up to
         my couch!

5 "Simeon and Levi are brothers;
     weapons of violence are their
         swords.
6 Let my soul come not into their
       council;
     O my glory, be not joined to their
         company.
   For in their anger they killed men,
     and in their willfulness they ham-
         strung oxen.
7 Cursed be their anger, for it is fierce,
     and their wrath, for it is cruel!
   I will divide them in Jacob
     and scatter them in Israel.

8 "Judah, your brothers shall praise
       you;
     your hand shall be on the neck of
         your enemies;
     your father's sons shall bow down
         before you.
9 Judah is a lion's cub;
     from the prey, my son, you have
         gone up.
   He stooped down; he crouched as a
       lion
     and as a lioness; who dares rouse
         him?
10 The scepter shall not depart from
       Judah,
     nor the ruler's staff from between
         his feet,
   until tribute comes to him;[1]
     and to him shall be the obedience
         of the peoples.
11 Binding his foal to the vine
     and his donkey's colt to the choice
         vine,
   he has washed his garments in wine
     and his vesture in the blood of
         grapes.
12 His eyes are darker than wine,
     and his teeth whiter than milk.

13 "Zebulun shall dwell at the shore of the
       sea;
     he shall become a haven for ships,
     and his border shall be at Sidon.

14 "Issachar is a strong donkey,
     crouching between the sheep-
         folds.[2]
15 He saw that a resting place was good,
     and that the land was pleasant,
   so he bowed his shoulder to bear,
     and became a servant at forced
         labor.

16 "Dan shall judge his people
     as one of the tribes of Israel.
17 Dan shall be a serpent in the way,
     a viper by the path,
   that bites the horse's heels
     so that his rider falls backward.
18 I wait for your salvation, O LORD.

19 "Raiders shall raid Gad,[3]
     but he shall raid at their heels.

20 "Asher's food shall be rich,
     and he shall yield royal delicacies.

21 "Naphtali is a doe let loose
     that bears beautiful fawns.[4]

22 "Joseph is a fruitful bough,
     a fruitful bough by a spring;
     his branches run over the wall.[5]
23 The archers bitterly attacked him,
     shot at him, and harassed him
         severely,
24 yet his bow remained unmoved;
     his arms[6] were made agile
   by the hands of the Mighty One of
       Jacob
     (from there is the Shepherd,[7] the
         Stone of Israel),
25 by the God of your father who will
       help you,
     by the Almighty[8] who will bless
         you
   with blessings of heaven above,
     blessings of the deep that crouches
         beneath,
     blessings of the breasts and of the
         womb.

---

[1] By a slight revocalization; a slight emendation yields (compare Septuagint, Syriac, Targum) *until he comes to whom it belongs;* Hebrew *until Shiloh comes,* or *until he comes to Shiloh* [2] Or *between its saddlebags* [3] *Gad* sounds like the Hebrew for *raiders* and *raid* [4] Or *he gives beautiful words,* or *that bears fawns of the fold* [5] Or *Joseph is a wild donkey, a wild donkey beside a spring, his wild colts beside the wall* [6] Hebrew *the arms of his hands* [7] Or *by the name of the Shepherd* [8] Hebrew *Shaddai*

26   The blessings of your father
     are mighty beyond the blessings of
       my parents,
     up to the bounties of the everlast-
       ing hills.[1]
   May they be on the head of Joseph,
     and on the brow of him who was
       set apart from his brothers.

27   "Benjamin is a ravenous wolf,
     in the morning devouring the prey
     and at evening dividing the spoil."

Jacob's Death and Burial

28 All these are the twelve tribes of Israel. This is what their father said to them as he blessed them, blessing each with the blessing suitable to him. 29 Then he commanded them and said to them, "I am to be gathered to my people; bury me with my fathers in the cave that is in the field of Ephron the Hittite, 30 in the cave that is in the field at Machpelah, to the east of Mamre, in the land of Canaan, which Abraham bought with the field from Ephron the Hittite to possess as a burying place. 31 There they buried Abraham and Sarah his wife. There they buried Isaac and Rebekah his wife, and there I buried Leah— 32 the field and the cave that is in it were bought from the Hittites." 33 When Jacob finished commanding his sons, he drew up his feet into the bed and breathed his last and was gathered to his people.

50 Then Joseph fell on his father's face and wept over him and kissed him. 2 And Joseph commanded his servants the physicians to embalm his father. So the physicians embalmed Israel. 3 Forty days were required for it, for that is how many are required for embalming. And the Egyptians wept for him seventy days.

4 And when the days of weeping for him were past, Joseph spoke to the household of Pharaoh, saying, "If now I have found favor in your eyes, please speak in the ears of Pharaoh, saying, 5 'My father made me swear, saying, "I am about to die: in my tomb that I hewed out for myself in the land of Canaan, there shall you bury me." Now therefore, let me please go up and bury my father. Then I will return.'" 6 And Pharaoh answered, "Go up, and bury your father, as he made you swear." 7 So

Joseph went up to bury his father. With him went up all the servants of Pharaoh, the elders of his household, and all the elders of the land of Egypt, 8 as well as all the household of Joseph, his brothers, and his father's household. Only their children, their flocks, and their herds were left in the land of Goshen. 9 And there went up with him both chariots and horsemen. It was a very great company. 10 When they came to the threshing floor of Atad, which is beyond the Jordan, they lamented there with a very great and grievous lamentation, and he made a mourning for his father seven days. 11 When the inhabitants of the land, the Canaanites, saw the mourning on the threshing floor of Atad, they said, "This is a grievous mourning by the Egyptians." Therefore the place was named Abel-mizraim;[2] it is beyond the Jordan. 12 Thus his sons did for him as he had commanded them, 13 for his sons carried him to the land of Canaan and buried him in the cave of the field at Machpelah, to the east of Mamre, which Abraham bought with the field from Ephron the Hittite to possess as a burying place. 14 After he had buried his father, Joseph returned to Egypt with his brothers and all who had gone up with him to bury his father.

God's Good Purposes

15 When Joseph's brothers saw that their father was dead, they said, "It may be that Joseph will hate us and pay us back for all the evil that we did to him." 16 So they sent a message to Joseph, saying, "Your father gave this command before he died: 17 'Say to Joseph, "Please forgive the transgression of your brothers and their sin, because they did evil to you." ' And now, please forgive the transgression of the servants of the God of your father." Joseph wept when they spoke to him. 18 His brothers also came and fell down before him and said, "Behold, we are your servants." 19 But Joseph said to them, "Do not fear, for am I in the place of God? 20 As for you, you meant evil against me, but God meant it for good, to bring it about that many people[3] should be kept alive, as they are today. 21 So do not fear; I will provide for you and your little ones." Thus he comforted them and spoke kindly to them.

---

[1] A slight emendation yields (compare Septuagint) *the blessings of the eternal mountains, the bounties of the everlasting hills*
[2] *Abel-mizraim* means *mourning* (or *meadow*) *of Egypt* [3] Or *a numerous people*

The Death of Joseph

22 So Joseph remained in Egypt, he and his father's house. Joseph lived 110 years. 23 And Joseph saw Ephraim's children of the third generation. The children also of Machir the son of Manasseh were counted as Joseph's own.[1] 24 And Joseph said to his brothers, "I am about to die, but God will visit you and bring you up out of this land to the land that he swore to Abraham, to Isaac, and to Jacob." 25 Then Joseph made the sons of Israel swear, saying, "God will surely visit you, and you shall carry up my bones from here." 26 So Joseph died, being 110 years old. They embalmed him, and he was put in a coffin in Egypt.

[1] Hebrew were born on Joseph's knees

Know True Happiness

verses to read
Genesis 50:15–21

Good can come out of the evil others plan. Don't limit your life by thinking that when bad things happen, your life is ruined or things are out of control. Bad things don't always mean your end. People might plan to hurt you, but no one can hurt you apart from God's wise and fatherly care for you. How you think about who is ultimately in control of life, and what trials are for, will determine how much they can hurt you. You can be attacked on all sides, trapped, and wounded, but if you trust that God is who he says he is, and decide that nothing matters except pleasing him, then you won't be destroyed—you'll only become stronger!

Suffering builds the life of the God Girl; it doesn't tear her down. She knows that suffering can lead to pure joy because it builds her perseverance and character. She knows it is through suffering that her faith is proven and her strength increased. Resistance, not ease, makes you stronger. So consider adversity to be only a part of your training. When you look at life from this perspective, no one can control you or hurt you.

This trial is only meant to make you better. So rise above your human nature that whines and complains and pushes back against trials, and trust in your heavenly Father who knows all, sees all, and ultimately controls all. As you stand on the solid Rock of your salvation, you will overcome anything the world might throw at you. Whatever others plan for evil, God will use for good.

The Death of Joseph

26 So Joseph remained in Egypt, he and his father's house. Joseph lived 110 years. 23 And Joseph saw Ephraim's children of the third generation. The children also of Machir the son of Manasseh were counted as Joseph's own. 24 And Joseph said to his brothers, "I am about to die, but God will

visit you and bring you up out of this land to the land that he swore to Abraham, to Isaac and to Jacob." 25 Then Joseph made the sons of Israel swear, saying, "God will surely visit you, and you shall carry up my bones from here." 26 So Joseph died, being 110 years old. They embalmed him, and he was put in a coffin in Egypt.

Know Your Happiness

INTRODUCTION TO

Exodus

Author: Moses

Time: Probably around the fifteenth century B.C.

Place: The wilderness of Sinai

Written to: The children of God

The gist

The book of Exodus is the story of God's people's salvation from slavery and their journey to the Promised Land.

Things to look for

- The ten plagues on Egypt (see Ex. 7:14–12:30)

- The parting of the Red Sea (see Ex. 14:13–15:21)

- The Ten Commandments (see Ex. 20:1–17)

- The golden calf (see Exodus 32)

Be Still

"The LORD will fight for you, and you have only to be silent."

Exodus 14:14

The book of Exodus is full of amazing encounters with God. In this book we see the Israelites almost three hundred years after Joseph died. They are growing in number and living the good life in Egypt, so much so that the new Pharaoh is afraid they will overtake the native Egyptians. So to make sure that doesn't happen, Pharaoh makes the Israelites slaves. He even goes so far as to try to have all the baby boys born to Israelite women killed off. But when the Israelites start to cry out in agony, God hears his people and comes to their rescue by freeing them from captivity.

Exodus means the "exit" or "way out," and this book shows God coming to the rescue of his people. From the plagues to the parting of the Red Sea to manna from heaven, God was with the Israelites every step of the way. God would have been amazingly real to these people, since it was obvious that no one else but God could do such miracles. But Exodus also shows us that, no matter how much God revealed himself, his people still managed to reject him. Amazing!

Exodus emphasizes obedience in response to grace. God gives this law to his people *after* he rescues them, not *before*. In his law, God shows us how to live as his redeemed children. In Exodus he makes promises to his people, and in return he asks for their obedience to his instructions.

Exodus is not only about God setting his people free. It is also about his coming and living in their midst. God is always present in the life of a God Girl, guiding and protecting you through his Holy Spirit. It's easy to look at the life of the Israelites and laugh at their disobedience and complaining, but look at your own life— how many times has God proven himself to you and you have still questioned his love, his presence, and his provision? Have we really changed over the centuries, or do we too demand more of God before we'll believe him?

As you read Exodus, notice how many times God shows up for his people, in spite of their silliness and disobedience. Look at all the things he does to prove not only his love for his people but his justice for those who stand against him.

Must-Know Terms

✑ *Aaron* ✑

Moses' brother, who served as his assistant in speaking for him (see Ex. 4:16) and was also the first high priest.

✑ *Adultery* ✑

Sexual relations with someone other than the person you are married to.

✑ *Ark* ✑

"The ark of the covenant" was the box-like container used to hold and to carry the two tablets of the covenant, the Ten Commandments.

✑ *Feast of Harvest* ✑

A one-day festival to celebrate the end of the harvest, during which the Israelites offered two loaves of bread and ten animals. Also known as "the Feast of Weeks," "the Day of the Firstfruits," or "Pentecost."

✑ *Law* ✑

God's instructions to his people on how to live a life that honors and loves God.

✑ *Mercy Seat* ✑

The golden lid of the ark of the covenant, seen as the "place of propitiation" or the removal of God's wrath. It points forward to the saving gift of Christ.

✑ *Mosaic Covenant* ✑

The covenant given to Moses on Mount Sinai, including the Ten Commandments. The sign of this covenant was to be the observance of the Sabbath (see Ex. 31:13). This is also called the Sinai covenant.

✑ *Passover* ✑

Also known as "the Feast of Unleavened Bread" (see Ex. 12:17), this is an important Jewish festival in remembrance of the Lord passing over the homes of the Israelites when he killed the firstborn sons of the Egyptians. During the festival only unleavened bread (bread made without yeast) is allowed in the house.

✑ *Yahweh Nissi* ✑

A name for God meaning "The LORD Is My Banner" (see Ex. 17:15).

Exodus

Israel Increases Greatly in Egypt

1 These are the names of the sons of Israel who came to Egypt with Jacob, each with his household: ²Reuben, Simeon, Levi, and Judah, ³Issachar, Zebulun, and Benjamin, ⁴Dan and Naphtali, Gad and Asher. ⁵All the descendants of Jacob were seventy persons; Joseph was already in Egypt. ⁶Then Joseph died, and all his brothers and all that generation. ⁷But the people of Israel were fruitful and increased greatly; they multiplied and grew exceedingly strong, so that the land was filled with them.

Pharaoh Oppresses Israel

⁸ Now there arose a new king over Egypt, who did not know Joseph. ⁹And he said to his people, "Behold, the people of Israel are too many and too mighty for us. ¹⁰Come, let us deal shrewdly with them, lest they multiply, and, if war breaks out, they join our enemies and fight against us and escape from the land." ¹¹Therefore they set taskmasters over them to afflict them with heavy burdens. They built for Pharaoh store cities, Pithom and Raamses. ¹²But the more they were oppressed, the more they multiplied and the more they spread abroad. And the Egyptians were in dread of the people of Israel. ¹³So they ruthlessly made the people of Israel work as slaves ¹⁴and made their lives bitter with hard service, in mortar and brick, and in all kinds of work in the field. In all their work they ruthlessly made them work as slaves.

¹⁵Then the king of Egypt said to the Hebrew midwives, one of whom was named Shiphrah and the other Puah, ¹⁶"When you serve as midwife to the Hebrew women and see them on the birthstool, if it is a son, you shall kill him, but if it is a daughter, she shall live." ¹⁷But the midwives feared God and did not do as the king of Egypt commanded them, but let the male children live. ¹⁸So the king of Egypt called the midwives and said to them, "Why have you done this, and let the male children live?" ¹⁹The midwives said to Pharaoh, "Because the Hebrew women are not like the Egyptian women, for they are vigorous and give birth before the midwife comes to them." ²⁰So God dealt well with the midwives. And the people multiplied and grew very strong. ²¹And because the midwives feared God, he gave them families. ²²Then Pharaoh commanded all his people, "Every son that is born to the Hebrews¹ you shall cast into the Nile, but you shall let every daughter live."

The Birth of Moses

2 Now a man from the house of Levi went and took as his wife a Levite woman. ²The woman conceived and bore a son, and when she saw that he was a fine child, she hid him three months. ³When she could hide him no longer, she took for him a basket made of bulrushes² and daubed it with bitumen and pitch. She put the child in it and placed it among the reeds by the river bank. ⁴And his sister stood at a distance to know what would be done to him. ⁵Now the daughter of Pharaoh came down to bathe at the river, while her young women walked beside the river. She saw the basket among the reeds and sent her servant woman, and she took it. ⁶When she opened it, she saw the child, and behold, the baby was crying. She took pity on him and said, "This is one of the Hebrews' children." ⁷Then his sister said to Pharaoh's daughter, "Shall I go and call you a nurse from the Hebrew women to nurse the child for you?" ⁸And Pharaoh's daughter said to her, "Go." So the girl went and called the child's mother. ⁹And Pharaoh's daughter said to her, "Take this child away and nurse him for me, and I will give you your wages." So the woman took the child and nursed him.

---

¹Samaritan, Septuagint, Targum; Hebrew lacks *to the Hebrews* ²Hebrew *papyrus reeds*

Jochebed

Read this God Girl story in Exodus 2:1–10; 6:20;
and Numbers 26:59.

> When she could hide him no longer, she took for him a basket
> made of bulrushes and daubed it with bitumen and pitch. She put
> the child in it and placed it among the reeds by the river bank.
>
> Exodus 2:3

If you love someone, set them free. It's a cliché for a reason: it's true to life.
For centuries it has happened, and for centuries it has been true that part
of loving is being able to walk away. When Jochebed gave birth to Moses,
she knew he was a special boy. So when the Pharaoh ordered all the baby
boys to be killed, she hid Moses away in order to protect him. But when he
got too old to hide, something had to be done, and giving him up was the
answer. It must have been hard to put the son she loved in a basket and offer him to another, but since that was the only chance he had to survive, she
did what she had to do.

You will have times in your life when you will be faced with two options:
either holding on tight to someone whom you were meant to let go of, or
trusting God with them and letting them float away. The choice is much easier
when your heart is consumed with pleasing God rather than yourself. When
you know that God can be trusted and that you can't hold on to what was
never yours in the first place, then you can take hold of what is truly yours:
a steadfast faith in the God who gives and who takes away (see Job 1:21).
Letting go hurts, no doubt, but holding on hurts more than just you—it hurts
the one you love. If you truly love someone, you have to know when to let go
and when to hold on tight.

[10] When the child grew older, she brought him to Pharaoh's daughter, and he became her son. She named him Moses, "Because," she said, "I drew him out of the water."[1]

Moses Flees to Midian

[11] One day, when Moses had grown up, he went out to his people and looked on their burdens, and he saw an Egyptian beating a Hebrew, one of his people.[2] [12] He looked this way and that, and seeing no one, he struck down the Egyptian and hid him in the sand. [13] When he went out the next day, behold, two Hebrews were struggling together. And he said to the man in the wrong, "Why do you strike your companion?" [14] He answered, "Who made you a prince and a judge over us? Do you mean to kill me as you killed the Egyptian?" Then Moses was afraid, and thought, "Surely the thing is known." [15] When Pharaoh heard of it, he sought to kill Moses. But Moses fled from Pharaoh and stayed in the land of Midian. And he sat down by a well.

[16] Now the priest of Midian had seven daughters, and they came and drew water and filled the troughs to water their father's flock. [17] The shepherds came and drove them away, but Moses stood up and saved them, and watered their flock. [18] When they came home to their father Reuel, he said, "How is it that you have come home so soon today?" [19] They said, "An Egyptian delivered us out of the hand of the shepherds and even drew water for us and watered the flock." [20] He said to his daughters, "Then where is he? Why have you left the man? Call him, that he may eat bread." [21] And Moses was content to dwell with the man, and he gave Moses his daughter Zipporah. [22] She gave birth to a son, and he called his name Gershom, for he said, "I have been a sojourner[3] in a foreign land."

God Hears Israel's Groaning

[23] During those many days the king of Egypt died, and the people of Israel groaned because of their slavery and cried out for help. Their cry for rescue from slavery came up to God. [24] And God heard their groaning, and God remembered his covenant with Abraham, with Isaac, and with Jacob. [25] God saw the people of Israel—and God knew.

The Burning Bush

3 Now Moses was keeping the flock of his father-in-law, Jethro, the priest of Midian, and he led his flock to the west side of the wilderness and came to Horeb, the mountain of God. [2] And the angel of the LORD appeared to him in a flame of fire out of the midst of a bush. He looked, and behold, the bush was burning, yet it was not consumed. [3] And Moses said, "I will turn aside to see this great sight, why the bush is not burned." [4] When the LORD saw that he turned aside to see, God called to him out of the bush, "Moses, Moses!" And he said, "Here I am." [5] Then he said, "Do not come near; take your sandals off your feet, for the place on which you are standing is holy ground." [6] And he said, "I am the God of your father, the God of Abraham, the God of Isaac, and the God of Jacob." And Moses hid his face, for he was afraid to look at God.

[7] Then the LORD said, "I have surely seen the affliction of my people who are in Egypt and have heard their cry because of their taskmasters. I know their sufferings, [8] and I have come down to deliver them out of the hand of the Egyptians and to bring them up out of that land to a good and broad land, a land flowing with milk and honey, to the place of the Canaanites, the Hittites, the Amorites, the Perizzites, the Hivites, and the Jebusites. [9] And now, behold, the cry of the people of Israel has come to me, and I have also seen the oppression with which the Egyptians oppress them. [10] Come, I will send you to Pharaoh that you may bring my people, the children of Israel, out of Egypt." [11] But Moses said to God, "Who am I that I should go to Pharaoh and bring the children of Israel out of Egypt?" [12] He said, "But I will be with you, and this shall be the sign for you, that I have sent you: when you have brought the people out of Egypt, you shall serve God on this mountain."

[13] Then Moses said to God, "If I come to the people of Israel and say to them, 'The God of your fathers has sent me to you,' and they ask me, 'What is his name?' what shall I say to them?" [14] God said to Moses, "I AM WHO I AM."[4] And he said, "Say this to the

---

[1] Moses sounds like the Hebrew for draw out [2] Hebrew brothers [3] Gershom sounds like the Hebrew for sojourner [4] Or I AM WHAT I AM, or I WILL BE WHAT I WILL BE

people of Israel, 'I AM has sent me to you.' "
¹⁵ God also said to Moses, "Say this to the people of Israel, 'The LORD,¹ the God of your fathers, the God of Abraham, the God of Isaac, and the God of Jacob, has sent me to you.' This is my name forever, and thus I am to be remembered throughout all generations. ¹⁶ Go and gather the elders of Israel together and say to them, 'The LORD, the God of your fathers, the God of Abraham, of Isaac, and of Jacob, has appeared to me, saying, "I have observed you and what has been done to you in Egypt, ¹⁷ and I promise that I will bring you up out of the affliction of Egypt to the land of the Canaanites, the Hittites, the Amorites, the Perizzites, the Hivites, and the Jebusites, a land flowing with milk and honey."' ¹⁸ And they will listen to your voice, and you and the elders of Israel shall go to the king of Egypt and say to him, 'The LORD, the God of the Hebrews, has met with us; and now, please let us go a three days' journey into the wilderness, that we may sacrifice to the LORD our God.' ¹⁹ But I know that the king of Egypt will not let you go unless compelled by a mighty hand.² ²⁰ So I will stretch out my hand and strike Egypt with all the wonders that I will do in it; after that he will let you go. ²¹ And I will give this people favor in the sight of the Egyptians; and when you go, you shall not go empty, ²² but each woman shall ask of her neighbor, and any woman who lives in her house, for silver and gold jewelry, and for clothing. You shall put them on your sons and on your daughters. So you shall plunder the Egyptians."

Moses Given Powerful Signs

4 Then Moses answered, "But behold, they will not believe me or listen to my voice, for they will say, 'The LORD did not appear to you.' " ² The LORD said to him, "What is that in your hand?" He said, "A staff." ³ And he said, "Throw it on the ground." So he threw it on the ground, and it became a serpent, and Moses ran from it. ⁴ But the LORD said to Moses, "Put out your hand and catch it by the tail"—so he put out his hand and caught it, and it became a staff in his hand— ⁵ "that they may believe that the LORD, the God of their fathers, the God of Abraham, the God of Isaac, and the

God of Jacob, has appeared to you." ⁶ Again the LORD said to him, "Put your hand inside your cloak."³ And he put his hand inside his cloak, and when he took it out, behold, his hand was leprous⁴ like snow. ⁷ Then God said, "Put your hand back inside your cloak." So he put his hand back inside his cloak, and when he took it out, behold, it was restored like the rest of his flesh. ⁸ "If they will not believe you," God said, "or listen to the first sign, they may believe the latter sign. ⁹ If they will not believe even these two signs or listen to your voice, you shall take some water from the Nile and pour it on the dry ground, and the water that you shall take from the Nile will become blood on the dry ground."

¹⁰ But Moses said to the LORD, "Oh, my Lord, I am not eloquent, either in the past or since you have spoken to your servant, but I am slow of speech and of tongue." ¹¹ Then the LORD said to him, "Who has made man's mouth? Who makes him mute, or deaf, or seeing, or blind? Is it not I, the LORD? ¹² Now therefore go, and I will be with your mouth and teach you what you shall speak." ¹³ But he said, "Oh, my Lord, please send someone else." ¹⁴ Then the anger of the LORD was kindled against Moses and he said, "Is there not Aaron, your brother, the Levite? I know that he can speak well. Behold, he is coming out to meet you, and when he sees you, he will be glad in his heart. ¹⁵ You shall speak to him and put the words in his mouth, and I will be with your mouth and with his mouth and will teach you both what to do. ¹⁶ He shall speak for you to the people, and he shall be your mouth, and you shall be as God to him. ¹⁷ And take in your hand this staff, with which you shall do the signs."

Moses Returns to Egypt

¹⁸ Moses went back to Jethro his father-in-law and said to him, "Please let me go back to my brothers in Egypt to see whether they are still alive." And Jethro said to Moses, "Go in peace." ¹⁹ And the LORD said to Moses in Midian, "Go back to Egypt, for all the men who were seeking your life are dead." ²⁰ So Moses took his wife and his sons and had them ride on a donkey, and went back to the land of

¹ The word LORD, when spelled with capital letters, stands for the divine name, YHWH, which is here connected with the verb *hayah*, "to be" in verse 14 ² Septuagint, Vulgate; Hebrew *go, not by a mighty hand* ³ Hebrew *into your bosom*; also verse 7 ⁴ *Leprosy* was a term for several skin diseases; see Leviticus 13

Egypt. And Moses took the staff of God in his hand.

²¹ And the LORD said to Moses, "When you go back to Egypt, see that you do before Pharaoh all the miracles that I have put in your power. But I will harden his heart, so that he will not let the people go. ²² Then you shall say to Pharaoh, 'Thus says the LORD, Israel is my firstborn son, ²³ and I say to you, "Let my son go that he may serve me." If you refuse to let him go, behold, I will kill your firstborn son.' "

²⁴ At a lodging place on the way the LORD met him and sought to put him to death. ²⁵ Then Zipporah took a flint and cut off her son's foreskin and touched Moses'[1] feet with it and said, "Surely you are a bridegroom of blood to me!" ²⁶ So he let him alone. It was then that she said, "A bridegroom of blood," because of the circumcision.

²⁷ The LORD said to Aaron, "Go into the wilderness to meet Moses." So he went and met him at the mountain of God and kissed him. ²⁸ And Moses told Aaron all the words of the LORD with which he had

sent him to speak, and all the signs that he had commanded him to do. ²⁹ Then Moses and Aaron went and gathered together all the elders of the people of Israel. ³⁰ Aaron spoke all the words that the LORD had spoken to Moses and did the signs in the sight of the people. ³¹ And the people believed; and when they heard that the LORD had visited the people of Israel and that he had seen their affliction, they bowed their heads and worshiped.

Making Bricks Without Straw

5 Afterward Moses and Aaron went and said to Pharaoh, "Thus says the LORD, the God of Israel, 'Let my people go, that they may hold a feast to me in the wilderness.' " ² But Pharaoh said, "Who is the LORD, that I should obey his voice and let Israel go? I do not know the LORD, and moreover, I will not let Israel go." ³ Then they said, "The God of the Hebrews has met with us. Please let us go a three days' journey into the wilderness that we may sacrifice to the LORD our God, lest he fall upon us with pestilence or with the sword." ⁴ But the king

[1] Hebrew *his*

Know How to Communicate

verses to read
Exodus 4:1-17

Shyness is never an excuse for sin. Just because you don't feel capable of reaching out to love and serve others doesn't mean you can disobey God's call. Nothing should keep you from reaching out to the world around you—not your tendency to fear rejection or to assume they all hate you, and not your fear of social situations—nothing is bigger than the God who commands you to go.

This should be good news to the shy girl, not something that freaks you out. It means that, contrary to popular belief, you don't have to be controlled by your shyness. You don't have to panic or be afraid of people, because God promises to help you do the things he tells you to do. God's people are called to have compassion and empathy, to treat others as we would want to be treated, to teach, and to share truth with others—yes, even with strangers. That means that if shyness is getting in the way of these commands on your life, then it is leading you to sin, and so you must not give in to it. You're a God Girl—you serve the one true God and not the god of fear. There is your freedom!

The cure for your fear is the love of the Father. When God's will is your will, nothing anyone says or does can hurt you, and that's the source of your confidence. You are truly free when you label yourself a God Girl instead of a shy girl and when, by his enabling grace, you choose his will over your own!

of Egypt said to them, "Moses and Aaron, why do you take the people away from their work? Get back to your burdens." [5]And Pharaoh said, "Behold, the people of the land are now many,[1] and you make them rest from their burdens!" [6]The same day Pharaoh commanded the taskmasters of the people and their foremen, [7]"You shall no longer give the people straw to make bricks, as in the past; let them go and gather straw for themselves. [8]But the number of bricks that they made in the past you shall impose on them, you shall by no means reduce it, for they are idle. Therefore they cry, 'Let us go and offer sacrifice to our God.' [9]Let heavier work be laid on the men that they may labor at it and pay no regard to lying words."

[10]So the taskmasters and the foremen of the people went out and said to the people, "Thus says Pharaoh, 'I will not give you straw. [11]Go and get your straw yourselves wherever you can find it, but your work will not be reduced in the least.'" [12]So the people were scattered throughout all the land of Egypt to gather stubble for straw. [13]The taskmasters were urgent, saying, "Complete your work, your daily task each day, as when there was straw." [14]And the foremen of the people of Israel, whom Pharaoh's taskmasters had set over them, were beaten and were asked, "Why have you not done all your task of making bricks today and yesterday, as in the past?"

[15]Then the foremen of the people of Israel came and cried to Pharaoh, "Why do you treat your servants like this? [16]No straw is given to your servants, yet they say to us, 'Make bricks!' And behold, your servants are beaten; but the fault is in your own people." [17]But he said, "You are idle, you are idle; that is why you say, 'Let us go and sacrifice to the LORD.' [18]Go now and work. No straw will be given you, but you must still deliver the same number of bricks." [19]The foremen of the people of Israel saw that they were in trouble when they said, "You shall by no means reduce your number of bricks, your daily task each day." [20]They met Moses and Aaron, who were waiting for them, as they came out from Pharaoh; [21]and they said to them, "The LORD look on you and judge, because you have made us stink in the sight of Pharaoh and his servants, and have put a sword in their hand to kill us."

[22]Then Moses turned to the LORD and said, "O Lord, why have you done evil to this people? Why did you ever send me? [23]For since I came to Pharaoh to speak in your name, he has done evil to this people, and you have not delivered your people at all."

God Promises Deliverance

6 But the LORD said to Moses, "Now you shall see what I will do to Pharaoh; for with a strong hand he will send them out, and with a strong hand he will drive them out of his land."

[2]God spoke to Moses and said to him, "I am the LORD. [3]I appeared to Abraham, to Isaac, and to Jacob, as God Almighty,[2] but by my name the LORD I did not make myself known to them. [4]I also established my covenant with them to give them the land of Canaan, the land in which they lived as sojourners. [5]Moreover, I have heard the groaning of the people of Israel whom the Egyptians hold as slaves, and I have remembered my covenant. [6]Say therefore to the people of Israel, 'I am the LORD, and I will bring you out from under the burdens of the Egyptians, and I will deliver you from slavery to them, and I will redeem you with an outstretched arm and with great acts of judgment. [7]I will take you to be my people, and I will be your God, and you shall know that I am the LORD your God, who has brought you out from under the burdens of the Egyptians. [8]I will bring you into the land that I swore to give to Abraham, to Isaac, and to Jacob. I will give it to you for a possession. I am the LORD.'" [9]Moses spoke thus to the people of Israel, but they did not listen to Moses, because of their broken spirit and harsh slavery.

[10]So the LORD said to Moses, [11]"Go in, tell Pharaoh king of Egypt to let the people of Israel go out of his land." [12]But Moses said to the LORD, "Behold, the people of Israel have not listened to me. How then shall Pharaoh listen to me, for I am of uncircumcised lips?" [13]But the LORD spoke to Moses and Aaron and gave them a charge about the people of Israel and about Pharaoh king of Egypt: to bring the people of Israel out of the land of Egypt.

[1]Samaritan *they are now more numerous than the people of the land* [2]Hebrew *El Shaddai*

The Genealogy of Moses and Aaron

¹⁴These are the heads of their fathers' houses: the sons of Reuben, the firstborn of Israel: Hanoch, Pallu, Hezron, and Carmi; these are the clans of Reuben. ¹⁵The sons of Simeon: Jemuel, Jamin, Ohad, Jachin, Zohar, and Shaul, the son of a Canaanite woman; these are the clans of Simeon. ¹⁶These are the names of the sons of Levi according to their generations: Gershon, Kohath, and Merari, the years of the life of Levi being 137 years. ¹⁷The sons of Gershon: Libni and Shimei, by their clans. ¹⁸The sons of Kohath: Amram, Izhar, Hebron, and Uzziel, the years of the life of Kohath being 133 years. ¹⁹The sons of Merari: Mahli and Mushi. These are the clans of the Levites according to their generations. ²⁰Amram took as his wife Jochebed his father's sister, and she bore him Aaron and Moses, the years of the life of Amram being 137 years. ²¹The sons of Izhar: Korah, Nepheg, and Zichri. ²²The sons of Uzziel: Mishael, Elzaphan, and Sithri. ²³Aaron took as his wife Elisheba, the daughter of Amminadab and the sister of Nahshon, and she bore him Nadab, Abihu, Eleazar, and Ithamar. ²⁴The sons of Korah: Assir, Elkanah, and Abiasaph; these are the clans of the Korahites. ²⁵Eleazar, Aaron's son, took as his wife one of the daughters of Putiel, and she bore him Phinehas. These are the heads of the fathers' houses of the Levites by their clans.

²⁶These are the Aaron and Moses to whom the LORD said: "Bring out the people of Israel from the land of Egypt by their hosts." ²⁷It was they who spoke to Pharaoh king of Egypt about bringing out the people of Israel from Egypt, this Moses and this Aaron.

²⁸On the day when the LORD spoke to Moses in the land of Egypt, ²⁹the LORD said to Moses, "I am the LORD; tell Pharaoh king of Egypt all that I say to you." ³⁰But Moses said to the LORD, "Behold, I am of uncircumcised lips. How will Pharaoh listen to me?"

Moses and Aaron Before Pharaoh

7 And the LORD said to Moses, "See, I have made you like God to Pharaoh, and your brother Aaron shall be your prophet. ²You shall speak all that I command you, and your brother Aaron shall tell Pharaoh to let the people of Israel go out of his land. ³But I will harden Pharaoh's heart, and though I multiply my signs and wonders in the land of Egypt, ⁴Pharaoh will not listen to you. Then I will lay my hand on Egypt and bring my hosts, my people the children of Israel, out of the land of Egypt by great acts of judgment. ⁵The Egyptians shall know that I am the LORD, when I stretch out my hand against Egypt and bring out the people of Israel from among them." ⁶Moses and Aaron did so; they did just as the LORD commanded them. ⁷Now Moses was eighty years old, and Aaron eighty-three years old, when they spoke to Pharaoh.

⁸Then the LORD said to Moses and Aaron, ⁹"When Pharaoh says to you, 'Prove yourselves by working a miracle,' then you shall say to Aaron, 'Take your staff and cast it down before Pharaoh, that it may become a serpent.'" ¹⁰So Moses and Aaron went to Pharaoh and did just as the LORD commanded. Aaron cast down his staff before Pharaoh and his servants, and it became a serpent. ¹¹Then Pharaoh summoned the wise men and the sorcerers, and they, the magicians of Egypt, also did the same by their secret arts. ¹²For each man cast down his staff, and they became serpents. But Aaron's staff swallowed up their staffs. ¹³Still Pharaoh's heart was hardened, and he would not listen to them, as the LORD had said.

The First Plague: Water Turned to Blood

¹⁴Then the LORD said to Moses, "Pharaoh's heart is hardened; he refuses to let the people go. ¹⁵Go to Pharaoh in the morning, as he is going out to the water. Stand on the bank of the Nile to meet him, and take in your hand the staff that turned into a serpent. ¹⁶And you shall say to him, 'The LORD, the God of the Hebrews, sent me to you, saying, "Let my people go, that they may serve me in the wilderness." But so far, you have not obeyed. ¹⁷Thus says the LORD, "By this you shall know that I am the LORD: behold, with the staff that is in my hand I will strike the water that is in the Nile, and it shall turn into blood. ¹⁸The fish in the Nile shall die, and the Nile will stink, and the Egyptians will grow weary of drinking water from the Nile."'" ¹⁹And the LORD said to Moses, "Say to Aaron, 'Take your staff and stretch out your hand over the waters of Egypt, over their rivers, their canals, and their ponds, and all their pools

of water, so that they may become blood, and there shall be blood throughout all the land of Egypt, even in vessels of wood and in vessels of stone.'"

²⁰Moses and Aaron did as the LORD commanded. In the sight of Pharaoh and in the sight of his servants he lifted up the staff and struck the water in the Nile, and all the water in the Nile turned into blood. ²¹And the fish in the Nile died, and the Nile stank, so that the Egyptians could not drink water from the Nile. There was blood throughout all the land of Egypt. ²²But the magicians of Egypt did the same by their secret arts. So Pharaoh's heart remained hardened, and he would not listen to them, as the LORD had said. ²³Pharaoh turned and went into his house, and he did not take even this to heart. ²⁴And all the Egyptians dug along the Nile for water to drink, for they could not drink the water of the Nile.

²⁵Seven full days passed after the LORD had struck the Nile.

The Second Plague: Frogs

8 ¹ Then the LORD said to Moses, "Go in to Pharaoh and say to him, 'Thus says the LORD, "Let my people go, that they may serve me. ²But if you refuse to let them go, behold, I will plague all your country with frogs. ³The Nile shall swarm with frogs that shall come up into your house and into your bedroom and on your bed and into the houses of your servants and your people,² and into your ovens and your kneading bowls. ⁴The frogs shall come up on you and on your people and on all your servants."'"⁵³ And the LORD said to Moses, "Say to Aaron, 'Stretch out your hand with your staff over the rivers, over the canals and over the pools, and make frogs come up on the land of Egypt!'" ⁶ So Aaron stretched out his hand over the waters of Egypt, and the frogs came up and covered the land of Egypt. ⁷But the magicians did the same by their secret arts and made frogs come up on the land of Egypt.

⁸Then Pharaoh called Moses and Aaron and said, "Plead with the LORD to take away the frogs from me and from my people, and I will let the people go to sacrifice to the LORD." ⁹Moses said to Pharaoh, "Be pleased to command me when I am to plead for you and for your servants and for your people,

that the frogs be cut off from you and your houses and be left only in the Nile." ¹⁰And he said, "Tomorrow." Moses said, "Be it as you say, so that you may know that there is no one like the LORD our God. ¹¹The frogs shall go away from you and your houses and your servants and your people. They shall be left only in the Nile." ¹²So Moses and Aaron went out from Pharaoh, and Moses cried to the LORD about the frogs, as he had agreed with Pharaoh.⁴ ¹³And the LORD did according to the word of Moses. The frogs died out in the houses, the courtyards, and the fields. ¹⁴And they gathered them together in heaps, and the land stank. ¹⁵But when Pharaoh saw that there was a respite, he hardened his heart and would not listen to them, as the LORD had said.

The Third Plague: Gnats

¹⁶Then the LORD said to Moses, "Say to Aaron, 'Stretch out your staff and strike the dust of the earth, so that it may become gnats in all the land of Egypt.'" ¹⁷And they did so. Aaron stretched out his hand with his staff and struck the dust of the earth, and there were gnats on man and beast. All the dust of the earth became gnats in all the land of Egypt. ¹⁸The magicians tried by their secret arts to produce gnats, but they could not. So there were gnats on man and beast. ¹⁹Then the magicians said to Pharaoh, "This is the finger of God." But Pharaoh's heart was hardened, and he would not listen to them, as the LORD had said.

The Fourth Plague: Flies

²⁰Then the LORD said to Moses, "Rise up early in the morning and present yourself to Pharaoh, as he goes out to the water, and say to him, 'Thus says the LORD, "Let my people go, that they may serve me. ²¹Or else, if you will not let my people go, behold, I will send swarms of flies on you and your servants and your people, and into your houses. And the houses of the Egyptians shall be filled with swarms of flies, and also the ground on which they stand. ²²But on that day I will set apart the land of Goshen, where my people dwell, so that no swarms of flies shall be there, that you may know that I am the LORD in the midst of the earth.⁵ ²³Thus I will put a divi-

¹Ch 7:26 in Hebrew ²Or among your people ³Ch 8:1 in Hebrew ⁴Or which he had brought upon Pharaoh ⁵Or that I the LORD am in the land

sion[1] between my people and your people. Tomorrow this sign shall happen.'"" [24] And the LORD did so. There came great swarms of flies into the house of Pharaoh and into his servants' houses. Throughout all the land of Egypt the land was ruined by the swarms of flies.

[25] Then Pharaoh called Moses and Aaron and said, "Go, sacrifice to your God within the land." [26] But Moses said, "It would not be right to do so, for the offerings we shall sacrifice to the LORD our God are an abomination to the Egyptians. If we sacrifice offerings abominable to the Egyptians before their eyes, will they not stone us? [27] We must go three days' journey into the wilderness and sacrifice to the LORD our God as he tells us." [28] So Pharaoh said, "I will let you go to sacrifice to the LORD your God in the wilderness; only you must not go very far away. Plead for me." [29] Then Moses said, "Behold, I am going out from you and I will plead with the LORD that the swarms of flies may depart from Pharaoh, from his servants, and from his people, tomorrow. Only let not Pharaoh cheat again by not letting the people go to sacrifice to the LORD." [30] So Moses went out from Pharaoh and prayed to the LORD. [31] And the LORD did as Moses asked, and removed the swarms of flies from Pharaoh, from his servants, and from his people; not one remained. [32] But Pharaoh hardened his heart this time also, and did not let the people go.

The Fifth Plague: Egyptian Livestock Die

9 Then the LORD said to Moses, "Go in to Pharaoh and say to him, 'Thus says the LORD, the God of the Hebrews, "Let my people go, that they may serve me. [2] For if you refuse to let them go and still hold them, [3] behold, the hand of the LORD will fall with a very severe plague upon your livestock that are in the field, the horses, the donkeys, the camels, the herds, and the flocks. [4] But the LORD will make a distinction between the livestock of Israel and the livestock of Egypt, so that nothing of all that belongs to the people of Israel shall die."'" [5] And the LORD set a time, saying, "Tomorrow the LORD will do this thing in the land." [6] And the next day the LORD did this thing. All the livestock of the Egyptians died, but not one of the livestock of the people of Israel died. [7] And Pharaoh sent, and behold, not one of the livestock of Israel was dead. But the heart of Pharaoh was hardened, and he did not let the people go.

The Sixth Plague: Boils

[8] And the LORD said to Moses and Aaron, "Take handfuls of soot from the kiln, and let Moses throw them in the air in the sight of Pharaoh. [9] It shall become fine dust over all the land of Egypt, and become boils breaking out in sores on man and beast throughout all the land of Egypt." [10] So they took soot from the kiln and stood before Pharaoh. And Moses threw it in the air, and it became boils breaking out in sores on man and beast. [11] And the magicians could not stand before Moses because of the boils, for the boils came upon the magicians and upon all the Egyptians. [12] But the LORD hardened the heart of Pharaoh, and he did not listen to them, as the LORD had spoken to Moses.

The Seventh Plague: Hail

[13] Then the LORD said to Moses, "Rise up early in the morning and present yourself before Pharaoh and say to him, 'Thus says the LORD, the God of the Hebrews, "Let my people go, that they may serve me. [14] For this time I will send all my plagues on you yourself,[2] and on your servants and your people, so that you may know that there is none like me in all the earth. [15] For by now I could have put out my hand and struck you and your people with pestilence, and you would have been cut off from the earth. [16] But for this purpose I have raised you up, to show you my power, so that my name may be proclaimed in all the earth. [17] You are still exalting yourself against my people and will not let them go. [18] Behold, about this time tomorrow I will cause very heavy hail to fall, such as never has been in Egypt from the day it was founded until now. [19] Now therefore send, get your livestock and all that you have in the field into safe shelter, for every man and beast that is in the field and is not brought home will die when the hail falls on them."'" [20] Then whoever feared the word of the LORD among the servants of Pharaoh hurried his slaves and his livestock into the houses, [21] but whoever did not pay attention to the word

[1] Septuagint, Vulgate; Hebrew *set redemption* [2] Hebrew *on your heart*

of the LORD left his slaves and his livestock in the field.

²²Then the LORD said to Moses, "Stretch out your hand toward heaven, so that there may be hail in all the land of Egypt, on man and beast and every plant of the field, in the land of Egypt." ²³Then Moses stretched out his staff toward heaven, and the LORD sent thunder and hail, and fire ran down to the earth. And the LORD rained hail upon the land of Egypt. ²⁴There was hail and fire flashing continually in the midst of the hail, very heavy hail, such as had never been in all the land of Egypt since it became a nation. ²⁵The hail struck down everything that was in the field in all the land of Egypt, both man and beast. And the hail struck down every plant of the field and broke every tree of the field. ²⁶Only in the land of Goshen, where the people of Israel were, was there no hail.

²⁷Then Pharaoh sent and called Moses and Aaron and said to them, "This time I have sinned; the LORD is in the right, and I and my people are in the wrong. ²⁸Plead with the LORD, for there has been enough of God's thunder and hail. I will let you go, and you shall stay no longer." ²⁹Moses said to him, "As soon as I have gone out of the city, I will stretch out my hands to the LORD. The thunder will cease, and there will be no more hail, so that you may know that the earth is the LORD's. ³⁰But as for you and your servants, I know that you do not yet fear the LORD God." ³¹(The flax and the barley were struck down, for the barley was in the ear and the flax was in bud. ³²But the wheat and the emmer[1] were not struck down, for they are late in coming up.) ³³So Moses went out of the city from Pharaoh and stretched out his hands to the LORD, and the thunder and the hail ceased, and the rain no longer poured upon the earth. ³⁴But when Pharaoh saw that the rain and the hail and the thunder had ceased, he sinned yet again and hardened his heart, he and his servants. ³⁵So the heart of Pharaoh was hardened, and he did not let the people of Israel go, just as the LORD had spoken through Moses.

The Eighth Plague: Locusts

10 Then the LORD said to Moses, "Go in to Pharaoh, for I have hardened his heart and the heart of his servants, that I may show these signs of mine among them, ²and that you may tell in the hearing of your son and of your grandson how I have dealt harshly with the Egyptians and what signs I have done among them, that you may know that I am the LORD."

³So Moses and Aaron went in to Pharaoh and said to him, "Thus says the LORD, the God of the Hebrews, 'How long will you refuse to humble yourself before me? Let my people go, that they may serve me. ⁴For if you refuse to let my people go, behold, tomorrow I will bring locusts into your country, ⁵and they shall cover the face of the land, so that no one can see the land. And they shall eat what is left to you after the hail, and they shall eat every tree of yours that grows in the field, ⁶and they shall fill your houses and the houses of all your servants and of all the Egyptians, as neither your fathers nor your grandfathers have seen, from the day they came on earth to this day.'" Then he turned and went out from Pharaoh.

⁷Then Pharaoh's servants said to him, "How long shall this man be a snare to us? Let the men go, that they may serve the LORD their God. Do you not yet understand that Egypt is ruined?" ⁸So Moses and Aaron were brought back to Pharaoh. And he said to them, "Go, serve the LORD your God. But which ones are to go?" ⁹Moses said, "We will go with our young and our old. We will go with our sons and daughters and with our flocks and herds, for we must hold a feast to the LORD." ¹⁰But he said to them, "The LORD be with you, if ever I let you and your little ones go! Look, you have some evil purpose in mind.[2] ¹¹No! Go, the men among you, and serve the LORD, for that is what you are asking." And they were driven out from Pharaoh's presence.

¹²Then the LORD said to Moses, "Stretch out your hand over the land of Egypt for the locusts, so that they may come upon the land of Egypt and eat every plant in the land, all that the hail has left." ¹³So Moses stretched out his staff over the land of Egypt, and the LORD brought an east wind upon the land all that day and all that night. When it was morning, the east wind had brought the locusts. ¹⁴The locusts came up over all the land of Egypt and settled on the whole country of Egypt, such a dense swarm of locusts as had never been before,

[1] A type of wheat [2] Hebrew *before your face*

nor ever will be again. **15** They covered the face of the whole land, so that the land was darkened, and they ate all the plants in the land and all the fruit of the trees that the hail had left. Not a green thing remained, neither tree nor plant of the field, through all the land of Egypt. **16** Then Pharaoh hastily called Moses and Aaron and said, "I have sinned against the LORD your God, and against you. **17** Now therefore, forgive my sin, please, only this once, and plead with the LORD your God only to remove this death from me." **18** So he went out from Pharaoh and pleaded with the LORD. **19** And the LORD turned the wind into a very strong west wind, which lifted the locusts and drove them into the Red Sea. Not a single locust was left in all the country of Egypt. **20** But the LORD hardened Pharaoh's heart, and he did not let the people of Israel go.

The Ninth Plague: Darkness

21 Then the LORD said to Moses, "Stretch out your hand toward heaven, that there may be darkness over the land of Egypt, a darkness to be felt." **22** So Moses stretched out his hand toward heaven, and there was pitch darkness in all the land of Egypt three days. **23** They did not see one another, nor did anyone rise from his place for three days, but all the people of Israel had light where they lived. **24** Then Pharaoh called Moses and said, "Go, serve the LORD; your little ones also may go with you; only let your flocks and your herds remain behind." **25** But Moses said, "You must also let us have sacrifices and burnt offerings, that we may sacrifice to the LORD our God. **26** Our livestock also must go with us; not a hoof shall be left behind, for we must take of them to serve the LORD our God, and we do not know with what we must serve the LORD until we arrive there." **27** But the LORD hardened Pharaoh's heart, and he would not let them go. **28** Then Pharaoh said to him, "Get away from me; take care never to see my face again, for on the day you see my face you shall die." **29** Moses said, "As you say! I will not see your face again."

A Final Plague Threatened

11 The LORD said to Moses, "Yet one plague more I will bring upon Pharaoh and upon Egypt. Afterward he will let you go from here. When he lets

verses to read
Exodus 10:1–2

When you are faced with impossible odds, just think of it as a chance for God to show up. Nothing that happens in the life of the God Girl is failure; everything is an opportunity. Adversity is a good thing when you use it to help you turn to the only God who can save you.

Don't let terrible situations or stubborn or angry people keep you from believing that God can and will do as he pleases on this earth. After all, he is all-powerful and always present, remember? His will ultimately wins. Even though times might look tough, you can be sure that he is still God and is still in control.

So don't fear what others fear. Just look at a trial as an opportunity for God to do what God does best: perform miracles. When you look at the world from that perspective, nothing can get you down, nothing can scare you, because you are sure of one thing, and that is God's presence and power. Relax and let others who don't know him do all the worrying. You are a God Girl and you are a child of the King. His hand is always on you to protect you and to guide you. Just look to him, trust him, and be sure that nothing happens without his ultimate permission. Because of that, you can be sure that you are able to overcome any tough situation.

you go, he will drive you away completely. ²Speak now in the hearing of the people, that they ask, every man of his neighbor and every woman of her neighbor, for silver and gold jewelry." ³And the LORD gave the people favor in the sight of the Egyptians. Moreover, the man Moses was very great in the land of Egypt, in the sight of Pharaoh's servants and in the sight of the people.

⁴So Moses said, "Thus says the LORD: 'About midnight I will go out in the midst of Egypt, ⁵and every firstborn in the land of Egypt shall die, from the firstborn of Pharaoh who sits on his throne, even to the firstborn of the slave girl who is behind the handmill, and all the firstborn of the cattle. ⁶There shall be a great cry throughout all the land of Egypt, such as there has never been, nor ever will be again. ⁷But not a dog shall growl against any of the people of Israel, either man or beast, that you may know that the LORD makes a distinction between Egypt and Israel.' ⁸And all these your servants shall come down to me and bow down to me, saying, 'Get out, you and all the people who follow you.' And after that I will go out." And he went out from Pharaoh in hot anger. ⁹Then the LORD said to Moses, "Pharaoh will not listen to you, that my wonders may be multiplied in the land of Egypt."

¹⁰Moses and Aaron did all these wonders before Pharaoh, and the LORD hardened Pharaoh's heart, and he did not let the people of Israel go out of his land.

Know Yourself

verse to read
Exodus 12:6

Since the cross, sacrifice no longer has to be made for our sins (see Heb. 10:18–19). Today, sacrifice for a God Girl is associated with giving up something that matters to you, and it is a part of how you worship God. When the Israelites were told to sacrifice a lamb for the Passover, they were told to select one that was special, with no defects, a.k.a. perfect. This perfect little lamb was to be cared for by the family for four days and then was to be slaughtered. So why didn't God tell them any old animal would do? Why didn't he just say kill a pigeon or a rat? Because the sacrifice was not just about killing the animal but also about people giving up what they needed and loved so that God would have first place in their hearts. Sacrifice isn't about giving up things that are easy to give up; it's about giving up what is hard to give up, so that we never forget the greatest treasure of our lives: God himself.

A lot of times we say we're giving up stuff or making sacrifices for God when we're really not, like saying we won't date anymore even though we haven't had a date in a year. In that case, saying that not dating is your sacrifice to God is not technically true, since you weren't dating anyway. But giving up any daydreaming or thinking about dating *would* be a great sacrifice, if that would be almost impossible for you without God's help. So whatever you want to give up for God, make sure that it's yours before you give it. In other words, if giving it up hurts, and you'll notice its absence, then that's a sacrifice.

While sacrifice is no longer a requirement, many use it as a way to deny their sinful nature and practice self-control. If there is something good in your life that you are willing to give up to prove your love for God, then that is sacrifice. Missionaries around the world give up the comforts of home in order to serve God more faithfully. Whatever you are feeling called to give up, do it out of a love for God. The joy you will experience as you trust God in this way will outweigh whatever you are giving up.

The Passover

12 The LORD said to Moses and Aaron in the land of Egypt, ²"This month shall be for you the beginning of months. It shall be the first month of the year for you. ³Tell all the congregation of Israel that on the tenth day of this month every man shall take a lamb according to their fathers' houses, a lamb for a household. ⁴And if the household is too small for a lamb, then he and his nearest neighbor shall take according to the number of persons; according to what each can eat you shall make your count for the lamb. ⁵Your lamb shall be without blemish, a male a year old. You may take it from the sheep or from the goats, ⁶and you shall keep it until the fourteenth day of this month, when the whole assembly of the congregation of Israel shall kill their lambs at twilight.¹

⁷"Then they shall take some of the blood and put it on the two doorposts and the lintel of the houses in which they eat it. ⁸They shall eat the flesh that night, roasted on the fire; with unleavened bread and bitter herbs they shall eat it. ⁹Do not eat any of it raw or boiled in water, but roasted, its head with its legs and its inner parts. ¹⁰And you shall let none of it remain until the morning; anything that remains until the morning you shall burn. ¹¹In this manner you shall eat it: with your belt fastened, your sandals on your feet, and your staff in your hand. And you shall eat it in haste. It is the LORD's Passover. ¹²For I will pass through the land of Egypt that night, and I will strike all the firstborn in the land of Egypt, both man and beast; and on all the gods of Egypt I will execute judgments: I am the LORD. ¹³The blood shall be a sign for you, on the houses where you are. And when I see the blood, I will pass over you, and no plague will befall you to destroy you, when I strike the land of Egypt.

¹⁴"This day shall be for you a memorial day, and you shall keep it as a feast to the LORD; throughout your generations, as a statute forever, you shall keep it as a feast. ¹⁵Seven days you shall eat unleavened bread. On the first day you shall remove leaven out of your houses, for if anyone eats what is leavened, from the first day until the seventh day, that person shall be cut off from Israel. ¹⁶On the first day you shall hold a holy assembly, and on the seventh day a holy assembly. No work shall be done on those days. But what everyone needs to eat, that alone may be prepared by you. ¹⁷And you shall observe the Feast of Unleavened Bread, for on this very day I brought your hosts out of the land of Egypt. Therefore you shall observe this day, throughout your generations, as a statute forever. ¹⁸In the first month, from the fourteenth day of the month at evening, you shall eat unleavened bread until the twenty-first day of the month at evening. ¹⁹For seven days no leaven is to be found in your houses. If anyone eats what is leavened, that person will be cut off from the congregation of Israel, whether he is a sojourner or a native of the land. ²⁰You shall eat nothing leavened; in all your dwelling places you shall eat unleavened bread."

Ask Yourself . . .

ABOUT SACRIFICE

- What are three things I feel like I can't live without?
- Which of them could I give up for God?
- Are they good things? Or are they bad for me?
- If they are bad, is giving them up a sacrifice—or a sign of my repentance?

²¹Then Moses called all the elders of Israel and said to them, "Go and select lambs for yourselves according to your clans, and kill the Passover lamb. ²²Take a bunch of hyssop and dip it in the blood that is in the basin, and touch the lintel and the two doorposts with the blood that is in the basin. None of you shall go out of the door of his house until the morning. ²³For the LORD will pass through to strike the Egyptians, and when he sees the blood on the lintel and on the two doorposts, the LORD will pass over the door and will not

¹ Hebrew *between the two evenings*

allow the destroyer to enter your houses to strike you. [24] You shall observe this rite as a statute for you and for your sons forever. [25] And when you come to the land that the LORD will give you, as he has promised, you shall keep this service. [26] And when your children say to you, 'What do you mean by this service?' [27] you shall say, 'It is the sacrifice of the LORD's Passover, for he passed over the houses of the people of Israel in Egypt, when he struck the Egyptians but spared our houses.'" And the people bowed their heads and worshiped.

[28] Then the people of Israel went and did so; as the LORD had commanded Moses and Aaron, so they did.

The Tenth Plague: Death of the Firstborn

[29] At midnight the LORD struck down all the firstborn in the land of Egypt, from the firstborn of Pharaoh who sat on his throne to the firstborn of the captive who was in the dungeon, and all the firstborn of the livestock. [30] And Pharaoh rose up in the night, he and all his servants and all the Egyptians. And there was a great cry in Egypt, for there was not a house where someone was not dead. [31] Then he summoned Moses and Aaron by night and said, "Up, go out from among my people, both you and the people of Israel; and go, serve the LORD, as you have said. [32] Take your flocks and your herds, as you have said, and be gone, and bless me also!"

The Exodus

[33] The Egyptians were urgent with the people to send them out of the land in haste. For they said, "We shall all be dead." [34] So the people took their dough before it was leavened, their kneading bowls being bound up in their cloaks on their shoulders. [35] The people of Israel had also done as Moses told them, for they had asked the Egyptians for silver and gold jewelry and for clothing. [36] And the LORD had given the people favor in the sight of the Egyptians, so that they let them have what they asked. Thus they plundered the Egyptians.

[37] And the people of Israel journeyed from Rameses to Succoth, about six hundred thousand men on foot, besides women and children. [38] A mixed multitude also went up with them, and very much livestock, both flocks and herds. [39] And they baked unleavened cakes of the dough that they had brought out of Egypt, for it was not leavened, because they were thrust out of Egypt and could not wait, nor had they prepared any provisions for themselves.

[40] The time that the people of Israel lived in Egypt was 430 years. [41] At the end of 430 years, on that very day, all the hosts of the LORD went out from the land of Egypt. [42] It was a night of watching by the LORD, to bring them out of the land of Egypt; so this same night is a night of watching kept to the LORD by all the people of Israel throughout their generations.

Institution of the Passover

[43] And the LORD said to Moses and Aaron, "This is the statute of the Passover: no foreigner shall eat of it, [44] but every slave[1] that is bought for money may eat of it after you have circumcised him. [45] No foreigner or hired worker may eat of it. [46] It shall be eaten in one house; you shall not take any of the flesh outside the house, and you shall not break any of its bones. [47] All the congregation of Israel shall keep it. [48] If a stranger shall sojourn with you and would keep the Passover to the LORD, let all his males be circumcised. Then he may come near and keep it; he shall be as a native of the land. But no uncircumcised person shall eat of it. [49] There shall be one law for the native and for the stranger who sojourns among you."

[50] All the people of Israel did just as the LORD commanded Moses and Aaron. [51] And on that very day the LORD brought the people of Israel out of the land of Egypt by their hosts.

Consecration of the Firstborn

13 The LORD said to Moses, [2] "Consecrate to me all the firstborn. Whatever is the first to open the womb among the people of Israel, both of man and of beast, is mine."

The Feast of Unleavened Bread

[3] Then Moses said to the people, "Remember this day in which you came out from Egypt, out of the house of slavery, for by a strong hand the LORD brought you out from this place. No leavened bread shall be eaten. [4] Today, in the month of Abib, you are going out. [5] And when the LORD brings you into the land of the Canaanites, the

---

[1] Or *servant*; the Hebrew term *'ebed* designates a range of social and economic roles (see About the ESV)

Hittites, the Amorites, the Hivites, and the Jebusites, which he swore to your fathers to give you, a land flowing with milk and honey, you shall keep this service in this month. [6] Seven days you shall eat unleavened bread, and on the seventh day there shall be a feast to the LORD. [7] Unleavened bread shall be eaten for seven days; no leavened bread shall be seen with you, and no leaven shall be seen with you in all your territory. [8] You shall tell your son on that day, 'It is because of what the LORD did for me when I came out of Egypt.' [9] And it shall be to you as a sign on your hand and as a memorial between your eyes, that the law of the LORD may be in your mouth. For with a strong hand the LORD has brought you out of Egypt. [10] You shall therefore keep this statute at its appointed time from year to year.

[11] "When the LORD brings you into the land of the Canaanites, as he swore to you and your fathers, and shall give it to you, [2] you shall set apart to the LORD all that first opens the womb. All the firstborn of your animals that are males shall be the LORD's. [13] Every firstborn of a donkey you shall redeem with a lamb, or if you will not redeem it you shall break its neck. Every firstborn of man among your sons you shall redeem. [14] And when in time to come your son asks you, 'What does this mean?' you shall say to him, 'By a strong hand the LORD brought us out of Egypt, from the house of slavery. [15] For when Pharaoh stubbornly refused to let us go, the LORD killed all the firstborn in the land of Egypt, both the firstborn of man and the firstborn of animals. Therefore I sacrifice to the LORD all the males that first open the womb, but all the firstborn of my sons I redeem.' [16] It shall be as a mark on your hand or frontlets between your eyes, for by a strong hand the LORD brought us out of Egypt."

Pillars of Cloud and Fire

[17] When Pharaoh let the people go, God did not lead them by way of the land of the Philistines, although that was near. For God said, "Lest the people change their minds when they see war and return to Egypt." [18] But God led the people around by the way of the wilderness toward the Red Sea. And the people of Israel went up out of the land of Egypt equipped for battle.

[19] Moses took the bones of Joseph with him, for Joseph[1] had made the sons of Israel solemnly swear, saying, "God will surely visit you, and you shall carry up my bones with you from here." [20] And they moved on from Succoth and encamped at Etham, on the edge of the wilderness. [21] And the LORD went before them by day in a pillar of cloud to lead them along the way, and by night in a pillar of fire to give them light, that they might travel by day and by night. [22] The pillar of cloud by day and the pillar of fire by night did not depart from before the people.

Crossing the Red Sea

14 Then the LORD said to Moses, [2] "Tell the people of Israel to turn back and encamp in front of Pi-hahiroth, between Migdol and the sea, in front of Baal-zephon; you shall encamp facing it, by the sea. [3] For Pharaoh will say of the people of Israel, 'They are wandering in the land; the wilderness has shut them in.' [4] And I will harden Pharaoh's heart, and he will pursue them, and I will get glory over Pharaoh and all his host, and the Egyptians shall know that I am the LORD." And they did so.

[5] When the king of Egypt was told that the people had fled, the mind of Pharaoh and his servants was changed toward the people, and they said, "What is this we have done, that we have let Israel go from serving us?" [6] So he made ready his chariot and took his army with him, [7] and took six hundred chosen chariots and all the other chariots of Egypt with officers over all of them. [8] And the LORD hardened the heart of Pharaoh king of Egypt, and he pursued the people of Israel while the people of Israel were going out defiantly. [9] The Egyptians pursued them, all Pharaoh's horses and chariots and his horsemen and his army, and overtook them encamped at the sea, by Pi-hahiroth, in front of Baal-zephon.

[10] When Pharaoh drew near, the people of Israel lifted up their eyes, and behold, the Egyptians were marching after them, and they feared greatly. And the people of Israel cried out to the LORD. [11] They said to Moses, "Is it because there are no graves in Egypt that you have taken us away to die in the wilderness? What have you done to us in bringing us out of Egypt? [12] Is not this what we said to you in Egypt: 'Leave

[1] Samaritan, Septuagint; Hebrew *he*

us alone that we may serve the Egyptians'? For it would have been better for us to serve the Egyptians than to die in the wilderness." ¹³ And Moses said to the people, "Fear not, stand firm, and see the salvation of the LORD, which he will work for you today. For the Egyptians whom you see today, you shall never see again. ¹⁴ The LORD will fight for you, and you have only to be silent."

¹⁵ The LORD said to Moses, "Why do you cry to me? Tell the people of Israel to go forward. ¹⁶ Lift up your staff, and stretch out your hand over the sea and divide it, that the people of Israel may go through the sea on dry ground. ¹⁷ And I will harden the hearts of the Egyptians so that they shall go in after them, and I will get glory over Pharaoh and all his host, his chariots, and his horsemen. ¹⁸ And the Egyptians shall know that I am the LORD, when I have gotten glory over Pharaoh, his chariots, and his horsemen."

¹⁹ Then the angel of God who was going before the host of Israel moved and went behind them, and the pillar of cloud moved from before them and stood behind them, ²⁰ coming between the host of Egypt and the host of Israel. And there was the cloud and the darkness. And it lit up the night[1] without one coming near the other all night.

²¹ Then Moses stretched out his hand over the sea, and the LORD drove the sea back by a strong east wind all night and made the sea dry land, and the waters were divided. ²² And the people of Israel went into the midst of the sea on dry ground, the waters being a wall to them on their right hand and on their left. ²³ The Egyptians pursued and went in after them into the midst of the sea, all Pharaoh's horses, his chariots, and his horsemen. ²⁴ And in the morning watch the LORD in the pillar of fire and of cloud looked down on the Egyptian forces and threw the Egyptian forces into a panic, ²⁵ clogging[2] their chariot wheels so that they drove heavily. And the Egyptians said, "Let us flee from before Israel, for the LORD fights for them against the Egyptians."

²⁶ Then the LORD said to Moses, "Stretch out your hand over the sea, that the water may come back upon the Egyptians, upon their chariots, and upon their horsemen."

²⁷ So Moses stretched out his hand over the sea, and the sea returned to its normal course when the morning appeared. And as the Egyptians fled into it, the LORD threw[3] the Egyptians into the midst of the sea. ²⁸ The waters returned and covered the chariots and the horsemen; of all the host of Pharaoh that had followed them into the sea, not one of them remained. ²⁹ But the people of Israel walked on dry ground through the sea, the waters being a wall to them on their right hand and on their left.

³⁰ Thus the LORD saved Israel that day from the hand of the Egyptians, and Israel saw the Egyptians dead on the seashore. ³¹ Israel saw the great power that the LORD used against the Egyptians, so the people feared the LORD, and they believed in the LORD and in his servant Moses.

The Song of Moses

15 Then Moses and the people of Israel sang this song to the LORD, saying,

"I will sing to the LORD, for he has
   triumphed gloriously;
  the horse and his rider[4] he has
   thrown into the sea.
² The LORD is my strength and my song,
  and he has become my salvation;
  this is my God, and I will praise him,
  my father's God, and I will exalt him.
³ The LORD is a man of war;
  the LORD is his name.

⁴ "Pharaoh's chariots and his host he
   cast into the sea,
  and his chosen officers were sunk
   in the Red Sea.
⁵ The floods covered them;
  they went down into the depths
   like a stone.
⁶ Your right hand, O LORD, glorious in
   power,
  your right hand, O LORD, shatters
   the enemy.
⁷ In the greatness of your majesty you
   overthrow your adversaries;
  you send out your fury; it consumes them like stubble.
⁸ At the blast of your nostrils the
   waters piled up;
  the floods stood up in a heap;
  the deeps congealed in the heart of
   the sea.

---

[1] Septuagint *and the night passed* [2] Or *binding* (compare Samaritan, Septuagint, Syriac); Hebrew *removing* [3] Hebrew *shook off* [4] Or *its chariot*; also verse 21

9 The enemy said, 'I will pursue, I will
   overtake,
   I will divide the spoil, my desire
     shall have its fill of them.
   I will draw my sword; my hand
     shall destroy them.'
0 You blew with your wind; the sea
     covered them;
   they sank like lead in the mighty
     waters.

11 "Who is like you, O LORD, among the
     gods?
   Who is like you, majestic in holi-
     ness,
   awesome in glorious deeds, doing
     wonders?
12 You stretched out your right hand;
   the earth swallowed them.

13 "You have led in your steadfast love
     the people whom you have
     redeemed;
   you have guided them by your
     strength to your holy abode.
14 The peoples have heard; they
     tremble;
   pangs have seized the inhabitants
     of Philistia.
15 Now are the chiefs of Edom dis-
     mayed;
   trembling seizes the leaders of
     Moab;
   all the inhabitants of Canaan have
     melted away.
16 Terror and dread fall upon them;
   because of the greatness of your
     arm, they are still as a stone,
   till your people, O LORD, pass by,
   till the people pass by whom you
     have purchased.
17 You will bring them in and plant
     them on your own mountain,
   the place, O LORD, which you have
     made for your abode,
   the sanctuary, O Lord, which your
     hands have established.
18 The LORD will reign forever and
     ever."

19 For when the horses of Pharaoh with
his chariots and his horsemen went into
the sea, the LORD brought back the waters
of the sea upon them, but the people of
Israel walked on dry ground in the midst
of the sea. 20 Then Miriam the prophetess,
the sister of Aaron, took a tambourine in
her hand, and all the women went out after
her with tambourines and dancing. 21 And
Miriam sang to them:

"Sing to the LORD, for he has tri-
     umphed gloriously;
   the horse and his rider he has
     thrown into the sea."

Bitter Water Made Sweet

22 Then Moses made Israel set out from
the Red Sea, and they went into the wilderness of Shur. They went three days
in the wilderness and found no water.
23 When they came to Marah, they could
not drink the water of Marah because it
was bitter; therefore it was named Marah.[1]
24 And the people grumbled against Moses,
saying, "What shall we drink?" 25 And he
cried to the LORD, and the LORD showed
him a log,[2] and he threw it into the water,
and the water became sweet.

There the LORD[3] made for them a statute
and a rule, and there he tested them, 26 saying, "If you will diligently listen to the voice
of the LORD your God, and do that which is
right in his eyes, and give ear to his commandments and keep all his statutes, I will
put none of the diseases on you that I put
on the Egyptians, for I am the LORD, your
healer."

27 Then they came to Elim, where there
were twelve springs of water and seventy
palm trees, and they encamped there by
the water.

Bread from Heaven

16 They set out from Elim, and all the
congregation of the people of Israel
came to the wilderness of Sin, which is
between Elim and Sinai, on the fifteenth
day of the second month after they had
departed from the land of Egypt. 2 And
the whole congregation of the people of
Israel grumbled against Moses and Aaron
in the wilderness, 3 and the people of Israel
said to them, "Would that we had died by
the hand of the LORD in the land of Egypt,
when we sat by the meat pots and ate
bread to the full, for you have brought us
out into this wilderness to kill this whole
assembly with hunger."

4 Then the LORD said to Moses, "Behold,
I am about to rain bread from heaven for

[1] Marah means bitterness [2] Or tree [3] Hebrew he

you, and the people shall go out and gather a day's portion every day, that I may test them, whether they will walk in my law or not. ⁵ On the sixth day, when they prepare what they bring in, it will be twice as much as they gather daily." ⁶ So Moses and Aaron said to all the people of Israel, "At evening you shall know that it was the LORD who brought you out of the land of Egypt, ⁷ and in the morning you shall see the glory of the LORD, because he has heard your grumbling against the LORD. For what are we, that you grumble against us?" ⁸ And Moses said, "When the LORD gives you in the evening meat to eat and in the morning bread to the full, because the LORD has heard your grumbling that you grumble against him— what are we? Your grumbling is not against us but against the LORD."

⁹ Then Moses said to Aaron, "Say to the whole congregation of the people of Israel, 'Come near before the LORD, for he has heard your grumbling.'" ¹⁰ And as soon as Aaron spoke to the whole congregation of the people of Israel, they looked toward the wilderness, and behold, the glory of the LORD appeared in the cloud. ¹¹ And the LORD said to Moses, ¹² "I have heard the grumbling of the people of Israel. Say to them, 'At twilight you shall eat meat, and in the morning you shall be filled with bread. Then you shall know that I am the LORD your God.'"

¹³ In the evening quail came up and covered the camp, and in the morning dew lay around the camp. ¹⁴ And when the dew had gone up, there was on the face of the wilderness a fine, flake-like thing, fine as frost on the ground. ¹⁵ When the people of Israel

---

Know True Happiness

verses to read
Exodus 16:1-3

Are there times when you hate your life? That was the case for the Israelites in the desert. "We're sick of this food," they complained. "We need meat." Really? God has just brought you out of slavery, and you're going to complain? What's up with that? From where we stand it all seems so crazy, doesn't it—complaining after what God had just done?

But have things really changed? And isn't complaining about your lot in life—like having a big nose or not being popular—the same as accusing the God of not giving you enough? Did you know that everything that happens to you has to come through God to get to you? Does that make him a tyrant in your eyes? It might, if you don't know the big picture.

The truth is that God has a purpose for everything in your life. And he promises to work all things together for your good. All your aches, pains, and emptiness—he'll use it all for good if you'll do just one thing: trust him. Can you trust that the place where you are in life right now is exactly where you should be? Everything that he gives or takes away is for your benefit. Even if it feels like the exact opposite, don't believe your feelings but trust him. When you do, you will find a life filled with hope and direction. You won't be wandering in the dark, dry desert, but you'll find your Promised Land, the place where you can be content no matter what happens.

Are you tired of being unhappy? Do you want victory? Then surrender yourself to God, by faith, holding nothing back. Determine, in reliance on the Spirit, to trust God and believe that your life is under his control no matter how lost you feel. You must believe God's Word when it says, "for those who love God all things work together for good" (Rom. 8:28).

w it, they said to one another, "What is ?"[1] For they did not know what it was. And oses said to them, "It is the bread that the ORD has given you to eat. [16] This is what ne LORD has commanded: 'Gather of it, ach one of you, as much as he can eat. You nall each take an omer,[2] according to the umber of the persons that each of you has i his tent.'" [17] And the people of Israel did). They gathered, some more, some less. But when they measured it with an omer, 'hoever gathered much had nothing left ver, and whoever gathered little had no .ck. Each of them gathered as much as he uld eat. [19] And Moses said to them, "Let o one leave any of it over till the morn-ig." [20] But they did not listen to Moses. ome left part of it till the morning, and bred worms and stank. And Moses was igry with them. [21] Morning by morning tey gathered it, each as much as he could at; but when the sun grew hot, it melted. [22] On the sixth day they gathered twice as uch bread, two omers each. And when all ie leaders of the congregation came and old Moses, [23] he said to them, "This is what ie LORD has commanded: 'Tomorrow is a ay of solemn rest, a holy Sabbath to the ORD; bake what you will bake and boil 'hat you will boil, and all that is left over y aside to be kept till the morning.'" [24] So iey laid it aside till the morning, as Moses ommanded them, and it did not stink, nd there were no worms in it. [25] Moses aid, "Eat it today, for today is a Sabbath to ie LORD; today you will not find it in the eld. [26] Six days you shall gather it, but on ie seventh day, which is a Sabbath, there 'ill be none."

[27] On the seventh day some of the people 'ent out to gather, but they found none. And the LORD said to Moses, "How long 'ill you refuse to keep my commandments nd my laws? [29] See! The LORD has given ou the Sabbath; therefore on the sixth day e gives you bread for two days. Remain ach of you in his place; let no one go out f his place on the seventh day." [30] So the eople rested on the seventh day.

[31] Now the house of Israel called its name anna. It was like coriander seed, white, nd the taste of it was like wafers made 'ith honey. [32] Moses said, "This is what the ORD has commanded: 'Let an omer of it be

kept throughout your generations, so that they may see the bread with which I fed you in the wilderness, when I brought you out of the land of Egypt.'" [33] And Moses said to Aaron, "Take a jar, and put an omer of manna in it, and place it before the LORD to be kept throughout your generations." [34] As the LORD commanded Moses, so Aaron placed it before the testimony to be kept. [35] The people of Israel ate the manna forty years, till they came to a habitable land. They ate the manna till they came to the border of the land of Canaan. [36] (An omer is the tenth part of an ephah.)[3]

Water from the Rock

17 All the congregation of the people of Israel moved on from the wilderness of Sin by stages, according to the commandment of the LORD, and camped at Rephidim, but there was no water for the people to drink. [2] Therefore the people quarreled with Moses and said, "Give us water to drink." And Moses said to them, "Why do you quarrel with me? Why do you test the LORD?" [3] But the people thirsted there for water, and the people grumbled against Moses and said, "Why did you bring us up out of Egypt, to kill us and our children and our livestock with thirst?" [4] So Moses cried to the LORD, "What shall I do with this people? They are almost ready to stone me." [5] And the LORD said to Moses, "Pass on before the people, taking with you some of the elders of Israel, and take in your hand the staff with which you struck the Nile, and go. [6] Behold, I will stand before you there on the rock at Horeb, and you shall strike the rock, and water shall come out of it, and the people will drink." And Moses did so, in the sight of the elders of Israel. [7] And he called the name of the place Massah[4] and Meribah,[5] because of the quarreling of the people of Israel, and because they tested the LORD by saying, "Is the LORD among us or not?"

Israel Defeats Amalek

[8] Then Amalek came and fought with Israel at Rephidim. [9] So Moses said to Joshua, "Choose for us men, and go out and fight with Amalek. Tomorrow I will stand on the top of the hill with the staff of God in my hand." [10] So Joshua did as Moses told

Dr "It is manna." Hebrew man hu [2] An omer was about 2 quarts or 2 liters [3] An ephah was about 3/5 bushel or 22 liters [4] Massah eans testing [5] Meribah means quarreling him, and fought with Amalek, while Moses, Aaron, and Hur went up to the top of the hill. [11] Whenever Moses held up his hand, Israel prevailed, and whenever he lowered his hand, Amalek prevailed. [12] But Moses' hands grew weary, so they took a stone and put it under him, and he sat on it, while Aaron and Hur held up his hands, one on one side, and the other on the other side. So his hands were steady until the going down of the sun. [13] And Joshua overwhelmed Amalek and his people with the sword.

[14] Then the LORD said to Moses, "Write this as a memorial in a book and recite it in the ears of Joshua, that I will utterly blot out the memory of Amalek from under heaven." [15] And Moses built an altar and called the name of it, The LORD Is My Banner, [16] saying, "A hand upon the throne[1] of the LORD! The LORD will have war with Amalek from generation to generation."

Jethro's Advice

18 Jethro, the priest of Midian, Moses' father-in-law, heard of all that God had done for Moses and for Israel his people, how the LORD had brought Israel out of Egypt. [2] Now Jethro, Moses' father-in-law, had taken Zipporah, Moses' wife, after he had sent her home, [3] along with her two sons. The name of the one was Gershom (for he said, "I have been a sojourner[2] in a foreign land"), [4] and the name of the other, Eliezer[3] (for he said, "The God of my father was my help, and delivered me from the sword of Pharaoh"). [5] Jethro, Moses' father-in-law, came with his sons and his wife to Moses in the wilderness where he was encamped at the mountain of God. [6] And when he sent word to Moses, "I,[4] your father-in-law Jethro, am coming to you with your wife and her two sons with her," [7] Moses went out to meet his father-in-law and bowed down and kissed him. And they asked each other of their welfare and went into the tent. [8] Then Moses told his father-in-law all that the LORD had done to Pharaoh and to the Egyptians for Israel's sake, all the hardship that had come upon them in the way, and how the LORD had delivered them. [9] And Jethro rejoiced for all the good that the LORD had done to Israel, in that he had delivered them out of the hand of the Egyptians.

[10] Jethro said, "Blessed be the LORD, wh has delivered you out of the hand of th Egyptians and out of the hand of Pharao and has delivered the people from unde the hand of the Egyptians. [11] Now I know that the LORD is greater than all gods because in this affair they dealt arrogantl with the people."[5] [12] And Jethro, Moses father-in-law, brought a burnt offering and sacrifices to God; and Aaron came with all the elders of Israel to eat bread with Moses' father-in-law before God.

[13] The next day Moses sat to judge th people, and the people stood around Mose from morning till evening. [14] When Moses father-in-law saw all that he was doing for the people, he said, "What is this tha you are doing for the people? Why do yo sit alone, and all the people stand around you from morning till evening?" [15] An Moses said to his father-in-law, "Becaus the people come to me to inquire of God [16] when they have a dispute, they come to me and I decide between one person an another, and I make them know the stat utes of God and his laws." [17] Moses' father in-law said to him, "What you are doing i not good. [18] You and the people with yo will certainly wear yourselves out, for th thing is too heavy for you. You are not able to do it alone. [19] Now obey my voice; I wil give you advice, and God be with you! You shall represent the people before God and bring their cases to God, [20] and you shall warn them about the statutes and the laws and make them know the way in which they must walk and what they must do [21] Moreover, look for able men from all the people, men who fear God, who are trust worthy and hate a bribe, and place such men over the people as chiefs of thousands of hundreds, of fifties, and of tens. [22] And let them judge the people at all times. Every great matter they shall bring to you, but any small matter they shall decide them selves. So it will be easier for you, and they will bear the burden with you. [23] If you do this, God will direct you, you will be able to endure, and all this people also will go to their place in peace."

[24] So Moses listened to the voice of his father-in-law and did all that he had said [25] Moses chose able men out of all Israel and made them heads over the people

---

[1] A slight change would yield *upon the banner* [2] *Gershom* sounds like the Hebrew word for *sojourner* [3] *Eliezer* means *My God is help*
[4] Hebrew; Samaritan, Septuagint, Syriac *behold* [5] Hebrew *with them*

chiefs of thousands, of hundreds, of fifties, and of tens. ²⁶ And they judged the people at all times. Any hard case they brought to Moses, but any small matter they decided themselves. ²⁷ Then Moses let his father-in-law depart, and he went away to his own country.

Israel at Mount Sinai

19 On the third new moon after the people of Israel had gone out of the land of Egypt, on that day they came into the wilderness of Sinai. ² They set out from Rephidim and came into the wilderness of Sinai, and they encamped in the wilderness. There Israel encamped before the mountain, ³ while Moses went up to God. The LORD called to him out of the mountain, saying, "Thus you shall say to the house of Jacob, and tell the people of Israel: ⁴ You yourselves have seen what I did to the Egyptians, and how I bore you on eagles' wings and brought you to myself. ⁵ Now therefore, if you will indeed obey my voice and keep my covenant, you shall be my treasured possession among all peoples,

for all the earth is mine; ⁶ and you shall be to me a kingdom of priests and a holy nation. These are the words that you shall speak to the people of Israel."

⁷ So Moses came and called the elders of the people and set before them all these words that the LORD had commanded him. ⁸ All the people answered together and said, "All that the LORD has spoken we will do." And Moses reported the words of the people to the LORD. ⁹ And the LORD said to Moses, "Behold, I am coming to you in a thick cloud, that the people may hear when I speak with you, and may also believe you forever."

When Moses told the words of the people to the LORD, ¹⁰ the LORD said to Moses, "Go to the people and consecrate them today and tomorrow, and let them wash their garments ¹¹ and be ready for the third day. For on the third day the LORD will come down on Mount Sinai in the sight of all the people. ¹² And you shall set limits for the people all around, saying, 'Take care not to go up into the mountain or touch the edge of it. Whoever touches the

Know God

verses to read
Exodus 19:1–6

You've read your Bible a thousand times and still nothing. What does it all mean? Where is God when I need him? Why do I feel so empty? Am I missing something? Then suddenly you obey him in some way and poof! That same verse you've read over and over before—it finally means something! Why didn't you get it before?

The reason may be that, when you read God's Word and then do what it says to do, something funny happens: he shows you more truth. He blesses you, as his Word says he will. Just as God asked the Israelites in Exodus 19 to obey him because of his outrageous grace in rescuing them from slavery to the Egyptians, so he is asking you to obey him because of his outrageous grace in rescuing you from slavery to sin, death, and hell. If you just aren't finding God and want something more, then consider just doing it—whatever God commands. Do what he is asking you to do, and you'll find more of him than you've ever found before. Obedience, the art of just doing it, brings you face-to-face with God. You won't ever have that connection you want to have until you do what he says. He's not a tyrant who tells you to do something only to punish you and wreck your life. No, he's your Father who tells you to do stuff so that your life will be better, because you will know him more deeply. Don't expect the worst from obedience; believe in the best. His Word promises it. Don't wait another minute; do what God is asking you to do today, and you'll see more of God than you are seeing right now.

mountain shall be put to death. ¹³No hand shall touch him, but he shall be stoned or shot;¹ whether beast or man, he shall not live.' When the trumpet sounds a long blast, they shall come up to the mountain." ¹⁴So Moses went down from the mountain to the people and consecrated the people; and they washed their garments. ¹⁵And he said to the people, "Be ready for the third day; do not go near a woman."

¹⁶On the morning of the third day there were thunders and lightnings and a thick cloud on the mountain and a very loud trumpet blast, so that all the people in the camp trembled. ¹⁷Then Moses brought the people out of the camp to meet God, and they took their stand at the foot of the mountain. ¹⁸Now Mount Sinai was wrapped in smoke because the Lord had descended on it in fire. The smoke of it went up like the smoke of a kiln, and the whole mountain trembled greatly. ¹⁹And as the sound of the trumpet grew louder and louder, Moses spoke, and God answered him in thunder. ²⁰The Lord came down on Mount Sinai, to the top of the mountain. And the Lord called Moses to the top of the mountain, and Moses went up.

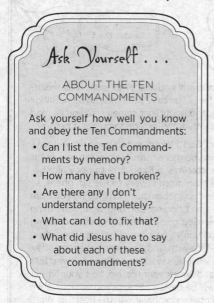

Ask Yourself . . .

ABOUT THE TEN COMMANDMENTS

Ask yourself how well you know and obey the Ten Commandments:

- Can I list the Ten Commandments by memory?
- How many have I broken?
- Are there any I don't understand completely?
- What can I do to fix that?
- What did Jesus have to say about each of these commandments?

²¹And the Lord said to Moses, "Go down and warn the people, lest they break through to the Lord to look and many of them perish. ²²Also let the priests who come near to the Lord consecrate themselves, lest the Lord break out against them." ²³And Moses said to the Lord, "The people cannot come up to Mount Sinai, for you yourself warned us, saying, 'Set limits around the mountain and consecrate it.'" ²⁴And the Lord said to him, "Go down, and come up bringing Aaron with you. But do not let the priests and the people break through to come up to the Lord, lest he break out against them." ²⁵So Moses went down to the people and told them.

The Ten Commandments

20 And God spoke all these words, saying,

²"I am the Lord your God, who brought you out of the land of Egypt, out of the house of slavery.

³"You shall have no other gods before² me.

⁴"You shall not make for yourself a carved image, or any likeness of anything that is in heaven above, or that is in the earth beneath, or that is in the water under the earth. ⁵You shall not bow down to them or serve them, for I the Lord your God am a jealous God, visiting the iniquity of the fathers on the children to the third and the fourth generation of those who hate me, ⁶but showing steadfast love to thousands³ of those who love me and keep my commandments.

⁷"You shall not take the name of the Lord your God in vain, for the Lord will not hold him guiltless who takes his name in vain.

⁸"Remember the Sabbath day, to keep it holy. ⁹Six days you shall labor, and do all your work, ¹⁰but the seventh day is a Sabbath to the Lord your God. On it you shall not do any work, you, or your son, or your daughter, your male servant, or your female servant, or your livestock, or the sojourner who is within your gates. ¹¹For in six days the Lord made heaven and earth, the sea, and all that is in them, and rested on the seventh day. Therefore the Lord blessed the Sabbath day and made it holy.

¹²"Honor your father and your mother, that your days may be long in the land that the Lord your God is giving you.

¹That is, shot with an arrow ²Or *besides* ³Or *to the thousandth generation*

[13] "You shall not murder.[1]

[14] "You shall not commit adultery.

[15] "You shall not steal.

[16] "You shall not bear false witness against your neighbor.

[17] "You shall not covet your neighbor's house; you shall not covet your neighbor's wife, or his male servant, or his female servant, or his ox, or his donkey, or anything that is your neighbor's."

[18] Now when all the people saw the thunder and the flashes of lightning and the sound of the trumpet and the mountain smoking, the people were afraid[2] and trembled, and they stood far off [19] and said to Moses, "You speak to us, and we will listen; but do not let God speak to us, lest we die." [20] Moses said to the people, "Do not fear, for God has come to test you, that the fear of him may be before you, that you may not sin." [21] The people stood far off, while Moses drew near to the thick darkness where God was.

Laws About Altars

[22] And the LORD said to Moses, "Thus you shall say to the people of Israel: 'You have seen for yourselves that I have talked with you from heaven. [23] You shall not make gods of silver to be with me, nor shall you make for yourselves gods of gold. [24] An altar of earth you shall make for me and sacrifice on it your burnt offerings and your peace offerings, your sheep and your oxen. In every place where I cause my name to be remembered I will come to you and bless you. [25] If you make me an altar of stone, you shall not build it of hewn stones, for if you wield your tool on it you profane it. [26] And you shall not go up by steps to my altar, that your nakedness be not exposed on it.'

Laws About Slaves

21 "Now these are the rules that you shall set before them. [2] When you buy a Hebrew slave,[3] he shall serve six years, and in the seventh he shall go out

[1] The Hebrew word also covers causing human death through carelessness or negligence [2] Samaritan, Septuagint, Syriac, Vulgate; Masoretic Text *the people saw* [3] Or *servant*; the Hebrew term *'ebed* designates a range of social and economic roles; also verses 5, 6, 7, 20, 21, 26, 27, 32 (see About the ESV)

verses to read
Exodus 20:1-17

Know Love

Sometimes the hardest people to love are the ones closest to you. It's easier to love people you see only from a distance, but the ones you see up close can be unimpressive, even unkind. But the truth is that we're all like that up close. No one is perfect, and the closer you get, the more you see those imperfections. And that's why parents can be so much trouble. Not only do you see all their blemishes and smell all their stinks, but you have to deal with all their emotional, spiritual, and mental weaknesses. When they tell you what to do, it can be hard to respect them, hard not to roll your eyes or to laugh. But then God knew that, didn't he? "Honor your father and your mother" (Ex. 20:12). It was such an important command that it made the Top Ten list!

Your parents were given to you to make you stronger. And though they might sometimes do that by godly example and insight, sometimes they do it by accident. No matter what your parents do, the most spiritual response to them is honor and respect, if only for their position as parents. Knowing this can help you to stop taking everything that comes from them as insanity or old age setting in and start thinking about it as direction from God. Each time you give up what you want to do, to do whatever your parents want, you build your spiritual strength and show God and the world that his desires are more important to you than your own. God is glorified, and you find that you are happier!

free, for nothing. [3] If he comes in single, he shall go out single; if he comes in married, then his wife shall go out with him. [4] If his master gives him a wife and she bears him sons or daughters, the wife and her children shall be her master's, and he shall go out alone. [5] But if the slave plainly says, 'I love my master, my wife, and my children; I will not go out free,' [6] then his master shall bring him to God, and he shall bring him to the door or the doorpost. And his master shall bore his ear through with an awl, and he shall be his slave forever.

[7] "When a man sells his daughter as a slave, she shall not go out as the male slaves do. [8] If she does not please her master, who has designated her[1] for himself, then he shall let her be redeemed. He shall have no right to sell her to a foreign people, since he has broken faith with her. [9] If he designates her for his son, he shall deal with her as with a daughter. [10] If he takes another wife to himself, he shall not diminish her food, her clothing, or her marital rights. [11] And if he does not do these three things for her, she shall go out for nothing, without payment of money.

[12] "Whoever strikes a man so that he dies shall be put to death. [13] But if he did not lie in wait for him, but God let him fall into his hand, then I will appoint for you a place to which he may flee. [14] But if a man willfully attacks another to kill him by cunning, you shall take him from my altar, that he may die.

[15] "Whoever strikes his father or his mother shall be put to death.

[16] "Whoever steals a man and sells him, and anyone found in possession of him, shall be put to death.

[17] "Whoever curses[2] his father or his mother shall be put to death.

[18] "When men quarrel and one strikes the other with a stone or with his fist and the man does not die but takes to his bed, [19] then if the man rises again and walks outdoors with his staff, he who struck him shall be clear; only he shall pay for the loss of his time, and shall have him thoroughly healed.

[20] "When a man strikes his slave, male or female, with a rod and the slave dies under his hand, he shall be avenged. [21] But if the slave survives a day or two, he is not to be avenged, for the slave is his money.

[22] "When men strive together and hit a pregnant woman, so that her children come out, but there is no harm, the one who hit her shall surely be fined, as the woman's husband shall impose on him, and he shall pay as the judges determine. [23] But if there is harm,[3] then you shall pay life for life, [24] eye for eye, tooth for tooth, hand for hand, foot for foot, [25] burn for burn, wound for wound, stripe for stripe.

[26] "When a man strikes the eye of his slave, male or female, and destroys it, he shall let the slave go free because of his eye. [27] If he knocks out the tooth of his slave, male or female, he shall let the slave go free because of his tooth.

[28] "When an ox gores a man or a woman to death, the ox shall be stoned, and its flesh shall not be eaten, but the owner of the ox shall not be liable. [29] But if the ox has been accustomed to gore in the past, and its owner has been warned but has not kept it in, and it kills a man or a woman, the ox shall be stoned, and its owner also shall be put to death. [30] If a ransom is imposed on him, then he shall give for the redemption of his life whatever is imposed on him. [31] If it gores a man's son or daughter, he shall be dealt with according to this same rule. [32] If the ox gores a slave, male or female, the owner shall give to their master thirty shekels[4] of silver, and the ox shall be stoned.

Laws About Restitution

[33] "When a man opens a pit, or when a man digs a pit and does not cover it, and an ox or a donkey falls into it, [34] the owner of the pit shall make restoration. He shall give money to its owner, and the dead beast shall be his.

[35] "When one man's ox butts another's, so that it dies, then they shall sell the live ox and share its price, and the dead beast also they shall share. [36] Or if it is known that the ox has been accustomed to gore in the past, and its owner has not kept it in, he shall repay ox for ox, and the dead beast shall be his.

---

[1] Or so that he has not designated her [2] Or dishonors; Septuagint reviles [3] Or so that her children come out and it is clear who was to blame, he shall be fined as the woman's husband shall impose on him, and he alone shall pay. If it is unclear who was to blame … [4] A shekel was about 2/5 ounce or 11 grams

22 ^{1} "If a man steals an ox or a sheep, and kills it or sells it, he shall repay five oxen for an ox, and four sheep for a sheep. ^{2} If a thief is found breaking in and is struck so that he dies, there shall be no bloodguilt for him, ^{3} but if the sun has risen on him, there shall be bloodguilt for him. He shall surely pay. If he has nothing, then he shall be sold for his theft. ^{4} If the stolen beast is found alive in his possession, whether it is an ox or a donkey or a sheep, he shall pay double.

^{5} "If a man causes a field or vineyard to be grazed over, or lets his beast loose and it feeds in another man's field, he shall make restitution from the best in his own field and in his own vineyard.

^{6} "If fire breaks out and catches in thorns so that the stacked grain or the standing grain or the field is consumed, he who started the fire shall make full restitution.

^{7} "If a man gives to his neighbor money or goods to keep safe, and it is stolen from the man's house, then, if the thief is found, he shall pay double. ^{8} If the thief is not found, the owner of the house shall come near to God to show whether or not he has put his hand to his neighbor's property. ^{9} For every breach of trust, whether it is for an ox, for a donkey, for a sheep, for a cloak, or for any kind of lost thing, of which one says, 'This is it,' the case of both parties shall come before God. The one whom God condemns shall pay double to his neighbor.

^{10} "If a man gives to his neighbor a donkey or an ox or a sheep or any beast to keep safe, and it dies or is injured or is driven away, without anyone seeing it, ^{11} an oath by the LORD shall be between them both to see whether or not he has put his hand to his neighbor's property. The owner shall accept the oath, and he shall not make restitution. ^{12} But if it is stolen from him, he shall make restitution to its owner. ^{13} If it is torn by beasts, let him bring it as evidence. He shall not make restitution for what has been torn.

^{14} "If a man borrows anything of his neighbor, and it is injured or dies, the owner not being with it, he shall make full restitution. ^{15} If the owner was with it, he shall not make restitution; if it was hired, it came for its hiring fee.^{3}

Laws About Social Justice

^{16} "If a man seduces a virgin^4 who is not betrothed and lies with her, he shall give the bride-price^5 for her and make her his wife. ^{17} If her father utterly refuses to give her to him, he shall pay money equal to the bride-price for virgins.

^{18} "You shall not permit a sorceress to live.

^{19} "Whoever lies with an animal shall be put to death.

^{20} "Whoever sacrifices to any god, other than the LORD alone, shall be devoted to destruction.^{6}

^{21} "You shall not wrong a sojourner or oppress him, for you were sojourners in the land of Egypt. ^{22} You shall not mistreat any widow or fatherless child. ^{23} If you do mistreat them, and they cry out to me, I will surely hear their cry, ^{24} and my wrath will burn, and I will kill you with the sword, and your wives shall become widows and your children fatherless.

^{25} "If you lend money to any of my people with you who is poor, you shall not be like a moneylender to him, and you shall not exact interest from him. ^{26} If ever you take your neighbor's cloak in pledge, you shall return it to him before the sun goes down, ^{27} for that is his only covering, and it is his cloak for his body; in what else shall he sleep? And if he cries to me, I will hear, for I am compassionate.

^{28} "You shall not revile God, nor curse a ruler of your people.

^{29} "You shall not delay to offer from the fullness of your harvest and from the outflow of your presses. The firstborn of your sons you shall give to me. ^{30} You shall do the same with your oxen and with your sheep: seven days it shall be with its mother; on the eighth day you shall give it to me.

^{31} "You shall be consecrated to me. Therefore you shall not eat any flesh that is torn by beasts in the field; you shall throw it to the dogs.

23 "You shall not spread a false report. You shall not join hands with a wicked man to be a malicious witness. ^{2} You shall not fall in with the many to do evil, nor shall you bear witness in a lawsuit, siding with the many, so as to pervert justice; ^{3} nor shall you be partial to a poor man in his lawsuit.

---

^{1} Ch 21:37 in Hebrew ^{2} Ch 22:1 in Hebrew ^{3} Or *it is reckoned in* (Hebrew *comes into*) *its hiring fee* ^{4} Or *a girl of marriageable age*; also verse 17 ^{5} Or *engagement present*; also verse 17 ^{6} That is, set apart (devoted) as an offering to the Lord (for destruction)

[4] "If you meet your enemy's ox or his donkey going astray, you shall bring it back to him. [5] If you see the donkey of one who hates you lying down under its burden, you shall refrain from leaving him with it; you shall rescue it with him.

[6] "You shall not pervert the justice due to your poor in his lawsuit. [7] Keep far from a false charge, and do not kill the innocent and righteous, for I will not acquit the wicked. [8] And you shall take no bribe, for a bribe blinds the clear-sighted and subverts the cause of those who are in the right.

[9] "You shall not oppress a sojourner. You know the heart of a sojourner, for you were sojourners in the land of Egypt.

Laws About the Sabbath and Festivals

[10] "For six years you shall sow your land and gather in its yield, [11] but the seventh year you shall let it rest and lie fallow, that the poor of your people may eat; and what they leave the beasts of the field may eat. You shall do likewise with your vineyard, and with your olive orchard.

[12] "Six days you shall do your work, but on the seventh day you shall rest; that your ox and your donkey may have rest, and the son of your servant woman, and the alien, may be refreshed.

[13] "Pay attention to all that I have said to you, and make no mention of the names of other gods, nor let it be heard on your lips.

[14] "Three times in the year you shall keep a feast to me. [15] You shall keep the Feast of Unleavened Bread. As I commanded you, you shall eat unleavened bread for seven days at the appointed time in the month of Abib, for in it you came out of Egypt. None shall appear before me empty-handed. [16] You shall keep the Feast of Harvest, of the firstfruits of your labor, of what you sow in the field. You shall keep the Feast of Ingathering at the end of the year, when you gather in from the field the fruit of your labor. [17] Three times in the year shall all your males appear before the Lord GOD.

[18] "You shall not offer the blood of my sacrifice with anything leavened, or let the fat of my feast remain until the morning.

[19] "The best of the firstfruits of your ground you shall bring into the house of the LORD your God.

"You shall not boil a young goat in its mother's milk.

Conquest of Canaan Promised

[20] "Behold, I send an angel before you to guard you on the way and to bring you to the place that I have prepared. [21] Pay careful attention to him and obey his voice; do not rebel against him, for he will not pardon your transgression, for my name is in him.

[22] "But if you carefully obey his voice and do all that I say, then I will be an enemy to your enemies and an adversary to your adversaries.

[23] "When my angel goes before you and brings you to the Amorites and the Hittites and the Perizzites and the Canaanites, the Hivites and the Jebusites, and I blot them out, [24] you shall not bow down to their gods nor serve them, nor do as they do, but you shall utterly overthrow them and break their pillars in pieces. [25] You shall serve the LORD your God, and he[1] will bless your bread and your water, and I will take sickness away from among you. [26] None shall miscarry or be barren in your land; I will fulfill the number of your days. [27] I will send my terror before you and will throw into confusion all the people against whom you shall come, and I will make all your enemies turn their backs to you. [28] And I will send hornets[2] before you, which shall drive out the Hivites, the Canaanites, and the Hittites from before you. [29] I will not drive them out from before you in one year, lest the land become desolate and the wild beasts multiply against you. [30] Little by little I will drive them out from before you, until you have increased and possess the land. [31] And I will set your border from the Red Sea to the Sea of the Philistines, and from the wilderness to the Euphrates,[3] for I will give the inhabitants of the land into your hand, and you shall drive them out before you. [32] You shall make no covenant with them and their gods. [33] They shall not dwell in your land, lest they make you sin against me; for if you serve their gods, it will surely be a snare to you."

The Covenant Confirmed

24 Then he said to Moses, "Come up to the LORD, you and Aaron, Nadab, and Abihu, and seventy of the elders of Israel, and worship from afar. [2] Moses alone shall come near to the LORD, but the others

---

[1] Septuagint, Vulgate / [2] Or the hornet / [3] Hebrew the River

shall not come near, and the people shall not come up with him."

³Moses came and told the people all the words of the LORD and all the rules.¹ And all the people answered with one voice and said, "All the words that the LORD has spoken we will do." ⁴And Moses wrote down all the words of the LORD. He rose early in the morning and built an altar at the foot of the mountain, and twelve pillars, according to the twelve tribes of Israel. ⁵And he sent young men of the people of Israel, who offered burnt offerings and sacrificed peace offerings of oxen to the LORD. ⁶And Moses took half of the blood and put it in basins, and half of the blood he threw against the altar. ⁷Then he took the Book of the Covenant and read it in the hearing of the people. And they said, "All that the LORD has spoken we will do, and we will be obedient." ⁸And Moses took the blood and threw it on the people and said, "Behold the blood of the covenant that the LORD has made with you in accordance with all these words."

⁹Then Moses and Aaron, Nadab, and Abihu, and seventy of the elders of Israel went up, ¹⁰and they saw the God of Israel. There was under his feet as it were a pavement of sapphire stone, like the very heaven for clearness. ¹¹And he did not lay his hand on the chief men of the people of Israel; they beheld God, and ate and drank.

¹²The LORD said to Moses, "Come up to me on the mountain and wait there, that I may give you the tablets of stone, with the law and the commandment, which I have written for their instruction." ¹³So Moses rose with his assistant Joshua, and Moses went up into the mountain of God. ¹⁴And he said to the elders, "Wait here for us until we return to you. And behold, Aaron and Hur are with you. Whoever has a dispute, let him go to them."

¹⁵Then Moses went up on the mountain, and the cloud covered the mountain. ¹⁶The glory of the LORD dwelt on Mount Sinai, and the cloud covered it six days. And on the seventh day he called to Moses out of the midst of the cloud. ¹⁷Now the appearance of the glory of the LORD was like a devouring fire on the top of the mountain in the sight of the people of Israel. ¹⁸Moses entered the cloud and went up on the mountain. And Moses was on the mountain forty days and forty nights.

Contributions for the Sanctuary

25 The LORD said to Moses, ²"Speak to the people of Israel, that they take for me a contribution. From every man whose heart moves him you shall receive the contribution for me. ³And this is the contribution that you shall receive from them: gold, silver, and bronze, ⁴blue and purple and scarlet yarns and fine twined linen, goats' hair, ⁵tanned rams' skins, goatskins,² acacia wood, ⁶oil for the lamps, spices for the anointing oil and for the fragrant incense, ⁷onyx stones, and stones for setting, for the ephod and for the breastpiece. ⁸And let them make me a sanctuary, that I may dwell in their midst. ⁹Exactly as I show you concerning the pattern of the tabernacle, and of all its furniture, so you shall make it.

The Ark of the Covenant

¹⁰"They shall make an ark of acacia wood. Two cubits³ and a half shall be its length, a cubit and a half its breadth, and a cubit and a half its height. ¹¹You shall overlay it with pure gold, inside and outside shall you overlay it, and you shall make on it a molding of gold around it. ¹²You shall cast four rings of gold for it and put them on its four feet, two rings on the one side of it, and two rings on the other side of it. ¹³You shall make poles of acacia wood and overlay them with gold. ¹⁴And you shall put the poles into the rings on the sides of the ark to carry the ark by them. ¹⁵The poles shall remain in the rings of the ark; they shall not be taken from it. ¹⁶And you shall put into the ark the testimony that I shall give you.

¹⁷"You shall make a mercy seat⁴ of pure gold. Two cubits and a half shall be its length, and a cubit and a half its breadth. ¹⁸And you shall make two cherubim of gold; of hammered work shall you make them, on the two ends of the mercy seat. ¹⁹Make one cherub on the one end, and one cherub on the other end. Of one piece with the mercy seat shall you make the cherubim on its two ends. ²⁰The cherubim shall spread out their wings above, overshadowing the mercy seat with their wings, their

---

¹Or *all the just decrees* ²Uncertain; possibly *dolphin skins*, or *dugong skins*; compare 26:14 ³A *cubit* was about 18 inches or 45 centimeters ⁴Or *cover*

faces one to another; toward the mercy seat shall the faces of the cherubim be. ²¹ And you shall put the mercy seat on the top of the ark, and in the ark you shall put the testimony that I shall give you. ²² There I will meet with you, and from above the mercy seat, from between the two cherubim that are on the ark of the testimony, I will speak with you about all that I will give you in commandment for the people of Israel.

The Table for Bread

²³ "You shall make a table of acacia wood. Two cubits shall be its length, a cubit its breadth, and a cubit and a half its height. ²⁴ You shall overlay it with pure gold and make a molding of gold around it. ²⁵ And you shall make a rim around it a handbreadth[1] wide, and a molding of gold around the rim. ²⁶ And you shall make for it four rings of gold, and fasten the rings to the four corners at its four legs. ²⁷ Close to the frame the rings shall lie, as holders for the poles to carry the table. ²⁸ You shall make the poles of acacia wood, and overlay them with gold, and the table shall be carried with these. ²⁹ And you shall make its plates and dishes for incense, and its flagons and bowls with which to pour drink offerings; you shall make them of pure gold. ³⁰ And you shall set the bread of the Presence on the table before me regularly.

The Golden Lampstand

³¹ "You shall make a lampstand of pure gold. The lampstand shall be made of hammered work: its base, its stem, its cups, its calyxes, and its flowers shall be of one piece with it. ³² And there shall be six branches going out of its sides, three branches of the lampstand out of one side of it and three branches of the lampstand out of the other side of it; ³³ three cups made like almond blossoms, each with calyx and flower, on one branch, and three cups made like almond blossoms, each with calyx and flower, on the other branch—so for the six branches going out of the lampstand. ³⁴ And on the lampstand itself there shall be four cups made like almond blossoms, with their calyxes and flowers, ³⁵ and a calyx of one piece with it under each pair of the six branches going out from the lampstand.

³⁶ Their calyxes and their branches shall be of one piece with it, the whole of it a single piece of hammered work of pure gold. ³⁷ You shall make seven lamps for it. And the lamps shall be set up so as to give light on the space in front of it. ³⁸ Its tongs and their trays shall be of pure gold. ³⁹ It shall be made, with all these utensils, out of a talent[2] of pure gold. ⁴⁰ And see that you make them after the pattern for them, which is being shown you on the mountain.

The Tabernacle

26 "Moreover, you shall make the tabernacle with ten curtains of fine twined linen and blue and purple and scarlet yarns; you shall make them with cherubim skillfully worked into them. ² The length of each curtain shall be twenty-eight cubits,[3] and the breadth of each curtain four cubits; all the curtains shall be the same size. ³ Five curtains shall be coupled to one another, and the other five curtains shall be coupled to one another. ⁴ And you shall make loops of blue on the edge of the outermost curtain in the first set. Likewise you shall make loops on the edge of the outermost curtain in the second set. ⁵ Fifty loops you shall make on the one curtain, and fifty loops you shall make on the edge of the curtain that is in the second set; the loops shall be opposite one another. ⁶ And you shall make fifty clasps of gold, and couple the curtains one to the other with the clasps, so that the tabernacle may be a single whole.

⁷ "You shall also make curtains of goats' hair for a tent over the tabernacle; eleven curtains shall you make. ⁸ The length of each curtain shall be thirty cubits, and the breadth of each curtain four cubits. The eleven curtains shall be the same size. ⁹ You shall couple five curtains by themselves, and six curtains by themselves, and the sixth curtain you shall double over at the front of the tent. ¹⁰ You shall make fifty loops on the edge of the curtain that is outermost in one set, and fifty loops on the edge of the curtain that is outermost in the second set.

¹¹ "You shall make fifty clasps of bronze, and put the clasps into the loops, and couple the tent together that it may be a single whole. ¹² And the part that remains of the

---

[1] A *handbreadth* was about 3 inches or 7.5 centimeters [2] A *talent* was about 75 pounds or 34 kilograms [3] A *cubit* was about 18 inches or 45 centimeters

curtains of the tent, the half curtain that remains, shall hang over the back of the tabernacle. [13] And the extra that remains in the length of the curtains, the cubit on the one side, and the cubit on the other side, shall hang over the sides of the tabernacle, on this side and that side, to cover it. [14] And you shall make for the tent a covering of tanned rams' skins and a covering of goatskins on top.

[15] "You shall make upright frames for the tabernacle of acacia wood. [16] Ten cubits shall be the length of a frame, and a cubit and a half the breadth of each frame. [17] There shall be two tenons in each frame, for fitting together. So shall you do for all the frames of the tabernacle. [18] You shall make the frames for the tabernacle: twenty frames for the south side; [19] and forty bases of silver you shall make under the twenty frames, two bases under one frame for its two tenons, and two bases under the next frame for its two tenons; [20] and for the second side of the tabernacle, on the north side twenty frames, [21] and their forty bases of silver, two bases under one frame, and two bases under the next frame. [22] And for the rear of the tabernacle westward you shall make six frames. [23] And you shall make two frames for corners of the tabernacle in the rear; [24] they shall be separate beneath, but joined at the top, at the first ring. Thus shall it be with both of them; they shall form the two corners. [25] And there shall be eight frames, with their bases of silver, sixteen bases; two bases under one frame, and two bases under another frame.

[26] "You shall make bars of acacia wood, five for the frames of the one side of the tabernacle, [27] and five bars for the frames of the other side of the tabernacle, and five bars for the frames of the side of the tabernacle at the rear westward. [28] The middle bar, halfway up the frames, shall run from end to end. [29] You shall overlay the frames with gold and shall make their rings of gold for holders for the bars, and you shall overlay the bars with gold. [30] Then you shall erect the tabernacle according to the plan for it that you were shown on the mountain.

[31] "And you shall make a veil of blue and purple and scarlet yarns and fine twined linen. It shall be made with cherubim skillfully worked into it. [32] And you shall hang it on four pillars of acacia overlaid with gold, with hooks of gold, on four bases of silver. [33] And you shall hang the veil from the clasps, and bring the ark of the testimony in there within the veil. And the veil shall separate for you the Holy Place from the Most Holy. [34] You shall put the mercy seat on the ark of the testimony in the Most Holy Place. [35] And you shall set the table outside the veil, and the lampstand on the south side of the tabernacle opposite the table, and you shall put the table on the north side.

[36] "You shall make a screen for the entrance of the tent, of blue and purple and scarlet yarns and fine twined linen, embroidered with needlework. [37] And you shall make for the screen five pillars of acacia, and overlay them with gold. Their hooks shall be of gold, and you shall cast five bases of bronze for them.

The Bronze Altar

27 "You shall make the altar of acacia wood, five cubits[1] long and five cubits broad. The altar shall be square, and its height shall be three cubits. [2] And you shall make horns for it on its four corners; its horns shall be of one piece with it, and you shall overlay it with bronze. [3] You shall make pots for it to receive its ashes, and shovels and basins and forks and fire pans. You shall make all its utensils of bronze. [4] You shall also make for it a grating, a network of bronze, and on the net you shall make four bronze rings at its four corners. [5] And you shall set it under the ledge of the altar so that the net extends halfway down the altar. [6] And you shall make poles for the altar, poles of acacia wood, and overlay them with bronze. [7] And the poles shall be put through the rings, so that the poles are on the two sides of the altar when it is carried. [8] You shall make it hollow, with boards. As it has been shown you on the mountain, so shall it be made.

The Court of the Tabernacle

[9] "You shall make the court of the tabernacle. On the south side the court shall have hangings of fine twined linen a hundred cubits long for one side. [10] Its twenty pillars and their twenty bases shall be of bronze, but the hooks of the pillars and their fillets shall be of silver. [11] And likewise for

[1] A *cubit* was about 18 inches or 45 centimeters

its length on the north side there shall be hangings a hundred cubits long, its pillars twenty and their bases twenty, of bronze, but the hooks of the pillars and their fillets shall be of silver. ¹²And for the breadth of the court on the west side there shall be hangings for fifty cubits, with ten pillars and ten bases. ¹³The breadth of the court on the front to the east shall be fifty cubits. ¹⁴The hangings for the one side of the gate shall be fifteen cubits, with their three pillars and three bases. ¹⁵On the other side the hangings shall be fifteen cubits, with their three pillars and three bases. ¹⁶For the gate of the court there shall be a screen twenty cubits long, of blue and purple and scarlet yarns and fine twined linen, embroidered with needlework. It shall have four pillars and with them four bases. ¹⁷All the pillars around the court shall be filleted with silver. Their hooks shall be of silver, and their bases of bronze. ¹⁸The length of the court shall be a hundred cubits, the breadth fifty, and the height five cubits, with hangings of fine twined linen and bases of bronze. ¹⁹All

the utensils of the tabernacle for every use and all its pegs and all the pegs of the court, shall be of bronze.

Oil for the Lamp

²⁰"You shall command the people of Israel that they bring to you pure beaten olive oil for the light, that a lamp may regularly be set up to burn. ²¹In the tent of meeting, outside the veil that is before the testimony, Aaron and his sons shall tend it from evening to morning before the LORD. It shall be a statute forever to be observed throughout their generations by the people of Israel.

The Priests' Garments

28 "Then bring near to you Aaron your brother, and his sons with him, from among the people of Israel, to serve me as priests—Aaron and Aaron's sons, Nadab and Abihu, Eleazar and Ithamar. ²And you shall make holy garments for Aaron your brother, for glory and for beauty. ³You shall speak to all the skillful, whom I have filled with a spirit of skill, that they make

Know Love

verses to read
Exodus 27:20-21

Light is a symbol of God and godliness. Before God created the seas teeming with creatures, the land growing with plants, and the first people, he turned on the light. "And God said, 'Let there be light,' and there was light" (Gen. 1:3). Light is always associated with goodness. God is said to be dressed in a robe of light (see Ps. 104:2), and 1 John 1:5 says he *is* light. His Word is a light that helps us to see where to walk (see Ps. 119:105). And the gospel itself is considered light to a dying world (see 2 Cor. 4:4).

God wants his people to live in the light. He wants the light to keep burning continually. There was a time when we lived in darkness, but when we met Jesus the lights were turned on and everything that was hidden was seen. As a God Girl you can't let yourself go back into darkness. Darkness is the opposite of light. In darkness evil lurks, sneaks, and pounces. Sin hides in the dark, but when we shine the light on our lives, sin can no longer hide. And that is why the light should always be on.

God Girl, you too are a light to the world, revealing truth to those who are lost and shining light on what people do in secret (see Matt. 5:14). But if you put your light out, hide it, or are ashamed of it, then you are giving in to the darkness. You have to trust that truth is what this earth needs, and that truth is found in the light. Remember, you have been united to the one who said he is the light of the world (see John 8:12)!

Aaron's garments to consecrate him for my priesthood. ⁴These are the garments that they shall make: a breastpiece, an ephod, a robe, a coat of checker work, a turban, and a sash. They shall make holy garments for Aaron your brother and his sons to serve me as priests. ⁵They shall receive gold, blue and purple and scarlet yarns, and fine twined linen.

⁶"And they shall make the ephod of gold, of blue and purple and scarlet yarns, and of fine twined linen, skillfully worked. ⁷It shall have two shoulder pieces attached to its two edges, so that it may be joined together. ⁸And the skillfully woven band on it shall be made like it and be of one piece with it, of gold, blue and purple and scarlet yarns, and fine twined linen. ⁹You shall take two onyx stones, and engrave on them the names of the sons of Israel, ¹⁰six of their names on the one stone, and the names of the remaining six on the other stone, in the order of their birth. ¹¹As a jeweler engraves signets, so shall you engrave the two stones with the names of the sons of Israel. You shall enclose them in settings of gold filigree. ¹²And you shall set the two stones on the shoulder pieces of the ephod, as stones of remembrance for the sons of Israel. And Aaron shall bear their names before the Lord on his two shoulders for remembrance. ¹³You shall make settings of gold filigree, ¹⁴and two chains of pure gold, twisted like cords; and you shall attach the corded chains to the settings.

¹⁵"You shall make a breastpiece of judgment, in skilled work. In the style of the ephod you shall make it— of gold, blue and purple and scarlet yarns, and fine twined linen shall you make it. ¹⁶It shall be square and doubled, a span¹ its length and a span its breadth. ¹⁷You shall set in it four rows of stones. A row of sardius,² topaz, and carbuncle shall be the first row; ¹⁸and the second row an emerald, a sapphire, and a diamond; ¹⁹and the third row a jacinth, an agate, and an amethyst; ²⁰and the fourth row a beryl, an onyx, and a jasper. They shall be set in gold filigree. ²¹There shall be twelve stones with their names according to the names of the sons of Israel. They shall be like signets, each engraved with its name, for the twelve tribes. ²²You shall make for the breastpiece twisted chains like cords, of pure gold. ²³And you shall make for the breastpiece two rings of gold, and put the two rings on the two edges of the breastpiece. ²⁴And you shall put the two cords of gold in the two rings at the edges of the breastpiece. ²⁵The two ends of the two cords you shall attach to the two settings of filigree, and so attach it in front to the shoulder pieces of the ephod. ²⁶You shall make two rings of gold, and put them at the two ends of the breastpiece, on its inside edge next to the ephod. ²⁷And you shall make two rings of gold, and attach them in front to the lower part of the two shoulder pieces of the ephod, at its seam above the skillfully woven band of the ephod. ²⁸And they shall bind the breastpiece by its rings to the rings of the ephod with a lace of blue, so that it may lie on the skillfully woven band of the ephod, so that the breastpiece shall not come loose from the ephod. ²⁹So Aaron shall bear the names of the sons of Israel in the breastpiece of judgment on his heart, when he goes into the Holy Place, to bring them to regular remembrance before the Lord. ³⁰And in the breastpiece of judgment you shall put the Urim and the Thummim, and they shall be on Aaron's heart, when he goes in before the Lord. Thus Aaron shall bear the judgment of the people of Israel on his heart before the Lord regularly.

³¹"You shall make the robe of the ephod all of blue. ³²It shall have an opening for the head in the middle of it, with a woven binding around the opening, like the opening in a garment,³ so that it may not tear. ³³On its hem you shall make pomegranates of blue and purple and scarlet yarns, around its hem, with bells of gold between them, ³⁴a golden bell and a pomegranate, a golden bell and a pomegranate, around the hem of the robe. ³⁵And it shall be on Aaron when he ministers, and its sound shall be heard when he goes into the Holy Place before the Lord, and when he comes out, so that he does not die.

³⁶"You shall make a plate of pure gold and engrave on it, like the engraving of a signet, 'Holy to the Lord.' ³⁷And you shall fasten it on the turban by a cord of blue. It shall be on the front of the turban. ³⁸It shall be on Aaron's forehead, and Aaron shall bear any guilt from the holy things that the

---

¹ A *span* was about 9 inches or 22 centimeters ² The identity of some of these stones is uncertain ³ The meaning of the Hebrew word is uncertain; possibly *coat of mail*

people of Israel consecrate as their holy gifts. It shall regularly be on his forehead, that they may be accepted before the LORD.

39 "You shall weave the coat in checker work of fine linen, and you shall make a turban of fine linen, and you shall make a sash embroidered with needlework.

40 "For Aaron's sons you shall make coats and sashes and caps. You shall make them for glory and beauty. 41 And you shall put them on Aaron your brother, and on his sons with him, and shall anoint them and ordain them and consecrate them, that they may serve me as priests. 42 You shall make for them linen undergarments to cover their naked flesh. They shall reach from the hips to the thighs; 43 and they shall be on Aaron and on his sons when they go into the tent of meeting or when they come near the altar to minister in the Holy Place, lest they bear guilt and die. This shall be a statute forever for him and for his offspring after him.

Consecration of the Priests

29 "Now this is what you shall do to them to consecrate them, that they may serve me as priests. Take one bull of the herd and two rams without blemish, 2 and unleavened bread, unleavened cakes mixed with oil, and unleavened wafers smeared with oil. You shall make them of fine wheat flour. 3 You shall put them in one basket and bring them in the basket, and bring the bull and the two rams. 4 You shall bring Aaron and his sons to the entrance of the tent of meeting and wash them with water. 5 Then you shall take the garments, and put on Aaron the coat and the robe of the ephod, and the ephod, and the breastpiece, and gird him with the skillfully woven band of the ephod. 6 And you shall set the turban on his head and put the holy crown on the turban. 7 You shall take the anointing oil and pour it on his head and anoint him. 8 Then you shall bring his sons and put coats on them, 9 and you shall gird Aaron and his sons with sashes and bind caps on them. And the priesthood shall be theirs by a statute forever. Thus you shall ordain Aaron and his sons.

10 "Then you shall bring the bull before the tent of meeting. Aaron and his sons shall lay their hands on the head of the bull. 11 Then you shall kill the bull before the LORD at the entrance of the tent of meet-

ing, 12 and shall take part of the blood of the bull and put it on the horns of the altar with your finger, and the rest of[1] the blood you shall pour out at the base of the altar. 13 And you shall take all the fat that covers the entrails, and the long lobe of the liver and the two kidneys with the fat that is on them, and burn them on the altar. 14 But the flesh of the bull and its skin and its dung you shall burn with fire outside the camp; it is a sin offering.

15 "Then you shall take one of the rams, and Aaron and his sons shall lay their hands on the head of the ram, 16 and you shall kill the ram and shall take its blood and throw it against the sides of the altar. 17 Then you shall cut the ram into pieces, and wash its entrails and its legs, and put them with its pieces and its head, 18 and burn the whole ram on the altar. It is a burnt offering to the LORD. It is a pleasing aroma, a food offering[2] to the LORD.

19 "You shall take the other ram, and Aaron and his sons shall lay their hands on the head of the ram, 20 and you shall kill the ram and take part of its blood and put it on the tip of the right ear of Aaron and on the tips of the right ears of his sons, and on the thumbs of their right hands and on the great toes of their right feet, and throw the rest of the blood against the sides of the altar. 21 Then you shall take part of the blood that is on the altar, and of the anointing oil, and sprinkle it on Aaron and his garments, and on his sons and his sons' garments with him. He and his garments shall be holy, and his sons and his sons' garments with him.

22 "You shall also take the fat from the ram and the fat tail and the fat that covers the entrails, and the long lobe of the liver and the two kidneys with the fat that is on them, and the right thigh (for it is a ram of ordination), 23 and one loaf of bread and one cake of bread made with oil, and one wafer out of the basket of unleavened bread that is before the LORD. 24 You shall put all these on the palms of Aaron and on the palms of his sons, and wave them for a wave offering before the LORD. 25 Then you shall take them from their hands and burn them on the altar on top of the burnt offering, as a pleasing aroma before the LORD. It is a food offering to the LORD.

26 "You shall take the breast of the ram of Aaron's ordination and wave it for a

---

[1] Hebrew all [2] Or an offering by fire; also verses 25, 41

wave offering before the Lord, and it shall be your portion. 27 And you shall consecrate the breast of the wave offering that is waved and the thigh of the priests' portion that is contributed from the ram of ordination, from what was Aaron's and his sons'. 28 It shall be for Aaron and his sons as a perpetual due from the people of Israel, for it is a contribution. It shall be a contribution from the people of Israel from their peace offerings, their contribution to the Lord.

29 "The holy garments of Aaron shall be for his sons after him; they shall be anointed in them and ordained in them. 30 The son who succeeds him as priest, who comes into the tent of meeting to minister in the Holy Place, shall wear them seven days.

31 "You shall take the ram of ordination and boil its flesh in a holy place. 32 And Aaron and his sons shall eat the flesh of the ram and the bread that is in the basket in the entrance of the tent of meeting. 33 They shall eat those things with which atonement was made at their ordination and consecration, but an outsider shall not eat of them, because they are holy. 34 And if any of the flesh for the ordination or of the bread remain until the morning, then you shall burn the remainder with fire. It shall not be eaten, because it is holy.

35 "Thus you shall do to Aaron and to his sons, according to all that I have commanded you. Through seven days shall you ordain them, 36 and every day you shall offer a bull as a sin offering for atonement. Also you shall purify the altar, when you make atonement for it, and shall anoint it to consecrate it. 37 Seven days you shall make atonement for the altar and consecrate it, and the altar shall be most holy. Whatever touches the altar shall become holy.

38 "Now this is what you shall offer on the altar: two lambs a year old day by day regularly. 39 One lamb you shall offer in the morning, and the other lamb you shall offer at twilight. 40 And with the first lamb a tenth measure[1] of fine flour mingled with a fourth of a hin[2] of beaten oil, and a fourth of a hin of wine for a drink offering. 41 The other lamb you shall offer at twilight, and shall offer with it a grain offering and its drink offering, as in the morning, for a pleasing aroma, a food offering to the Lord. 42 It shall be a regular burnt offering throughout your generations at the entrance of the tent of meeting before the Lord, where I will meet with you, to speak to you there. 43 There I will meet with the people of Israel, and it shall be sanctified by my glory. 44 I will consecrate the tent of meeting and the altar. Aaron also and his sons I will consecrate to serve me as priests. 45 I will dwell among the people of Israel and will be their God. 46 And they shall know that I am the Lord their God, who brought them out of the land of Egypt that I might dwell among them. I am the Lord their God.

The Altar of Incense

30 "You shall make an altar on which to burn incense; you shall make it of acacia wood. 2 A cubit[3] shall be its length, and a cubit its breadth. It shall be square, and two cubits shall be its height. Its horns shall be of one piece with it. 3 You shall overlay it with pure gold, its top and around its sides and its horns. And you shall make a molding of gold around it. 4 And you shall make two golden rings for it. Under its molding on two opposite sides of it you shall make them, and they shall be holders for poles with which to carry it. 5 You shall make the poles of acacia wood and overlay them with gold. 6 And you shall put it in front of the veil that is above the ark of the testimony, in front of the mercy seat that is above the testimony, where I will meet with you. 7 And Aaron shall burn fragrant incense on it. Every morning when he dresses the lamps he shall burn it, 8 and when Aaron sets up the lamps at twilight, he shall burn it, a regular incense offering before the Lord throughout your generations. 9 You shall not offer unauthorized incense on it, or a burnt offering, or a grain offering, and you shall not pour a drink offering on it. 10 Aaron shall make atonement on its horns once a year. With the blood of the sin offering of atonement he shall make atonement for it once in the year throughout your generations. It is most holy to the Lord."

The Census Tax

11 The Lord said to Moses, 12 "When you take the census of the people of Israel, then each shall give a ransom for his life to the Lord when you number them, that there

---

[1] Possibly an ephah (about 3/5 bushel or 22 liters) [2] A *hin* was about 4 quarts or 3.5 liters [3] A *cubit* was about 18 inches or 45 centimeters

be no plague among them when you number them. [13] Each one who is numbered in the census shall give this: half a shekel[1] according to the shekel of the sanctuary (the shekel is twenty gerahs),[2] half a shekel as an offering to the LORD. [14] Everyone who is numbered in the census, from twenty years old and upward, shall give the LORD's offering. [15] The rich shall not give more, and the poor shall not give less, than the half shekel, when you give the LORD's offering to make atonement for your lives. [16] You shall take the atonement money from the people of Israel and shall give it for the service of the tent of meeting, that it may bring the people of Israel to remembrance before the LORD, so as to make atonement for your lives."

The Bronze Basin

[17] The LORD said to Moses, [18] "You shall also make a basin of bronze, with its stand of bronze, for washing. You shall put it between the tent of meeting and the altar, and you shall put water in it, [19] with which Aaron and his sons shall wash their hands and their feet. [20] When they go into the tent of meeting, or when they come near the altar to minister, to burn a food offering[3] to the LORD, they shall wash with water, so that they may not die. [21] They shall wash their hands and their feet, so that they may not die. It shall be a statute forever to them, even to him and to his offspring throughout their generations."

The Anointing Oil and Incense

[22] The LORD said to Moses, [23] "Take the finest spices: of liquid myrrh 500 shekels, and of sweet-smelling cinnamon half as much, that is, 250, and 250 of aromatic cane, [24] and 500 of cassia, according to the shekel of the sanctuary, and a hin[4] of olive oil. [25] And you shall make of these a sacred anointing oil blended as by the perfumer; it shall be a holy anointing oil. [26] With it you shall anoint the tent of meeting and the ark of the testimony, [27] and the table and all its utensils, and the lampstand and its utensils, and the altar of incense, [28] and the altar of burnt offering with all its utensils and the basin and its stand. [29] You shall consecrate them, that they may be most holy. Whatever touches them will become holy.

[30] You shall anoint Aaron and his sons, and consecrate them, that they may serve me as priests. [31] And you shall say to the people of Israel, 'This shall be my holy anointing oil throughout your generations. [32] It shall not be poured on the body of an ordinary person, and you shall make no other like it in composition. It is holy, and it shall be holy to you. [33] Whoever compounds any like it or whoever puts any of it on an outsider shall be cut off from his people.' "

[34] The LORD said to Moses, "Take sweet spices, stacte, and onycha, and galbanum, sweet spices with pure frankincense (of each shall there be an equal part), [35] and make an incense blended as by the perfumer, seasoned with salt, pure and holy. [36] You shall beat some of it very small, and put part of it before the testimony in the tent of meeting where I shall meet with you. It shall be most holy for you. [37] And the incense that you shall make according to its composition, you shall not make for yourselves. It shall be for you holy to the LORD. [38] Whoever makes any like it to use as perfume shall be cut off from his people."

Oholiab and Bezalel

31 The LORD said to Moses, [2] "See, I have called by name Bezalel the son of Uri, son of Hur, of the tribe of Judah, [3] and I have filled him with the Spirit of God, with ability and intelligence, with knowledge and all craftsmanship, [4] to devise artistic designs, to work in gold, silver, and bronze, [5] in cutting stones for setting, and in carving wood, to work in every craft. [6] And behold, I have appointed with him Oholiab, the son of Ahisamach, of the tribe of Dan. And I have given to all able men ability, that they may make all that I have commanded you: [7] the tent of meeting, and the ark of the testimony, and the mercy seat that is on it, and all the furnishings of the tent, [8] the table and its utensils, and the pure lampstand with all its utensils, and the altar of incense, [9] and the altar of burnt offering with all its utensils, and the basin and its stand, [10] and the finely worked garments,[5] the holy garments for Aaron the priest and the garments of his sons, for their service as priests, [11] and the anointing oil and the fragrant incense for the Holy Place. According to all that I have commanded you, they shall do."

---

[1] A *shekel* was about 2/5 ounce or 11 grams [2] A *gerah* was about 1/50 ounce or 0.6 gram [3] Or *an offering by fire* [4] A *hin* was about 4 quarts or 3.5 liters [5] Or *garments for worship*

he Sabbath

¹²And the Lord said to Moses, ¹³"You are o speak to the people of Israel and say, Above all you shall keep my Sabbaths, for his is a sign between me and you through-ut your generations, that you may know hat I, the Lord, sanctify you. ¹⁴You shall keep the Sabbath, because it is holy for ou. Everyone who profanes it shall be put o death. Whoever does any work on it, hat soul shall be cut off from among his eople. ¹⁵Six days shall work be done, but he seventh day is a Sabbath of solemn est, holy to the Lord. Whoever does any vork on the Sabbath day shall be put to leath. ¹⁶Therefore the people of Israel shall keep the Sabbath, observing the Sabbath hroughout their generations, as a covenant orever. ¹⁷It is a sign forever between me nd the people of Israel that in six days the ,ord made heaven and earth, and on the eventh day he rested and was refreshed.'"

¹⁸And he gave to Moses, when he had inished speaking with him on Mount Sinai, he two tablets of the testimony, tablets of tone, written with the finger of God.

The Golden Calf

32 When the people saw that Moses delayed to come down from the mountain, the people gathered themselves ogether to Aaron and said to him, "Up, nake us gods who shall go before us. As or this Moses, the man who brought us up ut of the land of Egypt, we do not know vhat has become of him." ²So Aaron said o them, "Take off the rings of gold that are n the ears of your wives, your sons, and our daughters, and bring them to me." ³So all the people took off the rings of gold hat were in their ears and brought them o Aaron. ⁴And he received the gold from heir hand and fashioned it with a grav-ng tool and made a golden¹ calf. And they said, "These are your gods, O Israel, who prought you up out of the land of Egypt!" ⁵When Aaron saw this, he built an altar pefore it. And Aaron made a proclamation nd said, "Tomorrow shall be a feast to the Lord." ⁶And they rose up early the next day and offered burnt offerings and brought peace offerings. And the people sat down to eat and drink and rose up to play.

⁷And the Lord said to Moses, "Go down, for your people, whom you brought up out

of the land of Egypt, have corrupted them-selves. ⁸They have turned aside quickly out of the way that I commanded them. They have made for themselves a golden calf and have worshiped it and sacrificed to it and said, 'These are your gods, O Israel, who brought you up out of the land of Egypt!'" ⁹And the Lord said to Moses, "I have seen this people, and behold, it is a stiff-necked people. ¹⁰Now therefore let me alone, that my wrath may burn hot against them and I may consume them, in order that I may make a great nation of you."

¹¹But Moses implored the Lord his God and said, "O Lord, why does your wrath burn hot against your people, whom you have brought out of the land of Egypt with great power and with a mighty hand? ¹²Why should the Egyptians say, 'With evil intent did he bring them out, to kill them in the mountains and to consume them from the face of the earth'? Turn from your burning anger and relent from this disaster against your people. ¹³Remember Abraham, Isaac, and Israel, your servants, to whom you swore by your own self, and said to them, 'I will multiply your offspring as the stars of heaven, and all this land that I have promised I will give to your offspring, and they shall inherit it forever.'" ¹⁴And the Lord relented from the disaster that he had spoken of bringing on his people.

¹⁵Then Moses turned and went down from the mountain with the two tablets of the testimony in his hand, tablets that were written on both sides; on the front and on the back they were written. ¹⁶The tablets were the work of God, and the writing was the writing of God, engraved on the tab-lets. ¹⁷When Joshua heard the noise of the people as they shouted, he said to Moses, "There is a noise of war in the camp." ¹⁸But he said, "It is not the sound of shouting for victory, or the sound of the cry of defeat, but the sound of singing that I hear." ¹⁹And as soon as he came near the camp and saw the calf and the dancing, Moses' anger burned hot, and he threw the tablets out of his hands and broke them at the foot of the mountain. ²⁰He took the calf that they had made and burned it with fire and ground it to powder and scattered it on the water and made the people of Israel drink it.

²¹And Moses said to Aaron, "What did this people do to you that you have brought

¹ Hebrew *cast metal*; also verse 8

such a great sin upon them?" [22] And Aaron said, "Let not the anger of my lord burn hot. You know the people, that they are set on evil. [23] For they said to me, 'Make us gods who shall go before us. As for this Moses, the man who brought us up out of the land of Egypt, we do not know what has become of him.' [24] So I said to them, 'Let any who have gold take it off.' So they gave it to me, and I threw it into the fire, and out came this calf."

[25] And when Moses saw that the people had broken loose (for Aaron had let them break loose, to the derision of their enemies), [26] then Moses stood in the gate of the camp and said, "Who is on the LORD's side? Come to me." And all the sons of Levi gathered around him. [27] And he said to them, "Thus says the LORD God of Israel, 'Put your sword on your side each of you, and go to and fro from gate to gate throughout the camp, and each of you kill his brother and his companion and his neighbor.'" [28] And the sons of Levi did according to the word of Moses. And that day about three thousand men of the people fell. [29] And Moses said, "Today you have been ordained for the service of the LORD, each one at the cost of his son and of his brother, so that he might bestow a blessing upon you this day."

[30] The next day Moses said to the people, "You have sinned a great sin. And now I will go up to the LORD; perhaps I can make atonement for your sin." [31] So Moses returned to the LORD and said, "Alas, this people has sinned a great sin. They have made for themselves gods of gold. [32] But now, if you will forgive their sin—but if not, please blot me out of your book that you have written." [33] But the LORD said to Moses, "Whoever has sinned against me, I will blot out of my book. [34] But now go, lead the people to the place about which I have spoken to you; behold, my angel shall go before you. Nevertheless, in the day when I visit, I will visit their sin upon them." [35] Then the LORD sent a plague on the people, because they made the calf, the one that Aaron made.

The Command to Leave Sinai

33 The LORD said to Moses, "Depart; go up from here, you and the people whom you have brought up out of the land of Egypt, to the land of which I swore to Abraham, Isaac, and Jacob, saying, 'To your offspring I will give it.' [2] I will send an angel before you, and I will drive out the Canaanites, the Amorites, the Hittites, the Perizzites, the Hivites, and the Jebusites. [3] Go up to a land flowing with milk and honey; but I will not go up among you lest I consume you on the way, for you are a stiff-necked people."

[4] When the people heard this disastrous word, they mourned, and no one put on his ornaments. [5] For the LORD had said to Moses, "Say to the people of Israel, 'You are a stiff-necked people; if for a single moment I should go up among you, I would consume you. So now take off your ornaments, that I may know what to do with you.'" [6] Therefore the people of Israel stripped themselves of their ornaments, from Mount Horeb onward.

The Tent of Meeting

[7] Now Moses used to take the tent and pitch it outside the camp, far off from the camp, and he called it the tent of meeting. And everyone who sought the LORD would go out to the tent of meeting, which was outside the camp. [8] Whenever Moses went out to the tent, all the people would rise up, and each would stand at his tent door and watch Moses until he had gone into the tent. [9] When Moses entered the tent, the pillar of cloud would descend and stand at the entrance of the tent, and the LORD[1] would speak with Moses. [10] And when all the people saw the pillar of cloud standing at the entrance of the tent, all the people would rise up and worship, each at his tent door. [11] Thus the LORD used to speak to Moses face to face, as a man speaks to his friend. When Moses turned again into the camp, his assistant Joshua the son of Nun, a young man, would not depart from the tent.

Moses' Intercession

[12] Moses said to the LORD, "See, you say to me, 'Bring up this people,' but you have not let me know whom you will send with me. Yet you have said, 'I know you by name, and you have also found favor in my sight.' [13] Now therefore, if I have found favor in your sight, please show me now your ways, that I may know you in order to find favor in your sight. Consider too that this nation

[1] Hebrew *he*

is your people." ¹⁴And he said, "My presence will go with you, and I will give you rest." ¹⁵And he said to him, "If your presence will not go with me, do not bring us up from here. ¹⁶For how shall it be known that I have found favor in your sight, I and your people? Is it not in your going with us, so that we are distinct, I and your people, from every other people on the face of the earth?"

¹⁷And the LORD said to Moses, "This very thing that you have spoken I will do, for you have found favor in my sight, and I know you by name." ¹⁸Moses said, "Please show me your glory." ¹⁹And he said, "I will make all my goodness pass before you and will proclaim before you my name 'The LORD.' And I will be gracious to whom I will be gracious, and will show mercy on whom I will show mercy. ²⁰But," he said, "you cannot see my face, for man shall not see me and live." ²¹And the LORD said, "Behold, there is a place by me where you shall stand on the rock, ²²and while my glory passes by I will put you in a cleft of the rock, and I will cover you with my hand until I have passed by. ²³Then I will take away my hand, and you shall see my back, but my face shall not be seen."

Moses Makes New Tablets

34 The LORD said to Moses, "Cut for yourself two tablets of stone like the first, and I will write on the tablets the words that were on the first tablets, which you broke. ²Be ready by the morning, and come up in the morning to Mount Sinai, and present yourself there to me on the top of the mountain. ³No one shall come up with you, and let no one be seen throughout all the mountain. Let no flocks or herds graze opposite that mountain." ⁴So Moses cut two tablets of stone like the first. And he rose early in the morning and went up on Mount Sinai, as the LORD had commanded him, and took in his hand two tablets of stone. ⁵The LORD descended in the cloud and stood with him there, and proclaimed the name of the LORD. ⁶The LORD passed before him and proclaimed, "The LORD, the LORD, a God merciful and gracious, slow to anger, and abounding in steadfast love and faithfulness, ⁷keeping steadfast love for thousands,¹ forgiving iniquity and transgression and sin, but who will by no means

clear the guilty, visiting the iniquity of the fathers on the children and the children's children, to the third and the fourth generation." ⁸And Moses quickly bowed his head toward the earth and worshiped. ⁹And he said, "If now I have found favor in your sight, O Lord, please let the Lord go in the midst of us, for it is a stiff-necked people, and pardon our iniquity and our sin, and take us for your inheritance."

The Covenant Renewed

¹⁰And he said, "Behold, I am making a covenant. Before all your people I will do marvels, such as have not been created in all the earth or in any nation. And all the people among whom you are shall see the work of the LORD, for it is an awesome thing that I will do with you.

¹¹"Observe what I command you this day. Behold, I will drive out before you the Amorites, the Canaanites, the Hittites, the Perizzites, the Hivites, and the Jebusites. ¹²Take care, lest you make a covenant with the inhabitants of the land to which you go, lest it become a snare in your midst. ¹³You shall tear down their altars and break their pillars and cut down their Asherim ¹⁴(for you shall worship no other god, for the LORD, whose name is Jealous, is a jealous God), ¹⁵lest you make a covenant with the inhabitants of the land, and when they whore after their gods and sacrifice to their gods and you are invited, you eat of his sacrifice, ¹⁶and you take of their daughters for your sons, and their daughters whore after their gods and make your sons whore after their gods.

¹⁷"You shall not make for yourself any gods of cast metal.

¹⁸"You shall keep the Feast of Unleavened Bread. Seven days you shall eat unleavened bread, as I commanded you, at the time appointed in the month Abib, for in the month Abib you came out from Egypt. ¹⁹All that open the womb are mine, all your male² livestock, the firstborn of cow and sheep. ²⁰The firstborn of a donkey you shall redeem with a lamb, or if you will not redeem it you shall break its neck. All the firstborn of your sons you shall redeem. And none shall appear before me empty-handed.

²¹"Six days you shall work, but on the seventh day you shall rest. In plowing

---

¹Or *to the thousandth generation* ²Septuagint, Theodotion, Vulgate, Targum; the meaning of the Hebrew is uncertain

time and in harvest you shall rest. ²²You shall observe the Feast of Weeks, the firstfruits of wheat harvest, and the Feast of Ingathering at the year's end. ²³Three times in the year shall all your males appear before the LORD God, the God of Israel. ²⁴For I will cast out nations before you and enlarge your borders; no one shall covet your land, when you go up to appear before the LORD your God three times in the year.

²⁵"You shall not offer the blood of my sacrifice with anything leavened, or let the sacrifice of the Feast of the Passover remain until the morning. ²⁶The best of the firstfruits of your ground you shall bring to the house of the LORD your God. You shall not boil a young goat in its mother's milk."

²⁷And the LORD said to Moses, "Write these words, for in accordance with these words I have made a covenant with you and with Israel." ²⁸So he was there with the LORD forty days and forty nights. He neither ate bread nor drank water. And he wrote on the tablets the words of the covenant, the Ten Commandments.[1]

The Shining Face of Moses

²⁹When Moses came down from Mount Sinai, with the two tablets of the testimony in his hand as he came down from the mountain, Moses did not know that the skin of his face shone because he had been talking with God.[2] ³⁰Aaron and all the people of Israel saw Moses, and behold, the skin of his face shone, and they were afraid to come near him. ³¹But Moses called to them, and Aaron and all the leaders of the congregation returned to him, and Moses talked with them. ³²Afterward all the people of Israel came near, and he commanded them all that the LORD had spoken with him in Mount Sinai. ³³And when Moses had finished speaking with them, he put a veil over his face.

³⁴Whenever Moses went in before the LORD to speak with him, he would remove the veil, until he came out. And when he came out and told the people of Israel what he was commanded, ³⁵the people of Israel would see the face of Moses, that the skin of Moses' face was shining. And Moses would put the veil over his face again, until he went in to speak with him.

Sabbath Regulations

35 Moses assembled all the congregation of the people of Israel and said to them, "These are the things that the LORD has commanded you to do. ²Six days work shall be done, but on the seventh day you shall have a Sabbath of solemn rest, holy to the LORD. Whoever does any work on it shall be put to death. ³You shall kindle no fire in all your dwelling places on the Sabbath day."

Contributions for the Tabernacle

⁴Moses said to all the congregation of the people of Israel, "This is the thing that the LORD has commanded. ⁵Take from among you a contribution to the LORD. Whoever is of a generous heart, let him bring the LORD's contribution: gold, silver, and bronze; ⁶blue and purple and scarlet yarns and fine twined linen; goats' hair, ⁷tanned rams' skins, and goatskins;[3] acacia wood, ⁸oil for the light, spices for the anointing oil and for the fragrant incense, ⁹and onyx stones and stones for setting, for the ephod and for the breastpiece.

¹⁰"Let every skillful craftsman among you come and make all that the LORD has commanded: ¹¹the tabernacle, its tent and its covering, its hooks and its frames, its bars, its pillars, and its bases; ¹²the ark with its poles, the mercy seat, and the veil of the screen; ¹³the table with its poles and all its utensils, and the bread of the Presence; ¹⁴the lampstand also for the light, with its utensils and its lamps, and the oil for the light; ¹⁵and the altar of incense, with its poles, and the anointing oil and the fragrant incense, and the screen for the door, at the door of the tabernacle; ¹⁶the altar of burnt offering, with its grating of bronze, its poles, and all its utensils, the basin and its stand; ¹⁷the hangings of the court, its pillars and its bases, and the screen for the gate of the court; ¹⁸the pegs of the tabernacle and the pegs of the court, and their cords; ¹⁹the finely worked garments for ministering[4] in the Holy Place, the holy garments for Aaron the priest, and the garments of his sons, for their service as priests."

²⁰Then all the congregation of the people of Israel departed from the presence of Moses. ²¹And they came, everyone whose heart stirred him, and everyone whose spirit moved him, and brought the LORD's

---

[1] Hebrew the ten words [2] Hebrew him [3] The meaning of the Hebrew word is uncertain; also verse 23; compare 25:5 [4] Or garments for worship; see 31:10

contribution to be used for the tent of meeting, and for all its service, and for the holy garments. ²² So they came, both men and women. All who were of a willing heart brought brooches and earrings and signet rings and armlets, all sorts of gold objects, every man dedicating an offering of gold to the LORD. ²³ And every one who possessed blue or purple or scarlet yarns or fine linen or goats' hair or tanned rams' skins or goatskins brought them. ²⁴ Everyone who could make a contribution of silver or bronze brought it as the LORD's contribution. And every one who possessed acacia wood of any use in the work brought it. ²⁵ And every skillful woman spun with her hands, and they all brought what they had spun in blue and purple and scarlet yarns and fine twined linen. ²⁶ All the women whose hearts stirred them to use their skill spun the goats' hair. ²⁷ And the leaders brought onyx stones and stones to be set, for the ephod and for the breastpiece, ²⁸ and spices and oil for the light, and for the anointing oil, and for the fragrant incense. ²⁹ All the men and women, the people of Israel, whose heart moved them to bring anything for the work that the LORD had commanded by Moses to be done brought it as a freewill offering to the LORD.

Construction of the Tabernacle

³⁰ Then Moses said to the people of Israel, "See, the LORD has called by name Bezalel the son of Uri, son of Hur, of the tribe of Judah; ³¹ and he has filled him with the Spirit of God, with skill, with intelligence, with knowledge, and with all craftsmanship, ³² to devise artistic designs, to work in gold and silver and bronze, ³³ in cutting stones for setting, and in carving wood, for work in every skilled craft. ³⁴ And he has inspired him to teach, both him and Oholiab the son of Ahisamach of the tribe of Dan. ³⁵ He has filled them with skill to do every sort of work done by an engraver or by a designer or by an embroiderer in blue and purple and scarlet yarns and fine twined linen, or by a weaver—by any sort of workman or skilled designer.

Know Yourself

verses to read
Exodus 35:4–9

Is there something you can't part with? If someone asked you to give it up, could you do it? The thing you say you can't give up is the very thing you must be willing to give up, for God's sake. When something you own becomes the most important thing in your life, it becomes idolatry. An idol is anything that you obsess about, that you need, that you can't live without. The only thing that you truly can't live without, other than food and water, is the presence of God in your life. And when things overshadow that need or try to fill it, danger is in the air, and you will be miserable.

God asked the Israelites to give something of their own to him. Do you think he meant "your least favorite thing" or "the one thing you don't really like, use, or want"? Or do you think he was looking for something important that they really loved or thought they "needed"? Look at the things listed in Exodus 35:5: gold, silver, bronze. Do you think they were important to the people? Worth something? Yep, they were. In fact, all the things on that list would have been very valuable in their time, and hard to part with. Why do you think God asked for this contribution? Why would he want his followers to give up what they love most?

Look at the things in your life and see what you worship. What can you not live without or give up? Think about what that thing means to you and how it could be meeting some of the needs in your life that God wants to meet—for comfort, physical needs, hope, or joy. In what way do you worship things rather than God?

36

"Bezalel and Oholiab and every craftsman in whom the LORD has put skill and intelligence to know how to do any work in the construction of the sanctuary shall work in accordance with all that the LORD has commanded."

[2] And Moses called Bezalel and Oholiab and every craftsman in whose mind the LORD had put skill, everyone whose heart stirred him up to come to do the work. [3] And they received from Moses all the contribution that the people of Israel had brought for doing the work on the sanctuary. They still kept bringing him freewill offerings every morning, [4] so that all the craftsmen who were doing every sort of task on the sanctuary came, each from the task that he was doing, [5] and said to Moses, "The people bring much more than enough for doing the work that the LORD has commanded us to do." [6] So Moses gave command, and word was proclaimed throughout the camp, "Let no man or woman do anything more for the contribution for the sanctuary." So the people were restrained from bringing, [7] for the material they had was sufficient to do all the work, and more.

[8] And all the craftsmen among the workmen made the tabernacle with ten curtains. They were made of fine twined linen and blue and purple and scarlet yarns, with cherubim skillfully worked. [9] The length of each curtain was twenty-eight cubits,[1] and the breadth of each curtain four cubits. All the curtains were the same size.

[10] He[2] coupled five curtains to one another, and the other five curtains he coupled to one another. [11] He made loops of blue on the edge of the outermost curtain of the first set. Likewise he made them on the edge of the outermost curtain of the second set. [12] He made fifty loops on the one curtain, and he made fifty loops on the edge of the curtain that was in the second set. The loops were opposite one another. [13] And he made fifty clasps of gold, and coupled the curtains one to the other with clasps. So the tabernacle was a single whole.

[14] He also made curtains of goats' hair for a tent over the tabernacle. He made eleven curtains. [15] The length of each curtain was thirty cubits, and the breadth of each curtain four cubits. The eleven curtains were the same size. [16] He coupled five curtains by themselves, and six curtains by themselves. [17] And he made fifty loops on the edge of the outermost curtain of the one set, and fifty loops on the edge of the other connecting curtain. [18] And he made fifty clasps of bronze to couple the tent together that it might be a single whole. [19] And he made for the tent a covering of tanned rams' skins and goatskins.

[20] Then he made the upright frames for the tabernacle of acacia wood. [21] Ten cubits was the length of a frame, and a cubit and a half the breadth of each frame. [22] Each frame had two tenons for fitting together. He did this for all the frames of the tabernacle. [23] The frames for the tabernacle he made thus: twenty frames for the south side. [24] And he made forty bases of silver under the twenty frames, two bases under one frame for its two tenons, and two bases under the next frame for its two tenons. [25] For the second side of the tabernacle, on the north side, he made twenty frames [26] and their forty bases of silver, two bases under one frame and two bases under the next frame. [27] For the rear of the tabernacle westward he made six frames. [28] He made two frames for corners of the tabernacle in the rear. [29] And they were separate beneath but joined at the top, at the first ring. He made two of them this way for the two corners. [30] There were eight frames with their bases of silver: sixteen bases, under every frame two bases.

[31] He made bars of acacia wood, five for the frames of the one side of the tabernacle, [32] and five bars for the frames of the other side of the tabernacle, and five bars for the frames of the tabernacle at the rear westward. [33] And he made the middle bar to run from end to end halfway up the frames. [34] And he overlaid the frames with gold, and made their rings of gold for holders for the bars, and overlaid the bars with gold.

[35] He made the veil of blue and purple and scarlet yarns and fine twined linen; with cherubim skillfully worked into it he made it. [36] And for it he made four pillars of acacia and overlaid them with gold. Their hooks were of gold, and he cast for them four bases of silver. [37] He also made a screen for the entrance of the tent, of blue and purple and scarlet yarns and fine twined

---

[1] A *cubit* was about 18 inches or 45 centimeters [2] Probably Bezalel (compare 35:30; 37:1)

linen, embroidered with needlework, **38**and its five pillars with their hooks. He overlaid their capitals, and their fillets were of gold, but their five bases were of bronze.

Making the Ark

37 Bezalel made the ark of acacia wood. Two cubits[1] and a half was its length, a cubit and a half its breadth, and a cubit and a half its height. **2**And he overlaid it with pure gold inside and outside, and made a molding of gold around it. **3**And he cast for it four rings of gold for its four feet, two rings on its one side and two rings on its other side. **4**And he made poles of acacia wood and overlaid them with gold **5**and put the poles into the rings on the sides of the ark to carry the ark. **6**And he made a mercy seat of pure gold. Two cubits and a half was its length, and a cubit and a half its breadth. **7**And he made two cherubim of gold. He made them of hammered work on the two ends of the mercy seat, **8**one cherub on the one end, and one cherub on the other end. Of one piece with the mercy seat he made the cherubim on its two ends. **9**The cherubim spread out their wings above, overshadowing the mercy seat with their wings, with their faces one to another; toward the mercy seat were the faces of the cherubim.

Making the Table

10 He also made the table of acacia wood. Two cubits was its length, a cubit its breadth, and a cubit and a half its height. **11**And he overlaid it with pure gold, and made a molding of gold around it. **12**And he made a rim around it a handbreadth[2] wide, and made a molding of gold around the rim. **13**He cast for it four rings of gold and fastened the rings to the four corners at its four legs. **14**Close to the frame were the rings, as holders for the poles to carry the table. **15**He made the poles of acacia wood to carry the table, and overlaid them with gold. **16**And he made the vessels of pure gold that were to be on the table, its plates and dishes for incense, and its bowls and flagons with which to pour drink offerings.

Making the Lampstand

17 He also made the lampstand of pure gold. He made the lampstand of hammered work. Its base, its stem, its cups, its calyxes, and its flowers were of one piece with it. **18**And there were six branches going out of its sides, three branches of the lampstand out of one side of it and three branches of the lampstand out of the other side of it; **19**three cups made like almond blossoms, each with calyx and flower, on one branch, and three cups made like almond blossoms, each with calyx and flower, on the other branch— so for the six branches going out of the lampstand. **20**And on the lampstand itself were four cups made like almond blossoms, with their calyxes and flowers, **21**and a calyx of one piece with it under each pair of the six branches going out of it. **22**Their calyxes and their branches were of one piece with it. The whole of it was a single piece of hammered work of pure gold. **23**And he made its seven lamps and its tongs and its trays of pure gold. **24**He made it and all its utensils out of a talent[3] of pure gold.

Making the Altar of Incense

25 He made the altar of incense of acacia wood. Its length was a cubit, and its breadth was a cubit. It was square, and two cubits was its height. Its horns were of one piece with it. **26**He overlaid it with pure gold, its top and around its sides and its horns. And he made a molding of gold around it, **27**and made two rings of gold on it under its molding, on two opposite sides of it, as holders for the poles with which to carry it. **28**And he made the poles of acacia wood and overlaid them with gold.

29He made the holy anointing oil also, and the pure fragrant incense, blended as by the perfumer.

Making the Altar of Burnt Offering

38 He made the altar of burnt offering of acacia wood. Five cubits[4] was its length, and five cubits its breadth. It was square, and three cubits was its height. **2**He made horns for it on its four corners. Its horns were of one piece with it, and he overlaid it with bronze. **3**And he made all the utensils of the altar, the pots, the shovels, the basins, the forks, and the fire pans. He made all its utensils of bronze. **4**And he made for the altar a grating, a network of bronze, under its ledge, extending halfway

[1] A *cubit* was about 18 inches or 45 centimeters [2] A *handbreadth* was about 3 inches or 7.5 centimeters [3] A *talent* was about 75 pounds or 34 kilograms [4] A *cubit* was about 18 inches or 45 centimeters

down. ⁵He cast four rings on the four corners of the bronze grating as holders for the poles. ⁶He made the poles of acacia wood and overlaid them with bronze. ⁷And he put the poles through the rings on the sides of the altar to carry it with them. He made it hollow, with boards.

Making the Bronze Basin

⁸He made the basin of bronze and its stand of bronze, from the mirrors of the ministering women who ministered in the entrance of the tent of meeting.

Making the Court

⁹And he made the court. For the south side the hangings of the court were of fine twined linen, a hundred cubits; ¹⁰their twenty pillars and their twenty bases were of bronze, but the hooks of the pillars and their fillets were of silver. ¹¹And for the north side there were hangings of a hundred cubits, their twenty pillars, their twenty bases were of bronze, but the hooks of the pillars and their fillets were of silver. ¹²And for the west side were hangings of fifty cubits, their ten pillars, and their ten bases; the hooks of the pillars and their fillets were of silver. ¹³And for the front to the east, fifty cubits. ¹⁴The hangings for one side of the gate were fifteen cubits, with their three pillars and three bases. ¹⁵And so for the other side. On both sides of the gate of the court were hangings of fifteen cubits, with their three pillars and their three bases. ¹⁶All the hangings around the court were of fine twined linen. ¹⁷And the bases for the pillars were of bronze, but the hooks of the pillars and their fillets were of silver. The overlaying of their capitals was also of silver, and all the pillars of the court were filleted with silver. ¹⁸And the screen for the gate of the court was embroidered with needlework in blue and purple and scarlet yarns and fine twined linen. It was twenty cubits long and five cubits high in its breadth, corresponding to the hangings of the court. ¹⁹And their pillars were four in number. Their four bases were of bronze, their hooks of silver, and the overlaying of their capitals and their fillets of silver. ²⁰And all the pegs for the tabernacle and for the court all around were of bronze.

Materials for the Tabernacle

²¹These are the records of the tabernacle, the tabernacle of the testimony, as they were recorded at the commandment of Moses, the responsibility of the Levites under the direction of Ithamar the son of Aaron the priest. ²²Bezalel the son of Uri, son of Hur, of the tribe of Judah, made all that the Lord commanded Moses; ²³and with him was Oholiab the son of Ahisamach, of the tribe of Dan, an engraver and designer and embroiderer in blue and purple and scarlet yarns and fine twined linen. ²⁴All the gold that was used for the work, in all the construction of the sanctuary, the gold from the offering, was twenty-nine talents and 730 shekels,[1] by the shekel of the sanctuary. ²⁵The silver from those of the congregation who were recorded was a hundred talents and 1,775 shekels, by the shekel of the sanctuary: ²⁶a beka[2] a head (that is, half a shekel, by the shekel of the sanctuary), for everyone who was listed in the records, from twenty years old and upward, for 603,550 men. ²⁷The hundred talents of silver were for casting the bases of the sanctuary and the bases of the veil; a hundred bases for the hundred talents, a talent a base. ²⁸And of the 1,775 shekels he made hooks for the pillars and overlaid their capitals and made fillets for them. ²⁹The bronze that was offered was seventy talents and 2,400 shekels; ³⁰with it he made the bases for the entrance of the tent of meeting, the bronze altar and the bronze grating for it and all the utensils of the altar, ³¹the bases around the court, and the bases of the gate of the court, all the pegs of the tabernacle, and all the pegs around the court.

Making the Priestly Garments

39 From the blue and purple and scarlet yarns they made finely woven garments,[3] for ministering in the Holy Place. They made the holy garments for Aaron, as the Lord had commanded Moses.

²He made the ephod of gold, blue and purple and scarlet yarns, and fine twined linen. ³And they hammered out gold leaf, and he cut it into threads to work into the blue and purple and the scarlet yarns, and into the fine twined linen, in skilled design. ⁴They made for the ephod attach-

[1] A *talent* was about 75 pounds or 34 kilograms; a *shekel* was about 2/5 ounce or 11 grams [2] A *beka* was about 1/5 ounce or 5.5 grams [3] Or *garments for worship*

ing shoulder pieces, joined to it at its two edges. ⁵And the skillfully woven band on it was of one piece with it and made like it, of gold, blue and purple and scarlet yarns, and fine twined linen, as the LORD had commanded Moses.

⁶They made the onyx stones, enclosed in settings of gold filigree, and engraved like the engravings of a signet, according to the names of the sons of Israel. ⁷And he set them on the shoulder pieces of the ephod to be stones of remembrance for the sons of Israel, as the LORD had commanded Moses.

⁸He made the breastpiece, in skilled work, in the style of the ephod, of gold, blue and purple and scarlet yarns, and fine twined linen. ⁹It was square. They made the breastpiece doubled, a span¹ its length and a span its breadth when doubled. ¹⁰And they set in it four rows of stones. A row of sardius, topaz, and carbuncle was the first row; ¹¹and the second row, an emerald, a sapphire, and a diamond; ¹²and the third row, a jacinth, an agate, and an amethyst; ¹³and the fourth row, a beryl, an onyx, and a jasper. They were enclosed in settings of gold filigree. ¹⁴There were twelve stones with their names according to the names of the sons of Israel. They were like signets, each engraved with its name, for the twelve tribes. ¹⁵And they made on the breastpiece twisted chains like cords, of pure gold. ¹⁶And they made two settings of gold filigree and two gold rings, and put the two rings on the two edges of the breastpiece. ¹⁷And they put the two cords of gold in the two rings at the edges of the breastpiece. ¹⁸They attached the two ends of the two cords to the two settings of filigree. Thus they attached it in front to the shoulder pieces of the ephod. ¹⁹Then they made two rings of gold, and put them at the two ends of the breastpiece, on its inside edge next to the ephod. ²⁰And they made two rings of gold, and attached them in front to the lower part of the two shoulder pieces of the ephod, at its seam above the skillfully woven band of the ephod. ²¹And they bound the breastpiece by its rings to the rings of the ephod with a lace of blue, so that it should lie on the skillfully woven band of the ephod, and that the breastpiece should not come

loose from the ephod, as the LORD had commanded Moses.

²²He also made the robe of the ephod woven all of blue, ²³and the opening of the robe in it was like the opening in a garment, with a binding around the opening, so that it might not tear. ²⁴On the hem of the robe they made pomegranates of blue and purple and scarlet yarns and fine twined linen. ²⁵They also made bells of pure gold, and put the bells between the pomegranates all around the hem of the robe, between the pomegranates— ²⁶a bell and a pomegranate, a bell and a pomegranate around the hem of the robe for ministering, as the LORD had commanded Moses.

²⁷They also made the coats, woven of fine linen, for Aaron and his sons, ²⁸and the turban of fine linen, and the caps of fine linen, and the linen undergarments of fine twined linen, ²⁹and the sash of fine twined linen and of blue and purple and scarlet yarns, embroidered with needlework, as the LORD had commanded Moses.

³⁰They made the plate of the holy crown of pure gold, and wrote on it an inscription, like the engraving of a signet, "Holy to the LORD." ³¹And they tied to it a cord of blue to fasten it on the turban above, as the LORD had commanded Moses.

³²Thus all the work of the tabernacle of the tent of meeting was finished, and the people of Israel did according to all that the LORD had commanded Moses; so they did. ³³Then they brought the tabernacle to Moses, the tent and all its utensils, its hooks, its frames, its bars, its pillars, and its bases; ³⁴the covering of tanned rams' skins and goatskins, and the veil of the screen; ³⁵the ark of the testimony with its poles and the mercy seat; ³⁶the table with all its utensils, and the bread of the Presence; ³⁷the lampstand of pure gold and its lamps with the lamps set and all its utensils, and the oil for the light; ³⁸the golden altar, the anointing oil and the fragrant incense, and the screen for the entrance of the tent; ³⁹the bronze altar, and its grating of bronze, its poles, and all its utensils; the basin and its stand; ⁴⁰the hangings of the court, its pillars, and its bases, and the screen for the gate of the court, its cords, and its pegs; and all the utensils for the service of the tabernacle, for the tent of meeting; ⁴¹the finely

¹A *span* was about 9 inches or 22 centimeters

worked garments for ministering in the Holy Place, the holy garments for Aaron the priest, and the garments of his sons for their service as priests. ⁴²According to all that the LORD had commanded Moses, so the people of Israel had done all the work. ⁴³And Moses saw all the work, and behold, they had done it; as the LORD had commanded, so had they done it. Then Moses blessed them.

The Tabernacle Erected

40 The LORD spoke to Moses, saying, ²"On the first day of the first month you shall erect the tabernacle of the tent of meeting. ³And you shall put in it the ark of the testimony, and you shall screen the ark with the veil. ⁴And you shall bring in the table and arrange it, and you shall bring in the lampstand and set up its lamps. ⁵And you shall put the golden altar for incense before the ark of the testimony, and set up the screen for the door of the tabernacle. ⁶You shall set the altar of burnt offering before the door of the tabernacle of the tent of meeting, ⁷and place the basin between the tent of meeting and the altar, and put water in it. ⁸And you shall set up the court all around, and hang up the screen for the gate of the court.

⁹"Then you shall take the anointing oil and anoint the tabernacle and all that is in it, and consecrate it and all its furniture, so that it may become holy. ¹⁰You shall also anoint the altar of burnt offering and all its utensils, and consecrate the altar, so that the altar may become most holy. ¹¹You shall also anoint the basin and its stand, and consecrate it. ¹²Then you shall bring Aaron and his sons to the entrance of the tent of meeting and shall wash them with water ¹³and put on Aaron the holy garments. And you shall anoint him and consecrate him, that he may serve me as priest. ¹⁴You shall bring his sons also and put coats on them, ¹⁵and anoint them, as you anointed their father, that they may serve me as priests. And their anointing shall admit them to a perpetual priesthood throughout their generations."

¹⁶This Moses did; according to all that the LORD commanded him, so he did. ¹⁷In the first month in the second year, on the first day of the month, the tabernacle was erected. ¹⁸Moses erected the tabernacle. He laid its bases, and set up its frames, and put in its poles, and raised up its pillars. ¹⁹And he spread the tent over the tabernacle and put the covering of the tent over it, as the LORD had commanded Moses. ²⁰He took the testimony and put it into the ark, and put the poles on the ark and set the mercy seat above on the ark. ²¹And he brought the ark into the tabernacle and set up the veil of the screen, and screened the ark of the testimony, as the LORD had commanded Moses. ²²He put the table in the tent of meeting, on the north side of the tabernacle, outside the veil, ²³and arranged the bread on it before the LORD, as the LORD had commanded Moses. ²⁴He put the lampstand in the tent of meeting, opposite the table on the south side of the tabernacle, ²⁵and set up the lamps before the LORD, as the LORD had commanded Moses. ²⁶He put the golden altar in the tent of meeting before the veil, ²⁷and burned fragrant incense on it, as the LORD had commanded Moses. ²⁸He put in place the screen for the door of the tabernacle. ²⁹And he set the altar of burnt offering at the entrance of the tabernacle of the tent of meeting, and offered on it the burnt offering and the grain offering, as the LORD had commanded Moses. ³⁰He set the basin between the tent of meeting and the altar, and put water in it for washing, ³¹with which Moses and Aaron and his sons washed their hands and their feet. ³²When they went into the tent of meeting, and when they approached the altar, they washed, as the LORD commanded Moses. ³³And he erected the court around the tabernacle and the altar, and set up the screen of the gate of the court. So Moses finished the work.

The Glory of the LORD

³⁴Then the cloud covered the tent of meeting, and the glory of the LORD filled the tabernacle. ³⁵And Moses was not able to enter the tent of meeting because the cloud settled on it, and the glory of the LORD filled the tabernacle. ³⁶Throughout all their journeys, whenever the cloud was taken up from over the tabernacle, the people of Israel would set out. ³⁷But if the cloud was not taken up, then they did not set out till the day that it was taken up. ³⁸For the cloud of the LORD was on the tabernacle by day, and fire was in it by night, in the sight of all the house of Israel throughout all their journeys.

INTRODUCTION TO
Leviticus

Be Holy

"I am the LORD your God. Consecrate yourselves therefore, and be holy, for I am holy."

Leviticus 11:44

Author: Moses

Time: Probably around the
fifteenth century B.C.

Place: Probably the wilderness
of Sinai

Written to: The Israelites

The gist

Leviticus was written to show
God's people that God loved
them so much that he wanted
to provide a way to atone for
their sins. God also wanted to
teach the people how to live
clean and holy lives before
him. It is a list of rules that
they needed to follow—not
to be saved but because they
had been saved and were
now called to be God's special
people. Leviticus teaches us
how holy God is and shows us
the honor and respect that he
is due. Though we don't have
to follow these regulations any
longer, Leviticus still helps us
fully understand how gracious
God is to provide ways for
sin to be taken care of as we
serve him.

Things to look for

The different kinds of offerings: the burnt offering (see
Lev. 1:3–17), the grain offering
(see Leviticus 2), the fellowship (or peace) offering (see
Leviticus 3), the offering for
unintentional wrongdoing (see
Leviticus 4; 5:14–19), and the
sin offering (see Lev. 6:1–7)

The book of Leviticus is a reminder of what being "friends"
with a holy God means. God commanded his people to be
holy and set apart. That meant they had to do good and be
different from the rest of the world, who didn't worship him.
They needed to work at guarding their cleanliness and obeying all of the law so that they would live in an appropriate
way toward a holy God.

But since Jesus came, a lot has changed. He fulfilled the
laws in Leviticus, because he made the atoning sacrifice
toward which all the sacrifices in Leviticus pointed. Leviticus
prepares us for Jesus! His sacrifice set you free from sin. As
you approach God, never forget the amazing gift of the cross.
Just knowing what he gave you leads you to live in holy reverence and awe of him.

As you read this book, think about the way God has always
provided atonement for his people, and how he did this
supremely by giving up his own Son. Think also about how
important it was and still is for us to be set apart and holy.
Even though we don't have the same restrictions as the
Israelites had in Leviticus, we still have the call to holiness
and obedience that comes through Christ. Choose to see God
for the holy being he is, and never, ever forget the greatest
sacrifice ever made: the death of the Son of God. The Holy
One has made you his own. Never forget what that means in
your life and in your worship.

Must-Know Terms and Verses

∼ Feasts ∼

Regularly scheduled community worship times for the people of Israel. Also called festivals.

∼ Levites ∼

Descendants of Levi who were set apart as religious workers. They were commanded to serve the name of the Lord forever (see Deut. 18:1–8).

∼ Unclean ∼

Not fit for ceremonial worship, impure, unholy, dirty, foul, or morally unacceptable. The Old Testament teaches what God considers to be unclean and therefore not spiritually pure.

"Every one of you shall revere his mother and his father, and you shall keep my Sabbaths: I am the LORD your God." *Leviticus 19:3*

"You shall stand up before the gray head and honor the face of an old man, and you shall fear your God: I am the LORD." *Leviticus 19:32*

"I will make my dwelling among you, and my soul shall not abhor you. And I will walk among you and will be your God, and you shall be my people." *Leviticus 26:11–12*

Leviticus

Laws for Burnt Offerings

1 The LORD called Moses and spoke to him from the tent of meeting, saying, [2] "Speak to the people of Israel and say to them, When any one of you brings an offering to the LORD, you shall bring your offering of livestock from the herd or from the flock.

[3] "If his offering is a burnt offering from the herd, he shall offer a male without blemish. He shall bring it to the entrance of the tent of meeting, that he may be accepted before the LORD. [4] He shall lay his hand on the head of the burnt offering, and it shall be accepted for him to make atonement for him. [5] Then he shall kill the bull before the LORD, and Aaron's sons the priests shall bring the blood and throw the blood against the sides of the altar that is at the entrance of the tent of meeting. [6] Then he shall flay the burnt offering and cut it into pieces, [7] and the sons of Aaron the priest shall put fire on the altar and arrange wood on the fire. [8] And Aaron's sons the priests shall arrange the pieces, the head, and the fat, on the wood that is on the fire on the altar; [9] but its entrails and its legs he shall wash with water. And the priest shall burn all of it on the altar, as a burnt offering, a food offering[1] with a pleasing aroma to the LORD.

[10] "If his gift for a burnt offering is from the flock, from the sheep or goats, he shall bring a male without blemish, [11] and he shall kill it on the north side of the altar before the LORD, and Aaron's sons the priests shall throw its blood against the sides of the altar. [12] And he shall cut it into pieces, with its head and its fat, and the priest shall arrange them on the wood that is on the fire on the altar, [13] but the entrails and the legs he shall wash with water. And the priest shall offer all of it and burn it on the altar; it is a burnt offering, a food offering with a pleasing aroma to the LORD.

[14] "If his offering to the LORD is a burnt offering of birds, then he shall bring his offering of turtledoves or pigeons. [15] And the priest shall bring it to the altar and wring off its head and burn it on the altar. Its blood shall be drained out on the side of the altar. [16] He shall remove its crop with its contents[2] and cast it beside the altar on the east side, in the place for ashes. [17] He shall tear it open by its wings, but shall not sever it completely. And the priest shall burn it on the altar, on the wood that is on the fire. It is a burnt offering, a food offering with a pleasing aroma to the LORD.

Laws for Grain Offerings

2 "When anyone brings a grain offering as an offering to the LORD, his offering shall be of fine flour. He shall pour oil on it and put frankincense on it [2] and bring it to Aaron's sons the priests. And he shall take from it a handful of the fine flour and oil, with all of its frankincense, and the priest shall burn this as its memorial portion on the altar, a food offering with a pleasing aroma to the LORD. [3] But the rest of the grain offering shall be for Aaron and his sons; it is a most holy part of the LORD's food offerings.

[4] "When you bring a grain offering baked in the oven as an offering, it shall be unleavened loaves of fine flour mixed with oil or unleavened wafers smeared with oil. [5] And if your offering is a grain offering baked on a griddle, it shall be of fine flour unleavened, mixed with oil. [6] You shall break it in pieces and pour oil on it; it is a grain offering. [7] And if your offering is a grain offering cooked in a pan, it shall be made of fine flour with oil. [8] And you shall bring the grain offering that is made of these things to the LORD, and when it is presented to the priest, he shall bring it to

[1] Or an offering by fire; so throughout Leviticus [2] Or feathers

the altar. **9**And the priest shall take from the grain offering its memorial portion and burn this on the altar, a food offering with a pleasing aroma to the LORD. **10**But the rest of the grain offering shall be for Aaron and his sons; it is a most holy part of the LORD's food offerings.

11"No grain offering that you bring to the LORD shall be made with leaven, for you shall burn no leaven nor any honey as a food offering to the LORD. **12**As an offering of firstfruits you may bring them to the LORD, but they shall not be offered on the altar for a pleasing aroma. **13**You shall season all your grain offerings with salt. You shall not let the salt of the covenant with your God be missing from your grain offering; with all your offerings you shall offer salt.

14"If you offer a grain offering of first-fruits to the LORD, you shall offer for the grain offering of your firstfruits fresh ears, roasted with fire, crushed new grain. **15**And you shall put oil on it and lay frankincense on it; it is a grain offering. **16**And the priest shall burn as its memorial portion some of the crushed grain and some of the oil with all of its frankincense; it is a food offering to the LORD.

Laws for Peace Offerings

3 "If his offering is a sacrifice of peace offering, if he offers an animal from the herd, male or female, he shall offer it without blemish before the LORD. **2**And he shall lay his hand on the head of his offering and kill it at the entrance of the tent of meeting, and Aaron's sons the priests shall throw the blood against the sides of the altar. **3**And from the sacrifice of the peace offering, as a food offering to the LORD, he

verses to read
Leviticus 1:1–2

Imagine giving up something you need or love to God every morning and every evening. This was the system the Israelites lived under. Each morning and evening the community sacrificed things like food, grains, and animals (see Num. 28:1–8).

The guilt or sin offering was made to clear people of all the sins they had committed prior to the sacrifice. There was also the burnt offering, where they would burn up entire animals into ashes. This offering represented their total dedication to God, giving him their all. A third offering was the fellowship or peace offering. This was basically a family meal where everyone enjoyed fellowship and peace with one another and with God.

Let's look a little closer at those three things: You have the forgiveness of sin, complete dedication to him who forgave the sin, and then fellowship. And that pattern still exists today. The sacrifice of Jesus is your guilt offering, but it only had to happen once—forgiveness in full, once and for all. All that is required for forgiveness is for you to confess, repent, and accept Christ's blood as all you need. Then comes your complete dedication, and then fellowship and peace with God (see Rom. 5:1).

If you were completely holy as God is, then there would be no separation between the two of you. But since that isn't the case, something had to happen to get you together, and that was the sacrifice of Jesus. He is your one and only sacrifice. He is all that you need to be made holy in the eyes of God. No longer do you need to bring your choicest items to the altar in order to come near to God, but you now have full access to him because of your position in Christ. As you read the book of Leviticus, consider how much God requires of those who worship him.

Know God

shall offer the fat covering the entrails and all the fat that is on the entrails, **4**and the two kidneys with the fat that is on them at the loins, and the long lobe of the liver that he shall remove with the kidneys. **5**Then Aaron's sons shall burn it on the altar on top of the burnt offering, which is on the wood on the fire; it is a food offering with a pleasing aroma to the LORD.

6"If his offering for a sacrifice of peace offering to the LORD is an animal from the flock, male or female, he shall offer it without blemish. **7**If he offers a lamb for his offering, then he shall offer it before the LORD, **8**lay his hand on the head of his offering, and kill it in front of the tent of meeting; and Aaron's sons shall throw its blood against the sides of the altar. **9**Then from the sacrifice of the peace offering he shall offer as a food offering to the LORD its fat; he shall remove the whole fat tail, cut off close to the backbone, and the fat that covers the entrails and all the fat that is on the entrails **10**and the two kidneys with the fat that is on them at the loins and the long lobe of the liver that he shall remove with the kidneys. **11**And the priest shall burn it on the altar as a food offering to the LORD.

12"If his offering is a goat, then he shall offer it before the LORD **13**and lay his hand on its head and kill it in front of the tent of meeting, and the sons of Aaron shall throw its blood against the sides of the altar. **14**Then he shall offer from it, as his offering for a food offering to the LORD, the fat covering the entrails and all the fat that is on the entrails **15**and the two kidneys with the fat that is on them at the loins and the long lobe of the liver that he shall remove with the kidneys. **16**And the priest shall burn them on the altar as a food offering with a pleasing aroma. All fat is the LORD's. **17**It shall be a statute forever throughout your generations, in all your dwelling places, that you eat neither fat nor blood."

Laws for Sin Offerings

4 And the LORD spoke to Moses, saying, **2**"Speak to the people of Israel, saying, If anyone sins unintentionally[1] in any of the LORD's commandments about things not to be done, and does any one of them, **3**if it is the anointed priest who sins, thus bringing guilt on the people, then he shall offer for the sin that he has committed a bull from the herd without blemish to the LORD for a sin offering. **4**He shall bring the bull to the entrance of the tent of meeting before the LORD and lay his hand on the head of the bull and kill the bull before the LORD. **5**And the anointed priest shall take some of the blood of the bull and bring it into the tent of meeting, **6**and the priest shall dip his finger in the blood and sprinkle part of the blood seven times before the LORD in front of the veil of the sanctuary. **7**And the priest shall put some of the blood on the horns of the altar of fragrant incense before the LORD that is in the tent of meeting, and all the rest of the blood of the bull he shall pour out at the base of the altar of burnt offering that is at the entrance of the tent of meeting. **8**And all the fat of the bull of the sin offering he shall remove from it, the fat that covers the entrails and all the fat that is on the entrails **9**and the two kidneys with the fat that is on them at the loins and the long lobe of the liver that he shall remove with the kidneys **10**(just as these are taken from the ox of the sacrifice of the peace offerings); and the priest shall burn them on the altar of burnt offering. **11**But the skin of the bull and all its flesh, with its head, its legs, its entrails, and its dung— **12**all the rest of the bull— he shall carry outside the camp to a clean place, to the ash heap, and shall burn it up on a fire of wood. On the ash heap it shall be burned up.

13"If the whole congregation of Israel sins unintentionally[2] and the thing is hidden from the eyes of the assembly, and they do any one of the things that by the LORD's commandments ought not to be done, and they realize their guilt,[3] **14**when the sin which they have committed becomes known, the assembly shall offer a bull from the herd for a sin offering and bring it in front of the tent of meeting. **15**And the elders of the congregation shall lay their hands on the head of the bull before the LORD, and the bull shall be killed before the LORD. **16**Then the anointed priest shall bring some of the blood of the bull into the tent of meeting, **17**and the priest shall dip his finger in the blood and sprinkle it seven times before the LORD in front of the veil. **18**And he shall put some of the blood on the horns of the altar that is in the tent

[1] Or *by mistake*; so throughout Leviticus [2] Or *makes a mistake* [3] Or *suffer for their guilt*, or *are guilty*; also verses 22, 27, and chapter 5

of meeting before the LORD, and the rest of the blood he shall pour out at the base of the altar of burnt offering that is at the entrance of the tent of meeting. ¹⁹ And all its fat he shall take from it and burn on the altar. ²⁰ Thus shall he do with the bull. As he did with the bull of the sin offering, so shall he do with this. And the priest shall make atonement for them, and they shall be forgiven. ²¹ And he shall carry the bull outside the camp and burn it up as he burned the first bull; it is the sin offering for the assembly.

²² "When a leader sins, doing unintentionally any one of all the things that by the commandments of the LORD his God ought not to be done, and realizes his guilt, ²³ or the sin which he has committed is made known to him, he shall bring as his offering a goat, a male without blemish, ²⁴ and shall lay his hand on the head of the goat and kill it in the place where they kill the burnt offering before the LORD; it is a sin offering. ²⁵ Then the priest shall take some of the blood of the sin offering with his finger and put it on the horns of the altar of burnt offering and pour out the rest of its blood at the base of the altar of burnt offering. ²⁶ And all its fat he shall burn on the altar, like the fat of the sacrifice of peace offerings. So the priest shall make atonement for him for his sin, and he shall be forgiven.

²⁷ "If anyone of the common people sins unintentionally in doing any one of the things that by the LORD's commandments ought not to be done, and realizes his guilt, ²⁸ or the sin which he has committed is made known to him, he shall bring for his offering a goat, a female without blemish, for his sin which he has committed. ²⁹ And he shall lay his hand on the head of the sin offering and kill the sin offering in the place of burnt offering. ³⁰ And the priest shall take some of its blood with his finger and put it on the horns of the altar of burnt offering and pour out all the rest of its blood at the base of the altar. ³¹ And all its fat he shall remove, as the fat is removed from the peace offerings, and the priest shall burn it on the altar for a pleasing aroma to the LORD. And the priest shall make atonement for him, and he shall be forgiven.

³² "If he brings a lamb as his offering for a sin offering, he shall bring a female without blemish ³³ and lay his hand on the head of the sin offering and kill it for a sin offering in the place where they kill the burnt offering. ³⁴ Then the priest shall take some of the blood of the sin offering with his finger and put it on the horns of the altar of burnt offering and pour out all the rest of its blood at the base of the altar. ³⁵ And all its fat he shall remove as the fat of the lamb is removed from the sacrifice of peace offerings, and the priest shall burn it on the altar, on top of the LORD's food offerings. And the priest shall make atonement for him for the sin which he has committed, and he shall be forgiven.

5 "If anyone sins in that he hears a public adjuration to testify, and though he is a witness, whether he has seen or come to know the matter, yet does not speak, he shall bear his iniquity; ² or if anyone touches an unclean thing, whether a carcass of an unclean wild animal or a carcass of unclean livestock or a carcass of unclean swarming things, and it is hidden from him and he has become unclean, and he realizes his guilt; ³ or if he touches human uncleanness, of whatever sort the uncleanness may be with which one becomes unclean, and it is hidden from him, when he comes to know it, and realizes his guilt; ⁴ or if anyone utters with his lips a rash oath to do evil or to do good, any sort of rash oath that people swear, and it is hidden from him, when he comes to know it, and he realizes his guilt in any of these; ⁵ when he realizes his guilt in any of these and confesses the sin he has committed, ⁶ he shall bring to the LORD as his compensation¹ for the sin that he has committed, a female from the flock, a lamb or a goat, for a sin offering. And the priest shall make atonement for him for his sin.

⁷ "But if he cannot afford a lamb, then he shall bring to the LORD as his compensation for the sin that he has committed two turtledoves or two pigeons,² one for a sin offering and the other for a burnt offering. ⁸ He shall bring them to the priest, who shall offer first the one for the sin offering. He shall wring its head from its neck but shall not sever it completely, ⁹ and he shall sprinkle some of the blood of the sin offering on the side of the altar, while the rest of the blood shall be drained out at the base of the altar; it is a sin offering. ¹⁰ Then he shall offer the second for a burnt offering

¹ Hebrew *his guilt penalty*; so throughout Leviticus ² Septuagint *two young pigeons*; also verse 11

according to the rule. And the priest shall make atonement for him for the sin that he has committed, and he shall be forgiven.

11 "But if he cannot afford two turtledoves or two pigeons, then he shall bring as his offering for the sin that he has committed a tenth of an ephah[1] of fine flour for a sin offering. He shall put no oil on it and shall put no frankincense on it, for it is a sin offering. 12 And he shall bring it to the priest, and the priest shall take a handful of it as its memorial portion and burn this on the altar, on the LORD's food offerings; it is a sin offering. 13 Thus the priest shall make atonement for him for the sin which he has committed in any one of these things, and he shall be forgiven. And the remainder[2] shall be for the priest, as in the grain offering."

Laws for Guilt Offerings

14 The LORD spoke to Moses, saying, 15 "If anyone commits a breach of faith and sins unintentionally in any of the holy things of the LORD, he shall bring to the LORD as his compensation, a ram without blemish out of the flock, valued[3] in silver shekels,[4] according to the shekel of the sanctuary, for a guilt offering. 16 He shall also make restitution for what he has done amiss in the holy thing and shall add a fifth to it and give it to the priest. And the priest shall make atonement for him with the ram of the guilt offering, and he shall be forgiven.

17 "If anyone sins, doing any of the things that by the LORD's commandments ought not to be done, though he did not know it, then realizes his guilt, he shall bear his iniquity. 18 He shall bring to the priest a ram without blemish out of the flock, or its equivalent for a guilt offering, and the priest shall make atonement for him for the mistake that he made unintentionally, and he shall be forgiven. 19 It is a guilt offering; he has indeed incurred guilt before[5] the LORD."

6 ⁶ The LORD spoke to Moses, saying, 2 "If anyone sins and commits a breach of faith against the LORD by deceiving his neighbor in a matter of deposit or security, or through robbery, or if he has oppressed his neighbor 3 or has found something lost and lied about it, swearing falsely— in any of all the things that people do and sin

thereby— 4 if he has sinned and has realized his guilt and will restore what he took by robbery or what he got by oppression or the deposit that was committed to him or the lost thing that he found 5 or anything about which he has sworn falsely, he shall restore it in full and shall add a fifth to it, and give it to him to whom it belongs on the day he realizes his guilt. 6 And he shall bring to the priest as his compensation to the LORD a ram without blemish out of the flock, or its equivalent for a guilt offering. 7 And the priest shall make atonement for him before the LORD, and he shall be forgiven for any of the things that one may do and thereby become guilty."

The Priests and the Offerings

8 ⁷ The LORD spoke to Moses, saying, 9 "Command Aaron and his sons, saying, This is the law of the burnt offering. The burnt offering shall be on the hearth on the altar all night until the morning, and the fire of the altar shall be kept burning on it. 10 And the priest shall put on his linen garment and put his linen undergarment on his body, and he shall take up the ashes to which the fire has reduced the burnt offering on the altar and put them beside the altar. 11 Then he shall take off his garments and put on other garments and carry the ashes outside the camp to a clean place. 12 The fire on the altar shall be kept burning on it; it shall not go out. The priest shall burn wood on it every morning, and he shall arrange the burnt offering on it and shall burn on it the fat of the peace offerings. 13 Fire shall be kept burning on the altar continually; it shall not go out.

14 "And this is the law of the grain offering. The sons of Aaron shall offer it before the LORD in front of the altar. 15 And one shall take from it a handful of the fine flour of the grain offering and its oil and all the frankincense that is on the grain offering and burn this as its memorial portion on the altar, a pleasing aroma to the LORD. 16 And the rest of it Aaron and his sons shall eat. It shall be eaten unleavened in a holy place. In the court of the tent of meeting they shall eat it. 17 It shall not be baked with leaven. I have given it as their portion of my food offerings. It is a thing most holy, like the sin offering and the guilt

---

[1] An *ephah* was about 3/5 bushel or 22 liters [2] Septuagint; Hebrew *it* [3] Or *flock, or its equivalent* [4] A *shekel* was about 2/5 ounce or 11 grams [5] Or *he has paid full compensation to* [6] Ch 5:20 in Hebrew [7] Ch 6:1 in Hebrew

offering. [18] Every male among the children of Aaron may eat of it, as decreed forever throughout your generations, from the LORD's food offerings. Whatever touches them shall become holy."

[19] The LORD spoke to Moses, saying, [20] "This is the offering that Aaron and his sons shall offer to the LORD on the day when he is anointed: a tenth of an ephah[1] of fine flour as a regular grain offering, half of it in the morning and half in the evening. [21] It shall be made with oil on a griddle. You shall bring it well mixed, in baked[2] pieces like a grain offering, and offer it for a pleasing aroma to the LORD. [22] The priest from among Aaron's sons, who is anointed to succeed him, shall offer it to the LORD as decreed forever. The whole of it shall be burned. [23] Every grain offering of a priest shall be wholly burned. It shall not be eaten."

[24] The LORD spoke to Moses, saying, [25] "Speak to Aaron and his sons, saying, This is the law of the sin offering. In the place where the burnt offering is killed shall the sin offering be killed before the LORD; it is most holy. [26] The priest who offers it for sin shall eat it. In a holy place it shall be eaten, in the court of the tent of meeting. [27] Whatever touches its flesh shall be holy, and when any of its blood is splashed on a garment, you shall wash that on which it was splashed in a holy place. [28] And the earthenware vessel in which it is boiled shall be broken. But if it is boiled in a bronze vessel, that shall be scoured and rinsed in water. [29] Every male among the priests may eat of it; it is most holy. [30] But no sin offering shall be eaten from which any blood is brought into the tent of meeting to make atonement in the Holy Place; it shall be burned up with fire.

7 "This is the law of the guilt offering. It is most holy. [2] In the place where they kill the burnt offering they shall kill the guilt offering, and its blood shall be thrown against the sides of the altar. [3] And all its fat shall be offered, the fat tail, the fat that covers the entrails, [4] the two kidneys with the fat that is on them at the loins, and the long lobe of the liver that he shall remove with the kidneys. [5] The priest shall burn them on the altar as a food offering to the LORD; it is a guilt offering. [6] Every male among the priests may eat of it. It shall be eaten

in a holy place. It is most holy. [7] The guilt offering is just like the sin offering; there is one law for them. The priest who makes atonement with it shall have it. [8] And the priest who offers any man's burnt offering shall have for himself the skin of the burnt offering that he has offered. [9] And every grain offering baked in the oven and all that is prepared on a pan or a griddle shall belong to the priest who offers it. [10] And every grain offering, mixed with oil or dry, shall be shared equally among all the sons of Aaron.

[11] "And this is the law of the sacrifice of peace offerings that one may offer to the LORD. [12] If he offers it for a thanksgiving, then he shall offer with the thanksgiving sacrifice unleavened loaves mixed with oil, unleavened wafers smeared with oil, and loaves of fine flour well mixed with oil. [13] With the sacrifice of his peace offerings for thanksgiving he shall bring his offering with loaves of leavened bread. [14] And from it he shall offer one loaf from each offering, as a gift to the LORD. It shall belong to the priest who throws the blood of the peace offerings. [15] And the flesh of the sacrifice of his peace offerings for thanksgiving shall be eaten on the day of his offering. He shall not leave any of it until the morning. [16] But if the sacrifice of his offering is a vow offering or a freewill offering, it shall be eaten on the day that he offers his sacrifice, and on the next day what remains of it shall be eaten. [17] But what remains of the flesh of the sacrifice on the third day shall be burned up with fire. [18] If any of the flesh of the sacrifice of his peace offering is eaten on the third day, he who offers it shall not be accepted, neither shall it be credited to him. It is tainted, and he who eats of it shall bear his iniquity.

[19] "Flesh that touches any unclean thing shall not be eaten. It shall be burned up with fire. All who are clean may eat flesh, [20] but the person who eats of the flesh of the sacrifice of the LORD's peace offerings while an uncleanness is on him, that person shall be cut off from his people. [21] And if anyone touches an unclean thing, whether human uncleanness or an unclean beast or any unclean detestable creature, and then eats some flesh from the sacrifice of the LORD's peace offerings, that person shall be cut off from his people."

---

[1] An *ephah* was about 3/5 bushel or 22 liters [2] The meaning of the Hebrew is uncertain

²²The LORD spoke to Moses, saying, ²³"Speak to the people of Israel, saying, You shall eat no fat, of ox or sheep or goat. ²⁴The fat of an animal that dies of itself and the fat of one that is torn by beasts may be put to any other use, but on no account shall you eat it. ²⁵For every person who eats of the fat of an animal of which a food offering may be made to the LORD shall be cut off from his people. ²⁶Moreover, you shall eat no blood whatever, whether of fowl or of animal, in any of your dwelling places. ²⁷Whoever eats any blood, that person shall be cut off from his people."

²⁸The LORD spoke to Moses, saying, ²⁹"Speak to the people of Israel, saying, Whoever offers the sacrifice of his peace offerings to the LORD shall bring his offering to the LORD from the sacrifice of his peace offerings. ³⁰His own hands shall bring the LORD's food offerings. He shall bring the fat with the breast, that the breast may be waved as a wave offering before the LORD. ³¹The priest shall burn the fat on the altar, but the breast shall be for Aaron and his sons. ³²And the right thigh you shall give to the priest as a contribution from the sacrifice of your peace offerings. ³³Whoever among the sons of Aaron offers the blood of the peace offerings and the fat shall have the right thigh for a portion. ³⁴For the breast that is waved and the thigh that is contributed I have taken from the people of Israel, out of the sacrifices of their peace offerings, and have given them to Aaron the priest and to his sons, as a perpetual due from the people of Israel. ³⁵This is the portion of Aaron and of his sons from the LORD's food offerings, from the day they were presented to serve as priests of the LORD. ³⁶The LORD commanded this to be given them by the people of Israel, from the day that he anointed them. It is a perpetual due throughout their generations."

³⁷This is the law of the burnt offering, of the grain offering, of the sin offering, of the guilt offering, of the ordination offering, and of the peace offering, ³⁸which the LORD commanded Moses on Mount Sinai, on the day that he commanded the people of Israel to bring their offerings to the LORD, in the wilderness of Sinai.

Consecration of Aaron and His Sons

8 The LORD spoke to Moses, saying, ²"Take Aaron and his sons with him, and the garments and the anointing oil and the bull of the sin offering and the two rams and the basket of unleavened bread. ³And assemble all the congregation at the entrance of the tent of meeting." ⁴And Moses did as the LORD commanded him, and the congregation was assembled at the entrance of the tent of meeting.

⁵And Moses said to the congregation, "This is the thing that the LORD has commanded to be done." ⁶And Moses brought Aaron and his sons and washed them with water. ⁷And he put the coat on him and tied the sash around his waist and clothed him with the robe and put the ephod on him and tied the skillfully woven band of the ephod around him, binding it to him with the band.[1] ⁸And he placed the breastpiece on him, and in the breastpiece he put the Urim and the Thummim. ⁹And he set the turban on his head, and on the turban, in front, he set the golden plate, the holy crown, as the LORD commanded Moses.

¹⁰Then Moses took the anointing oil and anointed the tabernacle and all that was in it, and consecrated them. ¹¹And he sprinkled some of it on the altar seven times, and anointed the altar and all its utensils and the basin and its stand, to consecrate them. ¹²And he poured some of the anointing oil on Aaron's head and anointed him to consecrate him. ¹³And Moses brought Aaron's sons and clothed them with coats and tied sashes around their waists and bound caps on them, as the LORD commanded Moses.

¹⁴Then he brought the bull of the sin offering, and Aaron and his sons laid their hands on the head of the bull of the sin offering. ¹⁵And he[2] killed it, and Moses took the blood, and with his finger put it on the horns of the altar around it and purified the altar and poured out the blood at the base of the altar and consecrated it to make atonement for it. ¹⁶And he took all the fat that was on the entrails and the long lobe of the liver and the two kidneys with their fat, and Moses burned them on the altar. ¹⁷But the bull and its skin and its flesh and its dung he burned up with fire outside the camp, as the LORD commanded Moses.

[1] Hebrew with it [2] Probably Aaron or his representative; possibly Moses; also verses 16–23

¹⁸ Then he presented the ram of the burnt offering, and Aaron and his sons laid their hands on the head of the ram. ¹⁹ And he killed it, and Moses threw the blood against the sides of the altar. ²⁰ He cut the ram into pieces, and Moses burned the head and the pieces and the fat. ²¹ He washed the entrails and the legs with water, and Moses burned the whole ram on the altar. It was a burnt offering with a pleasing aroma, a food offering for the LORD, as the LORD commanded Moses.

²² Then he presented the other ram, the ram of ordination, and Aaron and his sons laid their hands on the head of the ram. ²³ And he killed it, and Moses took some of its blood and put it on the lobe of Aaron's right ear and on the thumb of his right hand and on the big toe of his right foot. ²⁴ Then he presented Aaron's sons, and Moses put some of the blood on the lobes of their right ears and on the thumbs of their right hands and on the big toes of their right feet. And Moses threw the blood against the sides of the altar. ²⁵ Then he took the fat and the fat tail and all the fat that was on the entrails and the long lobe of the liver and the two kidneys with their fat and the right thigh, ²⁶ and out of the basket of unleavened bread that was before the LORD he took one unleavened loaf and one loaf of bread with oil and one wafer and placed them on the pieces of fat and on the right thigh. ²⁷ And he put all these in the hands of Aaron and in the hands of his sons and waved them as a wave offering before the LORD. ²⁸ Then Moses took them from their hands and burned them on the altar with the burnt offering. This was an ordination offering with a pleasing aroma, a food offering to the LORD. ²⁹ And Moses took the breast and waved it for a wave offering before the LORD. It was Moses' portion of the ram of ordination, as the LORD commanded Moses.

³⁰ Then Moses took some of the anointing oil and of the blood that was on the altar and sprinkled it on Aaron and his garments, and also on his sons and his sons' garments. So he consecrated Aaron and his garments, and his sons and his sons' garments with him.

³¹ And Moses said to Aaron and his sons, "Boil the flesh at the entrance of the tent of meeting, and there eat it and the bread that is in the basket of ordination offerings, as I commanded, saying, 'Aaron and his sons shall eat it.' ³² And what remains of the flesh and the bread you shall burn up with fire. ³³ And you shall not go outside the entrance of the tent of meeting for seven days, until the days of your ordination are completed, for it will take seven days to ordain you. ³⁴ As has been done today, the LORD has commanded to be done to make atonement for you. ³⁵ At the entrance of the tent of meeting you shall remain day and night for seven days, performing what the LORD has charged, so that you do not die, for so I have been commanded." ³⁶ And Aaron and his sons did all the things that the LORD commanded by Moses.

The LORD Accepts Aaron's Offering

9 On the eighth day Moses called Aaron and his sons and the elders of Israel, ² and he said to Aaron, "Take for yourself a bull calf for a sin offering and a ram for a burnt offering, both without blemish, and offer them before the LORD. ³ And say to the people of Israel, 'Take a male goat for a sin offering, and a calf and a lamb, both a year old without blemish, for a burnt offering, ⁴ and an ox and a ram for peace offerings, to sacrifice before the LORD, and a grain offering mixed with oil, for today the LORD will appear to you.' " ⁵ And they brought what Moses commanded in front of the tent of meeting, and all the congregation drew near and stood before the LORD. ⁶ And Moses said, "This is the thing that the LORD commanded you to do, that the glory of the LORD may appear to you." ⁷ Then Moses said to Aaron, "Draw near to the altar and offer your sin offering and your burnt offering and make atonement for yourself and for the people, and bring the offering of the people and make atonement for them, as the LORD has commanded."

⁸ So Aaron drew near to the altar and killed the calf of the sin offering, which was for himself. ⁹ And the sons of Aaron presented the blood to him, and he dipped his finger in the blood and put it on the horns of the altar and poured out the blood at the base of the altar. ¹⁰ But the fat and the kidneys and the long lobe of the liver from the sin offering he burned on the altar, as the LORD commanded Moses. ¹¹ The flesh and the skin he burned up with fire outside the camp.

¹²Then he killed the burnt offering, and Aaron's sons handed him the blood, and he threw it against the sides of the altar. ¹³And they handed the burnt offering to him, piece by piece, and the head, and he burned them on the altar. ¹⁴And he washed the entrails and the legs and burned them with the burnt offering on the altar.

¹⁵Then he presented the people's offering and took the goat of the sin offering that was for the people and killed it and offered it as a sin offering, like the first one. ¹⁶And he presented the burnt offering and offered it according to the rule. ¹⁷And he presented the grain offering, took a handful of it, and burned it on the altar, besides the burnt offering of the morning.

¹⁸Then he killed the ox and the ram, the sacrifice of peace offerings for the people. And Aaron's sons handed him the blood, and he threw it against the sides of the altar. ¹⁹But the fat pieces of the ox and of the ram, the fat tail and that which covers the entrails and the kidneys and the long lobe of the liver— ²⁰they put the fat pieces on the breasts, and he burned the fat pieces on the altar, ²¹but the breasts and the right thigh Aaron waved for a wave offering before the LORD, as Moses commanded.

²²Then Aaron lifted up his hands toward the people and blessed them, and he came down from offering the sin offering and the burnt offering and the peace offerings. ²³And Moses and Aaron went into the tent of meeting, and when they came out they blessed the people, and the glory of the LORD appeared to all the people. ²⁴And fire came out from before the LORD and consumed the burnt offering and the pieces of fat on the altar, and when all the people saw it, they shouted and fell on their faces.

The Death of Nadab and Abihu

10 Now Nadab and Abihu, the sons of Aaron, each took his censer and put fire in it and laid incense on it and offered unauthorized[1] fire before the LORD, which he had not commanded them. ²And fire came out from before the LORD and consumed them, and they died before the LORD. ³Then Moses said to Aaron, "This is what the LORD has said: 'Among those who are near me I will be sanctified, and before all the people I will be glorified.'" And Aaron held his peace.

⁴And Moses called Mishael and Elzaphan, the sons of Uzziel the uncle of Aaron, and said to them, "Come near; carry your brothers away from the front of the sanctuary and out of the camp." ⁵So they came near and carried them in their coats out of the camp, as Moses had said. ⁶And Moses said to Aaron and to Eleazar and Ithamar his sons, "Do not let the hair of your heads hang loose, and do not tear your clothes, lest you die, and wrath come upon all the congregation; but let your brothers, the whole house of Israel, bewail the burning that the LORD has kindled. ⁷And do not go outside the entrance of the tent of meeting, lest you die, for the anointing oil of the LORD is upon you." And they did according to the word of Moses.

⁸And the LORD spoke to Aaron, saying, ⁹"Drink no wine or strong drink, you or your sons with you, when you go into the tent of meeting, lest you die. It shall be a statute forever throughout your generations. ¹⁰You are to distinguish between the holy and the common, and between the unclean and the clean, ¹¹and you are to teach the people of Israel all the statutes that the LORD has spoken to them by Moses."

¹²Moses spoke to Aaron and to Eleazar and Ithamar, his surviving sons: "Take the grain offering that is left of the LORD's food offerings, and eat it unleavened beside the altar, for it is most holy. ¹³You shall eat it in a holy place, because it is your due and your sons' due, from the LORD's food offerings, for so I am commanded. ¹⁴But the breast that is waved and the thigh that is contributed you shall eat in a clean place, you and your sons and your daughters with you, for they are given as your due and your sons' due from the sacrifices of the peace offerings of the people of Israel. ¹⁵The thigh that is contributed and the breast that is waved they shall bring with the food offerings of the fat pieces to wave for a wave offering before the LORD, and it shall be yours and your sons' with you as a due forever, as the LORD has commanded."

¹⁶Now Moses diligently inquired about the goat of the sin offering, and behold, it was burned up! And he was angry with Eleazar and Ithamar, the surviving sons of Aaron, saying, ¹⁷"Why have you not eaten the sin offering in the place of the

---

¹Or *strange*

sanctuary, since it is a thing most holy and has been given to you that you may bear the iniquity of the congregation, to make atonement for them before the LORD? ¹⁸ Behold, its blood was not brought into the inner part of the sanctuary. You certainly ought to have eaten it in the sanctuary, as I commanded." ¹⁹ And Aaron said to Moses, "Behold, today they have offered their sin offering and their burnt offering before the LORD, and yet such things as these have happened to me! If I had eaten the sin offering today, would the LORD have approved?" ²⁰ And when Moses heard that, he approved.

Clean and Unclean Animals

11 And the LORD spoke to Moses and Aaron, saying to them, ² "Speak to the people of Israel, saying, These are the living things that you may eat among all the animals that are on the earth. ³ Whatever parts the hoof and is cloven-footed and chews the cud, among the animals, you may eat. ⁴ Nevertheless, among those that chew the cud or part the hoof, you shall not eat these: The camel, because it chews the cud but does not part the hoof, is unclean to you. ⁵ And the rock badger, because it chews the cud but does not part the hoof, is unclean to you. ⁶ And the hare, because it chews the cud but does not part the hoof, is unclean to you. ⁷ And the pig, because it parts the hoof and is cloven-footed but does not chew the cud, is unclean to you. ⁸ You shall not eat any of their flesh, and you shall not touch their carcasses; they are unclean to you.

⁹ "These you may eat, of all that are in the waters. Everything in the waters that has fins and scales, whether in the seas or in the rivers, you may eat. ¹⁰ But anything in the seas or the rivers that does not have fins and scales, of the swarming creatures in the waters and of the living creatures that are in the waters, is detestable to you. ¹¹ You shall regard them as detestable; you shall not eat any of their flesh, and you shall detest their carcasses. ¹² Everything in the waters that does not have fins and scales is detestable to you.

¹³ "And these you shall detest among the birds;¹ they shall not be eaten; they are detestable: the eagle,² the bearded vulture, the black vulture, ¹⁴ the kite, the falcon of any kind, ¹⁵ every raven of any kind, ¹⁶ the

ostrich, the nighthawk, the sea gull, the hawk of any kind, ¹⁷ the little owl, the cormorant, the short-eared owl, ¹⁸ the barn owl, the tawny owl, the carrion vulture, ¹⁹ the stork, the heron of any kind, the hoopoe, and the bat.

²⁰ "All winged insects that go on all fours are detestable to you. ²¹ Yet among the winged insects that go on all fours you may eat those that have jointed legs above their feet, with which to hop on the ground. ²² Of them you may eat: the locust of any kind, the bald locust of any kind, the cricket of any kind, and the grasshopper of any kind. ²³ But all other winged insects that have four feet are detestable to you.

²⁴ "And by these you shall become unclean. Whoever touches their carcass shall be unclean until the evening, ²⁵ and whoever carries any part of their carcass shall wash his clothes and be unclean until the evening. ²⁶ Every animal that parts the hoof but is not cloven-footed or does not chew the cud is unclean to you. Everyone who touches them shall be unclean. ²⁷ And all that walk on their paws, among the animals that go on all fours, are unclean to you. Whoever touches their carcass shall be unclean until the evening, ²⁸ and he who carries their carcass shall wash his clothes and be unclean until the evening; they are unclean to you.

²⁹ "And these are unclean to you among the swarming things that swarm on the ground: the mole rat, the mouse, the great lizard of any kind, ³⁰ the gecko, the monitor lizard, the lizard, the sand lizard, and the chameleon. ³¹ These are unclean to you among all that swarm. Whoever touches them when they are dead shall be unclean until the evening. ³² And anything on which any of them falls when they are dead shall be unclean, whether it is an article of wood or a garment or a skin or a sack, any article that is used for any purpose. It must be put into water, and it shall be unclean until the evening; then it shall be clean. ³³ And if any of them falls into any earthenware vessel, all that is in it shall be unclean, and you shall break it. ³⁴ Any food in it that could be eaten, on which water comes, shall be unclean. And all drink that could be drunk from every such vessel shall be unclean. ³⁵ And everything on which any part of their carcass falls shall be unclean.

¹ Or *things that fly*; compare Genesis 1:20 ² The identity of many of these birds is uncertain

Whether oven or stove, it shall be broken in pieces. They are unclean and shall remain unclean for you. [36] Nevertheless, a spring or a cistern holding water shall be clean, but whoever touches a carcass in them shall be unclean. [37] And if any part of their carcass falls upon any seed grain that is to be sown, it is clean, [38] but if water is put on the seed and any part of their carcass falls on it, it is unclean to you.

[39] "And if any animal which you may eat dies, whoever touches its carcass shall be unclean until the evening, [40] and whoever eats of its carcass shall wash his clothes and be unclean until the evening. And whoever carries the carcass shall wash his clothes and be unclean until the evening.

[41] "Every swarming thing that swarms on the ground is detestable; it shall not be eaten. [42] Whatever goes on its belly, and whatever goes on all fours, or whatever has many feet, any swarming thing that swarms on the ground, you shall not eat, for they are detestable. [43] You shall not make yourselves detestable with any swarming thing that swarms, and you shall not defile yourselves with them, and become unclean through them. [44] For I am the LORD your God. Consecrate yourselves therefore, and be holy, for I am holy. You shall not defile yourselves with any swarming thing that crawls on the ground. [45] For I am the LORD who brought you up out of the land of Egypt to be your God. You shall therefore be holy, for I am holy."

[46] This is the law about beast and bird and every living creature that moves through the waters and every creature that swarms on the ground, [47] to make a distinction between the unclean and the clean and between the living creature that may be eaten and the living creature that may not be eaten.

Purification After Childbirth

12 The LORD spoke to Moses, saying, [2] "Speak to the people of Israel, saying, If a woman conceives and bears a male child, then she shall be unclean seven days. As at the time of her menstruation, she shall be unclean. [3] And on the eighth day

verses to read
Leviticus 11:44–45

Know God

Seven times in the book of Leviticus, God commands us to be holy because he is holy (see Lev. 11:44, 45; 19:2; 20:7, 26; 21:8; 22:32). Holiness isn't something to be watched from a distance. It isn't a goal that you're allowed to avoid because of the abundance of kindness poured out on you. God's grace isn't something that excuses you from holiness but something that helps you get holiness. Grace shouldn't be reserved for the occasional offense; it should be accepted as the very hand of God on your life, giving you the ability to do what is holy instead of being a slave to sin. The kindness of God brings mercy and forgiveness, but just as importantly, it brings his help. You can't live a holy life without the Holy Spirit on your side. And it is through the help of that Spirit that you have the ability to do what God commands, to be holy. If holiness feels like a totally unattainable goal, it's because you've tried to get there in your own power. Holiness can't be attained by the flesh. No act of strength can muster it. But you can willingly reach out and accept the gift of God's grace and his Holy Spirit, and through that gift you then can cultivate holiness.

The God Girl can't dismiss the idea of holiness as an unattainable goal, one that is better ignored than pursued because of her inability to be perfect. Holiness is your calling, God Girl, and you can start pursuing it today if you are willing to trust that it's through Christ's sacrifice and not through your own power that the Holy Spirit will make you holy.

the flesh of his foreskin shall be circumcised. [4] Then she shall continue for thirty-three days in the blood of her purifying. She shall not touch anything holy, nor come into the sanctuary, until the days of her purifying are completed. [5] But if she bears a female child, then she shall be unclean two weeks, as in her menstruation. And she shall continue in the blood of her purifying for sixty-six days.

[6] "And when the days of her purifying are completed, whether for a son or for a daughter, she shall bring to the priest at the entrance of the tent of meeting a lamb a year old for a burnt offering, and a pigeon or a turtledove for a sin offering, [7] and he shall offer it before the LORD and make atonement for her. Then she shall be clean from the flow of her blood. This is the law for her who bears a child, either male or female. [8] And if she cannot afford a lamb, then she shall take two turtledoves or two pigeons,[1] one for a burnt offering and the other for a sin offering. And the priest shall make atonement for her, and she shall be clean."

Laws About Leprosy

13 The LORD spoke to Moses and Aaron, saying, [2] "When a person has on the skin of his body a swelling or an eruption or a spot, and it turns into a case of leprous[2] disease on the skin of his body, then he shall be brought to Aaron the priest or to one of his sons the priests, [3] and the priest shall examine the diseased area on the skin of his body. And if the hair in the diseased area has turned white and the disease appears to be deeper than the skin of his body, it is a case of leprous disease. When the priest has examined him, he shall pronounce him unclean. [4] But if the spot is white in the skin of his body and appears no deeper than the skin, and the hair in it has not turned white, the priest shall shut up the diseased person for seven days. [5] And the priest shall examine him on the seventh day, and if in his eyes the disease is checked and the disease has not spread in the skin, then the priest shall shut him up for another seven days. [6] And the priest shall examine him again on the seventh day, and if the diseased area has faded and the disease has not spread in the skin, then the priest shall pronounce him clean; it is only

an eruption. And he shall wash his clothes and be clean. [7] But if the eruption spreads in the skin, after he has shown himself to the priest for his cleansing, he shall appear again before the priest. [8] And the priest shall look, and if the eruption has spread in the skin, then the priest shall pronounce him unclean; it is a leprous disease.

[9] "When a man is afflicted with a leprous disease, he shall be brought to the priest, [10] and the priest shall look. And if there is a white swelling in the skin that has turned the hair white, and there is raw flesh in the swelling, [11] it is a chronic leprous disease in the skin of his body, and the priest shall pronounce him unclean. He shall not shut him up, for he is unclean. [12] And if the leprous disease breaks out in the skin, so that the leprous disease covers all the skin of the diseased person from head to foot, so far as the priest can see, [13] then the priest shall look, and if the leprous disease has covered all his body, he shall pronounce him clean of the disease; it has all turned white, and he is clean. [14] But when raw flesh appears on him, he shall be unclean. [15] And the priest shall examine the raw flesh and pronounce him unclean. Raw flesh is unclean, for it is a leprous disease. [16] But if the raw flesh recovers and turns white again, then he shall come to the priest, [17] and the priest shall examine him, and if the disease has turned white, then the priest shall pronounce the diseased person clean; he is clean.

[18] "If there is in the skin of one's body a boil and it heals, [19] and in the place of the boil there comes a white swelling or a reddish-white spot, then it shall be shown to the priest. [20] And the priest shall look, and if it appears deeper than the skin and its hair has turned white, then the priest shall pronounce him unclean. It is a case of leprous disease that has broken out in the boil. [21] But if the priest examines it and there is no white hair in it and it is not deeper than the skin, but has faded, then the priest shall shut him up seven days. [22] And if it spreads in the skin, then the priest shall pronounce him unclean; it is a disease. [23] But if the spot remains in one place and does not spread, it is the scar of the boil, and the priest shall pronounce him clean.

[24] "Or, when the body has a burn on its skin and the raw flesh of the burn becomes

---

[1] Septuagint *two young pigeons* [2] *Leprosy* was a term for several skin diseases

a spot, reddish-white or white, [25] the priest shall examine it, and if the hair in the spot has turned white and it appears deeper than the skin, then it is a leprous disease. It has broken out in the burn, and the priest shall pronounce him unclean; it is a case of leprous disease. [26] But if the priest examines it and there is no white hair in the spot and it is no deeper than the skin, but has faded, the priest shall shut him up seven days, [27] and the priest shall examine him the seventh day. If it is spreading in the skin, then the priest shall pronounce him unclean; it is a case of leprous disease. [28] But if the spot remains in one place and does not spread in the skin, but has faded, it is a swelling from the burn, and the priest shall pronounce him clean, for it is the scar of the burn.

[29] "When a man or woman has a disease on the head or the beard, [30] the priest shall examine the disease. And if it appears deeper than the skin, and the hair in it is yellow and thin, then the priest shall pronounce him unclean. It is an itch, a leprous disease of the head or the beard. [31] And if the priest examines the itching disease and it appears no deeper than the skin and there is no black hair in it, then the priest shall shut up the person with the itching disease for seven days, [32] and on the seventh day the priest shall examine the disease. If the itch has not spread, and there is in it no yellow hair, and the itch appears to be no deeper than the skin, [33] then he shall shave himself, but the itch he shall not shave; and the priest shall shut up the person with the itching disease for another seven days. [34] And on the seventh day the priest shall examine the itch, and if the itch has not spread in the skin and it appears to be no deeper than the skin, then the priest shall pronounce him clean. And he shall wash his clothes and be clean. [35] But if the itch spreads in the skin after his cleansing, [36] then the priest shall examine him, and if the itch has spread in the skin, the priest need not seek for the yellow hair; he is unclean. [37] But if in his eyes the itch is unchanged and black hair has grown in it, the itch is healed and he is clean, and the priest shall pronounce him clean.

[38] "When a man or a woman has spots on the skin of the body, white spots, [39] the priest shall look, and if the spots on the skin of the body are of a dull white, it is leukoderma that has broken out in the skin; he is clean.

[40] "If a man's hair falls out from his head, he is bald; he is clean. [41] And if a man's hair falls out from his forehead, he has baldness of the forehead; he is clean. [42] But if there is on the bald head or the bald forehead a reddish-white diseased area, it is a leprous disease breaking out on his bald head or his bald forehead. [43] Then the priest shall examine him, and if the diseased swelling is reddish-white on his bald head or on his bald forehead, like the appearance of leprous disease in the skin of the body, [44] he is a leprous man, he is unclean. The priest must pronounce him unclean; his disease is on his head.

[45] "The leprous person who has the disease shall wear torn clothes and let the hair of his head hang loose, and he shall cover his upper lip[1] and cry out, 'Unclean, unclean.' [46] He shall remain unclean as long as he has the disease. He is unclean. He shall live alone. His dwelling shall be outside the camp.

[47] "When there is a case of leprous disease in a garment, whether a woolen or a linen garment, [48] in warp or woof of linen or wool, or in a skin or in anything made of skin, [49] if the disease is greenish or reddish in the garment, or in the skin or in the warp or the woof or in any article made of skin, it is a case of leprous disease, and it shall be shown to the priest. [50] And the priest shall examine the disease and shut up that which has the disease for seven days. [51] Then he shall examine the disease on the seventh day. If the disease has spread in the garment, in the warp or the woof, or in the skin, whatever be the use of the skin, the disease is a persistent leprous disease; it is unclean. [52] And he shall burn the garment, or the warp or the woof, the wool or the linen, or any article made of skin that is diseased, for it is a persistent leprous disease. It shall be burned in the fire.

[53] "And if the priest examines, and if the disease has not spread in the garment, in the warp or the woof or in any article made of skin, [54] then the priest shall command that they wash the thing in which is the disease, and he shall shut it up for another seven days. [55] And the priest shall examine the diseased thing after it has been

[1] Or mustache

washed. And if the appearance of the diseased area has not changed, though the disease has not spread, it is unclean. You shall burn it in the fire, whether the rot is on the back or on the front.

⁵⁶ "But if the priest examines, and if the diseased area has faded after it has been washed, he shall tear it out of the garment or the skin or the warp or the woof. ⁵⁷ Then if it appears again in the garment, in the warp or the woof, or in any article made of skin, it is spreading. You shall burn with fire whatever has the disease. ⁵⁸ But the garment, or the warp or the woof, or any article made of skin from which the disease departs when you have washed it, shall then be washed a second time, and be clean."

⁵⁹ This is the law for a case of leprous disease in a garment of wool or linen, either in the warp or the woof, or in any article made of skin, to determine whether it is clean or unclean.

Laws for Cleansing Lepers

14 The LORD spoke to Moses, saying, ² "This shall be the law of the leprous person for the day of his cleansing. He shall be brought to the priest, ³ and the priest shall go out of the camp, and the priest shall look. Then, if the case of leprous disease is healed in the leprous person, ⁴ the priest shall command them to take for him who is to be cleansed two live¹ clean birds and cedarwood and scarlet yarn and hyssop. ⁵ And the priest shall command them to kill one of the birds in an earthenware vessel over fresh² water. ⁶ He shall take the live bird with the cedarwood and the scarlet yarn and the hyssop, and dip them and the live bird in the blood of the bird that was killed over the fresh water. ⁷ And he shall sprinkle it seven times on him who is to be cleansed of the leprous disease. Then he shall pronounce him clean and shall let the living bird go into the open field. ⁸ And he who is to be cleansed shall wash his clothes and shave off all his hair and bathe himself in water, and he shall be clean. And after that he may come into the camp, but live outside his tent seven days. ⁹ And on the seventh day he shall shave off all his hair from his head, his beard, and his eyebrows. He shall shave off all his hair, and then he shall wash his clothes and bathe his body in water, and he shall be clean.

¹⁰ "And on the eighth day he shall take two male lambs without blemish, and one ewe lamb a year old without blemish, and a grain offering of three tenths of an ephah³ of fine flour mixed with oil, and one log⁴ of oil. ¹¹ And the priest who cleanses him shall set the man who is to be cleansed and these things before the LORD, at the entrance of the tent of meeting. ¹² And the priest shall take one of the male lambs and offer it for a guilt offering, along with the log of oil, and wave them for a wave offering before the LORD. ¹³ And he shall kill the lamb in the place where they kill the sin offering and the burnt offering, in the place of the sanctuary. For the guilt offering, like the sin offering, belongs to the priest; it is most holy. ¹⁴ The priest shall take some of the blood of the guilt offering, and the priest shall put it on the lobe of the right ear of him who is to be cleansed and on the thumb of his right hand and on the big toe of his right foot. ¹⁵ Then the priest shall take some of the log of oil and pour it into the palm of his own left hand ¹⁶ and dip his right finger in the oil that is in his left hand and sprinkle some oil with his finger seven times before the LORD. ¹⁷ And some of the oil that remains in his hand the priest shall put on the lobe of the right ear of him who is to be cleansed and on the thumb of his right hand and on the big toe of his right foot, on top of the blood of the guilt offering. ¹⁸ And the rest of the oil that is in the priest's hand he shall put on the head of him who is to be cleansed. Then the priest shall make atonement for him before the LORD. ¹⁹ The priest shall offer the sin offering, to make atonement for him who is to be cleansed from his uncleanness. And afterward he shall kill the burnt offering. ²⁰ And the priest shall offer the burnt offering and the grain offering on the altar. Thus the priest shall make atonement for him, and he shall be clean.

²¹ "But if he is poor and cannot afford so much, then he shall take one male lamb for a guilt offering to be waved, to make atonement for him, and a tenth of an ephah of fine flour mixed with oil for a grain offering, and a log of oil; ²² also two turtledoves or two pigeons, whichever he can afford. The

¹ Or *wild* ² Or *running*; Hebrew *living*; also verses 6, 50, 51, 52 ³ An *ephah* was about 3/5 bushel or 22 liters ⁴ A *log* was about 1/3 quart or 0.3 liter

one shall be a sin offering and the other a burnt offering. ²³ And on the eighth day he shall bring them for his cleansing to the priest, to the entrance of the tent of meeting, before the LORD. ²⁴ And the priest shall take the lamb of the guilt offering and the log of oil, and the priest shall wave them for a wave offering before the LORD. ²⁵ And he shall kill the lamb of the guilt offering. And the priest shall take some of the blood of the guilt offering and put it on the lobe of the right ear of him who is to be cleansed, and on the thumb of his right hand and on the big toe of his right foot. ²⁶ And the priest shall pour some of the oil into the palm of his own left hand, ²⁷ and shall sprinkle with his right finger some of the oil that is in his left hand seven times before the LORD. ²⁸ And the priest shall put some of the oil that is in his hand on the lobe of the right ear of him who is to be cleansed and on the thumb of his right hand and on the big toe of his right foot, in the place where the blood of the guilt offering was put. ²⁹ And the rest of the oil that is in the priest's hand he shall put on the head of him who is to be cleansed, to make atonement for him before the LORD. ³⁰ And he shall offer, of the turtledoves or pigeons, whichever he can afford, ³¹ one¹ for a sin offering and the other for a burnt offering, along with a grain offering. And the priest shall make atonement before the LORD for him who is being cleansed. ³² This is the law for him in whom is a case of leprous disease, who cannot afford the offerings for his cleansing."

Laws for Cleansing Houses

³³ The LORD spoke to Moses and Aaron, saying, ³⁴ "When you come into the land of Canaan, which I give you for a possession, and I put a case of leprous disease in a house in the land of your possession, ³⁵ then he who owns the house shall come and tell the priest, 'There seems to me to be some case of disease in my house.' ³⁶ Then the priest shall command that they empty the house before the priest goes to examine the disease, lest all that is in the house be declared unclean. And afterward the priest shall go in to see the house. ³⁷ And he shall examine the disease. And if the disease is in the walls of the house with greenish or reddish spots, and if it appears to be deeper than the surface, ³⁸ then the

priest shall go out of the house to the door of the house and shut up the house seven days. ³⁹ And the priest shall come again on the seventh day, and look. If the disease has spread in the walls of the house, ⁴⁰ then the priest shall command that they take out the stones in which is the disease and throw them into an unclean place outside the city. ⁴¹ And he shall have the inside of the house scraped all around, and the plaster that they scrape off they shall pour out in an unclean place outside the city. ⁴² Then they shall take other stones and put them in the place of those stones, and he shall take other plaster and plaster the house.

⁴³ "If the disease breaks out again in the house, after he has taken out the stones and scraped the house and plastered it, ⁴⁴ then the priest shall go and look. And if the disease has spread in the house, it is a persistent leprous disease in the house; it is unclean. ⁴⁵ And he shall break down the house, its stones and timber and all the plaster of the house, and he shall carry them out of the city to an unclean place. ⁴⁶ Moreover, whoever enters the house while it is shut up shall be unclean until the evening, ⁴⁷ and whoever sleeps in the house shall wash his clothes, and whoever eats in the house shall wash his clothes.

⁴⁸ "But if the priest comes and looks, and if the disease has not spread in the house after the house was plastered, then the priest shall pronounce the house clean, for the disease is healed. ⁴⁹ And for the cleansing of the house he shall take two small birds, with cedarwood and scarlet yarn and hyssop, ⁵⁰ and shall kill one of the birds in an earthenware vessel over fresh water ⁵¹ and shall take the cedarwood and the hyssop and the scarlet yarn, along with the live bird, and dip them in the blood of the bird that was killed and in the fresh water and sprinkle the house seven times. ⁵² Thus he shall cleanse the house with the blood of the bird and with the fresh water and with the live bird and with the cedarwood and hyssop and scarlet yarn. ⁵³ And he shall let the live bird go out of the city into the open country. So he shall make atonement for the house, and it shall be clean."

⁵⁴ This is the law for any case of leprous disease: for an itch, ⁵⁵ for leprous disease in a garment or in a house, ⁵⁶ and for a swelling or an eruption or a spot, ⁵⁷ to show

¹ Septuagint, Syriac; Hebrew *afford,* ³¹*such as he can afford, one*

when it is unclean and when it is clean. This is the law for leprous disease.

Laws About Bodily Discharges

15 The LORD spoke to Moses and Aaron, saying, [2] "Speak to the people of Israel and say to them, When any man has a discharge from his body,[1] his discharge is unclean. [3] And this is the law of his uncleanness for a discharge: whether his body runs with his discharge, or his body is blocked up by his discharge, it is his uncleanness. [4] Every bed on which the one with the discharge lies shall be unclean, and everything on which he sits shall be unclean. [5] And anyone who touches his bed shall wash his clothes and bathe himself in water and be unclean until the evening. [6] And whoever sits on anything on which the one with the discharge has sat shall wash his clothes and bathe himself in water and be unclean until the evening. [7] And whoever touches the body of the one with the discharge shall wash his clothes and bathe himself in water and be unclean until the evening. [8] And if the one with the discharge spits on someone who is clean, then he shall wash his clothes and bathe himself in water and be unclean until the evening. [9] And any saddle on which the one with the discharge rides shall be unclean. [10] And whoever touches anything that was under him shall be unclean until the evening. And whoever carries such things shall wash his clothes and bathe himself in water and be unclean until the evening. [11] Anyone whom the one with the discharge touches without having rinsed his hands in water shall wash his clothes and bathe himself in water and be unclean until the evening. [12] And an earthenware vessel that the one with the discharge touches shall be broken, and every vessel of wood shall be rinsed in water.

[13] "And when the one with a discharge is cleansed of his discharge, then he shall count for himself seven days for his cleansing, and wash his clothes. And he shall bathe his body in fresh water and shall be clean. [14] And on the eighth day he shall take two turtledoves or two pigeons and come before the LORD to the entrance of the tent of meeting and give them to the priest. [15] And the priest shall use them, one for a sin offering and the other for a burnt offer-

ing. And the priest shall make atonemen for him before the LORD for his discharge

[16] "If a man has an emission of semen, h shall bathe his whole body in water and b unclean until the evening. [17] And every gar ment and every skin on which the seme comes shall be washed with water and be unclean until the evening. [18] If a ma lies with a woman and has an emission o semen, both of them shall bathe themselve in water and be unclean until the evening

[19] "When a woman has a discharge and the discharge in her body is blood she shall be in her menstrual impurity for seven days, and whoever touches he shall be unclean until the evening. [20] An everything on which she lies during he menstrual impurity shall be unclean Everything also on which she sits shall b unclean. [21] And whoever touches her be shall wash his clothes and bathe himsel in water and be unclean until the evening [22] And whoever touches anything on whic she sits shall wash his clothes and bath himself in water and be unclean until th evening. [23] Whether it is the bed or any thing on which she sits, when he touche it he shall be unclean until the evening [24] And if any man lies with her and he menstrual impurity comes upon him, h shall be unclean seven days, and every be on which he lies shall be unclean.

[25] "If a woman has a discharge of bloo for many days, not at the time of her men strual impurity, or if she has a discharg beyond the time of her impurity, all th days of the discharge she shall continue i uncleanness. As in the days of her impu rity, she shall be unclean. [26] Every be on which she lies, all the days of her dis charge, shall be to her as the bed of he impurity. And everything on which she sit shall be unclean, as in the uncleanness o her menstrual impurity. [27] And whoeve touches these things shall be unclean, and shall wash his clothes and bathe himsel in water and be unclean until the evening [28] But if she is cleansed of her discharge, sh shall count for herself seven days, and afte that she shall be clean. [29] And on the eighth day she shall take two turtledoves or tw pigeons and bring them to the priest, t the entrance of the tent of meeting. [30] An the priest shall use one for a sin offering and the other for a burnt offering. And th

[1] Hebrew *flesh*; also verse 3

priest shall make atonement for her before the LORD for her unclean discharge.

31 "Thus you shall keep the people of Israel separate from their uncleanness, lest they die in their uncleanness by defiling my tabernacle that is in their midst."

32 This is the law for him who has a discharge and for him who has an emission of semen, becoming unclean thereby; 33 also for her who is unwell with her menstrual impurity, that is, for anyone, male or female, who has a discharge, and for the man who lies with a woman who is unclean.

The Day of Atonement

16 The LORD spoke to Moses after the death of the two sons of Aaron, when they drew near before the LORD and died, 2 and the LORD said to Moses, "Tell Aaron your brother not to come at any time into the Holy Place inside the veil, before the mercy seat that is on the ark, so that he may not die. For I will appear in the cloud over the mercy seat. 3 But in this way Aaron shall come into the Holy Place: with a bull from the herd for a sin offering and a ram for a burnt offering. 4 He shall put on the holy linen coat and shall have the linen undergarment on his body, and he shall tie the linen sash around his waist, and wear the linen turban; these are the holy garments. He shall bathe his body in water and then put them on. 5 And he shall take from the congregation of the people of Israel two male goats for a sin offering, and one ram for a burnt offering.

6 "Aaron shall offer the bull as a sin offering for himself and shall make atonement for himself and for his house. 7 Then he shall take the two goats and set them before the LORD at the entrance of the tent of meeting. 8 And Aaron shall cast lots over the two goats, one lot for the LORD and the other lot for Azazel.[1] 9 And Aaron shall present the goat on which the lot fell for the LORD and use it as a sin offering, 10 but the goat on which the lot fell for Azazel shall be presented alive before the LORD to make atonement over it, that it may be sent away into the wilderness to Azazel.

11 "Aaron shall present the bull as a sin offering for himself, and shall make atonement for himself and for his house. He shall kill the bull as a sin offering for himself. 12 And he shall take a censer full of coals of fire from the altar before the LORD, and two handfuls of sweet incense beaten small, and he shall bring it inside the veil 13 and put the incense on the fire before the LORD, that the cloud of the incense may cover the mercy seat that is over the testimony, so that he does not die. 14 And he shall take some of the blood of the bull and sprinkle it with his finger on the front of the mercy seat on the east side, and in front of the mercy seat he shall sprinkle some of the blood with his finger seven times.

> ## Ask Yourself . . .
>
> ### ABOUT HOLINESS
>
> - What does it mean to be holy?
> - In what ways has God been enabling me recently to grow in holiness?
> - What are some ways that I can practice holiness?
> - What does the New Testament say about holiness? (Check out 1 Thess. 3:13; 4:7; Heb. 12:14; 1 Peter 1:15–16; 2:5.)

15 "Then he shall kill the goat of the sin offering that is for the people and bring its blood inside the veil and do with its blood as he did with the blood of the bull, sprinkling it over the mercy seat and in front of the mercy seat. 16 Thus he shall make atonement for the Holy Place, because of the uncleannesses of the people of Israel and because of their transgressions, all their sins. And so he shall do for the tent of meeting, which dwells with them in the midst of their uncleannesses. 17 No one may be in the tent of meeting from the time he enters to make atonement in the Holy Place until he comes out and has made atonement for himself and for his house and for all the assembly of Israel. 18 Then he shall go out to the altar that is before the LORD and make atonement for it, and shall take some of the blood of the bull and some of the blood of

[1] The meaning of *Azazel* is uncertain; possibly the name of a place or a demon, traditionally a scapegoat; also verses 10, 26

the goat, and put it on the horns of the altar all around. ¹⁹And he shall sprinkle some of the blood on it with his finger seven times, and cleanse it and consecrate it from the uncleannesses of the people of Israel.

²⁰ "And when he has made an end of atoning for the Holy Place and the tent of meeting and the altar, he shall present the live goat. ²¹ And Aaron shall lay both his hands on the head of the live goat, and confess over it all the iniquities of the people of Israel, and all their transgressions, all their sins. And he shall put them on the head of the goat and send it away into the wilderness by the hand of a man who is in readiness. ²² The goat shall bear all their iniquities on itself to a remote area, and he shall let the goat go free in the wilderness.

²³ "Then Aaron shall come into the tent of meeting and shall take off the linen garments that he put on when he went into the Holy Place and shall leave them there. ²⁴ And he shall bathe his body in water in a holy place and put on his garments and come out and offer his burnt offering and the burnt offering of the people and make atonement for himself and for the people. ²⁵ And the fat of the sin offering he shall burn on the altar. ²⁶ And he who lets the goat go to Azazel shall wash his clothes and bathe his body in water, and afterward he may come into the camp. ²⁷ And the bull for the sin offering and the goat for the sin offering, whose blood was brought in to make atonement in the Holy Place, shall be carried outside the camp. Their skin and their flesh and their dung shall be burned up with fire. ²⁸ And he who burns them shall wash his clothes and bathe his body in water, and afterward he may come into the camp.

²⁹ "And it shall be a statute to you forever that in the seventh month, on the tenth day of the month, you shall afflict yourselves[1] and shall do no work, either the native or the stranger who sojourns among you. ³⁰ For on this day shall atonement be made for you to cleanse you. You shall be clean before the LORD from all your sins. ³¹ It is a Sabbath of solemn rest to you, and you shall afflict yourselves; it is a statute forever. ³² And the priest who is anointed and consecrated as priest in his father's place shall make atonement, wearing the holy linen garments. ³³ He shall make atonement for the holy sanctuary, and he shall make atonement for the tent of meeting and for the altar, and he shall make atonement for the priests and for all the people of the assembly. ³⁴ And this shall be a statute forever for you, that atonement may be made for the people of Israel once in the year because of all their sins." And Aaron[2] did as the LORD commanded Moses.

The Place of Sacrifice

17 And the LORD spoke to Moses, saying, ² "Speak to Aaron and his sons and to all the people of Israel and say to them, This is the thing that the LORD has commanded. ³ If any one of the house of Israel kills an ox or a lamb or a goat in the camp, or kills it outside the camp, ⁴ and does not bring it to the entrance of the tent of meeting to offer it as a gift to the LORD in front of the tabernacle of the LORD, bloodguilt shall be imputed to that man. He has shed blood, and that man shall be cut off from among his people. ⁵ This is to the end that the people of Israel may bring their sacrifices that they sacrifice in the open field, that they may bring them to the LORD, to the priest at the entrance of the tent of meeting, and sacrifice them as sacrifices of peace offerings to the LORD. ⁶ And the priest shall throw the blood on the altar of the LORD at the entrance of the tent of meeting and burn the fat for a pleasing aroma to the LORD. ⁷ So they shall no more sacrifice their sacrifices to goat demons, after whom they whore. This shall be a statute forever for them throughout their generations.

⁸ "And you shall say to them, Any one of the house of Israel, or of the strangers who sojourn among them, who offers a burnt offering or sacrifice ⁹ and does not bring it to the entrance of the tent of meeting to offer it to the LORD, that man shall be cut off from his people.

Laws Against Eating Blood

¹⁰ "If any one of the house of Israel or of the strangers who sojourn among them eats any blood, I will set my face against that person who eats blood and will cut him off from among his people. ¹¹ For the life of the flesh is in the blood, and I have given it for you on the altar to make atonement for your souls, for it is the blood that makes atonement by the life. ¹² Therefore I have said to the people of Israel, No per-

---

¹ Or *shall fast*; also verse 31   ² Hebrew *he*

son among you shall eat blood, neither shall any stranger who sojourns among you eat blood.

¹³ "Any one also of the people of Israel, or of the strangers who sojourn among them, who takes in hunting any beast or bird that may be eaten shall pour out its blood and cover it with earth. ¹⁴ For the life of every creature[1] is its blood: its blood is its life.[2] Therefore I have said to the people of Israel, You shall not eat the blood of any creature, for the life of every creature is its blood. Whoever eats it shall be cut off. ¹⁵ And every person who eats what dies of itself or what is torn by beasts, whether he is a native or a sojourner, shall wash his clothes and bathe himself in water and be unclean until the evening; then he shall be clean. ¹⁶ But if he does not wash them or bathe his flesh, he shall bear his iniquity."

Unlawful Sexual Relations

18 And the LORD spoke to Moses, saying, ² "Speak to the people of Israel and say to them, I am the LORD your God. ³ You shall not do as they do in the land of Egypt, where you lived, and you shall not do as they do in the land of Canaan, to which I am bringing you. You shall not walk in their statutes. ⁴ You shall follow my rules[3] and keep my statutes and walk in them. I am the LORD your God. ⁵ You shall therefore keep my statutes and my rules; if a person does them, he shall live by them: I am the LORD.

⁶ "None of you shall approach any one of his close relatives to uncover nakedness. I am the LORD. ⁷ You shall not uncover the nakedness of your father, which is the nakedness of your mother; she is your mother, you shall not uncover her nakedness. ⁸ You shall not uncover the nakedness of your father's wife; it is your father's nakedness. ⁹ You shall not uncover the nakedness of your sister, your father's daughter or your mother's daughter, whether brought up in the family or in another home. ¹⁰ You shall not uncover the nakedness of your son's daughter or of your daughter's daughter, for their nakedness is your own nakedness. ¹¹ You shall not uncover the nakedness of your father's wife's daughter, brought up in your father's family, since she is your sister. ¹² You shall

¹ Hebrew *all flesh* ² Hebrew *it is in its life* ³ Or *my just decrees*; also verse 5

Know God

verses to read
Leviticus 18:1-5

The world, or God—which will it be? How easy it is to listen to the ideas of the world and to fall in line with them, agreeing that they are right and even good. But the world has always had a different standard than God. What's morally encouraged in one society is punishable by death in the next. Even the standards of purity for drinking water in your city may be more strict or lax than in the neighboring town. But God's Word says, don't live by the standards set when you lived in Egypt, Canaan, or California; remember that you are a citizen of the kingdom of heaven. Live by those standards. You can't allow the standards of the world to creep into the truth of Scripture.

Understand God's call on the life of a believer and the great privilege it is to live as a member of his people—as his own child! See what Christ has saved you from and consider how you can gratefully respond, with your whole heart. Appreciate the history of our faith and the gift of God's grace. Read the Old Testament as preparing for the New Testament, considering how the whole Bible is a saving message of what God has done in Christ for us. The truth of the Old Testament has not been rejected but has been fulfilled in the life of Christ. Learn what that means by reading your Bible. Study God's Word, and make it your way of life.

not uncover the nakedness of your father's sister; she is your father's relative. ¹³You shall not uncover the nakedness of your mother's sister, for she is your mother's relative. ¹⁴ You shall not uncover the nakedness of your father's brother, that is, you shall not approach his wife; she is your aunt. ¹⁵You shall not uncover the nakedness of your daughter-in-law; she is your son's wife, you shall not uncover her nakedness. ¹⁶You shall not uncover the nakedness of your brother's wife; it is your brother's nakedness. ¹⁷You shall not uncover the nakedness of a woman and of her daughter, and you shall not take her son's daughter or her daughter's daughter to uncover her nakedness; they are relatives; it is depravity. ¹⁸And you shall not take a woman as a rival wife to her sister, uncovering her nakedness while her sister is still alive.

¹⁹ "You shall not approach a woman to uncover her nakedness while she is in her menstrual uncleanness. ²⁰And you shall not lie sexually with your neighbor's wife and so make yourself unclean with her. ²¹You shall not give any of your children to offer them[1] to Molech, and so profane the name of your God: I am the LORD. ²²You shall not lie with a male as with a woman; it is an abomination. ²³And you shall not lie with any animal and so make yourself unclean with it, neither shall any woman give herself to an animal to lie with it: it is perversion.

²⁴ "Do not make yourselves unclean by any of these things, for by all these the nations I am driving out before you have become unclean, ²⁵and the land became unclean, so that I punished its iniquity, and the land vomited out its inhabitants. ²⁶But you shall keep my statutes and my rules and do none of these abominations, either the native or the stranger who sojourns among you ²⁷(for the people of the land, who were before you, did all of these abominations, so that the land became unclean), ²⁸lest the land vomit you out when you make it unclean, as it vomited out the nation that was before you. ²⁹For everyone who does any of these abominations, the persons who do them shall be cut off from among their people. ³⁰So keep my charge never to practice any of these abominable customs that were practiced

before you, and never to make yourselves unclean by them: I am the LORD your God."

The LORD Is Holy

19 And the LORD spoke to Moses, saying, ² "Speak to all the congregation of the people of Israel and say to them, You shall be holy, for I the LORD your God am holy. ³Every one of you shall revere his mother and his father, and you shall keep my Sabbaths: I am the LORD your God. ⁴Do not turn to idols or make for yourselves any gods of cast metal: I am the LORD your God.

⁵ "When you offer a sacrifice of peace offerings to the LORD, you shall offer it so that you may be accepted. ⁶It shall be eaten the same day you offer it or on the day after, and anything left over until the third day shall be burned up with fire. ⁷If it is eaten at all on the third day, it is tainted; it will not be accepted, ⁸and everyone who eats it shall bear his iniquity, because he has profaned what is holy to the LORD, and that person shall be cut off from his people.

Love Your Neighbor as Yourself

⁹ "When you reap the harvest of your land, you shall not reap your field right up to its edge, neither shall you gather the gleanings after your harvest. ¹⁰And you shall not strip your vineyard bare, neither shall you gather the fallen grapes of your vineyard. You shall leave them for the poor and for the sojourner: I am the LORD your God.

¹¹ "You shall not steal; you shall not deal falsely; you shall not lie to one another. ¹²You shall not swear by my name falsely, and so profane the name of your God: I am the LORD.

¹³ "You shall not oppress your neighbor or rob him. The wages of a hired worker shall not remain with you all night until the morning. ¹⁴You shall not curse the deaf or put a stumbling block before the blind, but you shall fear your God: I am the LORD.

¹⁵ "You shall do no injustice in court. You shall not be partial to the poor or defer to the great, but in righteousness shall you judge your neighbor. ¹⁶You shall not go around as a slanderer among your people, and you shall not stand up against the life[2] of your neighbor: I am the LORD.

¹⁷ "You shall not hate your brother in your heart, but you shall reason frankly with your neighbor, lest you incur sin

[1] Hebrew *to make them pass through* [the fire] [2] Hebrew *blood*

because of him. **18** You shall not take vengeance or bear a grudge against the sons of your own people, but you shall love your neighbor as yourself: I am the LORD.

You Shall Keep My Statutes

19 "You shall keep my statutes. You shall not let your cattle breed with a different kind. You shall not sow your field with two kinds of seed, nor shall you wear a garment of cloth made of two kinds of material.

20 "If a man lies sexually with a woman who is a slave, assigned to another man and not yet ransomed or given her freedom, a distinction shall be made. They shall not be put to death, because she was not free; **21** but he shall bring his compensation to the LORD, to the entrance of the tent of meeting, a ram for a guilt offering. **22** And the priest shall make atonement for him with the ram of the guilt offering before the LORD for his sin that he has committed, and he shall be forgiven for the sin that he has committed.

23 "When you come into the land and plant any kind of tree for food, then you shall regard its fruit as forbidden.[1] Three years it shall be forbidden to you; it must not be eaten. **24** And in the fourth year all its fruit shall be holy, an offering of praise to the LORD. **25** But in the fifth year you may eat of its fruit, to increase its yield for you: I am the LORD your God.

26 "You shall not eat any flesh with the blood in it. You shall not interpret omens or tell fortunes. **27** You shall not round off the hair on your temples or mar the edges of your beard. **28** You shall not make any cuts on your body for the dead or tattoo yourselves: I am the LORD.

29 "Do not profane your daughter by making her a prostitute, lest the land fall into prostitution and the land become full of depravity. **30** You shall keep my Sabbaths and reverence my sanctuary: I am the LORD.

31 "Do not turn to mediums or necromancers; do not seek them out, and so make yourselves unclean by them: I am the LORD your God.

32 "You shall stand up before the gray head and honor the face of an old man, and you shall fear your God: I am the LORD.

33 "When a stranger sojourns with you in your land, you shall not do him wrong. **34** You shall treat the stranger who sojourns with you as the native among you, and you shall love him as yourself, for you were strangers in the land of Egypt: I am the LORD your God.

35 "You shall do no wrong in judgment, in measures of length or weight or quantity. **36** You shall have just balances, just weights, a just ephah, and a just hin:[2] I am the LORD your God, who brought you out of the land of Egypt. **37** And you shall observe all my statutes and all my rules, and do them: I am the LORD."

Punishment for Child Sacrifice

20 The LORD spoke to Moses, saying, **2** "Say to the people of Israel, Any one of the people of Israel or of the strangers who sojourn in Israel who gives any of his children to Molech shall surely be put to death. The people of the land shall stone him with stones. **3** I myself will set my face against that man and will cut him off from among his people, because he has given one of his children to Molech, to make my sanctuary unclean and to profane my holy name. **4** And if the people of the land do at all close their eyes to that man when he gives one of his children to Molech, and do not put him to death, **5** then I will set my face against that man and against his clan and will cut them off from among their people, him and all who follow him in whoring after Molech.

6 "If a person turns to mediums and necromancers, whoring after them, I will set my face against that person and will cut him off from among his people. **7** Consecrate yourselves, therefore, and be holy, for I am the LORD your God. **8** Keep my statutes and do them; I am the LORD who sanctifies you. **9** For anyone who curses his father or his mother shall surely be put to death; he has cursed his father or his mother; his blood is upon him.

Punishments for Sexual Immorality

10 "If a man commits adultery with the wife of[3] his neighbor, both the adulterer and the adulteress shall surely be put to death. **11** If a man lies with his father's wife, he has uncovered his father's nakedness; both of them shall surely be put to death; their blood is upon them. **12** If a man lies with his daughter-in-law, both of them

---

[1] Hebrew *as its uncircumcision* [2] An *ephah* was about 3/5 bushel or 22 liters; a *hin* was about 4 quarts or 3.5 liters [3] Hebrew repeats *if a man commits adultery with the wife of*

shall surely be put to death; they have committed perversion; their blood is upon them. [13] If a man lies with a male as with a woman, both of them have committed an abomination; they shall surely be put to death; their blood is upon them. [14] If a man takes a woman and her mother also, it is depravity; he and they shall be burned with fire, that there may be no depravity among you. [15] If a man lies with an animal, he shall surely be put to death, and you shall kill the animal. [16] If a woman approaches any animal and lies with it, you shall kill the woman and the animal; they shall surely be put to death; their blood is upon them.

[17] "If a man takes his sister, a daughter of his father or a daughter of his mother, and sees her nakedness, and she sees his nakedness, it is a disgrace, and they shall be cut off in the sight of the children of their people. He has uncovered his sister's nakedness, and he shall bear his iniquity. [18] If a man lies with a woman during her menstrual period and uncovers her nakedness, he has made naked her fountain, and she has uncovered the fountain of her blood. Both of them shall be cut off from among their people. [19] You shall not uncover the nakedness of your mother's sister or of your father's sister, for that is to make naked one's relative; they shall bear their iniquity. [20] If a man lies with his uncle's wife, he has uncovered his uncle's nakedness; they shall bear their sin; they shall die childless. [21] If a man takes his brother's wife, it is impurity.[1] He has uncovered his brother's nakedness; they shall be childless.

You Shall Be Holy

[22] "You shall therefore keep all my statutes and all my rules and do them, that the land where I am bringing you to live may not vomit you out. [23] And you shall not walk in the customs of the nation that I am driving out before you, for they did all these things, and therefore I detested them. [24] But I have said to you, 'You shall inherit their land, and I will give it to you to possess, a land flowing with milk and honey.' I am the LORD your God, who has separated you from the peoples. [25] You shall therefore separate the clean beast from the unclean, and the unclean bird from the clean. You shall not make yourselves detestable by beast or by bird or by anything which

the ground crawls, which I have set apart for you to hold unclean. [26] You shall be holy to me, for I the LORD am holy and have separated you from the peoples, that you should be mine.

[27] "A man or a woman who is a medium or a necromancer shall surely be put to death. They shall be stoned with stones; their blood shall be upon them."

Holiness and the Priests

21 And the LORD said to Moses, "Speak to the priests, the sons of Aaron, and say to them, No one shall make himself unclean for the dead among his people, [2] except for his closest relatives, his mother, his father, his son, his daughter, his brother, [3] or his virgin sister (who is near to him because she has had no husband; for her he may make himself unclean). [4] He shall not make himself unclean as a husband among his people and so profane himself. [5] They shall not make bald patches on their heads, nor shave off the edges of their beards, nor make any cuts on their body. [6] They shall be holy to their God and not profane the name of their God. For they offer the LORD's food offerings, the bread of their God; therefore they shall be holy. [7] They shall not marry a prostitute or a woman who has been defiled, neither shall they marry a woman divorced from her husband, for the priest is holy to his God. [8] You shall sanctify him, for he offers the bread of your God. He shall be holy to you, for I, the LORD, who sanctify you, am holy. [9] And the daughter of any priest, if she profanes herself by whoring, profanes her father; she shall be burned with fire.

[10] "The priest who is chief among his brothers, on whose head the anointing oil is poured and who has been consecrated to wear the garments, shall not let the hair of his head hang loose nor tear his clothes. [11] He shall not go in to any dead bodies nor make himself unclean, even for his father or for his mother. [12] He shall not go out of the sanctuary, lest he profane the sanctuary of his God, for the consecration of the anointing oil of his God is on him: I am the LORD. [13] And he shall take a wife in her virginity.[2] [14] A widow, or a divorced woman, or a woman who has been defiled, or a prostitute, these he shall not marry. But he shall take as his wife a virgin[3] of his

---

[1] Literally *menstrual impurity* [2] Or *a young wife* [3] Hebrew *young woman*

own people, ¹⁵that he may not profane his offspring among his people, for I am the Lord who sanctifies him."

¹⁶And the Lord spoke to Moses, saying, ¹⁷"Speak to Aaron, saying, None of your offspring throughout their generations who has a blemish may approach to offer the bread of his God. ¹⁸For no one who has a blemish shall draw near, a man blind or lame, or one who has a mutilated face or a limb too long, ¹⁹or a man who has an injured foot or an injured hand, ²⁰or a hunchback or a dwarf or a man with a defect in his sight or an itching disease or scabs or crushed testicles. ²¹No man of the offspring of Aaron the priest who has a blemish shall come near to offer the Lord's food offerings; since he has a blemish, he shall not come near to offer the bread of his God. ²²He may eat the bread of his God, both of the most holy and of the holy things, ²³but he shall not go through the veil or approach the altar, because he has a blemish, that he may not profane my sanctuaries, for I am the Lord who sanctifies them." ²⁴So Moses spoke to Aaron and to his sons and to all the people of Israel.

22 And the Lord spoke to Moses, saying, ²"Speak to Aaron and his sons so that they abstain from the holy things of the people of Israel, which they dedicate to me, so that they do not profane my holy name: I am the Lord. ³Say to them, 'If any one of all your offspring throughout your generations approaches the holy things that the people of Israel dedicate to the Lord, while he has an uncleanness, that person shall be cut off from my presence: I am the Lord. ⁴None of the offspring of Aaron who has a leprous disease or a discharge may eat of the holy things until he is clean. Whoever touches anything that is unclean through contact with the dead or a man who has had an emission of semen, ⁵and whoever touches a swarming thing by which he may be made unclean or a person from whom he may take uncleanness, whatever his uncleanness may be— ⁶the person who touches such a thing shall be unclean until the evening and shall not eat of the holy things unless he has bathed his body in water. ⁷When the sun goes down he shall be clean, and afterward he may eat of the holy things, because they are his food. ⁸He shall not eat what dies of itself

or is torn by beasts, and so make himself unclean by it: I am the Lord.' ⁹They shall therefore keep my charge, lest they bear sin for it and die thereby when they profane it: I am the Lord who sanctifies them.

¹⁰"A lay person shall not eat of a holy thing; no foreign guest of the priest or hired worker shall eat of a holy thing, ¹¹but if a priest buys a slave¹ as his property for money, the slave² may eat of it, and anyone born in his house may eat of his food. ¹²If a priest's daughter marries a layman, she shall not eat of the contribution of the holy things. ¹³But if a priest's daughter is widowed or divorced and has no child and returns to her father's house, as in her youth, she may eat of her father's food; yet no lay person shall eat of it. ¹⁴And if anyone eats of a holy thing unintentionally, he shall add the fifth of its value to it and give the holy thing to the priest. ¹⁵They shall not profane the holy things of the people of Israel, which they contribute to the Lord, ¹⁶and so cause them to bear iniquity and guilt, by eating their holy things: for I am the Lord who sanctifies them."

Acceptable Offerings

¹⁷And the Lord spoke to Moses, saying, ¹⁸"Speak to Aaron and his sons and all the people of Israel and say to them, When any one of the house of Israel or of the sojourners in Israel presents a burnt offering as his offering, for any of their vows or freewill offerings that they offer to the Lord, ¹⁹if it is to be accepted for you it shall be a male without blemish, of the bulls or the sheep or the goats. ²⁰You shall not offer anything that has a blemish, for it will not be acceptable for you. ²¹And when anyone offers a sacrifice of peace offerings to the Lord to fulfill a vow or as a freewill offering from the herd or from the flock, to be accepted it must be perfect; there shall be no blemish in it. ²²Animals blind or disabled or mutilated or having a discharge or an itch or scabs you shall not offer to the Lord or give them to the Lord as a food offering on the altar. ²³You may present a bull or a lamb that has a part too long or too short for a freewill offering, but for a vow offering it cannot be accepted. ²⁴Any animal that has its testicles bruised or crushed or torn or cut you shall not offer to the Lord; you shall not do it within your land, ²⁵neither

¹Or *servant*; twice in this verse ²Hebrew *he*

shall you offer as the bread of your God any such animals gotten from a foreigner. Since there is a blemish in them, because of their mutilation, they will not be accepted for you."

[26] And the LORD spoke to Moses, saying, [27] "When an ox or sheep or goat is born, it shall remain seven days with its mother, and from the eighth day on it shall be acceptable as a food offering to the LORD. [28] But you shall not kill an ox or a sheep and her young in one day. [29] And when you sacrifice a sacrifice of thanksgiving to the LORD, you shall sacrifice it so that you may be accepted. [30] It shall be eaten on the same day; you shall leave none of it until morning: I am the LORD.

[31] "So you shall keep my commandments and do them: I am the LORD. [32] And you shall not profane my holy name, that I may be sanctified among the people of Israel. I am the LORD who sanctifies you, [33] who brought you out of the land of Egypt to be your God: I am the LORD."

Feasts of the LORD

23 The LORD spoke to Moses, saying, [2] "Speak to the people of Israel and say to them, These are the appointed feasts of the LORD that you shall proclaim as holy convocations; they are my appointed feasts.

The Sabbath

[3] "Six days shall work be done, but on the seventh day is a Sabbath of solemn rest, a holy convocation. You shall do no work. It is a Sabbath to the LORD in all your dwelling places.

The Passover

[4] "These are the appointed feasts of the LORD, the holy convocations, which you shall proclaim at the time appointed for them. [5] In the first month, on the fourteenth day of the month at twilight,[1] is the LORD's Passover. [6] And on the fifteenth day of the same month is the Feast of Unleavened Bread to the LORD; for seven days you shall eat unleavened bread. [7] On the first day you shall have a holy convocation; you shall not do any ordinary work. [8] But you shall present a food offering to the LORD for seven days. On the seventh day is a holy convocation; you shall not do any ordinary work."

The Feast of Firstfruits

[9] And the LORD spoke to Moses, saying, [10] "Speak to the people of Israel and say to them, When you come into the land that I give you and reap its harvest, you shall bring the sheaf of the firstfruits of your harvest to the priest, [11] and he shall wave the sheaf before the LORD, so that you may be accepted. On the day after the Sabbath the priest shall wave it. [12] And on the day when you wave the sheaf, you shall offer a male lamb a year old without blemish as a burnt offering to the LORD. [13] And the grain offering with it shall be two tenths of an ephah[2] of fine flour mixed with oil, a food offering to the LORD with a pleasing aroma, and the drink offering with it shall be of wine, a fourth of a hin.[3] [14] And you shall eat neither bread nor grain parched or fresh until this same day, until you have brought the offering of your God: it is a statute forever throughout your generations in all your dwellings.

The Feast of Weeks

[15] "You shall count seven full weeks from the day after the Sabbath, from the day that you brought the sheaf of the wave offering. [16] You shall count fifty days to the day after the seventh Sabbath. Then you shall present a grain offering of new grain to the LORD. [17] You shall bring from your dwelling places two loaves of bread to be waved, made of two tenths of an ephah. They shall be of fine flour, and they shall be baked with leaven, as firstfruits to the LORD. [18] And you shall present with the bread seven lambs a year old without blemish, and one bull from the herd and two rams. They shall be a burnt offering to the LORD, with their grain offering and their drink offerings, a food offering with a pleasing aroma to the LORD. [19] And you shall offer one male goat for a sin offering, and two male lambs a year old as a sacrifice of peace offerings. [20] And the priest shall wave them with the bread of the firstfruits as a wave offering before the LORD, with the two lambs. They shall be holy to the LORD for the priest. [21] And you shall make a proclamation on the same day. You shall hold a holy convocation. You shall not do any ordinary work. It is a statute forever in all your dwelling places throughout your generations.

[22] "And when you reap the harvest of

[1] Hebrew *between the two evenings* [2] An *ephah* was about 3/5 bushel or 22 liters [3] A *hin* was about 4 quarts or 3.5 liters

your land, you shall not reap your field right up to its edge, nor shall you gather the gleanings after your harvest. You shall leave them for the poor and for the sojourner: I am the LORD your God."

The Feast of Trumpets

23 And the LORD spoke to Moses, saying, 24 "Speak to the people of Israel, saying, In the seventh month, on the first day of the month, you shall observe a day of solemn rest, a memorial proclaimed with blast of trumpets, a holy convocation. 25 You shall not do any ordinary work, and you shall present a food offering to the LORD."

The Day of Atonement

26 And the LORD spoke to Moses, saying, 27 "Now on the tenth day of this seventh month is the Day of Atonement. It shall be for you a time of holy convocation, and you shall afflict yourselves[1] and present a food offering to the LORD. 28 And you shall not do any work on that very day, for it is a Day of Atonement, to make atonement for you before the LORD your God. 29 For whoever is not afflicted on that very day shall be cut off from his people. 30 And whoever does any work on that very day, that person I will destroy from among his people. 31 You shall not do any work. It is a statute forever throughout your generations in all your dwelling places. 32 It shall be to you a Sabbath of solemn rest, and you shall afflict yourselves. On the ninth day of the month beginning at evening, from evening to evening shall you keep your Sabbath."

The Feast of Booths

33 And the LORD spoke to Moses, saying, 34 "Speak to the people of Israel, saying, On the fifteenth day of this seventh month and for seven days is the Feast of Booths[2] to the LORD. 35 On the first day shall be a holy convocation; you shall not do any ordinary work. 36 For seven days you shall present food offerings to the LORD. On the eighth day you shall hold a holy convocation and present a food offering to the LORD. It is a solemn assembly; you shall not do any ordinary work.

37 "These are the appointed feasts of the LORD, which you shall proclaim as times of holy convocation, for presenting to the LORD food offerings, burnt offerings and grain offerings, sacrifices and drink offerings, each on its proper day, 38 besides the LORD's Sabbaths and besides your gifts and besides all your vow offerings and besides all your freewill offerings, which you give to the LORD.

39 "On the fifteenth day of the seventh month, when you have gathered in the produce of the land, you shall celebrate the feast of the LORD seven days. On the first day shall be a solemn rest, and on the eighth day shall be a solemn rest. 40 And you shall take on the first day the fruit of splendid trees, branches of palm trees and boughs of leafy trees and willows of the brook, and you shall rejoice before the LORD your God seven days. 41 You shall celebrate it as a feast to the LORD for seven days in the year. It is a statute forever throughout your generations; you shall celebrate it in the seventh month. 42 You shall dwell in booths for seven days. All native Israelites shall dwell in booths, 43 that your generations may know that I made the people of Israel dwell in booths when I brought them out of the land of Egypt: I am the LORD your God."

44 Thus Moses declared to the people of Israel the appointed feasts of the LORD.

The Lamps

24 The LORD spoke to Moses, saying, 2 "Command the people of Israel to bring you pure oil from beaten olives for the lamp, that a light may be kept burning regularly. 3 Outside the veil of the testimony, in the tent of meeting, Aaron shall arrange it from evening to morning before the LORD regularly. It shall be a statute forever throughout your generations. 4 He shall arrange the lamps on the lampstand of pure gold[3] before the LORD regularly.

Bread for the Tabernacle

5 "You shall take fine flour and bake twelve loaves from it; two tenths of an ephah[4] shall be in each loaf. 6 And you shall set them in two piles, six in a pile, on the table of pure gold[5] before the LORD. 7 And you shall put pure frankincense on each pile, that it may go with the bread as a memorial portion as a food offering to the LORD. 8 Every Sabbath day Aaron shall

---

[1] Or shall fast; also verse 32   [2] Or tabernacles   [3] Hebrew the pure lampstand   [4] An ephah was about 3/5 bushel or 22 liters   [5] Hebrew the pure table

arrange it before the LORD regularly; it is from the people of Israel as a covenant forever. [9] And it shall be for Aaron and his sons, and they shall eat it in a holy place, since it is for him a most holy portion out of the LORD's food offerings, a perpetual due."

Punishment for Blasphemy

[10] Now an Israelite woman's son, whose father was an Egyptian, went out among the people of Israel. And the Israelite woman's son and a man of Israel fought in the camp, [11] and the Israelite woman's son blasphemed the Name, and cursed. Then they brought him to Moses. His mother's name was Shelomith, the daughter of Dibri, of the tribe of Dan. [12] And they put him in custody, till the will of the LORD should be clear to them.

[13] Then the LORD spoke to Moses, saying, [14] "Bring out of the camp the one who cursed, and let all who heard him lay their hands on his head, and let all the congregation stone him. [15] And speak to the people of Israel, saying, Whoever curses his God shall bear his sin. [16] Whoever blasphemes the name of the LORD shall surely be put to death. All the congregation shall stone him. The sojourner as well as the native, when he blasphemes the Name, shall be put to death.

An Eye for an Eye

[17] "Whoever takes a human life shall surely be put to death. [18] Whoever takes an animal's life shall make it good, life for life. [19] If anyone injures his neighbor, as he has done it shall be done to him, [20] fracture for fracture, eye for eye, tooth for tooth; whatever injury he has given a person shall be given to him. [21] Whoever kills an animal shall make it good, and whoever kills a person shall be put to death. [22] You shall have the same rule for the sojourner and for the native, for I am the LORD your God." [23] So Moses spoke to the people of Israel, and they brought out of the camp the one who had cursed and stoned him with stones. Thus the people of Israel did as the LORD commanded Moses.

The Sabbath Year

25 The LORD spoke to Moses on Mount Sinai, saying, [2] "Speak to the people of Israel and say to them, When you come into the land that I give you, the land shall keep a Sabbath to the LORD. [3] For six years you shall sow your field, and for six years you shall prune your vineyard and gather in its fruits, [4] but in the seventh year there shall be a Sabbath of solemn rest for the land, a Sabbath to the LORD. You shall not sow your field or prune your vineyard.

Know How to Communicate

verses to read
Leviticus 24:15-16

Many laws found in the Old Testament are no longer required. A lot of commandments are no longer commanded. A lot of the Old Testament law is ancient history this side of the cross, but some commandments will never, ever be removed. Some sins will always be sinful, and this is one: to curse the Lord's name.

Though death is no longer the punishment for sin in the life of the believer, using the name of the Lord as a curse word is still sinful. When you use his name in anger, frustration, pain, or even excitement, it's a sinful and ugly thing. In the time before Christ, this sin was considered so ugly that, unlike a lot of other sins mentioned, there was no sacrifice to atone for it. The punishment was death. This shows you what an ugly and unacceptable sin it is in the eyes of God.

God's name must be honored and respected, not used as a curse. As a God Girl, your faith should be obvious to all, and cursing God's name proves your disobedience. Don't let God's name be used in vain. Get rid of all that kind of talk, and honor God by honoring his name. Give God the respect he deserves.

5 You shall not reap what grows of itself in your harvest, or gather the grapes of your undressed vine. It shall be a year of solemn rest for the land. 6 The Sabbath of the land[1] shall provide food for you, for yourself and for your male and female slaves[2] and for your hired worker and the sojourner who lives with you, 7 and for your cattle and for the wild animals that are in your land: all its yield shall be for food.

The Year of Jubilee

8 "You shall count seven weeks[3] of years, seven times seven years, so that the time of the seven weeks of years shall give you forty-nine years. 9 Then you shall sound the loud trumpet on the tenth day of the seventh month. On the Day of Atonement you shall sound the trumpet throughout all your land. 10 And you shall consecrate the fiftieth year, and proclaim liberty throughout the land to all its inhabitants. It shall be a jubilee for you, when each of you shall return to his property and each of you shall return to his clan. 11 That fiftieth year shall be a jubilee for you; in it you shall neither sow nor reap what grows of itself nor gather the grapes from the undressed vines. 12 For it is a jubilee. It shall be holy to you. You may eat the produce of the field.[4]

13 "In this year of jubilee each of you shall return to his property. 14 And if you make a sale to your neighbor or buy from your neighbor, you shall not wrong one another. 15 You shall pay your neighbor according to the number of years after the jubilee, and he shall sell to you according to the number of years for crops. 16 If the years are many, you shall increase the price, and if the years are few, you shall reduce the price, for it is the number of the crops that he is selling to you. 17 You shall not wrong one another, but you shall fear your God, for I am the LORD your God.

18 "Therefore you shall do my statutes and keep my rules and perform them, and you will dwell in the land securely. 19 The land will yield its fruit, and you will eat your fill and dwell in it securely. 20 And if you say, 'What shall we eat in the seventh year, if we may not sow or gather in our crop?' 21 I will command my blessing on you in the sixth year, so that it will produce a crop sufficient for three years. 22 When you sow in the eighth year, you will be eating some of the old crop; you shall eat the old until the ninth year, when its crop arrives.

Redemption of Property

23 "The land shall not be sold in perpetuity, for the land is mine. For you are strangers and sojourners with me. 24 And in all the country you possess, you shall allow a redemption of the land.

25 "If your brother becomes poor and sells part of his property, then his nearest redeemer shall come and redeem what his brother has sold. 26 If a man has no one to redeem it and then himself becomes prosperous and finds sufficient means to redeem it, 27 let him calculate the years since he sold it and pay back the balance to the man to whom he sold it, and then return to his property. 28 But if he does not have sufficient means to recover it, then what he sold shall remain in the hand of the buyer until the year of jubilee. In the jubilee it shall be released, and he shall return to his property.

29 "If a man sells a dwelling house in a walled city, he may redeem it within a year of its sale. For a full year he shall have the right of redemption. 30 If it is not redeemed within a full year, then the house in the walled city shall belong in perpetuity to the buyer, throughout his generations; it shall not be released in the jubilee. 31 But the houses of the villages that have no wall around them shall be classified with the fields of the land. They may be redeemed, and they shall be released in the jubilee. 32 As for the cities of the Levites, the Levites may redeem at any time the houses in the cities they possess. 33 And if one of the Levites exercises his right of redemption, then the house that was sold in a city they possess shall be released in the jubilee. For the houses in the cities of the Levites are their possession among the people of Israel. 34 But the fields of pastureland belonging to their cities may not be sold, for that is their possession forever.

Kindness for Poor Brothers

35 "If your brother becomes poor and cannot maintain himself with you, you shall support him as though he were a stranger and a sojourner, and he shall live with you. 36 Take no interest from him or profit, but fear your God, that your brother may live

---

[1] That is, the Sabbath produce of the land [2] Or *servants* [3] Or *Sabbaths* [4] Or *countryside*

beside you. [37] You shall not lend him your money at interest, nor give him your food for profit. [38] I am the LORD your God, who brought you out of the land of Egypt to give you the land of Canaan, and to be your God.

[39] "If your brother becomes poor beside you and sells himself to you, you shall not make him serve as a slave: [40] he shall be with you as a hired worker and as a sojourner. He shall serve with you until the year of the jubilee. [41] Then he shall go out from you, he and his children with him, and go back to his own clan and return to the possession of his fathers. [42] For they are my servants,[1] whom I brought out of the land of Egypt; they shall not be sold as slaves. [43] You shall not rule over him ruthlessly but shall fear your God. [44] As for your male and female slaves whom you may have: you may buy male and female slaves from among the nations that are around you. [45] You may also buy from among the strangers who sojourn with you and their clans that are with you, who have been born in your land, and they may be your property. [46] You may bequeath them to your sons after you to inherit as a possession forever. You may make slaves of them, but over your brothers the people of Israel you shall not rule, one over another ruthlessly.

Redeeming a Poor Man

[47] "If a stranger or sojourner with you becomes rich, and your brother beside him becomes poor and sells himself to the stranger or sojourner with you or to a member of the stranger's clan, [48] then after he is sold he may be redeemed. One of his brothers may redeem him, [49] or his uncle or his cousin may redeem him, or a close relative from his clan may redeem him. Or if he grows rich he may redeem himself. [50] He shall calculate with his buyer from the year when he sold himself to him until the year of jubilee, and the price of his sale shall vary with the number of years. The time he was with his owner shall be rated as the time of a hired worker. [51] If there are still many years left, he shall pay proportionately for his redemption some of his sale price. [52] If there remain but a few years until the year of jubilee, he shall calculate and pay for his redemption in proportion to his years of service. [53] He shall treat him as a worker hired year by year. He shall not rule ruth-

lessly over him in your sight. [54] And if he is not redeemed by these means, then he and his children with him shall be released in the year of jubilee. [55] For it is to me that the people of Israel are servants.[2] They are my servants whom I brought out of the land of Egypt: I am the LORD your God.

Blessings for Obedience

26 "You shall not make idols for yourselves or erect an image or pillar, and you shall not set up a figured stone in your land to bow down to it, for I am the LORD your God. [2] You shall keep my Sabbaths and reverence my sanctuary: I am the LORD.

[3] "If you walk in my statutes and observe my commandments and do them, [4] then I will give you your rains in their season, and the land shall yield its increase, and the trees of the field shall yield their fruit. [5] Your threshing shall last to the time of the grape harvest, and the grape harvest shall last to the time for sowing. And you shall eat your bread to the full and dwell in your land securely. [6] I will give peace in the land, and you shall lie down, and none shall make you afraid. And I will remove harmful beasts from the land, and the sword shall not go through your land. [7] You shall chase your enemies, and they shall fall before you by the sword. [8] Five of you shall chase a hundred, and a hundred of you shall chase ten thousand, and your enemies shall fall before you by the sword. [9] I will turn to you and make you fruitful and multiply you and will confirm my covenant with you. [10] You shall eat old store long kept, and you shall clear out the old to make way for the new. [11] I will make my dwelling[3] among you, and my soul shall not abhor you. [12] And I will walk among you and will be your God, and you shall be my people. [13] I am the LORD your God, who brought you out of the land of Egypt, that you should not be their slaves. And I have broken the bars of your yoke and made you walk erect.

Punishment for Disobedience

[14] "But if you will not listen to me and will not do all these commandments, [15] if you spurn my statutes, and if your soul abhors my rules, so that you will not do all my commandments, but break my covenant, [16] then I will do this to you: I will visit you with panic, with wasting disease and fever

[1] Hebrew *slaves* [2] Or *slaves* [3] Hebrew *tabernacle*

that consume the eyes and make the heart ache. And you shall sow your seed in vain, for your enemies shall eat it. [17] I will set my face against you, and you shall be struck down before your enemies. Those who hate you shall rule over you, and you shall flee when none pursues you. [18] And if in spite of this you will not listen to me, then I will discipline you again sevenfold for your sins, [19] and I will break the pride of your power, and I will make your heavens like iron and your earth like bronze. [20] And your strength shall be spent in vain, for your land shall not yield its increase, and the trees of the land shall not yield their fruit.

[21] "Then if you walk contrary to me and will not listen to me, I will continue striking you, sevenfold for your sins. [22] And I will let loose the wild beasts against you, which shall bereave you of your children and destroy your livestock and make you few in number, so that your roads shall be deserted.

[23] "And if by this discipline you are not turned to me but walk contrary to me, [24] then I also will walk contrary to you, and I myself will strike you sevenfold for your sins. [25] And I will bring a sword upon you, that shall execute vengeance for the covenant. And if you gather within your cities, I will send pestilence among you, and you shall be delivered into the hand of the enemy. [26] When I break your supply[1] of bread, ten women shall bake your bread in a single oven and shall dole out your bread again by weight, and you shall eat and not be satisfied.

[27] "But if in spite of this you will not listen to me, but walk contrary to me, [28] then I will walk contrary to you in fury, and I myself will discipline you sevenfold for your sins. [29] You shall eat the flesh of your sons, and you shall eat the flesh of your daughters. [30] And I will destroy your high places and cut down your incense altars and cast your dead bodies upon the dead bodies of your idols, and my soul will abhor you. [31] And I will lay your cities waste and will make your sanctuaries desolate, and I will not smell your pleasing aromas. [32] And I myself will devastate the land, so that your enemies who settle in it shall be appalled at it. [33] And I will scatter you among the nations, and I will unsheathe the sword after you, and your land shall be a desolation, and your cities shall be a waste.

[34] "Then the land shall enjoy[2] its Sabbaths as long as it lies desolate, while you are in your enemies' land; then the land shall rest, and enjoy its Sabbaths. [35] As long as it lies desolate it shall have rest, the rest that it did not have on your Sabbaths when you were dwelling in it. [36] And as for those of you who are left, I will send faintness into their hearts in the lands of their enemies. The sound of a driven leaf shall put them to flight, and they shall flee as one flees from the sword, and they shall fall when none pursues. [37] They shall stumble over one another, as if to escape a sword, though none pursues. And you shall have no power to stand before your enemies. [38] And you shall perish among the nations, and the land of your enemies shall eat you up. [39] And those of you who are left shall rot away in your enemies' lands because of their iniquity, and also because of the iniquities of their fathers they shall rot away like them.

[40] "But if they confess their iniquity and the iniquity of their fathers in their treachery that they committed against me, and also in walking contrary to me, [41] so that I walked contrary to them and brought them into the land of their enemies—if then their uncircumcised heart is humbled and they make amends for their iniquity, [42] then I will remember my covenant with Jacob, and I will remember my covenant with Isaac and my covenant with Abraham, and I will remember the land. [43] But the land shall be abandoned by them and enjoy its Sabbaths while it lies desolate without them, and they shall make amends for their iniquity, because they spurned my rules and their soul abhorred my statutes. [44] Yet for all that, when they are in the land of their enemies, I will not spurn them, neither will I abhor them so as to destroy them utterly and break my covenant with them, for I am the LORD their God. [45] But I will for their sake remember the covenant with their forefathers, whom I brought out of the land of Egypt in the sight of the nations, that I might be their God: I am the LORD."

[46] These are the statutes and rules and laws that the LORD made between himself and the people of Israel through Moses on Mount Sinai.

---

[1] Hebrew *staff* [2] Or *pay for*; twice in this verse; also verse 43

Laws About Vows

27 The LORD spoke to Moses, saying, [2] "Speak to the people of Israel and say to them, If anyone makes a special vow to the LORD involving the valuation of persons, [3] then the valuation of a male from twenty years old up to sixty years old shall be fifty shekels[1] of silver, according to the shekel of the sanctuary. [4] If the person is a female, the valuation shall be thirty shekels. [5] If the person is from five years old up to twenty years old, the valuation shall be for a male twenty shekels, and for a female ten shekels. [6] If the person is from a month old up to five years old, the valuation shall be for a male five shekels of silver, and for a female the valuation shall be three shekels of silver. [7] And if the person is sixty years old or over, then the valuation for a male shall be fifteen shekels, and for a female ten shekels. [8] And if someone is too poor to pay the valuation, then he shall be made to stand before the priest, and the priest shall value him; the priest shall value him according to what the vower can afford.

[9] "If the vow[2] is an animal that may be offered as an offering to the LORD, all of it that he gives to the LORD is holy. [10] He shall not exchange it or make a substitute for it, good for bad, or bad for good; and if he does in fact substitute one animal for another, then both it and the substitute shall be holy. [11] And if it is any unclean animal that may not be offered as an offering to the LORD, then he shall stand the animal before the priest, [12] and the priest shall value it as either good or bad; as the priest values it, so it shall be. [13] But if he wishes to redeem it, he shall add a fifth to the valuation.

[14] "When a man dedicates his house as a holy gift to the LORD, the priest shall value it as either good or bad; as the priest values it, so it shall stand. [15] And if the donor wishes to redeem his house, he shall add a fifth to the valuation price, and it shall be his.

[16] "If a man dedicates to the LORD part of the land that is his possession, then the valuation shall be in proportion to its seed. A homer[3] of barley seed shall be valued at fifty shekels of silver. [17] If he dedicates his field from the year of jubilee, the valuation shall stand, [18] but if he dedicates his field after the jubilee, then the priest shall calculate the price according to the years that remain until the year of jubilee, and a deduction shall be made from the valuation. [19] And if he who dedicates the field wishes to redeem it, then he shall add a fifth to its valuation price, and it shall remain his. [20] But if he does not wish to redeem the field, or if he has sold the field to another man, it shall not be redeemed anymore. [21] But the field, when it is released in the jubilee, shall be a holy gift to the LORD, like a field that has been devoted. The priest shall be in possession of it. [22] If he dedicates to the LORD a field that he has bought, which is not a part of his possession, [23] then the priest shall calculate the amount of the valuation for it up to the year of jubilee, and the man shall give the valuation on that day as a holy gift to the LORD. [24] In the year of jubilee the field shall return to him from whom it was bought, to whom the land belongs as a possession. [25] Every valuation shall be according to the shekel of the sanctuary: twenty gerahs[4] shall make a shekel.

[26] "But a firstborn of animals, which as a firstborn belongs to the LORD, no man may dedicate; whether ox or sheep, it is the LORD's. [27] And if it is an unclean animal, then he shall buy it back at the valuation, and add a fifth to it; or, if it is not redeemed, it shall be sold at the valuation.

[28] "But no devoted thing that a man devotes to the LORD, of anything that he has, whether man or beast, or of his inherited field, shall be sold or redeemed; every devoted thing is most holy to the LORD. [29] No one devoted, who is to be devoted for destruction[5] from mankind, shall be ransomed; he shall surely be put to death.

[30] "Every tithe of the land, whether of the seed of the land or of the fruit of the trees, is the LORD's; it is holy to the LORD. [31] If a man wishes to redeem some of his tithe, he shall add a fifth to it. [32] And every tithe of herds and flocks, every tenth animal of all that pass under the herdsman's staff, shall be holy to the LORD. [33] One shall not differentiate between good or bad, neither shall he make a substitute for it; and if he does substitute for it, then both it and the substitute shall be holy; it shall not be redeemed."

[34] These are the commandments that the LORD commanded Moses for the people of Israel on Mount Sinai.

[1] A *shekel* was about 2/5 ounce or 11 grams [2] Hebrew *it* [3] A *homer* was about 6 bushels or 220 liters [4] A *gerah* was about 1/50 ounce or 0.6 gram [5] That is, set apart (devoted) as an offering to the Lord (for destruction)

INTRODUCTION TO
Numbers

Author: Moses

Time: Around the fifteenth century B.C.

Place: The plains of Moab

Written to: The children of God

The gist

Numbers tells us what happened right before the Israelites entered the Promised Land.

Things to look for

- The demands of the Israelites (see Numbers 11)
- The jealousy of Miriam and Aaron (see Numbers 12)
- The story of the spies (see Numbers 13)

Believe the Truth

"How long shall this wicked congregation grumble against me? I have heard the grumblings of the people of Israel, which they grumble against me. Say to them, 'As I live, declares the LORD, what you have said in my hearing I will do to you.'"

Numbers 14:27–28

Complaining is disbelief—disbelief that God is who he says he is and is alive and well in your life. When you complain, you dishonor God by telling him that it is not enough for you to have God—you also have to have other things just right. It's shortsighted and naive to act like God has in some way swindled you out of something you should have gotten, but it is not unusual. The Israelites had been freed from slavery and set free to enter the Promised Land, but when life got dry and the desert got hot, they complained. They started to doubt God's faithfulness and love. We tend to do the same things today.

When God gives you a vision of things to come, when he shows you a path you've got to take, don't be surprised when you're tested along that journey. And don't run in the opposite direction when the testing comes, but stand firm, knowing that you are God's own child. Even if everything in the world says he's wrong or absent, your heart and your mind have to hold fast to the truth that only God brings into your life what is best for you, even if it is painful.

Must-Know Terms and Verses

∞ *Census* ∞

A counting of the people, usually to prepare for war or taxation.

∞ *Nazirites* ∞

"Dedicated" or "consecrated" men or women who were set apart, sometimes before their birth, to be devoted to the service of God. They were not allowed to drink wine, cut their hair, or go near a dead body.

∞ *Ransom* ∞

A sum paid to set someone free from slavery or bondage, also known as redemption. Jesus paid the ransom for us by dying on the cross, which set us free from sin and the fear of death.

"The LORD bless you and keep you;
   the LORD make his face to shine upon you and be gracious to you;
   the LORD lift up his countenance upon you and give you peace."
Numbers 6:24–26

"Only do not rebel against the LORD. And do not fear the people of the land."
Numbers 14:9

Numbers

A Census of Israel's Warriors

1 The LORD spoke to Moses in the wilderness of Sinai, in the tent of meeting, on the first day of the second month, in the second year after they had come out of the land of Egypt, saying, ²"Take a census of all the congregation of the people of Israel, by clans, by fathers' houses, according to the number of names, every male, head by head. ³From twenty years old and upward, all in Israel who are able to go to war, you and Aaron shall list them, company by company. ⁴And there shall be with you a man from each tribe, each man being the head of the house of his fathers. ⁵And these are the names of the men who shall assist you. From Reuben, Elizur the son of Shedeur; ⁶from Simeon, Shelumiel the son of Zurishaddai; ⁷from Judah, Nahshon the son of Amminadab; ⁸from Issachar, Nethanel the son of Zuar; ⁹from Zebulun, Eliab the son of Helon; ¹⁰from the sons of Joseph, from Ephraim, Elishama the son of Ammihud, and from Manasseh, Gamaliel the son of Pedahzur; ¹¹from Benjamin, Abidan the son of Gideoni; ¹²from Dan, Ahiezer the son of Ammishaddai; ¹³from Asher, Pagiel the son of Ochran; ¹⁴from Gad, Eliasaph the son of Deuel; ¹⁵from Naphtali, Ahira the son of Enan." ¹⁶These were the ones chosen from the congregation, the chiefs of their ancestral tribes, the heads of the clans of Israel.

¹⁷Moses and Aaron took these men who had been named, ¹⁸and on the first day of the second month, they assembled the whole congregation together, who registered themselves by clans, by fathers' houses, according to the number of names from twenty years old and upward, head by head, ¹⁹as the LORD commanded Moses. So he listed them in the wilderness of Sinai.

²⁰The people of Reuben, Israel's firstborn, their generations, by their clans, by their fathers' houses, according to the number of names, head by head, every male from twenty years old and upward, all who were able to go to war: ²¹those listed of the tribe of Reuben were 46,500.

²²Of the people of Simeon, their generations, by their clans, by their fathers' houses, those of them who were listed, according to the number of names, head by head, every male from twenty years old and upward, all who were able to go to war: ²³those listed of the tribe of Simeon were 59,300.

²⁴Of the people of Gad, their generations, by their clans, by their fathers' houses, according to the number of the names, from twenty years old and upward, all who were able to go to war: ²⁵those listed of the tribe of Gad were 45,650.

²⁶Of the people of Judah, their generations, by their clans, by their fathers' houses, according to the number of names, from twenty years old and upward, every man able to go to war: ²⁷those listed of the tribe of Judah were 74,600.

²⁸Of the people of Issachar, their generations, by their clans, by their fathers' houses, according to the number of names, from twenty years old and upward, every man able to go to war: ²⁹those listed of the tribe of Issachar were 54,400.

³⁰Of the people of Zebulun, their generations, by their clans, by their fathers' houses, according to the number of names, from twenty years old and upward, every man able to go to war: ³¹those listed of the tribe of Zebulun were 57,400.

³²Of the people of Joseph, namely, of the people of Ephraim, their generations, by their clans, by their fathers' houses, according to the number of names, from twenty years old and upward, every man able to go to war: ³³those listed of the tribe of Ephraim were 40,500.

³⁴Of the people of Manasseh, their generations, by their clans, by their fathers' houses, according to the number of names, from twenty years old and upward, every

man able to go to war: ³⁵those listed of the tribe of Manasseh were 32,200.

³⁶Of the people of Benjamin, their generations, by their clans, by their fathers' houses, according to the number of names, from twenty years old and upward, every man able to go to war: ³⁷those listed of the tribe of Benjamin were 35,400.

³⁸Of the people of Dan, their generations, by their clans, by their fathers' houses, according to the number of names, from twenty years old and upward, every man able to go to war: ³⁹those listed of the tribe of Dan were 62,700.

⁴⁰Of the people of Asher, their generations, by their clans, by their fathers' houses, according to the number of names, from twenty years old and upward, every man able to go to war: ⁴¹those listed of the tribe of Asher were 41,500.

⁴²Of the people of Naphtali, their generations, by their clans, by their fathers' houses, according to the number of names, from twenty years old and upward, every man able to go to war: ⁴³those listed of the tribe of Naphtali were 53,400.

⁴⁴These are those who were listed, whom Moses and Aaron listed with the help of the chiefs of Israel, twelve men, each representing his fathers' house. ⁴⁵So all those listed of the people of Israel, by their fathers' houses, from twenty years old and upward, every man able to go to war in Israel— ⁴⁶all those listed were 603,550.

Levites Exempted

⁴⁷But the Levites were not listed along with them by their ancestral tribe. ⁴⁸For the LORD spoke to Moses, saying, ⁴⁹"Only the tribe of Levi you shall not list, and you shall not take a census of them among the people of Israel. ⁵⁰But appoint the Levites over the tabernacle of the testimony, and over all its furnishings, and over all that belongs to it. They are to carry the tabernacle and all its furnishings, and they shall take care of it and shall camp around the tabernacle. ⁵¹When the tabernacle is to set out, the Levites shall take it down, and when the tabernacle is to be pitched, the Levites shall set it up. And if any outsider comes near, he shall be put to death. ⁵²The people of Israel shall pitch their tents by their companies, each man in his own camp and each man by his own standard. ⁵³But the Levites shall camp around the

tabernacle of the testimony, so that ther may be no wrath on the congregation o the people of Israel. And the Levites sha keep guard over the tabernacle of the tes timony." ⁵⁴Thus did the people of Israe they did according to all that the LOR commanded Moses.

Arrangement of the Camp

2 The LORD spoke to Moses and Aaron saying, ²"The people of Israel sha camp each by his own standard, with th banners of their fathers' houses. The shall camp facing the tent of meeting o every side. ³Those to camp on the eas side toward the sunrise shall be of th standard of the camp of Judah by thei companies, the chief of the people of Juda being Nahshon the son of Amminadab, ⁴hi company as listed being 74,600. ⁵Thos to camp next to him shall be the tribe o Issachar, the chief of the people of Issacha being Nethanel the son of Zuar, ⁶his com pany as listed being 54,400. ⁷Then th tribe of Zebulun, the chief of the peopl of Zebulun being Eliab the son of Helon ⁸his company as listed being 57,400. ⁹A those listed of the camp of Judah, by thei companies, were 186,400. They shall se out first on the march.

¹⁰"On the south side shall be the stan dard of the camp of Reuben by their com panies, the chief of the people of Reube being Elizur the son of Shedeur, ¹¹his com pany as listed being 46,500. ¹²And thos to camp next to him shall be the tribe o Simeon, the chief of the people of Simeor being Shelumiel the son of Zurishaddai ¹³his company as listed being 59,300 ¹⁴Then the tribe of Gad, the chief of th people of Gad being Eliasaph the so of Reuel, ¹⁵his company as listed bein 45,650. ¹⁶All those listed of the camp o Reuben, by their companies, were 151,450 They shall set out second.

¹⁷"Then the tent of meeting shall set out with the camp of the Levites in the midst o the camps; as they camp, so shall they se out, each in position, standard by standard

¹⁸"On the west side shall be the standar of the camp of Ephraim by their compa nies, the chief of the people of Ephraim being Elishama the son of Ammihud, ¹⁹hi company as listed being 40,500. ²⁰An next to him shall be the tribe of Manasseh the chief of the people of Manasseh being

amaliel the son of Pedahzur, [21] his com-
any as listed being 32,200. [22] Then the
ribe of Benjamin, the chief of the people of
enjamin being Abidan the son of Gideoni,
his company as listed being 35,400. [24] All
hose listed of the camp of Ephraim, by
heir companies, were 108,100. They shall
et out third on the march.

[25] "On the north side shall be the standard
f the camp of Dan by their companies, the
hief of the people of Dan being Ahiezer
he son of Ammishaddai, [26] his company as
sted being 62,700. [27] And those to camp
ext to him shall be the tribe of Asher, the
hief of the people of Asher being Pagiel
he son of Ochran, [28] his company as listed
eing 41,500. [29] Then the tribe of Naphtali,
he chief of the people of Naphtali being
hira the son of Enan, [30] his company as
sted being 53,400. [31] All those listed of the
amp of Dan were 157,600. They shall set
ut last, standard by standard."

[32] These are the people of Israel as listed
y their fathers' houses. All those listed
n the camps by their companies were
03,550. [33] But the Levites were not listed
mong the people of Israel, as the LORD
ommanded Moses.

[34] Thus did the people of Israel. According
o all that the LORD commanded Moses, so
hey camped by their standards, and so
hey set out, each one in his clan, according
o his fathers' house.

he Sons of Aaron

3 These are the generations of Aaron and
Moses at the time when the LORD spoke
vith Moses on Mount Sinai. [2] These are
he names of the sons of Aaron: Nadab the
irstborn, and Abihu, Eleazar, and Ithamar.
These are the names of the sons of Aaron,
he anointed priests, whom he ordained
o serve as priests. [4] But Nadab and Abihu
lied before the LORD when they offered
inauthorized fire before the LORD in the
vilderness of Sinai, and they had no chil-
lren. So Eleazar and Ithamar served as
riests in the lifetime of Aaron their father.

)uties of the Levites

[5] And the LORD spoke to Moses, saying,
"Bring the tribe of Levi near, and set them
efore Aaron the priest, that they may
ninister to him. [7] They shall keep guard
ver him and over the whole congregation

before the tent of meeting, as they minister
at the tabernacle. [8] They shall guard all
the furnishings of the tent of meeting, and
keep guard over the people of Israel as they
minister at the tabernacle. [9] And you shall
give the Levites to Aaron and his sons; they
are wholly given to him from among the
people of Israel. [10] And you shall appoint
Aaron and his sons, and they shall guard
their priesthood. But if any outsider comes
near, he shall be put to death."

[11] And the LORD spoke to Moses, saying,
[12] "Behold, I have taken the Levites from
among the people of Israel instead of every
firstborn who opens the womb among the
people of Israel. The Levites shall be mine,
[13] for all the firstborn are mine. On the day
that I struck down all the firstborn in the
land of Egypt, I consecrated for my own all
the firstborn in Israel, both of man and of
beast. They shall be mine: I am the LORD."

[14] And the LORD spoke to Moses in the
wilderness of Sinai, saying, [15] "List the
sons of Levi, by fathers' houses and by
clans; every male from a month old and
upward you shall list." [16] So Moses listed
them according to the word of the LORD,
as he was commanded. [17] And these were
the sons of Levi by their names: Gershon
and Kohath and Merari. [18] And these are
the names of the sons of Gershon by their
clans: Libni and Shimei. [19] And the sons
of Kohath by their clans: Amram, Izhar,
Hebron, and Uzziel. [20] And the sons of
Merari by their clans: Mahli and Mushi.
These are the clans of the Levites, by their
fathers' houses.

[21] To Gershon belonged the clan of the
Libnites and the clan of the Shimeites;
these were the clans of the Gershonites.
[22] Their listing according to the number
of all the males from a month old and
upward was[1] 7,500. [23] The clans of the
Gershonites were to camp behind the tabernacle on the west, [24] with Eliasaph, the
son of Lael as chief of the fathers' house of
the Gershonites. [25] And the guard duty of
the sons of Gershon in the tent of meeting
involved the tabernacle, the tent with its
covering, the screen for the entrance of
the tent of meeting, [26] the hangings of the
court, the screen for the door of the court
that is around the tabernacle and the altar,
and its cords— all the service connected
with these.

---

[1] Hebrew *their listing was*

²⁷ To Kohath belonged the clan of the Amramites and the clan of the Izharites and the clan of the Hebronites and the clan of the Uzzielites; these are the clans of the Kohathites. ²⁸ According to the number of all the males, from a month old and upward, there were 8,600, keeping guard over the sanctuary. ²⁹ The clans of the sons of Kohath were to camp on the south side of the tabernacle, ³⁰ with Elizaphan the son of Uzziel as chief of the fathers' house of the clans of the Kohathites. ³¹ And their guard duty involved the ark, the table, the lampstand, the altars, the vessels of the sanctuary with which the priests minister, and the screen; all the service connected with these. ³² And Eleazar the son of Aaron the priest was to be chief over the chiefs of the Levites, and to have oversight of those who kept guard over the sanctuary.

³³ To Merari belonged the clan of the Mahlites and the clan of the Mushites: these are the clans of Merari. ³⁴ Their listing according to the number of all the males from a month old and upward was 6,200. ³⁵ And the chief of the fathers' house of the clans of Merari was Zuriel the son of Abihail. They were to camp on the north side of the tabernacle. ³⁶ And the appointed guard duty of the sons of Merari involved the frames of the tabernacle, the bars, the pillars, the bases, and all their accessories; all the service connected with these; ³⁷ also the pillars around the court, with their bases and pegs and cords.

³⁸ Those who were to camp before the tabernacle on the east, before the tent of meeting toward the sunrise, were Moses and Aaron and his sons, guarding the sanctuary itself, to protect[1] the people of Israel. And any outsider who came near was to be put to death. ³⁹ All those listed among the Levites, whom Moses and Aaron listed at the commandment of the LORD, by clans, all the males from a month old and upward, were 22,000.

Redemption of the Firstborn

⁴⁰ And the LORD said to Moses, "List all the firstborn males of the people of Israel, from a month old and upward, taking the number of their names. ⁴¹ And you shall take the Levites for me—I am the LORD—instead of all the firstborn among the peo-

ple of Israel, and the cattle of the Levite instead of all the firstborn among the cattl of the people of Israel." ⁴² So Moses liste all the firstborn among the people of Israe as the LORD commanded him. ⁴³ And all th firstborn males, according to the numbe of names, from a month old and upward a listed were 22,273.

⁴⁴ And the LORD spoke to Moses, saying ⁴⁵ "Take the Levites instead of all the first born among the people of Israel, and th cattle of the Levites instead of their cattle The Levites shall be mine: I am the LORD ⁴⁶ And as the redemption price for the 27: of the firstborn of the people of Israel, ove and above the number of the male Levites ⁴⁷ you shall take five shekels[2] per head; yo shall take them according to the sheke of the sanctuary (the shekel of twent gerahs[3]), ⁴⁸ and give the money to Aaro and his sons as the redemption price fo those who are over." ⁴⁹ So Moses took th redemption money from those who wer over and above those redeemed by th Levites. ⁵⁰ From the firstborn of the peopl of Israel he took the money, 1,365 shekels by the shekel of the sanctuary. ⁵¹ And Mose gave the redemption money to Aaron an his sons, according to the word of the LORI as the LORD commanded Moses.

Duties of the Kohathites

4 The LORD spoke to Moses and Aaron saying, ² "Take a census of the sons o Kohath from among the sons of Levi, b their clans and their fathers' houses, ³ from thirty years old up to fifty years old, a who can come on duty, to do the work i the tent of meeting. ⁴ This is the servic of the sons of Kohath in the tent of meet ing: the most holy things. ⁵ When the cam is to set out, Aaron and his sons shall g in and take down the veil of the scree and cover the ark of the testimony wit it. ⁶ Then they shall put on it a covering o goatskin[4] and spread on top of that a clot all of blue, and shall put in its poles. ⁷ An over the table of the bread of the Presenc they shall spread a cloth of blue and pu on it the plates, the dishes for incense, the bowls, and the flagons for the drink offer ing; the regular showbread also shall b on it. ⁸ Then they shall spread over then a cloth of scarlet and cover the same wit

---

[1] Hebrew guard   [2] A shekel was about 2/5 ounce or 11 grams   [3] A gerah was about 1/50 ounce or 0.6 gram   [4] The meaning of the Hebrew word is uncertain; compare Exodus 25:5

covering of goatskin, and shall put in its poles. ⁹And they shall take a cloth of blue and cover the lampstand for the light, with its lamps, its tongs, its trays, and all the vessels for oil with which it is supplied. And they shall put it with all its utensils in a covering of goatskin and put it on the carrying frame. ¹¹And over the golden altar they shall spread a cloth of blue and cover it with a covering of goatskin, and shall put in its poles. ¹²And they shall take all the vessels of the service that are used in the sanctuary and put them in a cloth of blue and cover them with a covering of goatskin and put them on the carrying frame. ¹³And they shall take away the ashes from the altar and spread a purple cloth over it. And they shall put on it all the utensils of the altar, which are used for the service there, the fire pans, the forks, the shovels, and the basins, all the utensils of the altar; and they shall spread on it a covering of goatskin, and shall put in its poles. ¹⁵And when Aaron and his sons have finished

covering the sanctuary and all the furnishings of the sanctuary, as the camp sets out, after that the sons of Kohath shall come to carry these, but they must not touch the holy things, lest they die. These are the things of the tent of meeting that the sons of Kohath are to carry.

¹⁶"And Eleazar the son of Aaron the priest shall have charge of the oil for the light, the fragrant incense, the regular grain offering, and the anointing oil, with the oversight of the whole tabernacle and all that is in it, of the sanctuary and its vessels."

¹⁷The LORD spoke to Moses and Aaron, saying, ¹⁸"Let not the tribe of the clans of the Kohathites be destroyed from among the Levites, ¹⁹but deal thus with them, that they may live and not die when they come near to the most holy things: Aaron and his sons shall go in and appoint them each to his task and to his burden, ²⁰but they shall not go in to look on the holy things even for a moment, lest they die."

verses to read
Numbers 3:44–51

Know True Happiness

Sinning is as easy as breathing. Without Christ, we can't help but sin. That's why God says that no one has God's approval, not one person is righteous, and everyone has turned away and fallen short of the glory of God (see Rom. 3:10–12). And so a price has to be paid to get your life back, just like a ransom to a kidnapper. Sin kidnaps you and puts you into slavery and bondage to itself. Sin calls out your name and says, "Come on, I will make you happy." But as soon as you turn to it, it grabs you and chains you down, making it impossible to get free. The sad thing is, many times we enjoy those chains and think they are more satisfying than life with God.

But there's a way out of those chains, and it is called redemption, the ransom for your soul. When God opens your eyes, bringing you from death to life, and you receive Jesus as your Lord and as the one who paid for your sins, your ransom is paid and you are set free. That means you're not only free from the penalty of sin but free from its bondage as well. Sin doesn't have power over you anymore (see Rom. 6:14). So you don't have to keep saying yes to it, giving in to it, or being weak because of it. God set you free. He doesn't save you just to give you a one-way ticket to heaven but to set you free. The only reason you continue to struggle with the same sin you fought before your redemption is because you choose to go back to it, like an abused wife goes back to her abusive husband. It's not right or good. It makes no sense; you've been set free, so why do you return to the place of torment? You don't have to! Turn to God and be free.

[21] The LORD spoke to Moses, saying, [22] "Take a census of the sons of Gershon also, by their fathers' houses and by their clans. [23] From thirty years old up to fifty years old, you shall list them, all who can come to do duty, to do service in the tent of meeting. [24] This is the service of the clans of the Gershonites, in serving and bearing burdens: [25] they shall carry the curtains of the tabernacle and the tent of meeting with its covering and the covering of goatskin that is on top of it and the screen for the entrance of the tent of meeting [26] and the hangings of the court and the screen for the entrance of the gate of the court that is around the tabernacle and the altar, and their cords and all the equipment for their service. And they shall do all that needs to be done with regard to them. [27] All the service of the sons of the Gershonites shall be at the command of Aaron and his sons, in all that they are to carry and in all that they have to do. And you shall assign to their charge all that they are to carry. [28] This is the service of the clans of the sons of the Gershonites in the tent of meeting, and their guard duty is to be under the direction of Ithamar the son of Aaron the priest.

[29] "As for the sons of Merari, you shall list them by their clans and their fathers' houses. [30] From thirty years old up to fifty years old, you shall list them, everyone who can come on duty, to do the service of the tent of meeting. [31] And this is what they are charged to carry, as the whole of their service in the tent of meeting: the frames of the tabernacle, with its bars, pillars, and bases, [32] and the pillars around the court with their bases, pegs, and cords, with all their equipment and all their accessories. And you shall list by name the objects that they are required to carry. [33] This is the service of the clans of the sons of Merari, the whole of their service in the tent of meeting, under the direction of Ithamar the son of Aaron the priest."

[34] And Moses and Aaron and the chiefs of the congregation listed the sons of the Kohathites, by their clans and their fathers' houses, [35] from thirty years old up to fifty years old, everyone who could come on duty, for service in the tent of meeting; [36] and those listed by clans were 2,750. [37] This was the list of the clans of the Kohathites, all who served in the tent of meeting, whom Moses and Aaron listed according to the commandment of the LORD by Moses.

[38] Those listed of the sons of Gershon, by their clans and their fathers' houses, [39] from thirty years old up to fifty years old, everyone who could come on duty for service in the tent of meeting— [40] those listed by their clans and their fathers' houses were 2,630. [41] This was the list of the clans of the sons of Gershon, all who served in the tent of meeting, whom Moses and Aaron listed according to the commandment of the LORD.

[42] Those listed of the clans of the sons of Merari, by their clans and their fathers' houses, [43] from thirty years old up to fifty years old, everyone who could come on duty, for service in the tent of meeting— [44] those listed by clans were 3,200. [45] This was the list of the clans of the sons of Merari, whom Moses and Aaron listed according to the commandment of the LORD by Moses.

[46] All those who were listed of the Levites, whom Moses and Aaron and the chiefs of Israel listed, by their clans and their fathers' houses, [47] from thirty years old up to fifty years old, everyone who could come to do the service of ministry and the service of bearing burdens in the tent of meeting, [48] those listed were 8,580. [49] According to the commandment of the LORD through Moses they were listed, each one with his task of serving or carrying. Thus they were listed by him, as the LORD commanded Moses.

Unclean People

5 The LORD spoke to Moses, saying, [2] "Command the people of Israel that they put out of the camp everyone who is leprous[1] or has a discharge and everyone who is unclean through contact with the dead. [3] You shall put out both male and female, putting them outside the camp, that they may not defile their camp, in the midst of which I dwell." [4] And the people of Israel did so, and put them outside the camp; as the LORD said to Moses, so the people of Israel did.

Confession and Restitution

[5] And the LORD spoke to Moses, saying, [6] "Speak to the people of Israel, When a

---

[1] *Leprosy* was a term for several skin diseases; see Leviticus 13

man or woman commits any of the sins that people commit by breaking faith with the LORD, and that person realizes his guilt, [7] he shall confess his sin that he has committed.[1] And he shall make full restitution for his wrong, adding a fifth to it and giving it to him to whom he did the wrong. [8] But if the man has no next of kin to whom restitution may be made for the wrong, the restitution for wrong shall go to the LORD for the priest, in addition to the ram of atonement with which atonement is made for him. [9] And every contribution, all the holy donations of the people of Israel, which they bring to the priest, shall be his. [10] Each one shall keep his holy donations: whatever anyone gives to the priest shall be his."

A Test for Adultery

[11] And the LORD spoke to Moses, saying, [12] "Speak to the people of Israel, If any man's wife goes astray and breaks faith with him, [13] if a man lies with her sexually, and it is hidden from the eyes of her husband, and she is undetected though she has defiled herself, and there is no witness against her, since she was not taken in the act, [14] and if the spirit of jealousy comes over him and he is jealous of his wife who has defiled herself, or if the spirit of jealousy comes over him and he is jealous of his wife, though she has not defiled herself, [15] then the man shall bring his wife to the priest and bring the offering required of her, a tenth of an ephah[2] of barley flour. He shall pour no oil on it and put no frankincense on it, for it is a grain offering of jealousy, a grain offering of remembrance, bringing iniquity to remembrance.

[16] "And the priest shall bring her near and set her before the LORD. [17] And the priest shall take holy water in an earthenware vessel and take some of the dust that is on the floor of the tabernacle and put it into the water. [18] And the priest shall set the woman before the LORD and unbind the hair of the woman's head and place in her hands the grain offering of remembrance, which is the grain offering of jealousy. And in his hand the priest shall have the water of bitterness that brings the curse. [19] Then the priest shall make her take an oath, saying, 'If no man has lain with you, and if you have not turned aside to uncleanness while you were under your husband's authority, be free from this water of bitterness that brings the curse. [20] But if you have gone astray, though you are under your husband's authority, and if you have defiled yourself, and some man other than your husband has lain with you, [21] then' (let the priest make the woman take the oath of the curse, and say to the woman) 'the LORD make you a curse and an oath among your people, when the LORD makes your thigh fall away and your body swell. [22] May this water that brings the curse pass into your bowels and make your womb swell and your thigh fall away.' And the woman shall say, 'Amen, Amen.'

[23] "Then the priest shall write these curses in a book and wash them off into the water of bitterness. [24] And he shall make the woman drink the water of bitterness that brings the curse, and the water that brings the curse shall enter into her and cause bitter pain. [25] And the priest shall take the grain offering of jealousy out of the woman's hand and shall wave the grain offering before the LORD and bring it to the altar. [26] And the priest shall take a handful of the grain offering, as its memorial portion, and burn it on the altar, and afterward shall make the woman drink the water. [27] And when he has made her drink the water, then, if she has defiled herself and has broken faith with her husband, the water that brings the curse shall enter into her and cause bitter pain, and her womb shall swell, and her thigh shall fall away, and the woman shall become a curse among her people. [28] But if the woman has not defiled herself and is clean, then she shall be free and shall conceive children.

[29] "This is the law in cases of jealousy, when a wife, though under her husband's authority, goes astray and defiles herself, [30] or when the spirit of jealousy comes over a man and he is jealous of his wife. Then he shall set the woman before the LORD, and the priest shall carry out for her all this law. [31] The man shall be free from iniquity, but the woman shall bear her iniquity."

The Nazirite Vow

6 And the LORD spoke to Moses, saying, [2] "Speak to the people of Israel and say to them, When either a man or a woman makes a special vow, the vow of a

---

[1] Hebrew *they shall confess their sin that they have committed* [2] An *ephah* was about 3/5 bushel or 22 liters

Nazirite,[1] to separate himself to the LORD, [3] he shall separate himself from wine and strong drink. He shall drink no vinegar made from wine or strong drink and shall not drink any juice of grapes or eat grapes, fresh or dried. [4] All the days of his separation[2] he shall eat nothing that is produced by the grapevine, not even the seeds or the skins.

[5] "All the days of his vow of separation, no razor shall touch his head. Until the time is completed for which he separates himself to the LORD, he shall be holy. He shall let the locks of hair of his head grow long.

[6] "All the days that he separates himself to the LORD he shall not go near a dead body. [7] Not even for his father or for his mother, for brother or sister, if they die, shall he make himself unclean, because his separation to God is on his head. [8] All the days of his separation he is holy to the LORD.

[9] "And if any man dies very suddenly beside him and he defiles his consecrated head, then he shall shave his head on the day of his cleansing; on the seventh day he shall shave it. [10] On the eighth day he shall bring two turtledoves or two pigeons to the priest to the entrance of the tent of meeting, [11] and the priest shall offer one for a sin offering and the other for a burnt offering, and make atonement for him, because he sinned by reason of the dead body. And he shall consecrate his head that same day [12] and separate himself to the LORD for the days of his separation and bring a male lamb a year old for a guilt offering. But the previous period shall be void, because his separation was defiled.

[13] "And this is the law for the Nazirite, when the time of his separation has been completed: he shall be brought to the entrance of the tent of meeting, [14] and he shall bring his gift to the LORD, one male lamb a year old without blemish for a burnt offering, and one ewe lamb a year old without blemish as a sin offering, and one ram without blemish as a peace offering, [15] and a basket of unleavened bread, loaves of fine flour mixed with oil, and unleavened wafers smeared with oil, and their grain offering and their drink offerings. [16] And the priest shall bring them before the LORD and offer his sin offering and his burnt offering, [17] and he shall offer the ram as

a sacrifice of peace offering to the LORD, with the basket of unleavened bread. The priest shall offer also its grain offering and its drink offering. [18] And the Nazirite shall shave his consecrated head at the entrance of the tent of meeting and shall take the hair from his consecrated head and put it on the fire that is under the sacrifice of the peace offering. [19] And the priest shall take the shoulder of the ram, when it is boiled, and one unleavened loaf out of the basket and one unleavened wafer, and shall put them on the hands of the Nazirite, after he has shaved the hair of his consecration, [20] and the priest shall wave them for a wave offering before the LORD. They are a holy portion for the priest, together with the breast that is waved and the thigh that is contributed. And after that the Nazirite may drink wine.

[21] "This is the law of the Nazirite. But if he vows an offering to the LORD above his Nazirite vow, as he can afford, in exact accordance with the vow that he takes, then he shall do in addition to the law of the Nazirite."

Aaron's Blessing

[22] The LORD spoke to Moses, saying, [23] "Speak to Aaron and his sons, saying, Thus you shall bless the people of Israel: you shall say to them,

[24]   The LORD bless you and keep you;
[25]   the LORD make his face to shine upon
            you and be gracious to you;
[26]   the LORD lift up his countenance[3]
            upon you and give you peace.

[27] "So shall they put my name upon the people of Israel, and I will bless them."

Offerings at the Tabernacle's Consecration

7 On the day when Moses had finished setting up the tabernacle and had anointed and consecrated it with all its furnishings and had anointed and consecrated the altar with all its utensils, [2] the chiefs of Israel, heads of their fathers' houses, who were the chiefs of the tribes, who were over those who were listed, approached [3] and brought their offerings before the LORD, six wagons and twelve oxen, a wagon for every two of the chiefs, and for each one an ox. They brought them before the tabernacle. [4] Then the LORD said to Moses,

---

[1] Nazirite means one separated, or one consecrated [2] Or Naziriteship [3] Or face

⁵"Accept these from them, that they may be used in the service of the tent of meeting, and give them to the Levites, to each man according to his service." ⁶So Moses took the wagons and the oxen and gave them to the Levites. ⁷Two wagons and four oxen he gave to the sons of Gershon, according to their service. ⁸And four wagons and eight oxen he gave to the sons of Merari, according to their service, under the direction of Ithamar the son of Aaron the priest. ⁹But to the sons of Kohath he gave none, because they were charged with the service of the holy things that had to be carried on the shoulder. ¹⁰And the chiefs offered offerings for the dedication of the altar on the day it was anointed; and the chiefs offered their offering before the altar. ¹¹And the LORD said to Moses, "They shall offer their offerings, one chief each day, for the dedication of the altar."

Ask Yourself . . .

ABOUT YOUR FAVORITE SIN

The problem with sin is that it can be fun. And that can make it hard to part with. Ask yourself:

- What are my favorite sins?
- What do I have the most trouble stopping?
- What did the sacrifice of Jesus do for my freedom from sin? (Check out Rom. 6:6–7, 18; Eph. 1:7; 1 John 5:18.)
- What sins will I determine, by the grace of God, to give up today?

¹²He who offered his offering the first day was Nahshon the son of Amminadab, of the tribe of Judah. ¹³And his offering was one silver plate whose weight was 130 shekels,¹ one silver basin of 70 shekels, according to the shekel of the sanctuary, both of them full of fine flour mixed with oil for a grain offering; ¹⁴one golden dish of 10 shekels, full of incense; ¹⁵one bull from the herd, one ram, one male lamb a year old, for a burnt offering; ¹⁶one male goat for a sin offering; ¹⁷and for the sacrifice of peace offerings, two oxen, five rams, five male goats, and five male lambs a year old. This was the offering of Nahshon the son of Amminadab.

¹⁸On the second day Nethanel the son of Zuar, the chief of Issachar, made an offering. ¹⁹He offered for his offering one silver plate whose weight was 130 shekels, one silver basin of 70 shekels, according to the shekel of the sanctuary, both of them full of fine flour mixed with oil for a grain offering; ²⁰one golden dish of 10 shekels, full of incense; ²¹one bull from the herd, one ram, one male lamb a year old, for a burnt offering; ²²one male goat for a sin offering; ²³and for the sacrifice of peace offerings, two oxen, five rams, five male goats, and five male lambs a year old. This was the offering of Nethanel the son of Zuar.

²⁴On the third day Eliab the son of Helon, the chief of the people of Zebulun: ²⁵his offering was one silver plate whose weight was 130 shekels, one silver basin of 70 shekels, according to the shekel of the sanctuary, both of them full of fine flour mixed with oil for a grain offering; ²⁶one golden dish of 10 shekels, full of incense; ²⁷one bull from the herd, one ram, one male lamb a year old, for a burnt offering; ²⁸one male goat for a sin offering; ²⁹and for the sacrifice of peace offerings, two oxen, five rams, five male goats, and five male lambs a year old. This was the offering of Eliab the son of Helon.

³⁰On the fourth day Elizur the son of Shedeur, the chief of the people of Reuben: ³¹his offering was one silver plate whose weight was 130 shekels, one silver basin of 70 shekels, according to the shekel of the sanctuary, both of them full of fine flour mixed with oil for a grain offering; ³²one golden dish of 10 shekels, full of incense; ³³one bull from the herd, one ram, one male lamb a year old, for a burnt offering; ³⁴one male goat for a sin offering; ³⁵and for the sacrifice of peace offerings, two oxen, five rams, five male goats, and five male lambs a year old. This was the offering of Elizur the son of Shedeur.

³⁶On the fifth day Shelumiel the son of Zurishaddai, the chief of the people of

¹A *shekel* was about 2/5 ounce or 11 grams

Simeon: [37] his offering was one silver plate whose weight was 130 shekels, one silver basin of 70 shekels, according to the shekel of the sanctuary, both of them full of fine flour mixed with oil for a grain offering; [38] one golden dish of 10 shekels, full of incense; [39] one bull from the herd, one ram, one male lamb a year old, for a burnt offering; [40] one male goat for a sin offering; [41] and for the sacrifice of peace offerings, two oxen, five rams, five male goats, and five male lambs a year old. This was the offering of Shelumiel the son of Zurishaddai.

[42] On the sixth day Eliasaph the son of Deuel, the chief of the people of Gad: [43] his offering was one silver plate whose weight was 130 shekels, one silver basin of 70 shekels, according to the shekel of the sanctuary, both of them full of fine flour mixed with oil for a grain offering; [44] one golden dish of 10 shekels, full of incense; [45] one bull from the herd, one ram, one male lamb a year old, for a burnt offering; [46] one male goat for a sin offering; [47] and for the sacrifice of peace offerings, two oxen, five rams, five male goats, and five male lambs a year old. This was the offering of Eliasaph the son of Deuel.

[48] On the seventh day Elishama the son of Ammihud, the chief of the people of Ephraim: [49] his offering was one silver plate whose weight was 130 shekels, one silver basin of 70 shekels, according to the shekel of the sanctuary, both of them full of fine flour mixed with oil for a grain offering; [50] one golden dish of 10 shekels, full of incense; [51] one bull from the herd, one ram, one male lamb a year old, for a burnt offering; [52] one male goat for a sin offering; [53] and for the sacrifice of peace offerings, two oxen, five rams, five male goats, and five male lambs a year old. This was the offering of Elishama the son of Ammihud.

[54] On the eighth day Gamaliel the son of Pedahzur, the chief of the people of Manasseh: [55] his offering was one silver plate whose weight was 130 shekels, one silver basin of 70 shekels, according to the shekel of the sanctuary, both of them full of fine flour mixed with oil for a grain offering; [56] one golden dish of 10 shekels, full of incense; [57] one bull from the herd, one ram, one male lamb a year old, for a burnt offering; [58] one male goat for a sin offering; [59] and for the sacrifice of peace offerings, two oxen, five rams, five male goats, and five male lambs a year old. This was the offering of Gamaliel the son of Pedahzur.

[60] On the ninth day Abidan the son of Gideoni, the chief of the people of Benjamin: [61] his offering was one silver plate whose weight was 130 shekels, one silver basin of 70 shekels, according to the shekel of the sanctuary, both of them full of fine flour mixed with oil for a grain offering; [62] one golden dish of 10 shekels, full of incense; [63] one bull from the herd, one ram, one male lamb a year old, for a burnt offering; [64] one male goat for a sin offering; [65] and for the sacrifice of peace offerings, two oxen, five rams, five male goats, and five male lambs a year old. This was the offering of Abidan the son of Gideoni.

[66] On the tenth day Ahiezer the son of Ammishaddai, the chief of the people of Dan: [67] his offering was one silver plate whose weight was 130 shekels, one silver basin of 70 shekels, according to the shekel of the sanctuary, both of them full of fine flour mixed with oil for a grain offering; [68] one golden dish of 10 shekels, full of incense; [69] one bull from the herd, one ram, one male lamb a year old, for a burnt offering; [70] one male goat for a sin offering; [71] and for the sacrifice of peace offerings, two oxen, five rams, five male goats, and five male lambs a year old. This was the offering of Ahiezer the son of Ammishaddai.

[72] On the eleventh day Pagiel the son of Ochran, the chief of the people of Asher: [73] his offering was one silver plate whose weight was 130 shekels, one silver basin of 70 shekels, according to the shekel of the sanctuary, both of them full of fine flour mixed with oil for a grain offering; [74] one golden dish of 10 shekels, full of incense; [75] one bull from the herd, one ram, one male lamb a year old, for a burnt offering; [76] one male goat for a sin offering; [77] and for the sacrifice of peace offerings, two oxen, five rams, five male goats, and five male lambs a year old. This was the offering of Pagiel the son of Ochran.

[78] On the twelfth day Ahira the son of Enan, the chief of the people of Naphtali: [79] his offering was one silver plate whose weight was 130 shekels, one silver basin of 70 shekels, according to the shekel of the sanctuary, both of them full of fine flour mixed with oil for a grain offering; [80] one golden dish of 10 shekels, full of incense; [81] one bull from the herd, one ram, one

male lamb a year old, for a burnt offering; [82] one male goat for a sin offering; [83] and for the sacrifice of peace offerings, two oxen, five rams, five male goats, and five male lambs a year old. This was the offering of Ahira the son of Enan.

[84] This was the dedication offering for the altar on the day when it was anointed, from the chiefs of Israel: twelve silver plates, twelve silver basins, twelve golden dishes, [85] each silver plate weighing 130 shekels and each basin 70, all the silver of the vessels 2,400 shekels according to the shekel of the sanctuary, [86] the twelve golden dishes, full of incense, weighing 10 shekels apiece according to the shekel of the sanctuary, all the gold of the dishes being 120 shekels; [87] all the cattle for the burnt offering twelve bulls, twelve rams, twelve male lambs a year old, with their grain offering; and twelve male goats for a sin offering; [88] and all the cattle for the sacrifice of peace offerings twenty-four bulls, the rams sixty, the male goats sixty, the male lambs a year old sixty. This was the dedication offering for the altar after it was anointed.

[89] And when Moses went into the tent of meeting to speak with the LORD, he heard the voice speaking to him from above the mercy seat that was on the ark of the testimony, from between the two cherubim; and it spoke to him.

The Seven Lamps

8 Now the LORD spoke to Moses, saying, [2] "Speak to Aaron and say to him, When you set up the lamps, the seven lamps shall give light in front of the lampstand." [3] And Aaron did so: he set up its lamps in front of the lampstand, as the LORD commanded Moses. [4] And this was the workmanship of the lampstand, hammered work of gold. From its base to its flowers, it was hammered work; according to the pattern that the LORD had shown Moses, so he made the lampstand.

Cleansing of the Levites

[5] And the LORD spoke to Moses, saying, [6] "Take the Levites from among the people of Israel and cleanse them. [7] Thus you shall do to them to cleanse them: sprinkle the water of purification upon them, and let them go with a razor over all their body, and wash their clothes and cleanse themselves. [8] Then let them take a bull from the herd and its grain offering of fine flour mixed with oil, and you shall take another bull from the herd for a sin offering. [9] And you shall bring the Levites before the tent of meeting and assemble the whole congregation of the people of Israel. [10] When you bring the Levites before the LORD, the people of Israel shall lay their hands on the Levites, [11] and Aaron shall offer the Levites before the LORD as a wave offering from the people of Israel, that they may do the service of the LORD. [12] Then the Levites shall lay their hands on the heads of the bulls, and you shall offer the one for a sin offering and the other for a burnt offering to the LORD to make atonement for the Levites. [13] And you shall set the Levites before Aaron and his sons, and shall offer them as a wave offering to the LORD.

[14] "Thus you shall separate the Levites from among the people of Israel, and the Levites shall be mine. [15] And after that the Levites shall go in to serve at the tent of meeting, when you have cleansed them and offered them as a wave offering. [16] For they are wholly given to me from among the people of Israel. Instead of all who open the womb, the firstborn of all the people of Israel, I have taken them for myself. [17] For all the firstborn among the people of Israel are mine, both of man and of beast. On the day that I struck down all the firstborn in the land of Egypt I consecrated them for myself, [18] and I have taken the Levites instead of all the firstborn among the people of Israel. [19] And I have given the Levites as a gift to Aaron and his sons from among the people of Israel, to do the service for the people of Israel at the tent of meeting and to make atonement for the people of Israel, that there may be no plague among the people of Israel when the people of Israel come near the sanctuary."

[20] Thus did Moses and Aaron and all the congregation of the people of Israel to the Levites. According to all that the LORD commanded Moses concerning the Levites, the people of Israel did to them. [21] And the Levites purified themselves from sin and washed their clothes, and Aaron offered them as a wave offering before the LORD, and Aaron made atonement for them to cleanse them. [22] And after that the Levites went in to do their service in the tent of meeting before Aaron and his sons; as the

LORD had commanded Moses concerning the Levites, so they did to them.

Retirement of the Levites

²³ And the LORD spoke to Moses, saying, ²⁴ "This applies to the Levites: from twenty-five years old and upward they[1] shall come to do duty in the service of the tent of meeting. ²⁵ And from the age of fifty years they shall withdraw from the duty of the service and serve no more. ²⁶ They minister[2] to their brothers in the tent of meeting by keeping guard, but they shall do no service. Thus shall you do to the Levites in assigning their duties."

The Passover Celebrated

9 And the LORD spoke to Moses in the wilderness of Sinai, in the first month of the second year after they had come out of the land of Egypt, saying, ² "Let the people of Israel keep the Passover at its appointed time. ³ On the fourteenth day of this month, at twilight, you shall keep it at its appointed time; according to all its statutes and all its rules you shall keep it." ⁴ So Moses told the people of Israel that they should keep the Passover. ⁵ And they kept the Passover in the first month, on the fourteenth day of the month, at twilight, in the wilderness of Sinai; according to all that the LORD commanded Moses, so the people of Israel did. ⁶ And there were certain men who were unclean through touching a dead body, so that they could not keep the Passover on that day, and they came before Moses and Aaron on that day. ⁷ And those men said to him, "We are unclean through touching a dead body. Why are we kept from bringing the LORD's offering at its appointed time among the people of Israel?" ⁸ And Moses said to them, "Wait, that I may hear what the LORD will command concerning you."

⁹ The LORD spoke to Moses, saying, ¹⁰ "Speak to the people of Israel, saying, If any one of you or of your descendants is unclean through touching a dead body, or is on a long journey, he shall still keep the Passover to the LORD. ¹¹ In the second month on the fourteenth day at twilight they shall keep it. They shall eat it with unleavened bread and bitter herbs. ¹² They shall leave none of it until the morning, nor break any of its bones; according to all the

statute for the Passover they shall keep it ¹³ But if anyone who is clean and is not or a journey fails to keep the Passover, that person shall be cut off from his people because he did not bring the LORD's offering at its appointed time; that man shall bear his sin. ¹⁴ And if a stranger sojourns among you and would keep the Passover to the LORD, according to the statute of the Passover and according to its rule, so shall he do. You shall have one statute, both for the sojourner and for the native."

The Cloud Covering the Tabernacle

¹⁵ On the day that the tabernacle was set up, the cloud covered the tabernacle, the tent of the testimony. And at evening it was over the tabernacle like the appearance of fire until morning. ¹⁶ So it was always: the cloud covered it by day[3] and the appearance of fire by night. ¹⁷ And whenever the cloud lifted from over the tent, after that the people of Israel set out, and in the place where the cloud settled down, there the people of Israel camped. ¹⁸ At the command of the LORD the people of Israel set out, and at the command of the LORD they camped. As long as the cloud rested over the tabernacle, they remained in camp. ¹⁹ Even when the cloud continued over the tabernacle many days, the people of Israel kept the charge of the LORD and did not set out. ²⁰ Sometimes the cloud was a few days over the tabernacle, and according to the command of the LORD they remained in camp; then according to the command of the LORD they set out. ²¹ And sometimes the cloud remained from evening until morning. And when the cloud lifted in the morning, they set out, or if it continued for a day and a night, when the cloud lifted they set out. ²² Whether it was two days, or a month, or a longer time, that the cloud continued over the tabernacle, abiding there, the people of Israel remained in camp and did not set out, but when it lifted they set out. ²³ At the command of the LORD they camped, and at the command of the LORD they set out. They kept the charge of the LORD, at the command of the LORD by Moses.

The Silver Trumpets

10 The LORD spoke to Moses, saying, ² "Make two silver trumpets. Of hammered work you shall make them, and you

[1] Hebrew *he*; also verses 25, 26 [2] Hebrew *He ministers* [3] Septuagint, Syriac, Vulgate; Hebrew lacks *by day*

shall use them for summoning the congregation and for breaking camp. ³And when both are blown, all the congregation shall gather themselves to you at the entrance of the tent of meeting. ⁴But if they blow only one, then the chiefs, the heads of the tribes of Israel, shall gather themselves to you. ⁵When you blow an alarm, the camps that are on the east side shall set out. ⁶And when you blow an alarm the second time, the camps that are on the south side shall set out. An alarm is to be blown whenever they are to set out. ⁷But when the assembly is to be gathered together, you shall blow a long blast, but you shall not sound an alarm. ⁸And the sons of Aaron, the priests, shall blow the trumpets. The trumpets shall be to you for a perpetual statute throughout your generations. ⁹And when you go to war in your land against the adversary who oppresses you, then you shall sound an alarm with the trumpets, that you may be remembered before the LORD your God, and you shall be saved from your enemies. ¹⁰On the day of your gladness also, and at your appointed feasts and at the beginnings of your months, you shall blow the trumpets over your burnt offerings and over the sacrifices of your peace offerings. They shall be a reminder of you before your God: I am the LORD your God."

Israel Leaves Sinai

¹¹In the second year, in the second month, on the twentieth day of the month, the cloud lifted from over the tabernacle of the testimony, ¹²and the people of Israel set out by stages from the wilderness of Sinai. And the cloud settled down in the wilderness of Paran. ¹³They set out for the first time at the command of the LORD by Moses. ¹⁴The standard of the camp of the people of Judah set out first by their companies, and over their company was Nahshon the son of Amminadab. ¹⁵And over the company of the tribe of the people of Issachar was Nethanel the son of Zuar. ¹⁶And over the company of the tribe of the people of Zebulun was Eliab the son of Helon.

¹⁷And when the tabernacle was taken down, the sons of Gershon and the sons of Merari, who carried the tabernacle, set out. ¹⁸And the standard of the camp of Reuben set out by their companies, and over their company was Elizur the son of Shedeur. ¹⁹And over the company of the tribe of the people of Simeon was Shelumiel the son of Zurishaddai. ²⁰And over the company of the tribe of the people of Gad was Eliasaph the son of Deuel.

²¹Then the Kohathites set out, carrying the holy things, and the tabernacle was set up before their arrival. ²²And the standard of the camp of the people of Ephraim set out by their companies, and over their company was Elishama the son of Ammihud. ²³And over the company of the tribe of the people of Manasseh was Gamaliel the son of Pedahzur. ²⁴And over the company of the tribe of the people of Benjamin was Abidan the son of Gideoni.

²⁵Then the standard of the camp of the people of Dan, acting as the rear guard of all the camps, set out by their companies, and over their company was Ahiezer the son of Ammishaddai. ²⁶And over the company of the tribe of the people of Asher was Pagiel the son of Ochran. ²⁷And over the company of the tribe of the people of Naphtali was Ahira the son of Enan. ²⁸This was the order of march of the people of Israel by their companies, when they set out.

²⁹And Moses said to Hobab the son of Reuel the Midianite, Moses' father-in-law, "We are setting out for the place of which the LORD said, 'I will give it to you.' Come with us, and we will do good to you, for the LORD has promised good to Israel." ³⁰But he said to him, "I will not go. I will depart to my own land and to my kindred." ³¹And he said, "Please do not leave us, for you know where we should camp in the wilderness, and you will serve as eyes for us. ³²And if you do go with us, whatever good the LORD will do to us, the same will we do to you."

³³So they set out from the mount of the LORD three days' journey. And the ark of the covenant of the LORD went before them three days' journey, to seek out a resting place for them. ³⁴And the cloud of the LORD was over them by day, whenever they set out from the camp.

³⁵And whenever the ark set out, Moses said, "Arise, O LORD, and let your enemies be scattered, and let those who hate you flee before you." ³⁶And when it rested, he said, "Return, O LORD, to the ten thousand thousands of Israel."

The People Complain

11 And the people complained in the hearing of the LORD about their misfortunes, and when the LORD heard it, his anger was kindled, and the fire of the LORD burned among them and consumed some outlying parts of the camp. [2] Then the people cried out to Moses, and Moses prayed to the LORD, and the fire died down. [3] So the name of that place was called Taberah,[1] because the fire of the LORD burned among them.

[4] Now the rabble that was among them had a strong craving. And the people of Israel also wept again and said, "Oh that we had meat to eat! [5] We remember the fish we ate in Egypt that cost nothing, the cucumbers, the melons, the leeks, the onions, and the garlic. [6] But now our strength is dried up, and there is nothing at all but this manna to look at."

[7] Now the manna was like coriander seed, and its appearance like that of bdellium. [8] The people went about and gathered it

---

[1] *Taberah* means *burning*

---

and ground it in handmills or beat it in mortars and boiled it in pots and made cakes of it. And the taste of it was like the taste of cakes baked with oil. [9] When the dew fell upon the camp in the night, the manna fell with it.

[10] Moses heard the people weeping throughout their clans, everyone at the door of his tent. And the anger of the LORD blazed hotly, and Moses was displeased. [11] Moses said to the LORD, "Why have you dealt ill with your servant? And why have I not found favor in your sight, that you lay the burden of all this people on me? [12] Did I conceive all this people? Did I give them birth, that you should say to me, 'Carry them in your bosom, as a nurse carries a nursing child,' to the land that you swore to give their fathers? [13] Where am I to get meat to give to all this people? For they weep before me and say, 'Give us meat, that we may eat.' [14] I am not able to carry all this people alone; the burden is too heavy for me. [15] If you will treat me like this, kill me at

---

Know Yourself

verses to read
Numbers 11:10–15

The normal human reaction to failure is despair. You feel like there's no way to fix the mess you've found yourself in, so like Moses you say, "It's all over. I might as well give up now." But you can't let that despair beat you. You have to realize that there's nothing special about your particular drama. Missing an opportunity to do something right is a really ordinary thing that happens to all of us. If you ignore that and think something tremendously unique has happened to you, you're probably going to sink into the pit of despair and not know how to get out, or even be willing to. The solution is in Jesus' words to his disciples, who were just as depressed about their lot in life. He said, "In the world you will have tribulation. But take heart; I have overcome the world" (John 16:33).

So what's the next thing in your life? What is Jesus calling you to get over and to get on with? If you wallow in your past and refuse to move on, you dishonor the Lord by closing your heart to his incredible promises, and you will probably fail all over again. Only when you trust him enough to get moving do you lessen the sting and the power of your past failure.

If you don't know what the next thing for you is, then let it be this and this alone: to trust Jesus completely and to pray continually. Then ultimately you can know that he works all things together for good—even your failures (see Rom. 8:28). By doing these things, you let this failure move you forward into his loving arms instead of backward into hopeless despair.

nce, if I find favor in your sight, that I may not see my wretchedness."

Elders Appointed to Aid Moses

[16] Then the LORD said to Moses, "Gather for me seventy men of the elders of Israel, whom you know to be the elders of the people and officers over them, and bring them to the tent of meeting, and let them take their stand there with you. [17] And I will come down and talk with you there. And I will take some of the Spirit that is on you and put it on them, and they shall bear the burden of the people with you, so that you may not bear it yourself alone. [18] And say to the people, 'Consecrate yourselves for tomorrow, and you shall eat meat, for you have wept in the hearing of the LORD, saying, "Who will give us meat to eat? For it was better for us in Egypt." Therefore the LORD will give you meat, and you shall eat. [19] You shall not eat just one day, or two days, or five days, or ten days, or twenty days, [20] but a whole month, until it comes out at your nostrils and becomes loathsome to you, because you have rejected the LORD who is among you and have wept before him, saying, "Why did we come out of Egypt?" ' " [21] But Moses said, "The people among whom I am number six hundred thousand on foot, and you have said, 'I will give them meat, that they may eat a whole month!' [22] Shall flocks and herds be slaughtered for them, and be enough for them? Or shall all the fish of the sea be gathered together for them, and be enough for them?" [23] And the LORD said to Moses, "Is the LORD's hand shortened? Now you shall see whether my word will come true for you or not."

[24] So Moses went out and told the people the words of the LORD. And he gathered seventy men of the elders of the people and placed them around the tent. [25] Then the LORD came down in the cloud and spoke to him, and took some of the Spirit that was on him and put it on the seventy elders. And as soon as the Spirit rested on them, they prophesied. But they did not continue doing it.

[26] Now two men remained in the camp, one named Eldad, and the other named Medad, and the Spirit rested on them. They were among those registered, but they had not gone out to the tent, and so they prophesied in the camp. [27] And a young man ran and told Moses, "Eldad and Medad are prophesying in the camp." [28] And Joshua the son of Nun, the assistant of Moses from his youth, said, "My lord Moses, stop them." [29] But Moses said to him, "Are you jealous for my sake? Would that all the LORD's people were prophets, that the LORD would put his Spirit on them!" [30] And Moses and the elders of Israel returned to the camp.

Quail and a Plague

[31] Then a wind from the LORD sprang up, and it brought quail from the sea and let them fall beside the camp, about a day's journey on this side and a day's journey on the other side, around the camp, and about two cubits[1] above the ground. [32] And the people rose all that day and all night and all the next day, and gathered the quail. Those who gathered least gathered ten homers.[2] And they spread them out for themselves all around the camp. [33] While the meat was yet between their teeth, before it was consumed, the anger of the LORD was kindled against the people, and the LORD struck down the people with a very great plague. [34] Therefore the name of that place was called Kibroth-hattaavah,[3] because there they buried the people who had the craving. [35] From Kibroth-hattaavah the people journeyed to Hazeroth, and they remained at Hazeroth.

Miriam and Aaron Oppose Moses

12 Miriam and Aaron spoke against Moses because of the Cushite woman whom he had married, for he had married a Cushite woman. [2] And they said, "Has the LORD indeed spoken only through Moses? Has he not spoken through us also?" And the LORD heard it. [3] Now the man Moses was very meek, more than all people who were on the face of the earth. [4] And suddenly the LORD said to Moses and to Aaron and Miriam, "Come out, you three, to the tent of meeting." And the three of them came out. [5] And the LORD came down in a pillar of cloud and stood at the entrance of the tent and called Aaron and Miriam, and they both came forward. [6] And he said, "Hear my words: If there is a prophet among you, I the LORD make

---

[1] A *cubit* was about 18 inches or 45 centimeters [2] A *homer* was about 6 bushels or 220 liters [3] *Kibroth-hattaavah* means *graves of craving*

Miriam

Read this God Girl story in Exodus 2:1–10;
15:20–21; Numbers 12:1–15; and 20:1.

> Miriam and Aaron spoke against Moses. . . . And they said, "Has
> the LORD indeed spoken only through Moses? Has he not spoken
> through us also?" And the LORD heard it.
>
> Numbers 12:1–2

No matter how close someone is to God and no matter how wise they are,
they are not immune to sin. Some of the greatest men and women of God
have found themselves faced with the fact that they royally messed up. And
Miriam is one of them. Miriam, the sister of Moses, the one who watched his
mother put him in that basket and into the river to be found by the Pharaoh's
daughter, grew up to become a prophetess, one who was gifted by God to
tell people God's thoughts. She loved God and served him well, but she also
sinned. Her jealousy and complaint were heard by God, and because of that
she suffered (see Num. 12:1–15).

Like Miriam, we all have the tendency to think more highly of ourselves
than we should. It's easy to look around you and say, "Why does God use
them for his work when I'm just as willing to be used?" But the complaint
you express isn't against other people so much as it is against God. As a
God Girl you must beware of criticizing God. And you must also be aware
that your sin is nothing new. When you sin, be quick to confess it and to
turn away from it, but don't let it become the end of your story. Don't let it
be the thing you are most remembered for. The way to do that is to move
forward in faith and obedience. Listen to what God wants; read his Word and
make it a part of your today from now on. Don't look back. Look forward
and keep your eye on the prize, Jesus himself, and your life will be of good
service to the King.

myself known to him in a vision; I speak with him in a dream. [7] Not so with my servant Moses. He is faithful in all my house. [3] With him I speak mouth to mouth, clearly, and not in riddles, and he beholds the form of the LORD. Why then were you not afraid to speak against my servant Moses?" [9] And the anger of the LORD was kindled against them, and he departed.

[10] When the cloud removed from over the tent, behold, Miriam was leprous,[1] like snow. And Aaron turned toward Miriam, and behold, she was leprous. [11] And Aaron said to Moses, "Oh, my lord, do not punish us[2] because we have done foolishly and have sinned. [12] Let her not be as one dead, whose flesh is half eaten away when he comes out of his mother's womb." [13] And Moses cried to the LORD, "O God, please heal her—please." [14] But the LORD said to Moses, "If her father had but spit in her face, should she not be shamed seven days? Let her be shut outside the camp seven days, and after that she may be brought in again." [15] So Miriam was shut outside the camp seven days, and the people did not set out on the march till Miriam was brought in again. [16] After that the people set out from Hazeroth, and camped in the wilderness of Paran.

Spies Sent into Canaan

13 The LORD spoke to Moses, saying, [2] "Send men to spy out the land of Canaan, which I am giving to the people of Israel. From each tribe of their fathers you shall send a man, every one a chief among them." [3] So Moses sent them from the wilderness of Paran, according to the command of the LORD, all of them men who were heads of the people of Israel. [4] And these were their names: From the tribe of Reuben, Shammua the son of Zaccur; [5] from the tribe of Simeon, Shaphat the son of Hori; [6] from the tribe of Judah, Caleb the son of Jephunneh; [7] from the tribe of Issachar, Igal the son of Joseph; [8] from the tribe of Ephraim, Hoshea the son of Nun; [9] from the tribe of Benjamin, Palti the son of Raphu; [10] from the tribe of Zebulun, Gaddiel the son of Sodi; [11] from the tribe of Joseph (that is, from the tribe of Manasseh), Gaddi the son of Susi; [12] from the tribe of Dan, Ammiel the son of Gemalli; [13] from the tribe of Asher, Sethur the son of Michael;

[14] from the tribe of Naphtali, Nahbi the son of Vophsi; [15] from the tribe of Gad, Geuel the son of Machi. [16] These were the names of the men whom Moses sent to spy out the land. And Moses called Hoshea the son of Nun Joshua.

[17] Moses sent them to spy out the land of Canaan and said to them, "Go up into the Negeb and go up into the hill country, [18] and see what the land is, and whether the people who dwell in it are strong or weak, whether they are few or many, [19] and whether the land that they dwell in is good or bad, and whether the cities that they dwell in are camps or strongholds, [20] and whether the land is rich or poor, and whether there are trees in it or not. Be of good courage and bring some of the fruit of the land." Now the time was the season of the first ripe grapes.

[21] So they went up and spied out the land from the wilderness of Zin to Rehob, near Lebo-hamath. [22] They went up into the Negeb and came to Hebron. Ahiman, Sheshai, and Talmai, the descendants of Anak, were there. (Hebron was built seven years before Zoan in Egypt.) [23] And they came to the Valley of Eshcol and cut down from there a branch with a single cluster of grapes, and they carried it on a pole between two of them; they also brought some pomegranates and figs. [24] That place was called the Valley of Eshcol,[3] because of the cluster that the people of Israel cut down from there.

Report of the Spies

[25] At the end of forty days they returned from spying out the land. [26] And they came to Moses and Aaron and to all the congregation of the people of Israel in the wilderness of Paran, at Kadesh. They brought back word to them and to all the congregation, and showed them the fruit of the land. [27] And they told him, "We came to the land to which you sent us. It flows with milk and honey, and this is its fruit. [28] However, the people who dwell in the land are strong, and the cities are fortified and very large. And besides, we saw the descendants of Anak there. [29] The Amalekites dwell in the land of the Negeb. The Hittites, the Jebusites, and the Amorites dwell in the hill country. And the Canaanites dwell by the sea, and along the Jordan."

[1] *Leprosy* was a term for several skin diseases; see Leviticus 13 [2] Hebrew *do not lay sin upon us* [3] *Eshcol* means *cluster*

³⁰ But Caleb quieted the people before Moses and said, "Let us go up at once and occupy it, for we are well able to overcome it." ³¹ Then the men who had gone up with him said, "We are not able to go up against the people, for they are stronger than we are." ³² So they brought to the people of Israel a bad report of the land that they had spied out, saying, "The land, through which we have gone to spy it out, is a land that devours its inhabitants, and all the people that we saw in it are of great height. ³³ And there we saw the Nephilim (the sons of Anak, who come from the Nephilim), and we seemed to ourselves like grasshoppers, and so we seemed to them."

The People Rebel

14 Then all the congregation raised a loud cry, and the people wept that night. ² And all the people of Israel grumbled against Moses and Aaron. The whole congregation said to them, "Would that we had died in the land of Egypt! Or would that we had died in this wilderness! ³ Why is the LORD bringing us into this land, to fall by the sword? Our wives and our little ones will become a prey. Would it not be better for us to go back to Egypt?" ⁴ And they said to one another, "Let us choose a leader and go back to Egypt."

⁵ Then Moses and Aaron fell on their faces before all the assembly of the congregation of the people of Israel. ⁶ And Joshua the son of Nun and Caleb the son of Jephunneh, who were among those who had spied out the land, tore their clothes ⁷ and said to all the congregation of the people of Israel, "The land, which we passed through to spy it out, is an exceedingly good land. ⁸ If the LORD delights in us, he will bring us into this land and give it to us, a land that flows with milk and honey. ⁹ Only do not rebel against the LORD. And do not fear the people of the land, for they are bread for us. Their protection is removed from them, and the LORD is with us; do not fear them." ¹⁰ Then all the con-

Know God

verses to read
Numbers 14:17–19

God's law says that when parents sin, those sins will be punished for generations to come. And so if one parent serves the idol of drunkenness, you see that pattern repeated for generations. Sin seems to be passed on in the DNA, but that doesn't have to be the case for you.

As a God Girl, you are no longer a slave to sin. You're no longer controlled by its power. While some children may continue on in the sinful ways of their parents, forever condemned to a life of bondage, you, God Girl, are now set free. Jesus came to set the captives free, and that means even you who used to be captive to the sins of your family. You might not have realized you're free, and you might have been living under the deception that your parents' sins will be your own, but that is rubbish. The price for those sins in your DNA has been paid. You are no longer living under the curse, because "Christ redeemed us from the curse of the law by becoming a curse for us" (Gal. 3:13).

When you read the Old Testament, you also have to take into consideration the New Testament. Yes, God curses the kids of sinners, but he also offers freedom from the curse to all those who are willing to repent and surrender to Jesus as the Lord of their lives. If there's a familial sin in your family, confess that sin as if it were your own, and then promise God that you will turn from it and never do it, trusting him for grace and strength to do so. You can be sure that, as you do, you will be set free from the curse and given a new life in the area where your family has previously been in bondage.

gregation said to stone them with stones. But the glory of the LORD appeared at the ent of meeting to all the people of Israel.

¹¹ And the LORD said to Moses, "How long vill this people despise me? And how long vill they not believe in me, in spite of all he signs that I have done among them? ² I will strike them with the pestilence and lisinherit them, and I will make of you nation greater and mightier than they."

Moses Intercedes for the People

¹³ But Moses said to the LORD, "Then the Egyptians will hear of it, for you brought p this people in your might from among hem, ¹⁴ and they will tell the inhabitants f this land. They have heard that you,) LORD, are in the midst of this people. 'or you, O LORD, are seen face to face, and 'our cloud stands over them and you go)efore them, in a pillar of cloud by day and n a pillar of fire by night. ¹⁵ Now if you kill his people as one man, then the nations vho have heard your fame will say, ¹⁶ 'It is)ecause the LORD was not able to bring this)eople into the land that he swore to give o them that he has killed them in the wil- lerness.' ¹⁷ And now, please let the power of the Lord be great as you have promised, ;aying, ¹⁸ 'The LORD is slow to anger and ıbounding in steadfast love, forgiving iniq- uity and transgression, but he will by no neans clear the guilty, visiting the iniquity of the fathers on the children, to the third ınd the fourth generation.' ¹⁹ Please pardon he iniquity of this people, according to the ;reatness of your steadfast love, just as 'ou have forgiven this people, from Egypt until now."

God Promises Judgment

²⁰ Then the LORD said, "I have pardoned, ıccording to your word. ²¹ But truly, as live, and as all the earth shall be filled with he glory of the LORD, ²² none of the men vho have seen my glory and my signs that did in Egypt and in the wilderness, and 'et have put me to the test these ten times ınd have not obeyed my voice, ²³ shall see he land that I swore to give to their fathers. And none of those who despised me shall ;ee it. ²⁴ But my servant Caleb, because he ıas a different spirit and has followed me ully, I will bring into the land into which ıe went, and his descendants shall pos- ;ess it. ²⁵ Now, since the Amalekites and

the Canaanites dwell in the valleys, turn tomorrow and set out for the wilderness by the way to the Red Sea."

Ask Yourself . . .

ABOUT YOUR FAMILY SIN

Familial sin is a real thing. It is bad habits, obsessions, and addictions that are passed on from generation to generation. Ask yourself:

- Do I see any familial sins when I look at my family?
- Do I have a problem with the same thing?
- Have I confessed the sin for myself and my family?
- How can I break the cycle of familial sin?

²⁶ And the LORD spoke to Moses and to Aaron, saying, ²⁷ "How long shall this wicked congregation grumble against me? I have heard the grumblings of the people of Israel, which they grumble against me. ²⁸ Say to them, 'As I live, declares the LORD, what you have said in my hearing I will do to you: ²⁹ your dead bodies shall fall in this wilderness, and of all your number, listed in the census from twenty years old and upward, who have grumbled against me, ³⁰ not one shall come into the land where I swore that I would make you dwell, except Caleb the son of Jephunneh and Joshua the son of Nun. ³¹ But your little ones, who you said would become a prey, I will bring in, and they shall know the land that you have rejected. ³² But as for you, your dead bod- ies shall fall in this wilderness. ³³ And your children shall be shepherds in the wilder- ness forty years and shall suffer for your faithlessness, until the last of your dead bodies lies in the wilderness. ³⁴ According to the number of the days in which you spied out the land, forty days, a year for each day, you shall bear your iniquity forty years, and you shall know my displeasure.' ³⁵ I, the LORD, have spoken. Surely this will

I do to all this wicked congregation who are gathered together against me: in this wilderness they shall come to a full end, and there they shall die."

³⁶ And the men whom Moses sent to spy out the land, who returned and made all the congregation grumble against him by bringing up a bad report about the land— ³⁷ the men who brought up a bad report of the land— died by plague before the LORD. ³⁸ Of those men who went to spy out the land, only Joshua the son of Nun and Caleb the son of Jephunneh remained alive.

Israel Defeated in Battle

³⁹ When Moses told these words to all the people of Israel, the people mourned greatly. ⁴⁰ And they rose early in the morning and went up to the heights of the hill country, saying, "Here we are. We will go up to the place that the LORD has promised, for we have sinned." ⁴¹ But Moses said, "Why now are you transgressing the command of the LORD, when that will not succeed? ⁴² Do not go up, for the Lord is not among you, lest you be struck down before your enemies. ⁴³ For there the Amalekites and the Canaanites are facing you, and you shall fall by the sword. Because you have turned back from following the LORD, the LORD will not be with you." ⁴⁴ But they presumed to go up to the heights of the hill country, although neither the ark of the covenant of the LORD nor Moses departed out of the camp. ⁴⁵ Then the Amalekites and the Canaanites who lived in that hill country came down and defeated them and pursued them, even to Hormah.

Laws About Sacrifices

15 The LORD spoke to Moses, saying, ² "Speak to the people of Israel and say to them, When you come into the land you are to inhabit, which I am giving you, ³ and you offer to the LORD from the herd or from the flock a food offering[1] or a burnt offering or a sacrifice, to fulfill a vow or as a freewill offering or at your appointed feasts, to make a pleasing aroma to the LORD, ⁴ then he who brings his offering shall offer to the LORD a grain offering of a tenth of an ephah[2] of fine flour, mixed with a quarter of a hin[3] of oil; ⁵ and you shall offer with the burnt offering, or for

the sacrifice, a quarter of a hin of wine for the drink offering for each lamb. ⁶ Or for a ram, you shall offer for a grain offering two tenths of an ephah of fine flour mixed with a third of a hin of oil. ⁷ And for the drink offering you shall offer a third of a hin of wine, a pleasing aroma to the LORD. ⁸ And when you offer a bull as a burnt offering or sacrifice, to fulfill a vow or for peace offerings to the LORD, ⁹ then one shall offer with the bull a grain offering of three tenths of an ephah of fine flour, mixed with half a hin of oil. ¹⁰ And you shall offer for the drink offering half a hin of wine, as a food offering, a pleasing aroma to the LORD.

¹¹ "Thus it shall be done for each bull or ram, or for each lamb or young goat. ¹² As many as you offer, so shall you do with each one, as many as there are. ¹³ Every native Israelite shall do these things in this way, in offering a food offering, with a pleasing aroma to the LORD. ¹⁴ And if a stranger is sojourning with you, or anyone is living permanently among you, and he wishes to offer a food offering, with a pleasing aroma to the LORD, he shall do as you do. ¹⁵ For the assembly, there shall be one statute for you and for the stranger who sojourns with you, a statute forever throughout your generations. You and the sojourner shall be alike before the LORD. ¹⁶ One law and one rule shall be for you and for the stranger who sojourns with you."

¹⁷ The LORD spoke to Moses, saying, ¹⁸ "Speak to the people of Israel and say to them, When you come into the land to which I bring you ¹⁹ and when you eat of the bread of the land, you shall present a contribution to the LORD. ²⁰ Of the first of your dough you shall present a loaf as a contribution; like a contribution from the threshing floor, so shall you present it. ²¹ Some of the first of your dough you shall give to the LORD as a contribution throughout your generations.

Laws About Unintentional Sins

²² "But if you sin unintentionally,[4] and do not observe all these commandments that the LORD has spoken to Moses, ²³ all that the LORD has commanded you by Moses, from the day that the LORD gave commandment, and onward throughout your generations, ²⁴ then if it was done unintentionally

---

[1] Or *an offering by fire*; so throughout Numbers [2] An *ephah* was about 3/5 bushel or 22 liters [3] A *hin* was about 4 quarts or 3.5 liters [4] Or *by mistake*; also verses 24, 27, 28, 29

without the knowledge of the congregation, all the congregation shall offer one
bull from the herd for a burnt offering, a
pleasing aroma to the LORD, with its grain
offering and its drink offering, according to
the rule, and one male goat for a sin offering. ²⁵And the priest shall make atonement
for all the congregation of the people of
Israel, and they shall be forgiven, because
it was a mistake, and they have brought
their offering, a food offering to the LORD,
and their sin offering before the LORD for
their mistake. ²⁶And all the congregation
of the people of Israel shall be forgiven,
and the stranger who sojourns among
them, because the whole population was
involved in the mistake.

²⁷"If one person sins unintentionally, he
shall offer a female goat a year old for a sin
offering. ²⁸And the priest shall make atonement before the LORD for the person who
makes a mistake, when he sins unintentionally, to make atonement for him, and he
shall be forgiven. ²⁹You shall have one law
for him who does anything unintentionally,
for him who is native among the people of
Israel and for the stranger who sojourns
among them. ³⁰But the person who does
anything with a high hand, whether he is
native or a sojourner, reviles the LORD, and
that person shall be cut off from among
his people. ³¹Because he has despised the
word of the LORD and has broken his commandment, that person shall be utterly cut
off; his iniquity shall be on him."

A Sabbathbreaker Executed

³²While the people of Israel were in the
wilderness, they found a man gathering
sticks on the Sabbath day. ³³And those who
found him gathering sticks brought him to
Moses and Aaron and to all the congrega-
tion. ³⁴They put him in custody, because it
had not been made clear what should be
done to him. ³⁵And the LORD said to Moses,
"The man shall be put to death; all the
congregation shall stone him with stones
outside the camp." ³⁶And all the congregation brought him outside the camp and
stoned him to death with stones, as the
LORD commanded Moses.

Tassels on Garments

³⁷The LORD said to Moses, ³⁸"Speak to
the people of Israel, and tell them to make
tassels on the corners of their garments
throughout their generations, and to put
a cord of blue on the tassel of each corner.
³⁹And it shall be a tassel for you to look at
and remember all the commandments of
the LORD, to do them, not to follow[1] after
your own heart and your own eyes, which
you are inclined to whore after. ⁴⁰So you
shall remember and do all my command-
ments, and be holy to your God. ⁴¹I am the
LORD your God, who brought you out of
the land of Egypt to be your God: I am the
LORD your God."

Korah's Rebellion

16 Now Korah the son of Izhar, son of
Kohath, son of Levi, and Dathan and
Abiram the sons of Eliab, and On the son
of Peleth, sons of Reuben, took men. ²And
they rose up before Moses, with a number
of the people of Israel, 250 chiefs of the
congregation, chosen from the assembly,
well-known men. ³They assembled themselves together against Moses and against
Aaron and said to them, "You have gone
too far! For all in the congregation are holy,
every one of them, and the LORD is among
them. Why then do you exalt yourselves
above the assembly of the LORD?" ⁴When
Moses heard it, he fell on his face, ⁵and
he said to Korah and all his company, "In
the morning the LORD will show who is
his,[2] and who is holy, and will bring him
near to him. The one whom he chooses he
will bring near to him. ⁶Do this: take censers, Korah and all his company; ⁷put fire
in them and put incense on them before
the LORD tomorrow, and the man whom
the LORD chooses shall be the holy one.
You have gone too far, sons of Levi!" ⁸And
Moses said to Korah, "Hear now, you sons
of Levi: ⁹is it too small a thing for you that
the God of Israel has separated you from
the congregation of Israel, to bring you
near to himself, to do service in the tabernacle of the LORD and to stand before the
congregation to minister to them, ¹⁰and
that he has brought you near him, and all
your brothers the sons of Levi with you?
And would you seek the priesthood also?
¹¹Therefore it is against the LORD that
you and all your company have gathered
together. What is Aaron that you grumble
against him?"

¹Hebrew to spy out ²Septuagint The LORD knows those who are his

¹²And Moses sent to call Dathan and Abiram the sons of Eliab, and they said, "We will not come up. ¹³Is it a small thing that you have brought us up out of a land flowing with milk and honey, to kill us in the wilderness, that you must also make yourself a prince over us? ¹⁴Moreover, you have not brought us into a land flowing with milk and honey, nor given us inheritance of fields and vineyards. Will you put out the eyes of these men? We will not come up." ¹⁵And Moses was very angry and said to the LORD, "Do not respect their offering. I have not taken one donkey from them, and I have not harmed one of them."

¹⁶And Moses said to Korah, "Be present, you and all your company, before the LORD, you and they, and Aaron, tomorrow. ¹⁷And let every one of you take his censer and put incense on it, and every one of you bring before the LORD his censer, 250 censers; you also, and Aaron, each his censer." ¹⁸So every man took his censer and put fire in them and laid incense on them and stood at the entrance of the tent of meeting with Moses and Aaron. ¹⁹Then Korah assembled all the congregation against them at the entrance of the tent of meeting. And the glory of the LORD appeared to all the congregation.

²⁰And the LORD spoke to Moses and to Aaron, saying, ²¹"Separate yourselves from among this congregation, that I may consume them in a moment." ²²And they fell on their faces and said, "O God, the God of the spirits of all flesh, shall one man sin, and will you be angry with all the congregation?" ²³And the LORD spoke to Moses, saying, ²⁴"Say to the congregation, Get away from the dwelling of Korah, Dathan, and Abiram."

²⁵Then Moses rose and went to Dathan and Abiram, and the elders of Israel followed him. ²⁶And he spoke to the congregation, saying, "Depart, please, from the tents of these wicked men, and touch nothing of theirs, lest you be swept away with all their sins." ²⁷So they got away from the dwelling of Korah, Dathan, and Abiram. And Dathan and Abiram came out and stood at the door of their tents, together with their wives, their sons, and their little ones. ²⁸And Moses said, "Hereby you shall know that the LORD has sent me to do all these works, and that it has not been of my own accord. ²⁹If these men die as all men die, or if they are visited by the fate of all mankind, then the LORD has not sent me. ³⁰But if the LORD creates something new, and the ground opens its mouth and swallows them up with all that belongs to them, and they go down alive into Sheol, then you shall know that these men have despised the LORD."

³¹And as soon as he had finished speaking all these words, the ground under them split apart. ³²And the earth opened its mouth and swallowed them up, with their households and all the people who belonged to Korah and all their goods. ³³So they and all that belonged to them went down alive into Sheol, and the earth closed over them, and they perished from the midst of the assembly. ³⁴And all Israel who were around them fled at their cry, for they said, "Lest the earth swallow us up!" ³⁵And fire came out from the LORD and consumed the 250 men offering the incense.

³⁶¹ Then the LORD spoke to Moses, saying, ³⁷"Tell Eleazar the son of Aaron the priest to take up the censers out of the blaze. Then scatter the fire far and wide, for they have become holy. ³⁸As for the censers of these men who have sinned at the cost of their lives, let them be made into hammered plates as a covering for the altar, for they offered them before the LORD, and they became holy. Thus they shall be a sign to the people of Israel." ³⁹So Eleazar the priest took the bronze censers, which those who were burned had offered, and they were hammered out as a covering for the altar, ⁴⁰to be a reminder to the people of Israel, so that no outsider who is not of the descendants of Aaron should draw near to burn incense before the LORD, lest he become like Korah and his company—as the LORD said to him through Moses.

⁴¹But on the next day all the congregation of the people of Israel grumbled against Moses and against Aaron, saying, "You have killed the people of the LORD." ⁴²And when the congregation had assembled against Moses and against Aaron, they turned toward the tent of meeting. And behold, the cloud covered it, and the glory of the LORD appeared. ⁴³And Moses and Aaron came to the front of the tent of meeting, ⁴⁴and the LORD spoke to Moses, saying, ⁴⁵"Get away

from the midst of this congregation, that I may consume them in a moment." And they fell on their faces. ⁴⁶ And Moses said to Aaron, "Take your censer, and put fire on it from off the altar and lay incense on it and carry it quickly to the congregation and make atonement for them, for wrath has gone out from the Lord; the plague has begun." ⁴⁷ So Aaron took it as Moses said and ran into the midst of the assembly. And behold, the plague had already begun among the people. And he put on the incense and made atonement for the people. ⁴⁸ And he stood between the dead and the living, and the plague was stopped. ⁴⁹ Now those who died in the plague were 14,700, besides those who died in the affair of Korah. ⁵⁰ And Aaron returned to Moses at the entrance of the tent of meeting, when the plague was stopped.

Aaron's Staff Buds

17 ¹ The Lord spoke to Moses, saying, ² "Speak to the people of Israel, and get from them staffs, one for each fathers' house, from all their chiefs according to their fathers' houses, twelve staffs. Write each man's name on his staff, ³ and write Aaron's name on the staff of Levi. For there shall be one staff for the head of each fathers' house. ⁴ Then you shall deposit them in the tent of meeting before the testimony, where I meet with you. ⁵ And the staff of the man whom I choose shall sprout. Thus I will make to cease from me the grumblings of the people of Israel, which they grumble against you." ⁶ Moses spoke to the people of Israel. And all their chiefs gave him staffs, one for each chief, according to their fathers' houses, twelve staffs. And the staff of Aaron was among their staffs. ⁷ And Moses deposited the staffs before the Lord in the tent of the testimony.

⁸ On the next day Moses went into the tent of the testimony, and behold, the staff of Aaron for the house of Levi had sprouted and put forth buds and produced blossoms, and it bore ripe almonds. ⁹ Then Moses brought out all the staffs from before the Lord to all the people of Israel. And they looked, and each man took his staff. ¹⁰ And the Lord said to Moses, "Put back the staff of Aaron before the testimony, to be kept as a sign for the rebels, that you may make

an end of their grumblings against me, lest they die." ¹¹ Thus did Moses; as the Lord commanded him, so he did.

¹² And the people of Israel said to Moses, "Behold, we perish, we are undone, we are all undone. ¹³ Everyone who comes near, who comes near to the tabernacle of the Lord, shall die. Are we all to perish?"

Duties of Priests and Levites

18 ¹ So the Lord said to Aaron, "You and your sons and your father's house with you shall bear iniquity connected with the sanctuary, and you and your sons with you shall bear iniquity connected with your priesthood. ² And with you bring your brothers also, the tribe of Levi, the tribe of your father, that they may join you and minister to you while you and your sons with you are before the tent of the testimony. ³ They shall keep guard over you and over the whole tent, but shall not come near to the vessels of the sanctuary or to the altar lest they, and you, die. ⁴ They shall join you and keep guard over the tent of meeting for all the service of the tent, and no outsider shall come near you. ⁵ And you shall keep guard over the sanctuary and over the altar, that there may never again be wrath on the people of Israel. ⁶ And behold, I have taken your brothers the Levites from among the people of Israel. They are a gift to you, given to the Lord, to do the service of the tent of meeting. ⁷ And you and your sons with you shall guard your priesthood for all that concerns the altar and that is within the veil; and you shall serve. I give your priesthood as a gift,² and any outsider who comes near shall be put to death."

⁸ Then the Lord spoke to Aaron, "Behold, I have given you charge of the contributions made to me, all the consecrated things of the people of Israel. I have given them to you as a portion and to your sons as a perpetual due. ⁹ This shall be yours of the most holy things, reserved from the fire: every offering of theirs, every grain offering of theirs and every sin offering of theirs and every guilt offering of theirs, which they render to me, shall be most holy to you and to your sons. ¹⁰ In a most holy place shall you eat it. Every male may eat it; it is holy to you. ¹¹ This also is yours: the contribution of their gift, all the wave

---

¹ Ch 17:16 in Hebrew ² Hebrew *service of gift*

offerings of the people of Israel. I have given them to you, and to your sons and daughters with you, as a perpetual due. Everyone who is clean in your house may eat it. [12] All the best of the oil and all the best of the wine and of the grain, the firstfruits of what they give to the LORD, I give to you. [13] The first ripe fruits of all that is in their land, which they bring to the LORD, shall be yours. Everyone who is clean in your house may eat it. [14] Every devoted thing in Israel shall be yours. [15] Everything that opens the womb of all flesh, whether man or beast, which they offer to the LORD, shall be yours. Nevertheless, the firstborn of man you shall redeem, and the firstborn of unclean animals you shall redeem. [16] And their redemption price (at a month old you shall redeem them) you shall fix at five shekels[1] in silver, according to the shekel of the sanctuary, which is twenty gerahs. [17] But the firstborn of a cow, or the firstborn of a sheep, or the firstborn of a goat, you shall not redeem; they are holy. You shall sprinkle their blood on the altar and shall burn their fat as a food offering, with a pleasing aroma to the LORD. [18] But their flesh shall be yours, as the breast that is waved and as the right thigh are yours. [19] All the holy contributions that the people of Israel present to the LORD I give to you, and to your sons and daughters with you, as a perpetual due. It is a covenant of salt forever before the LORD for you and for your offspring with you." [20] And the LORD said to Aaron, "You shall have no inheritance in their land, neither shall you have any portion among them. I am your portion and your inheritance among the people of Israel.

[21] "To the Levites I have given every tithe in Israel for an inheritance, in return for their service that they do, their service in the tent of meeting, [22] so that the people of Israel do not come near the tent of meeting, lest they bear sin and die. [23] But the Levites shall do the service of the tent of meeting, and they shall bear their iniquity. It shall be a perpetual statute throughout your generations, and among the people of Israel they shall have no inheritance. [24] For the tithe of the people of Israel, which they present as a contribution to the LORD, I have given to the Levites for an inheritance. Therefore I have said of them that

they shall have no inheritance among the people of Israel."

[25] And the LORD spoke to Moses, saying, [26] "Moreover, you shall speak and say to the Levites, 'When you take from the people of Israel the tithe that I have given you from them for your inheritance, then you shall present a contribution from it to the LORD, a tithe of the tithe. [27] And your contribution shall be counted to you as though it were the grain of the threshing floor, and as the fullness of the winepress. [28] So you shall also present a contribution to the LORD from all your tithes, which you receive from the people of Israel. And from it you shall give the LORD's contribution to Aaron the priest. [29] Out of all the gifts to you, you shall present every contribution due to the LORD; from each its best part is to be dedicated.' [30] Therefore you shall say to them, 'When you have offered from it the best of it, then the rest shall be counted to the Levites as produce of the threshing floor, and as produce of the winepress. [31] And you may eat it in any place, you and your households, for it is your reward in return for your service in the tent of meeting. [32] And you shall bear no sin by reason of it, when you have contributed the best of it. But you shall not profane the holy things of the people of Israel, lest you die.'"

Laws for Purification

19 Now the LORD spoke to Moses and to Aaron, saying, [2] "This is the statute of the law that the LORD has commanded: Tell the people of Israel to bring you a red heifer without defect, in which there is no blemish, and on which a yoke has never come. [3] And you shall give it to Eleazar the priest, and it shall be taken outside the camp and slaughtered before him. [4] And Eleazar the priest shall take some of its blood with his finger, and sprinkle some of its blood toward the front of the tent of meeting seven times. [5] And the heifer shall be burned in his sight. Its skin, its flesh, and its blood, with its dung, shall be burned. [6] And the priest shall take cedarwood and hyssop and scarlet yarn, and throw them into the fire burning the heifer. [7] Then the priest shall wash his clothes and bathe his body in water, and afterward he may come into the camp. But the priest shall be unclean until evening. [8] The one

[1] A *shekel* was about 2/5 ounce or 11 grams

who burns the heifer shall wash his clothes in water and bathe his body in water and shall be unclean until evening. ⁹And a man who is clean shall gather up the ashes of the heifer and deposit them outside the camp in a clean place. And they shall be kept for the water for impurity for the congregation of the people of Israel; it is a sin offering. ¹⁰And the one who gathers the ashes of the heifer shall wash his clothes and be unclean until evening. And this shall be a perpetual statute for the people of Israel, and for the stranger who sojourns among them.

¹¹ "Whoever touches the dead body of any person shall be unclean seven days. ¹²He shall cleanse himself with the water on the third day and on the seventh day, and so be clean. But if he does not cleanse himself on the third day and on the seventh day, he will not become clean. ¹³Whoever touches a dead person, the body of anyone who has died, and does not cleanse himself, defiles the tabernacle of the LORD, and that person shall be cut off from Israel; because the water for impurity was not thrown on him, he shall be unclean. His uncleanness is still on him.

¹⁴ "This is the law when someone dies in a tent: everyone who comes into the tent and everyone who is in the tent shall be unclean seven days. ¹⁵And every open vessel that has no cover fastened on it is unclean. ¹⁶Whoever in the open field touches someone who was killed with a sword or who died naturally, or touches a human bone or a grave, shall be unclean seven days. ¹⁷For the unclean they shall take some ashes of the burnt sin offering, and fresh¹ water shall be added in a vessel. ¹⁸Then a clean person shall take hyssop and dip it in the water and sprinkle it on the tent and on all the furnishings and on the persons who were there and on whoever touched the bone, or the slain or the dead or the grave. ¹⁹And the clean person shall sprinkle it on the unclean on the third day and on the seventh day. Thus on the seventh day he shall cleanse him, and he shall wash his clothes and bathe himself in water, and at evening he shall be clean. ²⁰ "If the man who is unclean does not cleanse himself, that person shall be cut off from the midst of the assembly, since he has defiled the sanctuary of the LORD.

Because the water for impurity has not been thrown on him, he is unclean. ²¹And it shall be a statute forever for them. The one who sprinkles the water for impurity shall wash his clothes, and the one who touches the water for impurity shall be unclean until evening. ²²And whatever the unclean person touches shall be unclean, and anyone who touches it shall be unclean until evening."

The Death of Miriam

20 And the people of Israel, the whole congregation, came into the wilderness of Zin in the first month, and the people stayed in Kadesh. And Miriam died there and was buried there.

The Waters of Meribah

²Now there was no water for the congregation. And they assembled themselves together against Moses and against Aaron. ³And the people quarreled with Moses and said, "Would that we had perished when our brothers perished before the LORD! ⁴Why have you brought the assembly of the LORD into this wilderness, that we should die here, both we and our cattle? ⁵And why have you made us come up out of Egypt to bring us to this evil place? It is no place for grain or figs or vines or pomegranates, and there is no water to drink." ⁶Then Moses and Aaron went from the presence of the assembly to the entrance of the tent of meeting and fell on their faces. And the glory of the LORD appeared to them, ⁷and the LORD spoke to Moses, saying, ⁸ "Take the staff, and assemble the congregation, you and Aaron your brother, and tell the rock before their eyes to yield its water. So you shall bring water out of the rock for them and give drink to the congregation and their cattle." ⁹And Moses took the staff from before the LORD, as he commanded him.

Moses Strikes the Rock

¹⁰Then Moses and Aaron gathered the assembly together before the rock, and he said to them, "Hear now, you rebels: shall we bring water for you out of this rock?" ¹¹And Moses lifted up his hand and struck the rock with his staff twice, and water came out abundantly, and the congregation drank, and their livestock. ¹²And the LORD

---

¹ Hebrew *living*

said to Moses and Aaron, "Because you did not believe in me, to uphold me as holy in the eyes of the people of Israel, therefore you shall not bring this assembly into the land that I have given them." [13] These are the waters of Meribah,[1] where the people of Israel quarreled with the LORD, and through them he showed himself holy.

Edom Refuses Passage

[14] Moses sent messengers from Kadesh to the king of Edom: "Thus says your brother Israel: You know all the hardship that we have met: [15] how our fathers went down to Egypt, and we lived in Egypt a long time. And the Egyptians dealt harshly with us and our fathers. [16] And when we cried to the LORD, he heard our voice and sent an angel and brought us out of Egypt. And here we are in Kadesh, a city on the edge of your territory. [17] Please let us pass through your land. We will not pass through field or vineyard, or drink water from a well. We will go along the King's Highway. We will not turn aside to the right hand or to the left until we have passed through your territory." [18] But Edom said to him, "You shall not pass through, lest I come out with the sword against you." [19] And the people of Israel said to him, "We will go up by the highway, and if we drink of your water, I and my livestock, then I will pay for it. Let me only pass through on foot, nothing more." [20] But he said, "You shall not pass through." And Edom came out against them with a large army and with a strong force. [21] Thus Edom refused to give Israel passage through his territory, so Israel turned away from him.

The Death of Aaron

[22] And they journeyed from Kadesh, and the people of Israel, the whole congrega-

[1] Meribah means quarreling

Know God

verses to read
Numbers 20:2–5

God never does anything stupid. What he does might seem crazy, like taking you out of a perfectly good job as a slave and moving you into the middle of the desert with nothing to eat but manna. But it's not stupid. God has a plan. And when you complain about your circumstances, you're not trusting God's wisdom, kindness, and love.

The Israelites were saved from bondage to the Egyptians, yet still they wondered if God had saved them just to kill them. Even after seeing so many miracles (the parting of the Red Sea alone should have been proof of God's hand in their lives!), they still refused to trust that God could protect them and save them.

When your life seems hopeless and your world is a barren desert, remember the Israelites. Remember that they could only see today, not tomorrow or the next day. They didn't know what God had in store. And they weren't considering that God's best was far better than anything the world could have offered.

Even if you have to live in the desert for a time, trust him. After all, how weak is your faith if you trust him only in the garden or on the high mountaintop? No, trust is most commendable when it is practiced in the face of adversity. Each trial you live through is your chance to grow in faith and to know God better. Use it—don't lose it by complaining about where you are or what you are being told to do, like the Israelites did. Maybe if they had learned to trust sooner, that first generation would have made it to the Promised Land. Instead they wandered around for the rest of their lives, only to leave the Land of Promise to their children (see Num. 14:22–23). Don't make that same mistake. Learn to trust today.

tion, came to Mount Hor. 23 And the LORD said to Moses and Aaron at Mount Hor, on the border of the land of Edom, 24 "Let Aaron be gathered to his people, for he shall not enter the land that I have given to the people of Israel, because you rebelled against my command at the waters of Meribah. 25 Take Aaron and Eleazar his son and bring them up to Mount Hor. 26 And strip Aaron of his garments and put them on Eleazar his son. And Aaron shall be gathered to his people and shall die there." 27 Moses did as the LORD commanded. And they went up Mount Hor in the sight of all the congregation. 28 And Moses stripped Aaron of his garments and put them on Eleazar his son. And Aaron died there on the top of the mountain. Then Moses and Eleazar came down from the mountain. 29 And when all the congregation saw that Aaron had perished, all the house of Israel wept for Aaron thirty days.

Arad Destroyed

21 When the Canaanite, the king of Arad, who lived in the Negeb, heard that Israel was coming by the way of Atharim, he fought against Israel, and took some of them captive. 2 And Israel vowed a vow to the LORD and said, "If you will indeed give this people into my hand, then I will devote their cities to destruction."[1] 3 And the LORD heeded the voice of Israel and gave over the Canaanites, and they devoted them and their cities to destruction. So the name of the place was called Hormah.[2]

The Bronze Serpent

4 From Mount Hor they set out by the way to the Red Sea, to go around the land of Edom. And the people became impatient on the way. 5 And the people spoke against God and against Moses, "Why have you brought us up out of Egypt to die in the wilderness? For there is no food and no water, and we loathe this worthless food." 6 Then the LORD sent fiery serpents among the people, and they bit the people, so that many people of Israel died. 7 And the people came to Moses and said, "We have sinned, for we have spoken against the LORD and against you. Pray to the LORD, that he take away the serpents from us."

So Moses prayed for the people. 8 And the LORD said to Moses, "Make a fiery serpent and set it on a pole, and everyone who is bitten, when he sees it, shall live." 9 So Moses made a bronze[3] serpent and set it on a pole. And if a serpent bit anyone, he would look at the bronze serpent and live.

The Song of the Well

10 And the people of Israel set out and camped in Oboth. 11 And they set out from Oboth and camped at Iye-abarim, in the wilderness that is opposite Moab, toward the sunrise. 12 From there they set out and camped in the Valley of Zered. 13 From there they set out and camped on the other side of the Arnon, which is in the wilderness that extends from the border of the Amorites, for the Arnon is the border of Moab, between Moab and the Amorites. 14 Therefore it is said in the Book of the Wars of the LORD,

> "Waheb in Suphah, and the valleys of the Arnon,
> 15   and the slope of the valleys
> that extends to the seat of Ar,
> and leans to the border of Moab."

16 And from there they continued to Beer;[4] that is the well of which the LORD said to Moses, "Gather the people together, so that I may give them water." 17 Then Israel sang this song:

> "Spring up, O well!—Sing to it!—
> 18   the well that the princes made,
> that the nobles of the people dug,
> with the scepter and with their staffs."

And from the wilderness they went on to Mattanah, 19 and from Mattanah to Nahaliel, and from Nahaliel to Bamoth, 20 and from Bamoth to the valley lying in the region of Moab by the top of Pisgah that looks down on the desert.[5]

King Sihon Defeated

21 Then Israel sent messengers to Sihon king of the Amorites, saying, 22 "Let me pass through your land. We will not turn aside into field or vineyard. We will not drink the water of a well. We will go by the King's Highway until we have passed through your territory." 23 But Sihon would not allow Israel to pass through his territory.

---

[1] That is, set apart (devote) as an offering to the Lord (for destruction); also verse 3   [2] *Hormah* means *destruction*   [3] Or *copper*   [4] *Beer* means *well*   [5] Or *Jeshimon*

He gathered all his people together and went out against Israel to the wilderness and came to Jahaz and fought against Israel. ²⁴And Israel defeated him with the edge of the sword and took possession of his land from the Arnon to the Jabbok, as far as to the Ammonites, for the border of the Ammonites was strong. ²⁵And Israel took all these cities, and Israel settled in all the cities of the Amorites, in Heshbon, and in all its villages. ²⁶For Heshbon was the city of Sihon the king of the Amorites, who had fought against the former king of Moab and taken all his land out of his hand, as far as the Arnon. ²⁷Therefore the ballad singers say,

"Come to Heshbon, let it be built;
    let the city of Sihon be established.
²⁸ For fire came out from Heshbon,
        flame from the city of Sihon.
    It devoured Ar of Moab,
        and swallowed¹ the heights of the
        Arnon.
²⁹ Woe to you, O Moab!
    You are undone, O people of
        Chemosh!
    He has made his sons fugitives,
        and his daughters captives,
        to an Amorite king, Sihon.
³⁰ So we overthrew them;
    Heshbon, as far as Dibon, per-
        ished;
    and we laid waste as far as
        Nophah;
    fire spread as far as Medeba."²

King Og Defeated

³¹Thus Israel lived in the land of the Amorites. ³²And Moses sent to spy out Jazer, and they captured its villages and dispossessed the Amorites who were there. ³³Then they turned and went up by the way to Bashan. And Og the king of Bashan came out against them, he and all his people, to battle at Edrei. ³⁴But the LORD said to Moses, "Do not fear him, for I have given him into your hand, and all his people, and his land. And you shall do to him as you did to Sihon king of the Amorites, who lived at Heshbon." ³⁵So they defeated him and his sons and all his people, until he had no survivor left. And they possessed his land.

Balak Summons Balaam

22 Then the people of Israel set out and camped in the plains of Moab beyond the Jordan at Jericho. ²And Balak the son of Zippor saw all that Israel had done to the Amorites. ³And Moab was in great dread of the people, because they were many. Moab was overcome with fear of the people of Israel. ⁴And Moab said to the elders of Midian, "This horde will now lick up all that is around us, as the ox licks up the grass of the field." So Balak the son of Zippor, who was king of Moab at that time, ⁵sent messengers to Balaam the son of Beor at Pethor, which is near the River in the land of the people of Amaw,³ to call him, saying, "Behold, a people has come out of Egypt. They cover the face of the earth, and they are dwelling opposite me. ⁶Come now, curse this people for me, since they are too mighty for me. Perhaps I shall be able to defeat them and drive them from the land, for I know that he whom you bless is blessed, and he whom you curse is cursed."

⁷So the elders of Moab and the elders of Midian departed with the fees for divination in their hand. And they came to Balaam and gave him Balak's message. ⁸And he said to them, "Lodge here tonight, and I will bring back word to you, as the LORD speaks to me." So the princes of Moab stayed with Balaam. ⁹And God came to Balaam and said, "Who are these men with you?" ¹⁰And Balaam said to God, "Balak the son of Zippor, king of Moab, has sent to me, saying, ¹¹'Behold, a people has come out of Egypt, and it covers the face of the earth. Now come, curse them for me. Perhaps I shall be able to fight against them and drive them out.'" ¹²God said to Balaam, "You shall not go with them. You shall not curse the people, for they are blessed." ¹³So Balaam rose in the morning and said to the princes of Balak, "Go to your own land, for the LORD has refused to let me go with you." ¹⁴So the princes of Moab rose and went to Balak and said, "Balaam refuses to come with us."

¹⁵Once again Balak sent princes, more in number and more honorable than these. ¹⁶And they came to Balaam and said to him, "Thus says Balak the son of Zippor: 'Let nothing hinder you from coming to me, ¹⁷for I will surely do you great honor,

¹Septuagint; Hebrew *the lords of* ²Compare Samaritan and Septuagint; Hebrew *and we laid waste as far as Nophah, which is as far as Medeba* ³Or *the people of his kindred*

and whatever you say to me I will do. Come, curse this people for me.'" ¹⁸But Balaam answered and said to the servants of Balak, "Though Balak were to give me his house full of silver and gold, I could not go beyond the command of the Lord my God to do less or more. ¹⁹So you, too, please stay here tonight, that I may know what more the Lord will say to me." ²⁰And God came to Balaam at night and said to him, "If the men have come to call you, rise, go with them; but only do what I tell you." ²¹So Balaam rose in the morning and saddled his donkey and went with the princes of Moab.

Balaam's Donkey and the Angel

²²But God's anger was kindled because he went, and the angel of the Lord took his stand in the way as his adversary. Now he was riding on the donkey, and his two servants were with him. ²³And the donkey saw the angel of the Lord standing in the road, with a drawn sword in his hand. And the donkey turned aside out of the road and went into the field. And Balaam struck the donkey, to turn her into the road. ²⁴Then the angel of the Lord stood in a narrow path between the vineyards, with a wall on either side. ²⁵And when the donkey saw the angel of the Lord, she pushed against the wall and pressed Balaam's foot against the wall. So he struck her again. ²⁶Then the angel of the Lord went ahead and stood in a narrow place, where there was no way to turn either to the right or to the left. ²⁷When the donkey saw the angel of the Lord, she lay down under Balaam. And Balaam's anger was kindled, and he struck the donkey with his staff. ²⁸Then the Lord opened the mouth of the donkey, and she said to Balaam, "What have I done to you, that you have struck me these three times?" ²⁹And Balaam said to the donkey, "Because you have made a fool of me. I wish I had a sword in my hand, for then I would kill you." ³⁰And the donkey said to Balaam, "Am I not your donkey, on which you have ridden all your life long to this day? Is it my habit to treat you this way?" And he said, "No."

³¹Then the Lord opened the eyes of Balaam, and he saw the angel of the Lord standing in the way, with his drawn sword in his hand. And he bowed down and fell on his face. ³²And the angel of the Lord said to him, "Why have you struck your donkey these three times? Behold, I have come out to oppose you because your way is perverse¹ before me. ³³The donkey saw me and turned aside before me these three times. If she had not turned aside from me, surely just now I would have killed you and let her live." ³⁴Then Balaam said to the angel of the Lord, "I have sinned, for I did not know that you stood in the road against me. Now therefore, if it is evil in your sight, I will turn back." ³⁵And the angel of the Lord said to Balaam, "Go with the men, but speak only the word that I tell you." So Balaam went on with the princes of Balak.

³⁶When Balak heard that Balaam had come, he went out to meet him at the city of Moab, on the border formed by the Arnon, at the extremity of the border. ³⁷And Balak said to Balaam, "Did I not send to you to call you? Why did you not come to me? Am I not able to honor you?" ³⁸Balaam said to Balak, "Behold, I have come to you! Have I now any power of my own to speak anything? The word that God puts in my mouth, that must I speak." ³⁹Then Balaam went with Balak, and they came to Kiriath-huzoth. ⁴⁰And Balak sacrificed oxen and sheep, and sent for Balaam and for the princes who were with him.

⁴¹And in the morning Balak took Balaam and brought him up to Bamoth-baal, and from there he saw a fraction of the people.

Balaam's First Oracle

23 And Balaam said to Balak, "Build for me here seven altars, and prepare for me here seven bulls and seven rams." ²Balak did as Balaam had said. And Balak and Balaam offered on each altar a bull and a ram. ³And Balaam said to Balak, "Stand beside your burnt offering, and I will go. Perhaps the Lord will come to meet me, and whatever he shows me I will tell you." And he went to a bare height, ⁴and God met Balaam. And Balaam said to him, "I have arranged the seven altars and I have offered on each altar a bull and a ram." ⁵And the Lord put a word in Balaam's mouth and said, "Return to Balak, and thus you shall speak." ⁶And he returned to him, and behold, he and all the princes of Moab were standing beside his burnt offering. ⁷And Balaam took up his discourse and said,

¹Or reckless

"From Aram Balak has brought me,
 the king of Moab from the eastern
  mountains:
'Come, curse Jacob for me,
 and come, denounce Israel!'
[8] How can I curse whom God has not
  cursed?
How can I denounce whom the
  LORD has not denounced?
[9] For from the top of the crags I see
  him,
 from the hills I behold him;
behold, a people dwelling alone,
 and not counting itself among the
  nations!
[10] Who can count the dust of Jacob
 or number the fourth part[1] of
  Israel?
Let me die the death of the upright,
 and let my end be like his!"

[11] And Balak said to Balaam, "What have
you done to me? I took you to curse my
enemies, and behold, you have done nothing but bless them." [12] And he answered and
said, "Must I not take care to speak what
the LORD puts in my mouth?"

Balaam's Second Oracle

[13] And Balak said to him, "Please come
with me to another place, from which
you may see them. You shall see only a
fraction of them and shall not see them
all. Then curse them for me from there."
[14] And he took him to the field of Zophim,
to the top of Pisgah, and built seven altars
and offered a bull and a ram on each altar.
[15] Balaam said to Balak, "Stand here beside
your burnt offering, while I meet the LORD
over there." [16] And the LORD met Balaam
and put a word in his mouth and said,
"Return to Balak, and thus shall you speak."
[17] And he came to him, and behold, he was
standing beside his burnt offering, and the
princes of Moab with him. And Balak said
to him, "What has the LORD spoken?" [18] And
Balaam took up his discourse and said,

"Rise, Balak, and hear;
 give ear to me, O son of Zippor:
[19] God is not man, that he should lie,
 or a son of man, that he should
  change his mind.
Has he said, and will he not do it?
 Or has he spoken, and will he not
  fulfill it?

[20] Behold, I received a command to
  bless:
he has blessed, and I cannot
  revoke it.
[21] He has not beheld misfortune in
  Jacob,
 nor has he seen trouble in Israel.
The LORD their God is with them,
 and the shout of a king is among
  them.
[22] God brings them out of Egypt
 and is for them like the horns of
  the wild ox.
[23] For there is no enchantment against
  Jacob,
 no divination against Israel;
now it shall be said of Jacob and
  Israel,
 'What has God wrought!'
[24] Behold, a people! As a lioness it
  rises up
 and as a lion it lifts itself;
it does not lie down until it has
  devoured the prey
 and drunk the blood of the slain."

[25] And Balak said to Balaam, "Do not
curse them at all, and do not bless them
at all." [26] But Balaam answered Balak, "Did
I not tell you, 'All that the LORD says, that
I must do'?" [27] And Balak said to Balaam,
"Come now, I will take you to another
place. Perhaps it will please God that you
may curse them for me from there." [28] So
Balak took Balaam to the top of Peor, which
overlooks the desert.[2] [29] And Balaam said
to Balak, "Build for me here seven altars
and prepare for me here seven bulls and
seven rams." [30] And Balak did as Balaam
had said, and offered a bull and a ram on
each altar.

Balaam's Third Oracle

24 When Balaam saw that it pleased
the LORD to bless Israel, he did not
go, as at other times, to look for omens, but
set his face toward the wilderness. [2] And
Balaam lifted up his eyes and saw Israel
camping tribe by tribe. And the Spirit of
God came upon him, [3] and he took up his
discourse and said,

"The oracle of Balaam the son of
  Beor,
 the oracle of the man whose eye is
  opened,[3]

[1] Or dust clouds [2] Or Jeshimon [3] Or closed, or perfect; also verse 15

4   the oracle of him who hears the
          words of God,
        who sees the vision of the Almighty,
          falling down with his eyes uncov-
          ered:
5   How lovely are your tents, O Jacob,
          your encampments, O Israel!
6   Like palm groves[1] that stretch afar,
          like gardens beside a river,
        like aloes that the LORD has planted,
          like cedar trees beside the waters.
7   Water shall flow from his buckets,
          and his seed shall be in many
          waters;
        his king shall be higher than Agag,
          and his kingdom shall be exalted.
8   God brings him out of Egypt
          and is for him like the horns of the
          wild ox;
        he shall eat up the nations, his adver-
          saries,
          and shall break their bones in
          pieces
          and pierce them through with his
          arrows.
9   He crouched, he lay down like a lion
          and like a lioness; who will rouse
          him up?
        Blessed are those who bless you,
          and cursed are those who curse
          you."

10 And Balak's anger was kindled against
Balaam, and he struck his hands together.
And Balak said to Balaam, "I called you to
curse my enemies, and behold, you have
blessed them these three times. 11 Therefore
now flee to your own place. I said, 'I will certainly honor you,' but the LORD has held you
back from honor." 12 And Balaam said to Balak, "Did I not tell your messengers whom
you sent to me, 13 'If Balak should give me his
house full of silver and gold, I would not be
able to go beyond the word of the LORD, to
do either good or bad of my own will. What
the LORD speaks, that will I speak'? 14 And
now, behold, I am going to my people. Come,
I will let you know what this people will do
to your people in the latter days."

Balaam's Final Oracle

15 And he took up his discourse and said,

        "The oracle of Balaam the son of Beor,
          the oracle of the man whose eye is
          opened,

16   the oracle of him who hears the
          words of God,
          and knows the knowledge of the
          Most High,
        who sees the vision of the Almighty,
          falling down with his eyes uncov-
          ered:
17   I see him, but not now;
          I behold him, but not near:
        a star shall come out of Jacob,
          and a scepter shall rise out of
          Israel;
        it shall crush the forehead[2] of Moab
          and break down all the sons of
          Sheth.
18   Edom shall be dispossessed;
          Seir also, his enemies, shall be
          dispossessed.
          Israel is doing valiantly.
19   And one from Jacob shall exercise
          dominion
          and destroy the survivors of cit-
          ies!"

20 Then he looked on Amalek and took up
his discourse and said,

        "Amalek was the first among the
          nations,
          but its end is utter destruction."

21 And he looked on the Kenite, and took
up his discourse and said,

        "Enduring is your dwelling place,
          and your nest is set in the rock.
22   Nevertheless, Kain shall be burned
          when Asshur takes you away cap-
          tive."

23 And he took up his discourse and said,

        "Alas, who shall live when God does
          this?
24   But ships shall come from Kittim
          and shall afflict Asshur and Eber;
          and he too shall come to utter
          destruction."

25 Then Balaam rose and went back to his
place. And Balak also went his way.

Baal Worship at Peor

25 While Israel lived in Shittim, the people began to whore with the daughters of Moab. 2 These invited the people to
the sacrifices of their gods, and the people

---

[1] Or valleys [2] Hebrew corners [of the head]

ate and bowed down to their gods. ³So Israel yoked himself to Baal of Peor. And the anger of the LORD was kindled against Israel. ⁴And the LORD said to Moses, "Take all the chiefs of the people and hang¹ them in the sun before the LORD, that the fierce anger of the LORD may turn away from Israel." ⁵And Moses said to the judges of Israel, "Each of you kill those of his men who have yoked themselves to Baal of Peor."

⁶And behold, one of the people of Israel came and brought a Midianite woman to his family, in the sight of Moses and in the sight of the whole congregation of the people of Israel, while they were weeping in the entrance of the tent of meeting. ⁷When Phinehas the son of Eleazar, son of Aaron the priest, saw it, he rose and left the congregation and took a spear in his hand ⁸and went after the man of Israel into the chamber and pierced both of them, the man of Israel and the woman through her belly. Thus the plague on the people of Israel was stopped. ⁹Nevertheless, those who died by the plague were twenty-four thousand.

The Zeal of Phinehas

¹⁰And the LORD said to Moses, ¹¹"Phinehas the son of Eleazar, son of Aaron the priest, has turned back my wrath from the people of Israel, in that he was jealous with my jealousy among them, so that I did not consume the people of Israel in my jealousy. ¹²Therefore say, 'Behold, I give to him my covenant of peace, ¹³and it shall be to him and to his descendants after him the covenant of a perpetual priesthood, because he was jealous for his God and made atonement for the people of Israel.'" ¹⁴The name of the slain man of Israel, who was killed with the Midianite woman, was Zimri the son of Salu, chief of a father's house belonging to the Simeonites. ¹⁵And the name of the Midianite woman who was killed was Cozbi the daughter of Zur, who was the tribal head of a father's house in Midian.

¹⁶And the LORD spoke to Moses, saying, ¹⁷"Harass the Midianites and strike them down, ¹⁸for they have harassed you with their wiles, with which they beguiled you in the matter of Peor, and in the matter of Cozbi, the daughter of the chief of Midian, their sister, who was killed on the day of the plague on account of Peor."

Census of the New Generation

26 After the plague, the LORD said to Moses and to Eleazar the son of Aaron, the priest, ²"Take a census of all the congregation of the people of Israel, from twenty years old and upward, by their fathers' houses, all in Israel who are able to go to war." ³And Moses and Eleazar the priest spoke with them in the plains of Moab by the Jordan at Jericho, saying, ⁴"Take a census of the people,² from twenty years old and upward," as the LORD commanded Moses. The people of Israel who came out of the land of Egypt were:

⁵Reuben, the firstborn of Israel; the sons of Reuben: of Hanoch, the clan of the Hanochites; of Pallu, the clan of the Palluites; ⁶of Hezron, the clan of the Hezronites; of Carmi, the clan of the Carmites. ⁷These are the clans of the Reubenites, and those listed were 43,730. ⁸And the sons of Pallu: Eliab. ⁹The sons of Eliab: Nemuel, Dathan, and Abiram. These are the Dathan and Abiram, chosen from the congregation, who contended against Moses and Aaron in the company of Korah, when they contended against the LORD ¹⁰and the earth opened its mouth and swallowed them up together with Korah, when that company died, when the fire devoured 250 men, and they became a warning. ¹¹But the sons of Korah did not die.

¹²The sons of Simeon according to their clans: of Nemuel, the clan of the Nemuelites; of Jamin, the clan of the Jaminites; of Jachin, the clan of the Jachinites; ¹³of Zerah, the clan of the Zerahites; of Shaul, the clan of the Shaulites. ¹⁴These are the clans of the Simeonites, 22,200.

¹⁵The sons of Gad according to their clans: of Zephon, the clan of the Zephonites; of Haggi, the clan of the Haggites; of Shuni, the clan of the Shunites; ¹⁶of Ozni, the clan of the Oznites; of Eri, the clan of the Erites; ¹⁷of Arod, the clan of the Arodites; of Areli, the clan of the Arelites. ¹⁸These are the clans of the sons of Gad as they were listed, 40,500.

¹⁹The sons of Judah were Er and Onan; and Er and Onan died in the land of Canaan. ²⁰And the sons of Judah according to their clans were: of Shelah, the clan of the Shelanites; of Perez, the clan of the Perezites; of Zerah, the clan of the Zerahites.

¹Or impale ²Take a census of the people is implied (compare verse 2)

²¹ And the sons of Perez were: of Hezron, the clan of the Hezronites; of Hamul, the clan of the Hamulites. ²² These are the clans of Judah as they were listed, 76,500.

²³ The sons of Issachar according to their clans: of Tola, the clan of the Tolaites; of Puvah, the clan of the Punites; ²⁴ of Jashub, the clan of the Jashubites; of Shimron, the clan of the Shimronites. ²⁵ These are the clans of Issachar as they were listed, 64,300.

²⁶ The sons of Zebulun, according to their clans: of Sered, the clan of the Seredites; of Elon, the clan of the Elonites; of Jahleel, the clan of the Jahleelites. ²⁷ These are the clans of the Zebulunites as they were listed, 60,500.

²⁸ The sons of Joseph according to their clans: Manasseh and Ephraim. ²⁹ The sons of Manasseh: of Machir, the clan of the Machirites; and Machir was the father of Gilead; of Gilead, the clan of the Gileadites. ³⁰ These are the sons of Gilead: of Iezer, the clan of the Iezerites; of Helek, the clan of the Helekites; ³¹ and of Asriel, the clan of the Asrielites; and of Shechem, the clan of the Shechemites; ³² and of Shemida, the clan of the Shemidaites; and of Hepher, the clan of the Hepherites. ³³ Now Zelophehad the son of Hepher had no sons, but daughters. And the names of the daughters of Zelophehad were Mahlah, Noah, Hoglah, Milcah, and Tirzah. ³⁴ These are the clans of Manasseh, and those listed were 52,700.

³⁵ These are the sons of Ephraim according to their clans: of Shuthelah, the clan of the Shuthelahites; of Becher, the clan of the Becherites; of Tahan, the clan of the Tahanites. ³⁶ And these are the sons of Shuthelah: of Eran, the clan of the Eranites. ³⁷ These are the clans of the sons of Ephraim as they were listed, 32,500. These are the sons of Joseph according to their clans.

³⁸ The sons of Benjamin according to their clans: of Bela, the clan of the Belaites; of Ashbel, the clan of the Ashbelites; of Ahiram, the clan of the Ahiramites; ³⁹ of Shephupham, the clan of the Shuphamites; of Hupham, the clan of the Huphamites. ⁴⁰ And the sons of Bela were Ard and Naaman: of Ard, the clan of the Ardites; of Naaman, the clan of the Naamites. ⁴¹ These are the sons of Benjamin according to their clans, and those listed were 45,600.

⁴² These are the sons of Dan according to their clans: of Shuham, the clan of the Shuhamites. These are the clans of Dan according to their clans. ⁴³ All the clans of the Shuhamites, as they were listed, were 64,400.

⁴⁴ The sons of Asher according to their clans: of Imnah, the clan of the Imnites; of Ishvi, the clan of the Ishvites; of Beriah, the clan of the Beriites. ⁴⁵ Of the sons of Beriah: of Heber, the clan of the Heberites; of Malchiel, the clan of the Malchielites. ⁴⁶ And the name of the daughter of Asher was Serah. ⁴⁷ These are the clans of the sons of Asher as they were listed, 53,400.

⁴⁸ The sons of Naphtali according to their clans: of Jahzeel, the clan of the Jahzeelites; of Guni, the clan of the Gunites; ⁴⁹ of Jezer, the clan of the Jezerites; of Shillem, the clan of the Shillemites. ⁵⁰ These are the clans of Naphtali according to their clans, and those listed were 45,400.

⁵¹ This was the list of the people of Israel, 601,730.

⁵² The LORD spoke to Moses, saying, ⁵³ "Among these the land shall be divided for inheritance according to the number of names. ⁵⁴ To a large tribe you shall give a large inheritance, and to a small tribe you shall give a small inheritance; every tribe shall be given its inheritance in proportion to its list. ⁵⁵ But the land shall be divided by lot. According to the names of the tribes of their fathers they shall inherit. ⁵⁶ Their inheritance shall be divided according to lot between the larger and the smaller."

⁵⁷ This was the list of the Levites according to their clans: of Gershon, the clan of the Gershonites; of Kohath, the clan of the Kohathites; of Merari, the clan of the Merarites. ⁵⁸ These are the clans of Levi: the clan of the Libnites, the clan of the Hebronites, the clan of the Mahlites, the clan of the Mushites, the clan of the Korahites. And Kohath was the father of Amram. ⁵⁹ The name of Amram's wife was Jochebed the daughter of Levi, who was born to Levi in Egypt. And she bore to Amram Aaron and Moses and Miriam their sister. ⁶⁰ And to Aaron were born Nadab, Abihu, Eleazar, and Ithamar. ⁶¹ But Nadab and Abihu died when they offered unauthorized fire before the LORD. ⁶² And those listed were 23,000, every male from a month old and upward. For they were not listed among the people of Israel, because there was no inheritance given to them among the people of Israel.

⁶³ These were those listed by Moses and Eleazar the priest, who listed the people of

Israel in the plains of Moab by the Jordan at Jericho. ⁶⁴ But among these there was not one of those listed by Moses and Aaron the priest, who had listed the people of Israel in the wilderness of Sinai. ⁶⁵ For the LORD had said of them, "They shall die in the wilderness." Not one of them was left, except Caleb the son of Jephunneh and Joshua the son of Nun.

The Daughters of Zelophehad

27 Then drew near the daughters of Zelophehad the son of Hepher, son of Gilead, son of Machir, son of Manasseh, from the clans of Manasseh the son of Joseph. The names of his daughters were: Mahlah, Noah, Hoglah, Milcah, and Tirzah. ² And they stood before Moses and before Eleazar the priest and before the chiefs and all the congregation, at the entrance of the tent of meeting, saying, ³ "Our father died in the wilderness. He was not among the company of those who gathered themselves together against the LORD in the company of Korah, but died for his own sin. And he had no sons. ⁴ Why should the name of our father be taken away from his clan because he had no son? Give to us a possession among our father's brothers."

⁵ Moses brought their case before the LORD. ⁶ And the LORD said to Moses, ⁷ "The daughters of Zelophehad are right. You shall give them possession of an inheritance among their father's brothers and transfer the inheritance of their father to them. ⁸ And you shall speak to the people of Israel, saying, 'If a man dies and has no son, then you shall transfer his inheritance to his daughter. ⁹ And if he has no daughter, then you shall give his inheritance to his brothers. ¹⁰ And if he has no brothers, then you shall give his inheritance to his father's brothers. ¹¹ And if his father has no brothers, then you shall give his inheritance to the nearest kinsman of his clan, and he shall possess it. And it shall be for the people of Israel a statute and rule, as the LORD commanded Moses.'"

Joshua to Succeed Moses

¹² The LORD said to Moses, "Go up into this mountain of Abarim and see the land that I have given to the people of Israel. ¹³ When you have seen it, you also shall be gathered to your people, as your brother Aaron was, ¹⁴ because you rebelled against my word in the wilderness of Zin when the congregation quarreled, failing to uphold me as holy at the waters before their eyes." (These are the waters of Meribah of Kadesh in the wilderness of Zin.) ¹⁵ Moses spoke to the LORD, saying, ¹⁶ "Let the LORD, the God of the spirits of all flesh, appoint a man over the congregation ¹⁷ who shall go out before them and come in before them, who shall lead them out and bring them in, that the congregation of the LORD may not be as sheep that have no shepherd." ¹⁸ So the LORD said to Moses, "Take Joshua the son of Nun, a man in whom is the Spirit, and lay your hand on him. ¹⁹ Make him stand before Eleazar the priest and all the congregation, and you shall commission him in their sight. ²⁰ You shall invest him with some of your authority, that all the congregation of the people of Israel may obey. ²¹ And he shall stand before Eleazar the priest, who shall inquire for him by the judgment of the Urim before the LORD. At his word they shall go out, and at his word they shall come in, both he and all the people of Israel with him, the whole congregation." ²² And Moses did as the LORD commanded him. He took Joshua and made him stand before Eleazar the priest and the whole congregation, ²³ and he laid his hands on him and commissioned him as the LORD directed through Moses.

Daily Offerings

28 The LORD spoke to Moses, saying, ² "Command the people of Israel and say to them, 'My offering, my food for my food offerings, my pleasing aroma, you shall be careful to offer to me at its appointed time.' ³ And you shall say to them, This is the food offering that you shall offer to the LORD: two male lambs a year old without blemish, day by day, as a regular offering. ⁴ The one lamb you shall offer in the morning, and the other lamb you shall offer at twilight; ⁵ also a tenth of an ephah[1] of fine flour for a grain offering, mixed with a quarter of a hin[2] of beaten oil. ⁶ It is a regular burnt offering, which was ordained at Mount Sinai for a pleasing aroma, a food offering to the LORD. ⁷ Its drink offering shall be a quarter of a hin for each lamb. In the Holy Place you shall pour out a drink offering of strong drink

---

[1] An *ephah* was about 3/5 bushel or 22 liters　[2] A *hin* was about 4 quarts or 3.5 liters

to the LORD. [8] The other lamb you shall offer at twilight. Like the grain offering of the morning, and like its drink offering, you shall offer it as a food offering, with a pleasing aroma to the LORD.

Sabbath Offerings

[9] "On the Sabbath day, two male lambs a year old without blemish, and two tenths of an ephah of fine flour for a grain offering, mixed with oil, and its drink offering: [10] this is the burnt offering of every Sabbath, besides the regular burnt offering and its drink offering.

Monthly Offerings

[11] "At the beginnings of your months, you shall offer a burnt offering to the LORD: two bulls from the herd, one ram, seven male lambs a year old without blemish; [12] also three tenths of an ephah of fine flour for a grain offering, mixed with oil, for each bull, and two tenths of fine flour for a grain offering, mixed with oil, for the one ram; [13] and a tenth of fine flour mixed with oil as a grain offering for every lamb; for a burnt offering with a pleasing aroma, a food offering to the LORD. [14] Their drink offerings shall be half a hin of wine for a bull, a third of a hin for a ram, and a quarter of a hin for a lamb. This is the burnt offering of each month throughout the months of the year. [15] Also one male goat for a sin offering to the LORD; it shall be offered besides the regular burnt offering and its drink offering.

Passover Offerings

[16] "On the fourteenth day of the first month is the LORD's Passover, [17] and on the fifteenth day of this month is a feast. Seven days shall unleavened bread be eaten. [18] On the first day there shall be a holy convocation. You shall not do any ordinary work, [19] but offer a food offering, a burnt offering to the LORD: two bulls from the herd, one ram, and seven male lambs a year old; see that they are without blemish; [20] also their grain offering of fine flour mixed with oil; three tenths of an ephah shall you offer for a bull, and two tenths for a ram; [21] a tenth shall you offer for each of the seven lambs; [22] also one male goat for a sin offering, to make atonement for you. [23] You shall offer these besides the burnt offering of the morning, which is for a regular burnt offering. [24] In the same way you shall offer daily, for seven days, the food of a food offering, with a pleasing aroma to the LORD. It shall be offered besides the regular burnt offering and its drink offering. [25] And on the seventh day you shall have a holy convocation. You shall not do any ordinary work.

Offerings for the Feast of Weeks

[26] "On the day of the firstfruits, when you offer a grain offering of new grain to the LORD at your Feast of Weeks, you shall have a holy convocation. You shall not do any ordinary work, [27] but offer a burnt offering, with a pleasing aroma to the LORD: two bulls from the herd, one ram, seven male lambs a year old; [28] also their grain offering of fine flour mixed with oil, three tenths of an ephah for each bull, two tenths for one ram, [29] a tenth for each of the seven lambs; [30] with one male goat, to make atonement for you. [31] Besides the regular burnt offering and its grain offering, you shall offer them and their drink offering. See that they are without blemish.

Offerings for the Feast of Trumpets

29 "On the first day of the seventh month you shall have a holy convocation. You shall not do any ordinary work. It is a day for you to blow the trumpets, [2] and you shall offer a burnt offering, for a pleasing aroma to the LORD: one bull from the herd, one ram, seven male lambs a year old without blemish; [3] also their grain offering of fine flour mixed with oil, three tenths of an ephah[1] for the bull, two tenths for the ram, [4] and one tenth for each of the seven lambs; [5] with one male goat for a sin offering, to make atonement for you; [6] besides the burnt offering of the new moon, and its grain offering, and the regular burnt offering and its grain offering, and their drink offering, according to the rule for them, for a pleasing aroma, a food offering to the LORD.

Offerings for the Day of Atonement

[7] "On the tenth day of this seventh month you shall have a holy convocation and afflict yourselves.[2] You shall do no work, [8] but you shall offer a burnt offering to the LORD, a pleasing aroma: one bull from the herd, one ram, seven male lambs a year

---

[1] An *ephah* was about 3/5 bushel or 22 liters   [2] Or *and fast*

old: see that they are without blemish. ⁹ And their grain offering shall be of fine flour mixed with oil, three tenths of an ephah for the bull, two tenths for the one ram, ¹⁰ a tenth for each of the seven lambs: ¹¹ also one male goat for a sin offering, besides the sin offering of atonement, and the regular burnt offering and its grain offering, and their drink offerings.

Offerings for the Feast of Booths

¹² "On the fifteenth day of the seventh month you shall have a holy convocation. You shall not do any ordinary work, and you shall keep a feast to the LORD seven days. ¹³ And you shall offer a burnt offering, a food offering, with a pleasing aroma to the LORD, thirteen bulls from the herd, two rams, fourteen male lambs a year old; they shall be without blemish; ¹⁴ and their grain offering of fine flour mixed with oil, three tenths of an ephah for each of the thir-

teen bulls, two tenths for each of the two rams, ¹⁵ and a tenth for each of the fourteen lambs; ¹⁶ also one male goat for a sin offering, besides the regular burnt offering, its grain offering and its drink offering.

¹⁷ "On the second day twelve bulls from the herd, two rams, fourteen male lambs a year old without blemish, ¹⁸ with the grain offering and the drink offerings for the bulls, for the rams, and for the lambs, in the prescribed quantities; ¹⁹ also one male goat for a sin offering, besides the regular burnt offering and its grain offering, and their drink offerings.

²⁰ "On the third day eleven bulls, two rams, fourteen male lambs a year old without blemish, ²¹ with the grain offering and the drink offerings for the bulls, for the rams, and for the lambs, in the prescribed quantities; ²² also one male goat for a sin offering, besides the regular burnt offering and its grain offering and its drink offering.

Know Yourself

verses to read
Numbers 28:26–31

Scent is an amazing thing. It can affect your mood, your emotions, and your thoughts. Smelling is so powerful that it can make you feel just like you felt the last time you smelled the same thing. Good smells have a way of calming us, and some say certain scents even help us to concentrate. But smells can also be disgusting. A lot of scents leave you running in the opposite direction. They can hit you like a slap in the face and make you want to cover your nose and mouth in self-protection.

In the spiritual realm, think of obedience to God as a good smell that God loves to inhale. Love, kindness, selflessness, giving, and serving all are soothing aromas to God. God delights to see these in the lives of his children. But sin is a stench that makes him turn his head and disregard even the prayers of the stinky (see Prov. 28:9). What is the aroma of your life? Remember that sin in God's children stinks to him for that very reason—they are his children. He loves them too much to see them waste their lives enjoying the tiny pleasures of sin when infinite joy is offered to them in God (see Ps. 16:11).

If you aren't sure, then check your thoughts and your actions. Do they match God's Word, or are they in conflict with it? A life in conflict with God is an unpleasant aroma. But a heart set on pleasing God is a soothing aroma. Love the Lord your God with all your heart. May he be charmed by the fragrance of your faith. But never forget that even when we are stinky because of our sin, Jesus went to a cross and suffered for sinners, so that our smelliness never causes God to turn his love away from us. Our obedience pleases God, since he is our Father; and precisely because he is our Father, our sin will never cause him to forsake us.

²³"On the fourth day ten bulls, two rams, fourteen male lambs a year old without blemish, ²⁴with the grain offering and the drink offerings for the bulls, for the rams, and for the lambs, in the prescribed quantities; ²⁵also one male goat for a sin offering, besides the regular burnt offering, its grain offering and its drink offering.

²⁶"On the fifth day nine bulls, two rams, fourteen male lambs a year old without blemish, ²⁷with the grain offering and the drink offerings for the bulls, for the rams, and for the lambs, in the prescribed quantities; ²⁸also one male goat for a sin offering; besides the regular burnt offering and its grain offering and its drink offering.

²⁹"On the sixth day eight bulls, two rams, fourteen male lambs a year old without blemish, ³⁰with the grain offering and the drink offerings for the bulls, for the rams, and for the lambs, in the prescribed quantities; ³¹also one male goat for a sin offering; besides the regular burnt offering, its grain offering, and its drink offerings.

³²"On the seventh day seven bulls, two rams, fourteen male lambs a year old without blemish, ³³with the grain offering and the drink offerings for the bulls, for the rams, and for the lambs, in the prescribed quantities; ³⁴also one male goat for a sin offering; besides the regular burnt offering, its grain offering, and its drink offering.

³⁵"On the eighth day you shall have a solemn assembly. You shall not do any ordinary work, ³⁶but you shall offer a burnt offering, a food offering, with a pleasing aroma to the LORD: one bull, one ram, seven male lambs a year old without blemish, ³⁷and the grain offering and the drink offerings for the bull, for the ram, and for the lambs, in the prescribed quantities; ³⁸also one male goat for a sin offering; besides the regular burnt offering and its grain offering and its drink offering.

³⁹"These you shall offer to the LORD at your appointed feasts, in addition to your vow offerings and your freewill offerings, for your burnt offerings, and for your grain offerings, and for your drink offerings, and for your peace offerings."

⁴⁰ ¹ So Moses told the people of Israel everything just as the LORD had commanded Moses.

Men and Vows

30 Moses spoke to the heads of the tribes of the people of Israel, saying, "This is what the LORD has commanded. ²If a man vows a vow to the LORD, or swears an oath to bind himself by a pledge, he shall not break his word. He shall do according to all that proceeds out of his mouth.

Women and Vows

³"If a woman vows a vow to the LORD and binds herself by a pledge, while within her father's house in her youth, ⁴and her father hears of her vow and of her pledge by which she has bound herself and says nothing to her, then all her vows shall stand, and every pledge by which she has bound herself shall stand. ⁵But if her father opposes her on the day that he hears of it, no vow of hers, no pledge by which she has bound herself shall stand. And the LORD will forgive her, because her father opposed her.

⁶"If she marries a husband, while under her vows or any thoughtless utterance of her lips by which she has bound herself, ⁷and her husband hears of it and says nothing to her on the day that he hears, then her vows shall stand, and her pledges by which she has bound herself shall stand. ⁸But if, on the day that her husband comes to hear of it, he opposes her, then he makes void her vow that was on her, and the thoughtless utterance of her lips by which she bound herself. And the LORD will forgive her. ⁹(But any vow of a widow or of a divorced woman, anything by which she has bound herself, shall stand against her.) ¹⁰And if she vowed in her husband's house or bound herself by a pledge with an oath, ¹¹and her husband heard of it and said nothing to her and did not oppose her, then all her vows shall stand, and every pledge by which she bound herself shall stand. ¹²But if her husband makes them null and void on the day that he hears them, then whatever proceeds out of her lips concerning her vows or concerning her pledge of herself shall not stand. Her husband has made them void, and the LORD will forgive her. ¹³Any vow and any binding oath to afflict herself,² her husband may establish,³ or her husband may make void. ¹⁴But if her husband says nothing to her from day to day, then he establishes all her vows or

all her pledges that are upon her. He has established them, because he said nothing to her on the day that he heard of them. [15] But if he makes them null and void after he has heard of them, then he shall bear her iniquity."

[16] These are the statutes that the LORD commanded Moses about a man and his wife and about a father and his daughter while she is in her youth within her father's house.

Vengeance on Midian

31 The LORD spoke to Moses, saying, [2] "Avenge the people of Israel on the Midianites. Afterward you shall be gathered to your people." [3] So Moses spoke to the people, saying, "Arm men from among you for the war, that they may go against Midian to execute the LORD's vengeance on Midian. [4] You shall send a thousand from each of the tribes of Israel to the war." [5] So there were provided, out of the thousands of Israel, a thousand from each tribe, twelve thousand armed for war. [6] And Moses sent them to the war, a thousand from each tribe, together with Phinehas the son of Eleazar the priest, with the vessels of the sanctuary and the trumpets for the alarm in his hand. [7] They warred against Midian, as the LORD commanded Moses, and killed every male. [8] They killed the kings of Midian with the rest of their slain, Evi, Rekem, Zur, Hur, and Reba, the five kings of Midian. And they also killed Balaam the son of Beor with the sword. [9] And the people of Israel took captive the women of Midian and their little ones, and they took as plunder all their cattle, their flocks, and all their goods. [10] All their cities in the places where they lived, and all their encampments, they burned with fire, [11] and took all the spoil and all the plunder, both of man and of beast. [12] Then they brought the captives and the plunder and the spoil to Moses, and to Eleazar the priest, and to the congregation of the people of Israel, at the camp on the plains of Moab by the Jordan at Jericho.

[13] Moses and Eleazar the priest and all the chiefs of the congregation went to meet them outside the camp. [14] And Moses was angry with the officers of the army, the commanders of thousands and the commanders of hundreds, who had come from service in the war. [15] Moses said to them, "Have you let all the women live? [16] Behold, these, on Balaam's advice, caused the people of Israel to act treacherously against the LORD in the incident of Peor, and so the plague came among the congregation of the LORD. [17] Now therefore, kill every male among the little ones, and kill every woman who has known man by lying with him. [18] But all the young girls who have not known man by lying with him keep alive for yourselves. [19] Encamp outside the camp seven days. Whoever of you has killed any person and whoever has touched any slain, purify yourselves and your captives on the third day and on the seventh day. [20] You shall purify every garment, every article of skin, all work of goats' hair, and every article of wood."

[21] Then Eleazar the priest said to the men in the army who had gone to battle: "This is the statute of the law that the LORD has commanded Moses: [22] only the gold, the silver, the bronze, the iron, the tin, and the lead, [23] everything that can stand the fire, you shall pass through the fire, and it shall be clean. Nevertheless, it shall also be purified with the water for impurity. And whatever cannot stand the fire, you shall pass through the water. [24] You must wash your clothes on the seventh day, and you shall be clean. And afterward you may come into the camp."

[25] The LORD said to Moses, [26] "Take the count of the plunder that was taken, both of man and of beast, you and Eleazar the priest and the heads of the fathers' houses of the congregation, [27] and divide the plunder into two parts between the warriors who went out to battle and all the congregation. [28] And levy for the LORD a tribute from the men of war who went out to battle, one out of five hundred, of the people and of the oxen and of the donkeys and of the flocks. [29] Take it from their half and give it to Eleazar the priest as a contribution to the LORD. [30] And from the people of Israel's half you shall take one drawn out of every fifty, of the people, of the oxen, of the donkeys, and of the flocks, of all the cattle, and give them to the Levites who keep guard over the tabernacle of the LORD." [31] And Moses and Eleazar the priest did as the LORD commanded Moses.

[32] Now the plunder remaining of the spoil that the army took was 675,000 sheep, [33] 72,000 cattle, [34] 61,000 donkeys, [35] and 32,000 persons in all, women who had not

known man by lying with him. 36 And the half, the portion of those who had gone out in the army, numbered 337,500 sheep, 37 and the LORD's tribute of sheep was 675. 38 The cattle were 36,000, of which the LORD's tribute was 72. 39 The donkeys were 30,500, of which the LORD's tribute was 61. 40 The persons were 16,000, of which the LORD's tribute was 32 persons. 41 And Moses gave the tribute, which was the contribution for the LORD, to Eleazar the priest, as the LORD commanded Moses.

42 From the people of Israel's half, which Moses separated from that of the men who had served in the army— 43 now the congregation's half was 337,500 sheep, 44 36,000 cattle, 45 and 30,500 donkeys, 46 and 16,000 persons— 47 from the people of Israel's half Moses took one of every 50, both of persons and of beasts, and gave them to the Levites who kept guard over the tabernacle of the LORD, as the LORD commanded Moses.

48 Then the officers who were over the thousands of the army, the commanders of thousands and the commanders of hundreds, came near to Moses 49 and said to Moses, "Your servants have counted the men of war who are under our command, and there is not a man missing from us. 50 And we have brought the LORD's offering, what each man found, articles of gold, armlets and bracelets, signet rings, earrings, and beads, to make atonement for ourselves before the LORD." 51 And Moses and Eleazar the priest received from them the gold, all crafted articles. 52 And all the gold of the contribution that they presented to the LORD, from the commanders of thousands and the commanders of hundreds, was 16,750 shekels.[1] 53 (The men in the army had each taken plunder for himself.) 54 And Moses and Eleazar the priest received the gold from the commanders of thousands and of hundreds, and brought it into the tent of meeting, as a memorial for the people of Israel before the LORD.

Reuben and Gad Settle in Gilead

32 Now the people of Reuben and the people of Gad had a very great number of livestock. And they saw the land of Jazer and the land of Gilead, and behold, the place was a place for livestock. 2 So the people of Gad and the people of Reuben came and said to Moses and to Eleazar the priest and to the chiefs of the congregation, 3 "Ataroth, Dibon, Jazer, Nimrah, Heshbon, Elealeh, Sebam, Nebo, and Beon, 4 the land that the LORD struck down before the congregation of Israel, is a land for livestock, and your servants have livestock." 5 And they said, "If we have found favor in your sight, let this land be given to your servants for a possession. Do not take us across the Jordan."

6 But Moses said to the people of Gad and to the people of Reuben, "Shall your brothers go to the war while you sit here? 7 Why will you discourage the heart of the people of Israel from going over into the land that the LORD has given them? 8 Your fathers did this, when I sent them from Kadesh-barnea to see the land. 9 For when they went up to the Valley of Eshcol and saw the land, they discouraged the heart of the people of Israel from going into the land that the LORD had given them. 10 And the LORD's anger was kindled on that day, and he swore, saying, 11 'Surely none of the men who came up out of Egypt, from twenty years old and upward, shall see the land that I swore to give to Abraham, to Isaac, and to Jacob, because they have not wholly followed me, 12 none except Caleb the son of Jephunneh the Kenizzite and Joshua the son of Nun, for they have wholly followed the LORD.' 13 And the LORD's anger was kindled against Israel, and he made them wander in the wilderness forty years, until all the generation that had done evil in the sight of the LORD was gone. 14 And behold, you have risen in your fathers' place, a brood of sinful men, to increase still more the fierce anger of the LORD against Israel! 15 For if you turn away from following him, he will again abandon them in the wilderness, and you will destroy all this people."

16 Then they came near to him and said, "We will build sheepfolds here for our livestock, and cities for our little ones, 17 but we will take up arms, ready to go before the people of Israel, until we have brought them to their place. And our little ones shall live in the fortified cities because of the inhabitants of the land. 18 We will not return to our homes until each of the people of Israel has gained his inheritance. 19 For we will not inherit with them on the other side of the Jordan and beyond,

[1] A *shekel* was about 2/5 ounce or 11 grams

because our inheritance has come to us on this side of the Jordan to the east." [20] So Moses said to them, "If you will do this, if you will take up arms to go before the LORD for the war, [21] and every armed man of you will pass over the Jordan before the LORD, until he has driven out his enemies from before him [22] and the land is subdued before the LORD; then after that you shall return and be free of obligation to the LORD and to Israel, and this land shall be your possession before the LORD. [23] But if you will not do so, behold, you have sinned against the LORD, and be sure your sin will find you out. [24] Build cities for your little ones and folds for your sheep, and do what you have promised." [25] And the people of Gad and the people of Reuben said to Moses, "Your servants will do as my lord commands. [26] Our little ones, our wives, our livestock, and all our cattle shall remain there in the cities of Gilead, [27] but your servants will pass over, every man who is armed for war, before the LORD to battle, as my lord orders."

[28] So Moses gave command concerning them to Eleazar the priest and to Joshua the son of Nun and to the heads of the fathers' houses of the tribes of the people of Israel. [29] And Moses said to them, "If the people of Gad and the people of Reuben, every man who is armed to battle before the LORD, will pass with you over the Jordan and the land shall be subdued before you, then you shall give them the land of Gilead for a possession. [30] However, if they will not pass over with you armed, they shall have possessions among you in the land of Canaan." [31] And the people of Gad and the people of Reuben answered, "What the LORD has said to your servants, we will do. [32] We will pass over armed before the LORD into the land of Canaan, and the possession of our inheritance shall remain with us beyond the Jordan."

[33] And Moses gave to them, to the people of Gad and to the people of Reuben and to the half-tribe of Manasseh the son of Joseph, the kingdom of Sihon king of the Amorites and the kingdom of Og king of Bashan, the land and its cities with their territories, the cities of the land throughout the country. [34] And the people of Gad built Dibon, Ataroth, Aroer, [35] Atroth-shophan, Jazer, Jogbehah, [36] Beth-nimrah

and Beth-haran, fortified cities, and folds for sheep. [37] And the people of Reuben built Heshbon, Elealeh, Kiriathaim, [38] Nebo, and Baal-meon (their names were changed), and Sibmah. And they gave other names to the cities that they built. [39] And the sons of Machir the son of Manasseh went to Gilead and captured it, and dispossessed the Amorites who were in it. [40] And Moses gave Gilead to Machir the son of Manasseh, and he settled in it. [41] And Jair the son of Manasseh went and captured their villages, and called them Havvoth-jair.[1] [42] And Nobah went and captured Kenath and its villages, and called it Nobah, after his own name.

Recounting Israel's Journey

33 These are the stages of the people of Israel, when they went out of the land of Egypt by their companies under the leadership of Moses and Aaron. [2] Moses wrote down their starting places, stage by stage, by command of the LORD, and these are their stages according to their starting places. [3] They set out from Rameses in the first month, on the fifteenth day of the first month. On the day after the Passover, the people of Israel went out triumphantly in the sight of all the Egyptians, [4] while the Egyptians were burying all their firstborn, whom the LORD had struck down among them. On their gods also the LORD executed judgments.

[5] So the people of Israel set out from Rameses and camped at Succoth. [6] And they set out from Succoth and camped at Etham, which is on the edge of the wilderness. [7] And they set out from Etham and turned back to Pi-hahiroth, which is east of Baal-zephon, and they camped before Migdol. [8] And they set out from before Hahiroth[2] and passed through the midst of the sea into the wilderness, and they went a three days' journey in the wilderness of Etham and camped at Marah. [9] And they set out from Marah and came to Elim; at Elim there were twelve springs of water and seventy palm trees, and they camped there. [10] And they set out from Elim and camped by the Red Sea. [11] And they set out from the Red Sea and camped in the wilderness of Sin. [12] And they set out from the wilderness of Sin and camped at Dophkah. [13] And they set out from Dophkah and camped at Alush. [14] And they set out from Alush and camped

---

[1] *Havvoth-jair* means *the villages of Jair* [2] Some manuscripts and versions *Pi-hahiroth*

at Rephidim, where there was no water for the people to drink. ¹⁵ And they set out from Rephidim and camped in the wilderness of Sinai. ¹⁶ And they set out from the wilderness of Sinai and camped at Kibroth-hattaavah. ¹⁷ And they set out from Kibroth-hattaavah and camped at Hazeroth. ¹⁸ And they set out from Hazeroth and camped at Rithmah. ¹⁹ And they set out from Rithmah and camped at Rimmon-perez. ²⁰ And they set out from Rimmon-perez and camped at Libnah. ²¹ And they set out from Libnah and camped at Rissah. ²² And they set out from Rissah and camped at Kehelathah. ²³ And they set out from Kehelathah and camped at Mount Shepher. ²⁴ And they set out from Mount Shepher and camped at Haradah. ²⁵ And they set out from Haradah and camped at Makheloth. ²⁶ And they set out from Makheloth and camped at Tahath. ²⁷ And they set out from Tahath and camped at Terah. ²⁸ And they set out from Terah and camped at Mithkah. ²⁹ And they set out from Mithkah and camped at Hashmonah. ³⁰ And they set out from Hashmonah and camped at Moseroth. ³¹ And they set out from Moseroth and camped at Bene-jaakan. ³² And they set out from Bene-jaakan and camped at Hor-haggidgad. ³³ And they set out from Hor-haggidgad and camped at Jotbathah. ³⁴ And they set out from Jotbathah and camped at Abronah. ³⁵ And they set out from Abronah and camped at Ezion-geber. ³⁶ And they set out from Ezion-geber and camped in the wilderness of Zin (that is, Kadesh). ³⁷ And they set out from Kadesh and camped at Mount Hor, on the edge of the land of Edom.

³⁸ And Aaron the priest went up Mount Hor at the command of the LORD and died there, in the fortieth year after the people of Israel had come out of the land of Egypt, on the first day of the fifth month. ³⁹ And Aaron was 123 years old when he died on Mount Hor.

⁴⁰ And the Canaanite, the king of Arad, who lived in the Negeb in the land of Canaan, heard of the coming of the people of Israel.

⁴¹ And they set out from Mount Hor and camped at Zalmonah. ⁴² And they set out from Zalmonah and camped at Punon. ⁴³ And they set out from Punon and camped at Oboth. ⁴⁴ And they set out from Oboth and camped at Iye-abarim, in the territory of Moab. ⁴⁵ And they set out from Iyim and camped at Dibon-gad. ⁴⁶ And they set out from Dibon-gad and camped at Almon-diblathaim. ⁴⁷ And they set out from Almon-diblathaim and camped in the mountains of Abarim, before Nebo. ⁴⁸ And they set out from the mountains of Abarim and camped in the plains of Moab by the Jordan at Jericho; ⁴⁹ they camped by the Jordan from Beth-jeshimoth as far as Abel-shittim in the plains of Moab.

Drive Out the Inhabitants

⁵⁰ And the LORD spoke to Moses in the plains of Moab by the Jordan at Jericho, saying, ⁵¹ "Speak to the people of Israel and say to them, When you pass over the Jordan into the land of Canaan, ⁵² then you shall drive out all the inhabitants of the land from before you and destroy all their figured stones and destroy all their metal images and demolish all their high places. ⁵³ And you shall take possession of the land and settle in it, for I have given the land to you to possess it. ⁵⁴ You shall inherit the land by lot according to your clans. To a large tribe you shall give a large inheritance, and to a small tribe you shall give a small inheritance. Wherever the lot falls for anyone, that shall be his. According to the tribes of your fathers you shall inherit. ⁵⁵ But if you do not drive out the inhabitants of the land from before you, then those of them whom you let remain shall be as barbs in your eyes and thorns in your sides, and they shall trouble you in the land where you dwell. ⁵⁶ And I will do to you as I thought to do to them."

Boundaries of the Land

34 The LORD spoke to Moses, saying, ² "Command the people of Israel, and say to them, When you enter the land of Canaan (this is the land that shall fall to you for an inheritance, the land of Canaan as defined by its borders), ³ your south side shall be from the wilderness of Zin alongside Edom, and your southern border shall run from the end of the Salt Sea on the east. ⁴ And your border shall turn south of the ascent of Akrabbim, and cross to Zin, and its limit shall be south of Kadesh-barnea. Then it shall go on to Hazar-addar, and pass along to Azmon. ⁵ And the border shall turn from Azmon to the Brook of Egypt, and its limit shall be at the sea.

6 "For the western border, you shall have the Great Sea and its[1] coast. This shall be your western border.

7 "This shall be your northern border: from the Great Sea you shall draw a line to Mount Hor. 8 From Mount Hor you shall draw a line to Lebo-hamath, and the limit of the border shall be at Zedad. 9 Then the border shall extend to Ziphron, and its limit shall be at Hazar-enan. This shall be your northern border.

10 "You shall draw a line for your eastern border from Hazar-enan to Shepham. 11 And the border shall go down from Shepham to Riblah on the east side of Ain. And the border shall go down and reach to the shoulder of the Sea of Chinnereth on the east. 12 And the border shall go down to the Jordan, and its limit shall be at the Salt Sea. This shall be your land as defined by its borders all around."

13 Moses commanded the people of Israel, saying, "This is the land that you shall inherit by lot, which the LORD has commanded to give to the nine tribes and to the half-tribe. 14 For the tribe of the people of Reuben by fathers' houses and the tribe of the people of Gad by their fathers' houses have received their inheritance, and also the half-tribe of Manasseh. 15 The two tribes and the half-tribe have received their inheritance beyond the Jordan east of Jericho, toward the sunrise."

List of Tribal Chiefs

16 The LORD spoke to Moses, saying, 17 "These are the names of the men who shall divide the land to you for inheritance: Eleazar the priest and Joshua the son of Nun. 18 You shall take one chief from every tribe to divide the land for inheritance. 19 These are the names of the men: Of the tribe of Judah, Caleb the son of Jephunneh. 20 Of the tribe of the people of Simeon, Shemuel the son of Ammihud. 21 Of the tribe of Benjamin, Elidad the son of Chislon. 22 Of the tribe of the people of Dan a chief, Bukki the son of Jogli. 23 Of the people of Joseph: of the tribe of the people of Manasseh a chief, Hanniel the son of Ephod. 24 And of the tribe of the people of Ephraim a chief, Kemuel the son of Shiphtan. 25 Of the tribe of the people of Zebulun a chief, Elizaphan the son of Parnach. 26 Of the tribe of the people of Issachar a chief, Paltiel the son of Azzan. 27 And of the tribe of the people of Asher a chief, Ahihud the son of Shelomi. 28 Of the tribe of the people of Naphtali a chief, Pedahel the son of Ammihud. 29 These are the men whom the LORD commanded to divide the inheritance for the people of Israel in the land of Canaan."

Cities for the Levites

35 The LORD spoke to Moses in the plains of Moab by the Jordan at Jericho, saying, 2 "Command the people of Israel to give to the Levites some of the inheritance of their possession as cities for them to dwell in. And you shall give to the Levites pasturelands around the cities. 3 The cities shall be theirs to dwell in, and their pasturelands shall be for their cattle and for their livestock and for all their beasts. 4 The pasturelands of the cities, which you shall give to the Levites, shall reach from the wall of the city outward a thousand cubits[2] all around. 5 And you shall measure, outside the city, on the east side two thousand cubits, and on the south side two thousand cubits, and on the west side two thousand cubits, and on the north side two thousand cubits, the city being in the middle. This shall belong to them as pastureland for their cities.

6 "The cities that you give to the Levites shall be the six cities of refuge, where you shall permit the manslayer to flee, and in addition to them you shall give forty-two cities. 7 All the cities that you give to the Levites shall be forty-eight, with their pasturelands. 8 And as for the cities that you shall give from the possession of the people of Israel, from the larger tribes you shall take many, and from the smaller tribes you shall take few; each, in proportion to the inheritance that it inherits, shall give of its cities to the Levites."

Cities of Refuge

9 And the LORD spoke to Moses, saying, 10 "Speak to the people of Israel and say to them, When you cross the Jordan into the land of Canaan, 11 then you shall select cities to be cities of refuge for you, that the manslayer who kills any person without intent may flee there. 12 The cities shall be for you a refuge from the avenger, that the manslayer may not die until he stands before the congregation for judgment.

[1] Syriac; Hebrew lacks *its*   [2] A *cubit* was about 18 inches or 45 centimeters

¹³And the cities that you give shall be your six cities of refuge. ¹⁴You shall give three cities beyond the Jordan, and three cities in the land of Canaan, to be cities of refuge. ¹⁵These six cities shall be for refuge for the people of Israel, and for the stranger and for the sojourner among them, that anyone who kills any person without intent may flee there.

¹⁶"But if he struck him down with an iron object, so that he died, he is a murderer. The murderer shall be put to death. ¹⁷And if he struck him down with a stone tool that could cause death, and he died, he is a murderer. The murderer shall be put to death. ¹⁸Or if he struck him down with a wooden tool that could cause death, and he died, he is a murderer. The murderer shall be put to death. ¹⁹The avenger of blood shall himself put the murderer to death; when he meets him, he shall put him to death. ²⁰And if he pushed him out of hatred or hurled something at him, lying in wait, so that he died, ²¹or in enmity struck him down with his hand, so that he died, then he who struck the blow shall be put to death. He is a murderer. The avenger of blood shall put the murderer to death when he meets him.

²²"But if he pushed him suddenly without enmity, or hurled anything on him without lying in wait ²³or used a stone that could cause death, and without seeing him dropped it on him, so that he died, though he was not his enemy and did not seek his harm, ²⁴then the congregation shall judge between the manslayer and the avenger of blood, in accordance with these rules. ²⁵And the congregation shall rescue the manslayer from the hand of the avenger of blood, and the congregation shall restore him to his city of refuge to which he had fled, and he shall live in it until the death of the high priest who was anointed with the holy oil. ²⁶But if the manslayer shall at any time go beyond the boundaries of his city of refuge to which he fled, ²⁷and the avenger of blood finds him outside the boundaries of his city of refuge, and the avenger of blood kills the manslayer, he shall not be guilty of blood. ²⁸For he must remain in his city of refuge until the death of the high priest, but after the death of the high priest the manslayer may return to the land of his possession. ²⁹And these things shall be for a statute and rule for you

throughout your generations in all your dwelling places.

³⁰"If anyone kills a person, the murderer shall be put to death on the evidence of witnesses. But no person shall be put to death on the testimony of one witness. ³¹Moreover, you shall accept no ransom for the life of a murderer, who is guilty of death, but he shall be put to death. ³²And you shall accept no ransom for him who has fled to his city of refuge, that he may return to dwell in the land before the death of the high priest. ³³You shall not pollute the land in which you live, for blood pollutes the land, and no atonement can be made for the land for the blood that is shed in it, except by the blood of the one who shed it. ³⁴You shall not defile the land in which you live, in the midst of which I dwell, for I the Lord dwell in the midst of the people of Israel."

Marriage of Female Heirs

36 The heads of the fathers' houses of the clan of the people of Gilead the son of Machir, son of Manasseh, from the clans of the people of Joseph, came near and spoke before Moses and before the chiefs, the heads of the fathers' houses of the people of Israel. ²They said, "The Lord commanded my lord to give the land for inheritance by lot to the people of Israel, and my lord was commanded by the Lord to give the inheritance of Zelophehad our brother to his daughters. ³But if they are married to any of the sons of the other tribes of the people of Israel, then their inheritance will be taken from the inheritance of our fathers and added to the inheritance of the tribe into which they marry. So it will be taken away from the lot of our inheritance. ⁴And when the jubilee of the people of Israel comes, then their inheritance will be added to the inheritance of the tribe into which they marry, and their inheritance will be taken from the inheritance of the tribe of our fathers."

⁵And Moses commanded the people of Israel according to the word of the Lord, saying, "The tribe of the people of Joseph is right. ⁶This is what the Lord commands concerning the daughters of Zelophehad: 'Let them marry whom they think best, only they shall marry within the clan of the tribe of their father. ⁷The inheritance of the people of Israel shall not

be transferred from one tribe to another, for every one of the people of Israel shall hold on to the inheritance of the tribe of his fathers. ⁸ And every daughter who possesses an inheritance in any tribe of the people of Israel shall be wife to one of the clan of the tribe of her father, so that every one of the people of Israel may possess the inheritance of his fathers. ⁹ So no inheritance shall be transferred from one tribe to another, for each of the tribes of the people of Israel shall hold on to its own inheritance.'"

¹⁰ The daughters of Zelophehad did as the LORD commanded Moses, ¹¹ for Mahlah, Tirzah, Hoglah, Milcah, and Noah, the daughters of Zelophehad, were married to sons of their father's brothers. ¹² They were married into the clans of the people of Manasseh the son of Joseph, and their inheritance remained in the tribe of their father's clan.

¹³ These are the commandments and the rules that the LORD commanded through Moses to the people of Israel in the plains of Moab by the Jordan at Jericho.

Deuteronomy

Remember What God Has Done

> "If you obey the commandments of the LORD your God that I command you today, by loving the LORD your God, by walking in his ways, and by keeping his commandments and his statutes and his rules, then you shall live and multiply, and the LORD your God will bless you in the land that you are entering to take possession of it."
>
> *Deuteronomy 30:16*

Author: Moses

Time: The end of the fifteenth century B.C.

Place: The plains east of the Jordan River

Written to: The Israelites

The gist

The Israelites were just about to enter the Promised Land without Moses. And before they did, he wanted to give them one last lesson on who God is, what he had done to redeem Israel, and how they were to respond in grateful obedience.

Things to look for

- The Ten Commandments (see Deuteronomy 5)
- Commands for loving God (see Deuteronomy 6)
- God's mercy to his people (see Deuteronomy 9)
- Teachings on obedience (see Deut. 10:12–12:1, 28; 13:4; and many other places)

You're not a Christian just because your parents are Christians. Your faith has to be your own, and in order for that to happen, you have to know what you believe and why you believe it. When the Israelites were about to enter the Promised Land, Moses was about to die. This new generation of Israelites wasn't there when Moses was given the Ten Commandments. They weren't familiar with God's covenant and commands, and they needed to be taught all over again what God had done for them and what he wanted from them.

Deuteronomy is Moses' testimony about God's character and law. He wanted this new generation to know how important it was to remember everything that had happened to their people in the land of Egypt and in the exodus, and he wanted to prepare them to honor their agreement with the Lord once they crossed the river into the Promised Land. Deuteronomy can be a testimony to you today as you remember all that God has done for you in the past and as by faith you look forward to all that he'll do for you in the future. His call on your life is not so different from his call on the lives of those Israelites so long ago: love the Lord your God, trusting him completely in all things. Then, in gratitude, as someone who has been redeemed in mercy, obey his commands, laws, and rules.

Must-Know Terms and Verses

❧ Ammonites ❧

The descendants of Ben Ammi, who was the son of Lot and his younger daughter (see Gen. 19:30–38). They refused to help the Israelites when they came out of Egypt (see Deut. 23:3–4).

❧ Edomites ❧

Edom was another name for Esau, the brother of Jacob, who gave up his inheritance for a bowl of soup. His descendants, the Edomites, refused to help the people of Judah when they were being attacked by the Babylonians (see Obadiah).

❧ El ❧

A Hebrew word meaning God.

❧ Moabites ❧

The descendants of Moab, who was the son of Lot and his older daughter (see Gen. 19:30–38). They refused to help the Israelites when they came out of Egypt (see Deut. 23:3–4).

"Then I said to you, 'Do not be in dread or afraid of them. The LORD your God who goes before you will himself fight for you, just as he did for you in Egypt before your eyes, and in the wilderness.'" *Deuteronomy 1:29–31*

"But from there you will seek the LORD your God and you will find him, if you search after him with all your heart and with all your soul." *Deuteronomy 4:29*

"You shall love the LORD your God with all your heart and with all your soul and with all your might." *Deuteronomy 6:5*

"You shall tithe all the yield of your seed that comes from the field year by year." *Deuteronomy 14:22*

Deuteronomy

The Command to Leave Horeb

1 These are the words that Moses spoke to all Israel beyond the Jordan in the wilderness, in the Arabah opposite Suph, between Paran and Tophel, Laban, Hazeroth, and Dizahab. ²It is eleven days' journey from Horeb by the way of Mount Seir to Kadesh-barnea. ³In the fortieth year, on the first day of the eleventh month, Moses spoke to the people of Israel according to all that the LORD had given him in commandment to them, ⁴after he had defeated Sihon the king of the Amorites, who lived in Heshbon, and Og the king of Bashan, who lived in Ashtaroth and in Edrei. ⁵Beyond the Jordan, in the land of Moab, Moses undertook to explain this law, saying, ⁶"The LORD our God said to us in Horeb, 'You have stayed long enough at this mountain. ⁷Turn and take your journey, and go to the hill country of the Amorites and to all their neighbors in the Arabah, in the hill country and in the lowland and in the Negeb and by the seacoast, the land of the Canaanites, and Lebanon, as far as the great river, the river Euphrates. ⁸See, I have set the land before you. Go in and take possession of the land that the LORD swore to your fathers, to Abraham, to Isaac, and to Jacob, to give to them and to their offspring after them.'

Leaders Appointed

⁹"At that time I said to you, 'I am not able to bear you by myself. ¹⁰The LORD your God has multiplied you, and behold, you are today as numerous as the stars of heaven. ¹¹May the LORD, the God of your fathers, make you a thousand times as many as you are and bless you, as he has promised you! ¹²How can I bear by myself the weight and burden of you and your strife? ¹³Choose for your tribes wise, understanding, and experienced men, and I will appoint them as your heads.' ¹⁴And you answered me, 'The thing that you have spoken is good for us to do.' ¹⁵So I took the heads of your tribes, wise and experienced men, and set them as heads over you, commanders of thousands, commanders of hundreds, commanders of fifties, commanders of tens, and officers, throughout your tribes. ¹⁶And I charged your judges at that time, 'Hear the cases between your brothers, and judge righteously between a man and his brother or the alien who is with him. ¹⁷You shall not be partial in judgment. You shall hear the small and the great alike. You shall not be intimidated by anyone, for the judgment is God's. And the case that is too hard for you, you shall bring to me, and I will hear it.' ¹⁸And I commanded you at that time all the things that you should do.

Israel's Refusal to Enter the Land

¹⁹"Then we set out from Horeb and went through all that great and terrifying wilderness that you saw, on the way to the hill country of the Amorites, as the LORD our God commanded us. And we came to Kadesh-barnea. ²⁰And I said to you, 'You have come to the hill country of the Amorites, which the LORD our God is giving us. ²¹See, the LORD your God has set the land before you. Go up, take possession, as the LORD, the God of your fathers, has told you. Do not fear or be dismayed.' ²²Then all of you came near me and said, 'Let us send men before us, that they may explore the land for us and bring us word again of the way by which we must go up and the cities into which we shall come.' ²³The thing seemed good to me, and I took twelve men from you, one man from each tribe. ²⁴And they turned and went up into the hill country, and came to the Valley of Eshcol and spied it out. ²⁵And they took in their hands some of the fruit of the land and brought it down to us, and brought us word again and said, 'It is a good land that the LORD our God is giving us.'

²⁶"Yet you would not go up, but rebelled

against the command of the LORD your God. ²⁷And you murmured in your tents and said, 'Because the LORD hated us he has brought us out of the land of Egypt, to give us into the hand of the Amorites, to destroy us. ²⁸Where are we going up? Our brothers have made our hearts melt, saying, "The people are greater and taller than we. The cities are great and fortified up to heaven. And besides, we have seen the sons of the Anakim there."' ²⁹Then I said to you, 'Do not be in dread or afraid of them. ³⁰The LORD your God who goes before you will himself fight for you, just as he did for you in Egypt before your eyes, ³¹and in the wilderness, where you have seen how the LORD your God carried you, as a man carries his son, all the way that you went until you came to this place.' ³²Yet in spite of this word you did not believe the LORD your God, ³³who went before you in the way to seek you out a place to pitch your tents, in fire by night and in the cloud by day, to show you by what way you should go.

The Penalty for Israel's Rebellion

³⁴"And the LORD heard your words and was angered, and he swore, ³⁵'Not one of these men of this evil generation sha see the good land that I swore to give t your fathers, ³⁶except Caleb the son o Jephunneh. He shall see it, and to him an to his children I will give the land on whic he has trodden, because he has wholly fol lowed the LORD!' ³⁷Even with me the LOR was angry on your account and said, 'Yo also shall not go in there. ³⁸Joshua the so of Nun, who stands before you, he sha enter. Encourage him, for he shall caus Israel to inherit it. ³⁹And as for your littl ones, who you said would become a prey and your children, who today have n knowledge of good or evil, they shall go i there. And to them I will give it, and the shall possess it. ⁴⁰But as for you, turn, an journey into the wilderness in the direc tion of the Red Sea.'

⁴¹"Then you answered me, 'We hav sinned against the LORD. We ourselves wi go up and fight, just as the LORD our Go commanded us.' And every one of you fas tened on his weapons of war and though it easy to go up into the hill country. ⁴²An the LORD said to me, 'Say to them, Do no go up or fight, for I am not in your midst

Know Yourself

verses to read
Deuteronomy 1:1-5

The Israelites took forty years to make a trip that should have taken eleven days. Forty years! Can you imagine? It seems impossible, doesn't it? But what about you—how long does it take you to learn what God wants to teach you? Have you been tested in the same thing over and over again? Do you see the same trials coming to you on a regular basis? If you say to yourself, "This keeps happening to me!" then it might be time to consider that you may be wandering in the desert because of your disobedience, and you aren't going to get out until you hand your life over to God and trust him completely.

So look at your life. If there's something you can't get past, get over, or get away from, then it might just be time to take a fresh look at it from the perspective of God's Word. Find out how you could act more like someone who agrees with Scripture and less like someone who agrees with their own sin. Talk to God. Ask him what lesson you need to learn so that you can get out of your desert wanderings. Remember, not all pain is a direct result of our disobedience; sometimes adversity comes simply because God in his great love wants to draw us closer to himself. Whatever the cause of your wilderness wandering, stop asking, "Why me?" and start asking, "What about God and his goodness is he trying to teach me?" Let God's Word be your guide.

lest you be defeated before your enemies.' [43] So I spoke to you, and you would not listen; but you rebelled against the command of the LORD and presumptuously went up into the hill country. [44] Then the Amorites who lived in that hill country came out against you and chased you as bees do and beat you down in Seir as far as Hormah. [45] And you returned and wept before the LORD, but the LORD did not listen to your voice or give ear to you. [46] So you remained at Kadesh many days, the days that you remained there.

The Wilderness Years

2 "Then we turned and journeyed into the wilderness in the direction of the Red Sea, as the LORD told me. And for many days we traveled around Mount Seir. [2] Then the LORD said to me, [3] 'You have been traveling around this mountain country long enough. Turn northward [4] and command the people, "You are about to pass through the territory of your brothers, the people of Esau, who live in Seir; and they will be afraid of you. So be very careful. [5] Do not contend with them, for I will not give you any of their land, no, not so much as for the sole of the foot to tread on, because I have given Mount Seir to Esau as a possession. [6] You shall purchase food from them with money, that you may eat, and you shall also buy water from them with money, that you may drink. [7] For the LORD your God has blessed you in all the work of your hands. He knows your going through this great wilderness. These forty years the LORD your God has been with you. You have lacked nothing."' [8] So we went on, away from our brothers, the people of Esau, who live in Seir, away from the Arabah road from Elath and Ezion-geber.

"And we turned and went in the direction of the wilderness of Moab. [9] And the LORD said to me, 'Do not harass Moab or contend with them in battle, for I will not give you any of their land for a possession, because I have given Ar to the people of Lot for a possession.' [10] (The Emim formerly lived there, a people great and many, and tall as the Anakim. [11] Like the Anakim they are also counted as Rephaim, but the Moabites call them Emim. [12] The Horites also lived in Seir formerly, but the people of Esau dispossessed them and destroyed them from

before them and settled in their place, as Israel did to the land of their possession, which the LORD gave to them.) [13] 'Now rise up and go over the brook Zered.' So we went over the brook Zered. [14] And the time from our leaving Kadesh-barnea until we crossed the brook Zered was thirty-eight years, until the entire generation, that is, the men of war, had perished from the camp, as the LORD had sworn to them. [15] For indeed the hand of the LORD was against them, to destroy them from the camp, until they had perished.

[16] "So as soon as all the men of war had perished and were dead from among the people, [17] the LORD said to me, [18] 'Today you are to cross the border of Moab at Ar. [19] And when you approach the territory of the people of Ammon, do not harass them or contend with them, for I will not give you any of the land of the people of Ammon as a possession, because I have given it to the sons of Lot for a possession.' [20] (It is also counted as a land of Rephaim. Rephaim formerly lived there— but the Ammonites call them Zamzummim— [21] a people great and many, and tall as the Anakim; but the LORD destroyed them before the Ammonites,[1] and they dispossessed them and settled in their place, [22] as he did for the people of Esau, who live in Seir, when he destroyed the Horites before them and they dispossessed them and settled in their place even to this day. [23] As for the Avvim, who lived in villages as far as Gaza, the Caphtorim, who came from Caphtor, destroyed them and settled in their place.) [24] 'Rise up, set out on your journey and go over the Valley of the Arnon. Behold, I have given into your hand Sihon the Amorite, king of Heshbon, and his land. Begin to take possession, and contend with him in battle. [25] This day I will begin to put the dread and fear of you on the peoples who are under the whole heaven, who shall hear the report of you and shall tremble and be in anguish because of you.'

The Defeat of King Sihon

[26] "So I sent messengers from the wilderness of Kedemoth to Sihon the king of Heshbon, with words of peace, saying, [27] 'Let me pass through your land. I will go only by the road; I will turn aside neither to the right nor to the left. [28] You shall sell

[1] Hebrew *them*

me food for money, that I may eat, and give me water for money, that I may drink. Only let me pass through on foot, 29 as the sons of Esau who live in Seir and the Moabites who live in Ar did for me, until I go over the Jordan into the land that the LORD our God is giving to us.' 30 But Sihon the king of Heshbon would not let us pass by him, for the LORD your God hardened his spirit and made his heart obstinate, that he might give him into your hand, as he is this day. 31 And the LORD said to me, 'Behold, I have begun to give Sihon and his land over to you. Begin to take possession, that you may occupy his land.' 32 Then Sihon came out against us, he and all his people, to battle at Jahaz. 33 And the LORD our God gave him over to us, and we defeated him and his sons and all his people. 34 And we captured all his cities at that time and devoted to destruction[1] every city, men, women, and children. We left no survivors. 35 Only the livestock we took as spoil for ourselves, with the plunder of the cities that we captured. 36 From Aroer, which is on the edge of the Valley of the Arnon, and from the city that is in the valley, as far as Gilead, there was not a city too high for us. The LORD our God gave all into our hands. 37 Only to the land of the sons of Ammon you did not draw near, that is, to all the banks of the river Jabbok and the cities of the hill country, whatever the LORD our God had forbidden us.

The Defeat of King Og

3 "Then we turned and went up the way to Bashan. And Og the king of Bashan came out against us, he and all his people, to battle at Edrei. 2 But the LORD said to me, 'Do not fear him, for I have given him and all his people and his land into your hand. And you shall do to him as you did to Sihon the king of the Amorites, who lived at Heshbon.' 3 So the LORD our God gave into our hand Og also, the king of Bashan, and all his people, and we struck him down until he had no survivor left. 4 And we took all his cities at that time—there was not a city that we did not take from them—sixty cities, the whole region of Argob, the kingdom of Og in Bashan. 5 All these were cities fortified with high walls, gates, and bars, besides very many unwalled villages. 6 And

we devoted them to destruction,[2] as we did to Sihon the king of Heshbon, devoting to destruction every city, men, women, and children. 7 But all the livestock and the spoil of the cities we took as our plunder. 8 So we took the land at that time out of the hand of the two kings of the Amorites who were beyond the Jordan, from the Valley of the Arnon to Mount Hermon 9 (the Sidonians call Hermon Sirion, while the Amorites call it Senir), 10 all the cities of the tableland and all Gilead and all Bashan, as far as Salecah and Edrei, cities of the kingdom of Og in Bashan. 11 (For only Og the king of Bashan was left of the remnant of the Rephaim. Behold, his bed was a bed of iron. Is it not in Rabbah of the Ammonites? Nine cubits[3] was its length, and four cubits its breadth, according to the common cubit.[4])

12 "When we took possession of this land at that time, I gave to the Reubenites and the Gadites the territory beginning at Aroer, which is on the edge of the Valley of the Arnon, and half the hill country of Gilead with its cities. 13 The rest of Gilead, and all Bashan, the kingdom of Og, that is, all the region of Argob, I gave to the half-tribe of Manasseh. (All that portion of Bashan is called the land of Rephaim. 14 Jair the Manassite took all the region of Argob, that is, Bashan, as far as the border of the Geshurites and the Maacathites, and called the villages after his own name, Havvoth-jair, as it is to this day.) 15 To Machir I gave Gilead, 16 and to the Reubenites and the Gadites I gave the territory from Gilead as far as the Valley of the Arnon, with the middle of the valley as a border, as far over as the river Jabbok, the border of the Ammonites; 17 the Arabah also, with the Jordan as the border, from Chinnereth as far as the Sea of the Arabah, the Salt Sea, under the slopes of Pisgah on the east.

18 "And I commanded you at that time, saying, 'The LORD your God has given you this land to possess. All your men of valor shall cross over armed before your brothers, the people of Israel. 19 Only your wives, your little ones, and your livestock (I know that you have much livestock) shall remain in the cities that I have given you, 20 until the LORD gives rest to your brothers, as to you, and they also occupy the land that the LORD your God gives them beyond the

---

[1] That is, set apart (devoted) as an offering to the Lord (for destruction) [2] That is, set apart (devoted) as an offering to the Lord (for destruction); twice in this verse [3] A *cubit* was about 18 inches or 45 centimeters [4] Hebrew *cubit of a man*

Jordan. Then each of you may return to his possession which I have given you.' [21] And I commanded Joshua at that time, 'Your eyes have seen all that the LORD your God has done to these two kings. So will the LORD do to all the kingdoms into which you are crossing. [22] You shall not fear them, for it is the LORD your God who fights for you.'

Moses Forbidden to Enter the Land

[23] "And I pleaded with the LORD at that time, saying, [24] 'O Lord GOD, you have only begun to show your servant your greatness and your mighty hand. For what god is there in heaven or on earth who can do such works and mighty acts as yours? [25] Please let me go over and see the good land beyond the Jordan, that good hill country and Lebanon.' [26] But the LORD was angry with me because of you and would not listen to me. And the LORD said to me, 'Enough from you; do not speak to me of this matter again. [27] Go up to the top of Pisgah and lift up your eyes westward and northward and southward and eastward, and look at it with your eyes, for you shall not go over this Jordan. [28] But charge Joshua, and encourage and strengthen him, for he shall go over at the head of this people, and he shall put them in possession of the land that you shall see.' [29] So we remained in the valley opposite Beth-peor.

Moses Commands Obedience

4 "And now, O Israel, listen to the statutes and the rules[1] that I am teaching you, and do them, that you may live, and go in and take possession of the land that the LORD, the God of your fathers, is giving you. [2] You shall not add to the word that I command you, nor take from it, that you may keep the commandments of the LORD your God that I command you. [3] Your eyes have seen what the LORD did at Baal-peor, for the LORD your God destroyed from among you all the men who followed the Baal of Peor. [4] But you who held fast to the LORD your God are all alive today. [5] See, I have taught you statutes and rules, as the LORD my God commanded me, that you should do them in the land that you are entering to take possession of it. [6] Keep them and do them, for that will be your wisdom and your understanding in the sight of the peoples, who, when they hear all these

statutes, will say, 'Surely this great nation is a wise and understanding people.' [7] For what great nation is there that has a god so near to it as the LORD our God is to us, whenever we call upon him? [8] And what great nation is there, that has statutes and rules so righteous as all this law that I set before you today?

[9] "Only take care, and keep your soul diligently, lest you forget the things that your eyes have seen, and lest they depart from your heart all the days of your life. Make them known to your children and your children's children— [10] how on the day that you stood before the LORD your God at Horeb, the LORD said to me, 'Gather the people to me, that I may let them hear my words, so that they may learn to fear me all the days that they live on the earth, and that they may teach their children so.' [11] And you came near and stood at the foot of the mountain, while the mountain burned with fire to the heart of heaven, wrapped in darkness, cloud, and gloom. [12] Then the LORD spoke to you out of the midst of the fire. You heard the sound of words, but saw no form; there was only a voice. [13] And he declared to you his covenant, which he commanded you to perform, that is, the Ten Commandments,[2] and he wrote them on two tablets of stone. [14] And the LORD commanded me at that time to teach you statutes and rules, that you might do them in the land that you are going over to possess.

Idolatry Forbidden

[15] "Therefore watch yourselves very carefully. Since you saw no form on the day that the LORD spoke to you at Horeb out of the midst of the fire, [16] beware lest you act corruptly by making a carved image for yourselves, in the form of any figure, the likeness of male or female, [17] the likeness of any animal that is on the earth, the likeness of any winged bird that flies in the air, [18] the likeness of anything that creeps on the ground, the likeness of any fish that is in the water under the earth. [19] And beware lest you raise your eyes to heaven, and when you see the sun and the moon and the stars, all the host of heaven, you be drawn away and bow down to them and serve them, things that the LORD your God has allotted to all the peoples under

[1] Or just decrees; also verses 5, 8, 14, 45 [2] Hebrew words

the whole heaven. ²⁰ But the LORD has taken you and brought you out of the iron furnace, out of Egypt, to be a people of his own inheritance, as you are this day. ²¹ Furthermore, the LORD was angry with me because of you, and he swore that I should not cross the Jordan, and that I should not enter the good land that the LORD your God is giving you for an inheritance. ²² For I must die in this land; I must not go over the Jordan. But you shall go over and take possession of that good land. ²³ Take care, lest you forget the covenant of the LORD your God, which he made with you, and make a carved image, the form of anything that the LORD your God has forbidden you. ²⁴ For the LORD your God is a consuming fire, a jealous God.

²⁵ "When you father children and children's children, and have grown old in the land, if you act corruptly by making a carved image in the form of anything, and by doing what is evil in the sight of the LORD your God, so as to provoke him to anger, ²⁶ I call heaven and earth to witness against you today, that you will soon utterly perish from the land that you are going over the Jordan to possess. You will not live long in it, but will be utterly destroyed. ²⁷ And the LORD will scatter you among the peoples, and you will be left few in number among the nations where the LORD will drive you. ²⁸ And there you will serve gods of wood and stone, the work of human hands, that neither see, nor hear, nor eat, nor smell. ²⁹ But from there you will seek the LORD your God and you will find him, if you search after him with all your heart and with all your soul. ³⁰ When you are in tribulation, and all these things come upon you in the latter days, you will return to the LORD your God and obey his voice. ³¹ For the LORD your God is a merciful God. He will not leave you or destroy you or forget the covenant with your fathers that he swore to them.

The LORD Alone Is God

³² "For ask now of the days that are past, which were before you, since the day that God created man on the earth, and ask from one end of heaven to the other, whether such a great thing as this has ever happened or was ever heard of. ³³ Did any people ever hear the voice of a god speaking out of the midst of the fire, as you have heard, and still live? ³⁴ Or has any god ever attempted to go and take a nation for himself from the midst of another nation, by trials, by signs, by wonders, and by war,

Know How to Communicate

verses to read
Deuteronomy 4:29-31

Do you find it hard to connect with God? Hard to hear his voice? Don't worry, this is to be expected. This is a fallen world, and for various reasons God sometimes feels distant. But no matter what you may feel like, you can always know that God loves you and has only the best in store for you—after all, he gave his only Son for us (see Rom. 8:32)!

God promises you that you will find him, but he makes the point that it will take energy—in fact, all the energy your heart has to give. Have you run after God with all your heart? Or is part of your heart somewhere else? It takes time to get your heart to concentrate, so don't give up when it doesn't focus immediately. And whatever happens, never forget how wonderfully patient God is with his children.

A lot of people just go to God for direction: "Which way is best for me?" But God is more concerned with you knowing him than he is with getting you what you want and where you want to go. So if you're having trouble hearing him, don't give up. Just trust that if you are persistent in wanting to know him, you will find him.

by a mighty hand and an outstretched arm, and by great deeds of terror, all of which the LORD your God did for you in Egypt before your eyes? ³⁵ To you it was shown, that you might know that the LORD is God; there is no other besides him. ³⁶ Out of heaven he let you hear his voice, that he might discipline you. And on earth he let you see his great fire, and you heard his words out of the midst of the fire. ³⁷ And because he loved your fathers and chose their offspring after them[1] and brought you out of Egypt with his own presence, by his great power, ³⁸ driving out before you nations greater and mightier than you, to bring you in, to give you their land for an inheritance, as it is this day, ³⁹ know therefore today, and lay it to your heart, that the LORD is God in heaven above and on the earth beneath; there is no other. ⁴⁰ Therefore you shall keep his statutes and his commandments, which I command you today, that it may go well with you and with your children after you, and that you may prolong your days in the land that the LORD your God is giving you for all time."

Cities of Refuge

⁴¹ Then Moses set apart three cities in the east beyond the Jordan, ⁴² that the manslayer might flee there, anyone who kills his neighbor unintentionally, without being at enmity with him in time past; he may flee to one of these cities and save his life: ⁴³ Bezer in the wilderness on the tableland for the Reubenites, Ramoth in Gilead for the Gadites, and Golan in Bashan for the Manassites.

Introduction to the Law

⁴⁴ This is the law that Moses set before the people of Israel. ⁴⁵ These are the testimonies, the statutes, and the rules, which Moses spoke to the people of Israel when they came out of Egypt, ⁴⁶ beyond the Jordan in the valley opposite Beth-peor, in the land of Sihon the king of the Amorites, who lived at Heshbon, whom Moses and the people of Israel defeated when they came out of Egypt. ⁴⁷ And they took possession of his land and the land of Og, the king of Bashan, the two kings of the Amorites, who lived to the east beyond the Jordan; ⁴⁸ from Aroer, which is on the edge of the Valley of the Arnon, as far as Mount Sirion[2]

(that is, Hermon), ⁴⁹ together with all the Arabah on the east side of the Jordan as far as the Sea of the Arabah, under the slopes of Pisgah.

The Ten Commandments

5 And Moses summoned all Israel and said to them, "Hear, O Israel, the statutes and the rules that I speak in your hearing today, and you shall learn them and be careful to do them. ² The LORD our God made a covenant with us in Horeb. ³ Not with our fathers did the LORD make this covenant, but with us, who are all of us here alive today. ⁴ The LORD spoke with you face to face at the mountain, out of the midst of the fire, ⁵ while I stood between the LORD and you at that time, to declare to you the word of the LORD. For you were afraid because of the fire, and you did not go up into the mountain. He said:

⁶ "'I am the LORD your God, who brought you out of the land of Egypt, out of the house of slavery.

⁷ "'You shall have no other gods before[3] me.

⁸ "'You shall not make for yourself a carved image, or any likeness of anything that is in heaven above, or that is on the earth beneath, or that is in the water under the earth. ⁹ You shall not bow down to them or serve them; for I the LORD your God am a jealous God, visiting the iniquity of the fathers on the children to the third and fourth generation of those who hate me, ¹⁰ but showing steadfast love to thousands[4] of those who love me and keep my commandments.

¹¹ "'You shall not take the name of the LORD your God in vain, for the LORD will not hold him guiltless who takes his name in vain.

¹² "'Observe the Sabbath day, to keep it holy, as the LORD your God commanded you. ¹³ Six days you shall labor and do all your work, ¹⁴ but the seventh day is a Sabbath to the LORD your God. On it you shall not do any work, you or your son or your daughter or your male servant or your female servant, or your ox or your donkey or any of your livestock, or the sojourner who is within your gates, that your male servant and your female servant may rest as well as you. ¹⁵ You shall remember that you were a slave[5] in the land of

Hebrew *his offspring after him* [2] Syriac; Hebrew *Sion* [3] Or *besides* [4] Or *to the thousandth generation* [5] Or *servant*

Egypt, and the LORD your God brought you out from there with a mighty hand and an outstretched arm. Therefore the LORD your God commanded you to keep the Sabbath day.

¹⁶ " 'Honor your father and your mother, as the LORD your God commanded you, that your days may be long, and that it may go well with you in the land that the LORD your God is giving you.

¹⁷ " 'You shall not murder.'¹

¹⁸ " 'And you shall not commit adultery.

¹⁹ " 'And you shall not steal.

²⁰ " 'And you shall not bear false witness against your neighbor.

²¹ " 'And you shall not covet your neighbor's wife. And you shall not desire your neighbor's house, his field, or his male servant, or his female servant, his ox, or his donkey, or anything that is your neighbor's.'

²² "These words the LORD spoke to all your assembly at the mountain out of the midst of the fire, the cloud, and the thick darkness, with a loud voice; and he added no more. And he wrote them on two tablets of stone and gave them to me. ²³ And as soon as you heard the voice out of the midst of the darkness, while the mountain was burning with fire, you came near to me, all the heads of your tribes, and your elders. ²⁴ And you said, 'Behold, the LORD our God has shown us his glory and greatness, and we have heard his voice out of the midst of the fire. This day we have seen God speak with man, and man still live. ²⁵ Now therefore why should we die? For this great fire will consume us. If we hear the voice of the LORD our God any more, we shall die. ²⁶ For who is there of all flesh, that has heard the voice of the living God speaking out of the midst of fire as we have, and has still lived? ²⁷ Go near and hear all that the LORD our God will say, and speak to us all that the LORD our God will speak to you, and we will hear and do it.'

²⁸ "And the LORD heard your words, when you spoke to me. And the LORD said to me, 'I have heard the words of this people, which they have spoken to you. They are right in all that they have spoken. ²⁹ Oh that they had such a heart as this always, to fear me and to keep all my commandments, that it might go well with them and with their descendants² forever! ³⁰ Go and say

to them, "Return to your tents." ³¹ But you stand here by me, and I will tell you the whole commandment and the statutes and the rules that you shall teach them, that they may do them in the land that I am giving them to possess.' ³² You shall be careful therefore to do as the LORD your God has commanded you. You shall not turn aside to the right hand or to the left. ³³ You shall walk in all the way that the LORD your God has commanded you, that you may live, and that it may go well with you, and that you may live long in the land that you shall possess.

The Greatest Commandment

6 "Now this is the commandment—the statutes and the rules³— that the LORD your God commanded me to teach you, that you may do them in the land to which you are going over, to possess it, ² that you may fear the LORD your God, you and your son and your son's son, by keeping all his statutes and his commandments, which I command you, all the days of your life, and that your days may be long. ³ Hear therefore, O Israel, and be careful to do them, that it may go well with you, and that you may multiply greatly, as the LORD, the God of your fathers, has promised you, in a land flowing with milk and honey.

⁴ "Hear, O Israel: The LORD our God, the LORD is one.⁴ ⁵ You shall love the LORD your God with all your heart and with all your soul and with all your might. ⁶ And these words that I command you today shall be on your heart. ⁷ You shall teach them diligently to your children, and shall talk of them when you sit in your house, and when you walk by the way, and when you lie down, and when you rise. ⁸ You shall bind them as a sign on your hand, and they shall be as frontlets between your eyes. ⁹ You shall write them on the doorposts of your house and on your gates.

¹⁰ "And when the LORD your God brings you into the land that he swore to your fathers, to Abraham, to Isaac, and to Jacob, to give you—with great and good cities that you did not build, ¹¹ and houses full of all good things that you did not fill, and cisterns that you did not dig, and vineyards and olive trees that you did not plant—and when you eat and are full, ¹² then take care

¹ The Hebrew word also covers causing human death through carelessness or negligence ² Or *sons* ³ Or *just decrees*; also verse 20
⁴ Or *The LORD our God is one LORD*; or *The LORD is our God, the LORD is one*; or *The LORD is our God, the LORD alone*

lest you forget the LORD, who brought you out of the land of Egypt, out of the house of slavery. [13] It is the LORD your God you shall fear. Him you shall serve and by his name you shall swear. [14] You shall not go after other gods, the gods of the peoples who are around you— [15] for the LORD your God in your midst is a jealous God—lest the anger of the LORD your God be kindled against you, and he destroy you from off the face of the earth.

[16] "You shall not put the LORD your God to the test, as you tested him at Massah. [17] You shall diligently keep the commandments of the LORD your God, and his testimonies and his statutes, which he has commanded you. [18] And you shall do what is right and good in the sight of the LORD, that it may go well with you, and that you may go in and take possession of the good land that the LORD swore to give to your fathers [19] by thrusting out all your enemies from before you, as the LORD has promised.

[20] "When your son asks you in time to come, 'What is the meaning of the testimonies and the statutes and the rules that the LORD our God has commanded you?' [21] then you shall say to your son, 'We were Pharaoh's slaves in Egypt. And the LORD brought us out of Egypt with a mighty hand. [22] And the LORD showed signs and wonders, great and grievous, against Egypt and against Pharaoh and all his household, before our eyes. [23] And he brought us out from there, that he might bring us in and give us the land that he swore to give to our fathers. [24] And the LORD commanded us to do all these statutes, to fear the LORD our God, for our good always, that he might preserve us alive, as we are this day. [25] And it will be righteousness for us, if we are careful to do all this commandment before the LORD our God, as he has commanded us.'

A Chosen People

7 "When the LORD your God brings you into the land that you are entering to take possession of it, and clears away many nations before you, the Hittites, the Girgashites, the Amorites, the Canaanites, the Perizzites, the Hivites, and the Jebusites, seven nations more numerous and mightier than you, [2] and when the LORD your God gives them over to you, and you defeat them, then you must devote them to complete destruction.[1] You shall make no covenant with them and show no mercy to them. [3] You shall not intermarry with them, giving your daughters to their sons or taking their daughters for your sons, [4] for they would turn away your sons from following me, to serve other gods. Then the anger of the LORD would be kindled against you, and he would destroy you quickly. [5] But thus shall you deal with them: you shall break down their altars and dash in pieces their pillars and chop down their Asherim and burn their carved images with fire.

[6] "For you are a people holy to the LORD your God. The LORD your God has chosen you to be a people for his treasured possession, out of all the peoples who are on the face of the earth. [7] It was not because you were more in number than any other people that the LORD set his love on you and chose you, for you were the fewest of all peoples, [8] but it is because the LORD loves you and is keeping the oath that he swore to your fathers, that the LORD has brought you out with a mighty hand and redeemed you from the house of slavery, from the hand of Pharaoh king of Egypt. [9] Know therefore that the LORD your God is God, the faithful God who keeps covenant and steadfast love with those who love him and keep his commandments, to a thousand generations, [10] and repays to their face those who hate him, by destroying them. He will not be slack with one who hates him. He will repay him to his face. [11] You shall therefore be careful to do the commandment and the statutes and the rules that I command you today.

[12] "And because you listen to these rules and keep and do them, the LORD your God will keep with you the covenant and the steadfast love that he swore to your fathers. [13] He will love you, bless you, and multiply you. He will also bless the fruit of your womb and the fruit of your ground, your grain and your wine and your oil, the increase of your herds and the young of your flock, in the land that he swore to your fathers to give you. [14] You shall be blessed above all peoples. There shall not be male or female barren among you or among your livestock. [15] And the LORD will take away from you all sickness, and none of the evil diseases of Egypt, which you knew, will he inflict on you, but he will lay

---

[1] That is, set apart (devote) as an offering to the Lord (for destruction)

them on all who hate you. [16] And you shall consume all the peoples that the LORD your God will give over to you. Your eye shall not pity them, neither shall you serve their gods, for that would be a snare to you.

[17] "If you say in your heart, 'These nations are greater than I. How can I dispossess them?' [18] you shall not be afraid of them but you shall remember what the LORD your God did to Pharaoh and to all Egypt, [19] the great trials that your eyes saw, the signs, the wonders, the mighty hand, and the outstretched arm, by which the LORD your God brought you out. So will the LORD your God do to all the peoples of whom you are afraid. [20] Moreover, the LORD your God will send hornets among them, until those who are left and hide themselves from you are destroyed. [21] You shall not be in dread of them, for the LORD your God is in your midst, a great and awesome God. [22] The LORD your God will clear away these nations before you little by little. You may not make an end of them at once,[1] lest the wild beasts grow too numerous for you. [23] But the LORD your God will give them over to you and throw them into great confusion, until they are destroyed. [24] And he will give their kings into your hand, and you shall make their name perish from under heaven. No one shall be able to stand against you until you have destroyed them. [25] The carved images of their gods you shall burn with fire. You shall not covet the silver or the gold that is on them or take it for yourselves, lest you be ensnared by it, for it is an abomination to the LORD your God. [26] And you shall not bring an abominable thing into your house and become devoted to destruction[2] like it. You shall utterly detest and abhor it, for it is devoted to destruction.

Remember the LORD Your God

8 "The whole commandment that I command you today you shall be careful to do, that you may live and multiply, and go in and possess the land that the LORD swore to give to your fathers. [2] And you shall remember the whole way that the LORD your God has led you these forty years in the wilderness, that he might humble you, testing you to know what was in your heart, whether you would keep his commandments or not. [3] And he

humbled you and let you hunger and fed you with manna, which you did not know, nor did your fathers know, that he might make you know that man does not live by bread alone, but man lives by every word[3] that comes from the mouth of the LORD. [4] Your clothing did not wear out on you and your foot did not swell these forty years. [5] Know then in your heart that, as a man disciplines his son, the LORD your God disciplines you. [6] So you shall keep the commandments of the LORD your God by walking in his ways and by fearing him. [7] For the LORD your God is bringing you into a good land, a land of brooks of water, of fountains and springs, flowing out in the valleys and hills, [8] a land of wheat and barley, of vines and fig trees and pomegranates, a land of olive trees and honey, [9] a land in which you will eat bread without scarcity, in which you will lack nothing, a land whose stones are iron, and out of whose hills you can dig copper. [10] And you shall eat and be full, and you shall bless the LORD your God for the good land he has given you.

[11] "Take care lest you forget the LORD your God by not keeping his commandments and his rules and his statutes, which I command you today, [12] lest, when you have eaten and are full and have built good houses and live in them, [13] and when your herds and flocks multiply and your silver and gold is multiplied and all that you have is multiplied, [14] then your heart be lifted up, and you forget the LORD your God, who brought you out of the land of Egypt, out of the house of slavery, [15] who led you through the great and terrifying wilderness, with its fiery serpents and scorpions and thirsty ground where there was no water, who brought you water out of the flinty rock, [16] who fed you in the wilderness with manna that your fathers did not know, that he might humble you and test you, to do you good in the end. [17] Beware lest you say in your heart, 'My power and the might of my hand have gotten me this wealth.' [18] You shall remember the LORD your God, for it is he who gives you power to get wealth, that he may confirm his covenant that he swore to your fathers, as it is this day. [19] And if you forget the LORD your God and go after other gods and serve them and worship them, I solemnly warn you today that you shall surely perish. [20] Like

---

[1] Or *quickly* [2] That is, set apart (devoted) as an offering to the Lord (for destruction); twice in this verse [3] Hebrew *by all*

he nations that the LORD makes to perish before you, so shall you perish, because you would not obey the voice of the LORD your God.

Not Because of Righteousness

9 "Hear, O Israel: you are to cross over the Jordan today, to go in to dispossess nations greater and mightier than you, cities great and fortified up to heaven, a people great and tall, the sons of the Anakim, whom you know, and of whom you have heard it said, 'Who can stand before the sons of Anak?' ³Know therefore today that he who goes over before you is a consuming fire is the LORD your God. He will destroy them and subdue them before you. So you shall drive them out and make them perish quickly, as the LORD has promised you.

⁴ "Do not say in your heart, after the LORD your God has thrust them out before you, 'It is because of my righteousness that the LORD has brought me in to possess this land,' whereas it is because of the wickedness of these nations that the LORD is driving them out before you. ⁵Not because of your righteousness or the uprightness of your heart are you going in to possess their land, but because of the wickedness of these nations the LORD your God is driving them out from before you, and that he may confirm the word that the LORD swore to your fathers, to Abraham, to Isaac, and to Jacob.

⁶ "Know, therefore, that the LORD your God is not giving you this good land to possess because of your righteousness, for you are a stubborn people. ⁷Remember and do not forget how you provoked the LORD your God to wrath in the wilderness. From the day you came out of the land of Egypt until you came to this place, you have been rebellious against the LORD. ⁸Even at Horeb you provoked the LORD to wrath, and the LORD was so angry with you that he was ready to destroy you. ⁹When I went up the mountain to receive the tablets of stone, the tablets of the covenant that the LORD made with you, I remained on the mountain forty days and forty nights. I neither ate bread nor drank water. ¹⁰And the LORD gave me the two tablets of stone written with the finger of God, and on them were all the words that the LORD had spoken

with you on the mountain out of the midst of the fire on the day of the assembly. ¹¹And at the end of forty days and forty nights the LORD gave me the two tablets of stone, the tablets of the covenant. ¹²Then the LORD said to me, 'Arise, go down quickly from here, for your people whom you have brought from Egypt have acted corruptly. They have turned aside quickly out of the way that I commanded them; they have made themselves a metal image.'

The Golden Calf

¹³ "Furthermore, the LORD said to me, 'I have seen this people, and behold, it is a stubborn people. ¹⁴Let me alone, that I may destroy them and blot out their name from under heaven. And I will make of you a nation mightier and greater than they.' ¹⁵So I turned and came down from the mountain, and the mountain was burning with fire. And the two tablets of the covenant were in my two hands. ¹⁶And I looked, and behold, you had sinned against the LORD your God. You had made yourselves a golden¹ calf. You had turned aside quickly from the way that the LORD had commanded you. ¹⁷So I took hold of the two tablets and threw them out of my two hands and broke them before your eyes. ¹⁸Then I lay prostrate before the LORD as before, forty days and forty nights. I neither ate bread nor drank water, because of all the sin that you had committed, in doing what was evil in the sight of the LORD to provoke him to anger. ¹⁹For I was afraid of the anger and hot displeasure that the LORD bore against you, so that he was ready to destroy you. But the LORD listened to me that time also. ²⁰And the LORD was so angry with Aaron that he was ready to destroy him. And I prayed for Aaron also at the same time. ²¹Then I took the sinful thing, the calf that you had made, and burned it with fire and crushed it, grinding it very small, until it was as fine as dust. And I threw the dust of it into the brook that ran down from the mountain.

²² "At Taberah also, and at Massah and at Kibroth-hattaavah you provoked the LORD to wrath. ²³And when the LORD sent you from Kadesh-barnea, saying, 'Go up and take possession of the land that I have given you,' then you rebelled against the commandment of the LORD your God and

¹ Hebrew cast metal

did not believe him or obey his voice. [24] You have been rebellious against the LORD from the day that I knew you.

[25] "So I lay prostrate before the LORD for these forty days and forty nights, because the LORD had said he would destroy you. [26] And I prayed to the LORD, 'O Lord GOD, do not destroy your people and your heritage, whom you have redeemed through your greatness, whom you have brought out of Egypt with a mighty hand. [27] Remember your servants, Abraham, Isaac, and Jacob. Do not regard the stubbornness of this people, or their wickedness or their sin, [28] lest the land from which you brought us say, "Because the LORD was not able to bring them into the land that he promised them, and because he hated them, he has brought them out to put them to death in the wilderness." [29] For they are your people and your heritage, whom you brought out by your great power and by your outstretched arm.'

New Tablets of Stone

10 "At that time the LORD said to me, 'Cut for yourself two tablets of stone like the first, and come up to me on the mountain and make an ark of wood. [2] And I will write on the tablets the words that were on the first tablets that you broke, and you shall put them in the ark.' [3] So I made an ark of acacia wood, and cut two tablets of stone like the first, and went up the mountain with the two tablets in my hand. [4] And he wrote on the tablets, in the same writing as before, the Ten Commandments[1] that the LORD had spoken to you on the mountain out of the midst of the fire on the day of the assembly. And the LORD gave them to me. [5] Then I turned and came down from the mountain and put the tablets in the ark that I had made. And there they are, as the LORD commanded me."

[6] (The people of Israel journeyed from Beeroth Bene-jaakan[2] to Moserah. There Aaron died, and there he was buried. And his son Eleazar ministered as priest in his place. [7] From there they journeyed to Gudgodah, and from Gudgodah to Jotbathah, a land with brooks of water. [8] At that time the LORD set apart the tribe of Levi to carry the ark of the covenant of the LORD to stand before the LORD to minister to him and to bless in his name,

to this day. [9] Therefore Levi has no portion or inheritance with his brothers. The LORD is his inheritance, as the LORD your God said to him.)

[10] "I myself stayed on the mountain, as at the first time, forty days and forty nights, and the LORD listened to me that time also. The LORD was unwilling to destroy you. [11] And the LORD said to me, 'Arise, go on your journey at the head of the people, so that they may go in and possess the land which I swore to their fathers to give them.'

Circumcise Your Heart

[12] "And now, Israel, what does the LORD your God require of you, but to fear the LORD your God, to walk in all his ways, to love him, to serve the LORD your God with all your heart and with all your soul, [13] and to keep the commandments and statutes of the LORD, which I am commanding you today for your good? [14] Behold, to the LORD your God belong heaven and the heaven of heavens, the earth with all that is in it. [15] Yet the LORD set his heart in love on your fathers and chose their offspring after them, you above all peoples, as you are this day. [16] Circumcise therefore the foreskin of your heart, and be no longer stubborn. [17] For the LORD your God is God of gods and Lord of lords, the great, the mighty, and the awesome God, who is not partial and takes no bribe. [18] He executes justice for the fatherless and the widow, and loves the sojourner, giving him food and clothing. [19] Love the sojourner, therefore, for you were sojourners in the land of Egypt. [20] You shall fear the LORD your God. You shall serve him and hold fast to him and by his name you shall swear. [21] He is your praise. He is your God, who has done for you these great and terrifying things that your eyes have seen. [22] Your fathers went down to Egypt seventy persons, and now the LORD your God has made you as numerous as the stars of heaven.

Love and Serve the LORD

11 "You shall therefore love the LORD your God and keep his charge, his statutes, his rules, and his commandments always. [2] And consider today (since I am not speaking to your children who have not known or seen it), consider the discipline of the LORD your God, his greatness, his

[1] Hebrew *words* [2] Or *the wells of the Bene-jaakan* [3] Or *instruction*

mighty hand and his outstretched arm, ³his signs and his deeds that he did in Egypt to Pharaoh the king of Egypt and to all his land, ⁴and what he did to the army of Egypt, to their horses and to their chariots, how he made the water of the Red Sea flow over them as they pursued after you, and how the LORD has destroyed them to this day, ⁵and what he did to you in the wilderness, until you came to this place, ⁶and what he did to Dathan and Abiram the sons of Eliab, son of Reuben, how the earth opened its mouth and swallowed them up, with their households, their tents, and every living thing that followed them, in the midst of all Israel. ⁷For your eyes have seen all the great work of the LORD that he did.

⁸"You shall therefore keep the whole commandment that I command you today, that you may be strong, and go in and take possession of the land that you are going over to possess, ⁹and that you may live long in the land that the LORD swore to your fathers to give to them and to their offspring, a land flowing with milk and honey. ¹⁰For the land that you are entering to take possession of it is not like the land of Egypt, from which you have come, where you sowed your seed and irrigated it,¹ like a garden of vegetables. ¹¹But the land that you are going over to possess is a land of hills and valleys, which drinks water by the rain from heaven, ¹²a land that the LORD your God cares for. The eyes of the LORD your God are always upon it, from the beginning of the year to the end of the year.

¹³"And if you will indeed obey my commandments that I command you today, to love the LORD your God, and to serve him with all your heart and with all your soul, ¹⁴he² will give the rain for your land in its season, the early rain and the later rain, that you may gather in your grain and your wine and your oil. ¹⁵And he will give grass in your fields for your livestock, and you shall eat and be full. ¹⁶Take care lest your heart be deceived, and you turn aside and serve other gods and worship them; ¹⁷then the anger of the LORD will be kindled against you, and he will shut up the heavens, so that there will be no rain, and the land will yield no fruit, and you

will perish quickly off the good land that the LORD is giving you.

¹⁸"You shall therefore lay up these words of mine in your heart and in your soul, and you shall bind them as a sign on your hand, and they shall be as frontlets between your eyes. ¹⁹You shall teach them to your children, talking of them when you are sitting in your house, and when you are walking by the way, and when you lie down, and when you rise. ²⁰You shall write them on the doorposts of your house and on your gates, ²¹that your days and the days of your children may be multiplied in the land that the LORD swore to your fathers to give them, as long as the heavens are above the earth. ²²For if you will be careful to do all this commandment that I command you to do, loving the LORD your God, walking in all his ways, and holding fast to him, ²³then the LORD will drive out all these nations before you, and you will dispossess nations greater and mightier than you. ²⁴Every place on which the sole of your foot treads shall be yours. Your territory shall be from the wilderness to³ the Lebanon and from the River, the river Euphrates, to the western sea. ²⁵No one shall be able to stand against you. The LORD your God will lay the fear of you and the dread of you on all the land that you shall tread, as he promised you.

²⁶"See, I am setting before you today a blessing and a curse: ²⁷the blessing, if you obey the commandments of the LORD your God, which I command you today, ²⁸and the curse, if you do not obey the commandments of the LORD your God, but turn aside from the way that I am commanding you today, to go after other gods that you have not known. ²⁹And when the LORD your God brings you into the land that you are entering to take possession of it, you shall set the blessing on Mount Gerizim and the curse on Mount Ebal. ³⁰Are they not beyond the Jordan, west of the road, toward the going down of the sun, in the land of the Canaanites who live in the Arabah, opposite Gilgal, beside the oak⁴ of Moreh? ³¹For you are to cross over the Jordan to go in to take possession of the land that the LORD your God is giving you. And when you possess it and live in it, ³²you shall be careful to

do all the statutes and the rules that I am setting before you today.

The LORD's Chosen Place of Worship

12 "These are the statutes and rules that you shall be careful to do in the land that the LORD, the God of your fathers, has given you to possess, all the days that you live on the earth. ²You shall surely destroy all the places where the nations whom you shall dispossess served their gods, on the high mountains and on the hills and under every green tree. ³You shall tear down their altars and dash in pieces their pillars and burn their Asherim with fire. You shall chop down the carved images of their gods and destroy

¹ Or *name as its habitation*

their name out of that place. ⁴You shall no worship the LORD your God in that way ⁵But you shall seek the place that the LORD your God will choose out of all your tribe to put his name and make his habitation there. There you shall go, ⁶and there yo shall bring your burnt offerings and you sacrifices, your tithes and the contribution that you present, your vow offerings, you freewill offerings, and the firstborn of you herd and of your flock. ⁷And there you sha eat before the LORD your God, and you shal rejoice, you and your households, in all tha you undertake, in which the LORD your God has blessed you.

⁸"You shall not do according to all tha we are doing here today, everyone doin

Know Love

verses to read
Deuteronomy 11:26–32

Love and fear are archenemies in the life of the God Girl. Love is a blessing and fear is a curse: complete opposites. As the children of Israel grouped up near the land of Shechem, they were shown the mountain of blessings (Mount Gerizim) and the mountain of curses (Mount Ebal), and God gave them a choice between the two. The choice before them was obedience or disobedience. If they obeyed God, then blessings would be theirs; but if they chose the opposite, then they would receive the curse.

Today you have the same kind of choice: you can choose between disobedience (fear) or obedience (love). One comes with a curse while the other comes with blessing. Most of the time, fear promises safety and pretends to come from wisdom, but the truth is that it's a thief. It steals your peace and your hope, and it weakens your will. But love provides you all the hope, peace, and happiness you could ever handle. Fear leads to slavery; love leads to freedom. The Enemy tells you that love is dangerous and leaves you vulnerable. And when you buy that lie, choosing love seems like a dangerous choice. But the God Girl doesn't need to protect herself from what God says to do. His call to love is to be obeyed no matter the cost. When you make decisions out of fear or self-protection, you push God off of the throne and stand on it with your hands on your hips in total defiance.

Fear should never be a barometer for action, telling you when the weather's right for you to do this or that. That includes the fear of losing something you love and the fear of loving someone you don't even like. If you trust God and his Word, fear will never be your master, but God's Word will be. Learn the truth about loving as God loves by reading in 1 Corinthians 13. This kind of love isn't dysfunctional. It doesn't love for what you get out of it. Study God's Word, look for truth, and make it a part of who you are, and you will be set free from the bondage of fear.

whatever is right in his own eyes, **9**for you have not as yet come to the rest and to the inheritance that the LORD your God is giving you. **10**But when you go over the Jordan and live in the land that the LORD your God is giving you to inherit, and when he gives you rest from all your enemies around, so that you live in safety, **11**then to the place that the LORD your God will choose, to make his name dwell there, there you shall bring all that I command you: your burnt offerings and your sacrifices, your tithes and the contribution that you present, and all your finest vow offerings that you vow to the LORD. **12**And you shall rejoice before the LORD your God, you and your sons and your daughters, your male servants and your female servants, and the Levite that is within your towns, since he has no portion or inheritance with you. **13**Take care that you do not offer your burnt offerings at any place that you see, **14**but at the place that the LORD will choose in one of your tribes, there you shall offer your burnt offerings, and there you shall do all that I am commanding you.

15 "However, you may slaughter and eat meat within any of your towns, as much as you desire, according to the blessing of the LORD your God that he has given you. The unclean and the clean may eat of it, as of the gazelle and as of the deer. **16**Only you shall not eat the blood; you shall pour it out on the earth like water. **17**You may not eat within your towns the tithe of your grain or of your wine or of your oil, or the firstborn of your herd or of your flock, or any of your vow offerings that you vow, or your freewill offerings or the contribution that you present, **18**but you shall eat them before the LORD your God in the place that the LORD your God will choose, you and your son and your daughter, your male servant and your female servant, and the Levite who is within your towns. And you shall rejoice before the LORD your God in all that you undertake. **19**Take care that you do not neglect the Levite as long as you live in your land.

20 "When the LORD your God enlarges your territory, as he has promised you, and you say, 'I will eat meat,' because you crave meat, you may eat meat whenever you desire. **21**If the place that the LORD your God will choose to put his name there

is too far from you, then you may kill any of your herd or your flock, which the LORD has given you, as I have commanded you, and you may eat within your towns whenever you desire. **22**Just as the gazelle or the deer is eaten, so you may eat of it. The unclean and the clean alike may eat of it. **23**Only be sure that you do not eat the blood, for the blood is the life, and you shall not eat the life with the flesh. **24**You shall not eat it; you shall pour it out on the earth like water. **25**You shall not eat it, that all may go well with you and with your children after you, when you do what is right in the sight of the LORD. **26**But the holy things that are due from you, and your vow offerings, you shall take, and you shall go to the place that the LORD will choose, **27**and offer your burnt offerings, the flesh and the blood, on the altar of the LORD your God. The blood of your sacrifices shall be poured out on the altar of the LORD your God, but the flesh you may eat. **28**Be careful to obey all these words that I command you, that it may go well with you and with your children after you forever, when you do what is good and right in the sight of the LORD your God.

Warning Against Idolatry

29 "When the LORD your God cuts off before you the nations whom you go in to dispossess, and you dispossess them and dwell in their land, **30**take care that you be not ensnared to follow them, after they have been destroyed before you, and that you do not inquire about their gods, saying, 'How did these nations serve their gods?— that I also may do the same.' **31**You shall not worship the LORD your God in that way, for every abominable thing that the LORD hates they have done for their gods, for they even burn their sons and their daughters in the fire to their gods.

32[1] "Everything that I command you, you shall be careful to do. You shall not add to it or take from it.

13 "If a prophet or a dreamer of dreams arises among you and gives you a sign or a wonder, **2**and the sign or wonder that he tells you comes to pass, and if he says, 'Let us go after other gods,' which you have not known, 'and let us serve them,' **3**you shall not listen to the words of that prophet or that dreamer of dreams. For

[1] Ch 13:1 in Hebrew

the LORD your God is testing you, to know whether you love the LORD your God with all your heart and with all your soul. [4] You shall walk after the LORD your God and fear him and keep his commandments and obey his voice, and you shall serve him and hold fast to him. [5] But that prophet or that dreamer of dreams shall be put to death, because he has taught rebellion against the LORD your God, who brought you out of the land of Egypt and redeemed you out of the house of slavery, to make you leave the way in which the LORD your God commanded you to walk. So you shall purge the evil[1] from your midst.

[6] "If your brother, the son of your mother, or your son or your daughter or the wife you embrace[2] or your friend who is as your own soul entices you secretly, saying, 'Let us go and serve other gods,' which neither you nor your fathers have known, [7] some of the gods of the peoples who are around you, whether near you or far off from you, from the one end of the earth to the other, [8] you shall not yield to him or listen to him, nor shall your eye pity him, nor shall you spare him, nor shall you conceal him. [9] But you shall kill him. Your hand shall be first against him to put him to death, and afterward the hand of all the people. [10] You shall stone him to death with stones, because he sought to draw you away from the LORD your God, who brought you out of the land of Egypt, out of the house of slavery. [11] And all Israel shall hear and fear and never again do any such wickedness as this among you.

[12] "If you hear in one of your cities, which the LORD your God is giving you to dwell there, [13] that certain worthless fellows have gone out among you and have drawn away the inhabitants of their city, saying, 'Let us go and serve other gods,' which you have not known, [14] then you shall inquire and make search and ask diligently. And behold, if it be true and certain that such an abomination has been done among you, [15] you shall surely put the inhabitants of that city to the sword, devoting it to destruction,[3] all who are in it and its cattle, with the edge of the sword. [16] You shall gather all its spoil into the midst of its open square and burn the city and all its spoil with fire, as a whole burnt offering to the LORD your God. It shall be a heap forever. It shall not be built again. [17] None of the devoted things shall stick to your hand, that the LORD may turn from the fierceness of his anger and show you mercy and have compassion on you and multiply you, as he swore to your fathers, [18] if you obey the voice of the LORD your God, keeping all his commandments that I am commanding you today, and doing what is right in the sight of the LORD your God.

Clean and Unclean Food

14 "You are the sons of the LORD your God. You shall not cut yourselves or make any baldness on your foreheads for the dead. [2] For you are a people holy to the LORD your God, and the LORD has chosen you to be a people for his treasured possession, out of all the peoples who are on the face of the earth.

[3] "You shall not eat any abomination. [4] These are the animals you may eat: the ox, the sheep, the goat, [5] the deer, the gazelle, the roebuck, the wild goat, the ibex,[4] the antelope, and the mountain sheep. [6] Every animal that parts the hoof and has the hoof cloven in two and chews the cud, among the animals, you may eat. [7] Yet of those that chew the cud or have the hoof cloven you shall not eat these: the camel, the hare, and the rock badger, because they chew the cud but do not part the hoof, are unclean for you. [8] And the pig, because it parts the hoof but does not chew the cud, is unclean for you. Their flesh you shall not eat, and their carcasses you shall not touch.

[9] "Of all that are in the waters you may eat these: whatever has fins and scales you may eat. [10] And whatever does not have fins and scales you shall not eat; it is unclean for you.

[11] "You may eat all clean birds. [12] But these are the ones that you shall not eat: the eagle,[5] the bearded vulture, the black vulture, [13] the kite, the falcon of any kind; [14] every raven of any kind; [15] the ostrich, the nighthawk, the sea gull, the hawk of any kind; [16] the little owl and the short-eared owl, the barn owl [17] and the tawny owl, the carrion vulture and the cormorant, [18] the stork, the heron of any kind; the hoopoe and the bat. [19] And all winged insects are

---

[1] Or *evil person* [2] Hebrew *the wife of your bosom* [3] That is, setting apart (devoting) as an offering to the Lord (for destruction) [4] Or *addax*
[5] The identity of many of these birds is uncertain

nclean for you; they shall not be eaten.
⁰All clean winged things you may eat.

21 "You shall not eat anything that has died naturally. You may give it to the sojourner who is within your towns, that he may eat it, or you may sell it to a foreigner. For you are a people holy to the LORD your God.

"You shall not boil a young goat in its mother's milk.

Ask Yourself . . .

ABOUT YOUR DEVOTION

Do you tithe? Do you think ten percent is too much to give to the God who gave it all to you in the first place? Tithing is essential for the God Girl. It teaches your soul and proves to your heart that God is more important than possessions. But have you ever thought about what is most valuable to you? Is it your time?

Do you give your time to God the same way you give your money? You might not have a lot of cash, but we all have the same amount of time in a day—twenty-four hours. How much of your time do you give God? Ten percent? Five percent? Two percent? One percent? Give God more of your time and you'll find that you'll have more time to do what needs to be done. It's the law of tithing: give, and you will get back.

The God Girl makes God her life. He is her obsession, and everything in her life is meant for God's glory. So why wouldn't you give the thing that is the most precious of all—your time—to the one you worship? Begin the practice of tithing your time today, and you will grow in faith and hope with each minute that you give up for your God.

Tithes

22 "You shall tithe all the yield of your seed that comes from the field year by year. 23 And before the LORD your God, in the place that he will choose, to make his name dwell there, you shall eat the tithe of your grain, of your wine, and of your oil, and the firstborn of your herd and flock, that you may learn to fear the LORD your God always. 24 And if the way is too long for you, so that you are not able to carry the tithe, when the LORD your God blesses you, because the place is too far from you, which the LORD your God chooses, to set his name there, 25 then you shall turn it into money and bind up the money in your hand and go to the place that the LORD your God chooses 26 and spend the money for whatever you desire—oxen or sheep or wine or strong drink, whatever your appetite craves. And you shall eat there before the LORD your God and rejoice, you and your household. 27 And you shall not neglect the Levite who is within your towns, for he has no portion or inheritance with you.

28 "At the end of every three years you shall bring out all the tithe of your produce in the same year and lay it up within your towns. 29 And the Levite, because he has no portion or inheritance with you, and the sojourner, the fatherless, and the widow, who are within your towns, shall come and eat and be filled, that the LORD your God may bless you in all the work of your hands that you do.

The Sabbatical Year

15 "At the end of every seven years you shall grant a release. 2 And this is the manner of the release: every creditor shall release what he has lent to his neighbor. He shall not exact it of his neighbor, his brother, because the LORD's release has been proclaimed. 3 Of a foreigner you may exact it, but whatever of yours is with your brother your hand shall release. 4 But there will be no poor among you; for the LORD will bless you in the land that the LORD your God is giving you for an inheritance to possess— 5 if only you will strictly obey the voice of the LORD your God, being careful to do all this commandment that I command you today. 6 For the LORD your God will bless you, as he promised you, and you shall lend to many nations, but you shall not borrow, and you shall rule over many nations, but they shall not rule over you.

[7] "If among you, one of your brothers should become poor, in any of your towns within your land that the LORD your God is giving you, you shall not harden your heart or shut your hand against your poor brother, [8] but you shall open your hand to him and lend him sufficient for his need, whatever it may be. [9] Take care lest there be an unworthy thought in your heart and you say, 'The seventh year, the year of release is near,' and your eye look grudgingly[1] on your poor brother, and you give him nothing, and he cry to the LORD against you, and you be guilty of sin. [10] You shall give to him freely, and your heart shall not be grudging when you give to him, because for this the LORD your God will bless you in all your work and in all that you undertake. [11] For there will never cease to be poor in the land. Therefore I command you, 'You shall open wide your hand to your brother, to the needy and to the poor, in your land.'

[12] "If your brother, a Hebrew man or a Hebrew woman, is sold[2] to you, he shall serve you six years, and in the seventh year you shall let him go free from you. [13] And when you let him go free from you, you shall not let him go empty-handed. [14] You shall furnish him liberally out of your flock, out of your threshing floor, and out of your winepress. As the LORD your God has blessed you, you shall give to him. [15] You shall remember that you were a slave in the land of Egypt, and the LORD your God redeemed you; therefore I command you this today. [16] But if he says to you, 'I will not go out from you,' because he loves you and your household, since he is well-off with you, [17] then you shall take an awl, and put it through his ear into the door, and he shall be your slave[3] forever. And to your female slave[4] you shall do the same. [18] It shall not seem hard to you when you let him go free from you, for at half the cost of a hired worker he has served you six years. So the LORD your God will bless you in all that you do.

[19] "All the firstborn males that are born of your herd and flock you shall dedicate to the LORD your God. You shall do no work with the firstborn of your herd, nor shear the firstborn of your flock. [20] You shall eat it, you and your household, before the LORD your God year by year at the place that the LORD will choose. [21] But if it has any blemish, if it is lame or blind or has any serious blemish whatever, you shall not sacrifice it to the LORD your God. [22] You shall eat it within your towns. The unclean and the clean alike may eat it, as though it were a gazelle or a deer. [23] Only you shall not eat its blood; you shall pour it out on the ground like water.

Passover

16 "Observe the month of Abib and keep the Passover to the LORD your God, for in the month of Abib the LORD your God brought you out of Egypt by night. [2] And you shall offer the Passover sacrifice to the LORD your God, from the flock or the herd, at the place that the LORD will choose, to make his name dwell there. [3] You shall eat no leavened bread with it. Seven days you shall eat it with unleavened bread, the bread of affliction—for you came out of the land of Egypt in haste—that all the days of your life you may remember the day when you came out of the land of Egypt. [4] No leaven shall be seen with you in all your territory for seven days, nor shall any of the flesh that you sacrifice on the evening of the first day remain all night until morning. [5] You may not offer the Passover sacrifice within any of your towns that the LORD your God is giving you, [6] but at the place that the LORD your God will choose, to make his name dwell in it, there you shall offer the Passover sacrifice, in the evening at sunset, at the time you came out of Egypt. [7] And you shall cook it and eat it at the place that the LORD your God will choose. And in the morning you shall turn and go to your tents. [8] For six days you shall eat unleavened bread, and on the seventh day there shall be a solemn assembly to the LORD your God. You shall do no work on it.

The Feast of Weeks

[9] "You shall count seven weeks. Begin to count the seven weeks from the time the sickle is first put to the standing grain. [10] Then you shall keep the Feast of Weeks to the LORD your God with the tribute of a freewill offering from your hand, which you shall give as the LORD your God blesses you. [11] And you shall rejoice before the LORD your

God, you and your son and your daughter, your male servant and your female servant, the Levite who is within your towns, the sojourner, the fatherless, and the widow who are among you, at the place that the LORD your God will choose, to make his name dwell there. [12] You shall remember that you were a slave in Egypt; and you shall be careful to observe these statutes.

The Feast of Booths

[13] "You shall keep the Feast of Booths seven days, when you have gathered in the produce from your threshing floor and your winepress. [14] You shall rejoice in your feast, you and your son and your daughter, your male servant and your female servant, the Levite, the sojourner, the fatherless, and the widow who are within your towns. [15] For seven days you shall keep the feast to the LORD your God at the place that the LORD will choose, because the LORD your God will bless you in all your produce and in all the work of your hands, so that you will be altogether joyful.

[16] "Three times a year all your males shall appear before the LORD your God at the place that he will choose: at the Feast of Unleavened Bread, at the Feast of Weeks, and at the Feast of Booths. They shall not appear before the LORD empty-handed. [17] Every man shall give as he is able, according to the blessing of the LORD your God that he has given you.

Justice

[18] "You shall appoint judges and officers in all your towns that the LORD your God is giving you, according to your tribes, and they shall judge the people with righteous judgment. [19] You shall not pervert justice. You shall not show partiality, and you shall not accept a bribe, for a bribe blinds the eyes of the wise and subverts the cause of the righteous. [20] Justice, and only justice, you shall follow, that you may live and inherit the land that the LORD your God is giving you.

Forbidden Forms of Worship

[21] "You shall not plant any tree as an Asherah beside the altar of the LORD your God that you shall make. [22] And you shall not set up a pillar, which the LORD your God hates.

17 "You shall not sacrifice to the LORD your God an ox or a sheep in which is a blemish, any defect whatever, for that is an abomination to the LORD your God.

[2] "If there is found among you, within any of your towns that the LORD your God is giving you, a man or woman who does what is evil in the sight of the LORD your God, in transgressing his covenant, [3] and has gone and served other gods and worshiped them, or the sun or the moon or any of the host of heaven, which I have forbidden, [4] and it is told you and you hear of it, then you shall inquire diligently, and if it is true and certain that such an abomination has been done in Israel, [5] then you shall bring out to your gates that man or woman who has done this evil thing, and you shall stone that man or woman to death with stones. [6] On the evidence of two witnesses or of three witnesses the one who is to die shall be put to death; a person shall not be put to death on the evidence of one witness. [7] The hand of the witnesses shall be first against him to put him to death, and afterward the hand of all the people. So you shall purge[1] the evil[2] from your midst.

Legal Decisions by Priests and Judges

[8] "If any case arises requiring decision between one kind of homicide and another, one kind of legal right and another, or one kind of assault and another, any case within your towns that is too difficult for you, then you shall arise and go up to the place that the LORD your God will choose. [9] And you shall come to the Levitical priests and to the judge who is in office in those days, and you shall consult them, and they shall declare to you the decision. [10] Then you shall do according to what they declare to you from that place that the LORD will choose. And you shall be careful to do according to all that they direct you. [11] According to the instructions that they give you, and according to the decision which they pronounce to you, you shall do. You shall not turn aside from the verdict that they declare to you, either to the right hand or to the left. [12] The man who acts presumptuously by not obeying the priest who stands to minister there before the LORD your God, or the judge, that man shall die. So you shall purge the evil from Israel.

---

[1] Septuagint *drive out*; also verse 12 [2] Or *evil person*; also verse 12

[13] And all the people shall hear and fear and not act presumptuously again.

Laws Concerning Israel's Kings

[14] "When you come to the land that the LORD your God is giving you, and you possess it and dwell in it and then say, 'I will set a king over me, like all the nations that are around me,' [15] you may indeed set a king over you whom the LORD your God will choose. One from among your brothers you shall set as king over you. You may not put a foreigner over you, who is not your brother. [16] Only he must not acquire many horses for himself or cause the people to return to Egypt in order to acquire many horses, since the LORD has said to you, 'You shall never return that way again.' [17] And he shall not acquire many wives for himself, lest his heart turn away, nor shall he acquire for himself excessive silver and gold.

[18] "And when he sits on the throne of his kingdom, he shall write for himself in a book a copy of this law, approved by[1] the Levitical priests. [19] And it shall be with him, and he shall read in it all the days of his life, that he may learn to fear the LORD his God by keeping all the words of this law and these statutes, and doing them, [20] that his heart may not be lifted up above his brothers, and that he may not turn aside from the commandment, either to the right hand or to the left, so that he may continue long in his kingdom, he and his children, in Israel.

Provision for Priests and Levites

18 "The Levitical priests, all the tribe of Levi, shall have no portion or inheritance with Israel. They shall eat the LORD's food offerings[2] as their[3] inheritance. [2] They shall have no inheritance among their brothers; the LORD is their inheritance, as he promised them. [3] And this shall be the priests' due from the people, from those offering a sacrifice, whether an ox or a sheep: they shall give to the priest the shoulder and the two cheeks and the stomach. [4] The firstfruits of your grain, of your wine and of your oil, and the first fleece of your sheep, you shall give him. [5] For the LORD your God has chosen him out of all your tribes to stand and minister

in the name of the LORD, him and his sons for all time.

[6] "And if a Levite comes from any of your towns out of all Israel, where he lives— and he may come when he desires[4]—to the place that the LORD will choose, [7] and ministers in the name of the LORD his God like all his fellow Levites who stand to minister there before the LORD, [8] then he may have equal portions to eat, besides what he receives from the sale of his patrimony.

Abominable Practices

[9] "When you come into the land that the LORD your God is giving you, you shall not learn to follow the abominable practices of those nations. [10] There shall not be found among you anyone who burns his son or his daughter as an offering,[6] anyone who practices divination or tells fortunes or interprets omens, or a sorcerer [11] or a charmer or a medium or a necromancer or one who inquires of the dead, [12] for whoever does these things is an abomination to the LORD. And because of these abominations the LORD your God is driving them out before you. [13] You shall be blameless before the LORD your God, [14] for these nations, which you are about to dispossess, listen to fortune-tellers and to diviners. But as for you, the LORD your God has not allowed you to do this.

A New Prophet like Moses

[15] "The LORD your God will raise up for you a prophet like me from among you, from your brothers—it is to him you shall listen— [16] just as you desired of the LORD your God at Horeb on the day of the assembly, when you said, 'Let me not hear again the voice of the LORD my God or see this great fire any more, lest I die.' [17] And the LORD said to me, 'They are right in what they have spoken. [18] I will raise up for them a prophet like you from among their brothers. And I will put my words in his mouth, and he shall speak to them all that I command him. [19] And whoever will not listen to my words that he shall speak in my name, I myself will require it of him. [20] But the prophet who presumes to speak a word in my name that I have not commanded him to speak, or[7] who speaks in the name of other gods, that same prophet shall die.

[1] Hebrew *from before* [2] Or *the offerings by fire to the LORD* [3] Hebrew *his* [4] Or *lives—if he comes enthusiastically* [5] The meaning of the Hebrew is uncertain [6] Hebrew *makes his son or his daughter pass through the fire* [7] Or *and*

[1] And if you say in your heart, 'How may we know the word that the LORD has not spoken?'— [22] when a prophet speaks in the name of the LORD, if the word does not come to pass or come true, that is a word that the LORD has not spoken; the prophet has spoken it presumptuously. You need not be afraid of him.

Laws Concerning Cities of Refuge

19 "When the LORD your God cuts off the nations whose land the LORD your God is giving you, and you dispossess them and dwell in their cities and in their houses, [2] you shall set apart three cities for yourselves in the land that the LORD your God is giving you to possess. [3] You shall measure the distances[1] and divide into three parts the area of the land that the LORD your God gives you as a possession, so that any manslayer can flee to them.

[4] "This is the provision for the manslayer, who by fleeing there may save his life. If anyone kills his neighbor unintentionally without having hated him in the past— [5] as when someone goes into the forest with his neighbor to cut wood, and his hand swings the axe to cut down a tree, and the head slips from the handle and strikes his neighbor so that he dies—he may flee to one of these cities and live, [6] lest the avenger of blood in hot anger pursue the manslayer and overtake him, because the way is long, and strike him fatally, though the man did not deserve to die, since he had not hated his neighbor in the past. [7] Therefore I command you, You shall set apart three cities. [8] And if the LORD your God enlarges your territory, as he has sworn to your fathers, and gives you all the land that he promised to give to your fathers— [9] provided you are careful to keep all this commandment, which I command you today, by loving the LORD your God and by walking ever in his ways—then you shall add three other cities to these three, [10] lest innocent blood be shed in your land that the LORD your God is giving you for an inheritance, and so the guilt of bloodshed be upon you.

[11] "But if anyone hates his neighbor and lies in wait for him and attacks him and strikes him fatally so that he dies, and he flees into one of these cities, [12] then the elders of his city shall send and take him

Hebrew *road*

Know God

verses to read
Deuteronomy 18:21–22

Have you ever been sure that you were doing just what God wanted, only to be shut down by a door slammed in your face? Would God tell you to do something that he knew wouldn't happen? Or was that not the voice of God but your own hopes? What is more possible, that you heard him wrong or that he lied? How do you know when it's God's voice and when it's just your own wishful thinking?

Maybe it just takes time. If what you think you are hearing agrees with Scripture, if you see the doors open to you as you move forward, and if other people actually agree with what you are hearing, then it might just be the voice of God. But what if it's just mass hysteria or high hopes? How can you really know you are tapped into God? The only answer is to look at his Word. What does his Word command? What does it say for you to do, God Girl? Stick to that, and you will be sure to do the will of God. And if for some reason a door that you've been knocking on doesn't open, or it opens for a time then slams in your face, it may be that you mistook *your* voice for God's, or maybe it was God's plan all along to teach you through this denial. Just remember to take note of the voice of your desires versus the voice of God, so that next time you'll more quickly recognize the difference.

from there, and hand him over to the avenger of blood, so that he may die. [13] Your eye shall not pity him, but you shall purge the guilt of innocent blood[1] from Israel, so that it may be well with you.

Property Boundaries

[14] "You shall not move your neighbor's landmark, which the men of old have set, in the inheritance that you will hold in the land that the LORD your God is giving you to possess.

Laws Concerning Witnesses

[15] "A single witness shall not suffice against a person for any crime or for any wrong in connection with any offense that he has committed. Only on the evidence of two witnesses or of three witnesses shall a charge be established. [16] If a malicious witness arises to accuse a person of wrongdoing, [17] then both parties to the dispute shall appear before the LORD, before the priests and the judges who are in office in those days. [18] The judges shall inquire diligently, and if the witness is a false witness and has accused his brother falsely, [19] then you shall do to him as he had meant to do to his brother. So you shall purge the evil[2] from your midst. [20] And the rest shall hear and fear, and shall never again commit any such evil among you. [21] Your eye shall not pity. It shall be life for life, eye for eye, tooth for tooth, hand for hand, foot for foot.

Laws Concerning Warfare

20 "When you go out to war against your enemies, and see horses and chariots and an army larger than your own, you shall not be afraid of them, for the LORD your God is with you, who brought you up out of the land of Egypt. [2] And when you draw near to the battle, the priest shall come forward and speak to the people [3] and shall say to them, 'Hear, O Israel, today you are drawing near for battle against your enemies: let not your heart faint. Do not fear or panic or be in dread of them, [4] for the LORD your God is he who goes with you to fight for you against your enemies, to give you the victory.' [5] Then the officers shall speak to the people, saying, 'Is there any man who has built a new house and has not dedicated it? Let him go back to his house, lest he die in the battle and another

man dedicate it. [6] And is there any man who has planted a vineyard and has not enjoyed its fruit? Let him go back to his house, lest he die in the battle and another man enjoy its fruit. [7] And is there any man who has betrothed a wife and has not taken her? Let him go back to his house, lest he die in the battle and another man take her.' [8] And the officers shall speak further to the people and say, 'Is there any man who is fearful and fainthearted? Let him go back to his house, lest he make the heart of his fellows melt like his own.' [9] And when the officers have finished speaking to the people, then commanders shall be appointed at the head of the people.

[10] "When you draw near to a city to fight against it, offer terms of peace to it. [11] And if it responds to you peaceably and it opens to you, then all the people who are found in it shall do forced labor for you and shall serve you. [12] But if it makes no peace with you, but makes war against you, then you shall besiege it. [13] And when the LORD your God gives it into your hand, you shall put all its males to the sword, [14] but the women and the little ones, the livestock, and everything else in the city, all its spoil, you shall take as plunder for yourselves. And you shall enjoy the spoil of your enemies, which the LORD your God has given you. [15] Thus you shall do to all the cities that are very far from you, which are not cities of the nations here. [16] But in the cities of these peoples that the LORD your God is giving you for an inheritance, you shall save alive nothing that breathes, [17] but you shall devote them to complete destruction,[3] the Hittites and the Amorites, the Canaanites and the Perizzites, the Hivites and the Jebusites, as the LORD your God has commanded, [18] that they may not teach you to do according to all their abominable practices that they have done for their gods, and so you sin against the LORD your God.

[19] "When you besiege a city for a long time, making war against it in order to take it, you shall not destroy its trees by wielding an axe against them. You may eat from them, but you shall not cut them down. Are the trees in the field human, that they should be besieged by you? [20] Only the trees that you know are not trees for food you may destroy and cut down, that you

---

[1] Or *the blood of the innocent* [2] Or *evil person* [3] That is, set apart (devote) as an offering to the Lord (for destruction)

…ay build siegeworks against the city that …akes war with you, until it falls.

tonement for Unsolved Murders

21 "If in the land that the LORD your God is giving you to possess some-…e is found slain, lying in the open coun-…y, and it is not known who killed him, …hen your elders and your judges shall …ome out, and they shall measure the dis-…nce to the surrounding cities. ³ And the …ders of the city that is nearest to the slain …an shall take a heifer that has never been …orked and that has not pulled in a yoke. …nd the elders of that city shall bring the …eifer down to a valley with running water, …hich is neither plowed nor sown, and …all break the heifer's neck there in the …alley. ⁵ Then the priests, the sons of Levi, …all come forward, for the LORD your God …as chosen them to minister to him and … bless in the name of the LORD, and by …eir word every dispute and every assault …all be settled. ⁶ And all the elders of that …ty nearest to the slain man shall wash …eir hands over the heifer whose neck was …roken in the valley, ⁷ and they shall testify, …ur hands did not shed this blood, nor did …ur eyes see it shed. ⁸ Accept atonement, … LORD, for your people Israel, whom you …ave redeemed, and do not set the guilt of …nocent blood in the midst of your people …rael, so that their blood guilt be atoned …r.' ⁹ So you shall purge the guilt of inno-…ent blood from your midst, when you do …hat is right in the sight of the LORD.

…arrying Female Captives

¹⁰ "When you go out to war against your …nemies, and the LORD your God gives …em into your hand and you take them …aptive, ¹¹ and you see among the captives … beautiful woman, and you desire to take …er to be your wife, ¹² and you bring her …ome to your house, she shall shave her …ead and pare her nails. ¹³ And she shall …ake off the clothes in which she was cap-…ured and shall remain in your house and …ment her father and her mother a full …onth. After that you may go in to her …nd be her husband, and she shall be your …ife. ¹⁴ But if you no longer delight in her, …ou shall let her go where she wants. But …ou shall not sell her for money, nor shall

you treat her as a slave, since you have humiliated her.

Inheritance Rights of the Firstborn

¹⁵ "If a man has two wives, the one loved and the other unloved, and both the loved and the unloved have borne him chil-dren, and if the firstborn son belongs to the unloved,[1] ¹⁶ then on the day when he assigns his possessions as an inheritance to his sons, he may not treat the son of the loved as the firstborn in preference to the son of the unloved, who is the firstborn, ¹⁷ but he shall acknowledge the firstborn, the son of the unloved, by giving him a double portion of all that he has, for he is the firstfruits of his strength. The right of the firstborn is his.

A Rebellious Son

¹⁸ "If a man has a stubborn and rebel-lious son who will not obey the voice of his father or the voice of his mother, and, though they discipline him, will not listen to them, ¹⁹ then his father and his mother shall take hold of him and bring him out to the elders of his city at the gate of the place where he lives, ²⁰ and they shall say to the elders of his city, 'This our son is stubborn and rebellious; he will not obey our voice; he is a glutton and a drunkard.' ²¹ Then all the men of the city shall stone him to death with stones. So you shall purge the evil from your midst, and all Israel shall hear, and fear.

A Man Hanged on a Tree Is Cursed

²² "And if a man has committed a crime punishable by death and he is put to death, and you hang him on a tree, ²³ his body shall not remain all night on the tree, but you shall bury him the same day, for a hanged man is cursed by God. You shall not defile your land that the LORD your God is giving you for an inheritance.

Various Laws

22 "You shall not see your brother's ox or his sheep going astray and ignore them. You shall take them back to your brother. ² And if he does not live near you and you do not know who he is, you shall bring it home to your house, and it shall stay with you until your brother seeks it. Then you shall restore it to him. ³ And you shall do the same with his donkey or with his garment, or with any lost thing of your brother's, which he loses and you find; you may not ignore it. [4] You shall not see your brother's donkey or his ox fallen down by the way and ignore them. You shall help him to lift them up again.

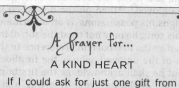

A Prayer for...
A KIND HEART

If I could ask for just one gift from you, let it be the spirit of kindness. Let others have fame and fortune and jewels and palaces, if I can just have a kind spirit. Give greatness and power to people who want them, but give me sisterly kindness. Make somebody else be beautiful, if only I can have a kind face.

May I never wound the heart of any of your struggling children. Help me do the little unremembered things that quietly help without intending to. Give me the unconscious radiance of a life that knows no grudge but loves all people because they are children of my Father, who loved them enough to send his Son to save them.

Amen.

[5] "A woman shall not wear a man's garment, nor shall a man put on a woman's cloak, for whoever does these things is an abomination to the LORD your God.

[6] "If you come across a bird's nest in any tree or on the ground, with young ones or eggs and the mother sitting on the young or on the eggs, you shall not take the mother with the young. [7] You shall let the mother go, but the young you may take for yourself, that it may go well with you, and that you may live long.

[8] "When you build a new house, you shall make a parapet for your roof, that you may not bring the guilt of blood upon your house, if anyone should fall from it.

[9] "You shall not sow your vineyard with two kinds of seed, lest the whole yield be forfeited,[1] the crop that you have sown an the yield of the vineyard. [10] You shall n plow with an ox and a donkey togethe [11] You shall not wear cloth of wool and line mixed together.

[12] "You shall make yourself tassels on th four corners of the garment with whic you cover yourself.

Laws Concerning Sexual Immorality

[13] "If any man takes a wife and goes i to her and then hates her [14] and accuse her of misconduct and brings a bad nam upon her, saying, 'I took this woman, an when I came near her, I did not find in he evidence of virginity,' [15] then the father o the young woman and her mother shal take and bring out the evidence of her vir ginity to the elders of the city in the gate [16] And the father of the young woman shal say to the elders, 'I gave my daughter t this man to marry, and he hates her; [17] an behold, he has accused her of misconduct saying, "I did not find in your daughter evi dence of virginity." And yet this is the evi dence of my daughter's virginity.' And the shall spread the cloak before the elder of the city. [18] Then the elders of that cit shall take the man and whip[2] him, [19] an they shall fine him a hundred shekels[3] o silver and give them to the father of the young woman, because he has brough a bad name upon a virgin[4] of Israel. An she shall be his wife. He may not divorce her all his days. [20] But if the thing is true that evidence of virginity was not found i the young woman, [21] then they shall bring out the young woman to the door of her father's house, and the men of her city shal stone her to death with stones, because she has done an outrageous thing in Israel by whoring in her father's house. So you shall purge the evil from your midst.

[22] "If a man is found lying with the wife of another man, both of them shall die, the man who lay with the woman, and the woman. So you shall purge the evil from Israel.

[23] "If there is a betrothed virgin, and a man meets her in the city and lies with her, [24] then you shall bring them both out to the gate of that city, and you shall stone them to death with stones, the young woman because she did not cry for help though she was in the city, and the man because

[1] Hebrew *become holy* [2] Or *discipline* [3] A *shekel* was about 2/5 ounce or 11 grams [4] Or *girl of marriageable age*

he violated his neighbor's wife. So you shall purge the evil from your midst.

²⁵ "But if in the open country a man meets a young woman who is betrothed, and the man seizes her and lies with her, then only the man who lay with her shall die. ²⁶ But you shall do nothing to the young woman; she has committed no offense punishable by death. For this case is like that of a man attacking and murdering his neighbor, ²⁷ because he met her in the open country, and though the betrothed young woman cried for help there was no one to rescue her.

²⁸ "If a man meets a virgin who is not betrothed, and seizes her and lies with her, and they are found, ²⁹ then the man who lay with her shall give to the father of the young woman fifty shekels of silver, and she shall be his wife, because he has violated her. He may not divorce her all his days.

³⁰¹ "A man shall not take his father's wife, so that he does not uncover his father's nakedness.²

Those Excluded from the Assembly

23 "No one whose testicles are crushed or whose male organ is cut off shall enter the assembly of the LORD.

² "No one born of a forbidden union may enter the assembly of the LORD. Even to the tenth generation, none of his descendants may enter the assembly of the LORD.

³ "No Ammonite or Moabite may enter the assembly of the LORD. Even to the tenth generation, none of them may enter the assembly of the LORD forever, ⁴ because they did not meet you with bread and with water on the way, when you came out of Egypt, and because they hired against you Balaam the son of Beor from Pethor of Mesopotamia, to curse you. ⁵ But the LORD your God would not listen to Balaam; instead the LORD your God turned the curse into a blessing for you, because the LORD your God loved you. ⁶ You shall not seek their peace or their prosperity all your days forever.

⁷ "You shall not abhor an Edomite, for he is your brother. You shall not abhor an Egyptian, because you were a sojourner in his land. ⁸ Children born to them in the third generation may enter the assembly of the LORD.

Uncleanness in the Camp

⁹ "When you are encamped against your enemies, then you shall keep yourself from every evil thing. ¹⁰ "If any man among you becomes unclean because of a nocturnal emission, then he shall go outside the camp. He shall not come inside the camp, ¹¹ but when evening comes, he shall bathe himself in water, and as the sun sets, he may come inside the camp. ¹² "You shall have a place outside the camp, and you shall go out to it. ¹³ And you shall have a trowel with your tools, and when you sit down outside, you shall dig a hole with it and turn back and cover up your excrement. ¹⁴ Because the LORD your God walks in the midst of your camp, to deliver you and to give up your enemies before you, therefore your camp must be holy, so that he may not see anything indecent among you and turn away from you.

Miscellaneous Laws

¹⁵ "You shall not give up to his master a slave³ who has escaped from his master to you. ¹⁶ He shall dwell with you, in your midst, in the place that he shall choose within one of your towns, wherever it suits him. You shall not wrong him.

¹⁷ "None of the daughters of Israel shall be a cult prostitute, and none of the sons of Israel shall be a cult prostitute. ¹⁸ You shall not bring the fee of a prostitute or the wages of a dog⁴ into the house of the LORD your God in payment for any vow, for both of these are an abomination to the LORD your God.

¹⁹ "You shall not charge interest on loans to your brother, interest on money, interest on food, interest on anything that is lent for interest. ²⁰ You may charge a foreigner interest, but you may not charge your brother interest, that the LORD your God may bless you in all that you undertake in the land that you are entering to take possession of it.

²¹ "If you make a vow to the LORD your God, you shall not delay fulfilling it, for the LORD your God will surely require it of you, and you will be guilty of sin. ²² But if you

---

¹ Ch 23:1 in Hebrew ² Hebrew *uncover his father's skirt* ³ Or *servant*; the Hebrew term *'ebed* designates a range of social and economic roles (see About the ESV) ⁴ Or *male prostitute*

refrain from vowing, you will not be guilty of sin. [23] You shall be careful to do what has passed your lips, for you have voluntarily vowed to the LORD your God what you have promised with your mouth.

[24] "If you go into your neighbor's vineyard, you may eat your fill of grapes, as many as you wish, but you shall not put any in your bag. [25] If you go into your neighbor's standing grain, you may pluck the ears with your hand, but you shall not put a sickle to your neighbor's standing grain.

Laws Concerning Divorce

24 "When a man takes a wife and marries her, if then she finds no favor in his eyes because he has found some indecency in her, and he writes her a certificate of divorce and puts it in her hand and sends her out of his house, and she departs out of his house, [2] and if she goes and becomes another man's wife, [3] and the latter man hates her and writes her a certificate of divorce and puts it in her hand and sends her out of his house, or if the latter man dies, who took her to be his wife, [4] then her former husband, who sent her away, may not take her again to be his wife, after she has been defiled, for that is an abomination before the LORD. And you shall not bring sin upon the land that the LORD your God is giving you for an inheritance.

Miscellaneous Laws

[5] "When a man is newly married, he shall not go out with the army or be liable for any other public duty. He shall be free at home one year to be happy with his wife whom he has taken.

[6] "No one shall take a mill or an upper millstone in pledge, for that would be taking a life in pledge.

[7] "If a man is found stealing one of his brothers of the people of Israel, and if he treats him as a slave or sells him, then that thief shall die. So you shall purge the evil from your midst.

[8] "Take care, in a case of leprous[1] disease, to be very careful to do according to all that the Levitical priests shall direct you. As I commanded them, so you shall be careful to do. [9] Remember what the LORD your God did to Miriam on the way as you came out of Egypt.

[10] "When you make your neighbor a loan of any sort, you shall not go into his house to collect his pledge. [11] You shall stand outside, and the man to whom you make the loan shall bring the pledge out to you. [12] And if he is a poor man, you shall not sleep in his pledge. [13] You shall restore to him the pledge as the sun sets, that he may sleep in his cloak and bless you. And it shall be righteousness for you before the LORD your God.

[14] "You shall not oppress a hired worker who is poor and needy, whether he is one of your brothers or one of the sojourners who are in your land within your towns. [15] You shall give him his wages on the same day, before the sun sets (for he is poor and counts on it), lest he cry against you to the LORD, and you be guilty of sin.

[16] "Fathers shall not be put to death because of their children, nor shall children be put to death because of their fathers. Each one shall be put to death for his own sin.

[17] "You shall not pervert the justice due to the sojourner or to the fatherless, or take a widow's garment in pledge, [18] but you shall remember that you were a slave in Egypt and the LORD your God redeemed you from there; therefore I command you to do this.

[19] "When you reap your harvest in your field and forget a sheaf in the field, you shall not go back to get it. It shall be for the sojourner, the fatherless, and the widow, that the LORD your God may bless you in all the work of your hands. [20] When you beat your olive trees, you shall not go over them again. It shall be for the sojourner, the fatherless, and the widow. [21] When you gather the grapes of your vineyard, you shall not strip it afterward. It shall be for the sojourner, the fatherless, and the widow. [22] You shall remember that you were a slave in the land of Egypt; therefore I command you to do this.

25 "If there is a dispute between men and they come into court and the judges decide between them, acquitting the innocent and condemning the guilty, [2] then if the guilty man deserves to be beaten, the judge shall cause him to lie down and be beaten in his presence with a number of stripes in proportion to his offense. [3] Forty stripes may be given him, but not more, lest, if one should go on to

---

[1] *Leprosy* was a term for several skin diseases; see Leviticus 13

beat him with more stripes than these, your brother be degraded in your sight. ⁴"You shall not muzzle an ox when it is treading out the grain.

Laws Concerning Levirate Marriage

⁵"If brothers dwell together, and one of them dies and has no son, the wife of the dead man shall not be married outside the family to a stranger. Her husband's brother shall go in to her and take her as his wife and perform the duty of a husband's brother to her. ⁶And the first son whom she bears shall succeed to the name of his dead brother, that his name may not be blotted out of Israel. ⁷And if the man does not wish to take his brother's wife, then his brother's wife shall go up to the gate to the elders and say, 'My husband's brother refuses to perpetuate his brother's name in Israel; he will not perform the duty of a husband's brother to me.' ⁸Then the elders of his city shall call him and speak to him, and if he persists, saying, 'I do not wish to take her,' ⁹then his brother's wife shall go up to him in the presence of the elders and pull his sandal off his foot and spit in his face. And she shall answer and say, 'So shall it be done to the man who does not build up his brother's house.' ¹⁰And the name of his house¹ shall be called in Israel, 'The house of him who had his sandal pulled off.'

Miscellaneous Laws

¹¹"When men fight with one another and the wife of the one draws near to rescue her husband from the hand of him who is beating him and puts out her hand and seizes him by the private parts, ¹²then you shall cut off her hand. Your eye shall have no pity.

¹³"You shall not have in your bag two kinds of weights, a large and a small. ¹⁴You shall not have in your house two kinds of measures, a large and a small. ¹⁵A full and fair² weight you shall have, a full and fair measure you shall have, that your days may be long in the land that the LORD your God is giving you. ¹⁶For all who do such things, all who act dishonestly, are an abomination to the LORD your God.

¹⁷"Remember what Amalek did to you on the way as you came out of Egypt, ¹⁸how he attacked you on the way when you were faint and weary, and cut off your tail, those who were lagging behind you, and he did not fear God. ¹⁹Therefore when the LORD your God has given you rest from all your enemies around you, in the land that the LORD your God is giving you for an inheritance to possess, you shall blot out the memory of Amalek from under heaven; you shall not forget.

Offerings of Firstfruits and Tithes

26 "When you come into the land that the LORD your God is giving you for an inheritance and have taken possession of it and live in it, ²you shall take some of the first of all the fruit of the ground, which you harvest from your land that the LORD your God is giving you, and you shall put it in a basket, and you shall go to the place that the LORD your God will choose, to make his name to dwell there. ³And you shall go to the priest who is in office at that time and say to him, 'I declare today to the LORD your God that I have come into the land that the LORD swore to our fathers to give us.' ⁴Then the priest shall take the basket from your hand and set it down before the altar of the LORD your God.

⁵"And you shall make response before the LORD your God, 'A wandering Aramean was my father. And he went down into Egypt and sojourned there, few in number, and there he became a nation, great, mighty, and populous. ⁶And the Egyptians treated us harshly and humiliated us and laid on us hard labor. ⁷Then we cried to the LORD, the God of our fathers, and the LORD heard our voice and saw our affliction, our toil, and our oppression. ⁸And the LORD brought us out of Egypt with a mighty hand and an outstretched arm, with great deeds of terror,³ with signs and wonders. ⁹And he brought us into this place and gave us this land, a land flowing with milk and honey. ¹⁰And behold, now I bring the first of the fruit of the ground, which you, O LORD, have given me.' And you shall set it down before the LORD your God and worship before the LORD your God. ¹¹And you shall rejoice in all the good that the LORD your God has given to you and to your house, you, and the Levite, and the sojourner who is among you.

¹²"When you have finished paying all the tithe of your produce in the third year, which is the year of tithing, giving it to the

¹Hebrew *its name* ²Or *just*, or *righteous*; twice in this verse ³Hebrew *with great terror*

Levite, the sojourner, the fatherless, and the widow, so that they may eat within your towns and be filled, [13] then you shall say before the LORD your God, 'I have removed the sacred portion out of my house, and moreover, I have given it to the Levite, the sojourner, the fatherless, and the widow, according to all your commandment that you have commanded me. I have not transgressed any of your commandments, nor have I forgotten them. [14] I have not eaten of the tithe while I was mourning, or removed any of it while I was unclean, or offered any of it to the dead. I have obeyed the voice of the LORD my God. I have done according to all that you have commanded me. [15] Look down from your holy habitation, from heaven, and bless your people Israel and the ground that you have given us, as you swore to our fathers, a land flowing with milk and honey.'

[16] "This day the LORD your God commands you to do these statutes and rules. You shall therefore be careful to do them with all your heart and with all your soul. [17] You have declared today that the LORD is your God, and that you will walk in his ways, and keep his statutes and his commandments and his rules, and will obey his voice. [18] And the LORD has declared today that you are a people for his treasured possession, as he has promised you, and that you are to keep all his commandments, [19] and that he will set you in praise and in fame and in honor high above all nations that he has made, and that you shall be a people holy to the LORD your God, as he promised."

The Altar on Mount Ebal

27 Now Moses and the elders of Israel commanded the people, saying, "Keep the whole commandment that I command you today. [2] And on the day you cross over the Jordan to the land that the LORD your God is giving you, you shall set up large stones and plaster them with plaster. [3] And you shall write on them all the words of this law, when you cross over to enter the land that the LORD your God is giving you, a land flowing with milk and honey, as the LORD, the God of your fathers, has promised you. [4] And when you have crossed over the Jordan, you shall set up these stones, concerning which I command you today, on Mount Ebal, and you shall

plaster them with plaster. [5] And there you shall build an altar to the LORD your God, an altar of stones. You shall wield no iron tool on them; [6] you shall build an altar to the LORD your God of uncut[1] stones. And you shall offer burnt offerings on it to the LORD your God, [7] and you shall sacrifice peace offerings and shall eat there, and you shall rejoice before the LORD your God. [8] And you shall write on the stones all the words of this law very plainly."

Curses from Mount Ebal

[9] Then Moses and the Levitical priests said to all Israel, "Keep silence and hear, O Israel: this day you have become the people of the LORD your God. [10] You shall therefore obey the voice of the LORD your God, keeping his commandments and his statutes, which I command you today."

[11] That day Moses charged the people, saying, [12] "When you have crossed over the Jordan, these shall stand on Mount Gerizim to bless the people: Simeon, Levi, Judah, Issachar, Joseph, and Benjamin. [13] And these shall stand on Mount Ebal for the curse: Reuben, Gad, Asher, Zebulun, Dan, and Naphtali. [14] And the Levites shall declare to all the men of Israel in a loud voice:

[15] "'Cursed be the man who makes a carved or cast metal image, an abomination to the LORD, a thing made by the hands of a craftsman, and sets it up in secret.' And all the people shall answer and say, 'Amen.'

[16] "'Cursed be anyone who dishonors his father or his mother.' And all the people shall say, 'Amen.'

[17] "'Cursed be anyone who moves his neighbor's landmark.' And all the people shall say, 'Amen.'

[18] "'Cursed be anyone who misleads a blind man on the road.' And all the people shall say, 'Amen.'

[19] "'Cursed be anyone who perverts the justice due to the sojourner, the fatherless, and the widow.' And all the people shall say, 'Amen.'

[20] "'Cursed be anyone who lies with his father's wife, because he has uncovered his father's nakedness.'[2] And all the people shall say, 'Amen.'

[21] "'Cursed be anyone who lies with any kind of animal.' And all the people shall say, 'Amen.'

[1] Hebrew *whole* [2] Hebrew *uncovered his father's skirt*

²² "'Cursed be anyone who lies with his sister, whether the daughter of his father or the daughter of his mother.' And all the people shall say, 'Amen.'

²³ "'Cursed be anyone who lies with his mother-in-law.' And all the people shall say, 'Amen.'

²⁴ "'Cursed be anyone who strikes down his neighbor in secret.' And all the people shall say, 'Amen.'

²⁵ "'Cursed be anyone who takes a bribe to shed innocent blood.' And all the people shall say, 'Amen.'

²⁶ "'Cursed be anyone who does not confirm the words of this law by doing them.' And all the people shall say, 'Amen.'

Blessings for Obedience

28 "And if you faithfully obey the voice of the LORD your God, being careful to do all his commandments that I command you today, the LORD your God will set you high above all the nations of the earth. ² And all these blessings shall come upon you and overtake you, if you obey the voice of the LORD your God. ³ Blessed shall you be in the city, and blessed shall you be in the field. ⁴ Blessed shall be the fruit of your womb and the fruit of your ground and the fruit of your cattle, the increase of your herds and the young of your flock. ⁵ Blessed shall be your basket and your kneading bowl. ⁶ Blessed shall you be when you come in, and blessed shall you be when you go out.

⁷ "The LORD will cause your enemies who rise against you to be defeated before you. They shall come out against you one way and flee before you seven ways. ⁸ The LORD will command the blessing on you in your barns and in all that you undertake. And he will bless you in the land that the LORD your God is giving you. ⁹ The LORD will establish you as a people holy to himself, as he has sworn to you, if you keep the commandments of the LORD your God and walk in his ways. ¹⁰ And all the peoples of the earth shall see that you are called by the name of the LORD, and they shall be afraid of you. ¹¹ And the LORD will make you abound in prosperity, in the fruit of your womb and in the fruit of your livestock and in the fruit of your ground, within the land that the LORD swore to your fathers to give you. ¹² The LORD will open to you his good treasury, the heavens, to give the rain to your land in its season and to bless all the work of your hands. And you shall lend to many nations, but you shall not borrow. ¹³ And the LORD will make you the head and not the tail, and you shall only go up and not down, if you obey the commandments of the LORD your God, which I command you today, being careful to do them, ¹⁴ and if you do not turn aside from any of the words that I command you today, to the right hand or to the left, to go after other gods to serve them.

Curses for Disobedience

¹⁵ "But if you will not obey the voice of the LORD your God or be careful to do all his commandments and his statutes that I command you today, then all these curses shall come upon you and overtake you. ¹⁶ Cursed shall you be in the city, and cursed shall you be in the field. ¹⁷ Cursed shall be your basket and your kneading bowl. ¹⁸ Cursed shall be the fruit of your womb and the fruit of your ground, the increase of your herds and the young of your flock. ¹⁹ Cursed shall you be when you come in, and cursed shall you be when you go out.

²⁰ "The LORD will send on you curses, confusion, and frustration in all that you undertake to do, until you are destroyed and perish quickly on account of the evil of your deeds, because you have forsaken me. ²¹ The LORD will make the pestilence stick to you until he has consumed you off the land that you are entering to take possession of it. ²² The LORD will strike you with wasting disease and with fever, inflammation and fiery heat, and with drought¹ and with blight and with mildew. They shall pursue you until you perish. ²³ And the heavens over your head shall be bronze, and the earth under you shall be iron. ²⁴ The LORD will make the rain of your land powder. From heaven dust shall come down on you until you are destroyed.

²⁵ "The LORD will cause you to be defeated before your enemies. You shall go out one way against them and flee seven ways before them. And you shall be a horror to all the kingdoms of the earth. ²⁶ And your dead body shall be food for all birds of the air and for the beasts of the earth, and there shall be no one to frighten them away. ²⁷ The LORD will strike you with

---

¹ Or *sword*

the boils of Egypt, and with tumors and scabs and itch, of which you cannot be healed. [28] The LORD will strike you with madness and blindness and confusion of mind, [29] and you shall grope at noonday, as the blind grope in darkness, and you shall not prosper in your ways.[1] And you shall be only oppressed and robbed continually, and there shall be no one to help you. [30] You shall betroth a wife, but another man shall ravish her. You shall build a house, but you shall not dwell in it. You shall plant a vineyard, but you shall not enjoy its fruit. [31] Your ox shall be slaughtered before your eyes, but you shall not eat any of it. Your donkey shall be seized before your face, but shall not be restored to you. Your sheep shall be given to your enemies, but there shall be no one to help you. [32] Your sons and your daughters shall be given to another people, while your eyes look on and fail with longing for them all day long, but you shall be helpless. [33] A nation that you have not known shall eat up the fruit of your ground and of all your labors, and you shall be only oppressed and crushed continually, [34] so that you are driven mad by the sights that your eyes see. [35] The LORD will strike you on the knees and on the legs with grievous boils of which you cannot be healed, from the sole of your foot to the crown of your head.

[36] "The LORD will bring you and your king whom you set over you to a nation that neither you nor your fathers have known. And there you shall serve other gods of wood and stone. [37] And you shall become a horror, a proverb, and a byword among all the peoples where the LORD will lead you away. [38] You shall carry much seed into the field and shall gather in little, for the locust shall consume it. [39] You shall plant vineyards and dress them, but you shall neither drink of the wine nor gather the grapes, for the worm shall eat them. [40] You shall have olive trees throughout all your territory, but you shall not anoint yourself with the oil, for your olives shall drop off. [41] You shall father sons and daughters, but they shall not be yours, for they shall go into captivity. [42] The cricket[2] shall possess all your trees and the fruit of your ground. [43] The sojourner who is among you shall rise higher and higher above you, and you shall come down lower and lower. [44] He

shall lend to you, and you shall not lend to him. He shall be the head, and you shall be the tail.

[45] "All these curses shall come upon you and pursue you and overtake you till you are destroyed, because you did not obey the voice of the LORD your God, to keep his commandments and his statutes that he commanded you. [46] They shall be a sign and a wonder against you and your offspring forever. [47] Because you did not serve the LORD your God with joyfulness and gladness of heart, because of the abundance of all things, [48] therefore you shall serve your enemies whom the LORD will send against you, in hunger and thirst, in nakedness, and lacking everything. And he will put a yoke of iron on your neck until he has destroyed you. [49] The LORD will bring a nation against you from far away, from the end of the earth, swooping down like the eagle, a nation whose language you do not understand, [50] a hard-faced nation who shall not respect the old or show mercy to the young. [51] It shall eat the offspring of your cattle and the fruit of your ground, until you are destroyed; it also shall not leave you grain, wine, or oil, the increase of your herds or the young of your flock, until they have caused you to perish.

[52] "They shall besiege you in all your towns, until your high and fortified walls, in which you trusted, come down throughout all your land. And they shall besiege you in all your towns throughout all your land, which the LORD your God has given you. [53] And you shall eat the fruit of your womb, the flesh of your sons and daughters, whom the LORD your God has given you, in the siege and in the distress with which your enemies shall distress you. [54] The man who is the most tender and refined among you will begrudge food to his brother, to the wife he embraces,[3] and to the last of the children whom he has left, [55] so that he will not give to any of them any of the flesh of his children whom he is eating, because he has nothing else left, in the siege and in the distress with which your enemy shall distress you in all your towns. [56] The most tender and refined woman among you, who would not venture to set the sole of her foot on the ground because she is so delicate and tender, will begrudge to the husband she embraces,[4] to her son

---

[1] Or *shall not succeed in finding your ways* [2] Identity uncertain [3] Hebrew *the wife of his bosom* [4] Hebrew *the husband of her bosom*

and to her daughter, [57] her afterbirth that comes out from between her feet and her children whom she bears, because lacking everything she will eat them secretly, in the siege and in the distress with which your enemy shall distress you in your towns.

[58] "If you are not careful to do all the words of this law that are written in this book, that you may fear this glorious and awesome name, the LORD your God, [59] then the LORD will bring on you and your offspring extraordinary afflictions, afflictions severe and lasting, and sicknesses grievous and lasting. [60] And he will bring upon you again all the diseases of Egypt, of which you were afraid, and they shall cling to you. [61] Every sickness also and every affliction that is not recorded in the book of this law, the LORD will bring upon you, until you are destroyed. [62] Whereas you were as numerous as the stars of heaven, you shall be left few in number, because you did not obey the voice of the LORD your God. [63] And as the LORD took delight in doing you good and multiplying you, so the LORD will take delight in bringing ruin upon you and destroying you. And you shall be plucked off the land that you are entering to take possession of it.

[64] "And the LORD will scatter you among all peoples, from one end of the earth to the other, and there you shall serve other gods of wood and stone, which neither you nor your fathers have known. [65] And among these nations you shall find no respite, and there shall be no resting place for the sole of your foot, but the LORD will give you there a trembling heart and failing eyes and a languishing soul. [66] Your life shall hang in doubt before you. Night and day you shall be in dread and have no assurance of your life. [67] In the morning you shall say, 'If only it were evening!' and at evening you shall say, 'If only it were morning!' because of the dread that your heart shall feel, and the sights that your eyes shall see. [68] And the LORD will bring you back in ships to Egypt, a journey that I promised that you should never make again; and there you shall offer yourselves for sale to your enemies as male and female slaves, but there will be no buyer."

The Covenant Renewed in Moab

29 [1] These are the words of the covenant that the LORD commanded Moses to make with the people of Israel in the land of Moab, besides the covenant that he had made with them at Horeb.

[2] And Moses summoned all Israel and said to them: "You have seen all that the LORD did before your eyes in the land of Egypt, to Pharaoh and to all his servants and to all his land, [3] the great trials that your eyes saw, the signs, and those great wonders. [4] But to this day the LORD has not given you a heart to understand or eyes to see or ears to hear. [5] I have led you forty years in the wilderness. Your clothes have not worn out on you, and your sandals have not worn off your feet. [6] You have not eaten bread, and you have not drunk wine or strong drink, that you may know that I am the LORD your God. [7] And when you came to this place, Sihon the king of Heshbon and Og the king of Bashan came out against us to battle, but we defeated them. [8] We took their land and gave it for an inheritance to the Reubenites, the Gadites, and the half-tribe of the Manassites. [9] Therefore keep the words of this covenant and do them, that you may prosper[3] in all that you do.

[10] "You are standing today all of you before the LORD your God: the heads of your tribes,[4] your elders, and your officers, all the men of Israel, [11] your little ones, your wives, and the sojourner who is in your camp, from the one who chops your wood to the one who draws your water, [12] so that you may enter into the sworn covenant of the LORD your God, which the LORD your God is making with you today, [13] that he may establish you today as his people, and that he may be your God, as he promised you, and as he swore to your fathers, to Abraham, to Isaac, and to Jacob. [14] It is not with you alone that I am making this sworn covenant, [15] but with whoever is standing here with us today before the LORD our God, and with whoever is not here with us today.

[16] "You know how we lived in the land of Egypt, and how we came through the midst of the nations through which you passed. [17] And you have seen their detestable things, their idols of wood and stone,

[1] Ch 28:69 in Hebrew   [2] Ch 29:1 in Hebrew   [3] Or *deal wisely*   [4] Septuagint, Syriac; Hebrew *your heads, your tribes*

of silver and gold, which were among them. [18] Beware lest there be among you a man or woman or clan or tribe whose heart is turning away today from the LORD our God to go and serve the gods of those nations. Beware lest there be among you a root bearing poisonous and bitter fruit, [19] one who, when he hears the words of this sworn covenant, blesses himself in his heart, saying, 'I shall be safe, though I walk in the stubbornness of my heart.' This will lead to the sweeping away of moist and dry alike. [20] The LORD will not be willing to forgive him, but rather the anger of the LORD and his jealousy will smoke against that man, and the curses written in this book will settle upon him, and the LORD will blot out his name from under heaven. [21] And the LORD will single him out from all the tribes of Israel for calamity, in accordance with all the curses of the covenant written in this Book of the Law. [22] And the next generation, your children who rise up after you, and the foreigner who comes from a far land, will say, when they see the afflictions of that land and the sicknesses with which the LORD has made it sick— [23] the whole land burned out with brimstone and salt, nothing sown and nothing growing, where no plant can sprout, an overthrow like that of Sodom and Gomorrah, Admah, and Zeboiim, which the LORD overthrew in his anger and wrath— [24] all the nations will say, 'Why has the LORD done thus to this land? What caused the heat of this great anger?' [25] Then people will say, 'It is because they abandoned the covenant of the LORD, the God of their fathers, which he made with them when he brought them out of the land of Egypt, [26] and went and served other gods and worshiped them, gods whom they had not known and whom he had not allotted to them. [27] Therefore the anger of the LORD was kindled against this land, bringing upon it all the curses written in this book, [28] and the LORD uprooted them from their land in anger and fury and great wrath, and cast them into another land, as they are this day.'

[29] "The secret things belong to the LORD our God, but the things that are revealed belong to us and to our children forever, that we may do all the words of this law.

Repentance and Forgiveness

30 "And when all these things come upon you, the blessing and the curse, which I have set before you, and you call them to mind among all the nations where the LORD your God has driven you, [2] and return to the LORD your God, you and your children, and obey his voice in all that I command you today, with all your heart and with all your soul, [3] then the LORD your God will restore your fortunes and have mercy on you, and he will gather you again from all the peoples where the LORD your God has scattered you. [4] If your outcasts are in the uttermost parts of heaven, from there the LORD your God will gather you, and from there he will take you. [5] And the LORD your God will bring you into the land that your fathers possessed, that you may possess it. And he will make you more prosperous and numerous than your fathers. [6] And the LORD your God will circumcise your heart and the heart of your offspring, so that you will love the LORD your God with all your heart and with all your soul, that you may live. [7] And the LORD your God will put all these curses on your foes and enemies who persecuted you. [8] And you shall again obey the voice of the LORD and keep all his commandments that I command you today. [9] The LORD your God will make you abundantly prosperous in all the work of your hand, in the fruit of your womb and in the fruit of your cattle and in the fruit of your ground. For the LORD will again take delight in prospering you, as he took delight in your fathers, [10] when you obey the voice of the LORD your God, to keep his commandments and his statutes that are written in this Book of the Law, when you turn to the LORD your God with all your heart and with all your soul.

The Choice of Life and Death

[11] "For this commandment that I command you today is not too hard for you, neither is it far off. [12] It is not in heaven, that you should say, 'Who will ascend to heaven for us and bring it to us, that we may hear it and do it?' [13] Neither is it beyond the sea, that you should say, 'Who will go over the sea for us and bring it to us, that we may hear it and do it?' [14] But the word is very near you. It is in your mouth and in your heart, so that you can do it.

¹⁵ "See, I have set before you today life and good, death and evil. ¹⁶ If you obey the commandments of the Lᴏʀᴅ your God[1] that I command you today, by loving the Lᴏʀᴅ your God, by walking in his ways, and by keeping his commandments and his statutes and his rules,[2] then you shall live and multiply, and the Lᴏʀᴅ your God will bless you in the land that you are entering to take possession of it. ¹⁷ But if your heart turns away, and you will not hear, but are drawn away to worship other gods and serve them, ¹⁸ I declare to you today, that you shall surely perish. You shall not live long in the land that you are going over the Jordan to enter and possess. ¹⁹ I call heaven and earth to witness against you today, that I have set before you life and death, blessing and curse. Therefore choose life, that you and your offspring may live, ²⁰ loving the Lᴏʀᴅ your God, obeying his voice and holding fast to him, for he is your life and length of days, that you may dwell in the land that the Lᴏʀᴅ swore to your fathers, to Abraham, to Isaac, and to Jacob, to give them."

Ask Yourself . . .

ABOUT MAKING DECISIONS

How do you make decisions about life? Think about it for a minute and ask yourself:

- Do I follow God's directions?
- When I have a big choice to make, how much do I rely on God's Word?
- Are there times when I choose not to listen to God before I make a decision? If so, why?
- Am I always loyal to God in my choices?

Joshua to Succeed Moses

31 So Moses continued to speak these words to all Israel. ² And he said to them, "I am 120 years old today. I am no longer able to go out and come in. The Lᴏʀᴅ has said to me, 'You shall not go over this Jordan.' ³ The Lᴏʀᴅ your God himself will go over before you. He will destroy these nations before you, so that you shall dispossess them, and Joshua will go over at your head, as the Lᴏʀᴅ has spoken. ⁴ And the Lᴏʀᴅ will do to them as he did to Sihon and Og, the kings of the Amorites, and to their land, when he destroyed them. ⁵ And the Lᴏʀᴅ will give them over to you, and you shall do to them according to the whole commandment that I have commanded you. ⁶ Be strong and courageous. Do not fear or be in dread of them, for it is the Lᴏʀᴅ your God who goes with you. He will not leave you or forsake you."

⁷ Then Moses summoned Joshua and said to him in the sight of all Israel, "Be strong and courageous, for you shall go with this people into the land that the Lᴏʀᴅ has sworn to their fathers to give them, and you shall put them in possession of it. ⁸ It is the Lᴏʀᴅ who goes before you. He will be with you; he will not leave you or forsake you. Do not fear or be dismayed."

The Reading of the Law

⁹ Then Moses wrote this law and gave it to the priests, the sons of Levi, who carried the ark of the covenant of the Lᴏʀᴅ, and to all the elders of Israel. ¹⁰ And Moses commanded them, "At the end of every seven years, at the set time in the year of release, at the Feast of Booths, ¹¹ when all Israel comes to appear before the Lᴏʀᴅ your God at the place that he will choose, you shall read this law before all Israel in their hearing. ¹² Assemble the people, men, women, and little ones, and the sojourner within your towns, that they may hear and learn to fear the Lᴏʀᴅ your God, and be careful to do all the words of this law, ¹³ and that their children, who have not known it, may hear and learn to fear the Lᴏʀᴅ your God, as long as you live in the land that you are going over the Jordan to possess."

Joshua Commissioned to Lead Israel

¹⁴ And the Lᴏʀᴅ said to Moses, "Behold, the days approach when you must die. Call Joshua and present yourselves in the tent of meeting, that I may commission him." And Moses and Joshua went and presented themselves in the tent of meeting. ¹⁵ And the Lᴏʀᴅ appeared in the tent in a pillar

[1] Septuagint; Hebrew lacks *If you obey the commandments of the Lᴏʀᴅ your God* [2] Or *his just decrees*

of cloud. And the pillar of cloud stood over the entrance of the tent.

[16] And the LORD said to Moses, "Behold, you are about to lie down with your fathers. Then this people will rise and whore after the foreign gods among them in the land that they are entering, and they will forsake me and break my covenant that I have made with them. [17] Then my anger will be kindled against them in that day, and I will forsake them and hide my face from them, and they will be devoured. And many evils and troubles will come upon them, so that they will say in that day, 'Have not these evils come upon us because our God is not among us?' [18] And I will surely hide my face in that day because of all the evil that they have done, because they have turned to other gods.

[19] "Now therefore write this song and teach it to the people of Israel. Put it in their mouths, that this song may be a witness for me against the people of Israel. [20] For when I have brought them into the land flowing with milk and honey, which I swore to give to their fathers, and they have eaten and are full and grown fat, they will turn to other gods and serve them, and despise me and break my covenant. [21] And when many evils and troubles have come upon them, this song shall confront them as a witness (for it will live unforgotten in the mouths of their offspring). For I know what they are inclined to do even today, before I have brought them into the land that I swore to give." [22] So Moses wrote this song the same day and taught it to the people of Israel.

[23] And the LORD[1] commissioned Joshua the son of Nun and said, "Be strong and courageous, for you shall bring the people of Israel into the land that I swore to give them. I will be with you."

[24] When Moses had finished writing the words of this law in a book to the very end, [25] Moses commanded the Levites who carried the ark of the covenant of the LORD, [26] "Take this Book of the Law and put it by the side of the ark of the covenant of the LORD your God, that it may be there for a witness against you. [27] For I know how rebellious and stubborn you are. Behold, even today while I am yet alive with you, you have been rebellious against the LORD. How much more after my death!

[28] Assemble to me all the elders of your tribes and your officers, that I may speak these words in their ears and call heaven and earth to witness against them. [29] For I know that after my death you will surely act corruptly and turn aside from the way that I have commanded you. And in the days to come evil will befall you, because you will do what is evil in the sight of the LORD, provoking him to anger through the work of your hands."

The Song of Moses

[30] Then Moses spoke the words of this song until they were finished, in the ears of all the assembly of Israel:

32 "Give ear, O heavens, and I will speak,
　　and let the earth hear the words of my mouth.
[2]　May my teaching drop as the rain,
　　my speech distill as the dew,
　like gentle rain upon the tender grass,
　　and like showers upon the herb.
[3]　For I will proclaim the name of the LORD;
　　ascribe greatness to our God!

[4]　"The Rock, his work is perfect,
　　for all his ways are justice.
　A God of faithfulness and without iniquity,
　　just and upright is he.
[5]　They have dealt corruptly with him;
　　they are no longer his children
　　　because they are blemished;
　　they are a crooked and twisted generation.
[6]　Do you thus repay the LORD,
　　you foolish and senseless people?
　Is not he your father, who created you,
　　who made you and established you?
[7]　Remember the days of old;
　　consider the years of many generations;
　ask your father, and he will show you,
　　your elders, and they will tell you.
[8]　When the Most High gave to the nations their inheritance,
　　when he divided mankind,

---

[1] Hebrew *he*

he fixed the borders[1] of the peoples
   according to the number of the
     sons of God.[2]

9 But the LORD's portion is his people,
   Jacob his allotted heritage.

10 "He found him in a desert land,
   and in the howling waste of the
     wilderness;
   he encircled him, he cared for him,
     he kept him as the apple of his eye.

11 Like an eagle that stirs up its nest,
   that flutters over its young,
   spreading out its wings, catching
     them,
   bearing them on its pinions,

12 the LORD alone guided him,
   no foreign god was with him.

13 He made him ride on the high places
     of the land,
   and he ate the produce of the field,
   and he suckled him with honey out
     of the rock,
   and oil out of the flinty rock.

14 Curds from the herd, and milk from
     the flock,
   with fat[3] of lambs,
   rams of Bashan and goats,
   with the very finest[4] of the
     wheat—
   and you drank foaming wine made
     from the blood of the grape.

15 "But Jeshurun grew fat, and kicked;
   you grew fat, stout, and sleek;
   then he forsook God who made him
   and scoffed at the Rock of his
     salvation.

16 They stirred him to jealousy with
     strange gods;
   with abominations they provoked
     him to anger.

17 They sacrificed to demons that were
     no gods,
   to gods they had never known,
   to new gods that had come recently,
   whom your fathers had never
     dreaded.

18 You were unmindful of the Rock that
     bore[5] you,
   and you forgot the God who gave
     you birth.

19 "The LORD saw it and spurned them,
   because of the provocation of his
     sons and his daughters.

20 And he said, 'I will hide my face from
     them;
   I will see what their end will be,
   for they are a perverse generation,
   children in whom is no faithful-
     ness.

21 They have made me jealous with
     what is no god;
   they have provoked me to anger
     with their idols.
   So I will make them jealous with
     those who are no people;
   I will provoke them to anger with a
     foolish nation.

22 For a fire is kindled by my anger,
   and it burns to the depths of Sheol,
   devours the earth and its increase,
   and sets on fire the foundations of
     the mountains.

23 "'And I will heap disasters upon them;
   I will spend my arrows on them;

24 they shall be wasted with hunger,
   and devoured by plague
   and poisonous pestilence;
   I will send the teeth of beasts against
     them,
   with the venom of things that
     crawl in the dust.

25 Outdoors the sword shall bereave,
   and indoors terror,
   for young man and woman alike,
   the nursing child with the man of
     gray hairs.

26 I would have said, "I will cut them to
     pieces;
   I will wipe them from human
     memory,"

27 had I not feared provocation by the
     enemy,
   lest their adversaries should mis-
     understand,
   lest they should say, "Our hand is
     triumphant,
   it was not the LORD who did all
     this."'

28 "For they are a nation void of counsel,
   and there is no understanding in
     them.

[1] Or *territories* [2] Compare Dead Sea Scroll, Septuagint; Masoretic Text *sons of Israel* [3] That is, with the best [4] Hebrew *with the kidney fat* [5] Or *fathered*

29 If they were wise, they would under-
         stand this;
      they would discern their latter
         end!
30 How could one have chased a thou-
         sand,
      and two have put ten thousand to
         flight,
      unless their Rock had sold them,
      and the LORD had given them up?
31 For their rock is not as our Rock;
      our enemies are by themselves.
32 For their vine comes from the vine of
         Sodom
      and from the fields of Gomorrah;
      their grapes are grapes of poison;
      their clusters are bitter;
33 their wine is the poison of serpents
      and the cruel venom of asps.

34 "'Is not this laid up in store with me,
      sealed up in my treasuries?
35 Vengeance is mine, and recompense,[1]
      for the time when their foot shall
         slip;
      for the day of their calamity is at
         hand,
      and their doom comes swiftly.'
36 For the LORD will vindicate[2] his
         people
      and have compassion on his ser-
         vants,
      when he sees that their power is
         gone
      and there is none remaining, bond
         or free.
37 Then he will say, 'Where are their
         gods,
      the rock in which they took refuge,
38 who ate the fat of their sacrifices
      and drank the wine of their drink
         offering?
      Let them rise up and help you;
      let them be your protection!

39 "'See now that I, even I, am he,
      and there is no god beside me;
      I kill and I make alive;
      I wound and I heal;
      and there is none that can deliver
         out of my hand.
40 For I lift up my hand to heaven
      and swear, As I live forever,

41 if I sharpen my flashing sword[3]
      and my hand takes hold on judg-
         ment,
   I will take vengeance on my adver-
         saries
      and will repay those who hate me.
42 I will make my arrows drunk with
         blood,
      and my sword shall devour flesh—
   with the blood of the slain and the
         captives,
      from the long-haired heads of the
         enemy.'

43 "Rejoice with him, O heavens;[4]
      bow down to him, all gods,[5]
   for he avenges the blood of his chil-
         dren[6]
      and takes vengeance on his adver-
         saries.
   He repays those who hate him[7]
      and cleanses[8] his people's land."[9]

44 Moses came and recited all the words
of this song in the hearing of the people,
he and Joshua[10] the son of Nun. 45 And
when Moses had finished speaking all
these words to all Israel, 46 he said to them,
"Take to heart all the words by which I am
warning you today, that you may command
them to your children, that they may be
careful to do all the words of this law. 47 For
it is no empty word for you, but your very
life, and by this word you shall live long in
the land that you are going over the Jordan
to possess."

Moses' Death Foretold

48 That very day the LORD spoke to
Moses, 49 "Go up this mountain of the
Abarim, Mount Nebo, which is in the land
of Moab, opposite Jericho, and view the
land of Canaan, which I am giving to the
people of Israel for a possession. 50 And
die on the mountain which you go up, and
be gathered to your people, as Aaron your
brother died in Mount Hor and was gathered to his people, 51 because you broke
faith with me in the midst of the people
of Israel at the waters of Meribah-kadesh,
in the wilderness of Zin, and because you
did not treat me as holy in the midst of
the people of Israel. 52 For you shall see

[1] Septuagint *and I will repay* [2] Septuagint *judge* [3] Hebrew *the lightning of my sword* [4] Dead Sea Scroll, Septuagint; Masoretic Text *Rejoice his people, O nations* [5] Masoretic Text lacks *bow down to him, all gods* [6] Dead Sea Scroll, Septuagint; Masoretic Text *servants* [7] Dead Sea Scroll, Septuagint; Masoretic Text lacks *He repays those who hate him* [8] Or *atones for* [9] Septuagint, Vulgate; Hebrew *his land his people* [10] Septuagint, Syriac, Vulgate; Hebrew *Hoshea*

he land before you, but you shall not go here, into the land that I am giving to the people of Israel."

Moses' Final Blessing on Israel

33 This is the blessing with which Moses the man of God blessed the people of Israel before his death. ²He said,

"The LORD came from Sinai
and dawned from Seir upon us;¹
he shone forth from Mount Paran;
he came from the ten thousands of
    holy ones,
with flaming fire² at his right hand.
³ Yes, he loved his people,³
all his holy ones were in his⁴ hand;
so they followed⁵ in your steps,
receiving direction from you,
⁴ when Moses commanded us a law,
as a possession for the assembly of
    Jacob.
⁵ Thus the LORD⁶ became king in
    Jeshurun,
when the heads of the people were
    gathered,
all the tribes of Israel together.

⁶ "Let Reuben live, and not die,
but let his men be few."

⁷And this he said of Judah:

"Hear, O LORD, the voice of Judah,
and bring him in to his people.
With your hands contend⁷ for him,
and be a help against his adversar-
    ies."

⁸And of Levi he said,

"Give to Levi⁸ your Thummim,
and your Urim to your godly one,
whom you tested at Massah,
with whom you quarreled at the
    waters of Meribah;
⁹ who said of his father and mother,
'I regard them not';
he disowned his brothers
and ignored his children.
For they observed your word
and kept your covenant.
¹⁰ They shall teach Jacob your rules
and Israel your law;

they shall put incense before you
and whole burnt offerings on your
    altar.
¹¹ Bless, O LORD, his substance,
and accept the work of his hands;
crush the loins of his adversaries,
of those who hate him, that they
    rise not again."

¹²Of Benjamin he said,

"The beloved of the LORD dwells in
    safety.
The High God⁹ surrounds him all day
    long,
and dwells between his shoulders."

¹³And of Joseph he said,

"Blessed by the LORD be his land,
with the choicest gifts of heaven
    above,¹⁰
and of the deep that crouches
    beneath,
¹⁴ with the choicest fruits of the sun
and the rich yield of the months,
¹⁵ with the finest produce of the
    ancient mountains
and the abundance of the everlast-
    ing hills,
¹⁶ with the best gifts of the earth and
    its fullness
and the favor of him who dwells in
    the bush.
May these rest on the head of Joseph,
on the pate of him who is prince
    among his brothers.
¹⁷ A firstborn bull¹¹—he has majesty,
and his horns are the horns of a
    wild ox;
with them he shall gore the peoples,
all of them, to the ends of the
    earth;
they are the ten thousands of
    Ephraim,
and they are the thousands of
    Manasseh."

¹⁸And of Zebulun he said,

"Rejoice, Zebulun, in your going out,
and Issachar, in your tents.

---

¹ Septuagint, Syriac, Vulgate; Hebrew *them* ² The meaning of the Hebrew word is uncertain ³ Septuagint; Hebrew *peoples* ⁴ Hebrew *your* ⁵ The meaning of the Hebrew word is uncertain ⁶ Hebrew *Thus he* ⁷ Probable reading; Hebrew *With his hands he contended* ⁸ Dead Sea Scroll, Septuagint; Masoretic Text lacks *Give to Levi* ⁹ Septuagint; Hebrew *dwells in safety by him. He* ¹⁰ Two Hebrew manuscripts and Targum; Hebrew *with the dew* ¹¹ Dead Sea Scroll, Septuagint, Samaritan; Masoretic Text *His firstborn bull*

19 They shall call peoples to their
         mountain;
      there they offer right sacrifices;
      for they draw from the abundance of
         the seas
         and the hidden treasures of the
            sand."

20 And of Gad he said,

   "Blessed be he who enlarges Gad!
      Gad crouches like a lion;
      he tears off arm and scalp.
21 He chose the best of the land for
         himself,
      for there a commander's portion
         was reserved;
      and he came with the heads of the
         people,
      with Israel he executed the justice
         of the LORD,
      and his judgments for Israel."

22 And of Dan he said,

   "Dan is a lion's cub
      that leaps from Bashan."

23 And of Naphtali he said,

   "O Naphtali, sated with favor,
      and full of the blessing of the LORD,
      possess the lake[1] and the south."

24 And of Asher he said,

   "Most blessed of sons be Asher;
      let him be the favorite of his broth-
         ers,
      and let him dip his foot in oil.
25 Your bars shall be iron and bronze,
      and as your days, so shall your
         strength be.

26 "There is none like God, O Jeshurun,
      who rides through the heavens to
         your help,
      through the skies in his majesty.
27 The eternal God is your dwelling
         place,[2]
      and underneath are the everlast-
         ing arms.[3]
   And he thrust out the enemy before
         you
      and said, 'Destroy.'

28 So Israel lived in safety,
      Jacob lived alone,[4]
   in a land of grain and wine,
      whose heavens drop down dew.
29 Happy are you, O Israel! Who is like
         you,
      a people saved by the LORD,
   the shield of your help,
      and the sword of your triumph!
   Your enemies shall come fawning to
         you,
      and you shall tread upon their
         backs."

The Death of Moses

34 Then Moses went up from the plains
      of Moab to Mount Nebo, to the top of
Pisgah, which is opposite Jericho. And the
LORD showed him all the land, Gilead as far
as Dan, 2 all Naphtali, the land of Ephraim
and Manasseh, all the land of Judah as far as
the western sea, 3 the Negeb, and the Plain,
that is, the Valley of Jericho the city of palm
trees, as far as Zoar. 4 And the LORD said to
him, "This is the land of which I swore to
Abraham, to Isaac, and to Jacob, 'I will give
it to your offspring.' I have let you see it
with your eyes, but you shall not go over
there." 5 So Moses the servant of the LORD
died there in the land of Moab, according to
the word of the LORD, 6 and he buried him
in the valley in the land of Moab opposite
Beth-peor; but no one knows the place of
his burial to this day. 7 Moses was 120 years
old when he died. His eye was undimmed,
and his vigor unabated. 8 And the people of
Israel wept for Moses in the plains of Moab
thirty days. Then the days of weeping and
mourning for Moses were ended.

9 And Joshua the son of Nun was full of
the spirit of wisdom, for Moses had laid
his hands on him. So the people of Israel
obeyed him and did as the LORD had commanded Moses. 10 And there has not arisen
a prophet since in Israel like Moses, whom
the LORD knew face to face, 11 none like him
for all the signs and the wonders that the
LORD sent him to do in the land of Egypt,
to Pharaoh and to all his servants and to all
his land, 12 and for all the mighty power and
all the great deeds of terror that Moses did
in the sight of all Israel.

[1] Or west [2] Or a dwelling place [3] Revocalization of verse 27 yields He subdues the ancient gods, and shatters the forces of old [4] Hebrew the abode of Jacob was alone

INTRODUCTION TO
Joshua

Author: Unknown

Time: Unknown

Place: Unknown

Written to: God's people, the Israelites

the gist

The Israelites enter the Promised Land under the command of Joshua. They do something that on the surface seems impossible, but through all you see that it really isn't they who do it but God. Watch for all the impossible things he will do with a willing people.

things to look for

God fulfilling his promises about the Promised Land (see Josh. 1:13–15; 10:40; 11:23; 21:44–45; 22:4; 23:9–15)

The working out of the covenant of God (see Josh. 1:7–8; 8:30–35; 22:5; 23:6, 15–16; 24:1–28)

The crossing of the Jordan River (see Joshua 3)

The destruction of Jericho (see Joshua 6)

Be Strong and Courageous

"Do not be afraid or dismayed; be strong and courageous. For thus the LORD will do to all your enemies against whom you fight."

Joshua 10:25

God always delivers on his promises, but when God says he'll do something and then doesn't do it immediately but waits one, two, or forty years, it can be easy to start doubting the promise. God isn't FedEx—when he makes a promise, he doesn't give an exact delivery date—but the God Girl knows she can trust God anyway, and that makes all the difference in the world.

When the Israelites left Egypt, God promised he would lead them to a land flowing with milk and honey (see Ex. 3:8). It was all they'd ever dreamed of: a land of their own, where they wouldn't be told by other nations what to do and when to do it, and where they could own their own homes and protect their families from the enemies of God. But it took forty years of wandering in a no-man's-land for that dream to come true.

Could that promise have been fulfilled sooner? Most definitely. In fact, the Israelites themselves were responsible for the delay of the fulfillment. Their distrust, disobedience, and disbelief in God's power and his protection put the promise on hold. God wanted to give them freedom and give them the land, but everyone reacted in fear—all except two, and Joshua was one of those two. Joshua saw the giants living in the land, but he was sure that God would give the Israelites the power to defeat them (see Num. 14:6–9).

God's promises aren't always clear, but you can be sure of them. And God's biggest promise to you, God Girl, is to love you and to keep you as his own, no matter how much of a mess you've made out of your life—if only you will trust him. Just like Joshua, you can take hold of the promises that everyone else missed out on because they doubted. With the power of God on his side, Joshua led his people to overwhelm those who should have been too powerful for them to conquer. When you are afraid to do what God has commanded you to do, you have to know that he will give you the power to do it. Then you, just like the Israelites led by Joshua, will find the rest that is promised to those who trust and obey (see Josh. 21:44).

Must-Know Terms and Verses

∽ Jericho ∽

The great walled city that the Israelites conquered by walking around it as God ordered them to do. The only inhabitants of Jericho who survived the attack were Rahab and her family.

∽ Jerusalem ∽

The central city of Israel and capital of the southern kingdom of Judah. The name means "possession of peace."

∽ Promised Land ∽

The land that God promised to Abraham and his descendants (Gen. 15:18–21).

Now the priests bearing the ark of the covenant of the LORD stood firmly on dry ground in the midst of the Jordan, and all Israel was passing over on dry ground until all the nation finished passing over the Jordan. *Joshua 3:17*

And the LORD said to Joshua, "See, I have given Jericho into your hand, with its king and mighty men of valor." *Joshua 6:2*

For it was the LORD's doing to harden their hearts that they should come against Israel in battle, in order that they should be devoted to destruction and should receive no mercy but be destroyed, just as the LORD commanded Moses. *Joshua 11:20*

"How long will you put off going in to take possession of the land, which the LORD, the God of your fathers, has given you?" *Joshua 18:3*

"Only be very careful to observe the commandment and the law that Moses the servant of the LORD commanded you, to love the LORD your God, and to walk in all his ways and to keep his commandments and to cling to him and to serve him with all your heart and with all your soul." *Joshua 22:5*

Joshua

God Commissions Joshua

1 After the death of Moses the servant of the Lord, the Lord said to Joshua the son of Nun, Moses' assistant, ²"Moses my servant is dead. Now therefore arise, go over this Jordan, you and all this people, into the land that I am giving to them, to the people of Israel. ³Every place that the sole of your foot will tread upon I have given to you, just as I promised to Moses. ⁴From the wilderness and this Lebanon as far as the great river, the river Euphrates, all the land of the Hittites to the Great Sea toward the going down of the sun shall be your territory. ⁵No man shall be able to stand before you all the days of your life. Just as I was with Moses, so I will be with you. I will not leave you or forsake you. ⁶Be strong and courageous, for you shall cause this people to inherit the land that I swore to their fathers to give them. ⁷Only be strong and very courageous, being careful to do according to all the law that Moses my servant commanded you. Do not turn from it to the right hand or to the left, that you may have good success¹ wherever you go. ⁸This Book of the Law shall not depart from your mouth, but you shall meditate on it day and night, so that you may be careful to do according to all that is written in it. For then you will make your way prosperous, and then you will have good success. ⁹Have I not commanded you? Be strong and courageous. Do not be frightened, and do not be dismayed, for the Lord your God is with you wherever you go."

Joshua Assumes Command

¹⁰And Joshua commanded the officers of the people, ¹¹"Pass through the midst of the camp and command the people, 'Prepare your provisions, for within three days you are to pass over this Jordan to go in to take possession of the land that the Lord your God is giving you to possess.'"

¹²And to the Reubenites, the Gadites, and the half-tribe of Manasseh Joshua said, ¹³"Remember the word that Moses the servant of the Lord commanded you, saying, 'The Lord your God is providing you a place of rest and will give you this land.' ¹⁴Your wives, your little ones, and your livestock shall remain in the land that Moses gave you beyond the Jordan, but all the men of valor among you shall pass over armed before your brothers and shall help them, ¹⁵until the Lord gives rest to your brothers as he has to you, and they also take possession of the land that the Lord your God is giving them. Then you shall return to the land of your possession and shall possess it, the land that Moses the servant of the Lord gave you beyond the Jordan toward the sunrise."

¹⁶And they answered Joshua, "All that you have commanded us we will do, and wherever you send us we will go. ¹⁷Just as we obeyed Moses in all things, so we will obey you. Only may the Lord your God be with you, as he was with Moses! ¹⁸Whoever rebels against your commandment and disobeys your words, whatever you command him, shall be put to death. Only be strong and courageous."

Rahab Hides the Spies

2 And Joshua the son of Nun sent² two men secretly from Shittim as spies, saying, "Go, view the land, especially Jericho." And they went and came into the house of a prostitute whose name was Rahab and lodged there. ²And it was told to the king of Jericho, "Behold, men of Israel have come here tonight to search out the land." ³Then the king of Jericho sent to Rahab, saying, "Bring out the men who have come to you, who entered your house, for they have come to search out all the land." ⁴But the woman had taken the two men and hidden them. And she said, "True, the men

¹ Or may act wisely ² Or had sent

Rahab

Read this God Girl story in Joshua 2; 6:15–25;
Matthew 1:5; Hebrews 11:31; and James 2:25.

There is therefore now no condemnation for those who are in
Christ Jesus.

Romans 8:1

God uses imperfect people! Throughout history he has used people just like you to deliver his message, to go into battle, to give birth to prophets, and even to give birth to his own Son. He uses imperfect people because that is all there is in this world. Every human being on earth is imperfect, flawed, and good at sinning. So you can be sure that your sin does not disqualify you from serving any more than theirs did. It doesn't keep you from salvation, and it also doesn't keep you from changing the world. Just look at the family line of David, the line that would one day give us Jesus, and you'll see it was filled with broken and imperfect people. And Rahab was one of those. Though she was a prostitute and a Gentile, she still believed in the God of Israel, and because of that she was blessed to become the mother of Boaz and the great-grandmother of Jesse (see Matt. 1:5). Then many generations later from Jesse came Jesus. Such a noble position for a messed-up woman! But her sins weren't counted against her, when she decided to trust God instead of humans.

God has to use imperfect people if he wants to use people at all, because there are no perfect people, not now or ever, except Jesus himself. When your imperfection leads you to believe that God can't use you, remember all the people he's used before you. Though he can't stand sin, Jesus Christ has paid the penalty your sin deserves, so that as you trust in Christ, God looks on you as perfectly righteous and delights to use you, in all your weakness. As a God Girl, you need not fear punishment or condemnation for your sins. You can know that when you are willing and God is ready to use you, you can do great things for the kingdom.

came to me, but I did not know where they were from. [5]And when the gate was about to be closed at dark, the men went out. I do not know where the men went. Pursue them quickly, for you will overtake them." [6]But she had brought them up to the roof and hid them with the stalks of flax that she had laid in order on the roof. [7]So the men pursued after them on the way to the Jordan as far as the fords. And the gate was shut as soon as the pursuers had gone out.

[8]Before the men[1] lay down, she came up to them on the roof [9]and said to the men, "I know that the LORD has given you the land, and that the fear of you has fallen upon us, and that all the inhabitants of the land melt away before you. [10]For we have heard how the LORD dried up the water of the Red Sea before you when you came out of Egypt, and what you did to the two kings of the Amorites who were beyond the Jordan, to Sihon and Og, whom you devoted to destruction.[2] [11]And as soon as we heard it, our hearts melted, and there was no spirit left in any man because of you, for the LORD your God, he is God in the heavens above and on the earth beneath. [12]Now then, please swear to me by the LORD that, as I have dealt kindly with you, you also will deal kindly with my father's house, and give me a sure sign [13]that you will save alive my father and mother, my brothers and sisters, and all who belong to them, and deliver our lives from death." [14]And the men said to her, "Our life for yours even to death! If you do not tell this business of ours, then when the LORD gives us the land we will deal kindly and faithfully with you."

[15]Then she let them down by a rope through the window, for her house was built into the city wall, so that she lived in the wall. [16]And she said[3] to them, "Go into the hills, or the pursuers will encounter you, and hide there three days until the pursuers have returned. Then afterward you may go your way." [17]The men said to her, "We will be guiltless with respect to this oath of yours that you have made us swear. [18]Behold, when we come into the land, you shall tie this scarlet cord in the window through which you let us down, and you shall gather into your house your father and mother, your brothers, and all

your father's household. [19]Then if anyone goes out of the doors of your house into the street, his blood shall be on his own head, and we shall be guiltless. But if a hand is laid on anyone who is with you in the house, his blood shall be on our head. [20]But if you tell this business of ours, then we shall be guiltless with respect to your oath that you have made us swear." [21]And she said, "According to your words, so be it." Then she sent them away, and they departed. And she tied the scarlet cord in the window.

[22]They departed and went into the hills and remained there three days until the pursuers returned, and the pursuers searched all along the way and found nothing. [23]Then the two men returned. They came down from the hills and passed over and came to Joshua the son of Nun, and they told him all that had happened to them. [24]And they said to Joshua, "Truly the LORD has given all the land into our hands. And also, all the inhabitants of the land melt away because of us."

Israel Crosses the Jordan

3 Then Joshua rose early in the morning and they set out from Shittim. And they came to the Jordan, he and all the people of Israel, and lodged there before they passed over. [2]At the end of three days the officers went through the camp [3]and commanded the people, "As soon as you see the ark of the covenant of the LORD your God being carried by the Levitical priests, then you shall set out from your place and follow it. [4]Yet there shall be a distance between you and it, about 2,000 cubits[4] in length. Do not come near it, in order that you may know the way you shall go, for you have not passed this way before." [5]Then Joshua said to the people, "Consecrate yourselves, for tomorrow the LORD will do wonders among you." [6]And Joshua said to the priests, "Take up the ark of the covenant and pass on before the people." So they took up the ark of the covenant and went before the people.

[7]The LORD said to Joshua, "Today I will begin to exalt you in the sight of all Israel, that they may know that, as I was with Moses, so I will be with you. [8]And as for you, command the priests who bear the

---

[1] Hebrew *they* [2] That is, set apart (devoted) as an offering to the Lord (for destruction) [3] Or *had said* [4] A *cubit* was about 18 inches or 45 centimeters

ark of the covenant, 'When you come to the brink of the waters of the Jordan, you shall stand still in the Jordan.'" [9] And Joshua said to the people of Israel, "Come here and listen to the words of the Lord your God." [10] And Joshua said, "Here is how you shall know that the living God is among you and that he will without fail drive out from before you the Canaanites, the Hittites, the Hivites, the Perizzites, the Girgashites, the Amorites, and the Jebusites. [11] Behold, the ark of the covenant of the Lord of all the earth[1] is passing over before you into the Jordan. [12] Now therefore take twelve men from the tribes of Israel, from each tribe a man. [13] And when the soles of the feet of the priests bearing the ark of the Lord, the Lord of all the earth, shall rest in the waters of the Jordan, the waters of the Jordan shall be cut off from flowing, and the waters coming down from above shall stand in one heap."

[14] So when the people set out from their tents to pass over the Jordan with the priests bearing the ark of the covenant before the people, [15] and as soon as those bearing the ark had come as far as the Jordan, and the feet of the priests bearing the ark were dipped in the brink of the water (now the Jordan overflows all its banks throughout the time of harvest), [16] the waters coming down from above stood and rose up in a heap very far away, at Adam, the city that is beside Zarethan, and those flowing down toward the Sea of the Arabah, the Salt Sea, were completely cut off. And the people passed over opposite Jericho. [17] Now the priests bearing the ark of the covenant of the Lord stood firmly on dry ground in the midst of the Jordan, and all Israel was passing over on dry ground until all the nation finished passing over the Jordan.

Twelve Memorial Stones from the Jordan

4 When all the nation had finished passing over the Jordan, the Lord said to Joshua, [2] "Take twelve men from the people, from each tribe a man, [3] and command them, saying, 'Take twelve stones from here out of the midst of the Jordan, from the very place where the priests' feet stood firmly, and bring them over with you and lay them down in the place where you lodge tonight.'" [4] Then Joshua called

the twelve men from the people of Israel, whom he had appointed, a man from each tribe. [5] And Joshua said to them, "Pass on before the ark of the Lord your God into the midst of the Jordan, and take up each of you a stone upon his shoulder, according to the number of the tribes of the people of Israel, [6] that this may be a sign among you. When your children ask in time to come, 'What do those stones mean to you?' [7] then you shall tell them that the waters of the Jordan were cut off before the ark of the covenant of the Lord. When it passed over the Jordan, the waters of the Jordan were cut off. So these stones shall be to the people of Israel a memorial forever."

[8] And the people of Israel did just as Joshua commanded and took up twelve stones out of the midst of the Jordan, according to the number of the tribes of the people of Israel, just as the Lord told Joshua. And they carried them over with them to the place where they lodged and laid them down[2] there. [9] And Joshua set up twelve stones in the midst of the Jordan, in the place where the feet of the priests bearing the ark of the covenant had stood; and they are there to this day. [10] For the priests bearing the ark stood in the midst of the Jordan until everything was finished that the Lord commanded Joshua to tell the people, according to all that Moses had commanded Joshua.

The people passed over in haste. [11] And when all the people had finished passing over, the ark of the Lord and the priests passed over before the people. [12] The sons of Reuben and the sons of Gad and the half-tribe of Manasseh passed over armed before the people of Israel, as Moses had told them. [13] About 40,000 ready for war passed over before the Lord for battle, to the plains of Jericho. [14] On that day the Lord exalted Joshua in the sight of all Israel, and they stood in awe of him just as they had stood in awe of Moses, all the days of his life.

[15] And the Lord said to Joshua, [16] "Command the priests bearing the ark of the testimony to come up out of the Jordan." [17] So Joshua commanded the priests, "Come up out of the Jordan." [18] And when the priests bearing the ark of the covenant of the Lord came up from the midst of the Jordan, and the soles of the priests' feet were lifted up

---

[1] Hebrew *the ark of the covenant, the Lord of all the earth* [2] Or *to rest* [3] Or *Joshua had set up*

on dry ground, the waters of the Jordan returned to their place and overflowed all its banks, as before.

¹⁹The people came up out of the Jordan on the tenth day of the first month, and they encamped at Gilgal on the east border of Jericho. ²⁰And those twelve stones, which they took out of the Jordan, Joshua set up at Gilgal. ²¹And he said to the people of Israel, "When your children ask their fathers in times to come, 'What do these stones mean?' ²²then you shall let your children know, 'Israel passed over this Jordan on dry ground.' ²³For the LORD your God dried up the waters of the Jordan for you until you passed over, as the LORD your God did to the Red Sea, which he dried up for us until we passed over, ²⁴so that all the peoples of the earth may know that the hand of the LORD is mighty, that you may fear the LORD your God forever."[1]

The New Generation Circumcised

5 As soon as all the kings of the Amorites who were beyond the Jordan to the west, and all the kings of the Canaanites who were by the sea, heard that the LORD had dried up the waters of the Jordan for the people of Israel until they had crossed over, their hearts melted and there was no longer any spirit in them because of the people of Israel.

²At that time the LORD said to Joshua, "Make flint knives and circumcise the sons of Israel a second time." ³So Joshua made flint knives and circumcised the sons of Israel at Gibeath-haaraloth.[2] ⁴And this is the reason why Joshua circumcised them: all the males of the people who came out of Egypt, all the men of war, had died in the wilderness on the way after they had come out of Egypt. ⁵Though all the people who came out had been circumcised, yet all the people who were born on the way in the wilderness after they had come out of Egypt had not been circumcised. ⁶For the people of Israel walked forty years in the wilderness, until all the nation, the men of war who came out of Egypt, perished, because they did not obey the voice of the LORD; the LORD swore to them that he would not let them see the land that the LORD had sworn to their fathers to give to us, a land flowing with milk and honey. ⁷So it was their children, whom he raised

up in their place, that Joshua circumcised. For they were uncircumcised, because they had not been circumcised on the way.

⁸When the circumcising of the whole nation was finished, they remained in their places in the camp until they were healed. ⁹And the LORD said to Joshua, "Today I have rolled away the reproach of Egypt from you." And so the name of that place is called Gilgal[3] to this day.

First Passover in Canaan

¹⁰While the people of Israel were encamped at Gilgal, they kept the Passover on the fourteenth day of the month in the evening on the plains of Jericho. ¹¹And the day after the Passover, on that very day, they ate of the produce of the land, unleavened cakes and parched grain. ¹²And the manna ceased the day after they ate of the produce of the land. And there was no longer manna for the people of Israel, but they ate of the fruit of the land of Canaan that year.

The Commander of the LORD's Army

¹³When Joshua was by Jericho, he lifted up his eyes and looked, and behold, a man was standing before him with his drawn sword in his hand. And Joshua went to him and said to him, "Are you for us, or for our adversaries?" ¹⁴And he said, "No; but I am the commander of the army of the LORD. Now I have come." And Joshua fell on his face to the earth and worshiped and said to him, "What does my lord say to his servant?" ¹⁵And the commander of the LORD's army said to Joshua, "Take off your sandals from your feet, for the place where you are standing is holy." And Joshua did so.

The Fall of Jericho

6 Now Jericho was shut up inside and outside because of the people of Israel. None went out, and none came in. ²And the LORD said to Joshua, "See, I have given Jericho into your hand, with its king and mighty men of valor. ³You shall march around the city, all the men of war going around the city once. Thus shall you do for six days. ⁴Seven priests shall bear seven trumpets of rams' horns before the ark. On the seventh day you shall march around the city seven times, and the priests shall blow the trumpets. ⁵And when they make a long blast with the ram's horn, when you

---

[1] Or all the days   [2] Gibeath-haaraloth means the hill of the foreskins   [3] Gilgal sounds like the Hebrew for to roll

hear the sound of the trumpet, then all the people shall shout with a great shout, and the wall of the city will fall down flat,[1] and the people shall go up, everyone straight before him." [6] So Joshua the son of Nun called the priests and said to them, "Take up the ark of the covenant and let seven priests bear seven trumpets of rams' horns before the ark of the LORD." [7] And he said to the people, "Go forward. March around the city and let the armed men pass on before the ark of the LORD."

[8] And just as Joshua had commanded the people, the seven priests bearing the seven trumpets of rams' horns before the LORD went forward, blowing the trumpets, with the ark of the covenant of the LORD following them. [9] The armed men were walking before the priests who were blowing the trumpets, and the rear guard was walking after the ark, while the trumpets blew continually. [10] But Joshua commanded the people, "You shall not shout or make your voice heard, neither shall any word go out of your mouth, until the day I tell you to shout. Then you shall shout." [11] So he caused the ark of the LORD to circle the city,

going about it once. And they came into the camp and spent the night in the camp

[12] Then Joshua rose early in the morning and the priests took up the ark of the LORD [13] And the seven priests bearing the seven trumpets of rams' horns before the ark of the LORD walked on, and they blew the trumpets continually. And the armed men were walking before them, and the rear guard was walking after the ark of the LORD, while the trumpets blew continually. [14] And the second day they marched around the city once, and returned into the camp. So they did for six days.

[15] On the seventh day they rose early at the dawn of day, and marched around the city in the same manner seven times. It was only on that day that they marched around the city seven times. [16] And at the seventh time, when the priests had blown the trumpets, Joshua said to the people "Shout, for the LORD has given you the city [17] And the city and all that is within it shall be devoted to the LORD for destruction. Only Rahab the prostitute and all who are with her in her house shall live, because she hid the messengers whom we sent [18] But you, keep yourselves from the thing

[1] Hebrew *under itself*; also verse 20　[2] That is, set apart (devoted) as an offering to the Lord (for destruction); also verses 18, 21

Know God

verses to read
Joshua 6:1–21

Are you facing a battle that you have to fight? Do you have a big trial in front of you that you aren't sure how you're going to overcome? Then take a look at God's Word for help. Look at the life of the people of Israel. In almost every challenge they faced, all Israel did was move forward in faith, looking to God for the victory, and God himself did all the fighting. When you count on God against all odds and take that step of faith, God will do what he does so well: win the battle for you!

This doesn't mean that, when you see something that has to be done, you can sit on your couch waiting for God to do his thing. You are called to participate, like the Israelites walking around Jericho. You have to move and trust that, when you get moving, God does miracles. Why would God repeatedly ask the Israelites to step out in faith and do things that ultimately he himself would do for them? It was a test of their faith. Moving, acting, doing what God calls the God Girl to do proves that you trust and believe in him. You have to know that God does the work through you, but he works through you when *you* start to work. So even if the job ahead of you seems ridiculous or scary, get up and get going so that you can see the hand of God at work in your life.

evoted to destruction, lest when you have devoted them you take any of the devoted things and make the camp of Israel a thing for destruction and bring trouble upon it. [19]But all silver and gold, and every vessel of bronze and iron, are holy to the LORD; they shall go into the treasury of the LORD." [20]So the people shouted, and the trumpets were blown. As soon as the people heard the sound of the trumpet, the people shouted a great shout, and the wall fell down flat, so that the people went up into the city, every man straight before him, and they captured the city. [21]Then they devoted all in the city to destruction, both men and women, young and old, oxen, sheep, and donkeys, with the edge of the sword.

[22]But to the two men who had spied out the land, Joshua said, "Go into the prostitute's house and bring out from there the woman and all who belong to her, as you swore to her." [23]So the young men who had been spies went in and brought out Rahab and her father and mother and brothers and all who belonged to her. And they brought all her relatives and put them outside the camp of Israel. [24]And they burned the city with fire, and everything in it. Only the silver and gold, and the vessels of bronze and of iron, they put into the treasury of the house of the LORD. [25]But Rahab the prostitute and her father's household and all who belonged to her, Joshua saved alive. And she has lived in Israel to this day, because she hid the messengers whom Joshua sent to spy out Jericho.

[26]Joshua laid an oath on them at that time, saying, "Cursed before the LORD be the man who rises up and rebuilds this city, Jericho.

"At the cost of his firstborn shall he
     lay its foundation,
  and at the cost of his youngest son
     shall he set up its gates."

[27]So the LORD was with Joshua, and his fame was in all the land.

Israel Defeated at Ai

7 But the people of Israel broke faith in regard to the devoted things, for Achan the son of Carmi, son of Zabdi, son of Zerah, of the tribe of Judah, took some of the devoted things. And the anger of the LORD burned against the people of Israel.

[2]Joshua sent men from Jericho to Ai, which is near Beth-aven, east of Bethel, and said to them, "Go up and spy out the land." And the men went up and spied out Ai. [3]And they returned to Joshua and said to him, "Do not have all the people go up, but let about two or three thousand men go up and attack Ai. Do not make the whole people toil up there, for they are few." [4]So about three thousand men went up there from the people. And they fled before the men of Ai, [5]and the men of Ai killed about thirty-six of their men and chased them before the gate as far as Shebarim and struck them at the descent. And the hearts of the people melted and became as water.

[6]Then Joshua tore his clothes and fell to the earth on his face before the ark of the LORD until the evening, he and the elders of Israel. And they put dust on their heads. [7]And Joshua said, "Alas, O Lord GOD, why have you brought this people over the Jordan at all, to give us into the hands of the Amorites, to destroy us? Would that we had been content to dwell beyond the Jordan! [8]O Lord, what can I say, when Israel has turned their backs before their enemies! [9]For the Canaanites and all the inhabitants of the land will hear of it and will surround us and cut off our name from the earth. And what will you do for your great name?"

The Sin of Achan

[10]The LORD said to Joshua, "Get up! Why have you fallen on your face? [11]Israel has sinned; they have transgressed my covenant that I commanded them; they have taken some of the devoted things; they have stolen and lied and put them among their own belongings. [12]Therefore the people of Israel cannot stand before their enemies. They turn their backs before their enemies, because they have become devoted for destruction.[1] I will be with you no more, unless you destroy the devoted things from among you. [13]Get up! Consecrate the people and say, 'Consecrate yourselves for tomorrow; for thus says the LORD, God of Israel, "There are devoted things in your midst, O Israel. You cannot stand before your enemies until you take away the devoted things from among you." [14]In the morning therefore you shall be brought near by your tribes. And the tribe

That is, set apart (devoted) as an offering to the Lord (for destruction)

that the LORD takes by lot shall come near by clans. And the clan that the LORD takes shall come near by households. And the household that the LORD takes shall come near man by man. ¹⁵And he who is taken with the devoted things shall be burned with fire, he and all that he has, because he has transgressed the covenant of the LORD, and because he has done an outrageous thing in Israel.' "

¹⁶So Joshua rose early in the morning and brought Israel near tribe by tribe, and the tribe of Judah was taken. ¹⁷And he brought near the clans of Judah, and the clan of the Zerahites was taken. And he brought near the clan of the Zerahites man by man, and Zabdi was taken. ¹⁸And he brought near his household man by man, and Achan the son of Carmi, son of Zabdi, son of Zerah, of the tribe of Judah, was taken. ¹⁹Then Joshua said to Achan, "My son, give glory to the LORD God of Israel and give praise[1] to him. And tell me now what you have done; do not hide it from me." ²⁰And Achan answered Joshua, "Truly I have sinned against the LORD God of Israel, and this is what I did: ²¹when I saw among the spoil a beautiful cloak from Shinar, and 200 shekels of silver, and a bar of gold weighing 50 shekels,[2] then I coveted them and took them. And see, they are hidden in the earth inside my tent, with the silver underneath."

²²So Joshua sent messengers, and they ran to the tent; and behold, it was hidden in his tent with the silver underneath. ²³And they took them out of the tent and brought them to Joshua and to all the people of Israel. And they laid them down before the LORD. ²⁴And Joshua and all Israel with him took Achan the son of Zerah, and the silver and the cloak and the bar of gold, and his sons and daughters and his oxen and donkeys and sheep and his tent and all that he had. And they brought them up to the Valley of Achor. ²⁵And Joshua said, "Why did you bring trouble on us? The LORD brings trouble on you today." And all Israel stoned him with stones. They burned them with fire and stoned them with stones. ²⁶And they raised over him a great heap of stones that remains to this day. Then the LORD turned from his burning anger. Therefore, to this day the name of that place is called the Valley of Achor.[3]

The Fall of Ai

8 And the LORD said to Joshua, "Do no fear and do not be dismayed. Take all the fighting men with you, and arise, go up to Ai. See, I have given into your hand the king of Ai, and his people, his city, and his land. ²And you shall do to Ai and its king as you did to Jericho and its king. Only its spoil and its livestock you shall take as plunder for yourselves. Lay an ambush against the city, behind it."

³So Joshua and all the fighting men arose to go up to Ai. And Joshua chose 30,000 mighty men of valor and sent them out by night. ⁴And he commanded them, "Behold, you shall lie in ambush against the city behind it. Do not go very far from the city, but all of you remain ready. ⁵And I and all the people who are with me will approach the city. And when they come out against us just as before, we shall flee before them. ⁶And they will come out after us, until we have drawn them away from the city. For they will say, 'They are fleeing from us just as before.' So we will flee before them. ⁷Then you shall rise up from the ambush and seize the city, for the LORD your God will give it into your hand. ⁸And as soon as you have taken the city, you shall set the city on fire. You shall do according to the word of the LORD. See, I have commanded you." ⁹So Joshua sent them out. And they went to the place of ambush and lay between Bethel and Ai, to the west of Ai, but Joshua spent that night among the people.

¹⁰Joshua arose early in the morning and mustered the people and went up, he and the elders of Israel, before the people to Ai. ¹¹And all the fighting men who were with him went up and drew near before the city and encamped on the north side of Ai, with a ravine between them and Ai. ¹²He took about 5,000 men and set them in ambush between Bethel and Ai, to the west of the city. ¹³So they stationed the forces, the main encampment that was north of the city and its rear guard west of the city. But Joshua spent that night in the valley. ¹⁴And as soon as the king of Ai saw this, he and all his people, the men of the city, hurried and went out early to the appointed place[4] toward the Arabah to meet Israel in battle. But he did not know that there was an ambush against him behind the

---

[1] Or *and make confession* [2] A *shekel* was about 2/5 ounce or 11 grams [3] *Achor* means *trouble* [4] Hebrew *appointed time*

city. [15] And Joshua and all Israel pretended to be beaten before them and fled in the direction of the wilderness. [16] So all the people who were in the city were called together to pursue them, and as they pursued Joshua they were drawn away from the city. [17] Not a man was left in Ai or Bethel who did not go out after Israel. They left the city open and pursued Israel.

[18] Then the LORD said to Joshua, "Stretch out the javelin that is in your hand toward Ai, for I will give it into your hand." And Joshua stretched out the javelin that was in his hand toward the city. [19] And the men in the ambush rose quickly out of their place, and as soon as he had stretched out his hand, they ran and entered the city and captured it. And they hurried to set the city on fire. [20] So when the men of Ai looked back, behold, the smoke of the city went up to heaven, and they had no power to flee this way or that, for the people who fled to the wilderness turned back against the pursuers. [21] And when Joshua and all Israel saw that the ambush had captured the city, and that the smoke of the city went up, then they turned back and struck down the men of Ai. [22] And the others came out from the city against them, so they were in the midst of Israel, some on this side, and some on that side. And Israel struck them down, until there was left none that survived or escaped. [23] But the king of Ai they took alive, and brought him near to Joshua.

[24] When Israel had finished killing all the inhabitants of Ai in the open wilderness where they pursued them, and all of them to the very last had fallen by the edge of the sword, all Israel returned to Ai and struck it down with the edge of the sword. [25] And all who fell that day, both men and women, were 12,000, all the people of Ai. [26] But Joshua did not draw back his hand with which he stretched out the javelin until he had devoted all the inhabitants of Ai to destruction.[1] [27] Only the livestock and the

[1] That is, set apart (devoted) as an offering to the Lord (for destruction)

Know Yourself

verses to read
Joshua 8:1-8

If God promised to help you do something that sounded impossible in the same way that he promised to help the Israelites capture Jericho and Ai, would you step out in trust and do what he said, or would you doubt his ability to deliver on his promise? Doing the things that God asks can seem totally impossible. "Walk around the city, and the walls are gonna crumble"? "Just walk onto the land, and I will take it from them and give it to you"? The Israelites must have had a hard time believing that everything God told them to do could actually be done, but history proves that he came through. Never once did God fail to fulfill his promise or work things out for the people who trusted him.

God would never call you to do something that couldn't be done. Knowing that, you can be sure that he's going to help you do whatever he asks, so you will have success. So if there is something in your life that seems impossible or something you know you should do but you just can't seem to do, know that you're not alone. God promises to help you. You just need to call on him and trust him to answer. Then move out in trust. Take the first step, walk, enter the door—don't wait but get moving. Your life can change for the better today. You can walk away from whatever is plaguing you or bringing you down. Freedom can be yours, but you've got to get moving. Walk out the door; it's unlocked. Take off the shackles; he's released you. Today, take back your life by giving it over to God. And remember, you can do everything through Christ who strengthens you (see Phil. 4:13).

spoil of that city Israel took as their plunder, according to the word of the LORD that he commanded Joshua. [28]So Joshua burned Ai and made it forever a heap of ruins, as it is to this day. [29]And he hanged the king of Ai on a tree until evening. And at sunset Joshua commanded, and they took his body down from the tree and threw it at the entrance of the gate of the city and raised over it a great heap of stones, which stands there to this day.

Joshua Renews the Covenant

[30]At that time Joshua built an altar to the LORD, the God of Israel, on Mount Ebal, [31]just as Moses the servant of the LORD had commanded the people of Israel, as it is written in the Book of the Law of Moses, "an altar of uncut stones, upon which no man has wielded an iron tool." And they offered on it burnt offerings to the LORD and sacrificed peace offerings. [32]And there, in the presence of the people of Israel, he wrote on the stones a copy of the law of Moses, which he had written. [33]And all Israel, sojourner as well as native born, with their elders and officers and their judges, stood on opposite sides of the ark before the Levitical priests who carried the ark of the covenant of the LORD, half of them in front of Mount Gerizim and half of them in front of Mount Ebal, just as Moses the servant of the LORD had commanded at the first, to bless the people of Israel. [34]And afterward he read all the words of the law, the blessing and the curse, according to all that is written in the Book of the Law. [35]There was not a word of all that Moses commanded that Joshua did not read before all the assembly of Israel, and the women, and the little ones, and the sojourners who lived[1] among them.

The Gibeonite Deception

9 As soon as all the kings who were beyond the Jordan in the hill country and in the lowland all along the coast of the Great Sea toward Lebanon, the Hittites, the Amorites, the Canaanites, the Perizzites, the Hivites, and the Jebusites, heard of this, [2]they gathered together as one to fight against Joshua and Israel.

[3]But when the inhabitants of Gibeon heard what Joshua had done to Jericho and to Ai, [4]they on their part acted with cunning and went and made ready provisions and took worn-out sacks for their donkeys, and wineskins, worn-out and torn and mended, [5]with worn-out, patched sandals on their feet, and worn-out clothes. And all their provisions were dry and crumbly. [6]And they went to Joshua in the camp at Gilgal and said to him and to the men of Israel, "We have come from a distant country, so now make a covenant with us." [7]But the men of Israel said to the Hivites, "Perhaps you live among us; then how can we make a covenant with you?" [8]They said to Joshua, "We are your servants." And Joshua said to them, "Who are you? And where do you come from?" [9]They said to him, "From a very distant country your servants have come, because of the name of the LORD your God. For we have heard a report of him, and all that he did in Egypt, [10]and all that he did to the two kings of the Amorites who were beyond the Jordan, to Sihon the king of Heshbon, and to Og king of Bashan, who lived in Ashtaroth. [11]So our elders and all the inhabitants of our country said to us, 'Take provisions in your hand for the journey and go to meet them and say to them, "We are your servants. Come now, make a covenant with us."' [12]Here is our bread. It was still warm when we took it from our houses as our food for the journey on the day we set out to come to you, but now, behold, it is dry and crumbly. [13]These wineskins were new when we filled them, and behold, they have burst. And these garments and sandals of ours are worn out from the very long journey." [14]So the men took some of their provisions, but did not ask counsel from the LORD. [15]And Joshua made peace with them and made a covenant with them, to let them live, and the leaders of the congregation swore to them.

[16]At the end of three days after they had made a covenant with them, they heard that they were their neighbors and that they lived among them. [17]And the people of Israel set out and reached their cities on the third day. Now their cities were Gibeon, Chephirah, Beeroth, and Kiriath-jearim. [18]But the people of Israel did not attack them, because the leaders of the congregation had sworn to them by the LORD, the God of Israel. Then all the congregation

---

[1] Or *traveled*

murmured against the leaders. [19] But all the leaders said to all the congregation, "We have sworn to them by the LORD, the God of Israel, and now we may not touch them. [20] This we will do to them: let them live, lest wrath be upon us, because of the oath that we swore to them." [21] And the leaders said to them, "Let them live." So they became cutters of wood and drawers of water for all the congregation, just as the leaders had said of them.

[22] Joshua summoned them, and he said to them, "Why did you deceive us, saying, 'We are very far from you,' when you dwell among us? [23] Now therefore you are cursed, and some of you shall never be anything but servants, cutters of wood and drawers of water for the house of my God." [24] They answered Joshua, "Because it was told to your servants for a certainty that the LORD your God had commanded his servant Moses to give you all the land and to destroy all the inhabitants of the land from before you—so we feared greatly for our lives because of you and did this thing. [25] And now, behold, we are in your hand. Whatever seems good and right in your sight to do to us, do it." [26] So he did this to them and delivered them out of the hand of the people of Israel, and they did not kill them. [27] But Joshua made them that day cutters of wood and drawers of water for the congregation and for the altar of the LORD, to this day, in the place that he should choose.

The Sun Stands Still

10 As soon as Adoni-zedek, king of Jerusalem, heard how Joshua had captured Ai and had devoted it to destruction,[1] doing to Ai and its king as he had done to Jericho and its king, and how the inhabitants of Gibeon had made peace with Israel and were among them, [2] he[2] feared greatly, because Gibeon was a great city, like one of the royal cities, and because it was greater than Ai, and all its men were warriors. [3] So Adoni-zedek king of Jerusalem sent to Hoham king of Hebron, to Piram king of Jarmuth, to Japhia king of Lachish, and to Debir king of Eglon, saying, [4] "Come up to me and help me, and let us strike Gibeon. For it has made peace with Joshua and with the people of Israel."

[5] Then the five kings of the Amorites, the king of Jerusalem, the king of Hebron, the king of Jarmuth, the king of Lachish, and the king of Eglon, gathered their forces and went up with all their armies and encamped against Gibeon and made war against it.

[6] And the men of Gibeon sent to Joshua at the camp in Gilgal, saying, "Do not relax your hand from your servants. Come up to us quickly and save us and help us, for all the kings of the Amorites who dwell in the hill country are gathered against us." [7] So Joshua went up from Gilgal, he and all the people of war with him, and all the mighty men of valor. [8] And the LORD said to Joshua, "Do not fear them, for I have given them into your hands. Not a man of them shall stand before you." [9] So Joshua came upon them suddenly, having marched up all night from Gilgal. [10] And the LORD threw them into a panic before Israel, who[3] struck them with a great blow at Gibeon and chased them by the way of the ascent of Beth-horon and struck them as far as Azekah and Makkedah. [11] And as they fled before Israel, while they were going down the ascent of Beth-horon, the LORD threw down large stones from heaven on them as far as Azekah, and they died. There were more who died because of the hailstones than the sons of Israel killed with the sword.

[12] At that time Joshua spoke to the LORD in the day when the LORD gave the Amorites over to the sons of Israel, and he said in the sight of Israel,

"Sun, stand still at Gibeon,
    and moon, in the Valley of Aijalon."
[13]   And the sun stood still, and the moon
        stopped,
    until the nation took vengeance on
        their enemies.

Is this not written in the Book of Jashar? The sun stopped in the midst of heaven and did not hurry to set for about a whole day. [14] There has been no day like it before or since, when the LORD heeded the voice of a man, for the LORD fought for Israel.

[15] So Joshua returned, and all Israel with him, to the camp at Gilgal.

[1] That is, set apart (devoted) as an offering to the Lord (for destruction); also verses 28, 35, 37, 39, 40 [2] One Hebrew manuscript, Vulgate (compare Syriac); most Hebrew manuscripts *they* [3] Or *and he*

Five Amorite Kings Executed

¹⁶ These five kings fled and hid themselves in the cave at Makkedah. ¹⁷ And it was told to Joshua, "The five kings have been found, hidden in the cave at Makkedah." ¹⁸ And Joshua said, "Roll large stones against the mouth of the cave and set men by it to guard them, ¹⁹ but do not stay there yourselves. Pursue your enemies; attack their rear guard. Do not let them enter their cities, for the LORD your God has given them into your hand." ²⁰ When Joshua and the sons of Israel had finished striking them with a great blow until they were wiped out, and when the remnant that remained of them had entered into the fortified cities, ²¹ then all the people returned safe to Joshua in the camp at Makkedah. Not a man moved his tongue against any of the people of Israel.

²² Then Joshua said, "Open the mouth of the cave and bring those five kings out to me from the cave." ²³ And they did so, and brought those five kings out to him from the cave, the king of Jerusalem, the king of Hebron, the king of Jarmuth, the king of Lachish, and the king of Eglon. ²⁴ And when they brought those kings out to Joshua, Joshua summoned all the men of Israel and said to the chiefs of the men of war who had gone with him, "Come near; put your feet on the necks of these kings." Then they came near and put their feet on their necks. ²⁵ And Joshua said to them, "Do not be afraid or dismayed; be strong and courageous. For thus the LORD will do to all your enemies against whom you fight." ²⁶ And afterward Joshua struck them and put them to death, and he hanged them on five trees. And they hung on the trees until evening. ²⁷ But at the time of the going down of the sun, Joshua commanded, and they took them down from the trees and threw them into the cave where they had hidden themselves, and they set large stones against the mouth of the cave, which remain to this very day.

²⁸ As for Makkedah, Joshua captured it on that day and struck it, and its king, with the edge of the sword. He devoted to destruction every person in it; he left none remaining. And he did to the king of Makkedah just as he had done to the king of Jericho.

Conquest of Southern Canaan

²⁹ Then Joshua and all Israel with him passed on from Makkedah to Libnah and fought against Libnah. ³⁰ And the LORD gave it also and its king into the hand of Israel. And he struck it with the edge of the sword, and every person in it; he left none remaining in it. And he did to its king as he had done to the king of Jericho.

³¹ Then Joshua and all Israel with him passed on from Libnah to Lachish and laid siege to it and fought against it. ³² And the LORD gave Lachish into the hand of Israel, and he captured it on the second day and struck it with the edge of the sword, and every person in it, as he had done to Libnah.

³³ Then Horam king of Gezer came up to help Lachish. And Joshua struck him and his people, until he left none remaining.

³⁴ Then Joshua and all Israel with him passed on from Lachish to Eglon. And they laid siege to it and fought against it. ³⁵ And they captured it on that day, and struck it with the edge of the sword. And he devoted every person in it to destruction that day, as he had done to Lachish.

³⁶ Then Joshua and all Israel with him went up from Eglon to Hebron. And they fought against it ³⁷ and captured it and struck it with the edge of the sword, and its king and its towns, and every person in it. He left none remaining, as he had done to Eglon, and devoted it to destruction and every person in it.

³⁸ Then Joshua and all Israel with him turned back to Debir and fought against it ³⁹ and he captured it with its king and all its towns. And they struck them with the edge of the sword and devoted to destruction every person in it; he left none remaining. Just as he had done to Hebron and to Libnah and its king, so he did to Debir and to its king.

⁴⁰ So Joshua struck the whole land, the hill country and the Negeb and the lowland and the slopes, and all their kings. He left none remaining, but devoted to destruction all that breathed, just as the LORD God of Israel commanded. ⁴¹ And Joshua struck them from Kadesh-barnea as far as Gaza, and all the country of Goshen, as far as Gibeon. ⁴² And Joshua captured all these kings and their land at one time, because the LORD God of Israel fought for Israel. ⁴³ Then Joshua returned, and all Israel with him, to the camp at Gilgal.

Conquests in Northern Canaan

11 When Jabin, king of Hazor, heard of this, he sent to Jobab king of Madon, and to the king of Shimron, and to the king of Achshaph, ²and to the kings who were in the northern hill country, and in the Arabah south of Chinneroth, and in the lowland, and in Naphoth-dor on the west, ³to the Canaanites in the east and the west, the Amorites, the Hittites, the Perizzites, and the Jebusites in the hill country, and the Hivites under Hermon in the land of Mizpah. ⁴And they came out with all their troops, a great horde, in number like the sand that is on the seashore, with very many horses and chariots. ⁵And all these kings joined their forces and came and encamped together at the waters of Merom to fight against Israel.

⁶And the LORD said to Joshua, "Do not be afraid of them, for tomorrow at this time I will give over all of them, slain, to Israel. You shall hamstring their horses and burn their chariots with fire." ⁷So Joshua and all his warriors came suddenly against them by the waters of Merom and fell upon them. ⁸And the LORD gave them into the hand of Israel, who struck them and chased them as far as Great Sidon and Misrephoth-maim, and eastward as far as the Valley of Mizpeh. And they struck them until he left none remaining. ⁹And Joshua did to them just as the LORD said to him: he hamstrung their horses and burned their chariots with fire.

¹⁰And Joshua turned back at that time and captured Hazor and struck its king with the sword, for Hazor formerly was the head of all those kingdoms. ¹¹And they struck with the sword all who were in it, devoting them to destruction;¹ there was none left that breathed. And he burned Hazor with fire. ¹²And all the cities of those kings, and all their kings, Joshua captured, and struck them with the edge of the sword, devoting them to destruction, just as Moses the servant of the LORD had commanded. ¹³But none of the cities that stood on mounds did Israel burn, except Hazor alone; that Joshua burned. ¹⁴And all the spoil of these cities and the livestock, the people of Israel took for their plunder. But every person they struck with the edge of the sword until they had destroyed them,

and they did not leave any who breathed. ¹⁵Just as the LORD had commanded Moses his servant, so Moses commanded Joshua, and so Joshua did. He left nothing undone of all that the LORD had commanded Moses.

¹⁶So Joshua took all that land, the hill country and all the Negeb and all the land of Goshen and the lowland and the Arabah and the hill country of Israel and its lowland ¹⁷from Mount Halak, which rises toward Seir, as far as Baal-gad in the Valley of Lebanon below Mount Hermon. And he captured all their kings and struck them and put them to death. ¹⁸Joshua made war a long time with all those kings. ¹⁹There was not a city that made peace with the people of Israel except the Hivites, the inhabitants of Gibeon. They took them all in battle. ²⁰For it was the LORD's doing to harden their hearts that they should come against Israel in battle, in order that they should be devoted to destruction and should receive no mercy but be destroyed, just as the LORD commanded Moses.

²¹And Joshua came at that time and cut off the Anakim from the hill country, from Hebron, from Debir, from Anab, and from all the hill country of Judah, and from all the hill country of Israel. Joshua devoted them to destruction with their cities. ²²There was none of the Anakim left in the land of the people of Israel. Only in Gaza, in Gath, and in Ashdod did some remain. ²³So Joshua took the whole land, according to all that the LORD had spoken to Moses. And Joshua gave it for an inheritance to Israel according to their tribal allotments. And the land had rest from war.

Kings Defeated by Moses

12 Now these are the kings of the land whom the people of Israel defeated and took possession of their land beyond the Jordan toward the sunrise, from the Valley of the Arnon to Mount Hermon, with all the Arabah eastward: ²Sihon king of the Amorites who lived at Heshbon and ruled from Aroer, which is on the edge of the Valley of the Arnon, and from the middle of the valley as far as the river Jabbok, the boundary of the Ammonites, that is, half of Gilead, ³and the Arabah to the Sea of Chinneroth eastward, and in the direction of Beth-jeshimoth, to the Sea of the Arabah, the Salt Sea, southward

¹ That is, setting apart (devoting) as an offering to the Lord (for destruction); also verses 12, 20, 21

to the foot of the slopes of Pisgah; ⁴and Og[1] king of Bashan, one of the remnant of the Rephaim, who lived at Ashtaroth and at Edrei ⁵and ruled over Mount Hermon and Salecah and all Bashan to the boundary of the Geshurites and the Maacathites, and over half of Gilead to the boundary of Sihon king of Heshbon. ⁶Moses, the servant of the LORD, and the people of Israel defeated them. And Moses the servant of the LORD gave their land for a possession to the Reubenites and the Gadites and the half-tribe of Manasseh.

Kings Defeated by Joshua

⁷And these are the kings of the land whom Joshua and the people of Israel defeated on the west side of the Jordan, from Baal-gad in the Valley of Lebanon to Mount Halak, that rises toward Seir (and Joshua gave their land to the tribes of Israel as a possession according to their allotments, ⁸in the hill country, in the lowland, in the Arabah, in the slopes, in the wilderness, and in the Negeb, the land of the Hittites, the Amorites, the Canaanites, the Perizzites, the Hivites, and the Jebusites): ⁹the king of Jericho, one; the king of Ai, which is beside Bethel, one; ¹⁰the king of Jerusalem, one; the king of Hebron, one; ¹¹the king of Jarmuth, one; the king of Lachish, one; ¹²the king of Eglon, one; the king of Gezer, one; ¹³the king of Debir, one; the king of Geder, one; ¹⁴the king of Hormah, one; the king of Arad, one; ¹⁵the king of Libnah, one; the king of Adullam, one; ¹⁶the king of Makkedah, one; the king of Bethel, one; ¹⁷the king of Tappuah, one; the king of Hepher, one; ¹⁸the king of Aphek, one; the king of Lasharon, one; ¹⁹the king of Madon, one; the king of Hazor, one; ²⁰the king of Shimron-meron, one; the king of Achshaph, one; ²¹the king of Taanach, one; the king of Megiddo, one; ²²the king of Kedesh, one; the king of Jokneam in Carmel, one; ²³the king of Dor in Naphath-dor, one; the king of Goiim in Galilee,[2] one; ²⁴the king of Tirzah, one: in all, thirty-one kings.

[1] Septuagint; Hebrew *the boundary of Og* [2] Septuagint; Hebrew *Gilgal*

Know God

verses to read
Joshua 11:16–20

When your enemies are relentless and just won't back down, don't be so quick to freak out. Obviously it's no fun to be attacked and made fun of. It's no pleasure cruise to have enemies, but when you've looked for peace, when you've loved them and nothing has changed, when you've humbled yourself and done things God's way rather than your way and they still are after you, you might want to consider whether their aggression might be part of God's plan. God doesn't want to hurt you, but he does want to teach you.

We always have something to learn in the trials of life, and this situation is no exception. What will you take from this relentless enemy of yours? How are you going to grow in faith instead of in anger and bitterness? Find out what reaction to your trials pleases God instead of trying to please your human nature. When you believe that God lets mean people into your life for a reason, you take away their power to hurt you and instead allow God to shape you. So don't be afraid of your enemy, but trust God to show you the path of righteousness in how you react to them.

In this life you're going to have enemies. You're going to run into people who hate you and people whose goal it is to punish you for whatever bothers them. But take heart: God is still God, and no one, not even a mean person, can take away his power in your life.

Land Still to Be Conquered

13 Now Joshua was old and advanced in years, and the LORD said to him, "You are old and advanced in years, and there remains yet very much land to possess. ²This is the land that yet remains: all the regions of the Philistines, and all those of the Geshurites ³(from the Shihor, which is east of Egypt, northward to the boundary of Ekron, it is counted as Canaanite; there are five rulers of the Philistines, those of Gaza, Ashdod, Ashkelon, Gath, and Ekron), and those of the Avvim, ⁴in the south, all the land of the Canaanites, and Mearah that belongs to the Sidonians, to Aphek, to the boundary of the Amorites, ⁵and the land of the Gebalites, and all Lebanon, toward the sunrise, from Baal-gad below Mount Hermon to Lebo-hamath, ⁶all the inhabitants of the hill country from Lebanon to Misrephoth-maim, even all the Sidonians. I myself will drive them out from before the people of Israel. Only allot the land to Israel for an inheritance, as I have commanded you. ⁷Now therefore divide this land for an inheritance to the nine tribes and half the tribe of Manasseh."

The Inheritance East of the Jordan

⁸With the other half of the tribe of Manasseh[1] the Reubenites and the Gadites received their inheritance, which Moses gave them, beyond the Jordan eastward, as Moses the servant of the LORD gave them: ⁹from Aroer, which is on the edge of the Valley of the Arnon, and the city that is in the middle of the valley, and all the tableland of Medeba as far as Dibon; ¹⁰and all the cities of Sihon king of the Amorites, who reigned in Heshbon, as far as the boundary of the Ammonites; ¹¹and Gilead, and the region of the Geshurites and Maacathites, and all Mount Hermon, and all Bashan to Salecah; ¹²all the kingdom of Og in Bashan, who reigned in Ashtaroth and in Edrei (he alone was left of the remnant of the Rephaim); these Moses had struck and driven out. ¹³Yet the people of Israel did not drive out the Geshurites or the Maacathites, but Geshur and Maacath dwell in the midst of Israel to this day.

¹⁴To the tribe of Levi alone Moses gave no inheritance. The offerings by fire to the LORD God of Israel are their inheritance, as he said to him.

¹⁵And Moses gave an inheritance to the tribe of the people of Reuben according to their clans. ¹⁶So their territory was from Aroer, which is on the edge of the Valley of the Arnon, and the city that is in the middle of the valley, and all the tableland by Medeba; ¹⁷with Heshbon, and all its cities that are in the tableland; Dibon, and Bamoth-baal, and Beth-baal-meon, ¹⁸and Jahaz, and Kedemoth, and Mephaath, ¹⁹and Kiriathaim, and Sibmah, and Zereth-shahar on the hill of the valley, ²⁰and Beth-peor, and the slopes of Pisgah, and Beth-jeshimoth, ²¹that is, all the cities of the tableland, and all the kingdom of Sihon king of the Amorites, who reigned in Heshbon, whom Moses defeated with the leaders of Midian, Evi and Rekem and Zur and Hur and Reba, the princes of Sihon, who lived in the land. ²²Balaam also, the son of Beor, the one who practiced divination, was killed with the sword by the people of Israel among the rest of their slain. ²³And the border of the people of Reuben was the Jordan as a boundary. This was the inheritance of the people of Reuben, according to their clans with their cities and villages.

²⁴Moses gave an inheritance also to the tribe of Gad, to the people of Gad, according to their clans. ²⁵Their territory was Jazer, and all the cities of Gilead, and half the land of the Ammonites, to Aroer, which is east of Rabbah, ²⁶and from Heshbon to Ramath-mizpeh and Betonim, and from Mahanaim to the territory of Debir;[2] ²⁷and in the valley Beth-haram, Beth-nimrah, Succoth, and Zaphon, the rest of the kingdom of Sihon king of Heshbon, having the Jordan as a boundary, to the lower end of the Sea of Chinnereth, eastward beyond the Jordan. ²⁸This is the inheritance of the people of Gad according to their clans, with their cities and villages.

²⁹And Moses gave an inheritance to the half-tribe of Manasseh. It was allotted to the half-tribe of the people of Manasseh according to their clans. ³⁰Their region extended from Mahanaim, through all Bashan, the whole kingdom of Og king of Bashan, and all the towns of Jair, which are in Bashan, sixty cities, ³¹and half Gilead, and Ashtaroth, and Edrei, the cities of the kingdom of Og in Bashan. These were allotted to the people of Machir the son

of Manasseh for the half of the people of Machir according to their clans.

32 These are the inheritances that Moses distributed in the plains of Moab, beyond the Jordan east of Jericho. 33 But to the tribe of Levi Moses gave no inheritance; the LORD God of Israel is their inheritance, just as he said to them.

The Inheritance West of the Jordan

14 These are the inheritances that the people of Israel received in the land of Canaan, which Eleazar the priest and Joshua the son of Nun and the heads of the fathers' houses of the tribes of the people of Israel gave them to inherit. 2 Their inheritance was by lot, just as the LORD had commanded by the hand of Moses for the nine and one-half tribes. 3 For Moses had given an inheritance to the two and one-half tribes beyond the Jordan, but to the Levites he gave no inheritance among them. 4 For the people of Joseph were two tribes, Manasseh and Ephraim. And no portion was given to the Levites in the land, but only cities to dwell in, with their pasturelands for their livestock and their substance. 5 The people of Israel did as the LORD commanded Moses; they allotted the land.

Caleb's Request and Inheritance

6 Then the people of Judah came to Joshua at Gilgal. And Caleb the son of Jephunneh the Kenizzite said to him, "You know what the LORD said to Moses the man of God in Kadesh-barnea concerning you and me. 7 I was forty years old when Moses the servant of the LORD sent me from Kadesh-barnea to spy out the land, and I brought him word again as it was in my heart. 8 But my brothers who went up with me made the heart of the people melt; yet I wholly followed the LORD my God. 9 And Moses swore on that day, saying, 'Surely the land on which your foot has trodden shall be an inheritance for you and your children forever, because you have wholly followed the LORD my God.' 10 And now, behold, the LORD has kept me alive, just as he said, these forty-five years since the time that the LORD spoke this word to Moses, while Israel walked in the wilderness. And now, behold, I am this day eighty-five years old. 11 I am still as strong today as I was in the day that Moses sent me; my strength now is as my strength was then, for war and for going and coming. 12 So now give me this hill country of which the LORD spoke on that day, for you heard on that day how the Anakim were there, with great fortified cities. It may be that the LORD will be with me, and I shall drive them out just as the LORD said."

13 Then Joshua blessed him, and he gave Hebron to Caleb the son of Jephunneh for an inheritance. 14 Therefore Hebron became the inheritance of Caleb the son of Jephunneh the Kenizzite to this day, because he wholly followed the LORD, the God of Israel. 15 Now the name of Hebron formerly was Kiriath-arba.[1] (Arba[2] was the greatest man among the Anakim.) And the land had rest from war.

The Allotment for Judah

15 The allotment for the tribe of the people of Judah according to their clans reached southward to the boundary of Edom, to the wilderness of Zin at the farthest south. 2 And their south boundary ran from the end of the Salt Sea, from the bay that faces southward. 3 It goes out southward of the ascent of Akrabbim, passes along to Zin, and goes up south of Kadesh-barnea, along by Hezron, up to Addar, turns about to Karka, 4 passes along to Azmon, goes out by the Brook of Egypt, and comes to its end at the sea. This shall be your south boundary. 5 And the east boundary is the Salt Sea, to the mouth of the Jordan. And the boundary on the north side runs from the bay of the sea at the mouth of the Jordan. 6 And the boundary goes up to Beth-hoglah and passes along north of Beth-arabah. And the boundary goes up to the stone of Bohan the son of Reuben. 7 And the boundary goes up to Debir from the Valley of Achor, and so northward, turning toward Gilgal, which is opposite the ascent of Adummim, which is on the south side of the valley. And the boundary passes along to the waters of En-shemesh and ends at En-rogel. 8 Then the boundary goes up by the Valley of the Son of Hinnom at the southern shoulder of the Jebusite (that is, Jerusalem). And the boundary goes up to the top of the mountain that lies over against the Valley of Hinnom, on the west, at the northern end of the

---

[1] Kiriath-arba means the city of Arba [2] Hebrew He

Valley of Rephaim. ⁹Then the boundary extends from the top of the mountain to the spring of the waters of Nephtoah, and from there to the cities of Mount Ephron. Then the boundary bends around to Baalah (that is, Kiriath-jearim). ¹⁰And the boundary circles west of Baalah to Mount Seir, passes along to the northern shoulder of Mount Jearim (that is, Chesalon), and goes down to Beth-shemesh and passes along by Timnah. ¹¹The boundary goes out to the shoulder of the hill north of Ekron, then the boundary bends around to Shikkeron and passes along to Mount Baalah and goes out to Jabneel. Then the boundary comes to an end at the sea. ¹²And the west boundary was the Great Sea with its coastline. This is the boundary around the people of Judah according to their clans.

¹³According to the commandment of the LORD to Joshua, he gave to Caleb the son of Jephunneh a portion among the people of Judah, Kiriath-arba, that is, Hebron (Arba was the father of Anak). ¹⁴And Caleb drove out from there the three sons of Anak, Sheshai and Ahiman and Talmai, the descendants of Anak. ¹⁵And he went up from there against the inhabitants of Debir. Now the name of Debir formerly was Kiriath-sepher. ¹⁶And Caleb said, "Whoever strikes Kiriath-sepher and captures it, to him will I give Achsah my daughter as wife." ¹⁷And Othniel the son of Kenaz, the brother of Caleb, captured it. And he gave him Achsah his daughter as wife. ¹⁸When she came to him, she urged him to ask her father for a field. And she got off her donkey, and Caleb said to her, "What do you want?" ¹⁹She said to him, "Give me a blessing. Since you have given me the land of the Negeb, give me also springs of water." And he gave her the upper springs and the lower springs.

²⁰This is the inheritance of the tribe of the people of Judah according to their clans. ²¹The cities belonging to the tribe of the people of Judah in the extreme south, toward the boundary of Edom, were Kabzeel, Eder, Jagur, ²²Kinah, Dimonah, Adadah, ²³Kedesh, Hazor, Ithnan, ²⁴Ziph, Telem, Bealoth, ²⁵Hazor-hadattah, Kerioth-hezron (that is, Hazor), ²⁶Amam, Shema, Moladah, ²⁷Hazar-gaddah, Heshmon, Beth-pelet, ²⁸Hazar-shual, Beersheba, Biziothiah, ²⁹Baalah, Iim, Ezem, ³⁰Eltolad, Chesil, Hormah, ³¹Ziklag, Madmannah, Sansannah,

³²Lebaoth, Shilhim, Ain, and Rimmon: in all, twenty-nine cities with their villages.

³³And in the lowland, Eshtaol, Zorah, Ashnah, ³⁴Zanoah, En-gannim, Tappuah, Enam, ³⁵Jarmuth, Adullam, Socoh, Azekah, ³⁶Shaaraim, Adithaim, Gederah, Gederothaim: fourteen cities with their villages.

³⁷Zenan, Hadashah, Migdal-gad, ³⁸Dilean, Mizpeh, Joktheel, ³⁹Lachish, Bozkath, Eglon, ⁴⁰Cabbon, Lahmam, Chitlish, ⁴¹Gederoth, Beth-dagon, Naamah, and Makkedah: sixteen cities with their villages.

⁴²Libnah, Ether, Ashan, ⁴³Iphtah, Ashnah, Nezib, ⁴⁴Keilah, Achzib, and Mareshah: nine cities with their villages.

⁴⁵Ekron, with its towns and its villages; ⁴⁶from Ekron to the sea, all that were by the side of Ashdod, with their villages.

⁴⁷Ashdod, its towns and its villages; Gaza, its towns and its villages; to the Brook of Egypt, and the Great Sea with its coastline.

⁴⁸And in the hill country, Shamir, Jattir, Socoh, ⁴⁹Dannah, Kiriath-sannah (that is, Debir), ⁵⁰Anab, Eshtemoh, Anim, ⁵¹Goshen, Holon, and Giloh: eleven cities with their villages.

⁵²Arab, Dumah, Eshan, ⁵³Janim, Beth-tappuah, Aphekah, ⁵⁴Humtah, Kiriath-arba (that is, Hebron), and Zior: nine cities with their villages.

⁵⁵Maon, Carmel, Ziph, Juttah, ⁵⁶Jezreel, Jokdeam, Zanoah, ⁵⁷Kain, Gibeah, and Timnah: ten cities with their villages.

⁵⁸Halhul, Beth-zur, Gedor, ⁵⁹Maarath, Beth-anoth, and Eltekon: six cities with their villages.

⁶⁰Kiriath-baal (that is, Kiriath-jearim), and Rabbah: two cities with their villages.

⁶¹In the wilderness, Beth-arabah, Middin, Secacah, ⁶²Nibshan, the City of Salt, and Engedi: six cities with their villages.

⁶³But the Jebusites, the inhabitants of Jerusalem, the people of Judah could not drive out, so the Jebusites dwell with the people of Judah at Jerusalem to this day.

The Allotment for Ephraim and Manasseh

16 The allotment of the people of Joseph went from the Jordan by Jericho, east of the waters of Jericho, into the wilderness, going up from Jericho into the hill country to Bethel. ²Then going from Bethel to Luz, it passes along to Ataroth, the territory of the Archites. ³Then it goes down westward to the territory of the Japhletites, as far as the territory of Lower Beth-horon, then to Gezer, and it ends at the sea.

⁴ The people of Joseph, Manasseh and Ephraim, received their inheritance.

⁵ The territory of the people of Ephraim by their clans was as follows: the boundary of their inheritance on the east was Ataroth-addar as far as Upper Beth-horon, ⁶ and the boundary goes from there to the sea. On the north is Michmethath. Then on the east the boundary turns around toward Taanath-shiloh and passes along beyond it on the east to Janoah, ⁷ then it goes down from Janoah to Ataroth and to Naarah, and touches Jericho, ending at the Jordan. ⁸ From Tappuah the boundary goes westward to the brook Kanah and ends at the sea. Such is the inheritance of the tribe of the people of Ephraim by their clans, ⁹ together with the towns that were set apart for the people of Ephraim within the inheritance of the Manassites, all those towns with their villages. ¹⁰ However, they did not drive out the Canaanites who lived in Gezer, so the Canaanites have lived in the midst of Ephraim to this day but have been made to do forced labor.

17 Then allotment was made to the people of Manasseh, for he was the firstborn of Joseph. To Machir the firstborn of Manasseh, the father of Gilead, were allotted Gilead and Bashan, because he was a man of war. ² And allotments were made to the rest of the people of Manasseh by their clans, Abiezer, Helek, Asriel, Shechem, Hepher, and Shemida. These were the male descendants of Manasseh the son of Joseph, by their clans.

³ Now Zelophehad the son of Hepher, son of Gilead, son of Machir, son of Manasseh, had no sons, but only daughters, and these are the names of his daughters: Mahlah, Noah, Hoglah, Milcah, and Tirzah. ⁴ They approached Eleazar the priest and Joshua the son of Nun and the leaders and said, "The LORD commanded Moses to give us an inheritance along with our brothers." So according to the mouth of the LORD he gave them an inheritance among the brothers of their father. ⁵ Thus there fell to Manasseh ten portions, besides the land of Gilead and Bashan, which is on the other side of the Jordan, ⁶ because the daughters of Manasseh received an inheritance along

with his sons. The land of Gilead was allotted to the rest of the people of Manasseh.

⁷ The territory of Manasseh reached from Asher to Michmethath, which is east of Shechem. Then the boundary goes along southward to the inhabitants of En-tappuah. ⁸ The land of Tappuah belonged to Manasseh, but the town of Tappuah on the boundary of Manasseh belonged to the people of Ephraim. ⁹ Then the boundary went down to the brook Kanah. These cities, to the south of the brook, among the cities of Manasseh, belong to Ephraim. Then the boundary of Manasseh goes on the north side of the brook and ends at the sea, ¹⁰ the land to the south being Ephraim's and that to the north being Manasseh's, with the sea forming its boundary. On the north Asher is reached, and on the east Issachar. ¹¹ Also in Issachar and in Asher Manasseh had Beth-shean and its villages, and Ibleam and its villages, and the inhabitants of Dor and its villages, and the inhabitants of En-dor and its villages, and the inhabitants of Taanach and its villages, and the inhabitants of Megiddo and its villages; the third is Naphath.[1] ¹² Yet the people of Manasseh could not take possession of those cities, but the Canaanites persisted in dwelling in that land. ¹³ Now when the people of Israel grew strong, they put the Canaanites to forced labor, but did not utterly drive them out.

¹⁴ Then the people of Joseph spoke to Joshua, saying, "Why have you given me but one lot and one portion as an inheritance, although I am a numerous people, since all along the LORD has blessed me?" ¹⁵ And Joshua said to them, "If you are a numerous people, go up by yourselves to the forest, and there clear ground for yourselves in the land of the Perizzites and the Rephaim, since the hill country of Ephraim is too narrow for you." ¹⁶ The people of Joseph said, "The hill country is not enough for us. Yet all the Canaanites who dwell in the plain have chariots of iron, both those in Beth-shean and its villages and those in the Valley of Jezreel." ¹⁷ Then Joshua said to the house of Joseph, to Ephraim and Manasseh, "You are a numerous people and have great power. You shall not have one allotment only, ¹⁸ but the hill country shall be yours, for though it is a forest, you shall clear it

[1] The meaning of the Hebrew is uncertain

and possess it to its farthest borders. For you shall drive out the Canaanites, though they have chariots of iron, and though they are strong."

Allotment of the Remaining Land

18 Then the whole congregation of the people of Israel assembled at Shiloh and set up the tent of meeting there. The land lay subdued before them.

² There remained among the people of Israel seven tribes whose inheritance had not yet been apportioned. ³ So Joshua said to the people of Israel, "How long will you put off going in to take possession of the land, which the LORD, the God of your fathers, has given you? ⁴ Provide three men from each tribe, and I will send them out that they may set out and go up and down the land. They shall write a description of it with a view to their inheritances, and then come to me. ⁵ They shall divide it into seven portions. Judah shall continue in his territory on the south, and the house of Joseph shall continue in their territory on the north. ⁶ And you shall describe the land in seven divisions and bring the description here to me. And I will cast lots for you here before the LORD our God. ⁷ The Levites have no portion among you, for the priesthood of the LORD is their heritage. And Gad and Reuben and half the tribe of Manasseh have received their inheritance beyond the Jordan eastward, which Moses the servant of the LORD gave them."

⁸ So the men arose and went, and Joshua charged those who went to write the description of the land, saying, "Go up and down in the land and write a description and return to me. And I will cast lots for you here before the LORD in Shiloh." ⁹ So the men went and passed up and down in the land and wrote in a book a description of it by towns in seven divisions. Then they came to Joshua to the camp at Shiloh, ¹⁰ and Joshua cast lots for them in Shiloh before the LORD. And there Joshua apportioned the land to the people of Israel, to each his portion.

Know Yourself

verses to read
Joshua 18:1–10

How long are you going to keep on worrying about something that the Lord has already given you? How long are you going to stress about your salvation or believe you are "too bad" to be forgiven? Holding on to discipline or punishment in order to "serve your time" like some common criminal is unbelief. Rejecting the promises of God because you believe you are "not worthy" to receive them is not trusting him. God wants your faith and your trust, but unless you let go of your fears and doubts, you will never be set free.

God had given the land to the Israelites, but seven tribes had failed to move into it. They just wasted their time trying to get the land God had already given them. From where we sit, that seems like insanity, but at the time it made total sense to them. And the things you believe about yourself and your God might make sense to you, but don't let your feelings fool you—if your feelings disagree with God's Word, then they are wrong. You can't get anywhere playing God, and that's what you're doing when you insist that God's promises don't apply to you because of your past or even your present. His promises always stand true, and if you want to get in on them, all you have to do is to believe them. The land is yours and all that goes with it—freedom, safety, and hope—but not until you reach out and take it. Your salvation requires something of you, but it's a simple thing: let go of any judgment you've brought down on yourself and accept the forgiveness of God, which is freely yours because of Christ's work.

The Inheritance for Benjamin

¹¹ The lot of the tribe of the people of Benjamin according to its clans came up, and the territory allotted to it fell between the people of Judah and the people of Joseph. ¹² On the north side their boundary began at the Jordan. Then the boundary goes up to the shoulder north of Jericho, then up through the hill country westward, and it ends at the wilderness of Beth-aven. ¹³ From there the boundary passes along southward in the direction of Luz, to the shoulder of Luz (that is, Bethel), then the boundary goes down to Ataroth-addar, on the mountain that lies south of Lower Beth-horon. ¹⁴ Then the boundary goes in another direction, turning on the western side southward from the mountain that lies to the south, opposite Beth-horon, and it ends at Kiriath-baal (that is, Kiriath-jearim), a city belonging to the people of Judah. This forms the western side. ¹⁵ And the southern side begins at the outskirts of Kiriath-jearim. And the boundary goes from there to Ephron,¹ to the spring of the waters of Nephtoah. ¹⁶ Then the boundary goes down to the border of the mountain that overlooks the Valley of the Son of Hinnom, which is at the north end of the Valley of Rephaim. And it then goes down the Valley of Hinnom, south of the shoulder of the Jebusites, and downward to En-rogel. ¹⁷ Then it bends in a northerly direction going on to En-shemesh, and from there goes to Geliloth, which is opposite the ascent of Adummim. Then it goes down to the stone of Bohan the son of Reuben, ¹⁸ and passing on to the north of the shoulder of Beth-arabah² it goes down to the Arabah. ¹⁹ Then the boundary passes on to the north of the shoulder of Beth-hoglah. And the boundary ends at the northern bay of the Salt Sea, at the south end of the Jordan: this is the southern border. ²⁰ The Jordan forms its boundary on the eastern side. This is the inheritance of the people of Benjamin, according to their clans, boundary by boundary all around.

²¹ Now the cities of the tribe of the people of Benjamin according to their clans were Jericho, Beth-hoglah, Emek-keziz, ²² Beth-arabah, Zemaraim, Bethel, ²³ Avvim, Parah, Ophrah, ²⁴ Chephar-ammoni, Ophni, Geba—twelve cities with their villages: ²⁵ Gibeon, Ramah, Beeroth, ²⁶ Mizpeh, Chephirah, Mozah, ²⁷ Rekem, Irpeel, Taralah, ²⁸ Zela, Haeleph, Jebus³ (that is, Jerusalem), Gibeah⁴ and Kiriath-jearim⁵—fourteen cities with their villages. This is the inheritance of the people of Benjamin according to its clans.

The Inheritance for Simeon

19 The second lot came out for Simeon, for the tribe of the people of Simeon, according to their clans, and their inheritance was in the midst of the inheritance of the people of Judah. ² And they had for their inheritance Beersheba, Sheba, Moladah, ³ Hazar-shual, Balah, Ezem, ⁴ Eltolad, Bethul, Hormah, ⁵ Ziklag, Beth-marcaboth, Hazar-susah, ⁶ Beth-lebaoth, and Sharuhen—thirteen cities with their villages; ⁷ Ain, Rimmon, Ether, and Ashan—four cities with their villages, ⁸ together with all the villages around these cities as far as Baalath-beer, Ramah of the Negeb. This was the inheritance of the tribe of the people of Simeon according to their clans. ⁹ The inheritance of the people of Simeon formed part of the territory of the people of Judah. Because the portion of the people of Judah was too large for them, the people of Simeon obtained an inheritance in the midst of their inheritance.

The Inheritance for Zebulun

¹⁰ The third lot came up for the people of Zebulun, according to their clans. And the territory of their inheritance reached as far as Sarid. ¹¹ Then their boundary goes up westward and on to Mareal and touches Dabbesheth, then the brook that is east of Jokneam. ¹² From Sarid it goes in the other direction eastward toward the sunrise to the boundary of Chisloth-tabor. From there it goes to Daberath, then up to Japhia. ¹³ From there it passes along on the east toward the sunrise to Gath-hepher, to Eth-kazin, and going on to Rimmon it bends toward Neah, ¹⁴ then on the north the boundary turns about to Hannathon, and it ends at the Valley of Iphtahel; ¹⁵ and Kattath, Nahalal, Shimron, Idalah, and Bethlehem—twelve cities with their villages. ¹⁶ This is the inheritance of the people of Zebulun, according to their clans—these cities with their villages.

¹ See 15:9; Hebrew *westward* ² Septuagint; Hebrew *to the shoulder over against the Arabah* ³ Septuagint, Syriac, Vulgate; Hebrew *the Jebusite* ⁴ Hebrew *Gibeath* ⁵ Septuagint; Hebrew *Kiriath*

The Inheritance for Issachar

17 The fourth lot came out for Issachar, for the people of Issachar, according to their clans. **18** Their territory included Jezreel, Chesulloth, Shunem, **19** Hapharaim, Shion, Anaharath, **20** Rabbith, Kishion, Ebez, **21** Remeth, En-gannim, En-haddah, Beth-pazzez. **22** The boundary also touches Tabor, Shahazumah, and Beth-shemesh, and its boundary ends at the Jordan— sixteen cities with their villages. **23** This is the inheritance of the tribe of the people of Issachar, according to their clans— the cities with their villages.

The Inheritance for Asher

24 The fifth lot came out for the tribe of the people of Asher according to their clans. **25** Their territory included Helkath, Hali, Beten, Achshaph, **26** Allammelech, Amad, and Mishal. On the west it touches Carmel and Shihor-libnath, **27** then it turns eastward, it goes to Beth-dagon, and touches Zebulun and the Valley of Iphtahel northward to Beth-emek and Neiel. Then it continues in the north to Cabul, **28** Ebron, Rehob, Hammon, Kanah, as far as Sidon the Great. **29** Then the boundary turns to Ramah, reaching to the fortified city of Tyre. Then the boundary turns to Hosah, and it ends at the sea; Mahalab,[1] Achzib, **30** Ummah, Aphek and Rehob— twenty-two cities with their villages. **31** This is the inheritance of the tribe of the people of Asher according to their clans— these cities with their villages.

The Inheritance for Naphtali

32 The sixth lot came out for the people of Naphtali, for the people of Naphtali, according to their clans. **33** And their boundary ran from Heleph, from the oak in Zaanannim, and Adami-nekeb, and Jabneel, as far as Lakkum, and it ended at the Jordan. **34** Then the boundary turns westward to Aznoth-tabor and goes from there to Hukkok, touching Zebulun at the south and Asher on the west and Judah on the east at the Jordan. **35** The fortified cities are Ziddim, Zer, Hammath, Rakkath, Chinnereth, **36** Adamah, Ramah, Hazor, **37** Kedesh, Edrei, En-hazor, **38** Yiron, Migdal-el, Horem, Beth-anath, and Beth-shemesh— nineteen cities with their villages. **39** This is the inheritance of the tribe of the people of Naphtali according to their clans— the cities with their villages.

The Inheritance for Dan

40 The seventh lot came out for the tribe of the people of Dan, according to their clans. **41** And the territory of its inheritance included Zorah, Eshtaol, Ir-shemesh, **42** Shaalabbin, Aijalon, Ithlah, **43** Elon, Timnah, Ekron, **44** Eltekeh, Gibbethon, Baalath, **45** Jehud, Bene-berak, Gath-rimmon, **46** and Me-jarkon and Rakkon with the territory over against Joppa. **47** When the territory of the people of Dan was lost to them, the people of Dan went up and fought against Leshem, and after capturing it and striking it with the sword they took possession of it and settled in it, calling Leshem, Dan, after the name of Dan their ancestor. **48** This is the inheritance of the tribe of the people of Dan, according to their clans— these cities with their villages.

The Inheritance for Joshua

49 When they had finished distributing the several territories of the land as inheritances, the people of Israel gave an inheritance among them to Joshua the son of Nun. **50** By command of the LORD they gave him the city that he asked, Timnath-serah in the hill country of Ephraim. And he rebuilt the city and settled in it.

51 These are the inheritances that Eleazar the priest and Joshua the son of Nun and the heads of the fathers' houses of the tribes of the people of Israel distributed by lot at Shiloh before the LORD, at the entrance of the tent of meeting. So they finished dividing the land.

The Cities of Refuge

20 Then the LORD said to Joshua, **2** "Say to the people of Israel, 'Appoint the cities of refuge, of which I spoke to you through Moses, **3** that the manslayer who strikes any person without intent or unknowingly may flee there. They shall be for you a refuge from the avenger of blood. **4** He shall flee to one of these cities and shall stand at the entrance of the gate of the city and explain his case to the elders of that city. Then they shall take him into the city and give him a place, and he shall remain with them. **5** And if the avenger of blood pursues him, they shall not give up

---

[1] Compare Septuagint; Hebrew *Mehebel*

the manslayer into his hand, because he struck his neighbor unknowingly, and did not hate him in the past. [6] And he shall remain in that city until he has stood before the congregation for judgment, until the death of him who is high priest at the time. Then the manslayer may return to his own town and his own home, to the town from which he fled.' "

[7] So they set apart Kedesh in Galilee in the hill country of Naphtali, and Shechem in the hill country of Ephraim, and Kiriath-arba (that is, Hebron) in the hill country of Judah. [8] And beyond the Jordan east of Jericho, they appointed Bezer in the wilderness on the tableland, from the tribe of Reuben, and Ramoth in Gilead, from the tribe of Gad, and Golan in Bashan, from the tribe of Manasseh. [9] These were the cities designated for all the people of Israel and for the stranger sojourning among them, that anyone who killed a person without intent could flee there, so that he might not die by the hand of the avenger of blood, till he stood before the congregation.

Cities and Pasturelands Allotted to Levi

21 Then the heads of the fathers' houses of the Levites came to Eleazar the priest and to Joshua the son of Nun and to the heads of the fathers' houses of the tribes of the people of Israel. [2] And they said to them at Shiloh in the land of Canaan, "The Lord commanded through Moses that we be given cities to dwell in, along with their pasturelands for our livestock." [3] So by command of the Lord the people of Israel gave to the Levites the following cities and pasturelands out of their inheritance.

[4] The lot came out for the clans of the Kohathites. So those Levites who were descendants of Aaron the priest received by lot from the tribes of Judah, Simeon, and Benjamin, thirteen cities. [5] And the rest of the Kohathites received by lot from the clans of the tribe of Ephraim, from the tribe of Dan and the half-tribe of Manasseh, ten cities. [6] The Gershonites received by lot from the clans of the tribe of Issachar, from the tribe of Asher, from the tribe of Naphtali, and from the half-tribe of Manasseh in Bashan, thirteen cities. [7] The Merarites according to their clans received from the tribe of Reuben, the tribe of Gad, and the tribe of Zebulun, twelve cities.

[8] These cities and their pasturelands the people of Israel gave by lot to the Levites, as the Lord had commanded through Moses.

[9] Out of the tribe of the people of Judah and the tribe of the people of Simeon they gave the following cities mentioned by name, [10] which went to the descendants of Aaron, one of the clans of the Kohathites who belonged to the people of Levi; since the lot fell to them first. [11] They gave them Kiriath-arba (Arba being the father of Anak), that is Hebron, in the hill country of Judah, along with the pasturelands around it. [12] But the fields of the city and its villages had been given to Caleb the son of Jephunneh as his possession.

[13] And to the descendants of Aaron the priest they gave Hebron, the city of refuge for the manslayer, with its pasturelands, Libnah with its pasturelands, [14] Jattir with its pasturelands, Eshtemoa with its pasturelands, [15] Holon with its pasturelands, Debir with its pasturelands, [16] Ain with its pasturelands, Juttah with its pasturelands, Beth-shemesh with its pasturelands—nine cities out of these two tribes; [17] then out of the tribe of Benjamin, Gibeon with its pasturelands, Geba with its pasturelands, [18] Anathoth with its pasturelands, and Almon with its pasturelands—four cities. [19] The cities of the descendants of Aaron, the priests, were in all thirteen cities with their pasturelands.

[20] As to the rest of the Kohathites belonging to the Kohathite clans of the Levites, the cities allotted to them were out of the tribe of Ephraim. [21] To them were given Shechem, the city of refuge for the manslayer, with its pasturelands in the hill country of Ephraim, Gezer with its pasturelands, [22] Kibzaim with its pasturelands, Beth-horon with its pasturelands—four cities; [23] and out of the tribe of Dan, Elteke with its pasturelands, Gibbethon with its pasturelands, [24] Aijalon with its pasturelands, Gath-rimmon with its pasturelands—four cities; [25] and out of the half-tribe of Manasseh, Taanach with its pasturelands, and Gath-rimmon with its pasturelands—two cities. [26] The cities of the clans of the rest of the Kohathites were ten in all with their pasturelands.

[27] And to the Gershonites, one of the clans of the Levites, were given out of the

half-tribe of Manasseh, Golan in Bashan with its pasturelands, the city of refuge for the manslayer, and Beeshterah with its pasturelands—two cities; ²⁸ and out of the tribe of Issachar, Kishion with its pasturelands, Daberath with its pasturelands, ²⁹ Jarmuth with its pasturelands, En-gannim with its pasturelands—four cities; ³⁰ and out of the tribe of Asher, Mishal with its pasturelands, Abdon with its pasturelands, ³¹ Helkath with its pasturelands, and Rehob with its pasturelands—four cities; ³² and out of the tribe of Naphtali, Kedesh in Galilee with its pasturelands, the city of refuge for the manslayer, Hammoth-dor with its pasturelands, and Kartan with its pasturelands—three cities. ³³ The cities of the several clans of the Gershonites were in all thirteen cities with their pasturelands.

³⁴ And to the rest of the Levites, the Merarite clans, were given out of the tribe of Zebulun, Jokneam with its pasturelands, Kartah with its pasturelands, ³⁵ Dimnah with its pasturelands, Nahalal with its pasturelands—four cities; ³⁶ and out of the tribe of Reuben, Bezer with its pasturelands, Jahaz with its pasturelands, ³⁷ Kedemoth with its pasturelands, and Mephaath with its pasturelands—four cities; ³⁸ and out of the tribe of Gad, Ramoth in Gilead with its pasturelands, the city of refuge for the manslayer, Mahanaim with its pasturelands, ³⁹ Heshbon with its pasturelands, Jazer with its pasturelands—four cities in all. ⁴⁰ As for the cities of the several Merarite clans, that is, the remainder of the clans of the Levites, those allotted to them were in all twelve cities.

⁴¹ The cities of the Levites in the midst of the possession of the people of Israel were in all forty-eight cities with their pasturelands. ⁴² These cities each had its pasturelands around it. So it was with all these cities.

⁴³ Thus the LORD gave to Israel all the land that he swore to give to their fathers. And they took possession of it, and they settled there. ⁴⁴ And the LORD gave them rest on every side just as he had sworn to their fathers. Not one of all their enemies had withstood them, for the LORD had given all their enemies into their hands. ⁴⁵ Not one word of all the good promises that the LORD had made to the house of Israel had failed; all came to pass.

A Prayer of...
NEED

Like the sun is full of light, the ocean full of water, heaven full of glory, may my heart be full of you, I pray. All love is in vain unless you are at work within me, regenerating me by your power, giving me eyes to see Jesus, showing me the realities of the unseen world. Give me yourself without measure, as an unimpaired fountain, an inexhaustible wealth.

I hate my coldness, poverty, emptiness, imperfect vision, weak service, prayerless prayers, praiseless praises. Don't let me grieve or resist you. Come as power, to get rid of every earthly desire, to reign as King of my heart, and to keep me yours. Come as teacher, leading me into all truth, filling me with all understanding. Come as love, so that I can adore the Father and love him as my all. Come as joy, to dwell in me, move in me, animate me. Come as light, illuminating the Scripture, molding me by its laws. Come as sanctifier, making my body, soul, and spirit wholly yours. Come as helper, with strength to bless and keep, directing my every step. Come as beautifier, bringing order out of confusion, loveliness out of chaos. Magnify your glory in me and make me a soothing fragrance.

Amen.

The Eastern Tribes Return Home

22 At that time Joshua summoned the Reubenites and the Gadites and the half-tribe of Manasseh, ² and said to them, "You have kept all that Moses the servant of the LORD commanded you and have obeyed my voice in all that I have commanded you. ³ You have not forsaken your brothers these many days, down to this day, but have been careful to keep the charge of the LORD your God. ⁴ And now the LORD your God has given rest to your brothers, as he promised them. Therefore turn and go to your tents in the land where your possession lies, which Moses the servant of the Lord gave you on the other side of the Jordan. ⁵Only be very careful to observe the commandment and the law that Moses the servant of the Lord commanded you, to love the Lord your God, and to walk in all his ways and to keep his commandments and to cling to him and to serve him with all your heart and with all your soul." ⁶So Joshua blessed them and sent them away, and they went to their tents.

⁷Now to the one half of the tribe of Manasseh Moses had given a possession in Bashan, but to the other half Joshua had given a possession beside their brothers in the land west of the Jordan. And when Joshua sent them away to their homes and blessed them, ⁸he said to them, "Go back to your tents with much wealth and with very much livestock, with silver, gold, bronze, and iron, and with much clothing. Divide the spoil of your enemies with your brothers." ⁹So the people of Reuben and the people of Gad and the half-tribe of Manasseh returned home, parting from the people of Israel at Shiloh, which is in the land of Canaan, to go to the land of Gilead, their own land of which they had possessed themselves by command of the Lord through Moses.

The Eastern Tribes' Altar of Witness

¹⁰And when they came to the region of the Jordan that is in the land of Canaan, the people of Reuben and the people of Gad and the half-tribe of Manasseh built there an altar by the Jordan, an altar of imposing size. ¹¹And the people of Israel heard it said, "Behold, the people of Reuben and the people of Gad and the half-tribe of Manasseh have built the altar at the frontier of the land of Canaan, in the region about the Jordan, on the side that belongs to the people of Israel." ¹²And when the people of Israel heard of it, the whole assembly of the people of Israel gathered at Shiloh to make war against them.

¹³Then the people of Israel sent to the people of Reuben and the people of Gad and the half-tribe of Manasseh, in the land of Gilead, Phinehas the son of Eleazar the priest, ¹⁴and with him ten chiefs, one from each of the tribal families of Israel, every one of them the head of a family among the clans of Israel. ¹⁵And they came to the people of Reuben, the people of Gad, and the half-tribe of Manasseh, in the land of Gilead, and they said to them, ¹⁶"Thus says the whole congregation of the Lord, 'What is this breach of faith that you have committed against the God of Israel in turning away this day from following the Lord by building yourselves an altar this day in rebellion against the Lord? ¹⁷Have we not had enough of the sin at Peor from which even yet we have not cleansed ourselves, and for which there came a plague upon the congregation of the Lord, ¹⁸that you too must turn away this day from following the Lord? And if you too rebel against the Lord today then tomorrow he will be angry with the whole congregation of Israel. ¹⁹But now, if the land of your possession is unclean, pass over into the Lord's land where the Lord's tabernacle stands, and take for yourselves a possession among us. Only do not rebel against the Lord or make us as rebels by building for yourselves an altar other than the altar of the Lord our God. ²⁰Did not Achan the son of Zerah break faith in the matter of the devoted things, and wrath fell upon all the congregation of Israel? And he did not perish alone for his iniquity.' "

²¹Then the people of Reuben, the people of Gad, and the half-tribe of Manasseh said in answer to the heads of the families of Israel, ²²"The Mighty One, God, the Lord! The Mighty One, God, the Lord! He knows; and let Israel itself know! If it was in rebellion or in breach of faith against the Lord, do not spare us today ²³for building an altar to turn away from following the Lord. Or if we did so to offer burnt offerings or grain offerings or peace offerings on it, may the Lord himself take vengeance. ²⁴No, but we did it from fear that in time to come your children might say to our children, 'What have you to do with the Lord, the God of Israel? ²⁵For the Lord has made the Jordan a boundary between us and you, you people of Reuben and people of Gad. You have no portion in the Lord.' So your children might make our children cease to worship the Lord. ²⁶Therefore we said, 'Let us now build an altar, not for burnt offering, nor for sacrifice, ²⁷but to be a witness between us and you, and between our generations after us, that we do perform the service of the Lord in his presence with our burnt offerings and sacrifices and peace offerings, so your children will not

ay to our children in time to come, "You have no portion in the LORD."' **28** And we thought, 'If this should be said to us or to our descendants in time to come, we should say, "Behold, the copy of the altar of the LORD, which our fathers made, not for burnt offerings, nor for sacrifice, but to be a witness between us and you."' **29** Far be it from us that we should rebel against the LORD and turn away this day from following the LORD by building an altar for burnt offering, grain offering, or sacrifice, other than the altar of the LORD our God that stands before his tabernacle!"

30 When Phinehas the priest and the chiefs of the congregation, the heads of the families of Israel who were with him, heard the words that the people of Reuben and the people of Gad and the people of Manasseh spoke, it was good in their eyes. **31** And Phinehas the son of Eleazar the priest said to the people of Reuben and the people of Gad and the people of Manasseh, "Today we know that the LORD is in our midst, because you have not committed this breach of faith against the LORD. Now you have delivered the people of Israel from the hand of the LORD."

32 Then Phinehas the son of Eleazar the priest, and the chiefs, returned from the people of Reuben and the people of Gad in the land of Gilead to the land of Canaan, to the people of Israel, and brought back word to them. **33** And the report was good in the eyes of the people of Israel. And the people of Israel blessed God and spoke no more of making war against them to destroy the land where the people of Reuben and the people of Gad were settled. **34** The people of Reuben and the people of Gad called the altar Witness, "For," they said, "it is a witness between us that the LORD is God."

Joshua's Charge to Israel's Leaders

23 A long time afterward, when the LORD had given rest to Israel from all their surrounding enemies, and Joshua was old and well advanced in years, **2** Joshua summoned all Israel, its elders and heads, its judges and officers, and said to them, "I am now old and well advanced in years. **3** And you have seen all that the LORD your God has done to all these nations for your sake, for it is the LORD your God who has fought for you. **4** Behold, I have allotted to you as an inheritance for your tribes those nations that remain, along with all the nations that I have already cut off, from the Jordan to the Great Sea in the west. **5** The LORD your God will push them back before you and drive them out of your sight. And you shall possess their land, just as the LORD your God promised you. **6** Therefore, be very strong to keep and to do all that is written in the Book of the Law of Moses, turning aside from it neither to the right hand nor to the left, **7** that you may not mix with these nations remaining among you or make mention of the names of their gods or swear by them or serve them or bow down to them, **8** but you shall cling to the LORD your God just as you have done to this day. **9** For the LORD has driven out before you great and strong nations. And as for you, no man has been able to stand before you to this day. **10** One man of you puts to flight a thousand, since it is the LORD your God who fights for you, just as he promised you. **11** Be very careful, therefore, to love the LORD your God. **12** For if you turn back and cling to the remnant of these nations remaining among you and make marriages with them, so that you associate with them and they with you, **13** know for certain that the LORD your God will no longer drive out these nations before you, but they shall be a snare and a trap for you, a whip on your sides and thorns in your eyes, until you perish from off this good ground that the LORD your God has given you.

14 "And now I am about to go the way of all the earth, and you know in your hearts and souls, all of you, that not one word has failed of all the good things[1] that the LORD your God promised concerning you. All have come to pass for you; not one of them has failed. **15** But just as all the good things that the LORD your God promised concerning you have been fulfilled for you, so the LORD will bring upon you all the evil things, until he has destroyed you from off this good land that the LORD your God has given you, **16** if you transgress the covenant of the LORD your God, which he commanded you, and go and serve other gods and bow down to them. Then the anger of the LORD will be kindled against you, and you shall perish quickly from off the good land that he has given to you."

Or *words*; also twice in verse 15

The Covenant Renewal at Shechem

24 Joshua gathered all the tribes of Israel to Shechem and summoned the elders, the heads, the judges, and the officers of Israel. And they presented themselves before God. [2] And Joshua said to all the people, "Thus says the LORD, the God of Israel, 'Long ago, your fathers lived beyond the Euphrates,[1] Terah, the father of Abraham and of Nahor; and they served other gods. [3] Then I took your father Abraham from beyond the River and led him through all the land of Canaan, and made his offspring many. I gave him Isaac. [4] And to Isaac I gave Jacob and Esau. And I gave Esau the hill country of Seir to possess, but Jacob and his children went down to Egypt. [5] And I sent Moses and Aaron, and I plagued Egypt with what I did in the midst of it, and afterward I brought you out.

[6] "Then I brought your fathers out of Egypt, and you came to the sea. And the Egyptians pursued your fathers with chariots and horsemen to the Red Sea. [7] And when they cried to the LORD, he put darkness between you and the Egyptians and made the sea come upon them and cover them; and your eyes saw what I did in Egypt. And you lived in the wilderness a long time. [8] Then I brought you to the land of the Amorites, who lived on the other side of the Jordan. They fought with you, and I gave them into your hand, and you took possession of their land, and I destroyed them before you. [9] Then Balak the son of Zippor, king of Moab, arose and fought against Israel. And he sent and invited Balaam the son of Beor to curse you, [10] but I would not listen to Balaam. Indeed, he blessed you. So I delivered you out of his hand. [11] And you went over the Jordan and came to Jericho, and the leaders of Jericho fought against you, and also the Amorites, the Perizzites, the Canaanites, the Hittites, the Girgashites, the Hivites, and the Jebusites. And I gave them into your hand. [12] And I sent the hornet before you, which drove them out before you, the two kings of the Amorites; it was not by your sword or by your bow. [13] I gave you a land on which you had not labored and cities that you had not built, and you dwell in them. You eat the fruit of vineyards and olive orchards that you did not plant.'

Choose Whom You Will Serve

[14] "Now therefore fear the LORD an serve him in sincerity and in faithfulnes: Put away the gods that your fathers serve beyond the River and in Egypt, and serv the LORD. [15] And if it is evil in your eyes t serve the LORD, choose this day whom yo will serve, whether the gods your father served in the region beyond the River, o the gods of the Amorites in whose land yo dwell. But as for me and my house, we wil serve the LORD."

[16] Then the people answered, "Far b it from us that we should forsake th LORD to serve other gods, [17] for it is th LORD our God who brought us and ou fathers up from the land of Egypt, out o the house of slavery, and who did thos great signs in our sight and preserved u in all the way that we went, and amon all the peoples through whom we passec [18] And the LORD drove out before us al the peoples, the Amorites who lived i the land. Therefore we also will serve th LORD, for he is our God."

[19] But Joshua said to the people, "Yo are not able to serve the LORD, for he is holy God. He is a jealous God; he will nc forgive your transgressions or your sins [20] If you forsake the LORD and serve foreig gods, then he will turn and do you harr and consume you, after having done yo good." [21] And the people said to Joshua "No, but we will serve the LORD." [22] The Joshua said to the people, "You are wit nesses against yourselves that you hav chosen the LORD, to serve him." And the said, "We are witnesses." [23] He said, "The put away the foreign gods that are amon; you, and incline your heart to the LORI the God of Israel." [24] And the people said t Joshua, "The LORD our God we will serve and his voice we will obey." [25] So Joshu made a covenant with the people tha day, and put in place statutes and rule for them at Shechem. [26] And Joshua wrot these words in the Book of the Law of Goc And he took a large stone and set it u] there under the terebinth that was by th sanctuary of the LORD. [27] And Joshua saic to all the people, "Behold, this stone shal be a witness against us, for it has heard al the words of the LORD that he spoke to us Therefore it shall be a witness against you

---

[1] Hebrew *the River*

est you deal falsely with your God." ²⁸ So Joshua sent the people away, every man to his inheritance.

Joshua's Death and Burial

²⁹ After these things Joshua the son of Nun, the servant of the LORD, died, being 110 years old. ³⁰ And they buried him in his own inheritance at Timnath-serah, which is in the hill country of Ephraim, north of the mountain of Gaash.

³¹ Israel served the LORD all the days of Joshua, and all the days of the elders who outlived Joshua and had known all the work that the LORD did for Israel.

³² As for the bones of Joseph, which the people of Israel brought up from Egypt, they buried them at Shechem, in the piece of land that Jacob bought from the sons of Hamor the father of Shechem for a hundred pieces of money.[1] It became an inheritance of the descendants of Joseph.

³³ And Eleazar the son of Aaron died, and they buried him at Gibeah, the town of Phinehas his son, which had been given him in the hill country of Ephraim.

---

[1] Hebrew *for a hundred qesitah*; a unit of money of unknown value

INTRODUCTION TO

Judges

Author: Unknown
Time: Unknown
Place: Unknown
Written to: God's people, the Israelites

The gist

In the book of Judges you see the goodness of God and the rebelliousness of his people. Time and again they would wander, complain, and forget God, but he was true to his promises and always rescued them. Judges were what the people needed for help and protection, and this book is the story of the flawed men and women whom God used to deliver his people.

Things to look for

- The explanation of why the judges were needed (see Judg. 2:6–3:6)
- The story of Deborah (see Judg. 4:4–5:31)
- The story of Gideon (see Judg. 6:11–8:32)

Return to Him

> So the anger of the LORD was kindled against Israel, and he gave them over to plunderers, who plundered them. And he sold them into the hand of their surrounding enemies.
>
> *Judges 2:14*

The wake-up call: something that happens in your life to get your attention. Hard times may come from the world, from your sinful choices, and even from God—but their cure is always God's presence. Trials and suffering should never make you freak out or give up but should be a time to look to God and his Word, a time to rest in his never-failing grace. Wherever this detour or roadblock came from, only resting in who God is and what he has done to redeem you will get you back on track.

No matter how many times you sin, God is going to give you a way out. All through the history of Israel you can see a people bouncing back and forth from faith to disbelief. A lot of times they would get off track by looking only at what they could see instead of at the invisible hand of God. But the beauty of history is that you get to see God's hand at work in the lives of other people and learn about his nature and his love for his children from what you see thousands of years later. Though God never saved his people from the consequences of their actions, he was always willing to send help their way. In the book of Judges you see just that—help, in the form of judges who would lead the Israelites in battle and guide them back to God. They were God's response to Israel's weakness and pleas for help, and they were evidence that God is never far from his people or deaf to their cries.

When your life takes a detour and you find yourself somewhere you never thought you'd be, don't give up hope: God is near and is ready to take you back. You might not know today how to change your life and get closer to the God you love, but as you read his Word you'll find that you're not alone. Millions before you have turned their backs on him, and many have had the strength to turn around and set things right. You just have to be willing to cry out to him, confess your sins to him, and then wait for him to do what only God can do: save you from your sin and the mess it's gotten you into.

Must-Know Verses

Whenever the LORD raised up judges for them, the LORD was with the judge, and he saved them from the hand of their enemies all the days of the judge. For the LORD was moved to pity by their groaning because of those who afflicted and oppressed them. *Judges 2:18*

"I will no longer drive out before them any of the nations that Joshua left when he died, in order to test Israel by them, whether they will take care to walk in the way of the LORD as their fathers did, or not." *Judges 2:21–22*

Then the people of Israel cried out to the LORD, and the LORD raised up for them a deliverer. *Judges 3:15*

Judges

The Continuing Conquest of Canaan

1 After the death of Joshua, the people of Israel inquired of the LORD, "Who shall go up first for us against the Canaanites, to fight against them?" ² The LORD said, "Judah shall go up; behold, I have given the land into his hand." ³ And Judah said to Simeon his brother, "Come up with me into the territory allotted to me, that we may fight against the Canaanites. And I likewise will go with you into the territory allotted to you." So Simeon went with him. ⁴ Then Judah went up and the LORD gave the Canaanites and the Perizzites into their hand, and they defeated 10,000 of them at Bezek. ⁵ They found Adoni-bezek at Bezek and fought against him and defeated the Canaanites and the Perizzites. ⁶ Adoni-bezek fled, but they pursued him and caught him and cut off his thumbs and his big toes. ⁷ And Adoni-bezek said, "Seventy kings with their thumbs and their big toes cut off used to pick up scraps under my table. As I have done, so God has repaid me." And they brought him to Jerusalem, and he died there.

⁸ And the men of Judah fought against Jerusalem and captured it and struck it with the edge of the sword and set the city on fire. ⁹ And afterward the men of Judah went down to fight against the Canaanites who lived in the hill country, in the Negeb, and in the lowland. ¹⁰ And Judah went against the Canaanites who lived in Hebron (now the name of Hebron was formerly Kiriath-arba), and they defeated Sheshai and Ahiman and Talmai.

¹¹ From there they went against the inhabitants of Debir. The name of Debir was formerly Kiriath-sepher. ¹² And Caleb said, "He who attacks Kiriath-sepher and captures it, I will give him Achsah my daughter for a wife." ¹³ And Othniel the son of Kenaz, Caleb's younger brother, captured it. And he gave him Achsah his daughter for a wife. ¹⁴ When she came to him, she urged him to ask her father for a field. And she dismounted from her donkey, and Caleb said to her, "What do you want?" ¹⁵ She said to him, "Give me a blessing. Since you have set me in the land of the Negeb, give me also springs of water." And Caleb gave her the upper springs and the lower springs.

¹⁶ And the descendants of the Kenite, Moses' father-in-law, went up with the people of Judah from the city of palms into the wilderness of Judah, which lies in the Negeb near Arad, and they went and settled with the people. ¹⁷ And Judah went with Simeon his brother, and they defeated the Canaanites who inhabited Zephath and devoted it to destruction. So the name of the city was called Hormah.[1] ¹⁸ Judah also captured Gaza with its territory, and Ashkelon with its territory, and Ekron with its territory. ¹⁹ And the LORD was with Judah, and he took possession of the hill country, but he could not drive out the inhabitants of the plain because they had chariots of iron. ²⁰ And Hebron was given to Caleb, as Moses had said. And he drove out from it the three sons of Anak. ²¹ But the people of Benjamin did not drive out the Jebusites who lived in Jerusalem, so the Jebusites have lived with the people of Benjamin in Jerusalem to this day.

²² The house of Joseph also went up against Bethel, and the LORD was with them. ²³ And the house of Joseph scouted out Bethel. (Now the name of the city was formerly Luz.) ²⁴ And the spies saw a man coming out of the city, and they said to him, "Please show us the way into the city, and we will deal kindly with you." ²⁵ And he showed them the way into the city. And they struck the city with the edge of the sword, but they let the man and all his family go. ²⁶ And the man went to the land

---

[1] *Hormah means utter destruction*

of the Hittites and built a city and called its name Luz. That is its name to this day.

Failure to Complete the Conquest

[27] Manasseh did not drive out the inhabitants of Beth-shean and its villages, or Taanach and its villages, or the inhabitants of Dor and its villages, or the inhabitants of Ibleam and its villages, or the inhabitants of Megiddo and its villages, for the Canaanites persisted in dwelling in that land. [28] When Israel grew strong, they put the Canaanites to forced labor, but did not drive them out completely.

[29] And Ephraim did not drive out the Canaanites who lived in Gezer, so the Canaanites lived in Gezer among them.

[30] Zebulun did not drive out the inhabitants of Kitron, or the inhabitants of Nahalol, so the Canaanites lived among them, but became subject to forced labor.

[31] Asher did not drive out the inhabitants of Acco, or the inhabitants of Sidon or of Ahlab or of Achzib or of Helbah or of Aphik or of Rehob, [32] so the Asherites lived among the Canaanites, the inhabitants of the land, for they did not drive them out.

[33] Naphtali did not drive out the inhabitants of Beth-shemesh, or the inhabitants of Beth-anath, so they lived among the Canaanites, the inhabitants of the land. Nevertheless, the inhabitants of Beth-shemesh and of Beth-anath became subject to forced labor for them.

[34] The Amorites pressed the people of Dan back into the hill country, for they did not allow them to come down to the plain. [35] The Amorites persisted in dwelling in Mount Heres, in Aijalon, and in Shaalbim, but the hand of the house of Joseph rested heavily on them, and they became subject to forced labor. [36] And the border of the Amorites ran from the ascent of Akrabbim, from Sela and upward.

Israel's Disobedience

2 Now the angel of the LORD went up from Gilgal to Bochim. And he said, "I brought you up from Egypt and brought you into the land that I swore to give to your fathers. I said, 'I will never break my covenant with you, [2] and you shall make no covenant with the inhabitants of this land; you shall break down their altars.' But you have not obeyed my voice. What is this you

have done? [3] So now I say, I will not drive them out before you, but they shall become thorns in your sides, and their gods shall be a snare to you." [4] As soon as the angel of the LORD spoke these words to all the people of Israel, the people lifted up their voices and wept. [5] And they called the name of that place Bochim.[1] And they sacrificed there to the LORD.

The Death of Joshua

[6] When Joshua dismissed the people, the people of Israel went each to his inheritance to take possession of the land. [7] And the people served the LORD all the days of Joshua, and all the days of the elders who outlived Joshua, who had seen all the great work that the LORD had done for Israel. [8] And Joshua the son of Nun, the servant of the LORD, died at the age of 110 years. [9] And they buried him within the boundaries of his inheritance in Timnath-heres, in the hill country of Ephraim, north of the mountain of Gaash. [10] And all that generation also were gathered to their fathers. And there arose another generation after them who did not know the LORD or the work that he had done for Israel.

Israel's Unfaithfulness

[11] And the people of Israel did what was evil in the sight of the LORD and served the Baals. [12] And they abandoned the LORD, the God of their fathers, who had brought them out of the land of Egypt. They went after other gods, from among the gods of the peoples who were around them, and bowed down to them. And they provoked the LORD to anger. [13] They abandoned the LORD and served the Baals and the Ashtaroth. [14] So the anger of the LORD was kindled against Israel, and he gave them over to plunderers, who plundered them. And he sold them into the hand of their surrounding enemies, so that they could no longer withstand their enemies. [15] Whenever they marched out, the hand of the LORD was against them for harm, as the LORD had warned, and as the LORD had sworn to them. And they were in terrible distress.

The LORD Raises Up Judges

[16] Then the LORD raised up judges, who saved them out of the hand of those who plundered them. [17] Yet they did not listen

---

[1] Bochim means weepers

to their judges, for they whored after other gods and bowed down to them. They soon turned aside from the way in which their fathers had walked, who had obeyed the commandments of the LORD, and they did not do so. ¹⁸ Whenever the LORD raised up judges for them, the LORD was with the judge, and he saved them from the hand of their enemies all the days of the judge. For the LORD was moved to pity by their groaning because of those who afflicted and oppressed them. ¹⁹ But whenever the judge died, they turned back and were more corrupt than their fathers, going after other gods, serving them and bowing down to them. They did not drop any of their practices or their stubborn ways. ²⁰ So the anger of the LORD was kindled against Israel, and he said, "Because this people have transgressed my covenant that I commanded their fathers and have not obeyed my voice, ²¹ I will no longer drive out before them any of the nations that Joshua left when he died, ²² in order to test Israel by them, whether they will take care to walk in the way of the LORD as their fathers did, or not." ²³ So the LORD left those nations, not driving them out quickly, and he did not give them into the hand of Joshua.

3 Now these are the nations that the LORD left, to test Israel by them, that is, all in Israel who had not experienced all the wars in Canaan. ² It was only in order that the generations of the people of Israel might know war, to teach war to those who had not known it before. ³ These are the nations: the five lords of the Philistines and all the Canaanites and the Sidonians and the Hivites who lived on Mount Lebanon, from Mount Baal-hermon as far as Lebo-hamath. ⁴ They were for the testing of Israel, to know whether Israel would obey the commandments of the LORD, which he commanded their fathers by the hand of Moses. ⁵ So the people of Israel lived among the Canaanites, the Hittites, the Amorites, the Perizzites, the Hivites, and the Jebusites. ⁶ And their daughters they took to themselves for wives, and their own daughters they gave to their sons, and they served their gods.

Othniel

⁷ And the people of Israel did what was evil in the sight of the LORD. They forgot the LORD their God and served the Baals and the Asheroth. ⁸ Therefore the anger of the LORD was kindled against Israel, and he sold them into the hand of Cushan-rishathaim king of Mesopotamia. And the people of Israel served Cushan-rishathaim eight years. ⁹ But when the people of Israel cried out to the LORD, the LORD raised up a deliverer for the people of Israel, who saved them, Othniel the son of Kenaz, Caleb's younger brother. ¹⁰ The Spirit of the LORD was upon him, and he judged Israel. He went out to war, and the LORD gave Cushan-rishathaim king of Mesopotamia into his hand. And his hand prevailed over Cushan-rishathaim. ¹¹ So the land had rest forty years. Then Othniel the son of Kenaz died.

Ehud

¹² And the people of Israel again did what was evil in the sight of the LORD, and the LORD strengthened Eglon the king of Moab against Israel, because they had done what was evil in the sight of the LORD. ¹³ He gathered to himself the Ammonites and the Amalekites, and went and defeated Israel. And they took possession of the city of palms. ¹⁴ And the people of Israel served Eglon the king of Moab eighteen years.

¹⁵ Then the people of Israel cried out to the LORD, and the LORD raised up for them a deliverer, Ehud, the son of Gera, the Benjaminite, a left-handed man. The people of Israel sent tribute by him to Eglon the king of Moab. ¹⁶ And Ehud made for himself a sword with two edges, a cubit¹ in length, and he bound it on his right thigh under his clothes. ¹⁷ And he presented the tribute to Eglon king of Moab. Now Eglon was a very fat man. ¹⁸ And when Ehud had finished presenting the tribute, he sent away the people who carried the tribute. ¹⁹ But he himself turned back at the idols near Gilgal and said, "I have a secret message for you, O king." And he commanded, "Silence." And all his attendants went out from his presence. ²⁰ And Ehud came to him as he was sitting alone in his cool roof chamber. And Ehud said, "I have a message from God for you." And he arose from his seat. ²¹ And Ehud reached with his left hand, took the sword from his right thigh, and thrust it into his belly. ²² And the hilt also went in after the blade, and the fat closed over the blade, for he did not pull

¹ A *cubit* was about 18 inches or 45 centimeters

the sword out of his belly; and the dung came out. ²³ Then Ehud went out into the porch¹ and closed the doors of the roof chamber behind him and locked them.

²⁴ When he had gone, the servants came, and when they saw that the doors of the roof chamber were locked, they thought, "Surely he is relieving himself in the closet of the cool chamber." ²⁵ And they waited till they were embarrassed. But when he still did not open the doors of the roof chamber, they took the key and opened them, and there lay their lord dead on the floor.

²⁶ Ehud escaped while they delayed, and he passed beyond the idols and escaped to Seirah. ²⁷ When he arrived, he sounded the trumpet in the hill country of Ephraim. Then the people of Israel went down with him from the hill country, and he was their leader. ²⁸ And he said to them, "Follow after me, for the Lord has given your enemies the Moabites into your hand." So they went down after him and seized the fords of the Jordan against the Moabites and did not allow anyone to pass over. ²⁹ And they killed at that time about 10,000 of the Moabites, all strong, able-bodied men; not a man escaped. ³⁰ So Moab was subdued that day under the hand of Israel. And the land had rest for eighty years.

Shamgar

³¹ After him was Shamgar the son of Anath, who killed 600 of the Philistines with an oxgoad, and he also saved Israel.

Deborah and Barak

4 And the people of Israel again did what was evil in the sight of the Lord after Ehud died. ² And the Lord sold them into the hand of Jabin king of Canaan, who reigned in Hazor. The commander of his army was Sisera, who lived in Harosheth-hagoyim. ³ Then the people of Israel cried out to the Lord for help, for he had 900 chariots of iron and he oppressed the people of Israel cruelly for twenty years.

⁴ Now Deborah, a prophetess, the wife of Lappidoth, was judging Israel at that time. ⁵ She used to sit under the palm of Deborah between Ramah and Bethel in the hill country of Ephraim, and the people of Israel came up to her for judgment. ⁶ She sent and summoned Barak the son of Abinoam from Kedesh-naphtali and said to

him, "Has not the Lord, the God of Israel, commanded you, 'Go, gather your men at Mount Tabor, taking 10,000 from the people of Naphtali and the people of Zebulun. ⁷ And I will draw out Sisera, the general of Jabin's army, to meet you by the river Kishon with his chariots and his troops, and I will give him into your hand'?" ⁸ Barak said to her, "If you will go with me, I will go, but if you will not go with me, I will not go." ⁹ And she said, "I will surely go with you. Nevertheless, the road on which you are going will not lead to your glory, for the Lord will sell Sisera into the hand of a woman." Then Deborah arose and went with Barak to Kedesh. ¹⁰ And Barak called out Zebulun and Naphtali to Kedesh. And 10,000 men went up at his heels, and Deborah went up with him.

¹¹ Now Heber the Kenite had separated from the Kenites, the descendants of Hobab the father-in-law of Moses, and had pitched his tent as far away as the oak in Zaanannim, which is near Kedesh.

¹² When Sisera was told that Barak the son of Abinoam had gone up to Mount Tabor, ¹³ Sisera called out all his chariots, 900 chariots of iron, and all the men who were with him, from Harosheth-hagoyim to the river Kishon. ¹⁴ And Deborah said to Barak, "Up! For this is the day in which the Lord has given Sisera into your hand. Does not the Lord go out before you?" So Barak went down from Mount Tabor with 10,000 men following him. ¹⁵ And the Lord routed Sisera and all his chariots and all his army before Barak by the edge of the sword. And Sisera got down from his chariot and fled away on foot. ¹⁶ And Barak pursued the chariots and the army to Harosheth-hagoyim, and all the army of Sisera fell by the edge of the sword; not a man was left.

¹⁷ But Sisera fled away on foot to the tent of Jael, the wife of Heber the Kenite, for there was peace between Jabin the king of Hazor and the house of Heber the Kenite. ¹⁸ And Jael came out to meet Sisera and said to him, "Turn aside, my lord; turn aside to me; do not be afraid." So he turned aside to her into the tent, and she covered him with a rug. ¹⁹ And he said to her, "Please give me a little water to drink, for I am thirsty." So she opened a skin of milk and gave him a drink and covered him. ²⁰ And

¹ The meaning of the Hebrew word is uncertain

he said to her, "Stand at the opening of the tent, and if any man comes and asks you, 'Is anyone here?' say, 'No.'" ²¹But Jael the wife of Heber took a tent peg, and took a hammer in her hand. Then she went softly to him and drove the peg into his temple until it went down into the ground while he was lying fast asleep from weariness. So he died. ²²And behold, as Barak was pursuing Sisera, Jael went out to meet him and said to him, "Come, and I will show you the man whom you are seeking." So he went in to her tent, and there lay Sisera dead, with the tent peg in his temple.

²³So on that day God subdued Jabin the king of Canaan before the people of Israel. ²⁴And the hand of the people of Israel pressed harder and harder against Jabin the king of Canaan, until they destroyed Jabin king of Canaan.

The Song of Deborah and Barak

5 Then sang Deborah and Barak the son of Abinoam on that day:

² "That the leaders took the lead in Israel,
  that the people offered themselves willingly,
  bless the LORD!

³ "Hear, O kings; give ear, O princes;
  to the LORD I will sing;
  I will make melody to the LORD,
    the God of Israel.

⁴ "LORD, when you went out from Seir,
  when you marched from the region of Edom,
  the earth trembled
  and the heavens dropped,
  yes, the clouds dropped water.
⁵ The mountains quaked before the LORD,
  even Sinai before the LORD, the God of Israel.

⁶ "In the days of Shamgar, son of Anath, in the days of Jael, the highways were abandoned,
  and travelers kept to the byways.
⁷ The villagers ceased in Israel;
  they ceased to be until I arose;
  I, Deborah, arose as a mother in Israel.

⁸ When new gods were chosen,
  then war was in the gates.
  Was shield or spear to be seen
    among forty thousand in Israel?
⁹ My heart goes out to the commanders of Israel
  who offered themselves willingly among the people.
  Bless the LORD.

¹⁰ "Tell of it, you who ride on white donkeys,
  you who sit on rich carpets¹
  and you who walk by the way.
¹¹ To the sound of musicians² at the watering places,
  there they repeat the righteous triumphs of the LORD,
  the righteous triumphs of his villagers in Israel.

"Then down to the gates marched the people of the LORD.

¹² "Awake, awake, Deborah!
  Awake, awake, break out in a song!
  Arise, Barak, lead away your captives, O son of Abinoam.
¹³ Then down marched the remnant of the noble;
  the people of the LORD marched down for me against the mighty.
¹⁴ From Ephraim their root they marched down into the valley,³
  following you, Benjamin, with your kinsmen;
  from Machir marched down the commanders,
  and from Zebulun those who bear the lieutenant's⁴ staff;
¹⁵ the princes of Issachar came with Deborah,
  and Issachar faithful to Barak;
  into the valley they rushed at his heels.
  Among the clans of Reuben there were great searchings of heart.
¹⁶ Why did you sit still among the sheepfolds,
  to hear the whistling for the flocks?
  Among the clans of Reuben there were great searchings of heart.

¹ The meaning of the Hebrew word is uncertain; it may connote *saddle blankets* ² Or *archers*; the meaning of the Hebrew word is uncertain ³ Septuagint; Hebrew *in Amalek* ⁴ Hebrew *commander's*

> Like a gold ring or an ornament of gold
> is a wise reprover to a listening ear.
>
> *Proverbs 25:12*

You need someone who fearlessly speaks truth into your life, someone who isn't afraid to offend you or to lose your friendship but will look you in the eye and tell you when things are out of whack. As a God Girl, you've got to let the presence of a prophet into your life—someone who will speak God's Word to you and not be silenced by your complaining or even your rejection. This prophet, or discipler, will remind you of your humanity, recognize sin where you might be too close to see it, and love you enough to risk your not liking them in the process.

When the Israelites sinned and followed after other gods, God (with a big G) allowed them to run around in ignorance for a while, but when they repented he would send them judges like Deborah. These judges would listen to their problems and then teach and admonish them, leading them back to truth. Deborah had an intimate relationship with God, and because of that she was able to help her people figure things out.

In your life you have to find a Deborah, someone who is connected to God and ready to help you understand your own faith. Prophets who speak God's Word to the people, reprimanding and correcting them and reminding them of God's commands as well as God's grace, are usually hated or at the very least avoided. No one wants to have their sins pointed out to them, but the wise girl ignores the pain in pursuit of the truth. Even though the truth hurts, she'd rather feel the sting of admonishment than live with the agony of unrepented sin. When others correct you, trust God enough to resist the urge to argue. Swallow your pride—it only wants to take you away from the truth. Accept correction with joy, knowing that it will only benefit you and make you into the woman you were meant to be.

7 Gilead stayed beyond the Jordan;
 and Dan, why did he stay with the
   ships?
Asher sat still at the coast of the sea,
 staying by his landings.
8 Zebulun is a people who risked their
   lives to the death;
Naphtali, too, on the heights of the
   field.

9 "The kings came, they fought;
 then fought the kings of Canaan,
at Taanach, by the waters of
   Megiddo;
 they got no spoils of silver.
10 From heaven the stars fought,
 from their courses they fought
   against Sisera.
21 The torrent Kishon swept them
   away,
 the ancient torrent, the torrent
   Kishon.
March on, my soul, with might!

22 "Then loud beat the horses' hoofs
 with the galloping, galloping of his
   steeds.

23 "Curse Meroz, says the angel of the
   LORD,
 curse its inhabitants thoroughly,
because they did not come to the
   help of the LORD,
 to the help of the LORD against the
   mighty.

24 "Most blessed of women be Jael,
 the wife of Heber the Kenite,
of tent-dwelling women most
   blessed.
25 He asked for water and she gave him
   milk;
 she brought him curds in a noble's
   bowl.
26 She sent her hand to the tent peg
 and her right hand to the workmen's mallet;
she struck Sisera;
 she crushed his head;
she shattered and pierced his
   temple.
27 Between her feet
 he sank, he fell, he lay still;
between her feet
 he sank, he fell;
where he sank,
 there he fell—dead.

28 "Out of the window she peered,
 the mother of Sisera wailed
   through the lattice:
'Why is his chariot so long in coming?
 Why tarry the hoofbeats of his
   chariots?'
29 Her wisest princesses answer,
 indeed, she answers herself,
30 'Have they not found and divided the
   spoil?—
 A womb or two for every man;
spoil of dyed materials for Sisera,
 spoil of dyed materials embroidered,
two pieces of dyed work embroidered for the neck as spoil?'

31 "So may all your enemies perish,
   O LORD!
 But your friends be like the sun as
   he rises in his might."

And the land had rest for forty years.

Midian Oppresses Israel

6 The people of Israel did what was evil in the sight of the LORD, and the LORD gave them into the hand of Midian seven years. ²And the hand of Midian overpowered Israel, and because of Midian the people of Israel made for themselves the dens that are in the mountains and the caves and the strongholds. ³For whenever the Israelites planted crops, the Midianites and the Amalekites and the people of the East would come up against them. ⁴They would encamp against them and devour the produce of the land, as far as Gaza, and leave no sustenance in Israel and no sheep or ox or donkey. ⁵For they would come up with their livestock and their tents; they would come like locusts in number—both they and their camels could not be counted—so that they laid waste the land as they came in. ⁶And Israel was brought very low because of Midian. And the people of Israel cried out for help to the LORD.

⁷When the people of Israel cried out to the LORD on account of the Midianites, ⁸the LORD sent a prophet to the people of Israel. And he said to them, "Thus says the LORD, the God of Israel: I led you up from Egypt and brought you out of the house of slavery. ⁹And I delivered you from the hand of the Egyptians and from the hand of all who oppressed you, and drove them out before you and gave you their land. ¹⁰And

I said to you, 'I am the Lord your God; you shall not fear the gods of the Amorites in whose land you dwell.' But you have not obeyed my voice."

The Call of Gideon

[11] Now the angel of the Lord came and sat under the terebinth at Ophrah, which belonged to Joash the Abiezrite, while his son Gideon was beating out wheat in the winepress to hide it from the Midianites. [12] And the angel of the Lord appeared to him and said to him, "The Lord is with you, O mighty man of valor." [13] And Gideon said to him, "Please, sir,[1] if the Lord is with us, why then has all this happened to us? And where are all his wonderful deeds that our fathers recounted to us, saying, 'Did not the Lord bring us up from Egypt?' But now the Lord has forsaken us and given us into the hand of Midian." [14] And the Lord[2] turned to him and said, "Go in this might of yours and save Israel from the hand of Midian; do not I send you?" [15] And he said to him, "Please, Lord, how can I save Israel? Behold, my clan is the weakest in Manasseh, and I am the least in my father's house." [16] And the Lord said to him, "But I will be with you, and you shall strike the Midianites as one man." [17] And he said to him, "If now I have found favor in your eyes, then show me a sign that it is you who speak with me. [18] Please do not depart from here until I come to you and bring out my present and set it before you." And he said, "I will stay till you return."

[19] So Gideon went into his house and prepared a young goat and unleavened cakes from an ephah[3] of flour. The meat he put in a basket, and the broth he put in a pot, and brought them to him under the terebinth and presented them. [20] And the angel of God said to him, "Take the meat and the unleavened cakes, and put them on this rock, and pour the broth over them." And he did so. [21] Then the angel of the Lord reached out the tip of the staff that was in his hand and touched the meat and the unleavened cakes. And fire sprang up from the rock and consumed the meat and the unleavened cakes. And the angel of the Lord vanished from his sight. [22] Then Gideon perceived that he was the angel of the Lord. And Gideon said, "Alas, O Lord God! For now I have seen the angel of the Lord face to face." [23] But the Lord said to him, "Peace

be to you. Do not fear; you shall not die." [24] Then Gideon built an altar there to the Lord and called it, The Lord Is Peace. To this day it still stands at Ophrah, which belongs to the Abiezrites.

[25] That night the Lord said to him, "Take your father's bull, and the second bull seven years old, and pull down the altar of Baal that your father has, and cut down the Asherah that is beside it [26] and build an altar to the Lord your God on the top of the stronghold here, with stones laid in due order. Then take the second bull and offer it as a burnt offering with the wood of the Asherah that you shall cut down." [27] So Gideon took ten men of his servants and did as the Lord had told him. But because he was too afraid of his family and the men of the town to do it by day, he did it by night.

Gideon Destroys the Altar of Baal

[28] When the men of the town rose early in the morning, behold, the altar of Baal was broken down, and the Asherah beside it was cut down, and the second bull was offered on the altar that had been built. [29] And they said to one another, "Who has done this thing?" And after they had searched and inquired, they said, "Gideon the son of Joash has done this thing." [30] Then the men of the town said to Joash, "Bring out your son, that he may die, for he has broken down the altar of Baal and cut down the Asherah beside it." [31] But Joash said to all who stood against him, "Will you contend for Baal? Or will you save him? Whoever contends for him shall be put to death by morning. If he is a god, let him contend for himself, because his altar has been broken down." [32] Therefore on that day Gideon[4] was called Jerubbaal, that is to say, "Let Baal contend against him," because he broke down his altar.

[33] Now all the Midianites and the Amalekites and the people of the East came together, and they crossed the Jordan and encamped in the Valley of Jezreel. [34] But the Spirit of the Lord clothed Gideon, and he sounded the trumpet, and the Abiezrites were called out to follow him. [35] And he sent messengers throughout all Manasseh, and they too were called out to follow him. And he sent messengers to Asher, Zebulun, and Naphtali, and they went up to meet them.

[1] Or Please, my Lord [2] Septuagint the angel of the Lord; also verse 16 [3] An ephah was about 3/5 bushel or 22 liters [4] Hebrew he

The Sign of the Fleece

36 Then Gideon said to God, "If you will save Israel by my hand, as you have said, **37** behold, I am laying a fleece of wool on the threshing floor. If there is dew on the fleece alone, and it is dry on all the ground, then I shall know that you will save Israel by my hand, as you have said." **38** And it was so. When he rose early next morning and squeezed the fleece, he wrung enough dew from the fleece to fill a bowl with water. **39** Then Gideon said to God, "Let not your anger burn against me; let me speak just once more. Please let me test just once more with the fleece. Please let it be dry on the fleece only, and on all the ground let there be dew." **40** And God did so that night; and it was dry on the fleece only, and on all the ground there was dew.

Gideon's Three Hundred Men

7 Then Jerubbaal (that is, Gideon) and all the people who were with him rose early and encamped beside the spring of Harod. And the camp of Midian was north of them, by the hill of Moreh, in the valley. **2** The LORD said to Gideon, "The people with you are too many for me to give the Midianites into their hand, lest Israel boast over me, saying, 'My own hand has saved me.' **3** Now therefore proclaim in the ears of the people, saying, 'Whoever is fearful and trembling, let him return home and hurry away from Mount Gilead.'" Then 22,000 of the people returned, and 10,000 remained.

4 And the LORD said to Gideon, "The people are still too many. Take them down to the water, and I will test them for you there, and anyone of whom I say to you, 'This one shall go with you,' shall go with you, and anyone of whom I say to you, 'This one shall not go with you,' shall not go." **5** So he brought the people down to the water. And the LORD said to Gideon, "Every one who laps the water with his tongue, as a dog laps, you shall set by himself. Likewise, every one who kneels down to drink." **6** And the number of those who lapped, putting their hands to their mouths, was 300 men,

Know God

verses to read
Judges 6:33–40

Are you waiting for a sign from God? Do you believe you are supposed to do something but are still waiting for proof? Beware of putting God to some kind of test, making him jump through hoops to prove himself to you. The only sign you need is the sign of his Word. What he says in it is true and doesn't need more proof. If God is asking you, through his Word, to do something, then you have to do it as soon as he asks you. To demand first some kind of a sign cheapens the Word of God.

In Judges 6 God comes to Gideon several times and tells him what he wants him to do. But Gideon asks God for a sign, a reassurance that what God said to do is really what God wanted him to do. God's words to him weren't enough; he, like a lot of us, wanted a miracle. Because of his fear or doubt, Gideon felt like he needed more. We learn from this story the kindness of God, the mercy that extends to us even in our weak faith.

Most demands for signs come out of fear—the fear of being wrong or the fear of doing whatever God has asked. Fear doesn't come from God; it comes from the Enemy. Satan would love to destroy the life of a believer by convincing him or her that God's Word has to be proven, backed up, and supported with signs to reassure us. But as a God Girl, you should have no question that following the Word of God is the right direction for your life. So don't stall any longer, and don't operate in the same fear that Gideon lived in. If you've been redeemed by God and called by his Word to do something, then get to doing it.

but all the rest of the people knelt down to drink water. [7] And the LORD said to Gideon, "With the 300 men who lapped I will save you and give the Midianites into your hand, and let all the others go every man to his home." [8] So the people took provisions in their hands, and their trumpets. And he sent all the rest of Israel every man to his tent, but retained the 300 men. And the camp of Midian was below him in the valley.

[9] That same night the LORD said to him, "Arise, go down against the camp, for I have given it into your hand. [10] But if you are afraid to go down, go down to the camp with Purah your servant. [11] And you shall hear what they say, and afterward your hands shall be strengthened to go down against the camp." Then he went down with Purah his servant to the outposts of the armed men who were in the camp. [12] And the Midianites and the Amalekites and all the people of the East lay along the valley like locusts in abundance, and their camels were without number, as the sand that is on the seashore in abundance. [13] When Gideon came, behold, a man was telling a dream to his comrade. And he said, "Behold, I dreamed a dream, and behold, a cake of barley bread tumbled into the camp of Midian and came to the tent and struck it so that it fell and turned it upside down, so that the tent lay flat." [14] And his comrade answered, "This is no other than the sword of Gideon the son of Joash, a man of Israel; God has given into his hand Midian and all the camp."

[15] As soon as Gideon heard the telling of the dream and its interpretation, he worshiped. And he returned to the camp of Israel and said, "Arise, for the LORD has given the host of Midian into your hand." [16] And he divided the 300 men into three companies and put trumpets into the hands of all of them and empty jars, with torches inside the jars. [17] And he said to them, "Look at me, and do likewise. When I come to the outskirts of the camp, do as I do. [18] When I blow the trumpet, I and all who are with me, then blow the trumpets also on every side of all the camp and shout, 'For the LORD and for Gideon.'"

Gideon Defeats Midian

[19] So Gideon and the hundred men who were with him came to the outskirts of the camp at the beginning of the middle watch, when they had just set the watch. And they blew the trumpets and smashed the jars that were in their hands. [20] Then the three companies blew the trumpets and broke the jars. They held in their left hands the torches, and in their right hands the trumpets to blow. And they cried out, "A sword for the LORD and for Gideon!" [21] Every man stood in his place around the camp, and all the army ran. They cried out and fled. [22] When they blew the 300 trumpets, the LORD set every man's sword against his comrade and against all the army. And the army fled as far as Beth-shittah toward Zererah,[1] as far as the border of Abel-meholah, by Tabbath. [23] And the men of Israel were called out from Naphtali and from Asher and from all Manasseh, and they pursued after Midian.

[24] Gideon sent messengers throughout all the hill country of Ephraim, saying, "Come down against the Midianites and capture the waters against them, as far as Beth-barah, and also the Jordan." So all the men of Ephraim were called out, and they captured the waters as far as Beth-barah, and also the Jordan. [25] And they captured the two princes of Midian, Oreb and Zeeb. They killed Oreb at the rock of Oreb, and Zeeb they killed at the winepress of Zeeb. Then they pursued Midian, and they brought the heads of Oreb and Zeeb to Gideon across the Jordan.

Gideon Defeats Zebah and Zalmunna

8 Then the men of Ephraim said to him, "What is this that you have done to us, not to call us when you went to fight against Midian?" And they accused him fiercely. [2] And he said to them, "What have I done now in comparison with you? Is not the gleaning of the grapes of Ephraim better than the grape harvest of Abiezer? [3] God has given into your hands the princes of Midian, Oreb and Zeeb. What have I been able to do in comparison with you?" Then their anger against him subsided when he said this.

[4] And Gideon came to the Jordan and crossed over, he and the 300 men who were with him, exhausted yet pursuing. [5] So he said to the men of Succoth, "Please give loaves of bread to the people who follow me, for they are exhausted, and I am pursuing after Zebah and Zalmunna,

[1] Some Hebrew manuscripts *Zeredah* [2] Hebrew *their spirit*

he kings of Midian." ⁶ And the officials f Succoth said, "Are the hands of Zebah nd Zalmunna already in your hand, that ve should give bread to your army?" ⁷ So ideon said, "Well then, when the LORD as given Zebah and Zalmunna into my and, I will flail your flesh with the thorns f the wilderness and with briers." ⁸ And rom there he went up to Penuel, and poke to them in the same way, and the nen of Penuel answered him as the men f Succoth had answered. ⁹ And he said to he men of Penuel, "When I come again in eace, I will break down this tower."

¹⁰ Now Zebah and Zalmunna were in Karkor with their army, about 15,000 nen, all who were left of all the army of he people of the East, for there had fallen 20,000 men who drew the sword. ¹¹ And ideon went up by the way of the tent wellers east of Nobah and Jogbehah and ttacked the army, for the army felt secure. ² And Zebah and Zalmunna fled, and he ursued them and captured the two kings f Midian, Zebah and Zalmunna, and he hrew all the army into a panic.

¹³ Then Gideon the son of Joash returned rom the battle by the ascent of Heres. ⁴ And he captured a young man of Succoth nd questioned him. And he wrote down or him the officials and elders of Succoth, eventy-seven men. ¹⁵ And he came to the nen of Succoth and said, "Behold Zebah nd Zalmunna, about whom you taunted ne, saying, 'Are the hands of Zebah and almunna already in your hand, that we hould give bread to your men who are xhausted?'" ¹⁶ And he took the elders of he city, and he took thorns of the wilder-ess and briers and with them taught the nen of Succoth a lesson. ¹⁷ And he broke lown the tower of Penuel and killed the nen of the city.

¹⁸ Then he said to Zebah and Zalmunna, Where are the men whom you killed at abor?" They answered, "As you are, so vere they. Every one of them resembled he son of a king." ¹⁹ And he said, "They vere my brothers, the sons of my mother. As the LORD lives, if you had saved them live, I would not kill you." ²⁰ So he said to ether his firstborn, "Rise and kill them!" But the young man did not draw his sword, or he was afraid, because he was still a oung man. ²¹ Then Zebah and Zalmunna

said, "Rise yourself and fall upon us, for as the man is, so is his strength." And Gideon arose and killed Zebah and Zalmunna, and he took the crescent ornaments that were on the necks of their camels.

Gideon's Ephod

²² Then the men of Israel said to Gideon, "Rule over us, you and your son and your grandson also, for you have saved us from the hand of Midian." ²³ Gideon said to them, "I will not rule over you, and my son will not rule over you; the LORD will rule over you." ²⁴ And Gideon said to them, "Let me make a request of you: every one of you give me the earrings from his spoil." (For they had golden earrings, because they were Ishmaelites.) ²⁵ And they answered, "We will willingly give them." And they spread a cloak, and every man threw in it the earrings of his spoil. ²⁶ And the weight of the golden earrings that he requested was 1,700 shekels¹ of gold, besides the crescent ornaments and the pendants and the purple garments worn by the kings of Midian, and besides the collars that were around the necks of their camels. ²⁷ And Gideon made an ephod of it and put it in his city, in Ophrah. And all Israel whored after it there, and it became a snare to Gideon and to his family. ²⁸ So Midian was subdued before the people of Israel, and they raised their heads no more. And the land had rest forty years in the days of Gideon.

The Death of Gideon

²⁹ Jerubbaal the son of Joash went and lived in his own house. ³⁰ Now Gideon had seventy sons, his own offspring,² for he had many wives. ³¹ And his concubine who was in Shechem also bore him a son, and he called his name Abimelech. ³² And Gideon the son of Joash died in a good old age and was buried in the tomb of Joash his father, at Ophrah of the Abiezrites.

³³ As soon as Gideon died, the people of Israel turned again and whored after the Baals and made Baal-berith their god. ³⁴ And the people of Israel did not remem-ber the LORD their God, who had delivered them from the hand of all their enemies on every side, ³⁵ and they did not show stead-fast love to the family of Jerubbaal (that is, Gideon) in return for all the good that he had done to Israel.

¹ shekel was about 2/5 ounce or 11 grams ² Hebrew who came from his own loins

Abimelech's Conspiracy

9 Now Abimelech the son of Jerubbaal went to Shechem to his mother's relatives and said to them and to the whole clan of his mother's family, ²"Say in the ears of all the leaders of Shechem, 'Which is better for you, that all seventy of the sons of Jerubbaal rule over you, or that one rule over you?' Remember also that I am your bone and your flesh."

³And his mother's relatives spoke all these words on his behalf in the ears of all the leaders of Shechem, and their hearts inclined to follow Abimelech, for they said, "He is our brother." ⁴And they gave him seventy pieces of silver out of the house of Baal-berith with which Abimelech hired worthless and reckless fellows, who followed him. ⁵And he went to his father's house at Ophrah and killed his brothers the sons of Jerubbaal, seventy men, on one stone. But Jotham the youngest son of Jerubbaal was left, for he hid himself. ⁶And all the leaders of Shechem came together, and all Beth-millo, and they went and made Abimelech king, by the oak of the pillar at Shechem.

⁷When it was told to Jotham, he went and stood on top of Mount Gerizim and cried aloud and said to them, "Listen to me, you leaders of Shechem, that God may listen to you. ⁸The trees once went out to anoint a king over them, and they said to the olive tree, 'Reign over us.' ⁹But the olive tree said to them, 'Shall I leave my abundance, by which gods and men are honored, and go hold sway over the trees?' ¹⁰And the trees said to the fig tree, 'You come and reign over us.' ¹¹But the fig tree said to them, 'Shall I leave my sweetness and my good fruit and go hold sway over the trees?' ¹²And the trees said to the vine, 'You come and reign over us.' ¹³But the vine said to them, 'Shall I leave my wine that cheers God and men and go hold sway over the trees?' ¹⁴Then all the trees said to the bramble, 'You come and reign over us.' ¹⁵And the bramble said to the trees, 'If in good faith you are anointing me king over you, then come and take refuge in my shade, but if not, let fire come out of the bramble and devour the cedars of Lebanon.'

¹⁶"Now therefore, if you acted in good faith and integrity when you made Abimelech king, and if you have dealt well wit[h] Jerubbaal and his house and have done t[o] him as his deeds deserved— ¹⁷for my fathe[r] fought for you and risked his life and deliv[-] ered you from the hand of Midian, ¹⁸and yo[u] have risen up against my father's house thi[s] day and have killed his sons, seventy me[n] on one stone, and have made Abimelec[h] the son of his female servant, king ove[r] the leaders of Shechem, because he is you[r] relative— ¹⁹if you then have acted in goo[d] faith and integrity with Jerubbaal and wit[h] his house this day, then rejoice in Abime[-] lech, and let him also rejoice in you. ²⁰Bu[t] if not, let fire come out from Abimelec[h] and devour the leaders of Shechem an[d] Beth-millo; and let fire come out from th[e] leaders of Shechem and from Beth-mill[o] and devour Abimelech." ²¹And Jotham ra[n] away and fled and went to Beer and live[d] there, because of Abimelech his brother.

The Downfall of Abimelech

²²Abimelech ruled over Israel thre[e] years. ²³And God sent an evil spirit betwee[n] Abimelech and the leaders of Shechem, an[d] the leaders of Shechem dealt treacherousl[y] with Abimelech, ²⁴that the violence done t[o] the seventy sons of Jerubbaal might com[e] and their blood be laid on Abimelech thei[r] brother, who killed them, and on the me[n] of Shechem, who strengthened his hand[s] to kill his brothers. ²⁵And the leaders o[f] Shechem put men in ambush against hi[m] on the mountaintops, and they robbed al[l] who passed by them along that way. An[d] it was told to Abimelech.

²⁶And Gaal the son of Ebed moved int[o] Shechem with his relatives, and the lead[-] ers of Shechem put confidence in hi[m] ²⁷And they went out into the field an[d] gathered the grapes from their vineyard[s] and trod them and held a festival; an[d] they went into the house of their god an[d] ate and drank and reviled Abimelec[h] ²⁸And Gaal the son of Ebed said, "Who i[s] Abimelech, and who are we of Sheche[m] that we should serve him? Is he not th[e] son of Jerubbaal, and is not Zebul his offi[-] cer? Serve the men of Hamor the father o[f] Shechem; but why should we serve him[?] ²⁹Would that this people were under m[y] hand! Then I would remove Abimelec[h] I would say¹ to Abimelech, 'Increase you[r] army, and come out.'"

---

¹Septuagint; Hebrew *and he said*

30 When Zebul the ruler of the city heard the words of Gaal the son of Ebed, his anger was kindled. 31 And he sent messengers to Abimelech secretly,[1] saying, "Behold, Gaal the son of Ebed and his relatives have come to Shechem, and they are stirring up[2] the city against you. 32 Now therefore, go by night, you and the people who are with you, and set an ambush in the field. 33 Then in the morning, as soon as the sun is up, rise early and rush upon the city. And when he and the people who are with him come out against you, you may do to them as your hand finds to do."

34 So Abimelech and all the men who were with him rose up by night and set an ambush against Shechem in four companies. 35 And Gaal the son of Ebed went out and stood in the entrance of the gate of the city, and Abimelech and the people who were with him rose from the ambush. 36 And when Gaal saw the people, he said to Zebul, "Look, people are coming down from the mountaintops!" And Zebul said to him, "You mistake[3] the shadow of the mountains for men." 37 Gaal spoke again and said, "Look, people are coming down from the center of the land, and one company is coming from the direction of the Diviners' Oak." 38 Then Zebul said to him, "Where is your mouth now, you who said, 'Who is Abimelech, that we should serve him?' Are not these the people whom you despised? Go out now and fight with them." 39 And Gaal went out at the head of the leaders of Shechem and fought with Abimelech. 40 And Abimelech chased him, and he fled before him. And many fell wounded, up to the entrance of the gate. 41 And Abimelech lived at Arumah, and Zebul drove out Gaal and his relatives, so that they could not dwell at Shechem.

42 On the following day, the people went out into the field, and Abimelech was told. 43 He took his people and divided them into three companies and set an ambush in the fields. And he looked and saw the people coming out of the city. So he rose against them and killed them. 44 Abimelech and the company that was with him rushed forward and stood at the entrance of the gate of the city, while the two companies rushed upon all who were in the field and killed them. 45 And Abimelech fought against the city all that day. He captured the city and killed the people who were in it, and he razed the city and sowed it with salt.

46 When all the leaders of the Tower of Shechem heard of it, they entered the stronghold of the house of El-berith. 47 Abimelech was told that all the leaders of the Tower of Shechem were gathered together. 48 And Abimelech went up to Mount Zalmon, he and all the people who were with him. And Abimelech took an axe in his hand and cut down a bundle of brushwood and took it up and laid it on his shoulder. And he said to the men who were with him, "What you have seen me do, hurry and do as I have done." 49 So every one of the people cut down his bundle and following Abimelech put it against the stronghold, and they set the stronghold on fire over them, so that all the people of the Tower of Shechem also died, about 1,000 men and women.

50 Then Abimelech went to Thebez and encamped against Thebez and captured it. 51 But there was a strong tower within the city, and all the men and women and all the leaders of the city fled to it and shut themselves in, and they went up to the roof of the tower. 52 And Abimelech came to the tower and fought against it and drew near to the door of the tower to burn it with fire. 53 And a certain woman threw an upper millstone on Abimelech's head and crushed his skull. 54 Then he called quickly to the young man his armor-bearer and said to him, "Draw your sword and kill me, lest they say of me, 'A woman killed him.'" And his young man thrust him through, and he died. 55 And when the men of Israel saw that Abimelech was dead, everyone departed to his home. 56 Thus God returned the evil of Abimelech, which he committed against his father in killing his seventy brothers. 57 And God also made all the evil of the men of Shechem return on their heads, and upon them came the curse of Jotham the son of Jerubbaal.

Tola and Jair

10 After Abimelech there arose to save Israel Tola the son of Puah, son of Dodo, a man of Issachar, and he lived at Shamir in the hill country of Ephraim. 2 And he judged Israel twenty-three years. Then he died and was buried at Shamir.

---

[1] Or at Tormah [2] Hebrew besieging, or closing up [3] Hebrew You see

³After him arose Jair the Gileadite, who judged Israel twenty-two years. ⁴And he had thirty sons who rode on thirty donkeys, and they had thirty cities, called Havvoth-jair to this day, which are in the land of Gilead. ⁵And Jair died and was buried in Kamon.

Further Disobedience and Oppression

⁶The people of Israel again did what was evil in the sight of the LORD and served the Baals and the Ashtaroth, the gods of Syria, the gods of Sidon, the gods of Moab, the gods of the Ammonites, and the gods of the Philistines. And they forsook the LORD and did not serve him. ⁷So the anger of the LORD was kindled against Israel, and he sold them into the hand of the Philistines and into the hand of the Ammonites, ⁸and they crushed and oppressed the people of Israel that year. For eighteen years they oppressed all the people of Israel who were beyond the Jordan in the land of the Amorites, which is in Gilead. ⁹And the Ammonites crossed the Jordan to fight also against Judah and against Benjamin and against the house of Ephraim, so that Israel was severely distressed.

¹⁰And the people of Israel cried out to the LORD, saying, "We have sinned against you, because we have forsaken our God and have served the Baals." ¹¹And the LORD said to the people of Israel, "Did I not save you from the Egyptians and from the Amorites, from the Ammonites and from the Philistines? ¹²The Sidonians also, and the Amalekites and the Maonites oppressed you, and you cried out to me, and I saved you out of their hand. ¹³Yet you have forsaken me and served other gods; therefore I will save you no more. ¹⁴Go and cry out to the gods whom you have chosen; let them save you in the time of your distress." ¹⁵And the people of Israel said to the LORD, "We have sinned; do to us whatever seems good to you. Only please deliver us this day." ¹⁶So they put away the foreign gods from among them and served the LORD, and he became impatient over the misery of Israel.

¹⁷Then the Ammonites were called to arms, and they encamped in Gilead. And the people of Israel came together, and they encamped at Mizpah. ¹⁸And the people, the leaders of Gilead, said one to another, "Who is the man who will begin to fight against the Ammonites? He shall be head over all the inhabitants of Gilead.

Jephthah Delivers Israel

11 Now Jephthah the Gileadite was a mighty warrior, but he was the son of a prostitute. Gilead was the father of Jephthah. ²And Gilead's wife also bore him sons. And when his wife's sons grew up, they drove Jephthah out and said to him, "You shall not have an inheritance in our father's house, for you are the son of another woman." ³Then Jephthah fled from his brothers and lived in the land of Tob, and worthless fellows collected around Jephthah and went out with him.

⁴After a time the Ammonites made war against Israel. ⁵And when the Ammonites made war against Israel, the elders of Gilead went to bring Jephthah from the land of Tob. ⁶And they said to Jephthah, "Come and be our leader, that we may fight against the Ammonites." ⁷But Jephthah said to the elders of Gilead, "Did you not hate me and drive me out of my father's house? Why have you come to me now when you are in distress?" ⁸And the elders of Gilead said to Jephthah, "That is why we have turned to you now, that you may go with us and fight against the Ammonites and be our head over all the inhabitants of Gilead." ⁹Jephthah said to the elders of Gilead, "If you bring me home again to fight against the Ammonites, and the LORD gives them over to me, I will be your head." ¹⁰And the elders of Gilead said to Jephthah, "The LORD will be witness between us, if we do not do as you say." ¹¹So Jephthah went with the elders of Gilead, and the people made him head and leader over them. And Jephthah spoke all his words before the LORD at Mizpah.

¹²Then Jephthah sent messengers to the king of the Ammonites and said, "What do you have against me, that you have come to me to fight against my land?" ¹³And the king of the Ammonites answered the messengers of Jephthah, "Because Israel on coming up from Egypt took away my land from the Arnon to the Jabbok and to the Jordan; now therefore restore it peaceably." ¹⁴Jephthah again sent messengers to the king of the Ammonites ¹⁵and said to him, "Thus says Jephthah: Israel did not take away the land of Moab or the land of the Ammonites, ¹⁶but when they came up from Egypt, Israel went through the

wilderness to the Red Sea and came to Kadesh. [17] Israel then sent messengers to the king of Edom, saying, 'Please let us pass through your land,' but the king of Edom would not listen. And they sent also to the king of Moab, but he would not consent. So Israel remained at Kadesh.

[18] "Then they journeyed through the wilderness and went around the land of Edom and the land of Moab and arrived on the east side of the land of Moab and camped on the other side of the Arnon. But they did not enter the territory of Moab, for the Arnon was the boundary of Moab. [19] Israel then sent messengers to Sihon king of the Amorites, king of Heshbon, and Israel said to him, 'Please let us pass through your land to our country,' [20] but Sihon did not trust Israel to pass through his territory, so Sihon gathered all his people together and encamped at Jahaz and fought with Israel. [21] And the LORD, the God of Israel, gave Sihon and all his people into the hand of Israel, and they defeated them. So Israel took possession of all the land of the Amorites, who inhabited that country. [22] And they took possession of all the territory of the Amorites from the Arnon to the Jabbok and from the wilderness to the Jordan. [23] So then the LORD, the God of Israel, dispossessed the Amorites from before his people Israel; and are you to take possession of them? [24] Will you not possess what Chemosh your god gives you to possess? And all that the LORD our God has dispossessed before us, we will possess. [25] Now are you any better than Balak the son of Zippor, king of Moab? Did he ever contend against Israel, or did he ever go to war with them? [26] While Israel lived in Heshbon and its villages, and in Aroer and its villages, and in all the cities that are on the banks of the Arnon, 300 years, why did you not deliver them within that time? [27] I therefore have not sinned against you, and you do me wrong by making war on me. The LORD, the Judge, decide this day between the people of Israel and the people of Ammon." [28] But the king of the Ammonites did not listen to the words of Jephthah that he sent to him.

Jephthah's Tragic Vow

[29] Then the Spirit of the LORD was upon Jephthah, and he passed through Gilead and Manasseh and passed on to Mizpah of Gilead, and from Mizpah of Gilead he passed on to the Ammonites. [30] And Jephthah made a vow to the LORD and said, "If you will give the Ammonites into my hand, [31] then whatever[1] comes out from the doors of my house to meet me when I return in peace from the Ammonites shall be the LORD's, and I will offer it[2] up for a burnt offering." [32] So Jephthah crossed over to the Ammonites to fight against them, and the LORD gave them into his hand. [33] And he struck them from Aroer to the neighborhood of Minnith, twenty cities, and as far as Abel-keramim, with a great blow. So the Ammonites were subdued before the people of Israel.

[34] Then Jephthah came to his home at Mizpah. And behold, his daughter came out to meet him with tambourines and with dances. She was his only child; besides her he had neither son nor daughter. [35] And as soon as he saw her, he tore his clothes and said, "Alas, my daughter! You have brought me very low, and you have become the cause of great trouble to me. For I have opened my mouth to the LORD, and I cannot take back my vow." [36] And she said to him, "My father, you have opened your mouth to the LORD; do to me according to what has gone out of your mouth, now that the LORD has avenged you on your enemies, on the Ammonites." [37] So she said to her father, "Let this thing be done for me: leave me alone two months, that I may go up and down on the mountains and weep for my virginity, I and my companions." [38] So he said, "Go." Then he sent her away for two months, and she departed, she and her companions, and wept for her virginity on the mountains. [39] And at the end of two months, she returned to her father, who did with her according to his vow that he had made. She had never known a man, and it became a custom in Israel [40] that the daughters of Israel went year by year to lament the daughter of Jephthah the Gileadite four days in the year.

Jephthah's Conflict with Ephraim

12 The men of Ephraim were called to arms, and they crossed to Zaphon and said to Jephthah, "Why did you cross over to fight against the Ammonites and did not call us to go with you? We will burn your house over you with fire." [2] And

[1] Or whoever [2] Or him

Jephthah said to them, "I and my people had a great dispute with the Ammonites, and when I called you, you did not save me from their hand. ³ And when I saw that you would not save me, I took my life in my hand and crossed over against the Ammonites, and the LORD gave them into my hand. Why then have you come up to me this day to fight against me?" ⁴ Then Jephthah gathered all the men of Gilead and fought with Ephraim. And the men of Gilead struck Ephraim, because they said, "You are fugitives of Ephraim, you Gileadites, in the midst of Ephraim and Manasseh." ⁵ And the Gileadites captured the fords of the Jordan against the Ephraimites. And when any of the fugitives of Ephraim said, "Let me go over," the men of Gilead said to him, "Are you an Ephraimite?" When he said, "No," ⁶ they said to him, "Then say Shibboleth," and he said, "Sibboleth," for he could not pronounce it right. Then they seized him and slaughtered him at the fords of the Jordan. At that time 42,000 of the Ephraimites fell.

⁷ Jephthah judged Israel six years. Then Jephthah the Gileadite died and was buried in his city in Gilead.[1]

Ibzan, Elon, and Abdon

⁸ After him Ibzan of Bethlehem judged Israel. ⁹ He had thirty sons, and thirty daughters he gave in marriage outside his clan, and thirty daughters he brought in from outside for his sons. And he judged Israel seven years. ¹⁰ Then Ibzan died and was buried at Bethlehem.

¹¹ After him Elon the Zebulunite judged Israel, and he judged Israel ten years. ¹² Then Elon the Zebulunite died and was buried at Aijalon in the land of Zebulun.

¹³ After him Abdon the son of Hillel the Pirathonite judged Israel. ¹⁴ He had forty sons and thirty grandsons, who rode on seventy donkeys, and he judged Israel eight years. ¹⁵ Then Abdon the son of Hillel the Pirathonite died and was buried at Pirathon in the land of Ephraim, in the hill country of the Amalekites.

The Birth of Samson

13 And the people of Israel again did what was evil in the sight of the LORD, so the LORD gave them into the hand of the Philistines for forty years.

² There was a certain man of Zorah, o the tribe of the Danites, whose name wa Manoah. And his wife was barren and ha no children. ³ And the angel of the LORD appeared to the woman and said to he "Behold, you are barren and have no borne children, but you shall conceiv and bear a son. ⁴ Therefore be careful an drink no wine or strong drink, and ea nothing unclean, ⁵ for behold, you shal conceive and bear a son. No razor shal come upon his head, for the child shall b a Nazirite to God from the womb, and h shall begin to save Israel from the hand o the Philistines." ⁶ Then the woman cam and told her husband, "A man of God cam to me, and his appearance was like th appearance of the angel of God, very awe some. I did not ask him where he was from and he did not tell me his name, ⁷ but h said to me, 'Behold, you shall conceiv and bear a son. So then drink no wine o strong drink, and eat nothing unclean, fo the child shall be a Nazirite to God from th womb to the day of his death.'"

⁸ Then Manoah prayed to the LORD an said, "O Lord, please let the man of Go whom you sent come again to us and teac us what we are to do with the child wh will be born." ⁹ And God listened to th voice of Manoah, and the angel of Go came again to the woman as she sat in th field. But Manoah her husband was no with her. ¹⁰ So the woman ran quickly an told her husband, "Behold, the man wh came to me the other day has appeared t me." ¹¹ And Manoah arose and went afte his wife and came to the man and sai to him, "Are you the man who spoke t this woman?" And he said, "I am." ¹² An Manoah said, "Now when your words com true, what is to be the child's manner o life, and what is his mission?" ¹³ And th angel of the LORD said to Manoah, "Of al that I said to the woman let her be carefu ¹⁴ She may not eat of anything that come from the vine, neither let her drink win or strong drink, or eat any unclean thing All that I commanded her let her observe

¹⁵ Manoah said to the angel of the LORD "Please let us detain you and prepare young goat for you." ¹⁶ And the angel o the LORD said to Manoah, "If you detai me, I will not eat of your food. But if yo prepare a burnt offering, then offer it to th

---

[1] Septuagint; Hebrew *in the cities of Gilead*

ORD." (For Manoah did not know that he as the angel of the LORD.) [17] And Manoah aid to the angel of the LORD, "What is your ame, so that, when your words come true, e may honor you?" [18] And the angel of e LORD said to him, "Why do you ask my ame, seeing it is wonderful?" [19] So Manoah ok the young goat with the grain offering, nd offered it on the rock to the LORD, to e one who works[1] wonders, and Manoah nd his wife were watching. [20] And when e flame went up toward heaven from the tar, the angel of the LORD went up in the ame of the altar. Now Manoah and his ife were watching, and they fell on their ces to the ground.

[21] The angel of the LORD appeared no ore to Manoah and to his wife. Then anoah knew that he was the angel of the ORD. [22] And Manoah said to his wife, "We all surely die, for we have seen God." But his wife said to him, "If the LORD ad meant to kill us, he would not have ccepted a burnt offering and a grain offer-g at our hands, or shown us all these ings, or now announced to us such things s these." [24] And the woman bore a son and lled his name Samson. And the young an grew, and the LORD blessed him. [25] And e Spirit of the LORD began to stir him in ahaneh-dan, between Zorah and Eshtaol.

amson's Marriage

L4 Samson went down to Timnah, and at Timnah he saw one of the aughters of the Philistines. [2] Then he came p and told his father and mother, "I saw he of the daughters of the Philistines at imnah. Now get her for me as my wife." But his father and mother said to him, "Is ere not a woman among the daughters f your relatives, or among all our people, at you must go to take a wife from the ncircumcised Philistines?" But Samson aid to his father, "Get her for me, for she right in my eyes."

[4] His father and mother did not know that was from the LORD, for he was seeking 1 opportunity against the Philistines. At at time the Philistines ruled over Israel. [5] Then Samson went down with his ther and mother to Timnah, and they ame to the vineyards of Timnah. And ehold, a young lion came toward him aring. [6] Then the Spirit of the LORD

rushed upon him, and although he had nothing in his hand, he tore the lion in pieces as one tears a young goat. But he did not tell his father or his mother what he had done. [7] Then he went down and talked with the woman, and she was right in Samson's eyes.

[8] After some days he returned to take her. And he turned aside to see the carcass of the lion, and behold, there was a swarm of bees in the body of the lion, and honey. [9] He scraped it out into his hands and went on, eating as he went. And he came to his father and mother and gave some to them, and they ate. But he did not tell them that he had scraped the honey from the carcass of the lion.

[10] His father went down to the woman, and Samson prepared a feast there, for so the young men used to do. [11] As soon as the people saw him, they brought thirty companions to be with him. [12] And Samson said to them, "Let me now put a riddle to you. If you can tell me what it is, within the seven days of the feast, and find it out, then I will give you thirty linen garments and thirty changes of clothes, [13] but if you can-not tell me what it is, then you shall give me thirty linen garments and thirty changes of clothes." And they said to him, "Put your riddle, that we may hear it." [14] And he said to them,

"Out of the eater came something to eat.
Out of the strong came something sweet."

And in three days they could not solve the riddle.

[15] On the fourth[2] day they said to Samson's wife, "Entice your husband to tell us what the riddle is, lest we burn you and your father's house with fire. Have you invited us here to impoverish us?" [16] And Samson's wife wept over him and said, "You only hate me; you do not love me. You have put a riddle to my people, and you have not told me what it is." And he said to her, "Behold, I have not told my father nor my mother, and shall I tell you?" [17] She wept before him the seven days that their feast lasted, and on the seventh day he told her, because she pressed him hard. Then she told the riddle to her people. [18] And the

eptuagint, Vulgate; Hebrew LORD, and working [2] Septuagint, Syriac; Hebrew seventh men of the city said to him on the seventh day before the sun went down,

> "What is sweeter than honey?
> What is stronger than a lion?"

And he said to them,

> "If you had not plowed with my heifer,
> you would not have found out my
> riddle."

[19] And the Spirit of the LORD rushed upon him, and he went down to Ashkelon and struck down thirty men of the town and took their spoil and gave the garments to those who had told the riddle. In hot anger he went back to his father's house. [20] And Samson's wife was given to his companion, who had been his best man.

Samson Defeats the Philistines

15 After some days, at the time of wheat harvest, Samson went to visit his wife with a young goat. And he said, "I will go in to my wife in the chamber." But her father would not allow him to go in. [2] And her father said, "I really thought that you utterly hated her, so I gave her to your companion. Is not her younger sister more beautiful than she? Please take her instead." [3] And Samson said to them, "This time I shall be innocent in regard to the Philistines, when I do them harm." [4] So Samson went and caught 300 foxes and took torches. And he turned them tail to tail and put a torch between each pair of tails. [5] And when he had set fire to the torches, he let the foxes go into the standing grain of the Philistines and set fire to the stacked grain and the standing grain, as well as the olive orchards. [6] Then the Philistines said, "Who has done this?" And they said, "Samson, the son-in-law of the Timnite, because he has taken his wife and given her to his companion." And the Philistines came up and burned her and her father with fire. [7] And Samson said to them, "If this is what you do, I swear I will be avenged on you, and after that I will quit." [8] And he struck them hip and thigh with a great blow, and he went down and stayed in the cleft of the rock of Etam.

[9] Then the Philistines came up and encamped in Judah and made a raid on Lehi. [10] And the men of Judah said, "Why

have you come up against us?" They said, "We have come up to bind Samson, to do to him as he did to us." [11] Then 3,000 men of Judah went down to the cleft of the rock of Etam, and said to Samson, "Do you not know that the Philistines are rulers over us? What then is this that you have done to us?" And he said to them, "As they did to me, so have I done to them." [12] And they said to him, "We have come down to bind you, that we may give you into the hands of the Philistines." And Samson said to them, "Swear to me that you will not attack me yourselves." [13] They said to him, "No; we will only bind you and give you into their hands. We will surely not kill you." So they bound him with two new ropes and brought him up from the rock.

[14] When he came to Lehi, the Philistines came shouting to meet him. Then the Spirit of the LORD rushed upon him, and the ropes that were on his arms became as flax that has caught fire, and his bonds melted off his hands. [15] And he found a fresh jawbone of a donkey, and put out his hand and took it, and with it he struck 1,000 men. [16] And Samson said,

> "With the jawbone of a donkey,
> heaps upon heaps,
> with the jawbone of a donkey
> have I struck down a thousand
> men."

[17] As soon as he had finished speaking, he threw away the jawbone out of his hand. And that place was called Ramath-lehi.[1]

[18] And he was very thirsty, and he called upon the LORD and said, "You have granted this great salvation by the hand of your servant, and shall I now die of thirst and fall into the hands of the uncircumcised?" [19] And God split open the hollow place that is at Lehi, and water came out from it. And when he drank, his spirit returned, and he revived. Therefore the name of it was called En-hakkore;[2] it is at Lehi to this day. [20] And he judged Israel in the days of the Philistines twenty years.

Samson and Delilah

16 Samson went to Gaza, and there he saw a prostitute, and he went in to her. [2] The Gazites were told, "Samson has come here." And they surrounded the place and set an ambush for him all night

---

[1] *Ramath-lehi* means *the hill of the jawbone* [2] *En-hakkore* means *the spring of him who called*

at the gate of the city. They kept quiet all night, saying, "Let us wait till the light of the morning; then we will kill him." ³But Samson lay till midnight, and at midnight he arose and took hold of the doors of the gate of the city and the two posts, and pulled them up, bar and all, and put them on his shoulders and carried them to the top of the hill that is in front of Hebron.

Ask Yourself . . .

ABOUT YOUR WEAKNESSES

Weaknesses. We all have them—those things that just seem to beat us every time. It's dangerous to be faced with the thing that is so hard for us to resist, so even the temptation should be avoided. Like an alcoholic who stays away from bars, so must you avoid those things that weaken your defenses against sin. Samson was weak in love; he gave in to Delilah in order to keep her, but she used his weakness against him. Have you ever been fooled in love? Ask yourself about your weakness and how to protect yourself in that area:

- Where is my faith weak?
- What do I need to avoid in order to stay strong?
- Do I have people in my life who want to lead me into temptation?
- How can I avoid sharing my weaknesses with the wrong people?

---

⁴After this he loved a woman in the Valley of Sorek, whose name was Delilah. ⁵And the lords of the Philistines came up to her and said to her, "Seduce him, and see where his great strength lies, and by what means we may overpower him, that we may bind him to humble him. And we will each give you 1,100 pieces of silver."

⁶So Delilah said to Samson, "Please tell me where your great strength lies, and how you might be bound, that one could subdue you."

⁷Samson said to her, "If they bind me with seven fresh bowstrings that have not been dried, then I shall become weak and be like any other man." ⁸Then the lords of the Philistines brought up to her seven fresh bowstrings that had not been dried, and she bound him with them. ⁹Now she had men lying in ambush in an inner chamber. And she said to him, "The Philistines are upon you, Samson!" But he snapped the bowstrings, as a thread of flax snaps when it touches the fire. So the secret of his strength was not known.

¹⁰Then Delilah said to Samson, "Behold, you have mocked me and told me lies. Please tell me how you might be bound." ¹¹And he said to her, "If they bind me with new ropes that have not been used, then I shall become weak and be like any other man." ¹²So Delilah took new ropes and bound him with them and said to him, "The Philistines are upon you, Samson!" And the men lying in ambush were in an inner chamber. But he snapped the ropes off his arms like a thread.

¹³Then Delilah said to Samson, "Until now you have mocked me and told me lies. Tell me how you might be bound." And he said to her, "If you weave the seven locks of my head with the web and fasten it tight with the pin, then I shall become weak and be like any other man." ¹⁴So while he slept, Delilah took the seven locks of his head and wove them into the web.[1] And she made them tight with the pin and said to him, "The Philistines are upon you, Samson!" But he awoke from his sleep and pulled away the pin, the loom, and the web.

¹⁵And she said to him, "How can you say, 'I love you,' when your heart is not with me? You have mocked me these three times, and you have not told me where your great strength lies." ¹⁶And when she pressed him hard with her words day after day, and urged him, his soul was vexed to death. ¹⁷And he told her all his heart, and said to her, "A razor has never come upon my head, for I have been a Nazirite to God from my mother's womb. If my head is shaved, then my strength will leave me,

---

¹ Compare Septuagint; Hebrew lacks *and fasten it tight . . . into the web*

and I shall become weak and be like any other man." ¹⁸When Delilah saw that he had told her all his heart, she sent and called the lords of the Philistines, saying, "Come up again, for he has told me all his heart." Then the lords of the Philistines came up to her and brought the money in their hands. ¹⁹She made him sleep on her knees. And she called a man and had him shave off the seven locks of his head. Then she began to torment him, and his strength left him. ²⁰And she said, "The Philistines are upon you, Samson!" And he awoke from his sleep and said, "I will go out as at other times and shake myself free." But he did not know that the LORD had left him. ²¹And the Philistines seized him and gouged out his eyes and brought him down to Gaza and bound him with bronze shackles. And he ground at the mill in the prison. ²²But the hair of his head began to grow again after it had been shaved.

The Death of Samson

²³Now the lords of the Philistines gathered to offer a great sacrifice to Dagon their god and to rejoice, and they said, "Our god has given Samson our enemy into our hand." ²⁴And when the people saw him, they praised their god. For they said, "Our god has given our enemy into our hand, the ravager of our country, who has killed many of us."[1] ²⁵And when their hearts were merry, they said, "Call Samson, that he may entertain us." So they called Samson out of the prison, and he entertained them. They made him stand between the pillars. ²⁶And Samson said to the young man who held him by the hand, "Let me feel the pillars on which the house rests, that I may lean against them." ²⁷Now the house was full of men and women. All the lords of the Philistines were there, and on the roof there were about 3,000 men and women, who looked on while Samson entertained. ²⁸Then Samson called to the LORD and said, "O Lord GOD, please remember me and please strengthen me only this once, O God, that I may be avenged on the Philistines for my two eyes." ²⁹And Samson grasped the two middle pillars on which the house rested, and he leaned his weight against them, his right hand on the one and his left hand on the other. ³⁰And Samson

said, "Let me die with the Philistines." Then he bowed with all his strength, and the house fell upon the lords and upon all the people who were in it. So the dead whom he killed at his death were more than those whom he had killed during his life. ³¹Then his brothers and all his family came down and took him and brought him up and buried him between Zorah and Eshtaol in the tomb of Manoah his father. He had judged Israel twenty years.

Micah and the Levite

17 There was a man of the hill country of Ephraim, whose name was Micah. ²And he said to his mother, "The 1,100 pieces of silver that were taken from you, about which you uttered a curse, and also spoke it in my ears, behold, the silver is with me; I took it." And his mother said, "Blessed be my son by the LORD." ³And he restored the 1,100 pieces of silver to his mother. And his mother said, "I dedicate the silver to the LORD from my hand for my son, to make a carved image and a metal image. Now therefore I will restore it to you." ⁴So when he restored the money to his mother, his mother took 200 pieces of silver and gave it to the silversmith, who made it into a carved image and a metal image. And it was in the house of Micah. ⁵And the man Micah had a shrine, and he made an ephod and household gods, and ordained[2] one of his sons, who became his priest. ⁶In those days there was no king in Israel. Everyone did what was right in his own eyes.

⁷Now there was a young man of Bethlehem in Judah, of the family of Judah, who was a Levite, and he sojourned there. ⁸And the man departed from the town of Bethlehem in Judah to sojourn where he could find a place. And as he journeyed, he came to the hill country of Ephraim to the house of Micah. ⁹And Micah said to him, "Where do you come from?" And he said to him, "I am a Levite of Bethlehem in Judah, and I am going to sojourn where I may find a place." ¹⁰And Micah said to him, "Stay with me, and be to me a father and a priest, and I will give you ten pieces of silver a year and a suit of clothes and your living." And the Levite went in. ¹¹And the Levite was content to dwell with the man, and the young man became to him like one of his

[1] Or who has multiplied our slain [2] Hebrew filled the hand of; also verse 12

ons. ¹²And Micah ordained the Levite, and the young man became his priest, and was in the house of Micah. ¹³Then Micah said, "Now I know that the LORD will prosper me, because I have a Levite as priest."

Danites Take the Levite and the Idol

18 In those days there was no king in Israel. And in those days the tribe of the people of Dan was seeking for itself an inheritance to dwell in, for until then no inheritance among the tribes of Israel had fallen to them. ²So the people of Dan sent five able men from the whole number of their tribe, from Zorah and from Eshtaol, to spy out the land and to explore it. And they said to them, "Go and explore the land." And they came to the hill country of Ephraim, to the house of Micah, and lodged there. ³When they were by the house of Micah, they recognized the voice of the young Levite. And they turned aside and said to him, "Who brought you here? What are you doing in this place? What is your business here?" ⁴And he said to them, "This is how Micah dealt with me: he has hired me, and I have become his priest." ⁵And they said to him, "Inquire of God, please, that we may know whether the journey on which we are setting out will succeed." ⁶And the priest said to them, "Go in peace. The journey on which you go is under the eye of the LORD."

⁷Then the five men departed and came to Laish and saw the people who were there, how they lived in security, after the manner of the Sidonians, quiet and unsuspecting, lacking¹ nothing that is in the earth and possessing wealth, and how they were far from the Sidonians and had no dealings with anyone. ⁸And when they came to their brothers at Zorah and Eshtaol, their brothers said to them, "What do you report?" ⁹They said, "Arise, and let us go up against them, for we have seen the land, and behold, it is very good. And will you do nothing? Do not be slow to go, to enter in and possess the land. ¹⁰As soon as you go, you will come to an unsuspecting people. The land is spacious, for God has given it into your hands, a place where there is no lack of anything that is in the earth."

¹¹So 600 men of the tribe of Dan, armed with weapons of war, set out from Zorah and Eshtaol, ¹²and went up and encamped at Kiriath-jearim in Judah. On this account that place is called Mahaneh-dan² to this day; behold, it is west of Kiriath-jearim. ¹³And they passed on from there to the hill country of Ephraim, and came to the house of Micah.

¹⁴Then the five men who had gone to scout out the country of Laish said to their brothers, "Do you know that in these houses there are an ephod, household gods, a carved image, and a metal image? Now therefore consider what you will do." ¹⁵And they turned aside there and came to the house of the young Levite, at the home of Micah, and asked him about his welfare. ¹⁶Now the 600 men of the Danites, armed with their weapons of war, stood by the entrance of the gate. ¹⁷And the five men who had gone to scout out the land went up and entered and took the carved image, the ephod, the household gods, and the metal image, while the priest stood by the entrance of the gate with the 600 men armed with weapons of war. ¹⁸And when these went into Micah's house and took the carved image, the ephod, the household gods, and the metal image, the priest said to them, "What are you doing?" ¹⁹And they said to him, "Keep quiet; put your hand on your mouth and come with us and be to us a father and a priest. Is it better for you to be priest to the house of one man, or to be priest to a tribe and clan in Israel?" ²⁰And the priest's heart was glad. He took the ephod and the household gods and the carved image and went along with the people.

²¹So they turned and departed, putting the little ones and the livestock and the goods in front of them. ²²When they had gone a distance from the home of Micah, the men who were in the houses near Micah's house were called out, and they overtook the people of Dan. ²³And they shouted to the people of Dan, who turned around and said to Micah, "What is the matter with you, that you come with such a company?" ²⁴And he said, "You take my gods that I made and the priest, and go away, and what have I left? How then do you ask me, 'What is the matter with you?'" ²⁵And the people of Dan said to him, "Do not let your voice be heard among us, lest angry fellows fall upon you, and you lose your life with the lives of your household."

---

¹Compare 18:10; the meaning of the Hebrew word is uncertain ²*Mahaneh-dan* means *camp of Dan*

26 Then the people of Dan went their way. And when Micah saw that they were too strong for him, he turned and went back to his home. 27 But the people of Dan took what Micah had made, and the priest who belonged to him, and they came to Laish, to a people quiet and unsuspecting, and struck them with the edge of the sword and burned the city with fire. 28 And there was no deliverer because it was far from Sidon, and they had no dealings with anyone. It was in the valley that belongs to Beth-rehob. Then they rebuilt the city and lived in it. 29 And they named the city Dan, after the name of Dan their ancestor, who was born to Israel; but the name of the city was Laish at the first. 30 And the people of Dan set up the carved image for themselves, and Jonathan the son of Gershom, son of Moses,[1] and his sons were priests to the tribe of the Danites until the day of the captivity of the land. 31 So they set up Micah's carved image that he made, as long as the house of God was at Shiloh.

A Levite and His Concubine

19 In those days, when there was no king in Israel, a certain Levite was sojourning in the remote parts of the hill country of Ephraim, who took to himself a concubine from Bethlehem in Judah. 2 And his concubine was unfaithful to[2] him, and she went away from him to her father's house at Bethlehem in Judah, and was there some four months. 3 Then her husband arose and went after her, to speak kindly to her and bring her back. He had with him his servant and a couple of donkeys. And she brought him into her father's house. And when the girl's father saw him, he came with joy to meet him. 4 And his father-in-law, the girl's father, made him stay, and he remained with him three days. So they ate and drank and spent the night there. 5 And on the fourth day they arose early in the morning, and he prepared to go, but the girl's father said to his son-in-law, "Strengthen your heart with a morsel of bread, and after that you may go." 6 So the two of them sat and ate and drank together. And the girl's father said to the man, "Be pleased to spend the night, and let your heart be merry." 7 And when the man rose up to go, his father-in-law pressed him,

till he spent the night there again. 8 And on the fifth day he arose early in the morning to depart. And the girl's father said, "Strengthen your heart and wait until the day declines." So they ate, both of them. 9 And when the man and his concubine and his servant rose up to depart, his father-in-law, the girl's father, said to him, "Behold, now the day has waned toward evening. Please, spend the night. Behold, the day draws to its close. Lodge here and let your heart be merry, and tomorrow you shall arise early in the morning for your journey, and go home." 10 But the man would not spend the night. He rose up and departed and arrived opposite Jebus (that is, Jerusalem). He had with him a couple of saddled donkeys, and his concubine was with him. 11 When they were near Jebus, the day was nearly over, and the servant said to his master, "Come now, let us turn aside to this city of the Jebusites and spend the night in it." 12 And his master said to him, "We will not turn aside into the city of foreigners, who do not belong to the people of Israel, but we will pass on to Gibeah." 13 And he said to his young man, "Come and let us draw near to one of these places and spend the night at Gibeah or at Ramah." 14 So they passed on and went their way. And the sun went down on them near Gibeah, which belongs to Benjamin, 15 and they turned aside there to go in and spend the night at Gibeah. And he went in and sat down in the open square of the city, for no one took them into his house to spend the night.

16 And behold, an old man was coming from his work in the field at evening. The man was from the hill country of Ephraim, and he was sojourning in Gibeah. The men of the place were Benjaminites. 17 And he lifted up his eyes and saw the traveler in the open square of the city. And the old man said, "Where are you going? And where do you come from?" 18 And he said to him, "We are passing from Bethlehem in Judah to the remote parts of the hill country of Ephraim, from which I come. I went to Bethlehem in Judah, and I am going to the house of the Lord,[3] but no one has taken me into his house. 19 We have straw and feed for our donkeys, with bread and wine for me and your female servant and the young man with your servants

---

[1] Or Manasseh [2] Septuagint, Old Latin *became angry with* [3] Septuagint *my home*; compare verse 29

there is no lack of anything." **20** And the old man said, "Peace be to you; I will care for all your wants. Only, do not spend the night in the square." **21** So he brought him into his house and gave the donkeys feed. And they washed their feet, and ate and drank.

Gibeah's Crime

22 As they were making their hearts merry, behold, the men of the city, worthless fellows, surrounded the house, beating on the door. And they said to the old man, the master of the house, "Bring out the man who came into your house, that we may know him." **23** And the man, the master of the house, went out to them and said to them, "No, my brothers, do not act so wickedly; since this man has come into my house, do not do this vile thing. **24** Behold, here are my virgin daughter and his concubine. Let me bring them out now. Violate them and do with them what seems good to you, but against this man do not do this outrageous thing." **25** But the men would not listen to him. So the man seized his concubine and made her go out to them. And they knew her and abused her all night until the morning. And as the dawn began to break, they let her go. **26** And as morning appeared, the woman came and fell down at the door of the man's house where her master was, until it was light.

27 And her master rose up in the morning, and when he opened the doors of the house and went out to go on his way, behold, there was his concubine lying at the door of the house, with her hands on the threshold. **28** He said to her, "Get up, let us be going." But there was no answer. Then he put her on the donkey, and the man rose up and went away to his home. **29** And when he entered his house, he took a knife, and taking hold of his concubine he divided her, limb by limb, into twelve pieces, and sent her throughout all the territory of Israel. **30** And all who saw it said, "Such a thing has never happened or been seen from the day that the people of Israel came up out of the land of Egypt until this day; consider it, take counsel, and speak."

Israel's War with the Tribe of Benjamin

20 Then all the people of Israel came out, from Dan to Beersheba, including the land of Gilead, and the congregation assembled as one man to the Lord at Mizpah. **2** And the chiefs of all the people, of all the tribes of Israel, presented themselves in the assembly of the people of God, 400,000 men on foot that drew the sword. **3** (Now the people of Benjamin heard that the people of Israel had gone up to Mizpah.) And the people of Israel said, "Tell us, how did this evil happen?" **4** And the Levite, the husband of the woman who was murdered, answered and said, "I came to Gibeah that belongs to Benjamin, I and my concubine, to spend the night. **5** And the leaders of Gibeah rose against me and surrounded the house against me by night. They meant to kill me, and they violated my concubine, and she is dead. **6** So I took hold of my concubine and cut her in pieces and sent her throughout all the country of the inheritance of Israel, for they have committed abomination and outrage in Israel. **7** Behold, you people of Israel, all of you, give your advice and counsel here."

8 And all the people arose as one man, saying, "None of us will go to his tent, and none of us will return to his house. **9** But now this is what we will do to Gibeah: we will go up against it by lot, **10** and we will take ten men of a hundred throughout all the tribes of Israel, and a hundred of a thousand, and a thousand of ten thousand, to bring provisions for the people, that when they come they may repay Gibeah of Benjamin, for all the outrage that they have committed in Israel." **11** So all the men of Israel gathered against the city, united as one man.

12 And the tribes of Israel sent men through all the tribe of Benjamin, saying, "What evil is this that has taken place among you? **13** Now therefore give up the men, the worthless fellows in Gibeah, that we may put them to death and purge evil from Israel." But the Benjaminites would not listen to the voice of their brothers, the people of Israel. **14** Then the people of Benjamin came together out of the cities to Gibeah to go out to battle against the people of Israel. **15** And the people of Benjamin mustered out of their cities on that day 26,000 men who drew the sword, besides the inhabitants of Gibeah, who mustered 700 chosen men. **16** Among all these were 700 chosen men who were left-handed; every one could sling a stone at a hair and not miss. **17** And the men of Israel, apart from Benjamin, mustered 400,000 men who drew the sword; all these were men of war.

18 The people of Israel arose and went up to Bethel and inquired of God, "Who shall go up first for us to fight against the people of Benjamin?" And the Lord said, "Judah shall go up first."

19 Then the people of Israel rose in the morning and encamped against Gibeah. **20** And the men of Israel went out to fight against Benjamin, and the men of Israel drew up the battle line against them at Gibeah. **21** The people of Benjamin came out of Gibeah and destroyed on that day 22,000 men of the Israelites. **22** But the people, the men of Israel, took courage, and again formed the battle line in the same place where they had formed it on the first day. **23** And the people of Israel went up and wept before the Lord until the evening. And they inquired of the Lord, "Shall we again draw near to fight against our brothers, the people of Benjamin?" And the Lord said, "Go up against them."

24 So the people of Israel came near against the people of Benjamin the second day. **25** And Benjamin went against them out of Gibeah the second day, and destroyed 18,000 men of the people of Israel. All these were men who drew the sword. **26** Then all the people of Israel, the whole army, went up and came to Bethel and wept. They sat there before the Lord and fasted that day until evening, and offered burnt offerings and peace offerings before the Lord. **27** And the people of Israel inquired of the Lord (for the ark of the covenant of God was there in those days, **28** and Phinehas the son of Eleazar, son of Aaron, ministered before it in those days), saying, "Shall we go out once more to battle against our brothers, the people of Benjamin, or shall we cease?" And the Lord said, "Go up, for tomorrow I will give them into your hand."

29 So Israel set men in ambush around Gibeah. **30** And the people of Israel went up against the people of Benjamin on the third day and set themselves in array against Gibeah, as at other times. **31** And the people of Benjamin went out against the people and were drawn away from the city. And as at other times they began to strike and kill some of the people in the highways, one of which goes up to Bethel and the other

to Gibeah, and in the open country, abou thirty men of Israel. **32** And the people c Benjamin said, "They are routed befor us, as at the first." But the people of Israe said, "Let us flee and draw them away fron the city to the highways." **33** And all the mer of Israel rose up out of their place and se themselves in array at Baal-tamar, and th men of Israel who were in ambush rushec out of their place from Maareh-geba.[1] **34** An there came against Gibeah 10,000 choser men out of all Israel, and the battle wa hard, but the Benjaminites did not knov that disaster was close upon them. **35** An the Lord defeated Benjamin before Israe and the people of Israel destroyed 25,10 men of Benjamin that day. All these wer men who drew the sword. **36** So the peopl of Benjamin saw that they were defeated

The men of Israel gave ground t Benjamin, because they trusted the mer in ambush whom they had set agains Gibeah. **37** Then the men in ambush hur ried and rushed against Gibeah; the mer in ambush moved out and struck all th city with the edge of the sword. **38** Now th appointed signal between the men of Israe and the men in the main ambush was tha when they made a great cloud of smok rise up out of the city **39** the men of Israe should turn in battle. Now Benjamin hac begun to strike and kill about thirty men o Israel. They said, "Surely they are defeatec before us, as in the first battle." **40** But wher the signal began to rise out of the city in column of smoke, the Benjaminites looke behind them, and behold, the whole of th city went up in smoke to heaven. **41** The the men of Israel turned, and the men o Benjamin were dismayed, for they saw tha disaster was close upon them. **42** Therefor they turned their backs before the men o Israel in the direction of the wilderness but the battle overtook them. And those who came out of the cities were destroy ing them in their midst. **43** Surrounding th Benjaminites, they pursued them and trod them down from Nohah[2] as far as opposite Gibeah on the east. **44** Eighteen thousanc men of Benjamin fell, all of them men o valor. **45** And they turned and fled towarc the wilderness to the rock of Rimmon. Five thousand men of them were cut down ir the highways. And they were pursued harc to Gidom, and 2,000 men of them were

---

[1] Some Septuagint manuscripts *place west of Geba*   [2] Septuagint; Hebrew [at their] *resting place*

struck down. ⁴⁶So all who fell that day of Benjamin were 25,000 men who drew the sword, all of them men of valor. ⁴⁷But 600 men turned and fled toward the wilderness to the rock of Rimmon and remained at the rock of Rimmon four months. ⁴⁸And the men of Israel turned back against the people of Benjamin and struck them with the edge of the sword, the city, men and beasts and all that they found. And all the towns that they found they set on fire.

Wives Provided for the Tribe of Benjamin

21 Now the men of Israel had sworn at Mizpah, "No one of us shall give his daughter in marriage to Benjamin." ²And the people came to Bethel and sat there till evening before God, and they lifted up their voices and wept bitterly. ³And they said, "O LORD, the God of Israel, why has this happened in Israel, that today there should be one tribe lacking in Israel?" ⁴And the next day the people rose early and built there an altar and offered burnt offerings and peace offerings. ⁵And the people of Israel said, "Which of all the tribes of Israel did not come up in the assembly to the LORD?" For they had taken a great oath concerning him who did not come up to the LORD to Mizpah, saying, "He shall surely be put to death." ⁶And the people of Israel had compassion for Benjamin their brother and said, "One tribe is cut off from Israel this day. ⁷What shall we do for wives for those who are left, since we have sworn by the LORD that we will not give them any of our daughters for wives?"

⁸And they said, "What one is there of the tribes of Israel that did not come up to the LORD to Mizpah?" And behold, no one had come to the camp from Jabesh-gilead, to the assembly. ⁹For when the people were mustered, behold, not one of the inhabitants of Jabesh-gilead was there. ¹⁰So the congregation sent 12,000 of their bravest men there and commanded them, "Go and strike the inhabitants of Jabesh-gilead with the edge of the sword; also the women and the little ones. ¹¹This is what you shall do: every male and every woman that has lain with a male you shall devote to destruction." ¹²And they found among the inhabitants of Jabesh-gilead 400 young virgins who had not known a man by lying with him, and they brought them to the camp at Shiloh, which is in the land of Canaan.

¹³Then the whole congregation sent word to the people of Benjamin who were at the rock of Rimmon and proclaimed peace to them. ¹⁴And Benjamin returned at that time. And they gave them the women whom they had saved alive of the women of Jabesh-gilead, but they were not enough for them. ¹⁵And the people had compassion on Benjamin because the LORD had made a breach in the tribes of Israel.

¹⁶Then the elders of the congregation said, "What shall we do for wives for those who are left, since the women are destroyed out of Benjamin?" ¹⁷And they said, "There must be an inheritance for the survivors of Benjamin, that a tribe not be blotted out from Israel. ¹⁸Yet we cannot give them wives from our daughters." For the people of Israel had sworn, "Cursed be he who gives a wife to Benjamin." ¹⁹So they said, "Behold, there is the yearly feast of the LORD at Shiloh, which is north of Bethel, on the east of the highway that goes up from Bethel to Shechem, and south of Lebonah." ²⁰And they commanded the people of Benjamin, saying, "Go and lie in ambush in the vineyards ²¹and watch. If the daughters of Shiloh come out to dance in the dances, then come out of the vineyards and snatch each man his wife from the daughters of Shiloh, and go to the land of Benjamin. ²²And when their fathers or their brothers come to complain to us, we will say to them, 'Grant them graciously to us, because we did not take for each man of them his wife in battle, neither did you give them to them, else you would now be guilty.'" ²³And the people of Benjamin did so and took their wives, according to their number, from the dancers whom they carried off. Then they went and returned to their inheritance and rebuilt the towns and lived in them. ²⁴And the people of Israel departed from there at that time, every man to his tribe and family, and they went out from there every man to his inheritance.

²⁵In those days there was no king in Israel. Everyone did what was right in his own eyes.

INTRODUCTION TO

Ruth

Author: Unknown
Time: Unknown
Place: Unknown
Written to: God's people

The gist

This book is about the life of Ruth, who lost her husband and then chose to follow her mother-in-law, which meant leaving her homeland and also choosing to follow the God whom her mother-in-law believe in. It is also the story of Boaz, who was the kinsman redeemer for Naomi and Ruth. A kinsman redeemer in ancient Israel was a close relative who was responsible for taking care of women who had no other male protectors. So Ruth is a story of redemption, echoing God's love for not only his people but anyone who would call on him.

Things to look for

The story of Boaz, the kinsman redeemer (see Ruth 2)

How God brings Ruth and Boaz together (see Ruth 3:1–4:12)

Fear Not

> "Where you go I will go, and where you lodge I will lodge. Your people shall be my people, and your God my God."
>
> *Ruth 1:16*

No matter how bad things get, you can be sure that what God wants to happen will happen. A lot of times God gets his people to do what they need to do by letting them suffer. Naomi moved to Moab because her family suffered from a famine, and famine was also the reason Jacob and his sons went to Egypt. Even though things seemed to be the worst they could be, it turned out to be all part of God's plan.

In the midst of trials you never know what good is going to come, but if you only concentrate on the bad parts of life, then bad is all you're going to see. When you can see your trials and suffering as just a crucial step to where you were meant to go, then nothing can get in your way. So instead of focusing on being free of depression, worry, or loneliness, focus on being full of Christ. Fill yourself with love, joy, service, and sacrifice. Fill yourself with God. A humbling example is when believers are imprisoned and beaten for their faith. They can't be "free" of many depressing and oppressive things, far worse than many of the trials we may face. So how do they get through it all? They fill themselves with the promises of God. They sing and pray with joy and with thankfulness that they are loved by the God of the universe. They're faithful to God and his Word.

If you allow your trials to seem bigger than God, they always grow into something bigger than you can handle on your own. But Scripture promises that God is not a distant observer but an active participant. He has plans for the lives of his kids, like he had for Ruth, and all you need to do is trust him, even when life is painful and you cannot understand what he is doing with your life.

Ruth was not from the family of faith. She didn't know Naomi's God, but she chose to trust him and to commit to following Naomi to her homeland. Even though Ruth didn't know what would happen to her, she was not going to give up her devotion to her mother-in-law, her people, and her God. Through the fearless faithfulness of Ruth, God would bring David and then Jesus himself from her lineage. And because of that, you are reading about her today.

Though fear and doubt may surround you at times, and all seems to be lost, take heart, God Girl—God is in control, and he allows suffering for a purpose. And if you are only willing to trust him, you will one day see that purpose. Just cling to the truth and refuse the sins of worry and fear, and you will be set free to soar.

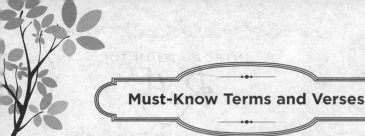

❧ *Moabite* ❧

A descendant from the tribe of Moab, who was a son of Lot and his daughter (see Gen. 19:36–37). The Moabites and the Israelites didn't always get along and often fought one another.

But Ruth said, "Do not urge me to leave you or to return from following you. For where you go I will go, and where you lodge I will lodge. Your people shall be my people, and your God my God." *Ruth 1:16*

"Wash therefore and anoint yourself, and put on your cloak and go down to the threshing floor, but do not make yourself known to the man until he has finished eating and drinking." *Ruth 3:3*

And he said, "May you be blessed by the LORD, my daughter. You have made this last kindness greater than the first in that you have not gone after young men, whether poor or rich." *Ruth 3:10*

Ruth

Naomi Widowed

1 In the days when the judges ruled there was a famine in the land, and a man of Bethlehem in Judah went to sojourn in the country of Moab, he and his wife and his two sons. **2** The name of the man was Elimelech and the name of his wife Naomi, and the names of his two sons were Mahlon and Chilion. They were Ephrathites from Bethlehem in Judah. They went into the country of Moab and remained there. **3** But Elimelech, the husband of Naomi, died, and she was left with her two sons. **4** These took Moabite wives; the name of the one was Orpah and the name of the other Ruth. They lived there about ten years, **5** and both Mahlon and Chilion died, so that the woman was left without her two sons and her husband.

Ruth's Loyalty to Naomi

6 Then she arose with her daughters-in-law to return from the country of Moab, for she had heard in the fields of Moab that the Lord had visited his people and given them food. **7** So she set out from the place where she was with her two daughters-in-law, and they went on the way to return to the land of Judah. **8** But Naomi said to her two daughters-in-law, "Go, return each of you to her mother's house. May the Lord deal kindly with you, as you have dealt with the dead and with me. **9** The Lord grant that you may find rest, each of you in the house of her husband!" Then she kissed them, and they lifted up their voices and wept. **10** And they said to her, "No, we will return with you to your people." **11** But Naomi said, "Turn back, my daughters; why will you go with me? Have I yet sons in my womb that they may become your husbands? **12** Turn back, my daughters; go your way, for I am too old to have a husband. If I should say I have hope, even if I should have a husband this night and should bear sons, **13** would you therefore wait till they were grown? Would you therefore refrain from marrying? No, my daughters, for it is exceedingly bitter to me for your sake that the hand of the Lord has gone out against me." **14** Then they lifted up their voices and wept again. And Orpah kissed her mother-in-law, but Ruth clung to her.

15 And she said, "See, your sister-in-law has gone back to her people and to her gods; return after your sister-in-law." **16** But Ruth said, "Do not urge me to leave you or to return from following you. For where you go I will go, and where you lodge I will lodge. Your people shall be my people, and your God my God. **17** Where you die I will die, and there will I be buried. May the Lord do so to me and more also if anything but death parts me from you." **18** And when Naomi saw that she was determined to go with her, she said no more.

Naomi and Ruth Return

19 So the two of them went on until they came to Bethlehem. And when they came to Bethlehem, the whole town was stirred because of them. And the women said, "Is this Naomi?" **20** She said to them, "Do not call me Naomi;[1] call me Mara,[2] for the Almighty has dealt very bitterly with me. **21** I went away full, and the Lord has brought me back empty. Why call me Naomi, when the Lord has testified against me and the Almighty has brought calamity upon me?"

22 So Naomi returned, and Ruth the Moabite her daughter-in-law with her, who returned from the country of Moab. And they came to Bethlehem at the beginning of barley harvest.

Ruth Meets Boaz

2 Now Naomi had a relative of her husband's, a worthy man of the clan of Elimelech, whose name was Boaz. **2** And

---

[1] *Naomi* means *pleasant* [2] *Mara* means *bitter*

Ruth

Read about her in the book of Ruth and
Matthew 1:5.

> We know that for those who love God all things work together for
> good, for those who are called according to his purpose.
>
> *Romans 8:28*

When life looks like it's over, when the one you love is gone and you have
nowhere to go, what do you do? Curl up and die? Or get up and get going?
For Ruth the answer was obvious: she would get up and get going. Her destiny
was tied to her husband's mother, and no matter how hard it would be, she
would not walk away. So instead of staying home to be with her family, where
things were familiar and safe, she decided to leave Moab with Naomi. This
trip would have been scary. How would they survive? What would they do?
But Ruth accepted Naomi and her God as her own and didn't look back. This
confidence in a God she barely knew and her willingness to do whatever her
mother-in-law asked her to do gave Ruth a brand-new life.

When all looks lost, when your dreams have been destroyed and you
wonder what to do next, your eyes are probably going to be on what you've
lost, but the only way to move forward is to trust in the God who will never
let you down. You are going to face times in your life when doing the right
thing seems like a waste of time, and following God rather than following your
feelings seems impossible. But in these times you have the privilege of casting
all your hopes on God, who cares more deeply for you than you know. Ruth is
a good example of a girl who fearlessly did what she had to do even though
she didn't know what would happen next. Now her name is written for all to
remember as being an ancestor of Jesse and King David, which is the lineage
of Christ himself (see Matt. 1:5). You never know what your pain will give way
to, but you can know that God will watch over you with wonderful tenderness
when you put your faith in the God who never fails.

uth the Moabite said to Naomi, "Let me o to the field and glean among the ears f grain after him in whose sight I shall nd favor." And she said to her, "Go, my aughter." ³So she set out and went and leaned in the field after the reapers, and he happened to come to the part of the eld belonging to Boaz, who was of the lan of Elimelech. ⁴And behold, Boaz came om Bethlehem. And he said to the reap-rs, "The LORD be with you!" And they nswered, "The LORD bless you." ⁵Then oaz said to his young man who was in harge of the reapers, "Whose young voman is this?" ⁶And the servant who was n charge of the reapers answered, "She is he young Moabite woman, who came back vith Naomi from the country of Moab. ⁷She aid, 'Please let me glean and gather among he sheaves after the reapers.' So she came, nd she has continued from early morning ntil now, except for a short rest."¹

⁸Then Boaz said to Ruth, "Now, listen, ny daughter, do not go to glean in another eld or leave this one, but keep close to ny young women. ⁹Let your eyes be on he field that they are reaping, and go fter them. Have I not charged the young nen not to touch you? And when you are hirsty, go to the vessels and drink what he young men have drawn." ¹⁰Then she ell on her face, bowing to the ground, and aid to him, "Why have I found favor in our eyes, that you should take notice of ne, since I am a foreigner?" ¹¹But Boaz nswered her, "All that you have done for our mother-in-law since the death of our husband has been fully told to me, nd how you left your father and mother nd your native land and came to a people hat you did not know before. ¹²The LORD epay you for what you have done, and full reward be given you by the LORD, he God of Israel, under whose wings you lave come to take refuge!" ¹³Then she said, I have found favor in your eyes, my lord, or you have comforted me and spoken kindly to your servant, though I am not one f your servants."

¹⁴And at mealtime Boaz said to her, Come here and eat some bread and dip our morsel in the wine." So she sat beside he reapers, and he passed to her roasted grain. And she ate until she was satisfied, nd she had some left over. ¹⁵When she

rose to glean, Boaz instructed his young men, saying, "Let her glean even among the sheaves, and do not reproach her. ¹⁶And also pull out some from the bundles for her and leave it for her to glean, and do not rebuke her."

¹⁷So she gleaned in the field until evening. Then she beat out what she had gleaned, and it was about an ephah² of barley. ¹⁸And she took it up and went into the city. Her mother-in-law saw what she had gleaned. She also brought out and gave her what food she had left over after being satisfied. ¹⁹And her mother-in-law said to her, "Where did you glean today? And where have you worked? Blessed be the man who took notice of you." So she told her mother-in-law with whom she had worked and said, "The man's name with whom I worked today is Boaz." ²⁰And Naomi said to her daughter-in-law, "May he be blessed by the LORD, whose kindness has not forsaken the living or the dead!" Naomi also said to her, "The man is a close relative of ours, one of our redeemers." ²¹And Ruth the Moabite said, "Besides, he said to me, 'You shall keep close by my young men until they have finished all my harvest.'" ²²And Naomi said to Ruth, her daughter-in-law, "It is good, my daughter, that you go out with his young women, lest in another field you be assaulted." ²³So she kept close to the young women of Boaz, gleaning until the end of the barley and wheat harvests. And she lived with her mother-in-law.

Ruth and Boaz at the Threshing Floor

3 Then Naomi her mother-in-law said to her, "My daughter, should I not seek rest for you, that it may be well with you? ²Is not Boaz our relative, with whose young women you were? See, he is winnowing barley tonight at the threshing floor. ³Wash therefore and anoint yourself, and put on your cloak and go down to the threshing floor, but do not make yourself known to the man until he has finished eating and drinking. ⁴But when he lies down, observe the place where he lies. Then go and uncover his feet and lie down, and he will tell you what to do." ⁵And she replied, "All that you say I will do."

⁶So she went down to the threshing floor and did just as her mother-in-law had commanded her. ⁷And when Boaz had eaten

¹Compare Septuagint, Vulgate; the meaning of the Hebrew phrase is uncertain ²An *ephah* was about 3/5 bushel or 22 liters

and drunk, and his heart was merry, he went to lie down at the end of the heap of grain. Then she came softly and uncovered his feet and lay down. [8] At midnight the man was startled and turned over, and behold, a woman lay at his feet! [9] He said, "Who are you?" And she answered, "I am Ruth, your servant. Spread your wings[1] over your servant, for you are a redeemer." [10] And he said, "May you be blessed by the LORD, my daughter. You have made this last kindness greater than the first in that you have not gone after young men, whether poor or rich. [11] And now, my daughter, do not fear. I will do for you all that you ask, for all my fellow townsmen know that you are a worthy woman. [12] And now it is true that I am a redeemer. Yet there is a redeemer nearer than I. [13] Remain tonight, and in the morning, if he will redeem you, good; let him do it. But if he is not willing to redeem you, then, as the LORD lives, I will redeem you. Lie down until the morning."

[14] So she lay at his feet until the morning, but arose before one could recognize another. And he said, "Let it not be known that the woman came to the threshing floor." [15] And he said, "Bring the garment you are wearing and hold it out." So she held it, and he measured out six measures of barley and put it on her. Then she went into the city. [16] And when she came to her mother-in-law, she said, "How did you fare, my daughter?" Then she told her all that the man had done for her, [17] saying, "These six measures of barley he gave to me, for he said to me, 'You must not go back empty-handed to your mother-in-law.'" [18] She replied, "Wait, my daughter, until you learn how the matter turns out, for the man will not rest but will settle the matter today."

Boaz Redeems Ruth

4 Now Boaz had gone up to the gate and sat down there. And behold, the redeemer, of whom Boaz had spoken, came by. So Boaz said, "Turn aside, friend; sit down here." And he turned aside and sat down. [2] And he took ten men of the elders of the city and said, "Sit down here." So they sat down. [3] Then he said to the redeemer, "Naomi, who has come back from the country of Moab, is selling the parcel of land that belonged to our relative Elimelech. [4] So I thought I would tell you of it and say,

'Buy it in the presence of those sitting her and in the presence of the elders of m people.' If you will redeem it, redeem it. Bu if you[2] will not, tell me, that I may know, fo there is no one besides you to redeem i and I come after you." And he said, "I wi redeem it." [5] Then Boaz said, "The day yo buy the field from the hand of Naomi, yo also acquire Ruth[3] the Moabite, the widow of the dead, in order to perpetuate th name of the dead in his inheritance." [6] The the redeemer said, "I cannot redeem it fo myself, lest I impair my own inheritance Take my right of redemption yourself, fo I cannot redeem it."

[7] Now this was the custom in forme times in Israel concerning redeeming an exchanging: to confirm a transaction, on one drew off his sandal and gave it to th other, and this was the manner of attestin in Israel. [8] So when the redeemer said t Boaz, "Buy it for yourself," he drew off hi sandal. [9] Then Boaz said to the elders an all the people, "You are witnesses this da that I have bought from the hand of Naom all that belonged to Elimelech and all tha belonged to Chilion and to Mahlon. [10] Als Ruth the Moabite, the widow of Mahlor I have bought to be my wife, to perpetu ate the name of the dead in his inheri tance, that the name of the dead may no be cut off from among his brothers an from the gate of his native place. You ar witnesses this day." [11] Then all the peopl who were at the gate and the elders said "We are witnesses. May the LORD make th woman, who is coming into your house like Rachel and Leah, who together built u the house of Israel. May you act worthily i Ephrathah and be renowned in Bethlehem [12] and may your house be like the house o Perez, whom Tamar bore to Judah, becaus of the offspring that the LORD will give yo by this young woman."

Ruth and Boaz Marry

[13] So Boaz took Ruth, and she becam his wife. And he went in to her, and th LORD gave her conception, and she bor a son. [14] Then the women said to Naomi "Blessed be the LORD, who has not left yo this day without a redeemer, and may hi name be renowned in Israel! [15] He shall b to you a restorer of life and a nourisher o your old age, for your daughter-in-law wh

---

[1] Compare 2:12; the word for *wings* can also mean *corners of a garment* [2] Hebrew *he* [3] Masoretic Text *you also buy it from Ruth*

ves you, who is more to you than seven
ons, has given birth to him." [16] Then Naomi
ook the child and laid him on her lap and
ecame his nurse. [17] And the women of the
eighborhood gave him a name, saying, "A
on has been born to Naomi." They named
im Obed. He was the father of Jesse, the
ather of David.

The Genealogy of David

[18] Now these are the generations of
Perez: Perez fathered Hezron, [19] Hezron
fathered Ram, Ram fathered Amminadab,
[20] Amminadab fathered Nahshon, Nahshon
fathered Salmon, [21] Salmon fathered Boaz,
Boaz fathered Obed, [22] Obed fathered Jesse,
and Jesse fathered David.

Author: Unknown
Time: Unknown
Place: Unknown
Written to: God's people, the Israelites

the gist

The book of 1 Samuel is the story of King Saul's life, from the time he was chosen to be king to his tragic downfall. Saul was the first king of the Israelites, after the time of the judges.

things to look for

- The story of Hannah (see 1 Sam. 1:1–2:10, 18–21)
- The call of Samuel (see 1 Samuel 3)

Rise Above

> But the LORD said to Samuel, "Do not look on his appearance or on the height of his stature, because I have rejected him. For the LORD sees not as man sees: man looks on the outward appearance, but the LORD looks on the heart."
>
> *1 Samuel 16:7*

Some of the hardest times in your life can also be your best times. Your trials and suffering prove who you are: when the going gets tough, will you run toward God or away from him? When you run to him you end up on your knees, which doesn't sound so great, but in the end the payoff is awesome. From the ground, it's easier to look up to God and miraculously find the comfort you need. Through this process you discover not only who he is but who you are: a child of the living God.

David, whose story starts here in 1 Samuel, is a good example of the stress and strain of suffering making a kid into a strong and powerful man of faith. His time on the run from Saul didn't destroy him; it made him into a man who understood the hand of God in his life. The same can be true for the God Girl: she grows in faith when she doesn't look for the easy way out and doesn't spend all her time daydreaming about the good life or whining about her own miserable life. The God Girl looks at all the things that come to her as an opportunity to get stronger and not as reasons to fear or to worry. It takes a lot of reps for your body to get stronger, and it takes a lot of reps of faith for your trust to get stronger.

When you're young, life comes at you guns blazing, but it's only temporary. Who you are today is not who you are going to be tomorrow, and that's because of the tests and trials you are going through right now. These are going to shape you into either a victim or a victor. So what's it gonna be?

If you want to avoid being the victim, then don't run in fear the next time suffering knocks on the door. Just look it dead in the eyes and know that its arrival means a chance for you to get your spiritual exercise. Look at the lives of the people who have gone before you, like David. The greatest people in history had to be tested and proven faithful before they could do the things they did in the name of God. So don't let your pain go unused, but turn to God and promise to trust him whenever storms hit.

Must-Know Terms and Verses

✍ *Glory of Israel* ✍

Netsah Yisrael, also translated as "the Strength of Israel," is another name for the Lord (see 1 Sam. 15:29).

✍ *Lord of Hosts* ✍

Yahweh Tsebaoth, also translated as "the Lord of Armies," describes God as the leader and commander of all armies of the world, both spiritual and earthly (hosts can mean either armies, good or bad angels, or the stars in heaven).

And she vowed a vow and said, "O LORD of hosts, if you will indeed look on the affliction of your servant and remember me and not forget your servant, but will give to your servant a son, then I will give him to the LORD all the days of his life, and no razor shall touch his head." *1 Samuel 1:11*

And the LORD came and stood, calling as at other times, "Samuel! Samuel!" And Samuel said, "Speak, for your servant hears." *1 Samuel 3:10*

"Has the LORD as great delight in burnt offerings and sacrifices,
    as in obeying the voice of the LORD?
Behold, to obey is better than sacrifice." *1 Samuel 15:22*

"Do not look on his appearance or on the height of his stature, because I have rejected him. For the LORD sees not as man sees: man looks on the outward appearance, but the LORD looks on the heart." *1 Samuel 16:7*

Then David said to the Philistine, "You come to me with a sword and with a spear and with a javelin, but I come to you in the name of the LORD of hosts, the God of the armies of Israel, whom you have defied. This day the LORD will deliver you into my hand." *1 Samuel 17:45–46*

He said to David, "You are more righteous than I, for you have repaid me good, whereas I have repaid you evil. And you have declared this day how you have dealt well with me, in that you did not kill me when the LORD put me into your hands. For if a man finds his enemy, will he let him go away safe? So may the LORD reward you with good for what you have done to me this day." *1 Samuel 24:17–19*

1 Samuel

The Birth of Samuel

1 There was a certain man of Ramathaim-zophim of the hill country of Ephraim whose name was Elkanah the son of Jeroham, son of Elihu, son of Tohu, son of Zuph, an Ephrathite. ²He had two wives. The name of the one was Hannah, and the name of the other, Peninnah. And Peninnah had children, but Hannah had no children.

³Now this man used to go up year by year from his city to worship and to sacrifice to the LORD of hosts at Shiloh, where the two sons of Eli, Hophni and Phinehas, were priests of the LORD. ⁴On the day when Elkanah sacrificed, he would give portions to Peninnah his wife and to all her sons and daughters. ⁵But to Hannah he gave a double portion, because he loved her, though the LORD had closed her womb.¹ ⁶And her rival used to provoke her grievously to irritate her, because the LORD had closed her womb. ⁷So it went on year by year. As often as she went up to the house of the LORD, she used to provoke her. Therefore Hannah wept and would not eat. ⁸And Elkanah, her husband, said to her, "Hannah, why do you weep? And why do you not eat? And why is your heart sad? Am I not more to you than ten sons?"

⁹After they had eaten and drunk in Shiloh, Hannah rose. Now Eli the priest was sitting on the seat beside the doorpost of the temple of the LORD. ¹⁰She was deeply distressed and prayed to the LORD and wept bitterly. ¹¹And she vowed a vow and said, "O LORD of hosts, if you will indeed look on the affliction of your servant and remember me and not forget your servant, but will give to your servant a son, then I will give him to the LORD all the days of his life, and no razor shall touch his head."

¹²As she continued praying before the LORD, Eli observed her mouth. ¹³Hannah was speaking in her heart; only her lips moved, and her voice was not heard. Therefore Eli took her to be a drunken woman. ¹⁴And Eli said to her, "How long will you go on being drunk? Put your wine away from you." ¹⁵But Hannah answered, "No, my lord, I am a woman troubled in spirit. I have drunk neither wine nor strong drink, but I have been pouring out my soul before the LORD. ¹⁶Do not regard your servant as a worthless woman, for all along I have been speaking out of my great anxiety and vexation." ¹⁷Then Eli answered, "Go in peace, and the God of Israel grant your petition that you have made to him." ¹⁸And she said, "Let your servant find favor in your eyes." Then the woman went her way and ate, and her face was no longer sad.

¹⁹They rose early in the morning and worshiped before the LORD; then they went back to their house at Ramah. And Elkanah knew Hannah his wife, and the LORD remembered her. ²⁰And in due time Hannah conceived and bore a son, and she called his name Samuel, for she said, "I have asked for him from the LORD."²

Samuel Given to the LORD

²¹The man Elkanah and all his house went up to offer to the LORD the yearly sacrifice and to pay his vow. ²²But Hannah did not go up, for she said to her husband, "As soon as the child is weaned, I will bring him, so that he may appear in the presence of the LORD and dwell there forever." ²³Elkanah her husband said to her, "Do what seems best to you; wait until you have weaned him; only, may the LORD establish his word." So the woman remained and nursed her son until she weaned him. ²⁴And when she had weaned him, she took him up with her, along with a three-year-old bull,³ an ephah⁴ of flour,

---

¹ Syriac; the meaning of the Hebrew is uncertain. Septuagint *And, although he loved Hannah, he would give Hannah only one portion, because the LORD had closed her womb* ² *Samuel* sounds like the Hebrew for *heard of God* ³ Dead Sea Scroll, Septuagint, Syriac; Masoretic Text *three bulls* ⁴ An *ephah* was about 3/5 bushel or 22 liters

and a skin of wine, and she brought him to the house of the LORD at Shiloh. And the child was young. ²⁵ Then they slaughtered the bull, and they brought the child to Eli. ²⁶ And she said, "Oh, my lord! As you live, my lord, I am the woman who was standing here in your presence, praying to the LORD. ²⁷ For this child I prayed, and the LORD has granted me my petition that I made to him. ²⁸ Therefore I have lent him to the LORD. As long as he lives, he is lent to the LORD."

And he worshiped the LORD there.

Hannah's Prayer

2 And Hannah prayed and said,

"My heart exults in the LORD;
  my horn is exalted in the LORD.
My mouth derides my enemies,
  because I rejoice in your salvation.

² "There is none holy like the LORD:
  for there is none besides you;
  there is no rock like our God.
³ Talk no more so very proudly,
  let not arrogance come from your
    mouth;
for the LORD is a God of knowledge,
  and by him actions are weighed.

⁴ The bows of the mighty are broken,
  but the feeble bind on strength.
⁵ Those who were full have hired
    themselves out for bread,
  but those who were hungry have
    ceased to hunger.
The barren has borne seven,
  but she who has many children is
    forlorn.
⁶ The LORD kills and brings to life;
  he brings down to Sheol and raises
    up.
⁷ The LORD makes poor and makes
    rich;
  he brings low and he exalts.
⁸ He raises up the poor from the dust;
  he lifts the needy from the ash
    heap
to make them sit with princes
  and inherit a seat of honor.
For the pillars of the earth are the
    LORD's,
  and on them he has set the world.

⁹ "He will guard the feet of his faithful
    ones,
  but the wicked shall be cut off in
    darkness,
  for not by might shall a man pre-
    vail.

verses to read
1 Samuel 2:6–8

Know True Happiness

Blaming all the hard times in your life on Satan can be easy; after all, he's out to get you and all of God's kids. But remember, it wasn't Satan who sent Jesus to the cross. It wasn't his idea to torture and kill Jesus—it was God's. So when something totally painful happens to you, don't blame it on the Enemy, because that's making it about him. Just focus on the one who will give you hope and peace; trust God and make it about him. Each attack and each abuse you experience should be a stepping-stone to lead you closer to God and not closer to the Enemy.

As you watch the world fall apart around you, remember that God is in control and that out of this misery can come something beautiful, just like salvation came from the bloody cross. That's just what Hannah was acknowledging in her prayer. Don't let the Enemy take what can be a tool in the hand of God and make it a weapon to cripple you. Rise above the pain into the realm of holiness and know that God lets suffering in your life to help make you holy. Don't allow your pain to be wasted or to be used against you, but harness it and take advantage of the perfecting power of it by looking to Christ all along the way. Then and only then will you be set free from the power of the Enemy.

⁰   The adversaries of the Lord shall be
         broken to pieces;
      against them he will thunder in
         heaven.
    The Lord will judge the ends of the
         earth;
      he will give strength to his king
         and exalt the horn of his anointed."

¹¹ Then Elkanah went home to Ramah. And the boy¹ was ministering to the Lord in the presence of Eli the priest.

Eli's Worthless Sons

¹² Now the sons of Eli were worthless men. They did not know the Lord. ¹³ The custom of the priests with the people was that when any man offered sacrifice, the priest's servant would come, while the meat was boiling, with a three-pronged fork in his hand, ¹⁴ and he would thrust it into the pan or kettle or cauldron or pot. All that the fork brought up the priest would take for himself. This is what they did at Shiloh to all the Israelites who came there. ¹⁵ Moreover, before the fat was burned, the priest's servant would come and say to the man who was sacrificing, "Give meat for the priest to roast, for he will not accept boiled meat from you but only raw." ¹⁶ And if the man said to him, "Let them burn the fat first, and then take as much as you wish," he would say, "No, you must give it now, and if not, I will take it by force." ¹⁷ Thus the sin of the young men was very great in the sight of the Lord, for the men treated the offering of the Lord with contempt.

¹⁸ Samuel was ministering before the Lord, a boy clothed with a linen ephod. ¹⁹ And his mother used to make for him a little robe and take it to him each year when she went up with her husband to offer the yearly sacrifice. ²⁰ Then Eli would bless Elkanah and his wife, and say, "May the Lord give you children by this woman for the petition she asked of the Lord." So then they would return to their home. ²¹ Indeed the Lord visited Hannah, and she conceived and bore three sons and two daughters. And the boy Samuel grew in the presence of the Lord.

Eli Rebukes His Sons

²² Now Eli was very old, and he kept hearing all that his sons were doing to all Israel, and how they lay with the women who were serving at the entrance to the tent of meeting. ²³ And he said to them, "Why do you do such things? For I hear of your evil dealings from all these people. ²⁴ No, my sons; it is no good report that I hear the people of the Lord spreading abroad. ²⁵ If someone sins against a man, God will mediate for him, but if someone sins against the Lord, who can intercede for him?" But they would not listen to the voice of their father, for it was the will of the Lord to put them to death.

²⁶ Now the boy Samuel continued to grow both in stature and in favor with the Lord and also with man.

The Lord Rejects Eli's Household

²⁷ And there came a man of God to Eli and said to him, "Thus says the Lord, 'Did I indeed reveal myself to the house of your father when they were in Egypt subject to the house of Pharaoh? ²⁸ Did I choose him out of all the tribes of Israel to be my priest, to go up to my altar, to burn incense, to wear an ephod before me? I gave to the house of your father all my offerings by fire from the people of Israel. ²⁹ Why then do you scorn² my sacrifices and my offerings that I commanded for my dwelling, and honor your sons above me by fattening yourselves on the choicest parts of every offering of my people Israel?' ³⁰ Therefore the Lord, the God of Israel, declares: 'I promised that your house and the house of your father should go in and out before me forever,' but now the Lord declares: 'Far be it from me, for those who honor me I will honor, and those who despise me shall be lightly esteemed. ³¹ Behold, the days are coming when I will cut off your strength and the strength of your father's house, so that there will not be an old man in your house. ³² Then in distress you will look with envious eye on all the prosperity that shall be bestowed on Israel, and there shall not be an old man in your house forever. ³³ The only one of you whom I shall not cut off from my altar shall be spared to weep his³ eyes out to grieve his heart, and all the descendants⁴ of your house shall die by the

¹ Hebrew *na'ar* can be rendered *boy* (2:11, 18, 21, 26; 3:1, 8), *servant* (2:13, 15), or *young man* (2:17), depending on the context ² Hebrew *kick at* ³ Septuagint; Hebrew *your*; twice in this verse ⁴ Hebrew *increase*

> You ask and do not receive, because you ask wrongly, to spend
> it on your passions.
>
> *James 4:3*

For years Hannah lived in misery, pleading to God for a baby and being picked on by the mean girl in her life, Peninnah. Her days were filled with tears. She begged God all the time to hear her prayers and to give her a son, but nothing happened until the fateful day when she suddenly made it not about her but about him: when she said she would give the baby to God, she finally got what she asked for. At that point, instead of clinging to her obsession to have a baby boy, she turned her attention to serving God and promised to give the boy to him to serve him all the days of his life. This one gift, this one dream she had, she promised to give away as soon as she got it. Wow, can you imagine?

The powerful lesson to be found here is that the power of prayer is released when the girl who prays changes her heart's focus from self-obsession to God-obsession. A lot of times you pray for things out of selfishness: "Me, me, me." And that's because you want the things this world tells you that you should want and not the things God wants. When that's your focus, prayer is pointless; it doesn't give you what you want because God doesn't answer selfish prayers. He knows your motives, and they mean a great deal to him.

When your prayer life is weak and ineffective, think about your motives. Are you praying so that your life will be better or so that your faith will be stronger? Your own sinful desires should never be the goal of your prayers (see James 4:3). When Hannah's focus went from serving her own need to serving God, he changed his no to yes. Sometimes going from self-obsession to God-obsession will change your prayers completely. The things you used to think were must-haves won't be so important anymore, or maybe you will just gain a more faithful motive for the things you want. Either way, your prayers will become more effective when you start to pray for God's will instead of your own. If you want to know God's will, look at his Word. As you do, your prayers will start to change, and so will his answers.

word of men.[1] [34] And this that shall come upon your two sons, Hophni and Phinehas, shall be the sign to you: both of them shall die on the same day. [35] And I will raise up for myself a faithful priest, who shall do according to what is in my heart and in my mind. And I will build him a sure house, and he shall go in and out before my anointed forever. [36] And everyone who is left in your house shall come to implore him for a piece of silver or a loaf of bread and shall say, 'Please put me in one of the priests' places, that I may eat a morsel of bread.'"

The LORD Calls Samuel

3 Now the boy Samuel was ministering to the LORD in the presence of Eli. And the word of the LORD was rare in those days; there was no frequent vision.

[2] At that time Eli, whose eyesight had begun to grow dim so that he could not see, was lying down in his own place. [3] The lamp of God had not yet gone out, and Samuel was lying down in the temple of the LORD, where the ark of God was.

[4] Then the LORD called Samuel, and he said, "Here I am!" [5] and ran to Eli and said, "Here I am, for you called me." But he said, "I did not call; lie down again." So he went and lay down.

[6] And the LORD called again, "Samuel!" and Samuel arose and went to Eli and said, "Here I am, for you called me." But he said, "I did not call, my son; lie down again." [7] Now Samuel did not yet know the LORD, and the word of the LORD had not yet been revealed to him.

[8] And the LORD called Samuel again the third time. And he arose and went to Eli and said, "Here I am, for you called me." Then Eli perceived that the LORD was calling the boy. [9] Therefore Eli said to Samuel, "Go, lie down, and if he calls you, you shall say, 'Speak, LORD, for your servant hears.'" So Samuel went and lay down in his place.

[10] And the LORD came and stood, calling as at other times, "Samuel! Samuel!" And Samuel said, "Speak, for your servant hears." [11] Then the LORD said to Samuel, "Behold, I am about to do a thing in Israel at which the two ears of everyone who hears it will tingle. [12] On that day I will fulfill against Eli all that I have spoken concerning his house, from beginning to end. [13] And I declare to him that I am about to punish his house forever, for the iniquity that he knew, because his sons were blaspheming God,[2] and he did not restrain them. [14] Therefore I swear to the house of Eli that the iniquity of Eli's house shall not be atoned for by sacrifice or offering forever."

[15] Samuel lay until morning; then he opened the doors of the house of the LORD. And Samuel was afraid to tell the vision to Eli. [16] But Eli called Samuel and said, "Samuel, my son." And he said, "Here I am." [17] And Eli said, "What was it that he told you? Do not hide it from me. May God do so to you and more also if you hide anything from me of all that he told you." [18] So Samuel told him everything and hid nothing from him. And he said, "It is the LORD. Let him do what seems good to him."

[19] And Samuel grew, and the LORD was with him and let none of his words fall to the ground. [20] And all Israel from Dan to Beersheba knew that Samuel was established as a prophet of the LORD. [21] And the LORD appeared again at Shiloh, for the LORD revealed himself to Samuel at Shiloh by the word of the LORD.

The Philistines Capture the Ark

4 And the word of Samuel came to all Israel.

Now Israel went out to battle against the Philistines. They encamped at Ebenezer, and the Philistines encamped at Aphek. [2] The Philistines drew up in line against Israel, and when the battle spread, Israel was defeated before the Philistines, who killed about four thousand men on the field of battle. [3] And when the people came to the camp, the elders of Israel said, "Why has the LORD defeated us today before the Philistines? Let us bring the ark of the covenant of the LORD here from Shiloh, that it[3] may come among us and save us from the power of our enemies." [4] So the people sent to Shiloh and brought from there the ark of the covenant of the LORD of hosts, who is enthroned on the cherubim. And the two sons of Eli, Hophni and Phinehas, were there with the ark of the covenant of God.

[5] As soon as the ark of the covenant of the LORD came into the camp, all Israel gave a mighty shout, so that the earth resounded. [6] And when the Philistines heard the noise of the shouting, they said, "What does this great shouting in the camp of the Hebrews

[1] Septuagint; Hebrew *die as men* [2] Or *blaspheming for themselves* [3] Or *he*

mean?" And when they learned that the ark of the LORD had come to the camp, [7] the Philistines were afraid, for they said, "A god has come into the camp." And they said, "Woe to us! For nothing like this has happened before. [8] Woe to us! Who can deliver us from the power of these mighty gods? These are the gods who struck the Egyptians with every sort of plague in the wilderness. [9] Take courage, and be men, O Philistines, lest you become slaves to the Hebrews as they have been to you; be men and fight."

[10] So the Philistines fought, and Israel was defeated, and they fled, every man to his home. And there was a very great slaughter, for thirty thousand foot soldiers of Israel fell. [11] And the ark of God was captured, and the two sons of Eli, Hophni and Phinehas, died.

The Death of Eli

[12] A man of Benjamin ran from the battle line and came to Shiloh the same day, with his clothes torn and with dirt on his head. [13] When he arrived, Eli was sitting on his seat by the road watching, for his heart trembled for the ark of God. And when the man came into the city and told the news, all the city cried out. [14] When Eli heard the sound of the outcry, he said, "What is this uproar?" Then the man hurried and came and told Eli. [15] Now Eli was ninety-eight years old and his eyes were set so that he could not see. [16] And the man said to Eli, "I am he who has come from the battle; I fled from the battle today." And he said, "How did it go, my son?" [17] He who brought the news answered and said, "Israel has fled before the Philistines, and there has also been a great defeat among the people. Your two sons also, Hophni and Phinehas, are dead, and the ark of God has been captured." [18] As soon as he mentioned the ark of God, Eli fell over backward from his seat by the side of the gate, and his neck was broken and he died, for the man was old and heavy. He had judged Israel forty years.

[19] Now his daughter-in-law, the wife of Phinehas, was pregnant, about to give birth. And when she heard the news that the ark of God was captured, and that her father-in-law and her husband were dead, she bowed and gave birth, for her pains came upon her. [20] And about the time of her death the women attending her said to her, "Do not be afraid, for you have borne a son." But she did not answer or pay attention. [21] And she named the child Ichabod, saying, "The glory has departed from Israel!" because the ark of God had been captured and because of her father-in-law and her husband. [22] And she said, "The glory has departed from Israel, for the ark of God has been captured."

The Philistines and the Ark

5 When the Philistines captured the ark of God, they brought it from Ebenezer to Ashdod. [2] Then the Philistines took the ark of God and brought it into the house of Dagon and set it up beside Dagon. [3] And when the people of Ashdod rose early the next day, behold, Dagon had fallen face downward on the ground before the ark of the LORD. So they took Dagon and put him back in his place. [4] But when they rose early on the next morning, behold, Dagon had fallen face downward on the ground before the ark of the LORD, and the head of Dagon and both his hands were lying cut off on the threshold. Only the trunk of Dagon was left to him. [5] This is why the priests of Dagon and all who enter the house of Dagon do not tread on the threshold of Dagon in Ashdod to this day.

[6] The hand of the LORD was heavy against the people of Ashdod, and he terrified and afflicted them with tumors, both Ashdod and its territory. [7] And when the men of Ashdod saw how things were, they said, "The ark of the God of Israel must not remain with us, for his hand is hard against us and against Dagon our god." [8] So they sent and gathered together all the lords of the Philistines and said, "What shall we do with the ark of the God of Israel?" They answered, "Let the ark of the God of Israel be brought around to Gath." So they brought the ark of the God of Israel there. [9] But after they had brought it around, the hand of the LORD was against the city, causing a very great panic, and he afflicted the men of the city, both young and old, so that tumors broke out on them. [10] So they sent the ark of God to Ekron. But as soon as the ark of God came to Ekron, the people of Ekron cried out, "They have brought around to us the ark of the God of Israel to kill us and our people." [11] They sent there-

[1] Or *gone into exile*; also verse 22

fore and gathered together all the lords of the Philistines and said, "Send away the ark of the God of Israel, and let it return to its own place, that it may not kill us and our people." For there was a deathly panic throughout the whole city. The hand of God was very heavy there. [12] The men who did not die were struck with tumors, and the cry of the city went up to heaven.

The Ark Returned to Israel

6 The ark of the LORD was in the country of the Philistines seven months. [2] And the Philistines called for the priests and the diviners and said, "What shall we do with the ark of the LORD? Tell us with what we shall send it to its place." [3] They said, "If you send away the ark of the God of Israel, do not send it empty, but by all means return him a guilt offering. Then you will be healed, and it will be known to you why his hand does not turn away from you." [4] And they said, "What is the guilt offering that we shall return to him?" They answered, "Five golden tumors and five golden mice, according to the number of the lords of the Philistines, for the same plague was on all of you and on your lords. [5] So you must make images of your tumors and images of your mice that ravage the land, and give glory to the God of Israel. Perhaps he will lighten his hand from off you and your gods and your land. [6] Why should you harden your hearts as the Egyptians and Pharaoh hardened their hearts? After he had dealt severely with them, did they not send the people away, and they departed? [7] Now then, take and prepare a new cart and two milk cows on which there has never come a yoke, and yoke the cows to the cart, but take their calves home, away from them. [8] And take the ark of the LORD and place it on the cart and put in a box at its side the figures of gold, which you are returning to him as a guilt offering. Then send it off and let it go its way and watch. [9] If it goes up on the way to its own land, to Beth-shemesh, then it is he who has done us this great harm, but if not, then we shall know that it is not his hand that struck us; it happened to us by coincidence."

[10] The men did so, and took two milk cows and yoked them to the cart and shut up their calves at home. [11] And they put the ark of the LORD on the cart and the box with the golden mice and the images of their tumors. [12] And the cows went straight in the direction of Beth-shemesh along one highway, lowing as they went. They turned neither to the right nor to the left, and the lords of the Philistines went after them as far as the border of Beth-shemesh. [13] Now the people of Beth-shemesh were reaping their wheat harvest in the valley. And when they lifted up their eyes and saw the ark, they rejoiced to see it. [14] The cart came into the field of Joshua of Beth-shemesh and stopped there. A great stone was there. And they split up the wood of the cart and offered the cows as a burnt offering to the LORD. [15] And the Levites took down the ark of the LORD and the box that was beside it, in which were the golden figures, and set them upon the great stone. And the men of Beth-shemesh offered burnt offerings and sacrificed sacrifices on that day to the LORD. [16] And when the five lords of the Philistines saw it, they returned that day to Ekron.

[17] These are the golden tumors that the Philistines returned as a guilt offering to the LORD: one for Ashdod, one for Gaza, one for Ashkelon, one for Gath, one for Ekron, [18] and the golden mice, according to the number of all the cities of the Philistines belonging to the five lords, both fortified cities and unwalled villages. The great stone beside which they set down the ark of the LORD is a witness to this day in the field of Joshua of Beth-shemesh.

[19] And he struck some of the men of Beth-shemesh, because they looked upon the ark of the LORD. He struck seventy men of them,[1] and the people mourned because the LORD had struck the people with a great blow. [20] Then the men of Beth-shemesh said, "Who is able to stand before the LORD, this holy God? And to whom shall he go up away from us?" [21] So they sent messengers to the inhabitants of Kiriath-jearim, saying, "The Philistines have returned the ark of the LORD. Come down and take it up to you."

7 And the men of Kiriath-jearim came and took up the ark of the LORD and brought it to the house of Abinadab on the hill. And they consecrated his son Eleazar to have charge of the ark of the LORD. [2] From the day that the ark was lodged at Kiriath-jearim, a long time passed, some

---

[1] Most Hebrew manuscripts *struck of the people seventy men, fifty thousand men*

twenty years, and all the house of Israel lamented after the LORD.

Ask Yourself . . .

ABOUT YOUR UNCONFESSED SIN

Samuel taught the Israelites that when they sinned they were to admit it, that is, to confess. After you confess and agree with God that you shouldn't have done what you did, the next step is repentance—never doing it again. Ask yourself about your unconfessed sin:

- Do I have some sins I have failed to confess?
- Do I go to bed with unconfessed sins in my life?
- What does God say about sin and confession? What precedes forgiveness? (See 1 John 1:9.)
- Are there any sins I have confessed but have failed to repent of?
- If my answer is yes, then what does God want me to do about them?

Samuel Judges Israel

³ And Samuel said to all the house of Israel, "If you are returning to the LORD with all your heart, then put away the foreign gods and the Ashtaroth from among you and direct your heart to the LORD and serve him only, and he will deliver you out of the hand of the Philistines." ⁴ So the people of Israel put away the Baals and the Ashtaroth, and they served the LORD only.

⁵ Then Samuel said, "Gather all Israel at Mizpah, and I will pray to the LORD for you." ⁶ So they gathered at Mizpah and drew water and poured it out before the LORD and fasted on that day and said there, "We have sinned against the LORD." And Samuel judged the people of Israel at Mizpah. ⁷ Now when the Philistines heard that the people of Israel had gathered a Mizpah, the lords of the Philistines wen up against Israel. And when the people of Israel heard of it, they were afraid o the Philistines. ⁸ And the people of Israel said to Samuel, "Do not cease to cry out to the LORD our God for us, that he may save us from the hand of the Philistines." ⁹ So Samuel took a nursing lamb and offered it as a whole burnt offering to the LORD. And Samuel cried out to the LORD for Israel, and the LORD answered him. ¹⁰ As Samuel was offering up the burnt offering the Philistines drew near to attack Israel But the LORD thundered with a mighty sound that day against the Philistines and threw them into confusion, and they were defeated before Israel. ¹¹ And the men o Israel went out from Mizpah and pursued the Philistines and struck them, as far as below Beth-car.

¹² Then Samuel took a stone and set i up between Mizpah and Shen[1] and called its name Ebenezer;[2] for he said, "Till now the LORD has helped us." ¹³ So the Philis tines were subdued and did not again enter the territory of Israel. And the hand of the LORD was against the Philistines all the days of Samuel. ¹⁴ The cities that the Phil istines had taken from Israel were restored to Israel, from Ekron to Gath, and Israel delivered their territory from the hand of the Philistines. There was peace also between Israel and the Amorites.

¹⁵ Samuel judged Israel all the days o his life. ¹⁶ And he went on a circuit year by year to Bethel, Gilgal, and Mizpah. And he judged Israel in all these places. ¹⁷ Then he would return to Ramah, for his home wa: there, and there also he judged Israel. And he built there an altar to the LORD.

Israel Demands a King

8 When Samuel became old, he made his sons judges over Israel. ² The name o his firstborn son was Joel, and the name of his second, Abijah; they were judges in Beersheba. ³ Yet his sons did not walk in hi: ways but turned aside after gain. They took bribes and perverted justice.

⁴ Then all the elders of Israel gathered together and came to Samuel at Ramah ⁵ and said to him, "Behold, you are old and your sons do not walk in your ways. Now appoint for us a king to judge us like all the

[1] Hebrew; Septuagint, Syriac *Jeshanah* [2] *Ebenezer* means *stone of help*

nations." [6] But the thing displeased Samuel when they said, "Give us a king to judge us." And Samuel prayed to the LORD. [7] And the LORD said to Samuel, "Obey the voice of the people in all that they say to you, for they have not rejected you, but they have rejected me from being king over them. [8] According to all the deeds that they have done, from the day I brought them up out of Egypt even to this day, forsaking me and serving other gods, so they are also doing to you. [9] Now then, obey their voice; only you shall solemnly warn them and show them the ways of the king who shall reign over them."

Samuel's Warning Against Kings

[10] So Samuel told all the words of the LORD to the people who were asking for a king from him. [11] He said, "These will be the ways of the king who will reign over you: he will take your sons and appoint them to his chariots and to be his horsemen and to run before his chariots. [12] And he will appoint for himself commanders of thousands and commanders of fifties, and some to plow his ground and to reap his harvest, and to make his implements of war and the equipment of his chariots. [13] He will take your daughters to be perfumers and cooks and bakers. [14] He will take the best of your fields and vineyards and olive orchards and give them to his servants. [15] He will take the tenth of your grain and of your vineyards and give it to his officers and to his servants. [16] He will take your male servants and female servants and the best of your young men[1] and your donkeys, and put them to his work. [17] He will take the tenth of your flocks, and you shall be his slaves. [18] And in that day you will cry out because of your king, whom you have chosen for yourselves, but the LORD will not answer you in that day."

The LORD Grants Israel's Request

[19] But the people refused to obey the voice of Samuel. And they said, "No! But there shall be a king over us, [20] that we also may be like all the nations, and that our king may judge us and go out before us and fight our battles." [21] And when Samuel had heard all the words of the people, he repeated them in the ears of the LORD. [22] And the LORD said to Samuel, "Obey their voice and make them a king." Samuel then said to the men of Israel, "Go every man to his city."

Saul Chosen to Be King

9 There was a man of Benjamin whose name was Kish, the son of Abiel, son of Zeror, son of Becorath, son of Aphiah, a Benjaminite, a man of wealth. [2] And he had a son whose name was Saul, a handsome young man. There was not a man among the people of Israel more handsome than he. From his shoulders upward he was taller than any of the people.

[3] Now the donkeys of Kish, Saul's father, were lost. So Kish said to Saul his son, "Take one of the young men with you, and arise, go and look for the donkeys." [4] And he passed through the hill country of Ephraim and passed through the land of Shalishah, but they did not find them. And they passed through the land of Shaalim, but they were not there. Then they passed through the land of Benjamin, but did not find them.

[5] When they came to the land of Zuph, Saul said to his servant[2] who was with him, "Come, let us go back, lest my father cease to care about the donkeys and become anxious about us." [6] But he said to him, "Behold, there is a man of God in this city, and he is a man who is held in honor; all that he says comes true. So now let us go there. Perhaps he can tell us the way we should go." [7] Then Saul said to his servant, "But if we go, what can we bring the man? For the bread in our sacks is gone, and there is no present to bring to the man of God. What do we have?" [8] The servant answered Saul again, "Here, I have with me a quarter of a shekel[3] of silver, and I will give it to the man of God to tell us our way." [9] (Formerly in Israel, when a man went to inquire of God, he said, "Come, let us go to the seer," for today's "prophet" was formerly called a seer.) [10] And Saul said to his servant, "Well said; come, let us go." So they went to the city where the man of God was.

[11] As they went up the hill to the city, they met young women coming out to draw water and said to them, "Is the seer here?" [12] They answered, "He is; behold, he is just ahead of you. Hurry. He has come just now to the city, because the people have a sacrifice today on the high place. [13] As soon as

---

[1] Septuagint cattle [2] Hebrew young man; also verses 7, 8, 10, 27 [3] A shekel was about 2/5 ounce or 11 grams

you enter the city you will find him, before he goes up to the high place to eat. For the people will not eat till he comes, since he must bless the sacrifice; afterward those who are invited will eat. Now go up, for you will meet him immediately." [14] So they went up to the city. As they were entering the city, they saw Samuel coming out toward them on his way up to the high place.

[15] Now the day before Saul came, the LORD had revealed to Samuel: [16] "Tomorrow about this time I will send to you a man from the land of Benjamin, and you shall anoint him to be prince[1] over my people Israel. He shall save my people from the hand of the Philistines. For I have seen[2] my people, because their cry has come to me." [17] When Samuel saw Saul, the LORD told him, "Here is the man of whom I spoke to you! He it is who shall restrain my people." [18] Then Saul approached Samuel in the gate and said, "Tell me where is the house of the seer?" [19] Samuel answered Saul, "I am the seer. Go up before me to the high place, for today you shall eat with me, and in the morning I will let you go and will tell you all that is on your mind. [20] As for your donkeys that were lost three days ago, do not set your mind on them, for they have been found. And for whom is all that is desirable in Israel? Is it not for you and for all your father's house?" [21] Saul answered, "Am I not a Benjaminite, from the least of the tribes of Israel? And is not my clan the humblest of all the clans of the tribe of Benjamin? Why then have you spoken to me in this way?"

[22] Then Samuel took Saul and his young man and brought them into the hall and gave them a place at the head of those who had been invited, who were about thirty persons. [23] And Samuel said to the cook, "Bring the portion I gave you, of which I said to you, 'Put it aside.'" [24] So the cook took up the leg and what was on it and set them before Saul. And Samuel said, "See, what was kept is set before you. Eat, because it was kept for you until the hour appointed, that you might eat with the guests."[3]

So Saul ate with Samuel that day. [25] And when they came down from the high place into the city, a bed was spread for Saul[4] on the roof, and he lay down to sleep. [26] Then at the break of dawn[5] Samuel called to Saul on the roof, "Up, that I may send you on your way." So Saul arose, and both he and Samuel went out into the street.

[27] As they were going down to the outskirts of the city, Samuel said to Saul, "Tell the servant to pass on before us, and when he has passed on, stop here yourself for a while, that I may make known to you the word of God."

Saul Anointed King

10 Then Samuel took a flask of oil and poured it on his head and kissed him and said, "Has not the LORD anointed you to be prince[6] over his people Israel? And you shall reign over the people of the LORD and you will save them from the hand of their surrounding enemies. And this shall be the sign to you that the LORD has anointed you to be prince[7] over his heritage. [2] When you depart from me today, you will meet two men by Rachel's tomb in the territory of Benjamin at Zelzah, and they will say to you, 'The donkeys that you went to seek are found, and now your father has ceased to care about the donkeys and is anxious about you, saying, "What shall I do about my son?"' [3] Then you shall go on from there farther and come to the oak of Tabor. Three men going up to God at Bethel will meet you there, one carrying three young goats, another carrying three loaves of bread, and another carrying a skin of wine. [4] And they will greet you and give you two loaves of bread, which you shall accept from their hand. [5] After that you shall come to Gibeath-elohim,[8] where there is a garrison of the Philistines. And there, as soon as you come to the city, you will meet a group of prophets coming down from the high place with harp, tambourine, flute, and lyre before them, prophesying. [6] Then the Spirit of the LORD will rush upon you, and you will prophesy with them and be turned into another man. [7] Now when these signs meet you, do what your hand finds to do, for God is with you. [8] Then go down before me to Gilgal. And behold, I am coming down to you to offer burnt offerings and to sacrifice peace offerings. Seven days you shall wait, until I come to you and show you what you shall do."

---

[1] Or leader [2] Septuagint adds the affliction of [3] Hebrew appointed, saying, 'I have invited the people' [4] Septuagint; Hebrew and he spoke with Saul [5] Septuagint; Hebrew And they arose early and at the break of dawn [6] Or leader [7] Septuagint; Hebrew lacks over his people Israel? And you shall. . . . to be prince [8] Gibeath-elohim means the hill of God

⁹ When he turned his back to leave Samuel, God gave him another heart. And all these signs came to pass that day. ¹⁰ When they came to Gibeah,¹ behold, a group of prophets met him, and the Spirit of God rushed upon him, and he prophesied among them. ¹¹ And when all who knew him previously saw how he prophesied with the prophets, the people said to one another, "What has come over the son of Kish? Is Saul also among the prophets?" ¹² And a man of the place answered, "And who is their father?" Therefore it became a proverb, "Is Saul also among the prophets?" ¹³ When he had finished prophesying, he came to the high place.

¹⁴ Saul's uncle said to him and to his servant, "Where did you go?" And he said, "To seek the donkeys. And when we saw they were not to be found, we went to Samuel." ¹⁵ And Saul's uncle said, "Please tell me what Samuel said to you." ¹⁶ And Saul said to his uncle, "He told us plainly that the donkeys had been found." But about the matter of the kingdom, of which Samuel had spoken, he did not tell him anything.

Saul Proclaimed King

¹⁷ Now Samuel called the people together to the LORD at Mizpah. ¹⁸ And he said to the people of Israel, "Thus says the LORD, the God of Israel, 'I brought up Israel out of Egypt, and I delivered you from the hand of the Egyptians and from the hand of all the kingdoms that were oppressing you.' ¹⁹ But today you have rejected your God, who saves you from all your calamities and your distresses, and you have said to him, 'Set a king over us.' Now therefore present yourselves before the LORD by your tribes and by your thousands."

²⁰ Then Samuel brought all the tribes of Israel near, and the tribe of Benjamin was taken by lot. ²¹ He brought the tribe of Benjamin near by its clans, and the clan of the Matrites was taken by lot;² and Saul the son of Kish was taken by lot. But when they sought him, he could not be found. ²² So they inquired again of the LORD, "Is there a man still to come?" and the LORD said, "Behold, he has hidden himself among the baggage." ²³ Then they ran and took him from there. And when he stood among the people, he was taller than any of the people from his shoulders upward. ²⁴ And

Samuel said to all the people, "Do you see him whom the LORD has chosen? There is none like him among all the people." And all the people shouted, "Long live the king!"

²⁵ Then Samuel told the people the rights and duties of the kingship, and he wrote them in a book and laid it up before the LORD. Then Samuel sent all the people away, each one to his home. ²⁶ Saul also went to his home at Gibeah, and with him went men of valor whose hearts God had touched. ²⁷ But some worthless fellows said, "How can this man save us?" And they despised him and brought him no present. But he held his peace.

Saul Defeats the Ammonites

11 Then Nahash the Ammonite went up and besieged Jabesh-gilead, and all the men of Jabesh said to Nahash, "Make a treaty with us, and we will serve you." ² But Nahash the Ammonite said to them, "On this condition I will make a treaty with you, that I gouge out all your right eyes, and thus bring disgrace on all Israel." ³ The elders of Jabesh said to him, "Give us seven days' respite that we may send messengers through all the territory of Israel. Then, if there is no one to save us, we will give ourselves up to you." ⁴ When the messengers came to Gibeah of Saul, they reported the matter in the ears of the people, and all the people wept aloud.

⁵ Now, behold, Saul was coming from the field behind the oxen. And Saul said, "What is wrong with the people, that they are weeping?" So they told him the news of the men of Jabesh. ⁶ And the Spirit of God rushed upon Saul when he heard these words, and his anger was greatly kindled. ⁷ He took a yoke of oxen and cut them in pieces and sent them throughout all the territory of Israel by the hand of the messengers, saying, "Whoever does not come out after Saul and Samuel, so shall it be done to his oxen!" Then the dread of the LORD fell upon the people, and they came out as one man. ⁸ When he mustered them at Bezek, the people of Israel were three hundred thousand, and the men of Judah thirty thousand. ⁹ And they said to the messengers who had come, "Thus shall you say to the men of Jabesh-gilead: 'Tomorrow, by the time the sun is hot, you shall have salvation.' "

¹ *Gibeah* means *the hill* ² Septuagint adds *finally he brought the family of the Matrites near, man by man*

When the messengers came and told the men of Jabesh, they were glad. [10]Therefore the men of Jabesh said, "Tomorrow we will give ourselves up to you, and you may do to us whatever seems good to you." [11]And the next day Saul put the people in three companies. And they came into the midst of the camp in the morning watch and struck down the Ammonites until the heat of the day. And those who survived were scattered, so that no two of them were left together.

The Kingdom Is Renewed

[12]Then the people said to Samuel, "Who is it that said, 'Shall Saul reign over us?' Bring the men, that we may put them to death." [13]But Saul said, "Not a man shall be put to death this day, for today the LORD has worked salvation in Israel." [14]Then Samuel said to the people, "Come, let us go to Gilgal and there renew the kingdom." [15]So all the people went to Gilgal, and there they made Saul king before the LORD in Gilgal. There they sacrificed peace offerings before the LORD, and there Saul and all the men of Israel rejoiced greatly.

Samuel's Farewell Address

12 And Samuel said to all Israel, "Behold, I have obeyed your voice in all that you have said to me and have made a king over you. [2]And now, behold, the king walks before you, and I am old and gray; and behold, my sons are with you. I have walked before you from my youth until this day. [3]Here I am; testify against me before the LORD and before his anointed. Whose ox have I taken? Or whose donkey have I taken? Or whom have I defrauded? Whom have I oppressed? Or from whose hand have I taken a bribe to blind my eyes with it? Testify against me[1] and I will restore it to you." [4]They said, "You have not defrauded us or oppressed us or taken anything from any man's hand." [5]And he said to them, "The LORD is witness against you, and his anointed is witness this day, that you have not found anything in my hand." And they said, "He is witness."

[6]And Samuel said to the people, "The LORD is witness,[2] who appointed Moses and Aaron and brought your fathers up out of the land of Egypt. [7]Now therefore stand still that I may plead with you before the LORD concerning all the righteous deeds of the LORD that he performed for you and for your fathers. [8]When Jacob went into Egypt, and the Egyptians oppressed them,[3] then your fathers cried out to the LORD, and the LORD sent Moses and Aaron, who brought your fathers out of Egypt and made them dwell in this place. [9]But they forgot the LORD their God. And he sold them into the hand of Sisera, commander of the army of Hazor,[4] and into the hand of the Philistines, and into the hand of the king of Moab. And they fought against them. [10]And they cried out to the LORD and said, 'We have sinned, because we have forsaken the LORD and have served the Baals and the Ashtaroth. But now deliver us out of the hand of our enemies, that we may serve you.' [11]And the LORD sent Jerubbaal and Barak[5] and Jephthah and Samuel and delivered you out of the hand of your enemies on every side, and you lived in safety. [12]And when you saw that Nahash the king of the Ammonites came against you, you said to me, 'No, but a king shall reign over us,' when the LORD your God was your king. [13]And now behold the king whom you have chosen, for whom you have asked; behold, the LORD has set a king over you. [14]If you will fear the LORD and serve him and obey his voice and not rebel against the commandment of the LORD, and if both you and the king who reigns over you will follow the LORD your God, it will be well. [15]But if you will not obey the voice of the LORD, but rebel against the commandment of the LORD, then the hand of the LORD will be against you and your king.[6] [16]Now therefore stand still and see this great thing that the LORD will do before your eyes. [17]Is it not wheat harvest today? I will call upon the LORD, that he may send thunder and rain. And you shall know and see that your wickedness is great, which you have done in the sight of the LORD, in asking for yourselves a king." [18]So Samuel called upon the LORD, and the LORD sent thunder and rain that day, and all the people greatly feared the LORD and Samuel.

[19]And all the people said to Samuel, "Pray for your servants to the LORD your God, that we may not die, for we have added to all our sins this evil, to ask for

---

[1]Septuagint; Hebrew lacks *Testify against me* [2]Septuagint; Hebrew lacks *is witness* [3]Septuagint; Hebrew lacks *and the Egyptians oppressed them* [4]Septuagint *the army of Jabin king of Hazor* [5]Septuagint, Syriac; Hebrew *Bedan* [6]Septuagint *fathers*

ourselves a king." 20 And Samuel said to the people, "Do not be afraid; you have done all this evil. Yet do not turn aside from following the LORD, but serve the LORD with all your heart. 21 And do not turn aside after empty things that cannot profit or deliver, for they are empty. 22 For the LORD will not forsake his people, for his great name's sake, because it has pleased the LORD to make you a people for himself. 23 Moreover, as for me, far be it from me that I should sin against the LORD by ceasing to pray for you, and I will instruct you in the good and the right way. 24 Only fear the LORD and serve him faithfully with all your heart. For consider what great things he has done for you. 25 But if you still do wickedly, you shall be swept away, both you and your king."

Saul Fights the Philistines

13 Saul lived for one year and then became king, and when he had reigned for two years over Israel,[1] 2 Saul chose three thousand men of Israel. Two thousand were with Saul in Michmash and the hill country of Bethel, and a thousand were with Jonathan in Gibeah of Benjamin. The rest of the people he sent home, every man to his tent. 3 Jonathan defeated the garrison of the Philistines that was at Geba, and the Philistines heard of it. And Saul blew the trumpet throughout all the land, saying, "Let the Hebrews hear." 4 And all Israel heard it said that Saul had defeated the garrison of the Philistines, and also that Israel had become a stench to the Philistines. And the people were called out to join Saul at Gilgal.

5 And the Philistines mustered to fight with Israel, thirty thousand chariots and six thousand horsemen and troops like the sand on the seashore in multitude. They came up and encamped in Michmash, to the east of Beth-aven. 6 When the men of Israel saw that they were in trouble (for the people were hard pressed), the people hid themselves in caves and in holes and in rocks and in tombs and in cisterns, 7 and some Hebrews crossed the fords of the Jordan to the land of Gad and Gilead. Saul was still at Gilgal, and all the people followed him trembling.

Saul's Unlawful Sacrifice

8 He waited seven days, the time appointed by Samuel. But Samuel did not come to Gilgal, and the people were scattering from him. 9 So Saul said, "Bring the burnt offering here to me, and the peace offerings." And he offered the burnt offering. 10 As soon as he had finished offering the burnt offering, behold, Samuel came. And Saul went out to meet him and greet him. 11 Samuel said, "What have you done?" And Saul said, "When I saw that the people were scattering from me, and that you did not come within the days appointed, and that the Philistines had mustered at Michmash, 12 I said, 'Now the Philistines will come down against me at Gilgal, and I have not sought the favor of the LORD.' So I forced myself, and offered the burnt offering." 13 And Samuel said to Saul, "You have done foolishly. You have not kept the command of the LORD your God, with which he commanded you. For then the LORD would have established your kingdom over Israel forever. 14 But now your kingdom shall not continue. The LORD has sought out a man after his own heart, and the LORD has commanded him to be prince[2] over his people, because you have not kept what the LORD commanded you." 15 And Samuel arose and went up from Gilgal. The rest of the people went up after Saul to meet the army; they went up from Gilgal[3] to Gibeah of Benjamin.

And Saul numbered the people who were present with him, about six hundred men. 16 And Saul and Jonathan his son and the people who were present with them stayed in Geba of Benjamin, but the Philistines encamped in Michmash. 17 And raiders came out of the camp of the Philistines in three companies. One company turned toward Ophrah, to the land of Shual; 18 another company turned toward Beth-horon; and another company turned toward the border that looks down on the Valley of Zeboim toward the wilderness.

19 Now there was no blacksmith to be found throughout all the land of Israel, for the Philistines said, "Lest the Hebrews make themselves swords or spears." 20 But every one of the Israelites went down to the Philistines to sharpen his plowshare, his mattock, his axe, or his sickle,[4] 21 and

---

[1] Hebrew *Saul was one year old when he became king, and he reigned two years over Israel* (see 1 Samuel 10:6); some Greek manuscripts give Saul's age when he began to reign as thirty years [2] Or *leader* [3] Septuagint; Hebrew lacks *The rest of the people . . . from Gilgal* [4] Septuagint; Hebrew *plowshare*

the charge was two-thirds of a shekel[1] for the plowshares and for the mattocks, and a third of a shekel[2] for sharpening the axes and for setting the goads.[3] **22** So on the day of the battle there was neither sword nor spear found in the hand of any of the people with Saul and Jonathan, but Saul and Jonathan his son had them. **23** And the garrison of the Philistines went out to the pass of Michmash.

Jonathan Defeats the Philistines

14 One day Jonathan the son of Saul said to the young man who carried his armor, "Come, let us go over to the Philistine garrison on the other side." But he did not tell his father. **2** Saul was staying in the outskirts of Gibeah in the pomegranate cave[4] at Migron. The people who were with him were about six hundred men, **3** including Ahijah the son of Ahitub, Ichabod's brother, son of Phinehas, son of Eli, the priest of the LORD in Shiloh, wearing an ephod. And the people did not know that Jonathan had gone. **4** Within the passes, by which Jonathan sought to go over to the Philistine garrison, there was a rocky crag on the one side and a rocky crag on the other side. The name of the one was Bozez, and the name of the other Seneh. **5** The one crag rose on the north in front of Michmash, and the other on the south in front of Geba.

6 Jonathan said to the young man who carried his armor, "Come, let us go over to the garrison of these uncircumcised. It may be that the LORD will work for us, for nothing can hinder the LORD from saving by many or by few." **7** And his armor-bearer said to him, "Do all that is in your heart. Do as you wish.[5] Behold, I am with you heart and soul." **8** Then Jonathan said, "Behold, we will cross over to the men, and we will show ourselves to them. **9** If they say to us, 'Wait until we come to you,' then we will stand still in our place, and we will not go up to them. **10** But if they say, 'Come up to us,' then we will go up, for the LORD has given them into our hand. And this shall be the sign to us." **11** So both of them showed themselves to the garrison of the Philistines. And the Philistines said, "Look, Hebrews are coming out of the holes where

they have hidden themselves." **12** And the men of the garrison hailed Jonathan and his armor-bearer and said, "Come up to us, and we will show you a thing." And Jonathan said to his armor-bearer, "Come up after me, for the LORD has given them into the hand of Israel." **13** Then Jonathan climbed up on his hands and feet, and his armor-bearer after him. And they fell before Jonathan, and his armor-bearer killed them after him. **14** And that first strike, which Jonathan and his armor-bearer made, killed about twenty men within as it were half a furrow's length in an acre[6] of land. **15** And there was a panic in the camp, in the field, and among all the people. The garrison and even the raiders trembled, the earth quaked, and it became a very great panic.[7]

16 And the watchmen of Saul in Gibeah of Benjamin looked, and behold, the multitude was dispersing here and there.[8] **17** Then Saul said to the people who were with him, "Count and see who has gone from us." And when they had counted, behold, Jonathan and his armor-bearer were not there. **18** So Saul said to Ahijah, "Bring the ark of God here." For the ark of God went at that time with the people[9] of Israel. **19** Now while Saul was talking to the priest, the tumult in the camp of the Philistines increased more and more. So Saul said to the priest, "Withdraw your hand." **20** Then Saul and all the people who were with him rallied and went into the battle. And behold, every Philistine's sword was against his fellow, and there was very great confusion. **21** Now the Hebrews who had been with the Philistines before that time and who had gone up with them into the camp, even they also turned to be with the Israelites who were with Saul and Jonathan. **22** Likewise, when all the men of Israel who had hidden themselves in the hill country of Ephraim heard that the Philistines were fleeing, they too followed hard after them in the battle. **23** So the LORD saved Israel that day. And the battle passed beyond Beth-aven.

Saul's Rash Vow

24 And the men of Israel had been hard pressed that day, so Saul had laid an oath

---

[1] Hebrew *was a pim* [2] A *shekel* was about 2/5 ounce or 11 grams [3] The meaning of the Hebrew verse is uncertain [4] Or *under the pomegranate* [tree] [5] Septuagint *Do all that your mind inclines to* [6] Hebrew *a yoke* [7] Or *became a panic from God* [8] Septuagint; Hebrew *they went here and there* [9] Hebrew; Septuagint *"Bring the ephod." For at that time he wore the ephod before the people*

on the people, saying, "Cursed be the man who eats food until it is evening and I am avenged on my enemies." So none of the people had tasted food. ²⁵ Now when all the people[1] came to the forest, behold, there was honey on the ground. ²⁶ And when the people entered the forest, behold, the honey was dropping, but no one put his hand to his mouth, for the people feared the oath. ²⁷ But Jonathan had not heard his father charge the people with the oath, so he put out the tip of the staff that was in his hand and dipped it in the honeycomb and put his hand to his mouth, and his eyes became bright. ²⁸ Then one of the people said, "Your father strictly charged the people with an oath, saying, 'Cursed be the man who eats food this day.'" And the people were faint. ²⁹ Then Jonathan said, "My father has troubled the land. See how my eyes have become bright because I tasted a little of this honey. ³⁰ How much better if the people had eaten freely today of the spoil of their enemies that they found. For now the defeat among the Philistines has not been great."

³¹ They struck down the Philistines that day from Michmash to Aijalon. And the people were very faint. ³² The people pounced on the spoil and took sheep and oxen and calves and slaughtered them on the ground. And the people ate them with the blood. ³³ Then they told Saul, "Behold, the people are sinning against the LORD by eating with the blood." And he said, "You have dealt treacherously; roll a great stone to me here."[2] ³⁴ And Saul said, "Disperse yourselves among the people and say to them, 'Let every man bring his ox or his sheep and slaughter them here and eat, and do not sin against the LORD by eating with the blood.'" So every one of the people brought his ox with him that night and they slaughtered them there. ³⁵ And Saul built an altar to the LORD; it was the first altar that he built to the LORD.

³⁶ Then Saul said, "Let us go down after the Philistines by night and plunder them until the morning light; let us not leave a man of them." And they said, "Do whatever seems good to you." But the priest said, "Let us draw near to God here." ³⁷ And Saul inquired of God, "Shall I go down after the Philistines? Will you give them into the hand of Israel?" But he did not answer him that day. ³⁸ And Saul said, "Come here, all you leaders of the people, and know and see how this sin has arisen today. ³⁹ For as the LORD lives who saves Israel, though it be in Jonathan my son, he shall surely die." But there was not a man among all the people who answered him. ⁴⁰ Then he said to all Israel, "You shall be on one side, and I and Jonathan my son will be on the other side." And the people said to Saul, "Do what seems good to you." ⁴¹ Therefore Saul said, "O LORD God of Israel, why have you not answered your servant this day? If this guilt is in me or in Jonathan my son, O LORD, God of Israel, give Urim. But if this guilt is in your people Israel, give Thummim."[3] And Jonathan and Saul were taken, but the people escaped. ⁴² Then Saul said, "Cast the lot between me and my son Jonathan." And Jonathan was taken.

⁴³ Then Saul said to Jonathan, "Tell me what you have done." And Jonathan told him, "I tasted a little honey with the tip of the staff that was in my hand. Here I am; I will die." ⁴⁴ And Saul said, "God do so to me and more also; you shall surely die, Jonathan." ⁴⁵ Then the people said to Saul, "Shall Jonathan die, who has worked this great salvation in Israel? Far from it! As the LORD lives, there shall not one hair of his head fall to the ground, for he has worked with God this day." So the people ransomed Jonathan, so that he did not die. ⁴⁶ Then Saul went up from pursuing the Philistines, and the Philistines went to their own place.

Saul Fights Israel's Enemies

⁴⁷ When Saul had taken the kingship over Israel, he fought against all his enemies on every side, against Moab, against the Ammonites, against Edom, against the kings of Zobah, and against the Philistines. Wherever he turned he routed them. ⁴⁸ And he did valiantly and struck the Amalekites and delivered Israel out of the hands of those who plundered them.

⁴⁹ Now the sons of Saul were Jonathan, Ishvi, and Malchi-shua. And the names of his two daughters were these: the name of the firstborn was Merab, and the name of the younger Michal. ⁵⁰ And the name of Saul's wife was Ahinoam the daughter of Ahimaaz. And the name of the commander

¹ Hebrew *land* ² Septuagint; Hebrew *this day* ³ Vulgate and Septuagint; Hebrew *Therefore Saul said to the LORD, the God of Israel, "Give Thummim."*

of his army was Abner the son of Ner, Saul's uncle. [51] Kish was the father of Saul, and Ner the father of Abner was the son of Abiel.

[52] There was hard fighting against the Philistines all the days of Saul. And when Saul saw any strong man, or any valiant man, he attached him to himself.

The Lord Rejects Saul

15 And Samuel said to Saul, "The Lord sent me to anoint you king over his people Israel; now therefore listen to the words of the Lord. [2] Thus says the Lord of hosts, 'I have noted what Amalek did to Israel in opposing them on the way when they came up out of Egypt. [3] Now go and strike Amalek and devote to destruction[1] all that they have. Do not spare them, but kill both man and woman, child and infant, ox and sheep, camel and donkey.'"

[4] So Saul summoned the people and numbered them in Telaim, two hundred thousand men on foot, and ten thousand men of Judah. [5] And Saul came to the city of Amalek and lay in wait in the valley. [6] Then Saul said to the Kenites, "Go, depart; go down from among the Amalekites, lest I destroy you with them. For you showed kindness to all the people of Israel when they came up out of Egypt." So the Kenites departed from among the Amalekites. [7] And Saul defeated the Amalekites from Havilah as far as Shur, which is east of Egypt. [8] And he took Agag the king of the Amalekites alive and devoted to destruction all the people with the edge of the sword. [9] But Saul and the people spared Agag and the best of the sheep and of the oxen and of the fattened calves[2] and the lambs, and all that was good, and would not utterly destroy them. All that was despised and worthless they devoted to destruction.

[10] The word of the Lord came to Samuel: [11] "I regret[3] that I have made Saul king, for he has turned back from following me and has not performed my commandments." And Samuel was angry, and he cried to the Lord all night. [12] And Samuel rose early to meet Saul in the morning. And it was told Samuel, "Saul came to Carmel, and behold, he set up a monument for himself and turned and passed on and went down to Gilgal." [13] And Samuel came to Saul, and Saul said to him, "Blessed be you to the Lord. I have performed the commandment of the Lord." [14] And Samuel said, "What then is this bleating of the sheep in my ears and the lowing of the oxen that I hear?" [15] Saul said, "They have brought them from the Amalekites, for the people spared the best of the sheep and of the oxen to sacrifice to the Lord your God, and the rest we have devoted to destruction." [16] Then Samuel said to Saul, "Stop! I will tell you what the Lord said to me this night." And he said to him, "Speak."

[17] And Samuel said, "Though you are little in your own eyes, are you not the head of the tribes of Israel? The Lord anointed you king over Israel. [18] And the Lord sent you on a mission and said, 'Go, devote to destruction the sinners, the Amalekites, and fight against them until they are consumed.' [19] Why then did you not obey the voice of the Lord? Why did you pounce on the spoil and do what was evil in the sight of the Lord?" [20] And Saul said to Samuel, "I have obeyed the voice of the Lord. I have gone on the mission on which the Lord sent me. I have brought Agag the king of Amalek, and I have devoted the Amalekites to destruction. [21] But the people took of the spoil, sheep and oxen, the best of the things devoted to destruction, to sacrifice to the Lord your God in Gilgal." [22] And Samuel said,

"Has the Lord as great delight in
  burnt offerings and sacrifices,
 as in obeying the voice of the
  Lord?
Behold, to obey is better than sacrifice,
 and to listen than the fat of rams.
[23] For rebellion is as the sin of divination,
  and presumption is as iniquity and
   idolatry.
Because you have rejected the word
  of the Lord,
 he has also rejected you from
  being king."

[24] Saul said to Samuel, "I have sinned, for I have transgressed the commandment of the Lord and your words, because I feared the people and obeyed their voice. [25] Now therefore, please pardon my sin and return with me that I may bow before the Lord." [26] And Samuel said to Saul, "I will

---

[1] That is, set apart (devote) as an offering to the Lord (for destruction); also verses 8, 9, 15, 18, 20, 21 [2] The meaning of the Hebrew term is uncertain [3] See also verses 29, 35

not return with you. For you have rejected the word of the LORD, and the LORD has rejected you from being king over Israel." [27] As Samuel turned to go away, Saul seized the skirt of his robe, and it tore. [28] And Samuel said to him, "The LORD has torn the kingdom of Israel from you this day and has given it to a neighbor of yours, who is better than you. [29] And also the Glory of Israel will not lie or have regret, for he is not a man, that he should have regret." [30] Then he said, "I have sinned; yet honor me now before the elders of my people and before Israel, and return with me, that I may bow before the LORD your God." [31] So Samuel turned back after Saul, and Saul bowed before the LORD.

[32] Then Samuel said, "Bring here to me Agag the king of the Amalekites." And Agag came to him cheerfully.[1] Agag said, "Surely the bitterness of death is past." [33] And Samuel said, "As your sword has made women childless, so shall your mother be childless among women." And Samuel hacked Agag to pieces before the LORD in Gilgal.

[34] Then Samuel went to Ramah, and Saul went up to his house in Gibeah of Saul. [35] And Samuel did not see Saul again until the day of his death, but Samuel grieved over Saul. And the LORD regretted that he had made Saul king over Israel.

David Anointed King

16 The LORD said to Samuel, "How long will you grieve over Saul, since I have rejected him from being king over Israel? Fill your horn with oil, and go. I will send you to Jesse the Bethlehemite, for I have provided for myself a king among his sons." [2] And Samuel said, "How can I go? If Saul hears it, he will kill me." And the LORD said, "Take a heifer with you and say, 'I have come to sacrifice to the LORD.' [3] And invite Jesse to the sacrifice, and I will

Or *haltingly* (compare Septuagint); the Hebrew is uncertain

verses to read
1 Samuel 16:1-13

Think about all the ways that God has led you. Your life has been filled with times when God pulled you out of trouble, led you to safety, and kept you from harm. He was never far away, even when you felt like he was. He pulled you out of trouble and kept you from death. Best of all, he has forgiven all your sins in Christ.

It's easy to look at life as one freak accident after another and to see people as in control instead of God. But God isn't a distant observer who created you and then let you go. He keeps you from things that could hurt you. He's always present and always powerful. He is forever standing beside you, asking you to look his way and take his hand. As a God Girl you are never truly alone. If there is a gulf between you and God, it's because of your refusal to accept his outstretched hand, not because he's disinterested in your life. He is supremely interested in everything that happens to you. And he is forever ready to make something beautiful of your pain and suffering. He is the only one who can.

David was once just a humble shepherd boy, but everything in his life—even down to being a shepherd who defended the sheep—was used by God to prepare David to be king. The girl who has the watchful eye of God on her can't fail to make something amazing out of her life when she is willing to consider God's power, his love, and his hand in her life. Let go of your urge to blame your situation on outside influences, and instead search for God's influences on your life. He is, after all, the one ultimately in control. And that's a good thing, even if it doesn't look like it right now. In the end you're gonna see how he used it all for good.

show you what you shall do. And you shall anoint for me him whom I declare to you." [4] Samuel did what the LORD commanded and came to Bethlehem. The elders of the city came to meet him trembling and said, "Do you come peaceably?" [5] And he said, "Peaceably; I have come to sacrifice to the LORD. Consecrate yourselves, and come with me to the sacrifice." And he consecrated Jesse and his sons and invited them to the sacrifice.

[6] When they came, he looked on Eliab and thought, "Surely the LORD's anointed is before him." [7] But the LORD said to Samuel, "Do not look on his appearance or on the height of his stature, because I have rejected him. For the LORD sees not as man sees: man looks on the outward appearance, but the LORD looks on the heart." [8] Then Jesse called Abinadab and made him pass before Samuel. And he said, "Neither has the LORD chosen this one." [9] Then Jesse made Shammah pass by. And he said, "Neither has the LORD chosen this one." [10] And Jesse made seven of his sons pass before Samuel. And Samuel said to Jesse, "The LORD has not chosen these." [11] Then Samuel said to Jesse, "Are all your sons here?" And he said, "There remains yet the youngest,[1] but behold, he is keeping the sheep." And Samuel said to Jesse, "Send and get him, for we will not sit down till he comes here." [12] And he sent and brought him in. Now he was ruddy and had beautiful eyes and was handsome. And the LORD said, "Arise, anoint him, for this is he." [13] Then Samuel took the horn of oil and anointed him in the midst of his brothers. And the Spirit of the LORD rushed upon David from that day forward. And Samuel rose up and went to Ramah.

David in Saul's Service

[14] Now the Spirit of the LORD departed from Saul, and a harmful spirit from the LORD tormented him. [15] And Saul's servants said to him, "Behold now, a harmful spirit from God is tormenting you. [16] Let our lord now command your servants who are before you to seek out a man who is skillful in playing the lyre, and when the harmful spirit from God is upon you, he will play it, and you will be well." [17] So Saul said to his servants, "Provide for me a man

who can play well and bring him to me." [18] One of the young men answered, "Behold, I have seen a son of Jesse the Bethlehemite who is skillful in playing, a man of valor, a man of war, prudent in speech, and a man of good presence, and the LORD is with him." [19] Therefore Saul sent messengers to Jesse and said, "Send me David your son who is with the sheep." [20] And Jesse took a donkey laden with bread and a skin of wine and a young goat and sent them by David his son to Saul. [21] And David came to Saul and entered his service. And Saul loved him greatly, and he became his armor-bearer. [22] And Saul sent to Jesse, saying, "Let David remain in my service, for he has found favor in my sight." [23] And whenever the harmful spirit from God was upon Saul, David took the lyre and played it with his hand. So Saul was refreshed and was well, and the harmful spirit departed from him.

David and Goliath

17 Now the Philistines gathered their armies for battle. And they were gathered at Socoh, which belongs to Judah, and encamped between Socoh and Azekah, in Ephes-dammim. [2] And Saul and the men of Israel were gathered, and encamped in the Valley of Elah, and drew up in line of battle against the Philistines. [3] And the Philistines stood on the mountain on the one side, and Israel stood on the mountain on the other side, with a valley between them. [4] And there came out from the camp of the Philistines a champion named Goliath of Gath, whose height was six[2] cubits[3] and a span. [5] He had a helmet of bronze on his head, and he was armed with a coat of mail, and the weight of the coat was five thousand shekels[4] of bronze. [6] And he had bronze armor on his legs, and a javelin of bronze slung between his shoulders. [7] The shaft of his spear was like a weaver's beam, and his spear's head weighed six hundred shekels of iron. And his shield-bearer went before him. [8] He stood and shouted to the ranks of Israel, "Why have you come out to draw up for battle? Am I not a Philistine, and are you not servants of Saul? Choose a man for yourselves, and let him come down to me. [9] If he is able to fight with me and kill me, then we will be your servants. But if I prevail against him

---

[1] Or *smallest* [2] Hebrew; Septuagint, Dead Sea Scroll and Josephus *four* [3] A *cubit* was about 18 inches or 45 centimeters [4] A *shekel* was about 2/5 ounce or 11 grams

and kill him, then you shall be our servants and serve us." ¹⁰ And the Philistine said, "I defy the ranks of Israel this day. Give me a man, that we may fight together." ¹¹ When Saul and all Israel heard these words of the Philistine, they were dismayed and greatly afraid.

¹² Now David was the son of an Ephrathite of Bethlehem in Judah, named Jesse, who had eight sons. In the days of Saul the man was already old and advanced in years.¹ ¹³ The three oldest sons of Jesse had followed Saul to the battle. And the names of his three sons who went to the battle were Eliab the firstborn, and next to him Abinadab, and the third Shammah. ⁴ David was the youngest. The three eldest followed Saul, ¹⁵ but David went back and forth from Saul to feed his father's sheep at Bethlehem. ¹⁶ For forty days the Philistine came forward and took his stand, morning and evening.

¹⁷ And Jesse said to David his son, "Take for your brothers an ephah² of this parched grain, and these ten loaves, and carry them quickly to the camp to your brothers. ¹⁸ Also take these ten cheeses to the commander of their thousand. See if your brothers are well, and bring some token from them."

¹⁹ Now Saul and they and all the men of Israel were in the Valley of Elah, fighting with the Philistines. ²⁰ And David rose early in the morning and left the sheep with a keeper and took the provisions and went, as Jesse had commanded him. And he came to the encampment as the host was going out to the battle line, shouting the war cry. ²¹ And Israel and the Philistines drew up for battle, army against army. ²² And David left the things in charge of the keeper of the baggage and ran to the ranks and went and greeted his brothers. ²³ As he talked with them, behold, the champion, the Philistine of Gath, Goliath by name, came up out of the ranks of the Philistines and spoke the same words as before. And David heard him.

²⁴ All the men of Israel, when they saw the man, fled from him and were much afraid. ²⁵ And the men of Israel said, "Have you seen this man who has come up? Surely he has come up to defy Israel. And the king will enrich the man who kills him with great riches and will give him his daughter and make his father's house

free in Israel." ²⁶ And David said to the men who stood by him, "What shall be done for the man who kills this Philistine and takes away the reproach from Israel? For who is this uncircumcised Philistine, that he should defy the armies of the living God?" ²⁷ And the people answered him in the same way, "So shall it be done to the man who kills him."

²⁸ Now Eliab his eldest brother heard when he spoke to the men. And Eliab's anger was kindled against David, and he said, "Why have you come down? And with whom have you left those few sheep in the wilderness? I know your presumption and the evil of your heart, for you have come down to see the battle." ²⁹ And David said, "What have I done now? Was it not but a word?" ³⁰ And he turned away from him toward another, and spoke in the same way, and the people answered him again as before.

³¹ When the words that David spoke were heard, they repeated them before Saul, and he sent for him. ³² And David said to Saul, "Let no man's heart fail because of him. Your servant will go and fight with this Philistine." ³³ And Saul said to David, "You are not able to go against this Philistine to fight with him, for you are but a youth, and he has been a man of war from his youth." ³⁴ But David said to Saul, "Your servant used to keep sheep for his father. And when there came a lion, or a bear, and took a lamb from the flock, ³⁵ I went after him and struck him and delivered it out of his mouth. And if he arose against me, I caught him by his beard and struck him and killed him. ³⁶ Your servant has struck down both lions and bears, and this uncircumcised Philistine shall be like one of them, for he has defied the armies of the living God." ³⁷ And David said, "The LORD who delivered me from the paw of the lion and from the paw of the bear will deliver me from the hand of this Philistine." And Saul said to David, "Go, and the LORD be with you!"

³⁸ Then Saul clothed David with his armor. He put a helmet of bronze on his head and clothed him with a coat of mail, ³⁹ and David strapped his sword over his armor. And he tried in vain to go, for he had not tested them. Then David said to Saul, "I cannot go with these, for I have not tested them." So David put them off.

---

¹ Septuagint, Syriac; Hebrew *advanced among men* ² An *ephah* was about 3/5 bushel or 22 liters

40 Then he took his staff in his hand and chose five smooth stones from the brook and put them in his shepherd's pouch. His sling was in his hand, and he approached the Philistine. **41** And the Philistine moved forward and came near to David, with his shield-bearer in front of him. **42** And when the Philistine looked and saw David, he disdained him, for he was but a youth, ruddy and handsome in appearance. **43** And the Philistine said to David, "Am I a dog, that you come to me with sticks?" And the Philistine cursed David by his gods. **44** The Philistine said to David, "Come to me, and I will give your flesh to the birds of the air and to the beasts of the field." **45** Then David said to the Philistine, "You come to me with a sword and with a spear and with a javelin, but I come to you in the name of the LORD of hosts, the God of the armies of Israel, whom you have defied. **46** This day the LORD will deliver you into my hand, and I will strike you down and cut off your head. And I will give the dead bodies of the host of the Philistines this day to the birds of the air and to the wild beasts of the earth, that all the earth may know that there is a God in Israel, **47** and that all this assembly may know that the LORD saves not with sword and spear. For the battle is the LORD's, and he will give you into our hand."

48 When the Philistine arose and came and drew near to meet David, David ran quickly toward the battle line to meet the Philistine. **49** And David put his hand in his bag and took out a stone and slung it and struck the Philistine on his forehead. The stone sank into his forehead, and he fell on his face to the ground.

50 So David prevailed over the Philistine with a sling and with a stone, and struck the Philistine and killed him. There was no sword in the hand of David. **51** Then David ran and stood over the Philistine and took his sword and drew it out of its sheath and killed him and cut off his head with it. When the Philistines saw that their champion was dead, they fled. **52** And the men of Israel and Judah rose with a shout and pursued the Philistines as far as Gath[1] and the gates of Ekron, so that the wounded Philistines fell on the way from Shaaraim as far as Gath and Ekron. **53** And the people of Israel came back from chasing the Philistines, and they plundered their camp. **54** And David took the head of the Philistine and brought it to Jerusalem, but he put his armor in his tent.

55 As soon as Saul saw David go out against the Philistine, he said to Abner, the commander of the army, "Abner, whose son is this youth?" And Abner said, "As your soul lives, O king, I do not know." **56** And the king said, "Inquire whose son the boy is." **57** And as soon as David returned from the striking down of the Philistine, Abner took him, and brought him before Saul with the head of the Philistine in his hand. **58** And Saul said to him, "Whose son are you, young man?" And David answered, "I am the son of your servant Jesse the Bethlehemite."

David and Jonathan's Friendship

18 As soon as he had finished speaking to Saul, the soul of Jonathan was knit to the soul of David, and Jonathan loved him as his own soul. **2** And Saul took him that day and would not let him return to his father's house. **3** Then Jonathan made a covenant with David, because he loved him as his own soul. **4** And Jonathan stripped himself of the robe that was on him and gave it to David, and his armor, and even his sword and his bow and his belt. **5** And David went out and was successful wherever Saul sent him, so that Saul set him over the men of war. And this was good in the sight of all the people and also in the sight of Saul's servants.

Saul's Jealousy of David

6 As they were coming home, when David returned from striking down the Philistine, the women came out of all the cities of Israel, singing and dancing, to meet King Saul, with tambourines, with songs of joy, and with musical instruments.[2] **7** And the women sang to one another as they celebrated,

"Saul has struck down his thousands,
        and David his ten thousands."

8 And Saul was very angry, and this saying displeased him. He said, "They have ascribed to David ten thousands, and to me they have ascribed thousands, and what more can he have but the kingdom?" **9** And Saul eyed David from that day on.

---

[1] Septuagint; Hebrew *Gai* [2] Or *triangles*, or *three-stringed instruments*

¹⁰ The next day a harmful spirit from God rushed upon Saul, and he raved within his house while David was playing the lyre, as he did day by day. Saul had his spear in his hand. ¹¹ And Saul hurled the spear, for he thought, "I will pin David to the wall." But David evaded him twice.

¹² Saul was afraid of David because the LORD was with him but had departed from Saul. ¹³ So Saul removed him from his presence and made him a commander of a thousand. And he went out and came in before the people. ¹⁴ And David had success in all his undertakings, for the LORD was with him. ¹⁵ And when Saul saw that he had great success, he stood in fearful awe of him. ¹⁶ But all Israel and Judah loved David, for he went out and came in before them.

David Marries Michal

¹⁷ Then Saul said to David, "Here is my elder daughter Merab. I will give her to you for a wife. Only be valiant for me and fight the LORD's battles." For Saul thought, "Let not my hand be against him, but let the hand of the Philistines be against him." ¹⁸ And David said to Saul, "Who am I, and who are my relatives, my father's clan in Israel, that I should be son-in-law to the king?" ¹⁹ But at the time when Merab, Saul's daughter, should have been given to David, she was given to Adriel the Meholathite for a wife.

²⁰ Now Saul's daughter Michal loved David. And they told Saul, and the thing pleased him. ²¹ Saul thought, "Let me give her to him, that she may be a snare for him and that the hand of the Philistines may be against him." Therefore Saul said to David a second time,[1] "You shall now be my son-in-law." ²² And Saul commanded his servants, "Speak to David in private and say, 'Behold, the king has delight in you, and all his servants love you. Now then become the king's son-in-law.'" ²³ And Saul's servants spoke those words in the ears of David. And David said, "Does it seem to you a little thing to become the king's son-in-law, since I am a poor man and have no reputation?" ²⁴ And the servants of Saul told him, "Thus and so did David speak." ²⁵ Then Saul said, "Thus shall you say to David, 'The king desires no bride-price except a hundred foreskins of the Philistines, that he may be avenged of the king's enemies.'"

Now Saul thought to make David fall by the hand of the Philistines. ²⁶ And when his servants told David these words, it pleased David well to be the king's son-in-law. Before the time had expired, ²⁷ David arose and went, along with his men, and killed two hundred of the Philistines. And David brought their foreskins, which were given in full number to the king, that he might become the king's son-in-law. And Saul gave him his daughter Michal for a wife. ²⁸ But when Saul saw and knew that the LORD was with David, and that Michal, Saul's daughter, loved him, ²⁹ Saul was even more afraid of David. So Saul was David's enemy continually.

³⁰ Then the commanders of the Philistines came out to battle, and as often as they came out David had more success than all the servants of Saul, so that his name was highly esteemed.

Saul Tries to Kill David

19 And Saul spoke to Jonathan his son and to all his servants, that they should kill David. But Jonathan, Saul's son, delighted much in David. ² And Jonathan told David, "Saul my father seeks to kill you. Therefore be on your guard in the morning. Stay in a secret place and hide yourself. ³ And I will go out and stand beside my father in the field where you are, and I will speak to my father about you. And if I learn anything I will tell you." ⁴ And Jonathan spoke well of David to Saul his father and said to him, "Let not the king sin against his servant David, because he has not sinned against you, and because his deeds have brought good to you. ⁵ For he took his life in his hand and he struck down the Philistine, and the LORD worked a great salvation for all Israel. You saw it, and rejoiced. Why then will you sin against innocent blood by killing David without cause?" ⁶ And Saul listened to the voice of Jonathan. Saul swore, "As the LORD lives, he shall not be put to death." ⁷ And Jonathan called David, and Jonathan reported to him all these things. And Jonathan brought David to Saul, and he was in his presence as before.

⁸ And there was war again. And David went out and fought with the Philistines and struck them with a great blow, so that they fled before him. ⁹ Then a harmful spirit

---

[1] Hebrew *by two*

from the LORD came upon Saul, as he sat in his house with his spear in his hand. And David was playing the lyre. [10] And Saul sought to pin David to the wall with the spear, but he eluded Saul, so that he struck the spear into the wall. And David fled and escaped that night.

[11] Saul sent messengers to David's house to watch him, that he might kill him in the morning. But Michal, David's wife, told him, "If you do not escape with your life tonight, tomorrow you will be killed." [12] So Michal let David down through the window, and he fled away and escaped. [13] Michal took an image[1] and laid it on the bed and put a pillow of goats' hair at its head and covered it with the clothes. [14] And when Saul sent messengers to take David, she said, "He is sick." [15] Then Saul sent the messengers to see David, saying, "Bring him up to me in the bed, that I may kill him." [16] And when the messengers came in, behold, the image was in the bed, with the pillow of goats' hair at its head. [17] Saul said to Michal, "Why have you deceived me thus and let my enemy go, so that he has escaped?" And Michal answered Saul, "He said to me, 'Let me go. Why should I kill you?'"

[18] Now David fled and escaped, and he came to Samuel at Ramah and told him all that Saul had done to him. And he and Samuel went and lived at Naioth. [19] And it was told Saul, "Behold, David is at Naioth in Ramah." [20] Then Saul sent messengers to take David, and when they saw the company of the prophets prophesying, and Samuel standing as head over them, the Spirit of God came upon the messengers of Saul, and they also prophesied. [21] When it was told Saul, he sent other messengers, and they also prophesied. And Saul sent messengers again the third time, and they also prophesied. [22] Then he himself went to Ramah and came to the great well that is in Secu. And he asked, "Where are Samuel and David?" And one said, "Behold, they are at Naioth in Ramah." [23] And he went there to Naioth in Ramah. And the Spirit of God came upon him also, and as he went he prophesied until he came to Naioth in Ramah. [24] And he too stripped off his clothes, and he too prophesied before Samuel and lay naked all that day and all that night. Thus it is said, "Is Saul also among the prophets?"

Jonathan Warns David

20 Then David fled from Naioth in Ramah and came and said before Jonathan, "What have I done? What is my guilt? And what is my sin before your father, that he seeks my life?" [2] And he said to him, "Far from it! You shall not die. Behold, my father does nothing either great or small without disclosing it to me. And why should my father hide this from me? It is not so." [3] But David vowed again, saying, "Your father knows well that I have found favor in your eyes, and he thinks, 'Do not let Jonathan know this, lest he be grieved.' But truly, as the LORD lives and as your soul lives, there is but a step between me and death." [4] Then Jonathan said to David, "Whatever you say, I will do for you." [5] David said to Jonathan, "Behold, tomorrow is the new moon, and I should not fail to sit at table with the king. But let me go, that I may hide myself in the field till the third day at evening. [6] If your father misses me at all, then say, 'David earnestly asked leave of me to run to Bethlehem his city, for there is a yearly sacrifice there for all the clan.' [7] If he says, 'Good!' it will be well with your servant, but if he is angry, then know that harm is determined by him. [8] Therefore deal kindly with your servant, for you have brought your servant into a covenant of the LORD with you. But if there is guilt in me, kill me yourself, for why should you bring me to your father?" [9] And Jonathan said, "Far be it from you! If I knew that it was determined by my father that harm should come to you, would I not tell you?" [10] Then David said to Jonathan, "Who will tell me if your father answers you roughly?" [11] And Jonathan said to David, "Come, let us go out into the field." So they both went out into the field.

[12] And Jonathan said to David, "The LORD, the God of Israel, be witness![2] When I have sounded out my father, about this time tomorrow, or the third day, behold, if he is well disposed toward David, shall I not then send and disclose it to you? [13] But should it please my father to do you harm, the LORD do so to Jonathan and more also if I do not disclose it to you and send you away, that you may go in safety. May the LORD be with you, as he has been with my father. [14] If I am still alive, show me the

---

[1] Or *a household god* [2] Hebrew lacks *be witness*

steadfast love of the LORD, that I may not die; ¹⁵ and do not cut off[1] your steadfast love from my house forever, when the LORD cuts off every one of the enemies of David from the face of the earth." ¹⁶ And Jonathan made a covenant with the house of David, saying, "May[2] the LORD take vengeance on David's enemies." ¹⁷ And Jonathan made David swear again by his love for him, for he loved him as he loved his own soul.

Ask Yourself . . .

ABOUT YOUR DEVOTION TO OTHERS

Scripture tells us to humbly think of others as better than ourselves (see Phil. 2:3). Humility isn't self-hate or being a glutton for punishment; it is loving others as much as you love yourself. Jonathan loved David as much as he loved himself, and that is what defined him as a true friend. Ask yourself about your devotion to your friends and family:

- Do I love others as much as I love myself?
- Am I willing to give up things I want so that others can be happy?
- What is the value of considering other people as well as my own desires?
- What scares me about not standing up for myself and letting others be right, or letting them have what I want for myself?
- In what ways can I start showing others that I love them as much as I love myself?

¹⁸ Then Jonathan said to him, "Tomorrow is the new moon, and you will be missed, because your seat will be empty. ¹⁹ On the third day go down quickly to the place where you hid yourself when the matter was in hand, and remain beside the stone heap.[3] ²⁰ And I will shoot three arrows to the side of it, as though I shot at a mark. ²¹ And behold, I will send the boy, saying, 'Go, find the arrows.' If I say to the boy, 'Look, the arrows are on this side of you, take them,' then you are to come, for, as the LORD lives, it is safe for you and there is no danger. ²² But if I say to the youth, 'Look, the arrows are beyond you,' then go, for the LORD has sent you away. ²³ And as for the matter of which you and I have spoken, behold, the LORD is between you and me forever."

²⁴ So David hid himself in the field. And when the new moon came, the king sat down to eat food. ²⁵ The king sat on his seat, as at other times, on the seat by the wall. Jonathan sat opposite,[4] and Abner sat by Saul's side, but David's place was empty. ²⁶ Yet Saul did not say anything that day, for he thought, "Something has happened to him. He is not clean; surely he is not clean." ²⁷ But on the second day, the day after the new moon, David's place was empty. And Saul said to Jonathan his son, "Why has not the son of Jesse come to the meal, either yesterday or today?" ²⁸ Jonathan answered Saul, "David earnestly asked leave of me to go to Bethlehem. ²⁹ He said, 'Let me go, for our clan holds a sacrifice in the city, and my brother has commanded me to be there. So now, if I have found favor in your eyes, let me get away and see my brothers.' For this reason he has not come to the king's table."

³⁰ Then Saul's anger was kindled against Jonathan, and he said to him, "You son of a perverse, rebellious woman, do I not know that you have chosen the son of Jesse to your own shame, and to the shame of your mother's nakedness? ³¹ For as long as the son of Jesse lives on the earth, neither you nor your kingdom shall be established. Therefore send and bring him to me, for he shall surely die." ³² Then Jonathan answered Saul his father, "Why should he be put to death? What has he done?" ³³ But Saul hurled his spear at him to strike him. So Jonathan knew that his father was determined to put David to death. ³⁴ And Jonathan rose from the table in fierce anger and ate no food the second day of

---

[1] Or but if I die, do not cut off   [2] Septuagint earth, ¹⁶let not the name of Jonathan be cut off from the house of David. And may   [3] Septuagint; Hebrew the stone Ezel   [4] Compare Septuagint; Hebrew stood up

the month, for he was grieved for David, because his father had disgraced him.

[35] In the morning Jonathan went out into the field to the appointment with David, and with him a little boy. [36] And he said to his boy, "Run and find the arrows that I shoot." As the boy ran, he shot an arrow beyond him. [37] And when the boy came to the place of the arrow that Jonathan had shot, Jonathan called after the boy and said, "Is not the arrow beyond you?" [38] And Jonathan called after the boy, "Hurry! Be quick! Do not stay!" So Jonathan's boy gathered up the arrows and came to his master. [39] But the boy knew nothing. Only Jonathan and David knew the matter. [40] And Jonathan gave his weapons to his boy and said to him, "Go and carry them to the city." [41] And as soon as the boy had gone, David rose from beside the stone heap[1] and fell on his face to the ground and bowed three times. And they kissed one another and wept with one another, David weeping the most. [42] Then Jonathan said to David, "Go in peace, because we have sworn both of us in the name of the LORD, saying, 'The LORD shall be between me and you, and between my offspring and your offspring, forever.'" And he rose and departed, and Jonathan went into the city.[2]

David and the Holy Bread

21 [3] Then David came to Nob to Ahimelech the priest. And Ahimelech came to meet David trembling and said to him, "Why are you alone, and no one with you?" [2] And David said to Ahimelech the priest, "The king has charged me with a matter and said to me, 'Let no one know anything of the matter about which I send you, and with which I have charged you.' I have made an appointment with the young men for such and such a place. [3] Now then, what do you have on hand? Give me five loaves of bread, or whatever is here." [4] And the priest answered David, "I have no common bread on hand, but there is holy bread—if the young men have kept themselves from women." [5] And David answered the priest, "Truly women have been kept from us as always when I go on an expedition. The vessels of the young men are holy even when it is an ordinary journey. How much more today will their vessels be holy?" [6] So the priest gave him the holy

bread, for there was no bread there but the bread of the Presence, which is removed from before the LORD, to be replaced by hot bread on the day it is taken away.

[7] Now a certain man of the servants of Saul was there that day, detained before the LORD. His name was Doeg the Edomite, the chief of Saul's herdsmen.

[8] Then David said to Ahimelech, "Then have you not here a spear or a sword at hand? For I have brought neither my sword nor my weapons with me, because the king's business required haste." [9] And the priest said, "The sword of Goliath the Philistine, whom you struck down in the Valley of Elah, behold, it is here wrapped in a cloth behind the ephod. If you will take that, take it, for there is none but that here." And David said, "There is none like that; give it to me."

David Flees to Gath

[10] And David rose and fled that day from Saul and went to Achish the king of Gath. [11] And the servants of Achish said to him, "Is not this David the king of the land? Did they not sing to one another of him in dances,

> 'Saul has struck down his thousands, and David his ten thousands'?"

[12] And David took these words to heart and was much afraid of Achish the king of Gath. [13] So he changed his behavior before them and pretended to be insane in their hands and made marks on the doors of the gate and let his spittle run down his beard. [14] Then Achish said to his servants, "Behold, you see the man is mad. Why then have you brought him to me? [15] Do I lack madmen, that you have brought this fellow to behave as a madman in my presence? Shall this fellow come into my house?"

David at the Cave of Adullam

22 David departed from there and escaped to the cave of Adullam. And when his brothers and all his father's house heard it, they went down there to him. [2] And everyone who was in distress, and everyone who was in debt, and everyone who was bitter in soul,[4] gathered to him. And he became commander over them. And there were with him about four hundred men.

---

[1] Septuagint; Hebrew *from beside the south* [2] This sentence is 21:1 in Hebrew [3] Ch 21:2 in Hebrew [4] Or *discontented*

³ And David went from there to Mizpeh of Moab. And he said to the king of Moab, "Please let my father and my mother stay[1] with you, till I know what God will do for me." ⁴ And he left them with the king of Moab, and they stayed with him all the time that David was in the stronghold. ⁵ Then the prophet Gad said to David, "Do not remain in the stronghold; depart, and go into the land of Judah." So David departed and went into the forest of Hereth.

Saul Kills the Priests at Nob

⁶ Now Saul heard that David was discovered, and the men who were with him. Saul was sitting at Gibeah under the tamarisk tree on the height with his spear in his hand, and all his servants were standing about him. ⁷ And Saul said to his servants who stood about him, "Hear now, people of Benjamin; will the son of Jesse give every one of you fields and vineyards, will he make you all commanders of thousands and commanders of hundreds, ⁸ that all of you have conspired against me? No one discloses to me when my son makes a covenant with the son of Jesse. None of you is sorry for me or discloses to me that my son has stirred up my servant against me, to lie in wait, as at this day." ⁹ Then answered Doeg the Edomite, who stood by the servants of Saul, "I saw the son of Jesse coming to Nob, to Ahimelech the son of Ahitub, ¹⁰ and he inquired of the LORD for him and gave him provisions and gave him the sword of Goliath the Philistine."

¹¹ Then the king sent to summon Ahimelech the priest, the son of Ahitub, and all his father's house, the priests who were at Nob, and all of them came to the king. ¹² And Saul said, "Hear now, son of Ahitub." And he answered, "Here I am, my lord." ¹³ And Saul said to him, "Why have you conspired against me, you and the son of Jesse, in that you have given him bread and a sword and have inquired of God for him, so that he has risen against me, to lie in wait, as at this day?" ¹⁴ Then Ahimelech answered the king, "And who among all your servants is so faithful as David, who is the king's son-in-law, and captain over[2] your bodyguard, and honored in your house? ¹⁵ Is today the first time that I have inquired of God for him? No! Let not the king impute anything to his servant or to

all the house of my father, for your servant has known nothing of all this, much or little." ¹⁶ And the king said, "You shall surely die, Ahimelech, you and all your father's house." ¹⁷ And the king said to the guard who stood about him, "Turn and kill the priests of the LORD, because their hand also is with David, and they knew that he fled and did not disclose it to me." But the servants of the king would not put out their hand to strike the priests of the LORD. ¹⁸ Then the king said to Doeg, "You turn and strike the priests." And Doeg the Edomite turned and struck down the priests, and he killed on that day eighty-five persons who wore the linen ephod. ¹⁹ And Nob, the city of the priests, he put to the sword; both man and woman, child and infant, ox, donkey and sheep, he put to the sword.

²⁰ But one of the sons of Ahimelech the son of Ahitub, named Abiathar, escaped and fled after David. ²¹ And Abiathar told David that Saul had killed the priests of the LORD. ²² And David said to Abiathar, "I knew on that day, when Doeg the Edomite was there, that he would surely tell Saul. I have occasioned the death of all the persons of your father's house. ²³ Stay with me; do not be afraid, for he who seeks my life seeks your life. With me you shall be in safekeeping."

David Saves the City of Keilah

23 Now they told David, "Behold, the Philistines are fighting against Keilah and are robbing the threshing floors." ² Therefore David inquired of the LORD, "Shall I go and attack these Philistines?" And the LORD said to David, "Go and attack the Philistines and save Keilah." ³ But David's men said to him, "Behold, we are afraid here in Judah; how much more then if we go to Keilah against the armies of the Philistines?" ⁴ Then David inquired of the LORD again. And the LORD answered him, "Arise, go down to Keilah, for I will give the Philistines into your hand." ⁵ And David and his men went to Keilah and fought with the Philistines and brought away their livestock and struck them with a great blow. So David saved the inhabitants of Keilah.

⁶ When Abiathar the son of Ahimelech had fled to David to Keilah, he had come down with an ephod in his hand. ⁷ Now it was told Saul that David had come to

---

¹ Syriac, Vulgate; Hebrew *go out* ² Septuagint, Targum; Hebrew *and has turned aside to*

Keilah. And Saul said, "God has given him into my hand, for he has shut himself in by entering a town that has gates and bars." [8] And Saul summoned all the people to war, to go down to Keilah, to besiege David and his men. [9] David knew that Saul was plotting harm against him. And he said to Abiathar the priest, "Bring the ephod here." [10] Then David said, "O LORD, the God of Israel, your servant has surely heard that Saul seeks to come to Keilah, to destroy the city on my account. [11] Will the men of Keilah surrender me into his hand? Will Saul come down, as your servant has heard? O LORD, the God of Israel, please tell your servant." And the LORD said, "He will come down." [12] Then David said, "Will the men of Keilah surrender me and my men into the hand of Saul?" And the LORD said, "They will surrender you." [13] Then David and his men, who were about six hundred, arose and departed from Keilah, and they went wherever they could go. When Saul was told that David had escaped from Keilah, he gave up the expedition. [14] And David remained in the strongholds in the wilderness, in the hill country of the wilderness of Ziph. And Saul sought him every day, but God did not give him into his hand.

Saul Pursues David

[15] David saw that Saul had come out to seek his life. David was in the wilderness of Ziph at Horesh. [16] And Jonathan, Saul's son, rose and went to David at Horesh, and strengthened his hand in God. [17] And he said to him, "Do not fear, for the hand of Saul my father shall not find you. You shall be king over Israel, and I shall be next to you. Saul my father also knows this." [18] And the two of them made a covenant before the LORD. David remained at Horesh, and Jonathan went home.

[19] Then the Ziphites went up to Saul at Gibeah, saying, "Is not David hiding among us in the strongholds at Horesh, on the hill of Hachilah, which is south of Jeshimon? [20] Now come down, O king, according to all your heart's desire to come down, and our part shall be to surrender him into the king's hand." [21] And Saul said, "May you be blessed by the LORD, for you have had compassion on me. [22] Go, make yet more sure. Know and see the place where his foot is, and who has seen him there, for

it is told me that he is very cunning. [23] Se therefore and take note of all the lurkin places where he hides, and come back t me with sure information. Then I will g with you. And if he is in the land, I wi search him out among all the thousands o Judah." [24] And they arose and went to Zip ahead of Saul.

Now David and his men were in the wi derness of Maon, in the Arabah to the sout of Jeshimon. [25] And Saul and his men wen to seek him. And David was told, so he wen down to the rock and lived in the wilder ness of Maon. And when Saul heard tha he pursued after David in the wilderness of Maon. [26] Saul went on one side of th mountain, and David and his men on th other side of the mountain. And David wa hurrying to get away from Saul. As Saul an his men were closing in on David and hi men to capture them, [27] a messenger cam to Saul, saying, "Hurry and come, for th Philistines have made a raid against th land." [28] So Saul returned from pursuin after David and went against the Philistine: Therefore that place was called the Rock o Escape.[1] [29] [2] And David went up from ther and lived in the strongholds of Engedi.

David Spares Saul's Life

24 [3] When Saul returned from followin the Philistines, he was told, "Beholc David is in the wilderness of Engedi." [2] The Saul took three thousand chosen men ou of all Israel and went to seek David an his men in front of the Wildgoats' Rock: [3] And he came to the sheepfolds by the way where there was a cave, and Saul went i to relieve himself.[4] Now David and his me were sitting in the innermost parts of th cave. [4] And the men of David said to him "Here is the day of which the LORD said t you, 'Behold, I will give your enemy int your hand, and you shall do to him as i shall seem good to you.'" Then David aros and stealthily cut off a corner of Saul' robe. [5] And afterward David's heart strucl him, because he had cut off a corner o Saul's robe. [6] He said to his men, "The LOR forbid that I should do this thing to m lord, the LORD's anointed, to put out m hand against him, seeing he is the LORD' anointed." [7] So David persuaded his me with these words and did not permit then

---

[1] Or *Rock of Divisions* [2] Ch 24:1 in Hebrew [3] Ch 24:2 in Hebrew [4] Hebrew *cover his feet*

o attack Saul. And Saul rose up and left the ave and went on his way.

⁸ Afterward David also arose and went ut of the cave, and called after Saul, "My ord the king!" And when Saul looked ehind him, David bowed with his face to he earth and paid homage. ⁹ And David aid to Saul, "Why do you listen to the vords of men who say, 'Behold, David eeks your harm'? ¹⁰ Behold, this day your yes have seen how the LORD gave you oday into my hand in the cave. And some old me to kill you, but I spared you.¹ I said, will not put out my hand against my lord, or he is the LORD's anointed.' ¹¹ See, my ather, see the corner of your robe in my and. For by the fact that I cut off the cor- er of your robe and did not kill you, you nay know and see that there is no wrong r treason in my hands. I have not sinned gainst you, though you hunt my life to ake it. ¹² May the LORD judge between me nd you, may the LORD avenge me against ou, but my hand shall not be against you. ¹³ As the proverb of the ancients says, 'Out f the wicked comes wickedness.' But ny hand shall not be against you. ¹⁴ After vhom has the king of Israel come out? fter whom do you pursue? After a dead og! After a flea! ¹⁵ May the LORD therefore e judge and give sentence between me nd you, and see to it and plead my cause nd deliver me from your hand."

¹⁶ As soon as David had finished speaking hese words to Saul, Saul said, "Is this your oice, my son David?" And Saul lifted up his oice and wept. ¹⁷ He said to David, "You re more righteous than I, for you have epaid me good, whereas I have repaid ou evil. ¹⁸ And you have declared this day ow you have dealt well with me, in that ou did not kill me when the LORD put me nto your hands. ¹⁹ For if a man finds his nemy, will he let him go away safe? So nay the LORD reward you with good for vhat you have done to me this day. ²⁰ And ow, behold, I know that you shall surely e king, and that the kingdom of Israel hall be established in your hand. ²¹ Swear o me therefore by the LORD that you will ot cut off my offspring after me, and that ou will not destroy my name out of my ather's house." ²² And David swore this to aul. Then Saul went home, but David and is men went up to the stronghold.

The Death of Samuel

25 Now Samuel died. And all Israel assembled and mourned for him, and they buried him in his house at Ramah.

David and Abigail

Then David rose and went down to the wilderness of Paran. ² And there was a man in Maon whose business was in Carmel. The man was very rich; he had three thou- sand sheep and a thousand goats. He was shearing his sheep in Carmel. ³ Now the name of the man was Nabal, and the name of his wife Abigail. The woman was discern- ing and beautiful, but the man was harsh and badly behaved; he was a Calebite. ⁴ David heard in the wilderness that Nabal was shearing his sheep. ⁵ So David sent ten young men. And David said to the young men, "Go up to Carmel, and go to Nabal and greet him in my name. ⁶ And thus you shall greet him: 'Peace be to you, and peace be to your house, and peace be to all that you have. ⁷ I hear that you have shearers. Now your shepherds have been with us, and we did them no harm, and they missed nothing all the time they were in Carmel. ⁸ Ask your young men, and they will tell you. Therefore let my young men find favor in your eyes, for we come on a feast day. Please give whatever you have at hand to your servants and to your son David.'"

⁹ When David's young men came, they said all this to Nabal in the name of David, and then they waited. ¹⁰ And Nabal answered David's servants, "Who is David? Who is the son of Jesse? There are many servants these days who are breaking away from their masters. ¹¹ Shall I take my bread and my water and my meat that I have killed for my shearers and give it to men who come from I do not know where?" ¹² So David's young men turned away and came back and told him all this. ¹³ And David said to his men, "Every man strap on his sword!" And every man of them strapped on his sword. David also strapped on his sword. And about four hundred men went up after David, while two hundred remained with the baggage.

¹⁴ But one of the young men told Abigail, Nabal's wife, "Behold, David sent messen- gers out of the wilderness to greet our master, and he railed at them. ¹⁵ Yet the men were very good to us, and we suffered

Septuagint, Syriac, Targum; Hebrew it [my eye] *spared you*

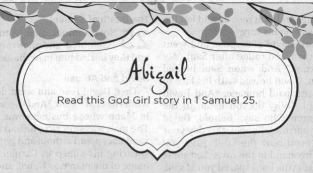

Abigail

Read this God Girl story in 1 Samuel 25.

She fell at his feet and said, "On me alone, my lord, be the guilt."

1 Samuel 25:24

Where there is sin, confession paves the way for forgiveness (see 1 John 1:9). But a lot of times people who are close to you refuse to confess their sin; in fact, they don't even acknowledge they've done anything sinful. They continue to live in ignorant bliss, bringing pain and suffering on everyone they love. Scripture shows us several instances where people actually confess sins for the people they love. The prophet Ezra saw the sins of his people and confessed them like he was a part of their evil even though he had nothing to do with it, and Abigail confessed the mistakes of her husband, Nabal, on his behalf, even though she wasn't even there when he said what he said.

It can be easy to judge and to resent what your family, friends, church, or even nation does, but what if you would stand in fellowship and confess the sin instead of just condemning it? God has been offended—that's really the point. The sin was against him and him alone, and confession is your gift to him, not to the offender.

And remember, when Jesus hung on the cross, he was taking the sins of others, too. Abigail and David and others who absorbed the sins of others were anticipating the greatest absorption of sin the universe could ever know—the Son of God taking on your sins and mine. It is true that some of the sins of the people you love might be hurting you. They might be causing you a lot of pain. But forgive them as you have been forgiven.

no harm, and we did not miss anything when we were in the fields, as long as we went with them. ¹⁶ They were a wall to us both by night and by day, all the while we were with them keeping the sheep. ¹⁷ Now therefore know this and consider what you should do, for harm is determined against our master and against all his house, and he is such a worthless man that one cannot speak to him."

¹⁸ Then Abigail made haste and took two hundred loaves and two skins of wine and five sheep already prepared and five seahs¹ of parched grain and a hundred clusters of raisins and two hundred cakes of figs, and laid them on donkeys. ¹⁹ And she said to her young men, "Go on before me; behold, I come after you." But she did not tell her husband Nabal. ²⁰ And as she rode on the donkey and came down under cover of the mountain, behold, David and his men came down toward her, and she met them. ²¹ Now David had said, "Surely in vain have I guarded all that this fellow has in the wilderness, so that nothing was missed of all that belonged to him, and he has returned me evil for good. ²² God do so to the enemies of David² and more also, if by morning I leave so much as one male of all who belong to him."

²³ When Abigail saw David, she hurried and got down from the donkey and fell before David on her face and bowed to the ground. ²⁴ She fell at his feet and said, "On me alone, my lord, be the guilt. Please let your servant speak in your ears, and hear the words of your servant. ²⁵ Let not my lord regard this worthless fellow, Nabal, for as his name is, so is he. Nabal³ is his name, and folly is with him. But I your servant did not see the young men of my lord, whom you sent. ²⁶ Now then, my lord, as the LORD lives, and as your soul lives, because the LORD has restrained you from bloodguilt and from saving with your own hand, now then let your enemies and those who seek to do evil to my lord be as Nabal. ²⁷ And now let this present that your servant has brought to my lord be given to the young men who follow my lord. ²⁸ Please forgive the trespass of your servant. For the LORD will certainly make my lord a sure house, because my lord is fighting the battles of the LORD, and evil shall not be found in you so long as you live. ²⁹ If men rise up to

pursue you and to seek your life, the life of my lord shall be bound in the bundle of the living in the care of the LORD your God. And the lives of your enemies he shall sling out as from the hollow of a sling. ³⁰ And when the LORD has done to my lord according to all the good that he has spoken concerning you and has appointed you prince⁴ over Israel, ³¹ my lord shall have no cause of grief or pangs of conscience for having shed blood without cause or for my lord working salvation himself. And when the LORD has dealt well with my lord, then remember your servant."

³² And David said to Abigail, "Blessed be the LORD, the God of Israel, who sent you this day to meet me! ³³ Blessed be your discretion, and blessed be you, who have kept me this day from bloodguilt and from working salvation with my own hand! ³⁴ For as surely as the LORD, the God of Israel, lives, who has restrained me from hurting you, unless you had hurried and come to meet me, truly by morning there had not been left to Nabal so much as one male." ³⁵ Then David received from her hand what she had brought him. And he said to her, "Go up in peace to your house. See, I have obeyed your voice, and I have granted your petition."

³⁶ And Abigail came to Nabal, and behold, he was holding a feast in his house, like the feast of a king. And Nabal's heart was merry within him, for he was very drunk. So she told him nothing at all until the morning light. ³⁷ In the morning, when the wine had gone out of Nabal, his wife told him these things, and his heart died within him, and he became as a stone. ³⁸ And about ten days later the LORD struck Nabal, and he died.

³⁹ When David heard that Nabal was dead, he said, "Blessed be the LORD who has avenged the insult I received at the hand of Nabal, and has kept back his servant from wrongdoing. The LORD has returned the evil of Nabal on his own head." Then David sent and spoke to Abigail, to take her as his wife. ⁴⁰ When the servants of David came to Abigail at Carmel, they said to her, "David has sent us to you to take you to him as his wife." ⁴¹ And she rose and bowed with her face to the ground and said, "Behold, your handmaid is a servant to wash the feet of the servants of my lord." ⁴² And Abigail

---

¹ A *seah* was about 7 quarts or 7.3 liters   ² Septuagint *to David*   ³ *Nabal* means *fool*   ⁴ Or *leader*

hurried and rose and mounted a donkey, and her five young women attended her. She followed the messengers of David and became his wife. ⁴³David also took Ahinoam of Jezreel, and both of them became his wives. ⁴⁴Saul had given Michal his daughter, David's wife, to Palti the son of Laish, who was of Gallim.

David Spares Saul Again

26 Then the Ziphites came to Saul at Gibeah, saying, "Is not David hiding himself on the hill of Hachilah, which is on the east of Jeshimon?" ²So Saul arose and went down to the wilderness of Ziph with three thousand chosen men of Israel to seek David in the wilderness of Ziph. ³And Saul encamped on the hill of Hachilah, which is beside the road on the east of Jeshimon. But David remained in the wilderness. When he saw that Saul came after him into the wilderness, ⁴David sent out spies and learned that Saul had indeed come. ⁵Then David rose and came to the place where Saul had encamped. And David saw the place where Saul lay, with Abner the son of Ner, the commander of his army. Saul was lying within the encampment, while the army was encamped around him.

⁶Then David said to Ahimelech the Hittite, and to Joab's brother Abishai the son of Zeruiah, "Who will go down with me into the camp to Saul?" And Abishai said, "I will go down with you." ⁷So David and Abishai went to the army by night. And there lay Saul sleeping within the encampment, with his spear stuck in the ground at his head, and Abner and the army lay around him. ⁸Then Abishai said to David, "God has given your enemy into your hand this day. Now please let me pin him to the earth with one stroke of the spear, and I will not strike him twice." ⁹But David said to Abishai, "Do not destroy him, for who can put out his hand against the LORD's anointed and be guiltless?" ¹⁰And David said, "As the LORD lives, the LORD will strike him, or his day will come to die, or he will go down into battle and perish. ¹¹The LORD forbid that I should put out my hand against the LORD's anointed. But take now the spear that is at his head and the jar of water, and let us go." ¹²So David took the spear and the jar of water from Saul's head, and they went away. No man saw it or knew it, nor did any awake, for they

were all asleep, because a deep sleep from the LORD had fallen upon them.

¹³Then David went over to the other side and stood far off on the top of the hill with a great space between them. ¹⁴And David called to the army, and to Abner the son of Ner, saying, "Will you not answer, Abner?" Then Abner answered, "Who are you who calls to the king?" ¹⁵And David said to Abner, "Are you not a man? Who is like you in Israel? Why then have you not kept watch over your lord the king? For one of the people came in to destroy the king your lord. ¹⁶This thing that you have done is not good. As the LORD lives, you deserve to die, because you have not kept watch over your lord, the LORD's anointed. And now see where the king's spear is and the jar of water that was at his head."

¹⁷Saul recognized David's voice and said, "Is this your voice, my son David?" And David said, "It is my voice, my lord, O king." ¹⁸And he said, "Why does my lord pursue after his servant? For what have I done? What evil is on my hands? ¹⁹Now therefore let my lord the king hear the words of his servant. If it is the LORD who has stirred you up against me, may he accept an offering, but if it is men, may they be cursed before the LORD, for they have driven me out this day that I should have no share in the heritage of the LORD, saying, 'Go, serve other gods.' ²⁰Now therefore, let not my blood fall to the earth away from the presence of the LORD, for the king of Israel has come out to seek a single flea like one who hunts a partridge in the mountains."

²¹Then Saul said, "I have sinned. Return, my son David, for I will no more do you harm, because my life was precious in your eyes this day. Behold, I have acted foolishly, and have made a great mistake." ²²And David answered and said, "Here is the spear, O king! Let one of the young men come over and take it. ²³The LORD rewards every man for his righteousness and his faithfulness, for the LORD gave you into my hand today, and I would not put out my hand against the LORD's anointed. ²⁴Behold, as your life was precious this day in my sight, so may my life be precious in the sight of the LORD, and may he deliver me out of all tribulation." ²⁵Then Saul said to David, "Blessed be you, my son David! You will do many things and will succeed in them." So David went his way, and Saul returned to his place.

David Flees to the Philistines

27 Then David said in his heart, "Now I shall perish one day by the hand of Saul. There is nothing better for me than that I should escape to the land of the Philistines. Then Saul will despair of seeking me any longer within the borders of Israel, and I shall escape out of his hand." ²So David arose and went over, he and the six hundred men who were with him, to Achish the son of Maoch, king of Gath. ³And David lived with Achish at Gath, he and his men, every man with his household, and David with his two wives, Ahinoam of Jezreel, and Abigail of Carmel, Nabal's widow. ⁴And when it was told Saul that David had fled to Gath, he no longer sought him.

⁵Then David said to Achish, "If I have found favor in your eyes, let a place be given me in one of the country towns, that I may dwell there. For why should your servant dwell in the royal city with you?" ⁶So that day Achish gave him Ziklag. Therefore Ziklag has belonged to the kings of Judah to this day. ⁷And the number of the days that David lived in the country of the Philistines was a year and four months.

⁸Now David and his men went up and made raids against the Geshurites, the Girzites, and the Amalekites, for these were the inhabitants of the land from of old, as far as Shur, to the land of Egypt. ⁹And David would strike the land and would leave neither man nor woman alive, but would take away the sheep, the oxen, the donkeys, the camels, and the garments, and come back to Achish. ¹⁰When Achish asked, "Where have you made a raid today?" David would say, "Against the Negeb of Judah," or, "Against the Negeb of the Jerahmeelites," or, "Against the Negeb of the Kenites." ¹¹And David would leave neither man nor woman alive to bring news to Gath, thinking, "lest they should tell about us and say, 'So David has done.'" Such was his custom all the while he lived in the country of the Philistines. ¹²And Achish trusted David, thinking, "He has made himself an utter stench to his people Israel; therefore he shall always be my servant."

Saul and the Medium of En-dor

28 In those days the Philistines gathered their forces for war, to fight against Israel. And Achish said to David, "Understand that you and your men are to go out with me in the army." ²David said to Achish, "Very well, you shall know what your servant can do." And Achish said to David, "Very well, I will make you my bodyguard for life."

Ask Yourself . . .

ABOUT THE OCCULT

The occult can be very alluring. The dark arts can draw you in, offering you a taste of excitement. But God forbids his people to practice it (see Deut. 18:10–12; see also 1 Sam. 28:3–20). How do you feel about the occult? Ask yourself:

- Am I impressed with things of the occult like witchcraft, mediums, fortune-telling, or spells?
- What does God have to say about involvement in that kind of stuff?
- Have I done any of the following: read my horoscope, played with a Ouija board, gone to a séance, prayed to the dead, practiced witchcraft, talked to a psychic, or gotten my cards read?
- Have I confessed my sin and repented of it?
- Do any of my friends do these things?
- Have I told them that these things are not biblical?
- How will I deal with these things in the future?

³Now Samuel had died, and all Israel had mourned for him and buried him in Ramah, his own city. And Saul had put the mediums and the necromancers out of the land. ⁴The Philistines assembled and came and encamped at Shunem. And Saul gathered all Israel, and they encamped at Gilboa. ⁵When Saul saw the army of the Philistines, he was afraid, and his heart

trembled greatly. [6]And when Saul inquired of the LORD, the LORD did not answer him, either by dreams, or by Urim, or by prophets. [7]Then Saul said to his servants, "Seek out for me a woman who is a medium, that I may go to her and inquire of her." And his servants said to him, "Behold, there is a medium at En-dor."

[8]So Saul disguised himself and put on other garments and went, he and two men with him. And they came to the woman by night. And he said, "Divine for me by a spirit and bring up for me whomever I shall name to you." [9]The woman said to him, "Surely you know what Saul has done, how he has cut off the mediums and the necromancers from the land. Why then are you laying a trap for my life to bring about my death?" [10]But Saul swore to her by the LORD, "As the LORD lives, no punishment shall come upon you for this thing." [11]Then the woman said, "Whom shall I bring up for you?" He said, "Bring up Samuel for me." [12]When the woman saw Samuel, she cried out with a loud voice. And the woman said to Saul, "Why have you deceived me? You are Saul." [13]The king said to her, "Do not be afraid. What do you see?" And the woman said to Saul, "I see a god coming up out of the earth." [14]He said to her, "What is his appearance?" And she said, "An old man is coming up, and he is wrapped in a robe." And Saul knew that it was Samuel, and he bowed with his face to the ground and paid homage.

[15]Then Samuel said to Saul, "Why have you disturbed me by bringing me up?" Saul answered, "I am in great distress, for the Philistines are warring against me, and God has turned away from me and answers me no more, either by prophets or by dreams. Therefore I have summoned you to tell me what I shall do." [16]And Samuel said, "Why then do you ask me, since the LORD has turned from you and become your enemy? [17]The LORD has done to you as he spoke by me, for the LORD has torn the kingdom out of your hand and given it to your neighbor, David. [18]Because you did not obey the voice of the LORD and did not carry out his fierce wrath against Amalek, therefore the LORD has done this thing to you this day. [19]Moreover, the LORD will give Israel also with you into the hand of the Philistines, and tomorrow you and your sons shall be with me. The LORD will give the army of Israel also into the hand of the Philistines."

[20]Then Saul fell at once full length on the ground, filled with fear because of the words of Samuel. And there was no strength in him, for he had eaten nothing all day and all night. [21]And the woman came to Saul, and when she saw that he was terrified, she said to him, "Behold, your servant has obeyed you. I have taken my life in my hand and have listened to what you have said to me. [22]Now therefore, you also obey your servant. Let me set a morsel of bread before you; and eat, that you may have strength when you go on your way." [23]He refused and said, "I will not eat." But his servants, together with the woman, urged him, and he listened to their words. So he arose from the earth and sat on the bed. [24]Now the woman had a fattened calf in the house, and she quickly killed it, and she took flour and kneaded it and baked unleavened bread of it, [25]and she put it before Saul and his servants, and they ate. Then they rose and went away that night.

The Philistines Reject David

29 Now the Philistines had gathered all their forces at Aphek. And the Israelites were encamped by the spring that is in Jezreel. [2]As the lords of the Philistines were passing on by hundreds and by thousands, and David and his men were passing on in the rear with Achish, [3]the commanders of the Philistines said, "What are these Hebrews doing here?" And Achish said to the commanders of the Philistines, "Is this not David, the servant of Saul, king of Israel, who has been with me now for days and years, and since he deserted to me I have found no fault in him to this day." [4]But the commanders of the Philistines were angry with him. And the commanders of the Philistines said to him, "Send the man back, that he may return to the place to which you have assigned him. He shall not go down with us to battle, lest in the battle he become an adversary to us. For how could this fellow reconcile himself to his lord? Would it not be with the heads of the men here? [5]Is not this David, of whom they sing to one another in dances,

'Saul has struck down his thousands,
  and David his ten thousands'?"

⁶ Then Achish called David and said to him, "As the LORD lives, you have been honest, and to me it seems right that you should march out and in with me in the campaign. For I have found nothing wrong in you from the day of your coming to me to this day. Nevertheless, the lords do not approve of you. ⁷ So go back now; and go peaceably, that you may not displease the lords of the Philistines." ⁸ And David said to Achish, "But what have I done? What have you found in your servant from the day I entered your service until now, that I may not go and fight against the enemies of my lord the king?" ⁹ And Achish answered David and said, "I know that you are as blameless in my sight as an angel of God. Nevertheless, the commanders of the Philistines have said, 'He shall not go up with us to the battle.' ¹⁰ Now then rise early in the morning with the servants of your lord who came with you, and start early in the morning, and depart as soon as you have light." ¹¹ So David set out with his men early in the morning to return to the land of the Philistines. But the Philistines went up to Jezreel.

David's Wives Are Captured

30 Now when David and his men came to Ziklag on the third day, the Amalekites had made a raid against the Negeb and against Ziklag. They had overcome Ziklag and burned it with fire ² and taken captive the women and all[1] who were in it, both small and great. They killed no one, but carried them off and went their way. ³ And when David and his men came to the city, they found it burned with fire, and their wives and sons and daughters taken captive. ⁴ Then David and the people who were with him raised their voices and wept until they had no more strength to weep. ⁵ David's two wives also had been taken captive, Ahinoam of Jezreel and Abigail the widow of Nabal of Carmel. ⁶ And David was greatly distressed, for the people spoke of stoning him, because all the people were bitter in soul,[2] each for his sons and daughters. But David strengthened himself in the LORD his God.

⁷ And David said to Abiathar the priest, the son of Ahimelech, "Bring me the ephod." So Abiathar brought the ephod to David. ⁸ And David inquired of the LORD, "Shall I pursue after this band? Shall I overtake them?" He answered him, "Pursue, for you shall surely overtake and shall surely rescue." ⁹ So David set out, and the six hundred men who were with him, and they came to the brook Besor, where those who were left behind stayed. ¹⁰ But David pursued, he and four hundred men. Two hundred stayed behind, who were too exhausted to cross the brook Besor.

¹¹ They found an Egyptian in the open country and brought him to David. And they gave him bread and he ate. They gave him water to drink, ¹² and they gave him a piece of a cake of figs and two clusters of raisins. And when he had eaten, his spirit revived, for he had not eaten bread or drunk water for three days and three nights. ¹³ And David said to him, "To whom do you belong? And where are you from?" He said, "I am a young man of Egypt, servant to an Amalekite, and my master left me behind because I fell sick three days ago. ¹⁴ We had made a raid against the Negeb of the Cherethites and against that which belongs to Judah and against the Negeb of Caleb, and we burned Ziklag with fire." ¹⁵ And David said to him, "Will you take me down to this band?" And he said, "Swear to me by God that you will not kill me or deliver me into the hands of my master, and I will take you down to this band."

David Defeats the Amalekites

¹⁶ And when he had taken him down, behold, they were spread abroad over all the land, eating and drinking and dancing, because of all the great spoil they had taken from the land of the Philistines and from the land of Judah. ¹⁷ And David struck them down from twilight until the evening of the next day, and not a man of them escaped, except four hundred young men, who mounted camels and fled. ¹⁸ David recovered all that the Amalekites had taken, and David rescued his two wives. ¹⁹ Nothing was missing, whether small or great, sons or daughters, spoil or anything that had been taken. David brought back all. ²⁰ David also captured all the flocks and herds, and the people drove the livestock before him,[3] and said, "This is David's spoil."

²¹ Then David came to the two hundred men who had been too exhausted to follow David, and who had been left at the brook

---

[1] Septuagint; Hebrew lacks *and all* [2] Compare 22:2 [3] The meaning of the Hebrew clause is uncertain

Besor. And they went out to meet David and to meet the people who were with him. And when David came near to the people he greeted them. ²² Then all the wicked and worthless fellows among the men who had gone with David said, "Because they did not go with us, we will not give them any of the spoil that we have recovered, except that each man may lead away his wife and children, and depart." ²³ But David said, "You shall not do so, my brothers, with what the LORD has given us. He has preserved us and given into our hand the band that came against us. ²⁴ Who would listen to you in this matter? For as his share is who goes down into the battle, so shall his share be who stays by the baggage. They shall share alike." ²⁵ And he made it a statute and a rule for Israel from that day forward to this day.

²⁶ When David came to Ziklag, he sent part of the spoil to his friends, the elders of Judah, saying, "Here is a present for you from the spoil of the enemies of the LORD." ²⁷ It was for those in Bethel, in Ramoth of the Negeb, in Jattir, ²⁸ in Aroer, in Siphmoth, in Eshtemoa, ²⁹ in Racal, in the cities of the Jerahmeelites, in the cities of the Kenites, ³⁰ in Hormah, in Bor-ashan, in Athach, ³¹ in Hebron, for all the places where David and his men had roamed.

The Death of Saul

31 Now the Philistines were fighting against Israel, and the men of Israel fled before the Philistines and fell slain on Mount Gilboa. ² And the Philistines overtook Saul and his sons, and the Philistines struck down Jonathan and Abinadab and Malchi-shua, the sons of Saul. ³ The battle pressed hard against Saul, and the archers found him, and he was badly wounded by the archers. ⁴ Then Saul said to his armor-bearer, "Draw your sword, and thrust me through with it, lest these uncircumcised come and thrust me through, and mistreat me." But his armor-bearer would not, for he feared greatly. Therefore Saul took his own sword and fell upon it. ⁵ And when his armor-bearer saw that Saul was dead, he also fell upon his sword and died with him. ⁶ Thus Saul died, and his three sons, and his armor-bearer, and all his men, on the same day together. ⁷ And when the men of Israel who were on the other side of the valley and those beyond the Jordan saw that the men of Israel had fled and that Saul and his sons were dead, they abandoned their cities and fled. And the Philistines came and lived in them.

⁸ The next day, when the Philistines came to strip the slain, they found Saul and his three sons fallen on Mount Gilboa. ⁹ So they cut off his head and stripped off his armor and sent messengers throughout the land of the Philistines, to carry the good news to the house of their idols and to the people. ¹⁰ They put his armor in the temple of Ashtaroth, and they fastened his body to the wall of Beth-shan. ¹¹ But when the inhabitants of Jabesh-gilead heard what the Philistines had done to Saul, ¹² all the valiant men arose and went all night and took the body of Saul and the bodies of his sons from the wall of Beth-shan, and they came to Jabesh and burned them there. ¹³ And they took their bones and buried them under the tamarisk tree in Jabesh and fasted seven days.

INTRODUCTION TO
2 Samuel

Author: Unknown

Time: Unknown

Place: Unknown

Written to: God's people, the Israelites

The gist

The book of 2 Samuel is about the life of King David, from the death of Saul through David's kingship. God rejected Saul because he didn't obey God, and he chose David because of David's heart for God. But even David failed to be the fully obedient king Israel longed for.

Things to look for

- God's covenant with David (see 2 Samuel 7)
- The story of David and Bathsheba (see 2 Samuel 11–12)
- David's song of deliverance (see 2 Samuel 22)

Know Forgiveness

> David said to Nathan, "I have sinned against the LORD."
>
> 2 Samuel 12:13

David was called a man after God's own heart (see 1 Sam. 13:14), but he sinned in a big way by having an affair with Bathsheba and then having her husband killed to cover it up. How could a man after God's own heart do something like that? And how could a righteous God keep on blessing him when all he deserved was punishment?

The answer starts with David's confession. When the prophet Nathan confronted King David on his evil choices, David was quick to confess the whole thing (see 2 Sam. 12:13). And what's most important is that he recognized that ultimately his sin was against God more than against any human person. David didn't argue for himself; he got right to the confession and agreed with God that he was a total sinner. And that one confession proved that even though he had sinned in such an awful way, he still loved God and wanted what God wanted.

Immediately after David's confession, the prophet Nathan told him that the Lord had taken away all his sins, but that didn't mean that God would also take away the consequences of his sin (see 2 Sam. 12:13–14). Sin has consequences regardless of how sorry you are for what you did. Once you confess your sins to God, you can know that you are forgiven and set free from the punishment that usually comes along with them in the spiritual world. But that doesn't mean you are free from the consequences of your sins in the physical world. Sin is never the best choice—not ever. Even though it promises all kinds of payoffs and perks, in the end its payoff is just death and destruction.

As you read 2 Samuel, look closely at the life of a man after God's own heart. See how he lived and how God delighted to pour out favor on David. See how his choices affected not only his life but his kids' lives. And think about how your sin can bring others down with it. As a God Girl, you can't let the temptations you face draw you into the cycle of sin that you used to like riding. Your heart can be a heart after God's own heart if you will give yourself over to what God wants, allowing your own desires to die. The crazy thing is, when you die to yourself, it is *then* that you really begin knowing true joy.

Must-Know Terms and Verses

➣ Anoint ➣

To pour oil on someone, as in anointing a king as a symbol of his power (see Ex. 29:7; 1 Sam. 16:13; Luke 4:18). It can also be a spiritual anointing done by the presence of the Holy Spirit. "The Lord's Anointed" in Hebrew is Messiah.

➣ Davidic Covenant ➣

The covenant that God made with David that his kingdom would continue for future generations (see 2 Sam. 7:12; 22:51). This covenant was considered unconditional and was fulfilled in the life of Christ (see Matt. 1:1; 2:4–6; Luke 1:30–33).

And David danced before the LORD with all his might. And David was wearing a linen ephod. So David and all the house of Israel brought up the ark of the LORD with shouting and with the sound of the horn. *2 Samuel 6:14–15*

"I will celebrate before the LORD. I will make myself yet more contemptible than this, and I will be abased in your eyes. But by the female servants of whom you have spoken, by them I shall be held in honor." *2 Samuel 6:21–22*

David said to Nathan, "I have sinned against the LORD." *2 Samuel 12:13*

But the king said to Araunah, "No, but I will buy it from you for a price. I will not offer burnt offerings to the LORD my God that cost me nothing." *2 Samuel 24:24*

2 Samuel

David Hears of Saul's Death

1 After the death of Saul, when David had returned from striking down the Amalekites, David remained two days in Ziklag. ²And on the third day, behold, a man came from Saul's camp, with his clothes torn and dirt on his head. And when he came to David, he fell to the ground and paid homage. ³David said to him, "Where do you come from?" And he said to him, "I have escaped from the camp of Israel." ⁴And David said to him, "How did it go? Tell me." And he answered, "The people fled from the battle, and also many of the people have fallen and are dead, and Saul and his son Jonathan are also dead." ⁵Then David said to the young man who told him, "How do you know that Saul and his son Jonathan are dead?" ⁶And the young man who told him said, "By chance I happened to be on Mount Gilboa, and there was Saul leaning on his spear, and behold, the chariots and the horsemen were close upon him. ⁷And when he looked behind him, he saw me, and called to me. And I answered, 'Here I am.' ⁸And he said to me, 'Who are you?' I answered him, 'I am an Amalekite.' ⁹And he said to me, 'Stand beside me and kill me, for anguish has seized me, and yet my life still lingers.' ¹⁰So I stood beside me and killed him, because I was sure that he could not live after he had fallen. And I took the crown that was on his head and the armlet that was on his arm, and I have brought them here to my lord."

¹¹Then David took hold of his clothes and tore them, and so did all the men who were with him. ¹²And they mourned and wept and fasted until evening for Saul and for Jonathan his son and for the people of the LORD and for the house of Israel, because they had fallen by the sword. ¹³And David said to the young man who told him, "Where do you come from?" And he answered, "I am the son of a sojourner, an Amalekite." ¹⁴David said to him, "How is it you were not afraid to put out your hand to destroy the LORD's anointed?" ¹⁵Then David called one of the young men and said, "Go, execute him." And he struck him down so that he died. ¹⁶And David said to him, "Your blood be on your head, for your own mouth has testified against you, saying, 'I have killed the LORD's anointed.'"

David's Lament for Saul and Jonathan

¹⁷And David lamented with this lamentation over Saul and Jonathan his son, ¹⁸and he said it[1] should be taught to the people of Judah; behold, it is written in the Book of Jashar:[2] He said:

¹⁹ "Your glory, O Israel, is slain on your
    high places!
  How the mighty have fallen!
²⁰ Tell it not in Gath,
    publish it not in the streets of
      Ashkelon,
  lest the daughters of the Philistines
      rejoice,
  lest the daughters of the uncircumcised exult.

²¹ "You mountains of Gilboa,
    let there be no dew or rain upon
      you,
    nor fields of offerings![3]
  For there the shield of the mighty
      was defiled,
    the shield of Saul, not anointed
      with oil.

²² "From the blood of the slain,
    from the fat of the mighty,
  the bow of Jonathan turned not
      back,
    and the sword of Saul returned not
      empty.

---

[1] Septuagint; Hebrew *the Bow*, which may be the name of the lament's tune   [2] Or *of the upright*   [3] Septuagint *firstfruits*

23 "Saul and Jonathan, beloved and
        lovely!
    In life and in death they were not
        divided;
    they were swifter than eagles;
        they were stronger than lions.

24 "You daughters of Israel, weep over
        Saul,
    who clothed you luxuriously in
        scarlet,
    who put ornaments of gold on
        your apparel.

25 "How the mighty have fallen
        in the midst of the battle!

    "Jonathan lies slain on your high
        places.
26   I am distressed for you, my
        brother Jonathan;
    very pleasant have you been to me;
        your love to me was extraordi-
        nary,
    surpassing the love of women.

27 "How the mighty have fallen,
        and the weapons of war perished!"

David Anointed King of Judah

2 After this David inquired of the LORD,
  "Shall I go up into any of the cities of
Judah?" And the LORD said to him, "Go up."
David said, "To which shall I go up?" And
he said, "To Hebron." ² So David went up
there, and his two wives also, Ahinoam of
Jezreel and Abigail the widow of Nabal of
Carmel. ³ And David brought up his men
who were with him, everyone with his
household, and they lived in the towns of
Hebron. ⁴ And the men of Judah came, and
there they anointed David king over the
house of Judah.

When they told David, "It was the men
of Jabesh-gilead who buried Saul," ⁵ David
sent messengers to the men of Jabesh-
gilead and said to them, "May you be
blessed by the LORD, because you showed
this loyalty to Saul your lord and buried
him. ⁶ Now may the LORD show steadfast
love and faithfulness to you. And I will do
good to you because you have done this
thing. ⁷ Now therefore let your hands be
strong, and be valiant, for Saul your lord is
dead, and the house of Judah has anointed
me king over them."

Ish-bosheth Made King of Israel

⁸ But Abner the son of Ner, commander
of Saul's army, took Ish-bosheth the son of
Saul and brought him over to Mahanaim,
⁹ and he made him king over Gilead and
the Ashurites and Jezreel and Ephraim
and Benjamin and all Israel. ¹⁰ Ish-bosheth,
Saul's son, was forty years old when he
began to reign over Israel, and he reigned
two years. But the house of Judah followed
David. ¹¹ And the time that David was king
in Hebron over the house of Judah was
seven years and six months.

The Battle of Gibeon

¹² Abner the son of Ner, and the servants
of Ish-bosheth the son of Saul, went out
from Mahanaim to Gibeon. ¹³ And Joab the
son of Zeruiah and the servants of David
went out and met them at the pool of
Gibeon. And they sat down, the one on
the one side of the pool, and the other on
the other side of the pool. ¹⁴ And Abner
said to Joab, "Let the young men arise and
compete before us." And Joab said, "Let
them arise." ¹⁵ Then they arose and passed
over by number, twelve for Benjamin and
Ish-bosheth the son of Saul, and twelve of
the servants of David. ¹⁶ And each caught
his opponent by the head and thrust his
sword in his opponent's side, so they fell
down together. Therefore that place was
called Helkath-hazzurim,[1] which is at
Gibeon. ¹⁷ And the battle was very fierce
that day. And Abner and the men of Israel
were beaten before the servants of David.

¹⁸ And the three sons of Zeruiah were
there, Joab, Abishai, and Asahel. Now
Asahel was as swift of foot as a wild gazelle.
¹⁹ And Asahel pursued Abner, and as he
went, he turned neither to the right hand
nor to the left from following Abner. ²⁰ Then
Abner looked behind him and said, "Is it
you, Asahel?" And he answered, "It is I."
²¹ Abner said to him, "Turn aside to your
right hand or to your left, and seize one
of the young men and take his spoil." But
Asahel would not turn aside from following him. ²² And Abner said again to Asahel,
"Turn aside from following me. Why should
I strike you to the ground? How then could
I lift up my face to your brother Joab?"
²³ But he refused to turn aside. Therefore
Abner struck him in the stomach with the
butt of his spear, so that the spear came

[1] Helkath-hazzurim means *the field of sword-edges*

ut at his back. And he fell there and died ...where he was. And all who came to the ...lace where Asahel had fallen and died, ...tood still.

A Prayer for...
FRIENDS

Dear God of love, in you alone I live. Please kindle the fire of love in my soul. Help me to lay myself aside and to think of others as I kneel before you. Don't let me selfishly keep you to myself, but remind me to bring others to the throne of hope and healing.

I ask your blessing, the best gift on earth, for those you have given me who are as dear to me as my own soul.

If they are far away right now, so that I can't say loving things to them today, be near them. Give them your joy; order their ways; keep them from sickness, from sorrow, and from sin; and let all things bring them closer to you.

If they are near me, give us wisdom and grace to be true helpers of one another, serving in love's service all day long.

Let nothing come between us to cloud our perfect trust, but help each of us to love more truly, more steadfastly, and more unselfishly.

And not only for those I love, but for others: for all who are lonely, or weary, or sad; for all who are turning away from the light; for all who have forgotten you, I pray, Lord, have pity on them.

Keep me from all the hard and bitter thoughts that I like too well, from envy and jealousy and pride, and give me the mind of Christ to rejoice in the lowest place where loving souls may serve.

Amen.

²⁴ But Joab and Abishai pursued Abner. And as the sun was going down they came to the hill of Ammah, which lies before Giah on the way to the wilderness of Gibeon.

²⁵ And the people of Benjamin gathered themselves together behind Abner and became one group and took their stand on the top of a hill. ²⁶ Then Abner called to Joab, "Shall the sword devour forever? Do you not know that the end will be bitter? How long will it be before you tell your people to turn from the pursuit of their brothers?" ²⁷ And Joab said, "As God lives, if you had not spoken, surely the men would not have given up the pursuit of their brothers until the morning." ²⁸ So Joab blew the trumpet, and all the men stopped and pursued Israel no more, nor did they fight anymore.

²⁹ And Abner and his men went all that night through the Arabah. They crossed the Jordan, and marching the whole morning, they came to Mahanaim. ³⁰ Joab returned from the pursuit of Abner. And when he had gathered all the people together, there were missing from David's servants nineteen men besides Asahel. ³¹ But the servants of David had struck down of Benjamin 360 of Abner's men. ³² And they took up Asahel and buried him in the tomb of his father, which was at Bethlehem. And Joab and his men marched all night, and the day broke upon them at Hebron.

Abner Joins David

3 There was a long war between the house of Saul and the house of David. And David grew stronger and stronger, while the house of Saul became weaker and weaker.

² And sons were born to David at Hebron: his firstborn was Amnon, of Ahinoam of Jezreel; ³ and his second, Chileab, of Abigail the widow of Nabal of Carmel; and the third, Absalom the son of Maacah the daughter of Talmai king of Geshur; ⁴ and the fourth, Adonijah the son of Haggith; and the fifth, Shephatiah the son of Abital; ⁵ and the sixth, Ithream, of Eglah, David's wife. These were born to David in Hebron.

⁶ While there was war between the house of Saul and the house of David, Abner was making himself strong in the house of Saul. ⁷ Now Saul had a concubine whose name was Rizpah, the daughter of Aiah. And Ish-bosheth said to Abner, "Why have you gone in to my father's concubine?" ⁸ Then Abner was very angry over the words of Ish-bosheth and said, "Am I a dog's head of Judah? To this day I keep showing steadfast

love to the house of Saul your father, to his brothers, and to his friends, and have not given you into the hand of David. And yet you charge me today with a fault concerning a woman. [9] God do so to Abner and more also, if I do not accomplish for David what the LORD has sworn to him, [10] to transfer the kingdom from the house of Saul and set up the throne of David over Israel and over Judah, from Dan to Beersheba." [11] And Ishbosheth could not answer Abner another word, because he feared him.

[12] And Abner sent messengers to David on his behalf,[1] saying, "To whom does the land belong? Make your covenant with me, and behold, my hand shall be with you to bring over all Israel to you." [13] And he said, "Good; I will make a covenant with you. But one thing I require of you; that is, you shall not see my face unless you first bring Michal, Saul's daughter, when you come to see my face." [14] Then David sent messengers to Ish-bosheth, Saul's son, saying, "Give me my wife Michal, for whom I paid the bridal price of a hundred foreskins of the Philistines." [15] And Ish-bosheth sent and took her from her husband Paltiel the son of Laish. [16] But her husband went with her, weeping after her all the way to Bahurim. Then Abner said to him, "Go, return." And he returned.

[17] And Abner conferred with the elders of Israel, saying, "For some time past you have been seeking David as king over you. [18] Now then bring it about, for the LORD has promised David, saying, 'By the hand of my servant David I will save my people Israel from the hand of the Philistines, and from the hand of all their enemies.'" [19] Abner also spoke to Benjamin. And then Abner went to tell David at Hebron all that Israel and the whole house of Benjamin thought good to do.

[20] When Abner came with twenty men to David at Hebron, David made a feast for Abner and the men who were with him. [21] And Abner said to David, "I will arise and go and will gather all Israel to my lord the king, that they may make a covenant with you, and that you may reign over all that your heart desires." So David sent Abner away, and he went in peace.

[22] Just then the servants of David arrived with Joab from a raid, bringing much spoil with them. But Abner was not with David

at Hebron, for he had sent him away, an he had gone in peace. [23] When Joab an all the army that was with him came, was told Joab, "Abner the son of Ner cam to the king, and he has let him go, and h has gone in peace." [24] Then Joab went t the king and said, "What have you done Behold, Abner came to you. Why is it tha you have sent him away, so that he is gone [25] You know that Abner the son of Ner cam to deceive you and to know your going ou and your coming in, and to know all tha you are doing."

Joab Murders Abner

[26] When Joab came out from David' presence, he sent messengers after Abne and they brought him back from the cister of Sirah. But David did not know about i [27] And when Abner returned to Hebro Joab took him aside into the midst of th gate to speak with him privately, and ther he struck him in the stomach, so that h died, for the blood of Asahel his brothe [28] Afterward, when David heard of it, h said, "I and my kingdom are forever guil less before the LORD for the blood of Abne the son of Ner. [29] May it fall upon the hea of Joab and upon all his father's house, an may the house of Joab never be withou one who has a discharge or who is leprou or who holds a spindle or who falls by th sword or who lacks bread!" [30] So Joab an Abishai his brother killed Abner, becaus he had put their brother Asahel to death i the battle at Gibeon.

David Mourns Abner

[31] Then David said to Joab and to all th people who were with him, "Tear you clothes and put on sackcloth and mour before Abner." And King David followe the bier. [32] They buried Abner at Hebro And the king lifted up his voice and wept a the grave of Abner, and all the people wep [33] And the king lamented for Abner, sayin

"Should Abner die as a fool dies?
[34]   Your hands were not bound;
         your feet were not fettered;
     as one falls before the wicked
         you have fallen."

And all the people wept again over him [35] Then all the people came to persuad David to eat bread while it was yet day. Bu

[1] Or where he was; Septuagint at Hebron

avid swore, saying, "God do so to me and
ore also, if I taste bread or anything else
ll the sun goes down!" ³⁶ And all the peo-
le took notice of it, and it pleased them,
s everything that the king did pleased all
ne people. ³⁷ So all the people and all Israel
nderstood that day that it had not been
ne king's will to put to death Abner the
on of Ner. ³⁸ And the king said to his ser-
ants, "Do you not know that a prince and
great man has fallen this day in Israel?
And I was gentle today, though anointed
ing. These men, the sons of Zeruiah, are
ore severe than I. The LORD repay the
vildoer according to his wickedness!"

h-bosheth Murdered

When Ish-bosheth, Saul's son, heard
that Abner had died at Hebron, his
ourage failed, and all Israel was dismayed.
Now Saul's son had two men who were
aptains of raiding bands; the name of
ne one was Baanah, and the name of the
ther Rechab, sons of Rimmon a man of
enjamin from Beeroth (for Beeroth also is
ounted part of Benjamin; ³ the Beerothites
ed to Gittaim and have been sojourners
nere to this day).

⁴ Jonathan, the son of Saul, had a son
rho was crippled in his feet. He was five
ears old when the news about Saul and
onathan came from Jezreel, and his nurse
ook him up and fled, and as she fled in
er haste, he fell and became lame. And
is name was Mephibosheth.

⁵ Now the sons of Rimmon the Beeroth-
e, Rechab and Baanah, set out, and about
ne heat of the day they came to the house
f Ish-bosheth as he was taking his noon-
ay rest. ⁶ And they came into the midst
f the house as if to get wheat, and they
tabbed him in the stomach. Then Rechab
nd Baanah his brother escaped.[1] ⁷ When
ney came into the house, as he lay on his
ed in his bedroom, they struck him and
ut him to death and beheaded him. They
ook his head and went by the way of the
rabah all night, ⁸ and brought the head of
sh-bosheth to David at Hebron. And they
aid to the king, "Here is the head of Ish-
osheth, the son of Saul, your enemy, who
ought your life. The LORD has avenged my
ord the king this day on Saul and on his
ffspring." ⁹ But David answered Rechab

and Baanah his brother, the sons of Rimmon the Beerothite, "As the LORD lives,
who has redeemed my life out of every
adversity, ¹⁰ when one told me, 'Behold,
Saul is dead,' and thought he was bringing
good news, I seized him and killed him at
Ziklag, which was the reward I gave him for
his news. ¹¹ How much more, when wicked
men have killed a righteous man in his own
house on his bed, shall I not now require
his blood at your hand and destroy you
from the earth?" ¹² And David commanded
his young men, and they killed them and
cut off their hands and feet and hanged
them beside the pool at Hebron. But they
took the head of Ish-bosheth and buried it
in the tomb of Abner at Hebron.

David Anointed King of Israel

Then all the tribes of Israel came to
David at Hebron and said, "Behold, we
are your bone and flesh. ² In times past,
when Saul was king over us, it was you who
led out and brought in Israel. And the LORD
said to you, 'You shall be shepherd of my
people Israel, and you shall be prince[2] over
Israel.'" ³ So all the elders of Israel came to
the king at Hebron, and King David made
a covenant with them at Hebron before the
LORD, and they anointed David king over
Israel. ⁴ David was thirty years old when he
began to reign, and he reigned forty years.
⁵ At Hebron he reigned over Judah seven
years and six months, and at Jerusalem he
reigned over all Israel and Judah thirty-
three years.[3]

⁶ And the king and his men went to
Jerusalem against the Jebusites, the inhabitants of the land, who said to David, "You
will not come in here, but the blind and
the lame will ward you off"—thinking,
"David cannot come in here." ⁷ Nevertheless,
David took the stronghold of Zion, that is,
the city of David. ⁸ And David said on that
day, "Whoever would strike the Jebusites,
let him get up the water shaft to attack
'the lame and the blind,' who are hated by
David's soul." Therefore it is said, "The blind
and the lame shall not come into the house."
⁹ And David lived in the stronghold and
called it the city of David. And David built
the city all around from the Millo inward.
¹⁰ And David became greater and greater, for
the LORD, the God of hosts, was with him.

¹ Septuagint *And behold, the doorkeeper of the house had been cleaning wheat, but she grew drowsy and slept. So Rechab and Baanah his
other slipped in* ² Or *leader* ³ Dead Sea Scroll lacks verses 4–5

[11] And Hiram king of Tyre sent messengers to David, and cedar trees, also carpenters and masons who built David a house. [12] And David knew that the LORD had established him king over Israel, and that he had exalted his kingdom for the sake of his people Israel.

[13] And David took more concubines and wives from Jerusalem, after he came from Hebron, and more sons and daughters were born to David. [14] And these are the names of those who were born to him in Jerusalem: Shammua, Shobab, Nathan, Solomon, [15] Ibhar, Elishua, Nepheg, Japhia, [16] Elishama, Eliada, and Eliphelet.

Ask Yourself . . .

ABOUT GOD'S WILL

When you are faced with a big decision, what do you do? Ask yourself these questions to see where God fits into your choices:

- How often have I made a major decision without asking God about it first?
- Have I ever asked others to help me seek God on big decisions?
- Do I trust myself to hear God's answers to my prayers?
- What can I do so that I become better at hearing God's promptings in my life?

David Defeats the Philistines

[17] When the Philistines heard that David had been anointed king over Israel, all the Philistines went up to search for David. But David heard of it and went down to the stronghold. [18] Now the Philistines had come and spread out in the Valley of Rephaim. [19] And David inquired of the LORD, "Shall I go up against the Philistines? Will you give them into my hand?" And the LORD said to David, "Go up, for I will certainly give the Philistines into you hand." [20] And David came to Baal-perazim and David defeated them there. And h said, "The LORD has broken through m enemies before me like a breaking flood Therefore the name of that place is calle Baal-perazim.[1] [21] And the Philistines le their idols there, and David and his me carried them away.

[22] And the Philistines came up yet agai and spread out in the Valley of Reph aim. [23] And when David inquired of th LORD, he said, "You shall not go up; g around to their rear, and come again them opposite the balsam trees. [24] An when you hear the sound of marching the tops of the balsam trees, then rous yourself, for then the LORD has gone ou before you to strike down the army of th Philistines." [25] And David did as the LOR commanded him, and struck down th Philistines from Geba to Gezer.

The Ark Brought to Jerusalem

6 David again gathered all the chose men of Israel, thirty thousand. [2] An David arose and went with all the peopl who were with him from Baale-judah t bring up from there the ark of God, whic is called by the name of the LORD of hos who sits enthroned on the cherubi [3] And they carried the ark of God on a ne cart and brought it out of the house Abinadab, which was on the hill. And Uzza and Ahio,[2] the sons of Abinadab, were dri ing the new cart,[3] [4] with the ark of God, an Ahio went before the ark.

Uzzah and the Ark

[5] And David and all the house of Isra were celebrating before the LORD, wit songs[4] and lyres and harps and tambou rines and castanets and cymbals. [6] An when they came to the threshing floor Nacon, Uzzah put out his hand to the ar of God and took hold of it, for the oxe stumbled. [7] And the anger of the LORD wa kindled against Uzzah, and God struc him down there because of his error, an he died there beside the ark of God. [8] An David was angry because the LORD ha broken out against Uzzah. And that place called Perez-uzzah[5] to this day. [9] And Davi

[1] *Baal-perazim* means *lord of bursting through* [2] *Or and his brother;* also verse 4 [3] Compare Septuagint; Hebrew *the new cart, and broug it out of the house of Abinadab, which was on the hill* [4] Septuagint, 1 Chronicles 13:8; Hebrew *fir trees* [5] *Perez-uzzah* means *the breaking out against Uzzah*

as afraid of the LORD that day, and he
id, "How can the ark of the LORD come to
e?" ¹⁰So David was not willing to take the
'k of the LORD into the city of David. But
avid took it aside to the house of Obed-
lom the Gittite. ¹¹And the ark of the LORD
:mained in the house of Obed-edom the
ittite three months, and the LORD blessed
bed-edom and all his household.

¹²And it was told King David, "The LORD
as blessed the household of Obed-edom
nd all that belongs to him, because of the
'k of God." So David went and brought
p the ark of God from the house of Obed-
lom to the city of David with rejoicing.
And when those who bore the ark of
e LORD had gone six steps, he sacrificed
1 ox and a fattened animal. ¹⁴And David
anced before the LORD with all his might.
nd David was wearing a linen ephod. ¹⁵So
avid and all the house of Israel brought
p the ark of the LORD with shouting and
ith the sound of the horn.

avid and Michal

¹⁶As the ark of the LORD came into the
ty of David, Michal the daughter of Saul
oked out of the window and saw King
avid leaping and dancing before the LORD,
nd she despised him in her heart. ¹⁷And
ey brought in the ark of the LORD and
t it in its place, inside the tent that David
ad pitched for it. And David offered burnt
fferings and peace offerings before the
ORD. ¹⁸And when David had finished offer-
g the burnt offerings and the peace offer-
gs, he blessed the people in the name
f the LORD of hosts ¹⁹and distributed
mong all the people, the whole multitude
f Israel, both men and women, a cake of
read, a portion of meat,¹ and a cake of
iisins to each one. Then all the people
eparted, each to his house.

²⁰And David returned to bless his house-
old. But Michal the daughter of Saul came
ut to meet David and said, "How the king
f Israel honored himself today, uncover-
g himself today before the eyes of his
ervants' female servants, as one of the
ulgar fellows shamelessly uncovers him-
elf!" ²¹And David said to Michal, "It was
efore the LORD, who chose me above your
ither and above all his house, to appoint
e as prince² over Israel, the people of

the LORD— and I will celebrate before the
LORD. ²²I will make myself yet more contemptible than this, and I will be abased in
your³ eyes. But by the female servants of
whom you have spoken, by them I shall be
held in honor." ²³And Michal the daughter
of Saul had no child to the day of her death.

The LORD's Covenant with David

7 Now when the king lived in his house
and the LORD had given him rest from
all his surrounding enemies, ²the king said
to Nathan the prophet, "See now, I dwell in
a house of cedar, but the ark of God dwells
in a tent." ³And Nathan said to the king,
"Go, do all that is in your heart, for the
LORD is with you."

⁴But that same night the word of the
LORD came to Nathan, ⁵"Go and tell my
servant David, 'Thus says the LORD: Would
you build me a house to dwell in? ⁶I have
not lived in a house since the day I brought
up the people of Israel from Egypt to this
day, but I have been moving about in a
tent for my dwelling. ⁷In all places where
I have moved with all the people of Israel,
did I speak a word with any of the judges⁴
of Israel, whom I commanded to shepherd
my people Israel, saying, "Why have you
not built me a house of cedar?"' ⁸Now,
therefore, thus you shall say to my servant
David, 'Thus says the LORD of hosts, I took
you from the pasture, from following the
sheep, that you should be prince⁵ over my
people Israel. ⁹And I have been with you
wherever you went and have cut off all
your enemies from before you. And I will
make for you a great name, like the name
of the great ones of the earth. ¹⁰And I will
appoint a place for my people Israel and
will plant them, so that they may dwell
in their own place and be disturbed no
more. And violent men shall afflict them
no more, as formerly, ¹¹from the time
that I appointed judges over my people
Israel. And I will give you rest from all your
enemies. Moreover, the LORD declares to
you that the LORD will make you a house.
¹²When your days are fulfilled and you lie
down with your fathers, I will raise up your
offspring after you, who shall come from
your body, and I will establish his kingdom.
¹³He shall build a house for my name, and
I will establish the throne of his kingdom

¹ulgate; the meaning of the Hebrew term is uncertain ²Or *leader* ³Septuagint; Hebrew *my* ⁴Compare 1 Chronicles 17:6; Hebrew
bes ⁵Or *leader*

forever. [14] I will be to him a father, and he shall be to me a son. When he commits iniquity, I will discipline him with the rod of men, with the stripes of the sons of men, [15] but my steadfast love will not depart from him, as I took it from Saul, whom I put away from before you. [16] And your house and your kingdom shall be made sure forever before me.[1] Your throne shall be established forever.'" [17] In accordance with all these words, and in accordance with all this vision, Nathan spoke to David.

David's Prayer of Gratitude

[18] Then King David went in and sat before the LORD and said, "Who am I, O Lord GOD, and what is my house, that you have brought me thus far? [19] And yet this was a small thing in your eyes, O Lord GOD. You have spoken also of your servant's house for a great while to come, and this is instruction for mankind, O Lord GOD! [20] And what more can David say to you? For you know your servant, O Lord GOD! [21] Because of your promise, and according to your own heart, you have brought about all this greatness, to make your servant know it. [22] Therefore you are great, O LORD God. For there is none like you, and there is no God besides you, according to all that we have heard with our ears. [23] And who is like your people Israel, the one nation on earth whom God went to redeem to be his people, making himself a name and doing for them[2] great and awesome things by driving out[3] before your people, whom you redeemed for yourself from Egypt, a nation and its gods? [24] And you established for yourself your people Israel to be your people forever. And you, O LORD, became their God. [25] And now, O LORD God, confirm forever the word that you have spoken concerning your servant and concerning his house, and do as you have spoken. [26] And your name will be magnified forever, saying, 'The LORD of hosts is God over Israel,' and the house of your servant David will be established before you. [27] For you, O LORD of hosts, the God of Israel, have made this revelation to your servant, saying, 'I will build you a house.' Therefore your servant has found courage to pray this prayer to you. [28] And now, O Lord GOD, you are God, and your words are true, and you have promised this good thing to your servant. [29] Now therefo may it please you to bless the house of yo servant, so that it may continue forev before you. For you, O Lord GOD, have sp ken, and with your blessing shall the hous of your servant be blessed forever."

David's Victories

8 After this David defeated the Phili tines and subdued them, and Dav took Metheg-ammah out of the hand the Philistines.

[2] And he defeated Moab and he measure them with a line, making them lie dow on the ground. Two lines he measured be put to death, and one full line to spared. And the Moabites became servan to David and brought tribute.

[3] David also defeated Hadadezer th son of Rehob, king of Zobah, as he went restore his power at the river Euphrate [4] And David took from him 1,700 horseme and 20,000 foot soldiers. And David han strung all the chariot horses but left enoug for 100 chariots. [5] And when the Syrians Damascus came to help Hadadezer ki of Zobah, David struck down 22,000 me of the Syrians. [6] Then David put garrisons Aram of Damascus, and the Syrians becan servants to David and brought tribute. Ar the LORD gave victory to David wherev he went. [7] And David took the shields gold that were carried by the servants Hadadezer and brought them to Jerusale [8] And from Betah and from Berothai, citi of Hadadezer, King David took very muc bronze.

[9] When Toi king of Hamath heard tha David had defeated the whole army of Ha adezer, [10] Toi sent his son Joram to Kir David, to ask about his health and to ble him because he had fought against Ha adezer and defeated him, for Hadadez had often been at war with Toi. And Jora brought with him articles of silver, of gol and of bronze. [11] These also King Davi dedicated to the LORD, together with th silver and gold that he dedicated fro all the nations he subdued, [12] from Edor Moab, the Ammonites, the Philistine Amalek, and from the spoil of Hadadez the son of Rehob, king of Zobah.

[13] And David made a name for himse when he returned from striking dow

[1] Septuagint; Hebrew you [2] With a few Targums, Vulgate, Syriac; Hebrew you [3] Septuagint (compare 1 Chronicles 17:21); Hebrew for your land

8,000 Edomites in the Valley of Salt. Then he put garrisons in Edom; through-out all Edom he put garrisons, and all the Edomites became David's servants. And the LORD gave victory to David wherever he went.

David's Officials

¹⁵ So David reigned over all Israel. And David administered justice and equity to all his people. ¹⁶ Joab the son of Zeruiah was over the army, and Jehoshaphat the son of Ahilud was recorder, ¹⁷ and Zadok the son of Ahitub and Ahimelech the son of Abiathar were priests, and Seraiah was secretary, ¹⁸ and Benaiah the son of Jehoiada was over¹ the Cherethites and the Pelethites, and David's sons were priests.

David's Kindness to Mephibosheth

9 And David said, "Is there still anyone left of the house of Saul, that I may show him kindness for Jonathan's sake?" ² Now there was a servant of the house of Saul whose name was Ziba, and they called him to David. And the king said to him, "Are you Ziba?" And he said, "I am your servant." ³ And the king said, "Is there not still someone of the house of Saul, that I may show the kindness of God to him?" Ziba said to the king, "There is still a son of Jonathan; he is crippled in his feet." ⁴ The king said to him, "Where is he?" And Ziba said to the king, "He is in the house of Machir the son of Ammiel, at Lo-debar." ⁵ Then King David sent and brought him from the house of Machir the son of Ammiel, at Lo-debar. ⁶ And Mephibosheth the son of Jonathan, son of Saul, came to David and fell on his face and paid homage. And David said, "Mephibosheth!" And he answered, "Behold, I am your servant." ⁷ And David said to him, "Do not fear, for I will show you kindness for the sake of your father Jonathan, and I will restore to you all the land of Saul your father, and you shall eat at my table always." ⁸ And he paid homage and said, "What is your servant, that you should show regard for a dead dog such as I?"

⁹ Then the king called Ziba, Saul's servant, and said to him, "All that belonged to Saul and to all his house I have given to your master's grandson. ¹⁰ And you and

your sons and your servants shall till the land for him and shall bring in the produce, that your master's grandson may have bread to eat. But Mephibosheth your master's grandson shall always eat at my table." Now Ziba had fifteen sons and twenty servants. ¹¹ Then Ziba said to the king, "According to all that my lord the king commands his servant, so will your servant do." So Mephibosheth ate at David's² table, like one of the king's sons. ¹² And Mephibosheth had a young son, whose name was Mica. And all who lived in Ziba's house became Mephibosheth's servants. ¹³ So Mephibosheth lived in Jerusalem, for he ate always at the king's table. Now he was lame in both his feet.

David Defeats Ammon and Syria

10 After this the king of the Ammonites died, and Hanun his son reigned in his place. ² And David said, "I will deal loyally³ with Hanun the son of Nahash, as his father dealt loyally with me." So David sent by his servants to console him concerning his father. And David's servants came into the land of the Ammonites. ³ But the princes of the Ammonites said to Hanun their lord, "Do you think, because David has sent comforters to you, that he is honoring your father? Has not David sent his servants to you to search the city and to spy it out and to overthrow it?" ⁴ So Hanun took David's servants and shaved off half the beard of each and cut off their garments in the middle, at their hips, and sent them away. ⁵ When it was told David, he sent to meet them, for the men were greatly ashamed. And the king said, "Remain at Jericho until your beards have grown and then return."

⁶ When the Ammonites saw that they had become a stench to David, the Ammonites sent and hired the Syrians of Beth-rehob, and the Syrians of Zobah, 20,000 foot soldiers, and the king of Maacah with 1,000 men, and the men of Tob, 12,000 men. ⁷ And when David heard of it, he sent Joab and all the host of the mighty men. ⁸ And the Ammonites came out and drew up in battle array at the entrance of the gate, and the Syrians of Zobah and of Rehob and the men of Tob and Maacah were by themselves in the open country.

¹ Compare 20:23, 1 Chronicles 18:17, Syriac, Targum, Vulgate; Hebrew lacks *was over* ² Septuagint; Hebrew *my* ³ Or *kindly*; twice in this verse

[9] When Joab saw that the battle was set against him both in front and in the rear, he chose some of the best men of Israel and arrayed them against the Syrians. [10] The rest of his men he put in the charge of Abishai his brother, and he arrayed them against the Ammonites. [11] And he said, "If the Syrians are too strong for me, then you shall help me, but if the Ammonites are too strong for you, then I will come and help you. [12] Be of good courage, and let us be courageous for our people, and for the cities of our God, and may the LORD do what seems good to him." [13] So Joab and the people who were with him drew near to battle against the Syrians, and they fled before him. [14] And when the Ammonites saw that the Syrians fled, they likewise fled before Abishai and entered the city. Then Joab returned from fighting against the Ammonites and came to Jerusalem.

[15] But when the Syrians saw that they had been defeated by Israel, they gathered themselves together. [16] And Hadadezer sent and brought out the Syrians who were beyond the Euphrates.[1] They came to Helam, with Shobach the commander of the army of Hadadezer at their head. [17] And when it was told David, he gathered all Israel together and crossed the Jordan and came to Helam. The Syrians arrayed themselves against David and fought with him. [18] And the Syrians fled before Israel, and David killed of the Syrians the men of 700 chariots, and 40,000 horsemen, and wounded Shobach the commander of their army, so that he died there. [19] And when all the kings who were servants of Hadadezer saw that they had been defeated by Israel, they made peace with Israel and became subject to them. So the Syrians were afraid to save the Ammonites anymore.

David and Bathsheba

11 In the spring of the year, the time when kings go out to battle, David sent Joab, and his servants with him, and all Israel. And they ravaged the Ammonites and besieged Rabbah. But David remained at Jerusalem.

[2] It happened, late one afternoon, when David arose from his couch and was walking on the roof of the king's house, that he saw from the roof a woman bathing; and the woman was very beautiful. [3] And David

sent and inquired about the woman. An[d] one said, "Is not this Bathsheba, the daug[h]ter of Eliam, the wife of Uriah the Hittite[?]" [4] So David sent messengers and took he[r,] and she came to him, and he lay with he[r.] (Now she had been purifying herself fro[m] her uncleanness.) Then she returned to he[r] house. [5] And the woman conceived, and sh[e] sent and told David, "I am pregnant."

Ask Yourself . . .

ABOUT LAZINESS

In ancient times, in the springtime kings would go off to war. But on one occasion King David sent his men out while he stayed behind. Then, while David should have been on the battlefield, he was on the roof admiring the wife of one of his men, and this led to destruction in his life and family. Ask yourself about the times when you have done something similar and gotten into trouble:

- Have I been somewhere I shouldn't have been and ended up making a mess of things?
- What are some things I don't do because I'm just too lazy?
- What kinds of things do I do in my idle time?
- How much of that time do I spend on heavenly things?
- How could my time be better spent?

---

[6] So David sent word to Joab, "Send m[e] Uriah the Hittite." And Joab sent Uriah t[o] David. [7] When Uriah came to him, Davi[d] asked how Joab was doing and how th[e] people were doing and how the war wa[s] going. [8] Then David said to Uriah, "G[o] down to your house and wash your feet[."] And Uriah went out of the king's hous[e,] and there followed him a present fro[m] the king. [9] But Uriah slept at the door o[f] the king's house with all the servant[s]

---

[1] Hebrew *the River*

of his lord, and did not go down to his house. ¹⁰When they told David, "Uriah did not go down to his house," David said to Uriah, "Have you not come from a journey? Why did you not go down to your house?" ¹¹Uriah said to David, "The ark and Israel and Judah dwell in booths, and my lord Joab and the servants of my lord are camping in the open field. Shall I then go to my house, to eat and to drink and to lie with my wife? As you live, and as your soul lives, I will not do this thing." ¹²Then David said to Uriah, "Remain here today also, and tomorrow I will send you back." So Uriah remained in Jerusalem that day and the next. ¹³And David invited him, and he ate in his presence and drank, so that he made him drunk. And in the evening he went out to lie on his couch with the servants of his lord, but he did not go down to his house.

¹⁴In the morning David wrote a letter to Joab and sent it by the hand of Uriah. ¹⁵In the letter he wrote, "Set Uriah in the forefront of the hardest fighting, and then draw back from him, that he may be struck down, and die." ¹⁶And as Joab was besieging the city, he assigned Uriah to the place where he knew there were valiant men. ¹⁷And the men of the city came out and fought with Joab, and some of the servants of David among the people fell. Uriah the Hittite also died. ¹⁸Then Joab sent and told David all the news about the fighting. ¹⁹And he instructed the messenger, "When you have finished telling all the news about the fighting to the king, ²⁰then, if the king's anger rises, and if he says to you, 'Why did you go so near the city to fight? Did you not know that they would shoot from the wall? ²¹Who killed Abimelech the son of Jerubbesheth? Did not a woman cast an upper millstone on him from the wall, so that he died at Thebez? Why did you go so near the wall?' then you shall say, 'Your servant Uriah the Hittite is dead also.'"

²²So the messenger went and came and told David all that Joab had sent him to tell. ²³The messenger said to David, "The men gained an advantage over us and came out against us in the field, but we drove them back to the entrance of the gate. ²⁴Then the archers shot at your servants from the wall. Some of the king's servants are dead, and your servant Uriah the Hittite is dead also." ²⁵David said to the messenger, "Thus shall you say to Joab, 'Do not let this matter displease you, for the sword devours now one and now another. Strengthen your attack against the city and overthrow it.' And encourage him."

²⁶When the wife of Uriah heard that Uriah her husband was dead, she lamented over her husband. ²⁷And when the mourning was over, David sent and brought her to his house, and she became his wife and bore him a son. But the thing that David had done displeased the LORD.

Nathan Rebukes David

12 And the LORD sent Nathan to David. He came to him and said to him, "There were two men in a certain city, the one rich and the other poor. ²The rich man had very many flocks and herds, ³but the poor man had nothing but one little ewe lamb, which he had bought. And he brought it up, and it grew up with him and with his children. It used to eat of his morsel and drink from his cup and lie in his arms,¹ and it was like a daughter to him. ⁴Now there came a traveler to the rich man, and he was unwilling to take one of his own flock or herd to prepare for the guest who had come to him, but he took the poor man's lamb and prepared it for the man who had come to him." ⁵Then David's anger was greatly kindled against the man, and he said to Nathan, "As the LORD lives, the man who has done this deserves to die, ⁶and he shall restore the lamb fourfold, because he did this thing, and because he had no pity."

⁷Nathan said to David, "You are the man! Thus says the LORD, the God of Israel, 'I anointed you king over Israel, and I delivered you out of the hand of Saul. ⁸And I gave you your master's house and your master's wives into your arms and gave you the house of Israel and of Judah. And if this were too little, I would add to you as much more. ⁹Why have you despised the word of the LORD, to do what is evil in his sight? You have struck down Uriah the Hittite with the sword and have taken his wife to be your wife and have killed him with the sword of the Ammonites. ¹⁰Now therefore the sword shall never depart from your house, because you have

despised me and have taken the wife of Uriah the Hittite to be your wife.' ¹¹Thus says the Lord, 'Behold, I will raise up evil against you out of your own house. And I will take your wives before your eyes and give them to your neighbor, and he shall lie with your wives in the sight of this sun. ¹²For you did it secretly, but I will do this thing before all Israel and before the sun.'" ¹³David said to Nathan, "I have sinned against the Lord." And Nathan said to David, "The Lord also has put away your sin; you shall not die. ¹⁴Nevertheless, because by this deed you have utterly scorned the Lord,[1] the child who is born to you shall die." ¹⁵Then Nathan went to his house.

David's Child Dies

And the Lord afflicted the child that Uriah's wife bore to David, and he became sick. ¹⁶David therefore sought God on behalf of the child. And David fasted and went in and lay all night on the ground. ¹⁷And the elders of his house stood beside him, to raise him from the ground, but he would not, nor did he eat food with them. ¹⁸On the seventh day the child died. And the servants of David were afraid to tell him that the child was dead, for they said, "Behold, while the child was yet alive, we spoke to him, and he did not listen to us. How then can we say to him the child is dead? He may do himself some harm." ¹⁹But when David saw that his servants were whispering together, David understood that the child was dead. And David said to his servants, "Is the child dead?" They said, "He is dead." ²⁰Then David arose from the earth and washed and anointed himself and changed his clothes. And he went into the house of the Lord and worshiped. He then went to his own house. And when he asked, they set food before him, and he ate. ²¹Then his servants said to him, "What is this thing that you have done? You fasted and wept for the child while he was alive; but when the child died, you arose and ate food." ²²He said, "While the child was still alive, I fasted and wept, for I said, 'Who knows whether the Lord will be gracious to me, that the child may live?' ²³But now he is dead. Why should I fast? Can I bring him

back again? I shall go to him, but he will not return to me."

Solomon's Birth

²⁴Then David comforted his wife, Bathsheba, and went in to her and lay with her, and she bore a son, and he called his name Solomon. And the Lord loved him ²⁵and sent a message by Nathan the prophet. So he called his name Jedidiah,[2] because of the Lord.

Rabbah Is Captured

²⁶Now Joab fought against Rabbah of the Ammonites and took the royal city. ²⁷And Joab sent messengers to David and said, "I have fought against Rabbah; moreover, I have taken the city of waters. ²⁸Now then gather the rest of the people together and encamp against the city and take it, lest I take the city and it be called by my name." ²⁹So David gathered all the people together and went to Rabbah and fought against it and took it. ³⁰And he took the crown of their king from his head. The weight of it was a talent[3] of gold, and in it was a precious stone, and it was placed on David's head. And he brought out the spoil of the city, a very great amount. ³¹And he brought out the people who were in it and set them to labor with saws and iron picks and iron axes and made them toil at[4] the brick kilns. And thus he did to all the cities of the Ammonites. Then David and all the people returned to Jerusalem.

Amnon and Tamar

13 Now Absalom, David's son, had a beautiful sister, whose name was Tamar. And after a time Amnon, David's son, loved her. ²And Amnon was so tormented that he made himself ill because of his sister Tamar, for she was a virgin, and it seemed impossible to Amnon to do anything to her. ³But Amnon had a friend, whose name was Jonadab, the son of Shimeah, David's brother. And Jonadab was a very crafty man. ⁴And he said to him, "O son of the king, why are you so haggard morning after morning? Will you not tell me?" Amnon said to him, "I love Tamar, my brother Absalom's sister." ⁵Jonadab said to him, "Lie down on your bed and pretend to be ill. And when your

---

[1] Masoretic Text *the enemies of the Lord*; Dead Sea Scroll *the word of the Lord* [2] *Jedidiah* means *beloved of the Lord* [3] A *talent* was about 75 pounds or 34 kilograms [4] Hebrew *pass through*

father comes to see you, say to him, 'Let my sister Tamar come and give me bread to eat, and prepare the food in my sight, that I may see it and eat it from her hand.'" ⁶ So Amnon lay down and pretended to be ill. And when the king came to see him, Amnon said to the king, "Please let my sister Tamar come and make a couple of cakes in my sight, that I may eat from her hand."

⁷ Then David sent home to Tamar, saying, "Go to your brother Amnon's house and prepare food for him." ⁸ So Tamar went to her brother Amnon's house, where he was lying down. And she took dough and kneaded it and made cakes in his sight and baked the cakes. ⁹ And she took the pan and emptied it out before him, but he refused to eat. And Amnon said, "Send out everyone from me." So everyone went out from him. ¹⁰ Then Amnon said to Tamar, "Bring the food into the chamber, that I may eat from your hand." And Tamar took the cakes she had made and brought them into the chamber to Amnon her brother. ¹¹ But when she brought them near him to eat, he took hold of her and said to her, "Come, lie with me, my sister." ¹² She answered him, "No, my brother, do not violate¹ me, for such a thing is not done in Israel; do not do this outrageous thing. ¹³ As for me, where could I carry my shame? And as for you, you would be as one of the outrageous fools in Israel. Now therefore, please speak to the king, for he will not withhold me from you." ¹⁴ But he would not listen to her, and being stronger than she, he violated her and lay with her.

¹⁵ Then Amnon hated her with very great hatred, so that the hatred with which he hated her was greater than the love with which he had loved her. And Amnon said to her, "Get up! Go!" ¹⁶ But she said to him, "No, my brother, for this wrong in sending me away is greater than the other that you did to me."² But he would not listen to her. ¹⁷ He called the young man who served him and said, "Put this woman out of my presence and bolt the door after her." ¹⁸ Now she was wearing a long robe³ with sleeves, for thus were the virgin daughters of the king dressed. So his servant put her out and bolted the door after her. ¹⁹ And Tamar put ashes on her head and tore the long robe that she wore. And she laid her hand on her head and went away, crying aloud as she went.

²⁰ And her brother Absalom said to her, "Has Amnon your brother been with you? Now hold your peace, my sister. He is your brother; do not take this to heart." So Tamar lived, a desolate woman, in her brother Absalom's house. ²¹ When King David heard of all these things, he was very angry.⁴ ²² But Absalom spoke to Amnon neither good nor bad, for Absalom hated Amnon, because he had violated his sister Tamar.

Absalom Murders Amnon

²³ After two full years Absalom had sheepshearers at Baal-hazor, which is near Ephraim, and Absalom invited all the king's sons. ²⁴ And Absalom came to the king and said, "Behold, your servant has sheepshearers. Please let the king and his servants go with your servant." ²⁵ But the king said to Absalom, "No, my son, let us not all go, lest we be burdensome to you." He pressed him, but he would not go but gave him his blessing. ²⁶ Then Absalom said, "If not, please let my brother Amnon go with us." And the king said to him, "Why should he go with you?" ²⁷ But Absalom pressed him until he let Amnon and all the king's sons go with him. ²⁸ Then Absalom commanded his servants, "Mark when Amnon's heart is merry with wine, and when I say to you, 'Strike Amnon,' then kill him. Do not fear; have I not commanded you? Be courageous and be valiant." ²⁹ So the servants of Absalom did to Amnon as Absalom had commanded. Then all the king's sons arose, and each mounted his mule and fled.

³⁰ While they were on the way, news came to David, "Absalom has struck down all the king's sons, and not one of them is left." ³¹ Then the king arose and tore his garments and lay on the earth. And all his servants who were standing by tore their garments. ³² But Jonadab the son of Shimeah, David's brother, said, "Let not my lord suppose that they have killed all the young men, the king's sons, for Amnon alone is dead. For by the command of Absalom this has been determined from

¹ Or humiliate; also verses 14, 22, 32 ² Compare Septuagint, Vulgate; the meaning of the Hebrew is uncertain ³ Or a robe of many colors (compare Genesis 37:3); also verse 19 ⁴ Dead Sea Scroll, Septuagint add But he would not punish his son Amnon, because he loved him, since he was his firstborn

the day he violated his sister Tamar. [33] Now therefore let not my lord the king so take it to heart as to suppose that all the king's sons are dead, for Amnon alone is dead."

Absalom Flees to Geshur

[34] But Absalom fled. And the young man who kept the watch lifted up his eyes and looked, and behold, many people were coming from the road behind him[1] by the side of the mountain. [35] And Jonadab said to the king, "Behold, the king's sons have come; as your servant said, so it has come about." [36] And as soon as he had finished speaking, behold, the king's sons came and lifted up their voice and wept. And the king also and all his servants wept very bitterly.

[37] But Absalom fled and went to Talmai the son of Ammihud, king of Geshur. And David mourned for his son day after day. [38] So Absalom fled and went to Geshur, and was there three years. [39] And the spirit of the king[2] longed to go out[3] to Absalom, because he was comforted about Amnon, since he was dead.

Absalom Returns to Jerusalem

14 Now Joab the son of Zeruiah knew that the king's heart went out to Absalom. [2] And Joab sent to Tekoa and brought from there a wise woman and said to her, "Pretend to be a mourner and put on mourning garments. Do not anoint yourself with oil, but behave like a woman who has been mourning many days for the dead. [3] Go to the king and speak thus to him." So Joab put the words in her mouth.

[4] When the woman of Tekoa came to the king, she fell on her face to the ground and paid homage and said, "Save me, O king." [5] And the king said to her, "What is your trouble?" She answered, "Alas, I am a widow; my husband is dead. [6] And your servant had two sons, and they quarreled with one another in the field. There was no one to separate them, and one struck the other and killed him. [7] And now the whole clan has risen against your servant, and they say, 'Give up the man who struck his brother, that we may put him to death for the life of his brother whom he killed.' And so they would destroy the heir also. Thus they would quench my coal that is left and leave to my husband neither name nor remnant on the face of the earth."

[8] Then the king said to the woman, "Go to your house, and I will give orders concerning you." [9] And the woman of Tekoa said to the king, "On me be the guilt, my lord the king, and on my father's house; let the king and his throne be guiltless." [10] The king said, "If anyone says anything to you, bring him to me, and he shall never touch you again." [11] Then she said, "Please let the king invoke the LORD your God, that the avenger of blood kill no more, and my son be not destroyed." He said, "As the LORD lives, not one hair of your son shall fall to the ground."

[12] Then the woman said, "Please let your servant speak a word to my lord the king." He said, "Speak." [13] And the woman said, "Why then have you planned such a thing against the people of God? For in giving this decision the king convicts himself, inasmuch as the king does not bring his banished one home again. [14] We must all die; we are like water spilled on the ground, which cannot be gathered up again. But God will not take away life, and he devises means so that the banished one will not remain an outcast. [15] Now I have come to say this to my lord the king because the people have made me afraid, and your servant thought, 'I will speak to the king; it may be that the king will perform the request of his servant. [16] For the king will hear and deliver his servant from the hand of the man who would destroy me and my son together from the heritage of God.' [17] And your servant thought, 'The word of my lord the king will set me at rest,' for my lord the king is like the angel of God to discern good and evil. The LORD your God be with you!"

[18] Then the king answered the woman, "Do not hide from me anything I ask you." And the woman said, "Let my lord the king speak." [19] The king said, "Is the hand of Joab with you in all this?" The woman answered and said, "As surely as you live, my lord the king, one cannot turn to the right hand or to the left from anything that my lord the king has said. It was your servant Joab who commanded me; it was he who put all these words in the mouth of your servant. [20] In order to change the course of things your servant Joab did this. But my lord has wisdom like the wisdom of the angel of God to know all things that are on the earth."

[21] Then the king said to Joab, "Behold now, I grant this; go, bring back the young

---

[1] Septuagint *the Horonaim Road* [2] Dead Sea Scroll, Septuagint; Hebrew *David* [3] Compare Vulgate *ceased to go out*

man Absalom." ²²And Joab fell on his face to the ground and paid homage and blessed the king. And Joab said, "Today your servant knows that I have found favor in your sight, my lord the king, in that the king has granted the request of his servant." ²³So Joab arose and went to Geshur and brought Absalom to Jerusalem. ²⁴And the king said, "Let him dwell apart in his own house; he is not to come into my presence." So Absalom lived apart in his own house and did not come into the king's presence.

²⁵Now in all Israel there was no one so much to be praised for his handsome appearance as Absalom. From the sole of his foot to the crown of his head there was no blemish in him. ²⁶And when he cut the hair of his head (for at the end of every year he used to cut it; when it was heavy on him, he cut it), he weighed the hair of his head, two hundred shekels¹ by the king's weight. ²⁷There were born to Absalom three sons, and one daughter whose name was Tamar. She was a beautiful woman.

²⁸So Absalom lived two full years in Jerusalem, without coming into the king's presence. ²⁹Then Absalom sent for Joab, to send him to the king, but Joab would not come to him. And he sent a second time, but Joab would not come. ³⁰Then he said to his servants, "See, Joab's field is next to mine, and he has barley there; go and set it on fire." So Absalom's servants set the field on fire.² ³¹Then Joab arose and went to Absalom at his house and said to him, "Why have your servants set my field on fire?" ³²Absalom answered Joab, "Behold, I sent word to you, 'Come here, that I may send you to the king, to ask, "Why have I come from Geshur? It would be better for me to be there still." Now therefore let me go into the presence of the king, and if there is guilt in me, let him put me to death.'" ³³Then Joab went to the king and told him, and he summoned Absalom. So he came to the king and bowed himself on his face to the ground before the king, and the king kissed Absalom.

Absalom's Conspiracy

15 After this Absalom got himself a chariot and horses, and fifty men to run before him. ²And Absalom used to rise early and stand beside the way of the gate. And when any man had a dispute to come before the king for judgment, Absalom would call to him and say, "From what city are you?" And when he said, "Your servant is of such and such a tribe in Israel," ³Absalom would say to him, "See, your claims are good and right, but there is no man designated by the king to hear you." ⁴Then Absalom would say, "Oh that I were judge in the land! Then every man with a dispute or cause might come to me, and I would give him justice." ⁵And whenever a man came near to pay homage to him, he would put out his hand and take hold of him and kiss him. ⁶Thus Absalom did to all of Israel who came to the king for judgment. So Absalom stole the hearts of the men of Israel.

⁷And at the end of four³ years Absalom said to the king, "Please let me go and pay my vow, which I have vowed to the LORD, in Hebron. ⁸For your servant vowed a vow while I lived at Geshur in Aram, saying, 'If the LORD will indeed bring me back to Jerusalem, then I will offer worship to⁴ the LORD.'" ⁹The king said to him, "Go in peace." So he arose and went to Hebron. ¹⁰But Absalom sent secret messengers throughout all the tribes of Israel, saying, "As soon as you hear the sound of the trumpet, then say, 'Absalom is king at Hebron!'" ¹¹With Absalom went two hundred men from Jerusalem who were invited guests, and they went in their innocence and knew nothing. ¹²And while Absalom was offering the sacrifices, he sent for⁵ Ahithophel the Gilonite, David's counselor, from his city Giloh. And the conspiracy grew strong, and the people with Absalom kept increasing.

David Flees Jerusalem

¹³And a messenger came to David, saying, "The hearts of the men of Israel have gone after Absalom." ¹⁴Then David said to all his servants who were with him at Jerusalem, "Arise, and let us flee, or else there will be no escape for us from Absalom. Go quickly, lest he overtake us quickly and bring down ruin on us and strike the city with the edge of the sword." ¹⁵And the king's servants said to the king, "Behold, your servants are ready to do whatever my lord the king decides." ¹⁶So the king went out, and all his household after him. And the king left ten concubines to keep the house. ¹⁷And the

¹A *shekel* was about 2/5 ounce or 11 grams ²Septuagint, Dead Sea Scroll add *So Joab's servants came to him with their clothes torn, and they said to him, "The servants of Absalom have set your field on fire."* ³Septuagint, Syriac; Hebrew *forty* ⁴Or *will serve* ⁵Or *sent*

king went out, and all the people after him. And they halted at the last house. [18] And all his servants passed by him, and all the Cherethites, and all the Pelethites, and all the six hundred Gittites who had followed him from Gath, passed on before the king. [19] Then the king said to Ittai the Gittite, "Why do you also go with us? Go back and stay with the king, for you are a foreigner and also an exile from your home. [20] You came only yesterday, and shall I today make you wander about with us, since I go I know not where? Go back and take your brothers with you, and may the LORD show[1] steadfast love and faithfulness to you." [21] But Ittai answered the king, "As the LORD lives, and as my lord the king lives, wherever my lord the king shall be, whether for death or for life, there also will your servant be." [22] And David said to Ittai, "Go then, pass on." So Ittai the Gittite passed on with all his men and all the little ones who were with him. [23] And all the land wept aloud as all the people passed by, and the king crossed the brook Kidron, and all the people passed on toward the wilderness.

[24] And Abiathar came up, and behold, Zadok came also with all the Levites, bearing the ark of the covenant of God. And they set down the ark of God until the people had all passed out of the city. [25] Then the king said to Zadok, "Carry the ark of God back into the city. If I find favor in the eyes of the LORD, he will bring me back and let me see both it and his dwelling place. [26] But if he says, 'I have no pleasure in you,' behold, here I am, let him do to me what seems good to him." [27] The king also said to Zadok the priest, "Are you not a seer? Go back[2] to the city in peace, with your two sons, Ahimaaz your son, and Jonathan the son of Abiathar. [28] See, I will wait at the fords of the wilderness until word comes from you to inform me." [29] So Zadok and Abiathar carried the ark of God back to Jerusalem, and they remained there.

[30] But David went up the ascent of the Mount of Olives, weeping as he went, barefoot and with his head covered. And all the people who were with him covered their heads, and they went up, weeping as they went. [31] And it was told David, "Ahithophel is among the conspirators

with Absalom." And David said, "O LORD please turn the counsel of Ahithophel into foolishness."

[32] While David was coming to the summit, where God was worshiped, behold, Hushai the Archite came to meet him with his coat torn and dirt on his head. [33] David said to him, "If you go on with me, you will be a burden to me. [34] But if you return to the city and say to Absalom, 'I will be your servant, O king; as I have been your father's servant in time past, so now I will be your servant,' then you will defeat for me the counsel of Ahithophel. [35] Are not Zadok and Abiathar the priests with you there? So whatever you hear from the king's house, tell it to Zadok and Abiathar the priests. [36] Behold, their two sons are with them there, Ahimaaz, Zadok's son, and Jonathan, Abiathar's son, and by them you shall send to me everything you hear." [37] So Hushai, David's friend, came into the city, just as Absalom was entering Jerusalem.

A Prayer for...
PEACE IN TRIALS

Dear God, in all your dealings with me, whether I am in joy or in pain, in light or in darkness, let me be brought to you.

Don't let me judge my life as good or bad just because it makes me happy or makes me sad, or because I get or don't get what I want. I pray that, instead, everything you let happen in my life will draw me closer to you, so that by knowing that you are perfect, I can be sure in everything that you are still perfectly loving me, and in every darkness that you are still enlightening me, and in every boring moment that you are still using me. And may I be sure that in all my misery and suffering, you are giving me life, just like you gave me life through the death of your Son, our Savior, Jesus Christ.

Amen.

[1] Septuagint; Hebrew lacks *may the LORD show*   [2] Septuagint *The king also said to Zadok the priest, "Look, go back*

David and Ziba

16 When David had passed a little beyond the summit, Ziba the servant of Mephibosheth met him, with a couple of donkeys saddled, bearing two hundred loaves of bread, a hundred bunches of raisins, a hundred of summer fruits, and a skin of wine. ²And the king said to Ziba, "Why have you brought these?" Ziba answered, "The donkeys are for the king's household to ride on, the bread and summer fruit for the young men to eat, and the wine for those who faint in the wilderness to drink." ³And the king said, "And where is your master's son?" Ziba said to the king, "Behold, he remains in Jerusalem, for he said, 'Today the house of Israel will give me back the kingdom of my father.'" ⁴Then the king said to Ziba, "Behold, all that belonged to Mephibosheth is now yours." And Ziba said, "I pay homage; let me ever find favor in your sight, my lord the king."

Shimei Curses David

⁵When King David came to Bahurim, there came out a man of the family of the house of Saul, whose name was Shimei, the son of Gera, and as he came he cursed continually. ⁶And he threw stones at David and at all the servants of King David, and all the people and all the mighty men were on his right hand and on his left. ⁷And Shimei said as he cursed, "Get out, get out, you man of blood, you worthless man! ⁸The LORD has avenged on you all the blood of the house of Saul, in whose place you have reigned, and the LORD has given the kingdom into the hand of your son Absalom. See, your evil is on you, for you are a man of blood."

⁹Then Abishai the son of Zeruiah said to the king, "Why should this dead dog curse my lord the king? Let me go over and take off his head." ¹⁰But the king said, "What have I to do with you, you sons of Zeruiah? If he is cursing because the LORD has said to him, 'Curse David,' who then shall say, 'Why have you done so?'" ¹¹And David said to Abishai and to all his servants, "Behold, my own son seeks my life; how much more now may this Benjaminite! Leave him alone, and let him curse, for the LORD has told him to. ¹²It may be that the LORD will look on the wrong done to me,¹ and that the LORD will repay me with good for

his cursing today." ¹³So David and his men went on the road, while Shimei went along on the hillside opposite him and cursed as he went and threw stones at him and flung dust. ¹⁴And the king, and all the people who were with him, arrived weary at the Jordan.² And there he refreshed himself.

Absalom Enters Jerusalem

¹⁵Now Absalom and all the people, the men of Israel, came to Jerusalem, and Ahithophel with him. ¹⁶And when Hushai the Archite, David's friend, came to Absalom, Hushai said to Absalom, "Long live the king! Long live the king!" ¹⁷And Absalom said to Hushai, "Is this your loyalty to your friend? Why did you not go with your friend?" ¹⁸And Hushai said to Absalom, "No, for whom the LORD and this people and all the men of Israel have chosen, his I will be, and with him I will remain. ¹⁹And again, whom should I serve? Should it not be his son? As I have served your father, so I will serve you."

²⁰Then Absalom said to Ahithophel, "Give your counsel. What shall we do?" ²¹Ahithophel said to Absalom, "Go in to your father's concubines, whom he has left to keep the house, and all Israel will hear that you have made yourself a stench to your father, and the hands of all who are with you will be strengthened." ²²So they pitched a tent for Absalom on the roof. And Absalom went in to his father's concubines in the sight of all Israel. ²³Now in those days the counsel that Ahithophel gave was as if one consulted the word of God; so was all the counsel of Ahithophel esteemed, both by David and by Absalom.

Hushai Saves David

17 Moreover, Ahithophel said to Absalom, "Let me choose twelve thousand men, and I will arise and pursue David tonight. ²I will come upon him while he is weary and discouraged and throw him into a panic, and all the people who are with him will flee. I will strike down only the king, ³and I will bring all the people back to you as a bride comes home to her husband. You seek the life of only one man,³ and all the people will be at peace." ⁴And the advice seemed right in the eyes of Absalom and all the elders of Israel.

¹Septuagint, Vulgate *will look upon my affliction* ²Septuagint; Hebrew lacks *at the Jordan* ³Septuagint; Hebrew *back to you. Like the return of the whole is the man whom you seek*

⁵ Then Absalom said, "Call Hushai the Archite also, and let us hear what he has to say." ⁶ And when Hushai came to Absalom, Absalom said to him, "Thus has Ahithophel spoken; shall we do as he says? If not, you speak." ⁷ Then Hushai said to Absalom, "This time the counsel that Ahithophel has given is not good." ⁸ Hushai said, "You know that your father and his men are mighty men, and that they are enraged,¹ like a bear robbed of her cubs in the field. Besides, your father is expert in war; he will not spend the night with the people. ⁹ Behold, even now he has hidden himself in one of the pits or in some other place. And as soon as some of the people fall² at the first attack, whoever hears it will say, 'There has been a slaughter among the people who follow Absalom.' ¹⁰ Then even the valiant man, whose heart is like the heart of a lion, will utterly melt with fear, for all Israel knows that your father is a mighty man, and that those who are with him are valiant men. ¹¹ But my counsel is that all Israel be gathered to you, from Dan to Beersheba, as the sand by the sea for multitude, and that you go to battle in person. ¹² So we shall come upon him in some place where he is to be found, and we shall light upon him as the dew falls on the ground, and of him and all the men with him not one will be left. ¹³ If he withdraws into a city, then all Israel will bring ropes to that city, and we shall drag it into the valley, until not even a pebble is to be found there." ¹⁴ And Absalom and all the men of Israel said, "The counsel of Hushai the Archite is better than the counsel of Ahithophel." For the Lord had ordained³ to defeat the good counsel of Ahithophel, so that the Lord might bring harm upon Absalom.

¹⁵ Then Hushai said to Zadok and Abiathar the priests, "Thus and so did Ahithophel counsel Absalom and the elders of Israel, and thus and so have I counseled. ¹⁶ Now therefore send quickly and tell David, 'Do not stay tonight at the fords of the wilderness, but by all means pass over, lest the king and all the people who are with him be swallowed up.'" ¹⁷ Now Jonathan and Ahimaaz were waiting at En-rogel. A female servant was to go and tell them, and they were to go and tell King David, for they were not to be seen entering the city. ¹⁸ But a young man saw them and told Absalom. So both of them went away quickly and came to the house of a man at Bahurim, who had a well in his courtyard. And they went down into it. ¹⁹ And the woman took and spread a covering over the well's mouth and scattered grain on it, and nothing was known of it. ²⁰ When Absalom's servants came to the woman at the house, they said, "Where are Ahimaaz and Jonathan?" And the woman said to them, "They have gone over the brook⁴ of water." And when they had sought and could not find them, they returned to Jerusalem.

²¹ After they had gone, the men came up out of the well, and went and told King David. They said to David, "Arise, and go quickly over the water, for thus and so has Ahithophel counseled against you." ²² Then David arose, and all the people who were with him, and they crossed the Jordan. By daybreak not one was left who had not crossed the Jordan.

²³ When Ahithophel saw that his counsel was not followed, he saddled his donkey and went off home to his own city. He set his house in order and hanged himself, and he died and was buried in the tomb of his father.

²⁴ Then David came to Mahanaim. And Absalom crossed the Jordan with all the men of Israel. ²⁵ Now Absalom had set Amasa over the army instead of Joab. Amasa was the son of a man named Ithra the Ishmaelite,⁵ who had married Abigal the daughter of Nahash, sister of Zeruiah, Joab's mother. ²⁶ And Israel and Absalom encamped in the land of Gilead.

²⁷ When David came to Mahanaim, Shobi the son of Nahash from Rabbah of the Ammonites, and Machir the son of Ammiel from Lo-debar, and Barzillai the Gileadite from Rogelim, ²⁸ brought beds, basins, and earthen vessels, wheat, barley, flour, parched grain, beans and lentils,⁶ ²⁹ honey and curds and sheep and cheese from the herd, for David and the people with him to eat, for they said, "The people are hungry and weary and thirsty in the wilderness."

Absalom Killed

18 Then David mustered the men who were with him and set over them commanders of thousands and command

---

¹ Hebrew *bitter of soul* ² Or *And as he falls on them* ³ Hebrew *commanded* ⁴ The meaning of the Hebrew word is uncertain ⁵ Compare 1 Chronicles 2:17; Hebrew *Israelite* ⁶ Hebrew adds *and parched grain*

ers of hundreds. [2] And David sent out the army, one third under the command of Joab, one third under the command of Abishai the son of Zeruiah, Joab's brother, and one third under the command of Ittai the Gittite. And the king said to the men, "I myself will also go out with you." [3] But the men said, "You shall not go out. For if we flee, they will not care about us. If half of us die, they will not care about us. But you are worth ten thousand of us. Therefore it is better that you send us help from the city." [4] The king said to them, "Whatever seems best to you I will do." So the king stood at the side of the gate, while all the army marched out by hundreds and by thousands. [5] And the king ordered Joab and Abishai and Ittai, "Deal gently for my sake with the young man Absalom." And all the people heard when the king gave orders to all the commanders about Absalom.

[6] So the army went out into the field against Israel, and the battle was fought in the forest of Ephraim. [7] And the men of Israel were defeated there by the servants of David, and the loss there was great on that day, twenty thousand men. [8] The battle spread over the face of all the country, and the forest devoured more people that day than the sword.

[9] And Absalom happened to meet the servants of David. Absalom was riding on his mule, and the mule went under the thick branches of a great oak,[1] and his head caught fast in the oak, and he was suspended between heaven and earth, while the mule that was under him went on. [10] And a certain man saw it and told Joab, "Behold, I saw Absalom hanging in an oak." [11] Joab said to the man who told him, "What, you saw him! Why then did you not strike him there to the ground? I would have been glad to give you ten pieces of silver and a belt." [12] But the man said to Joab, "Even if I felt in my hand the weight of a thousand pieces of silver, I would not reach out my hand against the king's son, for in our hearing the king commanded you and Abishai and Ittai, 'For my sake protect the young man Absalom.' [13] On the other hand, if I had dealt treacherously against his life[2] (and there is nothing hidden from the king), then you yourself would have stood aloof." [14] Joab said, "I will not waste time like this with you." And he took three

javelins in his hand and thrust them into the heart of Absalom while he was still alive in the oak. [15] And ten young men, Joab's armor-bearers, surrounded Absalom and struck him and killed him.

[16] Then Joab blew the trumpet, and the troops came back from pursuing Israel, for Joab restrained them. [17] And they took Absalom and threw him into a great pit in the forest and raised over him a very great heap of stones. And all Israel fled every one to his own home. [18] Now Absalom in his lifetime had taken and set up for himself the pillar that is in the King's Valley, for he said, "I have no son to keep my name in remembrance." He called the pillar after his own name, and it is called Absalom's monument[3] to this day.

David Hears of Absalom's Death

[19] Then Ahimaaz the son of Zadok said, "Let me run and carry news to the king that the LORD has delivered him from the hand of his enemies." [20] And Joab said to him, "You are not to carry news today. You may carry news another day, but today you shall carry no news, because the king's son is dead." [21] Then Joab said to the Cushite, "Go, tell the king what you have seen." The Cushite bowed before Joab, and ran. [22] Then Ahimaaz the son of Zadok said again to Joab, "Come what may, let me also run after the Cushite." And Joab said, "Why will you run, my son, seeing that you will have no reward for the news?" [23] "Come what may," he said, "I will run." So he said to him, "Run." Then Ahimaaz ran by the way of the plain, and outran the Cushite.

[24] Now David was sitting between the two gates, and the watchman went up to the roof of the gate by the wall, and when he lifted up his eyes and looked, he saw a man running alone. [25] The watchman called out and told the king. And the king said, "If he is alone, there is news in his mouth." And he drew nearer and nearer. [26] The watchman saw another man running. And the watchman called to the gate and said, "See, another man running alone!" The king said, "He also brings news." [27] The watchman said, "I think the running of the first is like the running of Ahimaaz the son of Zadok." And the king said, "He is a good man and comes with good news."

---

[1] Or terebinth; also verses 10, 14   [2] Or at the risk of my life   [3] Or Absalom's hand

²⁸ Then Ahimaaz cried out to the king, "All is well." And he bowed before the king with his face to the earth and said, "Blessed be the LORD your God, who has delivered up the men who raised their hand against my lord the king." ²⁹ And the king said, "Is it well with the young man Absalom?" Ahimaaz answered, "When Joab sent the king's servant, your servant, I saw a great commotion, but I do not know what it was." ³⁰ And the king said, "Turn aside and stand here." So he turned aside and stood still.

David's Grief

³¹ And behold, the Cushite came, and the Cushite said, "Good news for my lord the king! For the LORD has delivered you this day from the hand of all who rose up against you." ³² The king said to the Cushite, "Is it well with the young man Absalom?" And the Cushite answered, "May the enemies of my lord the king and all who rise up against you for evil be like that young man." ³³ ¹ And the king was deeply moved and went up to the chamber over the gate and wept. And as he went, he said, "O my son Absalom, my son, my son Absalom! Would I had died instead of you, O Absalom, my son, my son!"

Joab Rebukes David

19 It was told Joab, "Behold, the king is weeping and mourning for Absalom." ² So the victory that day was turned into mourning for all the people, for the people heard that day, "The king is grieving for his son." ³ And the people stole into the city that day as people steal in who are ashamed when they flee in battle. ⁴ The king covered his face, and the king cried with a loud voice, "O my son Absalom, O Absalom, my son, my son!" ⁵ Then Joab came into the house to the king and said, "You have today covered with shame the faces of all your servants, who have this day saved your life and the lives of your sons and your daughters and the lives of your wives and your concubines, ⁶ because you love those who hate you and hate those who love you. For you have made it clear today that commanders and servants are nothing to you, for today I know that if Absalom were alive and all of us were dead today, then you would be pleased. ⁷ Now therefore arise, go out and speak

kindly to your servants, for I swear by the LORD, if you do not go, not a man will stay with you this night, and this will be worse for you than all the evil that has come upon you from your youth until now." ⁸ Then the king arose and took his seat in the gate. And the people were all told, "Behold, the king is sitting in the gate." And all the people came before the king.

David Returns to Jerusalem

Now Israel had fled every man to his own home. ⁹ And all the people were arguing throughout all the tribes of Israel, saying, "The king delivered us from the hand of our enemies and saved us from the hand of the Philistines, and now he has fled out of the land from Absalom. ¹⁰ But Absalom, whom we anointed over us, is dead in battle. Now therefore why do you say nothing about bringing the king back?"

¹¹ And King David sent this message to Zadok and Abiathar the priests: "Say to the elders of Judah, 'Why should you be the last to bring the king back to his house, when the word of all Israel has come to the king?² ¹² You are my brothers; you are my bone and my flesh. Why then should you be the last to bring back the king?' ¹³ And say to Amasa, 'Are you not my bone and my flesh? God do so to me and more also, if you are not commander of my army from now on in place of Joab.'" ¹⁴ And he swayed the heart of all the men of Judah as one man, so that they sent word to the king, "Return, both you and all your servants." ¹⁵ So the king came back to the Jordan, and Judah came to Gilgal to meet the king and to bring the king over the Jordan.

David Pardons His Enemies

¹⁶ And Shimei the son of Gera, the Benjaminite, from Bahurim, hurried to come down with the men of Judah to meet King David. ¹⁷ And with him were a thousand men from Benjamin. And Ziba the servant of the house of Saul, with his fifteen sons and his twenty servants, rushed down to the Jordan before the king, ¹⁸ and they crossed the ford to bring over the king's household and to do his pleasure. And Shimei the son of Gera fell down before the king, as he was about to cross the Jordan, ¹⁹ and said to the king, "Let not my lord hold me guilty or remember how your servant

¹ Ch 19:1 in Hebrew ² Septuagint; Hebrew to the king, to his house

did wrong on the day my lord the king left Jerusalem. Do not let the king take it to heart. [20] For your servant knows that I have sinned. Therefore, behold, I have come this day, the first of all the house of Joseph to come down to meet my lord the king." [21] Abishai the son of Zeruiah answered, "Shall not Shimei be put to death for this, because he cursed the LORD's anointed?" [22] But David said, "What have I to do with you, you sons of Zeruiah, that you should this day be as an adversary to me? Shall anyone be put to death in Israel this day? For do I not know that I am this day king over Israel?" [23] And the king said to Shimei, "You shall not die." And the king gave him his oath.

[24] And Mephibosheth the son of Saul came down to meet the king. He had neither taken care of his feet nor trimmed his beard nor washed his clothes, from the day the king departed until the day he came back in safety. [25] And when he came to Jerusalem to meet the king, the king said to him, "Why did you not go with me, Mephibosheth?" [26] He answered, "My lord, O king, my servant deceived me, for your servant said to him, 'I will saddle a donkey for myself,[1] that I may ride on it and go with the king.' For your servant is lame. [27] He has slandered your servant to my lord the king. But my lord the king is like the angel of God; do therefore what seems good to you. [28] For all my father's house were but men doomed to death before my lord the king, but you set your servant among those who eat at your table. What further right have I, then, to cry to the king?" [29] And the king said to him, "Why speak any more of your affairs? I have decided: you and Ziba shall divide the land." [30] And Mephibosheth said to the king, "Oh, let him take it all, since my lord the king has come safely home."

[31] Now Barzillai the Gileadite had come down from Rogelim, and he went on with the king to the Jordan, to escort him over the Jordan. [32] Barzillai was a very aged man, eighty years old. He had provided the king with food while he stayed at Mahanaim, for he was a very wealthy man. [33] And the king said to Barzillai, "Come over with me, and I will provide for you with me in Jerusalem." [34] But Barzillai said to the king, "How many years have I still to live, that I should go up with the king to Jerusalem?

[35] I am this day eighty years old. Can I discern what is pleasant and what is not? Can your servant taste what he eats or what he drinks? Can I still listen to the voice of singing men and singing women? Why then should your servant be an added burden to my lord the king? [36] Your servant will go a little way over the Jordan with the king. Why should the king repay me with such a reward? [37] Please let your servant return, that I may die in my own city near the grave of my father and my mother. But here is your servant Chimham. Let him go over with my lord the king, and do for him whatever seems good to you." [38] And the king answered, "Chimham shall go over with me, and I will do for him whatever seems good to you, and all that you desire of me I will do for you." [39] Then all the people went over the Jordan, and the king went over. And the king kissed Barzillai and blessed him, and he returned to his own home. [40] The king went on to Gilgal, and Chimham went on with him. All the people of Judah, and also half the people of Israel, brought the king on his way.

[41] Then all the men of Israel came to the king and said to the king, "Why have our brothers the men of Judah stolen you away and brought the king and his household over the Jordan, and all David's men with him?" [42] All the men of Judah answered the men of Israel, "Because the king is our close relative. Why then are you angry over this matter? Have we eaten at all at the king's expense? Or has he given us any gift?" [43] And the men of Israel answered the men of Judah, "We have ten shares in the king, and in David also we have more than you. Why then did you despise us? Were we not the first to speak of bringing back our king?" But the words of the men of Judah were fiercer than the words of the men of Israel.

The Rebellion of Sheba

20 Now there happened to be there a worthless man, whose name was Sheba, the son of Bichri, a Benjaminite. And he blew the trumpet and said,

"We have no portion in David,
  and we have no inheritance in the
    son of Jesse;
  every man to his tents, O Israel!"

---

[1] Septuagint, Syriac, Vulgate *Saddle a donkey for me*

[2] So all the men of Israel withdrew from David and followed Sheba the son of Bichri. But the men of Judah followed their king steadfastly from the Jordan to Jerusalem.

[3] And David came to his house at Jerusalem. And the king took the ten concubines whom he had left to care for the house and put them in a house under guard and provided for them, but did not go in to them. So they were shut up until the day of their death, living as if in widowhood.

[4] Then the king said to Amasa, "Call the men of Judah together to me within three days, and be here yourself." [5] So Amasa went to summon Judah, but he delayed beyond the set time that had been appointed him. [6] And David said to Abishai, "Now Sheba the son of Bichri will do us more harm than Absalom. Take your lord's servants and pursue him, lest he get himself to fortified cities and escape from us."[1] [7] And there went out after him Joab's men and the Cherethites and the Pelethites, and all the mighty men. They went out from Jerusalem to pursue Sheba the son of Bichri. [8] When they were at the great stone that is in Gibeon, Amasa came to meet them. Now Joab was wearing a soldier's garment, and over it was a belt with a sword in its sheath fastened on his thigh, and as he went forward it fell out. [9] And Joab said to Amasa, "Is it well with you, my brother?" And Joab took Amasa by the beard with his right hand to kiss him. [10] But Amasa did not observe the sword that was in Joab's hand. So Joab struck him with it in the stomach and spilled his entrails to the ground without striking a second blow, and he died.

Then Joab and Abishai his brother pursued Sheba the son of Bichri. [11] And one of Joab's young men took his stand by Amasa and said, "Whoever favors Joab, and whoever is for David, let him follow Joab." [12] And Amasa lay wallowing in his blood in the highway. And anyone who came by, seeing him, stopped. And when the man saw that all the people stopped, he carried Amasa out of the highway into the field and threw a garment over him. [13] When he was taken out of the highway, all the people went on after Joab to pursue Sheba the son of Bichri.

[14] And Sheba passed through all the tribes of Israel to Abel of Beth-maacah,[2] and all the Bichrites[3] assembled and followed him in. [15] And all the men who were with Joab came and besieged him in Abel of Beth-maacah. They cast up a mound against the city, and it stood against the rampart, and they were battering the wall to throw it down. [16] Then a wise woman called from the city, "Listen! Listen! Tell Joab, 'Come here, that I may speak to you.'" [17] And he came near her, and the woman said, "Are you Joab?" He answered, "I am." Then she said to him, "Listen to the words of your servant." And he answered, "I am listening." [18] Then she said, "They used to say in former times, 'Let them but ask counsel at Abel,' and so they settled a matter. [19] I am one of those who are peaceable and faithful in Israel. You seek to destroy a city that is a mother in Israel. Why will you swallow up the heritage of the LORD?" [20] Joab answered, "Far be it from me, far be it, that I should swallow up or destroy! [21] That is not true. But a man of the hill country of Ephraim, called Sheba the son of Bichri, has lifted up his hand against King David. Give up him alone, and I will withdraw from the city." And the woman said to Joab, "Behold, his head shall be thrown to you over the wall." [22] Then the woman went to all the people in her wisdom. And they cut off the head of Sheba the son of Bichri and threw it out to Joab. So he blew the trumpet, and they dispersed from the city, every man to his home. And Joab returned to Jerusalem to the king.

[23] Now Joab was in command of all the army of Israel; and Benaiah the son of Jehoiada was in command of the Cherethites and the Pelethites; [24] and Adoram was in charge of the forced labor; and Jehoshaphat the son of Ahilud was the recorder; [25] and Sheva was secretary; and Zadok and Abiathar were priests; [26] and Ira the Jairite was also David's priest.

David Avenges the Gibeonites

21 Now there was a famine in the days of David for three years, year after year. And David sought the face of the LORD. And the LORD said, "There is bloodguilt on Saul and on his house, because he put the Gibeonites to death." [2] So the king called the Gibeonites and spoke to them. Now the Gibeonites were not of

---

[1] Hebrew *and snatch away our eyes* [2] Compare 20:15; Hebrew *and Beth-maacah* [3] Hebrew *Berites*

he people of Israel but of the remnant of the Amorites. Although the people of Israel had sworn to spare them, Saul had sought to strike them down in his zeal for the people of Israel and Judah. ³ And David said to the Gibeonites, "What shall I do for you? And how shall I make atonement, that you may bless the heritage of the LORD?" ⁴ The Gibeonites said to him, "It is not a matter of silver or gold between us and Saul or his house; neither is it for us to put any man to death in Israel." And he said, "What do you say that I shall do for you?" ⁵ They said to the king, "The man who consumed us and planned to destroy us, so that we should have no place in all the territory of Israel, ⁶ let seven of his sons be given to us, so that we may hang them before the LORD at Gibeah of Saul, the chosen of the LORD." And the king said, "I will give them."

⁷ But the king spared Mephibosheth, the son of Saul's son Jonathan, because of the oath of the LORD that was between them, between David and Jonathan the son of Saul. ⁸ The king took the two sons of Rizpah the daughter of Aiah, whom she bore to Saul, Armoni and Mephibosheth; and the five sons of Merab¹ the daughter of Saul, whom she bore to Adriel the son of Barzillai the Meholathite; ⁹ and he gave them into the hands of the Gibeonites, and they hanged them on the mountain before the LORD, and the seven of them perished together. They were put to death in the first days of harvest, at the beginning of barley harvest.

¹⁰ Then Rizpah the daughter of Aiah took sackcloth and spread it for herself on the rock, from the beginning of harvest until rain fell upon them from the heavens. And she did not allow the birds of the air to come upon them by day, or the beasts of the field by night. ¹¹ When David was told what Rizpah the daughter of Aiah, the concubine of Saul, had done, ¹² David went and took the bones of Saul and the bones of his son Jonathan from the men of Jabesh-gilead, who had stolen them from the public square of Beth-shan, where the Philistines had hanged them, on the day the Philistines killed Saul on Gilboa. ¹³ And he brought up from there the bones of Saul and the bones of his son Jonathan; and they gathered the bones of those who were hanged. ¹⁴ And they buried the bones of Saul and his son Jonathan in the land of Benjamin in Zela, in the tomb of Kish his father. And they did all that the king commanded. And after that God responded to the plea for the land.

War with the Philistines

¹⁵ There was war again between the Philistines and Israel, and David went down together with his servants, and they fought against the Philistines. And David grew weary. ¹⁶ And Ishbi-benob, one of the descendants of the giants, whose spear weighed three hundred shekels² of bronze, and who was armed with a new sword, thought to kill David. ¹⁷ But Abishai the son of Zeruiah came to his aid and attacked the Philistine and killed him. Then David's men swore to him, "You shall no longer go out with us to battle, lest you quench the lamp of Israel."

¹⁸ After this there was again war with the Philistines at Gob. Then Sibbecai the Hushathite struck down Saph, who was one of the descendants of the giants. ¹⁹ And there was again war with the Philistines at Gob, and Elhanan the son of Jaare-oregim, the Bethlehemite, struck down Goliath the Gittite, the shaft of whose spear was like a weaver's beam.³ ²⁰ And there was again war at Gath, where there was a man of great stature, who had six fingers on each hand, and six toes on each foot, twenty-four in number, and he also was descended from the giants. ²¹ And when he taunted Israel, Jonathan the son of Shimei, David's brother, struck him down. ²² These four were descended from the giants in Gath, and they fell by the hand of David and by the hand of his servants.

David's Song of Deliverance

22 And David spoke to the LORD the words of this song on the day when the LORD delivered him from the hand of all his enemies, and from the hand of Saul. ² He said,

> "The LORD is my rock and my fortress
> and my deliverer,
³ my⁴ God, my rock, in whom I take
> refuge,

---

¹ Two Hebrew manuscripts, Septuagint; most Hebrew manuscripts *Michal* ² A *shekel* was about 2/5 ounce or 11 grams ³ Contrast 1 Chronicles 20:5, which may preserve the original reading ⁴ Septuagint (compare Psalm 18:2); Hebrew lacks *my*

my shield, and the horn of my salvation,
    my stronghold and my refuge,
    my savior; you save me from violence.
4 I call upon the Lord, who is worthy
      to be praised,
    and I am saved from my enemies.

5 "For the waves of death encompassed
    me,
    the torrents of destruction
      assailed me;[1]
6 the cords of Sheol entangled me;
    the snares of death confronted me.

7 "In my distress I called upon the Lord;
    to my God I called.
    From his temple he heard my voice,
    and my cry came to his ears.

8 "Then the earth reeled and rocked;
    the foundations of the heavens
      trembled
    and quaked, because he was angry.
9 Smoke went up from his nostrils,[2]
    and devouring fire from his mouth;
    glowing coals flamed forth from
      him.
10 He bowed the heavens and came
      down;
    thick darkness was under his feet.
11 He rode on a cherub and flew;
    he was seen on the wings of the
      wind.
12 He made darkness around him his
      canopy,
    thick clouds, a gathering of water.
13 Out of the brightness before him
    coals of fire flamed forth.
14 The Lord thundered from heaven,
    and the Most High uttered his voice.
15 And he sent out arrows and scattered them;
    lightning, and routed them.
16 Then the channels of the sea were
      seen;
    the foundations of the world were
      laid bare,
    at the rebuke of the Lord,
    at the blast of the breath of his
      nostrils.

17 "He sent from on high, he took me;
    he drew me out of many waters.

18 He rescued me from my strong
      enemy,
    from those who hated me,
    for they were too mighty for me.
19 They confronted me in the day of my
      calamity,
    but the Lord was my support.
20 He brought me out into a broad place;
    he rescued me, because he
      delighted in me.

21 "The Lord dealt with me according to
    my righteousness;
    according to the cleanness of my
      hands he rewarded me.
22 For I have kept the ways of the Lord
    and have not wickedly departed
      from my God.
23 For all his rules were before me,
    and from his statutes I did not turn
      aside.
24 I was blameless before him,
    and I kept myself from guilt.
25 And the Lord has rewarded me
    according to my righteousness,
    according to my cleanness in his
      sight.

26 "With the merciful you show yourself
      merciful;
    with the blameless man you show
      yourself blameless;
27 with the purified you deal purely,
    and with the crooked you make
      yourself seem tortuous.
28 You save a humble people,
    but your eyes are on the haughty
      to bring them down.
29 For you are my lamp, O Lord,
    and my God lightens my darkness.
30 For by you I can run against a troop,
    and by my God I can leap over a
      wall.
31 This God—his way is perfect;
    the word of the Lord proves true;
    he is a shield for all those who take
      refuge in him.

32 "For who is God, but the Lord?
    And who is a rock, except our God?
33 This God is my strong refuge
    and has made my[3] way blameless.[4]
34 He made my feet like the feet of a deer
    and set me secure on the heights.

[1] Or terrified me [2] Or in his wrath [3] Or his; also verse 34 [4] Compare Psalm 18:32; Hebrew he has blamelessly set my way free, or he has made my way spring up blamelessly

He trains my hands for war,
  so that my arms can bend a bow of bronze.
You have given me the shield of your salvation,
  and your gentleness made me great.
You gave a wide place for my steps under me,
  and my feet[1] did not slip;
I pursued my enemies and destroyed them,
  and did not turn back until they were consumed.
I consumed them; I thrust them through, so that they did not rise;
  they fell under my feet.
For you equipped me with strength for the battle;
  you made those who rise against me sink under me.
You made my enemies turn their backs to me,[2]
  those who hated me, and I destroyed them.
They looked, but there was none to save;
  they cried to the LORD, but he did not answer them.
I beat them fine as the dust of the earth;
  I crushed them and stamped them down like the mire of the streets.

"You delivered me from strife with my people;[3]
  you kept me as the head of the nations;
people whom I had not known served me.
Foreigners came cringing to me;
  as soon as they heard of me, they obeyed me.
Foreigners lost heart
  and came trembling[4] out of their fortresses.

"The LORD lives, and blessed be my rock,
  and exalted be my God, the rock of my salvation,
the God who gave me vengeance
  and brought down peoples under me,

who brought me out from my enemies;
  you exalted me above those who rose against me;
  you delivered me from men of violence.

50 "For this I will praise you, O LORD, among the nations,
  and sing praises to your name.
51 Great salvation he brings[5] to his king,
  and shows steadfast love to his anointed,
  to David and his offspring forever."

The Last Words of David

23 Now these are the last words of David:

The oracle of David, the son of Jesse,
  the oracle of the man who was raised on high,
the anointed of the God of Jacob,
  the sweet psalmist of Israel:[6]

2 "The Spirit of the LORD speaks by me;
  his word is on my tongue.
3 The God of Israel has spoken;
  the Rock of Israel has said to me:
When one rules justly over men,
  ruling in the fear of God,
4 he dawns on them like the morning light,
  like the sun shining forth on a cloudless morning,
like rain[7] that makes grass to sprout from the earth.

5 "For does not my house stand so with God?
For he has made with me an everlasting covenant,
  ordered in all things and secure.
For will he not cause to prosper
  all my help and my desire?
6 But worthless men[8] are all like thorns that are thrown away,
  for they cannot be taken with the hand;
7 but the man who touches them
  arms himself with iron and the shaft of a spear,
and they are utterly consumed with fire."[9]

David's Mighty Men

[8] These are the names of the mighty men whom David had: Josheb-basshebeth a Tahchemonite; he was chief of the three.[1] He wielded his spear[2] against eight hundred whom he killed at one time.

[9] And next to him among the three mighty men was Eleazar the son of Dodo, son of Ahohi. He was with David when they defied the Philistines who were gathered there for battle, and the men of Israel withdrew. [10] He rose and struck down the Philistines until his hand was weary, and his hand clung to the sword. And the LORD brought about a great victory that day, and the men returned after him only to strip the slain.

[11] And next to him was Shammah, the son of Agee the Hararite. The Philistines gathered together at Lehi, where there was a plot of ground full of lentils, and the men fled from the Philistines. [12] But he took his stand in the midst of the plot and defended it and struck down the Philistines, and the LORD worked a great victory.

[13] And three of the thirty chief men went down and came about harvest time to David at the cave of Adullam, when a band of Philistines was encamped in the Valley of Rephaim. [14] David was then in the stronghold, and the garrison of the Philistines was then at Bethlehem. [15] And David said longingly, "Oh, that someone would give me water to drink from the well of Bethlehem that is by the gate!" [16] Then the three mighty men broke through the camp of the Philistines and drew water out of the well of Bethlehem that was by the gate and carried and brought it to David. But he would not drink of it. He poured it out to the LORD [17] and said, "Far be it from me, O LORD, that I should do this. Shall I drink the blood of the men who went at the risk of their lives?" Therefore he would not drink it. These things the three mighty men did.

[18] Now Abishai, the brother of Joab, the son of Zeruiah, was chief of the thirty.[3] And he wielded his spear against three hundred men[4] and killed them and won a name beside the three. [19] He was the most renowned of the thirty[5] and became their commander, but he did not attain to the three.

[20] And Benaiah the son of Jehoiada was a valiant man[6] of Kabzeel, a doer of great deeds. He struck down two ariels[7] of Moab. He also went down and struck down a lion in a pit on a day when snow had fallen. [21] And he struck down an Egyptian, a handsome man. The Egyptian had a spear in his hand, but Benaiah went down to him with a staff and snatched the spear out of the Egyptian's hand and killed him with his own spear. [22] These things did Benaiah the son of Jehoiada, and won a name beside the three mighty men. [23] He was renowned among the thirty, but he did not attain to the three. And David set him over his bodyguard.

[24] Asahel the brother of Joab was one of the thirty; Elhanan the son of Dodo of Bethlehem, [25] Shammah of Harod, Elika of Harod, [26] Helez the Paltite, Ira the son of Ikkesh of Tekoa, [27] Abiezer of Anathoth, Mebunnai the Hushathite, [28] Zalmon the Ahohite, Maharai of Netophah, [29] Heleb the son of Baanah of Netophah, Ittai the son of Ribai of Gibeah of the people of Benjamin, [30] Benaiah of Pirathon, Hiddai of the brooks of Gaash, [31] Abi-albon the Arbathite, Azmaveth of Bahurim, [32] Eliahba the Shaalbonite, the sons of Jashen, Jonathan, [33] Shammah the Hararite, Ahiam the son of Sharar the Hararite, [34] Eliphelet the son of Ahasbai of Maacah, Eliam the son of Ahithophel of Gilo, [35] Hezro[8] of Carmel, Paarai the Arbite, [36] Igal the son of Nathan of Zobah, Bani the Gadite, [37] Zelek the Ammonite, Naharai of Beeroth, the armor-bearer of Joab the son of Zeruiah, [38] Ira the Ithrite, Gareb the Ithrite, [39] Uriah the Hittite: thirty-seven in all.

David's Census

24 Again the anger of the LORD was kindled against Israel, and he incited David against them, saying, "Go, number Israel and Judah." [2] So the king said to Joab, the commander of the army, who was with him, "Go through all the tribes of Israel, from Dan to Beersheba, and number the people, that I may know the number of the people." [3] But Joab said to the king, "May the LORD your God add

---

[1] Or of the captains [2] Compare 1 Chronicles 11:11; the meaning of the Hebrew expression is uncertain [3] Two Hebrew manuscripts, Syriac; most Hebrew manuscripts three [4] Or slain ones [5] Compare 1 Chronicles 11:25; Hebrew Was he the most renowned of the three? [6] Or the son of Ishhai [7] The meaning of the word ariel is unknown [8] Or Hezrai [9] Septuagint to Joab and the commanders of the army

o the people a hundred times as many as they are, while the eyes of my lord the king still see it, but why does my lord the king delight in this thing?" ⁴But the king's word prevailed against Joab and the commanders of the army. So Joab and the commanders of the army went out from the presence of the king to number the people of Israel. ⁵They crossed the Jordan and began from Aroer,¹ and from the city that is in the middle of the valley, toward Gad and on to Jazer. ⁶Then they came to Gilead, and to Kadesh in the land of the Hittites;² and they came to Dan, and from Dan³ they went around to Sidon, ⁷and came to the fortress of Tyre and to all the cities of the Hivites and Canaanites; and they went out to the Negeb of Judah at Beersheba. ⁸So when they had gone through all the land, they came to Jerusalem at the end of nine months and twenty days. ⁹And Joab gave the sum of the numbering of the people to the king: in Israel there were 800,000 valiant men who drew the sword, and the men of Judah were 500,000.

The LORD's Judgment of David's Sin

¹⁰But David's heart struck him after he had numbered the people. And David said to the LORD, "I have sinned greatly in what I have done. But now, O LORD, please take away the iniquity of your servant, for I have done very foolishly." ¹¹And when David arose in the morning, the word of the LORD came to the prophet Gad, David's seer, saying, ¹²"Go and say to David, 'Thus says the LORD, Three things I offer⁴ you. Choose one of them, that I may do it to you.'" ¹³So Gad came to David and told him, and said to him, "Shall three⁵ years of famine come to you in your land? Or will you flee three months before your foes while they pursue you? Or shall there be three days' pestilence in your land? Now consider, and decide what answer I shall return to him who sent me." ¹⁴Then David said to Gad, "I am in great distress. Let us fall into the hand of the LORD, for his mercy is great; but let me not fall into the hand of man."

¹⁵So the LORD sent a pestilence on Israel from the morning until the appointed time.

¹Septuagint; Hebrew *encamped in Aroer* ²Septuagint; Hebrew *to the land of Tahtim-hodshi* ³Septuagint; Hebrew *they came to Dan-jaan* ⁴Or *hold over* ⁵Compare 1 Chronicles 21:12, Septuagint; Hebrew *seven*

verses to read
2 Samuel 24:18–25

Know God

King David said, "I will not offer burnt offerings to the LORD my God that cost me nothing" (2 Sam. 24:24). Why? Because in order for something to be a sacrifice, it has to cost you something. It's no sacrifice if it doesn't hurt you somehow. Giving up something that's easy to give up isn't what makes you holy, but giving up the very thing you don't want to—that is what makes you holy. Look at the things you won't let go of in your life, and then think about whether they should be sacrificed to the Lord.

For the God Girl, the act of sacrifice is an act of cleansing. It cleanses your heart and brings it back in line with God's will. When you don't allow your natural desires to rule your choices, you are free to obey God's Word and to worship him. But when you reserve those things you love for yourself and never give them up to God, then you've gotten off track.

As a God Girl, you've got to learn to identify what God is asking you to sacrifice. You will find the power to do this only as you remember that you are not the only one making a sacrifice—God himself sent his Son to make the greatest sacrifice of all. As you enjoy God's favor, won for you through Jesus' sacrificial death, you will begin to be able to let go of the things in life that you are holding on to more tightly than God.

And there died of the people from Dan to Beersheba 70,000 men. [16] And when the angel stretched out his hand toward Jerusalem to destroy it, the LORD relented from the calamity and said to the angel who was working destruction among the people, "It is enough; now stay your hand." And the angel of the LORD was by the threshing floor of Araunah the Jebusite. [17] Then David spoke to the LORD when he saw the angel who was striking the people, and said, "Behold, I have sinned, and I have done wickedly. But these sheep, what have they done? Please let your hand be against me and against my father's house."

David Builds an Altar

[18] And Gad came that day to David and said to him, "Go up, raise an altar to the LORD on the threshing floor of Araunah the Jebusite." [19] So David went up at Gad's word, as the LORD commanded. [20] And when Araunah looked down, he saw the king and his servants coming on toward him. And Araunah went out and paid homage to the king with his face to the ground. [21] And Araunah said, "Why has my lord the king come to his servant?" David said, "To buy the threshing floor from you, in order to build an altar to the LORD, that the plague may be averted from the people." [22] Then Araunah said to David, "Let my lord the king take and offer up what seems good to him. Here are the oxen for the burnt offering and the threshing sledges and the yokes of the oxen for the wood. [23] All this, O king, Araunah gives to the king." And Araunah said to the king, "May the LORD your God accept you." [24] But the king said to Araunah, "No, but I will buy it from you for a price. I will not offer burnt offerings to the LORD my God that cost me nothing." So David bought the threshing floor and the oxen for fifty shekels[1] of silver. [25] And David built there an altar to the LORD and offered burnt offerings and peace offerings. So the LORD responded to the plea for the land, and the plague was averted from Israel.

---

[1] A *shekel* was about 2/5 ounce or 11 grams

1 Kings

Judge between Right and Wrong

> "Keep the charge of the LORD your God, walking in his
> ways and keeping his statutes, his commandments, his
> rules, and his testimonies, as it is written in the Law
> of Moses, that you may prosper in all that you do and
> wherever you turn."
>
> *1 Kings 2:3*

Author: Unknown
Time: 561–538 B.C.
Place: Possibly Babylon
Written to: God's people, the
Israelites

The gist

The book of 1 Kings picks up
where 2 Samuel ends, with the
death of David. It follows the
split of the kingdom into Judah
and Israel. It centers on all the
kings, both good and bad, who
ruled during this time.

Things to look for

- The reign of King Solomon
  (see 1 Kings 2–11)

- The divided kingdom (see
  1 Kings 12–22)

The books of the Kings were written to show people why
God sent Judah into exile. Though the Israelites were God's
chosen people, their kings weren't all godly men. Some of
them fell away from God and gave up on serving him, while
others were more devoted. We wonder how God had such
patience with such a wild group of men, but what you learn
as you read this book is that ultimately no man decides
what God is going to do. No matter how bad they are or how
hard they try, God's will always wins. This can be hard to
swallow when you see bad people succeed and even harder
when you see them getting mercy and compassion. But as
you read these books you'll see how much God demands of
his people, and also how much mercy he shows so that his
promises will always stand.

As a God Girl, you must understand that man's sinfulness
never controls God's actions. When people in power pervert
that power and use it for their own good, God isn't looking
the other way; he is allowing their evil for some other good
that you can be sure is part of his plan. You might ask why
God has used so many sinful men and women to fulfill his
plans, but you might just as easily ask where he could find
perfect and sinless people to use instead! Of course no one
is completely righteous (see Rom. 3:10–12), so God has to
use broken and sinful people if he's going to use people at all.

As you read the book of 1 Kings, watch how the lives of
these great men and women seemed to order history, but also
understand that it wasn't them but *God* who determined the
ultimate direction for his people. Notice how their disobedience would affect their nations and how God's power to
show mercy to whomever he wants to show mercy has been
going on forever. But also notice how the men and women
who obeyed God found their own success. There is only one
God, and he's the one who ultimately decides the way things
are going to go.

Must-Know Facts and Verses

✛ The books of 1 and 2 Kings cover almost four hundred years of history.

"Keep the charge of the LORD your God, walking in his ways and keeping his statutes, his commandments, his rules, and his testimonies, as it is written in the Law of Moses, that you may prosper in all that you do and wherever you turn." *1 Kings 2:3*

And God said to him, "Because you have asked this, and have not asked for yourself long life or riches or the life of your enemies, but have asked for yourself understanding to discern what is right, behold, I now do according to your word. Behold, I give you a wise and discerning mind, so that none like you has been before you and none like you shall arise after you. I give you also what you have not asked, both riches and honor, so that no other king shall compare with you, all your days. And if you will walk in my ways, keeping my statutes and my commandments, as your father David walked, then I will lengthen your days." *1 Kings 3:11–14*

Now when the queen of Sheba heard of the fame of Solomon concerning the name of the LORD, she came to test him with hard questions. *1 Kings 10:1*

Then the fire of the LORD fell and consumed the burnt offering and the wood and the stones and the dust, and licked up the water that was in the trench. And when all the people saw it, they fell on their faces and said, "The LORD, he is God; the LORD, he is God." *1 Kings 18:38–39*

1 Kings

David in His Old Age

1 Now King David was old and advanced in years. And although they covered him with clothes, he could not get warm. ²Therefore his servants said to him, "Let a young woman be sought for my lord the king, and let her wait on the king and be in his service. Let her lie in your arms,[1] that my lord the king may be warm." ³So they sought for a beautiful young woman throughout all the territory of Israel, and found Abishag the Shunammite, and brought her to the king. ⁴The young woman was very beautiful, and she was of service to the king and attended to him, but the king knew her not.

Adonijah Sets Himself Up as King

⁵Now Adonijah the son of Haggith exalted himself, saying, "I will be king." And he prepared for himself chariots and horsemen, and fifty men to run before him. ⁶His father had never at any time displeased him by asking, "Why have you done thus and so?" He was also a very handsome man, and he was born next after Absalom. ⁷He conferred with Joab the son of Zeruiah and with Abiathar the priest. And they followed Adonijah and helped him. ⁸But Zadok the priest and Benaiah the son of Jehoiada and Nathan the prophet and Shimei and Rei and David's mighty men were not with Adonijah.

⁹Adonijah sacrificed sheep, oxen, and fattened cattle by the Serpent's Stone, which is beside En-rogel, and he invited all his brothers, the king's sons, and all the royal officials of Judah, ¹⁰but he did not invite Nathan the prophet or Benaiah or the mighty men or Solomon his brother.

Nathan and Bathsheba Before David

¹¹Then Nathan said to Bathsheba the mother of Solomon, "Have you not heard that Adonijah the son of Haggith has become king and David our lord does not know it? ¹²Now therefore come, let me give you advice, that you may save your own life and the life of your son Solomon. ¹³Go in at once to King David, and say to him, 'Did you not, my lord the king, swear to your servant, saying, "Solomon your son shall reign after me, and he shall sit on my throne"? Why then is Adonijah king?' ¹⁴Then while you are still speaking with the king, I also will come in after you and confirm[2] your words."

¹⁵So Bathsheba went to the king in his chamber (now the king was very old, and Abishag the Shunammite was attending to the king). ¹⁶Bathsheba bowed and paid homage to the king, and the king said, "What do you desire?" ¹⁷She said to him, "My lord, you swore to your servant by the LORD your God, saying, 'Solomon your son shall reign after me, and he shall sit on my throne.' ¹⁸And now, behold, Adonijah is king, although you, my lord the king, do not know it. ¹⁹He has sacrificed oxen, fattened cattle, and sheep in abundance, and has invited all the sons of the king, Abiathar the priest, and Joab the commander of the army, but Solomon your servant he has not invited. ²⁰And now, my lord the king, the eyes of all Israel are on you, to tell them who shall sit on the throne of my lord the king after him. ²¹Otherwise it will come to pass, when my lord the king sleeps with his fathers, that I and my son Solomon will be counted offenders."

²²While she was still speaking with the king, Nathan the prophet came in. ²³And they told the king, "Here is Nathan the prophet." And when he came in before the king, he bowed before the king, with his face to the ground. ²⁴And Nathan said, "My lord the king, have you said, 'Adonijah shall reign after me, and he shall sit on my throne'? ²⁵For he has gone down this day

¹Or in your bosom ²Or expand on

and has sacrificed oxen, fattened cattle, and sheep in abundance, and has invited all the king's sons, the commanders[1] of the army, and Abiathar the priest. And behold, they are eating and drinking before him, and saying, 'Long live King Adonijah!' ²⁶But me, your servant, and Zadok the priest, and Benaiah the son of Jehoiada, and your servant Solomon he has not invited. ²⁷Has this thing been brought about by my lord the king and you have not told your servants who should sit on the throne of my lord the king after him?"

Solomon Anointed King

²⁸Then King David answered, "Call Bathsheba to me." So she came into the king's presence and stood before the king. ²⁹And the king swore, saying, "As the LORD lives, who has redeemed my soul out of every adversity, ³⁰as I swore to you by the LORD, the God of Israel, saying, 'Solomon your son shall reign after me, and he shall sit on my throne in my place,' even so will I do this day." ³¹Then Bathsheba bowed with her face to the ground and paid homage to the king and said, "May my lord King David live forever!"

³²King David said, "Call to me Zadok the priest, Nathan the prophet, and Benaiah the son of Jehoiada." So they came before the king. ³³And the king said to them, "Take with you the servants of your lord and have Solomon my son ride on my own mule, and bring him down to Gihon. ³⁴And let Zadok the priest and Nathan the prophet there anoint him king over Israel. Then blow the trumpet and say, 'Long live King Solomon!' ³⁵You shall then come up after him, and he shall come and sit on my throne, for he shall be king in my place. And I have appointed him to be ruler over Israel and over Judah." ³⁶And Benaiah the son of Jehoiada answered the king, "Amen! May the LORD, the God of my lord the king, say so. ³⁷As the LORD has been with my lord the king, even so may he be with Solomon, and make his throne greater than the throne of my lord King David."

³⁸So Zadok the priest, Nathan the prophet, and Benaiah the son of Jehoiada, and the Cherethites and the Pelethites went down and had Solomon ride on King David's mule and brought him to Gihon. ³⁹There Zadok the priest took the horn of oil from the tent and anointed Solomon. The they blew the trumpet, and all the peopl said, "Long live King Solomon!" ⁴⁰And a the people went up after him, playing o pipes, and rejoicing with great joy, so tha the earth was split by their noise.

⁴¹Adonijah and all the guests who wer with him heard it as they finished feast ing. And when Joab heard the sound of th trumpet, he said, "What does this uproar i the city mean?" ⁴²While he was still speak ing, behold, Jonathan the son of Abiatha the priest came. And Adonijah sai "Come in, for you are a worthy man an bring good news." ⁴³Jonathan answere Adonijah, "No, for our lord King David ha made Solomon king, ⁴⁴and the king ha sent with him Zadok the priest, Nathan th prophet, and Benaiah the son of Jehoiad and the Cherethites and the Pelethite And they had him ride on the king's mul ⁴⁵And Zadok the priest and Nathan th prophet have anointed him king at Gihor and they have gone up from there rejoic ing, so that the city is in an uproar. This the noise that you have heard. ⁴⁶Solomo sits on the royal throne. ⁴⁷Moreover, th king's servants came to congratulate ou lord King David, saying, 'May your Go make the name of Solomon more famou than yours, and make his throne greate than your throne.' And the king bowed him self on the bed. ⁴⁸And the king also sai 'Blessed be the LORD, the God of Israel, wh has granted someone[2] to sit on my thron this day, my own eyes seeing it.'"

⁴⁹Then all the guests of Adonijah trem bled and rose, and each went his own wa ⁵⁰And Adonijah feared Solomon. So h arose and went and took hold of the horn of the altar. ⁵¹Then it was told Solomor "Behold, Adonijah fears King Solomor for behold, he has laid hold of the horn of the altar, saying, 'Let King Solomo swear to me first that he will not put hi servant to death with the sword.'" ⁵²An Solomon said, "If he will show himself worthy man, not one of his hairs shall fa to the earth, but if wickedness is found i him, he shall die." ⁵³So King Solomon sen and they brought him down from the alta And he came and paid homage to Kin Solomon, and Solomon said to him, "Go t your house."

¹Hebrew; Septuagint *Joab the commander* ²Septuagint *one of my offspring*

David's Instructions to Solomon

2 When David's time to die drew near, he commanded Solomon his son, saying, [2]"I am about to go the way of all the earth. Be strong, and show yourself a man, [3]and keep the charge of the LORD your God, walking in his ways and keeping his statutes, his commandments, his rules, and his testimonies, as it is written in the Law of Moses, that you may prosper in all that you do and wherever you turn, [4]that the LORD may establish his word that he spoke concerning me, saying, 'If your sons pay close attention to their way, to walk before me in faithfulness with all their heart and with all their soul, you shall not lack[1] a man on the throne of Israel.'

[5]"Moreover, you also know what Joab the son of Zeruiah did to me, how he dealt with the two commanders of the armies of Israel, Abner the son of Ner, and Amasa the son of Jether, whom he killed, avenging[2] in time of peace for blood that had been shed in war, and putting the blood of war[3] on the belt around his[4] waist and on the sandals on his feet. [6]Act therefore according to your wisdom, but do not let his gray head go down to Sheol in peace. [7]But deal loyally with the sons of Barzillai the Gileadite, and let them be among those who eat at your table, for with such loyalty[5] they met me when I fled from Absalom your brother. [8]And there is also with you Shimei the son of Gera, the Benjaminite from Bahurim, who cursed me with a grievous curse on the day when I went to Mahanaim. But when he came down to meet me at the Jordan, I swore to him by the LORD, saying, 'I will not put you to death with the sword.' [9]Now therefore do not hold him guiltless, for you are a wise man. You will know what you ought to do to him, and you shall bring his gray head down with blood to Sheol."

The Death of David

[10]Then David slept with his fathers and was buried in the city of David. [11]And the time that David reigned over Israel was forty years. He reigned seven years in Hebron and thirty-three years in Jerusalem. [12]So Solomon sat on the throne of David his father, and his kingdom was firmly established.

A Prayer for... CONSECRATION

God, you're good when you give and when you take away, when the sun shines on me and when night falls on me. You loved me before the foundation of the world, and in love you restored my soul. You love me still, in spite of my hard heart, ingratitude, and distrust. Your goodness has been with me during another year, leading me though a twisting wilderness—in retreat, helping me to advance; when beaten back, giving me progress. Your goodness will be with me next year too. I hoist the sail and pull up anchor with you as the pilot of my future, as you have been of my past. I thank you that you have covered my eyes to the waters ahead. If you have appointed storms of testing, you will be with me in them. If I have to pass through tempests of persecution and temptation, I won't drown. If I die, I will see your face all the sooner. If a painful end is in store for me, give me enough grace so that my faith won't falter. If I am turned away from doing what I love, I won't complain. Please be glorified in me whether I am in comfort or in trial. As a chosen vessel, use me as I was made to be used.

Amen.

Solomon's Reign Established

[13]Then Adonijah the son of Haggith came to Bathsheba the mother of Solomon. And she said, "Do you come peacefully?" He said, "Peacefully." [14]Then he said, "I have something to say to you." She said, "Speak." [15]He said, "You know that the kingdom was mine, and that all Israel fully expected me to reign. However, the kingdom has turned about and become my brother's, for it was his from the LORD. [16]And now I have one request to make of you; do not refuse me." She said to him, "Speak." [17]And

---

[1] Hebrew *there shall not be cut off for you* [2] Septuagint; Hebrew *placing* [3] Septuagint *innocent blood* [4] Septuagint *my*; twice in this verse [5] Or *steadfast love*

he said, "Please ask King Solomon—he will not refuse you—to give me Abishag the Shunammite as my wife." [18]Bathsheba said, "Very well; I will speak for you to the king."

[19]So Bathsheba went to King Solomon to speak to him on behalf of Adonijah. And the king rose to meet her and bowed down to her. Then he sat on his throne and had a seat brought for the king's mother, and she sat on his right. [20]Then she said, "I have one small request to make of you; do not refuse me." And the king said to her, "Make your request, my mother, for I will not refuse you." [21]She said, "Let Abishag the Shunammite be given to Adonijah your brother as his wife." [22]King Solomon answered his mother, "And why do you ask Abishag the Shunammite for Adonijah? Ask for him the kingdom also, for he is my older brother, and on his side are Abiathar[1] the priest and Joab the son of Zeruiah." [23]Then King Solomon swore by the LORD, saying, "God do so to me and more also if this word does not cost Adonijah his life! [24]Now therefore as the LORD lives, who has established me and placed me on the throne of David my father, and who has made me a house, as he promised, Adonijah shall be put to death today." [25]So King Solomon sent Benaiah the son of Jehoiada, and he struck him down, and he died.

[26]And to Abiathar the priest the king said, "Go to Anathoth, to your estate, for you deserve death. But I will not at this time put you to death, because you carried the ark of the Lord GOD before David my father, and because you shared in all my father's affliction." [27]So Solomon expelled Abiathar from being priest to the LORD, thus fulfilling the word of the LORD that he had spoken concerning the house of Eli in Shiloh.

[28]When the news came to Joab—for Joab had supported Adonijah although he had not supported Absalom—Joab fled to the tent of the LORD and caught hold of the horns of the altar. [29]And when it was told King Solomon, "Joab has fled to the tent of the LORD, and behold, he is beside the altar," Solomon sent Benaiah the son of Jehoiada, saying, "Go, strike him down." [30]So Benaiah came to the tent of the LORD and said to him, "The king commands, 'Come out.'" But he said, "No, I will die here." Then Benaiah brought the king word

again, saying, "Thus said Joab, and thus he answered me." [31]The king replied to him, "Do as he has said, strike him down and bury him, and thus take away from me and from my father's house the guilt for the blood that Joab shed without cause. [32]The LORD will bring back his bloody deeds on his own head, because, without the knowledge of my father David, he attacked and killed with the sword two men more righteous and better than himself, Abner the son of Ner, commander of the army of Israel, and Amasa the son of Jether, commander of the army of Judah. [33]So shall their blood come back on the head of Joab and on the head of his descendants forever. But for David and for his descendants and for his house and for his throne there shall be peace from the LORD forevermore. [34]Then Benaiah the son of Jehoiada went up and struck him down and put him to death. And he was buried in his own house in the wilderness. [35]The king put Benaiah the son of Jehoiada over the army in place of Joab, and the king put Zadok the priest in the place of Abiathar.

[36]Then the king sent and summoned Shimei and said to him, "Build yourself a house in Jerusalem and dwell there, and do not go out from there to any place whatever. [37]For on the day you go out and cross the brook Kidron, know for certain that you shall die. Your blood shall be on your own head." [38]And Shimei said to the king, "What you say is good; as my lord the king has said, so will your servant do." So Shimei lived in Jerusalem many days.

[39]But it happened at the end of three years that two of Shimei's servants ran away to Achish, son of Maacah, king of Gath. And when it was told Shimei, "Behold, your servants are in Gath," [40]Shimei arose and saddled a donkey and went to Gath to Achish to seek his servants. Shimei went and brought his servants from Gath. [41]And when Solomon was told that Shimei had gone from Jerusalem to Gath and returned, [42]the king sent and summoned Shimei and said to him, "Did I not make you swear by the LORD and solemnly warn you, saying, 'Know for certain that on the day you go out and go to any place whatever, you shall die'? And you said to me, 'What you say is good; I will obey.' [43]Why then have you not kept your oath to the LORD and the

---

[1] Septuagint, Syriac, Vulgate; Hebrew *and for him and for Abiathar*

commandment with which I commanded you?" ⁴⁴The king also said to Shimei, "You know in your own heart all the harm that you did to David my father. So the LORD will bring back your harm on your own head. ⁴⁵But King Solomon shall be blessed, and the throne of David shall be established before the LORD forever." ⁴⁶Then the king commanded Benaiah the son of Jehoiada, and he went out and struck him down, and he died.

So the kingdom was established in the hand of Solomon.

Solomon's Prayer for Wisdom

3 Solomon made a marriage alliance with Pharaoh king of Egypt. He took Pharaoh's daughter and brought her into the city of David until he had finished building his own house and the house of the LORD and the wall around Jerusalem. ²The people were sacrificing at the high places, however, because no house had yet been built for the name of the LORD.

³Solomon loved the LORD, walking in the statutes of David his father, only he sacrificed and made offerings at the high places. ⁴And the king went to Gibeon to sacrifice there, for that was the great high place. Solomon used to offer a thousand burnt offerings on that altar. ⁵At Gibeon the LORD appeared to Solomon in a dream by night, and God said, "Ask what I shall give you." ⁶And Solomon said, "You have shown great and steadfast love to your servant David my father, because he walked before you in faithfulness, in righteousness, and in uprightness of heart toward you. And you have kept for him this great and steadfast love and have given him a son to sit on his throne this day. ⁷And now, O LORD my God, you have made your servant king in place of David my father, although I am but a little child. I do not know how to go out or come in. ⁸And your servant is in the midst of your people whom you have chosen, a great people, too many to be numbered or counted for multitude. ⁹Give your servant therefore an understanding mind to govern your people, that I may discern between good and evil, for who is able to govern this your great people?"

¹⁰It pleased the Lord that Solomon had asked this. ¹¹And God said to him, "Because you have asked this, and have not asked for yourself long life or riches or the life of your enemies, but have asked for yourself understanding to discern what is right, ¹²behold, I now do according to your word. Behold, I give you a wise and discerning mind, so that none like you has been before you and none like you shall arise after you. ¹³I give you also what you have not asked, both riches and honor, so that no other king shall compare with you, all your days. ¹⁴And if you will walk in my ways, keeping my statutes and my commandments, as your father David walked, then I will lengthen your days."

¹⁵And Solomon awoke, and behold, it was a dream. Then he came to Jerusalem and stood before the ark of the covenant of the Lord, and offered up burnt offerings and peace offerings, and made a feast for all his servants.

Solomon's Wisdom

¹⁶Then two prostitutes came to the king and stood before him. ¹⁷The one woman said, "Oh, my lord, this woman and I live in the same house, and I gave birth to a child while she was in the house. ¹⁸Then on the third day after I gave birth, this woman also gave birth. And we were alone. There was no one else with us in the house; only we two were in the house. ¹⁹And this woman's son died in the night, because she lay on him. ²⁰And she arose at midnight and took my son from beside me, while your servant slept, and laid him at her breast, and laid her dead son at my breast. ²¹When I rose in the morning to nurse my child, behold, he was dead. But when I looked at him closely in the morning, behold, he was not the child that I had borne." ²²But the other woman said, "No, the living child is mine, and the dead child is yours." The first said, "No, the dead child is yours, and the living child is mine." Thus they spoke before the king.

²³Then the king said, "The one says, 'This is my son that is alive, and your son is dead'; and the other says, 'No; but your son is dead, and my son is the living one.'" ²⁴And the king said, "Bring me a sword." So a sword was brought before the king. ²⁵And the king said, "Divide the living child in two, and give half to the one and half to the other." ²⁶Then the woman whose son was alive said to the king, because her heart yearned for her son, "Oh, my lord, give her the living child, and by no means

put him to death." But the other said, "He shall be neither mine nor yours; divide him." ²⁷Then the king answered and said, "Give the living child to the first woman, and by no means put him to death; she is his mother." ²⁸And all Israel heard of the judgment that the king had rendered, and they stood in awe of the king, because they perceived that the wisdom of God was in him to do justice.

Solomon's Officials

4 King Solomon was king over all Israel, ²and these were his high officials: Azariah the son of Zadok was the priest; ³Elihoreph and Ahijah the sons of Shisha were secretaries; Jehoshaphat the son of Ahilud was recorder; ⁴Benaiah the son of Jehoiada was in command of the army; Zadok and Abiathar were priests; ⁵Azariah the son of Nathan was over the officers; Zabud the son of Nathan was priest and king's friend; ⁶Ahishar was in charge of the palace; and Adoniram the son of Abda was in charge of the forced labor.

⁷Solomon had twelve officers over all Israel, who provided food for the king and his household. Each man had to make provision for one month in the year. ⁸These were their names: Ben-hur, in the hill country of Ephraim; ⁹Ben-deker, in Makaz, Shaalbim, Beth-shemesh, and Elonbeth-hanan; ¹⁰Ben-hesed, in Arubboth (to him belonged Socoh and all the land of Hepher); ¹¹Ben-abinadab, in all Naphath-dor (he had Taphath the daughter of Solomon as his wife); ¹²Baana the son of Ahilud, in Taanach, Megiddo, and all Beth-shean that is beside Zarethan below Jezreel, and from Beth-shean to Abel-meholah, as far as the other side of Jokmeam; ¹³Ben-geber, in Ramoth-gilead (he had the villages of Jair the son of Manasseh, which are in Gilead, and he had the region of Argob, which is in Bashan, sixty great cities with walls and bronze bars); ¹⁴Ahinadab the son of Iddo, in Mahanaim; ¹⁵Ahimaaz, in Naphtali (he had taken Basemath the daughter of Solomon as his wife); ¹⁶Baana the son of Hushai, in Asher and Bealoth; ¹⁷Jehoshaphat the son of Paruah, in Issachar; ¹⁸Shimei the son of Ela, in Benjamin; ¹⁹Geber the son of Uri, in the land of Gilead, the country of Sihon king of the Amorites and of Og king of Bashan. And there was one governor who was over the land.

Solomon's Wealth and Wisdom

²⁰Judah and Israel were as many as the sand by the sea. They ate and drank and were happy. ²¹ ¹ Solomon ruled over all the kingdoms from the Euphrates² to the land of the Philistines and to the border of Egypt. They brought tribute and served Solomon all the days of his life.

²²Solomon's provision for one day was thirty cors³ of fine flour and sixty cors of meal, ²³ten fat oxen, and twenty pasture-fed cattle, a hundred sheep, besides deer, gazelles, roebucks, and fattened fowl. ²⁴For he had dominion over all the region west of the Euphrates⁴ from Tiphsah to Gaza, over all the kings west of the Euphrates. And he had peace on all sides around him. ²⁵And Judah and Israel lived in safety, from Dan even to Beersheba, every man under his vine and under his fig tree, all the days of Solomon. ²⁶Solomon also had 40,000⁵ stalls of horses for his chariots, and 12,000 horsemen. ²⁷And those officers supplied provisions for King Solomon, and for all who came to King Solomon's table, each one in his month. They let nothing be lacking. ²⁸Barley also and straw for the horses and swift steeds they brought to the place where it was required, each according to his duty.

²⁹And God gave Solomon wisdom and understanding beyond measure, and breadth of mind like the sand on the seashore, ³⁰so that Solomon's wisdom surpassed the wisdom of all the people of the east and all the wisdom of Egypt. ³¹For he was wiser than all other men, wiser than Ethan the Ezrahite, and Heman, Calcol, and Darda, the sons of Mahol, and his fame was in all the surrounding nations. ³²He also spoke 3,000 proverbs, and his songs were 1,005. ³³He spoke of trees, from the cedar that is in Lebanon to the hyssop that grows out of the wall. He spoke also of beasts, and of birds, and of reptiles, and of fish. ³⁴And people of all nations came to hear the wisdom of Solomon, and from all the kings of the earth, who had heard of his wisdom.

¹Ch 5:1 in Hebrew ²Hebrew *the River* ³A *cor* was about 6 bushels or 220 liters ⁴Hebrew *the River*; twice in this verse ⁵Hebrew; one Hebrew manuscript (see 2 Chron. 9:25 and Septuagint of 1 Kings 10:26) *4,000*

Ask Yourself . . .

ABOUT WISDOM

One definition of wisdom is good sense or judgment. How is yours? Ask yourself:

- Do I generally make wise decisions?
- What are some of the wise decisions I have made?
- What was I thinking when I made them?
- What are some of the not-so-wise decisions I've made?
- What was I thinking when I made them?
- If wisdom comes from God, then what are some ways I could get more wisdom?

Preparations for Building the Temple

5 ¹ Now Hiram king of Tyre sent his servants to Solomon when he heard that they had anointed him king in place of his father, for Hiram always loved David. ² And Solomon sent word to Hiram, ³ "You know that David my father could not build a house for the name of the LORD his God because of the warfare with which his enemies surrounded him, until the LORD put them under the soles of his feet. ⁴ But now the LORD my God has given me rest on every side. There is neither adversary nor misfortune. ⁵ And so I intend to build a house for the name of the LORD my God, as the LORD said to David my father, 'Your son, whom I will set on your throne in your place, shall build the house for my name.' ⁶ Now therefore command that cedars of Lebanon be cut for me. And my servants will join your servants, and I will pay you for your servants such wages as you set, for you know that there is no one among us who knows how to cut timber like the Sidonians."

⁷ As soon as Hiram heard the words of Solomon, he rejoiced greatly and said, "Blessed be the LORD this day, who has given to David a wise son to be over this great people." ⁸ And Hiram sent to Solomon, saying, "I have heard the message that you have sent to me. I am ready to do all you desire in the matter of cedar and cypress timber. ⁹ My servants shall bring it down to the sea from Lebanon, and I will make it into rafts to go by sea to the place you direct. And I will have them broken up there, and you shall receive it. And you shall meet my wishes by providing food for my household." ¹⁰ So Hiram supplied Solomon with all the timber of cedar and cypress that he desired, ¹¹ while Solomon gave Hiram 20,000 cors² of wheat as food for his household, and 20,000³ cors of beaten oil. Solomon gave this to Hiram year by year. ¹² And the LORD gave Solomon wisdom, as he promised him. And there was peace between Hiram and Solomon, and the two of them made a treaty.

¹³ King Solomon drafted forced labor out of all Israel, and the draft numbered 30,000 men. ¹⁴ And he sent them to Lebanon, 10,000 a month in shifts. They would be a month in Lebanon and two months at home. Adoniram was in charge of the draft. ¹⁵ Solomon also had 70,000 burden-bearers and 80,000 stonecutters in the hill country, ¹⁶ besides Solomon's 3,300 chief officers who were over the work, who had charge of the people who carried on the work. ¹⁷ At the king's command they quarried out great, costly stones in order to lay the foundation of the house with dressed stones. ¹⁸ So Solomon's builders and Hiram's builders and the men of Gebal did the cutting and prepared the timber and the stone to build the house.

Solomon Builds the Temple

6 In the four hundred and eightieth year after the people of Israel came out of the land of Egypt, in the fourth year of Solomon's reign over Israel, in the month of Ziv, which is the second month, he began to build the house of the LORD. ² The house that King Solomon built for the LORD was sixty cubits⁴ long, twenty cubits wide, and thirty cubits high. ³ The vestibule in front of the nave of the house was twenty

---

¹ Ch 5:15 in Hebrew ² A *cor* was about 6 bushels or 220 liters ³ Septuagint; Hebrew *twenty* ⁴ A *cubit* was about 18 inches or 45 centimeters

cubits long, equal to the width of the house, and ten cubits deep in front of the house. ⁴And he made for the house windows with recessed frames.¹ ⁵He also built a structure² against the wall of the house, running around the walls of the house, both the nave and the inner sanctuary. And he made side chambers all around. ⁶The lowest story³ was five cubits broad, the middle one was six cubits broad, and the third was seven cubits broad. For around the outside of the house he made offsets on the wall in order that the supporting beams should not be inserted into the walls of the house. ⁷When the house was built, it was with stone prepared at the quarry, so that neither hammer nor axe nor any tool of iron was heard in the house while it was being built.

⁸The entrance for the lowest⁴ story was on the south side of the house, and one went up by stairs to the middle story, and from the middle story to the third. ⁹So he built the house and finished it, and he made the ceiling of the house of beams and planks of cedar. ¹⁰He built the structure against the whole house, five cubits high, and it was joined to the house with timbers of cedar.

¹¹Now the word of the LORD came to Solomon, ¹²"Concerning this house that you are building, if you will walk in my statutes and obey my rules and keep all my commandments and walk in them, then I will establish my word with you, which I spoke to David your father. ¹³And I will dwell among the children of Israel and will not forsake my people Israel."

¹⁴So Solomon built the house and finished it. ¹⁵He lined the walls of the house on the inside with boards of cedar. From the floor of the house to the walls of the ceiling, he covered them on the inside with wood, and he covered the floor of the house with boards of cypress. ¹⁶He built twenty cubits of the rear of the house with boards of cedar from the floor to the walls, and he built this within as an inner sanctuary, as the Most Holy Place. ¹⁷The house, that is, the nave in front of the inner sanctuary, was forty cubits long. ¹⁸The cedar within the house was carved in the form of gourds and open flowers. All was cedar; no stone was seen. ¹⁹The inner sanctuary he prepared in the innermost part of the house, to set there the ark of the covenant of the LORD. ²⁰The inner sanctuary⁵ was twenty cubits long, twenty cubits wide, and twenty cubits high, and he overlaid it with pure gold. He also overlaid⁶ an altar of cedar. ²¹And Solomon overlaid the inside of the house with pure gold, and he drew chains of gold across, in front of the inner sanctuary, and overlaid it with gold. ²²And he overlaid the whole house with gold, until all the house was finished. Also the whole altar that belonged to the inner sanctuary he overlaid with gold.

²³In the inner sanctuary he made two cherubim of olivewood, each ten cubits high. ²⁴Five cubits was the length of one wing of the cherub, and five cubits the length of the other wing of the cherub; it was ten cubits from the tip of one wing to the tip of the other. ²⁵The other cherub also measured ten cubits; both cherubim had the same measure and the same form. ²⁶The height of one cherub was ten cubits, and so was that of the other cherub. ²⁷He put the cherubim in the innermost part of the house. And the wings of the cherubim were spread out so that a wing of one touched the one wall, and a wing of the other cherub touched the other wall; their other wings touched each other in the middle of the house. ²⁸And he overlaid the cherubim with gold.

²⁹Around all the walls of the house he carved engraved figures of cherubim and palm trees and open flowers, in the inner and outer rooms. ³⁰The floor of the house he overlaid with gold in the inner and outer rooms.

³¹For the entrance to the inner sanctuary he made doors of olivewood; the lintel and the doorposts were five-sided.⁷ ³²He covered the two doors of olivewood with carvings of cherubim, palm trees, and open flowers. He overlaid them with gold and spread gold on the cherubim and on the palm trees.

³³So also he made for the entrance to the nave doorposts of olivewood, in the form of a square, ³⁴and two doors of cypress wood. The two leaves of the one door were folding, and the two leaves of the other door were folding. ³⁵On them he carved cherubim and palm trees and open flowers, and he overlaid them with gold evenly applied

---

¹Or *blocked lattice windows* ²Or *platform*; also verse 10 ³Septuagint; Hebrew *structure*, or *platform* ⁴Septuagint, Targum; Hebrew *middle* ⁵Vulgate; Hebrew *and before the inner sanctuary* ⁶Septuagint *made* ⁷The meaning of the Hebrew phrase is uncertain

on the carved work. ³⁶ He built the inner court with three courses of cut stone and one course of cedar beams.

³⁷ In the fourth year the foundation of the house of the LORD was laid, in the month of Ziv. ³⁸ And in the eleventh year, in the month of Bul, which is the eighth month, the house was finished in all its parts, and according to all its specifications. He was seven years in building it.

Solomon Builds His Palace

7 Solomon was building his own house thirteen years, and he finished his entire house.

² He built the House of the Forest of Lebanon. Its length was a hundred cubits[1] and its breadth fifty cubits and its height thirty cubits, and it was built on four[2] rows of cedar pillars, with cedar beams on the pillars. ³ And it was covered with cedar above the chambers that were on the forty-five pillars, fifteen in each row. ⁴ There were window frames in three rows, and window opposite window in three tiers. ⁵ All the doorways and windows[3] had square frames, and window was opposite window in three tiers.

⁶ And he made the Hall of Pillars; its length was fifty cubits, and its breadth thirty cubits. There was a porch in front with pillars, and a canopy in front of them.

⁷ And he made the Hall of the Throne where he was to pronounce judgment, even the Hall of Judgment. It was finished with cedar from floor to rafters.[4]

⁸ His own house where he was to dwell, in the other court back of the hall, was of like workmanship. Solomon also made a house like this hall for Pharaoh's daughter whom he had taken in marriage.

⁹ All these were made of costly stones, cut according to measure, sawed with saws, back and front, even from the foundation to the coping, and from the outside to the great court. ¹⁰ The foundation was of costly stones, huge stones, stones of eight and ten cubits. ¹¹ And above were costly stones, cut according to measurement, and cedar. ¹² The great court had three courses of cut stone all around, and a course of cedar beams; so had the inner court of the house of the LORD and the vestibule of the house.

The Temple Furnishings

¹³ And King Solomon sent and brought Hiram from Tyre. ¹⁴ He was the son of a widow of the tribe of Naphtali, and his father was a man of Tyre, a worker in bronze. And he was full of wisdom, understanding, and skill for making any work in bronze. He came to King Solomon and did all his work.

¹⁵ He cast two pillars of bronze. Eighteen cubits was the height of one pillar, and a line of twelve cubits measured its circumference. It was hollow, and its thickness was four fingers. The second pillar was the same.[5] ¹⁶ He also made two capitals of cast bronze to set on the tops of the pillars. The height of the one capital was five cubits, and the height of the other capital was five cubits. ¹⁷ There were lattices of checker work with wreaths of chain work for the capitals on the tops of the pillars, a lattice[6] for the one capital and a lattice for the other capital. ¹⁸ Likewise he made pomegranates[7] in two rows around the one latticework to cover the capital that was on the top of the pillar, and he did the same with the other capital. ¹⁹ Now the capitals that were on the tops of the pillars in the vestibule were of lily-work, four cubits. ²⁰ The capitals were on the two pillars and also above the rounded projection which was beside the latticework. There were two hundred pomegranates in two rows all around, and so with the other capital. ²¹ He set up the pillars at the vestibule of the temple. He set up the pillar on the south and called its name Jachin, and he set up the pillar on the north and called its name Boaz. ²² And on the tops of the pillars was lily-work. Thus the work of the pillars was finished.

²³ Then he made the sea of cast metal. It was round, ten cubits from brim to brim, and five cubits high, and a line of thirty cubits measured its circumference. ²⁴ Under its brim were gourds, for ten cubits, compassing the sea all around. The gourds were in two rows, cast with it when it was cast. ²⁵ It stood on twelve oxen, three facing north, three facing west, three facing south, and three facing east. The sea was

---

[1] A *cubit* was about 18 inches or 45 centimeters [2] Septuagint *three* [3] Septuagint; Hebrew *posts* [4] Syriac, Vulgate; Hebrew *floor* [5] Targum, Syriac (compare Septuagint and Jeremiah 52:21); Hebrew *fingers. And a line of twelve cubits measured the circumference of the second pillar* [6] Septuagint; Hebrew *seven*; twice in this verse [7] Two manuscripts (compare Septuagint); Hebrew *pillars*

set on them, and all their rear parts were inward. ²⁶Its thickness was a handbreadth,[1] and its brim was made like the brim of a cup, like the flower of a lily. It held two thousand baths.[2]

²⁷He also made the ten stands of bronze. Each stand was four cubits long, four cubits wide, and three cubits high. ²⁸This was the construction of the stands: they had panels, and the panels were set in the frames, ²⁹and on the panels that were set in the frames were lions, oxen, and cherubim. On the frames, both above and below the lions and oxen, there were wreaths of beveled work. ³⁰Moreover, each stand had four bronze wheels and axles of bronze, and at the four corners were supports for a basin. The supports were cast with wreaths at the side of each. ³¹Its opening was within a crown that projected upward one cubit. Its opening was round, as a pedestal is made, a cubit and a half deep. At its opening there were carvings, and its panels were square, not round. ³²And the four wheels were underneath the panels. The axles of the wheels were of one piece with the stands, and the height of a wheel was a cubit and a half. ³³The wheels were made like a chariot wheel; their axles, their rims, their spokes, and their hubs were all cast. ³⁴There were four supports at the four corners of each stand. The supports were of one piece with the stands. ³⁵And on the top of the stand there was a round band half a cubit high; and on the top of the stand its stays and its panels were of one piece with it. ³⁶And on the surfaces of its stays and on its panels, he carved cherubim, lions, and palm trees, according to the space of each, with wreaths all around. ³⁷After this manner he made the ten stands. All of them were cast alike, of the same measure and the same form.

³⁸And he made ten basins of bronze. Each basin held forty baths, each basin measured four cubits, and there was a basin for each of the ten stands. ³⁹And he set the stands, five on the south side of the house, and five on the north side of the house. And he set the sea at the southeast corner of the house.

⁴⁰Hiram also made the pots, the shovels, and the basins. So Hiram finished all the work that he did for King Solomon on the house of the LORD: ⁴¹the two pillars, the two bowls of the capitals that were on the tops of the pillars, and the two latticeworks to cover the two bowls of the capitals that were on the tops of the pillars; ⁴²and the four hundred pomegranates for the two latticeworks, two rows of pomegranates for each latticework, to cover the two bowls of the capitals that were on the pillars; ⁴³the ten stands, and the ten basins on the stands; ⁴⁴and the one sea, and the twelve oxen underneath the sea.

⁴⁵Now the pots, the shovels, and the basins, all these vessels in the house of the LORD, which Hiram made for King Solomon, were of burnished bronze. ⁴⁶In the plain of the Jordan the king cast them, in the clay ground between Succoth and Zarethan. ⁴⁷And Solomon left all the vessels unweighed, because there were so many of them; the weight of the bronze was not ascertained.

⁴⁸So Solomon made all the vessels that were in the house of the LORD: the golden altar, the golden table for the bread of the Presence, ⁴⁹the lampstands of pure gold, five on the south side and five on the north, before the inner sanctuary; the flowers, the lamps, and the tongs, of gold; ⁵⁰the cups, snuffers, basins, dishes for incense, and fire pans, of pure gold; and the sockets of gold, for the doors of the innermost part of the house, the Most Holy Place, and for the doors of the nave of the temple.

⁵¹Thus all the work that King Solomon did on the house of the LORD was finished. And Solomon brought in the things that David his father had dedicated, the silver, the gold, and the vessels, and stored them in the treasuries of the house of the LORD.

The Ark Brought into the Temple

8 Then Solomon assembled the elders of Israel and all the heads of the tribes, the leaders of the fathers' houses of the people of Israel, before King Solomon in Jerusalem, to bring up the ark of the covenant of the LORD out of the city of David, which is Zion. ²And all the men of Israel assembled to King Solomon at the feast in the month Ethanim, which is the seventh month. ³And all the elders of Israel came, and the priests took up the ark. ⁴And they brought up the ark of the LORD, the tent of meeting, and all the holy vessels that were in the tent; the priests and the Levites

---

[1] A *handbreadth* was about 3 inches or 7.5 centimeters [2] A *bath* was about 6 gallons or 22 liters

brought them up. ⁵ And King Solomon and all the congregation of Israel, who had assembled before him, were with him before the ark, sacrificing so many sheep and oxen that they could not be counted or numbered. ⁶ Then the priests brought the ark of the covenant of the LORD to its place in the inner sanctuary of the house, in the Most Holy Place, underneath the wings of the cherubim. ⁷ For the cherubim spread out their wings over the place of the ark, so that the cherubim overshadowed the ark and its poles. ⁸ And the poles were so long that the ends of the poles were seen from the Holy Place before the inner sanctuary; but they could not be seen from outside. And they are there to this day. ⁹ There was nothing in the ark except the two tablets of stone that Moses put there at Horeb, where the LORD made a covenant with the people of Israel, when they came out of the land of Egypt. ¹⁰ And when the priests came out of the Holy Place, a cloud filled the house of the LORD, ¹¹ so that the priests could not stand to minister because of the cloud, for the glory of the LORD filled the house of the LORD.

Solomon Blesses the LORD

¹² Then Solomon said, "The LORD¹ has said that he would dwell in thick darkness. ¹³ I have indeed built you an exalted house, a place for you to dwell in forever." ¹⁴ Then the king turned around and blessed all the assembly of Israel, while all the assembly of Israel stood. ¹⁵ And he said, "Blessed be the LORD, the God of Israel, who with his hand has fulfilled what he promised with his mouth to David my father, saying, ¹⁶ 'Since the day that I brought my people Israel out of Egypt, I chose no city out of all the tribes of Israel in which to build a house, that my name might be there. But I chose David to be over my people Israel.' ¹⁷ Now it was in the heart of David my father to build a house for the name of the LORD, the God of Israel. ¹⁸ But the LORD said to David my father, 'Whereas it was in your heart to build a house for my name, you did well that it was in your heart. ¹⁹ Nevertheless, you shall not build the house, but your son who shall be born to you shall build the house for my name.' ²⁰ Now the LORD has fulfilled his promise that he made. For I have risen in the place of David my father,

and sit on the throne of Israel, as the LORD promised, and I have built the house for the name of the LORD, the God of Israel. ²¹ And there I have provided a place for the ark, in which is the covenant of the LORD that he made with our fathers, when he brought them out of the land of Egypt."

Solomon's Prayer of Dedication

²² Then Solomon stood before the altar of the LORD in the presence of all the assembly of Israel and spread out his hands toward heaven, ²³ and said, "O LORD, God of Israel, there is no God like you, in heaven above or on earth beneath, keeping covenant and showing steadfast love to your servants who walk before you with all their heart; ²⁴ you have kept with your servant David my father what you declared to him. You spoke with your mouth, and with your hand have fulfilled it this day. ²⁵ Now therefore, O LORD, God of Israel, keep for your servant David my father what you have promised him, saying, 'You shall not lack a man to sit before me on the throne of Israel, if only your sons pay close attention to their way, to walk before me as you have walked before me.' ²⁶ Now therefore, O God of Israel, let your word be confirmed, which you have spoken to your servant David my father.

²⁷ "But will God indeed dwell on the earth? Behold, heaven and the highest heaven cannot contain you; how much less this house that I have built! ²⁸ Yet have regard to the prayer of your servant and to his plea, O LORD my God, listening to the cry and to the prayer that your servant prays before you this day, ²⁹ that your eyes may be open night and day toward this house, the place of which you have said, 'My name shall be there,' that you may listen to the prayer that your servant offers toward this place. ³⁰ And listen to the plea of your servant and of your people Israel, when they pray toward this place. And listen in heaven your dwelling place, and when you hear, forgive.

³¹ "If a man sins against his neighbor and is made to take an oath and comes and swears his oath before your altar in this house, ³² then hear in heaven and act and judge your servants, condemning the guilty by bringing his conduct on his own head,

¹ Septuagint *The LORD has set the sun in the heavens, but*

and vindicating the righteous by rewarding him according to his righteousness.

[33] "When your people Israel are defeated before the enemy because they have sinned against you, and if they turn again to you and acknowledge your name and pray and plead with you in this house, [34] then hear in heaven and forgive the sin of your people Israel and bring them again to the land that you gave to their fathers.

[35] "When heaven is shut up and there is no rain because they have sinned against you, if they pray toward this place and acknowledge your name and turn from their sin, when you afflict them, [36] then hear in heaven and forgive the sin of your servants, your people Israel, when you teach them the good way in which they should walk, and grant rain upon your land, which you have given to your people as an inheritance.

[37] "If there is famine in the land, if there is pestilence or blight or mildew or locust or caterpillar, if their enemy besieges them in the land at their gates,[1] whatever plague, whatever sickness there is, [38] whatever prayer, whatever plea is made by any man or by all your people Israel, each knowing the affliction of his own heart and stretching out his hands toward this house, [39] then hear in heaven your dwelling place and forgive and act and render to each whose heart you know, according to all his ways (for you, you only, know the hearts of all the children of mankind), [40] that they may fear you all the days that they live in the land that you gave to our fathers.

[41] "Likewise, when a foreigner, who is not of your people Israel, comes from a far country for your name's sake [42] (for they shall hear of your great name and your mighty hand, and of your outstretched arm), when he comes and prays toward this house, [43] hear in heaven your dwelling place and do according to all for which the foreigner calls to you, in order that all the peoples of the earth may know your name and fear you, as do your people Israel, and that they may know that this house that I have built is called by your name.

[44] "If your people go out to battle against their enemy, by whatever way you shall send them, and they pray to the LORD toward the city that you have chosen and the house that I have built for your name,

[45] then hear in heaven their prayer and their plea, and maintain their cause.

[46] "If they sin against you—for there is no one who does not sin—and you are angry with them and give them to an enemy, so that they are carried away captive to the land of the enemy, far off or near, [47] yet if they turn their heart in the land to which they have been carried captive, and repent and plead with you in the land of their captors, saying, 'We have sinned and have acted perversely and wickedly,' [48] if they repent with all their mind and with all their heart in the land of their enemies, who carried them captive, and pray to you toward their land, which you gave to their fathers, the city that you have chosen, and the house that I have built for your name, [49] then hear in heaven your dwelling place their prayer and their plea, and maintain their cause [50] and forgive your people who have sinned against you, and all their transgressions that they have committed against you, and grant them compassion in the sight of those who carried them captive, that they may have compassion on them [51] (for they are your people, and your heritage, which you brought out of Egypt, from the midst of the iron furnace). [52] Let your eyes be open to the plea of your servant and to the plea of your people Israel, giving ear to them whenever they call to you. [53] For you separated them from among all the peoples of the earth to be your heritage, as you declared through Moses your servant, when you brought our fathers out of Egypt, O Lord GOD."

Solomon's Benediction

[54] Now as Solomon finished offering all this prayer and plea to the LORD, he arose from before the altar of the LORD, where he had knelt with hands outstretched toward heaven. [55] And he stood and blessed all the assembly of Israel with a loud voice, saying, [56] "Blessed be the LORD who has given rest to his people Israel, according to all that he promised. Not one word has failed of all his good promise, which he spoke by Moses his servant. [57] The LORD our God be with us, as he was with our fathers. May he not leave us or forsake us, [58] that he may incline our hearts to him, to walk in all his ways and to keep his commandments, his statutes, and his rules, which he com-

---

[1] Septuagint, Syriac *in any of their cities*

manded our fathers. **59** Let these words of mine, with which I have pleaded before the LORD, be near to the LORD our God day and night, and may he maintain the cause of his servant and the cause of his people Israel, as each day requires, **60** that all the peoples of the earth may know that the LORD is God; there is no other. **61** Let your heart therefore be wholly true to the LORD our God, walking in his statutes and keeping his commandments, as at this day."

Solomon's Sacrifices

62 Then the king, and all Israel with him, offered sacrifice before the LORD. **63** Solomon offered as peace offerings to the LORD 22,000 oxen and 120,000 sheep. So the king and all the people of Israel dedicated the house of the LORD. **64** The same day the king consecrated the middle of the court that was before the house of the LORD, for there he offered the burnt offering and the grain offering and the fat pieces of the peace offerings, because the bronze altar that was before the LORD was too small to receive the burnt offering and the grain offering and the fat pieces of the peace offerings.

65 So Solomon held the feast at that time, and all Israel with him, a great assembly, from Lebo-hamath to the Brook of Egypt, before the LORD our God, seven days.[1] **66** On the eighth day he sent the people away, and they blessed the king and went to their homes joyful and glad of heart for all the goodness that the LORD had shown to David his servant and to Israel his people.

The LORD Appears to Solomon

9 As soon as Solomon had finished building the house of the LORD and the king's house and all that Solomon desired to build, **2** the LORD appeared to Solomon a second time, as he had appeared to him at Gibeon. **3** And the LORD said to him, "I have heard your prayer and your plea, which you have made before me. I have consecrated this house that you have built, by putting my name there forever. My eyes and my heart will be there for all time. **4** And as for you, if you will walk before me, as David your father walked, with integrity of heart and uprightness, doing according to all that I have commanded you, and keeping my statutes and my rules, **5** then I will establish your royal throne over Israel forever, as I promised David your father, saying, 'You shall not lack a man on the throne of Israel.' **6** But if you turn aside from following me, you or your children, and do not keep my commandments and my statutes that I have set before you, but go and serve other gods and worship them, **7** then I will cut off Israel from the land that I have given them, and the house that I have consecrated for my name I will cast out of my sight, and Israel will become a proverb and a byword among all peoples. **8** And this house will become a heap of ruins.[2] Everyone passing by it will be astonished and will hiss, and they will say, 'Why has the LORD done thus to this land and to this house?' **9** Then they will say, 'Because they abandoned the LORD their God who brought their fathers out of the land of Egypt and laid hold on other gods and worshiped them and served them. Therefore the LORD has brought all this disaster on them.'"

Solomon's Other Acts

10 At the end of twenty years, in which Solomon had built the two houses, the house of the LORD and the king's house, **11** and Hiram king of Tyre had supplied Solomon with cedar and cypress timber and gold, as much as he desired, King Solomon gave to Hiram twenty cities in the land of Galilee. **12** But when Hiram came from Tyre to see the cities that Solomon had given him, they did not please him. **13** Therefore he said, "What kind of cities are these that you have given me, my brother?" So they are called the land of Cabul to this day. **14** Hiram had sent to the king 120 talents[3] of gold.

15 And this is the account of the forced labor that King Solomon drafted to build the house of the LORD and his own house and the Millo and the wall of Jerusalem and Hazor and Megiddo and Gezer **16** (Pharaoh king of Egypt had gone up and captured Gezer and burned it with fire, and had killed the Canaanites who lived in the city, and had given it as dowry to his daughter, Solomon's wife; **17** so Solomon rebuilt Gezer) and Lower Beth-horon **18** and Baalath and Tamar in the wilderness, in the land of Judah,[4] **19** and all the

---

[1] Septuagint; Hebrew *seven days and seven days, fourteen days* [2] Syriac, Old Latin; Hebrew *will become high* [3] A *talent* was about 75 pounds or 34 kilograms [4] Hebrew lacks *of Judah*

store cities that Solomon had, and the cities for his chariots, and the cities for his horsemen, and whatever Solomon desired to build in Jerusalem, in Lebanon, and in all the land of his dominion. **20** All the people who were left of the Amorites, the Hittites, the Perizzites, the Hivites, and the Jebusites, who were not of the people of Israel— **21** their descendants who were left after them in the land, whom the people of Israel were unable to devote to destruction[1]—these Solomon drafted to be slaves, and so they are to this day. **22** But of the people of Israel Solomon made no slaves. They were the soldiers, they were his officials, his commanders, his captains, his chariot commanders and his horsemen.

23 These were the chief officers who were over Solomon's work: 550 who had charge of the people who carried on the work.

24 But Pharaoh's daughter went up from the city of David to her own house that Solomon had built for her. Then he built the Millo.

25 Three times a year Solomon used to offer up burnt offerings and peace offerings on the altar that he built to the LORD, making offerings with it[2] before the LORD. So he finished the house.

26 King Solomon built a fleet of ships at Ezion-geber, which is near Eloth on the shore of the Red Sea, in the land of Edom. **27** And Hiram sent with the fleet his servants, seamen who were familiar with the sea, together with the servants of Solomon. **28** And they went to Ophir and brought from there gold, 420 talents, and they brought it to King Solomon.

The Queen of Sheba

10 Now when the queen of Sheba heard of the fame of Solomon concerning the name of the LORD, she came to test him with hard questions. **2** She came to Jerusalem with a very great retinue, with camels bearing spices and very much gold and precious stones. And when she came to Solomon, she told him all that was on her mind. **3** And Solomon answered all her questions; there was nothing hidden from the king that he could not explain to her. **4** And when the queen of Sheba had seen all the wisdom of Solomon, the house that he had built, **5** the food of his table, the seating

of his officials, and the attendance of his servants, their clothing, his cupbearers, and his burnt offerings that he offered at the house of the LORD, there was no more breath in her.

6 And she said to the king, "The report was true that I heard in my own land of your words and of your wisdom, **7** but I did not believe the reports until I came and my own eyes had seen it. And behold, the half was not told me. Your wisdom and prosperity surpass the report that I heard. **8** Happy are your men! Happy are your servants, who continually stand before you and hear your wisdom! **9** Blessed be the LORD your God, who has delighted in you and set you on the throne of Israel! Because the LORD loved Israel forever, he has made you king, that you may execute justice and righteousness." **10** Then she gave the king 120 talents[3] of gold, and a very great quantity of spices and precious stones. Never again came such an abundance of spices as these that the queen of Sheba gave to King Solomon.

11 Moreover, the fleet of Hiram, which brought gold from Ophir, brought from Ophir a very great amount of almug wood and precious stones. **12** And the king made of the almug wood supports for the house of the LORD and for the king's house, also lyres and harps for the singers. No such almug wood has come or been seen to this day.

13 And King Solomon gave to the queen of Sheba all that she desired, whatever she asked besides what was given her by the bounty of King Solomon. So she turned and went back to her own land with her servants.

Solomon's Great Wealth

14 Now the weight of gold that came to Solomon in one year was 666 talents of gold, **15** besides that which came from the explorers and from the business of the merchants, and from all the kings of the west and from the governors of the land. **16** King Solomon made 200 large shields of beaten gold; 600 shekels[4] of gold went into each shield. **17** And he made 300 shields of beaten gold; three minas[5] of gold went into each shield. And the king put them in the House of the Forest of Lebanon. **18** The king also made a great ivory throne and overlaid it with the finest gold. [19] The throne had six steps, and the throne had a round top,[1] and on each side of the seat were armrests and two lions standing beside the armrests, [20] while twelve lions stood there, one on each end of a step on the six steps. The like of it was never made in any kingdom. [21] All King Solomon's drinking vessels were of gold, and all the vessels of the House of the Forest of Lebanon were of pure gold. None were of silver; silver was not considered as anything in the days of Solomon. [22] For the king had a fleet of ships of Tarshish at sea with the fleet of Hiram. Once every three years the fleet of ships of Tarshish used to come bringing gold, silver, ivory, apes, and peacocks.[2]

[23] Thus King Solomon excelled all the kings of the earth in riches and in wisdom. [24] And the whole earth sought the presence of Solomon to hear his wisdom, which God had put into his mind. [25] Every one of them brought his present, articles of silver and gold, garments, myrrh, spices, horses, and mules, so much year by year.

[26] And Solomon gathered together chariots and horsemen. He had 1,400 chariots and 12,000 horsemen, whom he stationed in the chariot cities and with the king in Jerusalem. [27] And the king made silver as common in Jerusalem as stone, and he made cedar as plentiful as the sycamore of the Shephelah. [28] And Solomon's import of horses was from Egypt and Kue, and the king's traders received them from Kue at a price. [29] A chariot could be imported from Egypt for 600 shekels of silver and a horse for 150, and so through the king's traders they were exported to all the kings of the Hittites and the kings of Syria.

Solomon Turns from the LORD

11 Now King Solomon loved many foreign women, along with the daughter of Pharaoh: Moabite, Ammonite, Edomite, Sidonian, and Hittite women, [2] from the nations concerning which the LORD had said to the people of Israel, "You shall not enter into marriage with them, neither shall they with you, for surely they will turn away your heart after their gods." Solomon clung to these in love. [3] He had 700 wives, who were princesses, and 300 concubines. And his wives turned away his heart. [4] For when Solomon was old his wives turned away his heart after other

[1] Or at the back of the throne was a calf's head [2] Or baboons

Know Love

verses to read
1 Kings 11:1–8

As a God Girl, you can never let chasing boys get to be more important than chasing God. When anything in your life becomes more important to your heart than God, it's called an idol. Idolatry rips God from the throne of your life by making someone or something else the main focus. Boys should never be so important that getting one is your number one thought. Chasing love can quickly distract you from what's really important, especially if the one you're chasing doesn't love God the same way you do, or even at all. Any love that you find at the cost of devotion to God isn't healthy spiritually or emotionally.

Loving people is a good thing, but real love is about serving God and not yourself or your hormones. When loving is more about getting than giving, it isn't love at all; it's selfishness. As a God Girl you have to make sure that the love you chase is a love that serves God. All of your worth and your hope is in the hands of God, not in the dream of a boy. Guys are almost always going to disappoint you in some way or another, but God won't. When you trust in the one who never fails, you are preparing yourself to love the way the Father created you to—not out of your need but out of your faith in the one who is love (see 1 John 4:8).

gods, and his heart was not wholly true to the LORD his God, as was the heart of David his father. [5] For Solomon went after Ashtoreth the goddess of the Sidonians, and after Milcom the abomination of the Ammonites. [6] So Solomon did what was evil in the sight of the LORD and did not wholly follow the LORD, as David his father had done. [7] Then Solomon built a high place for Chemosh the abomination of Moab, and for Molech the abomination of the Ammonites, on the mountain east of Jerusalem. [8] And so he did for all his foreign wives, who made offerings and sacrificed to their gods.

The LORD Raises Adversaries

[9] And the LORD was angry with Solomon, because his heart had turned away from the LORD, the God of Israel, who had appeared to him twice [10] and had commanded him concerning this thing, that he should not go after other gods. But he did not keep what the LORD commanded. [11] Therefore the LORD said to Solomon, "Since this has been your practice and you have not kept my covenant and my statutes that I have commanded you, I will surely tear the kingdom from you and will give it to your servant. [12] Yet for the sake of David your father I will not do it in your days, but I will tear it out of the hand of your son. [13] However, I will not tear away all the kingdom, but I will give one tribe to your son, for the sake of David my servant and for the sake of Jerusalem that I have chosen."

[14] And the LORD raised up an adversary against Solomon, Hadad the Edomite. He was of the royal house in Edom. [15] For when David was in Edom, and Joab the commander of the army went up to bury the slain, he struck down every male in Edom [16] (for Joab and all Israel remained there six months, until he had cut off every male in Edom). [17] But Hadad fled to Egypt, together with certain Edomites of his father's servants, Hadad still being a little child. [18] They set out from Midian and came to Paran and took men with them from Paran and came to Egypt, to Pharaoh king of Egypt, who gave him a house and assigned him an allowance of food and gave him land. [19] And Hadad found great favor in the sight of Pharaoh, so that he gave him in marriage the sister of his own wife, the sister of Tahpenes the queen. [20] And the sister of Tahpenes bore him Genubath his son, whom Tahpenes weaned in Pharaoh's house. And Genubath was in Pharaoh's house among the sons of Pharaoh. [21] But when Hadad heard in Egypt that David slept with his fathers and that Joab the commander of the army was dead, Hadad said to Pharaoh, "Let me depart, that I may go to my own country." [22] But Pharaoh said to him, "What have you lacked with me that you are now seeking to go to your own country?" And he said to him, "Only let me depart."

[23] God also raised up as an adversary to him, Rezon the son of Eliada, who had fled from his master Hadadezer king of Zobah. [24] And he gathered men about him and became leader of a marauding band, after the killing by David. And they went to Damascus and lived there and made him king in Damascus. [25] He was an adversary of Israel all the days of Solomon, doing harm as Hadad did. And he loathed Israel and reigned over Syria.

[26] Jeroboam the son of Nebat, an Ephraimite of Zeredah, a servant of Solomon, whose mother's name was Zeruah, a widow, also lifted up his hand against the king. [27] And this was the reason why he lifted up his hand against the king. Solomon built the Millo, and closed up the breach of the city of David his father. [28] The man Jeroboam was very able, and when Solomon saw that the young man was industrious he gave him charge over all the forced labor of the house of Joseph. [29] And at that time, when Jeroboam went out of Jerusalem, the prophet Ahijah the Shilonite found him on the road. Now Ahijah had dressed himself in a new garment, and the two of them were alone in the open country. [30] Then Ahijah laid hold of the new garment that was on him, and tore it into twelve pieces. [31] And he said to Jeroboam, "Take for yourself ten pieces, for thus says the LORD, the God of Israel, 'Behold, I am about to tear the kingdom from the hand of Solomon and will give you ten tribes [32] (but he shall have one tribe, for the sake of my servant David and for the sake of Jerusalem, the city that I have chosen out of all the tribes of Israel), [33] because they have[1] forsaken me and worshiped Ashtoreth the goddess of the Sidonians, Chemosh the god of Moab,

---

[1] Septuagint, Syriac, Vulgate *he has*; twice in this verse

and Milcom the god of the Ammonites, and they have not walked in my ways, doing what is right in my sight and keeping my statutes and my rules, as David his father did. ³⁴ Nevertheless, I will not take the whole kingdom out of his hand, but I will make him ruler all the days of his life, for the sake of David my servant whom I chose, who kept my commandments and my statutes. ³⁵ But I will take the kingdom out of his son's hand and will give it to you, ten tribes. ³⁶ Yet to his son I will give one tribe, that David my servant may always have a lamp before me in Jerusalem, the city where I have chosen to put my name. ³⁷ And I will take you, and you shall reign over all that your soul desires, and you shall be king over Israel. ³⁸ And if you will listen to all that I command you, and will walk in my ways, and do what is right in my eyes by keeping my statutes and my commandments, as David my servant did, I will be with you and will build you a sure house, as I built for David, and I will give Israel to you. ³⁹ And I will afflict the offspring of David because of this, but not forever.'" ⁴⁰ Solomon sought therefore to kill Jeroboam. But Jeroboam arose and fled into Egypt, to Shishak king of Egypt, and was in Egypt until the death of Solomon.

⁴¹ Now the rest of the acts of Solomon, and all that he did, and his wisdom, are they not written in the Book of the Acts of Solomon? ⁴² And the time that Solomon reigned in Jerusalem over all Israel was forty years. ⁴³ And Solomon slept with his fathers and was buried in the city of David his father. And Rehoboam his son reigned in his place.

Rehoboam's Folly

12 Rehoboam went to Shechem, for all Israel had come to Shechem to make him king. ² And as soon as Jeroboam the son of Nebat heard of it (for he was still in Egypt, where he had fled from King Solomon), then Jeroboam returned from¹ Egypt. ³ And they sent and called him, and Jeroboam and all the assembly of Israel came and said to Rehoboam, ⁴ "Your father made our yoke heavy. Now therefore lighten the hard service of your father and his heavy yoke on us, and we will serve you." ⁵ He said to them, "Go away for three

days, then come again to me." So the people went away.

⁶ Then King Rehoboam took counsel with the old men, who had stood before Solomon his father while he was yet alive, saying, "How do you advise me to answer this people?" ⁷ And they said to him, "If you will be a servant to this people today and serve them, and speak good words to them when you answer them, then they will be your servants forever." ⁸ But he abandoned the counsel that the old men gave him and took counsel with the young men who had grown up with him and stood before him. ⁹ And he said to them, "What do you advise that we answer this people who have said to me, 'Lighten the yoke that your father put on us'?" ¹⁰ And the young men who had grown up with him said to him, "Thus shall you speak to this people who said to you, 'Your father made our yoke heavy, but you lighten it for us,' thus shall you say to them, 'My little finger is thicker than my father's thighs. ¹¹ And now, whereas my father laid on you a heavy yoke, I will add to your yoke. My father disciplined you with whips, but I will discipline you with scorpions.'"

¹² So Jeroboam and all the people came to Rehoboam the third day, as the king said, "Come to me again the third day." ¹³ And the king answered the people harshly, and forsaking the counsel that the old men had given him, ¹⁴ he spoke to them according to the counsel of the young men, saying, "My father made your yoke heavy, but I will add to your yoke. My father disciplined you with whips, but I will discipline you with scorpions." ¹⁵ So the king did not listen to the people, for it was a turn of affairs brought about by the LORD that he might fulfill his word, which the LORD spoke by Ahijah the Shilonite to Jeroboam the son of Nebat.

The Kingdom Divided

¹⁶ And when all Israel saw that the king did not listen to them, the people answered the king, "What portion do we have in David? We have no inheritance in the son of Jesse. To your tents, O Israel! Look now to your own house, David." So Israel went to their tents. ¹⁷ But Rehoboam reigned over the people of Israel who lived in the cities of Judah. ¹⁸ Then King Rehoboam sent Adoram, who was taskmaster over

¹ Septuagint, Vulgate (compare 2 Chronicles 10:2); Hebrew *lived in*

the forced labor, and all Israel stoned him to death with stones. And King Rehoboam hurried to mount his chariot to flee to Jerusalem. [19] So Israel has been in rebellion against the house of David to this day. [20] And when all Israel heard that Jeroboam had returned, they sent and called him to the assembly and made him king over all Israel. There was none that followed the house of David but the tribe of Judah only.

[21] When Rehoboam came to Jerusalem, he assembled all the house of Judah and the tribe of Benjamin, 180,000 chosen warriors, to fight against the house of Israel, to restore the kingdom to Rehoboam the son of Solomon. [22] But the word of God came to Shemaiah the man of God: [23] "Say to Rehoboam the son of Solomon, king of Judah, and to all the house of Judah and Benjamin, and to the rest of the people, [24] 'Thus says the LORD, You shall not go up or fight against your relatives the people of Israel. Every man return to his home, for this thing is from me.'" So they listened to the word of the LORD and went home again, according to the word of the LORD.

Jeroboam's Golden Calves

[25] Then Jeroboam built Shechem in the hill country of Ephraim and lived there. And he went out from there and built Penuel. [26] And Jeroboam said in his heart, "Now the kingdom will turn back to the house of David. [27] If this people go up to offer sacrifices in the temple of the LORD at Jerusalem, then the heart of this people will turn again to their lord, to Rehoboam king of Judah, and they will kill me and return to Rehoboam king of Judah." [28] So the king took counsel and made two calves of gold. And he said to the people, "You have gone up to Jerusalem long enough. Behold your gods, O Israel, who brought you up out of the land of Egypt." [29] And he set one in Bethel, and the other he put in Dan. [30] Then this thing became a sin, for the people went as far as Dan to be before one.[1] [31] He also made temples on high places and appointed priests from among all the people, who were not of the Levites. [32] And Jeroboam appointed a feast on the fifteenth day of the eighth month like the feast that was in Judah, and he offered sacrifices on the altar. So he did in Bethel, sacrificing to the calves that he

made. And he placed in Bethel the priests of the high places that he had made. [33] He went up to the altar that he had made in Bethel on the fifteenth day in the eighth month, in the month that he had devised from his own heart. And he instituted a feast for the people of Israel and went up to the altar to make offerings.

A Man of God Confronts Jeroboam

13 And behold, a man of God came out of Judah by the word of the LORD to Bethel. Jeroboam was standing by the altar to make offerings. [2] And the man cried against the altar by the word of the LORD and said, "O altar, altar, thus says the LORD: 'Behold, a son shall be born to the house of David, Josiah by name, and he shall sacrifice on you the priests of the high places who make offerings on you, and human bones shall be burned on you.'" [3] And he gave a sign the same day, saying, "This is the sign that the LORD has spoken: 'Behold, the altar shall be torn down, and the ashes that are on it shall be poured out.'" [4] And when the king heard the saying of the man of God, which he cried against the altar at Bethel, Jeroboam stretched out his hand from the altar, saying, "Seize him." And his hand, which he stretched out against him, dried up, so that he could not draw it back to himself. [5] The altar also was torn down, and the ashes poured out from the altar, according to the sign that the man of God had given by the word of the LORD. [6] And the king said to the man of God, "Entreat now the favor of the LORD your God, and pray for me, that my hand may be restored to me." And the man of God entreated the LORD, and the king's hand was restored to him and became as it was before. [7] And the king said to the man of God, "Come home with me, and refresh yourself, and I will give you a reward." [8] And the man of God said to the king, "If you give me half your house, I will not go in with you. And I will not eat bread or drink water in this place, [9] for so was it commanded me by the word of the LORD, saying, 'You shall neither eat bread nor drink water nor return by the way that you came.'" [10] So he went another way and did not return by the way that he came to Bethel.

---

[1] Septuagint *went to the one at Bethel and to the other as far as Dan*

The Prophet's Disobedience

[11] Now an old prophet lived in Bethel. And his sons[1] came and told him all that the man of God had done that day in Bethel. They also told to their father the words that he had spoken to the king. [12] And their father said to them, "Which way did he go?" And his sons showed him the way that the man of God who came from Judah had gone. [13] And he said to his sons, "Saddle the donkey for me." So they saddled the donkey for him and he mounted it. [14] And he went after the man of God and found him sitting under an oak. And he said to him, "Are you the man of God who came from Judah?" And he said, "I am." [15] Then he said to him, "Come home with me and eat bread." [16] And he said, "I may not return with you, or go in with you, neither will I eat bread nor drink water with you in this place, [17] for it was said to me by the word of the LORD, 'You shall neither eat bread nor drink water there, nor return by the way that you came.'" [18] And he said to him, "I also am a prophet as you are, and an angel spoke to me by the word of the LORD, saying, 'Bring him back with you into your house that he may eat bread and drink water.'" But he lied to him. [19] So he went back with him and ate bread in his house and drank water.

[20] And as they sat at the table, the word of the LORD came to the prophet who had brought him back. [21] And he cried to the man of God who came from Judah, "Thus says the LORD, 'Because you have disobeyed the word of the LORD and have not kept the command that the LORD your God commanded you, [22] but have come back and have eaten bread and drunk water in the place of which he said to you, "Eat no bread and drink no water," your body shall not come to the tomb of your fathers.'" [23] And after he had eaten bread and drunk, he saddled the donkey for the prophet whom he had brought back. [24] And as he went away a lion met him on the road and killed him. And his body was thrown in the road, and the donkey stood beside it; the lion also stood beside the body. [25] And behold, men passed by and saw the body thrown in the road and the lion standing by the body. And they came and told it in the city where the old prophet lived.

[26] And when the prophet who had brought him back from the way heard of it, he said, "It is the man of God who disobeyed the word of the LORD; therefore the LORD has given him to the lion, which has torn him and killed him, according to the word that the LORD spoke to him." [27] And he said to his sons, "Saddle the donkey for me." And they saddled it. [28] And he went and found his body thrown in the road, and the donkey and the lion standing beside the body. The lion had not eaten the body or torn the donkey. [29] And the prophet took up the body of the man of God and laid it on the donkey and brought it back to the city[2] to mourn and to bury him. [30] And he laid the body in his own grave. And they mourned over him, saying, "Alas, my brother!" [31] And after he had buried him, he said to his sons, "When I die, bury me in the grave in which the man of God is buried; lay my bones beside his bones. [32] For the saying that he called out by the word of the LORD against the altar in Bethel and against all the houses of the high places that are in the cities of Samaria shall surely come to pass."

[33] After this thing Jeroboam did not turn from his evil way, but made priests for the high places again from among all the people. Any who would, he ordained to be priests of the high places. [34] And this thing became sin to the house of Jeroboam, so as to cut it off and to destroy it from the face of the earth.

Prophecy Against Jeroboam

14 At that time Abijah the son of Jeroboam fell sick. [2] And Jeroboam said to his wife, "Arise, and disguise yourself, that it not be known that you are the wife of Jeroboam, and go to Shiloh. Behold, Ahijah the prophet is there, who said of me that I should be king over this people. [3] Take with you ten loaves, some cakes, and a jar of honey, and go to him. He will tell you what shall happen to the child."

[4] Jeroboam's wife did so. She arose and went to Shiloh and came to the house of Ahijah. Now Ahijah could not see, for his eyes were dim because of his age. [5] And the LORD said to Ahijah, "Behold, the wife of Jeroboam is coming to inquire of you concerning her son, for he is sick. Thus and thus shall you say to her."

---

[1] Septuagint, Syriac, Vulgate; Hebrew *son* [2] Septuagint; Hebrew *he came to the city of the old prophet*

When she came, she pretended to be another woman. [6] But when Ahijah heard the sound of her feet, as she came in at the door, he said, "Come in, wife of Jeroboam. Why do you pretend to be another? For I am charged with unbearable news for you. [7] Go, tell Jeroboam, 'Thus says the LORD, the God of Israel: "Because I exalted you from among the people and made you leader over my people Israel [8] and tore the kingdom away from the house of David and gave it to you, and yet you have not been like my servant David, who kept my commandments and followed me with all his heart, doing only that which was right in my eyes, [9] but you have done evil above all who were before you and have gone and made for yourself other gods and metal images, provoking me to anger, and have cast me behind your back, [10] therefore behold, I will bring harm upon the house of Jeroboam and will cut off from Jeroboam every male, both bond and free in Israel, and will burn up the house of Jeroboam, as a man burns up dung until it is all gone. [11] Anyone belonging to Jeroboam who dies in the city the dogs shall eat, and anyone who dies in the open country the birds of the heavens shall eat, for the LORD has spoken it."' [12] Arise therefore, go to your house. When your feet enter the city, the child shall die. [13] And all Israel shall mourn for him and bury him, for he only of Jeroboam shall come to the grave, because in him there is found something pleasing to the LORD, the God of Israel, in the house of Jeroboam. [14] Moreover, the LORD will raise up for himself a king over Israel who shall cut off the house of Jeroboam today. And henceforth, [15] the LORD will strike Israel as a reed is shaken in the water, and root up Israel out of this good land that he gave to their fathers and scatter them beyond the Euphrates,[1] because they have made their Asherim, provoking the LORD to anger. [16] And he will give Israel up because of the sins of Jeroboam, which he sinned and made Israel to sin."

[17] Then Jeroboam's wife arose and departed and came to Tirzah. And as she came to the threshold of the house, the child died. [18] And all Israel buried him and mourned for him, according to the word of the LORD, which he spoke by his servant Ahijah the prophet.

The Death of Jeroboam

[19] Now the rest of the acts of Jeroboam, how he warred and how he reigned, behold, they are written in the Book of the Chronicles of the Kings of Israel. [20] And the time that Jeroboam reigned was twenty-two years. And he slept with his fathers, and Nadab his son reigned in his place.

Rehoboam Reigns in Judah

[21] Now Rehoboam the son of Solomon reigned in Judah. Rehoboam was forty-one years old when he began to reign, and he reigned seventeen years in Jerusalem, the city that the LORD had chosen out of all the tribes of Israel, to put his name there. His mother's name was Naamah the Ammonite. [22] And Judah did what was evil in the sight of the LORD, and they provoked him to jealousy with their sins that they committed, more than all that their fathers had done. [23] For they also built for themselves high places and pillars and Asherim on every high hill and under every green tree, [24] and there were also male cult prostitutes in the land. They did according to all the abominations of the nations that the LORD drove out before the people of Israel.

[25] In the fifth year of King Rehoboam, Shishak king of Egypt came up against Jerusalem. [26] He took away the treasures of the house of the LORD and the treasures of the king's house. He took away everything. He also took away all the shields of gold that Solomon had made, [27] and King Rehoboam made in their place shields of bronze, and committed them to the hands of the officers of the guard, who kept the door of the king's house. [28] And as often as the king went into the house of the LORD, the guard carried them and brought them back to the guardroom.

[29] Now the rest of the acts of Rehoboam and all that he did, are they not written in the Book of the Chronicles of the Kings of Judah? [30] And there was war between Rehoboam and Jeroboam continually. [31] And Rehoboam slept with his fathers and was buried with his fathers in the city of David. His mother's name was Naamah the Ammonite. And Abijam his son reigned in his place.

---

[1] Hebrew the River

Abijam Reigns in Judah

15 Now in the eighteenth year of King Jeroboam the son of Nebat, Abijam began to reign over Judah. ² He reigned for three years in Jerusalem. His mother's name was Maacah the daughter of Abishalom. ³ And he walked in all the sins that his father did before him, and his heart was not wholly true to the LORD his God, as the heart of David his father. ⁴ Nevertheless, for David's sake the LORD his God gave him a lamp in Jerusalem, setting up his son after him, and establishing Jerusalem, ⁵ because David did what was right in the eyes of the LORD and did not turn aside from anything that he commanded him all the days of his life, except in the matter of Uriah the Hittite. ⁶ Now there was war between Rehoboam and Jeroboam all the days of his life. ⁷ The rest of the acts of Abijam and all that he did, are they not written in the Book of the Chronicles of the Kings of Judah? And there was war between Abijam and Jeroboam. ⁸ And Abijam slept with his fathers, and they buried him in the city of David. And Asa his son reigned in his place.

Asa Reigns in Judah

⁹ In the twentieth year of Jeroboam king of Israel, Asa began to reign over Judah, ¹⁰ and he reigned forty-one years in Jerusalem. His mother's name was Maacah the daughter of Abishalom. ¹¹ And Asa did what was right in the eyes of the LORD, as David his father had done. ¹² He put away the male cult prostitutes out of the land and removed all the idols that his fathers had made. ¹³ He also removed Maacah his mother from being queen mother because she had made an abominable image for Asherah. And Asa cut down her image and burned it at the brook Kidron. ¹⁴ But the high places were not taken away. Nevertheless, the heart of Asa was wholly true to the LORD all his days. ¹⁵ And he brought into the house of the LORD the sacred gifts of his father and his own sacred gifts, silver, and gold, and vessels.

¹⁶ And there was war between Asa and Baasha king of Israel all their days. ¹⁷ Baasha king of Israel went up against Judah and built Ramah, that he might permit no one to go out or come in to Asa king of Judah. ¹⁸ Then Asa took all the silver and the gold that were left in the treasures of the house of the LORD and the treasures of the king's house and gave them into the hands of his servants. And King Asa sent them to Ben-hadad the son of Tabrimmon, the son of Hezion, king of Syria, who lived in Damascus, saying, ¹⁹ "Let there be a covenant¹ between me and you, as there was between my father and your father. Behold, I am sending to you a present of silver and gold. Go, break your covenant with Baasha king of Israel, that he may withdraw from me." ²⁰ And Ben-hadad listened to King Asa and sent the commanders of his armies against the cities of Israel and conquered Ijon, Dan, Abel-beth-maacah, and all Chinneroth, with all the land of Naphtali. ²¹ And when Baasha heard of it, he stopped building Ramah, and he lived in Tirzah. ²² Then King Asa made a proclamation to all Judah, none was exempt, and they carried away the stones of Ramah and its timber, with which Baasha had been building, and with them King Asa built Geba of Benjamin and Mizpah. ²³ Now the rest of all the acts of Asa, all his might, and all that he did, and the cities that he built, are they not written in the Book of the Chronicles of the Kings of Judah? But in his old age he was diseased in his feet. ²⁴ And Asa slept with his fathers and was buried with his fathers in the city of David his father, and Jehoshaphat his son reigned in his place.

Nadab Reigns in Israel

²⁵ Nadab the son of Jeroboam began to reign over Israel in the second year of Asa king of Judah, and he reigned over Israel two years. ²⁶ He did what was evil in the sight of the LORD and walked in the way of his father, and in his sin which he made Israel to sin.

²⁷ Baasha the son of Ahijah, of the house of Issachar, conspired against him. And Baasha struck him down at Gibbethon, which belonged to the Philistines, for Nadab and all Israel were laying siege to Gibbethon. ²⁸ So Baasha killed him in the third year of Asa king of Judah and reigned in his place. ²⁹ And as soon as he was king, he killed all the house of Jeroboam. He left to the house of Jeroboam not one that breathed, until he had destroyed it, according to the word of the LORD that he spoke by his servant Ahijah the Shilonite.

¹ Or treaty; twice in this verse

[30] It was for the sins of Jeroboam that he sinned and that he made Israel to sin, and because of the anger to which he provoked the LORD, the God of Israel.

[31] Now the rest of the acts of Nadab and all that he did, are they not written in the Book of the Chronicles of the Kings of Israel? [32] And there was war between Asa and Baasha king of Israel all their days.

Baasha Reigns in Israel

[33] In the third year of Asa king of Judah, Baasha the son of Ahijah began to reign over all Israel at Tirzah, and he reigned twenty-four years. [34] He did what was evil in the sight of the LORD and walked in the way of Jeroboam and in his sin which he made Israel to sin.

16 And the word of the LORD came to Jehu the son of Hanani against Baasha, saying, [2] "Since I exalted you out of the dust and made you leader over my people Israel, and you have walked in the way of Jeroboam and have made my people Israel to sin, provoking me to anger with their sins, [3] behold, I will utterly sweep away Baasha and his house, and I will make your house like the house of Jeroboam the son of Nebat. [4] Anyone belonging to Baasha who dies in the city the dogs shall eat, and anyone of his who dies in the field the birds of the heavens shall eat."

[5] Now the rest of the acts of Baasha and what he did, and his might, are they not written in the Book of the Chronicles of the Kings of Israel? [6] And Baasha slept with his fathers and was buried at Tirzah, and Elah his son reigned in his place. [7] Moreover, the word of the LORD came by the prophet Jehu the son of Hanani against Baasha and his house, both because of all the evil that he did in the sight of the LORD, provoking him to anger with the work of his hands, in being like the house of Jeroboam, and also because he destroyed it.

Elah Reigns in Israel

[8] In the twenty-sixth year of Asa king of Judah, Elah the son of Baasha began to reign over Israel in Tirzah, and he reigned two years. [9] But his servant Zimri, commander of half his chariots, conspired against him. When he was at Tirzah, drinking himself drunk in the house of Arza, who was over the household in Tirzah, [10] Zimri came in and struck him down and kille[d] him, in the twenty-seventh year of Asa kin[g] of Judah, and reigned in his place.

[11] When he began to reign, as soon as h[e] had seated himself on his throne, he struc[k] down all the house of Baasha. He did n[ot] leave him a single male of his relatives o[r] his friends. [12] Thus Zimri destroyed all th[e] house of Baasha, according to the word o[f] the LORD, which he spoke against Baash[a] by Jehu the prophet, [13] for all the sins o[f] Baasha and the sins of Elah his son, whic[h] they sinned and which they made Israe[l] to sin, provoking the LORD God of Israel t[o] anger with their idols. [14] Now the rest of th[e] acts of Elah and all that he did, are they n[ot] written in the Book of the Chronicles of th[e] Kings of Israel?

Zimri Reigns in Israel

[15] In the twenty-seventh year of As[a] king of Judah, Zimri reigned seven day[s] in Tirzah. Now the troops were encampe[d] against Gibbethon, which belonged t[o] the Philistines, [16] and the troops wh[o] were encamped heard it said, "Zimri ha[s] conspired, and he has killed the king[."] Therefore all Israel made Omri, the com[-] mander of the army, king over Israel tha[t] day in the camp. [17] So Omri went up fro[m] Gibbethon, and all Israel with him, an[d] they besieged Tirzah. [18] And when Zim[ri] saw that the city was taken, he went int[o] the citadel of the king's house and burne[d] the king's house over him with fire an[d] died, [19] because of his sins that he com[-] mitted, doing evil in the sight of the LOR[D,] walking in the way of Jeroboam, and fo[r] his sin which he committed, making Israe[l] to sin. [20] Now the rest of the acts of Zimr[i] and the conspiracy that he made, are the[y] not written in the Book of the Chronicle[s] of the Kings of Israel?

Omri Reigns in Israel

[21] Then the people of Israel were divide[d] into two parts. Half of the people followe[d] Tibni the son of Ginath, to make him kin[g,] and half followed Omri. [22] But the peopl[e] who followed Omri overcame the peopl[e] who followed Tibni the son of Ginath. S[o] Tibni died, and Omri became king. [23] In th[e] thirty-first year of Asa king of Judah, Omr[i] began to reign over Israel, and he reigne[d] for twelve years; six years he reigned i[n] Tirzah. [24] He bought the hill of Samari[a]

rom Shemer for two talents[1] of silver, and
e fortified the hill and called the name
f the city that he built Samaria, after the
ame of Shemer, the owner of the hill.

²⁵ Omri did what was evil in the sight
f the LORD, and did more evil than all
vho were before him. ²⁶ For he walked in
ll the way of Jeroboam the son of Nebat,
nd in the sins that he made Israel to sin,
rovoking the LORD, the God of Israel, to
nger by their idols. ²⁷ Now the rest of the
cts of Omri that he did, and the might
hat he showed, are they not written in
he Book of the Chronicles of the Kings of
srael? ²⁸ And Omri slept with his fathers
nd was buried in Samaria, and Ahab his
on reigned in his place.

Ahab Reigns in Israel

²⁹ In the thirty-eighth year of Asa king
f Judah, Ahab the son of Omri began to
eign over Israel, and Ahab the son of Omri
eigned over Israel in Samaria twenty-two
ears. ³⁰ And Ahab the son of Omri did evil
n the sight of the LORD, more than all who
vere before him. ³¹ And as if it had been a
ight thing for him to walk in the sins of
eroboam the son of Nebat, he took for his
vife Jezebel the daughter of Ethbaal king
f the Sidonians, and went and served Baal
nd worshiped him. ³² He erected an altar
or Baal in the house of Baal, which he built
n Samaria. ³³ And Ahab made an Asherah.
Ahab did more to provoke the LORD, the
God of Israel, to anger than all the kings
f Israel who were before him. ³⁴ In his
ays Hiel of Bethel built Jericho. He laid
ts foundation at the cost of Abiram his
irstborn, and set up its gates at the cost
f his youngest son Segub, according to
he word of the LORD, which he spoke by
oshua the son of Nun.

Elijah Predicts a Drought

17 Now Elijah the Tishbite, of Tishbe[2]
in Gilead, said to Ahab, "As the
LORD, the God of Israel, lives, before whom
stand, there shall be neither dew nor rain
hese years, except by my word." ² And the
vord of the LORD came to him: ³ "Depart
rom here and turn eastward and hide
ourself by the brook Cherith, which is
ast of the Jordan. ⁴ You shall drink from
he brook, and I have commanded the
avens to feed you there." ⁵ So he went and

did according to the word of the LORD.
He went and lived by the brook Cherith
that is east of the Jordan. ⁶ And the ravens
brought him bread and meat in the morning, and bread and meat in the evening,
and he drank from the brook. ⁷ And after
a while the brook dried up, because there
was no rain in the land.

The Widow of Zarephath

⁸ Then the word of the LORD came to him,
⁹ "Arise, go to Zarephath, which belongs to
Sidon, and dwell there. Behold, I have commanded a widow there to feed you." ¹⁰ So
he arose and went to Zarephath. And when
he came to the gate of the city, behold, a
widow was there gathering sticks. And he
called to her and said, "Bring me a little
water in a vessel, that I may drink." ¹¹ And
as she was going to bring it, he called to
her and said, "Bring me a morsel of bread
in your hand." ¹² And she said, "As the LORD
your God lives, I have nothing baked, only
a handful of flour in a jar and a little oil in
a jug. And now I am gathering a couple of
sticks that I may go in and prepare it for
myself and my son, that we may eat it and
die." ¹³ And Elijah said to her, "Do not fear;
go and do as you have said. But first make
me a little cake of it and bring it to me,
and afterward make something for yourself and your son. ¹⁴ For thus says the LORD,
the God of Israel, 'The jar of flour shall not
be spent, and the jug of oil shall not be
empty, until the day that the LORD sends
rain upon the earth.'" ¹⁵ And she went and
did as Elijah said. And she and he and her
household ate for many days. ¹⁶ The jar of
flour was not spent, neither did the jug of
oil become empty, according to the word
of the LORD that he spoke by Elijah.

Elijah Raises the Widow's Son

¹⁷ After this the son of the woman, the
mistress of the house, became ill. And his
illness was so severe that there was no
breath left in him. ¹⁸ And she said to Elijah,
"What have you against me, O man of God?
You have come to me to bring my sin to
remembrance and to cause the death of my
son!" ¹⁹ And he said to her, "Give me your
son." And he took him from her arms and
carried him up into the upper chamber
where he lodged, and laid him on his own
bed. ²⁰ And he cried to the LORD, "O LORD

A *talent* was about 75 pounds or 34 kilograms ²Septuagint; Hebrew *of the settlers* my God, have you brought calamity even upon the widow with whom I sojourn, by killing her son?" [21] Then he stretched himself upon the child three times and cried to the LORD, "O LORD my God, let this child's life[1] come into him again." [22] And the LORD listened to the voice of Elijah. And the life of the child came into him again, and he revived. [23] And Elijah took the child and brought him down from the upper chamber into the house and delivered him to his mother. And Elijah said, "See, your son lives." [24] And the woman said to Elijah, "Now I know that you are a man of God, and that the word of the LORD in your mouth is truth."

Elijah Confronts Ahab

18 After many days the word of the LORD came to Elijah, in the third year, saying, "Go, show yourself to Ahab, and I will send rain upon the earth." [2] So Elijah went to show himself to Ahab. Now the famine was severe in Samaria. [3] And Ahab called Obadiah, who was over the household. (Now Obadiah feared the LORD greatly, [4] and when Jezebel cut off the prophets of the LORD, Obadiah took a hundred prophets and hid them by fifties in a cave and fed them with bread and water.) [5] And Ahab said to Obadiah, "Go through the land to all the springs of water and to all the valleys. Perhaps we may find grass and save the horses and mules alive, and not lose some of the animals." [6] So they divided the land between them to pass through it. Ahab went in one direction by himself, and Obadiah went in another direction by himself.

[7] And as Obadiah was on the way, behold, Elijah met him. And Obadiah recognized him and fell on his face and said, "Is it you, my lord Elijah?" [8] And he answered him, "It is I. Go, tell your lord, 'Behold, Elijah is here.'" [9] And he said, "How have I sinned, that you would give your servant into the hand of Ahab, to kill me? [10] As the LORD your God lives, there is no nation or kingdom where my lord has not sent to seek you. And when they would say, 'He is not here,' he would take an oath of the kingdom or nation, that they had not found you. [11] And now you say, 'Go, tell your lord, "Behold, Elijah is here."' [12] And as soon as I have gone from you, the Spirit of the LORD will carry

you I know not where. And so, when I com[e] and tell Ahab and he cannot find you, h[e] will kill me, although I your servant hav[e] feared the LORD from my youth. [13] Has it no[t] been told my lord what I did when Jezebe[l] killed the prophets of the LORD, how I hi[d] a hundred men of the LORD's prophets b[y] fifties in a cave and fed them with brea[d] and water? [14] And now you say, 'Go, te[ll] your lord, "Behold, Elijah is here"'; an[d] he will kill me." [15] And Elijah said, "As th[e] LORD of hosts lives, before whom I stan[d], I will surely show myself to him today." [16] S[o] Obadiah went to meet Ahab, and told hi[m]. And Ahab went to meet Elijah.

[17] When Ahab saw Elijah, Ahab said t[o] him, "Is it you, you troubler of Israel?" [18] And he answered, "I have not trouble[d] Israel, but you have, and your father'[s] house, because you have abandoned th[e] commandments of the LORD and followe[d] the Baals. [19] Now therefore send and gathe[r] all Israel to me at Mount Carmel, and th[e] 450 prophets of Baal and the 400 prophet[s] of Asherah, who eat at Jezebel's table."

The Prophets of Baal Defeated

[20] So Ahab sent to all the people of Israe[l] and gathered the prophets together a[t] Mount Carmel. [21] And Elijah came near t[o] all the people and said, "How long will yo[u] go limping between two different opin[i]ons? If the LORD is God, follow him; bu[t] if Baal, then follow him." And the peopl[e] did not answer him a word. [22] Then Elija[h] said to the people, "I, even I only, am lef[t] a prophet of the LORD, but Baal's proph[e]ets are 450 men. [23] Let two bulls be give[n] to us, and let them choose one bull fo[r] themselves and cut it in pieces and la[y] it on the wood, but put no fire to it. An[d] I will prepare the other bull and lay it o[n] the wood and put no fire to it. [24] And yo[u] call upon the name of your god, and I wi[ll] call upon the name of the LORD, and th[e] God who answers by fire, he is God." An[d] all the people answered, "It is well spo[ken." [25] Then Elijah said to the prophet[s] of Baal, "Choose for yourselves one bu[ll] and prepare it first, for you are many, an[d] call upon the name of your god, but pu[t] no fire to it." [26] And they took the bull tha[t] was given them, and they prepared it an[d] called upon the name of Baal from morn[ing until noon, saying, "O Baal, answe[r

---

[1] Or *soul*; also verse 22

s!" But there was no voice, and no one answered. And they limped around the altar that they had made. ²⁷ And at noon Elijah mocked them, saying, "Cry aloud, for he is a god. Either he is musing, or he is relieving himself, or he is on a journey, or perhaps he is asleep and must be awakened." ²⁸ And they cried aloud and cut themselves after their custom with swords and lances, until the blood gushed out upon them. ²⁹ And as midday passed, they raved on until the time of the offering of the oblation, but there was no voice. No one answered; no one paid attention.

³⁰ Then Elijah said to all the people, "Come near to me." And all the people came near to him. And he repaired the altar of the LORD that had been thrown down. ³¹ Elijah took twelve stones, according to the number of the tribes of the sons of Jacob, to whom the word of the LORD came, saying, "Israel shall be your name," ³² and with the stones he built an altar in the name of the LORD. And he made a trench about the altar, as great as would contain two seahs¹ of seed. ³³ And he put the wood in order and cut the bull in pieces and laid it on the wood. And he said, "Fill four jars with water and pour it on the burnt offering and on the wood." ³⁴ And he said, "Do it a second time." And they did it a second time. And he said, "Do it a third time." And they did it a third time. ³⁵ And the water ran around the altar and filled the trench also with water.

³⁶ And at the time of the offering of the oblation, Elijah the prophet came near and said, "O LORD, God of Abraham, Isaac, and Israel, let it be known this day that you are God in Israel, and that I am your servant, and that I have done all these things at your word. ³⁷ Answer me, O LORD, answer me, that this people may know that you, O LORD, are God, and that you have turned their hearts back." ³⁸ Then the fire of the LORD fell and consumed the burnt offering and the wood and the stones and the dust, and licked up the water that was in the trench. ³⁹ And when all the people saw it, they fell on their faces and said, "The LORD, he is God; the LORD, he is God." ⁴⁰ And Elijah said to them, "Seize the prophets of Baal; let not one of them escape." And they seized them. And Elijah brought them down to the brook Kishon and slaughtered them there.

The LORD Sends Rain

⁴¹ And Elijah said to Ahab, "Go up, eat and drink, for there is a sound of the rushing of rain." ⁴² So Ahab went up to eat and to drink. And Elijah went up to the top of Mount Carmel. And he bowed himself down on the earth and put his face between his knees. ⁴³ And he said to his servant, "Go up now, look toward the sea." And he went up and looked and said, "There is nothing." And he said, "Go again," seven times. ⁴⁴ And at the seventh time he said, "Behold, a little cloud like a man's hand is rising from the sea." And he said, "Go up, say to Ahab, 'Prepare your chariot and go down, lest the rain stop you.'" ⁴⁵ And in a little while the heavens grew black with clouds and wind, and there was a great rain. And Ahab rode and went to Jezreel. ⁴⁶ And the hand of the LORD was on Elijah, and he gathered up his garment and ran before Ahab to the entrance of Jezreel.

Elijah Flees Jezebel

19 Ahab told Jezebel all that Elijah had done, and how he had killed all the prophets with the sword. ² Then Jezebel sent a messenger to Elijah, saying, "So may the gods do to me and more also, if I do not make your life as the life of one of them by this time tomorrow." ³ Then he was afraid, and he arose and ran for his life and came to Beersheba, which belongs to Judah, and left his servant there.

⁴ But he himself went a day's journey into the wilderness and came and sat down under a broom tree. And he asked that he might die, saying, "It is enough; now, O LORD, take away my life, for I am no better than my fathers." ⁵ And he lay down and slept under a broom tree. And behold, an angel touched him and said to him, "Arise and eat." ⁶ And he looked, and behold, there was at his head a cake baked on hot stones and a jar of water. And he ate and drank and lay down again. ⁷ And the angel of the LORD came again a second time and touched him and said, "Arise and eat, for the journey is too great for you." ⁸ And he arose and ate and drank, and went in the strength of that food forty days and forty nights to Horeb, the mount of God.

¹ A *seah* was about 7 quarts or 7.3 liters

The LORD Speaks to Elijah

⁹ There he came to a cave and lodged in it. And behold, the word of the LORD came to him, and he said to him, "What are you doing here, Elijah?" ¹⁰ He said, "I have been very jealous for the LORD, the God of hosts. For the people of Israel have forsaken your covenant, thrown down your altars, and killed your prophets with the sword, and I, even I only, am left, and they seek my life, to take it away." ¹¹ And he said, "Go out and stand on the mount before the LORD." And behold, the LORD passed by, and a great and strong wind tore the mountains and broke in pieces the rocks before the LORD, but the LORD was not in the wind. And after the wind an earthquake, but the LORD was not in the earthquake. ¹² And after the earthquake a fire, but the LORD was not in the fire. And after the fire the sound of a low whisper.¹ ¹³ And when Elijah heard it, he wrapped his face in his cloak and went out and stood at the entrance of the cave. And behold, there came a voice to him and said, "What are you doing here, Elijah?" ¹⁴ He said, "I have been very jealous for the LORD, the God of hosts. For the people of Israel have forsaken your covenant, thrown down your altars, and killed your prophets with the sword, and I, even I only, am left, and they seek my life to take it away." ¹⁵ And the LORD said to him, "Go, return on your way to the wilderness of Damascus. And when you arrive, you shall anoint Hazael to be king over Syria, ¹⁶ And Jehu the son of Nimshi you shall anoint to be king over Israel, and Elisha the son of Shaphat of Abel-meholah you shall anoint to be prophet in your place. ¹⁷ And the one who escapes from the sword of Hazael shall Jehu put to death, and the one who escapes from the sword of Jehu shall Elisha put to death. ¹⁸ Yet I will leave seven thousand in Israel, all the knees that have not bowed to Baal, and every mouth that has not kissed him."

The Call of Elisha

¹⁹ So he departed from there and found Elisha the son of Shaphat, who was plowing with twelve yoke of oxen in front of

¹ Or a sound, a thin silence

Know Yourself

verses to read
1 Kings 19:1–8

If you never felt depressed, then you wouldn't be human. It's the nature of a rock to never get depressed, but you're not a rock; you're a human, and humans have emotions. The lows of life are what give you the ability to feel the highs. This world includes some bad things that are depressing. Don't get mad at yourself when those things show up in your life and sometimes get the best of you.

Elijah was depressed in this story. The world seemed to be out to get him, and he wanted nothing to do with it any longer. But look how God intervened. He didn't give Elijah some big revelation; he commanded him to do something simple but powerful: "Arise and eat" (1 Kings 19:5). Elijah didn't have a vision. He didn't see God in all his glory at that moment. But God met him where he was at, and Elijah just did what he was told to do.

Depression doesn't have to win. If you're willing to do what God asks you to do the minute he asks you, you can kick depression before it becomes too much for you to overcome. If God shows you that you have to do something like get out of bed and eat, then you've got to do it. When you get up and do something, you might see the depression start to lift. You have to make the effort to decide today whom you will follow—the voice of depression or the voice of God. Above all, remember God's great heart of tenderness toward you, even when all is darkness.

im, and he was with the twelfth. Elijah passed by him and cast his cloak upon him. ²⁰And he left the oxen and ran after Elijah and said, "Let me kiss my father and my mother, and then I will follow you." And he said to him, "Go back again, for what have I done to you?" ²¹And he returned from following him and took the yoke of oxen and sacrificed them and boiled their flesh with the yokes of the oxen and gave it to the people, and they ate. Then he arose and went after Elijah and assisted him.

Ahab's Wars with Syria

20 Ben-hadad the king of Syria gathered all his army together. Thirty-two kings were with him, and horses and chariots. And he went up and closed in on Samaria and fought against it. ²And he sent messengers into the city to Ahab king of Israel and said to him, "Thus says Ben-hadad: ³'Your silver and your gold are mine; your best wives and children also are mine.'" ⁴And the king of Israel answered, "As you say, my lord, O king, I am yours, and all that I have." ⁵The messengers came again and said, "Thus says Ben-hadad: 'I sent to you, saying, "Deliver to me your silver and your gold, your wives and your children." ⁶Nevertheless I will send my servants to you tomorrow about this time, and they shall search your house and the houses of your servants and lay hands on whatever pleases you and take it away.'"

⁷Then the king of Israel called all the elders of the land and said, "Mark, now, and see how this man is seeking trouble, for he sent to me for my wives and my children, and for my silver and my gold, and I did not refuse him." ⁸And all the elders and all the people said to him, "Do not listen or consent." ⁹So he said to the messengers of Ben-hadad, "Tell my lord the king, 'All that you first demanded of your servant I will do, but this thing I cannot do.'" And the messengers departed and brought him word again. ¹⁰Ben-hadad sent to him and said, "The gods do so to me and more also, if the dust of Samaria shall suffice for handfuls for all the people who follow me." ¹¹And the king of Israel answered, "Tell him, 'Let not him who straps on his armor boast himself as he who takes it off.'" ¹²When Ben-hadad heard this message as he was drinking with the kings in the booths, he said to his men, "Take your positions." And they took their positions against the city.

Ahab Defeats Ben-hadad

¹³And behold, a prophet came near to Ahab king of Israel and said, "Thus says the LORD, Have you seen all this great multitude? Behold, I will give it into your hand this day, and you shall know that I am the LORD." ¹⁴And Ahab said, "By whom?" He said, "Thus says the LORD, By the servants of the governors of the districts." Then he said, "Who shall begin the battle?" He answered, "You." ¹⁵Then he mustered the servants of the governors of the districts, and they were 232. And after them he mustered all the people of Israel, seven thousand.

¹⁶And they went out at noon, while Ben-hadad was drinking himself drunk in the booths, he and the thirty-two kings who helped him. ¹⁷The servants of the governors of the districts went out first. And Ben-hadad sent out scouts, and they reported to him, "Men are coming out from Samaria." ¹⁸He said, "If they have come out for peace, take them alive. Or if they have come out for war, take them alive."

¹⁹So these went out of the city, the servants of the governors of the districts and the army that followed them. ²⁰And each struck down his man. The Syrians fled, and Israel pursued them, but Ben-hadad king of Syria escaped on a horse with horsemen. ²¹And the king of Israel went out and struck the horses and chariots, and struck the Syrians with a great blow.

²²Then the prophet came near to the king of Israel and said to him, "Come, strengthen yourself, and consider well what you have to do, for in the spring the king of Syria will come up against you."

²³And the servants of the king of Syria said to him, "Their gods are gods of the hills, and so they were stronger than we. But let us fight against them in the plain, and surely we shall be stronger than they. ²⁴And do this: remove the kings, each from his post, and put commanders in their places, ²⁵and muster an army like the army that you have lost, horse for horse, and chariot for chariot. Then we will fight against them in the plain, and surely we shall be stronger than they." And he listened to their voice and did so.

Ahab Defeats Ben-hadad Again

²⁶ In the spring, Ben-hadad mustered the Syrians and went up to Aphek to fight against Israel. ²⁷ And the people of Israel were mustered and were provisioned and went against them. The people of Israel encamped before them like two little flocks of goats, but the Syrians filled the country. ²⁸ And a man of God came near and said to the king of Israel, "Thus says the LORD, 'Because the Syrians have said, "The LORD is a god of the hills but he is not a god of the valleys," therefore I will give all this great multitude into your hand, and you shall know that I am the LORD.'" ²⁹ And they encamped opposite one another seven days. Then on the seventh day the battle was joined. And the people of Israel struck down of the Syrians 100,000 foot soldiers in one day. ³⁰ And the rest fled into the city of Aphek, and the wall fell upon 27,000 men who were left.

Ben-hadad also fled and entered an inner chamber in the city. ³¹ And his servants said to him, "Behold now, we have heard that the kings of the house of Israel are merciful kings. Let us put sackcloth around our waists and ropes on our heads and go out to the king of Israel. Perhaps he will spare your life." ³² So they tied sackcloth around their waists and put ropes on their heads and went to the king of Israel and said, "Your servant Ben-hadad says, 'Please, let me live.'" And he said, "Does he still live? He is my brother." ³³ Now the men were watching for a sign, and they quickly took it up from him and said, "Yes, your brother Ben-hadad." Then he said, "Go and bring him." Then Ben-hadad came out to him, and he caused him to come up into the chariot. ³⁴ And Ben-hadad said to him, "The cities that my father took from your father I will restore, and you may establish bazaars for yourself in Damascus, as my father did in Samaria." And Ahab said, "I will let you go on these terms." So he made a covenant with him and let him go.

A Prophet Condemns Ben-hadad's Release

³⁵ And a certain man of the sons of the prophets said to his fellow at the command of the LORD, "Strike me, please." But the man refused to strike him. ³⁶ Then he said to him, "Because you have not obeyed the voice of the LORD, behold, as soon as you

have gone from me, a lion shall strike you down." And as soon as he had departed from him, a lion met him and struck him down. ³⁷ Then he found another man and said, "Strike me, please." And the man struck him—struck him and wounded him. ³⁸ So the prophet departed and waited for the king by the way, disguising himself with a bandage over his eyes. ³⁹ And as the king passed, he cried to the king and said, "Your servant went out into the midst of the battle, and behold, a soldier turned and brought a man to me and said, 'Guard this man; if by any means he is missing, your life shall be for his life, or else you shall pay a talent[1] of silver.' ⁴⁰ And as your servant was busy here and there, he was gone." The king of Israel said to him, "So shall your judgment be; you yourself have decided it." ⁴¹ Then he hurried to take the bandage away from his eyes, and the king of Israel recognized him as one of the prophets. ⁴² And he said to him, "Thus says the LORD, 'Because you have let go out of your hand the man whom I had devoted to destruction,[2] therefore your life shall be for his life and your people for his people.'" ⁴³ And the king of Israel went to his house vexed and sullen and came to Samaria.

Naboth's Vineyard

21 Now Naboth the Jezreelite had a vineyard in Jezreel, beside the palace of Ahab king of Samaria. ² And after this Ahab said to Naboth, "Give me your vineyard, that I may have it for a vegetable garden, because it is near my house, and I will give you a better vineyard for it; or if it seems good to you, I will give you its value in money." ³ But Naboth said to Ahab, "The LORD forbid that I should give you the inheritance of my fathers." ⁴ And Ahab went into his house vexed and sullen because of what Naboth the Jezreelite had said to him, for he had said, "I will not give you the inheritance of my fathers." And he lay down on his bed and turned away his face and would not eat food.

⁵ But Jezebel his wife came to him and said to him, "Why is your spirit so vexed that you eat no food?" ⁶ And he said to her, "Because I spoke to Naboth the Jezreelite and said to him, 'Give me your vineyard for money, or else, if it please you, I will give you another vineyard for it.' And he

---

[1] A *talent* was about 75 pounds or 34 kilograms [2] That is, set apart (devoted) as an offering to the Lord (for destruction)

answered, 'I will not give you my vineyard.'" [7] And Jezebel his wife said to him, "Do you now govern Israel? Arise and eat bread and let your heart be cheerful; I will give you the vineyard of Naboth the Jezreelite."

[8] So she wrote letters in Ahab's name and sealed them with his seal, and she sent the letters to the elders and the leaders who lived with Naboth in his city. [9] And she wrote in the letters, "Proclaim a fast, and set Naboth at the head of the people. [10] And set two worthless men opposite him, and let them bring a charge against him, saying, 'You have cursed[1] God and the king.' Then take him out and stone him to death." [11] And the men of his city, the elders and the leaders who lived in his city, did as Jezebel had sent word to them. As it was written in the letters that she had sent to them, [12] they proclaimed a fast and set Naboth at the head of the people. [13] And the two worthless men came in and sat opposite him. And the worthless men brought a charge against Naboth in the presence of the people, saying, "Naboth cursed God and the king." So they took him outside the city and stoned him to death with stones. [14] Then they sent to Jezebel, saying, "Naboth has been stoned; he is dead."

[15] As soon as Jezebel heard that Naboth had been stoned and was dead, Jezebel said to Ahab, "Arise, take possession of the vineyard of Naboth the Jezreelite, which he refused to give you for money, for Naboth is not alive, but dead." [16] And as soon as Ahab heard that Naboth was dead, Ahab arose to go down to the vineyard of Naboth the Jezreelite, to take possession of it.

The Lord Condemns Ahab

[17] Then the word of the Lord came to Elijah the Tishbite, saying, [18] "Arise, go down to meet Ahab king of Israel, who is in Samaria; behold, he is in the vineyard of Naboth, where he has gone to take possession. [19] And you shall say to him, 'Thus says the Lord, "Have you killed and also taken possession?"' And you shall say to him, 'Thus says the Lord: "In the place where dogs licked up the blood of Naboth shall dogs lick your own blood."'"

[20] Ahab said to Elijah, "Have you found me, O my enemy?" He answered, "I have found you, because you have sold yourself to do what is evil in the sight of the Lord.

[21] Behold, I will bring disaster upon you. I will utterly burn you up, and will cut off from Ahab every male, bond or free, in Israel. [22] And I will make your house like the house of Jeroboam the son of Nebat, and like the house of Baasha the son of Ahijah, for the anger to which you have provoked me, and because you have made Israel to sin. [23] And of Jezebel the Lord also said, 'The dogs shall eat Jezebel within the walls of Jezreel.' [24] Anyone belonging to Ahab who dies in the city the dogs shall eat, and anyone of his who dies in the open country the birds of the heavens shall eat."

Ahab's Repentance

[25] (There was none who sold himself to do what was evil in the sight of the Lord like Ahab, whom Jezebel his wife incited. [26] He acted very abominably in going after idols, as the Amorites had done, whom the Lord cast out before the people of Israel.)

[27] And when Ahab heard those words, he tore his clothes and put sackcloth on his flesh and fasted and lay in sackcloth and went about dejectedly. [28] And the word of the Lord came to Elijah the Tishbite, saying, [29] "Have you seen how Ahab has humbled himself before me? Because he has humbled himself before me, I will not bring the disaster in his days; but in his son's days I will bring the disaster upon his house."

Ahab and the False Prophets

22 For three years Syria and Israel continued without war. [2] But in the third year Jehoshaphat the king of Judah came down to the king of Israel. [3] And the king of Israel said to his servants, "Do you know that Ramoth-gilead belongs to us, and we keep quiet and do not take it out of the hand of the king of Syria?" [4] And he said to Jehoshaphat, "Will you go with me to battle at Ramoth-gilead?" And Jehoshaphat said to the king of Israel, "I am as you are, my people as your people, my horses as your horses."

[5] And Jehoshaphat said to the king of Israel, "Inquire first for the word of the Lord." [6] Then the king of Israel gathered the prophets together, about four hundred men, and said to them, "Shall I go to battle against Ramoth-gilead, or shall I refrain?" And they said, "Go up, for the

---

[1] Hebrew *blessed*; also verse 13

Lord will give it into the hand of the king." ⁷ But Jehoshaphat said, "Is there not here another prophet of the LORD of whom we may inquire?" ⁸ And the king of Israel said to Jehoshaphat, "There is yet one man by whom we may inquire of the LORD, Micaiah the son of Imlah, but I hate him, for he never prophesies good concerning me, but evil." And Jehoshaphat said, "Let not the king say so." ⁹ Then the king of Israel summoned an officer and said, "Bring quickly Micaiah the son of Imlah." ¹⁰ Now the king of Israel and Jehoshaphat the king of Judah were sitting on their thrones, arrayed in their robes, at the threshing floor at the entrance of the gate of Samaria, and all the prophets were prophesying before them. ¹¹ And Zedekiah the son of Chenaanah made for himself horns of iron and said, "Thus says the LORD, 'With these you shall push the Syrians until they are destroyed.' " ¹² And all the prophets prophesied so and said, "Go up to Ramoth-gilead and triumph; the LORD will give it into the hand of the king."

Micaiah Prophesies Against Ahab

¹³ And the messenger who went to summon Micaiah said to him, "Behold, the words of the prophets with one accord are favorable to the king. Let your word be like the word of one of them, and speak favorably." ¹⁴ But Micaiah said, "As the LORD lives, what the LORD says to me, that I will speak." ¹⁵ And when he had come to the king, the king said to him, "Micaiah, shall we go to Ramoth-gilead to battle, or shall we refrain?" And he answered him, "Go up and triumph; the LORD will give it into the hand of the king." ¹⁶ But the king said to him, "How many times shall I make you swear that you speak to me nothing but the truth in the name of the LORD?" ¹⁷ And he said, "I saw all Israel scattered on the mountains, as sheep that have no shepherd. And the LORD said, 'These have no master; let each return to his home in peace.' " ¹⁸ And the king of Israel said to Jehoshaphat, "Did I not tell you that he would not prophesy good concerning me, but evil?" ¹⁹ And Micaiah said, "Therefore hear the word of the LORD: I saw the LORD sitting on his throne, and all the host of heaven standing beside him on his right hand and on his left; ²⁰ and the LORD said, 'Who will entice Ahab, that he may go up and fall at Ramoth-gilead?' And one said one thing, and another said another. ²¹ Then a spirit came forward and stood before the LORD, saying, 'I will entice him.' ²² And the LORD said to him, 'By what means?' And he said, 'I will go out, and will be a lying spirit in the mouth of all his prophets.' And he said, 'You are to entice him, and you shall succeed; go out and do so.' ²³ Now therefore behold, the LORD has put a lying spirit in the mouth of all these your prophets; the LORD has declared disaster for you."

²⁴ Then Zedekiah the son of Chenaanah came near and struck Micaiah on the cheek and said, "How did the Spirit of the LORD go from me to speak to you?" ²⁵ And Micaiah said, "Behold, you shall see on that day when you go into an inner chamber to hide yourself." ²⁶ And the king of Israel said, "Seize Micaiah, and take him back to Amon the governor of the city and to Joash the king's son, ²⁷ and say, 'Thus says the king, "Put this fellow in prison and feed him meager rations of bread and water, until I come in peace."' " ²⁸ And Micaiah said, "If you return in peace, the LORD has not spoken by me." And he said, "Hear, all you peoples!"

Ahab Killed in Battle

²⁹ So the king of Israel and Jehoshaphat the king of Judah went up to Ramoth-gilead. ³⁰ And the king of Israel said to Jehoshaphat, "I will disguise myself and go into battle, but you wear your robes." And the king of Israel disguised himself and went into battle. ³¹ Now the king of Syria had commanded the thirty-two captains of his chariots, "Fight with neither small nor great, but only with the king of Israel." ³² And when the captains of the chariots saw Jehoshaphat, they said, "It is surely the king of Israel." So they turned to fight against him. And Jehoshaphat cried out. ³³ And when the captains of the chariots saw that it was not the king of Israel, they turned back from pursuing him. ³⁴ But a certain man drew his bow at random[1] and struck the king of Israel between the scale armor and the breastplate. Therefore he said to the driver of his chariot, "Turn around and carry me out of the battle, for I am wounded." ³⁵ And the battle continued that day, and the king was propped up in his chariot facing the Syrians, until at eve-

[1] Hebrew in his innocence

ning he died. And the blood of the wound flowed into the bottom of the chariot. ³⁶ And about sunset a cry went through the army, "Every man to his city, and every man to his country!"

³⁷ So the king died, and was brought to Samaria. And they buried the king in Samaria. ³⁸ And they washed the chariot by the pool of Samaria, and the dogs licked up his blood, and the prostitutes washed themselves in it, according to the word of the LORD that he had spoken. ³⁹ Now the rest of the acts of Ahab and all that he did, and the ivory house that he built and all the cities that he built, are they not written in the Book of the Chronicles of the Kings of Israel? ⁴⁰ So Ahab slept with his fathers, and Ahaziah his son reigned in his place.

Jehoshaphat Reigns in Judah

⁴¹ Jehoshaphat the son of Asa began to reign over Judah in the fourth year of Ahab king of Israel. ⁴² Jehoshaphat was thirty-five years old when he began to reign, and he reigned twenty-five years in Jerusalem. His mother's name was Azubah the daughter of Shilhi. ⁴³ He walked in all the way of Asa his father. He did not turn aside from it, doing what was right in the sight of the LORD. Yet the high places were not taken away, and the people still sacrificed and made offerings on the high places. ⁴⁴ Jehoshaphat also made peace with the king of Israel.

⁴⁵ Now the rest of the acts of Jehoshaphat, and his might that he showed, and how he warred, are they not written in the Book of the Chronicles of the Kings of Judah? ⁴⁶ And from the land he exterminated the remnant of the male cult prostitutes who remained in the days of his father Asa.

⁴⁷ There was no king in Edom; a deputy was king. ⁴⁸ Jehoshaphat made ships of Tarshish to go to Ophir for gold, but they did not go, for the ships were wrecked at Ezion-geber. ⁴⁹ Then Ahaziah the son of Ahab said to Jehoshaphat, "Let my servants go with your servants in the ships," but Jehoshaphat was not willing. ⁵⁰ And Jehoshaphat slept with his fathers and was buried with his fathers in the city of David his father, and Jehoram his son reigned in his place.

Ahaziah Reigns in Israel

⁵¹ Ahaziah the son of Ahab began to reign over Israel in Samaria in the seventeenth year of Jehoshaphat king of Judah, and he reigned two years over Israel. ⁵² He did what was evil in the sight of the LORD and walked in the way of his father and in the way of his mother and in the way of Jeroboam the son of Nebat, who made Israel to sin. ⁵³ He served Baal and worshiped him and provoked the LORD, the God of Israel, to anger in every way that his father had done.

INTRODUCTION TO

2 Kings

Author: Unknown
Time: 561–538 B.C.
Place: Possibly Babylon
Written to: God's people, the Israelites

the gist

The book of 2 Kings continues the account of the divided kingdoms of Israel and Judah. Though many of the kings were evil and did stupid things, 2 Kings shows that God will still do what he promised to do. He doesn't let the sins of his people keep him from his plans.

things to look for

- The good kings (see 2 Kings 9–10; 11:21–12:21; 14:1–22; 15:1–7, 32–38; 18–20; 22:1–23:30)

- The bad kings (see 2 Kings 3–8; 13; 14:23–29; 15:8–31; 16–17; 21; 23:31–25:30)

- How even the good kings messed up sometimes (see 2 Kings 10:30–31)

Trust God's Presence

He said, "Do not be afraid, for those who are with us are more than those who are with them." Then Elisha prayed and said, "O LORD, please open his eyes that he may see." So the LORD opened the eyes of the young man, and he saw, and behold, the mountain was full of horses and chariots of fire all around Elisha.

2 Kings 6:16–17

There are times in life when everything looks lost. But when things look their worst, don't always be so sure. For the God Girl, the only thing that is sure is that God is always present and his promises can be trusted. If you know the gospel, then you know what God has promised to those who love him. And though we all mess up so often, he will always be faithful and his Word will always be true.

In 2 Kings we see the people of God in the same mess as in 1 Kings. They were one nation, divided. Foreign armies were invading and conquering, and many times all looked lost, but for the prophet Elisha one thing was sure: God was still in control. So when the king of Aram sent his army to destroy Elisha, he was able to rest in the confidence that God would fight for him. Though the naked eye could not see the forces of God surrounding them, the spiritual eye could, and so Elisha prayed that his fearful servant would see what others couldn't see.

When all around you is falling down, look up. Use your spiritual eyes to see the truth that God is always with you and always protecting you. All you have to do is trust him. Trust him to do what needs to be done in order to save you. And trust that no matter how painful life becomes, he is still all-knowing, all-good, and totally taking care of everything.

As you read 2 Kings, notice the pattern of a people struggling spiritually but being repeatedly drawn back to the Father. See how shortsighted they were when they doubted and looked away from God, and how faithful he was whenever they called on his name. Though the book has a rather unhappy ending, it's not the end of the story. Read this, as you do all other Bible books, in the light of the New Testament and the coming of Christ, remembering all that God has done for his people no matter how sinful they are.

Must-Know Verses

And when the Syrians came down against him, Elisha prayed to the LORD and said, "Please strike this people with blindness." So he struck them with blindness in accordance with the prayer of Elisha. *2 Kings 6:18*

" 'In the territory of Jezreel the dogs shall eat the flesh of Jezebel, and the corpse of Jezebel shall be as dung on the face of the field in the territory of Jezreel, so that no one can say, This is Jezebel.' " *2 Kings 9:36–37*

But Jehu was not careful to walk in the law of the LORD, the God of Israel, with all his heart. He did not turn from the sins of Jeroboam, which he made Israel to sin. *2 Kings 10:31*

"Thus says the LORD, the God of David your father: I have heard your prayer; I have seen your tears. Behold, I will heal you." *2 Kings 20:5*

2 Kings

Elijah Denounces Ahaziah

1 After the death of Ahab, Moab rebelled against Israel.

²Now Ahaziah fell through the lattice in his upper chamber in Samaria, and lay sick; so he sent messengers, telling them, "Go, inquire of Baal-zebub, the god of Ekron, whether I shall recover from this sickness." ³But the angel of the LORD said to Elijah the Tishbite, "Arise, go up to meet the messengers of the king of Samaria, and say to them, 'Is it because there is no God in Israel that you are going to inquire of Baal-zebub, the god of Ekron? ⁴Now therefore thus says the LORD, You shall not come down from the bed to which you have gone up, but you shall surely die.'" So Elijah went.

⁵The messengers returned to the king, and he said to them, "Why have you returned?" ⁶And they said to him, "There came a man to meet us, and said to us, 'Go back to the king who sent you, and say to him, Thus says the LORD, Is it because there is no God in Israel that you are sending to inquire of Baal-zebub, the god of Ekron? Therefore you shall not come down from the bed to which you have gone up, but you shall surely die.'" ⁷He said to them, "What kind of man was he who came to meet you and told you these things?" ⁸They answered him, "He wore a garment of hair, with a belt of leather about his waist." And he said, "It is Elijah the Tishbite."

⁹Then the king sent to him a captain of fifty men with his fifty. He went up to Elijah, who was sitting on the top of a hill, and said to him, "O man of God, the king says, 'Come down.'" ¹⁰But Elijah answered the captain of fifty, "If I am a man of God, let fire come down from heaven and consume you and your fifty." Then fire came down from heaven and consumed him and his fifty.

¹¹Again the king sent to him another captain of fifty men with his fifty. And he answered and said to him, "O man of God, this is the king's order, 'Come down quickly!'" ¹²But Elijah answered them, "If I am a man of God, let fire come down from heaven and consume you and your fifty." Then the fire of God came down from heaven and consumed him and his fifty.

¹³Again the king sent the captain of a third fifty with his fifty. And the third captain of fifty went up and came and fell on his knees before Elijah and entreated him, "O man of God, please let my life, and the life of these fifty servants of yours, be precious in your sight. ¹⁴Behold, fire came down from heaven and consumed the two former captains of fifty men with their fifties, but now let my life be precious in your sight." ¹⁵Then the angel of the LORD said to Elijah, "Go down with him; do not be afraid of him." So he arose and went down with him to the king ¹⁶and said to him, "Thus says the LORD, 'Because you have sent messengers to inquire of Baal-zebub, the god of Ekron—is it because there is no God in Israel to inquire of his word?—therefore you shall not come down from the bed to which you have gone up, but you shall surely die.'"

¹⁷So he died according to the word of the LORD that Elijah had spoken. Jehoram became king in his place in the second year of Jehoram the son of Jehoshaphat, king of Judah, because Ahaziah had no son. ¹⁸Now the rest of the acts of Ahaziah that he did, are they not written in the Book of the Chronicles of the Kings of Israel?

Elijah Taken to Heaven

2 Now when the LORD was about to take Elijah up to heaven by a whirlwind, Elijah and Elisha were on their way from Gilgal. ²And Elijah said to Elisha, "Please stay here, for the LORD has sent me as far as Bethel." But Elisha said, "As the LORD lives, and as you yourself live, I will not leave you." So they went down to Bethel. ³And the sons of the prophets who were in

Bethel came out to Elisha and said to him, "Do you know that today the LORD will take away your master from over you?" And he said, "Yes, I know it; keep quiet."

⁴Elijah said to him, "Elisha, please stay here, for the LORD has sent me to Jericho." But he said, "As the LORD lives, and as you yourself live, I will not leave you." So they came to Jericho. ⁵The sons of the prophets who were at Jericho drew near to Elisha and said to him, "Do you know that today the LORD will take away your master from over you?" And he answered, "Yes, I know it; keep quiet."

⁶Then Elijah said to him, "Please stay here, for the LORD has sent me to the Jordan." But he said, "As the LORD lives, and as you yourself live, I will not leave you." So the two of them went on. ⁷Fifty men of the sons of the prophets also went and stood at some distance from them, as they both were standing by the Jordan. ⁸Then Elijah took his cloak and rolled it up and struck the water, and the water was parted to the one side and to the other, till the two of them could go over on dry ground.

Ask Yourself . . .

ABOUT YOUR WISHES

- If God asked me what one thing I wanted, what would it be?
- How would my life change if I got what I wished for?
- How would that change my relationship with God?
- What do I think of Elisha's request in 2 Kings 2:9?

⁹When they had crossed, Elijah said to Elisha, "Ask what I shall do for you, before I am taken from you." And Elisha said, "Please let there be a double portion of your spirit on me." ¹⁰And he said, "You have asked a hard thing; yet, if you see me as I am being taken from you, it shall be so for you, but if you do not see me, it shall not be so." ¹¹And as they still went on and talked, behold, chariots of fire and horses of fire

separated the two of them. And Elijah went up by a whirlwind into heaven. ¹²And Elisha saw it and he cried, "My father, my father! The chariots of Israel and its horsemen!" And he saw him no more.

Then he took hold of his own clothes and tore them in two pieces. ¹³And he took up the cloak of Elijah that had fallen from him and went back and stood on the bank of the Jordan. ¹⁴Then he took the cloak of Elijah that had fallen from him and struck the water, saying, "Where is the LORD, the God of Elijah?" And when he had struck the water, the water was parted to the one side and to the other, and Elisha went over.

Elisha Succeeds Elijah

¹⁵Now when the sons of the prophets who were at Jericho saw him opposite them, they said, "The spirit of Elijah rests on Elisha." And they came to meet him and bowed to the ground before him. ¹⁶And they said to him, "Behold now, there are with your servants fifty strong men. Please let them go and seek your master. It may be that the Spirit of the LORD has caught him up and cast him upon some mountain or into some valley." And he said, "You shall not send." ¹⁷But when they urged him till he was ashamed, he said, "Send." They sent therefore fifty men. And for three days they sought him but did not find him. ¹⁸And they came back to him while he was staying at Jericho, and he said to them, "Did I not say to you, 'Do not go'?"

¹⁹Now the men of the city said to Elisha, "Behold, the situation of this city is pleasant, as my lord sees, but the water is bad, and the land is unfruitful." ²⁰He said, "Bring me a new bowl, and put salt in it." So they brought it to him. ²¹Then he went out to the spring of water and threw salt in it and said, "Thus says the LORD, I have healed this water; from now on neither death nor miscarriage shall come from it." ²²So the water has been healed to this day, according to the word that Elisha spoke.

²³He went up from there to Bethel, and while he was going up on the way, some small boys came out of the city and jeered at him, saying, "Go up, you baldhead! Go up, you baldhead!" ²⁴And he turned around, and when he saw them, he cursed them in the name of the LORD. And two she-bears came out of the woods and tore forty-two of the boys. ²⁵From there he went on to

Mount Carmel, and from there he returned to Samaria.

Moab Rebels Against Israel

3 In the eighteenth year of Jehoshaphat king of Judah, Jehoram the son of Ahab became king over Israel in Samaria, and he reigned twelve years. ² He did what was evil in the sight of the LORD, though not like his father and mother, for he put away the pillar of Baal that his father had made. ³ Nevertheless, he clung to the sin of Jeroboam the son of Nebat, which he made Israel to sin; he did not depart from it.

⁴ Now Mesha king of Moab was a sheep breeder, and he had to deliver to the king of Israel 100,000 lambs and the wool of 100,000 rams. ⁵ But when Ahab died, the king of Moab rebelled against the king of Israel. ⁶ So King Jehoram marched out of Samaria at that time and mustered all Israel. ⁷ And he went and sent word to Jehoshaphat king of Judah, "The king of Moab has rebelled against me. Will you go with me to battle against Moab?" And he said, "I will go. I am as you are, my people as your people, my horses as your horses." ⁸ Then he said, "By which way shall we march?" Jehoram answered, "By the way of the wilderness of Edom."

⁹ So the king of Israel went with the king of Judah and the king of Edom. And when they had made a circuitous march of seven days, there was no water for the army or for the animals that followed them. ¹⁰ Then the king of Israel said, "Alas! The LORD has called these three kings to give them into the hand of Moab." ¹¹ And Jehoshaphat said, "Is there no prophet of the LORD here, through whom we may inquire of the LORD?" Then one of the king of Israel's servants answered, "Elisha the son of Shaphat is here, who poured water on the hands of Elijah." ¹² And Jehoshaphat said, "The word of the LORD is with him." So the king of Israel and Jehoshaphat and the king of Edom went down to him.

¹³ And Elisha said to the king of Israel, "What have I to do with you? Go to the prophets of your father and to the prophets of your mother." But the king of Israel said to him, "No; it is the LORD who has called these three kings to give them into the hand of Moab." ¹⁴ And Elisha said, "As the LORD of hosts lives, before whom

I stand, were it not that I have regard for Jehoshaphat the king of Judah, I would neither look at you nor see you. ¹⁵ But now bring me a musician." And when the musician played, the hand of the LORD came upon him. ¹⁶ And he said, "Thus says the LORD, 'I will make this dry streambed full of pools.' ¹⁷ For thus says the LORD, 'You shall not see wind or rain, but that streambed shall be filled with water, so that you shall drink, you, your livestock, and your animals.' ¹⁸ This is a light thing in the sight of the LORD. He will also give the Moabites into your hand, ¹⁹ and you shall attack every fortified city and every choice city, and shall fell every good tree and stop up all springs of water and ruin every good piece of land with stones." ²⁰ The next morning, about the time of offering the sacrifice, behold, water came from the direction of Edom, till the country was filled with water.

²¹ When all the Moabites heard that the kings had come up to fight against them, all who were able to put on armor, from the youngest to the oldest, were called out and were drawn up at the border. ²² And when they rose early in the morning and the sun shone on the water, the Moabites saw the water opposite them as red as blood. ²³ And they said, "This is blood; the kings have surely fought together and struck one another down. Now then, Moab, to the spoil!" ²⁴ But when they came to the camp of Israel, the Israelites rose and struck the Moabites, till they fled before them. And they went forward, striking the Moabites as they went.¹ ²⁵ And they overthrew the cities, and on every good piece of land every man threw a stone until it was covered. They stopped every spring of water and felled all the good trees, till only its stones were left in Kir-hareseth, and the slingers surrounded and attacked it. ²⁶ When the king of Moab saw that the battle was going against him, he took with him 700 swordsmen to break through, opposite the king of Edom, but they could not. ²⁷ Then he took his oldest son who was to reign in his place and offered him for a burnt offering on the wall. And there came great wrath against Israel. And they withdrew from him and returned to their own land.

¹ Septuagint; the meaning of the Hebrew is uncertain

Elisha and the Widow's Oil

4 Now the wife of one of the sons of the prophets cried to Elisha, "Your servant my husband is dead, and you know that your servant feared the LORD, but the creditor has come to take my two children to be his slaves." ²And Elisha said to her, "What shall I do for you? Tell me; what have you in the house?" And she said, "Your servant has nothing in the house except a jar of oil." ³Then he said, "Go outside, borrow vessels from all your neighbors, empty vessels and not too few. ⁴Then go in and shut the door behind yourself and your sons and pour into all these vessels. And when one is full, set it aside." ⁵So she went from him and shut the door behind herself and her sons. And as she poured they brought the vessels to her. ⁶When the vessels were full, she said to her son, "Bring me another vessel." And he said to her, "There is not another." Then the oil stopped flowing. ⁷She came and told the man of God, and he said, "Go, sell the oil and pay your debts, and you and your sons can live on the rest."

Elisha and the Shunammite Woman

⁸One day Elisha went on to Shunem, where a wealthy woman lived, who urged him to eat some food. So whenever he passed that way, he would turn in there to eat food. ⁹And she said to her husband, "Behold now, I know that this is a holy man of God who is continually passing our way. ¹⁰Let us make a small room on the roof with walls and put there for him a bed, a table, a chair, and a lamp, so that whenever he comes to us, he can go in there."

¹¹One day he came there, and he turned into the chamber and rested there. ¹²And he said to Gehazi his servant, "Call this Shunammite." When he had called her, she stood before him. ¹³And he said to him, "Say now to her, 'See, you have taken all this trouble for us; what is to be done for you? Would you have a word spoken on your behalf to the king or to the commander of the army?'" She answered, "I dwell among my own people." ¹⁴And he said, "What then is to be done for her?" Gehazi answered, "Well, she has no son, and her husband is old." ¹⁵He said, "Call her." And when he had called her, she stood in the doorway. ¹⁶And he said, "At this season, about this time next year, you shall embrace a son." And she said, "No, my lord, O man of God; do

not lie to your servant." ¹⁷But the woma conceived, and she bore a son about th time the following spring, as Elisha ha said to her.

Elisha Raises the Shunammite's Son

¹⁸When the child had grown, he went o one day to his father among the reaper ¹⁹And he said to his father, "Oh, my hea my head!" The father said to his servan "Carry him to his mother." ²⁰And whe he had lifted him and brought him to h mother, the child sat on her lap till noo and then he died. ²¹And she went up an laid him on the bed of the man of God an shut the door behind him and went ou ²²Then she called to her husband and sai "Send me one of the servants and one the donkeys, that I may quickly go to th man of God and come back again." ²³An he said, "Why will you go to him today It is neither new moon nor Sabbath." Sh said, "All is well." ²⁴Then she saddled th donkey, and she said to her servant, "Urg the animal on; do not slacken the pace f me unless I tell you." ²⁵So she set out an came to the man of God at Mount Carme

When the man of God saw her comin he said to Gehazi his servant, "Look, ther is the Shunammite. ²⁶Run at once to mee her and say to her, 'Is all well with you? all well with your husband? Is all well wit the child?'" And she answered, "All is well ²⁷And when she came to the mountain t the man of God, she caught hold of his fee And Gehazi came to push her away. But th man of God said, "Leave her alone, for sh is in bitter distress, and the LORD has hid den it from me and has not told me." ²⁸The she said, "Did I ask my lord for a son? Di I not say, 'Do not deceive me?'" ²⁹He sai to Gehazi, "Tie up your garment and tak my staff in your hand and go. If you mee anyone, do not greet him, and if anyon greets you, do not reply. And lay my sta on the face of the child." ³⁰Then the mothe of the child said, "As the LORD lives and a you yourself live, I will not leave you." S he arose and followed her. ³¹Gehazi wer on ahead and laid the staff on the face the child, but there was no sound or sign life. Therefore he returned to meet him an told him, "The child has not awakened."

³²When Elisha came into the house, h saw the child lying dead on his bed. ³³So h went in and shut the door behind the tw

f them and prayed to the LORD. **34** Then
e went up and lay on the child, putting
is mouth on his mouth, his eyes on his
yes, and his hands on his hands. And as
e stretched himself upon him, the flesh
f the child became warm. **35** Then he got
p again and walked once back and forth
i the house, and went up and stretched
imself upon him. The child sneezed
even times, and the child opened his eyes.
Then he summoned Gehazi and said, "Call
is Shunammite." So he called her. And
^hen she came to him, he said, "Pick up
our son." **37** She came and fell at his feet,
owing to the ground. Then she picked up
er son and went out.

lisha Purifies the Deadly Stew

38 And Elisha came again to Gilgal when
ere was a famine in the land. And as the
ons of the prophets were sitting before
im, he said to his servant, "Set on the
rge pot, and boil stew for the sons of the
rophets." **39** One of them went out into
e field to gather herbs, and found a wild
ine and gathered from it his lap full of
ild gourds, and came and cut them up
to the pot of stew, not knowing what they
ere. **40** And they poured out some for the
en to eat. But while they were eating of
e stew, they cried out, "O man of God,
ere is death in the pot!" And they could
ot eat it. **41** He said, "Then bring flour." And
e threw it into the pot and said, "Pour
ome out for the men, that they may eat."
nd there was no harm in the pot.

42 A man came from Baal-shalishah,
ringing the man of God bread of the first-
uits, twenty loaves of barley and fresh
ars of grain in his sack. And Elisha said,
Give to the men, that they may eat." **43** But
is servant said, "How can I set this before
hundred men?" So he repeated, "Give
em to the men, that they may eat, for
hus says the LORD, 'They shall eat and
ave some left.'" **44** So he set it before them.
nd they ate and had some left, according
o the word of the LORD.

aaman Healed of Leprosy

Naaman, commander of the army of the
king of Syria, was a great man with his
aster and in high favor, because by him
e LORD had given victory to Syria. He was
a mighty man of valor, but he was a leper.[1]
2 Now the Syrians on one of their raids
had carried off a little girl from the land
of Israel, and she worked in the service of
Naaman's wife. **3** She said to her mistress,
"Would that my lord were with the prophet
who is in Samaria! He would cure him of
his leprosy." **4** So Naaman went in and told
his lord, "Thus and so spoke the girl from
the land of Israel." **5** And the king of Syria
said, "Go now, and I will send a letter to the
king of Israel."

So he went, taking with him ten talents
of silver, six thousand shekels[2] of gold, and
ten changes of clothing. **6** And he brought
the letter to the king of Israel, which read,
"When this letter reaches you, know that
I have sent to you Naaman my servant,
that you may cure him of his leprosy." **7** And
when the king of Israel read the letter, he
tore his clothes and said, "Am I God, to
kill and to make alive, that this man sends
word to me to cure a man of his leprosy?
Only consider, and see how he is seeking a
quarrel with me."

8 But when Elisha the man of God heard
that the king of Israel had torn his clothes,
he sent to the king, saying, "Why have
you torn your clothes? Let him come now
to me, that he may know that there is a
prophet in Israel." **9** So Naaman came with
his horses and chariots and stood at the
door of Elisha's house. **10** And Elisha sent a
messenger to him, saying, "Go and wash in
the Jordan seven times, and your flesh shall
be restored, and you shall be clean." **11** But
Naaman was angry and went away, saying,
"Behold, I thought that he would surely
come out to me and stand and call upon
the name of the LORD his God, and wave
his hand over the place and cure the leper.
12 Are not Abana[3] and Pharpar, the rivers
of Damascus, better than all the waters of
Israel? Could I not wash in them and be
clean?" So he turned and went away in a
rage. **13** But his servants came near and said
to him, "My father, it is a great word the
prophet has spoken to you; will you not do
it? Has he actually said to you, 'Wash, and
be clean'?" **14** So he went down and dipped
himself seven times in the Jordan, according to the word of the man of God, and his
flesh was restored like the flesh of a little
child, and he was clean.

eprosy was a term for several skin diseases; see Leviticus 13 [2] A *talent* was about 75 pounds or 34 kilograms; a *shekel* was about
5 ounce or 11 grams [3] Or *Amana*

Naaman's Servant Girl

Read this God Girl story in 2 Kings 5:1–4.

> She said to her mistress, "Would that my lord were with the prophet who is in Samaria! He would cure him of his leprosy."
>
> 2 Kings 5:3

How much faith do you have in God? Enough to share with others? If Christ can save you, then he can save others as well, but only if you are willing to open your mouth and say something. There once was a little girl from Israel who was kidnapped and taken as a slave for the wife of a Syrian military officer named Naaman. This man had a terrible skin disease. No one could cure it, or at least so they thought until this little girl opened her mouth, risking punishment, and told Naaman's wife about a prophet in Israel who could cure her husband. Her faith in God and his prophet was so strong that she had the courage to speak up and offer help.

Is your faith that strong? Are you willing to offer the hand of God to people in distress? Your voice might be the only taste of salvation another person gets. Your words might be the beginning of their new life. You don't need a lot of words or all the answers, just a willingness to offer help where help is needed. As a God Girl, let yourself be known as a person with the courage to speak up when speaking up is required. Don't stand silently by while others miss out on the hand of God in their lives. Don't let people hurt those near you without hearing you say something. And don't walk away when strangers are in need. When you are willing to be rejected by others, your fearlessness will bring great honor to God and joy to you. Let God become more important to you than your image, and be a God Girl who stands up for the sick, the needy, and the brokenhearted.

ehazi's Greed and Punishment

¹⁵Then he returned to the man of God,
e and all his company, and he came and
ood before him. And he said, "Behold,
know that there is no God in all the earth
ut in Israel; so accept now a present from
ur servant." ¹⁶But he said, "As the LORD
ves, before whom I stand, I will receive
one." And he urged him to take it, but
e refused. ¹⁷Then Naaman said, "If not,
lease let there be given to your servant
vo mule loads of earth, for from now on
ur servant will not offer burnt offering
r sacrifice to any god but the LORD. ¹⁸In
is matter may the LORD pardon your ser-
ant: when my master goes into the house
f Rimmon to worship there, leaning on
y arm, and I bow myself in the house of
immon, when I bow myself in the house of
immon, the LORD pardon your servant in
is matter." ¹⁹He said to him, "Go in peace."

But when Naaman had gone from him
short distance, ²⁰Gehazi, the servant of
lisha the man of God, said, "See, my mas-
r has spared this Naaman the Syrian,
not accepting from his hand what he
rought. As the LORD lives, I will run
fter him and get something from him."
So Gehazi followed Naaman. And when
aaman saw someone running after him,
e got down from the chariot to meet him
nd said, "Is all well?" ²²And he said, "All is
ell. My master has sent me to say, 'There
ave just now come to me from the hill
ountry of Ephraim two young men of the
ons of the prophets. Please give them a
alent of silver and two changes of cloth-
g.' " ²³And Naaman said, "Be pleased to
ccept two talents." And he urged him and
ed up two talents of silver in two bags,
ith two changes of clothing, and laid them
n two of his servants. And they carried
hem before Gehazi. ²⁴And when he came
o the hill, he took them from their hand
nd put them in the house, and he sent
he men away, and they departed. ²⁵He
vent in and stood before his master, and
lisha said to him, "Where have you been,
ehazi?" And he said, "Your servant went
owhere." ²⁶But he said to him, "Did not
ny heart go when the man turned from his
hariot to meet you? Was it a time to accept
noney and garments, olive orchards and
ineyards, sheep and oxen, male servants
nd female servants? ²⁷Therefore the lep-
osy of Naaman shall cling to you and to

your descendants forever." So he went out
from his presence a leper, like snow.

The Axe Head Recovered

6 Now the sons of the prophets said to
Elisha, "See, the place where we dwell
under your charge is too small for us. ²Let
us go to the Jordan and each of us get there
a log, and let us make a place for us to dwell
there." And he answered, "Go." ³Then one
of them said, "Be pleased to go with your
servants." And he answered, "I will go." ⁴So
he went with them. And when they came
to the Jordan, they cut down trees. ⁵But
as one was felling a log, his axe head fell
into the water, and he cried out, "Alas, my
master! It was borrowed." ⁶Then the man
of God said, "Where did it fall?" When he
showed him the place, he cut off a stick and
threw it in there and made the iron float.
⁷And he said, "Take it up." So he reached
out his hand and took it.

Horses and Chariots of Fire

⁸Once when the king of Syria was warring against Israel, he took counsel with his
servants, saying, "At such and such a place
shall be my camp." ⁹But the man of God
sent word to the king of Israel, "Beware
that you do not pass this place, for the
Syrians are going down there." ¹⁰And the
king of Israel sent to the place about which
the man of God told him. Thus he used to
warn him, so that he saved himself there
more than once or twice.

¹¹And the mind of the king of Syria was
greatly troubled because of this thing, and
he called his servants and said to them,
"Will you not show me who of us is for the
king of Israel?" ¹²And one of his servants
said, "None, my lord, O king; but Elisha,
the prophet who is in Israel, tells the king
of Israel the words that you speak in your
bedroom." ¹³And he said, "Go and see
where he is, that I may send and seize him."
It was told him, "Behold, he is in Dothan."
¹⁴So he sent there horses and chariots and
a great army, and they came by night and
surrounded the city.

¹⁵When the servant of the man of God
rose early in the morning and went out,
behold, an army with horses and chariots
was all around the city. And the servant
said, "Alas, my master! What shall we do?"
¹⁶He said, "Do not be afraid, for those who
are with us are more than those who are

with them." [17] Then Elisha prayed and said, "O LORD, please open his eyes that he may see." So the LORD opened the eyes of the young man, and he saw, and behold, the mountain was full of horses and chariots of fire all around Elisha. [18] And when the Syrians came down against him, Elisha prayed to the LORD and said, "Please strike this people with blindness." So he struck them with blindness in accordance with the prayer of Elisha. [19] And Elisha said to them, "This is not the way, and this is not the city. Follow me, and I will bring you to the man whom you seek." And he led them to Samaria.

[20] As soon as they entered Samaria, Elisha said, "O LORD, open the eyes of these men, that they may see." So the LORD opened their eyes and they saw, and behold, they were in the midst of Samaria. [21] As soon as the king of Israel saw them, he said to Elisha, "My father, shall I strike them down? Shall I strike them down?" [22] He answered, "You shall not strike them down. Would you strike down those whom you have taken captive with your sword and with your bow? Set bread and water before them, that they may eat and drink and go to their master." [23] So he prepared for them a great feast, and when they had eaten and drunk, he sent them away, and they went to their master. And the Syrians did not come again on raids into the land of Israel.

Ben-hadad's Siege of Samaria

[24] Afterward Ben-hadad king of Syria mustered his entire army and went up and besieged Samaria. [25] And there was a great famine in Samaria, as they besieged it, until a donkey's head was sold for eighty shekels of silver, and the fourth part of a kab[1] of dove's dung for five shekels of silver. [26] Now as the king of Israel was passing by on the wall, a woman cried out to him, saying, "Help, my lord, O king!" [27] And he said, "If the LORD will not help you, how shall I help you? From the threshing floor, or from the winepress?" [28] And the king asked her, "What is your trouble?" She answered, "This woman said to me, 'Give your so

[1] A *shekel* was about 2/5 ounce or 11 grams; a *kab* was about 1 quart or 1 liter

Know God

verses to read
2 Kings 6:15–17

When life starts to get hard, it's not a bad thing to have God and no one else *but* him. When everyone has walked away, you can't find a friend, and no human arms are there to hold you, then you can know that God has cleared a path straight to his arms, through his Son Jesus. Because when you have all kinds of people to comfort you and everything you need to be soothed, then you don't really need God, do you?

Jesus didn't come to save the healthy people who have everything they need but to save the sick, the frightened, and the worried. People who have it all don't think they need Jesus. But people who want something deeper, people who are being tested, who have been left alone, and who are living on a steady diet of pain and insecurity—these kinds of people are the ones who know what it means to need Jesus and to be kept alive by him and him alone.

Each time you feel the sting of your "so-called life," thank God that he is pulling you closer to him instead of to some earthly comfort that would just distract you from his presence. Don't pray for more of what you want but for more of what you need. The truth is that what you need isn't always the same thing as what you want. God's desire for you equals your need. And what God wants is always the best. His love for you shows up in the tough times just as much as in the amazing times—sometimes even more.

at we may eat him today, and we will eat
y son tomorrow.' ²⁹So we boiled my son
d ate him. And on the next day I said to
r, 'Give your son, that we may eat him.'
t she has hidden her son." ³⁰When the
ng heard the words of the woman,
re his clothes—now he was passing by
the wall—and the people looked, and
hold, he had sackcloth beneath on his
dy— ³¹and he said, "May God do so to me
d more also, if the head of Elisha the son
Shaphat remains on his shoulders today."
³²Elisha was sitting in his house, and the
ders were sitting with him. Now the king
d dispatched a man from his presence,
t before the messenger arrived Elisha
id to the elders, "Do you see how this
urderer has sent to take off my head?
ok, when the messenger comes, shut the
or and hold the door fast against him. Is
t the sound of his master's feet behind
m?" ³³And while he was still speaking
ith them, the messenger came down to
m and said, "This trouble is from the
RD! Why should I wait for the LORD any
nger?"

sha Promises Food

But Elisha said, "Hear the word of the
LORD: thus says the LORD, Tomorrow
out this time a seah¹ of fine flour shall be
ld for a shekel,² and two seahs of barley
r a shekel, at the gate of Samaria." ²Then
e captain on whose hand the king leaned
id to the man of God, "If the LORD himself
ould make windows in heaven, could this
ing be?" But he said, "You shall see it with
ur own eyes, but you shall not eat of it."

e Syrians Flee

³Now there were four men who were
pers³ at the entrance to the gate. And
ey said to one another, "Why are we sit-
ng here until we die? ⁴If we say, 'Let us
ter the city,' the famine is in the city,
d we shall die there. And if we sit here,
e die also. So now come, let us go over to
e camp of the Syrians. If they spare our
es we shall live, and if they kill us we
all but die." ⁵So they arose at twilight to
to the camp of the Syrians. But when
ey came to the edge of the camp of the
rians, behold, there was no one there.
or the Lord had made the army of the

Syrians hear the sound of chariots and of
horses, the sound of a great army, so that
they said to one another, "Behold, the king
of Israel has hired against us the kings
of the Hittites and the kings of Egypt to
come against us." ⁷So they fled away in the
twilight and abandoned their tents, their
horses, and their donkeys, leaving the
camp as it was, and fled for their lives.
⁸And when these lepers came to the edge
of the camp, they went into a tent and ate
and drank, and they carried off silver and
gold and clothing and went and hid them.
Then they came back and entered another
tent and carried off things from it and went
and hid them.

Ask Yourself . . .

ABOUT YOUR LIFE

- Is God trying to get my attention?
- Have I gone to God with my problems, or have I only gone to other people instead?
- Does a certain problem keep coming up in my life?
- Could I be doing something that keeps making this thing happen to me?

---

⁹Then they said to one another, "We are
not doing right. This day is a day of good
news. If we are silent and wait until the
morning light, punishment will overtake
us. Now therefore come; let us go and tell
the king's household." ¹⁰So they came and
called to the gatekeepers of the city and
told them, "We came to the camp of the
Syrians, and behold, there was no one to
be seen or heard there, nothing but the
horses tied and the donkeys tied and the
tents as they were." ¹¹Then the gatekeepers
called out, and it was told within the king's
household. ¹²And the king rose in the night
and said to his servants, "I will tell you

---

seah was about 7 quarts or 7.3 liters ²A *shekel* was about 2/5 ounce or 11 grams ³*Leprosy* was a term for several skin diseases; see
viticus 13

what the Syrians have done to us. They know that we are hungry. Therefore they have gone out of the camp to hide themselves in the open country, thinking, 'When they come out of the city, we shall take them alive and get into the city.'" [13] And one of his servants said, "Let some men take five of the remaining horses, seeing that those who are left here will fare like the whole multitude of Israel who have already perished. Let us send and see." [14] So they took two horsemen, and the king sent them after the army of the Syrians, saying, "Go and see." [15] So they went after them as far as the Jordan, and behold, all the way was littered with garments and equipment that the Syrians had thrown away in their haste. And the messengers returned and told the king.

[16] Then the people went out and plundered the camp of the Syrians. So a seah of fine flour was sold for a shekel, and two seahs of barley for a shekel, according to the word of the LORD. [17] Now the king had appointed the captain on whose hand he leaned to have charge of the gate. And the people trampled him in the gate, so that he died, as the man of God had said when the king came down to him. [18] For when the man of God had said to the king, "Two seahs of barley shall be sold for a shekel, and a seah of fine flour for a shekel, about this time tomorrow in the gate of Samaria," [19] the captain had answered the man of God, "If the LORD himself should make windows in heaven, could such a thing be?" And he had said, "You shall see it with your own eyes, but you shall not eat of it." [20] And so it happened to him, for the people trampled him in the gate and he died.

The Shunammite's Land Restored

8 Now Elisha had said to the woman whose son he had restored to life, "Arise, and depart with your household, and sojourn wherever you can, for the LORD has called for a famine, and it will come upon the land for seven years." [2] So the woman arose and did according to the word of the man of God. She went with her household and sojourned in the land of the Philistines seven years. [3] And at the end of the seven years, when the woman returned from the land of the Philistines, she went to appeal to the king for her house and

her land. [4] Now the king was talking wi Gehazi the servant of the man of God, sa ing, "Tell me all the great things that Elis has done." [5] And while he was telling t king how Elisha had restored the dead life, behold, the woman whose son he ha restored to life appealed to the king for h house and her land. And Gehazi said, "M lord, O king, here is the woman, and he is her son whom Elisha restored to lif [6] And when the king asked the woma she told him. So the king appointed official for her, saying, "Restore all th was hers, together with all the produ of the fields from the day that she left t land until now."

Hazael Murders Ben-hadad

[7] Now Elisha came to Damascus. Be hadad the king of Syria was sick. A when it was told him, "The man of G has come here," [8] the king said to Haza "Take a present with you and go to me the man of God, and inquire of the LO through him, saying, 'Shall I recover fro this sickness?'" [9] So Hazael went to me him, and took a present with him, all kin of goods of Damascus, forty camels' load When he came and stood before him, said, "Your son Ben-hadad king of Syr has sent me to you, saying, 'Shall I recov from this sickness?'" [10] And Elisha said him, "Go, say to him, 'You shall certain recover,' but[1] the LORD has shown me th he shall certainly die." [11] And he fixed h gaze and stared at him, until he was emba rassed. And the man of God wept. [12] Ar Hazael said, "Why does my lord weep?" answered, "Because I know the evil th you will do to the people of Israel. Yo will set on fire their fortresses, and yo will kill their young men with the swo and dash in pieces their little ones and r open their pregnant women." [13] And Haza said, "What is your servant, who is but dog, that he should do this great thing Elisha answered, "The LORD has shown n that you are to be king over Syria." [14] The he departed from Elisha and came to h master, who said to him, "What did Elish say to you?" And he answered, "He told n that you would certainly recover." [15] But th next day he took the bed cloth[2] and dippe it in water and spread it over his face, till died. And Hazael became king in his plac

---

[1] Some manuscripts say, 'You shall certainly not recover,' for [2] The meaning of the Hebrew is uncertain

Jehoram Reigns in Judah

[16] In the fifth year of Joram the son of Ahab, king of Israel, when Jehoshaphat was king of Judah,[1] Jehoram the son of Jehoshaphat, king of Judah, began to reign. [17] He was thirty-two years old when he became king, and he reigned eight years in Jerusalem. [18] And he walked in the way of the kings of Israel, as the house of Ahab had done, for the daughter of Ahab was his wife. And he did what was evil in the sight of the LORD. [19] Yet the LORD was not willing to destroy Judah, for the sake of David his servant, since he promised to give a lamp to him and to his sons forever.

[20] In his days Edom revolted from the rule of Judah and set up a king of their own. [21] Then Joram[2] passed over to Zair with all his chariots and rose by night, and he and his chariot commanders struck the Edomites who had surrounded him, but his army fled home. [22] So Edom revolted from the rule of Judah to this day. Then Libnah revolted at the same time. [23] Now the rest of the acts of Joram, and all that he did, are they not written in the Book of the Chronicles of the Kings of Judah? [24] So Joram slept with his fathers and was buried with his fathers in the city of David, and Ahaziah his son reigned in his place.

Ahaziah Reigns in Judah

[25] In the twelfth year of Joram the son of Ahab, king of Israel, Ahaziah the son of Jehoram, king of Judah, began to reign. [26] Ahaziah was twenty-two years old when he began to reign, and he reigned one year in Jerusalem. His mother's name was Athaliah; she was a granddaughter of Omri king of Israel. [27] He also walked in the way of the house of Ahab and did what was evil in the sight of the LORD, as the house of Ahab had done, for he was son-in-law to the house of Ahab.

[28] He went with Joram the son of Ahab to make war against Hazael king of Syria at Ramoth-gilead, and the Syrians wounded Joram. [29] And King Joram returned to be healed in Jezreel of the wounds that the Syrians had given him at Ramah, when he fought against Hazael king of Syria. And Ahaziah the son of Jehoram king of Judah went down to see Joram the son of Ahab in Jezreel, because he was sick.

Jehu Anointed King of Israel

9 Then Elisha the prophet called one of the sons of the prophets and said to him, "Tie up your garments, and take this flask of oil in your hand, and go to Ramoth-gilead. [2] And when you arrive, look there for Jehu the son of Jehoshaphat, son of Nimshi. And go in and have him rise from among his fellows, and lead him to an inner chamber. [3] Then take the flask of oil and pour it on his head and say, 'Thus says the LORD, I anoint you king over Israel.' Then open the door and flee; do not linger."

[4] So the young man, the servant of the prophet, went to Ramoth-gilead. [5] And when he came, behold, the commanders of the army were in council. And he said, "I have a word for you, O commander." And Jehu said, "To which of us all?" And he said, "To you, O commander." [6] So he arose and went into the house. And the young man poured the oil on his head, saying to him, "Thus says the LORD, the God of Israel, I anoint you king over the people of the LORD, over Israel. [7] And you shall strike down the house of Ahab your master, so that I may avenge on Jezebel the blood of my servants the prophets, and the blood of all the servants of the LORD. [8] For the whole house of Ahab shall perish, and I will cut off from Ahab every male, bond or free, in Israel. [9] And I will make the house of Ahab like the house of Jeroboam the son of Nebat, and like the house of Baasha the son of Ahijah. [10] And the dogs shall eat Jezebel in the territory of Jezreel, and none shall bury her." Then he opened the door and fled.

[11] When Jehu came out to the servants of his master, they said to him, "Is all well? Why did this mad fellow come to you?" And he said to them, "You know the fellow and his talk." [12] And they said, "That is not true; tell us now." And he said, "Thus and so he spoke to me, saying, 'Thus says the LORD, I anoint you king over Israel.'" [13] Then in haste every man of them took his garment and put it under him on the bare[3] steps, and they blew the trumpet and proclaimed, "Jehu is king."

Jehu Assassinates Joram and Ahaziah

[14] Thus Jehu the son of Jehoshaphat the son of Nimshi conspired against Joram.

---

[1] Septuagint, Syriac lack *when Jehoshaphat was king of Judah* [2] *Joram* is an alternate spelling of *Jehoram* (the son of Jehoshaphat) as in verse 16; also verses 23, 24 [3] The meaning of the Hebrew word is uncertain

(Now Joram with all Israel had been on guard at Ramoth-gilead against Hazael king of Syria, [15]but King Joram had returned to be healed in Jezreel of the wounds that the Syrians had given him, when he fought with Hazael king of Syria.) So Jehu said, "If this is your decision, then let no one slip out of the city to go and tell the news in Jezreel." [16]Then Jehu mounted his chariot and went to Jezreel, for Joram lay there. And Ahaziah king of Judah had come down to visit Joram.

[17]Now the watchman was standing on the tower in Jezreel, and he saw the company of Jehu as he came and said, "I see a company." And Joram said, "Take a horseman and send to meet them, and let him say, 'Is it peace?'" [18]So a man on horseback went to meet him and said, "Thus says the king, 'Is it peace?'" And Jehu said, "What do you have to do with peace? Turn around and ride behind me." And the watchman reported, saying, "The messenger reached them, but he is not coming back." [19]Then he sent out a second horseman, who came to them and said, "Thus the king has said, 'Is it peace?'" And Jehu answered, "What do you have to do with peace? Turn around and ride behind me." [20]Again the watchman reported, "He reached them, but he is not coming back. And the driving is like the driving of Jehu the son of Nimshi, for he drives furiously."

[21]Joram said, "Make ready." And they made ready his chariot. Then Joram king of Israel and Ahaziah king of Judah set out, each in his chariot, and went to meet Jehu, and met him at the property of Naboth the Jezreelite. [22]And when Joram saw Jehu, he said, "Is it peace, Jehu?" He answered, "What peace can there be, so long as the whorings and the sorceries of your mother Jezebel are so many?" [23]Then Joram reined about and fled, saying to Ahaziah, "Treachery, O Ahaziah!" [24]And Jehu drew his bow with his full strength, and shot Joram between the shoulders, so that the arrow pierced his heart, and he sank in his chariot. [25]Jehu said to Bidkar his aide, "Take him up and throw him on the plot of ground belonging to Naboth the Jezreelite. For remember, when you and I rode side by side behind Ahab his father, how the LORD made this pronouncement

against him: [26]'As surely as I saw yesterday the blood of Naboth and the blood of his sons—declares the LORD—I will repay you on this plot of ground.' Now therefore take him up and throw him on the plot of ground, in accordance with the word of the LORD."

[27]When Ahaziah the king of Judah saw this, he fled in the direction of Beth-haggan. And Jehu pursued him and said, "Shoot him also." And they shot him[1] in the chariot at the ascent of Gur, which is by Ibleam. And he fled to Megiddo and died there. [28]His servants carried him in a chariot to Jerusalem, and buried him in his tomb with his fathers in the city of David. [29]In the eleventh year of Joram the son of Ahab, Ahaziah began to reign over Judah.

Jehu Executes Jezebel

[30]When Jehu came to Jezreel, Jezebel heard of it. And she painted her eyes and adorned her head and looked out of the window. [31]And as Jehu entered the gate, she said, "Is it peace, you Zimri, murderer of your master?" [32]And he lifted up his face to the window and said, "Who is on my side? Who?" Two or three eunuchs looked out at him. [33]He said, "Throw her down." So they threw her down. And some of her blood spattered on the wall and on the horses, and they trampled on her. [34]Then he went in and ate and drank. And he said, "See now to this cursed woman and bury her, for she is a king's daughter." [35]But when they went to bury her, they found no more of her than the skull and the feet and the palms of her hands. [36]When they came back and told him, he said, "This is the word of the LORD, which he spoke by his servant Elijah the Tishbite: 'In the territory of Jezreel the dogs shall eat the flesh of Jezebel, [37]and the corpse of Jezebel shall be as dung on the face of the field in the territory of Jezreel, so that no one can say, This is Jezebel.'"

Jehu Slaughters Ahab's Descendants

10 Now Ahab had seventy sons in Samaria. So Jehu wrote letters and sent them to Samaria, to the rulers of the city,[2] to the elders, and to the guardians of the sons[3] of Ahab, saying, [2]"Now then, as soon as this letter comes to you, see-

---

[1] Syriac, Vulgate (compare Septuagint); Hebrew lacks *and they shot him* [2] Septuagint, Vulgate; Hebrew *rulers of Jezreel* [3] Hebrew lacks *of the sons*

ng your master's sons are with you, and here are with you chariots and horses, fortified cities also, and weapons, ³select the best and fittest of your master's sons and set him on his father's throne and fight for your master's house." ⁴But they were exceedingly afraid and said, "Behold, the two kings could not stand before him. How then can we stand?" ⁵So he who was over the palace, and he who was over the city, together with the elders and the guardians, sent to Jehu, saying, "We are your servants, and we will do all that you tell us. We will not make anyone king. Do whatever is good in your eyes." ⁶Then he wrote to them a second letter, saying, "If you are on my side, and if you are ready to obey me, take the heads of your master's sons and come to me at Jezreel tomorrow at this time." Now the king's sons, seventy persons, were with the great men of the city, who were bringing them up. ⁷And as soon as the letter came to them, they took the king's sons and slaughtered them, seventy persons, and put their heads in baskets and sent them to him at Jezreel. ⁸When the messenger came and told him, "They have brought the heads of the king's sons," he said, "Lay them in two heaps at the entrance of the gate until the morning." ⁹Then in the morning, when he went out, he stood and said to all the people, "You are innocent. It was I who conspired against my master and killed him, but who struck down all these? ¹⁰Know then that there shall fall to the earth nothing of the word of the Lord, which the Lord spoke concerning the house of Ahab, for the Lord has done what he said by his servant Elijah." ¹¹So Jehu struck down all who remained of the house of Ahab in Jezreel, all his great men and his close friends and his priests, until he left him none remaining.

¹²Then he set out and went to Samaria. On the way, when he was at Beth-eked of the Shepherds, ¹³Jehu met the relatives of Ahaziah king of Judah, and he said, "Who are you?" And they answered, "We are the relatives of Ahaziah, and we came down to visit the royal princes and the sons of the queen mother." ¹⁴He said, "Take them alive." And they took them alive and slaughtered them at the pit of Beth-eked, forty-two persons, and he spared none of them.

A Prayer for... FORGIVENESS

Everlasting Creator and Father,

I have messed up, my nature is sinful, my faith is weakened; I am a mess, miserable and powerless, but my hope is in you. If I am saved it is because of your undeserved and amazing grace; it is not simply by mercy but by abundant mercy; not just by grace but by amazing grace. You have made the way to save me from sin's control and to restore my happiness, honor, and safety. Thank you for the everlasting covenant and for the appointment of Jesus as my Mediator. I am so thankful that he didn't fail, though he was totally discouraged. I'm thankful that he did the work you gave him to do and said on the cross, "It is finished." In him your justice is satisfied, your truth established, your law magnified, and a solid foundation is laid for my hope. I know he has taken my grief, carried my sorrow, won my peace, and healed my soul. I am justified by his blood and saved by his life. Having his Spirit, I have his mind in me. Please don't let my faith be a part-time thing, but may it be continual, influential, and effective. And help me to always continue in your words as well as your works, so that I can reach my end in peace.

Amen.

¹⁵And when he departed from there, he met Jehonadab the son of Rechab coming to meet him. And he greeted him and said to him, "Is your heart true to my heart as mine is to yours?" And Jehonadab answered, "It is." Jehu said,¹ "If it is, give me your hand." So he gave him his hand. And Jehu took him up with him into the chariot. ¹⁶And he said, "Come with me, and see my zeal for the Lord." So he² had him ride in his chariot. ¹⁷And when he came to Samaria, he struck down all who remained to Ahab in Samaria, till he had wiped them

¹Septuagint; Hebrew lacks *Jehu said* ²Septuagint, Syriac, Targum; Hebrew *they*

out, according to the word of the LORD that he spoke to Elijah.

Jehu Strikes Down the Prophets of Baal

[18] Then Jehu assembled all the people and said to them, "Ahab served Baal a little, but Jehu will serve him much. [19] Now therefore call to me all the prophets of Baal, all his worshipers and all his priests. Let none be missing, for I have a great sacrifice to offer to Baal. Whoever is missing shall not live." But Jehu did it with cunning in order to destroy the worshipers of Baal. [20] And Jehu ordered, "Sanctify a solemn assembly for Baal." So they proclaimed it. [21] And Jehu sent throughout all Israel, and all the worshipers of Baal came, so that there was not a man left who did not come. And they entered the house of Baal, and the house of Baal was filled from one end to the other. [22] He said to him who was in charge of the wardrobe, "Bring out the vestments for all the worshipers of Baal." So he brought out the vestments for them. [23] Then Jehu went into the house of Baal with Jehonadab the son of Rechab, and he said to the worshipers of Baal, "Search, and see that there is no servant of the LORD here among you, but only the worshipers of Baal." [24] Then they[1] went in to offer sacrifices and burnt offerings.

Now Jehu had stationed eighty men outside and said, "The man who allows any of those whom I give into your hands to escape shall forfeit his life." [25] So as soon as he had made an end of offering the burnt offering, Jehu said to the guard and to the officers, "Go in and strike them down; let not a man escape." So when they put them to the sword, the guard and the officers cast them out and went into the inner room of the house of Baal, [26] and they brought out the pillar that was in the house of Baal and burned it. [27] And they demolished the pillar of Baal, and demolished the house of Baal, and made it a latrine to this day.

Jehu Reigns in Israel

[28] Thus Jehu wiped out Baal from Israel. [29] But Jehu did not turn aside from the sins of Jeroboam the son of Nebat, which he made Israel to sin—that is, the golden calves that were in Bethel and in Dan. [30] And the LORD said to Jehu, "Because you have done well in carrying out what is right

in my eyes, and have done to the house of Ahab according to all that was in my heart, your sons of the fourth generation shall sit on the throne of Israel." [31] But Jehu was not careful to walk in the law of the LORD, the God of Israel, with all his heart. He did not turn from the sins of Jeroboam, which he made Israel to sin.

[32] In those days the LORD began to cut off parts of Israel. Hazael defeated them throughout the territory of Israel: [33] from the Jordan eastward, all the land of Gilead, the Gadites, and the Reubenites, and the Manassites, from Aroer, which is by the Valley of the Arnon, that is, Gilead and Bashan. [34] Now the rest of the acts of Jehu and all that he did, and all his might, are they not written in the Book of the Chronicles of the Kings of Israel? [35] So Jehu slept with his fathers, and they buried him in Samaria. And Jehoahaz his son reigned in his place. [36] The time that Jehu reigned over Israel in Samaria was twenty-eight years.

Athaliah Reigns in Judah

11 Now when Athaliah the mother of Ahaziah saw that her son was dead, she arose and destroyed all the royal family. [2] But Jehosheba, the daughter of King Joram, sister of Ahaziah, took Joash the son of Ahaziah and stole him away from among the king's sons who were being put to death, and she put[2] him and his nurse in a bedroom. Thus they[3] hid him from Athaliah, so that he was not put to death. [3] And he remained with her six years, hidden in the house of the LORD, while Athaliah reigned over the land.

Joash Anointed King in Judah

[4] But in the seventh year Jehoiada sent and brought the captains of the Carites and of the guards, and had them come to him in the house of the LORD. And he made a covenant with them and put them under oath in the house of the LORD, and he showed them the king's son. [5] And he commanded them, "This is the thing that you shall do: one third of you, those who come off duty on the Sabbath and guard the king's house [6] (another third being at the gate Sur and a third at the gate behind the guards) shall guard the palace.[4] [7] And the two divisions of you, which come on duty in force on the

---

[1] Septuagint *he* (compare verse 25) [2] Compare 2 Chronicles 22:11; Hebrew lacks *and she put* [3] Septuagint, Syriac, Vulgate (compare 2 Chronicles 22:11) *she* [4] The meaning of the Hebrew word is uncertain

Sabbath and guard the house of the LORD on behalf of the king, [8]shall surround the king, each with his weapons in his hand. And whoever approaches the ranks is to be put to death. Be with the king when he goes out and when he comes in."

[9]The captains did according to all that Jehoiada the priest commanded, and they each brought his men who were to go off duty on the Sabbath, with those who were to come on duty on the Sabbath, and came to Jehoiada the priest. [10]And the priest gave to the captains the spears and shields that had been King David's, which were in the house of the LORD. [11]And the guards stood, every man with his weapons in his hand, from the south side of the house to the north side of the house, around the altar and the house on behalf of the king. [12]Then he brought out the king's son and put the crown on him and gave him the testimony. And they proclaimed him king and anointed him, and they clapped their hands and said, "Long live the king!"

[13]When Athaliah heard the noise of the guard and of the people, she went into the house of the LORD to the people. [14]And when she looked, there was the king standing by the pillar, according to the custom, and the captains and the trumpeters beside the king, and all the people of the land rejoicing and blowing trumpets. And Athaliah tore her clothes and cried, "Treason! Treason!" [15]Then Jehoiada the priest commanded the captains who were set over the army, "Bring her out between the ranks, and put to death with the sword anyone who follows her." For the priest said, "Let her not be put to death in the house of the LORD." [16]So they laid hands on her; and she went through the horses' entrance to the king's house, and there she was put to death.

[17]And Jehoiada made a covenant between the LORD and the king and people, that they should be the LORD's people, and also between the king and the people. [18]Then all the people of the land went to the house of Baal and tore it down; his altars and his images they broke in pieces, and they killed Mattan the priest of Baal before the altars. And the priest posted watchmen over the house of the LORD. [19]And he took the captains, the Carites, the guards, and all the people of the land, and they brought the king down from the house of the LORD, marching through the gate of the guards to the king's house. And he took his seat on the throne of the kings. [20]So all the people of the land rejoiced, and the city was quiet after Athaliah had been put to death with the sword at the king's house.

Ask Yourself . . .

ABOUT THE NEW YOU

Before you turned your life over to God, you probably had some bad habits and sinful ideas, and you did some stupid things. Ask yourself about how you have changed:

- How has my faith changed me since I was saved?
- Are there old habits I'm holding on to?
- If I'm really a "new creation" (2 Cor. 5:17), why am I doing the same old stuff?
- What does God's Word say about overcoming my sin?
- Am I enjoying the gospel of free forgiveness every day?

Jehoash Reigns in Judah

[21][1] Jehoash[2] was seven years old when he began to reign.

12 In the seventh year of Jehu, Jehoash[3] began to reign, and he reigned forty years in Jerusalem. His mother's name was Zibiah of Beersheba. [2]And Jehoash did what was right in the eyes of the LORD all his days, because Jehoiada the priest instructed him. [3]Nevertheless, the high places were not taken away; the people continued to sacrifice and make offerings on the high places.

Jehoash Repairs the Temple

[4]Jehoash said to the priests, "All the money of the holy things that is brought

---

[1]Ch 12:1 in Hebrew [2]*Jehoash* is an alternate spelling of *Joash* (son of Ahaziah) as in verse 2 [3]*Jehoash* is an alternate spelling of *Joash* (son of Ahaziah) as in 11:2; also verses 2, 4, 6, 7, 18

into the house of the LORD, the money for which each man is assessed—the money from the assessment of persons—and the money that a man's heart prompts him to bring into the house of the LORD, [5] let the priests take, each from his donor, and let them repair the house wherever any need of repairs is discovered." [6] But by the twenty-third year of King Jehoash, the priests had made no repairs on the house. [7] Therefore King Jehoash summoned Jehoiada the priest and the other priests and said to them, "Why are you not repairing the house? Now therefore take no more money from your donors, but hand it over for the repair of the house." [8] So the priests agreed that they should take no more money from the people, and that they should not repair the house.

[9] Then Jehoiada the priest took a chest and bored a hole in the lid of it and set it beside the altar on the right side as one entered the house of the LORD. And the priests who guarded the threshold put in it all the money that was brought into the house of the LORD. [10] And whenever they saw that there was much money in the chest, the king's secretary and the high priest came up and they bagged and counted the money that was found in the house of the LORD. [11] Then they would give the money that was weighed out into the hands of the workmen who had the oversight of the house of the LORD. And they paid it out to the carpenters and the builders who worked on the house of the LORD, [12] and to the masons and the stonecutters, as well as to buy timber and quarried stone for making repairs on the house of the LORD, and for any outlay for the repairs of the house. [13] But there were not made for the house of the LORD basins of silver, snuffers, bowls, trumpets, or any vessels of gold, or of silver, from the money that was brought into the house of the LORD, [14] for that was given to the workmen who were repairing the house of the LORD with it. [15] And they did not ask for an accounting from the men into whose hand they delivered the money to pay out to the workmen, for they dealt honestly. [16] The money from the guilt offerings and the money from the sin offerings was not brought into the house of the LORD; it belonged to the priests.

[17] At that time Hazael king of Syria went up and fought against Gath and took it. But when Hazael set his face to go up against Jerusalem, [18] Jehoash king of Judah took all the sacred gifts that Jehoshaphat and Jehoram and Ahaziah his fathers, the kings of Judah, had dedicated, and his own sacred gifts, and all the gold that was found in the treasuries of the house of the LORD and of the king's house, and sent these to Hazael king of Syria. Then Hazael went away from Jerusalem.

The Death of Joash

[19] Now the rest of the acts of Joash and all that he did, are they not written in the Book of the Chronicles of the Kings of Judah? [20] His servants arose and made a conspiracy and struck down Joash in the house of Millo, on the way that goes down to Silla. [21] It was Jozacar the son of Shimeath and Jehozabad the son of Shomer, his servants, who struck him down, so that he died. And they buried him with his fathers in the city of David, and Amaziah his son reigned in his place.

Jehoahaz Reigns in Israel

13 In the twenty-third year of Joash the son of Ahaziah, king of Judah, Jehoahaz the son of Jehu began to reign over Israel in Samaria, and he reigned seventeen years. [2] He did what was evil in the sight of the LORD and followed the sins of Jeroboam the son of Nebat, which he made Israel to sin; he did not depart from them. [3] And the anger of the LORD was kindled against Israel, and he gave them continually into the hand of Hazael king of Syria and into the hand of Ben-hadad the son of Hazael. [4] Then Jehoahaz sought the favor of the LORD, and the LORD listened to him, for he saw the oppression of Israel, how the king of Syria oppressed them. [5] (Therefore the LORD gave Israel a savior, so that they escaped from the hand of the Syrians, and the people of Israel lived in their homes as formerly. [6] Nevertheless, they did not depart from the sins of the house of Jeroboam, which he made Israel to sin, but walked[1] in them; and the Asherah also remained in Samaria.) [7] For there was not left to Jehoahaz an army of more than fifty horsemen and ten chariots and ten thousand footmen, for the king of Syria had

---

[1] Septuagint, Syriac, Targum, Vulgate; Hebrew *he walked*

destroyed them and made them like the dust at threshing. ⁸ Now the rest of the acts of Jehoahaz and all that he did, and his might, are they not written in the Book of the Chronicles of the Kings of Israel? ⁹ So Jehoahaz slept with his fathers, and they buried him in Samaria, and Joash his son reigned in his place.

Jehoash Reigns in Israel

¹⁰ In the thirty-seventh year of Joash king of Judah, Jehoash[1] the son of Jehoahaz began to reign over Israel in Samaria, and he reigned sixteen years. ¹¹ He also did what was evil in the sight of the LORD. He did not depart from all the sins of Jeroboam the son of Nebat, which he made Israel to sin, but he walked in them. ¹² Now the rest of the acts of Joash and all that he did, and the might with which he fought against Amaziah king of Judah, are they not written in the Book of the Chronicles of the Kings of Israel? ¹³ So Joash slept with his fathers, and Jeroboam sat on his throne. And Joash was buried in Samaria with the kings of Israel.

The Death of Elisha

¹⁴ Now when Elisha had fallen sick with the illness of which he was to die, Joash king of Israel went down to him and wept before him, crying, "My father, my father! The chariots of Israel and its horsemen!" ¹⁵ And Elisha said to him, "Take a bow and arrows." So he took a bow and arrows. ¹⁶ Then he said to the king of Israel, "Draw the bow," and he drew it. And Elisha laid his hands on the king's hands. ¹⁷ And he said, "Open the window eastward," and he opened it. Then Elisha said, "Shoot," and he shot. And he said, "The LORD's arrow of victory, the arrow of victory over Syria! For you shall fight the Syrians in Aphek until you have made an end of them." ¹⁸ And he said, "Take the arrows," and he took them. And he said to the king of Israel, "Strike the ground with them." And he struck three times and stopped. ¹⁹ Then the man of God was angry with him and said, "You should have struck five or six times; then you would have struck down Syria until you had made an end of it, but now you will strike down Syria only three times."

²⁰ So Elisha died, and they buried him. Now bands of Moabites used to invade the land in the spring of the year. ²¹ And as a man was being buried, behold, a marauding band was seen and the man was thrown into the grave of Elisha, and as soon as the man touched the bones of Elisha, he revived and stood on his feet.

²² Now Hazael king of Syria oppressed Israel all the days of Jehoahaz. ²³ But the LORD was gracious to them and had compassion on them, and he turned toward them, because of his covenant with Abraham, Isaac, and Jacob, and would not destroy them, nor has he cast them from his presence until now.

²⁴ When Hazael king of Syria died, Ben-hadad his son became king in his place. ²⁵ Then Jehoash the son of Jehoahaz took again from Ben-hadad the son of Hazael the cities that he had taken from Jehoahaz his father in war. Three times Joash defeated him and recovered the cities of Israel.

Amaziah Reigns in Judah

14 In the second year of Joash the son of Joahaz, king of Israel, Amaziah the son of Joash, king of Judah, began to reign. ² He was twenty-five years old when he began to reign, and he reigned twenty-nine years in Jerusalem. His mother's name was Jehoaddin of Jerusalem. ³ And he did what was right in the eyes of the LORD, yet not like David his father. He did in all things as Joash his father had done. ⁴ But the high places were not removed; the people still sacrificed and made offerings on the high places. ⁵ And as soon as the royal power was firmly in his hand, he struck down his servants who had struck down the king his father. ⁶ But he did not put to death the children of the murderers, according to what is written in the Book of the Law of Moses, where the LORD commanded, "Fathers shall not be put to death because of their children, nor shall children be put to death because of their fathers. But each one shall die for his own sin."

⁷ He struck down ten thousand Edomites in the Valley of Salt and took Sela by storm, and called it Joktheel, which is its name to this day.

⁸ Then Amaziah sent messengers to Jehoash[2] the son of Jehoahaz, son of Jehu,

---

[1] *Jehoash* is an alternate spelling of *Joash* (son of Jehoahaz) as in verses 9, 12–14; also verse 25 [2] *Jehoash* is an alternate spelling of *Joash* (son of Jehoahaz) as in 13:9, 12–14; also verses 9, 11–16

king of Israel, saying, "Come, let us look one another in the face." [9] And Jehoash king of Israel sent word to Amaziah king of Judah, "A thistle on Lebanon sent to a cedar on Lebanon, saying, 'Give your daughter to my son for a wife,' and a wild beast of Lebanon passed by and trampled down the thistle. [10] You have indeed struck down Edom, and your heart has lifted you up. Be content with your glory, and stay at home, for why should you provoke trouble so that you fall, you and Judah with you?"

[11] But Amaziah would not listen. So Jehoash king of Israel went up, and he and Amaziah king of Judah faced one another in battle at Beth-shemesh, which belongs to Judah. [12] And Judah was defeated by Israel, and every man fled to his home. [13] And Jehoash king of Israel captured Amaziah king of Judah, the son of Jehoash, son of Ahaziah, at Beth-shemesh, and came to Jerusalem and broke down the wall of Jerusalem for four hundred cubits,[1] from the Ephraim Gate to the Corner Gate. [14] And he seized all the gold and silver, and all the vessels that were found in the house of the LORD and in the treasuries of the king's house, also hostages, and he returned to Samaria.

[15] Now the rest of the acts of Jehoash that he did, and his might, and how he fought with Amaziah king of Judah, are they not written in the Book of the Chronicles of the Kings of Israel? [16] And Jehoash slept with his fathers and was buried in Samaria with the kings of Israel, and Jeroboam his son reigned in his place.

[17] Amaziah the son of Joash, king of Judah, lived fifteen years after the death of Jehoash son of Jehoahaz, king of Israel. [18] Now the rest of the deeds of Amaziah, are they not written in the Book of the Chronicles of the Kings of Judah? [19] And they made a conspiracy against him in Jerusalem, and he fled to Lachish. But they sent after him to Lachish and put him to death there. [20] And they brought him on horses; and he was buried in Jerusalem with his fathers in the city of David. [21] And all the people of Judah took Azariah, who was sixteen years old, and made him king instead of his father Amaziah. [22] He built Elath and restored it to Judah, after the king slept with his fathers.

Jeroboam II Reigns in Israel

[23] In the fifteenth year of Amaziah the son of Joash, king of Judah, Jeroboam the son of Joash, king of Israel, began to reign in Samaria, and he reigned forty-one years. [24] And he did what was evil in the sight of the LORD. He did not depart from all the sins of Jeroboam the son of Nebat, which he made Israel to sin. [25] He restored the border of Israel from Lebo-hamath as far as the Sea of the Arabah, according to the word of the LORD, the God of Israel, which he spoke by his servant Jonah the son of Amittai, the prophet, who was from Gath-hepher. [26] For the LORD saw that the affliction of Israel was very bitter, for there was none left, bond or free, and there was none to help Israel. [27] But the LORD had not said that he would blot out the name of Israel from under heaven, so he saved them by the hand of Jeroboam the son of Joash.

[28] Now the rest of the acts of Jeroboam and all that he did, and his might, how he fought, and how he restored Damascus and Hamath to Judah in Israel, are they not written in the Book of the Chronicles of the Kings of Israel? [29] And Jeroboam slept with his fathers, the kings of Israel, and Zechariah his son reigned in his place.

Azariah Reigns in Judah

15 In the twenty-seventh year of Jeroboam king of Israel, Azariah the son of Amaziah, king of Judah, began to reign. [2] He was sixteen years old when he began to reign, and he reigned fifty-two years in Jerusalem. His mother's name was Jecoliah of Jerusalem. [3] And he did what was right in the eyes of the LORD, according to all that his father Amaziah had done. [4] Nevertheless, the high places were not taken away. The people still sacrificed and made offerings on the high places. [5] And the LORD touched the king, so that he was a leper[2] to the day of his death, and he lived in a separate house.[3] And Jotham the king's son was over the household, governing the people of the land. [6] Now the rest of the acts of Azariah, and all that he did, are they not written in the Book of the Chronicles of the Kings of Judah? [7] And Azariah slept with his fathers, and they buried him with his fathers in the city of David, and Jotham his son reigned in his place.

---

[1] A *cubit* was about 18 inches or 45 centimeters [2] *Leprosy* was a term for several skin diseases; see Leviticus 13 [3] The meaning of the Hebrew word is uncertain

Zechariah Reigns in Israel

[8] In the thirty-eighth year of Azariah king of Judah, Zechariah the son of Jeroboam reigned over Israel in Samaria six months. [9] And he did what was evil in the sight of the LORD, as his fathers had done. He did not depart from the sins of Jeroboam the son of Nebat, which he made Israel to sin. [10] Shallum the son of Jabesh conspired against him and struck him down at Ibleam and put him to death and reigned in his place. [11] Now the rest of the deeds of Zechariah, behold, they are written in the Book of the Chronicles of the Kings of Israel. [12] (This was the promise of the LORD that he gave to Jehu, "Your sons shall sit on the throne of Israel to the fourth generation." And so it came to pass.)

Shallum Reigns in Israel

[13] Shallum the son of Jabesh began to reign in the thirty-ninth year of Uzziah[1] king of Judah, and he reigned one month in Samaria. [14] Then Menahem the son of Gadi came up from Tirzah and came to Samaria, and he struck down Shallum the son of Jabesh in Samaria and put him to death and reigned in his place. [15] Now the rest of the deeds of Shallum, and the conspiracy that he made, behold, they are written in the Book of the Chronicles of the Kings of Israel. [16] At that time Menahem sacked Tiphsah and all who were in it and its territory from Tirzah on, because they did not open it to him. Therefore he sacked it, and he ripped open all the women in it who were pregnant.

Menahem Reigns in Israel

[17] In the thirty-ninth year of Azariah king of Judah, Menahem the son of Gadi began to reign over Israel, and he reigned ten years in Samaria. [18] And he did what was evil in the sight of the LORD. He did not depart all his days from all the sins of Jeroboam the son of Nebat, which he made Israel to sin. [19] Pul[2] the king of Assyria came against the land, and Menahem gave Pul a thousand talents[3] of silver, that he might help him to confirm his hold on the royal power. [20] Menahem exacted the money from Israel, that is, from all the wealthy men, fifty shekels[4] of silver from every man, to give to the king of Assyria. So the king of Assyria turned back and did not stay there in the land. [21] Now the rest of the deeds of Menahem and all that he did, are they not written in the Book of the Chronicles of the Kings of Israel? [22] And Menahem slept with his fathers, and Pekahiah his son reigned in his place.

Pekahiah Reigns in Israel

[23] In the fiftieth year of Azariah king of Judah, Pekahiah the son of Menahem began to reign over Israel in Samaria, and he reigned two years. [24] And he did what was evil in the sight of the LORD. He did not turn away from the sins of Jeroboam the son of Nebat, which he made Israel to sin. [25] And Pekah the son of Remaliah, his captain, conspired against him with fifty men of the people of Gilead, and struck him down in Samaria, in the citadel of the king's house with Argob and Arieh; he put him to death and reigned in his place. [26] Now the rest of the deeds of Pekahiah and all that he did, behold, they are written in the Book of the Chronicles of the Kings of Israel.

Pekah Reigns in Israel

[27] In the fifty-second year of Azariah king of Judah, Pekah the son of Remaliah began to reign over Israel in Samaria, and he reigned twenty years. [28] And he did what was evil in the sight of the LORD. He did not depart from the sins of Jeroboam the son of Nebat, which he made Israel to sin.

[29] In the days of Pekah king of Israel, Tiglath-pileser king of Assyria came and captured Ijon, Abel-beth-maacah, Janoah, Kedesh, Hazor, Gilead, and Galilee, all the land of Naphtali, and he carried the people captive to Assyria. [30] Then Hoshea the son of Elah made a conspiracy against Pekah the son of Remaliah and struck him down and put him to death and reigned in his place, in the twentieth year of Jotham the son of Uzziah. [31] Now the rest of the acts of Pekah and all that he did, behold, they are written in the Book of the Chronicles of the Kings of Israel.

Jotham Reigns in Judah

[32] In the second year of Pekah the son of Remaliah, king of Israel, Jotham the son of Uzziah, king of Judah, began to reign. [33] He was twenty-five years old when he began

---

[1] Another name for *Azariah* [2] Another name for *Tiglath-pileser III* (compare verse 29) [3] A *talent* was about 75 pounds or 34 kilograms [4] A *shekel* was about 2/5 ounce or 11 grams

to reign, and he reigned sixteen years in Jerusalem. His mother's name was Jerusha the daughter of Zadok. [34] And he did what was right in the eyes of the LORD, according to all that his father Uzziah had done. [35] Nevertheless, the high places were not removed. The people still sacrificed and made offerings on the high places. He built the upper gate of the house of the LORD. [36] Now the rest of the acts of Jotham and all that he did, are they not written in the Book of the Chronicles of the Kings of Judah? [37] In those days the LORD began to send Rezin the king of Syria and Pekah the son of Remaliah against Judah. [38] Jotham slept with his fathers and was buried with his fathers in the city of David his father, and Ahaz his son reigned in his place.

Ahaz Reigns in Judah

16 In the seventeenth year of Pekah the son of Remaliah, Ahaz the son of Jotham, king of Judah, began to reign. [2] Ahaz was twenty years old when he began to reign, and he reigned sixteen years in Jerusalem. And he did not do what was right in the eyes of the LORD his God, as his father David had done, [3] but he walked in the way of the kings of Israel. He even burned his son as an offering,[1] according to the despicable practices of the nations whom the LORD drove out before the people of Israel. [4] And he sacrificed and made offerings on the high places and on the hills and under every green tree.

[5] Then Rezin king of Syria and Pekah the son of Remaliah, king of Israel, came up to wage war on Jerusalem, and they besieged Ahaz but could not conquer him. [6] At that time Rezin the king of Syria recovered Elath for Syria and drove the men of Judah from Elath, and the Edomites came to Elath, where they dwell to this day. [7] So Ahaz sent messengers to Tiglath-pileser king of Assyria, saying, "I am your servant and your son. Come up and rescue me from the hand of the king of Syria and from the hand of the king of Israel, who are attacking me." [8] Ahaz also took the silver and gold that was found in the house of the LORD and in the treasures of the king's house and sent a present to the king of Assyria. [9] And the king of Assyria listened to him. The king of Assyria marched up

against Damascus and took it, carrying it people captive to Kir, and he killed Rezin

[10] When King Ahaz went to Damascu to meet Tiglath-pileser king of Assyria he saw the altar that was at Damascus And King Ahaz sent to Uriah the priest model of the altar, and its pattern, exact i all its details. [11] And Uriah the priest buil the altar; in accordance with all that Kin Ahaz had sent from Damascus, so Uriah th priest made it, before King Ahaz arrive from Damascus. [12] And when the kin came from Damascus, the king viewed th altar. Then the king drew near to the alta and went up on it [13] and burned his burn offering and his grain offering and poure his drink offering and threw the blood o his peace offerings on the altar. [14] And th bronze altar that was before the LORD h removed from the front of the house, fror the place between his altar and the hous of the LORD, and put it on the north sid of his altar. [15] And King Ahaz commande Uriah the priest, saying, "On the great alta burn the morning burnt offering and th evening grain offering and the king's burn offering and his grain offering, with th burnt offering of all the people of the lanc and their grain offering and their drin offering. And throw on it all the blood o the burnt offering and all the blood of th sacrifice, but the bronze altar shall be fo me to inquire by." [16] Uriah the priest did al this, as King Ahaz commanded.

[17] And King Ahaz cut off the frames of th stands and removed the basin from them and he took down the sea[2] from off th bronze oxen that were under it and put i on a stone pedestal. [18] And the covered wa for the Sabbath that had been built insid the house and the outer entrance for th king he caused to go around the house o the LORD, because of the king of Assyria [19] Now the rest of the acts of Ahaz tha he did, are they not written in the Boo of the Chronicles of the Kings of Judah [20] And Ahaz slept with his fathers and wa buried with his fathers in the city of David and Hezekiah his son reigned in his place

Hoshea Reigns in Israel

17 In the twelfth year of Ahaz king of Judah, Hoshea the son of Ela began to reign in Samaria over Israel, an he reigned nine years. [2] And he did wha

[1] Or *made his son pass through the fire* [2] Compare 1 Kings 7:23

was evil in the sight of the Lord, yet not as he kings of Israel who were before him. Against him came up Shalmaneser king of Assyria. And Hoshea became his vassal and paid him tribute. ⁴But the king of Assyria found treachery in Hoshea, for he had sent messengers to So, king of Egypt, and offered no tribute to the king of Assyria, as he had done year by year. Therefore the king of Assyria shut him up and bound him in prison. ⁵Then the king of Assyria invaded all the land and came to Samaria, and for three years he besieged it.

The Fall of Israel

⁶In the ninth year of Hoshea, the king of Assyria captured Samaria, and he carried the Israelites away to Assyria and placed them in Halah, and on the Habor, the river of Gozan, and in the cities of the Medes.

Exile Because of Idolatry

⁷And this occurred because the people of Israel had sinned against the Lord their God, who had brought them up out of the land of Egypt from under the hand of Pharaoh king of Egypt, and had feared other gods ⁸and walked in the customs of the nations whom the Lord drove out before the people of Israel, and in the customs that the kings of Israel had practiced. ⁹And the people of Israel did secretly against the Lord their God things that were not right. They built for themselves high places in all their towns, from watchtower to fortified city. ¹⁰They set up for themselves pillars and Asherim on every high hill and under every green tree, ¹¹and there they made offerings on all the high places, as the nations did whom the Lord carried away before them. And they did wicked things, provoking the Lord to anger, ¹²and they served idols, of which the Lord had said to them, "You shall not do this." ¹³Yet the Lord warned Israel and Judah by every prophet and every seer, saying, "Turn from your evil ways and keep my commandments and my statutes, in accordance with all the Law that I commanded your fathers, and that I sent to you by my servants the prophets."

¹⁴But they would not listen, but were stubborn, as their fathers had been, who did not believe in the Lord their God. ¹⁵They despised his statutes and his cov-enant that he made with their fathers and the warnings that he gave them. They went after false idols and became false, and they followed the nations that were around them, concerning whom the Lord had commanded them that they should not do like them. ¹⁶And they abandoned all the commandments of the Lord their God, and made for themselves metal images of two calves; and they made an Asherah and worshiped all the host of heaven and served Baal. ¹⁷And they burned their sons and their daughters as offerings¹ and used divination and omens and sold themselves to do evil in the sight of the Lord, provoking him to anger. ¹⁸Therefore the Lord was very angry with Israel and removed them out of his sight. None was left but the tribe of Judah only.

¹⁹Judah also did not keep the commandments of the Lord their God, but walked in the customs that Israel had introduced. ²⁰And the Lord rejected all the descendants of Israel and afflicted them and gave them into the hand of plunderers, until he had cast them out of his sight.

²¹When he had torn Israel from the house of David, they made Jeroboam the son of Nebat king. And Jeroboam drove Israel from following the Lord and made them commit great sin. ²²The people of Israel walked in all the sins that Jeroboam did. They did not depart from them, ²³until the Lord removed Israel out of his sight, as he had spoken by all his servants the prophets. So Israel was exiled from their own land to Assyria until this day.

Assyria Resettles Samaria

²⁴And the king of Assyria brought people from Babylon, Cuthah, Avva, Hamath, and Sepharvaim, and placed them in the cities of Samaria instead of the people of Israel. And they took possession of Samaria and lived in its cities. ²⁵And at the beginning of their dwelling there, they did not fear the Lord. Therefore the Lord sent lions among them, which killed some of them. ²⁶So the king of Assyria was told, "The nations that you have carried away and placed in the cities of Samaria do not know the law of the god of the land. Therefore he has sent lions among them, and behold, they are killing them, because they do not know the law of the god of the land." ²⁷Then the

¹Or made their sons and their daughters pass through the fire

king of Assyria commanded, "Send there one of the priests whom you carried away from there, and let him[1] go and dwell there and teach them the law of the god of the land." [28] So one of the priests whom they had carried away from Samaria came and lived in Bethel and taught them how they should fear the LORD.

[29] But every nation still made gods of its own and put them in the shrines of the high places that the Samaritans had made, every nation in the cities in which they lived. [30] The men of Babylon made Succoth-benoth, the men of Cuth made Nergal, the men of Hamath made Ashima, [31] and the Avvites made Nibhaz and Tartak; and the Sepharvites burned their children in the fire to Adrammelech and Anammelech, the gods of Sepharvaim. [32] They also feared the LORD and appointed from among themselves all sorts of people as priests of the high places, who sacrificed for them in the shrines of the high places. [33] So they feared the LORD but also served their own gods, after the manner of the nations from among whom they had been carried away.

[34] To this day they do according to the former manner. They do not fear the LORD, and they do not follow the statutes or the rules or the law or the commandment that the LORD commanded the children of Jacob, whom he named Israel. [35] The LORD made a covenant with them and commanded them, "You shall not fear other gods or bow yourselves to them or serve them or sacrifice to them, [36] but you shall fear the LORD, who brought you out of the land of Egypt with great power and with an outstretched arm. You shall bow yourselves to him, and to him you shall sacrifice. [37] And the statutes and the rules and the law and the commandment that he wrote for you, you shall always be careful to do. You shall not fear other gods, [38] and you shall not forget the covenant that I have made with you. You shall not fear other gods, [39] but you shall fear the LORD your God, and he will deliver you out of the hand of all your enemies." [40] However, they would not listen, but they did according to their former manner.

[41] So these nations feared the LORD and also served their carved images. Their children did likewise, and their children's children—as their fathers did, so they do to this day.

Hezekiah Reigns in Judah

18 In the third year of Hoshea son o Elah, king of Israel, Hezekiah th son of Ahaz, king of Judah, began to reig [2] He was twenty-five years old when h began to reign, and he reigned twenty nine years in Jerusalem. His mother's nam was Abi the daughter of Zechariah. [3] An he did what was right in the eyes of th LORD, according to all that David his fathe had done. [4] He removed the high place and broke the pillars and cut down th Asherah. And he broke in pieces the bronz serpent that Moses had made, for unt those days the people of Israel had mad offerings to it (it was called Nehushtan) [5] He trusted in the LORD, the God of Israe so that there was none like him among a the kings of Judah after him, nor amon those who were before him. [6] For he hel fast to the LORD. He did not depart from fo lowing him, but kept the commandment that the LORD commanded Moses. [7] An the LORD was with him; wherever he wer out, he prospered. He rebelled against th king of Assyria and would not serve hin [8] He struck down the Philistines as far a Gaza and its territory, from watchtower t fortified city.

[9] In the fourth year of King Hezekiah which was the seventh year of Hoshea so of Elah, king of Israel, Shalmaneser kin of Assyria came up against Samaria an besieged it, [10] and at the end of three year he took it. In the sixth year of Hezekiah which was the ninth year of Hoshea kin of Israel, Samaria was taken. [11] The kin of Assyria carried the Israelites away t Assyria and put them in Halah, and on th Habor, the river of Gozan, and in the citie of the Medes, [12] because they did not obe the voice of the LORD their God but trans gressed his covenant, even all that Mose the servant of the LORD commanded. The neither listened nor obeyed.

Sennacherib Attacks Judah

[13] In the fourteenth year of King Heze kiah, Sennacherib king of Assyria came u against all the fortified cities of Judah an took them. [14] And Hezekiah king of Judal sent to the king of Assyria at Lachish, say ing, "I have done wrong; withdraw fron me. Whatever you impose on me I wil bear." And the king of Assyria required o

---

[1] Syriac, Vulgate; Hebrew *them* [2] *Nehushtan* sounds like the Hebrew for both *bronze* and *serpent*

ezekiah king of Judah three hundred tal-
nts[1] of silver and thirty talents of gold.
And Hezekiah gave him all the silver that
vas found in the house of the LORD and
a the treasuries of the king's house. **16** At
1at time Hezekiah stripped the gold from
1e doors of the temple of the LORD and
om the doorposts that Hezekiah king of
1dah had overlaid and gave it to the king of
ssyria. **17** And the king of Assyria sent the
artan, the Rab-saris, and the Rabshakeh
vith a great army from Lachish to King
ezekiah at Jerusalem. And they went up
nd came to Jerusalem. When they arrived,
1ey came and stood by the conduit of the
pper pool, which is on the highway to the
Vasher's Field. **18** And when they called for
1e king, there came out to them Eliakim
1e son of Hilkiah, who was over the house-
old, and Shebnah the secretary, and Joah
1e son of Asaph, the recorder.

19 And the Rabshakeh said to them, "Say
o Hezekiah, 'Thus says the great king, the
ing of Assyria: On what do you rest this
ust of yours? **20** Do you think that mere
ords are strategy and power for war?
1 whom do you now trust, that you have
ebelled against me? **21** Behold, you are
usting now in Egypt, that broken reed
f a staff, which will pierce the hand of
ny man who leans on it. Such is Pharaoh
ing of Egypt to all who trust in him. **22** But
' you say to me, "We trust in the LORD our
od," is it not he whose high places and
Itars Hezekiah has removed, saying to
1dah and to Jerusalem, "You shall worship
efore this altar in Jerusalem"? **23** Come
ow, make a wager with my master the
ing of Assyria: I will give you two thou-
nd horses, if you are able on your part
o set riders on them. **24** How then can you
epulse a single captain among the least
f my master's servants, when you trust
1 Egypt for chariots and for horsemen?
⁵ Moreover, is it without the LORD that
have come up against this place to destroy
:? The LORD said to me, Go up against this
and, and destroy it.'"

26 Then Eliakim the son of Hilkiah, and
hebnah, and Joah, said to the Rabshakeh,
Please speak to your servants in Aramaic,
or we understand it. Do not speak to us in
he language of Judah within the hearing of
he people who are on the wall." **27** But the
abshakeh said to them, "Has my master

sent me to speak these words to your master and to you, and not to the men sitting
on the wall, who are doomed with you to
eat their own dung and to drink their own
urine?"

28 Then the Rabshakeh stood and called
out in a loud voice in the language of Judah:
"Hear the word of the great king, the king
of Assyria! **29** Thus says the king: 'Do not
let Hezekiah deceive you, for he will not
be able to deliver you out of my[2] hand.
30 Do not let Hezekiah make you trust in
the LORD by saying, The LORD will surely
deliver us, and this city will not be given
into the hand of the king of Assyria.' **31** Do
not listen to Hezekiah, for thus says the
king of Assyria: 'Make your peace with me[3]
and come out to me. Then each one of you
will eat of his own vine, and each one of
his own fig tree, and each one of you will
drink the water of his own cistern, **32** until
I come and take you away to a land like
your own land, a land of grain and wine, a
land of bread and vineyards, a land of olive
trees and honey, that you may live, and not
die. And do not listen to Hezekiah when
he misleads you by saying, "The LORD will
deliver us." **33** Has any of the gods of the
nations ever delivered his land out of the
hand of the king of Assyria? **34** Where are
the gods of Hamath and Arpad? Where
are the gods of Sepharvaim, Hena, and
Ivvah? Have they delivered Samaria out
of my hand? **35** Who among all the gods of
the lands have delivered their lands out
of my hand, that the LORD should deliver
Jerusalem out of my hand?'"

36 But the people were silent and answered him not a word, for the king's command was, "Do not answer him." **37** Then
Eliakim the son of Hilkiah, who was over
the household, and Shebna the secretary,
and Joah the son of Asaph, the recorder,
came to Hezekiah with their clothes torn
and told him the words of the Rabshakeh.

Isaiah Reassures Hezekiah

19 As soon as King Hezekiah heard
it, he tore his clothes and covered
himself with sackcloth and went into the
house of the LORD. **2** And he sent Eliakim,
who was over the household, and Shebna
the secretary, and the senior priests, covered with sackcloth, to the prophet Isaiah
the son of Amoz. **3** They said to him, "Thus

A *talent* was about 75 pounds or 34 kilograms ²Hebrew *his* ³Hebrew *Make a blessing with me* says Hezekiah, This day is a day of distress, of rebuke, and of disgrace; children have come to the point of birth, and there is no strength to bring them forth. ⁴It may be that the LORD your God heard all the words of the Rabshakeh, whom his master the king of Assyria has sent to mock the living God, and will rebuke the words that the LORD your God has heard; therefore lift up your prayer for the remnant that is left." ⁵When the servants of King Hezekiah came to Isaiah, ⁶Isaiah said to them, "Say to your master, 'Thus says the LORD: Do not be afraid because of the words that you have heard, with which the servants of the king of Assyria have reviled me. ⁷Behold, I will put a spirit in him, so that he shall hear a rumor and return to his own land, and I will make him fall by the sword in his own land.'"

Sennacherib Defies the LORD

⁸The Rabshakeh returned, and found the king of Assyria fighting against Libnah, for he heard that the king had left Lachish. ⁹Now the king heard concerning Tirhakah king of Cush, "Behold, he has set out to fight against you." So he sent messengers again to Hezekiah, saying, ¹⁰"Thus shall you speak to Hezekiah king of Judah: 'Do not let your God in whom you trust deceive you by promising that Jerusalem will not be given into the hand of the king of Assyria. ¹¹Behold, you have heard what the kings of Assyria have done to all lands, devoting them to destruction. And shall you be delivered? ¹²Have the gods of the nations delivered them, the nations that my fathers destroyed, Gozan, Haran, Rezeph, and the people of Eden who were in Telassar? ¹³Where is the king of Hamath, the king of Arpad, the king of the city of Sepharvaim, the king of Hena, or the king of Ivvah?'"

Hezekiah's Prayer

¹⁴Hezekiah received the letter from the hand of the messengers and read it; and Hezekiah went up to the house of the LORD and spread it before the LORD. ¹⁵And Hezekiah prayed before the LORD and said: "O LORD, the God of Israel, enthroned above the cherubim, you are the God, you alone, of all the kingdoms of the earth; you have made heaven and earth. ¹⁶Incline your ear, O LORD, and hear; open your eyes, O LORD, and see; and hear the

words of Sennacherib, which he has se[nt] to mock the living God. ¹⁷Truly, O LOR[D] the kings of Assyria have laid waste th[e] nations and their lands ¹⁸and have cas[t] their gods into the fire, for they were n[o] gods, but the work of men's hands, woo[d] and stone. Therefore they were destroye[d] ¹⁹So now, O LORD our God, save us, pleas[e] from his hand, that all the kingdoms o[f] the earth may know that you, O LORD, ar[e] God alone."

Isaiah Prophesies Sennacherib's Fall

²⁰Then Isaiah the son of Amoz sent t[o] Hezekiah, saying, "Thus says the LOR[D] the God of Israel: Your prayer to me abou[t] Sennacherib king of Assyria I have hear[d] ²¹This is the word that the LORD has sp[o]ken concerning him:

> "She despises you, she scorns you—
>   the virgin daughter of Zion;
> she wags her head behind you—
>   the daughter of Jerusalem.
>
> ²² "Whom have you mocked and reviled
>   Against whom have you raised
>   your voice
>   and lifted your eyes to the heights?
>   Against the Holy One of Israel!
> ²³ By your messengers you have
>   mocked the Lord,
>   and you have said, 'With my many
>   chariots
>   I have gone up the heights of the
>   mountains,
>   to the far recesses of Lebanon;
>   I felled its tallest cedars,
>   its choicest cypresses;
>   I entered its farthest lodging place,
>   its most fruitful forest.
> ²⁴ I dug wells
>   and drank foreign waters,
>   and I dried up with the sole of my
>   foot
>   all the streams of Egypt.'
>
> ²⁵ "Have you not heard
>   that I determined it long ago?
>   I planned from days of old
>   what now I bring to pass,
>   that you should turn fortified cities
>   into heaps of ruins,
> ²⁶ while their inhabitants, shorn of
>   strength,
>   are dismayed and confounded,

and have become like plants of the
    field
    and like tender grass,
    like grass on the housetops,
    blighted before it is grown.

"But I know your sitting down
    and your going out and coming in,
    and your raging against me.
Because you have raged against me
    and your complacency has come
        into my ears,
I will put my hook in your nose
    and my bit in your mouth,
and I will turn you back on the way
    by which you came.

29 "And this shall be the sign for you: this
ear eat what grows of itself, and in the
econd year what springs of the same.
hen in the third year sow and reap and
lant vineyards, and eat their fruit. 30 And
e surviving remnant of the house of
dah shall again take root downward and
ear fruit upward. 31 For out of Jerusalem
hall go a remnant, and out of Mount Zion
band of survivors. The zeal of the LORD
ill do this.

32 "Therefore thus says the LORD con-
erning the king of Assyria: He shall not
ome into this city or shoot an arrow there,
r come before it with a shield or cast up a
ege mound against it. 33 By the way that
e came, by the same he shall return, and
e shall not come into this city, declares the
ORD. 34 For I will defend this city to save
, for my own sake and for the sake of my
ervant David."

35 And that night the angel of the LORD
ent out and struck down 185,000 in the
amp of the Assyrians. And when people
rose early in the morning, behold, these
ere all dead bodies. 36 Then Sennacherib
ing of Assyria departed and went home
nd lived at Nineveh. 37 And as he was
orshiping in the house of Nisroch his
od, Adrammelech and Sharezer, his sons,
truck him down with the sword and
scaped into the land of Ararat. And Esar-
addon his son reigned in his place.

ezekiah's Illness and Recovery

20 In those days Hezekiah became sick
and was at the point of death. And
aiah the prophet the son of Amoz came to
im and said to him, "Thus says the LORD,
et your house in order, for you shall die;

you shall not recover.'" 2 Then Hezekiah
turned his face to the wall and prayed to
the LORD, saying, 3 "Now, O LORD, please
remember how I have walked before you
in faithfulness and with a whole heart, and
have done what is good in your sight." And
Hezekiah wept bitterly. 4 And before Isaiah
had gone out of the middle court, the word
of the LORD came to him: 5 "Turn back, and
say to Hezekiah the leader of my people,
Thus says the LORD, the God of David your
father: I have heard your prayer; I have
seen your tears. Behold, I will heal you. On
the third day you shall go up to the house
of the LORD, 6 and I will add fifteen years
to your life. I will deliver you and this city
out of the hand of the king of Assyria, and
I will defend this city for my own sake and
for my servant David's sake." 7 And Isaiah
said, "Bring a cake of figs. And let them take
and lay it on the boil, that he may recover."

8 And Hezekiah said to Isaiah, "What
shall be the sign that the LORD will heal
me, and that I shall go up to the house of
the LORD on the third day?" 9 And Isaiah
said, "This shall be the sign to you from
the LORD, that the LORD will do the thing
that he has promised: shall the shadow go
forward ten steps, or go back ten steps?"
10 And Hezekiah answered, "It is an easy
thing for the shadow to lengthen ten steps.
Rather let the shadow go back ten steps."
11 And Isaiah the prophet called to the
LORD, and he brought the shadow back
ten steps, by which it had gone down on
the steps of Ahaz.

Hezekiah and the Babylonian Envoys

12 At that time Merodach-baladan the son
of Baladan, king of Babylon, sent envoys
with letters and a present to Hezekiah,
for he heard that Hezekiah had been sick.
13 And Hezekiah welcomed them, and he
showed them all his treasure house, the
silver, the gold, the spices, the precious
oil, his armory, all that was found in his
storehouses. There was nothing in his
house or in all his realm that Hezekiah did
not show them. 14 Then Isaiah the prophet
came to King Hezekiah, and said to him,
"What did these men say? And from where
did they come to you?" And Hezekiah said,
"They have come from a far country, from
Babylon." 15 He said, "What have they seen
in your house?" And Hezekiah answered,
"They have seen all that is in my house;

there is nothing in my storehouses that I did not show them."

¹⁶ Then Isaiah said to Hezekiah, "Hear the word of the LORD: ¹⁷ Behold, the days are coming, when all that is in your house, and that which your fathers have stored up till this day, shall be carried to Babylon. Nothing shall be left, says the LORD. ¹⁸ And some of your own sons, who shall be born to you, shall be taken away, and they shall be eunuchs in the palace of the king of Babylon." ¹⁹ Then Hezekiah said to Isaiah, "The word of the LORD that you have spoken is good." For he thought, "Why not, if there will be peace and security in my days?"

²⁰ The rest of the deeds of Hezekiah and all his might and how he made the pool and the conduit and brought water into the city, are they not written in the Book of the Chronicles of the Kings of Judah? ²¹ And Hezekiah slept with his fathers, and Manasseh his son reigned in his place.

Manasseh Reigns in Judah

21 Manasseh was twelve years old when he began to reign, and he reigned fifty-five years in Jerusalem. His mother's name was Hephzibah. ² And he did what was evil in the sight of the LORD, according to the despicable practices of the nations whom the LORD drove out before the people of Israel. ³ For he rebuilt the high places that Hezekiah his father had destroyed, and he erected altars for Baal and made an Asherah, as Ahab king of Israel had done, and worshiped all the host of heaven and served them. ⁴ And he built altars in the house of the LORD, of which the LORD had said, "In Jerusalem will I put my name." ⁵ And he built altars for all the host of heaven in the two courts of the house of the LORD. ⁶ And he burned his son as an offering[1] and used fortune-telling and omens and dealt with mediums and with necromancers. He did much evil in the sight of the LORD, provoking him to anger. ⁷ And the carved image of Asherah that he had made he set in the house of which the LORD said to David and to Solomon his son, "In this house, and in Jerusalem, which I have chosen out of all the tribes of Israel, I will put my name forever. ⁸ And I will not cause the feet of Israel to wander anymore out of the land that I gave to their fathers, if only they will be careful to do

according to all that I have commanded them, and according to all the Law that my servant Moses commanded them." ⁹ But they did not listen, and Manasseh led them astray to do more evil than the nations had done whom the LORD destroyed before the people of Israel.

Manasseh's Idolatry Denounced

¹⁰ And the LORD said by his servants the prophets, ¹¹ "Because Manasseh king of Judah has committed these abominations and has done things more evil than all that the Amorites did, who were before him, and has made Judah also to sin with his idols, ¹² therefore thus says the LORD, the God of Israel: Behold, I am bringing upon Jerusalem and Judah such disaster[2] that the ears of everyone who hears of it will tingle. ¹³ And I will stretch over Jerusalem the measuring line of Samaria, and the plumb line of the house of Ahab, and I will wipe Jerusalem as one wipes a dish, wiping it and turning it upside down. ¹⁴ And I will forsake the remnant of my heritage and give them into the hand of their enemies, and they shall become a prey and a spoil to all their enemies, ¹⁵ because they have done what is evil in my sight and have provoked me to anger, since the day their fathers came out of Egypt, even to this day."

¹⁶ Moreover, Manasseh shed very much innocent blood, till he had filled Jerusalem from one end to another, besides the sin that he made Judah to sin so that they did what was evil in the sight of the LORD.

¹⁷ Now the rest of the acts of Manasseh and all that he did, and the sin that he committed, are they not written in the Book of the Chronicles of the Kings of Judah? ¹⁸ And Manasseh slept with his fathers and was buried in the garden of his house, in the garden of Uzza, and Amon his son reigned in his place.

Amon Reigns in Judah

¹⁹ Amon was twenty-two years old when he began to reign, and he reigned two years in Jerusalem. His mother's name was Meshullemeth the daughter of Haruz of Jotbah. ²⁰ And he did what was evil in the sight of the LORD, as Manasseh his father had done. ²¹ He walked in all the way in which his father walked and served the idols that his father served and worshiped

[1] Hebrew *made his son pass through the fire* [2] Or *evil*

hem. ²²He abandoned the LORD, the God of his fathers, and did not walk in the way of the LORD. ²³And the servants of Amon conspired against him and put the king to death in his house. ²⁴But the people of the land struck down all those who had conspired against King Amon, and the people of the land made Josiah his son king in his place. ²⁵Now the rest of the acts of Amon that he did, are they not written in the Book of the Chronicles of the Kings of Judah? ²⁶And he was buried in his tomb in the garden of Uzza, and Josiah his son reigned in his place.

Josiah Reigns in Judah

22 Josiah was eight years old when he began to reign, and he reigned thirty-one years in Jerusalem. His mother's name was Jedidah the daughter of Adaiah of Bozkath. ²And he did what was right in the eyes of the LORD and walked in all the way of David his father, and he did not turn aside to the right or to the left.

Josiah Repairs the Temple

³In the eighteenth year of King Josiah, the king sent Shaphan the son of Azaliah, son of Meshullam, the secretary, to the house of the LORD, saying, ⁴"Go up to Hilkiah the high priest, that he may count the money that has been brought into the house of the LORD, which the keepers of the threshold have collected from the people. ⁵And let it be given into the hand of the workmen who have the oversight of the house of the LORD, and let them give it to the workmen who are at the house of the LORD, repairing the house ⁶(that is, to the carpenters, and to the builders, and to the masons), and let them use it for buying timber and quarried stone to repair the house. ⁷But no accounting shall be asked from them for the money that is delivered into their hand, for they deal honestly."

Hilkiah Finds the Book of the Law

⁸And Hilkiah the high priest said to Shaphan the secretary, "I have found the Book of the Law in the house of the LORD." And Hilkiah gave the book to Shaphan, and he read it. ⁹And Shaphan the secretary came to the king, and reported to the king, "Your servants have emptied out the money that was found in the house and have delivered it into the hand of the workmen who have the oversight of the house

of the LORD." ¹⁰Then Shaphan the secretary told the king, "Hilkiah the priest has given me a book." And Shaphan read it before the king.

> ### Ask Yourself . . .
> #### ABOUT GOD'S WORD
> When the priests found the book of Moses' teachings, King Josiah tore his clothes. He was upset because the people hadn't followed God and he knew that God was angry because of it (see 2 Kings 22:8–13). Ask yourself:
> - How important to me is God's Word and following it?
> - Do I grieve when I mess up?
> - What can I do today to prove to God that his Word really matters to me?
> - When I mess up, can I then rest in the grace of God in the gospel?

¹¹When the king heard the words of the Book of the Law, he tore his clothes. ¹²And the king commanded Hilkiah the priest, and Ahikam the son of Shaphan, and Achbor the son of Micaiah, and Shaphan the secretary, and Asaiah the king's servant, saying, ¹³"Go, inquire of the LORD for me, and for the people, and for all Judah, concerning the words of this book that has been found. For great is the wrath of the LORD that is kindled against us, because our fathers have not obeyed the words of this book, to do according to all that is written concerning us."

¹⁴So Hilkiah the priest, and Ahikam, and Achbor, and Shaphan, and Asaiah went to Huldah the prophetess, the wife of Shallum the son of Tikvah, son of Harhas, keeper of the wardrobe (now she lived in Jerusalem in the Second Quarter), and they talked with her. ¹⁵And she said to them, "Thus says the LORD, the God of Israel: 'Tell the man who sent you to me, ¹⁶Thus says the

LORD, Behold, I will bring disaster upon this place and upon its inhabitants, all the words of the book that the king of Judah has read. [17] Because they have forsaken me and have made offerings to other gods, that they might provoke me to anger with all the work of their hands, therefore my wrath will be kindled against this place, and it will not be quenched. [18] But to the king of Judah, who sent you to inquire of the LORD, thus shall you say to him, Thus says the LORD, the God of Israel: Regarding the words that you have heard, [19] because your heart was penitent, and you humbled yourself before the LORD, when you heard how I spoke against this place and against its inhabitants, that they should become a desolation and a curse, and you have torn your clothes and wept before me, I also have heard you, declares the LORD. [20] Therefore, behold, I will gather you to your fathers, and you shall be gathered to your grave in peace, and your eyes shall not see all the disaster that I will bring upon this place.'" And they brought back word to the king.

Josiah's Reforms

23 Then the king sent, and all the elders of Judah and Jerusalem were gathered to him. [2] And the king went up to the house of the LORD, and with him all the men of Judah and all the inhabitants of Jerusalem and the priests and the prophets, all the people, both small and great. And he read in their hearing all the words of the Book of the Covenant that had been found in the house of the LORD. [3] And the king stood by the pillar and made a covenant before the LORD, to walk after the LORD and to keep his commandments and his testimonies and his statutes with all his heart and all his soul, to perform the words of this covenant that were written in this book. And all the people joined in the covenant.

[4] And the king commanded Hilkiah the high priest and the priests of the second order and the keepers of the threshold to bring out of the temple of the LORD all the vessels made for Baal, for Asherah, and for all the host of heaven. He burned them outside Jerusalem in the fields of the Kidron and carried their ashes to Bethel.

[5] And he deposed the priests whom the kings of Judah had ordained to make offerings in the high places at the cities of Judah and around Jerusalem; those also who burned incense to Baal, to the sun and the moon and the constellations and all the host of the heavens. [6] And he brought out the Asherah from the house of the LORD, outside Jerusalem, to the brook Kidron, and burned it at the brook Kidron and beat it to dust and cast the dust of it upon the graves of the common people. [7] And he broke down the houses of the male cult prostitutes who were in the house of the LORD, where the women wove hangings for the Asherah. [8] And he brought all the priests out of the cities of Judah, and defiled the high places where the priests had made offerings, from Geba to Beersheba. And he broke down the high places of the gates that were at the entrance of the gate of Joshua the governor of the city, which were on one's left at the gate of the city. [9] However, the priests of the high places did not come up to the altar of the LORD in Jerusalem, but they ate unleavened bread among their brothers. [10] And he defiled Topheth, which is in the Valley of the Son of Hinnom, that no one might burn his son or his daughter as an offering to Molech.[1] [11] And he removed the horses that the kings of Judah had dedicated to the sun, at the entrance to the house of the LORD, by the chamber of Nathan-melech the chamberlain, which was in the precincts.[2] And he burned the chariots of the sun with fire. [12] And the altars on the roof of the upper chamber of Ahaz, which the kings of Judah had made, and the altars that Manasseh had made in the two courts of the house of the LORD, he pulled down and broke in pieces[3] and cast the dust of them into the brook Kidron. [13] And the king defiled the high places that were east of Jerusalem, to the south of the mount of corruption, which Solomon the king of Israel had built for Ashtoreth the abomination of the Sidonians, and for Chemosh the abomination of Moab, and for Milcom the abomination of the Ammonites. [14] And he broke in pieces the pillars and cut down the Asherim and filled their places with the bones of men.

---

[1] Hebrew *might cause his son or daughter to pass through the fire for Molech* [2] The meaning of the Hebrew word is uncertain [3] Hebrew *pieces from there*

¹⁵ Moreover, the altar at Bethel, the high place erected by Jeroboam the son of Nebat, who made Israel to sin, that altar with the high place he pulled down and burned,¹ reducing it to dust. He also burned the Asherah. ¹⁶ And as Josiah turned, he saw the tombs there on the mount. And he sent and took the bones out of the tombs and burned them on the altar and defiled it, according to the word of the LORD that the man of God proclaimed, who had predicted these things. ¹⁷ Then he said, "What is that monument that I see?" And the men of the city told him, "It is the tomb of the man of God who came from Judah and predicted² these things that you have done against the altar at Bethel." ¹⁸ And he said, "Let him be; let no man move his bones." So they let his bones alone, with the bones of the prophet who came out of Samaria. ¹⁹ And Josiah removed all the shrines also of the high places that were in the cities of Samaria, which kings of Israel had made, provoking the LORD to anger. He did to them according to all that he had done at Bethel. ²⁰ And he sacrificed all the priests of the high places who were there, on the altars, and burned human bones on them. Then he returned to Jerusalem.

Josiah Restores the Passover

²¹ And the king commanded all the people, "Keep the Passover to the LORD your God, as it is written in this Book of the Covenant." ²² For no such Passover had been kept since the days of the judges who judged Israel, or during all the days of the kings of Israel or of the kings of Judah. ²³ But in the eighteenth year of King Josiah this Passover was kept to the LORD in Jerusalem.

²⁴ Moreover, Josiah put away the mediums and the necromancers and the household gods and the idols and all the abominations that were seen in the land of Judah and in Jerusalem, that he might establish the words of the law that were written in the book that Hilkiah the priest found in the house of the LORD. ²⁵ Before him there was no king like him, who turned to the LORD with all his heart and with all his soul and with all his might, according to all the Law of Moses, nor did any like him arise after him.

²⁶ Still the LORD did not turn from the burning of his great wrath, by which his anger was kindled against Judah, because of all the provocations with which Manasseh had provoked him. ²⁷ And the LORD said, "I will remove Judah also out of my sight, as I have removed Israel, and I will cast off this city that I have chosen, Jerusalem, and the house of which I said, My name shall be there."

Josiah's Death in Battle

²⁸ Now the rest of the acts of Josiah and all that he did, are they not written in the Book of the Chronicles of the Kings of Judah? ²⁹ In his days Pharaoh Neco king of Egypt went up to the king of Assyria to the river Euphrates. King Josiah went to meet him, and Pharaoh Neco killed him at Megiddo, as soon as he saw him. ³⁰ And his servants carried him dead in a chariot from Megiddo and brought him to Jerusalem and buried him in his own tomb. And the people of the land took Jehoahaz the son of Josiah, and anointed him, and made him king in his father's place.

Jehoahaz's Reign and Captivity

³¹ Jehoahaz was twenty-three years old when he began to reign, and he reigned three months in Jerusalem. His mother's name was Hamutal the daughter of Jeremiah of Libnah. ³² And he did what was evil in the sight of the LORD, according to all that his fathers had done. ³³ And Pharaoh Neco put him in bonds at Riblah in the land of Hamath, that he might not reign in Jerusalem, and laid on the land a tribute of a hundred talents³ of silver and a talent of gold. ³⁴ And Pharaoh Neco made Eliakim the son of Josiah king in the place of Josiah his father, and changed his name to Jehoiakim. But he took Jehoahaz away, and he came to Egypt and died there. ³⁵ And Jehoiakim gave the silver and the gold to Pharaoh, but he taxed the land to give the money according to the command of Pharaoh. He exacted the silver and the gold of the people of the land, from everyone according to his assessment, to give it to Pharaoh Neco.

Jehoiakim Reigns in Judah

³⁶ Jehoiakim was twenty-five years old when he began to reign, and he reigned

eleven years in Jerusalem. His mother's name was Zebidah the daughter of Pedaiah of Rumah. [37]And he did what was evil in the sight of the LORD, according to all that his fathers had done.

24 In his days, Nebuchadnezzar king of Babylon came up, and Jehoiakim became his servant for three years. Then he turned and rebelled against him. [2]And the LORD sent against him bands of the Chaldeans and bands of the Syrians and bands of the Moabites and bands of the Ammonites, and sent them against Judah to destroy it, according to the word of the LORD that he spoke by his servants the prophets. [3]Surely this came upon Judah at the command of the LORD, to remove them out of his sight, for the sins of Manasseh, according to all that he had done, [4]and also for the innocent blood that he had shed. For he filled Jerusalem with innocent blood, and the LORD would not pardon. [5]Now the rest of the deeds of Jehoiakim and all that he did, are they not written in the Book of the Chronicles of the Kings of Judah? [6]So Jehoiakim slept with his fathers, and Jehoiachin his son reigned in his place. [7]And the king of Egypt did not come again out of his land, for the king of Babylon had taken all that belonged to the king of Egypt from the Brook of Egypt to the river Euphrates.

Jehoiachin Reigns in Judah

[8]Jehoiachin was eighteen years old when he became king, and he reigned three months in Jerusalem. His mother's name was Nehushta the daughter of Elnathan of Jerusalem. [9]And he did what was evil in the sight of the LORD, according to all that his father had done.

Jerusalem Captured

[10]At that time the servants of Nebuchadnezzar king of Babylon came up to Jerusalem, and the city was besieged. [11]And Nebuchadnezzar king of Babylon came to the city while his servants were besieging it, [12]and Jehoiachin the king of Judah gave himself up to the king of Babylon, himself and his mother and his servants and his officials and his palace officials. The king of Babylon took him prisoner in the eighth year of his reign [13]and carried off all the treasures of the house of the LORD and the treasures of the king's house, and

cut in pieces all the vessels of gold in the temple of the LORD, which Solomon king of Israel had made, as the LORD had foretold. [14]He carried away all Jerusalem and all the officials and all the mighty men of valor, 10,000 captives, and all the craftsmen and the smiths. None remained, except the poorest people of the land. [15]And he carried away Jehoiachin to Babylon. The king's mother, the king's wives, his officials, and the chief men of the land he took into captivity from Jerusalem to Babylon. [16]And the king of Babylon brought captive to Babylon all the men of valor, 7,000, and the craftsmen and the metal workers, 1,000, all of them strong and fit for war. [17]And the king of Babylon made Mattaniah, Jehoiachin's uncle, king in his place, and changed his name to Zedekiah.

Zedekiah Reigns in Judah

[18]Zedekiah was twenty-one years old when he became king, and he reigned eleven years in Jerusalem. His mother's name was Hamutal the daughter of Jeremiah of Libnah. [19]And he did what was evil in the sight of the LORD, according to all that Jehoiakim had done. [20]For because of the anger of the LORD it came to the point in Jerusalem and Judah that he cast them out from his presence.

And Zedekiah rebelled against the king of Babylon.

Fall and Captivity of Judah

25 And in the ninth year of his reign, in the tenth month, on the tenth day of the month, Nebuchadnezzar king of Babylon came with all his army against Jerusalem and laid siege to it. And they built siegeworks all around it. [2]So the city was besieged till the eleventh year of King Zedekiah. [3]On the ninth day of the fourth month the famine was so severe in the city that there was no food for the people of the land. [4]Then a breach was made in the city, and all the men of war fled by night by the way of the gate between the two walls, by the king's garden, and the Chaldeans were around the city. And they went in the direction of the Arabah. [5]But the army of the Chaldeans pursued the king and overtook him in the plains of Jericho, and all his army was scattered from him. [6]Then they captured the king and brought him up to the king of Babylon at Riblah, and they passed sentence on him. **7** They slaughtered the sons of Zedekiah before his eyes, and put out the eyes of Zedekiah and bound him in chains and took him to Babylon.

8 In the fifth month, on the seventh day of the month—that was the nineteenth year of King Nebuchadnezzar, king of Babylon—Nebuzaradan, the captain of the bodyguard, a servant of the king of Babylon, came to Jerusalem. **9** And he burned the house of the LORD and the king's house and all the houses of Jerusalem; every great house he burned down. **10** And all the army of the Chaldeans, who were with the captain of the guard, broke down the walls around Jerusalem. **11** And the rest of the people who were left in the city and the deserters who had deserted to the king of Babylon, together with the rest of the multitude, Nebuzaradan the captain of the guard carried into exile. **12** But the captain of the guard left some of the poorest of the land to be vinedressers and plowmen.

13 And the pillars of bronze that were in the house of the LORD, and the stands and the bronze sea that were in the house of the LORD, the Chaldeans broke in pieces and carried the bronze to Babylon. **14** And they took away the pots and the shovels and the snuffers and the dishes for incense and all the vessels of bronze used in the temple service, **15** the fire pans also and the bowls. What was of gold the captain of the guard took away as gold, and what was of silver, as silver. **16** As for the two pillars, the one sea, and the stands that Solomon had made for the house of the LORD, the bronze of all these vessels was beyond weight. **17** The height of the one pillar was eighteen cubits,[1] and on it was a capital of bronze. The height of the capital was three cubits. A latticework and pomegranates, all of bronze, were all around the capital. And the second pillar had the same, with the latticework.

18 And the captain of the guard took Seraiah the chief priest and Zephaniah the second priest and the three keepers of the threshold; **19** and from the city he took an officer who had been in command of the men of war, and five men of the king's council who were found in the city; and the secretary of the commander of the army, who mustered the people of the land; and sixty men of the people of the land, who were found in the city. **20** And Nebuzaradan the captain of the guard took them and brought them to the king of Babylon at Riblah. **21** And the king of Babylon struck them down and put them to death at Riblah in the land of Hamath. So Judah was taken into exile out of its land.

Gedaliah Made Governor of Judah

22 And over the people who remained in the land of Judah, whom Nebuchadnezzar king of Babylon had left, he appointed Gedaliah the son of Ahikam, son of Shaphan, governor. **23** Now when all the captains and their men heard that the king of Babylon had appointed Gedaliah governor, they came with their men to Gedaliah at Mizpah, namely, Ishmael the son of Nethaniah, and Johanan the son of Kareah, and Seraiah the son of Tanhumeth the Netophathite, and Jaazaniah the son of the Maacathite. **24** And Gedaliah swore to them and their men, saying, "Do not be afraid because of the Chaldean officials. Live in the land and serve the king of Babylon, and it shall be well with you." **25** But in the seventh month, Ishmael the son of Nethaniah, son of Elishama, of the royal family, came with ten men and struck down Gedaliah and put him to death along with the Jews and the Chaldeans who were with him at Mizpah. **26** Then all the people, both small and great, and the captains of the forces arose and went to Egypt, for they were afraid of the Chaldeans.

Jehoiachin Released from Prison

27 And in the thirty-seventh year of the exile of Jehoiachin king of Judah, in the twelfth month, on the twenty-seventh day of the month, Evil-merodach king of Babylon, in the year that he began to reign, graciously freed[2] Jehoiachin king of Judah from prison. **28** And he spoke kindly to him and gave him a seat above the seats of the kings who were with him in Babylon. **29** So Jehoiachin put off his prison garments. And every day of his life he dined regularly at the king's table, **30** and for his allowance, a regular allowance was given him by the king, according to his daily needs, as long as he lived.

A *cubit* was about 18 inches or 45 centimeters [2] Hebrew *reign, lifted up the head of*

INTRODUCTION TO
1 Chronicles

Author: Unknown
Time: Possibly around 400 B.C.
Place: Unknown
Written to: The Israelites

The gist

The purpose of the Chronicles was to remind the Israelites of God's faithfulness in their past, and that's why genealogies fill the first part of the book. But it was also written to tell about the accomplishments and acts of King David. David led the people not only as a king but also in spiritual matters, and this book shows how he led his people to worship God.

Things to look for

- The ark of the covenant (see 1 Chron. 6:31; 13:1-14; 15:1-17:2)
- The death of Saul (see 1 Chronicles 10)
- David as a spiritual leader (see 1 Chronicles 15)

Know Your History

> And the fame of David went out into all lands, and the LORD brought the fear of him upon all nations.
>
> *1 Chronicles 14:17*

What's your legacy going to be? When you're dead and gone, what are people going to remember about you and what will they treasure that was yours? How will they be better because you existed? How will your family be different generations from now because of who you are and who you're becoming?

When you're young, you can have a feeling of powerlessness over your destiny, like you have no control over future generations. But then something starts to change in you, and you start to think about things like how your life will make a difference. You start to see that every decision you've made affects not only you but also the people who love you and even the ones who will never ever know you but will hear stories about you generations from now. Starting with you, your family history is changing. It's either getting holier and healthier or getting more uninspiring and unhealthy. The Israelites had a noble heritage of God's grace and promises to David that God wanted them to remember, so God had it recorded in 1 and 2 Chronicles. Even though history can sometimes be boring, we need it so that we don't forget where we've come from and where we should be going.

As a God Girl, you can give hope not only to your family but to your generation by being a shining light in the darkness, a girl of peace and hope. Think about how one man, David, changed the world, and then think about how your life can make a difference to your generation and even generations to come. So: are you going to change and start thinking of your devotion to the Savior as something that can empower you to make life matter, or are you going to stay lost in your own powerlessness and need? For the God Girl the answer is clear: change today and every day, by God's grace, to move in the direction of faith. Know what you believe and why you believe it. Learn to live up to the name of God Girl, and the impact you have on the world will last into eternity.

Must-Know Terms and Verses

Burnt Offering

An offering in which the entire sacrificial animal was to be burned as an offering to the Lord. This was a permanent requirement on the Jews and was to take place day and night (see Lev. 6:8–23).

City of David

The royal city that David captured and named Jerusalem (also known as Zion). It can also refer to the city of Bethlehem, where Jesus was born (see John 7:42).

Genealogy

A record of the descent of a family or group from their ancestors.

Peace Offering

Also known as the fellowship offering, this offering was made to God, and then part of the offering was fed to the worshipers in attendance.

Jabez called upon the God of Israel, saying, "Oh that you would bless me and enlarge my border, and that your hand might be with me, and that you would keep me from harm so that it might not bring me pain!" And God granted what he asked. *1 Chronicles 4:10*

"Who is like your people Israel, the one nation on earth whom God went to redeem to be his people, making for yourself a name for great and awesome things?" *1 Chronicles 17:21*

"And you, Solomon my son, know the God of your father and serve him with a whole heart and with a willing mind, for the LORD searches all hearts and understands every plan and thought. If you seek him, he will be found by you, but if you forsake him, he will cast you off forever. Be careful now, for the LORD has chosen you to build a house for the sanctuary; be strong and do it." *1 Chronicles 28:9–10*

1 Chronicles

From Adam to Abraham

1 ^{1} Adam, Seth, Enosh; ^{2} Kenan, Mahalalel, Jared; ^{3} Enoch, Methuselah, Lamech; Noah, Shem, Ham, and Japheth.

^{5} The sons of Japheth: Gomer, Magog, Madai, Javan, Tubal, Meshech, and Tiras. The sons of Gomer: Ashkenaz, Riphath,^{2} and Togarmah. ^{7} The sons of Javan: Elishah, Tarshish, Kittim, and Rodanim.

^{8} The sons of Ham: Cush, Egypt, Put, and Canaan. ^{9} The sons of Cush: Seba, Havilah, Sabta, Raama, and Sabteca. The sons of Raamah: Sheba and Dedan. ^{10} Cush fathered Nimrod. He was the first on earth to be a mighty man.^{3}

^{11} Egypt fathered Ludim, Anamim, Lehabim, Naphtuhim, ^{12} Pathrusim, Casluhim (from whom the Philistines came), and Caphtorim.

^{13} Canaan fathered Sidon his firstborn and Heth, ^{14} and the Jebusites, the Amorites, the Girgashites, ^{15} the Hivites, the Arkites, the Sinites, ^{16} the Arvadites, the Zemarites, and the Hamathites.

^{17} The sons of Shem: Elam, Asshur, Arpachshad, Lud, and Aram. And the sons of Aram:^{4} Uz, Hul, Gether, and Meshech. ^{18} Arpachshad fathered Shelah, and Shelah fathered Eber. ^{19} To Eber were born two sons: the name of the one was Peleg^5 (for in his days the earth was divided), and his brother's name was Joktan. ^{20} Joktan fathered Almodad, Sheleph, Hazarmaveth, Jerah, ^{21} Hadoram, Uzal, Diklah, ^{22} Obal,^{6} Abimael, Sheba, ^{23} Ophir, Havilah, and Jobab; all these were the sons of Joktan.

^{24} Shem, Arpachshad, Shelah; ^{25} Eber, Peleg, Reu; ^{26} Serug, Nahor, Terah; ^{27} Abram, that is, Abraham.

From Abraham to Jacob

^{28} The sons of Abraham: Isaac and Ishmael. ^{29} These are their genealogies: the firstborn of Ishmael, Nebaioth, and Kedar, Adbeel, Mibsam, ^{30} Mishma, Dumah, Massa, Hadad, Tema, ^{31} Jetur, Naphish, and Kedemah. These are the sons of Ishmael. ^{32} The sons of Keturah, Abraham's concubine: she bore Zimran, Jokshan, Medan, Midian, Ishbak, and Shuah. The sons of Jokshan: Sheba and Dedan. ^{33} The sons of Midian: Ephah, Epher, Hanoch, Abida, and Eldaah. All these were the descendants of Keturah.

^{34} Abraham fathered Isaac. The sons of Isaac: Esau and Israel. ^{35} The sons of Esau: Eliphaz, Reuel, Jeush, Jalam, and Korah. ^{36} The sons of Eliphaz: Teman, Omar, Zepho, Gatam, Kenaz, and of Timna,^{7} Amalek. ^{37} The sons of Reuel: Nahath, Zerah, Shammah, and Mizzah.

^{38} The sons of Seir: Lotan, Shobal, Zibeon, Anah, Dishon, Ezer, and Dishan. ^{39} The sons of Lotan: Hori and Hemam;^{8} and Lotan's sister was Timna. ^{40} The sons of Shobal: Alvan,^{9} Manahath, Ebal, Shepho,^{10} and Onam. The sons of Zibeon: Aiah and Anah. ^{41} The son^{11} of Anah: Dishon. The sons of Dishon: Hemdan,^{12} Eshban, Ithran, and Cheran. ^{42} The sons of Ezer: Bilhan, Zaavan, and Akan.^{13} The sons of Dishan: Uz and Aran.

^{43} These are the kings who reigned in the land of Edom before any king reigned over the people of Israel: Bela the son of Beor, the name of his city being Dinhabah. ^{44} Bela died, and Jobab the son of Zerah of Bozrah reigned in his place. ^{45} Jobab died, and Husham of the land of the Temanites reigned in his place. ^{46} Husham died, and Hadad the son of Bedad, who defeated Midian in the country of Moab, reigned in

^{1} Many names in these genealogies are spelled differently in other biblical books ^{2} Septuagint; Hebrew *Diphath* ^{3} Or *He began to be a mighty man on the earth* ^{4} Septuagint; Hebrew lacks *And the sons of Aram* ^{5} *Peleg* means *division* ^{6} Septuagint, Syriac compare Genesis 10:28); Hebrew *Ebal* ^{7} Septuagint (compare Genesis 36:12); Hebrew lacks *and of* ^{8} Septuagint (compare Genesis 6:22); Hebrew *Homam* ^{9} Septuagint (compare Genesis 36:23); Hebrew *Alian* ^{10} Septuagint (compare Genesis 36:23); Hebrew *hephi* ^{11} Hebrew *sons* ^{12} Septuagint (compare Genesis 36:26); Hebrew *Hamran* ^{13} Septuagint (compare Genesis 36:27); Hebrew *aakan* his place, the name of his city being Avith. ⁴⁷Hadad died, and Samlah of Masrekah reigned in his place. ⁴⁸Samlah died, and Shaul of Rehoboth on the Euphrates¹ reigned in his place. ⁴⁹Shaul died, and Baal-hanan, the son of Achbor, reigned in his place. ⁵⁰Baal-hanan died, and Hadad reigned in his place, the name of his city being Pai; and his wife's name was Mehetabel, the daughter of Matred, the daughter of Mezahab. ⁵¹And Hadad died.

The chiefs of Edom were: chiefs Timna, Alvah, Jetheth, ⁵²Oholibamah, Elah, Pinon, ⁵³Kenaz, Teman, Mibzar, ⁵⁴Magdiel, and Iram; these are the chiefs of Edom.

A Genealogy of David

2 These are the sons of Israel: Reuben, Simeon, Levi, Judah, Issachar, Zebulun, ²Dan, Joseph, Benjamin, Naphtali, Gad, and Asher. ³The sons of Judah: Er, Onan and Shelah; these three Bath-shua the Canaanite bore to him. Now Er, Judah's firstborn, was evil in the sight of the LORD, and he put him to death. ⁴His daughter-in-law Tamar also bore him Perez and Zerah. Judah had five sons in all.

⁵The sons of Perez: Hezron and Hamul. ⁶The sons of Zerah: Zimri, Ethan, Heman, Calcol, and Dara, five in all. ⁷The son² of Carmi: Achan, the troubler of Israel, who broke faith in the matter of the devoted thing; ⁸and Ethan's son was Azariah.

⁹The sons of Hezron that were born to him: Jerahmeel, Ram, and Chelubai. ¹⁰Ram fathered Amminadab, and Amminadab fathered Nahshon, prince of the sons of Judah. ¹¹Nahshon fathered Salmon,³ Salmon fathered Boaz, ¹²Boaz fathered Obed, Obed fathered Jesse. ¹³Jesse fathered Eliab his firstborn, Abinadab the second, Shimea the third, ¹⁴Nethanel the fourth, Raddai the fifth, ¹⁵Ozem the sixth, David the seventh. ¹⁶And their sisters were Zeruiah and Abigail. The sons of Zeruiah: Abishai, Joab, and Asahel, three. ¹⁷Abigail bore Amasa, and the father of Amasa was Jether the Ishmaelite.

¹⁸Caleb the son of Hezron fathered children by his wife Azubah, and by Jerioth; and these were her sons: Jesher, Shobab, and Ardon. ¹⁹When Azubah died, Caleb married Ephrath, who bore him Hur. ²⁰Hur fathered Uri, and Uri fathered Bezalel.

²¹Afterward Hezron went in to the daughter of Machir the father of Gilead, whom he married when he was sixty years old, and she bore him Segub. ²²And Segub fathered Jair, who had twenty-three cities in the land of Gilead. ²³But Geshur and Aram took from them Havvoth-jair, Kenath and its villages, sixty towns. All these were descendants of Machir, the father of Gilead. ²⁴After the death of Hezron, Caleb went in to Ephrathah,⁴ the wife of Hezron his father, and she bore him Ashhur, the father of Tekoa.

²⁵The sons of Jerahmeel, the firstborn of Hezron: Ram, his firstborn, Bunah, Oren, Ozem, and Ahijah. ²⁶Jerahmeel also had another wife, whose name was Atarah; she was the mother of Onam. ²⁷The sons of Ram, the firstborn of Jerahmeel: Maaz, Jamin, and Eker. ²⁸The sons of Onam: Shammai and Jada. The sons of Shammai: Nadab and Abishur. ²⁹The name of Abishur's wife was Abihail, and she bore him Ahban and Molid. ³⁰The sons of Nadab: Seled and Appaim; and Seled died childless. ³¹The son⁵ of Appaim: Ishi. The son of Ishi: Sheshan. The son of Sheshan: Ahlai. ³²The sons of Jada, Shammai's brother: Jether and Jonathan; and Jether died childless. ³³The sons of Jonathan: Peleth and Zaza. These were the descendants of Jerahmeel. ³⁴Now Sheshan had no sons, only daughters, but Sheshan had an Egyptian slave whose name was Jarha. ³⁵So Sheshan gave his daughter in marriage to Jarha his slave, and she bore him Attai. ³⁶Attai fathered Nathan, and Nathan fathered Zabad. ³⁷Zabad fathered Ephlal, and Ephlal fathered Obed. ³⁸Obed fathered Jehu, and Jehu fathered Azariah. ³⁹Azariah fathered Helez, and Helez fathered Eleasah. ⁴⁰Eleasah fathered Sismai, and Sismai fathered Shallum. ⁴¹Shallum fathered Jekamiah, and Jekamiah fathered Elishama.

⁴²The sons of Caleb the brother of Jerahmeel: Mareshah⁶ his firstborn, who fathered Ziph. The son⁷ of Mareshah: Hebron.⁸ ⁴³The sons of Hebron: Korah, Tappuah, Rekem and Shema. ⁴⁴Shema fathered Raham, the father of Jorkeam; and Rekem fathered Shammai. ⁴⁵The son of Shammai: Maon; and Maon fathered Beth-zur. ⁴⁶Ephah also, Caleb's concubine, bore Haran, Moza, and Gazez; and Haran fathered Gazez. ⁴⁷The

¹Hebrew the River ²Hebrew sons ³Septuagint (compare Ruth 4:21); Hebrew Salma ⁴Septuagint, Vulgate; Hebrew in Caleb Ephrathah ⁵Hebrew sons; three times in this verse ⁶Septuagint; Hebrew Mesha ⁷Hebrew sons ⁸Hebrew the father of Hebron

sons of Jahdai: Regem, Jotham, Geshan, Pelet, Ephah, and Shaaph. [48]Maacah, Caleb's concubine, bore Sheber and Tirhanah. [49]She also bore Shaaph the father of Madmannah, Sheva the father of Machbenah and the father of Gibea; and the daughter of Caleb was Achsah. [50]These were the descendants of Caleb.

The sons[1] of Hur the firstborn of Ephrathah: Shobal the father of Kiriath-jearim, [51]Salma, the father of Bethlehem, and Hareph the father of Beth-gader. [52]Shobal the father of Kiriath-jearim had other sons: Haroeh, half of the Menuhoth. [53]And the clans of Kiriath-jearim: the Ithrites, the Puthites, the Shumathites, and the Mishraites; from these came the Zorathites and the Eshtaolites. [54]The sons of Salma: Bethlehem, the Netophathites, Atrothbeth-joab and half of the Manahathites, the Zorites. [55]The clans also of the scribes who lived at Jabez: the Tirathites, the

Shimeathites and the Sucathites. These are the Kenites who came from Hammath, the father of the house of Rechab.

Descendants of David

3 These are the sons of David who were born to him in Hebron: the firstborn, Amnon, by Ahinoam the Jezreelite; the second, Daniel, by Abigail the Carmelite, [2]the third, Absalom, whose mother was Maacah, the daughter of Talmai, king of Geshur; the fourth, Adonijah, whose mother was Haggith; [3]the fifth, Shephatiah, by Abital; the sixth, Ithream, by his wife Eglah; [4]six were born to him in Hebron, where he reigned for seven years and six months. And he reigned thirty-three years in Jerusalem. [5]These were born to him in Jerusalem: Shimea, Shobab, Nathan and Solomon, four by Bath-shua, the daughter of Ammiel; [6]then Ibhar, Elishama, Eliphelet, [7]Nogah, Nepheg, Japhia, [8]Elishama, Eliada, and Eliphelet, nine. [9]All these were David's sons, besides the sons of the concubines, and Tamar was their sister.

[10]The son of Solomon was Rehoboam, Abijah his son, Asa his son, Jehoshaphat his son, [11]Joram his son, Ahaziah his son, Joash his son, [12]Amaziah his son, Azariah his son, Jotham his son, [13]Ahaz his son, Hezekiah his son, Manasseh his son, [14]Amon his son, Josiah his son. [15]The sons of Josiah: Johanan the firstborn, the second Jehoiakim, the third Zedekiah, the fourth Shallum. [16]The descendants of Jehoiakim: Jeconiah his son, Zedekiah his son; [17]and the sons of Jeconiah, the captive: Shealtiel his son, [18]Malchiram, Pedaiah, Shenazzar, Jekamiah, Hoshama and Nedabiah; [19]and the sons of Pedaiah: Zerubbabel and Shimei; and the sons of Zerubbabel: Meshullam and Hananiah, and Shelomith was their sister; [20]and Hashubah, Ohel, Berechiah, Hasadiah, and Jushab-hesed, five. [21]The sons of Hananiah: Pelatiah and Jeshaiah, his son[2] Rephaiah, his son Arnan, his son Obadiah, his son Shecaniah. [22]The son[3] of Shecaniah: Shemaiah. And the sons of Shemaiah: Hattush, Igal, Bariah, Neariah, and Shaphat, six. [23]The sons of Neariah: Elioenai, Hizkiah, and Azrikam, three. [24]The sons of Elioenai: Hodaviah, Eliashib, Pelaiah, Akkub, Johanan, Delaiah, and Anani, seven.

Ask Yourself . . .

ABOUT YOUR FAMILY

God proves the importance of family and heritage when he lists all the names of the Israelites in the line of David. Who you are has something to do with the people you come from. Ask yourself about your family tree and how it might affect who you are:

- What good habits can I see coming from my family tree?
- Are there certain sins that have been accepted by my family?
- Do I accept those same sins?
- Does my salvation make my family tree look any different?
- Am I placing sins I have inherited under the blood of Jesus, or am I giving in to feelings of condemnation?

[1] Septuagint, Vulgate; Hebrew son [2] Septuagint (compare Syriac, Vulgate); Hebrew sons of; four times in this verse [3] Hebrew sons

Descendants of Judah

4 The sons of Judah: Perez, Hezron, Carmi, Hur, and Shobal. ²Reaiah the son of Shobal fathered Jahath, and Jahath fathered Ahumai and Lahad. These were the clans of the Zorathites. ³These were the sons[1] of Etam: Jezreel, Ishma, and Idbash; and the name of their sister was Hazzelelponi, ⁴and Penuel fathered Gedor, and Ezer fathered Hushah. These were the sons of Hur, the firstborn of Ephrathah, the father of Bethlehem. ⁵Ashhur, the father of Tekoa, had two wives, Helah and Naarah; ⁶Naarah bore him Ahuzzam, Hepher, Temeni, and Haahashtari. These were the sons of Naarah. ⁷The sons of Helah: Zereth, Izhar, and Ethnan. ⁸Koz fathered Anub, Zobebah, and the clans of Aharhel, the son of Harum. ⁹Jabez was more honorable than his brothers; and his mother called his name Jabez, saying, "Because I bore him in pain."[2] ¹⁰Jabez called upon the God of Israel, saying, "Oh that you would bless me and enlarge my border, and that your hand might be with me, and that you would keep me from harm[3] so that it might not bring me pain!" And God granted what he asked. ¹¹Chelub, the brother of Shuhah, fathered Mehir, who fathered Eshton. ¹²Eshton fathered Beth-rapha, Paseah, and Tehinnah, the father of Ir-nahash. These are the men of Recah. ¹³The sons of Kenaz: Othniel and Seraiah; and the sons of Othniel: Hathath and Meonothai.[4] ¹⁴Meonothai fathered Ophrah; and Seraiah fathered Joab, the father of Ge-harashim,[5] so-called because they were craftsmen. ¹⁵The sons of Caleb the son of Jephunneh: Iru, Elah, and Naam; and the son[6] of Elah: Kenaz. ¹⁶The sons of Jehallelel: Ziph, Ziphah, Tiria, and Asarel. ¹⁷The sons of Ezrah: Jether, Mered, Epher, and Jalon. These are the sons of Bithiah, the daughter of Pharaoh, whom Mered married;[7] and she conceived and bore[8] Miriam, Shammai, and Ishbah, the father of Eshtemoa. ¹⁸And his Judahite wife bore Jered the father of Gedor, Heber the father of Soco, and Jekuthiel the father of Zanoah. ¹⁹The sons of the wife of Hodiah, the sister of Naham, were the fathers of Keilah the Garmite and Eshtemoa the Maacathite. ²⁰The sons of Shimon: Amnon, Rinnah, Ben-hanan, and Tilon. The sons of Ishi: Zoheth and Ben-zoheth. ²¹The sons of Shelah the son of Judah: Er the father of Lecah, Laadah the father of Mareshah, and the clans of the house of linen workers at Beth-ashbea, ²²and Jokim, and the men of Cozeba, and Joash, and Saraph, who ruled in Moab and returned to Lehem[9] (now the records[10] are ancient). ²³These were the potters who were inhabitants of Netaim and Gederah. They lived there in the king's service.

Descendants of Simeon

²⁴The sons of Simeon: Nemuel, Jamin, Jarib, Zerah, Shaul; ²⁵Shallum was his son, Mibsam his son, Mishma his son. ²⁶The sons of Mishma: Hammuel his son, Zaccur his son, Shimei his son. ²⁷Shimei had sixteen sons and six daughters; but his brothers did not have many children, nor did all their clan multiply like the men of Judah. ²⁸They lived in Beersheba, Moladah, Hazar-shual, ²⁹Bilhah, Ezem, Tolad, ³⁰Bethuel, Hormah, Ziklag, ³¹Beth-marcaboth, Hazar-susim, Beth-biri, and Shaaraim. These were their cities until David reigned. ³²And their villages were Etam, Ain, Rimmon, Tochen, and Ashan, five cities, ³³along with all their villages that were around these cities as far as Baal. These were their settlements, and they kept a genealogical record.

³⁴Meshobab, Jamlech, Joshah the son of Amaziah, ³⁵Joel, Jehu the son of Joshibiah, son of Seraiah, son of Asiel, ³⁶Elioenai, Jaakobah, Jeshohaiah, Asaiah, Adiel, Jesimiel, Benaiah, ³⁷Ziza the son of Shiphi, son of Allon, son of Jedaiah, son of Shimri, son of Shemaiah— ³⁸these mentioned by name were princes in their clans, and their fathers' houses increased greatly. ³⁹They journeyed to the entrance of Gedor, to the east side of the valley, to seek pasture for their flocks, ⁴⁰where they found rich, good pasture, and the land was very broad, quiet, and peaceful, for the former inhabitants there belonged to Ham. ⁴¹These, registered by name, came in the days of Hezekiah, king of Judah, and destroyed their tents and the Meunites who were found there, and marked them for destruction to this day, and settled in their place, because there was pasture there for their flocks. ⁴²And some of them, five hundred

---

[1] Septuagint (compare Vulgate); Hebrew *father* [2] *Jabez* sounds like the Hebrew for *pain* [3] Or *evil* [4] Septuagint, Vulgate; Hebrew lacks *Meonothai* [5] *Ge-harashim* means *valley of craftsmen* [6] Hebrew *sons* [7] The clause *These are . . . married* is transposed from verse 18 [8] Hebrew lacks *and bore* [9] Vulgate (compare Septuagint); Hebrew *and Jashubi-lahem* [10] Or *matters*

men of the Simeonites, went to Mount Seir, having as their leaders Pelatiah, Neariah, Rephaiah, and Uzziel, the sons of Ishi. ⁴³ And they defeated the remnant of the Amalekites who had escaped, and they have lived there to this day.

Descendants of Reuben

5 The sons of Reuben the firstborn of Israel (for he was the firstborn, but because he defiled his father's couch, his birthright was given to the sons of Joseph the son of Israel, so that he could not be enrolled as the oldest son; ² though Judah became strong among his brothers and a chief came from him, yet the birthright belonged to Joseph), ³ the sons of Reuben, the firstborn of Israel: Hanoch, Pallu, Hezron, and Carmi. ⁴ The sons of Joel: Shemaiah his son, Gog his son, Shimei his son, ⁵ Micah his son, Reaiah his son, Baal his son, ⁶ Beerah his son, whom Tiglath-pileser¹ king of Assyria carried away into exile; he was a chief of the Reubenites. ⁷ And his kinsmen by their clans, when the genealogy of their generations was recorded: the chief, Jeiel, and Zechariah, ⁸ and Bela the son of Azaz, son of Shema, son of Joel, who lived in Aroer, as far as Nebo and Baal-meon. ⁹ He also lived to the east as far as the entrance of the desert this side of the Euphrates, because their livestock had multiplied in the land of Gilead. ¹⁰ And in the days of Saul they waged war against the Hagrites, who fell into their hand. And they lived in their tents throughout all the region east of Gilead.

Descendants of Gad

¹¹ The sons of Gad lived over against them in the land of Bashan as far as Salecah: ¹² Joel the chief, Shapham the second, Janai, and Shaphat in Bashan. ¹³ And their kinsmen according to their fathers' houses: Michael, Meshullam, Sheba, Jorai, Jacan, Zia and Eber, seven. ¹⁴ These were the sons of Abihail the son of Huri, son of Jaroah, son of Gilead, son of Michael, son of Jeshishai, son of Jahdo, son of Buz. ¹⁵ Ahi the son of Abdiel, son of Guni, was chief in their fathers' houses, ¹⁶ and they lived in Gilead, in Bashan and in its towns, and in all the pasturelands of Sharon to their limits. ¹⁷ All of these were recorded in genealogies in the days of Jotham king of Judah, and in the days of Jeroboam king of Israel.

¹⁸ The Reubenites, the Gadites, and the half-tribe of Manasseh had valiant men who carried shield and sword, and drew the bow, expert in war, 44,760, able to go to war. ¹⁹ They waged war against the Hagrites, Jetur, Naphish, and Nodab. ²⁰ And when they prevailed² over them, the Hagrites and all who were with them were given into their hands, for they cried out to God in the battle, and he granted their urgent plea because they trusted in him. ²¹ They carried off their livestock: 50,000 of their camels, 250,000 sheep, 2,000 donkeys, and 100,000 men alive. ²² For many fell, because the war was of God. And they lived in their place until the exile.

The Half-Tribe of Manasseh

²³ The members of the half-tribe of Manasseh lived in the land. They were very numerous from Bashan to Baal-hermon, Senir, and Mount Hermon. ²⁴ These were the heads of their fathers' houses: Epher,³ Ishi, Eliel, Azriel, Jeremiah, Hodaviah, and Jahdiel, mighty warriors, famous men, heads of their fathers' houses. ²⁵ But they broke faith with the God of their fathers, and whored after the gods of the peoples of the land, whom God had destroyed before them. ²⁶ So the God of Israel stirred up the spirit of Pul king of Assyria, the spirit of Tiglath-pileser king of Assyria, and he took them into exile, namely, the Reubenites, the Gadites, and the half-tribe of Manasseh, and brought them to Halah, Habor, Hara, and the river Gozan, to this day.

Descendants of Levi

6 ⁴ The sons of Levi: Gershon, Kohath, and Merari. ² The sons of Kohath: Amram, Izhar, Hebron, and Uzziel. ³ The children of Amram: Aaron, Moses, and Miriam. The sons of Aaron: Nadab, Abihu, Eleazar, and Ithamar. ⁴ Eleazar fathered Phinehas, Phinehas fathered Abishua, ⁵ Abishua fathered Bukki, Bukki fathered Uzzi, ⁶ Uzzi fathered Zerahiah, Zerahiah fathered Meraioth, ⁷ Meraioth fathered Amariah, Amariah fathered Ahitub, ⁸ Ahitub fathered Zadok, Zadok fathered Ahimaaz, ⁹ Ahimaaz fathered Azariah, Azariah fathered Johanan, ¹⁰ and Johanan fathered Azariah (it was he who served as priest

¹ Hebrew *Tilgath-pilneser*; also verse 26   ² Or *they were helped to prevail*   ³ Septuagint, Vulgate; Hebrew *and Epher*   ⁴ Ch 5:27 in Hebrew

in the house that Solomon built in Jerusalem). [11] Azariah fathered Amariah, Amariah fathered Ahitub, [12] Ahitub fathered Zadok, Zadok fathered Shallum, [13] Shallum fathered Hilkiah, Hilkiah fathered Azariah, [14] Azariah fathered Seraiah, Seraiah fathered Jehozadak; [15] and Jehozadak went into exile when the LORD sent Judah and Jerusalem into exile by the hand of Nebuchadnezzar.

[16] [1] The sons of Levi: Gershom, Kohath, and Merari. [17] And these are the names of the sons of Gershom: Libni and Shimei. [18] The sons of Kohath: Amram, Izhar, Hebron and Uzziel. [19] The sons of Merari: Mahli and Mushi. These are the clans of the Levites according to their fathers. [20] Of Gershom: Libni his son, Jahath his son, Zimmah his son, [21] Joah his son, Iddo his son, Zerah his son, Jeatherai his son. [22] The sons of Kohath: Amminadab his son, Korah his son, Assir his son, [23] Elkanah his son, Ebiasaph his son, Assir his son, [24] Tahath his son, Uriel his son, Uzziah his son, and Shaul his son. [25] The sons of Elkanah: Amasai and Ahimoth, [26] Elkanah his son, Zophai his son, Nahath his son, [27] Eliab his son, Jeroham his son, Elkanah his son. [28] The sons of Samuel: Joel[2] his firstborn, the second Abijah.[3] [29] The sons of Merari: Mahli, Libni his son, Shimei his son, Uzzah his son, [30] Shimea his son, Haggiah his son, and Asaiah his son.

[31] These are the men whom David put in charge of the service of song in the house of the LORD after the ark rested there. [32] They ministered with song before the tabernacle of the tent of meeting until Solomon built the house of the LORD in Jerusalem, and they performed their service according to their order. [33] These are the men who served and their sons. Of the sons of the Kohathites: Heman the singer the son of Joel, son of Samuel, [34] son of Elkanah, son of Jeroham, son of Eliel, son of Toah, [35] son of Zuph, son of Elkanah, son of Mahath, son of Amasai, [36] son of Elkanah, son of Joel, son of Azariah, son of Zephaniah, [37] son of Tahath, son of Assir, son of Ebiasaph, son of Korah, [38] son of Izhar, son of Kohath, son of Levi, son of Israel; [39] and his brother Asaph, who stood on his right hand, namely, Asaph the son of Berechiah, son of Shimea, [40] son of Michael,

son of Baaseiah, son of Malchijah, [41] son of Ethni, son of Zerah, son of Adaiah, [42] son of Ethan, son of Zimmah, son of Shimei, [43] son of Jahath, son of Gershom, son of Levi. [44] On the left hand were their brothers, the sons of Merari: Ethan the son of Kishi, son of Abdi, son of Malluch, [45] son of Hashabiah, son of Amaziah, son of Hilkiah, [46] son of Amzi, son of Bani, son of Shemer, [47] son of Mahli, son of Mushi, son of Merari, son of Levi. [48] And their brothers the Levites were appointed for all the service of the tabernacle of the house of God.

[49] But Aaron and his sons made offerings on the altar of burnt offering and on the altar of incense for all the work of the Most Holy Place, and to make atonement for Israel, according to all that Moses the servant of God had commanded. [50] These are the sons of Aaron: Eleazar his son, Phinehas his son, Abishua his son, [51] Bukki his son, Uzzi his son, Zerahiah his son, [52] Meraioth his son, Amariah his son, Ahitub his son, [53] Zadok his son, Ahimaaz his son.

[54] These are their dwelling places according to their settlements within their borders: to the sons of Aaron of the clans of Kohathites, for theirs was the first lot, [55] to them they gave Hebron in the land of Judah and its surrounding pasturelands, [56] but the fields of the city and its villages they gave to Caleb the son of Jephunneh. [57] To the sons of Aaron they gave the cities of refuge: Hebron, Libnah with its pasturelands, Jattir, Eshtemoa with its pasturelands, [58] Hilen with its pasturelands, Debir with its pasturelands, [59] Ashan with its pasturelands, and Beth-shemesh with its pasturelands; [60] and from the tribe of Benjamin, Gibeon,[4] Geba with its pasturelands, Alemeth with its pasturelands, and Anathoth with its pasturelands. All their cities throughout their clans were thirteen.

[61] To the rest of the Kohathites were given by lot out of the clan of the tribe, out of the half-tribe, the half of Manasseh, ten cities. [62] To the Gershomites according to their clans were allotted thirteen cities out of the tribes of Issachar, Asher, Naphtali and Manasseh in Bashan. [63] To the Merarites according to their clans were allotted twelve cities out of the tribes of Reuben, Gad, and Zebulun. [64] So the people of Israel gave the Levites the cities with their pas-

---

[1] Ch 6:1 in Hebrew [2] Septuagint, Syriac (compare verse 33 and 1 Samuel 8:2); Hebrew lacks *Joel* [3] Hebrew *and Abijah* [4] Septuagint, Syriac (compare Joshua 21:17); Hebrew lacks *Gibeon*

turelands. ⁶⁵They gave by lot out of the tribes of Judah, Simeon, and Benjamin these cities that are mentioned by name.

⁶⁶And some of the clans of the sons of Kohath had cities of their territory out of the tribe of Ephraim. ⁶⁷They were given the cities of refuge: Shechem with its pasturelands in the hill country of Ephraim, Gezer with its pasturelands, ⁶⁸Jokmeam with its pasturelands, Beth-horon with its pasturelands, ⁶⁹Aijalon with its pasturelands, Gath-rimmon with its pasturelands, ⁷⁰and out of the half-tribe of Manasseh, Aner with its pasturelands, and Bileam with its pasturelands, for the rest of the clans of the Kohathites.

⁷¹To the Gershomites were given out of the clan of the half-tribe of Manasseh: Golan in Bashan with its pasturelands and Ashtaroth with its pasturelands; ⁷²and out of the tribe of Issachar: Kedesh with its pasturelands, Daberath with its pasturelands, ⁷³Ramoth with its pasturelands, and Anem with its pasturelands; ⁷⁴out of the tribe of Asher: Mashal with its pasturelands, Abdon with its pasturelands, ⁷⁵Hukok with its pasturelands, and Rehob with its pasturelands; ⁷⁶and out of the tribe of Naphtali: Kedesh in Galilee with its pasturelands, Hammon with its pasturelands, and Kiriathaim with its pasturelands. ⁷⁷To the rest of the Merarites were allotted out of the tribe of Zebulun: Rimmono with its pasturelands, Tabor with its pasturelands, ⁷⁸and beyond the Jordan at Jericho, on the east side of the Jordan, out of the tribe of Reuben: Bezer in the wilderness with its pasturelands, Jahzah with its pasturelands, ⁷⁹Kedemoth with its pasturelands, and Mephaath with its pasturelands; ⁸⁰and out of the tribe of Gad: Ramoth in Gilead with its pasturelands, Mahanaim with its pasturelands, ⁸¹Heshbon with its pasturelands, and Jazer with its pasturelands.

Descendants of Issachar

7 The sons[1] of Issachar: Tola, Puah, Jashub, and Shimron, four. ²The sons of Tola: Uzzi, Rephaiah, Jeriel, Jahmai, Ibsam, and Shemuel, heads of their fathers' houses, namely of Tola, mighty warriors of their generations, their number in the days of David being 22,600. ³The son[2] of Uzzi: Izrahiah. And the sons of Izrahiah: Michael, Obadiah, Joel, and Isshiah, all five of them

were chief men. ⁴And along with them, by their generations, according to their fathers' houses, were units of the army for war, 36,000, for they had many wives and sons. ⁵Their kinsmen belonging to all the clans of Issachar were in all 87,000 mighty warriors, enrolled by genealogy.

Descendants of Benjamin

⁶The sons of Benjamin: Bela, Becher, and Jediael, three. ⁷The sons of Bela: Ezbon, Uzzi, Uzziel, Jerimoth, and Iri, five, heads of fathers' houses, mighty warriors. And their enrollment by genealogies was 22,034. ⁸The sons of Becher: Zemirah, Joash, Eliezer, Elioenai, Omri, Jeremoth, Abijah, Anathoth, and Alemeth. All these were the sons of Becher. ⁹And their enrollment by genealogies, according to their generations, as heads of their fathers' houses, mighty warriors, was 20,200. ¹⁰The son of Jediael: Bilhan. And the sons of Bilhan: Jeush, Benjamin, Ehud, Chenaanah, Zethan, Tarshish, and Ahishahar. ¹¹All these were the sons of Jediael according to the heads of their fathers' houses, mighty warriors, 17,200, able to go to war. ¹²And Shuppim and Huppim were the sons of Ir, Hushim the son of Aher.

Descendants of Naphtali

¹³The sons of Naphtali: Jahziel, Guni, Jezer and Shallum, the descendants of Bilhah.

Descendants of Manasseh

¹⁴The sons of Manasseh: Asriel, whom his Aramean concubine bore; she bore Machir the father of Gilead. ¹⁵And Machir took a wife for Huppim and for Shuppim. The name of his sister was Maacah. And the name of the second was Zelophehad, and Zelophehad had daughters. ¹⁶And Maacah the wife of Machir bore a son, and she called his name Peresh; and the name of his brother was Sheresh; and his sons were Ulam and Rakem. ¹⁷The son of Ulam: Bedan. These were the sons of Gilead the son of Machir, son of Manasseh. ¹⁸And his sister Hammolecheth bore Ishhod, Abiezer and Mahlah. ¹⁹The sons of Shemida were Ahian, Shechem, Likhi, and Aniam.

Descendants of Ephraim

²⁰The sons of Ephraim: Shuthelah, and Bered his son, Tahath his son, Eleadah

¹Syriac (compare Vulgate); Hebrew *And to the sons* ²Hebrew *sons;* also verses 10, 12, 17

his son, Tahath his son, [21] Zabad his son, Shuthelah his son, and Ezer and Elead, whom the men of Gath who were born in the land killed, because they came down to raid their livestock. [22] And Ephraim their father mourned many days, and his brothers came to comfort him. [23] And Ephraim went in to his wife, and she conceived and bore a son. And he called his name Beriah, because disaster had befallen his house.[1] [24] His daughter was Sheerah, who built both Lower and Upper Beth-horon, and Uzzen-sheerah. [25] Rephah was his son, Resheph his son, Telah his son, Tahan his son, [26] Ladan his son, Ammihud his son, Elishama his son, [27] Nun[2] his son, Joshua his son. [28] Their possessions and settlements were Bethel and its towns, and to the east Naaran, and to the west Gezer and its towns, Shechem and its towns, and Ayyah and its towns; [29] also in possession of the Manassites, Beth-shean and its towns, Taanach and its towns, Megiddo and its towns, Dor and its towns. In these lived the sons of Joseph the son of Israel.

Descendants of Asher

[30] The sons of Asher: Imnah, Ishvah, Ishvi, Beriah, and their sister Serah. [31] The sons of Beriah: Heber, and Malchiel, who fathered Birzaith. [32] Heber fathered Japhlet, Shomer, Hotham, and their sister Shua. [33] The sons of Japhlet: Pasach, Bimhal, and Ashvath. These are the sons of Japhlet. [34] The sons of Shemer his brother: Rohgah, Jehubbah, and Aram. [35] The sons of Helem his brother: Zophah, Imna, Shelesh, and Amal. [36] The sons of Zophah: Suah, Harnepher, Shual, Beri, Imrah. [37] Bezer, Hod, Shamma, Shilshah, Ithran, and Beera. [38] The sons of Jether: Jephunneh, Pispa, and Ara. [39] The sons of Ulla: Arah, Hanniel, and Rizia. [40] All of these were men of Asher, heads of fathers' houses, approved, mighty warriors, chiefs of the princes. Their number enrolled by genealogies, for service in war, was 26,000 men.

A Genealogy of Saul

8 Benjamin fathered Bela his firstborn, Ashbel the second, Aharah the third, [2] Nohah the fourth, and Rapha the fifth. [3] And Bela had sons: Addar, Gera, Abihud, [4] Abishua, Naaman, Ahoah, [5] Gera, Shephuphan, and Huram. [6] These are the sons of Ehud (they were heads of fathers' houses of the inhabitants of Geba, and they were carried into exile to Manahath): [7] Naaman,[3] Ahijah, and Gera, that is, Heglam,[4] who fathered Uzza and Ahihud. [8] And Shaharaim fathered sons in the country of Moab after he had sent away Hushim and Baara his wives. [9] He fathered sons by Hodesh his wife: Jobab, Zibia, Mesha, Malcam, [10] Jeuz, Sachia, and Mirmah. These were his sons, heads of fathers' houses. [11] He also fathered sons by Hushim: Abitub and Elpaal. [12] The sons of Elpaal: Eber, Misham, and Shemed, who built Ono and Lod with its towns, [13] and Beriah and Shema (they were heads of fathers' houses of the inhabitants of Aijalon, who caused the inhabitants of Gath to flee); [14] and Ahio, Shashak, and Jeremoth. [15] Zebadiah, Arad, Eder, [16] Michael, Ishpah, and Joha were sons of Beriah. [17] Zebadiah, Meshullam, Hizki, Heber, [18] Ishmerai, Izliah, and Jobab were the sons of Elpaal. [19] Jakim, Zichri, Zabdi, [20] Elienai, Zillethai, Eliel, [21] Adaiah, Beraiah, and Shimrath were the sons of Shimei. [22] Ishpan, Eber, Eliel, [23] Abdon, Zichri, Hanan, [24] Hananiah, Elam, Anthothijah, [25] Iphdeiah, and Penuel were the sons of Shashak. [26] Shamsherai, Shehariah, Athaliah, [27] Jaareshiah, Elijah, and Zichri were the sons of Jeroham. [28] These were the heads of fathers' houses, according to their generations, chief men. These lived in Jerusalem.

[29] Jeiel[5] the father of Gibeon lived in Gibeon, and the name of his wife was Maacah. [30] His firstborn son: Abdon, then Zur, Kish, Baal, Nadab, [31] Gedor, Ahio, Zecher, [32] and Mikloth (he fathered Shimeah). Now these also lived opposite their kinsmen in Jerusalem, with their kinsmen. [33] Ner was the father of Kish, Kish of Saul, Saul of Jonathan, Malchi-shua, Abinadab and Eshbaal; [34] and the son of Jonathan was Merib-baal; and Merib-baal was the father of Micah. [35] The sons of Micah: Pithon, Melech, Tarea, and Ahaz. [36] Ahaz fathered Jehoaddah, and Jehoaddah fathered Alemeth, Azmaveth, and Zimri. Zimri fathered Moza. [37] Moza fathered Binea; Raphah was his son, Eleasah his son, Azel his son. [38] Azel had six sons, and these are their names: Azrikam, Bocheru, Ishmael, Sheariah, Obadiah, and Hanan.

---

[1] *Beriah* sounds like the Hebrew for *disaster*   [2] Hebrew *Non*   [3] Hebrew *and Naaman*   [4] Or *he carried them into exile*   [5] Compare 9:35; Hebrew lacks *Jeiel*

All these were the sons of Azel. ³⁹The sons of Eshek his brother: Ulam his firstborn, Jeush the second, and Eliphelet the third. ⁴⁰The sons of Ulam were men who were mighty warriors, bowmen, having many sons and grandsons, 150. All these were Benjaminites.

A Genealogy of the Returned Exiles

9 So all Israel was recorded in genealogies, and these are written in the Book of the Kings of Israel. And Judah was taken into exile in Babylon because of their breach of faith. ²Now the first to dwell again in their possessions in their cities were Israel, the priests, the Levites, and the temple servants. ³And some of the people of Judah, Benjamin, Ephraim, and Manasseh lived in Jerusalem: ⁴Uthai the son of Ammihud, son of Omri, son of Imri, son of Bani, from the sons of Perez the son of Judah. ⁵And of the Shilonites: Asaiah the firstborn, and his sons. ⁶Of the sons of Zerah: Jeuel and their kinsmen, 690. ⁷Of the Benjaminites: Sallu the son of Meshullam, son of Hodaviah, son of Hassenuah, ⁸Ibneiah the son of Jeroham, Elah the son of Uzzi, son of Michri, and Meshullam the son of Shephatiah, son of Reuel, son of Ibnijah; ⁹and their kinsmen according to their generations, 956. All these were heads of fathers' houses according to their fathers' houses.

¹⁰Of the priests: Jedaiah, Jehoiarib, Jachin, ¹¹and Azariah the son of Hilkiah, son of Meshullam, son of Zadok, son of Meraioth, son of Ahitub, the chief officer of the house of God; ¹²and Adaiah the son of Jeroham, son of Pashhur, son of Malchijah, and Maasai the son of Adiel, son of Jahzerah, son of Meshullam, son of Meshillemith, son of Immer; ¹³besides their kinsmen, heads of their fathers' houses, 1,760, mighty men for the work of the service of the house of God.

¹⁴Of the Levites: Shemaiah the son of Hasshub, son of Azrikam, son of Hashabiah, of the sons of Merari; ¹⁵and Bakbakkar, Heresh, Galal and Mattaniah the son of Mica, son of Zichri, son of Asaph; ¹⁶and Obadiah the son of Shemaiah, son of Galal, son of Jeduthun, and Berechiah the son of Asa, son of Elkanah, who lived in the villages of the Netophathites.

¹⁷The gatekeepers were Shallum, Akkub, Talmon, Ahiman, and their kinsmen (Shallum was the chief); ¹⁸until then they were in the king's gate on the east side as the gatekeepers of the camps of the Levites. ¹⁹Shallum the son of Kore, son of Ebiasaph, son of Korah, and his kinsmen of his fathers' house, the Korahites, were in charge of the work of the service, keepers of the thresholds of the tent, as their fathers had been in charge of the camp of the LORD, keepers of the entrance. ²⁰And Phinehas the son of Eleazar was the chief officer over them in time past; the LORD was with him. ²¹Zechariah the son of Meshelemiah was gatekeeper at the entrance of the tent of meeting. ²²All these, who were chosen as gatekeepers at the thresholds, were 212. They were enrolled by genealogies in their villages. David and Samuel the seer established them in their office of trust. ²³So they and their sons were in charge of the gates of the house of the LORD, that is, the house of the tent, as guards. ²⁴The gatekeepers were on the four sides, east, west, north, and south. ²⁵And their kinsmen who were in their villages were obligated to come in every seven days, in turn, to be with these, ²⁶for the four chief gatekeepers, who were Levites, were entrusted to be over the chambers and the treasures of the house of God. ²⁷And they lodged around the house of God, for on them lay the duty of watching, and they had charge of opening it every morning.

²⁸Some of them had charge of the utensils of service, for they were required to count them when they were brought in and taken out. ²⁹Others of them were appointed over the furniture and over all the holy utensils, also over the fine flour, the wine, the oil, the incense, and the spices. ³⁰Others, of the sons of the priests, prepared the mixing of the spices, ³¹and Mattithiah, one of the Levites, the firstborn of Shallum the Korahite, was entrusted with making the flat cakes. ³²Also some of their kinsmen of the Kohathites had charge of the showbread, to prepare it every Sabbath.

³³Now these, the singers, the heads of fathers' houses of the Levites, were in the chambers of the temple free from other service, for they were on duty day and night. ³⁴These were heads of fathers' houses of the Levites, according to their generations, leaders. These lived in Jerusalem.

Saul's Genealogy Repeated

35 In Gibeon lived the father of Gibeon, Jeiel, and the name of his wife was Maacah, 36 and his firstborn son Abdon, then Zur, Kish, Baal, Ner, Nadab, 37 Gedor, Ahio, Zechariah, and Mikloth; 38 and Mikloth was the father of Shimeam; and these also lived opposite their kinsmen in Jerusalem, with their kinsmen. 39 Ner fathered Kish, Kish fathered Saul, Saul fathered Jonathan, Malchi-shua, Abinadab, and Eshbaal. 40 And the son of Jonathan was Merib-baal, and Merib-baal fathered Micah. 41 The sons of Micah: Pithon, Melech, Tahrea, and Ahaz.[1] 42 And Ahaz fathered Jarah, and Jarah fathered Alemeth, Azmaveth, and Zimri. And Zimri fathered Moza. 43 Moza fathered Binea, and Rephaiah was his son, Eleasah his son, Azel his son. 44 Azel had six sons and these are their names: Azrikam, Bocheru, Ishmael, Sheariah, Obadiah, and Hanan; these were the sons of Azel.

The Death of Saul and His Sons

10 Now the Philistines fought against Israel, and the men of Israel fled before the Philistines and fell slain on Mount Gilboa. 2 And the Philistines overtook Saul and his sons, and the Philistines struck down Jonathan and Abinadab and Malchi-shua, the sons of Saul. 3 The battle pressed hard against Saul, and the archers found him, and he was wounded by the archers. 4 Then Saul said to his armorbearer, "Draw your sword and thrust me through with it, lest these uncircumcised come and mistreat me." But his armorbearer would not, for he feared greatly. Therefore Saul took his own sword and fell upon it. 5 And when his armor-bearer saw that Saul was dead, he also fell upon his sword and died. 6 Thus Saul died; he and his three sons and all his house died together. 7 And when all the men of Israel who were in the valley saw that the army[2] had fled and that Saul and his sons were dead, they abandoned their cities and fled, and the Philistines came and lived in them.

8 The next day, when the Philistines came to strip the slain, they found Saul and his sons fallen on Mount Gilboa. 9 And they stripped him and took his head and his armor, and sent messengers throughout the land of the Philistines to carry the good news to their idols and to the people. 10 And they put his armor in the temple of their gods and fastened his head in the temple of Dagon. 11 But when all Jabesh-gilead heard all that the Philistines had done to Saul, 12 all the valiant men arose and took away the body of Saul and the bodies of his sons, and brought them to Jabesh. And they buried their bones under the oak in Jabesh and fasted seven days.

13 So Saul died for his breach of faith. He broke faith with the LORD in that he did not keep the command of the LORD, and also consulted a medium, seeking guidance. 14 He did not seek guidance from the LORD. Therefore the LORD put him to death and turned the kingdom over to David the son of Jesse.

David Anointed King

11 Then all Israel gathered together to David at Hebron and said, "Behold, we are your bone and flesh. 2 In times past, even when Saul was king, it was you who led out and brought in Israel. And the LORD your God said to you, 'You shall be shepherd of my people Israel, and you shall be prince over my people Israel.'" 3 So all the elders of Israel came to the king at Hebron, and David made a covenant with them at Hebron before the LORD. And they anointed David king over Israel, according to the word of the LORD by Samuel.

David Takes Jerusalem

4 And David and all Israel went to Jerusalem, that is, Jebus, where the Jebusites were, the inhabitants of the land. 5 The inhabitants of Jebus said to David, "You will not come in here." Nevertheless, David took the stronghold of Zion, that is, the city of David. 6 David said, "Whoever strikes the Jebusites first shall be chief and commander." And Joab the son of Zeruiah went up first, so he became chief. 7 And David lived in the stronghold; therefore it was called the city of David. 8 And he built the city all around from the Millo in complete circuit, and Joab repaired the rest of the city. 9 And David became greater and greater, for the LORD of hosts was with him.

David's Mighty Men

10 Now these are the chiefs of David's mighty men, who gave him strong support in his kingdom, together with all Israel, to

---

[1] Compare 8:35; Hebrew lacks *and Ahaz* [2] Hebrew *they*

make him king, according to the word of the LORD concerning Israel. [11] This is an account of David's mighty men: Jashobeam, a Hachmonite, was chief of the three.[1] He wielded his spear against 300 whom he killed at one time.

[12] And next to him among the three mighty men was Eleazar the son of Dodo, the Ahohite. [13] He was with David at Pasdammim when the Philistines were gathered there for battle. There was a plot of ground full of barley, and the men fled from the Philistines. [14] But he took his[2] stand in the midst of the plot and defended it and killed the Philistines. And the LORD saved them by a great victory.

[15] Three of the thirty chief men went down to the rock to David at the cave of Adullam, when the army of Philistines was encamped in the Valley of Rephaim. [16] David was then in the stronghold, and the garrison of the Philistines was then at Bethlehem. [17] And David said longingly, "Oh that someone would give me water to drink from the well of Bethlehem that is by the gate!" [18] Then the three mighty men broke through the camp of the Philistines and drew water out of the well of Bethlehem that was by the gate and took it and brought it to David. But David would not drink it. He poured it out to the LORD [19] and said, "Far be it from me before my God that I should do this. Shall I drink the lifeblood of these men? For at the risk of their lives they brought it." Therefore he would not drink it. These things did the three mighty men.

[20] Now Abishai, the brother of Joab, was chief of the thirty.[3] And he wielded his spear against 300 men and killed them and won a name beside the three. [21] He was the most renowned[4] of the thirty[5] and became their commander, but he did not attain to the three.

[22] And Benaiah the son of Jehoiada was a valiant man[6] of Kabzeel, a doer of great deeds. He struck down two heroes of Moab. He also went down and struck down a lion in a pit on a day when snow had fallen. [23] And he struck down an Egyptian, a man of great stature, five cubits[7] tall. The Egyptian had in his hand a spear like a weaver's beam, but Benaiah went down to him with a staff and snatched the spear out of the Egyptian's hand and killed him with his own spear. [24] These things did Benaiah the son of Jehoiada and won a name beside the three mighty men. [25] He was renowned among the thirty, but he did not attain to the three. And David set him over his bodyguard.

[26] The mighty men were Asahel the brother of Joab, Elhanan the son of Dodo of Bethlehem, [27] Shammoth of Harod,[8] Helez the Pelonite, [28] Ira the son of Ikkesh of Tekoa, Abiezer of Anathoth, [29] Sibbecai the Hushathite, Ilai the Ahohite, [30] Maharai of Netophah, Heled the son of Baanah of Netophah, [31] Ithai the son of Ribai of Gibeah of the people of Benjamin, Benaiah of Pirathon, [32] Hurai of the brooks of Gaash, Abiel the Arbathite, [33] Azmaveth of Baharum, Eliahba the Shaalbonite, [34] Hashem[9] the Gizonite, Jonathan the son of Shagee the Hararite, [35] Ahiam the son of Sachar the Hararite, Eliphal the son of Ur, [36] Hepher the Mecherathite, Ahijah the Pelonite, [37] Hezro of Carmel, Naarai the son of Ezbai, [38] Joel the brother of Nathan, Mibhar the son of Hagri, [39] Zelek the Ammonite, Naharai of Beeroth, the armorbearer of Joab the son of Zeruiah, [40] Ira the Ithrite, Gareb the Ithrite, [41] Uriah the Hittite, Zabad the son of Ahlai, [42] Adina the son of Shiza the Reubenite, a leader of the Reubenites, and thirty with him, [43] Hanan the son of Maacah, and Joshaphat the Mithnite, [44] Uzzia the Ashterathite, Shama and Jeiel the sons of Hotham the Aroerite, [45] Jediael the son of Shimri, and Joha his brother, the Tizite, [46] Eliel the Mahavite, and Jeribai, and Joshaviah, the sons of Elnaam, and Ithmah the Moabite, [47] Eliel, and Obed, and Jaasiel the Mezobaite.

The Mighty Men Join David

12 Now these are the men who came to David at Ziklag, while he could not move about freely because of Saul the son of Kish. And they were among the mighty men who helped him in war. [2] They were bowmen and could shoot arrows and sling stones with either the right or the left hand; they were Benjaminites, Saul's kinsmen. [3] The chief was Ahiezer, then

---

[1] Compare 2 Samuel 23:8; Hebrew *thirty*, or *captains*　[2] Compare 2 Samuel 23:12; Hebrew *they . . . their*　[3] Syriac; Hebrew *three*　[4] Compare 2 Samuel 23:19; Hebrew *more renowned among the two*　[5] Syriac; Hebrew *three*　[6] Syriac; Hebrew *the son of a valiant man*　[7] A *cubit* was about 18 inches or 45 centimeters　[8] Compare 2 Samuel 23:25; Hebrew *the Harorite*　[9] Compare Septuagint and 2 Samuel 23:32; Hebrew *the sons of Hashem*

Joash, both sons of Shemaah of Gibeah; also Jeziel and Pelet, the sons of Azmaveth; Beracah, Jehu of Anathoth, [4] Ishmaiah of Gibeon, a mighty man among the thirty and a leader over the thirty; Jeremiah,[1] Jahaziel, Johanan, Jozabad of Gederah, [5] Eluzai,[2] Jerimoth, Bealiah, Shemariah, Shephatiah the Haruphite; [6] Elkanah, Isshiah, Azarel, Joezer, and Jashobeam, the Korahites; [7] And Joelah and Zebadiah, the sons of Jeroham of Gedor.

[8] From the Gadites there went over to David at the stronghold in the wilderness mighty and experienced warriors, expert with shield and spear, whose faces were like the faces of lions and who were swift as gazelles upon the mountains: [9] Ezer the chief, Obadiah second, Eliab third, [10] Mishmannah fourth, Jeremiah fifth, [11] Attai sixth, Eliel seventh, [12] Johanan eighth, Elzabad ninth, [13] Jeremiah tenth, Machbannai eleventh. [14] These Gadites were officers of the army; the least was a match for a hundred men and the greatest for a thousand. [15] These are the men who crossed the Jordan in the first month, when it was overflowing all its banks, and put to flight all those in the valleys, to the east and to the west.

[16] And some of the men of Benjamin and Judah came to the stronghold to David. [17] David went out to meet them and said to them, "If you have come to me in friendship to help me, my heart will be joined to you; but if to betray me to my adversaries, although there is no wrong in my hands, then may the God of our fathers see and rebuke you." [18] Then the Spirit clothed Amasai, chief of the thirty, and he said,

"We are yours, O David,
    and with you, O son of Jesse!
Peace, peace to you,
    and peace to your helpers!
For your God helps you."

Then David received them and made them officers of his troops.

[19] Some of the men of Manasseh deserted to David when he came with the Philistines for the battle against Saul. (Yet he did not help them, for the rulers of the Philistines took counsel and sent him away, saying, "At peril to our heads he will desert to his master Saul.") [20] As he went to Ziklag, these men of Manasseh deserted to him: Adnah, Jozabad, Jediael, Michael, Jozabad, Elihu, and Zillethai, chiefs of thousands in Manasseh. [21] They helped David against the band of raiders, for they were all mighty men of valor and were commanders in the army. [22] For from day to day men came to David to help him, until there was a great army, like an army of God.

[23] These are the numbers of the divisions of the armed troops who came to David in Hebron to turn the kingdom of Saul over to him, according to the word of the LORD. [24] The men of Judah bearing shield and spear were 6,800 armed troops. [25] Of the Simeonites, mighty men of valor for war, 7,100. [26] Of the Levites 4,600. [27] The prince Jehoiada, of the house of Aaron, and with him 3,700. [28] Zadok, a young man mighty in valor, and twenty-two commanders from his own fathers' house. [29] Of the Benjaminites, the kinsmen of Saul, 3,000, of whom the majority had to that point kept their allegiance to the house of Saul. [30] Of the Ephraimites 20,800, mighty men of valor, famous men in their fathers' houses. [31] Of the half-tribe of Manasseh 18,000, who were expressly named to come and make David king. [32] Of Issachar, men who had understanding of the times, to know what Israel ought to do, 200 chiefs, and all their kinsmen under their command. [33] Of Zebulun 50,000 seasoned troops, equipped for battle with all the weapons of war, to help David[3] with singleness of purpose. [34] Of Naphtali 1,000 commanders with whom were 37,000 men armed with shield and spear. [35] Of the Danites 28,600 men equipped for battle. [36] Of Asher 40,000 seasoned troops ready for battle. [37] Of the Reubenites and Gadites and the half-tribe of Manasseh from beyond the Jordan, 120,000 men armed with all the weapons of war.

[38] All these, men of war, arrayed in battle order, came to Hebron with a whole heart to make David king over all Israel. Likewise, all the rest of Israel were of a single mind to make David king. [39] And they were there with David for three days, eating and drinking, for their brothers had made preparation for them. [40] And also their relatives, from as far as Issachar and Zebulun and Naphtali, came bringing food on donkeys and on camels and on mules

[1] Hebrew verse 5 [2] Hebrew verse 6 [3] Septuagint; Hebrew lacks David

and on oxen, abundant provisions of flour, cakes of figs, clusters of raisins, and wine and oil, oxen and sheep, for there was joy in Israel.

The Ark Brought from Kiriath-Jearim

13 David consulted with the commanders of thousands and of hundreds, with every leader. [2] And David said to all the assembly of Israel, "If it seems good to you and from the LORD our God, let us send abroad to our brothers who remain in all the lands of Israel, as well as to the priests and Levites in the cities that have pasturelands, that they may be gathered to us. [3] Then let us bring again the ark of our God to us, for we did not seek it[1] in the days of Saul." [4] All the assembly agreed to do so, for the thing was right in the eyes of all the people.

Uzzah and the Ark

[5] So David assembled all Israel from the Nile[2] of Egypt to Lebo-hamath, to bring the ark of God from Kiriath-jearim. [6] And David and all Israel went up to Baalah, that is, to Kiriath-jearim that belongs to Judah, to bring up from there the ark of God, which is called by the name of the LORD who sits enthroned above the cherubim. [7] And they carried the ark of God on a new cart, from the house of Abinadab, and Uzzah and Ahio[3] were driving the cart. [8] And David and all Israel were celebrating before God with all their might, with song and lyres and harps and tambourines and cymbals and trumpets.

[9] And when they came to the threshing floor of Chidon, Uzzah put out his hand to take hold of the ark, for the oxen stumbled. [10] And the anger of the LORD was kindled against Uzzah, and he struck him down because he put out his hand to the ark, and he died there before God. [11] And David was angry because the LORD had broken out against Uzzah. And that place is called Perez-uzza[4] to this day. [12] And David was afraid of God that day, and he said, "How can I bring the ark of God home to me?" [13] So David did not take the ark home into the city of David, but took it aside to the house of Obed-edom the Gittite. [14] And the ark of God remained with the household of Obed-edom in his house three months.

And the LORD blessed the household of Obed-edom and all that he had.

David's Wives and Children

14 And Hiram king of Tyre sent messengers to David, and cedar trees, also masons and carpenters to build a house for him. [2] And David knew that the LORD had established him as king over Israel, and that his kingdom was highly exalted for the sake of his people Israel.

[3] And David took more wives in Jerusalem, and David fathered more sons and daughters. [4] These are the names of the children born to him in Jerusalem: Shammua, Shobab, Nathan, Solomon, [5] Ibhar, Elishua, Elpelet, [6] Nogah, Nepheg, Japhia, [7] Elishama, Beeliada and Eliphelet.

Philistines Defeated

[8] When the Philistines heard that David had been anointed king over all Israel, all the Philistines went up to search for David. But David heard of it and went out against them. [9] Now the Philistines had come and made a raid in the Valley of Rephaim. [10] And David inquired of God, "Shall I go up against the Philistines? Will you give them into my hand?" And the LORD said to him, "Go up, and I will give them into your hand." [11] And he went up to Baal-perazim, and David struck them down there. And David said, "God has broken through[5] my enemies by my hand, like a bursting flood." Therefore the name of that place is called Baal-perazim. [12] And they left their gods there, and David gave command, and they were burned.

[13] And the Philistines yet again made a raid in the valley. [14] And when David again inquired of God, God said to him, "You shall not go up after them; go around and come against them opposite the balsam trees. [15] And when you hear the sound of marching in the tops of the balsam trees, then go out to battle, for God has gone out before you to strike down the army of the Philistines." [16] And David did as God commanded him, and they struck down the Philistine army from Gibeon to Gezer. [17] And the fame of David went out into all lands, and the LORD brought the fear of him upon all nations.

[1] Or him [2] Hebrew Shihor [3] Or and his brother [4] Perez-uzza means the breaking out against Uzzah [5] Baal-perazim means Lord of breaking through

The Ark Brought to Jerusalem

15 David[1] built houses for himself in the city of David. And he prepared a place for the ark of God and pitched a tent for it. [2] Then David said that no one but the Levites may carry the ark of God, for the LORD had chosen them to carry the ark of the LORD and to minister to him forever. [3] And David assembled all Israel at Jerusalem to bring up the ark of the LORD to its place, which he had prepared for it. [4] And David gathered together the sons of Aaron and the Levites: [5] of the sons of Kohath, Uriel the chief, with 120 of his brothers; [6] of the sons of Merari, Asaiah the chief, with 220 of his brothers; [7] of the sons of Gershom, Joel the chief, with 130 of his brothers; [8] of the sons of Elizaphan, Shemaiah the chief, with 200 of his brothers; [9] of the sons of Hebron, Eliel the chief, with 80 of his brothers; [10] of the sons of Uzziel, Amminadab the chief, with 112 of his brothers. [11] Then David summoned the priests Zadok and Abiathar, and the Levites Uriel, Asaiah, Joel, Shemaiah, Eliel, and Amminadab, [12] and said to them, "You are the heads of the fathers' houses of the Levites. Consecrate yourselves, you and your brothers, so that you may bring up the ark of the LORD, the God of Israel, to the place that I have prepared for it. [13] Because you did not carry it the first time, the LORD our God broke out against us, because we did not seek him according to the rule." [14] So the priests and the Levites consecrated themselves to bring up the ark of the LORD, the God of Israel. [15] And the Levites carried the ark of God on their shoulders with the poles, as Moses had commanded according to the word of the LORD.

[16] David also commanded the chiefs of the Levites to appoint their brothers as the singers who should play loudly on musical instruments, on harps and lyres and cymbals, to raise sounds of joy. [17] So the Levites appointed Heman the son of Joel; and of his brothers Asaph the son of Berechiah; and of the sons of Merari, their brothers, Ethan the son of Kushaiah; [18] and with them their brothers of the second order, Zechariah, Jaaziel, Shemiramoth, Jehiel, Unni, Eliab, Benaiah, Maaseiah, Mattithiah, Eliphelehu, and Mikneiah, and the gatekeepers Obed-edom and Jeiel. [19] The singers, Heman, Asaph, and Ethan, were to sound bronze cymbals; [20] Zechariah, Aziel, Shemiramoth, Jehiel, Unni, Eliab, Maaseiah, and Benaiah were to play harps according to Alamoth [21] but Mattithiah, Eliphelehu, Mikneiah, Obed-edom, Jeiel, and Azaziah were to lead with lyres according to the Sheminith. [22] Chenaniah, leader of the Levites in music, should direct the music, for he understood it. [23] Berechiah and Elkanah were to be gatekeepers for the ark. [24] Shebaniah, Joshaphat, Nethanel, Amasai, Zechariah, Benaiah, and Eliezer, the priests, should blow the trumpets before the ark of God. Obed-edom and Jehiah were to be gatekeepers for the ark.

[25] So David and the elders of Israel and the commanders of thousands went to bring up the ark of the covenant of the LORD from the house of Obed-edom with rejoicing. [26] And because God helped the Levites who were carrying the ark of the covenant of the LORD, they sacrificed seven bulls and seven rams. [27] David was clothed with a robe of fine linen, as also were all the Levites who were carrying the ark, and the singers and Chenaniah the leader of the music of the singers. And David wore a linen ephod. [28] So all Israel brought up the ark of the covenant of the LORD with shouting, to the sound of the horn, trumpets, and cymbals, and made loud music on harps and lyres.

[29] And as the ark of the covenant of the LORD came to the city of David, Michal the daughter of Saul looked out of the window and saw King David dancing and celebrating, and she despised him in her heart.

The Ark Placed in a Tent

16 And they brought in the ark of God and set it inside the tent that David had pitched for it, and they offered burnt offerings and peace offerings before God. [2] And when David had finished offering the burnt offerings and the peace offerings, he blessed the people in the name of the LORD [3] and distributed to all Israel, both men and women, to each a loaf of bread, a portion of meat,[2] and a cake of raisins.

[4] Then he appointed some of the Levites as ministers before the ark of the LORD, to invoke, to thank, and to praise the LORD, the God of Israel. [5] Asaph was the chief, and second to him were Zechariah, Jeiel, She-

[1] Hebrew *He* [2] Compare Septuagint, Syriac, Vulgate; the meaning of the Hebrew is uncertain

miramoth, Jehiel, Mattithiah, Eliab, Benaiah, Obed-edom, and Jeiel, who were to play harps and lyres; Asaph was to sound the cymbals, 6 and Benaiah and Jahaziel the priests were to blow trumpets regularly before the ark of the covenant of God. 7 Then on that day David first appointed that thanksgiving be sung to the LORD by Asaph and his brothers.

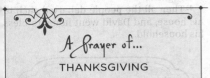

A Prayer of...
THANKSGIVING

Giver of all good,

Streams upon streams of love overflow my path.

You have made me out of nothing; you have recalled me from a far country; you have taken me from ignorance to knowledge, from darkness to light, from death to life, from misery to peace, from folly to wisdom, from error to truth, from sin to victory. Thank you for my high and holy calling. I thank you for ministering angels, for the comfort of your church, for the law of your Word, for the teaching of your Spirit, for Christian fellowship, for the holy lives lived before me, for examples that teach, and for examples that warn. Your will is in everything you provide to allow me to grow in grace. My heaven-born faith gives promise of eternal sight, my new birth a pledge of never-ending life. I come near to you, knowing you will draw near to me.

I ask of you, believing you have already given. I entrust myself to you, because you have restored me. I bless and adore you, the eternal God, for the comfort of these thoughts, the joy of these hopes.

Amen.

David's Song of Thanks

8   Oh give thanks to the LORD; call upon
         his name;
      make known his deeds among the
         peoples!
9   Sing to him, sing praises to him;
      tell of all his wondrous works!
10 Glory in his holy name;
      let the hearts of those who seek
         the LORD rejoice!
11 Seek the LORD and his strength;
      seek his presence continually!
12 Remember the wondrous works that
         he has done,
      his miracles and the judgments he
         uttered,
13 O offspring of Israel his servant,
      children of Jacob, his chosen ones!
14 He is the LORD our God;
      his judgments are in all the earth.
15 Remember his covenant forever,
      the word that he commanded, for
         a thousand generations,
16 the covenant that he made with
         Abraham,
      his sworn promise to Isaac,
17 which he confirmed to Jacob as a
         statute,
      to Israel as an everlasting covenant,
18 saying, "To you I will give the land of
         Canaan,
      as your portion for an inheritance."
19 When you were few in number,
      of little account, and sojourners in
         it,
20 wandering from nation to nation,
      from one kingdom to another
         people,
21 he allowed no one to oppress them;
      he rebuked kings on their account,
22 saying, "Touch not my anointed ones,
      do my prophets no harm!"
23 Sing to the LORD, all the earth!
      Tell of his salvation from day to
         day.
24 Declare his glory among the nations,
      his marvelous works among all the
         peoples!
25 For great is the LORD, and greatly to
         be praised,
      and he is to be feared above all
         gods.
26 For all the gods of the peoples are
         worthless idols,
      but the LORD made the heavens.
27 Splendor and majesty are before
         him;
      strength and joy are in his place.

28 Ascribe to the LORD, O families of the
     peoples,
        ascribe to the LORD glory and
          strength!
29 Ascribe to the LORD the glory due his
     name;
        bring an offering and come before
          him!
     Worship the LORD in the splendor of
       holiness;[1]
30   tremble before him, all the earth;
        yes, the world is established; it
          shall never be moved.
31 Let the heavens be glad, and let the
     earth rejoice,
        and let them say among the
          nations, "The LORD reigns!"
32 Let the sea roar, and all that fills it;
        let the field exult, and everything
          in it!
33 Then shall the trees of the forest sing
     for joy
        before the LORD, for he comes to
          judge the earth.
34 Oh give thanks to the LORD, for he is
     good;
        for his steadfast love endures
          forever!

35 Say also:

     "Save us, O God of our salvation,
        and gather and deliver us from
          among the nations,
     that we may give thanks to your holy
       name
        and glory in your praise.
36   Blessed be the LORD, the God of Israel,
        from everlasting to everlasting!"

Then all the people said, "Amen!" and
praised the LORD.

Worship Before the Ark

37 So David left Asaph and his brothers there before the ark of the covenant
of the LORD to minister regularly before
the ark as each day required, 38 and also
Obed-edom and his[2] sixty-eight brothers,
while Obed-edom, the son of Jeduthun, and
Hosah were to be gatekeepers. 39 And he
left Zadok the priest and his brothers the
priests before the tabernacle of the LORD
in the high place that was at Gibeon 40 to
offer burnt offerings to the LORD on the
altar of burnt offering regularly morning

and evening, to do all that is written in the
Law of the LORD that he commanded Israel.
41 With them were Heman and Jeduthun
and the rest of those chosen and expressly
named to give thanks to the LORD, for his
steadfast love endures forever. 42 Heman
and Jeduthun had trumpets and cymbals
for the music and instruments for sacred
song. The sons of Jeduthun were appointed
to the gate.

43 Then all the people departed each to
his house, and David went home to bless
his household.

Ask Yourself . . .

ABOUT WORSHIP

• How well do I worship God?

• What are some ways that I can
  worship him more?

• Do I ever brag about God?

• How often do I seek his
  presence? Always? Sometimes?
  Often?

The LORD's Covenant with David

17 Now when David lived in his house,
David said to Nathan the prophet,
"Behold, I dwell in a house of cedar, but the
ark of the covenant of the LORD is under a
tent." 2 And Nathan said to David, "Do all
that is in your heart, for God is with you."

3 But that same night the word of the
LORD came to Nathan, 4 "Go and tell my
servant David, 'Thus says the LORD: It
is not you who will build me a house to
dwell in. 5 For I have not lived in a house
since the day I brought up Israel to this
day, but I have gone from tent to tent and
from dwelling to dwelling. 6 In all places
where I have moved with all Israel, did
I speak a word with any of the judges of
Israel, whom I commanded to shepherd
my people, saying, "Why have you not built
me a house of cedar?"' 7 Now, therefore,
thus shall you say to my servant David,

---

[1] Or in holy attire [2] Hebrew their

hus says the LORD of hosts, I took you
om the pasture, from following the sheep,
» be prince over my people Israel, **8** and
have been with you wherever you have
one and have cut off all your enemies
om before you. And I will make for you
name, like the name of the great ones of
e earth. **9** And I will appoint a place for
y people Israel and will plant them, that
ey may dwell in their own place and be
isturbed no more. And violent men shall
aste them no more, as formerly, **10** from
e time that I appointed judges over my
eople Israel. And I will subdue all your
nemies. Moreover, I declare to you that
e LORD will build you a house. **11** When
ur days are fulfilled to walk with your
thers, I will raise up your offspring after
ou, one of your own sons, and I will estab-
sh his kingdom. **12** He shall build a house
or me, and I will establish his throne for-
ver. **13** I will be to him a father, and he shall
e to me a son. I will not take my steadfast
we from him, as I took it from him who
as before you, **14** but I will confirm him in
y house and in my kingdom forever, and
s throne shall be established forever.'"
In accordance with all these words, and
accordance with all this vision, Nathan
poke to David.

avid's Prayer

16 Then King David went in and sat before
e LORD and said, "Who am I, O LORD
od, and what is my house, that you have
rought me thus far? **17** And this was a
mall thing in your eyes, O God. You have
lso spoken of your servant's house for a
reat while to come, and have shown me
ture generations,[1] O LORD God! **18** And
hat more can David say to you for hon-
ring your servant? For you know your
ervant. **19** For your servant's sake, O LORD,
nd according to your own heart, you have
one all this greatness, in making known
ll these great things. **20** There is none like
ou, O LORD, and there is no God besides
ou, according to all that we have heard
ith our ears. **21** And who is like your peo-
le Israel, the one[2] nation on earth whom
od went to redeem to be his people, mak-
g for yourself a name for great and awe-
ome things, in driving out nations before
our people whom you redeemed from

Egypt? **22** And you made your people Israel
to be your people forever, and you, O LORD,
became their God. **23** And now, O LORD, let
the word that you have spoken concerning
your servant and concerning his house be
established forever, and do as you have
spoken, **24** and your name will be established and magnified forever, saying, 'The
LORD of hosts, the God of Israel, is Israel's
God,' and the house of your servant David
will be established before you. **25** For you,
my God, have revealed to your servant that
you will build a house for him. Therefore
your servant has found courage to pray
before you. **26** And now, O LORD, you are
God, and you have promised this good
thing to your servant. **27** Now you have been
pleased to bless the house of your servant,
that it may continue forever before you, for
it is you, O LORD, who have blessed, and it
is blessed forever."

David Defeats His Enemies

18 After this David defeated the Philistines and subdued them, and he
took Gath and its villages out of the hand
of the Philistines.

2 And he defeated Moab, and the Moabites became servants to David and brought
tribute.

3 David also defeated Hadadezer king of
Zobah-Hamath, as he went to set up his
monument[3] at the river Euphrates. **4** And
David took from him 1,000 chariots, 7,000
horsemen, and 20,000 foot soldiers. And
David hamstrung all the chariot horses, but
left enough for 100 chariots. **5** And when
the Syrians of Damascus came to help
Hadadezer king of Zobah, David struck
down 22,000 men of the Syrians. **6** Then
David put garrisons[4] in Syria of Damascus,
and the Syrians became servants to David
and brought tribute. And the LORD gave
victory to David[5] wherever he went. **7** And
David took the shields of gold that were
carried by the servants of Hadadezer and
brought them to Jerusalem. **8** And from
Tibhath and from Cun, cities of Hadadezer,
David took a large amount of bronze. With
it Solomon made the bronze sea and the
pillars and the vessels of bronze.

9 When Tou king of Hamath heard that
David had defeated the whole army of
Hadadezer, king of Zobah, **10** he sent his son

he meaning of the Hebrew is uncertain [2]Septuagint, Vulgate *other* [3]Hebrew *hand* [4]Septuagint, Vulgate, 2 Samuel 8:6 (compare
riac); Hebrew lacks *garrisons* [5]Hebrew *the* LORD *saved David*; also verse 13

Hadoram to King David, to ask about his health and to bless him because he had fought against Hadadezer and defeated him; for Hadadezer had often been at war with Tou. And he sent all sorts of articles of gold, of silver, and of bronze. [11] These also King David dedicated to the LORD, together with the silver and gold that he had carried off from all the nations, from Edom, Moab, the Ammonites, the Philistines, and Amalek. [12] And Abishai, the son of Zeruiah, killed 18,000 Edomites in the Valley of Salt. [13] Then he put garrisons in Edom, and all the Edomites became David's servants. And the LORD gave victory to David wherever he went.

David's Administration

[14] So David reigned over all Israel, and he administered justice and equity to all his people. [15] And Joab the son of Zeruiah was over the army; and Jehoshaphat the son of Ahilud was recorder; [16] and Zadok the son of Ahitub and Ahimelech the son of Abiathar were priests; and Shavsha was secretary; [17] and Benaiah the son of Jehoiada was over the Cherethites and the Pelethites; and David's sons were the chief officials in the service of the king.

The Ammonites Disgrace David's Men

19 Now after this Nahash the king of the Ammonites died, and his son reigned in his place. [2] And David said, "I will deal kindly with Hanun the son of Nahash, for his father dealt kindly with me." So David sent messengers to console him concerning his father. And David's servants came to the land of the Ammonites to Hanun to console him. [3] But the princes of the Ammonites said to Hanun, "Do you think, because David has sent comforters to you, that he is honoring your father? Have not his servants come to you to search and to overthrow and to spy out the land?" [4] So Hanun took David's servants and shaved them and cut off their garments in the middle, at their hips, and sent them away; [5] and they departed. When David was told concerning the men, he sent messengers to meet them, for the men were greatly ashamed. And the king said, "Remain at Jericho until your beards have grown and then return."

[6] When the Ammonites saw that the had become a stench to David, Hanun an the Ammonites sent 1,000 talents[1] of si ver to hire chariots and horsemen fro Mesopotamia, from Aram-maacah, an from Zobah. [7] They hired 32,000 charic and the king of Maacah with his army, wh came and encamped before Medeba. An the Ammonites were mustered from the cities and came to battle. [8] When Davi heard of it, he sent Joab and all the arm of the mighty men. [9] And the Ammonite came out and drew up in battle array the entrance of the city, and the kings wh had come were by themselves in the ope country.

Ammonites and Syrians Defeated

[10] When Joab saw that the battle was s against him both in front and in the rea he chose some of the best men of Israel an arrayed them against the Syrians. [11] Th rest of his men he put in the charge Abishai his brother, and they were arraye against the Ammonites. [12] And he said, " the Syrians are too strong for me, then yo shall help me, but if the Ammonites are to strong for you, then I will help you. [13] B strong, and let us use our strength for ou people and for the cities of our God, an may the LORD do what seems good to him [14] So Joab and the people who were wit him drew near before the Syrians for ba tle, and they fled before him. [15] And whe the Ammonites saw that the Syrians fle they likewise fled before Abishai, Joab brother, and entered the city. Then Joa came to Jerusalem.

[16] But when the Syrians saw that the had been defeated by Israel, they se messengers and brought out the Syria who were beyond the Euphrates,[2] wit Shophach the commander of the army Hadadezer at their head. [17] And when was told to David, he gathered all Isra together and crossed the Jordan and cam to them and drew up his forces agains them. And when David set the battle array against the Syrians, they fought wit him. [18] And the Syrians fled before Israe and David killed of the Syrians the men 7,000 chariots and 40,000 foot soldier and put to death also Shophach the com mander of their army. [19] And when th servants of Hadadezer saw that they ha

---

[1] A *talent* was about 75 pounds or 34 kilograms [2] Hebrew *the River*

...een defeated by Israel, they made peace with David and became subject to him. So the Syrians were not willing to save the Ammonites anymore.

The Capture of Rabbah

20 In the spring of the year, the time when kings go out to battle, Joab led out the army and ravaged the country of the Ammonites and came and besieged Rabbah. But David remained at Jerusalem. And Joab struck down Rabbah and overthrew it. ²And David took the crown of their king from his head. He found that it weighed a talent¹ of gold, and in it was a precious stone. And it was placed on David's head. And he brought out the spoil of the city, a very great amount. ³And he brought out the people who were in it and set them to labor² with saws and iron picks and axes.³ And thus David did to all the cities of the Ammonites. Then David and all the people returned to Jerusalem.

Philistine Giants Killed

⁴And after this there arose war with the Philistines at Gezer. Then Sibbecai the Hushathite struck down Sippai, who was one of the descendants of the giants, and the Philistines were subdued. ⁵And there was again war with the Philistines, and Elhanan the son of Jair struck down Lahmi the brother of Goliath the Gittite, the shaft of whose spear was like a weaver's beam. ⁶And there was again war at Gath, where there was a man of great stature, who had six fingers on each hand and six toes on each foot, twenty-four in number, and he also was descended from the giants. ⁷And when he taunted Israel, Jonathan the son of Shimea, David's brother, struck him down. These were descended from the giants in Gath, and they fell by the hand of David and by the hand of his servants.

David's Census Brings Pestilence

21 Then Satan stood against Israel and incited David to number Israel. ²So David said to Joab and the commanders of the army, "Go, number Israel, from Beersheba to Dan, and bring me a report, that I may know their number." ³But Joab said, "May the LORD add to his people a hundred times as many as they are! Are they not, my lord the king, all of them my

lord's servants? Why then should my lord require this? Why should it be a cause of guilt for Israel?" ⁴But the king's word prevailed against Joab. So Joab departed and went throughout all Israel and came back to Jerusalem. ⁵And Joab gave the sum of the numbering of the people to David. In all Israel there were 1,100,000 men who drew the sword, and in Judah 470,000 who drew the sword. ⁶But he did not include Levi and Benjamin in the numbering, for the king's command was abhorrent to Joab.

⁷But God was displeased with this thing, and he struck Israel. ⁸And David said to God, "I have sinned greatly in that I have done this thing. But now, please take away the iniquity of your servant, for I have acted very foolishly." ⁹And the LORD spoke to Gad, David's seer, saying, ¹⁰"Go and say to David, 'Thus says the LORD, Three things I offer you; choose one of them, that I may do it to you.'" ¹¹So Gad came to David and said to him, "Thus says the LORD, 'Choose what you will: ¹²either three years of famine, or three months of devastation by your foes while the sword of your enemies overtakes you, or else three days of the sword of the LORD, pestilence on the land, with the angel of the LORD destroying throughout all the territory of Israel.' Now decide what answer I shall return to him who sent me." ¹³Then David said to Gad, "I am in great distress. Let me fall into the hand of the LORD, for his mercy is very great, but do not let me fall into the hand of man."

¹⁴So the LORD sent a pestilence on Israel, and 70,000 men of Israel fell. ¹⁵And God sent the angel to Jerusalem to destroy it, but as he was about to destroy it, the LORD saw, and he relented from the calamity. And he said to the angel who was working destruction, "It is enough; now stay your hand." And the angel of the LORD was standing by the threshing floor of Ornan the Jebusite. ¹⁶And David lifted his eyes and saw the angel of the LORD standing between earth and heaven, and in his hand a drawn sword stretched out over Jerusalem. Then David and the elders, clothed in sackcloth, fell upon their faces. ¹⁷And David said to God, "Was it not I who gave command to number the people? It is I who have sinned and done great evil. But these sheep, what have they done? Please let your hand, O LORD my

---

¹ A *talent* was about 75 pounds or 34 kilograms   ² Compare 2 Samuel 12:31; Hebrew *he sawed*   ³ Compare 2 Samuel 12:31; Hebrew *saws*

God, be against me and against my father's house. But do not let the plague be on your people."

David Builds an Altar

[18] Now the angel of the LORD had commanded Gad to say to David that David should go up and raise an altar to the LORD on the threshing floor of Ornan the Jebusite. [19] So David went up at Gad's word, which he had spoken in the name of the LORD. [20] Now Ornan was threshing wheat. He turned and saw the angel, and his four sons who were with him hid themselves. [21] As David came to Ornan, Ornan looked and saw David and went out from the threshing floor and paid homage to David with his face to the ground. [22] And David said to Ornan, "Give me the site of the threshing floor that I may build on it an altar to the LORD—give it to me at its full price—that the plague may be averted from the people." [23] Then Ornan said to David, "Take it, and let my lord the king do what seems good to him. See, I give the oxen for burnt offerings and the threshing sledges for the wood and the wheat for a grain offering; I give it all." [24] But King David said to Ornan, "No, but I will buy them for the full price. I will not take for the LORD what is yours, nor offer burnt offerings that cost me nothing." [25] So David paid Ornan 600 shekels[1] of gold by weight for the site. [26] And David built there an altar to the LORD and presented burnt offerings and peace offerings and called on the LORD, and the LORD[2] answered him with fire from heaven upon the altar of burnt offering. [27] Then the LORD commanded the angel, and he put his sword back into its sheath.

[28] At that time, when David saw that the LORD had answered him at the threshing floor of Ornan the Jebusite, he sacrificed there. [29] For the tabernacle of the LORD, which Moses had made in the wilderness, and the altar of burnt offering were at that time in the high place at Gibeon, [30] but David could not go before it to inquire of God, for he was afraid of the sword of the angel of the LORD.

22 Then David said, "Here shall be the house of the LORD God and here the altar of burnt offering for Israel."

David Prepares for Temple Building

[2] David commanded to gather togethe the resident aliens who were in the land of Israel, and he set stonecutters to prepar dressed stones for building the house of God. [3] David also provided great quantitie of iron for nails for the doors of the gate and for clamps, as well as bronze in quanti ties beyond weighing, [4] and cedar timber without number, for the Sidonians and Tyrians brought great quantities of ceda to David. [5] For David said, "Solomon m son is young and inexperienced, and th house that is to be built for the LORD mus be exceedingly magnificent, of fame and glory throughout all lands. I will therefor make preparation for it." So David pro vided materials in great quantity befor his death.

Solomon Charged to Build the Temple

[6] Then he called for Solomon his son an charged him to build a house for the LOR the God of Israel. [7] David said to Solomor "My son, I had it in my heart to build house to the name of the LORD my God [8] But the word of the LORD came to me, say ing, 'You have shed much blood and hav waged great wars. You shall not build house to my name, because you have shed so much blood before me on the earth [9] Behold, a son shall be born to you who shall be a man of rest. I will give him res from all his surrounding enemies. For hi name shall be Solomon, and I will giv peace and quiet to Israel in his days. [10] H shall build a house for my name. He shal be my son, and I will be his father, and I wil establish his royal throne in Israel forever

[11] "Now, my son, the LORD be with you, s that you may succeed in building the hous of the LORD your God, as he has spoke concerning you. [12] Only, may the LORD gran you discretion and understanding, tha when he gives you charge over Israel yo may keep the law of the LORD your God [13] Then you will prosper if you are carefu to observe the statutes and the rules tha the LORD commanded Moses for Israel. B strong and courageous. Fear not; do not b dismayed. [14] With great pains I have pro vided for the house of the LORD 100,00 talents[3] of gold, a million talents of silve and bronze and iron beyond weighing, fo there is so much of it; timber and stone

---

[1] A *shekel* was about 2/5 ounce or 11 grams [2] Hebrew *he* [3] A *talent* was about 75 pounds or 34 kilograms

oo, I have provided. To these you must dd. ¹⁵You have an abundance of workmen: tonecutters, masons, carpenters, and all inds of craftsmen without number, skilled n working ¹⁶gold, silver, bronze, and iron. rise and work! The LORD be with you!"

¹⁷David also commanded all the leaders f Israel to help Solomon his son, saying, ³"Is not the LORD your God with you? And as he not given you peace on every side? or he has delivered the inhabitants of the and into my hand, and the land is subdued efore the LORD and his people. ¹⁹Now set our mind and heart to seek the LORD your God. Arise and build the sanctuary of the LORD God, so that the ark of the covenant f the LORD and the holy vessels of God nay be brought into a house built for the ame of the LORD."

David Organizes the Levites

23 When David was old and full of days, he made Solomon his son king over srael.

²David¹ assembled all the leaders of srael and the priests and the Levites. ³The evites, thirty years old and upward, were umbered, and the total was 38,000 men. "Twenty-four thousand of these," David aid,² "shall have charge of the work in the ouse of the LORD, 6,000 shall be officers nd judges, ⁵4,000 gatekeepers, and 4,000 hall offer praises to the LORD with the nstruments that I have made for praise." And David organized them in divisions orresponding to the sons of Levi: Gershon, Kohath, and Merari.

⁷The sons of Gershon³ were Ladan and himei. ⁸The sons of Ladan: Jehiel the chief, nd Zetham, and Joel, three. ⁹The sons of himei: Shelomoth, Haziel, and Haran, hree. These were the heads of the fathers' ouses of Ladan. ¹⁰And the sons of Shimei: ahath, Zina, and Jeush and Beriah. These our were the sons of Shimei. ¹¹Jahath vas the chief, and Zizah the second; but eush and Beriah did not have many sons, herefore they became counted as a single ather's house.

¹²The sons of Kohath: Amram, Izhar, Iebron, and Uzziel, four. ¹³The sons of mram: Aaron and Moses. Aaron was set part to dedicate the most holy things, hat he and his sons forever should make fferings before the LORD and minister to

him and pronounce blessings in his name forever. ¹⁴But the sons of Moses the man of God were named among the tribe of Levi. ¹⁵The sons of Moses: Gershom and Eliezer. ¹⁶The sons of Gershom: Shebuel the chief. ¹⁷The sons of Eliezer: Rehabiah the chief. Eliezer had no other sons, but the sons of Rehabiah were very many. ¹⁸The sons of Izhar: Shelomith the chief. ¹⁹The sons of Hebron: Jeriah the chief, Amariah the second, Jahaziel the third, and Jekameam the fourth. ²⁰The sons of Uzziel: Micah the chief and Isshiah the second.

²¹The sons of Merari: Mahli and Mushi. The sons of Mahli: Eleazar and Kish. ²²Eleazar died having no sons, but only daughters; their kinsmen, the sons of Kish, married them. ²³The sons of Mushi: Mahli, Eder, and Jeremoth, three.

²⁴These were the sons of Levi by their fathers' houses, the heads of fathers' houses as they were listed according to the number of the names of the individuals from twenty years old and upward who were to do the work for the service of the house of the LORD. ²⁵For David said, "The LORD, the God of Israel, has given rest to his people, and he dwells in Jerusalem forever. ²⁶And so the Levites no longer need to carry the tabernacle or any of the things for its service." ²⁷For by the last words of David the sons of Levi were numbered from twenty years old and upward. ²⁸For their duty was to assist the sons of Aaron for the service of the house of the LORD, having the care of the courts and the chambers, the cleansing of all that is holy, and any work for the service of the house of God. ²⁹Their duty was also to assist with the showbread, the flour for the grain offering, the wafers of unleavened bread, the baked offering, the offering mixed with oil, and all measures of quantity or size. ³⁰And they were to stand every morning, thanking and praising the LORD, and likewise at evening, ³¹and whenever burnt offerings were offered to the LORD on Sabbaths, new moons, and feast days, according to the number required of them, regularly before the LORD. ³²Thus they were to keep charge of the tent of meeting and the sanctuary, and to attend the sons of Aaron, their brothers, for the service of the house of the LORD.

¹Hebrew He ²Hebrew lacks David said ³Vulgate (compare Septuagint, Syriac); Hebrew to the Gershonite

David Organizes the Priests

24 The divisions of the sons of Aaron were these. The sons of Aaron: Nadab, Abihu, Eleazar, and Ithamar. ²But Nadab and Abihu died before their father and had no children, so Eleazar and Ithamar became the priests. ³With the help of Zadok of the sons of Eleazar, and Ahimelech of the sons of Ithamar, David organized them according to the appointed duties in their service. ⁴Since more chief men were found among the sons of Eleazar than among the sons of Ithamar, they organized them under sixteen heads of fathers' houses of the sons of Eleazar, and eight of the sons of Ithamar. ⁵They divided them by lot, all alike, for there were sacred officers and officers of God among both the sons of Eleazar and the sons of Ithamar. ⁶And the scribe Shemaiah, the son of Nethanel, a Levite, recorded them in the presence of the king and the princes and Zadok the priest and Ahimelech the son of Abiathar and the heads of the fathers' houses of the priests and of the Levites, one father's house being chosen for Eleazar and one chosen for Ithamar.

⁷The first lot fell to Jehoiarib, the second to Jedaiah, ⁸the third to Harim, the fourth to Seorim, ⁹the fifth to Malchijah, the sixth to Mijamin, ¹⁰the seventh to Hakkoz, the eighth to Abijah, ¹¹the ninth to Jeshua, the tenth to Shecaniah, ¹²the eleventh to Eliashib, the twelfth to Jakim, ¹³the thirteenth to Huppah, the fourteenth to Jeshebeab, ¹⁴the fifteenth to Bilgah, the sixteenth to Immer, ¹⁵the seventeenth to Hezir, the eighteenth to Happizzez, ¹⁶the nineteenth to Pethahiah, the twentieth to Jehezkel, ¹⁷the twenty-first to Jachin, the twenty-second to Gamul, ¹⁸the twenty-third to Delaiah, the twenty-fourth to Maaziah. ¹⁹These had as their appointed duty in their service to come into the house of the LORD according to the procedure established for them by Aaron their father, as the LORD God of Israel had commanded him.

²⁰And of the rest of the sons of Levi: of the sons of Amram, Shubael; of the sons of Shubael, Jehdeiah. ²¹Of Rehabiah: of the sons of Rehabiah, Isshiah the chief. ²²Of the Izharites, Shelomoth; of the sons of Shelomoth, Jahath. ²³The sons of Hebron:[1] Jeriah the chief,[2] Amariah the second,

Jahaziel the third, Jekameam the fourth. ²⁴The sons of Uzziel, Micah; of the son of Micah, Shamir. ²⁵The brother of Micah Isshiah; of the sons of Isshiah, Zechariah. ²⁶The sons of Merari: Mahli and Mushi. The sons of Jaaziah: Beno.[3] ²⁷The sons of Merari of Jaaziah, Beno, Shoham, Zaccur, and Ibr ²⁸Of Mahli: Eleazar, who had no sons. ²⁹O Kish, the sons of Kish: Jerahmeel. ³⁰Th sons of Mushi: Mahli, Eder, and Jerimoth These were the sons of the Levites according to their fathers' houses. ³¹These also the head of each father's house and hi younger brother alike, cast lots, just a their brothers the sons of Aaron, in th presence of King David, Zadok, Ahimelech and the heads of fathers' houses of th priests and of the Levites.

David Organizes the Musicians

25 David and the chiefs of the service also set apart for the service the sons of Asaph, and of Heman, and o Jeduthun, who prophesied with lyres with harps, and with cymbals. The list c those who did the work and of their dutie was: ²Of the sons of Asaph: Zaccur, Joseph Nethaniah, and Asharelah, sons of Asaph under the direction of Asaph, who prophesied under the direction of the king. ³O Jeduthun, the sons of Jeduthun: Gedaliah Zeri, Jeshaiah, Shimei,[4] Hashabiah, an Mattithiah, six, under the direction of thei father Jeduthun, who prophesied with th lyre in thanksgiving and praise to the LORD ⁴Of Heman, the sons of Heman: Bukkiah Mattaniah, Uzziel, Shebuel and Jerimoth Hananiah, Hanani, Eliathah, Giddalti, an Romamti-ezer, Joshbekashah, Malloth Hothir, Mahazioth. ⁵All these were th sons of Heman the king's seer, according to the promise of God to exalt him, fo God had given Heman fourteen sons an three daughters. ⁶They were all under th direction of their father in the music in th house of the LORD with cymbals, harps and lyres for the service of the house o God. Asaph, Jeduthun, and Heman wer under the order of the king. ⁷The numbe of them along with their brothers, wh were trained in singing to the LORD, all wh were skillful, was 288. ⁸And they cast lot for their duties, small and great, teache and pupil alike.

[1] Compare 23:19; Hebrew lacks *Hebron* [2] Compare 23:19; Hebrew lacks *the chief* [3] Or *his son*; also verse 27 [4] One Hebrew manuscript, Septuagint; most Hebrew manuscripts lack *Shimei*

⁹The first lot fell for Asaph to Joseph; the second to Gedaliah, to him and his brothers and his sons, twelve; ¹⁰the third to Zaccur, his sons and his brothers, twelve; ¹¹the fourth to Izri, his sons and his brothers, twelve; ¹²the fifth to Nethaniah, his sons and his brothers, twelve; ¹³the sixth to Bukkiah, his sons and his brothers, twelve; ¹⁴the seventh to Jesharelah, his sons and his brothers, twelve; ¹⁵the eighth to Jeshaiah, his sons and his brothers, twelve; ¹⁶the ninth to Mattaniah, his sons and his brothers, twelve; ¹⁷the tenth to Shimei, his sons and his brothers, twelve; ¹⁸the eleventh to Azarel, his sons and his brothers, twelve; ¹⁹the twelfth to Hashabiah, his sons and his brothers, twelve; ²⁰to the thirteenth, Shubael, his sons and his brothers, twelve; ²¹to the fourteenth, Mattithiah, his sons and his brothers, twelve; ²²to the fifteenth, to Jeremoth, his sons and his brothers, twelve; ²³to the sixteenth, to Hananiah, his sons and his brothers, twelve; ²⁴to the seventeenth, to Joshbekashah, his sons and his brothers, twelve; ²⁵to the eighteenth, to Hanani, his sons and his brothers, twelve; ²⁶to the nineteenth, to Mallothi, his sons and his brothers, twelve; ²⁷to the twentieth, to Eliathah, his sons and his brothers, twelve; ²⁸to the twenty-first, to Hothir, his sons and his brothers, twelve; ²⁹to the twenty-second, to Giddalti, his sons and his brothers, twelve; ³⁰to the twenty-third, Mahazioth, his sons and his brothers, twelve; ³¹to the twenty-fourth, to Romamti-ezer, his sons and his brothers, twelve.

Divisions of the Gatekeepers

26 As for the divisions of the gatekeepers: of the Korahites, Meshelemiah the son of Kore, of the sons of Asaph. ²And Meshelemiah had sons: Zechariah the firstborn, Jediael the second, Zebadiah the third, Jathniel the fourth, ³Elam the fifth, Jehohanan the sixth, Eliehoenai the seventh. ⁴And Obed-edom had sons: Shemaiah the firstborn, Jehozabad the second, Joah the third, Sachar the fourth, Nethanel the fifth, ⁵Ammiel the sixth, Issachar the seventh, Peullethai the eighth, for God blessed him. ⁶Also to his son Shemaiah were sons born who were rulers in their fathers' houses, for they were men of great ability. The sons of Shemaiah: Othni, Rephael,

Obed and Elzabad, whose brothers were able men, Elihu and Semachiah. ⁸All these were of the sons of Obed-edom with their sons and brothers, able men qualified for the service; sixty-two of Obed-edom. ⁹And Meshelemiah had sons and brothers, able men, eighteen. ¹⁰And Hosah, of the sons of Merari, had sons: Shimri the chief (for though he was not the firstborn, his father made him chief), ¹¹Hilkiah the second, Tebaliah the third, Zechariah the fourth: all the sons and brothers of Hosah were thirteen.

¹²These divisions of the gatekeepers, corresponding to their chief men, had duties, just as their brothers did, ministering in the house of the LORD. ¹³And they cast lots by fathers' houses, small and great alike, for their gates. ¹⁴The lot for the east fell to Shelemiah. They cast lots also for his son Zechariah, a shrewd counselor, and his lot came out for the north. ¹⁵Obed-edom's came out for the south, and to his sons was allotted the gatehouse. ¹⁶For Shuppim and Hosah it came out for the west, at the gate of Shallecheth on the road that goes up. Watch corresponded to watch. ¹⁷On the east there were six each day,¹ on the north four each day, on the south four each day, as well as two and two at the gatehouse. ¹⁸And for the colonnade² on the west there were four at the road and two at the colonnade. ¹⁹These were the divisions of the gatekeepers among the Korahites and the sons of Merari.

Treasurers and Other Officials

²⁰And of the Levites, Ahijah had charge of the treasuries of the house of God and the treasuries of the dedicated gifts. ²¹The sons of Ladan, the sons of the Gershonites belonging to Ladan, the heads of the fathers' houses belonging to Ladan the Gershonite: Jehieli.³ ²²The sons of Jehieli, Zetham, and Joel his brother, were in charge of the treasuries of the house of the LORD. ²³Of the Amramites, the Izharites, the Hebronites, and the Uzzielites— ²⁴and Shebuel the son of Gershom, son of Moses, was chief officer in charge of the treasuries. ²⁵His brothers: from Eliezer were his son Rehabiah, and his son Jeshaiah, and his son Joram, and his son Zichri, and his son Shelomoth.

[26] This Shelomoth and his brothers were in charge of all the treasuries of the dedicated gifts that David the king and the heads of the fathers' houses and the officers of the thousands and the hundreds and the commanders of the army had dedicated. [27] From spoil won in battles they dedicated gifts for the maintenance of the house of the LORD. [28] Also all that Samuel the seer and Saul the son of Kish and Abner the son of Ner and Joab the son of Zeruiah had dedicated—all dedicated gifts were in the care of Shelomoth[1] and his brothers.

[29] Of the Izharites, Chenaniah and his sons were appointed to external duties for Israel, as officers and judges. [30] Of the Hebronites, Hashabiah and his brothers, 1,700 men of ability, had the oversight of Israel westward of the Jordan for all the work of the LORD and for the service of the king. [31] Of the Hebronites, Jerijah was chief of the Hebronites of whatever genealogy or fathers' houses. (In the fortieth year of David's reign search was made and men of great ability among them were found at Jazer in Gilead.) [32] King David appointed him and his brothers, 2,700 men of ability, heads of fathers' houses, to have the oversight of the Reubenites, the Gadites and the half-tribe of the Manassites for everything pertaining to God and for the affairs of the king.

Military Divisions

27 This is the number of the people of Israel, the heads of fathers' houses, the commanders of thousands and hundreds, and their officers who served the king in all matters concerning the divisions that came and went, month after month throughout the year, each division numbering 24,000:

[2] Jashobeam the son of Zabdiel was in charge of the first division in the first month; in his division were 24,000. [3] He was a descendant of Perez and was chief of all the commanders. He served for the first month. [4] Dodai the Ahohite[2] was in charge of the division of the second month; in his division were 24,000. [5] The third commander, for the third month, was Benaiah, the son of Jehoiada the chief priest; in his division were 24,000. [6] This is the Benaiah who was a mighty man of the thirty and

in command of the thirty; Ammizabad hi son was in charge of his division.[3] [7] Asahe the brother of Joab was fourth, for th fourth month, and his son Zebadiah afte him; in his division were 24,000. [8] Th fifth commander, for the fifth month, wa Shamhuth the Izrahite; in his division wer 24,000. [9] Sixth, for the sixth month, wa Ira, the son of Ikkesh the Tekoite; in hi division were 24,000. [10] Seventh, for th seventh month, was Helez the Pelonite, o the sons of Ephraim; in his division wer 24,000. [11] Eighth, for the eighth month, wa Sibbecai the Hushathite, of the Zerahites in his division were 24,000. [12] Ninth, for th ninth month, was Abiezer of Anathoth, Benjaminite; in his division were 24,00([13] Tenth, for the tenth month, was Mahara of Netophah, of the Zerahites; in his divi sion were 24,000. [14] Eleventh, for the elev enth month, was Benaiah of Pirathon, o the sons of Ephraim; in his division wer 24,000. [15] Twelfth, for the twelfth month was Heldai the Netophathite, of Othnie in his division were 24,000.

Leaders of Tribes

[16] Over the tribes of Israel, for the Reu benites, Eliezer the son of Zichri was chie officer; for the Simeonites, Shephatiah the son of Maacah; [17] for Levi, Hashabia the son of Kemuel; for Aaron, Zadok; [18] fo Judah, Elihu, one of David's brothers for Issachar, Omri the son of Michael; [19] fo Zebulun, Ishmaiah the son of Obadiah for Naphtali, Jeremoth the son of Azrie [20] for the Ephraimites, Hoshea the son o Azaziah; for the half-tribe of Manasseh, Joe the son of Pedaiah; [21] for the half-tribe o Manasseh in Gilead, Iddo the son of Zecha riah; for Benjamin, Jaasiel the son of Abne [22] for Dan, Azarel the son of Jeroham. Thes were the leaders of the tribes of Israel [23] David did not count those below twenty years of age, for the LORD had promised t make Israel as many as the stars of heaven [24] Joab the son of Zeruiah began to count but did not finish. Yet wrath came upo Israel for this, and the number was no entered in the chronicles of King David.

[25] Over the king's treasuries was Azma veth the son of Adiel; and over the trea suries in the country, in the cities, in th villages, and in the towers, was Jonatha

---

[1] Hebrew *Shelomith* [2] Septuagint; Hebrew *Ahohite and his division and Mikloth the chief officer* [3] Septuagint, Vulgate; Hebrew *was his division*

the son of Uzziah; ²⁶and over those who did the work of the field for tilling the soil was Ezri the son of Chelub; ²⁷and over the vineyards was Shimei the Ramathite; and over the produce of the vineyards for the wine cellars was Zabdi the Shiphmite. ²⁸Over the olive and sycamore trees in the Shephelah was Baal-hanan the Gederite; and over the stores of oil was Joash. ²⁹Over the herds that pastured in Sharon was Shitrai the Sharonite; over the herds in the valleys was Shaphat the son of Adlai. ³⁰Over the camels was Obil the Ishmaelite; and over the donkeys was Jehdeiah the Meronothite. Over the flocks was Jaziz the Hagrite. ³¹All these were stewards of King David's property.

³²Jonathan, David's uncle, was a counselor, being a man of understanding and a scribe. He and Jehiel the son of Hachmoni attended the king's sons. ³³Ahithophel was the king's counselor, and Hushai the Archite was the king's friend. ³⁴Ahithophel was succeeded by Jehoiada the son of Benaiah, and Abiathar. Joab was commander of the king's army.

David's Charge to Israel

28 David assembled at Jerusalem all the officials of Israel, the officials of the tribes, the officers of the divisions that served the king, the commanders of thousands, the commanders of hundreds, the stewards of all the property and livestock of the king and his sons, together with the palace officials, the mighty men and all the seasoned warriors. ²Then King David rose to his feet and said: "Hear me, my brothers and my people. I had it in my heart to build a house of rest for the ark of the covenant of the LORD and for the footstool of our God, and I made preparations for building. ³But God said to me, 'You may not build a house for my name, for you are a man of war and have shed blood.' ⁴Yet the LORD God of Israel chose me from all my father's house to be king over Israel forever. For he chose Judah as leader, and in the house of Judah my father's house, and among my father's sons he took pleasure in me to make me king over all Israel. ⁵And of all my sons (for the LORD has given me many sons) he has chosen Solomon my son to sit on the throne of the kingdom of the LORD over Israel. ⁶He said to me, 'It is Solomon your son who shall build my house and my

courts, for I have chosen him to be my son, and I will be his father. ⁷I will establish his kingdom forever if he continues strong in keeping my commandments and my rules, as he is today.' ⁸Now therefore in the sight of all Israel, the assembly of the LORD, and in the hearing of our God, observe and seek out all the commandments of the LORD your God, that you may possess this good land and leave it for an inheritance to your children after you forever.

David's Charge to Solomon

⁹"And you, Solomon my son, know the God of your father and serve him with a whole heart and with a willing mind, for the LORD searches all hearts and understands every plan and thought. If you seek him, he will be found by you, but if you forsake him, he will cast you off forever. ¹⁰Be careful now, for the LORD has chosen you to build a house for the sanctuary; be strong and do it."

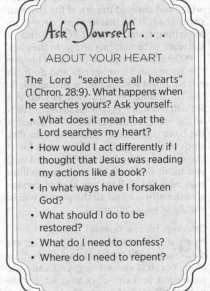

Ask Yourself . . .

ABOUT YOUR HEART

The Lord "searches all hearts" (1 Chron. 28:9). What happens when he searches yours? Ask yourself:

- What does it mean that the Lord searches my heart?
- How would I act differently if I thought that Jesus was reading my actions like a book?
- In what ways have I forsaken God?
- What should I do to be restored?
- What do I need to confess?
- Where do I need to repent?

¹¹Then David gave Solomon his son the plan of the vestibule of the temple,¹ and of its houses, its treasuries, its upper rooms, and its inner chambers, and of the room

---

¹Hebrew lacks *of the temple*

for the mercy seat; [12] and the plan of all that he had in mind for the courts of the house of the Lord, all the surrounding chambers, the treasuries of the house of God, and the treasuries for dedicated gifts; [13] for the divisions of the priests and of the Levites, and all the work of the service in the house of the Lord; for all the vessels for the service in the house of the Lord, [14] the weight of gold for all golden vessels for each service, the weight of silver vessels for each service, [15] the weight of the golden lampstands and their lamps, the weight of gold for each lampstand and its lamps, the weight of silver for a lampstand and its lamps, according to the use of each lampstand in the service, [16] the weight of gold for each table for the showbread, the silver for the silver tables, [17] and pure gold for the forks, the basins and the cups; for the golden bowls and the weight of each; for the silver bowls and the weight of each; [18] for the altar of incense made of refined gold, and its weight; also his plan for the golden chariot of the cherubim that spread their wings and covered the ark of the covenant of the Lord. [19] "All this he made clear to me in writing from the hand of the Lord, all the work to be done according to the plan."

[20] Then David said to Solomon his son, "Be strong and courageous and do it. Do not be afraid and do not be dismayed, for the Lord God, even my God, is with you. He will not leave you or forsake you, until all the work for the service of the house of the Lord is finished. [21] And behold the divisions of the priests and the Levites for all the service of the house of God; and with you in all the work will be every willing man who has skill for any kind of service; also the officers and all the people will be wholly at your command."

Offerings for the Temple

29 And David the king said to all the assembly, "Solomon my son, whom alone God has chosen, is young and inexperienced, and the work is great, for the palace will not be for man but for the Lord God. [2] So I have provided for the house of my God, so far as I was able, the gold for the things of gold, the silver for the things of silver, and the bronze for the things of bronze, the iron for the things of iron, and

wood for the things of wood, besides great quantities of onyx and stones for setting, antimony, colored stones, all sorts of precious stones and marble. [3] Moreover, in addition to all that I have provided for the holy house, I have a treasure of my own of gold and silver, and because of my devotion to the house of my God I give it to the house of my God: [4] 3,000 talents[1] of gold, of the gold of Ophir, and 7,000 talents of refined silver, for overlaying the walls of the house,[2] [5] and for all the work to be done by craftsmen, gold for the things of gold and silver for the things of silver. Who then will offer willingly, consecrating himself[3] today to the Lord?"

[6] Then the leaders of fathers' houses made their freewill offerings, as did also the leaders of the tribes, the commanders of thousands and of hundreds, and the officers over the king's work. [7] They gave for the service of the house of God 5,000 talents and 10,000 darics[4] of gold, 10,000 talents of silver, 18,000 talents of bronze, and 100,000 talents of iron. [8] And whoever had precious stones gave them to the treasury of the house of the Lord, in the care of Jehiel the Gershonite. [9] Then the people rejoiced because they had given willingly, for with a whole heart they had offered freely to the Lord. David the king also rejoiced greatly.

David Prays in the Assembly

[10] Therefore David blessed the Lord in the presence of all the assembly. And David said: "Blessed are you, O Lord, the God of Israel our father, forever and ever. [11] Yours, O Lord, is the greatness and the power and the glory and the victory and the majesty, for all that is in the heavens and in the earth is yours. Yours is the kingdom, O Lord, and you are exalted as head above all. [12] Both riches and honor come from you, and you rule over all. In your hand are power and might, and in your hand it is to make great and to give strength to all. [13] And now we thank you, our God, and praise your glorious name.

[14] "But who am I, and what is my people, that we should be able thus to offer willingly? For all things come from you, and of your own have we given you. [15] For we are strangers before you and sojourners, as

[1] A *talent* was about 75 pounds or 34 kilograms [2] Septuagint; Hebrew *houses* [3] Or *ordaining himself*; Hebrew *filling his hand* [4] A *daric* was a coin weighing about 1/4 ounce or 8.5 grams

all our fathers were. Our days on the earth are like a shadow, and there is no abiding.[1] [16] O LORD our God, all this abundance that we have provided for building you a house for your holy name comes from your hand and is all your own. [17] I know, my God, that you test the heart and have pleasure in uprightness. In the uprightness of my heart I have freely offered all these things, and now I have seen your people, who are present here, offering freely and joyously to you. [18] O LORD, the God of Abraham, Isaac, and Israel, our fathers, keep forever such purposes and thoughts in the hearts of your people, and direct their hearts toward you. [19] Grant to Solomon my son a whole heart that he may keep your commandments, your testimonies, and your statutes, performing all, and that he may build the palace for which I have made provision."

[20] Then David said to all the assembly, "Bless the LORD your God." And all the assembly blessed the LORD, the God of their fathers, and bowed their heads and paid homage to the LORD and to the king. [21] And they offered sacrifices to the LORD, and on the next day offered burnt offerings to the LORD, 1,000 bulls, 1,000 rams, and 1,000 lambs, with their drink offerings, and sacrifices in abundance for all Israel. [22] And they ate and drank before the LORD on that day with great gladness.

Solomon Anointed King

And they made Solomon the son of David king the second time, and they anointed him as prince for the LORD, and Zadok as priest. [23] Then Solomon sat on the throne of the LORD as king in place of David his father. And he prospered, and all Israel obeyed him. [24] All the leaders and the mighty men, and also all the sons of King David, pledged their allegiance to King Solomon. [25] And the LORD made Solomon very great in the sight of all Israel and bestowed on him such royal majesty as had not been on any king before him in Israel.

The Death of David

[26] Thus David the son of Jesse reigned over all Israel. [27] The time that he reigned over Israel was forty years. He reigned seven years in Hebron and thirty-three years in Jerusalem. [28] Then he died at a good age, full of days, riches, and honor. And Solomon his son reigned in his place. [29] Now the acts of King David, from first to last, are written in the Chronicles of Samuel the seer, and in the Chronicles of Nathan the prophet, and in the Chronicles of Gad the seer, [30] with accounts of all his rule and his might and of the circumstances that came upon him and upon Israel and upon all the kingdoms of the countries.

---

[1] Septuagint, Vulgate; Hebrew *hope*, or *prospect*

INTRODUCTION TO
2 Chronicles

Author: Unknown
Time: Possibly around 400 B.C.
Place: Unknown
Written to: The Israelites

The gist

The Chronicles were written to help the Israelites better understand and believe that God was still the God of David and Abraham. The chronicler wrote to remind them that the covenant that God made with David was also with his descendants, and that even though it seemed like God had forsaken them, he hadn't.

Things to look for

- The division of the kingdom (see 2 Chronicles 10–11)
- Description of the temple and the role of the priests (see 2 Chron. 20:5–9, 13, 27–28; 23:12–21; 24:4–14; 29:1–31:21; 34:1–35:19)

Humble Yourself

> "If my people who are called by my name humble themselves, and pray and seek my face and turn from their wicked ways, then I will hear from heaven and will forgive their sin and heal their land."
>
> 2 Chronicles 7:14

Sin has a cure, and the cure is the gospel. And one of the main ways believing the gospel changes us is by humbling us. Humility is crucial to joy-filled walking with God. Humility sounds like weakness, sounds uncomfortable, and even dangerous. But humility is just acknowledging your complete dependence on God and making a deliberate decision to make life not about you but about him. When your life is centered on your wants and needs, humility sneaks out the back door and danger sneaks in.

We see this in 2 Chronicles. When the Israelites' military and financial victories puffed them up, they lost their humility, and then they stopped worshiping the true God. But God didn't write them off like you might think he would; he kept his promise to David to bring him success for generations to come. But even so, his hand of protection was withdrawn from David's heirs while they lived their prideful and evil lives.

It's easy to let pride in your own abilities color your vision of what you were meant to be or to do. All day long you live with thoughts about yourself, your feelings, your wants, your needs, and your experiences, and it's easy to get all self-occupied. But you've gotta be careful. When things start to look bad, then it's time to stop all the self-centered thoughts and start looking up. Turn away from the sin of self-obsession and toward the strength of humility. When you walk humbly, without any regard for yourself or your wants but with an eye on God and what he wants, your life will be blessed. You'll find that your prayers are more effective, forgiveness is yours, and your life is healed.

Take a look at the lives of those who have turned their back on God and have tried to make their own way in this life, and let their lives be a warning. Let their destruction be a constant reminder of what a life turned away from God's face will give you. Trust God enough to humble yourself as the godly men and women who have lived before you have done.

Must-Know Terms and Verses

∞ *Covenant* ∞

A permanent agreement between two parties, often used by God to give his promises or favor to his people. A covenant usually requires some kind of obligation to be fulfilled by each of the parties involved.

∞ *Most Holy Place* ∞

The part of the tabernacle and temple where the ark of the covenant was kept.

"If my people who are called by my name humble themselves, and pray and seek my face and turn from their wicked ways, then I will hear from heaven and will forgive their sin and heal their land." *2 Chronicles 7:14*

"Thus says the LORD to you, 'Do not be afraid and do not be dismayed at this great horde, for the battle is not yours but God's.'" *2 Chronicles 20:15*

2 Chronicles

Solomon Worships at Gibeon

1 Solomon the son of David established himself in his kingdom, and the LORD his God was with him and made him exceedingly great.

²Solomon spoke to all Israel, to the commanders of thousands and of hundreds, to the judges, and to all the leaders in all Israel, the heads of fathers' houses. ³And Solomon, and all the assembly with him, went to the high place that was at Gibeon, for the tent of meeting of God, which Moses the servant of the LORD had made in the wilderness, was there. ⁴(But David had brought up the ark of God from Kiriath-jearim to the place that David had prepared for it, for he had pitched a tent for it in Jerusalem.) ⁵Moreover, the bronze altar that Bezalel the son of Uri, son of Hur, had made, was there before the tabernacle of the LORD. And Solomon and the assembly sought it¹ out. ⁶And Solomon went up there to the bronze altar before the LORD, which was at the tent of meeting, and offered a thousand burnt offerings on it.

Solomon Prays for Wisdom

⁷In that night God appeared to Solomon, and said to him, "Ask what I shall give you." ⁸And Solomon said to God, "You have shown great and steadfast love to David my father, and have made me king in his place. ⁹O LORD God, let your word to David my father be now fulfilled, for you have made me king over a people as numerous as the dust of the earth. ¹⁰Give me now wisdom and knowledge to go out and come in before this people, for who can govern this people of yours, which is so great?" ¹¹God answered Solomon, "Because this was in your heart, and you have not asked for possessions, wealth, honor, or the life of those who hate you, and have not even asked for long life, but have asked for wisdom and knowledge for yourself that you may govern my people over whom I have made you king, ¹²wisdom and knowledge are granted to you. I will also give you riches, possessions, and honor, such as none of the kings had who were before you, and none after you shall have the like." ¹³So Solomon came from² the high place at Gibeon, from before the tent of meeting, to Jerusalem. And he reigned over Israel.

Solomon Given Wealth

¹⁴Solomon gathered together chariots and horsemen. He had 1,400 chariots and 12,000 horsemen, whom he stationed in the chariot cities and with the king in Jerusalem. ¹⁵And the king made silver and gold as common in Jerusalem as stone, and he made cedar as plentiful as the sycamore of the Shephelah. ¹⁶And Solomon's import of horses was from Egypt and Kue, and the king's traders would buy them from Kue for a price. ¹⁷They imported a chariot from Egypt for 600 shekels³ of silver, and a horse for 150. Likewise through them these were exported to all the kings of the Hittites and the kings of Syria.

Preparing to Build the Temple

2⁴ Now Solomon purposed to build a temple for the name of the LORD, and a royal palace for himself. ²⁵ And Solomon assigned 70,000 men to bear burdens and 80,000 to quarry in the hill country, and 3,600 to oversee them. ³And Solomon sent word to Hiram the king of Tyre: "As you dealt with David my father and sent him cedar to build himself a house to dwell in, so deal with me. ⁴Behold, I am about to build a house for the name of the LORD my God and dedicate it to him for the burning of incense of sweet spices before him, and for the regular arrangement of the showbread, and for burnt offerings morning and evening, on the Sabbaths and the new moons and the appointed feasts of

---

¹Or *him* ²Septuagint, Vulgate; Hebrew *to* ³A *shekel* was about 2/5 ounce or 11 grams ⁴Ch 1:18 in Hebrew ⁵Ch 2:1 in Hebrew

the Lᴏʀᴅ our God, as ordained forever for Israel. **5**The house that I am to build will be great, for our God is greater than all gods. **6**But who is able to build him a house, since heaven, even highest heaven, cannot contain him? Who am I to build a house for him, except as a place to make offerings before him? **7**So now send me a man skilled to work in gold, silver, bronze, and iron, and in purple, crimson, and blue fabrics, trained also in engraving, to be with the skilled workers who are with me in Judah and Jerusalem, whom David my father provided. **8**Send me also cedar, cypress, and algum timber from Lebanon, for I know that your servants know how to cut timber in Lebanon. And my servants will be with your servants, **9**to prepare timber for me in abundance, for the house I am to build will be great and wonderful. **10**I will give for your servants, the woodsmen who cut timber, 20,000 cors[1] of crushed wheat, 20,000 cors of barley, 20,000 baths[2] of wine, and 20,000 baths of oil."

11Then Hiram the king of Tyre answered in a letter that he sent to Solomon, "Because the Lᴏʀᴅ loves his people, he has made you king over them." **12**Hiram also said, "Blessed be the Lᴏʀᴅ God of Israel, who made heaven and earth, who has given King David a wise son, who has discretion and understanding, who will build a temple for the Lᴏʀᴅ and a royal palace for himself. **13**"Now I have sent a skilled man, who has understanding, Huram-abi, **14**the son of a woman of the daughters of Dan, and his father was a man of Tyre. He is trained to work in gold, silver, bronze, iron, stone, and wood, and in purple, blue, and crimson fabrics and fine linen, and to do all sorts of engraving and execute any design that may be assigned him, with your craftsmen, the craftsmen of my lord, David your father. **15**Now therefore the wheat and barley, oil and wine, of which my lord has spoken, let him send to his servants. **16**And we will cut whatever timber you need from Lebanon and bring it to you in rafts by sea to Joppa, so that you may take it up to Jerusalem."

17Then Solomon counted all the resident aliens who were in the land of Israel, after the census of them that David his father had taken, and there were found 153,600. **18**Seventy thousand of them he assigned to bear burdens, 80,000 to quarry in the hill country, and 3,600 as overseers to make the people work.

Solomon Builds the Temple

3 Then Solomon began to build the house of the Lᴏʀᴅ in Jerusalem on Mount Moriah, where the Lᴏʀᴅ[3] had appeared to David his father, at the place that David had appointed, on the threshing floor of Ornan the Jebusite. **2**He began to build in the second month of the fourth year of his reign. **3**These are Solomon's measurements[4] for building the house of God: the length, in cubits[5] of the old standard, was sixty cubits, and the breadth twenty cubits. **4**The vestibule in front of the nave of the house was twenty cubits long, equal to the width of the house,[6] and its height was 120 cubits. He overlaid it on the inside with pure gold. **5**The nave he lined with cypress and covered it with fine gold and made palms and chains on it. **6**He adorned the house with settings of precious stones. The gold was gold of Parvaim. **7**So he lined the house with gold—its beams, its thresholds, its walls, and its doors—and he carved cherubim on the walls.

8And he made the Most Holy Place. Its length, corresponding to the breadth of the house, was twenty cubits, and its breadth was twenty cubits. He overlaid it with 600 talents[7] of fine gold. **9**The weight of gold for the nails was fifty shekels.[8] And he overlaid the upper chambers with gold.

10In the Most Holy Place he made two cherubim of wood[9] and overlaid[10] them with gold. **11**The wings of the cherubim together extended twenty cubits: one wing of the one, of five cubits, touched the wall of the house, and its other wing, of five cubits, touched the wing of the other cherub; **12**and of this cherub, one wing, of five cubits, touched the wall of the house, and the other wing, also of five cubits, was joined to the wing of the first cherub. **13**The wings of these cherubim extended twenty cubits. The cherubim[11] stood on their feet, facing the nave. **14**And he made the veil of

[1]A cor was about 6 bushels or 220 liters [2]A bath was about 6 gallons or 22 liters [3]Septuagint; Hebrew lacks the Lᴏʀᴅ [4]Syriac; Hebrew foundations [5]A cubit was about 18 inches or 45 centimeters [6]Compare 1 Kings 6:3; the meaning of the Hebrew is uncertain [7]A talent was about 75 pounds or 34 kilograms [8]A shekel was about 2/5 ounce or 11 grams [9]Septuagint; the meaning of the Hebrew is uncertain [10]Hebrew they overlaid [11]Hebrew they

ue and purple and crimson fabrics and
ne linen, and he worked cherubim on it.
¹⁵ In front of the house he made two pil-
rs thirty-five cubits high, with a capital
ʾ five cubits on the top of each. ¹⁶ He made
ains like a necklace¹ and put them on
e tops of the pillars, and he made a hun-
red pomegranates and put them on the
ains. ¹⁷ He set up the pillars in front of
e temple, one on the south, the other
n the north; that on the south he called
chin, and that on the north Boaz.

e Temple's Furnishings

He made an altar of bronze, twenty
cubits² long and twenty cubits wide
nd ten cubits high. ² Then he made the
ea of cast metal. It was round, ten cubits
om brim to brim, and five cubits high,
nd a line of thirty cubits measured its
rcumference. ³ Under it were figures of
ourds,³ for ten cubits, compassing the sea
l around. The gourds were in two rows,
ast with it when it was cast. ⁴ It stood
n twelve oxen, three facing north, three
cing west, three facing south, and three
cing east. The sea was set on them, and
l their rear parts were inward. ⁵ Its thick-
ess was a handbreadth.⁴ And its brim was
ade like the brim of a cup, like the flower
ʾ a lily. It held 3,000 baths.⁵ ⁶ He also made
n basins in which to wash, and set five on
e south side, and five on the north side.
these they were to rinse off what was
sed for the burnt offering, and the sea was
r the priests to wash in.

⁷ And he made ten golden lampstands
s prescribed, and set them in the temple,
ve on the south side and five on the north.
Ie also made ten tables and placed them
the temple, five on the south side and
ve on the north. And he made a hundred
asins of gold. ⁹ He made the court of the
riests and the great court and doors for
e court and overlaid their doors with
ronze. ¹⁰ And he set the sea at the south-
ast corner of the house.

¹¹ Hiram also made the pots, the shovels,
nd the basins. So Hiram finished the work
nat he did for King Solomon on the house
f God: ¹² the two pillars, the bowls, and
ne two capitals on the top of the pillars;
nd the two latticeworks to cover the two

bowls of the capitals that were on the top
of the pillars; ¹³ and the 400 pomegranates for the two latticeworks, two rows
of pomegranates for each latticework, to
cover the two bowls of the capitals that
were on the pillars. ¹⁴ He made the stands
also, and the basins on the stands, ¹⁵ and
the one sea, and the twelve oxen underneath it. ¹⁶ The pots, the shovels, the forks,
and all the equipment for these Huram-
abi made of burnished bronze for King
Solomon for the house of the LORD. ¹⁷ In
the plain of the Jordan the king cast them,
in the clay ground between Succoth and
Zeredah.⁶ ¹⁸ Solomon made all these things
in great quantities, for the weight of the
bronze was not sought.

¹⁹ So Solomon made all the vessels that
were in the house of God: the golden altar,
the tables for the bread of the Presence,
²⁰ the lampstands and their lamps of pure
gold to burn before the inner sanctuary, as
prescribed; ²¹ the flowers, the lamps, and
the tongs, of purest gold; ²² the snuffers,
basins, dishes for incense, and fire pans, of
pure gold, and the sockets⁷ of the temple,
for the inner doors to the Most Holy Place
and for the doors of the nave of the temple
were of gold.

5 Thus all the work that Solomon did for
the house of the LORD was finished.
And Solomon brought in the things that
David his father had dedicated, and stored
the silver, the gold, and all the vessels in the
treasuries of the house of God.

The Ark Brought to the Temple

² Then Solomon assembled the elders
of Israel and all the heads of the tribes,
the leaders of the fathers' houses of the
people of Israel, in Jerusalem, to bring up
the ark of the covenant of the LORD out
of the city of David, which is Zion. ³ And
all the men of Israel assembled before
the king at the feast that is in the seventh
month. ⁴ And all the elders of Israel came,
and the Levites took up the ark. ⁵ And they
brought up the ark, the tent of meeting,
and all the holy vessels that were in the
tent; the Levitical priests brought them up.
⁶ And King Solomon and all the congregation of Israel, who had assembled before
him, were before the ark, sacrificing so

---

lebrew *chains in the inner sanctuary* ²A *cubit* was about 18 inches or 45 centimeters ³Compare 1 Kings 7:24; Hebrew *oxen*; twice in
s verse ⁴A *handbreadth* was about 3 inches or 7.5 centimeters ⁵A *bath* was about 6 gallons or 22 liters ⁶Spelled *Zarethan* in 1 Kings
6 ⁷Compare 1 Kings 7:50; Hebrew *the entrance of the house*

many sheep and oxen that they could not be counted or numbered. [7] Then the priests brought the ark of the covenant of the LORD to its place, in the inner sanctuary of the house, in the Most Holy Place, underneath the wings of the cherubim. [8] The cherubim spread out their wings over the place of the ark, so that the cherubim made a covering above the ark and its poles. [9] And the poles were so long that the ends of the poles were seen from the Holy Place before the inner sanctuary, but they could not be seen from outside. And they are[1] there to this day. [10] There was nothing in the ark except the two tablets that Moses put there at Horeb, where the LORD made a covenant with the people of Israel, when they came out of Egypt. [11] And when the priests came out of the Holy Place (for all the priests who were present had consecrated themselves, without regard to their divisions, [12] and all the Levitical singers, Asaph, Heman, and Jeduthun, their sons and kinsmen, arrayed in fine linen, with cymbals, harps, and lyres, stood east of the altar with 120 priests who were trumpeters; [13] and it was the duty of the trumpeters and singers to make themselves heard in unison in praise and thanksgiving to the LORD), and when the song was raised, with trumpets and cymbals and other musical instruments, in praise to the LORD,

"For he is good,
for his steadfast love endures
forever,"

the house, the house of the LORD, was filled with a cloud, [14] so that the priests could not stand to minister because of the cloud, for the glory of the LORD filled the house of God.

Solomon Blesses the People

6 Then Solomon said, "The LORD has said that he would dwell in thick darkness. [2] But I have built you an exalted house, a place for you to dwell in forever." [3] Then the king turned around and blessed all the assembly of Israel, while all the assembly of Israel stood. [4] And he said, "Blessed be the LORD, the God of Israel, who with his hand has fulfilled what he promised with his mouth to David my father, saying, [5] 'Since the day that I brought my people out of the land of Egypt, I chose no city out

of all the tribes of Israel in which to bui a house, that my name might be there, ar I chose no man as prince over my peop Israel; [6] but I have chosen Jerusalem th my name may be there, and I have chose David to be over my people Israel.' [7] No it was in the heart of David my father build a house for the name of the LORD, th God of Israel. [8] But the LORD said to Dav my father, 'Whereas it was in your hea to build a house for my name, you did we that it was in your heart. [9] Nevertheles it is not you who shall build the hous but your son who shall be born to yo shall build the house for my name.' [10] No the LORD has fulfilled his promise that h made. For I have risen in the place of Dav my father and sit on the throne of Israe as the LORD promised, and I have built th house for the name of the LORD, the Go of Israel. [11] And there I have set the ark, which is the covenant of the LORD that h made with the people of Israel."

Solomon's Prayer of Dedication

[12] Then Solomon stood before the altar the LORD in the presence of all the assen bly of Israel and spread out his hand [13] Solomon had made a bronze platfor five cubits[2] long, five cubits wide, and thr cubits high, and had set it in the court, ar he stood on it. Then he knelt on his kne in the presence of all the assembly of Isra and spread out his hands toward heave [14] and said, "O LORD, God of Israel, the is no God like you, in heaven or on eart keeping covenant and showing steadfa love to your servants who walk befo you with all their heart, [15] who have ke with your servant David my father wh you declared to him. You spoke with yo mouth, and with your hand have fulfille it this day. [16] Now therefore, O LORD, Go of Israel, keep for your servant David m father what you have promised him, sa ing, 'You shall not lack a man to sit befo me on the throne of Israel, if only your so pay close attention to their way, to wa in my law as you have walked before m [17] Now therefore, O LORD, God of Israel, le your word be confirmed, which you hav spoken to your servant David.

[18] "But will God indeed dwell with ma on the earth? Behold, heaven and the hig est heaven cannot contain you, how muc

---

[1] Hebrew *it is*   [2] A *cubit* was about 18 inches or 45 centimeters

ss this house that I have built! [19] Yet have egard to the prayer of your servant and to is plea, O LORD my God, listening to the ry and to the prayer that your servant rays before you, [20] that your eyes may e open day and night toward this house, he place where you have promised to et your name, that you may listen to the rayer that your servant offers toward is place. [21] And listen to the pleas of your ervant and of your people Israel, when ey pray toward this place. And listen om heaven your dwelling place, and hen you hear, forgive.

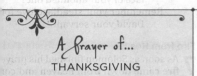

A Prayer of...
THANKSGIVING

Dear God, even though I am allowed to come near to you, I am not ignorant of my sin that should bar me from your presence. I don't deny my guilt. I confess my sinfulness and quickly thank you for your forgiveness. I pray that, like Moses, I would choose to suffer rather than enjoy the pleasures of sin. Help me to always put myself under your guiding hand; to take hold of the amazing covenant that binds me to you; to feel more of the purifying and softening faith that I profess; to have more compassion, love, pity, and kindness; to always remember the honor of being used as an instrument in your hands, ready to take any chance to be useful and willing to offer all my talents to your service.

You have done all things right for me, remembered me, saved me, and forgiven me. I haven't gotten everything that I want, but you have kept things from me when getting them would have meant my ruin or my injury. You repeatedly wipe away my tears, give me peace when my heart is broken, and discipline me for my good. All your work for me is perfect, and I praise you.

Amen.

[22] "If a man sins against his neighbor and is made to take an oath and comes and swears his oath before your altar in this house, [23] then hear from heaven and act and judge your servants, repaying the guilty by bringing his conduct on his own head, and vindicating the righteous by rewarding him according to his righteousness.

[24] "If your people Israel are defeated before the enemy because they have sinned against you, and they turn again and acknowledge your name and pray and plead with you in this house, [25] then hear from heaven and forgive the sin of your people Israel and bring them again to the land that you gave to them and to their fathers.

[26] "When heaven is shut up and there is no rain because they have sinned against you, if they pray toward this place and acknowledge your name and turn from their sin, when you afflict[1] them, [27] then hear in heaven and forgive the sin of your servants, your people Israel, when you teach them the good way[2] in which they should walk, and grant rain upon your land, which you have given to your people as an inheritance.

[28] "If there is famine in the land, if there is pestilence or blight or mildew or locust or caterpillar, if their enemies besiege them in the land at their gates, whatever plague, whatever sickness there is, [29] whatever prayer, whatever plea is made by any man or by all your people Israel, each knowing his own affliction and his own sorrow and stretching out his hands toward this house, [30] then hear from heaven your dwelling place and forgive and render to each whose heart you know, according to all his ways, for you, you only, know the hearts of the children of mankind, [31] that they may fear you and walk in your ways all the days that they live in the land that you gave to our fathers.

[32] "Likewise, when a foreigner, who is not of your people Israel, comes from a far country for the sake of your great name and your mighty hand and your outstretched arm, when he comes and prays toward this house, [33] hear from heaven your dwelling place and do according to all for which the foreigner calls to you, in order that all the peoples of the earth may know your name and fear you, as do your people Israel, and that they may know that

eptuagint, Vulgate; Hebrew *answer* [2] Septuagint, Syriac, Vulgate (compare 1 Kings 8:36); Hebrew *toward the good way* this house that I have built is called by your name. ³⁴"If your people go out to battle against their enemies, by whatever way you shall send them, and they pray to you toward this city that you have chosen and the house that I have built for your name, ³⁵then hear from heaven their prayer and their plea, and maintain their cause.

³⁶"If they sin against you—for there is no one who does not sin—and you are angry with them and give them to an enemy, so that they are carried away captive to a land far or near, ³⁷yet if they turn their heart in the land to which they have been carried captive, and repent and plead with you in the land of their captivity, saying, 'We have sinned and have acted perversely and wickedly,' ³⁸if they repent with all their mind and with all their heart in the land of their captivity to which they were carried captive, and pray toward their land, which you gave to their fathers, the city that you have chosen and the house that I have built for your name, ³⁹then hear from heaven your dwelling place their prayer and their

pleas, and maintain their cause and forgiv your people who have sinned against yo ⁴⁰Now, O my God, let your eyes be ope and your ears attentive to the prayer ‹ this place.

⁴¹ "And now arise, O Lord God, and go ‹
        your resting place,
      you and the ark of your might.
    Let your priests, O Lord God, be
        clothed with salvation,
      and let your saints rejoice in your
        goodness.
⁴² O Lord God, do not turn away the
        face of your anointed one!
      Remember your steadfast love fo
        David your servant."

Fire from Heaven

7 As soon as Solomon finished his praye fire came down from heaven and co sumed the burnt offering and the sacri fices, and the glory of the Lord filled th temple. ²And the priests could not ent the house of the Lord, because the glory ‹ the Lord filled the Lord's house. ³When ‹

Know Yourself

verses to read
2 Chronicles 6:24–25

To understand how much God hates your sin, you have only to look as far as the cross. Everything in you that is selfish, envious, bitter, resentful, or angry— everything in you that is not part of the character of God—is what put Christ on that cross.

When you confess your sin every day, you agree with God that a lot of you is broken and at odds with godliness, and so you honor the cross. But when you forget or skip over that very crucial part of each day, you start to take Christ's death for granted and so dishonor the cross. Don't let yourself get so comfortable with your sin, which was Christ's death sentence, that you can't see it anymore. Confess everything that doesn't come from God and agree that it's what sent his Son to the cross. God promises that when his people turn away from sin and pray to him in repentance, he will listen. When you do that, you will also find that your relationship with God grows in depth and power and peace. Confession is good for the soul.

Above all, never forget that while the cross shows us how much God hates sin, it also shows us how much he loves us. Our sin required nothing less than the horrible curse of the cross; but God's love sent nothing less than his own Son to bear that curse. As you consider the weight of sin each day, be sure also to consider the wonder of free grace, won through Jesus for you.

e people of Israel saw the fire come down
d the glory of the LORD on the temple,
ey bowed down with their faces to the
ound on the pavement and worshiped
d gave thanks to the LORD, saying, "For
e is good, for his steadfast love endures
rever."

he Dedication of the Temple

4 Then the king and all the people offered
crifice before the LORD. **5** King Solomon
fered as a sacrifice 22,000 oxen and
20,000 sheep. So the king and all the
ople dedicated the house of God. **6** The
iests stood at their posts; the Levites
so, with the instruments for music to the
RD that King David had made for giving
anks to the LORD—for his steadfast love
dures forever—whenever David offered
aises by their ministry;[1] opposite them
e priests sounded trumpets, and all
rael stood.

7 And Solomon consecrated the middle
the court that was before the house of
e LORD, for there he offered the burnt
fering and the fat of the peace offerings,
cause the bronze altar Solomon had
ade could not hold the burnt offering
d the grain offering and the fat.

8 At that time Solomon held the feast for
ven days, and all Israel with him, a very
eat assembly, from Lebo-hamath to the
rook of Egypt. **9** And on the eighth day
ey held a solemn assembly, for they had
pt the dedication of the altar seven days
d the feast seven days. **10** On the twenty-
ird day of the seventh month he sent the
ople away to their homes, joyful and glad
heart for the prosperity that the LORD
d granted to David and to Solomon and
Israel his people.

My People Pray

11 Thus Solomon finished the house of
e LORD and the king's house. All that
olomon had planned to do in the house
the LORD and in his own house he suc-
ssfully accomplished. **12** Then the LORD
peared to Solomon in the night and said
him: "I have heard your prayer and have
osen this place for myself as a house of
crifice. **13** When I shut up the heavens
that there is no rain, or command the
cust to devour the land, or send pesti-
nce among my people, **14** if my people who

are called by my name humble themselves,
and pray and seek my face and turn from
their wicked ways, then I will hear from
heaven and will forgive their sin and heal
their land. **15** Now my eyes will be open and
my ears attentive to the prayer that is made
in this place. **16** For now I have chosen and
consecrated this house that my name may
be there forever. My eyes and my heart will
be there for all time. **17** And as for you, if you
will walk before me as David your father
walked, doing according to all that I have
commanded you and keeping my statutes
and my rules, **18** then I will establish your
royal throne, as I covenanted with David
your father, saying, 'You shall not lack a
man to rule Israel.'

19 "But if you[2] turn aside and forsake
my statutes and my commandments that
I have set before you, and go and serve
other gods and worship them, **20** then I will
pluck you[3] up from my land that I have
given you, and this house that I have consecrated for my name, I will cast out of my
sight, and I will make it a proverb and a
byword among all peoples. **21** And at this
house, which was exalted, everyone passing by will be astonished and say, 'Why
has the LORD done thus to this land and to
this house?' **22** Then they will say, 'Because
they abandoned the LORD, the God of
their fathers who brought them out of the
land of Egypt, and laid hold on other gods
and worshiped them and served them.
Therefore he has brought all this disaster
on them.'"

Solomon's Accomplishments

8 At the end of twenty years, in which
Solomon had built the house of the
LORD and his own house, **2** Solomon rebuilt
the cities that Hiram had given to him, and
settled the people of Israel in them.

3 And Solomon went to Hamath-zobah
and took it. **4** He built Tadmor in the wilderness and all the store cities that he built in
Hamath. **5** He also built Upper Beth-horon
and Lower Beth-horon, fortified cities with
walls, gates, and bars, **6** and Baalath, and
all the store cities that Solomon had and
all the cities for his chariots and the cities
for his horsemen, and whatever Solomon
desired to build in Jerusalem, in Lebanon,
and in all the land of his dominion. **7** All
the people who were left of the Hittites,

the Amorites, the Perizzites, the Hivites, and the Jebusites, who were not of Israel, [8] from their descendants who were left after them in the land, whom the people of Israel had not destroyed—these Solomon drafted as forced labor, and so they are to this day. [9] But of the people of Israel Solomon made no slaves for his work; they were soldiers, and his officers, the commanders of his chariots, and his horsemen. [10] And these were the chief officers of King Solomon, 250, who exercised authority over the people.

[11] Solomon brought Pharaoh's daughter up from the city of David to the house that he had built for her, for he said, "My wife shall not live in the house of David king of Israel, for the places to which the ark of the LORD has come are holy."

[12] Then Solomon offered up burnt offerings to the LORD on the altar of the LORD that he had built before the vestibule, [13] as the duty of each day required, offering according to the commandment of Moses for the Sabbaths, the new moons, and the three annual feasts—the Feast of Unleavened Bread, the Feast of Weeks, and the Feast of Booths. [14] According to the ruling of David his father, he appointed the divisions of the priests for their service, and the Levites for their offices of praise and ministry before the priests as the duty of each day required, and the gatekeepers in their divisions at each gate, for so David the man of God had commanded. [15] And they did not turn aside from what the king had commanded the priests and Levites concerning any matter and concerning the treasuries.

[16] Thus was accomplished all the work of Solomon from[1] the day the foundation of the house of the LORD was laid until it was finished. So the house of the LORD was completed.

[17] Then Solomon went to Ezion-geber and Eloth on the shore of the sea, in the land of Edom. [18] And Hiram sent to him by the hand of his servants ships and servants familiar with the sea, and they went to Ophir together with the servants of Solomon and brought from there 450 talents[2] of gold and brought it to King Solomon.

The Queen of Sheba

9 Now when the queen of Sheba heard of the fame of Solomon, she came to Jerusalem to test him with hard questions, having a very great retinue and camels bearing spices and very much gold and precious stones. And when she came to Solomon, she told him all that was on her mind. [2] And Solomon answered all her questions. There was nothing hidden from Solomon that he could not explain to her. [3] And when the queen of Sheba had seen the wisdom of Solomon, the house that he had built, [4] the food of his table, the seating of his officials, and the attendance of his servants, and their clothing, his cupbearers, and their clothing, and his burnt offerings that he offered at the house of the LORD, there was no more breath in her.

[5] And she said to the king, "The report was true that I heard in my own land of your words and of your wisdom, [6] but I did not believe the[3] reports until I came and my own eyes had seen it. And behold, half the greatness of your wisdom was not told me; you surpass the report that I heard. [7] Happy are your wives![4] Happy are these your servants, who continually stand before you and hear your wisdom! [8] Blessed be the LORD your God, who has delighted in you and set you on his throne as king for the LORD your God! Because your God loved Israel and would establish them forever, he has made you king over them, that you may execute justice and righteousness." [9] Then she gave the king 120 talents[5] of gold, and a very great quantity of spices, and precious stones. There were no spices such as those that the queen of Sheba gave to King Solomon.

[10] Moreover, the servants of Hiram and the servants of Solomon, who brought gold from Ophir, brought algum wood and precious stones. [11] And the king made from the algum wood supports for the house of the LORD and for the king's house, lyres also and harps for the singers. There never was seen the like of them before in the land of Judah.

[12] And King Solomon gave to the queen of Sheba all that she desired, whatever she asked besides what she had brought to the king. So she turned and went back to her own land with her servants.

---

[1] Septuagint, Syriac, Vulgate; Hebrew *to* [2] A *talent* was about 75 pounds or 34 kilograms [3] Hebrew *their* [4] Septuagint (compare 1 Kings 10:8); Hebrew *men* [5] A *talent* was about 75 pounds or 34 kilograms

lomon's Wealth

13 Now the weight of gold that came to lomon in one year was 666 talents of ld, **14** besides that which the explorers d merchants brought. And all the kings Arabia and the governors of the land ought gold and silver to Solomon. **15** King lomon made 200 large shields of beaten ld; 600 shekels[1] of beaten gold went into ch shield. **16** And he made 300 shields beaten gold; 300 shekels of gold went to each shield; and the king put them in e House of the Forest of Lebanon. **17** The ng also made a great ivory throne and erlaid it with pure gold. **18** The throne d six steps and a footstool of gold, which ere attached to the throne, and on each le of the seat were armrests and two ns standing beside the armrests, **19** while elve lions stood there, one on each end a step on the six steps. Nothing like was ever made for any kingdom. **20** All ng Solomon's drinking vessels were of ld, and all the vessels of the House of the rest of Lebanon were of pure gold. Silver as not considered as anything in the days Solomon. **21** For the king's ships went to rshish with the servants of Hiram. Once ery three years the ships of Tarshish ed to come bringing gold, silver, ivory, es, and peacocks.[2]

22 Thus King Solomon excelled all the ngs of the earth in riches and in wisdom. And all the kings of the earth sought the esence of Solomon to hear his wisdom, nich God had put into his mind. **24** Every ne of them brought his present, articles of ver and of gold, garments, myrrh, spices, rses, and mules, so much year by year. And Solomon had 4,000 stalls for horses d chariots, and 12,000 horsemen, whom e stationed in the chariot cities and with e king in Jerusalem. **26** And he ruled over l the kings from the Euphrates[3] to the nd of the Philistines and to the border of ypt. **27** And the king made silver as com- on in Jerusalem as stone, and he made dar as plentiful as the sycamore of the ephelah. **28** And horses were imported r Solomon from Egypt and from all lands.

lomon's Death

29 Now the rest of the acts of Solomon, om first to last, are they not written in e history of Nathan the prophet, and in

the prophecy of Ahijah the Shilonite, and in the visions of Iddo the seer concern- ing Jeroboam the son of Nebat? **30** Solomon reigned in Jerusalem over all Israel forty years. **31** And Solomon slept with his fathers and was buried in the city of David his father, and Rehoboam his son reigned in his place.

The Revolt Against Rehoboam

10 Rehoboam went to Shechem, for all Israel had come to Shechem to make him king. **2** And as soon as Jeroboam the son of Nebat heard of it (for he was in Egypt, where he had fled from King Solomon), then Jeroboam returned from Egypt. **3** And they sent and called him. And Jeroboam and all Israel came and said to Rehoboam, **4** "Your father made our yoke heavy. Now therefore lighten the hard service of your father and his heavy yoke on us, and we will serve you." **5** He said to them, "Come to me again in three days." So the people went away.

6 Then King Rehoboam took counsel with the old men,[4] who had stood before Solomon his father while he was yet alive, saying, "How do you advise me to answer this people?" **7** And they said to him, "If you will be good to this people and please them and speak good words to them, then they will be your servants forever." **8** But he abandoned the counsel that the old men gave him, and took counsel with the young men who had grown up with him and stood before him. **9** And he said to them, "What do you advise that we answer this people who have said to me, 'Lighten the yoke that your father put on us'?" **10** And the young men who had grown up with him said to him, "Thus shall you speak to the people who said to you, 'Your father made our yoke heavy, but you lighten it for us'; thus shall you say to them, 'My little finger is thicker than my father's thighs. **11** And now, whereas my father laid on you a heavy yoke, I will add to your yoke. My father disciplined you with whips, but I will discipline you with scorpions.'"

12 So Jeroboam and all the people came to Rehoboam the third day, as the king said, "Come to me again the third day." **13** And the king answered them harshly; and for- saking the counsel of the old men, **14** King Rehoboam spoke to them according to

---

shekel was about 2/5 ounce or 11 grams [2] Or *baboons* [3] Hebrew *the River* [4] Or *the elders*; also verses 8, 13 the counsel of the young men, saying, "My father made your yoke heavy, but I will add to it. My father disciplined you with whips, but I will discipline you with scorpions." ¹⁵ So the king did not listen to the people, for it was a turn of affairs brought about by God that the LORD might fulfill his word, which he spoke by Ahijah the Shilonite to Jeroboam the son of Nebat.

¹⁶ And when all Israel saw that the king did not listen to them, the people answered the king, "What portion have we in David? We have no inheritance in the son of Jesse. Each of you to your tents, O Israel! Look now to your own house, David." So all Israel went to their tents. ¹⁷ But Rehoboam reigned over the people of Israel who lived in the cities of Judah. ¹⁸ Then King Rehoboam sent Hadoram,¹

¹ Spelled *Adoram* in 1 Kings 12:18

who was taskmaster over the forced lab and the people of Israel stoned him death with stones. And King Rehoboa quickly mounted his chariot to flee Jerusalem. ¹⁹ So Israel has been in rebe lion against the house of David to this d

Rehoboam Secures His Kingdom

11 When Rehoboam came to Jerusale he assembled the house of Jud and Benjamin, 180,000 chosen warrio to fight against Israel, to restore the kin dom to Rehoboam. ² But the word of t LORD came to Shemaiah the man of Go ³ "Say to Rehoboam the son of Solomo king of Judah, and to all Israel in Judah an Benjamin, ⁴ 'Thus says the LORD, You sh not go up or fight against your relativ Return every man to his home, for th thing is from me.'" So they listened to t

Know Yourself

verses to read
2 Chronicles 10:6–8

Faith isn't just about communion with God; it's also about being part of God's people. When you have a big decision to make or when troubles hit you from all sides and you don't know what to do, God doesn't want you to play the fool. The fool is the one who won't seek godly advice but chooses to listen to the crowd. The fool goes to her peers, who may have little or no wisdom, and does whatever they say she should do. But that's a stupid move.

True wisdom comes from people who are older and more mature than you are and who can see things from a broader perspective. You might not like what they say, and you might even blame their response on their being "out of touch" or "too conservative," but it's foolish to ignore them and just do what your friends say.

Friends are a good thing, and they can make your life so much better, but their wisdom isn't always mature. Usually they give advice with self-protection in mind— they either want to agree with your bad decisions in order to make you happy, or they encourage you to believe a sinful response is the only alternative because they are just as heated about things as you are. You can't let a friend or anyone else tell you that sin is the way to deal with your problems. No, you've gotta go to people who are more removed from the situation and have nothing to gain or lose by your ultimate decision. Then don't play the fool by returning to your friends and choosing their more immature and earthly response.

Friends are not always out to get you, and they aren't completely clueless, but they just don't always have the wisdom that comes with age. So think about where you get your advice, and look for godly counsel when you have a decision to make, especially one about spiritual matters.

word of the LORD and returned and did not go against Jeroboam.

⁵ Rehoboam lived in Jerusalem, and he built cities for defense in Judah. ⁶ He built Bethlehem, Etam, Tekoa, ⁷ Beth-zur, Soco, Adullam, ⁸ Gath, Mareshah, Ziph, ⁹ Adoraim, Lachish, Azekah, ¹⁰ Zorah, Aijalon, and Hebron, fortified cities that are in Judah and in Benjamin. ¹¹ He made the fortresses strong, and put commanders in them, and stores of food, oil, and wine. ¹² And he put shields and spears in all the cities and made them very strong. So he held Judah and Benjamin.

Priests and Levites Come to Jerusalem

¹³ And the priests and the Levites who were in all Israel presented themselves to him from all places where they lived. ¹⁴ For the Levites left their common lands and their holdings and came to Judah and Jerusalem, because Jeroboam and his sons cast them out from serving as priests of the LORD, ¹⁵ and he appointed his own priests for the high places and for the goat idols and for the calves that he had made. ¹⁶ And those who had set their hearts to seek the LORD God of Israel came after them from all the tribes of Israel to Jerusalem to sacrifice to the LORD, the God of their fathers. ¹⁷ They strengthened the kingdom of Judah, and for three years they made Rehoboam the son of Solomon secure, for they walked for three years in the way of David and Solomon.

Rehoboam's Family

¹⁸ Rehoboam took as wife Mahalath the daughter of Jerimoth the son of David, and of Abihail the daughter of Eliab the son of Jesse, ¹⁹ and she bore him sons, Jeush, Shemariah, and Zaham. ²⁰ After her he took Maacah the daughter of Absalom, who bore him Abijah, Attai, Ziza, and Shelomith. ²¹ Rehoboam loved Maacah the daughter of Absalom above all his wives and concubines (he took eighteen wives and sixty concubines, and fathered twenty-eight sons and sixty daughters). ²² And Rehoboam appointed Abijah the son of Maacah as chief prince among his brothers, for he intended to make him king. ²³ And he dealt wisely and distributed some of his sons through all the districts of Judah and Benjamin, in all the fortified cities,

and he gave them abundant provisions and procured wives for them.[1]

Ask Yourself . . .

ABOUT WINNING

Sometimes, getting what you want can be the worst thing that could happen. When times are good—when you are successful, popular, and happy—it can be easy to forget all about God. So ask yourself about winning:

- When things are going my way, how do I respond?
- Am I closer to God when I'm going through a trial or when I've had a big win?
- How could I make sure I stay close to God the next time life is going great?
- In what ways could I appreciate, honor, worship, or love him when life is going great?

Egypt Plunders Jerusalem

12 When the rule of Rehoboam was established and he was strong, he abandoned the law of the LORD, and all Israel with him. ² In the fifth year of King Rehoboam, because they had been unfaithful to the LORD, Shishak king of Egypt came up against Jerusalem ³ with 1,200 chariots and 60,000 horsemen. And the people were without number who came with him from Egypt—Libyans, Sukkiim, and Ethiopians. ⁴ And he took the fortified cities of Judah and came as far as Jerusalem. ⁵ Then Shemaiah the prophet came to Rehoboam and to the princes of Judah, who had gathered at Jerusalem because of Shishak, and said to them, "Thus says the LORD, 'You abandoned me, so I have abandoned you to the hand of Shishak.'" ⁶ Then the princes of Israel and the king humbled themselves and said, "The LORD is

---

[1] Hebrew *and sought a multitude of wives*

righteous." [7] When the LORD saw that they humbled themselves, the word of the LORD came to Shemaiah: "They have humbled themselves. I will not destroy them, but I will grant them some deliverance, and my wrath shall not be poured out on Jerusalem by the hand of Shishak. [8] Nevertheless, they shall be servants to him, that they may know my service and the service of the kingdoms of the countries."

[9] So Shishak king of Egypt came up against Jerusalem. He took away the treasures of the house of the LORD and the treasures of the king's house. He took away everything. He also took away the shields of gold that Solomon had made, [10] and King Rehoboam made in their place shields of bronze and committed them to the hands of the officers of the guard, who kept the door of the king's house. [11] And as often as the king went into the house of the LORD, the guard came and carried them and brought them back to the guardroom. [12] And when he humbled himself the wrath of the LORD turned from him, so as not to make a complete destruction. Moreover, conditions were good[1] in Judah.

[13] So King Rehoboam grew strong in Jerusalem and reigned. Rehoboam was forty-one years old when he began to reign, and he reigned seventeen years in Jerusalem, the city that the LORD had chosen out of all the tribes of Israel to put his name there. His mother's name was Naamah the Ammonite. [14] And he did evil, for he did not set his heart to seek the LORD.

[15] Now the acts of Rehoboam, from first to last, are they not written in the chronicles of Shemaiah the prophet and of Iddo the seer?[2] There were continual wars between Rehoboam and Jeroboam. [16] And Rehoboam slept with his fathers and was buried in the city of David, and Abijah[3] his son reigned in his place.

Abijah Reigns in Judah

13 In the eighteenth year of King Jeroboam, Abijah began to reign over Judah. [2] He reigned for three years in Jerusalem. His mother's name was Micaiah[4] the daughter of Uriel of Gibeah.

Now there was war between Abijah and Jeroboam. [3] Abijah went out to battle, having an army of valiant men of war, 400,000

chosen men. And Jeroboam drew up his line of battle against him with 800,000 chosen mighty warriors. [4] Then Abijah stood up on Mount Zemaraim that is in the hill country of Ephraim and said, "Hear me, O Jeroboam and all Israel! [5] Ought you not to know that the LORD God of Israel gave the kingship over Israel forever to David and his sons by a covenant of salt? [6] Yet Jeroboam the son of Nebat, a servant of Solomon the son of David, rose up and rebelled against his lord, [7] and certain worthless scoundrels gathered about him and defied Rehoboam the son of Solomon, when Rehoboam was young and irresolute[5] and could not withstand them.

[8] "And now you think to withstand the kingdom of the LORD in the hand of the sons of David, because you are a great multitude and have with you the golden calves that Jeroboam made you for gods. [9] Have you not driven out the priests of the LORD, the sons of Aaron, and the Levites, and made priests for yourselves like the peoples of other lands? Whoever comes for ordination[6] with a young bull or seven rams becomes a priest of what are no gods. [10] But as for us, the LORD is our God, and we have not forsaken him. We have priests ministering to the LORD who are sons of Aaron, and Levites for their service. [11] They offer to the LORD every morning and every evening burnt offerings and incense of sweet spices, set out the showbread on the table of pure gold, and care for the golden lampstand that its lamps may burn every evening. For we keep the charge of the LORD our God, but you have forsaken him. [12] Behold, God is with us at our head, and his priests with their battle trumpets to sound the call to battle against you. O sons of Israel, do not fight against the LORD, the God of your fathers, for you cannot succeed."

[13] Jeroboam had sent an ambush around to come upon them from behind. Thus his troops[7] were in front of Judah, and the ambush was behind them. [14] And when Judah looked, behold, the battle was in front of and behind them. And they cried to the LORD, and the priests blew the trumpets. [15] Then the men of Judah raised the battle shout. And when the men of Judah shouted, God defeated Jeroboam and all

---

[1] Hebrew *good things were found* [2] After *seer*, Hebrew adds *according to genealogy* [3] Spelled *Abijam* in 1 Kings 14:31 [4] Spelled *Maacah* in 1 Kings 15:2 [5] Hebrew *soft of heart* [6] Hebrew *to fill his hand* [7] Hebrew *they*

srael before Abijah and Judah. [16] The men of Israel fled before Judah, and God gave them into their hand. [17] Abijah and his people struck them with great force, so there fell slain of Israel 500,000 chosen men. [18] Thus the men of Israel were subdued at that time, and the men of Judah prevailed, because they relied on the LORD, the God of their fathers. [19] And Abijah pursued Jeroboam and took cities from him, Bethel with its villages and Jeshanah with its villages and Ephron[1] with its villages. [20] Jeroboam did not recover his power in the days of Abijah. And the LORD struck him down, and he died. [21] But Abijah grew mighty. And he took fourteen wives and had twenty-two sons and sixteen daughters. [22] The rest of the acts of Abijah, his ways and his sayings, are written in the story of the prophet Iddo.

Asa Reigns in Judah

14 [2] Abijah slept with his fathers, and they buried him in the city of David. And Asa his son reigned in his place. In his days the land had rest for ten years. [2] [3] And Asa did what was good and right in the eyes of the LORD his God. [3] He took away the foreign altars and the high places and broke down the pillars and cut down the Asherim [4] and commanded Judah to seek the LORD, the God of their fathers, and to keep the law and the commandment. [5] He also took out of all the cities of Judah the high places and the incense altars. And the kingdom had rest under him. [6] He built fortified cities in Judah, for the land had rest. He had no war in those years, for the LORD gave him peace. [7] And he said to Judah, "Let us build these cities and surround them with walls and towers, gates and bars. The land is still ours, because we have sought the LORD our God. We have sought him, and he has given us peace on every side." So they built and prospered. [8] And Asa had an army of 300,000 from Judah, armed with large shields and spears, and 280,000 men from Benjamin that carried shields and drew bows. All these were mighty men of valor.

[9] Zerah the Ethiopian came out against them with an army of a million men and 300 chariots, and came as far as Mareshah. [10] And Asa went out to meet him, and they drew up their lines of battle in the Valley of Zephathah at Mareshah. [11] And Asa cried to the LORD his God, "O LORD, there is none like you to help, between the mighty and the weak. Help us, O LORD our God, for we rely on you, and in your name we have come against this multitude. O LORD, you are our God; let not man prevail against you." [12] So the LORD defeated the Ethiopians before Asa and before Judah, and the Ethiopians fled. [13] Asa and the people who were with him pursued them as far as Gerar, and the Ethiopians fell until none remained alive, for they were broken before the LORD and his army. The men of Judah[4] carried away very much spoil. [14] And they attacked all the cities around Gerar, for the fear of the LORD was upon them. They plundered all the cities, for there was much plunder in them. [15] And they struck down the tents of those who had livestock and carried away sheep in abundance and camels. Then they returned to Jerusalem.

Asa's Religious Reforms

15 The Spirit of God came upon Azariah the son of Oded, [2] and he went out to meet Asa and said to him, "Hear me, Asa, and all Judah and Benjamin: The LORD is with you while you are with him. If you seek him, he will be found by you, but if you forsake him, he will forsake you. [3] For a long time Israel was without the true God, and without a teaching priest and without law, [4] but when in their distress they turned to the LORD, the God of Israel, and sought him, he was found by them. [5] In those times there was no peace to him who went out or to him who came in, for great disturbances afflicted all the inhabitants of the lands. [6] They were broken in pieces. Nation was crushed by nation and city by city, for God troubled them with every sort of distress. [7] But you, take courage! Do not let your hands be weak, for your work shall be rewarded."

[8] As soon as Asa heard these words, the prophecy of Azariah the son of Oded, he took courage and put away the detestable idols from all the land of Judah and Benjamin and from the cities that he had taken in the hill country of Ephraim, and he repaired the altar of the LORD that was in front of the vestibule of the house of the LORD.[5] [9] And he gathered all Judah and Benjamin, and those from Ephraim,

Manasseh, and Simeon who were residing with them, for great numbers had deserted to him from Israel when they saw that the LORD his God was with him. [10] They were gathered at Jerusalem in the third month of the fifteenth year of the reign of Asa. [11] They sacrificed to the LORD on that day from the spoil that they had brought 700 oxen and 7,000 sheep. [12] And they entered into a covenant to seek the LORD, the God of their fathers, with all their heart and with all their soul, [13] but that whoever would not seek the LORD, the God of Israel, should be put to death, whether young or old, man or woman. [14] They swore an oath to the LORD with a loud voice and with shouting and with trumpets and with horns. [15] And all Judah rejoiced over the oath, for they had sworn with all their heart and had sought him with their whole desire, and he was found by them, and the LORD gave them rest all around.

[16] Even Maacah, his mother, King Asa removed from being queen mother because she had made a detestable image for Asherah. Asa cut down her image, crushed it, and burned it at the brook Kidron. [17] But the high places were not taken out of Israel. Nevertheless, the heart of Asa was wholly true all his days. [18] And he brought into the house of God the sacred gifts of his father and his own sacred gifts, silver, and gold, and vessels. [19] And there was no more war until the thirty-fifth year of the reign of Asa.

Asa's Last Years

16 In the thirty-sixth year of the reign of Asa, Baasha king of Israel went up against Judah and built Ramah, that he might permit no one to go out or come in to Asa king of Judah. [2] Then Asa took silver and gold from the treasures of the house of the LORD and the king's house and sent them to Ben-hadad king of Syria, who lived in Damascus, saying, [3] "There is a covenant[1] between me and you, as there was between my father and your father. Behold, I am sending to you silver and gold. Go, break your covenant with Baasha king of Israel, that he may withdraw from me." [4] And Ben-hadad listened to King Asa and sent the commanders of his armies against the cities of Israel, and they conquered Ijon, Dan, Abel-maim, and all the store cities of Naphtali. [5] And when Baasha heard

of it, he stopped building Ramah and let his work cease. [6] Then King Asa took all Judah, and they carried away the stones of Ramah and its timber, with which Baasha had been building, and with them he built Geba and Mizpah.

[7] At that time Hanani the seer came to Asa king of Judah and said to him, "Because you relied on the king of Syria, and did not rely on the LORD your God, the army of the king of Syria has escaped you. [8] Were not the Ethiopians and the Libyans a huge army with very many chariots and horsemen? Yet because you relied on the LORD, he gave them into your hand. [9] For the eyes of the LORD run to and fro throughout the whole earth, to give strong support to those whose heart is blameless[2] toward him. You have done foolishly in this, for from now on you will have wars." [10] Then Asa was angry with the seer and put him in the stocks in prison, for he was in a rage with him because of this. And Asa inflicted cruelties upon some of the people at the same time.

[11] The acts of Asa, from first to last, are written in the Book of the Kings of Judah and Israel. [12] In the thirty-ninth year of his reign Asa was diseased in his feet, and his disease became severe. Yet even in his disease he did not seek the LORD, but sought help from physicians. [13] And Asa slept with his fathers, dying in the forty-first year of his reign. [14] They buried him in the tomb that he had cut for himself in the city of David. They laid him on a bier that had been filled with various kinds of spices prepared by the perfumer's art, and they made a very great fire in his honor.

Jehoshaphat Reigns in Judah

17 Jehoshaphat his son reigned in his place and strengthened himself against Israel. [2] He placed forces in all the fortified cities of Judah and set garrisons in the land of Judah, and in the cities of Ephraim that Asa his father had captured. [3] The LORD was with Jehoshaphat, because he walked in the earlier ways of his father David. He did not seek the Baals, [4] but sought the God of his father and walked in his commandments, and not according to the practices of Israel. [5] Therefore the LORD established the kingdom in his hand. And all Judah brought tribute to Jehoshaphat,

[1] Or *treaty*; twice in this verse [2] Or *whole*

and he had great riches and honor. [6] His heart was courageous in the ways of the LORD. And furthermore, he took the high places and the Asherim out of Judah.

[7] In the third year of his reign he sent his officials, Ben-hail, Obadiah, Zechariah, Nethanel, and Micaiah, to teach in the cities of Judah; [8] and with them the Levites, Shemaiah, Nethaniah, Zebadiah, Asahel, Shemiramoth, Jehonathan, Adonijah, Tobijah, and Tobadonijah; and with these Levites, the priests Elishama and Jehoram. [9] And they taught in Judah, having the Book of the Law of the LORD with them. They went about through all the cities of Judah and taught among the people.

[10] And the fear of the LORD fell upon all the kingdoms of the lands that were around Judah, and they made no war against Jehoshaphat. [11] Some of the Philistines brought Jehoshaphat presents and silver for tribute, and the Arabians also brought him 7,700 rams and 7,700 goats. [12] And Jehoshaphat grew steadily greater. He built in Judah fortresses and store cities, [13] and he had large supplies in the cities of Judah. He had soldiers, mighty men of valor, in Jerusalem. [14] This was the muster of them by fathers' houses: Of Judah, the commanders of thousands: Adnah the commander, with 300,000 mighty men of valor; [15] and next to him Jehohanan the commander, with 280,000; [16] and next to him Amasiah the son of Zichri, a volunteer for the service of the LORD, with 200,000 mighty men of valor. [17] Of Benjamin: Eliada, a mighty man of valor, with 200,000 men armed with bow and shield; [18] and next to him Jehozabad with 180,000 armed for war. [19] These were in the service of the king, besides those whom the king had placed in the fortified cities throughout all Judah.

Jehoshaphat Allies with Ahab

18 Now Jehoshaphat had great riches and honor, and he made a marriage alliance with Ahab. [2] After some years he went down to Ahab in Samaria. And Ahab killed an abundance of sheep and oxen for him and for the people who were with him, and induced him to go up against Ramoth-gilead. [3] Ahab king of Israel said to Jehoshaphat king of Judah, "Will you go with me to Ramoth-gilead?" He answered

him, "I am as you are, my people as your people. We will be with you in the war."

[4] And Jehoshaphat said to the king of Israel, "Inquire first for the word of the LORD." [5] Then the king of Israel gathered the prophets together, four hundred men, and said to them, "Shall we go to battle against Ramoth-gilead, or shall I refrain?" And they said, "Go up, for God will give it into the hand of the king." [6] But Jehoshaphat said, "Is there not here another prophet of the LORD of whom we may inquire?" [7] And the king of Israel said to Jehoshaphat, "There is yet one man by whom we may inquire of the LORD, Micaiah the son of Imlah; but I hate him, for he never prophesies good concerning me, but always evil." And Jehoshaphat said, "Let not the king say so." [8] Then the king of Israel summoned an officer and said, "Bring quickly Micaiah the son of Imlah." [9] Now the king of Israel and Jehoshaphat the king of Judah were sitting on their thrones, arrayed in their robes. And they were sitting at the threshing floor at the entrance of the gate of Samaria, and all the prophets were prophesying before them. [10] And Zedekiah the son of Chenaanah made for himself horns of iron and said, "Thus says the LORD, 'With these you shall push the Syrians until they are destroyed.'" [11] And all the prophets prophesied so and said, "Go up to Ramoth-gilead and triumph. The LORD will give it into the hand of the king."

[12] And the messenger who went to summon Micaiah said to him, "Behold, the words of the prophets with one accord are favorable to the king. Let your word be like the word of one of them, and speak favorably." [13] But Micaiah said, "As the LORD lives, what my God says, that I will speak." [14] And when he had come to the king, the king said to him, "Micaiah, shall we go to Ramoth-gilead to battle, or shall I refrain?" And he answered, "Go up and triumph; they will be given into your hand." [15] But the king said to him, "How many times shall I make you swear that you speak to me nothing but the truth in the name of the LORD?" [16] And he said, "I saw all Israel scattered on the mountains, as sheep that have no shepherd. And the LORD said, 'These have no master; let each return to his home in peace.'" [17] And the king of Israel said to Jehoshaphat, "Did I not tell you that he would not prophesy good concerning me,

but evil?" [18] And Micaiah said, "Therefore hear the word of the LORD: I saw the LORD sitting on his throne, and all the host of heaven standing on his right hand and on his left. [19] And the LORD said, 'Who will entice Ahab the king of Israel, that he may go up and fall at Ramoth-gilead?' And one said one thing, and another said another. [20] Then a spirit came forward and stood before the LORD, saying, 'I will entice him.' And the LORD said to him, 'By what means?' [21] And he said, 'I will go out, and will be a lying spirit in the mouth of all his prophets.' And he said, 'You are to entice him, and you shall succeed; go out and do so.' [22] Now therefore behold, the LORD has put a lying spirit in the mouth of these your prophets. The LORD has declared disaster concerning you."

[23] Then Zedekiah the son of Chenaanah came near and struck Micaiah on the cheek and said, "Which way did the Spirit of the LORD go from me to speak to you?" [24] And Micaiah said, "Behold, you shall see on that day when you go into an inner chamber to hide yourself." [25] And the king of Israel said, "Seize Micaiah and take him back to Amon the governor of the city and to Joash the king's son, [26] and say, 'Thus says the king, Put this fellow in prison and feed him with meager rations of bread and water until I return in peace.'" [27] And Micaiah said, "If you return in peace, the LORD has not spoken by me." And he said, "Hear, all you peoples!"

The Defeat and Death of Ahab

[28] So the king of Israel and Jehoshaphat the king of Judah went up to Ramoth-gilead. [29] And the king of Israel said to Jehoshaphat, "I will disguise myself and go into battle, but you wear your robes." And the king of Israel disguised himself, and they went into battle. [30] Now the king of Syria had commanded the captains of his chariots, "Fight with neither small nor great, but only with the king of Israel." [31] As soon as the captains of the chariots saw Jehoshaphat, they said, "It is the king of Israel." So they turned to fight against him. And Jehoshaphat cried out, and the LORD helped him; God drew them away from him. [32] For as soon as the captains of the chariots saw that it was not the king of Israel, they turned back from pursuing

him. [33] But a certain man drew his bow at random[1] and struck the king of Israel between the scale armor and the breastplate. Therefore he said to the driver of his chariot, "Turn around and carry me out of the battle, for I am wounded." [34] And the battle continued that day, and the king of Israel was propped up in his chariot facing the Syrians until evening. Then at sunset he died.

Jehoshaphat's Reforms

19 Jehoshaphat the king of Judah returned in safety to his house in Jerusalem. [2] But Jehu the son of Hanani the seer went out to meet him and said to King Jehoshaphat, "Should you help the wicked and love those who hate the LORD? Because of this, wrath has gone out against you from the LORD. [3] Nevertheless, some good is found in you, for you destroyed the Asheroth out of the land, and have set your heart to seek God."

[4] Jehoshaphat lived at Jerusalem. And he went out again among the people, from Beersheba to the hill country of Ephraim, and brought them back to the LORD, the God of their fathers. [5] He appointed judges in the land in all the fortified cities of Judah, city by city, [6] and said to the judges, "Consider what you do, for you judge not for man but for the LORD. He is with you in giving judgment. [7] Now then, let the fear of the LORD be upon you. Be careful what you do, for there is no injustice with the LORD our God, or partiality or taking bribes."

[8] Moreover, in Jerusalem Jehoshaphat appointed certain Levites and priests and heads of families of Israel, to give judgment for the LORD and to decide disputed cases. They had their seat at Jerusalem. [9] And he charged them: "Thus you shall do in the fear of the LORD, in faithfulness, and with your whole heart: [10] whenever a case comes to you from your brothers who live in their cities, concerning bloodshed, law or commandment, statutes or rules, then you shall warn them, that they may not incur guilt before the LORD and wrath may not come upon you and your brothers. Thus you shall do, and you will not incur guilt. [11] And behold, Amariah the chief priest is over you in all matters of the LORD; and Zebadiah the son of Ishmael, the governor of the house of Judah, in all

---

[1] Hebrew *in his innocence*

the king's matters, and the Levites will serve you as officers. Deal courageously, and may the LORD be with the upright!"[1]

Jehoshaphat's Prayer

20 After this the Moabites and Ammonites, and with them some of the Meunites,[2] came against Jehoshaphat for battle. ²Some men came and told Jehoshaphat, "A great multitude is coming against you from Edom,[3] from beyond the sea; and, behold, they are in Hazazon-tamar" (that is, Engedi). ³Then Jehoshaphat was afraid and set his face to seek the LORD, and proclaimed a fast throughout all Judah. ⁴And Judah assembled to seek help from the LORD; from all the cities of Judah they came to seek the LORD.

⁵And Jehoshaphat stood in the assembly of Judah and Jerusalem, in the house of the LORD, before the new court, ⁶and said, "O LORD, God of our fathers, are you not God in heaven? You rule over all the kingdoms of the nations. In your hand are power and might, so that none is able to withstand you. ⁷Did you not, our God, drive out the inhabitants of this land before your people Israel, and give it forever to the descendants of Abraham your friend? ⁸And they have lived in it and have built for you in it a sanctuary for your name, saying, ⁹'If disaster comes upon us, the sword, judgment,[4] or pestilence, or famine, we will stand before this house and before you—for your name is in this house—and cry out to you in our affliction, and you will hear and save.' ¹⁰And now behold, the men of Ammon and Moab and Mount Seir, whom you would not let Israel invade when they came from the land of Egypt, and whom they avoided and did not destroy—¹¹behold, they reward us by coming to drive us out of your possession, which you have given us to inherit. ¹²O our God, will you not execute judgment on them? For we are powerless against this great horde that is coming against us. We do not know what to do, but our eyes are on you."

¹³Meanwhile all Judah stood before the LORD, with their little ones, their wives, and their children. ¹⁴And the Spirit of the LORD came upon Jahaziel the son of Zechariah, son of Benaiah, son of Jeiel, son of Mattaniah, a Levite of the sons of Asaph, in the midst of the assembly. ¹⁵And he said, "Listen, all Judah and inhabitants of Jerusalem and King Jehoshaphat: Thus says the LORD to you, 'Do not be afraid and do not be dismayed at this great horde, for the battle is not yours but God's. ¹⁶Tomorrow go down against them. Behold, they will come up by the ascent of Ziz. You will find them at the end of the valley, east of the wilderness of Jeruel. ¹⁷You will not need to fight in this battle. Stand firm, hold your position, and see the salvation of the LORD on your behalf, O Judah and Jerusalem.' Do not be afraid and do not be dismayed. Tomorrow go out against them, and the LORD will be with you."

¹⁸Then Jehoshaphat bowed his head with his face to the ground, and all Judah and the inhabitants of Jerusalem fell down before the LORD, worshiping the LORD. ¹⁹And the Levites, of the Kohathites and the Korahites, stood up to praise the LORD, the God of Israel, with a very loud voice.

²⁰And they rose early in the morning and went out into the wilderness of Tekoa. And when they went out, Jehoshaphat stood and said, "Hear me, Judah and inhabitants of Jerusalem! Believe in the LORD your God, and you will be established; believe his prophets, and you will succeed." ²¹And when he had taken counsel with the people, he appointed those who were to sing to the LORD and praise him in holy attire, as they went before the army, and say,

> "Give thanks to the LORD,
>   for his steadfast love endures
>   forever."

²²And when they began to sing and praise, the LORD set an ambush against the men of Ammon, Moab, and Mount Seir, who had come against Judah, so that they were routed. ²³For the men of Ammon and Moab rose against the inhabitants of Mount Seir, devoting them to destruction, and when they had made an end of the inhabitants of Seir, they all helped to destroy one another.

The LORD Delivers Judah

²⁴When Judah came to the watchtower of the wilderness, they looked toward the horde, and behold, there[5] were dead bodies lying on the ground; none had escaped. ²⁵When Jehoshaphat and his people came

---

[1] Hebrew *the good* [2] Compare 26:7; Hebrew *Ammonites* [3] One Hebrew manuscript; most Hebrew manuscripts *Aram (Syria)* [4] Or *the sword of judgment* [5] Hebrew *they*

to take their spoil, they found among them, in great numbers, goods, clothing, and precious things, which they took for themselves until they could carry no more. They were three days in taking the spoil, it was so much. [26] On the fourth day they assembled in the Valley of Beracah,[1] for there they blessed the LORD. Therefore the name of that place has been called the Valley of Beracah to this day. [27] Then they returned, every man of Judah and Jerusalem, and Jehoshaphat at their head, returning to Jerusalem with joy, for the LORD had made them rejoice over their enemies. [28] They came to Jerusalem with harps and lyres and trumpets, to the house of the LORD. [29] And the fear of God came on all the kingdoms of the countries when they heard that the LORD had fought against the enemies of Israel. [30] So the realm of Jehoshaphat was quiet, for his God gave him rest all around.

[31] Thus Jehoshaphat reigned over Judah. He was thirty-five years old when he began to reign, and he reigned twenty-five years in Jerusalem. His mother's name was Azubah the daughter of Shilhi. [32] He walked in the way of Asa his father and did not turn aside from it, doing what was right in the sight of the LORD. [33] The high places, however, were not taken away; the people had not yet set their hearts upon the God of their fathers.

[34] Now the rest of the acts of Jehoshaphat, from first to last, are written in the chronicles of Jehu the son of Hanani, which are recorded in the Book of the Kings of Israel.

The End of Jehoshaphat's Reign

[35] After this Jehoshaphat king of Judah joined with Ahaziah king of Israel, who acted wickedly. [36] He joined him in building ships to go to Tarshish, and they built the ships in Ezion-geber. [37] Then Eliezer the son of Dodavahu of Mareshah prophesied against Jehoshaphat, saying, "Because you have joined with Ahaziah, the LORD will destroy what you have made." And the ships were wrecked and were not able to go to Tarshish.

Jehoram Reigns in Judah

21 Jehoshaphat slept with his fathers and was buried with his fathers in the city of David, and Jehoram his

---

[1] *Beracah* means *blessing*

Know How to Communicate

verses to read
2 Chronicles 20:15–17

Do you ever feel the need for vindication—to defend or justify yourself to others? Sometimes people get you wrong. They misunderstand you or they lie about you. But what do you do next?

Vindication is your attempt to fight the battle yourself, to fix things and to prove yourself to everyone who has you wrong. But God never asked you to vindicate yourself. This obsession to prove to other people that they're wrong and you're right is never an act of faith. When you say to yourself, "I have to explain myself, and they have to listen," you are forgetting that in the gospel you already have all the approval and justification you will ever need. When you see that someone is wrong or misunderstanding you, you've got to remember that God, not other people, determines what is most true of you. The God Girl has to trust God to intervene where he's going to intervene, and then she has to refuse to criticize his creation by complaining about people. Her job at this point is prayer, not judgment. This means that you have to remain calm and let people misunderstand you. What they think doesn't define you, so don't get all up in arms. Your job is to stay fixed on the gospel of grace and just keep trusting God, knowing that in Christ he delights in you no matter what others think.

on reigned in his place. ² He had brothers, the sons of Jehoshaphat: Azariah, Jehiel, Zechariah, Azariah, Michael, and Shephatiah; all these were the sons of Jehoshaphat king of Israel.¹ ³ Their father gave them great gifts of silver, gold, and valuable possessions, together with fortified cities in Judah, but he gave the kingdom to Jehoram, because he was the firstborn. ⁴ When Jehoram had ascended the throne of his father and was established, he killed all his brothers with the sword, and also some of the princes of Israel. ⁵ Jehoram was thirty-two years old when he became king, and he reigned eight years in Jerusalem. ⁶ And he walked in the way of the kings of Israel, as the house of Ahab had done, for the daughter of Ahab was his wife. And he did what was evil in the sight of the LORD. ⁷ Yet the LORD was not willing to destroy the house of David, because of the covenant that he had made with David, and since he had promised to give a lamp to him and to his sons forever.

⁸ In his days Edom revolted from the rule of Judah and set up a king of their own. Then Jehoram passed over with his commanders and all his chariots, and he rose by night and struck the Edomites who had surrounded him and his chariot commanders. ¹⁰ So Edom revolted from the rule of Judah to this day. At that time Libnah also revolted from his rule, because he had forsaken the LORD, the God of his fathers.

¹¹ Moreover, he made high places in the hill country of Judah and led the inhabitants of Jerusalem into whoredom and made Judah go astray. ¹² And a letter came to him from Elijah the prophet, saying, "Thus says the LORD, the God of David your father, 'Because you have not walked in the ways of Jehoshaphat your father, or in the ways of Asa king of Judah, ¹³ but have walked in the way of the kings of Israel and have enticed Judah and the inhabitants of Jerusalem into whoredom, as the house of Ahab led Israel into whoredom, and also you have killed your brothers, of your father's house, who were better than you, ¹⁴ behold, the LORD will bring a great plague on your people, your children, your wives, and all your possessions, ¹⁵ and you yourself will have a severe sickness with a disease of your bowels, until your bowels come out because of the disease, day by day.'"

¹⁶ And the LORD stirred up against Jehoram the anger² of the Philistines and of the Arabians who are near the Ethiopians. ¹⁷ And they came up against Judah and invaded it and carried away all the possessions they found that belonged to the king's house, and also his sons and his wives, so that no son was left to him except Jehoahaz, his youngest son.

¹⁸ And after all this the LORD struck him in his bowels with an incurable disease. ¹⁹ In the course of time, at the end of two years, his bowels came out because of the disease, and he died in great agony. His people made no fire in his honor, like the fires made for his fathers. ²⁰ He was thirty-two years old when he began to reign, and he reigned eight years in Jerusalem. And he departed with no one's regret. They buried him in the city of David, but not in the tombs of the kings.

Ahaziah Reigns in Judah

22 And the inhabitants of Jerusalem made Ahaziah, his youngest son, king in his place, for the band of men that came with the Arabians to the camp had killed all the older sons. So Ahaziah the son of Jehoram king of Judah reigned. ² Ahaziah was twenty-two³ years old when he began to reign, and he reigned one year in Jerusalem. His mother's name was Athaliah, the granddaughter of Omri. ³ He also walked in the ways of the house of Ahab, for his mother was his counselor in doing wickedly. ⁴ He did what was evil in the sight of the LORD, as the house of Ahab had done. For after the death of his father they were his counselors, to his undoing. ⁵ He even followed their counsel and went with Jehoram the son of Ahab king of Israel to make war against Hazael king of Syria at Ramoth-gilead. And the Syrians wounded Joram, ⁶ and he returned to be healed in Jezreel of the wounds that he had received at Ramah, when he fought against Hazael king of Syria. And Ahaziah the son of Jehoram king of Judah went down to see Joram the son of Ahab in Jezreel, because he was wounded.

⁷ But it was ordained by God that the downfall of Ahaziah should come about through his going to visit Joram. For when

---

¹ That is, Judah ² Hebrew *spirit* ³ See 2 Kings 8:26; Hebrew *forty-two*; Septuagint *twenty*

he came there, he went out with Jehoram to meet Jehu the son of Nimshi, whom the LORD had anointed to destroy the house of Ahab. [8] And when Jehu was executing judgment on the house of Ahab, he met the princes of Judah and the sons of Ahaziah's brothers, who attended Ahaziah, and he killed them. [9] He searched for Ahaziah, and he was captured while hiding in Samaria, and he was brought to Jehu and put to death. They buried him, for they said, "He is the grandson of Jehoshaphat, who sought the LORD with all his heart." And the house of Ahaziah had no one able to rule the kingdom.

Athaliah Reigns in Judah

[10] Now when Athaliah the mother of Ahaziah saw that her son was dead, she arose and destroyed all the royal family of the house of Judah. [11] But Jehoshabeath,[1] the daughter of the king, took Joash the son of Ahaziah and stole him away from among the king's sons who were about to be put to death, and she put him and his nurse in a bedroom. Thus Jehoshabeath, the daughter of King Jehoram and wife of Jehoiada the priest, because she was a sister of Ahaziah, hid him[2] from Athaliah, so that she did not put him to death. [12] And he remained with them six years, hidden in the house of God, while Athaliah reigned over the land.

Joash Made King

23 But in the seventh year Jehoiada took courage and entered into a covenant with the commanders of hundreds, Azariah the son of Jeroham, Ishmael the son of Jehohanan, Azariah the son of Obed, Maaseiah the son of Adaiah, and Elishaphat the son of Zichri. [2] And they went about through Judah and gathered the Levites from all the cities of Judah, and the heads of fathers' houses of Israel, and they came to Jerusalem. [3] And all the assembly made a covenant with the king in the house of God. And Jehoiada[3] said to them, "Behold, the king's son! Let him reign, as the LORD spoke concerning the sons of David. [4] This is the thing that you shall do: of you priests and Levites who come off duty on the Sabbath, one third shall be gatekeepers, [5] and one third shall be at the king's house and one third at the

Gate of the Foundation. And all the people shall be in the courts of the house of the LORD. [6] Let no one enter the house of the LORD except the priests and ministering Levites. They may enter, for they are holy, but all the people shall keep the charge of the LORD. [7] The Levites shall surround the king, each with his weapons in his hand. And whoever enters the house shall be put to death. Be with the king when he comes in and when he goes out."

[8] The Levites and all Judah did according to all that Jehoiada the priest commanded, and they each brought his men, who were to go off duty on the Sabbath, with those who were to come on duty on the Sabbath, for Jehoiada the priest did not dismiss the divisions. [9] And Jehoiada the priest gave to the captains the spears and the large and small shields that had been King David's, which were in the house of God. [10] And he set all the people as a guard for the king, every man with his weapon in his hand, from the south side of the house to the north side of the house, around the altar and the house. [11] Then they brought out the king's son and put the crown on him and gave him the testimony. And they proclaimed him king, and Jehoiada and his sons anointed him, and they said, "Long live the king."

Athaliah Executed

[12] When Athaliah heard the noise of the people running and praising the king, she went into the house of the LORD to the people. [13] And when she looked, there was the king standing by his pillar at the entrance, and the captains and the trumpeters beside the king, and all the people of the land rejoicing and blowing trumpets, and the singers with their musical instruments leading in the celebration. And Athaliah tore her clothes and cried, "Treason! Treason!" [14] Then Jehoiada the priest brought out the captains who were set over the army, saying to them, "Bring her out between the ranks, and anyone who follows her is to be put to death with the sword." For the priest said, "Do not put her to death in the house of the LORD." [15] So they laid hands on her,[4] and she went into the entrance of the horse gate of the king's house, and they put her to death there.

---

[1] Spelled *Jehosheba* in 2 Kings 11:2 [2] That is, Joash [3] Hebrew *he* [4] Or *they made a passage for her*

Jehoiada's Reforms

¹⁶ And Jehoiada made a covenant between himself and all the people and the king that they should be the LORD's people. ¹⁷ Then all the people went to the house of Baal and tore it down; his altars and his images they broke in pieces, and they killed Mattan the priest of Baal before the altars. ¹⁸ And Jehoiada posted watchmen for the house of the LORD under the direction of the Levitical priests and the Levites whom David had organized to be in charge of the house of the LORD, to offer burnt offerings to the LORD, as it is written in the Law of Moses, with rejoicing and with singing, according to the order of David. ¹⁹ He stationed the gatekeepers at the gates of the house of the LORD so that no one should enter who was in any way unclean. ²⁰ And he took the captains, the nobles, the governors of the people, and all the people of the land, and they brought the king down from the house of the LORD, marching through the upper gate to the king's house. And they set the king on the royal throne. ²¹ So all the people of the land rejoiced, and the city was quiet after Athaliah had been put to death with the sword.

Joash Repairs the Temple

24 Joash[1] was seven years old when he began to reign, and he reigned forty years in Jerusalem. His mother's name was Zibiah of Beersheba. ² And Joash did what was right in the eyes of the LORD all the days of Jehoiada the priest. ³ Jehoiada got for him two wives, and he had sons and daughters.

⁴ After this Joash decided to restore the house of the LORD. ⁵ And he gathered the priests and the Levites and said to them, 'Go out to the cities of Judah and gather from all Israel money to repair the house of your God from year to year, and see that you act quickly." But the Levites did not act quickly. ⁶ So the king summoned Jehoiada the chief and said to him, "Why have you not required the Levites to bring in from Judah and Jerusalem the tax levied by Moses, the servant of the LORD, and the congregation of Israel for the tent of testimony?" ⁷ For the sons of Athaliah, that wicked woman, had broken into the house of God, and had also used all the dedicated things of the house of the LORD for the Baals.

⁸ So the king commanded, and they made a chest and set it outside the gate of the house of the LORD. ⁹ And proclamation was made throughout Judah and Jerusalem to bring in for the LORD the tax that Moses the servant of God laid on Israel in the wilderness. ¹⁰ And all the princes and all the people rejoiced and brought their tax and dropped it into the chest until they had finished.[2] ¹¹ And whenever the chest was brought to the king's officers by the Levites, when they saw that there was much money in it, the king's secretary and the officer of the chief priest would come and empty the chest and take it and return it to its place. Thus they did day after day, and collected money in abundance. ¹² And the king and Jehoiada gave it to those who had charge of the work of the house of the LORD, and they hired masons and carpenters to restore the house of the LORD, and also workers in iron and bronze to repair the house of the LORD. ¹³ So those who were engaged in the work labored, and the repairing went forward in their hands, and they restored the house of God to its proper condition and strengthened it. ¹⁴ And when they had finished, they brought the rest of the money before the king and Jehoiada, and with it were made utensils for the house of the LORD, both for the service and for the burnt offerings, and dishes for incense and vessels of gold and silver. And they offered burnt offerings in the house of the LORD regularly all the days of Jehoiada.

¹⁵ But Jehoiada grew old and full of days, and died. He was 130 years old at his death. ¹⁶ And they buried him in the city of David among the kings, because he had done good in Israel, and toward God and his house.

¹⁷ Now after the death of Jehoiada the princes of Judah came and paid homage to the king. Then the king listened to them. ¹⁸ And they abandoned the house of the LORD, the God of their fathers, and served the Asherim and the idols. And wrath came upon Judah and Jerusalem for this guilt of theirs. ¹⁹ Yet he sent prophets among them to bring them back to the LORD. These testified against them, but they would not pay attention.

Joash's Treachery

²⁰ Then the Spirit of God clothed Zechariah the son of Jehoiada the priest, and

---

[1] Spelled *Jehoash* in 2 Kings 12:1 [2] Or *until it was full*

he stood above the people, and said to them, "Thus says God, 'Why do you break the commandments of the LORD, so that you cannot prosper? Because you have forsaken the LORD, he has forsaken you.'" [21] But they conspired against him, and by command of the king they stoned him with stones in the court of the house of the LORD. [22] Thus Joash the king did not remember the kindness that Jehoiada, Zechariah's father, had shown him, but killed his son. And when he was dying, he said, "May the LORD see and avenge!"[1]

Joash Assassinated

[23] At the end of the year the army of the Syrians came up against Joash. They came to Judah and Jerusalem and destroyed all the princes of the people from among the people and sent all their spoil to the king of Damascus. [24] Though the army of the Syrians had come with few men, the LORD delivered into their hand a very great army, because Judah[2] had forsaken the LORD, the God of their fathers. Thus they executed judgment on Joash.

[25] When they had departed from him, leaving him severely wounded, his servants conspired against him because of the blood of the son[3] of Jehoiada the priest, and killed him on his bed. So he died, and they buried him in the city of David, but they did not bury him in the tombs of the kings. [26] Those who conspired against him were Zabad the son of Shimeath the Ammonite, and Jehozabad the son of Shimrith the Moabite. [27] Accounts of his sons and of the many oracles against him and of the rebuilding[4] of the house of God are written in the Story of the Book of the Kings. And Amaziah his son reigned in his place.

Amaziah Reigns in Judah

25 Amaziah was twenty-five years old when he began to reign, and he reigned twenty-nine years in Jerusalem. His mother's name was Jehoaddan of Jerusalem. [2] And he did what was right in the eyes of the LORD, yet not with a whole heart. [3] And as soon as the royal power was firmly his, he killed his servants who had struck down the king his father. [4] But he did not put their children to death, according to what is written in the Law, in the Book of Moses, where the LORD commanded, "Fathers shall not die because of their children, nor children die because of their fathers, but each one shall die for his own sin."

Amaziah's Victories

[5] Then Amaziah assembled the men of Judah and set them by fathers' houses under commanders of thousands and of hundreds for all Judah and Benjamin. He mustered those twenty years old and upward, and found that they were 300,000 choice men, fit for war, able to handle spear and shield. [6] He hired also 100,000 mighty men of valor from Israel for 100 talents[5] of silver. [7] But a man of God came to him and said, "O king, do not let the army of Israel go with you, for the LORD is not with Israel, with all these Ephraimites. [8] But go, act, be strong for the battle. Why should you suppose that God will cast you down before the enemy? For God has power to help or to cast down." [9] And Amaziah said to the man of God, "But what shall we do about the hundred talents that I have given to the army of Israel?" The man of God answered, "The LORD is able to give you much more than this." [10] Then Amaziah discharged the army that had come to him from Ephraim to go home again. And they became very angry with Judah and returned home in fierce anger. [11] But Amaziah took courage and led out his people and went to the Valley of Salt and struck down 10,000 men of Seir. [12] The men of Judah captured another 10,000 alive and took them to the top of a rock and threw them down from the top of the rock, and they were all dashed to pieces. [13] But the men of the army whom Amaziah sent back, not letting them go with him to battle, raided the cities of Judah, from Samaria to Beth-horon, and struck down 3,000 people in them and took much spoil.

Amaziah's Idolatry

[14] After Amaziah came from striking down the Edomites, he brought the gods of the men of Seir and set them up as his gods and worshiped them, making offerings to them. [15] Therefore the LORD was angry with Amaziah and sent to him a prophet, who said to him, "Why have you

[1] Hebrew and seek [2] Hebrew they [3] Septuagint, Vulgate; Hebrew sons [4] Hebrew founding [5] A talent was about 75 pounds or 34 kilograms

ought the gods of a people who did not eliver their own people from your hand?" But as he was speaking, the king said to im, "Have we made you a royal counselor? top! Why should you be struck down?" o the prophet stopped, but said, "I know hat God has determined to destroy you, ecause you have done this and have not stened to my counsel."

srael Defeats Amaziah

17 Then Amaziah king of Judah took ounsel and sent to Joash the son of Jehohaz, son of Jehu, king of Israel, saying, Come, let us look one another in the face." 18 And Joash the king of Israel sent word o Amaziah king of Judah, "A thistle on ebanon sent to a cedar on Lebanon, sayng, 'Give your daughter to my son for a vife,' and a wild beast of Lebanon passed y and trampled down the thistle. 19 You ay, 'See, I¹ have struck down Edom,' and

your heart has lifted you up in boastfulness. But now stay at home. Why should you provoke trouble so that you fall, you and Judah with you?"

20 But Amaziah would not listen, for it was of God, in order that he might give them into the hand of their enemies, because they had sought the gods of Edom. 21 So Joash king of Israel went up, and he and Amaziah king of Judah faced one another in battle at Beth-shemesh, which belongs to Judah. 22 And Judah was defeated by Israel, and every man fled to his home. 23 And Joash king of Israel captured Amaziah king of Judah, the son of Joash, son of Ahaziah, at Beth-shemesh, and brought him to Jerusalem and broke down the wall of Jerusalem for 400 cubits,² from the Ephraim Gate to the Corner Gate. 24 And he seized all the gold and silver, and all the vessels that were found in the house of God, in the care of Obed-edom. He seized

¹Hebrew you ²A cubit was about 18 inches or 45 centimeters

verses to read
2 Chronicles 25:14–15

Know Yourself

Has God ever sent you a "prophet," a voice of reason sent to point out the sin in your life that you have chosen to ignore? When he does, it can hurt something awful, and your first response can be the common one: that is, to argue with them and to totally reject their warnings. But don't be so quick to fight for your sinfulness! Don't be so quick to try to prove you're right when others say you're wrong. Just stop and listen, thank them for their insight, and take it home with you. Then don't let another day go by without asking God for *his* word on the subject.

In order to have this kind of response, you have to tear down the wall of self-protection that you have built around your life. This takes a large dose of humility, but ignoring your sinfulness was really not self-protection in the first place. The wise girl refuses to lie to herself anymore and really wants to figure out where she's getting it wrong. Getting it wrong, after all, is a cause for concern. Do you want to live your life in ignorant bliss, or would you rather turn on the lights and see into all the dark places of your life, letting the grace of God flood into every corner? The best way to destroy the arguments of the Enemy in your life is by turning on the light and confronting the lies you have been accepting as truth.

Ignorant bliss is really no bliss at all; it's just a down payment on destruction. Sin's payoff isn't happiness; it's death. So don't trust your own deceitful heart anymore, but be willing to listen when others correct you. Even though it tears at your heart, listen. Even though it sounds absurd, listen. You'll have a teachable heart, and a teachable heart is a peaceful heart.

also the treasuries of the king's house, also hostages, and he returned to Samaria.

²⁵ Amaziah the son of Joash, king of Judah, lived fifteen years after the death of Joash the son of Jehoahaz, king of Israel. ²⁶ Now the rest of the deeds of Amaziah, from first to last, are they not written in the Book of the Kings of Judah and Israel? ²⁷ From the time when he turned away from the LORD they made a conspiracy against him in Jerusalem, and he fled to Lachish. But they sent after him to Lachish and put him to death there. ²⁸ And they brought him upon horses, and he was buried with his fathers in the city of David.[1]

Uzziah Reigns in Judah

26 And all the people of Judah took Uzziah, who was sixteen years old, and made him king instead of his father Amaziah. ² He built Eloth and restored it to Judah, after the king slept with his fathers. ³ Uzziah was sixteen years old when he began to reign, and he reigned fifty-two years in Jerusalem. His mother's name was Jecoliah of Jerusalem. ⁴ And he did what was right in the eyes of the LORD, according to all that his father Amaziah had done. ⁵ He set himself to seek God in the days of Zechariah, who instructed him in the fear of God, and as long as he sought the LORD, God made him prosper.

⁶ He went out and made war against the Philistines and broke through the wall of Gath and the wall of Jabneh and the wall of Ashdod, and he built cities in the territory of Ashdod and elsewhere among the Philistines. ⁷ God helped him against the Philistines and against the Arabians who lived in Gurbaal and against the Meunites. ⁸ The Ammonites paid tribute to Uzziah, and his fame spread even to the border of Egypt, for he became very strong. ⁹ Moreover, Uzziah built towers in Jerusalem at the Corner Gate and at the Valley Gate and at the Angle, and fortified them. ¹⁰ And he built towers in the wilderness and cut out many cisterns, for he had large herds, both in the Shephelah and in the plain, and he had farmers and vinedressers in the hills and in the fertile lands, for he loved the soil. ¹¹ Moreover, Uzziah had an army of soldiers, fit for war, in divisions according to the numbers in the muster made by Jeiel the secretary and Maaseiah the officer, under the direction of Hananiah, one of the king's commanders. ¹² The whole number of the heads of fathers' houses of mighty men of valor was 2,600. ¹³ Under their command was an army of 307,500, who could make war with mighty power, to help the king against the enemy. ¹⁴ And Uzziah prepared for all the army shields, spears, helmets, coats of mail, bows, and stones for slinging. ¹⁵ In Jerusalem he made machines, invented by skillful men, to be on the towers and the corners, to shoot arrows and great stones. And his fame spread far, for he was marvelously helped, till he was strong.

Uzziah's Pride and Punishment

¹⁶ But when he was strong, he grew proud, to his destruction. For he was unfaithful to the LORD his God and entered the temple of the LORD to burn incense on the altar of incense. ¹⁷ But Azariah the priest went in after him, with eighty priests of the LORD who were men of valor, ¹⁸ and they withstood King Uzziah and said to him, "It is not for you, Uzziah, to burn incense to the LORD, but for the priests the sons of Aaron, who are consecrated to burn incense. Go out of the sanctuary, for you have done wrong, and it will bring you no honor from the LORD God." ¹⁹ Then Uzziah was angry. Now he had a censer in his hand to burn incense, and when he became angry with the priests, leprosy broke out on his forehead in the presence of the priests in the house of the LORD, by the altar of incense. ²⁰ And Azariah the chief priest and all the priests looked at him, and behold, he was leprous in his forehead! And they rushed him out quickly, and he himself hurried to go out, because the LORD had struck him. ²¹ And King Uzziah was a leper to the day of his death, and being a leper lived in a separate house, for he was excluded from the house of the LORD. And Jotham his son was over the king's household, governing the people of the land.

²² Now the rest of the acts of Uzziah, from first to last, Isaiah the prophet the son of Amoz wrote. ²³ And Uzziah slept with his fathers, and they buried him with his fathers in the burial field that belonged to the kings, for they said, "He is a leper." And Jotham his son reigned in his place.

[1] Hebrew *of Judah* [2] *Leprosy* was a term for several skin diseases; see Leviticus 13

Jotham Reigns in Judah

27 Jotham was twenty-five years old when he began to reign, and he reigned sixteen years in Jerusalem. His mother's name was Jerushah the daughter of Zadok. [2] And he did what was right in the eyes of the LORD according to all that his father Uzziah had done, except he did not enter the temple of the LORD. But the people still followed corrupt practices. [3] He built the upper gate of the house of the LORD and did much building on the wall of Ophel. [4] Moreover, he built cities in the hill country of Judah, and forts and towers on the wooded hills. [5] He fought with the king of the Ammonites and prevailed against them. And the Ammonites gave him that year 100 talents[1] of silver, and 10,000 cors[2] of wheat and 10,000 of barley. The Ammonites paid him the same amount in the second and the third years. [6] So Jotham became mighty, because he ordered his ways before the LORD his God. [7] Now the rest of the acts of Jotham, and all his wars and his ways, behold, they are written in the Book of the Kings of Israel and Judah. [8] He was twenty-five years old when he began to reign, and he reigned sixteen years in Jerusalem. [9] And Jotham slept with his fathers, and they buried him in the city of David, and Ahaz his son reigned in his place.

Ahaz Reigns in Judah

28 Ahaz was twenty years old when he began to reign, and he reigned sixteen years in Jerusalem. And he did not do what was right in the eyes of the LORD, as his father David had done, [2] but he walked in the ways of the kings of Israel. He even made metal images for the Baals, [3] and made offerings in the Valley of the Son of Hinnom and burned his sons as an offering,[3] according to the abominations of the nations whom the LORD drove out before the people of Israel. [4] And he sacrificed and made offerings on the high places and on the hills and under every green tree.

Judah Defeated

[5] Therefore the LORD his God gave him into the hand of the king of Syria, who defeated him and took captive a great number of his people and brought them to Damascus. He was also given into the hand of the king of Israel, who struck him with great force. [6] For Pekah the son of Remaliah killed 120,000 from Judah in one day, all of them men of valor, because they had forsaken the LORD, the God of their fathers. [7] And Zichri, a mighty man of Ephraim, killed Maaseiah the king's son and Azrikam the commander of the palace and Elkanah the next in authority to the king.

[8] The men of Israel took captive 200,000 of their relatives, women, sons, and daughters. They also took much spoil from them and brought the spoil to Samaria. [9] But a prophet of the LORD was there, whose name was Oded, and he went out to meet the army that came to Samaria and said to them, "Behold, because the LORD, the God of your fathers, was angry with Judah, he gave them into your hand, but you have killed them in a rage that has reached up to heaven. [10] And now you intend to subjugate the people of Judah and Jerusalem, male and female, as your slaves. Have you not sins of your own against the LORD your God? [11] Now hear me, and send back the captives from your relatives whom you have taken, for the fierce wrath of the LORD is upon you."

[12] Certain chiefs also of the men of Ephraim, Azariah the son of Johanan, Berechiah the son of Meshillemoth, Jehizkiah the son of Shallum, and Amasa the son of Hadlai, stood up against those who were coming from the war [13] and said to them, "You shall not bring the captives in here, for you propose to bring upon us guilt against the LORD in addition to our present sins and guilt. For our guilt is already great, and there is fierce wrath against Israel." [14] So the armed men left the captives and the spoil before the princes and all the assembly. [15] And the men who have been mentioned by name rose and took the captives, and with the spoil they clothed all who were naked among them. They clothed them, gave them sandals, provided them with food and drink, and anointed them, and carrying all the feeble among them on donkeys, they brought them to their kinsfolk at Jericho, the city of palm trees. Then they returned to Samaria.

---

[1] talent was about 75 pounds or 34 kilograms [2] A cor was about 6 bushels or 220 liters [3] Hebrew made his sons pass through the fire

[16] At that time King Ahaz sent to the king[1] of Assyria for help. [17] For the Edomites had again invaded and defeated Judah and carried away captives. [18] And the Philistines had made raids on the cities in the Shephelah and the Negeb of Judah, and had taken Beth-shemesh, Aijalon, Gederoth, Soco with its villages, Timnah with its villages, and Gimzo with its villages. And they settled there. [19] For the LORD humbled Judah because of Ahaz king of Israel, for he had made Judah act sinfully[2] and had been very unfaithful to the LORD. [20] So Tiglath-pileser[3] king of Assyria came against him and afflicted him instead of strengthening him. [21] For Ahaz took a portion from the house of the LORD and the house of the king and of the princes, and gave tribute to the king of Assyria, but it did not help him.

Ahaz's Idolatry

[22] In the time of his distress he became yet more faithless to the LORD—this same King Ahaz. [23] For he sacrificed to the gods of Damascus that had defeated him and said, "Because the gods of the kings of Syria helped them, I will sacrifice to them that they may help me." But they were the ruin of him and of all Israel. [24] And Ahaz gathered together the vessels of the house of God and cut in pieces the vessels of the house of God, and he shut up the doors of the house of the LORD, and he made himself altars in every corner of Jerusalem. [25] In every city of Judah he made high places to make offerings to other gods, provoking to anger the LORD, the God of his fathers. [26] Now the rest of his acts and all his ways, from first to last, behold, they are written in the Book of the Kings of Judah and Israel. [27] And Ahaz slept with his fathers, and they buried him in the city, in Jerusalem, for they did not bring him into the tombs of the kings of Israel. And Hezekiah his son reigned in his place.

Hezekiah Reigns in Judah

29 Hezekiah began to reign when he was twenty-five years old, and he reigned twenty-nine years in Jerusalem. His mother's name was Abijah[4] the daughter of Zechariah. [2] And he did what was right in the eyes of the LORD, according to all that David his father had done.

Hezekiah Cleanses the Temple

[3] In the first year of his reign, in th first month, he opened the doors of th house of the LORD and repaired them. [4] H brought in the priests and the Levites an assembled them in the square on the ea [5] and said to them, "Hear me, Levites! No consecrate yourselves, and consecrate th house of the LORD, the God of your father and carry out the filth from the Holy Plac [6] For our fathers have been unfaithful an have done what was evil in the sight of th LORD our God. They have forsaken hi and have turned away their faces from th habitation of the LORD and turned the backs. [7] They also shut the doors of th vestibule and put out the lamps and hav not burned incense or offered burnt offe ings in the Holy Place to the God of Israe [8] Therefore the wrath of the LORD cam on Judah and Jerusalem, and he has mad them an object of horror, of astonishmen and of hissing, as you see with your ow eyes. [9] For behold, our fathers have falle by the sword, and our sons and our daugh ters and our wives are in captivity for th [10] Now it is in my heart to make a covena with the LORD, the God of Israel, in orde that his fierce anger may turn away fro us. [11] My sons, do not now be negligen for the LORD has chosen you to stand i his presence, to minister to him and to b his ministers and make offerings to him.

[12] Then the Levites arose, Mahath th son of Amasai, and Joel the son of Azaria of the sons of the Kohathites; and of th sons of Merari, Kish the son of Abdi, an Azariah the son of Jehallelel; and of th Gershonites, Joah the son of Zimmah, an Eden the son of Joah; [13] and of the sons elizaphan, Shimri and Jeuel; and of th sons of Asaph, Zechariah and Mattania [14] and of the sons of Heman, Jehuel an Shimei; and of the sons of Jeduthun, She maiah and Uzziel. [15] They gathered thei brothers and consecrated themselves an went in as the king had commanded, by th words of the LORD, to cleanse the house the LORD. [16] The priests went into the inne part of the house of the LORD to cleanse i and they brought out all the uncleannes that they found in the temple of the LOR into the court of the house of the LORD. An the Levites took it and carried it out to th

---

[1] Septuagint, Syriac, Vulgate (compare 2 Kings 16:7); Hebrew *kings* [2] Or *wildly* [3] Hebrew *Tilgath-pilneser* [4] Spelled *Abi* in 2 Kings 18:2

brook Kidron. ¹⁷They began to consecrate on the first day of the first month, and on the eighth day of the month they came to the vestibule of the LORD. Then for eight days they consecrated the house of the LORD, and on the sixteenth day of the first month they finished. ¹⁸Then they went in to Hezekiah the king and said, "We have cleansed all the house of the LORD, the altar of burnt offering and all its utensils, and the table for the showbread and all its utensils. ¹⁹All the utensils that King Ahaz discarded in his reign when he was faithless, we have made ready and consecrated, and behold, they are before the altar of the LORD."

Hezekiah Restores Temple Worship

²⁰Then Hezekiah the king rose early and gathered the officials of the city and went up to the house of the LORD. ²¹And they brought seven bulls, seven rams, seven lambs, and seven male goats for a sin offering for the kingdom and for the sanctuary and for Judah. And he commanded the priests, the sons of Aaron, to offer them on the altar of the LORD. ²²So they slaughtered the bulls, and the priests received the blood and threw it against the altar. And they slaughtered the rams, and their blood was thrown against the altar. And they slaughtered the lambs, and their blood was thrown against the altar. ²³Then the goats for the sin offering were brought to the king and the assembly, and they laid their hands on them, ²⁴and the priests slaughtered them and made a sin offering with their blood on the altar, to make atonement for all Israel. For the king commanded that the burnt offering and the sin offering should be made for all Israel.

²⁵And he stationed the Levites in the house of the LORD with cymbals, harps, and lyres, according to the commandment of David and of Gad the king's seer and of Nathan the prophet, for the commandment was from the LORD through his prophets. ²⁶The Levites stood with the instruments of David, and the priests with the trumpets. ²⁷Then Hezekiah commanded that the burnt offering be offered on the altar. And when the burnt offering began, the song to the LORD began also, and the trumpets, accompanied by the instruments of David king of Israel. ²⁸The whole assembly worshiped, and the singers sang, and the trumpeters sounded. All this continued until the burnt offering was finished. ²⁹When the offering was finished, the king and all who were present with him bowed themselves and worshiped. ³⁰And Hezekiah the king and the officials commanded the Levites to sing praises to the LORD with the words of David and of Asaph the seer. And they sang praises with gladness, and they bowed down and worshiped.

³¹Then Hezekiah said, "You have now consecrated yourselves to¹ the LORD. Come near; bring sacrifices and thank offerings to the house of the LORD." And the assembly brought sacrifices and thank offerings, and all who were of a willing heart brought burnt offerings. ³²The number of the burnt offerings that the assembly brought was 70 bulls, 100 rams, and 200 lambs; all these were for a burnt offering to the LORD. ³³And the consecrated offerings were 600 bulls and 3,000 sheep. ³⁴But the priests were too few and could not flay all the burnt offerings, so until other priests had consecrated themselves, their brothers the Levites helped them, until the work was finished—for the Levites were more upright in heart than the priests in consecrating themselves. ³⁵Besides the great number of burnt offerings, there was the fat of the peace offerings, and there were the drink offerings for the burnt offerings. Thus the service of the house of the LORD was restored. ³⁶And Hezekiah and all the people rejoiced because God had provided for the people, for the thing came about suddenly.

Passover Celebrated

30 Hezekiah sent to all Israel and Judah, and wrote letters also to Ephraim and Manasseh, that they should come to the house of the LORD at Jerusalem to keep the Passover to the LORD, the God of Israel. ²For the king and his princes and all the assembly in Jerusalem had taken counsel to keep the Passover in the second month— ³for they could not keep it at that time because the priests had not consecrated themselves in sufficient number, nor had the people assembled in Jerusalem— ⁴and the plan seemed right to the king and all the assembly. ⁵So they decreed to make a proclamation throughout all Israel, from Beersheba to Dan, that the people should come and keep the Passover to the LORD, the God of Israel, at Jerusalem, for they had not kept it as often as prescribed. [6] So couriers went throughout all Israel and Judah with letters from the king and his princes, as the king had commanded, saying, "O people of Israel, return to the LORD, the God of Abraham, Isaac, and Israel, that he may turn again to the remnant of you who have escaped from the hand of the kings of Assyria. [7] Do not be like your fathers and your brothers, who were faithless to the LORD God of their fathers, so that he made them a desolation, as you see. [8] Do not now be stiff-necked as your fathers were, but yield yourselves to the LORD and come to his sanctuary, which he has consecrated forever, and serve the LORD your God, that his fierce anger may turn away from you. [9] For if you return to the LORD, your brothers and your children will find compassion with their captors and return to this land. For the LORD your God is gracious and merciful and will not turn away his face from you, if you return to him."

[10] So the couriers went from city to city through the country of Ephraim and Manasseh, and as far as Zebulun, but they laughed them to scorn and mocked them. [11] However, some men of Asher, of Manasseh, and of Zebulun humbled themselves and came to Jerusalem. [12] The hand of God was also on Judah to give them one heart to do what the king and the princes commanded by the word of the LORD.

[13] And many people came together in Jerusalem to keep the Feast of Unleavened Bread in the second month, a very great assembly. [14] They set to work and removed the altars that were in Jerusalem, and all the altars for burning incense they took away and threw into the brook Kidron. [15] And they slaughtered the Passover lamb on the fourteenth day of the second month. And the priests and the Levites were ashamed, so that they consecrated themselves and brought burnt offerings into the house of the LORD. [16] They took their accustomed posts according to the Law of Moses the man of God. The priests threw the blood that they received from the hand of the Levites. [17] For there were many in the assembly who had not consecrated themselves. Therefore the Levites had to slaughter the Passover lamb for everyone who was not clean, to consecrate it to the LORD. [18] For a majority of the people, many of them from Ephraim, Manasseh, Issachar, and Zebulun, had not cleansed themselves, yet they ate the Passover otherwise than as prescribed. For Hezekiah had prayed for them, saying, "May the good LORD pardon everyone [19] who sets his heart to seek God, the LORD, the God of his fathers, even though not according to the sanctuary's rules of cleanness."[1] [20] And the LORD heard Hezekiah and healed the people. [21] And the people of Israel who were present at Jerusalem kept the Feast of Unleavened Bread seven days with great gladness, and the Levites and the priests praised the LORD day by day, singing with all their might[2] to the LORD. [22] And Hezekiah spoke encouragingly to all the Levites who showed good skill in the service of the LORD. So they ate the food of the festival for seven days, sacrificing peace offerings and giving thanks to the LORD, the God of their fathers.

[23] Then the whole assembly agreed together to keep the feast for another seven days. So they kept it for another seven days with gladness. [24] For Hezekiah king of Judah gave the assembly 1,000 bulls and 7,000 sheep for offerings, and the princes gave the assembly 1,000 bulls and 10,000 sheep. And the priests consecrated themselves in great numbers. [25] The whole assembly of Judah, and the priests and the Levites, and the whole assembly that came out of Israel, and the sojourners who came out of the land of Israel, and the sojourners who lived in Judah, rejoiced. [26] So there was great joy in Jerusalem, for since the time of Solomon the son of David king of Israel there had been nothing like this in Jerusalem. [27] Then the priests and the Levites arose and blessed the people, and their voice was heard, and their prayer came to his holy habitation in heaven.

Hezekiah Organizes the Priests

31 Now when all this was finished, all Israel who were present went out to the cities of Judah and broke in pieces the pillars and cut down the Asherim and broke down the high places and the altars throughout all Judah and Benjamin, and in Ephraim and Manasseh, until they had destroyed them all. Then all the people of

[1] Hebrew *not according to the cleanness of holiness* [2] Compare 1 Chronicles 13:8; Hebrew *with instruments of might*

Israel returned to their cities, every man to his possession.

[2] And Hezekiah appointed the divisions of the priests and of the Levites, division by division, each according to his service, the priests and the Levites, for burnt offerings and peace offerings, to minister in the gates of the camp of the LORD and to give thanks and praise. [3] The contribution of the king from his own possessions was for the burnt offerings: the burnt offerings of morning and evening, and the burnt offerings for the Sabbaths, the new moons, and the appointed feasts, as it is written in the Law of the LORD. [4] And he commanded the people who lived in Jerusalem to give the portion due to the priests and the Levites, that they might give themselves to the Law of the LORD. [5] As soon as the command was spread abroad, the people of Israel gave in abundance the firstfruits of grain, wine, oil, honey, and of all the produce of the field. And they brought in abundantly the tithe of everything. [6] And the people of Israel and Judah who lived in the cities of Judah also brought in the tithe of cattle and sheep, and the tithe of the dedicated things that had been dedicated to the LORD their God, and laid them in heaps. [7] In the third month they began to pile up the heaps, and finished them in the seventh month. [8] When Hezekiah and the princes came and saw the heaps, they blessed the LORD and his people Israel. And Hezekiah questioned the priests and the Levites about the heaps. [10] Azariah the chief priest, who was of the house of Zadok, answered him, "Since they began to bring the contributions into the house of the LORD, we have eaten and had enough and have plenty left, for the LORD has blessed his people, so that we have this large amount left."

[11] Then Hezekiah commanded them to prepare chambers in the house of the LORD, and they prepared them. [12] And they faithfully brought in the contributions, the tithes, and the dedicated things. The chief officer in charge of them was Conaniah the Levite, with Shimei his brother as second, [13] while Jehiel, Azaziah, Nahath, Asahel, Jerimoth, Jozabad, Eliel, Ismachiah, Mahath, and Benaiah were overseers assisting Conaniah and Shimei his brother, by the appointment of Hezekiah the king and Azariah the chief officer of the house of God. [14] And Kore the son of Imnah the Levite, keeper of the east gate, was over the freewill offerings to God, to apportion the contribution reserved for the LORD and the most holy offerings. [15] Eden, Miniamin, Jeshua, Shemaiah, Amariah, and Shecaniah were faithfully assisting him in the cities of the priests, to distribute the portions to their brothers, old and young alike, by divisions, [16] except those enrolled by genealogy, males from three years old and upward—all who entered the house of the LORD as the duty of each day required—for their service according to their offices, by their divisions. [17] The enrollment of the priests was according to their fathers' houses; that of the Levites from twenty years old and upward was according to their offices, by their divisions. [18] They were enrolled with all their little children, their wives, their sons, and their daughters, the whole assembly, for they were faithful in keeping themselves holy. [19] And for the sons of Aaron, the priests, who were in the fields of common land belonging to their cities, there were men in the several cities who were designated by name to distribute portions to every male among the priests and to everyone among the Levites who was enrolled.

[20] Thus Hezekiah did throughout all Judah, and he did what was good and right and faithful before the LORD his God. [21] And every work that he undertook in the service of the house of God and in accordance with the law and the commandments, seeking his God, he did with all his heart, and prospered.

Sennacherib Invades Judah

32 After these things and these acts of faithfulness, Sennacherib king of Assyria came and invaded Judah and encamped against the fortified cities, thinking to win them for himself. [2] And when Hezekiah saw that Sennacherib had come and intended to fight against Jerusalem, [3] he planned with his officers and his mighty men to stop the water of the springs that were outside the city; and they helped him. [4] A great many people were gathered, and they stopped all the springs and the brook that flowed through the land, saying, "Why should the kings of Assyria come and find much water?" [5] He set to work resolutely and built up all the wall that was broken down and raised towers upon it,[1] and outside it he built another wall, and he strengthened the Millo in the city of David. He also made weapons and shields in abundance. [6] And he set combat commanders over the people and gathered them together to him in the square at the gate of the city and spoke encouragingly to them, saying, [7] "Be strong and courageous. Do not be afraid or dismayed before the king of Assyria and all the horde that is with him, for there are more with us than with him. [8] With him is an arm of flesh, but with us is the LORD our God, to help us and to fight our battles." And the people took confidence from the words of Hezekiah king of Judah.

Sennacherib Blasphemes

[9] After this, Sennacherib king of Assyria, who was besieging Lachish with all his forces, sent his servants to Jerusalem to Hezekiah king of Judah and to all the people of Judah who were in Jerusalem, saying, [10] "Thus says Sennacherib king of Assyria, 'On what are you trusting, that you endure the siege in Jerusalem? [11] Is not Hezekiah misleading you, that he may give you over to die by famine and by thirst, when he tells you, "The LORD our God will deliver us from the hand of the king of Assyria"? [12] Has not this same Hezekiah taken away his high places and his altars and commanded Judah and Jerusalem, "Before one altar you shall worship, and on it you shall burn your sacrifices"? [13] Do you not know what I and my fathers have done to all the peoples of other lands? Were the gods of the nations of those lands at all able to deliver their lands out of my hand? [14] Who among all the gods of those nations that my fathers devoted to destruction was able to deliver his people from my hand, that your God should be able to deliver you from my hand? [15] Now, therefore, do not let Hezekiah deceive you or mislead you in this fashion, and do not believe him, for no god of any nation or kingdom has been able to deliver his people from my hand or from the hand of my fathers. How much less will your God deliver you out of my hand!'"

[16] And his servants said still more against the LORD God and against his servant Hezekiah. [17] And he wrote letters to cast contempt on the LORD, the God of Israel, and to speak against him, saying, "Like the gods of the nations of the lands who have not delivered their people from my hand, so the God of Hezekiah will not deliver his people from my hand." [18] And they shouted it with a loud voice in the language of Judah to the people of Jerusalem who were on the wall, to frighten and terrify them, in order that they might take the city. [19] And they spoke of the God of Jerusalem as they spoke of the gods of the peoples of the earth, which are the work of men's hands.

The LORD Delivers Jerusalem

[20] Then Hezekiah the king and Isaiah the prophet, the son of Amoz, prayed because of this and cried to heaven. [21] And the LORD sent an angel, who cut off all the mighty warriors and commanders and officers in the camp of the king of Assyria. So he returned with shame of face to his own land. And when he came into the house of his god, some of his own sons struck him down there with the sword. [22] So the LORD saved Hezekiah and the inhabitants of Jerusalem from the hand of Sennacherib king of Assyria and from the hand of all his enemies, and he provided for them on every side. [23] And many brought gifts to the LORD to Jerusalem and precious things to Hezekiah king of Judah, so that he was exalted in the sight of all nations from that time onward.

Hezekiah's Pride and Achievements

[24] In those days Hezekiah became sick and was at the point of death, and he prayed to the LORD, and he answered him and gave him a sign. [25] But Hezekiah did not make return according to the benefit done to him, for his heart was proud. Therefore wrath came upon him and Judah and Jerusalem. [26] But Hezekiah humbled himself for the pride of his heart, both he and the inhabitants of Jerusalem, so that the wrath of the LORD did not come upon them in the days of Hezekiah.

[27] And Hezekiah had very great riches and honor, and he made for himself treasuries for silver, for gold, for precious stones, for spices, for shields, and for all kinds of costly vessels; [28] storehouses also for the yield of grain, wine, and oil; and stalls for all kinds of cattle, and sheepfolds. [29] He likewise provided cities for himself

---

[1] Vulgate; Hebrew *and raised upon the towers*

nd flocks and herds in abundance, for God had given him very great possessions. ³⁰This same Hezekiah closed the upper outlet of the waters of Gihon and directed them down to the west side of the city of David. And Hezekiah prospered in all his works. ³¹And so in the matter of the envoys of the princes of Babylon, who had been sent to him to inquire about the sign that had been done in the land, God left him to himself, in order to test him and to know all that was in his heart.

³²Now the rest of the acts of Hezekiah and his good deeds, behold, they are written in the vision of Isaiah the prophet the son of Amoz, in the Book of the Kings of Judah and Israel. ³³And Hezekiah slept with his fathers, and they buried him in the upper part of the tombs of the sons of David, and all Judah and the inhabitants of Jerusalem did him honor at his death. And Manasseh his son reigned in his place.

Manasseh Reigns in Judah

33 Manasseh was twelve years old when he began to reign, and he reigned fifty-five years in Jerusalem. ²And he did what was evil in the sight of the LORD, according to the abominations of the nations whom the LORD drove out before the people of Israel. ³For he rebuilt the high places that his father Hezekiah had broken down, and he erected altars to the Baals, and made Asheroth, and worshiped all the host of heaven and served them. ⁴And he built altars in the house of the LORD, of which the LORD had said, "In Jerusalem shall my name be forever." ⁵And he built altars for all the host of heaven in the two courts of the house of the LORD. ⁶And he burned his sons as an offering in the Valley of the Son of Hinnom, and used fortune-telling and omens and sorcery, and dealt with mediums and with necromancers. He did much evil in the sight of the LORD, provoking him to anger. ⁷And the carved image of the idol that he had made he set in the house of God, of which God said to David and to Solomon his son, "In this house, and in Jerusalem, which I have chosen out of all the tribes of Israel, I will put my name forever, ⁸and I will no more remove the foot of Israel from the land that I appointed for your fathers, if only they will be careful to do all that I have commanded them, all

the law, the statutes, and the rules given through Moses." ⁹Manasseh led Judah and the inhabitants of Jerusalem astray, to do more evil than the nations whom the LORD destroyed before the people of Israel.

Manasseh's Repentance

¹⁰The LORD spoke to Manasseh and to his people, but they paid no attention. ¹¹Therefore the LORD brought upon them the commanders of the army of the king of Assyria, who captured Manasseh with hooks and bound him with chains of bronze and brought him to Babylon. ¹²And when he was in distress, he entreated the favor of the LORD his God and humbled himself greatly before the God of his fathers. ¹³He prayed to him, and God was moved by his entreaty and heard his plea and brought him again to Jerusalem into his kingdom. Then Manasseh knew that the LORD was God.

¹⁴Afterward he built an outer wall for the city of David west of Gihon, in the valley, and for the entrance into the Fish Gate, and carried it around Ophel, and raised it to a very great height. He also put commanders of the army in all the fortified cities in Judah. ¹⁵And he took away the foreign gods and the idol from the house of the LORD, and all the altars that he had built on the mountain of the house of the LORD and in Jerusalem, and he threw them outside of the city. ¹⁶He also restored the altar of the LORD and offered on it sacrifices of peace offerings and of thanksgiving, and he commanded Judah to serve the LORD, the God of Israel. ¹⁷Nevertheless, the people still sacrificed at the high places, but only to the LORD their God.

¹⁸Now the rest of the acts of Manasseh, and his prayer to his God, and the words of the seers who spoke to him in the name of the LORD, the God of Israel, behold, they are in the Chronicles of the Kings of Israel. ¹⁹And his prayer, and how God was moved by his entreaty, and all his sin and his faithlessness, and the sites on which he built high places and set up the Asherim and the images, before he humbled himself, behold, they are written in the Chronicles of the Seers.¹ ²⁰So Manasseh slept with his fathers, and they buried him in his house, and Amon his son reigned in his place.

One Hebrew manuscript, Septuagint; most Hebrew manuscripts *of Hozai*

Amon's Reign and Death

[21] Amon was twenty-two years old when he began to reign, and he reigned two years in Jerusalem. [22] And he did what was evil in the sight of the LORD, as Manasseh his father had done. Amon sacrificed to all the images that Manasseh his father had made, and served them. [23] And he did not humble himself before the LORD, as Manasseh his father had humbled himself, but this Amon incurred guilt more and more. [24] And his servants conspired against him and put him to death in his house. [25] But the people of the land struck down all those who had conspired against King Amon. And the people of the land made Josiah his son king in his place.

Josiah Reigns in Judah

34 Josiah was eight years old when he began to reign, and he reigned thirty-one years in Jerusalem. [2] And he did what was right in the eyes of the LORD, and walked in the ways of David his father; and he did not turn aside to the right hand or to the left. [3] For in the eighth year of his reign, while he was yet a boy, he began to seek the God of David his father, and in the twelfth year he began to purge Judah and Jerusalem of the high places, the Asherim, and the carved and the metal images. [4] And they chopped down the altars of the Baals in his presence, and he cut down the incense altars that stood above them. And he broke in pieces the Asherim and the carved and the metal images, and he made dust of them and scattered it over the graves of those who had sacrificed to them. [5] He also burned the bones of the priests on their altars and cleansed Judah and Jerusalem. [6] And in the cities of Manasseh, Ephraim, and Simeon, and as far as Naphtali, in their ruins[1] all around, [7] he broke down the altars and beat the Asherim and the images into powder and cut down all the incense altars throughout all the land of Israel. Then he returned to Jerusalem.

The Book of the Law Found

[8] Now in the eighteenth year of his reign, when he had cleansed the land and the house, he sent Shaphan the son of Azaliah, and Maaseiah the governor of the city, and Joah the son of Joahaz, the recorder, to repair the house of the LORD his God. [9] The came to Hilkiah the high priest and gav him the money that had been brought int the house of God, which the Levites, th keepers of the threshold, had collecte from Manasseh and Ephraim and from al the remnant of Israel and from all Juda and Benjamin and from the inhabitants o Jerusalem. [10] And they gave it to the work men who were working in the house of th LORD. And the workmen who were work ing in the house of the LORD gave it fo repairing and restoring the house. [11] The gave it to the carpenters and the build ers to buy quarried stone, and timber fo binders and beams for the buildings tha the kings of Judah had let go to ruin. [12] An the men did the work faithfully. Over then were set Jahath and Obadiah the Levites of the sons of Merari, and Zechariah an Meshullam, of the sons of the Kohathites, t have oversight. The Levites, all who wer skillful with instruments of music, [13] wer over the burden-bearers and directed al who did work in every kind of service and some of the Levites were scribes an officials and gatekeepers.

[14] While they were bringing out th money that had been brought into th house of the LORD, Hilkiah the priest foun the Book of the Law of the LORD give through Moses. [15] Then Hilkiah answere and said to Shaphan the secretary, "I hav found the Book of the Law in the house o the LORD." And Hilkiah gave the book t Shaphan. [16] Shaphan brought the book t the king, and further reported to the king "All that was committed to your servant they are doing. [17] They have emptied ou the money that was found in the house of the LORD and have given it into th hand of the overseers and the workmen. [18] Then Shaphan the secretary told the king "Hilkiah the priest has given me a book. And Shaphan read from it before the king

[19] And when the king heard the words o the Law, he tore his clothes. [20] And the king commanded Hilkiah, Ahikam the son o Shaphan, Abdon the son of Micah, Shaphan the secretary, and Asaiah the king's ser vant, saying, [21] "Go, inquire of the LORD for me and for those who are left in Israe and in Judah, concerning the words of the book that has been found. For great is the wrath of the LORD that is poured out on us

---

[1] The meaning of the Hebrew is uncertain

because our fathers have not kept the word of the LORD, to do according to all that is written in this book."

Huldah Prophesies Disaster

²²So Hilkiah and those whom the king had sent[1] went to Huldah the prophetess, the wife of Shallum the son of Tokhath, son of Hasrah, keeper of the wardrobe (now she lived in Jerusalem in the Second Quarter) and spoke to her to that effect. ²³And she said to them, "Thus says the LORD, the God of Israel: 'Tell the man who sent you to me, ²⁴Thus says the LORD, Behold, I will bring disaster upon this place and upon its inhabitants, all the curses that are written in the book that was read before the king of Judah. ²⁵Because they have forsaken me and have made offerings to other gods, that they might provoke me to anger with all the works of their hands, therefore my wrath will be poured out on this place and will not be quenched. ²⁶But to the king of Judah, who sent you to inquire of the LORD, thus shall you say to him, Thus says the LORD, the God of Israel: Regarding the words that you have heard, ²⁷because your heart was tender and you humbled yourself before God when you heard his words against this place and its inhabitants, and you have humbled yourself before me and have torn your clothes and wept before me, I also have heard you, declares the LORD. ²⁸Behold, I will gather you to your fathers, and you shall be gathered to your grave in peace, and your eyes shall not see all the disaster that I will bring upon this place and its inhabitants.'" And they brought back word to the king.

²⁹Then the king sent and gathered together all the elders of Judah and Jerusalem. ³⁰And the king went up to the house of the LORD, with all the men of Judah and the inhabitants of Jerusalem and the priests and the Levites, all the people both great and small. And he read in their hearing all the words of the Book of the Covenant that had been found in the house of the LORD. ³¹And the king stood in his place and made a covenant before the LORD, to walk after the LORD and to keep his commandments and his testimonies and his statutes, with all his heart and all his soul, to perform the words of the covenant that were written in this book.

³²Then he made all who were present in Jerusalem and in Benjamin join in it. And the inhabitants of Jerusalem did according to the covenant of God, the God of their fathers. ³³And Josiah took away all the abominations from all the territory that belonged to the people of Israel and made all who were present in Israel serve the LORD their God. All his days they did not turn away from following the LORD, the God of their fathers.

Josiah Keeps the Passover

35 Josiah kept a Passover to the LORD in Jerusalem. And they slaughtered the Passover lamb on the fourteenth day of the first month. ²He appointed the priests to their offices and encouraged them in the service of the house of the LORD. ³And he said to the Levites who taught all Israel and who were holy to the LORD, "Put the holy ark in the house that Solomon the son of David, king of Israel, built. You need not carry it on your shoulders. Now serve the LORD your God and his people Israel. ⁴Prepare yourselves according to your fathers' houses by your divisions, as prescribed in the writing of David king of Israel and the document of Solomon his son. ⁵And stand in the Holy Place according to the groupings of the fathers' houses of your brothers the lay people, and according to the division of the Levites by fathers' household. ⁶And slaughter the Passover lamb, and consecrate yourselves, and prepare for your brothers, to do according to the word of the LORD by Moses."

⁷Then Josiah contributed to the lay people, as Passover offerings for all who were present, lambs and young goats from the flock to the number of 30,000, and 3,000 bulls; these were from the king's possessions. ⁸And his officials contributed willingly to the people, to the priests, and to the Levites. Hilkiah, Zechariah, and Jehiel, the chief officers of the house of God, gave to the priests for the Passover offerings 2,600 Passover lambs and 300 bulls. ⁹Conaniah also, and Shemaiah and Nethanel his brothers, and Hashabiah and Jeiel and Jozabad, the chiefs of the Levites, gave to the Levites for the Passover offerings 5,000 lambs and young goats and 500 bulls.

¹⁰When the service had been prepared for, the priests stood in their place, and

[1] Syriac, Vulgate; Hebrew lacks *had sent*

the Levites in their divisions according to the king's command. [11] And they slaughtered the Passover lamb, and the priests threw the blood that they received from them while the Levites flayed the sacrifices. [12] And they set aside the burnt offerings that they might distribute them according to the groupings of the fathers' houses of the lay people, to offer to the LORD, as it is written in the Book of Moses. And so they did with the bulls. [13] And they roasted the Passover lamb with fire according to the rule; and they boiled the holy offerings in pots, in cauldrons, and in pans, and carried them quickly to all the lay people. [14] And afterward they prepared for themselves and for the priests, because the priests, the sons of Aaron, were offering the burnt offerings and the fat parts until night; so the Levites prepared for themselves and for the priests, the sons of Aaron. [15] The singers, the sons of Asaph, were in their place according to the command of David, and Asaph, and Heman, and Jeduthun the king's seer; and the gatekeepers were at each gate. They did not need to depart from their service, for their brothers the Levites prepared for them.

[16] So all the service of the LORD was prepared that day, to keep the Passover and to offer burnt offerings on the altar of the LORD, according to the command of King Josiah. [17] And the people of Israel who were present kept the Passover at that time, and the Feast of Unleavened Bread seven days. [18] No Passover like it had been kept in Israel since the days of Samuel the prophet. None of the kings of Israel had kept such a Passover as was kept by Josiah, and the priests and the Levites, and all Judah and Israel who were present, and the inhabitants of Jerusalem. [19] In the eighteenth year of the reign of Josiah this Passover was kept.

Josiah Killed in Battle

[20] After all this, when Josiah had prepared the temple, Neco king of Egypt went up to fight at Carchemish on the Euphrates, and Josiah went out to meet him. [21] But he sent envoys to him, saying, "What have we to do with each other, king of Judah? I am not coming against you this day, but against the house with which I am at war. And God has commanded me to hurry. Cease opposing

God, who is with me, lest he destroy you." [22] Nevertheless, Josiah did not turn away from him, but disguised himself in order to fight with him. He did not listen to the words of Neco from the mouth of God, but came to fight in the plain of Megiddo. [23] And the archers shot King Josiah. And the king said to his servants, "Take me away, for I am badly wounded." [24] So his servants took him out of the chariot and carried him in his second chariot and brought him to Jerusalem. And he died and was buried in the tombs of his fathers. All Judah and Jerusalem mourned for Josiah. [25] Jeremiah also uttered a lament for Josiah; and all the singing men and singing women have spoken of Josiah in their laments to this day. They made these a rule in Israel; behold, they are written in the Laments. [26] Now the rest of the acts of Josiah, and his good deeds according to what is written in the Law of the LORD, [27] and his acts, first and last, behold, they are written in the Book of the Kings of Israel and Judah.

Judah's Decline

36 The people of the land took Jehoahaz the son of Josiah and made him king in his father's place in Jerusalem. [2] Jehoahaz was twenty-three years old when he began to reign, and he reigned three months in Jerusalem. [3] Then the king of Egypt deposed him in Jerusalem and laid on the land a tribute of a hundred talents of silver and a talent[1] of gold. [4] And the king of Egypt made Eliakim his brother king over Judah and Jerusalem, and changed his name to Jehoiakim. But Neco took Jehoahaz his brother and carried him to Egypt.

[5] Jehoiakim was twenty-five years old when he began to reign, and he reigned eleven years in Jerusalem. He did what was evil in the sight of the LORD his God. [6] Against him came up Nebuchadnezzar king of Babylon and bound him in chains to take him to Babylon. [7] Nebuchadnezzar also carried part of the vessels of the house of the LORD to Babylon and put them in his palace in Babylon. [8] Now the rest of the acts of Jehoiakim, and the abominations that he did, and what was found against him, behold, they are written in the Book of the Kings of Israel and Judah. And Jehoiachin his son reigned in his place.

---

[1] A *talent* was about 75 pounds or 34 kilograms

⁹ Jehoiachin was eighteen¹ years old when he became king, and he reigned three months and ten days in Jerusalem. He did what was evil in the sight of the LORD. ¹⁰ In the spring of the year King Nebuchadnezzar sent and brought him to Babylon, with the precious vessels of the house of the LORD, and made his brother Zedekiah king over Judah and Jerusalem.

¹¹ Zedekiah was twenty-one years old when he began to reign, and he reigned eleven years in Jerusalem. ¹² He did what was evil in the sight of the LORD his God. He did not humble himself before Jeremiah the prophet, who spoke from the mouth of the LORD. ¹³ He also rebelled against King Nebuchadnezzar, who had made him swear by God. He stiffened his neck and hardened his heart against turning to the LORD, the God of Israel. ¹⁴ All the officers of the priests and the people likewise were exceedingly unfaithful, following all the abominations of the nations. And they polluted the house of the LORD that he had made holy in Jerusalem.

¹⁵ The LORD, the God of their fathers, sent persistently to them by his messengers, because he had compassion on his people and on his dwelling place. ¹⁶ But they kept mocking the messengers of God, despising his words and scoffing at his prophets, until the wrath of the LORD rose against his people, until there was no remedy.

Jerusalem Captured and Burned

¹⁷ Therefore he brought up against them the king of the Chaldeans, who killed their young men with the sword in the house of their sanctuary and had no compassion on young man or virgin, old man or aged. He gave them all into his hand. ¹⁸ And all the vessels of the house of God, great and small, and the treasures of the house of the LORD, and the treasures of the king and of his princes, all these he brought to Babylon. ¹⁹ And they burned the house of God and broke down the wall of Jerusalem and burned all its palaces with fire and destroyed all its precious vessels. ²⁰ He took into exile in Babylon those who had escaped from the sword, and they became servants to him and to his sons until the establishment of the kingdom of Persia, ²¹ to fulfill the word of the LORD by the mouth of Jeremiah, until the land had enjoyed its Sabbaths. All the days that it lay desolate it kept Sabbath, to fulfill seventy years.

The Proclamation of Cyrus

²² Now in the first year of Cyrus king of Persia, that the word of the LORD by the mouth of Jeremiah might be fulfilled, the LORD stirred up the spirit of Cyrus king of Persia, so that he made a proclamation throughout all his kingdom and also put it in writing: ²³ "Thus says Cyrus king of Persia, 'The LORD, the God of heaven, has given me all the kingdoms of the earth, and he has charged me to build him a house at Jerusalem, which is in Judah. Whoever is among you of all his people, may the LORD his God be with him. Let him go up.' "

¹ Septuagint (compare 2 Kings 24:8); most Hebrew manuscripts *eight*

INTRODUCTION TO

Ezra

Trust God's Promises

> And they sang responsively, praising and giving thanks to the LORD,
>
> "For he is good,
> for his steadfast love endures forever toward Israel."
>
> And all the people shouted with a great shout when they praised the LORD, because the foundation of the house of the LORD was laid.
>
> *Ezra 3:11*

Author: Unknown, possibly Ezra

Time: Sometime after 450 B.C.

Place: Probably Judah

Written to: The Israelites in Judah

The gist

Along with the book of Nehemiah, Ezra tells about the return of the Israelites from captivity in Babylon. Ezra was written to encourage them to continue to worship God, now that they were free, and to stick to obeying his commands even when the going got tough.

Things to look for

- The decree from Cyrus that freed the Jews from Babylon (see Ezra 1:1–4)
- The sins of the Israelites returning from captivity (see Ezra 9)
- The people's confession of sin (see Ezra 10)

Nothing happens that God can't use to get things done in the lives of his people. Through the most horrible and trying circumstances God cleanses, teaches, and delivers his people. Things might look lost and the end might seem to be near, but when God promises to rescue you, you can be sure he's going to do it.

When the Israelites went into exile and were taken away from everything that they knew, it seemed like the end for them. But God had a plan: "They shall be carried to Babylon and remain there until the day when I visit them, declares the LORD. Then I will bring them back and restore them to this place" (Jer. 27:22). In the middle of a trial, it might look like God has forgotten you. You might say something like, "This always happens to me," or, "I'm sure it's something I've done wrong." You might see only the bad in it, blame yourself, and think that God has "left the building." But you might just want to look closer. God uses these times for your good. Look at the lives of the Israelites: they were sent into captivity, but it wasn't for nothing. While they were there, they learned to look at their God in a new light. Instead of thinking of him as absent, they began to see him as involved with them. And so when they returned home from exile they were changed people, ready to serve God by rebuilding the temple that had been destroyed.

The book of Ezra stands as an example to all of us that God will restore us if we are willing to come back to him and trust him. He is ready to rebuild your relationship even after you have sinned in a big way. He isn't a God who holds a grudge; because of the gospel, he doesn't reject you and refuse to hear your cries. So read this book with your eyes on God and his incredible grace. Consider how faithful he is to his promises and how he works everything together for good.

Must-Know Facts and Verses

⚜ The books of Ezra and Nehemiah were originally one book.

⚜ The book was written in two languages: Aramaic for the royal letters, and Hebrew for all the rest.

" 'The hand of our God is for good on all who seek him, and the power of his wrath is against all who forsake him.' " *Ezra 8:22*

"O my God, I am ashamed and blush to lift my face to you, my God, for our iniquities have risen higher than our heads, and our guilt has mounted up to the heavens." *Ezra 9:6*

While Ezra prayed and made confession, weeping and casting himself down before the house of God, a very great assembly of men, women, and children, gathered to him out of Israel, for the people wept bitterly. *Ezra 10:1*

The Proclamation of Cyrus

1 In the first year of Cyrus king of Persia, that the word of the Lord by the mouth of Jeremiah might be fulfilled, the Lord stirred up the spirit of Cyrus king of Persia, so that he made a proclamation throughout all his kingdom and also put it in writing:

² "Thus says Cyrus king of Persia: The Lord, the God of heaven, has given me all the kingdoms of the earth, and he has charged me to build him a house at Jerusalem, which is in Judah. ³ Whoever is among you of all his people, may his God be with him, and let him go up to Jerusalem, which is in Judah, and rebuild the house of the Lord, the God of Israel—he is the God who is in Jerusalem. ⁴ And let each survivor, in whatever place he sojourns, be assisted by the men of his place with silver and gold, with goods and with beasts, besides freewill offerings for the house of God that is in Jerusalem."

⁵ Then rose up the heads of the fathers' houses of Judah and Benjamin, and the priests and the Levites, everyone whose spirit God had stirred to go up to rebuild the house of the Lord that is in Jerusalem. ⁶ And all who were about them aided them with vessels of silver, with gold, with goods, with beasts, and with costly wares, besides all that was freely offered. ⁷ Cyrus the king also brought out the vessels of the house of the Lord that Nebuchadnezzar had carried away from Jerusalem and placed in the house of his gods. ⁸ Cyrus king of Persia brought these out in the charge of Mithredath the treasurer, who counted them out to Sheshbazzar the prince of Judah. ⁹ And this was the number of them: 30 basins of gold, 1,000 basins of silver, 29 censers, ¹⁰ 30 bowls of gold, 410 bowls of silver, and 1,000 other vessels; ¹¹ all the vessels of gold and of silver were 5,400. All these did Sheshbazzar bring up, when the exiles were brought up from Babylonia to Jerusalem.

The Exiles Return

2 Now these were the people of the province who came up out of the captivity of those exiles whom Nebuchadnezzar the king of Babylon had carried captive to Babylonia. They returned to Jerusalem and Judah, each to his own town. ² They came with Zerubbabel, Jeshua, Nehemiah, Seraiah, Reelaiah, Mordecai, Bilshan, Mispar, Bigvai, Rehum, and Baanah.

The number of the men of the people of Israel: ³ the sons of Parosh, 2,172. ⁴ The sons of Shephatiah, 372. ⁵ The sons of Arah, 775. ⁶ The sons of Pahath-moab, namely the sons of Jeshua and Joab, 2,812. ⁷ The sons of Elam, 1,254. ⁸ The sons of Zattu, 945. ⁹ The sons of Zaccai, 760. ¹⁰ The sons of Bani, 642. ¹¹ The sons of Bebai, 623. ¹² The sons of Azgad, 1,222. ¹³ The sons of Adonikam, 666. ¹⁴ The sons of Bigvai, 2,056. ¹⁵ The sons of Adin, 454. ¹⁶ The sons of Ater, namely of Hezekiah, 98. ¹⁷ The sons of Bezai, 323. ¹⁸ The sons of Jorah, 112. ¹⁹ The sons of Hashum, 223. ²⁰ The sons of Gibbar, 95. ²¹ The sons of Bethlehem, 123. ²² The men of Netophah, 56. ²³ The men of Anathoth, 128. ²⁴ The sons of Azmaveth, 42. ²⁵ The sons of Kiriath-arim, Chephirah, and Beeroth, 743. ²⁶ The sons of Ramah and Geba, 621. ²⁷ The men of Michmas, 122. ²⁸ The men of Bethel and Ai, 223. ²⁹ The sons of Nebo, 52. ³⁰ The sons of Magbish, 156. ³¹ The sons of the other Elam, 1,254. ³² The sons of Harim, 320. ³³ The sons of Lod, Hadid, and Ono, 725. ³⁴ The sons of Jericho, 345. ³⁵ The sons of Senaah, 3,630.

³⁶ The priests: the sons of Jedaiah, of the house of Jeshua, 973. ³⁷ The sons of Immer, 1,052. ³⁸ The sons of Pashhur, 1,247. ³⁹ The sons of Harim, 1,017.

⁴⁰ The Levites: the sons of Jeshua and Kadmiel, of the sons of Hodaviah, 74. ⁴¹ The singers: the sons of Asaph, 128. ⁴² The sons of the gatekeepers: the sons of Shallum, the sons of Ater, the sons of Talmon, the sons

of Akkub, the sons of Hatita, and the sons of Shobai, in all 139.

⁴³The temple servants: the sons of Ziha, the sons of Hasupha, the sons of Tabbaoth, ⁴⁴the sons of Keros, the sons of Siaha, the sons of Padon, ⁴⁵the sons of Lebanah, the sons of Hagabah, the sons of Akkub, ⁴⁶the sons of Hagab, the sons of Shamlai, the sons of Hanan, ⁴⁷the sons of Giddel, the sons of Gahar, the sons of Reaiah, ⁴⁸the sons of Rezin, the sons of Nekoda, the sons of Gazzam, ⁴⁹the sons of Uzza, the sons of Paseah, the sons of Besai, ⁵⁰the sons of Asnah, the sons of Meunim, the sons of Nephisim, ⁵¹the sons of Bakbuk, the sons of Hakupha, the sons of Harhur, ⁵²the sons of Bazluth, the sons of Mehida, the sons of Harsha, ⁵³the sons of Barkos, the sons of Sisera, the sons of Temah, ⁵⁴the sons of Neziah, and the sons of Hatipha.

⁵⁵The sons of Solomon's servants: the sons of Sotai, the sons of Hassophereth, the sons of Peruda, ⁵⁶the sons of Jaalah, the sons of Darkon, the sons of Giddel, ⁵⁷the sons of Shephatiah, the sons of Hattil, the sons of Pochereth-hazzebaim, and the sons of Ami. ⁵⁸All the temple servants and the sons of Solomon's servants were 392.

⁵⁹The following were those who came up from Tel-melah, Tel-harsha, Cherub, Addan, and Immer, though they could not prove their fathers' houses or their descent, whether they belonged to Israel: ⁶⁰the sons of Delaiah, the sons of Tobiah, and the sons of Nekoda, 652. ⁶¹Also, of the sons of the priests: the sons of Habaiah, the sons of Hakkoz, and the sons of Barzillai (who had taken a wife from the daughters of Barzillai the Gileadite, and was called by their name). ⁶²These sought their registration among those enrolled in the genealogies, but they were not found there, and so they were excluded from the priesthood as unclean. ⁶³The governor told them that they were not to partake of the most holy food, until there should be a priest to consult Urim and Thummim.

⁶⁴The whole assembly together was 42,360, ⁶⁵besides their male and female servants, of whom there were 7,337, and they had 200 male and female singers. ⁶⁶Their horses were 736, their mules were 245, ⁶⁷their camels were 435, and their donkeys were 6,720.

⁶⁸Some of the heads of families, when they came to the house of the Lord that is in Jerusalem, made freewill offerings for the house of God, to erect it on its site. ⁶⁹According to their ability they gave to the treasury of the work 61,000 darics[1] of gold, 5,000 minas[2] of silver, and 100 priests' garments.

⁷⁰Now the priests, the Levites, some of the people, the singers, the gatekeepers, and the temple servants lived in their towns, and all the rest of Israel[3] in their towns.

Rebuilding the Altar

3 When the seventh month came, and the children of Israel were in the towns, the people gathered as one man to Jerusalem. ²Then arose Jeshua the son of Jozadak with his fellow priests, and Zerubbabel the son of Shealtiel with his kinsmen, and they built the altar of the God of Israel, to offer burnt offerings on it, as it is written in the Law of Moses the man of God. ³They set the altar in its place, for fear was on them because of the peoples of the lands, and they offered burnt offerings on it to the Lord, burnt offerings morning and evening. ⁴And they kept the Feast of Booths, as it is written, and offered the daily burnt offerings by number according to the rule, as each day required, ⁵and after that the regular burnt offerings, the offerings at the new moon and at all the appointed feasts of the Lord, and the offerings of everyone who made a freewill offering to the Lord. ⁶From the first day of the seventh month they began to offer burnt offerings to the Lord. But the foundation of the temple of the Lord was not yet laid. ⁷So they gave money to the masons and the carpenters, and food, drink, and oil to the Sidonians and the Tyrians to bring cedar trees from Lebanon to the sea, to Joppa, according to the grant that they had from Cyrus king of Persia.

Rebuilding the Temple

⁸Now in the second year after their coming to the house of God at Jerusalem, in the second month, Zerubbabel the son of Shealtiel and Jeshua the son of Jozadak made a beginning, together with the rest of their kinsmen, the priests and the Levites and all who had come to Jerusalem from the captivity. They appointed the Levites,

[1] A *daric* was a coin weighing about 1/4 ounce or 8.5 grams [2] A *mina* was about 1 1/4 pounds or 0.6 kilogram [3] Hebrew *all Israel*

from twenty years old and upward, to supervise the work of the house of the LORD. ⁹ And Jeshua with his sons and his brothers, and Kadmiel and his sons, the sons of Judah, together supervised the workmen in the house of God, along with the sons of Henadad and the Levites, their sons and brothers.

¹⁰ And when the builders laid the foundation of the temple of the LORD, the priests in their vestments came forward with trumpets, and the Levites, the sons of Asaph, with cymbals, to praise the LORD, according to the directions of David king of Israel. ¹¹ And they sang responsively, praising and giving thanks to the LORD,

> "For he is good,
>   for his steadfast love endures
>   forever toward Israel."

And all the people shouted with a great shout when they praised the LORD, because the foundation of the house of the LORD was laid. ¹² But many of the priests and Levites and heads of fathers' houses, old men who had seen the first house, wept with a loud voice when they saw the foundation of this house being laid, though many shouted aloud for joy, ¹³ so that the people could not distinguish the sound of the joyful shout from the sound of the people's weeping, for the people shouted with a great shout, and the sound was heard far away.

Adversaries Oppose the Rebuilding

4 Now when the adversaries of Judah and Benjamin heard that the returned exiles were building a temple to the LORD, the God of Israel, ² they approached Zerubbabel and the heads of fathers' houses and said to them, "Let us build with you, for we worship your God as you do, and we have been sacrificing to him ever since the days of Esarhaddon king of Assyria who brought us here." ³ But Zerubbabel, Jeshua, and the rest of the heads of fathers' houses in Israel said to them, "You have nothing to do with us in building a house to our God; but we alone will build to the LORD, the God of Israel, as King Cyrus the king of Persia has commanded us."

⁴ Then the people of the land discouraged the people of Judah and made them afraid to build ⁵ and bribed counselors against them to frustrate their purpose, all the days of Cyrus king of Persia, even until the reign of Darius king of Persia.

⁶ And in the reign of Ahasuerus, in the beginning of his reign, they wrote an accusation against the inhabitants of Judah and Jerusalem.

The Letter to King Artaxerxes

⁷ In the days of Artaxerxes, Bishlam and Mithredath and Tabeel and the rest of their associates wrote to Artaxerxes king of Persia. The letter was written in Aramaic and translated.[1] ⁸ Rehum the commander and Shimshai the scribe wrote a letter against Jerusalem to Artaxerxes the king as follows: ⁹ Rehum the commander, Shimshai the scribe, and the rest of their associates, the judges, the governors, the officials, the Persians, the men of Erech, the Babylonians, the men of Susa, that is, the Elamites, ¹⁰ and the rest of the nations whom the great and noble Osnappar deported and settled in the cities of Samaria and in the rest of the province Beyond the River. ¹¹ (This is a copy of the letter that they sent.) "To Artaxerxes the king: Your servants, the men of the province Beyond the River, send greeting. And now ¹² be it known to the king that the Jews who came up from you to us have gone to Jerusalem. They are rebuilding that rebellious and wicked city. They are finishing the walls and repairing the foundations. ¹³ Now be it known to the king that if this city is rebuilt and the walls finished, they will not pay tribute, custom, or toll, and the royal revenue will be impaired. ¹⁴ Now because we eat the salt of the palace and it is not fitting for us to witness the king's dishonor, therefore we send and inform the king, ¹⁵ in order that search may be made in the book of the records of your fathers. You will find in the book of the records and learn that this city is a rebellious city, hurtful to kings and provinces, and that sedition was stirred up in it from of old. That was why this city was laid waste. ¹⁶ We make known to the king that if this city is rebuilt and its walls finished, you will then

---

[1] Hebrew written in Aramaic and translated in Aramaic, indicating that 4:8–6:18 is in Aramaic; another interpretation is *The letter was written in the Aramaic script and set forth in the Aramaic language*

have no possession in the province Beyond the River."

The King Orders the Work to Cease

[17] The king sent an answer: "To Rehum the commander and Shimshai the scribe and the rest of their associates who live in Samaria and in the rest of the province Beyond the River, greeting. And now [18] the letter that you sent to us has been plainly read before me. [19] And I made a decree, and search has been made, and it has been found that this city from of old has risen against kings, and that rebellion and sedition have been made in it. [20] And mighty kings have been over Jerusalem, who ruled over the whole province Beyond the River, to whom tribute, custom, and toll were paid. [21] Therefore make a decree that these men be made to cease, and that this city be not rebuilt, until a decree is made by me. [22] And take care not to be slack in this matter. Why should damage grow to the hurt of the king?"

[23] Then, when the copy of King Artaxerxes' letter was read before Rehum and Shimshai the scribe and their associates, they went in haste to the Jews at Jerusalem and by force and power made them cease. [24] Then the work on the house of God that is in Jerusalem stopped, and it ceased until the second year of the reign of Darius king of Persia.

Rebuilding Begins Anew

5 Now the prophets, Haggai and Zechariah the son of Iddo, prophesied to the Jews who were in Judah and Jerusalem, in the name of the God of Israel who was over them. [2] Then Zerubbabel the son of Shealtiel and Jeshua the son of Jozadak arose and began to rebuild the house of God that is in Jerusalem, and the prophets of God were with them, supporting them.

[3] At the same time Tattenai the governor of the province Beyond the River and Shethar-bozenai and their associates came to them and spoke to them thus: "Who gave you a decree to build this house and to finish this structure?" [4] They[1] also asked them this: "What are the names of the men who are building this building?" [5] But the eye of their God was on the elders of the Jews, and they did not stop them until the report should reach Darius and then an answer be returned by letter concerning it.

Tattenai's Letter to King Darius

[6] This is a copy of the letter that Tattenai the governor of the province Beyond the River and Shethar-bozenai and his associates, the governors who were in the province Beyond the River, sent to Darius the king. [7] They sent him a report, in which was written as follows: "To Darius the king, all peace. [8] Be it known to the king that we went to the province of Judah, to the house of the great God. It is being built with huge stones, and timber is laid in the walls. This work goes on diligently and prospers in their hands. [9] Then we asked those elders and spoke to them thus: 'Who gave you a decree to build this house and to finish this structure?' [10] We also asked them their names, for your information, that we might write down the names of their leaders.[2] [11] And this was their reply to us: 'We are the servants of the God of heaven and earth, and we are rebuilding the house that was built many years ago, which a great king of Israel built and finished. [12] But because our fathers had angered the God of heaven, he gave them into the hand of Nebuchadnezzar king of Babylon, the Chaldean, who destroyed this house and carried away the people to Babylonia. [13] However, in the first year of Cyrus king of Babylon, Cyrus the king made a decree that this house of God should be rebuilt. [14] And the gold and silver vessels of the house of God, which Nebuchadnezzar had taken out of the temple that was in Jerusalem and brought into the temple of Babylon, these Cyrus the king took out of the temple of Babylon, and they were delivered to one whose name was Sheshbazzar, whom he had made governor; [15] and he said to him, "Take these vessels, go and put them in the temple that is in Jerusalem, and let the house of God be rebuilt on its site." [16] Then this Sheshbazzar came and laid the foundations of the house of God that is in Jerusalem, and from that time until now it has been in building, and it is not yet finished.' [17] Therefore, if it seems good to the king, let search be made in the royal archives there in Babylon, to see whether a decree was issued by Cyrus the king for the rebuilding of this house of God

---

[1] Septuagint, Syriac; Aramaic *We* [2] Aramaic *of the men at their heads*

in Jerusalem. And let the king send us his pleasure in this matter."

The Decree of Darius

6 Then Darius the king made a decree, and search was made in Babylonia, in the house of the archives where the documents were stored. ²And in Ecbatana, the citadel that is in the province of Media, a scroll was found on which this was written: "A record. ³In the first year of Cyrus the king, Cyrus the king issued a decree: Concerning the house of God at Jerusalem, let the house be rebuilt, the place where sacrifices were offered, and let its foundations be retained. Its height shall be sixty cubits¹ and its breadth sixty cubits, ⁴with three layers of great stones and one layer of timber. Let the cost be paid from the royal treasury. ⁵And also let the gold and silver vessels of the house of God, which Nebuchadnezzar took out of the temple that is in Jerusalem and brought to Babylon, be restored and brought back to the temple that is in Jerusalem, each to its place. You shall put them in the house of God."

⁶"Now therefore, Tattenai, governor of the province Beyond the River, Shethar-bozenai, and your² associates the governors who are in the province Beyond the River, keep away. ⁷Let the work on this house of God alone. Let the governor of the Jews and the elders of the Jews rebuild this house of God on its site. ⁸Moreover, I make a decree regarding what you shall do for these elders of the Jews for the rebuilding of this house of God. The cost is to be paid to these men in full and without delay from the royal revenue, the tribute of the province from Beyond the River. ⁹And whatever is needed—bulls, rams, or sheep for burnt offerings to the God of heaven, wheat, salt, wine, or oil, as the priests at Jerusalem require—let that be given to them day by day without fail, ¹⁰that they may offer pleasing sacrifices to the God of heaven and pray for the life of the king and his sons. ¹¹Also I make a decree that if anyone alters this edict, a beam shall be pulled out of his house, and he shall be impaled on it, and his house shall be made a dunghill. ¹²May the God who has caused his name to dwell there overthrow any king or people who shall put out a hand to alter this, or to destroy this house of

God that is in Jerusalem. I Darius make a decree; let it be done with all diligence."

The Temple Finished and Dedicated

¹³Then, according to the word sent by Darius the king, Tattenai, the governor of the province Beyond the River, Shethar-bozenai, and their associates did with all diligence what Darius the king had ordered. ¹⁴And the elders of the Jews built and prospered through the prophesying of Haggai the prophet and Zechariah the son of Iddo. They finished their building by decree of the God of Israel and by decree of Cyrus and Darius and Artaxerxes king of Persia; ¹⁵and this house was finished on the third day of the month of Adar, in the sixth year of the reign of Darius the king.

¹⁶And the people of Israel, the priests and the Levites, and the rest of the returned exiles, celebrated the dedication of this house of God with joy. ¹⁷They offered at the dedication of this house of God 100 bulls, 200 rams, 400 lambs, and as a sin offering for all Israel 12 male goats, according to the number of the tribes of Israel. ¹⁸And they set the priests in their divisions and the Levites in their divisions, for the service of God at Jerusalem, as it is written in the Book of Moses.

Passover Celebrated

¹⁹On the fourteenth day of the first month, the returned exiles kept the Passover. ²⁰For the priests and the Levites had purified themselves together; all of them were clean. So they slaughtered the Passover lamb for all the returned exiles, for their fellow priests, and for themselves. ²¹It was eaten by the people of Israel who had returned from exile, and also by every one who had joined them and separated himself from the uncleanness of the peoples of the land to worship the LORD, the God of Israel. ²²And they kept the Feast of Unleavened Bread seven days with joy, for the LORD had made them joyful and had turned the heart of the king of Assyria to them, so that he aided them in the work of the house of God, the God of Israel.

Ezra Sent to Teach the People

7 Now after this, in the reign of Arta-xerxes king of Persia, Ezra the son of Seraiah, son of Azariah, son of Hilkiah,

¹ A *cubit* was about 18 inches or 45 centimeters ² Aramaic *their*

²son of Shallum, son of Zadok, son of Ahitub, ³son of Amariah, son of Azariah, son of Meraioth, ⁴son of Zerahiah, son of Uzzi, son of Bukki, ⁵son of Abishua, son of Phinehas, son of Eleazar, son of Aaron the chief priest— ⁶this Ezra went up from Babylonia. He was a scribe skilled in the Law of Moses that the LORD, the God of Israel, had given, and the king granted him all that he asked, for the hand of the LORD his God was on him.

⁷And there went up also to Jerusalem, in the seventh year of Artaxerxes the king, some of the people of Israel, and some of the priests and Levites, the singers and gatekeepers, and the temple servants. ⁸And Ezra¹ came to Jerusalem in the fifth month, which was in the seventh year of the king. ⁹For on the first day of the first month he began to go up from Babylonia, and on the first day of the fifth month he came to Jerusalem, for the good hand of his God was on him. ¹⁰For Ezra had set his heart to study the Law of the LORD, and to do it and to teach his statutes and rules in Israel.

¹¹This is a copy of the letter that King Artaxerxes gave to Ezra the priest, the scribe, a man learned in matters of the commandments of the LORD and his statutes for Israel: ¹²"Artaxerxes, king of kings, to Ezra the priest, the scribe of the Law of the God of heaven. Peace.² And now ¹³I make a decree that anyone of the people of Israel or their priests or Levites in my kingdom, who freely offers to go to Jerusalem, may go with you. ¹⁴For you are sent by the king and his seven counselors to make inquiries about Judah and Jerusalem according to the Law of your God, which is in your hand, ¹⁵and also to carry the silver and gold that the king and his counselors have freely offered to the God of Israel, whose dwelling is in Jerusalem, ¹⁶with all the silver and gold that you shall find in the whole province of Babylonia, and with the freewill offerings of the people and the priests, vowed willingly for the house of their God that is in Jerusalem. ¹⁷With this money, then, you shall with all diligence buy bulls, rams, and lambs, with their grain offerings and their drink offerings, and you shall offer them on the altar of the house of your God that is in Jerusalem. ¹⁸Whatever seems good to you and your brothers to do with the rest of the silver and gold, you may do, according to the will of your God. ¹⁹The vessels that have been given you for the service of the house of your God, you shall deliver before the God of Jerusalem. ²⁰And whatever else is required for the house of your God, which it falls to you to provide, you may provide it out of the king's treasury.

²¹"And I, Artaxerxes the king, make a decree to all the treasurers in the province Beyond the River: Whatever Ezra the priest, the scribe of the Law of the God of heaven, requires of you, let it be done with all diligence, ²²up to 100 talents³ of silver, 100 cors⁴ of wheat, 100 baths⁵ of wine, 100 baths of oil, and salt without prescribing how much. ²³Whatever is decreed by the God of heaven, let it be done in full for the house of the God of heaven, lest his wrath be against the realm of the king and his sons. ²⁴We also notify you that it shall not be lawful to impose tribute, custom, or toll on anyone of the priests, the Levites, the singers, the doorkeepers, the temple servants, or other servants of this house of God.

²⁵"And you, Ezra, according to the wisdom of your God that is in your hand, appoint magistrates and judges who may judge all the people in the province Beyond the River, all such as know the laws of your God. And those who do not know them, you shall teach. ²⁶Whoever will not obey the law of your God and the law of the king, let judgment be strictly executed on him, whether for death or for banishment or for confiscation of his goods or for imprisonment."

²⁷Blessed be the LORD, the God of our fathers, who put such a thing as this into the heart of the king, to beautify the house of the LORD that is in Jerusalem, ²⁸and who extended to me his steadfast love before the king and his counselors, and before all the king's mighty officers. I took courage, for the hand of the LORD my God was on me, and I gathered leading men from Israel to go up with me.

Genealogy of Those Who Returned with Ezra

8 These are the heads of their fathers' houses, and this is the genealogy of those who went up with me from Bab-

¹Aramaic *he* ²Aramaic *Perfect* (probably a greeting) ³A *talent* was about 75 pounds or 34 kilograms ⁴A *cor* was about 6 bushels or 220 liters ⁵A *bath* was about 6 gallons or 22 liters

ylonia, in the reign of Artaxerxes the king: [2] Of the sons of Phinehas, Gershom. Of the sons of Ithamar, Daniel. Of the sons of David, Hattush. [3] Of the sons of Shecaniah, who was of the sons of Parosh, Zechariah, with whom were registered 150 men. [4] Of the sons of Pahath-moab, Eliehoenai the son of Zerahiah, and with him 200 men. [5] Of the sons of Zattu,[1] Shecaniah the son of Jahaziel, and with him 300 men. [6] Of the sons of Adin, Ebed the son of Jonathan, and with him 50 men. [7] Of the sons of Elam, Jeshaiah the son of Athaliah, and with him 70 men. [8] Of the sons of Shephatiah, Zebadiah the son of Michael, and with him 80 men. [9] Of the sons of Joab, Obadiah the son of Jehiel, and with him 218 men. [10] Of the sons of Bani,[2] Shelomith the son of Josiphiah, and with him 160 men. [11] Of the sons of Bebai, Zechariah, the son of Bebai, and with him 28 men. [12] Of the sons of Azgad, Johanan the son of Hakkatan, and with him 110 men. [13] Of the sons of Adonikam, those who came later, their names being Eliphelet, Jeuel, and Shemaiah, and with them 60 men. [14] Of the sons of Bigvai, Uthai and Zaccur, and with them 70 men.

Ezra Sends for Levites

[15] I gathered them to the river that runs to Ahava, and there we camped three days. As I reviewed the people and the priests, I found there none of the sons of Levi. [16] Then I sent for Eliezer, Ariel, Shemaiah, Elnathan, Jarib, Elnathan, Nathan, Zechariah, and Meshullam, leading men, and for Joiarib and Elnathan, who were men of insight, [17] and sent them to Iddo, the leading man at the place Casiphia, telling them what to say to Iddo and his brothers and[3] the temple servants at the place Casiphia, namely, to send us ministers for the house of our God. [18] And by the good hand of our God on us, they brought us a man of discretion, of the sons of Mahli the son of Levi, son of Israel, namely Sherebiah with his sons and kinsmen, 18; [19] also Hashabiah, and with him Jeshaiah of the sons of Merari, with his kinsmen and their sons, 20; [20] besides 220 of the temple servants, whom David and his officials had set apart to attend the Levites. These were all mentioned by name.

Fasting and Prayer for Protection

[21] Then I proclaimed a fast there, at the river Ahava, that we might humble ourselves before our God, to seek from him a safe journey for ourselves, our children, and all our goods. [22] For I was ashamed to ask the king for a band of soldiers and horsemen to protect us against the enemy on our way, since we had told the king, "The hand of our God is for good on all who seek him, and the power of his wrath is against all who forsake him." [23] So we fasted and implored our God for this, and he listened to our entreaty.

Priests to Guard Offerings

[24] Then I set apart twelve of the leading priests: Sherebiah, Hashabiah, and ten of their kinsmen with them. [25] And I weighed out to them the silver and the gold and the vessels, the offering for the house of our God that the king and his counselors and his lords and all Israel there present had offered. [26] I weighed out into their hand 650 talents[4] of silver, and silver vessels worth 200 talents,[5] and 100 talents of gold, [27] 20 bowls of gold worth 1,000 darics,[6] and two vessels of fine bright bronze as precious as gold. [28] And I said to them, "You are holy to the Lord, and the vessels are holy, and the silver and the gold are a freewill offering to the Lord, the God of your fathers. [29] Guard them and keep them until you weigh them before the chief priests and the Levites and the heads of fathers' houses in Israel at Jerusalem, within the chambers of the house of the Lord." [30] So the priests and the Levites took over the weight of the silver and the gold and the vessels, to bring them to Jerusalem, to the house of our God.

[31] Then we departed from the river Ahava on the twelfth day of the first month, to go to Jerusalem. The hand of our God was on us, and he delivered us from the hand of the enemy and from ambushes by the way. [32] We came to Jerusalem, and there we remained three days. [33] On the fourth day, within the house of our God, the silver and the gold and the vessels were weighed into the hands of Meremoth the priest, son of Uriah, and with him was Eleazar the son of Phinehas, and with them were the Levites, Jozabad the son of Jeshua and Noadiah the son of Binnui. [34] The whole was counted

---

[1] Septuagint; Hebrew lacks *of Zattu* [2] Septuagint; Hebrew lacks *Bani* [3] Hebrew lacks *and* [4] A *talent* was about 75 pounds or 34 kilograms [5] Revocalization; the number is missing in the Masoretic Text [6] A *daric* was a coin weighing about 1/4 ounce or 8.5 grams

and weighed, and the weight of everything was recorded.

[35] At that time those who had come from captivity, the returned exiles, offered burnt offerings to the God of Israel, twelve bulls for all Israel, ninety-six rams, seventy-seven lambs, and as a sin offering twelve male goats. All this was a burnt offering to the LORD. [36] They also delivered the king's commissions to the king's satraps[1] and to the governors of the province Beyond the River, and they aided the people and the house of God.

Ask Yourself . . .

ABOUT PRAYER

Do you have a good prayer life? Do you experience the answers to your prayers? Do you see God's hand on your life because of your prayers? If you want more from your prayer life, then here are some questions to consider:

- What does God's Word promise about prayer?
- Whose prayers does God listen to?
- Is there a sin I haven't confessed?
- Do I trust God to answer my prayers with the perfect answer?
- Do I live a life of prayer, or is my life too busy for me to pray?
- Is prayerlessness a sin?

Check out Prayer in the Quick Relief guide at the back of this Bible for help with these Qs.

Ezra Prays About Intermarriage

9 After these things had been done, the officials approached me and said, "The people of Israel and the priests and the Levites have not separated themselves from the peoples of the lands with their abominations, from the Canaanites, the Hittites, the Perizzites, the Jebusites, the Ammonites, the Moabites, the Egyptians, and the Amorites. [2] For they have taken some of their daughters to be wives for themselves and for their sons, so that the holy race[2] has mixed itself with the peoples of the lands. And in this faithlessness the hand of the officials and chief men has been foremost." [3] As soon as I heard this, I tore my garment and my cloak and pulled hair from my head and beard and sat appalled. [4] Then all who trembled at the words of the God of Israel, because of the faithlessness of the returned exiles, gathered around me while I sat appalled until the evening sacrifice. [5] And at the evening sacrifice I rose from my fasting, with my garment and my cloak torn, and fell upon my knees and spread out my hands to the LORD my God, [6] saying:

"O my God, I am ashamed and blush to lift my face to you, my God, for our iniquities have risen higher than our heads, and our guilt has mounted up to the heavens. [7] From the days of our fathers to this day we have been in great guilt. And for our iniquities we, our kings, and our priests have been given into the hand of the kings of the lands, to the sword, to captivity, to plundering, and to utter shame, as it is today. [8] But now for a brief moment favor has been shown by the LORD our God, to leave us a remnant and to give us a secure hold[3] within his holy place, that our God may brighten our eyes and grant us a little reviving in our slavery. [9] For we are slaves. Yet our God has not forsaken us in our slavery, but has extended to us his steadfast love before the kings of Persia, to grant us some reviving to set up the house of our God, to repair its ruins, and to give us protection[4] in Judea and Jerusalem.

[10] "And now, O our God, what shall we say after this? For we have forsaken your commandments, [11] which you commanded by your servants the prophets, saying, 'The land that you are entering, to take possession of it, is a land impure with the impurity of the peoples of the lands, with their abominations that have filled it from end to end with their uncleanness. [12] Therefore do not give your daughters to their sons, neither take their daughters for your sons, and never seek their peace or prosperity,

---

[1] A *satrap* was a Persian official   [2] Hebrew *offspring*   [3] Hebrew *nail*, or *tent-pin*   [4] Hebrew *a wall*

that you may be strong and eat the good of the land and leave it for an inheritance to your children forever.' ¹³ And after all that has come upon us for our evil deeds and for our great guilt, seeing that you, our God, have punished us less than our iniquities deserved and have given us such a remnant as this, ¹⁴ shall we break your commandments again and intermarry with the peoples who practice these abominations? Would you not be angry with us until you consumed us, so that there should be no remnant, nor any to escape? ¹⁵ O LORD, the God of Israel, you are just, for we are left a remnant that has escaped, as it is today. Behold, we are before you in our guilt, for none can stand before you because of this."

The People Confess Their Sin

10 While Ezra prayed and made confession, weeping and casting himself down before the house of God, a very great

assembly of men, women, and children, gathered to him out of Israel, for the people wept bitterly. ² And Shecaniah the son of Jehiel, of the sons of Elam, addressed Ezra: "We have broken faith with our God and have married foreign women from the peoples of the land, but even now there is hope for Israel in spite of this. ³ Therefore let us make a covenant with our God to put away all these wives and their children, according to the counsel of my lord¹ and of those who tremble at the commandment of our God, and let it be done according to the Law. ⁴ Arise, for it is your task, and we are with you; be strong and do it." ⁵ Then Ezra arose and made the leading priests and Levites and all Israel take an oath that they would do as had been said. So they took the oath.

⁶ Then Ezra withdrew from before the house of God and went to the chamber of Jehohanan the son of Eliashib, where he spent the night,² neither eating bread

¹ Or of the Lord ² Probable reading; Hebrew where he went

verses to read
Ezra 9:6-15

When all the people around Ezra sinned, Ezra confessed their sins as "our" sins and said, "Our guilt has mounted up to the heavens" (Ezra 9:6). He'd had nothing to do with their disobedience in mixing with pagans and turning their backs on God, but that didn't stop him from making himself a part of the confession. They were, after all, his people, and he was well aware of what their acts meant to a holy God. And so Ezra grieved as if he were the one who had walked away from God, and he prayed as though his very life depended on it.

How often have you shared the burden of the sins of the people you love, even confessing their sins as if they were your own? Probably never. It's not a normal thing to do, but think about what Ezra did and why he did it. Then think about how often you have judged the sins of others with disgust and revulsion. Which reaction is more holy? The next time you see the sins of the people you love, think about standing in spiritual grief with them, pleading with God to forgive "our" sins and to heal "us" of our unfaithfulness.

After the people saw Ezra crying in front of God's temple, they were so moved that they "wept bitterly" and confessed their unfaithfulness to God (Ezra 10:1). Ezra didn't force them to do this, but he influenced them by taking on their condition as his own and responding as a godly person would after coming face-to-face with sin in his own life. As a God Girl, you play a role in the spiritual lives of those in your family, community, and nation. Don't stand by as an observer, but become active in prayer and confession.

nor drinking water, for he was mourning over the faithlessness of the exiles. [7] And a proclamation was made throughout Judah and Jerusalem to all the returned exiles that they should assemble at Jerusalem, [8] and that if anyone did not come within three days, by order of the officials and the elders all his property should be forfeited, and he himself banned from the congregation of the exiles.

[9] Then all the men of Judah and Benjamin assembled at Jerusalem within the three days. It was the ninth month, on the twentieth day of the month. And all the people sat in the open square before the house of God, trembling because of this matter and because of the heavy rain. [10] And Ezra the priest stood up and said to them, "You have broken faith and married foreign women, and so increased the guilt of Israel. [11] Now then make confession to the LORD, the God of your fathers and do his will. Separate yourselves from the peoples of the land and from the foreign wives." [12] Then all the assembly answered with a loud voice, "It is so; we must do as you have said. [13] But the people are many, and it is a time of heavy rain; we cannot stand in the open. Nor is this a task for one day or for two, for we have greatly transgressed in this matter. [14] Let our officials stand for the whole assembly. Let all in our cities who have taken foreign wives come at appointed times, and with them the elders and judges of every city, until the fierce wrath of our God over this matter is turned away from us." [15] Only Jonathan the son of Asahel and Jahzeiah the son of Tikvah opposed this, and Meshullam and Shabbethai the Levite supported them.

[16] Then the returned exiles did so. Ezra the priest selected men,[1] heads of fathers' houses, according to their fathers' houses, each of them designated by name. On the first day of the tenth month they sat down to examine the matter; [17] and by the first day of the first month they had come to the end of all the men who had married foreign women.

Those Guilty of Intermarriage

[18] Now there were found some of the sons of the priests who had married foreign women: Maaseiah, Eliezer, Jarib, and Gedaliah, some of the sons of Jeshua the son of Jozadak and his brothers. [19] They pledged themselves to put away their wives, and their guilt offering was a ram of the flock for their guilt.[2] [20] Of the sons of Immer: Hanani and Zebadiah. [21] Of the sons of Harim: Maaseiah, Elijah, Shemaiah, Jehiel, and Uzziah. [22] Of the sons of Pashhur: Elioenai, Maaseiah, Ishmael, Nethanel, Jozabad, and Elasah.

[23] Of the Levites: Jozabad, Shimei, Kelaiah (that is, Kelita), Pethahiah, Judah, and Eliezer. [24] Of the singers: Eliashib. Of the gatekeepers: Shallum, Telem, and Uri.

[25] And of Israel: of the sons of Parosh: Ramiah, Izziah, Malchijah, Mijamin, Eleazar, Hashabiah,[3] and Benaiah. [26] Of the sons of Elam: Mattaniah, Zechariah, Jehiel, Abdi, Jeremoth, and Elijah. [27] Of the sons of Zattu: Elioenai, Eliashib, Mattaniah, Jeremoth, Zabad, and Aziza. [28] Of the sons of Bebai were Jehohanan, Hananiah, Zabbai, and Athlai. [29] Of the sons of Bani were Meshullam, Malluch, Adaiah, Jashub, Sheal, and Jeremoth. [30] Of the sons of Pahath-moab: Adna, Chelal, Benaiah, Maaseiah, Mattaniah, Bezalel, Binnui, and Manasseh. [31] Of the sons of Harim: Eliezer, Isshijah, Malchijah, Shemaiah, Shimeon, [32] Benjamin, Malluch, and Shemariah. [33] Of the sons of Hashum: Mattenai, Mattattah, Zabad, Eliphelet, Jeremai, Manasseh, and Shimei. [34] Of the sons of Bani: Maadai, Amram, Uel, [35] Benaiah, Bedeiah, Cheluhi, [36] Vaniah, Meremoth, Eliashib, [37] Mattaniah, Mattenai, Jaasu. [38] Of the sons of Binnui:[4] Shimei, [39] Shelemiah, Nathan, Adaiah, [40] Machnadebai, Shashai, Sharai, [41] Azarel, Shelemiah, Shemariah, [42] Shallum, Amariah, and Joseph. [43] Of the sons of Nebo: Jeiel, Mattithiah, Zabad, Zebina, Jaddai, Joel, and Benaiah. [44] All these had married foreign women, and some of the women had even borne children.[5]

---

[1] Syriac; Hebrew *And there were selected Ezra …* [2] Or *as their reparation* [3] Septuagint; Hebrew *Malchijah* [4] Septuagint; Hebrew *Bani, Binnui* [5] Or *and they put them away with their children*

INTRODUCTION TO
Nehemiah

Author: Unknown, possibly Ezra

Time: Sometime after 400 B.C.

Place: Probably in Jerusalem

Written to: The Israelites after their Babylonian captivity

The gist

While Ezra was the spiritual leader for the returned Israelites, Nehemiah was more of a political leader. In this book you can read about how he led the people to rebuild the walls of Jerusalem in order to be safe and protected. You can also read about the revival that happened once the Israelites moved home and how the lives of the people were restored after being so badly destroyed in captivity. No matter how badly God's people mess up, God continues to forgive them and fix them back up, and the book of Nehemiah is a good example of his doing just that.

Things to look for

- Nehemiah's return to Jerusalem (see Nehemiah 2)
- The walls of Jerusalem (see Neh. 1:3; 2:17–3:32; 4:6; 12:27, 30)

Be Set Apart

> "Shall we then listen to you and do all this great evil and act treacherously against our God by marrying foreign women?"
>
> Nehemiah 13:27

When God led his people out of captivity and restored them to their land, he wanted them to get things cleaned up. The temple was soon rebuilt, but the city remained defenseless without walls, and the people had strayed from God's law. Ezra and Nehemiah were called by God to lead the Israelites in the right direction and keep their focus on God instead of on themselves. God wanted and still wants his people to focus. He wants them to stop looking at all the pretty things and people around them and to set themselves apart, to be different, to be faithful.

Staying true to God in a world filled with all kinds of temptations can be hard. The Israelites had gotten used to the world and all its charms and sin. Instead of staying away from the temptation all around them, they gave in to it, even marrying women they weren't supposed to marry and letting the enemies of God become part of their bloodline. But God wouldn't stand for this, so in one bold move, Nehemiah told all the Israelites that they had to leave their wives and even kids who were not Israelites in order to set themselves apart. Can you imagine the horror of hearing those words? But it had to be done.

God doesn't break up families today. He doesn't command a believing wife to leave her nonbelieving husband, but he does command us not to marry nonbelievers in the first place. God still wants us to be set apart, and making yourself one with someone who hates or could care less about God isn't a holy act but a sinful one.

As you read the book of Nehemiah, think about why God wanted his people to work so hard to be kept apart from others who were not his own. Look at the faithfulness of God in taking back his disbelieving and sinful children over and over again, and see how, no matter what you might do, God's promises can be trusted, both the beautiful ones and the curses.

Must-Know Facts and Verses

⁑ Many scholars believe that Ezra wrote the book of Nehemiah.

⁑ In the Hebrew Bible, Ezra and Nehemiah are one book.

⁑ Nehemiah is about the restoration of Jerusalem after the exile in Babylon.

⁑ Nehemiah was a cupbearer to the king, which meant he had access to the king in a way others never would (see Neh. 1:11).

"I now pray before you day and night for the people of Israel your servants, confessing the sins of the people of Israel, which we have sinned against you. Even I and my father's house have sinned. We have acted very corruptly against you and have not kept the commandments, the statutes, and the rules that you commanded your servant Moses." *Nehemiah 1:6–7*

"O Lord, let your ear be attentive to the prayer of your servant, and to the prayer of your servants who delight to fear your name, and give success to your servant today, and grant him mercy in the sight of this man." *Nehemiah 1:11*

So Ezra the priest brought the Law before the assembly. . . . And he read from it facing the square before the Water Gate from early morning until midday. *Nehemiah 8:2–3*

And Ezra blessed the LORD, the great God, and all the people answered, "Amen, Amen," lifting up their hands. And they bowed their heads and worshiped the LORD with their faces to the ground. *Nehemiah 8:6*

Nehemiah

Report from Jerusalem

1 The words of Nehemiah the son of Hacaliah.

Now it happened in the month of Chislev, in the twentieth year, as I was in Susa the citadel, ²that Hanani, one of my brothers, came with certain men from Judah. And I asked them concerning the Jews who escaped, who had survived the exile, and concerning Jerusalem. ³And they said to me, "The remnant there in the province who had survived the exile is in great trouble and shame. The wall of Jerusalem is broken down, and its gates are destroyed by fire."

Nehemiah's Prayer

⁴As soon as I heard these words I sat down and wept and mourned for days, and continued fasting and praying before the God of heaven. ⁵And I said, "O LORD God of heaven, the great and awesome God who keeps covenant and steadfast love with those who love him and keep his commandments, ⁶let your ear be attentive and your eyes open, to hear the prayer of your servant that I now pray before you day and night for the people of Israel your servants, confessing the sins of the people of Israel, which we have sinned against you. Even I and my father's house have sinned. ⁷We have acted very corruptly against you and have not kept the commandments, the statutes, and the rules that you commanded your servant Moses. ⁸Remember the word that you commanded your servant Moses, saying, 'If you are unfaithful, I will scatter you among the peoples, ⁹but if you return to me and keep my commandments and do them, though your outcasts are in the uttermost parts of heaven, from there I will gather them and bring them to the place that I have chosen, to make my name dwell there.' ¹⁰They are your servants and your people, whom you have redeemed by your great power and by your strong hand. ¹¹O

Lord, let your ear be attentive to the prayer of your servant, and to the prayer of your servants who delight to fear your name, and give success to your servant today, and grant him mercy in the sight of this man."

Now I was cupbearer to the king.

Nehemiah Sent to Judah

2 In the month of Nisan, in the twentieth year of King Artaxerxes, when wine was before him, I took up the wine and gave it to the king. Now I had not been sad in his presence. ²And the king said to me, "Why is your face sad, seeing you are not sick? This is nothing but sadness of the heart." Then I was very much afraid. ³I said to the king, "Let the king live forever! Why should not my face be sad, when the city, the place of my fathers' graves, lies in ruins, and its gates have been destroyed by fire?" ⁴Then the king said to me, "What are you requesting?" So I prayed to the God of heaven. ⁵And I said to the king, "If it pleases the king, and if your servant has found favor in your sight, that you send me to Judah, to the city of my fathers' graves, that I may rebuild it." ⁶And the king said to me (the queen sitting beside him), "How long will you be gone, and when will you return?" So it pleased the king to send me when I had given him a time. ⁷And I said to the king, "If it pleases the king, let letters be given me to the governors of the province Beyond the River, that they may let me pass through until I come to Judah, ⁸and a letter to Asaph, the keeper of the king's forest, that he may give me timber to make beams for the gates of the fortress of the temple, and for the wall of the city, and for the house that I shall occupy." And the king granted me what I asked, for the good hand of my God was upon me.

Nehemiah Inspects Jerusalem's Walls

⁹Then I came to the governors of the province Beyond the River and gave them

the king's letters. Now the king had sent with me officers of the army and horse-men. [10] But when Sanballat the Horonite and Tobiah the Ammonite servant heard this, it displeased them greatly that some-one had come to seek the welfare of the people of Israel.

[11] So I went to Jerusalem and was there three days. [12] Then I arose in the night, I and a few men with me. And I told no one what my God had put into my heart to do for Jerusalem. There was no ani-mal with me but the one on which I rode. [13] I went out by night by the Valley Gate to the Dragon Spring and to the Dung Gate, and I inspected the walls of Jerusalem that were broken down and its gates that had been destroyed by fire. [14] Then I went on to the Fountain Gate and to the King's Pool, but there was no room for the ani-mal that was under me to pass. [15] Then I went up in the night by the valley and inspected the wall, and I turned back and entered by the Valley Gate, and so

returned. [16] And the officials did not know where I had gone or what I was doing, an I had not yet told the Jews, the priest the nobles, the officials, and the rest wh were to do the work.

[17] Then I said to them, "You see th trouble we are in, how Jerusalem lies i ruins with its gates burned. Come, let u build the wall of Jerusalem, that we may n longer suffer derision." [18] And I told them of the hand of my God that had been upo me for good, and also of the words that th king had spoken to me. And they said, "Le us rise up and build." So they strengthene their hands for the good work. [19] But whe Sanballat the Horonite and Tobiah th Ammonite servant and Geshem the Ara heard of it, they jeered at us and despise us and said, "What is this thing that yo are doing? Are you rebelling against th king?" [20] Then I replied to them, "The Go of heaven will make us prosper, and we hi servants will arise and build, but you hav no portion or right or claim[1] in Jerusalem

[1] Or memorial

verses to read
Nehemiah 1:4–11

Know God

Where you are and who is around you right now isn't just by chance. There's no such thing as chance in the life of a believer; chance would imply that God isn't in control and that things happen without any reason whatsoever. But God has a reason for everything that he allows. That means that he can bring you into rela-tionships that make no sense, that drive you crazy, and that you want to get out of, but if you look to him you might just find something amazing. Think about the people around you and ask yourself if God hasn't given them to you in order for you to intercede for them, to come to him with requests on their behalf, to help them, and even save them.

Praying for sinful people in your life isn't an option; it's a requirement for the God Girl. If they are in your life, then they need your prayers, even the bad people—es-pecially the bad ones. Pray for them, remembering your own badness that has been forgiven through Christ. Think about the fact that each person in your life needs your prayers just as must as you need their prayers. This prayer of intercession doesn't have to be hard; you don't have to get involved in their drama, but bring them before the throne of God and plead with him.

Don't ever think things happen by chance and that you weren't meant to be where you are. You were meant to be just where you are, and your prayers were meant to bring the freedom that others need.

Rebuilding the Wall

3 Then Eliashib the high priest rose up with his brothers the priests, and they built the Sheep Gate. They consecrated it and set its doors. They consecrated it as far as the Tower of the Hundred, as far as the Tower of Hananel. ²And next to him the men of Jericho built. And next to them¹ Zaccur the son of Imri built.

³The sons of Hassenaah built the Fish Gate. They laid its beams and set its doors, its bolts, and its bars. ⁴And next to them Jeremoth the son of Uriah, son of Hakkoz repaired. And next to them Meshullam the son of Berechiah, son of Meshezabel repaired. And next to them Zadok the son of Baana repaired. ⁵And next to them the Tekoites repaired, but their nobles would not stoop to serve their Lord.²

⁶Joiada the son of Paseah and Meshullam the son of Besodeiah repaired the Gate of Yeshanah.³ They laid its beams and set its doors, its bolts, and its bars. ⁷And next to them repaired Melatiah the Gibeonite and Jadon the Meronothite, the men of Gibeon and of Mizpah, the seat of the governor of the province Beyond the River. ⁸Next

to them Uzziel the son of Harhaiah, goldsmiths, repaired. Next to him Hananiah, one of the perfumers, repaired, and they restored Jerusalem as far as the Broad Wall. ⁹Next to them Rephaiah the son of Hur, ruler of half the district of⁴ Jerusalem, repaired. ¹⁰Next to them Jedaiah the son of Harumaph repaired opposite his house. And next to him Hattush the son of Hashabneiah repaired. ¹¹Malchijah the son of Harim and Hasshub the son of Pahath-moab repaired another section and the Tower of the Ovens. ¹²Next to him Shallum the son of Hallohesh, ruler of half the district of Jerusalem, repaired, he and his daughters.

¹³Hanun and the inhabitants of Zanoah repaired the Valley Gate. They rebuilt it and set its doors, its bolts, and its bars, and repaired a thousand cubits⁵ of the wall, as far as the Dung Gate.

¹⁴Malchijah the son of Rechab, ruler of the district of Beth-haccherem, repaired the Dung Gate. He rebuilt it and set its doors, its bolts, and its bars.

¹⁵And Shallum the son of Col-hozeh, ruler of the district of Mizpah, repaired

¹Hebrew *him* ²Or *lords* ³Or *of the old city* ⁴Or *foreman of half the portion assigned to*; also verses 12, 14, 15, 16, 17, 18 ⁵A *cubit* was about 18 inches or 45 centimeters

Know God

verses to read
Nehemiah 2:11–15

When God gives you a strong sense of his call for your life and future, you don't have to share it with everyone in order to make it more real. Sometimes your service to God will go unannounced and your devotion won't be seen or understood by anyone. You don't need to brag about the calling you've been given or explain why you're doing what you're doing. If it's really a calling from God, then it's gonna happen, and if not, then you won't have made a fool of yourself. As you spend more time in the presence of God, you will find yourself with all the encouragement you need to do what you are being asked to do. His approval is the only approval you need—and in the gospel, you have it.

A lot of callings in life are meant to be shared, but only at the right time. They have to be tested. They aren't served to you on a silver platter, but most often they are going to take some effort on your part, and a lot of times that effort is its own reward. It is also wise to seek the counsel of others as you discern what you think God is calling you to do. Other people, especially older ones who have had a chance to get to know you, will be able to point out things about you that you might not be aware of.

the Fountain Gate. He rebuilt it and covered it and set its doors, its bolts, and its bars. And he built the wall of the Pool of Shelah of the king's garden, as far as the stairs that go down from the city of David. [16] After him Nehemiah the son of Azbuk, ruler of half the district of Beth-zur, repaired to a point opposite the tombs of David, as far as the artificial pool, and as far as the house of the mighty men. [17] After him the Levites repaired: Rehum the son of Bani. Next to him Hashabiah, ruler of half the district of Keilah, repaired for his district. [18] After him their brothers repaired: Bavvai the son of Henadad, ruler of half the district of Keilah. [19] Next to him Ezer the son of Jeshua, ruler of Mizpah, repaired another section opposite the ascent to the armory at the buttress.[1] [20] After him Baruch the son of Zabbai repaired another section from the buttress to the door of the house of Eliashib the high priest. [21] After him Meremoth the son of Uriah, son of Hakkoz repaired another section from the door of the house of Eliashib to the end of the house of Eliashib. [22] After him the priests, the men of the surrounding area, repaired. [23] After them Benjamin and Hasshub repaired opposite their house. After them Azariah the son of Maaseiah, son of Ananiah repaired beside his own house. [24] After him Binnui the son of Henadad repaired another section, from the house of Azariah to the buttress [25] and to the corner. Palal the son of Uzai repaired opposite the buttress and the tower projecting from the upper house of the king at the court of the guard. After him Pedaiah the son of Parosh [26] and the temple servants living on Ophel repaired to a point opposite the Water Gate on the east and the projecting tower. [27] After him the Tekoites repaired another section opposite the great projecting tower as far as the wall of Ophel.

[28] Above the Horse Gate the priests repaired, each one opposite his own house. [29] After them Zadok the son of Immer repaired opposite his own house. After him Shemaiah the son of Shecaniah, the keeper of the East Gate, repaired. [30] After him Hananiah the son of Shelemiah and Hanun the sixth son of Zalaph repaired another section. After him Meshullam the son of Berechiah repaired opposite his chamber. [31] After him Malchijah, one of the goldsmiths, repaired as far as the house of the temple servants and of the merchants, opposite the Muster Gate,[2] and to the upper chamber of the corner. [32] And between the upper chamber of the corner and the Sheep Gate the goldsmiths and the merchants repaired.

Opposition to the Work

4 [3] Now when Sanballat heard that we were building the wall, he was angry and greatly enraged, and he jeered at the Jews. [2] And he said in the presence of his brothers and of the army of Samaria, "What are these feeble Jews doing? Will they restore it for themselves?[4] Will they sacrifice? Will they finish up in a day? Will they revive the stones out of the heaps of rubbish, and burned ones at that?" [3] Tobiah the Ammonite was beside him, and he said, "Yes, what they are building—if a fox goes up on it he will break down their stone wall!" [4] Hear, O our God, for we are despised. Turn back their taunt on their own heads and give them up to be plundered in a land where they are captives. [5] Do not cover their guilt, and let not their sin be blotted out from your sight, for they have provoked you to anger in the presence of the builders.

[6] So we built the wall. And all the wall was joined together to half its height, for the people had a mind to work.

[7] [5] But when Sanballat and Tobiah and the Arabs and the Ammonites and the Ashdodites heard that the repairing of the walls of Jerusalem was going forward and that the breaches were beginning to be closed, they were very angry. [8] And they all plotted together to come and fight against Jerusalem and to cause confusion in it. [9] And we prayed to our God and set a guard as a protection against them day and night.

[10] In Judah it was said,[6] "The strength of those who bear the burdens is failing. There is too much rubble. By ourselves we will not be able to rebuild the wall." [11] And our enemies said, "They will not know or see till we come among them and kill them and stop the work." [12] At that time the Jews who lived near them came from all directions and said to us ten times, "You must return to us."[7] [13] So in the lowest parts of the space

[1] Or *corner*; also verses 20, 24, 25 [2] Or *Hammiphkad Gate* [3] Ch 3:33 in Hebrew [4] Or *Will they commit themselves to God?* [5] Ch 4:1 in Hebrew [6] Hebrew *Judah said* [7] The meaning of the Hebrew is uncertain

behind the wall, in open places, I stationed the people by their clans, with their swords, their spears, and their bows. ¹⁴And I looked and arose and said to the nobles and to the officials and to the rest of the people, "Do not be afraid of them. Remember the Lord, who is great and awesome, and fight for your brothers, your sons, your daughters, your wives, and your homes."

The Work Resumes

¹⁵When our enemies heard that it was known to us and that God had frustrated their plan, we all returned to the wall, each to his work. ¹⁶From that day on, half of my servants worked on construction, and half held the spears, shields, bows, and coats of mail. And the leaders stood behind the whole house of Judah, ¹⁷who were building on the wall. Those who carried burdens were loaded in such a way that each labored on the work with one hand and held his weapon with the other. ¹⁸And each of the builders had his sword strapped at his side while he built. The man who sounded the trumpet was beside me. ¹⁹And I said to the nobles and to the officials and to the rest of the people, "The work is great and widely spread, and we are separated on the wall, far from one another. ²⁰In the place where you hear the sound of the trumpet, rally to us there. Our God will fight for us."

²¹So we labored at the work, and half of them held the spears from the break of dawn until the stars came out. ²²I also said to the people at that time, "Let every man and his servant pass the night within Jerusalem, that they may be a guard for us by night and may labor by day." ²³So neither I nor my brothers nor my servants nor the men of the guard who followed me, none of us took off our clothes; each kept his weapon at his right hand.¹

Nehemiah Stops Oppression of the Poor

5 Now there arose a great outcry of the people and of their wives against their Jewish brothers. ²For there were those who said, "With our sons and our daughters, we are many. So let us get grain, that we may eat and keep alive." ³There were also those who said, "We are mortgaging our fields, our vineyards, and our houses to get grain because of the famine." ⁴And there were those who said, "We have borrowed money for the king's tax on our fields and our vineyards. ⁵Now our flesh is as the flesh of our brothers, our children are as their children. Yet we are forcing our sons and our daughters to be slaves, and some of our daughters have already been enslaved, but it is not in our power to help it, for other men have our fields and our vineyards."

⁶I was very angry when I heard their outcry and these words. ⁷I took counsel with myself, and I brought charges against the nobles and the officials. I said to them, "You are exacting interest, each from his brother." And I held a great assembly against them ⁸and said to them, "We, as far as we are able, have bought back our Jewish brothers who have been sold to the nations, but you even sell your brothers that they may be sold to us!" They were silent and could not find a word to say. ⁹So I said, "The thing that you are doing is not good. Ought you not to walk in the fear of our God to prevent the taunts of the nations our enemies? ¹⁰Moreover, I and my brothers and my servants are lending them money and grain. Let us abandon this exacting of interest. ¹¹Return to them this very day their fields, their vineyards, their olive orchards, and their houses, and the percentage of money, grain, wine, and oil that you have been exacting from them." ¹²Then they said, "We will restore these and require nothing from them. We will do as you say." And I called the priests and made them swear to do as they had promised. ¹³I also shook out the fold² of my garment and said, "So may God shake out every man from his house and from his labor who does not keep this promise. So may he be shaken out and emptied." And all the assembly said "Amen" and praised the Lord. And the people did as they had promised.

Nehemiah's Generosity

¹⁴Moreover, from the time that I was appointed to be their governor in the land of Judah, from the twentieth year to the thirty-second year of Artaxerxes the king, twelve years, neither I nor my brothers ate the food allowance of the governor. ¹⁵The former governors who were before me laid heavy burdens on the people and took from them for their

¹Probable reading; Hebrew *each his weapon the water* ²Hebrew *bosom*

daily ration[1] forty shekels[2] of silver. Even their servants lorded it over the people. But I did not do so, because of the fear of God. [16] I also persevered in the work on this wall, and we acquired no land, and all my servants were gathered there for the work. [17] Moreover, there were at my table 150 men, Jews and officials, besides those who came to us from the nations that were around us. [18] Now what was prepared at my expense[3] for each day was one ox and six choice sheep and birds, and every ten days all kinds of wine in abundance. Yet for all this I did not demand the food allowance of the governor, because the service was too heavy on this people. [19] Remember for my good, O my God, all that I have done for this people.

Conspiracy Against Nehemiah

6 Now when Sanballat and Tobiah and Geshem the Arab and the rest of our enemies heard that I had built the wall and that there was no breach left in it (although up to that time I had not set up the doors in the gates), [2] Sanballat and Geshem sent to me, saying, "Come and let us meet together at Hakkephirim in the plain of Ono." But they intended to do me harm. [3] And I sent messengers to them, saying, "I am doing a great work and I cannot come down. Why should the work stop while I leave it and come down to you?" [4] And they sent to me four times in this way, and I answered them in the same manner. [5] In the same way Sanballat for the fifth time sent his servant to me with an open letter in his hand. [6] In it was written, "It is reported among the nations, and Geshem[4] also says it, that you and the Jews intend to rebel; that is why you are building the wall. And according to these reports you wish to become their king. [7] And you have also set up prophets to proclaim concerning you in Jerusalem 'There is a king in Judah.' And now the king

---

[1] Compare Vulgate; Hebrew *took from them with food and wine afterward* [2] *A shekel* was about 2/5 ounce or 11 grams [3] Or *prepared for me* [4] Hebrew *Gashmu*

Know Yourself

verses to read
Nehemiah 5:19; 6:9

When you pray, does God give you strength? If not, then take a look at your prayers. All of God's responses are good responses, including "no." If God doesn't give you what you ask for, then he has a very good reason. You have to trust him so much that, when your prayers seem to go unanswered or the answer is a loud "no," you can look up, smile, and say, "Thanks for knowing what's best for me." After all, what do *you* know about the future? How can you predict the outcome of this or that desire of your heart? You can't.

But as a God Girl, one thing you can be sure of is that God's will is the best possible will for your life. And if he sees fit not to give you something that you really, really want, then it's for a really, really good reason. So instead of worrying and freaking out about not getting what you want, think about why God might not want you to have it or, better yet, why he does want you to have exactly what he has given you and nothing more.

God will make you strong as you trust him. And he will answer every prayer you'll ever pray when you trust his Word. Find out about prayer. Do your homework and learn God's promises on the subject. Prayer is your lifeline, your hand reaching out to the Father who protects you, so why wouldn't you want to know everything about it that you could? And all you need to know is found in the pages of his Word. So go after the wisdom and truth in Scripture and become a God Girl who prays.

will hear of these reports. So now come and let us take counsel together." [8]Then I sent to him, saying, "No such things as you say have been done, for you are inventing them out of your own mind." [9]For they all wanted to frighten us, thinking, "Their hands will drop from the work, and it will not be done." But now, O God,[1] strengthen my hands.

[10]Now when I went into the house of Shemaiah the son of Delaiah, son of Mehetabel, who was confined to his home, he said, "Let us meet together in the house of God, within the temple. Let us close the doors of the temple, for they are coming to kill you. They are coming to kill you by night." [11]But I said, "Should such a man as I run away? And what man such as I could go into the temple and live?[2] I will not go in." [12]And I understood and saw that God had not sent him, but he had pronounced the prophecy against me because Tobiah and Sanballat had hired him. [13]For this purpose he was hired, that I should be afraid and act in this way and sin, and so they could give me a bad name in order to taunt me. [14]Remember Tobiah and Sanballat, O my God, according to these things that they did, and also the prophetess Noadiah and the rest of the prophets who wanted to make me afraid.

The Wall Is Finished

[15]So the wall was finished on the twenty-fifth day of the month Elul, in fifty-two days. [16]And when all our enemies heard of it, all the nations around us were afraid and fell greatly in their own esteem, for they perceived that this work had been accomplished with the help of our God. [17]Moreover, in those days the nobles of Judah sent many letters to Tobiah, and Tobiah's letters came to them. [18]For many in Judah were bound by oath to him, because he was the son-in-law of Shecaniah the son of Arah: and his son Jehohanan had taken the daughter of Meshullam the son of Berechiah as his wife. [19]Also they spoke of his good deeds in my presence and reported my words to him. And Tobiah sent letters to make me afraid.

7 Now when the wall had been built and I had set up the doors, and the gatekeepers, the singers, and the Levites had been appointed, [2]I gave my brother Hanani and Hananiah the governor of the castle charge over Jerusalem, for he was a more faithful and God-fearing man than many. [3]And I said to them, "Let not the gates of Jerusalem be opened until the sun is hot. And while they are still standing guard, let them shut and bar the doors. Appoint guards from among the inhabitants of Jerusalem, some at their guard posts and some in front of their own homes." [4]The city was wide and large, but the people within it were few, and no houses had been rebuilt.

Lists of Returned Exiles

[5]Then my God put it into my heart to assemble the nobles and the officials and the people to be enrolled by genealogy. And I found the book of the genealogy of those who came up at the first, and I found written in it:

[6]These were the people of the province who came up out of the captivity of those exiles whom Nebuchadnezzar the king of Babylon had carried into exile. They returned to Jerusalem and Judah, each to his town. [7]They came with Zerubbabel, Jeshua, Nehemiah, Azariah, Raamiah, Nahamani, Mordecai, Bilshan, Mispereth, Bigvai, Nehum, Baanah.

The number of the men of the people of Israel: [8]the sons of Parosh, 2,172. [9]The sons of Shephatiah, 372. [10]The sons of Arah, 652. [11]The sons of Pahath-moab, namely the sons of Jeshua and Joab, 2,818. [12]The sons of Elam, 1,254. [13]The sons of Zattu, 845. [14]The sons of Zaccai, 760. [15]The sons of Binnui, 648. [16]The sons of Bebai, 628. [17]The sons of Azgad, 2,322. [18]The sons of Adonikam, 667. [19]The sons of Bigvai, 2,067. [20]The sons of Adin, 655. [21]The sons of Ater, namely of Hezekiah, 98. [22]The sons of Hashum, 328. [23]The sons of Bezai, 324. [24]The sons of Hariph, 112. [25]The sons of Gibeon, 95. [26]The men of Bethlehem and Netophah, 188. [27]The men of Anathoth, 128. [28]The men of Beth-azmaveth, 42. [29]The men of Kiriath-jearim, Chephirah, and Beeroth, 743. [30]The men of Ramah and Geba, 621. [31]The men of Michmas, 122. [32]The men of Bethel and Ai, 123. [33]The men of the other Nebo, 52. [34]The sons of the other Elam, 1,254. [35]The sons of Harim, 320. [36]The sons of Jericho, 345. [37]The sons

[1] Hebrew lacks O God   [2] Or would go into the temple to save his life

of Lod, Hadid, and Ono, 721. [38]The sons of Senaah, 3,930.

[39]The priests: the sons of Jedaiah, namely the house of Jeshua, 973. [40]The sons of Immer, 1,052. [41]The sons of Pashhur, 1,247. [42]The sons of Harim, 1,017.

[43]The Levites: the sons of Jeshua, namely of Kadmiel of the sons of Hodevah, 74. [44]The singers: the sons of Asaph, 148. [45]The gatekeepers: the sons of Shallum, the sons of Ater, the sons of Talmon, the sons of Akkub, the sons of Hatita, the sons of Shobai, 138.

[46]The temple servants: the sons of Ziha, the sons of Hasupha, the sons of Tabbaoth, [47]the sons of Keros, the sons of Sia, the sons of Padon, [48]the sons of Lebana, the sons of Hagaba, the sons of Shalmai, [49]the sons of Hanan, the sons of Giddel, the sons of Gahar, [50]the sons of Reaiah, the sons of Rezin, the sons of Nekoda, [51]the sons of Gazzam, the sons of Uzza, the sons of Paseah, [52]the sons of Besai, the sons of Meunim, the sons of Nephushesim, [53]the sons of Bakbuk, the sons of Hakupha, the sons of Harhur, [54]the sons of Bazlith, the sons of Mehida, the sons of Harsha, [55]the sons of Barkos, the sons of Sisera, the sons of Temah, [56]the sons of Neziah, the sons of Hatipha.

[57]The sons of Solomon's servants: the sons of Sotai, the sons of Sophereth, the sons of Perida, [58]the sons of Jaala, the sons of Darkon, the sons of Giddel, [59]the sons of Shephatiah, the sons of Hattil, the sons of Pochereth-hazzebaim, the sons of Amon.

[60]All the temple servants and the sons of Solomon's servants were 392.

[61]The following were those who came up from Tel-melah, Tel-harsha, Cherub, Addon, and Immer, but they could not prove their fathers' houses nor their descent, whether they belonged to Israel: [62]the sons of Delaiah, the sons of Tobiah, the sons of Nekoda, 642. [63]Also, of the priests: the sons of Hobaiah, the sons of Hakkoz, the sons of Barzillai (who had taken a wife of the daughters of Barzillai the Gileadite and was called by their name). [64]These sought their registration among those enrolled in the genealogies, but it was not found there, so they were excluded from the priesthood as unclean. [65]The governor told them that they were not to partake of the most holy food until a priest with Urim and Thummim should arise.

Totals of People and Gifts

[66]The whole assembly together was 42,360, [67]besides their male and female servants, of whom there were 7,337. And they had 245 singers, male and female [68]Their horses were 736, their mules 245,[1] [69]their camels 435, and their donkeys 6,720.

[70]Now some of the heads of fathers' houses gave to the work. The governor gave to the treasury 1,000 darics[2] of gold, 50 basins, 30 priests' garments and 500 minas[3] of silver.[4] [71]And some of the heads of fathers' houses gave into the treasury of the work 20,000 darics of gold and 2,200 minas of silver. [72]And what the rest of the people gave was 20,000 darics of gold, 2,000 minas of silver, and 67 priests' garments.

[73]So the priests, the Levites, the gatekeepers, the singers, some of the people, the temple servants, and all Israel, lived in their towns.

And when the seventh month had come, the people of Israel were in their towns.

Ezra Reads the Law

8 And all the people gathered as one man into the square before the Water Gate. And they told Ezra the scribe to bring the Book of the Law of Moses that the LORD had commanded Israel. [2]So Ezra the priest brought the Law before the assembly, both men and women and all who could understand what they heard, on the first day of the seventh month. [3]And he read from it facing the square before the Water Gate from early morning until midday, in the presence of the men and the women and those who could understand. And the ears of all the people were attentive to the Book of the Law. [4]And Ezra the scribe stood on a wooden platform that they had made for the purpose. And beside him stood Mattithiah, Shema, Anaiah, Uriah, Hilkiah, and Maaseiah on his right hand, and Pedaiah, Mishael, Malchijah, Hashum, Hashbaddanah, Zechariah, and Meshullam on his left hand. [5]And Ezra opened the book in the sight of all the people, for he was above all the people, and as he opened it all the people stood. [6]And Ezra blessed the LORD, the great God, and all the people answered, "Amen, Amen," lifting up their hands. And they bowed their

---

[1] Compare Ezra 2:66 and the margins of some Hebrew manuscripts; Hebrew lacks *Their horses . . . 245* [2] A *daric* was a coin weighing about 1/4 ounce or 8.5 grams [3] A *mina* was about 1 1/4 pounds or 0.6 kilogram [4] Probable reading; Hebrew lacks *minas of silver*

heads and worshiped the LORD with their faces to the ground. [7] Also Jeshua, Bani, Sherebiah, Jamin, Akkub, Shabbethai, Hodiah, Maaseiah, Kelita, Azariah, Jozabad, Hanan, Pelaiah, the Levites,[1] helped the people to understand the Law, while the people remained in their places. [8] They read from the book, from the Law of God, clearly,[2] and they gave the sense, so that the people understood the reading.

This Day Is Holy

[9] And Nehemiah, who was the governor, and Ezra the priest and scribe, and the Levites who taught the people said to all the people, "This day is holy to the LORD your God; do not mourn or weep." For all the people wept as they heard the words of the Law. [10] Then he said to them, "Go your way. Eat the fat and drink sweet wine and send portions to anyone who has nothing ready, for this day is holy to our Lord. And do not be grieved, for the joy of the LORD is your strength." [11] So the Levites calmed all the people, saying, "Be quiet, for this day is holy; do not be grieved." [12] And all the people went their way to eat and drink and to send portions and to make great rejoicing, because they had understood the words that were declared to them.

Feast of Booths Celebrated

[13] On the second day the heads of fathers' houses of all the people, with the priests and the Levites, came together to Ezra the scribe in order to study the words of the Law. [14] And they found it written in the Law that the LORD had commanded by Moses that the people of Israel should dwell in booths[3] during the feast of the seventh month, [15] and that they should proclaim it and publish it in all their towns and in Jerusalem, "Go out to the hills and bring branches of olive, wild olive, myrtle, palm, and other leafy trees to make booths, as it is written." [16] So the people went out and brought them and made booths for themselves, each on his roof, and in their courts and in the courts of the house of God, and in the square at the Water Gate and in the square at the Gate of Ephraim. [17] And all the assembly of those who had returned from the captivity made booths and lived in the booths, for from the days of Jeshua the son of Nun to that day the

A Prayer for...
PURIFICATION

Lord Jesus, I sin. Please help me to never stop feeling bad because of it, never be content with myself, never think I have reached the point of perfection. Kill my envy, control my tongue, trample down my self. Give me grace to be holy, kind, gentle, pure, and peaceable; to live for you and not for myself; to copy your words and actions; to be transformed into your likeness; to be consecrated wholly to you; to live entirely to your glory.

Deliver me by your Holy Spirit from my attachment to unclean things, from wrong relationships, from the control of my evil passions, from the sugar of sin as well as its destruction, so that with deep repentance and earnest heart-searching I can come to you, throw myself on you, trust in you, cry to you, and be delivered by you.

O God, the Eternal All, help me to know that all things are shadows but you are substance; all things are quicksand but you are a mountain; all things are shifting but you are an anchor; all things are ignorance but you are wisdom.

If my life is to be a vessel tested in the burning heat, so be it, but sit at the furnace door and watch the ore so that nothing will be lost. If I sin willfully, grievously, and am in torment, please in your kindness take away my mourning and give me music, take away my misery and clothe me with beauty, hush my sighs and fill my heart with song, and then give me summer weather as your child.

Amen.

people of Israel had not done so. And there was very great rejoicing. [18] And day by day, from the first day to the last day, he read from the Book of the Law of God. They kept

---

[1] Vulgate; Hebrew *and the Levites*   [2] Or *with interpretation, or paragraph by paragraph*   [3] Or *temporary shelters*

the feast seven days, and on the eighth day there was a solemn assembly, according to the rule.

The People of Israel Confess Their Sin

9 Now on the twenty-fourth day of this month the people of Israel were assembled with fasting and in sackcloth, and with earth on their heads. [2] And the Israelites[1] separated themselves from all foreigners and stood and confessed their sins and the iniquities of their fathers. [3] And they stood up in their place and read from the Book of the Law of the LORD their God for a quarter of the day; for another quarter of it they made confession and worshiped the LORD their God. [4] On the stairs of the Levites stood Jeshua, Bani, Kadmiel, Shebaniah, Bunni, Sherebiah, Bani, and Chenani; and they cried with a loud voice to the LORD their God. [5] Then the Levites, Jeshua, Kadmiel, Bani, Hashabneiah, Sherebiah, Hodiah, Shebaniah, and Pethahiah, said, "Stand up and bless the LORD your God from everlasting to everlasting. Blessed be your glorious name, which is exalted above all blessing and praise.

[6] [2] "You are the LORD, you alone. You have made heaven, the heaven of heavens, with all their host, the earth and all that is on it, the seas and all that is in them; and you preserve all of them; and the host of heaven worships you. [7] You are the LORD, the God who chose Abram and brought him out of Ur of the Chaldeans and gave him the name Abraham. [8] You found his heart faithful before you, and made with him the covenant to give to his offspring the land of the Canaanite, the Hittite, the Amorite, the Perizzite, the Jebusite, and the Girgashite. And you have kept your promise, for you are righteous.

[9] "And you saw the affliction of our fathers in Egypt and heard their cry at the Red Sea, [10] and performed signs and wonders against Pharaoh and all his servants and all the people of his land, for you knew that they acted arrogantly against our fathers. And you made a name for yourself, as it is to this day. [11] And you divided the sea before them, so that they went through the midst of the sea on dry land, and you cast their pursuers into the depths, as a stone into mighty waters. [12] By a pillar of cloud you led them in the day, and by a pillar of fire in the night to light for them the way in which they should go. [13] You came down on Mount Sinai and spoke with them from heaven and gave them right rules and true laws, good statutes and commandments, [14] and you made known to them your holy Sabbath and commanded them commandments and statutes and a law by Moses your servant. [15] You gave them bread from heaven for their hunger and brought water for them out of the rock for their thirst, and you told them to go in to possess the land that you had sworn to give them.

[16] "But they and our fathers acted presumptuously and stiffened their neck and did not obey your commandments. [17] They refused to obey and were not mindful of the wonders that you performed among them, but they stiffened their neck and appointed a leader to return to their slavery in Egypt. But you are a God ready to forgive, gracious and merciful, slow to anger and abounding in steadfast love, and did not forsake them. [18] Even when they had made for themselves a golden[3] calf and said, 'This is your God who brought you up out of Egypt,' and had committed great blasphemies, [19] you in your great mercies did not forsake them in the wilderness. The pillar of cloud to lead them in the way did not depart from them by day, nor the pillar of fire by night to light for them the way by which they should go. [20] You gave your good Spirit to instruct them and did not withhold your manna from their mouth and gave them water for their thirst. [21] Forty years you sustained them in the wilderness, and they lacked nothing. Their clothes did not wear out and their feet did not swell.

[22] "And you gave them kingdoms and peoples and allotted to them every corner. So they took possession of the land of Sihon king of Heshbon and the land of Og king of Bashan. [23] You multiplied their children as the stars of heaven, and you brought them into the land that you had told their fathers to enter and possess. [24] So the descendants went in and possessed the land, and you subdued before them the inhabitants of the land, the Canaanites, and gave them into their hand, with their kings and the peoples of the land, that they might do with them as they would. [25] And they captured fortified cities and a rich land, and took possession of houses full

---

[1] Hebrew the offspring of Israel [2] Septuagint adds And Ezra said [3] Hebrew metal

of all good things, cisterns already hewn, vineyards, olive orchards and fruit trees in abundance. So they ate and were filled and became fat and delighted themselves in your great goodness.

²⁶"Nevertheless, they were disobedient and rebelled against you and cast your law behind their back and killed your prophets, who had warned them in order to turn them back to you, and they committed great blasphemies. ²⁷Therefore you gave them into the hand of their enemies, who made them suffer. And in the time of their suffering they cried out to you and you heard them from heaven, and according to your great mercies you gave them saviors who saved them from the hand of their enemies. ²⁸But after they had rest they did evil again before you, and you abandoned them to the hand of their enemies, so that they had dominion over them. Yet when they turned and cried to you, you heard from heaven, and many times you delivered them according to your mercies. ²⁹And you warned them in order to turn them back to your law. Yet they acted presumptuously and did not obey your commandments, but sinned against your rules, which if a person does them, he shall live by them, and they turned a stubborn shoulder and stiffened their neck and would not obey. ³⁰Many years you bore with them and warned them by your Spirit through your prophets. Yet they would not give ear. Therefore you gave them into the hand of the peoples of the lands. ³¹Nevertheless, in your great mercies you did not make an end of them or forsake them, for you are a gracious and merciful God.

³²"Now, therefore, our God, the great, the mighty, and the awesome God, who keeps covenant and steadfast love, let not all the hardship seem little to you that has come upon us, upon our kings, our princes, our priests, our prophets, our fathers, and all your people, since the time of the kings of Assyria until this day. ³³Yet you have been righteous in all that has come upon us, for you have dealt faithfully and we have acted wickedly. ³⁴Our kings, our princes, our priests, and our fathers have not kept your law or paid attention to your commandments and your warnings that you gave them. ³⁵Even in their own kingdom, and amid your great goodness that you gave

them, and in the large and rich land that you set before them, they did not serve you or turn from their wicked works. ³⁶Behold, we are slaves this day; in the land that you gave to our fathers to enjoy its fruit and its good gifts, behold, we are slaves. ³⁷And its rich yield goes to the kings whom you have set over us because of our sins. They rule over our bodies and over our livestock as they please, and we are in great distress.

³⁸¹"Because of all this we make a firm covenant in writing; on the sealed document are the names of² our princes, our Levites, and our priests.

The People Who Sealed the Covenant

10 ³"On the seals are the names of⁴ Nehemiah the governor, the son of Hacaliah, Zedekiah, ²Seraiah, Azariah, Jeremiah, ³Pashhur, Amariah, Malchijah, ⁴Hattush, Shebaniah, Malluch, ⁵Harim, Meremoth, Obadiah, ⁶Daniel, Ginnethon, Baruch, ⁷Meshullam, Abijah, Mijamin, ⁸Maaziah, Bilgai, Shemaiah; these are the priests. ⁹And the Levites: Jeshua the son of Azaniah, Binnui of the sons of Henadad, Kadmiel; ¹⁰and their brothers, Shebaniah, Hodiah, Kelita, Pelaiah, Hanan, ¹¹Mica, Rehob, Hashabiah, ¹²Zaccur, Sherebiah, Shebaniah, ¹³Hodiah, Bani, Beninu. ¹⁴The chiefs of the people: Parosh, Pahath-moab, Elam, Zattu, Bani, ¹⁵Bunni, Azgad, Bebai, ¹⁶Adonijah, Bigvai, Adin, ¹⁷Ater, Hezekiah, Azzur, ¹⁸Hodiah, Hashum, Bezai, ¹⁹Hariph, Anathoth, Nebai, ²⁰Magpiash, Meshullam, Hezir, ²¹Meshezabel, Zadok, Jaddua, ²²Pelatiah, Hanan, Anaiah, ²³Hoshea, Hananiah, Hasshub, ²⁴Hallohesh, Pilha, Shobek, ²⁵Rehum, Hashabnah, Maaseiah, ²⁶Ahiah, Hanan, Anan, ²⁷Malluch, Harim, Baanah.

The Obligations of the Covenant

²⁸"The rest of the people, the priests, the Levites, the gatekeepers, the singers, the temple servants, and all who have separated themselves from the peoples of the lands to the Law of God, their wives, their sons, their daughters, all who have knowledge and understanding, ²⁹join with their brothers, their nobles, and enter into a curse and an oath to walk in God's Law that was given by Moses the servant of God, and to observe and do all the commandments of the LORD our Lord and his rules and his statutes. ³⁰We will not give our daughters

¹Ch 10:1 in Hebrew ²Hebrew lacks *the names of* ³Ch 10:2 in Hebrew ⁴Hebrew lacks *the names of*

to the peoples of the land or take their daughters for our sons. [31] And if the peoples of the land bring in goods or any grain on the Sabbath day to sell, we will not buy from them on the Sabbath or on a holy day. And we will forego the crops of the seventh year and the exaction of every debt.

[32] "We also take on ourselves the obligation to give yearly a third part of a shekel[1] for the service of the house of our God: [33] for the showbread, the regular grain offering, the regular burnt offering, the Sabbaths, the new moons, the appointed feasts, the holy things, and the sin offerings to make atonement for Israel, and for all the work of the house of our God. [34] We, the priests, the Levites, and the people, have likewise cast lots for the wood offering, to bring it into the house of our God, according to our fathers' houses, at times appointed, year by year, to burn on the altar of the LORD our God, as it is written in the Law. [35] We obligate ourselves to bring the firstfruits of our ground and the firstfruits of all fruit of every tree, year by year, to the house of the LORD; [36] also to bring to the house of our God, to the priests who minister in the house of our God, the firstborn of our sons and of our cattle, as it is written in the Law, and the firstborn of our herds and of our flocks; [37] and to bring the first of our dough, and our contributions, the fruit of every tree, the wine and the oil, to the priests, to the chambers of the house of our God; and to bring to the Levites the tithes from our ground, for it is the Levites who collect the tithes in all our towns where we labor. [38] And the priest, the son of Aaron, shall be with the Levites when the Levites receive the tithes. And the Levites shall bring up the tithe of the tithes to the house of our God, to the chambers of the storehouse. [39] For the people of Israel and the sons of Levi shall bring the contribution of grain, wine, and oil to the chambers, where the vessels of the sanctuary are, as well as the priests who minister, and the gatekeepers and the singers. We will not neglect the house of our God."

The Leaders in Jerusalem

11 Now the leaders of the people lived in Jerusalem. And the rest of the people cast lots to bring one out of ten to live in Jerusalem the holy city, while nine out of ten[2] remained in the other towns. [2] And the people blessed all the men wh[...] willingly offered to live in Jerusalem.

[3] These are the chiefs of the provinc[...] who lived in Jerusalem; but in the towns of Judah everyone lived on his property i[n] their towns: Israel, the priests, the Levites the temple servants, and the descendants of Solomon's servants. [4] And in Jerusalem lived certain of the sons of Judah and o[f] the sons of Benjamin. Of the sons of Judah: Athaiah the son of Uzziah, son of Zechariah son of Amariah, son of Shephatiah, son of Mahalalel, of the sons of Perez; [5] and Maaseiah the son of Baruch, son of Colhozeh, son of Hazaiah, son of Adaiah, son of Joiarib, son of Zechariah, son of the Shilonite. [6] All the sons of Perez who lived in Jerusalem were 468 valiant men.

[7] And these are the sons of Benjamin: Sallu the son of Meshullam, son of Joed son of Pedaiah, son of Kolaiah, son o[f] Maaseiah, son of Ithiel, son of Jeshaiah [8] and his brothers, men of valor, 928.[3] [9] Joe[l] the son of Zichri was their overseer; and Judah the son of Hassenuah was second over the city.

[10] Of the priests: Jedaiah the son of Joiarib Jachin, [11] Seraiah the son of Hilkiah, son o[f] Meshullam, son of Zadok, son of Meraioth son of Ahitub, ruler of the house of God [12] and their brothers who did the work of the house, 822; and Adaiah the son o[f] Jeroham, son of Pelaliah, son of Amzi, son o[f] Zechariah, son of Pashhur, son of Malchijah, [13] and his brothers, heads of fathers' houses 242; and Amashsai, the son of Azarel, son o[f] Ahzai, son of Meshillemoth, son of Immer [14] and their brothers, mighty men of valor 128; their overseer was Zabdiel the son o[f] Haggedolim.

[15] And of the Levites: Shemaiah the son o[f] Hasshub, son of Azrikam, son of Hashabiah, son of Bunni; [16] and Shabbethai and Jozabad, of the chiefs of the Levites, who were over the outside work of the house of God; [17] and Mattaniah the son of Mica, son of Zabdi, son of Asaph, who was the leader of the praise,[4] who gave thanks, and Bakbukiah, the second among his brothers; and Abda the son of Shammua, son o[f] Galal, son of Jeduthun. [18] All the Levites in the holy city were 284.

---

[1] A *shekel* was about 2/5 ounce or 11 grams [2] Hebrew *nine hands* [3] Compare Septuagint; Hebrew *Jeshaiah, and after him Gabbai, Sallai, 928* [4] Compare Septuagint, Vulgate; Hebrew *beginning*

¹⁹ The gatekeepers, Akkub, Talmon and their brothers, who kept watch at the gates, were 172. ²⁰ And the rest of Israel, and of the priests and the Levites, were in all the towns of Judah, every one in his inheritance. ²¹ But the temple servants lived on Ophel; and Ziha and Gishpa were over the temple servants.

²² The overseer of the Levites in Jerusalem was Uzzi the son of Bani, son of Hashabiah, son of Mattaniah, son of Mica, of the sons of Asaph, the singers, over the work of the house of God. ²³ For there was a command from the king concerning them, and a fixed provision for the singers, as every day required. ²⁴ And Pethahiah the son of Meshezabel, of the sons of Zerah the son of Judah, was at the king's side¹ in all matters concerning the people.

Villages Outside Jerusalem

²⁵ And as for the villages, with their fields, some of the people of Judah lived in Kiriath-arba and its villages, and in Dibon and its villages, and in Jekabzeel and its villages, ²⁶ and in Jeshua and in Moladah and Beth-pelet, ²⁷ in Hazar-shual, in Beersheba and its villages, ²⁸ in Ziklag, in Meconah and its villages, ²⁹ in En-rimmon, in Zorah, in Jarmuth, ³⁰ Zanoah, Adullam, and their villages, Lachish and its fields, and Azekah and its villages. So they encamped from Beersheba to the Valley of Hinnom. ³¹ The people of Benjamin also lived from Geba onward, at Michmash, Aija, Bethel and its villages, ³² Anathoth, Nob, Ananiah, ³³ Hazor, Ramah, Gittaim, ³⁴ Hadid, Zeboim, Neballat, ³⁵ Lod, and Ono, the valley of craftsmen. ³⁶ And certain divisions of the Levites in Judah were assigned to Benjamin.

Priests and Levites

12 These are the priests and the Levites who came up with Zerubbabel the son of Shealtiel, and Jeshua: Seraiah, Jeremiah, Ezra, ² Amariah, Malluch, Hattush, ³ Shecaniah, Rehum, Meremoth, ⁴ Iddo, Ginnethoi, Abijah, ⁵ Mijamin, Maadiah, Bilgah, ⁶ Shemaiah, Joiarib, Jedaiah, ⁷ Sallu, Amok, Hilkiah, Jedaiah. These were the chiefs of the priests and of their brothers in the days of Jeshua.

⁸ And the Levites: Jeshua, Binnui, Kadmiel, Sherebiah, Judah, and Mattaniah, who with his brothers was in charge of the songs of thanksgiving. ⁹ And Bakbukiah and Unni and their brothers stood opposite them in the service. ¹⁰ And Jeshua was the father of Joiakim, Joiakim the father of Eliashib, Eliashib the father of Joiada, ¹¹ Joiada the father of Jonathan, and Jonathan the father of Jaddua.

¹² And in the days of Joiakim were priests, heads of fathers' houses: of Seraiah, Meraiah; of Jeremiah, Hananiah; ¹³ of Ezra, Meshullam; of Amariah, Jehohanan; ¹⁴ of Malluchi, Jonathan; of Shebaniah, Joseph; ¹⁵ of Harim, Adna; of Meraioth, Helkai; ¹⁶ of Iddo, Zechariah; of Ginnethon, Meshullam; ¹⁷ of Abijah, Zichri; of Miniamin, of Moadiah, Piltai; ¹⁸ of Bilgah, Shammua; of Shemaiah, Jehonathan; ¹⁹ of Joiarib, Mattenai; of Jedaiah, Uzzi; ²⁰ of Sallai, Kallai; of Amok, Eber; ²¹ of Hilkiah, Hashabiah; of Jedaiah, Nethanel.

²² In the days of Eliashib, Joiada, Johanan, and Jaddua, the Levites were recorded as heads of fathers' houses; so too were the priests in the reign of Darius the Persian. ²³ As for the sons of Levi, their heads of fathers' houses were written in the Book of the Chronicles until the days of Johanan the son of Eliashib. ²⁴ And the chiefs of the Levites: Hashabiah, Sherebiah, and Jeshua the son of Kadmiel, with their brothers who stood opposite them, to praise and to give thanks, according to the commandment of David the man of God, watch by watch. ²⁵ Mattaniah, Bakbukiah, Obadiah, Meshullam, Talmon, and Akkub were gatekeepers standing guard at the storehouses of the gates. ²⁶ These were in the days of Joiakim the son of Jeshua son of Jozadak, and in the days of Nehemiah the governor and of Ezra, the priest and scribe.

Dedication of the Wall

²⁷ And at the dedication of the wall of Jerusalem they sought the Levites in all their places, to bring them to Jerusalem to celebrate the dedication with gladness, with thanksgivings and with singing, with cymbals, harps, and lyres. ²⁸ And the sons of the singers gathered together from the district surrounding Jerusalem and from the villages of the Netophathites; ²⁹ also from Beth-gilgal and from the region of Geba and Azmaveth, for the singers had built for themselves villages around Jerusalem. ³⁰ And the priests and the Levites purified

themselves, and they purified the people and the gates and the wall.

31 Then I brought the leaders of Judah up onto the wall and appointed two great choirs that gave thanks. One went to the south on the wall to the Dung Gate. **32** And after them went Hoshaiah and half of the leaders of Judah, **33** and Azariah, Ezra, Meshullam, **34** Judah, Benjamin, Shemaiah, and Jeremiah, **35** and certain of the priests' sons with trumpets: Zechariah the son of Jonathan, son of Shemaiah, son of Mattaniah, son of Micaiah, son of Zaccur, son of Asaph; **36** and his relatives, Shemaiah, Azarel, Milalai, Gilalai, Maai, Nethanel, Judah, and Hanani, with the musical instruments of David the man of God. And Ezra the scribe went before them. **37** At the Fountain Gate they went up straight before them by the stairs of the city of David, at the ascent of the wall, above the house of David, to the Water Gate on the east.

38 The other choir of those who gave thanks went to the north, and I followed them with half of the people, on the wall, above the Tower of the Ovens, to the Broad Wall, **39** and above the Gate of Ephraim, and by the Gate of Yeshanah,[1] and by the Fish Gate and the Tower of Hananel and the Tower of the Hundred, to the Sheep Gate; and they came to a halt at the Gate of the Guard. **40** So both choirs of those who gave thanks stood in the house of God, and I and half of the officials with me; **41** and the priests Eliakim, Maaseiah, Miniamin, Micaiah, Elioenai, Zechariah, and Hananiah, with trumpets; **42** and Maaseiah, Shemaiah, Eleazar, Uzzi, Jehohanan, Malchijah, Elam, and Ezer. And the singers sang with Jezrahiah as their leader. **43** And they offered great sacrifices that day and rejoiced, for God had made them rejoice with great joy; the women and children also rejoiced. And the joy of Jerusalem was heard far away.

Service at the Temple

44 On that day men were appointed over the storerooms, the contributions, the first-fruits, and the tithes, to gather into them the portions required by the Law for the priests and for the Levites according to the fields of the towns, for Judah rejoiced over the priests and the Levites who ministered. **45** And they performed the service of their God and the service of purification, as did the singers and the gatekeepers, according to the command of David and his son Solomon. **46** For long ago in the days of David and Asaph there were directors of the singers, and there were songs[2] of praise and thanksgiving to God. **47** And all Israel in the days of Zerubbabel and in the days of Nehemiah gave the daily portions for the singers and the gatekeepers; and they set apart that which was for the Levites; and the Levites set apart that which was for the sons of Aaron.

Nehemiah's Final Reforms

13 On that day they read from the Book of Moses in the hearing of the people. And in it was found written that no Ammonite or Moabite should ever enter the assembly of God, **2** for they did not meet the people of Israel with bread and water, but hired Balaam against them to curse them—yet our God turned the curse into a blessing. **3** As soon as the people heard the law, they separated from Israel all those of foreign descent.

4 Now before this, Eliashib the priest, who was appointed over the chambers of the house of our God, and who was related to Tobiah, **5** prepared for Tobiah a large chamber where they had previously put the grain offering, the frankincense, the vessels, and the tithes of grain, wine, and oil, which were given by commandment to the Levites, singers, and gatekeepers, and the contributions for the priests. **6** While this was taking place, I was not in Jerusalem, for in the thirty-second year of Artaxerxes king of Babylon I went to the king. And after some time I asked leave of the king **7** and came to Jerusalem, and I then discovered the evil that Eliashib had done for Tobiah, preparing for him a chamber in the courts of the house of God. **8** And I was very angry, and I threw all the household furniture of Tobiah out of the chamber. **9** Then I gave orders, and they cleansed the chambers, and I brought back there the vessels of the house of God, with the grain offering and the frankincense.

10 I also found out that the portions of the Levites had not been given to them, so that the Levites and the singers, who did the work, had fled each to his field. **11** So I confronted the officials and said,

[1] Or of the old city [2] Or leaders

'Why is the house of God forsaken?" And I gathered them together and set them in their stations. [12] Then all Judah brought the tithe of the grain, wine, and oil into the storehouses. [13] And I appointed as treasurers over the storehouses Shelemiah the priest, Zadok the scribe, and Pedaiah of the Levites, and as their assistant Hanan the son of Zaccur, son of Mattaniah, for they were considered reliable, and their duty was to distribute to their brothers. [14] Remember me, O my God, concerning this, and do not wipe out my good deeds that I have done for the house of my God and for his service.

[15] In those days I saw in Judah people treading winepresses on the Sabbath, and bringing in heaps of grain and loading them on donkeys, and also wine, grapes, figs, and all kinds of loads, which they brought into Jerusalem on the Sabbath day. And I warned them on the day when they sold food. [16] Tyrians also, who lived in the city, brought in fish and all kinds of goods and sold them on the Sabbath to the people of Judah, in Jerusalem itself! [17] Then I confronted the nobles of Judah and said to them, "What is this evil thing that you are doing, profaning the Sabbath day? [18] Did not your fathers act in this way, and did not our God bring all this disaster[1] on us and on this city? Now you are bringing more wrath on Israel by profaning the Sabbath."

[19] As soon as it began to grow dark at the gates of Jerusalem before the Sabbath, I commanded that the doors should be shut and gave orders that they should not be opened until after the Sabbath. And I stationed some of my servants at the gates, that no load might be brought in on the Sabbath day. [20] Then the merchants and sellers of all kinds of wares lodged outside Jerusalem once or twice. [21] But I warned them and said to them, "Why do you lodge outside the wall? If you do so again, I will lay hands on you." From that time on they did not come on the Sabbath. [22] Then I commanded the Levites that they should purify themselves and come and guard the gates, to keep the Sabbath day holy. Remember this also in my favor, O my God, and spare me according to the greatness of your steadfast love.

[23] In those days also I saw the Jews who had married women of Ashdod, Ammon, and Moab. [24] And half of their children spoke the language of Ashdod, and they could not speak the language of Judah, but only the language of each people. [25] And I confronted them and cursed them and beat some of them and pulled out their hair. And I made them take an oath in the name of God, saying, "You shall not give your daughters to their sons, or take their daughters for your sons or for yourselves. [26] Did not Solomon king of Israel sin on account of such women? Among the many nations there was no king like him, and he was beloved by his God, and God made him king over all Israel. Nevertheless, foreign women made even him to sin. [27] Shall we then listen to you and do all this great evil and act treacherously against our God by marrying foreign women?"

[28] And one of the sons of Jehoiada, the son of Eliashib the high priest, was the son-in-law of Sanballat the Horonite. Therefore I chased him from me. [29] Remember them, O my God, because they have desecrated the priesthood and the covenant of the priesthood and the Levites.

[30] Thus I cleansed them from everything foreign, and I established the duties of the priests and Levites, each in his work; [31] and I provided for the wood offering at appointed times, and for the firstfruits.

Remember me, O my God, for good.

---

[1] The Hebrew word can mean *evil*, *harm*, or *disaster*, depending on the context

INTRODUCTION TO
Esther

uthor: Unknown
ime: Sometime after 465 B.C.
lace: Probably Persia
Vritten to: Unknown

the gist

sther is the story of a girl
rho became queen and how
od used her rise to such a
osition to save his people, the
raelites, from destruction.
sther is a reminder that God
s in control no matter what
olitical figure you might think
s holding all the power.

things to look for

How Esther became queen
(see Est. 2:1–18)

How Haman plotted to kill
the Jews (see Est. 3:1–4:3)

How Esther saved her
people (see Est. 4:4–9:19)

Seize the Opportunity

> "For if you keep silent at this time, relief and deliverance will rise for the Jews from another place, but you and your father's house will perish. And who knows whether you have not come to the kingdom for such a time as this?"
>
> Esther 4:14

A lot of stuff in the Bible can seem contradictory, but just because you can't conceive of something, that doesn't make it impossible. God can allow two opposites to both exist without contradicting each other. Think about the fact that God is completely sovereign over your life and all that happens in the universe, and yet at the same time he has made every human responsible for his or her actions (see Luke 22:22, for example). It's a paradox: it is hard to understand how both of these go together, but the Bible tells us that they do, and so we gladly trust the Lord at this point.

In the book of Esther you can see this paradox at work. Esther and her cousin, Mordecai, made decisions and took actions that affected an entire generation of Israelites, but you could also say that God had planned for them to do just that (see Est. 4:14). As you walk through life making real decisions and yet knowing that God has planned everything, rest in his unfailing care for you. Trust him, because in the gospel you are totally forgiven, so that every good thing and every hard thing that comes into your life can only be for your good.

God wants to use you to change a generation, and so he is inviting you to surrender all that you are to him. His purpose for you is clear, but what matters most is your daily worship and pursuit of holiness, not your perceived destiny. As you go after God every day, God's hand will be on your life, no matter what outward appearances may seem to indicate.

Faith knows there's more to life than meets the eye. The human mind can't easily conceive of human responsibility and divine sovereignty coexisting, but this is what Scripture teaches. Some things you have to believe without fully understanding. As a God Girl you have to know that what God wants to come to pass will come to pass, and if God has promised to protect his people, he's going to do it. As you read the book of Esther, look at how God saves his people and how he uses this young girl to do it.

Must-Know Facts, Terms, and Verses

☩ God is never mentioned in the book of Esther, nor is prayer.

☩ In Esther 3:8–11, King Xerxes signed a decree that all the Jews in the kingdom should be executed.

∾ Sovereignty ∾

This word describes God's supreme power and authority over all things (1 Tim. 6:15–16). He directs all things to carry out his good purposes for his people (Rom. 8:28–29).

And when Haman saw that Mordecai did not bow down or pay homage to him, Haman was filled with fury. But he disdained to lay hands on Mordecai alone. So, as they had made known to him the people of Mordecai, Haman sought to destroy all the Jews, the people of Mordecai, throughout the whole kingdom of Ahasuerus. *Esther 3:5–6*

"For if you keep silent at this time, relief and deliverance will rise for the Jews from another place, but you and your father's house will perish. And who knows whether you have not come to the kingdom for such a time as this?" *Esther 4:14*

"Go, gather all the Jews to be found in Susa, and hold a fast on my behalf, and do not eat or drink for three days, night or day. I and my young women will also fast as you do. Then I will go to the king, though it is against the law, and if I perish, I perish." *Esther 4:16*

Esther

The King's Banquets

1 Now in the days of Ahasuerus, the Ahasuerus who reigned from India to Ethiopia over 127 provinces, ²in those days when King Ahasuerus sat on his royal throne in Susa, the citadel, ³in the third year of his reign he gave a feast for all his officials and servants. The army of Persia and Media and the nobles and governors of the provinces were before him, ⁴while he showed the riches of his royal glory and the splendor and pomp of his greatness for many days, 180 days. ⁵And when these days were completed, the king gave for all the people present in Susa the citadel, both great and small, a feast lasting for seven days in the court of the garden of the king's palace. ⁶There were white cotton curtains and violet hangings fastened with cords of fine linen and purple to silver rods¹ and marble pillars, and also couches of gold and silver on a mosaic pavement of porphyry, marble, mother-of-pearl and precious stones. ⁷Drinks were served in golden vessels, vessels of different kinds, and the royal wine was lavished according to the bounty of the king. ⁸And drinking was according to this edict: "There is no compulsion." For the king had given orders to all the staff of his palace to do as each man desired. ⁹Queen Vashti also gave a feast for the women in the palace that belonged to King Ahasuerus.

Queen Vashti's Refusal

¹⁰On the seventh day, when the heart of the king was merry with wine, he commanded Mehuman, Biztha, Harbona, Bigtha and Abagtha, Zethar and Carkas, the seven eunuchs who served in the presence of King Ahasuerus, ¹¹to bring Queen Vashti before the king with her royal crown,² in order to show the peoples and the princes her beauty, for she was lovely to look at. ¹²But Queen Vashti refused to come at the king's command delivered by the eunuchs. At this the king became enraged, and his anger burned within him.

¹³Then the king said to the wise men who knew the times (for this was the king's procedure toward all who were versed in law and judgment, ¹⁴the men next to him being Carshena, Shethar, Admatha, Tarshish, Meres, Marsena, and Memucan, the seven princes of Persia and Media, who saw the king's face, and sat first in the kingdom): ¹⁵"According to the law, what is to be done to Queen Vashti, because she has not performed the command of King Ahasuerus delivered by the eunuchs?" ¹⁶Then Memucan said in the presence of the king and the officials, "Not only against the king has Queen Vashti done wrong, but also against all the officials and all the peoples who are in all the provinces of King Ahasuerus. ¹⁷For the queen's behavior will be made known to all women, causing them to look at their husbands with contempt, since they will say, 'King Ahasuerus commanded Queen Vashti to be brought before him, and she did not come.' ¹⁸This very day the noble women of Persia and Media who have heard of the queen's behavior will say the same to all the king's officials, and there will be contempt and wrath in plenty. ¹⁹If it please the king, let a royal order go out from him, and let it be written among the laws of the Persians and the Medes so that it may not be repealed, that Vashti is never again to come before King Ahasuerus. And let the king give her royal position to another who is better than she. ²⁰So when the decree made by the king is proclaimed throughout all his kingdom, for it is vast, all women will give honor to their husbands, high and low alike." ²¹This advice pleased the king and the princes, and the king did as Memucan proposed. ²²He sent letters to all

¹Or rings ²Or headdress

the royal provinces, to every province in its own script and to every people in its own language, that every man be master in his own household and speak according to the language of his people.

Esther Chosen Queen

2 After these things, when the anger of King Ahasuerus had abated, he remembered Vashti and what she had done and what had been decreed against her. ²Then the king's young men who attended him said, "Let beautiful young virgins be sought out for the king. ³And let the king appoint officers in all the provinces of his kingdom to gather all the beautiful young virgins to the harem in Susa the citadel, under custody of Hegai, the king's eunuch, who is in charge of the women. Let their cosmetics be given them. ⁴And let the young woman who pleases the king be queen instead of Vashti." This pleased the king, and he did so.

⁵Now there was a Jew in Susa the citadel whose name was Mordecai, the son of Jair, son of Shimei, son of Kish, a Benjaminite, ⁶who had been carried away from Jerusalem among the captives carried away with Jeconiah king of Judah, whom Nebuchadnezzar king of Babylon had carried away. ⁷He was bringing up Hadassah, that is Esther, the daughter of his uncle, for she had neither father nor mother. The young woman had a beautiful figure and was lovely to look at, and when her father and her mother died, Mordecai took her as his own daughter. ⁸So when the king's order and his edict were proclaimed, and when many young women were gathered in Susa the citadel in custody of Hegai, Esther also was taken into the king's palace and put in custody of Hegai, who had charge of the women. ⁹And the young woman pleased him and won his favor. And he quickly provided her with her cosmetics and her portion of food, and with seven chosen young women from the king's palace, and advanced her and her young women to the best place in the harem. ¹⁰Esther had not made known her people or kindred, for Mordecai had commanded her not to make it known. ¹¹And every day Mordecai walked in front of the court of the harem to learn how Esther was and what was happening to her.

¹²Now when the turn came for each young woman to go in to King Ahasuerus after being twelve months under the regulations for the women, since this was the regular period of their beautifying, six months with oil of myrrh and six months with spices and ointments for women– ¹³when the young woman went in to the king in this way, she was given whatever she desired to take with her from the harem to the king's palace. ¹⁴In the evening she would go in, and in the morning she would return to the second harem in custody of Shaashgaz, the king's eunuch who was in charge of the concubines. She would not go in to the king again, unless the king delighted in her and she was summoned by name.

¹⁵When the turn came for Esther the daughter of Abihail the uncle of Mordecai who had taken her as his own daughter to go in to the king, she asked for nothing except what Hegai the king's eunuch, who had charge of the women, advised. Now Esther was winning favor in the eyes of all who saw her. ¹⁶And when Esther was taken to King Ahasuerus, into his royal palace, in the tenth month, which is the month of Tebeth, in the seventh year of his reign, ¹⁷the king loved Esther more than all the women, and she won grace and favor in his sight more than all the virgins, so that he set the royal crown[1] on her head and made her queen instead of Vashti. ¹⁸Then the king gave a great feast for all his officials and servants; it was Esther's feast. He also granted a remission of taxes to the provinces and gave gifts with royal generosity.

Mordecai Discovers a Plot

¹⁹Now when the virgins were gathered together the second time, Mordecai was sitting at the king's gate. ²⁰Esther had not made known her kindred or her people, as Mordecai had commanded her, for Esther obeyed Mordecai just as when she was brought up by him. ²¹In those days, as Mordecai was sitting at the king's gate, Bigthan and Teresh, two of the king's eunuchs, who guarded the threshold, became angry and sought to lay hands on King Ahasuerus. ²²And this came to the knowledge of Mordecai, and he told it to Queen Esther, and Esther told the king in the name of Mordecai. ²³When the affair

[1] Or headdress

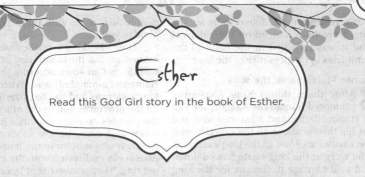

Esther

Read this God Girl story in the book of Esther.

"But seek first the kingdom of God and his righteousness, and all these things will be added to you."

Matthew 6:33

What comes first, God's provision or your prayer? It seems weird that the God who knows all your thoughts and sees everything you need asks you to ask him for what you need. Why would he need your words when he already knows what you're going to ask? Maybe he wants his people to learn to trust him as their heavenly Father. As you pray, your mind and soul get lined up with the things of the Spirit. Prayer draws you out of yourself and into things above. God wants to take care of his people, but he also wants them to ask.

You can really see this in the life of Esther. She was put in the palace through God's will. She got access to the king like no one else had, and when trouble hit for her people, she was the only one who could save them. But before she did anything, she asked her people to fast (see Est. 4:16). Though the story never mentions prayer, Jewish tradition connected fasting with prayer. So we can assume that Esther went before the Lord with prayer and fasting so that she could get his favor, because without it she didn't stand a chance.

Prayer isn't something to take lightly. It's of supreme value in the life of the believer. It's your lifeblood. Everything you do and everything that is done to you will be colored by the persistence or absence of your prayer. How sad it is to know God but to rarely talk with him or even think about him as your source of power and strength for all the issues in your life. When the Jews fasted and prayed, Esther was given a whole bunch of protection. What could have ended in total disaster for Mordecai and the Jewish people was turned around to become total success. As you read the story of Esther, think about how God allows the bad things in this world to pull his people to him and how, when you go after him in prayer, he's ready and able to change even the most horrific situations to good.

was investigated and found to be so, the men were both hanged on the gallows.[1] And it was recorded in the book of the chronicles in the presence of the king.

Haman Plots Against the Jews

3 After these things King Ahasuerus promoted Haman the Agagite, the son of Hammedatha, and advanced him and set his throne above all the officials who were with him. [2] And all the king's servants who were at the king's gate bowed down and paid homage to Haman, for the king had so commanded concerning him. But Mordecai did not bow down or pay homage. [3] Then the king's servants who were at the king's gate said to Mordecai, "Why do you transgress the king's command?" [4] And when they spoke to him day after day and he would not listen to them, they told Haman, in order to see whether Mordecai's words would stand, for he had told them that he was a Jew. [5] And when Haman saw that Mordecai did not bow down or pay homage to him, Haman was filled with fury. [6] But he disdained to lay hands on Mordecai alone. So, as they had made known to him the people of Mordecai, Haman sought to destroy all the Jews, the people of Mordecai, throughout the whole kingdom of Ahasuerus.

[7] In the first month, which is the month of Nisan, in the twelfth year of King Ahasuerus, they cast Pur (that is, they cast lots) before Haman day after day; and they cast it month after month till the twelfth month, which is the month of Adar. [8] Then Haman said to King Ahasuerus, "There is a certain people scattered abroad and dispersed among the peoples in all the provinces of your kingdom. Their laws are different from those of every other people, and they do not keep the king's laws, so that it is not to the king's profit to tolerate them. [9] If it please the king, let it be decreed that they be destroyed, and I will pay 10,000 talents[2] of silver into the hands of those who have charge of the king's business, that they may put it into the king's treasuries." [10] So the king took his signet ring from his hand and gave it to Haman the Agagite, the son of Hammedatha, the enemy of the Jews. [11] And the king said to Haman, "The money is given to you, the

people also, to do with them as it seem good to you."

[12] Then the king's scribes were sum moned on the thirteenth day of the fir month, and an edict, according to all tha Haman commanded, was written to th king's satraps and to the governors ove all the provinces and to the officials of a the peoples, to every province in its ow script and every people in its own lan guage. It was written in the name of Kin Ahasuerus and sealed with the king's sig net ring. [13] Letters were sent by couriers t all the king's provinces with instruction t destroy, to kill, and to annihilate all Jew young and old, women and children, i one day, the thirteenth day of the twelft month, which is the month of Adar, an to plunder their goods. [14] A copy of th document was to be issued as a decre in every province by proclamation to a the peoples to be ready for that day. [15] Th couriers went out hurriedly by order c the king, and the decree was issued in Sus the citadel. And the king and Haman sa down to drink, but the city of Susa wa thrown into confusion.

Esther Agrees to Help the Jews

4 When Mordecai learned all that ha been done, Mordecai tore his clothe and put on sackcloth and ashes, and wen out into the midst of the city, and he crie out with a loud and bitter cry. [2] He wen up to the entrance of the king's gate, fo no one was allowed to enter the king' gate clothed in sackcloth. [3] And in ever province, wherever the king's comman and his decree reached, there was grea mourning among the Jews, with fasting an weeping and lamenting, and many of ther lay in sackcloth and ashes.

[4] When Esther's young women and he eunuchs came and told her, the queen wa deeply distressed. She sent garments t clothe Mordecai, so that he might tak off his sackcloth, but he would not accep them. [5] Then Esther called for Hathach one of the king's eunuchs, who had bee appointed to attend her, and ordered hir to go to Mordecai to learn what this wa and why it was. [6] Hathach went out t Mordecai in the open square of the cit in front of the king's gate, [7] and Mordeca told him all that had happened to him, an

[1] Or *suspended on a stake* [2] A *talent* was about 75 pounds or 34 kilograms

e exact sum of money that Haman had romised to pay into the king's treasuries r the destruction of the Jews. [8] Mordecai so gave him a copy of the written decree ssued in Susa for their destruction, that e might show it to Esther and explain it her and command her to go to the king beg his favor and plead with him on ehalf of her people. [9] And Hathach went d told Esther what Mordecai had said. Then Esther spoke to Hathach and com- anded him to go to Mordecai and say, "All the king's servants and the people f the king's provinces know that if any an or woman goes to the king inside the ner court without being called, there is t one law—to be put to death, except the e to whom the king holds out the golden epter so that he may live. But as for me, have not been called to come in to the ng these thirty days."

[12] And they told Mordecai what Esther d said. [13] Then Mordecai told them to ply to Esther, "Do not think to yourself at in the king's palace you will escape y more than all the other Jews. [14] For you keep silent at this time, relief and eliverance will rise for the Jews from other place, but you and your father's use will perish. And who knows whether u have not come to the kingdom for such time as this?" [15] Then Esther told them reply to Mordecai, [16] "Go, gather all the ws to be found in Susa, and hold a fast my behalf, and do not eat or drink for ree days, night or day. I and my young omen will also fast as you do. Then I will to the king, though it is against the law, d if I perish, I perish." [17] Mordecai then ent away and did everything as Esther d ordered him.

sther Prepares a Banquet

On the third day Esther put on her royal robes and stood in the inner court of e king's palace, in front of the king's uarters, while the king was sitting on his yal throne inside the throne room oppo- te the entrance to the palace. [2] And when e king saw Queen Esther standing in the urt, she won favor in his sight, and he eld out to Esther the golden scepter that as in his hand. Then Esther approached nd touched the tip of the scepter. [3] And e king said to her, "What is it, Queen sther? What is your request? It shall be

given you, even to the half of my kingdom." [4] And Esther said, "If it please the king, let the king and Haman come today to a feast that I have prepared for the king." [5] Then the king said, "Bring Haman quickly, so that we may do as Esther has asked." So the king and Haman came to the feast that Esther had prepared. [6] And as they were drinking wine after the feast, the king said to Esther, "What is your wish? It shall be granted you. And what is your request? Even to the half of my kingdom, it shall be fulfilled." [7] Then Esther answered, "My wish and my request is: [8] If I have found favor in the sight of the king, and if it please the king to grant my wish and fulfill my request, let the king and Haman come to the feast that I will prepare for them, and tomorrow I will do as the king has said."

A Prayer for...

ACCEPTANCE

O God, giver of the world's joy, bearer of the world's pain, make me glad that as a believer I share in Christ's own suf- ferings; deliver me from the luxury of cheap sadness; and at the heart of all my trouble and sorrow, let unconquer- able gladness live through my Lord and Savior Jesus Christ.

May I quickly recognize your hand in my life. May I give you the praise whenever good things come to my doorstep, and may I give you the glory even when trouble moves in. Set me free from my broken way of thinking and clear my memory of the world's opinions and expectations so that I can rest in your approval, won for me by Christ.

Amen.

Haman Plans to Hang Mordecai

[9] And Haman went out that day joyful and glad of heart. But when Haman saw Mordecai in the king's gate, that he nei- ther rose nor trembled before him, he was filled with wrath against Mordecai. [10] Nevertheless, Haman restrained himself

and went home, and he sent and brought his friends and his wife Zeresh. ¹¹And Haman recounted to them the splendor of his riches, the number of his sons, all the promotions with which the king had honored him, and how he had advanced him above the officials and the servants of the king. ¹²Then Haman said, "Even Queen Esther let no one but me come with the king to the feast she prepared. And tomorrow also I am invited by her together with the king. ¹³Yet all this is worth nothing to me, so long as I see Mordecai the Jew sitting at the king's gate." ¹⁴Then his wife Zeresh and all his friends said to him, "Let a gallows¹ fifty cubits² high be made, and in the morning tell the king to have Mordecai hanged upon it. Then go joyfully with the king to the feast." This idea pleased Haman, and he had the gallows made.

The King Honors Mordecai

6 On that night the king could not sleep. And he gave orders to bring the book of memorable deeds, the chronicles, and they were read before the king. ²And it was found written how Mordecai had told about Bigthana³ and Teresh, two of the king's eunuchs, who guarded the threshold, and who had sought to lay hands on King Ahasuerus. ³And the king said, "What honor or distinction has been bestowed on Mordecai for this?" The king's young men who attended him said, "Nothing has been done for him." ⁴And the king said, "Who is in the court?" Now Haman had just entered the outer court of the king's palace to speak to the king about having Mordecai hanged on the gallows⁴ that he had prepared for him. ⁵And the king's young men told him, "Haman is there, standing in the court." And the king said, "Let him come in." ⁶So Haman came in, and the king said to him, "What should be done to the man whom the king delights to honor?" And Haman said to himself, "Whom would the king delight to honor more than me?" ⁷And Haman said to the king, "For the man whom the king delights to honor, ⁸let royal robes be brought, which the king has worn, and the horse that the king has ridden, and on whose head a royal crown⁵ is set. ⁹And let the robes and the horse be handed over to one of the king's most noble officials.

Let them dress the man whom the king delights to honor, and let them lead him on the horse through the square of the city, proclaiming before him: 'Thus shall it be done to the man whom the king delights to honor.' " ¹⁰Then the king said to Haman, "Hurry; take the robes and the horse, as you have said, and do so to Mordecai the Jew, who sits at the king's gate. Leave out nothing that you have mentioned." ¹¹So Haman took the robes and the horse, and he dressed Mordecai and led him through the square of the city, proclaiming before him, "Thus shall it be done to the man whom the king delights to honor."

¹²Then Mordecai returned to the king's gate. But Haman hurried to his house, mourning and with his head covered. ¹³And Haman told his wife Zeresh and all his friends everything that had happened to him. Then his wise men and his wife Zeresh said to him, "If Mordecai, before whom you have begun to fall, is of the Jewish people, you will not overcome him but will surely fall before him."

Esther Reveals Haman's Plot

¹⁴While they were yet talking with him, the king's eunuchs arrived and hurried to bring Haman to the feast that Esther had prepared.

7 So the king and Haman went in to feast with Queen Esther. ²And on the second day, as they were drinking wine after the feast, the king again said to Esther, "What is your wish, Queen Esther? It shall be granted you. And what is your request? Even to the half of my kingdom, it shall be fulfilled." ³Then Queen Esther answered, "If I have found favor in your sight, O king, and if it please the king, let my life be granted me for my wish, and my people for my request. ⁴For we have been sold, I and my people, to be destroyed, to be killed, and to be annihilated. If we had been sold merely as slaves, men and women, I would have been silent, for our affliction is not to be compared with the loss to the king." ⁵Then King Ahasuerus said to Queen Esther, "Who is he, and where is he, who has dared⁶ to do this?" ⁶And Esther said, "A foe and enemy! This wicked Haman!" Then Haman was terrified before the king and the queen.

---

¹Or *stake*; twice in this verse ²A *cubit* was about 18 inches or 45 centimeters ³*Bigthana* is an alternate spelling of *Bigthan* (see 2:21) ⁴Or *suspended on a stake* ⁵Or *headdress* ⁶Hebrew *whose heart has filled him*

Haman Is Hanged

⁷ And the king arose in his wrath from the wine-drinking and went into the palace garden, but Haman stayed to beg for his life from Queen Esther, for he saw that harm was determined against him by the king. ⁸ And the king returned from the palace garden to the place where they were drinking wine, as Haman was falling on the couch where Esther was. And the king said, "Will he even assault the queen in my presence, in my own house?" As the word left the mouth of the king, they covered Haman's face. ⁹ Then Harbona, one of the eunuchs in attendance on the king, said, Moreover, the gallows¹ that Haman has prepared for Mordecai, whose word saved the king, is standing at Haman's house, fifty cubits² high." ¹⁰ And the king said, "Hang him on that." So they hanged Haman on the gallows that he had prepared for Mordecai. Then the wrath of the king abated.

Esther Saves the Jews

8 On that day King Ahasuerus gave to Queen Esther the house of Haman, the enemy of the Jews. And Mordecai came before the king, for Esther had told what he was to her. ² And the king took off his signet ring, which he had taken from Haman, and gave it to Mordecai. And Esther set Mordecai over the house of Haman.

³ Then Esther spoke again to the king. She fell at his feet and wept and pleaded with him to avert the evil plan of Haman the Agagite and the plot that he had devised against the Jews. ⁴ When the king held out the golden scepter to Esther, ⁵ Esther rose and stood before the king. And she said, "If it please the king, and if I have found favor in his sight, and if the thing seems right before the king, and I am pleasing in his eyes, let an order be written to revoke the letters devised by Haman the Agagite, the son of Hammedatha, which he wrote to destroy the Jews who are in all the provinces of the king. ⁶ For how can I bear to see the calamity that is coming to my people? Or how can I bear to see the destruction of my kindred?" ⁷ Then King Ahasuerus said to Queen Esther and to Mordecai the Jew, "Behold, I have given Esther the house of Haman, and they have hanged him on the gallows,³ because he intended to lay hands on the Jews. ⁸ But you may write as you please with regard to the Jews, in the name of the king, and seal it with the king's ring, for an edict written in the name of the king and sealed with the king's ring cannot be revoked."

⁹ The king's scribes were summoned at that time, in the third month, which is the month of Sivan, on the twenty-third day. And an edict was written, according to all that Mordecai commanded concerning the Jews, to the satraps and the governors and the officials of the provinces from India to Ethiopia, 127 provinces, to each province in its own script and to each people in its own language, and also to the Jews in their script and their language. ¹⁰ And he wrote in the name of King Ahasuerus and sealed it with the king's signet ring. Then he sent the letters by mounted couriers riding on swift horses that were used in the king's service, bred from the royal stud, ¹¹ saying that the king allowed the Jews who were in every city to gather and defend their lives, to destroy, to kill, and to annihilate any armed force of any people or province that might attack them, children and women included, and to plunder their goods, ¹² on one day throughout all the provinces of King Ahasuerus, on the thirteenth day of the twelfth month, which is the month of Adar. ¹³ A copy of what was written was to be issued as a decree in every province, being publicly displayed to all peoples, and the Jews were to be ready on that day to take vengeance on their enemies. ¹⁴ So the couriers, mounted on their swift horses that were used in the king's service, rode out hurriedly, urged by the king's command. And the decree was issued in Susa the citadel.

¹⁵ Then Mordecai went out from the presence of the king in royal robes of blue and white, with a great golden crown⁴ and a robe of fine linen and purple, and the city of Susa shouted and rejoiced. ¹⁶ The Jews had light and gladness and joy and honor. ¹⁷ And in every province and in every city, wherever the king's command and his edict reached, there was gladness and joy among the Jews, a feast and a holiday. And many from the peoples of the country declared themselves Jews, for fear of the Jews had fallen on them.

---

¹ Or *stake*; also verse 10 ² A *cubit* was about 18 inches or 45 centimeters ³ Or *stake* ⁴ Or *headdress*

The Jews Destroy Their Enemies

9 Now in the twelfth month, which is the month of Adar, on the thirteenth day of the same, when the king's command and edict were about to be carried out, on the very day when the enemies of the Jews hoped to gain the mastery over them, the reverse occurred: the Jews gained mastery over those who hated them. [2] The Jews gathered in their cities throughout all the provinces of King Ahasuerus to lay hands on those who sought their harm. And no one could stand against them, for the fear of them had fallen on all peoples. [3] All the officials of the provinces and the satraps and the governors and the royal agents also helped the Jews, for the fear of Mordecai had fallen on them. [4] For Mordecai was great in the king's house, and his fame spread throughout all the provinces, for the man Mordecai grew more and more powerful. [5] The Jews struck all their enemies with the sword, killing and destroying them, and did as they pleased to those who hated them. [6] In Susa the citadel itself the Jews killed and destroyed 500 men, [7] and also killed Parshandatha and Dalphon and Aspatha [8] and Poratha and Adalia and Aridatha [9] and Parmashta and Arisai and Aridai and Vaizatha, [10] the ten sons of Haman the son of Hammedatha, the enemy of the Jews, but they laid no hand on the plunder.

[11] That very day the number of those killed in Susa the citadel was reported to the king. [12] And the king said to Queen Esther, "In Susa the citadel the Jews have killed and destroyed 500 men and also the ten sons of Haman. What then have they done in the rest of the king's provinces! Now what is your wish? It shall be granted you. And what further is your request? It shall be fulfilled." [13] And Esther said, "If it please the king, let the Jews who are in Susa be allowed tomorrow also to do according to this day's edict. And let the ten sons of Haman be hanged on the gallows."[1] [14] So the king commanded this to be done. A decree was issued in Susa, and the ten sons of Haman were hanged. [15] The Jews who were in Susa gathered also on the fourteenth day of the month of Adar and they killed 300 men in Susa, but they laid no hands on the plunder.

[16] Now the rest of the Jews who were in the king's provinces also gathered to defend their lives, and got relief from their enemies and killed 75,000 of those who hated them, but they laid no hands on the plunder. [17] This was on the thirteenth day of the month of Adar, and on the fourteenth day they rested and made that a day of feasting and gladness. [18] But the Jews who were in Susa gathered on the thirteenth day and on the fourteenth, and rested on the fifteenth day, making that a day of feasting and gladness. [19] Therefore the Jews of the villages, who live in the rural towns, hold the fourteenth day of the month of Adar as a day for gladness and feasting, as a holiday, and as a day on which they send gifts of food to one another.

The Feast of Purim Inaugurated

[20] And Mordecai recorded these things and sent letters to all the Jews who were in all the provinces of King Ahasuerus, both near and far, [21] obliging them to keep the fourteenth day of the month Adar and also the fifteenth day of the same, year by year, [22] as the days on which the Jews got relief from their enemies, and as the month that had been turned for them from sorrow into gladness and from mourning into a holiday; that they should make them days of feasting and gladness, days for sending gifts of food to one another and gifts to the poor.

[23] So the Jews accepted what they had started to do, and what Mordecai had written to them. [24] For Haman the Agagite, the son of Hammedatha, the enemy of all the Jews, had plotted against the Jews to destroy them, and had cast Pur (that is, cast lots), to crush and to destroy them. [25] But when it came before the king, he gave orders in writing that his evil plan that he had devised against the Jews should return on his own head, and that he and his sons should be hanged on the gallows.[2] [26] Therefore they called these days Purim, after the term Pur. Therefore, because of all that was written in this letter, and of what they had faced in this matter, and of what had happened to them, [27] the Jews firmly obligated themselves and their offspring and all who joined them, that without fail they would keep these two days according to what was written

[1] Or stake [2] Or suspended on a stake

and at the time appointed every year, [28] that these days should be remembered and kept throughout every generation, in every clan, province, and city, and that these days of Purim should never fall into disuse among the Jews, nor should the commemoration of these days cease among their descendants.

[29] Then Queen Esther, the daughter of Abihail, and Mordecai the Jew gave full written authority, confirming this second letter about Purim. [30] Letters were sent to all the Jews, to the 127 provinces of the kingdom of Ahasuerus, in words of peace and truth, [31] that these days of Purim should be observed at their appointed seasons, as Mordecai the Jew and Queen Esther obligated them, and as they had obligated themselves and their offspring, with regard to their fasts and their lamenting. [32] The command of Queen Esther confirmed these practices of Purim, and it was recorded in writing.

The Greatness of Mordecai

10 King Ahasuerus imposed tax on the land and on the coastlands of the sea. [2] And all the acts of his power and might, and the full account of the high honor of Mordecai, to which the king advanced him, are they not written in the Book of the Chronicles of the kings of Media and Persia? [3] For Mordecai the Jew was second in rank to King Ahasuerus, and he was great among the Jews and popular with the multitude of his brothers, for he sought the welfare of his people and spoke peace to all his people.

INTRODUCTION TO

Job

Author: Unknown
Time: Unknown
Place: Unknown
Written to: Unknown

The gist

The book of Job chronicles the trials and suffering of one man and what his friends said were the reasons for his trials. It shows us how Satan has to ask God for permission to harm God's people, and how God responds when his people suffer under his hand.

Things to look for

Satan's challenges to the Lord (see Job 1:6–12; 2:1–6)

Job's reaction to his suffering (see Job 3; 6–7; 9–10; 13:17–14:22; and many others)

Trust God with Your Suffering

"Naked I came from my mother's womb, and naked shall I return. The LORD gave, and the LORD has taken away; blessed be the name of the LORD."

Job 1:21

Nothing happens in your life that God didn't let happen. It's true that God gives only good and perfect gifts, but he also lets other things in your life like trials, persecution, and trouble happen for a reason. Job's life is a good example of this. Even though it was Satan who directly afflicted Job, he was able to do so only with God's permission—in fact, Job even said "the LORD has taken away," seeing God's own hand in his suffering.

When God brings hard things into your life, you may wonder why he would allow you to be hurt, but the answer can be found in the lives of people who have come before you, like Job. Because of Job's suffering, you now see that God rules in fatherly wisdom even over the most painful experiences in our lives. You can also see that God is never very far away, and all he wants is your faith in him and your trust in his Word. Above all, remember in your suffering that God's own Son experienced the ultimate suffering on the cross—condemnation and being forsaken by God—so that you and I never have to.

Must-Know Facts and Verses

✝ No one knows for sure who wrote Job.

✝ Job was not an Israelite but was from the land of Uz, yet he worshiped the one true God (see Job 1:1).

✝ The name Job means "enemy."

"Have you considered my servant Job, that there is none like him on the earth, a blameless and upright man, who fears God and turns away from evil?" *Job 1:8*

"Naked I came from my mother's womb, and naked shall I return. The LORD gave, and the LORD has taken away; blessed be the name of the LORD." *Job 1:21*

In all this Job did not sin or charge God with wrong. *Job 1:22*

"Shall we receive good from God, and shall we not receive evil?" *Job 2:10*

Job

Job's Character and Wealth

1 There was a man in the land of Uz whose name was Job, and that man was blameless and upright, one who feared God and turned away from evil. ²There were born to him seven sons and three daughters. ³He possessed 7,000 sheep, 3,000 camels, 500 yoke of oxen, and 500 female donkeys, and very many servants, so that this man was the greatest of all the people of the east. ⁴His sons used to go and hold a feast in the house of each one on his day, and they would send and invite their three sisters to eat and drink with them. ⁵And when the days of the feast had run their course, Job would send and consecrate them, and he would rise early in the morning and offer burnt offerings according to the number of them all. For Job said, "It may be that my children have sinned, and cursed[1] God in their hearts." Thus Job did continually.

Satan Allowed to Test Job

⁶Now there was a day when the sons of God came to present themselves before the LORD, and Satan[2] also came among them. ⁷The LORD said to Satan, "From where have you come?" Satan answered the LORD and said, "From going to and fro on the earth, and from walking up and down on it." ⁸And the LORD said to Satan, "Have you considered my servant Job, that there is none like him on the earth, a blameless and upright man, who fears God and turns away from evil?" ⁹Then Satan answered the LORD and said, "Does Job fear God for no reason? ¹⁰Have you not put a hedge around him and his house and all that he has, on every side? You have blessed the work of his hands, and his possessions have increased in the land. ¹¹But stretch out your hand and touch all that he has, and he will curse you to your face." ¹²And the LORD said to Satan,

"Behold, all that he has is in your hand. Only against him do not stretch out your hand." So Satan went out from the presence of the LORD.

Satan Takes Job's Property and Children

¹³Now there was a day when his sons and daughters were eating and drinking wine in their oldest brother's house, ¹⁴and there came a messenger to Job and said, "The oxen were plowing and the donkeys feeding beside them, ¹⁵and the Sabeans fell upon them and took them and struck down the servants[3] with the edge of the sword, and I alone have escaped to tell you." ¹⁶While he was yet speaking, there came another and said, "The fire of God fell from heaven and burned up the sheep and the servants and consumed them, and I alone have escaped to tell you." ¹⁷While he was yet speaking, there came another and said, "The Chaldeans formed three groups and made a raid on the camels and took them and struck down the servants with the edge of the sword, and I alone have escaped to tell you." ¹⁸While he was yet speaking, there came another and said, "Your sons and daughters were eating and drinking wine in their oldest brother's house, ¹⁹and behold, a great wind came across the wilderness and struck the four corners of the house, and it fell upon the young people, and they are dead, and I alone have escaped to tell you."

²⁰Then Job arose and tore his robe and shaved his head and fell on the ground and worshiped. ²¹And he said, "Naked I came from my mother's womb, and naked shall I return. The LORD gave, and the LORD has taken away; blessed be the name of the LORD."

²²In all this Job did not sin or charge God with wrong.

---

[1] The Hebrew word *bless* is used euphemistically for *curse* in 1:5, 11; 2:5, 9   [2] Hebrew *the Accuser* or *the Adversary*; so throughout chapters 1–2   [3] Hebrew *the young men*; also verses 16, 17

Satan Attacks Job's Health

2 Again there was a day when the sons of God came to present themselves before the LORD, and Satan also came among them to present himself before the LORD. ²And the LORD said to Satan, "From where have you come?" Satan answered the LORD and said, "From going to and fro on the earth, and from walking up and down on it." ³And the LORD said to Satan, "Have you considered my servant Job, that there is none like him on the earth, a blameless and upright man, who fears God and turns away from evil? He still holds fast his integrity, although you incited me against him to destroy him without reason." ⁴Then Satan answered the LORD and said, "Skin for skin! All that a man has he will give for his life. ⁵But stretch out your hand and touch his bone and his flesh, and he will curse you to your face." ⁶And the LORD said to Satan,

"Behold, he is in your hand; only spar[e] his life."

⁷So Satan went out from the presence o[f] the LORD and struck Job with loathsom[e] sores from the sole of his foot to the crow[n] of his head. ⁸And he took a piece of broke[n] pottery with which to scrape himself whil[e] he sat in the ashes.

⁹Then his wife said to him, "Do you sti[ll] hold fast your integrity? Curse God an[d] die." ¹⁰But he said to her, "You speak a[s] one of the foolish women would speak[.] Shall we receive good from God, and shal[l] we not receive evil?"¹ In all this Job did no[t] sin with his lips.

Job's Three Friends

¹¹Now when Job's three friends heard o[f] all this evil that had come upon him, the[y] came each from his own place, Eliphaz the Temanite, Bildad the Shuhite, and Zopha[r]

¹ Or *disaster*; also verse 11

verses to read
Job 1:13–22

God is found at the end of yourself. When you are beat down, worn out, bruised and battered, God becomes everything. The less you can rely on yourself or your past success, the clearer and more impressive his presence becomes. When the hard times hit, you often feel powerless, and with that there is less of you, and with less of you there is more room for him.

Prayer really takes wings and changes lives when it's not about you, your problems, or your fears but instead it's about God, his will, and his ways. At that point everything you want and need fades to the background. You don't need peace with where you are or how you feel. You don't need to feel comfortable with who you are or with who people think you are, because you know who *he* is. You'll find rest for your soul when you don't care if you are misunderstood, distrusted, rejected, or shamed. When you come to that point, you have found all you need in the one who knows what it is to be misunderstood, doubted, and horribly rejected. Remember that what you're lacking, or the trial you're facing, is nothing more than what millions before you have experienced. And remember that hardship is the fuel of faith. Faith proves itself in the hard times, not in the good times. Faith is born and grown through stress and turmoil, not through ease and comfort.

Whatever junk you're living through right now, just know that without this junk today, you might never find the need or passion for more of God. Don't let this stuff be wasted on your soul. Let it scrub you clean of any hint of self-obsession and sweeten you with a pure and humble God-obsession.

he Naamathite. They made an appoint-
nent together to come to show him sympa-
hy and comfort him. ¹²And when they saw
im from a distance, they did not recognize
im. And they raised their voices and wept,
nd they tore their robes and sprinkled
lust on their heads toward heaven. ¹³And
hey sat with him on the ground seven days
nd seven nights, and no one spoke a word
o him, for they saw that his suffering was
ery great.

ob Laments His Birth

3 After this Job opened his mouth and
cursed the day of his birth. ²And Job
aid:

³ "Let the day perish on which I was
        born,
    and the night that said,
    'A man is conceived.'
⁴ Let that day be darkness!
    May God above not seek it,
    nor light shine upon it.

5 Let gloom and deep darkness claim
        it.
    Let clouds dwell upon it;
    let the blackness of the day terrify
        it.
6 That night—let thick darkness seize
        it!
    Let it not rejoice among the days
        of the year;
    let it not come into the number of
        the months.
7 Behold, let that night be barren;
    let no joyful cry enter it.
8 Let those curse it who curse the day,
    who are ready to rouse up
        Leviathan.
9 Let the stars of its dawn be dark;
    let it hope for light, but have none,
    nor see the eyelids of the morn-
        ing,
10 because it did not shut the doors of
        my mother's womb,
    nor hide trouble from my eyes.

Know Yourself

verses to read
Job 3

You don't have to feel good to be godly. Everything in you might scream "Yuck!" Your emotions drag, your heart aches, and you feel like you can't go on, but God welcomes you into his presence no matter what you feel like, because through Jesus you have full access to the Father. You are his daughter! In spite of how things look, remember who you are, and focus on what is true and honorable and commendable (see Phil. 4:8).

You can't use your sadness as an excuse to be ungodly. Feelings lie and feelings manipulate, and if you let feelings be your guide, you're gonna spend more time off track than on the road to faithfulness. So listen to what your feelings have to say, but if they're bringing you down, like they did to Job when his trials first hit, then turn down the volume. You can acknowledge the feelings are there, you can even mourn and grieve as Job did, but then say, "Even so, I'm moving on as if everything's okay, because feelings aren't my god—and I know that, in Christ, all that happens is for my good" (see Rom. 8:28). When you act as if you feel good even when you don't, something amazing happens: you start to feel good! It's weird, but it happens. When you work at making what you know more important than how you feel, eventually your mind will be able to control your feelings and stop letting them control you. Then you'll be free.

People who are controlled by their feelings are like waves on the ocean, blown by the wind and tossed around by the sea. Want stability? Then take your life back from your emotions.

¹¹ "Why did I not die at birth,
    come out from the womb and
    expire?
¹² Why did the knees receive me?
    Or why the breasts, that I should
    nurse?
¹³ For then I would have lain down and
    been quiet;
    I would have slept; then I would
    have been at rest,
¹⁴ with kings and counselors of the
    earth
    who rebuilt ruins for themselves,
¹⁵ or with princes who had gold,
    who filled their houses with
    silver.
¹⁶ Or why was I not as a hidden still-
    born child,
    as infants who never see the
    light?
¹⁷ There the wicked cease from trou-
    bling,
    and there the weary are at rest.
¹⁸ There the prisoners are at ease
    together;
    they hear not the voice of the
    taskmaster.
¹⁹ The small and the great are there,
    and the slave is free from his mas-
    ter.

²⁰ "Why is light given to him who is in
    misery,
    and life to the bitter in soul,
²¹ who long for death, but it comes
    not,
    and dig for it more than for hidden
    treasures,
²² who rejoice exceedingly
    and are glad when they find the
    grave?
²³ Why is light given to a man whose
    way is hidden,
    whom God has hedged in?
²⁴ For my sighing comes instead of[1] my
    bread,
    and my groanings are poured out
    like water.
²⁵ For the thing that I fear comes upon
    me,
    and what I dread befalls me.
²⁶ I am not at ease, nor am I quiet;
    I have no rest, but trouble comes."

Eliphaz Speaks: The Innocent Prosper

4 Then Eliphaz the Temanite answered
and said:

² "If one ventures a word with you, will
    you be impatient?
    Yet who can keep from speaking?
³ Behold, you have instructed many,
    and you have strengthened the
    weak hands.
⁴ Your words have upheld him who
    was stumbling,
    and you have made firm the feeble
    knees.
⁵ But now it has come to you, and you
    are impatient;
    it touches you, and you are dis-
    mayed.
⁶ Is not your fear of God[2] your confi-
    dence,
    and the integrity of your ways
    your hope?

⁷ "Remember: who that was innocent
    ever perished?
    Or where were the upright cut off?
⁸ As I have seen, those who plow iniq-
    uity
    and sow trouble reap the same.
⁹ By the breath of God they perish,
    and by the blast of his anger they
    are consumed.
¹⁰ The roar of the lion, the voice of the
    fierce lion,
    the teeth of the young lions are
    broken.
¹¹ The strong lion perishes for lack of
    prey,
    and the cubs of the lioness are
    scattered.

¹² "Now a word was brought to me
    stealthily;
    my ear received the whisper of it.
¹³ Amid thoughts from visions of the
    night,
    when deep sleep falls on men,
¹⁴ dread came upon me, and trembling,
    which made all my bones shake.
¹⁵ A spirit glided past my face;
    the hair of my flesh stood up.
¹⁶ It stood still,
    but I could not discern its appear-
    ance.

---

[1] Or like; Hebrew before   [2] Hebrew lacks of God

A form was before my eyes;
  there was silence, then I heard a
    voice:

7 'Can mortal man be in the right
      before[1] God?
  Can a man be pure before his
      Maker?

8 Even in his servants he puts no trust,
    and his angels he charges with
      error;

9 how much more those who dwell in
      houses of clay,
  whose foundation is in the dust,
  who are crushed like the moth.

10 Between morning and evening they
      are beaten to pieces;
  they perish forever without any-
    one regarding it.

11 Is not their tent-cord plucked up
      within them,
  do they not die, and that without
      wisdom?'

5 "Call now; is there anyone who will
      answer you?
  To which of the holy ones will you
      turn?

2 Surely vexation kills the fool,
    and jealousy slays the simple.

3 I have seen the fool taking root,
    but suddenly I cursed his dwelling.

4 His children are far from safety;
    they are crushed in the gate,
    and there is no one to deliver
      them.

5 The hungry eat his harvest,
    and he takes it even out of thorns,[2]
    and the thirsty pant[3] after his[4]
      wealth.

6 For affliction does not come from the
      dust,
  nor does trouble sprout from the
      ground,

7 but man is born to trouble
    as the sparks fly upward.

8 "As for me, I would seek God,
    and to God would I commit my
      cause,

9 who does great things and unsearch-
      able,
  marvelous things without number:

10 he gives rain on the earth
    and sends waters on the fields;

11 he sets on high those who are lowly,
    and those who mourn are lifted to
      safety.

12 He frustrates the devices of the
      crafty,
  so that their hands achieve no suc-
      cess.

13 He catches the wise in their own
      craftiness,
  and the schemes of the wily are
    brought to a quick end.

14 They meet with darkness in the
      daytime
  and grope at noonday as in the
      night.

15 But he saves the needy from the
      sword of their mouth
  and from the hand of the mighty.

16 So the poor have hope,
    and injustice shuts her mouth.

17 "Behold, blessed is the one whom God
      reproves;
  therefore despise not the disci-
    pline of the Almighty.

18 For he wounds, but he binds up;
    he shatters, but his hands heal.

19 He will deliver you from six troubles;
    in seven no evil[5] shall touch you.

20 In famine he will redeem you from
      death,
  and in war from the power of the
      sword.

21 You shall be hidden from the lash of
      the tongue,
  and shall not fear destruction
    when it comes.

22 At destruction and famine you shall
      laugh,
  and shall not fear the beasts of the
      earth.

23 For you shall be in league with the
      stones of the field,
  and the beasts of the field shall be
    at peace with you.

24 You shall know that your tent is at
      peace,
  and you shall inspect your fold and
      miss nothing.

25 You shall know also that your off-
      spring shall be many,
  and your descendants as the grass
    of the earth.

[1] Or more than; twice in this verse [2] The meaning of the Hebrew is uncertain [3] Aquila, Symmachus, Syriac, Vulgate; Hebrew could be read as and the snare pants [4] Hebrew their [5] Or disaster

26 You shall come to your grave in ripe
   old age,
     like a sheaf gathered up in its
       season.
27 Behold, this we have searched out; it
   is true.
     Hear, and know it for your good."[1]

Job Replies: My Complaint Is Just

6 Then Job answered and said:

2 "Oh that my vexation were weighed,
     and all my calamity laid in the bal-
       ances!
3 For then it would be heavier than the
   sand of the sea;
     therefore my words have been
       rash.
4 For the arrows of the Almighty are in
   me;
     my spirit drinks their poison;
     the terrors of God are arrayed
       against me.
5 Does the wild donkey bray when he
   has grass,
     or the ox low over his fodder?
6 Can that which is tasteless be eaten
   without salt,
     or is there any taste in the juice of
       the mallow?[2]
7 My appetite refuses to touch them;
     they are as food that is loathsome
       to me.[3]

8 "Oh that I might have my request,
     and that God would fulfill my hope,
9 that it would please God to crush me,
     that he would let loose his hand
       and cut me off!
10 This would be my comfort;
     I would even exult[4] in pain unspar-
       ing,
     for I have not denied the words of
       the Holy One.
11 What is my strength, that I should
   wait?
     And what is my end, that I should
       be patient?
12 Is my strength the strength of stones,
     or is my flesh bronze?
13 Have I any help in me,
     when resource is driven from me?

14 "He who withholds[5] kindness from a
   friend
     forsakes the fear of the Almighty.
15 My brothers are treacherous as a
   torrent-bed,
     as torrential streams that pass
       away,
16 which are dark with ice,
     and where the snow hides itself.
17 When they melt, they disappear;
     when it is hot, they vanish from
       their place.
18 The caravans turn aside from their
   course;
     they go up into the waste and per-
       ish.
19 The caravans of Tema look,
     the travelers of Sheba hope.
20 They are ashamed because they
   were confident;
     they come there and are disap-
       pointed.
21 For you have now become nothing;
     you see my calamity and are
       afraid.
22 Have I said, 'Make me a gift'?
     Or, 'From your wealth offer a bribe
       for me'?
23 Or, 'Deliver me from the adversary's
   hand'?
     Or, 'Redeem me from the hand of
       the ruthless'?

24 "Teach me, and I will be silent;
     make me understand how I have
       gone astray.
25 How forceful are upright words!
     But what does reproof from you
       reprove?
26 Do you think that you can reprove
   words,
     when the speech of a despairing
       man is wind?
27 You would even cast lots over the
   fatherless,
     and bargain over your friend.

28 "But now, be pleased to look at me,
     for I will not lie to your face.
29 Please turn; let no injustice be done.
     Turn now; my vindication is at
       stake.
30 Is there any injustice on my tongue?
     Cannot my palate discern the
       cause of calamity?

---

[1] Hebrew for yourself [2] The meaning of the Hebrew word is uncertain [3] The meaning of the Hebrew is uncertain [4] The meaning of the Hebrew word is uncertain [5] Syriac, Vulgate (compare Targum); the meaning of the Hebrew word is uncertain

Job Continues: My Life Has No Hope

7 "Has not man a hard service on earth,
and are not his days like the days of
a hired hand?
Like a slave who longs for the
shadow,
and like a hired hand who looks
for his wages,
so I am allotted months of emptiness,
and nights of misery are apportioned to me.
When I lie down I say, 'When shall
I arise?'
But the night is long,
and I am full of tossing till the
dawn.
My flesh is clothed with worms and
dirt;
my skin hardens, then breaks out
afresh.
My days are swifter than a weaver's
shuttle
and come to their end without
hope.

"Remember that my life is a breath;
my eye will never again see good.
The eye of him who sees me will
behold me no more;
while your eyes are on me, I shall
be gone.
As the cloud fades and vanishes,
so he who goes down to Sheol
does not come up;
he returns no more to his house,
nor does his place know him anymore.

"Therefore I will not restrain my
mouth;
I will speak in the anguish of my
spirit;
I will complain in the bitterness of
my soul.
Am I the sea, or a sea monster,
that you set a guard over me?
When I say, 'My bed will comfort me,
my couch will ease my complaint,'
then you scare me with dreams
and terrify me with visions,
so that I would choose strangling
and death rather than my bones.
I loathe my life; I would not live
forever.
Leave me alone, for my days are a
breath.

17 What is man, that you make so much
of him,
and that you set your heart on him,
18 visit him every morning
and test him every moment?
19 How long will you not look away
from me,
nor leave me alone till I swallow
my spit?
20 If I sin, what do I do to you, you
watcher of mankind?
Why have you made me your
mark?
Why have I become a burden to
you?
21 Why do you not pardon my transgression
and take away my iniquity?
For now I shall lie in the earth;
you will seek me, but I shall not
be."

Bildad Speaks: Job Should Repent

8 Then Bildad the Shuhite answered and
said:

2 "How long will you say these things,
and the words of your mouth be a
great wind?
3 Does God pervert justice?
Or does the Almighty pervert the
right?
4 If your children have sinned against
him,
he has delivered them into the
hand of their transgression.
5 If you will seek God
and plead with the Almighty for
mercy,
6 if you are pure and upright,
surely then he will rouse himself
for you
and restore your rightful habitation.
7 And though your beginning was
small,
your latter days will be very great.

8 "For inquire, please, of bygone ages,
and consider what the fathers
have searched out.
9 For we are but of yesterday and
know nothing,
for our days on earth are a shadow.
10 Will they not teach you and tell you
and utter words out of their
understanding?

¹¹ "Can papyrus grow where there is no
     marsh?
     Can reeds flourish where there is
       no water?
¹² While yet in flower and not cut
       down,
     they wither before any other plant.
¹³ Such are the paths of all who forget
       God;
     the hope of the godless shall per-
       ish.
¹⁴ His confidence is severed,
     and his trust is a spider's web.[1]
¹⁵ He leans against his house, but it
       does not stand;
     he lays hold of it, but it does not
       endure.
¹⁶ He is a lush plant before the sun,
     and his shoots spread over his
       garden.
¹⁷ His roots entwine the stone heap;
     he looks upon a house of stones.
¹⁸ If he is destroyed from his place,
     then it will deny him, saying, 'I
       have never seen you.'
¹⁹ Behold, this is the joy of his way,
     and out of the soil others will
       spring.

²⁰ "Behold, God will not reject a blame-
       less man,
     nor take the hand of evildoers.
²¹ He will yet fill your mouth with
       laughter,
     and your lips with shouting.
²² Those who hate you will be clothed
       with shame,
     and the tent of the wicked will be
       no more."

Job Replies: There Is No Arbiter

9 Then Job answered and said:

² "Truly I know that it is so:
     But how can a man be in the right
       before God?
³ If one wished to contend with him,
     one could not answer him once in
       a thousand times.
⁴ He is wise in heart and mighty in
       strength
     —who has hardened himself
       against him, and succeeded?—

⁵ he who removes mountains, and
     they know it not,
     when he overturns them in his
       anger,
⁶ who shakes the earth out of its place,
     and its pillars tremble;
⁷ who commands the sun, and it does
       not rise;
     who seals up the stars;
⁸ who alone stretched out the heavens
     and trampled the waves of the sea;
⁹ who made the Bear and Orion,
     the Pleiades and the chambers of
       the south;
¹⁰ who does great things beyond
       searching out,
     and marvelous things beyond
       number.
¹¹ Behold, he passes by me, and I see
       him not;
     he moves on, but I do not perceive
       him.
¹² Behold, he snatches away; who can
       turn him back?
     Who will say to him, 'What are you
       doing?'

¹³ "God will not turn back his anger;
     beneath him bowed the helpers of
       Rahab.
¹⁴ How then can I answer him,
     choosing my words with him?
¹⁵ Though I am in the right, I cannot
       answer him;
     I must appeal for mercy to my
       accuser.[2]
¹⁶ If I summoned him and he answered
       me,
     I would not believe that he was
       listening to my voice.
¹⁷ For he crushes me with a tempest
     and multiplies my wounds without
       cause;
¹⁸ he will not let me get my breath,
     but fills me with bitterness.
¹⁹ If it is a contest of strength, behold,
       he is mighty!
     If it is a matter of justice, who can
       summon him?[3]
²⁰ Though I am in the right, my own
       mouth would condemn me;
     though I am blameless, he would
       prove me perverse.
²¹ I am blameless; I regard not myself;
     I loathe my life.

[1] Hebrew *house* [2] Or *to my judge* [3] Compare Septuagint; Hebrew *me*

It is all one; therefore I say,
'He destroys both the blameless
and the wicked.'
When disaster brings sudden death,
he mocks at the calamity[1] of the
innocent.
The earth is given into the hand of
the wicked;
he covers the faces of its judges—
if it is not he, who then is it?

"My days are swifter than a runner;
they flee away; they see no good.
They go by like skiffs of reed,
like an eagle swooping on the prey.
If I say, 'I will forget my complaint,
I will put off my sad face, and be of
good cheer,'
I become afraid of all my suffering,
for I know you will not hold me
innocent.
I shall be condemned;
why then do I labor in vain?
If I wash myself with snow
and cleanse my hands with lye,
yet you will plunge me into a pit,
and my own clothes will abhor me.
For he is not a man, as I am, that
I might answer him,
that we should come to trial
together.
There is no[2] arbiter between us,
who might lay his hand on us both.
Let him take his rod away from me,
and let not dread of him terrify me.
Then I would speak without fear of
him,
for I am not so in myself.

Job Continues: A Plea to God

10 "I loathe my life;
I will give free utterance to my
complaint;
I will speak in the bitterness of my
soul.
I will say to God, Do not condemn
me;
let me know why you contend
against me.
Does it seem good to you to oppress,
to despise the work of your hands
and favor the designs of the
wicked?
Have you eyes of flesh?
Do you see as man sees?

5 Are your days as the days of man,
or your years as a man's years,
6 that you seek out my iniquity
and search for my sin,
7 although you know that I am not
guilty,
and there is none to deliver out of
your hand?
8 Your hands fashioned and made me,
and now you have destroyed me
altogether.
9 Remember that you have made me
like clay;
and will you return me to the dust?
10 Did you not pour me out like milk
and curdle me like cheese?
11 You clothed me with skin and flesh,
and knit me together with bones
and sinews.
12 You have granted me life and steadfast love,
and your care has preserved my
spirit.
13 Yet these things you hid in your
heart;
I know that this was your purpose.
14 If I sin, you watch me
and do not acquit me of my iniquity.
15 If I am guilty, woe to me!
If I am in the right, I cannot lift up
my head,
for I am filled with disgrace
and look on my affliction.
16 And were my head lifted up,[3] you
would hunt me like a lion
and again work wonders against
me.
17 You renew your witnesses against me
and increase your vexation toward
me;
you bring fresh troops against me.

18 "Why did you bring me out from the
womb?
Would that I had died before any
eye had seen me
19 and were as though I had not been,
carried from the womb to the
grave.
20 Are not my days few?
Then cease, and leave me alone,
that I may find a little cheer

[1] The meaning of the Hebrew word is uncertain [2] Or *Would that there were an* [3] Hebrew lacks *my head*

²¹ before I go—and I shall not return—
    to the land of darkness and deep
        shadow,
²² the land of gloom like thick dark-
        ness,
    like deep shadow without any
        order,
    where light is as thick darkness."

Zophar Speaks: You Deserve Worse

11 Then Zophar the Naamathite an-
    swered and said:

² "Should a multitude of words go unan-
        swered,
    and a man full of talk be judged
        right?
³ Should your babble silence men,
    and when you mock, shall no one
        shame you?
⁴ For you say, 'My doctrine is pure,
    and I am clean in God's¹ eyes.'
⁵ But oh, that God would speak
    and open his lips to you,
⁶ and that he would tell you the
        secrets of wisdom!
    For he is manifold in understand-
        ing.²
    Know then that God exacts of you
        less than your guilt deserves.

⁷ "Can you find out the deep things of
        God?
    Can you find out the limit of the
        Almighty?
⁸ It is higher than heaven³—what can
        you do?
    Deeper than Sheol—what can you
        know?
⁹ Its measure is longer than the earth
    and broader than the sea.
¹⁰ If he passes through and imprisons
    and summons the court, who can
        turn him back?
¹¹ For he knows worthless men;
    when he sees iniquity, will he not
        consider it?
¹² But a stupid man will get understand-
        ing
    when a wild donkey's colt is born
        a man!

¹³ "If you prepare your heart,
    you will stretch out your hands
        toward him.

¹⁴ If iniquity is in your hand, put it far
        away,
    and let not injustice dwell in your
        tents.
¹⁵ Surely then you will lift up your face
        without blemish;
    you will be secure and will not fear.
¹⁶ You will forget your misery;
    you will remember it as waters
        that have passed away.
¹⁷ And your life will be brighter than
        the noonday;
    its darkness will be like the morn-
        ing.
¹⁸ And you will feel secure, because
        there is hope;
    you will look around and take your
        rest in security.
¹⁹ You will lie down, and none will
        make you afraid;
    many will court your favor.
²⁰ But the eyes of the wicked will fail;
    all way of escape will be lost to
        them,
    and their hope is to breathe their
        last."

Job Replies: The Lᴏʀᴅ Has Done This

12 Then Job answered and said:

² "No doubt you are the people,
    and wisdom will die with you.
³ But I have understanding as well as
        you;
    I am not inferior to you.
    Who does not know such things as
        these?
⁴ I am a laughingstock to my friends;
    I, who called to God and he
        answered me,
    a just and blameless man, am a
        laughingstock.
⁵ In the thought of one who is at ease
        there is contempt for misfor-
        tune;
    it is ready for those whose feet slip.
⁶ The tents of robbers are at peace,
    and those who provoke God are
        secure,
    who bring their god in their hand.

⁷ "But ask the beasts, and they will teach
        you;
    the birds of the heavens, and they
        will tell you;

¹ Hebrew *your* ² The meaning of the Hebrew is uncertain ³ Hebrew *The heights of heaven* ⁴ The meaning of the Hebrew is uncertain

12 Wisdom is with the aged,
    and understanding in length of
    days.
13 "With God[2] are wisdom and might;
    he has counsel and understanding.
14 If he tears down, none can rebuild;
    if he shuts a man in, none can
    open.
15 If he withholds the waters, they dry
    up;
    if he sends them out, they over-
    whelm the land.
16 With him are strength and sound
    wisdom;
    the deceived and the deceiver are
    his.
17 He leads counselors away stripped,
    and judges he makes fools.
18 He looses the bonds of kings
    and binds a waistcloth on their
    hips.
19 He leads priests away stripped
    and overthrows the mighty.
20 He deprives of speech those who are
    trusted
    and takes away the discernment of
    the elders.
21 He pours contempt on princes
    and loosens the belt of the strong.
22 He uncovers the deeps out of dark-
    ness
    and brings deep darkness to light.
23 He makes nations great, and he
    destroys them;
    he enlarges nations, and leads
    them away.
24 He takes away understanding from
    the chiefs of the people of the
    earth
    and makes them wander in a
    trackless waste.
25 They grope in the dark without light,
    and he makes them stagger like a
    drunken man.

Job Continues: Still I Will Hope in God

13 "Behold, my eye has seen all this,
    my ear has heard and under-
    stood it.
2   What you know, I also know;
    I am not inferior to you.
3   But I would speak to the Almighty,
    and I desire to argue my case with
    God.

Ask Yourself . . .

ABOUT OBEDIENCE

In the life of faith we all make wrong
choices. We get our advice from the
wrong place. We complain about
the things God has let into our lives.
We work to get out of trials instead
of to persevere through them, and
then we wonder why our faith is
so weak and our peace nonexistent. Think about these questions
and what they mean for your life.
Then consider God's thoughts on
the matter and ask yourself where
your life needs to change:

- Why do I exist? To satisfy
  myself or God?
- What is my number one
  goal—finding comfort or
  persevering?
- What do I ingest more of—TV
  or the Bible?
- When life gets hard, do I most
  often complain, or praise?
- Am I happy or worried?
- Am I content or fearful?
- Am I a believer or a doubter?
- Is there a sin I'm holding on to?
- Am I taking my disobedience
  to Jesus, letting him forgive
  me—completely?

8   or the bushes of the earth,[1] and they
    will teach you;
    and the fish of the sea will declare
    to you.
9   Who among all these does not know
    that the hand of the LORD has done
    this?
10 In his hand is the life of every living
    thing
    and the breath of all mankind.
11 Does not the ear test words
    as the palate tastes food?

[1] Or *speak to the earth* [2] Hebrew *him*

4   As for you, you whitewash with lies;
      worthless physicians are you all.
5   Oh that you would keep silent,
      and it would be your wisdom!
6   Hear now my argument
      and listen to the pleadings of my
        lips.
7   Will you speak falsely for God
      and speak deceitfully for him?
8   Will you show partiality toward him?
      Will you plead the case for God?
9   Will it be well with you when he
        searches you out?
      Or can you deceive him, as one
        deceives a man?
10 He will surely rebuke you
      if in secret you show partiality.
11 Will not his majesty terrify you,
      and the dread of him fall upon
        you?
12 Your maxims are proverbs of ashes;
      your defenses are defenses of clay.

13 "Let me have silence, and I will speak,
      and let come on me what may.
14 Why should I take my flesh in my
        teeth
      and put my life in my hand?
15 Though he slay me, I will hope in him;[1]
      yet I will argue my ways to his
        face.
16 This will be my salvation,
      that the godless shall not come
        before him.
17 Keep listening to my words,
      and let my declaration be in your
        ears.
18 Behold, I have prepared my case;
      I know that I shall be in the right.
19 Who is there who will contend with
        me?
      For then I would be silent and die.
20 Only grant me two things,
      then I will not hide myself from
        your face:
21 withdraw your hand far from me,
      and let not dread of you terrify me.
22 Then call, and I will answer;
      or let me speak, and you reply to
        me.
23 How many are my iniquities and my
        sins?
      Make me know my transgression
        and my sin.

24 Why do you hide your face
      and count me as your enemy?
25 Will you frighten a driven leaf
      and pursue dry chaff?
26 For you write bitter things against me
      and make me inherit the iniquities
        of my youth.
27 You put my feet in the stocks
      and watch all my paths;
      you set a limit for[2] the soles of my
        feet.
28 Man[3] wastes away like a rotten thing,
      like a garment that is moth-eaten.

Job Continues: Death Comes Soon to All

14 "Man who is born of a woman
      is few of days and full of trouble.
2   He comes out like a flower and with-
        ers;
      he flees like a shadow and contin-
        ues not.
3   And do you open your eyes on such a
        one
      and bring me into judgment with
        you?
4   Who can bring a clean thing out of an
        unclean?
      There is not one.
5   Since his days are determined,
      and the number of his months is
        with you,
      and you have appointed his limits
        that he cannot pass,
6   look away from him and leave him
        alone,[4]
      that he may enjoy, like a hired
        hand, his day.

7   "For there is hope for a tree,
      if it be cut down, that it will sprout
        again,
      and that its shoots will not cease.
8   Though its root grow old in the earth,
      and its stump die in the soil,
9   yet at the scent of water it will bud
      and put out branches like a young
        plant.
10 But a man dies and is laid low;
      man breathes his last, and where
        is he?
11 As waters fail from a lake
      and a river wastes away and dries
        up,

[1] Or Behold, he will slay me; I have no hope [2] Or you marked [3] Hebrew He [4] Probable reading; Hebrew look away from him, that he may cease

2 so a man lies down and rises not
again;
till the heavens are no more he will
not awake
or be roused out of his sleep.
13 Oh that you would hide me in Sheol,
that you would conceal me until
your wrath be past,
that you would appoint me a set
time, and remember me!
14 If a man dies, shall he live again?
All the days of my service I would
wait,
till my renewal[1] should come.
15 You would call, and I would answer
you;
you would long for the work of
your hands.
16 For then you would number my steps;
you would not keep watch over my
sin;
17 my transgression would be sealed up
in a bag,
and you would cover over my
iniquity.

18 "But the mountain falls and crumbles
away,
and the rock is removed from its
place;
19 the waters wear away the stones;
the torrents wash away the soil of
the earth;
so you destroy the hope of man.
20 You prevail forever against him, and
he passes;
you change his countenance, and
send him away.
21 His sons come to honor, and he does
not know it;
they are brought low, and he perceives it not.
22 He feels only the pain of his own
body,
and he mourns only for himself."

Eliphaz Accuses: Job Does Not Fear God

15 Then Eliphaz the Temanite answered and said:

2 "Should a wise man answer with
windy knowledge,
and fill his belly with the east wind?
3 Should he argue in unprofitable talk,
or in words with which he can do
no good?

4 But you are doing away with the fear
of God[2]
and hindering meditation before
God.
5 For your iniquity teaches your
mouth,
and you choose the tongue of the
crafty.
6 Your own mouth condemns you, and
not I;
your own lips testify against you.

7 "Are you the first man who was born?
Or were you brought forth before
the hills?
8 Have you listened in the council of
God?
And do you limit wisdom to yourself?
9 What do you know that we do not
know?
What do you understand that is
not clear to us?
10 Both the gray-haired and the aged
are among us,
older than your father.
11 Are the comforts of God too small for
you,
or the word that deals gently with
you?
12 Why does your heart carry you away,
and why do your eyes flash,
13 that you turn your spirit against God
and bring such words out of your
mouth?
14 What is man, that he can be pure?
Or he who is born of a woman, that
he can be righteous?
15 Behold, God[3] puts no trust in his holy
ones,
and the heavens are not pure in his
sight;
16 how much less one who is abominable and corrupt,
a man who drinks injustice like
water!

17 "I will show you; hear me,
and what I have seen I will declare
18 (what wise men have told,
without hiding it from their
fathers,
19 to whom alone the land was given,
and no stranger passed among
them).

[1] Or relief [2] Hebrew lacks of God [3] Hebrew he

20 The wicked man writhes in pain all
　　his days,
　　　through all the years that are laid
　　　up for the ruthless.
21 Dreadful sounds are in his ears;
　　in prosperity the destroyer will
　　come upon him.
22 He does not believe that he will
　　　return out of darkness,
　　and he is marked for the sword.
23 He wanders abroad for bread, saying,
　　'Where is it?'
　　He knows that a day of darkness is
　　ready at his hand;
24 distress and anguish terrify him;
　　they prevail against him, like a
　　king ready for battle.
25 Because he has stretched out his
　　hand against God
　　and defies the Almighty,
26 running stubbornly against him
　　with a thickly bossed shield;
27 because he has covered his face with
　　his fat
　　and gathered fat upon his waist
28 and has lived in desolate cities,
　　in houses that none should
　　inhabit,
　　which were ready to become
　　heaps of ruins;

[1] Or nor will his produce bend down to the earth

29 he will not be rich, and his wealth
　　will not endure,
　　nor will his possessions spread
　　over the earth;[1]
30 he will not depart from darkness;
　　the flame will dry up his shoots,
　　and by the breath of his mouth he
　　will depart.
31 Let him not trust in emptiness,
　　deceiving himself,
　　for emptiness will be his payment.
32 It will be paid in full before his time,
　　and his branch will not be green.
33 He will shake off his unripe grape
　　like the vine,
　　and cast off his blossom like the
　　olive tree.
34 For the company of the godless is
　　barren,
　　and fire consumes the tents of
　　bribery.
35 They conceive trouble and give birth
　　to evil,
　　and their womb prepares deceit."

Job Replies: Miserable Comforters Are You

16 Then Job answered and said:

2 "I have heard many such things;
　　miserable comforters are you all.

Know God

verses to read
Job 16:1-8

When Job's life was a miserable mess, his body was covered in painful sores, and he had lost everything, his friends were useless. They cut him down and blamed him for everything bad in his life. Job knew his friends were wrong, but he wasn't much better. He complained against God all the way through his suffering. When you are experiencing pain, the words of other people may make the pain worse, not better. And it may feel impossible not to complain against God. But he is calling you to trust him, even when you feel at a total loss to understand his ways.

Other people aren't ultimately responsible for your lot in life. So don't blame them for the things that happen to you, but look for God in everything. Where you are today isn't where you're going to be once you can find your way to God. After all, he knows all and sees all, and he promises never to abandon you or leave you (see Deut. 31:8). Nothing can separate you from his love, not even mean people. So choose to believe God rather than fear mean.

3 Shall windy words have an end?
    Or what provokes you that you
        answer?
4 I also could speak as you do,
    if you were in my place;
    I could join words together against
        you
    and shake my head at you.
5 I could strengthen you with my
        mouth,
    and the solace of my lips would
        assuage your pain.

6 "If I speak, my pain is not assuaged,
    and if I forbear, how much of it
        leaves me?
7 Surely now God has worn me out;
    he has[1] made desolate all my com-
        pany.
8 And he has shriveled me up,
    which is a witness against me,
    and my leanness has risen up against
        me;
    it testifies to my face.
9 He has torn me in his wrath and
        hated me;
    he has gnashed his teeth at me;
    my adversary sharpens his eyes
        against me.
10 Men have gaped at me with their
        mouth;
    they have struck me insolently on
        the cheek;
    they mass themselves together
        against me.
11 God gives me up to the ungodly
    and casts me into the hands of the
        wicked.
12 I was at ease, and he broke me apart;
    he seized me by the neck and
        dashed me to pieces;
    he set me up as his target;
13   his archers surround me.
    He slashes open my kidneys and
        does not spare;
    he pours out my gall on the ground.
14 He breaks me with breach upon
        breach;
    he runs upon me like a warrior.
15 I have sewed sackcloth upon my skin
    and have laid my strength in the
        dust.
16 My face is red with weeping,
    and on my eyelids is deep dark-
        ness,

17 although there is no violence in my
        hands,
    and my prayer is pure.

18 "O earth, cover not my blood,
    and let my cry find no resting place.
19 Even now, behold, my witness is in
        heaven,
    and he who testifies for me is on
        high.
20 My friends scorn me;
    my eye pours out tears to God,
21 that he would argue the case of a
        man with God,
    as[2] a son of man does with his
        neighbor.
22 For when a few years have come
    I shall go the way from which
        I shall not return.

Job Continues: Where Then Is My Hope?

17 "My spirit is broken; my days are
        extinct;
    the graveyard is ready for me.
2 Surely there are mockers about me,
    and my eye dwells on their provo-
        cation.

3 "Lay down a pledge for me with you;
    who is there who will put up secu-
        rity for me?
4 Since you have closed their hearts to
        understanding,
    therefore you will not let them
        triumph.
5 He who informs against his friends to
        get a share of their property—
    the eyes of his children will fail.

6 "He has made me a byword of the
        peoples,
    and I am one before whom men
        spit.
7 My eye has grown dim from vexa-
        tion,
    and all my members are like a
        shadow.
8 The upright are appalled at this,
    and the innocent stirs himself up
        against the godless.
9 Yet the righteous holds to his way,
    and he who has clean hands grows
        stronger and stronger.
10 But you, come on again, all of you,
    and I shall not find a wise man
        among you.

---

[1] Hebrew *you have*; also verse 8 [2] Hebrew *and*

11 My days are past; my plans are bro-
      ken off,
         the desires of my heart.
12 They make night into day:
         'The light,' they say, 'is near to the
            darkness.'[1]
13 If I hope for Sheol as my house,
         if I make my bed in darkness,
14 if I say to the pit, 'You are my father,'
         and to the worm, 'My mother,' or
            'My sister,'
15 where then is my hope?
         Who will see my hope?
16 Will it go down to the bars of Sheol?
         Shall we descend together into the
            dust?"

Bildad Speaks: God Punishes the Wicked

18 Then Bildad the Shuhite answered
and said:

2 "How long will you hunt for words?
         Consider, and then we will speak.
3 Why are we counted as cattle?
         Why are we stupid in your sight?
4 You who tear yourself in your anger,
         shall the earth be forsaken for you,
         or the rock be removed out of its
            place?

5 "Indeed, the light of the wicked is put
            out,
         and the flame of his fire does not
            shine.
6 The light is dark in his tent,
         and his lamp above him is put out.
7 His strong steps are shortened,
         and his own schemes throw him
            down.
8 For he is cast into a net by his own
            feet,
         and he walks on its mesh.
9 A trap seizes him by the heel;
         a snare lays hold of him.
10 A rope is hidden for him in the
            ground,
         a trap for him in the path.
11 Terrors frighten him on every side,
         and chase him at his heels.
12 His strength is famished,
         and calamity is ready for his stum-
            bling.
13 It consumes the parts of his skin;
         the firstborn of death consumes
            his limbs.

14 He is torn from the tent in which he
            trusted
         and is brought to the king of terrors.
15 In his tent dwells that which is none
            of his;
         sulfur is scattered over his habita-
            tion.
16 His roots dry up beneath,
         and his branches wither above.
17 His memory perishes from the earth,
         and he has no name in the street.
18 He is thrust from light into darkness,
         and driven out of the world.
19 He has no posterity or progeny
            among his people,
         and no survivor where he used to
            live.
20 They of the west are appalled at his
            day,
         and horror seizes them of the east.
21 Surely such are the dwellings of the
            unrighteous,
         such is the place of him who
            knows not God."

Job Replies: My Redeemer Lives

19 Then Job answered and said:

2 "How long will you torment me
         and break me in pieces with words?
3 These ten times you have cast
            reproach upon me;
         are you not ashamed to wrong me?
4 And even if it be true that I have erred,
         my error remains with myself.
5 If indeed you magnify yourselves
            against me
         and make my disgrace an argu-
            ment against me,
6 know then that God has put me in
            the wrong
         and closed his net about me.
7 Behold, I cry out, 'Violence!' but I am
            not answered;
         I call for help, but there is no justice.
8 He has walled up my way, so that
            I cannot pass,
         and he has set darkness upon my
            paths.
9 He has stripped from me my glory
         and taken the crown from my head.
10 He breaks me down on every side,
            and I am gone,
         and my hope has he pulled up like
            a tree.

---

[1] The meaning of the Hebrew is uncertain

11 He has kindled his wrath against me
       and counts me as his adversary.
12 His troops come on together;
       they have cast up their siege ramp[1]
           against me
       and encamp around my tent.

13 "He has put my brothers far from me,
       and those who knew me are
           wholly estranged from me.
14 My relatives have failed me,
       my close friends have forgotten
           me.
15 The guests in my house and my
           maidservants count me as a
           stranger;
       I have become a foreigner in their
           eyes.
16 I call to my servant, but he gives me
           no answer;
       I must plead with him with my
           mouth for mercy.
17 My breath is strange to my wife,
       and I am a stench to the children
           of my own mother.
18 Even young children despise me;
       when I rise they talk against me.
19 All my intimate friends abhor me,
       and those whom I loved have
           turned against me.
20 My bones stick to my skin and to my
           flesh,
       and I have escaped by the skin of
           my teeth.
21 Have mercy on me, have mercy on
           me, O you my friends,
       for the hand of God has touched
           me!
22 Why do you, like God, pursue me?
       Why are you not satisfied with my
           flesh?

23 "Oh that my words were written!
       Oh that they were inscribed in a
           book!
24 Oh that with an iron pen and lead
       they were engraved in the rock
           forever!
25 For I know that my Redeemer lives,
       and at the last he will stand upon
           the earth.[2]
26 And after my skin has been thus
           destroyed,
       yet in[3] my flesh I shall see God,

27 whom I shall see for myself,
       and my eyes shall behold, and not
           another.
       My heart faints within me!
28 If you say, 'How we will pursue him!'
       and, 'The root of the matter is
           found in him,'
29 be afraid of the sword,
       for wrath brings the punishment
           of the sword,
       that you may know there is a judg-
           ment."

Zophar Speaks: The Wicked Will Suffer

20 Then Zophar the Naamathite an-
       swered and said:

2 "Therefore my thoughts answer me,
       because of my haste within me.
3 I hear censure that insults me,
       and out of my understanding a
           spirit answers me.
4 Do you not know this from of old,
       since man was placed on earth,
5 that the exulting of the wicked is
           short,
       and the joy of the godless but for a
           moment?
6 Though his height mount up to the
           heavens,
       and his head reach to the clouds,
7 he will perish forever like his own
           dung;
       those who have seen him will say,
           'Where is he?'
8 He will fly away like a dream and not
           be found;
       he will be chased away like a
           vision of the night.
9 The eye that saw him will see him no
           more,
       nor will his place any more behold
           him.
10 His children will seek the favor of the
           poor,
       and his hands will give back his
           wealth.
11 His bones are full of his youthful
           vigor,
       but it will lie down with him in the
           dust.

12 "Though evil is sweet in his mouth,
       though he hides it under his
           tongue,

---

[1] Hebrew *their way* [2] Hebrew *dust* [3] Or *without*

13 though he is loath to let it go
    and holds it in his mouth,
14 yet his food is turned in his stomach;
    it is the venom of cobras within
    him.
15 He swallows down riches and vomits
    them up again;
    God casts them out of his belly.
16 He will suck the poison of cobras;
    the tongue of a viper will kill him.
17 He will not look upon the rivers,
    the streams flowing with honey
    and curds.
18 He will give back the fruit of his toil
    and will not swallow it down;
    from the profit of his trading
    he will get no enjoyment.
19 For he has crushed and abandoned
    the poor;
    he has seized a house that he did
    not build.

20 "Because he knew no contentment in
    his belly,
    he will not let anything in which
    he delights escape him.
21 There was nothing left after he had
    eaten;
    therefore his prosperity will not
    endure.
22 In the fullness of his sufficiency he
    will be in distress;
    the hand of everyone in misery
    will come against him.
23 To fill his belly to the full,
    God[1] will send his burning anger
    against him
    and rain it upon him into his body.
24 He will flee from an iron weapon;
    a bronze arrow will strike him
    through.
25 It is drawn forth and comes out of
    his body;
    the glittering point comes out of
    his gallbladder;
    terrors come upon him.
26 Utter darkness is laid up for his
    treasures;
    a fire not fanned will devour him;
    what is left in his tent will be con-
    sumed.
27 The heavens will reveal his iniquity,
    and the earth will rise up against
    him.

28 The possessions of his house will be
    carried away,
    dragged off in the day of God's[2]
    wrath.
29 This is the wicked man's portion
    from God,
    the heritage decreed for him by
    God."

Ask Yourself . . .

ABOUT SUFFERING

- What do I do when disaster hits?
- How can I make it more about God and less about other people next time?
- Am I mindful of the suffering of Jesus, especially his suffering on my behalf?
- What does the Bible say about trials and suffering? (See the Quick Relief guide in the back of this Bible for help.)

Job Replies: The Wicked Do Prosper

21 Then Job answered and said:

2 "Keep listening to my words,
    and let this be your comfort.
3 Bear with me, and I will speak,
    and after I have spoken, mock on.
4 As for me, is my complaint against
    man?
    Why should I not be impatient?
5 Look at me and be appalled,
    and lay your hand over your
    mouth.
6 When I remember, I am dismayed,
    and shuddering seizes my flesh.
7 Why do the wicked live,
    reach old age, and grow mighty in
    power?
8 Their offspring are established in
    their presence,
    and their descendants before their
    eyes.

---

[1] Hebrew he [2] Hebrew his

9 Their houses are safe from fear,
   and no rod of God is upon them.
10 Their bull breeds without fail;
   their cow calves and does not
      miscarry.
11 They send out their little boys like a
      flock,
   and their children dance.
12 They sing to the tambourine and the
      lyre
   and rejoice to the sound of the
      pipe.
13 They spend their days in prosperity,
   and in peace they go down to
      Sheol.
14 They say to God, 'Depart from us!
   We do not desire the knowledge of
      your ways.
15 What is the Almighty, that we should
      serve him?
   And what profit do we get if we
      pray to him?'
16 Behold, is not their prosperity in
      their hand?
   The counsel of the wicked is far
      from me.

17 "How often is it that the lamp of the
      wicked is put out?
   That their calamity comes upon
      them?
   That God[1] distributes pains in his
      anger?
18 That they are like straw before the
      wind,
   and like chaff that the storm car-
      ries away?
19 You say, 'God stores up their iniquity
      for their children.'
   Let him pay it out to them, that
      they may know it.
20 Let their own eyes see their destruc-
      tion,
   and let them drink of the wrath of
      the Almighty.
21 For what do they care for their
      houses after them,
   when the number of their months
      is cut off?
22 Will any teach God knowledge,
   seeing that he judges those who
      are on high?
23 One dies in his full vigor,
   being wholly at ease and secure,

24 his pails[2] full of milk
   and the marrow of his bones
      moist.
25 Another dies in bitterness of soul,
   never having tasted of prosperity.
26 They lie down alike in the dust,
   and the worms cover them.

27 "Behold, I know your thoughts
   and your schemes to wrong me.
28 For you say, 'Where is the house of
      the prince?
   Where is the tent in which the
      wicked lived?'
29 Have you not asked those who travel
      the roads,
   and do you not accept their testi-
      mony
30 that the evil man is spared in the day
      of calamity,
   that he is rescued in the day of
      wrath?
31 Who declares his way to his face,
   and who repays him for what he
      has done?
32 When he is carried to the grave,
   watch is kept over his tomb.
33 The clods of the valley are sweet to
      him;
   all mankind follows after him,
   and those who go before him are
      innumerable.
34 How then will you comfort me with
      empty nothings?
   There is nothing left of your
      answers but falsehood."

Eliphaz Speaks: Job's Wickedness Is Great

22 Then Eliphaz the Temanite answered and said:

2 "Can a man be profitable to God?
   Surely he who is wise is profitable
      to himself.
3 Is it any pleasure to the Almighty if
      you are in the right,
   or is it gain to him if you make
      your ways blameless?
4 Is it for your fear of him that he
      reproves you
   and enters into judgment with
      you?
5 Is not your evil abundant?
   There is no end to your iniquities.

[1] Hebrew he [2] The meaning of the Hebrew word is uncertain

6 For you have exacted pledges of your
    brothers for nothing
    and stripped the naked of their
    clothing.
7 You have given no water to the weary
    to drink,
    and you have withheld bread from
    the hungry.
8 The man with power possessed the
    land,
    and the favored man lived in it.
9 You have sent widows away empty,
    and the arms of the fatherless
    were crushed.
10 Therefore snares are all around you,
    and sudden terror overwhelms
    you,
11 or darkness, so that you cannot see,
    and a flood of water covers you.

12 "Is not God high in the heavens?
    See the highest stars, how lofty
    they are!
13 But you say, 'What does God know?
    Can he judge through the deep
    darkness?
14 Thick clouds veil him, so that he does
    not see,
    and he walks on the vault of
    heaven.'
15 Will you keep to the old way
    that wicked men have trod?
16 They were snatched away before
    their time;
    their foundation was washed away.
17 They said to God, 'Depart from us,'
    and 'What can the Almighty do to
    us?'[1]
18 Yet he filled their houses with good
    things—
    but the counsel of the wicked is far
    from me.
19 The righteous see it and are glad;
    the innocent one mocks at them,
20 saying, 'Surely our adversaries are
    cut off,
    and what they left the fire has
    consumed.'

21 "Agree with God, and be at peace;
    thereby good will come to you.
22 Receive instruction from his mouth,
    and lay up his words in your heart.

23 If you return to the Almighty you will
    be built up;
    if you remove injustice far from
    your tents,
24 if you lay gold in the dust,
    and gold of Ophir among the
    stones of the torrent-bed,
25 then the Almighty will be your gold
    and your precious silver.
26 For then you will delight yourself in
    the Almighty
    and lift up your face to God.
27 You will make your prayer to him,
    and he will hear you,
    and you will pay your vows.
28 You will decide on a matter, and it
    will be established for you,
    and light will shine on your ways.
29 For when they are humbled you say,
    'It is because of pride';[2]
    but he saves the lowly.
30 He delivers even the one who is not
    innocent,
    who will be delivered through the
    cleanness of your hands."

Job Replies: Where Is God?

23 Then Job answered and said:

2 "Today also my complaint is bitter;[3]
    my hand is heavy on account of my
    groaning.
3 Oh, that I knew where I might find
    him,
    that I might come even to his seat!
4 I would lay my case before him
    and fill my mouth with arguments.
5 I would know what he would
    answer me
    and understand what he would say
    to me.
6 Would he contend with me in the
    greatness of his power?
    No; he would pay attention to me.
7 There an upright man could argue
    with him,
    and I would be acquitted forever
    by my judge.

8 "Behold, I go forward, but he is not
    there,
    and backward, but I do not per-
    ceive him;

[1] Hebrew them [2] Or you say, 'It is exaltation' [3] Or defiant

9 on the left hand when he is working,
   I do not behold him;
   he turns to the right hand, but I do
      not see him.
10 But he knows the way that I take;
   when he has tried me, I shall come
      out as gold.
11 My foot has held fast to his steps;
   I have kept his way and have not
      turned aside.
12 I have not departed from the com-
      mandment of his lips;
   I have treasured the words of his
      mouth more than my portion
      of food.
13 But he is unchangeable,[1] and who
      can turn him back?
   What he desires, that he does.
14 For he will complete what he
      appoints for me,
   and many such things are in his
      mind.
15 Therefore I am terrified at his pres-
      ence;
   when I consider, I am in dread of
      him.
16 God has made my heart faint;
   the Almighty has terrified me;
17 yet I am not silenced because of the
      darkness,
   nor because thick darkness covers
      my face.

24 "Why are not times of judgment
      kept by the Almighty,
   and why do those who know him
      never see his days?
2 Some move landmarks;
   they seize flocks and pasture them.
3 They drive away the donkey of the
      fatherless;
   they take the widow's ox for a
      pledge.
4 They thrust the poor off the road;
   the poor of the earth all hide them-
      selves.
5 Behold, like wild donkeys in the
      desert
   the poor[2] go out to their toil, seek-
      ing game;
   the wasteland yields food for their
      children.
6 They gather their[3] fodder in the field,
   and they glean the vineyard of the
      wicked man.

7 They lie all night naked, without
      clothing,
   and have no covering in the cold.
8 They are wet with the rain of the
      mountains
   and cling to the rock for lack of
      shelter.
9 (There are those who snatch the
      fatherless child from the breast,
   and they take a pledge against the
      poor.)
10 They go about naked, without cloth-
      ing;
   hungry, they carry the sheaves;
11 among the olive rows of the wicked[4]
      they make oil;
   they tread the winepresses, but
      suffer thirst.
12 From out of the city the dying groan,
   and the soul of the wounded cries
      for help;
   yet God charges no one with wrong.

13 "There are those who rebel against the
      light,
   who are not acquainted with its
      ways,
   and do not stay in its paths.
14 The murderer rises before it is light,
   that he may kill the poor and
      needy,
   and in the night he is like a thief.
15 The eye of the adulterer also waits
      for the twilight,
   saying, 'No eye will see me';
   and he veils his face.
16 In the dark they dig through houses;
   by day they shut themselves up;
   they do not know the light.
17 For deep darkness is morning to all
      of them;
   for they are friends with the ter-
      rors of deep darkness.

18 "You say, 'Swift are they on the face of
      the waters;
   their portion is cursed in the land;
   no treader turns toward their
      vineyards.
19 Drought and heat snatch away the
      snow waters;
   so does Sheol those who have
      sinned.
20 The womb forgets them;
   the worm finds them sweet;

Or one   [2]Hebrew they   [3]Hebrew his   [4]Hebrew their olive rows

they are no longer remembered,
so wickedness is broken like a
tree.'

21 "They wrong the barren, childless
woman,
and do no good to the widow.
22 Yet God[1] prolongs the life of the
mighty by his power;
they rise up when they despair of
life.
23 He gives them security, and they are
supported,
and his eyes are upon their ways.
24 They are exalted a little while, and
then are gone;
they are brought low and gathered
up like all others;
they are cut off like the heads of
grain.
25 If it is not so, who will prove me a liar
and show that there is nothing in
what I say?"

Bildad Speaks: Man Cannot Be Righteous

25 Then Bildad the Shuhite answered
and said:

2 "Dominion and fear are with God;[2]
he makes peace in his high heaven.
3 Is there any number to his armies?
Upon whom does his light not
arise?
4 How then can man be in the right
before God?
How can he who is born of woman
be pure?
5 Behold, even the moon is not bright,
and the stars are not pure in his
eyes;
6 how much less man, who is a maggot,
and the son of man, who is a
worm!"

Job Replies: God's Majesty Is Unsearchable

26 Then Job answered and said:

2 "How you have helped him who has
no power!
How you have saved the arm that
has no strength!
3 How you have counseled him who
has no wisdom,
and plentifully declared sound
knowledge!

4 With whose help have you uttered
words,
and whose breath has come out
from you?
5 The dead tremble
under the waters and their inhabitants.
6 Sheol is naked before God,[3]
and Abaddon has no covering.
7 He stretches out the north over the
void
and hangs the earth on nothing.
8 He binds up the waters in his thick
clouds,
and the cloud is not split open
under them.
9 He covers the face of the full moon[4]
and spreads over it his cloud.
10 He has inscribed a circle on the face
of the waters
at the boundary between light and
darkness.
11 The pillars of heaven tremble
and are astounded at his rebuke.
12 By his power he stilled the sea;
by his understanding he shattered
Rahab.
13 By his wind the heavens were made
fair;
his hand pierced the fleeing serpent.
14 Behold, these are but the outskirts of
his ways,
and how small a whisper do we
hear of him!
But the thunder of his power who
can understand?"

Job Continues: I Will Maintain My Integrity

27 And Job again took up his discourse
and said:

2 "As God lives, who has taken away my
right,
and the Almighty, who has made
my soul bitter,
3 as long as my breath is in me,
and the spirit of God is in my nostrils,
4 my lips will not speak falsehood,
and my tongue will not utter deceit.
5 Far be it from me to say that you are
right;
till I die I will not put away my
integrity from me.

[1] Hebrew he [2] Hebrew him [3] Hebrew him [4] Or his throne

6 I hold fast my righteousness and will
        not let it go;
    my heart does not reproach me for
        any of my days.

7 "Let my enemy be as the wicked,
    and let him who rises up against
        me be as the unrighteous.
8 For what is the hope of the godless
        when God cuts him off,
    when God takes away his life?
9 Will God hear his cry
        when distress comes upon him?
10 Will he take delight in the Almighty?
    Will he call upon God at all times?
11 I will teach you concerning the hand
        of God;
    what is with the Almighty I will
        not conceal.
12 Behold, all of you have seen it your-
        selves;
    why then have you become alto-
        gether vain?

13 "This is the portion of a wicked man
        with God,
    and the heritage that oppressors
        receive from the Almighty:

14 If his children are multiplied, it is for
        the sword,
    and his descendants have not
        enough bread.
15 Those who survive him the pesti-
        lence buries,
    and his widows do not weep.
16 Though he heap up silver like dust,
    and pile up clothing like clay,
17 he may pile it up, but the righteous
        will wear it,
    and the innocent will divide the
        silver.
18 He builds his house like a moth's,
    like a booth that a watchman
        makes.
19 He goes to bed rich, but will do so no
        more;
    he opens his eyes, and his wealth
        is gone.
20 Terrors overtake him like a flood;
    in the night a whirlwind carries
        him off.
21 The east wind lifts him up and he is
        gone;
    it sweeps him out of his place.

Know Yourself

verses to read
Job 27:1-6

When you first start out as a God Girl, you are passionate, hopeful, and excited, but as the storms start to hit your life and the winds get to blowing, you start to bend under the stress of it all. When that happens you have two choices: you can either reject your first love, God, or hold on tightly to him. You can either forget all that you know about him and run for cover, or you can just keep on keepin' on, trusting him like you did in the beginning.

In the life of faith, trials are going to come. Your faith has to be tested, purified. You have to prove that your faith is real. So don't look at trials as something you've got to worry about but as a natural part of growing up. The strong tree isn't the one planted inside a warm, comfortable box in a climate-controlled building. No, the strong tree is the one planted outside in the elements, forced to live with extreme temperatures, drought, and snow. This hardy tree digs deep into the ground to keep itself alive, always reaching for more life-giving nutrients, always holding on. Your roots grow strong as you keep on getting those life-giving elements from the Father. A small little sapling grows into an enormous oak when it holds tightly to the soil that surrounds it. You too will grow in strength when you hold tightly to the Word of God. But remember, you will pull through ultimately not because of your hold on him but because of his hold on you.

²² It¹ hurls at him without pity;
      he flees from its² power in head-
         long flight.
²³ It claps its hands at him
      and hisses at him from its place.

Job Continues: Where Is Wisdom?

28 "Surely there is a mine for silver,
      and a place for gold that they
         refine.
² Iron is taken out of the earth,
      and copper is smelted from the ore.
³ Man puts an end to darkness
      and searches out to the farthest
         limit
      the ore in gloom and deep darkness.
⁴ He opens shafts in a valley away
         from where anyone lives;
      they are forgotten by travelers;
      they hang in the air, far away from
         mankind; they swing to and fro.
⁵ As for the earth, out of it comes
         bread,
      but underneath it is turned up as
         by fire.
⁶ Its stones are the place of sapphires,³
      and it has dust of gold.

⁷ "That path no bird of prey knows,
      and the falcon's eye has not seen it.
⁸ The proud beasts have not trodden it;
      the lion has not passed over it.

⁹ "Man puts his hand to the flinty rock
      and overturns mountains by the
         roots.
¹⁰ He cuts out channels in the rocks,
      and his eye sees every precious
         thing.
¹¹ He dams up the streams so that they
         do not trickle,
      and the thing that is hidden he
         brings out to light.

¹² "But where shall wisdom be found?
      And where is the place of under-
         standing?
¹³ Man does not know its worth,
      and it is not found in the land of
         the living.
¹⁴ The deep says, 'It is not in me,'
      and the sea says, 'It is not with me.'
¹⁵ It cannot be bought for gold,
      and silver cannot be weighed as its
         price.

¹⁶ It cannot be valued in the gold of
         Ophir,
      in precious onyx or sapphire.
¹⁷ Gold and glass cannot equal it,
      nor can it be exchanged for jewels
         of fine gold.
¹⁸ No mention shall be made of coral or
         of crystal;
      the price of wisdom is above
         pearls.
¹⁹ The topaz of Ethiopia cannot equal it,
      nor can it be valued in pure gold.

²⁰ "From where, then, does wisdom
         come?
      And where is the place of under-
         standing?
²¹ It is hidden from the eyes of all living
      and concealed from the birds of
         the air.
²² Abaddon and Death say,
      'We have heard a rumor of it with
         our ears.'

²³ "God understands the way to it,
      and he knows its place.
²⁴ For he looks to the ends of the earth
      and sees everything under the
         heavens.
²⁵ When he gave to the wind its weight
      and apportioned the waters by
         measure,
²⁶ when he made a decree for the rain
      and a way for the lightning of the
         thunder,
²⁷ then he saw it and declared it;
      he established it, and searched it
         out.
²⁸ And he said to man,
      'Behold, the fear of the Lord, that is
         wisdom,
      and to turn away from evil is
         understanding.'"

Job's Summary Defense

29 And Job again took up his discourse
      and said:

² "Oh, that I were as in the months of
         old,
      as in the days when God watched
         over me,
³ when his lamp shone upon my head,
      and by his light I walked through
         darkness,

¹Or *He* (that is, God); also verse 23 ²Or *his*; also verse 23 ³Or *lapis lazuli*; also verse 16

4   as I was in my prime,[1]
        when the friendship of God was
            upon my tent,
5   when the Almighty was yet with me,
        when my children were all around
            me,
6   when my steps were washed with
            butter,
        and the rock poured out for me
            streams of oil!
7   When I went out to the gate of the city,
        when I prepared my seat in the
            square,
8   the young men saw me and withdrew,
        and the aged rose and stood;
9   the princes refrained from talking
        and laid their hand on their mouth;
10 the voice of the nobles was hushed,
        and their tongue stuck to the roof
            of their mouth.
11 When the ear heard, it called me
            blessed,
        and when the eye saw, it approved,
12 because I delivered the poor who
            cried for help,
        and the fatherless who had none
            to help him.
13 The blessing of him who was about
            to perish came upon me,
        and I caused the widow's heart to
            sing for joy.
14 I put on righteousness, and it clothed
            me;
        my justice was like a robe and a
            turban.
15 I was eyes to the blind
        and feet to the lame.
16 I was a father to the needy,
        and I searched out the cause of
            him whom I did not know.
17 I broke the fangs of the unrighteous
        and made him drop his prey from
            his teeth.
18 Then I thought, 'I shall die in my nest,
        and I shall multiply my days as the
            sand,
19 my roots spread out to the waters,
        with the dew all night on my
            branches,
20 my glory fresh with me,
        and my bow ever new in my hand.'

21 "Men listened to me and waited
        and kept silence for my counsel.

22 After I spoke they did not speak
            again,
        and my word dropped upon them.
23 They waited for me as for the rain,
        and they opened their mouths as
            for the spring rain.
24 I smiled on them when they had no
            confidence,
        and the light of my face they did
            not cast down.
25 I chose their way and sat as chief,
        and I lived like a king among his
            troops,
        like one who comforts mourners.

30 "But now they laugh at me,
        men who are younger than I,
    whose fathers I would have dis-
            dained
        to set with the dogs of my flock.
2   What could I gain from the strength
            of their hands,
        men whose vigor is gone?
3   Through want and hard hunger
        they gnaw the dry ground by night
            in waste and desolation;
4   they pick saltwort and the leaves of
            bushes,
        and the roots of the broom tree for
            their food.[2]
5   They are driven out from human
            company;
        they shout after them as after a
            thief.
6   In the gullies of the torrents they
            must dwell,
        in holes of the earth and of the
            rocks.
7   Among the bushes they bray;
        under the nettles they huddle
            together.
8   A senseless, a nameless brood,
        they have been whipped out of the
            land.

9   "And now I have become their song;
        I am a byword to them.
10 They abhor me; they keep aloof from
            me;
        they do not hesitate to spit at the
            sight of me.
11 Because God has loosed my cord and
            humbled me,
        they have cast off restraint[3] in my
            presence.

---

[1] Hebrew *my autumn days* [2] Or *warmth* [3] Hebrew *the bridle*

12 On my right hand the rabble rise;
    they push away my feet;
    they cast up against me their ways
        of destruction.
13 They break up my path;
    they promote my calamity;
    they need no one to help them.
14 As through a wide breach they come;
    amid the crash they roll on.
15 Terrors are turned upon me;
    my honor is pursued as by the
        wind,
    and my prosperity has passed
        away like a cloud.

16 "And now my soul is poured out within
        me;
    days of affliction have taken hold
        of me.
17 The night racks my bones,
    and the pain that gnaws me takes
        no rest.
18 With great force my garment is dis-
        figured;
    it binds me about like the collar of
        my tunic.
19 God[1] has cast me into the mire,
    and I have become like dust and
        ashes.
20 I cry to you for help and you do not
        answer me;
    I stand, and you only look at me.
21 You have turned cruel to me;
    with the might of your hand you
        persecute me.
22 You lift me up on the wind; you make
        me ride on it,
    and you toss me about in the roar
        of the storm.
23 For I know that you will bring me to
        death
    and to the house appointed for all
        living.

24 "Yet does not one in a heap of ruins
        stretch out his hand,
    and in his disaster cry for help?[2]
25 Did not I weep for him whose day
        was hard?
    Was not my soul grieved for the
        needy?
26 But when I hoped for good, evil
        came,
    and when I waited for light, dark-
        ness came.

27 My inward parts are in turmoil and
        never still;
    days of affliction come to meet me.
28 I go about darkened, but not by the
        sun;
    I stand up in the assembly and cry
        for help.
29 I am a brother of jackals
    and a companion of ostriches.
30 My skin turns black and falls from me
    and my bones burn with heat.
31 My lyre is turned to mourning,
    and my pipe to the voice of those
        who weep.

Job's Final Appeal

31 "I have made a covenant with my
    eyes;
    how then could I gaze at a virgin?
2 What would be my portion from God
        above
    and my heritage from the Almighty
        on high?
3 Is not calamity for the unrighteous,
    and disaster for the workers of
        iniquity?
4 Does not he see my ways
    and number all my steps?

5 "If I have walked with falsehood
    and my foot has hastened to deceit
6 (Let me be weighed in a just balance,
    and let God know my integrity!)
7 if my step has turned aside from the
        way
    and my heart has gone after my
        eyes,
    and if any spot has stuck to my
        hands,
8 then let me sow, and another eat,
    and let what grows for me[3] be
        rooted out.

9 "If my heart has been enticed toward a
        woman,
    and I have lain in wait at my neigh-
        bor's door,
10 then let my wife grind for another,
    and let others bow down on her.
11 For that would be a heinous crime;
    that would be an iniquity to be
        punished by the judges;
12 for that would be a fire that con-
        sumes as far as Abaddon,
    and it would burn to the root all
        my increase.

[1] Hebrew He [2] The meaning of the Hebrew is uncertain [3] Or let my descendants

13 "If I have rejected the cause of my
    manservant or my maidservant,
   when they brought a complaint
    against me,
14 what then shall I do when God rises
    up?
   When he makes inquiry, what shall
    I answer him?
15 Did not he who made me in the
    womb make him?
   And did not one fashion us in the
    womb?

16 "If I have withheld anything that the
    poor desired,
   or have caused the eyes of the
    widow to fail,
17 or have eaten my morsel alone,
   and the fatherless has not eaten of it

18   (for from my youth the fatherless[1]
       grew up with me as with a
       father,
      and from my mother's womb
       I guided the widow[2]),
19 if I have seen anyone perish for lack
       of clothing,
      or the needy without covering,
20 if his body has not blessed me,[3]
      and if he was not warmed with the
       fleece of my sheep,
21 if I have raised my hand against the
       fatherless,
      because I saw my help in the gate,
22 then let my shoulder blade fall from
       my shoulder,
      and let my arm be broken from its
       socket.

[1]Hebrew he [2]Hebrew her [3]Hebrew if his loins have not blessed me

Know Yourself

verses to read
Job 31:1-8

Bad habits are like weeds. They dig down deep and wrap themselves around your heart, so removing them takes strength and wisdom. You could just yank them out by the roots, but if you've ever pulled weeds, you know how hard it can be to get those things out, especially if the roots have really dug in deep. But there's another way to kill the roots choking your spirit. Follow Job's example by asking yourself what sinful habits have crept into your life, and then begin to choke them out with something far better and more powerful—the beauty of Christ and the goodness of God in the gospel. The best way to suffocate a bad habit is to replace it with the good habit of enjoying the gospel of free grace. When you make Christ and his gospel the most important thing to you, the fruit of godliness will flow out through your life.

So don't sit around feeling bad about your bad habits or sins, and especially don't think about the sins of other people—that's a total waste of time. You need to spend your strength looking for the good in people and in your situations. When you find good things in people, try to imitate them. Watch how they overcome situations and feelings you aren't so good at overcoming. Refuse to be negative, always seeing the bad in things, and instead pay attention to the hand of God.

Bad habits can be uprooted by the Spirit of God as you stop treating them like they have more control over you than God does. When you made him Lord of your life, you became his slave. You can't be a slave to two masters. That means you aren't in chains to your bad habits and sinful way of living anymore. You are set free; all that's left to do is to step out of those old chains and run in the direction of God. You are no longer a prisoner but have been set free—so go ahead and act like it!

23 For I was in terror of calamity from
        God,
        and I could not have faced his
        majesty.

24 "If I have made gold my trust
        or called fine gold my confidence,
25 if I have rejoiced because my wealth
        was abundant
        or because my hand had found
        much,
26 if I have looked at the sun[1] when it
        shone,
        or the moon moving in splendor,
27 and my heart has been secretly
        enticed,
        and my mouth has kissed my hand,
28 this also would be an iniquity to be
        punished by the judges,
        for I would have been false to God
        above.

29 "If I have rejoiced at the ruin of him
        who hated me,
        or exulted when evil overtook him
30 (I have not let my mouth sin
        by asking for his life with a curse),
31 if the men of my tent have not said,
        'Who is there that has not been
        filled with his meat?'
32 (the sojourner has not lodged in the
        street;
        I have opened my doors to the
        traveler),
33 if I have concealed my transgressions
        as others do[2]
        by hiding my iniquity in my heart,
34 because I stood in great fear of the
        multitude,
        and the contempt of families terri-
        fied me,
        so that I kept silence, and did not
        go out of doors—
35 Oh, that I had one to hear me!
        (Here is my signature! Let the
        Almighty answer me!)
        Oh, that I had the indictment writ-
        ten by my adversary!
36 Surely I would carry it on my shoul-
        der;
        I would bind it on me as a crown;
37 I would give him an account of all my
        steps;
        like a prince I would approach him.

38 "If my land has cried out against me
        and its furrows have wept together,
39 if I have eaten its yield without pay-
        ment
        and made its owners breathe their
        last,
40 let thorns grow instead of wheat,
        and foul weeds instead of barley."

The words of Job are ended.

Elihu Rebukes Job's Three Friends

32 So these three men ceased to answer Job, because he was righteous in his own eyes. [2] Then Elihu the son of Barachel the Buzite, of the family of Ram, burned with anger. He burned with anger at Job because he justified himself rather than God. [3] He burned with anger also at Job's three friends because they had found no answer, although they had declared Job to be in the wrong. [4] Now Elihu had waited to speak to Job because they were older than he. [5] And when Elihu saw that there was no answer in the mouth of these three men, he burned with anger.

[6] And Elihu the son of Barachel the Buzite answered and said:

"I am young in years,
        and you are aged;
        therefore I was timid and afraid
        to declare my opinion to you.
7 I said, 'Let days speak,
        and many years teach wisdom.'
8 But it is the spirit in man,
        the breath of the Almighty, that
        makes him understand.
9 It is not the old[3] who are wise,
        nor the aged who understand
        what is right.
10 Therefore I say, 'Listen to me;
        let me also declare my opinion.'

11 "Behold, I waited for your words,
        I listened for your wise sayings,
        while you searched out what to
        say.
12 I gave you my attention,
        and, behold, there was none
        among you who refuted Job
        or who answered his words.
13 Beware lest you say, 'We have found
        wisdom;
        God may vanquish him, not a man.'

[1] Hebrew *the light* [2] Or *as Adam did* [3] Hebrew *many* [in years]

14 He has not directed his words
     against me,
  and I will not answer him with
     your speeches.

15 "They are dismayed; they answer no
     more;
  they have not a word to say.

16 And shall I wait, because they do not
     speak,
  because they stand there, and
     answer no more?

17 I also will answer with my share;
  I also will declare my opinion.

18 For I am full of words;
  the spirit within me constrains me.

19 Behold, my belly is like wine that has
     no vent;
  like new wineskins ready to burst.

20 I must speak, that I may find relief;
  I must open my lips and answer.

21 I will not show partiality to any man
  or use flattery toward any person.

22 For I do not know how to flatter,
  else my Maker would soon take me
     away.

Elihu Rebukes Job

33 "But now, hear my speech, O Job,
  and listen to all my words.

2 Behold, I open my mouth;
  the tongue in my mouth speaks.

3 My words declare the uprightness of
     my heart,
  and what my lips know they speak
     sincerely.

4 The Spirit of God has made me,
  and the breath of the Almighty
     gives me life.

5 Answer me, if you can;
  set your words in order before me;
     take your stand.

6 Behold, I am toward God as you are;
  I too was pinched off from a piece
     of clay.

7 Behold, no fear of me need terrify you;
  my pressure will not be heavy
     upon you.

8 "Surely you have spoken in my ears,
  and I have heard the sound of your
     words.

9 You say, 'I am pure, without trans-
     gression;
  I am clean, and there is no iniquity
     in me.

10 Behold, he finds occasions against me,
  he counts me as his enemy,

11 he puts my feet in the stocks
  and watches all my paths.'

12 "Behold, in this you are not right. I will
     answer you,
  for God is greater than man.

13 Why do you contend against him,
  saying, 'He will answer none of
     man's[1] words'?[2]

14 For God speaks in one way,
  and in two, though man does not
     perceive it.

15 In a dream, in a vision of the night,
  when deep sleep falls on men,
  while they slumber on their beds,

16 then he opens the ears of men
  and terrifies them with warnings,

17 that he may turn man aside from his
     deed
  and conceal pride from a man;

18 he keeps back his soul from the pit,
  his life from perishing by the sword.

19 "Man is also rebuked with pain on his
     bed
  and with continual strife in his
     bones,

20 so that his life loathes bread,
  and his appetite the choicest food.

21 His flesh is so wasted away that it
     cannot be seen,
  and his bones that were not seen
     stick out.

22 His soul draws near the pit,
  and his life to those who bring
     death.

23 If there be for him an angel,
  a mediator, one of the thousand,
  to declare to man what is right for
     him,

24 and he is merciful to him, and says,
  'Deliver him from going down into
     the pit;
  I have found a ransom;

25 let his flesh become fresh with youth;
  let him return to the days of his
     youthful vigor';

26 then man[3] prays to God, and he
     accepts him;
  he sees his face with a shout of joy,
  and he restores to man his righteous-
     ness.

27 He sings before men and says:

[1] Hebrew his [2] Or He will not answer for any of his own words [3] Hebrew he

'I sinned and perverted what was
  right,
  and it was not repaid to me.
28 He has redeemed my soul from going
  down into the pit,
  and my life shall look upon the
  light.'

29 "Behold, God does all these things,
  twice, three times, with a man,
30 to bring back his soul from the pit,
  that he may be lighted with the
  light of life.
31 Pay attention, O Job, listen to me;
  be silent, and I will speak.
32 If you have any words, answer me;
  speak, for I desire to justify you.
33 If not, listen to me;
  be silent, and I will teach you
  wisdom."

Elihu Asserts God's Justice

34 Then Elihu answered and said:

2 "Hear my words, you wise men,
  and give ear to me, you who know;
3 for the ear tests words
  as the palate tastes food.
4 Let us choose what is right;
  let us know among ourselves what
  is good.
5 For Job has said, 'I am in the right,
  and God has taken away my right;
6 in spite of my right I am counted a
  liar;
  my wound is incurable, though
  I am without transgression.'
7 What man is like Job,
  who drinks up scoffing like water,
8 who travels in company with evildoers
  and walks with wicked men?
9 For he has said, 'It profits a man
  nothing
  that he should take delight in God.'

10 "Therefore, hear me, you men of
  understanding:
  far be it from God that he should
  do wickedness,
  and from the Almighty that he
  should do wrong.
11 For according to the work of a man
  he will repay him,
  and according to his ways he will
  make it befall him.

12 Of a truth, God will not do wickedly,
  and the Almighty will not pervert
  justice.
13 Who gave him charge over the earth,
  and who laid on him[1] the whole
  world?
14 If he should set his heart to it
  and gather to himself his spirit and
  his breath,
15 all flesh would perish together,
  and man would return to dust.

16 "If you have understanding, hear this;
  listen to what I say.
17 Shall one who hates justice govern?
  Will you condemn him who is
  righteous and mighty,
18 who says to a king, 'Worthless one,'
  and to nobles, 'Wicked man,'
19 who shows no partiality to princes,
  nor regards the rich more than the
  poor,
  for they are all the work of his
  hands?
20 In a moment they die;
  at midnight the people are shaken
  and pass away,
  and the mighty are taken away by
  no human hand.

21 "For his eyes are on the ways of a man,
  and he sees all his steps.
22 There is no gloom or deep darkness
  where evildoers may hide themselves.
23 For God[2] has no need to consider a
  man further,
  that he should go before God in
  judgment.
24 He shatters the mighty without
  investigation
  and sets others in their place.
25 Thus, knowing their works,
  he overturns them in the night,
  and they are crushed.
26 He strikes them for their wickedness
  in a place for all to see,
27 because they turned aside from following him
  and had no regard for any of his
  ways,
28 so that they caused the cry of the
  poor to come to him,
  and he heard the cry of the
  afflicted—

---

[1] Hebrew lacks *on him* [2] Hebrew *he*

29 When he is quiet, who can condemn?
     When he hides his face, who can
          behold him,
        whether it be a nation or a man?—
30 that a godless man should not reign,
     that he should not ensnare the
          people.

31 "For has anyone said to God,
     'I have borne punishment; I will
          not offend any more;
32 teach me what I do not see;
     if I have done iniquity, I will do it
          no more'?
33 Will he then make repayment to suit
          you,
     because you reject it?
   For you must choose, and not I;
     therefore declare what you know.[1]
34 Men of understanding will say to me,
     and the wise man who hears me
          will say:
35 'Job speaks without knowledge;
     his words are without insight.'
36 Would that Job were tried to the end,
     because he answers like wicked
          men.
37 For he adds rebellion to his sin;
     he claps his hands among us
     and multiplies his words against
          God."

Elihu Condemns Job

35 And Elihu answered and said:

2 "Do you think this to be just?
     Do you say, 'It is my right before
          God,'
3 that you ask, 'What advantage have I?
     How am I better off than if I had
          sinned?'
4 I will answer you
     and your friends with you.
5 Look at the heavens, and see;
     and behold the clouds, which are
          higher than you.
6 If you have sinned, what do you
          accomplish against him?
     And if your transgressions are mul-
          tiplied, what do you do to him?
7 If you are righteous, what do you
          give to him?
     Or what does he receive from your
          hand?

8 Your wickedness concerns a man like
          yourself,
     and your righteousness a son of
          man.

9 "Because of the multitude of oppres-
          sions people cry out;
     they call for help because of the
          arm of the mighty.[2]
10 But none says, 'Where is God my
          Maker,
     who gives songs in the night,
11 who teaches us more than the beasts
          of the earth
     and makes us wiser than the birds
          of the heavens?'
12 There they cry out, but he does not
          answer,
     because of the pride of evil men.
13 Surely God does not hear an empty
          cry,
     nor does the Almighty regard it.
14 How much less when you say that
          you do not see him,
     that the case is before him, and
          you are waiting for him!
15 And now, because his anger does not
          punish,
     and he does not take much note of
          transgression,[3]
16 Job opens his mouth in empty talk;
     he multiplies words without
          knowledge."

Elihu Extols God's Greatness

36 And Elihu continued, and said:

2 "Bear with me a little, and I will show
          you,
     for I have yet something to say on
          God's behalf.
3 I will get my knowledge from afar
     and ascribe righteousness to my
          Maker.
4 For truly my words are not false;
     one who is perfect in knowledge is
          with you.

5 "Behold, God is mighty, and does not
          despise any;
     he is mighty in strength of under-
          standing.
6 He does not keep the wicked alive,
     but gives the afflicted their right.

[1] The meaning of the Hebrew in verses 29–33 is uncertain [2] Or the many [3] Theodotion, Symmachus (compare Vulgate); the meaning of the Hebrew word is uncertain

7   He does not withdraw his eyes from
the righteous,
     but with kings on the throne
     he sets them forever, and they are
exalted.

8   And if they are bound in chains
     and caught in the cords of affliction,

9   then he declares to them their work
     and their transgressions, that they
are behaving arrogantly.

10   He opens their ears to instruction
     and commands that they return
from iniquity.

11   If they listen and serve him,
     they complete their days in pros-
perity,
     and their years in pleasantness.

12   But if they do not listen, they perish
by the sword
     and die without knowledge.

13   "The godless in heart cherish anger;
     they do not cry for help when he
binds them.

14   They die in youth,
     and their life ends among the cult
prostitutes.

15   He delivers the afflicted by their
affliction
     and opens their ear by adversity.

16   He also allured you out of distress
     into a broad place where there was
no cramping,
     and what was set on your table
was full of fatness.

17   "But you are full of the judgment on
the wicked;
     judgment and justice seize you.

18   Beware lest wrath entice you into
scoffing,
     and let not the greatness of the
ransom turn you aside.

19   Will your cry for help avail to keep
you from distress,
     or all the force of your strength?

20   Do not long for the night,
     when peoples vanish in their
place.

21   Take care; do not turn to iniquity,
     for this you have chosen rather
than affliction.

22   Behold, God is exalted in his power;
     who is a teacher like him?

23   Who has prescribed for him his way,
     or who can say, 'You have done
wrong'?

24   "Remember to extol his work,
     of which men have sung.

25   All mankind has looked on it;
     man beholds it from afar.

26   Behold, God is great, and we know
him not;
     the number of his years is
unsearchable.

27   For he draws up the drops of water;
     they distill his mist in rain,

28   which the skies pour down
     and drop on mankind abundantly.

29   Can anyone understand the spreading of the clouds,
     the thunderings of his pavilion?

30   Behold, he scatters his lightning
about him
     and covers the roots of the sea.

31   For by these he judges peoples;
     he gives food in abundance.

32   He covers his hands with the lightning
     and commands it to strike the mark.

33   Its crashing declares his presence;[1]
     the cattle also declare that he rises.

Elihu Proclaims God's Majesty

37   "At this also my heart trembles
     and leaps out of its place.

2   Keep listening to the thunder of his
voice
     and the rumbling that comes from
his mouth.

3   Under the whole heaven he lets it go,
     and his lightning to the corners of
the earth.

4   After it his voice roars;
     he thunders with his majestic voice,
     and he does not restrain the light-
nings[2] when his voice is heard.

5   God thunders wondrously with his
voice;
     he does great things that we can-
not comprehend.

6   For to the snow he says, 'Fall on the
earth,'
     likewise to the downpour, his
mighty downpour.

7   He seals up the hand of every man,
     that all men whom he made may
know it.

---

[1] Hebrew *declares concerning him*   [2] Hebrew *them*

8 Then the beasts go into their lairs,
    and remain in their dens.
9 From its chamber comes the whirl-
    wind,
    and cold from the scattering winds.
10 By the breath of God ice is given,
    and the broad waters are frozen
        fast.
11 He loads the thick cloud with mois-
    ture;
    the clouds scatter his lightning.
12 They turn around and around by his
    guidance,
    to accomplish all that he com-
        mands them
    on the face of the habitable world.
13 Whether for correction or for his land
    or for love, he causes it to happen.

14 "Hear this, O Job;
    stop and consider the wondrous
        works of God.
15 Do you know how God lays his com-
    mand upon them
    and causes the lightning of his
        cloud to shine?
16 Do you know the balancings[1] of the
    clouds,
    the wondrous works of him who is
        perfect in knowledge,
17 you whose garments are hot
    when the earth is still because of
        the south wind?
18 Can you, like him, spread out the skies,
    hard as a cast metal mirror?
19 Teach us what we shall say to him;
    we cannot draw up our case
        because of darkness.
20 Shall it be told him that I would
    speak?
    Did a man ever wish that he would
        be swallowed up?

21 "And now no one looks on the light
    when it is bright in the skies,
    when the wind has passed and
        cleared them.
22 Out of the north comes golden splen-
    dor;
    God is clothed with awesome
        majesty.
23 The Almighty—we cannot find him;
    he is great in power;
    justice and abundant righteous-
        ness he will not violate.

24 Therefore men fear him;
    he does not regard any who are
        wise in their own conceit."[2]

The LORD Answers Job

38 Then the LORD answered Job out of
    the whirlwind and said:

2 "Who is this that darkens counsel by
    words without knowledge?
3 Dress for action[3] like a man;
    I will question you, and you make
        it known to me.

4 "Where were you when I laid the foun-
    dation of the earth?
    Tell me, if you have understanding.
5 Who determined its measure-
    ments—surely you know!
    Or who stretched the line upon it?
6 On what were its bases sunk,
    or who laid its cornerstone,
7 when the morning stars sang together
    and all the sons of God shouted for
        joy?

8 "Or who shut in the sea with doors
    when it burst out from the womb,
9 when I made clouds its garment
    and thick darkness its swaddling
        band,
10 and prescribed limits for it
    and set bars and doors,
11 and said, 'Thus far shall you come,
    and no farther,
    and here shall your proud waves
        be stayed'?

12 "Have you commanded the morning
    since your days began,
    and caused the dawn to know its
        place,
13 that it might take hold of the skirts of
    the earth,
    and the wicked be shaken out of it?
14 It is changed like clay under the seal,
    and its features stand out like a
        garment.
15 From the wicked their light is with-
    held,
    and their uplifted arm is broken.

16 "Have you entered into the springs of
    the sea,
    or walked in the recesses of the
        deep?

---

[1] Or hoverings [2] Hebrew in heart [3] Hebrew Gird up your loins

17 Have the gates of death been
        revealed to you,
        or have you seen the gates of deep
            darkness?
18 Have you comprehended the
        expanse of the earth?
        Declare, if you know all this.

19 "Where is the way to the dwelling of
        light,
        and where is the place of darkness,
20 that you may take it to its territory
        and that you may discern the
            paths to its home?
21 You know, for you were born then,
        and the number of your days is
            great!

22 "Have you entered the storehouses of
        the snow,
        or have you seen the storehouses
            of the hail,
23 which I have reserved for the time of
        trouble,
        for the day of battle and war?
24 What is the way to the place where
        the light is distributed,
        or where the east wind is scattered
            upon the earth?

25 "Who has cleft a channel for the tor-
        rents of rain
        and a way for the thunderbolt,
26 to bring rain on a land where no man
        is,
        on the desert in which there is no
            man,
27 to satisfy the waste and desolate
        land,
        and to make the ground sprout
            with grass?

28 "Has the rain a father,
        or who has begotten the drops of
            dew?
29 From whose womb did the ice come
        forth,
        and who has given birth to the
            frost of heaven?
30 The waters become hard like stone,
        and the face of the deep is frozen.

31 "Can you bind the chains of the
        Pleiades
        or loose the cords of Orion?

32 Can you lead forth the Mazzaroth[1] in
        their season,
        or can you guide the Bear with its
            children?
33 Do you know the ordinances of the
        heavens?
        Can you establish their rule on the
            earth?

34 "Can you lift up your voice to the
        clouds,
        that a flood of waters may cover
            you?
35 Can you send forth lightnings, that
        they may go
        and say to you, 'Here we are'?
36 Who has put wisdom in the inward
        parts[2]
        or given understanding to the
            mind?[3]
37 Who can number the clouds by wis-
        dom?
        Or who can tilt the waterskins of
            the heavens,
38 when the dust runs into a mass
        and the clods stick fast together?

39 "Can you hunt the prey for the lion,
        or satisfy the appetite of the young
            lions,
40 when they crouch in their dens
        or lie in wait in their thicket?
41 Who provides for the raven its prey,
        when its young ones cry to God for
            help,
        and wander about for lack of food?

39 "Do you know when the mountain
        goats give birth?
        Do you observe the calving of the
            does?
2 Can you number the months that
        they fulfill,
        and do you know the time when
            they give birth,
3 when they crouch, bring forth their
        offspring,
        and are delivered of their young?
4 Their young ones become strong;
        they grow up in the open;
        they go out and do not return to
            them.

5 "Who has let the wild donkey go free?
        Who has loosed the bonds of the
            swift donkey,

[1] Probably the name of a constellation [2] Or in the ibis [3] Or rooster

5 to whom I have given the arid plain
       for his home
     and the salt land for his dwelling
       place?
7 He scorns the tumult of the city;
     he hears not the shouts of the
       driver.
8 He ranges the mountains as his
       pasture,
     and he searches after every green
       thing.

9 "Is the wild ox willing to serve you?
     Will he spend the night at your
       manger?
10 Can you bind him in the furrow with
       ropes,
     or will he harrow the valleys after
       you?
11 Will you depend on him because his
       strength is great,
     and will you leave to him your
       labor?
12 Do you have faith in him that he will
       return your grain
     and gather it to your threshing
       floor?

13 "The wings of the ostrich wave
       proudly,
     but are they the pinions and plum-
       age of love?[1]
14 For she leaves her eggs to the earth
     and lets them be warmed on the
       ground,
15 forgetting that a foot may crush them
     and that the wild beast may
       trample them.
16 She deals cruelly with her young, as
       if they were not hers;
     though her labor be in vain, yet
       she has no fear,
17 because God has made her forget
       wisdom
     and given her no share in under-
       standing.
18 When she rouses herself to flee,[2]
     she laughs at the horse and his
       rider.

19 "Do you give the horse his might?
     Do you clothe his neck with a
       mane?
20 Do you make him leap like the
       locust?
     His majestic snorting is terrifying.

21 He paws[3] in the valley and exults in
       his strength;
     he goes out to meet the weapons.
22 He laughs at fear and is not dis-
       mayed;
     he does not turn back from the
       sword.
23 Upon him rattle the quiver,
     the flashing spear, and the javelin.
24 With fierceness and rage he swal-
       lows the ground;
     he cannot stand still at the sound
       of the trumpet.
25 When the trumpet sounds, he says
       'Aha!'
     He smells the battle from afar,
     the thunder of the captains, and
       the shouting.

26 "Is it by your understanding that the
       hawk soars
     and spreads his wings toward the
       south?
27 Is it at your command that the eagle
       mounts up
     and makes his nest on high?
28 On the rock he dwells and makes his
       home,
     on the rocky crag and stronghold.
29 From there he spies out the prey;
     his eyes behold it from far away.
30 His young ones suck up blood,
     and where the slain are, there is
       he."

40 And the Lord said to Job:

2 "Shall a faultfinder contend with the
       Almighty?
     He who argues with God, let him
       answer it."

Job Promises Silence
3 Then Job answered the Lord and said:

4 "Behold, I am of small account; what
       shall I answer you?
     I lay my hand on my mouth.
5 I have spoken once, and I will not
       answer;
     twice, but I will proceed no fur-
       ther."

The Lord Challenges Job
6 Then the Lord answered Job out of the
whirlwind and said:

The meaning of the Hebrew is uncertain [2] The meaning of the Hebrew is uncertain [3] Hebrew *They paw*

7 "Dress for action[1] like a man;
  I will question you, and you make
    it known to me.
8 Will you even put me in the wrong?
  Will you condemn me that you
    may be in the right?
9 Have you an arm like God,
  and can you thunder with a voice
    like his?

10 "Adorn yourself with majesty and
    dignity;
  clothe yourself with glory and
    splendor.
11 Pour out the overflowings of your
    anger,
  and look on everyone who is
    proud and abase him.
12 Look on everyone who is proud and
    bring him low
  and tread down the wicked where
    they stand.
13 Hide them all in the dust together;
  bind their faces in the world
    below.[2]
14 Then will I also acknowledge to you
  that your own right hand can save
    you.

15 "Behold, Behemoth,[3]
  which I made as I made you;
  he eats grass like an ox.
16 Behold, his strength in his loins,
  and his power in the muscles of his
    belly.
17 He makes his tail stiff like a cedar;
  the sinews of his thighs are knit
    together.
18 His bones are tubes of bronze,
  his limbs like bars of iron.

19 "He is the first of the works[4] of God;
  let him who made him bring near
    his sword!
20 For the mountains yield food for
    him
  where all the wild beasts play.
21 Under the lotus plants he lies,
  in the shelter of the reeds and in
    the marsh.
22 For his shade the lotus trees cover
    him;
  the willows of the brook surround
    him.

A Prayer of...

PRAISE

Dear Lord, the God of eternity: the heavens declare your glory.

The earth talks about your riches; the universe is your temple; your presence fills all the earth. You have created life for your pleasure and taught it happiness; you have made me what I am and given me what I have.

In you I live and move and have my being; your will has set the boundaries of my life and wisely takes care of all my affairs. Thank you for your riches to me in Jesus, for the unclouded revelation of him in your Word, where I see his person, character, kindness, glory, humiliation, sufferings, death, and resurrection. Help me to feel a need for his continual Saviorhood, and help me to cry with Job, "I am so insignificant"; with Peter, "Save me"; with the tax collector, "Be merciful to me, a sinner." Crush the love of sin in me. Let me know the need of renewal and forgiveness for my soul, so that I can serve and enjoy you forever. I come to you in the all-prevailing name of Jesus, with nothing of my own to plead.

Amen.

23 Behold, if the river is turbulent he is
    not frightened;
  he is confident though Jordan
    rushes against his mouth.
24 Can one take him by his eyes,[5]
  or pierce his nose with a snare?

41 [6] "Can you draw out Leviathan[7] with
    a fishhook
  or press down his tongue with a
    cord?
2 Can you put a rope in his nose
  or pierce his jaw with a hook?
3 Will he make many pleas to you?
  Will he speak to you soft words?

[1] Hebrew *Gird up your loins* [2] Hebrew *in the hidden place* [3] A large animal, exact identity unknown [4] Hebrew *ways* [5] Or *in his sight*
[6] Ch 40:25 in Hebrew [7] A large sea animal, exact identity unknown

⁴ Will he make a covenant with you
    to take him for your servant for-
       ever?
⁵ Will you play with him as with a bird,
    or will you put him on a leash for
       your girls?
⁶ Will traders bargain over him?
    Will they divide him up among the
       merchants?
⁷ Can you fill his skin with harpoons
    or his head with fishing spears?
⁸ Lay your hands on him;
    remember the battle—you will not
       do it again!
⁹¹ Behold, the hope of a man is false;
    he is laid low even at the sight of
       him.
¹⁰ No one is so fierce that he dares to
       stir him up.
    Who then is he who can stand
       before me?
¹¹ Who has first given to me, that
       I should repay him?
    Whatever is under the whole
       heaven is mine.

¹² "I will not keep silence concerning his
       limbs,
    or his mighty strength, or his
       goodly frame.
¹³ Who can strip off his outer garment?
    Who would come near him with a
       bridle?
¹⁴ Who can open the doors of his face?
    Around his teeth is terror.
¹⁵ His back is made of² rows of shields,
    shut up closely as with a seal.
¹⁶ One is so near to another
    that no air can come between them.
¹⁷ They are joined one to another;
    they clasp each other and cannot
       be separated.
¹⁸ His sneezings flash forth light,
    and his eyes are like the eyelids of
       the dawn.
¹⁹ Out of his mouth go flaming torches;
    sparks of fire leap forth.
²⁰ Out of his nostrils comes forth smoke,
    as from a boiling pot and burning
       rushes.
²¹ His breath kindles coals,
    and a flame comes forth from his
       mouth.
²² In his neck abides strength,
    and terror dances before him.

²³ The folds of his flesh stick together,
    firmly cast on him and immovable.
²⁴ His heart is hard as a stone,
    hard as the lower millstone.
²⁵ When he raises himself up the
       mighty³ are afraid;
    at the crashing they are beside
       themselves.
²⁶ Though the sword reaches him, it
       does not avail,
    nor the spear, the dart, or the
       javelin.
²⁷ He counts iron as straw,
    and bronze as rotten wood.
²⁸ The arrow cannot make him flee;
    for him sling stones are turned to
       stubble.
²⁹ Clubs are counted as stubble;
    he laughs at the rattle of javelins.
³⁰ His underparts are like sharp pot-
       sherds;
    he spreads himself like a threshing
       sledge on the mire.
³¹ He makes the deep boil like a pot;
    he makes the sea like a pot of oint-
       ment.
³² Behind him he leaves a shining wake;
    one would think the deep to be
       white-haired.
³³ On earth there is not his like,
    a creature without fear.
³⁴ He sees everything that is high;
    he is king over all the sons of pride."

Job's Confession and Repentance

42 Then Job answered the LORD and said:

² "I know that you can do all things,
    and that no purpose of yours can
       be thwarted.
³ 'Who is this that hides counsel with-
       out knowledge?'
    Therefore I have uttered what I did
       not understand,
    things too wonderful for me,
       which I did not know.
⁴ 'Hear, and I will speak;
    I will question you, and you make
       it known to me.'
⁵ I had heard of you by the hearing of
       the ear,
    but now my eye sees you;
⁶ therefore I despise myself,
    and repent⁴ in dust and ashes."

Ch 41:1 in Hebrew ²Or *His pride is in his* ³Or *gods* ⁴Or *and am comforted*

The LORD Rebukes Job's Friends

7 After the LORD had spoken these words to Job, the LORD said to Eliphaz the Temanite: "My anger burns against you and against your two friends, for you have not spoken of me what is right, as my servant Job has. **8** Now therefore take seven bulls and seven rams and go to my servant Job and offer up a burnt offering for yourselves. And my servant Job shall pray for you, for I will accept his prayer not to deal with you according to your folly. For you have not spoken of me what is right, as my servant Job has." **9** So Eliphaz the Temanite and Bildad the Shuhite and Zophar the Naamathite went and did what the LORD had told them, and the LORD accepted Job's prayer.

The LORD Restores Job's Fortunes

10 And the LORD restored the fortunes of Job, when he had prayed for his friends. And the LORD gave Job twice as much as

he had before. **11** Then came to him all his brothers and sisters and all who had known him before, and ate bread with him in his house. And they showed him sympathy and comforted him for all the evil[1] that the LORD had brought upon him. And each of them gave him a piece of money[2] and a ring of gold.

12 And the LORD blessed the latter days of Job more than his beginning. And he had 14,000 sheep, 6,000 camels, 1,000 yoke of oxen, and 1,000 female donkeys. **13** He had also seven sons and three daughters. **14** And he called the name of the first daughter Jemimah, and the name of the second Keziah, and the name of the third Keren-happuch. **15** And in all the land there were no women so beautiful as Job's daughters. And their father gave them an inheritance among their brothers. **16** And after this Job lived 140 years, and saw his sons, and his sons' sons, four generations. **17** And Job died, an old man, and full of days.

[1] Or *disaster* [2] Hebrew *a qesitah*; a unit of money of unknown value

Know God

verses to read
Job 42:7–10

Are you suffering? Your suffering will end when God is done using it for your good! Suffering isn't meant to destroy you, like you might think. It's meant to make you into something more than you are right now. Unless your suffering is self-inflicted, it will set you free if you will look in thankfulness to the one who allows it. Suffering is meant to lead you to worship and thankfulness, not to resentment and distrust. When the suffering God Girl trusts God instead of blaming him, her prayers are focused not on getting rid of the problem but on serving the one who is the Answer. The most effective prayers aren't the prayers begging for relief but the ones that look outside of yourself instead of inside.

The life of Job gives us a good example of powerful prayer. Job suffered a lot, but it wasn't until he prayed for his friends that his life was healed: "And the LORD restored the fortunes of Job, when he had prayed for his friends. And the LORD gave Job twice as much as he had before" (Job 42:10). The best and most powerful prayer is always the prayer for someone else. When you take your eyes off your own suffering and instead put them on serving others, you will find yourself free from grief and moving on to more important things—things that make a difference eternally.

Authors: David, Moses, Solomon, Ethan, Heman, Asaph, and many others

Time: Throughout the Old Testament period, but finalized after the Babylonian exile

Place: Unknown

Written to: God's people, or to God in worship

The gist

The book of Psalms is a collection of worship songs written at different times by a number of different men. They express the psalmists' thoughts and feelings about life and God. Each psalm was composed as the writer's response to the things going on in his life.

Things to look for

- The use of poetic language
- Different types of psalms:
  - Psalms of praise talk to God about how great he is
  - Messianic psalms anticipate the life of Jesus
  - Psalms of confession confess the sins of the psalmist
  - Historical psalms think back on the history of the nation of Israel (sometimes called Zion, the name of a mountain that represented God's promises to Israel)
  - "Imprecatory" psalms cry out for justice against those who have made God's people suffer
  - Psalms of lament or regret express sorrow
  - Psalms of thanksgiving recognize the blessings God has given

Sing to God

> In you, O LORD, do I take refuge;
>   let me never be put to shame;
>   in your righteousness deliver me!
>
> *Psalm 31:1*

Worship music is meant to help us do one thing, and that is to worship God. When you worship, you tell God how amazing he is, and you pour out your sense of awe, thanks, and reverence to him. It's like Christmas morning for God when you shower him with the gift of your praise. But what's amazing about worship is that it serves not only the God you sing to but also *you*, the one who sings. Worship was never meant to be a selfish act that you do so that you can feel better or feel inspired, but joy is indeed a side effect of genuine worship. A lot of times the songs you sing to God express your human emotions of fear, worry, and stress—at least that's what they did for King David. The book of Psalms is a collection of songs written by men like Moses, David, Ethan, Heman, and Asaph. They were written for many different reasons, but they did have one thing in common: they were all written to pour out their hearts to God.

Music isn't the only way you worship God. You worship him when you trust him by living in obedience to what he commands, when you thank him for all you've got, and when you talk with him about your life. Worship is more than just singing, but worship music can be a powerful way to connect your heart and soul to God. And the psalmists knew that, maybe better than anyone. As you read the book of Psalms, notice how the godly men who wrote the individual psalms were often scared, lonely, depressed, and suffering, but at the same time they always got back to hope and to a total belief that God would work it all out. Check out how the psalmist can spend most of his energy on complaining but wind up in worship when he finally remembers the truth. And remember that you are reading these psalms from this side of the empty tomb. Like all the books of the Old Testament, the book of Psalms should be read with the New Testament in mind. Always consider what the life, death, and resurrection of Jesus mean to your emotional life and how you relate to the Father.

Psalms can be a great way to speak with God. Read them out loud and make them your conversation with God. Trust the wisdom they speak, and know that communication with God is the most important thing in the life of a God Girl.

Must-Know Terms and Verses

✧ *Fear of the Lord* ✧

Refers to the awe, respect, love, and reverence that we are to have for God. It also means we fear his reaction or judgment more than anyone else's.

✧ *Mercy* ✧

Means not getting the punishment you really deserve. It is God's compassion for us though we have offended him; he sees us in our misery and sin and loves us anyway.

✧ *Selah* ✧

A musical term used in the book of Psalms. Its meaning is uncertain but may be "pause," "silence," "end," or even "louder."

✧ *Zion* ✧

Can mean many things, including fortress, citadel, the Temple Mount, God's holy mountain, the City of David, the City of God, the City of Jerusalem, the land of Judah, or the entire nation of Israel.

The LORD is my shepherd; I shall not want. *Psalm 23:1*

Wait for the LORD;
    be strong, and let your heart take courage;
    wait for the LORD! *Psalm 27:14*

The angel of the LORD encamps
    around those who fear him, and delivers them. *Psalm 34:7*

Delight yourself in the LORD,
    and he will give you the desires of your heart. *Psalm 37:4*

As a deer pants for flowing streams,
    so pants my soul for you, O God.
My soul thirsts for God,
    for the living God.
When shall I come and appear before God? *Psalm 42:1–2*

The Psalms

BOOK ONE

The Way of the Righteous and the Wicked

1 Blessed is the man[1]
　who walks not in the counsel of the
　　wicked,
nor stands in the way of sinners,
　nor sits in the seat of scoffers;
2 but his delight is in the law[2] of the
　　LORD,
　　and on his law he meditates day
　　and night.

3 He is like a tree
　planted by streams of water
that yields its fruit in its season,
　and its leaf does not wither.
In all that he does, he prospers.
4 The wicked are not so,
　　but are like chaff that the wind
　　drives away.

5 Therefore the wicked will not stand
　　in the judgment,
　　nor sinners in the congregation of
　　the righteous;
6 for the LORD knows the way of the
　　righteous,
　　but the way of the wicked will per-
　　ish.

The Reign of the LORD's Anointed

2 Why do the nations rage[3]
　and the peoples plot in vain?
2 The kings of the earth set themselves,
　and the rulers take counsel together,
　against the LORD and against his
　　Anointed, saying,
3 "Let us burst their bonds apart
　and cast away their cords from us."

4 He who sits in the heavens laughs;
　the Lord holds them in derision.

5 Then he will speak to them in his
　　wrath,
　and terrify them in his fury, saying,
6 "As for me, I have set my King
　on Zion, my holy hill."

7 I will tell of the decree:
　The LORD said to me, "You are my Son;
　today I have begotten you.
8 Ask of me, and I will make the
　　nations your heritage,
　　and the ends of the earth your pos-
　　session.
9 You shall break[4] them with a rod of
　　iron
　　and dash them in pieces like a pot-
　　ter's vessel."

10 Now therefore, O kings, be wise;
　be warned, O rulers of the earth.
11 Serve the LORD with fear,
　and rejoice with trembling.
12 Kiss the Son,
　lest he be angry, and you perish in
　　the way,
　for his wrath is quickly kindled.
Blessed are all who take refuge in
　him.

Save Me, O My God

3 A PSALM OF DAVID, WHEN HE FLED FROM
ABSALOM HIS SON.

1 O LORD, how many are my foes!
　Many are rising against me;
2 many are saying of my soul,
　there is no salvation for him in
　　God. *Selah*[5]

3 But you, O LORD, are a shield about
　me,
　my glory, and the lifter of my head.
4 I cried aloud to the LORD,
　and he answered me from his holy
　　hill. *Selah*

---

[1] The singular Hebrew word for *man* (*ish*) is used here to portray a representative example of a godly person; see About the ESV [2] Or *instruction* [3] Or *nations noisily assemble* [4] Revocalization yields (compare Septuagint) *You shall rule* [5] The meaning of the Hebrew word *Selah*, used frequently in the Psalms, is uncertain. It may be a musical or liturgical direction

5   I lay down and slept;
        I woke again, for the LORD sustained
            me.
6   I will not be afraid of many thou-
            sands of people
        who have set themselves against
            me all around.

7   Arise, O LORD!
        Save me, O my God!
    For you strike all my enemies on the
            cheek;
        you break the teeth of the wicked.

8   Salvation belongs to the LORD;
        your blessing be on your people!
                                        Selah

Answer Me When I Call

4 TO THE CHOIRMASTER: WITH STRINGED
    INSTRUMENTS. A PSALM OF DAVID.

1   Answer me when I call, O God of my
        righteousness!

¹Or *O men of rank* ²Or *Be agitated*

        You have given me relief when
            I was in distress.
        Be gracious to me and hear my
            prayer!

2   O men,¹ how long shall my honor be
            turned into shame?
        How long will you love vain words
            and seek after lies?   *Selah*
3   But know that the LORD has set apart
            the godly for himself;
        the LORD hears when I call to him.

4   Be angry,² and do not sin;
        ponder in your own hearts on your
            beds, and be silent.   *Selah*
5   Offer right sacrifices,
        and put your trust in the LORD.

6   There are many who say, "Who will
            show us some good?
        Lift up the light of your face upon
            us, O LORD!"

Know God

verses to read
Psalm 1

God is all about your life's process—walking with God day in and day out. It's easy to become concerned when you can't figure out your purpose in life, but God doesn't want you to focus on some great purpose off in the distance; he wants you to find him in the moment, right now. He wants you to trust him right now, not someday in the future when you find your purpose in life. God's purpose for your life isn't for later; it's for now. His purpose for you is the process of continually doing what he asks you to do, no matter how much it hurts. If you can move through the turmoil, stress, and strain of life by obeying God's Word and looking to him for each step and each action, then you will have found your purpose.

It can be a prideful thing to focus on looking for a "great" purpose. God doesn't need your grand accomplishments, but he wants your heart, fully devoted and trusting in him. When you give your life to him with that in mind, you'll see that every day you have fulfilled your purpose of loving the one who gave you life. The more you live with this goal in mind, the better your days will be and the more of an impact your life will have.

So don't think like other people think. Don't focus on yourself but focus on your God. Don't ask, "What's my purpose?" You know your purpose: to love and serve the one true God so that his will may be done on earth as it is in heaven (see Matt. 6:10). Line up your life with his, and your life will be filled with meaning.

7 You have put more joy in my heart
  than they have when their grain
  and wine abound.

8 In peace I will both lie down and
  sleep;
  for you alone, O LORD, make me
  dwell in safety.

Lead Me in Your Righteousness

5 TO THE CHOIRMASTER: FOR THE FLUTES.
A PSALM OF DAVID.

1 Give ear to my words, O LORD;
  consider my groaning.
2 Give attention to the sound of my cry,
  my King and my God,
  for to you do I pray.

Or I direct my prayer to you

3 O LORD, in the morning you hear my
  voice;
  in the morning I prepare a sacrifice for you[1] and watch.

4 For you are not a God who delights in
  wickedness;
  evil may not dwell with you.
5 The boastful shall not stand before
  your eyes;
  you hate all evildoers.
6 You destroy those who speak lies;
  the LORD abhors the bloodthirsty
  and deceitful man.

7 But I, through the abundance of your
  steadfast love,
  will enter your house.

Know Yourself

verses to read
Psalm 4:6–8

Sometimes you need to do more than just pray about things—your moods, for example. Don't just pray about your bad moods. Kick them out! Your mood comes from your way of thinking about the stuff in your life. The more you listen to your desires and feelings, the easier it is to miss the truth of Scripture. But the more you flat-out refuse to let the world around you decide your moods, looking instead to God and his incredible promises, the freer you become.

Growing into the God Girl you were meant to be means step-by-step, day-by-day grabbing your bad moods by the scruff of the neck and tossing them out the door. As you learn to make the Holy Spirit's thoughts your own, as you study God's Word and find out what pleases him, and as you want what he wants, then controlling your emotions becomes easier and easier. You start to recognize your bad moods more quickly, and sometimes you just refuse to let them live.

Your bad moods don't have to control you: you can control them. Consider what your mood is railing about: Is it your problem, your environment, or something someone said or did? Is it reacting to what God said? Does it care more about people or God? If it's caring more about the creation than the Creator, it's up to no good. Bad moods don't have to plague the God Girl because her mood is based not on her changing circumstances but on a God who never changes. Having a bad day? Think about how you can be happy in God even in the midst of the trial he has allowed. Having a hard time? Think how God has destined you to live with him forever in the new earth, totally by free grace.

As you grow from a God Girl into the woman you were meant to be, you'll get better at refusing to listen to your moods and instead choosing to listen to God. Each time you do, you'll build your strength, your character, and your faith.

I will bow down toward your holy
    temple
    in the fear of you.
8 Lead me, O LORD, in your righteous-
    ness
      because of my enemies;
      make your way straight before me.

9 For there is no truth in their mouth;
    their inmost self is destruction;
  their throat is an open grave;
    they flatter with their tongue.
10 Make them bear their guilt, O God;
    let them fall by their own counsels;
  because of the abundance of their
      transgressions cast them out,
    for they have rebelled against you.

11 But let all who take refuge in you
    rejoice;
      let them ever sing for joy,
  and spread your protection over
      them,
      that those who love your name
      may exult in you.
12 For you bless the righteous, O LORD;
    you cover him with favor as with a
      shield.

O LORD, Deliver My Life

6
TO THE CHOIRMASTER: WITH STRINGED
INSTRUMENTS; ACCORDING TO THE
SHEMINITH.[1] A PSALM OF DAVID.

1 O LORD, rebuke me not in your anger,
    nor discipline me in your wrath.
2 Be gracious to me, O LORD, for I am
    languishing;
    heal me, O LORD, for my bones are
      troubled.
3 My soul also is greatly troubled.
    But you, O LORD—how long?

4 Turn, O LORD, deliver my life;
    save me for the sake of your stead-
    fast love.
5 For in death there is no remem-
    brance of you;
    in Sheol who will give you praise?

6 I am weary with my moaning;
    every night I flood my bed with
      tears;
    I drench my couch with my weep-
    ing.

7 My eye wastes away because of
    grief;
    it grows weak because of all my
      foes.

8 Depart from me, all you workers of
    evil,
    for the LORD has heard the sound
      of my weeping.
9 The LORD has heard my plea;
    the LORD accepts my prayer.
10 All my enemies shall be ashamed
    and greatly troubled;
    they shall turn back and be put to
      shame in a moment.

In You Do I Take Refuge

7
A SHIGGAION[2] OF DAVID, WHICH HE SANG
TO THE LORD CONCERNING THE WORDS
OF CUSH, A BENJAMINITE.

1 O LORD my God, in you do I take
    refuge;
    save me from all my pursuers and
      deliver me,
2 lest like a lion they tear my soul
    apart,
    rending it in pieces, with none to
      deliver.

3 O LORD my God, if I have done this,
    if there is wrong in my hands,
4 if I have repaid my friend[3] with evil
    or plundered my enemy without
      cause,
5 let the enemy pursue my soul and
    overtake it,
    and let him trample my life to the
      ground
    and lay my glory in the dust. *Selah*

6 Arise, O LORD, in your anger;
    lift yourself up against the fury of
      my enemies;
    awake for me; you have appointed
      a judgment.
7 Let the assembly of the peoples be
    gathered about you;
    over it return on high.

8 The LORD judges the peoples;
    judge me, O LORD, according to my
      righteousness
    and according to the integrity that
      is in me.

---

[1] Probably a musical or liturgical term   [2] Probably a musical or liturgical term   [3] Hebrew *the one at peace with me*

⁹ Oh, let the evil of the wicked come to
　　an end,
　　and may you establish the righ-
　　　teous—
　you who test the minds and hearts,[1]
　　O righteous God!
¹⁰ My shield is with God,
　　who saves the upright in heart.
¹¹ God is a righteous judge,
　　and a God who feels indignation
　　　every day.

¹² If a man[2] does not repent, God[3] will
　　whet his sword;
　　he has bent and readied his bow;
¹³ he has prepared for him his deadly
　　weapons,
　　making his arrows fiery shafts.
¹⁴ Behold, the wicked man conceives evil
　　and is pregnant with mischief
　　and gives birth to lies.
¹⁵ He makes a pit, digging it out,
　　and falls into the hole that he has
　　　made.
¹⁶ His mischief returns upon his own
　　head,
　　and on his own skull his violence
　　　descends.

¹⁷ I will give to the LORD the thanks due
　　to his righteousness,
　　and I will sing praise to the name
　　　of the LORD, the Most High.

How Majestic Is Your Name

8 TO THE CHOIRMASTER: ACCORDING TO
THE GITTITH.[4] A PSALM OF DAVID.

¹ O LORD, our Lord,
　　how majestic is your name in all
　　　the earth!
　You have set your glory above the
　　heavens.
² Out of the mouth of babies and
　　infants,
　you have established strength
　　because of your foes,
　　to still the enemy and the avenger.

³ When I look at your heavens, the
　　work of your fingers,
　　the moon and the stars, which you
　　　have set in place,

⁴ what is man that you are mindful of
　　him,
　　and the son of man that you care
　　　for him?
⁵ Yet you have made him a little lower
　　than the heavenly beings[5]
　　and crowned him with glory and
　　　honor.
⁶ You have given him dominion over
　　the works of your hands;
　　you have put all things under his
　　　feet,
⁷ all sheep and oxen,
　　and also the beasts of the field,
⁸ the birds of the heavens, and the fish
　　of the sea,
　　whatever passes along the paths of
　　　the seas.

⁹ O LORD, our Lord,
　　how majestic is your name in all
　　　the earth!

I Will Recount Your Wonderful Deeds

9[6] TO THE CHOIRMASTER: ACCORDING TO
MUTH-LABBEN.[7] A PSALM OF DAVID.

¹ I will give thanks to the LORD with
　　my whole heart;
　　I will recount all of your wonderful
　　　deeds.
² I will be glad and exult in you;
　　I will sing praise to your name,
　　　O Most High.

³ When my enemies turn back,
　　they stumble and perish before[8]
　　　your presence.
⁴ For you have maintained my just
　　cause;
　　you have sat on the throne, giving
　　　righteous judgment.

⁵ You have rebuked the nations; you
　　have made the wicked perish;
　　you have blotted out their name
　　　forever and ever.
⁶ The enemy came to an end in ever-
　　lasting ruins;
　　their cities you rooted out;
　　the very memory of them has
　　　perished.

[1]Hebrew the hearts and kidneys [2]Hebrew he [3]Hebrew he [4]Probably a musical or liturgical term [5]Or than God; Septuagint than the angels [6]Psalms 9 and 10 together follow an acrostic pattern, each stanza beginning with the successive letters of the Hebrew alphabet. In the Septuagint they form one psalm [7]Probably a musical or liturgical term [8]Or because of

7 But the LORD sits enthroned forever;
     he has established his throne for
       justice,
8 and he judges the world with righ-
     teousness;
     he judges the peoples with
       uprightness.

9 The LORD is a stronghold for the
     oppressed,
     a stronghold in times of trouble.
10 And those who know your name put
     their trust in you,
     for you, O LORD, have not forsaken
       those who seek you.

11 Sing praises to the LORD, who sits
     enthroned in Zion!
     Tell among the peoples his deeds!
12 For he who avenges blood is mindful
     of them;
     he does not forget the cry of the
       afflicted.

13 Be gracious to me, O LORD!
     See my affliction from those who
       hate me,
     O you who lift me up from the
       gates of death,
14 that I may recount all your praises,
     that in the gates of the daughter of
       Zion
     I may rejoice in your salvation.

15 The nations have sunk in the pit that
     they made;
     in the net that they hid, their own
       foot has been caught.
16 The LORD has made himself known;
     he has executed judgment;
     the wicked are snared in the
       work of their own hands.
              Higgaion.[1] *Selah*

17 The wicked shall return to Sheol,
     all the nations that forget God.

18 For the needy shall not always be
     forgotten,
     and the hope of the poor shall not
       perish forever.

19 Arise, O LORD! Let not man prevail;
     let the nations be judged before
       you!

20 Put them in fear, O LORD!
     Let the nations know that they are
       but men!   *Selah*

Why Do You Hide Yourself?

10 Why, O LORD, do you stand far
     away?
     Why do you hide yourself in times
       of trouble?

2 In arrogance the wicked hotly pur-
     sue the poor;
     let them be caught in the schemes
       that they have devised.
3 For the wicked boasts of the desires
     of his soul,
     and the one greedy for gain curses
       and renounces the LORD.
4 In the pride of his face[3] the wicked
     does not seek him;[4]
     all his thoughts are, "There is no
       God."
5 His ways prosper at all times;
     your judgments are on high, out of
       his sight;
     as for all his foes, he puffs at them.
6 He says in his heart, "I shall not be
     moved;
     throughout all generations I shall
       not meet adversity."
7 His mouth is filled with cursing and
     deceit and oppression;
     under his tongue are mischief and
       iniquity.
8 He sits in ambush in the villages;
     in hiding places he murders the
       innocent.
     His eyes stealthily watch for the
       helpless;
9   he lurks in ambush like a lion in
       his thicket;
     he lurks that he may seize the poor;
     he seizes the poor when he draws
       him into his net.
10 The helpless are crushed, sink down,
     and fall by his might.
11 He says in his heart, "God has forgot-
     ten,
     he has hidden his face, he will
       never see it."

12 Arise, O LORD; O God, lift up your
     hand;
     forget not the afflicted.

---

[1] Probably a musical or liturgical term [2] Or *and he blesses the one greedy for gain* [3] Or *of his anger* [4] Or *the wicked says, "He will not call to account"*

3 Why does the wicked renounce God
        and say in his heart, "You will not
            call to account"?
4 But you do see, for you note mischief
        and vexation,
    that you may take it into your
        hands;
    to you the helpless commits himself;
        you have been the helper of the
            fatherless.
5 Break the arm of the wicked and
        evildoer;
    call his wickedness to account till
        you find none.

6 The LORD is king forever and ever;
        the nations perish from his land.
7 O LORD, you hear the desire of the
        afflicted;
    you will strengthen their heart;
        you will incline your ear
8 to do justice to the fatherless and the
        oppressed,
    so that man who is of the earth
        may strike terror no more.

The LORD Is in His Holy Temple

11 To the choirmaster. Of David.
    In the LORD I take refuge;
    how can you say to my soul,
        "Flee like a bird to your mountain,
2 for behold, the wicked bend the
        bow;
    they have fitted their arrow to the
        string
    to shoot in the dark at the upright
        in heart;
3 if the foundations are destroyed,
    what can the righteous do?"[1]

4 The LORD is in his holy temple;
    the LORD's throne is in heaven;
    his eyes see, his eyelids test the
        children of man.
5 The LORD tests the righteous,
    but his soul hates the wicked and
        the one who loves violence.
6 Let him rain coals on the wicked;
    fire and sulfur and a scorching
        wind shall be the portion of
            their cup.
7 For the LORD is righteous;
    he loves righteous deeds;
    the upright shall behold his face.

The Faithful Have Vanished

12 To the choirmaster: according to
    The Sheminith.[2] A Psalm of David.

1 Save, O LORD, for the godly one is
        gone;
    for the faithful have vanished from
        among the children of man.
2 Everyone utters lies to his neighbor;
    with flattering lips and a double
        heart they speak.

3 May the LORD cut off all flattering lips,
    the tongue that makes great boasts,
4 those who say, "With our tongue we
        will prevail,
    our lips are with us; who is master
        over us?"

5 "Because the poor are plundered,
        because the needy groan,
    I will now arise," says the LORD;
    "I will place him in the safety for
        which he longs."
6 The words of the LORD are pure
        words,
    like silver refined in a furnace on
        the ground,
    purified seven times.

7 You, O LORD, will keep them;
    you will guard us[3] from this gen-
        eration forever.
8 On every side the wicked prowl,
    as vileness is exalted among the
        children of man.

How Long, O LORD?

13 To the choirmaster. A Psalm of
    David.

1 How long, O LORD? Will you forget
        me forever?
    How long will you hide your face
        from me?
2 How long must I take counsel in my
        soul
    and have sorrow in my heart all
        the day?
    How long shall my enemy be exalted
        over me?

3 Consider and answer me, O LORD my
        God;
    light up my eyes, lest I sleep the
        sleep of death,

---

[1] Or for the foundations will be destroyed; what has the righteous done? [2] Probably a musical or liturgical term [3] Or guard him

4   lest my enemy say, "I have prevailed
        over him,"
            lest my foes rejoice because I am
                shaken.

5   But I have trusted in your steadfast
        love;
            my heart shall rejoice in your
                salvation.
6   I will sing to the LORD,
        because he has dealt bountifully
            with me.

The Fool Says, There Is No God

14 To the choirmaster. Of David.
        The fool says in his heart, "There
            is no God."
        They are corrupt, they do abomi-
            nable deeds,
        there is none who does good.

2   The LORD looks down from heaven
        on the children of man,
            to see if there are any who under-
                stand,[1]
            who seek after God.

3   They have all turned aside; together
        they have become corrupt;
            there is none who does good,
            not even one.

4   Have they no knowledge, all the
        evildoers
            who eat up my people as they eat
                bread
            and do not call upon the LORD?

5   There they are in great terror,
        for God is with the generation of
            the righteous.
6   You would shame the plans of the
        poor,
            but[2] the LORD is his refuge.

7   Oh, that salvation for Israel would
        come out of Zion!
            When the LORD restores the for-
                tunes of his people,
            let Jacob rejoice, let Israel be glad.

Who Shall Dwell on Your Holy Hill?

15 A Psalm of David.
        O LORD, who shall sojourn in
            your tent?
        Who shall dwell on your holy hill?

2   He who walks blamelessly and does
        what is right
            and speaks truth in his heart;
3   who does not slander with his
        tongue
            and does no evil to his neighbor,
            nor takes up a reproach against hi
                friend;
4   in whose eyes a vile person is
        despised,
            but who honors those who fear th
                LORD;
        who swears to his own hurt and doe
            not change;
5   who does not put out his money at
        interest
            and does not take a bribe against
                the innocent.
        He who does these things shall neve
            be moved.

You Will Not Abandon My Soul

16 A Miktam[3] of David.
        Preserve me, O God, for in you
            I take refuge.
2   I say to the LORD, "You are my Lord;
        I have no good apart from you."

3   As for the saints in the land, they are
        the excellent ones,
            in whom is all my delight.[4]

4   The sorrows of those who run after[5]
        another god shall multiply;
            their drink offerings of blood I will
                not pour out
            or take their names on my lips.

5   The LORD is my chosen portion and
        my cup;
            you hold my lot.
6   The lines have fallen for me in pleas-
        ant places;
            indeed, I have a beautiful inheri-
                tance.

7   I bless the LORD who gives me coun-
        sel;
            in the night also my heart instruct
                me.[6]
8   I have set the LORD always before
        me;
            because he is at my right hand,
            I shall not be shaken.

---

[1] Or that act wisely [2] Or for [3] Probably a musical or liturgical term [4] Or To the saints in the land, the excellent in whom is all my delight,
I say: [5] Or who acquire [6] Hebrew my kidneys instruct me

⁹ Therefore my heart is glad, and my
　　whole being¹ rejoices;
　my flesh also dwells secure.
¹⁰ For you will not abandon my soul to
　　Sheol,
　or let your holy one see corruption.²

¹¹ You make known to me the path of
　　life;
　in your presence there is fullness
　　of joy;
　　at your right hand are pleasures
　　forevermore.

In the Shadow of Your Wings

17 A Prayer of David.
　Hear a just cause, O Lord; attend
　　to my cry!
　Give ear to my prayer from lips
　　free of deceit!
² From your presence let my vindica-
　　tion come!
　Let your eyes behold the right!

³ You have tried my heart, you have
　　visited me by night,
　you have tested me, and you will
　　find nothing;
　I have purposed that my mouth
　　will not transgress.
⁴ With regard to the works of man, by
　　the word of your lips
　I have avoided the ways of the
　　violent.
⁵ My steps have held fast to your paths;
　my feet have not slipped.

⁶ I call upon you, for you will answer
　　me, O God;
　incline your ear to me; hear my
　　words.
⁷ Wondrously show³ your steadfast
　　love,
　O Savior of those who seek refuge
　　from their adversaries at your
　　right hand.

Hebrew *my glory* ² Or *see the pit* ³ Or *Distinguish me by*

verses to read
Psalm 16:1–6

Know God

Thinking that success is God's goal for your life is a total lie. When you pray, don't ask him to give you fame and fortune. Those worldly things mean nothing in the life of faith. God might give you success and fortune, but this success is never his ultimate goal or the goal of the God Girl.

God doesn't need you to be successful in order to save lives or to get done what he wants to get done. The cattle on a thousand hills are his (see Ps. 50:10). He created every living thing; they all belong to him (see Ps. 24:1). So it's wrong to believe that he needs your success or that you need success in order to serve him. God is concerned about your holiness more than your comfort. He wants you to be more like his Son, Jesus. His goal wasn't popularity, fame, or even success, but sacrifice. He's our living example. When your focus is success, your focus is yourself. But your focus should be God and his kingdom. Your first question should be, "Will this benefit the kingdom?" When your first thought is, "How will this benefit me?" you are showing that you worship not God but yourself. What a sad state it is to be more concerned with your own life than with the Life-giver! Instead, be one of those the psalmist talks about as "the saints in the land" (see Ps. 16:3).

As you realign your goals with the Father's, every minute becomes a success—even in your failures. Failure in the eyes of the world isn't always failure in God's eyes. Throughout time he has used the failed actions of his people to achieve his desired end. Don't let your failure to succeed in this world get you off track from the true success of following Jesus no matter how crazy that might seem.

⁸ Keep me as the apple of your eye;
    hide me in the shadow of your
        wings,
⁹ from the wicked who do me vio-
        lence,
    my deadly enemies who surround
        me.

¹⁰ They close their hearts to pity;
    with their mouths they speak
        arrogantly.
¹¹ They have now surrounded our
        steps;
    they set their eyes to cast us to the
        ground.
¹² He is like a lion eager to tear,
    as a young lion lurking in
        ambush.

¹³ Arise, O LORD! Confront him, subdue
        him!
    Deliver my soul from the wicked
        by your sword,
¹⁴ from men by your hand, O LORD,
    from men of the world whose por-
        tion is in this life.¹
    You fill their womb with treasure;²
    they are satisfied with children,
    and they leave their abundance to
        their infants.

¹⁵ As for me, I shall behold your face in
        righteousness;
    when I awake, I shall be satisfied
        with your likeness.

The LORD Is My Rock and My Fortress

18 TO THE CHOIRMASTER. A PSALM OF
DAVID, THE SERVANT OF THE LORD,
WHO ADDRESSED THE WORDS OF THIS
SONG TO THE LORD ON THE DAY WHEN
THE LORD RESCUED HIM FROM THE
HAND OF ALL HIS ENEMIES, AND FROM
THE HAND OF SAUL. HE SAID:

¹ I love you, O LORD, my strength.
² The LORD is my rock and my fortress
        and my deliverer,
    my God, my rock, in whom I take
        refuge,
    my shield, and the horn of my
        salvation, my stronghold.
³ I call upon the LORD, who is worthy
        to be praised,
    and I am saved from my enemies.

⁴ The cords of death encompassed me;
    the torrents of destruction
        assailed me;³
⁵ the cords of Sheol entangled me;
    the snares of death confronted me.

---

¹ Or from men whose portion in life is of the world ² Or As for your treasured ones, you fill their womb ³ Or terrified me

---

Know Yourself

verses to read
Psalm 17:10–15

Who are you? Do you know? When others laugh at what you do, make fun of you, or hate you, do you immediately look inside yourself to see if those mockers are right? Have you ever done that and felt like you just don't know yourself? Some people call knowing who you are "self-awareness," and they spend days, if not years, looking for it. Self-awareness isn't a sin, but constantly chasing after it means your heart is set on the wrong thing.

When things go wrong and when people cut you down, you don't need to find yourself: you need to find Jesus. Looking inward will only drag out the pain and dig you deeper into a pit, but if you look up to the source and goal of your faith (see Heb. 12:2), you're going to find freedom. Who you are on the inside isn't as important as who you believe Jesus is. When you've messed up, your only hope is to run to Jesus and to depend totally on him. Learn his thoughts. Study his Word and run to his throne. Then you will be set free from your failure and your self-preoccupation.

5 In my distress I called upon the LORD;
  to my God I cried for help.
  From his temple he heard my voice,
    and my cry to him reached his
      ears.

7 Then the earth reeled and rocked;
    the foundations also of the moun-
      tains trembled
  and quaked, because he was angry.
8 Smoke went up from his nostrils,[1]
    and devouring fire from his mouth;
    glowing coals flamed forth from
      him.
9 He bowed the heavens and came
      down;
    thick darkness was under his feet.
10 He rode on a cherub and flew;
    he came swiftly on the wings of
      the wind.
11 He made darkness his covering, his
      canopy around him,
    thick clouds dark with water.
12 Out of the brightness before him
    hailstones and coals of fire broke
      through his clouds.

13 The LORD also thundered in the
      heavens,
    and the Most High uttered his
      voice,
    hailstones and coals of fire.
14 And he sent out his arrows and scat-
      tered them;
    he flashed forth lightnings and
      routed them.
15 Then the channels of the sea were
      seen,
    and the foundations of the world
      were laid bare
  at your rebuke, O LORD,
    at the blast of the breath of your
      nostrils.

16 He sent from on high, he took me;
    he drew me out of many waters.
17 He rescued me from my strong enemy
    and from those who hated me,
    for they were too mighty for me.
18 They confronted me in the day of my
      calamity,
    but the LORD was my support.
19 He brought me out into a broad
      place;
    he rescued me, because he
      delighted in me.

20 The LORD dealt with me according to
      my righteousness;
    according to the cleanness of my
      hands he rewarded me.
21 For I have kept the ways of the LORD,
    and have not wickedly departed
      from my God.
22 For all his rules[2] were before me,
    and his statutes I did not put away
      from me.
23 I was blameless before him,
    and I kept myself from my guilt.
24 So the LORD has rewarded me
      according to my righteousness,
    according to the cleanness of my
      hands in his sight.

25 With the merciful you show yourself
      merciful;
    with the blameless man you show
      yourself blameless;
26 with the purified you show yourself
      pure;
    and with the crooked you make
      yourself seem tortuous.
27 For you save a humble people,
    but the haughty eyes you bring
      down.
28 For it is you who light my lamp;
    the LORD my God lightens my
      darkness.
29 For by you I can run against a troop,
    and by my God I can leap over a
      wall.
30 This God—his way is perfect;[3]
    the word of the LORD proves true;
    he is a shield for all those who take
      refuge in him.

31 For who is God, but the LORD?
    And who is a rock, except our
      God?—
32 the God who equipped me with
      strength
    and made my way blameless.
33 He made my feet like the feet of a deer
    and set me secure on the heights.
34 He trains my hands for war,
    so that my arms can bend a bow of
      bronze.
35 You have given me the shield of your
      salvation,
    and your right hand supported me,
    and your gentleness made me
      great.

[1] Or in his wrath [2] Or just decrees [3] Or blameless

³⁶ You gave a wide place for my steps
        under me,
    and my feet did not slip.
³⁷ I pursued my enemies and overtook
        them,
    and did not turn back till they
        were consumed.
³⁸ I thrust them through, so that they
        were not able to rise;
    they fell under my feet.
³⁹ For you equipped me with strength
        for the battle;
    you made those who rise against
        me sink under me.
⁴⁰ You made my enemies turn their
        backs to me,¹
    and those who hated me
        I destroyed.
⁴¹ They cried for help, but there was
        none to save;
    they cried to the Lord, but he did
        not answer them.
⁴² I beat them fine as dust before the
        wind;
    I cast them out like the mire of the
        streets.
⁴³ You delivered me from strife with the
        people;
    you made me the head of the
        nations;
    people whom I had not known
        served me.
⁴⁴ As soon as they heard of me they
        obeyed me;
    foreigners came cringing to me.
⁴⁵ Foreigners lost heart
    and came trembling out of their
        fortresses.
⁴⁶ The Lord lives, and blessed be my
        rock,
    and exalted be the God of my
        salvation—
⁴⁷ the God who gave me vengeance
    and subdued peoples under me,
⁴⁸ who delivered me from my enemies;
    yes, you exalted me above those
        who rose against me;
    you rescued me from the man of
        violence.
⁴⁹ For this I will praise you, O Lord,
        among the nations,
    and sing to your name.

⁵⁰ Great salvation he brings to his king,
    and shows steadfast love to his
        anointed,
    to David and his offspring forever.

The Law of the Lord Is Perfect

19 To the choirmaster. A Psalm of
     David.

¹ The heavens declare the glory of God,
    and the sky above² proclaims his
        handiwork.
² Day to day pours out speech,
    and night to night reveals knowl-
        edge.
³ There is no speech, nor are there
        words,
    whose voice is not heard.
⁴ Their voice³ goes out through all the
        earth,
    and their words to the end of the
        world.
 In them he has set a tent for the sun,
⁵   which comes out like a bride-
        groom leaving his chamber,
    and, like a strong man, runs its
        course with joy.
⁶ Its rising is from the end of the heav-
        ens,
    and its circuit to the end of them,
    and there is nothing hidden from
        its heat.

⁷ The law of the Lord is perfect,⁴
    reviving the soul;
 the testimony of the Lord is sure,
    making wise the simple;
⁸ the precepts of the Lord are right,
    rejoicing the heart;
 the commandment of the Lord is
        pure,
    enlightening the eyes;
⁹ the fear of the Lord is clean,
    enduring forever;
 the rules⁵ of the Lord are true,
    and righteous altogether.
¹⁰ More to be desired are they than gold,
    even much fine gold;
 sweeter also than honey
    and drippings of the honeycomb.
¹¹ Moreover, by them is your servant
        warned;
    in keeping them there is great
        reward.

¹Or You gave me my enemies' necks ²Hebrew the expanse; compare Genesis 1:6–8 ³Or Their measuring line ⁴Or blameless ⁵Or just
decrees

² Who can discern his errors?
    Declare me innocent from hidden
        faults.
³ Keep back your servant also from
        presumptuous sins;
    let them not have dominion over
        me!
Then I shall be blameless,
    and innocent of great transgression.

⁴ Let the words of my mouth and the
        meditation of my heart
    be acceptable in your sight,
    O LORD, my rock and my redeemer.

Trust in the Name of the LORD Our God

20 TO THE CHOIRMASTER. A PSALM OF
DAVID.

¹ May the LORD answer you in the day
        of trouble!
    May the name of the God of Jacob
        protect you!
² May he send you help from the sanc-
        tuary
    and give you support from Zion!

³ May he remember all your offerings
    and regard with favor your burnt
        sacrifices!   *Selah*

⁴ May he grant you your heart's desire
    and fulfill all your plans!
⁵ May we shout for joy over your
        salvation,
    and in the name of our God set up
        our banners!
May the LORD fulfill all your petitions!

⁶ Now I know that the LORD saves his
        anointed;
    he will answer him from his holy
        heaven
    with the saving might of his right
        hand.
⁷ Some trust in chariots and some in
        horses,
    but we trust in the name of the
        LORD our God.
⁸ They collapse and fall,
    but we rise and stand upright.

⁹ O LORD, save the king!
    May he answer us when we call.

---

verses to read
Psalm 19:12–14

Know Yourself

The God Girl doesn't give control of her life to anyone but God. And that means she only lets those who are assigned authority by God have authority over her. Certain authorities here on earth, set up by God, will control your life in certain seasons—like your parents, teachers, the police, or judges. But giving control to anyone whom God has not given control to is idolatry.

When you're young, it can be easy to look for people to tell you what to do. You don't have the answers, and you want help. You want to know how to dress and how to act. You want help, but help and advice can become control, and just as quickly your life can become less about pleasing God and more about pleasing people. When you make decisions and run your life based on what someone else wants you to do, you walk away from the will of God. No friend, no boyfriend, and no enemy should have control over your life. And when you do the things you do out of a fear of rejection or manipulation, you don't just make a mistake; you commit a sin.

Make it your prayer that no one should gain control over you but that you can learn to love others the way God has loved you. Work on humility instead of pride. Don't worry about what others might do or say; just always choose God's way and trust that he will truly work everything out for the good of those who love him (see Rom. 8:28).

The King Rejoices in the LORD's Strength

21 TO THE CHOIRMASTER. A PSALM OF DAVID.

1   O LORD, in your strength the king
        rejoices,
    and in your salvation how greatly
        he exults!
2   You have given him his heart's desire
    and have not withheld the request
        of his lips.   *Selah*
3   For you meet him with rich blessings;
    you set a crown of fine gold upon
        his head.
4   He asked life of you; you gave it to
        him,
    length of days forever and ever.
5   His glory is great through your salva-
        tion;
    splendor and majesty you bestow
        on him.
6   For you make him most blessed
        forever;[1]
    you make him glad with the joy of
        your presence.
7   For the king trusts in the LORD,
    and through the steadfast love of
        the Most High he shall not be
        moved.

8   Your hand will find out all your
        enemies;
    your right hand will find out those
        who hate you.
9   You will make them as a blazing
        oven
    when you appear.
    The LORD will swallow them up in
        his wrath,
    and fire will consume them.
10 You will destroy their descendants
        from the earth,
    and their offspring from among
        the children of man.
11 Though they plan evil against you,
    though they devise mischief, they
        will not succeed.
12 For you will put them to flight;
    you will aim at their faces with
        your bows.

13 Be exalted, O LORD, in your strength!
    We will sing and praise your
        power.

[1] Or *make him a source of blessing forever* [2] Or *dwelling in the praises*

Why Have You Forsaken Me?

22 TO THE CHOIRMASTER: ACCORDING TO THE DOE OF THE DAWN. A PSALM OF DAVID.

1   My God, my God, why have you for-
        saken me?
    Why are you so far from saving
        me, from the words of my
        groaning?
2   O my God, I cry by day, but you do
        not answer,
    and by night, but I find no rest.

3   Yet you are holy,
    enthroned on the praises[2] of Israel.
4   In you our fathers trusted;
    they trusted, and you delivered
        them.
5   To you they cried and were rescued;
    in you they trusted and were not
        put to shame.

6   But I am a worm and not a man,
    scorned by mankind and despised
        by the people.
7   All who see me mock me;
    they make mouths at me; they wag
        their heads;
8   "He trusts in the LORD; let him deliver
        him;
    let him rescue him, for he delights
        in him!"

9   Yet you are he who took me from the
        womb;
    you made me trust you at my
        mother's breasts.
10 On you was I cast from my birth,
    and from my mother's womb you
        have been my God.
11 Be not far from me,
    for trouble is near,
    and there is none to help.

12 Many bulls encompass me;
    strong bulls of Bashan surround
        me;
13 they open wide their mouths at me,
    like a ravening and roaring lion.

14 I am poured out like water,
    and all my bones are out of joint;
    my heart is like wax;
    it is melted within my breast;

my strength is dried up like a potsherd,
and my tongue sticks to my jaws;
  you lay me in the dust of death.

For dogs encompass me;
  a company of evildoers encircles
    me;
they have pierced my hands and
  feet[1]—

I can count all my bones—
  they stare and gloat over me;
they divide my garments among
  them,
  and for my clothing they cast lots.

But you, O LORD, do not be far off!
  O you my help, come quickly to my
    aid!

20   Deliver my soul from the sword,
       my precious life from the power of
         the dog!
21   Save me from the mouth of the lion!
     You have rescued[2] me from the horns
       of the wild oxen!

22   I will tell of your name to my broth-
       ers;
     in the midst of the congregation
       I will praise you:
23   You who fear the LORD, praise him!
       All you offspring of Jacob, glorify
         him,
       and stand in awe of him, all you
         offspring of Israel!

24   For he has despised or abhorred
       the affliction of the afflicted,

Some Hebrew manuscripts, Septuagint, Vulgate, Syriac; most Hebrew manuscripts *like a lion* [they are at] *my hands and feet* [2] Hebrew
answered

Know God

verses to read
Psalm 22

Whenever something turns out differently than you expected, it's easy to blame God. The first question is always "Why, God? Why me? Why this?" But those kinds of Qs can easily become a whine or a complaint. They can easily start to sound like an accusation: "I did what you asked—why didn't you hold up your end of the bargain?" Well, God isn't really concerned about making your life easy. He wants to make you holy. And the process of making you holy, which is called sanctification, doesn't always involve the easiest and most comfortable way.

When a trial comes into your life, your first response should be to ask God, "How can I serve you in this?" Any other response means you are trying to serve two masters—yourself and God. And that can't be done (see Matt. 6:24; Rom. 6:16). You have to focus completely on the end that God has in mind for your life. Once you do, living a godly life will become more like second nature. That's because God promises that as you trust him, he will give you peace. The apostle Paul puts it this way: "Aim for restoration, comfort one another, agree with one another, live in peace; and the God of love and peace will be with you" (2 Cor. 13:11). And again: "What you have learned and received and heard and seen in me—practice these things, and the God of peace will be with you" (Phil. 4:9).

When life gets tough, trust God, and he will grant you a peace and joy that goes beneath the tough situation. No matter what the results of your plans or dreams are, and even if it feels like God totally let you down, trust him, believe, and know that this too shall be used to make you a holy person if you will just let it. Like the psalmist, get good at knowing that even if things seem miserable, God is always there and is always in control. Let praise and not complaining be the final word in your talks with God.

and he has not hidden his face from
    him,
  but has heard, when he cried to
    him.

25 From you comes my praise in the
    great congregation;
  my vows I will perform before
    those who fear him.
26 The afflicted[1] shall eat and be satisfied;
    those who seek him shall praise
    the LORD!
  May your hearts live forever!

27 All the ends of the earth shall
    remember
  and turn to the LORD,
  and all the families of the nations
    shall worship before you.
28 For kingship belongs to the LORD,
    and he rules over the nations.

29 All the prosperous of the earth eat
    and worship;
  before him shall bow all who go
    down to the dust,
  even the one who could not keep
    himself alive.
30 Posterity shall serve him;
    it shall be told of the Lord to the
    coming generation;
31 they shall come and proclaim his
    righteousness to a people yet
    unborn,
  that he has done it.

The LORD Is My Shepherd

23 A PSALM OF DAVID.
    The LORD is my shepherd; I shall
    not want.
2   He makes me lie down in green
    pastures.
  He leads me beside still waters.[2]
3   He restores my soul.
  He leads me in paths of righteousness[3]
    for his name's sake.

4   Even though I walk through the val-
    ley of the shadow of death,[4]
    I will fear no evil,
  for you are with me;
    your rod and your staff,
    they comfort me.

5   You prepare a table before me
    in the presence of my enemies;

you anoint my head with oil;
    my cup overflows.
6 Surely[5] goodness and mercy[6] shall
    follow me
  all the days of my life,
  and I shall dwell[7] in the house of the
    LORD
  forever.[8]

A Prayer for...
BEDTIME

Stay with me tonight, God, so that the
brightness of your love will be around
me and so that the darkness won't be
so dark. Live with me, O Lord, tonight,
because I am not alone if you are here.

Stay with the sick, the sad, the forsaken, and the tired to strengthen, to
comfort, to cheer, and to give rest.

Protect me from the darkness of the
soul that I can't see and the loneliness
of heart where I can't hear your voice.
Live with me throughout my life, and
in the valley of the shadow of death,
don't walk out on me, but give me
courage, because you are still with me.

Amen.

The King of Glory

24 A PSALM OF DAVID.
    The earth is the LORD's and the
    fullness thereof,[9]
  the world and those who dwell
    therein,
2   for he has founded it upon the seas
    and established it upon the rivers.

3   Who shall ascend the hill of the
    LORD?
  And who shall stand in his holy
    place?
4   He who has clean hands and a pure
    heart,
  who does not lift up his soul to
    what is false
  and does not swear deceitfully.

[1] Or The meek [2] Hebrew beside waters of rest [3] Or in right paths [4] Or the valley of deep darkness [5] Or Only [6] Or steadfast love [7] Or shall
return to dwell [8] Hebrew for length of days [9] Or and all that fills it

He will receive blessing from the
    LORD
  and righteousness from the God of
    his salvation.
Such is the generation of those who
    seek him,
  who seek the face of the God of
    Jacob.[1]   *Selah*

Lift up your heads, O gates!
  And be lifted up, O ancient doors,
    that the King of glory may come in.
Who is this King of glory?
  The LORD, strong and mighty,
    the LORD, mighty in battle!
Lift up your heads, O gates!
  And lift them up, O ancient doors,
    that the King of glory may come in.
Who is this King of glory?
  The LORD of hosts,
    he is the King of glory!   *Selah*

Teach Me Your Paths

25 [2] OF DAVID.
    To you, O LORD, I lift up my soul.
  O my God, in you I trust;
    let me not be put to shame;
    let not my enemies exult over me.
  Indeed, none who wait for you shall
      be put to shame;
    they shall be ashamed who are
      wantonly treacherous.

  Make me to know your ways, O LORD;
    teach me your paths.
  Lead me in your truth and teach me,
    for you are the God of my salva-
      tion;
    for you I wait all the day long.

  Remember your mercy, O LORD, and
      your steadfast love,
    for they have been from of old.
  Remember not the sins of my youth
      or my transgressions;
    according to your steadfast love
      remember me,
    for the sake of your goodness,
      O LORD!

  Good and upright is the LORD;
    therefore he instructs sinners in
      the way.
  He leads the humble in what is right,
    and teaches the humble his way.

[10] All the paths of the LORD are stead-
      fast love and faithfulness,
    for those who keep his covenant
      and his testimonies.
[11] For your name's sake, O LORD,
    pardon my guilt, for it is great.
[12] Who is the man who fears the LORD?
    Him will he instruct in the way
      that he should choose.
[13] His soul shall abide in well-being,
    and his offspring shall inherit the
      land.
[14] The friendship[3] of the LORD is for
      those who fear him,
    and he makes known to them his
      covenant.
[15] My eyes are ever toward the LORD,
    for he will pluck my feet out of the
      net.

[16] Turn to me and be gracious to me,
    for I am lonely and afflicted.
[17] The troubles of my heart are
      enlarged;
    bring me out of my distresses.
[18] Consider my affliction and my trouble,
    and forgive all my sins.
[19] Consider how many are my foes,
    and with what violent hatred they
      hate me.
[20] Oh, guard my soul, and deliver me!
    Let me not be put to shame, for
      I take refuge in you.
[21] May integrity and uprightness pre-
      serve me,
    for I wait for you.
[22] Redeem Israel, O God,
    out of all his troubles.

I Will Bless the LORD

26 OF DAVID.
    Vindicate me, O LORD,
    for I have walked in my integrity,
    and I have trusted in the LORD
      without wavering.
[2] Prove me, O LORD, and try me;
    test my heart and my mind.[4]
[3] For your steadfast love is before my
      eyes,
    and I walk in your faithfulness.
[4] I do not sit with men of falsehood,
    nor do I consort with hypocrites.

---

eptuagint, Syriac, and two Hebrew manuscripts; Masoretic Text *Jacob, who seek your face* [2] This psalm is an acrostic poem, each verse
eginning with the successive letters of the Hebrew alphabet [3] Or *The secret counsel* [4] Hebrew *test my kidneys and my heart*

5 I hate the assembly of evildoers,
    and I will not sit with the wicked.

6 I wash my hands in innocence
    and go around your altar, O Lord,
7 proclaiming thanksgiving aloud,
    and telling all your wondrous
      deeds.

8 O Lord, I love the habitation of your
      house
    and the place where your glory
      dwells.

9 Do not sweep my soul away with sin-
      ners,
    nor my life with bloodthirsty men,
10 in whose hands are evil devices,
    and whose right hands are full of
      bribes.

11 But as for me, I shall walk in my
      integrity;
    redeem me, and be gracious to me.
12 My foot stands on level ground;
    in the great assembly I will bless
      the Lord.

The Lord Is My Light and My Salvation

27
Of David.
The Lord is my light and my
    salvation;
  whom shall I fear?
The Lord is the stronghold[1] of my life;
  of whom shall I be afraid?

2 When evildoers assail me
    to eat up my flesh,
  my adversaries and foes,
    it is they who stumble and fall.

3 Though an army encamp against me,
    my heart shall not fear;
  though war arise against me,
    yet[2] I will be confident.

4 One thing have I asked of the Lord,
    that will I seek after:
  that I may dwell in the house of the
    Lord
    all the days of my life,
  to gaze upon the beauty of the Lord
    and to inquire[3] in his temple.

5 For he will hide me in his shelter
    in the day of trouble;

he will conceal me under the cover
    his tent;
  he will lift me high upon a rock.

6 And now my head shall be lifted up
    above my enemies all around me,
  and I will offer in his tent
    sacrifices with shouts of joy;
  I will sing and make melody to the
    Lord.

7 Hear, O Lord, when I cry aloud;
    be gracious to me and answer me
8 You have said, "Seek[4] my face."
  My heart says to you,
    "Your face, Lord, do I seek."[5]
9 Hide not your face from me.
  Turn not your servant away in ange
    O you who have been my help.
  Cast me not off; forsake me not,
    O God of my salvation!
10 For my father and my mother have
      forsaken me,
    but the Lord will take me in.

11 Teach me your way, O Lord,
    and lead me on a level path
    because of my enemies.
12 Give me not up to the will of my
      adversaries;
  for false witnesses have risen
    against me,
  and they breathe out violence.

13 I believe[6] that I shall look upon the
      goodness of the Lord
    in the land of the living!
14 Wait for the Lord;
    be strong, and let your heart take
      courage;
    wait for the Lord!

The Lord Is My Strength and My Shield

28
Of David.
To you, O Lord, I call;
  my rock, be not deaf to me,
lest, if you be silent to me,
  I become like those who go down
    to the pit.
2 Hear the voice of my pleas for
      mercy,
    when I cry to you for help,
  when I lift up my hands
    toward your most holy sanctuary.[7]

[1] Or refuge [2] Or in this [3] Or meditate [4] The command (seek) is addressed to more than one person [5] The meaning of the Hebrew verse uncertain [6] Other Hebrew manuscripts Oh! Had I not believed [7] Hebrew your innermost sanctuary

3 Do not drag me off with the wicked,
  with the workers of evil,
 who speak peace with their neighbors
  while evil is in their hearts.
4 Give to them according to their work
  and according to the evil of their
   deeds;
 give to them according to the work of
  their hands;
  render them their due reward.
5 Because they do not regard the
   works of the LORD
  or the work of his hands,
 he will tear them down and build
  them up no more.

6 Blessed be the LORD!
  For he has heard the voice of my
   pleas for mercy.
7 The LORD is my strength and my
   shield;
  in him my heart trusts, and I am
   helped;
 my heart exults,
  and with my song I give thanks to
   him.

8 The LORD is the strength of his
   people;[1]
  he is the saving refuge of his
   anointed.
9 Oh, save your people and bless your
   heritage!
  Be their shepherd and carry them
   forever.

Ascribe to the LORD Glory

29 A PSALM OF DAVID.
  Ascribe to the LORD, O heavenly
   beings,[2]
 ascribe to the LORD glory and
  strength.
2 Ascribe to the LORD the glory due his
   name;
  worship the LORD in the splendor
   of holiness.[3]

3 The voice of the LORD is over the
   waters;
  the God of glory thunders,
  the LORD, over many waters.
4 The voice of the LORD is powerful;
  the voice of the LORD is full of
   majesty.

5 The voice of the LORD breaks the
   cedars;
  the LORD breaks the cedars of
   Lebanon.
6 He makes Lebanon to skip like a calf,
  and Sirion like a young wild ox.
7 The voice of the LORD flashes forth
   flames of fire.
8 The voice of the LORD shakes the
   wilderness;
  the LORD shakes the wilderness of
   Kadesh.
9 The voice of the LORD makes the
   deer give birth[4]
  and strips the forests bare,
  and in his temple all cry, "Glory!"

10 The LORD sits enthroned over the
   flood;
  the LORD sits enthroned as king
   forever.
11 May the LORD give strength to his
   people!
  May the LORD bless[5] his people
   with peace!

Joy Comes with the Morning

30 A PSALM OF DAVID. A SONG AT THE
  DEDICATION OF THE TEMPLE.

1 I will extol you, O LORD, for you have
   drawn me up
  and have not let my foes rejoice
   over me.
2 O LORD my God, I cried to you for
   help,
  and you have healed me.
3 O LORD, you have brought up my soul
   from Sheol;
  you restored me to life from
   among those who go down to
   the pit.[6]

4 Sing praises to the LORD, O you his
   saints,
  and give thanks to his holy name.[7]
5 For his anger is but for a moment,
  and his favor is for a lifetime.[8]
 Weeping may tarry for the night,
  but joy comes with the morning.

6 As for me, I said in my prosperity,
  "I shall never be moved."

---

[1] Some Hebrew manuscripts, Septuagint, Syriac; most Hebrew manuscripts *is their strength* [2] Hebrew *sons of God, or sons of might* [3] Or *in holy attire* [4] Revocalization yields *makes the oaks to shake* [5] Or *The LORD will give . . . The LORD will bless* [6] Or *to life, that I should not go down to the pit* [7] Hebrew *to the memorial of his holiness* (see Exodus 3:15) [8] Or *and in his favor is life*

7 By your favor, O LORD,
 you made my mountain stand strong;
 you hid your face;
 I was dismayed.

8 To you, O LORD, I cry,
 and to the Lord I plead for mercy:
9 "What profit is there in my death,[1]
 if I go down to the pit?[2]
Will the dust praise you?
 Will it tell of your faithfulness?
10 Hear, O LORD, and be merciful to me!
 O LORD, be my helper!"

11 You have turned for me my mourning into dancing;
 you have loosed my sackcloth
 and clothed me with gladness,
12 that my glory may sing your praise and not be silent.
 O LORD my God, I will give thanks to you forever!

Into Your Hand I Commit My Spirit

31 TO THE CHOIRMASTER. A PSALM OF DAVID.

1 In you, O LORD, do I take refuge;
 let me never be put to shame;
 in your righteousness deliver me!
2 Incline your ear to me;
 rescue me speedily!
Be a rock of refuge for me,
 a strong fortress to save me!

3 For you are my rock and my fortress;
 and for your name's sake you lead me and guide me;
4 you take me out of the net they have hidden for me,
 for you are my refuge.
5 Into your hand I commit my spirit;
 you have redeemed me, O LORD, faithful God.

6 I hate[3] those who pay regard to worthless idols,
 but I trust in the LORD.
7 I will rejoice and be glad in your steadfast love,
 because you have seen my affliction;
 you have known the distress of my soul,

8 and you have not delivered me into the hand of the enemy;
 you have set my feet in a broad place.

9 Be gracious to me, O LORD, for I am in distress;
 my eye is wasted from grief;
 my soul and my body also.
10 For my life is spent with sorrow,
 and my years with sighing;
my strength fails because of my iniquity,
 and my bones waste away.

11 Because of all my adversaries I have become a reproach,
 especially to my neighbors,
and an object of dread to my acquaintances;
 those who see me in the street flee from me.
12 I have been forgotten like one who is dead;
 I have become like a broken vessel.
13 For I hear the whispering of many—
 terror on every side!—
as they scheme together against me,
 as they plot to take my life.

14 But I trust in you, O LORD;
 I say, "You are my God."
15 My times are in your hand;
 rescue me from the hand of my enemies and from my persecutors!
16 Make your face shine on your servant;
 save me in your steadfast love!
17 O LORD, let me not be put to shame,
 for I call upon you;
let the wicked be put to shame;
 let them go silently to Sheol.
18 Let the lying lips be mute,
 which speak insolently against the righteous
 in pride and contempt.

19 Oh, how abundant is your goodness,
 which you have stored up for those who fear you
and worked for those who take refuge in you,
 in the sight of the children of mankind!

[1] Hebrew in my blood [2] Or to corruption [3] Masoretic Text; one Hebrew manuscript, Septuagint, Syriac, Jerome You hate

⁰ In the cover of your presence you
        hide them
     from the plots of men;
you store them in your shelter
     from the strife of tongues.

¹ Blessed be the LORD,
     for he has wondrously shown his
        steadfast love to me
     when I was in a besieged city.

² I had said in my alarm,[1]
     "I am cut off from your sight."
But you heard the voice of my pleas
        for mercy
     when I cried to you for help.

³ Love the LORD, all you his saints!
     The LORD preserves the faithful
     but abundantly repays the one
        who acts in pride.
⁴ Be strong, and let your heart take
        courage,
     all you who wait for the LORD!

Blessed Are the Forgiven

32 A MASKIL[2] OF DAVID.
      Blessed is the one whose trans-
        gression is forgiven,
     whose sin is covered.
² Blessed is the man against whom the
     LORD counts no iniquity,
     and in whose spirit there is no
        deceit.

³ For when I kept silent, my bones
        wasted away
     through my groaning all day long.
⁴ For day and night your hand was
        heavy upon me;
     my strength was dried up[3] as by
        the heat of summer.   *Selah*

⁵ I acknowledged my sin to you,
     and I did not cover my iniquity;
I said, "I will confess my transgres-
        sions to the LORD,"
     and you forgave the iniquity of my
        sin.   *Selah*

¹ Or *in my haste* ² Probably a musical or liturgical term ³ Hebrew *my vitality was changed*

Know God

verses to read
Psalm 31:14–24

The Lord never made a promise he's not going to keep. It's impossible for him to promise something and not do it, because that would make him a liar. If God were a liar, then he would not be holy but sinful. And God cannot sin; therefore, God cannot lie. Make sense? If you can believe that, you can be sure that any promise God makes, he's going to keep. You can trust that he will always protect, guard, and bless those who count on him, because he is holy and he promised it. He promises to never walk away from those who love him (see Heb. 13:5), and those who love him are the ones who do his will (see John 14:23; 1 John 2:5).

As a God Girl, you have to be confident in God's Word and sure of his promises. Then, when hard times come, you can rely on the truth and live in the peace of knowing that he will truly work everything together for your good (see Rom. 8:28). In this life a lot of people are gonna disappoint you. They will reject you, walk out on you, and even hate you. But God's character can't be compared to the sinful character of humanity. God can be trusted, even when things look completely bleak. When trials come and God seems silent, you can still be sure that he is present. If he weren't, then he wouldn't be God. By his very nature he knows everything (he's omniscient) and he is everywhere (he's omnipresent). The God Girl knows her God, so she knows that no matter how things look or feel, everything is well. She trusts that when she looks for God, she will find him, and that if she trusts him, he will bring her only what is good for her.

6 Therefore let everyone who is godly
   offer prayer to you at a time when
      you may be found;
   surely in the rush of great waters,
      they shall not reach him.
7 You are a hiding place for me;
   you preserve me from trouble;
   you surround me with shouts of
      deliverance.   *Selah*

8 I will instruct you and teach you in
      the way you should go;
   I will counsel you with my eye
      upon you.
9 Be not like a horse or a mule, with-
      out understanding,
   which must be curbed with bit and
      bridle,
   or it will not stay near you.

10 Many are the sorrows of the wicked,
   but steadfast love surrounds the
      one who trusts in the LORD.
11 Be glad in the LORD, and rejoice,
      O righteous,
   and shout for joy, all you upright in
      heart!

The Steadfast Love of the LORD

33 Shout for joy in the LORD, O you
   righteous!
   Praise befits the upright.
2 Give thanks to the LORD with the lyre;
   make melody to him with the harp
      of ten strings!

3 Sing to him a new song;
   play skillfully on the strings, with
      loud shouts.

4 For the word of the LORD is upright,
   and all his work is done in faithful
      ness.
5 He loves righteousness and justice;
   the earth is full of the steadfast
      love of the LORD.

6 By the word of the LORD the heavens
      were made,
   and by the breath of his mouth all
      their host.
7 He gathers the waters of the sea as a
      heap;
   he puts the deeps in storehouses.

8 Let all the earth fear the LORD;
   let all the inhabitants of the world
      stand in awe of him!
9 For he spoke, and it came to be;
   he commanded, and it stood firm.

10 The LORD brings the counsel of the
      nations to nothing;
   he frustrates the plans of the
      peoples.
11 The counsel of the LORD stands forever
   the plans of his heart to all genera-
      tions.
12 Blessed is the nation whose God is
      the LORD,
   the people whom he has chosen as
      his heritage!

Know God

verses to read
Psalm 32:1–5

Sin is an internal action that leads to an external result. You might think it's all external and say things like, "The Enemy is making me sin," or, "I can't control myself." You want change but you feel powerless. When you blame your actions on being addicted to something or on having an illness that makes you what you are, you are shifting the blame off of yourself and trying to justify yourself. But in the gospel, it is God who justifies you through Jesus—so you are free to admit your failings.

The beauty of the gospel is that you do not have to make yourself better in order for God to love you. He is totally for you, with you, on your side—all you bring to the table is your need. He does not want perfect people. He wants honest people. As long as you are willing to confess your sin, God Girl, the love and power of God is resting upon you. You are free!

3 The LORD looks down from heaven;
 he sees all the children of man;
4 from where he sits enthroned he
  looks out
 on all the inhabitants of the earth,
5 he who fashions the hearts of them
  all
 and observes all their deeds.
6 The king is not saved by his great
  army;
 a warrior is not delivered by his
  great strength.
7 The war horse is a false hope for
  salvation,
 and by its great might it cannot
  rescue.

8 Behold, the eye of the LORD is on
  those who fear him,
 on those who hope in his steadfast
  love,
9 that he may deliver their soul from
  death
 and keep them alive in famine.

10 Our soul waits for the LORD;
 he is our help and our shield.
11 For our heart is glad in him,
 because we trust in his holy name.
12 Let your steadfast love, O LORD, be
  upon us,
 even as we hope in you.

Taste and See That the LORD Is Good

34 1 OF DAVID, WHEN HE CHANGED HIS
BEHAVIOR BEFORE ABIMELECH, SO
THAT HE DROVE HIM OUT, AND HE
WENT AWAY.

1 I will bless the LORD at all times;
 his praise shall continually be in
  my mouth.
2 My soul makes its boast in the LORD;
 let the humble hear and be glad.
3 Oh, magnify the LORD with me,
 and let us exalt his name together!
4 I sought the LORD, and he
  answered me
 and delivered me from all my fears.
5 Those who look to him are radiant,
 and their faces shall never be
  ashamed.
6 This poor man cried, and the LORD
  heard him
 and saved him out of all his troubles.

7 The angel of the LORD encamps
 around those who fear him, and
  delivers them.

8 Oh, taste and see that the LORD is
  good!
 Blessed is the man who takes refuge in him!
9 Oh, fear the LORD, you his saints,
 for those who fear him have no
  lack!
10 The young lions suffer want and
  hunger;
 but those who seek the LORD lack
  no good thing.

11 Come, O children, listen to me;
 I will teach you the fear of the
  LORD.
12 What man is there who desires life
 and loves many days, that he may
  see good?
13 Keep your tongue from evil
 and your lips from speaking
  deceit.
14 Turn away from evil and do good;
 seek peace and pursue it.

15 The eyes of the LORD are toward the
  righteous
 and his ears toward their cry.
16 The face of the LORD is against those
  who do evil,
 to cut off the memory of them
  from the earth.
17 When the righteous cry for help, the
  LORD hears
 and delivers them out of all their
  troubles.
18 The LORD is near to the brokenhearted
 and saves the crushed in spirit.

19 Many are the afflictions of the righteous,
 but the LORD delivers him out of
  them all.
20 He keeps all his bones;
 not one of them is broken.
21 Affliction will slay the wicked,
 and those who hate the righteous
  will be condemned.
22 The LORD redeems the life of his
  servants;
 none of those who take refuge in
  him will be condemned.

1 This psalm is an acrostic poem, each verse beginning with the successive letters of the Hebrew alphabet

Great Is the Lord

35
Of David.

Contend, O Lord, with those who
  contend with me;
  fight against those who fight
    against me!
2 Take hold of shield and buckler
    and rise for my help!
3 Draw the spear and javelin[1]
    against my pursuers!
  Say to my soul,
    "I am your salvation!"

4 Let them be put to shame and dis-
    honor
    who seek after my life!
  Let them be turned back and disap-
    pointed
    who devise evil against me!
5 Let them be like chaff before the wind,
    with the angel of the Lord driving
    them away!
6 Let their way be dark and slippery,
    with the angel of the Lord pursu-
    ing them!

7 For without cause they hid their net
    for me;
  without cause they dug a pit for
    my life.[2]
8 Let destruction come upon him
    when he does not know it!
  And let the net that he hid ensnare
    him;
    let him fall into it—to his destruc-
    tion!

9 Then my soul will rejoice in the Lord,
    exulting in his salvation.
10 All my bones shall say,
    "O Lord, who is like you,
  delivering the poor
    from him who is too strong for him,
    the poor and needy from him who
    robs him?"

11 Malicious[3] witnesses rise up;
    they ask me of things that I do not
    know.
12 They repay me evil for good;
    my soul is bereft.[4]
13 But I, when they were sick—
    I wore sackcloth;
  I afflicted myself with fasting;

I prayed with head bowed[5] on my
    chest.
14 I went about as though I grieved
    for my friend or my brother;
  as one who laments his mother,
    I bowed down in mourning.

15 But at my stumbling they rejoiced
    and gathered;
    they gathered together against me
  wretches whom I did not know
    tore at me without ceasing;
16 like profane mockers at a feast,[6]
    they gnash at me with their teeth.

17 How long, O Lord, will you look on?
    Rescue me from their destruction,
    my precious life from the lions!
18 I will thank you in the great congre-
    gation;
    in the mighty throng I will praise
    you.

19 Let not those rejoice over me
    who are wrongfully my foes,
  and let not those wink the eye
    who hate me without cause.
20 For they do not speak peace,
    but against those who are quiet in
    the land
    they devise words of deceit.
21 They open wide their mouths against
    me;
    they say, "Aha, Aha!
    Our eyes have seen it!"

22 You have seen, O Lord; be not silent!
    O Lord, be not far from me!
23 Awake and rouse yourself for my
    vindication,
    for my cause, my God and my Lord!
24 Vindicate me, O Lord, my God,
    according to your righteousness,
    and let them not rejoice over me!
25 Let them not say in their hearts,
    "Aha, our heart's desire!"
  Let them not say, "We have swal-
    lowed him up."

26 Let them be put to shame and disap-
    pointed altogether
    who rejoice at my calamity!
  Let them be clothed with shame and
    dishonor
    who magnify themselves against me!

---

[1] Or and close the way [2] The word pit is transposed from the preceding line; Hebrew For without cause they hid the pit of their net for me;
without cause they dug for my life [3] Or Violent [4] Hebrew it is bereavement to my soul [5] Or my prayer shall turn back [6] The meaning of the
Hebrew phrase is uncertain

7 Let those who delight in my righ-
     teousness
   shout for joy and be glad
     and say evermore,
   "Great is the LORD,
     who delights in the welfare of his
     servant!"
8 Then my tongue shall tell of your
     righteousness
   and of your praise all the day long.

How Precious Is Your Steadfast Love

36 TO THE CHOIRMASTER. OF DAVID, THE
       SERVANT OF THE LORD.

1 Transgression speaks to the wicked
     deep in his heart;[1]
   there is no fear of God
     before his eyes.
2 For he flatters himself in his own eyes
     that his iniquity cannot be found
     out and hated.
3 The words of his mouth are trouble
     and deceit;
   he has ceased to act wisely and do
     good.
4 He plots trouble while on his bed;
   he sets himself in a way that is not
     good;
   he does not reject evil.

5 Your steadfast love, O LORD, extends
     to the heavens,
   your faithfulness to the clouds.
6 Your righteousness is like the moun-
     tains of God;
   your judgments are like the great
     deep;
   man and beast you save, O LORD.

7 How precious is your steadfast love,
     O God!
   The children of mankind take refuge
     in the shadow of your wings.
8 They feast on the abundance of your
     house,
   and you give them drink from the
     river of your delights.
9 For with you is the fountain of life;
   in your light do we see light.

10 Oh, continue your steadfast love to
     those who know you,
   and your righteousness to the
     upright of heart!

11 Let not the foot of arrogance come
     upon me,
   nor the hand of the wicked drive
     me away.
12 There the evildoers lie fallen;
   they are thrust down, unable to rise.

He Will Not Forsake His Saints

37[2] OF DAVID.
   Fret not yourself because of
     evildoers;
   be not envious of wrongdoers!
2 For they will soon fade like the grass
   and wither like the green herb.

3 Trust in the LORD, and do good;
   dwell in the land and befriend
     faithfulness.[3]
4 Delight yourself in the LORD,
   and he will give you the desires of
     your heart.

5 Commit your way to the LORD;
   trust in him, and he will act.
6 He will bring forth your righteous-
     ness as the light,
   and your justice as the noonday.

7 Be still before the LORD and wait
     patiently for him;
   fret not yourself over the one who
     prospers in his way,
   over the man who carries out evil
     devices!

8 Refrain from anger, and forsake
     wrath!
   Fret not yourself; it tends only to
     evil.
9 For the evildoers shall be cut off,
   but those who wait for the LORD
     shall inherit the land.

10 In just a little while, the wicked will
     be no more;
   though you look carefully at his
     place, he will not be there.
11 But the meek shall inherit the land
   and delight themselves in abun-
     dant peace.

12 The wicked plots against the righ-
     teous
   and gnashes his teeth at him,
13 but the Lord laughs at the wicked,
   for he sees that his day is coming.

---

[1] Some Hebrew manuscripts, Syriac, Jerome (compare Septuagint); most Hebrew manuscripts *in my heart* [2] This psalm is an acrostic poem, each stanza beginning with the successive letters of the Hebrew alphabet [3] Or *and feed on faithfulness*, or *and find safe pasture*

14 The wicked draw the sword and
        bend their bows
    to bring down the poor and needy,
    to slay those whose way is upright;
15 their sword shall enter their own
        heart,
    and their bows shall be broken.

16 Better is the little that the righteous
        has
    than the abundance of many wicked.
17 For the arms of the wicked shall be
        broken,
    but the LORD upholds the righteous.

18 The LORD knows the days of the
        blameless,
    and their heritage will remain
        forever;
19 they are not put to shame in evil times;
    in the days of famine they have
        abundance.

20 But the wicked will perish;
    the enemies of the LORD are like
        the glory of the pastures;
    they vanish—like smoke they van-
        ish away.

¹ Hebrew *by him*

21 The wicked borrows but does not
        pay back,
    but the righteous is generous and
        gives;
22 for those blessed by the LORD¹ shall
        inherit the land,
    but those cursed by him shall be
        cut off.

23 The steps of a man are established
        by the LORD,
    when he delights in his way;
24 though he fall, he shall not be cast
        headlong,
    for the LORD upholds his hand.

25 I have been young, and now am old,
    yet I have not seen the righteous
        forsaken
    or his children begging for bread.
26 He is ever lending generously,
    and his children become a bless-
        ing.

27 Turn away from evil and do good;
    so shall you dwell forever.
28 For the LORD loves justice;
    he will not forsake his saints.

Know Yourself

verses to read
Psalm 37:5–11

What are you most preoccupied with lately? What's the main thing you think about, worry about, and work so hard at? Have you asked God about it? Pleaded with him for help? Bugged him to death and gotten no reply? Do you want to know what might be the disconnect? Your focus. When your main issue is anything but the kingdom of God, then that's called worry, and worry separates you from God and messes up your relationship with him.

Jesus tells us to think about the lilies of the field. They don't worry about their lives, but they are so beautiful, just living where they were planted and not worrying about how nice the field across the street is. Don't you know that you are more important to God than the flowers? And don't you know that means that he will take care of you, no matter what (see Matt. 6:28–32)? After all, he gave his own Son for you. He could not prove his love for you any more than that! No matter what comes your way, God Girl, remember what God has done in the gospel and you can be sure that God is in control and no amount of complaining or whining will change that. So be satisfied with his omnipotence and rest in his care for you.

They are preserved forever,
  but the children of the wicked
    shall be cut off.
9 The righteous shall inherit the land
  and dwell upon it forever.

0 The mouth of the righteous utters
    wisdom,
  and his tongue speaks justice.
1 The law of his God is in his heart;
  his steps do not slip.

2 The wicked watches for the righteous
  and seeks to put him to death.
3 The LORD will not abandon him to
    his power
  or let him be condemned when he
    is brought to trial.

4 Wait for the LORD and keep his way,
  and he will exalt you to inherit the
    land;
  you will look on when the wicked
    are cut off.

5 I have seen a wicked, ruthless man,
  spreading himself like a green
    laurel tree.[1]
6 But he passed away,[2] and behold, he
    was no more;
  though I sought him, he could not
    be found.

7 Mark the blameless and behold the
    upright,
  for there is a future for the man of
    peace.
8 But transgressors shall be altogether
    destroyed;
  the future of the wicked shall be
    cut off.

9 The salvation of the righteous is from
    the LORD;
  he is their stronghold in the time
    of trouble.
40 The LORD helps them and delivers
    them;
  he delivers them from the wicked
    and saves them,
  because they take refuge in him.

Do Not Forsake Me, O Lord

38

A PSALM OF DAVID, FOR THE
MEMORIAL OFFERING.

1 O LORD, rebuke me not in your anger,
  nor discipline me in your wrath!

2 For your arrows have sunk into me,
  and your hand has come down on
    me.

3 There is no soundness in my flesh
    because of your indignation;
  there is no health in my bones
    because of my sin.
4 For my iniquities have gone over my
    head;
  like a heavy burden, they are too
    heavy for me.

5 My wounds stink and fester
  because of my foolishness,
6 I am utterly bowed down and pros-
    trate;
  all the day I go about mourning.
7 For my sides are filled with burning,
  and there is no soundness in my
    flesh.
8 I am feeble and crushed;
  I groan because of the tumult of
    my heart.

9 O Lord, all my longing is before you;
  my sighing is not hidden from you.
10 My heart throbs; my strength fails me,
  and the light of my eyes—it also
    has gone from me.
11 My friends and companions stand
    aloof from my plague,
  and my nearest kin stand far off.
12 Those who seek my life lay their
    snares;
  those who seek my hurt speak of
    ruin
  and meditate treachery all day long.

13 But I am like a deaf man; I do not hear,
  like a mute man who does not
    open his mouth.
14 I have become like a man who does
    not hear,
  and in whose mouth are no rebukes.

15 But for you, O LORD, do I wait;
  it is you, O Lord my God, who will
    answer.
16 For I said, "Only let them not rejoice
    over me,
  who boast against me when my
    foot slips!"

17 For I am ready to fall,
  and my pain is ever before me.

The identity of this tree is uncertain [2] Or But one passed by

18   I confess my iniquity;
     I am sorry for my sin.
19   But my foes are vigorous, they are
       mighty,
     and many are those who hate me
       wrongfully.
20   Those who render me evil for good
     accuse me because I follow after
       good.

21   Do not forsake me, O LORD!
     O my God, be not far from me!
22   Make haste to help me,
     O Lord, my salvation!

What Is the Measure of My Days?

39 To the choirmaster: to Jeduthun. A Psalm of David.

1   I said, "I will guard my ways,
     that I may not sin with my tongue;
    I will guard my mouth with a muzzle,
     so long as the wicked are in my
       presence."
2   I was mute and silent;
     I held my peace to no avail,
    and my distress grew worse.
3   My heart became hot within me.
    As I mused, the fire burned;
     then I spoke with my tongue:

4   "O LORD, make me know my end
     and what is the measure of my days;
     let me know how fleeting I am!
5   Behold, you have made my days a
       few handbreadths,
     and my lifetime is as nothing
       before you.
    Surely all mankind stands as a mere
       breath!   *Selah*
6   Surely a man goes about as a
       shadow!
    Surely for nothing[1] they are in turmoil;
     man heaps up wealth and does not
       know who will gather!

7   "And now, O Lord, for what do I wait?
     My hope is in you.
8   Deliver me from all my transgressions.
     Do not make me the scorn of the
       fool!
9   I am mute; I do not open my mouth,
     for it is you who have done it.
10   Remove your stroke from me;
     I am spent by the hostility of your
       hand.

11   When you discipline a man
     with rebukes for sin,
    you consume like a moth what is
       dear to him;
     surely all mankind is a mere
       breath!   *Selah*

12   "Hear my prayer, O LORD,
     and give ear to my cry;
     hold not your peace at my tears!
    For I am a sojourner with you,
     a guest, like all my fathers.
13   Look away from me, that I may smile
       again,
     before I depart and am no more!"

My Help and My Deliverer

40 To the choirmaster. A Psalm of David.

1   I waited patiently for the LORD;
     he inclined to me and heard my cry.
2   He drew me up from the pit of
       destruction,
     out of the miry bog,
    and set my feet upon a rock,
     making my steps secure.
3   He put a new song in my mouth,
     a song of praise to our God.
    Many will see and fear,
     and put their trust in the LORD.

4   Blessed is the man who makes
     the LORD his trust,
    who does not turn to the proud,
     to those who go astray after a lie!
5   You have multiplied, O LORD my God,
     your wondrous deeds and your
       thoughts toward us;
     none can compare with you!
    I will proclaim and tell of them,
     yet they are more than can be told.

6   In sacrifice and offering you have not
       delighted,
     but you have given me an open ear.[2]
    Burnt offering and sin offering
     you have not required.
7   Then I said, "Behold, I have come;
     in the scroll of the book it is writ-
       ten of me:
8   I delight to do your will, O my God;
     your law is within my heart."

9   I have told the glad news of deliver-
       ance[3]
     in the great congregation;

---

[1] Hebrew *Surely as a breath*   [2] Hebrew *ears you have dug for me*   [3] Hebrew *righteousness*; also verse 10

behold, I have not restrained my
lips,
    as you know, O LORD.
I have not hidden your deliverance
within my heart;
    I have spoken of your faithfulness
and your salvation;
I have not concealed your steadfast
love and your faithfulness
    from the great congregation.

1 As for you, O LORD, you will not
restrain
    your mercy from me;
your steadfast love and your faithfulness will
    ever preserve me!
2 For evils have encompassed me
beyond number;
my iniquities have overtaken me,
    and I cannot see;
they are more than the hairs of my
head;
    my heart fails me.

3 Be pleased, O LORD, to deliver me!
    O LORD, make haste to help me!
4 Let those be put to shame and disappointed altogether
    who seek to snatch away my life;
let those be turned back and brought
to dishonor
    who delight in my hurt!
5 Let those be appalled because of
their shame
    who say to me, "Aha, Aha!"

6 But may all who seek you
    rejoice and be glad in you;
may those who love your salvation
    say continually, "Great is the
LORD!"
7 As for me, I am poor and needy,
    but the Lord takes thought for me.
You are my help and my deliverer;
    do not delay, O my God!

O LORD, Be Gracious to Me

41

TO THE CHOIRMASTER. A PSALM OF
DAVID.

1 Blessed is the one who considers the
poor![1]
    In the day of trouble the LORD
delivers him;

2 the LORD protects him and keeps him
alive;
he is called blessed in the land;
    you do not give him up to the will
of his enemies.
3 The LORD sustains him on his sickbed;
    in his illness you restore him to
full health.[2]

4 As for me, I said, "O LORD, be gracious to me;
    heal me,[3] for I have sinned against
you!"
5 My enemies say of me in malice,
    "When will he die, and his name
perish?"
6 And when one comes to see me, he
utters empty words,
    while his heart gathers iniquity;
when he goes out, he tells it abroad.
7 All who hate me whisper together
about me;
    they imagine the worst for me.[4]
8 They say, "A deadly thing is poured
out[5] on him;
    he will not rise again from where
he lies."
9 Even my close friend in whom
I trusted,
    who ate my bread, has lifted his
heel against me.
10 But you, O LORD, be gracious to me,
    and raise me up, that I may repay
them!

11 By this I know that you delight in me:
    my enemy will not shout in tri-
umph over me.
12 But you have upheld me because of
my integrity,
    and set me in your presence forever.

13 Blessed be the LORD, the God of Israel,
    from everlasting to everlasting!
    Amen and Amen.

BOOK TWO

Why Are You Cast Down, O My Soul?

42

TO THE CHOIRMASTER. A MASKIL[6] OF
THE SONS OF KORAH.

1 As a deer pants for flowing streams,
    so pants my soul for you, O God.

Or weak ²Hebrew you turn all his bed ³Hebrew my soul ⁴Or they devise evil against me ⁵Or has fastened ⁶Probably a musical or
liturgical term

2 My soul thirsts for God,
 for the living God.
 When shall I come and appear before
  God?[1]

3 My tears have been my food
 day and night,
 while they say to me all the day
  long,
 "Where is your God?"

4 These things I remember,
 as I pour out my soul:
 how I would go with the throng
  and lead them in procession to the
   house of God
 with glad shouts and songs of
  praise,
  a multitude keeping festival.

5 Why are you cast down, O my soul,
 and why are you in turmoil within
  me?
 Hope in God; for I shall again praise
  him,
 my salvation[2] 6 and my God.

 My soul is cast down within me;
  therefore I remember you
 from the land of Jordan and of
  Hermon,
  from Mount Mizar.

7 Deep calls to deep
 at the roar of your waterfalls;
 all your breakers and your waves
  have gone over me.

8 By day the LORD commands his
  steadfast love,
 and at night his song is with me,
  a prayer to the God of my life.

9 I say to God, my rock:
 "Why have you forgotten me?
 Why do I go mourning
  because of the oppression of the
   enemy?"

10 As with a deadly wound in my bones,
 my adversaries taunt me,
 while they say to me all the day long,
 "Where is your God?"

11 Why are you cast down, O my soul,
 and why are you in turmoil within
  me?
 Hope in God; for I shall again praise
  him,
 my salvation and my God.

Send Out Your Light and Your Truth

43 Vindicate me, O God, and defend
 my cause
 against an ungodly people,
 from the deceitful and unjust man
  deliver me!

2 For you are the God in whom I take
  refuge;
 why have you rejected me?
 Why do I go about mourning
  because of the oppression of the
   enemy?

3 Send out your light and your truth;
 let them lead me;
 let them bring me to your holy hill
  and to your dwelling!

4 Then I will go to the altar of God,
 to God my exceeding joy,
 and I will praise you with the lyre,
  O God, my God.

5 Why are you cast down, O my soul,
 and why are you in turmoil within
  me?
 Hope in God; for I shall again praise
  him,
 my salvation and my God.

Come to Our Help

44 TO THE CHOIRMASTER. A MASKIL[3] OF
 THE SONS OF KORAH.

1 O God, we have heard with our ears,
 our fathers have told us,
 what deeds you performed in their
  days,
  in the days of old:

2 you with your own hand drove out
  the nations,
 but them you planted;
 you afflicted the peoples,
  but them you set free;

3 for not by their own sword did they
  win the land,
 nor did their own arm save them,
 but your right hand and your arm,
  and the light of your face,
  for you delighted in them.

4 You are my King, O God;
 ordain salvation for Jacob!

5 Through you we push down our foes;
 through your name we tread down
  those who rise up against us.

---

[1] Revocalization yields *and see the face of God* [2] Hebrew *the salvation of my face*; also verse 11 and 43:5 [3] Probably a musical or liturgical term

For not in my bow do I trust,
　nor can my sword save me.
But you have saved us from our foes
　and have put to shame those who
　　hate us.
In God we have boasted continually,
　and we will give thanks to your
　　name forever.　　　　　*Selah*

But you have rejected us and dis-
　　graced us
　and have not gone out with our
　　armies.
You have made us turn back from the
　　foe,
　and those who hate us have gotten
　　spoil.
You have made us like sheep for
　　slaughter
　and have scattered us among the
　　nations.
² You have sold your people for a
　　trifle,
　demanding no high price for them.
³ You have made us the taunt of our
　　neighbors,
　the derision and scorn of those
　　around us.
⁴ You have made us a byword among
　　the nations,
　a laughingstock¹ among the
　　peoples.
⁵ All day long my disgrace is before
　　me,
　and shame has covered my face
⁶ at the sound of the taunter and
　　reviler,
　at the sight of the enemy and the
　　avenger.

⁷ All this has come upon us,
　though we have not forgotten you,
　and we have not been false to your
　　covenant.
⁸ Our heart has not turned back,
　nor have our steps departed from
　　your way;
⁹ yet you have broken us in the place
　　of jackals
　and covered us with the shadow of
　　death.
⁰ If we had forgotten the name of our
　　God
　or spread out our hands to a for-
　　eign god,

²¹ would not God discover this?
　For he knows the secrets of the
　　heart.
²² Yet for your sake we are killed all the
　　day long;
　we are regarded as sheep to be
　　slaughtered.
²³ Awake! Why are you sleeping, O Lord?
　Rouse yourself! Do not reject us
　　forever!
²⁴ Why do you hide your face?
　Why do you forget our affliction
　　and oppression?
²⁵ For our soul is bowed down to the
　　dust;
　our belly clings to the ground.
²⁶ Rise up; come to our help!
　Redeem us for the sake of your
　　steadfast love!

Your Throne, O God, Is Forever

45 TO THE CHOIRMASTER: ACCORDING
TO LILIES. A MASKIL² OF THE SONS OF
KORAH; A LOVE SONG.

¹ My heart overflows with a pleasing
　　theme;
　I address my verses to the king;
　my tongue is like the pen of a
　　ready scribe.

² You are the most handsome of the
　　sons of men;
　grace is poured upon your lips;
　therefore God has blessed you
　　forever.
³ Gird your sword on your thigh,
　　O mighty one,
　in your splendor and majesty!

⁴ In your majesty ride out victoriously
　for the cause of truth and meek-
　　ness and righteousness;
　let your right hand teach you awe-
　　some deeds!
⁵ Your arrows are sharp
　in the heart of the king's enemies;
　the peoples fall under you.

⁶ Your throne, O God, is forever and
　　ever.
　The scepter of your kingdom is a
　　scepter of uprightness;
⁷ you have loved righteousness and
　　hated wickedness.

¹ Hebrew *a shaking of the head* ² Probably a musical or liturgical term

Therefore God, your God, has
    anointed you
  with the oil of gladness beyond
    your companions;
8 your robes are all fragrant with
    myrrh and aloes and cassia.
  From ivory palaces stringed instru-
    ments make you glad;
9 daughters of kings are among your
    ladies of honor;
  at your right hand stands the
    queen in gold of Ophir.

10 Hear, O daughter, and consider, and
    incline your ear:
  forget your people and your
    father's house,
11 and the king will desire your beauty.
  Since he is your lord, bow to him.
12 The people[1] of Tyre will seek your
    favor with gifts,
  the richest of the people.[2]
13 All glorious is the princess in her
    chamber, with robes interwo-
    ven with gold.
14 In many-colored robes she is led to
    the king,
  with her virgin companions fol-
    lowing behind her.
15 With joy and gladness they are led
    along
  as they enter the palace of the king.
16 In place of your fathers shall be your
    sons;
  you will make them princes in all
    the earth.
17 I will cause your name to be remem-
    bered in all generations;
  therefore nations will praise you
    forever and ever.

God Is Our Fortress

46
To the choirmaster. Of the Sons
of Korah. According to Alamoth.[3]
A Song.

1 God is our refuge and strength,
  a very present[4] help in trouble.
2 Therefore we will not fear though
    the earth gives way,
  though the mountains be moved
    into the heart of the sea,

3 though its waters roar and foam,
  though the mountains tremble at
    its swelling.   Sela

4 There is a river whose streams make
    glad the city of God,
  the holy habitation of the Most
    High.
5 God is in the midst of her; she shall
    not be moved;
  God will help her when morning
    dawns.
6 The nations rage, the kingdoms totte
  he utters his voice, the earth melt
7 The Lord of hosts is with us;
  the God of Jacob is our fortress.
                      Sela

8 Come, behold the works of the Lord
  how he has brought desolations o
    the earth.
9 He makes wars cease to the end of
    the earth;
  he breaks the bow and shatters
    the spear;
  he burns the chariots with fire.
10 "Be still, and know that I am God.
  I will be exalted among the nation
  I will be exalted in the earth!"
11 The Lord of hosts is with us;
  the God of Jacob is our fortress.
                      Sela

God Is King over All the Earth

47
To the choirmaster. A Psalm of
the Sons of Korah.

1 Clap your hands, all peoples!
  Shout to God with loud songs of joy
2 For the Lord, the Most High, is to be
    feared,
  a great king over all the earth.
3 He subdued peoples under us,
  and nations under our feet.
4 He chose our heritage for us,
  the pride of Jacob whom he loves.
                      Sela

5 God has gone up with a shout,
  the Lord with the sound of a trum
    pet.
6 Sing praises to God, sing praises!
  Sing praises to our King, sing
    praises!

[1] Hebrew *daughter* [2] Or *The daughter of Tyre is here with gifts, the richest of people seek your favor* [3] Probably a musical or liturgical term
[4] Or *well proved*

For God is the King of all the earth;
   sing praises with a psalm!¹

God reigns over the nations;
   God sits on his holy throne.
The princes of the peoples gather
   as the people of the God of
     Abraham.
For the shields of the earth belong to
   God;
   he is highly exalted!

ion, the City of Our God

48 A Song. A Psalm of the Sons of
   Korah.

Great is the LORD and greatly to be
   praised
   in the city of our God!
His holy mountain, ²beautiful in
   elevation,
   is the joy of all the earth,
Mount Zion, in the far north,
   the city of the great King.
Within her citadels God
   has made himself known as a
     fortress.

For behold, the kings assembled;
   they came on together.

ebrew *maskil*

5 As soon as they saw it, they were
   astounded;
   they were in panic; they took to
     flight.
6 Trembling took hold of them there,
   anguish as of a woman in labor.
7 By the east wind you shattered
   the ships of Tarshish.
8 As we have heard, so have we seen
   in the city of the LORD of hosts,
in the city of our God,
   which God will establish forever.
                 Selah

9 We have thought on your steadfast
   love, O God,
   in the midst of your temple.
10 As your name, O God,
   so your praise reaches to the ends
     of the earth.
Your right hand is filled with righteousness.
11 Let Mount Zion be glad!
Let the daughters of Judah rejoice
   because of your judgments!

12 Walk about Zion, go around her,
   number her towers,

verses to read
Psalm 46

Know True Happiness

You get closest to Jesus in the tough times, not the good times. That's when you learn who he is and what he can do to save you.

For a weak swimmer who doesn't understand the currents and the crashing waves, the surf is a scary thing to go into—deadly, even. But to the surfer who knows the waves and loves riding them, they are nothing to fear. Just like a surfer riding a wave that might destroy an ordinary person, you have to learn to look at the waves of your life, the tough times and hard relationships, as something to go through and not to fear. You are overwhelmingly victorious because of who God is (see Rom. 8:37), and not just in the easy things, but in all things. In the hard things of life, you can find not only his hand but the strength of your faith. Don't panic when the waves come; just see them as something you've got to ride on and go through in that season of your life.

Nothing can separate you from the love of God, not even your own weakness and failings (see Rom. 8:35–39). So hold on tight, keep your eyes on the Father, and enjoy the water!

13 consider well her ramparts,
   go through her citadels,
 that you may tell the next generation
14   that this is God,
   our God forever and ever.
   He will guide us forever.[1]

Why Should I Fear in Times of Trouble?

49 To the choirmaster. A Psalm of the Sons of Korah.

1 Hear this, all peoples!
   Give ear, all inhabitants of the
      world,
2 both low and high,
   rich and poor together!
3 My mouth shall speak wisdom;
   the meditation of my heart shall be
      understanding.
4 I will incline my ear to a proverb;
   I will solve my riddle to the music
      of the lyre.

5 Why should I fear in times of trouble,
   when the iniquity of those who
      cheat me surrounds me,
6 those who trust in their wealth
   and boast of the abundance of
      their riches?
7 Truly no man can ransom another,
   or give to God the price of his life,
8 for the ransom of their life is costly
   and can never suffice,
9 that he should live on forever
   and never see the pit.

10 For he sees that even the wise die;
   the fool and the stupid alike must
      perish
   and leave their wealth to others.
11 Their graves are their homes forever,[2]
   their dwelling places to all genera-
      tions,
   though they called lands by their
      own names.
12 Man in his pomp will not remain;
   he is like the beasts that perish.

13 This is the path of those who have
      foolish confidence;
   yet after them people approve of
      their boasts.[3]   *Selah*
14 Like sheep they are appointed for
      Sheol;
   death shall be their shepherd,

and the upright shall rule over them
   in the morning.
 Their form shall be consumed in
   Sheol, with no place to dwell.
15 But God will ransom my soul from
   the power of Sheol,
 for he will receive me.   *Sela*

16 Be not afraid when a man becomes
      rich,
 when the glory of his house
   increases.
17 For when he dies he will carry noth-
      ing away;
 his glory will not go down after
   him.
18 For though, while he lives, he counts
   himself blessed
 —and though you get praise when
   you do well for yourself—
19 his soul will go to the generation of
   his fathers,
 who will never again see light.
20 Man in his pomp yet without understanding is like the beasts that
   perish.

God Himself Is Judge

50 A Psalm of Asaph.
   The Mighty One, God the Lord,
 speaks and summons the earth
 from the rising of the sun to its
   setting.
2 Out of Zion, the perfection of beauty
 God shines forth.

3 Our God comes; he does not keep
   silence;[4]
 before him is a devouring fire,
 around him a mighty tempest.
4 He calls to the heavens above
 and to the earth, that he may judge
   his people:
5 "Gather to me my faithful ones,
 who made a covenant with me by
   sacrifice!"
6 The heavens declare his righteousness,
 for God himself is judge!   *Sela*

7 "Hear, O my people, and I will speak;
 O Israel, I will testify against you.
 I am God, your God.

---

[1] Septuagint; another reading is (compare Jerome, Syriac) *He will guide us beyond death* [2] Septuagint, Syriac, Targum; Hebrew *Their inward thought was that their homes were forever* [3] Or *and of those after them who approve of their boasts* [4] Or *May our God come, and not keep silence*

8   Not for your sacrifices do I rebuke
        you;
        your burnt offerings are continu-
        ally before me.
9   I will not accept a bull from your
        house
        or goats from your folds.
10 For every beast of the forest is mine,
        the cattle on a thousand hills.
11 I know all the birds of the hills,
        and all that moves in the field is
        mine.

12 "If I were hungry, I would not tell you,
        for the world and its fullness are
        mine.
13 Do I eat the flesh of bulls
        or drink the blood of goats?
14 Offer to God a sacrifice of thanksgiv-
        ing,[1]
        and perform your vows to the
        Most High,
15 and call upon me in the day of
        trouble;
        I will deliver you, and you shall
        glorify me."

16 But to the wicked God says:
        "What right have you to recite my
        statutes
        or take my covenant on your lips?
17 For you hate discipline,
        and you cast my words behind you.
18 If you see a thief, you are pleased
        with him,
        and you keep company with adul-
        terers.
19 "You give your mouth free rein for
        evil,
        and your tongue frames deceit.
20 You sit and speak against your
        brother;
        you slander your own mother's
        son.
21 These things you have done, and
        I have been silent;
        you thought that I[2] was one like
        yourself.
        But now I rebuke you and lay the
        charge before you.

22 "Mark this, then, you who forget God,
        lest I tear you apart, and there be
        none to deliver!

23 The one who offers thanksgiving as
        his sacrifice glorifies me;
        to one who orders his way rightly
        I will show the salvation of God!"

Create in Me a Clean Heart, O God

51 To the choirmaster. A Psalm of
David, when Nathan the prophet
went to him, after he had gone in
to Bathsheba.

1   Have mercy on me,[3] O God,
        according to your steadfast love;
        according to your abundant mercy
        blot out my transgressions.
2   Wash me thoroughly from my iniq-
        uity,
        and cleanse me from my sin!

3   For I know my transgressions,
        and my sin is ever before me.
4   Against you, you only, have I sinned
        and done what is evil in your sight,
        so that you may be justified in your
        words
        and blameless in your judgment.
5   Behold, I was brought forth in iniquity,
        and in sin did my mother conceive
        me.
6   Behold, you delight in truth in the
        inward being,
        and you teach me wisdom in the
        secret heart.

7   Purge me with hyssop, and I shall be
        clean;
        wash me, and I shall be whiter
        than snow.
8   Let me hear joy and gladness;
        let the bones that you have broken
        rejoice.
9   Hide your face from my sins,
        and blot out all my iniquities.
10 Create in me a clean heart, O God,
        and renew a right[4] spirit within me.
11 Cast me not away from your presence,
        and take not your Holy Spirit from
        me.
12 Restore to me the joy of your salva-
        tion,
        and uphold me with a willing spirit.
13 Then I will teach transgressors your
        ways,
        and sinners will return to you.

[1] Or Make thanksgiving your sacrifice to God [2] Or that the I AM [3] Or Be gracious to me [4] Or steadfast

¹⁴ Deliver me from bloodguiltiness,
     O God,
     O God of my salvation,
     and my tongue will sing aloud of
       your righteousness.
¹⁵ O Lord, open my lips,
     and my mouth will declare your
       praise.
¹⁶ For you will not delight in sacrifice,
     or I would give it;
     you will not be pleased with a
       burnt offering.
¹⁷ The sacrifices of God are a broken
       spirit;
     a broken and contrite heart, O God,
       you will not despise.

¹⁸ Do good to Zion in your good plea-
       sure;
     build up the walls of Jerusalem;
¹⁹ then will you delight in right sacri-
       fices,
     in burnt offerings and whole burnt
       offerings;
     then bulls will be offered on your
       altar.

¹ Probably a musical or liturgical term

The Steadfast Love of God Endures

52 To the choirmaster. A Maskil[1] of David, when Doeg, the Edomite, came and told Saul, "David has come to the house of Ahimelech."

¹ Why do you boast of evil, O mighty
       man?
     The steadfast love of God endures
       all the day.
² Your tongue plots destruction,
     like a sharp razor, you worker of
       deceit.
³ You love evil more than good,
     and lying more than speaking
         what is right.   *Selah*
⁴ You love all words that devour,
     O deceitful tongue.

⁵ But God will break you down forever;
     he will snatch and tear you from
       your tent;
     he will uproot you from the land of
       the living.   *Selah*
⁶ The righteous shall see and fear,
     and shall laugh at him, saying,

verses to read
Psalm 51

Know God

When you first come to Christ, you agree with him that what you used to believe was a lie. That's the first thing you must do in order to be forgiven and saved. The things the world told you, the pain you inflicted on yourself, the loneliness, the guilt, the emptiness—everything that a life without Christ gave you was a lie, and you finally agree with that. This is the beginning of repentance.

But repentance doesn't stop as soon as you accept Christ. It goes on every day. Every day, guaranteed, you do something sinful, something that proves you've bought the lies again. So every day you have to consciously repent of that stuff. Every day you have to clear the slate by calling a lie a lie and agreeing with God that you missed the mark. This doesn't mean that you have to feel unending guilt, but you do have to admit that you were a fool for being stupid enough to forget the truth yet again. It happens to everyone everywhere, and that's why God has made a way out: repentance.

God doesn't just put up with your junk. He isn't your best friend who overlooks your sins; he is God, and he requires holiness (see Matt. 5:48). Don't let your idea of a loving God cloud your need to recognize that he is a holy God and to agree with him about your sin. Confess your sin and repent, and then bask in the joy of his unending love.

7 "See the man who would not make
   God his refuge,
  but trusted in the abundance of his
     riches
   and sought refuge in his own
     destruction!"[1]

8 But I am like a green olive tree
   in the house of God.
  I trust in the steadfast love of God
   forever and ever.

9 I will thank you forever,
   because you have done it.
  I will wait for your name, for it is good,
   in the presence of the godly.

There Is None Who Does Good

53 To the choirmaster: according to
Mahalath. A Maskil[2] of David.

1 The fool says in his heart, "There is
   no God."
    They are corrupt, doing abomi-
      nable iniquity;
    there is none who does good.

2 God looks down from heaven
   on the children of man
  to see if there are any who under-
     stand,[3]
   who seek after God.

3 They have all fallen away;
   together they have become corrupt;
  there is none who does good,
   not even one.

4 Have those who work evil no knowl-
     edge,
   who eat up my people as they eat
     bread,
   and do not call upon God?

5 There they are, in great terror,
   where there is no terror!
  For God scatters the bones of him
   who encamps against you;
  you put them to shame, for God
   has rejected them.

6 Oh, that salvation for Israel would
   come out of Zion!
    When God restores the fortunes of
     his people,
    let Jacob rejoice, let Israel be glad.

The Lord Upholds My Life

54 To the choirmaster: with
stringed instruments. A Maskil[4]
of David, when the Ziphites went
and told Saul, "Is not David hiding
among us?"

1 O God, save me by your name,
   and vindicate me by your might.

2 O God, hear my prayer;
   give ear to the words of my mouth.

3 For strangers[5] have risen against me;
   ruthless men seek my life;
  they do not set God before them-
     selves.   *Selah*

4 Behold, God is my helper;
   the Lord is the upholder of my life.

5 He will return the evil to my enemies;
   in your faithfulness put an end to
     them.

6 With a freewill offering I will sacri-
     fice to you;
  I will give thanks to your name,
   O Lord, for it is good.

7 For he has delivered me from every
     trouble,
   and my eye has looked in triumph
     on my enemies.

Cast Your Burden on the Lord

55 To the choirmaster: with
stringed instruments. A Maskil[6]
of David.

1 Give ear to my prayer, O God,
   and hide not yourself from my plea
     for mercy!

2 Attend to me, and answer me;
   I am restless in my complaint and
     I moan,

3 because of the noise of the enemy,
   because of the oppression of the
     wicked.
  For they drop trouble upon me,
   and in anger they bear a grudge
     against me.

4 My heart is in anguish within me;
   the terrors of death have fallen
     upon me.

5 Fear and trembling come upon me,
   and horror overwhelms me.

[1] Or in his work of destruction [2] Probably musical or liturgical terms [3] Or who act wisely [4] Probably a musical or liturgical term [5] Some
Hebrew manuscripts and Targum insolent men (compare Psalm 86:14) [6] Probably a musical or liturgical term

6 And I say, "Oh, that I had wings like a
       dove!
     I would fly away and be at rest;
7 yes, I would wander far away;
     I would lodge in the wilderness; *Selah*
8 I would hurry to find a shelter
     from the raging wind and tempest."

9 Destroy, O Lord, divide their tongues;
     for I see violence and strife in the
       city.
10 Day and night they go around it
     on its walls,
   and iniquity and trouble are within it;
11   ruin is in its midst;
   oppression and fraud
     do not depart from its marketplace.

12 For it is not an enemy who taunts
     me—
     then I could bear it;
   it is not an adversary who deals
       insolently with me—
     then I could hide from him.
13 But it is you, a man, my equal,
     my companion, my familiar friend.
14 We used to take sweet counsel
       together;
     within God's house we walked in
       the throng.
15 Let death steal over them;
     let them go down to Sheol alive;
   for evil is in their dwelling place
     and in their heart.

16 But I call to God,
     and the LORD will save me.
17 Evening and morning and at noon
     I utter my complaint and moan,
     and he hears my voice.
18 He redeems my soul in safety
     from the battle that I wage,
     for many are arrayed against me.
19 God will give ear and humble them,
     he who is enthroned from of old, *Selah*
   because they do not change
     and do not fear God.

20 My companion[1] stretched out his
       hand against his friends;
     he violated his covenant.
21 His speech was smooth as butter,
     yet war was in his heart;

   his words were softer than oil,
     yet they were drawn swords.

22 Cast your burden on the LORD,
     and he will sustain you;
   he will never permit
     the righteous to be moved.

23 But you, O God, will cast them down
     into the pit of destruction;
   men of blood and treachery
     shall not live out half their days.
   But I will trust in you.

In God I Trust

56

TO THE CHOIRMASTER: ACCORDING TO
THE DOVE ON FAR-OFF TEREBINTHS.
A MIKTAM[2] OF DAVID, WHEN THE
PHILISTINES SEIZED HIM IN GATH.

1 Be gracious to me, O God, for man
       tramples on me;
     all day long an attacker oppresses
       me;
2 my enemies trample on me all day
       long,
     for many attack me proudly.
3 When I am afraid,
     I put my trust in you.
4 In God, whose word I praise,
     in God I trust; I shall not be afraid.
     What can flesh do to me?

5 All day long they injure my cause;[3]
     all their thoughts are against me
       for evil.
6 They stir up strife, they lurk;
     they watch my steps,
     as they have waited for my life.
7 For their crime will they escape?
     In wrath cast down the peoples,
       O God!

8 You have kept count of my tossings;[4]
     put my tears in your bottle.
     Are they not in your book?
9 Then my enemies will turn back
     in the day when I call.
     This I know, that[5] God is for me.
10 In God, whose word I praise,
     in the LORD, whose word I praise,
11 in God I trust; I shall not be afraid.
     What can man do to me?
12 I must perform my vows to you,
       O God;
     I will render thank offerings to you.

---

[1] Hebrew *He* [2] Probably a musical or liturgical term [3] Or *they twist my words* [4] Or *wanderings* [5] Or *because*

13 For you have delivered my soul from
        death,
    yes, my feet from falling,
  that I may walk before God
    in the light of life.

Let Your Glory Be over All the Earth

57

TO THE CHOIRMASTER: ACCORDING
TO DO NOT DESTROY. A MIKTAM[1] OF
DAVID, WHEN HE FLED FROM SAUL, IN
THE CAVE.

1 Be merciful to me, O God, be merciful
        to me,
    for in you my soul takes refuge;
  in the shadow of your wings I will
        take refuge,
    till the storms of destruction pass
        by.
2 I cry out to God Most High,
    to God who fulfills his purpose for
        me.
3 He will send from heaven and save
        me;
    he will put to shame him who
        tramples on me.   *Selah*
  God will send out his steadfast love
    and his faithfulness!

4 My soul is in the midst of lions;
    I lie down amid fiery beasts—
  the children of man, whose teeth are
        spears and arrows,
    whose tongues are sharp swords.

5 Be exalted, O God, above the heav-
        ens!
    Let your glory be over all the
        earth!

6 They set a net for my steps;
    my soul was bowed down.
  They dug a pit in my way,
    but they have fallen into it them-
        selves.   *Selah*
7 My heart is steadfast, O God,
    my heart is steadfast!
  I will sing and make melody!
8   Awake, my glory![2]
  Awake, O harp and lyre!
    I will awake the dawn!
9 I will give thanks to you, O Lord,
        among the peoples;
    I will sing praises to you among
        the nations.

10 For your steadfast love is great to the
        heavens,
    your faithfulness to the clouds.

11 Be exalted, O God, above the heavens!
    Let your glory be over all the earth!

God Who Judges the Earth

58

TO THE CHOIRMASTER: ACCORDING
TO DO NOT DESTROY. A MIKTAM[3] OF
DAVID.

1 Do you indeed decree what is right,
        you gods?[4]
    Do you judge the children of man
        uprightly?
2 No, in your hearts you devise wrongs;
    your hands deal out violence on
        earth.

3 The wicked are estranged from the
        womb;
    they go astray from birth, speaking
        lies.
4 They have venom like the venom of a
        serpent,
    like the deaf adder that stops its ear,
5 so that it does not hear the voice of
        charmers
    or of the cunning enchanter.

6 O God, break the teeth in their
        mouths;
    tear out the fangs of the young
        lions, O LORD!
7 Let them vanish like water that runs
        away;
    when he aims his arrows, let them
        be blunted.
8 Let them be like the snail that dis-
        solves into slime,
    like the stillborn child who never
        sees the sun.
9 Sooner than your pots can feel the
        heat of thorns,
    whether green or ablaze, may he
        sweep them away![5]

10 The righteous will rejoice when he
        sees the vengeance;
    he will bathe his feet in the blood
        of the wicked.
11 Mankind will say, "Surely there is a
        reward for the righteous;
    surely there is a God who judges
        on earth."

[1] Probably a musical or liturgical term [2] Or *my whole being* [3] Probably a musical or liturgical term [4] Or *you mighty lords* (by
revocalization; Hebrew *in silence*) [5] The meaning of the Hebrew verse is uncertain

Deliver Me from My Enemies

59

To the choirmaster: according to Do Not Destroy. A Miktam[1] of David, when Saul sent men to watch his house in order to kill him.

1 Deliver me from my enemies, O my God;
    protect me from those who rise up against me;
2 deliver me from those who work evil,
    and save me from bloodthirsty men.

3 For behold, they lie in wait for my life;
    fierce men stir up strife against me.
For no transgression or sin of mine, O Lord,
4 for no fault of mine, they run and make ready.
Awake, come to meet me, and see!
5 You, Lord God of hosts, are God of Israel.
Rouse yourself to punish all the nations;
    spare none of those who treacherously plot evil.   Selah

6 Each evening they come back,
    howling like dogs
    and prowling about the city.
7 There they are, bellowing with their mouths
    with swords in their lips—
    for "Who," they think,[2] "will hear us?"

8 But you, O Lord, laugh at them;
    you hold all the nations in derision.
9 O my Strength, I will watch for you,
    for you, O God, are my fortress.
10 My God in his steadfast love[3] will meet me;
    God will let me look in triumph on my enemies.

11 Kill them not, lest my people forget;
    make them totter[4] by your power and bring them down,
    O Lord, our shield!
12 For the sin of their mouths, the words of their lips,
    let them be trapped in their pride.

For the cursing and lies that they utter,
13   consume them in wrath;
    consume them till they are no more,
that they may know that God rules over Jacob
    to the ends of the earth.   Selah

14 Each evening they come back,
    howling like dogs
    and prowling about the city.
15 They wander about for food
    and growl if they do not get their fill.

16 But I will sing of your strength;
    I will sing aloud of your steadfast love in the morning.
For you have been to me a fortress
    and a refuge in the day of my distress.
17 O my Strength, I will sing praises to you,
    for you, O God, are my fortress,
    the God who shows me steadfast love.

He Will Tread Down Our Foes

60

To the choirmaster: according to Shushan Eduth. A Miktam[5] of David; for instruction; when he strove with Aram-naharaim and with Aram-zobah, and when Joab on his return struck down twelve thousand of Edom in the Valley of Salt.

1 O God, you have rejected us, broken our defenses;
    you have been angry; oh, restore us.
2 You have made the land to quake;
    you have torn it open;
    repair its breaches, for it totters.
3 You have made your people see hard things;
    you have given us wine to drink that made us stagger.

4 You have set up a banner for those who fear you,
    that they may flee to it from the bow.[6]   Selah

[1] Probably a musical or liturgical term [2] Hebrew lacks they think [3] Or The God who shows me steadfast love [4] Or wander [5] Probably musical or liturgical terms [6] Or that it may be displayed because of truth

5 That your beloved ones may be
    delivered,
      give salvation by your right hand
        and answer us!

6 God has spoken in his holiness:[1]
    "With exultation I will divide up
      Shechem
      and portion out the Vale of
        Succoth.
7 Gilead is mine; Manasseh is mine;
    Ephraim is my helmet;
    Judah is my scepter.
8 Moab is my washbasin;
    upon Edom I cast my shoe;
    over Philistia I shout in triumph."[2]

9 Who will bring me to the fortified
    city?
    Who will lead me to Edom?
10 Have you not rejected us, O God?
    You do not go forth, O God, with
      our armies.
11 Oh, grant us help against the foe,
    for vain is the salvation of man!
12 With God we shall do valiantly;
    it is he who will tread down our
      foes.

Lead Me to the Rock

61 To the choirmaster: with stringed instruments. Of David.

1 Hear my cry, O God,
    listen to my prayer;
2 from the end of the earth I call to you
    when my heart is faint.
    Lead me to the rock
    that is higher than I,
3 for you have been my refuge,
    a strong tower against the enemy.

4 Let me dwell in your tent forever!
    Let me take refuge under the shel-
      ter of your wings!   Selah
5 For you, O God, have heard my
    vows;
    you have given me the heritage of
      those who fear your name.

6 Prolong the life of the king;
    may his years endure to all genera-
      tions!
7 May he be enthroned forever before
    God;
    appoint steadfast love and faithful-
      ness to watch over him!

8 So will I ever sing praises to your
    name,
    as I perform my vows day after
      day.

My Soul Waits for God Alone

62 To the choirmaster: according to Jeduthun. A Psalm of David.

1 For God alone my soul waits in
    silence;
    from him comes my salvation.
2 He alone is my rock and my salvation,
    my fortress; I shall not be greatly
      shaken.

3 How long will all of you attack a man
    to batter him,
    like a leaning wall, a tottering
      fence?
4 They only plan to thrust him down
      from his high position.
    They take pleasure in falsehood.
  They bless with their mouths,
    but inwardly they curse.   Selah

5 For God alone, O my soul, wait in
    silence,
    for my hope is from him.
6 He only is my rock and my salvation,
    my fortress; I shall not be shaken.
7 On God rests my salvation and my
    glory;
    my mighty rock, my refuge is God.

8 Trust in him at all times, O people;
    pour out your heart before him;
    God is a refuge for us.   Selah

9 Those of low estate are but a breath;
    those of high estate are a delu-
      sion;
  in the balances they go up;
    they are together lighter than a
      breath.
10 Put no trust in extortion;
    set no vain hopes on robbery;
    if riches increase, set not your
      heart on them.

11 Once God has spoken;
    twice have I heard this:
  that power belongs to God,
12 and that to you, O Lord, belongs
      steadfast love.
  For you will render to a man
    according to his work.

---

[1] Or sanctuary [2] Revocalization (compare Psalm 108:10); Masoretic Text over me, O Philistia, shout in triumph

My Soul Thirsts for You

63 A Psalm of David, when he was in the wilderness of Judah.

1 O God, you are my God; earnestly
        I seek you;
    my soul thirsts for you;
    my flesh faints for you,
        as in a dry and weary land where
            there is no water.

2 So I have looked upon you in the
        sanctuary,
    beholding your power and glory.

3 Because your steadfast love is better
        than life,
    my lips will praise you.

4 So I will bless you as long as I live;
    in your name I will lift up my hands.

5 My soul will be satisfied as with fat
        and rich food,
    and my mouth will praise you with
        joyful lips,

6 when I remember you upon my bed,
    and meditate on you in the
        watches of the night;

7 for you have been my help,
    and in the shadow of your wings
        I will sing for joy.

8 My soul clings to you;
    your right hand upholds me.

9 But those who seek to destroy my life
    shall go down into the depths of
        the earth;

10 they shall be given over to the power
        of the sword;
    they shall be a portion for jackals.

11 But the king shall rejoice in God;
    all who swear by him shall exult,
    for the mouths of liars will be
        stopped.

Hide Me from the Wicked

64 To the choirmaster. A Psalm of David.

1 Hear my voice, O God, in my com-
        plaint;
    preserve my life from dread of the
        enemy.

2 Hide me from the secret plots of the
        wicked,
    from the throng of evildoers,

3 who whet their tongues like swords,
    who aim bitter words like arrows,

4 shooting from ambush at the blame-
        less,
    shooting at him suddenly and
        without fear.

5 They hold fast to their evil purpose;
    they talk of laying snares secretly,
    thinking, "Who can see them?"

6 They search out injustice,
    saying, "We have accomplished a
        diligent search."
    For the inward mind and heart of a
        man are deep.

7 But God shoots his arrow at them;
    they are wounded suddenly.

8 They are brought to ruin, with their
        own tongues turned against
            them;
    all who see them will wag their
        heads.

9 Then all mankind fears;
    they tell what God has brought
        about
    and ponder what he has done.

10 Let the righteous one rejoice in the
        Lord
    and take refuge in him!
    Let all the upright in heart exult!

O God of Our Salvation

65 To the choirmaster. A Psalm of David. A Song.

1 Praise is due to you,[1] O God, in Zion,
    and to you shall vows be per-
        formed.

2 O you who hear prayer,
    to you shall all flesh come.

3 When iniquities prevail against me,
    you atone for our transgressions.

4 Blessed is the one you choose and
        bring near,
    to dwell in your courts!
    We shall be satisfied with the good-
        ness of your house,
        the holiness of your temple!

5 By awesome deeds you answer us
        with righteousness,
    O God of our salvation,
    the hope of all the ends of the earth
    and of the farthest seas;

6 the one who by his strength estab-
        lished the mountains,
    being girded with might;

[1] Or Praise waits for you in silence

7   who stills the roaring of the seas,
       the roaring of their waves,
       the tumult of the peoples,
8   so that those who dwell at the ends
       of the earth are in awe at your
       signs.
    You make the going out of the morn-
       ing and the evening to shout
       for joy.

9   You visit the earth and water it;[1]
       you greatly enrich it;
    the river of God is full of water;
       you provide their grain,
       for so you have prepared it.
10 You water its furrows abundantly,
       settling its ridges,
    softening it with showers,
       and blessing its growth.
11 You crown the year with your bounty;
       your wagon tracks overflow with
       abundance.
12 The pastures of the wilderness over-
       flow,
       the hills gird themselves with joy,
13 the meadows clothe themselves with
       flocks,
       the valleys deck themselves with
       grain,
       they shout and sing together for joy.

How Awesome Are Your Deeds

66
TO THE CHOIRMASTER. A SONG.
A PSALM.

1   Shout for joy to God, all the earth;
2   sing the glory of his name;
       give to him glorious praise!
3   Say to God, "How awesome are your
       deeds!
    So great is your power that your
       enemies come cringing to you.
4   All the earth worships you
       and sings praises to you;
       they sing praises to your name."
                                      Selah

5   Come and see what God has done:
       he is awesome in his deeds toward
       the children of man.
6   He turned the sea into dry land;
       they passed through the river on
       foot.
    There did we rejoice in him,
7   who rules by his might forever,

whose eyes keep watch on the
       nations—
    let not the rebellious exalt them-
       selves.   Selah

8   Bless our God, O peoples;
       let the sound of his praise be
       heard,
9   who has kept our soul among the
       living
       and has not let our feet slip.
10 For you, O God, have tested us;
       you have tried us as silver is tried.
11 You brought us into the net;
       you laid a crushing burden on our
       backs;
12 you let men ride over our heads;
       we went through fire and through
       water;
    yet you have brought us out to a
       place of abundance.

13 I will come into your house with
       burnt offerings;
       I will perform my vows to you,
14 that which my lips uttered
       and my mouth promised when
       I was in trouble.
15 I will offer to you burnt offerings of
       fattened animals,
       with the smoke of the sacrifice of
       rams;
    I will make an offering of bulls and
       goats.   Selah

16 Come and hear, all you who fear
       God,
       and I will tell what he has done for
       my soul.
17 I cried to him with my mouth,
       and high praise was on[2] my
       tongue.[3]
18 If I had cherished iniquity in my
       heart,
       the Lord would not have listened.
19 But truly God has listened;
       he has attended to the voice of my
       prayer.
20 Blessed be God,
       because he has not rejected my
       prayer
       or removed his steadfast love from
       me!

[1] Or and make it overflow [2] Hebrew under [3] Or and he was exalted with my tongue

Make Your Face Shine upon Us

67 To the choirmaster: with stringed instruments. A Psalm. A Song.

1   May God be gracious to us and
        bless us
    and make his face to shine upon
        us,   *Selah*

2   that your way may be known on earth,
        your saving power among all
        nations.

3   Let the peoples praise you, O God;
        let all the peoples praise you!

4   Let the nations be glad and sing for
        joy,
        for you judge the peoples with
            equity
        and guide the nations upon earth.
                                               Selah

5   Let the peoples praise you, O God;
        let all the peoples praise you!

6   The earth has yielded its increase;
        God, our God, shall bless us.

7   God shall bless us;
        let all the ends of the earth fear
            him!

God Shall Scatter His Enemies

68 To the choirmaster. A Psalm of David. A Song.

1   God shall arise, his enemies shall be
        scattered;
        and those who hate him shall flee
            before him!

2   As smoke is driven away, so you shall
        drive them away;
        as wax melts before fire,
        so the wicked shall perish before
            God!

3   But the righteous shall be glad;
        they shall exult before God;
        they shall be jubilant with joy!

4   Sing to God, sing praises to his name;
        lift up a song to him who rides
            through the deserts;
        his name is the Lord;
        exult before him!

5   Father of the fatherless and protec-
        tor of widows
        is God in his holy habitation.

6   God settles the solitary in a home;
        he leads out the prisoners to pros-
            perity,
        but the rebellious dwell in a
            parched land.

7   O God, when you went out before
        your people,
        when you marched through the
            wilderness,   *Selah*

8   the earth quaked, the heavens
        poured down rain,
        before God, the One of Sinai,
        before God, the God of Israel.

9   Rain in abundance, O God, you shed
        abroad;
        you restored your inheritance as it
            languished;

10 your flock[1] found a dwelling in it;
        in your goodness, O God, you pro-
            vided for the needy.

11 The Lord gives the word;
        the women who announce the
            news are a great host:

12 "The kings of the armies—they flee
        they flee!"
    The women at home divide the spoil—

13 though you men lie among the
        sheepfolds—
    the wings of a dove covered with
        silver,
        its pinions with shimmering gold.

14 When the Almighty scatters kings
        there,
        let snow fall on Zalmon.

15 O mountain of God, mountain of
        Bashan;
        O many-peaked[2] mountain, moun-
            tain of Bashan!

16 Why do you look with hatred,
        O many-peaked mountain,
        at the mount that God desired for
            his abode,
        yes, where the Lord will dwell
            forever?

17 The chariots of God are twice ten
        thousand,
        thousands upon thousands;
        the Lord is among them; Sinai is
            now in the sanctuary.

18 You ascended on high,
        leading a host of captives in your
            train

[1] Or *your congregation* [2] Or *hunch-backed*; also verse 16

and receiving gifts among men,
even among the rebellious, that the
    LORD God may dwell there.

19 Blessed be the Lord,
        who daily bears us up;
    God is our salvation.   *Selah*
20 Our God is a God of salvation,
        and to GOD, the Lord, belong deliv-
            erances from death.
21 But God will strike the heads of his
            enemies,
        the hairy crown of him who walks
            in his guilty ways.
22 The Lord said,
        "I will bring them back from Bashan,
    I will bring them back from the
            depths of the sea,
23 that you may strike your feet in their
            blood,
        that the tongues of your dogs may
            have their portion from the foe."

24 Your procession is[1] seen, O God,
        the procession of my God, my King,
            into the sanctuary—
25 the singers in front, the musicians last,
        between them virgins playing
            tambourines:
26 "Bless God in the great congregation,
        the LORD, O you[2] who are of
            Israel's fountain!"
27 There is Benjamin, the least of them,
            in the lead,
        the princes of Judah in their throng,
        the princes of Zebulun, the princes
            of Naphtali.

28 Summon your power, O God,[3]
        the power, O God, by which you
            have worked for us.
29 Because of your temple at Jerusalem
        kings shall bear gifts to you.
30 Rebuke the beasts that dwell among
            the reeds,
        the herd of bulls with the calves of
            the peoples.
    Trample underfoot those who lust
            after tribute;
        scatter the peoples who delight in
            war.[4]
31 Nobles shall come from Egypt;
        Cush shall hasten to stretch out
            her hands to God.

32 O kingdoms of the earth, sing to
            God;
        sing praises to the Lord,   *Selah*
33 to him who rides in the heavens, the
            ancient heavens;
        behold, he sends out his voice, his
            mighty voice.
34 Ascribe power to God,
        whose majesty is over Israel,
        and whose power is in the skies.
35 Awesome is God from his[5] sanctuary;
        the God of Israel—he is the one
            who gives power and strength
                to his people.
    Blessed be God!

Save Me, O God

69 TO THE CHOIRMASTER: ACCORDING TO
        LILIES. OF DAVID.

1   Save me, O God!
        For the waters have come up to my
            neck.[6]
2   I sink in deep mire,
        where there is no foothold;
    I have come into deep waters,
        and the flood sweeps over me.
3   I am weary with my crying out;
        my throat is parched.
    My eyes grow dim
        with waiting for my God.

4   More in number than the hairs of my
            head
        are those who hate me without
            cause;
    mighty are those who would destroy
            me,
        those who attack me with lies.
    What I did not steal
        must I now restore?
5   O God, you know my folly;
        the wrongs I have done are not
            hidden from you.

6   Let not those who hope in you be put
            to shame through me,
        O Lord GOD of hosts;
    let not those who seek you be brought
            to dishonor through me,
        O God of Israel.
7   For it is for your sake that I have
            borne reproach,
        that dishonor has covered my face.

[1] Or *has been* [2] The Hebrew for *you* is plural here [3] By revocalization (compare Septuagint); Hebrew *Your God has summoned your power*
[4] The meaning of the Hebrew verse is uncertain [5] Septuagint; Hebrew *your* [6] Or *waters threaten my life*

8   I have become a stranger to my
    brothers,
        an alien to my mother's sons.

9   For zeal for your house has con-
    sumed me,
        and the reproaches of those who
        reproach you have fallen on
        me.

10 When I wept and humbled[1] my soul
    with fasting,
        it became my reproach.

11 When I made sackcloth my clothing,
        I became a byword to them.

12 I am the talk of those who sit in the
    gate,
        and the drunkards make songs
        about me.

13 But as for me, my prayer is to you,
    O LORD.
        At an acceptable time, O God,
        in the abundance of your steadfast
        love answer me in your saving
        faithfulness.

14 Deliver me
        from sinking in the mire;
    let me be delivered from my
        enemies
        and from the deep waters.

15 Let not the flood sweep over me,
        or the deep swallow me up,
        or the pit close its mouth over me.

16 Answer me, O LORD, for your stead-
    fast love is good;
        according to your abundant mercy,
        turn to me.

17 Hide not your face from your ser-
    vant;
        for I am in distress; make haste to
        answer me.

18 Draw near to my soul, redeem me;
        ransom me because of my
        enemies!

19 You know my reproach,
        and my shame and my dishonor;
        my foes are all known to you.

20 Reproaches have broken my heart,
        so that I am in despair.
    I looked for pity, but there was none,
        and for comforters, but I found
        none.

21 They gave me poison for food,
        and for my thirst they gave me
        sour wine to drink.

22 Let their own table before them
    become a snare;
        and when they are at peace, let it
        become a trap.[2]

23 Let their eyes be darkened, so that
    they cannot see,
        and make their loins tremble con-
        tinually.

24 Pour out your indignation upon them,
        and let your burning anger over-
        take them.

25 May their camp be a desolation;
        let no one dwell in their tents.

26 For they persecute him whom you
    have struck down,
        and they recount the pain of those
        you have wounded.

27 Add to them punishment upon pun-
    ishment;
        may they have no acquittal from
        you.[3]

28 Let them be blotted out of the book
    of the living;
        let them not be enrolled among
        the righteous.

29 But I am afflicted and in pain;
        let your salvation, O God, set me on
        high!

30 I will praise the name of God with a
    song;
        I will magnify him with thanksgiv-
        ing.

31 This will please the LORD more than
    an ox
        or a bull with horns and hoofs.

32 When the humble see it they will be
    glad;
        you who seek God, let your hearts
        revive.

33 For the LORD hears the needy
        and does not despise his own
        people who are prisoners.

34 Let heaven and earth praise him,
        the seas and everything that
        moves in them.

35 For God will save Zion
        and build up the cities of Judah,

---

[1] Hebrew lacks *and humbled* [2] Hebrew; a slight revocalization yields (compare Septuagint, Syriac, Jerome) *a snare, and retribution and a trap* [3] Hebrew *may they not come into your righteousness*

and people shall dwell there and
    possess it;
36 the offspring of his servants shall
    inherit it,
    and those who love his name shall
    dwell in it.

O Lord, Do Not Delay

70 To the choirmaster. Of David, for the memorial offering.

1 Make haste, O God, to deliver me!
    O Lord, make haste to help me!
2 Let them be put to shame and confu-
    sion
    who seek my life!
    Let them be turned back and brought
    to dishonor
    who delight in my hurt!
3 Let them turn back because of their
    shame
    who say, "Aha, Aha!"

4 May all who seek you
    rejoice and be glad in you!
    May those who love your salvation
    say evermore, "God is great!"
5 But I am poor and needy;
    hasten to me, O God!
    You are my help and my deliverer;
    O Lord, do not delay!

Forsake Me Not When My Strength Is Spent

71 In you, O Lord, do I take refuge;
    let me never be put to shame!
2 In your righteousness deliver me and
    rescue me;
    incline your ear to me, and save
    me!
3 Be to me a rock of refuge,
    to which I may continually come;
    you have given the command to save
    me,
    for you are my rock and my fortress.

4 Rescue me, O my God, from the hand
    of the wicked,
    from the grasp of the unjust and
    cruel man.
5 For you, O Lord, are my hope,
    my trust, O Lord, from my youth.
6 Upon you I have leaned from before
    my birth;
    you are he who took me from my
    mother's womb.
    My praise is continually of you.

7 I have been as a portent to many,
    but you are my strong refuge.
8 My mouth is filled with your praise,
    and with your glory all the day.
9 Do not cast me off in the time of old
    age;
    forsake me not when my strength
    is spent.
10 For my enemies speak concerning
    me;
    those who watch for my life con-
    sult together
11 and say, "God has forsaken him;
    pursue and seize him,
    for there is none to deliver him."

12 O God, be not far from me;
    O my God, make haste to help me!
13 May my accusers be put to shame
    and consumed;
    with scorn and disgrace may they
    be covered
    who seek my hurt.
14 But I will hope continually
    and will praise you yet more and
    more.
15 My mouth will tell of your righteous
    acts,
    of your deeds of salvation all the
    day,
    for their number is past my knowl-
    edge.
16 With the mighty deeds of the Lord
    God I will come;
    I will remind them of your righ-
    teousness, yours alone.

17 O God, from my youth you have
    taught me,
    and I still proclaim your wondrous
    deeds.
18 So even to old age and gray hairs,
    O God, do not forsake me,
    until I proclaim your might to
    another generation,
    your power to all those to come.
19 Your righteousness, O God,
    reaches the high heavens.
    You who have done great things,
    O God, who is like you?
20 You who have made me see many
    troubles and calamities
    will revive me again;
    from the depths of the earth
    you will bring me up again.

21 You will increase my greatness
    and comfort me again.

22 I will also praise you with the harp
    for your faithfulness, O my God;
  I will sing praises to you with the lyre,
    O Holy One of Israel.
23 My lips will shout for joy,
    when I sing praises to you;
  my soul also, which you have
    redeemed.
24 And my tongue will talk of your
    righteous help all the day
    long,
  for they have been put to shame and
    disappointed
  who sought to do me hurt.

Give the King Your Justice

72 OF SOLOMON.
Give the king your justice,
    O God,
  and your righteousness to the
    royal son!
2 May he judge your people with righ-
    teousness,
  and your poor with justice!
3 Let the mountains bear prosperity
    for the people,
  and the hills, in righteousness!
4 May he defend the cause of the poor
    of the people,
  give deliverance to the children of
    the needy,
  and crush the oppressor!

Know How to Communicate

verses to read
Psalm 71

Are you where God wants you? If you aren't, then get out of there! But if you *are* where he wants you to be, then stop complaining about it! As you trust him and walk with him, you can be sure that you are where you are so that God can work out his purpose in you, and so that you can become the very image and likeness of his Son (see Rom. 8:29).

Unless you have moved yourself, by sinning, into a situation or condition that God wants you out of to protect your soul, you are where God wants you. You can be sure that things are as they should be at this very moment—even if the place where you are is surrounded by strife, disease, pain, or suffering. When you let your experiences make you bitter, resentful, or sad, you can be sure that you have turned against the very God who ordained your life and on whom you depended even before you were born (see Ps. 71:6).

The freedom of being a God Girl is in knowing that everything in your life has a divine purpose. It's in knowing that you are never where you are by accident. It's in finding hope and opportunity, instead of despair, in your trials. Hope is what will distinguish you from those who are lost. You should never give up and surrender to emotional anguish. You have nothing to fear and nothing to complain about when you are where God wants you to be. He is your rock and your fortress (see Ps. 71:3). You can depend on him.

So don't complain about your circumstances or try to get out of them by doing something sinful, and you'll soon find a ton of spiritual growth and hopefulness. Resist the temptation to complain to others about your sad state. Don't dwell on it or worry about it. That's sin, and it's not fit for a God Girl. Sin never produces a healthier or happier life. All true pleasure is in Christ. Sin only pulls you farther away from the giver of life and threatens your perseverance. But thanking God for never leaving you, and trusting that he's got everything worked out, will do more for your healthy state of mind and emotions than any complaint ever could.

5 May they fear you[1] while the sun
  endures,
    and as long as the moon, through-
    out all generations!
6 May he be like rain that falls on the
  mown grass,
    like showers that water the earth!
7 In his days may the righteous flourish,
    and peace abound, till the moon be
    no more!

8 May he have dominion from sea to
  sea,
    and from the River[2] to the ends of
    the earth!
9 May desert tribes bow down before
  him,
    and his enemies lick the dust!
10 May the kings of Tarshish and of the
   coastlands
  render him tribute;
  may the kings of Sheba and Seba
  bring gifts!
11 May all kings fall down before him,
    all nations serve him!

12 For he delivers the needy when he
   calls,
    the poor and him who has no
    helper.
13 He has pity on the weak and the
   needy,
    and saves the lives of the needy.
14 From oppression and violence he
   redeems their life,
    and precious is their blood in his
    sight.

15 Long may he live;
    may gold of Sheba be given to him!
  May prayer be made for him continually,
    and blessings invoked for him all
    the day!
16 May there be abundance of grain in
   the land;
    on the tops of the mountains may
    it wave;
  may its fruit be like Lebanon;
  and may people blossom in the cities
  like the grass of the field!
17 May his name endure forever,
    his fame continue as long as the
    sun!
  May people be blessed in him,
    all nations call him blessed!

18 Blessed be the LORD, the God of
   Israel,
    who alone does wondrous things.
19 Blessed be his glorious name forever;
    may the whole earth be filled with
    his glory!
    Amen and Amen!

20 The prayers of David, the son of
   Jesse, are ended.

Ask Yourself . . .

ABOUT PROTECTION

In the Psalms God is often called
a refuge. What does that mean to
you today? Ask yourself about the
things that protect you:

- Where do I look for protection
  in this life?

- Do I have a refuge, a safe place
  I can go?

- What is good about refuge?

- How can I find the refuge of
  God in my life?

- Are there other people I
  know who have that kind of
  relationship with God? And if
  so, could I ask them to teach
  me what it means?

BOOK THREE

God Is My Strength and Portion Forever

73 A PSALM OF ASAPH.
    Truly God is good to Israel,
    to those who are pure in heart.
2 But as for me, my feet had almost
  stumbled,
    my steps had nearly slipped.
3 For I was envious of the arrogant
    when I saw the prosperity of the
    wicked.

4 For they have no pangs until death;
    their bodies are fat and sleek.

[1] Septuagint *He shall endure* [2] That is, the Euphrates

5 They are not in trouble as others are;
   they are not stricken like the rest
      of mankind.
6 Therefore pride is their necklace;
   violence covers them as a gar-
      ment.
7 Their eyes swell out through fatness;
   their hearts overflow with follies.
8 They scoff and speak with malice;
   loftily they threaten oppression.
9 They set their mouths against the
      heavens,
   and their tongue struts through
      the earth.
10 Therefore his people turn back to
      them,
   and find no fault in them.[1]
11 And they say, "How can God know?
   Is there knowledge in the Most
      High?"
12 Behold, these are the wicked;
   always at ease, they increase in
      riches.
13 All in vain have I kept my heart clean
   and washed my hands in inno-
      cence.
14 For all the day long I have been
      stricken
   and rebuked every morning.
15 If I had said, "I will speak thus,"
   I would have betrayed the genera-
      tion of your children.

16 But when I thought how to under-
      stand this,
   it seemed to me a wearisome task,
17 until I went into the sanctuary of
      God;
   then I discerned their end.

18 Truly you set them in slippery places;
   you make them fall to ruin.
19 How they are destroyed in a moment,
   swept away utterly by terrors!
20 Like a dream when one awakes,
   O Lord, when you rouse yourself,
      you despise them as phantoms.
21 When my soul was embittered,
   when I was pricked in heart,
22 I was brutish and ignorant;
   I was like a beast toward you.
23 Nevertheless, I am continually with
      you;
   you hold my right hand.

24 You guide me with your counsel,
   and afterward you will receive me
      to glory.
25 Whom have I in heaven but you?
   And there is nothing on earth that
      I desire besides you.
26 My flesh and my heart may fail,
   but God is the strength[2] of my
      heart and my portion forever.

27 For behold, those who are far from
      you shall perish;
   you put an end to everyone who is
      unfaithful to you.
28 But for me it is good to be near God;
   I have made the Lord GOD my
      refuge,
   that I may tell of all your works.

Arise, O God, Defend Your Cause

74 A MASKIL[3] OF ASAPH.
   O God, why do you cast us off
      forever?
   Why does your anger smoke
      against the sheep of your
      pasture?
2 Remember your congregation, which
      you have purchased of old,
   which you have redeemed to be
      the tribe of your heritage!
   Remember Mount Zion, where you
      have dwelt.
3 Direct your steps to the perpetual
      ruins;
   the enemy has destroyed every-
      thing in the sanctuary!

4 Your foes have roared in the midst of
      your meeting place;
   they set up their own signs for
      signs.
5 They were like those who swing axes
   in a forest of trees.[4]
6 And all its carved wood
   they broke down with hatchets
      and hammers.
7 They set your sanctuary on fire;
   they profaned the dwelling place
      of your name,
   bringing it down to the ground.
8 They said to themselves, "We will
      utterly subdue them";
   they burned all the meeting places
      of God in the land.

[1] Probable reading; Hebrew *the waters of a full cup are drained by them* [2] Hebrew *rock* [3] Probably a musical or liturgical term
[4] The meaning of the Hebrew is uncertain

9   We do not see our signs;
    there is no longer any prophet,
    and there is none among us who
    knows how long.

10 How long, O God, is the foe to scoff?
    Is the enemy to revile your name
    forever?

11 Why do you hold back your hand,
    your right hand?
    Take it from the fold of your gar-
    ment[1] and destroy them!

12 Yet God my King is from of old,
    working salvation in the midst of
    the earth.

13 You divided the sea by your might;
    you broke the heads of the sea
    monsters[2] on the waters.

14 You crushed the heads of Leviathan;
    you gave him as food for the crea-
    tures of the wilderness.

15 You split open springs and brooks;
    you dried up ever-flowing streams.

16 Yours is the day, yours also the night;
    you have established the heavenly
    lights and the sun.

17 You have fixed all the boundaries of
    the earth;
    you have made summer and winter.

18 Remember this, O Lord, how the
    enemy scoffs,
    and a foolish people reviles your
    name.

19 Do not deliver the soul of your dove
    to the wild beasts;
    do not forget the life of your poor
    forever.

20 Have regard for the covenant,
    for the dark places of the land
    are full of the habitations of
    violence.

21 Let not the downtrodden turn back
    in shame;
    let the poor and needy praise your
    name.

22 Arise, O God, defend your cause;
    remember how the foolish scoff at
    you all the day!

23 Do not forget the clamor of your foes,
    the uproar of those who rise
    against you, which goes up
    continually!

God Will Judge with Equity

75 To the choirmaster: according to Do Not Destroy. A Psalm of Asaph. A Song.

1 We give thanks to you, O God;
    we give thanks, for your name is
    near.
    We[3] recount your wondrous deeds.

2 "At the set time that I appoint
    I will judge with equity.

3 When the earth totters, and all its
    inhabitants,
    it is I who keep steady its pillars.
              Selah

4 I say to the boastful, 'Do not boast,'
    and to the wicked, 'Do not lift up
    your horn;

5 do not lift up your horn on high,
    or speak with haughty neck.'"

6 For not from the east or from the west
    and not from the wilderness
    comes lifting up,

7 but it is God who executes judgment,
    putting down one and lifting up
    another.

8 For in the hand of the Lord there is a
    cup
    with foaming wine, well mixed,
    and he pours out from it,
    and all the wicked of the earth
    shall drain it down to the dregs.

9 But I will declare it forever;
    I will sing praises to the God of
    Jacob.

10 All the horns of the wicked I will cut
    off,
    but the horns of the righteous shall
    be lifted up.

Who Can Stand Before You?

76 To the choirmaster: with stringed instruments. A Psalm of Asaph. A Song.

1 In Judah God is known;
    his name is great in Israel.

2 His abode has been established in
    Salem,
    his dwelling place in Zion.

3 There he broke the flashing arrows,
    the shield, the sword, and the
    weapons of war.   *Selah*

[1] Hebrew *from your bosom* [2] Or *the great sea creatures* [3] Hebrew *They*

⁴ Glorious are you, more majestic
   than the mountains full of prey.
⁵ The stouthearted were stripped of
      their spoil;
   they sank into sleep;
all the men of war
   were unable to use their hands.
⁶ At your rebuke, O God of Jacob,
   both rider and horse lay stunned.

⁷ But you, you are to be feared!
   Who can stand before you
   when once your anger is roused?
⁸ From the heavens you uttered judg-
      ment;
   the earth feared and was still,
⁹ when God arose to establish judgment,
   to save all the humble of the earth.
                                   Selah

¹⁰ Surely the wrath of man shall praise
      you;
   the remnant¹ of wrath you will put
      on like a belt.
¹¹ Make your vows to the LORD your
      God and perform them;
   let all around him bring gifts
   to him who is to be feared,
¹² who cuts off the spirit of princes,
   who is to be feared by the kings of
      the earth.

In the Day of Trouble I Seek the Lord

77 TO THE CHOIRMASTER: ACCORDING TO
     JEDUTHUN. A PSALM OF ASAPH.

¹ I cry aloud to God,
   aloud to God, and he will hear me.
² In the day of my trouble I seek the
      Lord;
   in the night my hand is stretched
      out without wearying;
   my soul refuses to be comforted.
³ When I remember God, I moan;
   when I meditate, my spirit faints.
                                   Selah

⁴ You hold my eyelids open;
   I am so troubled that I cannot
      speak.
⁵ I consider the days of old,
   the years long ago.
⁶ I said,² "Let me remember my song in
      the night;
   let me meditate in my heart."

Then my spirit made a diligent
   search:
⁷ "Will the Lord spurn forever,
   and never again be favorable?
⁸ Has his steadfast love forever ceased?
   Are his promises at an end for all
      time?
⁹ Has God forgotten to be gracious?
   Has he in anger shut up his com-
      passion?"   *Selah*

¹⁰ Then I said, "I will appeal to this,
   to the years of the right hand of
      the Most High."³
¹¹ I will remember the deeds of the LORD;
   yes, I will remember your wonders
      of old.
¹² I will ponder all your work,
   and meditate on your mighty
      deeds.
¹³ Your way, O God, is holy.
   What god is great like our God?
¹⁴ You are the God who works wonders;
   you have made known your might
      among the peoples.
¹⁵ You with your arm redeemed your
      people,
   the children of Jacob and Joseph.
                                   Selah

¹⁶ When the waters saw you, O God,
   when the waters saw you, they
      were afraid;
   indeed, the deep trembled.
¹⁷ The clouds poured out water;
   the skies gave forth thunder;
   your arrows flashed on every side.
¹⁸ The crash of your thunder was in the
      whirlwind;
   your lightnings lighted up the
      world;
   the earth trembled and shook.
¹⁹ Your way was through the sea,
   your path through the great waters;
   yet your footprints were unseen.⁴
²⁰ You led your people like a flock
   by the hand of Moses and Aaron.

Tell the Coming Generation

78 A MASKIL⁵ OF ASAPH.
     Give ear, O my people, to my
        teaching;
     incline your ears to the words of
        my mouth!

---

¹Or *extremity* ²Hebrew lacks *I said* ³Or *This is my grief: that the right hand of the Most High has changed* ⁴Hebrew *unknown* ⁵Probably a musical or liturgical term

2 I will open my mouth in a parable;
    I will utter dark sayings from of old,
3 things that we have heard and known,
    that our fathers have told us.
4 We will not hide them from their
        children,
    but tell to the coming generation
the glorious deeds of the Lord, and
        his might,
    and the wonders that he has done.

5 He established a testimony in Jacob
    and appointed a law in Israel,
which he commanded our fathers
    to teach to their children,
6 that the next generation might know
        them,
    the children yet unborn,
and arise and tell them to their chil-
        dren,
7   so that they should set their hope
        in God
and not forget the works of God,
    but keep his commandments;
8 and that they should not be like their
        fathers,
    a stubborn and rebellious genera-
        tion,
a generation whose heart was not
        steadfast,
    whose spirit was not faithful to God.

9 The Ephraimites, armed with[1] the
        bow,
    turned back on the day of battle.
10 They did not keep God's covenant,
    but refused to walk according to
        his law.
11 They forgot his works
    and the wonders that he had
        shown them.
12 In the sight of their fathers he per-
        formed wonders
    in the land of Egypt, in the fields of
        Zoan.
13 He divided the sea and let them pass
        through it,
    and made the waters stand like a
        heap.
14 In the daytime he led them with a
        cloud,
    and all the night with a fiery light.
15 He split rocks in the wilderness
    and gave them drink abundantly
        as from the deep.

16 He made streams come out of the rock
    and caused waters to flow down
        like rivers.
17 Yet they sinned still more against him,
    rebelling against the Most High in
        the desert.
18 They tested God in their heart
    by demanding the food they craved.
19 They spoke against God, saying,
    "Can God spread a table in the
        wilderness?
20 He struck the rock so that water
        gushed out
    and streams overflowed.
Can he also give bread
    or provide meat for his people?"

21 Therefore, when the Lord heard, he
        was full of wrath;
    a fire was kindled against Jacob;
    his anger rose against Israel,
22 because they did not believe in God
    and did not trust his saving power.
23 Yet he commanded the skies above
    and opened the doors of heaven,
24 and he rained down on them manna
        to eat
    and gave them the grain of heaven.
25 Man ate of the bread of the angels;
    he sent them food in abundance.
26 He caused the east wind to blow in
        the heavens,
    and by his power he led out the
        south wind;
27 he rained meat on them like dust,
    winged birds like the sand of the
        seas;
28 he let them fall in the midst of their
        camp,
    all around their dwellings.
29 And they ate and were well filled,
    for he gave them what they craved.
30 But before they had satisfied their
        craving,
    while the food was still in their
        mouths,
31 the anger of God rose against them,
    and he killed the strongest of them
    and laid low the young men of
        Israel.

32 In spite of all this, they still sinned;
    despite his wonders, they did not
        believe.

[1] Hebrew *armed and shooting*

33 So he made their days vanish like[1] a
   breath,[2]
     and their years in terror.
34 When he killed them, they sought
   him;
     they repented and sought God
     earnestly.
35 They remembered that God was
   their rock,
     the Most High God their redeemer.
36 But they flattered him with their
   mouths;
     they lied to him with their tongues.
37 Their heart was not steadfast toward
   him;
     they were not faithful to his cov-
     enant.
38 Yet he, being compassionate,
     atoned for their iniquity
     and did not destroy them;
   he restrained his anger often
     and did not stir up all his wrath.

39 He remembered that they were but
   flesh,
     a wind that passes and comes not
     again.
40 How often they rebelled against him
   in the wilderness
     and grieved him in the desert!
41 They tested God again and again
     and provoked the Holy One of
     Israel.
42 They did not remember his power[3]
     or the day when he redeemed
     them from the foe,
43 when he performed his signs in Egypt
     and his marvels in the fields of
     Zoan.
44 He turned their rivers to blood,
     so that they could not drink of
     their streams.
45 He sent among them swarms of flies,
     which devoured them,
     and frogs, which destroyed them.

[1] Hebrew *in* [2] Or *vapor* [3] Hebrew *hand*

Know True Happiness

verses to read
Psalm 78:29–31

Are you ever satisfied? Do you ever have enough? Or is there always something more you want or think you need? It's easy to see all that the world has to offer and to have a continual wish list. "I want this, and this, and that . . ." and the list goes on and on. But what does all this wanting say about you? And what does it sound like to the ears of God?

In the desert, the Israelites complained because they were tired of just eating manna all day every day, so God dropped all kinds of birds out of heaven for them to eat. But then they were bored with just birds and bread and wanted something different, and God got mad. Discontentment is disgusting. How awful it must feel to give and give and continually hear, "That's just not enough." Seems like if that happened to you, eventually you'd just want to give up trying—after all, the person is never going to be satisfied.

But when you love God and you know the lengths he went to in Christ to save you, you start to realize that, even though you really don't deserve anything, he has given you everything. Discontentment becomes a problem only when you get your head stuck in the world and lose your focus because you see pretty things and you want them. But when you can get your focus back on the big picture and the things that really matter, all that fades away into the background.

If you want to be free of the wanting and not getting, quit looking in front of you and start looking up. Forget what your eyes, ears, and mouth want and go after what your soul needs. When you do, God will be right there ready to give it to you.

6 He gave their crops to the destroying
locust
and the fruit of their labor to the
locust.
7 He destroyed their vines with hail
and their sycamores with frost.
8 He gave over their cattle to the hail
and their flocks to thunderbolts.
9 He let loose on them his burning
anger,
wrath, indignation, and distress,
a company of destroying angels.
0 He made a path for his anger;
he did not spare them from death,
but gave their lives over to the
plague.
1 He struck down every firstborn in
Egypt,
the firstfruits of their strength in
the tents of Ham.
2 Then he led out his people like sheep
and guided them in the wilderness
like a flock.
3 He led them in safety, so that they
were not afraid,
but the sea overwhelmed their
enemies.
4 And he brought them to his holy land,
to the mountain which his right
hand had won.
5 He drove out nations before them;
he apportioned them for a possession
and settled the tribes of Israel in
their tents.

6 Yet they tested and rebelled against
the Most High God
and did not keep his testimonies,
7 but turned away and acted treacherously like their fathers;
they twisted like a deceitful bow.
8 For they provoked him to anger with
their high places;
they moved him to jealousy with
their idols.
9 When God heard, he was full of wrath,
and he utterly rejected Israel.
0 He forsook his dwelling at Shiloh,
the tent where he dwelt among
mankind,
1 and delivered his power to captivity,
his glory to the hand of the foe.
2 He gave his people over to the sword
and vented his wrath on his heritage.

63 Fire devoured their young men,
and their young women had no
marriage song.
64 Their priests fell by the sword,
and their widows made no lamentation.
65 Then the Lord awoke as from sleep,
like a strong man shouting
because of wine.
66 And he put his adversaries to rout;
he put them to everlasting shame.

67 He rejected the tent of Joseph;
he did not choose the tribe of
Ephraim,
68 but he chose the tribe of Judah,
Mount Zion, which he loves.
69 He built his sanctuary like the high
heavens,
like the earth, which he has
founded forever.
70 He chose David his servant
and took him from the sheepfolds;
71 from following the nursing ewes he
brought him
to shepherd Jacob his people,
Israel his inheritance.
72 With upright heart he shepherded
them
and guided them with his skillful
hand.

How Long, O Lord?

79 A Psalm of Asaph.
O God, the nations have come
into your inheritance;
they have defiled your holy temple;
they have laid Jerusalem in ruins.
2 They have given the bodies of your
servants
to the birds of the heavens for food,
the flesh of your faithful to the
beasts of the earth.
3 They have poured out their blood
like water
all around Jerusalem,
and there was no one to bury them.
4 We have become a taunt to our
neighbors,
mocked and derided by those
around us.

5 How long, O Lord? Will you be angry
forever?
Will your jealousy burn like fire?
6 Pour out your anger on the nations
that do not know you,

and on the kingdoms
that do not call upon your name!

7 For they have devoured Jacob
and laid waste his habitation.

8 Do not remember against us our
former iniquities;[1]
let your compassion come speedily
to meet us,
for we are brought very low.

9 Help us, O God of our salvation,
for the glory of your name;
deliver us, and atone for our sins,
for your name's sake!

10 Why should the nations say,
"Where is their God?"
Let the avenging of the outpoured
blood of your servants
be known among the nations
before our eyes!

11 Let the groans of the prisoners come
before you;
according to your great power,
preserve those doomed to die!

12 Return sevenfold into the lap of our
neighbors
the taunts with which they have
taunted you, O Lord!

13 But we your people, the sheep of
your pasture,
will give thanks to you forever;
from generation to generation we
will recount your praise.

Restore Us, O God

80 To the choirmaster: according
to Lilies. A Testimony. Of Asaph,
a Psalm.

1 Give ear, O Shepherd of Israel,
you who lead Joseph like a flock.
You who are enthroned upon the
cherubim, shine forth.

2 Before Ephraim and Benjamin and
Manasseh,
stir up your might
and come to save us!

3 Restore us,[2] O God;
let your face shine, that we may be
saved!

4 O Lord God of hosts,
how long will you be angry with
your people's prayers?

5 You have fed them with the bread of
tears
and given them tears to drink in
full measure.

6 You make us an object of contention
for our neighbors,
and our enemies laugh among
themselves.

7 Restore us, O God of hosts;
let your face shine, that we may be
saved!

8 You brought a vine out of Egypt;
you drove out the nations and
planted it.

9 You cleared the ground for it;
it took deep root and filled the
land.

10 The mountains were covered with its
shade,
the mighty cedars with its
branches.

11 It sent out its branches to the sea
and its shoots to the River.[3]

12 Why then have you broken down its
walls,
so that all who pass along the way
pluck its fruit?

13 The boar from the forest ravages it,
and all that move in the field feed
on it.

14 Turn again, O God of hosts!
Look down from heaven, and see;
have regard for this vine,

15 the stock that your right hand
planted,
and for the son whom you made
strong for yourself.

16 They have burned it with fire; they
have cut it down;
may they perish at the rebuke of
your face!

17 But let your hand be on the man of
your right hand,
the son of man whom you have
made strong for yourself!

18 Then we shall not turn back from you;
give us life, and we will call upon
your name!

19 Restore us, O Lord God of hosts!
Let your face shine, that we may
be saved!

[1] Or the iniquities of former generations [2] Or Turn us again; also verses 7, 19 [3] That is, the Euphrates

Oh, That My People Would Listen to Me

81

TO THE CHOIRMASTER: ACCORDING TO THE GITTITH.[1] OF ASAPH.

1 Sing aloud to God our strength;
    shout for joy to the God of Jacob!
2 Raise a song; sound the tambourine,
    the sweet lyre with the harp.
3 Blow the trumpet at the new moon,
    at the full moon, on our feast day.
4 For it is a statute for Israel,
    a rule[2] of the God of Jacob.
5 He made it a decree in Joseph
    when he went out over[3] the land of
      Egypt.
    I hear a language I had not known:
6 "I relieved your[4] shoulder of the bur-
      den;
    your hands were freed from the
      basket.
7 In distress you called, and I delivered
      you;
    I answered you in the secret place
      of thunder;
    I tested you at the waters of
      Meribah.   *Selah*
8 Hear, O my people, while I admonish
      you!
    O Israel, if you would but listen to
      me!
9 There shall be no strange god among
      you;
    you shall not bow down to a for-
      eign god.
10 I am the LORD your God,
    who brought you up out of the
      land of Egypt.
    Open your mouth wide, and I will
      fill it.
11 "But my people did not listen to my
      voice;
    Israel would not submit to me.
12 So I gave them over to their stubborn
      hearts,
    to follow their own counsels.
13 Oh, that my people would listen to
      me,
    that Israel would walk in my ways!
14 I would soon subdue their enemies
    and turn my hand against their foes.
15 Those who hate the LORD would
      cringe toward him,
    and their fate would last forever.

16 But he would feed you[5] with the fin-
      est of the wheat,
    and with honey from the rock
      I would satisfy you."

Rescue the Weak and Needy

82

A PSALM OF ASAPH.

God has taken his place in the
    divine council;
    in the midst of the gods he holds
      judgment:
2 "How long will you judge unjustly
    and show partiality to the wicked?
                Selah
3 Give justice to the weak and the
      fatherless;
    maintain the right of the afflicted
      and the destitute.
4 Rescue the weak and the needy;
    deliver them from the hand of the
      wicked."

5 They have neither knowledge nor
      understanding,
    they walk about in darkness;
    all the foundations of the earth are
      shaken.

6 I said, "You are gods,
    sons of the Most High, all of you;
7 nevertheless, like men you shall die,
    and fall like any prince."[6]

8 Arise, O God, judge the earth;
    for you shall inherit all the nations!

O God, Do Not Keep Silence

83

A SONG. A PSALM OF ASAPH.

O God, do not keep silence;
    do not hold your peace or be still,
      O God!
2 For behold, your enemies make an
      uproar;
    those who hate you have raised
      their heads.
3 They lay crafty plans against your
      people;
    they consult together against your
      treasured ones.
4 They say, "Come, let us wipe them
      out as a nation;
    let the name of Israel be remem-
      bered no more!"
5 For they conspire with one accord;
    against you they make a covenant—

---

[1] Probably a musical or liturgical term [2] Or *just decree* [3] Or *against* [4] Hebrew *his*; also next line [5] That is, Israel; Hebrew *him* [6] Or *fall as one man, O princes*

6 the tents of Edom and the Ishmaelites,
      Moab and the Hagrites,
7 Gebal and Ammon and Amalek,
      Philistia with the inhabitants of
         Tyre;
8 Asshur also has joined them;
      they are the strong arm of the
         children of Lot.   *Selah*

9 Do to them as you did to Midian,
      as to Sisera and Jabin at the river
         Kishon,
10 who were destroyed at En-dor,
      who became dung for the ground.
11 Make their nobles like Oreb and Zeeb,
      all their princes like Zebah and
         Zalmunna,
12 who said, "Let us take possession for
         ourselves
      of the pastures of God."

13 O my God, make them like whirling
         dust,[1]
      like chaff before the wind.
14 As fire consumes the forest,
      as the flame sets the mountains
         ablaze,
15 so may you pursue them with your
         tempest
      and terrify them with your hur-
         ricane!
16 Fill their faces with shame,
      that they may seek your name,
         O Lord.
17 Let them be put to shame and dis-
         mayed forever;
      let them perish in disgrace,
18 that they may know that you alone,
      whose name is the Lord,
      are the Most High over all the earth.

My Soul Longs for the Courts of the Lord

84 To the choirmaster: according to
The Gittith.[2] A Psalm of the Sons
of Korah.

1 How lovely is your dwelling place,
      O Lord of hosts!
2 My soul longs, yes, faints
      for the courts of the Lord;
   my heart and flesh sing for joy
      to the living God.

3 Even the sparrow finds a home,
      and the swallow a nest for herself,
      where she may lay her young,

at your altars, O Lord of hosts,
      my King and my God.
4 Blessed are those who dwell in your
         house,
      ever singing your praise!   *Selah*

5 Blessed are those whose strength is
         in you,
      in whose heart are the highways to
         Zion.[3]
6 As they go through the Valley of Baca
      they make it a place of springs;
      the early rain also covers it with
         pools.
7 They go from strength to strength;
      each one appears before God in
         Zion.

8 O Lord God of hosts, hear my prayer;
      give ear, O God of Jacob!   *Selah*
9 Behold our shield, O God;
      look on the face of your anointed!

10 For a day in your courts is better
      than a thousand elsewhere.
   I would rather be a doorkeeper in
         the house of my God
      than dwell in the tents of wicked-
         ness.
11 For the Lord God is a sun and shield;
      the Lord bestows favor and honor.
   No good thing does he withhold
      from those who walk uprightly.
12 O Lord of hosts,
      blessed is the one who trusts in
         you!

Revive Us Again

85 To the choirmaster. A Psalm of
the Sons of Korah.

1 Lord, you were favorable to your
         land;
      you restored the fortunes of Jacob.
2 You forgave the iniquity of your
         people;
      you covered all their sin.   *Selah*
3 You withdrew all your wrath;
      you turned from your hot anger.

4 Restore us again, O God of our salva-
         tion,
      and put away your indignation
         toward us!
5 Will you be angry with us forever?
      Will you prolong your anger to all
         generations?

---

[1] Or *like a tumbleweed* [2] Probably a musical or liturgical term [3] Hebrew lacks *to Zion*

6 Will you not revive us again,
that your people may rejoice in
you?
7 Show us your steadfast love, O LORD,
and grant us your salvation.

A Prayer for...
OBEDIENCE

Dear God, Father of all, kindly give me the joy that comes from perfect agreement with your will. Help me bring every ungodly power in my soul into willing obedience. Give me the music of harmonious fellowship with you, so that all my powers can be like a united orchestra to praise and bless your holy name. And mercifully give me the joy of spiritual freedom.

Let the gospel become my song. Take the reluctance out of my obedience. Don't let me be in your house in the spirit of a bond-slave but in the spirit of a daughter, finding springs of comfort in your presence and considering your desire to be my delight.

Dear God, give me the holy joy of human sympathy. Recreate the part of my heart that has become insensitive to my sisters' successes and failures. If it is broken, graciously restore it out of the fullness of your love. Teach me to love no matter how I am loved back. And give me the desire to share your love with everyone, no matter how much they deserve it or do not.

Amen.

8 Let me hear what God the LORD will
speak,
for he will speak peace to his
people, to his saints;
but let them not turn back to folly.
9 Surely his salvation is near to those
who fear him,
that glory may dwell in our land.

10 Steadfast love and faithfulness meet;
righteousness and peace kiss each
other.

11 Faithfulness springs up from the
ground,
and righteousness looks down
from the sky.
12 Yes, the LORD will give what is good,
and our land will yield its increase.
13 Righteousness will go before him
and make his footsteps a way.

Great Is Your Steadfast Love

86 A PRAYER OF DAVID.
Incline your ear, O LORD, and
answer me,
for I am poor and needy.
2 Preserve my life, for I am godly;
save your servant, who trusts in
you—you are my God.
3 Be gracious to me, O Lord,
for to you do I cry all the day.
4 Gladden the soul of your servant,
for to you, O Lord, do I lift up my
soul.
5 For you, O Lord, are good and forgiving,
abounding in steadfast love to all
who call upon you.
6 Give ear, O LORD, to my prayer;
listen to my plea for grace.
7 In the day of my trouble I call upon
you,
for you answer me.

8 There is none like you among the
gods, O Lord,
nor are there any works like yours.
9 All the nations you have made shall
come
and worship before you, O Lord,
and shall glorify your name.
10 For you are great and do wondrous
things;
you alone are God.
11 Teach me your way, O LORD,
that I may walk in your truth;
unite my heart to fear your name.
12 I give thanks to you, O Lord my God,
with my whole heart,
and I will glorify your name forever.
13 For great is your steadfast love
toward me;
you have delivered my soul from
the depths of Sheol.

14 O God, insolent men have risen up
against me;
a band of ruthless men seeks my life,
and they do not set you before them.

15 But you, O Lord, are a God merciful
      and gracious,
   slow to anger and abounding in
      steadfast love and faithfulness.
16 Turn to me and be gracious to me;
   give your strength to your servant,
   and save the son of your maidser-
      vant.
17 Show me a sign of your favor,
   that those who hate me may see
      and be put to shame
   because you, LORD, have helped
      me and comforted me.

Glorious Things of You Are Spoken

87
A PSALM OF THE SONS OF KORAH.
A SONG.

1 On the holy mount stands the city he
      founded;
2   the LORD loves the gates of Zion
      more than all the dwelling places
      of Jacob.
3 Glorious things of you are spoken,
      O city of God.   *Selah*

4 Among those who know me I men-
      tion Rahab and Babylon;
   behold, Philistia and Tyre, with
      Cush[1]—
   "This one was born there," they say.
5 And of Zion it shall be said,
   "This one and that one were born in
      her";
   for the Most High himself will
      establish her.
6 The LORD records as he registers the
      peoples,
   "This one was born there."   *Selah*

7 Singers and dancers alike say,
   "All my springs are in you."

I Cry Out Day and Night Before You

88
A SONG. A PSALM OF THE SONS OF
KORAH. TO THE CHOIRMASTER:
ACCORDING TO MAHALATH LEANNOTH.
A MASKIL[2] OF HEMAN THE EZRAHITE.

1 O LORD, God of my salvation;
   I cry out day and night before you.
2 Let my prayer come before you;
   incline your ear to my cry!

3 For my soul is full of troubles,
   and my life draws near to Sheol.

4 I am counted among those who go
      down to the pit;
   I am a man who has no strength,
5 like one set loose among the dead,
   like the slain that lie in the grave,
   like those whom you remember no
      more,
   for they are cut off from your hand
6 You have put me in the depths of the
      pit,
   in the regions dark and deep.
7 Your wrath lies heavy upon me,
   and you overwhelm me with all
      your waves.   *Selah*

8 You have caused my companions to
      shun me;
   you have made me a horror[3] to
      them.
   I am shut in so that I cannot escape;
9   my eye grows dim through sorrow.
   Every day I call upon you, O LORD;
   I spread out my hands to you.
10 Do you work wonders for the dead?
   Do the departed rise up to praise
      you?   *Selah*
11 Is your steadfast love declared in the
      grave,
   or your faithfulness in Abaddon?
12 Are your wonders known in the
      darkness,
   or your righteousness in the land
      of forgetfulness?

13 But I, O LORD, cry to you;
   in the morning my prayer comes
      before you.
14 O LORD, why do you cast my soul
      away?
   Why do you hide your face from
      me?
15 Afflicted and close to death from my
      youth up,
   I suffer your terrors; I am help-
      less.[4]
16 Your wrath has swept over me;
   your dreadful assaults destroy me.
17 They surround me like a flood all day
      long;
   they close in on me together.
18 You have caused my beloved and my
      friend to shun me;
   my companions have become
      darkness.[5]

---

[1] Probably *Nubia* [2] Probably musical or liturgical terms [3] Or *an abomination* [4] The meaning of the Hebrew word is uncertain
[5] Or *darkness has become my only companion*

Will Sing of the Steadfast Love of the LORD

89 A MASKIL[1] OF ETHAN THE EZRAHITE.
I will sing of the steadfast love of
the LORD, forever;
  with my mouth I will make known
    your faithfulness to all genera-
    tions.
2 For I said, "Steadfast love will be
    built up forever;
  in the heavens you will establish
    your faithfulness."
3 You have said, "I have made a cov-
    enant with my chosen one;
  I have sworn to David my servant:
4 'I will establish your offspring forever,
    and build your throne for all gen-
    erations.'"   *Selah*

5 Let the heavens praise your won-
    ders, O LORD,
  your faithfulness in the assembly
    of the holy ones!

6 For who in the skies can be com-
    pared to the LORD?
  Who among the heavenly beings[2]
    is like the LORD,
7 a God greatly to be feared in the
    council of the holy ones,
  and awesome above all who are
    around him?
8 O LORD God of hosts,
  who is mighty as you are, O LORD,
    with your faithfulness all around
    you?
9 You rule the raging of the sea;
  when its waves rise, you still
    them.
10 You crushed Rahab like a carcass;
  you scattered your enemies with
    your mighty arm.
11 The heavens are yours; the earth also
    is yours;
  the world and all that is in it, you
    have founded them.

Probably a musical or liturgical term [2]Hebrew *the sons of God*, or *the sons of might*

Know Yourself

verses to read
Psalm 89:8–13

Are you suffering from a big strain on your life? Have you lost your sense of peace? Do you feel like your life is blown and tossed about by the wind and God has let go and left you adrift? Then take your eyes off the waves and look at his face. Every sailor knows that when a boat rises and falls on the ocean's waves, you can steady your stomach by looking at the steady horizon, not the side of the boat. When you look at something that is immovable, your stomach gets some peace. In the storms of life, your horizon is the face of God. He's the only one who can quiet the crashing waves. And if you keep your eyes on him, you won't get sick. If you look to his Word and don't stare at the rough waters, you can find peace.

If you aren't right with God, you can never get your mind off of yourself, and looking at yourself gets in the way of seeing his face. Are you looking to the horizon, to Jesus, right now in the problems in your life, or are you looking at the rough waters of life? If you look up to him, you can be sure you will find peace. The peace that only he can give is dependent not on circumstances or other people but only on what he himself has done to restore you to the Father. When you take your eyes off Jesus and worry, you get freaked out and depressed because you're thinking only about yourself. When you take time to talk things over with the Lord, to know him, and to worship him, your worries dry up and your only thought is how to stay near to him. Jesus is never stressed or freaked. So get close to him in your difficulties and let him say, "my peace I give to you" (John 14:27).

12 The north and the south, you have
      created them;
    Tabor and Hermon joyously praise
      your name.

13 You have a mighty arm;
    strong is your hand, high your
      right hand.

14 Righteousness and justice are the
      foundation of your throne;
    steadfast love and faithfulness go
      before you.

15 Blessed are the people who know
      the festal shout,
    who walk, O Lord, in the light of
      your face,

16 who exult in your name all the day
    and in your righteousness are
      exalted.

17 For you are the glory of their
      strength;
    by your favor our horn is exalted.

18 For our shield belongs to the Lord,
    our king to the Holy One of Israel.

19 Of old you spoke in a vision to your
      godly one,[1] and said:
    "I have granted help to one who is
      mighty;
    I have exalted one chosen from the
      people.

20 I have found David, my servant;
    with my holy oil I have anointed
      him,

21 so that my hand shall be established
      with him;
    my arm also shall strengthen him.

22 The enemy shall not outwit him;
    the wicked shall not humble him.

23 I will crush his foes before him
    and strike down those who hate
      him.

24 My faithfulness and my steadfast
      love shall be with him,
    and in my name shall his horn be
      exalted.

25 I will set his hand on the sea
    and his right hand on the rivers.

26 He shall cry to me, 'You are my
      Father,
    my God, and the Rock of my salva-
      tion.'

27 And I will make him the firstborn,
    the highest of the kings of the
      earth.

28 My steadfast love I will keep for him
      forever,
    and my covenant will stand firm[2]
      for him.

29 I will establish his offspring forever
    and his throne as the days of the
      heavens.

30 If his children forsake my law
    and do not walk according to my
      rules,[3]

31 if they violate my statutes
    and do not keep my command-
      ments,

32 then I will punish their transgression
      with the rod
    and their iniquity with stripes,

33 but I will not remove from him my
      steadfast love
    or be false to my faithfulness.

34 I will not violate my covenant
    or alter the word that went forth
      from my lips.

35 Once for all I have sworn by my holi-
      ness;
    I will not lie to David.

36 His offspring shall endure forever,
    his throne as long as the sun
      before me.

37 Like the moon it shall be established
      forever,
    a faithful witness in the skies."
                            Selah

38 But now you have cast off and
      rejected;
    you are full of wrath against your
      anointed.

39 You have renounced the covenant
      with your servant;
    you have defiled his crown in the
      dust.

40 You have breached all his walls;
    you have laid his strongholds in
      ruins.

41 All who pass by plunder him;
    he has become the scorn of his
      neighbors.

42 You have exalted the right hand of
      his foes;
    you have made all his enemies
      rejoice.

43 You have also turned back the edge
      of his sword,
    and you have not made him stand
      in battle.

[1] Some Hebrew manuscripts *godly ones* [2] Or *will remain faithful* [3] Or *my just decrees*

⁴⁴ You have made his splendor to cease
  and cast his throne to the ground.
⁴⁵ You have cut short the days of his
      youth;
    you have covered him with shame.
                                          Selah

⁴⁶ How long, O LORD? Will you hide
      yourself forever?
    How long will your wrath burn
      like fire?
⁴⁷ Remember how short my time is!
    For what vanity you have created
      all the children of man!
⁴⁸ What man can live and never see
      death?
    Who can deliver his soul from the
      power of Sheol?   *Selah*

⁴⁹ Lord, where is your steadfast love of
      old,
    which by your faithfulness you
      swore to David?
⁵⁰ Remember, O Lord, how your ser-
      vants are mocked,
    and how I bear in my heart the
      insults¹ of all the many nations,
⁵¹ with which your enemies mock,
      O LORD,
    with which they mock the foot-
      steps of your anointed.

⁵² Blessed be the LORD forever!
    Amen and Amen.

BOOK FOUR

From Everlasting to Everlasting

90 A PRAYER OF MOSES, THE MAN OF GOD.
    Lord, you have been our dwelling
      place²
    in all generations.
² Before the mountains were brought
      forth,
    or ever you had formed the earth
      and the world,
    from everlasting to everlasting you
      are God.

³ You return man to dust
    and say, "Return, O children of
      man!"³
⁴ For a thousand years in your sight
    are but as yesterday when it is past,
    or as a watch in the night.

⁵ You sweep them away as with a
      flood; they are like a dream,
    like grass that is renewed in the
      morning:
⁶ in the morning it flourishes and is
      renewed;
    in the evening it fades and withers.

⁷ For we are brought to an end by your
      anger;
    by your wrath we are dismayed.
⁸ You have set our iniquities before
      you,
    our secret sins in the light of your
      presence.

⁹ For all our days pass away under
      your wrath;
    we bring our years to an end like a
      sigh.
¹⁰ The years of our life are seventy,
    or even by reason of strength
      eighty;
    yet their span⁴ is but toil and
      trouble;
    they are soon gone, and we fly
      away.
¹¹ Who considers the power of your
      anger,
    and your wrath according to the
      fear of you?

¹² So teach us to number our days
    that we may get a heart of wisdom.
¹³ Return, O LORD! How long?
    Have pity on your servants!
¹⁴ Satisfy us in the morning with your
      steadfast love,
    that we may rejoice and be glad all
      our days.
¹⁵ Make us glad for as many days as you
      have afflicted us,
    and for as many years as we have
      seen evil.
¹⁶ Let your work be shown to your
      servants,
    and your glorious power to their
      children.
¹⁷ Let the favor⁵ of the Lord our God be
      upon us,
    and establish the work of our
      hands upon us;
    yes, establish the work of our
      hands!

¹Hebrew lacks *the insults* ²Some Hebrew manuscripts (compare Septuagint) *our refuge* ³Or *of Adam* ⁴Or *pride* ⁵Or *beauty*

My Refuge and My Fortress

91 He who dwells in the shelter of
the Most High
    will abide in the shadow of the
Almighty.
2 I will say[1] to the Lord, "My refuge
and my fortress,
    my God, in whom I trust."

3 For he will deliver you from the
snare of the fowler
    and from the deadly pestilence.
4 He will cover you with his pinions,
    and under his wings you will find
refuge;
    his faithfulness is a shield and
buckler.
5 You will not fear the terror of the
night,
    nor the arrow that flies by day,
6 nor the pestilence that stalks in
darkness,
    nor the destruction that wastes at
noonday.

7 A thousand may fall at your side,
    ten thousand at your right hand,
    but it will not come near you.
8 You will only look with your eyes
    and see the recompense of the
wicked.

9 Because you have made the Lord
your dwelling place—
    the Most High, who is my ref-
uge[2]—
10 no evil shall be allowed to befall
you,
    no plague come near your tent.

11 For he will command his angels
concerning you
    to guard you in all your ways.
12 On their hands they will bear you
up,
    lest you strike your foot against a
stone.
13 You will tread on the lion and the
adder;
    the young lion and the serpent you
will trample underfoot.

[1] Septuagint *He will say* [2] Or *For you, O Lord, are my refuge! You have made the Most High your dwelling place*

Know Love

verses to read
Psalm 91

There are a lot of places you can look for protection and rescue. A lot of people, things, and actions promise to save you from your life, your misery, and your pain, but the truth is that there's only one salvation, one rescuer, one protector, and that is God.

When life overwhelms you and when storms come, there is a safe harbor. God's hand is already on you if you are in Christ, and all he asks is that you receive his tender care for you. He's already here, and he's just waiting for you to take his hand. The only condition to this rescue is that you receive his love. For in Christ, you are his daughter. God is now your strong tower, your rock, your sure foundation. He is everything you need to build on and to grow. He is your source of strength and protection.

So when the storms come, when the attacks fall, don't look around for help but look up to the Helper. Trust his Word to be true; it will never steer you wrong. As soon as you are willing to accept his protection, you immediately have it. His Word is your lifeline, his Son is your salvation. Don't be so blind that you don't see the very hand of God reaching out to save you. Reach out in faith and grab hold of it. When you do, you will find all the protection you need, and your life will be saved from the pit of despair.

14 "Because he holds fast to me in love,
  I will deliver him;
  I will protect him, because he
    knows my name.
15 When he calls to me, I will answer
    him;
  I will be with him in trouble;
  I will rescue him and honor him.
16 With long life I will satisfy him
  and show him my salvation."

How Great Are Your Works

92 A Psalm. A Song for the Sabbath.
  It is good to give thanks to the
    Lord,
  to sing praises to your name,
    O Most High;
2 to declare your steadfast love in the
    morning,
  and your faithfulness by night,
3 to the music of the lute and the harp,
  to the melody of the lyre.
4 For you, O Lord, have made me glad
    by your work;
  at the works of your hands I sing
    for joy.

5 How great are your works, O Lord!
  Your thoughts are very deep!
6 The stupid man cannot know;
  the fool cannot understand this:
7 that though the wicked sprout like
    grass
  and all evildoers flourish,
  they are doomed to destruction
    forever;
8 but you, O Lord, are on high for-
    ever.
9 For behold, your enemies, O Lord,
  for behold, your enemies shall per-
    ish;
  all evildoers shall be scattered.

10 But you have exalted my horn like
    that of the wild ox;
  you have poured over me[1] fresh oil.
11 My eyes have seen the downfall of
    my enemies;
  my ears have heard the doom of
    my evil assailants.

12 The righteous flourish like the palm
    tree
  and grow like a cedar in Lebanon.

13 They are planted in the house of the
    Lord;
  they flourish in the courts of our
    God.
14 They still bear fruit in old age;
  they are ever full of sap and green,
15 to declare that the Lord is upright;
  he is my rock, and there is no
    unrighteousness in him.

The Lord Reigns

93 The Lord reigns; he is robed in
    majesty;
  the Lord is robed; he has put on
    strength as his belt.
  Yes, the world is established; it shall
    never be moved.
2 Your throne is established from of old;
  you are from everlasting.

3 The floods have lifted up, O Lord,
  the floods have lifted up their voice;
  the floods lift up their roaring.
4 Mightier than the thunders of many
    waters,
  mightier than the waves of the sea,
  the Lord on high is mighty!

5 Your decrees are very trustworthy;
  holiness befits your house,
  O Lord, forevermore.

The Lord Will Not Forsake His People

94 O Lord, God of vengeance,
  O God of vengeance, shine forth!
2 Rise up, O judge of the earth;
  repay to the proud what they
    deserve!
3 O Lord, how long shall the wicked,
  how long shall the wicked exult?
4 They pour out their arrogant words;
  all the evildoers boast.
5 They crush your people, O Lord,
  and afflict your heritage.
6 They kill the widow and the sojourner,
  and murder the fatherless;
7 and they say, "The Lord does not see;
  the God of Jacob does not perceive."

8 Understand, O dullest of the people!
  Fools, when will you be wise?
9 He who planted the ear, does he not
    hear?
  He who formed the eye, does he not
    see?

[1] Compare Syriac; the meaning of the Hebrew is uncertain

10 He who disciplines the nations, does
    he not rebuke?
   He who teaches man knowledge—
11   the LORD—knows the thoughts of
     man,
     that they are but a breath.[1]

12 Blessed is the man whom you disci-
    pline, O LORD,
    and whom you teach out of your
      law,
13 to give him rest from days of trouble,
    until a pit is dug for the wicked.
14 For the LORD will not forsake his
    people;
    he will not abandon his heritage;
15 for justice will return to the righteous,
    and all the upright in heart will
      follow it.

16 Who rises up for me against the
    wicked?
   Who stands up for me against
     evildoers?
17 If the LORD had not been my help,
    my soul would soon have lived in
      the land of silence.
18 When I thought, "My foot slips,"
    your steadfast love, O LORD, held
      me up.
19 When the cares of my heart are many,
    your consolations cheer my soul.
20 Can wicked rulers be allied with you,
    those who frame injustice by stat-
      ute?
21 They band together against the life of
    the righteous
    and condemn the innocent to death.[2]
22 But the LORD has become my strong-
    hold,
    and my God the rock of my refuge.
23 He will bring back on them their
    iniquity
    and wipe them out for their wick-
      edness;
    the LORD our God will wipe them
      out.

Let Us Sing Songs of Praise

95 Oh come, let us sing to the LORD;
    let us make a joyful noise to the
      rock of our salvation!
2 Let us come into his presence with
    thanksgiving;
    let us make a joyful noise to him
      with songs of praise!

3 For the LORD is a great God,
    and a great King above all gods.
4 In his hand are the depths of the
    earth;
    the heights of the mountains are
      his also.
5 The sea is his, for he made it,
    and his hands formed the dry land.

6 Oh come, let us worship and bow
    down;
    let us kneel before the LORD, our
      Maker!
7 For he is our God,
    and we are the people of his pas-
      ture,
    and the sheep of his hand.
   Today, if you hear his voice,
8   do not harden your hearts, as at
      Meribah,
    as on the day at Massah in the
      wilderness,
9 when your fathers put me to the test
    and put me to the proof, though
      they had seen my work.
10 For forty years I loathed that genera-
    tion
    and said, "They are a people who
      go astray in their heart,
    and they have not known my ways."
11 Therefore I swore in my wrath,
    "They shall not enter my rest."

Worship in the Splendor of Holiness

96 Oh sing to the LORD a new song;
    sing to the LORD, all the earth!
2 Sing to the LORD, bless his name;
    tell of his salvation from day to day.
3 Declare his glory among the nations,
    his marvelous works among all the
      peoples!
4 For great is the LORD, and greatly to
    be praised;
    he is to be feared above all gods.
5 For all the gods of the peoples are
    worthless idols,
    but the LORD made the heavens.
6 Splendor and majesty are before him;
    strength and beauty are in his
      sanctuary.

7 Ascribe to the LORD, O families of the
    peoples,
    ascribe to the LORD glory and
      strength!

[1] Septuagint they are futile [2] Hebrew condemn innocent blood

8 Ascribe to the LORD the glory due his
      name;
    bring an offering, and come into
      his courts!
9 Worship the LORD in the splendor of
      holiness;[1]
    tremble before him, all the earth!

0 Say among the nations, "The LORD
      reigns!
    Yes, the world is established; it
      shall never be moved;
    he will judge the peoples with
      equity."

1 Let the heavens be glad, and let the
      earth rejoice;
    let the sea roar, and all that fills it;
2   let the field exult, and everything
      in it!
    Then shall all the trees of the forest
      sing for joy
3   before the LORD, for he comes,
    for he comes to judge the earth.
    He will judge the world in righteous-
      ness,
    and the peoples in his faithful-
      ness.

The LORD Reigns

97 The LORD reigns, let the earth
      rejoice;
    let the many coastlands be glad!
2 Clouds and thick darkness are all
      around him;
    righteousness and justice are the
      foundation of his throne.
3 Fire goes before him
    and burns up his adversaries all
      around.
4 His lightnings light up the world;
    the earth sees and trembles.
5 The mountains melt like wax before
      the LORD,
    before the Lord of all the earth.

6 The heavens proclaim his righteous-
      ness,
    and all the peoples see his glory.
7 All worshipers of images are put to
      shame,
    who make their boast in worthless
      idols;
    worship him, all you gods!

8 Zion hears and is glad,
    and the daughters of Judah rejoice,
    because of your judgments,
      O LORD.
9 For you, O LORD, are most high over
      all the earth;
    you are exalted far above all gods.

10 O you who love the LORD, hate evil!
    He preserves the lives of his saints;
    he delivers them from the hand of
      the wicked.
11 Light is sown[2] for the righteous,
    and joy for the upright in heart.
12 Rejoice in the LORD, O you righteous,
    and give thanks to his holy name!

Make a Joyful Noise to the LORD

98 A PSALM.
      Oh sing to the LORD a new song,
    for he has done marvelous things!
    His right hand and his holy arm
      have worked salvation for him.
2   The LORD has made known his salva-
      tion;
    he has revealed his righteousness
      in the sight of the nations.
3   He has remembered his steadfast
      love and faithfulness
    to the house of Israel.
    All the ends of the earth have seen
      the salvation of our God.

4   Make a joyful noise to the LORD, all
      the earth;
    break forth into joyous song and
      sing praises!
5   Sing praises to the LORD with the lyre,
    with the lyre and the sound of
      melody!
6   With trumpets and the sound of the
      horn
    make a joyful noise before the
      King, the LORD!

7   Let the sea roar, and all that fills it;
    the world and those who dwell in it!
8   Let the rivers clap their hands;
    let the hills sing for joy together
9   before the LORD, for he comes
    to judge the earth.
    He will judge the world with righ-
      teousness,
    and the peoples with equity.

Or *in holy attire* [2]Most Hebrew manuscripts; one Hebrew manuscript, Septuagint, Syriac, Jerome *Light dawns*

The Lord Our God Is Holy

99 The Lord reigns; let the peoples
tremble!
He sits enthroned upon the cherubim; let the earth quake!
2 The Lord is great in Zion;
he is exalted over all the peoples.
3 Let them praise your great and awesome name!
Holy is he!
4 The King in his might loves justice.[1]
You have established equity;
you have executed justice
and righteousness in Jacob.
5 Exalt the Lord our God;
worship at his footstool!
Holy is he!

6 Moses and Aaron were among his
priests,
Samuel also was among those who
called upon his name.
They called to the Lord, and he
answered them.

7 In the pillar of the cloud he spoke to
them;
they kept his testimonies
and the statute that he gave them.

8 O Lord our God, you answered them
you were a forgiving God to them,
but an avenger of their wrongdoings
9 Exalt the Lord our God,
and worship at his holy mountain;
for the Lord our God is holy!

His Steadfast Love Endures Forever

100 A Psalm for giving thanks.
Make a joyful noise to the
Lord, all the earth!
2 Serve the Lord with gladness!
Come into his presence with sing-
ing!

3 Know that the Lord, he is God!
It is he who made us, and we are
his;[2]
we are his people, and the sheep o
his pasture.

[1] Or The might of the King loves justice [2] Or and not we ourselves

Know How to Communicate

verses to read
Psalm 100

Happiness and joy aren't the *goal* of faith, but they are the *symptoms* of faith. When your love of God is real, the natural result of that love in your life is happiness. His presence is like candy to a kid and a smile to a stranger. For the God Girl, coming into his presence after being in a war-torn world can be pure exhilaration, and that's where the shouts of joy come from. "Make a joyful noise to the Lord, all the earth!" (Ps. 100:1). Have you ever shouted for joy? The most expressive and passionate sounds to come out of the mouth of the God Girl are most often directed to her God. God's goodness fills her heart to overflowing, his power draws out her sense of awe and admiration, and she has to shout! And when she serves him it's with pure joy, because to serve the one you love is to truly live.

As a God Girl, you are called to come into God's presence with a joyful song (see Ps. 100:2). Is your song joyful? Or is it robotic? Do you mean it when you sing it? If not, then close your mouth. Don't lie to God as you worship him. Be honest as you sing; be loving as you praise. Believe what comes out of your mouth, or don't say it.

The fear of the Lord leads to a joy that must be expressed back to him. Experience more of God by learning more about him. As you learn how he thinks and what he has said, and as you do what pleases him, as your heavenly Father, you yourself will also be pleased.

⁴　Enter his gates with thanksgiving,
　　　and his courts with praise!
　　　Give thanks to him; bless his name!

⁵　For the LORD is good;
　　　his steadfast love endures forever,
　　　and his faithfulness to all genera-
　　　　tions.

I Will Walk with Integrity

101

A PSALM OF DAVID.
I will sing of steadfast love and
　justice;
to you, O LORD, I will make music.

²　I will ponder the way that is blame-
　　　less.
　　　Oh when will you come to me?
　　I will walk with integrity of heart
　　　within my house;

³　I will not set before my eyes
　　　anything that is worthless.
　　I hate the work of those who fall away;
　　　it shall not cling to me.

⁴　A perverse heart shall be far from me;
　　　I will know nothing of evil.

⁵　Whoever slanders his neighbor
　　　secretly
　　　I will destroy.
　　Whoever has a haughty look and an
　　　arrogant heart
　　　I will not endure.

⁶　I will look with favor on the faithful
　　　in the land,
　　　that they may dwell with me;
　　he who walks in the way that is
　　　blameless
　　　shall minister to me.

⁷　No one who practices deceit
　　　shall dwell in my house;
　　no one who utters lies
　　　shall continue before my eyes.

⁸　Morning by morning I will destroy
　　　all the wicked in the land,
　　cutting off all the evildoers
　　　from the city of the LORD.

Do Not Hide Your Face from Me

102

A PRAYER OF ONE AFFLICTED,
WHEN HE IS FAINT AND POURS OUT
HIS COMPLAINT BEFORE THE LORD.

¹　Hear my prayer, O LORD;
　　　let my cry come to you!

²　Do not hide your face from me
　　　in the day of my distress!
　　Incline your ear to me;
　　　answer me speedily in the day
　　　when I call!

³　For my days pass away like smoke,
　　　and my bones burn like a furnace.

⁴　My heart is struck down like grass
　　　and has withered;
　　　I forget to eat my bread.

⁵　Because of my loud groaning
　　　my bones cling to my flesh.

⁶　I am like a desert owl of the wilder-
　　　ness,
　　　like an owl¹ of the waste places;

⁷　I lie awake;
　　　I am like a lonely sparrow on the
　　　housetop.

⁸　All the day my enemies taunt me;
　　　those who deride me use my name
　　　for a curse.

⁹　For I eat ashes like bread
　　　and mingle tears with my drink,

¹⁰　because of your indignation and
　　　anger;
　　　for you have taken me up and
　　　thrown me down.

¹¹　My days are like an evening shadow;
　　　I wither away like grass.

¹²　But you, O LORD, are enthroned
　　　forever;
　　　you are remembered throughout
　　　all generations.

¹³　You will arise and have pity on Zion;
　　　it is the time to favor her;
　　　the appointed time has come.

¹⁴　For your servants hold her stones
　　　dear
　　　and have pity on her dust.

¹⁵　Nations will fear the name of the
　　　LORD,
　　　and all the kings of the earth will
　　　fear your glory.

¹⁶　For the LORD builds up Zion;
　　　he appears in his glory;

¹⁷　he regards the prayer of the desti-
　　　tute
　　　and does not despise their prayer.

¹⁸　Let this be recorded for a generation
　　　to come,
　　　so that a people yet to be created
　　　may praise the LORD:

¹ The precise identity of these birds is uncertain

19   that he looked down from his holy
       height;
       from heaven the Lord looked at
       the earth,
20   to hear the groans of the prisoners,
       to set free those who were
       doomed to die,
21   that they may declare in Zion the
       name of the Lord,
       and in Jerusalem his praise,
22   when peoples gather together,
       and kingdoms, to worship the
       Lord.

23   He has broken my strength in mid-
       course;
       he has shortened my days.
24   "O my God," I say, "take me not away
       in the midst of my days—
       you whose years endure
       throughout all generations!"

25   Of old you laid the foundation of the
       earth,
       and the heavens are the work of
       your hands.
26   They will perish, but you will
       remain;
       they will all wear out like a gar-
       ment.
       You will change them like a robe, and
       they will pass away,
27   but you are the same, and your
       years have no end.
28   The children of your servants shall
       dwell secure;
       their offspring shall be established
       before you.

Bless the Lord, O My Soul

103
Of David.
Bless the Lord, O my soul,
       and all that is within me,
       bless his holy name!
2   Bless the Lord, O my soul,
       and forget not all his benefits,
3   who forgives all your iniquity,
       who heals all your diseases,
4   who redeems your life from the pit,
       who crowns you with steadfast
       love and mercy,
5   who satisfies you with good
       so that your youth is renewed like
       the eagle's.

6   The Lord works righteousness
       and justice for all who are
       oppressed.
7   He made known his ways to Moses,
       his acts to the people of Israel.
8   The Lord is merciful and gracious,
       slow to anger and abounding in
       steadfast love.
9   He will not always chide,
       nor will he keep his anger forever.
10   He does not deal with us according
       to our sins,
       nor repay us according to our
       iniquities.
11   For as high as the heavens are above
       the earth,
       so great is his steadfast love
       toward those who fear him;
12   as far as the east is from the west,
       so far does he remove our trans-
       gressions from us.
13   As a father shows compassion to his
       children,
       so the Lord shows compassion to
       those who fear him.
14   For he knows our frame;[1]
       he remembers that we are dust.

15   As for man, his days are like grass;
       he flourishes like a flower of the
       field;
16   for the wind passes over it, and it is
       gone,
       and its place knows it no more.
17   But the steadfast love of the Lord is
       from everlasting to everlasting
       on those who fear him,
       and his righteousness to children's
       children,
18   to those who keep his covenant
       and remember to do his com-
       mandments.
19   The Lord has established his throne
       in the heavens,
       and his kingdom rules over all.

20   Bless the Lord, O you his angels,
       you mighty ones who do his word,
       obeying the voice of his word!
21   Bless the Lord, all his hosts,
       his ministers, who do his will!
22   Bless the Lord, all his works,
       in all places of his dominion.
       Bless the Lord, O my soul!

[1] Or knows how we are formed

O Lord My God, You Are Very Great

104 Bless the Lord, O my soul!
O Lord my God, you are very great!
You are clothed with splendor and majesty,

2 covering yourself with light as with a garment,
stretching out the heavens like a tent.

3 He lays the beams of his chambers on the waters;
he makes the clouds his chariot;
he rides on the wings of the wind;

4 he makes his messengers winds,
his ministers a flaming fire.

5 He set the earth on its foundations,
so that it should never be moved.

6 You covered it with the deep as with a garment;
the waters stood above the mountains.

7 At your rebuke they fled;
at the sound of your thunder they took to flight.

8 The mountains rose, the valleys sank down
to the place that you appointed for them.

9 You set a boundary that they may not pass,
so that they might not again cover the earth.

10 You make springs gush forth in the valleys;
they flow between the hills;

11 they give drink to every beast of the field;
the wild donkeys quench their thirst.

12 Beside them the birds of the heavens dwell;
they sing among the branches.

13 From your lofty abode you water the mountains;
the earth is satisfied with the fruit of your work.

14 You cause the grass to grow for the livestock
and plants for man to cultivate,
that he may bring forth food from the earth

15 and wine to gladden the heart of man,
oil to make his face shine
and bread to strengthen man's heart.

16 The trees of the Lord are watered abundantly,
the cedars of Lebanon that he planted.

17 In them the birds build their nests;
the stork has her home in the fir trees.

18 The high mountains are for the wild goats;
the rocks are a refuge for the rock badgers.

19 He made the moon to mark the seasons;[1]
the sun knows its time for setting.

20 You make darkness, and it is night,
when all the beasts of the forest creep about.

21 The young lions roar for their prey,
seeking their food from God.

[1] Or *the appointed times* (compare Genesis 1:14)

22 When the sun rises, they steal away
       and lie down in their dens.
23 Man goes out to his work
       and to his labor until the evening.

24 O Lord, how manifold are your works!
       In wisdom have you made them all;
       the earth is full of your creatures.
25 Here is the sea, great and wide,
       which teems with creatures innu-
           merable,
       living things both small and great.
26 There go the ships,
       and Leviathan, which you formed
           to play in it.[1]

27 These all look to you,
       to give them their food in due sea-
           son.
28 When you give it to them, they
       gather it up;
       when you open your hand, they
           are filled with good things.
29 When you hide your face, they are
       dismayed;
       when you take away their breath,
           they die
       and return to their dust.
30 When you send forth your Spirit,[2]
       they are created,
       and you renew the face of the
           ground.

31 May the glory of the Lord endure
       forever;
       may the Lord rejoice in his works,
32 who looks on the earth and it
       trembles,
       who touches the mountains and
           they smoke!
33 I will sing to the Lord as long as I live;
       I will sing praise to my God while
           I have being.
34 May my meditation be pleasing to him,
       for I rejoice in the Lord.
35 Let sinners be consumed from the
       earth,
       and let the wicked be no more!
   Bless the Lord, O my soul!
   Praise the Lord!

Tell of All His Wonderful Works

105 Oh give thanks to the Lord;
       call upon his name;
       make known his deeds among the
           peoples!

2 Sing to him, sing praises to him;
       tell of all his wondrous works!
3 Glory in his holy name;
       let the hearts of those who seek
           the Lord rejoice!
4 Seek the Lord and his strength;
       seek his presence continually!
5 Remember the wondrous works that
       he has done,
       his miracles, and the judgments he
           uttered,
6 O offspring of Abraham, his servant,
       children of Jacob, his chosen ones!

7 He is the Lord our God;
       his judgments are in all the earth.
8 He remembers his covenant forever,
       the word that he commanded, for
           a thousand generations,
9 the covenant that he made with
       Abraham,
       his sworn promise to Isaac,
10 which he confirmed to Jacob as a
       statute,
       to Israel as an everlasting covenant,
11 saying, "To you I will give the land of
       Canaan
       as your portion for an inheritance."

12 When they were few in number,
       of little account, and sojourners in
           it,
13 wandering from nation to nation,
       from one kingdom to another
           people,
14 he allowed no one to oppress them;
       he rebuked kings on their account,
15 saying, "Touch not my anointed ones,
       do my prophets no harm!"

16 When he summoned a famine on the
       land
       and broke all supply[3] of bread,
17 he had sent a man ahead of them,
       Joseph, who was sold as a slave.
18 His feet were hurt with fetters;
       his neck was put in a collar of iron;
19 until what he had said came to pass,
       the word of the Lord tested him.
20 The king sent and released him;
       the ruler of the peoples set him
           free;
21 he made him lord of his house
       and ruler of all his possessions,
22 to bind[4] his princes at his pleasure
       and to teach his elders wisdom.

[1] Or you formed to play with [2] Or breath [3] Hebrew staff [4] Septuagint, Syriac, Jerome instruct

23 Then Israel came to Egypt;
   Jacob sojourned in the land of Ham.
24 And the LORD made his people very
   fruitful
   and made them stronger than
   their foes.
25 He turned their hearts to hate his
   people,
   to deal craftily with his servants.
26 He sent Moses, his servant,
   and Aaron, whom he had chosen.
27 They performed his signs among
   them
   and miracles in the land of Ham.
28 He sent darkness, and made the land
   dark;
   they did not rebel[1] against his
   words.
29 He turned their waters into blood
   and caused their fish to die.
30 Their land swarmed with frogs,
   even in the chambers of their
   kings.
31 He spoke, and there came swarms of
   flies,
   and gnats throughout their country.
32 He gave them hail for rain,
   and fiery lightning bolts through
   their land.
33 He struck down their vines and fig
   trees,
   and shattered the trees of their
   country.
34 He spoke, and the locusts came,
   young locusts without number,
35 which devoured all the vegetation in
   their land
   and ate up the fruit of their ground.
36 He struck down all the firstborn in
   their land,
   the firstfruits of all their strength.

37 Then he brought out Israel with
   silver and gold,
   and there was none among his
   tribes who stumbled.
38 Egypt was glad when they departed,
   for dread of them had fallen upon it.
39 He spread a cloud for a covering,
   and fire to give light by night.
40 They asked, and he brought quail,
   and gave them bread from heaven
   in abundance.

41 He opened the rock, and water
   gushed out;
   it flowed through the desert like a
   river.
42 For he remembered his holy promise,
   and Abraham, his servant.

43 So he brought his people out with joy,
   his chosen ones with singing.
44 And he gave them the lands of the
   nations,
   and they took possession of the
   fruit of the peoples' toil,
45 that they might keep his statutes
   and observe his laws.
   Praise the LORD!

Give Thanks to the LORD, for He Is Good

106 Praise the LORD!
   Oh give thanks to the LORD, for
   he is good,
   for his steadfast love endures
   forever!
2 Who can utter the mighty deeds of
   the LORD,
   or declare all his praise?
3 Blessed are they who observe justice,
   who do righteousness at all times!

4 Remember me, O LORD, when you
   show favor to your people;
   help me when you save them,[2]
5 that I may look upon the prosperity
   of your chosen ones,
   that I may rejoice in the gladness
   of your nation,
   that I may glory with your inheritance.

6 Both we and our fathers have sinned;
   we have committed iniquity; we
   have done wickedness.
7 Our fathers, when they were in Egypt,
   did not consider your wondrous
   works;
   they did not remember the abundance of your steadfast love,
   but rebelled by the sea, at the Red
   Sea.
8 Yet he saved them for his name's sake,
   that he might make known his
   mighty power.
9 He rebuked the Red Sea, and it
   became dry,
   and he led them through the deep
   as through a desert.

Septuagint, Syriac omit not [2] Or Remember me, O LORD, with the favor you show to your people; help me with your salvation

10 So he saved them from the hand of
      the foe
   and redeemed them from the
      power of the enemy.
11 And the waters covered their adver-
      saries;
   not one of them was left.
12 Then they believed his words;
   they sang his praise.

13 But they soon forgot his works;
   they did not wait for his counsel.
14 But they had a wanton craving in the
      wilderness,
   and put God to the test in the
      desert;
15 he gave them what they asked,
   but sent a wasting disease among
      them.

16 When men in the camp were jealous
      of Moses
   and Aaron, the holy one of the LORD,
17 the earth opened and swallowed up
      Dathan,
   and covered the company of
      Abiram.
18 Fire also broke out in their company;
   the flame burned up the wicked.

19 They made a calf in Horeb
   and worshiped a metal image.
20 They exchanged the glory of God[1]
   for the image of an ox that eats
      grass.
21 They forgot God, their Savior,
   who had done great things in
      Egypt,
22 wondrous works in the land of Ham,
   and awesome deeds by the Red Sea.
23 Therefore he said he would destroy
      them—
   had not Moses, his chosen one,
   stood in the breach before him,
   to turn away his wrath from
      destroying them.

24 Then they despised the pleasant land,
   having no faith in his promise.
25 They murmured in their tents,
   and did not obey the voice of the
      LORD.
26 Therefore he raised his hand and
      swore to them
   that he would make them fall in
      the wilderness,

27 and would make their offspring fall
      among the nations,
   scattering them among the lands.

28 Then they yoked themselves to the
      Baal of Peor,
   and ate sacrifices offered to the
      dead;
29 they provoked the LORD to anger
      with their deeds,
   and a plague broke out among
      them.
30 Then Phinehas stood up and inter-
      vened,
   and the plague was stayed.
31 And that was counted to him as
      righteousness
   from generation to generation
      forever.

32 They angered him at the waters of
      Meribah,
   and it went ill with Moses on their
      account,
33 for they made his spirit bitter,[2]
   and he spoke rashly with his lips.

34 They did not destroy the peoples,
   as the LORD commanded them,
35 but they mixed with the nations
   and learned to do as they did.
36 They served their idols,
   which became a snare to them.
37 They sacrificed their sons
   and their daughters to the
      demons;
38 they poured out innocent blood,
   the blood of their sons and daugh-
      ters,
   whom they sacrificed to the idols of
      Canaan,
   and the land was polluted with
      blood.
39 Thus they became unclean by their
      acts,
   and played the whore in their
      deeds.

40 Then the anger of the LORD was
      kindled against his people,
   and he abhorred his heritage;
41 he gave them into the hand of the
      nations,
   so that those who hated them
      ruled over them.

[1] Hebrew exchanged their glory [2] Or they rebelled against God's Spirit

² Their enemies oppressed them,
   and they were brought into subjec-
      tion under their power.
³ Many times he delivered them,
   but they were rebellious in their
      purposes
   and were brought low through
      their iniquity.

⁴ Nevertheless, he looked upon their
      distress,
   when he heard their cry.
⁵ For their sake he remembered his
      covenant,
   and relented according to the
      abundance of his steadfast
      love.
⁶ He caused them to be pitied
   by all those who held them captive.

⁷ Save us, O LORD our God,
   and gather us from among the
      nations,
   that we may give thanks to your holy
      name
   and glory in your praise.

⁸ Blessed be the LORD, the God of Israel,
   from everlasting to everlasting!
   And let all the people say, "Amen!"
   Praise the LORD!

BOOK FIVE

Let the Redeemed of the LORD Say So

107 Oh give thanks to the LORD, for
          he is good,
   for his steadfast love endures
      forever!
² Let the redeemed of the LORD say so,
   whom he has redeemed from
      trouble¹
³ and gathered in from the lands,
   from the east and from the west,
   from the north and from the south.

⁴ Some wandered in desert wastes,
   finding no way to a city to dwell in;
⁵ hungry and thirsty,
   their soul fainted within them.
⁶ Then they cried to the LORD in their
      trouble,
   and he delivered them from their
      distress.
⁷ He led them by a straight way
   till they reached a city to dwell in.

⁸ Let them thank the LORD for his
      steadfast love,
   for his wondrous works to the
      children of man!
⁹ For he satisfies the longing soul,
   and the hungry soul he fills with
      good things.

A Prayer for...
THE FUTURE

O Lord, all the time in the world is of
no value to me unless the days are
spent in your presence, in your service,
to your glory. Give me a grace that
precedes, follows, guides, sustains,
sanctifies, and aids in every hour, so
that I won't be apart from you for one
moment but can rely on your Spirit
to supply my every thought, speak in
my every word, direct my every step,
prosper my every work, build up every
speck of faith, and give me a desire to
sing your praises, testify to your love,
and advance your kingdom.

I launch my boat on the unknown
waters of this year with you, O Father, as my harbor; you, O Son, at my
helm; you, O Holy Spirit, filling my
sails. Guide me to heaven with my full
armor on, my lamp burning, my ears
open to your call, my heart full of love,
and my soul free.

Give me your grace to sanctify me,
your comforts to cheer, your wisdom
to teach, your right hand to guide,
your counsel to instruct, your law to
judge, and your presence to stabilize.
May your awesomeness be my awe
and your triumphs my joy.

Amen.

¹⁰ Some sat in darkness and in the
      shadow of death,
   prisoners in affliction and in irons,
¹¹ for they had rebelled against the
      words of God,
   and spurned the counsel of the
      Most High.

¹ Or from the hand of the foe

¹² So he bowed their hearts down with
        hard labor;
    they fell down, with none to help.
¹³ Then they cried to the LORD in their
        trouble,
    and he delivered them from their
        distress.
¹⁴ He brought them out of darkness
        and the shadow of death,
    and burst their bonds apart.
¹⁵ Let them thank the LORD for his
        steadfast love,
    for his wondrous works to the
        children of man!
¹⁶ For he shatters the doors of bronze
    and cuts in two the bars of iron.

¹⁷ Some were fools through their sinful
        ways,
    and because of their iniquities suf-
        fered affliction;
¹⁸ they loathed any kind of food,
    and they drew near to the gates of
        death.
¹⁹ Then they cried to the LORD in their
        trouble,
    and he delivered them from their
        distress.
²⁰ He sent out his word and healed them,
    and delivered them from their
        destruction.
²¹ Let them thank the LORD for his
        steadfast love,
    for his wondrous works to the
        children of man!
²² And let them offer sacrifices of
        thanksgiving,
    and tell of his deeds in songs of joy!

²³ Some went down to the sea in ships,
    doing business on the great waters;
²⁴ they saw the deeds of the LORD,
    his wondrous works in the deep.
²⁵ For he commanded and raised the
        stormy wind,
    which lifted up the waves of the sea.
²⁶ They mounted up to heaven; they
        went down to the depths;
    their courage melted away in their
        evil plight;
²⁷ they reeled and staggered like
        drunken men
    and were at their wits' end.[1]

²⁸ Then they cried to the LORD in their
        trouble,
    and he delivered them from their
        distress.
²⁹ He made the storm be still,
    and the waves of the sea were
        hushed.
³⁰ Then they were glad that the waters
        were quiet,
    and he brought them to their
        desired haven.
³¹ Let them thank the LORD for his
        steadfast love,
    for his wondrous works to the
        children of man!
³² Let them extol him in the congrega-
        tion of the people,
    and praise him in the assembly of
        the elders.

³³ He turns rivers into a desert,
    springs of water into thirsty ground,
³⁴ a fruitful land into a salty waste,
    because of the evil of its inhabitants.
³⁵ He turns a desert into pools of water,
    a parched land into springs of
        water.
³⁶ And there he lets the hungry dwell,
    and they establish a city to live in;
³⁷ they sow fields and plant vineyards
    and get a fruitful yield.
³⁸ By his blessing they multiply greatly,
    and he does not let their livestock
        diminish.

³⁹ When they are diminished and
        brought low
    through oppression, evil, and sor-
        row,
⁴⁰ he pours contempt on princes
    and makes them wander in track-
        less wastes;
⁴¹ but he raises up the needy out of
        affliction
    and makes their families like
        flocks.
⁴² The upright see it and are glad,
    and all wickedness shuts its
        mouth.

⁴³ Whoever is wise, let him attend to
        these things;
    let them consider the steadfast
        love of the LORD.

[1] Hebrew and all their wisdom was swallowed up   [2] Hebrew they

With God We Shall Do Valiantly

108 A Song. A Psalm of David.

My heart is steadfast, O God!
I will sing and make melody with
all my being![1]
Awake, O harp and lyre!
I will awake the dawn!
I will give thanks to you, O Lord,
among the peoples;
I will sing praises to you among
the nations.
For your steadfast love is great above
the heavens;
your faithfulness reaches to the
clouds.

Be exalted, O God, above the heavens!
Let your glory be over all the earth!
That your beloved ones may be
delivered,
give salvation by your right hand
and answer me!

God has promised in his holiness:[2]
"With exultation I will divide up
Shechem
and portion out the Valley of
Succoth.
Gilead is mine; Manasseh is mine;
Ephraim is my helmet,
Judah my scepter.
Moab is my washbasin;
upon Edom I cast my shoe;
over Philistia I shout in triumph."

Who will bring me to the fortified city?
Who will lead me to Edom?
Have you not rejected us, O God?
You do not go out, O God, with our
armies.
Oh grant us help against the foe,
for vain is the salvation of man!
With God we shall do valiantly;
it is he who will tread down our
foes.

Help Me, O Lord My God

109 To the choirmaster. A Psalm of
David.

1 Be not silent, O God of my praise!
2 For wicked and deceitful mouths are
opened against me,
speaking against me with lying
tongues.

3 They encircle me with words of hate,
and attack me without cause.
4 In return for my love they accuse me,
but I give myself to prayer.[3]
5 So they reward me evil for good,
and hatred for my love.

6 Appoint a wicked man against him;
let an accuser stand at his right
hand.
7 When he is tried, let him come forth
guilty;
let his prayer be counted as sin!
8 May his days be few;
may another take his office!
9 May his children be fatherless
and his wife a widow!
10 May his children wander about and
beg,
seeking food far from the ruins
they inhabit!
11 May the creditor seize all that he has;
may strangers plunder the fruits of
his toil!
12 Let there be none to extend kindness
to him,
nor any to pity his fatherless children!
13 May his posterity be cut off;
may his name be blotted out in the
second generation!
14 May the iniquity of his fathers be
remembered before the Lord,
and let not the sin of his mother be
blotted out!
15 Let them be before the Lord continually,
that he may cut off the memory of
them from the earth!

16 For he did not remember to show
kindness,
but pursued the poor and needy
and the brokenhearted, to put
them to death.
17 He loved to curse; let curses come[4]
upon him!
He did not delight in blessing; may
it be far[5] from him!
18 He clothed himself with cursing as
his coat;
may it soak[6] into his body like
water,
like oil into his bones!

[1] Hebrew with my glory [2] Or sanctuary [3] Hebrew but I am prayer [4] Revocalization; Masoretic Text curses have come [5] Revocalization;
Masoretic Text it is far [6] Revocalization; Masoretic Text it has soaked

¹⁹ May it be like a garment that he
wraps around him,
like a belt that he puts on every day!
²⁰ May this be the reward of my accusers from the LORD,
of those who speak evil against my
life!

²¹ But you, O GOD my Lord,
deal on my behalf for your name's
sake;
because your steadfast love is
good, deliver me!
²² For I am poor and needy,
and my heart is stricken within me.
²³ I am gone like a shadow at evening;
I am shaken off like a locust.
²⁴ My knees are weak through fasting;
my body has become gaunt, with
no fat.
²⁵ I am an object of scorn to my accusers;
when they see me, they wag their
heads.

²⁶ Help me, O LORD my God!
Save me according to your steadfast love!
²⁷ Let them know that this is your hand;
you, O LORD, have done it!
²⁸ Let them curse, but you will bless!
They arise and are put to shame,
but your servant will be glad!
²⁹ May my accusers be clothed with
dishonor;
may they be wrapped in their own
shame as in a cloak!

³⁰ With my mouth I will give great
thanks to the LORD;
I will praise him in the midst of the
throng.
³¹ For he stands at the right hand of the
needy one,
to save him from those who condemn his soul to death.

Sit at My Right Hand

110 A PSALM OF DAVID.
The LORD says to my Lord:
"Sit at my right hand,
until I make your enemies your footstool."

² The LORD sends forth from Zion
your mighty scepter.
Rule in the midst of your enemies
³ Your people will offer themselves
freely
on the day of your power,¹
in holy garments;²
from the womb of the morning,
the dew of your youth will be
yours.³
⁴ The LORD has sworn
and will not change his mind,
"You are a priest forever
after the order of Melchizedek."

⁵ The Lord is at your right hand;
he will shatter kings on the day of
his wrath.
⁶ He will execute judgment among the
nations,
filling them with corpses;
he will shatter chiefs⁴
over the wide earth.
⁷ He will drink from the brook by the
way;
therefore he will lift up his head.

Great Are the LORD's Works

111⁵ Praise the LORD!
I will give thanks to the LORD
with my whole heart,
in the company of the upright, in
the congregation.
² Great are the works of the LORD,
studied by all who delight in them
³ Full of splendor and majesty is his
work,
and his righteousness endures
forever.
⁴ He has caused his wondrous works
to be remembered;
the LORD is gracious and merciful.
⁵ He provides food for those who fear
him;
he remembers his covenant forever
⁶ He has shown his people the power
of his works,
in giving them the inheritance of
the nations.
⁷ The works of his hands are faithful
and just;
all his precepts are trustworthy;

¹Or *on the day you lead your forces* ²Masoretic Text; some Hebrew manuscripts and Jerome *on the holy mountains* ³The meaning of the Hebrew is uncertain ⁴Or *the head* ⁵This psalm is an acrostic poem, each line beginning with the successive letters of the Hebrew alphabet

they are established forever and
    ever,
    to be performed with faithfulness
      and uprightness.
He sent redemption to his people;
    he has commanded his covenant
      forever.
    Holy and awesome is his name!
The fear of the LORD is the beginning
    of wisdom;
    all those who practice it have a
      good understanding.
    His praise endures forever!

The Righteous Will Never Be Moved

112 Praise the LORD!
    Blessed is the man who fears
      the LORD,
    who greatly delights in his com-
      mandments!
His offspring will be mighty in the
    land;
    the generation of the upright will
      be blessed.
Wealth and riches are in his house,
    and his righteousness endures
      forever.
Light dawns in the darkness for the
    upright;
    he is gracious, merciful, and righ-
      teous.
It is well with the man who deals
    generously and lends;
    who conducts his affairs with
      justice.
For the righteous will never be
    moved;
    he will be remembered forever.
He is not afraid of bad news;
    his heart is firm, trusting in the
      LORD.
His heart is steady; he will not be
    afraid,
    until he looks in triumph on his
      adversaries.
He has distributed freely; he has
    given to the poor;
    his righteousness endures forever;
    his horn is exalted in honor.
The wicked man sees it and is angry;
    he gnashes his teeth and melts
      away;
    the desire of the wicked will per-
      ish!

Who Is like the LORD Our God?

113 Praise the LORD!
    Praise, O servants of the LORD,
    praise the name of the LORD!

2 Blessed be the name of the LORD
    from this time forth and forever-
      more!
3 From the rising of the sun to its set-
    ting,
    the name of the LORD is to be
      praised!

4 The LORD is high above all nations,
    and his glory above the heavens!
5 Who is like the LORD our God,
    who is seated on high,
6 who looks far down
    on the heavens and the earth?
7 He raises the poor from the dust
    and lifts the needy from the ash
      heap,
8 to make them sit with princes,
    with the princes of his people.
9 He gives the barren woman a home,
    making her the joyous mother of
      children.
    Praise the LORD!

Tremble at the Presence of the Lord

114 When Israel went out from
    Egypt,
    the house of Jacob from a people of
      strange language,
2 Judah became his sanctuary,
    Israel his dominion.

3 The sea looked and fled;
    Jordan turned back.
4 The mountains skipped like rams,
    the hills like lambs.

5 What ails you, O sea, that you flee?
    O Jordan, that you turn back?
6 O mountains, that you skip like
    rams?
    O hills, like lambs?

7 Tremble, O earth, at the presence of
    the Lord,
    at the presence of the God of
      Jacob,
8 who turns the rock into a pool of
    water,
    the flint into a spring of water.

This psalm is an acrostic poem, each line beginning with the successive letters of the Hebrew alphabet

To Your Name Give Glory

115

Not to us, O Lord, not to us,
  but to your name give glory,
    for the sake of your steadfast love
    and your faithfulness!

2 Why should the nations say,
  "Where is their God?"
3 Our God is in the heavens;
  he does all that he pleases.

4 Their idols are silver and gold,
  the work of human hands.
5 They have mouths, but do not speak;
  eyes, but do not see.
6 They have ears, but do not hear;
  noses, but do not smell.
7 They have hands, but do not feel;
  feet, but do not walk;
  and they do not make a sound in
    their throat.
8 Those who make them become like
  them;
  so do all who trust in them.

9 O Israel,[1] trust in the Lord!
  He is their help and their shield.
10 O house of Aaron, trust in the Lord!
  He is their help and their shield.
11 You who fear the Lord, trust in the
  Lord!
  He is their help and their shield.

12 The Lord has remembered us; he
  will bless us;
  he will bless the house of Israel;
  he will bless the house of Aaron;
13 he will bless those who fear the Lord,
  both the small and the great.

14 May the Lord give you increase,
  you and your children!
15 May you be blessed by the Lord,
  who made heaven and earth!

16 The heavens are the Lord's heavens,
  but the earth he has given to the
    children of man.
17 The dead do not praise the Lord,
  nor do any who go down into
    silence.
18 But we will bless the Lord
  from this time forth and forever-
    more.
  Praise the Lord!

I Love the Lord

116

I love the Lord, because he ha
  heard
  my voice and my pleas for mercy.
2 Because he inclined his ear to me,
  therefore I will call on him as long
    as I live.
3 The snares of death encompassed m
  the pangs of Sheol laid hold on m
  I suffered distress and anguish.
4 Then I called on the name of the Lor
  "O Lord, I pray, deliver my soul!"

5 Gracious is the Lord, and righteous
  our God is merciful.
6 The Lord preserves the simple;
  when I was brought low, he saved
    me.
7 Return, O my soul, to your rest;
  for the Lord has dealt bountifully
    with you.

8 For you have delivered my soul from
  death,
  my eyes from tears,
  my feet from stumbling;
9 I will walk before the Lord
  in the land of the living.

10 I believed, even when[2] I spoke:
  "I am greatly afflicted";
11 I said in my alarm,
  "All mankind are liars."

12 What shall I render to the Lord
  for all his benefits to me?
13 I will lift up the cup of salvation
  and call on the name of the Lord,
14 I will pay my vows to the Lord
  in the presence of all his people.

15 Precious in the sight of the Lord
  is the death of his saints.
16 O Lord, I am your servant;
  I am your servant, the son of your
    maidservant.
  You have loosed my bonds.
17 I will offer to you the sacrifice of
  thanksgiving
  and call on the name of the Lord.
18 I will pay my vows to the Lord
  in the presence of all his people,
19 in the courts of the house of the Lor
  in your midst, O Jerusalem.
  Praise the Lord!

[1] Masoretic Text; many Hebrew manuscripts, Septuagint, Syriac O house of Israel [2] Or believed, indeed; Septuagint believed, therefore

The Lord's Faithfulness Endures Forever

117 Praise the Lord, all nations!
Extol him, all peoples!
For great is his steadfast love toward us,
and the faithfulness of the Lord endures forever.
Praise the Lord!

His Steadfast Love Endures Forever

118 Oh give thanks to the Lord, for he is good;
for his steadfast love endures forever!

Let Israel say,
"His steadfast love endures forever."
Let the house of Aaron say,
"His steadfast love endures forever."
Let those who fear the Lord say,
"His steadfast love endures forever."

Out of my distress I called on the Lord;
the Lord answered me and set me free.
The Lord is on my side; I will not fear.
What can man do to me?
The Lord is on my side as my helper;
I shall look in triumph on those who hate me.

It is better to take refuge in the Lord
than to trust in man.
It is better to take refuge in the Lord
than to trust in princes.

All nations surrounded me;
in the name of the Lord I cut them off!
They surrounded me, surrounded me on every side;
in the name of the Lord I cut them off!
They surrounded me like bees;
they went out like a fire among thorns;
in the name of the Lord I cut them off!
I was pushed hard,[1] so that I was falling,
but the Lord helped me.

The Lord is my strength and my song;
he has become my salvation.

15 Glad songs of salvation
are in the tents of the righteous:
"The right hand of the Lord does valiantly,
16 the right hand of the Lord exalts,
the right hand of the Lord does valiantly!"

17 I shall not die, but I shall live,
and recount the deeds of the Lord.
18 The Lord has disciplined me severely,
but he has not given me over to death.

19 Open to me the gates of righteousness,
that I may enter through them
and give thanks to the Lord.
20 This is the gate of the Lord;
the righteous shall enter through it.
21 I thank you that you have answered me
and have become my salvation.
22 The stone that the builders rejected
has become the cornerstone.[2]
23 This is the Lord's doing;
it is marvelous in our eyes.
24 This is the day that the Lord has made;
let us rejoice and be glad in it.

25 Save us, we pray, O Lord!
O Lord, we pray, give us success!

26 Blessed is he who comes in the name of the Lord!
We bless you from the house of the Lord.
27 The Lord is God,
and he has made his light to shine upon us.
Bind the festal sacrifice with cords,
up to the horns of the altar!

28 You are my God, and I will give thanks to you;
you are my God; I will extol you.
29 Oh give thanks to the Lord, for he is good;
for his steadfast love endures forever!

Your Word Is a Lamp to My Feet

Aleph

119[3] Blessed are those whose way is blameless,
who walk in the law of the Lord!

[1] Hebrew You (that is, the enemy) pushed me hard [2] Hebrew the head of the corner [3] This psalm is an acrostic poem of twenty-two stanzas, following the letters of the Hebrew alphabet; within a stanza, each verse begins with the same Hebrew letter

2 Blessed are those who keep his testi-
    monies,
  who seek him with their whole
   heart,
3 who also do no wrong,
  but walk in his ways!
4 You have commanded your precepts
  to be kept diligently.
5 Oh that my ways may be steadfast
  in keeping your statutes!
6 Then I shall not be put to shame,
  having my eyes fixed on all your
   commandments.
7 I will praise you with an upright heart,
  when I learn your righteous rules.[1]
8 I will keep your statutes;
  do not utterly forsake me!

Beth

9 How can a young man keep his way
  pure?
  By guarding it according to your
   word.
10 With my whole heart I seek you;
  let me not wander from your commandments!
11 I have stored up your word in my
  heart,
  that I might not sin against you.
12 Blessed are you, O Lord;
  teach me your statutes!
13 With my lips I declare
  all the rules[2] of your mouth.
14 In the way of your testimonies
  I delight
  as much as in all riches.
15 I will meditate on your precepts
  and fix my eyes on your ways.
16 I will delight in your statutes;
  I will not forget your word.

Gimel

17 Deal bountifully with your servant,
  that I may live and keep your word.
18 Open my eyes, that I may behold
  wondrous things out of your law.
19 I am a sojourner on the earth;
  hide not your commandments
   from me!
20 My soul is consumed with longing
  for your rules[3] at all times.
21 You rebuke the insolent, accursed
  ones,
  who wander from your commandments.

22 Take away from me scorn and contempt,
  for I have kept your testimonies.
23 Even though princes sit plotting
  against me,
  your servant will meditate on you
   statutes.
24 Your testimonies are my delight;
  they are my counselors.

Daleth

25 My soul clings to the dust;
  give me life according to your wor
26 When I told of my ways, you
  answered me;
  teach me your statutes!
27 Make me understand the way of you
  precepts,
  and I will meditate on your wondrous works.
28 My soul melts away for sorrow;
  strengthen me according to your
   word!
29 Put false ways far from me
  and graciously teach me your law!
30 I have chosen the way of faithfulnes
  I set your rules before me.
31 I cling to your testimonies, O Lord;
  let me not be put to shame!
32 I will run in the way of your commandments
  when you enlarge my heart![4]

He

33 Teach me, O Lord, the way of your
  statutes;
  and I will keep it to the end.[5]
34 Give me understanding, that I may
  keep your law
  and observe it with my whole hear
35 Lead me in the path of your commandments,
  for I delight in it.
36 Incline my heart to your testimonies
  and not to selfish gain!
37 Turn my eyes from looking at worth
  less things;
  and give me life in your ways.
38 Confirm to your servant your promise
  that you may be feared.
39 Turn away the reproach that I dread
  for your rules are good.
40 Behold, I long for your precepts;
  in your righteousness give me life!

[1] Or *your just and righteous decrees; also verses 62, 106, 160, 164* [2] Or *all the just decrees* [3] Or *your just decrees; also verses 30, 39, 43; 52, 75, 102, 108, 137, 156, 175* [4] Or *for you set my heart free* [5] Or *keep it as my reward*

Waw

Let your steadfast love come to me,
O Lord,
  your salvation according to your
  promise;
then shall I have an answer for him
  who taunts me,
  for I trust in your word.
And take not the word of truth
  utterly out of my mouth,
  for my hope is in your rules.
I will keep your law continually,
  forever and ever,
and I shall walk in a wide place,
  for I have sought your precepts.
I will also speak of your testimonies
  before kings
  and shall not be put to shame,
for I find my delight in your commandments,
  which I love.
I will lift up my hands toward your
  commandments, which I love,
  and I will meditate on your statutes.

Zayin

Remember your word to your servant,
  in which you have made me hope.
This is my comfort in my affliction,
  that your promise gives me life.

51 The insolent utterly deride me,
  but I do not turn away from your
  law.
52 When I think of your rules from of old,
  I take comfort, O Lord.
53 Hot indignation seizes me because of
  the wicked,
  who forsake your law.
54 Your statutes have been my songs
  in the house of my sojourning.
55 I remember your name in the night,
  O Lord,
  and keep your law.
56 This blessing has fallen to me,
  that I have kept your precepts.

Heth

57 The Lord is my portion;
  I promise to keep your words.
58 I entreat your favor with all my heart;
  be gracious to me according to
  your promise.
59 When I think on my ways,
  I turn my feet to your testimonies;
60 I hasten and do not delay
  to keep your commandments.
61 Though the cords of the wicked
  ensnare me,
  I do not forget your law.

Know True Happiness

verses to read
Psalm 119:33–40

Do your feelings control you? Are they your master? Your experiences and how you feel about them should never be your only guide in life. Moods, emotions, and feelings can be misleading. All they talk about is "me this" and "me that." They aren't focused on God. As a believer, you should never let your feelings get the better of your faith. Worry, fear, and loss of self-control can all be signs of a life that worships feelings instead of the Father.

How can you make decisions and take action based on faith in God instead of feelings? You have to learn to see past what you're experiencing right now and look to the Word of God. Just as people who are unable to see must feel for walls to guide them and obstacles to avoid as they walk, you have to steer clear of the obstacles in your path and instead reach out for what you know to be true and solid. Take your eyes off of the things that weaken your emotional state and draw you away from truth. You were meant to be a slave not to feelings but to the one true God. Trust God's written instructions to you—they aren't for show or just for reassurance but for guidance and direction. When your feelings falter, his Word will not.

62 At midnight I rise to praise you,
  because of your righteous rules.
63 I am a companion of all who fear you,
  of those who keep your precepts.
64 The earth, O Lord, is full of your
    steadfast love;
  teach me your statutes!

Teth

65 You have dealt well with your servant,
  O Lord, according to your word.
66 Teach me good judgment and knowl-
    edge,
  for I believe in your command-
    ments.
67 Before I was afflicted I went astray,
  but now I keep your word.
68 You are good and do good;
  teach me your statutes.
69 The insolent smear me with lies,
  but with my whole heart I keep
    your precepts;
70 their heart is unfeeling like fat,
  but I delight in your law.
71 It is good for me that I was afflicted,
  that I might learn your statutes.
72 The law of your mouth is better
    to me
  than thousands of gold and silver
    pieces.

Yodh

73 Your hands have made and fashioned
    me;
  give me understanding that I may
    learn your commandments.
74 Those who fear you shall see me and
    rejoice,
  because I have hoped in your word.
75 I know, O Lord, that your rules are
    righteous,
  and that in faithfulness you have
    afflicted me.
76 Let your steadfast love comfort me
  according to your promise to your
    servant.
77 Let your mercy come to me, that
    I may live;
  for your law is my delight.
78 Let the insolent be put to shame,
  because they have wronged me
    with falsehood;
  as for me, I will meditate on your
    precepts.

79 Let those who fear you turn to me,
  that they may know your testimo-
    nies.
80 May my heart be blameless in your
    statutes,
  that I may not be put to shame!

Kaph

81 My soul longs for your salvation;
  I hope in your word.
82 My eyes long for your promise;
  I ask, "When will you comfort me?"
83 For I have become like a wineskin in
    the smoke,
  yet I have not forgotten your stat-
    utes.
84 How long must your servant endure?[1]
  When will you judge those who
    persecute me?
85 The insolent have dug pitfalls for me;
  they do not live according to your
    law.
86 All your commandments are sure;
  they persecute me with falsehood;
    help me!
87 They have almost made an end of me
    on earth,
  but I have not forsaken your pre-
    cepts.
88 In your steadfast love give me life,
  that I may keep the testimonies of
    your mouth.

Lamedh

89 Forever, O Lord, your word
  is firmly fixed in the heavens.
90 Your faithfulness endures to all gen-
    erations;
  you have established the earth,
    and it stands fast.
91 By your appointment they stand this
    day,
  for all things are your servants.
92 If your law had not been my delight,
  I would have perished in my afflic-
    tion.
93 I will never forget your precepts,
  for by them you have given me life.
94 I am yours; save me,
  for I have sought your precepts.
95 The wicked lie in wait to destroy me,
  but I consider your testimonies.
96 I have seen a limit to all perfection,
  but your commandment is exceed-
    ingly broad.

[1] Hebrew *How many are the days of your servant?*

Mem

97 Oh how I love your law!
It is my meditation all the day.

98 Your commandment makes me wiser
than my enemies,
for it is ever with me.

99 I have more understanding than all
my teachers,
for your testimonies are my meditation.

100 I understand more than the aged,[1]
for I keep your precepts.

101 I hold back my feet from every evil
way,
in order to keep your word.

102 I do not turn aside from your rules,
for you have taught me.

103 How sweet are your words to my
taste,
sweeter than honey to my mouth!

104 Through your precepts I get understanding;
therefore I hate every false way.

Nun

105 Your word is a lamp to my feet
and a light to my path.

106 I have sworn an oath and confirmed
it,
to keep your righteous rules.

107 I am severely afflicted;
give me life, O Lord, according to
your word!

108 Accept my freewill offerings of
praise, O Lord,
and teach me your rules.

109 I hold my life in my hand continually,
but I do not forget your law.

110 The wicked have laid a snare for me,
but I do not stray from your precepts.

111 Your testimonies are my heritage
forever,
for they are the joy of my heart.

112 I incline my heart to perform your
statutes
forever, to the end.[2]

Samekh

113 I hate the double-minded,
but I love your law.

114 You are my hiding place and my
shield;
I hope in your word.

115 Depart from me, you evildoers,
that I may keep the commandments of my God.

116 Uphold me according to your promise, that I may live,
and let me not be put to shame in
my hope!

117 Hold me up, that I may be safe
and have regard for your statutes
continually!

118 You spurn all who go astray from
your statutes,
for their cunning is in vain.

119 All the wicked of the earth you dis-
card like dross,
therefore I love your testimonies.

120 My flesh trembles for fear of you,
and I am afraid of your judgments.

Ayin

121 I have done what is just and right;
do not leave me to my oppressors.

122 Give your servant a pledge of good;
let not the insolent oppress me.

123 My eyes long for your salvation
and for the fulfillment of your
righteous promise.

124 Deal with your servant according to
your steadfast love,
and teach me your statutes.

125 I am your servant; give me understanding,
that I may know your testimonies!

126 It is time for the Lord to act,
for your law has been broken.

127 Therefore I love your commandments
above gold, above fine gold.

128 Therefore I consider all your precepts to be right;
I hate every false way.

Pe

129 Your testimonies are wonderful;
therefore my soul keeps them.

130 The unfolding of your words gives
light;
it imparts understanding to the
simple.

131 I open my mouth and pant,
because I long for your commandments.

---

[1] Or the elders [2] Or statutes; the reward is eternal

132 Turn to me and be gracious to me,
  as is your way with those who love
    your name.
133 Keep steady my steps according to
    your promise,
  and let no iniquity get dominion
    over me.
134 Redeem me from man's oppression,
  that I may keep your precepts.
135 Make your face shine upon your
    servant,
  and teach me your statutes.
136 My eyes shed streams of tears,
  because people do not keep your
    law.

TSADHE

137 Righteous are you, O LORD,
  and right are your rules.
138 You have appointed your testimonies
    in righteousness
  and in all faithfulness.
139 My zeal consumes me,
  because my foes forget your
    words.

140 Your promise is well tried,
  and your servant loves it.
141 I am small and despised,
  yet I do not forget your precepts.
142 Your righteousness is righteous
    forever,
  and your law is true.
143 Trouble and anguish have found me
    out,
  but your commandments are my
    delight.
144 Your testimonies are righteous for-
    ever;
  give me understanding that I may
    live.

QOPH

145 With my whole heart I cry; answer
    me, O LORD!
  I will keep your statutes.
146 I call to you; save me,
  that I may observe your testimo-
    nies.
147 I rise before dawn and cry for help;
  I hope in your words.

Know God

verses to read
Psalm 119:129–136

Some people say that if things are going great in your life, look out, because something bad is coming. Sounds logical, right? No one has a perfect life without any
problems, so it makes sense that when it's been good for a while, something bad
must have to happen to keep up the law of averages. And besides, God promises
that we're going to have trials in this life, so we know bad stuff is going to happen.
But does that mean that you always have to be on alert for the next bad thing
that's about to happen? No way!

Expecting the worst is not trusting the God who promises to care for and protect
you. He promises to never abandon you or leave you and to use everything in your
life for your good if you are only willing to let him do that. That means that even
when bad things happen, they are ultimately for your good because of what he's
going to do with them.

So if your life is going great today, don't worry about tomorrow (see Matt.
6:25–34). Fear and worry are sinful, not holy. Don't let anyone scare you into
thinking that, if life is good, you'd better prepare for the worst. That cheapens the
gifts of God. Instead, learn to be content with whatever you have, enjoying what
he gives you and what he takes away. Fearfulness is never an acceptable character
trait for a believer unless it's the fear of the Lord, which means that nothing scares
you except walking away from him.

48 My eyes are awake before the
    watches of the night,
      that I may meditate on your prom-
      ise.
49 Hear my voice according to your
    steadfast love;
      O Lord, according to your justice
      give me life.
50 They draw near who persecute me
    with evil purpose;
      they are far from your law.
51 But you are near, O Lord,
    and all your commandments are
      true.
52 Long have I known from your testi-
    monies
      that you have founded them forever.

Resh

53 Look on my affliction and deliver me,
    for I do not forget your law.
54 Plead my cause and redeem me;
    give me life according to your
      promise!
55 Salvation is far from the wicked,
    for they do not seek your statutes.
56 Great is your mercy, O Lord;
    give me life according to your rules.
57 Many are my persecutors and my
    adversaries,
      but I do not swerve from your
      testimonies.
58 I look at the faithless with disgust,
    because they do not keep your
      commands.
59 Consider how I love your precepts!
    Give me life according to your
      steadfast love.
60 The sum of your word is truth,
    and every one of your righteous
      rules endures forever.

Sin and Shin

61 Princes persecute me without cause,
    but my heart stands in awe of your
      words.
62 I rejoice at your word
    like one who finds great spoil.
63 I hate and abhor falsehood,
    but I love your law.
64 Seven times a day I praise you
    for your righteous rules.
65 Great peace have those who love
    your law;
      nothing can make them stumble.
66 I hope for your salvation, O Lord,
    and I do your commandments.

167 My soul keeps your testimonies;
    I love them exceedingly.
168 I keep your precepts and testimonies,
    for all my ways are before you.

Taw

169 Let my cry come before you, O Lord;
    give me understanding according
      to your word!
170 Let my plea come before you;
    deliver me according to your word.
171 My lips will pour forth praise,
    for you teach me your statutes.
172 My tongue will sing of your word,
    for all your commandments are
      right.
173 Let your hand be ready to help me,
    for I have chosen your precepts.
174 I long for your salvation, O Lord,
    and your law is my delight.
175 Let my soul live and praise you,
    and let your rules help me.
176 I have gone astray like a lost sheep;
    seek your servant,
      for I do not forget your command-
      ments.

Deliver Me, O Lord

120 A Song of Ascents.
In my distress I called to the
    Lord,
    and he answered me.
2 Deliver me, O Lord,
    from lying lips,
    from a deceitful tongue.

3 What shall be given to you,
    and what more shall be done to you,
    you deceitful tongue?
4 A warrior's sharp arrows,
    with glowing coals of the broom
      tree!

5 Woe to me, that I sojourn in Meshech,
    that I dwell among the tents of
      Kedar!
6 Too long have I had my dwelling
    among those who hate peace.
7 I am for peace,
    but when I speak, they are for war!

My Help Comes from the Lord

121 A Song of Ascents.
I lift up my eyes to the hills.
    From where does my help come?
2 My help comes from the Lord,
    who made heaven and earth.

³ He will not let your foot be moved;
   he who keeps you will not slum-
   ber.

⁴ Behold, he who keeps Israel
   will neither slumber nor sleep.

⁵ The LORD is your keeper;
   the LORD is your shade on your
   right hand.

⁶ The sun shall not strike you by day,
   nor the moon by night.

⁷ The LORD will keep you from all evil;
   he will keep your life.

⁸ The LORD will keep
   your going out and your coming in
   from this time forth and forevermore.

Let Us Go to the House of the LORD

122 A SONG OF ASCENTS. OF DAVID.
   I was glad when they said to
   me,
   "Let us go to the house of the LORD!"

¹ Or *as a testimony for*

² Our feet have been standing
   within your gates, O Jerusalem!

³ Jerusalem—built as a city
   that is bound firmly together,

⁴ to which the tribes go up,
   the tribes of the LORD,
   as was decreed for¹ Israel,
   to give thanks to the name of the
   LORD.

⁵ There thrones for judgment were
   set,
   the thrones of the house of David.

⁶ Pray for the peace of Jerusalem!
   "May they be secure who love you!

⁷ Peace be within your walls
   and security within your towers!"

⁸ For my brothers and companions'
   sake
   I will say, "Peace be within you!"

⁹ For the sake of the house of the LORD
   our God,
   I will seek your good.

verses to read
Psalm 122

Are you glad when you get to go to the house of the Lord? Or is it something you have to do but aren't really excited about? Going to church shouldn't be something a believer does begrudgingly. Church is the place where you get to worship God like you will worship him in heaven, with a chorus of voices. Church is a place where you get to learn what pleases him, talk about how great he is, hear about the amazing things he's done, and read what he has to say. Church is the place where you get to be with others who think the same way as you do about God and where you can be free to praise him and give him thanks. So why is it so hard to get up in the morning and get out the door? Why do you feel so bummed about taking a day to do church?

The most common answer is, "I'm just not getting anything out of it." But that answer sounds like church is all about what you get out of it and not what the Lord gets. Change your way of thinking about church and maybe you'll change the way you feel about it. Instead of thinking of church as being only for your benefit, think of it as also being for God's benefit. Go there to give him your heart, your voice, your presence. Go there to serve him by loving other members of the faith. Go there to be taught how to obey God and how to minister to the lost. Go there to be trained to serve. Go to church for the one whose church it is, and church will no longer be a pain but a blast. When you make it all about him, it can't help but be all good.

Our Eyes Look to the Lord Our God

123 A Song of Ascents.
To you I lift up my eyes,
O you who are enthroned in the
heavens!
2 Behold, as the eyes of servants
look to the hand of their master,
as the eyes of a maidservant
to the hand of her mistress,
so our eyes look to the Lord our God,
till he has mercy upon us.

3 Have mercy upon us, O Lord, have
mercy upon us,
for we have had more than enough
of contempt.
4 Our soul has had more than enough
of the scorn of those who are at
ease,
of the contempt of the proud.

Our Help Is in the Name of the Lord

124 A Song of Ascents. Of David.
If it had not been the Lord
who was on our side—
let Israel now say—
2 if it had not been the Lord who was
on our side
when people rose up against us,
3 then they would have swallowed us
up alive,
when their anger was kindled
against us;
4 then the flood would have swept us
away,
the torrent would have gone over
us;
5 then over us would have gone
the raging waters.

6 Blessed be the Lord,
who has not given us
as prey to their teeth!
7 We have escaped like a bird
from the snare of the fowlers;
the snare is broken,
and we have escaped!

8 Our help is in the name of the Lord,
who made heaven and earth.

The Lord Surrounds His People

125 A Song of Ascents.
Those who trust in the Lord
are like Mount Zion,
which cannot be moved, but
abides forever.

2 As the mountains surround Jerusalem,
so the Lord surrounds his people,
from this time forth and forevermore.
3 For the scepter of wickedness shall
not rest
on the land allotted to the righteous,
lest the righteous stretch out
their hands to do wrong.
4 Do good, O Lord, to those who are
good,
and to those who are upright in
their hearts!
5 But those who turn aside to their
crooked ways
the Lord will lead away with evildoers!
Peace be upon Israel!

Restore Our Fortunes, O Lord

126 A Song of Ascents.
When the Lord restored the
fortunes of Zion,
we were like those who dream.
2 Then our mouth was filled with
laughter,
and our tongue with shouts of joy;
then they said among the nations,
"The Lord has done great things for
them."
3 The Lord has done great things for us;
we are glad.

4 Restore our fortunes, O Lord,
like streams in the Negeb!
5 Those who sow in tears
shall reap with shouts of joy!
6 He who goes out weeping,
bearing the seed for sowing,
shall come home with shouts of joy,
bringing his sheaves with him.

Unless the Lord Builds the House

127 A Song of Ascents. Of Solomon.
Unless the Lord builds the
house,
those who build it labor in vain.
Unless the Lord watches over the
city,
the watchman stays awake in vain.
2 It is in vain that you rise up early
and go late to rest,
eating the bread of anxious toil;
for he gives to his beloved sleep.

3 Behold, children are a heritage from
   the Lord,
     the fruit of the womb a reward.
4 Like arrows in the hand of a warrior
     are the children[1] of one's youth.
5 Blessed is the man
     who fills his quiver with them!
   He shall not be put to shame
     when he speaks with his enemies
       in the gate.[2]

Blessed Is Everyone Who Fears the Lord

128
A Song of Ascents.
Blessed is everyone who fears
   the Lord,
     who walks in his ways!
2 You shall eat the fruit of the labor of
     your hands;
       you shall be blessed, and it shall be
         well with you.
3 Your wife will be like a fruitful vine
     within your house;
       your children will be like olive shoots
         around your table.
4 Behold, thus shall the man be blessed
     who fears the Lord.
5 The Lord bless you from Zion!
   May you see the prosperity of
     Jerusalem
       all the days of your life!
6 May you see your children's children!
   Peace be upon Israel!

They Have Afflicted Me from My Youth

129
A Song of Ascents.
"Greatly[3] have they afflicted me
   from my youth"—
     let Israel now say—
2 "Greatly have they afflicted me from
     my youth,
       yet they have not prevailed against
         me.
3 The plowers plowed upon my back;
     they made long their furrows."
4 The Lord is righteous;
     he has cut the cords of the wicked.
5 May all who hate Zion
     be put to shame and turned back-
       ward!
6 Let them be like the grass on the
     housetops,
       which withers before it grows up,

7 with which the reaper does not fill
     his hand
       nor the binder of sheaves his arms,
8 nor do those who pass by say,
   "The blessing of the Lord be upon
     you!
   We bless you in the name of the
     Lord!"

My Soul Waits for the Lord

130
A Song of Ascents.
Out of the depths I cry to you,
   O Lord!
2 O Lord, hear my voice!
   Let your ears be attentive
     to the voice of my pleas for mercy!
3 If you, O Lord, should mark iniqui-
     ties,
   O Lord, who could stand?
4 But with you there is forgiveness,
     that you may be feared.
5 I wait for the Lord, my soul waits,
     and in his word I hope;
6 my soul waits for the Lord
     more than watchmen for the
       morning,
     more than watchmen for the
       morning.
7 O Israel, hope in the Lord!
   For with the Lord there is stead-
     fast love,
       and with him is plentiful redemp-
         tion.
8 And he will redeem Israel
     from all his iniquities.

I Have Calmed and Quieted My Soul

131
A Song of Ascents. Of David.
O Lord, my heart is not lifted
   up;
     my eyes are not raised too high;
   I do not occupy myself with things
     too great and too marvelous for me.
2 But I have calmed and quieted my
     soul,
       like a weaned child with its mother;
   like a weaned child is my soul
     within me.
3 O Israel, hope in the Lord
     from this time forth and forever-
       more.

[1] Or sons [2] Or They shall not be put to shame when they speak with their enemies in the gate [3] Or Often; also verse 2

he LORD Has Chosen Zion

132
A SONG OF ASCENTS.
Remember, O LORD, in David's
favor,
all the hardships he endured,

2 how he swore to the LORD
and vowed to the Mighty One of
Jacob,

3 "I will not enter my house
or get into my bed,

4 I will not give sleep to my eyes
or slumber to my eyelids,

5 until I find a place for the LORD,
a dwelling place for the Mighty
One of Jacob."

6 Behold, we heard of it in Ephrathah;
we found it in the fields of Jaar.

7 "Let us go to his dwelling place;
let us worship at his footstool!"

8 Arise, O LORD, and go to your resting
place,
you and the ark of your might.

9 Let your priests be clothed with
righteousness,
and let your saints shout for joy.

10 For the sake of your servant David,
do not turn away the face of your
anointed one.

11 The LORD swore to David a sure oath
from which he will not turn back:
"One of the sons of your body[1]
I will set on your throne.

12 If your sons keep my covenant
and my testimonies that I shall
teach them,
their sons also forever
shall sit on your throne."

13 For the LORD has chosen Zion;
he has desired it for his dwelling
place:

14 "This is my resting place forever;
here I will dwell, for I have desired
it.

15 I will abundantly bless her provisions;
I will satisfy her poor with bread.

16 Her priests I will clothe with salvation,
and her saints will shout for joy.

17 There I will make a horn to sprout
for David;
I have prepared a lamp for my
anointed.

18 His enemies I will clothe with shame,
but on him his crown will shine."

When Brothers Dwell in Unity

133
A SONG OF ASCENTS. OF DAVID.
Behold, how good and pleasant it is
when brothers dwell in unity![2]

2 It is like the precious oil on the head,
running down on the beard,
on the beard of Aaron,
running down on the collar of his
robes!

3 It is like the dew of Hermon,
which falls on the mountains of
Zion!
For there the LORD has commanded
the blessing,
life forevermore.

Come, Bless the Lord

134
A SONG OF ASCENTS.
Come, bless the LORD, all you
servants of the LORD,
who stand by night in the house of
the LORD!

2 Lift up your hands to the holy place
and bless the LORD!

3 May the LORD bless you from Zion,
he who made heaven and earth!

Your Name, O LORD, Endures Forever

135
Praise the LORD!
Praise the name of the LORD,
give praise, O servants of the LORD,

2 who stand in the house of the LORD,
in the courts of the house of our
God!

3 Praise the LORD, for the LORD is good;
sing to his name, for it is pleasant![3]

4 For the LORD has chosen Jacob for
himself,
Israel as his own possession.

5 For I know that the LORD is great,
and that our Lord is above all gods.

6 Whatever the LORD pleases, he does,
in heaven and on earth,
in the seas and all deeps.

7 He it is who makes the clouds rise at
the end of the earth,
who makes lightnings for the rain
and brings forth the wind from his
storehouses.

[1] Hebrew of your fruit of the womb [2] Or dwell together [3] Or for he is beautiful

8   He it was who struck down the first-
    born of Egypt,
        both of man and of beast;
9   who in your midst, O Egypt,
        sent signs and wonders
        against Pharaoh and all his ser-
        vants;
10 who struck down many nations
        and killed mighty kings,
11 Sihon, king of the Amorites,
        and Og, king of Bashan,
        and all the kingdoms of Canaan,
12 and gave their land as a heritage,
        a heritage to his people Israel.

13 Your name, O Lord, endures forever,
        your renown,[1] O Lord, throughout
        all ages.
14 For the Lord will vindicate his people
        and have compassion on his ser-
        vants.

15 The idols of the nations are silver
        and gold,
        the work of human hands.
16 They have mouths, but do not speak;
        they have eyes, but do not see;
17 they have ears, but do not hear,
        nor is there any breath in their
        mouths.
18 Those who make them become like
        them,
        so do all who trust in them.

19 O house of Israel, bless the Lord!
        O house of Aaron, bless the Lord!
20 O house of Levi, bless the Lord!
        You who fear the Lord, bless the
        Lord!
21 Blessed be the Lord from Zion,
        he who dwells in Jerusalem!
        Praise the Lord!

His Steadfast Love Endures Forever

136
1   Give thanks to the Lord, for he
    is good,
        for his steadfast love endures
        forever.
2   Give thanks to the God of gods,
        for his steadfast love endures
        forever.
3   Give thanks to the Lord of lords,
        for his steadfast love endures
        forever;

4   to him who alone does great won-
    ders,
        for his steadfast love endures
        forever;
5   to him who by understanding made
        the heavens,
        for his steadfast love endures
        forever;
6   to him who spread out the earth
        above the waters,
        for his steadfast love endures
        forever;
7   to him who made the great lights,
        for his steadfast love endures
        forever;
8   the sun to rule over the day,
        for his steadfast love endures
        forever;
9   the moon and stars to rule over the
        night,
        for his steadfast love endures
        forever;

10 to him who struck down the first-
    born of Egypt,
        for his steadfast love endures
        forever;
11 and brought Israel out from among
        them,
        for his steadfast love endures
        forever;
12 with a strong hand and an out-
        stretched arm,
        for his steadfast love endures
        forever;
13 to him who divided the Red Sea in
        two,
        for his steadfast love endures
        forever;
14 and made Israel pass through the
        midst of it,
        for his steadfast love endures
        forever;
15 but overthrew[2] Pharaoh and his host
        in the Red Sea,
        for his steadfast love endures
        forever;
16 to him who led his people through
        the wilderness,
        for his steadfast love endures
        forever;
17 to him who struck down great kings,
        for his steadfast love endures
        forever;

[1] Or remembrance [2] Hebrew shook off

8 and killed mighty kings,
  for his steadfast love endures
    forever;

9 Sihon, king of the Amorites,
  for his steadfast love endures
    forever;

0 and Og, king of Bashan,
  for his steadfast love endures
    forever;

¹ and gave their land as a heritage,
  for his steadfast love endures
    forever;

² a heritage to Israel his servant,
  for his steadfast love endures
    forever.

³ It is he who remembered us in our
    low estate,
  for his steadfast love endures
    forever;

⁴ and rescued us from our foes,
  for his steadfast love endures
    forever;

²5 he who gives food to all flesh,
  for his steadfast love endures
    forever.

²6 Give thanks to the God of heaven,
  for his steadfast love endures
    forever.

How Shall We Sing the Lord's Song?

137 By the waters of Babylon,
       there we sat down and wept,
  when we remembered Zion.

2 On the willows¹ there
  we hung up our lyres.

3 For there our captors
    required of us songs,
  and our tormentors, mirth, saying,
    "Sing us one of the songs of Zion!"

4 How shall we sing the Lord's song
    in a foreign land?

5 If I forget you, O Jerusalem,
    let my right hand forget its skill!

6 Let my tongue stick to the roof of my
      mouth,
    if I do not remember you,
  if I do not set Jerusalem
    above my highest joy!

7 Remember, O Lord, against the
      Edomites
  the day of Jerusalem,

how they said, "Lay it bare, lay it bare,
  down to its foundations!"

8 O daughter of Babylon, doomed to be
    destroyed,
  blessed shall he be who repays you
    with what you have done to us!

9 Blessed shall he be who takes your
    little ones
  and dashes them against the rock!

Give Thanks to the Lord

138 Of David.
       I give you thanks, O Lord, with
         my whole heart;
  before the gods I sing your praise;

2 I bow down toward your holy temple
  and give thanks to your name for
      your steadfast love and your
      faithfulness,
  for you have exalted above all things
    your name and your word.²

3 On the day I called, you answered me;
  my strength of soul you increased.³

4 All the kings of the earth shall give
      you thanks, O Lord,
  for they have heard the words of
      your mouth,

5 and they shall sing of the ways of the
      Lord,
  for great is the glory of the Lord.

6 For though the Lord is high, he
      regards the lowly,
  but the haughty he knows from afar.

7 Though I walk in the midst of trouble,
    you preserve my life;
  you stretch out your hand against
      the wrath of my enemies,
    and your right hand delivers me.

8 The Lord will fulfill his purpose for
      me;
  your steadfast love, O Lord,
    endures forever.
  Do not forsake the work of your
    hands.

Search Me, O God, and Know My Heart

139 To the choirmaster. A Psalm of
       David.

1 O Lord, you have searched me and
    known me!

2 You know when I sit down and when
    I rise up;
  you discern my thoughts from afar.

¹ Or poplars ² Or you have exalted your word above all your name ³ Hebrew you made me bold in my soul with strength

A Prayer for...

MORNING TIME

Compassionate Lord, your mercies have brought me to another day. My gifts will be in vain if I don't grow in grace, increase in knowledge, and ripen for spiritual harvest. Today, let me know you as you are, love you supremely, serve you wholly, admire you fully. Through your loving kindness let my will respond to you, knowing that the power to obey is not in me but that your free love alone enables me to serve you. Here is my empty heart; overflow it with your best gifts. Here is my ignorance; chase away its bliss, and replace it with wisdom.

O ever-watchful Shepherd, lead, guide, help me today. Without your hand to guide me, I mess up and wander off. Hedge up my path so that I don't wander off into sinful fun and indulge in its addictive flavor. Direct my feet so that I won't get entangled in Satan's secret snares or fall into his hidden traps. Defend me from people who attack, from evil circumstances, and even from myself. My enemies are a part of my nature; they cling to me like my skin. I can't get away from their contact. When I stand up and when I sit down, they shackle me. They lure me continually to sin. My enemy is close by. Come with almighty power and throw them out, and destroy every bit of sin that is in me today.

Amen.

3 You search out my path and my lying down
   and are acquainted with all my ways.
4 Even before a word is on my tongue,
   behold, O Lord, you know it altogether.
5 You hem me in, behind and before,
   and lay your hand upon me.

6 Such knowledge is too wonderful for me;
   it is high; I cannot attain it.

7 Where shall I go from your Spirit?
   Or where shall I flee from your presence?
8 If I ascend to heaven, you are there!
   If I make my bed in Sheol, you are there!
9 If I take the wings of the morning
   and dwell in the uttermost parts of the sea,
10 even there your hand shall lead me,
    and your right hand shall hold me.
11 If I say, "Surely the darkness shall cover me,
    and the light about me be night,"
12 even the darkness is not dark to you;
    the night is bright as the day,
    for darkness is as light with you.

13 For you formed my inward parts;
    you knitted me together in my mother's womb.
14 I praise you, for I am fearfully and wonderfully made.[1]
   Wonderful are your works;
    my soul knows it very well.
15 My frame was not hidden from you,
   when I was being made in secret,
    intricately woven in the depths of the earth.
16 Your eyes saw my unformed substance;
   in your book were written, every one of them,
    the days that were formed for me,
    when as yet there was none of them.

17 How precious to me are your thoughts, O God!
    How vast is the sum of them!
18 If I would count them, they are more than the sand.
    I awake, and I am still with you.

19 Oh that you would slay the wicked, O God!
    O men of blood, depart from me!
20 They speak against you with malicious intent;
    your enemies take your name in vain.[2]

[1] Or for I am fearfully set apart [2] Hebrew lacks your name

1 Do I not hate those who hate you,
       O Lord?
    And do I not loathe those who rise
       up against you?
2 I hate them with complete hatred;
    I count them my enemies.

3 Search me, O God, and know my
       heart!
    Try me and know my thoughts![1]
4 And see if there be any grievous way
       in me,
    and lead me in the way everlasting![2]

Deliver Me, O Lord, from Evil Men

140
To the choirmaster. A Psalm of David.

1 Deliver me, O Lord, from evil men;
    preserve me from violent men,
2 who plan evil things in their heart
    and stir up wars continually.
3 They make their tongue sharp as a
       serpent's,
    and under their lips is the venom
       of asps.   *Selah*

4 Guard me, O Lord, from the hands of
       the wicked;
    preserve me from violent men,
    who have planned to trip up my
       feet.
5 The arrogant have hidden a trap for
       me,
    and with cords they have spread a
       net;[3]
    beside the way they have set
       snares for me.   *Selah*

6 I say to the Lord, You are my God;
    give ear to the voice of my pleas
       for mercy, O Lord!
7 O Lord, my Lord, the strength of my
       salvation,
    you have covered my head in the
       day of battle.
8 Grant not, O Lord, the desires of the
       wicked;
    do not further their[4] evil plot, or
       they will be exalted!   *Selah*

9 As for the head of those who sur-
       round me,
    let the mischief of their lips over-
       whelm them!

10 Let burning coals fall upon them!
     Let them be cast into fire,
        into miry pits, no more to rise!
11 Let not the slanderer be established
        in the land;
     let evil hunt down the violent man
        speedily!

12 I know that the Lord will maintain
        the cause of the afflicted,
     and will execute justice for the
        needy.
13 Surely the righteous shall give thanks
        to your name;
     the upright shall dwell in your
        presence.

Give Ear to My Voice

141
A Psalm of David.
O Lord, I call upon you; hasten
        to me!
     Give ear to my voice when I call to
        you!
2 Let my prayer be counted as incense
        before you,
     and the lifting up of my hands as
        the evening sacrifice!

3 Set a guard, O Lord, over my mouth;
     keep watch over the door of my
        lips!
4 Do not let my heart incline to any evil,
     to busy myself with wicked deeds
  in company with men who work
        iniquity,
     and let me not eat of their delica-
        cies!

5 Let a righteous man strike me—it is
        a kindness;
     let him rebuke me—it is oil for my
        head;
     let my head not refuse it.
  Yet my prayer is continually against
        their evil deeds.
6 When their judges are thrown over
        the cliff,[5]
     then they shall hear my words, for
        they are pleasant.
7 As when one plows and breaks up
        the earth,
     so shall our bones be scattered at
        the mouth of Sheol.[6]

[1] Or *cares* [2] Or *in the ancient way* (compare Jeremiah 6:16) [3] Or *they have spread cords as a net* [4] Hebrew *his* [5] Or *When their judges fall into the hands of the Rock* [6] The meaning of the Hebrew in verses 6, 7 is uncertain

8 But my eyes are toward you, O GOD,
 my Lord;
  in you I seek refuge; leave me not
  defenseless![1]
9 Keep me from the trap that they have
 laid for me
  and from the snares of evildoers!
10 Let the wicked fall into their own nets,
 while I pass by safely.

You Are My Refuge

142 A MASKIL[2] OF DAVID, WHEN HE
 WAS IN THE CAVE. A PRAYER.

1 With my voice I cry out to the LORD;
  with my voice I plead for mercy to
  the LORD.
2 I pour out my complaint before him;
  I tell my trouble before him.

3 When my spirit faints within me,
  you know my way!
 In the path where I walk
  they have hidden a trap for me.
4 Look to the right and see:
  there is none who takes notice of
  me;
 no refuge remains to me;
  no one cares for my soul.

5 I cry to you, O LORD;
  I say, "You are my refuge,
  my portion in the land of the living."
6 Attend to my cry,
  for I am brought very low!
 Deliver me from my persecutors,
  for they are too strong for me!
7 Bring me out of prison,
  that I may give thanks to your
  name!
 The righteous will surround me,
  for you will deal bountifully with
  me.

My Soul Thirsts for You

143 A PSALM OF DAVID.
 Hear my prayer, O LORD;
  give ear to my pleas for mercy!
 In your faithfulness answer me, in
  your righteousness!
2 Enter not into judgment with your
 servant,
  for no one living is righteous
  before you.

3 For the enemy has pursued my soul;
  he has crushed my life to the
  ground;
 he has made me sit in darkness
  like those long dead.
4 Therefore my spirit faints within me;
  my heart within me is appalled.

5 I remember the days of old;
  I meditate on all that you have
  done;
 I ponder the work of your hands.
6 I stretch out my hands to you;
  my soul thirsts for you like a
  parched land.   *Selah*

7 Answer me quickly, O LORD!
  My spirit fails!
 Hide not your face from me,
  lest I be like those who go down to
  the pit.
8 Let me hear in the morning of your
  steadfast love,
  for in you I trust.
 Make me know the way I should go,
  for to you I lift up my soul.

9 Deliver me from my enemies, O LORD!
  I have fled to you for refuge.[3]
10 Teach me to do your will,
  for you are my God!
 Let your good Spirit lead me
  on level ground!

11 For your name's sake, O LORD, preserve my life!
  In your righteousness bring my
  soul out of trouble!
12 And in your steadfast love you will
  cut off my enemies,
  and you will destroy all the adversaries of my soul,
  for I am your servant.

My Rock and My Fortress

144 OF DAVID.
 Blessed be the LORD, my rock,
 who trains my hands for war,
  and my fingers for battle;
2 he is my steadfast love and my fortress,
  my stronghold and my deliverer,
 my shield and he in whom I take
  refuge,
  who subdues peoples[4] under me.

[1] Hebrew *refuge; do not pour out my life!* [2] Probably a musical or liturgical term [3] One Hebrew manuscript, Septuagint; most Hebrew manuscripts *To you I have covered* [4] Many Hebrew manuscripts, Dead Sea Scroll, Jerome, Syriac, Aquila; most Hebrew manuscripts *subdues my people*

A Prayer for...
STARTING THE DAY

Almighty God, as I start this day I commit my self, soul, body, tasks, and friends to you. Watch over, keep, guide, direct, sanctify, and bless me. Make my heart one with you. Mold me completely into the image of Jesus, like a potter molds clay. May my lips be a well-tuned instrument to sound your praise. Let those around see me living by your Spirit, trampling the world underfoot, refusing the lies of the world, being transformed by a renewed mind, wearing the full armor of God, shining as an always burning light, and showing holiness in everything I do. Don't let evil enter my thoughts, words, or hands. May I travel the dusty roads of life clean from spot or stain. In everything I do, let my affection be in heaven, my love fly upward in flames of fire, my gaze be fixed on unseen things, and my eyes be open to the emptiness, fragility, and mockery of earth and its pride. May I view all things in the mirror of eternity, waiting for the coming of my Lord, listening for the last trumpet call, finding hope in the new heaven and earth. Today, order all my communications according to your wisdom and for mutual good. Don't let me be used or use others. May I speak each word as if it were my last word and walk each step as if it were my final step. If my life should end today, let this be my best and holiest day ever.

Amen.

3 O Lord, what is man that you regard him,
   or the son of man that you think of him?
4 Man is like a breath;
   his days are like a passing shadow.

5 Bow your heavens, O Lord, and come down!
   Touch the mountains so that they smoke!
6 Flash forth the lightning and scatter them;
   send out your arrows and rout them!
7 Stretch out your hand from on high;
   rescue me and deliver me from the many waters,
   from the hand of foreigners,
8 whose mouths speak lies
   and whose right hand is a right hand of falsehood.

9 I will sing a new song to you, O God;
   upon a ten-stringed harp I will play to you,
10 who gives victory to kings,
   who rescues David his servant from the cruel sword.
11 Rescue me and deliver me
   from the hand of foreigners,
   whose mouths speak lies
   and whose right hand is a right hand of falsehood.

12 May our sons in their youth
   be like plants full grown,
   our daughters like corner pillars cut for the structure of a palace;
13 may our granaries be full,
   providing all kinds of produce;
   may our sheep bring forth thousands and ten thousands in our fields;
14 may our cattle be heavy with young,
   suffering no mishap or failure in bearing;[1]
   may there be no cry of distress in our streets!
15 Blessed are the people to whom such blessings fall!
   Blessed are the people whose God is the Lord!

Great Is the Lord
145 [2] A Song of Praise. Of David.
   I will extol you, my God and King,
   and bless your name forever and ever.
2 Every day I will bless you
   and praise your name forever and ever.

Hebrew *with no breaking in or going out* [2] This psalm is an acrostic poem, each verse beginning with the successive letters of the Hebrew alphabet

3 Great is the LORD, and greatly to be
   praised,
   and his greatness is unsearchable.

4 One generation shall commend your
   works to another,
   and shall declare your mighty acts.
5 On the glorious splendor of your
   majesty,
   and on your wondrous works,
   I will meditate.
6 They shall speak of the might of your
   awesome deeds,
   and I will declare your greatness.
7 They shall pour forth the fame of
   your abundant goodness
   and shall sing aloud of your righteousness.

8 The LORD is gracious and merciful,
   slow to anger and abounding in
   steadfast love.
9 The LORD is good to all,
   and his mercy is over all that he
   has made.

10 All your works shall give thanks to
   you, O LORD,
   and all your saints shall bless you!
11 They shall speak of the glory of your
   kingdom
   and tell of your power,
12 to make known to the children of
   man your[1] mighty deeds,
   and the glorious splendor of your
   kingdom.
13 Your kingdom is an everlasting kingdom,
   and your dominion endures
   throughout all generations.

   [The LORD is faithful in all his words
   and kind in all his works.][2]
14 The LORD upholds all who are falling
   and raises up all who are bowed
   down.
15 The eyes of all look to you,
   and you give them their food in
   due season.
16 You open your hand;
   you satisfy the desire of every living thing.
17 The LORD is righteous in all his ways
   and kind in all his works.

18 The LORD is near to all who call on
   him,
   to all who call on him in truth.
19 He fulfills the desire of those who
   fear him;
   he also hears their cry and saves
   them.
20 The LORD preserves all who love him,
   but all the wicked he will destroy.

21 My mouth will speak the praise of
   the LORD,
   and let all flesh bless his holy
   name forever and ever.

Put Not Your Trust in Princes

146
Praise the LORD!
Praise the LORD, O my soul!
2 I will praise the LORD as long as I live;
   I will sing praises to my God while
   I have my being.

3 Put not your trust in princes,
   in a son of man, in whom there is
   no salvation.
4 When his breath departs, he returns
   to the earth;
   on that very day his plans perish.

5 Blessed is he whose help is the God
   of Jacob,
   whose hope is in the LORD his God,
6 who made heaven and earth,
   the sea, and all that is in them,
   who keeps faith forever;
7 who executes justice for the
   oppressed,
   who gives food to the hungry.

   The LORD sets the prisoners free;
8 the LORD opens the eyes of the
   blind.
   The LORD lifts up those who are
   bowed down;
   the LORD loves the righteous.
9 The LORD watches over the sojourners;
   he upholds the widow and the
   fatherless,
   but the way of the wicked he
   brings to ruin.

10 The LORD will reign forever,
   your God, O Zion, to all generations.
   Praise the LORD!

[1] Hebrew *his*; also next line [2] These two lines are supplied by one Hebrew manuscript, Septuagint, Syriac (compare Dead Sea Scroll)

He Heals the Brokenhearted

147 Praise the LORD!
For it is good to sing praises to
our God;
for it is pleasant,[1] and a song of
praise is fitting.

2 The LORD builds up Jerusalem;
he gathers the outcasts of Israel.

3 He heals the brokenhearted
and binds up their wounds.

4 He determines the number of the
stars;
he gives to all of them their names.

5 Great is our Lord, and abundant in
power;
his understanding is beyond measure.

6 The LORD lifts up the humble;[2]
he casts the wicked to the ground.

7 Sing to the LORD with thanksgiving;
make melody to our God on the
lyre!

8 He covers the heavens with clouds;
he prepares rain for the earth;
he makes grass grow on the hills.

9 He gives to the beasts their food,
and to the young ravens that cry.

10 His delight is not in the strength of
the horse,
nor his pleasure in the legs of a
man,

11 but the LORD takes pleasure in those
who fear him,
in those who hope in his steadfast
love.

12 Praise the LORD, O Jerusalem!
Praise your God, O Zion!

13 For he strengthens the bars of your
gates;
he blesses your children within you.

14 He makes peace in your borders;
he fills you with the finest of the
wheat.

15 He sends out his command to the
earth;
his word runs swiftly.

16 He gives snow like wool;
he scatters frost like ashes.

17 He hurls down his crystals of ice like
crumbs;
who can stand before his cold?

18 He sends out his word, and melts
them;
he makes his wind blow and the
waters flow.

19 He declares his word to Jacob,
his statutes and rules[3] to Israel.

20 He has not dealt thus with any other
nation;
they do not know his rules.[4]
Praise the LORD!

Praise the Name of the LORD

148 Praise the LORD!
Praise the LORD from the heavens;
praise him in the heights!

2 Praise him, all his angels;
praise him, all his hosts!

3 Praise him, sun and moon,
praise him, all you shining stars!

4 Praise him, you highest heavens,
and you waters above the heavens!

5 Let them praise the name of the LORD!
For he commanded and they were
created.

6 And he established them forever and
ever;
he gave a decree, and it shall not
pass away.[5]

7 Praise the LORD from the earth,
you great sea creatures and all
deeps,

8 fire and hail, snow and mist,
stormy wind fulfilling his word!

9 Mountains and all hills,
fruit trees and all cedars!

10 Beasts and all livestock,
creeping things and flying birds!

11 Kings of the earth and all peoples,
princes and all rulers of the earth!

12 Young men and maidens together,
old men and children!

13 Let them praise the name of the LORD,
for his name alone is exalted;
his majesty is above earth and
heaven.

14 He has raised up a horn for his people,
praise for all his saints,
for the people of Israel who are
near to him.
Praise the LORD!

[1] Or for he is beautiful   [2] Or afflicted   [3] Or and just decrees   [4] Or his just decrees   [5] Or it shall not be transgressed

Sing to the LORD a New Song

149
Praise the LORD!
Sing to the LORD a new song,
his praise in the assembly of the
godly!

2 Let Israel be glad in his Maker;
let the children of Zion rejoice in
their King!

3 Let them praise his name with dancing,
making melody to him with tambourine and lyre!

4 For the LORD takes pleasure in his
people;
he adorns the humble with salvation.

5 Let the godly exult in glory;
let them sing for joy on their beds.

6 Let the high praises of God be in
their throats
and two-edged swords in their
hands,

7 to execute vengeance on the nations
and punishments on the peoples,

8 to bind their kings with chains
and their nobles with fetters of iron

9 to execute on them the judgment
written!
This is honor for all his godly ones.
Praise the LORD!

Let Everything Praise the LORD

150
Praise the LORD!
Praise God in his sanctuary;
praise him in his mighty heavens![1]

2 Praise him for his mighty deeds;
praise him according to his excellent greatness!

3 Praise him with trumpet sound;
praise him with lute and harp!

4 Praise him with tambourine and
dance;
praise him with strings and pipe!

5 Praise him with sounding cymbals;
praise him with loud clashing
cymbals!

6 Let everything that has breath praise
the LORD!
Praise the LORD!

[1] Hebrew *expanse* (compare Genesis 1:6–8)

INTRODUCTION TO
Proverbs

Authors: King Solomon, Agur, King Lemuel, and others

Time: Probably finalized sometime after 700 B.C.

Place: Unknown

Written to: Solomon's son, and all who seek wisdom

The gist

These proverbs were written to teach God's people wisdom. They are not just good ideas but eternal truths. Reading them and making them a part of your life will give you insight and discipline.

Things to look for

- The use of poetic language
- The purpose of the proverbs (see Prov. 1:1–7)

Seek Wisdom

> The proverbs of Solomon, son of David, king of Israel: . . .
>
> to give prudence to the simple,
> knowledge and discretion to the youth.
>
> *Proverbs 1:1, 4*

When God offered to make King Solomon's biggest wish come true, Solomon's request was kind of shocking. Of all the things in the world he could have asked for—more money, fame, a long life—he asked for wisdom. Amazing! What kind of person would think that, if they could ask for anything at all, they should ask for wisdom? But that's exactly what this man asked for, and his request was so impressive that God decided to give him more wisdom than anyone before or since, as well as riches and honor (see 2 Chron. 1:7–12).

Why would wisdom be the first thing out of Solomon's mouth? Why would he want that? Think about your life and how different it would be if you had the wisdom of God running through your veins. Wisdom changes everything. It changes how you think, how you feel, and how you act. Wisdom is of highest value. It's the secret to a truly meaningful life.

Wisdom should be the goal of every God Girl, and the book of Proverbs is a good place to start to find it. This collection of poetic truth, written by King Solomon as well as Agur the son of Jakeh (see Prov. 30:1) and King Lemuel (see Prov. 31:1), is the key to a lot of life's biggest questions. If you want to know what to do or how to act, you might just find your answer in these pages. Don't think of Proverbs as human wisdom but as the very wisdom of God and insight into what he wants for your life, as well as insight into the human condition. As you read and absorb these truths, your own wisdom will grow.

Must-Know Terms and Verses

✐ *Discipline* ✐
Correction or punishment for wrongdoing, or the act of training in obedience and self-control.

✐ *Proverb* ✐
A short general truth, written in a way that is easy to remember.

✐ *Wisdom* ✐
The ability to cope with life and to determine proper moral conduct in all situations.

Keep your heart with all vigilance,
  for from it flow the springs of life. *Proverbs 4:23*

Commit your work to the LORD,
  and your plans will be established. *Proverbs 16:3*

A friend loves at all times,
  and a brother is born for adversity. *Proverbs 17:17*

The reward for humility and fear of the LORD
  is riches and honor and life. *Proverbs 22:4*

Proverbs

The Beginning of Knowledge

1 The proverbs of Solomon, son of David, king of Israel:

2 To know wisdom and instruction,
   to understand words of insight,
3 to receive instruction in wise dealing,
   in righteousness, justice, and
   equity;
4 to give prudence to the simple,
   knowledge and discretion to the
   youth—
5 Let the wise hear and increase in
   learning,
   and the one who understands
   obtain guidance,
6 to understand a proverb and a saying,
   the words of the wise and their
   riddles.

7 The fear of the LORD is the beginning
   of knowledge;
   fools despise wisdom and instruction.

The Enticement of Sinners

8 Hear, my son, your father's instruction,
   and forsake not your mother's
   teaching,
9 for they are a graceful garland for
   your head
   and pendants for your neck.
10 My son, if sinners entice you,
   do not consent.
11 If they say, "Come with us, let us lie
   in wait for blood;
   let us ambush the innocent without reason;
12 like Sheol let us swallow them alive,
   and whole, like those who go down
   to the pit;
13 we shall find all precious goods,
   we shall fill our houses with plunder;

14 throw in your lot among us;
   we will all have one purse"—
15 my son, do not walk in the way with
   them;
   hold back your foot from their
   paths,
16 for their feet run to evil,
   and they make haste to shed blood.
17 For in vain is a net spread
   in the sight of any bird,
18 but these men lie in wait for their
   own blood;
   they set an ambush for their own
   lives.
19 Such are the ways of everyone who is
   greedy for unjust gain;
   it takes away the life of its possess-
   ors.

The Call of Wisdom

20 Wisdom cries aloud in the street,
   in the markets she raises her voice;
21 at the head of the noisy streets she
   cries out;
   at the entrance of the city gates
   she speaks:
22 "How long, O simple ones, will you love
   being simple?
   How long will scoffers delight in
   their scoffing
   and fools hate knowledge?
23 If you turn at my reproof,[1]
   behold, I will pour out my spirit to
   you;
   I will make my words known to you.
24 Because I have called and you
   refused to listen,
   have stretched out my hand and
   no one has heeded,
25 because you have ignored all my
   counsel
   and would have none of my reproof,
26 I also will laugh at your calamity;
   I will mock when terror strikes you,

[1] Or Will you turn away at my reproof?

27 when terror strikes you like a storm
   and your calamity comes like a
      whirlwind,
   when distress and anguish come
      upon you.
28 Then they will call upon me, but
      I will not answer;
   they will seek me diligently but
      will not find me.
29 Because they hated knowledge
   and did not choose the fear of the
      LORD,
30 would have none of my counsel
   and despised all my reproof,
31 therefore they shall eat the fruit of
      their way,
   and have their fill of their own
      devices.
32 For the simple are killed by their
      turning away,
   and the complacency of fools
      destroys them;
33 but whoever listens to me will dwell
      secure
   and will be at ease, without dread
      of disaster."

The Value of Wisdom

2 My son, if you receive my words
   and treasure up my commandments
      with you,
2 making your ear attentive to wisdom
   and inclining your heart to under-
      standing;
3 yes, if you call out for insight
   and raise your voice for under-
      standing,
4 if you seek it like silver
   and search for it as for hidden
      treasures,
5 then you will understand the fear of
      the LORD
   and find the knowledge of God.
6 For the LORD gives wisdom;
   from his mouth come knowledge
      and understanding;
7 he stores up sound wisdom for the
      upright;
   he is a shield to those who walk in
      integrity,
8 guarding the paths of justice
   and watching over the way of his
      saints.

9 Then you will understand righteous
      ness and justice
   and equity, every good path;
10 for wisdom will come into your heart
   and knowledge will be pleasant to
      your soul;
11 discretion will watch over you,
   understanding will guard you,
12 delivering you from the way of evil,
   from men of perverted speech,
13 who forsake the paths of uprightnes
   to walk in the ways of darkness,
14 who rejoice in doing evil
   and delight in the perverseness of
      evil,
15 men whose paths are crooked,
   and who are devious in their ways

16 So you will be delivered from the
      forbidden[1] woman,
   from the adulteress[2] with her
      smooth words,
17 who forsakes the companion of her
      youth
   and forgets the covenant of her God
18 for her house sinks down to death,
   and her paths to the departed;[3]
19 none who go to her come back,
   nor do they regain the paths of life
20 So you will walk in the way of the
      good
   and keep to the paths of the righ-
      teous.
21 For the upright will inhabit the land,
   and those with integrity will
      remain in it,
22 but the wicked will be cut off from
      the land,
   and the treacherous will be rooted
      out of it.

Trust in the LORD with All Your Heart

3 My son, do not forget my teaching,
   but let your heart keep my com-
      mandments,
2 for length of days and years of life
   and peace they will add to you.
3 Let not steadfast love and faithful-
      ness forsake you;
   bind them around your neck;
   write them on the tablet of your
      heart.

[1] Hebrew *strange* [2] Hebrew *foreign woman* [3] Hebrew *to the Rephaim*

4   So you will find favor and good suc-
       cess[1]
     in the sight of God and man.

5   Trust in the LORD with all your
       heart,
     and do not lean on your own
       understanding.

6   In all your ways acknowledge him,
     and he will make straight your
       paths.

7   Be not wise in your own eyes;
     fear the LORD, and turn away from
       evil.

8   It will be healing to your flesh[2]
     and refreshment[3] to your bones.

9   Honor the LORD with your wealth
     and with the firstfruits of all your
       produce;

10 then your barns will be filled with
       plenty,
     and your vats will be bursting with
       wine.

11 My son, do not despise the LORD's
       discipline
     or be weary of his reproof,

12 for the LORD reproves him whom he
       loves,
     as a father the son in whom he
       delights.

Blessed Is the One Who Finds Wisdom

13 Blessed is the one who finds wis-
       dom,
     and the one who gets understand-
       ing,

14 for the gain from her is better than
       gain from silver
     and her profit better than gold.

15 She is more precious than jewels,
     and nothing you desire can com-
       pare with her.

16 Long life is in her right hand;
     in her left hand are riches and
       honor.

17 Her ways are ways of pleasantness,
     and all her paths are peace.

18 She is a tree of life to those who lay
       hold of her;
     those who hold her fast are called
       blessed.

19 The LORD by wisdom founded the
       earth;
     by understanding he established
       the heavens;

20 by his knowledge the deeps broke
       open,
     and the clouds drop down the dew.

21 My son, do not lose sight of these—
     keep sound wisdom and discre-
       tion,

22 and they will be life for your soul
     and adornment for your neck.

23 Then you will walk on your way
       securely,
     and your foot will not stumble.

24 If you lie down, you will not be
       afraid;
     when you lie down, your sleep will
       be sweet.

25 Do not be afraid of sudden terror
     or of the ruin[4] of the wicked, when
       it comes,

26 for the LORD will be your confidence
     and will keep your foot from being
       caught.

27 Do not withhold good from those to
       whom it is due,[5]
     when it is in your power to do it.

28 Do not say to your neighbor, "Go, and
       come again,
     tomorrow I will give it"—when
       you have it with you.

29 Do not plan evil against your neighbor,
     who dwells trustingly beside you.

30 Do not contend with a man for no
       reason,
     when he has done you no harm.

31 Do not envy a man of violence
     and do not choose any of his ways,

32 for the devious person is an abomi-
       nation to the LORD,
     but the upright are in his confi-
       dence.

33 The LORD's curse is on the house of
       the wicked,
     but he blesses the dwelling of the
       righteous.

34 Toward the scorners he is scornful,
     but to the humble he gives favor.[6]

35 The wise will inherit honor,
     but fools get[7] disgrace.

[1] Or repute [2] Hebrew navel [3] Or medicine [4] Hebrew storm [5] Hebrew Do not withhold good from its owners [6] Or grace [7] The meaning of the Hebrew word is uncertain

A Father's Wise Instruction

4 Hear, O sons, a father's instruction,
and be attentive, that you may gain[1]
insight,

2 for I give you good precepts;
do not forsake my teaching.

3 When I was a son with my father,
tender, the only one in the sight of
my mother,

4 he taught me and said to me,
"Let your heart hold fast my words;
keep my commandments, and live.

5 Get wisdom; get insight;
do not forget, and do not turn away
from the words of my mouth.

6 Do not forsake her, and she will keep
you;
love her, and she will guard you.

7 The beginning of wisdom is this: Get
wisdom,
and whatever you get, get insight.

8 Prize her highly, and she will exalt
you;
she will honor you if you embrace
her.

9 She will place on your head a graceful garland;
she will bestow on you a beautiful
crown."

10 Hear, my son, and accept my words,
that the years of your life may be
many.

11 I have taught you the way of wisdom;
I have led you in the paths of
uprightness.

12 When you walk, your step will not be
hampered,
and if you run, you will not
stumble.

13 Keep hold of instruction; do not let
go;
guard her, for she is your life.

14 Do not enter the path of the wicked,
and do not walk in the way of the
evil.

15 Avoid it; do not go on it;
turn away from it and pass on.

16 For they cannot sleep unless they
have done wrong;
they are robbed of sleep unless
they have made someone
stumble.

17 For they eat the bread of wickedness
and drink the wine of violence.

18 But the path of the righteous is like
the light of dawn,
which shines brighter and brighter
until full day.

19 The way of the wicked is like deep
darkness;
they do not know over what they
stumble.

20 My son, be attentive to my words;
incline your ear to my sayings.

21 Let them not escape from your
sight;
keep them within your heart.

22 For they are life to those who find
them,
and healing to all their[2] flesh.

23 Keep your heart with all vigilance,
for from it flow the springs of life.

24 Put away from you crooked speech,
and put devious talk far from you.

25 Let your eyes look directly forward,
and your gaze be straight before
you.

26 Ponder[3] the path of your feet;
then all your ways will be sure.

27 Do not swerve to the right or to the
left;
turn your foot away from evil.

Warning Against Adultery

5 My son, be attentive to my wisdom;
incline your ear to my understanding,

2 that you may keep discretion,
and your lips may guard knowledge.

3 For the lips of a forbidden[4] woman
drip honey,
and her speech[5] is smoother than
oil,

4 but in the end she is bitter as wormwood,
sharp as a two-edged sword.

5 Her feet go down to death;
her steps follow the path to[6]
Sheol;

6 she does not ponder the path of life;
her ways wander, and she does not
know it.

[1] Hebrew *know* [2] Hebrew *his* [3] Or *Make level* [4] Hebrew *strange*; also verse 20 [5] Hebrew *palate* [6] Hebrew *lay hold of*

7   And now, O sons, listen to me,
        and do not depart from the words
        of my mouth.
8   Keep your way far from her,
        and do not go near the door of her
        house,
9   lest you give your honor to others
        and your years to the merciless,
10 lest strangers take their fill of your
        strength,
        and your labors go to the house of
        a foreigner,
11 and at the end of your life you groan,
        when your flesh and body are
        consumed,
12 and you say, "How I hated discipline,
        and my heart despised reproof!

13 I did not listen to the voice of my
        teachers
        or incline my ear to my instructors.
14 I am at the brink of utter ruin
        in the assembled congregation."

15 Drink water from your own cistern,
        flowing water from your own
        well.
16 Should your springs be scattered
        abroad,
        streams of water in the streets?
17 Let them be for yourself alone,
        and not for strangers with you.
18 Let your fountain be blessed,
        and rejoice in the wife of your
        youth,
19 a lovely deer, a graceful doe.

Know Love

verses to read
Proverbs 4:20-27

Your heart makes bad choices if left to its own devices, partly because it feels so deeply and those feelings insist on being heard. Like a spoiled child, your feelings demand immediate attention. They want what they want, when they want it. But just because your heart feels something, that doesn't make it true. A lot of times your heart lies. That's because feelings are often based on your experience of the world around you, not necessarily on God's truth. The beauty of knowing and obeying God's Word is that it is unchanging and sure; it doesn't go back and forth based on the actions or feelings of humanity. It doesn't tease you by saying one thing only to change to something else when the winds pick up. No, God's Word is constant, and its stability gives you a chance to rise above the storms of this life. It's an outstretched hand in the storm, and it helps you find your way safely through the fog of emotion.

God tells you in Proverbs 4:23 to guard your heart because the source of your life flows from it. The word "heart" here doesn't mean the beating organ in your chest; it means your mind, your thoughts, and your emotions—all that is you. You have to guard your thoughts and feelings because out of those come your love for God and his commands, and out of that comes your ability to serve, to find joy, and to trust God. If you let your heart be led astray, then your faith gets derailed. A lot of girls let emotions alone guide their decisions. They say, "I feel it, so it has to be real." But that isn't always true. Faith isn't about feeling; it's about knowing. We don't say, "I feel like I believe in Jesus." We either believe and follow him or we don't. Of course, our faith includes feelings, but feelings can be fickle. They rise and fall like the wind and are prone to rebellion, but your mind can and should overcome your feelings if you focus your thoughts on God's Word. When you guard your heart, you refuse to think things based solely on how you feel, and instead you judge everything based on God's Word. So guard your heart, and let truth be your guide instead of random experience.

Let her breasts fill you at all times
  with delight;
    be intoxicated[1] always in her love.
20 Why should you be intoxicated, my
      son, with a forbidden woman
    and embrace the bosom of an
      adulteress?[2]
21 For a man's ways are before the eyes
      of the Lord,
    and he ponders[3] all his paths.
22 The iniquities of the wicked ensnare
      him,
    and he is held fast in the cords of
      his sin.
23 He dies for lack of discipline,
    and because of his great folly he is
      led astray.

Practical Warnings

6 My son, if you have put up security
    for your neighbor,
      have given your pledge for a
        stranger,
2 if you are snared in the words of
        your mouth,
      caught in the words of your
        mouth,
3 then do this, my son, and save your-
        self,
      for you have come into the hand of
        your neighbor:
      go, hasten,[4] and plead urgently
        with your neighbor.
4 Give your eyes no sleep
      and your eyelids no slumber;
5 save yourself like a gazelle from the
        hand of the hunter,[5]
      like a bird from the hand of the
        fowler.

6 Go to the ant, O sluggard;
      consider her ways, and be wise.
7 Without having any chief,
      officer, or ruler,
8 she prepares her bread in summer
      and gathers her food in harvest.
9 How long will you lie there, O slug-
        gard?
      When will you arise from your
        sleep?
10 A little sleep, a little slumber,
      a little folding of the hands to
        rest,

11 and poverty will come upon you like
      a robber,
    and want like an armed man.

12 A worthless person, a wicked man,
      goes about with crooked speech,
13 winks with his eyes, signals[6] with his
      feet,
    points with his finger,
14 with perverted heart devises evil,
      continually sowing discord;
15 therefore calamity will come upon
      him suddenly;
    in a moment he will be broken
      beyond healing.

16 There are six things that the Lord
      hates,
    seven that are an abomination to
      him:
17 haughty eyes, a lying tongue,
    and hands that shed innocent
      blood,
18 a heart that devises wicked plans,
    feet that make haste to run to evil,
19 a false witness who breathes out lies,
    and one who sows discord among
      brothers.

Warnings Against Adultery

20 My son, keep your father's com-
      mandment,
    and forsake not your mother's
      teaching.
21 Bind them on your heart always;
    tie them around your neck.
22 When you walk, they[7] will lead you;
    when you lie down, they will
      watch over you;
    and when you awake, they will talk
      with you.
23 For the commandment is a lamp and
      the teaching a light,
    and the reproofs of discipline are
      the way of life,
24 to preserve you from the evil
      woman,[8]
    from the smooth tongue of the
      adulteress.[9]
25 Do not desire her beauty in your
      heart,
    and do not let her capture you
      with her eyelashes;

---

[1] Hebrew be led astray; also verse 20 [2] Hebrew a foreign woman [3] Or makes level [4] Or humble yourself [5] Hebrew lacks of the hunter
[6] Hebrew scrapes [7] Hebrew it; three times in this verse [8] Revocalization (compare Septuagint) yields from the wife of a neighbor
[9] Hebrew the foreign woman

26 for the price of a prostitute is only a
      loaf of bread,[1]
   but a married woman[2] hunts down
      a precious life.
27 Can a man carry fire next to his chest
      and his clothes not be burned?
28 Or can one walk on hot coals
      and his feet not be scorched?
29 So is he who goes in to his neighbor's
      wife;
   none who touches her will go
      unpunished.
30 People do not despise a thief if he
      steals
   to satisfy his appetite when he is
      hungry,
31 but if he is caught, he will pay seven-
      fold;
   he will give all the goods of his
      house.
32 He who commits adultery lacks sense;
   he who does it destroys himself.
33 He will get wounds and dishonor,
   and his disgrace will not be wiped
      away.
34 For jealousy makes a man furious,
   and he will not spare when he
      takes revenge.
35 He will accept no compensation;
   he will refuse though you multiply
      gifts.

Warning Against the Adulteress

7 My son, keep my words
   and treasure up my commandments
      with you;
2 keep my commandments and live;
   keep my teaching as the apple of
      your eye;
3 bind them on your fingers;
   write them on the tablet of your
      heart.
4 Say to wisdom, "You are my sister,"
   and call insight your intimate
      friend,
5 to keep you from the forbidden[3]
      woman,
   from the adulteress[4] with her
      smooth words.
6 For at the window of my house
   I have looked out through my lat-
      tice,

7 and I have seen among the simple,
   I have perceived among the youths,
      a young man lacking sense,
8 passing along the street near her
      corner;
   taking the road to her house
9 in the twilight, in the evening,
   at the time of night and darkness.
10 And behold, the woman meets him,
      dressed as a prostitute, wily of
      heart.[5]
11 She is loud and wayward;
   her feet do not stay at home;
12 now in the street, now in the market,
   and at every corner she lies in wait.
13 She seizes him and kisses him,
   and with bold face she says to him,
14 "I had to offer sacrifices,[6]
   and today I have paid my vows;
15 so now I have come out to meet you,
   to seek you eagerly, and I have
      found you.
16 I have spread my couch with cover-
      ings,
   colored linens from Egyptian linen;
17 I have perfumed my bed with myrrh,
      aloes, and cinnamon.
18 Come, let us take our fill of love till
      morning;
   let us delight ourselves with love.
19 For my husband is not at home;
   he has gone on a long journey;
20 he took a bag of money with him;
   at full moon he will come home."
21 With much seductive speech she
      persuades him;
   with her smooth talk she compels
      him.
22 All at once he follows her,
   as an ox goes to the slaughter,
   or as a stag is caught fast[7]
23   till an arrow pierces its liver;
   as a bird rushes into a snare;
      he does not know that it will cost
      him his life.
24 And now, O sons, listen to me,
   and be attentive to the words of
      my mouth.
25 Let not your heart turn aside to her
      ways;
   do not stray into her paths,

---

[1] Or (compare Septuagint, Syriac, Vulgate) *for a prostitute leaves a man with nothing but a loaf of bread* [2] Hebrew *a man's wife* [3] Hebrew *strange* [4] Hebrew *the foreign woman* [5] Hebrew *guarded in heart* [6] Hebrew *peace offerings* [7] Probable reading (compare Septuagint, Vulgate, Syriac); Hebrew *as an anklet for the discipline of a fool*

26 for many a victim has she laid low,
   and all her slain are a mighty
   throng.
27 Her house is the way to Sheol,
   going down to the chambers of
   death.

The Blessings of Wisdom

8 Does not wisdom call?
   Does not understanding raise her
   voice?
2 On the heights beside the way,
   at the crossroads she takes her
   stand;
3 beside the gates in front of the town,
   at the entrance of the portals she
   cries aloud:
4 "To you, O men, I call,
   and my cry is to the children of
   man.
5 O simple ones, learn prudence;
   O fools, learn sense.
6 Hear, for I will speak noble things,
   and from my lips will come what is
   right,
7 for my mouth will utter truth;
   wickedness is an abomination to
   my lips.
8 All the words of my mouth are righteous;
   there is nothing twisted or
   crooked in them.
9 They are all straight to him who
   understands,
   and right to those who find knowledge.
10 Take my instruction instead of silver,
   and knowledge rather than choice
   gold,
11 for wisdom is better than jewels,
   and all that you may desire cannot
   compare with her.

12 "I, wisdom, dwell with prudence,
   and I find knowledge and discretion.
13 The fear of the LORD is hatred of evil.
   Pride and arrogance and the way of
   evil
   and perverted speech I hate.
14 I have counsel and sound wisdom;
   I have insight; I have strength.
15 By me kings reign,
   and rulers decree what is just;

16 by me princes rule,
   and nobles, all who govern justly.[1]
17 I love those who love me,
   and those who seek me diligently
   find me.
18 Riches and honor are with me,
   enduring wealth and righteousness.
19 My fruit is better than gold, even fine
   gold,
   and my yield than choice silver.
20 I walk in the way of righteousness,
   in the paths of justice,
21 granting an inheritance to those who
   love me,
   and filling their treasuries.

22 "The LORD possessed[2] me at the beginning of his work,[3]
   the first of his acts of old.
23 Ages ago I was set up,
   at the first, before the beginning of
   the earth.
24 When there were no depths I was
   brought forth,
   when there were no springs
   abounding with water.
25 Before the mountains had been
   shaped,
   before the hills, I was brought forth,
26 before he had made the earth with
   its fields,
   or the first of the dust of the world.
27 When he established the heavens,
   I was there;
   when he drew a circle on the face
   of the deep,
28 when he made firm the skies above,
   when he established[4] the fountains
   of the deep,
29 when he assigned to the sea its limit,
   so that the waters might not transgress his command,
   when he marked out the foundations
   of the earth,
30 then I was beside him, like a master workman,
   and I was daily his[5] delight,
   rejoicing before him always,
31 rejoicing in his inhabited world
   and delighting in the children of
   man.

32 "And now, O sons, listen to me:
   blessed are those who keep my
   ways.

---

[1] Most Hebrew manuscripts; many Hebrew manuscripts, Septuagint *govern the earth* [2] Or *fathered*; Septuagint *created* [3] Hebrew *way*
[4] The meaning of the Hebrew is uncertain [5] Or *daily filled with*

33 Hear instruction and be wise,
        and do not neglect it.
34 Blessed is the one who listens to me,
        watching daily at my gates,
        waiting beside my doors.
35 For whoever finds me finds life
        and obtains favor from the LORD,
36 but he who fails to find me injures
        himself;
        all who hate me love death."

The Way of Wisdom

9 Wisdom has built her house;
        she has hewn her seven pillars.
2   She has slaughtered her beasts; she
        has mixed her wine;
        she has also set her table.
3   She has sent out her young women
        to call
        from the highest places in the town,
4   "Whoever is simple, let him turn in
        here!"
        To him who lacks sense she says,
5   "Come, eat of my bread
        and drink of the wine I have mixed.
6   Leave your simple ways,[1] and live,
        and walk in the way of insight."

7   Whoever corrects a scoffer gets
        himself abuse,
        and he who reproves a wicked
        man incurs injury.
8   Do not reprove a scoffer, or he will
        hate you;
        reprove a wise man, and he will
        love you.
9   Give instruction[2] to a wise man, and
        he will be still wiser;
        teach a righteous man, and he will
        increase in learning.
10 The fear of the LORD is the beginning
        of wisdom,
        and the knowledge of the Holy One
        is insight.
11 For by me your days will be multi-
        plied,
        and years will be added to your life.
12 If you are wise, you are wise for
        yourself;
        if you scoff, you alone will bear it.

The Way of Folly

13 The woman Folly is loud;
        she is seductive[3] and knows noth-
        ing.

14 She sits at the door of her house;
        she takes a seat on the highest
        places of the town,
15 calling to those who pass by,
        who are going straight on their
        way,
16 "Whoever is simple, let him turn in
        here!"
        And to him who lacks sense she
        says,
17 "Stolen water is sweet,
        and bread eaten in secret is pleas-
        ant."
18 But he does not know that the dead[4]
        are there,
        that her guests are in the depths of
        Sheol.

The Proverbs of Solomon

10 The proverbs of Solomon.

    A wise son makes a glad father,
        but a foolish son is a sorrow to his
        mother.
2   Treasures gained by wickedness do
        not profit,
        but righteousness delivers from
        death.
3   The LORD does not let the righteous
        go hungry,
        but he thwarts the craving of the
        wicked.
4   A slack hand causes poverty,
        but the hand of the diligent makes
        rich.
5   He who gathers in summer is a pru-
        dent son,
        but he who sleeps in harvest is a
        son who brings shame.
6   Blessings are on the head of the
        righteous,
        but the mouth of the wicked con-
        ceals violence.
7   The memory of the righteous is a
        blessing,
        but the name of the wicked will
        rot.
8   The wise of heart will receive com-
        mandments,
        but a babbling fool will come to
        ruin.
9   Whoever walks in integrity walks
        securely,
        but he who makes his ways
        crooked will be found out.

---

[1] Or Leave the company of the simple [2] Hebrew lacks instruction [3] Or full of simpleness [4] Hebrew Rephaim

10 Whoever winks the eye causes
      trouble,
   and a babbling fool will come to
      ruin.
11 The mouth of the righteous is a foun-
      tain of life,
   but the mouth of the wicked con-
      ceals violence.

Ask Yourself . . .

ABOUT YOUR WORDS

- What is foolish talk?
- Is my speech always honest?
- What does God's Word say
  about fighting with my words?
- How can I improve my use of
  words, to be more holy?
- How can the gospel transform
  the way I use words?

---

12 Hatred stirs up strife,
   but love covers all offenses.
13 On the lips of him who has under-
      standing, wisdom is found,
   but a rod is for the back of him
      who lacks sense.
14 The wise lay up knowledge,
   but the mouth of a fool brings ruin
      near.
15 A rich man's wealth is his strong city;
   the poverty of the poor is their
      ruin.
16 The wage of the righteous leads to life,
   the gain of the wicked to sin.
17 Whoever heeds instruction is on the
      path to life,
   but he who rejects reproof leads
      others astray.
18 The one who conceals hatred has
      lying lips,
   and whoever utters slander is a
      fool.
19 When words are many, transgression
      is not lacking,
   but whoever restrains his lips is
      prudent.

20 The tongue of the righteous is choice
      silver;
   the heart of the wicked is of little
      worth.
21 The lips of the righteous feed many,
   but fools die for lack of sense.
22 The blessing of the LORD makes rich,
   and he adds no sorrow with it.[1]
23 Doing wrong is like a joke to a fool,
   but wisdom is pleasure to a man of
      understanding.
24 What the wicked dreads will come
      upon him,
   but the desire of the righteous will
      be granted.
25 When the tempest passes, the
      wicked is no more,
   but the righteous is established
      forever.
26 Like vinegar to the teeth and smoke
      to the eyes,
   so is the sluggard to those who
      send him.
27 The fear of the LORD prolongs life,
   but the years of the wicked will be
      short.
28 The hope of the righteous brings joy,
   but the expectation of the wicked
      will perish.
29 The way of the LORD is a stronghold
      to the blameless,
   but destruction to evildoers.
30 The righteous will never be
      removed,
   but the wicked will not dwell in
      the land.
31 The mouth of the righteous brings
      forth wisdom,
   but the perverse tongue will be cut
      off.
32 The lips of the righteous know what
      is acceptable,
   but the mouth of the wicked, what
      is perverse.

11 A false balance is an abomination
      to the LORD,
   but a just weight is his delight.
2 When pride comes, then comes
      disgrace,
   but with the humble is wisdom.
3 The integrity of the upright guides
      them,
   but the crookedness of the treach-
      erous destroys them.

[1] Or and toil adds nothing to it

4   Riches do not profit in the day of
        wrath,
        but righteousness delivers from
        death.
5   The righteousness of the blameless
        keeps his way straight,
        but the wicked falls by his own
        wickedness.
6   The righteousness of the upright
        delivers them,
        but the treacherous are taken cap-
        tive by their lust.
7   When the wicked dies, his hope will
        perish,
        and the expectation of wealth[1]
        perishes too.
8   The righteous is delivered from
        trouble,
        and the wicked walks into it
        instead.
9   With his mouth the godless man
        would destroy his neighbor,
        but by knowledge the righteous
        are delivered.
10 When it goes well with the righteous,
        the city rejoices,
        and when the wicked perish there
        are shouts of gladness.
11 By the blessing of the upright a city
        is exalted,
        but by the mouth of the wicked it
        is overthrown.
12 Whoever belittles his neighbor lacks
        sense,
        but a man of understanding
        remains silent.
13 Whoever goes about slandering
        reveals secrets,
        but he who is trustworthy in spirit
        keeps a thing covered.
14 Where there is no guidance, a people
        falls,
        but in an abundance of counselors
        there is safety.
15 Whoever puts up security for a
        stranger will surely suffer harm,
        but he who hates striking hands in
        pledge is secure.
16 A gracious woman gets honor,
        and violent men get riches.
17 A man who is kind benefits himself,
        but a cruel man hurts himself.
18 The wicked earns deceptive wages,
        but one who sows righteousness
        gets a sure reward.

19 Whoever is steadfast in righteous-
        ness will live,
        but he who pursues evil will die.
20 Those of crooked heart are an
        abomination to the LORD,
        but those of blameless ways are
        his delight.
21 Be assured, an evil person will not go
        unpunished,
        but the offspring of the righteous
        will be delivered.
22 Like a gold ring in a pig's snout
        is a beautiful woman without
        discretion.
23 The desire of the righteous ends only
        in good;
        the expectation of the wicked in
        wrath.
24 One gives freely, yet grows all the
        richer;
        another withholds what he should
        give, and only suffers want.
25 Whoever brings blessing will be
        enriched,
        and one who waters will himself
        be watered.
26 The people curse him who holds
        back grain,
        but a blessing is on the head of
        him who sells it.
27 Whoever diligently seeks good seeks
        favor,[2]
        but evil comes to him who
        searches for it.
28 Whoever trusts in his riches will fall,
        but the righteous will flourish like
        a green leaf.
29 Whoever troubles his own house-
        hold will inherit the wind,
        and the fool will be servant to the
        wise of heart.
30 The fruit of the righteous is a tree of
        life,
        and whoever captures souls is wise.
31 If the righteous is repaid on earth,
        how much more the wicked and
        the sinner!

12
    Whoever loves discipline loves
        knowledge,
        but he who hates reproof is stupid.
2   A good man obtains favor from the
        LORD,
        but a man of evil devices he con-
        demns.

[1] Or of his strength, or of iniquity [2] Or acceptance

3   No one is established by wickedness,
        but the root of the righteous will
            never be moved.

4   An excellent wife is the crown of her
        husband,
        but she who brings shame is like
            rottenness in his bones.

5   The thoughts of the righteous are just;
        the counsels of the wicked are
            deceitful.

6   The words of the wicked lie in wait
        for blood,
        but the mouth of the upright deliv-
            ers them.

7   The wicked are overthrown and are
        no more,
        but the house of the righteous will
            stand.

8   A man is commended according to
        his good sense,
        but one of twisted mind is
            despised.

9   Better to be lowly and have a servant
        than to play the great man and
            lack bread.

10 Whoever is righteous has regard for
        the life of his beast,
        but the mercy of the wicked is cruel.

11 Whoever works his land will have
        plenty of bread,
        but he who follows worthless
            pursuits lacks sense.

12 Whoever is wicked covets the spoil
        of evildoers,
        but the root of the righteous bears
            fruit.

13 An evil man is ensnared by the trans-
        gression of his lips,
        but the righteous escapes from
            trouble.

14 From the fruit of his mouth a man is
        satisfied with good,
        and the work of a man's hand
            comes back to him.

15 The way of a fool is right in his own
        eyes,
        but a wise man listens to advice.

16 The vexation of a fool is known at
        once,
        but the prudent ignores an insult.

17 Whoever speaks[1] the truth gives
        honest evidence,
        but a false witness utters deceit.

18 There is one whose rash words are
        like sword thrusts,
        but the tongue of the wise brings
            healing.

19 Truthful lips endure forever,
        but a lying tongue is but for a
            moment.

20 Deceit is in the heart of those who
        devise evil,
        but those who plan peace have joy.

21 No ill befalls the righteous,
        but the wicked are filled with
            trouble.

22 Lying lips are an abomination to the
        Lord,
        but those who act faithfully are his
            delight.

23 A prudent man conceals knowledge,
        but the heart of fools proclaims
            folly.

24 The hand of the diligent will rule,
        while the slothful will be put to
            forced labor.

25 Anxiety in a man's heart weighs him
        down,
        but a good word makes him glad.

26 One who is righteous is a guide to his
        neighbor,[2]
        but the way of the wicked leads
            them astray.

27 Whoever is slothful will not roast his
        game,
        but the diligent man will get pre-
            cious wealth.[3]

28 In the path of righteousness is life,
        and in its pathway there is no death.

13 A wise son hears his father's
        instruction,
        but a scoffer does not listen to
            rebuke.

2   From the fruit of his mouth a man
        eats what is good,
        but the desire of the treacherous is
            for violence.

3   Whoever guards his mouth pre-
        serves his life;
        he who opens wide his lips comes
            to ruin.

4   The soul of the sluggard craves and
        gets nothing,
        while the soul of the diligent is
            richly supplied.

5   The righteous hates falsehood,
        but the wicked brings shame[4] and
            disgrace.

[1] Hebrew breathes out [2] Or The righteous chooses his friends carefully [3] Or but diligence is precious wealth [4] Or stench

6 Righteousness guards him whose
        way is blameless,
     but sin overthrows the wicked.
7 One pretends to be rich, yet has
        nothing;
     another pretends to be poor, yet
        has great wealth.
8 The ransom of a man's life is his
        wealth,
     but a poor man hears no threat.
9 The light of the righteous rejoices,
     but the lamp of the wicked will be
        put out.
10 By insolence comes nothing but strife,
     but with those who take advice is
        wisdom.
11 Wealth gained hastily[1] will dwindle,
     but whoever gathers little by little
        will increase it.
12 Hope deferred makes the heart sick,
     but a desire fulfilled is a tree of
        life.
13 Whoever despises the word brings
        destruction on himself,
     but he who reveres the command-
        ment will be rewarded.
14 The teaching of the wise is a fountain
        of life,
     that one may turn away from the
        snares of death.
15 Good sense wins favor,
     but the way of the treacherous is
        their ruin.[2]
16 In everything the prudent acts with
        knowledge,
     but a fool flaunts his folly.
17 A wicked messenger falls into
        trouble,
     but a faithful envoy brings healing.
18 Poverty and disgrace come to him
        who ignores instruction,
     but whoever heeds reproof is
        honored.
19 A desire fulfilled is sweet to the soul,
     but to turn away from evil is an
        abomination to fools.
20 Whoever walks with the wise
        becomes wise,
     but the companion of fools will
        suffer harm.
21 Disaster[3] pursues sinners,
     but the righteous are rewarded
        with good.

22 A good man leaves an inheritance to
        his children's children,
     but the sinner's wealth is laid up
        for the righteous.
23 The fallow ground of the poor would
        yield much food,
     but it is swept away through injus-
        tice.
24 Whoever spares the rod hates his son,
     but he who loves him is diligent to
        discipline him.[4]
25 The righteous has enough to satisfy
        his appetite,
     but the belly of the wicked suffers
        want.

14 The wisest of women builds her
        house,
     but folly with her own hands tears
        it down.
2 Whoever walks in uprightness fears
        the Lord,
     but he who is devious in his ways
        despises him.
3 By the mouth of a fool comes a rod
        for his back,[5]
     but the lips of the wise will pre-
        serve them.
4 Where there are no oxen, the manger
        is clean,
     but abundant crops come by the
        strength of the ox.
5 A faithful witness does not lie,
     but a false witness breathes out lies.
6 A scoffer seeks wisdom in vain,
     but knowledge is easy for a man of
        understanding.
7 Leave the presence of a fool,
     for there you do not meet words of
        knowledge.
8 The wisdom of the prudent is to
        discern his way,
     but the folly of fools is deceiving.
9 Fools mock at the guilt offering,
     but the upright enjoy acceptance.[6]
10 The heart knows its own bitterness,
     and no stranger shares its joy.
11 The house of the wicked will be
        destroyed,
     but the tent of the upright will
        flourish.
12 There is a way that seems right to a
        man,
     but its end is the way to death.[7]

[1] Or by fraud [2] Probable reading (compare Septuagint, Syriac, Vulgate); Hebrew is rugged, or is an enduring rut [3] Or Evil [4] Or who loves
him disciplines him early [5] Or In the mouth of a fool is a rod of pride [6] Hebrew but among the upright is acceptance [7] Hebrew ways of death

13 Even in laughter the heart may ache,
and the end of joy may be grief.
14 The backslider in heart will be filled
with the fruit of his ways,
and a good man will be filled with
the fruit of his ways.
15 The simple believes everything,
but the prudent gives thought to
his steps.
16 One who is wise is cautious[1] and
turns away from evil,
but a fool is reckless and careless.
17 A man of quick temper acts foolishly,
and a man of evil devices is hated.
18 The simple inherit folly,
but the prudent are crowned with
knowledge.
19 The evil bow down before the good,
the wicked at the gates of the
righteous.
20 The poor is disliked even by his
neighbor,
but the rich has many friends.
21 Whoever despises his neighbor is a
sinner,
but blessed is he who is generous
to the poor.
22 Do they not go astray who devise evil?
Those who devise good meet[2]
steadfast love and faithfulness.
23 In all toil there is profit,
but mere talk tends only to poverty.
24 The crown of the wise is their
wealth,
but the folly of fools brings folly.
25 A truthful witness saves lives,
but one who breathes out lies is
deceitful.
26 In the fear of the Lord one has
strong confidence,
and his children will have a refuge.
27 The fear of the Lord is a fountain of
life,
that one may turn away from the
snares of death.
28 In a multitude of people is the glory
of a king,
but without people a prince is
ruined.
29 Whoever is slow to anger has great
understanding,
but he who has a hasty temper
exalts folly.

30 A tranquil[3] heart gives life to the
flesh,
but envy[4] makes the bones rot.
31 Whoever oppresses a poor man
insults his Maker,
but he who is generous to the
needy honors him.
32 The wicked is overthrown through
his evildoing,
but the righteous finds refuge in
his death.
33 Wisdom rests in the heart of a man
of understanding,
but it makes itself known even in
the midst of fools.[5]
34 Righteousness exalts a nation,
but sin is a reproach to any
people.
35 A servant who deals wisely has the
king's favor,
but his wrath falls on one who acts
shamefully.

Ask Yourself . . .

ABOUT ENVY

Envy can eat you up inside and
make you crazy. "I want it, so why
can't I have it?" Ask yourself about
envy:

- What do I envy in others?

- Is that thing a result of sin?

- When I envy, am I accusing
  God of neglecting me or not
  caring for me?

- Would I want something that
  God didn't think was the best
  for me?

- Do I trust him to give me just
  what I need?

15 A soft answer turns away wrath,
but a harsh word stirs up anger.
2 The tongue of the wise commends
knowledge,
but the mouths of fools pour out
folly.

[1] Or fears [the Lord] [2] Or show [3] Or healing [4] Or jealousy [5] Or Wisdom rests quietly in the heart of a man of understanding, but makes itself known in the midst of fools

³ The eyes of the LORD are in every
      place,
  keeping watch on the evil and the
      good.
⁴ A gentle[1] tongue is a tree of life,
  but perverseness in it breaks the
      spirit.
⁵ A fool despises his father's instruction,
  but whoever heeds reproof is
      prudent.
⁶ In the house of the righteous there is
      much treasure,
  but trouble befalls the income of
      the wicked.
⁷ The lips of the wise spread knowl-
      edge;
  not so the hearts of fools.[2]
⁸ The sacrifice of the wicked is an
      abomination to the LORD,
  but the prayer of the upright is
      acceptable to him.
⁹ The way of the wicked is an abomi-
      nation to the LORD,
  but he loves him who pursues
      righteousness.
¹⁰ There is severe discipline for him
      who forsakes the way;
  whoever hates reproof will die.
¹¹ Sheol and Abaddon lie open before
      the LORD;
  how much more the hearts of the
      children of man!
¹² A scoffer does not like to be reproved;
  he will not go to the wise.
¹³ A glad heart makes a cheerful face,
  but by sorrow of heart the spirit is
      crushed.
¹⁴ The heart of him who has under-
      standing seeks knowledge,
  but the mouths of fools feed on folly.
¹⁵ All the days of the afflicted are evil,
  but the cheerful of heart has a
      continual feast.
¹⁶ Better is a little with the fear of the
      LORD
  than great treasure and trouble
      with it.
¹⁷ Better is a dinner of herbs where
      love is
  than a fattened ox and hatred with
      it.
¹⁸ A hot-tempered man stirs up strife,
  but he who is slow to anger quiets
      contention.

[1] Or healing [2] Or the hearts of fools are not steadfast

A Prayer for...
CONTENTMENT

Heavenly Father, if I should suffer from my needs, go without nice clothes, and live in poverty, make my heart prize your love, know it, and be hemmed in by it, though I miss out on all blessings. You have the right to afflict and test me with wants, because by these trials I can see my sins and learn to want nothing to do with them. Let me willingly accept misery, sorrows, and temptations if because of them I can see that sin is the greatest evil and be delivered from it, with thanks to you, acknowledging this as the highest testimony of your love.

When your Son, Jesus, came into my soul instead of sin, he became more dear to me than sin ever was; his kind rule replaced sin's tyranny. Teach me to believe that if I ever want to conquer sin, I must not only work to overcome it but invite Christ to live in the place of it, and he has to become more to me than my terrible lust had been, that his sweetness, power, and life may be there in its place. Teach me to seek kindness from him that is contrary to sin.

When I am afraid of evils to come, comfort me by showing me that in myself I am a dying, condemned wretch, but in Christ I am restored and alive; that in myself I find insufficiency and no rest, but in Christ I have satisfaction and peace; that in myself I am weak and unable to do good, but in Christ I have the ability to do all things. Though now I have his kindnesses in full, I enjoy them only in part; bring quickly the day when I shall have them perfectly in that state where I will be with you face to face, with all sin and darkness and sadness gone forever. O Lord, may that day come quickly!

Amen.

19 The way of a sluggard is like a hedge
        of thorns,
    but the path of the upright is a
        level highway.
20 A wise son makes a glad father,
    but a foolish man despises his
        mother.
21 Folly is a joy to him who lacks sense,
    but a man of understanding walks
        straight ahead.
22 Without counsel plans fail,
    but with many advisers they suc-
        ceed.
23 To make an apt answer is a joy to a
        man,
    and a word in season, how good it
        is!
24 The path of life leads upward for the
        prudent,
    that he may turn away from Sheol
        beneath.
25 The Lord tears down the house of
        the proud
    but maintains the widow's bound-
        aries.
26 The thoughts of the wicked are an
        abomination to the Lord,
    but gracious words are pure.
27 Whoever is greedy for unjust gain
        troubles his own household,
    but he who hates bribes will live.
28 The heart of the righteous ponders
        how to answer,
    but the mouth of the wicked pours
        out evil things.
29 The Lord is far from the wicked,
    but he hears the prayer of the
        righteous.
30 The light of the eyes rejoices the heart,
    and good news refreshes[1] the bones.
31 The ear that listens to life-giving
        reproof
    will dwell among the wise.
32 Whoever ignores instruction
        despises himself,
    but he who listens to reproof gains
        intelligence.
33 The fear of the Lord is instruction in
        wisdom,
    and humility comes before honor.

16 The plans of the heart belong to
        man,
    but the answer of the tongue is
        from the Lord.

2 All the ways of a man are pure in his
        own eyes,
    but the Lord weighs the spirit.
3 Commit your work to the Lord,
    and your plans will be established.
4 The Lord has made everything for
        its purpose,
    even the wicked for the day of
        trouble.
5 Everyone who is arrogant in heart is
        an abomination to the Lord;
    be assured, he will not go unpun-
        ished.
6 By steadfast love and faithfulness
        iniquity is atoned for,
    and by the fear of the Lord one
        turns away from evil.
7 When a man's ways please the Lord,
    he makes even his enemies to be at
        peace with him.
8 Better is a little with righteousness
    than great revenues with injustice.
9 The heart of man plans his way,
    but the Lord establishes his steps.
10 An oracle is on the lips of a king;
    his mouth does not sin in judgment
11 A just balance and scales are the
        Lord's;
    all the weights in the bag are his
        work.
12 It is an abomination to kings to do
        evil,
    for the throne is established by
        righteousness.
13 Righteous lips are the delight of a
        king,
    and he loves him who speaks what
        is right.
14 A king's wrath is a messenger of
        death,
    and a wise man will appease it.
15 In the light of a king's face there is life,
    and his favor is like the clouds that
        bring the spring rain.
16 How much better to get wisdom than
        gold!
    To get understanding is to be
        chosen rather than silver.
17 The highway of the upright turns
        aside from evil;
    whoever guards his way preserves
        his life.
18 Pride goes before destruction,
    and a haughty spirit before a fall.

[1] Hebrew makes fat

9 It is better to be of a lowly spirit with
the poor
than to divide the spoil with the
proud.

0 Whoever gives thought to the word[1]
will discover good,
and blessed is he who trusts in the
LORD.

1 The wise of heart is called discerning,
and sweetness of speech increases
persuasiveness.

2 Good sense is a fountain of life to
him who has it,
but the instruction of fools is folly.

3 The heart of the wise makes his
speech judicious
and adds persuasiveness to his lips.

4 Gracious words are like a honeycomb,
sweetness to the soul and health
to the body.

25 There is a way that seems right to a
man,
but its end is the way to death.[2]

26 A worker's appetite works for him;
his mouth urges him on.

27 A worthless man plots evil,
and his speech[3] is like a scorching
fire.

28 A dishonest man spreads strife,
and a whisperer separates close
friends.

29 A man of violence entices his neighbor
and leads him in a way that is not
good.

30 Whoever winks his eyes plans[4] dishonest things;
he who purses his lips brings evil
to pass.

31 Gray hair is a crown of glory;
it is gained in a righteous life.

Or to a matter [2]Hebrew ways of death [3]Hebrew what is on his lips [4]Hebrew to plan

Know How to Communicate

verses to read
Proverbs 16:18–19

Humility is the foundation of all godliness. Without it, you can't confess your sins or ask Jesus to save you. Humility is the beginning of all righteousness, and so it's crucial to the God Girl. But what about when you are humiliated by a bad or prideful person?

When you're faced with the sin of someone else's pride, your first instinct isn't holiness. The natural human reaction is retaliation or revenge. In fact, if you're not careful, other people's sin can become an excuse for your sin. "But she started it!" or "How dare he!" you say, and game on! When they sin, your sense of fairness kicks in, and the last thing on your mind is meekness and obedience. That's how things get started—fights, arguments, bitterness. Troubled relationships start with a lack of humility, which keeps us from finding peace when others are sin-ning. It's as if your mind decides that it's not fair that you have to be good when they're being so bad. But that's human thinking, not godly thinking. If God's law depended on the actions of others, then even the pagans would be considered obedient (check out Matt. 5:46–48). But God's law depends not on what *they do* but on *who he is.*

In any relationship it's crucial for you, as a God Girl, to know what God commands instead of relying on what other people do. In every battle you have to choose what God wants you to choose, even if the result will be your humiliation. It seems counterintuitive, but mean people are changed not by your retaliation but by your prayer. So go to God in prayer instead of going to them in anger. Trust that God's Word is good even if it seems unfair. And you will find yourself with more peace than you know what to do with.

32 Whoever is slow to anger is better
  than the mighty,
    and he who rules his spirit than he
    who takes a city.
33 The lot is cast into the lap,
    but its every decision is from the
    Lord.

17

Better is a dry morsel with quiet
than a house full of feasting[1] with
strife.
2 A servant who deals wisely will rule
    over a son who acts shamefully
    and will share the inheritance as
    one of the brothers.
3 The crucible is for silver, and the
    furnace is for gold,
    and the Lord tests hearts.
4 An evildoer listens to wicked lips,
    and a liar gives ear to a mischie-
    vous tongue.
5 Whoever mocks the poor insults his
    Maker;
    he who is glad at calamity will not
    go unpunished.
6 Grandchildren are the crown of the
    aged,
    and the glory of children is their
    fathers.
7 Fine speech is not becoming to a fool;
    still less is false speech to a prince.
8 A bribe is like a magic stone in the
    eyes of the one who gives it;
    wherever he turns he prospers.
9 Whoever covers an offense seeks love,
    but he who repeats a matter sepa-
    rates close friends.
10 A rebuke goes deeper into a man of
    understanding
    than a hundred blows into a fool.
11 An evil man seeks only rebellion,
    and a cruel messenger will be sent
    against him.
12 Let a man meet a she-bear robbed of
    her cubs
    rather than a fool in his folly.
13 If anyone returns evil for good,
    evil will not depart from his house.
14 The beginning of strife is like letting
    out water,
    so quit before the quarrel breaks
    out.
15 He who justifies the wicked and he
    who condemns the righteous
    are both alike an abomination to
    the Lord.

16 Why should a fool have money in his
    hand to buy wisdom
    when he has no sense?
17 A friend loves at all times,
    and a brother is born for adversity.
18 One who lacks sense gives a pledge
    and puts up security in the pres-
    ence of his neighbor.
19 Whoever loves transgression loves
    strife;
    he who makes his door high seeks
    destruction.
20 A man of crooked heart does not
    discover good,
    and one with a dishonest tongue
    falls into calamity.
21 He who sires a fool gets himself sor-
    row,
    and the father of a fool has no joy.
22 A joyful heart is good medicine,
    but a crushed spirit dries up the
    bones.
23 The wicked accepts a bribe in
    secret[2]
    to pervert the ways of justice.
24 The discerning sets his face toward
    wisdom,
    but the eyes of a fool are on the
    ends of the earth.
25 A foolish son is a grief to his father
    and bitterness to her who bore
    him.
26 To impose a fine on a righteous man
    is not good,
    nor to strike the noble for their
    uprightness.
27 Whoever restrains his words has
    knowledge,
    and he who has a cool spirit is a
    man of understanding.
28 Even a fool who keeps silent is con-
    sidered wise;
    when he closes his lips, he is
    deemed intelligent.

18

Whoever isolates himself seeks
his own desire;
he breaks out against all sound
judgment.
2 A fool takes no pleasure in under-
    standing,
    but only in expressing his opinion.
3 When wickedness comes, contempt
    comes also,
    and with dishonor comes disgrace.

---

[1] Hebrew sacrifices [2] Hebrew a bribe from the bosom

4 The words of a man's mouth are
      deep waters;
   the fountain of wisdom is a bub-
      bling brook.
5 It is not good to be partial to[1] the
      wicked
   or to deprive the righteous of
      justice.
6 A fool's lips walk into a fight,
   and his mouth invites a beating.
7 A fool's mouth is his ruin,
   and his lips are a snare to his soul.
8 The words of a whisperer are like
      delicious morsels;
   they go down into the inner parts
      of the body.
9 Whoever is slack in his work
   is a brother to him who destroys.
10 The name of the LORD is a strong
      tower;
   the righteous man runs into it and
      is safe.
11 A rich man's wealth is his strong city,
   and like a high wall in his imagina-
      tion.
12 Before destruction a man's heart is
      haughty,
   but humility comes before honor.
13 If one gives an answer before he
      hears,
   it is his folly and shame.
14 A man's spirit will endure sickness,
   but a crushed spirit who can bear?
15 An intelligent heart acquires knowl-
      edge,
   and the ear of the wise seeks
      knowledge.
16 A man's gift makes room for him
   and brings him before the great.
17 The one who states his case first
      seems right,
   until the other comes and exam-
      ines him.
18 The lot puts an end to quarrels
   and decides between powerful
      contenders.
19 A brother offended is more unyield-
      ing than a strong city,
   and quarreling is like the bars of a
      castle.
20 From the fruit of a man's mouth his
      stomach is satisfied;
   he is satisfied by the yield of his lips.

21 Death and life are in the power of the
      tongue,
   and those who love it will eat its
      fruits.
22 He who finds a wife finds a good thing
   and obtains favor from the LORD.
23 The poor use entreaties,
   but the rich answer roughly.
24 A man of many companions may
      come to ruin,
   but there is a friend who sticks
      closer than a brother.

19 Better is a poor person who
      walks in his integrity
   than one who is crooked in speech
      and is a fool.
2 Desire[2] without knowledge is not
      good,
   and whoever makes haste with his
      feet misses his way.
3 When a man's folly brings his way to
      ruin,
   his heart rages against the LORD.
4 Wealth brings many new friends,
   but a poor man is deserted by his
      friend.
5 A false witness will not go unpun-
      ished,
   and he who breathes out lies will
      not escape.
6 Many seek the favor of a generous
      man,[3]
   and everyone is a friend to a man
      who gives gifts.
7 All a poor man's brothers hate him;
   how much more do his friends go
      far from him!
He pursues them with words, but
      does not have them.[4]
8 Whoever gets sense loves his own
      soul;
   he who keeps understanding will
      discover good.
9 A false witness will not go unpun-
      ished,
   and he who breathes out lies will
      perish.
10 It is not fitting for a fool to live in
      luxury,
   much less for a slave to rule over
      princes.
11 Good sense makes one slow to anger,
   and it is his glory to overlook an
      offense.

---

[1] Hebrew *to lift the face of* [2] Or *A soul* [3] Or *of a noble* [4] The meaning of the Hebrew sentence is uncertain

12 A king's wrath is like the growling of
    a lion,
      but his favor is like dew on the
        grass.
13 A foolish son is ruin to his father,
      and a wife's quarreling is a con-
        tinual dripping of rain.
14 House and wealth are inherited from
    fathers,
      but a prudent wife is from the LORD.
15 Slothfulness casts into a deep sleep,
      and an idle person will suffer
        hunger.
16 Whoever keeps the commandment
      keeps his life;
      he who despises his ways will die.
17 Whoever is generous to the poor
      lends to the LORD,
      and he will repay him for his deed.
18 Discipline your son, for there is hope;
      do not set your heart on putting
        him to death.
19 A man of great wrath will pay the
    penalty,
      for if you deliver him, you will only
        have to do it again.
20 Listen to advice and accept instruction,
      that you may gain wisdom in the
        future.

21 Many are the plans in the mind of a
    man,
      but it is the purpose of the LORD
        that will stand.
22 What is desired in a man is steadfast
    love,
      and a poor man is better than a liar.
23 The fear of the LORD leads to life,
      and whoever has it rests satisfied;
      he will not be visited by harm.
24 The sluggard buries his hand in the
    dish
      and will not even bring it back to
        his mouth.
25 Strike a scoffer, and the simple will
      learn prudence;
      reprove a man of understanding,
        and he will gain knowledge.
26 He who does violence to his father
      and chases away his mother
    is a son who brings shame and
      reproach.
27 Cease to hear instruction, my son,
      and you will stray from the words
        of knowledge.
28 A worthless witness mocks at justice,
      and the mouth of the wicked
        devours iniquity.

Know God

verses to read
Proverbs 19:13–25

Are you spiritually lazy? It's easy to be so busy and so energetic in life that you have nothing left for spiritual stuff. But if you want more faith, more hope, more peace—if you want more of God and his presence—then you can't afford to be lazy. Your soul will go hungry if you let yourself be spiritually lazy (see Prov. 19:15).

Spiritual laziness starts when you don't have the energy to love God with all your heart, soul, mind, and strength. And it keeps going when you are too worn out or exhausted to get up and do what you know God is asking you to do. When you see a need and you don't fill it, when you hear a cry for help and you're too busy to answer, spiritual laziness will distract you and comfort you for the moment. But when you skip reading your Bible, you miss the chance to have more of him in your life. Every time you fall into the trap of spiritual laziness, you are refusing to feed your soul, and as a result your soul gets weak and fearful. Guard your heart, your mind, and your soul by becoming aware of your tendency to choose the easy way instead of devotion and discipline. But above all, remember that no matter how disciplined or lazy you are, you are God's daughter and his love for you is constant.

⁹ Condemnation is ready for scoffers,
  and beating for the backs of fools.

20 Wine is a mocker, strong drink a
       brawler,
   and whoever is led astray by it is
       not wise.[1]
² The terror of a king is like the growl-
     ing of a lion;
   whoever provokes him to anger
     forfeits his life.
³ It is an honor for a man to keep aloof
     from strife,
   but every fool will be quarreling.
⁴ The sluggard does not plow in the
     autumn;
   he will seek at harvest and have
     nothing.
⁵ The purpose in a man's heart is like
     deep water,
   but a man of understanding will
     draw it out.
⁶ Many a man proclaims his own
     steadfast love,
   but a faithful man who can find?
⁷ The righteous who walks in his
     integrity—
   blessed are his children after him!
⁸ A king who sits on the throne of
     judgment
   winnows all evil with his eyes.
⁹ Who can say, "I have made my heart
     pure;
   I am clean from my sin"?
¹⁰ Unequal[2] weights and unequal mea-
     sures
   are both alike an abomination to
     the LORD.
¹¹ Even a child makes himself known
     by his acts,
   by whether his conduct is pure
     and upright.[3]
¹² The hearing ear and the seeing eye,
   the LORD has made them both.
¹³ Love not sleep, lest you come to
     poverty;
   open your eyes, and you will have
     plenty of bread.
¹⁴ "Bad, bad," says the buyer,
   but when he goes away, then he
     boasts.
¹⁵ There is gold and abundance of
     costly stones,
   but the lips of knowledge are a
     precious jewel.

¹⁶ Take a man's garment when he has
     put up security for a stranger,
   and hold it in pledge when he puts
     up security for foreigners.[4]
¹⁷ Bread gained by deceit is sweet to a
     man,
   but afterward his mouth will be
     full of gravel.
¹⁸ Plans are established by counsel;
   by wise guidance wage war.
¹⁹ Whoever goes about slandering
     reveals secrets;
   therefore do not associate with a
     simple babbler.[5]
²⁰ If one curses his father or his mother,
   his lamp will be put out in utter
     darkness.
²¹ An inheritance gained hastily in the
     beginning
   will not be blessed in the end.
²² Do not say, "I will repay evil";
   wait for the LORD, and he will
     deliver you.
²³ Unequal weights are an abomination
     to the LORD,
   and false scales are not good.
²⁴ A man's steps are from the LORD;
   how then can man understand his
     way?
²⁵ It is a snare to say rashly, "It is holy,"
   and to reflect only after making
     vows.
²⁶ A wise king winnows the wicked
   and drives the wheel over them.
²⁷ The spirit[6] of man is the lamp of the
     LORD,
   searching all his innermost parts.
²⁸ Steadfast love and faithfulness pre-
     serve the king,
   and by steadfast love his throne is
     upheld.
²⁹ The glory of young men is their
     strength,
   but the splendor of old men is
     their gray hair.
³⁰ Blows that wound cleanse away evil;
   strokes make clean the innermost
     parts.

21 The king's heart is a stream of
       water in the hand of the LORD;
   he turns it wherever he will.
² Every way of a man is right in his
     own eyes,
   but the LORD weighs the heart.

¹ Or will not become wise ² Or Two kinds of; also verse 23 ³ Or Even a child can dissemble in his actions, though his conduct seems pure and upright ⁴ Or for an adulteress (compare 27:13) ⁵ Hebrew with one who is simple in his lips ⁶ Hebrew breath

3 To do righteousness and justice
  is more acceptable to the LORD
  than sacrifice.
4 Haughty eyes and a proud heart,
  the lamp[1] of the wicked, are sin.
5 The plans of the diligent lead surely
  to abundance,
  but everyone who is hasty comes
  only to poverty.

Ask Yourself . . .

ABOUT THOSE IN NEED

- Have I ever seen a stranger
  in need and walked right by
  because I was shy or afraid?

- If a stranger were crying on the
  bus next to me, would I try to
  comfort him or her?

- If I knew a girl who didn't
  have nice clothes and I knew
  she had nothing to wear to
  the dance, would I loan her
  something of mine?

- Am I too afraid to help people
  in need?

- What makes me afraid?

- What does God tell me
  will happen if I refuse to
  help people in need (see
  Prov. 21:13)?

- What did God do for me when
  he saw *me* in great need,
  because of sin?

---

6 The getting of treasures by a lying
  tongue
  is a fleeting vapor and a snare of
  death.[2]
7 The violence of the wicked will
  sweep them away,
  because they refuse to do what is
  just.
8 The way of the guilty is crooked,
  but the conduct of the pure is
  upright.

9 It is better to live in a corner of the
  housetop
  than in a house shared with a
  quarrelsome wife.
10 The soul of the wicked desires evil;
  his neighbor finds no mercy in his
  eyes.
11 When a scoffer is punished, the
  simple becomes wise;
  when a wise man is instructed, he
  gains knowledge.
12 The Righteous One observes the
  house of the wicked;
  he throws the wicked down to
  ruin.
13 Whoever closes his ear to the cry of
  the poor
  will himself call out and not be
  answered.
14 A gift in secret averts anger,
  and a concealed bribe,[3] strong
  wrath.
15 When justice is done, it is a joy to the
  righteous
  but terror to evildoers.
16 One who wanders from the way of
  good sense
  will rest in the assembly of the
  dead.
17 Whoever loves pleasure will be a
  poor man;
  he who loves wine and oil will not
  be rich.
18 The wicked is a ransom for the righteous,
  and the traitor for the upright.
19 It is better to live in a desert land
  than with a quarrelsome and fretful woman.
20 Precious treasure and oil are in a
  wise man's dwelling,
  but a foolish man devours it.
21 Whoever pursues righteousness and
  kindness
  will find life, righteousness, and
  honor.
22 A wise man scales the city of the
  mighty
  and brings down the stronghold in
  which they trust.
23 Whoever keeps his mouth and his
  tongue
  keeps himself out of trouble.

[1] Or *the plowing* [2] Some Hebrew manuscripts, Septuagint, Latin; most Hebrew manuscripts *vapor for those who seek death* [3] Hebrew *a bribe in the bosom*

4 "Scoffer" is the name of the arrogant,
    haughty man
    who acts with arrogant pride.
5 The desire of the sluggard kills him,
    for his hands refuse to labor.
6 All day long he craves and craves,
    but the righteous gives and does
    not hold back.
7 The sacrifice of the wicked is an
    abomination;
    how much more when he brings it
    with evil intent.
8 A false witness will perish,
    but the word of a man who hears
    will endure.
9 A wicked man puts on a bold face,
    but the upright gives thought to[1]
    his ways.
10 No wisdom, no understanding, no
    counsel
    can avail against the LORD.
11 The horse is made ready for the day
    of battle,
    but the victory belongs to the LORD.

22

A good name is to be chosen
    rather than great riches,
    and favor is better than silver or
    gold.
2 The rich and the poor meet together;
    the LORD is the maker of them all.
3 The prudent sees danger and hides
    himself,
    but the simple go on and suffer for
    it.
4 The reward for humility and fear of
    the LORD
    is riches and honor and life.[2]
5 Thorns and snares are in the way of
    the crooked;
    whoever guards his soul will keep
    far from them.
6 Train up a child in the way he should
    go;
    even when he is old he will not
    depart from it.
7 The rich rules over the poor,
    and the borrower is the slave of
    the lender.
8 Whoever sows injustice will reap
    calamity,
    and the rod of his fury will fail.
9 Whoever has a bountiful[3] eye will be
    blessed,
    for he shares his bread with the
    poor.

10 Drive out a scoffer, and strife will go
    out,
    and quarreling and abuse will
    cease.
11 He who loves purity of heart,
    and whose speech is gracious, will
    have the king as his friend.
12 The eyes of the LORD keep watch
    over knowledge,
    but he overthrows the words of
    the traitor.
13 The sluggard says, "There is a lion
    outside!
    I shall be killed in the streets!"
14 The mouth of forbidden[4] women is a
    deep pit;
    he with whom the LORD is angry
    will fall into it.
15 Folly is bound up in the heart of a
    child,
    but the rod of discipline drives it
    far from him.
16 Whoever oppresses the poor to
    increase his own wealth,
    or gives to the rich, will only come
    to poverty.

Words of the Wise

17 Incline your ear, and hear the words
    of the wise,
    and apply your heart to my knowl-
    edge,
18 for it will be pleasant if you keep
    them within you,
    if all of them are ready on your lips.
19 That your trust may be in the LORD,
    I have made them known to you
    today, even to you.
20 Have I not written for you thirty say-
    ings
    of counsel and knowledge,
21 to make you know what is right and
    true,
    that you may give a true answer to
    those who sent you?
22 Do not rob the poor, because he is
    poor,
    or crush the afflicted at the gate,
23 for the LORD will plead their cause
    and rob of life those who rob them.
24 Make no friendship with a man given
    to anger,
    nor go with a wrathful man,

[1] Or establishes [2] Or The reward for humility is the fear of the LORD, riches and honor and life [3] Hebrew good [4] Hebrew strange

25 lest you learn his ways
    and entangle yourself in a snare.
26 Be not one of those who give pledges,
    who put up security for debts.
27 If you have nothing with which to pay,
    why should your bed be taken
        from under you?
28 Do not move the ancient landmark
    that your fathers have set.
29 Do you see a man skillful in his work?
    He will stand before kings;
    he will not stand before obscure
        men.

23

When you sit down to eat with a
    ruler,
    observe carefully what[1] is before
        you,
2 and put a knife to your throat
    if you are given to appetite.
3 Do not desire his delicacies,
    for they are deceptive food.
4 Do not toil to acquire wealth;
    be discerning enough to desist.
5 When your eyes light on it, it is gone,
    for suddenly it sprouts wings,
    flying like an eagle toward heaven.
6 Do not eat the bread of a man who is
    stingy;[2]
    do not desire his delicacies,
7 for he is like one who is inwardly
    calculating.[3]
    "Eat and drink!" he says to you,
    but his heart is not with you.
8 You will vomit up the morsels that
    you have eaten,
    and waste your pleasant words.
9 Do not speak in the hearing of a fool,
    for he will despise the good sense
    of your words.
10 Do not move an ancient landmark
    or enter the fields of the fatherless,
11 for their Redeemer is strong;
    he will plead their cause against
        you.
12 Apply your heart to instruction
    and your ear to words of knowl-
        edge.
13 Do not withhold discipline from a
    child;
    if you strike him with a rod, he will
        not die.
14 If you strike him with the rod,
    you will save his soul from Sheol.

15 My son, if your heart is wise,
    my heart too will be glad.
16 My inmost being[4] will exult
    when your lips speak what is right

Ask Yourself . . .

ABOUT YOUR THOUGHTS

Your thoughts say a lot about your soul. If you love God and believe his Word is true, then ask yourself if there is any sin in your thoughts:

- Do I want what others have?
- Am I thinking anything that is a complaint?
- Am I lusting in my thoughts?
- Do I have any mean thoughts about any person?
- Do I think I am better than others?
- Do I think I have to be comfortable in order to be happy?
- Do I worry about things?
- Do I doubt God's power, protection, or forgiveness?

As you look into God's Word, you will start to see areas in your life where you have let sin move in. If you answered yes to any of these, then you must confess, repent, and get back to thinking about whatever is true, honorable, and commendable (see Phil. 4:8).

17 Let not your heart envy sinners,
    but continue in the fear of the
        Lord all the day.
18 Surely there is a future,
    and your hope will not be cut off.

19 Hear, my son, and be wise,
    and direct your heart in the way.
20 Be not among drunkards[5]
    or among gluttonous eaters of meat

[1] Or who [2] Hebrew whose eye is evil [3] Or for as he calculates in his soul, so is he [4] Hebrew My kidneys [5] Hebrew those who drink too much wine

¹ for the drunkard and the glutton will
   come to poverty,
   and slumber will clothe them with
   rags.

² Listen to your father who gave you
   life,
   and do not despise your mother
   when she is old.

³ Buy truth, and do not sell it;
   buy wisdom, instruction, and
   understanding.

⁴ The father of the righteous will
   greatly rejoice;
   he who fathers a wise son will be
   glad in him.

⁵ Let your father and mother be glad;
   let her who bore you rejoice.

⁶ My son, give me your heart,
   and let your eyes observe¹ my ways.

⁷ For a prostitute is a deep pit;
   an adulteress² is a narrow well.

⁸ She lies in wait like a robber
   and increases the traitors among
   mankind.

⁹ Who has woe? Who has sorrow?
   Who has strife? Who has com-
   plaining?
   Who has wounds without cause?
   Who has redness of eyes?

³⁰ Those who tarry long over wine;
   those who go to try mixed wine.

³¹ Do not look at wine when it is red,
   when it sparkles in the cup
   and goes down smoothly.

³² In the end it bites like a serpent
   and stings like an adder.

³³ Your eyes will see strange things,
   and your heart utter perverse
   things.

³⁴ You will be like one who lies down in
   the midst of the sea,
   like one who lies on the top of a
   mast.³

³⁵ "They struck me," you will say,⁴ "but
   I was not hurt;
   they beat me, but I did not feel it.
   When shall I awake?
   I must have another drink."

24

Be not envious of evil men,
   nor desire to be with them,

² for their hearts devise violence,
   and their lips talk of trouble.

³ By wisdom a house is built,
   and by understanding it is established;

⁴ by knowledge the rooms are filled
   with all precious and pleasant
   riches.

⁵ A wise man is full of strength,
   and a man of knowledge enhances
   his might,

⁶ for by wise guidance you can wage
   your war,
   and in abundance of counselors
   there is victory.

⁷ Wisdom is too high for a fool;
   in the gate he does not open his
   mouth.

⁸ Whoever plans to do evil
   will be called a schemer.

⁹ The devising⁵ of folly is sin,
   and the scoffer is an abomination
   to mankind.

¹⁰ If you faint in the day of adversity,
   your strength is small.

¹¹ Rescue those who are being taken
   away to death;
   hold back those who are stumbling
   to the slaughter.

¹² If you say, "Behold, we did not know
   this,"
   does not he who weighs the heart
   perceive it?
   Does not he who keeps watch over
   your soul know it,
   and will he not repay man according to his work?

¹³ My son, eat honey, for it is good,
   and the drippings of the honeycomb are sweet to your taste.

¹⁴ Know that wisdom is such to your
   soul;
   if you find it, there will be a future,
   and your hope will not be cut off.

¹⁵ Lie not in wait as a wicked man
   against the dwelling of the
   righteous;
   do no violence to his home;

¹⁶ for the righteous falls seven times
   and rises again,
   but the wicked stumble in times of
   calamity.

¹ Or *delight in* ² Hebrew *a foreign woman* ³ Or *of the rigging* ⁴ Hebrew lacks *you will say* ⁵ Or *scheming*

17 Do not rejoice when your enemy falls,
    and let not your heart be glad
        when he stumbles,
18 lest the Lord see it and be displeased,
    and turn away his anger from him.

19 Fret not yourself because of evildoers,
    and be not envious of the wicked,
20 for the evil man has no future;
    the lamp of the wicked will be put
        out.

21 My son, fear the Lord and the king,
    and do not join with those who do
        otherwise,
22 for disaster will arise suddenly from
        them,
    and who knows the ruin that will
        come from them both?

More Sayings of the Wise

23 These also are sayings of the wise.

Partiality in judging is not good.
24 Whoever says to the wicked, "You are
    in the right,"
    will be cursed by peoples,
        abhorred by nations,
25 but those who rebuke the wicked
    will have delight,
    and a good blessing will come
        upon them.
26 Whoever gives an honest answer
    kisses the lips.

27 Prepare your work outside;
    get everything ready for yourself
        in the field,
    and after that build your house.

28 Be not a witness against your neigh-
    bor without cause,
    and do not deceive with your lips.
29 Do not say, "I will do to him as he has
    done to me;
    I will pay the man back for what he
        has done."

30 I passed by the field of a sluggard,
    by the vineyard of a man lacking
        sense,
31 and behold, it was all overgrown
    with thorns;
    the ground was covered with
        nettles,
    and its stone wall was broken
        down.

32 Then I saw and considered it;
    I looked and received instruction.
33 A little sleep, a little slumber,
    a little folding of the hands to rest,
34 and poverty will come upon you like
    a robber,
    and want like an armed man.

More Proverbs of Solomon

25 These also are proverbs of Solomon
which the men of Hezekiah king of
Judah copied.

2 It is the glory of God to conceal
    things,
    but the glory of kings is to search
        things out.
3 As the heavens for height, and the
    earth for depth,
    so the heart of kings is unsearch-
        able.
4 Take away the dross from the silver,
    and the smith has material for a
        vessel;
5 take away the wicked from the pres-
    ence of the king,
    and his throne will be established
        in righteousness.
6 Do not put yourself forward in the
    king's presence
    or stand in the place of the great,
7 for it is better to be told, "Come up
    here,"
    than to be put lower in the pres-
        ence of a noble.

What your eyes have seen
8 do not hastily bring into court,
for[1] what will you do in the end,
    when your neighbor puts you to
        shame?
9 Argue your case with your neighbor
    himself,
    and do not reveal another's secret,
10 lest he who hears you bring shame
    upon you,
    and your ill repute have no end.

11 A word fitly spoken
    is like apples of gold in a setting of
        silver.
12 Like a gold ring or an ornament of
    gold
    is a wise reprover to a listening
        ear.

[1] Hebrew or else

3 Like the cold of snow in the time of
      harvest
      is a faithful messenger to those
      who send him;
      he refreshes the soul of his masters.

4 Like clouds and wind without rain
      is a man who boasts of a gift he
      does not give.

5 With patience a ruler may be per-
      suaded,
      and a soft tongue will break a bone.

6 If you have found honey, eat only
      enough for you,
      lest you have your fill of it and
      vomit it.

7 Let your foot be seldom in your
      neighbor's house,
      lest he have his fill of you and hate
      you.

8 A man who bears false witness
      against his neighbor
      is like a war club, or a sword, or a
      sharp arrow.

9 Trusting in a treacherous man in
      time of trouble
      is like a bad tooth or a foot that
      slips.

10 Whoever sings songs to a heavy heart
      is like one who takes off a garment
      on a cold day,
      and like vinegar on soda.

1 If your enemy is hungry, give him
      bread to eat,
      and if he is thirsty, give him water
      to drink,

2 for you will heap burning coals on
      his head,
      and the LORD will reward you.

3 The north wind brings forth rain,
      and a backbiting tongue, angry
      looks.

4 It is better to live in a corner of the
      housetop
      than in a house shared with a
      quarrelsome wife.

5 Like cold water to a thirsty soul,
      so is good news from a far country.

6 Like a muddied spring or a polluted
      fountain
      is a righteous man who gives way
      before the wicked.

7 It is not good to eat much honey,
      nor is it glorious to seek one's own
      glory.[1]

28 A man without self-control
      is like a city broken into and left
      without walls.

26

Like snow in summer or rain in
      harvest,
      so honor is not fitting for a fool.

2 Like a sparrow in its flitting, like a
      swallow in its flying,
      a curse that is causeless does not
      alight.

3 A whip for the horse, a bridle for the
      donkey,
      and a rod for the back of fools.

4 Answer not a fool according to his
      folly,
      lest you be like him yourself.

5 Answer a fool according to his folly,
      lest he be wise in his own eyes.

6 Whoever sends a message by the
      hand of a fool
      cuts off his own feet and drinks
      violence.

7 Like a lame man's legs, which hang
      useless,
      is a proverb in the mouth of fools.

8 Like one who binds the stone in the
      sling
      is one who gives honor to a fool.

9 Like a thorn that goes up into the
      hand of a drunkard
      is a proverb in the mouth of fools.

10 Like an archer who wounds every-
      one
      is one who hires a passing fool or
      drunkard.[2]

11 Like a dog that returns to his vomit
      is a fool who repeats his folly.

12 Do you see a man who is wise in his
      own eyes?
      There is more hope for a fool than
      for him.

13 The sluggard says, "There is a lion in
      the road!
      There is a lion in the streets!"

14 As a door turns on its hinges,
      so does a sluggard on his bed.

15 The sluggard buries his hand in the
      dish;
      it wears him out to bring it back to
      his mouth.

16 The sluggard is wiser in his own eyes
      than seven men who can answer
      sensibly.

[1] The meaning of the Hebrew line is uncertain [2] Or hires a fool or passersby

17 Whoever meddles in a quarrel not
   his own
      is like one who takes a passing dog
      by the ears.

18 Like a madman who throws firebrands, arrows, and death

19 is the man who deceives his neighbor
   and says, "I am only joking!"

20 For lack of wood the fire goes out,
   and where there is no whisperer,
      quarreling ceases.

21 As charcoal to hot embers and wood
   to fire,
      so is a quarrelsome man for kin-
      dling strife.

22 The words of a whisperer are like
   delicious morsels;
      they go down into the inner parts
      of the body.

23 Like the glaze[1] covering an earthen
   vessel
      are fervent lips with an evil heart.

24 Whoever hates disguises himself
   with his lips
      and harbors deceit in his heart;

25 when he speaks graciously, believe
   him not,
      for there are seven abominations
      in his heart;

26 though his hatred be covered with
   deception,
      his wickedness will be exposed in
      the assembly.

27 Whoever digs a pit will fall into it,
   and a stone will come back on him
      who starts it rolling.

28 A lying tongue hates its victims,
   and a flattering mouth works ruin.

27 Do not boast about tomorrow,
   for you do not know what a day
   may bring.

2 Let another praise you, and not your
   own mouth;
      a stranger, and not your own lips.

3 A stone is heavy, and sand is weighty,
   but a fool's provocation is heavier
   than both.

4 Wrath is cruel, anger is overwhelming,
   but who can stand before jealousy?

5 Better is open rebuke
   than hidden love.

6 Faithful are the wounds of a friend;
   profuse are the kisses of an enemy.

7 One who is full loathes honey,
   but to one who is hungry everything bitter is sweet.

8 Like a bird that strays from its nest
   is a man who strays from his
   home.

9 Oil and perfume make the heart glad,
   and the sweetness of a friend
      comes from his earnest coun-
      sel.[2]

10 Do not forsake your friend and your
   father's friend,
      and do not go to your brother's
      house in the day of your
      calamity.
   Better is a neighbor who is near
      than a brother who is far away.

11 Be wise, my son, and make my heart
   glad,
      that I may answer him who
      reproaches me.

12 The prudent sees danger and hides
   himself,
      but the simple go on and suffer for
      it.

13 Take a man's garment when he has
   put up security for a stranger,
      and hold it in pledge when he puts
      up security for an adulteress.[3]

14 Whoever blesses his neighbor with a
   loud voice,
      rising early in the morning,
      will be counted as cursing.

15 A continual dripping on a rainy day
   and a quarrelsome wife are alike;

16 to restrain her is to restrain the wind
   or to grasp[4] oil in one's right hand.

17 Iron sharpens iron,
   and one man sharpens another.[5]

18 Whoever tends a fig tree will eat its
   fruit,
      and he who guards his master will
      be honored.

19 As in water face reflects face,
   so the heart of man reflects the
   man.

20 Sheol and Abaddon are never satisfied,
      and never satisfied are the eyes of
      man.

21 The crucible is for silver, and the
   furnace is for gold,
      and a man is tested by his praise.

---

[1] By revocalization; Hebrew *silver of dross* [2] Or *and so does the sweetness of a friend that comes from his earnest counsel* [3] Hebrew *a foreign woman*; a slight emendation yields (compare Vulgate; see also 20:16) *foreigners* [4] Hebrew *to meet with* [5] Hebrew *sharpens the face of another*

22 Crush a fool in a mortar with a pestle
   along with crushed grain,
      yet his folly will not depart from
      him.

23 Know well the condition of your
   flocks,
      and give attention to your herds,
24 for riches do not last forever;
      and does a crown endure to all
      generations?
25 When the grass is gone and the new
   growth appears
      and the vegetation of the moun-
      tains is gathered,
26 the lambs will provide your clothing,
      and the goats the price of a field.
27 There will be enough goats' milk for
   your food,
      for the food of your household
      and maintenance for your girls.

28 The wicked flee when no one
      pursues,
      but the righteous are bold as a lion.
2 When a land transgresses, it has
   many rulers,
      but with a man of understanding
      and knowledge,
      its stability will long continue.
3 A poor man who oppresses the poor
      is a beating rain that leaves no
      food.
4 Those who forsake the law praise the
   wicked,
      but those who keep the law strive
      against them.
5 Evil men do not understand justice,
      but those who seek the LORD
      understand it completely.
6 Better is a poor man who walks in
   his integrity
      than a rich man who is crooked in
      his ways.
7 The one who keeps the law is a son
   with understanding,
      but a companion of gluttons
      shames his father.
8 Whoever multiplies his wealth by
   interest and profit[1]
      gathers it for him who is generous
      to the poor.
9 If one turns away his ear from hearing the law,
      even his prayer is an abomination.

10 Whoever misleads the upright into
    an evil way
      will fall into his own pit,
      but the blameless will have a
      goodly inheritance.

Ask Yourself . . .
ABOUT YOUR PRAYERS

- What do I pray for the most?
- If I get what I want, will I be more holy?
- Do I pray more for myself or for others?
- Are my prayers being answered?
- If not, then according to God's Word, why might that be?
- What is the purpose of my prayers?
- What should be the purpose of prayer?
- Am I aware that Jesus is interceding for me at God's right hand?

11 A rich man is wise in his own eyes,
      but a poor man who has under-
      standing will find him out.
12 When the righteous triumph, there is
   great glory,
      but when the wicked rise, people
      hide themselves.
13 Whoever conceals his transgressions
      will not prosper,
      but he who confesses and forsakes
      them will obtain mercy.
14 Blessed is the one who fears the
   LORD always,
      but whoever hardens his heart will
      fall into calamity.
15 Like a roaring lion or a charging bear
      is a wicked ruler over a poor people.
16 A ruler who lacks understanding is a
   cruel oppressor,
      but he who hates unjust gain will
      prolong his days.

[1] That is, profit that comes from charging interest to the poor

17 If one is burdened with the blood of
another,
   he will be a fugitive until death;[1]
   let no one help him.

18 Whoever walks in integrity will be
delivered,
   but he who is crooked in his ways
will suddenly fall.

19 Whoever works his land will have
plenty of bread,
   but he who follows worthless
pursuits will have plenty of
poverty.

20 A faithful man will abound with
blessings,
   but whoever hastens to be rich
will not go unpunished.

21 To show partiality is not good,
   but for a piece of bread a man will
do wrong.

22 A stingy man[2] hastens after wealth
   and does not know that poverty
will come upon him.

23 Whoever rebukes a man will afterward find more favor
   than he who flatters with his
tongue.

24 Whoever robs his father or his
mother
   and says, "That is no transgression,"
   is a companion to a man who
destroys.

25 A greedy man stirs up strife,
   but the one who trusts in the LORD
will be enriched.

[1] Hebrew *until the pit* [2] Hebrew *A man whose eye is evil*

Know Love

verses to read
Proverbs 28:12–14

"None is righteous, no, not one" (Rom. 3:10). No one is perfect. We all mess up and get it wrong, and there's nothing more ugly, nothing more ungodly than a person who says, "I haven't done anything wrong" and refuses to admit his or her mistakes.

Confession can feel as uncomfortable as being stripped of all your clothing. But confessing when you do something wrong is the foundation of all faith. Without confession you wouldn't be saved, because your confession is what first brought you to your knees and brought Jesus to your heart.

Confession of sin is crucial to the life of the believer, and so is apologizing when your sin hurts others. The fact is that when you apologize, you don't actually look vulnerable; you look strong. The strong girl is the one who can control herself enough to risk embarrassment or disdain from others in order to be godly. The strong girl isn't afraid of the wrath of people, but only of God. And the strong girl puts the feelings and needs of others first and refuses to be ruled by the fear of others finding out she's an imperfect person.

An apology turns away wrath. It turned away the wrath of God when you offered it to him, and it will turn away the wrath of the people you've wronged when you offer it to them. Apologizing when you've been wrong restores relationships. It builds trust and strengthens love.

A quick apology is like pulling a splinter out of your finger: it ends the pain, eliminates the danger of infection, and lets the healing begin. So be quick to apologize, and you will discover that truth never disappoints, and that confession is the foundation of all things pure and godly. Bring your darkness into the light, think about your sin, and let the words "I'm sorry, please forgive me" be your friend.

26 Whoever trusts in his own mind is a
 fool,
  but he who walks in wisdom will
  be delivered.
27 Whoever gives to the poor will not
 want,
  but he who hides his eyes will get
  many a curse.
28 When the wicked rise, people hide
 themselves,
  but when they perish, the righteous increase.

29 He who is often reproved, yet
 stiffens his neck,
  will suddenly be broken beyond
  healing.
2 When the righteous increase, the
 people rejoice,
  but when the wicked rule, the
  people groan.
3 He who loves wisdom makes his
 father glad,
  but a companion of prostitutes
  squanders his wealth.
4 By justice a king builds up the land,
  but he who exacts gifts[1] tears it
  down.
5 A man who flatters his neighbor
  spreads a net for his feet.
6 An evil man is ensnared in his transgression,
  but a righteous man sings and
  rejoices.
7 A righteous man knows the rights of
 the poor;
  a wicked man does not understand
  such knowledge.
8 Scoffers set a city aflame,
  but the wise turn away wrath.
9 If a wise man has an argument with a
 fool,
  the fool only rages and laughs, and
  there is no quiet.
10 Bloodthirsty men hate one who is
 blameless
  and seek the life of the upright.[2]
11 A fool gives full vent to his spirit,
  but a wise man quietly holds it back.
12 If a ruler listens to falsehood,
  all his officials will be wicked.
13 The poor man and the oppressor
 meet together;
  the LORD gives light to the eyes of
  both.

14 If a king faithfully judges the poor,
 his throne will be established
 forever.
15 The rod and reproof give wisdom,
  but a child left to himself brings
  shame to his mother.
16 When the wicked increase, transgression increases,
  but the righteous will look upon
  their downfall.
17 Discipline your son, and he will give
 you rest;
  he will give delight to your heart.
18 Where there is no prophetic vision
 the people cast off restraint,[3]
  but blessed is he who keeps the law.
19 By mere words a servant is not disciplined,
  for though he understands, he will
  not respond.
20 Do you see a man who is hasty in his
 words?
  There is more hope for a fool than
  for him.
21 Whoever pampers his servant from
 childhood
  will in the end find him his heir.[4]
22 A man of wrath stirs up strife,
  and one given to anger causes
  much transgression.
23 One's pride will bring him low,
  but he who is lowly in spirit will
  obtain honor.
24 The partner of a thief hates his own
 life;
  he hears the curse, but discloses
  nothing.
25 The fear of man lays a snare,
  but whoever trusts in the LORD is
  safe.
26 Many seek the face of a ruler,
  but it is from the LORD that a man
  gets justice.
27 An unjust man is an abomination to
 the righteous,
  but one whose way is straight is an
  abomination to the wicked.

The Words of Agur

30 The words of Agur son of Jakeh. The
 oracle.[5]

 The man declares, I am weary, O God;
  I am weary, O God, and worn out.[6]

---

[1] Or who taxes heavily [2] Or but the upright seek his soul [3] Or the people are discouraged [4] The meaning of the Hebrew word rendered his heir is uncertain [5] Or Jakeh, the man of Massa [6] Revocalization; Hebrew The man declares to Ithiel, to Ithiel and Ucal

2 Surely I am too stupid to be a man.
    I have not the understanding of a
    man.
3 I have not learned wisdom,
    nor have I knowledge of the Holy
    One.
4 Who has ascended to heaven and
    come down?
    Who has gathered the wind in his
    fists?
    Who has wrapped up the waters in a
    garment?
    Who has established all the ends
    of the earth?
    What is his name, and what is his
    son's name?
    Surely you know!

5 Every word of God proves true;
    he is a shield to those who take
    refuge in him.
6 Do not add to his words,
    lest he rebuke you and you be
    found a liar.

7 Two things I ask of you;
    deny them not to me before I die:

¹ Hebrew *There is a generation*; also verses 12, 13, 14

8 Remove far from me falsehood and
    lying;
    give me neither poverty nor riches
    feed me with the food that is need
    ful for me,
9 lest I be full and deny you
    and say, "Who is the LORD?"
    or lest I be poor and steal
    and profane the name of my God.

10 Do not slander a servant to his master
    lest he curse you, and you be held
    guilty.

11 There are those¹ who curse their
    fathers
    and do not bless their mothers.
12 There are those who are clean in
    their own eyes
    but are not washed of their filth.
13 There are those—how lofty are their
    eyes,
    how high their eyelids lift!
14 There are those whose teeth are
    swords,
    whose fangs are knives,
to devour the poor from off the earth
    the needy from among mankind.

Know God

verses to read
Proverbs 29:22–27

Fear of anything or anyone other than God is sin. People are afraid because they don't have the blood of Jesus in their veins. Worry and fear come from doubt, so how can anyone who trusts Jesus be filled with worry and fear? If you are a God Girl, by definition you are a believer, not a doubter. Doubt and belief cannot peacefully coexist. One will always conquer the other. Fear and worry are the symptoms of doubt, so they should be rejected in favor of faith.

If you tend to fear, think about this: the same God who saved you from your sin can save you from whatever you are afraid of. Are you more devoted to the voice of fear or the voice of God? In order to be free, you have to say no every time fear talks to your soul. Just say, "I trust my God," and leave it at that (see Prov. 29:25). Fear might never stop knocking at your door, but you don't ever have to answer again. Lock the dead bolt and cover the peephole!

Fear is a blatant disregard for the work that Christ has done for you. Don't call him a liar. Take his hand and trust him to hold you up as you climb the cliff and cross the canyon.

15 The leech has two daughters:
  Give and Give.[1]
Three things are never satisfied;
  four never say, "Enough":
16 Sheol, the barren womb,
  the land never satisfied with
    water,
  and the fire that never says,
    "Enough."

17 The eye that mocks a father
  and scorns to obey a mother
will be picked out by the ravens of
    the valley
  and eaten by the vultures.

18 Three things are too wonderful for
    me;
  four I do not understand:
19 the way of an eagle in the sky,
  the way of a serpent on a rock,
  the way of a ship on the high seas,
  and the way of a man with a vir-
    gin.

20 This is the way of an adulteress:
  she eats and wipes her mouth
  and says, "I have done no wrong."

21 Under three things the earth
    trembles;
  under four it cannot bear up:
22 a slave when he becomes king,
  and a fool when he is filled with
    food;
23 an unloved woman when she gets a
    husband,
  and a maidservant when she dis-
    places her mistress.

24 Four things on earth are small,
  but they are exceedingly wise:
25 the ants are a people not strong,
  yet they provide their food in the
    summer;
26 the rock badgers are a people not
    mighty,
  yet they make their homes in the
    cliffs;

[1] Or "Give, give," they cry

Know Yourself

verses to read
Proverbs 30:7-9

Do you consume more than you need? It's a simple question about a simple topic: stuff. How much stuff—clothes, food, and toys—do you use that you technically don't need in order to survive? When you overconsume, it's because of your focus. We tend to focus on what we consume, and consume to the degree of our obsession over a thing. In other words, if you love books and read them ravenously, your focus is knowledge. Or you may eat anything and everything because your focus is comfort or satisfaction.

When someone consumes more than they need, they run the risk of actually denying God by making what they consume more important than he is. The author of this proverb asked God to make him neither rich nor poor. Can you imagine praying for something like that? "Lord, don't give me lots of money so I can buy all the things I want." What a prayer!

Think about the impact of your consumption on your relationship with the Father. Where do you put most of your thoughts? What occupies most of your time, your energy, your heart? Have your obsessions, those things you can't live without, replaced God on the throne of your heart? If so, they are little idols, and they will suffocate your joy in God. If you want more of his hand and presence in your life, then take a look at what you consume and see if you don't spend too much time and energy on the things around you instead of the God above you.

27 the locusts have no king,
  yet all of them march in rank;
28 the lizard you can take in your hands,
  yet it is in kings' palaces.

29 Three things are stately in their tread;
  four are stately in their stride:
30 the lion, which is mightiest among
    beasts
  and does not turn back before any;
31 the strutting rooster,[1] the he-goat,
  and a king whose army is with him.[2]

32 If you have been foolish, exalting
    yourself,
  or if you have been devising evil,
  put your hand on your mouth.
33 For pressing milk produces curds,
  pressing the nose produces blood,
  and pressing anger produces
    strife.

The Words of King Lemuel

31 The words of King Lemuel. An oracle
that his mother taught him:

2 What are you doing, my son?[3] What
    are you doing, son of my womb?
  What are you doing, son of my
    vows?
3 Do not give your strength to women,
  your ways to those who destroy
    kings.
4 It is not for kings, O Lemuel,
  it is not for kings to drink wine,
  or for rulers to take strong drink,
5 lest they drink and forget what has
    been decreed
  and pervert the rights of all the
    afflicted.
6 Give strong drink to the one who is
    perishing,
  and wine to those in bitter dis-
    tress;[4]
7 let them drink and forget their pov-
    erty
  and remember their misery no
    more.
8 Open your mouth for the mute,
  for the rights of all who are desti-
    tute.[5]
9 Open your mouth, judge righteously,
  defend the rights of the poor and
    needy.

The Woman Who Fears the Lord

10[6] An excellent wife who can find?
  She is far more precious than
    jewels.
11 The heart of her husband trusts in
    her,
  and he will have no lack of gain.
12 She does him good, and not harm,
  all the days of her life.
13 She seeks wool and flax,
  and works with willing hands.
14 She is like the ships of the merchant;
  she brings her food from afar.
15 She rises while it is yet night
  and provides food for her house-
    hold
  and portions for her maidens.
16 She considers a field and buys it;
  with the fruit of her hands she
    plants a vineyard.
17 She dresses herself[7] with strength
  and makes her arms strong.
18 She perceives that her merchandise
    is profitable.
  Her lamp does not go out at night.
19 She puts her hands to the distaff,
  and her hands hold the spindle.
20 She opens her hand to the poor
  and reaches out her hands to the
    needy.
21 She is not afraid of snow for her
    household,
  for all her household are clothed in
    scarlet.[8]
22 She makes bed coverings for herself;
  her clothing is fine linen and
    purple.
23 Her husband is known in the gates
  when he sits among the elders of
    the land.
24 She makes linen garments and sells
    them;
  she delivers sashes to the mer-
    chant.
25 Strength and dignity are her clothing,
  and she laughs at the time to come.
26 She opens her mouth with wisdom,
  and the teaching of kindness is on
    her tongue.
27 She looks well to the ways of her
    household
  and does not eat the bread of idle-
    ness.

---

[1] Or the magpie, or the greyhound; Hebrew girt-of-loins [2] Or against whom there is no rising up [3] Hebrew What, my son? [4] Hebrew those bitter in soul [5] Hebrew are sons of passing away [6] Verses 10–31 are an acrostic poem, each verse beginning with the successive letters of the Hebrew alphabet [7] Hebrew She girds her loins [8] Or in double thickness

The Proverbs 31 Woman

Read this God Girl story in Proverbs 31:10–31.

> Strength and dignity are her clothing,
>   and she laughs at the time to come.

Proverbs 31:25

A God Girl, like the Proverbs 31 woman, is a blessing to those who know her. Her strong character and industrious spirit give where others only take. Having been rescued by sheer grace, her focus isn't on herself but on her God, and because of that she isn't easily offended when others play while she works or sleep while she labors. Her gift to those around her is her undying love for God, which takes her out of herself and gives her the confidence to create opportunities to prosper. Everything that she does, she does for the love of God, and because of that the people he has entrusted her with are well cared for. She is able, by the help of God, to do more than the average person could do—because she doesn't rely on her own strength but on his. When stress or worry rears its ugly head, she quickly looks the other way and returns to her purpose on earth: to serve a living God and not her emotions. She speaks with wisdom that comes from her faith in God and his Holy Spirit.

The words of the God Girl encourage and admonish and never belittle or despise. They are always colored with the love of God. She isn't afraid of teaching others the truth of Scripture because she is so confident in it herself. She is tireless in her efforts to serve the living God because she draws her power from him each day. Others are amazed at her tenacity and ability to overcome even the most difficult situations. She finds truth in the Word of God and application for her daily life, looking for all the answers to life's hard questions in its pages. Her life is enviable, not because she is so remarkable herself but because she knows God's remarkable love for her. Peace, hope, and love are hers, and because of that others call her, like the women who have come before her, blessed.

28   Her children rise up and call her
         blessed;
      her husband also, and he praises
         her:
29   "Many women have done excellently,
      but you surpass them all."

30   Charm is deceitful, and beauty is vain,
      but a woman who fears the LORD
         is to be praised.
31   Give her of the fruit of her hands,
      and let her works praise her in the
         gates.

INTRODUCTION TO
Ecclesiastes

Author: A son of King David, possibly Solomon

Time: Possibly the fifth century B.C.

Place: Probably Israel

Written to: Nonbelievers as well as the Israelites

the gist

Ecclesiastes is a king's thoughts on the futility of life without God as your number one concern. He had tried it all, done it all, and found out that "all" wasn't enough because without God "all" was nothing.

things to look for

The use of poetic language

Thoughts on happiness (see Eccles. 2:24–25; 3:12–13, 22; 5:18–20; 8:15; 9:7–9; 11:7–10)

Things that are pointless (see Eccles. 1:14; 2:1–2, 11, 15, 17, 26; 4:4, 7–8, 16; 5:10; 6:2, 12; 7:15; 8:14; 9:9; 11:10)

Fear God

> Fear God and keep his commandments, for this is the whole duty of man.
>
> *Ecclesiastes 12:13*

Do you want to be rich and famous? How do you think that would change your life? Would it make you happier, more at ease, more hopeful? The truth is that a lot of us look for our reason, our significance, in the hope of fame. It's easy to believe that it would be heaven on earth, or at least a ton better than your ordinary life. But if you think being famous would be great, then you're gonna have an interesting ride reading Ecclesiastes.

Solomon was the richest and most famous guy on earth. He was the king. He could buy or build, take or own anything he wanted. And since he had it all, he used his dough and fame to try to buy happiness. He owned everything he wanted to own and had the luxury to spend a ton of time just looking for fun things to do on this earth—or "under the sun," as he put it. He did find temporary pleasure, but he realized in his old age that it was all pointless—that none of it really mattered. All his parties and purchases, all his popularity and his ability to get other people to do whatever he wanted them to do was a total zero when he looked back on it all. In the end, he figured out that nothing under that big ol' yellow sun would make him happy and content the way God could.

Some people are uncomfortable with the book of Ecclesiastes because much of it seems to contradict the rest of Scripture. But as you read this book, remember that it is written from the perspective of a man looking for all his wants and needs to be fulfilled here on earth instead of looking to God. Look at Ecclesiastes as the ultimate study in hedonism, which is looking for pleasure as your main goal in life. It's easy, even as a God Girl to make pleasure your number one goal, but as Solomon found out, it doesn't really satisfy you unless you seek pleasure mainly in God. All the really solid joys of life are only in Jesus. When you find this out, you'll find everything you've ever needed.

Must-Know Verses

Then I considered all that my hands had done and the toil I had expended in doing it, and behold, all was vanity and a striving after wind, and there was nothing to be gained under the sun. *Ecclesiastes 2:11*

For everything there is a season, and a time for every matter under heaven. *Ecclesiastes 3:1*

Though a man might prevail against one who is alone, two will withstand him—a threefold cord is not quickly broken. *Ecclesiastes 4:12*

In the day of prosperity be joyful, and in the day of adversity consider: God has made the one as well as the other, so that man may not find out anything that will be after him. *Ecclesiastes 7:14*

Ecclesiastes

All Is Vanity

1 ¹ The words of the Preacher,[1] the son of David, king in Jerusalem.

² Vanity[2] of vanities, says the Preacher,
  vanity of vanities! All is vanity.
³ What does man gain by all the toil
  at which he toils under the sun?
⁴ A generation goes, and a generation comes,
  but the earth remains forever.
⁵ The sun rises, and the sun goes down,
  and hastens[3] to the place where it rises.
⁶ The wind blows to the south
  and goes around to the north;
around and around goes the wind,
  and on its circuits the wind returns.
⁷ All streams run to the sea,
  but the sea is not full;
to the place where the streams flow,
  there they flow again.
⁸ All things are full of weariness;
  a man cannot utter it;
the eye is not satisfied with seeing,
  nor the ear filled with hearing.
⁹ What has been is what will be,
  and what has been done is what will be done,
and there is nothing new under the sun.
¹⁰ Is there a thing of which it is said,
  "See, this is new"?
It has been already
  in the ages before us.
¹¹ There is no remembrance of former things,[4]
  nor will there be any remembrance

of later things[5] yet to be
  among those who come after.

The Vanity of Wisdom

¹² I the Preacher have been king over Israel in Jerusalem. ¹³ And I applied my heart[6] to seek and to search out by wisdom all that is done under heaven. It is an unhappy business that God has given to the children of man to be busy with. ¹⁴ I have seen everything that is done under the sun, and behold, all is vanity[7] and a striving after wind.[8]

¹⁵ What is crooked cannot be made straight,
  and what is lacking cannot be counted.

¹⁶ I said in my heart, "I have acquired great wisdom, surpassing all who were over Jerusalem before me, and my heart has had great experience of wisdom and knowledge." ¹⁷ And I applied my heart to know wisdom and to know madness and folly. I perceived that this also is but a striving after wind.

¹⁸ For in much wisdom is much vexation,
  and he who increases knowledge increases sorrow.

The Vanity of Self-Indulgence

2 ¹ I said in my heart, "Come now, I will test you with pleasure; enjoy yourself." But behold, this also was vanity.[9] ² I said of laughter, "It is mad," and of pleasure, "What use is it?" ³ I searched with my heart how to cheer my body with wine—my heart still guiding me with wisdom—and

---

[1] Or *Convener*, or *Collector*; Hebrew *Qoheleth* (so throughout Ecclesiastes) [2] The Hebrew term *hebel*, translated *vanity* or *vain*, refers concretely to a "mist," "vapor," or "mere breath," and metaphorically to something that is fleeting or elusive (with different nuances depending on the context). It appears five times in this verse and in 29 other verses in Ecclesiastes [3] Or *and returns panting* [4] Or *former people* [5] Or *later people* [6] The Hebrew term denotes the center of one's inner life, including mind, will, and emotions [7] The Hebrew term *hebel* can refer to a "vapor" or "mere breath" (see note on 1:2) [8] Or *a feeding on wind*; compare Hosea 12:1 (also in Ecclesiastes 1:17; 2:11, 17, 26; 4:4, 6, 16; 6:9) [9] The Hebrew term *hebel* can refer to a "vapor" or "mere breath"; also verses 11, 15, 17, 19, 21, 23, 26 (see note on 1:2)

how to lay hold on folly, till I might see what was good for the children of man to do under heaven during the few days of their life. ⁴I made great works. I built houses and planted vineyards for myself. ⁵I made myself gardens and parks, and planted in them all kinds of fruit trees. ⁶I made myself pools from which to water the forest of growing trees. ⁷I bought male and female slaves, and had slaves who were born in my house. I had also great possessions of herds and flocks, more than any who had been before me in Jerusalem. ⁸I also gathered for myself silver and gold and the treasure of kings and provinces. I got singers, both men and women, and many concubines,¹ the delight of the sons of man.

⁹So I became great and surpassed all who were before me in Jerusalem. Also my wisdom remained with me. ¹⁰And whatever my eyes desired I did not keep from them. I kept my heart from no pleasure, for my heart found pleasure in all my toil, and this was my reward for all my toil. ¹¹Then I considered all that my hands had done and the toil I had expended in doing it, and behold, all was vanity and a striving after wind, and there was nothing to be gained under the sun.

The Vanity of Living Wisely

¹²So I turned to consider wisdom and madness and folly. For what can the man do who comes after the king? Only what has already been done. ¹³Then I saw that there is more gain in wisdom than in folly, as there is more gain in light than in darkness. ¹⁴The wise person has his eyes in his head, but the fool walks in darkness. And yet I perceived that the same event happens to all of them. ¹⁵Then I said in my heart, "What happens to the fool will happen to me also. Why then have I been so very wise?" And I said in my heart that this also is vanity. ¹⁶For of the wise as of the fool there is no enduring remembrance, seeing that in the days to come all will have been long forgotten. How the wise dies just like the fool! ¹⁷So I hated life, because what is done under the sun was grievous to me, for all is vanity and a striving after wind.

The Vanity of Toil

¹⁸I hated all my toil in which I toil under the sun, seeing that I must leave it to the man who will come after me, ¹⁹and who knows whether he will be wise or a fool? Yet he will be master of all for which I toiled and used my wisdom under the sun. This also is vanity. ²⁰So I turned about and gave my heart up to despair over all the toil of my labors under the sun, ²¹because sometimes a person who has toiled with wisdom and knowledge and skill must leave everything to be enjoyed by someone who did not toil for it. This also is vanity and a great evil. ²²What has a man from all the toil and striving of heart with which he toils beneath the sun? ²³For all his days are full of sorrow, and his work is a vexation. Even in the night his heart does not rest. This also is vanity.

²⁴There is nothing better for a person than that he should eat and drink and find enjoyment² in his toil. This also, I saw, is from the hand of God, ²⁵for apart from him who can eat or who can have enjoyment? ²⁶For to the one who pleases him God has given wisdom and knowledge and joy, but to the sinner he has given the business of gathering and collecting, only to give to one who pleases God. This also is vanity and striving after wind.

A Time for Everything

3 For everything there is a season, and a time for every matter under heaven:

² a time to be born, and a time to die;
a time to plant, and a time to pluck up what is planted;
³ a time to kill, and a time to heal;
a time to break down, and a time to build up;
⁴ a time to weep, and a time to laugh;
a time to mourn, and a time to dance;
⁵ a time to cast away stones, and a time to gather stones together;
a time to embrace, and a time to refrain from embracing;
⁶ a time to seek, and a time to lose;
a time to keep, and a time to cast away;
⁷ a time to tear, and a time to sew;
a time to keep silence, and a time to speak;

¹The meaning of the Hebrew word is uncertain ²Or *and make his soul see good* ³Some Hebrew manuscripts, Septuagint, Syriac; most Hebrew manuscripts *apart from me*

³ a time to love, and a time to hate;
  a time for war, and a time for peace.

The God-Given Task

⁹What gain has the worker from his toil? ¹⁰I have seen the business that God has given to the children of man to be busy with. ¹¹He has made everything beautiful in its time. Also, he has put eternity into man's heart, yet so that he cannot find out what God has done from the beginning to the end. ¹²I perceived that there is nothing better for them than to be joyful and to do good as long as they live; ¹³also that everyone should eat and drink and take pleasure in all his toil—this is God's gift to man.

¹⁴I perceived that whatever God does endures forever; nothing can be added to it, nor anything taken from it. God has done it, so that people fear before him. ¹⁵That which is, already has been; that which is to be, already has been; and God seeks what has been driven away.¹

From Dust to Dust

¹⁶Moreover, I saw under the sun that in the place of justice, even there was wick-edness, and in the place of righteousness, even there was wickedness. ¹⁷I said in my heart, God will judge the righteous and the wicked, for there is a time for every matter and for every work. ¹⁸I said in my heart with regard to the children of man that God is testing them that they may see that they themselves are but beasts. ¹⁹For what happens to the children of man and what happens to the beasts is the same; as one dies, so dies the other. They all have the same breath, and man has no advantage over the beasts, for all is vanity.² ²⁰All go to one place. All are from the dust, and to dust all return. ²¹Who knows whether the spirit of man goes upward and the spirit of the beast goes down into the earth? ²²So I saw that there is nothing better than that a man should rejoice in his work, for that is his lot. Who can bring him to see what will be after him?

Evil Under the Sun

4 Again I saw all the oppressions that are done under the sun. And behold, the tears of the oppressed, and they had no one to comfort them! On the side of their

¹Hebrew what has been pursued ²The Hebrew term hebel can refer to a "vapor" or "mere breath" (see note on 1:2)

Know True Happiness

verses to read
Ecclesiastes 2:24–26

True happiness, or joy, as the Bible calls it, isn't dependent on what happens to you or around you. If it were, it would be just manufactured happiness, a fake imitation of the real thing. True happiness is something that comes right from God. When you concentrate and rely on his Spirit's presence in your life, you will get more happiness than you ever knew was possible.

It's easy to find shallow happiness in things and people and even easier to lose all hope of happiness when those things and people disappoint you or fail you. But the girl who doesn't rely on the stuff or situations around her to find joy is the girl who has found all she needs. Like Paul, you can find the secret of being content, or happy, in all situations if you're just willing to draw your happiness from the well of living water instead of from the things of life here on earth (see Phil. 4:10–14). When trials come, when boredom sets in, happiness can still be yours—when you take into account the Word of God and its truth in your life. A girl who never lets God's Word be too far from her mind and refuses to let one day go by without looking for him is a girl who knows the secret to true happiness. God promises true happiness to anyone who is willing to make him Lord of their life and then to continually focus their mind and heart on him daily.

oppressors there was power, and there was no one to comfort them. [2] And I thought the dead who are already dead more fortunate than the living who are still alive. [3] But better than both is he who has not yet been and has not seen the evil deeds that are done under the sun.

[4] Then I saw that all toil and all skill in work come from a man's envy of his neighbor. This also is vanity[1] and a striving after wind.

[5] The fool folds his hands and eats his own flesh.

[6] Better is a handful of quietness than two hands full of toil and a striving after wind.

[7] Again, I saw vanity under the sun: [8] one person who has no other, either son or brother, yet there is no end to all his toil, and his eyes are never satisfied with riches, so that he never asks, "For whom am I toiling and depriving myself of pleasure?" This also is vanity and an unhappy business.

[9] Two are better than one, because they have a good reward for their toil. [10] For if they fall, one will lift up his fellow. But woe to him who is alone when he falls and has not another to lift him up! [11] Again, if two lie together, they keep warm, but how can one keep warm alone? [12] And though a man might prevail against one who is alone, two will withstand him—a threefold cord is not quickly broken.

[13] Better was a poor and wise youth than an old and foolish king who no longer knew how to take advice. [14] For he went from prison to the throne, though in his own kingdom he had been born poor. [15] I saw all the living who move about under the sun, along with that[2] youth who was to stand in the king's[3] place. [16] There was no end of all the people, all of whom he led. Yet those who come later will not rejoice in him. Surely this also is vanity and a striving after wind.

Fear God

5 [4] Guard your steps when you go to the house of God. To draw near to listen is better than to offer the sacrifice of fools, for they do not know that they are doing evil. [2] [5] Be not rash with your mouth, nor let your heart be hasty to utter a word before

God, for God is in heaven and you are o earth. Therefore let your words be fev [3] For a dream comes with much busines and a fool's voice with many words.

[4] When you vow a vow to God, do no delay paying it, for he has no pleasure i fools. Pay what you vow. [5] It is better tha you should not vow than that you shoul vow and not pay. [6] Let not your mouth lea you[6] into sin, and do not say before th messenger[7] that it was a mistake. Wh should God be angry at your voice an destroy the work of your hands? [7] For whe dreams increase and words grow man there is vanity;[8] but[9] God is the one yo must fear.

The Vanity of Wealth and Honor

[8] If you see in a province the oppressio of the poor and the violation of justic and righteousness, do not be amazed a the matter, for the high official is watche by a higher, and there are yet higher one over them. [9] But this is gain for a land i every way: a king committed to culti vated fields.[10]

[10] He who loves money will not be satis fied with money, nor he who loves wealt with his income; this also is vanity. [11] Whe goods increase, they increase who ea them, and what advantage has their owne but to see them with his eyes? [12] Sweet i the sleep of a laborer, whether he eats littl or much, but the full stomach of the ric will not let him sleep.

[13] There is a grievous evil that I have see under the sun: riches were kept by thei owner to his hurt, [14] and those riches wer lost in a bad venture. And he is father of son, but he has nothing in his hand. [15] A he came from his mother's womb he sha go again, naked as he came, and shall tak nothing for his toil that he may carry awa in his hand. [16] This also is a grievous evi just as he came, so shall he go, and wha gain is there to him who toils for the wind [17] Moreover, all his days he eats in darknes in much vexation and sickness and anger

[18] Behold, what I have seen to be goo and fitting is to eat and drink and fin enjoyment[11] in all the toil with which on toils under the sun the few days of his lif

---

[1] The Hebrew term *hebel* can refer to a "vapor" or "mere breath"; also verses 7, 8, 16 (see note on 1:2) [2] Hebrew *the second* [3] Hebrew *his* [4] Ch 4:17 in Hebrew [5] Ch 5:1 in Hebrew [6] Hebrew *your flesh* [7] Or *angel* [8] The Hebrew term *hebel* can refer to a "vapor" or "mere breath" also verse 10 (see note on 1:2) [9] Or *For when dreams and vanities increase, words also grow many; but* [10] The meaning of the Hebrew verse is uncertain [11] Or *and see good*

at God has given him, for this is his lot. Everyone also to whom God has given wealth and possessions and power to enjoy them, and to accept his lot and rejoice in his toil—this is the gift of God. **20** For he will not much remember the days of his life because God keeps him occupied with joy in his heart.

A Prayer for...
THE MORNING

Dear God, author of everything good, I come to you for the grace I need for another day's duties and events. I step out into a crazy world; I carry about with me a sinful heart. I know that without you I can't do anything and that everything I'm worried about, however harmless in itself, might just be an opportunity for my sin or stupidity, unless you keep me in your power. Hold me up, and I will be safe.

Keep my mind clean and focused, my obsession away from idols, and my character from the stain of wrong choices. Please don't let me do anything that I can't ask you to bless and that I can't ask you to participate in. Give me success in all the godly things I do, or get my heart ready for disappointments. Give me neither poverty nor wealth. Give me just the food I need for life, so that I won't be full and deny you by saying, "Who is the Lord?" or be poor and steal and take your name in vain.

Please make everything that I encounter good for me by my prayer and your will. Teach me how to use the world and not abuse it, to improve my talents, to not waste my time, to walk wisely where people are in need and in kindness around other believers, to do good to all people and especially to my fellow Christians, and to give you the glory.

             Amen.

6 There is an evil that I have seen under the sun, and it lies heavy on mankind: **2** a man to whom God gives wealth, possessions, and honor, so that he lacks nothing of all that he desires, yet God does not give him power to enjoy them, but a stranger enjoys them. This is vanity;[1] it is a grievous evil. **3** If a man fathers a hundred children and lives many years, so that the days of his years are many, but his soul is not satisfied with life's good things, and he also has no burial, I say that a stillborn child is better off than he. **4** For it comes in vanity and goes in darkness, and in darkness its name is covered. **5** Moreover, it has not seen the sun or known anything, yet it finds rest rather than he. **6** Even though he should live a thousand years twice over, yet enjoy[2] no good—do not all go to the one place?

7 All the toil of man is for his mouth, yet his appetite is not satisfied.[3] **8** For what advantage has the wise man over the fool? And what does the poor man have who knows how to conduct himself before the living? **9** Better is the sight of the eyes than the wandering of the appetite: this also is vanity and a striving after wind.

10 Whatever has come to be has already been named, and it is known what man is, and that he is not able to dispute with one stronger than he. **11** The more words, the more vanity, and what is the advantage to man? **12** For who knows what is good for man while he lives the few days of his vain[4] life, which he passes like a shadow? For who can tell man what will be after him under the sun?

The Contrast of Wisdom and Folly

7 A good name is better than precious ointment,
     and the day of death than the day of birth.

2 It is better to go to the house of mourning
     than to go to the house of feasting,
     for this is the end of all mankind,
     and the living will lay it to heart.

3 Sorrow is better than laughter,
     for by sadness of face the heart is made glad.

The Hebrew term *hebel* can refer to a "vapor" or "mere breath"; also verses 4, 9, 11 (see note on 1:2) [2] Or *see* [3] Hebrew *filled*
The Hebrew term *hebel* can refer to a "vapor" or "mere breath" (see note on 1:2)

4   The heart of the wise is in the house
of mourning,
but the heart of fools is in the
house of mirth.
5   It is better for a man to hear the
rebuke of the wise
than to hear the song of fools.
6   For as the crackling of thorns under
a pot,
so is the laughter of the fools;
this also is vanity.[1]
7   Surely oppression drives the wise
into madness,
and a bribe corrupts the heart.
8   Better is the end of a thing than its
beginning,
and the patient in spirit is better
than the proud in spirit.
9   Be not quick in your spirit to become
angry,
for anger lodges in the heart[2] of
fools.
10   Say not, "Why were the former days
better than these?"
For it is not from wisdom that you
ask this.
11   Wisdom is good with an inheritance,
an advantage to those who see the
sun.
12   For the protection of wisdom is like
the protection of money,
and the advantage of knowledge is
that wisdom preserves the life
of him who has it.
13   Consider the work of God:
who can make straight what he
has made crooked?

14 In the day of prosperity be joyful, and in the day of adversity consider: God has made the one as well as the other, so that man may not find out anything that will be after him.

15 In my vain[3] life I have seen everything. There is a righteous man who perishes in his righteousness, and there is a wicked man who prolongs his life in his evildoing. 16 Be not overly righteous, and do not make yourself too wise. Why should you destroy yourself? 17 Be not overly wicked, neither be a fool. Why should you die before your time? 18 It is good that you should take hold of this, and from that withhold not your

hand, for the one who fears God shall come out from both of them.

19 Wisdom gives strength to the wise man more than ten rulers who are in a city.

20 Surely there is not a righteous man on earth who does good and never sins.

21 Do not take to heart all the things that people say, lest you hear your servant cursing you. 22 Your heart knows that many times you yourself have cursed others.

23 All this I have tested by wisdom. I said, "I will be wise," but it was far from me. 24 That which has been is far off, and deep, very deep; who can find it out?

25 I turned my heart to know and to search out and to seek wisdom and the scheme of things, and to know the wickedness of folly and the foolishness that is madness. 26 And I find something more bitter than death: the woman whose heart is snares and nets, and whose hands are fetters. He who pleases God escapes her, but the sinner is taken by her. 27 Behold, this is what I found, says the Preacher, while adding one thing to another to find the scheme of things— 28 which my soul has sought repeatedly, but I have not found. One man among a thousand I found, but a woman among all these I have not found. 29 See, this alone I found, that God made man upright, but they have sought out many schemes.

Keep the King's Command

8   Who is like the wise?
And who knows the interpretation
of a thing?
A man's wisdom makes his face
shine,
and the hardness of his face is
changed.

2 I say:[4] Keep the king's command, because of God's oath to him.[5] 3 Be not hasty to go from his presence. Do not take your stand in an evil cause, for he does whatever he pleases. 4 For the word of the king is supreme, and who may say to him, "What are you doing?" 5 Whoever keeps a command will know no evil thing, and the wise heart will know the proper time and the just way. 6 For there is a time and a way for everything, although man's trouble[6] lies heavy on him. 7 For he does

---

[1] The Hebrew term *hebel* can refer to a "vapor" or "mere breath" (see note on 1:2) [2] Hebrew *in the bosom* [3] The Hebrew term *hebel* can refer to a "vapor" or "mere breath" (see note on 1:2) [4] Hebrew lacks *say* [5] Or *because of your oath to God* [6] Or *evil*

not know what is to be, for who can tell him how it will be? **8** No man has power to retain the spirit, or power over the day of death. There is no discharge from war, nor will wickedness deliver those who are given to it. **9** All this I observed while applying my heart to all that is done under the sun, when man had power over man to his hurt.

Those Who Fear God Will Do Well

10 Then I saw the wicked buried. They used to go in and out of the holy place and were praised[1] in the city where they had done such things. This also is vanity.[2] **11** Because the sentence against an evil deed is not executed speedily, the heart of the children of man is fully set to do evil. **12** Though a sinner does evil a hundred times and prolongs his life, yet I know that it will be well with those who fear God, because they fear before him. **13** But it will not be well with the wicked, neither will he prolong his days like a shadow, because he does not fear before God.

Man Cannot Know God's Ways

14 There is a vanity that takes place on earth, that there are righteous people to whom it happens according to the deeds of the wicked, and there are wicked people to whom it happens according to the deeds of the righteous. I said that this also is vanity. **15** And I commend joy, for man has nothing better under the sun but to eat and drink and be joyful, for this will go with him in his toil through the days of his life that God has given him under the sun.

16 When I applied my heart to know wisdom, and to see the business that is done on earth, how neither day nor night do one's eyes see sleep, **17** then I saw all the work of God, that man cannot find out the work that is done under the sun. However much man may toil in seeking, he will not find it out. Even though a wise man claims to know, he cannot find it out.

Death Comes to All

9 But all this I laid to heart, examining it all, how the righteous and the wise and their deeds are in the hand of God. Whether it is love or hate, man does not know; both are before him. **2** It is the same

for all, since the same event happens to the righteous and the wicked, to the good and the evil,[3] to the clean and the unclean, to him who sacrifices and him who does not sacrifice. As the good one is, so is the sinner, and he who swears is as he who shuns an oath. **3** This is an evil in all that is done under the sun, that the same event happens to all. Also, the hearts of the children of man are full of evil, and madness is in their hearts while they live, and after that they go to the dead. **4** But he who is joined with all the living has hope, for a living dog is better than a dead lion. **5** For the living know that they will die, but the dead know nothing, and they have no more reward, for the memory of them is forgotten. **6** Their love and their hate and their envy have already perished, and forever they have no more share in all that is done under the sun.

Enjoy Life with the One You Love

7 Go, eat your bread with joy, and drink your wine with a merry heart, for God has already approved what you do.

8 Let your garments be always white. Let not oil be lacking on your head.

9 Enjoy life with the wife whom you love, all the days of your vain[4] life that he has given you under the sun, because that is your portion in life and in your toil at which you toil under the sun. **10** Whatever your hand finds to do, do it with your might,[5] for there is no work or thought or knowledge or wisdom in Sheol, to which you are going.

Wisdom Better than Folly

11 Again I saw that under the sun the race is not to the swift, nor the battle to the strong, nor bread to the wise, nor riches to the intelligent, nor favor to those with knowledge, but time and chance happen to them all. **12** For man does not know his time. Like fish that are taken in an evil net, and like birds that are caught in a snare, so the children of man are snared at an evil time, when it suddenly falls upon them.

13 I have also seen this example of wisdom under the sun, and it seemed great to me. **14** There was a little city with few men in it, and a great king came against it

[1] Some Hebrew manuscripts, Septuagint, Vulgate; most Hebrew manuscripts *forgotten* [2] The Hebrew term *hebel* can refer to a "vapor" or "mere breath"; also twice in verse 14 (see note on 1:2) [3] Septuagint, Syriac, Vulgate; Hebrew lacks *and the evil* [4] The Hebrew term *hebel* can refer to a "vapor" or "mere breath" (see note on 1:2) [5] Or *finds to do with your might, do it*

and besieged it, building great siegeworks against it. [15] But there was found in it a poor, wise man, and he by his wisdom delivered the city. Yet no one remembered that poor man. [16] But I say that wisdom is better than might, though the poor man's wisdom is despised and his words are not heard.

[17] The words of the wise heard in quiet are better than the shouting of a ruler among fools. [18] Wisdom is better than weapons of war, but one sinner destroys much good.

10 Dead flies make the perfumer's ointment give off a stench;
  so a little folly outweighs wisdom and honor.
[2] A wise man's heart inclines him to the right,
  but a fool's heart to the left.
[3] Even when the fool walks on the road, he lacks sense,
  and he says to everyone that he is a fool.
[4] If the anger of the ruler rises against you, do not leave your place,
  for calmness[1] will lay great offenses to rest.

[5] There is an evil that I have seen under the sun, as it were an error proceeding from the ruler: [6] folly is set in many high places, and the rich sit in a low place. [7] I have seen slaves on horses, and princes walking on the ground like slaves.

[8] He who digs a pit will fall into it,
  and a serpent will bite him who breaks through a wall.
[9] He who quarries stones is hurt by them,
  and he who splits logs is endangered by them.
[10] If the iron is blunt, and one does not sharpen the edge,
  he must use more strength,
  but wisdom helps one to succeed.[2]
[11] If the serpent bites before it is charmed,
  there is no advantage to the charmer.

[12] The words of a wise man's mouth win him favor,[3]
  but the lips of a fool consume him.

[13] The beginning of the words of his mouth is foolishness,
  and the end of his talk is evil madness.
[14] A fool multiplies words,
  though no man knows what is to be and who can tell him what will be after him?
[15] The toil of a fool wearies him,
  for he does not know the way to the city.

[16] Woe to you, O land, when your king is a child,
  and your princes feast in the morning!
[17] Happy are you, O land, when your king is the son of the nobility,
  and your princes feast at the proper time,
  for strength, and not for drunkenness!
[18] Through sloth the roof sinks in,
  and through indolence the house leaks.
[19] Bread is made for laughter,
  and wine gladdens life,
  and money answers everything.
[20] Even in your thoughts, do not curse the king,
  nor in your bedroom curse the rich,
  for a bird of the air will carry your voice,
  or some winged creature tell the matter.

Cast Your Bread upon the Waters

11 Cast your bread upon the waters, for you will find it after many days.
[2] Give a portion to seven, or even to eight,
  for you know not what disaster may happen on earth.
[3] If the clouds are full of rain,
  they empty themselves on the earth,
  and if a tree falls to the south or to the north,
  in the place where the tree falls, there it will lie.
[4] He who observes the wind will not sow,
  and he who regards the clouds will not reap.

[1] Hebrew *healing* [2] Or *wisdom is an advantage for success* [3] Or *are gracious*

⁵As you do not know the way the spirit comes to the bones in the womb[1] of a woman with child, so you do not know the work of God who makes everything.

⁶In the morning sow your seed, and at evening withhold not your hand, for you do not know which will prosper, this or that, or whether both alike will be good.

⁷Light is sweet, and it is pleasant for the eyes to see the sun.

⁸So if a person lives many years, let him rejoice in them all; but let him remember that the days of darkness will be many. All that comes is vanity.[2]

⁹Rejoice, O young man, in your youth, and let your heart cheer you in the days of your youth. Walk in the ways of your heart and the sight of your eyes. But know that for all these things God will bring you into judgment.

¹⁰Remove vexation from your heart, and put away pain[3] from your body, for youth and the dawn of life are vanity.

Remember Your Creator in Your Youth

12 Remember also your Creator in the days of your youth, before the evil days come and the years draw near of which you will say, "I have no pleasure in them"; ²before the sun and the light and the moon and the stars are darkened and the clouds return after the rain, ³in the day when the keepers of the house tremble, and the strong men are bent, and the grinders cease because they are few, and those who look through the windows are dimmed, ⁴and the doors on the street are shut—when the sound of the grinding is low, and one rises up at the sound of a bird, and all the daughters of song

[1] Some Hebrew manuscripts, Targum; most Hebrew manuscripts *As you do not know the way of the wind, or how the bones grow in the womb* [2] The Hebrew term *hebel* can refer to a "vapor" or "mere breath"; also verse 10 (see note on 1:2) [3] Or *evil*

verses to read
Ecclesiastes 12:1–8

Know God

What do you want in your spiritual life? What's your goal when it comes to worship? Your relationship with God was designed for something, but are you matching up with that design?

When you want things for yourself, when you come to the Lord just for peace or blessings, or when you want him to make you feel complete or happy, you miss out on the whole purpose for your salvation: for you to love him. Your faith didn't save you so that you could get all you want but so that you could get back to a right relationship with the Father. That relationship isn't only about getting: it is also about giving. Think of it like this: the two greatest commandments aren't about your peace or your happiness but about stepping outside yourself and loving God and your neighbor (see Matt. 22:34–40).

You weren't put here on earth to develop your spiritual life so that you could "arrive" and then just lie back and rest. No, you were made for much more, and that much more starts with a shift in your goals. What you want each morning when you get up will determine who you become each day. The God Girl makes her goal not her own emotional well-being but knowing her God—remembering her Creator while she is young (see Eccles. 12:1). When God is your goal, everything else falls into place, because no matter what painful things you experience, they cannot take God away from you. Nothing others do will faze you when your goal is not to feel good but to know God more. Each morning when you get up, tell yourself, "Today my goal is God himself—not happiness or peace in things, but in him and him alone."

are brought low— [5]they are afraid also of what is high, and terrors are in the way; the almond tree blossoms, the grasshopper drags itself along,[1] and desire fails, because man is going to his eternal home, and the mourners go about the streets— [6]before the silver cord is snapped, or the golden bowl is broken, or the pitcher is shattered at the fountain, or the wheel broken at the cistern, [7]and the dust returns to the earth as it was, and the spirit returns to God who gave it. [8]Vanity[2] of vanities, says the Preacher; all is vanity.

Fear God and Keep His Commandments

[9]Besides being wise, the Preacher also taught the people knowledge, weighing and studying and arranging many proverbs with great care. [10]The Preacher sought to find words of delight, and uprightly he wrote words of truth.

[11]The words of the wise are like goads, and like nails firmly fixed are the collected sayings; they are given by one Shepherd. [12]My son, beware of anything beyond these. Of making many books there is no end, and much study is a weariness of the flesh.

[13]The end of the matter; all has been heard. Fear God and keep his commandments, for this is the whole duty of man. [14]For God will bring every deed into judgment, with[4] every secret thing, whether good or evil.

---

[1]Or is a burden [2]The Hebrew term hebel can refer to a "vapor" or "mere breath" (three times in this verse); see note on 1:2 [3]Or the duty of all mankind [4]Or into the judgment on

INTRODUCTION TO THE
Song of Solomon

Author: King Solomon

Time: Between 971 and 931 B.C.

Place: Unknown

Written to: Unknown

The gist

The Song of Solomon is a poetic story about love and marriage. It may be based on the love of King Solomon and a young country girl he married. It shows the value of saving sex for marriage and of understanding commitment and loyalty in marriage.

Things to look for

- The use of poetic language
- The nature of love (see Song 3:5; 4:10; 8:6–7)
- The wedding (see Song 3:6–11)
- The wedding night (see Song 4:1–5:1)

Know Love

> I adjure you, O daughters of Jerusalem,
>   by the gazelles or the does of the field,
> that you not stir up or awaken love
>   until it pleases.

Song of Solomon 2:7

Romantic love is a two-way street. A lot of girls' hearts have been given to famous boys on stage and screen, but that kind of love is a one-way street. It's called unrequited love, and it's a kind of lie. A lot of well-meaning girls have convinced themselves that what they feel is so strong that it must be true. They dream of him and fantasize about his love. Then, over time, when he never calls, they start to think that maybe God lied or maybe they did something wrong. But nothing could be further from the truth. Love is a totally amazing experience, but it also has to be grounded in faith—and not faith in a feeling but in a God who never promises romantic bliss but most definitely promises holiness.

When all your energy is focused on how you feel, your focus is selfish, and true love isn't selfish. True love is not about being adored or romanced but about loving your neighbor, or in this case your significant other, as yourself. It's about thinking of others as better than yourself (see Phil. 2:3) and even about loving your enemies.

There is a season when love is ripe, and it is important that you know your season. Don't let what feels like love lie to you. Love isn't just a feeling. It is also how we act. God's Word never orders us to be fulfilled or to find our dream but to learn the secret of being content no matter what the situation.

Feelings of love are sure to come, but it's what you think about them that's going to prove how true they are. Don't let your life be about obeying your feelings instead of obeying your God. Feelings can be fun, but they aren't always trustworthy, so take every feeling captive to the Word of God and be careful not to call it love before its proper time.

As you read the Song of Solomon, don't get confused by the language, but think about how deep love can be and what an amazing gift from God it is. Understand how love, at its proper time, is incredible.

Must-Know Verses

He brought me to the banqueting house,
    and his banner over me was love.
Sustain me with raisins;
    refresh me with apples,
    for I am sick with love. *Song of Solomon 2:4–5*

A garden locked is my sister, my bride,
    a spring locked, a fountain sealed. *Song of Solomon 4:12*

I am my beloved's and my beloved is mine. *Song of Solomon 6:3*

The Song of Solomon

1

The Song of Songs, which is Solomon's.

The Bride Confesses Her Love

SHE[1]

2 Let him kiss me with the kisses of his
    mouth!
For your love is better than wine;
3   your anointing oils are fragrant;
your name is oil poured out;
    therefore virgins love you.
4 Draw me after you; let us run.
    The king has brought me into his
    chambers.

OTHERS

We will exult and rejoice in you;
    we will extol your love more than
    wine;
    rightly do they love you.

SHE

5 I am very dark, but lovely,
    O daughters of Jerusalem,
like the tents of Kedar,
    like the curtains of Solomon.
6 Do not gaze at me because I am dark,
    because the sun has looked upon
    me.
My mother's sons were angry with
    me;
    they made me keeper of the vine-
    yards,
    but my own vineyard I have not
    kept!
7 Tell me, you whom my soul loves,
    where you pasture your flock,
    where you make it lie down at
    noon;
for why should I be like one who
    veils herself
    beside the flocks of your compan-
    ions?

Solomon and His Bride Delight in Each Other

HE

8 If you do not know,
    O most beautiful among women,
follow in the tracks of the flock,
    and pasture your young goats
    beside the shepherds' tents.

9 I compare you, my love,
    to a mare among Pharaoh's chari-
    ots.
10 Your cheeks are lovely with orna-
    ments,
    your neck with strings of jewels.

OTHERS

11 We will make for you[2] ornaments of
    gold,
    studded with silver.

SHE

12 While the king was on his couch,
    my nard gave forth its fragrance.
13 My beloved is to me a sachet of myrrh
    that lies between my breasts.
14 My beloved is to me a cluster of
    henna blossoms
    in the vineyards of Engedi.

HE

15 Behold, you are beautiful, my love;
    behold, you are beautiful;
    your eyes are doves.

SHE

16 Behold, you are beautiful, my
    beloved, truly delightful.
Our couch is green;
17   the beams of our house are cedar;
    our rafters are pine.

2

I am a rose[3] of Sharon,
    a lily of the valleys.

[1] The translators have added speaker identifications based on the gender and number of the Hebrew words [2] The Hebrew for *you* is feminine singular [3] Probably a bulb, such as a crocus, asphodel, or narcissus

HE

2 As a lily among brambles,
      so is my love among the young
         women.

SHE

3 As an apple tree among the trees of
         the forest,
      so is my beloved among the young
         men.
 With great delight I sat in his
         shadow,
      and his fruit was sweet to my taste.
4 He brought me to the banqueting
         house,[1]
      and his banner over me was love.
5 Sustain me with raisins;
      refresh me with apples,
      for I am sick with love.
6 His left hand is under my head,
      and his right hand embraces me!

7 I adjure you,[2] O daughters of
         Jerusalem,
      by the gazelles or the does of the
         field,
   that you not stir up or awaken love
      until it pleases.

The Bride Adores Her Beloved

8 The voice of my beloved!
      Behold, he comes,
   leaping over the mountains,
      bounding over the hills.
9 My beloved is like a gazelle
      or a young stag.
   Behold, there he stands
      behind our wall,
   gazing through the windows,
      looking through the lattice.
10 My beloved speaks and says to me:
 "Arise, my love, my beautiful one,
      and come away,

[1] Hebrew *the house of wine* [2] That is, I put you on oath; so throughout the Song

---

Know Love

verses to read
Song of Solomon 1

True love can't hold itself back. When you're in love, your heart wants to tell the world, because it feels like if you don't it's just gonna burst. Love notes, love songs, and love poetry all come from a heart filled to overflowing with adoration and passion. But after a while it can be easy to forget to tell the people you love what you love about them. Life gets in the way, times get tough, tempers flare, and suddenly you aren't speaking all lovey to each other anymore. But love needs to be talked about; it needs to be given in the form of verbal appreciation and adoration. We have to tell the people we love why we love them, and tell them often. Song of Solomon is an example of this, and we need to do the same thing when it comes to our love for God.

In the life of faith, the God Girl wants to tell her God how much she adores him. She wants to tell him how much he means to her, not only to worship him but to remind her own heart of all that he is. If she doesn't do this, she can quickly forget all about God's goodness and holiness. As a God Girl you have to concentrate on the goodness of God. You have to remind yourself how you've been touched by his grace, his provision, and his power. You must tell him every day what his presence in your life means. The God Girl knows that the power of love rests in her ability to speak words of love.

God's love for you is expressed in his Word and in the life of his Son, the Word made flesh. Don't miss his love songs, love letters, and love gifts. Know love and know him. Speak love and be known by him.

[1] for behold, the winter is past;
  the rain is over and gone.
[2] The flowers appear on the earth,
  the time of singing[1] has come,
and the voice of the turtledove
  is heard in our land.
[3] The fig tree ripens its figs,
  and the vines are in blossom;
  they give forth fragrance.
Arise, my love, my beautiful one,
  and come away.
[4] O my dove, in the clefts of the rock,
  in the crannies of the cliff,
let me see your face,
  let me hear your voice,
for your voice is sweet,
  and your face is lovely.
[5] Catch the foxes[2] for us,
  the little foxes
that spoil the vineyards,
  for our vineyards are in blossom."

[6] My beloved is mine, and I am his;
  he grazes[3] among the lilies.
[7] Until the day breathes
  and the shadows flee,
turn, my beloved, be like a gazelle
  or a young stag on cleft mountains.[4]

The Bride's Dream

3 On my bed by night
  I sought him whom my soul loves;
  I sought him, but found him not.
[2] I will rise now and go about the city,
  in the streets and in the squares;
I will seek him whom my soul loves.
  I sought him, but found him not.
[3] The watchmen found me
  as they went about in the city.
"Have you seen him whom my soul
  loves?"
[4] Scarcely had I passed them
  when I found him whom my soul
  loves.
I held him, and would not let him go
  until I had brought him into my
  mother's house,
  and into the chamber of her who
  conceived me.
[5] I adjure you, O daughters of Jerusalem,
  by the gazelles or the does of the
  field,
that you not stir up or awaken love
  until it pleases.

> ### Ask Yourself . . .
> #### ABOUT LOVE
>
> - When is the proper time for love, according to my friends?
> - When is it according to my parents?
> - When is it according to God?
> - When it comes to love and the things I'll do for love, do my ideas line up more with God's or the world's?
> - How can I find out more about God's ideas on love and relationships?

Solomon Arrives for the Wedding

[6] What is that coming up from the
  wilderness
  like columns of smoke,
perfumed with myrrh and frankincense,
  with all the fragrant powders of a
  merchant?
[7] Behold, it is the litter[5] of Solomon!
Around it are sixty mighty men,
  some of the mighty men of Israel,
[8] all of them wearing swords
  and expert in war,
each with his sword at his thigh,
  against terror by night.
[9] King Solomon made himself a car-
  riage[6]
  from the wood of Lebanon.
[10] He made its posts of silver,
  its back of gold, its seat of purple;
its interior was inlaid with love
  by the daughters of Jerusalem.
[11] Go out, O daughters of Zion,
  and look upon King Solomon,
with the crown with which his
  mother crowned him
on the day of his wedding,
  on the day of the gladness of his
  heart.

[1] Or pruning [2] Or jackals [3] Or he pastures his flock [4] Or mountains of Bether [5] That is, the couch on which servants carry a king [6] Or sedan chair

Solomon Admires His Bride's Beauty

HE

4 Behold, you are beautiful, my love,
  behold, you are beautiful!
Your eyes are doves
  behind your veil.
Your hair is like a flock of goats
  leaping down the slopes of Gilead.
2 Your teeth are like a flock of shorn
  ewes
  that have come up from the wash-
    ing,
all of which bear twins,
  and not one among them has lost
    its young.
3 Your lips are like a scarlet thread,
  and your mouth is lovely.
Your cheeks are like halves of a
    pomegranate
  behind your veil.
4 Your neck is like the tower of David,
  built in rows of stone;[1]
on it hang a thousand shields,
  all of them shields of warriors.
5 Your two breasts are like two fawns,
  twins of a gazelle,
  that graze among the lilies.
6 Until the day breathes
  and the shadows flee,
I will go away to the mountain of
    myrrh
  and the hill of frankincense.
7 You are altogether beautiful, my love;
  there is no flaw in you.
8 Come with me from Lebanon, my
    bride;
  come with me from Lebanon.
Depart[2] from the peak of Amana,
  from the peak of Senir and
    Hermon,
from the dens of lions,
  from the mountains of leopards.

9 You have captivated my heart, my
    sister, my bride;
  you have captivated my heart with
    one glance of your eyes,
  with one jewel of your necklace.
10 How beautiful is your love, my sister,
    my bride!
  How much better is your love than
    wine,
  and the fragrance of your oils than
    any spice!

11 Your lips drip nectar, my bride;
  honey and milk are under your
    tongue;
  the fragrance of your garments is
    like the fragrance of Lebanon.
12 A garden locked is my sister, my
    bride,
a spring locked, a fountain sealed.
13 Your shoots are an orchard of pome-
    granates
  with all choicest fruits,
  henna with nard,
14 nard and saffron, calamus and cin-
    namon,
  with all trees of frankincense,
myrrh and aloes,
  with all choice spices—
15 a garden fountain, a well of living
    water,
  and flowing streams from Lebanon.

16 Awake, O north wind,
  and come, O south wind!
Blow upon my garden,
  let its spices flow.

Together in the Garden of Love

SHE

Let my beloved come to his garden,
  and eat its choicest fruits.

HE

5 I came to my garden, my sister, my
    bride,
  I gathered my myrrh with my spice,
  I ate my honeycomb with my
    honey,
  I drank my wine with my milk.

OTHERS

Eat, friends, drink,
  and be drunk with love!

The Bride Searches for Her Beloved

SHE

2 I slept, but my heart was awake.
A sound! My beloved is knocking.
"Open to me, my sister, my love,
  my dove, my perfect one,
for my head is wet with dew,
  my locks with the drops of the
    night."
3 I had put off my garment;
  how could I put it on?
I had bathed my feet;
  how could I soil them?

[1] The meaning of the Hebrew word is uncertain   [2] Or *Look*

⁴ My beloved put his hand to the latch,
  and my heart was thrilled within
  me.
⁵ I arose to open to my beloved,
  and my hands dripped with myrrh,
  my fingers with liquid myrrh,
  on the handles of the bolt.
⁶ I opened to my beloved,
  but my beloved had turned and
  gone.
  My soul failed me when he spoke.
  I sought him, but found him not;
  I called him, but he gave no answer.
⁷ The watchmen found me
  as they went about in the city;
  they beat me, they bruised me,
  they took away my veil,
  those watchmen of the walls.
⁸ I adjure you, O daughters of
  Jerusalem,
  if you find my beloved,
  that you tell him
  I am sick with love.

OTHERS
⁹ What is your beloved more than
  another beloved,
  O most beautiful among women?
  What is your beloved more than
  another beloved,
  that you thus adjure us?

The Bride Praises Her Beloved
SHE
⁰ My beloved is radiant and ruddy,
  distinguished among ten thousand.
¹ His head is the finest gold;
  his locks are wavy,
  black as a raven.
² His eyes are like doves
  beside streams of water,
  bathed in milk,
  sitting beside a full pool.¹
³ His cheeks are like beds of spices,
  mounds of sweet-smelling herbs.
  His lips are lilies,
  dripping liquid myrrh.
⁴ His arms are rods of gold,
  set with jewels.
  His body is polished ivory,²
  bedecked with sapphires.³
⁵ His legs are alabaster columns,
  set on bases of gold.

His appearance is like Lebanon,
  choice as the cedars.
¹⁶ His mouth⁴ is most sweet,
  and he is altogether desirable.
  This is my beloved and this is my
  friend,
  O daughters of Jerusalem.

OTHERS
6 Where has your beloved gone,
  O most beautiful among women?
  Where has your beloved turned,
  that we may seek him with you?

Together in the Garden of Love
SHE
² My beloved has gone down to his
  garden
  to the beds of spices,
  to graze⁵ in the gardens
  and to gather lilies.
³ I am my beloved's and my beloved is
  mine;
  he grazes among the lilies.

Solomon and His Bride Delight in Each Other
HE
⁴ You are beautiful as Tirzah, my love,
  lovely as Jerusalem,
  awesome as an army with banners.
⁵ Turn away your eyes from me,
  for they overwhelm me—
  Your hair is like a flock of goats
  leaping down the slopes of Gilead.
⁶ Your teeth are like a flock of ewes
  that have come up from the washing;
  all of them bear twins;
  not one among them has lost its
  young.
⁷ Your cheeks are like halves of a
  pomegranate
  behind your veil.
⁸ There are sixty queens and eighty
  concubines,
  and virgins without number.
⁹ My dove, my perfect one, is the only
  one,
  the only one of her mother,
  pure to her who bore her.
  The young women saw her and
  called her blessed;
  the queens and concubines also,
  and they praised her.

¹ The meaning of the Hebrew is uncertain ² The meaning of the Hebrew word is uncertain ³ Hebrew *lapis lazuli* ⁴ Hebrew *palate* ⁵ Or to
pasture his flock; also verse 3

¹⁰ "Who is this who looks down like the
dawn,
 beautiful as the moon, bright as
 the sun,
 awesome as an army with banners?"

SHE
¹¹ I went down to the nut orchard
 to look at the blossoms of the valley,
to see whether the vines had budded,
 whether the pomegranates were
 in bloom.
¹² Before I was aware, my desire set me
 among the chariots of my kinsman,
 a prince.[1]

OTHERS
¹³[2] Return, return, O Shulammite,
 return, return, that we may look
 upon you.

HE
Why should you look upon the
 Shulammite,
 as upon a dance before two
 armies?[3]

7 How beautiful are your feet in sandals,
 O noble daughter!
Your rounded thighs are like jewels,
 the work of a master hand.
² Your navel is a rounded bowl
 that never lacks mixed wine.
Your belly is a heap of wheat,
 encircled with lilies.
³ Your two breasts are like two fawns,
 twins of a gazelle.
⁴ Your neck is like an ivory tower.
Your eyes are pools in Heshbon,
 by the gate of Bath-rabbim.
Your nose is like a tower of Lebanon,
 which looks toward Damascus.
⁵ Your head crowns you like Carmel,
 and your flowing locks are like
 purple;
 a king is held captive in the tresses.

⁶ How beautiful and pleasant you are,
 O loved one, with all your delights![4]
⁷ Your stature is like a palm tree,
 and your breasts are like its clusters.
⁸ I say I will climb the palm tree
 and lay hold of its fruit.

Oh may your breasts be like clusters
 of the vine,
 and the scent of your breath like
 apples,
⁹ and your mouth[5] like the best wine.

SHE
It goes down smoothly for my
 beloved,
 gliding over lips and teeth.[6]

¹⁰ I am my beloved's,
 and his desire is for me.

The Bride Gives Her Love
¹¹ Come, my beloved,
 let us go out into the fields
 and lodge in the villages;[7]
¹² let us go out early to the vineyards
 and see whether the vines have
 budded,
 whether the grape blossoms have
 opened
 and the pomegranates are in bloom
There I will give you my love.
¹³ The mandrakes give forth fragrance,
 and beside our doors are all choice
 fruits,
 new as well as old,
 which I have laid up for you, O my
 beloved.

Longing for Her Beloved
8 Oh that you were like a brother to me
 who nursed at my mother's breasts!
If I found you outside, I would kiss
 you,
 and none would despise me.
² I would lead you and bring you
 into the house of my mother—
 she who used to teach me.
I would give you spiced wine to drink,
 the juice of my pomegranate.
³ His left hand is under my head,
 and his right hand embraces me!
⁴ I adjure you, O daughters of
 Jerusalem,
 that you not stir up or awaken love
 until it pleases.

⁵ Who is that coming up from the
 wilderness,
 leaning on her beloved?

Under the apple tree I awakened you.

---

[1] Or chariots of Ammi-Nadib [2] Ch 7:1 in Hebrew [3] Or dance of Mahanaim [4] Or among delights [5] Hebrew palate [6] Septuagint, Syriac,
Vulgate; Hebrew causing the lips of sleepers to speak [7] Or among the henna plants

There your mother was in labor with
    you;
        there she who bore you was in
        labor.

6 Set me as a seal upon your heart,
    as a seal upon your arm,
for love is strong as death,
    jealousy[1] is fierce as the grave.[2]
Its flashes are flashes of fire,
    the very flame of the LORD.
7 Many waters cannot quench love,
    neither can floods drown it.
If a man offered for love
    all the wealth of his house,
    he[3] would be utterly despised.

Final Advice

OTHERS

8 We have a little sister,
    and she has no breasts.
What shall we do for our sister
    on the day when she is spoken for?
9 If she is a wall,
    we will build on her a battlement
        of silver,
but if she is a door,
    we will enclose her with boards of
        cedar.

SHE

10 I was a wall,
    and my breasts were like towers;
then I was in his eyes
    as one who finds[4] peace.

11 Solomon had a vineyard at Baal-
        hamon;
    he let out the vineyard to keepers;
    each one was to bring for its fruit a
        thousand pieces of silver.
12 My vineyard, my very own, is before
        me;
    you, O Solomon, may have the
        thousand,
    and the keepers of the fruit two
        hundred.

HE

13 O you who dwell in the gardens,
    with companions listening for
        your voice;
    let me hear it.

SHE

14 Make haste, my beloved,
    and be like a gazelle
or a young stag
    on the mountains of spices.

[1] Or ardor [2] Hebrew as Sheol [3] Or it [4] Or brings out

INTRODUCTION TO
Isaiah

Author: Isaiah

Time: Probably around 740–680 B.C.

Place: Probably Jerusalem

Written to: The Israelites

The gist

This book is the prophecy of Isaiah. It explains how God disciplines his people for their sins. It also tells how, after the judgment, he has mercy and never forgets his promises. Isaiah wants his readers to understand that everything is under God's control, not the enemy's.

Things to look for

The use of prophetic poetry

God's case against his people (see Isa. 1:2–9)

God's judgment (see Isa. 3:1–4:1)

References to Christ (see Isa. 7:14; 9:6–7; 11:1–10; 42:1–4; 53:1–12; 61:1–3; 63:1–2)

Servant Songs (songs about Israel applied to Christ, the true Israel) (see Isa. 42:1–9; 49:1–13; 50:4–11; 52:13–53:12)

Words of comfort (see Isa. 12:1; 28:12; 40:1; 49:13; 51:3, 12; 52:9; 57:18; 61:2)

Wait on the Lord

> They who wait for the LORD shall renew their
> strength;
> they shall mount up with wings like eagles;
> they shall run and not be weary;
> they shall walk and not faint.
>
> *Isaiah 40:31*

Impatience is not a virtue. When you look at a situation in your life and decide to take matters into your own hands instead of waiting for God, you turn your back on the God who was going to do it for you or through you anyway. For a while this approach might work, and you might get things done. The attention you wanted might come your way, the dreams you had might be coming true. But if what you did was in your own strength and not the strength of the Lord, then your energy is going to run out and your success is going to turn to failure.

When you think you need something in this life, it's almost second nature to dive in headfirst and get things done. You take charge of your life and even the lives of others and do what you can to ward off loneliness and suffering. But maybe the loneliness and suffering that would come by waiting on God is just what your soul needs.

When you wait on God, your eyes aren't on yourself; they are looking upward in quiet trust in his promises. When that's your position, you're going to see his glory and his love start to work in your life. Eyes focused on God might see trials and even danger, but they aren't overwhelmed with fear. They are never weary and they never fail, because they see God's tender, loving care and ability to meet all your needs.

To wait on God means to trust him with every part of your life—especially the parts where you have to be patient. Patience *is* a virtue, because it teaches your heart not to rely on its own understanding but to trust in the Lord (see Prov. 3:5). As you read the book of Isaiah, watch how the Israelites failed to trust God and how God repeatedly promised to take them back, even promising a Messiah to take away the sins of the world.

Must-Know Terms and Verses

⟨⟩ *Sodom and Gomorrah* ⟨⟩

Notorious cities of evil, destroyed by God because of their sinfulness (see Genesis 18–19; Isa. 1:9–10; 3:9; 13:19; Ezek. 16:49–50).

"Though your sins are like scarlet,
   they shall be as white as snow." *Isaiah 1:18*

"Do not call conspiracy all that this people calls conspiracy, and do not fear what they fear, nor be in dread." *Isaiah 8:12*

Fear not, for I am with you;
   be not dismayed, for I am your God;
I will strengthen you, I will help you,
   I will uphold you with my righteous right hand. *Isaiah 41:10*

Surely he has borne our griefs
   and carried our sorrows;
yet we esteemed him stricken,
   smitten by God, and afflicted.
But he was pierced for our transgressions;
   he was crushed for our iniquities;
upon him was the chastisement that brought us peace,
   and with his wounds we are healed. *Isaiah 53:4–5*

Isaiah

1 The vision of Isaiah the son of Amoz, which he saw concerning Judah and Jerusalem in the days of Uzziah, Jotham, Ahaz, and Hezekiah, kings of Judah.

The Wickedness of Judah

2 Hear, O heavens, and give ear,
   O earth;
   for the LORD has spoken:
"Children[1] have I reared and brought up,
   but they have rebelled against me.
3 The ox knows its owner,
   and the donkey its master's crib,
but Israel does not know,
   my people do not understand."

4 Ah, sinful nation,
   a people laden with iniquity,
offspring of evildoers,
   children who deal corruptly!
They have forsaken the LORD,
   they have despised the Holy One of Israel,
   they are utterly estranged.

5 Why will you still be struck down?
   Why will you continue to rebel?
The whole head is sick,
   and the whole heart faint.
6 From the sole of the foot even to the head,
   there is no soundness in it,
but bruises and sores
   and raw wounds;
they are not pressed out or bound up
   or softened with oil.

7 Your country lies desolate;
   your cities are burned with fire;
in your very presence
   foreigners devour your land;
   it is desolate, as overthrown by foreigners.
8 And the daughter of Zion is left
   like a booth in a vineyard,
like a lodge in a cucumber field,
   like a besieged city.
9 If the LORD of hosts
   had not left us a few survivors,
we should have been like Sodom,
   and become like Gomorrah.

10 Hear the word of the LORD,
   you rulers of Sodom!
Give ear to the teaching[2] of our God,
   you people of Gomorrah!
11 "What to me is the multitude of your sacrifices?
   says the LORD;
I have had enough of burnt offerings of rams
   and the fat of well-fed beasts;
I do not delight in the blood of bulls,
   or of lambs, or of goats.

12 "When you come to appear before me,
   who has required of you
   this trampling of my courts?
13 Bring no more vain offerings;
   incense is an abomination to me.
New moon and Sabbath and the calling of convocations—
   I cannot endure iniquity and solemn assembly.
14 Your new moons and your appointed feasts
   my soul hates;
they have become a burden to me;
   I am weary of bearing them.
15 When you spread out your hands,
   I will hide my eyes from you;
even though you make many prayers,
   I will not listen;
your hands are full of blood.
16 Wash yourselves; make yourselves clean;
   remove the evil of your deeds from before my eyes;
cease to do evil,
17   learn to do good;

---

[1] Or *Sons*; also verse 4 [2] Or *law*

    seek justice,
        correct oppression;
    bring justice to the fatherless,
        plead the widow's cause.

18 "Come now, let us reason[1] together,
        says the LORD:
    though your sins are like scarlet,
        they shall be as white as snow;
    though they are red like crimson,
        they shall become like wool.
19 If you are willing and obedient,
        you shall eat the good of the land;
20 but if you refuse and rebel,
        you shall be eaten by the sword;
    for the mouth of the LORD has
        spoken."

The Unfaithful City

21 How the faithful city
        has become a whore,[2]
    she who was full of justice!
    Righteousness lodged in her,
        but now murderers.
22 Your silver has become dross,
        your best wine mixed with water.
23 Your princes are rebels
        and companions of thieves.
    Everyone loves a bribe
        and runs after gifts.
    They do not bring justice to the
        fatherless,
    and the widow's cause does not
        come to them.

24 Therefore the Lord declares,
        the LORD of hosts,
        the Mighty One of Israel:
    "Ah, I will get relief from my enemies
        and avenge myself on my foes.
25 I will turn my hand against you
        and will smelt away your dross as
        with lye
    and remove all your alloy.
26 And I will restore your judges as at
        the first,
    and your counselors as at the
        beginning.
    Afterward you shall be called the city
        of righteousness,
        the faithful city."

27 Zion shall be redeemed by justice,
        and those in her who repent, by
        righteousness.

28 But rebels and sinners shall be bro-
        ken together,
    and those who forsake the LORD
        shall be consumed.
29 For they[3] shall be ashamed of the
        oaks
        that you desired;
    and you shall blush for the gardens
        that you have chosen.
30 For you shall be like an oak
        whose leaf withers,
    and like a garden without water.
31 And the strong shall become tinder,
        and his work a spark,
    and both of them shall burn together,
        with none to quench them.

The Mountain of the LORD

2 The word that Isaiah the son of Amoz saw concerning Judah and Jerusalem.

2 It shall come to pass in the latter
        days
    that the mountain of the house of
        the LORD
    shall be established as the highest of
        the mountains,
    and shall be lifted up above the
        hills;
    and all the nations shall flow to it,
3   and many peoples shall come, and
        say:
  "Come, let us go up to the mountain of
        the LORD,
    to the house of the God of Jacob,
    that he may teach us his ways
        and that we may walk in his paths."
    For out of Zion shall go the law,[4]
        and the word of the LORD from
        Jerusalem.
4 He shall judge between the nations,
        and shall decide disputes for many
        peoples;
    and they shall beat their swords into
        plowshares,
        and their spears into pruning
        hooks;
    nation shall not lift up sword against
        nation,
    neither shall they learn war any-
        more.

5 O house of Jacob,
    come, let us walk
    in the light of the LORD.

[1] Or dispute [2] Or become unchaste [3] Some Hebrew manuscripts you [4] Or teaching

The Day of the Lord

6 For you have rejected your people,
    the house of Jacob,
  because they are full of things from
      the east
    and of fortune-tellers like the
        Philistines,
    and they strike hands with the
        children of foreigners.
7 Their land is filled with silver and
      gold,
    and there is no end to their trea-
        sures;
  their land is filled with horses,
    and there is no end to their chari-
        ots.
8 Their land is filled with idols;
    they bow down to the work of
        their hands,
    to what their own fingers have
        made.
9 So man is humbled,
    and each one is brought low—
    do not forgive them!
10 Enter into the rock
    and hide in the dust
  from before the terror of the Lord,
    and from the splendor of his maj-
        esty.
11 The haughty looks of man shall be
      brought low,
    and the lofty pride of men shall be
        humbled,
  and the Lord alone will be exalted in
      that day.

12 For the Lord of hosts has a day
    against all that is proud and lofty,
    against all that is lifted up—and it
        shall be brought low;
13 against all the cedars of Lebanon,
    lofty and lifted up;
    and against all the oaks of Bashan;
14 against all the lofty mountains,
    and against all the uplifted hills;
15 against every high tower,
    and against every fortified wall;
16 against all the ships of Tarshish,
    and against all the beautiful craft.
17 And the haughtiness of man shall be
      humbled,
    and the lofty pride of men shall be
        brought low,
  and the Lord alone will be exalted
      in that day.

18 And the idols shall utterly pass away.
19 And people shall enter the caves of
      the rocks
    and the holes of the ground,[1]
  from before the terror of the Lord,
    and from the splendor of his maj-
        esty,
  when he rises to terrify the earth.

20 In that day mankind will cast away
    their idols of silver and their idols
        of gold,
  which they made for themselves to
      worship,
    to the moles and to the bats,
21 to enter the caverns of the rocks
    and the clefts of the cliffs,
  from before the terror of the Lord,
    and from the splendor of his maj-
        esty,
  when he rises to terrify the earth.
22 Stop regarding man
    in whose nostrils is breath,
    for of what account is he?

Judgment on Judah and Jerusalem

3 For behold, the Lord God of hosts
    is taking away from Jerusalem and
        from Judah
  support and supply,[2]
    all support of bread,
    and all support of water;
2   the mighty man and the soldier,
      the judge and the prophet,
      the diviner and the elder,
3   the captain of fifty
      and the man of rank,
    the counselor and the skillful magi-
        cian
      and the expert in charms.
4 And I will make boys their princes,
    and infants[3] shall rule over them.
5 And the people will oppress one
      another,
      every one his fellow
      and every one his neighbor;
  the youth will be insolent to the
      elder,
    and the despised to the honorable.

6 For a man will take hold of his
      brother
    in the house of his father, saying:
  "You have a cloak;
    you shall be our leader,

---

[1] Hebrew dust [2] Hebrew staff [3] Or caprice

and this heap of ruins
    shall be under your rule";
7 in that day he will speak out, saying:
    "I will not be a healer;[1]
      in my house there is neither bread
        nor cloak;
    you shall not make me
      leader of the people."

8 For Jerusalem has stumbled,
    and Judah has fallen,
  because their speech and their deeds
      are against the LORD,
    defying his glorious presence.[2]

9 For the look on their faces bears wit-
      ness against them;
    they proclaim their sin like Sodom;
    they do not hide it.
  Woe to them!
    For they have brought evil on
      themselves.
10 Tell the righteous that it shall be well
    with them,
    for they shall eat the fruit of their
      deeds.
11 Woe to the wicked! It shall be ill with
    him,
    for what his hands have dealt out
      shall be done to him.
12 My people—infants are their
    oppressors,
    and women rule over them.
  O my people, your guides mislead you
    and they have swallowed up[3] the
      course of your paths.

13 The LORD has taken his place to
    contend;
    he stands to judge peoples.
14 The LORD will enter into judgment
    with the elders and princes of his
      people:
  "It is you who have devoured[4] the
      vineyard,
    the spoil of the poor is in your
      houses.
15 What do you mean by crushing my
    people,
    by grinding the face of the poor?"
      declares the Lord GOD of hosts.

16 The LORD said:
  Because the daughters of Zion are
    haughty
    and walk with outstretched necks,
    glancing wantonly with their eyes,

    mincing along as they go,
    tinkling with their feet,
17 therefore the Lord will strike with a
    scab
    the heads of the daughters of Zion
    and the LORD will lay bare their
      secret parts.

18 In that day the Lord will take away the finery of the anklets, the headbands, and the crescents; 19 the pendants, the bracelets, and the scarves; 20 the headdresses, the armlets, the sashes, the perfume boxes, and the amulets; 21 the signet rings and nose rings; 22 the festal robes, the mantles, the cloaks, and the handbags; 23 the mirrors, the linen garments, the turbans, and the veils.

24 Instead of perfume there will be rot-
    tenness;
    and instead of a belt, a rope;
  and instead of well-set hair, bald-
      ness;
    and instead of a rich robe, a skirt
      of sackcloth;
    and branding instead of beauty.
25 Your men shall fall by the sword
    and your mighty men in battle.
26 And her gates shall lament and
    mourn;
    empty, she shall sit on the ground.

4 And seven women shall take hold of one man in that day, saying, "We will eat our own bread and wear our own clothes, only let us be called by your name; take away our reproach."

The Branch of the LORD Glorified

2 In that day the branch of the LORD shall be beautiful and glorious, and the fruit of the land shall be the pride and honor of the survivors of Israel. 3 And he who is left in Zion and remains in Jerusalem will be called holy, everyone who has been recorded for life in Jerusalem, 4 when the Lord shall have washed away the filth of the daughters of Zion and cleansed the bloodstains of Jerusalem from its midst by a spirit of judgment and by a spirit of burning.[5] 5 Then the LORD will create over the whole site of Mount Zion and over her assemblies a cloud by day, and smoke and the shining of a flaming fire by night; for over all the glory there will be a canopy.

---

[1] Hebrew *binder of wounds* [2] Hebrew *the eyes of his glory* [3] Or *they have confused* [4] Or *grazed over; compare Exodus 22:5* [5] Or *purging*

There will be a booth for shade by day
from the heat, and for a refuge and a shelter from the storm and rain.

The Vineyard of the LORD Destroyed

5 Let me sing for my beloved
  my love song concerning his vine-
    yard:
My beloved had a vineyard
  on a very fertile hill.
² He dug it and cleared it of stones,
  and planted it with choice vines;
he built a watchtower in the midst of
    it,
  and hewed out a wine vat in it;
and he looked for it to yield grapes,
  but it yielded wild grapes.

³ And now, O inhabitants of Jerusalem
  and men of Judah,
judge between me and my vineyard.
⁴ What more was there to do for my
    vineyard,
  that I have not done in it?
When I looked for it to yield grapes,
  why did it yield wild grapes?

⁵ And now I will tell you
  what I will do to my vineyard.
I will remove its hedge,
  and it shall be devoured;¹
I will break down its wall,
  and it shall be trampled down.
⁶ I will make it a waste;
  it shall not be pruned or hoed,
  and briers and thorns shall grow
    up;
I will also command the clouds
  that they rain no rain upon it.

⁷ For the vineyard of the LORD of hosts
  is the house of Israel,
and the men of Judah
  are his pleasant planting;
and he looked for justice,
  but behold, bloodshed;²
for righteousness,
  but behold, an outcry!³

Woe to the Wicked

⁸ Woe to those who join house to
    house,
  who add field to field,

until there is no more room,
  and you are made to dwell alone
  in the midst of the land.
⁹ The LORD of hosts has sworn in my
    hearing:
"Surely many houses shall be deso-
    late,
  large and beautiful houses, with-
    out inhabitant.
¹⁰ For ten acres⁴ of vineyard shall yield
    but one bath,
  and a homer of seed shall yield but
    an ephah."⁵

¹¹ Woe to those who rise early in the
    morning,
  that they may run after strong
    drink,
who tarry late into the evening
  as wine inflames them!
¹² They have lyre and harp,
  tambourine and flute and wine at
    their feasts,
but they do not regard the deeds of
    the LORD,
  or see the work of his hands.

¹³ Therefore my people go into exile
  for lack of knowledge;⁶
their honored men go hungry,⁷
  and their multitude is parched
    with thirst.
¹⁴ Therefore Sheol has enlarged its
    appetite
  and opened its mouth beyond
    measure,
and the nobility of Jerusalem⁸ and
    her multitude will go down,
  her revelers and he who exults in
    her.
¹⁵ Man is humbled, and each one is
    brought low,
  and the eyes of the haughty⁹ are
    brought low.
¹⁶ But the LORD of hosts is exalted¹⁰ in
    justice,
  and the Holy God shows himself
    holy in righteousness.
¹⁷ Then shall the lambs graze as in their
    pasture,
  and nomads shall eat among the
    ruins of the rich.

¹Or *grazed over*; compare Exodus 22:5 ²The Hebrew words for *justice* and *bloodshed* sound alike ³The Hebrew words for *righteous* and *outcry* sound alike ⁴Hebrew *ten yoke*, the area ten yoke of oxen can plow in a day ⁵A *bath* was about 6 gallons or 22 liters; a *homer* was about 6 bushels or 220 liters; an *ephah* was about 3/5 bushel or 22 liters ⁶Or *without their knowledge* ⁷Or *die of hunger* ⁸Hebrew *her nobility* ⁹Hebrew *high* ¹⁰Hebrew *high*

18 Woe to those who draw iniquity with
  cords of falsehood,
  who draw sin as with cart ropes,
19 who say: "Let him be quick,
  let him speed his work
  that we may see it;
  let the counsel of the Holy One of
  Israel draw near,
  and let it come, that we may know
  it!"
20 Woe to those who call evil good
  and good evil,
  who put darkness for light
  and light for darkness,
  who put bitter for sweet
  and sweet for bitter!
21 Woe to those who are wise in their
  own eyes,
  and shrewd in their own sight!
22 Woe to those who are heroes at
  drinking wine,
  and valiant men in mixing strong
  drink,
23 who acquit the guilty for a bribe,
  and deprive the innocent of his
  right!

24 Therefore, as the tongue of fire
  devours the stubble,
  and as dry grass sinks down in the
  flame,
  so their root will be as rottenness,
  and their blossom go up like dust;
  for they have rejected the law of the
  LORD of hosts,
  and have despised the word of the
  Holy One of Israel.
25 Therefore the anger of the LORD was
  kindled against his people,
  and he stretched out his hand
  against them and struck them,
  and the mountains quaked;
  and their corpses were as refuse
  in the midst of the streets.
  For all this his anger has not turned
  away,
  and his hand is stretched out still.

26 He will raise a signal for nations far
  away,
  and whistle for them from the
  ends of the earth;
  and behold, quickly, speedily they
  come!

27 None is weary, none stumbles,
  none slumbers or sleeps,
  not a waistband is loose,
  not a sandal strap broken;
28 their arrows are sharp,
  all their bows bent,
  their horses' hoofs seem like flint,
  and their wheels like the whirlwind.
29 Their roaring is like a lion,
  like young lions they roar;
  they growl and seize their prey;
  they carry it off, and none can
  rescue.
30 They will growl over it on that day,
  like the growling of the sea.
  And if one looks to the land,
  behold, darkness and distress;
  and the light is darkened by its
  clouds.

Isaiah's Vision of the Lord

6 In the year that King Uzziah died I saw the Lord sitting upon a throne, high and lifted up; and the train[1] of his robe filled the temple. 2 Above him stood the seraphim. Each had six wings: with two he covered his face, and with two he covered his feet, and with two he flew. 3 And one called to another and said:

  "Holy, holy, holy is the LORD of hosts;
  the whole earth is full of his glory!"[2]

4 And the foundations of the threshold shook at the voice of him who called, and the house was filled with smoke. 5 And I said: "Woe is me! For I am lost; for I am a man of unclean lips, and I dwell in the midst of a people of unclean lips; for my eyes have seen the King, the LORD of hosts!

6 Then one of the seraphim flew to me, having in his hand a burning coal that he had taken with tongs from the altar. 7 And he touched my mouth and said: "Behold, this has touched your lips; your guilt is taken away, and your sin atoned for."

Isaiah's Commission from the Lord

8 And I heard the voice of the Lord say-ing, "Whom shall I send, and who will go for us?" Then I said, "Here I am! Send me." 9 And he said, "Go, and say to this people:

  "'Keep on hearing,[3] but do not understand;

[1] Or hem [2] Or may his glory fill the whole earth [3] Or Hear indeed

keep on seeing,[1] but do not perceive.'
10 Make the heart of this people dull,[2]
    and their ears heavy,
    and blind their eyes;
lest they see with their eyes,
    and hear with their ears,
and understand with their hearts,
    and turn and be healed."
11 Then I said, "How long, O Lord?"
And he said:
"Until cities lie waste
    without inhabitant,
and houses without people,
    and the land is a desolate waste,
12   and the Lord removes people far
      away,
    and the forsaken places are many
      in the midst of the land.
13 And though a tenth remain in it,
    it will be burned[3] again,

like a terebinth or an oak,
    whose stump remains
    when it is felled."
The holy seed[4] is its stump.

Isaiah Sent to King Ahaz

7 In the days of Ahaz the son of Jotham, son of Uzziah, king of Judah, Rezin the king of Syria and Pekah the son of Remaliah the king of Israel came up to Jerusalem to wage war against it, but could not yet mount an attack against it. [2]When the house of David was told, "Syria is in league with[5] Ephraim," the heart of Ahaz[6] and the heart of his people shook as the trees of the forest shake before the wind.

[3]And the Lord said to Isaiah, "Go out to meet Ahaz, you and Shear-jashub[7] your son, at the end of the conduit of the upper pool on the highway to the Washer's Field.

Or *see indeed* [2]Hebrew *fat* [3]Or *purged* [4]Or *offspring* [5]Hebrew *Syria has rested upon* [6]Hebrew *his heart* [7]*Shear-jashub* means *A remnant shall return*

Know God

verses to read
Isaiah 6:8–10

God is always speaking, but only a few are ever listening. Silence in the spiritual realm isn't the result of God's distance but of ours. God is forever asking, forever sending, and forever saving, but only those who are interested in his presence and listening for his voice will ever know it. In this case, Isaiah wasn't "called"—he was listening when God was calling anyone who would listen. By God's grace, Isaiah had his mind and ears on God and was ready and willing to do whatever needed to be done. God spoke, and Isaiah answered: "Here I am! Send me" (Isa. 6:8). Were there others who could have answered? Maybe, but Isaiah didn't hesitate to answer, and because of that, events in his life were set into motion that changed the course of history.

Your purpose in life isn't something you need to dig deep to discover. It isn't hidden and difficult to find. It is to know God, to listen to his voice, and to do whatever he commands. And nowhere is God's voice heard more clearly than in his Word. You can be sure of his voice when you read it in the pages of Scripture. All you have to do is make it a part of your life, your actions, and your thoughts. As you do, God's will for your life will become evident. If you have to make a choice between two things, the question you need to ask is, "Would one of the two choices be against God's will as seen in his Word?" If the answer is yes, then you know which choice to make, because sin is never an option.

If you want more of God, more guidance, and more direction, then learn his Word. Make it your goal to be alert to his voice and to stand up and say, "Here I am. Send me."

[4] And say to him, 'Be careful, be quiet, do not fear, and do not let your heart be faint because of these two smoldering stumps of firebrands, at the fierce anger of Rezin and Syria and the son of Remaliah. [5] Because Syria, with Ephraim and the son of Remaliah, has devised evil against you, saying, [6] "Let us go up against Judah and terrify it, and let us conquer it[1] for ourselves, and set up the son of Tabeel as king in the midst of it," [7] thus says the Lord GOD:

> " 'It shall not stand,
>   and it shall not come to pass.
> [8]   For the head of Syria is Damascus,
>   and the head of Damascus is Rezin.
>   And within sixty-five years
>   Ephraim will be shattered from
>   being a people.
> [9]   And the head of Ephraim is Samaria,
>   and the head of Samaria is the son
>   of Remaliah.
>   If you[2] are not firm in faith,
>   you will not be firm at all.' "

The Sign of Immanuel

[10] Again the LORD spoke to Ahaz, [11] "Ask a sign of the LORD your[3] God; let it be deep as Sheol or high as heaven." [12] But Ahaz said, "I will not ask, and I will not put the LORD to the test." [13] And he[4] said, "Hear then, O house of David! Is it too little for you to weary men, that you weary my God also? [14] Therefore the Lord himself will give you a sign. Behold, the virgin shall conceive and bear a son, and shall call his name Immanuel.[5] [15] He shall eat curds and honey when he knows how to refuse the evil and choose the good. [16] For before the boy knows how to refuse the evil and choose the good, the land whose two kings you dread will be deserted. [17] The LORD will bring upon you and upon your people and upon your father's house such days as have not come since the day that Ephraim departed from Judah—the king of Assyria."

[18] In that day the LORD will whistle for the fly that is at the end of the streams of Egypt, and for the bee that is in the land of Assyria. [19] And they will all come and settle in the steep ravines, and in the clefts of the rocks, and on all the thornbushes, and on all the pastures.[6]

[20] In that day the Lord will shave with a razor that is hired beyond the River—with the king of Assyria—the head and the hair of the feet, and it will sweep away the beard also.

[21] In that day a man will keep alive a young cow and two sheep, [22] and because of the abundance of milk that they give, he will eat curds, for everyone who is left in the land will eat curds and honey.

[23] In that day every place where there used to be a thousand vines, worth a thousand shekels[7] of silver, will become briers and thorns. [24] With bow and arrows a man will come there, for all the land will be briers and thorns. [25] And as for all the hills that used to be hoed with a hoe, you will not come there for fear of briers and thorns, but they will become a place where cattle are let loose and where sheep tread.

The Coming Assyrian Invasion

8 Then the LORD said to me, "Take a large tablet and write on it in common characters,[8] 'Belonging to Maher-shalal-hash-baz.'[9] [2] And I will get reliable witnesses, Uriah the priest and Zechariah the son of Jeberechiah, to attest for me."

[3] And I went to the prophetess, and she conceived and bore a son. Then the LORD said to me, "Call his name Maher-shalal-hash-baz; [4] for before the boy knows how to cry 'My father' or 'My mother,' the wealth of Damascus and the spoil of Samaria will be carried away before the king of Assyria."

[5] The LORD spoke to me again: [6] "Because this people has refused the waters of Shiloah that flow gently, and rejoice over Rezin and the son of Remaliah, [7] therefore, behold, the Lord is bringing up against them the waters of the River, mighty and many, the king of Assyria and all his glory. And it will rise over all its channels and go over all its banks, [8] and it will sweep on into Judah, it will overflow and pass on, reaching even to the neck, and its outspread wings will fill the breadth of your land, O Immanuel."

> [9]   Be broken,[10] you peoples, and be
>   shattered;[11]
>   give ear, all you far countries;

---

[1] Hebrew *let us split it open* [2] The Hebrew for *you* is plural in verses 9, 13, 14 [3] The Hebrew for *you* and *your* is singular in verses 11, 16, 17 [4] That is, Isaiah [5] *Immanuel* means *God is with us* [6] Or *watering holes*, or *brambles* [7] A *shekel* was about 2/5 ounce or 11 grams [8] Hebrew *with a man's stylus* [9] *Maher-shalal-hash-baz* means *The spoil speeds, the prey hastens* [10] Or *Be evil* [11] Or *dismayed*

strap on your armor and be shattered;
strap on your armor and be shattered.

[10] Take counsel together, but it will
come to nothing;
speak a word, but it will not stand,
for God is with us.[1]

Fear God, Wait for the Lord

[11] For the Lord spoke thus to me with his strong hand upon me, and warned me not to walk in the way of this people, saying: [12] "Do not call conspiracy all that this people calls conspiracy, and do not fear what they fear, nor be in dread. [13] But the Lord of hosts, him you shall honor as holy. Let him be your fear, and let him be your dread. [14] And he will become a sanctuary and a stone of offense and a rock of stumbling to both houses of Israel, a trap and a snare to the inhabitants of Jerusalem. [15] And many shall stumble on it. They shall fall and be broken; they shall be snared and taken."

[16] Bind up the testimony; seal the teaching[2] among my disciples. [17] I will wait for the Lord, who is hiding his face from the house of Jacob, and I will hope in him. [18] Behold, I and the children whom the Lord has given me are signs and portents in Israel from the Lord of hosts, who dwells on Mount Zion. [19] And when they say to you, "Inquire of the mediums and the necromancers who chirp and mutter," should not a people inquire of their God? Should they inquire of the dead on behalf of the living? [20] To the teaching and to the testimony! If they will not speak according to this word, it is because they have no dawn. [21] They will pass through the land,[3] greatly distressed and hungry. And when they are hungry, they will be enraged and will speak contemptuously against[4] their king and their God, and turn their faces upward. [22] And they will look to the earth, but behold, distress and darkness, the gloom of anguish. And they will be thrust into thick darkness.

For to Us a Child Is Born

9 [5] But there will be no gloom for her who was in anguish. In the former time he brought into contempt the land of Zebulun and the land of Naphtali, but in the latter time he has made glorious the way of the sea, the land beyond the Jordan, Galilee of the nations.[6]

[2][7] The people who walked in darkness
have seen a great light;
those who dwelt in a land of deep
darkness,
on them has light shone.
[3] You have multiplied the nation;
you have increased its joy;
they rejoice before you
as with joy at the harvest,
as they are glad when they divide
the spoil.
[4] For the yoke of his burden,
and the staff for his shoulder,
the rod of his oppressor,
you have broken as on the day of
Midian.
[5] For every boot of the tramping warrior in battle tumult
and every garment rolled in blood
will be burned as fuel for the fire.
[6] For to us a child is born,
to us a son is given;
and the government shall be upon[8]
his shoulder,
and his name shall be called[9]
Wonderful Counselor, Mighty God,
Everlasting Father, Prince of Peace.
[7] Of the increase of his government
and of peace
there will be no end,
on the throne of David and over his
kingdom,
to establish it and to uphold it
with justice and with righteousness
from this time forth and forevermore.
The zeal of the Lord of hosts will do
this.

Judgment on Arrogance and Oppression

[8] The Lord has sent a word against
Jacob,
and it will fall on Israel;
[9] and all the people will know,
Ephraim and the inhabitants of
Samaria,
who say in pride and in arrogance
of heart:
[10] "The bricks have fallen,
but we will build with dressed
stones;

---

[1] The Hebrew for *God is with us* is *Immanuel* [2] Or *law*; also verse 20 [3] Hebrew *it* [4] Or *speak contemptuously by* [5] Ch 8:23 in Hebrew [6] Or *of the Gentiles* [7] Ch 9:1 in Hebrew [8] Or *is upon* [9] Or *is called*

the sycamores have been cut down,
 but we will put cedars in their
  place."

11 But the LORD raises the adversaries
    of Rezin against him,
  and stirs up his enemies.
12 The Syrians on the east and the
     Philistines on the west
  devour Israel with open mouth.
  For all this his anger has not turned
   away,
  and his hand is stretched out still.

13 The people did not turn to him who
     struck them,
  nor inquire of the LORD of hosts.
14 So the LORD cut off from Israel head
    and tail,
  palm branch and reed in one day—
15 the elder and honored man is the
    head,
  and the prophet who teaches lies
   is the tail;
16 for those who guide this people have
     been leading them astray,
  and those who are guided by them
   are swallowed up.
17 Therefore the Lord does not rejoice
     over their young men,
  and has no compassion on their
   fatherless and widows;
  for everyone is godless and an evil-
    doer,
  and every mouth speaks folly.[1]
  For all this his anger has not turned
   away,
  and his hand is stretched out still.

18 For wickedness burns like a fire;
  it consumes briers and thorns;
  it kindles the thickets of the forest,
  and they roll upward in a column
   of smoke.
19 Through the wrath of the LORD of
    hosts
   the land is scorched,
  and the people are like fuel for the
   fire;
  no one spares another.
20 They slice meat on the right, but are
    still hungry,
  and they devour on the left, but
   are not satisfied;
  each devours the flesh of his own
   arm,

21 Manasseh devours Ephraim, and
    Ephraim devours Manasseh;
  together they are against Judah.
  For all this his anger has not turned
   away,
  and his hand is stretched out still.

Ask Yourself . . .

ABOUT HELPING

- Is there someone in need near
  me whom I can help?
- What do I have that someone
  else needs more than I do?
- Is there something that I won't
  give up? Why? What does that
  say about my understanding of
  all that God has done for me in
  the gospel?
- What keeps me from helping
  others who need my things or
  my time?
- Whom could I get to join me in
  serving those in need?

10 Woe to those who decree iniqui-
     tous decrees,
  and the writers who keep writing
   oppression,
2 to turn aside the needy from justice
  and to rob the poor of my people
   of their right,
  that widows may be their spoil,
  and that they may make the fatherless their prey!
3 What will you do on the day of pun-
    ishment,
  in the ruin that will come from
   afar?
  To whom will you flee for help,
  and where will you leave your
   wealth?
4 Nothing remains but to crouch
    among the prisoners
  or fall among the slain.

[1] Or speaks disgraceful things

For all this his anger has not turned
away,
    and his hand is stretched out still.

Judgment on Arrogant Assyria

5 Ah, Assyria, the rod of my anger;
        the staff in their hands is my fury!
6 Against a godless nation I send him,
        and against the people of my
            wrath I command him,
    to take spoil and seize plunder,
        and to tread them down like the
            mire of the streets.
7 But he does not so intend,
        and his heart does not so think;
    but it is in his heart to destroy,
        and to cut off nations not a few;
8 for he says:
    "Are not my commanders all kings?
9   Is not Calno like Carchemish?
        Is not Hamath like Arpad?
        Is not Samaria like Damascus?
10 As my hand has reached to the king-
            doms of the idols,
        whose carved images were greater
            than those of Jerusalem and
            Samaria,
11 shall I not do to Jerusalem and her
            idols
        as I have done to Samaria and her
            images?"

12 When the Lord has finished all his
work on Mount Zion and on Jerusalem,
he[1] will punish the speech of the arrogant
heart of the king of Assyria and the boastful look in his eyes. 13 For he says:

    "By the strength of my hand I have
            done it,
        and by my wisdom, for I have
            understanding;
    I remove the boundaries of peoples,
        and plunder their treasures;
        like a bull I bring down those who
            sit on thrones.
14 My hand has found like a nest
        the wealth of the peoples;
    and as one gathers eggs that have
            been forsaken,
        so I have gathered all the earth;
    and there was none that moved a
            wing
        or opened the mouth or chirped."

15 Shall the axe boast over him who
            hews with it,
        or the saw magnify itself against
            him who wields it?
    As if a rod should wield him who lifts
            it,
        or as if a staff should lift him who
            is not wood!
16 Therefore the Lord GOD of hosts
        will send wasting sickness among
            his stout warriors,
    and under his glory a burning will be
            kindled,
        like the burning of fire.
17 The light of Israel will become a fire,
        and his Holy One a flame,
    and it will burn and devour
        his thorns and briers in one day.
18 The glory of his forest and of his
            fruitful land
        the LORD will destroy, both soul
            and body,
        and it will be as when a sick man
            wastes away.
19 The remnant of the trees of his forest
            will be so few
        that a child can write them down.

The Remnant of Israel Will Return

20 In that day the remnant of Israel and
the survivors of the house of Jacob will
no more lean on him who struck them,
but will lean on the LORD, the Holy One of
Israel, in truth. 21 A remnant will return,
the remnant of Jacob, to the mighty God.
22 For though your people Israel be as the
sand of the sea, only a remnant of them will
return. Destruction is decreed, overflowing
with righteousness. 23 For the Lord GOD of
hosts will make a full end, as decreed, in
the midst of all the earth.

24 Therefore thus says the Lord GOD of
hosts: "O my people, who dwell in Zion,
be not afraid of the Assyrians when they
strike with the rod and lift up their staff
against you as the Egyptians did. 25 For in
a very little while my fury will come to an
end, and my anger will be directed to their
destruction. 26 And the LORD of hosts will
wield against them a whip, as when he
struck Midian at the rock of Oreb. And his
staff will be over the sea, and he will lift
it as he did in Egypt. 27 And in that day his
burden will depart from your shoulder, and

his yoke from your neck; and the yoke will be broken because of the fat."[1]

28 He has come to Aiath;
    he has passed through Migron;
        at Michmash he stores his baggage;
29 they have crossed over the pass;
        at Geba they lodge for the night;
    Ramah trembles;
        Gibeah of Saul has fled.
30 Cry aloud, O daughter of Gallim!
        Give attention, O Laishah!
        O poor Anathoth!
31 Madmenah is in flight;
        the inhabitants of Gebim flee for
            safety.
32 This very day he will halt at Nob;
        he will shake his fist
    at the mount of the daughter of
            Zion,
        the hill of Jerusalem.

33 Behold, the Lord GOD of hosts
        will lop the boughs with terrifying
            power;
    the great in height will be hewn down,
        and the lofty will be brought low.
34 He will cut down the thickets of the
            forest with an axe,
        and Lebanon will fall by the
            Majestic One.

Ask Yourself . . .

ABOUT GOD'S CALL

- What does the branch of Jesse refer to (see Isa. 11:1)?
- Why would people gather around a signal (see Isa. 11:10)?
- Where else does the book of Isaiah talk about the Messiah?
- How much do I know about the prophecies in this book and the life of Jesus in the New Testament?
- Where can I start today to learn more?

The Righteous Reign of the Branch

11 There shall come forth a shoot
        from the stump of Jesse,
    and a branch from his roots shall
            bear fruit.
2 And the Spirit of the LORD shall rest
            upon him,
    the Spirit of wisdom and under-
            standing,
    the Spirit of counsel and might,
    the Spirit of knowledge and the
            fear of the LORD.
3 And his delight shall be in the fear of
            the LORD.

He shall not judge by what his eyes
            see,
        or decide disputes by what his
            ears hear,
4 but with righteousness he shall judge
            the poor,
        and decide with equity for the
            meek of the earth;
    and he shall strike the earth with the
            rod of his mouth,
        and with the breath of his lips he
            shall kill the wicked.
5 Righteousness shall be the belt of his
            waist,
        and faithfulness the belt of his loins.

6 The wolf shall dwell with the lamb,
        and the leopard shall lie down
            with the young goat,
    and the calf and the lion and the fat-
            tened calf together;
        and a little child shall lead them.
7 The cow and the bear shall graze;
        their young shall lie down together;
        and the lion shall eat straw like the
            ox.
8 The nursing child shall play over the
            hole of the cobra,
        and the weaned child shall put his
            hand on the adder's den.
9 They shall not hurt or destroy
        in all my holy mountain;
    for the earth shall be full of the
            knowledge of the LORD
        as the waters cover the sea.

10 In that day the root of Jesse, who shall stand as a signal for the peoples—of him shall the nations inquire, and his resting place shall be glorious.

[1] The meaning of the Hebrew is uncertain

[11] In that day the Lord will extend his hand yet a second time to recover the remnant that remains of his people, from Assyria, from Egypt, from Pathros, from Cush,[1] from Elam, from Shinar, from Hamath, and from the coastlands of the sea.

[12] He will raise a signal for the nations
    and will assemble the banished of
        Israel,
and gather the dispersed of Judah
    from the four corners of the earth.
[13] The jealousy of Ephraim shall depart,
    and those who harass Judah shall
        be cut off;
Ephraim shall not be jealous of Judah,
    and Judah shall not harass Ephraim.
[14] But they shall swoop down on the
        shoulder of the Philistines in
        the west,
    and together they shall plunder
        the people of the east.
They shall put out their hand against
        Edom and Moab,
    and the Ammonites shall obey
        them.
[15] And the LORD will utterly destroy[2]
    the tongue of the Sea of Egypt,
and will wave his hand over the River
    with his scorching breath,[3]
and strike it into seven channels,
    and he will lead people across in
        sandals.
[16] And there will be a highway from
        Assyria
    for the remnant that remains of his
        people,
as there was for Israel
    when they came up from the land
        of Egypt.

The LORD Is My Strength and My Song

12 You[4] will say in that day:
    "I will give thanks to you, O LORD,
    for though you were angry with me,
your anger turned away,
    that you might comfort me.

[2] "Behold, God is my salvation;
    I will trust, and will not be afraid;
for the LORD GOD[5] is my strength and
        my song,
    and he has become my salvation."

[3] With joy you[6] will draw water from the wells of salvation. [4] And you will say in that day:

"Give thanks to the LORD,
    call upon his name,
make known his deeds among the
        peoples,
    proclaim that his name is exalted.
[5] "Sing praises to the LORD, for he has
        done gloriously;
    let this be made known[7] in all the
        earth.
[6] Shout, and sing for joy, O inhabitant
        of Zion,
    for great in your[8] midst is the Holy
        One of Israel."

The Judgment of Babylon

13 The oracle concerning Babylon which Isaiah the son of Amoz saw.

[2] On a bare hill raise a signal;
    cry aloud to them;
wave the hand for them to enter
    the gates of the nobles.
[3] I myself have commanded my conse-
        crated ones,
    and have summoned my mighty
        men to execute my anger,
    my proudly exulting ones.[9]
[4] The sound of a tumult is on the
        mountains
    as of a great multitude!
The sound of an uproar of kingdoms,
    of nations gathering together!
The LORD of hosts is mustering
    a host for battle.
[5] They come from a distant land,
    from the end of the heavens,
the LORD and the weapons of his
        indignation,
    to destroy the whole land.[10]
[6] Wail, for the day of the LORD is near;
    as destruction from the Almighty[11]
        it will come!
[7] Therefore all hands will be feeble,
    and every human heart will melt.
[8] They will be dismayed:
    pangs and agony will seize them;
    they will be in anguish like a
        woman in labor.

---

[1] Probably *Nubia* [2] Hebrew *devote to destruction* [3] Or *wind* [4] The Hebrew for *you* is singular in verse 1 [5] Hebrew *for Yah, the LORD*
[6] The Hebrew for *you* is plural in verses 3, 4 [7] Or *this is made known* [8] The Hebrew for *your* in verse 6 is singular, referring to the *inhabitant of Zion* [9] Or *those who exult in my majesty* [10] Or *earth*; also verse 9 [11] The Hebrew words for *destruction* and *almighty* sound alike

They will look aghast at one another;
  their faces will be aflame.

9 Behold, the day of the LORD comes,
  cruel, with wrath and fierce anger,
to make the land a desolation
  and to destroy its sinners from it.
10 For the stars of the heavens and their
    constellations
  will not give their light;
the sun will be dark at its rising,
  and the moon will not shed its light.
11 I will punish the world for its evil,
  and the wicked for their iniquity;
I will put an end to the pomp of the
    arrogant,
  and lay low the pompous pride of
    the ruthless.
12 I will make people more rare than
    fine gold,
  and mankind than the gold of Ophir.
13 Therefore I will make the heavens
    tremble,
  and the earth will be shaken out of
    its place,
at the wrath of the LORD of hosts
  in the day of his fierce anger.
14 And like a hunted gazelle,
  or like sheep with none to gather
    them,
each will turn to his own people,
  and each will flee to his own land.
15 Whoever is found will be thrust
    through,
  and whoever is caught will fall by
    the sword.
16 Their infants will be dashed in pieces[1]
  before their eyes;
their houses will be plundered
  and their wives ravished.

17 Behold, I am stirring up the Medes
  against them,
who have no regard for silver
  and do not delight in gold.
18 Their bows will slaughter[1] the young
    men;
  they will have no mercy on the
    fruit of the womb;
  their eyes will not pity children.
19 And Babylon, the glory of kingdoms,
  the splendor and pomp of the
    Chaldeans,
will be like Sodom and Gomorrah
  when God overthrew them.

20 It will never be inhabited
  or lived in for all generations;
no Arab will pitch his tent there;
  no shepherds will make their
    flocks lie down there.
21 But wild animals will lie down there,
  and their houses will be full of
    howling creatures;
there ostriches[2] will dwell,
  and there wild goats will dance.
22 Hyenas[3] will cry in its towers,
  and jackals in the pleasant palaces;
its time is close at hand
  and its days will not be prolonged.

The Restoration of Jacob

14 For the LORD will have compassion on Jacob and will again choose Israel, and will set them in their own land, and sojourners will join them and will attach themselves to the house of Jacob. 2 And the peoples will take them and bring them to their place, and the house of Israel will possess them in the LORD's land as male and female slaves.[4] They will take captive those who were their captors, and rule over those who oppressed them.

Israel's Remnant Taunts Babylon

3 When the LORD has given you rest from your pain and turmoil and the hard service with which you were made to serve, 4 you will take up this taunt against the king of Babylon:

"How the oppressor has ceased,
  the insolent fury[5] ceased!
5 The LORD has broken the staff of the
    wicked,
  the scepter of rulers,
6 that struck the peoples in wrath
  with unceasing blows,
that ruled the nations in anger
  with unrelenting persecution.
7 The whole earth is at rest and quiet;
  they break forth into singing.
8 The cypresses rejoice at you,
  the cedars of Lebanon, saying,
'Since you were laid low,
  no woodcutter comes up against us.'
9 Sheol beneath is stirred up
  to meet you when you come;
it rouses the shades to greet you,
  all who were leaders of the earth;

---

[1] Hebrew *dash in pieces* [2] Or *owls* [3] Or *foxes* [4] Or *servants* [5] Dead Sea Scroll (compare Septuagint, Syriac, Vulgate); the meaning of the word in the Masoretic Text is uncertain

it raises from their thrones
  all who were kings of the nations.
10 All of them will answer
  and say to you:
'You too have become as weak as we!
  You have become like us!'
11 Your pomp is brought down to Sheol,
  the sound of your harps;
maggots are laid as a bed beneath you,
  and worms are your covers.

12 "How you are fallen from heaven,
  O Day Star, son of Dawn!
How you are cut down to the ground,
  you who laid the nations low!
13 You said in your heart,
  'I will ascend to heaven;
above the stars of God
  I will set my throne on high;
I will sit on the mount of assembly
  in the far reaches of the north;[1]
14 I will ascend above the heights of the clouds;
  I will make myself like the Most High.'
15 But you are brought down to Sheol,
  to the far reaches of the pit.
16 Those who see you will stare at you
  and ponder over you:
'Is this the man who made the earth tremble,
  who shook kingdoms,
17 who made the world like a desert
  and overthrew its cities,
  who did not let his prisoners go home?'
18 All the kings of the nations lie in glory,
  each in his own tomb;[2]
19 but you are cast out, away from your grave,
  like a loathed branch,
clothed with the slain, those pierced by the sword,
  who go down to the stones of the pit,
  like a dead body trampled underfoot.
20 You will not be joined with them in burial,
  because you have destroyed your land,
  you have slain your people.

"May the offspring of evildoers
  nevermore be named!

21 Prepare slaughter for his sons
  because of the guilt of their fathers,
lest they rise and possess the earth,
  and fill the face of the world with cities."

22 "I will rise up against them," declares the LORD of hosts, "and will cut off from Babylon name and remnant, descendants and posterity," declares the LORD. 23 "And I will make it a possession of the hedgehog,[3] and pools of water, and I will sweep it with the broom of destruction," declares the LORD of hosts.

An Oracle Concerning Assyria
24 The LORD of hosts has sworn:
  "As I have planned,
    so shall it be,
  and as I have purposed,
    so shall it stand,
25 that I will break the Assyrian in my land,
  and on my mountains trample him underfoot;
and his yoke shall depart from them,
  and his burden from their shoulder."

26 This is the purpose that is purposed
  concerning the whole earth,
and this is the hand that is stretched out
  over all the nations.
27 For the LORD of hosts has purposed,
  and who will annul it?
His hand is stretched out,
  and who will turn it back?

An Oracle Concerning Philistia
28 In the year that King Ahaz died came this oracle:

29 Rejoice not, O Philistia, all of you,
  that the rod that struck you is broken,
for from the serpent's root will come forth an adder,
  and its fruit will be a flying fiery serpent.
30 And the firstborn of the poor will graze,
  and the needy lie down in safety;
but I will kill your root with famine,
  and your remnant it will slay.
31 Wail, O gate; cry out, O city;
  melt in fear, O Philistia, all of you!

[1] Or in the remote parts of Zaphon [2] Hebrew house [3] Possibly porcupine, or owl

For smoke comes out of the north,
and there is no straggler in his
ranks.

32 What will one answer the messengers of the nation?
"The Lord has founded Zion,
and in her the afflicted of his
people find refuge."

An Oracle Concerning Moab

15 An oracle concerning Moab.

Because Ar of Moab is laid waste in a
night,
Moab is undone;
because Kir of Moab is laid waste in
a night,
Moab is undone.
2 He has gone up to the temple,[1] and to
Dibon,
to the high places[2] to weep;
over Nebo and over Medeba
Moab wails.
On every head is baldness;
every beard is shorn;
3 in the streets they wear sackcloth;
on the housetops and in the squares
everyone wails and melts in tears.
4 Heshbon and Elealeh cry out;
their voice is heard as far as Jahaz;
therefore the armed men of Moab
cry aloud;
his soul trembles.
5 My heart cries out for Moab;
her fugitives flee to Zoar,
to Eglath-shelishiyah.
For at the ascent of Luhith
they go up weeping;
on the road to Horonaim
they raise a cry of destruction;
6 the waters of Nimrim
are a desolation;
the grass is withered, the vegetation
fails,
the greenery is no more.
7 Therefore the abundance they have
gained
and what they have laid up
they carry away
over the Brook of the Willows.
8 For a cry has gone
around the land of Moab;

her wailing reaches to Eglaim;
her wailing reaches to Beer-elim.
9 For the waters of Dibon[3] are full of
blood;
for I will bring upon Dibon even
more,
a lion for those of Moab who escape,
for the remnant of the land.

16 Send the lamb to the ruler of the
land,
from Sela, by way of the desert,
to the mount of the daughter of
Zion.
2 Like fleeing birds,
like a scattered nest,
so are the daughters of Moab
at the fords of the Arnon.

3 "Give counsel;
grant justice;
make your shade like night
at the height of noon;
shelter the outcasts;
do not reveal the fugitive;
4 let the outcasts of Moab
sojourn among you;
be a shelter to them[4]
from the destroyer.
When the oppressor is no more,
and destruction has ceased,
and he who tramples underfoot has
vanished from the land,
5 then a throne will be established in
steadfast love,
and on it will sit in faithfulness
in the tent of David
one who judges and seeks justice
and is swift to do righteousness."

6 We have heard of the pride of Moab—
how proud he is!—
of his arrogance, his pride, and his
insolence;
in his idle boasting he is not right.
7 Therefore let Moab wail for Moab,
let everyone wail.
Mourn, utterly stricken,
for the raisin cakes of Kir-hareseth.

8 For the fields of Heshbon languish,
and the vine of Sibmah;
the lords of the nations
have struck down its branches,

[1] Hebrew *the house* [2] Or *temple, even Dibon to the high places* [3] Dead Sea Scroll, Vulgate (compare Syriac); Masoretic Text *Dimon*; twice
in this verse [4] Some Hebrew manuscripts, Septuagint, Syriac; Masoretic Text *let my outcasts sojourn among you; as for Moab, be a shelter
to them*

which reached to Jazer
and strayed to the desert;
its shoots spread abroad
and passed over the sea.
9 Therefore I weep with the weeping
of Jazer
for the vine of Sibmah;
I drench you with my tears,
O Heshbon and Elealeh;
for over your summer fruit and your
harvest
the shout has ceased.
10 And joy and gladness are taken away
from the fruitful field,
and in the vineyards no songs are
sung,
no cheers are raised;
no treader treads out wine in the
presses;
I have put an end to the shouting.
11 Therefore my inner parts moan like a
lyre for Moab,
and my inmost self for Kir-hareseth.

12 And when Moab presents himself,
when he wearies himself on the high place,
when he comes to his sanctuary to pray, he
will not prevail.

13 This is the word that the LORD spoke
concerning Moab in the past. 14 But now the
LORD has spoken, saying, "In three years,
like the years of a hired worker, the glory
of Moab will be brought into contempt, in
spite of all his great multitude, and those
who remain will be very few and feeble."

An Oracle Concerning Damascus

17 An oracle concerning Damascus.

Behold, Damascus will cease to be a
city
and will become a heap of ruins.
2 The cities of Aroer are deserted;
they will be for flocks,
which will lie down, and none will
make them afraid.
3 The fortress will disappear from
Ephraim,
and the kingdom from Damascus;
and the remnant of Syria will be
like the glory of the children of
Israel,
declares the LORD of hosts.

4 And in that day the glory of Jacob
will be brought low,
and the fat of his flesh will grow
lean.
5 And it shall be as when the reaper
gathers standing grain
and his arm harvests the ears,
and as when one gleans the ears of
grain
in the Valley of Rephaim.
6 Gleanings will be left in it,
as when an olive tree is beaten—
two or three berries
in the top of the highest bough,
four or five
on the branches of a fruit tree,
declares the LORD God of Israel.

7 In that day man will look to his Maker,
and his eyes will look on the Holy One of
Israel. 8 He will not look to the altars, the
work of his hands, and he will not look on
what his own fingers have made, either the
Asherim or the altars of incense.

9 In that day their strong cities will be like
the deserted places of the wooded heights
and the hilltops, which they deserted
because of the children of Israel, and there
will be desolation.

10 For you have forgotten the God of
your salvation
and have not remembered the
Rock of your refuge;
therefore, though you plant pleasant
plants
and sow the vine-branch of a
stranger,
11 though you make them grow[1] on the
day that you plant them,
and make them blossom in the
morning that you sow,
yet the harvest will flee away[2]
in a day of grief and incurable pain.

12 Ah, the thunder of many peoples;
they thunder like the thundering
of the sea!
Ah, the roar of nations;
they roar like the roaring of
mighty waters!
13 The nations roar like the roaring of
many waters,
but he will rebuke them, and they
will flee far away,

---

[1] Or though you carefully fence them [2] Or will be a heap

chased like chaff on the mountains
before the wind
and whirling dust before the storm.
[14] At evening time, behold, terror!
Before morning, they are no more!
This is the portion of those who loot
us,
and the lot of those who plunder us.

An Oracle Concerning Cush

18 Ah, land of whirring wings
that is beyond the rivers of Cush,[1]
[2] which sends ambassadors by the sea,
in vessels of papyrus on the waters!
Go, you swift messengers,
to a nation tall and smooth,
to a people feared near and far,
a nation mighty and conquering,
whose land the rivers divide.

[3] All you inhabitants of the world,
you who dwell on the earth,
when a signal is raised on the mountains, look!
When a trumpet is blown, hear!
[4] For thus the Lord said to me:
"I will quietly look from my dwelling
like clear heat in sunshine,
like a cloud of dew in the heat of
harvest."
[5] For before the harvest, when the
blossom is over,
and the flower becomes a ripening
grape,
he cuts off the shoots with pruning
hooks,
and the spreading branches he
lops off and clears away.
[6] They shall all of them be left
to the birds of prey of the mountains
and to the beasts of the earth.
And the birds of prey will summer
on them,
and all the beasts of the earth will
winter on them.

[7] At that time tribute will be brought to
the Lord of hosts

from a people tall and smooth,
from a people feared near and far,
a nation mighty and conquering,
whose land the rivers divide,

to Mount Zion, the place of the name of the
Lord of hosts.

An Oracle Concerning Egypt

19 An oracle concerning Egypt.

Behold, the Lord is riding on a swift
cloud
and comes to Egypt;
and the idols of Egypt will tremble at
his presence,
and the heart of the Egyptians will
melt within them.
[2] And I will stir up Egyptians against
Egyptians,
and they will fight, each against
another
and each against his neighbor,
city against city, kingdom against
kingdom;
[3] and the spirit of the Egyptians within
them will be emptied out,
and I will confound[2] their counsel;
and they will inquire of the idols and
the sorcerers,
and the mediums and the necromancers;
[4] and I will give over the Egyptians
into the hand of a hard master,
and a fierce king will rule over them,
declares the Lord God of hosts.

[5] And the waters of the sea will be
dried up,
and the river will be dry and
parched,
[6] and its canals will become foul,
and the branches of Egypt's Nile
will diminish and dry up,
reeds and rushes will rot away.
[7] There will be bare places by the Nile,
on the brink of the Nile,
and all that is sown by the Nile will
be parched,
will be driven away, and will be no
more.
[8] The fishermen will mourn and
lament,
all who cast a hook in the Nile;
and they will languish
who spread nets on the water.
[9] The workers in combed flax will be
in despair,
and the weavers of white cotton.

[1] Probably *Nubia* [2] Or *I will swallow up*

10 Those who are the pillars of the land
        will be crushed,
        and all who work for pay will be
            grieved.

11 The princes of Zoan are utterly fool-
        ish;
        the wisest counselors of Pharaoh
            give stupid counsel.
    How can you say to Pharaoh,
        "I am a son of the wise,
        a son of ancient kings"?

12 Where then are your wise men?
        Let them tell you
        that they might know what the
            LORD of hosts has purposed
            against Egypt.

13 The princes of Zoan have become
        fools,
        and the princes of Memphis are
            deluded;
        those who are the cornerstones of
            her tribes
        have made Egypt stagger.

14 The LORD has mingled within her a
        spirit of confusion,
        and they will make Egypt stagger in
            all its deeds,
        as a drunken man staggers in his
            vomit.

15 And there will be nothing for Egypt
        that head or tail, palm branch or
            reed, may do.

Egypt, Assyria, Israel Blessed

16 In that day the Egyptians will be like
women, and tremble with fear before the
hand that the LORD of hosts shakes over
them. 17 And the land of Judah will become
a terror to the Egyptians. Everyone to
whom it is mentioned will fear because
of the purpose that the LORD of hosts has
purposed against them.

18 In that day there will be five cities
in the land of Egypt that speak the language of Canaan and swear allegiance to
the LORD of hosts. One of these will be
called the City of Destruction.[1]

19 In that day there will be an altar to
the LORD in the midst of the land of Egypt,
and a pillar to the LORD at its border. 20 It
will be a sign and a witness to the LORD
of hosts in the land of Egypt. When they
cry to the LORD because of oppressors, he
will send them a savior and defender, and

deliver them. 21 And the LORD will make
himself known to the Egyptians, and the
Egyptians will know the LORD in that day
and worship with sacrifice and offering,
and they will make vows to the LORD and
perform them. 22 And the LORD will strike
Egypt, striking and healing, and they will
return to the LORD, and he will listen to
their pleas for mercy and heal them.

23 In that day there will be a highway from
Egypt to Assyria, and Assyria will come
into Egypt, and Egypt into Assyria, and the
Egyptians will worship with the Assyrians.

24 In that day Israel will be the third with
Egypt and Assyria, a blessing in the midst
of the earth, 25 whom the LORD of hosts
has blessed, saying, "Blessed be Egypt my
people, and Assyria the work of my hands,
and Israel my inheritance."

A Sign Against Egypt and Cush

20 In the year that the commander in
chief, who was sent by Sargon the
king of Assyria, came to Ashdod and fought
against it and captured it— 2 at that time
the LORD spoke by Isaiah the son of Amoz,
saying, "Go, and loose the sackcloth from
your waist and take off your sandals from
your feet," and he did so, walking naked
and barefoot.

3 Then the LORD said, "As my servant
Isaiah has walked naked and barefoot for
three years as a sign and a portent against
Egypt and Cush,[2] 4 so shall the king of
Assyria lead away the Egyptian captives
and the Cushite exiles, both the young
and the old, naked and barefoot, with but-
tocks uncovered, the nakedness of Egypt.
5 Then they shall be dismayed and ashamed
because of Cush their hope and of Egypt
their boast. 6 And the inhabitants of this
coastland will say in that day, 'Behold, this
is what has happened to those in whom
we hoped and to whom we fled for help to
be delivered from the king of Assyria! And
we, how shall we escape?'"

Fallen, Fallen Is Babylon

21 The oracle concerning the wilderness of the sea.

    As whirlwinds in the Negeb sweep on,
        it comes from the wilderness,
        from a terrible land.

[1] Dead Sea Scroll and some other manuscripts *City of the Sun* [2] Probably *Nubia*

2 A stern vision is told to me;
   the traitor betrays,
   and the destroyer destroys.
   Go up, O Elam;
   lay siege, O Media;
   all the sighing she has caused
   I bring to an end.
3 Therefore my loins are filled with
      anguish;
   pangs have seized me,
   like the pangs of a woman in labor;
   I am bowed down so that I cannot
      hear;
   I am dismayed so that I cannot see.
4 My heart staggers; horror has
      appalled me;
   the twilight I longed for
   has been turned for me into trem-
      bling.
5 They prepare the table,
   they spread the rugs,[1]
   they eat, they drink.
   Arise, O princes;
   oil the shield!
6 For thus the Lord said to me:
   "Go, set a watchman;
   let him announce what he sees.
7 When he sees riders, horsemen in
      pairs,
   riders on donkeys, riders on camels,
   let him listen diligently,
   very diligently."
8 Then he who saw cried out:[2]
   "Upon a watchtower I stand, O Lord,
   continually by day,
   and at my post I am stationed
   whole nights.
9 And behold, here come riders,
   horsemen in pairs!"
   And he answered,
   "Fallen, fallen is Babylon;
   and all the carved images of her gods
   he has shattered to the ground."
10 O my threshed and winnowed one,
   what I have heard from the LORD
      of hosts,
   the God of Israel, I announce to you.

11 The oracle concerning Dumah.

   One is calling to me from Seir,
   "Watchman, what time of the night?
   Watchman, what time of the night?"
12 The watchman says:

   "Morning comes, and also the night.
   If you will inquire, inquire;
   come back again."

13 The oracle concerning Arabia.

   In the thickets in Arabia you will
      lodge,
   O caravans of Dedanites.
14 To the thirsty bring water;
   meet the fugitive with bread,
   O inhabitants of the land of Tema.
15 For they have fled from the swords,
   from the drawn sword,
   from the bent bow,
   and from the press of battle.

16 For thus the Lord said to me, "Within
a year, according to the years of a hired
worker, all the glory of Kedar will come to
an end. 17 And the remainder of the archers
of the mighty men of the sons of Kedar will
be few, for the LORD, the God of Israel, has
spoken."

An Oracle Concerning Jerusalem

22 The oracle concerning the valley of
vision.

   What do you mean that you have
      gone up,
   all of you, to the housetops,
2 you who are full of shoutings,
   tumultuous city, exultant town?
   Your slain are not slain with the sword
   or dead in battle.
3 All your leaders have fled together;
   without the bow they were cap-
      tured.
   All of you who were found were
      captured,
   though they had fled far away.
4 Therefore I said:
   "Look away from me;
   let me weep bitter tears;
   do not labor to comfort me
   concerning the destruction of the
      daughter of my people."

5 For the Lord GOD of hosts has a day
   of tumult and trampling and con-
      fusion
   in the valley of vision,
   a battering down of walls
   and a shouting to the mountains.

---

[1] Or they set the watchman [2] Dead Sea Scroll, Syriac; Masoretic Text Then a lion cried out, or Then he cried out like a lion

6   And Elam bore the quiver
        with chariots and horsemen,
        and Kir uncovered the shield.
7   Your choicest valleys were full of
            chariots,
        and the horsemen took their stand
            at the gates.
8   He has taken away the covering of
        Judah.

In that day you looked to the weapons of the House of the Forest, 9 and you saw that the breaches of the city of David are many. You collected the waters of the lower pool, 10 and you counted the houses of Jerusalem, and you broke down the houses to fortify the wall. 11 You made a reservoir between the two walls for the water of the old pool. But you did not look to him who did it, or see him who planned it long ago.

12 In that day the Lord God of hosts
        called for weeping and mourning,
        for baldness and wearing sackcloth;
13 and behold, joy and gladness,
        killing oxen and slaughtering sheep,
        eating flesh and drinking wine.
    "Let us eat and drink,
        for tomorrow we die."
14 The Lord of hosts has revealed him-
        self in my ears:
    "Surely this iniquity will not be
        atoned for you until you die,"
    says the Lord God of hosts.

15 Thus says the Lord God of hosts, "Come, go to this steward, to Shebna, who is over the household, and say to him: 16 What have you to do here, and whom have you here, that you have cut out here a tomb for yourself, you who cut out a tomb on the height and carve a dwelling for yourself in the rock? 17 Behold, the Lord will hurl you away violently, O you strong man. He will seize firm hold on you 18 and whirl you around and around, and throw you like a ball into a wide land. There you shall die, and there shall be your glorious chariots, you shame of your master's house. 19 I will thrust you from your office, and you will be pulled down from your station. 20 In that day I will call my servant Eliakim the son of Hilkiah, 21 and I will clothe him with your robe, and will bind your sash on him, and will commit your authority to his hand. And he shall be a father to the inhabitants of Jerusalem and to the house of Judah. 22 And I will place on his shoulder the key of the house of David. He shall open, and none shall shut; and he shall shut, and none shall open. 23 And I will fasten him like a peg in a secure place, and he will become a throne of honor to his father's house. 24 And they will hang on him the whole honor of his father's house, the offspring and issue, every small vessel, from the cups to all the flagons. 25 In that day, declares the Lord of hosts, the peg that was fastened in a secure place will give way, and it will be cut down and fall, and the load that was on it will be cut off, for the Lord has spoken."

An Oracle Concerning Tyre and Sidon

23 The oracle concerning Tyre.

    Wail, O ships of Tarshish,
        for Tyre is laid waste, without
            house or harbor!
    From the land of Cyprus[1]
        it is revealed to them.
2   Be still, O inhabitants of the coast;
        the merchants of Sidon, who cross
            the sea, have filled you.
3   And on many waters
    your revenue was the grain of Shihor,
        the harvest of the Nile;
        you were the merchant of the
            nations.
4   Be ashamed, O Sidon, for the sea has
            spoken,
        the stronghold of the sea, saying:
    "I have neither labored nor given birth,
        I have neither reared young men
        nor brought up young women."
5   When the report comes to Egypt,
        they will be in anguish[2] over the
            report about Tyre.
6   Cross over to Tarshish;
        wail, O inhabitants of the coast!
7   Is this your exultant city
        whose origin is from days of old,
    whose feet carried her
        to settle far away?
8   Who has purposed this
        against Tyre, the bestower of
            crowns,
    whose merchants were princes,
        whose traders were the honored
            of the earth?

[1] Hebrew *Kittim*; also verse 12   [2] Hebrew *they will have labor pains*

⁹ The LORD of hosts has purposed it,
    to defile the pompous pride of all
        glory,[1]
    to dishonor all the honored of the
        earth.
¹⁰ Cross over your land like the Nile,
    O daughter of Tarshish;
    there is no restraint anymore.
¹¹ He has stretched out his hand over
        the sea;
    he has shaken the kingdoms;
    the LORD has given command con-
        cerning Canaan
    to destroy its strongholds.
¹² And he said:
"You will no more exult,
    O oppressed virgin daughter of
        Sidon;
    arise, cross over to Cyprus,
        even there you will have no rest."

¹³Behold the land of the Chaldeans! This
is the people that was not;[2] Assyria destined it for wild beasts. They erected their
siege towers, they stripped her palaces
bare, they made her a ruin.

¹⁴ Wail, O ships of Tarshish,
    for your stronghold is laid waste.

¹⁵In that day Tyre will be forgotten for seventy years, like the days[3] of one king. At the
end of seventy years, it will happen to Tyre
as in the song of the prostitute:

¹⁶ "Take a harp;
    go about the city,
    O forgotten prostitute!
Make sweet melody;
    sing many songs,
    that you may be remembered."

¹⁷At the end of seventy years, the LORD will
visit Tyre, and she will return to her wages
and will prostitute herself with all the kingdoms of the world on the face of the earth.
¹⁸Her merchandise and her wages will be
holy to the LORD. It will not be stored or
hoarded, but her merchandise will supply
abundant food and fine clothing for those
who dwell before the LORD.

Judgment on the Whole Earth

24 Behold, the LORD will empty the
earth[4] and make it desolate,
    and he will twist its surface and
        scatter its inhabitants.

² And it shall be, as with the people, so
        with the priest;
    as with the slave, so with his mas-
        ter;
    as with the maid, so with her mis-
        tress;
as with the buyer, so with the seller;
    as with the lender, so with the bor-
        rower;
    as with the creditor, so with the
        debtor.
³ The earth shall be utterly empty and
        utterly plundered;
    for the LORD has spoken this
        word.

⁴ The earth mourns and withers;
    the world languishes and withers;
    the highest people of the earth
        languish.
⁵ The earth lies defiled
    under its inhabitants;
for they have transgressed the laws,
    violated the statutes,
    broken the everlasting covenant.
⁶ Therefore a curse devours the earth,
    and its inhabitants suffer for their
        guilt;
therefore the inhabitants of the earth
    are scorched,
    and few men are left.
⁷ The wine mourns,
    the vine languishes,
    all the merry-hearted sigh.
⁸ The mirth of the tambourines is
        stilled,
    the noise of the jubilant has
        ceased,
    the mirth of the lyre is stilled.
⁹ No more do they drink wine with
        singing;
    strong drink is bitter to those who
        drink it.
¹⁰ The wasted city is broken down;
    every house is shut up so that
        none can enter.
¹¹ There is an outcry in the streets for
        lack of wine;
    all joy has grown dark;
    the gladness of the earth is ban-
        ished.
¹² Desolation is left in the city;
    the gates are battered into ruins.

[1] The Hebrew words for *glory* and *hosts* sound alike [2] Or *that has become nothing* [3] Or *lifetime* [4] Or *land*; also throughout this chapter

13 For thus it shall be in the midst of the
        earth
     among the nations,
  as when an olive tree is beaten,
     as at the gleaning when the grape
        harvest is done.
14 They lift up their voices, they sing for
        joy;
     over the majesty of the LORD they
        shout from the west.[1]
15 Therefore in the east[2] give glory to
        the LORD;
     in the coastlands of the sea, give
        glory to the name of the LORD,
        the God of Israel.
16 From the ends of the earth we hear
        songs of praise,
     of glory to the Righteous One.
  But I say, "I waste away,
     I waste away. Woe is me!
  For the traitors have betrayed,
     with betrayal the traitors have
        betrayed."
17 Terror and the pit and the snare[3]
     are upon you, O inhabitant of the
        earth!
18 He who flees at the sound of the terror
     shall fall into the pit,
  and he who climbs out of the pit
     shall be caught in the snare.
  For the windows of heaven are
        opened,
     and the foundations of the earth
        tremble.
19 The earth is utterly broken,
     the earth is split apart,
     the earth is violently shaken.
20 The earth staggers like a drunken
        man;
     it sways like a hut;
  its transgression lies heavy upon it,
     and it falls, and will not rise again.

21 On that day the LORD will punish
     the host of heaven, in heaven,
     and the kings of the earth, on the
        earth.
22 They will be gathered together
     as prisoners in a pit;
  they will be shut up in a prison,
     and after many days they will be
        punished.
23 Then the moon will be confounded
     and the sun ashamed,

for the LORD of hosts reigns
     on Mount Zion and in Jerusalem,
  and his glory will be before his elders.

God Will Swallow Up Death Forever

25 O LORD, you are my God;
     I will exalt you; I will praise your
        name,
  for you have done wonderful things,
     plans formed of old, faithful and
        sure.
2 For you have made the city a heap,
     the fortified city a ruin;
  the foreigners' palace is a city no
        more;
     it will never be rebuilt.
3 Therefore strong peoples will glorify
        you;
     cities of ruthless nations will fear
        you.
4 For you have been a stronghold to
        the poor,
     a stronghold to the needy in his
        distress,
     a shelter from the storm and a
        shade from the heat;
  for the breath of the ruthless is like a
        storm against a wall,
5   like heat in a dry place.
  You subdue the noise of the foreign-
        ers;
     as heat by the shade of a cloud,
     so the song of the ruthless is put
        down.

6 On this mountain the LORD of hosts
     will make for all peoples
     a feast of rich food, a feast of well-
        aged wine,
     of rich food full of marrow, of aged
        wine well refined.
7 And he will swallow up on this
        mountain
     the covering that is cast over all
        peoples,
     the veil that is spread over all
        nations.
8 He will swallow up death forever;
  and the Lord GOD will wipe away
        tears from all faces,
     and the reproach of his people
        he will take away from all the
        earth,
  for the LORD has spoken.

[1] Hebrew from the sea [2] Hebrew in the realm of light [3] The Hebrew words for terror, pit, and snare sound alike

9 It will be said on that day,
  "Behold, this is our God; we have
    waited for him, that he might
    save us.
  This is the LORD; we have waited
    for him;
  let us be glad and rejoice in his
    salvation."
10 For the hand of the LORD will rest on
    this mountain,
  and Moab shall be trampled down
    in his place,
  as straw is trampled down in a
    dunghill.[1]
11 And he will spread out his hands in
    the midst of it
  as a swimmer spreads his hands
    out to swim,
  but the LORD will lay low his pomp-
    ous pride together with the
    skill[2] of his hands.
12 And the high fortifications of his
    walls he will bring down,
  lay low, and cast to the ground, to
    the dust.

You Keep Him in Perfect Peace

26 In that day this song will be sung in
    the land of Judah:

  "We have a strong city;
    he sets up salvation
    as walls and bulwarks.
2 Open the gates,
    that the righteous nation that
    keeps faith may enter in.
3 You keep him in perfect peace
    whose mind is stayed on you,
    because he trusts in you.
4 Trust in the LORD forever,
    for the LORD GOD is an everlasting
    rock.
5 For he has humbled
    the inhabitants of the height,
    the lofty city.
  He lays it low, lays it low to the ground,
    casts it to the dust.
6 The foot tramples it,
    the feet of the poor,
    the steps of the needy."

7 The path of the righteous is level;
    you make level the way of the
    righteous.
8 In the path of your judgments,
    O LORD, we wait for you;

your name and remembrance
    are the desire of our soul.
9 My soul yearns for you in the night;
    my spirit within me earnestly
    seeks you.
  For when your judgments are in the
    earth,
    the inhabitants of the world learn
    righteousness.
10 If favor is shown to the wicked,
    he does not learn righteousness;
  in the land of uprightness he deals
    corruptly
    and does not see the majesty of
    the LORD.

A prayer for...
SELF-CONTROL

Dear God, give me self-control! You say, "Be perfect, as your heavenly Father is perfect" (Matt. 5:48). But how can I be perfect when you can see every dark area of my heart? How do I avoid nasty words and irritated reactions unless you help me every minute? I want steadiness and quietness of heart, no matter how sudden the surprise or how great the strain.

Please make good your promise to keep me in perfect peace when my mind is set on you. Nothing can take you by surprise and nothing outlasts you. So help me, in this moment and always, to put the reins of my life into your hands. Let it be no longer me but Christ who lives in me.

Amen.

---

11 O LORD, your hand is lifted up,
    but they do not see it.
  Let them see your zeal for your
    people, and be ashamed.
  Let the fire for your adversaries
    consume them.
12 O LORD, you will ordain peace for
    us,
    for you have indeed done for us all
    our works.

[1] The Hebrew words for *dunghill* and for the Moabite town *Madmen* (Jeremiah 48:2) sound alike [2] Or *in spite of the skill*

3 O Lord our God,
> other lords besides you have ruled
> > over us,
> but your name alone we bring to
> > remembrance.

4 They are dead, they will not live;
> they are shades, they will not arise;
to that end you have visited them
> > with destruction
> and wiped out all remembrance of
> > them.

5 But you have increased the nation,
> > O Lord,
> you have increased the nation; you
> > are glorified;
> you have enlarged all the borders
> > of the land.

6 O Lord, in distress they sought you;
> they poured out a whispered
> > prayer
> when your discipline was upon
> > them.

7 Like a pregnant woman
> who writhes and cries out in her
> > pangs
> when she is near to giving birth,
so were we because of you, O Lord;

8 we were pregnant, we writhed,
> but we have given birth to wind.
We have accomplished no deliver-
> > ance in the earth,
> and the inhabitants of the world
> > have not fallen.

9 Your dead shall live; their bodies
> > shall rise.
> You who dwell in the dust, awake
> > and sing for joy!
For your dew is a dew of light,
> and the earth will give birth to the
> > dead.

10 Come, my people, enter your cham-
> > bers,
> and shut your doors behind you;
hide yourselves for a little while
> until the fury has passed by.

11 For behold, the Lord is coming out
> > from his place
> to punish the inhabitants of the
> > earth for their iniquity,
and the earth will disclose the blood
> > shed on it,
> and will no more cover its slain.

The Redemption of Israel

27 In that day the Lord with his hard
and great and strong sword will
punish Leviathan the fleeing serpent,
Leviathan the twisting serpent, and he will
slay the dragon that is in the sea.

2 In that day,
> "A pleasant vineyard,[1] sing of it!

3 I, the Lord, am its keeper;
> every moment I water it.
> Lest anyone punish it,
I keep it night and day;

4 I have no wrath.
Would that I had thorns and briers to
> > battle!
> I would march against them,
> I would burn them up together.

5 Or let them lay hold of my protection,
> let them make peace with me,
> let them make peace with me."

6 In days to come[2] Jacob shall take root,
> Israel shall blossom and put forth
> > shoots
> and fill the whole world with fruit.

7 Has he struck them as he struck
> > those who struck them?
> Or have they been slain as their
> > slayers were slain?

8 Measure by measure,[3] by exile you
> > contended with them;
he removed them with his fierce
> > breath[4] in the day of the east
> > wind.

9 Therefore by this the guilt of Jacob
> > will be atoned for,
> and this will be the full fruit of the
> > removal of his sin:[5]
when he makes all the stones of the
> > altars
> like chalkstones crushed to pieces,
> no Asherim or incense altars will
> > remain standing.

10 For the fortified city is solitary,
> a habitation deserted and for-
> > saken, like the wilderness;
there the calf grazes;
> there it lies down and strips its
> > branches.

11 When its boughs are dry, they are
> > broken;
> women come and make a fire of
> > them.

Many Hebrew manuscripts *A vineyard of wine* [2] Hebrew *In those to come* [3] Or *By driving her away*; the meaning of the Hebrew word is uncertain [4] Or *wind* [5] Septuagint *and this is the blessing when I take away his sin*

For this is a people without discern-
    ment;
  therefore he who made them will
      not have compassion on them;
  he who formed them will show
      them no favor.

¹² In that day from the river Euphrates¹
to the Brook of Egypt the Lord will thresh
out the grain, and you will be gleaned one
by one, O people of Israel. ¹³ And in that day
a great trumpet will be blown, and those
who were lost in the land of Assyria and
those who were driven out to the land of
Egypt will come and worship the Lord on
the holy mountain at Jerusalem.

Judgment on Ephraim and Jerusalem

28 Ah, the proud crown of the
    drunkards of Ephraim,
  and the fading flower of its glori-
      ous beauty,
  which is on the head of the rich
      valley of those overcome with
      wine!
² Behold, the Lord has one who is
      mighty and strong;
  like a storm of hail, a destroying
      tempest,
  like a storm of mighty, overflowing
      waters,
  he casts down to the earth with his
      hand.
³ The proud crown of the drunkards of
      Ephraim
  will be trodden underfoot;
⁴ and the fading flower of its glorious
      beauty,
  which is on the head of the rich
      valley,
  will be like a first-ripe fig before the
      summer:
  when someone sees it, he swal-
      lows it
  as soon as it is in his hand.

⁵ In that day the Lord of hosts will be
      a crown of glory,²
  and a diadem of beauty, to the
      remnant of his people,
⁶ and a spirit of justice to him who sits
      in judgment,
  and strength to those who turn
      back the battle at the gate.

⁷ These also reel with wine
  and stagger with strong drink;
the priest and the prophet reel with
      strong drink,
  they are swallowed by³ wine,
  they stagger with strong drink,
they reel in vision,
  they stumble in giving judgment.
⁸ For all tables are full of filthy vomit,
  with no space left.

⁹ "To whom will he teach knowledge,
  and to whom will he explain the
      message?
Those who are weaned from the milk,
  those taken from the breast?
¹⁰ For it is precept upon precept, pre-
      cept upon precept,
  line upon line, line upon line,
  here a little, there a little."

¹¹ For by people of strange lips
  and with a foreign tongue
the Lord will speak to this people,
¹² to whom he has said,
"This is rest;
  give rest to the weary;
and this is repose";
  yet they would not hear.
¹³ And the word of the Lord will be to
      them
  precept upon precept, precept upon
      precept,
  line upon line, line upon line,
  here a little, there a little,
that they may go, and fall backward,
  and be broken, and snared, and
      taken.

A Cornerstone in Zion

¹⁴ Therefore hear the word of the Lord,
      you scoffers,
  who rule this people in Jerusalem!
¹⁵ Because you have said, "We have
      made a covenant with death,
  and with Sheol we have an agree-
      ment,
when the overwhelming whip passes
      through
  it will not come to us,
for we have made lies our refuge,
  and in falsehood we have taken
      shelter";
¹⁶ therefore thus says the Lord God,

¹ Hebrew *from the River* ² The Hebrew words for *glory* and *hosts* sound alike ³ Or *confused by*

"Behold, I am the one who has laid[1] as
    a foundation in Zion,
    a stone, a tested stone,
a precious cornerstone, of a sure
    foundation:
    'Whoever believes will not be in
    haste.'
17 And I will make justice the line,
    and righteousness the plumb line;
and hail will sweep away the refuge
    of lies,
    and waters will overwhelm the
    shelter."
18 Then your covenant with death will
    be annulled,
    and your agreement with Sheol
    will not stand;
when the overwhelming scourge
    passes through,
    you will be beaten down by it.
19 As often as it passes through it will
    take you;
    for morning by morning it will
    pass through,
    by day and by night;
and it will be sheer terror to under-
    stand the message.
20 For the bed is too short to stretch
    oneself on,
    and the covering too narrow to
    wrap oneself in.
21 For the LORD will rise up as on
    Mount Perazim;
    as in the Valley of Gibeon he will
    be roused;
to do his deed—strange is his deed!
    and to work his work—alien is his
    work!
22 Now therefore do not scoff,
    lest your bonds be made strong;
for I have heard a decree of destruc-
    tion
    from the Lord GOD of hosts against
    the whole land.
23 Give ear, and hear my voice;
    give attention, and hear my speech.
24 Does he who plows for sowing plow
    continually?
    Does he continually open and har-
    row his ground?
25 When he has leveled its surface,
    does he not scatter dill, sow cumin,

and put in wheat in rows
    and barley in its proper place,
    and emmer[2] as the border?
26 For he is rightly instructed;
    his God teaches him.

27 Dill is not threshed with a threshing
    sledge,
    nor is a cart wheel rolled over
    cumin,
but dill is beaten out with a stick,
    and cumin with a rod.
28 Does one crush grain for bread?
    No, he does not thresh it forever;[3]
when he drives his cart wheel over it
    with his horses, he does not crush it.
29 This also comes from the LORD of
    hosts;
    he is wonderful in counsel
    and excellent in wisdom.

The Siege of Jerusalem

29 Ah, Ariel, Ariel,
    the city where David encamped!
Add year to year;
    let the feasts run their round.
2 Yet I will distress Ariel,
    and there shall be moaning and
    lamentation,
    and she shall be to me like an Ariel.[4]
3 And I will encamp against you all
    around,
    and will besiege you with towers
    and I will raise siegeworks against
    you.
4 And you will be brought low; from
    the earth you shall speak,
    and from the dust your speech will
    be bowed down;
your voice shall come from the
    ground like the voice of a ghost,
    and from the dust your speech
    shall whisper.

5 But the multitude of your foreign
    foes shall be like small dust,
    and the multitude of the ruthless
    like passing chaff.
And in an instant, suddenly,
6 you will be visited by the LORD of
    hosts
with thunder and with earthquake
    and great noise,
    with whirlwind and tempest, and
    the flame of a devouring fire.

[1] Dead Sea Scroll *I am laying* [2] A type of wheat [3] Or *Grain is crushed for bread; he will surely thresh it, but not forever* [4] *Ariel* could mean *lion of God*, or *hero* (2 Samuel 23:20), or *altar hearth* (Ezekiel 43:15–16)

7   And the multitude of all the nations
          that fight against Ariel,
       all that fight against her and her
          stronghold and distress her,
       shall be like a dream, a vision of
          the night.
8   As when a hungry man dreams, and
          behold, he is eating
       and awakes with his hunger not
          satisfied,
       or as when a thirsty man dreams,
          and behold, he is drinking
       and awakes faint, with his thirst
          not quenched,
       so shall the multitude of all the
          nations be
       that fight against Mount Zion.

9   Astonish yourselves[1] and be aston-
          ished;
       blind yourselves and be blind!
       Be drunk, but not with wine;
          stagger, but not with strong drink!
10   For the LORD has poured out upon
          you
       a spirit of deep sleep,
       and has closed your eyes (the proph-
          ets),
          and covered your heads (the
          seers).

11 And the vision of all this has become to
you like the words of a book that is sealed.
When men give it to one who can read, saying, "Read this," he says, "I cannot, for it is
sealed." 12 And when they give the book to
one who cannot read, saying, "Read this,"
he says, "I cannot read."

13   And the Lord said:
     "Because this people draw near with
          their mouth
       and honor me with their lips,
          while their hearts are far from
          me,
       and their fear of me is a command-
          ment taught by men,
14   therefore, behold, I will again
       do wonderful things with this
          people,
       with wonder upon wonder;
       and the wisdom of their wise men
          shall perish,
       and the discernment of their dis-
          cerning men shall be hidden."

15   Ah, you who hide deep from the
          LORD your counsel,
       whose deeds are in the dark,
       and who say, "Who sees us? Who
          knows us?"
16   You turn things upside down!
       Shall the potter be regarded as the
          clay,
       that the thing made should say of its
          maker,
       "He did not make me";
       or the thing formed say of him who
          formed it,
       "He has no understanding"?

17   Is it not yet a very little while
       until Lebanon shall be turned into
          a fruitful field,
       and the fruitful field shall be
          regarded as a forest?
18   In that day the deaf shall hear
       the words of a book,
       and out of their gloom and darkness
          the eyes of the blind shall see.
19   The meek shall obtain fresh joy in
          the LORD,
       and the poor among mankind shall
          exult in the Holy One of Israel.
20   For the ruthless shall come to nothing
          and the scoffer cease,
       and all who watch to do evil shall
          be cut off,
21   who by a word make a man out to be
          an offender,
       and lay a snare for him who
          reproves in the gate,
       and with an empty plea turn aside
          him who is in the right.

22 Therefore thus says the LORD, who
redeemed Abraham, concerning the house
of Jacob:

     "Jacob shall no more be ashamed,
       no more shall his face grow pale.
23   For when he sees his children,
       the work of my hands, in his midst,
          they will sanctify my name;
       they will sanctify the Holy One of
          Jacob
       and will stand in awe of the God of
          Israel.
24   And those who go astray in spirit will
          come to understanding,
       and those who murmur will accept
          instruction."

[1] Or Linger awhile

Do Not Go Down to Egypt

30 "Ah, stubborn children," declares
the LORD,
"who carry out a plan, but not mine,
and who make an alliance,[1] but not of
my Spirit,
that they may add sin to sin;
[2] who set out to go down to Egypt,
without asking for my direction,
to take refuge in the protection of
Pharaoh
and to seek shelter in the shadow
of Egypt!
[3] Therefore shall the protection of
Pharaoh turn to your shame,
and the shelter in the shadow of
Egypt to your humiliation.
[4] For though his officials are at Zoan
and his envoys reach Hanes,
[5] everyone comes to shame
through a people that cannot
profit them,
that brings neither help nor profit,
but shame and disgrace."

[6] An oracle on the beasts of the Negeb.

Through a land of trouble and
anguish,
from where come the lioness and
the lion,
the adder and the flying fiery
serpent,
they carry their riches on the backs
of donkeys,
and their treasures on the humps
of camels,
to a people that cannot profit them.
[7] Egypt's help is worthless and empty;
therefore I have called her
"Rahab who sits still."

A Rebellious People

[8] And now, go, write it before them on
a tablet
and inscribe it in a book,
that it may be for the time to come
as a witness forever.[2]
[9] For they are a rebellious people,
lying children,
children unwilling to hear
the instruction of the LORD;
[10] who say to the seers, "Do not see,"
and to the prophets, "Do not
prophesy to us what is right;

speak to us smooth things,
prophesy illusions,
[11] leave the way, turn aside from the
path,
let us hear no more about the Holy
One of Israel."

[12] Therefore thus says the Holy One of
Israel,
"Because you despise this word
and trust in oppression and perverseness
and rely on them,
[13] therefore this iniquity shall be to you
like a breach in a high wall, bulging
out, and about to collapse,
whose breaking comes suddenly,
in an instant;
[14] and its breaking is like that of a potter's vessel
that is smashed so ruthlessly
that among its fragments not a shard
is found
with which to take fire from the
hearth,
or to dip up water out of the cistern."

[15] For thus said the Lord GOD, the Holy
One of Israel,
"In returning[3] and rest you shall be
saved;
in quietness and in trust shall be
your strength."
But you were unwilling, [16] and you
said,
"No! We will flee upon horses";
therefore you shall flee away;
and, "We will ride upon swift steeds";
therefore your pursuers shall be
swift.
[17] A thousand shall flee at the threat of
one;
at the threat of five you shall flee,
till you are left
like a flagstaff on the top of a
mountain,
like a signal on a hill.

The LORD Will Be Gracious

[18] Therefore the LORD waits to be gracious to you,
and therefore he exalts himself to
show mercy to you.

[1] Hebrew *who weave a web* [2] Some Hebrew manuscripts, Syriac, Targum, Vulgate, and Greek versions; Masoretic Text *forever and ever*
[3] Or *repentance*

For the LORD is a God of justice;
blessed are all those who wait for
him.

¹⁹ For a people shall dwell in Zion, in
Jerusalem; you shall weep no more. He will
surely be gracious to you at the sound of
your cry. As soon as he hears it, he answers
you. ²⁰ And though the Lord give you the
bread of adversity and the water of affliction, yet your Teacher will not hide himself anymore, but your eyes shall see your
Teacher. ²¹ And your ears shall hear a word
behind you, saying, "This is the way, walk in
it," when you turn to the right or when you
turn to the left. ²² Then you will defile your
carved idols overlaid with silver and your
gold-plated metal images. You will scatter
them as unclean things. You will say to
them, "Be gone!"

²³ And he will give rain for the seed with
which you sow the ground, and bread,
the produce of the ground, which will be
rich and plenteous. In that day your livestock will graze in large pastures, ²⁴ and
the oxen and the donkeys that work the
ground will eat seasoned fodder, which
has been winnowed with shovel and fork.
²⁵ And on every lofty mountain and every
high hill there will be brooks running with
water, in the day of the great slaughter,
when the towers fall. ²⁶ Moreover, the light
of the moon will be as the light of the sun,
and the light of the sun will be sevenfold,
as the light of seven days, in the day when
the LORD binds up the brokenness of his
people, and heals the wounds inflicted by
his blow.

²⁷   Behold, the name of the LORD comes
            from afar,
        burning with his anger, and in
            thick rising smoke;[1]
    his lips are full of fury,
        and his tongue is like a devouring
            fire;
²⁸   his breath is like an overflowing
            stream
        that reaches up to the neck;
    to sift the nations with the sieve of
            destruction,
        and to place on the jaws of the
            peoples a bridle that leads
            astray.

²⁹ You shall have a song as in the night
when a holy feast is kept, and gladness of
heart, as when one sets out to the sound of
the flute to go to the mountain of the LORD,
to the Rock of Israel. ³⁰ And the LORD will
cause his majestic voice to be heard and
the descending blow of his arm to be seen,
in furious anger and a flame of devouring fire, with a cloudburst and storm and
hailstones. ³¹ The Assyrians will be terror-
stricken at the voice of the LORD, when he
strikes with his rod. ³² And every stroke of
the appointed staff that the LORD lays on
them will be to the sound of tambourines
and lyres. Battling with brandished arm,
he will fight with them. ³³ For a burning
place[2] has long been prepared; indeed, for
the king it is made ready, its pyre made
deep and wide, with fire and wood in abundance; the breath of the LORD, like a stream
of sulfur, kindles it.

Woe to Those Who Go Down to Egypt

31   Woe to those who go down to
            Egypt for help
        and rely on horses,
    who trust in chariots because they
            are many
        and in horsemen because they are
            very strong,
    but do not look to the Holy One of
            Israel
        or consult the LORD!
²   And yet he is wise and brings disaster;
        he does not call back his words,
    but will arise against the house of
            the evildoers
        and against the helpers of those
            who work iniquity.
³   The Egyptians are man, and not God,
        and their horses are flesh, and not
            spirit.
    When the LORD stretches out his
            hand,
        the helper will stumble, and he
            who is helped will fall,
        and they will all perish together.

⁴   For thus the LORD said to me,
    "As a lion or a young lion growls over
            his prey,
        and when a band of shepherds is
            called out against him
    he is not terrified by their shouting
        or daunted at their noise,

---

[1] Hebrew *in weight of uplifted clouds* [2] Or *For Topheth*

so the Lord of hosts will come down
to fight[1] on Mount Zion and on its
hill.

5 Like birds hovering, so the Lord of
hosts
will protect Jerusalem;
he will protect and deliver it;
he will spare and rescue it."

6 Turn to him from whom people[2] have
deeply revolted, O children of Israel. 7 For in
that day everyone shall cast away his idols
of silver and his idols of gold, which your
hands have sinfully made for you.

8 "And the Assyrian shall fall by a sword,
not of man;
and a sword, not of man, shall
devour him;
and he shall flee from the sword,
and his young men shall be put to
forced labor.

9 His rock shall pass away in terror,
and his officers desert the standard in panic,"
declares the Lord, whose fire is in
Zion,
and whose furnace is in Jerusalem.

Ask Yourself . . .

ABOUT PAMPERING

Isaiah said, "Rise up, you women
who are at ease, hear my voice"
(Isa. 32:9). Ask yourself:

- What does it mean to be
  pampered?
- Do I pamper myself?
- Why would pampered women
  be called out in this verse?
- What impact does pampering
  have on my spiritual life?
- What damage could it inflict?
- What does God's Word have to
  say about pampering yourself?
  (Hint: see what it says about
  dying to self, sanctification,
  and suffering.)

A King Will Reign in Righteousness

32 Behold, a king will reign in righteousness,
and princes will rule in justice.
2 Each will be like a hiding place from
the wind,
a shelter from the storm,
like streams of water in a dry place,
like the shade of a great rock in a
weary land.
3 Then the eyes of those who see will
not be closed,
and the ears of those who hear will
give attention.
4 The heart of the hasty will understand and know,
and the tongue of the stammerers
will hasten to speak distinctly.
5 The fool will no more be called noble,
nor the scoundrel said to be honorable.
6 For the fool speaks folly,
and his heart is busy with iniquity,
to practice ungodliness,
to utter error concerning the Lord,
to leave the craving of the hungry
unsatisfied,
and to deprive the thirsty of drink.
7 As for the scoundrel—his devices
are evil;
he plans wicked schemes
to ruin the poor with lying words,
even when the plea of the needy is
right.
8 But he who is noble plans noble
things,
and on noble things he stands.

Complacent Women Warned of Disaster

9 Rise up, you women who are at ease,
hear my voice;
you complacent daughters, give
ear to my speech.
10 In little more than a year
you will shudder, you complacent
women;
for the grape harvest fails,
the fruit harvest will not come.
11 Tremble, you women who are at ease,
shudder, you complacent ones;
strip, and make yourselves bare,
and tie sackcloth around your waist.
12 Beat your breasts for the pleasant
fields,
for the fruitful vine,

---

[1] The Hebrew words for *hosts* and *to fight* sound alike [2] Hebrew *they*

13 for the soil of my people
        growing up in thorns and briers,
    yes, for all the joyous houses
        in the exultant city.
14 For the palace is forsaken,
        the populous city deserted;
    the hill and the watchtower
        will become dens forever,
    a joy of wild donkeys,
        a pasture of flocks;
15 until the Spirit is poured upon us
        from on high,
    and the wilderness becomes a
        fruitful field,
    and the fruitful field is deemed a
        forest.
16 Then justice will dwell in the wilder-
        ness,
        and righteousness abide in the
        fruitful field.
17 And the effect of righteousness will
        be peace,
        and the result of righteousness,
        quietness and trust[1] forever.
18 My people will abide in a peaceful
        habitation,
        in secure dwellings, and in quiet
        resting places.
19 And it will hail when the forest falls
        down,
        and the city will be utterly laid low.
20 Happy are you who sow beside all
        waters,
        who let the feet of the ox and the
        donkey range free.

O Lord, Be Gracious to Us

33 Ah, you destroyer,
        who yourself have not been
        destroyed,
    you traitor,
        whom none has betrayed!
    When you have ceased to destroy,
        you will be destroyed;
    and when you have finished betraying,
        they will betray you.

2   O Lord, be gracious to us; we wait
        for you.
        Be our arm every morning,
        our salvation in the time of trouble.
3   At the tumultuous noise peoples flee;
        when you lift yourself up, nations
        are scattered,

4   and your spoil is gathered as the
        caterpillar gathers;
        as locusts leap, it is leapt upon.
5   The Lord is exalted, for he dwells on
        high;
        he will fill Zion with justice and
        righteousness,
6   and he will be the stability of your
        times,
        abundance of salvation, wisdom,
        and knowledge;
        the fear of the Lord is Zion's[2]
        treasure.

7   Behold, their heroes cry in the streets;
        the envoys of peace weep bitterly.
8   The highways lie waste;
        the traveler ceases.
    Covenants are broken;
        cities[3] are despised;
        there is no regard for man.
9   The land mourns and languishes;
        Lebanon is confounded and with-
        ers away;
    Sharon is like a desert,
        and Bashan and Carmel shake off
        their leaves.

10 "Now I will arise," says the Lord,
        "now I will lift myself up;
        now I will be exalted.
11 You conceive chaff; you give birth to
        stubble;
        your breath is a fire that will con-
        sume you.
12 And the peoples will be as if burned
        to lime,
        like thorns cut down, that are
        burned in the fire."

13 Hear, you who are far off, what I have
        done;
        and you who are near, acknowl-
        edge my might.
14 The sinners in Zion are afraid;
        trembling has seized the godless:
    "Who among us can dwell with the
        consuming fire?
        Who among us can dwell with
        everlasting burnings?"
15 He who walks righteously and
        speaks uprightly,
        who despises the gain of oppres-
        sions,

[1] Or security [2] Hebrew his [3] Masoretic Text; Dead Sea Scroll witnesses

who shakes his hands, lest they hold
   a bribe,
who stops his ears from hearing of
   bloodshed
and shuts his eyes from looking on
   evil,

¹⁶ he will dwell on the heights;
   his place of defense will be the
      fortresses of rocks;
   his bread will be given him; his
      water will be sure.

¹⁷ Your eyes will behold the king in his
      beauty;
   they will see a land that stretches
      afar.

¹⁸ Your heart will muse on the terror:
   "Where is he who counted, where is
      he who weighed the tribute?
   Where is he who counted the tow-
      ers?"

¹⁹ You will see no more the insolent
      people,
   the people of an obscure speech
      that you cannot comprehend,
   stammering in a tongue that you
      cannot understand.

²⁰ Behold Zion, the city of our
      appointed feasts!
   Your eyes will see Jerusalem,
   an untroubled habitation, an
      immovable tent,
   whose stakes will never be plucked
      up,
   nor will any of its cords be broken.

²¹ But there the LORD in majesty will be
      for us
   a place of broad rivers and streams,
   where no galley with oars can go,
   nor majestic ship can pass.

²² For the LORD is our judge; the LORD
      is our lawgiver;
   the LORD is our king; he will save us.

²³ Your cords hang loose;
   they cannot hold the mast firm in
      its place
   or keep the sail spread out.
   Then prey and spoil in abundance
      will be divided;
   even the lame will take the prey.

²⁴ And no inhabitant will say, "I am sick";
   the people who dwell there will be
      forgiven their iniquity.

Judgment on the Nations

34

Draw near, O nations, to hear,
   and give attention, O peoples!
Let the earth hear, and all that fills it;
   the world, and all that comes from
      it.

² For the LORD is enraged against all
      the nations,
   and furious against all their host;
   he has devoted them to destruc-
      tion,[1] has given them over for
      slaughter.

³ Their slain shall be cast out,
   and the stench of their corpses
      shall rise;
   the mountains shall flow with
      their blood.

⁴ All the host of heaven shall rot away,
   and the skies roll up like a scroll.
All their host shall fall,
   as leaves fall from the vine,
   like leaves falling from the fig tree.

⁵ For my sword has drunk its fill in the
      heavens;
   behold, it descends for judgment
      upon Edom,
   upon the people I have devoted to
      destruction.

⁶ The LORD has a sword; it is sated
      with blood;
   it is gorged with fat,
   with the blood of lambs and goats,
   with the fat of the kidneys of rams.
For the LORD has a sacrifice in Bozrah,
   a great slaughter in the land of
      Edom.

⁷ Wild oxen shall fall with them,
   and young steers with the mighty
      bulls.
Their land shall drink its fill of blood,
   and their soil shall be gorged with
      fat.

⁸ For the LORD has a day of vengeance,
   a year of recompense for the cause
      of Zion.

⁹ And the streams of Edom[2] shall be
      turned into pitch,
   and her soil into sulfur;
   her land shall become burning
      pitch.

¹⁰ Night and day it shall not be
      quenched;
   its smoke shall go up forever.

---

[1] That is, set apart (devoted) as an offering to the Lord (for destruction); also verse 5 [2] Hebrew *her streams*

From generation to generation it
shall lie waste;
none shall pass through it forever
and ever.
11 But the hawk and the porcupine[1]
shall possess it,
the owl and the raven shall dwell
in it.
He shall stretch the line of confusion[2]
over it,
and the plumb line of emptiness.
12 Its nobles—there is no one there to
call it a kingdom,
and all its princes shall be nothing.

13 Thorns shall grow over its strongholds,
nettles and thistles in its fortresses.
It shall be the haunt of jackals,
an abode for ostriches.[3]
14 And wild animals shall meet with
hyenas;
the wild goat shall cry to his fellow;
indeed, there the night bird[4] settles
and finds for herself a resting place.

15 There the owl nests and lays
and hatches and gathers her young
in her shadow;
indeed, there the hawks are gathered,
each one with her mate.
16 Seek and read from the book of the
LORD:
Not one of these shall be missing;
none shall be without her mate.
For the mouth of the LORD has commanded,
and his Spirit has gathered them.
17 He has cast the lot for them;
his hand has portioned it out to
them with the line;
they shall possess it forever;
from generation to generation
they shall dwell in it.

The Ransomed Shall Return

35 The wilderness and the dry land
shall be glad;
the desert shall rejoice and blossom like the crocus;
2 it shall blossom abundantly
and rejoice with joy and singing.
The glory of Lebanon shall be given
to it,
the majesty of Carmel and Sharon.

They shall see the glory of the LORD,
the majesty of our God.

3 Strengthen the weak hands,
and make firm the feeble knees.
4 Say to those who have an anxious
heart,
"Be strong; fear not!
Behold, your God
will come with vengeance,
with the recompense of God.
He will come and save you."

5 Then the eyes of the blind shall be
opened,
and the ears of the deaf unstopped;
6 then shall the lame man leap like a
deer,
and the tongue of the mute sing for
joy.
For waters break forth in the wilderness,
and streams in the desert;
7 the burning sand shall become a
pool,
and the thirsty ground springs of
water;
in the haunt of jackals, where they lie
down,
the grass shall become reeds and
rushes.

8 And a highway shall be there,
and it shall be called the Way of
Holiness;
the unclean shall not pass over it.
It shall belong to those who walk
on the way;
even if they are fools, they shall
not go astray.[5]
9 No lion shall be there,
nor shall any ravenous beast come
up on it;
they shall not be found there,
but the redeemed shall walk
there.
10 And the ransomed of the LORD shall
return
and come to Zion with singing;
everlasting joy shall be upon their
heads;
they shall obtain gladness and joy,
and sorrow and sighing shall flee
away.

[1] The identity of the animals rendered *hawk* and *porcupine* is uncertain [2] Hebrew *formlessness* [3] Or *owls* [4] Identity uncertain [5] Or *if they are fools, they shall not wander in it*

Sennacherib Invades Judah

36 In the fourteenth year of King Hezekiah, Sennacherib king of Assyria came up against all the fortified cities of Judah and took them. ²And the king of Assyria sent the Rabshakeh¹ from Lachish to King Hezekiah at Jerusalem, with a great army. And he stood by the conduit of the upper pool on the highway to the Washer's Field. ³And there came out to him Eliakim the son of Hilkiah, who was over the household, and Shebna the secretary, and Joah the son of Asaph, the recorder.

⁴And the Rabshakeh said to them, "Say to Hezekiah, 'Thus says the great king, the king of Assyria: On what do you rest this trust of yours? ⁵Do you think that mere words are strategy and power for war? In whom do you now trust, that you have rebelled against me? ⁶Behold, you are trusting in Egypt, that broken reed of a staff, which will pierce the hand of any man who leans on it. Such is Pharaoh king of Egypt to all who trust in him. ⁷But if you say to me, "We trust in the LORD our God," is it not he whose high places and altars Hezekiah has removed, saying to Judah and to Jerusalem, "You shall worship before this altar"? ⁸Come now, make a wager with my master the king of Assyria: I will give you two thousand horses, if you are able on your part to set riders on them. ⁹How then can you repulse a single captain among the least of my master's servants, when you trust in Egypt for chariots and for horsemen? ¹⁰Moreover, is it without the LORD that I have come up against this land to destroy it? The LORD said to me, Go up against this land and destroy it.'"

¹¹Then Eliakim, Shebna, and Joah said to the Rabshakeh, "Please speak to your servants in Aramaic, for we understand it. Do not speak to us in the language of Judah within the hearing of the people who are on the wall." ¹²But the Rabshakeh said, "Has my master sent me to speak these words to your master and to you, and not to the men sitting on the wall, who are doomed with you to eat their own dung and drink their own urine?"

¹³Then the Rabshakeh stood and called out in a loud voice in the language of Judah: "Hear the words of the great king, the king of Assyria! ¹⁴Thus says the king:

'Do not let Hezekiah deceive you, for he will not be able to deliver you. ¹⁵Do not let Hezekiah make you trust in the LORD by saying, "The LORD will surely deliver us. This city will not be given into the hand of the king of Assyria." ¹⁶Do not listen to Hezekiah. For thus says the king of Assyria: Make your peace with me² and come out to me. Then each one of you will eat of his own vine, and each one of his own fig tree, and each one of you will drink the water of his own cistern, ¹⁷until I come and take you away to a land like your own land, a land of grain and wine, a land of bread and vineyards. ¹⁸Beware lest Hezekiah mislead you by saying, "The LORD will deliver us." Has any of the gods of the nations delivered his land out of the hand of the king of Assyria? ¹⁹Where are the gods of Hamath and Arpad? Where are the gods of Sepharvaim? Have they delivered Samaria out of my hand? ²⁰Who among all the gods of these lands have delivered their lands out of my hand, that the LORD should deliver Jerusalem out of my hand?'"

²¹But they were silent and answered him not a word, for the king's command was, "Do not answer him." ²²Then Eliakim the son of Hilkiah, who was over the household, and Shebna the secretary, and Joah the son of Asaph, the recorder, came to Hezekiah with their clothes torn, and told him the words of the Rabshakeh.

Hezekiah Seeks Isaiah's Help

37 As soon as King Hezekiah heard it, he tore his clothes and covered himself with sackcloth and went into the house of the LORD. ²And he sent Eliakim, who was over the household, and Shebna the secretary, and the senior priests, covered with sackcloth, to the prophet Isaiah the son of Amoz. ³They said to him, "Thus says Hezekiah, 'This day is a day of distress, of rebuke, and of disgrace; children have come to the point of birth, and there is no strength to bring them forth. ⁴It may be that the LORD your God will hear the words of the Rabshakeh, whom his master the king of Assyria has sent to mock the living God, and will rebuke the words that the LORD your God has heard; therefore lift up your prayer for the remnant that is left.'"

---

¹ *Rabshakeh* is the title of a high-ranking Assyrian military officer   ² Hebrew *Make a blessing with me*

[5] When the servants of King Hezekiah came to Isaiah, [6] Isaiah said to them, "Say to your master, 'Thus says the LORD: Do not be afraid because of the words that you have heard, with which the young men of the king of Assyria have reviled me. [7] Behold, I will put a spirit in him, so that he shall hear a rumor and return to his own land, and I will make him fall by the sword in his own land.'"

[8] The Rabshakeh returned, and found the king of Assyria fighting against Libnah, for he had heard that the king had left Lachish. [9] Now the king heard concerning Tirhakah king of Cush,[1] "He has set out to fight against you." And when he heard it, he sent messengers to Hezekiah, saying, [10] "Thus shall you speak to Hezekiah king of Judah: 'Do not let your God in whom you trust deceive you by promising that Jerusalem will not be given into the hand of the king of Assyria. [11] Behold, you have heard what the kings of Assyria have done to all lands, devoting them to destruction. And shall you be delivered? [12] Have the gods of the nations delivered them, the nations that my fathers destroyed, Gozan, Haran, Rezeph, and the people of Eden who were in Telassar? [13] Where is the king of Hamath, the king of Arpad, the king of the city of Sepharvaim, the king of Hena, or the king of Ivvah?'"

Hezekiah's Prayer for Deliverance

[14] Hezekiah received the letter from the hand of the messengers, and read it; and Hezekiah went up to the house of the LORD, and spread it before the LORD. [15] And Hezekiah prayed to the LORD: [16] "O LORD of hosts, God of Israel, enthroned above the cherubim, you are the God, you alone, of all the kingdoms of the earth; you have made heaven and earth. [17] Incline your ear, O LORD, and hear; open your eyes, O LORD, and see; and hear all the words of Sennacherib, which he has sent to mock the living God. [18] Truly, O LORD, the kings of Assyria have laid waste all the nations and their lands, [19] and have cast their gods into the fire. For they were no gods, but the work of men's hands, wood and stone. Therefore they were destroyed. [20] So now, O LORD our God, save us from his hand, that all the kingdoms of the earth may know that you alone are the LORD."

Sennacherib's Fall

[21] Then Isaiah the son of Amoz sent to Hezekiah, saying, "Thus says the LORD, the God of Israel: Because you have prayed to me concerning Sennacherib king of Assyria, [22] this is the word that the LORD has spoken concerning him:

"'She despises you, she scorns you—
    the virgin daughter of Zion;
she wags her head behind you—
    the daughter of Jerusalem.

[23] "'Whom have you mocked and reviled?
    Against whom have you raised
        your voice
and lifted your eyes to the heights?
    Against the Holy One of Israel!
[24] By your servants you have mocked
        the Lord,
    and you have said, With my many
        chariots
I have gone up the heights of the
        mountains,
    to the far recesses of Lebanon,
to cut down its tallest cedars,
    its choicest cypresses,
to come to its remotest height,
    its most fruitful forest.
[25] I dug wells
    and drank waters,
to dry up with the sole of my foot
    all the streams of Egypt.

[26] "'Have you not heard
    that I determined it long ago?
I planned from days of old
    what now I bring to pass,
that you should make fortified cities
    crash into heaps of ruins,
[27] while their inhabitants, shorn of
        strength,
    are dismayed and confounded,
and have become like plants of the
        field
    and like tender grass,
like grass on the housetops,
    blighted[2] before it is grown.

[28] "'I know your sitting down
    and your going out and coming in,
    and your raging against me.
[29] Because you have raged against me
    and your complacency has come to
        my ears,

---

[1] Probably *Nubia* [2] Some Hebrew manuscripts and 2 Kings 19:26; most Hebrew manuscripts *like a field*

I will put my hook in your nose
  and my bit in your mouth,
and I will turn you back on the way
  by which you came.'

30 "And this shall be the sign for you: this year you shall eat what grows of itself, and in the second year what springs from that. Then in the third year sow and reap, and plant vineyards, and eat their fruit. 31 And the surviving remnant of the house of Judah shall again take root downward and bear fruit upward. 32 For out of Jerusalem shall go a remnant, and out of Mount Zion a band of survivors. The zeal of the LORD of hosts will do this.

33 "Therefore thus says the LORD concerning the king of Assyria: He shall not come into this city or shoot an arrow there or come before it with a shield or cast up a siege mound against it. 34 By the way that he came, by the same he shall return, and he shall not come into this city, declares the LORD. 35 For I will defend this city to save it, for my own sake and for the sake of my servant David."

36 And the angel of the LORD went out and struck down 185,000 in the camp of the Assyrians. And when people arose early in the morning, behold, these were all dead bodies. 37 Then Sennacherib king of Assyria departed and returned home and lived at Nineveh. 38 And as he was worshiping in the house of Nisroch his god, Adrammelech and Sharezer, his sons, struck him down with the sword. And after they escaped into the land of Ararat, Esarhaddon his son reigned in his place.

Hezekiah's Sickness and Recovery

38 In those days Hezekiah became sick and was at the point of death. And Isaiah the prophet the son of Amoz came to him, and said to him, "Thus says the LORD: Set your house in order, for you shall die, you shall not recover."[1] 2 Then Hezekiah turned his face to the wall and prayed to the LORD, 3 and said, "Please, O LORD, remember how I have walked before you in faithfulness and with a whole heart, and have done what is good in your sight." And Hezekiah wept bitterly.

4 Then the word of the LORD came to Isaiah: 5 "Go and say to Hezekiah, Thus says the LORD, the God of David your father: I have heard your prayer; I have seen your tears. Behold, I will add fifteen years to your life.[2] 6 I will deliver you and this city out of the hand of the king of Assyria, and will defend this city.

7 "This shall be the sign to you from the LORD, that the LORD will do this thing that he has promised: 8 Behold, I will make the shadow cast by the declining sun on the dial of Ahaz turn back ten steps." So the sun turned back on the dial the ten steps by which it had declined.[3]

9 A writing of Hezekiah king of Judah, after he had been sick and had recovered from his sickness:

10   I said, In the middle[4] of my days
      I must depart;
   I am consigned to the gates of Sheol
      for the rest of my years.
11   I said, I shall not see the LORD,
      the LORD in the land of the living;
   I shall look on man no more
      among the inhabitants of the world.
12   My dwelling is plucked up and
         removed from me
      like a shepherd's tent;
   like a weaver I have rolled up my life;
      he cuts me off from the loom;
   from day to night you bring me to an
         end;
13   I calmed myself[5] until morning;
   like a lion he breaks all my bones;
      from day to night you bring me to
         an end.
14   Like a swallow or a crane I chirp;
      I moan like a dove.
   My eyes are weary with looking
         upward.
   O Lord, I am oppressed; be my
         pledge of safety!
15   What shall I say? For he has spoken
         to me,
      and he himself has done it.
   I walk slowly all my years
      because of the bitterness of my soul.
16   O Lord, by these things men live,
      and in all these is the life of my
         spirit.
   Oh restore me to health and make
      me live!

[1] Or live; also verses 9, 21 [2] Hebrew to your days [3] The meaning of the Hebrew verse is uncertain [4] Or In the quiet [5] Or (with Targum) I cried for help

17 Behold, it was for my welfare
    that I had great bitterness;
but in love you have delivered my life
    from the pit of destruction,
for you have cast all my sins
    behind your back.
18 For Sheol does not thank you;
    death does not praise you;
those who go down to the pit do not
    hope
    for your faithfulness.
19 The living, the living, he thanks you,
    as I do this day;
the father makes known to the chil-
    dren
    your faithfulness.

20 The LORD will save me,
    and we will play my music on
        stringed instruments
all the days of our lives,
    at the house of the LORD.

21 Now Isaiah had said, "Let them take a cake of figs and apply it to the boil, that he may recover." 22 Hezekiah also had said, "What is the sign that I shall go up to the house of the LORD?"

Envoys from Babylon

39 At that time Merodach-baladan the son of Baladan, king of Babylon, sent envoys with letters and a present to Hezekiah, for he heard that he had been sick and had recovered. 2 And Hezekiah welcomed them gladly. And he showed them his treasure house, the silver, the gold, the spices, the precious oil, his whole armory, all that was found in his storehouses. There was nothing in his house or in all his realm that Hezekiah did not show them. 3 Then Isaiah the prophet came to King Hezekiah, and said to him, "What did these men say? And from where did they come to you?" Hezekiah said, "They have come to me from a far country, from Babylon." 4 He said, "What have they seen in your house?" Hezekiah answered, "They have seen all that is in my house. There is nothing in my storehouses that I did not show them."

5 Then Isaiah said to Hezekiah, "Hear the word of the LORD of hosts: 6 Behold, the days are coming, when all that is in your house, and that which your fathers have stored up till this day, shall be carried to Babylon. Nothing shall be left, says the LORD. 7 And some of your own sons, who will come from you, whom you will father, shall be taken away, and they shall be eunuchs in the palace of the king of Babylon." 8 Then Hezekiah said to Isaiah, "The word of the LORD that you have spoken is good." For he thought, "There will be peace and security in my days."

Comfort for God's People

40 Comfort, comfort my people,
    says your God.
2 Speak tenderly to Jerusalem,
    and cry to her
that her warfare[1] is ended,
    that her iniquity is pardoned,
that she has received from the
    LORD's hand
    double for all her sins.

3 A voice cries:[2]
"In the wilderness prepare the way of
    the LORD;
    make straight in the desert a high-
        way for our God.
4 Every valley shall be lifted up,
    and every mountain and hill be
        made low;
the uneven ground shall become level,
    and the rough places a plain.
5 And the glory of the LORD shall be
    revealed,
    and all flesh shall see it together,
for the mouth of the LORD has
    spoken."

The Word of God Stands Forever

6 A voice says, "Cry!"
    And I said,[3] "What shall I cry?"
All flesh is grass,
    and all its beauty[4] is like the flower
        of the field.
7 The grass withers, the flower fades
    when the breath of the LORD blows
        on it;
    surely the people are grass.
8 The grass withers, the flower fades,
    but the word of our God will stand
        forever.

The Greatness of God

9 Go on up to a high mountain,
    O Zion, herald of good news;[5]

---

[1] Or hardship [2] Or A voice of one crying [3] Revocalization based on Dead Sea Scroll, Septuagint, Vulgate; Masoretic Text And someone say.
[4] Or all its constancy [5] Or O herald of good news to Zion

lift up your voice with strength,
　O Jerusalem, herald of good news;[1]
　lift it up, fear not;
say to the cities of Judah,
　"Behold your God!"

10 Behold, the Lord God comes with
　　might,
　　and his arm rules for him;
behold, his reward is with him,
　　and his recompense before him.

11 He will tend his flock like a shepherd;
　he will gather the lambs in his arms;
he will carry them in his bosom,
　　and gently lead those that are with
　　young.

12 Who has measured the waters in the
　　hollow of his hand
　　and marked off the heavens with a
　　span,
enclosed the dust of the earth in a
　　measure
　　and weighed the mountains in
　　scales
　　and the hills in a balance?

13 Who has measured[2] the Spirit of the
　　Lord,
　　or what man shows him his coun-
　　sel?

14 Whom did he consult,
　　and who made him understand?
Who taught him the path of justice,
　　and taught him knowledge,
　　and showed him the way of under-
　　standing?

15 Behold, the nations are like a drop
　　from a bucket,
　　and are accounted as the dust on
　　the scales;
　　behold, he takes up the coastlands
　　like fine dust.

16 Lebanon would not suffice for fuel,
　　nor are its beasts enough for a
　　burnt offering.

17 All the nations are as nothing before
　　him,
　　they are accounted by him as less
　　than nothing and emptiness.

18 To whom then will you liken God,
　　or what likeness compare with him?

19 An idol! A craftsman casts it,
　　and a goldsmith overlays it with
　　gold
　　and casts for it silver chains.

20 He who is too impoverished for an
　　offering
　　chooses wood[3] that will not rot;
he seeks out a skillful craftsman
　　to set up an idol that will not move.

21 Do you not know? Do you not hear?
　　Has it not been told you from the
　　beginning?
　　Have you not understood from the
　　foundations of the earth?

22 It is he who sits above the circle of
　　the earth,
　　and its inhabitants are like grass-
　　hoppers;
who stretches out the heavens like a
　　curtain,
　　and spreads them like a tent to
　　dwell in;

23 who brings princes to nothing,
　　and makes the rulers of the earth
　　as emptiness.

24 Scarcely are they planted, scarcely
　　sown,
　　scarcely has their stem taken root
　　in the earth,
when he blows on them, and they
　　wither,
　　and the tempest carries them off
　　like stubble.

25 To whom then will you compare me,
　　that I should be like him? says the
　　Holy One.

26 Lift up your eyes on high and see:
　　who created these?
He who brings out their host by
　　number,
　　calling them all by name,
by the greatness of his might,
　　and because he is strong in power
　　not one is missing.

27 Why do you say, O Jacob,
　　and speak, O Israel,
"My way is hidden from the Lord,
　　and my right is disregarded by my
　　God"?

28 Have you not known? Have you not
　　heard?
The Lord is the everlasting God,
　　the Creator of the ends of the earth.
He does not faint or grow weary;
　　his understanding is unsearchable.

[1] Or O herald of good news to Jerusalem [2] Or has directed [3] Or He chooses valuable wood

29 He gives power to the faint,
      and to him who has no might he
          increases strength.
30 Even youths shall faint and be weary,
      and young men shall fall exhausted;
31 but they who wait for the LORD shall
          renew their strength;
      they shall mount up with wings
          like eagles;
    they shall run and not be weary;
      they shall walk and not faint.

Fear Not, for I Am with You

41 Listen to me in silence, O coast-
    lands;
      let the peoples renew their strength;
    let them approach, then let them
          speak;
      let us together draw near for judg-
          ment.

2 Who stirred up one from the east
      whom victory meets at every step?[1]
    He gives up nations before him,
      so that he tramples kings under-
          foot;
    he makes them like dust with his
          sword,
      like driven stubble with his bow.

[1] Or whom righteousness calls to follow?

3 He pursues them and passes on safely,
      by paths his feet have not trod.
4 Who has performed and done this,
      calling the generations from the
          beginning?
    I, the LORD, the first,
      and with the last; I am he.
5 The coastlands have seen and are
          afraid;
      the ends of the earth tremble;
      they have drawn near and come.
6 Everyone helps his neighbor
      and says to his brother, "Be strong!"
7 The craftsman strengthens the gold-
          smith,
      and he who smooths with the ham-
          mer him who strikes the anvil,
    saying of the soldering, "It is good";
      and they strengthen it with nails
          so that it cannot be moved.

8 But you, Israel, my servant,
      Jacob, whom I have chosen,
    the offspring of Abraham, my
          friend;
9 you whom I took from the ends of
          the earth,
      and called from its farthest corners,

Know True Happiness

verses to read
Isaiah 40:27–31

Do you ever feel like doing good is a giant waste of time because no one ever notices? Or worse yet, they think you are being bad when you are actually being good? You get no respect, and it's no fair. But never mind if you don't get the respect you deserve. Never mind if you work hard on something and never get the credit for it. Don't look for fame and approval from people. Don't scratch and fight to be recognized. In Christ, you already have all the approval you will ever need. You've already been discovered!

As a God Girl, your only goal should be doing the will of the God who has given you full and unchanging approval in Christ, not getting hollow approval from other people. He promises blessing to those who walk with him and trust him. When he says you will get your reward for whatever you do, he isn't lying. You have to trust the economy of God—everything you do will either build your inheritance in heaven or tear it down. Work for blessing by sowing goodness and mercy, by serving in peace and in hope, and by trusting him, rather than people, for your reward.

saying to you, "You are my servant,
    I have chosen you and not cast you
        off";
fear not, for I am with you;
    be not dismayed, for I am your God;
I will strengthen you, I will help you,
    I will uphold you with my righ-
        teous right hand.

Behold, all who are incensed against
        you
    shall be put to shame and con-
        founded;
those who strive against you
    shall be as nothing and shall perish.
You shall seek those who contend
        with you,
    but you shall not find them;
those who war against you
    shall be as nothing at all.
For I, the LORD your God,
    hold your right hand;
it is I who say to you, "Fear not,
    I am the one who helps you."

Fear not, you worm Jacob,
    you men of Israel!

I am the one who helps you, declares
        the LORD;
    your Redeemer is the Holy One of
        Israel.
15 Behold, I make of you a threshing
        sledge,
    new, sharp, and having teeth;
you shall thresh the mountains and
        crush them,
    and you shall make the hills like
        chaff;
16 you shall winnow them, and the
        wind shall carry them away,
    and the tempest shall scatter
        them.
And you shall rejoice in the LORD;
    in the Holy One of Israel you shall
        glory.

17 When the poor and needy seek
        water,
    and there is none,
    and their tongue is parched with
        thirst,
I the LORD will answer them;
    I the God of Israel will not forsake
        them.

verses to read
Isaiah 41:1–10

How hard is it to hear God? How hard is it to even know he's listening and watch-ing your every move? Hard sometimes, huh? That might just be because you don't know his voice. He's talking, but maybe you're confusing his voice with something else.

The truth is that a lot of times God talks through circumstances. Nothing happens to you that doesn't first go through his victorious hands. No matter how tragic the situation you're in, you have to get into the habit of listening to God's voice in the rumbling of circumstance. If you can stop and say, "Talk to me, God—I want to listen," and then really listen instead of worrying, whining, or complaining, your life will become amazing. Nothing will ever again be meaningless. And remember that the main way we listen to God is by listening to his Word, the Bible.

Life isn't like a series of events that God watches from a distance. It is more like a movie with a beginning, a middle, and an end; a hero, a villain, and a conflict. For those who believe, the ending is sure to be a good one, and the middle can be pure adventure if you are only willing to believe that God is talking. Believe and trust that what he says is true: he will strengthen you and help you; he will support you with his victorious right hand (see Isa. 41:10). Let these words be your strength, especially when all seems lost. Never forget that God is always involved.

18 I will open rivers on the bare heights,
   and fountains in the midst of the
      valleys.
   I will make the wilderness a pool of
      water,
   and the dry land springs of water.
19 I will put in the wilderness the cedar,
   the acacia, the myrtle, and the olive.
   I will set in the desert the cypress,
   the plane and the pine together,
20 that they may see and know,
   may consider and understand
      together,
   that the hand of the LORD has done
      this,
   the Holy One of Israel has created it.

The Futility of Idols

21 Set forth your case, says the LORD;
   bring your proofs, says the King of
      Jacob.
22 Let them bring them, and tell us
   what is to happen.
   Tell us the former things, what they
      are,
   that we may consider them,
   that we may know their outcome;
   or declare to us the things to come.
23 Tell us what is to come hereafter,
   that we may know that you are
      gods;
   do good, or do harm,
   that we may be dismayed and ter-
      rified.[1]
24 Behold, you are nothing,
   and your work is less than noth-
      ing;
   an abomination is he who chooses
      you.
25 I stirred up one from the north, and
      he has come,
   from the rising of the sun, and he
      shall call upon my name;
   he shall trample on rulers as on
      mortar,
   as the potter treads clay.
26 Who declared it from the beginning,
      that we might know,
   and beforehand, that we might say,
      "He is right"?
   There was none who declared it,
   none who proclaimed,
   none who heard your words.

27 I was the first to say[2] to Zion,
      "Behold, here they are!"
   and I give to Jerusalem a herald of
      good news.
28 But when I look, there is no one;
   among these there is no counselor
   who, when I ask, gives an answer.
29 Behold, they are all a delusion;
   their works are nothing;
   their metal images are empty wind.

The LORD's Chosen Servant

42 Behold my servant, whom
   I uphold,
   my chosen, in whom my soul
      delights;
   I have put my Spirit upon him;
   he will bring forth justice to the
      nations.
2 He will not cry aloud or lift up his
      voice,
   or make it heard in the street;
3 a bruised reed he will not break,
   and a faintly burning wick he will
      not quench;
   he will faithfully bring forth justice.
4 He will not grow faint or be discour-
      aged[3]
   till he has established justice in the
      earth;
   and the coastlands wait for his law.

5 Thus says God, the LORD,
   who created the heavens and
      stretched them out,
   who spread out the earth and what
      comes from it,
   who gives breath to the people on it
   and spirit to those who walk in it:
6 "I am the LORD; I have called you[4] in
      righteousness;
   I will take you by the hand and
      keep you;
   I will give you as a covenant for the
      people,
   a light for the nations,
7 to open the eyes that are blind,
   to bring out the prisoners from the
      dungeon,
   from the prison those who sit in
      darkness.
8 I am the LORD; that is my name;
   my glory I give to no other,
   nor my praise to carved idols.

---

[1] Or that we may both be dismayed and see [2] Or Formerly I said [3] Or bruised [4] The Hebrew for you is singular; four times in this verse

⁹ Behold, the former things have come
to pass,
  and new things I now declare;
before they spring forth
  I tell you of them."

Sing to the LORD a New Song
¹⁰ Sing to the LORD a new song,
  his praise from the end of the earth,
you who go down to the sea, and all
that fills it,
  the coastlands and their inhabitants.
¹¹ Let the desert and its cities lift up
their voice,
  the villages that Kedar inhabits;
let the habitants of Sela sing for joy,
  let them shout from the top of the
  mountains.
¹² Let them give glory to the LORD,
  and declare his praise in the coastlands.
¹³ The LORD goes out like a mighty man,
  like a man of war he stirs up his
  zeal;
he cries out, he shouts aloud,
  he shows himself mighty against
  his foes.

¹⁴ For a long time I have held my peace;
  I have kept still and restrained
  myself;
now I will cry out like a woman in
labor;
  I will gasp and pant.
¹⁵ I will lay waste mountains and hills,
  and dry up all their vegetation;
I will turn the rivers into islands,¹
  and dry up the pools.
¹⁶ And I will lead the blind
  in a way that they do not know,
in paths that they have not known
  I will guide them.
I will turn the darkness before them
  into light,
  the rough places into level ground.
These are the things I do,
  and I do not forsake them.
¹⁷ They are turned back and utterly put
to shame,
  who trust in carved idols,
who say to metal images,
  "You are our gods."

Israel's Failure to Hear and See
¹⁸ Hear, you deaf,
  and look, you blind, that you may
  see!
¹⁹ Who is blind but my servant,
  or deaf as my messenger whom
  I send?
Who is blind as my dedicated one,²
  or blind as the servant of the
  LORD?
²⁰ He sees many things, but does not
observe them;
  his ears are open, but he does not
  hear.
²¹ The LORD was pleased, for his righteousness' sake,
  to magnify his law and make it
  glorious.
²² But this is a people plundered and
looted;
  they are all of them trapped in holes
  and hidden in prisons;
they have become plunder with none
  to rescue,
  spoil with none to say, "Restore!"
²³ Who among you will give ear to this,
  will attend and listen for the time
  to come?
²⁴ Who gave up Jacob to the looter,
  and Israel to the plunderers?
Was it not the LORD, against whom
  we have sinned,
  in whose ways they would not walk,
  and whose law they would not
  obey?
²⁵ So he poured on him the heat of his
anger
  and the might of battle;
it set him on fire all around, but he
  did not understand;
  it burned him up, but he did not
  take it to heart.

Israel's Only Savior
43 But now thus says the LORD,
  he who created you, O Jacob,
he who formed you, O Israel:
"Fear not, for I have redeemed you;
  I have called you by name, you are
  mine.
² When you pass through the waters,
  I will be with you;
and through the rivers, they shall
  not overwhelm you;

when you walk through fire you shall
    not be burned,
  and the flame shall not consume
    you.
3 For I am the LORD your God,
  the Holy One of Israel, your Savior.
I give Egypt as your ransom,
  Cush and Seba in exchange for you.
4 Because you are precious in my
    eyes,
  and honored, and I love you,
I give men in return for you,
  peoples in exchange for your life.
5 Fear not, for I am with you;
  I will bring your offspring from the
    east,
  and from the west I will gather you.
6 I will say to the north, Give up,
  and to the south, Do not withhold;
bring my sons from afar
  and my daughters from the end of
    the earth,
7 everyone who is called by my name,
  whom I created for my glory,
  whom I formed and made."

8 Bring out the people who are blind,
    yet have eyes,
  who are deaf, yet have ears!
9 All the nations gather together,
  and the peoples assemble.
Who among them can declare this,
  and show us the former things?
Let them bring their witnesses to
    prove them right,
  and let them hear and say, It is true.
10 "You are my witnesses," declares the
    LORD,
  "and my servant whom I have cho-
    sen,
that you may know and believe me
  and understand that I am he.
Before me no god was formed,
  nor shall there be any after me.
11 I, I am the LORD,
  and besides me there is no savior.
12 I declared and saved and proclaimed,
  when there was no strange god
    among you;
  and you are my witnesses,"
    declares the LORD, "and I am
    God.
13 Also henceforth I am he;
  there is none who can deliver from
    my hand;
  I work, and who can turn it back?"

14 Thus says the LORD,
  your Redeemer, the Holy One of
    Israel:
"For your sake I send to Babylon
  and bring them all down as fugi-
    tives,
  even the Chaldeans, in the ships in
    which they rejoice.
15 I am the LORD, your Holy One,
  the Creator of Israel, your King."

16 Thus says the LORD,
  who makes a way in the sea,
  a path in the mighty waters,
17 who brings forth chariot and horse,
  army and warrior;
they lie down, they cannot rise,
  they are extinguished, quenched
    like a wick:
18 "Remember not the former things,
  nor consider the things of old.
19 Behold, I am doing a new thing;
  now it springs forth, do you not
    perceive it?
I will make a way in the wilderness
  and rivers in the desert.
20 The wild beasts will honor me,
  the jackals and the ostriches,
for I give water in the wilderness,
  rivers in the desert,
to give drink to my chosen people,
21   the people whom I formed for
    myself
that they might declare my praise.

22 "Yet you did not call upon me, O Jacob
  but you have been weary of me,
    O Israel!
23 You have not brought me your sheep
    for burnt offerings,
  or honored me with your sacrifices
I have not burdened you with offer-
    ings,
  or wearied you with frankincense.
24 You have not bought me sweet cane
    with money,
  or satisfied me with the fat of your
    sacrifices.
But you have burdened me with your
    sins;
  you have wearied me with your
    iniquities.

25 "I, I am he
  who blots out your transgressions
    for my own sake,
  and I will not remember your sins.

⁶ Put me in remembrance; let us argue together;
  set forth your case, that you may be proved right.
⁷ Your first father sinned,
  and your mediators transgressed against me.
⁸ Therefore I will profane the princes of the sanctuary,
  and deliver Jacob to utter destruction
  and Israel to reviling.

Israel the Lord's Chosen

44 "But now hear, O Jacob my servant,
  Israel whom I have chosen!
² Thus says the Lord who made you,
  who formed you from the womb
  and will help you:
Fear not, O Jacob my servant,
  Jeshurun whom I have chosen.
³ For I will pour water on the thirsty land,
  and streams on the dry ground;
I will pour my Spirit upon your offspring,
  and my blessing on your descendants.
⁴ They shall spring up among the grass
  like willows by flowing streams.
⁵ This one will say, 'I am the Lord's,'
  another will call on the name of Jacob,
and another will write on his hand, 'The Lord's,'
  and name himself by the name of Israel."

Besides Me There Is No God

⁶ Thus says the Lord, the King of Israel
  and his Redeemer, the Lord of hosts:
"I am the first and I am the last;
  besides me there is no god.
⁷ Who is like me? Let him proclaim it.[1]
  Let him declare and set it before me,
since I appointed an ancient people.
  Let them declare what is to come,
  and what will happen.
⁸ Fear not, nor be afraid;
  have I not told you from of old and declared it?
  And you are my witnesses!
Is there a God besides me?
  There is no Rock; I know not any."

The Folly of Idolatry

⁹ All who fashion idols are nothing, and the things they delight in do not profit. Their witnesses neither see nor know, that they may be put to shame. ¹⁰ Who fashions a god or casts an idol that is profitable for nothing? ¹¹ Behold, all his companions shall be put to shame, and the craftsmen are only human. Let them all assemble, let them stand forth. They shall be terrified; they shall be put to shame together.

¹² The ironsmith takes a cutting tool and works it over the coals. He fashions it with hammers and works it with his strong arm. He becomes hungry, and his strength fails; he drinks no water and is faint. ¹³ The carpenter stretches a line; he marks it out with a pencil. He shapes it with planes and marks it with a compass. He shapes it into the figure of a man, with the beauty of a man, to dwell in a house. ¹⁴ He cuts down cedars, or he chooses a cypress tree or an oak and lets it grow strong among the trees of the forest. He plants a cedar and the rain nourishes it. ¹⁵ Then it becomes fuel for a man. He takes a part of it and warms himself; he kindles a fire and bakes bread. Also he makes a god and worships it; he makes it an idol and falls down before it. ¹⁶ Half of it he burns in the fire. Over the half he eats meat; he roasts it and is satisfied. Also he warms himself and says, "Aha, I am warm, I have seen the fire!" ¹⁷ And the rest of it he makes into a god, his idol, and falls down to it and worships it. He prays to it and says, "Deliver me, for you are my god!"

¹⁸ They know not, nor do they discern, for he has shut their eyes, so that they cannot see, and their hearts, so that they cannot understand. ¹⁹ No one considers, nor is there knowledge or discernment to say, "Half of it I burned in the fire; I also baked bread on its coals; I roasted meat and have eaten. And shall I make the rest of it an abomination? Shall I fall down before a block of wood?" ²⁰ He feeds on ashes; a deluded heart has led him astray, and he cannot deliver himself or say, "Is there not a lie in my right hand?"

The Lord Redeems Israel

²¹ Remember these things, O Jacob,
  and Israel, for you are my servant;

Or Who like me can proclaim it?

I formed you; you are my servant;
O Israel, you will not be forgotten
by me.
22 I have blotted out your transgressions like a cloud
and your sins like mist;
return to me, for I have redeemed you.
23 Sing, O heavens, for the LORD has
done it;
shout, O depths of the earth;
break forth into singing, O mountains,
O forest, and every tree in it!
For the LORD has redeemed Jacob,
and will be glorified[1] in Israel.

24 Thus says the LORD, your Redeemer,
who formed you from the womb:
"I am the LORD, who made all things,
who alone stretched out the heavens,
who spread out the earth by
myself,
25 who frustrates the signs of liars
and makes fools of diviners,
who turns wise men back
and makes their knowledge foolish,
26 who confirms the word of his servant
and fulfills the counsel of his messengers,
who says of Jerusalem, 'She shall be
inhabited,'
and of the cities of Judah, 'They
shall be built,
and I will raise up their ruins';
27 who says to the deep, 'Be dry;
I will dry up your rivers';
28 who says of Cyrus, 'He is my shepherd,
and he shall fulfill all my purpose';
saying of Jerusalem, 'She shall be
built,'
and of the temple, 'Your foundation shall be laid.'"

Cyrus, God's Instrument

45 Thus says the LORD to his
anointed, to Cyrus,
whose right hand I have grasped,
to subdue nations before him
and to loose the belts of kings,
to open doors before him
that gates may not be closed:
2 "I will go before you
and level the exalted places,[2]

I will break in pieces the doors of
bronze
and cut through the bars of iron,
3 I will give you the treasures of darkness
and the hoards in secret places,
that you may know that it is I, the
LORD,
the God of Israel, who call you by
your name.
4 For the sake of my servant Jacob,
and Israel my chosen,
I call you by your name,
I name you, though you do not
know me.
5 I am the LORD, and there is no other,
besides me there is no God;
I equip you, though you do not
know me,
6 that people may know, from the rising of the sun
and from the west, that there is
none besides me;
I am the LORD, and there is no
other.
7 I form light and create darkness,
I make well-being and create
calamity,
I am the LORD, who does all these
things.

8 "Shower, O heavens, from above,
and let the clouds rain down righteousness;
let the earth open, that salvation and
righteousness may bear fruit;
let the earth cause them both to
sprout;
I the LORD have created it.

9 "Woe to him who strives with him who
formed him,
a pot among earthen pots!
Does the clay say to him who forms
it, 'What are you making?'
or 'Your work has no handles'?
10 Woe to him who says to a father,
'What are you begetting?'
or to a woman, 'With what are you
in labor?'"

11 Thus says the LORD,
the Holy One of Israel, and the one
who formed him:

[1] Or will display his beauty [2] Masoretic Text; Dead Sea Scroll, Septuagint level the mountains

"Ask me of things to come;
 will you command me concerning
   my children and the work of
   my hands?[1]
I made the earth
   and created man on it;
it was my hands that stretched out
   the heavens,
   and I commanded all their host.
I have stirred him up in righteousness,
   and I will make all his ways level;
he shall build my city
   and set my exiles free,
not for price or reward,"
   says the LORD of hosts.

The LORD, the Only Savior

Thus says the LORD:
"The wealth of Egypt and the merchandise of Cush,
   and the Sabeans, men of stature,
shall come over to you and be yours;
   they shall follow you;
   they shall come over in chains and
     bow down to you.
They will plead with you, saying:
   'Surely God is in you, and there is
     no other,
   no god besides him.'"

Truly, you are a God who hides himself,
   O God of Israel, the Savior.
All of them are put to shame and
   confounded;
   the makers of idols go in confusion
     together.
But Israel is saved by the LORD
   with everlasting salvation;
you shall not be put to shame or
   confounded
   to all eternity.

For thus says the LORD,
who created the heavens
   (he is God!),
who formed the earth and made it
   (he established it;
he did not create it empty,
   he formed it to be inhabited!):
"I am the LORD, and there is no other.
I did not speak in secret,
   in a land of darkness;
I did not say to the offspring of Jacob,
   'Seek me in vain.'[2]

I the LORD speak the truth;
   I declare what is right.

20 "Assemble yourselves and come;
   draw near together,
   you survivors of the nations!
They have no knowledge
   who carry about their wooden
     idols,
and keep on praying to a god
   that cannot save.
21 Declare and present your case;
   let them take counsel together!
Who told this long ago?
   Who declared it of old?
Was it not I, the LORD?
   And there is no other god besides
     me,
a righteous God and a Savior;
   there is none besides me.

22 "Turn to me and be saved,
   all the ends of the earth!
   For I am God, and there is no other.
23 By myself I have sworn;
   from my mouth has gone out in
     righteousness
   a word that shall not return:
'To me every knee shall bow,
   every tongue shall swear alle-
     giance.'[3]
24 "Only in the LORD, it shall be said of
     me,
   are righteousness and strength;
to him shall come and be ashamed
   all who were incensed against him.
25 In the LORD all the offspring of Israel
   shall be justified and shall glory."

The Idols of Babylon and the One True God

46 Bel bows down; Nebo stoops;
   their idols are on beasts and
     livestock;
these things you carry are borne
   as burdens on weary beasts.
2 They stoop; they bow down together;
   they cannot save the burden,
   but themselves go into captivity.

3 "Listen to me, O house of Jacob,
   all the remnant of the house of
     Israel,

---

[1] slight emendation yields *will you question me about my children, or command me concerning the work of my hands?* [2] Hebrew *in emptiness* [3] Septuagint *every tongue shall confess to God*

who have been borne by me from
before your birth,
carried from the womb;
4 even to your old age I am he,
and to gray hairs I will carry you.
I have made, and I will bear;
I will carry and will save.

5 "To whom will you liken me and make
me equal,
and compare me, that we may be
alike?
6 Those who lavish gold from the purse,
and weigh out silver in the scales,
hire a goldsmith, and he makes it
into a god;
then they fall down and worship!
7 They lift it to their shoulders, they
carry it,
they set it in its place, and it stands
there;
it cannot move from its place.
If one cries to it, it does not answer
or save him from his trouble.

8 "Remember this and stand firm,
recall it to mind, you transgressors,
9 remember the former things of old;
for I am God, and there is no other;
I am God, and there is none like me,
10 declaring the end from the beginning
and from ancient times things not
yet done,
saying, 'My counsel shall stand,
and I will accomplish all my purpose,'
11 calling a bird of prey from the east,
the man of my counsel from a far
country.
I have spoken, and I will bring it to
pass;
I have purposed, and I will do it.

12 "Listen to me, you stubborn of heart,
you who are far from righteousness:
13 I bring near my righteousness; it is
not far off,
and my salvation will not delay;
I will put salvation in Zion,
for Israel my glory."

The Humiliation of Babylon

47 Come down and sit in the dust,
O virgin daughter of Babylon;
sit on the ground without a throne,
O daughter of the Chaldeans!

For you shall no more be called
tender and delicate.
2 Take the millstones and grind flour,
put off your veil,
strip off your robe, uncover your leg,
pass through the rivers.
3 Your nakedness shall be uncovered,
and your disgrace shall be seen.
I will take vengeance,
and I will spare no one.
4 Our Redeemer—the LORD of hosts is
his name—
is the Holy One of Israel.

5 Sit in silence, and go into darkness,
O daughter of the Chaldeans;
for you shall no more be called
the mistress of kingdoms.
6 I was angry with my people;
I profaned my heritage;
I gave them into your hand;
you showed them no mercy;
on the aged you made your yoke
exceedingly heavy.
7 You said, "I shall be mistress forever,"
so that you did not lay these things
to heart
or remember their end.

8 Now therefore hear this, you lover of
pleasures,
who sit securely,
who say in your heart,
"I am, and there is no one besides
me;
I shall not sit as a widow
or know the loss of children":
9 These two things shall come to you
in a moment, in one day;
the loss of children and widowhood
shall come upon you in full measure,
in spite of your many sorceries
and the great power of your
enchantments.

10 You felt secure in your wickedness,
you said, "No one sees me";
your wisdom and your knowledge
led you astray,
and you said in your heart,
"I am, and there is no one besides
me."
11 But evil shall come upon you,
which you will not know how to
charm away;

disaster shall fall upon you,
  for which you will not be able to
    atone;
and ruin shall come upon you suddenly,
  of which you know nothing.

2 Stand fast in your enchantments
  and your many sorceries,
  with which you have labored from
    your youth;
perhaps you may be able to succeed;
  perhaps you may inspire terror.
3 You are wearied with your many
  counsels;
  let them stand forth and save you,
those who divide the heavens,
  who gaze at the stars,
who at the new moons make known
  what shall come upon you.

4 Behold, they are like stubble;
  the fire consumes them;
they cannot deliver themselves
  from the power of the flame.
No coal for warming oneself is this,
  no fire to sit before!
5 Such to you are those with whom
  you have labored,
  who have done business with you
    from your youth;
they wander about, each in his own
  direction;
  there is no one to save you.

Israel Refined for God's Glory

48 Hear this, O house of Jacob,
  who are called by the name of
    Israel,
and who came from the waters of
  Judah,
who swear by the name of the Lord
  and confess the God of Israel,
  but not in truth or right.
2 For they call themselves after the
  holy city,
  and stay themselves on the God of
    Israel;
  the Lord of hosts is his name.

3 "The former things I declared of old;
  they went out from my mouth, and
    I announced them;
  then suddenly I did them, and they
    came to pass.

4 Because I know that you are obstinate,
  and your neck is an iron sinew
  and your forehead brass,
5 I declared them to you from of old,
  before they came to pass
    I announced them to you,
lest you should say, 'My idol did them,
  my carved image and my metal
    image commanded them.'

6 "You have heard; now see all this;
  and will you not declare it?
From this time forth I announce to
  you new things,
  hidden things that you have not
    known.
7 They are created now, not long ago;
  before today you have never heard
    of them,
  lest you should say, 'Behold,
    I knew them.'
8 You have never heard, you have
  never known,
  from of old your ear has not been
    opened.
For I knew that you would surely
  deal treacherously,
  and that from before birth you
    were called a rebel.

9 "For my name's sake I defer my anger,
  for the sake of my praise I restrain
    it for you,
  that I may not cut you off.
10 Behold, I have refined you, but not as
  silver;
  I have tried[1] you in the furnace of
    affliction.
11 For my own sake, for my own sake,
  I do it,
  for how should my name[2] be pro-
    faned?
  My glory I will not give to another.

The Lord's Call to Israel
12 "Listen to me, O Jacob,
  and Israel, whom I called!
I am he; I am the first,
  and I am the last.
13 My hand laid the foundation of the
  earth,
  and my right hand spread out the
    heavens;
when I call to them,
  they stand forth together.

---

[1] Or I have chosen [2] Hebrew lacks my name

14 "Assemble, all of you, and listen!
    Who among them has declared
        these things?
The LORD loves him;
    he shall perform his purpose on
        Babylon,
    and his arm shall be against the
        Chaldeans.
15 I, even I, have spoken and called him;
    I have brought him, and he will
        prosper in his way.
16 Draw near to me, hear this:
    from the beginning I have not
        spoken in secret,
    from the time it came to be I have
        been there."
And now the Lord GOD has sent me,
    and his Spirit.

17 Thus says the LORD,
    your Redeemer, the Holy One of
        Israel:
"I am the LORD your God,
    who teaches you to profit,
    who leads you in the way you
        should go.
18 Oh that you had paid attention to my
        commandments!
    Then your peace would have been
        like a river,
    and your righteousness like the
        waves of the sea;
19 your offspring would have been like
        the sand,
    and your descendants like its
        grains;
    their name would never be cut off
        or destroyed from before me."

20 Go out from Babylon, flee from
        Chaldea,
    declare this with a shout of joy,
        proclaim it,
    send it out to the end of the earth;
    say, "The LORD has redeemed his
        servant Jacob!"
21 They did not thirst when he led them
        through the deserts;
    he made water flow for them from
        the rock;
    he split the rock and the water
        gushed out.
22 "There is no peace," says the LORD, "for
        the wicked."

The Servant of the LORD

49 Listen to me, O coastlands,
    and give attention, you peoples
        from afar.
The LORD called me from the womb,
    from the body of my mother he
        named my name.
2 He made my mouth like a sharp
        sword;
    in the shadow of his hand he hid
        me;
    he made me a polished arrow;
    in his quiver he hid me away.
3 And he said to me, "You are my ser-
        vant,
    Israel, in whom I will be glorified."[1]
4 But I said, "I have labored in vain;
    I have spent my strength for noth-
        ing and vanity;
    yet surely my right is with the LORD,
    and my recompense with my God."

5 And now the LORD says,
    he who formed me from the womb
        to be his servant,
to bring Jacob back to him;
    and that Israel might be gathered
        to him—
for I am honored in the eyes of the
        LORD,
    and my God has become my
        strength—
6 he says:
"It is too light a thing that you should
        be my servant
    to raise up the tribes of Jacob
    and to bring back the preserved of
        Israel;
I will make you as a light for the
        nations,
    that my salvation may reach to the
        end of the earth."

7 Thus says the LORD,
    the Redeemer of Israel and his
        Holy One,
to one deeply despised, abhorred by
        the nation,
    the servant of rulers:
"Kings shall see and arise;
    princes, and they shall prostrate
        themselves;
because of the LORD, who is faithful,
    the Holy One of Israel, who has
        chosen you."

[1] Or I will display my beauty

The Restoration of Israel

8 Thus says the LORD:

"In a time of favor I have answered
you;
in a day of salvation I have helped
you;
I will keep you and give you
as a covenant to the people,
to establish the land,
to apportion the desolate heritages,
9 saying to the prisoners, 'Come out,'
to those who are in darkness,
'Appear.'
They shall feed along the ways;
on all bare heights shall be their
pasture;
10 they shall not hunger or thirst,
neither scorching wind nor sun
shall strike them,
for he who has pity on them will lead
them,
and by springs of water will guide
them.
11 And I will make all my mountains a
road,
and my highways shall be raised
up.
12 Behold, these shall come from afar,
and behold, these from the north
and from the west,[1]
and these from the land of Syene."[2]

13 Sing for joy, O heavens, and exult,
O earth;
break forth, O mountains, into
singing!
For the LORD has comforted his
people
and will have compassion on his
afflicted.

14 But Zion said, "The LORD has forsaken me;
my Lord has forgotten me."

15 "Can a woman forget her nursing child,
that she should have no compassion on the son of her womb?
Even these may forget,
yet I will not forget you.
16 Behold, I have engraved you on the
palms of my hands;
your walls are continually before
me.

17 Your builders make haste;[3]
your destroyers and those who
laid you waste go out from you.
18 Lift up your eyes around and see;
they all gather, they come to you.
As I live, declares the LORD,
you shall put them all on as an
ornament;
you shall bind them on as a bride
does.

19 "Surely your waste and your desolate
places
and your devastated land—
surely now you will be too narrow
for your inhabitants,
and those who swallowed you up
will be far away.
20 The children of your bereavement
will yet say in your ears:
'The place is too narrow for me;
make room for me to dwell in.'
21 Then you will say in your heart:
'Who has borne me these?
I was bereaved and barren,
exiled and put away,
but who has brought up these?
Behold, I was left alone;
from where have these come?'"

22 Thus says the Lord GOD:

"Behold, I will lift up my hand to the
nations,
and raise my signal to the peoples;
and they shall bring your sons in
their arms,[4]
and your daughters shall be carried on their shoulders.
23 Kings shall be your foster fathers,
and their queens your nursing
mothers.
With their faces to the ground they
shall bow down to you,
and lick the dust of your feet.
Then you will know that I am the
LORD;
those who wait for me shall not be
put to shame."

24 Can the prey be taken from the
mighty,
or the captives of a tyrant[5] be
rescued?
25 For thus says the LORD:

Hebrew from the sea [2]Dead Sea Scroll; Masoretic Text Sinim [3]Dead Sea Scroll; Masoretic Text Your children make haste [4]Hebrew in
their bosom [5]Dead Sea Scroll, Syriac, Vulgate (see also verse 25); Masoretic Text of a righteous man

"Even the captives of the mighty shall
  be taken,
  and the prey of the tyrant be res-
    cued,
for I will contend with those who
  contend with you,
  and I will save your children.
26 I will make your oppressors eat their
  own flesh,
  and they shall be drunk with their
    own blood as with wine.
Then all flesh shall know
  that I am the LORD your Savior,
  and your Redeemer, the Mighty
    One of Jacob."

Israel's Sin and the Servant's Obedience

50 Thus says the LORD:
  "Where is your mother's certifi-
    cate of divorce,
  with which I sent her away?
Or which of my creditors is it
  to whom I have sold you?
Behold, for your iniquities you were
    sold,
  and for your transgressions your
    mother was sent away.
2 Why, when I came, was there no man;
  why, when I called, was there no
    one to answer?
Is my hand shortened, that it cannot
    redeem?
Or have I no power to deliver?
Behold, by my rebuke I dry up the sea,
  I make the rivers a desert;
their fish stink for lack of water
  and die of thirst.
3 I clothe the heavens with blackness
  and make sackcloth their covering."

4 The Lord GOD has given me
  the tongue of those who are taught,
that I may know how to sustain with
    a word
  him who is weary.
Morning by morning he awakens;
  he awakens my ear
  to hear as those who are taught.
5 The Lord GOD has opened my ear,
  and I was not rebellious;
  I turned not backward.
6 I gave my back to those who strike,
  and my cheeks to those who pull
    out the beard;
I hid not my face
  from disgrace and spitting.

7 But the Lord GOD helps me;
  therefore I have not been disgraced
therefore I have set my face like a
    flint,
  and I know that I shall not be put
    to shame.
8 He who vindicates me is near.
Who will contend with me?
  Let us stand up together.
Who is my adversary?
  Let him come near to me.
9 Behold, the Lord GOD helps me;
  who will declare me guilty?
Behold, all of them will wear out like
    a garment;
  the moth will eat them up.

10 Who among you fears the LORD
  and obeys the voice of his servant
Let him who walks in darkness
  and has no light
trust in the name of the LORD
  and rely on his God.
11 Behold, all you who kindle a fire,
  who equip yourselves with burn-
    ing torches!
Walk by the light of your fire,
  and by the torches that you have
    kindled!
This you have from my hand:
  you shall lie down in torment.

The LORD's Comfort for Zion

51 "Listen to me, you who pursue
    righteousness,
  you who seek the LORD:
look to the rock from which you
    were hewn,
  and to the quarry from which you
    were dug.
2 Look to Abraham your father
  and to Sarah who bore you;
for he was but one when I called
    him,
  that I might bless him and multiply
    him.
3 For the LORD comforts Zion;
  he comforts all her waste places
and makes her wilderness like Eden,
  her desert like the garden of the
    LORD;
joy and gladness will be found in her
  thanksgiving and the voice of song

4 "Give attention to me, my people,
  and give ear to me, my nation;

for a law[1] will go out from me,
and I will set my justice for a light
to the peoples.
My righteousness draws near,
my salvation has gone out,
and my arms will judge the
peoples;
the coastlands hope for me,
and for my arm they wait.
Lift up your eyes to the heavens,
and look at the earth beneath;
for the heavens vanish like smoke,
the earth will wear out like a garment,
and they who dwell in it will die in
like manner;[2]
but my salvation will be forever,
and my righteousness will never
be dismayed.

"Listen to me, you who know righteousness,
the people in whose heart is my
law;
fear not the reproach of man,
nor be dismayed at their revilings.
For the moth will eat them up like a
garment,
and the worm will eat them like
wool;
but my righteousness will be forever,
and my salvation to all generations."

Awake, awake, put on strength,
O arm of the LORD;
awake, as in days of old,
the generations of long ago.
Was it not you who cut Rahab in
pieces,
who pierced the dragon?
Was it not you who dried up the sea,
the waters of the great deep,
who made the depths of the sea a
way
for the redeemed to pass over?
And the ransomed of the LORD shall
return
and come to Zion with singing;
everlasting joy shall be upon their
heads;
they shall obtain gladness and joy,
and sorrow and sighing shall flee
away.

12 "I, I am he who comforts you;
who are you that you are afraid of
man who dies,
of the son of man who is made like
grass,
13 and have forgotten the LORD, your
Maker,
who stretched out the heavens
and laid the foundations of the
earth,
and you fear continually all the day
because of the wrath of the
oppressor,
when he sets himself to destroy?
And where is the wrath of the
oppressor?
14 He who is bowed down shall speedily be released;
he shall not die and go down to the
pit,
neither shall his bread be lacking.
15 I am the LORD your God,
who stirs up the sea so that its
waves roar—
the LORD of hosts is his name.
16 And I have put my words in your
mouth
and covered you in the shadow of
my hand,
establishing[3] the heavens
and laying the foundations of the
earth,
and saying to Zion, 'You are my
people.'"

17 Wake yourself, wake yourself,
stand up, O Jerusalem,
you who have drunk from the hand
of the LORD
the cup of his wrath,
who have drunk to the dregs
the bowl, the cup of staggering.
18 There is none to guide her
among all the sons she has borne;
there is none to take her by the hand
among all the sons she has
brought up.
19 These two things have happened to
you—
who will console you?—
devastation and destruction, famine
and sword;
who will comfort you?[4]

---

[1] Or for teaching; also verse 7 [2] Or will die like gnats [3] Or planting [4] Dead Sea Scroll, Septuagint, Syriac, Vulgate; Masoretic Text how shall
comfort you

20 Your sons have fainted;
    they lie at the head of every street
    like an antelope in a net;
  they are full of the wrath of the LORD,
    the rebuke of your God.

21 Therefore hear this, you who are
    afflicted,
    who are drunk, but not with wine:
22 Thus says your Lord, the LORD,
    your God who pleads the cause of
    his people:
  "Behold, I have taken from your hand
    the cup of staggering;
  the bowl of my wrath you shall drink
    no more;
23 and I will put it into the hand of your
    tormentors,
    who have said to you,
  'Bow down, that we may pass over';
  and you have made your back like
    the ground
    and like the street for them to pass
    over."

The LORD's Coming Salvation

52 Awake, awake,
    put on your strength, O Zion;
  put on your beautiful garments,
    O Jerusalem, the holy city;
  for there shall no more come into you
    the uncircumcised and the unclean.
2 Shake yourself from the dust and
    arise;
  be seated, O Jerusalem;
  loose the bonds from your neck,
    O captive daughter of Zion.

³For thus says the LORD: "You were sold
for nothing, and you shall be redeemed
without money." ⁴For thus says the Lord
GOD: "My people went down at the first
into Egypt to sojourn there, and the
Assyrian oppressed them for nothing.¹
⁵Now therefore what have I here," declares
the LORD, "seeing that my people are taken
away for nothing? Their rulers wail,"
declares the LORD, "and continually all the
day my name is despised. ⁶Therefore my
people shall know my name. Therefore in
that day they shall know that it is I who
speak; here I am."

7 How beautiful upon the mountains
    are the feet of him who brings
    good news,

  who publishes peace, who brings
    good news of happiness,
  who publishes salvation,
    who says to Zion, "Your God reigns."
8 The voice of your watchmen— they
    lift up their voice;
    together they sing for joy;
  for eye to eye they see
    the return of the LORD to Zion.
9 Break forth together into singing,
    you waste places of Jerusalem,
  for the LORD has comforted his
    people;
    he has redeemed Jerusalem.
10 The LORD has bared his holy arm
    before the eyes of all the nations,
  and all the ends of the earth shall see
    the salvation of our God.

11 Depart, depart, go out from there;
    touch no unclean thing;
  go out from the midst of her; purify
    yourselves,
    you who bear the vessels of the
    LORD.
12 For you shall not go out in haste,
    and you shall not go in flight,
  for the LORD will go before you,
    and the God of Israel will be your
    rear guard.

He Was Pierced for Our Transgressions

13 Behold, my servant shall act wisely;²
    he shall be high and lifted up,
    and shall be exalted.
14 As many were astonished at you—
    his appearance was so marred,
    beyond human semblance,
    and his form beyond that of the
    children of mankind—
15 so shall he sprinkle³ many nations;
    kings shall shut their mouths
    because of him;
  for that which has not been told
    them they see,
  and that which they have not
    heard they understand.

53 Who has believed what he has
    heard from us?⁴
  And to whom has the arm of the
    LORD been revealed?
2 For he grew up before him like a
    young plant,
    and like a root out of dry ground;

---

¹Or the Assyrian has oppressed them of late ²Or shall prosper ³Or startle ⁴Or Who has believed what we have heard?

he had no form or majesty that we
    should look at him,
  and no beauty that we should
    desire him.
3 He was despised and rejected[1] by
    men;
  a man of sorrows,[2] and acquainted
    with[3] grief;[4]
and as one from whom men hide
    their faces[5]
  he was despised, and we esteemed
    him not.

4 Surely he has borne our griefs
    and carried our sorrows;
yet we esteemed him stricken,
    smitten by God, and afflicted.
5 But he was pierced for our transgres-
    sions;
  he was crushed for our iniquities;
upon him was the chastisement that
    brought us peace,
  and with his wounds we are
    healed.

6 All we like sheep have gone astray;
    we have turned—every one—to
      his own way;
and the LORD has laid on him
    the iniquity of us all.

7 He was oppressed, and he was
    afflicted,
  yet he opened not his mouth;
like a lamb that is led to the slaughter,
  and like a sheep that before its
    shearers is silent,
  so he opened not his mouth.

8 By oppression and judgment he was
    taken away;
  and as for his generation, who
    considered
that he was cut off out of the land of
    the living,
  stricken for the transgression of
    my people?
9 And they made his grave with the
    wicked
  and with a rich man in his death,

Or forsaken [2]Or pains; also verse 4 [3]Or and knowing [4]Or sickness; also verse 4 [5]Or as one who hides his face from us

Know Yourself

verses to read
Isaiah 53

You've been misunderstood. Slammed. Lied about. Something is going around, and it isn't true. Your choice? Vindication! "I have to explain myself. I have to get them to understand," you say to yourself, and so off you go to fix things, manage the situation, get people to understand. And suddenly God slips from the throne of your life and up onto the throne you crawl to take your "rightful" place.

Screech. "Stop this ride! I wanna get off!" It's time to take a lesson from Jesus and get back on track. Listen, he wasn't in the habit of explaining everything when he was walking on earth. Almost unimaginably, he left misunderstandings to correct themselves—or better said, he left it to God to work things out in the lives of the people who misunderstood him, lied about him, or generally hated him. If you are righteous in God's eyes because of the work of Christ, having been adopted as his daughter, isn't that enough? Do you really need to defend yourself anymore?

Sure, it won't be easy, but godliness rarely is. As long as you are looking for vindication in the eyes of other human beings, you are going to be completely distracted from God. And that distraction will affect your heart, your mind, and your body. Get your focus off the world and onto God. What people think or say has no bearing on eternity. Don't give them more power over you than they deserve, but choose to make your investment in the eternal and let the King work out the temporary for himself.

although he had done no violence,
  and there was no deceit in his
      mouth.

10   Yet it was the will of the LORD to
          crush him;
      he has put him to grief;[1]
  when his soul makes[2] an offering for
      guilt,
  he shall see his offspring; he shall
      prolong his days;
  the will of the LORD shall prosper in
      his hand.

11   Out of the anguish of his soul he shall
          see[3] and be satisfied;
      by his knowledge shall the righteous
          one, my servant,
          make many to be accounted righ-
              teous,
      and he shall bear their iniquities.

12   Therefore I will divide him a portion
          with the many,[4]
      and he shall divide the spoil with
          the strong,[5]
  because he poured out his soul to
      death
      and was numbered with the trans-
          gressors;
  yet he bore the sin of many,
      and makes intercession for the
          transgressors.

The Eternal Covenant of Peace

54

"Sing, O barren one, who did not
    bear;
  break forth into singing and cry
      aloud,
  you who have not been in labor!
For the children of the desolate one
    will be more
  than the children of her who is
      married," says the LORD.

2   "Enlarge the place of your tent,
      and let the curtains of your habita-
          tions be stretched out;
  do not hold back; lengthen your cords
      and strengthen your stakes.
3   For you will spread abroad to the
          right and to the left,
      and your offspring will possess the
          nations
  and will people the desolate cities.

4   "Fear not, for you will not be ashamed;
      be not confounded, for you will not
          be disgraced;
  for you will forget the shame of your
      youth,
      and the reproach of your widow-
          hood you will remember no
          more.
5   For your Maker is your husband,
      the LORD of hosts is his name;
  and the Holy One of Israel is your
      Redeemer,
      the God of the whole earth he is
          called.
6   For the LORD has called you
      like a wife deserted and grieved in
          spirit,
  like a wife of youth when she is cast
      off,
      says your God.
7   For a brief moment I deserted you,
      but with great compassion I will
          gather you.
8   In overflowing anger for a moment
      I hid my face from you,
  but with everlasting love I will have
      compassion on you,"
      says the LORD, your Redeemer.

9   "This is like the days of Noah[6] to me:
      as I swore that the waters of Noah
          should no more go over the earth,
  so I have sworn that I will not be
      angry with you,
      and will not rebuke you.
10   For the mountains may depart
      and the hills be removed,
  but my steadfast love shall not
      depart from you,
      and my covenant of peace shall not
          be removed,"
      says the LORD, who has compas-
          sion on you.

11   "O afflicted one, storm-tossed and not
          comforted,
      behold, I will set your stones in
          antimony,
      and lay your foundations with sap-
          phires.[7]
12   I will make your pinnacles of agate,[8]
      your gates of carbuncles,[9]
      and all your wall of precious stones.

---

[1] Or he has made him sick [2] Or when you make his soul [3] Masoretic Text; Dead Sea Scroll he shall see light [4] Or with the great [5] Or with the numerous [6] Some manuscripts For this is as the waters of Noah [7] Or lapis lazuli [8] Or jasper, or ruby [9] Or crystal

3 All your children shall be taught by
    the Lord,
  and great shall be the peace of
    your children.
4 In righteousness you shall be estab-
    lished;
  you shall be far from oppression,
    for you shall not fear;
  and from terror, for it shall not
    come near you.
5 If anyone stirs up strife,
  it is not from me;
  whoever stirs up strife with you
    shall fall because of you.
6 Behold, I have created the smith
  who blows the fire of coals
  and produces a weapon for its
    purpose.
I have also created the ravager to
    destroy;
7 no weapon that is fashioned
    against you shall succeed,
  and you shall refute every tongue
    that rises against you in judg-
    ment.
This is the heritage of the servants of
    the Lord
  and their vindication[1] from me,
    declares the Lord."

The Compassion of the Lord

55 "Come, everyone who thirsts,
    come to the waters;
and he who has no money,
    come, buy and eat!
Come, buy wine and milk
    without money and without price.
2 Why do you spend your money for
    that which is not bread,
  and your labor for that which does
    not satisfy?
Listen diligently to me, and eat what
    is good,
  and delight yourselves in rich food.
3 Incline your ear, and come to me;
  hear, that your soul may live;
  and I will make with you an everlast-
    ing covenant,
    my steadfast, sure love for David.
4 Behold, I made him a witness to the
    peoples,
  a leader and commander for the
    peoples.

5 Behold, you shall call a nation that
    you do not know,
  and a nation that did not know you
    shall run to you,
because of the Lord your God, and of
    the Holy One of Israel,
  for he has glorified you.

6 "Seek the Lord while he may be found;
  call upon him while he is near;
7 let the wicked forsake his way,
  and the unrighteous man his
    thoughts;
  let him return to the Lord, that he
    may have compassion on him,
  and to our God, for he will abun-
    dantly pardon.
8 For my thoughts are not your
    thoughts,
  neither are your ways my ways,
    declares the Lord.
9 For as the heavens are higher than
    the earth,
  so are my ways higher than your
    ways
  and my thoughts than your
    thoughts.

10 "For as the rain and the snow come
    down from heaven
  and do not return there but water
    the earth,
making it bring forth and sprout,
  giving seed to the sower and bread
    to the eater,
11 so shall my word be that goes out
    from my mouth;
  it shall not return to me empty,
but it shall accomplish that which
    I purpose,
  and shall succeed in the thing for
    which I sent it.

12 "For you shall go out in joy
  and be led forth in peace;
the mountains and the hills before you
  shall break forth into singing,
  and all the trees of the field shall
    clap their hands.
13 Instead of the thorn shall come up
    the cypress;
  instead of the brier shall come up
    the myrtle;
and it shall make a name for the Lord,
  an everlasting sign that shall not
    be cut off."

[1] Or *righteousness*

Salvation for Foreigners

56 Thus says the LORD:
"Keep justice, and do righteousness,
for soon my salvation will come,
and my righteousness be revealed.
2 Blessed is the man who does this,
and the son of man who holds it
fast,
who keeps the Sabbath, not profaning it,
and keeps his hand from doing any
evil."

3 Let not the foreigner who has joined
himself to the LORD say,
"The LORD will surely separate me
from his people";
and let not the eunuch say,
"Behold, I am a dry tree."
4 For thus says the LORD:
"To the eunuchs who keep my
Sabbaths,
who choose the things that
please me
and hold fast my covenant,
5 I will give in my house and within my
walls
a monument and a name
better than sons and daughters;
I will give them an everlasting name
that shall not be cut off.

6 "And the foreigners who join themselves to the LORD,
to minister to him, to love the
name of the LORD,
and to be his servants,
everyone who keeps the Sabbath and
does not profane it,
and holds fast my covenant—
7 these I will bring to my holy mountain,
and make them joyful in my house
of prayer;
their burnt offerings and their sacrifices
will be accepted on my altar;
for my house shall be called a house
of prayer
for all peoples."
8 The Lord GOD,
who gathers the outcasts of Israel,
declares,

"I will gather yet others to him
besides those already gathered."

Israel's Irresponsible Leaders

9 All you beasts of the field, come to
devour—
all you beasts in the forest.
10 His watchmen are blind;
they are all without knowledge;
they are all silent dogs;
they cannot bark,
dreaming, lying down,
loving to slumber.
11 The dogs have a mighty appetite;
they never have enough.
But they are shepherds who have no
understanding;
they have all turned to their own
way,
each to his own gain, one and all.
12 "Come," they say, "let me get wine;
let us fill ourselves with strong
drink;
and tomorrow will be like this day,
great beyond measure."

Israel's Futile Idolatry

57 The righteous man perishes,
and no one lays it to heart;
devout men are taken away,
while no one understands.
For the righteous man is taken away
from calamity;
2 he enters into peace;
they rest in their beds
who walk in their uprightness.
3 But you, draw near,
sons of the sorceress,
offspring of the adulterer and the
loose woman.
4 Whom are you mocking?
Against whom do you open your
mouth wide
and stick out your tongue?
Are you not children of transgression,
the offspring of deceit,
5 you who burn with lust among the
oaks,[1]
under every green tree,
who slaughter your children in the
valleys,
under the clefts of the rocks?
6 Among the smooth stones of the valley is your portion;
they, they, are your lot;

[1] Or among the terebinths

to them you have poured out a drink
  offering,
    you have brought a grain offering.
    Shall I relent for these things?
7 On a high and lofty mountain
    you have set your bed,
    and there you went up to offer
      sacrifice.
8 Behind the door and the doorpost
    you have set up your memorial;
  for, deserting me, you have uncov-
    ered your bed,
    you have gone up to it,
    you have made it wide;
  and you have made a covenant for
    yourself with them,
    you have loved their bed,
    you have looked on nakedness.[1]
9 You journeyed to the king with oil
    and multiplied your perfumes;
  you sent your envoys far off,
    and sent down even to Sheol.
10 You were wearied with the length of
    your way,
    but you did not say, "It is hopeless";
  you found new life for your strength,
    and so you were not faint.[2]

11 Whom did you dread and fear,
    so that you lied,
  and did not remember me,
    did not lay it to heart?
  Have I not held my peace, even for a
    long time,
    and you do not fear me?
12 I will declare your righteousness and
    your deeds,
    but they will not profit you.
13 When you cry out, let your collection
    of idols deliver you!
  The wind will carry them all off,
    a breath will take them away.
  But he who takes refuge in me shall
    possess the land
    and shall inherit my holy mountain.

Comfort for the Contrite

14 And it shall be said,
  "Build up, build up, prepare the way,
    remove every obstruction from my
      people's way."
15 For thus says the One who is high
    and lifted up,
    who inhabits eternity, whose name
      is Holy:

"I dwell in the high and holy place,
    and also with him who is of a
      contrite and lowly spirit,
  to revive the spirit of the lowly,
    and to revive the heart of the con-
      trite.
16 For I will not contend forever,
    nor will I always be angry;
  for the spirit would grow faint before
    me,
    and the breath of life that I made.
17 Because of the iniquity of his unjust
    gain I was angry,
  I struck him; I hid my face and was
    angry,
    but he went on backsliding in the
      way of his own heart.
18 I have seen his ways, but I will heal
    him;
  I will lead him and restore comfort
    to him and his mourners,
19   creating the fruit of the lips.
  Peace, peace, to the far and to the
      near," says the LORD,
    "and I will heal him.
20 But the wicked are like the tossing
    sea;
  for it cannot be quiet,
    and its waters toss up mire and dirt.
21 There is no peace," says my God, "for
    the wicked."

True and False Fasting

58 "Cry aloud; do not hold back;
    lift up your voice like a trumpet;
  declare to my people their transgres-
    sion,
    to the house of Jacob their sins.
2 Yet they seek me daily
    and delight to know my ways,
  as if they were a nation that did
      righteousness
    and did not forsake the judgment
      of their God;
  they ask of me righteous judgments;
    they delight to draw near to God.
3 'Why have we fasted, and you see it
    not?
  Why have we humbled ourselves,
    and you take no knowledge of
      it?'
  Behold, in the day of your fast you
    seek your own pleasure,[3]
    and oppress all your workers.

Or on a monument (see 56:5); Hebrew on a hand [2] Hebrew and so you were not sick [3] Or pursue your own business

4 Behold, you fast only to quarrel and to fight
    and to hit with a wicked fist.
  Fasting like yours this day
    will not make your voice to be heard on high.
5 Is such the fast that I choose,
    a day for a person to humble himself?
  Is it to bow down his head like a reed,
    and to spread sackcloth and ashes under him?
  Will you call this a fast,
    and a day acceptable to the LORD?

6 "Is not this the fast that I choose:
    to loose the bonds of wickedness,
    to undo the straps of the yoke,
  to let the oppressed[1] go free,
    and to break every yoke?
7 Is it not to share your bread with the hungry
    and bring the homeless poor into your house;
  when you see the naked, to cover him,
    and not to hide yourself from your own flesh?
8 Then shall your light break forth like the dawn,
    and your healing shall spring up speedily;
  your righteousness shall go before you;
    the glory of the LORD shall be your rear guard.
9 Then you shall call, and the LORD will answer;
    you shall cry, and he will say, 'Here I am.'
  If you take away the yoke from your midst,
    the pointing of the finger, and speaking wickedness,
10 if you pour yourself out for the hungry
    and satisfy the desire of the afflicted,
  then shall your light rise in the darkness
    and your gloom be as the noonday.
11 And the LORD will guide you continually
    and satisfy your desire in scorched places
    and make your bones strong;

and you shall be like a watered garden,
    like a spring of water,
    whose waters do not fail.
12 And your ancient ruins shall be rebuilt;
    you shall raise up the foundations of many generations;
  you shall be called the repairer of the breach,
    the restorer of streets to dwell in.

13 "If you turn back your foot from the Sabbath,
    from doing your pleasure[2] on my holy day,
  and call the Sabbath a delight
    and the holy day of the LORD honorable;
  if you honor it, not going your own ways,
    or seeking your own pleasure,[3] or talking idly;[4]
14 then you shall take delight in the LORD,
    and I will make you ride on the heights of the earth;[5]
  I will feed you with the heritage of Jacob your father,
    for the mouth of the LORD has spoken."

Evil and Oppression

59 Behold, the LORD's hand is not shortened, that it cannot save,
    or his ear dull, that it cannot hear;
2 but your iniquities have made a separation
    between you and your God,
  and your sins have hidden his face from you
    so that he does not hear.
3 For your hands are defiled with blood
    and your fingers with iniquity;
  your lips have spoken lies;
    your tongue mutters wickedness.
4 No one enters suit justly;
    no one goes to law honestly;
  they rely on empty pleas, they speak lies,
    they conceive mischief and give birth to iniquity.
5 They hatch adders' eggs;
    they weave the spider's web;

[1] Or bruised [2] Or business [3] Or pursuing your own business [4] Hebrew or speaking a word [5] Or of the land

he who eats their eggs dies,
  and from one that is crushed a
    viper is hatched.
6 Their webs will not serve as cloth-
    ing;
  men will not cover themselves
    with what they make.
Their works are works of iniquity,
  and deeds of violence are in their
    hands.
7 Their feet run to evil,
  and they are swift to shed inno-
    cent blood;
their thoughts are thoughts of iniq-
    uity;
  desolation and destruction are in
    their highways.
8 The way of peace they do not know,
  and there is no justice in their
    paths;
they have made their roads
    crooked;
  no one who treads on them knows
    peace.

9 Therefore justice is far from us,
  and righteousness does not over-
    take us;

we hope for light, and behold, dark-
    ness,
  and for brightness, but we walk in
    gloom.
10 We grope for the wall like the blind;
  we grope like those who have no
    eyes;
we stumble at noon as in the twi-
    light,
  among those in full vigor we are
    like dead men.
11 We all growl like bears;
  we moan and moan like doves;
we hope for justice, but there is
    none;
  for salvation, but it is far from us.
12 For our transgressions are multi-
    plied before you,
  and our sins testify against us;
for our transgressions are with us,
  and we know our iniquities:
13 transgressing, and denying the
    LORD,
  and turning back from following
    our God,
speaking oppression and revolt,
  conceiving and uttering from the
    heart lying words.

verses to read
Isaiah 59:1–2

Know Love

Do you have a sin in your life that you just can't walk away from? If your answer is yes, then don't be surprised if life is miserable. When sin becomes so important to you that you won't give it up even though you've spotted it, then you've let that sin become more important than God. Life will be miserable as long as you are your own master.

God does not draw near to those who cherish secret sins that they know are wrong. Be careful not to say, "I've tried to stop it, but it's just too hard." That's like saying, "I know sin is bad, but it's worse to walk away from it than to keep it." By God's Spirit, through his enabling power, you are now able to say no to sin and discover what true pleasure—not the shallow pleasures of sin—really is.

Look for those areas where you struggle, and see if you aren't refusing to drop the hand of sin and reach for the hand of God. A lot of people say that it's too difficult to stop a particular sinful habit, but as a follower of Christ you are actually able to change. According to Jesus, sin is no longer your master—he is. When you disagree, you are saying that Jesus is wrong, and you are giving the sin in your life the role of master. Remember, you can't serve two masters. So choose today whom you're going to serve.

Judgment and Redemption

14 Justice is turned back,
    and righteousness stands far
      away;
  for truth has stumbled in the public
      squares,
    and uprightness cannot enter.
15 Truth is lacking,
    and he who departs from evil
      makes himself a prey.

  The Lord saw it, and it displeased
      him[1]
    that there was no justice.
16 He saw that there was no man,
    and wondered that there was no
      one to intercede;
  then his own arm brought him salva-
      tion,
    and his righteousness upheld him.
17 He put on righteousness as a breast-
      plate,
    and a helmet of salvation on his
      head;
  he put on garments of vengeance for
      clothing,
    and wrapped himself in zeal as a
      cloak.
18 According to their deeds, so will he
      repay,
    wrath to his adversaries, repay-
      ment to his enemies;
    to the coastlands he will render
      repayment.
19 So they shall fear the name of the
      Lord from the west,
    and his glory from the rising of the
      sun;
  for he will come like a rushing
      stream,[2]
    which the wind of the Lord drives.

20 "And a Redeemer will come to Zion,
    to those in Jacob who turn from
      transgression," declares the
      Lord.

21 "And as for me, this is my covenant with
them," says the Lord: "My Spirit that is
upon you, and my words that I have put in
your mouth, shall not depart out of your
mouth, or out of the mouth of your offspring, or out of the mouth of your children's offspring," says the Lord, "from this
time forth and forevermore."

The Future Glory of Israel

60

Arise, shine, for your light has
    come,
  and the glory of the Lord has risen
    upon you.
2 For behold, darkness shall cover the
    earth,
    and thick darkness the peoples;
  but the Lord will arise upon you,
    and his glory will be seen upon you.
3 And nations shall come to your light,
    and kings to the brightness of your
      rising.

4 Lift up your eyes all around, and see;
    they all gather together, they come
      to you;
  your sons shall come from afar,
    and your daughters shall be car-
      ried on the hip.
5 Then you shall see and be radiant;
    your heart shall thrill and exult,[3]
  because the abundance of the sea
      shall be turned to you,
    the wealth of the nations shall
      come to you.
6 A multitude of camels shall cover you,
    the young camels of Midian and
      Ephah;
    all those from Sheba shall come.
  They shall bring gold and frankin-
      cense,
    and shall bring good news, the
      praises of the Lord.
7 All the flocks of Kedar shall be gath-
      ered to you;
    the rams of Nebaioth shall minis-
      ter to you;
  they shall come up with acceptance
      on my altar,
    and I will beautify my beautiful
      house.

8 Who are these that fly like a cloud,
    and like doves to their windows?
9 For the coastlands shall hope for me,
    the ships of Tarshish first,
  to bring your children from afar,
    their silver and gold with them,
  for the name of the Lord your God,
    and for the Holy One of Israel,
    because he has made you beautiful.

10 Foreigners shall build up your walls,
    and their kings shall minister to
      you;

---

[1] Hebrew *and it was evil in his eyes* [2] Hebrew *a narrow river* [3] Hebrew *your heart shall tremble and grow wide*

for in my wrath I struck you,
    but in my favor I have had mercy
        on you.
Your gates shall be open continually;
    day and night they shall not be shut,
that people may bring to you the
        wealth of the nations,
    with their kings led in procession.
For the nation and kingdom
    that will not serve you shall perish;
    those nations shall be utterly laid
        waste.
The glory of Lebanon shall come to
        you,
    the cypress, the plane, and the pine,
to beautify the place of my sanctuary,
    and I will make the place of my
        feet glorious.
The sons of those who afflicted you
    shall come bending low to you,
and all who despised you
    shall bow down at your feet;
they shall call you the City of the LORD,
    the Zion of the Holy One of Israel.

Whereas you have been forsaken and
        hated,
    with no one passing through,
I will make you majestic forever,
    a joy from age to age.
You shall suck the milk of nations;
    you shall nurse at the breast of
        kings;
and you shall know that I, the LORD,
        am your Savior
    and your Redeemer, the Mighty
        One of Jacob.

Instead of bronze I will bring gold,
    and instead of iron I will bring
        silver;
instead of wood, bronze,
    instead of stones, iron.
I will make your overseers peace
    and your taskmasters righteous-
        ness.
Violence shall no more be heard in
        your land,
    devastation or destruction within
        your borders;
you shall call your walls Salvation,
    and your gates Praise.

The sun shall be no more
    your light by day,

nor for brightness shall the moon
    give you light;[1]
but the LORD will be your everlasting
        light,
    and your God will be your glory.[2]
20 Your sun shall no more go down,
    nor your moon withdraw itself;
for the LORD will be your everlasting
        light,
    and your days of mourning shall
        be ended.
21 Your people shall all be righteous;
    they shall possess the land forever,
the branch of my planting, the work
    of my hands,
    that I might be glorified.[3]
22 The least one shall become a clan,
    and the smallest one a mighty
        nation;
I am the LORD;
    in its time I will hasten it.

The Year of the LORD's Favor

61 The Spirit of the Lord GOD is
        upon me,
    because the LORD has anointed me
to bring good news to the poor;[4]
    he has sent me to bind up the
        brokenhearted,
to proclaim liberty to the captives,
    and the opening of the prison to
        those who are bound;[5]
2 to proclaim the year of the LORD's
        favor,
    and the day of vengeance of our
        God;
    to comfort all who mourn;
3 to grant to those who mourn in Zion—
    to give them a beautiful headdress
        instead of ashes,
the oil of gladness instead of mourn-
        ing,
    the garment of praise instead of a
        faint spirit;
that they may be called oaks of righ-
        teousness,
    the planting of the LORD, that he
        may be glorified.[6]
4 They shall build up the ancient ruins;
    they shall raise up the former
        devastations;
they shall repair the ruined cities,
    the devastations of many genera-
        tions.

Masoretic Text; Dead Sea Scroll, Septuagint, Targum add *by night* [2]Or *your beauty* [3]Or *that I might display my beauty* [4]Or *afflicted*
Or *the opening* [of the eyes] *to those who are blind*; Septuagint *and recovery of sight to the blind* [6]Or *that he may display his beauty*

5 Strangers shall stand and tend your
　　flocks;
　　　foreigners shall be your plowmen
　　　　and vinedressers;
6 but you shall be called the priests of
　　the LORD;
　　　they shall speak of you as the min-
　　　　isters of our God;
　　you shall eat the wealth of the
　　　　nations,
　　　and in their glory you shall boast.
7 Instead of your shame there shall be
　　a double portion;
　　　instead of dishonor they shall
　　　　rejoice in their lot;
　　therefore in their land they shall pos-
　　　　sess a double portion;
　　　they shall have everlasting joy.

8 For I the LORD love justice;
　　I hate robbery and wrong;[1]
　　I will faithfully give them their rec-
　　　　ompense,
　　　and I will make an everlasting cov-
　　　　enant with them.
9 Their offspring shall be known
　　among the nations,
　　　and their descendants in the midst
　　　　of the peoples;
　　all who see them shall acknowledge
　　　　them,
　　　that they are an offspring the LORD
　　　　has blessed.

10 I will greatly rejoice in the LORD;
　　my soul shall exult in my God,
　　for he has clothed me with the gar-
　　　　ments of salvation;
　　　he has covered me with the robe of
　　　　righteousness,
　　as a bridegroom decks himself like a
　　　　priest with a beautiful head-
　　　　dress,
　　　and as a bride adorns herself with
　　　　her jewels.
11 For as the earth brings forth its
　　sprouts,
　　　and as a garden causes what is
　　　　sown in it to sprout up,
　　so the Lord GOD will cause righteous-
　　　　ness and praise
　　　to sprout up before all the
　　　　nations.

Zion's Coming Salvation

62 For Zion's sake I will not keep
　　silent,
　　　and for Jerusalem's sake I will not
　　　　be quiet,
　　until her righteousness goes forth as
　　　　brightness,
　　　and her salvation as a burning
　　　　torch.
2 The nations shall see your righteous-
　　ness,
　　　and all the kings your glory,
　　and you shall be called by a new name
　　　that the mouth of the LORD will give.
3 You shall be a crown of beauty in the
　　hand of the LORD,
　　　and a royal diadem in the hand of
　　　　your God.
4 You shall no more be termed
　　Forsaken,[2]
　　　and your land shall no more be
　　　　termed Desolate,[3]
　　but you shall be called My Delight Is
　　　　in Her,[4]
　　　and your land Married;[5]
　　for the LORD delights in you,
　　　and your land shall be married.
5 For as a young man marries a young
　　woman,
　　　so shall your sons marry you,
　　and as the bridegroom rejoices over
　　　　the bride,
　　　so shall your God rejoice over you.

6 On your walls, O Jerusalem,
　　I have set watchmen;
　　all the day and all the night
　　　they shall never be silent.
　　You who put the LORD in remem-
　　　　brance,
　　　take no rest,
7 and give him no rest
　　　until he establishes Jerusalem
　　　and makes it a praise in the earth.
8 The LORD has sworn by his right
　　hand
　　　and by his mighty arm:
　　"I will not again give your grain
　　　to be food for your enemies,
　　and foreigners shall not drink your
　　　　wine
　　　for which you have labored;
9 but those who garner it shall eat it
　　and praise the LORD,

[1] Or robbery with a burnt offering　[2] Hebrew Azubah　[3] Hebrew Shemamah　[4] Hebrew Hephzibah　[5] Hebrew Beulah

and those who gather it shall drink it
   in the courts of my sanctuary."[1]

10 Go through, go through the gates;
   prepare the way for the people;
build up, build up the highway;
   clear it of stones;
lift up a signal over the peoples.
11 Behold, the LORD has proclaimed
   to the end of the earth:
Say to the daughter of Zion,
   "Behold, your salvation comes;
behold, his reward is with him,
   and his recompense before him."
12 And they shall be called The Holy
   People,
   The Redeemed of the LORD;
and you shall be called Sought Out,
   A City Not Forsaken.

The LORD's Day of Vengeance

63 Who is this who comes from
   Edom,
   in crimsoned garments from
   Bozrah,
he who is splendid in his apparel,
   marching in the greatness of his
   strength?
"It is I, speaking in righteousness,
   mighty to save."

2 Why is your apparel red,
   and your garments like his who
   treads in the winepress?

3 "I have trodden the winepress alone,
   and from the peoples no one was
   with me;
I trod them in my anger
   and trampled them in my wrath;
their lifeblood[2] spattered on my garments,
   and stained all my apparel.
4 For the day of vengeance was in my
   heart,
   and my year of redemption[3] had
   come.
5 I looked, but there was no one to help;
   I was appalled, but there was no
   one to uphold;

[1] Or *in my holy courts* [2] Or *their juice; also verse 6* [3] Or *the year of my redeemed*

verse to read
Isaiah 62:6

The strong Christian is the one who has a life filled with prayer. Prayerlessness leaves a believer weakened and fearful. When your heart is growing cold, when hope is lost, when emotions run wild, the first place to look is your prayerlessness. When a God Girl prays, she calls on the name of the Lord and he listens. She makes it clear to herself and to her God who is the most important person of all. She places more emphasis on communion with God than on pleasure, busyness, and distraction. Prayerlessness is one of the most common weaknesses in the life of a believer. But when you don't pray you are failing to worship the God who has rescued you. Prayerlessness can derail even the strongest believer. If your life isn't producing everything you imagined it would, then look at your prayer life. The amount of time you spend speaking with God, pleading with him, and seeking his mind directly affects your success in every area of your life.

When a God Girl prays, remembering that Jesus has given her full access to the Father, she finds doors that were slammed shut opening in front of her. She finds life changing all around her and within her. She releases the power of the Holy Spirit in her life and begins to find more hope and peace than she ever dreamed existed. You can't afford to accept prayerlessness in your life. Fight to devote your mind and time to the pursuit of communion with the Creator of the universe and Lover of your soul.

so my own arm brought me salvation,
  and my wrath upheld me.
6 I trampled down the peoples in my
    anger;
  I made them drunk in my wrath,
  and I poured out their lifeblood on
    the earth."

The Lord's Mercy Remembered

7 I will recount the steadfast love of
    the Lord,
  the praises of the Lord,
according to all that the Lord has
    granted us,
  and the great goodness to the
    house of Israel
that he has granted them according
    to his compassion,
  according to the abundance of his
    steadfast love.
8 For he said, "Surely they are my
    people,
  children who will not deal falsely."
  And he became their Savior.
9 In all their affliction he was afflicted,[1]
  and the angel of his presence
    saved them;
  in his love and in his pity he
    redeemed them;
  he lifted them up and carried them
    all the days of old.

10 But they rebelled
  and grieved his Holy Spirit;
therefore he turned to be their enemy,
  and himself fought against them.
11 Then he remembered the days of old,
    of Moses and his people.[2]
  Where is he who brought them up
    out of the sea
  with the shepherds of his flock?
  Where is he who put in the midst of
    them
  his Holy Spirit,
12 who caused his glorious arm
    to go at the right hand of Moses,
who divided the waters before them
    to make for himself an everlasting
      name,
13 who led them through the depths?
  Like a horse in the desert,
  they did not stumble.

14 Like livestock that go down into the
    valley,
  the Spirit of the Lord gave them
    rest.
So you led your people,
  to make for yourself a glorious
    name.

Prayer for Mercy

15 Look down from heaven and see,
  from your holy and beautiful[3]
    habitation.
  Where are your zeal and your might?
  The stirring of your inner parts
    and your compassion
  are held back from me.
16 For you are our Father,
  though Abraham does not know us,
  and Israel does not acknowledge us;
you, O Lord, are our Father,
  our Redeemer from of old is your
    name.
17 O Lord, why do you make us wander
    from your ways
  and harden our heart, so that we
    fear you not?
Return for the sake of your servants,
  the tribes of your heritage.
18 Your holy people held possession for
    a little while;[4]
  our adversaries have trampled
    down your sanctuary.
19 We have become like those over
    whom you have never ruled,
  like those who are not called by
    your name.

64 Oh that you would rend the heav-
    ens and come down,
  that the mountains might quake at
    your presence—
25 as when fire kindles brushwood
    and the fire causes water to boil—
to make your name known to your
    adversaries,
  and that the nations might tremble
    at your presence!
3 When you did awesome things that
    we did not look for,
  you came down, the mountains
    quaked at your presence.
4 From of old no one has heard
  or perceived by the ear,

---

[1] Or he did not afflict [2] Or Then his people remembered the days of old, of Moses [3] Or holy and glorious [4] Or They have dispossessed your holy people for a little while [5] Ch 64:1 in Hebrew

no eye has seen a God besides you,
    who acts for those who wait for
        him.

5 You meet him who joyfully works
     righteousness,
    those who remember you in your
        ways.
    Behold, you were angry, and we
        sinned;
    in our sins we have been a long
        time, and shall we be saved?[1]

6 We have all become like one who is
     unclean,
    and all our righteous deeds are
        like a polluted garment.
    We all fade like a leaf,
    and our iniquities, like the wind,
        take us away.

7 There is no one who calls upon your
     name,
    who rouses himself to take hold of
        you;
    for you have hidden your face from us,
    and have made us melt in[2] the
        hand of our iniquities.

8 But now, O LORD, you are our Father;
    we are the clay, and you are our
        potter;
    we are all the work of your hand.

9 Be not so terribly angry, O LORD,
    and remember not iniquity forever.
    Behold, please look, we are all
        your people.

10 Your holy cities have become a wil-
     derness;
    Zion has become a wilderness,
        Jerusalem a desolation.

11 Our holy and beautiful[3] house,
    where our fathers praised you,
        has been burned by fire,
    and all our pleasant places have
        become ruins.

12 Will you restrain yourself at these
     things, O LORD?
    Will you keep silent, and afflict us
        so terribly?

Judgment and Salvation

65 I was ready to be sought by those
    who did not ask for me;
    I was ready to be found by those
     who did not seek me.

I said, "Here I am, here I am,"
    to a nation that was not called by[4]
        my name.

2 I spread out my hands all the day
    to a rebellious people,
    who walk in a way that is not good,
        following their own devices;

3 a people who provoke me
    to my face continually,
    sacrificing in gardens
        and making offerings on bricks;

4 who sit in tombs,
    and spend the night in secret
        places;
    who eat pig's flesh,
    and broth of tainted meat is in
        their vessels;

5 who say, "Keep to yourself,
    do not come near me, for I am too
        holy for you."
    These are a smoke in my nostrils,
     a fire that burns all the day.

6 Behold, it is written before me:
    "I will not keep silent, but I will
        repay;
    I will indeed repay into their lap

7 both your iniquities and your
        fathers' iniquities together,
                says the LORD;
    because they made offerings on the
        mountains
    and insulted me on the hills,
    I will measure into their lap
        payment for their former deeds."[5]

8 Thus says the LORD:
"As the new wine is found in the
     cluster,
    and they say, 'Do not destroy it,
        for there is a blessing in it,'
    so I will do for my servants' sake,
     and not destroy them all.

9 I will bring forth offspring from Jacob,
    and from Judah possessors of my
        mountains;
    my chosen shall possess it,
    and my servants shall dwell there.

10 Sharon shall become a pasture for
     flocks,
    and the Valley of Achor a place for
        herds to lie down,
    for my people who have sought me.

11 But you who forsake the LORD,
    who forget my holy mountain,

---

[1] Or in your ways is continuance, that we might be saved   [2] Masoretic Text; Septuagint, Syriac, Targum *have delivered us into*   [3] Or holy and glorious   [4] Or that did not call upon   [5] Or I will first measure their payment into their lap

who set a table for Fortune
    and fill cups of mixed wine for
        Destiny,
[12] I will destine you to the sword,
    and all of you shall bow down to
        the slaughter,
because, when I called, you did not
    answer;
    when I spoke, you did not listen,
but you did what was evil in my eyes
    and chose what I did not delight in."

[13] Therefore thus says the Lord GOD:
"Behold, my servants shall eat,
    but you shall be hungry;
behold, my servants shall drink,
    but you shall be thirsty;
behold, my servants shall rejoice,
    but you shall be put to shame;
[14] behold, my servants shall sing for
        gladness of heart,
    but you shall cry out for pain of
        heart
    and shall wail for breaking of spirit.
[15] You shall leave your name to my
        chosen for a curse,
    and the Lord GOD will put you to
        death,
    but his servants he will call by
        another name.
[16] So that he who blesses himself in the
        land
    shall bless himself by the God of
        truth,
and he who takes an oath in the land
    shall swear by the God of truth;
because the former troubles are
        forgotten
    and are hidden from my eyes.

New Heavens and a New Earth

[17] "For behold, I create new heavens
        and a new earth,
    and the former things shall not be
        remembered
        or come into mind.
[18] But be glad and rejoice forever
    in that which I create;
for behold, I create Jerusalem to be a
        joy,
    and her people to be a gladness.
[19] I will rejoice in Jerusalem
    and be glad in my people;

no more shall be heard in it the
        sound of weeping
    and the cry of distress.
[20] No more shall there be in it
    an infant who lives but a few days,
    or an old man who does not fill out
        his days,
for the young man shall die a hun-
        dred years old,
    and the sinner a hundred years old
        shall be accursed.
[21] They shall build houses and inhabit
        them;
    they shall plant vineyards and eat
        their fruit.
[22] They shall not build and another
        inhabit;
    they shall not plant and another eat;
for like the days of a tree shall the
        days of my people be,
    and my chosen shall long enjoy[1]
        the work of their hands.
[23] They shall not labor in vain
    or bear children for calamity,[2]
for they shall be the offspring of the
        blessed of the LORD,
    and their descendants with them.
[24] Before they call I will answer;
    while they are yet speaking I will
        hear.
[25] The wolf and the lamb shall graze
        together;
    the lion shall eat straw like the ox,
    and dust shall be the serpent's food.
They shall not hurt or destroy
    in all my holy mountain,"
                    says the LORD.

The Humble and Contrite in Spirit

66 Thus says the LORD:
    "Heaven is my throne,
    and the earth is my footstool;
what is the house that you would
        build for me,
    and what is the place of my rest?
[2] All these things my hand has made,
    and so all these things came to be,
                    declares the LORD.
But this is the one to whom I will look:
    he who is humble and contrite in
        spirit
    and trembles at my word.

[1] Hebrew *shall wear out* [2] Or *for sudden terror*

3 "He who slaughters an ox is like one
      who kills a man;
   he who sacrifices a lamb, like one
      who breaks a dog's neck;
   he who presents a grain offering, like
      one who offers pig's blood;
   he who makes a memorial offering
      of frankincense, like one who
      blesses an idol.
 These have chosen their own ways,
   and their soul delights in their
      abominations;
4 I also will choose harsh treatment
      for them
   and bring their fears upon them,
 because when I called, no one
      answered,
   when I spoke, they did not listen;
 but they did what was evil in my eyes
   and chose that in which I did not
      delight."

5 Hear the word of the Lord,
   you who tremble at his word:
 "Your brothers who hate you
   and cast you out for my name's sake
 have said, 'Let the Lord be glorified,
   that we may see your joy';
   but it is they who shall be put to
      shame.

6 "The sound of an uproar from the city!
   A sound from the temple!
 The sound of the Lord,
   rendering recompense to his
      enemies!

Rejoice with Jerusalem

7 "Before she was in labor
   she gave birth;
 before her pain came upon her
   she delivered a son.
8 Who has heard such a thing?
   Who has seen such things?
 Shall a land be born in one day?
   Shall a nation be brought forth in
      one moment?
 For as soon as Zion was in labor
   she brought forth her children.
9 Shall I bring to the point of birth and
      not cause to bring forth?"
   says the Lord;
 "shall I, who cause to bring forth, shut
      the womb?"
   says your God.

10 "Rejoice with Jerusalem, and be glad
      for her,
   all you who love her;
 rejoice with her in joy,
   all you who mourn over her;
11 that you may nurse and be satisfied
      from her consoling breast;
 that you may drink deeply with
      delight
   from her glorious abundance."[1]

12 For thus says the Lord:
 "Behold, I will extend peace to her
      like a river,
   and the glory of the nations like an
      overflowing stream;
 and you shall nurse, you shall be car-
      ried upon her hip,
   and bounced upon her knees.
13 As one whom his mother comforts,
   so I will comfort you;
 you shall be comforted in
      Jerusalem.
14 You shall see, and your heart shall
      rejoice;
   your bones shall flourish like the
      grass;
 and the hand of the Lord shall be
      known to his servants,
   and he shall show his indignation
      against his enemies.

Final Judgment and Glory of the Lord

15 "For behold, the Lord will come in fire,
   and his chariots like the whirlwind,
 to render his anger in fury,
   and his rebuke with flames of fire.
16 For by fire will the Lord enter into
      judgment,
   and by his sword, with all flesh;
   and those slain by the Lord shall
      be many.

17 "Those who sanctify and purify themselves to go into the gardens, following
one in the midst, eating pig's flesh and the
abomination and mice, shall come to an
end together, declares the Lord.
18 "For I know[2] their works and their
thoughts, and the time is coming[3] to gather
all nations and tongues. And they shall
come and shall see my glory, 19and I will set
a sign among them. And from them I will
send survivors to the nations, to Tarshish,
Pul, and Lud, who draw the bow, to Tubal
and Javan, to the coastlands far away, that

[1] Or breast [2] Septuagint, Syriac; Hebrew lacks know [3] Hebrew and it is coming

have not heard my fame or seen my glory. And they shall declare my glory among the nations. [20] And they shall bring all your brothers from all the nations as an offering to the LORD, on horses and in chariots and in litters and on mules and on dromedaries, to my holy mountain Jerusalem, says the LORD, just as the Israelites bring their grain offering in a clean vessel to the house of the LORD. [21] And some of them also I will take for priests and for Levites, says the LORD.

[22]   "For as the new heavens and the new earth
      that I make

shall remain before me, says the LORD,
   so shall your offspring and your name remain.
[23]   From new moon to new moon,
      and from Sabbath to Sabbath,
   all flesh shall come to worship before me,
      declares the LORD.

[24] "And they shall go out and look on the dead bodies of the men who have rebelled against me. For their worm shall not die, their fire shall not be quenched, and they shall be an abhorrence to all flesh."

INTRODUCTION TO

Jeremiah

Accept Correction

> "To whom shall I speak and give warning,
>   that they may hear?
> Behold, their ears are uncircumcised,
>   they cannot listen."

Jeremiah 6:10

Authors: Jeremiah and his assistant Baruch

Time: Sometime after 586 B.C.

Place: Judah

Written to: The kingdom of Judah

The gist

Jeremiah wrote to show the people their idolatry in turning from serving God and the imminent destruction that would come because of it. But Jeremiah also points to their salvation, and to ours, as he prophesies about the coming Messiah.

Things to look for

- Jeremiah's anguish over the destruction of Judah (see Jer. 4:19–21)
- Jeremiah's extended description of God's coming restoration of his people (see Jeremiah 30–33)

When God talks, do you listen? Or do you change the subject? Hearing from God isn't always a good feeling and doesn't always sound heavenly. A lot of times it's a pain, and nothing you want to hear. It can be like a rude awakening to get an unwanted reminder of your own imperfection, and the easy response is to say, "So what?" "That's just how I am," or "Nobody's perfect." But the better way to handle a correction, whether it comes as a heavenly tap or as a rude slap from an unloving human being, is with humility and sanctification in mind. Brushing off correction or admonishment is never a good idea, so the smart girl thinks it over and compares it with God's Word to see if what she's hearing sounds like a message from God. Nobody grows in godliness without facing the ugly truth about themselves from time to time. So this isn't a reason to feel depressed or to freak out but a chance, by God's grace, to reset and think about a new path, a new way of thinking or acting.

The prophet Jeremiah warned God's people of the sinful path they were walking down, but even though he spoke for God, he was most often rejected and feared by the people, who didn't want to be told they were doing anything wrong. As you read Jeremiah, look at how easy it was for the people to choose their sin over God's correction, but also look at how God never gave up on his people, because of his great love for them and the covenant promises he had made.

Not everything that everyone tells you about yourself is true, but the God Girl looks at correction as a chance to find out more about what pleases God and really to look at her own motives and desires with regard to what she's hearing. When you are corrected, your best response is always to choose not to blame the person who's correcting you but to try to find some truth in their words. Humility is never a bad or even a weak choice but always a godly one. Don't be quick to be hurt or offended, but be quick to prayerfully and thoughtfully consider what God might be trying to tell you.

Must-Know Facts, Terms, and Verses

† Jeremiah didn't always like being a prophet. He complained a lot about how lonely it was, like in Jeremiah 15:10–21 and 20:7–18.

Branch of Righteousness or a Righteous Branch for David

A name referring to the Messiah who will come from the line of David (see Jer. 23:5–6).

Cistern

An underground tank or chamber for storing water. A dry one is used as a holding cell for prisoners in Jeremiah 38:6.

Queen of Heaven

The goddess Ishtar, goddess of war and fertility (see Jer. 44:18).

"Do not be afraid of them,
for I am with you to deliver you,
declares the LORD." *Jeremiah 1:8*

"'Obey my voice, and I will be your God, and you shall be my people. And walk in all the way that I command you, that it may be well with you.'" *Jeremiah 7:23*

The heart is deceitful above all things,
and desperately sick;
who can understand it? *Jeremiah 17:9*

"For I know the plans I have for you, declares the LORD, plans for welfare and not for evil, to give you a future and a hope." *Jeremiah 29:11*

"They shall be my people, and I will be their God. I will give them one heart and one way, that they may fear me forever, for their own good and the good of their children after them. I will make with them an everlasting covenant, that I will not turn away from doing good to them. And I will put the fear of me in their hearts, that they may not turn from me. I will rejoice in doing them good, and I will plant them in this land in faithfulness, with all my heart and all my soul." *Jeremiah 32:38–41*

Jeremiah

1

1 The words of Jeremiah, the son of Hilkiah, one of the priests who were in Anathoth in the land of Benjamin, ²to whom the word of the LORD came in the days of Josiah the son of Amon, king of Judah, in the thirteenth year of his reign. ³It came also in the days of Jehoiakim the son of Josiah, king of Judah, and until the end of the eleventh year of Zedekiah, the son of Josiah, king of Judah, until the captivity of Jerusalem in the fifth month.

The Call of Jeremiah

⁴Now the word of the LORD came to me, saying,

⁵ "Before I formed you in the womb
      I knew you,
   and before you were born I conse-
          crated you;
   I appointed you a prophet to the
          nations."

⁶Then I said, "Ah, Lord GOD! Behold, I do not know how to speak, for I am only a youth." ⁷But the LORD said to me,

   "Do not say, 'I am only a youth';
      for to all to whom I send you, you
          shall go,
   and whatever I command you, you
          shall speak.
⁸ Do not be afraid of them,
      for I am with you to deliver you,
          declares the LORD."

⁹Then the LORD put out his hand and touched my mouth. And the LORD said to me,

   "Behold, I have put my words in your
          mouth.
¹⁰ See, I have set you this day over
      nations and over kingdoms,
   to pluck up and to break down,

to destroy and to overthrow,
   to build and to plant."

¹¹And the word of the LORD came to me, saying, "Jeremiah, what do you see?" And I said, "I see an almond¹ branch." ¹²Then the LORD said to me, "You have seen well, for I am watching over my word to perform it."

¹³The word of the LORD came to me a second time, saying, "What do you see?" And I said, "I see a boiling pot, facing away from the north." ¹⁴Then the LORD said to me, "Out of the north disaster² shall be let loose upon all the inhabitants of the land. ¹⁵For behold, I am calling all the tribes of the kingdoms of the north, declares the LORD, and they shall come, and every one shall set his throne at the entrance of the gates of Jerusalem, against all its walls all around and against all the cities of Judah. ¹⁶And I will declare my judgments against them, for all their evil in forsaking me. They have made offerings to other gods and worshiped the works of their own hands. ¹⁷But you, dress yourself for work;³ arise, and say to them everything that I command you. Do not be dismayed by them, lest I dismay you before them. ¹⁸And I, behold, I make you this day a fortified city, an iron pillar, and bronze walls, against the whole land, against the kings of Judah, its officials, its priests, and the people of the land. ¹⁹They will fight against you, but they shall not prevail against you, for I am with you, declares the LORD, to deliver you."

Israel Forsakes the LORD

2 The word of the LORD came to me, saying, ²"Go and proclaim in the hearing of Jerusalem, Thus says the LORD,

   "I remember the devotion of your
          youth,
      your love as a bride,

¹ *Almond* sounds like the Hebrew for *watching* (compare verse 12) ² The Hebrew word can mean *evil, harm,* or *disaster,* depending on the context; so throughout Jeremiah ³ Hebrew *gird up your loins*

how you followed me in the wilderness,
in a land not sown.
3 Israel was holy to the LORD,
the firstfruits of his harvest.
All who ate of it incurred guilt;
disaster came upon them,
declares the LORD."

4 Hear the word of the LORD, O house of Jacob, and all the clans of the house of Israel. 5 Thus says the LORD:

"What wrong did your fathers find
in me
that they went far from me,
and went after worthlessness, and
became worthless?
6 They did not say, 'Where is the LORD
who brought us up from the land
of Egypt,
who led us in the wilderness,
in a land of deserts and pits,
in a land of drought and deep darkness,
in a land that none passes through,
where no man dwells?'
7 And I brought you into a plentiful land
to enjoy its fruits and its good
things.
But when you came in, you defiled
my land
and made my heritage an abomination.
8 The priests did not say, 'Where is the
LORD?'
Those who handle the law did not
know me;
the shepherds[1] transgressed against
me;
the prophets prophesied by Baal
and went after things that do not
profit.
9 "Therefore I still contend with you,
declares the LORD,
and with your children's children
I will contend.
10 For cross to the coasts of Cyprus and
see,
or send to Kedar and examine with
care;
see if there has been such a thing.
11 Has a nation changed its gods,
even though they are no gods?

But my people have changed their
glory
for that which does not profit.
12 Be appalled, O heavens, at this;
be shocked, be utterly desolate,
declares the LORD,
13 for my people have committed two
evils:
they have forsaken me,
the fountain of living waters,
and hewed out cisterns for themselves,
broken cisterns that can hold no
water.

14 "Is Israel a slave? Is he a homeborn
servant?
Why then has he become a prey?
15 The lions have roared against him;
they have roared loudly.
They have made his land a waste;
his cities are in ruins, without
inhabitant.
16 Moreover, the men of Memphis and
Tahpanhes
have shaved[2] the crown of your
head.
17 Have you not brought this upon
yourself
by forsaking the LORD your God,
when he led you in the way?
18 And now what do you gain by going
to Egypt
to drink the waters of the Nile?
Or what do you gain by going to
Assyria
to drink the waters of the
Euphrates?[3]
19 Your evil will chastise you,
and your apostasy will reprove
you.
Know and see that it is evil and bitter
for you to forsake the LORD your
God;
the fear of me is not in you,
declares the Lord GOD of hosts.

20 "For long ago I broke your yoke
and burst your bonds;
but you said, 'I will not serve.'
Yes, on every high hill
and under every green tree
you bowed down like a whore.
21 Yet I planted you a choice vine,
wholly of pure seed.

[1] Or rulers [2] Hebrew grazed [3] Hebrew the River

How then have you turned degener-
   ate
and become a wild vine?
22 Though you wash yourself with lye
   and use much soap,
      the stain of your guilt is still before
         me,
                      declares the Lord GOD.
23 How can you say, 'I am not unclean,
   I have not gone after the Baals'?
Look at your way in the valley;
   know what you have done—
a restless young camel running here
   and there,
24 a wild donkey used to the wilder-
      ness,
in her heat sniffing the wind!
   Who can restrain her lust?
None who seek her need weary
   themselves;
   in her month they will find her.
25 Keep your feet from going unshod
   and your throat from thirst.
But you said, 'It is hopeless,
   for I have loved foreigners,
   and after them I will go.'

26 "As a thief is shamed when caught,
      so the house of Israel shall be
         shamed:
they, their kings, their officials,
   their priests, and their prophets,
27 who say to a tree, 'You are my
         father,'
   and to a stone, 'You gave me birth.'
For they have turned their back to me,
   and not their face.
But in the time of their trouble they
      say,
   'Arise and save us!'
28 But where are your gods
   that you made for yourself?
Let them arise, if they can save you,
   in your time of trouble;
for as many as your cities
   are your gods, O Judah.

29 "Why do you contend with me?
   You have all transgressed against
      me,
                      declares the LORD.
30 In vain have I struck your children;
   they took no correction;

Know Yourself

verses to read
Jeremiah 2:1–13

Are you eager to please God, or are you more interested in expecting him to please you? Are you driven by a desire to serve him, or are you whining because things aren't going your way? Your soul will never be happy when it has forgotten what God wants from it, and that is your presence and adoration. How much of that do you give? How much do you rejoice to do what pleases God and to give him a good rep with your friends and family, in light of all the kindness he has shown you in Christ by forgiving you?

In Jeremiah 2, God is asking his people why they have walked away, forgotten they loved him, and gone after other gods. He can remember a time when they adored and trusted him, but somehow they have gotten away from that passion, hope, and love. Do you notice a difference in your life? Has your passion for God grown, or has it diminished? Can you remember a time when you cared more about him than anything? If you have gone backward instead of forward in your love relationship, then you will more than likely feel bad right now, and that's not what your Father in heaven wants. He welcomes you back into his arms, no matter how distant or lazy you have been lately.

Today is another chance to get back to your first love. Plan time today, tomorrow, and all week to devote to remembering what God has done for you in Jesus, to adoring him, and to just being in his presence.

your own sword devoured your
     prophets
   like a ravening lion.
31 And you, O generation, behold the
     word of the LORD.
Have I been a wilderness to Israel,
   or a land of thick darkness?
Why then do my people say, 'We are
     free,
   we will come no more to you'?
32 Can a virgin forget her ornaments,
   or a bride her attire?
Yet my people have forgotten me
   days without number.

33 "How well you direct your course
     to seek love!
So that even to wicked women
   you have taught your ways.
34 Also on your skirts is found
     the lifeblood of the guiltless poor;
you did not find them breaking in.
Yet in spite of all these things
35 you say, 'I am innocent;
   surely his anger has turned from
     me.'
Behold, I will bring you to judgment
   for saying, 'I have not sinned.'
36 How much you go about,
   changing your way!
You shall be put to shame by Egypt
   as you were put to shame by
     Assyria.
37 From it too you will come away
   with your hands on your head,
for the LORD has rejected those in
     whom you trust,
   and you will not prosper by them.

3 "If[1] a man divorces his wife
   and she goes from him
and becomes another man's wife,
   will he return to her?
Would not that land be greatly pol-
     luted?
You have played the whore with
     many lovers;
   and would you return to me?
               declares the LORD.
2 Lift up your eyes to the bare heights,
     and see!
   Where have you not been ravished?
By the waysides you have sat await-
     ing lovers
   like an Arab in the wilderness.

[1] Septuagint, Syriac; Hebrew *Saying, "If*

You have polluted the land
   with your vile whoredom.
3 Therefore the showers have been
     withheld,
   and the spring rain has not come;
yet you have the forehead of a
     whore;
   you refuse to be ashamed.
4 Have you not just now called to me,
   'My father, you are the friend of my
     youth—
5 will he be angry forever,
   will he be indignant to the end?'
Behold, you have spoken,
   but you have done all the evil that
     you could."

Ask Yourself . . .

ABOUT PURITY

When you sin, it can be hard to
forgive yourself. But the only forgiveness you need is from God. Ask
yourself about your purity:

- Is there something I can't
forgive myself for doing?
- According to his Word, can
God forgive me?
- Why do I have higher
standards for forgiveness than
God?
- What do I have to do to be
forgiven?
- Am I ready to accept God's
perfect forgiveness, won for
me by Jesus?

Faithless Israel Called to Repentance

6 The LORD said to me in the days of
King Josiah: "Have you seen what she did,
that faithless one, Israel, how she went up
on every high hill and under every green
tree, and there played the whore? 7 And
I thought, 'After she has done all this she
will return to me,' but she did not return,
and her treacherous sister Judah saw it.
8 She saw that for all the adulteries of that

faithless one, Israel, I had sent her away with a decree of divorce. Yet her treacherous sister Judah did not fear, but she too went and played the whore. ⁹Because she took her whoredom lightly, she polluted the land, committing adultery with stone and tree. ¹⁰Yet for all this her treacherous sister Judah did not return to me with her whole heart, but in pretense, declares the LORD."

¹¹And the LORD said to me, "Faithless Israel has shown herself more righteous than treacherous Judah. ¹²Go, and proclaim these words toward the north, and say,

"'Return, faithless Israel,
　　　　　　　declares the LORD.
I will not look on you in anger,
　for I am merciful,
　　　　　　　declares the LORD;
I will not be angry forever.
¹³ Only acknowledge your guilt,
　that you rebelled against the LORD
　　your God
and scattered your favors among
　　foreigners under every green
　　tree,
　and that you have not obeyed my
　　voice,
　　　　　　　declares the LORD.
¹⁴ Return, O faithless children,
　　　　　　　declares the LORD;
　for I am your master;
I will take you, one from a city and
　　two from a family,
　and I will bring you to Zion.

¹⁵"'And I will give you shepherds after my own heart, who will feed you with knowledge and understanding. ¹⁶And when you have multiplied and been fruitful in the land, in those days, declares the LORD, they shall no more say, "The ark of the covenant of the LORD." It shall not come to mind or be remembered or missed; it shall not be made again. ¹⁷At that time Jerusalem shall be called the throne of the LORD, and all nations shall gather to it, to the presence of the LORD in Jerusalem, and they shall no more stubbornly follow their own evil heart. ¹⁸In those days the house of Judah shall join the house of Israel, and together they shall come from the land of the north to the land that I gave your fathers for a heritage.

¹⁹ "'I said,
　How I would set you among my
　　sons,
and give you a pleasant land,
　a heritage most beautiful of all
　　nations.
And I thought you would call me, My
　　Father,
　and would not turn from following
　　me.
²⁰ Surely, as a treacherous wife leaves
　　her husband,
　so have you been treacherous to
　　me, O house of Israel,
　　　　　　declares the LORD.'"

²¹ A voice on the bare heights is heard,
　the weeping and pleading of
　　Israel's sons
because they have perverted their
　　way;
　they have forgotten the LORD their
　　God.
²² "Return, O faithless sons;
　I will heal your faithlessness."
"Behold, we come to you,
　for you are the LORD our God.
²³ Truly the hills are a delusion,
　the orgies¹ on the mountains.
Truly in the LORD our God
　is the salvation of Israel.

²⁴"But from our youth the shameful thing has devoured all for which our fathers labored, their flocks and their herds, their sons and their daughters. ²⁵Let us lie down in our shame, and let our dishonor cover us. For we have sinned against the LORD our God, we and our fathers, from our youth even to this day, and we have not obeyed the voice of the LORD our God."

4 "If you return, O Israel,
　　　　　　declares the LORD,
　to me you should return.
If you remove your detestable things
　　from my presence,
　and do not waver,
² and if you swear, 'As the LORD lives,'
　in truth, in justice, and in righ-
　　teousness,
then nations shall bless themselves
　　in him,
　and in him shall they glory."

¹Hebrew commotion

³ For thus says the LORD to the men of Judah and Jerusalem:

"Break up your fallow ground,
    and sow not among thorns.
⁴   Circumcise yourselves to the LORD;
    remove the foreskin of your hearts,
    O men of Judah and inhabitants of
        Jerusalem;
    lest my wrath go forth like fire,
    and burn with none to quench it,
    because of the evil of your deeds."

Ask Yourself . . .

ABOUT IDOLS

God's people forgot their first love and fell for idols—little gods that they thought would give them hope, happiness, and comfort. Ask yourself about your own idols that get between you and God:

- Do I have any idols?

- Do I obsess over anything or anyone?

- Is my mind happier thinking about my obsession than thinking about God?

- Do I have something that does for me what God wants to do for me (comfort me, help me, guide me)?

- Have I forgotten that God should be my first love, my only obsession?

- Am I willing to destroy or walk away from my idols and restore fellowship with the one true God?

Disaster from the North

⁵ Declare in Judah, and proclaim in Jerusalem, and say,

"Blow the trumpet through the land;
    cry aloud and say,
'Assemble, and let us go
    into the fortified cities!'

⁶   Raise a standard toward Zion,
    flee for safety, stay not,
for I bring disaster from the north,
    and great destruction.
⁷   A lion has gone up from his thicket,
    a destroyer of nations has set out;
he has gone out from his place
to make your land a waste;
    your cities will be ruins
        without inhabitant.
⁸   For this put on sackcloth,
    lament and wail,
for the fierce anger of the LORD
    has not turned back from us."

⁹ "In that day, declares the LORD, courage shall fail both king and officials. The priests shall be appalled and the prophets astounded." ¹⁰ Then I said, "Ah, Lord GOD, surely you have utterly deceived this people and Jerusalem, saying, 'It shall be well with you,' whereas the sword has reached their very life."

¹¹ At that time it will be said to this people and to Jerusalem, "A hot wind from the bare heights in the desert toward the daughter of my people, not to winnow or cleanse, ¹² a wind too full for this comes for me. Now it is I who speak in judgment upon them."

¹³   Behold, he comes up like clouds;
        his chariots like the whirlwind;
    his horses are swifter than eagles—
        woe to us, for we are ruined!
¹⁴   O Jerusalem, wash your heart from
        evil,
    that you may be saved.
    How long shall your wicked thoughts
        lodge within you?
¹⁵   For a voice declares from Dan
        and proclaims trouble from Mount
            Ephraim.
¹⁶   Warn the nations that he is coming;
        announce to Jerusalem,
    "Besiegers come from a distant land;
        they shout against the cities of
            Judah.
¹⁷   Like keepers of a field are they
        against her all around,
    because she has rebelled against
        me,
                declares the LORD.
¹⁸   Your ways and your deeds
        have brought this upon you.

This is your doom, and it is bitter;
 it has reached your very heart."

Anguish over Judah's Desolation

19 My anguish, my anguish! I writhe in
  pain!
 Oh the walls of my heart!
My heart is beating wildly;
 I cannot keep silent,
for I hear the sound of the trumpet,
 the alarm of war.
20 Crash follows hard on crash;
 the whole land is laid waste.
Suddenly my tents are laid waste,
 my curtains in a moment.
21 How long must I see the standard
 and hear the sound of the trumpet?

22 "For my people are foolish;
 they know me not;
they are stupid children;
 they have no understanding.
They are 'wise'—in doing evil!
 But how to do good they know not."

23 I looked on the earth, and behold, it
  was without form and void;
 and to the heavens, and they had
  no light.
24 I looked on the mountains, and
  behold, they were quaking,
 and all the hills moved to and fro.
25 I looked, and behold, there was no
  man,
 and all the birds of the air had fled.
26 I looked, and behold, the fruitful land
  was a desert,
 and all its cities were laid in ruins
 before the LORD, before his fierce
  anger.

27 For thus says the LORD, "The whole
land shall be a desolation; yet I will not
make a full end.

28 "For this the earth shall mourn,
 and the heavens above be dark;
for I have spoken; I have purposed;
 I have not relented, nor will I turn
  back."

29 At the noise of horseman and archer
 every city takes to flight;
they enter thickets; they climb
  among rocks;
 all the cities are forsaken,
 and no man dwells in them.
30 And you, O desolate one,

what do you mean that you dress in
  scarlet,
 that you adorn yourself with ornaments of gold,
 that you enlarge your eyes with
  paint?
In vain you beautify yourself.
 Your lovers despise you;
 they seek your life.
31 For I heard a cry as of a woman in
  labor,
 anguish as of one giving birth to
  her first child,
the cry of the daughter of Zion gasp-
  ing for breath,
 stretching out her hands,
"Woe is me! I am fainting before murderers."

Jerusalem Refused to Repent

5 Run to and fro through the streets
  of Jerusalem,
 look and take note!
Search her squares to see
 if you can find a man,
one who does justice
 and seeks truth,
that I may pardon her.
2 Though they say, "As the LORD lives,"
 yet they swear falsely.
3 O LORD, do not your eyes look for
  truth?
You have struck them down,
 but they felt no anguish;
you have consumed them,
 but they refused to take correction.
They have made their faces harder
  than rock;
 they have refused to repent.

4 Then I said, "These are only the poor;
 they have no sense;
for they do not know the way of the
  LORD,
 the justice of their God.
5 I will go to the great
 and will speak to them,
for they know the way of the LORD,
 the justice of their God."
But they all alike had broken the
  yoke;
 they had burst the bonds.

6 Therefore a lion from the forest shall
  strike them down,
 a wolf from the desert shall devastate them.

A leopard is watching their cities;
 everyone who goes out of them
  shall be torn in pieces,
because their transgressions are
  many,
 their apostasies are great.

7 "How can I pardon you?
 Your children have forsaken me
 and have sworn by those who are
  no gods.
When I fed them to the full,
 they committed adultery
 and trooped to the houses of
  whores.
8 They were well-fed, lusty stallions,
 each neighing for his neighbor's
  wife.
9 Shall I not punish them for these
  things?
      declares the LORD;
 and shall I not avenge myself
 on a nation such as this?

10 "Go up through her vine rows and
  destroy,
 but make not a full end;
strip away her branches,
 for they are not the LORD's.
11 For the house of Israel and the house
  of Judah
 have been utterly treacherous to
  me,
      declares the LORD.
12 They have spoken falsely of the
  LORD
 and have said, 'He will do nothing;
no disaster will come upon us,
 nor shall we see sword or famine.
13 The prophets will become wind;
 the word is not in them.
Thus shall it be done to them!'"

The LORD Proclaims Judgment

14 Therefore thus says the LORD, the
  God of hosts:
"Because you have spoken this word,
 behold, I am making my words in
  your mouth a fire,
 and this people wood, and the fire
  shall consume them.
15 Behold, I am bringing against you
 a nation from afar, O house of Israel,
      declares the LORD.
It is an enduring nation;
 it is an ancient nation,

a nation whose language you do not
  know,
 nor can you understand what they
  say.
16 Their quiver is like an open tomb;
 they are all mighty warriors.
17 They shall eat up your harvest and
  your food;
 they shall eat up your sons and
  your daughters;
 they shall eat up your flocks and
  your herds;
 they shall eat up your vines and
  your fig trees;
your fortified cities in which you
  trust
 they shall beat down with the
  sword."

18 "But even in those days, declares the LORD, I will not make a full end of you. 19 And when your people say, 'Why has the LORD our God done all these things to us?' you shall say to them, 'As you have forsaken me and served foreign gods in your land, so you shall serve foreigners in a land that is not yours.'"

20 Declare this in the house of Jacob;
 proclaim it in Judah:
21 "Hear this, O foolish and senseless
  people,
 who have eyes, but see not,
 who have ears, but hear not.
22 Do you not fear me? declares the
  LORD.
 Do you not tremble before me?
I placed the sand as the boundary for
  the sea,
 a perpetual barrier that it cannot
  pass;
though the waves toss, they cannot
  prevail;
 though they roar, they cannot pass
  over it.
23 But this people has a stubborn and
  rebellious heart;
 they have turned aside and gone
  away.
24 They do not say in their hearts,
 'Let us fear the LORD our God,
who gives the rain in its season,
 the autumn rain and the spring rain,
and keeps for us
 the weeks appointed for the harvest.'

25 Your iniquities have turned these
        away,
    and your sins have kept good from
        you.
26 For wicked men are found among my
        people;
    they lurk like fowlers lying in wait.[1]
    They set a trap;
        they catch men.
27 Like a cage full of birds,
    their houses are full of deceit;
    therefore they have become great
        and rich;
28 they have grown fat and sleek.
    They know no bounds in deeds of evil;
        they judge not with justice
    the cause of the fatherless, to make it
        prosper,
    and they do not defend the rights
        of the needy.
29 Shall I not punish them for these
        things?
                        declares the LORD,
    and shall I not avenge myself
        on a nation such as this?"

30 An appalling and horrible thing
        has happened in the land:
31 the prophets prophesy falsely,
    and the priests rule at their direc-
        tion;
    my people love to have it so,
        but what will you do when the end
            comes?

Impending Disaster for Jerusalem

6   Flee for safety, O people of Benjamin,
    from the midst of Jerusalem!
    Blow the trumpet in Tekoa,
        and raise a signal on Beth-
            haccherem,
    for disaster looms out of the north,
        and great destruction.
2   The lovely and delicately bred I will
        destroy,
        the daughter of Zion.[2]
3   Shepherds with their flocks shall
        come against her;
    they shall pitch their tents around
        her;
    they shall pasture, each in his
        place.
4   "Prepare war against her;
    arise, and let us attack at noon!

Woe to us, for the day declines,
    for the shadows of evening
        lengthen!
5   Arise, and let us attack by night
    and destroy her palaces!"

6   For thus says the LORD of hosts:
    "Cut down her trees;
        cast up a siege mound against
            Jerusalem.
    This is the city that must be pun-
        ished;
        there is nothing but oppression
            within her.
7   As a well keeps its water fresh,
        so she keeps fresh her evil;
    violence and destruction are heard
        within her;
    sickness and wounds are ever
        before me.
8   Be warned, O Jerusalem,
        lest I turn from you in disgust,
    lest I make you a desolation,
        an uninhabited land."

9   Thus says the LORD of hosts:
    "They shall glean thoroughly as a vine
        the remnant of Israel;
    like a grape gatherer pass your hand
        again
        over its branches."
10 To whom shall I speak and give warn-
        ing,
        that they may hear?
    Behold, their ears are uncircumcised,
        they cannot listen;
    behold, the word of the LORD is to
        them an object of scorn;
        they take no pleasure in it.
11 Therefore I am full of the wrath of
        the LORD;
        I am weary of holding it in.
    "Pour it out upon the children in the
        street,
        and upon the gatherings of young
            men, also;
    both husband and wife shall be taken,
        the elderly and the very aged.
12 Their houses shall be turned over to
        others,
        their fields and wives together,
    for I will stretch out my hand
        against the inhabitants of the land,"
                            declares the LORD.

[1] The meaning of the Hebrew is uncertain [2] Or *I have likened the daughter of Zion to the loveliest pasture*

¹³ "For from the least to the greatest of
    them,
    everyone is greedy for unjust gain;
and from prophet to priest,
    everyone deals falsely.
¹⁴ They have healed the wound of my
    people lightly,
    saying, 'Peace, peace,'
    when there is no peace.
¹⁵ Were they ashamed when they com-
    mitted abomination?
    No, they were not at all ashamed;
    they did not know how to blush.
Therefore they shall fall among those
    who fall;
    at the time that I punish them,
    they shall be overthrown,"
           says the LORD.

¹⁶ Thus says the LORD:
"Stand by the roads, and look,
    and ask for the ancient paths,
where the good way is; and walk in
    it,
    and find rest for your souls.
But they said, 'We will not walk in it.'
¹⁷ I set watchmen over you, saying,
    'Pay attention to the sound of the
    trumpet!'
But they said, 'We will not pay atten-
    tion.'
¹⁸ Therefore hear, O nations,
    and know, O congregation, what
    will happen to them.
¹⁹ Hear, O earth; behold, I am bringing
    disaster upon this people,
    the fruit of their devices,
because they have not paid attention
    to my words;
    and as for my law, they have
    rejected it.
²⁰ What use to me is frankincense that
    comes from Sheba,
    or sweet cane from a distant land?
Your burnt offerings are not accept-
    able,
    nor your sacrifices pleasing to me.
²¹ Therefore thus says the LORD:
'Behold, I will lay before this people
    stumbling blocks against which
    they shall stumble;
fathers and sons together,
    neighbor and friend shall perish.'"

²² Thus says the LORD:

"Behold, a people is coming from the
    north country,
    a great nation is stirring from the
    farthest parts of the earth.
²³ They lay hold on bow and javelin;
    they are cruel and have no mercy;
    the sound of them is like the roar-
    ing sea;
they ride on horses,
    set in array as a man for battle,
    against you, O daughter of Zion!"
²⁴ We have heard the report of it;
    our hands fall helpless;
anguish has taken hold of us,
    pain as of a woman in labor.
²⁵ Go not out into the field,
    nor walk on the road,
for the enemy has a sword;
    terror is on every side.
²⁶ O daughter of my people, put on
    sackcloth,
    and roll in ashes;
make mourning as for an only son,
    most bitter lamentation,
for suddenly the destroyer
    will come upon us.

²⁷ "I have made you a tester of metals
    among my people,
    that you may know and test their
    ways.
²⁸ They are all stubbornly rebellious,
    going about with slanders;
they are bronze and iron;
    all of them act corruptly.
²⁹ The bellows blow fiercely;
    the lead is consumed by the fire;
in vain the refining goes on,
    for the wicked are not removed.
³⁰ Rejected silver they are called,
    for the LORD has rejected them."

Evil in the Land

7 The word that came to Jeremiah from
the LORD: ² "Stand in the gate of the
LORD's house, and proclaim there this
word, and say, Hear the word of the LORD,
all you men of Judah who enter these gates
to worship the LORD. ³ Thus says the LORD
of hosts, the God of Israel: Amend your
ways and your deeds, and I will let you
dwell in this place. ⁴ Do not trust in these
deceptive words: 'This is the temple of the
LORD, the temple of the LORD, the temple
of the LORD.'

⁵ "For if you truly amend your ways and
your deeds, if you truly execute justice one

with another, ⁶ if you do not oppress the sojourner, the fatherless, or the widow, or shed innocent blood in this place, and if you do not go after other gods to your own harm, ⁷ then I will let you dwell in this place, in the land that I gave of old to your fathers forever.

⁸ "Behold, you trust in deceptive words to no avail. ⁹ Will you steal, murder, commit adultery, swear falsely, make offerings to Baal, and go after other gods that you have not known, ¹⁰ and then come and stand before me in this house, which is called by my name, and say, 'We are delivered!'—only to go on doing all these abominations? ¹¹ Has this house, which is called by my name, become a den of robbers in your eyes? Behold, I myself have seen it, declares the Lord. ¹² Go now to my place that was in Shiloh, where I made my name dwell at first, and see what I did to it because of the evil of my people Israel. ¹³ And now, because you have done all these things, declares the Lord, and when I spoke to you persistently you did not listen, and when I called you, you did not answer, ¹⁴ therefore I will do to the house that is called by my name, and in which you trust, and to the place that I gave to you and to your fathers, as I did to Shiloh. ¹⁵ And I will cast you out of my sight, as I cast out all your kinsmen, all the offspring of Ephraim.

¹⁶ "As for you, do not pray for this people, or lift up a cry or prayer for them, and do not intercede with me, for I will not hear you. ¹⁷ Do you not see what they are doing in the cities of Judah and in the streets of Jerusalem? ¹⁸ The children gather wood, the fathers kindle fire, and the women knead dough, to make cakes for the queen of heaven. And they pour out drink offerings to other gods, to provoke me to anger. ¹⁹ Is it I whom they provoke? declares the Lord. Is it not themselves, to their own shame? ²⁰ Therefore thus says the Lord God: Behold, my anger and my wrath will be poured out on this place, upon man and beast, upon the trees of the field and the fruit of the ground; it will burn and not be quenched."

²¹ Thus says the Lord of hosts, the God of Israel: "Add your burnt offerings to your sacrifices, and eat the flesh. ²² For in the day that I brought them out of the land of Egypt, I did not speak to your fathers or command them concerning burnt offerings and sacrifices. ²³ But this command I gave them: 'Obey my voice, and I will be your God, and you shall be my people. And walk in all the way that I command you, that it may be well with you.' ²⁴ But they did not obey or incline their ear, but walked in their own counsels and the stubbornness of their evil hearts, and went backward and not forward. ²⁵ From the day that your fathers came out of the land of Egypt to this day, I have persistently sent all my servants the prophets to them, day after day. ²⁶ Yet they did not listen to me or incline their ear, but stiffened their neck. They did worse than their fathers.

²⁷ "So you shall speak all these words to them, but they will not listen to you. You shall call to them, but they will not answer you. ²⁸ And you shall say to them, 'This is the nation that did not obey the voice of the Lord their God, and did not accept discipline; truth has perished; it is cut off from their lips.

²⁹ " 'Cut off your hair and cast it away;
        raise a lamentation on the bare
            heights,
        for the Lord has rejected and for-
            saken
        the generation of his wrath.'

The Valley of Slaughter

³⁰ "For the sons of Judah have done evil in my sight, declares the Lord. They have set their detestable things in the house that is called by my name, to defile it. ³¹ And they have built the high places of Topheth, which is in the Valley of the Son of Hinnom, to burn their sons and their daughters in the fire, which I did not command, nor did it come into my mind. ³² Therefore, behold, the days are coming, declares the Lord, when it will no more be called Topheth, or the Valley of the Son of Hinnom, but the Valley of Slaughter; for they will bury in Topheth, because there is no room elsewhere. ³³ And the dead bodies of this people will be food for the birds of the air, and for the beasts of the earth, and none will frighten them away. ³⁴ And I will silence in the cities of Judah and in the streets of Jerusalem the voice of mirth and the voice of gladness, the voice of the bridegroom and the voice of the bride, for the land shall become a waste.

8 "At that time, declares the LORD, the bones of the kings of Judah, the bones of its officials, the bones of the priests, the bones of the prophets, and the bones of the inhabitants of Jerusalem shall be brought out of their tombs. ² And they shall be spread before the sun and the moon and all the host of heaven, which they have loved and served, which they have gone after, and which they have sought and worshiped. And they shall not be gathered or buried. They shall be as dung on the surface of the ground. ³ Death shall be preferred to life by all the remnant that remains of this evil family in all the places where I have driven them, declares the LORD of hosts.

Sin and Treachery

4   "You shall say to them, Thus says the
    LORD:
    When men fall, do they not rise again?
      If one turns away, does he not
        return?
5   Why then has this people turned away
      in perpetual backsliding?
    They hold fast to deceit;
      they refuse to return.
6   I have paid attention and listened,
      but they have not spoken rightly;
    no man relents of his evil,
      saying, 'What have I done?'
    Everyone turns to his own course,
      like a horse plunging headlong
        into battle.
7   Even the stork in the heavens
      knows her times,
    and the turtledove, swallow, and
      crane[1]
      keep the time of their coming,
    but my people know not
      the rules[2] of the LORD.

8   "How can you say, 'We are wise,
      and the law of the LORD is with us'?
    But behold, the lying pen of the
      scribes
      has made it into a lie.
9   The wise men shall be put to shame;
      they shall be dismayed and taken;
    behold, they have rejected the word
      of the LORD,
      so what wisdom is in them?
10   Therefore I will give their wives to
      others
      and their fields to conquerors,

    because from the least to the great-
      est
    everyone is greedy for unjust gain;
    from prophet to priest,
      everyone deals falsely.
11   They have healed the wound of my
      people lightly,
      saying, 'Peace, peace,'
      when there is no peace.
12   Were they ashamed when they com-
      mitted abomination?
    No, they were not at all ashamed;
      they did not know how to blush.
    Therefore they shall fall among the
      fallen;
      when I punish them, they shall be
        overthrown,
            says the LORD.
13   When I would gather them, declares
      the LORD,
      there are no grapes on the vine,
      nor figs on the fig tree;
    even the leaves are withered,
      and what I gave them has passed
        away from them."[3]

14   Why do we sit still?
    Gather together; let us go into the
      fortified cities
      and perish there,
    for the LORD our God has doomed us
      to perish
      and has given us poisoned water
        to drink,
      because we have sinned against
        the LORD.
15   We looked for peace, but no good
      came;
      for a time of healing, but behold,
        terror.

16   "The snorting of their horses is heard
      from Dan;
      at the sound of the neighing of
        their stallions
      the whole land quakes.
    They come and devour the land and
      all that fills it,
      the city and those who dwell in it.
17   For behold, I am sending among you
      serpents,
      adders that cannot be charmed,
      and they shall bite you,"
            declares the LORD.

[1] The meaning of the Hebrew word is uncertain [2] Or just decrees [3] The meaning of the Hebrew is uncertain

Jeremiah Grieves for His People

18 My joy is gone; grief is upon me;[1]
    my heart is sick within me.
19 Behold, the cry of the daughter of my
        people
      from the length and breadth of the
        land:
    "Is the LORD not in Zion?
      Is her King not in her?"
    "Why have they provoked me to anger
        with their carved images
      and with their foreign idols?"
20 "The harvest is past, the summer is
        ended,
      and we are not saved."
21 For the wound of the daughter of my
        people is my heart wounded;
    I mourn, and dismay has taken
        hold on me.

22 Is there no balm in Gilead?
      Is there no physician there?
    Why then has the health of the
        daughter of my people
      not been restored?
9[2] Oh that my head were waters,
    and my eyes a fountain of tears,
    that I might weep day and night
      for the slain of the daughter of my
        people!
23 Oh that I had in the desert
      a travelers' lodging place,
    that I might leave my people
      and go away from them!
    For they are all adulterers,
      a company of treacherous men.
3 They bend their tongue like a bow;
      falsehood and not truth has grown
        strong[4] in the land;
    for they proceed from evil to evil,
      and they do not know me, declares
        the LORD.

4 Let everyone beware of his neighbor,
      and put no trust in any brother,
    for every brother is a deceiver,
      and every neighbor goes about as
        a slanderer.
5 Everyone deceives his neighbor,
      and no one speaks the truth;
    they have taught their tongue to
        speak lies;
      they weary themselves committing
        iniquity.

6 Heaping oppression upon oppres-
        sion, and deceit upon deceit,
    they refuse to know me, declares
        the LORD.

7 Therefore thus says the LORD of hosts:
    "Behold, I will refine them and test
        them,
      for what else can I do, because of
        my people?
8 Their tongue is a deadly arrow;
      it speaks deceitfully;
    with his mouth each speaks peace to
        his neighbor,
      but in his heart he plans an
        ambush for him.
9 Shall I not punish them for these
        things? declares the LORD,
      and shall I not avenge myself
        on a nation such as this?

10 "I will take up weeping and wailing for
        the mountains,
      and a lamentation for the pastures
        of the wilderness,
    because they are laid waste so that
        no one passes through,
      and the lowing of cattle is not
        heard;
    both the birds of the air and the
        beasts
      have fled and are gone.
11 I will make Jerusalem a heap of ruins,
      a lair of jackals,
    and I will make the cities of Judah a
        desolation,
      without inhabitant."

12 Who is the man so wise that he can
understand this? To whom has the mouth
of the LORD spoken, that he may declare
it? Why is the land ruined and laid waste
like a wilderness, so that no one passes
through? 13 And the LORD says: "Because
they have forsaken my law that I set before
them, and have not obeyed my voice or
walked in accord with it, 14 but have stubbornly followed their own hearts and have
gone after the Baals, as their fathers taught
them. 15 Therefore thus says the LORD of
hosts, the God of Israel: Behold, I will feed
this people with bitter food, and give them
poisonous water to drink. 16 I will scatter
them among the nations whom neither
they nor their fathers have known, and

---

[1] Compare Septuagint; the meaning of the Hebrew is uncertain [2] Ch 8:23 in Hebrew [3] Ch 9:1 in Hebrew [4] Septuagint; Hebrew *and not
for truth they have grown strong*

I will send the sword after them, until I have consumed them."

17 Thus says the LORD of hosts:
"Consider, and call for the mourning
     women to come;
  send for the skillful women to
     come;
18 let them make haste and raise a wail-
     ing over us,
  that our eyes may run down with
     tears
  and our eyelids flow with water.
19 For a sound of wailing is heard from
     Zion:
  'How we are ruined!
  We are utterly shamed,
because we have left the land,
  because they have cast down our
     dwellings.'"

20 Hear, O women, the word of the LORD,
  and let your ear receive the word
     of his mouth;
  teach to your daughters a lament,
  and each to her neighbor a dirge.
21 For death has come up into our win-
     dows;
  it has entered our palaces,
cutting off the children from the
     streets
  and the young men from the
     squares.
22 Speak: "Thus declares the LORD,
  'The dead bodies of men shall fall
     like dung upon the open field,
  like sheaves after the reaper,
     and none shall gather them.'"

23 Thus says the LORD: "Let not the wise man boast in his wisdom, let not the mighty man boast in his might, let not the rich man boast in his riches, 24 but let him who boasts boast in this, that he understands and knows me, that I am the LORD who practices steadfast love, justice, and righteousness in the earth. For in these things I delight, declares the LORD."

25 "Behold, the days are coming, declares the LORD, when I will punish all those who are circumcised merely in the flesh— 26 Egypt, Judah, Edom, the sons of Ammon, Moab, and all who dwell in the desert who cut the corners of their hair, for all these nations are uncircumcised, and all the house of Israel are uncircumcised in heart."

Idols and the Living God

10 Hear the word that the LORD speaks to you, O house of Israel. 2 Thus says the LORD:

"Learn not the way of the nations,
  nor be dismayed at the signs of the
     heavens
  because the nations are dismayed
     at them,
3 for the customs of the peoples are
     vanity.[1]
A tree from the forest is cut down
  and worked with an axe by the
     hands of a craftsman.
4 They decorate it with silver and gold;
  they fasten it with hammer and
     nails
  so that it cannot move.
5 Their idols[2] are like scarecrows in a
     cucumber field,
  and they cannot speak;
they have to be carried,
  for they cannot walk.
Do not be afraid of them,
  for they cannot do evil,
  neither is it in them to do good."

6 There is none like you, O LORD;
  you are great, and your name is
     great in might.
7 Who would not fear you, O King of
     the nations?
  For this is your due;
for among all the wise ones of the
     nations
  and in all their kingdoms
  there is none like you.
8 They are both stupid and foolish;
  the instruction of idols is but wood!
9 Beaten silver is brought from
     Tarshish,
  and gold from Uphaz.
They are the work of the craftsman
  and of the hands of the gold-
     smith;
  their clothing is violet and purple;
  they are all the work of skilled men.
10 But the LORD is the true God;
  he is the living God and the ever-
     lasting King.
At his wrath the earth quakes,
  and the nations cannot endure his
     indignation.

1 Or vapor, or mist 2 Hebrew They

¹¹ Thus shall you say to them: "The gods who did not make the heavens and the earth shall perish from the earth and from under the heavens."¹

¹² It is he who made the earth by his
power,
who established the world by his
wisdom,
and by his understanding
stretched out the heavens.
¹³ When he utters his voice, there is a
tumult of waters in the heav-
ens,
and he makes the mist rise from
the ends of the earth.
He makes lightning for the rain,
and he brings forth the wind from
his storehouses.
¹⁴ Every man is stupid and without
knowledge;
every goldsmith is put to shame by
his idols,
for his images are false,
and there is no breath in them.
¹⁵ They are worthless, a work of delu-
sion;
at the time of their punishment
they shall perish.
¹⁶ Not like these is he who is the por-
tion of Jacob,
for he is the one who formed all
things,
and Israel is the tribe of his inheritance;
the LORD of hosts is his name.

¹⁷ Gather up your bundle from the
ground,
O you who dwell under siege!
¹⁸ For thus says the LORD:
"Behold, I am slinging out the inhabitants of the land
at this time,
and I will bring distress on them,
that they may feel it."

¹⁹ Woe is me because of my hurt!
My wound is grievous.
But I said, "Truly this is an affliction,
and I must bear it."
²⁰ My tent is destroyed,
and all my cords are broken;
my children have gone from me,
and they are not;

¹ This verse is in Aramaic

there is no one to spread my tent
again
and to set up my curtains.
²¹ For the shepherds are stupid
and do not inquire of the LORD;
therefore they have not prospered,
and all their flock is scattered.

²² A voice, a rumor! Behold, it comes!—
a great commotion out of the
north country
to make the cities of Judah a desolation,
a lair of jackals.

²³ I know, O LORD, that the way of man
is not in himself,
that it is not in man who walks to
direct his steps.
²⁴ Correct me, O LORD, but in justice;
not in your anger, lest you bring
me to nothing.

²⁵ Pour out your wrath on the nations
that know you not,
and on the peoples that call not on
your name,
for they have devoured Jacob;
they have devoured him and consumed him,
and have laid waste his habitation.

The Broken Covenant

11 The word that came to Jeremiah from the LORD: ² "Hear the words of this covenant, and speak to the men of Judah and the inhabitants of Jerusalem. ³ You shall say to them, Thus says the LORD, the God of Israel: Cursed be the man who does not hear the words of this covenant ⁴ that I commanded your fathers when I brought them out of the land of Egypt, from the iron furnace, saying, Listen to my voice, and do all that I command you. So shall you be my people, and I will be your God, ⁵ that I may confirm the oath that I swore to your fathers, to give them a land flowing with milk and honey, as at this day." Then I answered, "So be it, LORD."

⁶ And the LORD said to me, "Proclaim all these words in the cities of Judah and in the streets of Jerusalem: Hear the words of this covenant and do them. ⁷ For I solemnly warned your fathers when I brought them up out of the land of Egypt, warning them persistently, even to this day, saying, Obey

my voice. ⁸Yet they did not obey or incline their ear, but everyone walked in the stubbornness of his evil heart. Therefore I brought upon them all the words of this covenant, which I commanded them to do, but they did not."

A Prayer for...
CONSISTENCY

Dear Lord, what's the matter with me that I am so emotional and moody, so quickly changing, one moment confessing my love for you and the next giving in to the temptations that draw me away from you? One minute I'm cheerful, smiling, and kind, and the next I'm bummed and irritable. God, I do not understand myself! What a strange creature I am! But I do not pray, my Father, that everything would always be the same, because I would get tired of unending sunshine and want a rain shower. I don't pray that my way will always be on level ground, because then I would miss the mountains. I don't pray that I would always hear music, because then I would want the blessing of silence.

But I do pray, Lord, that I would have some pattern of consistency in my relationship with you. Teach me balance, so that I can live a life of faith and trust in you and show kindness and love to others, and so that I will not be at one moment up in the sky and at the next at the bottom of a well. Help me to walk with my hand in your hand, knowing that you came down from the mountaintops to walk in the valleys—so that I won't give way to depression when I also have to return to the valley but will remember that the trail will go back up again. But whether I am on the mountaintop or in the valley, may I always be aware that you are walking beside me. And may I remember that if you are with me, it makes no difference where I am.

Amen.

---

⁹Again the LORD said to me, "A conspiracy exists among the men of Judah and the inhabitants of Jerusalem. ¹⁰They have turned back to the iniquities of their forefathers, who refused to hear my words. They have gone after other gods to serve them. The house of Israel and the house of Judah have broken my covenant that I made with their fathers. ¹¹Therefore, thus says the LORD, Behold, I am bringing disaster upon them that they cannot escape. Though they cry to me, I will not listen to them. ¹²Then the cities of Judah and the inhabitants of Jerusalem will go and cry to the gods to whom they make offerings, but they cannot save them in the time of their trouble. ¹³For your gods have become as many as your cities, O Judah, and as many as the streets of Jerusalem are the altars you have set up to shame, altars to make offerings to Baal.

¹⁴"Therefore do not pray for this people, or lift up a cry or prayer on their behalf, for I will not listen when they call to me in the time of their trouble. ¹⁵What right has my beloved in my house, when she has done many vile deeds? Can even sacrificial flesh avert your doom? Can you then exult? ¹⁶The LORD once called you 'a green olive tree, beautiful with good fruit.' But with the roar of a great tempest he will set fire to it, and its branches will be consumed. ¹⁷The LORD of hosts, who planted you, has decreed disaster against you, because of the evil that the house of Israel and the house of Judah have done, provoking me to anger by making offerings to Baal."

¹⁸ The LORD made it known to me and
    I knew;
    then you showed me their deeds.
¹⁹ But I was like a gentle lamb
    led to the slaughter.
  I did not know it was against me
    they devised schemes, saying,
  "Let us destroy the tree with its fruit,
    let us cut him off from the land of
      the living,
    that his name be remembered no
      more."
²⁰ But, O LORD of hosts, who judges
    righteously,
  who tests the heart and the mind,
  let me see your vengeance upon them,
    for to you have I committed my
      cause.

²¹ Therefore thus says the Lord concerning the men of Anathoth, who seek your life, and say, "Do not prophesy in the name of the Lord, or you will die by our hand"— ²² therefore thus says the Lord of hosts: Behold, I will punish them. The young men shall die by the sword, their sons and their daughters shall die by famine, ²³ and none of them shall be left. For I will bring disaster upon the men of Anathoth, the year of their punishment."

Jeremiah's Complaint

12 Righteous are you, O Lord,
    when I complain to you;
      yet I would plead my case before
        you.
Why does the way of the wicked prosper?
    Why do all who are treacherous
      thrive?
² You plant them, and they take root;
    they grow and produce fruit;
you are near in their mouth
    and far from their heart.
³ But you, O Lord, know me;
    you see me, and test my heart
      toward you.
Pull them out like sheep for the
      slaughter,
    and set them apart for the day of
      slaughter.
⁴ How long will the land mourn
    and the grass of every field
      wither?
For the evil of those who dwell in it
    the beasts and the birds are swept
      away,
    because they said, "He will not see
      our latter end."

The Lord Answers Jeremiah

⁵ "If you have raced with men on foot,
    and they have wearied you,
      how will you compete with horses?
And if in a safe land you are so trusting,
    what will you do in the thicket of
      the Jordan?
⁶ For even your brothers and the
      house of your father,
    even they have dealt treacherously
      with you;
    they are in full cry after you;

do not believe them,
    though they speak friendly words
      to you."

⁷ "I have forsaken my house;
    I have abandoned my heritage;
    I have given the beloved of my soul
      into the hands of her enemies.
⁸ My heritage has become to me
    like a lion in the forest;
she has lifted up her voice against me;
    therefore I hate her.
⁹ Is my heritage to me like a hyena's
      lair?
    Are the birds of prey against her
      all around?
Go, assemble all the wild beasts;
    bring them to devour.
¹⁰ Many shepherds have destroyed my
      vineyard;
    they have trampled down my portion;
they have made my pleasant portion
    a desolate wilderness.
¹¹ They have made it a desolation;
    desolate, it mourns to me.
The whole land is made desolate,
    but no man lays it to heart.
¹² Upon all the bare heights in the desert
    destroyers have come,
for the sword of the Lord devours
    from one end of the land to the
      other;
    no flesh has peace.
¹³ They have sown wheat and have
      reaped thorns;
    they have tired themselves out but
      profit nothing.
They shall be ashamed of their¹ harvests
    because of the fierce anger of the
      Lord."

¹⁴ Thus says the Lord concerning all my evil neighbors who touch the heritage that I have given my people Israel to inherit: "Behold, I will pluck them up from their land, and I will pluck up the house of Judah from among them. ¹⁵ And after I have plucked them up, I will again have compassion on them, and I will bring them again each to his heritage and each to his land. ¹⁶ And it shall come to pass, if they will diligently learn the ways of my people, to swear by my name, 'As the Lord lives,'

---

even as they taught my people to swear by Baal, then they shall be built up in the midst of my people. **17** But if any nation will not listen, then I will utterly pluck it up and destroy it, declares the LORD."

The Ruined Loincloth

13 Thus says the LORD to me, "Go and buy a linen loincloth and put it around your waist, and do not dip it in water." **2** So I bought a loincloth according to the word of the LORD, and put it around my waist. **3** And the word of the LORD came to me a second time, **4** "Take the loincloth that you have bought, which is around your waist, and arise, go to the Euphrates and hide it there in a cleft of the rock." **5** So I went and hid it by the Euphrates, as the LORD commanded me. **6** And after many days the LORD said to me, "Arise, go to the Euphrates, and take from there the loincloth that I commanded you to hide there." **7** Then I went to the Euphrates, and dug, and I took the loincloth from the place where I had hidden it. And behold, the loincloth was spoiled; it was good for nothing.

8 Then the word of the LORD came to me: **9** "Thus says the LORD: Even so will I spoil the pride of Judah and the great pride of Jerusalem. **10** This evil people, who refuse to hear my words, who stubbornly follow their own heart and have gone after other gods to serve them and worship them, shall be like this loincloth, which is good for nothing. **11** For as the loincloth clings to the waist of a man, so I made the whole house of Israel and the whole house of Judah cling to me, declares the LORD, that they might be for me a people, a name, a praise, and a glory, but they would not listen.

The Jars Filled with Wine

12 "You shall speak to them this word: 'Thus says the LORD, the God of Israel, "Every jar shall be filled with wine."' And they will say to you, 'Do we not indeed know that every jar will be filled with wine?' **13** Then you shall say to them, 'Thus says the LORD: Behold, I will fill with drunkenness all the inhabitants of this land: the kings who sit on David's throne, the priests, the prophets, and all the inhabitants of Jerusalem. **14** And I will dash them

one against another, fathers and sons together, declares the LORD. I will not pity or spare or have compassion, that I should not destroy them.' "

Exile Threatened

15   Hear and give ear; be not proud,
        for the LORD has spoken.
16   Give glory to the LORD your God
        before he brings darkness,
    before your feet stumble
        on the twilight mountains,
    and while you look for light
        he turns it into gloom
        and makes it deep darkness.
17   But if you will not listen,
        my soul will weep in secret for
            your pride;
    my eyes will weep bitterly and run
            down with tears,
        because the LORD's flock has been
            taken captive.

18   Say to the king and the queen mother:
        "Take a lowly seat,
    for your beautiful crown
        has come down from your head."
19   The cities of the Negeb are shut up,
        with none to open them;
    all Judah is taken into exile,
        wholly taken into exile.

20   "Lift up your eyes and see
        those who come from the north.
    Where is the flock that was given
            you,
        your beautiful flock?
21   What will you say when they set as
            head over you
        those whom you yourself have
            taught to be friends to you?
    Will not pangs take hold of you
        like those of a woman in labor?
22   And if you say in your heart,
        'Why have these things come upon
            me?'
    it is for the greatness of your iniquity
        that your skirts are lifted up
        and you suffer violence.
23   Can the Ethiopian change his skin
        or the leopard his spots?
    Then also you can do good
        who are accustomed to do evil.
24   I will scatter you[1] like chaff
        driven by the wind from the desert

---

[1] Hebrew *them*

²⁵ This is your lot,
 the portion I have measured out to
   you, declares the LORD,
because you have forgotten me
 and trusted in lies.
²⁶ I myself will lift up your skirts over
   your face,
 and your shame will be seen.
²⁷ I have seen your abominations,
 your adulteries and neighings,
  your lewd whorings,
 on the hills in the field.
Woe to you, O Jerusalem!
 How long will it be before you are
   made clean?"

Famine, Sword, and Pestilence

14 The word of the LORD that came to Jeremiah concerning the drought:

² "Judah mourns,
 and her gates languish;
her people lament on the ground,
 and the cry of Jerusalem goes up.
³ Her nobles send their servants for
   water;
 they come to the cisterns;
they find no water;
 they return with their vessels
   empty;
they are ashamed and confounded
 and cover their heads.
⁴ Because of the ground that is dismayed,
 since there is no rain on the land,
the farmers are ashamed;
 they cover their heads.
⁵ Even the doe in the field forsakes her
   newborn fawn
 because there is no grass.
⁶ The wild donkeys stand on the bare
   heights;
 they pant for air like jackals;
their eyes fail
 because there is no vegetation.

⁷ "Though our iniquities testify against
   us,
 act, O LORD, for your name's sake;
for our backslidings are many;
 we have sinned against you.
⁸ O you hope of Israel,
 its savior in time of trouble,
why should you be like a stranger in
   the land,
 like a traveler who turns aside to
   tarry for a night?

⁹ Why should you be like a man confused,
 like a mighty warrior who cannot
   save?
Yet you, O LORD, are in the midst of us,
 and we are called by your name;
  do not leave us."

¹⁰ Thus says the LORD concerning this
   people:
"They have loved to wander thus;
 they have not restrained their feet;
therefore the LORD does not accept
   them;
 now he will remember their iniquity
  and punish their sins."

¹¹ The LORD said to me: "Do not pray for the welfare of this people. ¹² Though they fast, I will not hear their cry, and though they offer burnt offering and grain offering, I will not accept them. But I will consume them by the sword, by famine, and by pestilence."

Lying Prophets

¹³ Then I said: "Ah, Lord GOD, behold, the prophets say to them, 'You shall not see the sword, nor shall you have famine, but I will give you assured peace in this place.'" ¹⁴ And the LORD said to me: "The prophets are prophesying lies in my name. I did not send them, nor did I command them or speak to them. They are prophesying to you a lying vision, worthless divination, and the deceit of their own minds. ¹⁵ Therefore thus says the LORD concerning the prophets who prophesy in my name although I did not send them, and who say, 'Sword and famine shall not come upon this land': By sword and famine those prophets shall be consumed. ¹⁶ And the people to whom they prophesy shall be cast out in the streets of Jerusalem, victims of famine and sword, with none to bury them— them, their wives, their sons, and their daughters. For I will pour out their evil upon them.

¹⁷ "You shall say to them this word:
'Let my eyes run down with tears
   night and day,
 and let them not cease,
for the virgin daughter of my people
 is shattered with a great
   wound,
 with a very grievous blow.

18 If I go out into the field,
  behold, those pierced by the sword!
And if I enter the city,
  behold, the diseases of famine!
For both prophet and priest ply their
    trade through the land
  and have no knowledge.' "

19 Have you utterly rejected Judah?
  Does your soul loathe Zion?
Why have you struck us down
  so that there is no healing for us?
We looked for peace, but no good
    came;
  for a time of healing, but behold,
    terror.
20 We acknowledge our wickedness,
    O Lord,
  and the iniquity of our fathers,
  for we have sinned against you.
21 Do not spurn us, for your name's sake;
  do not dishonor your glorious
    throne;
  remember and do not break your
    covenant with us.
22 Are there any among the false gods
    of the nations that can bring
    rain?
  Or can the heavens give showers?
Are you not he, O Lord our God?
  We set our hope on you,
  for you do all these things.

The Lord Will Not Relent

15 Then the Lord said to me, "Though
Moses and Samuel stood before me,
yet my heart would not turn toward this
people. Send them out of my sight, and let
them go! ²And when they ask you, 'Where
shall we go?' you shall say to them, 'Thus
says the Lord:

  " 'Those who are for pestilence, to pesti-
    lence,
  and those who are for the sword,
    to the sword;
  those who are for famine, to famine,
    and those who are for captivity, to
    captivity.'

³ I will appoint over them four kinds of
destroyers, declares the Lord: the sword to
kill, the dogs to tear, and the birds of the air
and the beasts of the earth to devour and
destroy. ⁴And I will make them a horror to
all the kingdoms of the earth because of

what Manasseh the son of Hezekiah, king
of Judah, did in Jerusalem.

5 "Who will have pity on you,
    O Jerusalem,
  or who will grieve for you?
Who will turn aside
  to ask about your welfare?
6 You have rejected me, declares the
    Lord;
  you keep going backward,
so I have stretched out my hand
    against you and destroyed
    you—
  I am weary of relenting.
7 I have winnowed them with a win-
    nowing fork
  in the gates of the land;
I have bereaved them; I have
    destroyed my people;
  they did not turn from their ways.
8 I have made their widows more in
    number
  than the sand of the seas;
I have brought against the mothers
    of young men
  a destroyer at noonday;
I have made anguish and terror
  fall upon them suddenly.
9 She who bore seven has grown feeble;
  she has fainted away;
her sun went down while it was yet
    day;
  she has been shamed and dis-
    graced.
And the rest of them I will give to the
    sword
  before their enemies,
            declares the Lord."

Jeremiah's Complaint

¹⁰Woe is me, my mother, that you bore
me, a man of strife and contention to the
whole land! I have not lent, nor have I borrowed, yet all of them curse me. ¹¹The
Lord said, "Have I not¹ set you free for
their good? Have I not pleaded for you
before the enemy in the time of trouble
and in the time of distress? ¹²Can one break
iron, iron from the north, and bronze?

¹³"Your wealth and your treasures I will
give as spoil, without price, for all your
sins, throughout all your territory. ¹⁴I will
make you serve your enemies in a land that

¹The meaning of the Hebrew is uncertain

you do not know, for in my anger a fire is
kindled that shall burn forever."

15 O Lord, you know;
    remember me and visit me,
      and take vengeance for me on my
        persecutors.
  In your forbearance take me not away;
    know that for your sake I bear
      reproach.
16 Your words were found, and I ate
      them,
    and your words became to me a joy
      and the delight of my heart,
  for I am called by your name,
    O Lord, God of hosts.
17 I did not sit in the company of revel-
      ers,
    nor did I rejoice;
  I sat alone, because your hand was
      upon me,
    for you had filled me with indigna-
      tion.
18 Why is my pain unceasing,
    my wound incurable,
      refusing to be healed?
  Will you be to me like a deceitful
      brook,
    like waters that fail?

19 Therefore thus says the Lord:
  "If you return, I will restore you,
    and you shall stand before me.
  If you utter what is precious, and not
      what is worthless,
    you shall be as my mouth.
  They shall turn to you,
    but you shall not turn to them.
20 And I will make you to this people
    a fortified wall of bronze;
  they will fight against you,
    but they shall not prevail over you,
  for I am with you
    to save you and deliver you,
                    declares the Lord.
21 I will deliver you out of the hand of
      the wicked,
    and redeem you from the grasp of
      the ruthless."

Famine, Sword, and Death

16 The word of the Lord came to me:
  2 "You shall not take a wife, nor shall
you have sons or daughters in this place.
3 For thus says the Lord concerning the
sons and daughters who are born in this
place, and concerning the mothers who

bore them and the fathers who fathered
them in this land: 4 They shall die of deadly
diseases. They shall not be lamented, nor
shall they be buried. They shall be as dung
on the surface of the ground. They shall
perish by the sword and by famine, and
their dead bodies shall be food for the
birds of the air and for the beasts of the
earth.

5 "For thus says the Lord: Do not enter
the house of mourning, or go to lament or
grieve for them, for I have taken away my
peace from this people, my steadfast love
and mercy, declares the Lord. 6 Both great
and small shall die in this land. They shall
not be buried, and no one shall lament for
them or cut himself or make himself bald
for them. 7 No one shall break bread for the
mourner, to comfort him for the dead, nor
shall anyone give him the cup of consolation to drink for his father or his mother.
8 You shall not go into the house of feasting
to sit with them, to eat and drink. 9 For thus
says the Lord of hosts, the God of Israel:
Behold, I will silence in this place, before
your eyes and in your days, the voice of
mirth and the voice of gladness, the voice of
the bridegroom and the voice of the bride.

10 "And when you tell this people all these
words, and they say to you, 'Why has the
Lord pronounced all this great evil against
us? What is our iniquity? What is the sin
that we have committed against the Lord
our God?' 11 then you shall say to them:
'Because your fathers have forsaken me,
declares the Lord, and have gone after
other gods and have served and worshiped
them, and have forsaken me and have not
kept my law, 12 and because you have done
worse than your fathers, for behold, every
one of you follows his stubborn, evil will,
refusing to listen to me. 13 Therefore I will
hurl you out of this land into a land that
neither you nor your fathers have known,
and there you shall serve other gods day
and night, for I will show you no favor.'

The Lord Will Restore Israel

14 "Therefore, behold, the days are coming, declares the Lord, when it shall no
longer be said, 'As the Lord lives who
brought up the people of Israel out of the
land of Egypt,' 15 but 'As the Lord lives who
brought up the people of Israel out of the
north country and out of all the countries
where he had driven them.' For I will bring

them back to their own land that I gave to their fathers.

¹⁶ "Behold, I am sending for many fishers, declares the LORD, and they shall catch them. And afterward I will send for many hunters, and they shall hunt them from every mountain and every hill, and out of the clefts of the rocks. ¹⁷ For my eyes are on all their ways. They are not hidden from me, nor is their iniquity concealed from my eyes. ¹⁸ But first I will doubly repay their iniquity and their sin, because they have polluted my land with the carcasses of their detestable idols, and have filled my inheritance with their abominations."

A Prayer for...
TRUST

Almighty God, please help me to be who you want me to be and to do what you want me to do. Help me to always listen to the voice of your Spirit inside of me and not to let one fault go unrepented of or one spot in my heart stay uncleaned. Help me to not hold on to even the sin that will cost me the most to part with; to not look back but forward; to not cast my eyes down to the ground but lift them up to heaven; to not lean on mortal man but on you, the Rock of Ages. And keep me loving all mankind, doing good to all people, loving you, and never doubting that you love me and will make all things work together for the good of those who trust in you, my Lord, my Father and my God.

Amen.

¹⁹ O LORD, my strength and my strong-
        hold,
    my refuge in the day of trouble,
to you shall the nations come
        from the ends of the earth and say:
"Our fathers have inherited nothing
            but lies,
        worthless things in which there is
            no profit.

²⁰ Can man make for himself gods?
        Such are not gods!"

²¹ "Therefore, behold, I will make them know, this once I will make them know my power and my might, and they shall know that my name is the LORD."

The Sin of Judah

17 "The sin of Judah is written with a pen of iron; with a point of diamond it is engraved on the tablet of their heart and on the horns of their altars, ² while their children remember their altars and their Asherim, beside every green tree and on the high hills, ³ on the mountains in the open country. Your wealth and all your treasures I will give for spoil as the price of your high places for sin throughout all your territory. ⁴ You shall loosen your hand from your heritage that I gave to you, and I will make you serve your enemies in a land that you do not know, for in my anger a fire is kindled that shall burn forever."

⁵ Thus says the LORD:
"Cursed is the man who trusts in man
        and makes flesh his strength,[1]
        whose heart turns away from the
            LORD.
⁶ He is like a shrub in the desert,
        and shall not see any good come.
He shall dwell in the parched places
            of the wilderness,
        in an uninhabited salt land.

⁷ "Blessed is the man who trusts in the
            LORD,
        whose trust is the LORD.
⁸ He is like a tree planted by water,
        that sends out its roots by the
            stream,
    and does not fear when heat comes,
        for its leaves remain green,
    and is not anxious in the year of
            drought,
        for it does not cease to bear fruit."

⁹ The heart is deceitful above all things,
        and desperately sick;
        who can understand it?
¹⁰ "I the LORD search the heart
        and test the mind,[2]
    to give every man according to his
            ways,
        according to the fruit of his deeds."

¹ Hebrew *arm* ² Hebrew *kidneys*

1 Like the partridge that gathers a
    brood that she did not hatch,
  so is he who gets riches but not by
    justice;
  in the midst of his days they will
    leave him,
  and at his end he will be a fool.

2 A glorious throne set on high from
    the beginning
  is the place of our sanctuary.

3 O LORD, the hope of Israel,
  all who forsake you shall be put to
    shame;
  those who turn away from you[1] shall
    be written in the earth,
  for they have forsaken the LORD,
    the fountain of living water.

Jeremiah Prays for Deliverance

4 Heal me, O LORD, and I shall be healed;
  save me, and I shall be saved,
    for you are my praise.
5 Behold, they say to me,
  "Where is the word of the LORD?
    Let it come!"
6 I have not run away from being your
    shepherd,
  nor have I desired the day of sick-
    ness.
  You know what came out of my lips;
    it was before your face.
7 Be not a terror to me;
  you are my refuge in the day of
    disaster.
8 Let those be put to shame who per-
    secute me,
  but let me not be put to shame;
  let them be dismayed,
    but let me not be dismayed;
  bring upon them the day of disaster;
    destroy them with double destruc-
      tion!

Keep the Sabbath Holy

19 Thus said the LORD to me: "Go and
stand in the People's Gate, by which the
kings of Judah enter and by which they go
out, and in all the gates of Jerusalem, 20 and
say: 'Hear the word of the LORD, you kings
of Judah, and all Judah, and all the inhabitants of Jerusalem, who enter by these
gates. 21 Thus says the LORD: Take care for
the sake of your lives, and do not bear a
burden on the Sabbath day or bring it in by
the gates of Jerusalem. 22 And do not carry a
burden out of your houses on the Sabbath
or do any work, but keep the Sabbath day
holy, as I commanded your fathers. 23 Yet
they did not listen or incline their ear, but
stiffened their neck, that they might not
hear and receive instruction.

24 "'But if you listen to me, declares the
LORD, and bring in no burden by the gates
of this city on the Sabbath day, but keep
the Sabbath day holy and do no work on it,
25 then there shall enter by the gates of this
city kings and princes who sit on the throne
of David, riding in chariots and on horses,
they and their officials, the men of Judah
and the inhabitants of Jerusalem. And this
city shall be inhabited forever. 26 And people
shall come from the cities of Judah and the
places around Jerusalem, from the land of
Benjamin, from the Shephelah, from the
hill country, and from the Negeb, bringing burnt offerings and sacrifices, grain
offerings and frankincense, and bringing
thank offerings to the house of the LORD.
27 But if you do not listen to me, to keep the
Sabbath day holy, and not to bear a burden
and enter by the gates of Jerusalem on the
Sabbath day, then I will kindle a fire in
its gates, and it shall devour the palaces
of Jerusalem and shall not be quenched.'"

The Potter and the Clay

18 The word that came to Jeremiah
from the LORD: 2 "Arise, and go down
to the potter's house, and there I will let
you hear my words." 3 So I went down to
the potter's house, and there he was working at his wheel. 4 And the vessel he was
making of clay was spoiled in the potter's
hand, and he reworked it into another vessel, as it seemed good to the potter to do.

5 Then the word of the LORD came to me:
6 "O house of Israel, can I not do with you
as this potter has done? declares the LORD.
Behold, like the clay in the potter's hand, so
are you in my hand, O house of Israel. 7 If at
any time I declare concerning a nation or
a kingdom, that I will pluck up and break
down and destroy it, 8 and if that nation,
concerning which I have spoken, turns
from its evil, I will relent of the disaster
that I intended to do to it. 9 And if at any
time I declare concerning a nation or a
kingdom that I will build and plant it, 10 and
if it does evil in my sight, not listening to

my voice, then I will relent of the good that I had intended to do to it. [11] Now, therefore, say to the men of Judah and the inhabitants of Jerusalem: 'Thus says the LORD, Behold, I am shaping disaster against you and devising a plan against you. Return, every one from his evil way, and amend your ways and your deeds.'

[12] "But they say, 'That is in vain! We will follow our own plans, and will every one act according to the stubbornness of his evil heart.'

[13]   "Therefore thus says the LORD:
Ask among the nations,
    Who has heard the like of this?
The virgin Israel
    has done a very horrible thing.
[14]   Does the snow of Lebanon leave
        the crags of Sirion?[1]
Do the mountain waters run dry,[2]
    the cold flowing streams?
[15]   But my people have forgotten me;
    they make offerings to false gods;
they made them stumble in their
        ways,
    in the ancient roads,
and to walk into side roads,
    not the highway,
[16]   making their land a horror,
        a thing to be hissed at forever.
Everyone who passes by it is horrified
    and shakes his head.
[17]   Like the east wind I will scatter them
        before the enemy.
I will show them my back, not my face,
    in the day of their calamity."

[18] Then they said, "Come, let us make plots against Jeremiah, for the law shall not perish from the priest, nor counsel from the wise, nor the word from the prophet. Come, let us strike him with the tongue, and let us not pay attention to any of his words."

[19]   Hear me, O LORD,
        and listen to the voice of my adversaries.
[20]   Should good be repaid with evil?
        Yet they have dug a pit for my life.
    Remember how I stood before you
        to speak good for them,
        to turn away your wrath from
            them.

[21]   Therefore deliver up their children
            to famine;
        give them over to the power of the
            sword;
    let their wives become childless and
        widowed.
    May their men meet death by
        pestilence,
        their youths be struck down by the
            sword in battle.
[22]   May a cry be heard from their houses
        when you bring the plunderer suddenly upon them!
    For they have dug a pit to take me
        and laid snares for my feet.
[23]   Yet you, O LORD, know
        all their plotting to kill me.
    Forgive not their iniquity,
        nor blot out their sin from your
            sight.
    Let them be overthrown before you;
        deal with them in the time of your
            anger.

The Broken Flask

19 Thus says the LORD, "Go, buy a potter's earthenware flask, and take some of the elders of the people and some of the elders of the priests, [2] and go out to the Valley of the Son of Hinnom at the entry of the Potsherd Gate, and proclaim there the words that I tell you. [3] You shall say, 'Hear the word of the LORD, O kings of Judah and inhabitants of Jerusalem. Thus says the LORD of hosts, the God of Israel, Behold, I am bringing such disaster upon this place that the ears of everyone who hears of it will tingle. [4] Because the people have forsaken me and have profaned this place by making offerings in it to other gods whom neither they nor their fathers nor the kings of Judah have known; and because they have filled this place with the blood of innocents, [5] and have built the high places of Baal to burn their sons in the fire as burnt offerings to Baal, which I did not command or decree, nor did it come into my mind— [6] therefore, behold, days are coming, declares the LORD, when this place shall no more be called Topheth, or the Valley of the Son of Hinnom, but the Valley of Slaughter. [7] And in this place I will make void the plans of Judah and Jerusalem, and will cause their people to fall by the sword before their enemies, and by the hand of

---

[1] Hebrew *of the field* [2] Hebrew *Are foreign waters plucked up*

those who seek their life. I will give their dead bodies for food to the birds of the air and to the beasts of the earth. ⁸And I will make this city a horror, a thing to be hissed at. Everyone who passes by it will be horrified and will hiss because of all its wounds. ⁹And I will make them eat the flesh of their sons and their daughters, and everyone shall eat the flesh of his neighbor in the siege and in the distress, with which their enemies and those who seek their life afflict them.'

¹⁰"Then you shall break the flask in the sight of the men who go with you, ¹¹and shall say to them, 'Thus says the Lord of hosts: So will I break this people and this city, as one breaks a potter's vessel, so that it can never be mended. Men shall bury in Topheth because there will be no place else to bury. ¹²Thus will I do to this place, declares the Lord, and to its inhabitants, making this city like Topheth. ¹³The houses of Jerusalem and the houses of the kings of Judah—all the houses on whose roofs offerings have been offered to all the host of heaven, and drink offerings have been poured out to other gods—shall be defiled like the place of Topheth.'"

¹⁴Then Jeremiah came from Topheth, where the Lord had sent him to prophesy, and he stood in the court of the Lord's house and said to all the people: ¹⁵"Thus says the Lord of hosts, the God of Israel, behold, I am bringing upon this city and upon all its towns all the disaster that I have pronounced against it, because they have stiffened their neck, refusing to hear my words."

Jeremiah Persecuted by Pashhur

20 Now Pashhur the priest, the son of Immer, who was chief officer in the house of the Lord, heard Jeremiah prophesying these things. ²Then Pashhur beat Jeremiah the prophet, and put him in the stocks that were in the upper Benjamin Gate of the house of the Lord. ³The next day, when Pashhur released Jeremiah from the stocks, Jeremiah said to him, "The Lord does not call your name Pashhur, but Terror on Every Side. ⁴For thus says the Lord: Behold, I will make you a terror to yourself and to all your friends. They shall fall by the sword of their enemies while you look on. And I will give all Judah

into the hand of the king of Babylon. He shall carry them captive to Babylon, and shall strike them down with the sword. ⁵Moreover, I will give all the wealth of the city, all its gains, all its prized belongings, and all the treasures of the kings of Judah into the hand of their enemies, who shall plunder them and seize them and carry them to Babylon. ⁶And you, Pashhur, and all who dwell in your house, shall go into captivity. To Babylon you shall go, and there you shall die, and there you shall be buried, you and all your friends, to whom you have prophesied falsely."

⁷ O Lord, you have deceived me,
      and I was deceived;
   you are stronger than I,
      and you have prevailed.
   I have become a laughingstock all the
         day;
      everyone mocks me.
⁸ For whenever I speak, I cry out,
      I shout, "Violence and destruction!"
   For the word of the Lord has become
         for me
      a reproach and derision all day long.
⁹ If I say, "I will not mention him,
      or speak any more in his name,"
   there is in my heart as it were a
         burning fire
      shut up in my bones,
   and I am weary with holding it in,
      and I cannot.
¹⁰ For I hear many whispering.
      Terror is on every side!
   "Denounce him! Let us denounce him!"
      say all my close friends,
      watching for my fall.
   "Perhaps he will be deceived;
      then we can overcome him
      and take our revenge on him."
¹¹ But the Lord is with me as a dread
         warrior;
      therefore my persecutors will
         stumble;
      they will not overcome me.
   They will be greatly shamed,
      for they will not succeed.
   Their eternal dishonor
      will never be forgotten.
¹² O Lord of hosts, who tests the righ-
         teous,
      who sees the heart and the mind,¹

¹ Hebrew *kidneys*

let me see your vengeance upon them,
    for to you have I committed my
        cause.

13 Sing to the Lord;
        praise the Lord!
    For he has delivered the life of the
        needy
        from the hand of evildoers.

14 Cursed be the day
        on which I was born!
    The day when my mother bore me,
        let it not be blessed!
15 Cursed be the man who brought the
        news to my father,
    "A son is born to you,"
        making him very glad.
16 Let that man be like the cities
        that the Lord overthrew without
        pity;
    let him hear a cry in the morning
        and an alarm at noon,
17 because he did not kill me in the
        womb;
    so my mother would have been my
        grave,
        and her womb forever great.
18 Why did I come out from the womb
        to see toil and sorrow,
        and spend my days in shame?

Jerusalem Will Fall to Nebuchadnezzar

21 This is the word that came to Jeremiah from the Lord, when King Zedekiah sent to him Pashhur the son of Malchiah and Zephaniah the priest, the son of Maaseiah, saying, [2] "Inquire of the Lord for us, for Nebuchadnezzar[1] king of Babylon is making war against us. Perhaps the Lord will deal with us according to all his wonderful deeds and will make him withdraw from us."

[3] Then Jeremiah said to them: "Thus you shall say to Zedekiah, [4] 'Thus says the Lord, the God of Israel: Behold, I will turn back the weapons of war that are in your hands and with which you are fighting against the king of Babylon and against the Chaldeans who are besieging you outside the walls. And I will bring them together into the midst of this city. [5] I myself will fight against you with outstretched hand and strong arm, in anger and in fury and in great wrath. [6] And I will strike down

the inhabitants of this city, both man and beast. They shall die of a great pestilence. [7] Afterward, declares the Lord, I will give Zedekiah king of Judah and his servants and the people in this city who survive the pestilence, sword, and famine into the hand of Nebuchadnezzar king of Babylon and into the hand of their enemies, into the hand of those who seek their lives. He shall strike them down with the edge of the sword. He shall not pity them or spare them or have compassion.'

[8] "And to this people you shall say: 'Thus says the Lord: Behold, I set before you the way of life and the way of death. [9] He who stays in this city shall die by the sword, by famine, and by pestilence, but he who goes out and surrenders to the Chaldeans who are besieging you shall live and shall have his life as a prize of war. [10] For I have set my face against this city for harm and not for good, declares the Lord: it shall be given into the hand of the king of Babylon, and he shall burn it with fire.'

Message to the House of David

[11] "And to the house of the king of Judah say, 'Hear the word of the Lord, [12] O house of David! Thus says the Lord:

" 'Execute justice in the morning,
        and deliver from the hand of the
        oppressor
    him who has been robbed,
    lest my wrath go forth like fire,
        and burn with none to quench it,
        because of your evil deeds.' "

13 "Behold, I am against you, O inhabitant
        of the valley,
        O rock of the plain,
                declares the Lord;
    you who say, 'Who shall come down
        against us,
        or who shall enter our habitations?'
14 I will punish you according to the
        fruit of your deeds,
                declares the Lord;
    I will kindle a fire in her forest,
        and it shall devour all that is
        around her."

22 Thus says the Lord: "Go down to the house of the king of Judah and speak there this word, [2] and say, 'Hear the

---

[1] Hebrew *Nebuchadrezzar*, an alternate spelling of *Nebuchadnezzar* (king of Babylon) occurring frequently from Jeremiah 21–52; this latter spelling is used throughout Jeremiah for consistency

word of the LORD, O king of Judah, who
sits on the throne of David, you, and your
servants, and your people who enter these
gates. ³ Thus says the LORD: Do justice
and righteousness, and deliver from the
hand of the oppressor him who has been
robbed. And do no wrong or violence to
the resident alien, the fatherless, and the
widow, nor shed innocent blood in this
place. ⁴ For if you will indeed obey this
word, then there shall enter the gates of
this house kings who sit on the throne of
David, riding in chariots and on horses,
they and their servants and their people.
⁵ But if you will not obey these words, I
swear by myself, declares the LORD, that
this house shall become a desolation. ⁶ For
thus says the LORD concerning the house
of the king of Judah:

> "'You are like Gilead to me,
>   like the summit of Lebanon,
> yet surely I will make you a desert,
>   an uninhabited city.¹
⁷ I will prepare destroyers against
>   you,
>   each with his weapons,
> and they shall cut down your choic-
>   est cedars
>   and cast them into the fire.

⁸ "'And many nations will pass by this
city, and every man will say to his neighbor, "Why has the LORD dealt thus with
this great city?" ⁹ And they will answer,
"Because they have forsaken the covenant
of the LORD their God and worshiped other
gods and served them."'"

¹⁰ Weep not for him who is dead,
>   nor grieve for him,
> but weep bitterly for him who goes
>   away,
>   for he shall return no more
>   to see his native land.

Message to the Sons of Josiah

¹¹ For thus says the LORD concerning
Shallum the son of Josiah, king of Judah,
who reigned instead of Josiah his father,
and who went away from this place: "He
shall return here no more, ¹² but in the
place where they have carried him captive,
there shall he die, and he shall never see
this land again."

Hebrew *cities*

¹³ "Woe to him who builds his house by
>   unrighteousness,
>   and his upper rooms by injustice,
> who makes his neighbor serve him
>   for nothing
>   and does not give him his wages,
¹⁴ who says, 'I will build myself a great
>   house
>   with spacious upper rooms,'
> who cuts out windows for it,
>   paneling it with cedar
>   and painting it with vermilion.
¹⁵ Do you think you are a king
>   because you compete in cedar?
> Did not your father eat and drink
>   and do justice and righteousness?
>   Then it was well with him.
¹⁶ He judged the cause of the poor and
>   needy;
>   then it was well.
> Is not this to know me?
>   declares the LORD.
¹⁷ But you have eyes and heart
>   only for your dishonest gain,
> for shedding innocent blood,
>   and for practicing oppression and
>   violence."

¹⁸ Therefore thus says the LORD concerning Jehoiakim the son of Josiah, king of
Judah:

> "They shall not lament for him, saying,
>   'Ah, my brother!' or 'Ah, sister!'
> They shall not lament for him, saying,
>   'Ah, lord!' or 'Ah, his majesty!'
¹⁹ With the burial of a donkey he shall
>   be buried,
>   dragged and dumped beyond the
>   gates of Jerusalem."

²⁰ "Go up to Lebanon, and cry out,
>   and lift up your voice in Bashan;
> cry out from Abarim,
>   for all your lovers are destroyed.
²¹ I spoke to you in your prosperity,
>   but you said, 'I will not listen.'
> This has been your way from your
>   youth,
>   that you have not obeyed my voice.
²² The wind shall shepherd all your
>   shepherds,
>   and your lovers shall go into cap-
>   tivity;

then you will be ashamed and confounded
because of all your evil.
23 O inhabitant of Lebanon,
nested among the cedars,
how you will be pitied when pangs
come upon you,
pain as of a woman in labor!"

24 "As I live, declares the LORD, though Coniah the son of Jehoiakim, king of Judah, were the signet ring on my right hand, yet I would tear you off 25 and give you into the hand of those who seek your life, into the hand of those of whom you are afraid, even into the hand of Nebuchadnezzar king of Babylon and into the hand of the Chaldeans. 26 I will hurl you and the mother who bore you into another country, where you were not born, and there you shall die. 27 But to the land to which they will long to return, there they shall not return."

28 Is this man Coniah a despised, broken pot,
a vessel no one cares for?
Why are he and his children hurled
and cast
into a land that they do not know?
29 O land, land, land,
hear the word of the LORD!
30 Thus says the LORD:
"Write this man down as childless,
a man who shall not succeed in his
days,
for none of his offspring shall succeed
in sitting on the throne of David
and ruling again in Judah."

The Righteous Branch

23 "Woe to the shepherds who destroy and scatter the sheep of my pasture!" declares the LORD. 2 Therefore thus says the LORD, the God of Israel, concerning the shepherds who care for my people: "You have scattered my flock and have driven them away, and you have not attended to them. Behold, I will attend to you for your evil deeds, declares the LORD. 3 Then I will gather the remnant of my flock out of all the countries where I have driven them, and I will bring them back to their fold, and they shall be fruitful and multiply. 4 I will set shepherds over them who will care for them, and they shall fear no more,

nor be dismayed, neither shall any be missing, declares the LORD.

5 "Behold, the days are coming, declares the LORD, when I will raise up for David a righteous Branch, and he shall reign as king and deal wisely, and shall execute justice and righteousness in the land. 6 In his days Judah will be saved, and Israel will dwell securely. And this is the name by which he will be called: 'The LORD is our righteousness.'

7 "Therefore, behold, the days are coming, declares the LORD, when they shall no longer say, 'As the LORD lives who brought up the people of Israel out of the land of Egypt,' 8 but 'As the LORD lives who brought up and led the offspring of the house of Israel out of the north country and out of all the countries where he[1] had driven them.' Then they shall dwell in their own land."

Lying Prophets

9 Concerning the prophets:

My heart is broken within me;
all my bones shake;
I am like a drunken man,
like a man overcome by wine,
because of the LORD
and because of his holy words.
10 For the land is full of adulterers;
because of the curse the land
mourns,
and the pastures of the wilderness
are dried up.
Their course is evil,
and their might is not right.
11 "Both prophet and priest are ungodly;
even in my house I have found
their evil,
declares the LORD.
12 Therefore their way shall be to them
like slippery paths in the darkness,
into which they shall be driven and
fall,
for I will bring disaster upon them
in the year of their punishment,
declares the LORD.
13 In the prophets of Samaria
I saw an unsavory thing:
they prophesied by Baal
and led my people Israel astray.
14 But in the prophets of Jerusalem
I have seen a horrible thing:

[1] Septuagint; Hebrew I

they commit adultery and walk in lies;
  they strengthen the hands of evil-
      doers,
  so that no one turns from his evil;
all of them have become like Sodom
      to me,
  and its inhabitants like Gomorrah."
¹⁵ Therefore thus says the LORD of
      hosts concerning the prophets:
"Behold, I will feed them with bitter
      food
  and give them poisoned water to
      drink,
for from the prophets of Jerusalem
  ungodliness has gone out into all
      the land."

¹⁶ Thus says the LORD of hosts: "Do not
listen to the words of the prophets who
prophesy to you, filling you with vain
hopes. They speak visions of their own
minds, not from the mouth of the LORD.
¹⁷ They say continually to those who
despise the word of the LORD, 'It shall be
well with you'; and to everyone who stubbornly follows his own heart, they say, 'No
disaster shall come upon you.'"

¹⁸ For who among them has stood in
          the council of the LORD
      to see and to hear his word,
      or who has paid attention to his
          word and listened?
¹⁹ Behold, the storm of the LORD!
      Wrath has gone forth,
    a whirling tempest;
      it will burst upon the head of the
          wicked.
²⁰ The anger of the LORD will not turn
          back
      until he has executed and accom-
          plished
      the intents of his heart.
    In the latter days you will under-
        stand it clearly.
²¹ "I did not send the prophets,
      yet they ran;
    I did not speak to them,
      yet they prophesied.
²² But if they had stood in my council,
      then they would have proclaimed
          my words to my people,
    and they would have turned them
          from their evil way,
      and from the evil of their deeds.

²³ "Am I a God at hand, declares the
LORD, and not a God far away? ²⁴ Can a
man hide himself in secret places so that
I cannot see him? declares the LORD. Do
I not fill heaven and earth? declares the
LORD. ²⁵ I have heard what the prophets
have said who prophesy lies in my name,
saying, 'I have dreamed, I have dreamed!'
²⁶ How long shall there be lies in the heart
of the prophets who prophesy lies, and
who prophesy the deceit of their own
heart, ²⁷ who think to make my people forget my name by their dreams that they tell
one another, even as their fathers forgot
my name for Baal? ²⁸ Let the prophet who
has a dream tell the dream, but let him
who has my word speak my word faithfully.
What has straw in common with wheat?
declares the LORD. ²⁹ Is not my word like
fire, declares the LORD, and like a hammer
that breaks the rock in pieces? ³⁰ Therefore,
behold, I am against the prophets, declares
the LORD, who steal my words from one
another. ³¹ Behold, I am against the prophets, declares the LORD, who use their
tongues and declare, 'declares the LORD.'
³² Behold, I am against those who prophesy
lying dreams, declares the LORD, and who
tell them and lead my people astray by
their lies and their recklessness, when I did
not send them or charge them. So they
do not profit this people at all, declares
the LORD.

³³ "When one of this people, or a prophet
or a priest asks you, 'What is the bur-
den of the LORD?' you shall say to them,
'You are the burden,[1] and I will cast you
off, declares the LORD.' ³⁴ And as for the
prophet, priest, or one of the people who
says, 'The burden of the LORD,' I will punish that man and his household. ³⁵ Thus
shall you say, every one to his neighbor
and every one to his brother, 'What has the
LORD answered?' or 'What has the LORD
spoken?' ³⁶ But 'the burden of the LORD'
you shall mention no more, for the burden
is every man's own word, and you pervert
the words of the living God, the LORD of
hosts, our God. ³⁷ Thus you shall say to the
prophet, 'What has the LORD answered
you?' or 'What has the LORD spoken?'
³⁸ But if you say, 'The burden of the LORD,'
thus says the LORD, 'Because you have said
these words, "The burden of the LORD,"
when I sent to you, saying, "You shall not

¹ Septuagint, Vulgate; Hebrew *What burden?*

say, 'The burden of the LORD,' " [39] therefore, behold, I will surely lift you up and cast you away from my presence, you and the city that I gave to you and your fathers. [40] And I will bring upon you everlasting reproach and perpetual shame, which shall not be forgotten.' "

The Good Figs and the Bad Figs

24 After Nebuchadnezzar king of Babylon had taken into exile from Jerusalem Jeconiah the son of Jehoiakim, king of Judah, together with the officials of Judah, the craftsmen, and the metal workers, and had brought them to Babylon, the LORD showed me this vision: behold, two baskets of figs placed before the temple of the LORD. [2] One basket had very good figs, like first-ripe figs, but the other basket had very bad figs, so bad that they could not be eaten. [3] And the LORD said to me, "What do you see, Jeremiah?" I said, "Figs, the good figs very good, and the bad figs very bad, so bad that they cannot be eaten."

[4] Then the word of the LORD came to me: [5] "Thus says the LORD, the God of Israel: Like these good figs, so I will regard as good the exiles from Judah, whom I have sent away from this place to the land of the Chaldeans. [6] I will set my eyes on them for good, and I will bring them back to this land. I will build them up, and not tear them down; I will plant them, and not pluck them up. [7] I will give them a heart to know that I am the LORD, and they shall be my people and I will be their God, for they shall return to me with their whole heart.

[8] "But thus says the LORD: Like the bad figs that are so bad they cannot be eaten, so will I treat Zedekiah the king of Judah, his officials, the remnant of Jerusalem who remain in this land, and those who dwell in the land of Egypt. [9] I will make them a horror[1] to all the kingdoms of the earth, to be a reproach, a byword, a taunt, and a curse in all the places where I shall drive them. [10] And I will send sword, famine, and pestilence upon them, until they shall be utterly destroyed from the land that I gave to them and their fathers."

Seventy Years of Captivity

25 The word that came to Jeremiah concerning all the people of Judah, in the fourth year of Jehoiakim the son of Josiah, king of Judah (that was the first year of Nebuchadnezzar king of Babylon), [2] which Jeremiah the prophet spoke to all the people of Judah and all the inhabitants of Jerusalem: [3] "For twenty-three years, from the thirteenth year of Josiah the son of Amon, king of Judah, to this day, the word of the LORD has come to me, and I have spoken persistently to you, but you have not listened. [4] You have neither listened nor inclined your ears to hear although the LORD persistently sent to you all his servants the prophets, [5] saying, 'Turn now, every one of you, from his evil way and evil deeds, and dwell upon the land that the LORD has given to you and your fathers from of old and forever. [6] Do not go after other gods to serve and worship them, or provoke me to anger with the work of your hands. Then I will do you no harm.' [7] Yet you have not listened to me, declares the LORD, that you might provoke me to anger with the work of your hands to your own harm.

[8] "Therefore thus says the LORD of hosts: Because you have not obeyed my words, [9] behold, I will send for all the tribes of the north, declares the LORD, and for Nebuchadnezzar the king of Babylon, my servant, and I will bring them against this land and its inhabitants, and against all these surrounding nations. I will devote them to destruction, and make them a horror, a hissing, and an everlasting desolation. [10] Moreover, I will banish from them the voice of mirth and the voice of gladness, the voice of the bridegroom and the voice of the bride, the grinding of the millstones and the light of the lamp. [11] This whole land shall become a ruin and a waste, and these nations shall serve the king of Babylon seventy years. [12] Then after seventy years are completed, I will punish the king of Babylon and that nation, the land of the Chaldeans, for their iniquity, declares the LORD, making the land an everlasting waste. [13] I will bring upon that land all the words that I have uttered against it, everything written in this book, which Jeremiah prophesied against all the nations. [14] For many nations and great kings shall make slaves even of them, and I will recompense them according to their deeds and the work of their hands."

[1] Compare Septuagint; Hebrew *horror for evil*

The Cup of the Lord's Wrath

[15] Thus the Lord, the God of Israel, said to me: "Take from my hand this cup of the wine of wrath, and make all the nations to whom I send you drink it. [16] They shall drink and stagger and be crazed because of the sword that I am sending among them."

[17] So I took the cup from the Lord's hand, and made all the nations to whom he Lord sent me drink it: [18] Jerusalem and the cities of Judah, its kings and officials, to make them a desolation and a waste, a hissing and a curse, as at this day; [19] Pharaoh king of Egypt, his servants, his officials, all his people, [20] and all the mixed tribes among them; all the kings of the land of Uz and all the kings of the land of the Philistines (Ashkelon, Gaza, Ekron, and the remnant of Ashdod); [21] Edom, Moab, and the sons of Ammon; [22] all the kings of Tyre, all the kings of Sidon, and the kings of the coastland across the sea; [23] Dedan, Tema, Buz, and all who cut the corners of their hair; [24] all the kings of Arabia and all the kings of the mixed tribes who dwell in the desert; [25] all the kings of Zimri, all the kings of Elam, and all the kings of Media; [26] all the kings of the north, far and near, one after another, and all the kingdoms of the world that are on the face of the earth. And after them the king of Babylon[1] shall drink.

[27] "Then you shall say to them, 'Thus says the Lord of hosts, the God of Israel: Drink, be drunk and vomit, fall and rise no more, because of the sword that I am sending among you.'

[28] "And if they refuse to accept the cup from your hand to drink, then you shall say to them, 'Thus says the Lord of hosts: You must drink! [29] For behold, I begin to work disaster at the city that is called by my name, and shall you go unpunished? You shall not go unpunished, for I am summoning a sword against all the inhabitants of the earth, declares the Lord of hosts.'

[30] "You, therefore, shall prophesy against them all these words, and say to them:

" 'The Lord will roar from on high,
    and from his holy habitation utter
        his voice;

he will roar mightily against his fold,
    and shout, like those who tread
        grapes,
    against all the inhabitants of the
        earth.
[31]   The clamor will resound to the ends
            of the earth,
    for the Lord has an indictment
        against the nations;
he is entering into judgment with all
        flesh,
    and the wicked he will put to the
        sword,
                    declares the Lord.'

[32]   "Thus says the Lord of hosts:
    Behold, disaster is going forth
        from nation to nation,
    and a great tempest is stirring
        from the farthest parts of the earth!

[33] "And those pierced by the Lord on that day shall extend from one end of the earth to the other. They shall not be lamented, or gathered, or buried; they shall be dung on the surface of the ground.

[34]   "Wail, you shepherds, and cry out,
        and roll in ashes, you lords of the
            flock,
    for the days of your slaughter and
            dispersion have come,
        and you shall fall like a choice ves-
            sel.
[35]   No refuge will remain for the shep-
            herds,
        nor escape for the lords of the flock.
[36]   A voice—the cry of the shepherds,
        and the wail of the lords of the
            flock!
    For the Lord is laying waste their
            pasture,
[37]   and the peaceful folds are devas-
            tated
        because of the fierce anger of the
            Lord.
[38]   Like a lion he has left his lair,
        for their land has become a waste
    because of the sword of the oppressor,
        and because of his fierce anger."

Jeremiah Threatened with Death

26 In the beginning of the reign of Jehoiakim the son of Josiah, king of Judah, this word came from the Lord: [2] "Thus says the Lord: Stand in the court of

---

Hebrew *Sheshach*, a code name for Babylon

the LORD's house, and speak to all the cities of Judah that come to worship in the house of the LORD all the words that I command you to speak to them; do not hold back a word. ³It may be they will listen, and every one turn from his evil way, that I may relent of the disaster that I intend to do to them because of their evil deeds. ⁴You shall say to them, 'Thus says the LORD: If you will not listen to me, to walk in my law that I have set before you, ⁵and to listen to the words of my servants the prophets whom I send to you urgently, though you have not listened, ⁶then I will make this house like Shiloh, and I will make this city a curse for all the nations of the earth.'"

⁷The priests and the prophets and all the people heard Jeremiah speaking these words in the house of the LORD. ⁸And when Jeremiah had finished speaking all that the LORD had commanded him to speak to all the people, then the priests and the prophets and all the people laid hold of him, saying, "You shall die! ⁹Why have you prophesied in the name of the LORD, saying, 'This house shall be like Shiloh, and this city shall be desolate, without inhabitant'?" And all the people gathered around Jeremiah in the house of the LORD.

¹⁰When the officials of Judah heard these things, they came up from the king's house to the house of the LORD and took their seat in the entry of the New Gate of the house of the LORD. ¹¹Then the priests and the prophets said to the officials and to all the people, "This man deserves the sentence of death, because he has prophesied against this city, as you have heard with your own ears."

¹²Then Jeremiah spoke to all the officials and all the people, saying, "The LORD sent me to prophesy against this house and this city all the words you have heard. ¹³Now therefore mend your ways and your deeds, and obey the voice of the LORD your God, and the LORD will relent of the disaster that he has pronounced against you. ¹⁴But as for me, behold, I am in your hands. Do with me as seems good and right to you. ¹⁵Only know for certain that if you put me to death, you will bring innocent blood upon yourselves and upon this city and its inhabitants, for in truth the LORD sent me to you to speak all these words in your ears."

Jeremiah Spared from Death

¹⁶Then the officials and all the people said to the priests and the prophets, "This man does not deserve the sentence of death, for he has spoken to us in the name of the LORD our God." ¹⁷And certain of the elders of the land arose and spoke to all the assembled people, saying, ¹⁸"Micah of Moresheth prophesied in the days of Hezekiah king of Judah, and said to all the people of Judah, 'Thus says the LORD of hosts,

"'Zion shall be plowed as a field;
    Jerusalem shall become a heap of
        ruins,
    and the mountain of the house a
        wooded height.'

¹⁹Did Hezekiah king of Judah and all Judah put him to death? Did he not fear the LORD and entreat the favor of the LORD, and did not the LORD relent of the disaster that he had pronounced against them? But we are about to bring great disaster upon ourselves."

²⁰There was another man who prophesied in the name of the LORD, Uriah the son of Shemaiah from Kiriath-jearim. He prophesied against this city and against this land in words like those of Jeremiah. ²¹And when King Jehoiakim, with all his warriors and all the officials, heard his words, the king sought to put him to death. But when Uriah heard of it, he was afraid and fled and escaped to Egypt. ²²Then King Jehoiakim sent to Egypt certain men, Elnathan the son of Achbor and others with him, ²³and they took Uriah from Egypt and brought him to King Jehoiakim, who struck him down with the sword and dumped his dead body into the burial place of the common people.

²⁴But the hand of Ahikam the son of Shaphan was with Jeremiah so that he was not given over to the people to be put to death.

The Yoke of Nebuchadnezzar

27 In the beginning of the reign of Zedekiah[1] the son of Josiah, king of Judah, this word came to Jeremiah from the LORD. ²Thus the LORD said to me: "Make yourself straps and yoke-bars, and put them on your neck. ³Send word[2] to the king of Edom, the king of Moab, the king of the sons of Ammon, the king of Tyre, and the king of Sidon by the hand of the envoys who have come to Jerusalem to Zedekiah king of Judah. **4**Give them this charge for their masters: 'Thus says the LORD of hosts, the God of Israel: This is what you shall say to your masters: **5**"It is I who by my great power and my outstretched arm have made the earth, with the men and animals that are on the earth, and I give it to whomever it seems right to me. **6**Now I have given all these lands into the hand of Nebuchadnezzar, the king of Babylon, my servant, and I have given him also the beasts of the field to serve him. **7**All the nations shall serve him and his son and his grandson, until the time of his own land comes. Then many nations and great kings shall make him their slave.

8"'"But if any nation or kingdom will not serve this Nebuchadnezzar king of Babylon, and put its neck under the yoke of the king of Babylon, I will punish that nation with the sword, with famine, and with pestilence, declares the LORD, until I have consumed it by his hand. **9**So do not listen to your prophets, your diviners, your dreamers, your fortune-tellers, or your sorcerers, who are saying to you, 'You shall not serve the king of Babylon.' **10**For it is a lie that they are prophesying to you, with the result that you will be removed far from your land, and I will drive you out, and you will perish. **11**But any nation that will bring its neck under the yoke of the king of Babylon and serve him, I will leave on its own land, to work it and dwell there, declares the LORD."'"

12To Zedekiah king of Judah I spoke in like manner: "Bring your necks under the yoke of the king of Babylon, and serve him and his people and live. **13**Why will you and your people die by the sword, by famine, and by pestilence, as the LORD has spoken concerning any nation that will not serve the king of Babylon? **14**Do not listen to the words of the prophets who are saying to you, 'You shall not serve the king of Babylon,' for it is a lie that they are prophesying to you. **15**I have not sent them, declares the LORD, but they are prophesying falsely in my name, with the result that I will drive you out and you will perish, you and the prophets who are prophesying to you."

16Then I spoke to the priests and to all this people, saying, "Thus says the LORD: Do not listen to the words of your prophets who are prophesying to you, saying, Behold, the vessels of the LORD's house

will now shortly be brought back from Babylon,' for it is a lie that they are prophesying to you. **17**Do not listen to them; serve the king of Babylon and live. Why should this city become a desolation? **18**If they are prophets, and if the word of the LORD is with them, then let them intercede with the LORD of hosts, that the vessels that are left in the house of the LORD, in the house of the king of Judah, and in Jerusalem may not go to Babylon. **19**For thus says the LORD of hosts concerning the pillars, the sea, the stands, and the rest of the vessels that are left in this city, **20**which Nebuchadnezzar king of Babylon did not take away, when he took into exile from Jerusalem to Babylon Jeconiah the son of Jehoiakim, king of Judah, and all the nobles of Judah and Jerusalem— **21**thus says the LORD of hosts, the God of Israel, concerning the vessels that are left in the house of the LORD, in the house of the king of Judah, and in Jerusalem: **22**They shall be carried to Babylon and remain there until the day when I visit them, declares the LORD. Then I will bring them back and restore them to this place."

Hananiah the False Prophet

28 In that same year, at the beginning of the reign of Zedekiah king of Judah, in the fifth month of the fourth year, Hananiah the son of Azzur, the prophet from Gibeon, spoke to me in the house of the LORD, in the presence of the priests and all the people, saying, **2**"Thus says the LORD of hosts, the God of Israel: I have broken the yoke of the king of Babylon. **3**Within two years I will bring back to this place all the vessels of the LORD's house, which Nebuchadnezzar king of Babylon took away from this place and carried to Babylon. **4**I will also bring back to this place Jeconiah the son of Jehoiakim, king of Judah, and all the exiles from Judah who went to Babylon, declares the LORD, for I will break the yoke of the king of Babylon."

5Then the prophet Jeremiah spoke to Hananiah the prophet in the presence of the priests and all the people who were standing in the house of the LORD, **6**and the prophet Jeremiah said, "Amen! May the LORD do so; may the LORD make the words that you have prophesied come true, and bring back to this place from Babylon the vessels of the house of the LORD, and all the exiles. **7**Yet hear now this word that I speak in your hearing and in the hearing of all the people. [8] The prophets who preceded you and me from ancient times prophesied war, famine, and pestilence against many countries and great kingdoms. [9] As for the prophet who prophesies peace, when the word of that prophet comes to pass, then it will be known that the LORD has truly sent the prophet."

[10] Then the prophet Hananiah took the yoke-bars from the neck of Jeremiah the prophet and broke them. [11] And Hananiah spoke in the presence of all the people, saying, "Thus says the LORD: Even so will I break the yoke of Nebuchadnezzar king of Babylon from the neck of all the nations within two years." But Jeremiah the prophet went his way.

[12] Sometime after the prophet Hananiah had broken the yoke-bars from off the neck of Jeremiah the prophet, the word of the LORD came to Jeremiah: [13] "Go, tell Hananiah, 'Thus says the LORD: You have broken wooden bars, but you have made in their place bars of iron. [14] For thus says the LORD of hosts, the God of Israel: I have put upon the neck of all these nations an iron yoke to serve Nebuchadnezzar king of Babylon, and they shall serve him, for I have given to him even the beasts of the field.' " [15] And Jeremiah the prophet said to the prophet Hananiah, "Listen, Hananiah, the LORD has not sent you, and you have made this people trust in a lie. [16] Therefore thus says the LORD: 'Behold, I will remove you from the face of the earth. This year you shall die, because you have uttered rebellion against the LORD.' "

[17] In that same year, in the seventh month, the prophet Hananiah died.

Jeremiah's Letter to the Exiles

29 These are the words of the letter that Jeremiah the prophet sent from Jerusalem to the surviving elders of the exiles, and to the priests, the prophets, and all the people, whom Nebuchadnezzar had taken into exile from Jerusalem to Babylon. [2] This was after King Jeconiah and the queen mother, the eunuchs, the officials of Judah and Jerusalem, the craftsmen, and the metal workers had departed from Jerusalem. [3] The letter was sent by the hand of Elasah the son of Shaphan and Gemariah the son of Hilkiah, whom Zedekiah king of Judah sent to Babylon to Nebuchadnezzar king of Babylon. It said: [4] "Thus says the LORD of hosts, the God of Israel, to all the exiles whom I have sent into exile from Jerusalem to Babylon: [5] Build houses and live in them; plant gardens and eat their produce. [6] Take wives and have sons and daughters; take wives for your sons, and give your daughters in marriage, that they may bear sons and daughters; multiply there, and do not decrease. [7] But seek the welfare of the city where I have sent you into exile, and pray to the LORD on its behalf, for in its welfare you will find your welfare. [8] For thus says the LORD of hosts, the God of Israel: Do not let your prophets and your diviners who are among you deceive you, and do not listen to the dreams that they dream,[1] [9] for it is a lie that they are prophesying to you in my name; I did not send them, declares the LORD.

[10] "For thus says the LORD: When seventy years are completed for Babylon, I will visit you, and I will fulfill to you my promise and bring you back to this place. [11] For I know the plans I have for you, declares the LORD, plans for welfare[2] and not for evil, to give you a future and a hope. [12] Then you will call upon me and come and pray to me, and I will hear you. [13] You will seek me and find me, when you seek me with all your heart. [14] I will be found by you, declares the LORD, and I will restore your fortunes and gather you from all the nations and all the places where I have driven you, declares the LORD, and I will bring you back to the place from which I sent you into exile.

[15] "Because you have said, 'The LORD has raised up prophets for us in Babylon,' [16] thus says the LORD concerning the king who sits on the throne of David, and concerning all the people who dwell in this city, your kinsmen who did not go out with you into exile: [17] 'Thus says the LORD of hosts, behold, I am sending on them sword, famine, and pestilence, and I will make them like vile figs that are so rotten they cannot be eaten. [18] I will pursue them with sword, famine, and pestilence, and will make them a horror to all the kingdoms of the earth, to be a curse, a terror, a hissing, and a reproach among all the nations where I have driven them, [19] because they did not pay attention to my words, declares the LORD, that I persistently sent to you by my

[1] Hebrew *your dreams, which you cause to dream* [2] Or *peace*

servants the prophets, but you would not listen, declares the LORD.' ²⁰ Hear the word of the LORD, all you exiles whom I sent away from Jerusalem to Babylon: ²¹ 'Thus says the LORD of hosts, the God of Israel, concerning Ahab the son of Kolaiah and Zedekiah the son of Maaseiah, who are prophesying a lie to you in my name: Behold, I will deliver them into the hand of Nebuchadnezzar king of Babylon, and he shall strike them down before your eyes. ²² Because of them this curse shall be used by all the exiles from Judah in Babylon: "The LORD make you like Zedekiah and Ahab, whom the king of Babylon roasted in the fire," ²³ because they have done an outrageous thing in Israel, they have committed adultery with their neighbors' wives, and they have spoken in my name lying words that I did not command them. I am the one who knows, and I am witness, declares the LORD.' "

Shemaiah's False Prophecy

²⁴ To Shemaiah of Nehelam you shall say: ²⁵ "Thus says the LORD of hosts, the God of Israel: You have sent letters in your name to all the people who are in Jerusalem, and to Zephaniah the son of Maaseiah the priest, and to all the priests, saying, ²⁶ 'The LORD has made you priest instead of Jehoiada the priest, to have charge in the house of the LORD over every madman who prophesies, to put him in the stocks and neck irons. ²⁷ Now why have you not rebuked Jeremiah of Anathoth who is prophesying to you? ²⁸ For he has sent to us in Babylon, saying, "Your exile will be long; build houses and live in them, and plant gardens and eat their produce." '"

²⁹ Zephaniah the priest read this letter in the hearing of Jeremiah the prophet. ³⁰ Then the word of the LORD came to Jeremiah: ³¹ "Send to all the exiles, saying, 'Thus says the LORD concerning Shemaiah of Nehelam: Because Shemaiah had prophesied to you when I did not send him, and has made you trust in a lie, ³² therefore thus says the LORD: Behold, I will punish Shemaiah of Nehelam and his descendants. He shall not have anyone living among this people, and

verses to read
Jeremiah 29:10–14

Have you ever heard how God took the day off? He got so tired from running the world and listening to everyone's prayers that he just clocked out. He didn't make the sun rise or set; he didn't set the wind in motion. The ocean flooded and the sky fell. It was a disaster. Never heard about that day? That's because it never happened. If God took the day off, more than a few things would get messed up.

Have you ever thought that God took the day off from hearing you? Felt like he was clueless about your life and your needs? How reliable you think God is depends on your understanding of the gospel. If you know God has given his own Son to suffer and be killed so that you can be restored to God, then how could God be uncaring about your life? Not possible. You'd have to change his name to "Bob" or to "god" with a little "g." The only reason he doesn't "feel" present is because you chose to believe he's AWOL—absent without official leave.

You want God to hear you? Then all you have to do is believe. Faith requires belief. Belief that he does have a plan for you. Belief that he's there and that he's working everything out for good. Belief that he knows best. When you have faith, suddenly you'll find that even bad stuff is good stuff in your life. What looks like disaster is actually protection. And what feels like failure is actually pure success. God says that his wisdom will look like nonsense to the world (see 1 Cor. 1:18), and the truth is, it will look like nonsense to you if you aren't willing to believe and to trust that he can make good out of anything and everything that happens to you.

he shall not see the good that I will do to my people, declares the LORD, for he has spoken rebellion against the LORD.'"

Restoration for Israel and Judah

30 The word that came to Jeremiah from the LORD: [2] "Thus says the LORD, the God of Israel: Write in a book all the words that I have spoken to you. [3] For behold, days are coming, declares the LORD, when I will restore the fortunes of my people, Israel and Judah, says the LORD, and I will bring them back to the land that I gave to their fathers, and they shall take possession of it."

[4] These are the words that the LORD spoke concerning Israel and Judah:

[5]　"Thus says the LORD:
　　We have heard a cry of panic,
　　　of terror, and no peace.
[6]　Ask now, and see,
　　　can a man bear a child?
　　Why then do I see every man
　　　with his hands on his stomach like
　　　　a woman in labor?
　　Why has every face turned pale?
[7]　Alas! That day is so great
　　　there is none like it;
　　it is a time of distress for Jacob;
　　　yet he shall be saved out of it.

[8] "And it shall come to pass in that day, declares the LORD of hosts, that I will break his yoke from off your neck, and I will burst your bonds, and foreigners shall no more make a servant of him.[1] [9] But they shall serve the LORD their God and David their king, whom I will raise up for them.

[10]　"Then fear not, O Jacob my servant,
　　　declares the LORD,
　　　nor be dismayed, O Israel;
　　for behold, I will save you from far
　　　away,
　　and your offspring from the land
　　　of their captivity.
　　Jacob shall return and have quiet and
　　　ease,
　　and none shall make him afraid.
[11]　For I am with you to save you,
　　　　declares the LORD;
　　I will make a full end of all the nations
　　　among whom I scattered you,
　　but of you I will not make a full end.

　　I will discipline you in just measure,
　　　and I will by no means leave you
　　　　unpunished.

[12]　"For thus says the LORD:
　　Your hurt is incurable,
　　　and your wound is grievous.
[13]　There is none to uphold your cause,
　　　no medicine for your wound,
　　　no healing for you.
[14]　All your lovers have forgotten you;
　　　they care nothing for you;
　　for I have dealt you the blow of an
　　　enemy,
　　　the punishment of a merciless foe,
　　because your guilt is great,
　　　because your sins are flagrant.
[15]　Why do you cry out over your hurt?
　　　Your pain is incurable.
　　Because your guilt is great,
　　　because your sins are flagrant,
　　I have done these things to you.
[16]　Therefore all who devour you shall
　　　be devoured,
　　　and all your foes, every one of
　　　　them, shall go into captivity;
　　those who plunder you shall be plun-
　　　dered,
　　　and all who prey on you I will
　　　　make a prey.
[17]　For I will restore health to you,
　　　and your wounds I will heal,
　　　　　　declares the LORD,
　　because they have called you an
　　　outcast:
　　　'It is Zion, for whom no one cares!'

[18]　"Thus says the LORD:
　　Behold, I will restore the fortunes of
　　　the tents of Jacob
　　　and have compassion on his dwell-
　　　　ings;
　　the city shall be rebuilt on its
　　　mound,
　　　and the palace shall stand where it
　　　　used to be.
[19]　Out of them shall come songs of
　　　thanksgiving,
　　　and the voices of those who cel-
　　　　ebrate.
　　I will multiply them, and they shall
　　　not be few;
　　　I will make them honored, and
　　　　they shall not be small.

[1] Or serve him

0 Their children shall be as they were
       of old,
       and their congregation shall be
         established before me,
       and I will punish all who oppress
         them.
1 Their prince shall be one of them-
       selves;
       their ruler shall come out from
         their midst;
     I will make him draw near, and he
       shall approach me,
       for who would dare of himself to
         approach me?
                    declares the LORD.
2 And you shall be my people,
       and I will be your God."

3 Behold the storm of the LORD!
       Wrath has gone forth,
     a whirling tempest;
       it will burst upon the head of the
         wicked.
4 The fierce anger of the LORD will not
       turn back
       until he has executed and accom-
         plished
       the intentions of his mind.
     In the latter days you will under-
       stand this.

The LORD Will Turn Mourning to Joy

31 "At that time, declares the LORD,
     I will be the God of all the clans of
Israel, and they shall be my people."

2 Thus says the LORD:
     "The people who survived the sword
       found grace in the wilderness;
     when Israel sought for rest,
3   the LORD appeared to him[1] from
         far away.
     I have loved you with an everlasting
       love;
       therefore I have continued my
         faithfulness to you.
4 Again I will build you, and you shall
       be built,
       O virgin Israel!
     Again you shall adorn yourself with
       tambourines
       and shall go forth in the dance of
         the merrymakers.
5 Again you shall plant vineyards
       on the mountains of Samaria;

     the planters shall plant
       and shall enjoy the fruit.
6 For there shall be a day when watch-
       men will call
       in the hill country of Ephraim:
     'Arise, and let us go up to Zion,
       to the LORD our God.' "

7 For thus says the LORD:
     "Sing aloud with gladness for Jacob,
       and raise shouts for the chief of
         the nations;
     proclaim, give praise, and say,
       'O LORD, save your people,
       the remnant of Israel.'
8 Behold, I will bring them from the
       north country
       and gather them from the farthest
         parts of the earth,
     among them the blind and the lame,
       the pregnant woman and she who
         is in labor, together;
     a great company, they shall return
       here.
9 With weeping they shall come,
       and with pleas for mercy I will
         lead them back,
     I will make them walk by brooks of
       water,
       in a straight path in which they
         shall not stumble,
     for I am a father to Israel,
       and Ephraim is my firstborn.

10 "Hear the word of the LORD,
       O nations,
       and declare it in the coastlands far
         away;
     say, 'He who scattered Israel will
       gather him,
       and will keep him as a shepherd
         keeps his flock.'
11 For the LORD has ransomed Jacob
       and has redeemed him from hands
         too strong for him.
12 They shall come and sing aloud on
       the height of Zion,
       and they shall be radiant over the
         goodness of the LORD,
     over the grain, the wine, and the oil,
       and over the young of the flock
         and the herd;
     their life shall be like a watered gar-
       den,
       and they shall languish no more.

Septuagint; Hebrew *me*

¹³ Then shall the young women rejoice
  in the dance,
     and the young men and the old
       shall be merry.
  I will turn their mourning into joy;
     I will comfort them, and give them
       gladness for sorrow.
¹⁴ I will feast the soul of the priests
  with abundance,
     and my people shall be satisfied
       with my goodness,
                    declares the LORD."

¹⁵ Thus says the LORD:
  "A voice is heard in Ramah,
     lamentation and bitter weeping.
  Rachel is weeping for her children;
     she refuses to be comforted for her
       children,
  because they are no more."

¹⁶ Thus says the LORD:
  "Keep your voice from weeping,
     and your eyes from tears,
  for there is a reward for your work,
                    declares the LORD,
     and they shall come back from the
       land of the enemy.
¹⁷ There is hope for your future,
                    declares the LORD,
     and your children shall come back
       to their own country.
¹⁸ I have heard Ephraim grieving,
  'You have disciplined me, and I was
     disciplined,
     like an untrained calf;
  bring me back that I may be restored,
     for you are the LORD my God.
¹⁹ For after I had turned away, I relented,
     and after I was instructed, I struck
       my thigh;
  I was ashamed, and I was confounded,
     because I bore the disgrace of my
       youth.'
²⁰ Is Ephraim my dear son?
     Is he my darling child?
  For as often as I speak against him,
     I do remember him still.
  Therefore my heart[1] yearns for him;
     I will surely have mercy on him,
                    declares the LORD.

²¹ "Set up road markers for yourself;
     make yourself guideposts;
  consider well the highway,
     the road by which you went.

Return, O virgin Israel,
     return to these your cities.
²² How long will you waver,
     O faithless daughter?
  For the LORD has created a new thing
     on the earth:
  a woman encircles a man."

²³ Thus says the LORD of hosts, the God
of Israel: "Once more they shall use these
words in the land of Judah and in its cities,
when I restore their fortunes:

  "'The LORD bless you, O habitation of
     righteousness,
     O holy hill!'

²⁴ And Judah and all its cities shall dwell
there together, and the farmers and those
who wander with their flocks. ²⁵ For I will
satisfy the weary soul, and every languishing soul I will replenish."

²⁶ At this I awoke and looked, and my
sleep was pleasant to me.

²⁷ "Behold, the days are coming, declares
the LORD, when I will sow the house of
Israel and the house of Judah with the seed
of man and the seed of beast. ²⁸ And it shall
come to pass that as I have watched over
them to pluck up and break down, to overthrow, destroy, and bring harm, so I will
watch over them to build and to plant,
declares the LORD. ²⁹ In those days they
shall no longer say:

  "'The fathers have eaten sour grapes,
     and the children's teeth are set on
       edge.'

³⁰ But everyone shall die for his own iniquity. Each man who eats sour grapes, his
teeth shall be set on edge.

The New Covenant

³¹ "Behold, the days are coming, declares
the LORD, when I will make a new covenant
with the house of Israel and the house of
Judah, ³² not like the covenant that I made
with their fathers on the day when I took
them by the hand to bring them out of the
land of Egypt, my covenant that they broke,
though I was their husband, declares the
LORD. ³³ For this is the covenant that I will
make with the house of Israel after those
days, declares the LORD: I will put my law
within them, and I will write it on their
hearts. And I will be their God, and they

[1] Hebrew bowels

Rachel

Read about her in Genesis 29:1–33:20; 35:16–20;
46:19–22; Jeremiah 31:15; and Matthew 2:18.

> Leah's eyes were weak, but Rachel was beautiful in form and appearance. Jacob loved Rachel.
>
> *Genesis 29:17–18*

Beauty is no sign of happiness or holiness. Though being beautiful can make a girl feel like she "has it made," it doesn't guarantee success. Rachel, the second wife of Jacob, was a beauty, and he adored her. But all the beauty in the world didn't make Rachel happy. She wanted more, and the more she wanted couldn't be gotten by a pretty face. Her life should have been blessed by all accounts. But Rachel was not content. She was envious, jealous, and bitter about her lack and her sister's abundance.

Beauty can give a false impression. On the surface, it seems to give success and peace. "She's pretty, so how can she be depressed?" It's as if we believe that beauty relieves us of all misery. But nothing could be further from the truth. Beauty is not our salvation. It can be a gift, but it isn't assurance of a life of contentment. Whether you are considered beautiful or not, thank God for giving you life and for filling that life with what is most important: his presence. When the God Girl is thankful for the life of Christ in her, she becomes the most beautiful thing on earth. Her calm assurance, her ability to reach out to others in need, her love for even her enemies spreads joy wherever she goes. The God Girl is beautiful regardless of her features because of the Spirit who lives within her and controls her every move. As you start to devote your heart to the one who loves you the most, he gives his strength to you, lifts you up above the fray, and plants your feet on solid ground. The beauty of a life focused on God and his Word is something to behold. Don't let your beauty or lack thereof be an excuse not to have a beautiful heart. True beauty comes from within and shines its light on everyone who looks at it. Become beautiful to the people around you, share the love of God with them, and you will be a true God Girl.

shall be my people. ³⁴And no longer shall each one teach his neighbor and each his brother, saying, 'Know the LORD,' for they shall all know me, from the least of them to the greatest, declares the LORD. For I will forgive their iniquity, and I will remember their sin no more."

³⁵   Thus says the LORD,
   who gives the sun for light by day
      and the fixed order of the moon
         and the stars for light by night,
   who stirs up the sea so that its waves
      roar—
      the LORD of hosts is his name:
³⁶   "If this fixed order departs
      from before me, declares the LORD,
   then shall the offspring of Israel cease
      from being a nation before me
         forever."

³⁷   Thus says the LORD:
   "If the heavens above can be mea-
      sured,

and the foundations of the earth
      below can be explored,
   then I will cast off all the offspring o
      Israel
   for all that they have done,
                  declares the LORD

³⁸"Behold, the days are coming, declare the LORD, when the city shall be rebuil for the LORD from the Tower of Hanane to the Corner Gate. ³⁹And the measurin line shall go out farther, straight to th hill Gareb, and shall then turn to Goah ⁴⁰The whole valley of the dead bodies an the ashes, and all the fields as far as th brook Kidron, to the corner of the Hors Gate toward the east, shall be sacred t the LORD. It shall not be plucked up o overthrown anymore forever."

Jeremiah Buys a Field During the Siege

32 The word that came to Jeremia from the LORD in the tenth yea of Zedekiah king of Judah, which was th

Know Yourself

verses to read
Jeremiah 31:31-34

God made a covenant, or an agreement, with the Israelites, and they broke it (see Jer. 11:10). They messed up royally! But God didn't give up on them; in fact, he gave them a second chance, a new covenant. But can you imagine if they wouldn't agree to it because they just couldn't get over their past mistakes? Sounds ridiculous, but how many times do you say, "I just can't get over what I did"? When you can't get over your sin or accept God's forgiveness, the past can haunt you and keep you living in your mistakes and traumas. But Jesus paid for all your failings. They're all taken care of.

Your past was never meant to be your present, but it should help you understand it. God lets you remember your mess-ups and your misery so they can be a light for the future. If you're brave enough to step out of the past and only look at it as a guide to the future, then you can be free to live in the present without the chains of your mistakes. Holding on to yesterday as if it's a part of today is craziness. God has offered you a second chance. Grace is his gift to the sinner in you—will you reject it today and choose to live in your sinful past? Or will you trust that he's big enough to help you get over your mistakes? Let go and refuse to continue to relive yesterday, and you will let God redeem your past. God is relentless in his love for you, and he will continue to call you back to himself no matter what you have done in the past. The only thing that stands between you and forgiveness is your inability to accept his forgiveness, not your inability to forgive yourself. You don't need your own forgiveness—God's is all-sufficient. So accept his forgiveness and move on. He is ready and waiting.

eighteenth year of Nebuchadnezzar. ²At that time the army of the king of Babylon was besieging Jerusalem, and Jeremiah the prophet was shut up in the court of the guard that was in the palace of the king of Judah. ³For Zedekiah king of Judah had imprisoned him, saying, "Why do you prophesy and say, 'Thus says the LORD: Behold, I am giving this city into the hand of the king of Babylon, and he shall capture it; ⁴Zedekiah king of Judah shall not escape out of the hand of the Chaldeans, but shall surely be given into the hand of the king of Babylon, and shall speak with him face to face and see him eye to eye. ⁵And he shall take Zedekiah to Babylon, and there he shall remain until I visit him, declares the LORD. Though you fight against the Chaldeans, you shall not succeed'?"

⁶Jeremiah said, "The word of the LORD came to me: ⁷Behold, Hanamel the son of Shallum your uncle will come to you and say, 'Buy my field that is at Anathoth, for the right of redemption by purchase is yours.' ⁸Then Hanamel my cousin came to me in the court of the guard, in accordance with the word of the LORD, and said to me, 'Buy my field that is at Anathoth in the land of Benjamin, for the right of possession and redemption is yours; buy it for yourself.' Then I knew that this was the word of the LORD.

⁹"And I bought the field at Anathoth from Hanamel my cousin, and weighed out the money to him, seventeen shekels of silver. ¹⁰I signed the deed, sealed it, got witnesses, and weighed the money on scales. ¹¹Then I took the sealed deed of purchase, containing the terms and conditions and the open copy. ¹²And I gave the deed of purchase to Baruch the son of Neriah son of Mahseiah, in the presence of Hanamel my cousin, in the presence of the witnesses who signed the deed of purchase, and in the presence of all the Judeans who were sitting in the court of the guard. ¹³I charged Baruch in their presence, saying, ¹⁴'Thus says the LORD of hosts, the God of Israel: Take these deeds, both this sealed deed of purchase and this open deed, and put them in an earthenware vessel, that they may last for a long time. ¹⁵For thus says the LORD of hosts, the God of Israel: Houses and fields and vineyards shall again be bought in this land.'

Jeremiah Prays for Understanding

¹⁶"After I had given the deed of purchase to Baruch the son of Neriah, I prayed to the LORD, saying: ¹⁷'Ah, Lord GOD! It is you who have made the heavens and the earth by your great power and by your outstretched arm! Nothing is too hard for you. ¹⁸You show steadfast love to thousands, but you repay the guilt of fathers to their children after them, O great and mighty God, whose name is the LORD of hosts, ¹⁹great in counsel and mighty in deed, whose eyes are open to all the ways of the children of man, rewarding each one according to his ways and according to the fruit of his deeds. ²⁰You have shown signs and wonders in the land of Egypt, and to this day in Israel and among all mankind, and have made a name for yourself, as at this day. ²¹You brought your people Israel out of the land of Egypt with signs and wonders, with a strong hand and outstretched arm, and with great terror. ²²And you gave them this land, which you swore to their fathers to give them, a land flowing with milk and honey. ²³And they entered and took possession of it. But they did not obey your voice or walk in your law. They did nothing of all you commanded them to do. Therefore you have made all this disaster come upon them. ²⁴Behold, the siege mounds have come up to the city to take it, and because of sword and famine and pestilence the city is given into the hands of the Chaldeans who are fighting against it. What you spoke has come to pass, and behold, you see it. ²⁵Yet you, O Lord GOD, have said to me, "Buy the field for money and get witnesses"—though the city is given into the hands of the Chaldeans.'"

²⁶The word of the LORD came to Jeremiah: ²⁷"Behold, I am the LORD, the God of all flesh. Is anything too hard for me? ²⁸Therefore, thus says the LORD: Behold, I am giving this city into the hands of the Chaldeans and into the hand of Nebuchadnezzar king of Babylon, and he shall capture it. ²⁹The Chaldeans who are fighting against this city shall come and set this city on fire and burn it, with the houses on whose roofs offerings have been made to Baal and drink offerings have been poured out to other gods, to provoke me to anger. ³⁰For the children of Israel and the children of Judah have done nothing but evil in my sight from their youth. The children of

Israel have done nothing but provoke me to anger by the work of their hands, declares the LORD. ³¹ This city has aroused my anger and wrath, from the day it was built to this day, so that I will remove it from my sight ³² because of all the evil of the children of Israel and the children of Judah that they did to provoke me to anger—their kings and their officials, their priests and their prophets, the men of Judah and the inhabitants of Jerusalem. ³³ They have turned to me their back and not their face. And though I have taught them persistently, they have not listened to receive instruction. ³⁴ They set up their abominations in the house that is called by my name, to defile it. ³⁵ They built the high places of Baal in the Valley of the Son of Hinnom, to offer up their sons and daughters to Molech, though I did not command them, nor did it enter into my mind, that they should do this abomination, to cause Judah to sin.

Ask Yourself . . .

ABOUT GOD'S LOVE

- What is God's "everlasting covenant" (see Jer. 32:40)?
- Do I believe God enjoys blessing me (see Jer. 32:41)?
- Can love hurt sometimes?
- Does God discipline me even though he loves me?
- If life gets rough, should I assume that God doesn't love me anymore?
- Was Jesus' life ever rough? Did God ever stop loving him?
- Do I feel like God doesn't love me right now? If so, what does the Bible say about that?

They Shall Be My People; I Will Be Their God

³⁶ "Now therefore thus says the LORD, the God of Israel, concerning this city of which

you say, 'It is given into the hand of the king of Babylon by sword, by famine, and by pestilence': ³⁷ Behold, I will gather them from all the countries to which I drove them in my anger and my wrath and in great indignation. I will bring them back to this place, and I will make them dwell in safety. ³⁸ And they shall be my people, and I will be their God. ³⁹ I will give them one heart and one way, that they may fear me forever, for their own good and the good of their children after them. ⁴⁰ I will make with them an everlasting covenant, that I will not turn away from doing good to them. And I will put the fear of me in their hearts, that they may not turn from me. ⁴¹ I will rejoice in doing them good, and I will plant them in this land in faithfulness, with all my heart and all my soul.

⁴² "For thus says the LORD: Just as I have brought all this great disaster upon this people, so I will bring upon them all the good that I promise them. ⁴³ Fields shall be bought in this land of which you are saying, 'It is a desolation, without man or beast; it is given into the hand of the Chaldeans.' ⁴⁴ Fields shall be bought for money, and deeds shall be signed and sealed and witnessed, in the land of Benjamin, in the places about Jerusalem, and in the cities of Judah, in the cities of the hill country, in the cities of the Shephelah, and in the cities of the Negeb; for I will restore their fortunes, declares the LORD."

The LORD Promises Peace

33 The word of the LORD came to Jeremiah a second time, while he was still shut up in the court of the guard: ² "Thus says the LORD who made the earth,¹ the LORD who formed it to establish it—the LORD is his name: ³ Call to me and I will answer you, and will tell you great and hidden things that you have not known. ⁴ For thus says the LORD, the God of Israel, concerning the houses of this city and the houses of the kings of Judah that were torn down to make a defense against the siege mounds and against the sword: ⁵ They are coming in to fight against the Chaldeans and to fill them² with the dead bodies of men whom I shall strike down in my anger and my wrath, for I have hidden my face from this city because of all their evil. ⁶ Behold, I will bring to it health and

¹ Septuagint; Hebrew *it* ² That is, the torn-down houses

healing, and I will heal them and reveal to them abundance of prosperity and security. [7] I will restore the fortunes of Judah and the fortunes of Israel, and rebuild them as they were at first. [8] I will cleanse them from all the guilt of their sin against me, and I will forgive all the guilt of their sin and rebellion against me. [9] And this city[1] shall be to me a name of joy, a praise and a glory before all the nations of the earth who shall hear of all the good that I do for them. They shall fear and tremble because of all the good and all the prosperity I provide for it.

[10] "Thus says the LORD: In this place of which you say, 'It is a waste without man or beast,' in the cities of Judah and the streets of Jerusalem that are desolate, without man or inhabitant or beast, there shall be heard again [11] the voice of mirth and the voice of gladness, the voice of the bridegroom and the voice of the bride, the voices of those who sing, as they bring thank offerings to the house of the LORD:

"'Give thanks to the LORD of hosts,
    for the LORD is good,
    for his steadfast love endures
        forever!'

For I will restore the fortunes of the land as at first, says the LORD.

[12] "Thus says the LORD of hosts: In this place that is waste, without man or beast, and in all of its cities, there shall again be habitations of shepherds resting their flocks. [13] In the cities of the hill country, in the cities of the Shephelah, and in the cities of the Negeb, in the land of Benjamin, the places about Jerusalem, and in the cities of Judah, flocks shall again pass under the hands of the one who counts them, says the LORD.

The LORD's Eternal Covenant with David

[14] "Behold, the days are coming, declares the LORD, when I will fulfill the promise I made to the house of Israel and the house of Judah. [15] In those days and at that time I will cause a righteous Branch to spring up for David, and he shall execute justice and righteousness in the land. [16] In those days Judah will be saved, and Jerusalem will dwell securely. And this is the name by which it will be called: 'The LORD is our righteousness.'

[17] "For thus says the LORD: David shall never lack a man to sit on the throne of the house of Israel, [18] and the Levitical priests shall never lack a man in my presence to offer burnt offerings, to burn grain offerings, and to make sacrifices forever."

[19] The word of the LORD came to Jeremiah: [20] "Thus says the LORD: If you can break my covenant with the day and my covenant with the night, so that day and night will not come at their appointed time, [21] then also my covenant with David my servant may be broken, so that he shall not have a son to reign on his throne, and my covenant with the Levitical priests my ministers. [22] As the host of heaven cannot be numbered and the sands of the sea cannot be measured, so I will multiply the offspring of David my servant, and the Levitical priests who minister to me."

[23] The word of the LORD came to Jeremiah: [24] "Have you not observed that these people are saying, 'The LORD has rejected the two clans that he chose'? Thus they have despised my people so that they are no longer a nation in their sight. [25] Thus says the LORD: If I have not established my covenant with day and night and the fixed order of heaven and earth, [26] then I will reject the offspring of Jacob and David my servant and will not choose one of his offspring to rule over the offspring of Abraham, Isaac, and Jacob. For I will restore their fortunes and will have mercy on them."

Zedekiah to Die in Babylon

34 The word that came to Jeremiah from the LORD, when Nebuchadnezzar king of Babylon and all his army and all the kingdoms of the earth under his dominion and all the peoples were fighting against Jerusalem and all of its cities: [2] "Thus says the LORD, the God of Israel: Go and speak to Zedekiah king of Judah and say to him, 'Thus says the LORD: Behold, I am giving this city into the hand of the king of Babylon, and he shall burn it with fire. [3] You shall not escape from his hand but shall surely be captured and delivered into his hand. You shall see the king of Babylon eye to eye and speak with him face to face. And you shall go to Babylon.' [4] Yet hear the word of the LORD, O Zedekiah king of Judah! Thus says the

[1] Hebrew *And it*

LORD concerning you: 'You shall not die by the sword. [5] You shall die in peace. And as spices were burned for your fathers, the former kings who were before you, so people shall burn spices for you and lament for you, saying, "Alas, lord!"' For I have spoken the word, declares the LORD."

[6] Then Jeremiah the prophet spoke all these words to Zedekiah king of Judah, in Jerusalem, [7] when the army of the king of Babylon was fighting against Jerusalem and against all the cities of Judah that were left, Lachish and Azekah, for these were the only fortified cities of Judah that remained.

[8] The word that came to Jeremiah from the LORD, after King Zedekiah had made a covenant with all the people in Jerusalem to make a proclamation of liberty to them, [9] that everyone should set free his Hebrew slaves, male and female, so that no one should enslave a Jew, his brother. [10] And they obeyed, all the officials and all the people who had entered into the covenant that everyone would set free his slave, male or female, so that they would not be enslaved again. They obeyed and set them free. [11] But afterward they turned around and took back the male and female slaves they had set free, and brought them into subjection as slaves. [12] The word of the LORD came to Jeremiah from the LORD: [13] "Thus says the LORD, the God of Israel: I myself made a covenant with your fathers when I brought them out of the land of Egypt, out of the house of slavery, saying, [14] 'At the end of seven years each of you must set free the fellow Hebrew who has been sold to you and has served you six years; you must set him free from your service.' But your fathers did not listen to me or incline their ears to me. [15] You recently repented and did what was right in my eyes by proclaiming liberty, each to his neighbor, and you made a covenant before me in the house that is called by my name, [16] but then you turned around and profaned my name when each of you took back his male and female slaves, whom you had set free according to their desire, and you brought them into subjection to be your slaves.

[17] "Therefore, thus says the LORD: You have not obeyed me by proclaiming liberty, every one to his brother and to his neighbor; behold, I proclaim to you liberty to the sword, to pestilence, and to

famine, declares the LORD. I will make yo[u] a horror to all the kingdoms of the earth. [18] And the men who transgressed my cov[e]nant and did not keep the terms of the covenant that they made before me, I wil[l] make them like[1] the calf that they cut in two and passed between its parts— [19] th[e] officials of Judah, the officials of Jerusalem, the eunuchs, the priests, and all the people of the land who passed between the part[s] of the calf. [20] And I will give them into the hand of their enemies and into the hand of those who seek their lives. Their dea[d] bodies shall be food for the birds of the ai[r] and the beasts of the earth. [21] And Zedekiah king of Judah and his officials I will giv[e] into the hand of their enemies and int[o] the hand of those who seek their lives, int[o] the hand of the army of the king of Babylo[n] which has withdrawn from you. [22] Behold, I will command, declares the LORD, an[d] will bring them back to this city. And they will fight against it and take it and burn i[t] with fire. I will make the cities of Judah [a] desolation without inhabitant."

The Obedience of the Rechabites

35 The word that came to Jeremia[h] from the LORD in the days of Jehoi[a]kim the son of Josiah, king of Judah[:] [2] "Go to the house of the Rechabites an[d] speak with them and bring them to th[e] house of the LORD, into one of the cham[-]bers; then offer them wine to drink." [3] S[o] I took Jaazaniah the son of Jeremiah, son of Habazziniah and his brothers and all hi[s] sons and the whole house of the Rechabites[.] [4] I brought them to the house of the LOR[D] into the chamber of the sons of Hanan the son of Igdaliah, the man of God, which wa[s] near the chamber of the officials, above th[e] chamber of Maaseiah the son of Shallum[,] keeper of the threshold. [5] Then I set befor[e] the Rechabites pitchers full of wine, an[d] cups, and I said to them, "Drink wine." [6] Bu[t] they answered, "We will drink no wine for Jonadab the son of Rechab, our father[,] commanded us, 'You shall not drink wine, neither you nor your sons forever. [7] You shall not build a house; you shall not sow seed; you shall not plant or have a vineyard[,] but you shall live in tents all your days, tha[t] you may live many days in the land where you sojourn.' [8] We have obeyed the voic[e] of Jonadab the son of Rechab, our father[,]

---

[1] Hebrew lacks *them like*

all that he commanded us, to drink no wine all our days, ourselves, our wives, our sons, or our daughters, ⁹and not to build houses to dwell in. We have no vineyard or field or seed, ¹⁰but we have lived in tents and have obeyed and done all that Jonadab our father commanded us. ¹¹But when Nebuchadnezzar king of Babylon came up against the land, we said, 'Come, and let us go to Jerusalem for fear of the army of the Chaldeans and the army of the Syrians.' So we are living in Jerusalem."

¹²Then the word of the LORD came to Jeremiah: ¹³"Thus says the LORD of hosts, the God of Israel: Go and say to the people of Judah and the inhabitants of Jerusalem, Will you not receive instruction and listen to my words? declares the LORD. ¹⁴The command that Jonadab the son of Rechab gave to his sons, to drink no wine, has been kept, and they drink none to this day, for they have obeyed their father's command. I have spoken to you persistently, but you have not listened to me. ¹⁵I have sent to you all my servants the prophets, sending them persistently, saying, 'Turn now every one of you from his evil way, and amend your deeds, and do not go after other gods to serve them, and then you shall dwell in the land that I gave to you and your fathers.' But you did not incline your ear or listen to me. ¹⁶The sons of Jonadab the son of Rechab have kept the command that their father gave them, but this people has not obeyed me. ¹⁷Therefore, thus says the LORD, the God of hosts, the God of Israel: Behold, I am bringing upon Judah and all the inhabitants of Jerusalem all the disaster that I have pronounced against them, because I have spoken to them and they have not listened, I have called to them and they have not answered."

¹⁸But to the house of the Rechabites Jeremiah said, "Thus says the LORD of hosts, the God of Israel: Because you have obeyed the command of Jonadab your father and kept all his precepts and done all that he commanded you, ¹⁹therefore thus says the LORD of hosts, the God of Israel: Jonadab the son of Rechab shall never lack a man to stand before me."

Jehoiakim Burns Jeremiah's Scroll

36 In the fourth year of Jehoiakim the son of Josiah, king of Judah, this word came to Jeremiah from the LORD:

²"Take a scroll and write on it all the words that I have spoken to you against Israel and Judah and all the nations, from the day I spoke to you, from the days of Josiah until today. ³It may be that the house of Judah will hear all the disaster that I intend to do to them, so that every one may turn from his evil way, and that I may forgive their iniquity and their sin."

⁴Then Jeremiah called Baruch the son of Neriah, and Baruch wrote on a scroll at the dictation of Jeremiah all the words of the LORD that he had spoken to him. ⁵And Jeremiah ordered Baruch, saying, "I am banned from going to the house of the LORD, ⁶so you are to go, and on a day of fasting in the hearing of all the people in the LORD's house you shall read the words of the LORD from the scroll that you have written at my dictation. You shall read them also in the hearing of all the men of Judah who come out of their cities. ⁷It may be that their plea for mercy will come before the LORD, and that every one will turn from his evil way, for great is the anger and wrath that the LORD has pronounced against this people." ⁸And Baruch the son of Neriah did all that Jeremiah the prophet ordered him about reading from the scroll the words of the LORD in the LORD's house.

⁹In the fifth year of Jehoiakim the son of Josiah, king of Judah, in the ninth month, all the people in Jerusalem and all the people who came from the cities of Judah to Jerusalem proclaimed a fast before the LORD. ¹⁰Then, in the hearing of all the people, Baruch read the words of Jeremiah from the scroll, in the house of the LORD, in the chamber of Gemariah the son of Shaphan the secretary, which was in the upper court, at the entry of the New Gate of the LORD's house.

¹¹When Micaiah the son of Gemariah, son of Shaphan, heard all the words of the LORD from the scroll, ¹²he went down to the king's house, into the secretary's chamber, and all the officials were sitting there: Elishama the secretary, Delaiah the son of Shemaiah, Elnathan the son of Achbor, Gemariah the son of Shaphan, Zedekiah the son of Hananiah, and all the officials. ¹³And Micaiah told them all the words that he had heard, when Baruch read the scroll in the hearing of the people. ¹⁴Then all the officials sent Jehudi the son of Nethaniah, son of Shelemiah, son of Cushi, to say to

Baruch, "Take in your hand the scroll that you read in the hearing of the people, and come." So Baruch the son of Neriah took the scroll in his hand and came to them. [15] And they said to him, "Sit down and read it." So Baruch read it to them. [16] When they heard all the words, they turned one to another in fear. And they said to Baruch, "We must report all these words to the king." [17] Then they asked Baruch, "Tell us, please, how did you write all these words? Was it at his dictation?" [18] Baruch answered them, "He dictated all these words to me, while I wrote them with ink on the scroll." [19] Then the officials said to Baruch, "Go and hide, you and Jeremiah, and let no one know where you are."

[20] So they went into the court to the king, having put the scroll in the chamber of Elishama the secretary, and they reported all the words to the king. [21] Then the king sent Jehudi to get the scroll, and he took it from the chamber of Elishama the secretary. And Jehudi read it to the king and all the officials who stood beside the king. [22] It was the ninth month, and the king was sitting in the winter house, and there was a fire burning in the fire pot before him. [23] As Jehudi read three or four columns, the king would cut them off with a knife and throw them into the fire in the fire pot, until the entire scroll was consumed in the fire that was in the fire pot. [24] Yet neither the king nor any of his servants who heard all these words was afraid, nor did they tear their garments. [25] Even when Elnathan and Delaiah and Gemariah urged the king not to burn the scroll, he would not listen to them. [26] And the king commanded Jerahmeel the king's son and Seraiah the son of Azriel and Shelemiah the son of Abdeel to seize Baruch the secretary and Jeremiah the prophet, but the LORD hid them.

[27] Now after the king had burned the scroll with the words that Baruch wrote at Jeremiah's dictation, the word of the LORD came to Jeremiah: [28] "Take another scroll and write on it all the former words that were in the first scroll, which Jehoiakim the king of Judah has burned. [29] And concerning Jehoiakim king of Judah you shall say, 'Thus says the LORD, You have burned this scroll, saying, "Why have you written in it that the king of Babylon will certainly come and destroy this land, and will cut

off from it man and beast?" [30] Therefore thus says the LORD concerning Jehoiakim king of Judah: He shall have none to sit on the throne of David, and his dead body shall be cast out to the heat by day and the frost by night. [31] And I will punish him and his offspring and his servants for their iniquity. I will bring upon them and upon the inhabitants of Jerusalem and upon the people of Judah all the disaster that I have pronounced against them, but they would not hear.' "

[32] Then Jeremiah took another scroll and gave it to Baruch the scribe, the son of Neriah, who wrote on it at the dictation of Jeremiah all the words of the scroll that Jehoiakim king of Judah had burned in the fire. And many similar words were added to them.

Jeremiah Warns Zedekiah

37 Zedekiah the son of Josiah, whom Nebuchadnezzar king of Babylon made king in the land of Judah, reigned instead of Coniah the son of Jehoiakim. [2] But neither he nor his servants nor the people of the land listened to the words of the LORD that he spoke through Jeremiah the prophet.

[3] King Zedekiah sent Jehucal the son of Shelemiah, and Zephaniah the priest, the son of Maaseiah, to Jeremiah the prophet, saying, "Please pray for us to the LORD our God." [4] Now Jeremiah was still going in and out among the people, for he had not yet been put in prison. [5] The army of Pharaoh had come out of Egypt. And when the Chaldeans who were besieging Jerusalem heard news about them, they withdrew from Jerusalem.

[6] Then the word of the LORD came to Jeremiah the prophet: [7] "Thus says the LORD, God of Israel: Thus shall you say to the king of Judah who sent you to me to inquire of me, 'Behold, Pharaoh's army that came to help you is about to return to Egypt, to its own land. [8] And the Chaldeans shall come back and fight against this city. They shall capture it and burn it with fire. [9] Thus says the LORD, Do not deceive yourselves, saying, "The Chaldeans will surely go away from us," for they will not go away. [10] For even if you should defeat the whole army of Chaldeans who are fighting against you, and there remained of them only wounded

men, every man in his tent, they would rise up and burn this city with fire.'"

Jeremiah Imprisoned

¹¹ Now when the Chaldean army had withdrawn from Jerusalem at the approach of Pharaoh's army, ¹² Jeremiah set out from Jerusalem to go to the land of Benjamin to receive his portion there among the people. ¹³ When he was at the Benjamin Gate, a sentry there named Irijah the son of Shelemiah, son of Hananiah, seized Jeremiah the prophet, saying, "You are deserting to the Chaldeans." ¹⁴ And Jeremiah said, "It is a lie; I am not deserting to the Chaldeans." But Irijah would not listen to him, and seized Jeremiah and brought him to the officials. ¹⁵ And the officials were enraged at Jeremiah, and they beat him and imprisoned him in the house of Jonathan the secretary, for it had been made a prison.

¹⁶ When Jeremiah had come to the dungeon cells and remained there many days, ¹⁷ King Zedekiah sent for him and received him. The king questioned him secretly in his house and said, "Is there any word from the LORD?" Jeremiah said, "There is." Then he said, "You shall be delivered into the hand of the king of Babylon." ¹⁸ Jeremiah also said to King Zedekiah, "What wrong have I done to you or your servants or this people, that you have put me in prison? ¹⁹ Where are your prophets who prophesied to you, saying, 'The king of Babylon will not come against you and against this land'? ²⁰ Now hear, please, O my lord the king: let my humble plea come before you and do not send me back to the house of Jonathan the secretary, lest I die there." ²¹ So King Zedekiah gave orders, and they committed Jeremiah to the court of the guard. And a loaf of bread was given him daily from the bakers' street, until all the bread of the city was gone. So Jeremiah remained in the court of the guard.

Jeremiah Cast into the Cistern

38 Now Shephatiah the son of Mattan, Gedaliah the son of Pashhur, Jucal the son of Shelemiah, and Pashhur the son of Malchiah heard the words that Jeremiah was saying to all the people, ² "Thus says the LORD: He who stays in this city shall die by the sword, by famine, and by pestilence, but he who goes out to the Chaldeans shall live. He shall have his life as a prize of war, and live. ³ Thus says the LORD: This city shall surely be given into the hand of the army of the king of Babylon and be taken." ⁴ Then the officials said to the king, "Let this man be put to death, for he is weakening the hands of the soldiers who are left in this city, and the hands of all the people, by speaking such words to them. For this man is not seeking the welfare of this people, but their harm." ⁵ King Zedekiah said, "Behold, he is in your hands, for the king can do nothing against you." ⁶ So they took Jeremiah and cast him into the cistern of Malchiah, the king's son, which was in the court of the guard, letting Jeremiah down by ropes. And there was no water in the cistern, but only mud, and Jeremiah sank in the mud.

Jeremiah Rescued from the Cistern

⁷ When Ebed-melech the Ethiopian, a eunuch who was in the king's house, heard that they had put Jeremiah into the cistern—the king was sitting in the Benjamin Gate— ⁸ Ebed-melech went from the king's house and said to the king, ⁹ "My lord the king, these men have done evil in all that they did to Jeremiah the prophet by casting him into the cistern, and he will die there of hunger, for there is no bread left in the city." ¹⁰ Then the king commanded Ebed-melech the Ethiopian, "Take thirty men with you from here, and lift Jeremiah the prophet out of the cistern before he dies." ¹¹ So Ebed-melech took the men with him and went to the house of the king, to a wardrobe in the storehouse, and took from there old rags and worn-out clothes, which he let down to Jeremiah in the cistern by ropes. ¹² Then Ebed-melech the Ethiopian said to Jeremiah, "Put the rags and clothes between your armpits and the ropes." Jeremiah did so. ¹³ Then they drew Jeremiah up with ropes and lifted him out of the cistern. And Jeremiah remained in the court of the guard.

Jeremiah Warns Zedekiah Again

¹⁴ King Zedekiah sent for Jeremiah the prophet and received him at the third entrance of the temple of the LORD. The king said to Jeremiah, "I will ask you a question; hide nothing from me." ¹⁵ Jeremiah said to Zedekiah, "If I tell you, will you not surely put me to death? And if

I give you counsel, you will not listen to me." **16** Then King Zedekiah swore secretly to Jeremiah, "As the LORD lives, who made our souls, I will not put you to death or deliver you into the hand of these men who seek your life."

17 Then Jeremiah said to Zedekiah, "Thus says the LORD, the God of hosts, the God of Israel: If you will surrender to the officials of the king of Babylon, then your life shall be spared, and this city shall not be burned with fire, and you and your house shall live. **18** But if you do not surrender to the officials of the king of Babylon, then this city shall be given into the hand of the Chaldeans, and they shall burn it with fire, and you shall not escape from their hand." **19** King Zedekiah said to Jeremiah, "I am afraid of the Judeans who have deserted to the Chaldeans, lest I be handed over to them and they deal cruelly with me." **20** Jeremiah said, "You shall not be given to them. Obey now the voice of the LORD in what I say to you, and it shall be well with you, and your life shall be spared. **21** But if you refuse to surrender, this is the vision which the LORD has shown to me: **22** Behold, all the women left in the house of the king of Judah were being led out to the officials of the king of Babylon and were saying,

"'Your trusted friends have deceived you
    and prevailed against you;
now that your feet are sunk in the mud,
    they turn away from you.'

23 All your wives and your sons shall be led out to the Chaldeans, and you yourself shall not escape from their hand, but shall be seized by the king of Babylon, and this city shall be burned with fire."

24 Then Zedekiah said to Jeremiah, "Let no one know of these words, and you shall not die. **25** If the officials hear that I have spoken with you and come to you and say to you, 'Tell us what you said to the king and what the king said to you; hide nothing from us and we will not put you to death,' **26** then you shall say to them, 'I made a humble plea to the king that he would not send me back to the house of Jonathan to die there.'" **27** Then all the officials came to Jeremiah and asked him, and he answered them as the king had instructed him. So they stopped speaking with him, for the conversation had not been overheard. **28** And Jeremiah remained in the court of the guard until the day that Jerusalem was taken.

The Fall of Jerusalem

39 In the ninth year of Zedekiah king of Judah, in the tenth month, Nebuchadnezzar king of Babylon and all his army came against Jerusalem and besieged it. **2** In the eleventh year of Zedekiah, in the fourth month, on the ninth day of the month, a breach was made in the city **3** Then all the officials of the king of Babylon came and sat in the middle gate: Nergal-sar-ezer of Samgar, Nebu-sar-sekim the Rab-saris, Nergal-sar-ezer the Rab-mag with all the rest of the officers of the king of Babylon. **4** When Zedekiah king of Judah and all the soldiers saw them, they fled, going out of the city at night by way of the king's garden through the gate between the two walls; and they went toward the Arabah. **5** But the army of the Chaldeans pursued them and overtook Zedekiah in the plains of Jericho. And when they had taken him, they brought him up to Nebuchadnezzar king of Babylon, at Riblah, in the land of Hamath; and he passed sentence on him. **6** The king of Babylon slaughtered the sons of Zedekiah at Riblah before his eyes, and the king of Babylon slaughtered all the nobles of Judah. **7** He put out the eyes of Zedekiah and bound him in chains to take him to Babylon. **8** The Chaldeans burned the king's house and the house of the people, and broke down the walls of Jerusalem. **9** Then Nebuzaradan, the captain of the guard, carried into exile to Babylon the rest of the people who were left in the city, those who had deserted to him, and the people who remained. **10** Nebuzaradan, the captain of the guard, left in the land of Judah some of the poor people who owned nothing, and gave them vineyards and fields at the same time.

The LORD Delivers Jeremiah

11 Nebuchadnezzar king of Babylon gave command concerning Jeremiah through Nebuzaradan, the captain of the guard, saying, **12** "Take him, look after him well, and do him no harm, but deal with him as he tells you." **13** So Nebuzaradan the captain of the guard, Nebushazban the Rab-saris, Nergal-sar-ezer the Rab-mag, and all the chief officers of the king of Babylon **14** sent nd took Jeremiah from the court of the guard. They entrusted him to Gedaliah the on of Ahikam, son of Shaphan, that he should take him home. So he lived among he people.

¹⁵ The word of the LORD came to Jeremiah while he was shut up in the court of the guard: ¹⁶ "Go, and say to Ebed-melech the Ethiopian, 'Thus says the LORD of hosts, he God of Israel: Behold, I will fulfill my words against this city for harm and not or good, and they shall be accomplished before you on that day. ¹⁷ But I will deliver you on that day, declares the LORD, and you shall not be given into the hand of men of whom you are afraid. ¹⁸ For I will surely save you, and you shall not fall by the sword, but you shall have your life as a prize of war, because you have put your trust in me, declares the LORD.'"

Jeremiah Remains in Judah

40 The word that came to Jeremiah from the LORD after Nebuzaradan the captain of the guard had let him go from Ramah, when he took him bound in chains along with all the captives of Jerusalem and Judah who were being exiled to Babylon. ² The captain of the guard took Jeremiah and said to him, "The LORD your God pronounced this disaster against this place. ³ The LORD has brought it about, and has done as he said. Because you sinned against the LORD and did not obey his voice, this thing has come upon you. ⁴ Now, behold, I release you today from the chains on your hands. If it seems good to you to come with me to Babylon, come, and I will look after you well, but if it seems wrong to you to come with me to Babylon, do not come. See, the whole land is before you; go wherever you think it good and right to go. ⁵ If you remain,¹ then return to Gedaliah the son of Ahikam, son of Shaphan, whom the king of Babylon appointed governor of the cities of Judah, and dwell with him among the people. Or go wherever you think it right to go." So the captain of the guard gave him an allowance of food and a present, and let him go. ⁶ Then Jeremiah went to Gedaliah the son of Ahikam, at Mizpah, and lived with him among the people who were left in the land.

⁷ When all the captains of the forces in the open country and their men heard

that the king of Babylon had appointed Gedaliah the son of Ahikam governor in the land and had committed to him men, women, and children, those of the poorest of the land who had not been taken into exile to Babylon, ⁸ they went to Gedaliah at Mizpah—Ishmael the son of Nethaniah, Johanan the son of Kareah, Seraiah the son of Tanhumeth, the sons of Ephai the Netophathite, Jezaniah the son of the Maacathite, they and their men. ⁹ Gedaliah the son of Ahikam, son of Shaphan, swore to them and their men, saying, "Do not be afraid to serve the Chaldeans. Dwell in the land and serve the king of Babylon, and it shall be well with you. ¹⁰ As for me, I will dwell at Mizpah, to represent you before the Chaldeans who will come to us. But as for you, gather wine and summer fruits and oil, and store them in your vessels, and dwell in your cities that you have taken." ¹¹ Likewise, when all the Judeans who were in Moab and among the Ammonites and in Edom and in other lands heard that the king of Babylon had left a remnant in Judah and had appointed Gedaliah the son of Ahikam, son of Shaphan, as governor over them, ¹² then all the Judeans returned from all the places to which they had been driven and came to the land of Judah, to Gedaliah at Mizpah. And they gathered wine and summer fruits in great abundance.

¹³ Now Johanan the son of Kareah and all the leaders of the forces in the open country came to Gedaliah at Mizpah ¹⁴ and said to him, "Do you know that Baalis the king of the Ammonites has sent Ishmael the son of Nethaniah to take your life?" But Gedaliah the son of Ahikam would not believe them. ¹⁵ Then Johanan the son of Kareah spoke secretly to Gedaliah at Mizpah, "Please let me go and strike down Ishmael the son of Nethaniah, and no one will know it. Why should he take your life, so that all the Judeans who are gathered about you would be scattered, and the remnant of Judah would perish?" ¹⁶ But Gedaliah the son of Ahikam said to Johanan the son of Kareah, "You shall not do this thing, for you are speaking falsely of Ishmael."

Gedaliah Murdered

41 In the seventh month, Ishmael the son of Nethaniah, son of Elishama, of the royal family, one of the chief officers

¹ Syriac; the meaning of the Hebrew phrase is uncertain

of the king, came with ten men to Gedaliah the son of Ahikam, at Mizpah. As they ate bread together there at Mizpah, [2]Ishmael the son of Nethaniah and the ten men with him rose up and struck down Gedaliah the son of Ahikam, son of Shaphan, with the sword, and killed him, whom the king of Babylon had appointed governor in the land. [3]Ishmael also struck down all the Judeans who were with Gedaliah at Mizpah, and the Chaldean soldiers who happened to be there.

[4]On the day after the murder of Gedaliah, before anyone knew of it, [5]eighty men arrived from Shechem and Shiloh and Samaria, with their beards shaved and their clothes torn, and their bodies gashed, bringing grain offerings and incense to present at the temple of the LORD. [6]And Ishmael the son of Nethaniah came out from Mizpah to meet them, weeping as he came. As he met them, he said to them, "Come in to Gedaliah the son of Ahikam." [7]When they came into the city, Ishmael the son of Nethaniah and the men with him slaughtered them and cast them into a cistern. [8]But there were ten men among them who said to Ishmael, "Do not put us to death, for we have stores of wheat, barley, oil, and honey hidden in the fields." So he refrained and did not put them to death with their companions.

[9]Now the cistern into which Ishmael had thrown all the bodies of the men whom he had struck down along with[1] Gedaliah was the large cistern that King Asa had made for defense against Baasha king of Israel; Ishmael the son of Nethaniah filled it with the slain. [10]Then Ishmael took captive all the rest of the people who were in Mizpah, the king's daughters and all the people who were left at Mizpah, whom Nebuzaradan, the captain of the guard, had committed to Gedaliah the son of Ahikam. Ishmael the son of Nethaniah took them captive and set out to cross over to the Ammonites.

[11]But when Johanan the son of Kareah and all the leaders of the forces with him heard of all the evil that Ishmael the son of Nethaniah had done, [12]they took all their men and went to fight against Ishmael the son of Nethaniah. They came upon him at the great pool that is in Gibeon. [13]And when all the people who were with

Ishmael saw Johanan the son of Kareah and all the leaders of the forces with him, they rejoiced. [14]So all the people whom Ishmael had carried away captive from Mizpah turned around and came back, and went to Johanan the son of Kareah. [15]But Ishmael the son of Nethaniah escaped from Johanan with eight men, and went to the Ammonites. [16]Then Johanan the son of Kareah and all the leaders of the forces with him took from Mizpah all the rest of the people whom he had recovered from Ishmael the son of Nethaniah, after he had struck down Gedaliah the son of Ahikam— soldiers, women, children, and eunuchs whom Johanan brought back from Gibeon. [17]And they went and stayed at Geruth Chimham near Bethlehem, intending to go to Egypt [18]because of the Chaldeans. For they were afraid of them, because Ishmael the son of Nethaniah had struck down Gedaliah the son of Ahikam, whom the king of Babylon had made governor over the land.

Warning Against Going to Egypt

42 Then all the commanders of the forces, and Johanan the son of Kareah and Jezaniah the son of Hoshaiah and all the people from the least to the greatest, came near [2]and said to Jeremiah the prophet, "Let our plea for mercy come before you, and pray to the LORD your God for us, for all this remnant—because we are left with but a few, as your eyes see us— [3]that the LORD your God may show us the way we should go, and the thing that we should do." [4]Jeremiah the prophet said to them, "I have heard you. Behold, I will pray to the LORD your God according to your request, and whatever the LORD answers you I will tell you. I will keep nothing back from you." [5]Then they said to Jeremiah, "May the LORD be a true and faithful witness against us if we do not act according to all the word with which the LORD your God sends you to us. [6]Whether it is good or bad, we will obey the voice of the LORD our God to whom we are sending you, that it may be well with us when we obey the voice of the LORD our God."

[7]At the end of ten days the word of the LORD came to Jeremiah. [8]Then he summoned Johanan the son of Kareah and all the commanders of the forces who were

[1]Hebrew *by the hand of*

with him, and all the people from the least to the greatest, ⁹and said to them, "Thus says the LORD, the God of Israel, to whom you sent me to present your plea for mercy before him: ¹⁰If you will remain in this land, then I will build you up and not pull you down; I will plant you, and not pluck you up; for I relent of the disaster that I did to you. ¹¹Do not fear the king of Babylon, of whom you are afraid. Do not fear him, declares the LORD, for I am with you, to save you and to deliver you from his hand. ¹²I will grant you mercy, that he may have mercy on you and let you remain in your own land. ¹³But if you say, 'We will not remain in this land,' disobeying the voice of the LORD your God ¹⁴and saying, 'No, we will go to the land of Egypt, where we shall not see war or hear the sound of the trumpet or be hungry for bread, and we will dwell there,' ¹⁵then hear the word of the LORD, O remnant of Judah. Thus says the LORD of hosts, the God of Israel: If you set your faces to enter Egypt and go to live there, ¹⁶then the sword that you fear shall overtake you there in the land of Egypt, and the famine of which you are afraid shall follow close after you to Egypt, and there you shall die. ¹⁷All the men who set their faces to go to Egypt to live there shall die by the sword, by famine, and by pestilence. They shall have no remnant or survivor from the disaster that I will bring upon them.

¹⁸"For thus says the LORD of hosts, the God of Israel: As my anger and my wrath were poured out on the inhabitants of Jerusalem, so my wrath will be poured out on you when you go to Egypt. You shall become an execration, a horror, a curse, and a taunt. You shall see this place no more. ¹⁹The LORD has said to you, O remnant of Judah, 'Do not go to Egypt.' Know for a certainty that I have warned you this day ²⁰that you have gone astray at the cost of your lives. For you sent me to the LORD your God, saying, 'Pray for us to the LORD our God, and whatever the LORD our God says declare to us and we will do it.' ²¹And I have this day declared it to you, but you have not obeyed the voice of the LORD your God in anything that he sent me to tell you. ²²Now therefore know for a certainty that you shall die by the sword, by famine, and by pestilence in the place where you desire to go to live."

Jeremiah Taken to Egypt

43 When Jeremiah finished speaking to all the people all these words of the LORD their God, with which the LORD their God had sent him to them, ²Azariah the son of Hoshaiah and Johanan the son of Kareah and all the insolent men said to Jeremiah, "You are telling a lie. The LORD our God did not send you to say, 'Do not go to Egypt to live there,' ³but Baruch the son of Neriah has set you against us, to deliver us into the hand of the Chaldeans, that they may kill us or take us into exile in Babylon." ⁴So Johanan the son of Kareah and all the commanders of the forces and all the people did not obey the voice of the LORD, to remain in the land of Judah. ⁵But Johanan the son of Kareah and all the commanders of the forces took all the remnant of Judah who had returned to live in the land of Judah from all the nations to which they had been driven— ⁶the men, the women, the children, the princesses, and every person whom Nebuzaradan the captain of the guard had left with Gedaliah the son of Ahikam, son of Shaphan; also Jeremiah the prophet and Baruch the son of Neriah. ⁷And they came into the land of Egypt, for they did not obey the voice of the LORD. And they arrived at Tahpanhes.

⁸Then the word of the LORD came to Jeremiah in Tahpanhes: ⁹"Take in your hands large stones and hide them in the mortar in the pavement that is at the entrance to Pharaoh's palace in Tahpanhes, in the sight of the men of Judah, ¹⁰and say to them, 'Thus says the LORD of hosts, the God of Israel: Behold, I will send and take Nebuchadnezzar the king of Babylon, my servant, and I will set his throne above these stones that I have hidden, and he will spread his royal canopy over them. ¹¹He shall come and strike the land of Egypt, giving over to the pestilence those who are doomed to the pestilence, to captivity those who are doomed to captivity, and to the sword those who are doomed to the sword. ¹²I shall kindle a fire in the temples of the gods of Egypt, and he shall burn them and carry them away captive. And he shall clean the land of Egypt as a shepherd cleans his cloak of vermin, and he shall go away from there in peace. ¹³He shall break the obelisks of Heliopolis, which is in the land of Egypt, and the temples of the gods of Egypt he shall burn with fire.'"

Judgment for Idolatry

44 The word that came to Jeremiah concerning all the Judeans who lived in the land of Egypt, at Migdol, at Tahpanhes, at Memphis, and in the land of Pathros, [2] "Thus says the LORD of hosts, the God of Israel: You have seen all the disaster that I brought upon Jerusalem and upon all the cities of Judah. Behold, this day they are a desolation, and no one dwells in them, [3] because of the evil that they committed, provoking me to anger, in that they went to make offerings and serve other gods that they knew not, neither they, nor you, nor your fathers. [4] Yet I persistently sent to you all my servants the prophets, saying, 'Oh, do not do this abomination that I hate!' [5] But they did not listen or incline their ear, to turn from their evil and make no offerings to other gods. [6] Therefore my wrath and my anger were poured out and kindled in the cities of Judah and in the streets of Jerusalem, and they became a waste and a desolation, as at this day. [7] And now thus says the LORD God of hosts, the God of Israel: Why do you commit this great evil against yourselves, to cut off from you man and woman, infant and child, from the midst of Judah, leaving you no remnant? [8] Why do you provoke me to anger with the works of your hands, making offerings to other gods in the land of Egypt where you have come to live, so that you may be cut off and become a curse and a taunt among all the nations of the earth? [9] Have you forgotten the evil of your fathers, the evil of the kings of Judah, the evil of their[1] wives, your own evil, and the evil of your wives, which they committed in the land of Judah and in the streets of Jerusalem? [10] They have not humbled themselves even to this day, nor have they feared, nor walked in my law and my statutes that I set before you and before your fathers.

[11] "Therefore thus says the LORD of hosts, the God of Israel: Behold, I will set my face against you for harm, to cut off all Judah. [12] I will take the remnant of Judah who have set their faces to come to the land of Egypt to live, and they shall all be consumed. In the land of Egypt they shall fall; by the sword and by famine they shall be consumed. From the least to the greatest, they shall die by the sword and by famine, and they shall become an oath, a horror, a curse, and a taunt. [13] I will punish those who dwell in the land of Egypt, as I have punished Jerusalem, with the sword, with famine, and with pestilence, [14] so that none of the remnant of Judah who have come to live in the land of Egypt shall escape or survive or return to the land of Judah, to which they desire to return to dwell there. For they shall not return, except some fugitives."

[15] Then all the men who knew that their wives had made offerings to other gods, and all the women who stood by, a great assembly, all the people who lived in Pathros in the land of Egypt, answered Jeremiah: [16] "As for the word that you have spoken to us in the name of the LORD, we will not listen to you. [17] But we will do everything that we have vowed, make offerings to the queen of heaven and pour out drink offerings to her, as we did, both we and our fathers, our kings and our officials, in the cities of Judah and in the streets of Jerusalem. For then we had plenty of food, and prospered, and saw no disaster. [18] But since we left off making offerings to the queen of heaven and pouring out drink offerings to her, we have lacked everything and have been consumed by the sword and by famine." [19] And the women said,[2] "When we made offerings to the queen of heaven and poured out drink offerings to her, was it without our husbands' approval that we made cakes for her bearing her image and poured out drink offerings to her?"

[20] Then Jeremiah said to all the people, men and women, all the people who had given him this answer: [21] "As for the offerings that you offered in the cities of Judah and in the streets of Jerusalem, you and your fathers, your kings and your officials and the people of the land, did not the LORD remember them? Did it not come into his mind? [22] The LORD could no longer bear your evil deeds and the abominations that you committed. Therefore your land has become a desolation and a waste and a curse, without inhabitant, as it is this day. [23] It is because you made offerings and because you sinned against the LORD and did not obey the voice of the LORD or walk in his law and in his statutes and in his testimonies that this disaster has happened to you, as at this day."

---

[1] Hebrew *his* [2] Compare Syriac; Hebrew lacks *And the women said*

24 Jeremiah said to all the people and all the women, "Hear the word of the Lord, all you of Judah who are in the land of Egypt. 25 Thus says the Lord of hosts, the God of Israel: You and your wives have declared with your mouths, and have fulfilled it with your hands, saying, 'We will surely perform our vows that we have made, to make offerings to the queen of heaven and to pour out drink offerings to her.' Then confirm your vows and perform your vows! 26 Therefore hear the word of the Lord, all you of Judah who dwell in the land of Egypt: Behold, I have sworn by my great name, says the Lord, that my name shall no more be invoked by the mouth of any man of Judah in all the land of Egypt, saying, 'As the Lord God lives.' 27 Behold, I am watching over them for disaster and not for good. All the men of Judah who are in the land of Egypt shall be consumed by the sword and by famine, until there is an end of them. 28 And those who escape the sword shall return from the land of Egypt to the land of Judah, few in number; and all the remnant of Judah, who came to the land of Egypt to live, shall know whose word will stand, mine or theirs. 29 This shall be the sign to you, declares the Lord, that I will punish you in this place, in order that you may know that my words will surely stand against you for harm: 30 Thus says the Lord, Behold, I will give Pharaoh Hophra king of Egypt into the hand of his enemies and into the hand of those who seek his life, as I gave Zedekiah king of Judah into the hand of Nebuchadnezzar king of Babylon, who was his enemy and sought his life."

Message to Baruch

45 The word that Jeremiah the prophet spoke to Baruch the son of Neriah, when he wrote these words in a book at the dictation of Jeremiah, in the fourth year of Jehoiakim the son of Josiah, king of Judah: 2 "Thus says the Lord, the God of Israel, to

Know True Happiness

verses to read
Jeremiah 45

Is your main goal happiness, or holiness? One of the great secrets to the Christian life is that you don't need to choose one over the other. God has made us to find true happiness *in* holiness, not instead of holiness. The only real, solid joy is in walking with God. While it is painful when God does not give us the things that we ask for, it may be that he is drawing us into greater holiness with his "no," and greater holiness always ultimately brings not less joy but more.

God's Word promises to give you what you ask, when you ask for what he wants. Ask yourself what you want from God and why. Is it something that would make you more holy and therefore more happy? If you're more concerned with shallow, worldly happiness, then you might want to rethink your wish list. Think about what you're asking God for and how you could start to want more of what he wants for your life. God's goal is always to strengthen your relationship with him, not to increase your comfort, popularity, or success. He wants to give you great things—far greater than you think—but it all has to do with your holiness and relationship with him.

So look at his Word and see what he wants for his kids. Think about his gifts, his life, his love. Think about what you want and what that says about you. Do you concentrate on the things of heaven? Are you content with the things God has given you—especially his own Son!—or do you need more? Can you find hope in your situation, knowing that God answers prayers not according to your will but according to his divine and perfect will? Because God is truly good, he will always give you what is the very best for you right now.

you, O Baruch: [3]You said, 'Woe is me! For the Lord has added sorrow to my pain. I am weary with my groaning, and I find no rest.' [4]Thus shall you say to him, Thus says the Lord: Behold, what I have built I am breaking down, and what I have planted I am plucking up—that is, the whole land. [5]And do you seek great things for yourself? Seek them not, for behold, I am bringing disaster upon all flesh, declares the Lord. But I will give you your life as a prize of war in all places to which you may go."

Judgment on Egypt

46 The word of the Lord that came to Jeremiah the prophet concerning the nations.

[2]About Egypt. Concerning the army of Pharaoh Neco, king of Egypt, which was by the river Euphrates at Carchemish and which Nebuchadnezzar king of Babylon defeated in the fourth year of Jehoiakim the son of Josiah, king of Judah:

[3] "Prepare buckler and shield,
    and advance for battle!
[4] Harness the horses;
    mount, O horsemen!
Take your stations with your helmets,
    polish your spears,
    put on your armor!
[5] Why have I seen it?
They are dismayed
    and have turned backward.
Their warriors are beaten down
    and have fled in haste;
they look not back—
    terror on every side!
        declares the Lord.

[6] "The swift cannot flee away,
    nor the warrior escape;
in the north by the river Euphrates
    they have stumbled and fallen.

[7] "Who is this, rising like the Nile,
    like rivers whose waters surge?
[8] Egypt rises like the Nile,
    like rivers whose waters surge.
He said, 'I will rise, I will cover the earth,
    I will destroy cities and their inhabitants.'
[9] Advance, O horses,
    and rage, O chariots!
Let the warriors go out:
    men of Cush and Put who handle the shield,
    men of Lud, skilled in handling the bow.
[10] That day is the day of the Lord God of hosts,
    a day of vengeance,
    to avenge himself on his foes.
The sword shall devour and be sated
    and drink its fill of their blood.
For the Lord God of hosts holds a sacrifice
    in the north country by the river Euphrates.
[11] Go up to Gilead, and take balm,
    O virgin daughter of Egypt!
In vain you have used many medicines;
    there is no healing for you.
[12] The nations have heard of your shame,
    and the earth is full of your cry;
for warrior has stumbled against warrior;
    they have both fallen together."

[13]The word that the Lord spoke to Jeremiah the prophet about the coming of Nebuchadnezzar king of Babylon to strike the land of Egypt:

[14] "Declare in Egypt, and proclaim in Migdol;
    proclaim in Memphis and Tahpanhes;
say, 'Stand ready and be prepared,
    for the sword shall devour around you.'
[15] Why are your mighty ones face down?
They do not stand[1]
    because the Lord thrust them down.
[16] He made many stumble, and they fell,
    and they said one to another,
'Arise, and let us go back to our own people
    and to the land of our birth,
    because of the sword of the oppressor.'
[17] Call the name of Pharaoh, king of Egypt,
    'Noisy one who lets the hour go by.'

[18] "As I live, declares the King,
    whose name is the Lord of hosts,

[1] Hebrew *He does not stand*

like Tabor among the mountains
   and like Carmel by the sea, shall
     one come.
Prepare yourselves baggage for exile,
   O inhabitants of Egypt!
For Memphis shall become a waste,
   a ruin, without inhabitant.

"A beautiful heifer is Egypt,
   but a biting fly from the north has
     come upon her.
Even her hired soldiers in her midst
   are like fattened calves;
yes, they have turned and fled
     together;
   they did not stand,
for the day of their calamity has
     come upon them,
   the time of their punishment.

"She makes a sound like a serpent glid-
     ing away;
   for her enemies march in force
and come against her with axes
   like those who fell trees.
They shall cut down her forest,
     declares the Lord,
   though it is impenetrable,
because they are more numerous
     than locusts;
   they are without number.
The daughter of Egypt shall be put to
     shame;
   she shall be delivered into the hand
     of a people from the north."

²⁵ The Lord of hosts, the God of Israel, said: "Behold, I am bringing punishment upon Amon of Thebes, and Pharaoh and Egypt and her gods and her kings, upon Pharaoh and those who trust in him. ²⁶ I will deliver them into the hand of those who seek their life, into the hand of Nebuchadnezzar king of Babylon and his officers. Afterward Egypt shall be inhabited as in the days of old, declares the Lord.

²⁷ "But fear not, O Jacob my servant,
   nor be dismayed, O Israel,
for behold, I will save you from far
     away,
   and your offspring from the land
     of their captivity.
Jacob shall return and have quiet and
     ease,
   and none shall make him afraid.

²⁸ Fear not, O Jacob my servant,
     declares the Lord,
   for I am with you.
I will make a full end of all the nations
   to which I have driven you,
   but of you I will not make a full end.
I will discipline you in just measure,
   and I will by no means leave you
     unpunished."

Judgment on the Philistines

47 The word of the Lord that came to Jeremiah the prophet concerning the Philistines, before Pharaoh struck down Gaza.

² "Thus says the Lord:
Behold, waters are rising out of the
     north,
   and shall become an overflowing
     torrent;
they shall overflow the land and all
     that fills it,
   the city and those who dwell in it.
Men shall cry out,
   and every inhabitant of the land
     shall wail.
³ At the noise of the stamping of the
     hoofs of his stallions,
   at the rushing of his chariots, at
     the rumbling of their wheels,
the fathers look not back to their
     children,
   so feeble are their hands,
⁴ because of the day that is coming to
     destroy
   all the Philistines,
to cut off from Tyre and Sidon
   every helper that remains.
For the Lord is destroying the
     Philistines,
   the remnant of the coastland of
     Caphtor.
⁵ Baldness has come upon Gaza;
   Ashkelon has perished.
O remnant of their valley,
   how long will you gash yourselves?
⁶ Ah, sword of the Lord!
   How long till you are quiet?
Put yourself into your scabbard;
   rest and be still!
⁷ How can it¹ be quiet
   when the Lord has given it a
     charge?

---

¹ Septuagint, Vulgate; Hebrew *you*

Against Ashkelon and against the
seashore
he has appointed it."

Judgment on Moab

48 Concerning Moab.
Thus says the Lord of hosts, the
God of Israel:

"Woe to Nebo, for it is laid waste!
Kiriathaim is put to shame, it is
taken;
the fortress is put to shame and
broken down;
²   the renown of Moab is no more.
In Heshbon they planned disaster
against her:
'Come, let us cut her off from being
a nation!'
You also, O Madmen, shall be brought
to silence;
the sword shall pursue you.

³   "A voice! A cry from Horonaim,
'Desolation and great destruction!'
⁴   Moab is destroyed;
her little ones have made a cry.
⁵   For at the ascent of Luhith
they go up weeping;[1]
for at the descent of Horonaim
they have heard the distressed cry[2]
of destruction.
⁶   Flee! Save yourselves!
You will be like a juniper in the
desert!
⁷   For, because you trusted in your
works and your treasures,
you also shall be taken;
and Chemosh shall go into exile
with his priests and his officials.
⁸   The destroyer shall come upon every
city,
and no city shall escape;
the valley shall perish,
and the plain shall be destroyed,
as the Lord has spoken.

⁹   "Give wings to Moab,
for she would fly away;
her cities shall become a desolation,
with no inhabitant in them.

¹⁰ "Cursed is he who does the work of
the Lord with slackness, and cursed is he
who keeps back his sword from bloodshed.

¹¹   "Moab has been at ease from his yout
and has settled on his dregs;
he has not been emptied from vesse
to vessel,
nor has he gone into exile;
so his taste remains in him,
and his scent is not changed.

¹² "Therefore, behold, the days are com
ing, declares the Lord, when I shall sen
to him pourers who will pour him, an
empty his vessels and break his[3] jars i
pieces. ¹³ Then Moab shall be ashame
of Chemosh, as the house of Israel wa
ashamed of Bethel, their confidence.

¹⁴   "How do you say, 'We are heroes
and mighty men of war'?
¹⁵   The destroyer of Moab and his cities
has come up,
and the choicest of his young men
have gone down to slaughter,
declares the King, whose name is
the Lord of hosts.
¹⁶   The calamity of Moab is near at hand
and his affliction hastens swiftly.
¹⁷   Grieve for him, all you who are
around him,
and all who know his name;
say, 'How the mighty scepter is broken,
the glorious staff.'

¹⁸   "Come down from your glory,
and sit on the parched ground,
O inhabitant of Dibon!
For the destroyer of Moab has come
up against you;
he has destroyed your strongholds
¹⁹   Stand by the way and watch,
O inhabitant of Aroer!
Ask him who flees and her who
escapes;
say, 'What has happened?'
²⁰   Moab is put to shame, for it is broken
wail and cry!
Tell it beside the Arnon,
that Moab is laid waste.

²¹ "Judgment has come upon the table
land, upon Holon, and Jahzah, and Meph
aath, ²² and Dibon, and Nebo, and
Beth-diblathaim, ²³ and Kiriathaim, and
Beth-gamul, and Beth-meon, ²⁴ and Kerioth
and Bozrah, and all the cities of the land o
Moab, far and near. ²⁵ The horn of Moab i

---

[1] Hebrew *weeping goes up with weeping*   [2] Septuagint (compare Isaiah 15:5) *heard the cry*   [3] Septuagint, Aquila; Hebrew *their*

cut off, and his arm is broken, declares the LORD. ²⁶ "Make him drunk, because he magnified himself against the LORD, so that Moab shall wallow in his vomit, and he too shall be held in derision. ²⁷ Was not Israel a derision to you? Was he found among thieves, that whenever you spoke of him you wagged your head?

²⁸ "Leave the cities, and dwell in the rock,
     O inhabitants of Moab!
Be like the dove that nests
     in the sides of the mouth of a gorge.
²⁹ We have heard of the pride of Moab—
     he is very proud—
of his loftiness, his pride, and his
     arrogance,
     and the haughtiness of his heart.
³⁰ I know his insolence, declares the
     LORD;
     his boasts are false,
     his deeds are false.
³¹ Therefore I wail for Moab;
     I cry out for all Moab;
     for the men of Kir-hareseth I mourn.
³² More than for Jazer I weep for you,
     O vine of Sibmah!
Your branches passed over the sea,
     reached to the Sea of Jazer;
on your summer fruits and your
     grapes
     the destroyer has fallen.
³³ Gladness and joy have been taken
     away
     from the fruitful land of Moab;
I have made the wine cease from the
     winepresses;
     no one treads them with shouts of
     joy;
     the shouting is not the shout of joy.

³⁴ "From the outcry at Heshbon even to Elealeh, as far as Jahaz they utter their voice, from Zoar to Horonaim and Eglath-shelishiyah. For the waters of Nimrim also have become desolate. ³⁵ And I will bring to an end in Moab, declares the LORD, him who offers sacrifice in the high place and makes offerings to his god. ³⁶ Therefore my heart moans for Moab like a flute, and my heart moans like a flute for the men of Kir-hareseth. Therefore the riches they gained have perished.

³⁷ "For every head is shaved and every beard cut off. On all the hands are gashes, and around the waist is sackcloth. ³⁸ On all the housetops of Moab and in the squares there is nothing but lamentation, for I have broken Moab like a vessel for which no one cares, declares the LORD. ³⁹ How it is broken! How they wail! How Moab has turned his back in shame! So Moab has become a derision and a horror to all that are around him."

⁴⁰ For thus says the LORD:
"Behold, one shall fly swiftly like an
     eagle
     and spread his wings against Moab;
⁴¹ the cities shall be taken
     and the strongholds seized.
The heart of the warriors of Moab
     shall be in that day
     like the heart of a woman in her
     birth pains;
⁴² Moab shall be destroyed and be no
     longer a people,
     because he magnified himself
     against the LORD.
⁴³ Terror, pit, and snare
     are before you, O inhabitant of
     Moab!
           declares the LORD.
⁴⁴ He who flees from the terror
     shall fall into the pit,
and he who climbs out of the pit
     shall be caught in the snare.
For I will bring these things upon
     Moab,
     the year of their punishment,
           declares the LORD.
⁴⁵ "In the shadow of Heshbon
     fugitives stop without strength,
for fire came out from Heshbon,
     flame from the house of Sihon;
it has destroyed the forehead of Moab,
     the crown of the sons of tumult.
⁴⁶ Woe to you, O Moab!
     The people of Chemosh are undone,
for your sons have been taken captive,
     and your daughters into captivity.
⁴⁷ Yet I will restore the fortunes of Moab
     in the latter days, declares the
     LORD."
Thus far is the judgment on Moab.

Judgment on Ammon

49 Concerning the Ammonites.
Thus says the LORD:

"Has Israel no sons?
     Has he no heir?

Why then has Milcom dispossessed
    Gad,
    and his people settled in its cities?
2   Therefore, behold, the days are com-
        ing,
    declares the LORD,
    when I will cause the battle cry to be
        heard
    against Rabbah of the Ammonites;
it shall become a desolate mound,
    and its villages shall be burned
        with fire;
then Israel shall dispossess those
    who dispossessed him,
    says the LORD.

3   "Wail, O Heshbon, for Ai is laid waste!
    Cry out, O daughters of Rabbah!
Put on sackcloth,
    lament, and run to and fro among
        the hedges!
For Milcom shall go into exile,
    with his priests and his officials.
4   Why do you boast of your valleys,[1]
    O faithless daughter,
who trusted in her treasures, saying,
    'Who will come against me?'
5   Behold, I will bring terror upon you,
    declares the Lord GOD of hosts,
    from all who are around you,
and you shall be driven out, every
        man straight before him,
    with none to gather the fugitives.

6 "But afterward I will restore the fortunes of the Ammonites, declares the LORD."

Judgment on Edom

7 Concerning Edom.
Thus says the LORD of hosts:

    "Is wisdom no more in Teman?
        Has counsel perished from the
            prudent?
        Has their wisdom vanished?
8   Flee, turn back, dwell in the depths,
        O inhabitants of Dedan!
    For I will bring the calamity of Esau
        upon him,
        the time when I punish him.
9   If grape gatherers came to you,
        would they not leave gleanings?
    If thieves came by night,
        would they not destroy only
            enough for themselves?

10 But I have stripped Esau bare;
        I have uncovered his hiding places,
        and he is not able to conceal him-
            self.
    His children are destroyed, and his
        brothers,
        and his neighbors; and he is no
            more.
11 Leave your fatherless children; I will
        keep them alive;
        and let your widows trust in me."

12 For thus says the LORD: "If those who
did not deserve to drink the cup must
drink it, will you go unpunished? You shall
not go unpunished, but you must drink.
13 For I have sworn by myself, declares the
LORD, that Bozrah shall become a horror,
a taunt, a waste, and a curse, and all her
cities shall be perpetual wastes."

14 I have heard a message from the LORD,
        and an envoy has been sent among
            the nations:
    "Gather yourselves together and come
            against her,
        and rise up for battle!
15 For behold, I will make you small
            among the nations,
        despised among mankind.
16 The horror you inspire has deceived
            you,
        and the pride of your heart,
    you who live in the clefts of the rock,[2]
        who hold the height of the hill.
    Though you make your nest as high
            as the eagle's,
        I will bring you down from there,
                    declares the LORD.

17 "Edom shall become a horror. Everyone
who passes by it will be horrified and will
hiss because of all its disasters. 18 As when
Sodom and Gomorrah and their neighboring cities were overthrown, says the LORD,
no man shall dwell there, no man shall
sojourn in her. 19 Behold, like a lion coming
up from the jungle of the Jordan against a
perennial pasture, I will suddenly make
him[3] run away from her. And I will appoint
over her whomever I choose. For who is
like me? Who will summon me? What shepherd can stand before me? 20 Therefore hear
the plan that the LORD has made against
Edom and the purposes that he has formed
against the inhabitants of Teman: Even the

---

[1] Hebrew boast of your valleys, your valley flows [2] Or of Sela [3] Septuagint, Syriac them

little ones of the flock shall be dragged away. Surely their fold shall be appalled at their fate. ²¹At the sound of their fall the earth shall tremble; the sound of their cry shall be heard at the Red Sea. ²²Behold, one shall mount up and fly swiftly like an eagle and spread his wings against Bozrah, and the heart of the warriors of Edom shall be in that day like the heart of a woman in her birth pains."

Judgment on Damascus

²³Concerning Damascus:

"Hamath and Arpad are confounded,
    for they have heard bad news;
they melt in fear,
    they are troubled like the sea that
        cannot be quiet.
²⁴ Damascus has become feeble, she
        turned to flee,
    and panic seized her;
anguish and sorrows have taken hold
        of her,
    as of a woman in labor.
²⁵ How is the famous city not forsaken,
    the city of my joy?
²⁶ Therefore her young men shall fall in
        her squares,
    and all her soldiers shall be
        destroyed in that day,
            declares the Lord of hosts.
²⁷ And I will kindle a fire in the wall of
        Damascus,
    and it shall devour the strongholds
        of Ben-hadad."

Judgment on Kedar and Hazor

²⁸Concerning Kedar and the kingdoms of Hazor that Nebuchadnezzar king of Babylon struck down.

Thus says the Lord:
"Rise up, advance against Kedar!
    Destroy the people of the east!
²⁹ Their tents and their flocks shall be
        taken,
    their curtains and all their goods;
their camels shall be led away from
        them,
    and men shall cry to them: 'Terror
        on every side!'
³⁰ Flee, wander far away, dwell in the
        depths,
    O inhabitants of Hazor!
            declares the Lord.

For Nebuchadnezzar king of Babylon
    has made a plan against you
    and formed a purpose against you.

³¹ "Rise up, advance against a nation at
        ease,
    that dwells securely,
            declares the Lord,
    that has no gates or bars,
        that dwells alone.
³² Their camels shall become plunder,
    their herds of livestock a spoil.
I will scatter to every wind
    those who cut the corners of their
        hair,
and I will bring their calamity
    from every side of them,
            declares the Lord.
³³ Hazor shall become a haunt of jackals,
    an everlasting waste;
no man shall dwell there;
    no man shall sojourn in her."

Judgment on Elam

³⁴The word of the Lord that came to Jeremiah the prophet concerning Elam, in the beginning of the reign of Zedekiah king of Judah.

³⁵Thus says the Lord of hosts: "Behold, I will break the bow of Elam, the mainstay of their might. ³⁶And I will bring upon Elam the four winds from the four quarters of heaven. And I will scatter them to all those winds, and there shall be no nation to which those driven out of Elam shall not come. ³⁷I will terrify Elam before their enemies and before those who seek their life. I will bring disaster upon them, my fierce anger, declares the Lord. I will send the sword after them, until I have consumed them, ³⁸and I will set my throne in Elam and destroy their king and officials, declares the Lord.

³⁹"But in the latter days I will restore the fortunes of Elam, declares the Lord."

Judgment on Babylon

50 The word that the Lord spoke concerning Babylon, concerning the land of the Chaldeans, by Jeremiah the prophet:

² "Declare among the nations and proclaim,
    set up a banner and proclaim,
    conceal it not, and say:

'Babylon is taken,
    Bel is put to shame,
    Merodach is dismayed.
Her images are put to shame,
    her idols are dismayed.'

³ "For out of the north a nation has come up against her, which shall make her land a desolation, and none shall dwell in it; both man and beast shall flee away.

⁴ "In those days and in that time, declares the LORD, the people of Israel and the people of Judah shall come together, weeping as they come, and they shall seek the LORD their God. ⁵ They shall ask the way to Zion, with faces turned toward it, saying, 'Come, let us join ourselves to the LORD in an everlasting covenant that will never be forgotten.'

⁶ "My people have been lost sheep. Their shepherds have led them astray, turning them away on the mountains. From mountain to hill they have gone. They have forgotten their fold. ⁷ All who found them have devoured them, and their enemies have said, 'We are not guilty, for they have sinned against the LORD, their habitation of righteousness, the LORD, the hope of their fathers.'

⁸ "Flee from the midst of Babylon, and go out of the land of the Chaldeans, and be as male goats before the flock. ⁹ For behold, I am stirring up and bringing against Babylon a gathering of great nations, from the north country. And they shall array themselves against her. From there she shall be taken. Their arrows are like a skilled warrior who does not return empty-handed. ¹⁰ Chaldea shall be plundered; all who plunder her shall be sated, declares the LORD.

¹¹   "Though you rejoice, though you exult,
    O plunderers of my heritage,
   though you frolic like a heifer in the
      pasture,
   and neigh like stallions,
¹²   your mother shall be utterly shamed,
   and she who bore you shall be
      disgraced.
  Behold, she shall be the last of the
    nations,
   a wilderness, a dry land, and a
    desert.

Ask Yourself . . .

ABOUT GOD'S PROVISION

- What does the Bible mean when it refers to people as sheep (see Jer. 50:6–7)?
- How is God meant to be our pasture?
- What do sheep get from their pasture? (See Psalm 23.)
- In what ways do I sin when I get my strength and nourishment from any place other than God?
- Is God my pasture? If not, how can I get back to him?

¹³   Because of the wrath of the LORD she
      shall not be inhabited
   but shall be an utter desolation;
  everyone who passes by Babylon
      shall be appalled,
   and hiss because of all her wounds.
¹⁴   Set yourselves in array against
      Babylon all around,
   all you who bend the bow;
  shoot at her, spare no arrows,
   for she has sinned against the LORD.
¹⁵   Raise a shout against her all around;
   she has surrendered;
  her bulwarks have fallen;
   her walls are thrown down.
  For this is the vengeance of the LORD:
   take vengeance on her;
   do to her as she has done.
¹⁶   Cut off from Babylon the sower,
   and the one who handles the sickle
      in time of harvest;
  because of the sword of the oppressor,
   every one shall turn to his own
      people,
   and every one shall flee to his own
      land.

¹⁷ "Israel is a hunted sheep driven away by lions. First the king of Assyria devoured him, and now at last Nebuchadnezzar king of Babylon has gnawed his bones. ¹⁸ Therefore, thus says the LORD of hosts,

the God of Israel: Behold, I am bringing punishment on the king of Babylon and his land, as I punished the king of Assyria. [19] I will restore Israel to his pasture, and he shall feed on Carmel and in Bashan, and his desire shall be satisfied on the hills of Ephraim and in Gilead. [20] In those days and in that time, declares the LORD, iniquity shall be sought in Israel, and there shall be none, and sin in Judah, and none shall be found, for I will pardon those whom I leave as a remnant.

[21] "Go up against the land of Merathaim,[1]
    and against the inhabitants of
        Pekod.[2]
Kill, and devote them to destruction,[3]
            declares the LORD,
    and do all that I have commanded
        you.
[22] The noise of battle is in the land,
    and great destruction!
[23] How the hammer of the whole earth
    is cut down and broken!
How Babylon has become
    a horror among the nations!
[24] I set a snare for you and you were
        taken, O Babylon,
    and you did not know it;
you were found and caught,
    because you opposed the LORD.
[25] The LORD has opened his armory
    and brought out the weapons of
        his wrath,
for the Lord GOD of hosts has a work
        to do
    in the land of the Chaldeans.
[26] Come against her from every quarter;
    open her granaries;
pile her up like heaps of grain, and
        devote her to destruction;
    let nothing be left of her.
[27] Kill all her bulls;
    let them go down to the slaughter.
Woe to them, for their day has come,
    the time of their punishment.

[28] "A voice! They flee and escape from the land of Babylon, to declare in Zion the vengeance of the LORD our God, vengeance for his temple.

[29] "Summon archers against Babylon, all those who bend the bow. Encamp around her; let no one escape. Repay her according to her deeds; do to her according to all that she has done. For she has proudly defied the LORD, the Holy One of Israel. [30] Therefore her young men shall fall in her squares, and all her soldiers shall be destroyed on that day, declares the LORD.

[31] "Behold, I am against you, O proud one,
        declares the Lord GOD of hosts,
    for your day has come,
        the time when I will punish you.
[32] The proud one shall stumble and fall,
    with none to raise him up,
and I will kindle a fire in his cities,
    and it will devour all that is around
        him.

[33] "Thus says the LORD of hosts: The people of Israel are oppressed, and the people of Judah with them. All who took them captive have held them fast; they refuse to let them go. [34] Their Redeemer is strong; the LORD of hosts is his name. He will surely plead their cause, that he may give rest to the earth, but unrest to the inhabitants of Babylon.

[35] "A sword against the Chaldeans,
        declares the LORD,
    and against the inhabitants of
        Babylon,
    and against her officials and her
        wise men!
[36] A sword against the diviners,
    that they may become fools!
A sword against her warriors,
    that they may be destroyed!
[37] A sword against her horses and
        against her chariots,
    and against all the foreign troops
        in her midst,
    that they may become women!
A sword against all her treasures,
    that they may be plundered!
[38] A drought against her waters,
    that they may be dried up!
For it is a land of images,
    and they are mad over idols.

[39] "Therefore wild beasts shall dwell with hyenas in Babylon, and ostriches shall dwell in her. She shall never again have people, nor be inhabited for all generations. [40] As when God overthrew Sodom and Gomorrah and their neighboring cities, declares the LORD, so no man shall dwell there, and no son of man shall sojourn in her.

[1] Merathaim means double rebellion [2] Pekod means punishment [3] That is, set apart (devote) as an offering to the Lord (for destruction)

41 "Behold, a people comes from the
      north;
   a mighty nation and many kings
   are stirring from the farthest parts
      of the earth.
42 They lay hold of bow and spear;
   they are cruel and have no mercy.
   The sound of them is like the roaring
      of the sea;
   they ride on horses,
   arrayed as a man for battle
   against you, O daughter of Babylon!

43 "The king of Babylon heard the report
      of them,
   and his hands fell helpless;
   anguish seized him,
   pain as of a woman in labor.

44 "Behold, like a lion coming up from the
thicket of the Jordan against a perennial
pasture, I will suddenly make them run
away from her, and I will appoint over her
whomever I choose. For who is like me?
Who will summon me? What shepherd can
stand before me? 45 Therefore hear the plan
that the LORD has made against Babylon,
and the purposes that he has formed
against the land of the Chaldeans: Surely
the little ones of their flock shall be dragged
away; surely their fold shall be appalled at
their fate. 46 At the sound of the capture of
Babylon the earth shall tremble, and her cry
shall be heard among the nations."

The Utter Destruction of Babylon

51 Thus says the LORD:
   "Behold, I will stir up the spirit of
      a destroyer
   against Babylon,
   against the inhabitants of Leb-
      kamai,[1]
2 and I will send to Babylon winnowers,
   and they shall winnow her,
   and they shall empty her land,
   when they come against her from
      every side
   on the day of trouble.
3 Let not the archer bend his bow,
   and let him not stand up in his
      armor.
   Spare not her young men;
   devote to destruction[2] all her army.
4 They shall fall down slain in the land
      of the Chaldeans,
   and wounded in her streets.

5 For Israel and Judah have not been
      forsaken
   by their God, the LORD of hosts,
   but the land of the Chaldeans[3] is full
      of guilt
   against the Holy One of Israel.

6 "Flee from the midst of Babylon;
   let every one save his life!
   Be not cut off in her punishment,
   for this is the time of the LORD's
      vengeance,
   the repayment he is rendering her.
7 Babylon was a golden cup in the
      LORD's hand,
   making all the earth drunken;
   the nations drank of her wine;
   therefore the nations went mad.
8 Suddenly Babylon has fallen and
      been broken;
   wail for her!
   Take balm for her pain;
   perhaps she may be healed.
9 We would have healed Babylon,
   but she was not healed.
   Forsake her, and let us go
   each to his own country,
   for her judgment has reached up to
      heaven
   and has been lifted up even to the
      skies.
10 The LORD has brought about our
      vindication;
   come, let us declare in Zion
   the work of the LORD our God.

11 "Sharpen the arrows!
   Take up the shields!

The LORD has stirred up the spirit of the
kings of the Medes, because his purpose
concerning Babylon is to destroy it, for
that is the vengeance of the LORD, the vengeance for his temple.

12 "Set up a standard against the walls of
      Babylon;
   make the watch strong;
   set up watchmen;
   prepare the ambushes;
   for the LORD has both planned and
      done
   what he spoke concerning the
      inhabitants of Babylon.
13 O you who dwell by many waters,
   rich in treasures,

---

[1] A code name for Chaldea [2] That is, set apart (devote) as an offering to the Lord (for destruction) [3] Hebrew their land

your end has come;
  the thread of your life is cut.
14 The LORD of hosts has sworn by
     himself:
  Surely I will fill you with men, as
     many as locusts,
    and they shall raise the shout of
     victory over you.

15 "It is he who made the earth by his
     power,
    who established the world by his
     wisdom,
  and by his understanding stretched
     out the heavens.
16 When he utters his voice there is a
     tumult of waters in the heavens,
    and he makes the mist rise from
     the ends of the earth.
  He makes lightning for the rain,
    and he brings forth the wind from
     his storehouses.
17 Every man is stupid and without
     knowledge;
    every goldsmith is put to shame by
     his idols,
  for his images are false,
    and there is no breath in them.
18 They are worthless, a work of delu-
     sion;
    at the time of their punishment
     they shall perish.
19 Not like these is he who is the por-
     tion of Jacob,
    for he is the one who formed all
     things,
  and Israel is the tribe of his inheri-
     tance;
    the LORD of hosts is his name.

20 "You are my hammer and weapon of
     war:
  with you I break nations in pieces;
    with you I destroy kingdoms;
21 with you I break in pieces the horse
     and his rider;
    with you I break in pieces the
     chariot and the charioteer;
22 with you I break in pieces man and
     woman;
    with you I break in pieces the old
     man and the youth;
    with you I break in pieces the young
     man and the young woman;
23   with you I break in pieces the
     shepherd and his flock;

  with you I break in pieces the farmer
     and his team;
    with you I break in pieces gover-
     nors and commanders.

24 "I will repay Babylon and all the inhabitants of Chaldea before your very eyes
for all the evil that they have done in Zion,
declares the LORD.

25 "Behold, I am against you, O destroying
     mountain,
             declares the LORD,
  which destroys the whole earth;
  I will stretch out my hand against you,
    and roll you down from the crags,
    and make you a burnt mountain.
26 No stone shall be taken from you for
     a corner
    and no stone for a foundation,
  but you shall be a perpetual waste,
    declares the LORD.

27 "Set up a standard on the earth;
    blow the trumpet among the
     nations;
  prepare the nations for war against
     her;
    summon against her the kingdoms,
    Ararat, Minni, and Ashkenaz;
  appoint a marshal against her;
    bring up horses like bristling
     locusts.
28 Prepare the nations for war against
     her,
    the kings of the Medes, with their
     governors and deputies,
    and every land under their domin-
     ion.
29 The land trembles and writhes in
     pain,
    for the LORD's purposes against
     Babylon stand,
  to make the land of Babylon a deso-
     lation,
    without inhabitant.
30 The warriors of Babylon have ceased
     fighting;
    they remain in their strongholds;
  their strength has failed;
    they have become women;
  her dwellings are on fire;
    her bars are broken.
31 One runner runs to meet another,
    and one messenger to meet another,
  to tell the king of Babylon
    that his city is taken on every side;

³² the fords have been seized,
  the marshes are burned with fire,
  and the soldiers are in panic.
³³ For thus says the LORD of hosts, the
    God of Israel:
  The daughter of Babylon is like a
    threshing floor
    at the time when it is trodden;
  yet a little while
    and the time of her harvest will
      come."

³⁴ "Nebuchadnezzar the king of Babylon
    has devoured me;
  he has crushed me;
  he has made me an empty vessel;
  he has swallowed me like a mon-
    ster;
  he has filled his stomach with my
    delicacies;
  he has rinsed me out.¹
³⁵ The violence done to me and to my
    kinsmen be upon Babylon,"
  let the inhabitant of Zion say.
  "My blood be upon the inhabitants of
    Chaldea,"
  let Jerusalem say.
³⁶ Therefore thus says the LORD:
  "Behold, I will plead your cause
    and take vengeance for you.
  I will dry up her sea
    and make her fountain dry,
³⁷ and Babylon shall become a heap of
    ruins,
    the haunt of jackals,
  a horror and a hissing,
    without inhabitant.

³⁸ "They shall roar together like lions;
    they shall growl like lions' cubs.
³⁹ While they are inflamed I will pre-
    pare them a feast
    and make them drunk, that they
      may become merry,
  then sleep a perpetual sleep
    and not wake, declares the LORD.
⁴⁰ I will bring them down like lambs to
    the slaughter,
    like rams and male goats.

⁴¹ "How Babylon² is taken,
    the praise of the whole earth seized!
  How Babylon has become
    a horror among the nations!

⁴² The sea has come up on Babylon;
    she is covered with its tumultuous
      waves.
⁴³ Her cities have become a horror,
    a land of drought and a desert,
  a land in which no one dwells,
    and through which no son of man
      passes.
⁴⁴ And I will punish Bel in Babylon,
    and take out of his mouth what he
      has swallowed.
  The nations shall no longer flow to
    him;
    the wall of Babylon has fallen.

⁴⁵ "Go out of the midst of her, my people!
    Let every one save his life
    from the fierce anger of the LORD!
⁴⁶ Let not your heart faint, and be not
    fearful
    at the report heard in the land,
  when a report comes in one year
    and afterward a report in another
      year,
  and violence is in the land,
    and ruler is against ruler.

⁴⁷ "Therefore, behold, the days are com-
    ing
    when I will punish the images of
      Babylon;
  her whole land shall be put to shame,
    and all her slain shall fall in the
      midst of her.
⁴⁸ Then the heavens and the earth,
    and all that is in them,
  shall sing for joy over Babylon,
    for the destroyers shall come
      against them out of the north,
        declares the LORD.
⁴⁹ Babylon must fall for the slain of
    Israel,
    just as for Babylon have fallen the
      slain of all the earth.

⁵⁰ "You who have escaped from the
    sword,
    go, do not stand still!
  Remember the LORD from far away,
    and let Jerusalem come into your
      mind:
⁵¹ 'We are put to shame, for we have
    heard reproach;
    dishonor has covered our face,

---

¹ Or *he has expelled me* ² Hebrew *Sheshach*, a code name for Babylon

for foreigners have come
   into the holy places of the Lord's
     house.'

52 "Therefore, behold, the days are com-
    ing, declares the Lord,
   when I will execute judgment upon
    her images,
and through all her land
   the wounded shall groan.

53 Though Babylon should mount up to
    heaven,
   and though she should fortify her
    strong height,
yet destroyers would come from me
   against her,
   declares the Lord.

54 "A voice! A cry from Babylon!
   The noise of great destruction
    from the land of the Chaldeans!

55 For the Lord is laying Babylon waste
   and stilling her mighty voice.
Their waves roar like many waters;
   the noise of their voice is raised,

56 for a destroyer has come upon her,
    upon Babylon;
her warriors are taken;
   their bows are broken in pieces,
for the Lord is a God of recompense;
   he will surely repay.

57 I will make drunk her officials and
    her wise men,
   her governors, her commanders,
    and her warriors;
they shall sleep a perpetual sleep
    and not wake,
   declares the King, whose name is
    the Lord of hosts.

58 "Thus says the Lord of hosts:
   The broad wall of Babylon
    shall be leveled to the ground,
and her high gates
    shall be burned with fire.
The peoples labor for nothing,
   and the nations weary themselves
    only for fire."

59 The word that Jeremiah the prophet commanded Seraiah the son of Neriah, son of Mahseiah, when he went with Zedekiah king of Judah to Babylon, in the fourth year of his reign. Seraiah was the quartermaster. **60** Jeremiah wrote in a book all the disaster that should come upon Babylon, all these words that are written concerning Babylon.

61 And Jeremiah said to Seraiah: "When you come to Babylon, see that you read all these words, **62** and say, 'O Lord, you have said concerning this place that you will cut it off, so that nothing shall dwell in it, neither man nor beast, and it shall be desolate forever.' **63** When you finish reading this book, tie a stone to it and cast it into the midst of the Euphrates, **64** and say, 'Thus shall Babylon sink, to rise no more, because of the disaster that I am bringing upon her, and they shall become exhausted.'"

Thus far are the words of Jeremiah.

The Fall of Jerusalem Recounted

52 Zedekiah was twenty-one years old when he became king, and he reigned eleven years in Jerusalem. His mother's name was Hamutal the daughter of Jeremiah of Libnah. **2** And he did what was evil in the sight of the Lord, according to all that Jehoiakim had done. **3** For because of the anger of the Lord it came to the point in Jerusalem and Judah that he cast them out from his presence.

And Zedekiah rebelled against the king of Babylon. **4** And in the ninth year of his reign, in the tenth month, on the tenth day of the month, Nebuchadnezzar king of Babylon came with all his army against Jerusalem, and laid siege to it. And they built siegeworks all around it. **5** So the city was besieged till the eleventh year of King Zedekiah. **6** On the ninth day of the fourth month the famine was so severe in the city that there was no food for the people of the land. **7** Then a breach was made in the city, and all the men of war fled and went out from the city by night by the way of a gate between the two walls, by the king's garden, and the Chaldeans were around the city. And they went in the direction of the Arabah. **8** But the army of the Chaldeans pursued the king and overtook Zedekiah in the plains of Jericho, and all his army was scattered from him. **9** Then they captured the king and brought him up to the king of Babylon at Riblah in the land of Hamath, and he passed sentence on him. **10** The king of Babylon slaughtered the sons of Zedekiah before his eyes, and also slaughtered all the officials of Judah at Riblah. **11** He put out the eyes of Zedekiah, and bound him in chains, and the king of Babylon took him to Babylon, and put him in prison till the day of his death.

The Temple Burned

[12] In the fifth month, on the tenth day of the month—that was the nineteenth year of King Nebuchadnezzar, king of Babylon—Nebuzaradan the captain of the bodyguard, who served the king of Babylon, entered Jerusalem. [13] And he burned the house of the LORD, and the king's house and all the houses of Jerusalem; every great house he burned down. [14] And all the army of the Chaldeans, who were with the captain of the guard, broke down all the walls around Jerusalem. [15] And Nebuzaradan the captain of the guard carried away captive some of the poorest of the people and the rest of the people who were left in the city and the deserters who had deserted to the king of Babylon, together with the rest of the artisans. [16] But Nebuzaradan the captain of the guard left some of the poorest of the land to be vinedressers and plowmen.

[17] And the pillars of bronze that were in the house of the LORD, and the stands and the bronze sea that were in the house of the LORD, the Chaldeans broke in pieces, and carried all the bronze to Babylon. [18] And they took away the pots and the shovels and the snuffers and the basins and the dishes for incense and all the vessels of bronze used in the temple service; [19] also the small bowls and the fire pans and the basins and the pots and the lampstands and the dishes for incense and the bowls for drink offerings. What was of gold the captain of the guard took away as gold, and what was of silver, as silver. [20] As for the two pillars, the one sea, the twelve bronze bulls that were under the sea,[1] and the stands, which Solomon the king had made for the house of the LORD, the bronze of all these things was beyond weight. [21] As for the pillars, the height of the one pillar was eighteen cubits,[2] its circumference was twelve cubits, and its thickness was four fingers, and it was hollow. [22] On it was a capital of bronze. The height of the one capital was five cubits. A network and pomegranates, all of bronze, were around the capital. And the second pillar had the same, with pomegranates. [23] There were ninety-six pomegranates on the sides; all the pomegranates were a hundred upon the network all around.

The People Exiled to Babylon

[24] And the captain of the guard took Seraiah the chief priest, and Zephaniah the second priest and the three keepers of the threshold; [25] and from the city he took an officer who had been in command of the men of war, and seven men of the king's council, who were found in the city, and the secretary of the commander of the army, who mustered the people of the land and sixty men of the people of the land who were found in the midst of the city. [26] And Nebuzaradan the captain of the guard took them and brought them to the king of Babylon at Riblah. [27] And the king of Babylon struck them down and put them to death at Riblah in the land of Hamath. So Judah was taken into exile out of its land.

[28] This is the number of the people whom Nebuchadnezzar carried away captive: in the seventh year, 3,023 Judeans; [29] in the eighteenth year of Nebuchadnezzar he carried away captive from Jerusalem 832 persons; [30] in the twenty-third year of Nebuchadnezzar, Nebuzaradan the captain of the guard carried away captive of the Judeans 745 persons; all the persons were 4,600.

Jehoiachin Released from Prison

[31] And in the thirty-seventh year of the exile of Jehoiachin king of Judah, in the twelfth month, on the twenty-fifth day of the month, Evil-merodach king of Babylon, in the year that he began to reign, graciously freed[3] Jehoiachin king of Judah and brought him out of prison. [32] And he spoke kindly to him and gave him a seat above the seats of the kings who were with him in Babylon. [33] So Jehoiachin put off his prison garments. And every day of his life he dined regularly at the king's table, [34] and for his allowance, a regular allowance was given him by the king, according to his daily needs, until the day of his death, as long as he lived.

[1] Hebrew lacks the sea [2] A cubit was about 18 inches or 45 centimeters [3] Hebrew king, lifted up the head of

INTRODUCTION TO

Lamentations

Author: Possibly Jeremiah

Time: Sometime after 586 B.C.

Place: Probably Judah

Written to: Israelites in exile, and to God as prayers

The gist

Lamentations was written to express grief for the people of Judah and their sinful choices which led to their destruction. Jerusalem had fallen to the Babylonians because of the sins of its people. But, though he grieved, the author clung to God's covenant promises to his people. The book's purpose is to help people face pain and not to fear it or to run away from it.

Things to look for

- The use of forceful poetic language
- The destruction of Jerusalem
- Hope in the middle of suffering (see Lam. 3:21–41)

Pray for Mercy

> Why should a living man complain,
> a man, about the punishment of his sins?
>
> Lamentations 3:39

When really, really bad things happen, even God's people complain about it. They moan about their lot in life and wonder where God is in it all. And the book of Lamentations is just that, a lament—a mourning over the horrible things that have happened in the lives of God's people—along with a confession of the sin that led them to their situation in the first place. Jerusalem had been destroyed; a lot of people had been killed, and many were dragged off like slaves into exile. The people were in misery and were wondering where God's hand was in it all. The author of this great book, who some think was Jeremiah, knew that this disaster came directly from God himself because of how bad the people had been living, and so he begged God for mercy.

When bad things happen because of the stupid things you've done, you can take the lead of the book of Lamentations and agree with God that he got it right and you got it wrong. And just like we see in Lamentations 3, you can also follow that up with a prayer—that God won't stay angry forever and that he will have mercy and compassion on you in the midst of the discipline you deserve.

As a modern-day God Girl, you may find it hard to understand why God lets such painful things happen to his people, but no matter what the answer, you have to be willing to concede that God loves you more than you could ever imagine, and if he saw fit to let something like this happen to you, well, then it must be for a very good reason. Lamentations might seem like an archaic book that means nothing to you today, but in it you just might find a lot that you can relate to. Lamentations is proof that you're not the first to ever feel like God has turned his back on you or to feel tormented by life and abandoned by everyone you love. Reading about the pain of others and understanding that you are not alone should give you hope. And remember, as the author points out: God's compassion is unlimited, and he is good to people who wait for him and trust that his will is the best will there is.

Must-Know Terms and Verses

❧ *Lamentation* ❧
A verbal expression of sorrow, grief, or pain.

———————

"The LORD is in the right,
 for I have rebelled against his word." *Lamentations 1:18*

But this I call to mind,
 and therefore I have hope:
The steadfast love of the LORD never ceases;
 his mercies never come to an end;
they are new every morning;
 great is your faithfulness. *Lamentations 3:21–23*

Is it not from the mouth of the Most High
 that good and bad come? *Lamentations 3:38*

Lamentations

How Lonely Sits the City

1 How lonely sits the city
    that was full of people!
How like a widow has she become,
    she who was great among the
        nations!
She who was a princess among the
        provinces
    has become a slave.

² She weeps bitterly in the night,
    with tears on her cheeks;
among all her lovers
    she has none to comfort her;
all her friends have dealt treacher-
        ously with her;
    they have become her enemies.

³ Judah has gone into exile because of
        affliction
    and hard servitude;
she dwells now among the nations,
    but finds no resting place;
her pursuers have all overtaken her
    in the midst of her distress.[1]

⁴ The roads to Zion mourn,
    for none come to the festival;
all her gates are desolate;
    her priests groan;
her virgins have been afflicted,[2]
    and she herself suffers bitterly.

⁵ Her foes have become the head;
    her enemies prosper,
because the Lord has afflicted her
    for the multitude of her transgres-
        sions;
her children have gone away,
    captives before the foe.

⁶ From the daughter of Zion
    all her majesty has departed.
Her princes have become like deer
    that find no pasture;

they fled without strength
    before the pursuer.

⁷ Jerusalem remembers
    in the days of her affliction and
        wandering
all the precious things
    that were hers from days of old.
When her people fell into the hand of
        the foe,
    and there was none to help her,
her foes gloated over her;
    they mocked at her downfall.

⁸ Jerusalem sinned grievously;
    therefore she became filthy;
all who honored her despise her,
    for they have seen her nakedness;
she herself groans
    and turns her face away.

⁹ Her uncleanness was in her skirts;
    she took no thought of her future;[3]
therefore her fall is terrible;
    she has no comforter.
"O Lord, behold my affliction,
    for the enemy has triumphed!"

¹⁰ The enemy has stretched out his
        hands
    over all her precious things;
for she has seen the nations
    enter her sanctuary,
those whom you forbade
    to enter your congregation.

¹¹ All her people groan
    as they search for bread;
they trade their treasures for food
    to revive their strength.
"Look, O Lord, and see,
    for I am despised."

¹² "Is it nothing to you, all you who pass
        by?
    Look and see

---

[1] Or *in the narrow passes* [2] Septuagint, Old Latin *dragged away* [3] Or *end*

if there is any sorrow like my sorrow,
    which was brought upon me,
which the Lord inflicted
    on the day of his fierce anger.

A Prayer about...
SUFFERING

Lord, high and holy, meek and lowly,

You have brought me to the valley of vision, where I live in the valley but see you in the heights. Though I'm closed in by mountains of sin, I can still see your glory. Let me learn the ironic lesson that the way down is the way up, that to be low is to be high, that the broken heart is the healed heart, that the contrite spirit is the rejoicing spirit, that the repenting soul is the victorious soul, that to have nothing is to own everything, that to bear the cross is to wear the crown, that to give is to receive, and that the valley is the place of vision. Lord, stars can be seen from inside even the deepest wells, and the deeper the wells, the brighter your stars shine. Please let me find your light in my darkness, your life in my death, your joy in my sorrow, your grace in my sin, your riches in my poverty, your glory in my valley.

Amen.

¹³ "From on high he sent fire;
    into my bones[1] he made it
        descend;
he spread a net for my feet;
    he turned me back;
he has left me stunned,
    faint all the day long.

¹⁴ "My transgressions were bound[2] into a
        yoke;
    by his hand they were fastened
        together;
they were set upon my neck;
    he caused my strength to fail;
the Lord gave me into the hands
    of those whom I cannot withstand.

¹⁵ "The Lord rejected
    all my mighty men in my midst;
he summoned an assembly
        against me
    to crush my young men;
the Lord has trodden as in a wine-
        press
    the virgin daughter of Judah.

¹⁶ "For these things I weep;
    my eyes flow with tears;
for a comforter is far from me,
    one to revive my spirit;
my children are desolate,
    for the enemy has prevailed."

¹⁷ Zion stretches out her hands,
    but there is none to comfort her;
the Lord has commanded against
        Jacob
    that his neighbors should be his
        foes;
Jerusalem has become
    a filthy thing among them.

¹⁸ "The Lord is in the right,
    for I have rebelled against his
        word;
but hear, all you peoples,
    and see my suffering;
my young women and my young
        men
    have gone into captivity.

¹⁹ "I called to my lovers,
    but they deceived me;
my priests and elders
    perished in the city,
while they sought food
    to revive their strength.

²⁰ "Look, O Lord, for I am in distress;
    my stomach churns;
my heart is wrung within me,
    because I have been very rebel-
        lious.
In the street the sword bereaves;
    in the house it is like death.

²¹ "They heard[3] my groaning,
    yet there is no one to comfort me.
All my enemies have heard of my
        trouble;
    they are glad that you have done it.
You have brought[4] the day you
        announced;
    now let them be as I am.

---

[1] Septuagint; Hebrew *bones and* [2] The meaning of the Hebrew is uncertain [3] Septuagint, Syriac *Hear* [4] Syriac *Bring*

22 "Let all their evildoing come before
       you,
     and deal with them
   as you have dealt with me
       because of all my transgressions;
   for my groans are many,
     and my heart is faint."

The Lord Has Destroyed Without Pity

2 How the Lord in his anger
     has set the daughter of Zion under a
       cloud!
   He has cast down from heaven to
       earth
     the splendor of Israel;
   he has not remembered his foot-
       stool
     in the day of his anger.

2   The Lord has swallowed up without
       mercy
     all the habitations of Jacob;
   in his wrath he has broken down
       the strongholds of the daughter of
         Judah;
   he has brought down to the ground
       in dishonor
     the kingdom and its rulers.

3   He has cut down in fierce anger
     all the might of Israel;
   he has withdrawn from them his
       right hand
     in the face of the enemy;
   he has burned like a flaming fire in
       Jacob,
     consuming all around.

4   He has bent his bow like an enemy,
     with his right hand set like a foe;
   and he has killed all who were
       delightful in our eyes
     in the tent of the daughter of Zion;
   he has poured out his fury like fire.

5   The Lord has become like an enemy;
     he has swallowed up Israel;
   he has swallowed up all its palaces;
     he has laid in ruins its strong-
       holds,
   and he has multiplied in the daugh-
       ter of Judah
     mourning and lamentation.

6   He has laid waste his booth like a
       garden,
     laid in ruins his meeting place;

   the LORD has made Zion forget
       festival and Sabbath,
   and in his fierce indignation has
       spurned king and priest.

7   The Lord has scorned his altar,
       disowned his sanctuary;
   he has delivered into the hand of the
       enemy
     the walls of her palaces;
   they raised a clamor in the house of
       the LORD
     as on the day of festival.

8   The LORD determined to lay in ruins
       the wall of the daughter of Zion;
   he stretched out the measuring line;
       he did not restrain his hand from
         destroying;
   he caused rampart and wall to
       lament;
     they languished together.

9   Her gates have sunk into the ground;
       he has ruined and broken her bars;
   her king and princes are among the
       nations;
     the law is no more,
   and her prophets find
     no vision from the LORD.

10 The elders of the daughter of Zion
       sit on the ground in silence;
   they have thrown dust on their
       heads
     and put on sackcloth;
   the young women of Jerusalem
     have bowed their heads to the
       ground.

11 My eyes are spent with weeping;
     my stomach churns;
   my bile is poured out to the ground
     because of the destruction of the
       daughter of my people,
   because infants and babies faint
     in the streets of the city.

12 They cry to their mothers,
     "Where is bread and wine?"
   as they faint like a wounded man
     in the streets of the city,
   as their life is poured out
     on their mothers' bosom.

13 What can I say for you, to what com-
       pare you,
     O daughter of Jerusalem?

What can I liken to you, that I may
  comfort you,
    O virgin daughter of Zion?
For your ruin is vast as the sea;
  who can heal you?

14 Your prophets have seen for you
  false and deceptive visions;
they have not exposed your iniquity
  to restore your fortunes,
but have seen for you oracles
  that are false and misleading.

15 All who pass along the way
  clap their hands at you;
they hiss and wag their heads
  at the daughter of Jerusalem:
"Is this the city that was called
  the perfection of beauty,
  the joy of all the earth?"

16 All your enemies
  rail against you;
they hiss, they gnash their teeth,
  they cry: "We have swallowed her!
Ah, this is the day we longed for;
  now we have it; we see it!"

17 The LORD has done what he purposed;
  he has carried out his word,
which he commanded long ago;
  he has thrown down without pity;
he has made the enemy rejoice over
    you
  and exalted the might of your foes.

18 Their heart cried to the Lord.
  O wall of the daughter of Zion,
let tears stream down like a torrent
  day and night!
Give yourself no rest,
  your eyes no respite!

19 "Arise, cry out in the night,
  at the beginning of the night
    watches!
Pour out your heart like water
  before the presence of the Lord!
Lift your hands to him
  for the lives of your children,
who faint for hunger
  at the head of every street."

20 Look, O LORD, and see!
  With whom have you dealt thus?
Should women eat the fruit of their
    womb,
  the children of their tender care?

Should priest and prophet be killed
  in the sanctuary of the Lord?

21 In the dust of the streets
  lie the young and the old;
my young women and my young men
  have fallen by the sword;
you have killed them in the day of
    your anger,
  slaughtering without pity.

22 You summoned as if to a festival day
  my terrors on every side,
and on the day of the anger of the
    LORD
  no one escaped or survived;
those whom I held and raised
  my enemy destroyed.

Great Is Your Faithfulness

3 I am the man who has seen affliction
  under the rod of his wrath;
2 he has driven and brought me
  into darkness without any light;
3 surely against me he turns his hand
  again and again the whole day long.

4 He has made my flesh and my skin
  waste away;
  he has broken my bones;
5 he has besieged and enveloped me
  with bitterness and tribulation;
6 he has made me dwell in darkness
  like the dead of long ago.

7 He has walled me about so that I can-
    not escape;
  he has made my chains heavy;
8 though I call and cry for help,
  he shuts out my prayer;
9 he has blocked my ways with blocks
  of stones;
  he has made my paths crooked.

10 He is a bear lying in wait for me,
  a lion in hiding;
11 he turned aside my steps and tore
  me to pieces;
  he has made me desolate;
12 he bent his bow and set me
  as a target for his arrow.

13 He drove into my kidneys
  the arrows of his quiver;
14 I have become the laughingstock of
  all peoples,
  the object of their taunts all day
    long.

¹⁵ He has filled me with bitterness;
    he has sated me with wormwood.

¹⁶ He has made my teeth grind on
      gravel,
    and made me cower in ashes;
¹⁷ my soul is bereft of peace;
    I have forgotten what happiness[1]
      is;
¹⁸ so I say, "My endurance has perished;
    so has my hope from the LORD."

¹⁹ Remember my affliction and my
      wanderings,
    the wormwood and the gall!
²⁰ My soul continually remembers it
    and is bowed down within me.

²¹ But this I call to mind,
    and therefore I have hope:

²² The steadfast love of the LORD never
      ceases;[2]
    his mercies never come to an end;
²³ they are new every morning;
    great is your faithfulness.
²⁴ "The LORD is my portion," says my soul,
    "therefore I will hope in him."

²⁵ The LORD is good to those who wait
      for him,
    to the soul who seeks him.
²⁶ It is good that one should wait qui-
      etly
    for the salvation of the LORD.

[1] Hebrew *good* [2] Syriac, Targum; Hebrew *Because of the steadfast love of the LORD, we are not cut off*

Know True Happiness

verses to read
Lamentations 3:21–38

Do you live by your emotions? Do you yell when you're angry, lash out when you're sad, and fight back when you're hurt? As a follower of Christ, you were never meant to blindly follow your emotions. That's what you did before you chose this path and were brought into the family. So why do you still get bossed around by your emotions at times, instead of listening to the voice of God?

Do you bow to your emotions just out of habit or weakness? Or do you some-times feel cheated because you didn't get out of a situation what you thought you should have gotten? "That's not fair!" you say. "I deserve more." Someone didn't do what you wanted, so you are angry. Someone didn't give you what you thought you were going to get, so you are sad. Frustrated expectations lead you down bad emotional paths, and more often than not you follow them.

But what if you could be free from your emotions' control and back under the control of Christ—wouldn't your life be better? Wouldn't your self-control improve and your emotions calm? After all, that's what he promises: "Come to me, all who labor and are heavy laden, and I will give you rest" (Matt. 11:28). He'll give you rest from what led you here and there, up and down. Rest from yourself.

A life completely turned over to Christ is a life where emotions complement but do not control. Unchecked, emotions are like a spoiled child, always demanding satisfaction. But a follower of Christ is like him: humble and gentle, not expecting everything to go her way but trusting that everything will work out in the end. You have to choose whom you are going to follow, your emotions or your God. For all human beings there will be heartache, grief, and great loss, but as you hand yourself over to God, your emotions will start to come under your control and will bring depth to your life instead of misery. Like the author of Lamentations, you can express grief and despair, but never to the point that it distracts you from who God is, and from what a life lived for him ultimately means.

27 It is good for a man that he bear
the yoke in his youth.

28 Let him sit alone in silence
when it is laid on him;
29 let him put his mouth in the dust—
there may yet be hope;
30 let him give his cheek to the one who
strikes,
and let him be filled with insults.

31 For the Lord will not
cast off forever,
32 but, though he cause grief, he will
have compassion
according to the abundance of his
steadfast love;
33 for he does not afflict from his heart
or grieve the children of men.

34 To crush underfoot
all the prisoners of the earth,
35 to deny a man justice
in the presence of the Most High,
36 to subvert a man in his lawsuit,
the Lord does not approve.

37 Who has spoken and it came to pass,
unless the Lord has commanded
it?
38 Is it not from the mouth of the Most
High
that good and bad come?
39 Why should a living man complain,
a man, about the punishment of
his sins?

40 Let us test and examine our ways,
and return to the LORD!
41 Let us lift up our hearts and hands
to God in heaven:
42 "We have transgressed and rebelled,
and you have not forgiven.

43 "You have wrapped yourself with
anger and pursued us,
killing without pity;
44 you have wrapped yourself with a
cloud
so that no prayer can pass through.
45 You have made us scum and garbage
among the peoples.

46 "All our enemies
open their mouths against us;

47 panic and pitfall have come upon us,
devastation and destruction;
48 my eyes flow with rivers of tears
because of the destruction of the
daughter of my people.

49 "My eyes will flow without ceasing,
without respite,
50 until the LORD from heaven
looks down and sees;
51 my eyes cause me grief
at the fate of all the daughters of
my city.

52 "I have been hunted like a bird
by those who were my enemies
without cause;
53 they flung me alive into the pit
and cast stones on me;
54 water closed over my head;
I said, 'I am lost.'

55 "I called on your name, O LORD,
from the depths of the pit;
56 you heard my plea, 'Do not close
your ear to my cry for help!'
57 You came near when I called on you;
you said, 'Do not fear!'

58 "You have taken up my cause, O Lord;
you have redeemed my life.
59 You have seen the wrong done to me,
O LORD;
judge my cause.
60 You have seen all their vengeance,
all their plots against me.

61 "You have heard their taunts, O LORD,
all their plots against me.
62 The lips and thoughts of my assail-
ants
are against me all the day long.
63 Behold their sitting and their rising;
I am the object of their taunts.

64 "You will repay them,[1] O LORD,
according to the work of their
hands.
65 You will give them[2] dullness of heart;
your curse will be[3] on them.
66 You will pursue them[4] in anger and
destroy them
from under your heavens,
O LORD."[5]

[1] Or Repay them [2] Or Give them [3] Or place your curse [4] Or Pursue them [5] Syriac (compare Septuagint, Vulgate); Hebrew the heavens of the LORD

The Holy Stones Lie Scattered

4 How the gold has grown dim,
   how the pure gold is changed!
  The holy stones lie scattered
   at the head of every street.

2 The precious sons of Zion,
   worth their weight in fine gold,
  how they are regarded as earthen
    pots,
   the work of a potter's hands!

3 Even jackals offer the breast;
   they nurse their young,
  but the daughter of my people has
    become cruel,
   like the ostriches in the wilder-
    ness.

4 The tongue of the nursing infant
    sticks
   to the roof of its mouth for thirst;
  the children beg for food,
   but no one gives to them.

5 Those who once feasted on delica-
    cies
   perish in the streets;
  those who were brought up in purple
   embrace ash heaps.

6 For the chastisement[1] of the daugh-
    ter of my people has been
    greater
   than the punishment[2] of Sodom,
  which was overthrown in a moment,
   and no hands were wrung for her.[3]

7 Her princes were purer than snow,
   whiter than milk;
  their bodies were more ruddy than
    coral,
   the beauty of their form[4] was like
    sapphire.[5]

8 Now their face is blacker than soot;
   they are not recognized in the
    streets;
  their skin has shriveled on their
    bones;
   it has become as dry as wood.

9 Happier were the victims of the
    sword
   than the victims of hunger,
  who wasted away, pierced
   by lack of the fruits of the field.

10 The hands of compassionate women
   have boiled their own children;
  they became their food
   during the destruction of the
    daughter of my people.

11 The LORD gave full vent to his wrath;
   he poured out his hot anger,
  and he kindled a fire in Zion
   that consumed its foundations.

12 The kings of the earth did not
    believe,
   nor any of the inhabitants of the
    world,
  that foe or enemy could enter
   the gates of Jerusalem.

13 This was for the sins of her prophets
   and the iniquities of her priests,
  who shed in the midst of her
   the blood of the righteous.

14 They wandered, blind, through the
    streets;
   they were so defiled with blood
  that no one was able to touch
   their garments.

15 "Away! Unclean!" people cried at them.
   "Away! Away! Do not touch!"
  So they became fugitives and wan-
    derers;
   people said among the nations,
  "They shall stay with us no longer."

16 The LORD himself[6] has scattered
    them;
   he will regard them no more;
  no honor was shown to the priests,
   no favor to the elders.

17 Our eyes failed, ever watching
   vainly for help;
  in our watching we watched
   for a nation which could not save.

18 They dogged our steps
   so that we could not walk in our
    streets;
  our end drew near; our days were
    numbered,
   for our end had come.

19 Our pursuers were swifter
   than the eagles in the heavens;

---

[1] Or iniquity   [2] Or sin   [3] The meaning of the Hebrew is uncertain   [4] The meaning of the Hebrew is uncertain   [5] Hebrew *lapis lazuli*
[6] Hebrew *The face of the* LORD

they chased us on the mountains;
  they lay in wait for us in the wil-
    derness.

20 The breath of our nostrils, the LORD's
  anointed,
  was captured in their pits,
of whom we said, "Under his shadow
  we shall live among the nations."

21 Rejoice and be glad, O daughter of
  Edom,
  you who dwell in the land of Uz;
but to you also the cup shall pass;
  you shall become drunk and strip
    yourself bare.

22 The punishment of your iniquity,
  O daughter of Zion, is accom-
    plished;
  he will keep you in exile no longer;[1]
but your iniquity, O daughter of
  Edom, he will punish;
  he will uncover your sins.

Restore Us to Yourself, O LORD

5 Remember, O LORD, what has
  befallen us;
  look, and see our disgrace!
2 Our inheritance has been turned
  over to strangers,
  our homes to foreigners.
3 We have become orphans, fatherless;
  our mothers are like widows.
4 We must pay for the water we drink;
  the wood we get must be bought.
5 Our pursuers are at our necks;[2]
  we are weary; we are given no rest.
6 We have given the hand to Egypt, and
  to Assyria,
  to get bread enough.
7 Our fathers sinned, and are no more;
  and we bear their iniquities.

8 Slaves rule over us;
  there is none to deliver us from
    their hand.
9 We get our bread at the peril of our
  lives,
  because of the sword in the wil-
    derness.
10 Our skin is hot as an oven
  with the burning heat of famine.
11 Women are raped in Zion,
  young women in the towns of
    Judah.
12 Princes are hung up by their hands;
  no respect is shown to the elders.
13 Young men are compelled to grind at
  the mill,
  and boys stagger under loads of
    wood.
14 The old men have left the city gate,
  the young men their music.
15 The joy of our hearts has ceased;
  our dancing has been turned to
    mourning.
16 The crown has fallen from our head;
  woe to us, for we have sinned!
17 For this our heart has become sick,
  for these things our eyes have
    grown dim,
18 for Mount Zion which lies desolate;
  jackals prowl over it.
19 But you, O LORD, reign forever;
  your throne endures to all genera-
    tions.
20 Why do you forget us forever,
  why do you forsake us for so many
    days?
21 Restore us to yourself, O LORD, that
  we may be restored!
  Renew our days as of old—
22 unless you have utterly rejected us,
  and you remain exceedingly angry
    with us.

[1] Or he will not exile you again [2] Symmachus With a yoke on our necks

INTRODUCTION TO
Ezekiel

Author: Ezekiel

Time: 593–571 B.C.

Place: Babylon

Written to: The Jews in captivity in Babylon

The gist

While Jeremiah warned the people of Judah about their coming destruction, Ezekiel was saying the same thing in Babylon. The sin of the Israelites would be their downfall, and Ezekiel's job was to let them know and to encourage them to repent. His message, like the messages of all the prophets, was about God's ultimate restoration of his people, in spite of their persistent waywardness and rebellion.

Things to look for

- Vivid descriptions of Ezekiel's visions (see Ezekiel 1–3; 8–11; 37; 40–48)

- References to God's end-time restoration of his people

- The many times God says "they will know that I am the LORD" (look for 17 times)

Repent and Live

"But if a wicked person turns away from all his sins that he has committed and keeps all my statutes and does what is just and right, he shall surely live; he shall not die. None of the transgressions that he has committed shall be remembered against him; for the righteousness that he has done he shall live. Have I any pleasure in the death of the wicked, declares the Lord GOD, and not rather that he should turn from his way and live?"

Ezekiel 18:21–23

The book of Ezekiel was written during some of the darkest days of God's people. The kingdoms had been attacked and destroyed, and a lot of people had been either killed or dragged off to exile. The priest and prophet Ezekiel was one of those exiles living in Babylon. God came to Ezekiel and told him what to do in order to get the attention of the Israelites, and some of it seems pretty wild. Some of the descriptions of his visions sound a lot like UFO sightings: enormous flying objects, inhuman figures, and glowing lights. One time he laid in public, all wrapped up with ropes, for 430 days. Another time he dug a hole in the wall of his house, packed his bags, and crawled out, pretending he was going into exile. Object lessons were definitely Ezekiel's thing. His prophecy was part words and part show, and because of that this book can be super hard to understand. What does it all mean? And how does it apply to you?

The most important message you can get out of all this is the disobedience of God's people, the discipline God used to show them who he is, and the grace God insisted on giving to his people no matter what. The Israelites had turned away to other gods and had forgotten him. They started acting like the people they lived with. But because of God's covenant promises, he couldn't let them keep on getting it wrong.

When bad times come, it's easy to feel like God has forgotten you. But even the most miserable times can be a chance for hope and for a change in the status quo. God isn't a distant figure who made the world and then just watches as it spins out of control, and the book of Ezekiel proves it. God lets people get into a mess only for so long, and then he does something to get their attention. These prophecies were written to show the people how they had walked away from God and to remind them that he would take them back if they would simply give themselves to him yet again. Sometimes the acts of God look strange and even cruel, but you have to remember that God always acts out of love and justice, and his goal is always bringing his people back to himself (see Ezek. 18:21–32).

Must-Know Terms and Verses

❧ The Lord Is There (or Yahweh Shammah) ❧
A phrase used by Ezekiel to describe the holy city of Jerusalem (see Ezek. 48:35).

❧ Oracle ❧
A message from God such as prophecy or guidance. Can also be used to describe the holy place in the temple.

"And I will give them one heart, and a new spirit I will put within them. I will remove the heart of stone from their flesh and give them a heart of flesh." *Ezekiel 11:19*

"Therefore say to the house of Israel, Thus says the Lord GOD: Repent and turn away from your idols, and turn away your faces from all your abominations." *Ezekiel 14:6*

Ezekiel

Ezekiel in Babylon

1 In the thirtieth year, in the fourth month, on the fifth day of the month, as I was among the exiles by the Chebar canal, the heavens were opened, and I saw visions of God.[1] [2] On the fifth day of the month (it was the fifth year of the exile of King Jehoiachin), [3] the word of the LORD came to Ezekiel the priest, the son of Buzi, in the land of the Chaldeans by the Chebar canal, and the hand of the LORD was upon him there.

The Glory of the LORD

[4] As I looked, behold, a stormy wind came out of the north, and a great cloud, with brightness around it, and fire flashing forth continually, and in the midst of the fire, as it were gleaming metal.[2] [5] And from the midst of it came the likeness of four living creatures. And this was their appearance: they had a human likeness, [6] but each had four faces, and each of them had four wings. [7] Their legs were straight, and the soles of their feet were like the sole of a calf's foot. And they sparkled like burnished bronze. [8] Under their wings on their four sides they had human hands. And the four had their faces and their wings thus: [9] their wings touched one another. Each one of them went straight forward, without turning as they went. [10] As for the likeness of their faces, each had a human face. The four had the face of a lion on the right side, the four had the face of an ox on the left side, and the four had the face of an eagle. [11] Such were their faces. And their wings were spread out above. Each creature had two wings, each of which touched the wing of another, while two covered their bodies. [12] And each went straight forward. Wherever the spirit[3] would go, they went, without turning as they went. [13] As for the likeness of the living creatures, their appearance was like burning coals of fire, like the appearance of torches moving to and fro among the living creatures. And the fire was bright, and out of the fire went forth lightning. [14] And the living creatures darted to and fro, like the appearance of a flash of lightning.

[15] Now as I looked at the living creatures, I saw a wheel on the earth beside the living creatures, one for each of the four of them.[4] [16] As for the appearance of the wheels and their construction: their appearance was like the gleaming of beryl. And the four had the same likeness, their appearance and construction being as it were a wheel within a wheel. [17] When they went, they went in any of their four directions[5] without turning as they went. [18] And their rims were tall and awesome, and the rims of all four were full of eyes all around. [19] And when the living creatures went, the wheels went beside them; and when the living creatures rose from the earth, the wheels rose. [20] Wherever the spirit wanted to go, they went, and the wheels rose along with them, for the spirit of the living creatures[6] was in the wheels. [21] When those went, these went; and when those stood, these stood; and when those rose from the earth, the wheels rose along with them, for the spirit of the living creatures was in the wheels.

[22] Over the heads of the living creatures there was the likeness of an expanse, shining like awe-inspiring crystal, spread out above their heads. [23] And under the expanse their wings were stretched out straight, one toward another. And each creature had two wings covering its body. [24] And when they went, I heard the sound of their wings like the sound of many waters, like the sound of the Almighty, a sound of tumult like the sound of an army. When they stood still, they let down their wings. [25] And there came a voice from above the

---

[1] Or *from God* [2] Or *amber*; also verse 27 [3] Or *Spirit*; also twice in verse 20 and once in verse 21 [4] Hebrew *of their faces* [5] Hebrew *on their four sides* [6] Or *the spirit of life*; also verse 21

expanse over their heads. When they stood still, they let down their wings.

²⁶ And above the expanse over their heads there was the likeness of a throne, in appearance like sapphire;[1] and seated above the likeness of a throne was a likeness with a human appearance. ²⁷ And upward from what had the appearance of his waist I saw as it were gleaming metal, like the appearance of fire enclosed all around. And downward from what had the appearance of his waist I saw as it were the appearance of fire, and there was brightness around him.[2] ²⁸ Like the appearance of the bow that is in the cloud on the day of rain, so was the appearance of the brightness all around.

Such was the appearance of the likeness of the glory of the LORD. And when I saw it, I fell on my face, and I heard the voice of one speaking.

Ezekiel's Call

2 And he said to me, "Son of man,[3] stand on your feet, and I will speak with you." ² And as he spoke to me, the Spirit entered into me and set me on my feet, and I heard him speaking to me. ³ And he said to me, "Son of man, I send you to the people of Israel, to nations of rebels, who have rebelled against me. They and their fathers have transgressed against me to this very day. ⁴ The descendants also are impudent and stubborn: I send you to them, and you shall say to them, 'Thus says the Lord GOD.' ⁵ And whether they hear or refuse to hear (for they are a rebellious house) they will know that a prophet has been among them. ⁶ And you, son of man, be not afraid of them, nor be afraid of their words, though briers and thorns are with you and you sit on scorpions.[4] Be not afraid of their words, nor be dismayed at their

---

[1] Or *lapis lazuli* [2] Or *it* [3] Or *Son of Adam*; so throughout Ezekiel [4] Or *on scorpion plants*

Know Yourself

verses to read
Ezekiel 2:3-8

Is being nice always the godly choice? Sometimes we're nice just to keep the peace. Your friend asks you if you think she has a problem with gossip, and while you know she does, you say "no way" so that she won't gossip about you. Or you have a friend who is mean to other people, but you don't say anything because you don't want a fight. When you are nice in order to protect yourself, look out, because you might just be putting yourself before God. Sometimes, like the prophet Ezekiel, we are called to speak up, and that might mean ticking people off. It's so much easier to just be nice and avoid the conflict altogether. But when sin is involved, being nice and not saying anything that would offend is contributing to that sin, even joining in.

As a God Girl, you need to be fearless in speaking God's Word. That means speaking the truth even when people don't want to hear it. They'll be expecting you to "love" them, meaning that you let them live in denial of their own sin. But that's not loving them, it's fearing them—and you are not to fear anyone but God (see Prov. 1:7; Matt. 10:28).

This isn't a free pass to go around criticizing everyone but a call to be honest when honesty is requested. When your friends ask your opinion on something, you have an obligation to tell them the truth, even when it might hurt. But you don't have to run around getting onto everyone's sin; that's like throwing pearls to pigs (see Matt. 7:6)—they just aren't interested. But when you have an opening or even an invitation, don't pass it up. Speak God's Word and risk the agitation and even anger of others so that you might serve God rather than yourself.

ooks, for they are a rebellious house. ⁷And you shall speak my words to them, whether they hear or refuse to hear, for they are a rebellious house.

⁸"But you, son of man, hear what I say to you. Be not rebellious like that rebellious house; open your mouth and eat what I give you." ⁹And when I looked, behold, a hand was stretched out to me, and behold, a scroll of a book was in it. ¹⁰And he spread it before me. And it had writing on the front and on the back, and there were written on it words of lamentation and mourning and woe.

3 And he said to me, "Son of man, eat whatever you find here. Eat this scroll, and go, speak to the house of Israel." ²So I opened my mouth, and he gave me this scroll to eat. ³And he said to me, "Son of man, feed your belly with this scroll that I give you and fill your stomach with it." Then I ate it, and it was in my mouth as sweet as honey.

⁴And he said to me, "Son of man, go to the house of Israel and speak with my words to them. ⁵For you are not sent to a people of foreign speech and a hard language, but to the house of Israel— ⁶not to many peoples of foreign speech and a hard language, whose words you cannot understand. Surely, if I sent you to such, they would listen to you. ⁷But the house of Israel will not be willing to listen to you, for they are not willing to listen to me: because all the house of Israel have a hard forehead and a stubborn heart. ⁸Behold, I have made your face as hard as their faces, and your forehead as hard as their foreheads. ⁹Like emery harder than flint have I made your forehead. Fear them not, nor be dismayed at their looks, for they are a rebellious house." ¹⁰Moreover, he said to me, "Son of man, all my words that I shall speak to you receive in your heart, and hear with your ears. ¹¹And go to the exiles, to your people, and speak to them and say to them, 'Thus says the Lord GOD,' whether they hear or refuse to hear."

¹²Then the Spirit[1] lifted me up, and I heard behind me the voice[2] of a great earthquake: "Blessed be the glory of the LORD from its place!" ¹³It was the sound of the wings of the living creatures as they touched one another, and the sound of the wheels beside them, and the sound of a great earthquake. ¹⁴The Spirit lifted me up and took me away, and I went in bitterness in the heat of my spirit, the hand of the LORD being strong upon me. ¹⁵And I came to the exiles at Tel-abib, who were dwelling by the Chebar canal, and I sat where they were dwelling.[3] And I sat there overwhelmed among them seven days.

A Watchman for Israel

¹⁶And at the end of seven days, the word of the LORD came to me: ¹⁷"Son of man, I have made you a watchman for the house of Israel. Whenever you hear a word from my mouth, you shall give them warning from me. ¹⁸If I say to the wicked, 'You shall surely die,' and you give him no warning, nor speak to warn the wicked from his wicked way, in order to save his life, that wicked person shall die for[4] his iniquity, but his blood I will require at your hand. ¹⁹But if you warn the wicked, and he does not turn from his wickedness, or from his wicked way, he shall die for his iniquity, but you will have delivered your soul. ²⁰Again, if a righteous person turns from his righteousness and commits injustice, and I lay a stumbling block before him, he shall die. Because you have not warned him, he shall die for his sin, and his righteous deeds that he has done shall not be remembered, but his blood I will require at your hand. ²¹But if you warn the righteous person not to sin, and he does not sin, he shall surely live, because he took warning, and you will have delivered your soul."

²²And the hand of the LORD was upon me there. And he said to me, "Arise, go out into the valley,[5] and there I will speak with you." ²³So I arose and went out into the valley, and behold, the glory of the LORD stood there, like the glory that I had seen by the Chebar canal, and I fell on my face. ²⁴But the Spirit entered into me and set me on my feet, and he spoke with me and said to me, "Go, shut yourself within your house. ²⁵And you, O son of man, behold, cords will be placed upon you, and you shall be bound with them, so that you cannot go out among the people. ²⁶And I will make your tongue cling to the roof of your mouth, so that you shall be mute and unable to reprove them, for they are a rebellious house. ²⁷But when I speak with you, I will open your mouth, and you shall

say to them, 'Thus says the Lord GOD.' He who will hear, let him hear; and he who will refuse to hear, let him refuse, for they are a rebellious house.

The Siege of Jerusalem Symbolized

4 "And you, son of man, take a brick and lay it before you, and engrave on it a city, even Jerusalem. ²And put siegeworks against it, and build a siege wall against it, and cast up a mound against it. Set camps also against it, and plant battering rams against it all around. ³And you, take an iron griddle, and place it as an iron wall between you and the city; and set your face toward it, and let it be in a state of siege, and press the siege against it. This is a sign for the house of Israel.

⁴"Then lie on your left side, and place the punishment[1] of the house of Israel upon it. For the number of the days that you lie on it, you shall bear their punishment. ⁵For I assign to you a number of days, 390 days, equal to the number of the years of their punishment. So long shall you bear the punishment of the house of Israel. ⁶And when you have completed these, you shall lie down a second time, but on your right side, and bear the punishment of the house of Judah. Forty days I assign you, a day for each year. ⁷And you shall set your face toward the siege of Jerusalem, with your arm bared, and you shall prophesy against the city. ⁸And behold, I will place cords upon you, so that you cannot turn from one side to the other, till you have completed the days of your siege.

⁹"And you, take wheat and barley, beans and lentils, millet and emmer,[2] and put them into a single vessel and make your bread from them. During the number of days that you lie on your side, 390 days, you shall eat it. ¹⁰And your food that you eat shall be by weight, twenty shekels[3] a day; from day to day[4] you shall eat it. ¹¹And water you shall drink by measure, the sixth part of a hin;[5] from day to day you shall drink. ¹²And you shall eat it as a barley cake, baking it in their sight on human dung." ¹³And the LORD said, "Thus shall the people of Israel eat their bread unclean, among the nations where I will drive them." ¹⁴Then I said, "Ah, Lord GOD! Behold, I have never defiled myself.[6]

From my youth up till now I have never eaten what died of itself or was torn by beasts, nor has tainted meat come into my mouth." ¹⁵Then he said to me, "See, I assign to you cow's dung instead of human dung on which you may prepare your bread. ¹⁶Moreover, he said to me, "Son of man behold, I will break the supply[7] of bread in Jerusalem. They shall eat bread by weight and with anxiety, and they shall drink water by measure and in dismay. ¹⁷I will do this that they may lack bread and water, and look at one another in dismay, and rot away because of their punishment.

Jerusalem Will Be Destroyed

5 "And you, O son of man, take a sharp sword. Use it as a barber's razor and pass it over your head and your beard. Then take balances for weighing and divide the hair. ²A third part you shall burn in the fire in the midst of the city, when the days of the siege are completed. And a third part you shall take and strike with the sword all around the city. And a third part you shall scatter to the wind, and I will unsheath the sword after them. ³And you shall take from these a small number and bind them in the skirts of your robe. ⁴And of these again you shall take some and cast them into the midst of the fire and burn them in the fire. From there a fire will come out into all the house of Israel.

⁵"Thus says the Lord GOD: This is Jerusalem. I have set her in the center of the nations, with countries all around her. ⁶And she has rebelled against my rules by doing wickedness more than the nations and against my statutes more than the countries all around her; for they have rejected my rules and have not walked in my statutes. ⁷Therefore thus says the Lord GOD: Because you are more turbulent than the nations that are all around you, and have not walked in my statutes or obeyed my rules, and have not[8] even acted according to the rules of the nations that are all around you, ⁸therefore thus says the Lord GOD: Behold, I, even I, am against you. And I will execute judgments[9] in your midst in the sight of the nations. ⁹And because of all your abominations I will do with you what I have never yet done, and the like

---

[1] Or *iniquity*; also verses 5, 6, 17   [2] A type of wheat   [3] A *shekel* was about 2/5 ounce or 11 grams   [4] Or *at a set time daily*; also verse 11
[5] A *hin* was about 4 quarts or 3.5 liters   [6] Hebrew *my soul* (or *throat*) *has never been made unclean*   [7] Hebrew *staff*   [8] Some Hebrew manuscripts and Syriac lack *not*   [9] The same Hebrew expression can mean *obey rules*, or *execute judgments*, depending on the context

of which I will never do again. [10] Therefore fathers shall eat their sons in your midst, and sons shall eat their fathers. And I will execute judgments on you, and any of you who survive I will scatter to all the winds. [11] Therefore, as I live, declares the Lord God, surely, because you have defiled my sanctuary with all your detestable things and with all your abominations, therefore I will withdraw.[1] My eye will not spare, and I will have no pity. [12] A third part of you shall die of pestilence and be consumed with famine in your midst; a third part shall fall by the sword all around you; and a third part I will scatter to all the winds and will unsheathe the sword after them.

[13] "Thus shall my anger spend itself, and I will vent my fury upon them and satisfy myself. And they shall know that I am the Lord— that I have spoken in my jealousy—when I spend my fury upon them. [14] Moreover, I will make you a desolation and an object of reproach among the nations all around you and in the sight of all who pass by. [15] You shall be[2] a reproach and a taunt, a warning and a horror, to the nations all around you, when I execute judgments on you in anger and fury, and with furious rebukes—I am the Lord; I have spoken— [16] when I send against you[3] the deadly arrows of famine, arrows for destruction, which I will send to destroy you, and when I bring more and more famine upon you and break your supply[4] of bread. [17] I will send famine and wild beasts against you, and they will rob you of your children. Pestilence and blood shall pass through you, and I will bring the sword upon you. I am the Lord; I have spoken."

Judgment Against Idolatry

6 The word of the Lord came to me: [2] "Son of man, set your face toward the mountains of Israel, and prophesy against them, [3] and say, You mountains of Israel, hear the word of the Lord God! Thus says the Lord God to the mountains and the hills, to the ravines and the valleys: Behold, I, even I, will bring a sword upon you, and I will destroy your high places. [4] Your altars shall become desolate, and your incense altars shall be broken, and I will cast down your slain before your idols. [5] And I will lay the dead bodies of the people of Israel

before their idols, and I will scatter your bones around your altars. [6] Wherever you dwell, the cities shall be waste and the high places ruined, so that your altars will be waste and ruined,[5] your idols broken and destroyed, your incense altars cut down, and your works wiped out. [7] And the slain shall fall in your midst, and you shall know that I am the Lord.

[8] "Yet I will leave some of you alive. When you have among the nations some who escape the sword, and when you are scattered through the countries, [9] then those of you who escape will remember me among the nations where they are carried captive, how I have been broken over their whoring heart that has departed from me and over their eyes that go whoring after their idols. And they will be loathsome in their own sight for the evils that they have committed, for all their abominations. [10] And they shall know that I am the Lord. I have not said in vain that I would do this evil to them."

[11] Thus says the Lord God: "Clap your hands and stamp your foot and say, Alas, because of all the evil abominations of the house of Israel, for they shall fall by the sword, by famine, and by pestilence. [12] He who is far off shall die of pestilence, and he who is near shall fall by the sword, and he who is left and is preserved shall die of famine. Thus I will spend my fury upon them. [13] And you shall know that I am the Lord, when their slain lie among their idols around their altars, on every high hill, on all the mountaintops, under every green tree, and under every leafy oak, wherever they offered pleasing aroma to all their idols. [14] And I will stretch out my hand against them and make the land desolate and waste, in all their dwelling places, from the wilderness to Riblah.[6] Then they will know that I am the Lord."

The Day of the Wrath of the Lord

7 The word of the Lord came to me: [2] "And you, O son of man, thus says the Lord God to the land of Israel: An end! The end has come upon the four corners of the land.[7] [3] Now the end is upon you, and I will send my anger upon you; I will judge you according to your ways, and I will punish you for all your abominations. [4] And

---

[1] Some Hebrew manuscripts *I will cut you down* [2] Dead Sea Scroll, Septuagint, Syriac, Vulgate, Targum; Masoretic Text *And it shall be*
[3] Hebrew *them* [4] Hebrew *staff* [5] Or *and punished* [6] Some Hebrew manuscripts; most Hebrew manuscripts *Diblah* [7] Or *earth*

my eye will not spare you, nor will I have pity, but I will punish you for your ways, while your abominations are in your midst. Then you will know that I am the LORD.

Ask Yourself . . .

ABOUT GOD'S ANGER

The book of Ezekiel is filled with angry words from God. The Israelites sinned and God got mad. Have you ever thought God was mad at you? Ask yourself:

- Do I feel like God is angry at me for something I've done?
- What does he require from people who make him angry with their sin?
- How did Jesus take care of that for me?
- What does God require in order to forgive those of us who have accepted the sacrifice of Jesus?
- How is life different this side of the cross?

⁵"Thus says the Lord GOD: Disaster after disaster![1] Behold, it comes. ⁶An end has come; the end has come; it has awakened against you. Behold, it comes. ⁷Your doom[2] has come to you, O inhabitant of the land. The time has come; the day is near, a day of tumult, and not of joyful shouting on the mountains. ⁸Now I will soon pour out my wrath upon you, and spend my anger against you, and judge you according to your ways, and I will punish you for all your abominations. ⁹And my eye will not spare, nor will I have pity. I will punish you according to your ways, while your abominations are in your midst. Then you will know that I am the LORD, who strikes.

¹⁰"Behold, the day! Behold, it comes! Your doom has come; the rod has blossomed;

pride has budded. ¹¹Violence has grown up into a rod of wickedness. None of them shall remain, nor their abundance, nor their wealth; neither shall there be preeminence among them.[3] ¹²The time has come; the day has arrived. Let not the buyer rejoice, nor the seller mourn, for wrath is upon all their multitude.[4] ¹³For the seller shall not return to what he has sold, while they live. For the vision concerns all their multitude; it shall not turn back; and because of his iniquity, none can maintain his life.[5]

¹⁴"They have blown the trumpet and made everything ready, but none goes to battle, for my wrath is upon all their multitude. ¹⁵The sword is without; pestilence and famine are within. He who is in the field dies by the sword, and him who is in the city famine and pestilence devour. ¹⁶And if any survivors escape, they will be on the mountains, like doves of the valleys, all of them moaning, each one over his iniquity. ¹⁷All hands are feeble, and all knees turn to water. ¹⁸They put on sackcloth, and horror covers them. Shame is on all faces, and baldness on all their heads. ¹⁹They cast their silver into the streets, and their gold is like an unclean thing. Their silver and gold are not able to deliver them in the day of the wrath of the LORD. They cannot satisfy their hunger or fill their stomachs with it. For it was the stumbling block of their iniquity. ²⁰His beautiful ornament they used for pride, and they made their abominable images and their detestable things of it. Therefore I make it an unclean thing to them. ²¹And I will give it into the hands of foreigners for prey, and to the wicked of the earth for spoil, and they shall profane it. ²²I will turn my face from them, and they shall profane my treasured[6] place. Robbers shall enter and profane it.

²³"Forge a chain![7] For the land is full of bloody crimes and the city is full of violence. ²⁴I will bring the worst of the nations to take possession of their houses. I will put an end to the pride of the strong, and their holy places[8] shall be profaned. ²⁵When anguish comes, they will seek peace, but there shall be none. ²⁶Disaster comes upon disaster; rumor follows rumor. They seek a vision from the prophet, while the law[9] perishes

---

[1] Some Hebrew manuscripts (compare Syriac, Targum); most Hebrew manuscripts *Disaster! A unique disaster!* [2] The meaning of the Hebrew word is uncertain; also verse 10 [3] The meaning of this last Hebrew sentence is uncertain [4] Or *abundance*; also verses 13, 14 [5] The meaning of this last Hebrew sentence is uncertain [6] Or *secret* [7] Probably refers to an instrument of captivity [8] By revocalization (compare Septuagint); Hebrew *and those who sanctify them* [9] Or *instruction*

from the priest and counsel from the elders. ²⁷The king mourns, the prince is wrapped in despair, and the hands of the people of the land are paralyzed by terror. According to their way I will do to them, and according to their judgments I will judge them, and they shall know that I am the LORD."

Abominations in the Temple

8 In the sixth year, in the sixth month, on the fifth day of the month, as I sat in my house, with the elders of Judah sitting before me, the hand of the Lord GOD fell upon me there. ²Then I looked, and behold, a form that had the appearance of a man.¹ Below what appeared to be his waist was fire, and above his waist was something like the appearance of brightness, like gleaming metal.² ³He put out the form of a hand and took me by a lock of my head, and the Spirit lifted me up between earth and heaven and brought me in visions of God to Jerusalem, to the entrance of the gateway of the inner court that faces north, where was the seat of the image of jealousy, which provokes to jealousy. ⁴And behold, the glory of the God of Israel was there, like the vision that I saw in the valley.

⁵Then he said to me, "Son of man, lift up your eyes now toward the north." So I lifted up my eyes toward the north, and behold, north of the altar gate, in the entrance, was this image of jealousy. ⁶And he said to me, "Son of man, do you see what they are doing, the great abominations that the house of Israel are committing here, to drive me far from my sanctuary? But you will see still greater abominations."

⁷And he brought me to the entrance of the court, and when I looked, behold, there was a hole in the wall. ⁸Then he said to me, "Son of man, dig in the wall." So I dug in the wall, and behold, there was an entrance. ⁹And he said to me, "Go in, and see the vile abominations that they are committing here." ¹⁰So I went in and saw. And there, engraved on

¹By revocalization (compare Septuagint); Hebrew *of fire* ²Or *amber*

Know God

verses to read
Ezekiel 8:9–12

God hates idols. He calls them wicked and disgusting. An idol is anything that leads you to obsession and anything that you look to for answers, for hope, for peace, for comfort, or for anything else God wants to provide for you. We all have idols; we just don't always know it. That's because they've become such a part of us. A lot of times they control us so much that we can't even distinguish them from our own personalities. They control what we think and what we do. They say things like, "You deserve more than that," "You've got to get what you want," and "Life isn't fair." They make big demands on our hearts and our lives, wanting us to serve them at all costs.

You might not recognize the voices of your idols, but chances are they are there, deep inside you. In order to love and serve God you have to refuse to serve your idols. You can't have two gods; it doesn't work that way. In order to spot your idols, just ask yourself what you think about the most, what you can't live without, and where you lack self-control. As you explore these areas of yourself, you will more than likely find places where something other than God controls you, and there you've found your idols.

Don't resist God's love by following idols. Dare to break free today. Reject, renounce, and refuse your idols. It's the only way to serve God and to experience joy, and it will be the answer to your bondage. Nothing can control the God Girl who has her mind set on God and God alone.

the wall all around, was every form of creeping things and loathsome beasts, and all the idols of the house of Israel. ¹¹ And before them stood seventy men of the elders of the house of Israel, with Jaazaniah the son of Shaphan standing among them. Each had his censer in his hand, and the smoke of the cloud of incense went up. ¹² Then he said to me, "Son of man, have you seen what the elders of the house of Israel are doing in the dark, each in his room of pictures? For they say, 'The LORD does not see us, the LORD has forsaken the land.'" ¹³ He said also to me, "You will see still greater abominations that they commit."

> ## Ask Yourself . . .
>
> ### ABOUT YOUR SECRETS
>
> What you do in secret says a lot about your idols—those things you do that you know are wrong but you don't want to give up. Ask yourself:
>
> - What things do I do that I don't want anyone else to know about?
> - Is my secret or my desire to hide it sinful?
> - What does Ezekiel 8:12 tell us about keeping secrets from God?
> - Do I believe that God sees all my secrets?
> - Have I confessed to him my desire to hide my sin?
> - How can I repent after I have confessed?

¹⁴ Then he brought me to the entrance of the north gate of the house of the LORD, and behold, there sat women weeping for Tammuz. ¹⁵ Then he said to me, "Have you seen this, O son of man? You will see still greater abominations than these."

¹⁶ And he brought me into the inner court of the house of the LORD. And behold, at the entrance of the temple of the LORD, between the porch and the altar, were about twenty-five men, with their backs to the temple of the LORD, and their faces toward the east, worshiping the sun toward the east. ¹⁷ Then he said to me, "Have you seen this, O son of man? Is it too light a thing for the house of Judah to commit the abominations that they commit here, that they should fill the land with violence and provoke me still further to anger? Behold, they put the branch to their¹ nose. ¹⁸ Therefore I will act in wrath. My eye will not spare, nor will I have pity. And though they cry in my ears with a loud voice, I will not hear them."

Idolaters Killed

9 Then he cried in my ears with a loud voice, saying, "Bring near the executioners of the city, each with his destroying weapon in his hand." ² And behold, six men came from the direction of the upper gate which faces north, each with his weapon for slaughter in his hand, and with them was a man clothed in linen, with a writing case at his waist. And they went in and stood beside the bronze altar.

³ Now the glory of the God of Israel had gone up from the cherub on which it rested to the threshold of the house. And he called to the man clothed in linen, who had the writing case at his waist. ⁴ And the LORD said to him, "Pass through the city, through Jerusalem, and put a mark on the foreheads of the men who sigh and groan over all the abominations that are committed in it." ⁵ And to the others he said in my hearing, "Pass through the city after him, and strike. Your eye shall not spare, and you shall show no pity. ⁶ Kill old men outright, young men and maidens, little children and women, but touch no one on whom is the mark. And begin at my sanctuary." So they began with the elders who were before the house. ⁷ Then he said to them, "Defile the house, and fill the courts with the slain. Go out." So they went out and struck in the city. ⁸ And while they were striking, and I was left alone, I fell upon my face, and cried, "Ah, Lord GOD! Will you destroy all the remnant of Israel in the outpouring of your wrath on Jerusalem?"

⁹ Then he said to me, "The guilt of the house of Israel and Judah is exceedingly

¹ Or my

great. The land is full of blood, and the city full of injustice. For they say, 'The LORD has forsaken the land, and the LORD does not see.' ¹⁰ As for me, my eye will not spare, nor will I have pity; I will bring their deeds upon their heads."

¹¹ And behold, the man clothed in linen, with the writing case at his waist, brought back word, saying, "I have done as you commanded me."

The Glory of the LORD Leaves the Temple

10 Then I looked, and behold, on the expanse that was over the heads of the cherubim there appeared above them something like a sapphire,¹ in appearance like a throne. ² And he said to the man clothed in linen, "Go in among the whirling wheels underneath the cherubim. Fill your hands with burning coals from between the cherubim, and scatter them over the city."

And he went in before my eyes. ³ Now the cherubim were standing on the south side of the house, when the man went in, and a cloud filled the inner court. ⁴ And the glory of the LORD went up from the cherub to the threshold of the house, and the house was filled with the cloud, and the court was filled with the brightness of the glory of the LORD. ⁵ And the sound of the wings of the cherubim was heard as far as the outer court, like the voice of God Almighty when he speaks.

⁶ And when he commanded the man clothed in linen, "Take fire from between the whirling wheels, from between the cherubim," he went in and stood beside a wheel. ⁷ And a cherub stretched out his hand from between the cherubim to the fire that was between the cherubim, and took some of it and put it into the hands of the man clothed in linen, who took it and went out. ⁸ The cherubim appeared to have the form of a human hand under their wings.

⁹ And I looked, and behold, there were four wheels beside the cherubim, one beside each cherub, and the appearance of the wheels was like sparkling beryl. ¹⁰ And as for their appearance, the four had the same likeness, as if a wheel were within a wheel. ¹¹ When they went, they went in any of their four directions² without turning

as they went, but in whatever direction the front wheel³ faced, the others followed without turning as they went. ¹² And their whole body, their rims, and their spokes, their wings,⁴ and the wheels were full of eyes all around—the wheels that the four of them had. ¹³ As for the wheels, they were called in my hearing "the whirling wheels." ¹⁴ And every one had four faces: the first face was the face of the cherub, and the second face was a human face, and the third the face of a lion, and the fourth the face of an eagle.

¹⁵ And the cherubim mounted up. These were the living creatures that I saw by the Chebar canal. ¹⁶ And when the cherubim went, the wheels went beside them. And when the cherubim lifted up their wings to mount up from the earth, the wheels did not turn from beside them. ¹⁷ When they stood still, these stood still, and when they mounted up, these mounted up with them, for the spirit of the living creatures⁵ was in them.

¹⁸ Then the glory of the LORD went out from the threshold of the house, and stood over the cherubim. ¹⁹ And the cherubim lifted up their wings and mounted up from the earth before my eyes as they went out, with the wheels beside them. And they stood at the entrance of the east gate of the house of the LORD, and the glory of the God of Israel was over them.

²⁰ These were the living creatures that I saw underneath the God of Israel by the Chebar canal; and I knew that they were cherubim. ²¹ Each had four faces, and each four wings, and underneath their wings the likeness of human hands. ²² And as for the likeness of their faces, they were the same faces whose appearance I had seen by the Chebar canal. Each one of them went straight forward.

Judgment on Wicked Counselors

11 The Spirit lifted me up and brought me to the east gate of the house of the LORD, which faces east. And behold, at the entrance of the gateway there were twenty-five men. And I saw among them Jaazaniah the son of Azzur, and Pelatiah the son of Benaiah, princes of the people. ² And he said to me, "Son of man, these are the men who devise iniquity and who

¹ Or lapis lazuli ² Hebrew to their four sides ³ Hebrew the head ⁴ Or their whole body, their backs, their hands, and their wings ⁵ Or spirit of life

give wicked counsel in this city; ³who say, "The time is not near¹ to build houses. This city is the cauldron, and we are the meat.' ⁴Therefore prophesy against them, prophesy, O son of man."

⁵And the Spirit of the Lord fell upon me, and he said to me, "Say, Thus says the Lord: So you think, O house of Israel. For I know the things that come into your mind. ⁶You have multiplied your slain in this city and have filled its streets with the slain. ⁷Therefore thus says the Lord God: Your slain whom you have laid in the midst of it, they are the meat, and this city is the cauldron, but you shall be brought out of the midst of it. ⁸You have feared the sword, and I will bring the sword upon you, declares the Lord God. ⁹And I will bring you out of the midst of it, and give you into the hands of foreigners, and execute judgments upon you. ¹⁰You shall fall by the sword. I will judge you at the border of Israel, and you shall know that I am the Lord. ¹¹This city shall not be your cauldron, nor shall you be the meat in the midst of it. I will judge you at the border of Israel, ¹²and you shall know that I am the Lord. For you have not walked in my statutes, nor obeyed my rules, but have acted according to the rules of the nations that are around you."

¹³And it came to pass, while I was prophesying, that Pelatiah the son of Benaiah died. Then I fell down on my face and cried out with a loud voice and said, "Ah, Lord God! Will you make a full end of the remnant of Israel?"

Israel's New Heart and Spirit

¹⁴And the word of the Lord came to me: ¹⁵"Son of man, your brothers, even your brothers, your kinsmen,² the whole house of Israel, all of them, are those of whom the inhabitants of Jerusalem have said, 'Go far from the Lord; to us this land is given for a possession.' ¹⁶Therefore say, 'Thus says the Lord God: Though I removed them far off among the nations, and though I scattered them among the countries, yet I have been a sanctuary to them for a while³ in the countries where they have gone.' ¹⁷Therefore say, 'Thus says the Lord God: I will gather you from the peoples and assemble you out of the countries where

you have been scattered, and I will give you the land of Israel.' ¹⁸And when they come there, they will remove from it all its detestable things and all its abominations. ¹⁹And I will give them one heart, and a new spirit I will put within them. I will remove the heart of stone from their flesh and give them a heart of flesh, ²⁰that they may walk in my statutes and keep my rules and obey them. And they shall be my people, and I will be their God. ²¹But as for those whose heart goes after their detestable things and their abominations, I will⁴ bring their deeds upon their own heads, declares the Lord God."

²²Then the cherubim lifted up their wings, with the wheels beside them, and the glory of the God of Israel was over them. ²³And the glory of the Lord went up from the midst of the city and stood on the mountain that is on the east side of the city. ²⁴And the Spirit lifted me up and brought me in the vision by the Spirit of God into Chaldea, to the exiles. Then the vision that I had seen went up from me. ²⁵And I told the exiles all the things that the Lord had shown me.

Judah's Captivity Symbolized

12

The word of the Lord came to me: ²"Son of man, you dwell in the midst of a rebellious house, who have eyes to see, but see not, who have ears to hear, but hear not, for they are a rebellious house. ³As for you, son of man, prepare for yourself an exile's baggage, and go into exile by day in their sight. You shall go like an exile from your place to another place in their sight. Perhaps they will understand, though⁵ they are a rebellious house. ⁴You shall bring out your baggage by day in their sight, as baggage for exile, and you shall go out yourself at evening in their sight, as those do who must go into exile. ⁵In their sight dig through the wall, and bring your baggage out through it. ⁶In their sight you shall lift the baggage upon your shoulder and carry it out at dusk. You shall cover your face that you may not see the land, for I have made you a sign for the house of Israel."

⁷And I did as I was commanded. I brought out my baggage by day, as baggage for exile, and in the evening I dug through the wall with my own hands.

---

¹Or Is not the time near . . . ? ²Hebrew the men of your redemption ³Or in small measure ⁴Hebrew To the heart of their detestable things and their abominations their heart goes; I will ⁵Or will see that

I brought out my baggage at dusk, carrying it on my shoulder in their sight.

⁸ In the morning the word of the LORD came to me: ⁹ "Son of man, has not the house of Israel, the rebellious house, said to you, 'What are you doing?' ¹⁰ Say to them, 'Thus says the Lord GOD: This oracle concerns[1] the prince in Jerusalem and all the house of Israel who are in it.'[2] ¹¹ Say, 'I am a sign for you: as I have done, so shall it be done to them. They shall go into exile, into captivity.' ¹² And the prince who is among them shall lift his baggage upon his shoulder at dusk, and shall go out. They shall dig through the wall to bring him out through it. He shall cover his face, that he may not see the land with his eyes. ¹³ And I will spread my net over him, and he shall be taken in my snare. And I will bring him to Babylon, the land of the Chaldeans, yet he shall not see it, and he shall die there. ¹⁴ And I will scatter toward every wind all who are around him, his helpers and all his troops, and I will unsheathe the sword after them. ¹⁵ And they shall know that I am the LORD, when I disperse them among the nations and scatter them among the countries. ¹⁶ But I will let a few of them escape from the sword, from famine and pestilence, that they may declare all their abominations among the nations where they go, and may know that I am the LORD."

¹⁷ And the word of the LORD came to me: ¹⁸ "Son of man, eat your bread with quaking, and drink water with trembling and with anxiety. ¹⁹ And say to the people of the land, Thus says the Lord GOD concerning the inhabitants of Jerusalem in the land of Israel: They shall eat their bread with anxiety, and drink water in dismay. In this way her land will be stripped of all it contains, on account of the violence of all those who dwell in it. ²⁰ And the inhabited cities shall be laid waste, and the land shall become a desolation; and you shall know that I am the LORD."

²¹ And the word of the LORD came to me: ²² "Son of man, what is this proverb that you[3] have about the land of Israel, saying, 'The days grow long, and every vision comes to nothing'? ²³ Tell them therefore, 'Thus says the Lord GOD: I will put an end to this proverb, and they shall no more use it as a proverb in Israel.' But say to them, The days are near, and the fulfillment[4] of every vision. ²⁴ For there shall be no more any false vision or flattering divination within the house of Israel. ²⁵ For I am the LORD; I will speak the word that I will speak, and it will be performed. It will no longer be delayed, but in your days, O rebellious house, I will speak the word and perform it, declares the Lord GOD."

²⁶ And the word of the LORD came to me: ²⁷ "Son of man, behold, they of the house of Israel say, 'The vision that he sees is for many days from now, and he prophesies of times far off.' ²⁸ Therefore say to them, Thus says the Lord GOD: None of my words will be delayed any longer, but the word that I speak will be performed, declares the Lord GOD."

False Prophets Condemned

13 The word of the LORD came to me: ² "Son of man, prophesy against the prophets of Israel, who are prophesying, and say to those who prophesy from their own hearts: 'Hear the word of the LORD!' ³ Thus says the Lord GOD, Woe to the foolish prophets who follow their own spirit, and have seen nothing! ⁴ Your prophets have been like jackals among ruins, O Israel. ⁵ You have not gone up into the breaches, or built up a wall for the house of Israel, that it might stand in battle in the day of the LORD. ⁶ They have seen false visions and lying divinations. They say, 'Declares the LORD,' when the LORD has not sent them, and yet they expect him to fulfill their word. ⁷ Have you not seen a false vision and uttered a lying divination, whenever you have said, 'Declares the LORD,' although I have not spoken?"

⁸ Therefore thus says the Lord GOD: "Because you have uttered falsehood and seen lying visions, therefore behold, I am against you, declares the Lord GOD. ⁹ My hand will be against the prophets who see false visions and who give lying divinations. They shall not be in the council of my people, nor be enrolled in the register of the house of Israel, nor shall they enter the land of Israel. And you shall know that I am the Lord GOD. ¹⁰ Precisely because they have misled my people, saying, 'Peace,' when there is no peace, and because, when the people build a wall, these prophets smear it with whitewash,[5] ¹¹ say to those who smear it with whitewash that it shall

---

[1] Or *This burden is* [2] Hebrew *in the midst of them* [3] The Hebrew for *you* is plural [4] Hebrew *word* [5] Or *plaster*; also verses 11, 14, 15

fall! There will be a deluge of rain, and you, O great hailstones, will fall, and a stormy wind break out. [12] And when the wall falls, will it not be said to you, 'Where is the coating with which you smeared it?' [13] Therefore thus says the Lord GOD: I will make a stormy wind break out in my wrath, and there shall be a deluge of rain in my anger, and great hailstones in wrath to make a full end. [14] And I will break down the wall that you have smeared with whitewash, and bring it down to the ground, so that its foundation will be laid bare. When it falls, you shall perish in the midst of it, and you shall know that I am the LORD. [15] Thus will I spend my wrath upon the wall and upon those who have smeared it with whitewash, and I will say to you, The wall is no more, nor those who smeared it, [16] the prophets of Israel who prophesied concerning Jerusalem and saw visions of peace for her, when there was no peace, declares the Lord GOD.

[17] "And you, son of man, set your face against the daughters of your people, who prophesy out of their own hearts. Prophesy against them [18] and say, Thus says the Lord GOD: Woe to the women who sew magic bands upon all wrists, and make veils for the heads of persons of every stature, in the hunt for souls! Will you hunt down souls belonging to my people and keep your own souls alive? [19] You have profaned me among my people for handfuls of barley and for pieces of bread, putting to death souls who should not die and keeping alive souls who should not live, by your lying to my people, who listen to lies.

[20] "Therefore thus says the Lord GOD: Behold, I am against your magic bands with which you hunt the souls like birds, and I will tear them from your arms, and I will let the souls whom you hunt go free, the souls like birds. [21] Your veils also I will tear off and deliver my people out of your hand, and they shall be no more in your hand as prey, and you shall know that I am the LORD. [22] Because you have disheartened the righteous falsely, although I have not grieved him, and you have encouraged the wicked, that he should not turn from his evil way to save his life, [23] therefore you shall no more see false visions nor practice divination. I will deliver my people out of

your hand. And you shall know that I am the LORD."

Idolatrous Elders Condemned

14 Then certain of the elders of Israel came to me and sat before me. [2] And the word of the LORD came to me: [3] "Son of man, these men have taken their idols into their hearts, and set the stumbling block of their iniquity before their faces. Should I indeed let myself be consulted by them? [4] Therefore speak to them and say to them, Thus says the Lord GOD: Any one of the house of Israel who takes his idols into his heart and sets the stumbling block of his iniquity before his face, and yet comes to the prophet, I the LORD will answer him as he comes with the multitude of his idols, [5] that I may lay hold of the hearts of the house of Israel, who are all estranged from me through their idols.

[6] "Therefore say to the house of Israel, Thus says the Lord GOD: Repent and turn away from your idols, and turn away your faces from all your abominations. [7] For any one of the house of Israel, or of the strangers who sojourn in Israel, who separates himself from me, taking his idols into his heart and putting the stumbling block of his iniquity before his face, and yet comes to a prophet to consult me through him, I the LORD will answer him myself. [8] And I will set my face against that man; I will make him a sign and a byword and cut him off from the midst of my people, and you shall know that I am the LORD. [9] And if the prophet is deceived and speaks a word, I, the LORD, have deceived that prophet, and I will stretch out my hand against him and will destroy him from the midst of my people Israel. [10] And they shall bear their punishment[1]—the punishment of the prophet and the punishment of the inquirer shall be alike— [11] that the house of Israel may no more go astray from me, nor defile themselves anymore with all their transgressions, but that they may be my people and I may be their God, declares the Lord GOD."

Jerusalem Will Not Be Spared

[12] And the word of the LORD came to me: [13] "Son of man, when a land sins against me by acting faithlessly, and I stretch out my hand against it and break its supply[2]

---

[1] Or *iniquity*; three times in this verse [2] Hebrew *staff*

of bread and send famine upon it, and cut off from it man and beast, ¹⁴even if these three men, Noah, Daniel, and Job, were in it, they would deliver but their own lives by their righteousness, declares the Lord GOD.

¹⁵"If I cause wild beasts to pass through the land, and they ravage it, and it be made desolate, so that no one may pass through because of the beasts, ¹⁶even if these three men were in it, as I live, declares the Lord GOD, they would deliver neither sons nor daughters. They alone would be delivered, but the land would be desolate.

¹⁷"Or if I bring a sword upon that land and say, Let a sword pass through the land, and I cut off from it man and beast, ¹⁸though these three men were in it, as I live, declares the Lord GOD, they would deliver neither sons nor daughters, but they alone would be delivered.

¹⁹"Or if I send a pestilence into that land and pour out my wrath upon it with blood, to cut off from it man and beast, ²⁰even if Noah, Daniel, and Job were in it, as I live, declares the Lord GOD, they would deliver neither son nor daughter. They would deliver but their own lives by their righteousness.

²¹"For thus says the Lord GOD: How much more when I send upon Jerusalem my four disastrous acts of judgment, sword, famine, wild beasts, and pestilence, to cut off from it man and beast! ²²But behold, some survivors will be left in it, sons and daughters who will be brought out; behold, when they come out to you, and you see their ways and their deeds, you will be consoled for the disaster that I have brought upon Jerusalem, for all that I have brought upon it. ²³They will console you, when you see their ways and their deeds, and you shall know that I have not done without cause all that I have done in it, declares the Lord GOD."

Jerusalem, a Useless Vine

15 And the word of the LORD came to me: ²"Son of man, how does the wood of the vine surpass any wood, the vine branch that is among the trees of the forest? ³Is wood taken from it to make anything? Do people take a peg from it to hang any vessel on it? ⁴Behold, it is given to the fire for fuel. When the fire has consumed both ends of it, and the middle

of it is charred, is it useful for anything? ⁵Behold, when it was whole, it was used for nothing. How much less, when the fire has consumed it and it is charred, can it ever be used for anything! ⁶Therefore thus says the Lord GOD: Like the wood of the vine among the trees of the forest, which I have given to the fire for fuel, so have I given up the inhabitants of Jerusalem. ⁷And I will set my face against them. Though they escape from the fire, the fire shall yet consume them, and you will know that I am the LORD, when I set my face against them. ⁸And I will make the land desolate, because they have acted faithlessly, declares the Lord GOD."

The LORD's Faithless Bride

16 Again the word of the LORD came to me: ²"Son of man, make known to Jerusalem her abominations, ³and say, Thus says the Lord GOD to Jerusalem: Your origin and your birth are of the land of the Canaanites; your father was an Amorite and your mother a Hittite. ⁴And as for your birth, on the day you were born your cord was not cut, nor were you washed with water to cleanse you, nor rubbed with salt, nor wrapped in swaddling cloths. ⁵No eye pitied you, to do any of these things to you out of compassion for you, but you were cast out on the open field, for you were abhorred, on the day that you were born.

⁶"And when I passed by you and saw you wallowing in your blood, I said to you in your blood, 'Live!' I said to you in your blood, 'Live!' ⁷I made you flourish like a plant of the field. And you grew up and became tall and arrived at full adornment. Your breasts were formed, and your hair had grown; yet you were naked and bare.

⁸"When I passed by you again and saw you, behold, you were at the age for love, and I spread the corner of my garment over you and covered your nakedness; I made my vow to you and entered into a covenant with you, declares the Lord GOD, and you became mine. ⁹Then I bathed you with water and washed off your blood from you and anointed you with oil. ¹⁰I clothed you also with embroidered cloth and shod you with fine leather. I wrapped you in fine linen and covered you with silk.¹ ¹¹And I adorned you with ornaments and put bracelets on your wrists and a

¹ Or with rich fabric

chain on your neck. ¹²And I put a ring on your nose and earrings in your ears and a beautiful crown on your head. ¹³Thus you were adorned with gold and silver, and your clothing was of fine linen and silk and embroidered cloth. You ate fine flour and honey and oil. You grew exceedingly beautiful and advanced to royalty. ¹⁴And your renown went forth among the nations because of your beauty, for it was perfect through the splendor that I had bestowed on you, declares the Lord God.

¹⁵"But you trusted in your beauty and played the whore¹ because of your renown and lavished your whorings² on any passerby; your beauty³ became his. ¹⁶You took some of your garments and made for yourself colorful shrines, and on them played the whore. The like has never been, nor ever shall be.⁴ ¹⁷You also took your beautiful jewels of my gold and of my silver, which I had given you, and made for yourself images of men, and with them played the whore. ¹⁸And you took your embroidered garments to cover them, and set my oil and my incense before them. ¹⁹Also my bread that I gave you—I fed you with fine flour and oil and honey—you set before them for a pleasing aroma; and so it was, declares the Lord God. ²⁰And you took your sons and your daughters, whom you had borne to me, and these you sacrificed to them to be devoured. Were your whorings so small a matter ²¹that you slaughtered my children and delivered them up as an offering by fire to them? ²²And in all your abominations and your whorings you did not remember the days of your youth, when you were naked and bare, wallowing in your blood.

²³"And after all your wickedness (woe, woe to you! declares the Lord God), ²⁴you built yourself a vaulted chamber and made yourself a lofty place in every square. ²⁵At the head of every street you built your lofty place and made your beauty an abomination, offering yourself⁵ to any passerby and multiplying your whoring. ²⁶You also played the whore with the Egyptians, your lustful neighbors, multiplying your whoring, to provoke me to anger. ²⁷Behold, therefore, I stretched out my hand against you and diminished your allotted portion and delivered you to the greed of your

enemies, the daughters of the Philistines who were ashamed of your lewd behavior. ²⁸You played the whore also with the Assyrians, because you were not satisfied, yes, you played the whore with them, and still you were not satisfied. ²⁹You multiplied your whoring also with the trading land of Chaldea, and even with this you were not satisfied.

³⁰"How sick is your heart,⁶ declares the Lord God, because you did all these things the deeds of a brazen prostitute, ³¹building your vaulted chamber at the head of every street, and making your lofty place in every square. Yet you were not like a prostitute, because you scorned payment ³²Adulterous wife, who receives strangers instead of her husband! ³³Men give gifts to all prostitutes, but you gave your gifts to all your lovers, bribing them to come to you from every side with your whorings. ³⁴So you were different from other women in your whorings. No one solicited you to play the whore, and you gave payment, while no payment was given to you; therefore you were different.

³⁵"Therefore, O prostitute, hear the word of the Lord: ³⁶Thus says the Lord God Because your lust was poured out and your nakedness uncovered in your whorings with your lovers, and with all your abominable idols, and because of the blood of your children that you gave to them ³⁷therefore, behold, I will gather all your lovers with whom you took pleasure, all those you loved and all those you hated I will gather them against you from every side and will uncover your nakedness to them, that they may see all your nakedness. ³⁸And I will judge you as women who commit adultery and shed blood are judged, and bring upon you the blood of wrath and jealousy. ³⁹And I will give you into their hands, and they shall throw down your vaulted chamber and break down your lofty places. They shall strip you of your clothes and take your beautiful jewels and leave you naked and bare ⁴⁰They shall bring up a crowd against you, and they shall stone you and cut you to pieces with their swords. ⁴¹And they shall burn your houses and execute judgments upon you in the sight of many women I will make you stop playing the whore,

¹Or were unfaithful; also verses 16, 17, 26, 28 ²Or unfaithfulness; also verses 20, 22, 25, 26, 29, 33, 34, 36 ³Hebrew it ⁴The meaning of this Hebrew sentence is uncertain ⁵Hebrew spreading your legs ⁶Revocalization yields How I am filled with anger against you

and you shall also give payment no more. ⁴²So will I satisfy my wrath on you, and my jealousy shall depart from you. I will be calm and will no more be angry. ⁴³Because you have not remembered the days of your youth, but have enraged me with all these things, therefore, behold, I have returned your deeds upon your head, declares the Lord GOD. Have you not committed lewdness in addition to all your abominations?

⁴⁴"Behold, everyone who uses proverbs will use this proverb about you: 'Like mother, like daughter.' ⁴⁵You are the daughter of your mother, who loathed her husband and her children; and you are the sister of your sisters, who loathed their husbands and their children. Your mother was a Hittite and your father an Amorite. ⁴⁶And your elder sister is Samaria, who lived with her daughters to the north of you; and your younger sister, who lived to the south of you, is Sodom with her daughters. ⁴⁷Not only did you walk in their ways and do according to their abominations; within a very little time you were more corrupt than they in all your ways. ⁴⁸As I live, declares the Lord GOD, your sister Sodom and her daughters have not done as you and your daughters have done. ⁴⁹Behold, this was the guilt of your sister Sodom: she and her daughters had pride, excess of food, and prosperous ease, but did not aid the poor and needy. ⁵⁰They were haughty and did an abomination before me. So I removed them, when I saw it. ⁵¹Samaria has not committed half your sins. You have committed more abominations than they, and have made your sisters appear righteous by all the abominations that you have committed. ⁵²Bear your disgrace, you also, for you have intervened on behalf of your sisters. Because of your sins in which you acted more abominably than they, they are more in the right than you. So be ashamed, you also, and bear your disgrace, for you have made your sisters appear righteous.

⁵³"I will restore their fortunes, both the fortunes of Sodom and her daughters, and the fortunes of Samaria and her daughters, and I will restore your own fortunes in their midst, ⁵⁴that you may bear your disgrace and be ashamed of all that you have done, becoming a consolation to them. ⁵⁵As for your sisters, Sodom and her daughters shall return to their former state, and Samaria and her daughters shall return to their former state, and you and your daughters shall return to your former state. ⁵⁶Was not your sister Sodom a byword in your mouth in the day of your pride, ⁵⁷before your wickedness was uncovered? Now you have become an object of reproach for the daughters of Syria[1] and all those around her, and for the daughters of the Philistines, those all around who despise you. ⁵⁸You bear the penalty of your lewdness and your abominations, declares the LORD.

The LORD's Everlasting Covenant

⁵⁹"For thus says the Lord GOD: I will deal with you as you have done, you who have despised the oath in breaking the covenant, ⁶⁰yet I will remember my covenant with you in the days of your youth, and I will establish for you an everlasting covenant. ⁶¹Then you will remember your ways and be ashamed when you take your sisters, both your elder and your younger, and I give them to you as daughters, but not on account of[2] the covenant with you. ⁶²I will establish my covenant with you, and you shall know that I am the LORD, ⁶³that you may remember and be confounded, and never open your mouth again because of your shame, when I atone for you for all that you have done, declares the Lord GOD."

Parable of Two Eagles and a Vine

17 The word of the LORD came to me: ²"Son of man, propound a riddle, and speak a parable to the house of Israel; ³say, Thus says the Lord GOD: A great eagle with great wings and long pinions, rich in plumage of many colors, came to Lebanon and took the top of the cedar. ⁴He broke off the topmost of its young twigs and carried it to a land of trade and set it in a city of merchants. ⁵Then he took of the seed of the land and planted it in fertile soil.[3] He placed it beside abundant waters. He set it like a willow twig, ⁶and it sprouted and became a low spreading vine, and its branches turned toward him, and its roots remained where it stood. So it became a vine and produced branches and put out boughs.

⁷"And there was another great eagle with great wings and much plumage, and

behold, this vine bent its roots toward him and shot forth its branches toward him from the bed where it was planted, that he might water it. [8] It had been planted on good soil by abundant waters, that it might produce branches and bear fruit and become a noble vine.

[9] "Say, Thus says the Lord GOD: Will it thrive? Will he not pull up its roots and cut off its fruit, so that it withers, so that all its fresh sprouting leaves wither? It will not take a strong arm or many people to pull it from its roots. [10] Behold, it is planted; will it thrive? Will it not utterly wither when the east wind strikes it—wither away on the bed where it sprouted?"

[11] Then the word of the LORD came to me: [12] "Say now to the rebellious house, Do you not know what these things mean? Tell them, behold, the king of Babylon came to Jerusalem, and took her king and her princes and brought them to him to Babylon. [13] And he took one of the royal offspring[1] and made a covenant with him, putting him under oath (the chief men of the land he had taken away), [14] that the kingdom might be humble and not lift itself up, and keep his covenant that it might stand. [15] But he rebelled against him by sending his ambassadors to Egypt, that they might give him horses and a large army. Will he thrive? Can one escape who does such things? Can he break the covenant and yet escape?

[16] "As I live, declares the Lord GOD, surely in the place where the king dwells who made him king, whose oath he despised, and whose covenant with him he broke, in Babylon he shall die. [17] Pharaoh with his mighty army and great company will not help him in war, when mounds are cast up and siege walls built to cut off many lives. [18] He despised the oath in breaking the covenant, and behold, he gave his hand and did all these things; he shall not escape. [19] Therefore thus says the Lord GOD: As I live, surely it is my oath that he despised, and my covenant that he broke. I will return it upon his head. [20] I will spread my net over him, and he shall be taken in my snare, and I will bring him to Babylon and enter into judgment with him there for the treachery he has committed against me. [21] And all the pick[2] of his troops shall fall by the sword, and the survivors shall be scattered to every wind, and you shall know that I am the LORD; I have spoken."

[22] Thus says the Lord GOD: "I myself will take a sprig from the lofty top of the cedar and will set it out. I will break off from the topmost of its young twigs a tender one, and I myself will plant it on a high and lofty mountain. [23] On the mountain height of Israel will I plant it, that it may bear branches and produce fruit and become a noble cedar. And under it will dwell every kind of bird; in the shade of its branches birds of every sort will nest. [24] And all the trees of the field shall know that I am the LORD; I bring low the high tree, and make high the low tree, dry up the green tree, and make the dry tree flourish. I am the LORD; I have spoken, and I will do it."

The Soul Who Sins Shall Die

18 The word of the LORD came to me: [2] "What do you[3] mean by repeating this proverb concerning the land of Israel, 'The fathers have eaten sour grapes, and the children's teeth are set on edge'? [3] As I live, declares the Lord GOD, this proverb shall no more be used by you in Israel. [4] Behold, all souls are mine; the soul of the father as well as the soul of the son is mine: the soul who sins shall die.

[5] "If a man is righteous and does what is just and right— [6] if he does not eat upon the mountains or lift up his eyes to the idols of the house of Israel, does not defile his neighbor's wife or approach a woman in her time of menstrual impurity, [7] does not oppress anyone, but restores to the debtor his pledge, commits no robbery, gives his bread to the hungry and covers the naked with a garment, [8] does not lend at interest or take any profit,[4] withholds his hand from injustice, executes true justice between man and man, [9] walks in my statutes, and keeps my rules by acting faithfully— he is righteous; he shall surely live, declares the Lord GOD.

[10] "If he fathers a son who is violent, a shedder of blood, who does any of these things [11] (though he himself did none of these things), who even eats upon the mountains, defiles his neighbor's wife, [12] oppresses the poor and needy, commits robbery, does not restore the pledge, lifts

---

[1] Hebrew *seed* [2] Some Hebrew manuscripts, Syriac, Targum; most Hebrew manuscripts *all the fugitives* [3] The Hebrew for *you* is plural
[4] That is, profit that comes from charging interest to the poor; also verses 13, 17 (compare Leviticus 25:36)

up his eyes to the idols, commits abomination, ¹³ lends at interest, and takes profit; shall he then live? He shall not live. He has done all these abominations; he shall surely die; his blood shall be upon himself.

¹⁴ "Now suppose this man fathers a son who sees all the sins that his father has done; he sees, and does not do likewise: ¹⁵ he does not eat upon the mountains or lift up his eyes to the idols of the house of Israel, does not defile his neighbor's wife, ¹⁶ does not oppress anyone, exacts no pledge, commits no robbery, but gives his bread to the hungry and covers the naked with a garment, ¹⁷ withholds his hand from iniquity,¹ takes no interest or profit, obeys my rules, and walks in my statutes; he shall not die for his father's iniquity; he shall surely live. ¹⁸ As for his father, because he practiced extortion, robbed his brother, and did what is not good among his people, behold, he shall die for his iniquity.

¹⁹ "Yet you say, 'Why should not the son suffer for the iniquity of the father?' When the son has done what is just and right, and has been careful to observe all my statutes, he shall surely live. ²⁰ The soul who sins shall die. The son shall not suffer for the iniquity of the father, nor the father suffer for the iniquity of the son. The righteousness of the righteous shall be upon himself, and the wickedness of the wicked shall be upon himself.

²¹ "But if a wicked person turns away from all his sins that he has committed and keeps all my statutes and does what is just and right, he shall surely live; he shall not die. ²² None of the transgressions that he has committed shall be remembered against him; for the righteousness that he has done he shall live. ²³ Have I any pleasure in the death of the wicked, declares the Lord God, and not rather that he should turn from his way and live? ²⁴ But when a righteous person turns away from his righteousness and does injustice and does the same abominations that the wicked person does, shall he live? None of the righteous deeds that he has done shall be remembered; for the treachery of which he is guilty and the sin he has committed, for them he shall die.

²⁵ "Yet you say, 'The way of the Lord is not just.' Hear now, O house of Israel: Is my way not just? Is it not your ways that are not just? ²⁶ When a righteous person turns away from his righteousness and does injustice, he shall die for it; for the injustice that he has done he shall die. ²⁷ Again, when a wicked person turns away from the wickedness he has committed and does what is just and right, he shall save his life. ²⁸ Because he considered and turned away from all the transgressions that he had committed, he shall surely live; he shall not die. ²⁹ Yet the house of Israel says, 'The way of the Lord is not just.' O house of Israel, are my ways not just? Is it not your ways that are not just?

³⁰ "Therefore I will judge you, O house of Israel, every one according to his ways, declares the Lord God. Repent and turn from all your transgressions, lest iniquity be your ruin.² ³¹ Cast away from you all the transgressions that you have committed, and make yourselves a new heart and a new spirit! Why will you die, O house of Israel? ³² For I have no pleasure in the death of anyone, declares the Lord God; so turn, and live."

A Lament for the Princes of Israel

19 And you, take up a lamentation for the princes of Israel, ² and say:

What was your mother? A lioness!
        Among lions she crouched;
in the midst of young lions
        she reared her cubs.
³   And she brought up one of her cubs;
        he became a young lion,
and he learned to catch prey;
        he devoured men.
⁴   The nations heard about him;
        he was caught in their pit,
and they brought him with hooks
        to the land of Egypt.
⁵   When she saw that she waited in vain,
        that her hope was lost,
she took another of her cubs
        and made him a young lion.
⁶   He prowled among the lions;
        he became a young lion,
and he learned to catch prey;
        he devoured men,
⁷   and seized³ their widows.
        He laid waste their cities,
and the land was appalled and all
            who were in it
        at the sound of his roaring.

¹ Septuagint; Hebrew *from the poor* ² Or *lest iniquity be your stumbling block* ³ Hebrew *knew*

8 Then the nations set against him
    from provinces on every side;
they spread their net over him;
    he was taken in their pit.
9 With hooks they put him in a cage[1]
    and brought him to the king of
        Babylon;
    they brought him into custody,
that his voice should no more be
        heard
    on the mountains of Israel.

10 Your mother was like a vine in a
        vineyard[2]
    planted by the water,
fruitful and full of branches
    by reason of abundant water.
11 Its strong stems became
    rulers' scepters;
it towered aloft
    among the thick boughs;[3]
it was seen in its height
    with the mass of its branches.
12 But the vine was plucked up in fury,
    cast down to the ground;
the east wind dried up its fruit;
    they were stripped off and with-
        ered.
As for its strong stem,
    fire consumed it.
13 Now it is planted in the wilderness,
    in a dry and thirsty land.
14 And fire has gone out from the stem
        of its shoots,
    has consumed its fruit,
so that there remains in it no strong
        stem,
    no scepter for ruling.

This is a lamentation and has become a
lamentation.

Israel's Continuing Rebellion

20 In the seventh year, in the fifth
month, on the tenth day of the
month, certain of the elders of Israel came
to inquire of the LORD, and sat before me.
2 And the word of the LORD came to me:
3 "Son of man, speak to the elders of Israel,
and say to them, Thus says the Lord GOD,
Is it to inquire of me that you come? As
I live, declares the Lord GOD, I will not be
inquired of by you. 4 Will you judge them,
son of man, will you judge them? Let them
know the abominations of their fathers,

5 and say to them, Thus says the Lord GOD:
On the day when I chose Israel, I swore[4] to
the offspring of the house of Jacob, making
myself known to them in the land of Egypt,
I swore to them, saying, I am the LORD
your God. 6 On that day I swore to them
that I would bring them out of the land of
Egypt into a land that I had searched out
for them, a land flowing with milk and
honey, the most glorious of all lands. 7 And
I said to them, Cast away the detestable
things your eyes feast on, every one of you
and do not defile yourselves with the idols
of Egypt; I am the LORD your God. 8 But they
rebelled against me and were not willing
to listen to me. None of them cast away the
detestable things their eyes feasted on, nor
did they forsake the idols of Egypt.

"Then I said I would pour out my wrath
upon them and spend my anger against
them in the midst of the land of Egypt.
9 But I acted for the sake of my name, that
it should not be profaned in the sight of
the nations among whom they lived, in
whose sight I made myself known to them
in bringing them out of the land of Egypt.
10 So I led them out of the land of Egypt and
brought them into the wilderness. 11 I gave
them my statutes and made known to them
my rules, by which, if a person does them,
he shall live. 12 Moreover, I gave them my
Sabbaths, as a sign between me and them
that they might know that I am the LORD
who sanctifies them. 13 But the house of
Israel rebelled against me in the wilderness. They did not walk in my statutes but
rejected my rules, by which, if a person
does them, he shall live; and my Sabbaths
they greatly profaned.

"Then I said I would pour out my wrath
upon them in the wilderness, to make a
full end of them. 14 But I acted for the sake
of my name, that it should not be profaned in the sight of the nations, in whose
sight I had brought them out. 15 Moreover,
I swore to them in the wilderness that I
would not bring them into the land that
I had given them, a land flowing with milk
and honey, the most glorious of all lands,
16 because they rejected my rules and did
not walk in my statutes, and profaned my
Sabbaths; for their heart went after their
idols. 17 Nevertheless, my eye spared them

---

[1] Or *in a wooden collar* [2] Some Hebrew manuscripts; most Hebrew manuscripts *in your blood* [3] Or *the clouds* [4] Hebrew *I lifted my hand*; twice in this verse; also verses 6, 15, 23, 28, 42

and I did not destroy them or make a full end of them in the wilderness.

¹⁸ "And I said to their children in the wilderness, Do not walk in the statutes of your fathers, nor keep their rules, nor defile yourselves with their idols. ¹⁹ I am the LORD your God; walk in my statutes, and be careful to obey my rules, ²⁰ and keep my Sabbaths holy that they may be a sign between me and you, that you may know that I am the LORD your God. ²¹ But the children rebelled against me. They did not walk in my statutes and were not careful to obey my rules, by which, if a person does them, he shall live; they profaned my Sabbaths.

"Then I said I would pour out my wrath upon them and spend my anger against them in the wilderness. ²² But I withheld my hand and acted for the sake of my name, that it should not be profaned in the sight of the nations, in whose sight I had brought them out. ²³ Moreover, I swore to them in the wilderness that I would scatter them among the nations and disperse them through the countries, ²⁴ because they had not obeyed my rules, but had rejected my statutes and profaned my Sabbaths, and their eyes were set on their fathers' idols. ²⁵ Moreover, I gave them statutes that were not good and rules by which they could not have life, ²⁶ and I defiled them through their very gifts in their offering up all their firstborn, that I might devastate them. I did it that they might know that I am the LORD.

²⁷ "Therefore, son of man, speak to the house of Israel and say to them, Thus says the Lord GOD: In this also your fathers blasphemed me, by dealing treacherously with me. ²⁸ For when I had brought them into the land that I swore to give them, then wherever they saw any high hill or any leafy tree, there they offered their sacrifices and there they presented the provocation of their offering; there they sent up their pleasing aromas, and there they poured out their drink offerings. ²⁹ (I said to them, What is the high place to which you go? So its name is called Bamah¹ to this day.)

³⁰ "Therefore say to the house of Israel, Thus says the Lord GOD: Will you defile yourselves after the manner of your fathers and go whoring after their detestable things? ³¹ When you present your gifts and offer up your children in fire,² you defile yourselves with all your idols to this day.

And shall I be inquired of by you, O house of Israel? As I live, declares the Lord GOD, I will not be inquired of by you.

³² "What is in your mind shall never happen—the thought, 'Let us be like the nations, like the tribes of the countries, and worship wood and stone.'

The LORD Will Restore Israel

³³ "As I live, declares the Lord GOD, surely with a mighty hand and an outstretched arm and with wrath poured out I will be king over you. ³⁴ I will bring you out from the peoples and gather you out of the countries where you are scattered, with a mighty hand and an outstretched arm, and with wrath poured out. ³⁵ And I will bring you into the wilderness of the peoples, and there I will enter into judgment with you face to face. ³⁶ As I entered into judgment with your fathers in the wilderness of the land of Egypt, so I will enter into judgment with you, declares the Lord GOD. ³⁷ I will make you pass under the rod, and I will bring you into the bond of the covenant. ³⁸ I will purge out the rebels from among you, and those who transgress against me. I will bring them out of the land where they sojourn, but they shall not enter the land of Israel. Then you will know that I am the LORD.

³⁹ "As for you, O house of Israel, thus says the Lord GOD: Go serve every one of you his idols, now and hereafter, if you will not listen to me; but my holy name you shall no more profane with your gifts and your idols.

⁴⁰ "For on my holy mountain, the mountain height of Israel, declares the Lord GOD, there all the house of Israel, all of them, shall serve me in the land. There I will accept them, and there I will require your contributions and the choicest of your gifts, with all your sacred offerings. ⁴¹ As a pleasing aroma I will accept you, when I bring you out from the peoples and gather you out of the countries where you have been scattered. And I will manifest my holiness among you in the sight of the nations. ⁴² And you shall know that I am the LORD, when I bring you into the land of Israel, the country that I swore to give to your fathers. ⁴³ And there you shall remember your ways and all your deeds with which you have defiled yourselves,

---

¹ Bamah means high place ² Hebrew and make your children pass through the fire

and you shall loathe yourselves for all the evils that you have committed. [44] And you shall know that I am the LORD, when I deal with you for my name's sake, not according to your evil ways, nor according to your corrupt deeds, O house of Israel, declares the LORD."

[45] [1] And the word of the LORD came to me: [46] "Son of man, set your face toward the southland;[2] preach against the south, and prophesy against the forest land in the Negeb. [47] Say to the forest of the Negeb, Hear the word of the LORD: Thus says the Lord GOD, Behold, I will kindle a fire in you, and it shall devour every green tree in you and every dry tree. The blazing flame shall not be quenched, and all faces from south to north shall be scorched by it. [48] All flesh shall see that I the LORD have kindled it; it shall not be quenched." [49] Then I said, "Ah, Lord GOD! They are saying of me, 'Is he not a maker of parables?'"

The LORD Has Drawn His Sword

21 [3] The word of the LORD came to me: [2] "Son of man, set your face toward Jerusalem and preach against the sanctuaries.[4] Prophesy against the land of Israel [3] and say to the land of Israel, Thus says the LORD: Behold, I am against you and will draw my sword from its sheath and will cut off from you both righteous and wicked. [4] Because I will cut off from you both righteous and wicked, therefore my sword shall be drawn from its sheath against all flesh from south to north. [5] And all flesh shall know that I am the LORD. I have drawn my sword from its sheath; it shall not be sheathed again.

[6] "As for you, son of man, groan; with breaking heart and bitter grief, groan before their eyes. [7] And when they say to you, 'Why do you groan?' you shall say, 'Because of the news that it is coming. Every heart will melt, and all hands will be feeble; every spirit will faint, and all knees will be weak as water. Behold, it is coming, and it will be fulfilled,'" declares the Lord GOD.

[8] And the word of the LORD came to me: [9] "Son of man, prophesy and say, Thus says the Lord, say:

"A sword, a sword is sharpened
    and also polished,
[10]   sharpened for slaughter,
        polished to flash like lightning!

(Or shall we rejoice? You have despised the rod, my son, with everything of wood.) [11] So the sword is given to be polished that it may be grasped in the hand. It is sharpened and polished to be given into the hand of the slayer. [12] Cry out and wail, son of man, for it is against my people. It is against all the princes of Israel. They are delivered over to the sword with my people. Strike therefore upon your thigh. [13] For it will not be a testing—what could it do if you despise the rod?"[6] declares the Lord GOD.

[14] "As for you, son of man, prophesy. Clap your hands and let the sword come down twice, yes, three times,[7] the sword for those to be slain. It is the sword for the great slaughter, which surrounds them, [15] that their hearts may melt, and many stumble. At all their gates I have given the glittering sword. Ah, it is made like lightning; it is taken up[9] for slaughter. [16] Cut sharply to the right; set yourself to the left, wherever your face is directed. [17] I also will clap my hands, and I will satisfy my fury; I the LORD have spoken."

[18] The word of the LORD came to me again: [19] "As for you, son of man, mark two ways for the sword of the king of Babylon to come. Both of them shall come from the same land. And make a signpost; make it at the head of the way to a city. [20] Mark a way for the sword to come to Rabbah of the Ammonites and to Judah, into Jerusalem the fortified. [21] For the king of Babylon stands at the parting of the way, at the head of the two ways, to use divination. He shakes the arrows; he consults the teraphim;[10] he looks at the liver. [22] Into his right hand comes the divination for Jerusalem, to set battering rams, to open the mouth with murder, to lift up the voice with shouting, to set battering rams against the gates, to cast up mounds, to build siege towers. [23] But to them it will seem like a false divination. They have sworn solemn oaths, but he brings their guilt to remembrance, that they may be taken.

---

[1] Ch 21:1 in Hebrew [2] Or *toward Teman* [3] Ch 21:6 in Hebrew [4] Some Hebrew manuscripts, compare Septuagint, Syriac *against their sanctuary* [5] Probable reading; Hebrew *The rod of my son despises everything of wood* [6] Or *For it is a testing; and what if even the rod despises? It shall not be!* [7] Hebrew *its third* [8] Hebrew *many stumbling blocks* [9] The meaning of the Hebrew word rendered *taken up* is uncertain [10] Or *household idols*

24 "Therefore thus says the Lord GOD: Because you have made your guilt to be remembered, in that your transgressions are uncovered, so that in all your deeds your sins appear—because you have come to remembrance, you shall be taken in hand. 25 And you, O profane[1] wicked one, prince of Israel, whose day has come, the time of your final punishment, 26 thus says the Lord GOD: Remove the turban and take off the crown. Things shall not remain as they are. Exalt that which is low, and bring low that which is exalted. 27 A ruin, ruin, ruin I will make it. This also shall not be, until he comes, the one to whom judgment belongs, and I will give it to him.

28 "And you, son of man, prophesy, and say, Thus says the Lord GOD concerning the Ammonites and concerning their reproach; say, A sword, a sword is drawn for the slaughter. It is polished to consume and to flash like lightning— 29 while they see for you false visions, while they divine lies for you— to place you on the necks of the profane wicked, whose day has come, the time of their final punishment. 30 Return it to its sheath. In the place where you were created, in the land of your origin, I will judge you. 31 And I will pour out my indignation upon you; I will blow upon you with the fire of my wrath, and I will deliver you into the hands of brutish men, skillful to destroy. 32 You shall be fuel for the fire. Your blood shall be in the midst of the land. You shall be no more remembered, for I the LORD have spoken."

Israel's Shedding of Blood

22 And the word of the LORD came to me, saying, 2 "And you, son of man, will you judge, will you judge the bloody city? Then declare to her all her abominations. 3 You shall say, Thus says the Lord GOD: A city that sheds blood in her midst, so that her time may come, and that makes idols to defile herself! 4 You have become guilty by the blood that you have shed, and defiled by the idols that you have made, and you have brought your days near, and the appointed time of[2] your years has come. Therefore I have made you a reproach to the nations, and a mockery to all the countries. 5 Those who are near and those who

are far from you will mock you; your name is defiled; you are full of tumult.

6 "Behold, the princes of Israel in you, every one according to his power, have been bent on shedding blood. 7 Father and mother are treated with contempt in you; the sojourner suffers extortion in your midst; the fatherless and the widow are wronged in you. 8 You have despised my holy things and profaned my Sabbaths. 9 There are men in you who slander to shed blood, and people in you who eat on the mountains; they commit lewdness in your midst. 10 In you men uncover their fathers' nakedness; in you they violate women who are unclean in their menstrual impurity. 11 One commits abomination with his neighbor's wife; another lewdly defiles his daughter-in-law; another in you violates his sister, his father's daughter. 12 In you they take bribes to shed blood; you take interest and profit[3] and make gain of your neighbors by extortion; but me you have forgotten, declares the Lord GOD.

13 "Behold, I strike my hand at the dishonest gain that you have made, and at the blood that has been in your midst. 14 Can your courage endure, or can your hands be strong, in the days that I shall deal with you? I the LORD have spoken, and I will do it. 15 I will scatter you among the nations and disperse you through the countries, and I will consume your uncleanness out of you. 16 And you shall be profaned by your own doing in the sight of the nations, and you shall know that I am the LORD."

17 And the word of the LORD came to me: 18 "Son of man, the house of Israel has become dross to me; all of them are bronze and tin and iron and lead in the furnace; they are dross of silver. 19 Therefore thus says the Lord GOD: Because you have all become dross, therefore, behold, I will gather you into the midst of Jerusalem. 20 As one gathers silver and bronze and iron and lead and tin into a furnace, to blow the fire on it in order to melt it, so I will gather you in my anger and in my wrath, and I will put you in and melt you. 21 I will gather you and blow on you with the fire of my wrath, and you shall be melted in the midst of it. 22 As silver is melted in a furnace, so you shall be melted in the midst of it, and

[1] Or slain; also verse 29 [2] Some Hebrew manuscripts, Septuagint, Syriac, Vulgate, Targum; most Hebrew manuscripts until [3] That is, profit that comes from charging interest to the poor (compare Leviticus 25:36)

you shall know that I am the LORD; I have poured out my wrath upon you."

²³ And the word of the LORD came to me: ²⁴ "Son of man, say to her, You are a land that is not cleansed or rained upon in the day of indignation. ²⁵ The conspiracy of her prophets in her midst is like a roaring lion tearing the prey; they have devoured human lives; they have taken treasure and precious things; they have made many widows in her midst. ²⁶ Her priests have done violence to my law and have profaned my holy things. They have made no distinction between the holy and the common, neither have they taught the difference between the unclean and the clean, and they have disregarded my Sabbaths, so that I am profaned among them. ²⁷ Her princes in her midst are like wolves tearing the prey, shedding blood, destroying lives to get dishonest gain. ²⁸ And her prophets have smeared whitewash for them, seeing false visions and divining lies for them, saying, 'Thus says the Lord GOD,' when the LORD has not spoken. ²⁹ The people of the land have practiced extortion and committed robbery. They have oppressed the poor and needy, and have extorted from the sojourner without justice. ³⁰ And I sought for a man among them who should build up the wall and stand in the breach before me for the land, that I should not destroy it, but I found none. ³¹ Therefore I have poured out my indignation upon them. I have consumed them with the fire of my wrath. I have returned their way upon their heads, declares the Lord GOD."

Oholah and Oholibah

23 The word of the LORD came to me: ² "Son of man, there were two women, the daughters of one mother. ³ They played the whore in Egypt; they played the whore in their youth; there their breasts were pressed and their virgin bosoms[1] handled. ⁴ Oholah was the name of the elder and Oholibah the name of her sister. They became mine, and they bore sons and daughters. As for their names, Oholah is Samaria, and Oholibah is Jerusalem.

⁵ "Oholah played the whore while she was mine, and she lusted after her lovers the Assyrians, warriors ⁶ clothed in purple, governors and commanders, all of them desirable young men, horsemen riding on horses. ⁷ She bestowed her whoring upon them, the choicest men of Assyria all of them, and she defiled herself with all the idols of everyone after whom she lusted. ⁸ She did not give up her whoring that she had begun in Egypt; for in her youth men had lain with her and handled her virgin bosom and poured out their whoring lust upon her. ⁹ Therefore I delivered her into the hands of her lovers, into the hands of the Assyrians, after whom she lusted. ¹⁰ These uncovered her nakedness; they seized her sons and her daughters; and as for her, they killed her with the sword; and she became a byword among women when judgment had been executed on her.

¹¹ "Her sister Oholibah saw this, and she became more corrupt than her sister[2] in her lust and in her whoring, which was worse than that of her sister. ¹² She lusted after the Assyrians, governors and commanders, warriors clothed in full armor, horsemen riding on horses, all of them desirable young men. ¹³ And I saw that she was defiled; they both took the same way. ¹⁴ But she carried her whoring further. She saw men portrayed on the wall, the images of the Chaldeans portrayed in vermilion, ¹⁵ wearing belts on their waists, with flowing turbans on their heads, all of them having the appearance of officers, a likeness of Babylonians whose native land was Chaldea. ¹⁶ When she saw them, she lusted after them and sent messengers to them in Chaldea. ¹⁷ And the Babylonians came to her into the bed of love, and they defiled her with their whoring lust. And after she was defiled by them, she turned from them in disgust. ¹⁸ When she carried on her whoring so openly and flaunted her nakedness, I turned in disgust from her, as I had turned in disgust from her sister. ¹⁹ Yet she increased her whoring, remembering the days of her youth, when she played the whore in the land of Egypt ²⁰ and lusted after her lovers there, whose members were like those of donkeys, and whose issue was like that of horses. ²¹ Thus you longed for the lewdness of your youth, when the Egyptians handled your bosom and pressed[3] your young breasts."

²² Therefore, O Oholibah, thus says the Lord GOD: "Behold, I will stir up against you your lovers from whom you turned in disgust, and I will bring them against you

---

[1] Hebrew *nipples*; also verses 8, 21   [2] Hebrew *than she*   [3] Vulgate, Syriac; Hebrew *bosom for the sake of*

rom every side: ²³ the Babylonians and all he Chaldeans, Pekod and Shoa and Koa, and all the Assyrians with them, desirable oung men, governors and commanders all of them, officers and men of renown, all of them riding on horses. ²⁴ And they hall come against you from the north[1] with chariots and wagons and a host of peoples. They shall set themselves against ou on every side with buckler, shield, and helmet; and I will commit the judgment to hem, and they shall judge you according o their judgments. ²⁵ And I will direct my ealousy against you, that they may deal vith you in fury. They shall cut off your nose and your ears, and your survivors hall fall by the sword. They shall seize our sons and your daughters, and your urvivors shall be devoured by fire. ²⁶ They hall also strip you of your clothes and ake away your beautiful jewels. ²⁷ Thus will put an end to your lewdness and your vhoring begun in the land of Egypt, so that ou shall not lift up your eyes to them or emember Egypt anymore.

²⁸ "For thus says the Lord God: Behold, will deliver you into the hands of those vhom you hate, into the hands of those rom whom you turned in disgust, ²⁹ and hey shall deal with you in hatred and take away all the fruit of your labor and leave ou naked and bare, and the nakedness of your whoring shall be uncovered. Your ewdness and your whoring ³⁰ have brought his upon you, because you played the vhore with the nations and defiled yourself vith their idols. ³¹ You have gone the way of your sister; therefore I will give her cup nto your hand. ³² Thus says the Lord God:

"You shall drink your sister's cup
    that is deep and large;
  you shall be laughed at and held in
      derision,
    for it contains much;
³   you will be filled with drunkenness
      and sorrow.
  A cup of horror and desolation,
    the cup of your sister Samaria;
⁴   you shall drink it and drain it out,
      and gnaw its shards,
      and tear your breasts;

or I have spoken, declares the Lord God.
⁵ Therefore thus says the Lord God:

Because you have forgotten me and cast me behind your back, you yourself must bear the consequences of your lewdness and whoring."

³⁶ The Lord said to me: "Son of man, will you judge Oholah and Oholibah? Declare to them their abominations. ³⁷ For they have committed adultery, and blood is on their hands. With their idols they have committed adultery, and they have even offered up[2] to them for food the children whom they had borne to me. ³⁸ Moreover, this they have done to me: they have defiled my sanctuary on the same day and profaned my Sabbaths. ³⁹ For when they had slaughtered their children in sacrifice to their idols, on the same day they came into my sanctuary to profane it. And behold, this is what they did in my house. ⁴⁰ They even sent for men to come from afar, to whom a messenger was sent; and behold, they came. For them you bathed yourself, painted your eyes, and adorned yourself with ornaments. ⁴¹ You sat on a stately couch, with a table spread before it on which you had placed my incense and my oil. ⁴² The sound of a carefree multitude was with her; and with men of the common sort, drunkards[3] were brought from the wilderness; and they put bracelets on the hands of the women, and beautiful crowns on their heads.

⁴³ "Then I said of her who was worn out by adultery, Now they will continue to use her for a whore, even her![4] ⁴⁴ For they have gone in to her, as men go in to a prostitute. Thus they went in to Oholah and to Oholibah, lewd women! ⁴⁵ But righteous men shall pass judgment on them with the sentence of adulteresses, and with the sentence of women who shed blood, because they are adulteresses, and blood is on their hands."

⁴⁶ For thus says the Lord God: "Bring up a vast host against them, and make them an object of terror and a plunder. ⁴⁷ And the host shall stone them and cut them down with their swords. They shall kill their sons and their daughters, and burn up their houses. ⁴⁸ Thus will I put an end to lewdness in the land, that all women may take warning and not commit lewdness as you have done. ⁴⁹ And they shall return your lewdness upon you, and you shall bear the

Septuagint; the meaning of the Hebrew word is unknown ² Or *have even made pass through the fire* ³ Or *Sabeans* ⁴ The meaning of the Hebrew verse is uncertain penalty for your sinful idolatry, and you shall know that I am the Lord God."

The Siege of Jerusalem

24 In the ninth year, in the tenth month, on the tenth day of the month, the word of the Lord came to me: [2] "Son of man, write down the name of this day, this very day. The king of Babylon has laid siege to Jerusalem this very day. [3] And utter a parable to the rebellious house and say to them, Thus says the Lord God:

"Set on the pot, set it on;
    pour in water also;
[4] put in it the pieces of meat,
    all the good pieces, the thigh and the shoulder;
    fill it with choice bones.
[5] Take the choicest one of the flock;
    pile the logs[1] under it;
  boil it well;
    seethe also its bones in it.

[6] "Therefore thus says the Lord God: Woe to the bloody city, to the pot whose corrosion is in it, and whose corrosion has not gone out of it! Take out of it piece after piece, without making any choice.[2] [7] For the blood she has shed is in her midst; she put it on the bare rock; she did not pour it out on the ground to cover it with dust. [8] To rouse my wrath, to take vengeance, I have set on the bare rock the blood she has shed, that it may not be covered. [9] Therefore thus says the Lord God: Woe to the bloody city! I also will make the pile great. [10] Heap on the logs, kindle the fire, boil the meat well, mix in the spices,[3] and let the bones be burned up. [11] Then set it empty upon the coals, that it may become hot, and its copper may burn, that its uncleanness may be melted in it, its corrosion consumed. [12] She has wearied herself with toil;[4] its abundant corrosion does not go out of it. Into the fire with its corrosion! [13] On account of your unclean lewdness, because I would have cleansed you and you were not cleansed from your uncleanness, you shall not be cleansed anymore till I have satisfied my fury upon you. [14] I am the Lord. I have spoken; it shall come to pass; I will do it. I will not go back; I will not spare; I will not relent; according to your ways and your deeds you will be judged, declares the Lord God."

Ezekiel's Wife Dies

[15] The word of the Lord came to me[16] "Son of man, behold, I am about to take the delight of your eyes away from you a a stroke; yet you shall not mourn or weep nor shall your tears run down. [17] Sigh, bu not aloud; make no mourning for the dead Bind on your turban, and put your shoes on your feet; do not cover your lips, no eat the bread of men." [18] So I spoke to th people in the morning, and at evening m wife died. And on the next morning I did a I was commanded.

[19] And the people said to me, "Will yo not tell us what these things mean for us that you are acting thus?" [20] Then I sai to them, "The word of the Lord came t me: [21] 'Say to the house of Israel, Thus say the Lord God: Behold, I will profane m sanctuary, the pride of your power, th delight of your eyes, and the yearning o your soul, and your sons and your daugh ters whom you left behind shall fall by th sword. [22] And you shall do as I have done you shall not cover your lips, nor eat th bread of men. [23] Your turbans shall be o your heads and your shoes on your fee you shall not mourn or weep, but you sha rot away in your iniquities and groan t one another. [24] Thus shall Ezekiel be to yo a sign; according to all that he has done yo shall do. When this comes, then you wi know that I am the Lord God.'

[25] "As for you, son of man, surely on th day when I take from them their strong hold, their joy and glory, the delight of thei eyes and their soul's desire, and also thei sons and daughters, [26] on that day a fugitiv will come to you to report to you the new [27] On that day your mouth will be opened t the fugitive, and you shall speak and be n longer mute. So you will be a sign to then and they will know that I am the Lord."

Prophecy Against Ammon

25 The word of the Lord came to me [2] "Son of man, set your face towar the Ammonites and prophesy against them [3] Say to the Ammonites, Hear the word o the Lord God: Thus says the Lord Go Because you said, 'Aha!' over my sanctuar when it was profaned, and over the land o Israel when it was made desolate, and ove the house of Judah when they went int

---

[1] Compare verse 10; Hebrew *the bones* [2] Hebrew *no lot has fallen upon it* [3] Or *empty out the broth* [4] The meaning of the Hebrew is uncertain

xile, ⁴therefore behold, I am handing you
ver to the people of the East for a posses-
ion, and they shall set their encampments
mong you and make their dwellings in
our midst. They shall eat your fruit, and
hey shall drink your milk. ⁵I will make
.abbah a pasture for camels and Ammon¹
fold for flocks. Then you will know that
am the LORD. ⁶For thus says the Lord GOD:
ecause you have clapped your hands and
tamped your feet and rejoiced with all the
nalice within your soul against the land of
srael, ⁷therefore, behold, I have stretched
ut my hand against you, and will hand
ou over as plunder to the nations. And
will cut you off from the peoples and will
nake you perish out of the countries; I will
estroy you. Then you will know that I am
he LORD.

Prophecy Against Moab and Seir

⁸"Thus says the Lord GOD: Because Moab
nd Seir² said, 'Behold, the house of Judah
s like all the other nations,' ⁹therefore
will lay open the flank of Moab from the
ities, from its cities on its frontier, the
lory of the country, Beth-jeshimoth, Baal-
neon, and Kiriathaim. ¹⁰I will give it along
vith the Ammonites to the people of the
Cast as a possession, that the Ammonites
nay be remembered no more among the
ations, ¹¹and I will execute judgments
pon Moab. Then they will know that I am
he LORD.

Prophecy Against Edom

¹²"Thus says the Lord GOD: Because
:dom acted revengefully against the house
f Judah and has grievously offended in
aking vengeance on them, ¹³therefore thus
ays the Lord GOD, I will stretch out my
and against Edom and cut off from it man
nd beast. And I will make it desolate; from
eman even to Dedan they shall fall by the
word. ¹⁴And I will lay my vengeance upon
:dom by the hand of my people Israel,
nd they shall do in Edom according to
ny anger and according to my wrath, and
hey shall know my vengeance, declares
he Lord GOD.

Prophecy Against Philistia

¹⁵"Thus says the Lord GOD: Because the
*hilistines acted revengefully and took
engeance with malice of soul to destroy

in never-ending enmity, ¹⁶therefore thus
says the Lord GOD, Behold, I will stretch out
my hand against the Philistines, and I will
cut off the Cherethites and destroy the rest
of the seacoast. ¹⁷I will execute great vengeance on them with wrathful rebukes.
Then they will know that I am the LORD,
when I lay my vengeance upon them."

Prophecy Against Tyre

26 In the eleventh year, on the first
day of the month, the word of the
LORD came to me: ²"Son of man, because
Tyre said concerning Jerusalem, 'Aha, the
gate of the peoples is broken; it has swung
open to me. I shall be replenished, now that
she is laid waste,' ³therefore thus says the
Lord GOD: Behold, I am against you, O Tyre,
and will bring up many nations against
you, as the sea brings up its waves. ⁴They
shall destroy the walls of Tyre and break
down her towers, and I will scrape her soil
from her and make her a bare rock. ⁵She
shall be in the midst of the sea a place
for the spreading of nets, for I have spoken, declares the Lord GOD. And she shall
become plunder for the nations, ⁶and her
daughters on the mainland shall be killed
by the sword. Then they will know that
I am the LORD.

⁷"For thus says the Lord GOD: Behold,
I will bring against Tyre from the north
Nebuchadnezzar³ king of Babylon, king of
kings, with horses and chariots, and with
horsemen and a host of many soldiers. ⁸He
will kill with the sword your daughters
on the mainland. He will set up a siege
wall against you and throw up a mound
against you, and raise a roof of shields
against you. ⁹He will direct the shock of
his battering rams against your walls, and
with his axes he will break down your towers. ¹⁰His horses will be so many that their
dust will cover you. Your walls will shake at
the noise of the horsemen and wagons and
chariots, when he enters your gates as men
enter a city that has been breached. ¹¹With
the hoofs of his horses he will trample
all your streets. He will kill your people
with the sword, and your mighty pillars
will fall to the ground. ¹²They will plunder your riches and loot your merchandise. They will break down your walls and
destroy your pleasant houses. Your stones
and timber and soil they will cast into the

Hebrew *and the Ammonites* ²Septuagint lacks *and Seir* ³Hebrew *Nebuchadrezzar*; so throughout Ezekiel midst of the waters. [13]And I will stop the music of your songs, and the sound of your lyres shall be heard no more. [14]I will make you a bare rock. You shall be a place for the spreading of nets. You shall never be rebuilt, for I am the Lord; I have spoken, declares the Lord God.

[15]"Thus says the Lord God to Tyre: Will not the coastlands shake at the sound of your fall, when the wounded groan, when slaughter is made in your midst? [16]Then all the princes of the sea will step down from their thrones and remove their robes and strip off their embroidered garments. They will clothe themselves with trembling; they will sit on the ground and tremble every moment and be appalled at you. [17]And they will raise a lamentation over you and say to you,

"'How you have perished,
　　you who were inhabited from the
　　　　seas,
　　O city renowned,
　　　who was mighty on the sea;
　　she and her inhabitants imposed
　　　　their terror
　　　on all her inhabitants!
[18]　Now the coastlands tremble
　　　on the day of your fall,
　　and the coastlands that are on the
　　　　sea
　　　are dismayed at your passing.'

[19]"For thus says the Lord God: When I make you a city laid waste, like the cities that are not inhabited, when I bring up the deep over you, and the great waters cover you, [20]then I will make you go down with those who go down to the pit, to the people of old, and I will make you to dwell in the world below, among ruins from of old, with those who go down to the pit, so that you will not be inhabited; but I will set beauty in the land of the living. [21]I will bring you to a dreadful end, and you shall be no more. Though you be sought for, you will never be found again, declares the Lord God."

A Lament for Tyre

27 The word of the Lord came to me: [2]"Now you, son of man, raise a lamentation over Tyre, [3]and say to Tyre, who dwells at the entrances to the sea, merchant of the peoples to many coastlands, thus says the Lord God:

"O Tyre, you have said,
　　'I am perfect in beauty.'
[4]　Your borders are in the heart of the
　　　　seas;
　　　your builders made perfect your
　　　　beauty.
[5]　They made all your planks
　　　of fir trees from Senir;
　　they took a cedar from Lebanon
　　　to make a mast for you.
[6]　Of oaks of Bashan
　　　they made your oars;
　　they made your deck of pines
　　　from the coasts of Cyprus,
　　　inlaid with ivory.
[7]　Of fine embroidered linen from
　　　　Egypt
　　　was your sail,
　　　serving as your banner;
　　blue and purple from the coasts of
　　　　Elishah
　　　was your awning.
[8]　The inhabitants of Sidon and Arvad
　　　were your rowers;
　　your skilled men, O Tyre, were in
　　　　you;
　　　they were your pilots.
[9]　The elders of Gebal and her skilled
　　　　men were in you,
　　　caulking your seams;
　　all the ships of the sea with their
　　　　mariners were in you
　　　to barter for your wares.

[10]"Persia and Lud and Put were in your army as your men of war. They hung the shield and helmet in you; they gave you splendor. [11]Men of Arvad and Helech were on your walls all around, and men of Gamad were in your towers. They hung their shields on your walls all around; they made perfect your beauty.

[12]"Tarshish did business with you because of your great wealth of every kind; silver, iron, tin, and lead they exchanged for your wares. [13]Javan, Tubal, and Meshech traded with you; they exchanged human beings and vessels of bronze for your merchandise. [14]From Beth-togarmah they exchanged horses, war horses, and mules for your wares. [15]The men of Dedan[1] traded with you. Many coastlands were your own special markets; they brought you in payment ivory tusks and ebony. [16]Syria did business with you because of your abun

---

[1] Hebrew; Septuagint *Rhodes*

ant goods; they exchanged for your wares emeralds, purple, embroidered work, fine linen, coral, and ruby. **17** Judah and the land of Israel traded with you; they exchanged for your merchandise wheat of Minnith, meal,[1] honey, oil, and balm. **18** Damascus did business with you for your abundant goods, because of your great wealth of every kind; wine of Helbon and wool of Sahar **19** and casks of wine[2] from Uzal they exchanged for your wares; wrought iron, cassia, and calamus were bartered for your merchandise. **20** Dedan traded with you in saddlecloths for riding. **21** Arabia and all the princes of Kedar were your favored dealers in lambs, rams, and goats; in these they did business with you. **22** The traders of Sheba and Raamah traded with you; they exchanged for your wares the best of all kinds of spices and all precious stones and gold. **23** Haran, Canneh, Eden, traders of Sheba, Asshur, and Chilmad traded with you. **24** In your market these traded with you in choice garments, in clothes of blue and embroidered work, and in carpets of colored material, bound with cords and made secure. **25** The ships of Tarshish traveled for you with your merchandise. So you were filled and heavily laden in the heart of the seas.

26 "Your rowers have brought you out
 into the high seas.
 The east wind has wrecked you
  in the heart of the seas.
27 Your riches, your wares, your merchandise,
 your mariners and your pilots,
your caulkers, your dealers in merchandise,
  and all your men of war who are in
   you,
 with all your crew
  that is in your midst,
sink into the heart of the seas
 on the day of your fall.
28 At the sound of the cry of your pilots
 the countryside shakes,
29 and down from their ships
 come all who handle the oar.
The mariners and all the pilots of the
  sea
 stand on the land
30 and shout aloud over you
 and cry out bitterly.

They cast dust on their heads
 and wallow in ashes;
31 they make themselves bald for you
 and put sackcloth on their waist,
and they weep over you in bitterness
  of soul,
 with bitter mourning.
32 In their wailing they raise a lamentation for you
 and lament over you:
'Who is like Tyre,
 like one destroyed in the midst of
  the sea?
33 When your wares came from the
  seas,
 you satisfied many peoples;
with your abundant wealth and
  merchandise
 you enriched the kings of the
  earth.
34 Now you are wrecked by the seas,
 in the depths of the waters;
your merchandise and all your crew
  in your midst
 have sunk with you.
35 All the inhabitants of the coastlands
 are appalled at you,
and the hair of their kings bristles
  with horror;
 their faces are convulsed.
36 The merchants among the peoples
  hiss at you;
 you have come to a dreadful end
 and shall be no more forever.'"

Prophecy Against the Prince of Tyre

28 The word of the LORD came to me: **2** "Son of man, say to the prince of Tyre, Thus says the Lord GOD:

"Because your heart is proud,
 and you have said, 'I am a god,
I sit in the seat of the gods,
 in the heart of the seas,'
yet you are but a man, and no god,
 though you make your heart like
  the heart of a god—
3 you are indeed wiser than Daniel;
 no secret is hidden from you;
4 by your wisdom and your understanding
 you have made wealth for yourself,
and have gathered gold and silver
 into your treasuries;

[1] The meaning of the Hebrew word is unknown [2] Probable reading; Hebrew *wool of Sahar, Vedan, and Javan*

5 by your great wisdom in your trade
    you have increased your wealth,
    and your heart has become proud
    in your wealth—
6 therefore thus says the Lord GOD:
    Because you make your heart
    like the heart of a god,
7 therefore, behold, I will bring for-
    eigners upon you,
    the most ruthless of the nations;
    and they shall draw their swords
    against the beauty of your
    wisdom
    and defile your splendor.
8 They shall thrust you down into the
    pit,
    and you shall die the death of the
    slain
    in the heart of the seas.
9 Will you still say, 'I am a god,'
    in the presence of those who kill
    you,
    though you are but a man, and no
    god,
    in the hands of those who slay
    you?
10 You shall die the death of the uncir-
    cumcised
    by the hand of foreigners;
    for I have spoken, declares the
    Lord GOD."

A Lament over the King of Tyre

11 Moreover, the word of the LORD came
to me: 12 "Son of man, raise a lamentation
over the king of Tyre, and say to him, Thus
says the Lord GOD:

"You were the signet of perfection,[1]
    full of wisdom and perfect in
    beauty.
13 You were in Eden, the garden of
    God;
    every precious stone was your
    covering,
    sardius, topaz, and diamond,
    beryl, onyx, and jasper,
    sapphire,[2] emerald, and carbuncle;
    and crafted in gold were your set-
    tings
    and your engravings.[3]
On the day that you were created
    they were prepared.

14 You were an anointed guardian
    cherub.
    I placed you;[4] you were on the holy
    mountain of God;
    in the midst of the stones of fire
    you walked.
15 You were blameless in your ways
    from the day you were created,
    till unrighteousness was found in
    you.
16 In the abundance of your trade
    you were filled with violence in
    your midst, and you sinned;
    so I cast you as a profane thing from
    the mountain of God,
    and I destroyed you,[5] O guardian
    cherub,
    from the midst of the stones of fire
17 Your heart was proud because of
    your beauty;
    you corrupted your wisdom for
    the sake of your splendor.
    I cast you to the ground;
    I exposed you before kings,
    to feast their eyes on you.
18 By the multitude of your iniquities,
    in the unrighteousness of your
    trade
    you profaned your sanctuaries;
    so I brought fire out from your
    midst;
    it consumed you,
    and I turned you to ashes on the
    earth
    in the sight of all who saw you.
19 All who know you among the
    peoples
    are appalled at you;
    you have come to a dreadful end
    and shall be no more forever."

Prophecy Against Sidon

20 The word of the LORD came to me:
21 "Son of man, set your face toward Sidon,
and prophesy against her 22 and say, Thus
says the Lord GOD:

"Behold, I am against you, O Sidon,
    and I will manifest my glory in
    your midst.
And they shall know that I am the
    LORD
    when I execute judgments in her
    and manifest my holiness in her;

---

[1] The meaning of the Hebrew phrase is uncertain [2] Or lapis lazuli [3] The meaning of the Hebrew phrase is uncertain [4] The meaning of the Hebrew phrase is uncertain [5] Or banished you

³ for I will send pestilence into her,
  and blood into her streets;
and the slain shall fall in her midst,
  by the sword that is against her on
    every side.
Then they will know that I am the
  LORD.

²⁴ "And for the house of Israel there shall
be no more a brier to prick or a thorn to
hurt them among all their neighbors who
have treated them with contempt. Then
they will know that I am the Lord GOD.

Israel Gathered in Security

²⁵ "Thus says the Lord GOD: When
I gather the house of Israel from the peoples among whom they are scattered, and
manifest my holiness in them in the sight
of the nations, then they shall dwell in
their own land that I gave to my servant
Jacob. ²⁶ And they shall dwell securely in
it, and they shall build houses and plant
vineyards. They shall dwell securely, when

I execute judgments upon all their neighbors who have treated them with contempt. Then they will know that I am the
LORD their God."

Prophecy Against Egypt

29 In the tenth year, in the tenth month,
on the twelfth day of the month, the
word of the LORD came to me: ² "Son of
man, set your face against Pharaoh king
of Egypt, and prophesy against him and
against all Egypt; ³ speak, and say, Thus
says the Lord GOD:

"Behold, I am against you,
    Pharaoh king of Egypt,
  the great dragon that lies
    in the midst of his streams,
  that says, 'My Nile is my own;
    I made it for myself.'
⁴   I will put hooks in your jaws,
    and make the fish of your streams
      stick to your scales;

verses to read
Ezekiel 28:11–16

Know God

It is easy to look around and think that you are all alone, but don't be so sure. There
just might be angels watching you right now. Just because you can't see them
doesn't mean they're less real. Contrary to what some people might say, they aren't
the ghosts of people who have died and now serve as messengers of God. They
are angelic beings created to do God's work, and part of that work is watching
over his people (see Ps. 34:7). There is more to your life than meets the eye. God
promises to guard those who fear him with an invisible protection. Even though
sometimes your life might look like a lonely disaster, as a God Girl you've got to
remember that you are never alone—you have the Spirit of God inside you and
his angels beside you.

Loneliness is a lie that pulls you inside of yourself to find emptiness and despair.
When you look at your loneliness and resent it, or when you think you are too bad
to be loved, you sin by calling God a liar. His promises are too many to list here,
but his Word is clear that we are not alone. Millions like you walk this earth and
share the same struggles every day, and millions more watch you from heaven (see
1 Cor. 10:13; Gal. 6:2; Heb. 12:1). Best of all, in Jesus you have a divine friend who
will never leave you or forsake you (see Heb. 13:5).

When you start to feel bad about your life, stop and look for things in your life that
prove God is there. Look beyond the physical world and trust the truth of Scripture
when it points you to the invisible world that is all around you. Look especially at
the cross of Christ, where God's great love for you was proven.

and I will draw you up out of the
midst of your streams,
with all the fish of your streams
that stick to your scales.
5 And I will cast you out into the wilderness,
you and all the fish of your
streams;
you shall fall on the open field,
and not be brought together or
gathered.
To the beasts of the earth and to the
birds of the heavens
I give you as food.

[6] Then all the inhabitants of Egypt shall know that I am the Lord.

"Because you[1] have been a staff of reed to the house of Israel, [7] when they grasped you with the hand, you broke and tore all their shoulders; and when they leaned on you, you broke and made all their loins to shake.[2] [8] Therefore thus says the Lord God: Behold, I will bring a sword upon you, and will cut off from you man and beast, [9] and the land of Egypt shall be a desolation and a waste. Then they will know that I am the Lord.

"Because you[3] said, 'The Nile is mine, and I made it,' [10] therefore, behold, I am against you and against your streams, and I will make the land of Egypt an utter waste and desolation, from Migdol to Syene, as far as the border of Cush. [11] No foot of man shall pass through it, and no foot of beast shall pass through it; it shall be uninhabited forty years. [12] And I will make the land of Egypt a desolation in the midst of desolated countries, and her cities shall be a desolation forty years among cities that are laid waste. I will scatter the Egyptians among the nations, and disperse them through the countries.

[13] "For thus says the Lord God: At the end of forty years I will gather the Egyptians from the peoples among whom they were scattered, [14] and I will restore the fortunes of Egypt and bring them back to the land of Pathros, the land of their origin, and there they shall be a lowly kingdom. [15] It shall be the most lowly of the kingdoms, and never again exalt itself above the nations. And I will make them so small that they will never again rule over the nations. [16] And

it shall never again be the reliance of the house of Israel, recalling their iniquity when they turn to them for aid. Then they will know that I am the Lord God."

[17] In the twenty-seventh year, in the first month, on the first day of the month, the word of the Lord came to me: [18] "Son of man, Nebuchadnezzar king of Babylon made his army labor hard against Tyre. Every head was made bald, and every shoulder was rubbed bare, yet neither he nor his army got anything from Tyre to pay for the labor that he had performed against her. [19] Therefore thus says the Lord God: Behold, I will give the land of Egypt to Nebuchadnezzar king of Babylon; and he shall carry off its wealth[4] and despoil it and plunder it; and it shall be the wages for his army. [20] I have given him the land of Egypt as his payment for which he labored, because they worked for me, declares the Lord God.

[21] "On that day I will cause a horn to spring up for the house of Israel, and I will open your lips among them. Then they will know that I am the Lord."

A Lament for Egypt

30 The word of the Lord came to me: [2] "Son of man, prophesy, and say, Thus says the Lord God:

"Wail, 'Alas for the day!'
3   For the day is near,
the day of the Lord is near;
it will be a day of clouds,
a time of doom for[5] the nations.
4   A sword shall come upon Egypt,
and anguish shall be in Cush,
when the slain fall in Egypt,
and her wealth[6] is carried away,
and her foundations are torn
down.

[5] Cush, and Put, and Lud, and all Arabia, and Libya,[7] and the people of the land that is in league,[8] shall fall with them by the sword.

6   "Thus says the Lord:
Those who support Egypt shall fall,
and her proud might shall come
down;
from Migdol to Syene
they shall fall within her by the
sword,

---

[1] Hebrew *they* [2] Syriac (compare Psalm 69:23); Hebrew *to stand* [3] Hebrew *he* [4] Or *multitude* [5] Hebrew lacks *doom for* [6] Or *multitude*; also verse 10 [7] With Septuagint; Hebrew *Cub* [8] Hebrew *and the sons of the land of the covenant*

declares the Lord GOD.

7 And they shall be desolated in the
      midst of desolated countries,
      and their cities shall be in the midst
         of cities that are laid waste.

8 Then they will know that I am the
      LORD,
      when I have set fire to Egypt,
      and all her helpers are broken.

9 "On that day messengers shall go out
from me in ships to terrify the unsuspecting people of Cush, and anguish shall come
upon them on the day of Egypt's doom;[1] for,
behold, it comes!

10 "Thus says the Lord GOD:

   "I will put an end to the wealth of
      Egypt,
      by the hand of Nebuchadnezzar
         king of Babylon.
11 He and his people with him, the most
      ruthless of nations,
      shall be brought in to destroy the
         land,
   and they shall draw their swords
      against Egypt
   and fill the land with the slain.
12 And I will dry up the Nile
      and will sell the land into the hand
         of evildoers;
   I will bring desolation upon the land
      and everything in it,
      by the hand of foreigners;
   I am the LORD; I have spoken.

13 "Thus says the Lord GOD:

   "I will destroy the idols
      and put an end to the images in
         Memphis;
   there shall no longer be a prince
      from the land of Egypt;
      so I will put fear in the land of
         Egypt.
14 I will make Pathros a desolation
      and will set fire to Zoan
      and will execute judgments on
         Thebes.
15 And I will pour out my wrath on
      Pelusium,
      the stronghold of Egypt,
      and cut off the multitude[2] of
         Thebes.
16 And I will set fire to Egypt;
      Pelusium shall be in great agony;

   Thebes shall be breached,
      and Memphis shall face enemies[3]
         by day.
17 The young men of On and of Pi-beseth
      shall fall by the sword,
      and the women[4] shall go into cap-
         tivity.
18 At Tehaphnehes the day shall be
      dark,
      when I break there the yoke bars
         of Egypt,
   and her proud might shall come to
      an end in her;
      she shall be covered by a cloud,
      and her daughters shall go into
         captivity.
19 Thus I will execute judgments on
      Egypt.
      Then they will know that I am the
         LORD."

Egypt Shall Fall to Babylon

20 In the eleventh year, in the first month,
on the seventh day of the month, the word
of the LORD came to me: 21 "Son of man,
I have broken the arm of Pharaoh king of
Egypt, and behold, it has not been bound
up, to heal it by binding it with a bandage,
so that it may become strong to wield the
sword. 22 Therefore thus says the Lord GOD:
Behold, I am against Pharaoh king of Egypt
and will break his arms, both the strong
arm and the one that was broken, and I will
make the sword fall from his hand. 23 I will
scatter the Egyptians among the nations
and disperse them through the countries.
24 And I will strengthen the arms of the
king of Babylon and put my sword in his
hand, but I will break the arms of Pharaoh,
and he will groan before him like a man
mortally wounded. 25 I will strengthen the
arms of the king of Babylon, but the arms
of Pharaoh shall fall. Then they shall know
that I am the LORD, when I put my sword
into the hand of the king of Babylon and he
stretches it out against the land of Egypt.
26 And I will scatter the Egyptians among
the nations and disperse them throughout
the countries. Then they will know that
I am the LORD."

Pharaoh to Be Slain

31 In the eleventh year, in the third
month, on the first day of the month,
the word of the LORD came to me: 2 "Son of

[1] Hebrew *the day of Egypt* [2] Or *wealth* [3] Or *distress* [4] Or *the cities*; Hebrew *they*

man, say to Pharaoh king of Egypt and to
his multitude:

> "Whom are you like in your greatness?
> 3 Behold, Assyria was a cedar in
> Lebanon,
> with beautiful branches and forest
> shade,
> and of towering height,
> its top among the clouds.[1]
> 4 The waters nourished it;
> the deep made it grow tall,
> making its rivers flow
> around the place of its planting,
> sending forth its streams
> to all the trees of the field.
> 5 So it towered high
> above all the trees of the field;
> its boughs grew large
> and its branches long
> from abundant water in its shoots.
> 6 All the birds of the heavens
> made their nests in its boughs;
> under its branches all the beasts of
> the field
> gave birth to their young,
> and under its shadow
> lived all great nations.
> 7 It was beautiful in its greatness,
> in the length of its branches;
> for its roots went down
> to abundant waters.
> 8 The cedars in the garden of God
> could not rival it,
> nor the fir trees equal its boughs;
> neither were the plane trees
> like its branches;
> no tree in the garden of God
> was its equal in beauty.
> 9 I made it beautiful
> in the mass of its branches,
> and all the trees of Eden envied it,
> that were in the garden of God.

10 "Therefore thus says the Lord God:
Because it[2] towered high and set its top
among the clouds, and its heart was proud
of its height, 11 I will give it into the hand of
a mighty one of the nations. He shall surely
deal with it as its wickedness deserves.
I have cast it out. 12 Foreigners, the most
ruthless of nations, have cut it down and
left it. On the mountains and in all the valleys its branches have fallen, and its boughs
have been broken in all the ravines of the
land, and all the peoples of the earth have
gone away from its shadow and left it. 13 On
its fallen trunk dwell all the birds of the
heavens, and on its branches are all the
beasts of the field. 14 All this is in order
that no trees by the waters may grow to
towering height or set their tops among the
clouds, and that no trees that drink water
may reach up to them in height. For they
are all given over to death, to the world
below, among the children of man,[3] with
those who go down to the pit.

15 "Thus says the Lord God: On the day
the cedar[4] went down to Sheol I caused
mourning; I closed the deep over it, and
restrained its rivers, and many waters
were stopped. I clothed Lebanon in gloom
for it, and all the trees of the field fainted
because of it. 16 I made the nations quake
at the sound of its fall, when I cast it down
to Sheol with those who go down to the pit.
And all the trees of Eden, the choice and
best of Lebanon, all that drink water, were
comforted in the world below. 17 They also
went down to Sheol with it, to those who
are slain by the sword; yes, those who were
its arm, who lived under its shadow among
the nations.

18 "Whom are you thus like in glory and
in greatness among the trees of Eden?
You shall be brought down with the trees
of Eden to the world below. You shall lie
among the uncircumcised, with those who
are slain by the sword.

"This is Pharaoh and all his multitude,
declares the Lord God."

A Lament over Pharaoh and Egypt

32 In the twelfth year, in the twelfth
month, on the first day of the month,
the word of the Lord came to me: 2 "Son
of man, raise a lamentation over Pharaoh
king of Egypt and say to him:

> "You consider yourself a lion of the
> nations,
> but you are like a dragon in the seas;
> you burst forth in your rivers,
> trouble the waters with your feet,
> and foul their rivers.
> 3 Thus says the Lord God:
> I will throw my net over you
> with a host of many peoples,
> and they will haul you up in my
> dragnet.

---

[1] Or *its top went through the thick boughs*; also verses 10, 14 [2] Syriac, Vulgate; Hebrew *you* [3] Or *of Adam* [4] Hebrew *it*

4 And I will cast you on the ground;
   on the open field I will fling you,
and will cause all the birds of the
   heavens to settle on you,
and I will gorge the beasts of the
   whole earth with you.
5 I will strew your flesh upon the
   mountains
and fill the valleys with your carcass.[1]
6 I will drench the land even to the
   mountains
   with your flowing blood,
and the ravines will be full of you.
7 When I blot you out, I will cover the
   heavens
   and make their stars dark;
I will cover the sun with a cloud,
   and the moon shall not give its
   light.
8 All the bright lights of heaven
   will I make dark over you,
   and put darkness on your land,
      declares the Lord God.

9 "I will trouble the hearts of many peoples, when I bring your destruction among the nations, into the countries that you have not known. 10 I will make many peoples appalled at you, and the hair of their kings shall bristle with horror because of you, when I brandish my sword before them. They shall tremble every moment, every one for his own life, on the day of your downfall.

11 "For thus says the Lord God: The sword of the king of Babylon shall come upon you. 12 I will cause your multitude to fall by the swords of mighty ones, all of them most ruthless of nations.

"They shall bring to ruin the pride of
   Egypt,
   and all its multitude[2] shall perish.
13 I will destroy all its beasts
   from beside many waters;
and no foot of man shall trouble
   them anymore,
   nor shall the hoofs of beasts
   trouble them.
14 Then I will make their waters clear,
   and cause their rivers to run like
   oil,
      declares the Lord God.

15 When I make the land of Egypt desolate,
and when the land is desolate of
   all that fills it,
when I strike down all who dwell in
   it,
   then they will know that I am the
   Lord.

16 This is a lamentation that shall be chanted; the daughters of the nations shall chant it; over Egypt, and over all her multitude, shall they chant it, declares the Lord God."

17 In the twelfth year, in the twelfth month,[3] on the fifteenth day of the month, the word of the Lord came to me: 18 "Son of man, wail over the multitude of Egypt, and send them down, her and the daughters of majestic nations, to the world below, to those who have gone down to the pit:

19   'Whom do you surpass in beauty?
    Go down and be laid to rest with
      the uncircumcised.'

20 They shall fall amid those who are slain by the sword. Egypt[4] is delivered to the sword; drag her away, and all her multitudes. 21 The mighty chiefs shall speak of them, with their helpers, out of the midst of Sheol: 'They have come down, they lie still, the uncircumcised, slain by the sword.'

22 "Assyria is there, and all her company, its graves all around it, all of them slain, fallen by the sword, 23 whose graves are set in the uttermost parts of the pit; and her company is all around her grave, all of them slain, fallen by the sword, who spread terror in the land of the living.

24 "Elam is there, and all her multitude around her grave; all of them slain, fallen by the sword, who went down uncircumcised into the world below, who spread their terror in the land of the living; and they bear their shame with those who go down to the pit. 25 They have made her a bed among the slain with all her multitude, her graves all around it, all of them uncircumcised, slain by the sword; for terror of them was spread in the land of the living, and they bear their shame with those who go down to the pit; they are placed among the slain.

26 "Meshech-Tubal is there, and all her multitude, her graves all around it, all of

Hebrew *your height* [2] Or *wealth* [3] Hebrew lacks *in the twelfth month* [4] Hebrew *She* them uncircumcised, slain by the sword; for they spread their terror in the land of the living. 27 And they do not lie with the mighty, the fallen from among the uncircumcised, who went down to Sheol with their weapons of war, whose swords were laid under their heads, and whose iniquities are upon their bones; for the terror of the mighty men was in the land of the living. 28 But as for you, you shall be broken and lie among the uncircumcised, with those who are slain by the sword.

29 "Edom is there, her kings and all her princes, who for all their might are laid with those who are killed by the sword; they lie with the uncircumcised, with those who go down to the pit.

30 "The princes of the north are there, all of them, and all the Sidonians, who have gone down in shame with the slain, for all the terror that they caused by their might; they lie uncircumcised with those who are slain by the sword, and bear their shame with those who go down to the pit.

31 "When Pharaoh sees them, he will be comforted for all his multitude, Pharaoh and all his army, slain by the sword, declares the Lord GOD. 32 For I spread terror in the land of the living; and he shall be laid to rest among the uncircumcised, with those who are slain by the sword, Pharaoh and all his multitude, declares the Lord GOD."

Ezekiel Is Israel's Watchman

33 The word of the LORD came to me: 2 "Son of man, speak to your people and say to them, If I bring the sword upon a land, and the people of the land take a man from among them, and make him their watchman, 3 and if he sees the sword coming upon the land and blows the trumpet and warns the people, 4 then if anyone who hears the sound of the trumpet does not take warning, and the sword comes and takes him away, his blood shall be upon his own head. 5 He heard the sound of the trumpet and did not take warning; his blood shall be upon himself. But if he had taken warning, he would have saved his life. 6 But if the watchman sees the sword coming and does not blow the trumpet, so that the people are not warned, and the sword comes and takes any one of them, that person is taken away in his iniquity,

but his blood I will require at the watchman's hand.

7 "So you, son of man, I have made a watchman for the house of Israel. Whenever you hear a word from my mouth, you shall give them warning from me. 8 If I say to the wicked, O wicked one, you shall surely die, and you do not speak to warn the wicked to turn from his way, that wicked person shall die in his iniquity, but his blood I will require at your hand. 9 But if you warn the wicked to turn from his way, and he does not turn from his way, that person shall die in his iniquity, but you will have delivered your soul.

Why Will You Die, Israel?

10 "And you, son of man, say to the house of Israel, Thus have you said: 'Surely our transgressions and our sins are upon us, and we rot away because of them. How then can we live?' 11 Say to them, As I live, declares the Lord GOD, I have no pleasure in the death of the wicked, but that the wicked turn from his way and live; turn back, turn back from your evil ways, for why will you die, O house of Israel?

12 "And you, son of man, say to your people, The righteousness of the righteous shall not deliver him when he transgresses, and as for the wickedness of the wicked, he shall not fall by it when he turns from his wickedness, and the righteous shall not be able to live by his righteousness[1] when he sins. 13 Though I say to the righteous that he shall surely live, yet if he trusts in his righteousness and does injustice, none of his righteous deeds shall be remembered, but in his injustice that he has done he shall die. 14 Again, though I say to the wicked, 'You shall surely die,' yet if he turns from his sin and does what is just and right, 15 if the wicked restores the pledge, gives back what he has taken by robbery, and walks in the statutes of life, not doing injustice, he shall surely live; he shall not die. 16 None of the sins that he has committed shall be remembered against him. He has done what is just and right; he shall surely live.

17 "Yet your people say, 'The way of the Lord is not just,' when it is their own way that is not just. 18 When the righteous turns from his righteousness and does injustice, he shall die for it. 19 And when the wicked turns from his wickedness and does what

---

[1] Hebrew *by it*

s just and right, he shall live by this. ²⁰Yet ou say, 'The way of the Lord is not just.' house of Israel, I will judge each of you according to his ways."

erusalem Struck Down

²¹In the twelfth year of our exile, in the enth month, on the fifth day of the month, fugitive from Jerusalem came to me and aid, "The city has been struck down." ²Now the hand of the LORD had been upon me the evening before the fugitive ame; and he had opened my mouth by the ime the man came to me in the morning, o my mouth was opened, and I was no onger mute.

²³The word of the LORD came to me: ⁴"Son of man, the inhabitants of these vaste places in the land of Israel keep aying, 'Abraham was only one man, yet te got possession of the land; but we re many; the land is surely given us to ossess.' ²⁵Therefore say to them, Thus ays the Lord GOD: You eat flesh with the lood and lift up your eyes to your idols nd shed blood; shall you then possess the and? ²⁶You rely on the sword, you commit bominations, and each of you defiles his teighbor's wife; shall you then possess the and? ²⁷Say this to them, Thus says the ord GOD: As I live, surely those who are n the waste places shall fall by the sword, nd whoever is in the open field I will give o the beasts to be devoured, and those vho are in strongholds and in caves shall lie by pestilence. ²⁸And I will make the and a desolation and a waste, and her roud might shall come to an end, and the nountains of Israel shall be so desolate hat none will pass through. ²⁹Then they vill know that I am the LORD, when I have nade the land a desolation and a waste because of all their abominations that they ave committed.

³⁰"As for you, son of man, your people vho talk together about you by the walls nd at the doors of the houses, say to one nother, each to his brother, 'Come, and tear what the word is that comes from the ORD.' ³¹And they come to you as people :ome, and they sit before you as my peo-le, and they hear what you say but they vill not do it; for with lustful talk in their nouths they act; their heart is set on their ;ain. ³²And behold, you are to them like

one who sings lustful songs with a beauti-ful voice and plays¹ well on an instrument, for they hear what you say, but they will not do it. ³³When this comes—and come it will!—then they will know that a prophet has been among them."

Prophecy Against the Shepherds of Israel

34 The word of the LORD came to me: ²"Son of man, prophesy against the shepherds of Israel; prophesy, and say to them, even to the shepherds, Thus says the Lord GOD: Ah, shepherds of Israel who have been feeding yourselves! Should not shepherds feed the sheep? ³You eat the fat, you clothe yourselves with the wool, you slaughter the fat ones, but you do not feed the sheep. ⁴The weak you have not strengthened, the sick you have not healed, the injured you have not bound up, the strayed you have not brought back, the lost you have not sought, and with force and harshness you have ruled them. ⁵So they were scattered, because there was no shepherd, and they became food for all the wild beasts. ⁶My sheep were scattered; they wandered over all the mountains and on every high hill. My sheep were scattered over all the face of the earth, with none to search or seek for them.

⁷"Therefore, you shepherds, hear the word of the LORD: ⁸As I live, declares the Lord GOD, surely because my sheep have become a prey, and my sheep have become food for all the wild beasts, since there was no shepherd, and because my shepherds have not searched for my sheep, but the shepherds have fed themselves, and have not fed my sheep, ⁹therefore, you shep-herds, hear the word of the LORD: ¹⁰Thus says the Lord GOD, Behold, I am against the shepherds, and I will require my sheep at their hand and put a stop to their feeding the sheep. No longer shall the shepherds feed themselves. I will rescue my sheep from their mouths, that they may not be food for them.

The Lord GOD Will Seek Them Out

¹¹"For thus says the Lord GOD: Behold, I, I myself will search for my sheep and will seek them out. ¹²As a shepherd seeks out his flock when he is among his sheep that have been scattered, so will I seek out my sheep, and I will rescue them from all

¹ Hebrew *like the singing of lustful songs with a beautiful voice and one who plays*

places where they have been scattered on a day of clouds and thick darkness. [13] And I will bring them out from the peoples and gather them from the countries, and will bring them into their own land. And I will feed them on the mountains of Israel, by the ravines, and in all the inhabited places of the country. [14] I will feed them with good pasture, and on the mountain heights of Israel shall be their grazing land. There they shall lie down in good grazing land, and on rich pasture they shall feed on the mountains of Israel. [15] I myself will be the shepherd of my sheep, and I myself will make them lie down, declares the Lord GOD. [16] I will seek the lost, and I will bring back the strayed, and I will bind up the injured, and I will strengthen the weak, and the fat and the strong I will destroy.[1] I will feed them in justice.

[17] "As for you, my flock, thus says the Lord GOD: Behold, I judge between sheep and sheep, between rams and male goats. [18] Is it not enough for you to feed on the good pasture, that you must tread down with your feet the rest of your pasture; and to drink of clear water, that you must muddy the rest of the water with your feet? [19] And must my sheep eat what you have trodden with your feet, and drink what you have muddied with your feet?

[20] "Therefore, thus says the Lord GOD to them: Behold, I, I myself will judge between the fat sheep and the lean sheep. [21] Because you push with side and shoulder, and thrust at all the weak with your horns, till you have scattered them abroad, [22] I will rescue[2] my flock; they shall no longer be a prey. And I will judge between sheep and sheep. [23] And I will set up over them one shepherd, my servant David, and he shall feed them: he shall feed them and be their shepherd. [24] And I, the LORD, will be their God, and my servant David shall be prince among them. I am the LORD; I have spoken.

The LORD's Covenant of Peace

[25] "I will make with them a covenant of peace and banish wild beasts from the land, so that they may dwell securely in the wilderness and sleep in the woods. [26] And I will make them and the places all around my hill a blessing, and I will send down the showers in their season; they shall be showers of blessing. [27] And the trees of the field shall yield their fruit, and the eart shall yield its increase, and they shall b secure in their land. And they shall know that I am the LORD, when I break the bar of their yoke, and deliver them from th hand of those who enslaved them. [28] The shall no more be a prey to the nations, no shall the beasts of the land devour them They shall dwell securely, and none sha make them afraid. [29] And I will provide fo them renowned plantations so that the shall no more be consumed with hunger i the land, and no longer suffer the reproacl of the nations. [30] And they shall know tha I am the LORD their God with them, an that they, the house of Israel, are my peo ple, declares the Lord GOD. [31] And you ar my sheep, human sheep of my pasture and I am your God, declares the Lord GOD

Prophecy Against Mount Seir

35 The word of the LORD came to me [2] "Son of man, set your face agains Mount Seir, and prophesy against it, [3] an say to it, Thus says the Lord GOD: Beholc I am against you, Mount Seir, and I wil stretch out my hand against you, an I will make you a desolation and a waste [4] I will lay your cities waste, and you sha become a desolation, and you shall know that I am the LORD. [5] Because you cher ished perpetual enmity and gave over th people of Israel to the power of the swor at the time of their calamity, at the tim of their final punishment, [6] therefore, a I live, declares the Lord GOD, I will pre pare you for blood, and blood shall pursu you; because you did not hate bloodshed therefore blood shall pursue you. [7] I wil make Mount Seir a waste and a desola tion, and I will cut off from it all who com and go. [8] And I will fill its mountains wit the slain. On your hills and in your valley and in all your ravines those slain wit the sword shall fall. [9] I will make you perpetual desolation, and your cities shal not be inhabited. Then you will know tha I am the LORD.

[10] "Because you said, 'These two nation and these two countries shall be mine and we will take possession of them'— although the LORD was there— [11] therefore as I live, declares the Lord GOD, I will dea with you according to the anger and envy that you showed because of your hatrec

---

[1] Septuagint, Syriac, Vulgate *I will watch over* [2] Or *save*

against them. And I will make myself known among them, when I judge you. ²And you shall know that I am the LORD.

"I have heard all the revilings that you uttered against the mountains of Israel, saying, 'They are laid desolate; they are given us to devour.' ¹³And you magnified yourselves against me with your mouth, and multiplied your words against me; I heard it. ¹⁴Thus says the Lord GOD: While the whole earth rejoices, I will make you desolate. ¹⁵As you rejoiced over the inheritance of the house of Israel, because it was desolate, so I will deal with you; you shall be desolate, Mount Seir, and all Edom, all of it. Then they will know that I am the LORD.

Prophecy to the Mountains of Israel

36 "And you, son of man, prophesy to the mountains of Israel, and say, O mountains of Israel, hear the word of the LORD. ²Thus says the Lord GOD: Because the enemy said of you, 'Aha!' and, 'The ancient heights have become our possession,' ³therefore prophesy, and say, Thus says the Lord GOD: Precisely because they made you desolate and crushed you from all sides, so that you became the possession of the rest of the nations, and you became the talk and evil gossip of the people, ⁴therefore, O mountains of Israel, hear the word of the Lord GOD: Thus says the Lord GOD to the mountains and the hills, the ravines and the valleys, the desolate wastes and the deserted cities, which have become a prey and derision to the rest of the nations all around, ⁵therefore thus says the Lord GOD: Surely I have spoken in my hot jealousy against the rest of the nations and against all Edom, who gave my land to themselves as a possession with wholehearted joy and utter contempt, that they might make its pasturelands a prey. Therefore prophesy concerning the land of Israel, and say to the mountains and hills, to the ravines and valleys, Thus says the Lord GOD: Behold, I have spoken in my jealous wrath, because you have suffered the reproach of the nations. ⁷Therefore thus says the Lord GOD: I swear that the nations that are all around you shall themselves suffer reproach.

⁸"But you, O mountains of Israel, shall shoot forth your branches and yield your fruit to my people Israel, for they will soon come home. ⁹For behold, I am for you, and I will turn to you, and you shall be tilled and sown. ¹⁰And I will multiply people on you, the whole house of Israel, all of it. The cities shall be inhabited and the waste places rebuilt. ¹¹And I will multiply on you man and beast, and they shall multiply and be fruitful. And I will cause you to be inhabited as in your former times, and will do more good to you than ever before. Then you will know that I am the LORD. ¹²I will let people walk on you, even my people Israel. And they shall possess you, and you shall be their inheritance, and you shall no longer bereave them of children. ¹³Thus says the Lord GOD: Because they say to you, 'You devour people, and you bereave your nation of children,' ¹⁴therefore you shall no longer devour people and no longer bereave your nation of children, declares the Lord GOD. ¹⁵And I will not let you hear anymore the reproach of the nations, and you shall no longer bear the disgrace of the peoples and no longer cause your nation to stumble, declares the Lord GOD."

The LORD's Concern for His Holy Name

¹⁶The word of the LORD came to me: ¹⁷"Son of man, when the house of Israel lived in their own land, they defiled it by their ways and their deeds. Their ways before me were like the uncleanness of a woman in her menstrual impurity. ¹⁸So I poured out my wrath upon them for the blood that they had shed in the land, for the idols with which they had defiled it. ¹⁹I scattered them among the nations, and they were dispersed through the countries. In accordance with their ways and their deeds I judged them. ²⁰But when they came to the nations, wherever they came, they profaned my holy name, in that people said of them, 'These are the people of the LORD, and yet they had to go out of his land.' ²¹But I had concern for my holy name, which the house of Israel had profaned among the nations to which they came.

I Will Put My Spirit Within You

²²"Therefore say to the house of Israel, Thus says the Lord GOD: It is not for your sake, O house of Israel, that I am about to act, but for the sake of my holy name, which you have profaned among the nations to which you came. ²³And I will vindicate the holiness of my great name, which has been profaned among the nations, and

which you have profaned among them. And the nations will know that I am the Lord, declares the Lord God, when through you I vindicate my holiness before their eyes. [24] I will take you from the nations and gather you from all the countries and bring you into your own land. [25] I will sprinkle clean water on you, and you shall be clean from all your uncleannesses, and from all your idols I will cleanse you. [26] And I will give you a new heart, and a new spirit I will put within you. And I will remove the heart of stone from your flesh and give you a heart of flesh. [27] And I will put my Spirit within you, and cause you to walk in my statutes and be careful to obey my rules.[1] [28] You shall dwell in the land that I gave to your fathers, and you shall be my people, and I will be your God. [29] And I will deliver you from all your uncleannesses. And I will summon the grain and make it abundant and lay no famine upon you. [30] I will make the fruit of the tree and the increase of the field abundant, that you may never again suffer the disgrace of famine among the nations. [31] Then you will remember your evil ways, and your deeds that were not good, and you will loathe yourselves for your iniquities and your abominations. [32] It is not for your sake that I will act, declares the Lord God; let that be known to you. Be ashamed and confounded for your ways, O house of Israel.

[33] "Thus says the Lord God: On the day that I cleanse you from all your iniquities, I will cause the cities to be inhabited, and the waste places shall be rebuilt. [34] And the land that was desolate shall be tilled, instead of being the desolation that it was in the sight of all who passed by. [35] And they will say, 'This land that was desolate has become like the garden of Eden, and the waste and desolate and ruined cities are now fortified and inhabited.' [36] Then the nations that are left all around you shall know that I am the Lord; I have rebuilt the ruined places and replanted that which was desolate. I am the Lord; I have spoken, and I will do it.

[37] "Thus says the Lord God: This also I will let the house of Israel ask me to do for them: to increase their people like a flock. [38] Like the flock for sacrifices,[2] like the flock at Jerusalem during her appointed feasts, so shall the waste cities be filled with flocks of people. Then they will know that I am the Lord."

The Valley of Dry Bones

37 The hand of the Lord was upon me and he brought me out in the Spirit of the Lord and set me down in the middle of the valley;[3] it was full of bones. [2] And he led me around among them, and behold, there were very many on the surface of the valley, and behold, they were very dry. [3] And he said to me, "Son of man, can these bones live?" And I answered, "O Lord God, you know." [4] Then he said to me, "Prophesy over these bones, and say to them, O dry bones, hear the word of the Lord. [5] Thus says the Lord God to these bones: Behold, I will cause breath[4] to enter you, and you shall live. [6] And I will lay sinews upon you, and will cause flesh to come upon you, and cover you with skin, and put breath in you, and you shall live, and you shall know that I am the Lord."

[7] So I prophesied as I was commanded. And as I prophesied, there was a sound, and behold, a rattling,[5] and the bones came together, bone to its bone. [8] And I looked, and behold, there were sinews on them, and flesh had come upon them, and skin had covered them. But there was no breath in them. [9] Then he said to me, "Prophesy to the breath; prophesy, son of man, and say to the breath, Thus says the Lord God: Come from the four winds, O breath, and breathe on these slain, that they may live." [10] So I prophesied as he commanded me, and the breath came into them, and they lived and stood on their feet, an exceedingly great army.

[11] Then he said to me, "Son of man, these bones are the whole house of Israel. Behold, they say, 'Our bones are dried up, and our hope is lost; we are indeed cut off.' [12] Therefore prophesy, and say to them, Thus says the Lord God: Behold, I will open your graves and raise you from your graves, O my people. And I will bring you into the land of Israel. [13] And you shall know that I am the Lord, when I open your graves, and raise you from your graves, O my people. [14] And I will put my Spirit within you, and you shall live, and I will place you in your own land. Then you shall

---

[1] Or *my just decrees* [2] Hebrew *flock of holy things* [3] Or *plain;* also verse 2 [4] Or *spirit;* also verses 6, 9, 10 [5] Or *an earthquake* (compare 3:12, 13)

know that I am the LORD; I have spoken, and I will do it, declares the LORD."

I Will Be Their God, They Shall Be My People

¹⁵ The word of the LORD came to me: ¹⁶ "Son of man, take a stick¹ and write on it, 'For Judah, and the people of Israel associated with him'; then take another stick and write on it, 'For Joseph (the stick of Ephraim) and all the house of Israel associated with him.' ¹⁷ And join them one to another into one stick, that they may become one in your hand. ¹⁸ And when your people say to you, 'Will you not tell us what you mean by these?' ¹⁹ say to them, Thus says the Lord GOD: Behold, I am about to take the stick of Joseph (that is in the hand of Ephraim) and the tribes of Israel associated with him. And I will join with it the stick of Judah,² and make them one stick, that they may be one in my hand. ²⁰ When the sticks on which you write are in your hand before their eyes, ²¹ then say to them, Thus says the Lord GOD: Behold, I will take the people of Israel from the nations among which they have gone, and will gather them from all around, and bring them to their own land. ²² And I will make them one nation in the land, on the mountains of Israel. And one king shall be king over them all, and they shall be no longer two nations, and no longer divided into two kingdoms. ²³ They shall not defile themselves anymore with their idols and their detestable things, or with any of their transgressions. But I will save them from all the backslidings³ in which they have

¹ Or *one piece of wood;* also verses 17, 19, 20   ² Hebrew *And I will place them on it, the stick of Judah*   ³ Many Hebrew manuscripts; other Hebrew manuscripts *dwellings*

Know God

verses to read
Ezekiel 37:21-23

God is a God of justice. That means he doesn't let evil or sin win. In the end, evil and sin require a price be paid, and that price is death. But God doesn't want you to die, so he made a way out for you. The way out is called the gospel—what God has done in the death and resurrection of his Son, Jesus, the benefits of which you receive with the empty hands of faith.

You might feel like you've done something so bad that you can't be forgiven even if you change your ways, but that's not true. People from the beginning of time have been sinning just as badly as you, and time and again God has proven that nothing is so bad that it can't be forgiven (nothing, that is, except completely rejecting him). Even the Israelites, who turned their back on the God of their ancestors and worshiped other gods, were taken back over and over again by the same God who will take you back. Of course, they did suffer the consequences of their sinful choices—disease, attack, slavery, and even exile—but still God was their God, and still he promised to take them back. Ultimately he sent his Son as a guilt offering so that no one would have to die but anyone could have eternal life, and that includes you.

Don't let your life slogan be that you're "just too bad to be forgiven" or "just too bad to be loved," because that's just not true. You are too loved to be forgotten and too prized to be given up on. But to be forgiven you've gotta confess and repent—a simple yet challenging task. So don't argue with God about your sinfulness; just agree with him and then accept his outstretched hand by saying, "Thank you." Today you are one step away from freedom. Take it now and get on with the better things God has waiting for you.

sinned, and will cleanse them; and they shall be my people, and I will be their God. **24** "My servant David shall be king over them, and they shall all have one shepherd. They shall walk in my rules and be careful to obey my statutes. **25** They shall dwell in the land that I gave to my servant Jacob, where your fathers lived. They and their children and their children's children shall dwell there forever, and David my servant shall be their prince forever. **26** I will make a covenant of peace with them. It shall be an everlasting covenant with them. And I will set them in their land[1] and multiply them, and will set my sanctuary in their midst forevermore. **27** My dwelling place shall be with them, and I will be their God, and they shall be my people. **28** Then the nations will know that I am the LORD who sanctifies Israel, when my sanctuary is in their midst forevermore."

Prophecy Against Gog

38 The word of the LORD came to me: **2** "Son of man, set your face toward Gog, of the land of Magog, the chief prince of Meshech[2] and Tubal, and prophesy against him **3** and say, Thus says the Lord GOD: Behold, I am against you, O Gog, chief prince of Meshech[3] and Tubal. **4** And I will turn you about and put hooks into your jaws, and I will bring you out, and all your army, horses and horsemen, all of them clothed in full armor, a great host, all of them with buckler and shield, wielding swords. **5** Persia, Cush, and Put are with them, all of them with shield and helmet; **6** Gomer and all his hordes; Beth-togarmah from the uttermost parts of the north with all his hordes—many peoples are with you.

7 "Be ready and keep ready, you and all your hosts that are assembled about you, and be a guard for them. **8** After many days you will be mustered. In the latter years you will go against the land that is restored from war, the land whose people were gathered from many peoples upon the mountains of Israel, which had been a continual waste. Its people were brought out from the peoples and now dwell securely, all of them. **9** You will advance, coming on like a storm. You will be like a cloud covering the land, you and all your hordes, and many peoples with you.

10 "Thus says the Lord GOD: On that day thoughts will come into your mind, and you will devise an evil scheme **11** and say, 'I will go up against the land of unwalled villages. I will fall upon the quiet people who dwell securely, all of them dwelling without walls, and having no bars or gates,' **12** to seize spoil and carry off plunder, to turn your hand against the waste places that are now inhabited, and the people who were gathered from the nations, who have acquired livestock and goods, who dwell at the center of the earth. **13** Sheba and Dedan and the merchants of Tarshish and all its leaders[4] will say to you, 'Have you come to seize spoil? Have you assembled your hosts to carry off plunder, to carry away silver and gold, to take away livestock and goods, to seize great spoil?'

14 "Therefore, son of man, prophesy, and say to Gog, Thus says the Lord GOD: On that day when my people Israel are dwelling securely, will you not know it? **15** You will come from your place out of the uttermost parts of the north, you and many peoples with you, all of them riding on horses, a great host, a mighty army. **16** You will come up against my people Israel, like a cloud covering the land. In the latter days I will bring you against my land, that the nations may know me, when through you, O Gog, I vindicate my holiness before their eyes.

17 "Thus says the Lord GOD: Are you he of whom I spoke in former days by my servants the prophets of Israel, who in those days prophesied for years that I would bring you against them? **18** But on that day, the day that Gog shall come against the land of Israel, declares the Lord GOD, my wrath will be roused in my anger. **19** For in my jealousy and in my blazing wrath I declare, On that day there shall be a great earthquake in the land of Israel. **20** The fish of the sea and the birds of the heavens and the beasts of the field and all creeping things that creep on the ground, and all the people who are on the face of the earth shall quake at my presence. And the mountains shall be thrown down, and the cliffs shall fall, and every wall shall tumble to the ground. **21** I will summon a sword against Gog[5] on all my mountains, declares the Lord GOD. Every man's sword will be against his brother. **22** With pestilence

[1] Hebrew lacks *in their land* [2] Or *Magog, the prince of Rosh, Meshech* [3] Or *Gog, prince of Rosh, Meshech* [4] Hebrew *young lions* [5] Hebrew *against him*

nd bloodshed I will enter into judgment ith him, and I will rain upon him and his ordes and the many peoples who are with im torrential rains and hailstones, fire and ulfur. ²³ So I will show my greatness and y holiness and make myself known in the yes of many nations. Then they will know at I am the LORD.

39 "And you, son of man, prophesy against Gog and say, Thus says the ord GOD: Behold, I am against you, O Gog, nief prince of Meshech[1] and Tubal. ² And will turn you about and drive you for- ard, and bring you up from the uttermost arts of the north, and lead you against e mountains of Israel. ³ Then I will strike our bow from your left hand, and will ake your arrows drop out of your right and. ⁴ You shall fall on the mountains of rael, you and all your hordes and the eoples who are with you. I will give you to irds of prey of every sort and to the beasts f the field to be devoured. ⁵ You shall fall in e open field, for I have spoken, declares e Lord GOD. ⁶ I will send fire on Magog nd on those who dwell securely in the oastlands, and they shall know that I am e LORD.

⁷ "And my holy name I will make known the midst of my people Israel, and I will ot let my holy name be profaned anymore. nd the nations shall know that I am the ORD, the Holy One in Israel. ⁸ Behold, it coming and it will be brought about, eclares the Lord GOD. That is the day of hich I have spoken.

⁹ "Then those who dwell in the cities of rael will go out and make fires of the eapons and burn them, shields and buck- rs, bow and arrows, clubs[2] and spears; nd they will make fires of them for seven ears, ¹⁰ so that they will not need to take ood out of the field or cut down any out f the forests, for they will make their fires f the weapons. They will seize the spoil of ose who despoiled them, and plunder ose who plundered them, declares the ord GOD.

¹¹ "On that day I will give to Gog a place r burial in Israel, the Valley of the ravelers, east of the sea. It will block the avelers, for there Gog and all his multi- ade will be buried. It will be called the alley of Hamon-gog.[3] ¹² For seven months e house of Israel will be burying them,

in order to cleanse the land. ¹³ All the peo- ple of the land will bury them, and it will bring them renown on the day that I show my glory, declares the Lord GOD. ¹⁴ They will set apart men to travel through the land regularly and bury those travelers remaining on the face of the land, so as to cleanse it. At[4] the end of seven months they will make their search. ¹⁵ And when these travel through the land and anyone sees a human bone, then he shall set up a sign by it, till the buriers have buried it in the Valley of Hamon-gog. ¹⁶ (Hamonah[5] is also the name of the city.) Thus shall they cleanse the land.

¹⁷ "As for you, son of man, thus says the Lord GOD: Speak to the birds of every sort and to all beasts of the field, 'Assemble and come, gather from all around to the sacrificial feast that I am preparing for you, a great sacrificial feast on the moun- tains of Israel, and you shall eat flesh and drink blood. ¹⁸ You shall eat the flesh of the mighty, and drink the blood of the princes of the earth—of rams, of lambs, and of he-goats, of bulls, all of them fat beasts of Bashan. ¹⁹ And you shall eat fat till you are filled, and drink blood till you are drunk, at the sacrificial feast that I am preparing for you. ²⁰ And you shall be filled at my table with horses and charioteers, with mighty men and all kinds of warriors,' declares the Lord GOD.

²¹ "And I will set my glory among the nations, and all the nations shall see my judgment that I have executed, and my hand that I have laid on them. ²² The house of Israel shall know that I am the LORD their God, from that day forward. ²³ And the nations shall know that the house of Israel went into captivity for their iniquity, because they dealt so treacherously with me that I hid my face from them and gave them into the hand of their adversaries, and they all fell by the sword. ²⁴ I dealt with them according to their uncleanness and their transgressions, and hid my face from them.

The LORD Will Restore Israel

²⁵ "Therefore thus says the Lord GOD: Now I will restore the fortunes of Jacob and have mercy on the whole house of Israel, and I will be jealous for my holy name. ²⁶ They shall forget their shame and all the

treachery they have practiced against me, when they dwell securely in their land with none to make them afraid, [27] when I have brought them back from the peoples and gathered them from their enemies' lands, and through them have vindicated my holiness in the sight of many nations. [28] Then they shall know that I am the LORD their God, because I sent them into exile among the nations and then assembled them into their own land. I will leave none of them remaining among the nations anymore. [29] And I will not hide my face anymore from them, when I pour out my Spirit upon the house of Israel, declares the Lord GOD."

Vision of the New Temple

40 In the twenty-fifth year of our exile, at the beginning of the year, on the tenth day of the month, in the fourteenth year after the city was struck down, on that very day, the hand of the LORD was upon me, and he brought me to the city.[1] [2] In visions of God he brought me to the land of Israel, and set me down on a very high mountain, on which was a structure like a city to the south. [3] When he brought me there, behold, there was a man whose appearance was like bronze, with a linen cord and a measuring reed in his hand. And he was standing in the gateway. [4] And the man said to me, "Son of man, look with your eyes, and hear with your ears, and set your heart upon all that I shall show you, for you were brought here in order that I might show it to you. Declare all that you see to the house of Israel."

The East Gate to the Outer Court

[5] And behold, there was a wall all around the outside of the temple area, and the length of the measuring reed in the man's hand was six long cubits, each being a cubit and a handbreadth[2] in length. So he measured the thickness of the wall, one reed; and the height, one reed. [6] Then he went into the gateway facing east, going up its steps, and measured the threshold of the gate, one reed deep.[3] [7] And the side rooms, one reed long and one reed broad; and the space between the side rooms, five cubits; and the threshold of the gate by the vestibule of the gate at the inner end, one

reed. [8] Then he measured the vestibule of the gateway, on the inside, one reed. [9] Then he measured the vestibule of the gateway, eight cubits; and its jambs, two cubits; and the vestibule of the gate was at the inner end. [10] And there were three side rooms on either side of the east gate. The three were of the same size, and the jambs on either side were of the same size. [11] Then he measured the width of the opening of the gateway, ten cubits; and the length of the gateway, thirteen cubits. [12] There was a barrier before the side rooms, one cubit on either side. And the side rooms were six cubits on either side. [13] Then he measured the gate from the ceiling of the one side room to the ceiling of the other, a breadth of twenty-five cubits; the openings faced each other. [14] He measured also the vestibule, twenty cubits. And around the vestibule of the gateway was the court.[4] [15] From the front of the gate at the entrance to the front of the inner vestibule of the gate was fifty cubits. [16] And the gateway had windows all around, narrowing inward toward the side rooms and toward their jambs, and likewise the vestibule had windows all around inside, and on the jambs were palm trees.

The Outer Court

[17] Then he brought me into the outer court. And behold, there were chambers and a pavement, all around the court. Thirty chambers faced the pavement. [18] And the pavement ran along the side of the gates, corresponding to the length of the gates. This was the lower pavement. [19] Then he measured the distance from the inner front of the lower gate to the outer front of the inner court,[5] a hundred cubits on the east side and on the north side.[6]

The North Gate

[20] As for the gate that faced toward the north, belonging to the outer court, he measured its length and its breadth. [21] Its side rooms, three on either side, and its jambs and its vestibule were of the same size as those of the first gate. Its length was fifty cubits, and its breadth twenty-five cubits. [22] And its windows, its vestibule, and its palm trees were of the same size as those

---

[1] Hebrew *brought me there* [2] A *cubit* was about 18 inches or 45 centimeters; a *handbreadth* was about 3 inches or 7.5 centimeters [3] Hebrew *deep, and one threshold, one reed deep* [4] Text uncertain; Hebrew *And he made the jambs sixty cubits, and to the jamb of the court was the gateway all around* [5] Hebrew *distance from before the low gate before the inner court to the outside* [6] Or *cubits. So far the eastern gate; now to the northern gate.*

of the gate that faced toward the east. And by seven steps people would go up to it, and find its vestibule before them. ²³ And opposite the gate on the north, as on the east, was a gate to the inner court. And he measured from gate to gate, a hundred cubits.

The South Gate

²⁴ And he led me toward the south, and behold, there was a gate on the south. And he measured its jambs and its vestibule; they had the same size as the others. ²⁵ Both it and its vestibule had windows all around, like the windows of the others. Its length was fifty cubits, and its breadth twenty-five cubits. ²⁶ And there were seven steps leading up to it, and its vestibule was before them, and it had palm trees on its jambs, one on either side. ²⁷ And there was a gate on the south of the inner court. And he measured from gate to gate toward the south, a hundred cubits.

The Inner Court

²⁸ Then he brought me to the inner court through the south gate, and he measured the south gate. It was of the same size as the others. ²⁹ Its side rooms, its jambs, and its vestibule were of the same size as the others, and both it and its vestibule had windows all around. Its length was fifty cubits, and its breadth twenty-five cubits. ³⁰ And there were vestibules all around, twenty-five cubits long and five cubits broad. ³¹ Its vestibule faced the outer court, and palm trees were on its jambs, and its stairway had eight steps.

³² Then he brought me to the inner court on the east side, and he measured the gate. It was of the same size as the others. ³³ Its side rooms, its jambs, and its vestibule were of the same size as the others, and both it and its vestibule had windows all around. Its length was fifty cubits, and its breadth twenty-five cubits. ³⁴ Its vestibule faced the outer court, and it had palm trees on its jambs, on either side, and its stairway had eight steps.

³⁵ Then he brought me to the north gate, and he measured it. It had the same size as the others. ³⁶ Its side rooms, its jambs, and its vestibule were of the same size as the others,[1] and it had windows all around.

Its length was fifty cubits, and its breadth twenty-five cubits. ³⁷ Its vestibule[2] faced the outer court, and it had palm trees on its jambs, on either side, and its stairway had eight steps.

³⁸ There was a chamber with its door in the vestibule of the gate,[3] where the burnt offering was to be washed. ³⁹ And in the vestibule of the gate were two tables on either side, on which the burnt offering and the sin offering and the guilt offering were to be slaughtered. ⁴⁰ And off to the side, on the outside as one goes up to the entrance of the north gate, were two tables; and off to the other side of the vestibule of the gate were two tables. ⁴¹ Four tables were on either side of the gate, eight tables, on which to slaughter. ⁴² And there were four tables of hewn stone for the burnt offering, a cubit and a half long, and a cubit and a half broad, and one cubit high, on which the instruments were to be laid with which the burnt offerings and the sacrifices were slaughtered. ⁴³ And hooks,[4] a handbreadth long, were fastened all around within. And on the tables the flesh of the offering was to be laid.

Chambers for the Priests

⁴⁴ On the outside of the inner gateway there were two chambers[5] in the inner court, one[6] at the side of the north gate facing south, the other at the side of the south[7] gate facing north. ⁴⁵ And he said to me, "This chamber that faces south is for the priests who have charge of the temple, ⁴⁶ and the chamber that faces north is for the priests who have charge of the altar. These are the sons of Zadok, who alone[8] among the sons of Levi may come near to the LORD to minister to him." ⁴⁷ And he measured the court, a hundred cubits long and a hundred cubits broad, a square. And the altar was in front of the temple.

The Vestibule of the Temple

⁴⁸ Then he brought me to the vestibule of the temple and measured the jambs of the vestibule, five cubits on either side. And the breadth of the gate was fourteen cubits, and the sidewalls of the gate[9] were three cubits on either side. ⁴⁹ The length of the vestibule was twenty cubits, and the

breadth twelve[1] cubits, and people would go up to it by ten steps.[2] And there were pillars beside the jambs, one on either side.

The Inner Temple

41 Then he brought me to the nave and measured the jambs. On each side six cubits[3] was the breadth of the jambs.[4] [2] And the breadth of the entrance was ten cubits, and the sidewalls of the entrance were five cubits on either side. And he measured the length of the nave,[5] forty cubits, and its breadth, twenty cubits. [3] Then he went into the inner room and measured the jambs of the entrance, two cubits; and the entrance, six cubits; and the sidewalls on either side[6] of the entrance, seven cubits. [4] And he measured the length of the room, twenty cubits, and its breadth, twenty cubits, across the nave. And he said to me, "This is the Most Holy Place."

[5] Then he measured the wall of the temple, six cubits thick, and the breadth of the side chambers, four cubits, all around the temple. [6] And the side chambers were in three stories, one over another, thirty in each story. There were offsets[7] all around the wall of the temple to serve as supports for the side chambers, so that they should not be supported by the wall of the temple. [7] And it became broader as it wound upward to the side chambers, because the temple was enclosed upward all around the temple. Thus the temple had a broad area upward, and so one went up from the lowest story to the top story through the middle story. [8] I saw also that the temple had a raised platform all around; the foundations of the side chambers measured a full reed of six long cubits. [9] The thickness of the outer wall of the side chambers was five cubits. The free space between the side chambers of the temple and the [10] other chambers was a breadth of twenty cubits all around the temple on every side. [11] And the doors of the side chambers opened on the free space, one door toward the north, and another door toward the south. And the breadth of the free space was five cubits all around.

[12] The building that was facing the separate yard on the west side was seventy cubits broad, and the wall of the building was five cubits thick all around, and its length ninety cubits.

[13] Then he measured the temple, a hundred cubits long; and the yard and the building with its walls, a hundred cubits long; [14] also the breadth of the east front of the temple and the yard, a hundred cubits.

[15] Then he measured the length of the building facing the yard that was at the back and its galleries[8] on either side, a hundred cubits.

The inside of the nave and the vestibules of the court, [16] the thresholds and the narrow windows and the galleries all around the three of them, opposite the threshold, were paneled with wood all around, from the floor up to the windows (now the windows were covered), [17] to the space above the door, even to the inner room, and on the outside. And on all the walls all around, inside and outside, was a measured pattern.[9] [18] It was carved of cherubim and palm trees, a palm tree between cherub and cherub. Every cherub had two faces: [19] a human face toward the palm tree on the one side, and the face of a young lion toward the palm tree on the other side. They were carved on the whole temple all around. [20] From the floor to above the door, cherubim and palm trees were carved; similarly the wall of the nave.

[21] The doorposts of the nave were squared, and in front of the Holy Place was something resembling [22] an altar of wood, three cubits high, two cubits long, and two cubits broad.[10] Its corners, its base,[11] and its walls were of wood. He said to me, "This is the table that is before the LORD." [23] The nave and the Holy Place had each a double door. [24] The double doors had two leaves apiece, two swinging leaves for each door. [25] And on the doors of the nave were carved cherubim and palm trees, such as were carved on the walls. And there was a canopy[12] of wood in front of the vestibule outside. [26] And there were narrow windows and palm trees on either side, on the sidewalls of the vestibule, the side chambers of the temple, and the canopies.

---

[1] Septuagint; Hebrew *eleven* [2] Septuagint; Hebrew *and by steps that would go up to it* [3] A *cubit* was about 18 inches or 45 centimeters [4] Compare Septuagint; Hebrew *tent* [5] Hebrew *its length* [6] Septuagint; Hebrew *and the breadth* [7] Septuagint, compare 1 Kings 6:6; the meaning of the Hebrew word is uncertain [8] The meaning of the Hebrew term is unknown; also verse 16 [9] Hebrew *were measurements* [10] Septuagint; Hebrew lacks *two cubits broad* [11] Septuagint; Hebrew *length* [12] The meaning of the Hebrew word is unknown; also verse 26

The Temple's Chambers

42 Then he led me out into the outer court, toward the north, and he brought me to the chambers that were opposite the separate yard and opposite the building on the north. ²The length of the building whose door faced north was a hundred cubits,[1] and the breadth fifty cubits. ³Facing the twenty cubits that belonged to the inner court, and facing the pavement that belonged to the outer court, was gallery[2] against gallery in three stories. ⁴And before the chambers was a passage inward, ten cubits wide and a hundred cubits long,[3] and their doors were on the north. ⁵Now the upper chambers were narrower, for the galleries took more away from them than from the lower and middle chambers of the building. ⁶For they were in three stories, and they had no pillars like the pillars of the courts. Thus the upper chambers were set back from the ground more than the lower and the middle ones. ⁷And there was a wall outside parallel to the chambers, toward the outer court, opposite the chambers, fifty cubits long. ⁸For the chambers on the outer court were fifty cubits long, while those opposite the nave[4] were a hundred cubits long. ⁹Below these chambers was an entrance on the east side, as one enters them from the outer court.

¹⁰In the thickness of the wall of the court, on the south[5] also, opposite the yard and opposite the building, there were chambers ¹¹with a passage in front of them. They were similar to the chambers on the north, of the same length and breadth, with the same exits[6] and arrangements and doors, ²as were the entrances of the chambers on the south. There was an entrance at the beginning of the passage, the passage before the corresponding wall on the east as one enters them.[7]

¹³Then he said to me, "The north chambers and the south chambers opposite the yard are the holy chambers, where the priests who approach the LORD shall eat the most holy offerings. There they shall put the most holy offerings—the grain offering, the sin offering, and the guilt offering—for the place is holy. ¹⁴When the priests enter the Holy Place, they shall not go out of it into the outer court without laying there the garments in which they minister, for these are holy. They shall put on other garments before they go near to that which is for the people."

¹⁵Now when he had finished measuring the interior of the temple area, he led me out by the gate that faced east, and measured the temple area all around. ¹⁶He measured the east side with the measuring reed, 500 cubits by the measuring reed all around. ¹⁷He measured the north side, 500 cubits by the measuring reed all around. ¹⁸He measured the south side, 500 cubits by the measuring reed. ¹⁹Then he turned to the west side and measured, 500 cubits by the measuring reed. ²⁰He measured it on the four sides. It had a wall around it, 500 cubits long and 500 cubits broad, to make a separation between the holy and the common.

The Glory of the LORD Fills the Temple

43 Then he led me to the gate, the gate facing east. ²And behold, the glory of the God of Israel was coming from the east. And the sound of his coming was like the sound of many waters, and the earth shone with his glory. ³And the vision I saw was just like the vision that I had seen when he[8] came to destroy the city, and just like the vision that I had seen by the Chebar canal. And I fell on my face. ⁴As the glory of the LORD entered the temple by the gate facing east, ⁵the Spirit lifted me up and brought me into the inner court; and behold, the glory of the LORD filled the temple.

⁶While the man was standing beside me, I heard one speaking to me out of the temple, ⁷and he said to me, "Son of man, this is the place of my throne and the place of the soles of my feet, where I will dwell in the midst of the people of Israel forever. And the house of Israel shall no more defile my holy name, neither they, nor their kings, by their whoring and by the dead bodies[9] of their kings at their high places,[10] ⁸by setting their threshold by my threshold and their doorposts beside my doorposts, with only a wall between me and them.

They have defiled my holy name by their abominations that they have committed, so I have consumed them in my anger. [9]Now let them put away their whoring and the dead bodies of their kings far from me, and I will dwell in their midst forever.

[10]"As for you, son of man, describe to the house of Israel the temple, that they may be ashamed of their iniquities; and they shall measure the plan. [11]And if they are ashamed of all that they have done, make known to them the design of the temple, its arrangement, its exits and its entrances, that is, its whole design; and make known to them as well all its statutes and its whole design and all its laws, and write it down in their sight, so that they may observe all its laws and all its statutes and carry them out. [12]This is the law of the temple: the whole territory on the top of the mountain all around shall be most holy. Behold, this is the law of the temple.

The Altar

[13]"These are the measurements of the altar by cubits (the cubit being a cubit and a handbreadth):[1] its base shall be one cubit high[2] and one cubit broad, with a rim of one span[3] around its edge. And this shall be the height of the altar: [14]from the base on the ground to the lower ledge, two cubits, with a breadth of one cubit; and from the smaller ledge to the larger ledge, four cubits, with a breadth of one cubit; [15]and the altar hearth, four cubits; and from the altar hearth projecting upward, four horns. [16]The altar hearth shall be square, twelve cubits long by twelve broad. [17]The ledge also shall be square, fourteen cubits long by fourteen broad, with a rim around it half a cubit broad, and its base one cubit all around. The steps of the altar shall face east."

[18]And he said to me, "Son of man, thus says the Lord GOD: These are the ordinances for the altar: On the day when it is erected for offering burnt offerings upon it and for throwing blood against it, [19]you shall give to the Levitical priests of the family of Zadok, who draw near to me to minister to me, declares the Lord GOD, a bull from the herd for a sin offering. [20]And you shall take some of its blood and put it on the four horns of the altar and on the four corners of the ledge and upon the rim all

around. Thus you shall purify the altar and make atonement for it. [21]You shall also take the bull of the sin offering, and it shall be burned in the appointed place belonging to the temple, outside the sacred area. [22]And on the second day you shall offer a male goat without blemish for a sin offering; and the altar shall be purified, as it was purified with the bull. [23]When you have finished purifying it, you shall offer a bull from the herd without blemish and a ram from the flock without blemish. [24]You shall present them before the LORD, and the priests shall sprinkle salt on them and offer them up as a burnt offering to the LORD. [25]For seven days you shall provide daily a male goat for a sin offering; also, a bull from the herd and a ram from the flock, without blemish, shall be provided. [26]Seven days shall they make atonement for the altar and cleanse it, and so consecrate it.[4] [27]And when they have completed these days, then from the eighth day onward the priests shall offer on the altar your burnt offerings and your peace offerings, and I will accept you, declares the Lord GOD."

The Gate for the Prince

44 Then he brought me back to the outer gate of the sanctuary, which faces east. And it was shut. [2]And the LORD said to me, "This gate shall remain shut; it shall not be opened, and no one shall enter by it, for the LORD, the God of Israel, has entered by it. Therefore it shall remain shut. [3]Only the prince may sit in it to eat bread before the LORD. He shall enter by way of the vestibule of the gate, and shall go out by the same way."

[4]Then he brought me by way of the north gate to the front of the temple, and I looked, and behold, the glory of the LORD filled the temple of the LORD. And I fell on my face. [5]And the LORD said to me, "Son of man, mark well, see with your eyes, and hear with your ears all that I shall tell you concerning all the statutes of the temple of the LORD and all its laws. And mark well the entrance to the temple and all the exits from the sanctuary. [6]And say to the rebellious house,[5] to the house of Israel, Thus says the Lord GOD: O house of Israel, enough of all your abominations, [7]in admitting foreigners, uncircumcised in heart and

[1]A *cubit* was about 18 inches or 45 centimeters; a *handbreadth* was about 3 inches or 7.5 centimeters [2]Or *its gutter shall be one cubit deep* [3]A *span* was about 9 inches or 22 centimeters [4]Hebrew *fill its hand* [5]Septuagint; Hebrew lacks *house*

flesh, to be in my sanctuary, profaning my temple, when you offer to me my food, the fat and the blood. You[1] have broken my covenant, in addition to all your abominations. And you have not kept charge of my holy things, but you have set others to keep my charge for you in my sanctuary.

9 "Thus says the Lord GOD: No foreigner, uncircumcised in heart and flesh, of all the foreigners who are among the people of Israel, shall enter my sanctuary. 10 But the Levites who went far from me, going astray from me after their idols when Israel went astray, shall bear their punishment.[2] 11 They shall be ministers in my sanctuary, having oversight at the gates of the temple and ministering in the temple. They shall slaughter the burnt offering and the sacrifice for the people, and they shall stand before the people, to minister to them. 12 Because they ministered to them before their idols and became a stumbling block of iniquity to the house of Israel, therefore I have sworn concerning them, declares the Lord GOD, and they shall bear their punishment. 13 They shall not come near to me, to serve me as priest, nor come near any of my holy things and the things that are most holy, but they shall bear their shame and the abominations that they have committed. 14 Yet I will appoint them to keep charge of the temple, to do all its service and all that is to be done in it.

Rules for Levitical Priests

15 "But the Levitical priests, the sons of Zadok, who kept the charge of my sanctuary when the people of Israel went astray from me, shall come near to me to minister to me. And they shall stand before me to offer me the fat and the blood, declares the Lord GOD. 16 They shall enter my sanctuary, and they shall approach my table, to minister to me, and they shall keep my charge. 17 When they enter the gates of the inner court, they shall wear linen garments. They shall have nothing of wool on them, while they minister at the gates of the inner court, and within. 18 They shall have linen turbans on their heads, and linen undergarments around their waists. They shall not bind themselves with anything that causes sweat. 19 And when they go out into the outer court to the people,

they shall put off the garments in which they have been ministering and lay them in the holy chambers. And they shall put on other garments, lest they transmit holiness to the people with their garments. 20 They shall not shave their heads or let their locks grow long; they shall surely trim the hair of their heads. 21 No priest shall drink wine when he enters the inner court. 22 They shall not marry a widow or a divorced woman, but only virgins of the offspring of the house of Israel, or a widow who is the widow of a priest. 23 They shall teach my people the difference between the holy and the common, and show them how to distinguish between the unclean and the clean. 24 In a dispute, they shall act as judges, and they shall judge it according to my judgments. They shall keep my laws and my statutes in all my appointed feasts, and they shall keep my Sabbaths holy. 25 They shall not defile themselves by going near to a dead person. However, for father or mother, for son or daughter, for brother or unmarried sister they may defile themselves. 26 After he[3] has become clean, they shall count seven days for him. 27 And on the day that he goes into the Holy Place, into the inner court, to minister in the Holy Place, he shall offer his sin offering, declares the Lord GOD.

28 "This shall be their inheritance: I am their inheritance: and you shall give them no possession in Israel; I am their possession. 29 They shall eat the grain offering, the sin offering, and the guilt offering, and every devoted thing in Israel shall be theirs. 30 And the first of all the firstfruits of all kinds, and every offering of all kinds from all your offerings, shall belong to the priests. You shall also give to the priests the first of your dough, that a blessing may rest on your house. 31 The priests shall not eat of anything, whether bird or beast, that has died of itself or is torn by wild animals.

The Holy District

45 "When you allot the land as an inheritance, you shall set apart for the LORD a portion of the land as a holy district, 25,000 cubits[4] long and 20,000[5] cubits broad. It shall be holy throughout its whole extent. 2 Of this a square plot of 500 by 500 cubits shall be for the sanctuary,

---

Septuagint, Syriac, Vulgate; Hebrew *They*   2 Or *iniquity*; also verse 12   3 That is, a priest   4 A *cubit* was about 18 inches or 45 centimeters   5 Septuagint; Hebrew *ten* with fifty cubits for an open space around it. [3] And from this measured district you shall measure off a section 25,000 cubits long and 10,000 broad, in which shall be the sanctuary, the Most Holy Place. [4] It shall be the holy portion of the land. It shall be for the priests, who minister in the sanctuary and approach the LORD to minister to him, and it shall be a place for their houses and a holy place for the sanctuary. [5] Another section, 25,000 cubits long and 10,000 cubits broad, shall be for the Levites who minister at the temple, as their possession for cities to live in.[1]

[6] "Alongside the portion set apart as the holy district you shall assign for the property of the city an area 5,000 cubits broad and 25,000 cubits long. It shall belong to the whole house of Israel.

The Portion for the Prince

[7] "And to the prince shall belong the land on both sides of the holy district and the property of the city, alongside the holy district and the property of the city, on the west and on the east, corresponding in length to one of the tribal portions, and extending from the western to the eastern boundary [8] of the land. It is to be his property in Israel. And my princes shall no more oppress my people, but they shall let the house of Israel have the land according to their tribes.

[9] "Thus says the Lord GOD: Enough, O princes of Israel! Put away violence and oppression, and execute justice and righteousness. Cease your evictions of my people, declares the Lord GOD.

[10] "You shall have just balances, a just ephah, and a just bath.[2] [11] The ephah and the bath shall be of the same measure, the bath containing one tenth of a homer;[3] and the ephah one tenth of a homer; the homer shall be the standard measure. [12] The shekel shall be twenty gerahs;[4] twenty shekels plus twenty-five shekels plus fifteen shekels shall be your mina.[5]

[13] "This is the offering that you shall make: one sixth of an ephah from each homer of wheat, and one sixth of an ephah from each homer of barley, [14] and as the fixed portion of oil, measured in baths, one tenth of a

bath from each cor[6] (the cor, like the homer, contains ten baths).[7] [15] And one sheep from every flock of two hundred, from the watering places of Israel for grain offering, burnt offering, and peace offerings, to make atonement for them, declares the Lord GOD. [16] All the people of the land shall be obliged to give this offering to the prince in Israel. [17] It shall be the prince's duty to furnish the burnt offerings, grain offerings, and drink offerings, at the feasts, the new moons, and the Sabbaths, all the appointed feasts of the house of Israel: he shall provide the sin offerings, grain offerings, burnt offerings, and peace offerings, to make atonement on behalf of the house of Israel.

[18] "Thus says the Lord GOD: In the first month, on the first day of the month, you shall take a bull from the herd without blemish, and purify the sanctuary. [19] The priest shall take some of the blood of the sin offering and put it on the doorposts of the temple, the four corners of the ledge of the altar, and the posts of the gate of the inner court. [20] You shall do the same on the seventh day of the month for anyone who has sinned through error or ignorance; so you shall make atonement for the temple.

[21] "In the first month, on the fourteenth day of the month, you shall celebrate the Feast of the Passover, and for seven days unleavened bread shall be eaten. [22] On that day the prince shall provide for himself and all the people of the land a young bull for a sin offering. [23] And on the seven days of the festival he shall provide as a burnt offering to the LORD seven young bulls and seven rams without blemish, on each of the seven days; and a male goat daily for a sin offering. [24] And he shall provide as a grain offering an ephah for each bull, an ephah for each ram, and a hin[8] of oil to each ephah. [25] In the seventh month, on the fifteenth day of the month and for the seven days of the feast, he shall make the same provision for sin offerings, burnt offerings, and grain offerings, and for the oil.

The Prince and the Feasts

46 "Thus says the Lord GOD: The gate of the inner court that faces east shall be shut on the six working days, but

---

[1] Septuagint; Hebrew *as their possession, twenty chambers* [2] An *ephah* was about 3/5 of a bushel or 22 liters; a *bath* was about 6 gallons or 22 liters [3] A *homer* was about 6 bushels or 220 liters [4] A *shekel* was about 2/5 ounce or 11 grams; a *gerah* was about 1/50 ounce or 0.6 gram [5] A *mina* was about 1 1/4 pounds or 0.6 kilogram [6] A *cor* was about 6 bushels or 220 liters [7] See Vulgate; Hebrew *(ten baths are a homer, for ten baths are a homer)* [8] A *hin* was about 4 quarts or 3.5 liters

on the Sabbath day it shall be opened, and on the day of the new moon it shall be opened. ²The prince shall enter by the vestibule of the gate from outside, and shall take his stand by the post of the gate. The priests shall offer his burnt offering and his peace offerings, and he shall worship at the threshold of the gate. Then he shall go out, but the gate shall not be shut until evening. ³The people of the land shall bow down at the entrance of that gate before the LORD on the Sabbaths and on the new moons. ⁴The burnt offering that the prince offers to the LORD on the Sabbath day shall be six lambs without blemish and a ram without blemish. ⁵And the grain offering with the ram shall be an ephah,¹ and the grain offering with the lambs shall be as much as he is able, together with a hin² of oil to each ephah. ⁶On the day of the new moon he shall offer a bull from the herd without blemish, and six lambs and a ram, which shall be without blemish. ⁷As a grain offering he shall provide an ephah with the bull and an ephah with the ram, and with the lambs as much as he is able, together with a hin of oil to each ephah. ⁸When the prince enters, he shall enter by the vestibule of the gate, and he shall go out by the same way.

⁹"When the people of the land come before the LORD at the appointed feasts, he who enters by the north gate to worship shall go out by the south gate, and he who enters by the south gate shall go out by the north gate: no one shall return by way of the gate by which he entered, but each shall go out straight ahead. ¹⁰When they enter, the prince shall enter with them, and when they go out, he shall go out.

¹¹"At the feasts and the appointed festivals, the grain offering with a young bull shall be an ephah, and with a ram an ephah, and with the lambs as much as one is able to give, together with a hin of oil to an ephah. ¹²When the prince provides a freewill offering, either a burnt offering or peace offerings as a freewill offering to the LORD, the gate facing east shall be opened for him. And he shall offer his burnt offering or his peace offerings as he does on the Sabbath day. Then he shall go out, and after he has gone out the gate shall be shut.

¹³"You shall provide a lamb a year old without blemish for a burnt offering to the LORD daily; morning by morning you shall provide it. ¹⁴And you shall provide a grain offering with it morning by morning, one sixth of an ephah, and one third of a hin of oil to moisten the flour, as a grain offering to the LORD. This is a perpetual statute. ¹⁵Thus the lamb and the meal offering and the oil shall be provided, morning by morning, for a regular burnt offering.

¹⁶"Thus says the Lord GOD: If the prince makes a gift to any of his sons as his inheritance, it shall belong to his sons. It is their property by inheritance. ¹⁷But if he makes a gift out of his inheritance to one of his servants, it shall be his to the year of liberty. Then it shall revert to the prince; surely it is his inheritance— it shall belong to his sons. ¹⁸The prince shall not take any of the inheritance of the people, thrusting them out of their property. He shall give his sons their inheritance out of his own property, so that none of my people shall be scattered from his property."

Boiling Places for Offerings

¹⁹Then he brought me through the entrance, which was at the side of the gate, to the north row of the holy chambers for the priests, and behold, a place was there at the extreme western end of them. ²⁰And he said to me, "This is the place where the priests shall boil the guilt offering and the sin offering, and where they shall bake the grain offering, in order not to bring them out into the outer court and so transmit holiness to the people."

²¹Then he brought me out to the outer court and led me around to the four corners of the court. And behold, in each corner of the court there was another court— ²²in the four corners of the court were small³ courts, forty cubits⁴ long and thirty broad; the four were of the same size. ²³On the inside, around each of the four courts was a row of masonry, with hearths made at the bottom of the rows all around. ²⁴Then he said to me, "These are the kitchens where those who minister at the temple shall boil the sacrifices of the people."

Water Flowing from the Temple

47 Then he brought me back to the door of the temple, and behold, water was issuing from below the threshold of the

---

¹An *ephah* was about 3/5 bushel or 22 liters ²A *hin* was about 4 quarts or 3.5 liters ³Septuagint, Syriac, Vulgate; the meaning of the Hebrew word is uncertain ⁴A *cubit* was about 18 inches or 45 centimeters

temple toward the east (for the temple faced east). The water was flowing down from below the south end of the threshold of the temple, south of the altar. ²Then he brought me out by way of the north gate and led me around on the outside to the outer gate that faces toward the east; and behold, the water was trickling out on the south side.

³Going on eastward with a measuring line in his hand, the man measured a thousand cubits,[1] and then led me through the water, and it was ankle-deep. ⁴Again he measured a thousand, and led me through the water, and it was knee-deep. Again he measured a thousand, and led me through the water, and it was waist-deep. ⁵Again he measured a thousand, and it was a river that I could not pass through, for the water had risen. It was deep enough to swim in, a river that could not be passed through. ⁶And he said to me, "Son of man, have you seen this?"

Then he led me back to the bank of the river. ⁷As I went back, I saw on the bank of the river very many trees on the one side and on the other. ⁸And he said to me, "This water flows toward the eastern region and goes down into the Arabah, and enters the sea;[2] when the water flows into the sea, the water will become fresh.[3] ⁹And wherever the river goes,[4] every living creature that swarms will live, and there will be very many fish. For this water goes there, that the waters of the sea[5] may become fresh; so everything will live where the river goes. ¹⁰Fishermen will stand beside the sea. From Engedi to Eneglaim it will be a place for the spreading of nets. Its fish will be of very many kinds, like the fish of the Great Sea.[6] ¹¹But its swamps and marshes will not become fresh; they are to be left for salt. ¹²And on the banks, on both sides of the river, there will grow all kinds of trees for food. Their leaves will not wither, nor their fruit fail, but they will bear fresh fruit every month, because the water for them flows from the sanctuary. Their fruit will be for food, and their leaves for healing."

Division of the Land

¹³Thus says the Lord GOD: "This is the boundary[7] by which you shall divide the land for inheritance among the twelve tribes of Israel. Joseph shall have two portions. ¹⁴And you shall divide equally what I swore to give to your fathers. This land shall fall to you as your inheritance.

¹⁵"This shall be the boundary of the land: On the north side, from the Great Sea by way of Hethlon to Lebo-hamath, and on to Zedad,[8] ¹⁶Berothah, Sibraim (which lies on the border between Damascus and Hamath), as far as Hazer-hatticon, which is on the border of Hauran. ¹⁷So the boundary shall run from the sea to Hazar-enan, which is on the northern border of Damascus, with the border of Hamath to the north.[9] This shall be the north side.[10]

¹⁸"On the east side, the boundary shall run between Hauran and Damascus; along the Jordan between Gilead and the land of Israel; to the eastern sea and as far as Tamar.[11] This shall be the east side.

¹⁹"On the south side, it shall run from Tamar as far as the waters of Meribah-kadesh, from there along the Brook of Egypt[12] to the Great Sea. This shall be the south side.

²⁰"On the west side, the Great Sea shall be the boundary to a point opposite Lebo-hamath. This shall be the west side.

²¹"So you shall divide this land among you according to the tribes of Israel. ²²You shall allot it as an inheritance for yourselves and for the sojourners who reside among you and have had children among you. They shall be to you as native-born children of Israel. With you they shall be allotted an inheritance among the tribes of Israel. ²³In whatever tribe the sojourner resides, there you shall assign him his inheritance, declares the Lord GOD.

48

"These are the names of the tribes: Beginning at the northern extreme, beside the way of Hethlon to Lebo-hamath, as far as Hazar-enan (which is on the northern border of Damascus over against Hamath), and[13] extending from the east side to the west,[14] Dan, one portion. ²Adjoining the territory of Dan, from the

---

[1] A *cubit* was about 18 inches or 45 centimeters [2] That is, the Dead Sea [3] Hebrew *will be healed*; also verses 9, 11 [4] Septuagint, Syriac, Vulgate, Targum; Hebrew *the two rivers go* [5] Hebrew lacks *the waters of the sea* [6] That is, the Mediterranean Sea; also verses 15, 19, 20 [7] Probable reading; Hebrew *The valley of the boundary* [8] Septuagint; Hebrew *the entrance of Zedad, Hamath* [9] The meaning of the Hebrew is uncertain [10] Probable reading; Hebrew *and as for the north side* [11] Compare Syriac; Hebrew *to the eastern sea you shall measure* [12] Hebrew lacks *of Egypt* [13] Probable reading; Hebrew *and they shall be his* [14] Septuagint (compare verses 2–8); Hebrew *the east side the west*

east side to the west, Asher, one portion. ³Adjoining the territory of Asher, from the east side to the west, Naphtali, one portion. ⁴Adjoining the territory of Naphtali, from the east side to the west, Manasseh, one portion. ⁵Adjoining the territory of Manasseh, from the east side to the west, Ephraim, one portion. ⁶Adjoining the territory of Ephraim, from the east side to the west, Reuben, one portion. ⁷Adjoining the territory of Reuben, from the east side to the west, Judah, one portion.

⁸"Adjoining the territory of Judah, from the east side to the west, shall be the portion which you shall set apart, 25,000 cubits[1] in breadth, and in length equal to one of the tribal portions, from the east side to the west, with the sanctuary in the midst of it. ⁹The portion that you shall set apart for the Lᴏʀᴅ shall be 25,000 cubits in length, and 20,000[2] in breadth. ¹⁰These shall be the allotments of the holy portion: the priests shall have an allotment measuring 25,000 cubits on the northern side, 10,000 cubits in breadth on the western side, 10,000 in breadth on the eastern side, and 25,000 in length on the southern side, with the sanctuary of the Lᴏʀᴅ in the midst of it. ¹¹This shall be for the consecrated priests, the sons of Zadok, who kept my charge, who did not go astray when the people of Israel went astray, as the Levites did. ¹²And it shall belong to them as a special portion from the holy portion of the land, a most holy place, adjoining the territory of the Levites. ¹³And alongside the territory of the priests, the Levites shall have an allotment 25,000 cubits in length and 10,000 in breadth. The whole length shall be 25,000 cubits and the breadth 20,000.[3] ¹⁴They shall not sell or exchange any of it. They shall not alienate this choice portion of the land, for it is holy to the Lᴏʀᴅ.

¹⁵"The remainder, 5,000 cubits in breadth and 25,000 in length, shall be for common use for the city, for dwellings and for open country. In the midst of it shall be the city, ¹⁶and these shall be its measurements: the north side 4,500 cubits, the south side 4,500, the east side 4,500, and the west side 4,500. ¹⁷And the city shall have open land: on the north 250 cubits, on the south 250, on the east 250, and on the west 250. ¹⁸The remainder of the length alongside the holy portion shall be 10,000 cubits to the east, and 10,000 to the west, and it shall be alongside the holy portion. Its produce shall be food for the workers of the city. ¹⁹And the workers of the city, from all the tribes of Israel, shall till it. ²⁰The whole portion that you shall set apart shall be 25,000 cubits square, that is, the holy portion together with the property of the city.

²¹"What remains on both sides of the holy portion and of the property of the city shall belong to the prince. Extending from the 25,000 cubits of the holy portion to the east border, and westward from the 25,000 cubits to the west border, parallel to the tribal portions, it shall belong to the prince. The holy portion with the sanctuary of the temple shall be in its midst. ²²It shall be separate from the property of the Levites and the property of the city, which are in the midst of that which belongs to the prince. The portion of the prince shall lie between the territory of Judah and the territory of Benjamin.

²³"As for the rest of the tribes: from the east side to the west, Benjamin, one portion. ²⁴Adjoining the territory of Benjamin, from the east side to the west, Simeon, one portion. ²⁵Adjoining the territory of Simeon, from the east side to the west, Issachar, one portion. ²⁶Adjoining the territory of Issachar, from the east side to the west, Zebulun, one portion. ²⁷Adjoining the territory of Zebulun, from the east side to the west, Gad, one portion. ²⁸And adjoining the territory of Gad to the south, the boundary shall run from Tamar to the waters of Meribah-kadesh, from there along the Brook of Egypt[4] to the Great Sea.[5] ²⁹This is the land that you shall allot as an inheritance among the tribes of Israel, and these are their portions, declares the Lord Gᴏᴅ.

The Gates of the City

³⁰"These shall be the exits of the city: On the north side, which is to be 4,500 cubits by measure, ³¹three gates, the gate of Reuben, the gate of Judah, and the gate of Levi, the gates of the city being named after the tribes of Israel. ³²On the east side, which is to be 4,500 cubits, three gates, the gate of Joseph, the gate of Benjamin,

---

[1] A *cubit* was about 18 inches or 45 centimeters [2] Compare 45:1; Hebrew *ten* [3] Septuagint; Hebrew *10,000* [4] Hebrew lacks *of Egypt* [5] That is, the Mediterranean Sea

and the gate of Dan. [33] On the south side, which is to be 4,500 cubits by measure, three gates, the gate of Simeon, the gate of Issachar, and the gate of Zebulun. [34] On the west side, which is to be 4,500 cubits, three gates,[1] the gate of Gad, the gate of Asher, and the gate of Naphtali. [35] The circumference of the city shall be 18,000 cubits. And the name of the city from that time on shall be, The LORD Is There."

[1] One Hebrew manuscript, Syriac (compare Septuagint); most Hebrew manuscripts *their gates three*

INTRODUCTION TO
Daniel

Author: Daniel
Time: Around 530 B.C.
Place: Babylon
Written to: The Israelites

The gist

When Daniel was just a kid, he was captured and dragged off to live in a foreign land as a slave. This book is about his life while living in Babylon: how he lived as a believer in a hostile land, how he was faithful to God no matter what the punishment, and how God protected him for his faithfulness. Daniel was a prophet, so he wrote to tell people about God's wrath and God's faithfulness. Daniel also prophesied about the future.

Things to look for

- How Daniel and his friends stayed faithful to God (see Daniel 1)
- Shadrach, Meshach, and Abednego in the fiery furnace (see Daniel 3)
- Daniel in the lions' den (see Daniel 6)

Keep Your Faith

> "If this be so, our God whom we serve is able to deliver us from the burning fiery furnace, and he will deliver us out of your hand, O king. But if not, be it known to you, O king, that we will not serve your gods or worship the golden image that you have set up."
>
> Daniel 3:17–18

When God shows you something, you can't let your common sense talk you out of it. Common sense is natural and faith is spiritual. When God's way totally contradicts your common sense, whom will you trust? For Daniel, it would have made more sense to join the crowd, but his faith said differently. If your common sense can't make sense of your faith, which wins out? It's easy in those great mountaintop moments to say, "I trust him and I'll do whatever he says," but what happens when you come down into the valley where it's all cold, dark, and damp, and everything you see argues against what you learned on the mountain?

When God shows something to you, it won't stay just an idea for long. Soon your vision will be tested, and to prove its truth you'll have to do what you know is right even when everything in you screams, "This doesn't make sense!" If you can hold on to what you heard God tell you and stay connected to him and his Word, your faith won't be just a good idea but a confident way of life.

When Daniel and his friends faced death, they refused to turn their backs on God and deny their faith. They knew who God was, and they would let nothing replace him or remove him from his throne in their lives. As you read the book of Daniel, notice the tests of faith the Israelites in Babylon faced, and see how God was with them every step of the way.

Is your faith being tested? Remember that this test will either prove God right or steal your faith. Jesus said, "Blessed is the one who is not offended by me" (Matt. 11:6). You have to trust God's faithfulness no matter what test you come up against. The tests aren't going to stop; they have to come in order to make your faith real. So keep fighting for the truth. Don't let your common sense or anybody else's sway you. Faith is a total trust in God that refuses to believe for a second that he will fail.

Must-Know Terms and Verses

✑ *The Abomination That Makes Desolate* ✑

Often called "the abomination of desolation," this is something done to the Jerusalem temple that will profane it, such as setting up altars to other gods in it or sacrificing unclean animals (see Dan. 11:31; 12:11; Matt. 24:15).

But Daniel resolved that he would not defile himself with the king's food, or with the wine that he drank. *Daniel 1:8*

So Daniel was taken up out of the den, and no kind of harm was found on him, because he had trusted in his God. *Daniel 6:23*

"I saw in the night visions,

    and behold, with the clouds of heaven
        there came one like a son of man,
    and he came to the Ancient of Days
        and was presented before him.
And to him was given dominion
        and glory and a kingdom,
that all peoples, nations, and languages
        should serve him;
his dominion is an everlasting dominion,
        which shall not pass away,
and his kingdom one
        that shall not be destroyed." *Daniel 7:13–14*

Daniel

Daniel Taken to Babylon

1 In the third year of the reign of Jehoiakim king of Judah, Nebuchadnezzar king of Babylon came to Jerusalem and besieged it. ²And the Lord gave Jehoiakim king of Judah into his hand, with some of the vessels of the house of God. And he brought them to the land of Shinar, to the house of his god, and placed the vessels in the treasury of his god. ³Then the king commanded Ashpenaz, his chief eunuch, to bring some of the people of Israel, both of the royal family[1] and of the nobility, ⁴youths without blemish, of good appearance and skillful in all wisdom, endowed with knowledge, understanding learning, and competent to stand in the king's palace, and to teach them the literature and language of the Chaldeans. ⁵The king assigned them a daily portion of the food that the king ate, and of the wine that he drank. They were to be educated for three years, and at the end of that time they were to stand before the king. ⁶Among these were Daniel, Hananiah, Mishael, and Azariah of the tribe of Judah. ⁷And the chief of the eunuchs gave them names: Daniel he called Belteshazzar, Hananiah he called Shadrach, Mishael he called Meshach, and Azariah he called Abednego.

Daniel's Faithfulness

⁸But Daniel resolved that he would not defile himself with the king's food, or with the wine that he drank. Therefore he asked the chief of the eunuchs to allow him not to defile himself. ⁹And God gave Daniel favor and compassion in the sight of the chief of the eunuchs, ¹⁰and the chief of the eunuchs said to Daniel, "I fear my lord the king, who assigned your food and your drink; for why should he see that you were in worse condition than the youths who are of your own age? So you would endanger my head with the king." ¹¹Then Daniel said to the steward whom the chief of the eunuchs had assigned over Daniel, Hananiah, Mishael, and Azariah, ¹²"Test your servants for ten days; let us be given vegetables to eat and water to drink. ¹³Then let our appearance and the appearance of the youths who eat the king's food be observed by you, and deal with your servants according to what you see." ¹⁴So he listened to them in this matter, and tested them for ten days. ¹⁵At the end of ten days it was seen that they were better in appearance and fatter in flesh than all the youths who ate the king's food. ¹⁶So the steward took away their food and the wine they were to drink, and gave them vegetables.

¹⁷As for these four youths, God gave them learning and skill in all literature and wisdom, and Daniel had understanding in all visions and dreams. ¹⁸At the end of the time, when the king had commanded that they should be brought in, the chief of the eunuchs brought them in before Nebuchadnezzar. ¹⁹And the king spoke with them, and among all of them none was found like Daniel, Hananiah, Mishael, and Azariah. Therefore they stood before the king. ²⁰And in every matter of wisdom and understanding about which the king inquired of them, he found them ten times better than all the magicians and enchanters that were in all his kingdom. ²¹And Daniel was there until the first year of King Cyrus.

Nebuchadnezzar's Dream

2 In the second year of the reign of Nebuchadnezzar, Nebuchadnezzar had dreams; his spirit was troubled, and his sleep left him. ²Then the king commanded that the magicians, the enchanters, the sorcerers, and the Chaldeans be summoned to tell the king his dreams. So they came in and stood before the king. ³And the king said to them, "I had a dream, and my spirit

---

[1] Hebrew *of the seed of the kingdom*

is troubled to know the dream." ⁴Then the Chaldeans said to the king in Aramaic,¹ "O king, live forever! Tell your servants the dream, and we will show the interpretation." ⁵The king answered and said to the Chaldeans, "The word from me is firm: if you do not make known to me the dream and its interpretation, you shall be torn limb from limb, and your houses shall be laid in ruins. ⁶But if you show the dream and its interpretation, you shall receive from me gifts and rewards and great honor. Therefore show me the dream and its interpretation." ⁷They answered a second time and said, "Let the king tell his servants the dream, and we will show its interpretation." ⁸The king answered and said, "I know with certainty that you are trying to gain time, because you see that the word from me is firm— ⁹if you do not make the dream known to me, there is but one sentence for you. You have agreed to speak lying and corrupt words before me till the times change. Therefore tell me the dream, and I shall know that you can show me its interpretation." ¹⁰The Chaldeans answered the king and said, "There is not a man on earth who can meet the king's demand, for no great and powerful king has asked such a thing of any magician or enchanter or Chaldean. ¹¹The thing that the king asks is difficult, and no one can show it to the king except the gods, whose dwelling is not with flesh."

¹²Because of this the king was angry and very furious, and commanded that all the wise men of Babylon be destroyed. ¹³So the decree went out, and the wise men were about to be killed; and they sought Daniel and his companions, to kill them. ¹⁴Then Daniel replied with prudence and discretion to Arioch, the captain of the king's guard, who had gone out to kill the wise men of Babylon. ¹⁵He declared² to Arioch, the king's captain, "Why is the decree of the king so urgent?" Then Arioch made the matter known to Daniel. ¹⁶And Daniel went in and requested the king to appoint him a time, that he might show the interpretation to the king.

God Reveals Nebuchadnezzar's Dream

¹⁷Then Daniel went to his house and made the matter known to Hananiah, Mishael, and Azariah, his companions,

¹⁸and told them to seek mercy from the God of heaven concerning this mystery, so that Daniel and his companions might not be destroyed with the rest of the wise men of Babylon. ¹⁹Then the mystery was revealed to Daniel in a vision of the night. Then Daniel blessed the God of heaven. ²⁰Daniel answered and said:

"Blessed be the name of God forever
    and ever,
  to whom belong wisdom and
    might.
²¹ He changes times and seasons;
  he removes kings and sets up
    kings;
he gives wisdom to the wise
  and knowledge to those who have
    understanding;
²² he reveals deep and hidden things;
  he knows what is in the darkness,
    and the light dwells with him.
²³ To you, O God of my fathers,
  I give thanks and praise,
for you have given me wisdom and
    might,
  and have now made known to me
    what we asked of you,
  for you have made known to us the
    king's matter."

²⁴Therefore Daniel went in to Arioch, whom the king had appointed to destroy the wise men of Babylon. He went and said thus to him: "Do not destroy the wise men of Babylon; bring me in before the king, and I will show the king the interpretation."

²⁵Then Arioch brought in Daniel before the king in haste and said thus to him: "I have found among the exiles from Judah a man who will make known to the king the interpretation." ²⁶The king declared to Daniel, whose name was Belteshazzar, "Are you able to make known to me the dream that I have seen and its interpretation?" ²⁷Daniel answered the king and said, "No wise men, enchanters, magicians, or astrologers can show to the king the mystery that the king has asked, ²⁸but there is a God in heaven who reveals mysteries, and he has made known to King Nebuchadnezzar what will be in the latter days. Your dream and the visions of your head as you lay in bed are these: ²⁹To you, O king, as you lay in bed came thoughts of what would be

¹The text from this point to the end of chapter 7 is in Aramaic ²Aramaic *answered and said*; also verse 26

after this, and he who reveals mysteries made known to you what is to be. [30] But as for me, this mystery has been revealed to me, not because of any wisdom that I have more than all the living, but in order that the interpretation may be made known to the king, and that you may know the thoughts of your mind.

Daniel Interprets the Dream

[31] "You saw, O king, and behold, a great image. This image, mighty and of exceeding brightness, stood before you, and its appearance was frightening. [32] The head of this image was of fine gold, its chest and arms of silver, its middle and thighs of bronze, [33] its legs of iron, its feet partly of iron and partly of clay. [34] As you looked, a stone was cut out by no human hand, and it struck the image on its feet of iron and clay, and broke them in pieces. [35] Then the iron, the clay, the bronze, the silver, and the gold, all together were broken in pieces, and became like the chaff of the summer threshing floors; and the wind carried them away, so that not a trace of them could be found. But the stone that struck the image became a great mountain and filled the whole earth.

[36] "This was the dream. Now we will tell the king its interpretation. [37] You, O king, the king of kings, to whom the God of heaven has given the kingdom, the power, and the might, and the glory, [38] and into whose hand he has given, wherever they dwell, the children of man, the beasts of the field, and the birds of the heavens, making you rule over them all—you are the head of gold. [39] Another kingdom inferior to you shall arise after you, and yet a third kingdom of bronze, which shall rule over all the earth. [40] And there shall be a fourth kingdom, strong as iron, because iron breaks to pieces and shatters all things. And like iron that crushes, it shall break and crush all these. [41] And as you saw the feet and toes, partly of potter's clay and partly of iron, it shall be a divided kingdom, but some of the firmness of iron shall be in it, just as you saw iron mixed with the soft clay. [42] And as the toes of the feet were partly iron and partly clay, so the kingdom shall be partly strong and partly brittle. [43] As you saw the iron mixed with soft clay, so they will mix with one another in marriage,[1]

but they will not hold together, just as iron does not mix with clay. [44] And in the days of those kings the God of heaven will set up a kingdom that shall never be destroyed, nor shall the kingdom be left to another people. It shall break in pieces all these kingdoms and bring them to an end, and it shall stand forever, [45] just as you saw that a stone was cut from a mountain by no human hand, and that it broke in pieces the iron, the bronze, the clay, the silver, and the gold. A great God has made known to the king what shall be after this. The dream is certain, and its interpretation sure."

Daniel Is Promoted

[46] Then King Nebuchadnezzar fell upon his face and paid homage to Daniel, and commanded that an offering and incense be offered up to him. [47] The king answered and said to Daniel, "Truly, your God is God of gods and Lord of kings, and a revealer of mysteries, for you have been able to reveal this mystery." [48] Then the king gave Daniel high honors and many great gifts, and made him ruler over the whole province of Babylon and chief prefect over all the wise men of Babylon. [49] Daniel made a request of the king, and he appointed Shadrach, Meshach, and Abednego over the affairs of the province of Babylon. But Daniel remained at the king's court.

Nebuchadnezzar's Golden Image

3 King Nebuchadnezzar made an image of gold, whose height was sixty cubits[2] and its breadth six cubits. He set it up on the plain of Dura, in the province of Babylon. [2] Then King Nebuchadnezzar sent to gather the satraps, the prefects, and the governors, the counselors, the treasurers, the justices, the magistrates, and all the officials of the provinces to come to the dedication of the image that King Nebuchadnezzar had set up. [3] Then the satraps, the prefects, and the governors, the counselors, the treasurers, the justices, the magistrates, and all the officials of the provinces gathered for the dedication of the image that King Nebuchadnezzar had set up. And they stood before the image that Nebuchadnezzar had set up. [4] And the herald proclaimed aloud, "You are commanded, O peoples, nations, and languages, [5] that when you hear the sound of

---

[1] Aramaic *by the seed of men* [2] A *cubit* was about 18 inches or 45 centimeters

the horn, pipe, lyre, trigon, harp, bagpipe, and every kind of music, you are to fall down and worship the golden image that King Nebuchadnezzar has set up. [6] And whoever does not fall down and worship shall immediately be cast into a burning fiery furnace." [7] Therefore, as soon as all the peoples heard the sound of the horn, pipe, lyre, trigon, harp, bagpipe, and every kind of music, all the peoples, nations, and languages fell down and worshiped the golden image that King Nebuchadnezzar had set up.

The Fiery Furnace

[8] Therefore at that time certain Chaldeans came forward and maliciously accused the Jews. [9] They declared[1] to King Nebuchadnezzar, "O king, live forever! [10] You, O king, have made a decree, that every man who hears the sound of the horn, pipe, lyre, trigon, harp, bagpipe, and every kind of music, shall fall down and worship the golden image. [11] And whoever does not fall down and worship shall be cast into a burning fiery furnace. [12] There are certain Jews whom you have appointed over the affairs of the province of Babylon: Shadrach, Meshach, and Abednego. These men, O king, pay no attention to you; they do not serve your gods or worship the golden image that you have set up."

[13] Then Nebuchadnezzar in furious rage commanded that Shadrach, Meshach, and Abednego be brought. So they brought these men before the king. [14] Nebuchadnezzar answered and said to them, "Is it true, O Shadrach, Meshach, and Abednego, that you do not serve my gods or worship the golden image that I have set up? [15] Now if you are ready when you hear the sound of the horn, pipe, lyre, trigon, harp, bagpipe, and every kind of music, to fall down and worship the image that I have made, well and good.[2] But if you do not worship, you shall immediately be cast into a burning fiery furnace. And who is the god who will deliver you out of my hands?"

[16] Shadrach, Meshach, and Abednego answered and said to the king, "O Nebuchadnezzar, we have no need to answer you in this matter. [17] If this be so, our God whom we serve is able to deliver us from the burning fiery furnace, and he will deliver us out of your hand, O king.[3] [18] But if not, be it known to you, O king, that we will not serve your gods or worship the golden image that you have set up."

Ask Yourself . . .

ABOUT YOUR FAITH

- If I knew that obeying God would mean my destruction, would I do it anyway?
- How does peer pressure affect my faith?
- Do I really believe that God can save me from anything I face?
- In what ways have I shown my lack of faith?
- How can I prove my faith in the future?

[19] Then Nebuchadnezzar was filled with fury, and the expression of his face was changed against Shadrach, Meshach, and Abednego. He ordered the furnace heated seven times more than it was usually heated. [20] And he ordered some of the mighty men of his army to bind Shadrach, Meshach, and Abednego, and to cast them into the burning fiery furnace. [21] Then these men were bound in their cloaks, their tunics,[4] their hats, and their other garments, and they were thrown into the burning fiery furnace. [22] Because the king's order was urgent and the furnace overheated, the flame of the fire killed those men who took up Shadrach, Meshach, and Abednego. [23] And these three men, Shadrach, Meshach, and Abednego, fell bound into the burning fiery furnace.

[24] Then King Nebuchadnezzar was astonished and rose up in haste. He declared to his counselors, "Did we not cast three men bound into the fire?" They answered and said to the king, "True, O king." [25] He

---

[1] Aramaic *answered and said*; also verses 24, 26 [2] Aramaic lacks *well and good* [3] Or *If our God whom we serve is able to deliver us, he will deliver us from the burning fiery furnace and out of your hand, O king.* [4] The meaning of the Aramaic words rendered *cloaks* and *tunics* is uncertain; also verse 27

answered and said, "But I see four men unbound, walking in the midst of the fire, and they are not hurt; and the appearance of the fourth is like a son of the gods."

²⁶ Then Nebuchadnezzar came near to the door of the burning fiery furnace; he declared, "Shadrach, Meshach, and Abednego, servants of the Most High God, come out, and come here!" Then Shadrach, Meshach, and Abednego came out from the fire. ²⁷ And the satraps, the prefects, the governors, and the king's counselors gathered together and saw that the fire had not had any power over the bodies of those men. The hair of their heads was not singed, their cloaks were not harmed, and no smell of fire had come upon them. ²⁸ Nebuchadnezzar answered and said, "Blessed be the God of Shadrach, Meshach, and Abednego, who has sent his angel and delivered his servants, who trusted in him, and set aside¹ the king's command, and yielded up their bodies rather than serve and worship any god except their own God. ²⁹ Therefore I make a decree: Any people, nation, or language that speaks anything against the God of Shadrach, Meshach, and Abednego shall be torn limb from limb, and their houses laid in ruins, for there is no other god who is able to rescue in this way." ³⁰ Then the king promoted Shadrach, Meshach, and Abednego in the province of Babylon.

Nebuchadnezzar Praises God

4 ² King Nebuchadnezzar to all peoples, nations, and languages, that dwell in all the earth: Peace be multiplied to you! ²It has seemed good to me to show the signs and wonders that the Most High God has done for me.

³   How great are his signs,
            how mighty his wonders!
      His kingdom is an everlasting king-
            dom,
            and his dominion endures from
                  generation to generation.

Nebuchadnezzar's Second Dream

⁴³ I, Nebuchadnezzar, was at ease in my house and prospering in my palace. ⁵I saw a dream that made me afraid. As I lay in bed the fancies and the visions of my head alarmed me. ⁶So I made a decree that all the wise men of Babylon should be brought before me, that they might make known to me the interpretation of the dream. ⁷ Then the magicians, the enchanters, the Chaldeans, and the astrologers came in, and I told them the dream, but they could not make known to me its interpretation. ⁸At last Daniel came in before me—he who was named Belteshazzar after the name of my god, and in whom is the spirit of the holy gods⁴—and I told him the dream, saying, ⁹"O Belteshazzar, chief of the magicians, because I know that the spirit of the holy gods is in you and that no mystery is too difficult for you, tell me the visions of my dream that I saw and their interpretation. ¹⁰The visions of my head as I lay in bed were these: I saw, and behold, a tree in the midst of the earth, and its height was great. ¹¹The tree grew and became strong, and its top reached to heaven, and it was visible to the end of the whole earth. ¹²Its leaves were beautiful and its fruit abundant, and in it was food for all. The beasts of the field found shade under it, and the birds of the heavens lived in its branches, and all flesh was fed from it.

¹³ "I saw in the visions of my head as I lay in bed, and behold, a watcher, a holy one, came down from heaven. ¹⁴He proclaimed aloud and said thus: 'Chop down the tree and lop off its branches, strip off its leaves and scatter its fruit. Let the beasts flee from under it and the birds from its branches. ¹⁵But leave the stump of its roots in the earth, bound with a band of iron and bronze, amid the tender grass of the field. Let him be wet with the dew of heaven. Let his portion be with the beasts in the grass of the earth. ¹⁶Let his mind be changed from a man's, and let a beast's mind be given to him; and let seven periods of time pass over him. ¹⁷The sentence is by the decree of the watchers, the decision by the word of the holy ones, to the end that the living may know that the Most High rules the kingdom of men and gives it to whom he will and sets over it the lowliest of men.' ¹⁸This dream I, King Nebuchadnezzar, saw. And you, O Belteshazzar, tell me the interpretation, because all the wise men of my kingdom are not able to make known to me the interpretation, but you are able, for the spirit of the holy gods is in you."

¹ Aramaic *and changed*   ² Ch 3:31 in Aramaic   ³ Ch 4:1 in Aramaic   ⁴ Or *Spirit of the holy God*; also verses 9, 18

Daniel Interprets the Second Dream

¹⁹ Then Daniel, whose name was Belteshazzar, was dismayed for a while, and his thoughts alarmed him. The king answered and said, "Belteshazzar, let not the dream or the interpretation alarm you." Belteshazzar answered and said, "My lord, may the dream be for those who hate you and its interpretation for your enemies! ²⁰ The tree you saw, which grew and became strong, so that its top reached to heaven, and it was visible to the end of the whole earth, ²¹ whose leaves were beautiful and its fruit abundant, and in which was food for all, under which beasts of the field found shade, and in whose branches the birds of the heavens lived— ²² it is you, O king, who have grown and become strong. Your greatness has grown and reaches to heaven, and your dominion to the ends of the earth. ²³ And because the king saw a watcher, a holy one, coming down from heaven and saying, 'Chop down the tree and destroy it, but leave the stump of its roots in the earth, bound with a band of iron and bronze, in the tender grass of the field, and let him be wet with the dew of heaven, and let his portion be with the beasts of the field, till seven periods of time pass over him,' ²⁴ this is the interpretation, O king: It is a decree of the Most High, which has come upon my lord the king, ²⁵ that you shall be driven from among men, and your dwelling shall be with the beasts of the field. You shall be made to eat grass like an ox, and you shall be wet with the dew of heaven, and seven periods of time shall pass over you, till you know that the Most High rules the kingdom of men and gives it to whom he will. ²⁶ And as it was commanded to leave the stump of the roots of the tree, your kingdom shall be confirmed for you from the time that you know that Heaven rules. ²⁷ Therefore, O king, let my counsel be acceptable to you: break off your sins by practicing righteousness, and your iniquities by showing mercy to the oppressed, that there may perhaps be a lengthening of your prosperity."

Nebuchadnezzar's Humiliation

²⁸ All this came upon King Nebuchadnezzar. ²⁹ At the end of twelve months he was walking on the roof of the royal palace of Babylon, ³⁰ and the king answered and said, "Is not this great Babylon, which I have built by my mighty power as a royal residence and for the glory of my majesty?" ³¹ While the words were still in the king's mouth, there fell a voice from heaven, "O King Nebuchadnezzar, to you it is spoken: The kingdom has departed from you, ³² and you shall be driven from among men, and your dwelling shall be with the beasts of the field. And you shall be made to eat grass like an ox, and seven periods of time shall pass over you, until you know that the Most High rules the kingdom of men and gives it to whom he will." ³³ Immediately the word was fulfilled against Nebuchadnezzar. He was driven from among men and ate grass like an ox, and his body was wet with the dew of heaven till his hair grew as long as eagles' feathers, and his nails were like birds' claws.

Nebuchadnezzar Restored

³⁴ At the end of the days I, Nebuchadnezzar, lifted my eyes to heaven, and my reason returned to me, and I blessed the Most High, and praised and honored him who lives forever,

> for his dominion is an everlasting
> dominion,
> and his kingdom endures from
> generation to generation;

³⁵ all the inhabitants of the earth are
> accounted as nothing,
> and he does according to his will
> among the host of heaven
> and among the inhabitants of the
> earth;
> and none can stay his hand
> or say to him, "What have you
> done?"

³⁶ At the same time my reason returned to me, and for the glory of my kingdom, my majesty and splendor returned to me. My counselors and my lords sought me, and I was established in my kingdom, and still more greatness was added to me. ³⁷ Now I, Nebuchadnezzar, praise and extol and honor the King of heaven, for all his works are right and his ways are just; and those who walk in pride he is able to humble.

The Handwriting on the Wall

5 King Belshazzar made a great feast for a thousand of his lords and drank wine in front of the thousand.

[2] Belshazzar, when he tasted the wine, commanded that the vessels of gold and of silver that Nebuchadnezzar his father[1] had taken out of the temple in Jerusalem be brought, that the king and his lords, his wives, and his concubines might drink from them. [3] Then they brought in the golden vessels that had been taken out of the temple, the house of God in Jerusalem, and the king and his lords, his wives, and his concubines drank from them. [4] They drank wine and praised the gods of gold and silver, bronze, iron, wood, and stone.

[5] Immediately the fingers of a human hand appeared and wrote on the plaster of the wall of the king's palace, opposite the lampstand. And the king saw the hand as it wrote. [6] Then the king's color changed, and his thoughts alarmed him; his limbs gave way, and his knees knocked together. [7] The king called loudly to bring in the enchanters, the Chaldeans, and the astrologers. The king declared[2] to the wise men of Babylon, "Whoever reads this writing, and shows me its interpretation, shall be clothed with purple and have a chain of gold around his neck and shall be the third ruler in the kingdom." [8] Then all the king's wise men came in, but they could not read the writing or make known to the king the interpretation. [9] Then King Belshazzar was greatly alarmed, and his color changed, and his lords were perplexed.

[10] The queen,[3] because of the words of the king and his lords, came into the banqueting hall, and the queen declared, "O king, live forever! Let not your thoughts alarm you or your color change. [11] There is a man in your kingdom in whom is the spirit of the holy gods.[4] In the days of your father, light and understanding and wisdom like the wisdom of the gods were found in him, and King Nebuchadnezzar, your father— your father the king—made him chief of the magicians, enchanters, Chaldeans, and astrologers, [12] because an excellent spirit, knowledge, and understanding to interpret dreams, explain riddles, and solve problems were found in this Daniel, whom the king named Belteshazzar. Now let Daniel be called, and he will show the interpretation."

Daniel Interprets the Handwriting

[13] Then Daniel was brought in before the king. The king answered and said to Daniel, "You are that Daniel, one of the exiles of Judah, whom the king my father brought from Judah. [14] I have heard of you that the spirit of the gods[5] is in you, and that light and understanding and excellent wisdom are found in you. [15] Now the wise men, the enchanters, have been brought in before me to read this writing and make known to me its interpretation, but they could not show the interpretation of the matter. [16] But I have heard that you can give interpretations and solve problems. Now if you can read the writing and make known to me its interpretation, you shall be clothed with purple and have a chain of gold around your neck and shall be the third ruler in the kingdom."

[17] Then Daniel answered and said before the king, "Let your gifts be for yourself, and give your rewards to another. Nevertheless, I will read the writing to the king and make known to him the interpretation. [18] O king, the Most High God gave Nebuchadnezzar your father kingship and greatness and glory and majesty. [19] And because of the greatness that he gave him, all peoples, nations, and languages trembled and feared before him. Whom he would, he killed, and whom he would, he kept alive; whom he would, he raised up, and whom he would, he humbled. [20] But when his heart was lifted up and his spirit was hardened so that he dealt proudly, he was brought down from his kingly throne, and his glory was taken from him. [21] He was driven from among the children of mankind, and his mind was made like that of a beast, and his dwelling was with the wild donkeys. He was fed grass like an ox, and his body was wet with the dew of heaven, until he knew that the Most High God rules the kingdom of mankind and sets over it whom he will. [22] And you his son,[6] Belshazzar, have not humbled your heart, though you knew all this, [23] but you have lifted up yourself against the Lord of heaven. And the vessels of his house have been brought in before you, and you and your lords, your wives, and your concubines have drunk wine from them. And you have praised the gods of silver and

---

[1] Or predecessor; also verses 11, 13, 18 [2] Aramaic answered and said; also verse 10 [3] Or queen mother; twice in this verse [4] Or Spirit of the holy God [5] Or Spirit of God [6] Or successor

gold, of bronze, iron, wood, and stone, which do not see or hear or know, but the God in whose hand is your breath, and whose are all your ways, you have not honored.

²⁴"Then from his presence the hand was sent, and this writing was inscribed. ²⁵And this is the writing that was inscribed: MENE, MENE, TEKEL, and PARSIN. ²⁶This is the interpretation of the matter: MENE, God has numbered¹ the days of your kingdom and brought it to an end; ²⁷TEKEL, you have been weighed² in the balances and found wanting; ²⁸PERES, your kingdom is divided and given to the Medes and Persians."³

²⁹Then Belshazzar gave the command, and Daniel was clothed with purple, a chain of gold was put around his neck, and a proclamation was made about him, that he should be the third ruler in the kingdom.

³⁰That very night Belshazzar the Chaldean king was killed. ³¹⁴And Darius the Mede received the kingdom, being about sixty-two years old.

Daniel and the Lions' Den

6 It pleased Darius to set over the kingdom 120 satraps, to be throughout the whole kingdom; ²and over them three high officials, of whom Daniel was one, to whom these satraps should give account, so that the king might suffer no loss. ³Then this Daniel became distinguished above all the other high officials and satraps, because an excellent spirit was in him. And the king planned to set him over the whole kingdom. ⁴Then the high officials and the satraps sought to find a ground for complaint against Daniel with regard to the kingdom, but they could find no ground for complaint or any fault, because he was faithful, and no error or fault was found in him. ⁵Then these men said, "We shall not find any ground for complaint against this Daniel unless we find it in connection with the law of his God."

⁶Then these high officials and satraps came by agreement⁵ to the king and said to him, "O King Darius, live forever! ⁷All the high officials of the kingdom, the prefects and the satraps, the counselors and the governors are agreed that the king should establish an ordinance and enforce an injunction, that whoever makes petition to any god or man for thirty days, except to you, O king, shall be cast into the den of lions. ⁸Now, O king, establish the injunction and sign the document, so that it cannot be changed, according to the law of the Medes and the Persians, which cannot be revoked." ⁹Therefore King Darius signed the document and injunction.

¹⁰When Daniel knew that the document had been signed, he went to his house where he had windows in his upper chamber open toward Jerusalem. He got down on his knees three times a day and prayed and gave thanks before his God, as he had done previously. ¹¹Then these men came by agreement and found Daniel making petition and plea before his God. ¹²Then they came near and said before the king, concerning the injunction, "O king! Did you not sign an injunction, that anyone who makes petition to any god or man within thirty days except to you, O king, shall be cast into the den of lions?" The king answered and said, "The thing stands fast, according to the law of the Medes and Persians, which cannot be revoked." ¹³Then they answered and said before the king, "Daniel, who is one of the exiles from Judah, pays no attention to you, O king, or the injunction you have signed, but makes his petition three times a day."

¹⁴Then the king, when he heard these words, was much distressed and set his mind to deliver Daniel. And he labored till the sun went down to rescue him. ¹⁵Then these men came by agreement to the king and said to the king, "Know, O king, that it is a law of the Medes and Persians that no injunction or ordinance that the king establishes can be changed."

¹⁶Then the king commanded, and Daniel was brought and cast into the den of lions. The king declared⁶ to Daniel, "May your God, whom you serve continually, deliver you!" ¹⁷And a stone was brought and laid on the mouth of the den, and the king sealed it with his own signet and with the signet of his lords, that nothing might be changed concerning Daniel. ¹⁸Then the king went to his palace and spent the night

---

¹MENE sounds like the Aramaic for numbered ²TEKEL sounds like the Aramaic for weighed ³PERES (the singular of Parsin) sounds like the Aramaic for divided and for Persia ⁴Ch 6:1 in Aramaic ⁵Or came thronging; also verses 11, 15 ⁶Aramaic answered and said; also verse 20

fasting; no diversions were brought to him, and sleep fled from him.

¹⁹ Then, at break of day, the king arose and went in haste to the den of lions. ²⁰ As he came near to the den where Daniel was, he cried out in a tone of anguish. The king declared to Daniel, "O Daniel, servant of the living God, has your God, whom you serve continually, been able to deliver you from the lions?" ²¹ Then Daniel said to the king, "O king, live forever! ²² My God sent his angel and shut the lions' mouths, and they have not harmed me, because I was found blameless before him; and also before you, O king, I have done no harm." ²³ Then the king was exceedingly glad, and commanded that Daniel be taken up out of the den. So Daniel was taken up out of the den, and no kind of harm was found on him, because he had trusted in his God. ²⁴ And the king commanded, and those men who had maliciously accused Daniel were brought and cast into the den of lions— they, their children, and their wives. And before they reached the bottom of the den, the lions overpowered them and broke all their bones in pieces.

²⁵ Then King Darius wrote to all the peoples, nations, and languages that dwell in all the earth: "Peace be multiplied to you. ²⁶ I make a decree, that in all my royal dominion people are to tremble and fear before the God of Daniel,

for he is the living God,
    enduring forever;
his kingdom shall never be destroyed,
    and his dominion shall be to the
        end.
²⁷ He delivers and rescues;
    he works signs and wonders
        in heaven and on earth,
    he who has saved Daniel
        from the power of the lions."

²⁸ So this Daniel prospered during the reign of Darius and the reign of Cyrus the Persian.

---

verses to read
Daniel 6

Prayer is to your soul what your pulse is to your body. A doctor can tell the condition of your heart by checking your pulse, and you can check the condition of your soul by checking your prayer. What percentage of your time does God get from you? How much prayer is too much? If you truly believed in the power of prayer, could you ever get enough? Would any effort to find the time for it be too much? This doesn't mean we should do nothing but pray, but it does mean that we continually develop a heart that delights in the presence of God our Father. The girl who believes in this power is the girl who finds strength in the presence of God. Instead of considering prayer a drudgery, she sees it as a joy and a necessity to her very soul. She finds in it the strength and ability to do more than she ever could without it.

The Enemy's goal is to keep you from communion with the Father. When you put off prayer for another time, you obey the Enemy's secret whispers. Don't let your life be controlled by his deceit. You cannot live without prayer—it is your lifeblood and the only thing that will set you free from the chaos of life.

Daniel had a choice to make: he could obey the king's decree not to worship God, or he could defy it and risk certain death. Knowing his God and his own need for prayer, he chose the better path. What might look different in your own prayer life, as you continue to surrender your life to God and step into the joys of glad communion with him? He is always eager to welcome us into his presence, because we are his children. He delights to hear our prayers and tenderly care for us.

Daniel's Vision of the Four Beasts

7 In the first year of Belshazzar king of Babylon, Daniel saw a dream and visions of his head as he lay in his bed. Then he wrote down the dream and told the sum of the matter. [2] Daniel declared,[1] "I saw in my vision by night, and behold, the four winds of heaven were stirring up the great sea. [3] And four great beasts came up out of the sea, different from one another. [4] The first was like a lion and had eagles' wings. Then as I looked its wings were plucked off, and it was lifted up from the ground and made to stand on two feet like a man, and the mind of a man was given to it. [5] And behold, another beast, a second one, like a bear. It was raised up on one side. It had three ribs in its mouth between its teeth; and it was told, 'Arise, devour much flesh.' [6] After this I looked, and behold, another, like a leopard, with four wings of a bird on its back. And the beast had four heads, and dominion was given to it. [7] After this I saw in the night visions, and behold, a fourth beast, terrifying and dreadful and exceedingly strong. It had great iron teeth; it devoured and broke in pieces and stamped what was left with its feet. It was different from all the beasts that were before it, and it had ten horns. [8] I considered the horns, and behold, there came up among them another horn, a little one, before which three of the first horns were plucked up by the roots. And behold, in this horn were eyes like the eyes of a man, and a mouth speaking great things.

The Ancient of Days Reigns

[9] "As I looked,

> thrones were placed,
>> and the Ancient of Days took his
>> seat;
> his clothing was white as snow,
>> and the hair of his head like pure
>> wool;
> his throne was fiery flames;
>> its wheels were burning fire.
[10] A stream of fire issued
>> and came out from before him;
> a thousand thousands served him,
>> and ten thousand times ten thou-
>> sand stood before him;
> the court sat in judgment,
>> and the books were opened.

[11] "I looked then because of the sound of the great words that the horn was speaking. And as I looked, the beast was killed, and its body destroyed and given over to be burned with fire. [12] As for the rest of the beasts, their dominion was taken away, but their lives were prolonged for a season and a time.

The Son of Man Is Given Dominion

[13] "I saw in the night visions,

> and behold, with the clouds of heaven
>> there came one like a son of man,
> and he came to the Ancient of Days
>> and was presented before him.
[14] And to him was given dominion
>> and glory and a kingdom,
> that all peoples, nations, and lan-
>> guages
>> should serve him;
> his dominion is an everlasting
>> dominion,
>> which shall not pass away,
> and his kingdom one
>> that shall not be destroyed.

Daniel's Vision Interpreted

[15] "As for me, Daniel, my spirit within me[2] was anxious, and the visions of my head alarmed me. [16] I approached one of those who stood there and asked him the truth concerning all this. So he told me and made known to me the interpretation of the things. [17] 'These four great beasts are four kings who shall arise out of the earth. [18] But the saints of the Most High shall receive the kingdom and possess the kingdom forever, forever and ever.'

[19] "Then I desired to know the truth about the fourth beast, which was different from all the rest, exceedingly terrifying, with its teeth of iron and claws of bronze, and which devoured and broke in pieces and stamped what was left with its feet, [20] and about the ten horns that were on its head, and the other horn that came up and before which three of them fell, the horn that had eyes and a mouth that spoke great things, and that seemed greater than its companions. [21] As I looked, this horn made war with the saints and prevailed over them, [22] until the Ancient of Days came, and judgment was given for the saints of the Most High, and the time came when the saints possessed the kingdom.

[1] Aramaic *answered and said* [2] Aramaic *within its sheath*

23 "Thus he said: 'As for the fourth beast,

there shall be a fourth kingdom on
    earth,
    which shall be different from all
        the kingdoms,
and it shall devour the whole earth,
    and trample it down, and break it
        to pieces.
24 As for the ten horns,
    out of this kingdom ten kings shall
        arise,
    and another shall arise after them;
he shall be different from the former
        ones,
    and shall put down three kings.
25 He shall speak words against the
        Most High,
    and shall wear out the saints of the
        Most High,
    and shall think to change the times
        and the law;
and they shall be given into his hand
    for a time, times, and half a time.
26 But the court shall sit in judgment,
    and his dominion shall be taken
        away,
    to be consumed and destroyed to
        the end.
27 And the kingdom and the dominion
    and the greatness of the kingdoms
        under the whole heaven
    shall be given to the people of the
        saints of the Most High;
his kingdom shall be an everlasting
        kingdom,
    and all dominions shall serve and
        obey him.'1

28 "Here is the end of the matter. As for
me, Daniel, my thoughts greatly alarmed
me, and my color changed, but I kept the
matter in my heart."

Daniel's Vision of the Ram and the Goat

8 In the third year of the reign of King
Belshazzar a vision appeared to me,
Daniel, after that which appeared to me
at the first. 2 And I saw in the vision; and
when I saw, I was in Susa the citadel, which
is in the province of Elam. And I saw in the
vision, and I was at the Ulai canal. 3 I raised
my eyes and saw, and behold, a ram standing on the bank of the canal. It had two
horns, and both horns were high, but one

was higher than the other, and the higher
one came up last. 4 I saw the ram charging
westward and northward and southward.
No beast could stand before him, and there
was no one who could rescue from his
power. He did as he pleased and became
great.

5 As I was considering, behold, a male
goat came from the west across the face
of the whole earth, without touching the
ground. And the goat had a conspicuous
horn between his eyes. 6 He came to the
ram with the two horns, which I had seen
standing on the bank of the canal, and he
ran at him in his powerful wrath. 7 I saw
him come close to the ram, and he was
enraged against him and struck the ram
and broke his two horns. And the ram had
no power to stand before him, but he cast
him down to the ground and trampled on
him. And there was no one who could rescue the ram from his power. 8 Then the goat
became exceedingly great, but when he
was strong, the great horn was broken, and
instead of it there came up four conspicuous horns toward the four winds of heaven.

9 Out of one of them came a little horn,
which grew exceedingly great toward the
south, toward the east, and toward the glorious land. 10 It grew great, even to the host
of heaven. And some of the host and some2
of the stars it threw down to the ground
and trampled on them. 11 It became great,
even as great as the Prince of the host. And
the regular burnt offering was taken away
from him, and the place of his sanctuary
was overthrown. 12 And a host will be given
over to it together with the regular burnt
offering because of transgression,3 and it
will throw truth to the ground, and it will
act and prosper. 13 Then I heard a holy one
speaking, and another holy one said to the
one who spoke, "For how long is the vision
concerning the regular burnt offering, the
transgression that makes desolate, and the
giving over of the sanctuary and host to
be trampled underfoot?" 14 And he said to
me,4 "For 2,300 evenings and mornings.
Then the sanctuary shall be restored to its
rightful state."

The Interpretation of the Vision

15 When I, Daniel, had seen the vision,
I sought to understand it. And behold,

---

1 Or their kingdom shall be an everlasting kingdom, and all dominions shall serve and obey them 2 Or host, that is, some 3 Or in an act of
rebellion 4 Hebrew; Septuagint, Theodotion, Vulgate to him

A Prayer of...

CONFESSION AND PETITION

Holy Lord, I have sinned more times than I can count and have been guilty of pride and doubt, of failure to find your will in your Word, of neglecting to look for you in my daily life. My failures and shortcomings prove me guilty, but I thank you that they aren't going to stand against me, because all of them have been laid on Christ. Please conquer my immorality and give me the grace to live above it. Please don't let my hormones or my lust for things I don't have enslave me again, but I ask you to rule over me in freedom and power.

I thank you for saying no to a lot of my prayers. I've asked with ungodly motives for what I do not have; I have prayed out of my own lust and have been rejected; I have prayed for Egypt and have been given a wilderness. Please keep being patient as you work on me. Answer no to my misguided prayers, and help me accept it. Take away my unfaithful desires, every human ambition, and everything that is contrary to your rule. Thank you for your wisdom and love, for all the acts of discipline that I deserve, and for putting me into the furnace to refine my gold and remove my impurities.

No trial is as hard to live through as seeing my own sinfulness. If you would give me the choice to live in pleasure and keep my sins or to have them burnt away through trials, I'd choose to be sanctified through trial. Set me free from every evil habit, all my acceptance of former sins, everything that dims the brightness of your grace in me, and everything that prevents me from finding my happiness in you. Then I will bless you, God of righteousness, for helping me to be righteous.

Amen.

there stood before me one having the appearance of a man. ¹⁶And I heard a man's voice between the banks of the Ulai, and it called, "Gabriel, make this man understand the vision." ¹⁷So he came near where I stood. And when he came, I was frightened and fell on my face. But he said to me, "Understand, O son of man, that the vision is for the time of the end."

¹⁸And when he had spoken to me, I fell into a deep sleep with my face to the ground. But he touched me and made me stand up. ¹⁹He said, "Behold, I will make known to you what shall be at the latter end of the indignation, for it refers to the appointed time of the end. ²⁰As for the ram that you saw with the two horns, these are the kings of Media and Persia. ²¹And the goat¹ is the king of Greece. And the great horn between his eyes is the first king. ²²As for the horn that was broken, in place of which four others arose, four kingdoms shall arise from his² nation, but not with his power. ²³And at the latter end of their kingdom, when the transgressors have reached their limit, a king of bold face, one who understands riddles, shall arise. ²⁴His power shall be great—but not by his own power; and he shall cause fearful destruction and shall succeed in what he does, and destroy mighty men and the people who are the saints. ²⁵By his cunning he shall make deceit prosper under his hand, and in his own mind he shall become great. Without warning he shall destroy many. And he shall even rise up against the Prince of princes, and he shall be broken—but by no human hand. ²⁶The vision of the evenings and the mornings that has been told is true, but seal up the vision, for it refers to many days from now."

²⁷And I, Daniel, was overcome and lay sick for some days. Then I rose and went about the king's business, but I was appalled by the vision and did not understand it.

Daniel's Prayer for His People

9 In the first year of Darius the son of Ahasuerus, by descent a Mede, who was made king over the realm of the Chaldeans— ²in the first year of his reign, I, Daniel, perceived in the books the number of years that, according to the word of the LORD to Jeremiah the prophet, must

¹ Or *the shaggy goat* ² Theodotion, Septuagint, Vulgate; Hebrew *the*

pass before the end of the desolations of Jerusalem, namely, seventy years.

³Then I turned my face to the Lord God, seeking him by prayer and pleas for mercy with fasting and sackcloth and ashes. ⁴I prayed to the Lᴏʀᴅ my God and made confession, saying, "O Lord, the great and awesome God, who keeps covenant and steadfast love with those who love him and keep his commandments, ⁵we have sinned and done wrong and acted wickedly and rebelled, turning aside from your commandments and rules. ⁶We have not listened to your servants the prophets, who spoke in your name to our kings, our princes, and our fathers, and to all the people of the land. ⁷To you, O Lord, belongs righteousness, but to us open shame, as at this day, to the men of Judah, to the inhabitants of Jerusalem, and to all Israel, those who are near and those who are far away, in all the lands to which you have driven them, because of the treachery that they have committed against you. ⁸To us, O Lᴏʀᴅ, belongs open shame, to our kings, to our princes, and to our fathers, because we have sinned against you. ⁹To the Lord our God belong mercy and forgiveness, for we have rebelled against him ¹⁰and have not obeyed the voice of the Lᴏʀᴅ our God by walking in his laws, which he set before us by his servants the prophets. ¹¹All Israel has transgressed your law and turned aside, refusing to obey your voice. And the curse and oath that are written in the Law of Moses the servant of God have been poured out upon us, because we have sinned against him. ¹²He has confirmed his words, which he spoke against us and against our rulers who ruled us,¹ by bringing upon us a great calamity. For under the whole heaven there has not been done anything like what has been done against Jerusalem. ¹³As it is written in the Law of Moses, all this calamity has come upon us; yet we have not entreated the favor of the Lᴏʀᴅ our God, turning from our iniquities and gaining insight by your truth. ¹⁴Therefore the Lᴏʀᴅ has kept ready the calamity and has brought it upon us, for the Lᴏʀᴅ our God is righteous in all the works that he has done, and we have not obeyed his voice. ¹⁵And now, O Lord our God, who brought your people out of the land of Egypt with a mighty hand, and have made a name for yourself, as at this day, we have sinned, we have done wickedly.

¹⁶"O Lord, according to all your righteous acts, let your anger and your wrath turn away from your city Jerusalem, your holy hill, because for our sins, and for the iniquities of our fathers, Jerusalem and your people have become a byword among all who are around us. ¹⁷Now therefore, O our God, listen to the prayer of your servant and to his pleas for mercy, and for your own sake, O Lord,² make your face to shine upon your sanctuary, which is desolate. ¹⁸O my God, incline your ear and hear. Open your eyes and see our desolations, and the city that is called by your name. For we do not present our pleas before you because of our righteousness, but because of your great mercy. ¹⁹O Lord, hear; O Lord, forgive. O Lord, pay attention and act. Delay not, for your own sake, O my God, because your city and your people are called by your name."

Gabriel Brings an Answer

²⁰While I was speaking and praying, confessing my sin and the sin of my people Israel, and presenting my plea before the Lᴏʀᴅ my God for the holy hill of my God, ²¹while I was speaking in prayer, the man Gabriel, whom I had seen in the vision at the first, came to me in swift flight at the time of the evening sacrifice. ²²He made me understand, speaking with me and saying, "O Daniel, I have now come out to give you insight and understanding. ²³At the beginning of your pleas for mercy a word went out, and I have come to tell it to you, for you are greatly loved. Therefore consider the word and understand the vision.

The Seventy Weeks

²⁴"Seventy weeks³ are decreed about your people and your holy city, to finish the transgression, to put an end to sin, and to atone for iniquity, to bring in everlasting righteousness, to seal both vision and prophet, and to anoint a most holy place.⁴ ²⁵Know therefore and understand that from the going out of the word to restore and build Jerusalem to the coming of an anointed one, a prince, there shall be seven weeks. Then for sixty-two weeks it shall be built again⁵ with squares and moat, but in

---

¹ Or our judges who judged us ² Hebrew for the Lord's sake ³ Or sevens; also twice in verse 25 and once in verse 26 ⁴ Or thing, or one ⁵ Or there shall be seven weeks and sixty-two weeks. It shall be built again

a troubled time. [26] And after the sixty-two weeks, an anointed one shall be cut off and shall have nothing. And the people of the prince who is to come shall destroy the city and the sanctuary. Its[1] end shall come with a flood, and to the end there shall be war. Desolations are decreed. [27] And he shall make a strong covenant with many for one week,[2] and for half of the week he shall put an end to sacrifice and offering. And on the wing of abominations shall come one who makes desolate, until the decreed end is poured out on the desolator."

Daniel's Terrifying Vision of a Man

10 In the third year of Cyrus king of Persia a word was revealed to Daniel, who was named Belteshazzar. And the word was true, and it was a great conflict.[3] And he understood the word and had understanding of the vision.

[2] In those days I, Daniel, was mourning for three weeks. [3] I ate no delicacies, no meat or wine entered my mouth, nor did I anoint myself at all, for the full three weeks. [4] On the twenty-fourth day of the first month, as I was standing on the bank of the great river (that is, the Tigris) [5] I lifted up my eyes and looked, and behold, a man clothed in linen, with a belt of fine gold from Uphaz around his waist. [6] His body was like beryl, his face like the appearance of lightning, his eyes like flaming torches, his arms and legs like the gleam of burnished bronze, and the sound of his words like the sound of a multitude. [7] And I, Daniel, alone saw the vision, for the men who were with me did not see the vision, but a great trembling fell upon them, and they fled to hide themselves. [8] So I was left alone and saw this great vision, and no strength was left in me. My radiant appearance was fearfully changed,[4] and I retained no strength. [9] Then I heard the sound of his words, and as I heard the sound of his words, I fell on my face in deep sleep with my face to the ground.

[10] And behold, a hand touched me and set me trembling on my hands and knees. [11] And he said to me, "O Daniel, man greatly loved, understand the words that I speak to you, and stand upright, for now I have been sent to you." And when he had spoken this word to me, I stood up trembling. [12] Then he said to me, "Fear not, Daniel, for from the first day that you set your heart to understand and humbled yourself before your God, your words have been heard, and I have come because of your words. [13] The prince of the kingdom of Persia withstood me twenty-one days, but Michael, one of the chief princes, came to help me, for I was left there with the kings of Persia, [14] and came to make you understand what is to happen to your people in the latter days. For the vision is for days yet to come."

[15] When he had spoken to me according to these words, I turned my face toward the ground and was mute. [16] And behold, one in the likeness of the children of man touched my lips. Then I opened my mouth and spoke. I said to him who stood before me, "O my lord, by reason of the vision pains have come upon me, and I retain no strength. [17] How can my lord's servant talk with my lord? For now no strength remains in me, and no breath is left in me."

[18] Again one having the appearance of a man touched me and strengthened me. [19] And he said, "O man greatly loved, fear not, peace be with you; be strong and of good courage." And as he spoke to me, I was strengthened and said, "Let my lord speak, for you have strengthened me." [20] Then he said, "Do you know why I have come to you? But now I will return to fight against the prince of Persia; and when I go out, behold, the prince of Greece will come. [21] But I will tell you what is inscribed in the book of truth: there is none who contends by my side against these except Michael, your prince.

The Kings of the South and the North

11 "And as for me, in the first year of Darius the Mede, I stood up to confirm and strengthen him.

[2] "And now I will show you the truth. Behold, three more kings shall arise in Persia, and a fourth shall be far richer than all of them. And when he has become strong through his riches, he shall stir up all against the kingdom of Greece. [3] Then a mighty king shall arise, who shall rule with great dominion and do as he wills. [4] And as soon as he has arisen, his kingdom shall be broken and divided toward the four winds of heaven, but not to his posterity, nor according to the authority with which he ruled, for his kingdom shall be plucked up and go to others besides these.

---

[1] Or His [2] Or seven; twice in this verse [3] Or and it was about a great conflict [4] Hebrew My splendor was changed to ruin

⁵"Then the king of the south shall be strong, but one of his princes shall be stronger than he and shall rule, and his authority shall be a great authority. ⁶After some years they shall make an alliance, and the daughter of the king of the south shall come to the king of the north to make an agreement. But she shall not retain the strength of her arm, and he and his arm shall not endure, but she shall be given up, and her attendants, he who fathered her, and he who supported¹ her in those times.

⁷"And from a branch from her roots one shall arise in his place. He shall come against the army and enter the fortress of the king of the north, and he shall deal with them and shall prevail. ⁸He shall also carry off to Egypt their gods with their metal images and their precious vessels of silver and gold, and for some years he shall refrain from attacking the king of the north. ⁹Then the latter shall come into the realm of the king of the south but shall return to his own land.

¹⁰"His sons shall wage war and assemble a multitude of great forces, which shall keep coming and overflow and pass through, and again shall carry the war as far as his fortress. ¹¹Then the king of the south, moved with rage, shall come out and fight against the king of the north. And he shall raise a great multitude, but it shall be given into his hand. ¹²And when the multitude is taken away, his heart shall be exalted, and he shall cast down tens of thousands, but he shall not prevail. ¹³For the king of the north shall again raise a multitude, greater than the first. And after some years² he shall come on with a great army and abundant supplies.

¹⁴"In those times many shall rise against the king of the south, and the violent among your own people shall lift themselves up in order to fulfill the vision, but they shall fail. ¹⁵Then the king of the north shall come and throw up siegeworks and take a well-fortified city. And the forces of the south shall not stand, or even his best troops, for there shall be no strength to stand. ¹⁶But he who comes against him shall do as he wills, and none shall stand before him. And he shall stand in the glorious land, with destruction in his hand. ¹⁷He shall set his face to come with the strength of his whole kingdom, and he shall bring

terms of an agreement and perform them. He shall give him the daughter of women to destroy the kingdom,³ but it shall not stand or be to his advantage. ¹⁸Afterward he shall turn his face to the coastlands and shall capture many of them, but a commander shall put an end to his insolence. Indeed,⁴ he shall turn his insolence back upon him. ¹⁹Then he shall turn his face back toward the fortresses of his own land, but he shall stumble and fall, and shall not be found.

²⁰"Then shall arise in his place one who shall send an exactor of tribute for the glory of the kingdom. But within a few days he shall be broken, neither in anger nor in battle. ²¹In his place shall arise a contemptible person to whom royal majesty has not been given. He shall come in without warning and obtain the kingdom by flatteries. ²²Armies shall be utterly swept away before him and broken, even the prince of the covenant. ²³And from the time that an alliance is made with him he shall act deceitfully, and he shall become strong with a small people. ²⁴Without warning he shall come into the richest parts⁵ of the province, and he shall do what neither his fathers nor his fathers' fathers have done, scattering among them plunder, spoil, and goods. He shall devise plans against strongholds, but only for a time. ²⁵And he shall stir up his power and his heart against the king of the south with a great army. And the king of the south shall wage war with an exceedingly great and mighty army, but he shall not stand, for plots shall be devised against him. ²⁶Even those who eat his food shall break him. His army shall be swept away, and many shall fall down slain. ²⁷And as for the two kings, their hearts shall be bent on doing evil. They shall speak lies at the same table, but to no avail, for the end is yet to be at the time appointed. ²⁸And he shall return to his land with great wealth, but his heart shall be set against the holy covenant. And he shall work his will and return to his own land.

²⁹"At the time appointed he shall return and come into the south, but it shall not be this time as it was before. ³⁰For ships of Kittim shall come against him, and he shall be afraid and withdraw, and shall turn back and be enraged and take action against the holy covenant. He shall turn back and pay attention to those who forsake the holy

---

¹Or *obtained* ²Hebrew *at the end of the times* ³Hebrew *her*, or *it* ⁴The meaning of the Hebrew is uncertain ⁵Or *among the richest men*

covenant. [31] Forces from him shall appear and profane the temple and fortress, and shall take away the regular burnt offering. And they shall set up the abomination that makes desolate. [32] He shall seduce with flattery those who violate the covenant, but the people who know their God shall stand firm and take action. [33] And the wise among the people shall make many understand, though for some days they shall stumble by sword and flame, by captivity and plunder. [34] When they stumble, they shall receive a little help. And many shall join themselves to them with flattery, [35] and some of the wise shall stumble, so that they may be refined, purified, and made white, until the time of the end, for it still awaits the appointed time.

[36] "And the king shall do as he wills. He shall exalt himself and magnify himself above every god, and shall speak astonishing things against the God of gods. He shall prosper till the indignation is accomplished; for what is decreed shall be done. [37] He shall pay no attention to the gods of his fathers, or to the one beloved by women. He shall not pay attention to any other god, for he shall magnify himself above all. [38] He shall honor the god of fortresses instead of these. A god whom his fathers did not know he shall honor with gold and silver, with precious stones and costly gifts. [39] He shall deal with the strongest fortresses with the help of a foreign god. Those who acknowledge him he shall load with honor. He shall make them rulers over many and shall divide the land for a price.[1]

[40] "At the time of the end, the king of the south shall attack[2] him, but the king of the north shall rush upon him like a whirlwind, with chariots and horsemen, and with many ships. And he shall come into countries and shall overflow and pass through. [41] He shall come into the glorious land. And tens of thousands shall fall, but these shall be delivered out of his hand: Edom and Moab and the main part of the Ammonites. [42] He shall stretch out his hand against the countries, and the land of Egypt shall not escape. [43] He shall become ruler of the treasures of gold and of silver, and all the precious things of Egypt, and the Libyans and the Cushites shall follow in his train. [44] But news from the east and the north shall alarm him, and he shall go out with great fury to destroy and devote many to destruction. [45] And he shall pitch his palatial tents between the sea and the glorious holy mountain. Yet he shall come to his end, with none to help him.

The Time of the End

12 "At that time shall arise Michael, the great prince who has charge of your people. And there shall be a time of trouble, such as never has been since there was a nation till that time. But at that time your people shall be delivered, everyone whose name shall be found written in the book. [2] And many of those who sleep in the dust of the earth shall awake, some to everlasting life, and some to shame and everlasting contempt. [3] And those who are wise shall shine like the brightness of the sky above;[3] and those who turn many to righteousness, like the stars forever and ever. [4] But you, Daniel, shut up the words and seal the book, until the time of the end. Many shall run to and fro, and knowledge shall increase."

[5] Then I, Daniel, looked, and behold, two others stood, one on this bank of the stream and one on that bank of the stream. [6] And someone said to the man clothed in linen, who was above the waters of the stream,[4] "How long shall it be till the end of these wonders?" [7] And I heard the man clothed in linen, who was above the waters of the stream; he raised his right hand and his left hand toward heaven and swore by him who lives forever that it would be for a time, times, and half a time, and that when the shattering of the power of the holy people comes to an end all these things would be finished. [8] I heard, but I did not understand. Then I said, "O my lord, what shall be the outcome of these things?" [9] He said, "Go your way, Daniel, for the words are shut up and sealed until the time of the end. [10] Many shall purify themselves and make themselves white and be refined, but the wicked shall act wickedly. And none of the wicked shall understand, but those who are wise shall understand. [11] And from the time that the regular burnt offering is taken away and the abomination that makes desolate is set up, there shall be 1,290 days. [12] Blessed is he who waits and arrives at the 1,335 days. [13] But go your way till the end. And you shall rest and shall stand in your allotted place at the end of the days."

---

[1] Or *land as payment* [2] Hebrew *thrust at* [3] Hebrew *the expanse*; compare Genesis 1:6–8 [4] Or *who was upstream*; also verse 7

INTRODUCTION TO
Hosea

Return to Your God

> Return, O Israel, to the LORD your God,
> for you have stumbled because of your iniquity.
>
> Hosea 14:1

Author: Hosea
Time: The eighth century B.C.
Place: Israel
Written to: The people of Israel

The gist

The book of Hosea begins with the story of the prophet who was told by God to marry a prostitute as a symbol of God's covenant faithfulness to Israel in spite of Israel's unfaithfulness. The story tells of their marriage and her cheating on him. God wanted his people to know that there would be consequences for sin but that he would remain faithful and always take them back if they repented.

Things to look for

- Israel's sin of idolatry (see Hos. 2:8, 13; 4:17; 8:4–6; 10:5; 11:2; 13:1–2)
- God's case against Israel (see Hos. 4:1–2; 6:4–10; 12:1–14)
- God's desire to take Israel back (see Hos. 2:14–23)

It's very easy to forget the Lord when the world calls. And it's even easier to want more of what you see that others have and so to forget your first love. But when your desire for anything—for love, acceptance, fame, happiness, or friendship—becomes more important than your love for God, you are in dangerous territory. When your desires for this life war against your desire to serve him, you are looking down a long, slippery hill. Most of the time it's easy to choose what you can see and feel and to ignore the one whom you can't see, but each time you choose the world over the Father, even just for a minute, you turn your back on him. And each time you turn your back, you forget his character, his power, and his commands. And you are cheating on the Lover of your soul.

That is just what the Israelites had done in the time of Hosea. Like a prostitute cheating on her husband, they forgot their first love. So God used Hosea as his example, and asked him to marry Gomer, a prostitute. This relationship would be an example to God's people of their unfaithfulness and his undying love.

In this little book you find out how much God hates it when his people prostitute themselves by running after other gods (idols), looking for something or someone other than God to complete them and make them happy. For the God Girl there can be nothing and no one more important than her God—not even herself. No reward, no achievement, no victory is so important that God should be shelved, put on hold, or forgotten.

When you tell yourself that you "deserve" something or that you "can't live without" something or someone, that's a red flag waving to warn you that you are about to turn your back and walk away from the one who saves. So if you see red, turn around immediately by confessing your tendency to serve your emotions and your desires. Stay near to your first love and refuse to be enticed by what the world has to offer.

Must-Know Verses

The LORD said to Hosea, "Go, take to yourself a wife of whoredom and have children of whoredom, for the land commits great whoredom by forsaking the LORD." *Hosea 1:2*

"[She] adorned herself with her ring and jewelry,
    and went after her lovers
    and forgot me, declares the LORD." *Hosea 2:13*

"I will betroth you to me forever. I will betroth you to me in righteousness and in justice, in steadfast love and in mercy. I will betroth you to me in faithfulness. And you shall know the LORD." *Hosea 2:19–20*

Woe to them, for they have strayed from me!
    Destruction to them, for they have rebelled against me!
I would redeem them,
    but they speak lies against me.
They do not cry to me from the heart,
    but they wail upon their beds. *Hosea 7:13–14*

I will love them freely,
    for my anger has turned from them. *Hosea 14:4*

Hosea

1 The word of the LORD that came to Hosea, the son of Beeri, in the days of Uzziah, Jotham, Ahaz, and Hezekiah, kings of Judah, and in the days of Jeroboam the son of Joash, king of Israel.

Hosea's Wife and Children

² When the LORD first spoke through Hosea, the LORD said to Hosea, "Go, take to yourself a wife of whoredom and have children of whoredom, for the land commits great whoredom by forsaking the LORD." ³ So he went and took Gomer, the daughter of Diblaim, and she conceived and bore him a son.

⁴ And the LORD said to him, "Call his name Jezreel, for in just a little while I will punish the house of Jehu for the blood of Jezreel, and I will put an end to the kingdom of the house of Israel. ⁵ And on that day I will break the bow of Israel in the Valley of Jezreel."

⁶ She conceived again and bore a daughter. And the LORD said to him, "Call her name No Mercy,¹ for I will no more have mercy on the house of Israel, to forgive them at all. ⁷ But I will have mercy on the house of Judah, and I will save them by the LORD their God. I will not save them by bow or by sword or by war or by horses or by horsemen."

⁸ When she had weaned No Mercy, she conceived and bore a son. ⁹ And the LORD said, "Call his name Not My People,² for you are not my people, and I am not your God."³

¹⁰⁴ Yet the number of the children of Israel shall be like the sand of the sea, which cannot be measured or numbered. And in the place where it was said to them, "You are not my people," it shall be said to them, "Children⁵ of the living God." ¹¹ And the children of Judah and the children of Israel shall be gathered together, and they shall appoint for themselves one head. And they shall go up from the land, for great shall be the day of Jezreel.

Israel's Unfaithfulness Punished

2 ⁶ Say to your brothers, "You are my people,"⁷ and to your sisters, "You have received mercy."⁸

² "Plead with your mother, plead—
    for she is not my wife,
    and I am not her husband—
that she put away her whoring from
        her face,
    and her adultery from between
        her breasts;
³ lest I strip her naked
    and make her as in the day she
        was born,
and make her like a wilderness,
    and make her like a parched land,
    and kill her with thirst.
⁴ Upon her children also I will have no
        mercy,
    because they are children of
        whoredom.
⁵ For their mother has played the
        whore;
    she who conceived them has acted
        shamefully.
For she said, 'I will go after my lov-
        ers,
    who give me my bread and my
        water,
    my wool and my flax, my oil and
        my drink.'
⁶ Therefore I will hedge up her⁹ way
        with thorns,
    and I will build a wall against her,
    so that she cannot find her paths.
⁷ She shall pursue her lovers
    but not overtake them,
and she shall seek them
    but shall not find them.

¹ Hebrew *Lo-ruhama*, which means *she has not received mercy* ² Hebrew *Lo-ammi*, which means *not my people* ³ Hebrew *I am not yours* ⁴ Ch 2:1 in Hebrew ⁵ Or *Sons* ⁶ Ch 2:3 in Hebrew ⁷ Hebrew *ammi*, which means *my people* ⁸ Hebrew *ruhama*, which means *she has received mercy* ⁹ Hebrew *your*

Then she shall say,
'I will go and return to my first
husband,
for it was better for me then than
now.'

Ask Yourself . . .

ABOUT LOVE

Love can be an all-consuming emotion. The one you love might seem
like all you need in this life, but as
a God Girl you have to beware of
putting any love above the love of
God. Boys can steal your thoughts,
occupy your mind, and consume
your emotions, so balance is the
key to real love. Ask yourself these
questions about love:

- What do I get from being in
  love?

- Have I let my love life become
  more important than my
  spiritual life?

- Whom do I spend more time
  thinking about, boys or God?

- What does God think about
  someone who is consumed
  with human love?

8 And she did not know
that it was I who gave her
the grain, the wine, and the oil,
and who lavished on her silver and
gold,
which they used for Baal.
9 Therefore I will take back
my grain in its time,
and my wine in its season,
and I will take away my wool and my
flax,
which were to cover her nakedness.
10 Now I will uncover her lewdness
in the sight of her lovers,
and no one shall rescue her out of
my hand.

11 And I will put an end to all her mirth,
her feasts, her new moons, her
Sabbaths,
and all her appointed feasts.
12 And I will lay waste her vines and
her fig trees,
of which she said,
'These are my wages,
which my lovers have given me.'
I will make them a forest,
and the beasts of the field shall
devour them.
13 And I will punish her for the feast
days of the Baals
when she burned offerings to them
and adorned herself with her ring
and jewelry,
and went after her lovers
and forgot me, declares the LORD.

The LORD's Mercy on Israel

14 "Therefore, behold, I will allure her,
and bring her into the wilderness,
and speak tenderly to her.
15 And there I will give her her vineyards
and make the Valley of Achor[1] a
door of hope.
And there she shall answer as in the
days of her youth,
as at the time when she came out
of the land of Egypt.

16 "And in that day, declares the LORD, you
will call me 'My Husband,' and no longer
will you call me 'My Baal.' 17 For I will
remove the names of the Baals from her
mouth, and they shall be remembered by
name no more. 18 And I will make for them
a covenant on that day with the beasts of
the field, the birds of the heavens, and the
creeping things of the ground. And I will
abolish[2] the bow, the sword, and war from
the land, and I will make you lie down
in safety. 19 And I will betroth you to me
forever. I will betroth you to me in righteousness and in justice, in steadfast love
and in mercy. 20 I will betroth you to me in
faithfulness. And you shall know the LORD.

21 "And in that day I will answer, declares
the LORD,
I will answer the heavens,
and they shall answer the earth,

---

[1] *Achor* means *trouble*; compare Joshua 7:26   [2] Hebrew *break*

22 and the earth shall answer the grain,
　　the wine, and the oil,
　　and they shall answer Jezreel,[1]
23 and I will sow her for myself in the
　　land.
　　And I will have mercy on No Mercy,[2]
　　and I will say to Not My People,[3]
　　　'You are my people';
　　and he shall say, 'You are my God.'"

Hosea Redeems His Wife

3 And the LORD said to me, "Go again, love a woman who is loved by another man and is an adulteress, even as the LORD loves the children of Israel, though they turn to other gods and love cakes of raisins." ²So I bought her for fifteen shekels of silver and a homer and a lethech[4] of barley. ³And I said to her, "You must dwell as mine for many days. You shall not play the whore, or belong to another man; so will I also be to you." ⁴For the children of Israel shall dwell many days without king or prince, without sacrifice or pillar, without ephod or household gods. ⁵Afterward the children of Israel shall return and seek the LORD their God, and David their king, and they shall come in fear to the LORD and to his goodness in the latter days.

The LORD Accuses Israel

4 Hear the word of the LORD, O children of Israel,
　　for the LORD has a controversy with
　　　the inhabitants of the land.
　　There is no faithfulness or steadfast
　　　love,
　　and no knowledge of God in the
　　　land;
2 there is swearing, lying, murder, stealing, and committing adultery;
　　they break all bounds, and bloodshed follows bloodshed.
3 Therefore the land mourns,
　　and all who dwell in it languish,
　　and also the beasts of the field
　　and the birds of the heavens,
　　and even the fish of the sea are
　　　taken away.
4 Yet let no one contend,
　　and let none accuse,
　　for with you is my contention,
　　　O priest.[5]

5 You shall stumble by day;
　　the prophet also shall stumble
　　　with you by night;
　　and I will destroy your mother.
6 My people are destroyed for lack of
　　knowledge;
　　because you have rejected knowledge,
　　I reject you from being a priest to
　　　me.
　　And since you have forgotten the law
　　　of your God,
　　I also will forget your children.
7 The more they increased,
　　the more they sinned against me;
　　I will change their glory into shame.
8 They feed on the sin[6] of my people;
　　they are greedy for their iniquity.
9 And it shall be like people, like priest;
　　I will punish them for their ways
　　and repay them for their deeds.
10 They shall eat, but not be satisfied;
　　they shall play the whore, but not
　　　multiply,
　　because they have forsaken the LORD
　　　to cherish ¹¹whoredom, wine, and
　　　new wine,
　　which take away the understanding.
12 My people inquire of a piece of wood,
　　and their walking staff gives them
　　　oracles.
　　For a spirit of whoredom has led
　　　them astray,
　　and they have left their God to play
　　　the whore.
13 They sacrifice on the tops of the
　　mountains
　　and burn offerings on the hills,
　　under oak, poplar, and terebinth,
　　because their shade is good.
　　Therefore your daughters play the
　　　whore,
　　and your brides commit adultery.
14 I will not punish your daughters
　　when they play the whore,
　　nor your brides when they commit
　　　adultery;
　　for the men themselves go aside with
　　　prostitutes
　　and sacrifice with cult prostitutes,
　　and a people without understanding
　　shall come to ruin.

[1] Jezreel means God will sow [2] Hebrew Lo-ruhama [3] Hebrew Lo-ammi [4] A shekel was about 2/5 ounce or 11 grams; a homer was about 6 bushels or 220 liters; a lethech was about 3 bushels or 110 liters [5] Or for your people are like those who contend with the priest [6] Or sin offering

¹⁵ Though you play the whore, O Israel,
   let not Judah become guilty.
Enter not into Gilgal,
   nor go up to Beth-aven,
   and swear not, "As the LORD lives."
¹⁶ Like a stubborn heifer,
   Israel is stubborn;
can the LORD now feed them
   like a lamb in a broad pasture?

¹⁷ Ephraim is joined to idols;
   leave him alone.
¹⁸ When their drink is gone, they give
      themselves to whoring;
   their rulers¹ dearly love shame.
¹⁹ A wind has wrapped them² in its
      wings,
   and they shall be ashamed because
      of their sacrifices.

Punishment Coming for Israel and Judah

5 Hear this, O priests!
   Pay attention, O house of Israel!
Give ear, O house of the king!
   For the judgment is for you;
for you have been a snare at Mizpah
   and a net spread upon Tabor.
² And the revolters have gone deep
      into slaughter,
   but I will discipline all of them.
³ I know Ephraim,
   and Israel is not hidden from me;
for now, O Ephraim, you have played
      the whore;
   Israel is defiled.
⁴ Their deeds do not permit them
   to return to their God.
For the spirit of whoredom is within
      them,
   and they know not the LORD.

⁵ The pride of Israel testifies to his face;³
   Israel and Ephraim shall stumble
      in his guilt;
   Judah also shall stumble with them.
⁶ With their flocks and herds they
      shall go
   to seek the LORD,
but they will not find him;
   he has withdrawn from them.
⁷ They have dealt faithlessly with the
      LORD;
   for they have borne alien children.
Now the new moon shall devour
   them with their fields.

⁸ Blow the horn in Gibeah,
   the trumpet in Ramah.
Sound the alarm at Beth-aven;
   we follow you,⁴ O Benjamin!
⁹ Ephraim shall become a desolation
   in the day of punishment;
among the tribes of Israel
   I make known what is sure.
¹⁰ The princes of Judah have become
   like those who move the land-
      mark;
upon them I will pour out
   my wrath like water.
¹¹ Ephraim is oppressed, crushed in
      judgment,
   because he was determined to go
      after filth.⁵
¹² But I am like a moth to Ephraim,
   and like dry rot to the house of
      Judah.

¹³ When Ephraim saw his sickness,
   and Judah his wound,
then Ephraim went to Assyria,
   and sent to the great king.⁶
But he is not able to cure you
   or heal your wound.
¹⁴ For I will be like a lion to Ephraim,
   and like a young lion to the house
      of Judah.
I, even I, will tear and go away;
   I will carry off, and no one shall
      rescue.

¹⁵ I will return again to my place,
   until they acknowledge their guilt
      and seek my face,
   and in their distress earnestly seek
      me.

Israel and Judah Are Unrepentant

6 "Come, let us return to the LORD;
   for he has torn us, that he may heal
      us;
   he has struck us down, and he will
      bind us up.
² After two days he will revive us;
   on the third day he will raise us up,
   that we may live before him.
³ Let us know; let us press on to know
      the LORD;
   his going out is sure as the dawn;
he will come to us as the showers,
   as the spring rains that water the
      earth."

¹Hebrew *shields* ²Hebrew *her* ³Or *in his presence* ⁴Or *after you* ⁵Or *to follow human precepts* ⁶Or *to King Jareb*

4 What shall I do with you, O Ephraim?
  What shall I do with you, O Judah?
  Your love is like a morning cloud,
    like the dew that goes early away.
5 Therefore I have hewn them by the
      prophets;
  I have slain them by the words of
      my mouth,
  and my judgment goes forth as the
      light.
6 For I desire steadfast love[1] and not
      sacrifice,
  the knowledge of God rather than
      burnt offerings.
7 But like Adam they transgressed the
      covenant;
  there they dealt faithlessly with
      me.
8 Gilead is a city of evildoers,
    tracked with blood.

9 As robbers lie in wait for a man,
    so the priests band together;
  they murder on the way to Shechem;
    they commit villainy.
10 In the house of Israel I have seen a
      horrible thing;
  Ephraim's whoredom is there;
    Israel is defiled.
11 For you also, O Judah, a harvest is
      appointed,
  when I restore the fortunes of my
      people.

7 When I would heal Israel,
  the iniquity of Ephraim is revealed,
    and the evil deeds of Samaria;
  for they deal falsely;
    the thief breaks in,
    and the bandits raid outside.
2 But they do not consider
    that I remember all their evil.

[1] Septuagint *mercy*

Know God

verses to read
Hosea 5:13–15

Confession is a requirement for forgiveness because it cleanses your soul. It's the same as with your body: if you don't clean your wounds, you will never heal. When you get a big, bloody cut, the first step is to stop the bleeding with some kind of bandage, but what then? Do you just wrap it up and go on with your life, or do you hop in the car, drive to the hospital, and go through the pain of letting them take off the bandage and clean the wound? Even though it doesn't sound like much fun, you've got to open it up. If you don't clean your wound, every little speck of dirt that might have gotten into your body through the gash can lead to infection. The small, invisible bacteria can easily go unnoticed and be ignored, but eventually they will flare up and attack not only the area of the wound but your entire body. And it's the same with your soul: it has to be cleaned and protected from small sins that can work their way into your bloodstream. Confession is the antibacterial cleanser for the job. "If we confess our sins, he is faithful and just to forgive us our sins and to cleanse us from all unrighteousness" (1 John 1:9).

So what about your unconfessed sins, those small bacteria that infect and cause trouble? A girl who covers over her sin is bound for a life of chaos and pain. God says that he won't give much success to those who do that (see Deut. 28:15–68), and in fact he also says he will ignore their prayers (see Prov. 28:9). As a God Girl, you have to confess daily. Every day, look over your life and agree with God that sin is sin. As soon as you confess, it's forgiven, and through the work of Christ you are all cleaned up, saved from infection. So admit your guilt, and God will be your protection and guide.

Now their deeds surround them;
  they are before my face.
3 By their evil they make the king glad,
  and the princes by their treachery.
4 They are all adulterers;
  they are like a heated oven
whose baker ceases to stir the fire,
  from the kneading of the dough
  until it is leavened.
5 On the day of our king, the princes
  became sick with the heat of wine;
  he stretched out his hand with
    mockers.
6 For with hearts like an oven they
    approach their intrigue;
  all night their anger smolders;
  in the morning it blazes like a
    flaming fire.
7 All of them are hot as an oven,
  and they devour their rulers.
All their kings have fallen,
  and none of them calls upon me.

8 Ephraim mixes himself with the
    peoples;
  Ephraim is a cake not turned.
9 Strangers devour his strength,
  and he knows it not;
gray hairs are sprinkled upon him,
  and he knows it not.
10 The pride of Israel testifies to his
    face;[1]
  yet they do not return to the Lord
    their God,
  nor seek him, for all this.

11 Ephraim is like a dove,
  silly and without sense,
  calling to Egypt, going to Assyria.
12 As they go, I will spread over them
    my net;
  I will bring them down like birds
    of the heavens;
  I will discipline them according
    to the report made to their
    congregation.
13 Woe to them, for they have strayed
    from me!
  Destruction to them, for they have
    rebelled against me!
I would redeem them,
  but they speak lies against me.

14 They do not cry to me from the
    heart,
  but they wail upon their beds;

for grain and wine they gash them-
    selves;
  they rebel against me.
15 Although I trained and strengthened
    their arms,
  yet they devise evil against me.
16 They return, but not upward;[2]
  they are like a treacherous bow;
their princes shall fall by the sword
  because of the insolence of their
    tongue.
This shall be their derision in the
    land of Egypt.

Israel Will Reap the Whirlwind

8 Set the trumpet to your lips!
  One like a vulture is over the house
    of the Lord,
because they have transgressed my
    covenant
  and rebelled against my law.
2 To me they cry,
  "My God, we—Israel—know you."
3 Israel has spurned the good;
  the enemy shall pursue him.

4 They made kings, but not through
    me.
  They set up princes, but I knew it
    not.
With their silver and gold they made
    idols
  for their own destruction.
5 I have[3] spurned your calf, O Samaria.
  My anger burns against them.
How long will they be incapable of
    innocence?
6 For it is from Israel;
a craftsman made it;
  it is not God.
The calf of Samaria
  shall be broken to pieces.[4]

7 For they sow the wind,
  and they shall reap the whirlwind.
The standing grain has no heads;
  it shall yield no flour;
if it were to yield,
  strangers would devour it.
8 Israel is swallowed up;
  already they are among the
    nations
  as a useless vessel.
9 For they have gone up to Assyria,
  a wild donkey wandering alone;
  Ephraim has hired lovers.

[1] Or in his presence [2] Or to the Most High [3] Hebrew He has [4] Or shall go up in flames

10 Though they hire allies among the
    nations,
  I will soon gather them up.
And the king and princes shall soon
    writhe
  because of the tribute.

11 Because Ephraim has multiplied
    altars for sinning,
  they have become to him altars for
    sinning.
12 Were I to write for him my laws by
    the ten thousands,
  they would be regarded as a
    strange thing.
13 As for my sacrificial offerings,
  they sacrifice meat and eat it,
    but the LORD does not accept them.
Now he will remember their iniquity
  and punish their sins;
    they shall return to Egypt.
14 For Israel has forgotten his Maker
  and built palaces,
and Judah has multiplied fortified cit-
    ies;
  so I will send a fire upon his cities,
  and it shall devour her strongholds.

The LORD Will Punish Israel

9 Rejoice not, O Israel!
  Exult not like the peoples;
for you have played the whore, for-
    saking your God.
  You have loved a prostitute's
    wages
  on all threshing floors.
2 Threshing floor and wine vat shall
    not feed them,
  and the new wine shall fail them.
3 They shall not remain in the land of
    the LORD,
  but Ephraim shall return to Egypt,
  and they shall eat unclean food in
    Assyria.

4 They shall not pour drink offerings
    of wine to the LORD,
  and their sacrifices shall not
    please him.
It shall be like mourners' bread to
    them;
  all who eat of it shall be defiled;
for their bread shall be for their
    hunger only;
  it shall not come to the house of
    the LORD.

5 What will you do on the day of the
    appointed festival,
  and on the day of the feast of the
    LORD?
6 For behold, they are going away from
    destruction;
  but Egypt shall gather them;
  Memphis shall bury them.
Nettles shall possess their precious
    things of silver;
  thorns shall be in their tents.

7 The days of punishment have come;
  the days of recompense have
    come;
  Israel shall know it.
The prophet is a fool;
  the man of the spirit is mad,
because of your great iniquity
  and great hatred.
8 The prophet is the watchman of
    Ephraim with my God;
  yet a fowler's snare is on all his
    ways,
  and hatred in the house of his
    God.
9 They have deeply corrupted them-
    selves
  as in the days of Gibeah:
he will remember their iniquity;
  he will punish their sins.

10 Like grapes in the wilderness,
  I found Israel.
Like the first fruit on the fig tree
  in its first season,
  I saw your fathers.
But they came to Baal-peor
  and consecrated themselves to the
    thing of shame,
  and became detestable like the
    thing they loved.
11 Ephraim's glory shall fly away like a
    bird—
  no birth, no pregnancy, no concep-
    tion!
12 Even if they bring up children,
  I will bereave them till none is left.
Woe to them
  when I depart from them!
13 Ephraim, as I have seen, was like
  a young palm[1] planted in a
    meadow;
  but Ephraim must lead his chil-
    dren out to slaughter.[2]

Or like Tyre [2] Hebrew to him who slaughters

14 Give them, O LORD—
      what will you give?
   Give them a miscarrying womb
      and dry breasts.

15 Every evil of theirs is in Gilgal;
      there I began to hate them.
   Because of the wickedness of their
         deeds
      I will drive them out of my house.
   I will love them no more;
      all their princes are rebels.

16 Ephraim is stricken;
      their root is dried up;
      they shall bear no fruit.
   Even though they give birth,
      I will put their beloved children to
         death.
17 My God will reject them
      because they have not listened to
         him;
      they shall be wanderers among the
         nations.

¹ Hebrew *He*

10 Israel is a luxuriant vine
      that yields its fruit.
   The more his fruit increased,
      the more altars he built;
   as his country improved,
      he improved his pillars.
2 Their heart is false;
      now they must bear their guilt.
   The LORD¹ will break down their
         altars
      and destroy their pillars.

3 For now they will say:
      "We have no king,
   for we do not fear the LORD;
      and a king—what could he do for
         us?"
4 They utter mere words;
      with empty oaths they make cov-
         enants;
   so judgment springs up like poison-
         ous weeds
      in the furrows of the field.

Know God

verses to read
Hosea 9:14–17

What good is a command if the one who gets it doesn't do it? When the Lord commands his people, they prove they heard him by trusting him enough to do what he said. If they don't, sooner or later he's going to do something about it. When people refuse to listen, or in other words refuse to obey, God's wrath goes into action. Thankfully, Christ's death and resurrection saves us from the wrath of God by giving us a sacrifice for our sins. He sets us free from punishment and rejection, but he doesn't set us free to sin to our heart's content. He sets us free from the wrath of God, but not from the *eye* of God. The God Girl can't let grace be her free pass to sin, any more than the forgiveness she gives other people is a free pass for them to hurt her again.

When you see a sin in your life, it's time to reject it, to turn around and go the other way. Confess what you've done wrong and decide to never do it again. Accept God's forgiveness, but also accept his strength that will help you to avoid the pattern of sin that led you to need to confess in the first place. As a God Girl you can call him Lord of your life, but it's your Spirit-led actions that prove whether that's true or not. Take a look at the life of the Israelites and their rejection of God's law and see how God drew them back to himself through discipline. If you are experiencing God's discipline, don't panic. Just look at it as a red flag warning you to turn around and go the other way. God's commands are good and therefore good for you to follow.

5 The inhabitants of Samaria tremble
    for the calf[1] of Beth-aven.
 Its people mourn for it, and so do its
    idolatrous priests—
  those who rejoiced over it and
    over its glory—
  for it has departed[2] from them.
6 The thing itself shall be carried to
    Assyria
  as tribute to the great king.[3]
 Ephraim shall be put to shame,
  and Israel shall be ashamed of his
    idol.[4]

7 Samaria's king shall perish
  like a twig on the face of the
    waters.
8 The high places of Aven, the sin of
    Israel,
  shall be destroyed.
 Thorn and thistle shall grow up
  on their altars,
 and they shall say to the mountains,
    "Cover us,"
  and to the hills, "Fall on us."

9 From the days of Gibeah, you have
    sinned, O Israel;
  there they have continued.
 Shall not the war against the
    unjust[5] overtake them in
    Gibeah?
10 When I please, I will discipline them,
  and nations shall be gathered
    against them
  when they are bound up for their
    double iniquity.

11 Ephraim was a trained calf
  that loved to thresh,
  and I spared her fair neck;
 but I will put Ephraim to the yoke;
  Judah must plow;
  Jacob must harrow for himself.
12 Sow for yourselves righteousness;
  reap steadfast love;
  break up your fallow ground,
 for it is the time to seek the LORD,
  that he may come and rain righ-
    teousness upon you.

13 You have plowed iniquity;
  you have reaped injustice;
  you have eaten the fruit of lies.

 Because you have trusted in your
    own way
  and in the multitude of your war-
    riors,
14 therefore the tumult of war shall
    arise among your people,
  and all your fortresses shall be
    destroyed,
 as Shalman destroyed Beth-arbel on
    the day of battle;
  mothers were dashed in pieces
    with their children.
15 Thus it shall be done to you,
    O Bethel,
  because of your great evil.
 At dawn the king of Israel
  shall be utterly cut off.

The LORD's Love for Israel

11 When Israel was a child, I loved
    him,
  and out of Egypt I called my son.
2 The more they were called,
  the more they went away;
 they kept sacrificing to the Baals
  and burning offerings to idols.

3 Yet it was I who taught Ephraim to
    walk;
  I took them up by their arms,
  but they did not know that
    I healed them.
4 I led them with cords of kindness,[6]
  with the bands of love,
 and I became to them as one who
    eases the yoke on their jaws,
  and I bent down to them and fed
    them.

5 They shall not[7] return to the land of
    Egypt,
  but Assyria shall be their king,
  because they have refused to
    return to me.
6 The sword shall rage against their
    cities,
  consume the bars of their gates,
  and devour them because of their
    own counsels.
7 My people are bent on turning away
    from me,
  and though they call out to the
    Most High,
  he shall not raise them up at all.

[1] Or calves [2] Or has gone into exile [3] Or to King Jareb [4] Or counsel [5] Hebrew the children of injustice [6] Or humaneness; Hebrew man [7] Or surely

8   How can I give you up, O Ephraim?
       How can I hand you over, O Israel?
   How can I make you like Admah?
       How can I treat you like Zeboiim?
   My heart recoils within me;
       my compassion grows warm and
           tender.
9   I will not execute my burning anger;
       I will not again destroy Ephraim;
   for I am God and not a man,
       the Holy One in your midst,
       and I will not come in wrath.[1]

10 They shall go after the LORD;
       he will roar like a lion;
   when he roars,
       his children shall come trembling
           from the west;
11 they shall come trembling like birds
           from Egypt,
       and like doves from the land of
           Assyria,
   and I will return them to their
       homes, declares the LORD.
12[2] Ephraim has surrounded me with
           lies,
       and the house of Israel with deceit,
   but Judah still walks with God
       and is faithful to the Holy One.

12

   Ephraim feeds on the wind
       and pursues the east wind all
           day long;
   they multiply falsehood and vio-
       lence;
       they make a covenant with Assyria,
       and oil is carried to Egypt.

The LORD's Indictment of Israel and Judah

2   The LORD has an indictment against
           Judah
       and will punish Jacob according to
           his ways;
       he will repay him according to his
           deeds.
3   In the womb he took his brother by
           the heel,
       and in his manhood he strove with
           God.
4   He strove with the angel and pre-
           vailed;
       he wept and sought his favor.
   He met God[3] at Bethel,
       and there God spoke with us—
5   the LORD, the God of hosts,
       the LORD is his memorial name:

6   "So you, by the help of your God,
           return,
       hold fast to love and justice,
       and wait continually for your God."

7   A merchant, in whose hands are false
           balances,
       he loves to oppress.
8   Ephraim has said, "Ah, but I am rich;
       I have found wealth for myself;
   in all my labors they cannot find in
       me iniquity or sin."
9   I am the LORD your God
       from the land of Egypt;
   I will again make you dwell in tents,
       as in the days of the appointed
           feast.

10 I spoke to the prophets;
       it was I who multiplied visions,
       and through the prophets gave
           parables.
11 If there is iniquity in Gilead,
       they shall surely come to nothing:
   in Gilgal they sacrifice bulls;
       their altars also are like stone
           heaps
       on the furrows of the field.
12 Jacob fled to the land of Aram;
       there Israel served for a wife,
       and for a wife he guarded sheep.
13 By a prophet the LORD brought Israel
           up from Egypt,
       and by a prophet he was guarded.
14 Ephraim has given bitter provoca-
           tion;
       so his Lord will leave his blood-
           guilt on him
       and will repay him for his dis-
           graceful deeds.

The LORD's Relentless Judgment on Israel

13

   When Ephraim spoke, there was
       trembling;
       he was exalted in Israel,
       but he incurred guilt through Baal
           and died.
2   And now they sin more and more,
       and make for themselves metal
           images,
   idols skillfully made of their silver,
       all of them the work of craftsmen.
   It is said of them,
       "Those who offer human sacrifice
           kiss calves!"

[1] Or into the city   [2] Ch 12:1 in Hebrew   [3] Hebrew him

3 Therefore they shall be like the
      morning mist
    or like the dew that goes early away,
like the chaff that swirls from the
      threshing floor
    or like smoke from a window.

4 But I am the Lord your God
    from the land of Egypt;
you know no God but me,
    and besides me there is no savior.

5 It was I who knew you in the wilder-
    ness,
    in the land of drought;

6 but when they had grazed,[1] they
      became full,
    they were filled, and their heart
      was lifted up;
    therefore they forgot me.

7 So I am to them like a lion;
    like a leopard I will lurk beside the
      way.

8 I will fall upon them like a bear
      robbed of her cubs;
    I will tear open their breast,
and there I will devour them like a
      lion,
      as a wild beast would rip them
      open.

9 He destroys[2] you, O Israel,
    for you are against me, against
      your helper.

10 Where now is your king, to save you
    in all your cities?
    Where are all your rulers—
those of whom you said,
    "Give me a king and princes"?

11 I gave you a king in my anger,
    and I took him away in my wrath.

12 The iniquity of Ephraim is bound up;
    his sin is kept in store.

13 The pangs of childbirth come for him,
    but he is an unwise son,
for at the right time he does not pre-
    sent himself
    at the opening of the womb.

14 Shall I ransom them from the power
    of Sheol?
    Shall I redeem them from Death?
O Death, where are your plagues?
    O Sheol, where is your sting?
    Compassion is hidden from my
      eyes.

15 Though he may flourish among his
      brothers,
    the east wind, the wind of the
      Lord, shall come,
    rising from the wilderness,
and his fountain shall dry up;
    his spring shall be parched;
it shall strip his treasury
    of every precious thing.

16[3] Samaria shall bear her guilt,
    because she has rebelled against
      her God;
they shall fall by the sword;
    their little ones shall be dashed in
      pieces,
    and their pregnant women ripped
      open.

A Plea to Return to the Lord

14 Return, O Israel, to the Lord your
    God,
    for you have stumbled because of
      your iniquity.

2 Take with you words
    and return to the Lord;
say to him,
   "Take away all iniquity;
accept what is good,
    and we will pay with bulls
    the vows[4] of our lips.

3 Assyria shall not save us;
    we will not ride on horses;
and we will say no more, 'Our God,'
    to the work of our hands.
In you the orphan finds mercy."

4 I will heal their apostasy;
    I will love them freely,
    for my anger has turned from
      them.

5 I will be like the dew to Israel;
    he shall blossom like the lily;
    he shall take root like the trees of
      Lebanon;

6 his shoots shall spread out;
    his beauty shall be like the olive,
    and his fragrance like Lebanon.

7 They shall return and dwell beneath
    my[5] shadow;
    they shall flourish like the grain;
they shall blossom like the vine;
    their fame shall be like the wine of
      Lebanon.

Hebrew *according to their pasture* [2] Or *I will destroy* [3] Ch 14:1 in Hebrew [4] Septuagint, Syriac *pay the fruit* [5] Hebrew *his*

8   O Ephraim, what have I to do with
         idols?
     It is I who answer and look after
         you.[1]
     I am like an evergreen cypress;
         from me comes your fruit.

9   Whoever is wise, let him understand
         these things;
     whoever is discerning, let him
         know them;
     for the ways of the LORD are right,
         and the upright walk in them,
         but transgressors stumble in them.

[1] Hebrew *him*

INTRODUCTION TO
Joel

Author: Joel

Time: Probably around 590 B.C.

Place: Israel

Written to: The people of Judah

The gist

Like most prophets, Joel was writing to warn his people. They had just experienced a natural disaster of locusts, so that they could understand the wrath of God. The Lord wanted them to know that their sin would lead to punishment, and so he exhorted them to repent and return to him.

Things to look for

Descriptions of God's grace (see Joel 2:12–14, 28–32)

Warnings about the day of the Lord (see Joel 1:15; 2:1, 11, 31; 3:14, 18)

Heed the Warning Signs

> For the day of the LORD is near,
> and as destruction from the Almighty it comes.
>
> Joel 1:15

God isn't happy when his people sin. And when things get really bad, God does something about it. In the Old Testament, God used things like plagues, invasion, and destruction to get his people to wake up and look up. The book of Joel was written to help the Israelites understand the destruction that had been coming their way and would soon come again because of the evil things they were doing.

Not long before Joel wrote to his people, a plague of locusts had hit them hard. Since you probably haven't seen a swarm of locusts, let me tell you what that meant: The locusts flow like a giant river, devouring every piece of vegetation in their way. And when they are gone, nothing is left standing. Israel was an agricultural society, so this invasion left the people with nothing to eat and nothing to feed their livestock. Things weren't looking so good from where they stood, yet the prophet didn't write to condemn them but to show them a way out of their misery. That way out was returning to God through repentance, prayer, and fasting. Joel wanted the people to understand that all that destruction had come because they had rejected God. And more destruction was on its way. Bad guys were about to invade from the north, and they weren't going to mess around.

God didn't want the attacks on Israel to be looked at as haphazard events. Nothing happens outside of God's control. And when he lets destruction come on his people, it's time for them to sit up and listen. When hard times come your way, don't worry over them, but look to God and trust him even if you don't understand why certain things are happening. Is he trying to get your attention? Is he allowing all this stuff in order to purify you or strengthen you? Not all destruction comes from your sin; a lot of it is because of the sin of other people, but that doesn't change your responsibility to ask, "Where is my sin, and how can I turn around and get things right?" God uses everything in your life for your good when you are willing to trust him and to turn your life over to him.

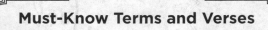

Must-Know Terms and Verses

☙ *Day of the Lord* ❧

A time in the future when God will judge everyone on earth, at which time God's enemies will be destroyed and his people will be exalted.

☙ *Valley of Decision* ❧

The valley where all the people who rejected God will one day be judged by him.

Return to the LORD your God,
    for he is gracious and merciful,
slow to anger, and abounding in steadfast love;
    and he relents over disaster. *Joel 2:13*

"And it shall come to pass afterward,
    that I will pour out my Spirit on all flesh;
your sons and your daughters shall prophesy,
    your old men shall dream dreams,
    and your young men shall see visions." *Joel 2:28*

Joel

1 The word of the LORD that came to Joel, the son of Pethuel:

An Invasion of Locusts

2 Hear this, you elders;
  give ear, all inhabitants of the land!
Has such a thing happened in your days,
  or in the days of your fathers?
3 Tell your children of it,
  and let your children tell their children,
  and their children to another generation.

4 What the cutting locust left,
  the swarming locust has eaten.
What the swarming locust left,
  the hopping locust has eaten,
and what the hopping locust left,
  the destroying locust has eaten.

5 Awake, you drunkards, and weep,
  and wail, all you drinkers of wine,
because of the sweet wine,
  for it is cut off from your mouth.
6 For a nation has come up against my land,
  powerful and beyond number;
its teeth are lions' teeth,
  and it has the fangs of a lioness.
7 It has laid waste my vine
  and splintered my fig tree;
it has stripped off their bark and thrown it down;
  their branches are made white.

8 Lament like a virgin[1] wearing sackcloth
  for the bridegroom of her youth.
9 The grain offering and the drink offering are cut off
  from the house of the LORD.
The priests mourn,
  the ministers of the LORD.

10 The fields are destroyed,
  the ground mourns,
because the grain is destroyed,
  the wine dries up,
  the oil languishes.

11 Be ashamed,[2] O tillers of the soil;
  wail, O vinedressers,
for the wheat and the barley,
  because the harvest of the field has perished.
12 The vine dries up;
  the fig tree languishes.
Pomegranate, palm, and apple,
  all the trees of the field are dried up,
and gladness dries up
  from the children of man.

A Call to Repentance

13 Put on sackcloth and lament,
  O priests;
wail, O ministers of the altar.
Go in, pass the night in sackcloth,
  O ministers of my God!
Because grain offering and drink offering
  are withheld from the house of your God.

14 Consecrate a fast;
  call a solemn assembly.
Gather the elders
  and all the inhabitants of the land
to the house of the LORD your God,
  and cry out to the LORD.

15 Alas for the day!
For the day of the LORD is near,
  and as destruction from the Almighty[3] it comes.
16 Is not the food cut off
  before our eyes,
joy and gladness
  from the house of our God?

Or *young woman* [2] The Hebrew words for *dry up* and *be ashamed* in verses 10–12, 17 sound alike [3] *Destruction* sounds like the Hebrew for *Almighty*

¹⁷ The seed shrivels under the clods;[1]
    the storehouses are desolate;
the granaries are torn down
    because the grain has dried up.
¹⁸ How the beasts groan!
    The herds of cattle are perplexed
because there is no pasture for them;
    even the flocks of sheep suffer.[2]

¹⁹ To you, O LORD, I call.
For fire has devoured
    the pastures of the wilderness,
and flame has burned
    all the trees of the field.
²⁰ Even the beasts of the field pant for
    you
    because the water brooks are
      dried up,
and fire has devoured
    the pastures of the wilderness.

The Day of the LORD

2 Blow a trumpet in Zion;
    sound an alarm on my holy moun-
      tain!
Let all the inhabitants of the land
      tremble,
    for the day of the LORD is coming;
      it is near,
² a day of darkness and gloom,
    a day of clouds and thick darkness
Like blackness there is spread upon
      the mountains
    a great and powerful people;
their like has never been before,
    nor will be again after them
    through the years of all genera-
      tions.

³ Fire devours before them,
    and behind them a flame burns.
The land is like the garden of Eden
      before them,
    but behind them a desolate wilder
      ness,
    and nothing escapes them.

⁴ Their appearance is like the appear-
      ance of horses,
    and like war horses they run.
⁵ As with the rumbling of chariots,
    they leap on the tops of the moun-
      tains,
like the crackling of a flame of fire
    devouring the stubble,
like a powerful army
    drawn up for battle.

⁶ Before them peoples are in anguish;
    all faces grow pale.
⁷ Like warriors they charge;
    like soldiers they scale the wall.
They march each on his way;
    they do not swerve from their
      paths.

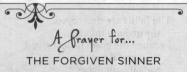

A Prayer for...

THE FORGIVEN SINNER

Wonderful God, thank you for letting me know you. I used to live in the world while being totally ignorant of its Creator. I took advantage of your gifts but didn't know the Giver. I was blind while I enjoyed the sunlight and was deaf to everything spiritual with voices all around me. I understood a lot of things, but I had no knowledge of your ways. I saw the world, but I didn't see Jesus.

I'm so thankful for the day when by your sovereignty you looked at me and called me by grace. At that point my dead heart started to beat, my darkened eye glimmered with light, my dull ear caught your echo, and I turned to you and found you, a God ready to hear and willing to save.

Then I found my heart was fighting with you, irritating your Spirit, and so I fell at your feet and heard you thunder, "The person who sins will die." But when grace let me know and love you, I saw your Son dying so that I could live, and in that death I found my all.

My soul sings as I remember that peace. May I never lose my hold on Christ or his hold on me. Please remind me always of the mercy I've found; let me tell others about you as long as I live—that you are a sin-pardoning God, taking up the blasphemer and the ungodly and washing them from their deepest stain.

Amen.

---

[1] The meaning of the Hebrew line is uncertain   [2] Or *are made desolate*

They do not jostle one another;
   each marches in his path;
they burst through the weapons
   and are not halted.
They leap upon the city,
   they run upon the walls,
they climb up into the houses,
   they enter through the windows
      like a thief.

The earth quakes before them;
   the heavens tremble.
The sun and the moon are darkened,
   and the stars withdraw their shin-
      ing.
The Lord utters his voice
   before his army,
for his camp is exceedingly great;
   he who executes his word is pow-
      erful.
For the day of the Lord is great and
      very awesome;
   who can endure it?

Return to the Lord

"Yet even now," declares the Lord,
   "return to me with all your heart,
with fasting, with weeping, and with
      mourning;
   and rend your hearts and not your
      garments."
Return to the Lord your God,
   for he is gracious and merciful,
slow to anger, and abounding in
      steadfast love;
   and he relents over disaster.
Who knows whether he will not turn
      and relent,
   and leave a blessing behind him,
a grain offering and a drink offering
   for the Lord your God?

Blow the trumpet in Zion;
   consecrate a fast;
call a solemn assembly;
   gather the people.
Consecrate the congregation;
   assemble the elders;
gather the children,
   even nursing infants.
Let the bridegroom leave his room,
   and the bride her chamber.

Between the vestibule and the altar
   let the priests, the ministers of the
      Lord, weep

and say, "Spare your people, O Lord,
   and make not your heritage a
      reproach,
   a byword among the nations.[1]
Why should they say among the
      peoples,
   'Where is their God?'"

The Lord Had Pity

18 Then the Lord became jealous for
      his land
   and had pity on his people.
19 The Lord answered and said to his
      people,
"Behold, I am sending to you
   grain, wine, and oil,
   and you will be satisfied;
and I will no more make you
   a reproach among the nations.

20 "I will remove the northerner far from
      you,
   and drive him into a parched and
      desolate land,
his vanguard[2] into the eastern sea,
   and his rear guard[3] into the west-
      ern sea;
the stench and foul smell of him will
      rise,
   for he has done great things.

21 "Fear not, O land;
   be glad and rejoice,
   for the Lord has done great things!
22 Fear not, you beasts of the field,
   for the pastures of the wilderness
      are green;
the tree bears its fruit;
   the fig tree and vine give their full
      yield.

23 "Be glad, O children of Zion,
   and rejoice in the Lord your God,
for he has given the early rain for
      your vindication;
he has poured down for you abun-
      dant rain,
   the early and the latter rain, as
      before.

24 "The threshing floors shall be full of
      grain;
   the vats shall overflow with wine
      and oil.
25 I will restore[4] to you the years
   that the swarming locust has eaten,

---

[1] Or reproach, that the nations should rule over them [2] Hebrew face [3] Hebrew his end [4] Or pay back

the hopper, the destroyer, and the
cutter,
   my great army, which I sent among
you.

26 "You shall eat in plenty and be satisfied,
   and praise the name of the LORD
your God,
   who has dealt wondrously with you.
And my people shall never again be
put to shame.
27 You shall know that I am in the midst
of Israel,
   and that I am the LORD your God
and there is none else.
And my people shall never again be
put to shame.

The LORD Will Pour Out His Spirit

28 [1] "And it shall come to pass afterward,
   that I will pour out my Spirit on all
flesh;
   your sons and your daughters shall
prophesy,
   your old men shall dream dreams,
   and your young men shall see
visions.
29 Even on the male and female servants
in those days I will pour out my
Spirit.

30 "And I will show wonders in the heavens and on the earth, blood and fire and columns of smoke. 31 The sun shall be turned to darkness, and the moon to blood, before the great and awesome day of the LORD comes. 32 And it shall come to pass that everyone who calls on the name of the LORD shall be saved. For in Mount Zion and in Jerusalem there shall be those who escape, as the LORD has said, and among the survivors shall be those whom the LORD calls.

The LORD Judges the Nations

3 [2] "For behold, in those days and at that time, when I restore the fortunes of Judah and Jerusalem, 2 I will gather all the nations and bring them down to the Valley of Jehoshaphat. And I will enter into judgment with them there, on behalf of my people and my heritage Israel, because they have scattered them among the nations and have divided up my land, 3 and have cast lots for my people, and have traded a boy for a prostitute, and have sold a girl for wine and have drunk it.

4 "What are you to me, O Tyre and Sidon, and all the regions of Philistia? Are you paying me back for something? If you are paying me back, I will return your payment on your own head swiftly and speedily. 5 For you have taken my silver and my gold, and have carried my rich treasures into your temples.[3] 6 You have sold the people of Judah and Jerusalem to the Greeks in order to remove them far from their own border. 7 Behold, I will stir them up from the place to which you have sold them, and I will return your payment on your own head. 8 I will sell your sons and your daughters into the hand of the people of Judah, and they will sell them to the Sabeans, to a nation far away, for the LORD has spoken."

9 Proclaim this among the nations:
Consecrate for war;[4]
   stir up the mighty men.
Let all the men of war draw near;
   let them come up.
10 Beat your plowshares into swords,
   and your pruning hooks into spears;
   let the weak say, "I am a warrior."

11 Hasten and come,
   all you surrounding nations,
   and gather yourselves there.
Bring down your warriors, O LORD.
12 Let the nations stir themselves up
   and come up to the Valley of
Jehoshaphat;
   for there I will sit to judge
   all the surrounding nations.

13 Put in the sickle,
   for the harvest is ripe.
Go in, tread,
   for the winepress is full.
The vats overflow,
   for their evil is great.

14 Multitudes, multitudes,
   in the valley of decision!
For the day of the LORD is near
   in the valley of decision.
15 The sun and the moon are darkened,
   and the stars withdraw their shining.
16 The LORD roars from Zion,
   and utters his voice from Jerusalem,
   and the heavens and the earth
quake.

---

1 Ch 3:1 in Hebrew   2 Ch 4:1 in Hebrew   3 Or palaces   4 Or Consecrate a war

But the Lord is a refuge to his
people,
  a stronghold to the people of
Israel.

The Glorious Future of Judah

7 "So you shall know that I am the Lord
your God,
  who dwells in Zion, my holy mountain.
And Jerusalem shall be holy,
  and strangers shall never again
pass through it.

8 "And in that day
  the mountains shall drip sweet wine,
  and the hills shall flow with milk,

and all the streambeds of Judah
  shall flow with water;
and a fountain shall come forth from
the house of the Lord
and water the Valley of Shittim.

19 "Egypt shall become a desolation
  and Edom a desolate wilderness,
for the violence done to the people of
Judah,
  because they have shed innocent
blood in their land.
20 But Judah shall be inhabited forever,
  and Jerusalem to all generations.
21 I will avenge their blood,
  blood I have not avenged,[1]
  for the Lord dwells in Zion."

---

[1] Or I will acquit their bloodguilt that I have not acquitted

INTRODUCTION TO
Amos

Amos 5:6

Author: Amos, a sheep farmer

Time: 762–754 B.C.

Place: Judah

Written to: The leaders of ancient Israel

The gist

Amos is a book about the universal justice of God. Israel fully expected that God would judge the wicked nations all around them, but they were not prepared for the fact that Israel, too, would be judged, due to their uncaring attitude toward the poor and the weak.

Things to look for

- The exploits of the rich (see Amos 2:6–7; 3:10–15; 5:7, 10–13; 6:4, 12; 8:4–6)

- God's restoration of his people despite their sin (see Amos 9:11–15)

Search for God

Seek the LORD and live.

Which would you rather be: blissfully ignorant or completely aware of the sin in your life? A lot of people would choose blissful ignorance because they think that it will somehow keep them from the pain of being convicted of sin and the need to do something about it. This made the job of the prophet a tough one. He had to point out people's sin so that they wouldn't die in blissful but deadly ignorance. Not the most fun job in the world.

In the book of Amos, the prophet wants to make sure that none of the Israelites are living with a false sense of security. Their sin was obvious, but they had chosen ignorant bliss over doing something about it. They were living immoral and greedy lives, stomping on the poor to get what they wanted while they lived the good life of the rich and famous. Taking a Sabbath seemed like an imposition on their busy workweek. And even though they looked "religious" on the outside, on the inside they were prideful and cruel.

God's justice can't stand immorality. He can't just let it slide but has to do something when his people turn away from him. Though most prophets were people who listened to God and then passed on what they heard to the people, a lot of times they would speak to God on the people's behalf, and in the book of Amos you find him interceding for the Israelites. As you read, you will see something that not a lot of people know, and that's that God will change his plans for man—God changes his plans twice after Amos intercedes (check it out in Amos 7:3, 6).

As a God Girl you can't just skim over these so-called Minor Prophets as if they don't apply to your life today. These short books have a lot to say about the character of God and even about the character of people. Look for ways that you can relate to the Israelites and how you might be religious on the outside but sinful on the inside. Then promise to make a change before it's too late. Take the prophet Amos's warning as a personal one. Don't ever dismiss the power of all of God's Word in the life of the modern believer.

Must-Know Terms and Verses

✑ *Horns of the Altar* ✑

Four large horns or projections that came out on either side of the altar. Cutting them off would mean that no further sacrifice could be made for sin (see Amos 3:14).

✑ *House of Jacob* ✑

Refers to the family of the Israelites, starting with Jacob's twelve sons.

✑ *Minor Prophet* ✑

The books of Hosea through Malachi are referred to as the Minor Prophets. This refers to the length of the books, not the importance of the prophets.

———•••———

"They have rejected the law of the LORD,
    and have not kept his statutes,
but their lies have led them astray,
    those after which their fathers walked.
So I will send a fire upon Judah,
    and it shall devour the strongholds of Jerusalem." *Amos 2:4–5*

"Do two walk together,
    unless they have agreed to meet?" *Amos 3:3*

Seek the LORD and live. *Amos 5:6*

Amos

1 The words of Amos, who was among the shepherds[1] of Tekoa, which he saw concerning Israel in the days of Uzziah king of Judah and in the days of Jeroboam the son of Joash, king of Israel, two years[2] before the earthquake.

Judgment on Israel's Neighbors

And he said:

> "The LORD roars from Zion
>   and utters his voice from Jerusalem;
> the pastures of the shepherds mourn,
>   and the top of Carmel withers."

Thus says the LORD:

> "For three transgressions of Damascus,
>   and for four, I will not revoke the
>   punishment,[3]
> because they have threshed Gilead
>   with threshing sledges of iron.
> ⁴ So I will send a fire upon the house
>   of Hazael,
>   and it shall devour the strongholds
>   of Ben-hadad.
> ⁵ I will break the gate-bar of Damascus,
>   and cut off the inhabitants from
>   the Valley of Aven,[4]
> and him who holds the scepter from
>   Beth-eden;
>   and the people of Syria shall go
>   into exile to Kir,"
> > says the LORD.

Thus says the LORD:

> "For three transgressions of Gaza,
>   and for four, I will not revoke the
>   punishment,
> because they carried into exile a
>   whole people
>   to deliver them up to Edom.
> ⁷ So I will send a fire upon the wall of
>   Gaza,
>   and it shall devour her strong-
>   holds.
> ⁸ I will cut off the inhabitants from
>   Ashdod,
>   and him who holds the scepter
>   from Ashkelon;
> I will turn my hand against Ekron,
>   and the remnant of the Philistines
>   shall perish,"
> > says the Lord GOD.

⁹ Thus says the LORD:

> "For three transgressions of Tyre,
>   and for four, I will not revoke the
>   punishment,
> because they delivered up a whole
>   people to Edom,
>   and did not remember the cov-
>   enant of brotherhood.
> ¹⁰ So I will send a fire upon the wall of
>   Tyre,
>   and it shall devour her strong-
>   holds."

¹¹ Thus says the LORD:

> "For three transgressions of Edom,
>   and for four, I will not revoke the
>   punishment,
> because he pursued his brother with
>   the sword
>   and cast off all pity,
> and his anger tore perpetually,
>   and he kept his wrath forever.
> ¹² So I will send a fire upon Teman,
>   and it shall devour the strongholds
>   of Bozrah."

¹³ Thus says the LORD:

> "For three transgressions of the
>   Ammonites,
>   and for four, I will not revoke the
>   punishment,
> because they have ripped open preg-
>   nant women in Gilead,
>   that they might enlarge their bor-
>   der.

---

[1] Or *sheep breeders* [2] Or *during two years* [3] Hebrew *I will not turn it back*; also verses 6, 9, 11, 13 [4] Or *On*

14 So I will kindle a fire in the wall of
        Rabbah,
    and it shall devour her strongholds,
    with shouting on the day of battle,
    with a tempest in the day of the
        whirlwind;
15 and their king shall go into exile,
    he and his princes[1] together,"
                    says the LORD.

2 Thus says the LORD:

    "For three transgressions of Moab,
        and for four, I will not revoke the
            punishment,[2]
    because he burned to lime
        the bones of the king of Edom.
2   So I will send a fire upon Moab,
        and it shall devour the strongholds
            of Kerioth,
    and Moab shall die amid uproar,
        amid shouting and the sound of
            the trumpet;
3   I will cut off the ruler from its midst,
        and will kill all its princes[3] with
            him,"
                    says the LORD.

Judgment on Judah
4 Thus says the LORD:

    "For three transgressions of Judah,
        and for four, I will not revoke the
            punishment,
    because they have rejected the law of
        the LORD,
        and have not kept his statutes,
    but their lies have led them astray,
        those after which their fathers
            walked.
5   So I will send a fire upon Judah,
        and it shall devour the strongholds
            of Jerusalem."

Judgment on Israel
6 Thus says the LORD:

    "For three transgressions of Israel,
        and for four, I will not revoke the
            punishment,
    because they sell the righteous for
        silver,
        and the needy for a pair of san-
            dals—

7   those who trample the head of the
        poor into the dust of the earth
        and turn aside the way of the
            afflicted;
    a man and his father go in to the
        same girl,
        so that my holy name is profaned;
8   they lay themselves down beside
        every altar
        on garments taken in pledge,
    and in the house of their God they
        drink
        the wine of those who have been
            fined.

9   "Yet it was I who destroyed the
        Amorite before them,
        whose height was like the height
            of the cedars
        and who was as strong as the oaks;
    I destroyed his fruit above
        and his roots beneath.
10 Also it was I who brought you up out
        of the land of Egypt
        and led you forty years in the
            wilderness,
        to possess the land of the Amorite.
11 And I raised up some of your sons for
        prophets,
        and some of your young men for
            Nazirites.
    Is it not indeed so, O people of
        Israel?"
                    declares the LORD.

12 "But you made the Nazirites drink
        wine,
        and commanded the prophets,
            saying, 'You shall not prophesy.'

13 "Behold, I will press you down in your
        place,
        as a cart full of sheaves presses
            down.
14 Flight shall perish from the swift,
        and the strong shall not retain his
            strength,
        nor shall the mighty save his life;
15 he who handles the bow shall not
        stand,
        and he who is swift of foot shall
            not save himself,
        nor shall he who rides the horse
            save his life;

---

[1] Or officials [2] Hebrew I will not turn it back; also verses 4, 6 [3] Or officials

6   and he who is stout of heart among
the mighty
    shall flee away naked in that day,"
                declares the LORD.

Israel's Guilt and Punishment

3 Hear this word that the LORD has spoken against you, O people of Israel, against the whole family that I brought up out of the land of Egypt:

2   "You only have I known
    of all the families of the earth;
  therefore I will punish you
    for all your iniquities.

3   "Do two walk together,
    unless they have agreed to meet?

4   Does a lion roar in the forest,
    when he has no prey?
  Does a young lion cry out from his
den,
    if he has taken nothing?

5   Does a bird fall in a snare on the earth,
    when there is no trap for it?
Does a snare spring up from the
ground,
    when it has taken nothing?

6   Is a trumpet blown in a city,
    and the people are not afraid?
Does disaster come to a city,
    unless the LORD has done it?

7   "For the Lord GOD does nothing
    without revealing his secret
    to his servants the prophets.

8   The lion has roared;
    who will not fear?
The Lord GOD has spoken;
    who can but prophesy?"

9   Proclaim to the strongholds in Ashdod
    and to the strongholds in the land
of Egypt,
and say, "Assemble yourselves on the
mountains of Samaria,
    and see the great tumults within
her,
    and the oppressed in her midst."

Know Love

verses to read
Amos 3:1–8

Amos 3:3 explains that when two people are friends, it's because they believe the same things; they have something in common. Two people don't walk together unless they've met, talked, and agreed that they both want to go in the same direction. But what happens when one of the two leaves the path of faith and refuses to walk in godliness? At this point one goes in one direction, toward godliness, while the other goes in another direction, toward sin. Then the friendship is in trouble.

When this happens, it can be easy to deviate from what you know is right just because you want to make your friend happy and keep walking together. But you have to remember that your ultimate goal is God and not the whims of a friend. The God Girl has to stay on the path of righteousness as she loves her friend, even if that means loving that friend only from a distance. She must refuse to change her own path, because her ultimate goal is to make God happy, even at the expense of friendship.

When you make a decision about what kind of friend you're going to be, decide to be one who doesn't just act on feelings but who lives by the facts of God's Word. Know that when you walk with someone and call them friend, you show your agreement with them. If your friend isn't living a godly life, then you might be on the wrong path too. You can't be friends for long and not end up on the same path. Take a look at all your friendships from God's perspective, and then fearlessly love them—or leave them—according to God's call on your life.

10 "They do not know how to do right,"
     declares the LORD,
   "those who store up violence and
     robbery in their strongholds."

11 Therefore thus says the Lord GOD:

   "An adversary shall surround the land
     and bring down[1] your defenses
       from you,
     and your strongholds shall be
       plundered."

12 Thus says the LORD: "As the shepherd
rescues from the mouth of the lion two legs,
or a piece of an ear, so shall the people of Israel who dwell in Samaria be rescued, with
the corner of a couch and part[2] of a bed.

13 "Hear, and testify against the house of
     Jacob,"
     declares the Lord GOD, the God of
       hosts,
14 "that on the day I punish Israel for his
     transgressions,
     I will punish the altars of Bethel,
   and the horns of the altar shall be cut
     off
     and fall to the ground.
15 I will strike the winter house along
     with the summer house,
     and the houses of ivory shall perish,
   and the great houses[3] shall come to
     an end,"
                     declares the LORD.

4 "Hear this word, you cows of Bashan,
     who are on the mountain of
       Samaria,
   who oppress the poor, who crush the
     needy,
   who say to your husbands, 'Bring,
     that we may drink!'
2 The Lord GOD has sworn by his holi-
     ness
     that, behold, the days are coming
       upon you,
   when they shall take you away with
     hooks,
     even the last of you with fishhooks.
3 And you shall go out through the
     breaches,
     each one straight ahead;
   and you shall be cast out into
     Harmon,"
                     declares the LORD.

4 "Come to Bethel, and transgress;
     to Gilgal, and multiply transgres-
       sion;
   bring your sacrifices every morning,
     your tithes every three days;
5 offer a sacrifice of thanksgiving of
     that which is leavened,
     and proclaim freewill offerings,
       publish them;
   for so you love to do, O people of
     Israel!"
                 declares the Lord GOD

Israel Has Not Returned to the LORD
6 "I gave you cleanness of teeth in all
     your cities,
     and lack of bread in all your
       places,
   yet you did not return to me,"
                         declares the LORD

7 "I also withheld the rain from you
     when there were yet three months
       to the harvest;
   I would send rain on one city,
     and send no rain on another city;
   one field would have rain,
     and the field on which it did not
       rain would wither;
8 so two or three cities would wander
     to another city
     to drink water, and would not be
       satisfied;
   yet you did not return to me,"
                         declares the LORD

9 "I struck you with blight and mildew;
     your many gardens and your vine-
       yards,
   your fig trees and your olive trees
     the locust devoured;
   yet you did not return to me,"
                         declares the LORD

10 "I sent among you a pestilence after
     the manner of Egypt;
   I killed your young men with the
     sword,
   and carried away your horses,[4]
     and I made the stench of your
       camp go up into your nostrils;
   yet you did not return to me,"
                         declares the LORD

[1] Hebrew *An adversary, one who surrounds the land—he shall bring down* [2] The meaning of the Hebrew word is uncertain [3] Or *and man, houses* [4] Hebrew *along with the captivity of your horses*

¹ "I overthrew some of you,
   as when God overthrew Sodom
     and Gomorrah,
  and you were as a brand¹ plucked
    out of the burning;
yet you did not return to me,"
              declares the LORD.

² "Therefore thus I will do to you,
    O Israel;
  because I will do this to you,
  prepare to meet your God,
    O Israel!"

³ For behold, he who forms the moun-
    tains and creates the wind,
  and declares to man what is his
    thought,
who makes the morning darkness,
  and treads on the heights of the
    earth—
  the LORD, the God of hosts, is his
    name!

Seek the LORD and Live

5 Hear this word that I take up over you
in lamentation, O house of Israel:

² "Fallen, no more to rise,
   is the virgin Israel;

That is, a burning stick ² Or to bitter fruit

forsaken on her land,
   with none to raise her up."

³ For thus says the Lord GOD:

"The city that went out a thousand
   shall have a hundred left,
and that which went out a hundred
   shall have ten left
to the house of Israel."

⁴ For thus says the LORD to the house of
Israel:

"Seek me and live;
⁵   but do not seek Bethel,
and do not enter into Gilgal
   or cross over to Beersheba;
for Gilgal shall surely go into exile,
   and Bethel shall come to nothing."

⁶ Seek the LORD and live,
   lest he break out like fire in the
     house of Joseph,
  and it devour, with none to quench
     it for Bethel,
⁷ O you who turn justice to worm-
     wood²
  and cast down righteousness to
    the earth!

Know True Happiness

verses to read
Amos 5:4–6

"Seek me and live," God says to you (Amos 5:4). Have you strayed from God? Done wrong in his eyes? Go back to him, ask his forgiveness, and live. When you look at some of the ways God punishes sin, you might think he's dangerous and not to be trusted. Thinking about all the wrath he has poured out on the earth can be scary. But the message that keeps repeating itself throughout the entire Bible is God's love for his people even when they mess up, because the wrath they deserve was ultimately put on God's own Son.

If your life is in a dark place, if you feel dead inside and don't know what to do, turn around and go to God to live. When you leave the things of this world in your rearview mirror and start heading as fast as you can toward God, you are headed toward real joy. The way to get your life back on track isn't hiding things under the rug but bringing them into the light so that you are free to run unencumbered back to him, our good Father. Don't worry about not being prepared or needing to get things right first—his love has no prerequisite. Know that whatever the condition of your heart today, you can go back to him and live.

8 He who made the Pleiades and
        Orion,
        and turns deep darkness into the
            morning
        and darkens the day into night,
    who calls for the waters of the sea
        and pours them out on the surface
            of the earth,
    the LORD is his name;
9 who makes destruction flash forth
        against the strong,
        so that destruction comes upon
            the fortress.

10 They hate him who reproves in the
        gate,
        and they abhor him who speaks
            the truth.
11 Therefore because you trample on[1]
        the poor
        and you exact taxes of grain from
            him,
    you have built houses of hewn stone,
        but you shall not dwell in them;
    you have planted pleasant vineyards,
        but you shall not drink their wine.
12 For I know how many are your trans-
        gressions
        and how great are your sins—
    you who afflict the righteous, who
        take a bribe,
        and turn aside the needy in the gate.
13 Therefore he who is prudent will
        keep silent in such a time,
        for it is an evil time.

14 Seek good, and not evil,
        that you may live;
    and so the LORD, the God of hosts,
        will be with you,
        as you have said.
15 Hate evil, and love good,
        and establish justice in the gate;
    it may be that the LORD, the God of
        hosts,
        will be gracious to the remnant of
            Joseph.

16 Therefore thus says the LORD, the God of
hosts, the Lord:

"In all the squares there shall be wail-
        ing,
        and in all the streets they shall say,
            'Alas! Alas!'

They shall call the farmers to mourn-
        ing
        and to wailing those who are
            skilled in lamentation,
17 and in all vineyards there shall be
        wailing,
        for I will pass through your midst,"
            says the LORD.

Let Justice Roll Down

18 Woe to you who desire the day of the
        LORD!
        Why would you have the day of the
            LORD?
    It is darkness, and not light,
19   as if a man fled from a lion,
        and a bear met him,
    or went into the house and leaned
            his hand against the wall,
        and a serpent bit him.
20 Is not the day of the LORD darkness,
        and not light,
        and gloom with no brightness in
            it?

21 "I hate, I despise your feasts,
        and I take no delight in your sol-
            emn assemblies.
22 Even though you offer me your burnt
        offerings and grain offerings,
        I will not accept them;
    and the peace offerings of your fat-
        tened animals,
        I will not look upon them.
23 Take away from me the noise of your
        songs;
        to the melody of your harps I will
            not listen.
24 But let justice roll down like waters,
        and righteousness like an ever-
            flowing stream.

25 "Did you bring to me sacrifices and
offerings during the forty years in the
wilderness, O house of Israel? 26 You shall
take up Sikkuth your king, and Kiyyun your
star-god—your images that you made for
yourselves, 27 and I will send you into exile
beyond Damascus," says the LORD, whose
name is the God of hosts.

Woe to Those at Ease in Zion

6 "Woe to those who are at ease in Zion,
        and to those who feel secure on
            the mountain of Samaria,

the notable men of the first of the
  nations,
    to whom the house of Israel
      comes!
2 Pass over to Calneh, and see,
    and from there go to Hamath the
      great;
      then go down to Gath of the
        Philistines.
    Are you better than these kingdoms?
      Or is their territory greater than
        your territory,
3 O you who put far away the day of
      disaster
    and bring near the seat of violence?

4 "Woe to those who lie on beds of
      ivory
    and stretch themselves out on
      their couches,
    and eat lambs from the flock
      and calves from the midst of the
        stall,
5 who sing idle songs to the sound of
      the harp
    and like David invent for them-
      selves instruments of music,
6 who drink wine in bowls
    and anoint themselves with the
      finest oils,
    but are not grieved over the ruin of
      Joseph!
7 Therefore they shall now be the first
      of those who go into exile,
    and the revelry of those who
      stretch themselves out shall
        pass away."

8 The Lord GOD has sworn by himself,
declares the LORD, the God of hosts:

  "I abhor the pride of Jacob
    and hate his strongholds,
    and I will deliver up the city and
      all that is in it."

9 And if ten men remain in one house,
they shall die. 10 And when one's relative,
the one who anoints him for burial, shall
take him up to bring the bones out of the
house, and shall say to him who is in the
innermost parts of the house, "Is there still
anyone with you?" he shall say, "No"; and
he shall say, "Silence! We must not mention
the name of the LORD."

11 For behold, the LORD commands,
    and the great house shall be struck
      down into fragments,
    and the little house into bits.
12 Do horses run on rocks?
    Does one plow there[1] with oxen?
    But you have turned justice into
      poison
    and the fruit of righteousness into
      wormwood[2]—
13 you who rejoice in Lo-debar,[3]
    who say, "Have we not by our own
      strength
    captured Karnaim[4] for ourselves?"
14 "For behold, I will raise up against you
      a nation,
    O house of Israel," declares the
      LORD, the God of hosts;
  "and they shall oppress you from
      Lebo-hamath
    to the Brook of the Arabah."

Warning Visions

7 This is what the Lord GOD showed
  me: behold, he was forming locusts
when the latter growth was just beginning
to sprout, and behold, it was the latter
growth after the king's mowings. 2 When
they had finished eating the grass of the
land, I said,

  "O Lord GOD, please forgive!
    How can Jacob stand?
    He is so small!"
3 The LORD relented concerning this:
    "It shall not be," said the LORD.

4 This is what the Lord GOD showed
me: behold, the Lord GOD was calling for
a judgment by fire, and it devoured the
great deep and was eating up the land.
5 Then I said,

  "O Lord GOD, please cease!
    How can Jacob stand?
    He is so small!"
6 The LORD relented concerning this:
    "This also shall not be," said the
      Lord GOD.

7 This is what he showed me: behold, the
Lord was standing beside a wall built with
a plumb line, with a plumb line in his hand.
8 And the LORD said to me, "Amos, what do
you see?" And I said, "A plumb line." Then
the Lord said,

Or the sea [2] Or into bitter fruit [3] Lo-debar means nothing [4] Karnaim means horns (a symbol of strength)

"Behold, I am setting a plumb line
   in the midst of my people Israel;
   I will never again pass by them;
9   the high places of Isaac shall be
     made desolate,
     and the sanctuaries of Israel shall
     be laid waste,
     and I will rise against the house of
     Jeroboam with the sword."

Amos Accused

10 Then Amaziah the priest of Bethel sent to Jeroboam king of Israel, saying, "Amos has conspired against you in the midst of the house of Israel. The land is not able to bear all his words. 11 For thus Amos has said,

"'Jeroboam shall die by the sword,
   and Israel must go into exile
   away from his land.'"

12 And Amaziah said to Amos, "O seer, go, flee away to the land of Judah, and eat bread there, and prophesy there, 13 but never again prophesy at Bethel, for it is the king's sanctuary, and it is a temple of the kingdom."

14 Then Amos answered and said to Amaziah, "I was[1] no prophet, nor a prophet's son, but I was a herdsman and a dresser of sycamore figs. 15 But the LORD took me from following the flock, and the LORD said to me, 'Go, prophesy to my people Israel.' 16 Now therefore hear the word of the LORD.

"You say, 'Do not prophesy against
   Israel,
   and do not preach against the
   house of Isaac.'

17 Therefore thus says the LORD:

"'Your wife shall be a prostitute in the
   city,
   and your sons and your daughters
     shall fall by the sword,
   and your land shall be divided up
     with a measuring line;
   you yourself shall die in an unclean
     land,
   and Israel shall surely go into exile
     away from its land.'"

The Coming Day of Bitter Mourning

8 This is what the Lord GOD showed me: behold, a basket of summer fruit. 2 And he said, "Amos, what do you see?" And I said, "A basket of summer fruit." Then the LORD said to me,

"The end[2] has come upon my people
   Israel;
   I will never again pass by them.
3 The songs of the temple[3] shall
     become wailings[4] in that day,"
       declares the Lord GOD
"So many dead bodies!"
"They are thrown everywhere!"
"Silence!"

4 Hear this, you who trample on the
     needy
   and bring the poor of the land to
     an end,
5 saying, "When will the new moon be
     over,
   that we may sell grain?
And the Sabbath,
   that we may offer wheat for sale,
that we may make the ephah small
     and the shekel[5] great
   and deal deceitfully with false bal-
     ances,
6 that we may buy the poor for silver
   and the needy for a pair of sandals
   and sell the chaff of the wheat?"

7 The LORD has sworn by the pride of
     Jacob:
"Surely I will never forget any of their
     deeds.
8 Shall not the land tremble on this
     account,
   and everyone mourn who dwells
     in it,
   and all of it rise like the Nile,
     and be tossed about and sink
     again, like the Nile of Egypt?"

9 "And on that day," declares the Lord
     GOD,
"I will make the sun go down at
     noon
   and darken the earth in broad
     daylight.
10 I will turn your feasts into mourning
   and all your songs into lamenta-
     tion;

---

[1] Or am; twice in this verse [2] The Hebrew words for end and summer fruit sound alike [3] Or palace [4] Or The singing women of the palace shall wail [5] An ephah was about 3/5 bushel or 22 liters; a shekel was about 2/5 ounce or 11 grams

I will bring sackcloth on every waist
   and baldness on every head;
I will make it like the mourning for
    an only son
   and the end of it like a bitter day.

1 "Behold, the days are coming," declares
    the Lord God,
  "when I will send a famine on the
    land—
not a famine of bread, nor a thirst for
    water,
  but of hearing the words of the
    Lord.
2 They shall wander from sea to sea,
   and from north to east;
they shall run to and fro, to seek the
    word of the Lord,
  but they shall not find it.
3 "In that day the lovely virgins and the
    young men
   shall faint for thirst.
4 Those who swear by the Guilt of
    Samaria,
   and say, 'As your god lives, O Dan,'
and, 'As the Way of Beersheba lives,'
   they shall fall, and never rise
    again."

The Destruction of Israel

9 I saw the Lord standing beside[1] the
  altar, and he said:

"Strike the capitals until the thresh-
    olds shake,
   and shatter them on the heads of
    all the people;[2]
and those who are left of them I will
    kill with the sword;
  not one of them shall flee away;
  not one of them shall escape.

2 "If they dig into Sheol,
   from there shall my hand take
    them;
  if they climb up to heaven,
   from there I will bring them down.
3 If they hide themselves on the top of
    Carmel,
   from there I will search them out
    and take them;
and if they hide from my sight at the
    bottom of the sea,
   there I will command the serpent,
    and it shall bite them.

4 And if they go into captivity before
    their enemies,
   there I will command the sword,
    and it shall kill them;
and I will fix my eyes upon them
   for evil and not for good."

5 The Lord God of hosts,
he who touches the earth and it
    melts,
   and all who dwell in it mourn,
and all of it rises like the Nile,
   and sinks again, like the Nile of
    Egypt;
6 who builds his upper chambers in
    the heavens
   and founds his vault upon the
    earth;
who calls for the waters of the sea
   and pours them out upon the
    surface of the earth—
the Lord is his name.

7 "Are you not like the Cushites to me,
   O people of Israel?" declares the
    Lord.
"Did I not bring up Israel from the
    land of Egypt,
   and the Philistines from Caphtor
    and the Syrians from Kir?
8 Behold, the eyes of the Lord God are
    upon the sinful kingdom,
   and I will destroy it from the sur-
    face of the ground,
   except that I will not utterly
    destroy the house of Jacob,"
           declares the Lord.

9 "For behold, I will command,
   and shake the house of Israel
    among all the nations
as one shakes with a sieve,
   but no pebble shall fall to the
    earth.
10 All the sinners of my people shall die
    by the sword,
   who say, 'Disaster shall not over-
    take or meet us.'

The Restoration of Israel

11 "In that day I will raise up
   the booth of David that is fallen
  and repair its breaches,
   and raise up its ruins
   and rebuild it as in the days of old,

12 that they may possess the remnant
        of Edom
    and all the nations who are called
        by my name,"[1]
    declares the LORD who does this.

13 "Behold, the days are coming," declares
        the LORD,
    "when the plowman shall overtake
        the reaper
    and the treader of grapes him who
        sows the seed;
    the mountains shall drip sweet wine,
    and all the hills shall flow with it.

14 I will restore the fortunes of my
        people Israel,
    and they shall rebuild the ruined
        cities and inhabit them;
    they shall plant vineyards and drink
        their wine,
    and they shall make gardens and
        eat their fruit.

15 I will plant them on their land,
    and they shall never again be
        uprooted
    out of the land that I have given
        them,"
                    says the LORD your God

[1] Hebrew; Septuagint (compare Acts 15:17) *that the remnant of mankind and all the nations who are called by my name may seek the Lord*

INTRODUCTION TO
Obadiah

Author: Obadiah

Time: Probably around 585 B.C.

Place: Probably Judah

Written to: Israelites/Edomites

the gist

This prophecy is directed at Edom because of their lack of care and concern for their brothers, the Israelites. Though the Edomites would probably never have seen or heard this book, it stands as a reminder to the Israelites of God's protection. When the Jews were being attacked and carried away to Babylon, the Edomites just laughed and even joined in on the attacks. God wanted the people to know that he was God over all, and their sin would not go unpunished.

things to look for

Descriptions of the Edomites (see Obad. 2–3, 10–14)

The danger of pride (see Obad. 2–4)

The judgment coming to the Edomites (see Obad. 8–9)

Don't Get Even

> As you have done, it shall be done to you;
>   your deeds shall return on your own head.
>
> *Obadiah 15*

If God treated you the way you treat other people, how happy would that make you feel? In Obadiah we see a family feud between the Israelites and the Edomites. They had a long-standing disdain for each other, so when the Israelites were in trouble, the Edomites were gloating instead of helping. And their actions got the attention of God so much that he had the prophet Obadiah say something about it. Obadiah warns the Edomites that they will soon experience God's anger and wrath because of their refusing to help their relatives and actually killing some of them. God wants his people, the Israelites, to know that justice will be served—that they can trust him to even accounts and to punish those who have hurt them.

No one can sin and get away with it. Look around, and it might seem like bad people are getting away with bad stuff, and for a time that may be true, but you can be sure that it isn't going to be that way forever. The thing the God Girl has to do is trust God with her pain. She has to trust that God gets better revenge than she ever could. And she has to know God's Word in order to understand how he operates. As you read the Bible, see how God's hand is always on his people and how even when things seem hopeless, he does restore the brokenhearted.

As you read this little book, you'll see how God is in charge of everything—even people who have rejected him. He will one day judge the whole earth. An important lesson for you to learn is that, no matter how others have sinned against you, violated you, or hurt you, God is righteous and just, and he is even more angry about the ways you've been wronged than you are. He will settle the score. In the meantime, trust him.

Must-Know Facts and Verses

✢ The Edomites are the descendants of Esau, Jacob's older brother.

✢ Obadiah means "servant of the Lord."

"The pride of your heart has deceived you,
    you who live in the clefts of the rock,
    in your lofty dwelling,
who say in your heart,
    'Who will bring me down to the ground?'" *Obadiah 3*

Do not gloat over the day of your brother
    in the day of his misfortune;
do not rejoice over the people of Judah
    in the day of their ruin. *Obadiah 12*

The day of the LORD is near upon all the nations.
As you have done, it shall be done to you;
    your deeds shall return on your own head. *Obadiah 15*

Obadiah

¹The vision of Obadiah.

Edom Will Be Humbled

Thus says the Lord GOD concerning
  Edom:
We have heard a report from the LORD,
  and a messenger has been sent
    among the nations:
"Rise up! Let us rise against her for
    battle!"
² Behold, I will make you small among
    the nations;
  you shall be utterly despised.¹
³ The pride of your heart has deceived
    you,
  you who live in the clefts of the
    rock,²
  in your lofty dwelling,
who say in your heart,
  "Who will bring me down to the
    ground?"
⁴ Though you soar aloft like the eagle,
  though your nest is set among the
    stars,
  from there I will bring you down,
              declares the LORD.

⁵ If thieves came to you,
  if plunderers came by night—
  how you have been destroyed!—
  would they not steal only enough
    for themselves?
If grape gatherers came to you,
  would they not leave gleanings?
⁶ How Esau has been pillaged,
  his treasures sought out!
⁷ All your allies have driven you to
    your border;
  those at peace with you have
    deceived you;
they have prevailed against you;
  those who eat your bread³ have set
    a trap beneath you—
you have⁴ no understanding.

⁸ Will I not on that day, declares the
    LORD,
  destroy the wise men out of Edom,
  and understanding out of Mount
    Esau?
⁹ And your mighty men shall be dis-
    mayed, O Teman,
  so that every man from Mount
    Esau will be cut off by slaugh-
    ter.

Edom's Violence Against Jacob
¹⁰ Because of the violence done to your
    brother Jacob,
  shame shall cover you,
  and you shall be cut off forever.
¹¹ On the day that you stood aloof,
  on the day that strangers carried
    off his wealth
and foreigners entered his gates
  and cast lots for Jerusalem,
  you were like one of them.
¹² But do not gloat over the day of your
    brother
  in the day of his misfortune;
do not rejoice over the people of
    Judah
  in the day of their ruin;
do not boast⁵
  in the day of distress.
¹³ Do not enter the gate of my people
  in the day of their calamity;
do not gloat over his disaster
  in the day of his calamity;
do not loot his wealth
  in the day of his calamity.
¹⁴ Do not stand at the crossroads
  to cut off his fugitives;
do not hand over his survivors
  in the day of distress.

The Day of the LORD Is Near
¹⁵ For the day of the LORD is near upon
    all the nations.

---

¹ Or *Behold, I have made you small among the nations; you are utterly despised* ² Or *Sela* ³ Hebrew lacks *those who eat* ⁴ Hebrew *he has*
⁵ Hebrew *do not enlarge your mouth*

As you have done, it shall be done to you;
> your deeds shall return on your own head.

16 For as you have drunk on my holy mountain,
> so all the nations shall drink continually;
they shall drink and swallow,
> and shall be as though they had never been.

17 But in Mount Zion there shall be those who escape,
> and it shall be holy,
and the house of Jacob shall possess their own possessions.

18 The house of Jacob shall be a fire,
> and the house of Joseph a flame,
> and the house of Esau stubble;
they shall burn them and consume them,
> and there shall be no survivor for the house of Esau,
>> for the LORD has spoken.

The Kingdom of the LORD

19 Those of the Negeb shall possess Mount Esau,
> and those of the Shephelah
>> shall possess the land of the Philistines;
they shall possess the land of Ephraim
> and the land of Samaria,
> and Benjamin shall possess Gilead.

20 The exiles of this host of the people of Israel
shall possess the land of the Canaanites as far as Zarephath,
and the exiles of Jerusalem who are in Sepharad
shall possess the cities of the Negeb.

21 Saviors shall go up to Mount Zion
> to rule Mount Esau,
> and the kingdom shall be the LORD's.

Know Yourself

verses to read
Obadiah 10–14

Somebody else's failure can never be your success. When you see someone who has failed and you say to yourself, "See, I'm smarter than she is," or, "He deserved it," all you are doing is bringing judgment on yourself, not on them. In Romans 2:1 Paul explains it this way: "Therefore you have no excuse, O man, every one of you who judges. For in passing judgment on another you condemn yourself, because you, the judge, practice the very same things." Their sin, whatever it might be, is theirs to deal with, but as soon as you make it an excuse for *your* sin, you bring the problem home with you. And focusing on their sin easily leads to your pride.

You have to learn to let God deal with others as he knows best, without being happy when they suffer. The most important thing for you is your relationship with God, not with people. Whatever you might think about another person can never lead you to break God's commandments. When all you want to do is obey him, suddenly you are free from the strain of worrying about human failure and attack because you want only what God wants. And all of a sudden you're getting happy when other people do well and sad when they fail. And that's a sure sign you're becoming a disciple who attracts people to God's side instead of being just another catty girl who pushes them away.

INTRODUCTION TO

Jonah

Author: Unknown
Time: Unknown
Place: Unknown
Written to: The people of God

The gist

Jonah heard God ask him to go warn the people he feared the most, that they would be saved from punishment if they would just repent. And when Jonah heard this command from God, he went the other way. He didn't want to do it. But God had other ideas. Jonah teaches us that God will save whomever he wants to save, and we can't get judgmental about it because we too need his grace as much as anyone, even the most wicked people in the world.

Things to look for

- Jonah's time at sea (see Jonah 1:3–2:10)
- The conversion of the Ninevites (see Jonah 3)

Love Your Enemies

"Should not I pity Nineveh, that great city, in which there are more than 120,000 persons who do not know their right hand from their left, and also much cattle?"

Jonah 4:11

Jonah was a prophet of Israel about seven hundred years before Christ. That meant he would speak for God and tell people about God's judgment and anger. But when God asked Jonah to love his enemies and tell them what God would do if they didn't straighten up, Jonah said, "No way!" Nineveh was a pagan nation. They were mean, evil, violent, and destructive—and proud of it. The Israelites were scared to death of them, and for good reason. And because of all that, Jonah didn't think that God should give them anything like forgiveness and compassion. After all, they weren't even a part of the nation of Israel. So he tried to run away from doing what God asked him to do.

It's a story you've probably heard before, and so you know who wins in the end. You might know that the people of Nineveh repent as soon as they hear what Jonah has to say, but you might not have known that years later, this nation would attack and destroy the nation of Israel. Ironic, isn't it? They repent because the God of Israel tells them to, and then they just forget all about him and decide to kill all his people.

There's more to this story than a tale of man meets fish. Through Jonah's story you can learn a lot about what happens when you run away from God and don't do what he says. But there's still more to learn: as you read Jonah, notice how God has the freedom to save whomever he wants to save, and how he has total power and sovereignty over the whole world. From this little book you can see that God can and will control all of nature—water, storms, fish, plants, worms, everything. God is all-powerful and all-knowing, and you can't run and hide from him. Even more than this, we learn that the grace of God is desperately needed not only by immoral people but also by moral people—not only by outsiders like the people of Nineveh but also by insiders like Jonah.

Must-Know Facts and Verses

✦ Jonah isn't just a fish story; it's a historical account of a real-life event. Jesus even referred to it in the New Testament (see Matt. 16:4; Luke 11:29–32).

Now the word of the LORD came to Jonah the son of Amittai, saying, "Arise, go to Nineveh, that great city, and call out against it, for their evil has come up before me." But Jonah rose to flee to Tarshish from the presence of the LORD. *Jonah 1:1–3*

He said to them, "Pick me up and hurl me into the sea; then the sea will quiet down for you, for I know it is because of me that this great tempest has come upon you." *Jonah 1:12*

"I called out to the LORD, out of my distress,
   and he answered me;
out of the belly of Sheol I cried,
   and you heard my voice." *Jonah 2:2*

"When my life was fainting away,
   I remembered the LORD,
and my prayer came to you,
   into your holy temple.
Those who pay regard to vain idols
   forsake their hope of steadfast love.
But I with the voice of thanksgiving
   will sacrifice to you;
what I have vowed I will pay.
   Salvation belongs to the LORD!" *Jonah 2:7–9*

When God saw what they did, how they turned from their evil way, God relented of the disaster that he had said he would do to them, and he did not do it. *Jonah 3:10*

"I knew that you are a gracious God and merciful, slow to anger and abounding in steadfast love, and relenting from disaster. Therefore now, O LORD, please take my life from me, for it is better for me to die than to live." And the LORD said, "Do you do well to be angry?" *Jonah 4:2–4*

Jonah

Jonah Flees the Presence of the Lord

1 Now the word of the Lord came to Jonah the son of Amittai, saying, ²"Arise, go to Nineveh, that great city, and call out against it, for their evil[1] has come up before me." ³But Jonah rose to flee to Tarshish from the presence of the Lord. He went down to Joppa and found a ship going to Tarshish. So he paid the fare and went down into it, to go with them to Tarshish, away from the presence of the Lord.

Ask Yourself . . .

ABOUT RUNNING FROM GOD

- Does God want you to do something that you are too afraid to do?

- What do you think will happen if you do what he wants?

- In a battle of wills, who do you think will win—you or God?

- What can you do to stop running?

⁴But the Lord hurled a great wind upon the sea, and there was a mighty tempest on the sea, so that the ship threatened to break up. ⁵Then the mariners were afraid, and each cried out to his god. And they hurled the cargo that was in the ship into the sea to lighten it for them. But Jonah had gone down into the inner part of the ship and had lain down and was fast asleep. ⁶So the captain came and said to him, "What do you mean, you sleeper? Arise, call out to your god! Perhaps the god will give a thought to us, that we may not perish."

Jonah Is Thrown into the Sea

⁷And they said to one another, "Come, let us cast lots, that we may know on whose account this evil has come upon us." So they cast lots, and the lot fell on Jonah. ⁸Then they said to him, "Tell us on whose account this evil has come upon us. What is your occupation? And where do you come from? What is your country? And of what people are you?" ⁹And he said to them, "I am a Hebrew, and I fear the Lord, the God of heaven, who made the sea and the dry land." ¹⁰Then the men were exceedingly afraid and said to him, "What is this that you have done!" For the men knew that he was fleeing from the presence of the Lord, because he had told them.

¹¹Then they said to him, "What shall we do to you, that the sea may quiet down for us?" For the sea grew more and more tempestuous. ¹²He said to them, "Pick me up and hurl me into the sea; then the sea will quiet down for you, for I know it is because of me that this great tempest has come upon you." ¹³Nevertheless, the men rowed hard[2] to get back to dry land, but they could not, for the sea grew more and more tempestuous against them. ¹⁴Therefore they called out to the Lord, "O Lord, let us not perish for this man's life, and lay not on us innocent blood, for you, O Lord, have done as it pleased you." ¹⁵So they picked up Jonah and hurled him into the sea, and the sea ceased from its raging. ¹⁶Then the men feared the Lord exceedingly, and they offered a sacrifice to the Lord and made vows.

[1] The same Hebrew word can mean *evil* or *disaster*, depending on the context; so throughout Jonah [2] Hebrew *the men dug in their oars*]

A Great Fish Swallows Jonah

¹⁷ ¹ And the LORD appointed[2] a great fish to swallow up Jonah. And Jonah was in the belly of the fish three days and three nights.

Jonah's Prayer

2 Then Jonah prayed to the LORD his God from the belly of the fish, ²saying,

"I called out to the LORD, out of my
distress,
and he answered me;
out of the belly of Sheol I cried,
and you heard my voice.

³ For you cast me into the deep,
into the heart of the seas,
and the flood surrounded me;
all your waves and your billows
passed over me.

⁴ Then I said, 'I am driven away
from your sight;
yet I shall again look
upon your holy temple.'

⁵ The waters closed in over me to take
my life;
the deep surrounded me;

weeds were wrapped about my head
⁶ at the roots of the mountains.
I went down to the land
whose bars closed upon me forever,
yet you brought up my life from the
pit,
O LORD my God.

⁷ When my life was fainting away,
I remembered the LORD,
and my prayer came to you,
into your holy temple.

⁸ Those who pay regard to vain idols
forsake their hope of steadfast
love.

⁹ But I with the voice of thanksgiving
will sacrifice to you;
what I have vowed I will pay.
Salvation belongs to the LORD!"

¹⁰ And the LORD spoke to the fish, and it vomited Jonah out upon the dry land.

Jonah Goes to Nineveh

3 Then the word of the LORD came to Jonah the second time, saying, ²"Arise, go to Nineveh, that great city, and call out

¹Ch 2:1 in Hebrew ²Or had appointed

Know God

verses to read
Jonah 2

God provided a giant fish for Jonah as protection from a watery grave. That cold, stinky, wet fish wouldn't have been a nice place. Jonah would have been terrified, sure that he was going to die. But being a prophet, Jonah knew something about God. And after the initial shock wore off and he took a look at the situation, he did the most important thing he could do: he thanked God. Yep, he thanked God from inside his fishy prison!

Thanking God in the midst of your stinky fish and suffering will save you a lot of pain. Nothing happens to you that God cannot and will not use for your good (see Rom. 8:28). When you believe that and trust him, you will be free to live without fear or worry. You'll be free to rest in a peace that goes beyond anything that you can imagine (see Phil. 4:7). No storm, no trial, no destruction can get to you unless God puts it there to rescue you from your choices.

In the belly of the fish, Jonah was brought to trust God in a deeper way than he ever had before. He was brought to say, "Salvation belongs to the LORD!" (Jonah 2:9). Jonah had to surrender to God once more, totally helpless and in need of God's mercy. Do you feel helpless in some way today? Perhaps God is asking you to trust him in a deeper way then ever before, bringing you into greater joys than you have yet known. Trust him. Salvation belongs to the Lord!

against it the message that I tell you." ³ So Jonah arose and went to Nineveh, according to the word of the LORD. Now Nineveh was an exceedingly great city,¹ three days' journey in breadth.² ⁴ Jonah began to go into the city, going a day's journey. And he called out, "Yet forty days, and Nineveh shall be overthrown!" ⁵ And the people of Nineveh believed God. They called for a fast and put on sackcloth, from the greatest of them to the least of them.

The People of Nineveh Repent

⁶ The word reached³ the king of Nineveh, and he arose from his throne, removed his robe, covered himself with sackcloth, and sat in ashes. ⁷ And he issued a proclamation and published through Nineveh, "By the decree of the king and his nobles: Let neither man nor beast, herd nor flock, taste anything. Let them not feed or drink water, ⁸ but let man and beast be covered with sackcloth, and let them call out mightily to God. Let everyone turn from his evil way and from the violence that is in his hands. ⁹ Who knows? God may turn and relent and turn from his fierce anger, so that we may not perish."

¹⁰ When God saw what they did, how they turned from their evil way, God relented of the disaster that he had said he would do to them, and he did not do it.

Jonah's Anger and the LORD's Compassion

4 But it displeased Jonah exceedingly,⁴ and he was angry. ² And he prayed to the LORD and said, "O LORD, is not this what I said when I was yet in my country? That is why I made haste to flee to Tarshish; for I knew that you are a gracious God and merciful, slow to anger and abounding in steadfast love, and relenting from disaster. ³ Therefore now, O LORD, please take my life from me, for it is better for me to die than to live." ⁴ And the LORD said, "Do you do well to be angry?"

¹ Hebrew *a great city to God* ² Or *a visit was a three days' journey* ³ Or *had reached* ⁴ Hebrew *it was exceedingly evil to Jonah*

Know True Happiness

verses to read
Jonah 4

Self-pity says, "I can't do this." It says, "This is too hard." Self-pity takes God off of the throne and puts you and your self-interests in his place. And self-pity makes decisions based on feelings instead of faith. This isn't an acceptable way of thinking for the God Girl. God wants you to decide the worth of your life based not on your circumstances but on his faithfulness. You can be sure that nothing can get you out of God's hands, and so whatever happens to you or around you won't be the end of you, any more than it's the end of God.

As a God Girl, you can't allow a hint of self-pity to get you off track from trusting the truth that God has everything under control. No challenge, no situation, no pain, no calling is too difficult for you to get over and through in faith instead of fear and self-pity. But no one finds God's glory till they stop staring at their miserable life. When negative thoughts start to creep in, and your mind starts to whine and complain, and you tell God, "I can't do this," just remember that he made you able to do it. You can and you have to. So instead of saying, "I can't do it," say, "Why not? Why shouldn't I suffer, since suffering is here to make me more like Jesus?" (see Phil. 3:10).

When you feel self-pity you start to think of yourself as a freak, a girl whose life just can't be fixed, but that's never true of the God Girl. God can use anything for good (see Rom. 8:28). You can survive anything, and if you trust God, you can grow and be happy even in the midst of suffering and trials.

⁵Jonah went out of the city and sat to the east of the city and made a booth for himself there. He sat under it in the shade, till he should see what would become of the city. ⁶Now the LORD God appointed a plant[1] and made it come up over Jonah, that it might be a shade over his head, to save him from his discomfort.[2] So Jonah was exceedingly glad because of the plant. ⁷But when dawn came up the next day, God appointed a worm that attacked the plant, so that it withered. ⁸When the sun rose, God appointed a scorching east wind, and the sun beat down on the head of Jonah so that he was faint. And he asked that he might die and said, "It is better for me to die than to live." ⁹But God said to Jonah, "Do you do well to be angry for the plant?" And he said, "Yes, I do well to be angry, angry enough to die." ¹⁰And the LORD said, "You pity the plant, for which you did not labor, nor did you make it grow, which came into being in a night and perished in a night. ¹¹And should not I pity Nineveh, that great city, in which there are more than 120,000 persons who do not know their right hand from their left, and also much cattle?"

---

[1] Hebrew qiqayon, probably the castor oil plant; also verses 7, 9, 10 [2] Or his evil

INTRODUCTION TO
Micah

Author: Micah

Time: The eighth century B.C.

Place: Probably the village of Moresheth in Judah

Written to: The people of Judah

The gist

The book of Micah is about the impending destruction of both Israel in the north and Judah in the south. The prophet warns the people that they have broken their covenant with God, and he tells them how God will send destruction for their sin. He talks about the future captivity as discipline—and discipline just shows that God loves them enough to teach them right from wrong.

Things to look for

- The three different prophecies (see Micah 1–2; 3–5; 6–7)

- God's ultimate redemption of his people (see Mic. 2:12; 4:7; 5:7–8; 7:18)

- The confession of God's people (see Micah 7)

Judgment and Mercy

> Who is a God like you, pardoning iniquity
>   and passing over transgression
>   for the remnant of his inheritance?
> He does not retain his anger forever,
>   because he delights in steadfast love.
>
> *Micah 7:18*

Face it: the things you can see are easier to trust than the things you can't see. But the idea that something or someone else could do the things that God himself promises to do is idiotic. It's giving too much credit and devotion to something or someone other than God, and in the Old Testament that's called idolatry. In the days of Micah, idolatry was rampant. The people were rebels, idolaters, and violent. They had messed with the temples and rejected God's law, and Micah was sent to warn them that disaster was on its way.

Your obsessions—those things that you can't stop thinking about, worrying over, or dreaming of—are idols too if they take up more of your mind space than thoughts of God. Those things and people you turn to for comfort, hope, peace, protection, and salvation are your little idols, and they will be your destruction. In this little book, Micah warns the people about their disregard for God and their stupid attachment to things other than him. And in no uncertain terms he spells out the destruction that will result from their unfaithfulness.

It's scary to think of the wrath of God being taken out on the people who reject him and turn to other gods. God is not someone to be trifled with. Think carefully about what you obsess over. Because of the infinite joy waiting for those who love and trust God above all else, you can get rid of those idols in your life.

Must-Know Terms and Verses

∽ *Judah* ∾

One of the twelve sons of Jacob, and the tribe made up of his descendants. After the division of Israel, it referred to the southern kingdom, made up of the tribes of Judah and Benjamin, whose capital was Jerusalem.

∽ *Samaria* ∾

The capital of the northern kingdom of Israel.

Woe to those who devise wickedness
 and work evil on their beds! *Micah 2:1*

The seers shall be disgraced,
 and the diviners put to shame;
they shall all cover their lips,
 for there is no answer from God. *Micah 3:7*

"He has told you, O man, what is good;
 and what does the LORD require of you
but to do justice, and to love kindness,
 and to walk humbly with your God?" *Micah 6:8*

But as for me, I will look to the LORD;
 I will wait for the God of my salvation;
 my God will hear me. *Micah 7:7*

Micah

1

1 The word of the LORD that came to Micah of Moresheth in the days of Jotham, Ahaz, and Hezekiah, kings of Judah, which he saw concerning Samaria and Jerusalem.

The Coming Destruction

2 Hear, you peoples, all of you;[1]
    pay attention, O earth, and all that
        is in it,
and let the Lord GOD be a witness
        against you,
    the Lord from his holy temple.

3 For behold, the LORD is coming out
        of his place,
    and will come down and tread
        upon the high places of the
        earth.

4 And the mountains will melt under
        him,
    and the valleys will split open,
like wax before the fire,
    like waters poured down a steep
        place.

5 All this is for the transgression of
        Jacob
    and for the sins of the house of
        Israel.
What is the transgression of Jacob?
    Is it not Samaria?
And what is the high place of Judah?
    Is it not Jerusalem?

6 Therefore I will make Samaria a heap
        in the open country,
    a place for planting vineyards,
and I will pour down her stones into
        the valley
    and uncover her foundations.

7 All her carved images shall be beaten
        to pieces,
    all her wages shall be burned with
        fire,
and all her idols I will lay waste,

for from the fee of a prostitute she
        gathered them,
    and to the fee of a prostitute they
        shall return.

8 For this I will lament and wail;
    I will go stripped and naked;
I will make lamentation like the jack-
        als,
    and mourning like the ostriches.

9 For her wound is incurable,
    and it has come to Judah;
it has reached to the gate of my
        people,
    to Jerusalem.

10 Tell it not in Gath;
    weep not at all;
in Beth-le-aphrah
    roll yourselves in the dust.

11 Pass on your way,
    inhabitants of Shaphir,
    in nakedness and shame;
the inhabitants of Zaanan
    do not come out;
the lamentation of Beth-ezel
    shall take away from you its stand-
        ing place.

12 For the inhabitants of Maroth
    wait anxiously for good,
because disaster has come down
        from the LORD
    to the gate of Jerusalem.

13 Harness the steeds to the chariots,
    inhabitants of Lachish;
it was the beginning of sin
    to the daughter of Zion,
for in you were found
    the transgressions of Israel.

14 Therefore you shall give parting
        gifts[2]
    to Moresheth-gath;
the houses of Achzib shall be a
        deceitful thing
    to the kings of Israel.

[1] Hebrew all of them [2] Or give dowry

¹⁵ I will again bring a conqueror to you,
    inhabitants of Mareshah;
  the glory of Israel
    shall come to Adullam.
¹⁶ Make yourselves bald and cut off
    your hair,

A Prayer for...
PURITY

Save me completely from sin. I know I am righteous only because of the righteousness of Another, but I pant and pine to be more like you. I am your child and should look like it. Help me to see my own sinfulness. When it tempts me, help me to be dead to its voice.

Deliver me from the attack as well as the control of sin. Help me to walk as Christ walked, to live in the newness of his life—the life of love, the life of faith, the life of holiness.

I hate my inclination toward the things that bring death: toward laziness, envy, meanness, pride. Forgive me and kill these vices; have mercy on my unbelief, on my corrupt and wandering heart.

When your blessings come, I start to idolize them and set my affection on some beloved object: friends, popularity, wealth, honor. Clean this spiritual adultery out of me and give me purity. Close my heart to all but you.

Help me to always be devoted, confident, obedient, and childlike in my trust of you; to love you with all my soul, mind, and strength; to love others as much as I love myself; to be saved from my stubborn temper, hard thoughts, slanderous words, meanness, and unkind manners; and to master my tongue.

Fill me with grace daily, so that my life will be a fountain of sweet water.

Amen.

---

  for the children of your delight;
make yourselves as bald as the eagle,
  for they shall go from you into exile.

Woe to the Oppressors

2 Woe to those who devise wickedness
    and work evil on their beds!
  When the morning dawns, they
    perform it,
    because it is in the power of their
      hand.
² They covet fields and seize them,
    and houses, and take them away;
  they oppress a man and his house,
    a man and his inheritance.
³ Therefore thus says the Lord:
  behold, against this family I am
    devising disaster,¹
    from which you cannot remove
      your necks,
  and you shall not walk haughtily,
    for it will be a time of disaster.
⁴ In that day they shall take up a taunt
      song against you
    and moan bitterly,
  and say, "We are utterly ruined;
    he changes the portion of my
      people;
  how he removes it from me!
    To an apostate he allots our fields."
⁵ Therefore you will have none to cast
      the line by lot
    in the assembly of the Lord.

⁶ "Do not preach"—thus they preach—
  "one should not preach of such
      things;
    disgrace will not overtake us."
⁷ Should this be said, O house of Jacob?
  Has the Lord grown impatient?²
    Are these his deeds?
  Do not my words do good
    to him who walks uprightly?
⁸ But lately my people have risen up as
      an enemy;
  you strip the rich robe from those
    who pass by trustingly
    with no thought of war.³
⁹ The women of my people you drive
      out
    from their delightful houses;
  from their young children you take
      away
    my splendor forever.

---

¹The same Hebrew word can mean *evil* or *disaster*, depending on the context ²Hebrew *Has the spirit of the Lord grown short?*
³Or *returning from war*

10 Arise and go,
　　for this is no place to rest,
because of uncleanness that destroys
　　with a grievous destruction.
11 If a man should go about and utter
　　　　wind and lies,
　　saying, "I will preach to you of
　　　　wine and strong drink,"
　　he would be the preacher for this
　　　　people!
12 I will surely assemble all of you,
　　　　O Jacob;
　　I will gather the remnant of Israel;
　I will set them together
　　like sheep in a fold,
like a flock in its pasture,
　　a noisy multitude of men.
13 He who opens the breach goes up
　　　　before them;
　　they break through and pass the
　　　　gate,

¹ Hebrew *from off them*

going out by it.
Their king passes on before them,
　　the LORD at their head.

Rulers and Prophets Denounced

3 And I said:
　　Hear, you heads of Jacob
　　　　and rulers of the house of Israel!
　　Is it not for you to know justice?—
2 　　you who hate the good and love
　　　　　　the evil,
　　who tear the skin from off my
　　　　　　people¹
　　and their flesh from off their
　　　　　　bones,
3 　　who eat the flesh of my people,
　　　　and flay their skin from off them,
　　and break their bones in pieces
　　　　and chop them up like meat in a
　　　　　　pot,
　　　　like flesh in a cauldron.

verses to read
Micah 3:1-4

Know Yourself

It can be hard not to pay attention to the world with all of its amazing sights and imaginative ideas, but every time you get all wrapped up in the world, you open yourself up to turning away from God. And suddenly you find yourself not living in him but in the world, and your prayer life suffers. See, God says he won't listen to people who love the world, which means those who put all their hope in it and get obsessed about it. The problem with obsession is that it means all your thoughts are caught up in getting the one thing you obsess about, even to the detriment of other things and people. When you obsess, you take a giant step toward hating good and loving evil (see Mic. 3:2), since evil is anything that draws your attention away from God in order to control you.

If your prayer life is weak and you never get the answers you want, then maybe the answer is in where you are living: are you living in the world or in faith? So think about your week. What do you do and think about most often? Is your life all wrapped up in Jesus and his Word, or do you spend the majority of your strength just keeping up with the world?

Prayer is your access to the Creator of all. It's your way to ask and to receive from the one who provides everything you need for life and for happiness. If you could have continual access to the God of the universe, because Jesus has opened the way, why wouldn't you take the opportunity and run with it? Sort out where your allegiance lies. Turn your back on the world, deny it, and head straight for the arms of God. Learn to live there, without giving the world a vote, and your prayer life will explode.

4 Then they will cry to the LORD,
　　but he will not answer them;
he will hide his face from them at
　　　that time,
　　　because they have made their
　　　　deeds evil.

5 Thus says the LORD concerning the
　　　prophets
　　who lead my people astray,
who cry "Peace"
　　when they have something to eat,
but declare war against him
　　who puts nothing into their
　　　mouths.

6 Therefore it shall be night to you,
　　without vision,
　　and darkness to you, without
　　　divination.
The sun shall go down on the proph-
　　ets,
　　and the day shall be black over
　　　them;

7 the seers shall be disgraced,
　　and the diviners put to shame;
they shall all cover their lips,
　　for there is no answer from God.

8 But as for me, I am filled with
　　power,
　　with the Spirit of the LORD,
　　and with justice and might,
to declare to Jacob his transgression
　　and to Israel his sin.

9 Hear this, you heads of the house of
　　Jacob
　　and rulers of the house of Israel,
who detest justice
　　and make crooked all that is
　　　straight,

10 who build Zion with blood
　　and Jerusalem with iniquity.

11 Its heads give judgment for a bribe;
　　its priests teach for a price;
　　its prophets practice divination for
　　　money;
yet they lean on the LORD and say,
　　"Is not the LORD in the midst of us?
　　No disaster shall come upon us."

12 Therefore because of you
　　Zion shall be plowed as a field;
Jerusalem shall become a heap of
　　ruins,
　　and the mountain of the house a
　　　wooded height.

The Mountain of the LORD

4 It shall come to pass in the latter days
that the mountain of the house of
　　the LORD
shall be established as the highest of
　　the mountains,
　　and it shall be lifted up above the
　　　hills;
and peoples shall flow to it,

2 　　and many nations shall come, and
　　　say:
"Come, let us go up to the mountain of
　　the LORD,
　　to the house of the God of Jacob,
that he may teach us his ways
　　and that we may walk in his paths."
For out of Zion shall go forth the law,[1]
　　and the word of the LORD from
　　　Jerusalem.

3 He shall judge between many peoples,
　　and shall decide for strong nations
　　　far away;
and they shall beat their swords into
　　plowshares,
　　and their spears into pruning
　　　hooks;
nation shall not lift up sword against
　　nation,
　　neither shall they learn war any-
　　　more;

4 but they shall sit every man under
　　　his vine and under his fig tree,
　　and no one shall make them afraid,
　　for the mouth of the LORD of hosts
　　　has spoken.

5 For all the peoples walk
　　each in the name of its god,
but we will walk in the name of the
　　LORD our God
　　forever and ever.

The LORD Shall Rescue Zion

6 In that day, declares the LORD,
　　I will assemble the lame
and gather those who have been
　　driven away
　　and those whom I have afflicted;

7 and the lame I will make the remnant,
　　and those who were cast off, a
　　　strong nation;
and the LORD will reign over them in
　　Mount Zion
　　from this time forth and forever-
　　　more.

[1] Or teaching

8 And you, O tower of the flock,
   hill of the daughter of Zion,
to you shall it come,
   the former dominion shall come,
   kingship for the daughter of
      Jerusalem.

9 Now why do you cry aloud?
   Is there no king in you?
Has your counselor perished,
   that pain seized you like a woman
      in labor?
10 Writhe and groan,[1] O daughter of Zion,
   like a woman in labor,
for now you shall go out from the
      city
   and dwell in the open country;
   you shall go to Babylon.
There you shall be rescued;
   there the LORD will redeem you
   from the hand of your enemies.

11 Now many nations
   are assembled against you,
saying, "Let her be defiled,
   and let our eyes gaze upon Zion."
12 But they do not know
   the thoughts of the LORD;
they do not understand his plan,
   that he has gathered them as
      sheaves to the threshing floor.
13 Arise and thresh,
   O daughter of Zion,
for I will make your horn iron,
   and I will make your hoofs bronze;
you shall beat in pieces many peoples;
   and shall devote[2] their gain to the
      LORD,
   their wealth to the Lord of the
      whole earth.

The Ruler to Be Born in Bethlehem

5 [3] Now muster your troops, O daughter[4] of troops;
   siege is laid against us;
with a rod they strike the judge of
      Israel
   on the cheek.
2 [5] But you, O Bethlehem Ephrathah,
   who are too little to be among the
      clans of Judah,
from you shall come forth for me
   one who is to be ruler in Israel,
   whose coming forth is from of old,
      from ancient days.

3 Therefore he shall give them up until
      the time
   when she who is in labor has given
      birth;
then the rest of his brothers shall
      return
   to the people of Israel.
4 And he shall stand and shepherd
      his flock in the strength of the
      LORD,
   in the majesty of the name of the
      LORD his God.
And they shall dwell secure, for now
      he shall be great
   to the ends of the earth.
5 And he shall be their peace.

When the Assyrian comes into our
      land
   and treads in our palaces,
then we will raise against him seven
      shepherds
   and eight princes of men;
6 they shall shepherd the land of
      Assyria with the sword,
   and the land of Nimrod at its
      entrances;
and he shall deliver us from the
      Assyrian
   when he comes into our land
   and treads within our border.

A Remnant Shall Be Delivered

7 Then the remnant of Jacob shall be
   in the midst of many peoples
like dew from the LORD,
   like showers on the grass,
which delay not for a man
   nor wait for the children of man.
8 And the remnant of Jacob shall be
      among the nations,
   in the midst of many peoples,
like a lion among the beasts of the
      forest,
   like a young lion among the flocks
      of sheep,
which, when it goes through, treads
      down
   and tears in pieces, and there is
      none to deliver.
9 Your hand shall be lifted up over
      your adversaries,
   and all your enemies shall be cut
      off.

[1] Or push [2] Hebrew devote to destruction [3] Ch 4:14 in Hebrew [4] That is, city [5] Ch 5:1 in Hebrew

10 And in that day, declares the LORD,
    I will cut off your horses from
        among you
    and will destroy your chariots;
11 and I will cut off the cities of your
        land
    and throw down all your strong-
        holds;
12 and I will cut off sorceries from your
        hand,
    and you shall have no more tellers
        of fortunes;
13 and I will cut off your carved images
    and your pillars from among you,
    and you shall bow down no more
    to the work of your hands;
14 and I will root out your Asherah
        images from among you
    and destroy your cities.
15 And in anger and wrath I will execute
        vengeance
    on the nations that did not obey.

The Indictment of the LORD

6 Hear what the LORD says:
    Arise, plead your case before the
        mountains,
    and let the hills hear your voice.
2 Hear, you mountains, the indictment
        of the LORD,
    and you enduring foundations of
        the earth,
    for the LORD has an indictment
        against his people,
    and he will contend with Israel.

3 "O my people, what have I done to
        you?
    How have I wearied you? Answer
        me!
4 For I brought you up from the land of
        Egypt
    and redeemed you from the house
        of slavery,
    and I sent before you Moses,
        Aaron, and Miriam.
5 O my people, remember what Balak
        king of Moab devised,
    and what Balaam the son of Beor
        answered him,
    and what happened from Shittim to
        Gilgal,
    that you may know the righteous
        acts of the LORD."

What Does the LORD Require?

6 "With what shall I come before the
        LORD,
    and bow myself before God on
        high?
    Shall I come before him with burnt
        offerings,
    with calves a year old?
7 Will the LORD be pleased with[1] thou-
        sands of rams,
    with ten thousands of rivers of oil?
    Shall I give my firstborn for my
        transgression,
    the fruit of my body for the sin of
        my soul?"
8 He has told you, O man, what is good;
    and what does the LORD require of
        you
    but to do justice, and to love kind-
        ness,[2]
    and to walk humbly with your
        God?

Destruction of the Wicked

9 The voice of the LORD cries to the
        city—
    and it is sound wisdom to fear
        your name:
    "Hear of the rod and of him who
        appointed it![3]
10 Can I forget any longer the trea-
        sures[4] of wickedness in the
        house of the wicked,
    and the scant measure that is
        accursed?
11 Shall I acquit the man with wicked
        scales
    and with a bag of deceitful
        weights?
12 Your[5] rich men are full of violence;
    your inhabitants speak lies,
    and their tongue is deceitful in
        their mouth.
13 Therefore I strike you with a griev-
        ous blow,
    making you desolate because of
        your sins.
14 You shall eat, but not be satisfied,
    and there shall be hunger within
        you;
    you shall put away, but not preserve,
    and what you preserve I will give
        to the sword.

[1] Or *Will the LORD accept* [2] Or *steadfast love* [3] The meaning of the Hebrew is uncertain [4] Or *Are there still treasures* [5] Hebrew *whose*

15 You shall sow, but not reap;
  you shall tread olives, but not
    anoint yourselves with oil;
  you shall tread grapes, but not
    drink wine.
16 For you have kept the statutes of
    Omri,[1]
  and all the works of the house of
    Ahab;
  and you have walked in their coun-
    sels,
  that I may make you a desolation,
    and your[2] inhabitants a hissing;
  so you shall bear the scorn of my
    people."

Wait for the God of Salvation

7 Woe is me! For I have become
  as when the summer fruit has been
    gathered,
  as when the grapes have been
    gleaned:
  there is no cluster to eat,
    no first-ripe fig that my soul desires.
2 The godly has perished from the
    earth,
  and there is no one upright among
    mankind;
  they all lie in wait for blood,
    and each hunts the other with a net.
3 Their hands are on what is evil, to do
    it well;
  the prince and the judge ask for a
    bribe,
  and the great man utters the evil
    desire of his soul;
    thus they weave it together.
4 The best of them is like a brier,
  the most upright of them a thorn
    hedge.
  The day of your watchmen, of your
    punishment, has come;
  now their confusion is at hand.
5 Put no trust in a neighbor;
  have no confidence in a friend;
  guard the doors of your mouth
    from her who lies in your arms;[3]
6 for the son treats the father with
    contempt,
  the daughter rises up against her
    mother,
  the daughter-in-law against her
    mother-in-law;
  a man's enemies are the men of his
    own house.

7 But as for me, I will look to the LORD;
  I will wait for the God of my salva-
    tion;
  my God will hear me.

8 Rejoice not over me, O my enemy;
  when I fall, I shall rise;
  when I sit in darkness,
    the LORD will be a light to me.
9 I will bear the indignation of the
    LORD
  because I have sinned against him,
  until he pleads my cause
    and executes judgment for me.
  He will bring me out to the light;
    I shall look upon his vindication.
10 Then my enemy will see,
  and shame will cover her who said
    to me,
  "Where is the LORD your God?"
  My eyes will look upon her;
  now she will be trampled down
    like the mire of the streets.

11 A day for the building of your walls!
  In that day the boundary shall be
    far extended.
12 In that day they[4] will come to you,
  from Assyria and the cities of
    Egypt,
  and from Egypt to the River,
  from sea to sea and from mountain
    to mountain.
13 But the earth will be desolate
  because of its inhabitants,
  for the fruit of their deeds.

14 Shepherd your people with your
    staff,
  the flock of your inheritance,
  who dwell alone in a forest
  in the midst of a garden land;[5]
  let them graze in Bashan and Gilead
    as in the days of old.
15 As in the days when you came out of
    the land of Egypt,
  I will show them[6] marvelous
    things.
16 The nations shall see and be
    ashamed of all their might;
  they shall lay their hands on their
    mouths;
    their ears shall be deaf;
17 they shall lick the dust like a serpent,
  like the crawling things of the
    earth;

---

[1] Hebrew For the statutes of Omri are kept [2] Hebrew its [3] Hebrew bosom [4] Hebrew he [5] Hebrew of Carmel [6] Hebrew him

they shall come trembling out of
 their strongholds;
they shall turn in dread to the
 LORD our God,
and they shall be in fear of you.

God's Steadfast Love and Compassion

18 Who is a God like you, pardoning
 iniquity
 and passing over transgression
 for the remnant of his inheritance?

He does not retain his anger forever,
 because he delights in steadfast
 love.
19 He will again have compassion on us;
 he will tread our iniquities underfoot.
You will cast all our[1] sins
 into the depths of the sea.
20 You will show faithfulness to Jacob
 and steadfast love to Abraham,
as you have sworn to our fathers
 from the days of old.

[1] Hebrew *their*

verses to read
Micah 7:18–20

Know God

Are you absolutely convinced that God can do anything he says he will do? If you are, then you have faith. If not, then you do not have faith; you have doubt. If you want to be forgiven for the junk you've done, then you have to believe in God's forgiveness in the gospel. You have to believe that no matter what you did, it's done, over, finished, and that you're forgiven—not because of how you fixed it or what you did but because you trust in what Christ has done on your behalf.

God promises to make you cleaned up, spotless, righteous, if you'll just cast yourself on his Son in faith. When you worry about your past sins, think about them all the time, and say stuff like, "I just can't get over it," you don't believe; you doubt. Did you know that only believers get forgiveness, not doubters? It's so simple that a lot of people miss it. Just believe in Christ, looking to him, and you've got it. Don't believe, and you've missed it. How simple, yet how difficult!

So here's how it's done: when you mess up, agree with God that you sinned. Tell him point-blank that you sinned against him, not anybody else. Then thank him for his forgiveness and promise you'll never do it again. If you can do that, then you've got it. Plain and simple.

See, forgiveness is grounded in faith, not works. It isn't about you but about him. All you have to do is have the guts to believe in Christ. Can you believe?

INTRODUCTION TO
Nahum

Author: Nahum
Time: 664–612 B.C.
Place: Judah
Written to: The people of Judah

The gist
A century after Jonah went to Nineveh, Nahum was called to prophesy about Nineveh's sin and future destruction.

Things to look for
• The description of Nineveh (see Nah. 1:12–14; 3:1, 4, 16)
• The description of God (see Nah. 1:2–7)

Expect Judgment for Sin

The LORD is slow to anger and great in power,
  and the LORD will by no means clear the guilty.

Nahum 1:3

Life isn't fair. Seems like it oughta be, but it isn't. Sometimes bad people are luckier than good people. They torture and even kill people, and yet life seems to go their way. They seem to have success in everything they do, even though they do it with an evil heart. But as a God Girl you can be sure of one thing: God doesn't let evil go unpunished. He doesn't look away and just allow bad people to win. Sure, it may look like it right now, but in the end everyone will have to pay for the evil that they do.

In the days of Nahum, the city of Nineveh was the greatest and most powerful city in the land. It was the capital of Assyria, and they ruled a lot of the world. The people who lived there were known for being bloodthirsty even to the point of burning children and cutting off the hands of their enemies. They had overthrown Israel and turned Judah into a vassal state. Now the same Nineveh that Jonah had reluctantly warned to repent was back at it again and refusing to change. But in the end Nineveh itself would be completely destroyed, never to be rebuilt.

In the New Testament, Jesus teaches that we are to love our enemies and do good to those who hate us, and at times this can seem like sheer insanity. But you have to remember that although you aren't allowed to get revenge, God is a God of justice, so he's not going to let evil be rewarded for long. When bad people win at your expense, don't complain; just thank God for the amazing gift of Jesus Christ and the forgiveness he offers for your sins. After all, you were once the enemy of God but he didn't taken vengeance on you—he gave his Son for you.

The book of Nahum is a short book, but it can be a challenge. If you want more background on Judah and its relationship to Nineveh before you read it, check out 2 Kings 17–19 and 2 Chronicles 32–33.

Must-Know Facts, Terms, and Verses

✝ Nahum was written to address the people of Nineveh, although they probably never would have heard or read it. It would have served as a comfort to the Israelites that God was still in control.

∽ *Nineveh* ∾

The capital of the pagan nation of Assyria. Considered to be one of the most evil cities of its time. Referred to in the books of Jonah, Nahum, 2 Kings 17–19, and 2 Chronicles 32–33.

> The LORD is slow to anger and great in power,
> and the LORD will by no means clear the guilty. *Nahum 1:3*

> The LORD is good,
> a stronghold in the day of trouble;
> he knows those who take refuge in him. *Nahum 1:7*

Nahum

1 An oracle concerning Nineveh. The book of the vision of Nahum of Elkosh.

God's Wrath Against Nineveh

2 The LORD is a jealous and avenging God;
  the LORD is avenging and wrathful;
 the LORD takes vengeance on his adversaries
  and keeps wrath for his enemies.
3 The LORD is slow to anger and great in power,
  and the LORD will by no means clear the guilty.
 His way is in whirlwind and storm,
  and the clouds are the dust of his feet.
4 He rebukes the sea and makes it dry;
  he dries up all the rivers;
 Bashan and Carmel wither;
  the bloom of Lebanon withers.
5 The mountains quake before him;
  the hills melt;
 the earth heaves before him,
  the world and all who dwell in it.
6 Who can stand before his indignation?
  Who can endure the heat of his anger?
 His wrath is poured out like fire,
  and the rocks are broken into pieces by him.
7 The LORD is good,
  a stronghold in the day of trouble;
 he knows those who take refuge in him.
8 But with an overflowing flood
 he will make a complete end of the adversaries,[1]
  and will pursue his enemies into darkness.
9 What do you plot against the LORD?
  He will make a complete end;
  trouble will not rise up a second time.
10 For they are like entangled thorns,
  like drunkards as they drink;
 they are consumed like stubble fully dried.
11 From you came one
  who plotted evil against the LORD,
  a worthless counselor.

12 Thus says the LORD,
 "Though they are at full strength and many,
  they will be cut down and pass away.
 Though I have afflicted you,
  I will afflict you no more.
13 And now I will break his yoke from off you
  and will burst your bonds apart."
14 The LORD has given commandment about you:
 "No more shall your name be perpetuated;
 from the house of your gods I will cut off
  the carved image and the metal image.
 I will make your grave, for you are vile."

15[2] Behold, upon the mountains, the feet of him
  who brings good news,
  who publishes peace!
 Keep your feasts, O Judah;
  fulfill your vows,
 for never again shall the worthless pass through you;
  he is utterly cut off.

The Destruction of Nineveh

2 The scatterer has come up against you.
  Man the ramparts;
  watch the road;

---

[1] Hebrew *of her place* [2] Ch 2:1 in Hebrew

dress for battle;[1]
　collect all your strength.

2　For the LORD is restoring the majesty
　　　of Jacob
　　as the majesty of Israel,
　for plunderers have plundered them
　　and ruined their branches.

3　The shield of his mighty men is red;
　　his soldiers are clothed in scarlet.
　The chariots come with flashing
　　　metal
　　on the day he musters them;
　　the cypress spears are brandished.
4　The chariots race madly through the
　　　streets;
　　they rush to and fro through the
　　　squares;
　they gleam like torches;
　　they dart like lightning.
5　He remembers his officers;
　　they stumble as they go,
　they hasten to the wall;
　　the siege tower[2] is set up.
6　The river gates are opened;
　　the palace melts away;
7　its mistress[3] is stripped;[4] she is car-
　　　ried off,
　her slave girls lamenting,
　moaning like doves
　　and beating their breasts.
8　Nineveh is like a pool
　　whose waters run away.[5]
　"Halt! Halt!" they cry,
　　but none turns back.
9　Plunder the silver,
　　plunder the gold!
　There is no end of the treasure
　　or of the wealth of all precious
　　　things.

10　Desolate! Desolation and ruin!
　　Hearts melt and knees tremble;
　anguish is in all loins;
　　all faces grow pale!
11　Where is the lions' den,
　　the feeding place of the young
　　　lions,
　where the lion and lioness went,
　　where his cubs were, with none to
　　　disturb?
12　The lion tore enough for his cubs
　　and strangled prey for his lion-
　　　esses;

he filled his caves with prey
　and his dens with torn flesh.

13　Behold, I am against you, declares the
LORD of hosts, and I will burn your[6] chariots in smoke, and the sword shall devour
your young lions. I will cut off your prey
from the earth, and the voice of your messengers shall no longer be heard.

Woe to Nineveh

3　Woe to the bloody city,
　all full of lies and plunder—
　　no end to the prey!
2　The crack of the whip, and rumble of
　　　the wheel,
　galloping horse and bounding
　　　chariot!
3　Horsemen charging,
　flashing sword and glittering
　　　spear,
　hosts of slain,
　　heaps of corpses,
　dead bodies without end—
　　they stumble over the bodies!
4　And all for the countless whorings of
　　　the prostitute,
　graceful and of deadly charms,
　who betrays nations with her whor-
　　　ings,
　　and peoples with her charms.

5　Behold, I am against you,
　　declares the LORD of hosts,
　and will lift up your skirts over
　　　your face;
　and I will make nations look at your
　　　nakedness
　　and kingdoms at your shame.
6　I will throw filth at you
　　and treat you with contempt
　　and make you a spectacle.
7　And all who look at you will shrink
　　　from you and say,
　"Wasted is Nineveh; who will grieve
　　　for her?"
　　Where shall I seek comforters for
　　　you?

8　Are you better than Thebes[7]
　　that sat by the Nile,
　with water around her,
　　her rampart a sea,
　　and water her wall?

---

[1] Hebrew gird your loins [2] Or the mantelet [3] The meaning of the Hebrew word rendered its mistress is uncertain [4] Or exiled [5] Compare Septuagint; the meaning of the Hebrew is uncertain [6] Hebrew her [7] Hebrew No-amon

9 Cush was her strength;
      Egypt too, and that without limit;
   Put and the Libyans were her[1]
      helpers.
10 Yet she became an exile;
      she went into captivity;
   her infants were dashed in pieces
      at the head of every street;
   for her honored men lots were cast,
      and all her great men were bound
         in chains.
11 You also will be drunken;
      you will go into hiding;
   you will seek a refuge from the enemy.
12 All your fortresses are like fig trees
      with first-ripe figs—
   if shaken they fall
      into the mouth of the eater.
13 Behold, your troops
      are women in your midst.
   The gates of your land
      are wide open to your enemies;
      fire has devoured your bars.

14 Draw water for the siege;
      strengthen your forts;
   go into the clay;
      tread the mortar;
      take hold of the brick mold!

15 There will the fire devour you;
      the sword will cut you off.
   It will devour you like the locust.
   Multiply yourselves like the locust;
      multiply like the grasshopper!
16 You increased your merchants
      more than the stars of the heavens.
   The locust spreads its wings and
      flies away.

17 Your princes are like grasshoppers,
      your scribes[2] like clouds of locusts
   settling on the fences
      in a day of cold—
   when the sun rises, they fly away;
      no one knows where they are.

18 Your shepherds are asleep,
      O king of Assyria;
      your nobles slumber.
   Your people are scattered on the
      mountains
      with none to gather them.
19 There is no easing your hurt;
      your wound is grievous.
   All who hear the news about you
      clap their hands over you.
   For upon whom has not come
      your unceasing evil?

---

[1] Hebrew your [2] Or marshals

INTRODUCTION TO
Habakkuk

Author: Habakkuk

Time: Around the seventh century B.C.

Place: Judah

Written to: The people of Judah

The gist

Habakkuk isn't your average prophet. Instead of getting on people for their sins, he turns to God and bugs him about why he lets evil people get away with stuff and why he uses evil people to punish his own people. Even though confronting God might sound like a dangerous thing to do, God still answers Habakkuk, and his answers are found in this little book. By the end of the book Habakkuk is encouraged because of the power and grace of God in the lives of his people. This is a book of questions, but it is also a book of hope.

Things to look for

- Habakkuk's questions (see Hab. 1:2–4, 12–17)
- God's answer (see Hab. 1:5–11; 2:2–20)
- Habakkuk's description of God (see Habakkuk 3)

Question God

> O LORD, how long shall I cry for help,
> and you will not hear?
>
> Habakkuk 1:2

Why is there evil in this world? Why does God let people hurt other people so much? You see it all the time and you wonder, what's going on? Why doesn't he step in and do something? Will bad people always be able to do whatever they want? We all have questions for God about things that we just can't understand, and the prophet Habakkuk wasn't any different. He wasn't your usual prophet; he didn't point out people's sin. He went to God and asked him why evil was going unpunished. He wondered, just like we do, why God seems to be so slow to punish bad people. Does he just allow sin? The answer is no, he doesn't just allow sin; and yes, he will punish bad people. In fact, in this book God promises a terrible punishment: invasion and captivity. So Habakkuk has even more questions: are the Israelites really so bad that the evil Babylonians should attack them and tear them away from their homes? God answers Habakkuk and tells him not to worry because the Babylonians also will be judged.

Habakkuk confronts God and asks for answers, but at the end of the day he knows that God is in control and that he is a good God. As a God Girl, you don't have to be afraid to ask God questions, but the answer is always going to be the same: he is in control, he does know what he is doing, and he will punish people for their sins. It's never your job to take those things into your own hands; he's more than capable of handling them. When bad people seem to succeed, know that truth will prevail and justice will be found, but it just might not come at your hands. As you read Habakkuk, trust in the Lord with fresh trust for today. All things must end in praise of the one who is working all things out in the end for the good of his children (see Rom. 8:28).

Must-Know Verses

O LORD, how long shall I cry for help,
and you will not hear? *Habakkuk 1:2*

You who are of purer eyes than to see evil
and cannot look at wrong,
why do you idly look at traitors
and remain silent when the wicked swallows up
the man more righteous than he? *Habakkuk 1:13*

"Behold, his soul is puffed up; it is not upright within him,
but the righteous shall live by his faith." *Habakkuk 2:4*

"Woe to him who heaps up what is not his own—
for how long?—
and loads himself with pledges!" *Habakkuk 2:6*

"The LORD is in his holy temple;
let all the earth keep silence before him." *Habakkuk 2:20*

O LORD, I have heard the report of you,
and your work, O LORD, do I fear.
In the midst of the years revive it;
in the midst of the years make it known;
in wrath remember mercy. *Habakkuk 3:2*

GOD, the Lord, is my strength;
he makes my feet like the deer's;
he makes me tread on my high places. *Habakkuk 3:19*

Habakkuk

1 The oracle that Habakkuk the prophet saw.

Habakkuk's Complaint

2 O LORD, how long shall I cry for help,
  and you will not hear?
Or cry to you "Violence!"
  and you will not save?
3 Why do you make me see iniquity,
  and why do you idly look at wrong?
Destruction and violence are before me;
  strife and contention arise.
4 So the law is paralyzed,
  and justice never goes forth.
For the wicked surround the righteous;
  so justice goes forth perverted.

The LORD's Answer

5 "Look among the nations, and see;
  wonder and be astounded.
For I am doing a work in your days
  that you would not believe if told.
6 For behold, I am raising up the Chaldeans,
  that bitter and hasty nation,
who march through the breadth of the earth,
  to seize dwellings not their own.
7 They are dreaded and fearsome;
  their justice and dignity go forth from themselves.
8 Their horses are swifter than leopards,
  more fierce than the evening wolves;
  their horsemen press proudly on.
Their horsemen come from afar;
  they fly like an eagle swift to devour.
9 They all come for violence,
  all their faces forward.
They gather captives like sand.
10 At kings they scoff,
  and at rulers they laugh.
They laugh at every fortress,
  for they pile up earth and take it.
11 Then they sweep by like the wind and go on,
  guilty men, whose own might is their god!"

Habakkuk's Second Complaint

12 Are you not from everlasting,
  O LORD my God, my Holy One?
  We shall not die.
O LORD, you have ordained them as a judgment,
  and you, O Rock, have established them for reproof.
13 You who are of purer eyes than to see evil
  and cannot look at wrong,
why do you idly look at traitors
  and remain silent when the wicked swallows up
the man more righteous than he?
14 You make mankind like the fish of the sea,
  like crawling things that have no ruler.
15 He[1] brings all of them up with a hook;
  he drags them out with his net;
he gathers them in his dragnet;
  so he rejoices and is glad.
16 Therefore he sacrifices to his net
  and makes offerings to his dragnet;
for by them he lives in luxury,[2]
  and his food is rich.
17 Is he then to keep on emptying his net
  and mercilessly killing nations forever?

2 I will take my stand at my watchpost
  and station myself on the tower,
and look out to see what he will say to me,
  and what I will answer concerning my complaint.

---

[1] That is, the wicked foe   [2] Hebrew *his portion is fat*

The Righteous Shall Live by His Faith

2 And the LORD answered me:

"Write the vision;
    make it plain on tablets,
    so he may run who reads it.
3 For still the vision awaits its
        appointed time;
    it hastens to the end—it will not
        lie.
    If it seems slow, wait for it;
    it will surely come; it will not
        delay.

4 "Behold, his soul is puffed up; it is not
        upright within him,
    but the righteous shall live by his
        faith.[1]

5 "Moreover, wine[2] is a traitor,
    an arrogant man who is never at
        rest.[3]
    His greed is as wide as Sheol;
    like death he has never enough.
    He gathers for himself all nations
    and collects as his own all
        peoples."

Woe to the Chaldeans

6 Shall not all these take up their taunt against him, with scoffing and riddles for him, and say,

"Woe to him who heaps up what is
        not his own—
    for how long?—
    and loads himself with pledges!"
7 Will not your debtors suddenly arise,
    and those awake who will make
        you tremble?
    Then you will be spoil for them.
8 Because you have plundered many
        nations,
    all the remnant of the peoples
        shall plunder you,
    for the blood of man and violence to
        the earth,
    to cities and all who dwell in them.

9 "Woe to him who gets evil gain for his
        house,
    to set his nest on high,
    to be safe from the reach of harm!
10 You have devised shame for your
        house
    by cutting off many peoples;
    you have forfeited your life.

11 For the stone will cry out from the
        wall,
    and the beam from the woodwork
        respond.

12 "Woe to him who builds a town with
        blood
    and founds a city on iniquity!
13 Behold, is it not from the LORD of
        hosts
    that peoples labor merely for fire,
    and nations weary themselves for
        nothing?
14 For the earth will be filled
    with the knowledge of the glory of
        the LORD
    as the waters cover the sea.

15 "Woe to him who makes his neighbors
        drink—
    you pour out your wrath and make
        them drunk,
    in order to gaze at their naked-
        ness!
16 You will have your fill of shame
        instead of glory.
    Drink, yourself, and show your
        uncircumcision!
The cup in the LORD's right hand
    will come around to you,
    and utter shame will come upon
        your glory!
17 The violence done to Lebanon will
        overwhelm you,
    as will the destruction of the
        beasts that terrified them,
for the blood of man and violence to
    the earth,
    to cities and all who dwell in them.

18 "What profit is an idol
    when its maker has shaped it,
    a metal image, a teacher of lies?
For its maker trusts in his own cre-
    ation
    when he makes speechless idols!
19 Woe to him who says to a wooden
        thing, Awake;
    to a silent stone, Arise!
Can this teach?
Behold, it is overlaid with gold and
    silver,
    and there is no breath at all in it.
20 But the LORD is in his holy temple;
    let all the earth keep silence before
        him."

---

[1] Or faithfulness [2] Masoretic Text; Dead Sea Scroll wealth [3] The meaning of the Hebrew of these two lines is uncertain

Habakkuk's Prayer

3 A prayer of Habakkuk the prophet, according to Shigionoth.

2 O Lord, I have heard the report of
    you,
  and your work, O Lord, do I fear.
In the midst of the years revive it;
  in the midst of the years make it
    known;
  in wrath remember mercy.

3 God came from Teman,
  and the Holy One from Mount
    Paran.   *Selah*
His splendor covered the heavens,
  and the earth was full of his praise.

4 His brightness was like the light;
  rays flashed from his hand;
  and there he veiled his power.

5 Before him went pestilence,
  and plague followed at his heels.[1]

6 He stood and measured the earth;
  he looked and shook the nations;

then the eternal mountains were
    scattered;
  the everlasting hills sank low.
  His were the everlasting ways.

7 I saw the tents of Cushan in affliction;
  the curtains of the land of Midian
    did tremble.

8 Was your wrath against the rivers,
    O Lord?
  Was your anger against the rivers,
  or your indignation against the
    sea,
when you rode on your horses,
  on your chariot of salvation?

9 You stripped the sheath from your
    bow,
  calling for many arrows.[2]   *Selah*
You split the earth with rivers.

10 The mountains saw you and writhed;
  the raging waters swept on;
the deep gave forth its voice;
  it lifted its hands on high.

---

[1] Hebrew *feet* [2] The meaning of the Hebrew line is uncertain

Know True Happiness

verses to read
Habakkuk 3:16–19

God can and will be your strength. He will give you the ability and the power to do hard things if you will just trust him. God has given you a promise, and that is that he will give you strength and feet like those of a deer and help you walk on mountains (see Hab. 3:19). Climbing a mountain isn't easy. There are brambles, loose rocks, and crevices. Your feet can get stuck and you can trip, skin your knees, and hurt your hands. Your body can be tormented by climbing up the mountains that fill your life. But if you are only willing to let him, he will help you to leap across large crevices, to climb swiftly without faltering, and to rise to mountain peaks where you can see the world from a totally new perspective.

Are you tired of being lost in the valley, unable to see the open sky above or the lay of the land beyond? Do you want the freshness of the mountaintop, the rush of the climb, and the protection of feet as sure as a deer's? Then pour everything into loving the one who loves you. Refuse to find your hope anywhere else. Walk away from things and people who control you. Turn your life over to the God who saves. Dig into his Word, beg him for his presence. Vow to serve him and him alone for the rest of your life, and you will have feet like a deer as you climb higher and higher out of the valley that surrounds you. Never fear, even if you walk through the dark valley of death, but turn to him and know that he will protect you and make your way straight. Walking with God involves pain and adversity, but it is a pain filled with joy and comfort, because we are sharing in Christ's own pain (2 Cor. 1:3–5; Phil. 3:9–10).

11 The sun and moon stood still in their
        place
      at the light of your arrows as they
        sped,
      at the flash of your glittering
        spear.
12 You marched through the earth in
        fury;
      you threshed the nations in anger.
13 You went out for the salvation of
        your people,
      for the salvation of your anointed.
    You crushed the head of the house of
        the wicked,
      laying him bare from thigh to
        neck.[1]   *Selah*
14 You pierced with his own arrows the
        heads of his warriors,
      who came like a whirlwind to scat-
        ter me,
      rejoicing as if to devour the poor in
        secret.
15 You trampled the sea with your
        horses,
      the surging of mighty waters.

16 I hear, and my body trembles;
      my lips quiver at the sound;
    rottenness enters into my bones;
      my legs tremble beneath me.
    Yet I will quietly wait for the day of
        trouble
      to come upon people who invade
        us.

Habakkuk Rejoices in the LORD

17 Though the fig tree should not blos-
        som,
      nor fruit be on the vines,
    the produce of the olive fail
      and the fields yield no food,
    the flock be cut off from the fold
      and there be no herd in the stalls,
18 yet I will rejoice in the LORD;
      I will take joy in the God of my
        salvation.
19 GOD, the Lord, is my strength;
      he makes my feet like the deer's;
      he makes me tread on my high
        places.

To the choirmaster: with stringed[2]
  instruments.

[1] The meaning of the Hebrew line is uncertain [2] Hebrew *my stringed*

INTRODUCTION TO Zephaniah

Author: Zephaniah

Time: 640–610 B.C.

Place: Judah

Written to: The people of Judah and Jerusalem

The gist

The Israelites had really done t this time. They turned their back on God and started to act like the nonbelievers around them. They worshiped other gods and had no sense of guilt for their sin. Zephaniah wrote to warn them of the coming day of the Lord and to assure them of God's never-failing covenant love for them (see Zeph. 3:17).

Things to look for

- God's judgment (see Zephaniah 1)
- The call to turn away from sin (see Zeph. 2:1–3:8)
- Hope for God's people (see Zeph. 3:9–20)

Search for Humility

> Seek the LORD, all you humble of the land,
> who do his just commands;
> seek righteousness; seek humility.
>
> *Zephaniah 2:3*

When a prophet came to town, the people didn't run out to greet him, because they didn't want to hear what he was going to say. But when God's people walk away from him, something has to happen. And it's the prophet who speaks for God on this kind of stuff. Have you ever known a prophet— someone who called you on your sin and told you what God's Word had to say about it? It's scary but good. It feels uncomfortable and invasive, unwanted and ugly, but you have to remember that when you run away from correction, you miss out on the chance to get things right. The God Girl should be ready to hear what God has to say, even if it sounds challenging to her way of life.

By the time the prophet Zephaniah came along, the people of Israel had turned away from God for generations. They worshiped other gods, practiced astrology, and even sacrificed their kids like the pagans did. And God had had enough, so he prepared something called "the day of the Lord"—judgment day—and he sent Zephaniah to let them know about it.

As you read about the wrath of God, don't miss the most beautiful part of Zephaniah's message: God's promise to protect people who turn back to him after messing up. When his people are willing to repent and not keep going the way they are going, God promises to take them back. That's good news!

It's easy to get off track into a mess of sin and sadness and sense God's hand of punishment on your life. But the prescription for your disobedience is found in Zephaniah 2:3: "seek righteousness; seek humility." These two things will get you out of the dark and into the light. No matter how bad your past is, you can look at the life of the people of Israel for hope. Know that God wants you to come back to him. He wants to restore your faith and redeem your life just like he did theirs. All sin leads to bad things in your life. Be happy when someone points it out, because now you have a chance to be free. So repent of your old way of doing things, and enter into true life.

Must-Know Terms and Verses

☙ *Humility* ☙

A lack of pride in yourself or your ability to do things without God. A belief that you aren't competing with the world for success but that you can trust God for everything.

Be silent before the Lord GOD!
    For the day of the LORD is near. *Zephaniah 1:7*

Seek the LORD, all you humble of the land,
    who do his just commands;
seek righteousness; seek humility;
    perhaps you may be hidden
    on the day of the anger of the LORD. *Zephaniah 2:3*

This shall be their lot in return for their pride,
    because they taunted and boasted
    against the people of the LORD of hosts.
The LORD will be awesome against them. *Zephaniah 2:10–11*

"At that time I will change the speech of the peoples
    to a pure speech,
that all of them may call upon the name of the LORD
    and serve him with one accord." *Zephaniah 3:9*

The LORD your God is in your midst,
    a mighty one who will save;
he will rejoice over you with gladness;
    he will quiet you by his love;
he will exult over you with loud singing. *Zephaniah 3:17*

"At that time I will bring you in,
    at the time when I gather you together;
for I will make you renowned and praised
    among all the peoples of the earth,
when I restore your fortunes
    before your eyes," says the LORD. *Zephaniah 3:20*

Zephaniah

1

1 The word of the LORD that came to Zephaniah the son of Cushi, son of Gedaliah, son of Amariah, son of Hezekiah, in the days of Josiah the son of Amon, king of Judah.

The Coming Judgment on Judah

2 "I will utterly sweep away everything
from the face of the earth,"
declares the LORD.
3 "I will sweep away man and beast;
I will sweep away the birds of the
heavens
and the fish of the sea,
and the rubble[1] with the wicked.
I will cut off mankind
from the face of the earth,"
declares the LORD.
4 "I will stretch out my hand against
Judah
and against all the inhabitants of
Jerusalem;
and I will cut off from this place the
remnant of Baal
and the name of the idolatrous
priests along with the priests,
5 those who bow down on the roofs
to the host of the heavens,
those who bow down and swear to
the LORD
and yet swear by Milcom,
6 those who have turned back from
following the LORD,
who do not seek the LORD or
inquire of him."

The Day of the LORD Is Near

7 Be silent before the Lord GOD!
For the day of the LORD is near;
the LORD has prepared a sacrifice
and consecrated his guests.
8 And on the day of the LORD's sacrifice—

"I will punish the officials and the
king's sons
and all who array themselves in
foreign attire.
9 On that day I will punish
everyone who leaps over the
threshold,
and those who fill their master's[2]
house
with violence and fraud.

10 "On that day," declares the LORD,
"a cry will be heard from the Fish
Gate,
a wail from the Second Quarter,
a loud crash from the hills.
11 Wail, O inhabitants of the Mortar!
For all the traders[3] are no more;
all who weigh out silver are cut off.
12 At that time I will search Jerusalem
with lamps,
and I will punish the men
who are complacent,[4]
those who say in their hearts,
'The LORD will not do good,
nor will he do ill.'
13 Their goods shall be plundered,
and their houses laid waste.
Though they build houses,
they shall not inhabit them;
though they plant vineyards,
they shall not drink wine from
them."

14 The great day of the LORD is near,
near and hastening fast;
the sound of the day of the LORD is
bitter;
the mighty man cries aloud there.
15 A day of wrath is that day,
a day of distress and anguish,
a day of ruin and devastation,
a day of darkness and gloom,

---

[1] Or *stumbling blocks* (that is, idols) [2] Or *their Lord's* [3] Or *all the people of Canaan* [4] Hebrew *are thickening on the dregs* [of their wine]

a day of clouds and thick darkness,
16 a day of trumpet blast and battle
cry
against the fortified cities
and against the lofty battlements.

17 I will bring distress on mankind,
so that they shall walk like the
blind,
because they have sinned against
the LORD;
their blood shall be poured out like
dust,
and their flesh like dung.
18 Neither their silver nor their gold
shall be able to deliver them
on the day of the wrath of the
LORD.
In the fire of his jealousy,
all the earth shall be consumed;
for a full and sudden end
he will make of all the inhabitants
of the earth.

Judgment on Judah's Enemies

2 Gather together, yes, gather,
O shameless nation,
2 before the decree takes effect[1]
—before the day passes away like
chaff—
before there comes upon you
the burning anger of the LORD,
before there comes upon you
the day of the anger of the LORD.
3 Seek the LORD, all you humble of the
land,
who do his just commands;[2]
seek righteousness; seek humility;
perhaps you may be hidden
on the day of the anger of the
LORD.

4 For Gaza shall be deserted,
and Ashkelon shall become a desolation;
Ashdod's people shall be driven out
at noon,
and Ekron shall be uprooted.
5 Woe to you inhabitants of the seacoast,
you nation of the Cherethites!
The word of the LORD is against you,
O Canaan, land of the Philistines;
and I will destroy you until no
inhabitant is left.

6 And you, O seacoast, shall be pastures,
with meadows[3] for shepherds
and folds for flocks.
7 The seacoast shall become the possession
of the remnant of the house of
Judah,
on which they shall graze,
and in the houses of Ashkelon
they shall lie down at evening.
For the LORD their God will be mindful of them
and restore their fortunes.

8 "I have heard the taunts of Moab
and the revilings of the
Ammonites,
how they have taunted my people
and made boasts against their territory.
9 Therefore, as I live," declares the
LORD of hosts,
the God of Israel,
"Moab shall become like Sodom,
and the Ammonites like Gomorrah,
a land possessed by nettles and salt
pits,
and a waste forever.
The remnant of my people shall
plunder them,
and the survivors of my nation
shall possess them."
10 This shall be their lot in return for
their pride,
because they taunted and boasted
against the people of the LORD of
hosts.
11 The LORD will be awesome against
them;
for he will famish all the gods of
the earth,
and to him shall bow down,
each in its place,
all the lands of the nations.

12 You also, O Cushites,
shall be slain by my sword.

13 And he will stretch out his hand
against the north
and destroy Assyria,
and he will make Nineveh a desolation,
a dry waste like the desert.

[1] Hebrew gives birth [2] Or who carry out his judgment [3] Or caves

Herds shall lie down in her midst,
    all kinds of beasts;[1]
even the owl and the hedgehog[2]
    shall lodge in her capitals;
a voice shall hoot in the window;
    devastation will be on the threshold;
        for her cedar work will be laid
            bare.
5 This is the exultant city
        that lived securely,
    that said in her heart,
        "I am, and there is no one else."
    What a desolation she has become,
        a lair for wild beasts!
    Everyone who passes by her
        hisses and shakes his fist.

Judgment on Jerusalem and the Nations

3 Woe to her who is rebellious and
        defiled,
            the oppressing city!
2 She listens to no voice;
        she accepts no correction.
    She does not trust in the LORD;
        she does not draw near to her God.

3 Her officials within her
        are roaring lions;
    her judges are evening wolves
        that leave nothing till the morning.
4 Her prophets are fickle, treacherous
        men;
    her priests profane what is holy;
        they do violence to the law.
5 The LORD within her is righteous;
        he does no injustice;
    every morning he shows forth his
        justice;
        each dawn he does not fail;
        but the unjust knows no shame.
6 "I have cut off nations;
        their battlements are in ruins;
    I have laid waste their streets
        so that no one walks in them;
    their cities have been made desolate,
        without a man, without an inhabitant.
7 I said, 'Surely you will fear me;
        you will accept correction.
    Then your[3] dwelling would not be
        cut off
            according to all that I have
                appointed against you.'[4]

But all the more they were eager
    to make all their deeds corrupt.
8 "Therefore wait for me," declares the
        LORD,
    "for the day when I rise up to seize
        the prey.
    For my decision is to gather nations,
        to assemble kingdoms,
    to pour out upon them my indignation,
        all my burning anger;
    for in the fire of my jealousy
        all the earth shall be consumed.

The Conversion of the Nations

9 "For at that time I will change the
        speech of the peoples
        to a pure speech,
    that all of them may call upon the
        name of the LORD
        and serve him with one accord.
10 From beyond the rivers of Cush
        my worshipers, the daughter of my
            dispersed ones,
        shall bring my offering.
11 "On that day you shall not be put to
        shame
        because of the deeds by which you
            have rebelled against me;
    for then I will remove from your midst
        your proudly exultant ones,
    and you shall no longer be haughty
        in my holy mountain.
12 But I will leave in your midst
        a people humble and lowly.
    They shall seek refuge in the name of
        the LORD,
13   those who are left in Israel;
    they shall do no injustice
        and speak no lies,
    nor shall there be found in their
        mouth
        a deceitful tongue.
    For they shall graze and lie down,
        and none shall make them afraid."

Israel's Joy and Restoration

14 Sing aloud, O daughter of Zion;
        shout, O Israel!
    Rejoice and exult with all your heart,
        O daughter of Jerusalem!
15 The LORD has taken away the judgments against you;
        he has cleared away your enemies.

---

[1] Hebrew *beasts of every nation* [2] The identity of the animals rendered *owl* and *hedgehog* is uncertain [3] Hebrew *her* [4] Hebrew *her*

The King of Israel, the LORD, is in
   your midst;
      you shall never again fear evil.
16 On that day it shall be said to
      Jerusalem:
   "Fear not, O Zion;
      let not your hands grow weak.
17 The LORD your God is in your midst,
      a mighty one who will save;
   he will rejoice over you with gladness;
      he will quiet you by his love;
   he will exult over you with loud sing-
      ing.
18 I will gather those of you who mourn
      for the festival,
   so that you will no longer suffer
      reproach.[1]

19 Behold, at that time I will deal
      with all your oppressors.
   And I will save the lame
      and gather the outcast,
   and I will change their shame into
      praise
      and renown in all the earth.
20 At that time I will bring you in,
      at the time when I gather you
         together;
   for I will make you renowned and
      praised
      among all the peoples of the
         earth,
   when I restore your fortunes
      before your eyes," says the LORD.

[1] The meaning of the Hebrew is uncertain

verses to read
Zephaniah 3:14–17

Know Love

The believer should never think that God is not involved or paying attention to her life. When you believe in God, you know that he is always present, and not only present but totally interested in and concerned with your well-being. His Word confirms his love for you. Even if your doubt and distraction cause you to miss the truth, it's still true that if you're far from him, he's not the one who walked away—you are.

If your God can't save you, then he isn't God. If you doubt his ability or desire to take care of you and love you, then you are doubting his very being. As a God Girl, you have to believe that God is concerned with your life and cares about you. Even when your world looks horrific, your soul is never lost, and your heart shouldn't be either.

Remember all that he's done. Rehearse it over and over in your head. Read his thoughts and his story of your redemption in his Word. When you do, you can make his Word a part of the way you think and therefore a part of how you feel as well. Don't forget your first love. When you come back to basics and let the cares of this world fade into the background, you'll find everything you need by just trusting in the God of the Bible no matter what the world looks like around you. Don't look anywhere else for him when he's right here calling you near. Trust that his Word is true and his intentions are holy and for your good, and you'll find more hope and peace than you ever thought possible.

INTRODUCTION TO
Haggai

Rebuild the Temple

Author: Haggai

Time: Around 520 B.C.

Place: Judah

Written to: The Jews returning from exile

The gist

When the Jews returned home after being in exile for so long, they knew they needed to rebuild the temple that had been destroyed, but when local political types started to apply pressure for them to stop, they gave in and gave up. The prophet Haggai wrote this book to convince the people to get back to worshiping God instead of fearing people.

Things to look for

God's message to his people (see Hag. 1:1–11)

How many times Haggai says his message is from God (see Hag. 1:1, 3, 13; 2:1, 20)

God telling the people to think about what they are doing (see Hag. 1:5, 7; 2:15, 18)

"Thus says the LORD of hosts: Consider your ways. You have sown much, and harvested little. You eat, but you never have enough; you drink, but you never have your fill. You clothe yourselves, but no one is warm. And he who earns wages does so to put them into a bag with holes."

Haggai 1:5–6

When you touch something clean, do your hands get clean? No? Okay, but if you touch something dirty, does the dirt get onto your hands? Oh yeah! Impurity is spread easily and quickly; holiness, not so much (see Hag. 2:12–13). For the people of Haggai's time, their spiritual laziness made everything they touched fail. They worked, but they never had enough. Their lives were mediocre, mundane, nothing special. They loved God and worshiped him, but most of their energy and time went into themselves. They were so obsessed with satisfying their own needs that they put God in the backseat. They lived by the rule that if something was too hard to do, then it wasn't time to do it. The result was that they did only things that were easy—because that made them happy. So instead of working on God's temple, they decorated their houses. And God was watching. Haggai's message is for people who spend all their time, money, and effort on themselves instead of on God. It's a dangerous thing, and one that God will not stand for.

Is there anything you don't do because it's just too hard? How about Bible study, prayer, or serving? Is doing what is right so much harder than following the crowd that you give up on the hard stuff and settle for the mediocre? Whether your life is spectacular or average, your devotion to God isn't proven by how much money you make or how successful you are but by the presence of the Holy Spirit in your life. That presence gives you things like peace, patience, hope, joy, and love. If your life is in emotional turmoil and you've moved away from God, then it's time to return to faith and to doing what God calls you to do. Above all, remember, when unclean people like us touch Jesus, we don't make him unclean: he makes us clean! Return to him, trust him, and let his cleansing grace flood into and through your life.

Must-Know Facts and Verses

- ⚜ Haggai's message was that the Israelites needed to rebuild the temple after returning from exile.

- ⚜ The danger of procrastination is a big theme of this book.

- ⚜ Haggai means "festival."

- ⚜ Haggai and Zechariah were prophets at the same time.

- ⚜ Haggai is filled with prophecy about the need for restored fellowship with God through the temple.

" 'Thus says the LORD of hosts: Yet once more, in a little while, I will shake the heavens and the earth and the sea and the dry land. And I will shake all nations, so that the treasures of all nations shall come in, and I will fill this house with glory, says the LORD of hosts.' " *Haggai 2:6–7*

Haggai

The Command to Rebuild the Temple

1 In the second year of Darius the king, in the sixth month, on the first day of the month, the word of the LORD came by the hand of Haggai the prophet to Zerubbabel the son of Shealtiel, governor of Judah, and to Joshua the son of Jehozadak, the high priest: ² "Thus says the LORD of hosts: These people say the time has not yet come to rebuild the house of the LORD." ³ Then the word of the LORD came by the hand of Haggai the prophet, ⁴ "Is it a time for you yourselves to dwell in your paneled houses, while this house lies in ruins? ⁵ Now, therefore, thus says the LORD of hosts: Consider your ways. ⁶ You have sown much, and harvested little. You eat, but you never have enough; you drink, but you never have your fill. You clothe yourselves, but no one is warm. And he who earns wages does so to put them into a bag with holes.

⁷ "Thus says the LORD of hosts: Consider your ways. ⁸ Go up to the hills and bring wood and build the house, that I may take pleasure in it and that I may be glorified, says the LORD. ⁹ You looked for much, and behold, it came to little. And when you brought it home, I blew it away. Why? declares the LORD of hosts. Because of my house that lies in ruins, while each of you busies himself with his own house.

Know True Happiness

verses to read
Haggai 1:3–7

Are you let down by your life and what you have or don't have? You do everything you think you need to do in order to be happy, but you aren't satisfied. Everything and everyone seems to disappoint you. You look for more but can't find it. And then when you do find what you were looking for, you still aren't satisfied. Why?

An unsatisfied life comes from a lack of agreeing with God, not from a lack of exciting stuff. When you decide to agree with Christ no matter what happens, you'll find more than the world could ever offer, but as long as you think that the riches of this world, all the fame it has to offer, and the comfort it promises are what you want and need, what you plant will never produce the fruit you want to be yours.

The answer to all discontentment is to be content in God. In Christ, he has given you a salvation and an inheritance that will one day make the millionaires of this world look poor and small. It's easy to think like the world around you and just accept things that seem to make sense to you, but in order to be content, the believer has to look at things differently—that is, with Scripture in mind. Run everything you think and accept as truth through the filter of God's Word, and don't let the lies of this world color your faith. The truth can set you free from a deceptive world and let you see things for what they really are. Truth heals, and the truth is found nowhere but in the pages of God's Word.

¹⁰Therefore the heavens above you have withheld the dew, and the earth has withheld its produce. ¹¹And I have called for a drought on the land and the hills, on the grain, the new wine, the oil, on what the ground brings forth, on man and beast, and on all their labors."

The People Obey the LORD

¹²Then Zerubbabel the son of Shealtiel, and Joshua the son of Jehozadak, the high priest, with all the remnant of the people, obeyed the voice of the LORD their God, and the words of Haggai the prophet, as the LORD their God had sent him. And the people feared the LORD. ¹³Then Haggai, the messenger of the LORD, spoke to the people with the LORD's message, "I am with you, declares the LORD." ¹⁴And the LORD stirred up the spirit of Zerubbabel the son of Shealtiel, governor of Judah, and the spirit of Joshua the son of Jehozadak, the high priest, and the spirit of all the remnant of the people. And they came and worked on the house of the LORD of hosts, their God, ¹⁵on the twenty-fourth day of the month, in the sixth month, in the second year of Darius the king.

The Coming Glory of the Temple

2 In the seventh month, on the twenty-first day of the month, the word of the LORD came by the hand of Haggai the prophet, ²"Speak now to Zerubbabel the son of Shealtiel, governor of Judah, and to Joshua the son of Jehozadak, the high priest, and to all the remnant of the people, and say, ³'Who is left among you who saw this house in its former glory? How do you see it now? Is it not as nothing in your eyes? ⁴Yet now be strong, O Zerubbabel, declares the LORD. Be strong, O Joshua, son of Jehozadak, the high priest. Be strong, all you people of the land, declares the LORD. Work, for I am with you, declares the LORD of hosts, ⁵according to the covenant that I made with you when you came out of Egypt. My Spirit remains in your midst. Fear not. ⁶For thus says the LORD of hosts: Yet once more, in a little while, I will shake the heavens and the earth and the sea and the dry land. ⁷And I will shake all nations, so that the treasures of all nations shall come in, and I will fill this house with glory, says the LORD of hosts. ⁸The silver is mine, and the gold is mine,

---

A Prayer for...

STRENGTH

O Lord, thank you that the battle between you and Satan has never been uncertain and will end in your victory. Calvary broke the dragon's head, and so I'm dealing with a defeated opponent who with all his subtlety and strength has already lost. When I feel the serpent at my heel, please help me to remember the one whose heel was bruised but who, when bruised, broke the Devil's head.

Heal me of any wounds that I get in the great conflict: if I have been corrupted, if my faith has suffered damage, if my hope is less than bright, if my love is not passionate, if some creature comfort occupies my heart, if my soul sinks under the pressure of the fight. O you whose every promise is salve, every touch life, draw near to your weary warrior and refresh me so I can rise again to wage war and never tire until my enemy is beaten down.

Give me such fellowship with you that I can disregard Satan, unbelief, and the world with delight that doesn't come from any human source and that no mere human can damage. Give me a drink from the eternal fountain that flows from your unchangeable, everlasting love and law. Then my hand will never weaken, my feet never stumble, my sword never rest, my shield never rust, my helmet never shatter, my breastplate never fall as my strength rests in the power of your might.

Amen.

---

declares the LORD of hosts. ⁹The latter glory of this house shall be greater than the former, says the LORD of hosts. And in this place I will give peace, declares the LORD of hosts.'"

Blessings for a Defiled People

¹⁰On the twenty-fourth day of the ninth month, in the second year of Darius, the

word of the Lord came by Haggai the prophet, [11] "Thus says the Lord of hosts: Ask the priests about the law: [12] 'If someone carries holy meat in the fold of his garment and touches with his fold bread or stew or wine or oil or any kind of food, does it become holy?'" The priests answered and said, "No." [13] Then Haggai said, "If someone who is unclean by contact with a dead body touches any of these, does it become unclean?" The priests answered and said, "It does become unclean." [14] Then Haggai answered and said, "So is it with this people, and with this nation before me, declares the Lord, and so with every work of their hands. And what they offer there is unclean. [15] Now then, consider from this day onward.[1] Before stone was placed upon stone in the temple of the Lord, [16] how did you fare? When[2] one came to a heap of twenty measures, there were but ten. When one came to the wine vat to draw fifty measures, there were but twenty. [17] I struck you and all the products of your toil with blight and with mildew and with hail, yet you did not turn to me, declares the Lord. [18] Consider from this day onward, from the twenty-fourth day of the ninth month. Since the day that the foundation of the Lord's temple was laid, consider: [19] Is the seed yet in the barn? Indeed, the vine, the fig tree, the pomegranate, and the olive tree have yielded nothing. But from this day on I will bless you."

Zerubbabel Chosen as a Signet

[20] The word of the Lord came a second time to Haggai on the twenty-fourth day of the month, [21] "Speak to Zerubbabel, governor of Judah, saying, I am about to shake the heavens and the earth, [22] and to overthrow the throne of kingdoms. I am about to destroy the strength of the kingdoms of the nations, and overthrow the chariots and their riders. And the horses and their riders shall go down, every one by the sword of his brother. [23] On that day, declares the Lord of hosts, I will take you, O Zerubbabel my servant, the son of Shealtiel, declares the Lord, and make you like a[3] signet ring, for I have chosen you, declares the Lord of hosts."

---

[1] Or backward; also verse 18 [2] Probable reading (compare Septuagint); Hebrew Lord, since they were. When [3] Hebrew the

INTRODUCTION TO
Zechariah

Author: Zechariah

Time: Around 520 B.C.

Place: Jerusalem

Written to: The exiles returning to Jerusalem

The gist

Like the book of Haggai, Zechariah's message was meant to encourage the people who had returned from exile in Babylon to rebuild the temple that had been destroyed. God confirms that the Israelites are his chosen people and also promises to come back to live with them. Zechariah also teaches about a future salvation coming in the form of the Messiah.

Things to look for

- Encouragement to rebuild the temple in Jerusalem (see Zech. 1:16–17; 4:9; 6:14–15)

- Prophecies about the Messiah (see Zech. 3:8; 6:12–13; 9:9–11)

- Description of the Messiah's second coming (see Zechariah 14)

Return to God

> "Therefore say to them, Thus declares the LORD of hosts: Return to me, says the LORD of hosts, and I will return to you, says the LORD of hosts."
>
> *Zechariah 1:3*

Life has a way of taking your mind off of God. At first he was all you could think about, but then something happened that got your attention, and then something else, and pretty soon you're saying, "God who?" Without continual contact, it's easy to get so far down another road that getting back to him seems almost impossible. And all of a sudden you don't sense his presence, or worse yet you fear his presence, because you've wandered so far away. But throughout history God has been a God of kindness and grace. He's always calling his people to come back to him, no matter what they've done or where they've been. "Return to me, says the LORD of hosts, and I will return to you" (Zech. 1:3). He is near, and all you have to do is turn around and look at him. When you are willing to come back to him no matter where you've been, fearlessly letting go of your mistakes and freely accepting his forgiveness, then you will be saved. You will be saved from your detour, your road to ruin. You can't let anyone lie to you. He's near, and he's ready for you to come back home. So don't let your sinfulness come between you and God, but find the power in the blood of Jesus that lets you return to him free of stain and wrinkle (see Eph. 5:27).

When the book of Zechariah was written, the Israelites had gotten distracted from their God and had forgotten their first love yet again. Their distractions and obsessions lessened their allegiance, and soon all their energy was focused anywhere but up. But God didn't forget his covenant with his people, nor has he forgotten you. Even in the time of Zechariah he promised you salvation through the Messiah, Jesus (see Zech. 9:9–11; 12:10–11; 13:7). He promised a way back to him and away from sin. As you read Zechariah, notice for how long God had planned this amazing gift of salvation.

Must-Know Facts and Verses

✦ Haggai, Malachi, and Zechariah all wrote to the Israelites who had been exiles in Babylon.

✦ Zechariah talks about the coming Messiah in 3:8; 6:12–13; 9:9; 12:10; and 13:1, 7.

"Not by might, nor by power, but by my Spirit, says the LORD of hosts."
Zechariah 4:6

"'Thus says the LORD of hosts, "Behold, the man whose name is the Branch: for he shall branch out from his place, and he shall build the temple of the LORD."'" *Zechariah 6:12*

"Thus says the LORD of hosts, Render true judgments, show kindness and mercy to one another, do not oppress the widow, the fatherless, the sojourner, or the poor, and let none of you devise evil against another in your heart."
Zechariah 7:9–10

"As I called, and they would not hear, so they called, and I would not hear," says the LORD of hosts. *Zechariah 7:13*

> Behold, your king is coming to you;
> righteous and having salvation is he,
> humble and mounted on a donkey,
> on a colt, the foal of a donkey. *Zechariah 9:9*

> I will set your prisoners free. *Zechariah 9:11*

"I will put this third into the fire,
and refine them as one refines silver,
and test them as gold is tested.
They will call upon my name,
and I will answer them.
I will say, 'They are my people';
and they will say, 'The LORD is my God.'" *Zechariah 13:9*

Zechariah

A Call to Return to the Lord

1 In the eighth month, in the second year of Darius, the word of the Lord came to the prophet Zechariah, the son of Berechiah, son of Iddo, saying, ² "The Lord was very angry with your fathers. ³ Therefore say to them, Thus declares the Lord of hosts: Return to me, says the Lord of hosts, and I will return to you, says the Lord of hosts. ⁴ Do not be like your fathers, to whom the former prophets cried out, Thus says the Lord of hosts, Return from your evil ways and from your evil deeds.' But they did not hear or pay attention to me, declares the Lord. ⁵ Your fathers, where are they? And the prophets, do they live forever? ⁶ But my words and my statutes, which I commanded my servants the prophets, did they not overtake your fathers? So they repented and said, 'As the Lord of hosts purposed to deal with us for our ways and deeds, so has he dealt with us.' "

A Vision of a Horseman

⁷ On the twenty-fourth day of the eleventh month, which is the month of Shebat, in the second year of Darius, the word of the Lord came to the prophet Zechariah, the son of Berechiah, son of Iddo, saying, ⁸ "I saw in the night, and behold, a man riding on a red horse! He was standing among the myrtle trees in the glen, and behind him were red, sorrel, and white horses. ⁹ Then I said, 'What are these, my lord?' The angel who talked with me said to me, 'I will show you what they are.' ¹⁰ So the man who was standing among the myrtle trees answered, 'These are they whom the Lord has sent to patrol the earth.' ¹¹ And they answered the angel of the Lord who was standing among the myrtle trees, and said, 'We have patrolled the earth, and behold, all the earth remains at rest.' ¹² Then the angel of the Lord said, 'O Lord of hosts, how long will you have no mercy on Jerusalem and

Ask Yourself . . .

ABOUT YOUR FAITH

Zechariah's book of prophecy starts out with God asking his people to return to him (see Zech. 1:3). They had wandered away, backslidden, and lost their way. Ask yourself if you can relate:

- Am I backslidden in some area of my life?
- What keeps me from asking forgiveness and getting back to God?
- What does his Word say about his willingness to take me back?
- Is there anything that God can't forgive? (For help, see "Forgiveness" in the Quick Relief section of this Bible.)

the cities of Judah, against which you have been angry these seventy years?' ¹³ And the Lord answered gracious and comforting words to the angel who talked with me. ¹⁴ So the angel who talked with me said to me, 'Cry out, Thus says the Lord of hosts: I am exceedingly jealous for Jerusalem and for Zion. ¹⁵ And I am exceedingly angry with the nations that are at ease; for while I was angry but a little, they furthered the disaster. ¹⁶ Therefore, thus says the Lord, I have returned to Jerusalem with mercy; my house shall be built in it, declares the Lord of hosts, and the measuring line shall be stretched out over Jerusalem. ¹⁷ Cry out again, Thus says the Lord of hosts: My cities shall again overflow with prosperity, and the LORD will again comfort Zion and again choose Jerusalem.' "

A Vision of Horns and Craftsmen

18 [1] And I lifted my eyes and saw, and behold, four horns! [19] And I said to the angel who talked with me, "What are these?" And he said to me, "These are the horns that have scattered Judah, Israel, and Jerusalem." [20] Then the LORD showed me four craftsmen. [21] And I said, "What are these coming to do?" He said, "These are the horns that scattered Judah, so that no one raised his head. And these have come to terrify them, to cast down the horns of the nations who lifted up their horns against the land of Judah to scatter it."

A Vision of a Man with a Measuring Line

2 [2] And I lifted my eyes and saw, and behold, a man with a measuring line in his hand! [2] Then I said, "Where are you going?" And he said to me, "To measure Jerusalem, to see what is its width and what is its length." [3] And behold, the angel who talked with me came forward, and another angel came forward to meet him [4] and said to him, "Run, say to that young man, 'Jerusalem shall be inhabited as villages without walls, because of the multitude of people and livestock in it. [5] And I will be to her a wall of fire all around, declares the LORD, and I will be the glory in her midst.' "

[6] Up! Up! Flee from the land of the north, declares the LORD. For I have spread you abroad as the four winds of the heavens, declares the LORD. [7] Up! Escape to Zion, you who dwell with the daughter of Babylon. [8] For thus said the LORD of hosts, after his glory sent me[3] to the nations who plundered you, for he who touches you touches the apple of his eye: [9] "Behold, I will shake my hand over them, and they shall become plunder for those who served them. Then you will know that the LORD of hosts has sent me. [10] Sing and rejoice, O daughter of Zion, for behold, I come and I will dwell in your midst, declares the LORD. [11] And many nations shall join themselves to the LORD in that day, and shall be my people. And I will dwell in your midst, and you shall know that the LORD of hosts has sent me

to you. [12] And the LORD will inherit Judah as his portion in the holy land, and will again choose Jerusalem."

[13] Be silent, all flesh, before the LORD, for he has roused himself from his holy dwelling.

A Vision of Joshua the High Priest

3 Then he showed me Joshua the high priest standing before the angel of the LORD, and Satan[4] standing at his right hand to accuse him. [2] And the LORD said to Satan, "The LORD rebuke you, O Satan! The LORD who has chosen Jerusalem rebuke you! Is not this a brand[5] plucked from the fire?" [3] Now Joshua was standing before the angel, clothed with filthy garments. [4] And the angel said to those who were standing before him, "Remove the filthy garments from him." And to him he said, "Behold, I have taken your iniquity away from you, and I will clothe you with pure vestments." [5] And I said, "Let them put a clean turban on his head." So they put a clean turban on his head and clothed him with garments. And the angel of the LORD was standing by.

[6] And the angel of the LORD solemnly assured Joshua, [7] "Thus says the LORD of hosts: If you will walk in my ways and keep my charge, then you shall rule my house and have charge of my courts, and I will give you the right of access among those who are standing here. [8] Hear now, O Joshua the high priest, you and your friends who sit before you, for they are men who are a sign: behold, I will bring my servant the Branch. [9] For behold, on the stone that I have set before Joshua, on a single stone with seven eyes,[6] I will engrave its inscription, declares the LORD of hosts, and I will remove the iniquity of this land in a single day. [10] In that day, declares the LORD of hosts, every one of you will invite his neighbor to come under his vine and under his fig tree."

A Vision of a Golden Lampstand

4 And the angel who talked with me came again and woke me, like a man who is awakened out of his sleep. [2] And he said to me, "What do you see?" I said, "I see, and behold, a lampstand all of gold, with a bowl on the top of it, and seven lamps on it, with seven lips on each of the lamps that are on

---

[1] Ch 2:1 in Hebrew [2] Ch 2:5 in Hebrew [3] Or *he sent me after glory* [4] Hebrew *the Accuser* or *the Adversary* [5] That is, a burning stick
[6] Or *facets*

the top of it. ³And there are two olive trees by it, one on the right of the bowl and the other on its left." ⁴And I said to the angel who talked with me, "What are these, my lord?" ⁵Then the angel who talked with me answered and said to me, "Do you not know what these are?" I said, "No, my lord." ⁶Then he said to me, "This is the word of the LORD to Zerubbabel: Not by might, nor by power, but by my Spirit, says the LORD of hosts. ⁷Who are you, O great mountain? Before Zerubbabel you shall become a plain. And he shall bring forward the top stone amid shouts of 'Grace, grace to it!' "

⁸Then the word of the LORD came to me, saying, ⁹"The hands of Zerubbabel have laid the foundation of this house; his hands shall also complete it. Then you will know that the LORD of hosts has sent me to you. ¹⁰For whoever has despised the day of small things shall rejoice, and shall see the plumb line in the hand of Zerubbabel.

"These seven are the eyes of the LORD, which range through the whole earth." ¹¹Then I said to him, "What are these two olive trees on the right and the left of the lampstand?" ¹²And a second time I answered and said to him, "What are these two branches of the olive trees, which are beside the two golden pipes from which the golden oil¹ is poured out?" ¹³He said to me, "Do you not know what these are?" I said, "No, my lord." ¹⁴Then he said, "These are the two anointed ones² who stand by the Lord of the whole earth."

A Vision of a Flying Scroll

5 Again I lifted my eyes and saw, and behold, a flying scroll! ²And he said to me, "What do you see?" I answered, "I see a flying scroll. Its length is twenty cubits, and its width ten cubits."³ ³Then he said to me, "This is the curse that goes out over the face of the whole land. For everyone who steals shall be cleaned out according to what is on one side, and everyone who swears falsely⁴ shall be cleaned out according to what is on the other side. ⁴I will send it out, declares the LORD of hosts, and it shall enter the house of the thief, and the house of him who swears falsely by my name. And it shall remain in his house and consume it, both timber and stones."

A Vision of a Woman in a Basket

⁵Then the angel who talked with me came forward and said to me, "Lift your eyes and see what this is that is going out." ⁶And I said, "What is it?" He said, "This is the basket⁵ that is going out." And he said, "This is their iniquity⁶ in all the land." ⁷And behold, the leaden cover was lifted, and there was a woman sitting in the basket! ⁸And he said, "This is Wickedness." And he thrust her back into the basket, and thrust down the leaden weight on its opening.

⁹Then I lifted my eyes and saw, and behold, two women coming forward! The wind was in their wings. They had wings like the wings of a stork, and they lifted up the basket between earth and heaven. ¹⁰Then I said to the angel who talked with me, "Where are they taking the basket?" ¹¹He said to me, "To the land of Shinar, to build a house for it. And when this is prepared, they will set the basket down there on its base."

A Vision of Four Chariots

6 Again I lifted my eyes and saw, and behold, four chariots came out from between two mountains. And the mountains were mountains of bronze. ²The first chariot had red horses, the second black horses, ³the third white horses, and the fourth chariot dappled horses—all of them strong.⁷ ⁴Then I answered and said to the angel who talked with me, "What are these, my lord?" ⁵And the angel answered and said to me, "These are going out to the four winds of heaven, after presenting themselves before the Lord of all the earth. ⁶The chariot with the black horses goes toward the north country, the white ones go after them, and the dappled ones go toward the south country." ⁷When the strong horses came out, they were impatient to go and patrol the earth. And he said, "Go, patrol the earth." So they patrolled the earth. ⁸Then he cried to me, "Behold, those who go toward the north country have set my Spirit at rest in the north country."

The Crown and the Temple

⁹And the word of the LORD came to me: ¹⁰"Take from the exiles Heldai, Tobijah, and Jedaiah, who have arrived from Babylon,

---

¹Hebrew lacks *oil* ²Hebrew *two sons of new oil* ³A *cubit* was about 18 inches or 45 centimeters ⁴Hebrew lacks *falsely* (supplied from verse 4) ⁵Hebrew *ephah*; also verses 7–11. An *ephah* was about 3/5 bushel or 22 liters ⁶One Hebrew manuscript, Septuagint, Syriac; most Hebrew manuscripts *eye* ⁷Or *and the fourth chariot strong dappled horses*

A Prayer for...

STRENGTH IN THE BATTLE OF LIFE

In the battle between good and evil, there are things that bring life, health, peace, and joy, and there are also things that cause fighting, disease, misery, and death. In this battle between good and evil, may the little that I can do be sweet, sound, just, and generous. And may all that I do be in line with your will and your desire to work all things together for the good of those who love you.

Whether a battle ends in victory or defeat, teach me to lay at your feet my burden of responsibility, knowing that the outcome is never the result of my single effort but is the result of thousands of forces, of which my act is only one.

When something that I do is successful, don't let me be prideful, but make me modestly thankful for the other conditions which make my success possible. May I be humbly grateful for the privilege of sharing in a victory that is mainly yours.

And when the battle seems to be a failure, may I have the assurance that it's because of things I had no part in and could not control. And may I know that, in spite of this particular defeat, the powers of good are much stronger, and the powers of evil are much weaker, because of your sovereign grace working in and through me.

Amen.

shall build the temple of the LORD. [13] It i he who shall build the temple of the LOR and shall bear royal honor, and shall s and rule on his throne. And there sha be a priest on his throne, and the counse of peace shall be between them both." [14] And the crown shall be in the temple o the LORD as a reminder to Helem,[1] Tobija Jedaiah, and Hen the son of Zephaniah.

[15] "And those who are far off shall com and help to build the temple of the LOR And you shall know that the LORD of host has sent me to you. And this shall come t pass, if you will diligently obey the voice o the LORD your God."

A Call for Justice and Mercy

7 In the fourth year of King Darius, th word of the LORD came to Zechariah o the fourth day of the ninth month, which i Chislev. [2] Now the people of Bethel had ser Sharezer and Regem-melech and their me to entreat the favor of the LORD, [3] sayin to the priests of the house of the LORD o hosts and the prophets, "Should I weep an abstain in the fifth month, as I have don for so many years?"

[4] Then the word of the LORD of host came to me: [5] "Say to all the people of th land and the priests, When you fasted an mourned in the fifth month and in the sev enth, for these seventy years, was it for m that you fasted? [6] And when you eat an when you drink, do you not eat for your selves and drink for yourselves? [7] Were no these the words that the LORD proclaime by the former prophets, when Jerusale was inhabited and prosperous, with he cities around her, and the South and th lowland were inhabited?"

[8] And the word of the LORD came t Zechariah, saying, [9] "Thus says the LOR of hosts, Render true judgments, show kindness and mercy to one another, [10] d not oppress the widow, the fatherless, th sojourner, or the poor, and let none of yo devise evil against another in your heart [11] But they refused to pay attention an turned a stubborn shoulder and stoppe their ears that they might not hear.[2] [12] The made their hearts diamond-hard lest the should hear the law and the words tha the LORD of hosts had sent by his Spir through the former prophets. Therefor great anger came from the LORD of host

and go the same day to the house of Josiah, the son of Zephaniah. [11] Take from them silver and gold, and make a crown, and set it on the head of Joshua, the son of Jehozadak, the high priest. [12] And say to him, 'Thus says the LORD of hosts, "Behold, the man whose name is the Branch: for he shall branch out from his place, and he

[1] An alternate spelling of *Heldai* (verse 10) [2] Hebrew *and made their ears too heavy to hear*

³ "As I¹ called, and they would not hear, so they called, and I would not hear," says the LORD of hosts, ¹⁴ "and I scattered them with a whirlwind among all the nations that they had not known. Thus the land they left was desolate, so that no one went to and fro, and the pleasant land was made desolate."

The Coming Peace and Prosperity of Zion

8 And the word of the LORD of hosts came, saying, ² "Thus says the LORD of hosts: I am jealous for Zion with great jealousy, and I am jealous for her with great wrath. ³ Thus says the LORD: I have returned to Zion and will dwell in the midst of Jerusalem, and Jerusalem shall be called the faithful city, and the mountain of the LORD of hosts, the holy mountain. ⁴ Thus says the LORD of hosts: Old men and old women shall again sit in the streets of Jerusalem, each with staff in hand because of great age. ⁵ And the streets of the city shall be full of boys and girls playing in its streets. ⁶ Thus says the LORD of hosts: If it is marvelous in the sight of the remnant of this people in those days, should it also be marvelous in my sight, declares the LORD of hosts? ⁷ Thus says the LORD of hosts: Behold, I will save my people from the east country and from the west country, ⁸ and I will bring them to dwell in the midst of Jerusalem. And they shall be my people, and I will be their God, in faithfulness and in righteousness."

⁹ Thus says the LORD of hosts: "Let your hands be strong, you who in these days have been hearing these words from the mouth of the prophets who were present on the day that the foundation of the house of the LORD of hosts was laid, that the temple might be built. ¹⁰ For before those days there was no wage for man or any wage for beast, neither was there any safety from the foe for him who went out or came in, for I set every man against his neighbor. ¹¹ But now I will not deal with the remnant of this people as in the former days, declares the LORD of hosts. ¹² For there shall be a sowing of peace. The vine shall give its fruit, and the ground shall give its produce, and the heavens shall give their dew. And I will cause the remnant of this people to possess all these things. ¹³ And as you have been a byword of cursing among the nations, O house of Judah and house of Israel, so will I save you, and you shall be a blessing. Fear not, but let your hands be strong."

¹⁴ For thus says the LORD of hosts: "As I purposed to bring disaster to you when your fathers provoked me to wrath, and I did not relent, says the LORD of hosts, ¹⁵ so again have I purposed in these days to bring good to Jerusalem and to the house of Judah; fear not. ¹⁶ These are the things that you shall do: Speak the truth to one another; render in your gates judgments that are true and make for peace; ¹⁷ do not devise evil in your hearts against one another, and love no false oath, for all these things I hate, declares the LORD."

¹⁸ And the word of the LORD of hosts came to me, saying, ¹⁹ "Thus says the LORD of hosts: The fast of the fourth month and the fast of the fifth and the fast of the seventh and the fast of the tenth shall be to the house of Judah seasons of joy and gladness and cheerful feasts. Therefore love truth and peace.

²⁰ "Thus says the LORD of hosts: Peoples shall yet come, even the inhabitants of many cities. ²¹ The inhabitants of one city shall go to another, saying, 'Let us go at once to entreat the favor of the LORD and to seek the LORD of hosts; I myself am going.' ²² Many peoples and strong nations shall come to seek the LORD of hosts in Jerusalem and to entreat the favor of the LORD. ²³ Thus says the LORD of hosts: In those days ten men from the nations of every tongue shall take hold of the robe of a Jew, saying, 'Let us go with you, for we have heard that God is with you.'"

Judgment on Israel's Enemies

9 The oracle of the word of the LORD
   is against the land of Hadrach
   and Damascus is its resting place.
For the LORD has an eye on mankind
   and on all the tribes of Israel,²
²   and on Hamath also, which borders
      on it,
   Tyre and Sidon, though they are
      very wise.
³ Tyre has built herself a rampart
   and heaped up silver like dust,
   and fine gold like the mud of the
      streets.

¹ Hebrew *he* ² Or *For the eye of mankind, especially of all the tribes of Israel, is toward the* LORD

4 But behold, the Lord will strip her of
    her possessions
      and strike down her power on the
        sea,
      and she shall be devoured by fire.
5 Ashkelon shall see it, and be afraid;
      Gaza too, and shall writhe in
        anguish;
      Ekron also, because its hopes are
        confounded.
    The king shall perish from Gaza;
      Ashkelon shall be uninhabited;
6 a mixed people[1] shall dwell in
      Ashdod,
    and I will cut off the pride of
      Philistia.
7 I will take away its blood from its
      mouth,
      and its abominations from
        between its teeth;
    it too shall be a remnant for our God;
      it shall be like a clan in Judah,
      and Ekron shall be like the
        Jebusites.
8 Then I will encamp at my house as a
      guard,
      so that none shall march to and
        fro;
    no oppressor shall again march over
      them,
      for now I see with my own eyes.

The Coming King of Zion

9 Rejoice greatly, O daughter of Zion!
      Shout aloud, O daughter of
        Jerusalem!
    Behold, your king is coming to you;
      righteous and having salvation is
        he,
    humble and mounted on a donkey,
      on a colt, the foal of a donkey.
10 I will cut off the chariot from
      Ephraim
      and the war horse from Jerusalem;
    and the battle bow shall be cut off,
      and he shall speak peace to the
        nations;
    his rule shall be from sea to sea,
      and from the River to the ends of
        the earth.
11 As for you also, because of the blood
      of my covenant with you,
    I will set your prisoners free from
      the waterless pit.

12 Return to your stronghold, O prison-
      ers of hope;
    today I declare that I will restore
      to you double.
13 For I have bent Judah as my bow;
      I have made Ephraim its arrow.
    I will stir up your sons, O Zion,
      against your sons, O Greece,
      and wield you like a warrior's
        sword.

The Lord Will Save His People

14 Then the Lord will appear over
      them,
      and his arrow will go forth like
        lightning;
    the Lord God will sound the trum-
      pet
      and will march forth in the whirl-
        winds of the south.
15 The Lord of hosts will protect them,
      and they shall devour, and tread
        down the sling stones,
    and they shall drink and roar as if
        drunk with wine,
      and be full like a bowl,
      drenched like the corners of the
        altar.

16 On that day the Lord their God will
      save them,
      as the flock of his people;
    for like the jewels of a crown
      they shall shine on his land.
17 For how great is his goodness, and
      how great his beauty!
    Grain shall make the young men
      flourish,
      and new wine the young women.

The Restoration for Judah and Israel

10 Ask rain from the Lord
      in the season of the spring rain,
    from the Lord who makes the storm
      clouds,
      and he will give them showers of
        rain,
      to everyone the vegetation in the
        field.
2 For the household gods utter non-
      sense,
      and the diviners see lies;
    they tell false dreams
      and give empty consolation.

[1] Or a foreign people; Hebrew a bastard

Therefore the people wander like
sheep;
   they are afflicted for lack of a shepherd.

3 "My anger is hot against the shepherds,
   and I will punish the leaders;[1]
for the Lord of hosts cares for his
flock, the house of Judah,
and will make them like his majestic steed in battle.
4 From him shall come the cornerstone,
   from him the tent peg,
from him the battle bow,
   from him every ruler—all of them
together.
5 They shall be like mighty men in
battle,
   trampling the foe in the mud of the
streets;
they shall fight because the Lord is
with them,
   and they shall put to shame the
riders on horses.

6 "I will strengthen the house of Judah,
   and I will save the house of Joseph.
I will bring them back because I have
compassion on them,
   and they shall be as though I had
not rejected them,
for I am the Lord their God and
I will answer them.
7 Then Ephraim shall become like a
mighty warrior,
   and their hearts shall be glad as
with wine.
Their children shall see it and be
glad;
   their hearts shall rejoice in the
Lord.

8 "I will whistle for them and gather
them in,
   for I have redeemed them,
and they shall be as many as they
were before.
9 Though I scattered them among the
nations,
   yet in far countries they shall
remember me,
and with their children they shall
live and return.

10 I will bring them home from the land
of Egypt,
   and gather them from Assyria,
and I will bring them to the land of
Gilead and to Lebanon,
   till there is no room for them.
11 He shall pass through the sea of
troubles
   and strike down the waves of the
sea,
and all the depths of the Nile shall
be dried up.
The pride of Assyria shall be laid low,
   and the scepter of Egypt shall
depart.
12 I will make them strong in the Lord,
   and they shall walk in his name,"
        declares the Lord.

The Flock Doomed to Slaughter

11 Open your doors, O Lebanon,
   that the fire may devour your
cedars!
2 Wail, O cypress, for the cedar has
fallen,
   for the glorious trees are ruined!
Wail, oaks of Bashan,
   for the thick forest has been felled!
3 The sound of the wail of the shepherds,
   for their glory is ruined!
The sound of the roar of the lions,
   for the thicket of the Jordan is
ruined!

4 Thus said the Lord my God: "Become shepherd of the flock doomed to slaughter. 5 Those who buy them slaughter them and go unpunished, and those who sell them say, 'Blessed be the Lord, I have become rich,' and their own shepherds have no pity on them. 6 For I will no longer have pity on the inhabitants of this land, declares the Lord. Behold, I will cause each of them to fall into the hand of his neighbor, and each into the hand of his king, and they shall crush the land, and I will deliver none from their hand." 7 So I became the shepherd of the flock doomed to be slaughtered by the sheep traders. And I took two staffs, one I named Favor, the other I named Union. And I tended the sheep. 8 In one month I destroyed the three shepherds. But I became impatient with them, and they

also detested me. ⁹So I said, "I will not be your shepherd. What is to die, let it die. What is to be destroyed, let it be destroyed. And let those who are left devour the flesh of one another." ¹⁰And I took my staff Favor, and I broke it, annulling the covenant that I had made with all the peoples. ¹¹So it was annulled on that day, and the sheep traders, who were watching me, knew that it was the word of the LORD. ¹²Then I said to them, "If it seems good to you, give me my wages; but if not, keep them." And they weighed out as my wages thirty pieces of silver. ¹³Then the LORD said to me, "Throw it to the potter"— the lordly price at which I was priced by them. So I took the thirty pieces of silver and threw them into the house of the LORD, to the potter. ¹⁴Then I broke my second staff Union, annulling the brotherhood between Judah and Israel.

¹⁵Then the LORD said to me, "Take once more the equipment of a foolish shepherd. ¹⁶For behold, I am raising up in the land a shepherd who does not care for those being destroyed, or seek the young or heal the maimed or nourish the healthy, but devours the flesh of the fat ones, tearing off even their hoofs.

¹⁷   "Woe to my worthless shepherd,
      who deserts the flock!
  May the sword strike his arm
      and his right eye!
  Let his arm be wholly withered,
      his right eye utterly blinded!"

The LORD Will Give Salvation

12 The oracle of the word of the LORD concerning Israel: Thus declares the LORD, who stretched out the heavens and founded the earth and formed the spirit of man within him: ²"Behold, I am about to make Jerusalem a cup of staggering to all the surrounding peoples. The siege of Jerusalem will also be against Judah. ³On that day I will make Jerusalem a heavy stone for all the peoples. All who lift it will surely hurt themselves. And all the nations of the earth will gather against it. ⁴On that day, declares the LORD, I will strike every horse with panic, and its rider with madness. But for the sake of the house of Judah I will keep my eyes open, when I strike every horse of the peoples with blindness. ⁵Then the clans of Judah shall say to

themselves, 'The inhabitants of Jerusalem have strength through the LORD of hosts, their God.'

⁶"On that day I will make the clans of Judah like a blazing pot in the midst of wood, like a flaming torch among sheaves. And they shall devour to the right and to the left all the surrounding peoples, while Jerusalem shall again be inhabited in its place, in Jerusalem.

⁷"And the LORD will give salvation to the tents of Judah first, that the glory of the house of David and the glory of the inhabitants of Jerusalem may not surpass that of Judah. ⁸On that day the LORD will protect the inhabitants of Jerusalem, so that the feeblest among them on that day shall be like David, and the house of David shall be like God, like the angel of the LORD, going before them. ⁹And on that day I will seek to destroy all the nations that come against Jerusalem.

Him Whom They Have Pierced

¹⁰"And I will pour out on the house of David and the inhabitants of Jerusalem a spirit of grace and pleas for mercy, so that, when they look on me, on him whom they have pierced, they shall mourn for him, as one mourns for an only child, and weep bitterly over him, as one weeps over a firstborn. ¹¹On that day the mourning in Jerusalem will be as great as the mourning for Hadad-rimmon in the plain of Megiddo. ¹²The land shall mourn, each family¹ by itself: the family of the house of David by itself, and their wives by themselves; the family of the house of Nathan by itself, and their wives by themselves; ¹³the family of the house of Levi by itself and their wives by themselves; the family of the Shimeites by itself, and their wives by themselves; ¹⁴and all the families that are left, each by itself, and their wives by themselves.

13 "On that day there shall be a fountain opened for the house of David and the inhabitants of Jerusalem, to cleanse them from sin and uncleanness.

Idolatry Cut Off

²"And on that day, declares the LORD of hosts, I will cut off the names of the idols from the land, so that they shall be remembered no more. And also I will

¹Or *clan*; also verses 13, 14

emove from the land the prophets and
he spirit of uncleanness. ³ And if anyone
gain prophesies, his father and mother
vho bore him will say to him, 'You shall
ot live, for you speak lies in the name of
he LORD.' And his father and mother who
ore him shall pierce him through when
e prophesies.

⁴ "On that day every prophet will be
shamed of his vision when he prophesies.
Ie will not put on a hairy cloak in order to
eceive, ⁵ but he will say, 'I am no prophet,
am a worker of the soil, for a man sold me
n my youth.'¹ ⁶ And if one asks him, 'What
re these wounds on your back?'² he will
ay, 'The wounds I received in the house
f my friends.'

The Shepherd Struck

⁷   "Awake, O sword, against my shep-
       herd,
       against the man who stands next
          to me,"
       declares the LORD of hosts.

     "Strike the shepherd, and the sheep
       will be scattered;
     I will turn my hand against the
       little ones.
⁸   In the whole land, declares the LORD,
     two thirds shall be cut off and per-
       ish,
     and one third shall be left alive.
⁹   And I will put this third into the fire,
     and refine them as one refines
       silver,
     and test them as gold is tested.
     They will call upon my name,
       and I will answer them.
     I will say, 'They are my people';
       and they will say, 'The LORD is my
         God.'"

The Coming Day of the LORD

14 Behold, a day is coming for the LORD,
when the spoil taken from you will
be divided in your midst. ² For I will gather
all the nations against Jerusalem to battle,
and the city shall be taken and the houses

---

¹ Or for the land has been my possession since my youth ² Or on your chest; Hebrew *wounds between your hands*

---

verses to read
Zechariah 13:7–9

Know Yourself

The grass is always greener in the neighbor's yard. Why does it seem like you
have a "blah" or even miserable life and everyone else's is so great? Life isn't
always fair, at least not to the human eye. But remember, in order for gold to be
purified and refined, it has to be heated to extreme temperatures. As the heat
rises, all the dross, or bad stuff, rises to the top, where it can be skimmed off.
It's next to impossible to identify your own "dross"—your own bad stuff—when
life is good. But when troubles hit and the heat goes up, then your dirt is easier
to see. And that's when you can start to scrape off all that junk once and for
all. As you are refined by the trials of life, you start to turn to the one who can
save you, the one you need more than anything or anyone else, and your life is
cleansed and made new.

So don't fear the fire. Don't worry when life goes wrong, but look to Jesus and
see if he might be revealing something that needs to be removed from your life.
When your focus is on improvement and purification instead of worldly questions
and worries, your Spirit-led ability to rise above and even overcome adversity
grows. No trial is a waste of time when your focus is on pleasing God instead of
yourself. When you see suffering as God's tool for your sanctification, it suddenly
doesn't control you or scare you. The goal of the God Girl is humility, thankfulness,
and praise. And when you practice those things in your life, the power your trials
used to have over you is gone.

plundered and the women raped. Half of the city shall go out into exile, but the rest of the people shall not be cut off from the city. ³ Then the LORD will go out and fight against those nations as when he fights on a day of battle. ⁴ On that day his feet shall stand on the Mount of Olives that lies before Jerusalem on the east, and the Mount of Olives shall be split in two from east to west by a very wide valley, so that one half of the Mount shall move northward, and the other half southward. ⁵ And you shall flee to the valley of my mountains, for the valley of the mountains shall reach to Azal. And you shall flee as you fled from the earthquake in the days of Uzziah king of Judah. Then the LORD my God will come, and all the holy ones with him.

⁶ On that day there shall be no light, cold, or frost.¹ ⁷ And there shall be a unique² day, which is known to the LORD, neither day nor night, but at evening time there shall be light.

⁸ On that day living waters shall flow out from Jerusalem, half of them to the eastern sea³ and half of them to the western sea.⁴ It shall continue in summer as in winter.

⁹ And the LORD will be king over all the earth. On that day the LORD will be one and his name one.

¹⁰ The whole land shall be turned into a plain from Geba to Rimmon south of Jerusalem. But Jerusalem shall remain aloft on its site from the Gate of Benjamin to the place of the former gate, to the Corner Gate, and from the Tower of Hananel to the king's winepresses. ¹¹ And it shall be inhabited, for there shall never again be a decree of utter destruction.⁵ Jerusalem shall dwell in security.

¹² And this shall be the plague with which the LORD will strike all the peoples that wage war against Jerusalem: their flesh will rot while they are still standing on their feet, their eyes will rot in their sockets, and their tongues will rot in their mouths.

¹³ And on that day a great panic from the LORD shall fall on them, so that each will seize the hand of another, and the hand of the one will be raised against the hand of the other. ¹⁴ Even Judah will fight at Jerusalem. And the wealth of all the surrounding nations shall be collected, gold, silver, and garments in great abundance. ¹⁵ And a plague like this plague shall fall on the horses, the mules, the camels, the donkeys, and whatever beasts may be in those camps.

¹⁶ Then everyone who survives of all the nations that have come against Jerusalem shall go up year after year to worship the King, the LORD of hosts, and to keep the Feast of Booths. ¹⁷ And if any of the families of the earth do not go up to Jerusalem to worship the King, the LORD of hosts, there will be no rain on them. ¹⁸ And if the family of Egypt does not go up and present themselves, then on them there shall be no rain;⁶ there shall be the plague with which the LORD afflicts the nations that do not go up to keep the Feast of Booths. ¹⁹ This shall be the punishment to Egypt and the punishment to all the nations that do not go up to keep the Feast of Booths.

²⁰ And on that day there shall be inscribed on the bells of the horses, "Holy to the LORD." And the pots in the house of the LORD shall be as the bowls before the altar. ²¹ And every pot in Jerusalem and Judah shall be holy to the LORD of hosts, so that all who sacrifice may come and take of them and boil the meat of the sacrifice in them. And there shall no longer be a trader⁷ in the house of the LORD of hosts on that day.

---

¹ Compare Septuagint, Syriac, Vulgate, Targum; the meaning of the Hebrew is uncertain ² Hebrew *one* ³ That is, the Dead Sea ⁴ That is, the Mediterranean Sea ⁵ The Hebrew term rendered *decree of utter destruction* refers to things devoted (or set apart) to the Lord (or by the Lord) for destruction ⁶ Hebrew lacks *rain* ⁷ Or *Canaanite*

INTRODUCTION TO
Malachi

Return to Your First Love

> "From the days of your fathers you have turned aside from my statutes and have not kept them. Return to me, and I will return to you, says the LORD of hosts."
>
> *Malachi 3:7*

Author: Malachi

Time: Possibly around 450–414 B.C.

Place: Judah

Written to: Israel

The gist

The book of Malachi is about how easy it is to forget the love of God and to accept a counterfeit kind of love. It talks to a people who have become hardened to the sin in their lives and have refused to repent and return to their first love. In this book the prophet talks about a Messiah who will make everything new and will restore the relationship between God and his people.

Things to look for

- Thoughts on marriage outside of your faith (see Mal. 2:11–12)

- Thoughts on divorce (see Mal. 2:13–16)

- Thoughts on cheating God (see Mal. 3:6–18)

In an ungodly world it can be easy to start to think of godliness as extremism. When you see the world around you living life however it wants to live, it's easy to then look at God's Word and say, "That's just asking too much." And that's exactly what happened to the Israelites after they returned from exile. They started to let things slide, to become less and less worried about gratefully obeying God and more preoccupied with the easy life. They still loved God, or so they said. They prayed to him and worshiped him, but they also worshiped other things like their dreams and wants. They started to question God's love for them and to question their definition of sin. And so their faith kind of fell apart, so God sent the prophet Malachi to warn them that things were going to get bad because they had walked away from their first love.

Centuries after Malachi wrote this book, the same kinds of things are still going on in the lives of believers around the world. A lot of believers look just like the culture around them. They see their salvation as a free pass to live like the rest of the world. But this side of the cross we still need to understand God's justice. He doesn't change his law like the world changes. He doesn't turn a blind eye to the sinful choices of the world. He will judge them. And he doesn't even turn a blind eye to the sinful choices of his own people. He will discipline them, for their own good, out of his great love for them.

As you read Malachi, don't just think about the life of the Israelites, but think about believers today and even about yourself. In what ways do you walk away from truth and accept the world's ideas of right and wrong? And what does God expect of his children, even today? The Old Testament wasn't just written for the olden days; there's good stuff in it that is for today as well (see Rom. 15:4), so read it with the cross and our present-day world in mind.

✝ Malachi means "my messenger."

✍ *Second Exodus* ✍

The Israelites' return from captivity in Babylon.

"A son honors his father, and a servant his master. If then I am a father, where is my honor? And if I am a master, where is my fear? says the LORD of hosts." *Malachi 1:6*

"And now, O priests, this command is for you. If you will not listen, if you will not take it to heart to give honor to my name, says the LORD of hosts, then I will send the curse upon you." *Malachi 2:1–2*

"Will man rob God? Yet you are robbing me." *Malachi 3:8*

"You have said, 'It is vain to serve God. What is the profit of our keeping his charge or of walking as in mourning before the LORD of hosts? And now we call the arrogant blessed. Evildoers not only prosper but they put God to the test and they escape.'" *Malachi 3:14–15*

Malachi

1 The oracle of the word of the LORD to Israel by Malachi.[1]

The LORD's Love for Israel

2 "I have loved you," says the LORD. But you say, "How have you loved us?" "Is not Esau Jacob's brother?" declares the LORD. "Yet I have loved Jacob 3 but Esau I have hated. I have laid waste his hill country and left his heritage to jackals of the desert." 4 If Edom says, "We are shattered but we will rebuild the ruins," the LORD of hosts says, "They may build, but I will tear down, and they will be called 'the wicked country,' and the people with whom the LORD is angry forever.'" 5 Your own eyes shall see this, and you shall say, "Great is the LORD beyond the border of Israel!"

The Priests' Polluted Offerings

6 "A son honors his father, and a servant his master. If then I am a father, where is my honor? And if I am a master, where is my fear? says the LORD of hosts to you, O priests, who despise my name. But you say, 'How have we despised your name?' 7 By offering polluted food upon my altar. But you say, 'How have we polluted you?' By saying that the LORD's table may be despised. 8 When you offer blind animals in sacrifice, is that not evil? And when you offer those that are lame or sick, is that not evil? Present that to your governor; will he accept you or show you favor? says the LORD of hosts. 9 And now entreat the favor of God, that he may be gracious to us. With such a gift from your hand, will he show favor to any of you? says the LORD of hosts. 10 Oh that there were one among you who would shut the doors, that you might not kindle fire on my altar in vain! I have no pleasure in you, says the LORD of hosts, and I will not accept an offering from your hand. 11 For from the rising of the sun to its setting my name will be[2] great among the nations, and in every place incense will be offered to my name, and a pure offering. For my name will be great among the nations, says the LORD of hosts. 12 But you profane it when you say that the Lord's table is polluted, and its fruit, that is, its food may be despised. 13 But you say, 'What a weariness this is,' and you snort at it, says the LORD of hosts. You bring what has been taken by violence or is lame or sick, and this you bring as your offering! Shall I accept that from your hand? says the LORD. 14 Cursed be the cheat who has a male in his flock, and vows it, and yet sacrifices to the Lord what is blemished. For I am a great King, says the LORD of hosts, and my name will be feared among the nations.

The LORD Rebukes the Priests

2 "And now, O priests, this command is for you. 2 If you will not listen, if you will not take it to heart to give honor to my name, says the LORD of hosts, then I will send the curse upon you and I will curse your blessings. Indeed, I have already cursed them, because you do not lay it to heart. 3 Behold, I will rebuke your offspring,[3] and spread dung on your faces, the dung of your offerings, and you shall be taken away with it.[4] 4 So shall you know that I have sent this command to you, that my covenant with Levi may stand, says the LORD of hosts. 5 My covenant with him was one of life and peace, and I gave them to him. It was a covenant of fear, and he feared me. He stood in awe of my name. 6 True instruction[5] was in his mouth, and no wrong was found on his lips. He walked with me in peace and uprightness, and he turned many from iniquity. 7 For the lips of a priest should guard knowledge, and people[6] should seek instruction from

---

Malachi means *my messenger* [2] Or *is* (three times in verse 11; also verse 14) [3] Hebrew *seed* [4] Or *to it* [5] Or *law*; also verses 7, 8, 9 [6] Hebrew *they*

his mouth, for he is the messenger of the LORD of hosts. [8] But you have turned aside from the way. You have caused many to stumble by your instruction. You have corrupted the covenant of Levi, says the LORD of hosts, [9] and so I make you despised and abased before all the people, inasmuch as you do not keep my ways but show partiality in your instruction."

Judah Profaned the Covenant

[10] Have we not all one Father? Has not one God created us? Why then are we faithless to one another, profaning the covenant of our fathers? [11] Judah has been faithless, and abomination has been committed in Israel and in Jerusalem. For Judah has profaned the sanctuary of the LORD, which he loves, and has married the daughter of a foreign god. [12] May the LORD cut off from the tents of Jacob any descendant[1] of the man who does this, who brings an offering to the LORD of hosts!

[13] And this second thing you do. You cover the LORD's altar with tears, with weeping and groaning because he no longer regards the offering or accepts it with favor from your hand. [14] But you say, "Why does he not?" Because the LORD was witness between you and the wife of your youth, to whom you have been faithless, though she is your companion and your wife by covenant. [15] Did he not make them one, with a portion of the Spirit in their union?[2] And what was the one God seeking?[4] Godly offspring. So guard yourselves[5] in your spirit, and let none of you be faithless to the wife of your youth. [16] "Fo

[1] Hebrew *any who wakes and answers* [2] Hebrew *in it* [3] Hebrew *the one* [4] Or *And not one has done this who has a portion of the Spirit. And what was that one seeking?* [5] Or *So take care*; also verse 16

verses to read
Malachi 1:6–14

Know True Happiness

What does it mean to honor the Father? How do you give him respect? You look to the life of the Son, Jesus, who honored and respected God better than anyone. In his life you can find the way to do what God wants and to give him honor and respect. One of the most important truths about the life of Jesus is that he never made decisions to serve himself. He was never self-determined or self-willed, but he was one with the Father. That means that it wasn't about him but what God wanted of him. And Jesus wants the same for you. He wants you to be one with him as he is one with the Father. But what does that mean?

Being one with Jesus means that you are not emotionally capsized by what people say or do, because you know that life isn't about you. Life is about him, and that gives you freedom from shame and embarrassment, because nothing you do is about you: you belong completely to Christ. When you submit to the will of God and lean on him, honoring him and humbling yourself as Christ humbled himself, you are living according to your new identify as his child. This is who you now are. And this is your true joy.

Don't stand on your right to do this or that. Don't work at godliness with your self-will, but rely on him, trusting that if you honor and respect him, he will lift you up. As you become one with Christ and you stop making life about you and start making it all about him, the life you've wanted will be yours—but it won't be the life of fame and comfort and ease, but of truly knowing God and being at peace with him and with yourself. You will experience more contentment, more hope, and more joy than you ever dreamed of, and all because of God's gracious purposes in your life.

he man who does not love his wife but divorces her,[1] says the LORD, the God of Israel, covers[2] his garment with violence, says the LORD of hosts. So guard yourselves in your spirit, and do not be faithless."

The Messenger of the LORD

[17] You have wearied the LORD with your words. But you say, "How have we wearied him?" By saying, "Everyone who does evil is good in the sight of the LORD, and he delights in them." Or by asking, "Where is the God of justice?"

Ask Yourself . . .

ABOUT SUCCESS

- What is my definition of success?
- Is there anyone whose success I envy?
- Are they living a godly life?
- If not, then what do I envy about them, and how does that align with God's Word?
- What would be God's definition of success?

3 "Behold, I send my messenger, and he will prepare the way before me. And the Lord whom you seek will suddenly come to his temple; and the messenger of the covenant in whom you delight, behold, he is coming, says the LORD of hosts. [2] But who can endure the day of his coming, and who can stand when he appears? For he is like a refiner's fire and like fullers' soap. [3] He will sit as a refiner and purifier of silver, and he will purify the sons of Levi and refine them like gold and silver, and they will bring offerings in righteousness to the LORD.[3] [4] Then the offering of Judah and Jerusalem will be pleasing to the LORD as in the days of old and as in former years.

[5] "Then I will draw near to you for judgment. I will be a swift witness against the sorcerers, against the adulterers, against those who swear falsely, against those who oppress the hired worker in his wages, the widow and the fatherless, against those who thrust aside the sojourner, and do not fear me, says the LORD of hosts.

Robbing God

[6] "For I the LORD do not change; therefore you, O children of Jacob, are not consumed. [7] From the days of your fathers you have turned aside from my statutes and have not kept them. Return to me, and I will return to you, says the LORD of hosts. But you say, 'How shall we return?' [8] Will man rob God? Yet you are robbing me. But you say, 'How have we robbed you?' In your tithes and contributions. [9] You are cursed with a curse, for you are robbing me, the whole nation of you. [10] Bring the full tithe into the storehouse, that there may be food in my house. And thereby put me to the test, says the LORD of hosts, if I will not open the windows of heaven for you and pour down for you a blessing until there is no more need. [11] I will rebuke the devourer[4] for you, so that it will not destroy the fruits of your soil, and your vine in the field shall not fail to bear, says the LORD of hosts. [12] Then all nations will call you blessed, for you will be a land of delight, says the LORD of hosts.

[13] "Your words have been hard against me, says the LORD. But you say, 'How have we spoken against you?' [14] You have said, 'It is vain to serve God. What is the profit of our keeping his charge or of walking as in mourning before the LORD of hosts? [15] And now we call the arrogant blessed. Evildoers not only prosper but they put God to the test and they escape.'"

The Book of Remembrance

[16] Then those who feared the LORD spoke with one another. The LORD paid attention and heard them, and a book of remembrance was written before him of those who feared the LORD and esteemed his name. [17] "They shall be mine, says the LORD of hosts, in the day when I make up my treasured possession, and I will spare them as a man spares his son who serves

[1] Hebrew *who hates and divorces* [2] Probable meaning (compare Septuagint and Deuteronomy 24:1–4); or *"The LORD, the God of Israel, says that he hates divorce, and him who covers"* [3] Or *and they will belong to the LORD, bringers of an offering in righteousness* [4] Probably a name for some crop-destroying pest or pests

him. [18] Then once more you shall see the distinction between the righteous and the wicked, between one who serves God and one who does not serve him.

The Great Day of the LORD

4 [1] "For behold, the day is coming, burning like an oven, when all the arrogant and all evildoers will be stubble. The day that is coming shall set them ablaze, says the LORD of hosts, so that it will leave them neither root nor branch. [2] But for you who fear my name, the sun of righteousness shall rise with healing in its wings. You shall go out leaping like calves from the stall. [3] And you shall tread down the wicked, for they will be ashes under the soles of your feet, on the day when I act, says the LORD of hosts.

[4] "Remember the law of my servant Moses, the statutes and rules[2] that I commanded him at Horeb for all Israel.

[5] "Behold, I will send you Elijah the prophet before the great and awesome day of the LORD comes. [6] And he will turn the hearts of fathers to their children and the hearts of children to their fathers, lest I come and strike the land with a decree of utter destruction."[3]

[1] Ch 4:1–6 is ch 3:19–24 in Hebrew [2] Or *and just decrees* [3] The Hebrew term rendered *decree of utter destruction* refers to things devoted (or set apart) to the Lord (or by the Lord) for destruction

---

verses to read
Malachi 3:14–15

Sometimes it seems pointless to obey God. Whether you do right or wrong, it's all the same, isn't it? It's easy to think so when you're tired of doing what's right.

But the more you think like this, the more the payoff of sin seems more appealing than obedience. Many famous people claw their way to the top, and we call them blessed. They disobey God's commands, and yet we envy them. Their success makes it look like their sin goes unpunished, but that's a lie. They might look successful on the outside, but on the inside they're empty.

Choosing the right path instead of the easy one is never a mistake. The life of a God Girl is not an easy life. You are going to see other people doing a lot of things that you want to do but can't. And because of that, it's going to look like they're getting away with more. But the easy life isn't the definition of success. God's Word says you are to find happiness in the trials, not in the easy life. Happiness (or joy) comes from knowing and enjoying God in all his beauty and goodness.

The prophets got on God's people because of their belief that the world and all its little gods were more valuable than God. They wandered off and got distracted with pretty things, happy things, and hopeful things. They turned away from God's law and picked up other laws or just made their own, and in the end they suffered. Let their error serve as a warning for your life. Refuse to serve the world, but serve God with all your heart, soul, mind, and strength. As you do, your life will have all that it needs—in fact, even more than you ever dreamed (see Eph. 3:20).

THE

New Testament

INTRODUCTION TO
Matthew

Author: Matthew, a tax collector and disciple of Jesus

Time: Around A.D. 55 to 80

Place: Either Palestine or Syria

Written to: Jewish Christians

the gist

Matthew was one of the guys who traveled with Jesus. He knew firsthand who Jesus was and what he had done. In his book, Matthew wants people to get the fact that Jesus was the Messiah who had been predicted, the one they all were waiting for. So look for all the times he proves how Jesus fulfilled the Old Testament prophecies about the coming Messiah.

things to look for

The use of the phrase "kingdom of heaven" 32 times

53 Old Testament references

13 places where Matthew shows how Jesus fulfilled the Old Testament prophecies

The ways Matthew defends the faith

The Great Commission (see Matt. 28:19–20)

Follow Jesus

> "If anyone would come after me, let him deny himself and take up his cross and follow me."
>
> Matthew 16:24

The stuff Jesus said while he walked this earth was, and still is, radical and sometimes even offensive to our ears. Deny yourself and take up your cross? What? Aren't we supposed to look out for number one and stand up for ourselves? Jesus' words made no sense to the natural mind. He encouraged things like forgetting about self-protection, self-interest, and self-promotion. He asked people to consider themselves significant only insofar as they serve the master (see Matt. 6:24). And he said that, if we get into that way of thinking, we'll find all kinds of good stuff like love, joy, and wisdom.

Before Jesus got here, humans had to offer animal sacrifices so that the blood of an animal could clear them of the wrong they had done. But now you have a permanent sacrifice for your sin: the blood from the lamb they call Jesus. And you now have a power that was not available before. That power is the Holy Spirit that God has sent to you. If you'll walk in step with the Spirit, he'll give you all the power you need to do just what needs to be done.

When he taught, Jesus pushed the envelope and said hard things—that anger is just as bad as murder, for example; or that lust is just as bad as adultery. He set such a high standard because God's Holy Spirit now lives in us. You are his temple, the place he stays, and your life is now a living sacrifice. Your life is no longer your own but has been given to him, and that is why your life needs to be focused not on yourself but on the God you live for.

The book of Matthew is filled with amazing stuff from the mouth of your Savior. Dig in to these pages. In them you will find his thoughts, and in his thoughts you will find his being.

Must-Know Terms and Verses

✎ *Pharisees* ✎

A group of Jews who strictly observed the law of the Old Testament. Many of them were very self-righteous and prideful, looking down on anyone who didn't keep every letter of the law, especially when it came to tithing and purity.

✎ *Repent* ✎

To turn away from sin and agree that God's commands are good. Repentance involves a change of your mind and your actions.

✎ *Sadducees* ✎

Members of an aristocratic sect of Judaism that rejected Jesus as well as the idea of the resurrection of the dead.

"In the same way, let your light shine before others, so that they may see your good works and give glory to your Father who is in heaven." *Matthew 5:16*

"I say to you that everyone who looks at a woman with lustful intent has already committed adultery with her in his heart." *Matthew 5:28*

"But I say to you, Do not resist the one who is evil. But if anyone slaps you on the right cheek, turn to him the other also." *Matthew 5:39*

"So whatever you wish that others would do to you, do also to them." *Matthew 7:12*

"Not everyone who says to me, 'Lord, Lord,' will enter the kingdom of heaven, but the one who does the will of my Father who is in heaven." *Matthew 7:21*

"The greatest among you shall be your servant. Whoever exalts himself will be humbled, and whoever humbles himself will be exalted." *Matthew 23:11–12*

The Gospel According to

Matthew

The Genealogy of Jesus Christ

1 The book of the genealogy of Jesus Christ, the son of David, the son of Abraham.

² Abraham was the father of Isaac, and Isaac the father of Jacob, and Jacob the father of Judah and his brothers, ³ and Judah the father of Perez and Zerah by Tamar, and Perez the father of Hezron, and Hezron the father of Ram,¹ ⁴ and Ram the father of Amminadab, and Amminadab the father of Nahshon, and Nahshon the father of Salmon, ⁵ and Salmon the father of Boaz by Rahab, and Boaz the father of Obed by Ruth, and Obed the father of Jesse, ⁶ and Jesse the father of David the king.

And David was the father of Solomon by the wife of Uriah, ⁷ and Solomon the father of Rehoboam, and Rehoboam the father of Abijah, and Abijah the father of Asaph,² ⁸ and Asaph the father of Jehoshaphat, and Jehoshaphat the father of Joram, and Joram the father of Uzziah, ⁹ and Uzziah the father of Jotham, and Jotham the father of Ahaz, and Ahaz the father of Hezekiah, ¹⁰ and Hezekiah the father of Manasseh, and Manasseh the father of Amos,³ and Amos the father of Josiah, ¹¹ and Josiah the father of Jechoniah and his brothers, at the time of the deportation to Babylon.

¹² And after the deportation to Babylon: Jechoniah was the father of Shealtiel,⁴ and Shealtiel the father of Zerubbabel, ¹³ and Zerubbabel the father of Abiud, and Abiud the father of Eliakim, and Eliakim the father of Azor, ¹⁴ and Azor the father of Zadok, and Zadok the father of Achim, and Achim the father of Eliud, ¹⁵ and Eliud the father of Eleazar, and Eleazar the father of Matthan, and Matthan the father of Jacob, ¹⁶ and Jacob the father of Joseph the husband of Mary, of whom Jesus was born, who is called Christ.

¹⁷ So all the generations from Abraham to David were fourteen generations, and from David to the deportation to Babylon fourteen generations, and from the deportation to Babylon to the Christ fourteen generations.

The Birth of Jesus Christ

¹⁸ Now the birth of Jesus Christ⁵ took place in this way. When his mother Mary had been betrothed⁶ to Joseph, before they came together she was found to be with child from the Holy Spirit. ¹⁹ And her husband Joseph, being a just man and unwilling to put her to shame, resolved to divorce her quietly. ²⁰ But as he considered these things, behold, an angel of the Lord appeared to him in a dream, saying, "Joseph, son of David, do not fear to take Mary as your wife, for that which is conceived in her is from the Holy Spirit. ²¹ She will bear a son, and you shall call his name Jesus, for he will save his people from their sins." ²² All this took place to fulfill what the Lord had spoken by the prophet:

²³ ᵃ"Behold, the virgin shall conceive and
bear a son,
and they shall call his name
Immanuel"

(which means, God with us). ²⁴ When Joseph woke from sleep, he did as the angel of the Lord commanded him: he took his wife, ²⁵ but knew her not until she had given birth to a son. And he called his name Jesus.

The Visit of the Wise Men

2 Now after Jesus was born in Bethlehem of Judea in the days of Herod the king, behold, wise men⁷ from the east came to Jerusalem, ² saying, "Where is he who has been born king of the Jews? For we saw

---

¹ Greek *Aram*; also verse 4 ² *Asaph* is probably an alternate spelling of *Asa*; some manuscripts *Asa*; also verse 8 ³ *Amos* is probably an alternate spelling of *Amon*; some manuscripts *Amon*; twice in this verse ⁴ Greek *Salathiel*; twice in this verse ⁵ Some manuscripts *of the Christ* ⁶ That is, legally pledged to be married ⁷ Greek *magi*; also verses 7, 16 ᵃ Isa. 7:14

Mary, Mother of Jesus

Read this God Girl story in Matthew 1–2; Luke 1–2; John 2:1–12; 19:25–27; and Acts 1:14.

> And Mary said, "Behold, I am the servant of the Lord; let it be to me according to your word."
>
> Luke 1:38

A lot of times, the things God promises to do in your life are less about happiness and more about testing, rejection, and sadness. But that doesn't make them less of a gift.

For Mary, the promise that she would have a child was both a blessing and a test. Pregnancy out of wedlock. Rejection from family and friends. And watching her son go to the cross. In human terms it was a real mess, but from God's perspective it was divine intervention that would end up saving the world. All of Mary's suffering would give way to blessing.

How hard it is in the midst of a trial to see any light at the end of the tunnel, and how hard it must have been for Mary to watch her child suffering on an ugly cross. Could she have imagined what would happen next? Was she so faithful that she was just waiting expectantly for his resurrection? Or was she too sad to even think?

When God makes a promise, the only thing you can do is hold on to it. Even in the face of doubt and pain, you have to hold on tight to what you were promised. You might never get a promise like Mary's, but you might be called to suffer a lot here on earth. When you suffer, like Mary, you have to keep your mind focused on the things you have heard from God. Be clear about who or what you will believe—your eyes, or God's promises.

No matter what this world throws at you, you can find a deep peace in knowing that God's will is the perfect will and that he never lets anything happen unless it will bring him glory. When his glory is your number one goal, you know you have nothing to fear when trials hit. When you courageously look suffering in the eyes and say, "God's will be done," your faith will be a rock to stand on and you will find relief where others can only find agony.

As you read about the life of Mary, think about how she felt and what she would have gone through emotionally as she lived out her role as the mother of the Savior. But also think about her devotion to God and how it kept her strong to the end.

his star when it rose[1] and have come to worship him." [3] When Herod the king heard this, he was troubled, and all Jerusalem with him; [4] and assembling all the chief priests and scribes of the people, he inquired of them where the Christ was to be born. [5] They told him, "In Bethlehem of Judea, for so it is written by the prophet:

> [6] a" 'And you, O Bethlehem, in the land of Judah,
>   are by no means least among the rulers of Judah;
>   for from you shall come a ruler
>   who will shepherd my people Israel.' "

[7] Then Herod summoned the wise men secretly and ascertained from them what time the star had appeared. [8] And he sent them to Bethlehem, saying, "Go and search diligently for the child, and when you have found him, bring me word, that I too may come and worship him." [9] After listening to the king, they went on their way. And behold, the star that they had seen when it rose went before them until it came to rest over the place where the child was. [10] When they saw the star, they rejoiced exceedingly with great joy. [11] And going into the house they saw the child with Mary his mother, and they fell down and worshiped him. Then, opening their treasures, they offered him gifts, gold and frankincense and myrrh. [12] And being warned in a dream not to return to Herod, they departed to their own country by another way.

The Flight to Egypt

[13] Now when they had departed, behold, an angel of the Lord appeared to Joseph in a dream and said, "Rise, take the child and his mother, and flee to Egypt, and remain there until I tell you, for Herod is about to search for the child, to destroy him." [14] And he rose and took the child and his mother by night and departed to Egypt [15] and remained there until the death of Herod. This was to fulfill what the Lord had spoken by the prophet, b"Out of Egypt I called my son."

Herod Kills the Children

[16] Then Herod, when he saw that he had been tricked by the wise men, became furi-

ous, and he sent and killed all the male children in Bethlehem and in all that region who were two years old or under, according to the time that he had ascertained from the wise men. [17] Then was fulfilled what was spoken by the prophet Jeremiah:

> [18] c"A voice was heard in Ramah,
>   weeping and loud lamentation,
>   Rachel weeping for her children;
>   she refused to be comforted,
>   because they are no more."

The Return to Nazareth

[19] But when Herod died, behold, an angel of the Lord appeared in a dream to Joseph in Egypt, [20] saying, "Rise, take the child and his mother and go to the land of Israel, for those who sought the child's life are dead." [21] And he rose and took the child and his mother and went to the land of Israel. [22] But when he heard that Archelaus was reigning over Judea in place of his father Herod, he was afraid to go there, and being warned in a dream he withdrew to the district of Galilee. [23] And he went and lived in a city called Nazareth, so that what was spoken by the prophets might be fulfilled, that he would be called a Nazarene.

John the Baptist Prepares the Way

3 [d] In those days John the Baptist came preaching in the wilderness of Judea, [2] "Repent, for the kingdom of heaven is at hand." [3] For this is he who was spoken of by the prophet Isaiah when he said,

> e"The voice of one crying in the wilderness:
> 'Prepare[2] the way of the Lord;
>   make his paths straight.' "

[4] Now John wore a garment of camel's hair and a leather belt around his waist, and his food was locusts and wild honey. [5] Then Jerusalem and all Judea and all the region about the Jordan were going out to him, [6] and they were baptized by him in the river Jordan, confessing their sins.

[7] But when he saw many of the Pharisees and Sadducees coming to his baptism, he said to them, "You brood of vipers! Who warned you to flee from the wrath to come? [8] Bear fruit in keeping with repentance. [9] And do not presume to say to yourselves,

---

[1] Or *in the east; also verse 9* [2] Or *crying: Prepare in the wilderness* [a] Mic. 5:2 [b] Hos. 11:1 [c] Jer. 31:15 [d] For 3:1-12 see parallels Mark 1:2-8; Luke 3:1-17 [e] Isa. 40:3

'We have Abraham as our father,' for I tell you, God is able from these stones to raise up children for Abraham. [10] Even now the axe is laid to the root of the trees. Every tree therefore that does not bear good fruit is cut down and thrown into the fire.

[11] "I baptize you with water for repentance, but he who is coming after me is mightier than I, whose sandals I am not worthy to carry. He will baptize you with the Holy Spirit and fire. [12] His winnowing fork is in his hand, and he will clear his threshing floor and gather his wheat into the barn, but the chaff he will burn with unquenchable fire."

The Baptism of Jesus

[13] [a] Then Jesus came from Galilee to the Jordan to John, to be baptized by him. [14] John would have prevented him, saying, "I need to be baptized by you, and do you come to me?" [15] But Jesus answered him, "Let it be so now, for thus it is fitting for us to fulfill all righteousness." Then he consented. [16] And when Jesus was baptized, immediately he went up from the water, and behold, the heavens were opened to him,[1] and he saw the Spirit of God descending like a dove and coming to rest on him; [17] and behold, a voice from heaven said, "This is my beloved Son,[2] with whom I am well pleased."

The Temptation of Jesus

4 [b] Then Jesus was led up by the Spirit into the wilderness to be tempted by the devil. [2] And after fasting forty days and forty nights, he was hungry. [3] And the tempter came and said to him, "If you are the Son of God, command these stones to become loaves of bread." [4] But he answered, "It is written,

[c] "'Man shall not live by bread alone,
    but by every word that comes
        from the mouth of God.'"

[5] Then the devil took him to the holy city and set him on the pinnacle of the temple [6] and said to him, "If you are the Son of God, throw yourself down, for it is written,

[d] "'He will command his angels concerning you,'

and

"'On their hands they will bear you up,
    lest you strike your foot against a
        stone.'"

[7] Jesus said to him, "Again it is written, [e] 'You shall not put the Lord your God to the test.'" [8] Again, the devil took him to a very high mountain and showed him all the kingdoms of the world and their glory. [9] And he said to him, "All these I will give you, if you will fall down and worship me." [10] Then Jesus said to him, "Be gone, Satan! For it is written,

[f] "'You shall worship the Lord your God
    and him only shall you serve.'"

[11] Then the devil left him, and behold, angels came and were ministering to him.

Jesus Begins His Ministry

[12] Now when he heard that John had been arrested, he withdrew into Galilee. [13] And leaving Nazareth he went and lived in Capernaum by the sea, in the territory of Zebulun and Naphtali, [14] so that what was spoken by the prophet Isaiah might be fulfilled:

[15] [g] "The land of Zebulun and the land of
        Naphtali,
    the way of the sea, beyond
        the Jordan, Galilee of the
        Gentiles—
[16]   the people dwelling in darkness
        have seen a great light,
    and for those dwelling in the region
        and shadow of death,
        on them a light has dawned."

[17] From that time Jesus began to preach, saying, "Repent, for the kingdom of heaven is at hand."

Jesus Calls the First Disciples

[18] [h] While walking by the Sea of Galilee, he saw two brothers, Simon (who is called Peter) and Andrew his brother, casting a net into the sea, for they were fishermen. [19] And he said to them, "Follow me, and I will make you fishers of men."[3] [20] Immediately they left their nets and followed him. [21] And going on from there he saw two other brothers, James the son of

[1] Some manuscripts omit *to him* [2] Or *my Son, my* (or *the*) *Beloved* [3] The Greek word *anthropoi* refers here to both men and women [a] For 3:13-17 see parallels Mark 1:9-11; Luke 3:21, 22 [b] For 4:1-11 see parallels Mark 1:12, 13; Luke 4:1-13 [c] Deut. 8:3 [d] Ps. 91:11, 12 [e] Deut. 6:16 [f] Deut. 6:13 [g] Isa. 9:1, 2 [h] For 4:18-22 see parallel Mark 1:16-20

Zebedee and John his brother, in the boat with Zebedee their father, mending their nets, and he called them. ²²Immediately they left the boat and their father and followed him.

Jesus Ministers to Great Crowds

²³And he went throughout all Galilee, teaching in their synagogues and proclaiming the gospel of the kingdom and healing every disease and every affliction among the people. ²⁴So his fame spread throughout all Syria, and they brought him all the sick, those afflicted with various diseases and pains, those oppressed by demons, epileptics, and paralytics, and he healed them. ²⁵And great crowds followed him from Galilee and the Decapolis, and from Jerusalem and Judea, and from beyond the Jordan.

The Sermon on the Mount

5 Seeing the crowds, he went up on the mountain, and when he sat down, his disciples came to him.

The Beatitudes

²And he opened his mouth and taught them, saying:

³"Blessed are the poor in spirit, for theirs is the kingdom of heaven.

⁴"Blessed are those who mourn, for they shall be comforted.

⁵"Blessed are the meek, for they shall inherit the earth.

⁶"Blessed are those who hunger and thirst for righteousness, for they shall be satisfied.

⁷"Blessed are the merciful, for they shall receive mercy.

⁸"Blessed are the pure in heart, for they shall see God.

⁹"Blessed are the peacemakers, for they shall be called sons¹ of God.

¹⁰"Blessed are those who are persecuted for righteousness' sake, for theirs is the kingdom of heaven.

¹¹"Blessed are you when others revile you and persecute you and utter all kinds of evil against you falsely on my account. ¹²Rejoice and be glad, for your reward is great in heaven, for so they persecuted the prophets who were before you.

Salt and Light

¹³"You are the salt of the earth, but if salt has lost its taste, how shall its saltiness be restored? It is no longer good for anything except to be thrown out and trampled under people's feet.

¹⁴"You are the light of the world. A city set on a hill cannot be hidden. ¹⁵Nor do people light a lamp and put it under a basket, but on a stand, and it gives light to all in the house. ¹⁶In the same way, let your light shine before others, so that² they may see your good works and give glory to your Father who is in heaven.

Christ Came to Fulfill the Law

¹⁷"Do not think that I have come to abolish the Law or the Prophets; I have not come to abolish them but to fulfill them. ¹⁸For truly, I say to you, until heaven and earth pass away, not an iota, not a dot, will pass from the Law until all is accomplished. ¹⁹Therefore whoever relaxes one of the least of these commandments and teaches others to do the same will be called least in the kingdom of heaven, but whoever does them and teaches them will be called great in the kingdom of heaven. ²⁰For I tell you, unless your righteousness exceeds that of the scribes and Pharisees, you will never enter the kingdom of heaven.

Anger

²¹"You have heard that it was said to those of old, ᵃ'You shall not murder; and whoever murders will be liable to judgment.' ²²But I say to you that everyone who is angry with his brother³ will be liable to judgment; whoever insults⁴ his brother will be liable to the council; and whoever says, 'You fool!' will be liable to the hell⁵ of fire. ²³So if you are offering your gift at the altar and there remember that your brother has something against you, ²⁴leave your gift there before the altar and go. First be reconciled to your brother, and then come and offer your gift. ²⁵Come to terms quickly with your accuser while you are going with him to court, lest your accuser hand you over to the judge, and the judge to the guard, and you be put in prison. ²⁶Truly, I say to you, you will never get out until you have paid the last penny.⁶

¹ Greek huioi; see About the ESV ² Or house. ¹⁶Let your light so shine before others that ³ Some manuscripts insert without cause ⁴ Greek says Raca to (a term of abuse) ⁵ Greek Gehenna; also verses 29, 30 ⁶ Greek kodrantes, Roman copper coin (Latin quadrans) worth about 1/64 of a denarius (which was a day's wage for a laborer) ᵃ Ex. 20:13; Deut. 5:17

Lust

27 "You have heard that it was said, ᵃ'You shall not commit adultery.' **28** But I say to you that everyone who looks at a woman with lustful intent has already committed adultery with her in his heart. **29** If your right eye causes you to sin, tear it out and throw it away. For it is better that you lose one of your members than that your whole body be thrown into hell. **30** And if your right hand causes you to sin, cut it off and throw it away. For it is better that you lose one of your members than that your whole body go into hell.

Divorce

31 "It was also said, ᵇ'Whoever divorces his wife, let him give her a certificate of divorce.' **32** But I say to you that everyone who divorces his wife, except on the ground of sexual immorality, makes her commit adultery, and whoever marries a divorced woman commits adultery.

Oaths

33 "Again you have heard that it was said to those of old, 'You shall not swear falsely, but shall perform to the Lord what you have sworn.' **34** But I say to you, Do not take an oath at all, either by heaven, for it is the throne of God, **35** or by the earth, for it is his footstool, or by Jerusalem, for it is the city of the great King. **36** And do not take an oath by your head, for you cannot make one hair white or black. **37** Let what you say be simply 'Yes' or 'No'; anything more than this comes from evil.¹

Retaliation

38 "You have heard that it was said, ᶜ'An eye for an eye and a tooth for a tooth.' **39** But I say to you, Do not resist the one who is evil. But ᵈif anyone slaps you on the right cheek, turn to him the other also. **40** And if anyone would sue you and take your tunic,² let him have your cloak as well. **41** And if anyone forces you to go one mile, go with

---

¹Or *the evil one* ²Greek *chiton*, a long garment worn under the cloak next to the skin ᵃEx. 20:14; Deut. 5:18 ᵇDeut. 24:1 ᶜEx. 21:24; Lev. 24:20; Deut. 19:21 ᵈFor 5:39-42 see parallel Luke 6:29, 30

Know Love

verses to read
Matthew 5:38–48

Love, according to Jesus, isn't picky. It's not just for the lovable ones, but for the unlovable as well. If you only love those who love you back, then what good is love to a world that is dying? Jesus puts it this way: "For if you love those who love you, what reward do you have? Do not even the tax collectors do the same? And if you greet only your brothers, what more are you doing than others? Do not even the Gentiles do the same?" (Matt. 5:46–47). Love doesn't exclude people who don't love you back. It includes them all, even your enemies. Jesus makes that clear when he says, "But I say to you, Love your enemies and pray for those who persecute you" (Matt. 5:44).

So what do you think? Can you do it? Can you love someone who is out to get you? Someone who wants to hurt you? If not, Jesus asks, then what good is your love? The God Girl loves others not because of who they are or what they do but because of how deeply God has loved her, even when she was an enemy of God.

When you learn to look at life from this perspective, what people do to you or around you doesn't hurt you like it used to. When your number one goal isn't getting the attention you want but loving as God has loved you, you can no longer be pulled down or hurt by anyone. God gives you the answer for bullies, mean girls, angry people, and the cruel world, and that answer is love. Just love. Love them. Hurt when they hurt, pray for them, care for them, and give to them, but above all love them as God loves you, because he does.

him two miles. ⁴²Give to the one who begs from you, and do not refuse the one who would borrow from you.

Love Your Enemies

⁴³"You have heard that it was said, ᵃ'You shall love your neighbor and hate your enemy.' ⁴⁴But I say to you, Love your enemies and pray for those who persecute you, ⁴⁵so that you may be sons of your Father who is in heaven. For he makes his sun rise on the evil and on the good, and sends rain on the just and on the unjust. ⁴⁶For if you love those who love you, what reward do you have? Do not even the tax collectors do the same? ⁴⁷And if you greet only your brothers,¹ what more are you doing than others? Do not even the Gentiles do the same? ⁴⁸You therefore must be perfect, as your heavenly Father is perfect.

Giving to the Needy

6 "Beware of practicing your righteousness before other people in order to be seen by them, for then you will have no reward from your Father who is in heaven. ²"Thus, when you give to the needy, sound no trumpet before you, as the hypocrites do in the synagogues and in the streets, that they may be praised by others. Truly, I say to you, they have received their reward. ³But when you give to the needy, do not let your left hand know what your right hand is doing, ⁴so that your giving may be in secret. And your Father who sees in secret will reward you.

The Lord's Prayer

⁵"And when you pray, you must not be like the hypocrites. For they love to stand and pray in the synagogues and at the street corners, that they may be seen by others. Truly, I say to you, they have received their reward. ⁶But when you pray, go into your room and shut the door and pray to your Father who is in secret. And your Father who sees in secret will reward you.

⁷"And when you pray, do not heap up empty phrases as the Gentiles do, for they think that they will be heard for their many words. ⁸Do not be like them, for your Father knows what you need before you ask him. ⁹Pray then like this:

"Our Father in heaven,
        hallowed be your name.²
¹⁰   Your kingdom come,
        your will be done,³
            on earth as it is in heaven.
¹¹   Give us this day our daily bread,⁴
¹²   and forgive us our debts,
            as we also have forgiven our debt-
            ors.
¹³   And lead us not into temptation,
            but deliver us from evil.⁵

¹⁴For if you forgive others their trespasses, your heavenly Father will also forgive you, ¹⁵but if you do not forgive others their trespasses, neither will your Father forgive your trespasses.

Fasting

¹⁶"And when you fast, do not look gloomy like the hypocrites, for they disfigure their faces that their fasting may be seen by others. Truly, I say to you, they have received their reward. ¹⁷But when you fast, anoint your head and wash your face, ¹⁸that your fasting may not be seen by others but by your Father who is in secret. And your Father who sees in secret will reward you.

Lay Up Treasures in Heaven

¹⁹"Do not lay up for yourselves treasures on earth, where moth and rust⁶ destroy and where thieves break in and steal, ²⁰but lay up for yourselves treasures in heaven, where neither moth nor rust destroys and where thieves do not break in and steal. ²¹For where your treasure is, there your heart will be also.

²²"The eye is the lamp of the body. So, if your eye is healthy, your whole body will be full of light, ²³but if your eye is bad, your whole body will be full of darkness. If then the light in you is darkness, how great is the darkness!

²⁴"No one can serve two masters, for either he will hate the one and love the other, or he will be devoted to the one and despise the other. You cannot serve God and money.⁷

---

¹Or brothers and sisters. The plural Greek word adelphoi (translated "brothers") refers to siblings in a family. In New Testament usage, depending on the context, adelphoi may refer either to brothers or to brothers and sisters ²Or Let your name be kept holy, or Let your name be treated with reverence ³Or Let your kingdom come, let your will be done ⁴Or our bread for tomorrow ⁵Or the evil one; some manuscripts add For yours is the kingdom and the power and the glory, forever. Amen ⁶Or worm; also verse 20 ⁷Greek mammon, a Semitic word for money or possessions ᵃLev. 19:18

Do Not Be Anxious

²⁵ ᵃ "Therefore I tell you, do not be anxious about your life, what you will eat or what you will drink, nor about your body, what you will put on. Is not life more than food, and the body more than clothing? ²⁶ Look at the birds of the air: they neither sow nor reap nor gather into barns, and yet your heavenly Father feeds them. Are you not of more value than they? ²⁷ And which of you by being anxious can add a single hour to his span of life?¹ ²⁸ And why are you anxious about clothing? Consider the lilies of the field, how they grow: they neither toil nor spin, ²⁹ yet I tell you, even Solomon in all his glory was not arrayed like one of these. ³⁰ But if God so clothes the grass of the field, which today is alive and tomorrow is thrown into the oven, will he not much more clothe you, O you of little faith? ³¹ Therefore do not be anxious, saying, 'What shall we eat?' or 'What shall we drink?' or 'What shall we wear?' ³² For the Gentiles seek after all these things, and your heavenly Father knows that you need them all. ³³ But seek first the kingdom of God and his righteousness, and all these things will be added to you.

³⁴ "Therefore do not be anxious about tomorrow, for tomorrow will be anxious for itself. Sufficient for the day is its own trouble.

Judging Others

7 ᵇ "Judge not, that you be not judged. ² For with the judgment you pronounce you will be judged, and with the measure you use it will be measured to you. ³ Why do you see the speck that is in your brother's eye, but do not notice the log that is in your own eye? ⁴ Or how can you say to your brother, 'Let me take the speck out of your eye,' when there is the log in your own eye? ⁵ You hypocrite, first take the log out of your own eye, and then you will see clearly to take the speck out of your brother's eye.

⁶ "Do not give dogs what is holy, and do not throw your pearls before pigs, lest they trample them underfoot and turn to attack you.

Ask, and It Will Be Given

⁷ ᶜ "Ask, and it will be given to you; seek, and you will find; knock, and it will be opened to you. ⁸ For everyone who asks receives, and the one who seeks finds, and to the one who knocks it will be opened. ⁹ Or which one of you, if his son asks him for bread, will give him a stone? ¹⁰ Or if he asks for a fish, will give him a serpent? ¹¹ If you then, who are evil, know how to give good gifts to your children, how much more will your Father who is in heaven give good things to those who ask him!

The Golden Rule

¹² "So whatever you wish that others would do to you, do also to them, for this is the Law and the Prophets.

¹³ "Enter by the narrow gate. For the gate is wide and the way is easy² that leads to destruction, and those who enter by it are many. ¹⁴ For the gate is narrow and the way is hard that leads to life, and those who find it are few.

A Tree and Its Fruit

¹⁵ "Beware of false prophets, who come to you in sheep's clothing but inwardly are ravenous wolves. ¹⁶ You will recognize them by their fruits. Are grapes gathered from thornbushes, or figs from thistles? ¹⁷ So, every healthy tree bears good fruit, but the diseased tree bears bad fruit. ¹⁸ A healthy tree cannot bear bad fruit, nor can a diseased tree bear good fruit. ¹⁹ Every tree that does not bear good fruit is cut down and thrown into the fire. ²⁰ Thus you will recognize them by their fruits.

I Never Knew You

²¹ "Not everyone who says to me, 'Lord, Lord,' will enter the kingdom of heaven, but the one who does the will of my Father who is in heaven. ²² On that day many will say to me, 'Lord, Lord, did we not prophesy in your name, and cast out demons in your name, and do many mighty works in your name?' ²³ And then will I declare to them, 'I never knew you; depart from me, you workers of lawlessness.'

Build Your House on the Rock

²⁴ ᵈ "Everyone then who hears these words of mine and does them will be like a wise man who built his house on the rock. ²⁵ And the rain fell, and the floods came, and the winds blew and beat on that

¹ Or *a single cubit to his stature*; a *cubit* was about 18 inches or 45 centimeters   ² Some manuscripts *For the way is wide and easy*
ᵃ For 6:25-33 see parallel Luke 12:22-31   ᵇ For 7:1-5 see parallel Luke 6:37, 38, 41, 42   ᶜ For 7:7-11 see parallel Luke 11:9-13   ᵈ For 7:24-27 see parallel Luke 6:47-49

house, but it did not fall, because it had been founded on the rock. [26] And everyone who hears these words of mine and does not do them will be like a foolish man who built his house on the sand. [27] And the rain fell, and the floods came, and the winds blew and beat against that house, and it fell, and great was the fall of it."

The Authority of Jesus

[28] And when Jesus finished these sayings, the crowds were astonished at his teaching, [29] for he was teaching them as one who had authority, and not as their scribes.

Jesus Cleanses a Leper

8 When he came down from the mountain, great crowds followed him. [2] [a] And behold, a leper[1] came to him and knelt before him, saying, "Lord, if you will, you can make me clean." [3] And Jesus[2] stretched

out his hand and touched him, saying, "I will; be clean." And immediately his leprosy was cleansed. [4] And Jesus said to him, "See that you say nothing to anyone, but go, show yourself to the priest and offer the gift that Moses commanded, for a proof to them."

The Faith of a Centurion

[5] [b] When he had entered Capernaum, a centurion came forward to him, appealing to him, [6] "Lord, my servant is lying paralyzed at home, suffering terribly." [7] And he said to him, "I will come and heal him." [8] But the centurion replied, "Lord, I am not worthy to have you come under my roof, but only say the word, and my servant will be healed. [9] For I too am a man under authority, with soldiers under me. And I say to one, 'Go,' and he goes, and to another, 'Come,' and he comes, and to my servant,[3]

---

[1] *Leprosy* was a term for several skin diseases; see Leviticus 13   [2] Greek *he*   [3] Greek *bondservant*   [a] For 8:2-4 see parallels Mark 1:40-44; Luke 5:12-14   [b] For 8:5-13 see parallel Luke 7:1-10

Know God

verses to read
Matthew 7:7–11

Is there something that God has promised in his Word that he has not yet done for you? Are you beginning to mistrust him, or at the very least are you doubting your ability to hear him?

If God is slow in bringing to pass one of his promises to you, there's a reason for it. Like a good father who knows what his kids need and when they need it, the Father above knows exactly what you need and when you need it. Sometimes not getting the thing you want is exactly what you need, but with your limited perspective you don't know that. That's why it should be such a relief to know that you have a Father God who can be trusted. Everything good that you have comes from him, and everything bad in your life is something he has allowed in order that it might bring glory to him as you learn to trust him more deeply.

Now, the only wild card in this situation is you. Will you stand on the truth of God's Word, acting upon it and living it? Or will you reject truth because what you want is slow in coming? A God Girl's faith must be grounded in the grace and infallibility of the Father. When you can trust him, then you can be set free. And that freedom will be the doorway to spiritual growth and maturity.

Every girl has moments of fear when she wonders, *Does my Father really care? Will he always be there?* Every girl needs a rock, a solid foundation that will never shake, and though her earthly father may never be any of those things, she has a heavenly Father who will *always* be those things. This should bring you a lot of joy! God can be trusted. He is not a liar; you can trust him with your heart.

'Do this,' and he does it." ¹⁰When Jesus heard this, he marveled and said to those who followed him, "Truly, I tell you, with no one in Israel¹ have I found such faith. ¹¹I tell you, many will come from east and west and recline at table with Abraham, Isaac, and Jacob in the kingdom of heaven, ¹²while the sons of the kingdom will be thrown into the outer darkness. In that place there will be weeping and gnashing of teeth." ¹³And to the centurion Jesus said, "Go; let it be done for you as you have believed." And the servant was healed at that very moment.

Jesus Heals Many

¹⁴ᵃAnd when Jesus entered Peter's house, he saw his mother-in-law lying sick with a fever. ¹⁵He touched her hand, and the fever left her, and she rose and began to serve him. ¹⁶That evening they brought to him many who were oppressed by demons, and he cast out the spirits with a word and healed all who were sick. ¹⁷This was to fulfill what was spoken by the prophet Isaiah: ᵇ"He took our illnesses and bore our diseases."

The Cost of Following Jesus

¹⁸Now when Jesus saw a crowd around him, he gave orders to go over to the other side. ¹⁹ᶜAnd a scribe came up and said to him, "Teacher, I will follow you wherever you go." ²⁰And Jesus said to him, "Foxes have holes, and birds of the air have nests, but the Son of Man has nowhere to lay his head." ²¹Another of the disciples said to him, "Lord, let me first go and bury my father." ²²And Jesus said to him, "Follow me, and leave the dead to bury their own dead."

Jesus Calms a Storm

²³ᵈAnd when he got into the boat, his disciples followed him. ²⁴And behold, there arose a great storm on the sea, so that the boat was being swamped by the waves; but he was asleep. ²⁵And they went and woke him, saying, "Save us, Lord; we are perishing." ²⁶And he said to them, "Why are you afraid, O you of little faith?" Then he rose and rebuked the winds and the sea, and there was a great calm. ²⁷And the men marveled, saying, "What sort of man is this, that even winds and sea obey him?"

Jesus Heals Two Men with Demons

²⁸ᵉAnd when he came to the other side, to the country of the Gadarenes,² two demon-possessed³ men met him, coming out of the tombs, so fierce that no one could pass that way. ²⁹And behold, they cried out, "What have you to do with us, O Son of God? Have you come here to torment us before the time?" ³⁰Now a herd of many pigs was feeding at some distance from them. ³¹And the demons begged him, saying, "If you cast us out, send us away into the herd of pigs." ³²And he said to them, "Go." So they came out and went into the pigs, and behold, the whole herd rushed down the steep bank into the sea and drowned in the waters. ³³The herdsmen fled, and going into the city they told everything, especially what had happened to the demon-possessed men. ³⁴And behold, all the city came out to meet Jesus, and when they saw him, they begged him to leave their region.

Jesus Heals a Paralytic

9 And getting into a boat he crossed over and came to his own city. ²ᶠAnd behold, some people brought to him a paralytic, lying on a bed. And when Jesus saw their faith, he said to the paralytic, "Take heart, my son; your sins are forgiven." ³And behold, some of the scribes said to themselves, "This man is blaspheming." ⁴But Jesus, knowing⁴ their thoughts, said, "Why do you think evil in your hearts? ⁵For which is easier, to say, 'Your sins are forgiven,' or to say, 'Rise and walk'? ⁶But that you may know that the Son of Man has authority on earth to forgive sins"—he then said to the paralytic—"Rise, pick up your bed and go home." ⁷And he rose and went home. ⁸When the crowds saw it, they were afraid, and they glorified God, who had given such authority to men.

Jesus Calls Matthew

⁹ᵍAs Jesus passed on from there, he saw a man called Matthew sitting at the tax booth, and he said to him, "Follow me." And he rose and followed him.

¹⁰And as Jesus⁵ reclined at table in the house, behold, many tax collectors and sinners came and were reclining with Jesus

---

¹Some manuscripts *not even in Israel* ²Some manuscripts *Gergesenes*; some *Gerasenes* ³Greek *daimonizomai*; also verse 33; elsewhere rendered *oppressed by demons* ⁴Some manuscripts *perceiving* ⁵Greek *he* ᵃFor 8:14-17 see parallels Mark 1:29-34; Luke 4:38-41 ᵇIsa. 53:4 ᶜFor 8:19-22 see parallel Luke 9:57-62 ᵈFor 8:23-27 see parallels Mark 4:35-41; Luke 8:22-25 ᵉFor 8:28-34 see parallels Mark 5:1-21; Luke 8:26-39 ᶠFor 9:2-8 see parallels Mark 2:1-12; Luke 5:17-26 ᵍFor 9:9-17 see parallels Mark 2:13-22; Luke 5:27-39

and his disciples. [11] And when the Pharisees saw this, they said to his disciples, "Why does your teacher eat with tax collectors and sinners?" [12] But when he heard it, he said, "Those who are well have no need of a physician, but those who are sick. [13] Go and learn what this means, [a]'I desire mercy, and not sacrifice.' For I came not to call the righteous, but sinners."

A Question About Fasting

[14] Then the disciples of John came to him, saying, "Why do we and the Pharisees fast,[1] but your disciples do not fast?" [15] And Jesus said to them, "Can the wedding guests mourn as long as the bridegroom is with them? The days will come when the bridegroom is taken away from them, and then they will fast. [16] No one puts a piece of unshrunk cloth on an old garment, for the patch tears away from the garment, and a worse tear is made. [17] Neither is new wine put into old wineskins. If it is, the skins burst and the wine is spilled and the skins are destroyed. But new wine is put into fresh wineskins, and so both are preserved."

A Girl Restored to Life and a Woman Healed

[18][b] While he was saying these things to them, behold, a ruler came in and knelt before him, saying, "My daughter has just died, but come and lay your hand on her, and she will live." [19] And Jesus rose and followed him, with his disciples. [20] And behold, a woman who had suffered from a discharge of blood for twelve years came up behind him and touched the fringe of his garment, [21] for she said to herself, "If I only touch his garment, I will be made well." [22] Jesus turned, and seeing her he said, "Take heart, daughter; your faith has made you well." And instantly[2] the woman was made well. [23] And when Jesus came to the ruler's house and saw the flute players and the crowd making a commotion, [24] he said, "Go away, for the girl is not dead but sleeping." And they laughed at him. [25] But when the crowd had been put outside, he went in and took her by the hand, and the girl arose. [26] And the report of this went through all that district.

Jesus Heals Two Blind Men

[27] And as Jesus passed on from there, two blind men followed him, crying aloud, "Have mercy on us, Son of David." [28] When he entered the house, the blind men came to him, and Jesus said to them, "Do you believe that I am able to do this?" They said to him, "Yes, Lord." [29] Then he touched their eyes, saying, "According to your faith be it done to you." [30] And their eyes were opened. And Jesus sternly warned them, "See that no one knows about it." [31] But they went away and spread his fame through all that district.

Jesus Heals a Man Unable to Speak

[32] As they were going away, behold, a demon-oppressed man who was mute was brought to him. [33] And when the demon had been cast out, the mute man spoke. And the crowds marveled, saying, "Never was anything like this seen in Israel." [34] But the Pharisees said, "He casts out demons by the prince of demons."

The Harvest Is Plentiful, the Laborers Few

[35] And Jesus went throughout all the cities and villages, teaching in their synagogues and proclaiming the gospel of the kingdom and healing every disease and every affliction. [36] When he saw the crowds, he had compassion for them, because they were harassed and helpless, like sheep without a shepherd. [37] Then he said to his disciples, "The harvest is plentiful, but the laborers are few; [38] therefore pray earnestly to the Lord of the harvest to send out laborers into his harvest."

The Twelve Apostles

10 And he called to him his twelve disciples and gave them authority over unclean spirits, to cast them out, and to heal every disease and every affliction. [2][c] The names of the twelve apostles are these: first, Simon, who is called Peter, and Andrew his brother; James the son of Zebedee, and John his brother; [3] Philip and Bartholomew; Thomas and Matthew the tax collector; James the son of Alphaeus, and Thaddaeus;[3] [4] Simon the Zealot,[4] and Judas Iscariot, who betrayed him.

---

[1] Some manuscripts add *much*, or *often* [2] Greek *from that hour* [3] Some manuscripts *Lebbaeus*, or *Lebbaeus called Thaddaeus* [4] Greek *kananaios*, meaning *zealot* [a] Hos. 6:6 [b] For 9:18-26 see parallels Mark 5:21-43; Luke 8:40-56 [c] For 10:2-4 see parallels Mark 3:16-19; Luke 6:13-16

The Woman with Chronic Bleeding

Read this God Girl story in Matthew 9:20-22;
Mark 5:25-34; and Luke 8:43-48.

> And he could do no mighty work there, except that he laid his
> hands on a few sick people and healed them. And he marveled
> because of their unbelief.
>
> Mark 6:5-6

When he was on this earth Jesus did a lot of miracles in the presence of faith, but when faith was gone, he didn't do them (see Mark 6:5). The doubts and disbelief of the people kept him from showing his power in their lives. What a tragedy to miss out on the power of God because you fear that he will not do for you the very thing that you need! To doubt is to remove the power of God from your life, but to believe is to have access to the miraculous. As a believer, you are by very definition not a doubter. But how many times have you doubted God's salvation in your life? How many times have you failed to believe that his power would be released for you?

In the middle of doubt Jesus does not do miracles, but in the middle of faith he shows up. The woman who touched his coat showed her faith as she reached out to connect with him, and two thousand years later you show your faith as you reach out to connect with him through prayer. Prayer is your fighting the crowds and reaching out to touch his garment. Prayer is your act of faith in who he is and what he can do. It is your proof that you will believe and not doubt. It is your outstretched arm trembling with hope and anticipation.

The woman with the chronic bleeding was sure of one thing, and that was that if she could just touch the hem of Jesus' clothing, his power would heal her. Her mind was made up: he was the healer. He had healed others, and he would heal her. And today you have to be sure of one thing, and that is that whether or not God gives you exactly what you want right now, he is good and therefore he can be trusted. Faith says, "Your will be done." It stands in eager anticipation of the miracle that God will choose to give you. And it believes that no matter what the condition of your life, the true miracle is that he forgives your sins and accepts you as his child.

Jesus Sends Out the Twelve Apostles

[5] These twelve Jesus sent out, instructing them, "Go nowhere among the Gentiles and enter no town of the Samaritans, [6] but go rather to the lost sheep of the house of Israel. [7] And proclaim as you go, saying, 'The kingdom of heaven is at hand.' [8] Heal the sick, raise the dead, cleanse lepers,[1] cast out demons. You received without paying; give without pay. [9] [a] Acquire no gold or silver or copper for your belts, [10] no bag for your journey, or two tunics[2] or sandals or a staff, for the laborer deserves his food. [11] And whatever town or village you enter, find out who is worthy in it and stay there until you depart. [12] As you enter the house, greet it. [13] And if the house is worthy, let your peace come upon it, but if it is not worthy, let your peace return to you. [14] And if anyone will not receive you or listen to your words, shake off the dust from your feet when you leave that house or town. [15] Truly, I say to you, it will be more bearable on the day of judgment for the land of Sodom and Gomorrah than for that town.

Persecution Will Come

[16] "Behold, I am sending you out as sheep in the midst of wolves, so be wise as serpents and innocent as doves. [17] Beware of men, for they will deliver you over to courts and flog you in their synagogues, [18] and you will be dragged before governors and kings for my sake, to bear witness before them and the Gentiles. [19] When they deliver you over, do not be anxious how you are to speak or what you are to say, for what you are to say will be given to you in that hour. [20] For it is not you who speak, but the Spirit of your Father speaking through you. [21] Brother will deliver brother over to death, and the father his child, and children will rise against parents and have them put to death, [22] and you will be hated by all for my name's sake. But the one who endures to the end will be saved. [23] When they persecute you in one town, flee to the next, for truly, I say to you, you will not have gone through all the towns of Israel before the Son of Man comes.

[24] "A disciple is not above his teacher, nor a servant[3] above his master. [25] It is enough for the disciple to be like his teacher, and the servant like his master. If they have called the master of the house Beelzebul, how much more will they malign[4] those of his household.

Have No Fear

[26] "So have no fear of them, [b] for nothing is covered that will not be revealed, or hidden that will not be known. [27] What I tell you in the dark, say in the light, and what you hear whispered, proclaim on the housetops. [28] And do not fear those who kill the body but cannot kill the soul. Rather fear him who can destroy both soul and body in hell.[5] [29] Are not two sparrows sold for a penny?[6] And not one of them will fall to the ground apart from your Father. [30] But even the hairs of your head are all numbered. [31] Fear not, therefore; you are of more value than many sparrows. [32] So everyone who acknowledges me before men, I also will acknowledge before my Father who is in heaven, [33] but whoever denies me before men, I also will deny before my Father who is in heaven.

Not Peace, but a Sword

[34] [c] "Do not think that I have come to bring peace to the earth. I have not come to bring peace, but a sword. [35] For I have come to set a man against his father, and a daughter against her mother, and a daughter-in-law against her mother-in-law. [36] And a person's enemies will be those of his own household. [37] Whoever loves father or mother more than me is not worthy of me, and whoever loves son or daughter more than me is not worthy of me. [38] And whoever does not take his cross and follow me is not worthy of me. [39] Whoever finds his life will lose it, and whoever loses his life for my sake will find it.

Rewards

[40] "Whoever receives you receives me, and whoever receives me receives him who sent me. [41] The one who receives a prophet because he is a prophet will receive a prophet's reward, and the one who receives a righteous person because he is a righteous person will receive a righteous person's reward. [42] And whoever gives one of

---

[1] *Leprosy* was a term for several skin diseases; see Leviticus 13 [2] Greek *chiton*, a long garment worn under the cloak next to the skin [3] Greek *bondservant*; also verse 25 [4] Greek lacks *will they malign* [5] Greek *Gehenna* [6] Greek *assarion*, Roman copper coin (Latin *quadrans*) worth about 1/16 of a *denarius* (which was a day's wage for a laborer) [a] For 10:9-15 see parallels Mark 6:8-11; Luke 9:3-5 [b] For 10:26-33 see parallel Luke 12:2-9 [c] For 10:34, 35 see parallel Luke 12:51-53

these little ones even a cup of cold water because he is a disciple, truly, I say to you, he will by no means lose his reward."

Messengers from John the Baptist

11 When Jesus had finished instructing his twelve disciples, he went on from there to teach and preach in their cities.

2[a]Now when John heard in prison about the deeds of the Christ, he sent word by his disciples 3and said to him, "Are you the one who is to come, or shall we look for another?" 4And Jesus answered them, "Go and tell John what you hear and see: 5the blind receive their sight and the lame walk, lepers[1] are cleansed and the deaf hear, and the dead are raised up, and the poor have good news preached to them. 6And blessed is the one who is not offended by me."

7As they went away, Jesus began to speak to the crowds concerning John: "What did you go out into the wilderness to see? A reed shaken by the wind? 8What then did you go out to see? A man[2] dressed in soft clothing? Behold, those who wear soft clothing are in kings' houses. 9What then

did you go out to see? A prophet?[3] Yes, I tell you, and more than a prophet. 10This is he of whom it is written,

[b]" 'Behold, I send my messenger before your face,
who will prepare your way before you.'

11Truly, I say to you, among those born of women there has arisen no one greater than John the Baptist. Yet the one who is least in the kingdom of heaven is greater than he. 12From the days of John the Baptist until now the kingdom of heaven has suffered violence,[4] and the violent take it by force. 13For all the Prophets and the Law prophesied until John, 14and if you are willing to accept it, he is Elijah who is to come. 15He who has ears to hear,[5] let him hear.

16"But to what shall I compare this generation? It is like children sitting in the marketplaces and calling to their playmates,

17 " 'We played the flute for you, and you did not dance;
we sang a dirge, and you did not mourn.'

---

[1] *Leprosy* was a term for several skin diseases; see Leviticus 13 [2] Or *Why then did you go out? To see a man . . .* [3] Some manuscripts *Why then did you go out? To see a prophet?* [4] Or *has been coming violently* [5] Some manuscripts omit *to hear* [a] For 11:2-19 see parallel Luke 7:18-35 [b] Mal. 3:1

Know How to Communicate

verses to read
Matthew 11:28-30

What does it mean to find the kind of rest talked about in Matthew 11:28? Have you found it, or are you lost in the stress of a particular problem? God promises to take that problem from you, but you have to be willing to hand it over. The longer you hold on to it and refuse to let go, the longer you make God wait. Part of believing in God is believing God's Word is true. And nothing is truer than the truth that God can and will handle your burden for you. But turning it over to him means more than just giving it up; it means giving it up and taking up his yoke. You make an exchange—your burden for his. And he promises that *his* burden is light.

So what is his burden, his yoke? It's simple. It's walking with him as a redeemed sinner. Give up your problems and start concerning yourself with doing just what he asks. It's easy, really. He promises it is, and that's because he has forgiven you and he promises to help you. He walks beside you and gives you the strength—his strength—to do it. The burden you are carrying right now is not his will for you. He wants you to be free to leave the heavy lifting to him. So walk with your divine Friend. Know that as you do, your burden becomes a whole lot lighter.

18 For John came neither eating nor drinking, and they say, 'He has a demon.' **19** The Son of Man came eating and drinking, and they say, 'Look at him! A glutton and a drunkard, a friend of tax collectors and sinners!' Yet wisdom is justified by her deeds."[1]

Woe to Unrepentant Cities

20 Then he began to denounce the cities where most of his mighty works had been done, because they did not repent. **21** a "Woe to you, Chorazin! Woe to you, Bethsaida! For if the mighty works done in you had been done in Tyre and Sidon, they would have repented long ago in sackcloth and ashes. **22** But I tell you, it will be more bearable on the day of judgment for Tyre and Sidon than for you. **23** And you, Capernaum, will you be exalted to heaven? You will be brought down to Hades. For if the mighty works done in you had been done in Sodom, it would have remained until this day. **24** But I tell you that it will be more tolerable on the day of judgment for the land of Sodom than for you."

Come to Me, and I Will Give You Rest

25 b At that time Jesus declared, "I thank you, Father, Lord of heaven and earth, that you have hidden these things from the wise and understanding and revealed them to little children; **26** yes, Father, for such was your gracious will.[2] **27** All things have been handed over to me by my Father, and no one knows the Son except the Father, and no one knows the Father except the Son and anyone to whom the Son chooses to reveal him. **28** Come to me, all who labor and are heavy laden, and I will give you rest. **29** Take my yoke upon you, and learn from me, for I am gentle and lowly in heart, and you will find rest for your souls. **30** For my yoke is easy, and my burden is light."

Jesus Is Lord of the Sabbath

12 At that time c Jesus went through the grainfields on the Sabbath. His disciples were hungry, and they began to pluck heads of grain and to eat. **2** But when the Pharisees saw it, they said to him, "Look, your disciples are doing what is not lawful to do on the Sabbath." **3** He said to them, "Have you not read what David did when he was hungry, and those who

were with him: **4** how he entered the house of God and ate the bread of the Presence, which it was not lawful for him to eat nor for those who were with him, but only for the priests? **5** Or have you not read in the Law how on the Sabbath the priests in the temple profane the Sabbath and are guiltless? **6** I tell you, something greater than the temple is here. **7** And if you had known what this means, d 'I desire mercy, and not sacrifice,' you would not have condemned the guiltless. **8** For the Son of Man is lord of the Sabbath."

A Man with a Withered Hand

9 He went on from there and e entered their synagogue. **10** And a man was there with a withered hand. And they asked him, "Is it lawful to heal on the Sabbath?"—so that they might accuse him. **11** He said to them, "Which one of you who has a sheep, if it falls into a pit on the Sabbath, will not take hold of it and lift it out? **12** Of how much more value is a man than a sheep! So it is lawful to do good on the Sabbath." **13** Then he said to the man, "Stretch out your hand." And the man stretched it out, and it was restored, healthy like the other. **14** But the Pharisees went out and conspired against him, how to destroy him.

God's Chosen Servant

15 Jesus, aware of this, withdrew from there. And many followed him, and he healed them all **16** and ordered them not to make him known. **17** This was to fulfill what was spoken by the prophet Isaiah:

18 f "Behold, my servant whom I have chosen,
　　　my beloved with whom my soul is well pleased.
　　I will put my Spirit upon him,
　　　and he will proclaim justice to the Gentiles.
19　He will not quarrel or cry aloud,
　　　nor will anyone hear his voice in the streets;
20　a bruised reed he will not break,
　　　and a smoldering wick he will not quench,
　　until he brings justice to victory;
21　　and in his name the Gentiles will hope."

---

[1] Some manuscripts *children* (compare Luke 7:35) [2] Or *for so it pleased you well* [a] For 11:21-24 see parallel Luke 10:13-15 [b] For 11:25-27 see parallel Luke 10:21, 22 [c] For 12:1-8 see parallels Mark 2:23-28; Luke 6:1-5 [d] Hos. 6:6 [e] For 12:9-14 see parallels Mark 3:1-6; Luke 6:6-11 [f] Isa. 42:1-3

Blasphemy Against the Holy Spirit

22 [a]Then a demon-oppressed man who was blind and mute was brought to him, and he healed him, so that the man spoke and saw. 23 And all the people were amazed, and said, "Can this be the Son of David?" 24 But when the Pharisees heard it, they said, "It is only by Beelzebul, the prince of demons, that this man casts out demons." 25 Knowing their thoughts, [b]he said to them, "Every kingdom divided against itself is laid waste, and no city or house divided against itself will stand. 26 And if Satan casts out Satan, he is divided against himself. How then will his kingdom stand? 27 And if I cast out demons by Beelzebul, by whom do your sons cast them out? Therefore they will be your judges. 28 But if it is by the Spirit of God that I cast out demons, then the kingdom of God has come upon you. 29 Or how can someone enter a strong man's house and plunder his goods, unless he first binds the strong man? Then indeed he may plunder his house. 30 Whoever is not with me is against me, and whoever does not gather with me scatters. 31 [c]Therefore I tell you, every sin and blasphemy will be forgiven people, but the blasphemy against the Spirit will not be forgiven. 32 And whoever speaks a word against the Son of Man will be forgiven, but whoever speaks against the Holy Spirit will not be forgiven, either in this age or in the age to come.

A Tree Is Known by Its Fruit

33 "Either make the tree good and its fruit good, or make the tree bad and its fruit bad, for the tree is known by its fruit. 34 You brood of vipers! How can you speak good, when you are evil? For out of the abundance of the heart the mouth speaks. 35 The good person out of his good treasure brings forth good, and the evil person out of his evil treasure brings forth evil. 36 I tell you, on the day of judgment people will give account for every careless word they speak, 37 for by your words you will be justified, and by your words you will be condemned."

The Sign of Jonah

38 Then some of the scribes and Pharisees answered him, saying, "Teacher, we wish to see a sign from you." 39 But he answered them, [d]"An evil and adulterous generation seeks for a sign, but no sign will be given to it except the sign of the prophet Jonah. 40 For just as Jonah was three days and three nights in the belly of the great fish, so will the Son of Man be three days and three nights in the heart of the earth. 41 The men of Nineveh will rise up at the judgment with this generation and condemn it, for they repented at the preaching of Jonah, and behold, something greater than Jonah is here. 42 The queen of the South will rise up at the judgment with this generation and condemn it, for she came from the ends of the earth to hear the wisdom of Solomon, and behold, something greater than Solomon is here.

Return of an Unclean Spirit

43 "When [e]the unclean spirit has gone out of a person, it passes through waterless places seeking rest, but finds none. 44 Then it says, 'I will return to my house from which I came.' And when it comes, it finds the house empty, swept, and put in order. 45 Then it goes and brings with it seven other spirits more evil than itself, and they enter and dwell there, and the last state of that person is worse than the first. So also will it be with this evil generation."

Jesus' Mother and Brothers

46 While he was still speaking to the people, behold, [f]his mother and his brothers stood outside, asking to speak to him.[1] 48 But he replied to the man who told him, "Who is my mother, and who are my brothers?" 49 And stretching out his hand toward his disciples, he said, "Here are my mother and my brothers! 50 For whoever does the will of my Father in heaven is my brother and sister and mother."

The Parable of the Sower

13 That same day Jesus went out of the house [g]and sat beside the sea. 2 And great crowds gathered about him, so that he got into a boat and sat down. And the whole crowd stood on the beach. 3 And he

---

[1] Some manuscripts insert verse 47: Someone told him, "Your mother and your brothers are standing outside, asking to speak to you"
[a] For 12:22-24 see parallel Luke 11:14, 15　[b] For 12:25-29 see parallels Mark 3:23-27; Luke 11:17-22　[c] For 12:31, 32 see parallel Mark 3:28-30　[d] For 12:39-42 see parallel Luke 11:29-32　[e] For 12:43-45 see parallel Luke 11:24-26　[f] For 12:46-50 see parallels Mark 3:31-35; Luke 8:19-21　[g] For 13:1-15 see parallels Mark 4:1-12; Luke 8:4-10

told them many things in parables, saying: "A sower went out to sow. ⁴And as he sowed, some seeds fell along the path, and the birds came and devoured them. ⁵Other seeds fell on rocky ground, where they did not have much soil, and immediately they sprang up, since they had no depth of soil, ⁶but when the sun rose they were scorched. And since they had no root, they withered away. ⁷Other seeds fell among thorns, and the thorns grew up and choked them. ⁸Other seeds fell on good soil and produced grain, some a hundredfold, some sixty, some thirty. ⁹He who has ears,¹ let him hear."

The Purpose of the Parables

¹⁰Then the disciples came and said to him, "Why do you speak to them in parables?" ¹¹And he answered them, "To you it has been given to know the secrets of the kingdom of heaven, but to them it has not been given. ¹²For to the one who has, more will be given, and he will have an abundance, but from the one who has not, even what he has will be taken away. ¹³This is why I speak to them in parables, because seeing they do not see, and hearing they do not hear, nor do they understand. ¹⁴Indeed, in their case the prophecy of Isaiah is fulfilled that says:

^a" "You will indeed hear but never understand,
     and you will indeed see but never perceive."
¹⁵   For this people's heart has grown dull,
          and with their ears they can barely hear,
     and their eyes they have closed,
     lest they should see with their eyes
          and hear with their ears
     and understand with their heart
          and turn, and I would heal them.'

¹⁶But blessed are your eyes, for they see, and your ears, for they hear. ¹⁷For truly, I say to you, many prophets and righteous people longed to see what you see, and did not see it, and to hear what you hear, and did not hear it.

The Parable of the Sower Explained

^{18 b}"Hear then the parable of the sower: ¹⁹When anyone hears the word of the kingdom and does not understand it, the evil one comes and snatches away what has been sown in his heart. This is what was sown along the path. ²⁰As for what was sown on rocky ground, this is the one who hears the word and immediately receives it with joy, ²¹yet he has no root in himself, but endures for a while, and when tribulation or persecution arises on account of the word, immediately he falls away.² ²²As for what was sown among thorns, this is the one who hears the word, but the cares of the world and the deceitfulness of riches choke the word, and it proves unfruitful. ²³As for what was sown on good soil, this is the one who hears the word and understands it. He indeed bears fruit and yields, in one case a hundredfold, in another sixty, and in another thirty."

The Parable of the Weeds

²⁴He put another parable before them, saying, "The kingdom of heaven may be compared to a man who sowed good seed in his field, ²⁵but while his men were sleeping, his enemy came and sowed weeds³ among the wheat and went away. ²⁶So when the plants came up and bore grain, then the weeds appeared also. ²⁷And the servants⁴ of the master of the house came and said to him, 'Master, did you not sow good seed in your field? How then does it have weeds?' ²⁸He said to them, 'An enemy has done this.' So the servants said to him, 'Then do you want us to go and gather them?' ²⁹But he said, 'No, lest in gathering the weeds you root up the wheat along with them. ³⁰Let both grow together until the harvest, and at harvest time I will tell the reapers, Gather the weeds first and bind them in bundles to be burned, but gather the wheat into my barn.' "

The Mustard Seed and the Leaven

³¹He put another parable before them, saying, ^c"The kingdom of heaven is like a grain of mustard seed that a man took and sowed in his field. ³²It is the smallest of all seeds, but when it has grown it is larger than all the garden plants and becomes a tree, so that the birds of the air come and make nests in its branches."

³³He told them another parable. "The kingdom of heaven is like leaven that a

¹Some manuscripts add here and in verse 43 to hear ²Or stumbles ³Probably darnel, a wheat-like weed ⁴Greek bondservants; also verse 28 ^aIsa. 6:9, 10 ^bFor 13:18-23 see parallels Mark 4:13-20; Luke 8:11-15 ^cFor 13:31, 32 see parallels Mark 4:30-32; Luke 13:18, 19

woman took and hid in three measures of flour, till it was all leavened."

Prophecy and Parables

34 All these things Jesus said to the crowds in parables; indeed, he said nothing to them without a parable. **35** This was to fulfill what was spoken by the prophet:[1]

> *a*"I will open my mouth in parables;
> I will utter what has been hidden
> since the foundation of the
> world."

The Parable of the Weeds Explained

36 Then he left the crowds and went into the house. And his disciples came to him, saying, "Explain to us the parable of the weeds of the field." **37** He answered, "The one who sows the good seed is the Son of Man. **38** The field is the world, and the good seed is the sons of the kingdom. The weeds are the sons of the evil one, **39** and the enemy who sowed them is the devil. The harvest is the end of the age, and the reapers are angels. **40** Just as the weeds are gathered and burned with fire, so will it be at the end of the age. **41** The Son of Man will send his angels, and they will gather out of his kingdom all causes of sin and all law-breakers, **42** and throw them into the fiery furnace. In that place there will be weeping and gnashing of teeth. **43** Then the righteous will shine like the sun in the kingdom of their Father. He who has ears, let him hear.

The Parable of the Hidden Treasure

44 "The kingdom of heaven is like treasure hidden in a field, which a man found and covered up. Then in his joy he goes and sells all that he has and buys that field.

---

[1] Some manuscripts *Isaiah the prophet* *a* Ps. 78:2

Know True Happiness

verses to read
Matthew 13:1–23

Did you notice in this parable what Jesus said will choke the word out of your life? Is it the Devil? No, he doesn't give the Devil that much credit. Read verse 22 again. What kills the truth of God's Word in your life is the worries of life—worries about things you wish you had, what people think of you, your look, your image, and your friends or lack thereof.

Worry tells God that you don't trust him to take care of the practical parts of your life. Sure, you trust him for salvation, but for food and clothing? Nope. When you were a child, you trusted your parents to provide everything you needed. You didn't worry about what you had or didn't have, because you knew all you had to do was ask them and your needs would be met. But now that you are older you wonder, Will there be enough for me? Will it be what I need? Worrying is accusing God of not taking care of his own. It's calling him a delinquent father and looking for insurance to protect you in case of disaster.

But the God Girl has assurance, not insurance. She has the assurance that God will never leave her and will always provide for her. The God Girl is the most content girl on the planet because she knows she has exactly what she needs, and that's why she doesn't allow worry to choke out the seed of God's Word in her life.

Remember that your fears and worries say more about your belief in God than they do about your lot in life. Freedom isn't just about resisting the Devil and his hold on your life; it's also about seeing the truth about the thoughts in your head. Practice seeing worry for what it is—a lie about God's goodness—and choose to trust your faithful Father instead.

The Parable of the Pearl of Great Value

[45] "Again, the kingdom of heaven is like a merchant in search of fine pearls, [46] who, on finding one pearl of great value, went and sold all that he had and bought it.

The Parable of the Net

[47] "Again, the kingdom of heaven is like a net that was thrown into the sea and gathered fish of every kind. [48] When it was full, men drew it ashore and sat down and sorted the good into containers but threw away the bad. [49] So it will be at the end of the age. The angels will come out and separate the evil from the righteous [50] and throw them into the fiery furnace. In that place there will be weeping and gnashing of teeth.

New and Old Treasures

[51] "Have you understood all these things?" They said to him, "Yes." [52] And he said to them, "Therefore every scribe who has been trained for the kingdom of heaven is like a master of a house, who brings out of his treasure what is new and what is old."

Jesus Rejected at Nazareth

[53] And when Jesus had finished these parables, he went away from there, [54][a] and coming to his hometown he taught them in their synagogue, so that they were astonished, and said, "Where did this man get this wisdom and these mighty works? [55] Is not this the carpenter's son? Is not his mother called Mary? And are not his brothers James and Joseph and Simon and Judas? [56] And are not all his sisters with us? Where then did this man get all these things?" [57] And they took offense at him. But Jesus said to them, "A prophet is not without honor except in his hometown and in his own household." [58] And he did not do many mighty works there, because of their unbelief.

The Death of John the Baptist

14 [b] At that time Herod the tetrarch heard about the fame of Jesus, [2] and he said to his servants, "This is John the Baptist. He has been raised from the dead; that is why these miraculous powers are at work in him." [3] For Herod had seized John and bound him and put him in prison for the sake of Herodias, his brother Philip's wife,[1] [4] because John had been saying to him, "It is not lawful for you to have her." [5] And though he wanted to put him to death, he feared the people, because they held him to be a prophet. [6] But when Herod's birthday came, the daughter of Herodias danced before the company and pleased Herod, [7] so that he promised with an oath to give her whatever she might ask. [8] Prompted by her mother, she said, "Give me the head of John the Baptist here on a platter." [9] And the king was sorry, but because of his oaths and his guests he commanded it to be given. [10] He sent and had John beheaded in the prison, [11] and his head was brought on a platter and given to the girl, and she brought it to her mother. [12] And his disciples came and took the body and buried it, and they went and told Jesus.

Jesus Feeds the Five Thousand

[13] Now when Jesus heard this, [c] he withdrew from there in a boat to a desolate place by himself. But when the crowds heard it, they followed him on foot from the towns. [14] When he went ashore he saw a great crowd, and he had compassion on them and healed their sick. [15] Now when it was evening, the disciples came to him and said, "This is a desolate place, and the day is now over; send the crowds away to go into the villages and buy food for themselves." [16] But Jesus said, "They need not go away; you give them something to eat." [17] They said to him, "We have only five loaves here and two fish." [18] And he said, "Bring them here to me." [19] Then he ordered the crowds to sit down on the grass, and taking the five loaves and the two fish, he looked up to heaven and said a blessing. Then he broke the loaves and gave them to the disciples, and the disciples gave them to the crowds. [20] And they all ate and were satisfied. And they took up twelve baskets full of the broken pieces left over. [21] And those who ate were about five thousand men, besides women and children.

Jesus Walks on the Water

[22][d] Immediately he made the disciples get into the boat and go before him to the other side, while he dismissed the crowds. [23] And after he had dismissed the crowds,

---

[1] Some manuscripts *his brother's wife* [a] For 13:54-58 see parallel Mark 6:1-6 [b] For 14:1-12 see parallels Mark 6:14-29; Luke 9:7-9 [c] For 14:13-21 see parallels Mark 6:32-44; Luke 9:10-17; John 6:1-13 [d] For 14:22-33 see parallels Mark 6:45-52; John 6:16-21

he went up on the mountain by himself to pray. When evening came, he was there alone, [24] but the boat by this time was a long way[1] from the land,[2] beaten by the waves, for the wind was against them. [25] And in the fourth watch of the night he came to them, walking on the sea. [26] But when the disciples saw him walking on the sea, they were terrified, and said, "It is a ghost!" and they cried out in fear. [27] But immediately Jesus spoke to them, saying, "Take heart; it is I. Do not be afraid."

[28] And Peter answered him, "Lord, if it is you, command me to come to you on the water." [29] He said, "Come." So Peter got out of the boat and walked on the water and came to Jesus. [30] But when he saw the wind,[3] he was afraid, and beginning to sink he cried out, "Lord, save me." [31] Jesus immediately reached out his hand and took hold of him, saying to him, "O you of little faith, why did you doubt?" [32] And when they got into the boat, the wind ceased. [33] And those in the boat worshiped him, saying, "Truly you are the Son of God."

Jesus Heals the Sick in Gennesaret

[34] [a] And when they had crossed over, they came to land at Gennesaret. [35] And when the men of that place recognized him, they sent around to all that region and brought to him all who were sick [36] and implored him that they might only touch the fringe of his garment. And as many as touched it were made well.

Traditions and Commandments

15 [b] Then Pharisees and scribes came to Jesus from Jerusalem and said, [2] "Why do your disciples break the tradition of the elders? For they do not wash their hands when they eat." [3] He answered them, "And why do you break the commandment of God for the sake of your tradition? [4] For God commanded, 'Honor your father and your mother,' and, [d] 'Whoever reviles father or mother must surely die.' [5] But you say, 'If anyone tells his father or his mother, "What you would have gained from me is given to God,"[4] [6] he need not honor his father.' So for the sake of your tradition you have made void the word[5] of God. [7] You

hypocrites! Well did Isaiah prophesy of you, when he said:

[8] [c] "'This people honors me with their
lips,
but their heart is far from me;
[9]   in vain do they worship me,
teaching as doctrines the commandments of men.'"

What Defiles a Person

[10] And he called the people to him and said to them, "Hear and understand: [11] it is not what goes into the mouth that defiles a person, but what comes out of the mouth; this defiles a person." [12] Then the disciples came and said to him, "Do you know that the Pharisees were offended when they heard this saying?" [13] He answered, "Every plant that my heavenly Father has not planted will be rooted up. [14] Let them alone; they are blind guides.[6] And if the blind lead the blind, both will fall into a pit." [15] But Peter said to him, "Explain the parable to us." [16] And he said, "Are you also still without understanding? [17] Do you not see that whatever goes into the mouth passes into the stomach and is expelled?[7] [18] But what comes out of the mouth proceeds from the heart, and this defiles a person. [19] For out of the heart come evil thoughts, murder, adultery, sexual immorality, theft, false witness, slander. [20] These are what defile a person. But to eat with unwashed hands does not defile anyone."

The Faith of a Canaanite Woman

[21] [f] And Jesus went away from there and withdrew to the district of Tyre and Sidon. [22] And behold, a Canaanite woman from that region came out and was crying, "Have mercy on me, O Lord, Son of David; my daughter is severely oppressed by a demon." [23] But he did not answer her a word. And his disciples came and begged him, saying, "Send her away, for she is crying out after us." [24] He answered, "I was sent only to the lost sheep of the house of Israel." [25] But she came and knelt before him, saying, "Lord, help me." [26] And he answered, "It is not right to take the children's bread and throw it to the dogs." [27] She said, "Yes, Lord, yet even the dogs eat the crumbs that fall from their mas-

---

[1] Greek *many stadia*, a *stadion* was about 607 feet or 185 meters [2] Some manuscripts *was out on the sea* [3] Some manuscripts *strong wind* [4] Or *is an offering* [5] Some manuscripts *law* [6] Some manuscripts add *of the blind* [7] Greek *is expelled into the latrine* [a] For 14:34-36 see parallel Mark 6:53-56 [b] For 15:1-20 see parallel Mark 7:1-23 [c] Ex. 20:12 [d] Ex. 21:17 [e] Isa. 29:13 [f] For 15:21-28 see parallel Mark 7:24-30

ters' table." [28] Then Jesus answered her, "O woman, great is your faith! Be it done for you as you desire." And her daughter was healed instantly.[1]

Jesus Heals Many

[29] Jesus went on from there and walked beside the Sea of Galilee. And he went up on the mountain and sat down there. [30] And great crowds came to him, bringing with them the lame, the blind, the crippled, the mute, and many others, and they put them at his feet, and he healed them, [31] so that the crowd wondered, when they saw the mute speaking, the crippled healthy, the lame walking, and the blind seeing. And they glorified the God of Israel.

Jesus Feeds the Four Thousand

[32] [a] Then Jesus called his disciples to him and said, "I have compassion on the crowd because they have been with me now three days and have nothing to eat. And I am unwilling to send them away hungry, lest they faint on the way." [33] And the disciples said to him, "Where are we to get enough bread in such a desolate place to feed so great a crowd?" [34] And Jesus said to them, "How many loaves do you have?" They said, "Seven, and a few small fish." [35] And directing the crowd to sit down on the ground, [36] he took the seven loaves and the fish, and having given thanks he broke them and gave them to the disciples, and the disciples gave them to the crowds. [37] And they all ate and were satisfied. And they took up seven baskets full of the broken pieces left over. [38] Those who ate were four thousand men, besides women and children. [39] And after sending away the crowds, he got into the boat and went to the region of Magadan.

The Pharisees and Sadducees Demand Signs

16 [b] And the Pharisees and Sadducees came, and to test him they asked him to show them a sign from heaven. [2] He answered them,[2] "When it is evening, you say, 'It will be fair weather, for the sky is red.' [3] And in the morning, 'It will be stormy today, for the sky is red and threatening.' You know how to interpret the appearance of the sky, but you cannot interpret the signs of the times. [4] An evil and adulterous generation seeks for a sign, but no sign will be given to it except the sign of Jonah." So he left them and departed.

The Leaven of the Pharisees and Sadducees

[5] When the disciples reached the other side, they had forgotten to bring any bread. [6] Jesus said to them, "Watch and beware of the leaven of the Pharisees and Sadducees." [7] And they began discussing it among themselves, saying, "We brought no bread." [8] But Jesus, aware of this, said, "O you of little faith, why are you discussing among yourselves the fact that you have no bread? [9] Do you not yet perceive? Do you not remember the five loaves for the five thousand, and how many baskets you gathered? [10] Or the seven loaves for the four thousand, and how many baskets you gathered? [11] How is it that you fail to understand that I did not speak about bread? Beware of the leaven of the Pharisees and Sadducees." [12] Then they understood that he did not tell them to beware of the leaven of bread, but of the teaching of the Pharisees and Sadducees.

Peter Confesses Jesus as the Christ

[13] [c] Now when Jesus came into the district of Caesarea Philippi, he asked his disciples, "Who do people say that the Son of Man is?" [14] And they said, "Some say John the Baptist, others say Elijah, and others Jeremiah or one of the prophets." [15] He said to them, "But who do you say that I am?" [16] Simon Peter replied, "You are the Christ, the Son of the living God." [17] And Jesus answered him, "Blessed are you, Simon Bar-Jonah! For flesh and blood has not revealed this to you, but my Father who is in heaven. [18] And I tell you, you are Peter, and on this rock[3] I will build my church, and the gates of hell[4] shall not prevail against it. [19] I will give you the keys of the kingdom of heaven, and whatever you bind on earth shall be bound in heaven, and whatever you loose on earth shall be loosed[5] in heaven." [20] Then he strictly charged the disciples to tell no one that he was the Christ.

[1] Greek *from that hour* [2] Some manuscripts omit the following words to the end of verse 3 [3] The Greek words for *Peter* and *rock* sound similar [4] Greek *the gates of Hades* [5] Or *shall have been bound . . . shall have been loosed* [a] For 15:32-39 see parallel Mark 8:1-10 [b] For 16:1-12 see parallel Mark 8:11-21 [c] For 16:13-16 see parallels Mark 8:27-29; Luke 9:18-20

Jesus Foretells His Death and Resurrection

²¹ ᵃFrom that time Jesus began to show his disciples that he must go to Jerusalem and suffer many things from the elders and chief priests and scribes, and be killed, and on the third day be raised. ²²And Peter took him aside and began to rebuke him, saying, "Far be it from you, Lord!¹ This shall never happen to you." ²³But he turned and said to Peter, "Get behind me, Satan! You are a hindrance² to me. For you are not setting your mind on the things of God, but on the things of man."

Take Up Your Cross and Follow Jesus

²⁴Then Jesus told his disciples, "If anyone would come after me, let him deny himself and take up his cross and follow me. ²⁵For whoever would save his life³ will lose it, but whoever loses his life for my sake will find it. ²⁶For what will it profit a man if he gains the whole world and forfeits his soul? Or what shall a man give in return for his soul? ²⁷For the Son of Man is going to come with his angels in the glory of his Father, and then he will repay each person according to what he has done. ²⁸Truly, I say to you, there are some standing here who will not taste death until they see the Son of Man coming in his kingdom."

The Transfiguration

17 ᵇAnd after six days Jesus took with him Peter and James, and John his brother, and led them up a high mountain by themselves. ²And he was transfigured before them, and his face shone like the sun, and his clothes became white as light. ³And behold, there appeared to them Moses and Elijah, talking with him. ⁴And Peter said to Jesus, "Lord, it is good that we are here. If you wish, I will make three tents here, one for you and one for Moses and one for Elijah." ⁵He was still speaking when, behold, a bright cloud overshadowed them, and a voice from the cloud said, "This is my beloved Son,⁴ with whom I am well pleased; listen to him." ⁶When the disciples heard this, they fell on their faces and were terrified. ⁷But Jesus came and touched them, saying, "Rise, and have no

fear." ⁸And when they lifted up their eyes, they saw no one but Jesus only.

⁹ ᶜAnd as they were coming down the mountain, Jesus commanded them, "Tell no one the vision, until the Son of Man is raised from the dead." ¹⁰And the disciples asked him, "Then why do the scribes say that first Elijah must come?" ¹¹He answered, "Elijah does come, and he will restore all things. ¹²But I tell you that Elijah has already come, and they did not recognize him, but did to him whatever they pleased. So also the Son of Man will certainly suffer at their hands." ¹³Then the disciples understood that he was speaking to them of John the Baptist.

Jesus Heals a Boy with a Demon

¹⁴ ᵈAnd when they came to the crowd, a man came up to him and, kneeling before him, ¹⁵said, "Lord, have mercy on my son, for he is an epileptic and he suffers terribly. For often he falls into the fire, and often into the water. ¹⁶And I brought him to your disciples, and they could not heal him." ¹⁷And Jesus answered, "O faithless and twisted generation, how long am I to be with you? How long am I to bear with you? Bring him here to me." ¹⁸And Jesus rebuked the demon,⁵ and it⁶ came out of him, and the boy was healed instantly.⁷ ¹⁹Then the disciples came to Jesus privately and said, "Why could we not cast it out?" ²⁰He said to them, "Because of your little faith. For truly, I say to you, if you have faith like a grain of mustard seed, you will say to this mountain, 'Move from here to there,' and it will move, and nothing will be impossible for you."⁸

Jesus Again Foretells Death, Resurrection

²² ᵉAs they were gathering⁹ in Galilee, Jesus said to them, "The Son of Man is about to be delivered into the hands of men, ²³and they will kill him, and he will be raised on the third day." And they were greatly distressed.

The Temple Tax

²⁴When they came to Capernaum, the collectors of the two-drachma tax went up to Peter and said, "Does your teacher not

---

¹ Or "[May God be] merciful to you, Lord!" ² Greek stumbling block ³ The same Greek word can mean either soul or life, depending on the context; twice in this verse and twice in verse 26 ⁴ Or My Son, my (or the) Beloved ⁵ Greek it ⁶ Greek the demon ⁷ Greek from that hour ⁸ Some manuscripts insert verse 21: But this kind never comes out except by prayer and fasting ⁹ Some manuscripts remained
ᵃ For 16:21-28 see parallels Mark 8:31–9:1; Luke 9:22-27 ᵇ For 17:1-8 see parallels Mark 9:2-8; Luke 9:28-36 ᶜ For 17:9-13 see parallel Mark 9:9-13 ᵈ For 17:14-19 see parallels Mark 9:14-28; Luke 9:37-42 ᵉ For 17:22, 23 see parallels Mark 9:30-32; Luke 9:43-45

pay the tax?" **25** He said, "Yes." And when he came into the house, Jesus spoke to him first, saying, "What do you think, Simon? From whom do kings of the earth take toll or tax? From their sons or from others?" **26** And when he said, "From others," Jesus said to him, "Then the sons are free. **27** However, not to give offense to them, go to the sea and cast a hook and take the first fish that comes up, and when you open its mouth you will find a shekel.[1] Take that and give it to them for me and for yourself."

Who Is the Greatest?

18 [a] At that time the disciples came to Jesus, saying, "Who is the greatest in the kingdom of heaven?" **2** And calling to him a child, he put him in the midst of them **3** and said, "Truly, I say to you, unless you turn and become like children, you will never enter the kingdom of heaven. **4** Whoever humbles himself like this child is the greatest in the kingdom of heaven.

5 "Whoever receives one such child in my name receives me, **6** but whoever causes one of these little ones who believe in me to sin,[2] it would be better for him to have a great millstone fastened around his neck and to be drowned in the depth of the sea.

Temptations to Sin

7 "Woe to the world for temptations to sin![3] For it is necessary that temptations come, but woe to the one by whom the temptation comes! **8** And if your hand or your foot causes you to sin, cut it off and throw it away. It is better for you to enter life crippled or lame than with two hands or two feet to be thrown into the eternal fire. **9** And if your eye causes you to sin, tear it out and throw it away. It is better for you to enter life with one eye than with two eyes to be thrown into the hell[4] of fire.

The Parable of the Lost Sheep

10 "See that you do not despise one of these little ones. For I tell you that in heaven their angels always see the face of my Father who is in heaven.[5] **12** What do you think? If a man has a hundred sheep, and one of them has gone astray, does he not leave the ninety-nine on the mountains and go in search of the one that went astray? **13** And if he finds it, truly, I say to you, he rejoices over it more than over the ninety-nine that never went astray. **14** So it is not the will of my[6] Father who is in heaven that one of these little ones should perish.

If Your Brother Sins Against You

15 "If your brother sins against you, go and tell him his fault, between you and him alone. If he listens to you, you have gained your brother. **16** But if he does not listen, take one or two others along with you, that every charge may be established by the evidence of two or three witnesses. **17** If he refuses to listen to them, tell it to the church. And if he refuses to listen even to the church, let him be to you as a Gentile and a tax collector. **18** Truly, I say to you, whatever you bind on earth shall be bound in heaven, and whatever you loose on earth shall be loosed[7] in heaven. **19** Again I say to you, if two of you agree on earth about anything they ask, it will be done for them by my Father in heaven. **20** For where two or three are gathered in my name, there am I among them."

The Parable of the Unforgiving Servant

21 Then Peter came up and said to him, "Lord, how often will my brother sin against me, and I forgive him? As many as seven times?" **22** Jesus said to him, "I do not say to you seven times, but seventy-seven times.

23 "Therefore the kingdom of heaven may be compared to a king who wished to settle accounts with his servants.[8] **24** When he began to settle, one was brought to him who owed him ten thousand talents.[9] **25** And since he could not pay, his master ordered him to be sold, with his wife and children and all that he had, and payment to be made. **26** So the servant[10] fell on his knees, imploring him, 'Have patience with me, and I will pay you everything.' **27** And out of pity for him, the master of that servant released him and forgave him the debt. **28** But when that same servant went out, he found one of his fellow servants who owed him a hundred denarii,[11] and seizing him, he began to choke him, saying, 'Pay what you

---

[1] Greek *stater*, a silver coin worth four drachmas or approximately one shekel   [2] Greek *causes . . . to stumble*; also verses 8, 9   [3] Greek *stumbling blocks*   [4] Greek *Gehenna*   [5] Some manuscripts add verse 11: *For the Son of Man came to save the lost*   [6] Some manuscripts *your*   [7] *Or shall have been bound . . . shall have been loosed*   [8] Greek *bondservants*; also verses 28, 31   [9] A *talent* was a monetary unit worth about twenty years' wages for a laborer   [10] Greek *bondservant*; also verses 27, 28, 29, 32, 33   [11] A *denarius* was a day's wage for a laborer
[a] For 18:1-5 see parallels Mark 9:33-37; Luke 9:46-48

owe.' ²⁹So his fellow servant fell down and pleaded with him, 'Have patience with me, and I will pay you.' ³⁰He refused and went and put him in prison until he should pay the debt. ³¹When his fellow servants saw what had taken place, they were greatly distressed, and they went and reported to their master all that had taken place. ³²Then his master summoned him and said to him, 'You wicked servant! I forgave you all that debt because you pleaded with me. ³³And should not you have had mercy on your fellow servant, as I had mercy on you?' ³⁴And in anger his master delivered him to the jailers,¹ until he should pay all his debt. ³⁵So also my heavenly Father will do to every one of you, if you do not forgive your brother from your heart."

Teaching About Divorce

19 Now when Jesus had finished these sayings, he went away from Galilee and ᵈentered the region of Judea beyond the Jordan. ²And large crowds followed him, and he healed them there.

³And Pharisees came up to him and tested him by asking, "Is it lawful to divorce one's wife for any cause?" ⁴He answered, "Have you not read that he who created them from the beginning made them male and female, ⁵and said, ᵇ'Therefore a man shall leave his father and his mother and hold fast to his wife, and the two shall become one flesh'? ⁶So they are no longer two but one flesh. What therefore God has joined together, let not man separate." ⁷They said to him, "Why then did Moses command one to give a certificate of divorce and to send her away?" ⁸He said to them, "Because of your hardness of heart Moses allowed you to divorce your wives, but from the beginning it was not so. ⁹And I say to you: whoever divorces his wife, except for sexual immorality, and marries another, commits adultery."²

¹⁰The disciples said to him, "If such is the case of a man with his wife, it is better not to marry." ¹¹But he said to them, "Not everyone can receive this saying, but only those to whom it is given. ¹²For there are eunuchs who have been so from birth, and there are eunuchs who have been made

eunuchs by men, and there are eunuchs who have made themselves eunuchs for the sake of the kingdom of heaven. Let the one who is able to receive this receive it."

Let the Children Come to Me

¹³ᶜThen children were brought to him that he might lay his hands on them and pray. The disciples rebuked the people, ¹⁴but Jesus said, "Let the little children come to me and do not hinder them, for to such belongs the kingdom of heaven." ¹⁵And he laid his hands on them and went away.

The Rich Young Man

¹⁶ᵈAnd behold, a man came up to him, saying, "Teacher, what good deed must I do to have eternal life?" ¹⁷And he said to him, "Why do you ask me about what is good? There is only one who is good. If you would enter life, keep the commandments." ¹⁸He said to him, "Which ones?" And Jesus said, ᵉ"You shall not murder, You shall not commit adultery, You shall not steal, You shall not bear false witness, ¹⁹Honor your father and mother, and, ᶠYou shall love your neighbor as yourself." ²⁰The young man said to him, "All these I have kept. What do I still lack?" ²¹Jesus said to him, "If you would be perfect, go, sell what you possess and give to the poor, and you will have treasure in heaven; and come, follow me." ²²When the young man heard this he went away sorrowful, for he had great possessions.

²³And Jesus said to his disciples, "Truly, I say to you, only with difficulty will a rich person enter the kingdom of heaven. ²⁴Again I tell you, it is easier for a camel to go through the eye of a needle than for a rich person to enter the kingdom of God." ²⁵When the disciples heard this, they were greatly astonished, saying, "Who then can be saved?" ²⁶But Jesus looked at them and said, "With man this is impossible, but with God all things are possible." ²⁷Then Peter said in reply, "See, we have left everything and followed you. What then will we have?" ²⁸Jesus said to them, "Truly, I say to you, in the new world,³ when the Son of Man will sit on his glorious throne, you who have followed me will also sit on twelve thrones, judging the twelve tribes of Israel. ²⁹And everyone who has left houses or brothers

or sisters or father or mother or children or lands, for my name's sake, will receive a hundredfold[1] and will inherit eternal life. [30] But many who are first will be last, and the last first.

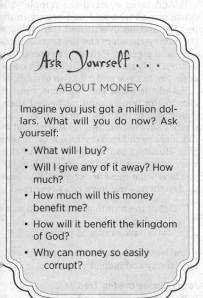

Ask Yourself . . .

ABOUT MONEY

Imagine you just got a million dollars. What will you do now? Ask yourself:

- What will I buy?
- Will I give any of it away? How much?
- How much will this money benefit me?
- How will it benefit the kingdom of God?
- Why can money so easily corrupt?

Laborers in the Vineyard

20 "For the kingdom of heaven is like a master of a house who went out early in the morning to hire laborers for his vineyard. [2] After agreeing with the laborers for a denarius[2] a day, he sent them into his vineyard. [3] And going out about the third hour he saw others standing idle in the marketplace, [4] and to them he said, 'You go into the vineyard too, and whatever is right I will give you.' [5] So they went. Going out again about the sixth hour and the ninth hour, he did the same. [6] And about the eleventh hour he went out and found others standing. And he said to them, 'Why do you stand here idle all day?' [7] They said to him, 'Because no one has hired us.' He said to them, 'You go into the vineyard too.' [8] And when evening came, the owner of the vineyard said to his foreman, 'Call the laborers and pay them their wages, beginning with the last, up to the first.' [9] And when those hired about the eleventh hour

came, each of them received a denarius. [10] Now when those hired first came, they thought they would receive more, but each of them also received a denarius. [11] And on receiving it they grumbled at the master of the house, [12] saying, 'These last worked only one hour, and you have made them equal to us who have borne the burden of the day and the scorching heat.' [13] But he replied to one of them, 'Friend, I am doing you no wrong. Did you not agree with me for a denarius? [14] Take what belongs to you and go. I choose to give to this last worker as I give to you. [15] Am I not allowed to do what I choose with what belongs to me? Or do you begrudge my generosity?'[3] [16] So the last will be first, and the first last."

Jesus Foretells His Death a Third Time

[17] [a] And as Jesus was going up to Jerusalem, he took the twelve disciples aside, and on the way he said to them, [18] "See, we are going up to Jerusalem. And the Son of Man will be delivered over to the chief priests and scribes, and they will condemn him to death [19] and deliver him over to the Gentiles to be mocked and flogged and crucified, and he will be raised on the third day."

A Mother's Request

[20] [b] Then the mother of the sons of Zebedee came up to him with her sons, and kneeling before him she asked him for something. [21] And he said to her, "What do you want?" She said to him, "Say that these two sons of mine are to sit, one at your right hand and one at your left, in your kingdom." [22] Jesus answered, "You do not know what you are asking. Are you able to drink the cup that I am to drink?" They said to him, "We are able." [23] He said to them, "You will drink my cup, but to sit at my right hand and at my left is not mine to grant, but it is for those for whom it has been prepared by my Father." [24] And when the ten heard it, they were indignant at the two brothers. [25] But Jesus called them to him and said, "You know that the rulers of the Gentiles lord it over them, and their great ones exercise authority over them. [26] It shall not be so among you. But whoever would be great among you must be your servant,[4] [27] and whoever would

be first among you must be your slave,[1] [28]even as the Son of Man came not to be served but to serve, and to give his life as a ransom for many."

Jesus Heals Two Blind Men

[29][a]And as they went out of Jericho, a great crowd followed him. [30]And behold, there were two blind men sitting by the roadside, and when they heard that Jesus was passing by, they cried out, "Lord,[2] have mercy on us, Son of David!" [31]The crowd rebuked them, telling them to be silent, but they cried out all the more, "Lord, have mercy on us, Son of David!" [32]And stopping, Jesus called them and said, "What do you want me to do for you?" [33]They said to him, "Lord, let our eyes be opened." [34]And Jesus in pity touched their eyes, and immediately they recovered their sight and followed him.

The Triumphal Entry

21 [b]Now when they drew near to Jerusalem and came to Bethphage, to the Mount of Olives, then Jesus sent two disciples, [2]saying to them, "Go into the village in front of you, and immediately you will find a donkey tied, and a colt with her. Untie them and bring them to me. [3]If anyone says anything to you, you shall say, 'The Lord needs them,' and he will send them at once." [4]This took place to fulfill what was spoken by the prophet, saying,

[5] [c]"Say to the daughter of Zion,
  'Behold, your king is coming to you,
    humble, and mounted on a donkey,
    on a colt,[3] the foal of a beast of
        burden.'"

[6]The disciples went and did as Jesus had directed them. [7]They brought the donkey and the colt and put on them their cloaks, and he sat on them. [8]Most of the crowd spread their cloaks on the road, and others cut branches from the trees and spread them on the road. [9]And the crowds that went before him and that followed him were shouting, "Hosanna to the Son of David! Blessed is he who comes in the name of the Lord! Hosanna in the highest!" [10]And when he entered Jerusalem, the whole city was stirred up, saying, "Who is this?" [11]And the crowds said, "This is the prophet Jesus, from Nazareth of Galilee."

Jesus Cleanses the Temple

[12][d]And Jesus entered the temple[4] and drove out all who sold and bought in the temple, and he overturned the tables of the money-changers and the seats of those who sold pigeons. [13]He said to them, "It is written, [e]'My house shall be called a house of prayer,' but you make it a den of robbers."

[14]And the blind and the lame came to him in the temple, and he healed them. [15]But when the chief priests and the scribes saw the wonderful things that he did, and the children crying out in the temple, "Hosanna to the Son of David!" they were indignant, [16]and they said to him, "Do you hear what these are saying?" And Jesus said to them, "Yes; have you never read,

[f]"'Out of the mouth of infants and nursing babies
    you have prepared praise'?"

[17]And leaving them, he went out of the city to Bethany and lodged there.

Jesus Curses the Fig Tree

[18][g]In the morning, as he was returning to the city, he became hungry. [19]And seeing a fig tree by the wayside, he went to it and found nothing on it but only leaves. And he said to it, "May no fruit ever come from you again!" And the fig tree withered at once. [20]When the disciples saw it, they marveled, saying, "How did the fig tree wither at once?" [21]And Jesus answered them, "Truly, I say to you, if you have faith and do not doubt, you will not only do what has been done to the fig tree, but even if you say to this mountain, 'Be taken up and thrown into the sea,' it will happen. [22]And whatever you ask in prayer, you will receive, if you have faith."

The Authority of Jesus Challenged

[23][h]And when he entered the temple, the chief priests and the elders of the people came up to him as he was teaching, and said, "By what authority are you doing these things, and who gave you this authority?" [24]Jesus answered them, "I also will ask

[1]Greek *bondservant (doulos)* [2]Some manuscripts omit *Lord* [3]Or *donkey, and on a colt,* [4]Some manuscripts add *of God* [a]For 20:29-34 see parallels Mark 10:46-52; Luke 18:35-43 [b]For 21:1-9 see parallels Mark 11:1-10; Luke 19:28-38; John 12:12-15 [c]Zech. 9:9 [d]For 21:12-16 see parallels Mark 11:15-18; Luke 19:45-47 [e]Isa. 56:7 [f]Ps. 8:2 (Gk.) [g]For 21:18-22 see parallel Mark 11:12-14, 20-24 [h]For 21:23-27 see parallels Mark 11:27-33; Luke 20:1-8

you one question, and if you tell me the answer, then I also will tell you by what authority I do these things. 25The baptism of John, from where did it come? From heaven or from man?" And they discussed it among themselves, saying, "If we say, 'From heaven,' he will say to us, 'Why then did you not believe him?' 26But if we say, 'From man,' we are afraid of the crowd, for they all hold that John was a prophet." 27So they answered Jesus, "We do not know." And he said to them, "Neither will I tell you by what authority I do these things.

The Parable of the Two Sons

28"What do you think? A man had two sons. And he went to the first and said, 'Son, go and work in the vineyard today.' 29And he answered, 'I will not,' but afterward he changed his mind and went. 30And he went to the other son and said the same. And he answered, 'I go, sir,' but did not go. 31Which of the two did the will of his father?" They said, "The first." Jesus said to them, "Truly, I say to you, the tax collectors and the prostitutes go into the kingdom of God before you. 32For John came to you in the way of righteousness, and you did not believe him, but the tax collectors and the prostitutes believed him. And even when you saw it, you did not afterward change your minds and believe him.

The Parable of the Tenants

33 a"Hear another parable. There was a master of a house who planted a vineyard and put a fence around it and dug a winepress in it and built a tower and leased it to tenants, and went into another country. 34When the season for fruit drew near, he sent his servants[1] to the tenants to get his fruit. 35And the tenants took his servants and beat one, killed another, and stoned another. 36Again he sent other servants, more than the first. And they did the same to them. 37Finally he sent his son to them, saying, 'They will respect my son.' 38But when the tenants saw the son, they said to themselves, 'This is the heir. Come, let us kill him and have his inheritance.' 39And they took him and threw him out of the vineyard and killed him. 40When therefore the owner of the vineyard comes, what will he do to those tenants?" 41They said

to him, "He will put those wretches to a miserable death and let out the vineyard to other tenants who will give him the fruits in their seasons."

42Jesus said to them, "Have you never read in the Scriptures:

b"'The stone that the builders rejected
     has become the cornerstone;[2]
   this was the Lord's doing,
     and it is marvelous in our eyes'?

43Therefore I tell you, the kingdom of God will be taken away from you and given to a people producing its fruits. 44And the one who falls on this stone will be broken to pieces; and when it falls on anyone, it will crush him."[3]

45When the chief priests and the Pharisees heard his parables, they perceived that he was speaking about them. 46And although they were seeking to arrest him, they feared the crowds, because they held him to be a prophet.

The Parable of the Wedding Feast

22 And again Jesus spoke to them in parables, saying, 2"The kingdom of heaven may be compared to a king who gave a wedding feast for his son, 3and sent his servants[4] to call those who were invited to the wedding feast, but they would not come. 4Again he sent other servants, saying, 'Tell those who are invited, "See, I have prepared my dinner, my oxen and my fat calves have been slaughtered, and everything is ready. Come to the wedding feast."' 5But they paid no attention and went off, one to his farm, another to his business, 6while the rest seized his servants, treated them shamefully, and killed them. 7The king was angry, and he sent his troops and destroyed those murderers and burned their city. 8Then he said to his servants, 'The wedding feast is ready, but those invited were not worthy. 9Go therefore to the main roads and invite to the wedding feast as many as you find.' 10And those servants went out into the roads and gathered all whom they found, both bad and good. So the wedding hall was filled with guests.

11"But when the king came in to look at the guests, he saw there a man who had no wedding garment. 12And he said to him, 'Friend, how did you get in here without a wedding garment?' And he was speechless. [13] Then the king said to the attendants, 'Bind him hand and foot and cast him into the outer darkness. In that place there will be weeping and gnashing of teeth.' [14] For many are called, but few are chosen."

Paying Taxes to Caesar

[15] [a] Then the Pharisees went and plotted how to entangle him in his words. [16] And they sent their disciples to him, along with the Herodians, saying, "Teacher, we know that you are true and teach the way of God truthfully, and you do not care about anyone's opinion, for you are not swayed by appearances.[1] [17] Tell us, then, what you think. Is it lawful to pay taxes to Caesar, or not?" [18] But Jesus, aware of their malice, said, "Why put me to the test, you hypocrites? [19] Show me the coin for the tax." And they brought him a denarius.[2] [20] And Jesus said to them, "Whose likeness and inscription is this?" [21] They said, "Caesar's." Then he said to them, "Therefore render to Caesar the things that are Caesar's, and to God the things that are God's." [22] When they heard it, they marveled. And they left him and went away.

Sadducees Ask About the Resurrection

[23] The same day Sadducees came to him, who say that there is no resurrection, and they asked him a question, [24] saying, "Teacher, Moses said, 'If a man dies having no children, his brother must marry the widow and raise up offspring for his brother.' [25] Now there were seven brothers among us. The first married and died, and having no offspring left his wife to his brother. [26] So too the second and third, down to the seventh. [27] After them all, the woman died. [28] In the resurrection, therefore, of the seven, whose wife will she be? For they all had her."

[29] But Jesus answered them, "You are wrong, because you know neither the Scriptures nor the power of God. [30] For in the resurrection they neither marry nor are given in marriage, but are like angels in heaven. [31] And as for the resurrection of the dead, have you not read what was said to you by God: [32] [b] 'I am the God of Abraham, and the God of Isaac, and the God of Jacob'?

He is not God of the dead, but of the living.'" [33] And when the crowd heard it, they were astonished at his teaching.

The Great Commandment

[34] [c] But when the Pharisees heard that he had silenced the Sadducees, they gathered together. [35] And one of them, a lawyer, asked him a question to test him. [36] "Teacher, which is the great commandment in the Law?" [37] And he said to him, "You shall love the Lord your God with all your heart and with all your soul and with all your mind. [38] This is the great and first commandment. [39] And a second is like it: You shall love your neighbor as yourself. [40] On these two commandments depend all the Law and the Prophets."

Whose Son Is the Christ?

[41] [d] Now while the Pharisees were gathered together, Jesus asked them a question, [42] saying, "What do you think about the Christ? Whose son is he?" They said to him, "The son of David." [43] He said to them, "How is it then that David, in the Spirit, calls him Lord, saying,

[44] [e] "'The Lord said to my Lord,
    "Sit at my right hand,
        until I put your enemies under
            your feet"'?

[45] If then David calls him Lord, how is he his son?" [46] And no one was able to answer him a word, nor from that day did anyone dare to ask him any more questions.

Seven Woes to the Scribes and Pharisees

23 Then Jesus [f] said to the crowds and to his disciples, [2] "The scribes and the Pharisees sit on Moses' seat, [3] so do and observe whatever they tell you, but not the works they do. For they preach, but do not practice. [4] They tie up heavy burdens, hard to bear;[3] and lay them on people's shoulders, but they themselves are not willing to move them with their finger. [5] They do all their deeds to be seen by others. For they make their phylacteries broad and their fringes long, [6] and they love the place of honor at feasts and the best seats in the synagogues [7] and greetings in the marketplaces and being called rabbi[4]

[1] Greek for you do not look at people's faces [2] A denarius was a day's wage for a laborer [3] Some manuscripts omit hard to bear [4] Rabbi means my teacher, or my master; also verse 8 [a] For 22:15-32 see parallels Mark 12:13-27; Luke 20:20-38 [b] Ex. 3:6 [c] For 22:34-40 see parallel Mark 12:28-33 [d] For 22:41-45 see parallels Mark 12:35-37; Luke 20:41-44 [e] Ps. 110:1 [f] For 23:1, 2, 5-7 see parallels Mark 12:38-40; Luke 20:45, 46

by others. [8] But you are not to be called rabbi, for you have one teacher, and you are all brothers.[1] [9] And call no man your father on earth, for you have one Father, who is in heaven. [10] Neither be called instructors, for you have one instructor, the Christ. [11] The greatest among you shall be your servant. [12] Whoever exalts himself will be humbled, and whoever humbles himself will be exalted.

[13] "But woe to you, scribes and Pharisees, hypocrites! For you shut the kingdom of heaven in people's faces. For you neither enter yourselves nor allow those who would enter to go in.[2] [15] Woe to you, scribes and Pharisees, hypocrites! For you travel across sea and land to make a single proselyte, and when he becomes a proselyte, you make him twice as much a child of hell[3] as yourselves.

[16] "Woe to you, blind guides, who say, 'If anyone swears by the temple, it is nothing, but if anyone swears by the gold of the temple, he is bound by his oath.' [17] You blind fools! For which is greater, the gold or the temple that has made the gold sacred? [18] And you say, 'If anyone swears by the altar, it is nothing, but if anyone swears by the gift that is on the altar, he is bound by his oath.' [19] You blind men! For which is greater, the gift or the altar that makes the gift sacred? [20] So whoever swears by the altar swears by it and by everything on it. [21] And whoever swears by the temple swears by it and by him who dwells in it. [22] And whoever swears by heaven swears by the throne of God and by him who sits upon it.

[23] "Woe to you, scribes and Pharisees, hypocrites! For you tithe the mint and dill and cumin, and have neglected the weightier matters of the law: justice and mercy and faithfulness. These you ought to have done, without neglecting the others. [24] You blind guides, straining out a gnat and swallowing a camel!

[25] "Woe to you, scribes and Pharisees, hypocrites! For you clean the outside of the cup and the plate, but inside they are full of greed and self-indulgence. [26] You blind Pharisee! First clean the inside of the cup and the plate, that the outside also may be clean.

[27] "Woe to you, scribes and Pharisees, hypocrites! For you are like whitewashed tombs, which outwardly appear beautiful, but within are full of dead people's bones and all uncleanness. [28] So you also outwardly appear righteous to others, but within you are full of hypocrisy and lawlessness.

[29] "Woe to you, scribes and Pharisees, hypocrites! For you build the tombs of the prophets and decorate the monuments of the righteous, [30] saying, 'If we had lived in the days of our fathers, we would not have taken part with them in shedding the blood of the prophets.' [31] Thus you witness against yourselves that you are sons of those who murdered the prophets. [32] Fill up, then, the measure of your fathers. [33] You serpents, you brood of vipers, how are you to escape being sentenced to hell? [34] Therefore I send you prophets and wise men and scribes, some of whom you will kill and crucify, and some you will flog in your synagogues and persecute from town to town, [35] so that on you may come all the righteous blood shed on earth, from the blood of righteous Abel to the blood of Zechariah the son of Barachiah,[4] whom you murdered between the sanctuary and the altar. [36] Truly, I say to you, all these things will come upon this generation.

Lament over Jerusalem

[37] [a] "O Jerusalem, Jerusalem, the city that kills the prophets and stones those who are sent to it! How often would I have gathered your children together as a hen gathers her brood under her wings, and you were not willing! [38] See, your house is left to you desolate. [39] For I tell you, you will not see me again, until you say, [b]'Blessed is he who comes in the name of the Lord.'"

Jesus Foretells Destruction of the Temple

24 [c] Jesus left the temple and was going away, when his disciples came to point out to him the buildings of the temple. [2] But he answered them, "You see all these, do you not? Truly, I say to you, there will not be left here one stone upon another that will not be thrown down."

---

[1] Or brothers and sisters [2] Some manuscripts add here (or after verse 12) verse 14: *Woe to you, scribes and Pharisees, hypocrites! For you devour widows' houses and for a pretense you make long prayers; therefore you will receive the greater condemnation* [3] Greek *Gehenna*; also verse 33 [4] Some manuscripts omit *the son of Barachiah* [a] For 23:37-39 see parallel Luke 13:34, 35 [b] Ps. 118:26 [c] For 24:1-51 see parallels Mark 13:1-37; Luke 21:5-36

Signs of the End of the Age

³ As he sat on the Mount of Olives, the disciples came to him privately, saying, "Tell us, when will these things be, and what will be the sign of your coming and of the end of the age?" ⁴ And Jesus answered them, "See that no one leads you astray. ⁵ For many will come in my name, saying, 'I am the Christ,' and they will lead many astray. ⁶ And you will hear of wars and rumors of wars. See that you are not alarmed, for this must take place, but the end is not yet. ⁷ For nation will rise against nation, and kingdom against kingdom, and there will be famines and earthquakes in various places. ⁸ All these are but the beginning of the birth pains.

⁹ "Then they will deliver you up to tribulation and put you to death, and you will be hated by all nations for my name's sake. ¹⁰ And then many will fall away[1] and betray one another and hate one another. ¹¹ And many false prophets will arise and lead many astray. ¹² And because lawlessness will be increased, the love of many will grow cold. ¹³ But the one who endures to the end will be saved. ¹⁴ And this gospel of the kingdom will be proclaimed throughout the whole world as a testimony to all nations, and then the end will come.

The Abomination of Desolation

¹⁵ "So when you see the abomination of desolation spoken of by the prophet Daniel, standing in the holy place (let the reader understand), ¹⁶ then let those who are in Judea flee to the mountains. ¹⁷ Let the one who is on the housetop not go down to take what is in his house, ¹⁸ and let the one who is in the field not turn back to take his cloak. ¹⁹ And alas for women who are pregnant and for those who are nursing infants in those days! ²⁰ Pray that your flight may not be in winter or on a Sabbath. ²¹ For then there will be great tribulation, such as has not been from the beginning of the world until now, no, and never will be. ²² And if those days had not been cut short, no human being would be saved. But for the sake of the elect those days will be cut short. ²³ Then if anyone says to you, 'Look, here is the Christ!' or 'There he is!' do not believe it. ²⁴ For false christs and false prophets will arise and perform great signs and wonders, so as to lead astray, if

possible, even the elect. ²⁵ See, I have told you beforehand. ²⁶ So, if they say to you, 'Look, he is in the wilderness,' do not go out. If they say, 'Look, he is in the inner rooms,' do not believe it. ²⁷ For as the lightning comes from the east and shines as far as the west, so will be the coming of the Son of Man. ²⁸ Wherever the corpse is, there the vultures will gather.

The Coming of the Son of Man

²⁹ "Immediately after the tribulation of those days the sun will be darkened, and the moon will not give its light, and the stars will fall from heaven, and the powers of the heavens will be shaken. ³⁰ Then will appear in heaven the sign of the Son of Man, and then all the tribes of the earth will mourn, and they will see the Son of Man coming on the clouds of heaven with power and great glory. ³¹ And he will send out his angels with a loud trumpet call, and they will gather his elect from the four winds, from one end of heaven to the other.

The Lesson of the Fig Tree

³² "From the fig tree learn its lesson: as soon as its branch becomes tender and puts out its leaves, you know that summer is near. ³³ So also, when you see all these things, you know that he is near, at the very gates. ³⁴ Truly, I say to you, this generation will not pass away until all these things take place. ³⁵ Heaven and earth will pass away, but my words will not pass away.

No One Knows That Day and Hour

³⁶ "But concerning that day and hour no one knows, not even the angels of heaven, nor the Son,[2] but the Father only. ³⁷ For as were the days of Noah, so will be the coming of the Son of Man. ³⁸ For as in those days before the flood they were eating and drinking, marrying and giving in marriage, until the day when Noah entered the ark, ³⁹ and they were unaware until the flood came and swept them all away, so will be the coming of the Son of Man. ⁴⁰ Then two men will be in the field; one will be taken and one left. ⁴¹ Two women will be grinding at the mill; one will be taken and one left. ⁴² Therefore, stay awake, for you do not know on what day your Lord is coming. ⁴³ But know this, that if the master of the house had known in what part of the night

[1] Or *stumble*　[2] Some manuscripts omit *nor the Son*

he thief was coming, he would have stayed awake and would not have let his house be broken into. **44** Therefore you also must be ready, for the Son of Man is coming at an hour you do not expect.

45 "Who then is the faithful and wise servant,[1] whom his master has set over his household, to give them their food at the proper time? **46** Blessed is that servant whom his master will find so doing when he comes. **47** Truly, I say to you, he will set him over all his possessions. **48** But if that wicked servant says to himself, 'My master is delayed,' **49** and begins to beat his fellow servants[2] and eats and drinks with drunkards, **50** the master of that servant will come on a day when he does not expect him and at an hour he does not know **51** and will cut him in pieces and put him with the hypocrites. In that place there will be weeping and gnashing of teeth.

The Parable of the Ten Virgins

25 "Then the kingdom of heaven will be like ten virgins who took their lamps[3] and went to meet the bridegroom.[4] **2** Five of them were foolish, and five were wise. **3** For when the foolish took their lamps, they took no oil with them, **4** but the wise took flasks of oil with their lamps. **5** As the bridegroom was delayed, they all became drowsy and slept. **6** But at midnight there was a cry, 'Here is the bridegroom! Come out to meet him.' **7** Then all those virgins rose and trimmed their lamps. **8** And the foolish said to the wise, 'Give us some of your oil, for our lamps are going out.' **9** But the wise answered, saying, 'Since there will not be enough for us and for you, go rather to the dealers and buy for yourselves.' **10** And while they were going to buy, the bridegroom came, and those who were ready went in with him to the marriage feast, and the door was shut. **11** Afterward the other virgins came also, saying, 'Lord, lord, open to us.' **12** But he answered, 'Truly, I say to you, I do not know you.' **13** Watch therefore, for you know neither the day nor the hour.

The Parable of the Talents

14 "For it will be like a man going on a journey, who called his servants[5] and entrusted to them his property. **15** To one he gave five talents,[6] to another two, to another one, to each according to his ability. Then he went away. **16** He who had

---

Greek *bondservant*; also verses 46, 48, 50 [2] Greek *bondservants* [3] Or *torches* [4] Some manuscripts add *and the bride* [5] Greek *bondservants*; also verse 19 [6] A *talent* was a monetary unit worth about twenty years' wages for a laborer

Know Yourself

verses to read
Matthew 25:14–30

What are you good at? Are you a good listener? A good promoter? Are you a good problem solver? A good teacher? What do you do well that could help a hurting world?

When you have a talent that can improve the lives of those around you and you don't use it, you lose it. In other words, God promises in Matthew 25 to increase what you already have whenever you invest it for the good of his children. When you use your talents to serve God, you will find yourself with more than you ever imagined. But if you refuse to use the talents he's given you for good and instead you just let them rust or be used for evil, look out—the results could be disastrous. God didn't give you your talent so that you could just go and bury it out of fear of rejection or failure. He gave it to you so that you could go out and do all that you can to invest it in the lives of those in need.

Don't feel talented? Everyone has talent in something. Figure out what you are good at. Take a personality test or spiritual gifts inventory. Find out who you are and what you do best, and then do all you can to use those skills to serve others.

received the five talents went at once and traded with them, and he made five talents more. ¹⁷ So also he who had the two talents made two talents more. ¹⁸ But he who had received the one talent went and dug in the ground and hid his master's money. ¹⁹ Now after a long time the master of those servants came and settled accounts with them. ²⁰ And he who had received the five talents came forward, bringing five talents more, saying, 'Master, you delivered to me five talents; here I have made five talents more.' ²¹ His master said to him, 'Well done, good and faithful servant.¹ You have been faithful over a little; I will set you over much. Enter into the joy of your master.' ²² And he also who had the two talents came forward, saying, 'Master, you delivered to me two talents; here I have made two talents more.' ²³ His master said to him, 'Well done, good and faithful servant. You have been faithful over a little; I will set you over much. Enter into the joy of your master.' ²⁴ He also who had received the one talent came forward, saying, 'Master, I knew you to be a hard man, reaping where you did not sow, and gathering where you scattered no seed, ²⁵ so I was afraid, and I went and hid your talent in the ground. Here you have what is yours.' ²⁶ But his master answered him, 'You wicked and slothful servant! You knew that I reap where I have not sown and gather where I scattered no seed? ²⁷ Then you ought to have invested my money with the bankers, and at my coming I should have received what was my own with interest. ²⁸ So take the talent from him and give it to him who has the ten talents. ²⁹ For to everyone who has will more be given, and he will have an abundance. But from the one who has not, even what he has will be taken away. ³⁰ And cast the worthless servant into the outer darkness. In that place there will be weeping and gnashing of teeth.'

The Final Judgment

³¹ "When the Son of Man comes in his glory, and all the angels with him, then he will sit on his glorious throne. ³² Before him will be gathered all the nations, and he will separate people one from another as a shepherd separates the sheep from the goats. ³³ And he will place the sheep on his right, but the goats on the left. ³⁴ Then the King will say to those on his right, 'Come you who are blessed by my Father, inherit the kingdom prepared for you from the foundation of the world. ³⁵ For I was hungry and you gave me food, I was thirsty and you gave me drink, I was a stranger and you welcomed me, ³⁶ I was naked and you clothed me, I was sick and you visited me, I was in prison and you came to me.' ³⁷ Then the righteous will answer him, saying, 'Lord, when did we see you hungry and feed you, or thirsty and give you drink? ³⁸ And when did we see you a stranger and welcome you, or naked and clothe you? ³⁹ And when did we see you sick or in prison and visit you?' ⁴⁰ And the King will answer them, 'Truly, I say to you, as you did it to one of the least of these my brothers, you did it to me.'

⁴¹ "Then he will say to those on his left, 'Depart from me, you cursed, into the eternal fire prepared for the devil and his angels. ⁴² For I was hungry and you gave me no food, I was thirsty and you gave me no drink, ⁴³ I was a stranger and you did not welcome me, naked and you did not clothe me, sick and in prison and you did not visit me.' ⁴⁴ Then they also will answer, saying, 'Lord, when did we see you hungry or thirsty or a stranger or naked or sick or in prison, and did not minister to you?' ⁴⁵ Then he will answer them, saying, 'Truly I say to you, as you did not do it to one of the least of these, you did not do it to me.' ⁴⁶ And these will go away into eternal punishment, but the righteous into eternal life.'

The Plot to Kill Jesus

26 When Jesus had finished all these sayings, he said to his disciples, ² ᵃ "You know that after two days the Passover is coming, and the Son of Man will be delivered up to be crucified."

³ Then the chief priests and the elders of the people gathered in the palace of the high priest, whose name was Caiaphas, ⁴ and plotted together in order to arrest Jesus by stealth and kill him. ⁵ But they said, "Not during the feast, lest there be an uproar among the people."

Jesus Anointed at Bethany

⁶ ᵇ Now when Jesus was at Bethany in the house of Simon the leper,³ ⁷ a woman came

---

¹ Greek *bondservant*; also verses 23, 26, 30   ² Or *brothers and sisters*   ³ *Leprosy* was a term for several skin diseases; see Leviticus 13
ᵃ For 26:2-5 see parallels Mark 14:1, 2; Luke 22:1, 2   ᵇ For 26:6-13 see parallels Mark 14:3-9; John 12:1-8

up to him with an alabaster flask of very expensive ointment, and she poured it on his head as he reclined at table. [8] And when the disciples saw it, they were indignant, saying, "Why this waste? [9] For this could have been sold for a large sum and given to the poor." [10] But Jesus, aware of this, said to them, "Why do you trouble the woman? For she has done a beautiful thing to me. [11] For you always have the poor with you, but you will not always have me. [12] In pouring this ointment on my body, she has done it to prepare me for burial. [13] Truly, I say to you, wherever this gospel is proclaimed in the whole world, what she has done will also be told in memory of her."

Judas to Betray Jesus

[14] [a] Then one of the twelve, whose name was Judas Iscariot, went to the chief priests [15] and said, "What will you give me if I deliver him over to you?" And they paid him thirty pieces of silver. [16] And from that moment he sought an opportunity to betray him.

The Passover with the Disciples

[17] [b] Now on the first day of Unleavened Bread the disciples came to Jesus, saying, "Where will you have us prepare for you to eat the Passover?" [18] He said, "Go into the city to a certain man and say to him, 'The Teacher says, My time is at hand. I will keep the Passover at your house with my disciples.'" [19] And the disciples did as Jesus had directed them, and they prepared the Passover.

[20] [c] When it was evening, he reclined at table with the twelve. [1] [21] And as they were eating, he said, "Truly, I say to you, one of you will betray me." [22] And they were very sorrowful and began to say to him one after another, "Is it I, Lord?" [23] He answered, "He who has dipped his hand in the dish with me will betray me. [24] The Son of Man goes as it is written of him, but woe to that man by whom the Son of Man is betrayed! It would have been better for that man if he had not been born." [25] Judas, who would betray him, answered, "Is it I, Rabbi?" He said to him, "You have said so."

Institution of the Lord's Supper

[26] [d] Now as they were eating, Jesus took bread, and after blessing it he broke it and gave it to the disciples, and said, "Take, eat; this is my body." [27] And he took a cup, and when he had given thanks he gave it to them, saying, "Drink of it, all of you, [28] for this is my blood of the[2] covenant, which is poured out for many for the forgiveness of sins. [29] I tell you I will not drink again of this fruit of the vine until that day when I drink it new with you in my Father's kingdom."

Jesus Foretells Peter's Denial

[30] [e] And when they had sung a hymn, they went out to the Mount of Olives. [31] Then Jesus said to them, "You will all fall away because of me this night. For it is written, 'I will [f] strike the shepherd, and the sheep of the flock will be scattered.' [32] But after I am raised up, I will go before you to Galilee." [33] Peter answered him, "Though they all fall away because of you, I will never fall away." [34] Jesus said to him, "Truly, I tell you, this very night, before the rooster crows, you will deny me three times." [35] Peter said to him, "Even if I must die with you, I will not deny you!" And all the disciples said the same.

Jesus Prays in Gethsemane

[36] [g] Then Jesus went with them to a place called Gethsemane, and he said to his disciples, "Sit here, while I go over there and pray." [37] And taking with him Peter and the two sons of Zebedee, he began to be sorrowful and troubled. [38] Then he said to them, "My soul is very sorrowful, even to death; remain here, and watch[3] with me." [39] And going a little farther he fell on his face and prayed, saying, "My Father, if it be possible, let this cup pass from me; nevertheless, not as I will, but as you will." [40] And he came to the disciples and found them sleeping. And he said to Peter, "So, could you not watch with me one hour? [41] Watch and pray that you may not enter into temptation. The spirit indeed is willing, but the flesh is weak." [42] Again, for the second time, he went away and prayed, "My Father, if this cannot pass unless I drink it, your will be done." [43] And again he came and found them sleeping, for their eyes were heavy.

[1] Some manuscripts add *disciples* [2] Some manuscripts insert *new* [3] Or *keep awake*; also verses 40, 41 [a] For 26:14-16 see parallels Mark 14:10, 11; Luke 22:3-6 [b] For 26:17-19 see parallels Mark 14:12-16; Luke 22:7-13 [c] For 26:20-24 see parallel Mark 14:17-21 [d] For 26:26-29 see parallels Mark 14:22-25; Luke 22:18-20 [e] For 26:30-35 see parallel Mark 14:26-31 [f] Zech. 13:7 [g] For 26:36-46 see parallels Mark 14:32-42; Luke 22:39-46

⁴⁴ So, leaving them again, he went away and prayed for the third time, saying the same words again. ⁴⁵ Then he came to the disciples and said to them, "Sleep and take your rest later on.¹ See, the hour is at hand, and the Son of Man is betrayed into the hands of sinners. ⁴⁶ Rise, let us be going; see, my betrayer is at hand."

Betrayal and Arrest of Jesus

⁴⁷ᵃ While he was still speaking, Judas came, one of the twelve, and with him a great crowd with swords and clubs, from the chief priests and the elders of the people. ⁴⁸ Now the betrayer had given them a sign, saying, "The one I will kiss is the man; seize him." ⁴⁹ And he came up to Jesus at once and said, "Greetings, Rabbi!" And he kissed him. ⁵⁰ Jesus said to him, "Friend, do what you came to do."² Then they came up and laid hands on Jesus and seized him. ⁵¹ And behold, one of those who were with Jesus stretched out his hand and drew his sword and struck the servant³ of the high priest and cut off his ear. ⁵² Then Jesus said to him, "Put your sword back into its place. For all who take the sword will perish by the sword. ⁵³ Do you think that I cannot appeal to my Father, and he will at once send me more than twelve legions of angels? ⁵⁴ But how then should the Scriptures be fulfilled, that it must be so?" ⁵⁵ At that hour Jesus said to the crowds, "Have you come out as against a robber, with swords and clubs to capture me? Day after day I sat in the temple teaching, and you did not seize me. ⁵⁶ But all this has taken place that the Scriptures of the prophets might be fulfilled." Then all the disciples left him and fled.

Jesus Before Caiaphas and the Council

⁵⁷ Then ᵇthose who had seized Jesus led him to Caiaphas the high priest, where the scribes and the elders had gathered. ⁵⁸ And Peter was following him at a distance, as far as the courtyard of the high priest, and going inside he sat with the guards to see the end. ⁵⁹ Now the chief priests and the whole council⁴ were seeking false testimony against Jesus that they might put him to death, ⁶⁰ but they found none, though many false witnesses came

forward. At last two came forward ⁶¹ and said, "This man said, 'I am able to destroy the temple of God, and to rebuild it in three days.'" ⁶² And the high priest stood up and said, "Have you no answer to make? What is it that these men testify against you?"⁵ ⁶³ But Jesus remained silent. And the high priest said to him, "I adjure you by the living God, tell us if you are the Christ, the Son of God." ⁶⁴ Jesus said to him, "You have said so. But I tell you, from now on you will see the Son of Man seated at the right hand of Power and coming on the clouds of heaven." ⁶⁵ Then the high priest tore his robes and said, "He has uttered blasphemy. What further witnesses do we need? You have now heard his blasphemy. ⁶⁶ What is your judgment?" They answered, "He deserves death." ⁶⁷ Then they spit in his face and struck him. And some slapped him, ⁶⁸ saying, "Prophesy to us, you Christ! Who is it that struck you?"

Peter Denies Jesus

⁶⁹ᶜ Now Peter was sitting outside in the courtyard. And a servant girl came up to him and said, "You also were with Jesus the Galilean." ⁷⁰ But he denied it before them all, saying, "I do not know what you mean." ⁷¹ And when he went out to the entrance, another servant girl saw him, and she said to the bystanders, "This man was with Jesus of Nazareth." ⁷² And again he denied it with an oath: "I do not know the man." ⁷³ After a little while the bystanders came up and said to Peter, "Certainly you too are one of them, for your accent betrays you." ⁷⁴ Then he began to invoke a curse on himself and to swear, "I do not know the man." And immediately the rooster crowed. ⁷⁵ And Peter remembered the saying of Jesus, "Before the rooster crows, you will deny me three times." And he went out and wept bitterly.

Jesus Delivered to Pilate

27 When morning came, all the chief priests and the elders of the people took counsel against Jesus to put him to death. ² And they bound him and led him away and delivered him over to Pilate the governor.

---

¹ Or Are you still sleeping and taking your rest? ² Or Friend, why are you here? ³ Greek bondservant ⁴ Greek Sanhedrin ⁵ Or Have you no answer to what these men testify against you? ᵃ For 26:47-56 see parallels Mark 14:43-50; Luke 22:47-53; John 18:3-11 ᵇ For 26:57-68 see parallel Mark 14:53-65 ᶜ For 26:69-75 see parallels Mark 14:66-72; Luke 22:55-62; John 18:16-18, 25-27

Judas Hangs Himself

[3] Then when Judas, his betrayer, saw that Jesus[1] was condemned, he changed his mind and brought back the thirty pieces of silver to the chief priests and the elders, [4] saying, "I have sinned by betraying innocent blood." They said, "What is that to us? See to it yourself." [5] And throwing down the pieces of silver into the temple, he departed, and he went and hanged himself. [6] But the chief priests, taking the pieces of silver, said, "It is not lawful to put them into the treasury, since it is blood money." [7] So they took counsel and bought with them the potter's field as a burial place for strangers. [8] Therefore that field has been called the Field of Blood to this day. [9] Then was fulfilled what had been spoken by the prophet Jeremiah, saying, [a] "And they took the thirty pieces of silver, the price of him on whom a price had been set by some of the sons of Israel, [10] and they gave them for the potter's field, as the Lord directed me."

Jesus Before Pilate

[11] [b] Now Jesus stood before the governor, and the governor asked him, "Are you the King of the Jews?" Jesus said, "You have said so." [12] But when he was accused by the chief priests and elders, he gave no answer. [13] Then Pilate said to him, "Do you not hear how many things they testify against you?" [14] But he gave him no answer, not even to a single charge, so that the governor was greatly amazed.

The Crowd Chooses Barabbas

[15] [c] Now at the feast the governor was accustomed to release for the crowd any one prisoner whom they wanted. [16] And they had then a notorious prisoner called Barabbas. [17] So when they had gathered, Pilate said to them, "Whom do you want me to release for you: Barabbas, or Jesus who is called Christ?" [18] For he knew that it was out of envy that they had delivered him up. [19] Besides, while he was sitting on the judgment seat, his wife sent word to him, "Have nothing to do with that righteous man, for I have suffered much because of him today in a dream." [20] Now the chief priests and the elders persuaded the crowd to ask for Barabbas and destroy Jesus. [21] The governor again said to them, "Which of the two do you want me to release for you?" And they said, "Barabbas." [22] Pilate said to them, "Then what shall I do with Jesus who is called Christ?" They all said, "Let him be crucified!" [23] And he said, "Why, what evil has he done?" But they shouted all the more, "Let him be crucified!"

Pilate Delivers Jesus to Be Crucified

[24] So when Pilate saw that he was gaining nothing, but rather that a riot was beginning, he took water and washed his hands before the crowd, saying, "I am innocent of this man's blood;[2] see to it yourselves." [25] And all the people answered, "His blood be on us and on our children!" [26] Then he released for them Barabbas, and having scourged[3] Jesus, delivered him to be crucified.

Jesus Is Mocked

[27] [d] Then the soldiers of the governor took Jesus into the governor's headquarters,[4] and they gathered the whole battalion[5] before him. [28] And they stripped him and put a scarlet robe on him, [29] and twisting together a crown of thorns, they put it on his head and put a reed in his right hand. And kneeling before him, they mocked him, saying, "Hail, King of the Jews!" [30] And they spit on him and took the reed and struck him on the head. [31] And when they had mocked him, they stripped him of the robe and put his own clothes on him and led him away to crucify him.

The Crucifixion

[32] As they went out, they found a man of Cyrene, Simon by name. They compelled this man to carry his cross. [33] [e] And when they came to a place called Golgotha (which means Place of a Skull), [34] they offered him wine to drink, mixed with gall, but when he tasted it, he would not drink it. [35] And when they had crucified him, they divided his garments among them by casting lots. [36] Then they sat down and kept watch over him there. [37] And over his head they put the charge against him, which read, "This is Jesus, the King of the

---

[1] Greek *he* [2] Some manuscripts *this righteous blood*, or *this righteous man's blood* [3] A Roman judicial penalty, consisting of a severe beating with a multi-lashed whip containing imbedded pieces of bone and metal [4] Greek *the praetorium* [5] Greek *cohort*; a tenth of a Roman legion, usually about 600 men　[a] Zech. 11:13　[b] For 27:11-14 see parallels Mark 15:1-5; Luke 23:1-3; John 18:28-38　[c] For 27:15-26 see parallels Mark 15:6-15; Luke 23:18-25; John 18:39, 40; 19:16　[d] For 27:27-31 see parallels Mark 15:16-20; John 19:2, 3　[e] For 27:33-51 see parallels Mark 15:22-38; Luke 23:32-38, 44-46; John 19:17-19, 23, 24, 28-30

Jews." **38** Then two robbers were crucified with him, one on the right and one on the left. **39** And those who passed by derided him, wagging their heads **40** and saying, "You who would destroy the temple and rebuild it in three days, save yourself! If you are the Son of God, come down from the cross." **41** So also the chief priests, with the scribes and elders, mocked him, saying, **42** "He saved others; he cannot save himself. He is the King of Israel; let him come down now from the cross, and we will believe in him. **43** He trusts in God; let God deliver him now, if he desires him. For he said, 'I am the Son of God.'" **44** And the robbers who were crucified with him also reviled him in the same way.

The Death of Jesus

45 Now from the sixth hour[1] there was darkness over all the land[2] until the ninth hour.[3] **46** And about the ninth hour Jesus cried out with a loud voice, saying, [a] "Eli, Eli, lema sabachthani?" that is, "My God, my God, why have you forsaken me?" **47** And some of the bystanders, hearing it, said, "This man is calling Elijah." **48** And one of them at once ran and took a sponge, filled it with sour wine, and put it on a reed and gave it to him to drink. **49** But the others said, "Wait, let us see whether Elijah will come to save him." **50** And Jesus cried out again with a loud voice and yielded up his spirit.

51 And behold, the curtain of the temple was torn in two, from top to bottom. And the earth shook, and the rocks were split. **52** The tombs also were opened. And many bodies of the saints who had fallen asleep were raised, **53** and coming out of the tombs after his resurrection they went into the holy city and appeared to many. **54** [b] When the centurion and those who were with him, keeping watch over Jesus, saw the earthquake and what took place, they were filled with awe and said, "Truly this was the Son[4] of God!"

55 There were also many women there, looking on from a distance, who had followed Jesus from Galilee, ministering to him, **56** among whom were Mary Magdalene and Mary the mother of James and Joseph and the mother of the sons of Zebedee.

Jesus Is Buried

57 [c] When it was evening, there came a rich man from Arimathea, named Joseph, who also was a disciple of Jesus. **58** He went to Pilate and asked for the body of Jesus. Then Pilate ordered it to be given to him. **59** And Joseph took the body and wrapped it in a clean linen shroud **60** and laid it in his own new tomb, which he had cut in the rock. And he rolled a great stone to the entrance of the tomb and went away. **61** Mary Magdalene and the other Mary were there, sitting opposite the tomb.

The Guard at the Tomb

62 The next day, that is, after the day of Preparation, the chief priests and the Pharisees gathered before Pilate **63** and said, "Sir, we remember how that impostor said, while he was still alive, 'After three days I will rise.' **64** Therefore order the tomb to be made secure until the third day, lest his disciples go and steal him away and tell the people, 'He has risen from the dead,' and the last fraud will be worse than the first." **65** Pilate said to them, "You have a guard[5] of soldiers. Go, make it as secure as you can." **66** So they went and made the tomb secure by sealing the stone and setting a guard.

The Resurrection

28 [d] Now after the Sabbath, toward the dawn of the first day of the week, Mary Magdalene and the other Mary went to see the tomb. **2** And behold, there was a great earthquake, for an angel of the Lord descended from heaven and came and rolled back the stone and sat on it. **3** His appearance was like lightning, and his clothing white as snow. **4** And for fear of him the guards trembled and became like dead men. **5** But the angel said to the women, "Do not be afraid, for I know that you seek Jesus who was crucified. **6** He is not here, for he has risen, as he said. Come, see the place where he[6] lay. **7** Then go quickly and tell his disciples that he has risen from the dead, and behold, he is going before you to Galilee; there you will see him. See, I have told you." **8** So they departed quickly from the tomb with fear and great joy, and ran to tell his disciples. **9** And behold, Jesus met

[1] That is, noon [2] Or *earth* [3] That is, 3 P.M. [4] Or *a son* [5] Or *Take a guard* [6] Some manuscripts *the Lord* [a] Ps. 22:1 [b] For 27:54-56 see parallels Mark 15:39-41; Luke 23:47, 49 [c] For 27:57-61 see parallels Mark 15:42-47; Luke 23:50-56; John 19:38-42 [d] For 28:1-8 see parallels Mark 16:1-8; Luke 24:1-10; John 20:1

hem and said, "Greetings!" And they came up and took hold of his feet and worshiped him. [10] Then Jesus said to them, "Do not be afraid; go and tell my brothers to go to Galilee, and there they will see me."

The Report of the Guard

[11] While they were going, behold, some of the guard went into the city and told the chief priests all that had taken place. [12] And when they had assembled with the elders and taken counsel, they gave a sufficient sum of money to the soldiers [13] and said, "Tell people, 'His disciples came by night and stole him away while we were asleep.' [14] And if this comes to the governor's ears, we will satisfy him and keep you out of trouble." [15] So they took the money and did as they were directed. And this story has been spread among the Jews to this day.

The Great Commission

[16] Now the eleven disciples went to Galilee, to the mountain to which Jesus had directed them. [17] And when they saw him they worshiped him, but some doubted. [18] And Jesus came and said to them, "All authority in heaven and on earth has been given to me. [19] Go therefore and make disciples of all nations, baptizing them in[1] the name of the Father and of the Son and of the Holy Spirit, [20] teaching them to observe all that I have commanded you. And behold, I am with you always, to the end of the age."

[1] Or into

INTRODUCTION TO Mark

Author: Probably Mark, a.k.a. John Mark, who traveled with Paul, Barnabas, and Peter. He was not one of the twelve disciples.

Time: Probably between A.D. 55 and 70

Place: Most likely in Rome

Written to: The Gentile Christians in Rome

The gist

Mark wrote this book to help Gentiles (non-Jews) understand who Jesus is, so he doesn't use a lot of religious lingo. He also wanted to help believers understand that their King is a suffering king.

Things to look for

- Action-packed tone and pace, vivid speech, and use of present tense

- A large number of miracles (18) and only 4 parables documented

- Many mentions of Jesus' death and betrayal (see Mark 8:31; 9:31; 10:33–34)

- Mark's descriptions of the disciples being kind of slow to catch on (see Mark 4:13; 6:52; 8:17, 21; 9:10, 32; 10:26)

- Many references to Jesus' emotional life (see Mark 1:41; 3:5; and many others)

Love God and Your Neighbors

> "But that you may know that the Son of Man has authority on earth to forgive sins"—he said to the paralytic— "I say to you, rise, pick up your bed, and go home."
>
> Mark 2:10–11

Have you seen a miracle in your life? We've all heard stories of people being healed of some incurable disease and have been amazed by the fact that only the hand of God could have done it. Miracles make people sit up and listen. They make them rethink any doubts they might have about God and his role in our world. So imagine being around when Jesus walked the earth. His miracles astounded people. They drew crowds. They freaked out the Pharisees. They convinced thousands that he was the Son of God. But the greatest miracle of all was not healing the blind man or the leper but forgiving them of their sins.

The book of Mark takes you on a wild ride through the amazing life of Jesus. He heals the sick and lame. He walks on water, feeds five thousand people, and calms a storm. And through miracle after miracle, he proves that he truly is the Son of God. But in all these miraculous events, don't lose sight of the most valuable miracle of all: his forgiveness of people like you and me.

Miracles happened daily as Jesus walked this earth, but if your life needs a miracle and you don't see one coming, don't be so quick to complain. If you want God's help, ask him; but no matter what the answer, know that your life is already a miracle. You have already been healed and given a new life by the saving blood of Jesus. Every time you sin, thank God for his forgiveness and realize what an amazing miracle it is.

The book of Mark was written to give you a taste of the life of Christ while he walked the earth. As you read it, watch the power of Jesus at work. Notice how much he cared not only for the souls of the people but also for their bodies and minds. And watch as he proves that he truly is the Son of God, able to do anything and everything that the Father himself can do.

Must-Know Verses

And a voice came from heaven, "You are my beloved Son; with you I am well pleased." *Mark 1:11*

And Jesus said to them, "Follow me, and I will make you become fishers of men." And immediately they left their nets and followed him. *Mark 1:17–18*

And he awoke and rebuked the wind and said to the sea, "Peace! Be still!" And the wind ceased, and there was a great calm. *Mark 4:39*

She had heard the reports about Jesus and came up behind him in the crowd and touched his garment. For she said, "If I touch even his garments, I will be made well." And immediately the flow of blood dried up, and she felt in her body that she was healed of her disease. *Mark 5:27–29*

"Whoever would be great among you must be your servant, and whoever would be first among you must be slave of all. For even the Son of Man came not to be served but to serve, and to give his life as a ransom for many." *Mark 10:43–45*

Jesus answered, "The most important is, 'Hear, O Israel: The Lord our God, the Lord is one. And you shall love the Lord your God with all your heart and with all your soul and with all your mind and with all your strength.' The second is this: 'You shall love your neighbor as yourself.' There is no other commandment greater than these." *Mark 12:29–31*

John the Baptist Prepares the Way

1 The beginning of the gospel of Jesus Christ, the Son of God.[1]

²ᵃAs it is written in Isaiah the prophet,[2]

ᵇ"Behold, I send my messenger before your face,
who will prepare your way,
³ ᶜ the voice of one crying in the wilderness:
'Prepare[3] the way of the Lord,
make his paths straight,'"

John appeared, baptizing in the wilderness and proclaiming a baptism of repentance for the forgiveness of sins. ⁵And all the country of Judea and all Jerusalem were going out to him and were being baptized by him in the river Jordan, confessing their sins. ⁶Now John was clothed with camel's hair and wore a leather belt around his waist and ate locusts and wild honey. ⁷And he preached, saying, "After me comes he who is mightier than I, the strap of whose sandals I am not worthy to stoop down and untie. ⁸I have baptized you with water, but he will baptize you with the Holy Spirit."

The Baptism of Jesus

⁹ᵈIn those days Jesus came from Nazareth of Galilee and was baptized by John in the Jordan. ¹⁰And when he came up out of the water, immediately he saw the heavens being torn open and the Spirit descending on him like a dove. ¹¹And a voice came from heaven, "You are my beloved Son;[4] with you I am well pleased."

The Temptation of Jesus

¹²The Spirit immediately drove him out into the wilderness. ¹³And he was in the wilderness forty days, being tempted by Satan. And he was with the wild animals, and the angels were ministering to him.

Jesus Begins His Ministry

¹⁴Now after John was arrested, Jesus came into Galilee, proclaiming the gospel of God, ¹⁵and saying, "The time is fulfilled, and the kingdom of God is at hand; repent and believe in the gospel."

Jesus Calls the First Disciples

¹⁶ᵉPassing alongside the Sea of Galilee, he saw Simon and Andrew the brother of Simon casting a net into the sea, for they were fishermen. ¹⁷And Jesus said to them, "Follow me, and I will make you become fishers of men."[5] ¹⁸And immediately they left their nets and followed him. ¹⁹And going on a little farther, he saw James the son of Zebedee and John his brother, who were in their boat mending the nets. ²⁰And immediately he called them, and they left their father Zebedee in the boat with the hired servants and followed him.

Jesus Heals a Man with an Unclean Spirit

²¹ᶠAnd they went into Capernaum, and immediately on the Sabbath he entered the synagogue and was teaching. ²²And they were astonished at his teaching, for he taught them as one who had authority, and not as the scribes. ²³And immediately there was in their synagogue a man with an unclean spirit. And he cried out, ²⁴"What have you to do with us, Jesus of Nazareth? Have you come to destroy us? I know who you are—the Holy One of God." ²⁵But Jesus rebuked him, saying, "Be silent, and come out of him!" ²⁶And the unclean spirit, convulsing him and crying out with a loud voice, came out of him. ²⁷And they were all amazed, so that they questioned among themselves, saying, "What is this?

¹ Some manuscripts omit *the Son of God* ² Some manuscripts *in the prophets* ³ Or *crying: Prepare in the wilderness* ⁴ Or *my Son, my (or the) Beloved* ⁵ The Greek word *anthropoi* refers here to both men and women ᵃFor 1:2-8 see parallels Matt. 3:1-12; Luke 3:2-17 ᵇMal. 3:1 ᶜIsa. 40:3 ᵈFor 1:9-11 see parallels Matt. 3:13-17; Luke 3:21, 22 ᵉFor 1:16-20 see parallel Matt. 4:18-22 ᶠFor 1:21-28 see parallel Luke 4:31-37

A new teaching with authority! He commands even the unclean spirits, and they obey him." ²⁸ And at once his fame spread everywhere throughout all the surrounding region of Galilee.

Jesus Heals Many

²⁹ᵃAnd immediately he¹ left the synagogue and entered the house of Simon and Andrew, with James and John. ³⁰ Now Simon's mother-in-law lay ill with a fever, and immediately they told him about her. ³¹ And he came and took her by the hand and lifted her up, and the fever left her, and she began to serve them.

³² That evening at sundown they brought to him all who were sick or oppressed by demons. ³³ And the whole city was gathered together at the door. ³⁴ And he healed many who were sick with various diseases, and cast out many demons. And he would not permit the demons to speak, because they knew him.

Jesus Preaches in Galilee

³⁵ᵇAnd rising very early in the morning, while it was still dark, he departed and went out to a desolate place, and there he prayed. ³⁶ And Simon and those who were with him searched for him, ³⁷ and they found him and said to him, "Everyone is looking for you." ³⁸ And he said to them, "Let us go on to the next towns, that I may preach there also, for that is why I came out." ³⁹ And he went throughout all Galilee, preaching in their synagogues and casting out demons.

Jesus Cleanses a Leper

⁴⁰ᶜAnd a leper² came to him, imploring him, and kneeling said to him, "If you will, you can make me clean." ⁴¹ Moved with pity, he stretched out his hand and touched him and said to him, "I will; be clean." ⁴² And immediately the leprosy left him, and he was made clean. ⁴³ And Jesus³ sternly charged him and sent him away at once ⁴⁴ and said to him, "See that you say noth-

¹Some manuscripts *they* ²*Leprosy* was a term for several skin diseases; see Leviticus 13 ³Greek *he*; also verse 45 ᵃFor 1:29-34 see parallels Matt. 8:14-16; Luke 4:38-41 ᵇFor 1:35-38 see parallel Luke 4:42, 43 ᶜFor 1:40-44 see parallels Matt. 8:2-4; Luke 5:12-14

Know God

verses to read
Mark 1:14–20

Are you a follower or a leader? When it comes to your life, who is in the lead? You or Jesus? In the Bible the disciples (Christians) were called "followers." A follower is someone who believes the Word of God, is saved by Jesus' sacrifice and filled with his Spirit, and trusts in Jesus. But just look at the word for a minute: follower. A follower isn't out in the lead saying, "Come on! Let's go!" A follower isn't picking the path and then trying to convince the leader that he should go where she wants. A follower comes along behind the leader. A follower does whatever the leader says and goes wherever the leader leads.

When you pray, are you in front of God, directing him to where you want to go next, or are you behind him, asking where he wants you to go next? It's really easy to try to direct God when you pray. It's easy to forget who's God and who's the follower. But do the words "stumbling around in the dark" mean anything to you? Does that ever sound like your life? Well, maybe that's because you've run ahead of the light. If you would fall back and follow the light, like walking through the dark with a flashlight in your hand, then you would be able to see better and stumble less.

Follow Jesus. Don't look back at him and say, "Are you keeping up?" Fall back and follow. Rest. Be calm. Wait. And move out as he moves out. When you follow God instead of trying to lead him, your steps will be more confident and firm.

ing to anyone, but go, show yourself to the priest and offer for your cleansing what Moses commanded, for a proof to them." ⁴⁵But he went out and began to talk freely about it, and to spread the news, so that Jesus could no longer openly enter a town, but was out in desolate places, and people were coming to him from every quarter.

Jesus Heals a Paralytic

2 And when he returned to Capernaum after some days, it was reported that he was at home. ²And many were gathered together, so that there was no more room, not even at the door. And he was preaching the word to them. ³ªAnd they came, bringing to him a paralytic carried by four men. ⁴And when they could not get near him because of the crowd, they removed the roof above him, and when they had made an opening, they let down the bed on which the paralytic lay. ⁵And when Jesus saw their faith, he said to the paralytic, "Son, your sins are forgiven." ⁶Now some of the scribes were sitting there, questioning in their hearts, ⁷"Why does this man speak like that? He is blaspheming! Who can forgive sins but God alone?" ⁸And immediately Jesus, perceiving in his spirit that they thus questioned within themselves, said to them, "Why do you question these things in your hearts? ⁹Which is easier, to say to the paralytic, 'Your sins are forgiven,' or to say, 'Rise, take up your bed and walk'? ¹⁰But that you may know that the Son of Man has authority on earth to forgive sins"—he said to the paralytic— ¹¹"I say to you, rise, pick up your bed, and go home." ¹²And he rose and immediately picked up his bed and went out before them all, so that they were all amazed and glorified God, saying, "We never saw anything like this!"

Jesus Calls Levi

¹³He went out again beside the sea, and all the crowd was coming to him, and he was teaching them. ¹⁴ᵇAnd as he passed by, he saw Levi the son of Alphaeus sitting at the tax booth, and he said to him, "Follow me." And he rose and followed him.

¹⁵And as he reclined at table in his house, many tax collectors and sinners were reclining with Jesus and his disciples, for there were many who followed him. ¹⁶And the scribes ofª the Pharisees, when they saw that he was eating with sinners and tax collectors, said to his disciples, "Why does he eat² with tax collectors and sinners?" ¹⁷And when Jesus heard it, he said to them, "Those who are well have no need of a physician, but those who are sick. I came not to call the righteous, but sinners."

A Question About Fasting

¹⁸Now John's disciples and the Pharisees were fasting. And people came and said to him, "Why do John's disciples and the disciples of the Pharisees fast, but your disciples do not fast?" ¹⁹And Jesus said to them, "Can the wedding guests fast while the bridegroom is with them? As long as they have the bridegroom with them, they cannot fast. ²⁰The days will come when the bridegroom is taken away from them, and then they will fast in that day. ²¹No one sews a piece of unshrunk cloth on an old garment. If he does, the patch tears away from it, the new from the old, and a worse tear is made. ²²And no one puts new wine into old wineskins. If he does, the wine will burst the skins—and the wine is destroyed, and so are the skins. But new wine is for fresh wineskins."³

Jesus Is Lord of the Sabbath

²³ᶜOne Sabbath he was going through the grainfields, and as they made their way, his disciples began to pluck heads of grain. ²⁴And the Pharisees were saying to him, "Look, why are they doing what is not lawful on the Sabbath?" ²⁵And he said to them, "Have you never read what David did, when he was in need and was hungry, he and those who were with him: ²⁶how he entered the house of God, in the time of⁴ Abiathar the high priest, and ate the bread of the Presence, which it is not lawful for any but the priests to eat, and also gave it to those who were with him?" ²⁷And he said to them, "The Sabbath was made for man, not man for the Sabbath. ²⁸So the Son of Man is lord even of the Sabbath."

A Man with a Withered Hand

3 ᵈAgain he entered the synagogue, and a man was there with a withered hand. ²And they watched Jesus,⁵ to see whether

---

¹Some manuscripts *and* ²Some manuscripts add *and drink* ³Some manuscripts omit *But new wine is for fresh wineskins* ⁴Or *in the passage about* ⁵Greek *him* ªFor 2:3-12 see parallels Matt. 9:2-8; Luke 5:17-26 ᵇFor 2:14-22 see parallels Matt. 9:9-17; Luke 5:27-39 ᶜFor 2:23-28 see parallels Matt. 12:1-8; Luke 6:1-5 ᵈFor 3:1-6 see parallels Matt. 12:9-14; Luke 6:6-11

he would heal him on the Sabbath, so that they might accuse him. ³And he said to the man with the withered hand, "Come here." ⁴And he said to them, "Is it lawful on the Sabbath to do good or to do harm, to save life or to kill?" But they were silent. ⁵And he looked around at them with anger, grieved at their hardness of heart, and said to the man, "Stretch out your hand." He stretched it out, and his hand was restored. ⁶The Pharisees went out and immediately held counsel with the Herodians against him, how to destroy him.

A Great Crowd Follows Jesus

⁷Jesus withdrew with his disciples to the sea, and a great crowd followed, from Galilee and Judea ⁸and Jerusalem and Idumea and from beyond the Jordan and from around Tyre and Sidon. When the great crowd heard all that he was doing, they came to him. ⁹And he told his disciples to have a boat ready for him because of the crowd, lest they crush him, ¹⁰for he had healed many, so that all who had diseases pressed around him to touch him. ¹¹And whenever the unclean spirits saw him, they fell down before him and cried out, "You are the Son of God." ¹²And he strictly ordered them not to make him known.

The Twelve Apostles

¹³And he went up on the mountain and called to him those whom he desired, and they came to him. ¹⁴And he appointed twelve (whom he also named apostles) so that they might be with him and he might send them out to preach ¹⁵and have authority to cast out demons. ¹⁶He appointed the twelve: ᵃSimon (to whom he gave the name Peter); ¹⁷James the son of Zebedee and John the brother of James (to whom he gave the name Boanerges, that is, Sons of Thunder); ¹⁸Andrew, and Philip, and Bartholomew, and Matthew, and Thomas, and James the son of Alphaeus, and Thaddaeus, and Simon the Zealot,¹ ¹⁹and Judas Iscariot, who betrayed him.

²⁰Then he went home, and the crowd gathered again, so that they could not even eat. ²¹And when his family heard it, they went out to seize him, for they were saying, "He is out of his mind."

Blasphemy Against the Holy Spirit

²²And the scribes who came down from Jerusalem were saying, "He is possessed by Beelzebul," and "by the prince of demons he casts out the demons." ²³ᵇAnd he called them to him and said to them in parables, "How can Satan cast out Satan? ²⁴If a kingdom is divided against itself, that kingdom cannot stand. ²⁵And if a house is divided against itself, that house will not be able to stand. ²⁶And if Satan has risen up against himself and is divided, he cannot stand, but is coming to an end. ²⁷But no one can enter a strong man's house and plunder his goods, unless he first binds the strong man. Then indeed he may plunder his house.

²⁸ᶜ"Truly, I say to you, all sins will be forgiven the children of man, and whatever blasphemies they utter, ²⁹but whoever blasphemes against the Holy Spirit never has forgiveness, but is guilty of an eternal sin"— ³⁰for they were saying, "He has an unclean spirit."

Jesus' Mother and Brothers

³¹ᵈAnd his mother and his brothers came, and standing outside they sent to him and called him. ³²And a crowd was sitting around him, and they said to him, "Your mother and your brothers² are outside, seeking you." ³³And he answered them, "Who are my mother and my brothers?" ³⁴And looking about at those who sat around him, he said, "Here are my mother and my brothers! ³⁵For whoever does the will of God, he is my brother and sister and mother."

The Parable of the Sower

4 Again ᵉhe began to teach beside the sea. And a very large crowd gathered about him, so that he got into a boat and sat in it on the sea, and the whole crowd was beside the sea on the land. ²And he was teaching them many things in parables, and in his teaching he said to them: ³"Listen! Behold, a sower went out to sow. ⁴And as he sowed, some seed fell along the path, and the birds came and devoured it. ⁵Other seed fell on rocky ground, where it did not have much soil, and immediately it sprang up, since it had no depth of soil. ⁶And when the sun rose, it was scorched, and since it

---

¹Greek *kananaios*, meaning *zealot* ²Other early manuscripts add *and your sisters* ᵃFor 3:16-19 see parallels Matt. 10:2-4; Luke 6:13-16 ᵇFor 3:23-27 see parallels Matt. 12:25-29; Luke 11:17-22 ᶜFor 3:28-30 see parallel Matt. 12:31, 32 ᵈFor 3:31-35 see parallels Matt. 12:46-50; Luke 8:19-21 ᵉFor 4:1-12 see parallels Matt. 13:1-15; Luke 8:4-10

...ad no root, it withered away. ⁷Other seed fell among thorns, and the thorns grew up and choked it, and it yielded no grain. ⁸And other seeds fell into good soil and produced grain, growing up and increasing and yielding thirtyfold and sixtyfold and a hundredfold." ⁹And he said, "He who has ears to hear, let him hear."

The Purpose of the Parables

¹⁰And when he was alone, those around him with the twelve asked him about the parables. ¹¹And he said to them, "To you has been given the secret of the kingdom of God, but for those outside everything is in parables, ¹²so that

> "they may indeed see but not per-
> ceive,
> and may indeed hear but not
> understand,
> lest they should turn and be for-
> given."

¹³ᵃAnd he said to them, "Do you not under-stand this parable? How then will you understand all the parables? ¹⁴The sower sows the word. ¹⁵And these are the ones along the path, where the word is sown: when they hear, Satan immediately comes and takes away the word that is sown in them. ¹⁶And these are the ones sown on rocky ground: the ones who, when they hear the word, immediately receive it with joy. ¹⁷And they have no root in themselves, but endure for a while; then, when tribula-tion or persecution arises on account of the word, immediately they fall away.¹ ¹⁸And others are the ones sown among thorns. They are those who hear the word, ¹⁹but the cares of the world and the deceitful-ness of riches and the desires for other things enter in and choke the word, and it proves unfruitful. ²⁰But those that were sown on the good soil are the ones who hear the word and accept it and bear fruit, thirtyfold and sixtyfold and a hundredfold."

A Lamp Under a Basket

²¹ᵇAnd he said to them, "Is a lamp brought in to be put under a basket, or under a bed, and not on a stand? ²²For nothing is hidden except to be made mani-fest; nor is anything secret except to come to light. ²³If anyone has ears to hear, let him hear." ²⁴And he said to them, "Pay attention

Or *stumble* ᵃFor 4:13-20 see parallels Matt. 13:18-23; Luke 8:11-15 ᵇFor 4:21-25 see parallel Luke 8:16-18

Know How to Communicate

verses to read
Mark 3:22-30

In this part of Scripture, people are calling Jesus the Devil. They are saying that the fact that demons are being released from people means that Satan is letting them go. They are blaming all of Jesus' work on Satan, and this is so obviously blasphemy (i.e., words that insult or devalue God to the point of bringing God's curse).

But what about when you blame stuff in your life on Satan? When you say stuff like "The Devil is doing this or that to me," could you possibly be blaming Satan for something that God is causing to happen in your life?

Remember, God disciplines those he loves. And sometimes discipline can look like an attack from the Enemy. You have to beware of giving Satan too much credit. When you do, you can miss out on what God is trying to do in your life. Not all bad things that happen to you are really bad—a lot are actually happening for your good. They are purifying you, teaching you, and leading you back to God. So don't be too quick to blame everything bad on the Enemy. He doesn't have that much power over you. Don't give the Holy Spirit any reason to be upset with you (see Eph. 4:30) by giving the bad guys credit where credit isn't due.

to what you hear: with the measure you use, it will be measured to you, and still more will be added to you. 25 For to the one who has, more will be given, and from the one who has not, even what he has will be taken away."

The Parable of the Seed Growing

26 And he said, "The kingdom of God is as if a man should scatter seed on the ground. 27 He sleeps and rises night and day, and the seed sprouts and grows; he knows not how. 28 The earth produces by itself, first the blade, then the ear, then the full grain in the ear. 29 But when the grain is ripe, at once he puts in the sickle, because the harvest has come."

The Parable of the Mustard Seed

30 a And he said, "With what can we compare the kingdom of God, or what parable shall we use for it? 31 It is like a grain of mustard seed, which, when sown on the ground, is the smallest of all the seeds on earth, 32 yet when it is sown it grows up and becomes larger than all the garden plants and puts out large branches, so that the birds of the air can make nests in its shade."

33 With many such parables he spoke the word to them, as they were able to hear it. 34 He did not speak to them without a parable, but privately to his own disciples he explained everything.

Jesus Calms a Storm

35 b On that day, when evening had come, he said to them, "Let us go across to the other side." 36 And leaving the crowd, they took him with them in the boat, just as he was. And other boats were with him. 37 And a great windstorm arose, and the waves were breaking into the boat, so that the boat was already filling. 38 But he was in the stern, asleep on the cushion. And they woke him and said to him, "Teacher, do you not care that we are perishing?" 39 And he awoke and rebuked the wind and said to the sea, "Peace! Be still!" And the wind ceased, and there was a great calm. 40 He said to them, "Why are you so afraid? Have you still no faith?" 41 And they were filled with great fear and said to one another, "Who then is this, that even the wind and the sea obey him?"

Jesus Heals a Man with a Demon

5 c They came to the other side of the sea, to the country of the Gerasenes. 2 And when Jesus[2] had stepped out of the boat, immediately there met him out of the tombs a man with an unclean spirit. 3 He lived among the tombs. And no one could bind him anymore, not even with a chain, 4 for he had often been bound with shackles and chains, but he wrenched the chains apart, and he broke the shackles in pieces. No one had the strength to subdue him. 5 Night and day among the tombs and on the mountains he was always crying out and cutting himself with stones. 6 And when he saw Jesus from afar, he ran and fell down before him. 7 And crying out with a loud voice, he said, "What have you to do with me, Jesus, Son of the Most High God? I adjure you by God, do not torment me." 8 For he was saying to him, "Come out of the man, you unclean spirit!" 9 And Jesus asked him, "What is your name?" He replied, "My name is Legion, for we are many." 10 And he begged him earnestly not to send them out of the country. 11 Now a great herd of pigs was feeding there on the hillside, 12 and they begged him, saying, "Send us to the pigs; let us enter them." 13 So he gave them permission. And the unclean spirits came out and entered the pigs; and the herd, numbering about two thousand, rushed down the steep bank into the sea and drowned in the sea.

14 The herdsmen fled and told it in the city and in the country. And people came to see what it was that had happened. 15 And they came to Jesus and saw the demon-possessed[3] man, the one who had had the legion, sitting there, clothed and in his right mind, and they were afraid. 16 And those who had seen it described to them what had happened to the demon-possessed man and to the pigs. 17 And they began to beg Jesus[4] to depart from their region. 18 As he was getting into the boat, the man who had been possessed with demons begged him that he might be with him. 19 And he did not permit him but said to him, "Go home to your friends and tell them how much the Lord has done for you, and how he has had mercy on you." 20 And he went away and began to proclaim in the

[1] Some manuscripts Gergesenes; some Gadarenes [2] Greek he; also verse 9 [3] Greek daimonizomai; also verses 16, 18; elsewhere rendered oppressed by demons [4] Greek him a For 4:30-32 see parallels Matt. 13:31, 32; Luke 13:18, 19 b For 4:35-41 see parallels Matt. 8:18, 23-27; Luke 8:22-25 c For 5:1-20 see parallels Matt. 8:28-34; Luke 8:26-39

ecapolis how much Jesus had done for
im, and everyone marveled.

Jesus Heals a Woman and Jairus's
Daughter

²¹ And when Jesus had crossed again in
the boat to the other side, a great crowd
gathered about him, and he was beside
the sea. ²² ᵃThen came one of the rulers of
the synagogue, Jairus by name, and seeing him, he fell at his feet ²³ and implored
him earnestly, saying, "My little daughter
is at the point of death. Come and lay your
hands on her, so that she may be made well
and live." ²⁴ And he went with him.

And a great crowd followed him and
thronged about him. ²⁵ And there was a
woman who had had a discharge of blood
for twelve years, ²⁶ and who had suffered
much under many physicians, and had
spent all that she had, and was no better
but rather grew worse. ²⁷ She had heard the
reports about Jesus and came up behind
him in the crowd and touched his garment.
²⁸ For she said, "If I touch even his garments, I will be made well." ²⁹ And immediately the flow of blood dried up, and she
felt in her body that she was healed of her
disease. ³⁰ And Jesus, perceiving in himself
that power had gone out from him, immediately turned about in the crowd and said,
"Who touched my garments?" ³¹ And his
disciples said to him, "You see the crowd
pressing around you, and yet you say, 'Who
touched me?'" ³² And he looked around to
see who had done it. ³³ But the woman,
knowing what had happened to her, came
in fear and trembling and fell down before
him and told him the whole truth. ³⁴ And
he said to her, "Daughter, your faith has
made you well; go in peace, and be healed
of your disease."

³⁵ While he was still speaking, there
came from the ruler's house some who
said, "Your daughter is dead. Why trouble
the Teacher any further?" ³⁶ But over-
hearing¹ what they said, Jesus said to the
ruler of the synagogue, "Do not fear, only
believe." ³⁷ And he allowed no one to follow
him except Peter and James and John the
brother of James. ³⁸ They came to the house
of the ruler of the synagogue, and Jesus²
saw a commotion, people weeping and
wailing loudly. ³⁹ And when he had entered,

he said to them, "Why are you making a
commotion and weeping? The child is not
dead but sleeping." ⁴⁰ And they laughed at
him. But he put them all outside and took
the child's father and mother and those
who were with him and went in where the
child was. ⁴¹ Taking her by the hand he said
to her, "Talitha cumi," which means, "Little
girl, I say to you, arise." ⁴² And immediately
the girl got up and began walking (for she
was twelve years of age), and they were
immediately overcome with amazement.
⁴³ And he strictly charged them that no one
should know this, and told them to give her
something to eat.

Jesus Rejected at Nazareth

6 ᵇHe went away from there and came
to his hometown, and his disciples followed him. ² And on the Sabbath he began
to teach in the synagogue, and many who
heard him were astonished, saying, "Where
did this man get these things? What is the
wisdom given to him? How are such mighty
works done by his hands? ³ Is not this the
carpenter, the son of Mary and brother
of James and Joses and Judas and Simon?
And are not his sisters here with us?" And
they took offense at him. ⁴ And Jesus said
to them, "A prophet is not without honor,
except in his hometown and among his relatives and in his own household." ⁵ And he
could do no mighty work there, except that
he laid his hands on a few sick people and
healed them. ⁶ And he marveled because of
their unbelief.

And he went about among the villages
teaching.

Jesus Sends Out the Twelve Apostles

⁷ ᶜAnd he called the twelve and began
to send them out two by two, and gave
them authority over the unclean spirits.
⁸ He charged them to take nothing for their
journey except a staff—no bread, no bag,
no money in their belts— ⁹ but to wear sandals and not put on two tunics.³ ¹⁰ And he
said to them, "Whenever you enter a house,
stay there until you depart from there.
¹¹ And if any place will not receive you and
they will not listen to you, when you leave,
shake off the dust that is on your feet as a
testimony against them." ¹² So they went
out and proclaimed that people should

repent. [13] And they cast out many demons and anointed with oil many who were sick and healed them.

The Death of John the Baptist

[14] [a] King Herod heard of it, for Jesus'[1] name had become known. Some[2] said, "John the Baptist[3] has been raised from the dead. That is why these miraculous powers are at work in him." [15] But others said, "He is Elijah." And others said, "He is a prophet, like one of the prophets of old." [16] But when Herod heard of it, he said, "John, whom I beheaded, has been raised." [17] For it was Herod who had sent and seized John and bound him in prison for the sake of Herodias, his brother Philip's wife, because he had married her. [18] For John had been saying to Herod, "It is not lawful for you to have your brother's wife." [19] And Herodias had a grudge against him and wanted to put him to death. But she could not, [20] for Herod feared John, knowing that he was a righteous and holy man, and he kept him safe. When he heard him, he was greatly perplexed, and yet he heard him gladly.

[21] But an opportunity came when Herod on his birthday gave a banquet for his nobles and military commanders and the leading men of Galilee. [22] For when Herodias's daughter came in and danced she pleased Herod and his guests. And the king said to the girl, "Ask me for whatever you wish, and I will give it to you." [23] And he vowed to her, "Whatever you ask me I will give you, up to half of my kingdom." [24] And she went out and said to her mother, "For what should I ask?" And she said, "The head of John the Baptist." [25] And she came in immediately with haste to the king and asked, saying, "I want you to give me at once the head of John the Baptist on a platter." [26] And the king was exceedingly sorry, but because of his oaths and his guests he did not want to break his word to her. [27] And immediately the king sent an executioner with orders to bring John's[4] head. He went and beheaded him in the prison [28] and brought his head on a platter and gave it to the girl, and the girl gave it to her mother. [29] When his disciples heard of it, they came and took his body and laid it in a tomb.

Jesus Feeds the Five Thousand

[30] The apostles returned to Jesus and told him all that they had done and taught. [31] And he said to them, "Come away by yourselves to a desolate place and rest

[1] Greek his [2] Some manuscripts He [3] Greek baptizer; also verse 24 [4] Greek his [a] For 6:14-29 see parallels Matt. 14:1-12; Luke 9:7-9

Know Yourself

verses to read
Mark 6:1–6

"I trust God, I just don't trust myself." When it comes to your life and the needs you have, do you believe God's Word? Do you perhaps trust everything he says, but, because you know yourself, you just aren't sure you'll get things right?

It's easy to be certain about who Jesus is and to believe in his power but still be unsure about yourself. But be careful of thinking like that. When you fear your future and worry about what you will do, what you will wear, and how you will survive, you aren't just doubting yourself—you're doubting him. When you think you just can't do something or survive something, you have to confess your doubt—not your doubt about your own abilities but your doubt about God's abilities. You have to say, "God, I confess that I don't trust you. I haven't truly believed your Word, and I am completely stressed out because of it. Please forgive me and help me to trust that what you say is true and that you are God, the one who provides for me and meets all my needs." Just like Jesus couldn't work many miracles in his hometown where so many doubted him, God can't work any miracle in your life until you believe that he can and will.

while." For many were coming and going, and they had no leisure even to eat. [32][d]And they went away in the boat to a desolate place by themselves. [33]Now many saw them going and recognized them, and they ran there on foot from all the towns and got there ahead of them. [34]When he went ashore he saw a great crowd, and he had compassion on them, because they were like sheep without a shepherd. And he began to teach them many things. [35]And when it grew late, his disciples came to him and said, "This is a desolate place, and the hour is now late. [36]Send them away to go into the surrounding countryside and villages and buy themselves something to eat." [37]But he answered them, "You give them something to eat." And they said to him, "Shall we go and buy two hundred denarii[1] worth of bread and give it to them to eat?" [38]And he said to them, "How many loaves do you have? Go and see." And when they had found out, they said, "Five, and two fish." [39]Then he commanded them all to sit down in groups on the green grass. [40]So they sat down in groups, by hundreds and by fifties. [41]And taking the five loaves and the two fish he looked up to heaven and said a blessing and broke the loaves and gave them to the disciples to set before the people. And he divided the two fish among them all. [42]And they all ate and were satisfied. [43]And they took up twelve baskets full of broken pieces and of the fish. [44]And those who ate the loaves were five thousand men.

Jesus Walks on the Water

[45][b]Immediately he made his disciples get into the boat and go before him to the other side, to Bethsaida, while he dismissed the crowd. [46]And after he had taken leave of them, he went up on the mountain to pray. [47]And when evening came, the boat was out on the sea, and he was alone on the land. [48]And he saw that they were making headway painfully, for the wind was against them. And about the fourth watch of the night[2] he came to them, walking on the sea. He meant to pass by them, [49]but when they saw him walking on the sea they thought it was a ghost, and cried out,

[50]for they all saw him and were terrified. But immediately he spoke to them and said, "Take heart; it is I. Do not be afraid." [51]And he got into the boat with them, and the wind ceased. And they were utterly astounded, [52]for they did not understand about the loaves, but their hearts were hardened.

Jesus Heals the Sick in Gennesaret

[53][c]When they had crossed over, they came to land at Gennesaret and moored to the shore. [54]And when they got out of the boat, the people immediately recognized him [55]and ran about the whole region and began to bring the sick people on their beds to wherever they heard he was. [56]And wherever he came, in villages, cities, or countryside, they laid the sick in the marketplaces and implored him that they might touch even the fringe of his garment. And as many as touched it were made well.

Traditions and Commandments

7 [d]Now when the Pharisees gathered to him, with some of the scribes who had come from Jerusalem, [2]they saw that some of his disciples ate with hands that were defiled, that is, unwashed. [3](For the Pharisees and all the Jews do not eat unless they wash their hands properly,[3] holding to the tradition of the elders, [4]and when they come from the marketplace, they do not eat unless they wash.[4] And there are many other traditions that they observe, such as the washing of cups and pots and copper vessels and dining couches.[5]) [5]And the Pharisees and the scribes asked him, "Why do your disciples not walk according to the tradition of the elders, but eat with defiled hands?" [6]And he said to them, "Well did Isaiah prophesy of you hypocrites, as it is written,

[e]"'This people honors me with their lips,
        but their heart is far from me;
[7]   in vain do they worship me,
        teaching as doctrines the commandments of men.'

[8]You leave the commandment of God and hold to the tradition of men."

---

[1]A *denarius* was a day's wage for a laborer [2]That is, between 3 A.M. and 6 A.M. [3]Greek *unless they wash the hands with a fist*, probably indicating a kind of ceremonial washing [4]Greek *unless they baptize*; some manuscripts *unless they purify themselves* [5]Some manuscripts omit *and dining couches* [a]For 6:32-44 see parallels Matt. 14:13-21; Luke 9:10-17; John 6:1-13 [b]For 6:45-52 see parallels Matt. 14:22-33; John 6:16-21 [c]For 6:53-56 see parallel Matt. 14:34-36 [d]For 7:1-30 see parallel Matt. 15:1-28 [e]Isa. 29:13

⁹And he said to them, "You have a fine way of rejecting the commandment of God in order to establish your tradition! ¹⁰For Moses said, ᵃ'Honor your father and your mother'; and, ᵇ'Whoever reviles father or mother must surely die.' ¹¹But you say, 'If a man tells his father or his mother, "Whatever you would have gained from me is Corban"' (that is, given to God)¹— ¹²then you no longer permit him to do anything for his father or mother, ¹³thus making void the word of God by your tradition that you have handed down. And many such things you do."

What Defiles a Person

¹⁴And he called the people to him again and said to them, "Hear me, all of you, and understand: ¹⁵There is nothing outside a person that by going into him can defile him, but the things that come out of a person are what defile him."² ¹⁷And when he had entered the house and left the people, his disciples asked him about the parable. ¹⁸And he said to them, "Then are you also without understanding? Do you not see that whatever goes into a person from outside cannot defile him, ¹⁹since it enters not his heart but his stomach, and is expelled?"³ (Thus he declared all foods clean.) ²⁰And he said, "What comes out of a person is what defiles him. ²¹For from within, out of the heart of man, come evil thoughts, sexual immorality, theft, murder, adultery, ²²coveting, wickedness, deceit, sensuality, envy, slander, pride, foolishness. ²³All these evil things come from within, and they defile a person."

The Syrophoenician Woman's Faith

²⁴And from there he arose and went away to the region of Tyre and Sidon.⁴ And he entered a house and did not want anyone to know, yet he could not be hidden. ²⁵But immediately a woman whose little daughter had an unclean spirit heard of him and came and fell down at his feet. ²⁶Now the woman was a Gentile, a Syrophoenician by birth. And she begged him to cast the demon out of her daughter. ²⁷And he said to her, "Let the children be fed first, for it is not right to take the children's bread and throw it to the dogs." ²⁸But she answered him, "Yes, Lord; yet even the dogs under the table eat the children's crumbs." ²⁹And he said to her, "For this statement you may go your way; the demon has left your daughter." ³⁰And she went home and found the child lying in bed and the demon gone.

Jesus Heals a Deaf Man

³¹Then he returned from the region of Tyre and went through Sidon to the Sea of Galilee, in the region of the Decapolis. ³²And they brought to him a man who was deaf and had a speech impediment, and they begged him to lay his hand on him. ³³And taking him aside from the crowd privately, he put his fingers into his ears, and after spitting touched his tongue. ³⁴And looking up to heaven, he sighed and said to him, "Ephphatha," that is, "Be opened." ³⁵And his ears were opened, his tongue was released, and he spoke plainly. ³⁶And Jesus⁵ charged them to tell no one. But the more he charged them, the more zealously they proclaimed it. ³⁷And they were astonished beyond measure, saying, "He has done all things well. He even makes the deaf hear and the mute speak."

Jesus Feeds the Four Thousand

8 ᶜIn those days, when again a great crowd had gathered, and they had nothing to eat, he called his disciples to him and said to them, ²"I have compassion on the crowd, because they have been with me now three days and have nothing to eat. ³And if I send them away hungry to their homes, they will faint on the way. And some of them have come from far away." ⁴And his disciples answered him, "How can one feed these people with bread here in this desolate place?" ⁵And he asked them, "How many loaves do you have?" They said, "Seven." ⁶And he directed the crowd to sit down on the ground. And he took the seven loaves, and having given thanks, he broke them and gave them to his disciples to set before the people; and they set them before the crowd. ⁷And they had a few small fish. And having blessed them, he said that these also should be set before them. ⁸And they ate and were satisfied. And they took up the broken pieces left over, seven baskets full. ⁹And there were about four thousand people. And he sent

---

¹Or an offering ²Some manuscripts add verse 16: If anyone has ears to hear, let him hear ³Greek goes out into the latrine ⁴Some manuscripts omit and Sidon ⁵Greek he ᵃEx. 20:12 ᵇEx. 21:17 ᶜFor 8:1-10 see parallel Matt. 15:32-39

them away. [10] And immediately he got into the boat with his disciples and went to the district of Dalmanutha.[1]

The Pharisees Demand a Sign

[11] [a] The Pharisees came and began to argue with him, seeking from him a sign from heaven to test him. [12] And he sighed deeply in his spirit and said, "Why does this generation seek a sign? Truly, I say to you, no sign will be given to this generation." [13] And he left them, got into the boat again, and went to the other side.

The Leaven of the Pharisees and Herod

[14] Now they had forgotten to bring bread, and they had only one loaf with them in the boat. [15] And he cautioned them, saying, "Watch out; beware of the leaven of the Pharisees and the leaven of Herod."[2] [16] And they began discussing with one another the fact that they had no bread. [17] And Jesus, aware of this, said to them, "Why are you discussing the fact that you have no bread? Do you not yet perceive or understand? Are your hearts hardened? [18] Having eyes do you not see, and having ears do you not hear? And do you not remember? [19] When I broke the five loaves for the five thousand, how many baskets full of broken pieces did you take up?" They said to him, "Twelve." [20] "And the seven for the four thousand, how many baskets full of broken pieces did you take up?" And they said to him, "Seven." [21] And he said to them, "Do you not yet understand?"

Jesus Heals a Blind Man at Bethsaida

[22] And they came to Bethsaida. And some people brought to him a blind man and begged him to touch him. [23] And he took the blind man by the hand and led him out of the village, and when he had spit on his eyes and laid his hands on him, he asked him, "Do you see anything?" [24] And he looked up and said, "I see people, but they look like trees, walking." [25] Then Jesus[3] laid his hands on his eyes again; and he opened his eyes, his sight was restored, and he saw everything clearly. [26] And he sent him to his home, saying, "Do not even enter the village."

Peter Confesses Jesus as the Christ

[27] [b] And Jesus went on with his disciples to the villages of Caesarea Philippi. And on the way he asked his disciples, "Who do people say that I am?" [28] And they told him, "John the Baptist; and others say, Elijah; and others, one of the prophets." [29] And he asked them, "But who do you say that I am?" Peter answered him, "You are the Christ." [30] And he strictly charged them to tell no one about him.

Jesus Foretells His Death and Resurrection

[31] [c] And he began to teach them that the Son of Man must suffer many things and be rejected by the elders and the chief priests and the scribes and be killed, and after three days rise again. [32] And he said this plainly. And Peter took him aside and began to rebuke him. [33] But turning and seeing his disciples, he rebuked Peter and said, "Get behind me, Satan! For you are not setting your mind on the things of God, but on the things of man."

[34] And calling the crowd to him with his disciples, he said to them, "If anyone would come after me, let him deny himself and take up his cross and follow me. [35] For whoever would save his life[4] will lose it, but whoever loses his life for my sake and the gospel's will save it. [36] For what does it profit a man to gain the whole world and forfeit his soul? [37] For what can a man give in return for his soul? [38] For whoever is ashamed of me and of my words in this adulterous and sinful generation, of him will the Son of Man also be ashamed when he comes in the glory of his Father with the holy angels."

9 And he said to them, "Truly, I say to you, there are some standing here who will not taste death until they see the kingdom of God after it has come with power."

The Transfiguration

[2] [d] And after six days Jesus took with him Peter and James and John, and led them up a high mountain by themselves. And he was transfigured before them, [3] and his clothes became radiant, intensely white, as no one[5] on earth could bleach them. [4] And there appeared to them Elijah with Moses, and they were talking with Jesus.

---

[1] Some manuscripts *Magadan*, or *Magdala* [2] Some manuscripts *the Herodians* [3] Greek *he* [4] The same Greek word can mean either *soul* or *life*, depending on the context; twice in this verse and once in verse 36 and once in verse 37 [5] Greek *launderer* (*gnapheus*)
[a] For 8:11-21 see parallel Matt. 16:1-12 [b] For 8:27-29 see parallels Matt. 16:13-16; Luke 9:18-20 [c] For 8:31–9:1 see parallels Matt. 16:21-28; Luke 9:22-27 [d] For 9:2-8 see parallels Matt. 17:1-8; Luke 9:28-36

[5] And Peter said to Jesus, "Rabbi,[1] it is good that we are here. Let us make three tents, one for you and one for Moses and one for Elijah." [6] For he did not know what to say, for they were terrified. [7] And a cloud overshadowed them, and a voice came out of the cloud, "This is my beloved Son;[2] listen to him." [8] And suddenly, looking around, they no longer saw anyone with them but Jesus only.

[9] [a] And as they were coming down the mountain, he charged them to tell no one what they had seen, until the Son of Man had risen from the dead. [10] So they kept the matter to themselves, questioning what this rising from the dead might mean. [11] And they asked him, "Why do the scribes say that first Elijah must come?" [12] And he said to them, "Elijah does come first to restore all things. And how is it written of the Son of Man that he should suffer many things and be treated with contempt? [13] But I tell you that Elijah has come, and they did to him whatever they pleased, as it is written of him."

Jesus Heals a Boy with an Unclean Spirit

[14] [b] And when they came to the disciples, they saw a great crowd around them, and scribes arguing with them. [15] And immediately all the crowd, when they saw him, were greatly amazed and ran up to him and greeted him. [16] And he asked them, "What are you arguing about with them?" [17] And someone from the crowd answered him, "Teacher, I brought my son to you, for he has a spirit that makes him mute. [18] And whenever it seizes him, it throws him down, and he foams and grinds his teeth and becomes rigid. So I asked your disciples to cast it out, and they were not able." [19] And he answered them, "O faithless generation, how long am I to be with you? How long am I to bear with you? Bring him to me." [20] And they brought the boy to him. And when the spirit saw him, immediately it convulsed the boy, and he fell on the ground and rolled about, foaming at the mouth. [21] And Jesus asked his father, "How long has this been happening to him?" And he said, "From childhood. [22] And it has often cast him into fire and into water, to destroy him. But if you can do anything, have compassion on us and help us." [23] And Jesus said to him, "'If you can'! All things are possible for one who believes." [24] Immediately the father of the child cried out[3] and said, "I believe; help my unbelief!" [25] And when Jesus saw that a crowd came running together, he rebuked the unclean spirit, saying to it, "You mute and deaf spirit, I command you, come out of him and never enter him again." [26] And after crying out and convulsing him terribly, it came out, and the boy was like a corpse, so that most of them said, "He is dead." [27] But Jesus took him by the hand and lifted him up, and he arose. [28] And when he had entered the house, his disciples asked him privately, "Why could we not cast it out?" [29] And he said to them, "This kind cannot be driven out by anything but prayer."[4]

Jesus Again Foretells Death, Resurrection

[30] [c] They went on from there and passed through Galilee. And he did not want anyone to know, [31] for he was teaching his disciples, saying to them, "The Son of Man is going to be delivered into the hands of men, and they will kill him. And when he is killed, after three days he will rise." [32] But they did not understand the saying, and were afraid to ask him.

Who Is the Greatest?

[33] And they came to Capernaum. And when he was in the house [d] he asked them, "What were you discussing on the way?" [34] But they kept silent, for on the way they had argued with one another about who was the greatest. [35] And he sat down and called the twelve. And he said to them, "If anyone would be first, he must be last of all and servant of all." [36] And he took a child and put him in the midst of them, and taking him in his arms, he said to them, [37] "Whoever receives one such child in my name receives me, and whoever receives me, receives not me but him who sent me."

Anyone Not Against Us Is for Us

[38] [e] John said to him, "Teacher, we saw someone casting out demons in your name,[5] and we tried to stop him, because he was not following us." [39] But Jesus said,

[1] *Rabbi* means *my teacher*, or *my master* [2] *Or my Son, my* (or *the*) *Beloved* [3] Some manuscripts add *with tears* [4] Some manuscripts add *and fasting* [5] Some manuscripts add *who does not follow us* [a] For 9:9-13 see parallel Matt. 17:9-13 [b] For 9:14-28 see parallels Matt. 17:14-19; Luke 9:37-42 [c] For 9:30-32 see parallels Matt. 17:22, 23; Luke 9:43-45 [d] For 9:33-37 see parallels Matt. 18:1-5; Luke 9:46-48 [e] For 9:38-40 see parallel Luke 9:49, 50

Do not stop him, for no one who does a mighty work in my name will be able soon afterward to speak evil of me. **40** For the one who is not against us is for us. **41** For truly, I say to you, whoever gives you a cup of water to drink because you belong to Christ will by no means lose his reward.

Temptations to Sin

42 "Whoever causes one of these little ones who believe in me to sin,[1] it would be better for him if a great millstone were hung around his neck and he were thrown into the sea. **43** And if your hand causes you to sin, cut it off. It is better for you to enter life crippled than with two hands to go to hell,[2] to the unquenchable fire.[3] **45** And if your foot causes you to sin, cut it off. It is better for you to enter life lame than with two feet to be thrown into hell. **47** And if your eye causes you to sin, tear it out. It is better for you to enter the kingdom of God with one eye than with two eyes to be thrown into hell, **48** 'where their worm does not die and the fire is not quenched.' **49** For everyone will be salted with fire.[4] **50** Salt is good, but if the salt has lost its saltiness, how will you make it salty again? Have salt in yourselves, and be at peace with one another."

Teaching About Divorce

10 [a] And he left there and went to the region of Judea and beyond the Jordan, and crowds gathered to him again. And again, as was his custom, he taught them.

2 And Pharisees came up and in order to test him asked, "Is it lawful for a man to divorce his wife?" **3** He answered them, "What did Moses command you?" **4** They said, "Moses allowed a man to write a certificate of divorce and to send her away." **5** And Jesus said to them, "Because of your hardness of heart he wrote you this commandment. **6** But from the beginning of creation, 'God made them [b] male and female.' **7** [c] 'Therefore a man shall leave his father and mother and hold fast to his wife,[5] **8** and the two shall become one flesh.' So they are no longer two but one flesh. **9** What

therefore God has joined together, let not man separate."

10 And in the house the disciples asked him again about this matter. **11** And he said to them, "Whoever divorces his wife and marries another commits adultery against her, **12** and if she divorces her husband and marries another, she commits adultery."

Let the Children Come to Me

13 [d] And they were bringing children to him that he might touch them, and the disciples rebuked them. **14** But when Jesus saw it, he was indignant and said to them, "Let the children come to me; do not hinder them, for to such belongs the kingdom of God. **15** Truly, I say to you, whoever does not receive the kingdom of God like a child shall not enter it." **16** And he took them in his arms and blessed them, laying his hands on them.

The Rich Young Man

17 [e] And as he was setting out on his journey, a man ran up and knelt before him and asked him, "Good Teacher, what must I do to inherit eternal life?" **18** And Jesus said to him, "Why do you call me good? No one is good except God alone. **19** You know the commandments: [f] 'Do not murder, Do not commit adultery, Do not steal, Do not bear false witness, Do not defraud, Honor your father and mother.'" **20** And he said to him, "Teacher, all these I have kept from my youth." **21** And Jesus, looking at him, loved him, and said to him, "You lack one thing: go, sell all that you have and give to the poor, and you will have treasure in heaven; and come, follow me." **22** Disheartened by the saying, he went away sorrowful, for he had great possessions.

23 And Jesus looked around and said to his disciples, "How difficult it will be for those who have wealth to enter the kingdom of God!" **24** And the disciples were amazed at his words. But Jesus said to them again, "Children, how difficult it is[6] to enter the kingdom of God! **25** It is easier for a camel to go through the eye of a needle than for a rich person to enter the kingdom of God." **26** And they were exceedingly astonished, and said to him,[7] "Then

---

[1] Greek *to stumble*; also verses 43, 45, 47 [2] Greek *Gehenna*; also verse 47 [3] Some manuscripts add verses 44 and 46 (which are identical with verse 48) [4] Some manuscripts add *and every sacrifice will be salted with salt* [5] Some manuscripts omit *and hold fast to his wife* [6] Some manuscripts add *for those who trust in riches* [7] Some manuscripts *to one another* [a] For 10:1-12 see parallel Matt. 19:1-9 [b] Gen. 1:27; 5:2 [c] Gen. 2:24 [d] For 10:13-16 see parallels Matt. 19:13-15; Luke 18:15-17 [e] For 10:17-31 see parallels Matt. 19:16-30; Luke 18:18-30 [f] Ex. 20:12-16; Deut. 5:16-20

who can be saved?" ²⁷ Jesus looked at them and said, "With man it is impossible, but not with God. For all things are possible with God." ²⁸ Peter began to say to him, "See, we have left everything and followed you." ²⁹ Jesus said, "Truly, I say to you, there is no one who has left house or brothers or sisters or mother or father or children or lands, for my sake and for the gospel, ³⁰ who will not receive a hundredfold now in this time, houses and brothers and sisters and mothers and children and lands, with persecutions, and in the age to come eternal life. ³¹ But many who are first will be last, and the last first."

Jesus Foretells His Death a Third Time

³² ªAnd they were on the road, going up to Jerusalem, and Jesus was walking ahead of them. And they were amazed, and those who followed were afraid. And taking the twelve again, he began to tell them what was to happen to him, ³³ saying, "See, we are going up to Jerusalem, and the Son of Man will be delivered over to the chief priests and the scribes, and they will condemn him to death and deliver him over to the Gentiles. ³⁴ And they will mock him and spit on him, and flog him and kill him. And after three days he will rise."

The Request of James and John

³⁵ ᵇAnd James and John, the sons of Zebedee, came up to him and said to him, "Teacher, we want you to do for us whatever we ask of you." ³⁶ And he said to them, "What do you want me to do for you?" ³⁷ And they said to him, "Grant us to sit, one at your right hand and one at your left, in your glory." ³⁸ Jesus said to them, "You do not know what you are asking. Are you able to drink the cup that I drink, or to be baptized with the baptism with which I am baptized?" ³⁹ And they said to him, "We are able." And Jesus said to them, "The cup that I drink you will drink, and with the baptism with which I am baptized, you will be baptized, ⁴⁰ but to sit at my right hand or at my left is not mine to grant, but it is for those for whom it has been prepared." ⁴¹ And when the ten heard it, they began to be indignant at James and John. ⁴² And Jesus called them to him and said to them, "You know that those who are considered rulers of the Gentiles lord it over them, and their great ones exercise authority over them. ⁴³ But it shall not be so among you. But whoever would be great among you must be your servant,[1] ⁴⁴ and whoever would be first among you must be slave[2] of

---

[1] Greek diakonos [2] Greek bondservant (doulos) ª For 10:32-34 see parallels Matt. 20:17-19; Luke 18:31-33 ᵇ For 10:35-45 see parallel Matt. 20:20-28

Know Yourself

verses to read
Mark 10:46–52

Jesus tells you to ask for anything in his name and it will be yours (see John 16:23–24), but if you don't have faith in him, then you won't even think about asking. It's your faith in him that will change your life, heal you, and take out the old and bring in the new. But when you choose worry over faith, you cut the very rope that was there to pull you up, and you stay in the messy goo of your worry and helplessness.

It's super easy to doubt God's ability to help you when you look at your past and think, "I've always had this problem." When it's a recurring issue, your mind starts to believe it's an irreversible problem, and so you are afraid to ask God to change it. But you have to remember that God likes doing what seems absolutely impossible. If you want to become like Christ, if you want his will to be done in your life, trust him. Exercise faith. After all, it is Christ, not our faith, that saves and helps us. The call on your life is not to muster up enough faith but simply to look to Christ, trusting him and resting on him.

all. **45**For even the Son of Man came not to be served but to serve, and to give his life as a ransom for many."

Jesus Heals Blind Bartimaeus

46[a]And they came to Jericho. And as he was leaving Jericho with his disciples and a great crowd, Bartimaeus, a blind beggar, the son of Timaeus, was sitting by the roadside. **47**And when he heard that it was Jesus of Nazareth, he began to cry out and say, "Jesus, Son of David, have mercy on me!" **48**And many rebuked him, telling him to be silent. But he cried out all the more, "Son of David, have mercy on me!" **49**And Jesus stopped and said, "Call him." And they called the blind man, saying to him, "Take heart. Get up; he is calling you." **50**And throwing off his cloak, he sprang up and came to Jesus. **51**And Jesus said to him, "What do you want me to do for you?" And the blind man said to him, "Rabbi, let me recover my sight." **52**And Jesus said to him, "Go your way; your faith has made you well." And immediately he recovered his sight and followed him on the way.

The Triumphal Entry

11 [b]Now when they drew near to Jerusalem, to Bethphage and Bethany, at the Mount of Olives, Jesus[1] sent two of his disciples **2**and said to them, "Go into the village in front of you, and immediately as you enter it you will find a colt tied, on which no one has ever sat. Untie it and bring it. **3**If anyone says to you, 'Why are you doing this?' say, 'The Lord has need of it and will send it back here immediately.'" **4**And they went away and found a colt tied at a door outside in the street, and they untied it. **5**And some of those standing there said to them, "What are you doing, untying the colt?" **6**And they told them what Jesus had said, and they let them go. **7**And they brought the colt to Jesus and threw their cloaks on it, and he sat on it. **8**And many spread their cloaks on the road, and others spread leafy branches that they had cut from the fields. **9**And those who went before and those who followed were shouting, "Hosanna! Blessed is he who comes in the name of the Lord! **10**Blessed is the coming kingdom of our father David! Hosanna in the highest!"

11And he entered Jerusalem and went into the temple. And when he had looked around at everything, as it was already late, he went out to Bethany with the twelve.

Jesus Curses the Fig Tree

12On the following day, when they came from Bethany, he was hungry. **13**And seeing in the distance a fig tree in leaf, he went to see if he could find anything on it. When he came to it, he found nothing but leaves, for it was not the season for figs. **14**And he said to it, "May no one ever eat fruit from you again." And his disciples heard it.

Jesus Cleanses the Temple

15[c]And they came to Jerusalem. And he entered the temple and began to drive out those who sold and those who bought in the temple, and he overturned the tables of the money-changers and the seats of those who sold pigeons. **16**And he would not allow anyone to carry anything through the temple. **17**And he was teaching them and saying to them, "Is it not written, [d]'My house shall be called a house of prayer for all the nations'? But you have made it a den of robbers." **18**And the chief priests and the scribes heard it and were seeking a way to destroy him, for they feared him, because all the crowd was astonished at his teaching. **19**And when evening came they[2] went out of the city.

The Lesson from the Withered Fig Tree

20[e]As they passed by in the morning, they saw the fig tree withered away to its roots. **21**And Peter remembered and said to him, "Rabbi, look! The fig tree that you cursed has withered." **22**And Jesus answered them, "Have faith in God. **23**Truly, I say to you, whoever says to this mountain, 'Be taken up and thrown into the sea,' and does not doubt in his heart, but believes that what he says will come to pass, it will be done for him. **24**Therefore I tell you, whatever you ask in prayer, believe that you have received[3] it, and it will be yours. **25**And whenever you stand praying, forgive, if you have anything against anyone, so that your

[1]Greek he [2]Some manuscripts he [3]Some manuscripts are receiving [a]For 10:46-52 see parallels Matt. 20:29-34; Luke 18:35-43 [b]For 11:1-10 see parallels Matt. 21:1-9; Luke 19:28-38; John 12:12-15 [c]For 11:15-18 see parallels Matt. 21:12-16; Luke 19:45-47 [d]Isa. 56:7 [e]For 11:20-24 see parallel Matt. 21:19-22

Father also who is in heaven may forgive you your trespasses."[1]

The Authority of Jesus Challenged

27 [a]And they came again to Jerusalem. And as he was walking in the temple, the chief priests and the scribes and the elders came to him, 28 and they said to him, "By what authority are you doing these things, or who gave you this authority to do them?" 29 Jesus said to them, "I will ask you one question; answer me, and I will tell you by what authority I do these things. 30 Was the baptism of John from heaven or from man? Answer me." 31 And they discussed it with one another, saying, "If we say, 'From heaven,' he will say, 'Why then did you not believe him?' 32 But shall we say, 'From man'?"— they were afraid of the people, for they all held that John really was a prophet. 33 So they answered Jesus, "We do not know." And Jesus said to them, "Neither will I tell you by what authority I do these things."

The Parable of the Tenants

12 [b]And he began to speak to them in parables. "A man planted a vineyard and put a fence around it and dug a pit for the winepress and built a tower, and leased it to tenants and went into another country. 2 When the season came, he sent a servant[2] to the tenants to get from them some of the fruit of the vineyard. 3 And they took him

[1] Some manuscripts add verse 26: *But if you do not forgive, neither will your Father who is in heaven forgive your trespasses* [2] Greek *bondservant*; also verse 4 [a] For 11:27-33 see parallels Matt. 21:23-27; Luke 20:1-8 [b] For 12:1-12 see parallels Matt. 21:33-46; Luke 20:9-18

Know Yourself

verses to read
Mark 11:15–19

The temple was considered the holy place where God would come to meet his people. Jesus was very protective of the temple when he walked this earth. The Jews had started to use it for a marketplace instead of a holy place, and when Jesus saw it, he was ticked. He became very angry, turning over tables and scattering their precious stuff all over the floor. He wasn't going to stand for his Father's temple being used by the people for their own good. It was meant to be reserved for the uses of God alone.

When Jesus left this earth and sent the Holy Spirit to live within us, we no longer needed the temple to meet God because now our bodies would be the temple of his Holy Spirit (see John 14:26; 1 Cor. 6:19). That was a game changer. Suddenly people didn't have to go to a certain place to be with God because they had God with them always.

So what does all this mean for your body, the new temple of the Holy Spirit? What kind of a temple are you keeping? Have you used your body for your own good? And would Jesus be pleased, or would he be kicking over tables and taking names? You have to beware of making your body a temple for your own pleasure and your own service, because when you do, it's just a matter of time before there will be consequences. No one owns your body but the Lord Jesus Christ. Period. End of story. He has instructed you to take care of the temple, not to act like you own it yourself—and not to share it with a man other than your husband.

When you belong to Jesus and his perfect record of obedience has become yours, your temple will be as clean as a bleach factory after a tank spill—clean, disinfected, and pure. We do not live in purity in order to *become* a clean temple; rather, we must be careful to remain pure, remembering that we are *already* our Lord's clean temple.

and beat him and sent him away empty-handed. [4] Again he sent to them another servant, and they struck him on the head and treated him shamefully. [5] And he sent another, and him they killed. And so with many others: some they beat, and some they killed. [6] He had still one other, a beloved son. Finally he sent him to them, saying, 'They will respect my son.' [7] But those tenants said to one another, 'This is the heir. Come, let us kill him, and the inheritance will be ours.' [8] And they took him and killed him and threw him out of the vineyard. [9] What will the owner of the vineyard do? He will come and destroy the tenants and give the vineyard to others. [10] Have you not read this Scripture:

[a] "'The stone that the builders rejected
        has become the cornerstone;[1]
[11]   this was the Lord's doing,
        and it is marvelous in our eyes'?"

[12] And they were seeking to arrest him but feared the people, for they perceived that he had told the parable against them. So they left him and went away.

Paying Taxes to Caesar

[13] [b] And they sent to him some of the Pharisees and some of the Herodians, to trap him in his talk. [14] And they came and said to him, "Teacher, we know that you are true and do not care about anyone's opinion. For you are not swayed by appearances,[2] but truly teach the way of God. Is it lawful to pay taxes to Caesar, or not? Should we pay them, or should we not?" [15] But, knowing their hypocrisy, he said to them, "Why put me to the test? Bring me a denarius[3] and let me look at it." [16] And they brought one. And he said to them, "Whose likeness and inscription is this?" They said to him, "Caesar's." [17] Jesus said to them, "Render to Caesar the things that are Caesar's, and to God the things that are God's." And they marveled at him.

The Sadducees Ask About the Resurrection

[18] And Sadducees came to him, who say that there is no resurrection. And they asked him a question, saying, [19] "Teacher, Moses wrote for us that if a man's brother dies and leaves a wife, but leaves no child, the man[4] must take the widow and raise up offspring for his brother. [20] There were seven brothers; the first took a wife, and when he died left no offspring. [21] And the second took her, and died, leaving no offspring. And the third likewise. [22] And the seven left no offspring. Last of all the woman also died. [23] In the resurrection, when they rise again, whose wife will she be? For the seven had her as wife."

[24] Jesus said to them, "Is this not the reason you are wrong, because you know neither the Scriptures nor the power of God? [25] For when they rise from the dead, they neither marry nor are given in marriage, but are like angels in heaven. [26] And as for the dead being raised, have you not read in the book of Moses, in the passage about the bush, how God spoke to him, saying, [c] 'I am the God of Abraham, and the God of Isaac, and the God of Jacob'? [27] He is not God of the dead, but of the living. You are quite wrong."

The Great Commandment

[28] [d] And one of the scribes came up and heard them disputing with one another, and seeing that he answered them well, asked him, "Which commandment is the most important of all?" [29] Jesus answered, "The most important is, [e] 'Hear, O Israel: The Lord our God, the Lord is one. [30] And you shall love the Lord your God with all your heart and with all your soul and with all your mind and with all your strength.' [31] The second is this: [f] 'You shall love your neighbor as yourself.' There is no other commandment greater than these." [32] And the scribe said to him, "You are right, Teacher. You have truly said that he is one, and there is no other besides him. [33] And to love him with all the heart and with all the understanding and with all the strength, and to love one's neighbor as oneself, is much more than all whole burnt offerings and sacrifices." [34] And when Jesus saw that he answered wisely, he said to him, "You are not far from the kingdom of God." And after that no one dared to ask him any more questions.

Whose Son Is the Christ?

[35] [g] And as Jesus taught in the temple, he said, "How can the scribes say that the

---

[1] Greek *the head of the corner* [2] Greek *you do not look at people's faces* [3] A *denarius* was a day's wage for a laborer [4] Greek *his brother*
[a] Ps. 118:22, 23 [b] For 12:13-27 see parallels Matt. 22:15-32; Luke 20:20-38 [c] Ex. 3:6 [d] For 12:28-34 see parallel Matt. 22:34-40, 46 [e] Deut. 6:4, 5 [f] Lev. 19:18 [g] For 12:35-37 see parallels Matt. 22:41-45; Luke 20:41-44

Christ is the son of David? [36]David himself, in the Holy Spirit, declared,

> [a]"'The Lord said to my Lord,
>   "Sit at my right hand,
>   until I put your enemies under
>   your feet."'

[37]David himself calls him Lord. So how is he his son?" And the great throng heard him gladly.

Beware of the Scribes

[38][b]And in his teaching he said, "Beware of the scribes, who like to walk around in long robes and like greetings in the marketplaces [39]and have the best seats in the synagogues and the places of honor at feasts, [40]who devour widows' houses and for a pretense make long prayers. They will receive the greater condemnation."

The Widow's Offering

[41][c]And he sat down opposite the treasury and watched the people putting money into the offering box. Many rich people put in large sums. [42]And a poor widow came and put in two small copper coins, which make a penny.[1] [43]And he called his disciples to him and said to them, "Truly, I say to you, this poor widow has put in more than all those who are contributing to the offering box. [44]For they all contributed out of their abundance, but she out of her poverty has put in everything she had, all she had to live on."

Jesus Foretells Destruction of the Temple

13 [d]And as he came out of the temple, one of his disciples said to him, "Look, Teacher, what wonderful stones and what wonderful buildings!" [2]And Jesus said to him, "Do you see these great buildings? There will not be left here one stone upon another that will not be thrown down."

Signs of the Close of the Age

[3]And as he sat on the Mount of Olives opposite the temple, Peter and James and John and Andrew asked him privately, [4]"Tell us, when will these things be, and what will be the sign when all these things are about to be accomplished?" [5]And Jesus began to say to them, "See that no one leads you astray. [6]Many will come in my name, saying, 'I am he!' and they will lead many astray. [7]And when you hear of wars and rumors of wars, do not be alarmed. This must take place, but the end is not yet. [8]For nation will rise against nation and kingdom against kingdom. There will be earthquakes in various places; there will be famines. These are but the beginning of the birth pains.

[9]"But be on your guard. For they will deliver you over to councils, and you will be beaten in synagogues, and you will stand before governors and kings for my sake, to bear witness before them. [10]And the gospel must first be proclaimed to all nations. [11]And when they bring you to trial and deliver you over, do not be anxious beforehand what you are to say, but say whatever is given you in that hour, for it is not you who speak, but the Holy Spirit. [12]And brother will deliver brother over to death, and the father his child, and children will rise against parents and have them put to death. [13]And you will be hated by all for my name's sake. But the one who endures to the end will be saved.

The Abomination of Desolation

[14]"But when you see the abomination of desolation standing where he ought not to be (let the reader understand), then let those who are in Judea flee to the mountains. [15]Let the one who is on the housetop not go down, nor enter his house, to take anything out, [16]and let the one who is in the field not turn back to take his cloak. [17]And alas for women who are pregnant and for those who are nursing infants in those days! [18]Pray that it may not happen in winter. [19]For in those days there will be such tribulation as has not been from the beginning of the creation that God created until now, and never will be. [20]And if the Lord had not cut short the days, no human being would be saved. But for the sake of the elect, whom he chose, he shortened the days. [21]And then if anyone says to you, 'Look, here is the Christ!' or 'Look, there he is!' do not believe it. [22]For false christs and false prophets will arise and perform signs and wonders, to lead astray, if possible, the elect. [23]But be on guard; I have told you all things beforehand.

---

[1]Greek two lepta, which make a kodrantes; a kodrantes (Latin quadrans) was a Roman copper coin worth about 1/64 of a denarius (which was a day's wage for a laborer) [a]Ps. 110:1 [b]For 12:38-40 see parallels Matt. 23:1, 2, 5-7; Luke 20:45, 46 [c]For 12:41-44 see parallel Luke 21:1-4 [d]For 13:1-37 see parallels Matt. 24:1-51; Luke 21:5-36

The Coming of the Son of Man

²⁴ "But in those days, after that tribulation, the sun will be darkened, and the moon will not give its light, ²⁵ and the stars will be falling from heaven, and the powers in the heavens will be shaken. ²⁶ And then they will see the Son of Man coming in clouds with great power and glory. ²⁷ And then he will send out the angels and gather his elect from the four winds, from the ends of the earth to the ends of heaven.

The Lesson of the Fig Tree

²⁸ "From the fig tree learn its lesson: as soon as its branch becomes tender and puts out its leaves, you know that summer is near. ²⁹ So also, when you see these things taking place, you know that he is near, at the very gates. ³⁰ Truly, I say to you, this generation will not pass away until all these things take place. ³¹ Heaven and earth will pass away, but my words will not pass away.

No One Knows That Day or Hour

³² "But concerning that day or that hour, no one knows, not even the angels in heaven, nor the Son, but only the Father. ³³ Be on guard, keep awake.¹ For you do not know when the time will come. ³⁴ It is like a man going on a journey, when he leaves home and puts his servants² in charge, each with his work, and commands the doorkeeper to stay awake. ³⁵ Therefore stay awake—for you do not know when the master of the house will come, in the evening, or at midnight, or when the rooster crows,³ or in the morning— ³⁶ lest he come suddenly and find you asleep. ³⁷ And what I say to you I say to all: Stay awake."

The Plot to Kill Jesus

14 ᵃ It was now two days before the Passover and the Feast of Unleavened Bread. And the chief priests and the scribes were seeking how to arrest him by stealth and kill him, ² for they said, "Not during the feast, lest there be an uproar from the people."

Jesus Anointed at Bethany

³ ᵇ And while he was at Bethany in the house of Simon the leper,⁴ as he was reclining at table, a woman came with an alabaster flask of ointment of pure nard, very costly, and she broke the flask and poured it over his head. ⁴ There were some who said to themselves indignantly, "Why was the ointment wasted like that? ⁵ For this ointment could have been sold for more than three hundred denarii⁵ and given to the poor." And they scolded her. ⁶ But Jesus said, "Leave her alone. Why do you trouble her? She has done a beautiful thing to me. ⁷ For you always have the poor with you, and whenever you want, you can do good for them. But you will not always have me. ⁸ She has done what she could; she has anointed my body beforehand for burial. ⁹ And truly, I say to you, wherever the gospel is proclaimed in the whole world, what she has done will be told in memory of her."

Judas to Betray Jesus

¹⁰ ᶜ Then Judas Iscariot, who was one of the twelve, went to the chief priests in order to betray him to them. ¹¹ And when they heard it, they were glad and promised to give him money. And he sought an opportunity to betray him.

The Passover with the Disciples

¹² ᵈ And on the first day of Unleavened Bread, when they sacrificed the Passover lamb, his disciples said to him, "Where will you have us go and prepare for you to eat the Passover?" ¹³ And he sent two of his disciples and said to them, "Go into the city, and a man carrying a jar of water will meet you. Follow him, ¹⁴ and wherever he enters, say to the master of the house, 'The Teacher says, Where is my guest room, where I may eat the Passover with my disciples?' ¹⁵ And he will show you a large upper room furnished and ready; there prepare for us." ¹⁶ And the disciples set out and went to the city and found it just as he had told them, and they prepared the Passover.

¹⁷ ᵉ And when it was evening, he came with the twelve. ¹⁸ And as they were reclining at table and eating, Jesus said, "Truly, I say to you, one of you will betray me, one who is eating with me." ¹⁹ They began to be sorrowful and to say to him one after another, "Is it I?" ²⁰ He said to them, "It is one of the twelve, one who is dipping bread

¹ Some manuscripts add *and pray* ² Greek *bondservants* ³ That is, the third watch of the night, between midnight and 3 A.M. ⁴ *Leprosy* was a term for several skin diseases; see Leviticus 13 ⁵ A *denarius* was a day's wage for a laborer ᵃ For 14:1, 2 see parallels Matt. 26:2-5; Luke 22:1, 2 ᵇ For 14:3-9 see parallels Matt. 26:6-13; John 12:1-8 ᶜ For 14:10, 11 see parallels Matt. 26:14-16; Luke 22:3-6 ᵈ For 14:12-16 see parallels Matt. 26:17-19; Luke 22:7-13 ᵉ For 14:17-21 see parallel Matt. 26:20-24

into the dish with me. ²¹ For the Son of Man goes as it is written of him, but woe to that man by whom the Son of Man is betrayed! It would have been better for that man if he had not been born."

Institution of the Lord's Supper

²² ᵃ And as they were eating, he took bread, and after blessing it broke it and gave it to them, and said, "Take; this is my body." ²³ And he took a cup, and when he had given thanks he gave it to them, and they all drank of it. ²⁴ And he said to them, "This is my blood of the¹ covenant, which is poured out for many. ²⁵ Truly, I say to you, I will not drink again of the fruit of the vine until that day when I drink it new in the kingdom of God."

Jesus Foretells Peter's Denial

²⁶ ᵇ And when they had sung a hymn, they went out to the Mount of Olives. ²⁷ And Jesus said to them, "You will all fall away, for it is written, 'I will ᶜ strike the shepherd, and the sheep will be scattered.' ²⁸ But after I am raised up, I will go before you to Galilee." ²⁹ Peter said to him, "Even though they all fall away, I will not." ³⁰ And Jesus said to him, "Truly, I tell you, this very night, before the rooster crows twice, you will deny me three times." ³¹ But he said emphatically, "If I must die with you, I will not deny you." And they all said the same.

Jesus Prays in Gethsemane

³² ᵈ And they went to a place called Gethsemane. And he said to his disciples, "Sit here while I pray." ³³ And he took with him Peter and James and John, and began to be greatly distressed and troubled. ³⁴ And he said to them, "My soul is very sorrowful, even to death. Remain here and watch."² ³⁵ And going a little farther, he fell on the ground and prayed that, if it were possible, the hour might pass from him. ³⁶ And he said, "Abba, Father, all things are possible

¹ Some manuscripts insert *new* ² Or *keep awake*; also verses 37, 38 ᵃ For 14:22-25 see parallels Matt. 26:26-29; Luke 22:18-20 ᵇ For 14:26-31 see parallel Matt. 26:30-35 ᶜ Zech. 13:7 ᵈ For 14:32-42 see parallels Matt. 26:36-46; Luke 22:39-46

Know True Happiness

verses to read
Mark 14:32-42

Nothing is wrong with asking God to take your suffering from you and give you peace. But in the same breath you have to let him know that, if he doesn't do what you ask, you still want whatever he wants. That's a hard statement to make, but that's what you say whenever you pray, as Jesus did, "your will be done" (Matt. 6:10).

God has a reason for everything he allows in your life, even the suffering part. That's why we are commanded to rejoice when we suffer (see James 1:2). Jesus knew what kind of suffering he would soon have to endure, and it overwhelmed him to the point of sweating blood (see Luke 22:44). Nothing has been that hard for you, ever! But let Jesus be your example, knowing that even if your suffering is almost unbearable, you can trust God's will for you in that suffering. Most importantly, don't just let Jesus be your example of suffering well but remember that, because Jesus suffered the greatest punishment possible—condemnation from the Father—you will never have to.

Suffering isn't your enemy or the worst thing that could ever happen to you. In fact, you can suffer and be happy at the same time! If you don't believe this, just take a look at what God says in 1 Peter 1:6. Suffering isn't something that has to trample you like a wild horse. Instead, it is something that you can climb on top of and ride to freedom. Suffering doesn't have to overwhelm you. Instead, it can help you grow and make you a whole lot better.

or you. Remove this cup from me. Yet not what I will, but what you will." [37] And he came and found them sleeping, and he said to Peter, "Simon, are you asleep? Could you not watch one hour? [38] Watch and pray that you may not enter into temptation. The spirit indeed is willing, but the flesh is weak." [39] And again he went away and prayed, saying the same words. [40] And again he came and found them sleeping, for their eyes were very heavy, and they did not know what to answer him. [41] And he came the third time and said to them, "Are you still sleeping and taking your rest? It is enough; the hour has come. The Son of Man is betrayed into the hands of sinners. [42] Rise, let us be going; see, my betrayer is at hand."

Betrayal and Arrest of Jesus

[43] [a]And immediately, while he was still speaking, Judas came, one of the twelve, and with him a crowd with swords and clubs, from the chief priests and the scribes and the elders. [44] Now the betrayer had given them a sign, saying, "The one I will kiss is the man. Seize him and lead him away under guard." [45] And when he came, he went up to him at once and said, "Rabbi!" And he kissed him. [46] And they laid hands on him and seized him. [47] But one of those who stood by drew his sword and struck the servant[1] of the high priest and cut off his ear. [48] And Jesus said to them, "Have you come out as against a robber, with swords and clubs to capture me? [49] Day after day I was with you in the temple teaching, and you did not seize me. But let the Scriptures be fulfilled." [50] And they all left him and fled.

A Young Man Flees

[51] And a young man followed him, with nothing but a linen cloth about his body. And they seized him, [52] but he left the linen cloth and ran away naked.

Jesus Before the Council

[53] [b]And they led Jesus to the high priest. And all the chief priests and the elders and the scribes came together. [54] And Peter had followed him at a distance, right into the courtyard of the high priest. And he was sitting with the guards and warming him-self at the fire. [55] Now the chief priests and the whole council[2] were seeking testimony against Jesus to put him to death, but they found none. [56] For many bore false witness against him, but their testimony did not agree. [57] And some stood up and bore false witness against him, saying, [58] "We heard him say, 'I will destroy this temple that is made with hands, and in three days I will build another, not made with hands.'" [59] Yet even about this their testimony did not agree. [60] And the high priest stood up in the midst and asked Jesus, "Have you no answer to make? What is it that these men testify against you?"[3] [61] But he remained silent and made no answer. Again the high priest asked him, "Are you the Christ, the Son of the Blessed?" [62] And Jesus said, "I am, and you will see the Son of Man seated at the right hand of Power, and coming with the clouds of heaven." [63] And the high priest tore his garments and said, "What further witnesses do we need? [64] You have heard his blasphemy. What is your decision?" And they all condemned him as deserving death. [65] And some began to spit on him and to cover his face and to strike him, saying to him, "Prophesy!" And the guards received him with blows.

Peter Denies Jesus

[66] [c]And as Peter was below in the court-yard, one of the servant girls of the high priest came, [67] and seeing Peter warming himself, she looked at him and said, "You also were with the Nazarene, Jesus." [68] But he denied it, saying, "I neither know nor understand what you mean." And he went out into the gateway[4] and the rooster crowed.[5] [69] And the servant girl saw him and began again to say to the bystanders, "This man is one of them." [70] But again he denied it. And after a little while the bystanders again said to Peter, "Certainly you are one of them, for you are a Galilean." [71] But he began to invoke a curse on himself and to swear, "I do not know this man of whom you speak." [72] And immediately the rooster crowed a second time. And Peter remembered how Jesus had said to him, "Before the rooster crows twice, you will deny me three times." And he broke down and wept.[6]

---

[1] Greek bondservant [2] Greek Sanhedrin [3] Or Have you no answer to what these men testify against you? [4] Or forecourt [5] Some manuscripts omit and the rooster crowed [6] Or And when he had thought about it, he wept [a] For 14:43-50 see parallels Matt. 26:47-56; Luke 22:47-53; John 18:3-11 [b] For 14:53-65 see parallel Matt. 26:57-68 [c] For 14:66-72 see parallels Matt. 26:69-75; Luke 22:55-62; John 18:16-18, 25-27

Jesus Delivered to Pilate

15 And as soon as it was morning, the chief priests held a consultation with the elders and scribes and the whole council. And they bound Jesus and led him away and delivered him over to Pilate. [2] [a]And Pilate asked him, "Are you the King of the Jews?" And he answered him, "You have said so." [3] And the chief priests accused him of many things. [4] And Pilate again asked him, "Have you no answer to make? See how many charges they bring against you." [5] But Jesus made no further answer, so that Pilate was amazed.

Pilate Delivers Jesus to Be Crucified

[6] [b]Now at the feast he used to release for them one prisoner for whom they asked. [7] And among the rebels in prison, who had committed murder in the insurrection, there was a man called Barabbas. [8] And the crowd came up and began to ask Pilate to do as he usually did for them. [9] And he answered them, saying, "Do you want me to release for you the King of the Jews?" [10] For he perceived that it was out of envy that the chief priests had delivered him up. [11] But the chief priests stirred up the crowd to have him release for them Barabbas instead. [12] And Pilate again said to them, "Then what shall I do with the man you call the King of the Jews?" [13] And they cried out again, "Crucify him." [14] And Pilate said to them, "Why, what evil has he done?" But they shouted all the more, "Crucify him." [15] So Pilate, wishing to satisfy the crowd, released for them Barabbas, and having scourged[1] Jesus, he delivered him to be crucified.

Jesus Is Mocked

[16] [c]And the soldiers led him away inside the palace (that is, the governor's headquarters),[2] and they called together the whole battalion.[3] [17] And they clothed him in a purple cloak, and twisting together a crown of thorns, they put it on him. [18] And they began to salute him, "Hail, King of the Jews!" [19] And they were striking his head with a reed and spitting on him and kneeling down in homage to him. [20] And when they had mocked him, they stripped him of the purple cloak and put his own clothes on him. And they led him out to crucify him.

The Crucifixion

[21] And they compelled a passerby, Simon of Cyrene, who was coming in from the country, the father of Alexander and Rufus, to carry his cross. [22] [d]And they brought him to the place called Golgotha (which means Place of a Skull). [23] And they offered him wine mixed with myrrh, but he did not take it. [24] And they crucified him and divided his garments among them, casting lots for them, to decide what each should take. [25] And it was the third hour[4] when they crucified him. [26] And the inscription of the charge against him read, "The King of the Jews." [27] And with him they crucified two robbers, one on his right and one on his left.[5] [29] And those who passed by derided him, wagging their heads and saying, "Aha! You who would destroy the temple and rebuild it in three days, [30] save yourself, and come down from the cross!" [31] So also the chief priests with the scribes mocked him to one another, saying, "He saved others; he cannot save himself. [32] Let the Christ, the King of Israel, come down now from the cross that we may see and believe." Those who were crucified with him also reviled him.

The Death of Jesus

[33] And when the sixth hour[6] had come, there was darkness over the whole land until the ninth hour.[7] [34] And at the ninth hour Jesus cried with a loud voice, [e]"Eloi, Eloi, lema sabachthani?" which means, "My God, my God, why have you forsaken me?" [35] And some of the bystanders hearing it said, "Behold, he is calling Elijah." [36] And someone ran and filled a sponge with sour wine, put it on a reed and gave it to him to drink, saying, "Wait, let us see whether Elijah will come to take him down." [37] And Jesus uttered a loud cry and breathed his last. [38] And the curtain of the temple was torn in two, from top to bottom. [39] [f]And when the centurion, who stood facing him

---

[1] A Roman judicial penalty, consisting of a severe beating with a multi-lashed whip containing imbedded pieces of bone and metal [2] Greek *the praetorium* [3] Greek *cohort*; a tenth of a Roman legion, usually about 600 men [4] That is, 9 A.M. [5] Some manuscripts insert verse 28: *And the Scripture was fulfilled that says, "He was numbered with the transgressors"* [6] That is, noon [7] That is, 3 P.M. [a] For 15:2-5 see parallels Matt. 27:11-14; Luke 23:1-3; John 18:28-38 [b] For 15:6-15 see parallels Matt. 27:15-26; Luke 23:18-25; John 18:39, 40; 19:16 [c] For 15:16-20 see parallels Matt. 27:27-31; John 19:2, 3 [d] For 15:22-38 see parallels Matt. 27:33-51; Luke 23:32-38, 44-46; John 19:17-19, 23, 24, 28-30 [e] Ps. 22:1 [f] For 15:39-41 see parallels Matt. 27:54-56; Luke 23:47, 49

aw that in this way he[1] breathed his last, he aid, "Truly this man was the Son[2] of God!"

[40] There were also women looking on rom a distance, among whom were Mary Magdalene, and Mary the mother of James he younger and of Joses, and Salome. [41] When he was in Galilee, they followed him and ministered to him, and there were also many other women who came up with him to Jerusalem.

Jesus Is Buried

[42] [a] And when evening had come, since it was the day of Preparation, that is, the day before the Sabbath, [43] Joseph of Arimathea, a respected member of the council, who was also himself looking for the kingdom of God, took courage and went to Pilate and asked for the body of Jesus. [44] Pilate was surprised to hear that he should have already died.[3] And summoning the centurion, he asked him whether he was already dead. [45] And when he learned from the centurion that he was dead, he granted the corpse to Joseph. [46] And Joseph[4] bought a linen shroud, and taking him down, wrapped him in the linen shroud and laid him in a tomb that had been cut out of the rock. And he rolled a stone against the entrance of the tomb. [47] Mary Magdalene and Mary the mother of Joses saw where he was laid.

The Resurrection

16 [b] When the Sabbath was past, Mary Magdalene, Mary the mother of James, and Salome bought spices, so that they might go and anoint him. [2] And very early on the first day of the week, when the sun had risen, they went to the tomb. [3] And they were saying to one another, "Who will roll away the stone for us from the entrance of the tomb?" [4] And looking up, they saw that the stone had been rolled back—it was very large. [5] And entering the tomb, they saw a young man sitting on the right side, dressed in a white robe, and they were alarmed. [6] And he said to them, "Do not be alarmed. You seek Jesus of Nazareth, who was crucified. He has risen; he is not here. See the place where they laid him. [7] But go, tell his disciples and

Peter that he is going before you to Galilee. There you will see him, just as he told you." [8] And they went out and fled from the tomb, for trembling and astonishment had seized them, and they said nothing to anyone, for they were afraid.

[SOME OF THE EARLIEST MANUSCRIPTS DO NOT INCLUDE 16:9–20.][5]

Jesus Appears to Mary Magdalene

[9] [[Now when he rose early on the first day of the week, he appeared first to Mary Magdalene, from whom he had cast out seven demons. [10] She went and told those who had been with him, as they mourned and wept. [11] But when they heard that he was alive and had been seen by her, they would not believe it.

Jesus Appears to Two Disciples

[12] After these things he appeared in another form to two of them, as they were walking into the country. [13] And they went back and told the rest, but they did not believe them.

The Great Commission

[14] Afterward he appeared to the eleven themselves as they were reclining at table, and he rebuked them for their unbelief and hardness of heart, because they had not believed those who saw him after he had risen. [15] And he said to them, "Go into all the world and proclaim the gospel to the whole creation. [16] Whoever believes and is baptized will be saved, but whoever does not believe will be condemned. [17] And these signs will accompany those who believe: in my name they will cast out demons; they will speak in new tongues; [18] they will pick up serpents with their hands; and if they drink any deadly poison, it will not hurt them; they will lay their hands on the sick, and they will recover."

[19] So then the Lord Jesus, after he had spoken to them, was taken up into heaven and sat down at the right hand of God. [20] And they went out and preached everywhere, while the Lord worked with them and confirmed the message by accompanying signs.]]

---

[1] Some manuscripts insert *cried out and* [2] Or *a son* [3] Or *Pilate wondered whether he had already died* [4] Greek *he* [5] Some manuscripts end the book with 16:8; others include verses 9–20 immediately after verse 8. At least one manuscript inserts additional material after verse 14; some manuscripts include after verse 8 the following: *But they reported briefly to Peter and those with him all that they had been told. And after this, Jesus himself sent out by means of them, from east to west, the sacred and imperishable proclamation of eternal salvation.* These manuscripts then continue with verses 9–20 [a] For 15:42-47 see parallels Matt. 27:57-61; Luke 23:50-56; John 19:38-42
For 16:1-8 see parallels Matt. 28:1-8; Luke 24:1-10; John 20:1

INTRODUCTION TO

Luke

Author: Luke, a Gentile doctor and a traveling companion of Paul.

Time: Between A.D. 62 and 80

Place: Unknown, possibly in Caesarea, Rome, or even Achaia (in Greece)

Written to: Theophilus (see Luke 1:3–4) and Gentile believers

The gist

Luke wanted to help Theophilus and his other readers know that God's plan of salvation had been fulfilled in Jesus and that the gospel was available to all kinds of people, especially those who were considered outsiders.

Things to look for

• Many mentions of forgiveness (see Luke 3:3; 5:18–26; 6:37; and many others)

• Repeated use of the words *save* or *salvation* (see Luke 1:69, 71, 77; 2:30; 3:6; 19:9)

• Luke's emphasis on prayer

• Luke's repetition of the concepts of happiness and joy

Love Your Enemies

> Love your enemies, do good to those who hate you, bless those who curse you, pray for those who abuse you.
>
> Luke 6:27–28

The Mosaic law includes this oldie but goodie: "an eye for an eye, a tooth for a tooth" (see Ex. 21:24). Getting even and standing up for yourself by giving as good as you got were allowed in the Old Testament days. As long as you didn't repay a wrong with a bigger wrong, you were okay. But then along came Christ with a radical message that turned this way of thinking on its head. He started telling people to love their enemies and even to be kind to those who hated them. What a shocking message! Imagine a world where everyone acted this way, where everyone loved other people as much as themselves. Heaven, maybe? But in the reality of earth, Jesus' teachings seem to make no sense; in fact, they sound downright insane. What about self-protection, defending your rights, and the all-important issue of fairness?

A lot of things the world says are important might make sense to you. Like Martha, you might worry about getting everything done (see Luke 10:38–42). Your eyes might be on the present problem and not the eternal God. But as a God Girl you can't allow the urgent to come before the essential. The essential of your faith, as taught by Jesus himself, is "Love the Lord your God with all your heart and with all your soul and with all your strength and with all your mind." And "Love . . . your neighbor as yourself" (Luke 10:27). You can't hate your enemies and obey Jesus. Not gonna happen. Nope, the answer is love.

As you read Luke's Gospel account of the life of Jesus, look at how Jesus loved his enemies, but don't confuse that with how he rejected *God's* enemies. And as you read Jesus' words, think about what a shock to the system his renegade message would have been to his listeners—and in fact, what a shock it is even today.

Must-Know Verses

"Love your enemies, do good to those who hate you, bless those who curse you, pray for those who abuse you." *Luke 6:27–28*

"If you love those who love you, what benefit is that to you? For even sinners love those who love them." *Luke 6:32*

"The harvest is plentiful, but the laborers are few. Therefore pray earnestly to the Lord of the harvest to send out laborers into his harvest. Go your way; behold, I am sending you out as lambs in the midst of wolves." *Luke 10:2–3*

"You shall love the Lord your God with all your heart and with all your soul and with all your strength and with all your mind, and your neighbor as yourself." *Luke 10:27*

"Martha, Martha, you are anxious and troubled about many things, but one thing is necessary. Mary has chosen the good portion, which will not be taken away from her." *Luke 10:41–42*

"Therefore I tell you, do not be anxious about your life, what you will eat, nor about your body, what you will put on. For life is more than food, and the body more than clothing. Consider the ravens: they neither sow nor reap, they have neither storehouse nor barn, and yet God feeds them. Of how much more value are you than the birds!" *Luke 12:22–24*

"The Son of Man came to seek and to save the lost." *Luke 19:10*

The Gospel According to

Luke

Dedication to Theophilus

1 Inasmuch as many have undertaken to compile a narrative of the things that have been accomplished among us, ²just as those who from the beginning were eyewitnesses and ministers of the word have delivered them to us, ³it seemed good to me also, having followed all things closely for some time past, to write an orderly account for you, most excellent Theophilus, ⁴that you may have certainty concerning the things you have been taught.

Birth of John the Baptist Foretold

⁵ In the days of Herod, king of Judea, there was a priest named Zechariah,¹ of the division of Abijah. And he had a wife from the daughters of Aaron, and her name was Elizabeth. ⁶And they were both righteous before God, walking blamelessly in all the commandments and statutes of the Lord. ⁷But they had no child, because Elizabeth was barren, and both were advanced in years.

⁸Now while he was serving as priest before God when his division was on duty, ⁹according to the custom of the priesthood, he was chosen by lot to enter the temple of the Lord and burn incense. ¹⁰And the whole multitude of the people were praying outside at the hour of incense. ¹¹And there appeared to him an angel of the Lord standing on the right side of the altar of incense. ¹²And Zechariah was troubled when he saw him, and fear fell upon him. ¹³But the angel said to him, "Do not be afraid, Zechariah, for your prayer has been heard, and your wife Elizabeth will bear you a son, and you shall call his name John. ¹⁴And you will have joy and gladness, and many will rejoice at his birth, ¹⁵for he will be great before the Lord. And he must not drink wine or strong drink, and he will be filled with the Holy Spirit, even from his mother's womb. ¹⁶And he will turn many of the children of Israel to the Lord their God, ¹⁷and he will go before him in the spirit and power of Elijah, to turn the hearts of the fathers to the children, and the disobedient to the wisdom of the just, to make ready for the Lord a people prepared."

¹⁸And Zechariah said to the angel, "How shall I know this? For I am an old man, and my wife is advanced in years." ¹⁹And the angel answered him, "I am Gabriel. I stand in the presence of God, and I was sent to speak to you and to bring you this good news. ²⁰And behold, you will be silent and unable to speak until the day that these things take place, because you did not believe my words, which will be fulfilled in their time." ²¹And the people were waiting for Zechariah, and they were wondering at his delay in the temple. ²²And when he came out, he was unable to speak to them, and they realized that he had seen a vision in the temple. And he kept making signs to them and remained mute. ²³And when his time of service was ended, he went to his home.

²⁴After these days his wife Elizabeth conceived, and for five months she kept herself hidden, saying, ²⁵"Thus the Lord has done for me in the days when he looked on me, to take away my reproach among people."

Birth of Jesus Foretold

²⁶ In the sixth month the angel Gabriel was sent from God to a city of Galilee named Nazareth, ²⁷to a virgin betrothed² to a man whose name was Joseph, of the house of David. And the virgin's name was Mary. ²⁸And he came to her and said, "Greetings, O favored one, the Lord is with you!"³ ²⁹But she was greatly troubled at the saying, and tried to discern what sort of greeting this might be. ³⁰And the angel said to her, "Do not be afraid, Mary, for you have found favor with God. ³¹And behold, you will conceive in your womb and bear a son, and you shall call his name Jesus. ³²He will

---

¹Greek *Zacharias* ²That is, legally pledged to be married ³Some manuscripts add *Blessed are you among women!*

be great and will be called the Son of the Most High. And the Lord God will give to him the throne of his father David, [33] and he will reign over the house of Jacob forever, and of his kingdom there will be no end."

[34] And Mary said to the angel, "How will this be, since I am a virgin?"[1]

[35] And the angel answered her, "The Holy Spirit will come upon you, and the power of the Most High will overshadow you; therefore the child to be born[2] will be called holy— the Son of God. [36] And behold, your relative Elizabeth in her old age has also conceived a son, and this is the sixth month with her who was called barren. [37] For nothing will be impossible with God." [38] And Mary said, "Behold, I am the servant[3] of the Lord; let it be to me according to your word." And the angel departed from her.

Mary Visits Elizabeth

[39] In those days Mary arose and went with haste into the hill country, to a town in Judah, [40] and she entered the house of Zechariah and greeted Elizabeth. [41] And when Elizabeth heard the greeting of Mary, the baby leaped in her womb. And Elizabeth was filled with the Holy Spirit, [42] and she exclaimed with a loud cry, "Blessed are you among women, and blessed is the fruit of your womb! [43] And why is this granted to me that the mother of my Lord should come to me? [44] For behold, when the sound of your greeting came to my ears, the baby in my womb leaped for joy. [45] And blessed is she who believed that there would be[4] a fulfillment of what was spoken to her from the Lord."

Mary's Song of Praise: The Magnificat

[46] And Mary said,

"My soul magnifies the Lord,
[47]   and my spirit rejoices in God my
          Savior,
[48]   for he has looked on the humble
          estate of his servant.
     For behold, from now on all gen-
          erations will call me blessed;
[49]   for he who is mighty has done great
          things for me,
          and holy is his name.
[50]   And his mercy is for those who fear
          him
          from generation to generation.

[51] He has shown strength with his arm;
          he has scattered the proud in the
               thoughts of their hearts;
[52]   he has brought down the mighty
               from their thrones
          and exalted those of humble
               estate;
[53]   he has filled the hungry with good
               things,
          and the rich he has sent away
               empty.
[54] He has helped his servant Israel,
          in remembrance of his mercy,
[55]   as he spoke to our fathers,
          to Abraham and to his offspring
               forever."

[56] And Mary remained with her about three months and returned to her home.

The Birth of John the Baptist

[57] Now the time came for Elizabeth to give birth, and she bore a son. [58] And her neighbors and relatives heard that the Lord had shown great mercy to her, and they rejoiced with her. [59] And on the eighth day they came to circumcise the child. And they would have called him Zechariah after his father, [60] but his mother answered, "No; he shall be called John." [61] And they said to her, "None of your relatives is called by this name." [62] And they made signs to his father, inquiring what he wanted him to be called. [63] And he asked for a writing tablet and wrote, "His name is John." And they all wondered. [64] And immediately his mouth was opened and his tongue loosed, and he spoke, blessing God. [65] And fear came on all their neighbors. And all these things were talked about through all the hill country of Judea, [66] and all who heard them laid them up in their hearts, saying, "What then will this child be?" For the hand of the Lord was with him.

Zechariah's Prophecy

[67] And his father Zechariah was filled with the Holy Spirit and prophesied, saying,

[68] "Blessed be the Lord God of Israel,
          for he has visited and redeemed
               his people
[69]   and has raised up a horn of salvation
               for us
          in the house of his servant David,

---

[1] Greek since I do not know a man [2] Some manuscripts add of you [3] Greek bondservant; also verse 48 [4] Or believed, for there will be

70 as he spoke by the mouth of his holy
      prophets from of old,
71 that we should be saved from our
      enemies
      and from the hand of all who hate
          us;
72 to show the mercy promised to our
      fathers
      and to remember his holy cov-
          enant,
73 the oath that he swore to our father
      Abraham, to grant us
74   that we, being delivered from the
          hand of our enemies,
      might serve him without fear,
75   in holiness and righteousness
          before him all our days.
76 And you, child, will be called the
      prophet of the Most High;
      for you will go before the Lord to
          prepare his ways,
77 to give knowledge of salvation to his
      people
      in the forgiveness of their sins,
78 because of the tender mercy of our
      God,
      whereby the sunrise shall visit us[1]
          from on high
79 to give light to those who sit in
      darkness and in the shadow of
          death,
      to guide our feet into the way of
          peace."

80 And the child grew and became strong in
spirit, and he was in the wilderness until
the day of his public appearance to Israel.

The Birth of Jesus Christ

2 In those days a decree went out from
Caesar Augustus that all the world
should be registered. ²This was the first
registration when[2] Quirinius was governor
of Syria. ³And all went to be registered,
each to his own town. ⁴And Joseph also
went up from Galilee, from the town of
Nazareth, to Judea, to the city of David,
which is called Bethlehem, because he was
of the house and lineage of David, ⁵to be
registered with Mary, his betrothed,[3] who
was with child. ⁶And while they were there,
the time came for her to give birth. ⁷And
she gave birth to her firstborn son and
wrapped him in swaddling cloths and laid
him in a manger, because there was no
place for them in the inn.

The Shepherds and the Angels

⁸And in the same region there were
shepherds out in the field, keeping watch
over their flock by night. ⁹And an angel of
the Lord appeared to them, and the glory
of the Lord shone around them, and they
were filled with great fear. ¹⁰And the angel
said to them, "Fear not, for behold, I bring
you good news of great joy that will be for
all the people. ¹¹For unto you is born this
day in the city of David a Savior, who is
Christ the Lord. ¹²And this will be a sign
for you: you will find a baby wrapped in
swaddling cloths and lying in a manger."
¹³And suddenly there was with the angel
a multitude of the heavenly host praising
God and saying,

14   "Glory to God in the highest,
          and on earth peace among those
              with whom he is pleased!"[4]

¹⁵When the angels went away from them
into heaven, the shepherds said to one
another, "Let us go over to Bethlehem and
see this thing that has happened, which
the Lord has made known to us." ¹⁶And
they went with haste and found Mary and
Joseph, and the baby lying in a manger.
¹⁷And when they saw it, they made known
the saying that had been told them concerning this child. ¹⁸And all who heard
it wondered at what the shepherds told
them. ¹⁹But Mary treasured up all these
things, pondering them in her heart.
²⁰And the shepherds returned, glorifying
and praising God for all they had heard and
seen, as it had been told them.

²¹And at the end of eight days, when he
was circumcised, he was called Jesus, the
name given by the angel before he was
conceived in the womb.

Jesus Presented at the Temple

²²And when the time came for their
purification according to the Law of
Moses, they brought him up to Jerusalem
to present him to the Lord ²³(as it is written in the Law of the Lord, [a]"Every male
who first opens the womb shall be called
holy to the Lord") ²⁴and to offer a sacrifice
according to what is said in the Law of

---

[1] Or when the sunrise shall dawn upon us; some manuscripts since the sunrise has visited us [2] Or This was the registration before [3] That is, one legally pledged to be married [4] Some manuscripts peace, good will among men [a] Ex. 13:2, 12

Elizabeth

Read this God Girl story in Luke 1:5–25, 36–45,
and 57–63.

> And they were both righteous before God, walking blamelessly
> in all the commandments and statutes of the Lord.
>
> Luke 1:6

Luke says Elizabeth followed God "blamelessly"—that doesn't mean perfectly, but with consistent uprightness and integrity. And in God's mercy, she was blessed with a baby. She had wanted a child for years—years that could have turned her bitter toward God and resentful of her life. Her childless state would have been grounds for divorce in her time, so Zechariah could have left her for another woman without any problem at all. But as they trusted God, they didn't part. Instead they prayed. They trusted God no matter what the circumstances. And in the end they were given their heart's desire.

When something amazing happens in your life, how do you react? Are you on cloud nine, thanking God for all he has done? Hopefully so. But what about when your something isn't as amazing as the something that has happened to someone else? That was the case for Elizabeth. She was going to have a baby boy, one who would become known as John the Baptist, a very important man by any standard. But her little cousin Mary showed up at her door with an even more amazing pregnancy. Mary would give birth to the child whom Elizabeth's son would serve. But when Elizabeth saw Mary and felt her own baby jump in the presence of Mary's child, she wasn't jealous as a lot of us would be. She was excited and ready for what God could and would do through these two babies.

It's easy to be excited about something amazing in your life until you see that someone else has something even more amazing—and then you start to resent that fact. But if you keep your eyes on the Messiah the way Elizabeth did, then you'll be happy when other people seem to be more blessed than you are. And you won't be burned or bummed if their success seems to outdo your own.

the Lord, [a]"a pair of turtledoves, or two young pigeons." [25] Now there was a man in Jerusalem, whose name was Simeon, and this man was righteous and devout, waiting for the consolation of Israel, and the Holy Spirit was upon him. [26] And it had been revealed to him by the Holy Spirit that he would not see death before he had seen the Lord's Christ. [27] And he came in the Spirit into the temple, and when the parents brought in the child Jesus, to do for him according to the custom of the Law, [28] he took him up in his arms and blessed God and said,

[29]   "Lord, now you are letting your ser-
         vant[1] depart in peace,
         according to your word;
[30]   for my eyes have seen your salvation
[31]   that you have prepared in the
         presence of all peoples,
[32]   a light for revelation to the Gentiles,
         and for glory to your people
         Israel."

[33] And his father and his mother marveled at what was said about him. [34] And Simeon blessed them and said to Mary his mother, "Behold, this child is appointed for the fall and rising of many in Israel, and for a sign that is opposed [35] (and a sword will pierce through your own soul also), so that thoughts from many hearts may be revealed."

[36] And there was a prophetess, Anna, the daughter of Phanuel, of the tribe of Asher. She was advanced in years, having lived with her husband seven years from when she was a virgin, [37] and then as a widow until she was eighty-four.[2] She did not depart from the temple, worshiping with fasting and prayer night and day. [38] And coming up at that very hour she began to give thanks to God and to speak of him to all who were waiting for the redemption of Jerusalem.

The Return to Nazareth

[39] And when they had performed everything according to the Law of the Lord, they returned into Galilee, to their own town of Nazareth. [40] And the child grew and became strong, filled with wisdom. And the favor of God was upon him.

The Boy Jesus in the Temple

[41] Now his parents went to Jerusalem every year at the Feast of the Passover. [42] And when he was twelve years old, they went up according to custom. [43] And when the feast was ended, as they were returning, the boy Jesus stayed behind in Jerusalem. His parents did not know it, [44] but supposing him to be in the group they went a day's journey, but then they began to search for him among their relatives and acquaintances, [45] and when they did not find him, they returned to Jerusalem, searching for him. [46] After three days they found him in the temple, sitting among the teachers, listening to them and asking them questions. [47] And all who heard him were amazed at his understanding and his answers. [48] And when his parents[3] saw him, they were astonished. And his mother said to him, "Son, why have you treated us so? Behold, your father and I have been searching for you in great distress." [49] And he said to them, "Why were you looking for me? Did you not know that I must be in my Father's house?"[4] [50] And they did not understand the saying that he spoke to them. [51] And he went down with them and came to Nazareth and was submissive to them. And his mother treasured up all these things in her heart.

[52] And Jesus increased in wisdom and in stature[5] and in favor with God and man.

John the Baptist Prepares the Way

3 In the fifteenth year of the reign of Tiberius Caesar, Pontius Pilate being governor of Judea, and Herod being tetrarch of Galilee, and his brother Philip tetrarch of the region of Ituraea and Trachonitis, and Lysanias tetrarch of Abilene, [2] during the high priesthood of Annas and Caiaphas, [b] the word of God came to John the son of Zechariah in the wilderness. [3] And he went into all the region around the Jordan, proclaiming a baptism of repentance for the forgiveness of sins. [4] As it is written in the book of the words of Isaiah the prophet,

[c] "The voice of one crying in the wilderness:
   'Prepare the way of the Lord,[6]
   make his paths straight.

---

[1] Greek bondservant [2] Or as a widow for eighty-four years [3] Greek they [4] Or about my Father's business [5] Or years [6] Or crying, Prepare in the wilderness the way of the Lord [a] Lev. 12:8 [b] For 3:2-17 see parallels Matt. 3:1-12; Mark 1:2-8 [c] Isa. 40:3-5

5   Every valley shall be filled,
        and every mountain and hill shall
            be made low,
     and the crooked shall become
            straight,
        and the rough places shall become
            level ways,
6   and all flesh shall see the salvation of
            God.' "

7 He said therefore to the crowds that came out to be baptized by him, "You brood of vipers! Who warned you to flee from the wrath to come? 8 Bear fruits in keeping with repentance. And do not begin to say to yourselves, 'We have Abraham as our father.' For I tell you, God is able from these stones to raise up children for Abraham. 9 Even now the axe is laid to the root of the trees. Every tree therefore that does not bear good fruit is cut down and thrown into the fire."

10 And the crowds asked him, "What then shall we do?" 11 And he answered them, "Whoever has two tunics[1] is to share with him who has none, and whoever has food is to do likewise." 12 Tax collectors also came to be baptized and said to him, "Teacher, what shall we do?" 13 And he said to them, "Collect no more than you are authorized to do." 14 Soldiers also asked him, "And we, what shall we do?" And he said to them, "Do not extort money from anyone by threats or by false accusation, and be content with your wages."

15 As the people were in expectation, and all were questioning in their hearts concerning John, whether he might be the Christ, 16 John answered them all, saying, "I baptize you with water, but he who is mightier than I is coming, the strap of whose sandals I am not worthy to untie. He will baptize you with the Holy Spirit and fire. 17 His winnowing fork is in his hand, to clear his threshing floor and to gather the wheat into his barn, but the chaff he will burn with unquenchable fire."

18 So with many other exhortations he preached good news to the people. 19 But Herod the tetrarch, who had been reproved by him for Herodias, his brother's wife, and for all the evil things that Herod had done,

20 added this to them all, that he locked up John in prison.

21 Now when all the people were baptized, and when [a] Jesus also had been baptized and was praying, the heavens were opened, 22 and the Holy Spirit descended on him in bodily form, like a dove; and a voice came from heaven, "You are my beloved Son;[2] with you I am well pleased."[3]

The Genealogy of Jesus Christ

23 Jesus, when he began his ministry, was about thirty years of age, being the son (as was supposed) of Joseph, the son of Heli, 24 the son of Matthat, the son of Levi, the son of Melchi, the son of Jannai, the son of Joseph, 25 the son of Mattathias, the son of Amos, the son of Nahum, the son of Esli, the son of Naggai, 26 the son of Maath, the son of Mattathias, the son of Semein, the son of Josech, the son of Joda, 27 the son of Joanan, the son of Rhesa, the son of Zerubbabel, the son of Shealtiel,[4] the son of Neri, 28 the son of Melchi, the son of Addi, the son of Cosam, the son of Elmadam, the son of Er, 29 the son of Joshua, the son of Eliezer, the son of Jorim, the son of Matthat, the son of Levi, 30 the son of Simeon, the son of Judah, the son of Joseph, the son of Jonam, the son of Eliakim, 31 the son of Melea, the son of Menna, the son of Mattatha, the son of Nathan, the son of David, 32 the son of Jesse, the son of Obed, the son of Boaz, the son of Sala, the son of Nahshon, 33 the son of Amminadab, the son of Admin, the son of Arni, the son of Hezron, the son of Perez, the son of Judah, 34 the son of Jacob, the son of Isaac, the son of Abraham, the son of Terah, the son of Nahor, 35 the son of Serug, the son of Reu, the son of Peleg, the son of Eber, the son of Shelah, 36 the son of Cainan, the son of Arphaxad, the son of Shem, the son of Noah, the son of Lamech, 37 the son of Methuselah, the son of Enoch, the son of Jared, the son of Mahalaleel, the son of Cainan, 38 the son of Enos, the son of Seth, the son of Adam, the son of God.

The Temptation of Jesus

4 [b] And Jesus, full of the Holy Spirit, returned from the Jordan and was led by the Spirit in the wilderness 2 for forty days, being tempted by the devil. And he

---

[1] Greek *chiton*, a long garment worn under the cloak next to the skin [2] Or *my Son, my* (or *the*) *Beloved* [3] Some manuscripts *beloved Son; today I have begotten you* [4] Greek *Salathiel* [a] For 3:21, 22 see parallels Matt. 3:13-17; Mark 1:9-11 [b] For 4:1-13 see parallels Matt. 4:1-11; Mark 1:12, 13

ate nothing during those days. And when they were ended, he was hungry. ³The devil said to him, "If you are the Son of God, command this stone to become bread." ⁴And Jesus answered him, "It is written, ᵃ'Man shall not live by bread alone.'" ⁵And the devil took him up and showed him all the kingdoms of the world in a moment of time, ⁶and said to him, "To you I will give all this authority and their glory, for it has been delivered to me, and I give it to whom I will. ⁷If you, then, will worship me, it will all be yours." ⁸And Jesus answered him, "It is written,

ᵇ'You shall worship the Lord your God,
and him only shall you serve.'"

⁹And he took him to Jerusalem and set him on the pinnacle of the temple and said to him, "If you are the Son of God, throw yourself down from here, ¹⁰for it is written,

ᶜ'He will command his angels concerning you,
to guard you,'

¹¹and

ᵈ'On their hands they will bear you up,
lest you strike your foot against a stone.'"

¹²And Jesus answered him, "It is said, ᵉ'You shall not put the Lord your God to the test.'" ¹³And when the devil had ended every temptation, he departed from him until an opportune time.

Jesus Begins His Ministry

¹⁴And Jesus returned in the power of the Spirit to Galilee, and a report about him went out through all the surrounding country. ¹⁵And he taught in their synagogues, being glorified by all.

Jesus Rejected at Nazareth

¹⁶And he came to Nazareth, where he had been brought up. And as was his custom, he went to the synagogue on the Sabbath day, and he stood up to read. ¹⁷And the scroll of the prophet Isaiah was given to him. He unrolled the scroll and found the place where it was written,

¹⁸ ᶠ"The Spirit of the Lord is upon me,
because he has anointed me
to proclaim good news to the poor.
He has sent me to proclaim liberty to the captives
and recovering of sight to the blind,
to set at liberty those who are oppressed,
¹⁹ to proclaim the year of the Lord's favor."

²⁰And he rolled up the scroll and gave it back to the attendant and sat down. And the eyes of all in the synagogue were fixed on him. ²¹And he began to say to them, "Today this Scripture has been fulfilled in your hearing." ²²And all spoke well of him and marveled at the gracious words that were coming from his mouth. And they said, "Is not this Joseph's son?" ²³And he said to them, "Doubtless you will quote to me this proverb, 'Physician, heal yourself.' What we have heard you did at Capernaum, do here in your hometown as well." ²⁴And he said, "Truly, I say to you, no prophet is acceptable in his hometown. ²⁵But in truth, I tell you, there were many widows in Israel in the days of Elijah, when the heavens were shut up three years and six months, and a great famine came over all the land, ²⁶and Elijah was sent to none of them but only to Zarephath, in the land of Sidon, to a woman who was a widow. ²⁷And there were many lepers¹ in Israel in the time of the prophet Elisha, and none of them was cleansed, but only Naaman the Syrian." ²⁸When they heard these things, all in the synagogue were filled with wrath. ²⁹And they rose up and drove him out of the town and brought him to the brow of the hill on which their town was built, so that they could throw him down the cliff. ³⁰But passing through their midst, he went away.

Jesus Heals a Man with an Unclean Demon

³¹ ᵍAnd he went down to Capernaum, a city of Galilee. And he was teaching them on the Sabbath, ³²and they were astonished at his teaching, for his word possessed authority. ³³And in the synagogue there was a man who had the spirit of an unclean demon, and he cried out with a loud voice,

---

¹ *Leprosy* was a term for several skin diseases; see Leviticus 13 ᵃDeut. 8:3 ᵇDeut. 6:13 ᶜPs. 91:11 ᵈPs. 91:12 ᵉDeut. 6:16 ᶠIsa. 61:1, 2
ᵍFor 4:31-37 see parallel Mark 1:21-28

34 "Ha![1] What have you to do with us, Jesus of Nazareth? Have you come to destroy us? I know who you are—the Holy One of God." **35** But Jesus rebuked him, saying, "Be silent and come out of him!" And when the demon had thrown him down in their midst, he came out of him, having done him no harm. **36** And they were all amazed and said to one another, "What is this word? For with authority and power he commands the unclean spirits, and they come out!" **37** And reports about him went out into every place in the surrounding region.

Jesus Heals Many

38 [d]And he arose and left the synagogue and entered Simon's house. Now Simon's mother-in-law was ill with a high fever, and they appealed to him on her behalf. **39** And he stood over her and rebuked the fever, and it left her, and immediately she rose and began to serve them.

40 Now when the sun was setting, all those who had any who were sick with various diseases brought them to him, and he laid his hands on every one of them and healed them. **41** And demons also came out of many, crying, "You are the Son of God!" But he rebuked them and would not allow them to speak, because they knew that he was the Christ.

Jesus Preaches in Synagogues

42 [b]And when it was day, he departed and went into a desolate place. And the people sought him and came to him, and would have kept him from leaving them, **43** but he said to them, "I must preach the good news of the kingdom of God to the other towns as well; for I was sent for this purpose." **44** And he was preaching in the synagogues of Judea.[2]

Jesus Calls the First Disciples

5 On one occasion, while the crowd was pressing in on him to hear the word of God, he was standing by the lake of Gennesaret, **2** and he saw two boats by the lake, but the fishermen had gone out of them and were washing their nets. **3** Getting into one of the boats, which was Simon's, he asked him to put out a little from the land. And he sat down and taught the

people from the boat. **4** And when he had finished speaking, he said to Simon, "Put out into the deep and let down your nets for a catch." **5** And Simon answered, "Master, we toiled all night and took nothing! But at your word I will let down the nets." **6** And when they had done this, they enclosed a large number of fish, and their nets were breaking. **7** They signaled to their partners in the other boat to come and help them. And they came and filled both the boats, so that they began to sink. **8** But when Simon Peter saw it, he fell down at Jesus' knees, saying, "Depart from me, for I am a sinful man, O Lord." **9** For he and all who were with him were astonished at the catch of fish that they had taken, **10** and so also were James and John, sons of Zebedee, who were partners with Simon. And Jesus said to Simon, "Do not be afraid; from now on you will be catching men."[3] **11** And when they had brought their boats to land, they left everything and followed him.

Jesus Cleanses a Leper

12 While he was in one of the cities, [c]there came a man full of leprosy.[4] And when he saw Jesus, he fell on his face and begged him, "Lord, if you will, you can make me clean." **13** And Jesus[5] stretched out his hand and touched him, saying, "I will; be clean." And immediately the leprosy left him. **14** And he charged him to tell no one, but "go and show yourself to the priest, and make an offering for your cleansing, as Moses commanded, for a proof to them." **15** But now even more the report about him went abroad, and great crowds gathered to hear him and to be healed of their infirmities. **16** But he would withdraw to desolate places and pray.

Jesus Heals a Paralytic

17 On one of those days, as he was teaching, Pharisees and teachers of the law were sitting there, who had come from every village of Galilee and Judea and from Jerusalem. And the power of the Lord was with him to heal.[6] **18** [d]And behold, some men were bringing on a bed a man who was paralyzed, and they were seeking to bring him in and lay him before Jesus, **19** but finding no way to bring him in, because of the

---

[1] Or *Leave us alone* [2] Some manuscripts *Galilee* [3] The Greek word *anthropoi* refers here to both men and women [4] *Leprosy* was a term for several skin diseases; see Leviticus 13 [5] Greek *he* [6] Some manuscripts *was present to heal them* [a] For 4:38-41 see parallels Matt. 8:14-17; Mark 1:29-34 [b] For 4:42, 43 see parallel Mark 1:35-38 [c] For 5:12-14 see parallels Matt. 8:2-4; Mark 1:40-44 [d] For 5:18-26 see parallels Matt. 9:2-8; Mark 2:1-12

crowd, they went up on the roof and let him down with his bed through the tiles into the midst before Jesus. ²⁰ And when he saw their faith, he said, "Man, your sins are forgiven you." ²¹ And the scribes and the Pharisees began to question, saying, "Who is this who speaks blasphemies? Who can forgive sins but God alone?" ²² When Jesus perceived their thoughts, he answered them, "Why do you question in your hearts? ²³ Which is easier, to say, 'Your sins are forgiven you,' or to say, 'Rise and walk'? ²⁴ But that you may know that the Son of Man has authority on earth to forgive sins"—he said to the man who was paralyzed—"I say to you, rise, pick up your bed and go home." ²⁵ And immediately he rose up before them and picked up what he had been lying on and went home, glorifying God. ²⁶ And amazement seized them all, and they glorified God and were filled with awe, saying, "We have seen extraordinary things today."

Jesus Calls Levi

²⁷ ᵃ After this he went out and saw a tax collector named Levi, sitting at the tax booth. And he said to him, "Follow me." ²⁸ And leaving everything, he rose and followed him.

²⁹ And Levi made him a great feast in his house, and there was a large company of tax collectors and others reclining at table with them. ³⁰ And the Pharisees and their scribes grumbled at his disciples, saying, "Why do you eat and drink with tax collectors and sinners?" ³¹ And Jesus answered them, "Those who are well have no need of a physician, but those who are sick. ³² I have not come to call the righteous but sinners to repentance."

A Question About Fasting

³³ And they said to him, "The disciples of John fast often and offer prayers, and so do the disciples of the Pharisees, but yours eat and drink." ³⁴ And Jesus said to them, "Can you make wedding guests fast while the bridegroom is with them? ³⁵ The days will come when the bridegroom is taken away from them, and then they will fast in those days." ³⁶ He also told them a parable: "No one tears a piece from a new garment and puts it on an old garment. If he does,

he will tear the new, and the piece from the new will not match the old. ³⁷ And no one puts new wine into old wineskins. If he does, the new wine will burst the skins and it will be spilled, and the skins will be destroyed. ³⁸ But new wine must be put into fresh wineskins. ³⁹ And no one after drinking old wine desires new, for he says, 'The old is good.'"[1]

A Prayer of... CONFESSION

God, help me to see the log in my own eye before I can even see the sawdust that's in my friend's eye. Let me see my offenses with my eyes wide open. Make them more obvious to me than the sins of others—as bright as the sun. But blind me to the offenses inflicted on me by the ones I love. Wipe them from my memory; take them out of my mind forever.

Let me carry and measure the balance of love, and let me be in my own eyes the most guilty of sin. Help me at the same time with your gift of grace, so that I won't be downcast when I grieve for my sin and so ruin my happiness or integrity. Touch me with fire from the altar, so that I might be up and working to rebuild the walls of my city.

Amen.

Jesus Is Lord of the Sabbath

6 ᵇ On a Sabbath,[2] while he was going through the grainfields, his disciples plucked and ate some heads of grain, rubbing them in their hands. ² But some of the Pharisees said, "Why are you doing what is not lawful to do on the Sabbath?" ³ And Jesus answered them, "Have you not read what David did when he was hungry, he and those who were with him: ⁴ how he entered the house of God and took and ate the bread of the Presence, which is not lawful for any but the priests to eat, and

---

¹ Some manuscripts *better* ² Some manuscripts *On the second first Sabbath* (that is, on the second Sabbath after the first) ᵃ For 5:27-38 see parallels Matt. 9:9-17; Mark 2:13-22 ᵇ For 6:1-5 see parallels Matt. 12:1-8; Mark 2:23-28

also gave it to those with him?" ⁵And he said to them, "The Son of Man is lord of the Sabbath."

A Man with a Withered Hand

⁶On another Sabbath, *a* he entered the synagogue and was teaching, and a man was there whose right hand was withered. ⁷And the scribes and the Pharisees watched him, to see whether he would heal on the Sabbath, so that they might find a reason to accuse him. ⁸But he knew their thoughts, and he said to the man with the withered hand, "Come and stand here." And he rose and stood there. ⁹And Jesus said to them, "I ask you, is it lawful on the Sabbath to do good or to do harm, to save life or to destroy it?" ¹⁰And after looking around at them all he said to him, "Stretch out your hand." And he did so, and his hand was restored. ¹¹But they were filled with fury and discussed with one another what they might do to Jesus.

The Twelve Apostles

¹²In these days he went out to the mountain to pray, and all night he continued in prayer to God. ¹³And when day came, he called his disciples *b* and chose from them twelve, whom he named apostles: ¹⁴Simon, whom he named Peter, and Andrew his brother, and James and John, and Philip, and Bartholomew, ¹⁵and Matthew, and Thomas, and James the son of Alphaeus, and Simon who was called the Zealot, ¹⁶and Judas the son of James, and Judas Iscariot, who became a traitor.

Jesus Ministers to a Great Multitude

¹⁷And he came down with them and stood on a level place, with a great crowd of his disciples and a great multitude of people from all Judea and Jerusalem and the seacoast of Tyre and Sidon, ¹⁸who came to hear him and to be healed of their diseases. And those who were troubled with unclean spirits were cured. ¹⁹And all the crowd sought to touch him, for power came out from him and healed them all.

The Beatitudes

²⁰And he lifted up his eyes on his disciples, and said:

"Blessed are you who are poor, for yours is the kingdom of God.

²¹"Blessed are you who are hungry now, for you shall be satisfied.

"Blessed are you who weep now, for you shall laugh.

²²"Blessed are you when people hate you and when they exclude you and revile you and spurn your name as evil, on account of the Son of Man! ²³Rejoice in that day, and leap for joy, for behold, your reward is great in heaven; for so their fathers did to the prophets.

Jesus Pronounces Woes

²⁴"But woe to you who are rich, for you have received your consolation.

²⁵"Woe to you who are full now, for you shall be hungry.

"Woe to you who laugh now, for you shall mourn and weep.

²⁶"Woe to you, when all people speak well of you, for so their fathers did to the false prophets.

Love Your Enemies

²⁷"But I say to you who hear, Love your enemies, do good to those who hate you, ²⁸bless those who curse you, pray for those who abuse you. ²⁹ *c*To one who strikes you on the cheek, offer the other also, and from one who takes away your cloak do not withhold your tunic¹ either. ³⁰Give to everyone who begs from you, and from one who takes away your goods do not demand them back. ³¹And as you wish that others would do to you, do so to them.

³²"If you love those who love you, what benefit is that to you? For even sinners love those who love them. ³³And if you do good to those who do good to you, what benefit is that to you? For even sinners do the same. ³⁴And if you lend to those from whom you expect to receive, what credit is that to you? Even sinners lend to sinners, to get back the same amount. ³⁵But love your enemies, and do good, and lend, expecting nothing in return, and your reward will be great, and you will be sons of the Most High, for he is kind to the ungrateful and the evil. ³⁶Be merciful, even as your Father is merciful.

Judging Others

³⁷ *d*"Judge not, and you will not be judged; condemn not, and you will not be con-

¹Greek *chiton*, a long garment worn under the cloak next to the skin *a*For 6:6-11 see parallels Matt. 12:9-14; Mark 3:1-6 *b*For 6:13-16 see parallels Matt. 10:2-4; Mark 3:16-19 *c*For 6:29, 30 see parallel Matt. 5:39-42 *d*For 6:37, 38, 41, 42 see parallel Matt. 7:1-5

demned; forgive, and you will be forgiven; [38] give, and it will be given to you. Good measure, pressed down, shaken together, running over, will be put into your lap. For with the measure you use it will be measured back to you."

[39] He also told them a parable: "Can a blind man lead a blind man? Will they not both fall into a pit? [40] A disciple is not above his teacher, but everyone when he is fully trained will be like his teacher. [41] Why do you see the speck that is in your brother's eye, but do not notice the log that is in your own eye? [42] How can you say to your brother, 'Brother, let me take out the speck that is in your eye,' when you yourself do not see the log that is in your own eye? You hypocrite, first take the log out of your own eye, and then you will see clearly to take out the speck that is in your brother's eye.

A Tree and Its Fruit

[43] "For [a] no good tree bears bad fruit, nor again does a bad tree bear good fruit, [44] for each tree is known by its own fruit. For figs are not gathered from thornbushes, nor are grapes picked from a bramble bush. [45] The good person out of the good treasure of his heart produces good, and the evil person out of his evil treasure produces evil, for out of the abundance of the heart his mouth speaks.

Build Your House on the Rock

[46] "Why do you call me 'Lord, Lord,' and not do what I tell you? [47][b] Everyone who comes to me and hears my words and does them, I will show you what he is like: [48] he is like a man building a house, who dug deep and laid the foundation on the rock. And when a flood arose, the stream broke against that house and could not shake it, because it had been well built.[1] [49] But the one who hears and does not do them is like a man who built a house on the ground without a foundation. When the stream broke against it, immediately it fell, and the ruin of that house was great."

Jesus Heals a Centurion's Servant

7 After he had finished all his sayings in the hearing of the people, [c] he entered Capernaum. [2] Now a centurion had a servant[2] who was sick and at the point of death, who was highly valued by him. [3] When the centurion[3] heard about Jesus, he sent to him elders of the Jews, asking him to come and heal his servant. [4] And when they came to Jesus, they pleaded with him earnestly, saying, "He is worthy to have you do this for him, [5] for he loves our nation, and he is the one who built us our synagogue." [6] And Jesus went with them. When he was not far from the house, the centurion sent friends, saying to him, "Lord, do not trouble yourself, for I am not worthy to have you come under my roof. [7] Therefore I did not presume to come to you. But say the word, and let my servant be healed. [8] For I too am a man set under authority, with soldiers under me: and I say to one, 'Go,' and he goes; and to another, 'Come,' and he comes; and to my servant, 'Do this,' and he does it." [9] When Jesus heard these things, he marveled at him, and turning to the crowd that followed him, said, "I tell you, not even in Israel have I found such faith." [10] And when those who had been sent returned to the house, they found the servant well.

Jesus Raises a Widow's Son

[11] Soon afterward[4] he went to a town called Nain, and his disciples and a great crowd went with him. [12] As he drew near to the gate of the town, behold, a man who had died was being carried out, the only son of his mother, and she was a widow, and a considerable crowd from the town was with her. [13] And when the Lord saw her, he had compassion on her and said to her, "Do not weep." [14] Then he came up and touched the bier, and the bearers stood still. And he said, "Young man, I say to you, arise." [15] And the dead man sat up and began to speak, and Jesus[5] gave him to his mother. [16] Fear seized them all, and they glorified God, saying, "A great prophet has arisen among us!" and "God has visited his people!" [17] And this report about him spread through the whole of Judea and all the surrounding country.

Messengers from John the Baptist

[18][d] The disciples of John reported all these things to him. And John, [19] calling two of his disciples to him, sent them to

---

[1] Some manuscripts *founded upon the rock* [2] Greek *bondservant*; also verses 3, 8, 10 [3] Greek *he* [4] Some manuscripts *The next day* [5] Greek *he* [a] For 6:43, 44 see parallel Matt. 7:16, 20 [b] For 6:47-49 see parallel Matt. 7:24-27 [c] For 7:1-10 see parallel Matt. 8:5-13 [d] For 7:18-35 see parallel Matt. 11:2-19

the Lord, saying, "Are you the one who is to come, or shall we look for another?" [20] And when the men had come to him, they said, "John the Baptist has sent us to you, saying, 'Are you the one who is to come, or shall we look for another?' " [21] In that hour he healed many people of diseases and plagues and evil spirits, and on many who were blind he bestowed sight. [22] And he answered them, "Go and tell John what you have seen and heard: the blind receive their sight, the lame walk, lepers[1] are cleansed, and the deaf hear, the dead are raised up, the poor have good news preached to them. [23] And blessed is the one who is not offended by me."

[24] When John's messengers had gone, Jesus[2] began to speak to the crowds concerning John: "What did you go out into the wilderness to see? A reed shaken by the wind? [25] What then did you go out to see? A man dressed in soft clothing? Behold, those who are dressed in splendid clothing and live in luxury are in kings' courts. [26] What then did you go out to see? A prophet? Yes, I tell you, and more than a prophet. [27] This is he of whom it is written,

[a]" 'Behold, I send my messenger before
    your face,
    who will prepare your way before
    you.'

[28] I tell you, among those born of women none is greater than John. Yet the one who is least in the kingdom of God is greater than he." [29] (When all the people heard this, and the tax collectors too, they declared God just,[3] having been baptized with the baptism of John, [30] but the Pharisees and the lawyers rejected the purpose of God for themselves, not having been baptized by him.)

[31] "To what then shall I compare the people of this generation, and what are they like? [32] They are like children sitting in the marketplace and calling to one another,

    " 'We played the flute for you, and you
        did not dance;
    we sang a dirge, and you did not
        weep.'

[33] For John the Baptist has come eating no bread and drinking no wine, and you say, 'He has a demon.' [34] The Son of Man has

come eating and drinking, and you say, 'Look at him! A glutton and a drunkard, a friend of tax collectors and sinners!' [35] Yet wisdom is justified by all her children."

A Sinful Woman Forgiven

[36] One of the Pharisees asked him to eat with him, and he went into the Pharisee's house and reclined at the table. [37] And behold, a woman of the city, who was a sinner, when she learned that he was reclining at table in the Pharisee's house, brought an alabaster flask of ointment, [38] and standing behind him at his feet, weeping, she began to wet his feet with her tears and wiped them with the hair of her head and kissed his feet and anointed them with the ointment. [39] Now when the Pharisee who had invited him saw this, he said to himself, "If this man were a prophet, he would have known who and what sort of woman this is who is touching him, for she is a sinner." [40] And Jesus answering said to him, "Simon, I have something to say to you." And he answered, "Say it, Teacher."

[41] "A certain moneylender had two debtors. One owed five hundred denarii, and the other fifty. [42] When they could not pay, he cancelled the debt of both. Now which of them will love him more?" [43] Simon answered, "The one, I suppose, for whom he cancelled the larger debt." And he said to him, "You have judged rightly." [44] Then turning toward the woman he said to Simon, "Do you see this woman? I entered your house; you gave me no water for my feet, but she has wet my feet with her tears and wiped them with her hair. [45] You gave me no kiss, but from the time I came in she has not ceased to kiss my feet. [46] You did not anoint my head with oil, but she has anointed my feet with ointment. [47] Therefore I tell you, her sins, which are many, are forgiven— for she loved much. But he who is forgiven little, loves little." [48] And he said to her, "Your sins are forgiven." [49] Then those who were at table with him began to say among[4] themselves, "Who is this, who even forgives sins?" [50] And he said to the woman, "Your faith has saved you; go in peace."

Women Accompanying Jesus

8 Soon afterward he went on through cities and villages, proclaiming and bringing the good news of the kingdom of

---

[1] *Leprosy* was a term for several skin diseases; see Leviticus 13 [2] Greek *he* [3] Greek *they justified God* [4] Or *to* [a] Mal. 3:1

God. And the twelve were with him, [2]and also some women who had been healed of evil spirits and infirmities: Mary, called Magdalene, from whom seven demons had gone out, [3]and Joanna, the wife of Chuza, Herod's household manager, and Susanna, and many others, who provided for them[1] out of their means.

The Parable of the Sower

[4][a]And when a great crowd was gathering and people from town after town came to him, he said in a parable, [5]"A sower went out to sow his seed. And as he sowed, some fell along the path and was trampled underfoot, and the birds of the air devoured it. [6]And some fell on the rock, and as it grew up, it withered away, because it had no moisture. [7]And some fell among thorns, and the thorns grew up with it and choked it. [8]And some fell into good soil and grew and yielded a hundredfold." As he said these things, he called out, "He who has ears to hear, let him hear."

The Purpose of the Parables

[9]And when his disciples asked him what this parable meant, [10]he said, "To you it has been given to know the secrets of the kingdom of God, but for others they are in parables, so [b]that 'seeing they may not see, and hearing they may not understand.' [11][c]Now the parable is this: The seed is the word of God. [12]The ones along the path are those who have heard; then the devil comes and takes away the word from their hearts, so that they may not believe and be saved. [13]And the ones on the rock are those who, when they hear the word, receive it with joy. But these have no root; they believe for a while, and in time of testing fall away. [14]And as for what fell among the thorns, they are those who hear, but as they go on their way they are choked by the cares and riches and pleasures of life, and their fruit does not mature. [15]As for that in the good soil, they are those who, hearing the word, hold it fast in an honest and good heart, and bear fruit with patience.

A Lamp Under a Jar

[16][d]"No one after lighting a lamp covers it with a jar or puts it under a bed, but puts it on a stand, so that those who enter may see the light. [17]For nothing is hidden that will not be made manifest, nor is anything secret that will not be known and come to light. [18]Take care then how you hear, for to the one who has, more will be given, and from the one who has not, even what he thinks that he has will be taken away."

Jesus' Mother and Brothers

[19][e]Then his mother and his brothers came to him, but they could not reach him because of the crowd. [20]And he was told, "Your mother and your brothers are standing outside, desiring to see you." [21]But he answered them, "My mother and my brothers are those who hear the word of God and do it."

Jesus Calms a Storm

[22][f]One day he got into a boat with his disciples, and he said to them, "Let us go across to the other side of the lake." So they set out, [23]and as they sailed he fell asleep. And a windstorm came down on the lake, and they were filling with water and were in danger. [24]And they went and woke him, saying, "Master, Master, we are perishing!" And he awoke and rebuked the wind and the raging waves, and they ceased, and there was a calm. [25]He said to them, "Where is your faith?" And they were afraid, and they marveled, saying to one another, "Who then is this, that he commands even winds and water, and they obey him?"

Jesus Heals a Man with a Demon

[26][g]Then they sailed to the country of the Gerasenes,[2] which is opposite Galilee. [27]When Jesus[3] had stepped out on land, there met him a man from the city who had demons. For a long time he had worn no clothes, and he had not lived in a house but among the tombs. [28]When he saw Jesus, he cried out and fell down before him and said with a loud voice, "What have you to do with me, Jesus, Son of the Most High God? I beg you, do not torment me." [29]For he had commanded the unclean spirit to come out of the man. (For many a time it had seized him. He was kept under guard and bound with chains and

Mary Magdalene

Read this God Girl story in Matthew 27:55–56, 61; 28:1–10; Mark 15:40, 47; 16:1–11; Luke 8:1–3; 24:1–12; and John 19:25; 20:1–2, 11–18.

"Therefore I tell you, her sins, which are many, are forgiven—for she loved much. But he who is forgiven little, loves little."

Luke 7:47

When you realize all that Jesus has forgiven in your life, love just gushes out of you. Like when you first fall in love, you can't contain all the appreciation and adoration. And the more Jesus forgives, the more you love him. That's what Jesus was saying in Luke 7 about the woman who washed his feet with her tears. And we see that same devotion in the life of Mary Magdalene.

Jesus freed Mary from seven demons. How her body became a haven for demons we don't know, but what really matters is their eviction and her salvation. When she was released and forgiven, she became completely devoted to Jesus. She followed him everywhere, along with the disciples, and even used her own money to help support his ministry. Mary was so sure of her love for Jesus that she, along with Jesus' mother, stayed at his feet even as he died on the cross. While others stood at a distance in fear and suspicion, Mary refused to look away or deny her love. And Mary was the first to witness his resurrection.

The truth is that all of us have been forgiven a lot. It doesn't take demons and other evil practices to make your story of salvation incredible. You don't have to look far to find all kinds of junk in your life: bitterness, self-obsession, worry, fear, greed, envy—and the list goes on. When you look at the life of Mary Magdalene, don't envy her friendship with Jesus or her incredible story, but consider why she was so in love: she knew just how much she had been saved from. Do you know how much you have been saved from? How much you *can* be saved from?

God Girl, you have been saved from much and you will be saved from much, much more. So take an honest look at yourself. As you start to see the bad parts of your life, grieve for your stupidity and the time you've wasted, but be quick to let it all go and trust God for his forgiveness. When you consider all that God has saved you from, your love for the Savior who continues to rescue you will grow to match or exceed that of Mary Magdalene.

shackles, but he would break the bonds and be driven by the demon into the desert.) [30] Jesus then asked him, "What is your name?" And he said, "Legion," for many demons had entered him. [31] And they begged him not to command them to depart into the abyss. [32] Now a large herd of pigs was feeding there on the hillside, and they begged him to let them enter these. So he gave them permission. [33] Then the demons came out of the man and entered the pigs, and the herd rushed down the steep bank into the lake and drowned.

[34] When the herdsmen saw what had happened, they fled and told it in the city and in the country. [35] Then people went out to see what had happened, and they came to Jesus and found the man from whom the demons had gone, sitting at the feet of Jesus, clothed and in his right mind, and they were afraid. [36] And those who had seen it told them how the demon-possessed[1] man had been healed. [37] Then all the people of the surrounding country of the Gerasenes asked him to depart from them, for they were seized with great fear. So he got into the boat and returned. [38] The man from whom the demons had gone begged that he might be with him, but Jesus sent him away, saying, [39] "Return to your home, and declare how much God has done for you." And he went away, proclaiming throughout the whole city how much Jesus had done for him.

Jesus Heals a Woman and Jairus's Daughter

[40] Now when Jesus returned, the crowd welcomed him, for they were all waiting for him. [41] [a] And there came a man named Jairus, who was a ruler of the synagogue. And falling at Jesus' feet, he implored him to come to his house, [42] for he had an only daughter, about twelve years of age, and she was dying.

As Jesus went, the people pressed around him. [43] And there was a woman who had had a discharge of blood for twelve years, and though she had spent all her living on physicians,[2] she could not be healed by anyone. [44] She came up behind him and touched the fringe of his garment, and immediately her discharge of blood ceased. [45] And Jesus said, "Who was it that touched me?" When all denied it, Peter[3] said, "Master, the crowds surround you and are pressing in on you!" [46] But Jesus said, "Someone touched me, for I perceive that power has gone out from me." [47] And when the woman saw that she was not hidden, she came trembling, and falling down before him declared in the presence of all the people why she had touched him, and how she had been immediately healed. [48] And he said to her, "Daughter, your faith has made you well; go in peace."

[49] While he was still speaking, someone from the ruler's house came and said, "Your daughter is dead; do not trouble the Teacher any more." [50] But Jesus on hearing this answered him, "Do not fear; only believe, and she will be well." [51] And when he came to the house, he allowed no one to enter with him, except Peter and John and James, and the father and mother of the child. [52] And all were weeping and mourning for her, but he said, "Do not weep, for she is not dead but sleeping." [53] And they laughed at him, knowing that she was dead. [54] But taking her by the hand he called, saying, "Child, arise." [55] And her spirit returned, and she got up at once. And he directed that something should be given her to eat. [56] And her parents were amazed, but he charged them to tell no one what had happened.

Jesus Sends Out the Twelve Apostles

9 And he called the twelve together and gave them power and authority over all demons and to cure diseases, [2] and he sent them out to proclaim the kingdom of God and to heal. [3] [b] And he said to them, "Take nothing for your journey, no staff, nor bag, nor bread, nor money; and do not have two tunics.[4] [4] And whatever house you enter, stay there, and from there depart. [5] And wherever they do not receive you, when you leave that town shake off the dust from your feet as a testimony against them." [6] And they departed and went through the villages, preaching the gospel and healing everywhere.

Herod Is Perplexed by Jesus

7 [a] Now Herod the tetrarch heard about all that was happening, and he was perplexed, because it was said by some that John had been raised from the dead, 8 by some that Elijah had appeared, and by others that one of the prophets of old had risen. 9 Herod said, "John I beheaded, but who is this about whom I hear such things?" And he sought to see him.

Jesus Feeds the Five Thousand

10 On their return the apostles told him all that they had done. [b] And he took them and withdrew apart to a town called Bethsaida. 11 When the crowds learned it, they followed him, and he welcomed them and spoke to them of the kingdom of God and cured those who had need of healing. 12 Now the day began to wear away, and the twelve came and said to him, "Send the crowd away to go into the surrounding villages and countryside to find lodging and get provisions, for we are here in a desolate place." 13 But he said to them, "You give them something to eat." They said, "We have no more than five loaves and two fish—unless we are to go and buy food for all these people." 14 For there were about five thousand men. And he said to his disciples, "Have them sit down in groups of about fifty each." 15 And they did so, and had them all sit down. 16 And taking the five loaves and the two fish, he looked up to heaven and said a blessing over them. Then he broke the loaves and gave them to the disciples to set before the crowd. 17 And they all ate and were satisfied. And what was left over was picked up, twelve baskets of broken pieces.

Peter Confesses Jesus as the Christ

18 [c] Now it happened that as he was praying alone, the disciples were with him. And he asked them, "Who do the crowds say that I am?" 19 And they answered, "John the Baptist. But others say, Elijah, and others, that one of the prophets of old has risen." 20 Then he said to them, "But who do you say that I am?" And Peter answered, "The Christ of God."

Jesus Foretells His Death

21 And he strictly charged and commanded them to tell this to no one, 22 [d] say-

ing, "The Son of Man must suffer many things and be rejected by the elders and chief priests and scribes, and be killed, and on the third day be raised."

Take Up Your Cross and Follow Jesus

23 And he said to all, "If anyone would come after me, let him deny himself and take up his cross daily and follow me. 24 For whoever would save his life will lose it, but whoever loses his life for my sake will save it. 25 For what does it profit a man if he gains the whole world and loses or forfeits himself? 26 For whoever is ashamed of me and of my words, of him will the Son of Man be ashamed when he comes in his glory and the glory of the Father and of the holy angels. 27 But I tell you truly, there are some standing here who will not taste death until they see the kingdom of God."

The Transfiguration

28 Now about eight days after these sayings he took with him Peter and John and James and went up on the mountain to pray. 29 And as he was praying, the appearance of his face was altered, and his clothing became dazzling white. 30 And behold, two men were talking with him, Moses and Elijah, 31 who appeared in glory and spoke of his departure,[1] which he was about to accomplish at Jerusalem. 32 Now Peter and those who were with him were heavy with sleep, but when they became fully awake they saw his glory and the two men who stood with him. 33 And as the men were parting from him, Peter said to Jesus, "Master, it is good that we are here. Let us make three tents, one for you and one for Moses and one for Elijah"—not knowing what he said. 34 As he was saying these things, a cloud came and overshadowed them, and they were afraid as they entered the cloud. 35 And a voice came out of the cloud, saying, "This is my Son, my Chosen One;[2] listen to him!" 36 And when the voice had spoken, Jesus was found alone. And they kept silent and told no one in those days anything of what they had seen.

Jesus Heals a Boy with an Unclean Spirit

37 On the next day, when they had come down from the mountain, a great crowd met him. 38 And behold, a man from the

---

[1] Greek exodus [2] Some manuscripts my Beloved [a] For 9:7-9 see parallels Matt. 14:1-12; Mark 6:14-29 [b] For 9:10-17 see parallels Matt. 14:13-21; Mark 6:32-44; John 6:1-13 [c] For 9:18-20 see parallels Matt. 16:13-16; Mark 8:27-29 [d] For 9:22-27 see parallels Matt. 16:21-28; Mark 8:31–9:1

crowd cried out, "Teacher, I beg you to look at my son, for he is my only child. [39] And behold, a spirit seizes him, and he suddenly cries out. It convulses him so that he foams at the mouth, and shatters him, and will hardly leave him. [40] And I begged your disciples to cast it out, but they could not." [41] Jesus answered, "O faithless and twisted generation, how long am I to be with you and bear with you? Bring your son here." [42] While he was coming, the demon threw him to the ground and convulsed him. But Jesus rebuked the unclean spirit and healed the boy, and gave him back to his father. [43] And all were astonished at the majesty of God.

Jesus Again Foretells His Death

But while they were all marveling at everything he was doing, Jesus[1] said to his disciples, [44] "Let these words sink into your ears: The Son of Man is about to be delivered into the hands of men." [45] But they did not understand this saying, and it was concealed from them, so that they might not perceive it. And they were afraid to ask him about this saying.

Who Is the Greatest?

[46] An argument arose among them as to which of them was the greatest. [47] But Jesus, knowing the reasoning of their hearts, took a child and put him by his side [48] and said to them, "Whoever receives this child in my name receives me, and whoever receives me receives him who sent me. For he who is least among you all is the one who is great."

Anyone Not Against Us Is For Us

[49] John answered, "Master, we saw someone casting out demons in your name, and we tried to stop him, because he does not follow with us." [50] But Jesus said to him, "Do not stop him, for the one who is not against you is for you."

A Samaritan Village Rejects Jesus

[51] When the days drew near for him to be taken up, he set his face to go to Jerusalem. [52] And he sent messengers ahead of him, who went and entered a village of the Samaritans, to make preparations for him. [53] But the people did not receive him,

because his face was set toward Jerusalem. [54] And when his disciples James and John saw it, they said, "Lord, do you want us to tell fire to come down from heaven and consume them?"[2] [55] But he turned and rebuked them.[3] [56] And they went on to another village.

The Cost of Following Jesus

[57] [a] As they were going along the road, someone said to him, "I will follow you wherever you go." [58] And Jesus said to him, "Foxes have holes, and birds of the air have nests, but the Son of Man has nowhere to lay his head." [59] To another he said, "Follow me." But he said, "Lord, let me first go and bury my father." [60] And Jesus[4] said to him, "Leave the dead to bury their own dead. But as for you, go and proclaim the kingdom of God." [61] Yet another said, "I will follow you, Lord, but let me first say farewell to those at my home." [62] Jesus said to him, "No one who puts his hand to the plow and looks back is fit for the kingdom of God."

Jesus Sends Out the Seventy-Two

10 After this the Lord appointed seventy-two[5] others and sent them on ahead of him, two by two, into every town and place where he himself was about to go. [2] And he said to them, "The harvest is plentiful, but the laborers are few. Therefore pray earnestly to the Lord of the harvest to send out laborers into his harvest. [3] Go your way; behold, I am sending you out as lambs in the midst of wolves. [4] Carry no moneybag, no knapsack, no sandals, and greet no one on the road. [5] Whatever house you enter, first say, 'Peace be to this house!' [6] And if a son of peace is there, your peace will rest upon him. But if not, it will return to you. [7] And remain in the same house, eating and drinking what they provide, for the laborer deserves his wages. Do not go from house to house. [8] Whenever you enter a town and they receive you, eat what is set before you. [9] Heal the sick in it and say to them, 'The kingdom of God has come near to you.' [10] But whenever you enter a town and they do not receive you, go into its streets and say, [11] 'Even the dust of your town that clings to our feet we wipe off against you.

---

[1] Greek he [2] Some manuscripts add as Elijah did [3] Some manuscripts add and he said, "You do not know what manner of spirit you are of; for the Son of Man came not to destroy people's lives but to save them" [4] Greek he [5] Some manuscripts seventy; also verse 17 [a] For 9:57-62 see parallel Matt. 8:19-22

Nevertheless know this, that the kingdom of God has come near.' [12] I tell you, it will be more bearable on that day for Sodom than for that town.

Woe to Unrepentant Cities

[13] [a] "Woe to you, Chorazin! Woe to you, Bethsaida! For if the mighty works done in you had been done in Tyre and Sidon, they would have repented long ago, sitting in sackcloth and ashes. [14] But it will be more bearable in the judgment for Tyre and Sidon than for you. [15] And you, Capernaum, will you be exalted to heaven? You shall be brought down to Hades.

[16] "The one who hears you hears me, and the one who rejects you rejects me, and the one who rejects me rejects him who sent me."

The Return of the Seventy-Two

[17] The seventy-two returned with joy, saying, "Lord, even the demons are subject to us in your name!" [18] And he said to them, "I saw Satan fall like lightning from heaven. [19] Behold, I have given you authority to tread on serpents and scorpions, and over all the power of the enemy, and nothing shall hurt you. [20] Nevertheless, do not rejoice in this, that the spirits are subject to you, but rejoice that your names are written in heaven."

Jesus Rejoices in the Father's Will

[21] [b] In that same hour he rejoiced in the Holy Spirit and said, "I thank you, Father, Lord of heaven and earth, that you have hidden these things from the wise and understanding and revealed them to little children; yes, Father, for such was your gracious will.[1] [22] All things have been handed over to me by my Father, and no one knows who the Son is except the Father, or who the Father is except the Son and anyone to whom the Son chooses to reveal him."

[23] Then turning to the disciples he said privately, "Blessed are the eyes that see what you see! [24] For I tell you that many prophets and kings desired to see what you see, and did not see it, and to hear what you hear, and did not hear it."

The Parable of the Good Samaritan

[25] And behold, a lawyer stood up to put him to the test, saying, "Teacher, what shall I do to inherit eternal life?" [26] He said to him, "What is written in the Law? How do you read it?" [27] And he answered, [c] "You shall love the Lord your God with all your heart and with all your soul and with all your strength and with all your mind, and [d] your neighbor as yourself." [28] And he said to him, "You have answered correctly; do this, and you will live."

[29] But he, desiring to justify himself, said to Jesus, "And who is my neighbor?" [30] Jesus replied, "A man was going down from Jerusalem to Jericho, and he fell among robbers, who stripped him and beat him and departed, leaving him half dead. [31] Now by chance a priest was going down that road, and when he saw him he passed by on the other side. [32] So likewise a Levite, when he came to the place and saw him, passed by on the other side. [33] But a Samaritan, as he journeyed, came to where he was, and when he saw him, he had compassion. [34] He went to him and bound up his wounds, pouring on oil and wine. Then he set him on his own animal and brought him to an inn and took care of him. [35] And the next day he took out two denarii[2] and gave them to the innkeeper, saying, 'Take care of him, and whatever more you spend, I will repay you when I come back.' [36] Which of these three, do you think, proved to be a neighbor to the man who fell among the robbers?" [37] He said, "The one who showed him mercy." And Jesus said to him, "You go, and do likewise."

Martha and Mary

[38] Now as they went on their way, Jesus[3] entered a village. And a woman named Martha welcomed him into her house. [39] And she had a sister called Mary, who sat at the Lord's feet and listened to his teaching. [40] But Martha was distracted with much serving. And she went up to him and said, "Lord, do you not care that my sister has left me to serve alone? Tell her then to help me." [41] But the Lord answered her, "Martha, Martha, you are anxious and troubled about many things, [42] but one thing is necessary.[4] Mary has chosen the good portion, which will not be taken away from her."

---

[1] Or for so it pleased you well   [2] A denarius was a day's wage for a laborer   [3] Greek he   [4] Some manuscripts few things are necessary, or only one   [a] For 10:13-15 see parallel Matt. 11:21-24   [b] For 10:21, 22 see parallel Matt. 11:25-27   [c] Deut. 6:5   [d] Lev. 19:18

The Lord's Prayer

11 Now Jesus[1] was praying in a certain place, and when he finished, one of his disciples said to him, "Lord, teach us to pray, as John taught his disciples." [2] And he said to them, "When you pray, say:

"Father, hallowed be your name.
Your kingdom come.
[3] Give us each day our daily bread,[2]
[4] and forgive us our sins,
for we ourselves forgive everyone
who is indebted to us.
And lead us not into temptation."

[5] And he said to them, "Which of you who has a friend will go to him at midnight and say to him, 'Friend, lend me three loaves, [6] for a friend of mine has arrived on a journey, and I have nothing to set before him'; [7] and he will answer from within, 'Do not bother me; the door is now shut, and my children are with me in bed. I cannot get up and give you anything'? [8] I tell you, though he will not get up and give him anything because he is his friend, yet because of his impudence[3] he will rise and give him whatever he needs. [9] And I tell you, [a] ask, and it will be given to you; seek, and you will find; knock, and it will be opened to you. [10] For everyone who asks receives, and the one who seeks finds, and to the one who knocks it will be opened. [11] What father among you, if his son asks for[4] a fish, will instead of a fish give him a serpent; [12] or if he asks for an egg, will give him a scorpion? [13] If you then, who are evil, know how to give good gifts to your children, how much more will the heavenly Father give the Holy Spirit to those who ask him!"

Jesus and Beelzebul

[14] [b] Now he was casting out a demon that was mute. When the demon had gone out,

---

[1] Greek *he* [2] Or *our bread for tomorrow* [3] Or *persistence* [4] Some manuscripts insert *bread, will give him a stone; or if he asks for*
[a] For 11:9-13 see parallel Matt. 7:7-11 [b] For 11:14, 15 see parallel Matt. 12:22-24

Know Love

verses to read
Luke 10:25–37

Is your love selfless, or selfish? Selfish love demands something in return. Love, acceptance, kindness, concern—something. It gives, therefore it wants to get. Selfish love is always thinking, "What's in it for me?" And it's always asking, "Why should I love you when you won't love me back?" But selfish love isn't really love at all, because true love thinks nothing of itself but focuses on loving others in order to serve them and Christ, who is our example of selfless love.

Unconditional love is something we all want as human beings. We want to be loved no matter what we do, but how often are we willing to return love in the same way? We make demands and set rules on our love, but true love doesn't make demands. It is given freely and abundantly. The only rule when it comes to giving love is that love for a human can never come before our love for God. Our love should never try to replace the Holy Spirit but should flow from his presence.

How many times do you give kindness and then scream when you get anger in return? How many times do you give advice and then complain when it isn't followed? Do you resent it when you give understanding and compassion and receive nothing of the kind in return? The love you give to others should never be conditional on what you get back, but it should come from knowing the God who first loved you. You should be compelled by his love, not by the response or lack of response from other people. You should be defined by God's love, not the actions of others. When your focus is not mainly getting but giving, then your love will grow. And through that love, all other virtues will flow.

the mute man spoke, and the people marveled. [15] But some of them said, "He casts out demons by Beelzebul, the prince of demons," [16] while others, to test him, kept seeking from him a sign from heaven. [17a] But he, knowing their thoughts, said to them, "Every kingdom divided against itself is laid waste, and a divided household falls. [18] And if Satan also is divided against himself, how will his kingdom stand? For you say that I cast out demons by Beelzebul. [19] And if I cast out demons by Beelzebul, by whom do your sons cast them out? Therefore they will be your judges. [20] But if it is by the finger of God that I cast out demons, then the kingdom of God has come upon you. [21] When a strong man, fully armed, guards his own palace, his goods are safe; [22] but when one stronger than he attacks him and overcomes him, he takes away his armor in which he trusted and divides his spoil. [23] Whoever is not with me is against me, and whoever does not gather with me scatters.

Return of an Unclean Spirit

[24b] "When the unclean spirit has gone out of a person, it passes through waterless places seeking rest, and finding none it says, 'I will return to my house from which I came.' [25] And when it comes, it finds the house swept and put in order. [26] Then it goes and brings seven other spirits more evil than itself, and they enter and dwell there. And the last state of that person is worse than the first."

True Blessedness

[27] As he said these things, a woman in the crowd raised her voice and said to him, "Blessed is the womb that bore you, and the breasts at which you nursed!" [28] But he said, "Blessed rather are those who hear the word of God and keep it!"

The Sign of Jonah

[29] When the crowds were increasing, he began to say, c "This generation is an evil generation. It seeks for a sign, but no sign will be given to it except the sign of Jonah. [30] For as Jonah became a sign to the people of Nineveh, so will the Son of Man be to this generation. [31] The queen of the South will rise up at the judgment with the men of this generation and condemn them, for she came from the ends of the earth to hear the wisdom of Solomon, and behold, something greater than Solomon is here. [32] The men of Nineveh will rise up at the judgment with this generation and condemn it, for they repented at the preaching of Jonah, and behold, something greater than Jonah is here.

The Light in You

[33] "No one after lighting a lamp puts it in a cellar or under a basket, but on a stand, so that those who enter may see the light. [34] Your eye is the lamp of your body. When your eye is healthy, your whole body is full of light, but when it is bad, your body is full of darkness. [35] Therefore be careful lest the light in you be darkness. [36] If then your whole body is full of light, having no part dark, it will be wholly bright, as when a lamp with its rays gives you light."

Woes to the Pharisees and Lawyers

[37] While Jesus[1] was speaking, a Pharisee asked him to dine with him, so he went in and reclined at table. [38] The Pharisee was astonished to see that he did not first wash before dinner. [39] And the Lord said to him, "Now you Pharisees cleanse the outside of the cup and of the dish, but inside you are full of greed and wickedness. [40] You fools! Did not he who made the outside make the inside also? [41] But give as alms those things that are within, and behold, everything is clean for you.

[42] "But woe to you Pharisees! For you tithe mint and rue and every herb, and neglect justice and the love of God. These you ought to have done, without neglecting the others. [43] Woe to you Pharisees! For you love the best seat in the synagogues and greetings in the marketplaces. [44] Woe to you! For you are like unmarked graves, and people walk over them without knowing it."

[45] One of the lawyers answered him, "Teacher, in saying these things you insult us also." [46] And he said, "Woe to you lawyers also! For you load people with burdens hard to bear, and you yourselves do not touch the burdens with one of your fingers. [47] Woe to you! For you build the tombs of the prophets whom your fathers killed. [48] So you are witnesses and you consent to the deeds of your fathers, for they

[1] Greek he a For 11:17-22 see parallels Matt. 12:25-29; Mark 3:23-27 b For 11:24-26 see parallel Matt. 12:43-45 c For 11:29-32 see parallel Matt. 12:39-42

killed them, and you build their tombs. ⁴⁹ Therefore also the Wisdom of God said, 'I will send them prophets and apostles, some of whom they will kill and persecute,' ⁵⁰ so that the blood of all the prophets, shed from the foundation of the world, may be charged against this generation, ⁵¹ from the blood of Abel to the blood of Zechariah, who perished between the altar and the sanctuary. Yes, I tell you, it will be required of this generation. ⁵² Woe to you lawyers! For you have taken away the key of knowledge. You did not enter yourselves, and you hindered those who were entering."

⁵³ As he went away from there, the scribes and the Pharisees began to press him hard and to provoke him to speak about many things, ⁵⁴ lying in wait for him, to catch him in something he might say.

ᵃ For 12:2-9 see parallel Matt. 10:26-33

Beware of the Leaven of the Pharisees

12 In the meantime, when so many thousands of the people had gathered together that they were trampling one another, he began to say to his disciples first, "Beware of the leaven of the Pharisees, which is hypocrisy. ² ᵃ Nothing is covered up that will not be revealed, or hidden that will not be known. ³ Therefore whatever you have said in the dark shall be heard in the light, and what you have whispered in private rooms shall be proclaimed on the housetops.

Have No Fear

⁴ "I tell you, my friends, do not fear those who kill the body, and after that have nothing more that they can do. ⁵ But I will warn you whom to fear: fear him who, after he

verses to read
Luke 11:27-32

Have you obeyed God and had it not turn out the way you thought it would? Have you done what he commanded and then been burned? When doing the right thing ends in the opposite of what you expected, does that mean that your obedience was wasted and there must have been a better option?

A lot of times you will be called to do some crazy things as a believer. Jonah thought preaching to the Ninevites would be crazy (see Jonah 1). Jesus says to love your enemies and do good to those who hate you (see Matt. 5:44). Huh? Sounds dangerous. Turn the other cheek—and get your feelings hurt? Submit—and be controlled? Preposterous! When you do these crazy things, a lot of the time nothing good seems to come of it. So over time you decide God's way just isn't working for you, and the next time you are hurt you retaliate instead of loving. When they say something you don't like, you criticize or refuse to do what you are told to do. You no longer do everything God asks but only what seems smart.

The real issue isn't whether doing the right thing has failed you but how you define failure. If your definition of failure is "not getting what you wanted," then yes, obeying God might lead to failure. But a more accurate definition of failure is "not trusting God enough to do what he asks you to do." So if you are obeying God, what looks like a total failure may actually be success in the spiritual realm. The God Girl knows that no matter what the outcome, her obedience will always produce godliness and therefore success, even when all things seem to say otherwise. When the promise seems to be broken and when the answer seems to be no, still she obeys, because she is aware of her eternal reward and spiritual destination. God promises that obedience will not disappoint, and the God Girl believes him.

has killed, has authority to cast into hell.[1] Yes, I tell you, fear him! [6]Are not five sparrows sold for two pennies?[2] And not one of them is forgotten before God. [7]Why, even the hairs of your head are all numbered. Fear not; you are of more value than many sparrows.

Acknowledge Christ Before Men

[8]"And I tell you, everyone who acknowledges me before men, the Son of Man also will acknowledge before the angels of God, [9]but the one who denies me before men will be denied before the angels of God. [10]And everyone who speaks a word against the Son of Man will be forgiven, but the one who blasphemes against the Holy Spirit will not be forgiven. [11]And when they bring you before the synagogues and the rulers and the authorities, do not be anxious about how you should defend yourself or what you should say, [12]for the Holy Spirit will teach you in that very hour what you ought to say."

The Parable of the Rich Fool

[13]Someone in the crowd said to him, "Teacher, tell my brother to divide the inheritance with me." [14]But he said to him, "Man, who made me a judge or arbitrator over you?" [15]And he said to them, "Take care, and be on your guard against all covetousness, for one's life does not consist in the abundance of his possessions." [16]And he told them a parable, saying, "The land of a rich man produced plentifully, [17]and he thought to himself, 'What shall I do, for I have nowhere to store my crops?' [18]And he said, 'I will do this: I will tear down my barns and build larger ones, and there I will store all my grain and my goods. [19]And I will say to my soul, "Soul, you have ample goods laid up for many years; relax, eat, drink, be merry."' [20]But God said to him, 'Fool! This night your soul is required of you, and the things you have prepared, whose will they be?' [21]So is the one who lays up treasure for himself and is not rich toward God."

Do Not Be Anxious

[22]And he said to his disciples, [a]"Therefore I tell you, do not be anxious about your life,

what you will eat, nor about your body, what you will put on. [23]For life is more than food, and the body more than clothing. [24]Consider the ravens: they neither sow nor reap, they have neither storehouse nor barn, and yet God feeds them. Of how much more value are you than the birds! [25]And which of you by being anxious can add a single hour to his span of life?[3] [26]If then you are not able to do as small a thing as that, why are you anxious about the rest? [27]Consider the lilies, how they grow: they neither toil nor spin,[4] yet I tell you, even Solomon in all his glory was not arrayed like one of these. [28]But if God so clothes the grass, which is alive in the field today, and tomorrow is thrown into the oven, how much more will he clothe you, O you of little faith! [29]And do not seek what you are to eat and what you are to drink, nor be worried. [30]For all the nations of the world seek after these things, and your Father knows that you need them. [31]Instead, seek his[5] kingdom, and these things will be added to you.

[32]"Fear not, little flock, for it is your Father's good pleasure to give you the kingdom. [33]Sell your possessions, and give to the needy. Provide yourselves with moneybags that do not grow old, with a treasure in the heavens that does not fail, where no thief approaches and no moth destroys. [34]For where your treasure is, there will your heart be also.

You Must Be Ready

[35]"Stay dressed for action[6] and keep your lamps burning, [36]and be like men who are waiting for their master to come home from the wedding feast, so that they may open the door to him at once when he comes and knocks. [37]Blessed are those servants[7] whom the master finds awake when he comes. Truly, I say to you, he will dress himself for service and have them recline at table, and he will come and serve them. [38]If he comes in the second watch, or in the third, and finds them awake, blessed are those servants! [39]But know this, that if the master of the house had known at what hour the thief was coming, he[8] would not have left his

house to be broken into. ⁴⁰ You also must be ready, for the Son of Man is coming at an hour you do not expect."

⁴¹ Peter said, "Lord, are you telling this parable for us or for all?" ⁴² And the Lord said, "Who then is the faithful and wise manager, whom his master will set over his household, to give them their portion of food at the proper time? ⁴³ Blessed is that servant¹ whom his master will find so doing when he comes. ⁴⁴ Truly, I say to you, he will set him over all his possessions. ⁴⁵ But if that servant says to himself, 'My master is delayed in coming,' and begins to beat the male and female servants, and to eat and drink and get drunk, ⁴⁶ the master of that servant will come on a day when he does not expect him and at an hour he does not know, and will cut him in pieces and put him with the unfaithful. ⁴⁷ And that servant who knew his master's will but did not get ready or act according to his will, will receive a severe beating. ⁴⁸ But the one who did not know, and did what deserved a beating, will receive a light beating. Everyone to whom much was given, of him much will be required, and from him to whom they entrusted much, they will demand the more.

Not Peace, but Division

⁴⁹ "I came to cast fire on the earth, and would that it were already kindled! ⁵⁰ I have a baptism to be baptized with, and how great is my distress until it is accomplished! ⁵¹ ᵃ Do you think that I have come to give peace on earth? No, I tell you, but rather division. ⁵² For from now on in one house there will be five divided, three against two and two against three. ⁵³ They will be divided, father against son and son against father, mother against daughter and daughter against mother, mother-in-law against her daughter-in-law and daughter-in-law against mother-in-law."

Interpreting the Time

⁵⁴ He also said to the crowds, "When you see a cloud rising in the west, you say at once, 'A shower is coming.' And so it happens. ⁵⁵ And when you see the south wind blowing, you say, 'There will be scorching heat,' and it happens. ⁵⁶ You hypocrites! You know how to interpret the appearance of

¹ Greek *bondservant*; also verses 45, 46, 47 ᵃ For 12:51-53 see parallel Matt. 10:34, 35

Know God

verses to read
Luke 12:29-34

Following Christ is not going to cost you something; it's going to cost you *everything*. Everything in you that isn't a part of the life of Christ in you has to be purified, cleaned out of your life. And purification hurts. Your heart and body may violently object when something you love is taken away. But the pain of giving up all that isn't Christ in you shouldn't be something to fear but something to look forward to. Because with each part of you that you give up, you get a part of him. And the more you get, the more you become like him.

Giving things up in order to come closer to God, to obey his Word, and to refuse to serve yourself any longer isn't only holy, it's healthy. The truly strong and successful girl is the one who has nothing to prove to anyone but God. She is the one who has said no to all that the world has to offer and yes to all that heaven holds and even demands.

When God shows you something that's got to go, be quick to get rid of it. Don't whine about how much you'll miss it. Don't wonder if it's really God asking you to give it up. Just give it up, knowing that a heart turned over completely to God is a happy heart. And your faith will be rewarded—guaranteed!

earth and sky, but why do you not know how to interpret the present time?

Settle with Your Accuser

[57] "And why do you not judge for yourselves what is right? [58] As you go with your accuser before the magistrate, make an effort to settle with him on the way, lest he drag you to the judge, and the judge hand you over to the officer, and the officer put you in prison. [59] I tell you, you will never get out until you have paid the very last penny."[1]

Repent or Perish

13 There were some present at that very time who told him about the Galileans whose blood Pilate had mingled with their sacrifices. [2] And he answered them, "Do you think that these Galileans were worse sinners than all the other Galileans, because they suffered in this way? [3] No, I tell you; but unless you repent, you will all likewise perish. [4] Or those eighteen on whom the tower in Siloam fell and killed them: do you think that they were worse offenders than all the others who lived in Jerusalem? [5] No, I tell you; but unless you repent, you will all likewise perish."

The Parable of the Barren Fig Tree

[6] And he told this parable: "A man had a fig tree planted in his vineyard, and he came seeking fruit on it and found none. [7] And he said to the vinedresser, 'Look, for three years now I have come seeking fruit on this fig tree, and I find none. Cut it down. Why should it use up the ground?' [8] And he answered him, 'Sir, let it alone this year also, until I dig around it and put on manure. [9] Then if it should bear fruit next year, well and good; but if not, you can cut it down.'"

A Woman with a Disabling Spirit

[10] Now he was teaching in one of the synagogues on the Sabbath. [11] And behold, there was a woman who had had a disabling spirit for eighteen years. She was bent over and could not fully straighten herself. [12] When Jesus saw her, he called her over and said to her, "Woman, you are freed from your disability." [13] And he laid his hands on her, and immediately she was made straight, and she glorified God. [14] But the ruler of the synagogue, indignant because Jesus had healed on the Sabbath, said to the people, "There are six days in which work ought to be done. Come on those days and be healed, and not on the Sabbath day." [15] Then the Lord answered him, "You hypocrites! Does not each of you on the Sabbath untie his ox or his donkey from the manger and lead it away to water it? [16] And ought not this woman, a daughter of Abraham whom Satan bound for eighteen years, be loosed from this bond on the Sabbath day?" [17] As he said these things, all his adversaries were put to shame, and all the people rejoiced at all the glorious things that were done by him.

The Mustard Seed and the Leaven

[18] [a] He said therefore, "What is the kingdom of God like? And to what shall I compare it? [19] It is like a grain of mustard seed that a man took and sowed in his garden, and it grew and became a tree, and the birds of the air made nests in its branches."

[20] And again he said, "To what shall I compare the kingdom of God? [21] It is like leaven that a woman took and hid in three measures of flour, until it was all leavened."

The Narrow Door

[22] He went on his way through towns and villages, teaching and journeying toward Jerusalem. [23] And someone said to him, "Lord, will those who are saved be few?" And he said to them, [24] "Strive to enter through the narrow door. For many, I tell you, will seek to enter and will not be able. [25] When once the master of the house has risen and shut the door, and you begin to stand outside and to knock at the door, saying, 'Lord, open to us,' then he will answer you, 'I do not know where you come from.' [26] Then you will begin to say, 'We ate and drank in your presence, and you taught in our streets.' [27] But he will say, 'I tell you, I do not know where you come from. Depart from me, all you workers of evil!' [28] In that place there will be weeping and gnashing of teeth, when you see Abraham and Isaac and Jacob and

[1] Greek *lepton*, a Jewish bronze or copper coin worth about 1/128 of a *denarius* (which was a day's wage for a laborer) [a] For 13:18, 19 see parallels Matt. 13:31, 32; Mark 4:30-32

all the prophets in the kingdom of God but you yourselves cast out. [29] And people will come from east and west, and from north and south, and recline at table in the kingdom of God. [30] And behold, some are last who will be first, and some are first who will be last."

Lament over Jerusalem

[31] At that very hour some Pharisees came and said to him, "Get away from here, for Herod wants to kill you." [32] And he said to them, "Go and tell that fox, 'Behold, I cast out demons and perform cures today and tomorrow, and the third day I finish my course. [33] Nevertheless, I must go on my way today and tomorrow and the day following, for it cannot be that a prophet should perish away from Jerusalem.' [34] [a] O Jerusalem, Jerusalem, the city that kills the prophets and stones those who are sent to it! How often would I have gathered your children together as a hen gathers her brood under her wings, and you were not willing! [35] Behold, your house is forsaken. And I tell you, you will not see me until you say, [b] 'Blessed is he who comes in the name of the Lord!' "

Healing of a Man on the Sabbath

14 One Sabbath, when he went to dine at the house of a ruler of the Pharisees, they were watching him carefully. [2] And behold, there was a man before him who had dropsy. [3] And Jesus responded to the lawyers and Pharisees, saying, "Is it lawful to heal on the Sabbath, or not?" [4] But they remained silent. Then he took him and healed him and sent him away. [5] And he said to them, "Which of you, having a son[1] or an ox that has fallen into a well on a Sabbath day, will not immediately pull him out?" [6] And they could not reply to these things.

The Parable of the Wedding Feast

[7] Now he told a parable to those who were invited, when he noticed how they chose the places of honor, saying to them, [8] "When you are invited by someone to a wedding feast, do not sit down in a place of honor, lest someone more distinguished than you be invited by him, [9] and he who invited you both will come and

say to you, 'Give your place to this person,' and then you will begin with shame to take the lowest place. [10] But when you are invited, go and sit in the lowest place, so that when your host comes he may say to you, 'Friend, move up higher.' Then you will be honored in the presence of all who sit at table with you. [11] For everyone who exalts himself will be humbled, and he who humbles himself will be exalted."

The Parable of the Great Banquet

[12] He said also to the man who had invited him, "When you give a dinner or a banquet, do not invite your friends or your brothers[2] or your relatives or rich neighbors, lest they also invite you in return and you be repaid. [13] But when you give a feast, invite the poor, the crippled, the lame, the blind, [14] and you will be blessed, because they cannot repay you. For you will be repaid at the resurrection of the just."

[15] When one of those who reclined at table with him heard these things, he said to him, "Blessed is everyone who will eat bread in the kingdom of God!" [16] But he said to him, "A man once gave a great banquet and invited many. [17] And at the time for the banquet he sent his servant[3] to say to those who had been invited, 'Come, for everything is now ready.' [18] But they all alike began to make excuses. The first said to him, 'I have bought a field, and I must go out and see it. Please have me excused.' [19] And another said, 'I have bought five yoke of oxen, and I go to examine them. Please have me excused.' [20] And another said, 'I have married a wife, and therefore I cannot come.' [21] So the servant came and reported these things to his master. Then the master of the house became angry and said to his servant, 'Go out quickly to the streets and lanes of the city, and bring in the poor and crippled and blind and lame.' [22] And the servant said, 'Sir, what you commanded has been done, and still there is room.' [23] And the master said to the servant, 'Go out to the highways and hedges and compel people to come in, that my house may be filled. [24] For I tell you,[4] none of those men who were invited shall taste my banquet.' "

---

[1] Some manuscripts *a donkey* [2] Or *your brothers and sisters*. The plural Greek word *adelphoi* (translated "brothers") refers to siblings in a family. In New Testament usage, depending on the context, *adelphoi* may refer either to *brothers* or to *brothers and sisters* [3] Greek *bondservant*; also verses 21, 22, 23 [4] The Greek word for *you* here is plural [a] For 13:34, 35 see parallel Matt. 23:37-39 [b] Ps. 118:26

The Cost of Discipleship

²⁵ Now great crowds accompanied him, and he turned and said to them, ²⁶ "If anyone comes to me and does not hate his own father and mother and wife and children and brothers and sisters, yes, and even his own life, he cannot be my disciple. ²⁷ Whoever does not bear his own cross and come after me cannot be my disciple. ²⁸ For which of you, desiring to build a tower, does not first sit down and count the cost, whether he has enough to complete it? ²⁹ Otherwise, when he has laid a foundation and is not able to finish, all who see it begin to mock him, ³⁰ saying, 'This man began to build and was not able to finish.' ³¹ Or what king, going out to encounter another king in war, will not sit down first and deliberate whether he is able with ten thousand to meet him who comes against him with twenty thousand? ³² And if not, while the other is yet a great way off, he sends a delegation and asks for terms of peace. ³³ So therefore, any one of you who does not renounce all that he has cannot be my disciple.

Salt Without Taste Is Worthless

³⁴ "Salt is good, but if salt has lost its taste, how shall its saltiness be restored? ³⁵ It is of no use either for the soil or for the manure pile. It is thrown away. He who has ears to hear, let him hear."

The Parable of the Lost Sheep

15 Now the tax collectors and sinners were all drawing near to hear him. ² And the Pharisees and the scribes grumbled, saying, "This man receives sinners and eats with them."

³ So he told them this parable: ⁴ "What man of you, having a hundred sheep, if he has lost one of them, does not leave the ninety-nine in the open country, and go after the one that is lost, until he finds it? ⁵ And when he has found it, he lays it on his shoulders, rejoicing. ⁶ And when he comes home, he calls together his friends and his neighbors, saying to them, 'Rejoice with me, for I have found my sheep that was lost.' ⁷ Just so, I tell you, there will be more joy in heaven over one sinner who repents than over

verses to read
Luke 14:25-33

What does it mean to love Jesus more than your own life? Not a lot of people really know the answer to that Q. It's human nature to think of yourself first, and thinking of someone else first is downright divine. After all, it's *your* feelings that race through your body, *your* eyes that see the world, and *your* heart that feels the pain of rejection, worry, fear, loneliness, and even love. With all these feelings and experiences, it's hard to focus on something other than yourself, yet that's what Jesus wants you to do—to think about him more than yourself. He wants you to love him with *all* of your heart, not just a part of it.

Anything in your heart that isn't holy is not from Jesus and is direct evidence that you love your own life more than his. But don't freak—that doesn't mean you're a lost cause. It just means you're human. Thank God that his grace is freely given to those who realize the error of their ways! So check your life and find those areas of unholiness that make your life miserable or broken. Find out where you need healing, and then ask him for grace to truly see that your desires aren't as important as his. Let go of anything that puts the focus on your own life rather than the life of Jesus in you. Make him, his Word, and his character the most important things in your life, and let him know it. Imitate him. Believe him and look at your life through his eyes instead of your own. When you do, you will find that your life and your spirit calm down.

ninety-nine righteous persons who need no repentance.

The Parable of the Lost Coin

8 "Or what woman, having ten silver coins,[1] if she loses one coin, does not light a lamp and sweep the house and seek diligently until she finds it? **9** And when she has found it, she calls together her friends and neighbors, saying, 'Rejoice with me, for I have found the coin that I had lost.' **10** Just so, I tell you, there is joy before the angels of God over one sinner who repents."

The Parable of the Prodigal Son

11 And he said, "There was a man who had two sons. **12** And the younger of them said to his father, 'Father, give me the share of property that is coming to me.' And he divided his property between them. **13** Not many days later, the younger son gathered all he had and took a journey into a far country, and there he squandered his property in reckless living. **14** And when he had spent everything, a severe famine arose in that country, and he began to be in need. **15** So he went and hired himself out to[2] one of the citizens of that country, who sent him into his fields to feed pigs. **16** And he was longing to be fed with the pods that the pigs ate, and no one gave him anything.

17 "But when he came to himself, he said, 'How many of my father's hired servants have more than enough bread, but I perish here with hunger! **18** I will arise and go to my father, and I will say to him, "Father, I have sinned against heaven and before you. **19** I am no longer worthy to be called your son. Treat me as one of your hired servants."' **20** And he arose and came to his father. But while he was still a long way off, his father saw him and felt compassion, and ran and embraced him and kissed him. **21** And the son said to him, 'Father, I have sinned against heaven and before you. I am no longer worthy to be called your son.'[3] **22** But the father said to his servants,[4] 'Bring quickly the best robe, and put it on him, and put a ring on his hand, and shoes on his feet. **23** And bring the fattened calf and kill it, and let us eat and celebrate. **24** For this my son was dead, and is alive again;

he was lost, and is found.' And they began to celebrate.

25 "Now his older son was in the field, and as he came and drew near to the house, he heard music and dancing. **26** And he called one of the servants and asked what these things meant. **27** And he said to him, 'Your brother has come, and your father has killed the fattened calf, because he has received him back safe and sound.' **28** But he was angry and refused to go in. His father came out and entreated him, **29** but he answered his father, 'Look, these many years I have served you, and I never disobeyed your command, yet you never gave me a young goat, that I might celebrate with my friends. **30** But when this son of yours came, who has devoured your property with prostitutes, you killed the fattened calf for him!' **31** And he said to him, 'Son, you are always with me, and all that is mine is yours. **32** It was fitting to celebrate and be glad, for this your brother was dead, and is alive; he was lost, and is found.' "

The Parable of the Dishonest Manager

16 He also said to the disciples, "There was a rich man who had a manager, and charges were brought to him that this man was wasting his possessions. **2** And he called him and said to him, 'What is this that I hear about you? Turn in the account of your management, for you can no longer be manager.' **3** And the manager said to himself, 'What shall I do, since my master is taking the management away from me? I am not strong enough to dig, and I am ashamed to beg. **4** I have decided what to do, so that when I am removed from management, people may receive me into their houses.' **5** So, summoning his master's debtors one by one, he said to the first, 'How much do you owe my master?' **6** He said, 'A hundred measures[5] of oil.' He said to him, 'Take your bill, and sit down quickly and write fifty.' **7** Then he said to another, 'And how much do you owe?' He said, 'A hundred measures[6] of wheat.' He said to him, 'Take your bill, and write eighty.' **8** The master commended the dishonest manager for his shrewdness. For the sons of this world[7] are more shrewd in dealing with their own generation than the sons of light. ⁹ And I tell you, make friends for yourselves by means of unrighteous wealth,¹ so that when it fails they may receive you into the eternal dwellings.

¹⁰ "One who is faithful in a very little is also faithful in much, and one who is dishonest in a very little is also dishonest in much. ¹¹ If then you have not been faithful in the unrighteous wealth, who will entrust to you the true riches? ¹² And if you have not been faithful in that which is another's, who will give you that which is your own? ¹³ No servant can serve two masters, for either he will hate the one and love the other, or he will be devoted to the one and despise the other. You cannot serve God and money."

The Law and the Kingdom of God

¹⁴ The Pharisees, who were lovers of money, heard all these things, and they ridiculed him. ¹⁵ And he said to them, "You are those who justify yourselves before men, but God knows your hearts. For what is exalted among men is an abomination in the sight of God.

¹⁶ "The Law and the Prophets were until John; since then the good news of the kingdom of God is preached, and everyone forces his way into it.² ¹⁷ But it is easier for heaven and earth to pass away than for one dot of the Law to become void.

Divorce and Remarriage

¹⁸ "Everyone who divorces his wife and marries another commits adultery, and he who marries a woman divorced from her husband commits adultery.

The Rich Man and Lazarus

¹⁹ "There was a rich man who was clothed in purple and fine linen and who feasted sumptuously every day. ²⁰ And at his gate was laid a poor man named Lazarus, covered with sores, ²¹ who desired to be fed with what fell from the rich man's table. Moreover, even the dogs came and licked his sores. ²² The poor man died and was carried by the angels to Abraham's side.³ The rich man also died and was buried, ²³ and in Hades, being in torment, he lifted up his eyes and saw Abraham far off and Lazarus at his side. ²⁴ And he called out, 'Father Abraham, have mercy on me, and

send Lazarus to dip the end of his finger in water and cool my tongue, for I am in anguish in this flame.' ²⁵ But Abraham said, 'Child, remember that you in your lifetime received your good things, and Lazarus in like manner bad things; but now he is comforted here, and you are in anguish. ²⁶ And besides all this, between us and you a great chasm has been fixed, in order that those who would pass from here to you may not be able, and none may cross from there to us.' ²⁷ And he said, 'Then I beg you, father, to send him to my father's house— ²⁸ for I have five brothers⁴— so that he may warn them, lest they also come into this place of torment.' ²⁹ But Abraham said, 'They have Moses and the Prophets; let them hear them.' ³⁰ And he said, 'No, father Abraham, but if someone goes to them from the dead, they will repent.' ³¹ He said to him, 'If they do not hear Moses and the Prophets, neither will they be convinced if someone should rise from the dead.'"

Temptations to Sin

17 And he said to his disciples, "Temptations to sin⁵ are sure to come, but woe to the one through whom they come! ² It would be better for him if a millstone were hung around his neck and he were cast into the sea than that he should cause one of these little ones to sin.⁶ ³ Pay attention to yourselves! If your brother sins, rebuke him, and if he repents, forgive him, ⁴ and if he sins against you seven times in the day, and turns to you seven times, saying, 'I repent,' you must forgive him."

Increase Our Faith

⁵ The apostles said to the Lord, "Increase our faith!" ⁶ And the Lord said, "If you had faith like a grain of mustard seed, you could say to this mulberry tree, 'Be uprooted and planted in the sea,' and it would obey you.

Unworthy Servants

⁷ "Will any one of you who has a servant⁷ plowing or keeping sheep say to him when he has come in from the field, 'Come at once and recline at table'? ⁸ Will he not rather say to him, 'Prepare supper for me, and dress properly,⁸ and serve me while I eat and drink, and afterward you will eat and drink'? ⁹ Does he thank the servant

¹ Greek *mammon*, a Semitic word for money or possessions; also verse 11; rendered *money* in verse 13 ² Or *everyone is forcefully urged into it* ³ Greek *bosom*; also verse 23 ⁴ Or *brothers and sisters* ⁵ Greek *Stumbling blocks* ⁶ Greek *stumble* ⁷ Greek *bondservant*; also verse 9 ⁸ Greek *gird yourself*

because he did what was commanded? **10**So you also, when you have done all that you were commanded, say, 'We are unworthy servants;[1] we have only done what was our duty.'"

Jesus Cleanses Ten Lepers

11On the way to Jerusalem he was passing along between Samaria and Galilee. **12**And as he entered a village, he was met by ten lepers,[2] who stood at a distance **13**and lifted up their voices, saying, "Jesus, Master, have mercy on us." **14**When he saw them he said to them, "Go and show yourselves to the priests." And as they went they were cleansed. **15**Then one of them, when he saw that he was healed, turned back, praising God with a loud voice; **16**and he fell on his face at Jesus' feet, giving him thanks. Now he was a Samaritan. **17**Then Jesus answered, "Were not ten cleansed? Where are the nine? **18**Was no one found to return and give praise to God except this foreigner?" **19**And he said to him, "Rise and go your way; your faith has made you well."[3]

The Coming of the Kingdom

20Being asked by the Pharisees when the kingdom of God would come, he answered them, "The kingdom of God is not coming in ways that can be observed, **21**nor will they say, 'Look, here it is!' or 'There!' for behold, the kingdom of God is in the midst of you."[4]

22And he said to the disciples, "The days are coming when you will desire to see one of the days of the Son of Man, and you will not see it. **23**And they will say to you, 'Look, there!' or 'Look, here!' Do not go out or follow them. **24**For as the lightning flashes and lights up the sky from one side to the other, so will the Son of Man be in his day.[5] **25**But first he must suffer many things and be rejected by this generation. **26**Just as it was in the days of Noah, so will it be in the days of the Son of Man. **27**They were eating and drinking and marrying and being given in marriage, until the day when Noah entered the ark, and the flood came and destroyed them all. **28**Likewise, just as it was in the days of Lot—they were eating and drinking, buying and selling, planting and building, **29**but on the day

when Lot went out from Sodom, fire and sulfur rained from heaven and destroyed them all— **30**so will it be on the day when the Son of Man is revealed. **31**On that day, let the one who is on the housetop, with his goods in the house, not come down to take them away, and likewise let the one who is in the field not turn back. **32**Remember Lot's wife. **33**Whoever seeks to preserve his life will lose it, but whoever loses his life will keep it. **34**I tell you, in that night there will be two in one bed. One will be taken and the other left. **35**There will be two women grinding together. One will be taken and the other left."[6] **37**And they said to him, "Where, Lord?" He said to them, "Where the corpse[7] is, there the vultures[8] will gather."

The Parable of the Persistent Widow

18 And he told them a parable to the effect that they ought always to pray and not lose heart. **2**He said, "In a certain city there was a judge who neither feared God nor respected man. **3**And there was a widow in that city who kept coming to him and saying, 'Give me justice against my adversary.' **4**For a while he refused, but afterward he said to himself, 'Though I neither fear God nor respect man, **5**yet because this widow keeps bothering me, I will give her justice, so that she will not beat me down by her continual coming.'" **6**And the Lord said, "Hear what the unrighteous judge says. **7**And will not God give justice to his elect, who cry to him day and night? Will he delay long over them? **8**I tell you, he will give justice to them speedily. Nevertheless, when the Son of Man comes, will he find faith on earth?"

The Pharisee and the Tax Collector

9He also told this parable to some who trusted in themselves that they were righteous, and treated others with contempt: **10**"Two men went up into the temple to pray, one a Pharisee and the other a tax collector. **11**The Pharisee, standing by himself, prayed[9] thus: 'God, I thank you that I am not like other men, extortioners, unjust, adulterers, or even like this tax collector. **12**I fast twice a week; I give tithes of all that I get.' **13**But the tax collector, standing

[1] Greek *bondservants* [2] *Leprosy* was a term for several skin diseases; see Leviticus 13 [3] Or *has saved you* [4] Or *within you*, or *within your grasp* [5] Some manuscripts omit *in his day* [6] Some manuscripts add verse 36: *Two men will be in the field; one will be taken and the other left* [7] Greek *body* [8] Or *eagles* [9] Or *standing, prayed to himself*

far off, would not even lift up his eyes to heaven, but beat his breast, saying, 'God, be merciful to me, a sinner!' ¹⁴ I tell you, this man went down to his house justified, rather than the other. For everyone who exalts himself will be humbled, but the one who humbles himself will be exalted."

Let the Children Come to Me

¹⁵*a* Now they were bringing even infants to him that he might touch them. And when the disciples saw it, they rebuked them. ¹⁶ But Jesus called them to him, saying, "Let the children come to me, and do not hinder them, for to such belongs the kingdom of God. ¹⁷ Truly, I say to you, whoever does not receive the kingdom of God like a child shall not enter it."

The Rich Ruler

¹⁸*b* And a ruler asked him, "Good Teacher, what must I do to inherit eternal life?" ¹⁹ And Jesus said to him, "Why do you call me good? No one is good except God alone. ²⁰ You know the commandments: *c* 'Do not commit adultery, Do not murder, Do not steal, Do not bear false witness, Honor your father and mother.'" ²¹ And he said, "All

these I have kept from my youth." ²² When Jesus heard this, he said to him, "One thing you still lack. Sell all that you have and distribute to the poor, and you will have treasure in heaven; and come, follow me." ²³ But when he heard these things, he became very sad, for he was extremely rich. ²⁴ Jesus, seeing that he had become sad, said, "How difficult it is for those who have wealth to enter the kingdom of God! ²⁵ For it is easier for a camel to go through the eye of a needle than for a rich person to enter the kingdom of God." ²⁶ Those who heard it said, "Then who can be saved?" ²⁷ But he said, "What is impossible with man is possible with God." ²⁸ And Peter said, "See, we have left our homes and followed you." ²⁹ And he said to them, "Truly, I say to you, there is no one who has left house or wife or brothers[1] or parents or children, for the sake of the kingdom of God, ³⁰ who will not receive many times more in this time, and in the age to come eternal life."

Jesus Foretells His Death a Third Time

³¹*d* And taking the twelve, he said to them, "See, we are going up to Jerusalem, and everything that is written about the Son of

[1] Or *wife or brothers and sisters*   *a* For 18:15-17 see parallels Matt. 19:13-15; Mark 10:13-16   *b* For 18:18-30 see parallels Matt. 19:16-30; Mark 10:17-31   *c* Ex. 20:12-16; Deut. 5:16-20   *d* For 18:31-33 see parallels Matt. 20:17-19; Mark 10:32-34

verses to read
Luke 18:9-14

Fame is not God's goal for your life. God isn't concerned about making people famous and adored. It's tempting to measure how successful you are as a person by how popular you are, but that's not God's measuring stick. His own Son wasn't born a king or even a rich man but a poor carpenter's son. He didn't run around with a marketing guy or a PR girl, looking for the limelight; he looked for the hearts of people.

When you are really in love with God, you don't look for the attention of the world but you look to give God all of your attention. Don't let fame become your goal. In your life, God should always be the famous one, because he's the one people need, the one they crave. God's goal is to humble you, not feed your big fat ego. Many people without the Spirit of God can't understand how to resist the call to fame and popularity, but when you have the Spirit in you, he gives you the strength to be perfectly happy when you are perfectly unnoticeable. Don't try to draw attention to your holiness or your amazing prayer life, but work to put all the attention on him so that whatever you do, you will do it all to the glory of God.

Man by the prophets will be accomplished. ³² For he will be delivered over to the Gentiles and will be mocked and shamefully treated and spit upon. ³³ And after flogging him, they will kill him, and on the third day he will rise." ³⁴ But they understood none of these things. This saying was hidden from them, and they did not grasp what was said.

Jesus Heals a Blind Beggar

³⁵ ªAs he drew near to Jericho, a blind man was sitting by the roadside begging. ³⁶ And hearing a crowd going by, he inquired what this meant. ³⁷ They told him, "Jesus of Nazareth is passing by." ³⁸ And he cried out, "Jesus, Son of David, have mercy on me!" ³⁹ And those who were in front rebuked him, telling him to be silent. But he cried out all the more, "Son of David, have mercy on me!" ⁴⁰ And Jesus stopped and commanded him to be brought to him. And when he came near, he asked him, ⁴¹ "What do you want me to do for you?" He said, "Lord, let me recover my sight." ⁴² And Jesus said to him, "Recover your sight; your faith has made you well." ⁴³ And immediately he recovered his sight and followed him, glorifying God. And all the people, when they saw it, gave praise to God.

Jesus and Zacchaeus

19 He entered Jericho and was passing through. ² And behold, there was a man named Zacchaeus. He was a chief tax collector and was rich. ³ And he was seeking to see who Jesus was, but on account of the crowd he could not, because he was small in stature. ⁴ So he ran on ahead and climbed up into a sycamore tree to see him, for he was about to pass that way. ⁵ And when Jesus came to the place, he looked up and said to him, "Zacchaeus, hurry and come down, for I must stay at your house today." ⁶ So he hurried and came down and received him joyfully. ⁷ And when they saw it, they all grumbled, "He has gone in to be the guest of a man who is a sinner." ⁸ And Zacchaeus stood and said to the Lord, "Behold, Lord, the half of my goods I give to the poor. And if I have defrauded anyone of anything, I restore it fourfold." ⁹ And Jesus said to him, "Today salvation

has come to this house, since he also is a son of Abraham. ¹⁰ For the Son of Man came to seek and to save the lost."

The Parable of the Ten Minas

¹¹ As they heard these things, he proceeded to tell a parable, because he was near to Jerusalem, and because they supposed that the kingdom of God was to appear immediately. ¹² He said therefore, "A nobleman went into a far country to receive for himself a kingdom and then return. ¹³ Calling ten of his servants,¹ he gave them ten minas,² and said to them, 'Engage in business until I come.' ¹⁴ But his citizens hated him and sent a delegation after him, saying, 'We do not want this man to reign over us.' ¹⁵ When he returned, having received the kingdom, he ordered these servants to whom he had given the money to be called to him, that he might know what they had gained by doing business. ¹⁶ The first came before him, saying, 'Lord, your mina has made ten minas more.' ¹⁷ And he said to him, 'Well done, good servant!³ Because you have been faithful in a very little, you shall have authority over ten cities.' ¹⁸ And the second came, saying, 'Lord, your mina has made five minas.' ¹⁹ And he said to him, 'And you are to be over five cities.' ²⁰ Then another came, saying, 'Lord, here is your mina, which I kept laid away in a handkerchief; ²¹ for I was afraid of you, because you are a severe man. You take what you did not deposit, and reap what you did not sow.' ²² He said to him, 'I will condemn you with your own words, you wicked servant! You knew that I was a severe man, taking what I did not deposit and reaping what I did not sow? ²³ Why then did you not put my money in the bank, and at my coming I might have collected it with interest?' ²⁴ And he said to those who stood by, 'Take the mina from him, and give it to the one who has the ten minas.' ²⁵ And they said to him, 'Lord, he has ten minas!' ²⁶ 'I tell you that to everyone who has, more will be given, but from the one who has not, even what he has will be taken away. ²⁷ But as for these enemies of mine, who did not want me to reign over them, bring them here and slaughter them before me.' "

---

¹ Greek *bondservants*; also verse 15 ² A *mina* was about three months' wages for a laborer ³ Greek *bondservant*; also verse 22
ª For 18:35-43 see parallels Matt. 20:29-34; Mark 10:46-52

The Triumphal Entry

²⁸ And when he had said these things, he went on ahead, going up to Jerusalem. ²⁹ ᵃ When he drew near to Bethphage and Bethany, at the mount that is called Olivet, he sent two of the disciples, ³⁰ saying, "Go into the village in front of you, where on entering you will find a colt tied, on which no one has ever yet sat. Untie it and bring it here. ³¹ If anyone asks you, 'Why are you untying it?' you shall say this: 'The Lord has need of it.'" ³² So those who were sent went away and found it just as he had told them. ³³ And as they were untying the colt, its owners said to them, "Why are you untying the colt?" ³⁴ And they said, "The Lord has need of it." ³⁵ And they brought it to Jesus, and throwing their cloaks on the colt, they set Jesus on it. ³⁶ And as he rode along, they spread their cloaks on the road. ³⁷ As he was drawing near—already on the way down the Mount of Olives—the whole multitude of his disciples began to rejoice and praise God with a loud voice for all the mighty works that they had seen, ³⁸ saying, "Blessed is the King who comes in the name of the Lord! Peace in heaven and glory in the highest!" ³⁹ And some of the Pharisees in the crowd said to him, "Teacher, rebuke your disciples." ⁴⁰ He answered, "I tell you, if these were silent, the very stones would cry out."

Jesus Weeps over Jerusalem

⁴¹ And when he drew near and saw the city, he wept over it, ⁴² saying, "Would that you, even you, had known on this day the things that make for peace! But now they are hidden from your eyes. ⁴³ For the days will come upon you, when your enemies will set up a barricade around you and surround you and hem you in on every side ⁴⁴ and tear you down to the ground, you and your children within you. And they will not leave one stone upon another in you, because you did not know the time of your visitation."

Jesus Cleanses the Temple

⁴⁵ ᵇ And he entered the temple and began to drive out those who sold, ⁴⁶ saying to them, "It is written, ᶜ 'My house shall be a house of prayer,' but you have made it a den of robbers."

⁴⁷ And he was teaching daily in the temple. The chief priests and the scribes and the principal men of the people were seeking to destroy him, ⁴⁸ but they did not find anything they could do, for all the people were hanging on his words.

The Authority of Jesus Challenged

20 ᵈ One day, as Jesus¹ was teaching the people in the temple and preaching the gospel, the chief priests and the scribes with the elders came up ² and said to him, "Tell us by what authority you do these things, or who it is that gave you this authority." ³ He answered them, "I also will ask you a question. Now tell me, ⁴ was the baptism of John from heaven or from man?" ⁵ And they discussed it with one another, saying, "If we say, 'From heaven,' he will say, 'Why did you not believe him?' ⁶ But if we say, 'From man,' all the people will stone us to death, for they are convinced that John was a prophet." ⁷ So they answered that they did not know where it came from. ⁸ And Jesus said to them, "Neither will I tell you by what authority I do these things."

The Parable of the Wicked Tenants

⁹ ᵉ And he began to tell the people this parable: "A man planted a vineyard and let it out to tenants and went into another country for a long while. ¹⁰ When the time came, he sent a servant² to the tenants, so that they would give him some of the fruit of the vineyard. But the tenants beat him and sent him away empty-handed. ¹¹ And he sent another servant. But they also beat and treated him shamefully, and sent him away empty-handed. ¹² And he sent yet a third. This one also they wounded and cast out. ¹³ Then the owner of the vineyard said, 'What shall I do? I will send my beloved son; perhaps they will respect him.' ¹⁴ But when the tenants saw him, they said to themselves, 'This is the heir. Let us kill him, so that the inheritance may be ours.' ¹⁵ And they threw him out of the vineyard and killed him. What then will the owner of the vineyard do to them? ¹⁶ He will come and destroy those tenants and give the vineyard to others." When they heard this, they said, "Surely not!" ¹⁷ But he looked

---

¹ Greek *he* ² Greek *bondservant*; also verse 11 ᵃ For 19:29-38 see parallels Matt. 21:1-9; Mark 11:1-10; John 12:12-15 ᵇ For 19:45-47 see parallels Matt. 21:12-16; Mark 11:15-18 ᶜ Isa. 56:7 ᵈ For 20:1-8 see parallels Matt. 21:23-27; Mark 11:27-33 ᵉ For 20:9-18 see parallels Matt. 21:33-46; Mark 12:1-12

directly at them and said, "What then is this that is written:

a"'The stone that the builders rejected has become the cornerstone'?[1]

[18] Everyone who falls on that stone will be broken to pieces, and when it falls on anyone, it will crush him."

Paying Taxes to Caesar

[19] The scribes and the chief priests sought to lay hands on him at that very hour, for they perceived that he had told this parable against them, but they feared the people. [20] *b*So they watched him and sent spies, who pretended to be sincere, that they might catch him in something he said, so as to deliver him up to the authority and jurisdiction of the governor. [21] So they asked him, "Teacher, we know that you speak and teach rightly, and show no partiality,[2] but truly teach the way of God. [22] Is it lawful for us to give tribute to Caesar, or not?" [23] But he perceived their craftiness, and said to them, [24] "Show me a denarius.[3] Whose likeness and inscription does it have?" They said, "Caesar's." [25] He said to them, "Then render to Caesar the things that are Caesar's, and to God the things that are God's." [26] And they were not able in the presence of the people to catch him in what he said, but marveling at his answer they became silent.

Sadducees Ask About the Resurrection

[27] There came to him some Sadducees, those who deny that there is a resurrection, [28] and they asked him a question, saying, "Teacher, Moses wrote for us that if a man's brother dies, having a wife but no children, the man[4] must take the widow and raise up offspring for his brother. [29] Now there were seven brothers. The first took a wife, and died without children. [30] And the second [31] and the third took her, and likewise all seven left no children and died. [32] Afterward the woman also died. [33] In the resurrection, therefore, whose wife will the woman be? For the seven had her as wife."

[34] And Jesus said to them, "The sons of this age marry and are given in marriage, [35] but those who are considered worthy to attain to that age and to the resurrection from the dead neither marry nor are given in marriage, [36] for they cannot die anymore, because they are equal to angels and are sons of God, being sons[5] of the resurrection. [37] But that the dead are raised, even Moses showed, in the passage about the bush, where he calls the Lord the God of Abraham and the God of Isaac and the God of Jacob. [38] Now he is not God of the dead, but of the living, for all live to him." [39] Then some of the scribes answered, "Teacher, you have spoken well." [40] For they no longer dared to ask him any question.

Whose Son Is the Christ?

[41] *c*But he said to them, "How can they say that the Christ is David's son? [42] For David himself says in the Book of Psalms,

d"'The Lord said to my Lord,
  "Sit at my right hand,
[43]   until I make your enemies your
      footstool."'

[44] David thus calls him Lord, so how is he his son?"

Beware of the Scribes

[45] *e*And in the hearing of all the people he said to his disciples, [46] "Beware of the scribes, who like to walk around in long robes, and love greetings in the marketplaces and the best seats in the synagogues and the places of honor at feasts, [47] who devour widows' houses and for a pretense make long prayers. They will receive the greater condemnation."

The Widow's Offering

21 *f*Jesus[6] looked up and saw the rich putting their gifts into the offering box, [2] and he saw a poor widow put in two small copper coins.[7] [3] And he said, "Truly, I tell you, this poor widow has put in more than all of them. [4] For they all contributed out of their abundance, but she out of her poverty put in all she had to live on."

Jesus Foretells Destruction of the Temple

[5] *g*And while some were speaking of the temple, how it was adorned with noble

---

[1] Greek *the head of the corner* [2] Greek *and do not receive a face* [3] A *denarius* was a day's wage for a laborer [4] Greek *his brother* [5] Greek *huioi*; see About the ESV [6] Greek *He* [7] Greek *two lepta*; a *lepton* was a Jewish bronze or copper coin worth about 1/128 of a *denarius* (which was a day's wage for a laborer) *a*Ps. 118:22 *b*For 20:20-38 see parallels Matt. 22:15-32; Mark 12:13-27 *c*For 20:41-44 see parallels Matt. 22:41-45; Mark 12:35-37 *d*Ps. 110:1 *e*For 20:45, 46 see parallels Matt. 23:1, 2, 5-7; Mark 12:38-40 *f*For 21:1-4 see parallel Mark 12:41-44 *g*For 21:5-36 see parallels Matt. 24:1-51; Mark 13:1-37

The Widow With Two Coins

Read this God Girl story in Luke 21:1–4.

"Truly, I tell you, this poor widow has put in more than all of them. For they all contributed out of their abundance, but she out of her poverty put in all she had to live on."

Luke 21:3–4

A lot of people would say that for your giving to be worth anything, it has to be the best there is to give—quality. But God doesn't compare the quality of your gift with another's. Nor does he compare quantities, because he's most concerned with the motives and the spiritual condition of those giving. The two coins the widow dropped into the offering box were unimpressive to everyone else. But for her, their quantity was impressive—the quantity of her gift was all she had. She didn't think about the insignificance of that amount or about how small her coins were. She simply wanted to give what she had—not just some of it, keeping the rest for herself, but all two coins of it.

To give all you have, no matter how unimpressive it is, is a very noble act. But this isn't just about money; this is also about your time and talents. You might not be a scholar, you might not be an intercessor, you might not even be very good with words, but the quantity of time that you give to God is of great value. The brilliant theologian may have deep insights about God, but that quality of knowledge means very little if he doesn't spend any quantity time with God. And the time you give to God might never lead to great sermons or amazing works of literature, but the time you spend says a lot about your degree of devotion to him.

We often think that relationships need quality time more than quantity, but ask a small child or someone in love if they would rather have a few moments of "quality time" or an entire day with their loved one, and the answer will be instant: "More time!" Even if all you do is go for a walk, toss a ball, or sit and stare at each other, in a relationship time means a lot. In your relationship with God, don't give up on quantity just because you're afraid that your quality isn't good enough. When your heart is in the right place, the time you spend with God will please him—and your relationship will grow.

stones and offerings, he said, [6]"As for these things that you see, the days will come when there will not be left here one stone upon another that will not be thrown down." [7]And they asked him, "Teacher, when will these things be, and what will be the sign when these things are about to take place?" [8]And he said, "See that you are not led astray. For many will come in my name, saying, 'I am he!' and, 'The time is at hand!' Do not go after them. [9]And when you hear of wars and tumults, do not be terrified, for these things must first take place, but the end will not be at once."

Jesus Foretells Wars and Persecution

[10]Then he said to them, "Nation will rise against nation, and kingdom against kingdom. [11]There will be great earthquakes, and in various places famines and pestilences. And there will be terrors and great signs from heaven. [12]But before all this they will lay their hands on you and persecute you, delivering you up to the synagogues and prisons, and you will be brought before kings and governors for my name's sake. [13]This will be your opportunity to bear witness. [14]Settle it therefore in your minds not to meditate beforehand how to answer, [15]for I will give you a mouth and wisdom, which none of your adversaries will be able to withstand or contradict. [16]You will be delivered up even by parents and brothers[1] and relatives and friends, and some of you they will put to death. [17]You will be hated by all for my name's sake. [18]But not a hair of your head will perish. [19]By your endurance you will gain your lives.

Jesus Foretells Destruction of Jerusalem

[20]"But when you see Jerusalem surrounded by armies, then know that its desolation has come near. [21]Then let those who are in Judea flee to the mountains, and let those who are inside the city depart, and let not those who are out in the country enter it, [22]for these are days of vengeance, to fulfill all that is written. [23]Alas for women who are pregnant and for those who are nursing infants in those days! For there will be great distress upon the earth and wrath against this people. [24]They will fall by the edge of the sword and be led captive among all nations, and Jerusalem will be trampled underfoot by the Gentiles, until the times of the Gentiles are fulfilled.

The Coming of the Son of Man

[25]"And there will be signs in sun and moon and stars, and on the earth distress of nations in perplexity because of the roaring of the sea and the waves, [26]people fainting with fear and with foreboding of what is coming on the world. For the powers of the heavens will be shaken. [27]And then they will see the Son of Man coming in a cloud with power and great glory. [28]Now when these things begin to take place, straighten up and raise your heads, because your redemption is drawing near."

The Lesson of the Fig Tree

[29]And he told them a parable: "Look at the fig tree, and all the trees. [30]As soon as they come out in leaf, you see for yourselves and know that the summer is already near. [31]So also, when you see these things taking place, you know that the kingdom of God is near. [32]Truly, I say to you, this generation will not pass away until all has taken place. [33]Heaven and earth will pass away, but my words will not pass away.

Watch Yourselves

[34]"But watch yourselves lest your hearts be weighed down with dissipation and drunkenness and cares of this life, and that day come upon you suddenly like a trap. [35]For it will come upon all who dwell on the face of the whole earth. [36]But stay awake at all times, praying that you may have strength to escape all these things that are going to take place, and to stand before the Son of Man."

[37]And every day he was teaching in the temple, but at night he went out and lodged on the mount called Olivet. [38]And early in the morning all the people came to him in the temple to hear him.

The Plot to Kill Jesus

22 Now the Feast of Unleavened Bread drew near, which is called the Passover. [2]And the chief priests and the scribes were seeking how to put him to death, for they feared the people.

Judas to Betray Jesus

[3][a]Then Satan entered into Judas called Iscariot, who was of the number of the

---

[1]Or parents and brothers and sisters [a]For 22:3-6 see parallels Matt. 26:14-16; Mark 14:10, 11

twelve. [4] He went away and conferred with the chief priests and officers how he might betray him to them. [5] And they were glad, and agreed to give him money. [6] So he consented and sought an opportunity to betray him to them in the absence of a crowd.

The Passover with the Disciples

[7] [a] Then came the day of Unleavened Bread, on which the Passover lamb had to be sacrificed. [8] So Jesus[1] sent Peter and John, saying, "Go and prepare the Passover for us, that we may eat it." [9] They said to him, "Where will you have us prepare it?" [10] He said to them, "Behold, when you have entered the city, a man carrying a jar of water will meet you. Follow him into the house that he enters [11] and tell the master of the house, 'The Teacher says to you, Where is the guest room, where I may eat the Passover with my disciples?' [12] And he will show you a large upper room furnished; prepare it there." [13] And they went and found it just as he had told them, and they prepared the Passover.

Institution of the Lord's Supper

[14] And when the hour came, he reclined at table, and the apostles with him. [15] And he said to them, "I have earnestly desired to eat this Passover with you before I suffer. [16] For I tell you I will not eat it[2] until it is fulfilled in the kingdom of God." [17] And he took a cup, and when he had given thanks he said, "Take this, and divide it among yourselves. [18] For I tell you that from now on I will not drink of the fruit of the vine until the kingdom of God comes." [19] [b] And he took bread, and when he had given thanks, he broke it and gave it to them, saying, "This is my body, which is given for you. Do this in remembrance of me." [20] And likewise the cup after they had eaten, saying, "This cup that is poured out for you is the new covenant in my blood.[3] [21] [c] But behold, the hand of him who betrays me is with me on the table. [22] For the Son of Man goes as it has been determined, but woe to that man by whom he is betrayed!" [23] And they began to question one another, which of them it could be who was going to do this.

Who Is the Greatest?

[24] A dispute also arose among them, as to which of them was to be regarded as the greatest. [25] And he said to them, "The kings of the Gentiles exercise lordship over them, and those in authority over them are called benefactors. [26] But not so with you. Rather, let the greatest among you become as the youngest, and the leader as one who serves. [27] For who is the greater, one who reclines at table or one who serves? Is it not the one who reclines at table? But I am among you as the one who serves.

[28] "You are those who have stayed with me in my trials, [29] and I assign to you, as my Father assigned to me, a kingdom, [30] that you may eat and drink at my table in my kingdom and sit on thrones judging the twelve tribes of Israel.

Jesus Foretells Peter's Denial

[31] "Simon, Simon, behold, Satan demanded to have you,[4] that he might sift you like wheat, [32] but I have prayed for you that your faith may not fail. And when you have turned again, strengthen your brothers." [33] Peter[5] said to him, "Lord, I am ready to go with you both to prison and to death." [34] Jesus[6] said, "I tell you, Peter, the rooster will not crow this day, until you deny three times that you know me."

Scripture Must Be Fulfilled in Jesus

[35] And he said to them, "When I sent you out with no moneybag or knapsack or sandals, did you lack anything?" They said, "Nothing." [36] He said to them, "But now let the one who has a moneybag take it, and likewise a knapsack. And let the one who has no sword sell his cloak and buy one. [37] For I tell you that this Scripture must be fulfilled in me: [d] 'And he was numbered with the transgressors.' For what is written about me has its fulfillment." [38] And they said, "Look, Lord, here are two swords." And he said to them, "It is enough."

Jesus Prays on the Mount of Olives

[39] And he came out and went, as was his custom, to the Mount of Olives, and the disciples followed him. [40] [e] And when he came to the place, he said to them, "Pray that you may not enter into temptation." [41] And

[1] Greek he [2] Some manuscripts never eat it again [3] Some manuscripts omit, in whole or in part, verses 19b-20 (which is given . . . in my blood) [4] The Greek word for you (twice in this verse) is plural; in verse 32, all four instances are singular [5] Greek He [6] Greek He
[a] For 22:7-13 see parallels Matt. 26:17-19; Mark 14:12-16 [b] For 22:19, 20 see parallels Matt. 26:26-28; Mark 14:22-24 [c] For 22:21-23 see parallels Matt. 26:21-24; Mark 14:18-21 [d] Isa. 53:12 [e] For 22:40-46 see parallels Matt. 26:36-46; Mark 14:32-42

he withdrew from them about a stone's throw, and knelt down and prayed, [42] saying, "Father, if you are willing, remove this cup from me. Nevertheless, not my will, but yours, be done." [43] And there appeared to him an angel from heaven, strengthening him. [44] And being in an agony he prayed more earnestly; and his sweat became like great drops of blood falling down to the ground.[1] [45] And when he rose from prayer, he came to the disciples and found them sleeping for sorrow, [46] and he said to them, "Why are you sleeping? Rise and pray that you may not enter into temptation."

Betrayal and Arrest of Jesus

[47] [a] While he was still speaking, there came a crowd, and the man called Judas, one of the twelve, was leading them. He drew near to Jesus to kiss him, [48] but Jesus said to him, "Judas, would you betray the Son of Man with a kiss?" [49] And when those who were around him saw what would follow, they said, "Lord, shall we strike with the sword?" [50] And one of them struck the servant[2] of the high priest and cut off his right ear. [51] But Jesus said, "No more of this!" And he touched his ear and healed him. [52] Then Jesus said to the chief priests and officers of the temple and elders, who had come out against him, "Have you come out as against a robber, with swords and clubs? [53] When I was with you day after day in the temple, you did not lay hands on me. But this is your hour, and the power of darkness."

Peter Denies Jesus

[54] Then they seized him and led him away, bringing him into the high priest's house, and Peter was following at a distance. [55] [b] And when they had kindled a fire in the middle of the courtyard and sat down together, Peter sat down among them. [56] Then a servant girl, seeing him as he sat in the light and looking closely at him, said, "This man also was with him." [57] But he denied it, saying, "Woman, I do not know him." [58] And a little later someone else saw him and said, "You also are one of them." But Peter said, "Man, I am not." [59] And after an interval of about an hour still another insisted, saying, "Certainly this man also was with him, for he too is a

Galilean." [60] But Peter said, "Man, I do not know what you are talking about." And immediately, while he was still speaking, the rooster crowed. [61] And the Lord turned and looked at Peter. And Peter remembered the saying of the Lord, how he had said to him, "Before the rooster crows today, you will deny me three times." [62] And he went out and wept bitterly.

Jesus Is Mocked

[63] Now the men who were holding Jesus in custody were mocking him as they beat him. [64] They also blindfolded him and kept asking him, "Prophesy! Who is it that struck you?" [65] And they said many other things against him, blaspheming him.

Jesus Before the Council

[66] When day came, the assembly of the elders of the people gathered together, both chief priests and scribes. And they led him away to their council, and they said, [67] "If you are the Christ, tell us." But he said to them, "If I tell you, you will not believe, [68] and if I ask you, you will not answer. [69] But from now on the Son of Man shall be seated at the right hand of the power of God." [70] So they all said, "Are you the Son of God, then?" And he said to them, "You say that I am." [71] Then they said, "What further testimony do we need? We have heard it ourselves from his own lips."

Jesus Before Pilate

23 Then the whole company of them arose and brought him before Pilate. [2] And they began to accuse him, saying, "We found this man misleading our nation and forbidding us to give tribute to Caesar, and saying that he himself is Christ, a king." [3] And Pilate asked him, "Are you the King of the Jews?" And he answered him, "You have said so." [4] Then Pilate said to the chief priests and the crowds, "I find no guilt in this man." [5] But they were urgent, saying, "He stirs up the people, teaching throughout all Judea, from Galilee even to this place."

Jesus Before Herod

[6] When Pilate heard this, he asked whether the man was a Galilean. [7] And when he learned that he belonged to Herod's jurisdiction, he sent him over to

[1] Some manuscripts omit verses 43 and 44 [2] Greek bondservant [a] For 22:47-53 see parallels Matt. 26:47-56; Mark 14:43-50; John 18:3-11 [b] For 22:55-62 see parallels Matt. 26:69-75; Mark 14:66-72; John 18:16-18, 25-27

Herod, who was himself in Jerusalem at that time. ⁸When Herod saw Jesus, he was very glad, for he had long desired to see him, because he had heard about him, and he was hoping to see some sign done by him. ⁹So he questioned him at some length, but he made no answer. ¹⁰The chief priests and the scribes stood by, vehemently accusing him. ¹¹And Herod with his soldiers treated him with contempt and mocked him. Then, arraying him in splendid clothing, he sent him back to Pilate. ¹²And Herod and Pilate became friends with each other that very day, for before this they had been at enmity with each other.

¹³Pilate then called together the chief priests and the rulers and the people, ¹⁴and said to them, "You brought me this man as one who was misleading the people. And after examining him before you, behold, I did not find this man guilty of any of your charges against him. ¹⁵Neither did Herod, for he sent him back to us. Look, nothing deserving death has been done by him. ¹⁶I will therefore punish and release him."[1]

Pilate Delivers Jesus to Be Crucified

¹⁸[a]But they all cried out together, "Away with this man, and release to us Barabbas"— ¹⁹a man who had been thrown into prison for an insurrection started in the city and for murder. ²⁰Pilate addressed them once more, desiring to release Jesus, ²¹but they kept shouting, "Crucify, crucify him!" ²²A third time he said to them, "Why, what evil has he done? I have found in him no guilt deserving death. I will therefore punish and release him." ²³But they were urgent, demanding with loud cries that he should be crucified. And their voices prevailed. ²⁴So Pilate decided that their demand should be granted. ²⁵He released the man who had been thrown into prison for insurrection and murder, for whom they asked, but he delivered Jesus over to their will.

The Crucifixion

²⁶And as they led him away, they seized one Simon of Cyrene, who was coming in from the country, and laid on him the cross, to carry it behind Jesus. ²⁷And there followed him a great multitude of the people

and of women who were mourning and lamenting for him. ²⁸But turning to them Jesus said, "Daughters of Jerusalem, do not weep for me, but weep for yourselves and for your children. ²⁹For behold, the days are coming when they will say, 'Blessed are the barren and the wombs that never bore and the breasts that never nursed!' ³⁰Then they will begin to say to the mountains, 'Fall on us,' and to the hills, 'Cover us.' ³¹For if they do these things when the wood is green, what will happen when it is dry?"

³²Two others, who were criminals, were led away to be put to death with him. ³³And when they came to the place that is called The Skull, there they crucified him, and the criminals, one on his right and one on his left. ³⁴And Jesus said, "Father, forgive them, for they know not what they do."[2] And they cast lots to divide his garments. ³⁵And the people stood by, watching, but the rulers scoffed at him, saying, "He saved others; let him save himself, if he is the Christ of God, his Chosen One!" ³⁶The soldiers also mocked him, coming up and offering him sour wine ³⁷and saying, "If you are the King of the Jews, save yourself!" ³⁸There was also an inscription over him,[3] "This is the King of the Jews."

³⁹One of the criminals who were hanged railed at him,[4] saying, "Are you not the Christ? Save yourself and us!" ⁴⁰But the other rebuked him, saying, "Do you not fear God, since you are under the same sentence of condemnation? ⁴¹And we indeed justly, for we are receiving the due reward of our deeds; but this man has done nothing wrong." ⁴²And he said, "Jesus, remember me when you come into your kingdom." ⁴³And he said to him, "Truly, I say to you, today you will be with me in Paradise."

The Death of Jesus

⁴⁴It was now about the sixth hour,[5] and there was darkness over the whole land until the ninth hour,[6] ⁴⁵while the sun's light failed. And the curtain of the temple was torn in two. ⁴⁶Then Jesus, calling out with a loud voice, said, "Father, into your hands I commit my spirit!" And having said this he breathed his last. ⁴⁷Now when the centurion saw what had taken place, he praised God, saying, "Certainly this man

[1] Here, or after verse 19, some manuscripts add verse 17: *Now he was obliged to release one man to them at the festival* [2] Some manuscripts omit the sentence *And Jesus . . . what they do* [3] Some manuscripts add *in letters of Greek and Latin and Hebrew* [4] Or *blasphemed him* [5] That is, noon [6] That is, 3 P.M. [a] For 23:18-25 see parallels Matt. 27:15-26; Mark 15:6-15; John 18:39, 40; 19:16

was innocent!" ⁴⁸ And all the crowds that had assembled for this spectacle, when they saw what had taken place, returned home beating their breasts. ⁴⁹ And all his acquaintances and the women who had followed him from Galilee stood at a distance watching these things.

Jesus Is Buried

⁵⁰ᵃ Now there was a man named Joseph, from the Jewish town of Arimathea. He was a member of the council, a good and righteous man, ⁵¹ who had not consented to their decision and action; and he was looking for the kingdom of God. ⁵² This man went to Pilate and asked for the body of Jesus. ⁵³ Then he took it down and wrapped it in a linen shroud and laid him in a tomb cut in stone, where no one had ever yet been laid. ⁵⁴ It was the day of Preparation, and the Sabbath was beginning.¹ ⁵⁵ The women who had come with him from Galilee followed and saw the tomb and how his body was laid. ⁵⁶ Then they returned and prepared spices and ointments.

On the Sabbath they rested according to the commandment.

The Resurrection

24 ᵇ But on the first day of the week, at early dawn, they went to the tomb, taking the spices they had prepared. ² And they found the stone rolled away from the tomb, ³ but when they went in they did not find the body of the Lord Jesus. ⁴ While they were perplexed about this, behold, two men stood by them in dazzling apparel. ⁵ And as they were frightened and bowed their faces to the ground, the men said to them, "Why do you seek the living among the dead? ⁶ He is not here, but has risen. Remember how he told you, while he was still in Galilee, ⁷ that the Son of Man must be delivered into the hands of sinful men and be crucified and on the third day rise." ⁸ And they remembered his words, and returning from the tomb they told all these things to the eleven and to all the rest. ¹⁰ Now it was Mary Magdalene and Joanna and Mary the mother of James and the other women with them who told these things to the apostles, ¹¹ but these words seemed to them an idle tale, and they did not believe them. ¹² But Peter rose

and ran to the tomb; stooping and looking in, he saw the linen cloths by themselves; and he went home marveling at what had happened.

A Prayer about...
THE CROSS

Heavenly Father, how can I thank you for the unspeakable gift of your Son on the cross? How can I thank you for my eternal salvation, made possible because of that death on the cross? He died for me so that I could live eternally. Through his death on the cross I am dead to sin and I live in the power of his life.

Father in heaven, teach me, I humbly ask you, what it means to say that I am dead with Christ and can live my life in him. Teach me to realize that my sinful flesh is totally corrupt and nailed to the cross, to be destroyed so that the life of Christ might be real in me.

Teach me, above all, to believe that I can't understand or experience this except through the continual working of the Holy Spirit living inside of me. Father, for his sake I ask it.

Amen.

On the Road to Emmaus

¹³ That very day two of them were going to a village named Emmaus, about seven miles² from Jerusalem, ¹⁴ and they were talking with each other about all these things that had happened. ¹⁵ While they were talking and discussing together, Jesus himself drew near and went with them. ¹⁶ But their eyes were kept from recognizing him. ¹⁷ And he said to them, "What is this conversation that you are holding with each other as you walk?" And they stood still, looking sad. ¹⁸ Then one of them, named Cleopas, answered him, "Are you the only visitor to Jerusalem who does not know the things that have happened there in these days?" ¹⁹ And he said

¹ Greek *was dawning* ² Greek *sixty stadia; a stadion* was about 607 feet or 185 meters ᵃ For 23:50-56 see parallels Matt. 27:57-61; Mark 15:42-47; John 19:38-42 ᵇ For 24:1-10 see parallels Matt. 28:1-8; Mark 16:1-8; John 20:1

to them, "What things?" And they said to him, "Concerning Jesus of Nazareth, a man who was a prophet mighty in deed and word before God and all the people, ²⁰ and how our chief priests and rulers delivered him up to be condemned to death, and crucified him. ²¹ But we had hoped that he was the one to redeem Israel. Yes, and besides all this, it is now the third day since these things happened. ²² Moreover, some women of our company amazed us. They were at the tomb early in the morning, ²³ and when they did not find his body, they came back saying that they had even seen a vision of angels, who said that he was alive. ²⁴ Some of those who were with us went to the tomb and found it just as the women had said, but him they did not see." ²⁵ And he said to them, "O foolish ones, and slow of heart to believe all that the prophets have spoken! ²⁶ Was it not necessary that the Christ should suffer these things and enter into his glory?" ²⁷ And beginning with Moses and all the Prophets, he interpreted to them in all the Scriptures the things concerning himself.

²⁸ So they drew near to the village to which they were going. He acted as if he were going farther, ²⁹ but they urged him strongly, saying, "Stay with us, for it is toward evening and the day is now far spent." So he went in to stay with them. ³⁰ When he was at table with them, he took the bread and blessed and broke it and gave it to them. ³¹ And their eyes were opened, and they recognized him. And he vanished from their sight. ³² They said to each other, "Did not our hearts burn within us while he talked to us on the road, while he opened to us the Scriptures?" ³³ And they rose that same hour and returned to Jerusalem. And they found the eleven and those who were with them gathered together, ³⁴ saying, "The Lord has risen indeed, and has appeared to Simon!" ³⁵ Then they told what had happened on the road, and how he was known to them in the breaking of the bread.

Jesus Appears to His Disciples

³⁶ As they were talking about these things, Jesus himself stood among them, and said to them, "Peace to you!" ³⁷ But

Know True Happiness

verses to read
Luke 24:13-35

If you are feeling depressed about life, it may be because you don't trust in God's providence or his power in this world. Depression is often a result of either getting what you want and realizing it wasn't what you thought it would be, or not getting what you want and being upset about it. Either way, it's all about you, not God. But it isn't something you have to live with. Unless you're dealing with a real medical condition, like clinical depression, feeling better about life has to do with God's grace changing what you want.

When your focus changes from loving what you want to loving whatever God wants to give you, then depression starts to fade away. When you trust that God is truly involved in the lives of those who love him, then you don't need to be all depressed—because suddenly you see things through new lenses. You see life—the good, the bad, the ugly, all of it—as a gift from him, one that you might not understand just yet but one that you trust you will someday appreciate.

Depression and moping around about life are often symptoms of spiritual sickness, and you can change your attitude if you are willing to trust God and look for him relentlessly. Take your focus off of what you want, need, or demand and put it onto looking for God and finding him in the middle of your mess and your emptiness.

they were startled and frightened and thought they saw a spirit. [38] And he said to them, "Why are you troubled, and why do doubts arise in your hearts? [39] See my hands and my feet, that it is I myself. Touch me, and see. For a spirit does not have flesh and bones as you see that I have." [40] And when he had said this, he showed them his hands and his feet. [41] And while they still disbelieved for joy and were marveling, he said to them, "Have you anything here to eat?" [42] They gave him a piece of broiled fish,[1] [43] and he took it and ate before them.

[44] Then he said to them, "These are my words that I spoke to you while I was still with you, that everything written about me in the Law of Moses and the Prophets and the Psalms must be fulfilled." [45] Then he opened their minds to understand the Scriptures, [46] and said to them, "Thus it is written, that the Christ should suffer and on the third day rise from the dead, [47] and that repentance and[2] forgiveness of sins should be proclaimed in his name to all nations, beginning from Jerusalem. [48] You are witnesses of these things. [49] And behold, I am sending the promise of my Father upon you. But stay in the city until you are clothed with power from on high."

The Ascension

[50] Then he led them out as far as Bethany, and lifting up his hands he blessed them. [51] While he blessed them, he parted from them and was carried up into heaven. [52] And they worshiped him and returned to Jerusalem with great joy, [53] and were continually in the temple blessing God.

Some manuscripts add *and some honeycomb* [2] Some manuscripts *for*

INTRODUCTION TO John

Know Jesus

Author: John, "the disciple whom Jesus loved," son of Zebedee the fisherman

Time: Between A.D. 85 and 95

Place: Ephesus

Written to: New believers and people curious about Jesus

the gist

John wrote to teach people that eternal life comes from believing in Jesus and that Jesus is God. One of the things John focuses on is all the amazing miracles of Jesus that prove that Jesus is God himself.

things to look for

The famous verse John 3:16

The use of the phrase "the Word" for Jesus (see John 1)

Jesus' many miracles

How the word *light* is used to refer to Jesus

> When they heard these words, some of the people said, "This really is the Prophet." Others said, "This is the Christ."
>
> *John 7:40–41*

A lot of people say Jesus was a prophet or a good man but not God. They'll listen to what he has to say and take some truth out of it, but they will not go so far as to believe that he was who he said he was. See, it's easy to believe only the human parts about Jesus, like recognizing his wisdom and his common sense, but it's another thing completely to believe that he is God, who became flesh and walked among us.

In the book of John, Jesus is called "the Word." The Word refers to Jesus as God fully expressing himself in human form (see John 1:1, 14–18). And John assures us that the Word was always alive—even before the world was created (see John 1:2–3). God not only made the universe and everything in it by his word but he speaks to us and brings us to himself through his Word, Jesus. When Jesus came to earth he was still the Word of God, come to set humanity free from sin. Nothing he said could be false.

We as believers need to be convinced of who Jesus is. If we only give him credit for being a good guy, we miss out on his very nature and we reject God himself. As you read the Gospel of John, you have to decide if Jesus was a wise man with some crazy tendencies or if he was truly the Son of God. It's hard to call him just a prophet or a wise teacher when he called himself God in several different ways: "the bread of life" (John 6:35, 48), "the light of the world" (John 8:12), the "I am" (John 8:58), "the door" (John 10:7), "the good shepherd" (John 10:11, 14), "the life" (John 11:25), and "the way, and the truth, and the life" (John 14:6). Saying stuff like this about himself made the people who didn't believe him angry enough to send him to the cross.

As you read through the Gospel of John, see how important the life of Jesus is to your salvation and notice all the ways he described himself. As a God Girl, you need to know this God whom you serve and love.

Must-Know Terms and Verses

✒ *Fall Asleep* ✒

This expression is often used as a metaphor for death, as in John 11:11.

✒ *The Light* ✒

Often used in Scripture to refer to Jesus (see John 1:9).

✒ *The Way* ✒

In John 14:6 Jesus calls himself "the way," because he is our path to God.

✒ *The Word* ✒

A term used in John to refer to Jesus.

In the beginning was the Word, and the Word was with God, and the Word was God. He was in the beginning with God. *John 1:1–2*

The Word became flesh and dwelt among us. *John 1:14*

"For God so loved the world, that he gave his only Son, that whoever believes in him should not perish but have eternal life." *John 3:16*

"I am the vine; you are the branches. Whoever abides in me and I in him, he it is that bears much fruit, for apart from me you can do nothing." *John 15:5*

The Gospel According to John

The Word Became Flesh

1 In the beginning was the Word, and the Word was with God, and the Word was God. ² He was in the beginning with God. ³ All things were made through him, and without him was not any thing made that was made. ⁴ In him was life,[1] and the life was the light of men. ⁵ The light shines in the darkness, and the darkness has not overcome it.

⁶ There was a man sent from God, whose name was John. ⁷ He came as a witness, to bear witness about the light, that all might believe through him. ⁸ He was not the light, but came to bear witness about the light.

⁹ The true light, which gives light to everyone, was coming into the world. ¹⁰ He was in the world, and the world was made through him, yet the world did not know him. ¹¹ He came to his own,[2] and his own people[3] did not receive him. ¹² But to all who did receive him, who believed in his name, he gave the right to become children of God, ¹³ who were born, not of blood nor of the will of the flesh nor of the will of man, but of God.

¹⁴ And the Word became flesh and dwelt among us, and we have seen his glory, glory as of the only Son from the Father, full of grace and truth. ¹⁵ (John bore witness about him, and cried out, "This was he of whom I said, 'He who comes after me ranks before me, because he was before me.' ") ¹⁶ For from his fullness we have all received, grace upon grace.[4] ¹⁷ For the law was given through Moses; grace and truth came through Jesus Christ. ¹⁸ No one has ever seen God; the only God,[5] who is at the Father's side,[6] he has made him known.

The Testimony of John the Baptist

¹⁹ And this is the testimony of John, when the Jews sent priests and Levites from Jerusalem to ask him, "Who are you?" ²⁰ He confessed, and did not deny, but confessed, "I am not the Christ." ²¹ And they asked him, "What then? Are you Elijah?" He said, "I am not." "Are you the Prophet?" And he answered, "No." ²² So they said to him, "Who are you? We need to give an answer to those who sent us. What do you say about yourself?" ²³ He said, "I am ᵃthe voice of one crying out in the wilderness, 'Make straight[7] the way of the Lord,' as the prophet Isaiah said."

²⁴ (Now they had been sent from the Pharisees.) ²⁵ They asked him, "Then why are you baptizing, if you are neither the Christ, nor Elijah, nor the Prophet?" ²⁶ John answered them, "I baptize with water, but among you stands one you do not know, ²⁷ even he who comes after me, the strap of whose sandal I am not worthy to untie." ²⁸ These things took place in Bethany across the Jordan, where John was baptizing.

Behold, the Lamb of God

²⁹ The next day he saw Jesus coming toward him, and said, "Behold, the Lamb of God, who takes away the sin of the world! ³⁰ This is he of whom I said, 'After me comes a man who ranks before me, because he was before me.' ³¹ I myself did not know him, but for this purpose I came baptizing with water, that he might be revealed to Israel." ³² And John bore witness: "I saw the Spirit descend from heaven like a dove, and it remained on him. ³³ I myself did not know him, but he who sent me to baptize with water said to me, 'He on whom you see the Spirit descend and remain, this is he who baptizes with the Holy Spirit.' ³⁴ And I have seen and have borne witness that this is the Son of God."

---

[1] Or was not any thing made. That which has been made was life in him [2] Greek to his own things; that is, to his own domain, or to his own people [3] People is implied in Greek [4] Or grace in place of grace [5] Or the only One, who is God; some manuscripts the only Son [6] Greek in the bosom of the Father [7] Or crying out, 'In the wilderness make straight ᵃ Isa. 40:3

Jesus Calls the First Disciples

[35] The next day again John was standing with two of his disciples, [36] and he looked at Jesus as he walked by and said, "Behold, the Lamb of God!" [37] The two disciples heard him say this, and they followed Jesus. [38] Jesus turned and saw them following and said to them, "What are you seeking?" And they said to him, "Rabbi" (which means Teacher), "where are you staying?" [39] He said to them, "Come and you will see." So they came and saw where he was staying, and they stayed with him that day, for it was about the tenth hour.[1] [40] One of the two who heard John speak and followed Jesus[2] was Andrew, Simon Peter's brother. [41] He first found his own brother Simon and said to him, "We have found the Messiah" (which means Christ). [42] He brought him to Jesus. Jesus looked at him and said, "You are Simon the son of John. You shall be called Cephas" (which means Peter[3]).

Jesus Calls Philip and Nathanael

[43] The next day Jesus decided to go to Galilee. He found Philip and said to him, "Follow me." [44] Now Philip was from Bethsaida, the city of Andrew and Peter. [45] Philip found Nathanael and said to him, "We have found him of whom Moses in the Law and also the prophets wrote, Jesus of Nazareth, the son of Joseph." [46] Nathanael said to him, "Can anything good come out of Nazareth?" Philip said to him, "Come and see." [47] Jesus saw Nathanael coming toward him and said of him, "Behold, an Israelite indeed, in whom there is no deceit!" [48] Nathanael said to him, "How do you know me?" Jesus answered him, "Before Philip called you, when you were under the fig tree, I saw you." [49] Nathanael answered him, "Rabbi, you are the Son of God! You are the King of Israel!" [50] Jesus answered him, "Because I said to you, 'I saw you under the fig tree,' do you believe? You will see greater things than these." [51] And he said to him, "Truly, truly, I say to you,[4] you will see heaven opened, and the angels of God ascending and descending on the Son of Man."

The Wedding at Cana

2 On the third day there was a wedding at Cana in Galilee, and the mother of Jesus was there. [2] Jesus also was invited to the wedding with his disciples. [3] When the wine ran out, the mother of Jesus said to him, "They have no wine." [4] And Jesus said to her, "Woman, what does this have to do with me? My hour has not yet come." [5] His mother said to the servants, "Do whatever he tells you."

[6] Now there were six stone water jars there for the Jewish rites of purification, each holding twenty or thirty gallons. [7] Jesus said to the servants, "Fill the jars with water." And they filled them up to the brim. [8] And he said to them, "Now draw some out and take it to the master of the feast." So they took it. [9] When the master of the feast tasted the water now become wine, and did not know where it came from (though the servants who had drawn the water knew), the master of the feast called the bridegroom [10] and said to him, "Everyone serves the good wine first, and when people have drunk freely, then the poor wine. But you have kept the good wine until now." [11] This, the first of his signs, Jesus did at Cana in Galilee, and manifested his glory. And his disciples believed in him.

[12] After this he went down to Capernaum, with his mother and his brothers[6] and his disciples, and they stayed there for a few days.

Jesus Cleanses the Temple

[13] The Passover of the Jews was at hand, and Jesus went up to Jerusalem. [14] In the temple he found those who were selling oxen and sheep and pigeons, and the money-changers sitting there. [15] And making a whip of cords, he drove them all out of the temple, with the sheep and oxen. And he poured out the coins of the money-changers and overturned their tables. [16] And he told those who sold the pigeons, "Take these things away; do not make my Father's house a house of trade." [17] His disciples remembered that it was written, [a] "Zeal for your house will consume me."

[1] That is, about 4 P.M. [2] Greek *him* [3] *Cephas* and *Peter* are from the word for *rock* in Aramaic and Greek, respectively [4] The Greek for *you* is plural; twice in this verse [5] Greek *two or three measures* (*metrētas*); a *metrētēs* was about 10 gallons or 35 liters [6] Or *brothers and sisters*. The plural Greek word *adelphoi* (translated "brothers") refers to siblings in a family. In New Testament usage, depending on the context, *adelphoi* may refer either to *brothers* or to *brothers and sisters* [a] Ps. 69:9

[18] So the Jews said to him, "What sign do you show us for doing these things?" [19] Jesus answered them, "Destroy this temple, and in three days I will raise it up." [20] The Jews then said, "It has taken forty-six years to build this temple,[1] and will you raise it up in three days?" [21] But he was speaking about the temple of his body. [22] When therefore he was raised from the dead, his disciples remembered that he had said this, and they believed the Scripture and the word that Jesus had spoken.

Jesus Knows What Is in Man

[23] Now when he was in Jerusalem at the Passover Feast, many believed in his name when they saw the signs that he was doing. [24] But Jesus on his part did not entrust himself to them, because he knew all people [25] and needed no one to bear witness about man, for he himself knew what was in man.

You Must Be Born Again

3 Now there was a man of the Pharisees named Nicodemus, a ruler of the Jews. [2] This man came to Jesus[2] by night and said to him, "Rabbi, we know that you are a teacher come from God, for no one can do these signs that you do unless God is with him." [3] Jesus answered him, "Truly, truly, I say to you, unless one is born again[3] he cannot see the kingdom of God." [4] Nicodemus said to him, "How can a man be born when he is old? Can he enter a second time into his mother's womb and be born?" [5] Jesus answered, "Truly, truly, I say to you, unless one is born of water and the Spirit, he cannot enter the kingdom of God. [6] That which is born of the flesh is flesh, and that which is born of the Spirit is spirit.[4] [7] Do not marvel that I said to you, 'You[5] must be born again.' [8] The wind[6] blows where it wishes, and you hear its sound, but you do not know where it comes from or where it goes. So it is with everyone who is born of the Spirit."

[9] Nicodemus said to him, "How can these things be?" [10] Jesus answered him, "Are you the teacher of Israel and yet you do not understand these things? [11] Truly, truly, I say to you, we speak of what we know, and bear witness to what we have seen, but you[7] do not receive our testimony. [12] If I have told you earthly things and you do not believe, how can you believe if I tell you heavenly things? [13] No one has ascended into heaven except he who descended from heaven, the Son of Man.[8] [14] And as Moses lifted up the serpent in the wilderness, so must the Son of Man be lifted up, [15] that whoever believes in him may have eternal life.[9]

For God So Loved the World

[16] "For God so loved the world,[10] that he gave his only Son, that whoever believes in him should not perish but have eternal life. [17] For God did not send his Son into the world to condemn the world, but in order that the world might be saved through him. [18] Whoever believes in him is not condemned, but whoever does not believe is condemned already, because he has not believed in the name of the only Son of God. [19] And this is the judgment: the light has come into the world, and people loved the darkness rather than the light because their works were evil. [20] For everyone who does wicked things hates the light and does not come to the light, lest his works should be exposed. [21] But whoever does what is true comes to the light, so that it may be clearly seen that his works have been carried out in God."

John the Baptist Exalts Christ

[22] After this Jesus and his disciples went into the Judean countryside, and he remained there with them and was baptizing. [23] John also was baptizing at Aenon near Salim, because water was plentiful there, and people were coming and being baptized [24] (for John had not yet been put in prison).

[25] Now a discussion arose between some of John's disciples and a Jew over purification. [26] And they came to John and said to him, "Rabbi, he who was with you across the Jordan, to whom you bore witness—look, he is baptizing, and all are going to him." [27] John answered, "A person cannot receive even one thing unless it is given him from heaven. [28] You yourselves bear me witness, that I said, 'I am not the Christ, but I have been sent before him.' [29] The one who has the bride is the bridegroom. The friend of the bridegroom, who stands and

---

[1] Or *This temple was built forty-six years ago* [2] Greek *him* [3] Or *from above*; the Greek is purposely ambiguous and can mean both *again* and *from above*; also verse 7 [4] The same Greek word means both *wind* and *spirit* [5] The Greek for *you* is plural here [6] The same Greek word means both *wind* and *spirit* [7] The Greek for *you* is plural here; also four times in verse 12 [8] Some manuscripts add *who is in heaven* [9] Some interpreters hold that the quotation ends at verse 15 [10] Or *For this is how God loved the world*

hears him, rejoices greatly at the bride-groom's voice. Therefore this joy of mine is now complete. ³⁰ He must increase, but I must decrease."¹

³¹ He who comes from above is above all. He who is of the earth belongs to the earth and speaks in an earthly way. He who comes from heaven is above all. ³² He bears witness to what he has seen and heard, yet no one receives his testimony. ³³ Whoever receives his testimony sets his seal to this, that God is true. ³⁴ For he whom God has sent utters the words of God, for he gives the Spirit without measure. ³⁵ The Father loves the Son and has given all things into his hand. ³⁶ Whoever believes in the Son has eternal life; whoever does not obey the Son shall not see life, but the wrath of God remains on him.

Jesus and the Woman of Samaria

4 Now when Jesus learned that the Pharisees had heard that Jesus was making and baptizing more disciples than John ² (although Jesus himself did not bap-tize, but only his disciples), ³ he left Judea and departed again for Galilee. ⁴ And he had to pass through Samaria. ⁵ So he came to a town of Samaria called Sychar, near the field that Jacob had given to his son Joseph. ⁶ Jacob's well was there; so Jesus, wearied as he was from his journey, was sitting beside the well. It was about the sixth hour.²

⁷ A woman from Samaria came to draw water. Jesus said to her, "Give me a drink." ⁸ (For his disciples had gone away into the city to buy food.) ⁹ The Samaritan woman said to him, "How is it that you, a Jew, ask for a drink from me, a woman of Samaria?" (For Jews have no dealings with Samaritans.) ¹⁰ Jesus answered her, "If you knew the gift of God, and who it is that is saying to you, 'Give me a drink,' you would have asked him, and he would have given you living water." ¹¹ The woman said to him, "Sir, you have nothing to draw water with, and the well is deep. Where do you get that living water? ¹² Are you greater than our father Jacob? He gave us

¹ Some interpreters hold that the quotation continues through verse 36 ² That is, about noon

verses to read
John 4:1-42

Know God

Have you ever felt like the well of your emotions was too deep for even Jesus to manage? Does your soul seem so out of whack, such a particularly depressing case, that not even Jesus himself can get to the bottom of things and heal you? Like the woman at the well, you think your troubles are too deep for him to give you any comfort. When Jesus tells you not to let your heart be troubled, you turn away from him and say, "It can't be done. My well of pain and agony is too deep."

But wait—isn't Jesus God Almighty? When you say he can't help you, you are denying the *Almighty* part of his name. There's a reason for that name, and it's that he's, well, "*all* mighty"—not partly mighty or almost mighty enough but *all* mighty.

Sure, it's easy for you to go to him as Comforter or Sympathizer, maybe even Provider. But you just can't call him Almighty, can you? The reason a lot of Christians don't feel Christ working in their lives is because they have refused to recognize that he is the Almighty. When you get into a particularly tough situation, don't mock the Almighty by saying, "Of course he can't do what I need. This is just too much for him to fix." Do you really think your problems are bigger than Almighty God? It may seem that way at times, but it's simply not true. So trust yourself to his care and give the Almighty back the power in your life. He has done some amazing things in history, and he can do an amazing work in your life, too.

the well and drank from it himself, as did his sons and his livestock." ¹³Jesus said to her, "Everyone who drinks of this water will be thirsty again, ¹⁴but whoever drinks of the water that I will give him will never be thirsty again.¹ The water that I will give him will become in him a spring of water welling up to eternal life." ¹⁵The woman said to him, "Sir, give me this water, so that I will not be thirsty or have to come here to draw water."

¹⁶Jesus said to her, "Go, call your husband, and come here." ¹⁷The woman answered him, "I have no husband." Jesus said to her, "You are right in saying, 'I have no husband'; ¹⁸for you have had five husbands, and the one you now have is not your husband. What you have said is true." ¹⁹The woman said to him, "Sir, I perceive that you are a prophet. ²⁰Our fathers worshiped on this mountain, but you say that in Jerusalem is the place where people ought to worship." ²¹Jesus said to her, "Woman, believe me, the hour is coming when neither on this mountain nor in Jerusalem will you worship the Father. ²²You worship what you do not know; we worship what we know, for salvation is from the Jews. ²³But the hour is coming, and is now here, when the true worshipers will worship the Father in spirit and truth, for the Father is seeking such people to worship him. ²⁴God is spirit, and those who worship him must worship in spirit and truth." ²⁵The woman said to him, "I know that Messiah is coming (he who is called Christ). When he comes, he will tell us all things." ²⁶Jesus said to her, "I who speak to you am he."

²⁷Just then his disciples came back. They marveled that he was talking with a woman, but no one said, "What do you seek?" or, "Why are you talking with her?" ²⁸So the woman left her water jar and went away into town and said to the people, ²⁹"Come, see a man who told me all that I ever did. Can this be the Christ?" ³⁰They went out of the town and were coming to him.

³¹Meanwhile the disciples were urging him, saying, "Rabbi, eat." ³²But he said to them, "I have food to eat that you do not know about." ³³So the disciples said to one another, "Has anyone brought him something to eat?" ³⁴Jesus said to them,

"My food is to do the will of him who sent me and to accomplish his work. ³⁵Do you not say, 'There are yet four months, then comes the harvest'? Look, I tell you, lift up your eyes, and see that the fields are white for harvest. ³⁶Already the one who reaps is receiving wages and gathering fruit for eternal life, so that sower and reaper may rejoice together. ³⁷For here the saying holds true, 'One sows and another reaps.' ³⁸I sent you to reap that for which you did not labor. Others have labored, and you have entered into their labor."

³⁹Many Samaritans from that town believed in him because of the woman's testimony, "He told me all that I ever did." ⁴⁰So when the Samaritans came to him, they asked him to stay with them, and he stayed there two days. ⁴¹And many more believed because of his word. ⁴²They said to the woman, "It is no longer because of what you said that we believe, for we have heard for ourselves, and we know that this is indeed the Savior of the world."

⁴³After the two days he departed for Galilee. ⁴⁴(For Jesus himself had testified that a prophet has no honor in his own hometown.) ⁴⁵So when he came to Galilee, the Galileans welcomed him, having seen all that he had done in Jerusalem at the feast. For they too had gone to the feast.

Jesus Heals an Official's Son

⁴⁶So he came again to Cana in Galilee, where he had made the water wine. And at Capernaum there was an official whose son was ill. ⁴⁷When this man heard that Jesus had come from Judea to Galilee, he went to him and asked him to come down and heal his son, for he was at the point of death. ⁴⁸So Jesus said to him, "Unless you² see signs and wonders you will not believe." ⁴⁹The official said to him, "Sir, come down before my child dies." ⁵⁰Jesus said to him, "Go; your son will live." The man believed the word that Jesus spoke to him and went on his way. ⁵¹As he was going down, his servants³ met him and told him that his son was recovering. ⁵²So he asked them the hour when he began to get better, and they said to him, "Yesterday at the seventh hour⁴ the fever left him." ⁵³The father knew that was the hour when Jesus had said to him, "Your son will live." And he himself believed, and all his household. ⁵⁴This was

---

¹Greek *forever* ²The Greek for *you* is plural; twice in this verse ³Greek *bondservants* ⁴That is, at 1 P.M.

now the second sign that Jesus did when he had come from Judea to Galilee.

The Healing at the Pool on the Sabbath

5 After this there was a feast of the Jews, and Jesus went up to Jerusalem. [2] Now there is in Jerusalem by the Sheep Gate a pool, in Aramaic[1] called Bethesda,[2] which has five roofed colonnades. [3] In these lay a multitude of invalids—blind, lame, and paralyzed.[3] [5] One man was there who had been an invalid for thirty-eight years. [6] When Jesus saw him lying there and knew that he had already been there a long time, he said to him, "Do you want to be healed?" [7] The sick man answered him, "Sir, I have no one to put me into the pool when the water is stirred up, and while I am going another steps down before me." [8] Jesus said to him, "Get up, take up your bed, and walk." [9] And at once the man was healed, and he took up his bed and walked.

Now that day was the Sabbath. [10] So the Jews[4] said to the man who had been healed, "It is the Sabbath, and it is not lawful for you to take up your bed." [11] But he answered them, "The man who healed me, that man said to me, 'Take up your bed, and walk.'" [12] They asked him, "Who is the man who said to you, 'Take up your bed and walk'?" [13] Now the man who had been healed did not know who it was, for Jesus had withdrawn, as there was a crowd in the place. [14] Afterward Jesus found him in the temple and said to him, "See, you are well! Sin no more, that nothing worse may happen to you." [15] The man went away and told the Jews that it was Jesus who had healed him. [16] And this was why the Jews were persecuting Jesus, because he was doing these things on the Sabbath. [17] But Jesus answered them, "My Father is working until now, and I am working."

Jesus Is Equal with God

[18] This was why the Jews were seeking all the more to kill him, because not only was he breaking the Sabbath, but he was even calling God his own Father, making himself equal with God.

The Authority of the Son

[19] So Jesus said to them, "Truly, truly, I say to you, the Son can do nothing of his own accord, but only what he sees the Father doing. For whatever the Father[5] does, that the Son does likewise. [20] For the Father loves the Son and shows him all that he himself is doing. And greater works than these will he show him, so that you may marvel. [21] For as the Father raises the dead and gives them life, so also the Son gives life to whom he will. [22] The Father judges no one, but has given all judgment to the Son, [23] that all may honor the Son, just as they honor the Father. Whoever does not honor the Son does not honor the Father who sent him. [24] Truly, truly, I say to you, whoever hears my word and believes him who sent me has eternal life. He does not come into judgment, but has passed from death to life.

[25] "Truly, truly, I say to you, an hour is coming, and is now here, when the dead will hear the voice of the Son of God, and those who hear will live. [26] For as the Father has life in himself, so he has granted the Son also to have life in himself. [27] And he has given him authority to execute judgment, because he is the Son of Man. [28] Do not marvel at this, for an hour is coming when all who are in the tombs will hear his voice [29] and come out, those who have done good to the resurrection of life, and those who have done evil to the resurrection of judgment.

Witnesses to Jesus

[30] "I can do nothing on my own. As I hear, I judge, and my judgment is just, because I seek not my own will but the will of him who sent me. [31] If I alone bear witness about myself, my testimony is not true. [32] There is another who bears witness about me, and I know that the testimony that he bears about me is true. [33] You sent to John, and he has borne witness to the truth. [34] Not that the testimony that I receive is from man, but I say these things so that you may be saved. [35] He was a burning and shining lamp, and you were willing to rejoice for a while in his light. [36] But the testimony that I have is greater than that

---

[1] Or Hebrew [2] Some manuscripts Bethsaida [3] Some manuscripts insert, wholly or in part, waiting for the moving of the water; [4] for an angel of the Lord went down at certain seasons into the pool, and stirred the water: whoever stepped in first after the stirring of the water was healed of whatever disease he had [4] The Greek word Ioudaioi refers specifically here to Jewish religious leaders, and others under their influence, who opposed Jesus in that time; also verses 15, 16, 18 [5] Greek he

The Woman at The Well

Read this God Girl story in John 4:4-42.

> Do not love the world or the things in the world. If anyone loves the world, the love of the Father is not in him. For all that is in the world—the desires of the flesh and the desires of the eyes and pride of life—is not from the Father but is from the world. And the world is passing away along with its desires, but whoever does the will of God abides forever.
>
> 1 John 2:15-17

You can look a lot of places for acceptance. You can look for it in the arms of a boy, in the eyes of your father, or in the applause of the crowd. But being accepted by a person, no matter how cute or kind he is, will never give you what you think it will. Soon something will happen, and he will fail you. He might even walk away from you because of his own human nature.

You might believe that you can't live without acceptance. You cringe when you think about the possibility of rejection and loneliness. And acceptance can easily become your number one goal. You search and fight for it at all costs. You give up your values and compromise your beliefs, thinking that the payoff of acceptance will make it all worthwhile.

This is what happened in the life of the Samaritan woman. She ravenously chased after acceptance in the arms of man after man. And each man left her empty and unsatisfied. She couldn't be alone, so she looked for another temporary high in the love of a man. But when she ran into Jesus at the well, this all changed. Her first instinct was to disagree with him and argue her case, but in the end he won her over, and she discovered an acceptance and love that would never abandon her or leave her. Then her entire life changed. Before this encounter she was isolated and lonely. She went for water in the heat of the day when other women wouldn't be around to see her in her disgrace. But when she left Jesus, she ran back to the people and told them all about him. She was so confident and outgoing that those who used to shun her now followed her out to see this most amazing man.

God Girl, you must know that no man on earth will accept you the way you want to be accepted. God saves that job for himself. It's a dangerous thing to place all your hope in a guy when God is the only one who was meant to be your hope. The love of the right guy can be a wonderful thing, but when he becomes your reason for living or the master of your feelings or actions, he has replaced God as the master of your soul. In Jesus you can find all the love and acceptance you need, and once you accept that, then and only then will you be able to accept the love of a guy and put it in the proper place in your life.

of John. For the works that the Father has given me to accomplish, the very works that I am doing, bear witness about me that the Father has sent me. [37] And the Father who sent me has himself borne witness about me. His voice you have never heard, his form you have never seen, [38] and you do not have his word abiding in you, for you do not believe the one whom he has sent. [39] You search the Scriptures because you think that in them you have eternal life; and it is they that bear witness about me, [40] yet you refuse to come to me that you may have life. [41] I do not receive glory from people. [42] But I know that you do not have the love of God within you. [43] I have come in my Father's name, and you do not receive me. If another comes in his own name, you will receive him. [44] How can you believe, when you receive glory from one another and do not seek the glory that comes from the only God? [45] Do not think that I will accuse you to the Father. There is one who accuses you: Moses, on whom you have set your hope. [46] For if you believed Moses, you would believe me; for he wrote of me. [47] But if you do not believe his writings, how will you believe my words?"

Jesus Feeds the Five Thousand

6 After this [a]Jesus went away to the other side of the Sea of Galilee, which is the Sea of Tiberias. [2] And a large crowd was following him, because they saw the signs that he was doing on the sick. [3] Jesus went up on the mountain, and there he sat down with his disciples. [4] Now the Passover, the feast of the Jews, was at hand. [5] Lifting up his eyes, then, and seeing that a large crowd was coming toward him, Jesus said to Philip, "Where are we to buy bread, so that these people may eat?" [6] He said this to test him, for he himself knew what he would do. [7] Philip answered him, "Two hundred denarii[1] worth of bread would not be enough for each of them to get a little." [8] One of his disciples, Andrew, Simon Peter's brother, said to him, [9] "There is a boy here who has five barley loaves and two fish, but what are they for so many?" [10] Jesus said, "Have the people sit down." Now there was much grass in the place. So the men sat down, about five thousand in number. [11] Jesus then took the loaves, and

when he had given thanks, he distributed them to those who were seated. So also the fish, as much as they wanted. [12] And when they had eaten their fill, he told his disciples, "Gather up the leftover fragments, that nothing may be lost." [13] So they gathered them up and filled twelve baskets with fragments from the five barley loaves left by those who had eaten. [14] When the people saw the sign that he had done, they said, "This is indeed the Prophet who is to come into the world!"

[15] Perceiving then that they were about to come and take him by force to make him king, Jesus [b]withdrew again to the mountain by himself.

Jesus Walks on Water

[16] When evening came, his disciples went down to the sea, [17] got into a boat, and started across the sea to Capernaum. It was now dark, and Jesus had not yet come to them. [18] The sea became rough because a strong wind was blowing. [19] When they had rowed about three or four miles,[2] they saw Jesus walking on the sea and coming near the boat, and they were frightened. [20] But he said to them, "It is I; do not be afraid." [21] Then they were glad to take him into the boat, and immediately the boat was at the land to which they were going.

I Am the Bread of Life

[22] On the next day the crowd that remained on the other side of the sea saw that there had been only one boat there, and that Jesus had not entered the boat with his disciples, but that his disciples had gone away alone. [23] Other boats from Tiberias came near the place where they had eaten the bread after the Lord had given thanks. [24] So when the crowd saw that Jesus was not there, nor his disciples, they themselves got into the boats and went to Capernaum, seeking Jesus.

[25] When they found him on the other side of the sea, they said to him, "Rabbi, when did you come here?" [26] Jesus answered them, "Truly, truly, I say to you, you are seeking me, not because you saw signs, but because you ate your fill of the loaves. [27] Do not work for the food that perishes, but for the food that endures to eternal life, which the Son of Man will give to you. For on him

---

[1] A *denarius* was a day's wage for a laborer   [2] Greek *twenty-five or thirty stadia*; a *stadion* was about 607 feet or 185 meters   [a] For 6:1-13 see parallels Matt. 14:13-21; Mark 6:32-44; Luke 9:10-17   [b] For 6:15-21 see parallels Matt. 14:22-33; Mark 6:45-52

God the Father has set his seal." [28] Then they said to him, "What must we do, to be doing the works of God?" [29] Jesus answered them, "This is the work of God, that you believe in him whom he has sent." [30] So they said to him, "Then what sign do you do, that we may see and believe you? What work do you perform? [31] Our fathers ate the manna in the wilderness; as it is written, [a]'He gave them bread from heaven to eat.'" [32] Jesus then said to them, "Truly, truly, I say to you, it was not Moses who gave you the bread from heaven, but my Father gives you the true bread from heaven. [33] For the bread of God is he who comes down from heaven and gives life to the world." [34] They said to him, "Sir, give us this bread always."

[35] Jesus said to them, "I am the bread of life; whoever comes to me shall not hunger, and whoever believes in me shall never thirst. [36] But I said to you that you have seen me and yet do not believe. [37] All that the Father gives me will come to me, and whoever comes to me I will never cast out. [38] For I have come down from heaven, not to do my own will but the will of him who sent me. [39] And this is the will of him who sent me, that I should lose nothing of all that he has given me, but raise it up on the last day. [40] For this is the will of my Father, that everyone who looks on the Son and believes in him should have eternal life, and I will raise him up on the last day."

[41] So the Jews grumbled about him, because he said, "I am the bread that came down from heaven." [42] They said, "Is not this Jesus, the son of Joseph, whose father and mother we know? How does he now say, 'I have come down from heaven'?" [43] Jesus answered them, "Do not grumble among yourselves. [44] No one can come to me unless the Father who sent me draws him. And I will raise him up on the last day. [45] It is written in the Prophets, [b]'And

[a] Neh. 9:15 [b] Isa. 54:13

Know Yourself

verses to read
John 6:32–58

"Feast your eyes on this." "You'll get an eyeful." "Eye candy." All of these expressions make the eyes sound like the place on your face where you put your food. And that isn't so far from the truth. You ingest things not just with your mouth but also with your eyes. Maybe that's what Jesus meant when he said, "I am the bread of life" (John 6:48) and talked about the person who "feeds on me" (John 6:57). After all, you can't literally eat him. So what's with this choice of words?

When you feed on something, you get your strength from it. Eat vegetables and meat, and you'll get strength from them. Without food you get weak and cranky, and eventually you're too worn out to think or even move. Food for the mouth is necessary for life. But another kind of food is essential for the spirit, and that is the Jesus kind. In John 1, Jesus is called the Word, and that's also what we call Scripture: the Word of God. No coincidence here. You feed on Jesus by feasting your eyes on his Word, the Bible.

When your emotional life is on edge, when you feel weak spiritually or your mind is weak and weary, feed it by drinking in the Word of God. Get your strength by devouring truth. When you do, the truth of the Word goes into your mind and through your heart until it nourishes you and teaches you all that you need to live a holy life. And that means a good life. When you devour the Word of God, instead of getting a sugar high or a little extra around the middle, you get things like peace, hope, contentment, and love. As your spiritual life gains nourishment through the Word, your soul is satisfied. So take a big bite and enjoy!

they will all be taught by God.' Everyone who has heard and learned from the Father comes to me— ⁴⁶not that anyone has seen the Father except he who is from God; he has seen the Father. ⁴⁷Truly, truly, I say to you, whoever believes has eternal life. ⁴⁸I am the bread of life. ⁴⁹Your fathers ate the manna in the wilderness, and they died. ⁵⁰This is the bread that comes down from heaven, so that one may eat of it and not die. ⁵¹I am the living bread that came down from heaven. If anyone eats of this bread, he will live forever. And the bread that I will give for the life of the world is my flesh."

⁵²The Jews then disputed among themselves, saying, "How can this man give us his flesh to eat?" ⁵³So Jesus said to them, "Truly, truly, I say to you, unless you eat the flesh of the Son of Man and drink his blood, you have no life in you. ⁵⁴Whoever feeds on my flesh and drinks my blood has eternal life, and I will raise him up on the last day. ⁵⁵For my flesh is true food, and my blood is true drink. ⁵⁶Whoever feeds on my flesh and drinks my blood abides in me, and I in him. ⁵⁷As the living Father sent me, and I live because of the Father, so whoever feeds on me, he also will live because of me. ⁵⁸This is the bread that came down from heaven, not like the bread¹ the fathers ate, and died. Whoever feeds on this bread will live forever." ⁵⁹Jesus² said these things in the synagogue, as he taught at Capernaum.

The Words of Eternal Life

⁶⁰When many of his disciples heard it, they said, "This is a hard saying; who can listen to it?" ⁶¹But Jesus, knowing in himself that his disciples were grumbling about this, said to them, "Do you take offense at this? ⁶²Then what if you were to see the Son of Man ascending to where he was before? ⁶³It is the Spirit who gives life; the flesh is no help at all. The words that I have spoken to you are spirit and life. ⁶⁴But there are some of you who do not believe." (For Jesus knew from the beginning who those were who did not believe, and who it was who would betray him.) ⁶⁵And he said, "This is why I told you that no one can come to me unless it is granted him by the Father."

⁶⁶After this many of his disciples turned back and no longer walked with him. ⁶⁷So Jesus said to the Twelve, "Do you want to go away as well?" ⁶⁸Simon Peter answered him, "Lord, to whom shall we go? You have the words of eternal life, ⁶⁹and we have believed, and have come to know, that you are the Holy One of God." ⁷⁰Jesus answered them, "Did I not choose you, the Twelve? And yet one of you is a devil." ⁷¹He spoke of Judas the son of Simon Iscariot, for he, one of the Twelve, was going to betray him.

Jesus at the Feast of Booths

7 After this Jesus went about in Galilee He would not go about in Judea, because the Jews³ were seeking to kill him. ²Now the Jews' Feast of Booths was at hand. ³So his brothers⁴ said to him, "Leave here and go to Judea, that your disciples also may see the works you are doing. ⁴For no one works in secret if he seeks to be known openly. If you do these things, show yourself to the world." ⁵For not even his brothers believed in him. ⁶Jesus said to them, "My time has not yet come, but your time is always here. ⁷The world cannot hate you, but it hates me because I testify about it that its works are evil. ⁸You go up to the feast. I am not⁵ going up to this feast, for my time has not yet fully come." ⁹After saying this, he remained in Galilee.

¹⁰But after his brothers had gone up to the feast, then he also went up, not publicly but in private. ¹¹The Jews were looking for him at the feast, and saying, "Where is he?" ¹²And there was much muttering about him among the people. While some said, "He is a good man," others said, "No, he is leading the people astray." ¹³Yet for fear of the Jews no one spoke openly of him.

¹⁴About the middle of the feast Jesus went up into the temple and began teaching. ¹⁵The Jews therefore marveled, saying, "How is it that this man has learning,⁶ when he has never studied?" ¹⁶So Jesus answered them, "My teaching is not mine, but his who sent me. ¹⁷If anyone's will is to do God's⁷ will, he will know whether the teaching is from God or whether I am speaking on my own authority. ¹⁸The one who speaks on his own authority seeks his own glory; but the one who seeks the glory of him who sent him is true, and in him there is no falsehood. ¹⁹Has not Moses given you the law? Yet none of you

¹Greek lacks the bread ²Greek He ³Or Judeans; Greek Ioudaioi probably refers here to Jewish religious leaders, and others under their influence, in that time ⁴Or brothers and sisters; also verses 5, 10 ⁵Some manuscripts add yet ⁶Or this man knows his letters ⁷Greek his

keeps the law. Why do you seek to kill me?" [20] The crowd answered, "You have a demon! Who is seeking to kill you?" [21] Jesus answered them, "I did one work, and you all marvel at it. [22] Moses gave you circumcision (not that it is from Moses, but from the fathers), and you circumcise a man on the Sabbath. [23] If on the Sabbath a man receives circumcision, so that the law of Moses may not be broken, are you angry with me because on the Sabbath I made a man's whole body well? [24] Do not judge by appearances, but judge with right judgment."

Can This Be the Christ?

[25] Some of the people of Jerusalem therefore said, "Is not this the man whom they seek to kill? [26] And here he is, speaking openly, and they say nothing to him! Can it be that the authorities really know that this is the Christ? [27] But we know where this man comes from, and when the Christ appears, no one will know where he comes from." [28] So Jesus proclaimed, as he taught in the temple, "You know me, and you know where I come from. But I have not come of my own accord. He who sent me is true, and him you do not know. [29] I know him, for I come from him, and he sent me." [30] So they were seeking to arrest him, but no one laid a hand on him, because his hour had not yet come. [31] Yet many of the people believed in him. They said, "When the Christ appears, will he do more signs than this man has done?"

Officers Sent to Arrest Jesus

[32] The Pharisees heard the crowd muttering these things about him, and the chief priests and Pharisees sent officers to arrest him. [33] Jesus then said, "I will be with you a little longer, and then I am going to him who sent me. [34] You will seek me and you will not find me. Where I am you cannot come." [35] The Jews said to one another, "Where does this man intend to go that we will not find him? Does he intend to go to the Dispersion among the Greeks and teach the Greeks? [36] What does he mean by saying, 'You will seek me and you will not find me,' and, 'Where I am you cannot come'?"

Rivers of Living Water

[37] On the last day of the feast, the great day, Jesus stood up and cried out, "If anyone thirsts, let him come to me and drink. [38] Whoever believes in me, as[1] the Scripture has said, 'Out of his heart will flow rivers of living water.'" [39] Now this he said about the Spirit, whom those who believed in him were to receive, for as yet the Spirit had not been given, because Jesus was not yet glorified.

Division Among the People

[40] When they heard these words, some of the people said, "This really is the Prophet." [41] Others said, "This is the Christ." But some said, "Is the Christ to come from Galilee? [42] Has not the Scripture said that the Christ comes from the offspring of David, and comes from Bethlehem, the village where David was?" [43] So there was a division among the people over him. [44] Some of them wanted to arrest him, but no one laid hands on him.

[45] The officers then came to the chief priests and Pharisees, who said to them, "Why did you not bring him?" [46] The officers answered, "No one ever spoke like this man!" [47] The Pharisees answered them, "Have you also been deceived? [48] Have any of the authorities or the Pharisees believed in him? [49] But this crowd that does not know the law is accursed." [50] Nicodemus, who had gone to him before, and who was one of them, said to them, [51] "Does our law judge a man without first giving him a hearing and learning what he does?" [52] They replied, "Are you from Galilee too? Search and see that no prophet arises from Galilee."

[THE EARLIEST MANUSCRIPTS DO NOT INCLUDE 7:53–8:11.][2]

The Woman Caught in Adultery

8 [53] [[They went each to his own house, [1] but Jesus went to the Mount of Olives. [2] Early in the morning he came again to the temple. All the people came to him, and he sat down and taught them. [3] The scribes and the Pharisees brought a woman who had been caught in adultery, and placing her in the midst [4] they said to him, "Teacher, this woman has been caught in the act of adultery. [5] Now in the Law Moses commanded us to stone such women. So what

---

[1] Or *let him come to me, and let him who believes in me drink. As* [2] Some manuscripts do not include 7:53–8:11; others add the passage here or after 7:36 or after 21:25 or after Luke 21:38, with variations in the text

do you say?" ⁶This they said to test him, that they might have some charge to bring against him. Jesus bent down and wrote with his finger on the ground. ⁷And as they continued to ask him, he stood up and said to them, "Let him who is without sin among you be the first to throw a stone at her." ⁸And once more he bent down and wrote on the ground. ⁹But when they heard it, they went away one by one, beginning with the older ones, and Jesus was left alone with the woman standing before him. ¹⁰Jesus stood up and said to her, "Woman, where are they? Has no one condemned you?" ¹¹She said, "No one, Lord." And Jesus said, "Neither do I condemn you; go, and from now on sin no more."]]

I Am the Light of the World

¹²Again Jesus spoke to them, saying, "I am the light of the world. Whoever follows me will not walk in darkness, but will have the light of life." ¹³So the Pharisees said to him, "You are bearing witness about yourself; your testimony is not true."

¹Some manuscripts *he*

¹⁴Jesus answered, "Even if I do bear witness about myself, my testimony is true, for I know where I came from and where I am going, but you do not know where I come from or where I am going. ¹⁵You judge according to the flesh; I judge no one. ¹⁶Yet even if I do judge, my judgment is true, for it is not I alone who judge, but I and the Father¹ who sent me. ¹⁷In your Law it is written that the testimony of two people is true. ¹⁸I am the one who bears witness about myself, and the Father who sent me bears witness about me." ¹⁹They said to him therefore, "Where is your Father?" Jesus answered, "You know neither me nor my Father. If you knew me, you would know my Father also." ²⁰These words he spoke in the treasury, as he taught in the temple; but no one arrested him, because his hour had not yet come.

²¹So he said to them again, "I am going away, and you will seek me, and you will die in your sin. Where I am going, you cannot come." ²²So the Jews said, "Will he kill himself, since he says, 'Where I am going

Know Yourself

verses to read
John 7:37-39

Jesus didn't say, "Whoever believes in me, deep in his heart will be a pool of living water." No, he's not talking about a green, stagnant pond, covered with lily pads and bugs where all the goodness and blessing stays comfortably inside of you, unmoved by the current. He's talking about a river with a current of blessing and goodness that flows right through you and out to everyone around you.

Contrary to popular belief, Jesus' teachings were never about "finding yourself" but rather about the life that comes out of you. It's a life that provides comfort and enjoyment not by seeking these things as ends in themselves but through service to the rest of the world. When you continually focus on yourself, you do the exact opposite of what Christ taught. Nowhere in Scripture are you called to elevate yourself. Instead you're told to live for others and not to think more highly of yourself than you should. Jesus' life is the model; he didn't live to find himself but gave all he was as an offering to the Father. And he died on that cross because he loved the world.

In your life, that means that you can and should let what God puts into your life freely flow out into the lives of others. When you do, you will find your life is no longer stagnant and murky but is becoming a great source of living water—of hope to the world around you.

ou cannot come'?" 23 He said to them, "You re from below; I am from above. You are f this world; I am not of this world. 24 I told ou that you would die in your sins, for ınless you believe that I am he you will die n your sins." 25 So they said to him, "Who ıre you?" Jesus said to them, "Just what have been telling you from the beginning. 6 I have much to say about you and much o judge, but he who sent me is true, and declare to the world what I have heard rom him." 27 They did not understand that ıe had been speaking to them about the 'ather. 28 So Jesus said to them, "When you ıave lifted up the Son of Man, then you will ‹now that I am he, and that I do nothing ›n my own authority, but speak just as the 'ather taught me. 29 And he who sent me s with me. He has not left me alone, for always do the things that are pleasing to ıim." 30 As he was saying these things, many ›elieved in him.

he Truth Will Set You Free

31 So Jesus said to the Jews who had ›elieved him, "If you abide in my word, you ıre truly my disciples, 32 and you will know he truth, and the truth will set you free." 3 They answered him, "We are offspring ›f Abraham and have never been enslaved o anyone. How is it that you say, 'You will ›ecome free'?"

34 Jesus answered them, "Truly, truly, say to you, everyone who practices sin is a ‹lave[1] to sin. 35 The slave does not remain in he house forever; the son remains forever. 6 So if the Son sets you free, you will be free ndeed. 37 I know that you are offspring of ٰbraham; yet you seek to kill me because ny word finds no place in you. 38 I speak of vhat I have seen with my Father, and you lo what you have heard from your father."

ou Are of Your Father the Devil

39 They answered him, "Abraham is our ather." Jesus said to them, "If you were ٰbraham's children, you would be doing he works Abraham did, 40 but now you seek to kill me, a man who has told you he truth that I heard from God. This is ot what Abraham did. 41 You are doing he works your father did." They said to ıim, "We were not born of sexual immo-ality. We have one Father—even God." 42 Jesus said to them, "If God were your

Father, you would love me, for I came from God and I am here. I came not of my own accord, but he sent me. 43 Why do you not understand what I say? It is because you cannot bear to hear my word. 44 You are of your father the devil, and your will is to do your father's desires. He was a murderer from the beginning, and does not stand in the truth, because there is no truth in him. When he lies, he speaks out of his own character, for he is a liar and the father of lies. 45 But because I tell the truth, you do not believe me. 46 Which one of you convicts me of sin? If I tell the truth, why do you not believe me? 47 Whoever is of God hears the words of God. The reason why you do not hear them is that you are not of God."

Before Abraham Was, I Am

48 The Jews answered him, "Are we not right in saying that you are a Samaritan and have a demon?" 49 Jesus answered, "I do not have a demon, but I honor my Father, and you dishonor me. 50 Yet I do not seek my own glory; there is One who seeks it, and he is the judge. 51 Truly, truly, I say to you, if anyone keeps my word, he will never see death." 52 The Jews said to him, "Now we know that you have a demon! Abraham died, as did the prophets, yet you say, 'If anyone keeps my word, he will never taste death.' 53 Are you greater than our father Abraham, who died? And the prophets died! Who do you make yourself out to be?" 54 Jesus answered, "If I glorify myself, my glory is nothing. It is my Father who glorifies me, of whom you say, 'He is our God.'[2] 55 But you have not known him. I know him. If I were to say that I do not know him, I would be a liar like you, but I do know him and I keep his word. 56 Your father Abraham rejoiced that he would see my day. He saw it and was glad." 57 So the Jews said to him, "You are not yet fifty years old, and have you seen Abraham?"[3] 58 Jesus said to them, "Truly, truly, I say to you, before Abraham was, I am." 59 So they picked up stones to throw at him, but Jesus hid himself and went out of the temple.

Jesus Heals a Man Born Blind

9 As he passed by, he saw a man blind from birth. 2 And his disciples asked him, "Rabbi, who sinned, this man or his

---

Greek bondservant; also verse 35 [2] Some manuscripts your God [3] Some manuscripts has Abraham seen you?

parents, that he was born blind?" ³Jesus answered, "It was not that this man sinned, or his parents, but that the works of God might be displayed in him. ⁴We must work the works of him who sent me while it is day; night is coming, when no one can work. ⁵As long as I am in the world, I am the light of the world." ⁶Having said these things, he spit on the ground and made mud with the saliva. Then he anointed the man's eyes with the mud ⁷and said to him, "Go, wash in the pool of Siloam" (which means Sent). So he went and washed and came back seeing.

⁸The neighbors and those who had seen him before as a beggar were saying, "Is this not the man who used to sit and beg?" ⁹Some said, "It is he." Others said, "No, but he is like him." He kept saying, "I am the man." ¹⁰So they said to him, "Then how were your eyes opened?" ¹¹He answered, "The man called Jesus made mud and anointed my eyes and said to me, 'Go to Siloam and wash.' So I went and washed and received my sight." ¹²They said to him, "Where is he?" He said, "I do not know."

¹³They brought to the Pharisees the man who had formerly been blind. ¹⁴Now it was a Sabbath day when Jesus made the mud and opened his eyes. ¹⁵So the Pharisees again asked him how he had received his sight. And he said to them, "He put mud on my eyes, and I washed, and I see." ¹⁶Some of the Pharisees said, "This man is not from God, for he does not keep the Sabbath." But others said, "How can a man who is a sinner do such signs?" And there was a division among them. ¹⁷So they said again to the blind man, "What do you say about him, since he has opened your eyes?" He said, "He is a prophet."

¹⁸The Jews[1] did not believe that he had been blind and had received his sight, until they called the parents of the man who had received his sight ¹⁹and asked them, "Is this your son, who you say was born blind? How then does he now see?" ²⁰His parents answered, "We know that this is our son and that he was born blind. ²¹But how he now sees we do not know, nor do we know who opened his eyes. Ask him; he is of age. He will speak for himself." ²²(His parents said these things because they feared the Jews, for the Jews had already agreed that

if anyone should confess Jesus[2] to be Christ, he was to be put out of the synagogue. ²³Therefore his parents said, "He is of age; ask him.")

²⁴So for the second time they called the man who had been blind and said to him, "Give glory to God. We know that this man is a sinner." ²⁵He answered, "Whether he is a sinner I do not know. One thing I do know, that though I was blind, now I see." ²⁶They said to him, "What did he do to you? How did he open your eyes?" ²⁷He answered them, "I have told you already, and you would not listen. Why do you want to hear it again? Do you also want to become his disciples?" ²⁸And they reviled him, saying, "You are his disciple, but we are disciples of Moses. ²⁹We know that God has spoken to Moses, but as for this man, we do not know where he comes from." ³⁰The man answered, "Why, this is an amazing thing! You do not know where he comes from, and yet he opened my eyes. ³¹We know that God does not listen to sinners, but if anyone is a worshiper of God and does his will, God listens to him. ³²Never since the world began has it been heard that anyone opened the eyes of a man born blind. ³³If this man were not from God, he could do nothing." ³⁴They answered him, "You were born in utter sin, and would you teach us?" And they cast him out.

³⁵Jesus heard that they had cast him out, and having found him he said, "Do you believe in the Son of Man?"[3] ³⁶He answered, "And who is he, sir, that I may believe in him?" ³⁷Jesus said to him, "You have seen him, and it is he who is speaking to you." ³⁸He said, "Lord, I believe," and he worshiped him. ³⁹Jesus said, "For judgment I came into this world, that those who do not see may see, and those who see may become blind." ⁴⁰Some of the Pharisees near him heard these things, and said to him, "Are we also blind?" ⁴¹Jesus said to them, "If you were blind, you would have no guilt;[4] but now that you say, 'We see,' your guilt remains.

I Am the Good Shepherd

10 "Truly, truly, I say to you, he who does not enter the sheepfold by the door but climbs in by another way, that man is a thief and a robber. ²But he

---

[1] Greek *Ioudaioi* probably refers here to Jewish religious leaders, and others under their influence, in that time; also verse 22 [2] Greek *him* [3] Some manuscripts *the Son of God* [4] Greek *you would not have sin*

who enters by the door is the shepherd of the sheep. ³ To him the gatekeeper opens. The sheep hear his voice, and he calls his own sheep by name and leads them out. ⁴ When he has brought out all his own, he goes before them, and the sheep follow him, for they know his voice. ⁵ A stranger they will not follow, but they will flee from him, for they do not know the voice of strangers." ⁶ This figure of speech Jesus used with them, but they did not understand what he was saying to them.

⁷ So Jesus again said to them, "Truly, truly, I say to you, I am the door of the sheep. ⁸ All who came before me are thieves and robbers, but the sheep did not listen to them. ⁹ I am the door. If anyone enters by me, he will be saved and will go in and out and find pasture. ¹⁰ The thief comes only to steal and kill and destroy. I came that they may have life and have it abundantly. ¹¹ I am the good shepherd. The good shepherd lays down his life for the sheep. ¹² He who is a hired hand and not a shepherd, who does not own the sheep, sees the wolf coming and leaves the sheep and flees, and the wolf snatches them and scatters them. ¹³ He flees because he is a hired hand and cares nothing for the sheep. ¹⁴ I am the good shepherd. I know my own and my own know me, ¹⁵ just as the Father knows me and I know the Father; and I lay down my life for the sheep. ¹⁶ And I have other sheep that are not of this fold. I must bring them also, and they will listen to my voice. So there will be one flock, one shepherd. ¹⁷ For this reason the Father loves me, because I lay down my life that I may take it up again. ⁸ No one takes it from me, but I lay it down of my own accord. I have authority to lay it down, and I have authority to take it up again. This charge I have received from my Father."

¹⁹ There was again a division among the Jews because of these words. ²⁰ Many of them said, "He has a demon, and is insane; why listen to him?" ²¹ Others said, "These are not the words of one who is oppressed by a demon. Can a demon open the eyes of the blind?"

and the Father Are One

²² At that time the Feast of Dedication took place at Jerusalem. It was winter,

²³ and Jesus was walking in the temple, in the colonnade of Solomon. ²⁴ So the Jews gathered around him and said to him, "How long will you keep us in suspense? If you are the Christ, tell us plainly." ²⁵ Jesus answered them, "I told you, and you do not believe. The works that I do in my Father's name bear witness about me, ²⁶ but you do not believe because you are not among my sheep. ²⁷ My sheep hear my voice, and I know them, and they follow me. ²⁸ I give them eternal life, and they will never perish, and no one will snatch them out of my hand. ²⁹ My Father, who has given them to me,¹ is greater than all, and no one is able to snatch them out of the Father's hand. ³⁰ I and the Father are one."

³¹ The Jews picked up stones again to stone him. ³² Jesus answered them, "I have shown you many good works from the Father; for which of them are you going to stone me?" ³³ The Jews answered him, "It is not for a good work that we are going to stone you but for blasphemy, because you, being a man, make yourself God." ³⁴ Jesus answered them, "Is it not written in your Law, ᵃ'I said, you are gods'? ³⁵ If he called them gods to whom the word of God came—and Scripture cannot be broken— ³⁶ do you say of him whom the Father consecrated and sent into the world, 'You are blaspheming,' because I said, 'I am the Son of God'? ³⁷ If I am not doing the works of my Father, then do not believe me; ³⁸ but if I do them, even though you do not believe me, believe the works, that you may know and understand that the Father is in me and I am in the Father." ³⁹ Again they sought to arrest him, but he escaped from their hands.

⁴⁰ He went away again across the Jordan to the place where John had been baptizing at first, and there he remained. ⁴¹ And many came to him. And they said, "John did no sign, but everything that John said about this man was true." ⁴² And many believed in him there.

The Death of Lazarus

11 Now a certain man was ill, Lazarus of Bethany, the village of Mary and her sister Martha. ² It was Mary who anointed the Lord with ointment and wiped his feet with her hair, whose brother Lazarus was ill. ³ So the sisters sent to him, saying, "Lord, he whom you love is ill." ⁴ But

Some manuscripts *What my Father has given to me*   ᵃ Ps. 82:6

when Jesus heard it he said, "This illness does not lead to death. It is for the glory of God, so that the Son of God may be glorified through it."

A Prayer for...

RESTING IN GOD

O God most high, most glorious, the thought of your infinite serenity makes me happy, because I'm struggling and stirring, troubled and distressed, but you are forever at perfect peace. Your plans don't cause any fear or worry; they are as sure and permanent as the eternal hills. Your power knows no bounds, your goodness no end. You bring order out of confusion, and my defeats are your victories. The Lord God omnipotent reigns!

I come to you as a sinner, with cares and sorrows, to leave every concern entirely to you and every sin for Christ's precious blood. Revive deep spirituality in my heart; let me live near to the Good Shepherd, hear his voice, know its tones, follow its calls. Keep me from deception by causing me to live in the truth and from harm by helping me to walk in the power of the Spirit. Give me intense faith in eternal truths, burning into me by experience the things I know. Let me never be ashamed of the truth of the gospel, that I may bear its disgrace, vindicate it, see Jesus as its essence, and know in it the power of the Spirit.

Lord, help me, for I am often lukewarm; doubt weakens my confidence, and sin makes me forget you. Let the weeds that grow in my soul be cut at their roots; allow me to know that I truly live only when I live for you, and all else is worthless. Your presence alone can make me holy, devout, strong, and happy. Live in me, gracious God.

Amen.

⁵ Now Jesus loved Martha and her sister and Lazarus. ⁶ So, when he heard that Lazarus[1] was ill, he stayed two days longer in the place where he was. ⁷ Then after this he said to the disciples, "Let us go to Judea again." ⁸ The disciples said to him, "Rabbi, the Jews were just now seeking to stone you, and are you going there again?" ⁹ Jesus answered, "Are there not twelve hours in the day? If anyone walks in the day, he does not stumble, because he sees the light of this world. ¹⁰ But if anyone walks in the night, he stumbles, because the light is not in him." ¹¹ After saying these things, he said to them, "Our friend Lazarus has fallen asleep, but I go to awaken him." ¹² The disciples said to him, "Lord, if he has fallen asleep, he will recover." ¹³ Now Jesus had spoken of his death, but they thought that he meant taking rest in sleep. ¹⁴ Then Jesus told them plainly, "Lazarus has died, ¹⁵ and for your sake I am glad that I was not there, so that you may believe. But let us go to him." ¹⁶ So Thomas, called the Twin,[2] said to his fellow disciples, "Let us also go, that we may die with him."

I Am the Resurrection and the Life

¹⁷ Now when Jesus came, he found that Lazarus had already been in the tomb four days. ¹⁸ Bethany was near Jerusalem, about two miles[3] off, ¹⁹ and many of the Jews had come to Martha and Mary to console them concerning their brother. ²⁰ So when Martha heard that Jesus was coming, she went and met him, but Mary remained seated in the house. ²¹ Martha said to Jesus, "Lord, if you had been here, my brother would not have died. ²² But even now I know that whatever you ask from God, God will give you." ²³ Jesus said to her, "Your brother will rise again." ²⁴ Martha said to him, "I know that he will rise again in the resurrection on the last day." ²⁵ Jesus said to her, "I am the resurrection and the life.[4] Whoever believes in me, though he die, yet shall he live, ²⁶ and everyone who lives and believes in me shall never die. Do you believe this?" ²⁷ She said to him, "Yes, Lord; I believe that you are the Christ, the Son of God, who is coming into the world."

[1] Greek *he*; also verse 17 [2] Greek *Didymus* [3] Greek *fifteen stadia*; a *stadion* was about 607 feet or 185 meters [4] Some manuscripts omit *and the life*

esus Weeps

28 When she had said this, she went and
alled her sister Mary, saying in private,
The Teacher is here and is calling for you."
9 And when she heard it, she rose quickly
nd went to him. 30 Now Jesus had not yet
ome into the village, but was still in the
lace where Martha had met him. 31 When
he Jews who were with her in the house,
onsoling her, saw Mary rise quickly and
o out, they followed her, supposing that
he was going to the tomb to weep there.
2 Now when Mary came to where Jesus
vas and saw him, she fell at his feet, say-
ng to him, "Lord, if you had been here,
ny brother would not have died." 33 When
esus saw her weeping, and the Jews who
ad come with her also weeping, he was
leeply moved[1] in his spirit and greatly
roubled. 34 And he said, "Where have you
aid him?" They said to him, "Lord, come
nd see." 35 Jesus wept. 36 So the Jews said,
See how he loved him!" 37 But some of
hem said, "Could not he who opened the
yes of the blind man also have kept this
nan from dying?"

esus Raises Lazarus

38 Then Jesus, deeply moved again, came
o the tomb. It was a cave, and a stone lay
gainst it. 39 Jesus said, "Take away the
tone." Martha, the sister of the dead man,
aid to him, "Lord, by this time there will
e an odor, for he has been dead four days."
0 Jesus said to her, "Did I not tell you that
f you believed you would see the glory
f God?" 41 So they took away the stone.
nd Jesus lifted up his eyes and said,
Father, I thank you that you have heard
ne. 42 I knew that you always hear me, but
said this on account of the people standing
round, that they may believe that you sent
ne." 43 When he had said these things, he
ried out with a loud voice, "Lazarus, come
ut." 44 The man who had died came out, his
ands and feet bound with linen strips, and
is face wrapped with a cloth. Jesus said to
hem, "Unbind him, and let him go."

he Plot to Kill Jesus

45 Many of the Jews therefore, who had
ome with Mary and had seen what he
lid, believed in him, 46 but some of them
vent to the Pharisees and told them what
Jesus had done. 47 So the chief priests and
the Pharisees gathered the council and
said, "What are we to do? For this man
performs many signs. 48 If we let him go
on like this, everyone will believe in him,
and the Romans will come and take away
both our place and our nation." 49 But one
of them, Caiaphas, who was high priest
that year, said to them, "You know noth-
ing at all. 50 Nor do you understand that it
is better for you that one man should die
for the people, not that the whole nation
should perish." 51 He did not say this of
his own accord, but being high priest that
year he prophesied that Jesus would die
for the nation, 52 and not for the nation only,
but also to gather into one the children of
God who are scattered abroad. 53 So from
that day on they made plans to put him
to death.

54 Jesus therefore no longer walked
openly among the Jews, but went from
there to the region near the wilderness, to
a town called Ephraim, and there he stayed
with the disciples.

55 Now the Passover of the Jews was at
hand, and many went up from the country
to Jerusalem before the Passover to purify
themselves. 56 They were looking for[2] Jesus
and saying to one another as they stood in
the temple, "What do you think? That he
will not come to the feast at all?" 57 Now
the chief priests and the Pharisees had
given orders that if anyone knew where he
was, he should let them know, so that they
might arrest him.

Mary Anoints Jesus at Bethany

12 Six days before the Passover, Jesus
therefore came to Bethany, where
Lazarus was, whom Jesus had raised from
the dead. 2 So they gave a dinner for him
there. Martha served, and Lazarus was
one of those reclining with him at table.
3 Mary therefore took a pound[3] of expen-
sive ointment made from pure nard, and
anointed the feet of Jesus and wiped his
feet with her hair. The house was filled
with the fragrance of the perfume. 4 But
Judas Iscariot, one of his disciples (he who
was about to betray him), said, 5 "Why was
this ointment not sold for three hundred
denarii[4] and given to the poor?" 6 He said
this, not because he cared about the poor,

Or *was indignant*; also verse 38 [2]Greek *were seeking for* [3]Greek *litra*; a *litra* (or Roman pound) was equal to about 11 1/2 ounces or
27 grams [4]A *denarius* was a day's wage for a laborer

Martha

Read this God Girl story in Luke 10:38–42 and
John 11:1–44; 12:1–2.

Do all things without grumbling or disputing.

Philippians 2:14

Martha's problem wasn't so much working too hard as it was complaining about it. The real issue wasn't her work ethic but the fact that she resented her sister Mary, who in her mind wasn't doing anything worth anything for anyone (see Luke 10:38–42). So the problem wasn't in her actions but in her thoughts and her words. If she would have just kept her mouth shut and her mind on the job at hand, would she have gotten such a harsh rebuke from Jesus? Maybe not.

In the life of faith, sometimes hard work has to be done. You may be called to serve, to work, and to labor while other people seem to be goofing off and having fun. But at the point when you complain about it, you are no longer serving anyone but yourself. Complaining is sin. Why would you whine to God about other people's selfishness when by whining you prove your own selfishness? When you work for God, you can't blame others for the hard work it requires. Your service is between you and God, and what others around you are doing is irrelevant. To complain is to judge the spiritual position of those you complain about, and who are you to judge (see Rom. 14:4)?

As a God Girl, you have to keep your commitment to God between you and God and not between you and others. When you start comparing, you start sliding down the slippery slope of resentment. Allow others to answer the call of God however they are going to. Don't expect them to serve the same way you do. And don't assume that your hard work somehow makes you better. Martha will forever be known as the workaholic complainer. She will forever be seen as the whiner, while her sister Mary will forever be seen as the gentle and wise one who took advantage of the presence of Jesus while she could. How will you be remembered?

but because he was a thief, and having charge of the moneybag he used to help himself to what was put into it. [7] Jesus said, "Leave her alone, so that she may keep it[1] for the day of my burial. [8] For the poor you always have with you, but you do not always have me."

The Plot to Kill Lazarus

[9] When the large crowd of the Jews learned that Jesus[2] was there, they came, not only on account of him but also to see Lazarus, whom he had raised from the dead. [10] So the chief priests made plans to put Lazarus to death as well, [11] because on account of him many of the Jews were going away and believing in Jesus.

The Triumphal Entry

[12] The next day [a] the large crowd that had come to the feast heard that Jesus was coming to Jerusalem. [13] So they took branches of palm trees and went out to meet him, crying out, "Hosanna! Blessed is he who comes in the name of the Lord, even the King of Israel!" [14] And Jesus found a young donkey and sat on it, just as it is written,

[15] [b] "Fear not, daughter of Zion;
    behold, your king is coming,
        sitting on a donkey's colt!"

[16] His disciples did not understand these things at first, but when Jesus was glorified, then they remembered that these things had been written about him and had been done to him. [17] The crowd that had been with him when he called Lazarus out of the tomb and raised him from the dead continued to bear witness. [18] The reason why the crowd went to meet him was that they heard he had done this sign. [19] So the Pharisees said to one another, "You see that you are gaining nothing. Look, the world has gone after him."

Some Greeks Seek Jesus

[20] Now among those who went up to worship at the feast were some Greeks. [21] So these came to Philip, who was from Bethsaida in Galilee, and asked him, "Sir, we wish to see Jesus." [22] Philip went and told Andrew; Andrew and Philip went and told Jesus. [23] And Jesus answered them, "The hour has come for the Son of Man to be glorified. [24] Truly, truly, I say to you, unless a grain of wheat falls into the earth and dies, it remains alone; but if it dies, it bears much fruit. [25] Whoever loves his life loses it, and whoever hates his life in this world will keep it for eternal life. [26] If anyone serves me, he must follow me; and where I am, there will my servant be also. If anyone serves me, the Father will honor him.

The Son of Man Must Be Lifted Up

[27] "Now is my soul troubled. And what shall I say? 'Father, save me from this hour'? But for this purpose I have come to this hour. [28] Father, glorify your name." Then a voice came from heaven: "I have glorified it, and I will glorify it again." [29] The crowd that stood there and heard it said that it had thundered. Others said, "An angel has spoken to him." [30] Jesus answered, "This voice has come for your sake, not mine. [31] Now is the judgment of this world; now will the ruler of this world be cast out. [32] And I, when I am lifted up from the earth, will draw all people to myself." [33] He said this to show by what kind of death he was going to die. [34] So the crowd answered him, "We have heard from the Law that the Christ remains forever. How can you say that the Son of Man must be lifted up? Who is this Son of Man?" [35] So Jesus said to them, "The light is among you for a little while longer. Walk while you have the light, lest darkness overtake you. The one who walks in the darkness does not know where he is going. [36] While you have the light, believe in the light, that you may become sons of light."

The Unbelief of the People

When Jesus had said these things, he departed and hid himself from them. [37] Though he had done so many signs before them, they still did not believe in him, [38] so that the word spoken by the prophet Isaiah might be fulfilled:

[c] "Lord, who has believed what he heard
        from us,
    and to whom has the arm of the
        Lord been revealed?"

[39] Therefore they could not believe. For again Isaiah said,

---

[1] Or Leave her alone; she intended to keep it   [2] Greek he   [a] For 12:12-15 see parallels Matt. 21:4-9; Mark 11:7-10; Luke 19:35-38   [b] Zech. 9:9   [c] Isa. 53:1

40 [a]"He has blinded their eyes
        and hardened their heart,
    lest they see with their eyes,
        and understand with their heart,
            and turn,
        and I would heal them."

41 Isaiah said these things because he saw his glory and spoke of him. 42 Nevertheless, many even of the authorities believed in him, but for fear of the Pharisees they did not confess it, so that they would not be put out of the synagogue; 43 for they loved the glory that comes from man more than the glory that comes from God.

Jesus Came to Save the World

44 And Jesus cried out and said, "Whoever believes in me, believes not in me but in him who sent me. 45 And whoever sees me sees him who sent me. 46 I have come into the world as light, so that whoever believes in me may not remain in darkness. 47 If anyone hears my words and does not keep them, I do not judge him; for I did not come to judge the world but to save the world. 48 The one who rejects me and does not receive my words has a judge; the word that I have spoken will judge him on the last day. 49 For I have not spoken on my own authority, but the Father who sent me has himself given me a commandment—what to say and what to speak. 50 And I know that his commandment is eternal life. What I say, therefore, I say as the Father has told me."

Jesus Washes the Disciples' Feet

13 Now before the Feast of the Passover, when Jesus knew that his hour had come to depart out of this world to the Father, having loved his own who were in the world, he loved them to the end. 2 During supper, when the devil had already put it into the heart of Judas Iscariot, Simon's son, to betray him, 3 Jesus, knowing that the Father had given all things into his hands, and that he had come from God and was going back to God, 4 rose from supper. He laid aside his outer garments, and taking a towel, tied it around his waist. 5 Then he poured water into a basin and began to wash the disciples' feet and to wipe them with the towel that was wrapped around him. 6 He came to Simon Peter, who said to

him, "Lord, do you wash my feet?" 7 Jesus answered him, "What I am doing you do not understand now, but afterward you will understand." 8 Peter said to him, "You shall never wash my feet." Jesus answered him, "If I do not wash you, you have no share with me." 9 Simon Peter said to him, "Lord, not my feet only but also my hands and my head!" 10 Jesus said to him, "The one who has bathed does not need to wash, except for his feet,[1] but is completely clean. And you[2] are clean, but not every one of you." 11 For he knew who was to betray him; that was why he said, "Not all of you are clean."

12 When he had washed their feet and put on his outer garments and resumed his place, he said to them, "Do you understand what I have done to you? 13 You call me Teacher and Lord, and you are right, for so I am. 14 If I then, your Lord and Teacher, have washed your feet, you also ought to wash one another's feet. 15 For I have given you an example, that you also should do just as I have done to you. 16 Truly, truly, I say to you, a servant[3] is not greater than his master, nor is a messenger greater than the one who sent him. 17 If you know these things, blessed are you if you do them. 18 I am not speaking of all of you; I know whom I have chosen. But the Scripture will be fulfilled,[4] [b]'He who ate my bread has lifted his heel against me.' 19 I am telling you this now, before it takes place, that when it does take place you may believe that I am he. 20 Truly, truly, I say to you, whoever receives the one I send receives me, and whoever receives me receives the one who sent me."

One of You Will Betray Me

21 After saying these things, Jesus was troubled in his spirit, and testified, "Truly, truly, I say to you, one of you will betray me." 22 The disciples looked at one another, uncertain of whom he spoke. 23 One of his disciples, whom Jesus loved, was reclining at table at Jesus' side,[5] 24 so Simon Peter motioned to him to ask Jesus[6] of whom he was speaking. 25 So that disciple, leaning back against Jesus, said to him, "Lord, who is it?" 26 Jesus answered, "It is he to whom I will give this morsel of bread when I have dipped it." So when he had dipped the morsel, he gave it to Judas, the son of

---

[1] Some manuscripts omit *except for his feet* [2] The Greek words for *you* in this verse are plural [3] Greek *bondservant* [4] Greek *But in order that the Scripture may be fulfilled* [5] Greek *in the bosom of Jesus* [6] Greek lacks *Jesus* [a] Isa. 6:10 [b] Ps. 41:9

Simon Iscariot. ²⁷Then after he had taken the morsel, Satan entered into him. Jesus said to him, "What you are going to do, do quickly." ²⁸Now no one at the table knew why he said this to him. ²⁹Some thought that, because Judas had the moneybag, Jesus was telling him, "Buy what we need for the feast," or that he should give something to the poor. ³⁰So, after receiving the morsel of bread, he immediately went out. And it was night.

A New Commandment

³¹When he had gone out, Jesus said, "Now is the Son of Man glorified, and God is glorified in him. ³²If God is glorified in him, God will also glorify him in himself, and glorify him at once. ³³Little children, yet a little while I am with you. You will seek me, and just as I said to the Jews, so now I also say to you, 'Where I am going you cannot come.' ³⁴A new commandment

¹ Or *You believe in God*

I give to you, that you love one another: just as I have loved you, you also are to love one another. ³⁵By this all people will know that you are my disciples, if you have love for one another."

Jesus Foretells Peter's Denial

³⁶Simon Peter said to him, "Lord, where are you going?" Jesus answered him, "Where I am going you cannot follow me now, but you will follow afterward." ³⁷Peter said to him, "Lord, why can I not follow you now? I will lay down my life for you." ³⁸Jesus answered, "Will you lay down your life for me? Truly, truly, I say to you, the rooster will not crow till you have denied me three times.

I Am the Way, and the Truth, and the Life

14 "Let not your hearts be troubled. Believe in God;¹ believe also in me. ²In my Father's house are many rooms. If it

Know Love

verses to read
John 13:34–35

Loving isn't just a suggestion; it's the command on which all other commands are based. As a believer, you have nothing without love—and that has to do not only with receiving love but also with giving love. It is super-duper important that you love other believers, and a lot of times that means giving in, being willing to lose, and turning the other cheek. If you are unwilling to do those things, you are unwilling to love. Love is selfless; it chooses to give no matter what it gets in return. When Christians love only people who love them, they don't prove to anyone anything about who God is. They only prove their hypocrisy. It doesn't make sense to accept the love of God, who doesn't owe us anything and whom we turn away from daily, and then refuse to love others when they hurt or reject us. Christian love is a sign to the world that God is greater than our needs and feelings. It is a sign of his great power in our lives.

If your love defines you, then who are you? Do you look like the God who loves you or like the world that surrounds you? When you understand the power of love and God's command to love, then you will truly be set free from the chains of rejection, fear, and loneliness. You will be able to see everything in the light of love, and out of that will come blessings for you and for those you love.

Take heart—love never fails. It might be rejected and it might give you pain, but that doesn't make it less valuable or rewarding to your soul. The God Girl will be known by her love. And the love that she offers will impact not only the hearts of those who receive it but also the heart of the girl who gives it.

were not so, would I have told you that I go to prepare a place for you?[1] ³And if I go and prepare a place for you, I will come again and will take you to myself, that where I am you may be also. ⁴And you know the way to where I am going."[2] ⁵Thomas said to him, "Lord, we do not know where you are going. How can we know the way?" ⁶Jesus said to him, "I am the way, and the truth, and the life. No one comes to the Father except through me. ⁷If you had known me, you would have known my Father also.[3] From now on you do know him and have seen him."

⁸Philip said to him, "Lord, show us the Father, and it is enough for us." ⁹Jesus said to him, "Have I been with you so long, and you still do not know me, Philip? Whoever has seen me has seen the Father. How can you say, 'Show us the Father'? ¹⁰Do you not believe that I am in the Father and the Father is in me? The words that I say to you I do not speak on my own authority, but the Father who dwells in me does his works. ¹¹Believe me that I am in the Father and the Father is in me, or else believe on account of the works themselves.

¹²"Truly, truly, I say to you, whoever believes in me will also do the works that I do; and greater works than these will he do, because I am going to the Father. ¹³Whatever you ask in my name, this I will do, that the Father may be glorified in the Son. ¹⁴If you ask me[4] anything in my name, I will do it.

Jesus Promises the Holy Spirit

¹⁵"If you love me, you will keep my commandments. ¹⁶And I will ask the Father, and he will give you another Helper,[5] to be with you forever, ¹⁷even the Spirit of truth, whom the world cannot receive, because it neither sees him nor knows him. You know him, for he dwells with you and will be[6] in you.

¹⁸"I will not leave you as orphans; I will come to you. ¹⁹Yet a little while and the world will see me no more, but you will see me. Because I live, you also will live. ²⁰In that day you will know that I am in my Father, and you in me, and I in you. ²¹Whoever has my commandments and keeps them, he it is who loves me. And he

who loves me will be loved by my Father, and I will love him and manifest myself to him." ²²Judas (not Iscariot) said to him, "Lord, how is it that you will manifest yourself to us, and not to the world?" ²³Jesus answered him, "If anyone loves me, he will keep my word, and my Father will love him, and we will come to him and make our home with him. ²⁴Whoever does not love me does not keep my words. And the word that you hear is not mine but the Father's who sent me.

²⁵"These things I have spoken to you while I am still with you. ²⁶But the Helper, the Holy Spirit, whom the Father will send in my name, he will teach you all things and bring to your remembrance all that I have said to you. ²⁷Peace I leave with you; my peace I give to you. Not as the world gives do I give to you. Let not your hearts be troubled, neither let them be afraid. ²⁸You heard me say to you, 'I am going away, and I will come to you.' If you loved me, you would have rejoiced, because I am going to the Father, for the Father is greater than I. ²⁹And now I have told you before it takes place, so that when it does take place you may believe. ³⁰I will no longer talk much with you, for the ruler of this world is coming. He has no claim on me, ³¹but I do as the Father has commanded me, so that the world may know that I love the Father. Rise, let us go from here.

I Am the True Vine

15 "I am the true vine, and my Father is the vinedresser. ²Every branch in me that does not bear fruit he takes away, and every branch that does bear fruit he prunes, that it may bear more fruit. ³Already you are clean because of the word that I have spoken to you. ⁴Abide in me, and I in you. As the branch cannot bear fruit by itself, unless it abides in the vine, neither can you, unless you abide in me. ⁵I am the vine; you are the branches. Whoever abides in me and I in him, he it is that bears much fruit, for apart from me you can do nothing. ⁶If anyone does not abide in me he is thrown away like a branch and withers; and the branches are gathered, thrown into the fire, and

[1] Or In my Father's house are many rooms; if it were not so, I would have told you; for I go to prepare a place for you　[2] Some manuscripts Where I am going you know, and the way you know　[3] Or If you know me, you will know my Father also, or If you have known me, you will know my Father also　[4] Some manuscripts omit me　[5] Or Advocate, or Counselor; also 14:26; 15:26; 16:7　[6] Some manuscripts and is

burned. [7] If you abide in me, and my words abide in you, ask whatever you wish, and it will be done for you. [8] By this my Father is glorified, that you bear much fruit and so prove to be my disciples. [9] As the Father has loved me, so have I loved you. Abide in my love. [10] If you keep my commandments, you will abide in my love, just as I have kept my Father's commandments and abide in his love. [11] These things I have spoken to you, that my joy may be in you, and that your joy may be full.

[12] "This is my commandment, that you love one another as I have loved you. [13] Greater love has no one than this, that someone lay down his life for his friends. [14] You are my friends if you do what I command you. [15] No longer do I call you servants,[1] for the servant[2] does not know what his master is doing; but I have called you friends, for all that I have heard from my Father I have made known to you. [16] You did not choose me, but I chose you and appointed you that you should go and bear fruit and that your fruit should abide, so that whatever you ask the Father in my name, he may give it to you. [17] These things I command you, so that you will love one another.

The Hatred of the World

[18] "If the world hates you, know that it has hated me before it hated you. [19] If you were of the world, the world would love you as its own; but because you are not of the world, but I chose you out of the world, therefore the world hates you. [20] Remember the word that I said to you: 'A servant is not greater than his master.' If they persecuted me, they will also persecute you. If they kept my word, they will also keep yours. [21] But all these things they will do to you on account of my name, because they do not know him who sent me. [22] If I had not come and spoken to them, they would not have been guilty of sin,[3] but now they have no excuse for their sin. [23] Whoever hates me hates my Father

[1] Greek bondservants [2] Greek bondservant; also verse 20 [3] Greek they would not have sin; also verse 24

Know God

verses to read
John 15:1–10

Jesus calls you to live in him. But how do you do that? What does it mean? How do you live "in" someone? How do you live with anyone who isn't physically with you?

The way you live with Jesus and stay attached to the vine is through your thoughts. That means the more time you spend studying, reading, praying, and thinking of him, the stronger your connection will be. When you find there are times that he slips off your already full plate, or you just don't have the strength to obey, you need to look at your thoughts. How much thought time do you really give to your God? Does he get ten minutes of uninterrupted thought a day? One hour?

Without spending a good amount of time thinking on Jesus, you will not live in him. Sure, you're busy. You have so many demands on you and so much to do, but without time spent with Jesus, you won't have the energy it takes to do it all. And you certainly won't have the power to handle the temptations that come your way every day. The truth is that you cannot afford to neglect spending time with Jesus. The more you have to do, the more time you need to spend with him. He is your source of strength. He is the one who will make you fruitful and productive. If you are feeling insufficient, then it's time to check your thought life. Are you living in him, or leaving him for other "more important" things? You don't have the strength to do it all by yourself. By grace, live in him.

also. ²⁴ If I had not done among them the works that no one else did, they would not be guilty of sin, but now they have seen and hated both me and my Father. ²⁵ But the word that is written in their Law must be fulfilled: ᵃ'They hated me without a cause.'

²⁶ "But when the Helper comes, whom I will send to you from the Father, the Spirit of truth, who proceeds from the Father, he will bear witness about me. ²⁷ And you also will bear witness, because you have been with me from the beginning.

16
"I have said all these things to you to keep you from falling away. ² They will put you out of the synagogues. Indeed, the hour is coming when whoever kills you will think he is offering service to God. ³ And they will do these things because they have not known the Father, nor me. ⁴ But I have said these things to you, that when their hour comes you may remember that I told them to you.

The Work of the Holy Spirit

"I did not say these things to you from the beginning, because I was with you. ⁵ But now I am going to him who sent me, and none of you asks me, 'Where are you going?' ⁶ But because I have said these things to you, sorrow has filled your heart. ⁷ Nevertheless, I tell you the truth: it is to your advantage that I go away, for if I do not go away, the Helper will not come to you. But if I go, I will send him to you. ⁸ And when he comes, he will convict the world concerning sin and righteousness and judgment: ⁹ concerning sin, because they do not believe in me; ¹⁰ concerning righteousness, because I go to the Father, and you will see me no longer; ¹¹ concerning judgment, because the ruler of this world is judged.

¹² "I still have many things to say to you, but you cannot bear them now. ¹³ When the Spirit of truth comes, he will guide you into all the truth, for he will not speak on his own authority, but whatever he hears he will speak, and he will declare to you the things that are to come. ¹⁴ He will glorify me, for he will take what is mine and declare it to you. ¹⁵ All that the Father has is mine; therefore I said that he will take what is mine and declare it to you.

Your Sorrow Will Turn into Joy

¹⁶ "A little while, and you will see me no longer; and again a little while, and you will see me." ¹⁷ So some of his disciples said to one another, "What is this that he says to us, 'A little while, and you will not see me, and again a little while, and you will see me'; and, 'because I am going to the Father'?" ¹⁸ So they were saying, "What does he mean by 'a little while'? We do not know what he is talking about." ¹⁹ Jesus knew that they wanted to ask him, so he said to them, "Is this what you are asking yourselves, what I meant by saying, 'A little while and you will not see me, and again a little while and you will see me'? ²⁰ Truly, truly, I say to you, you will weep and lament, but the world will rejoice. You will be sorrowful, but your sorrow will turn into joy. ²¹ When a woman is giving birth, she has sorrow because her hour has come, but when she has delivered the baby, she no longer remembers the anguish, for joy that a human being has been born into the world. ²² So also you have sorrow now, but I will see you again, and your hearts will rejoice, and no one will take your joy from you. ²³ In that day you will ask nothing of me. Truly, truly, I say to you, whatever you ask of the Father in my name, he will give it to you. ²⁴ Until now you have asked nothing in my name. Ask, and you will receive, that your joy may be full.

I Have Overcome the World

²⁵ "I have said these things to you in figures of speech. The hour is coming when I will no longer speak to you in figures of speech but will tell you plainly about the Father. ²⁶ In that day you will ask in my name, and I do not say to you that I will ask the Father on your behalf; ²⁷ for the Father himself loves you, because you have loved me and have believed that I came from God.¹ ²⁸ I came from the Father and have come into the world, and now I am leaving the world and going to the Father."

²⁹ His disciples said, "Ah, now you are speaking plainly and not using figurative speech! ³⁰ Now we know that you know all things and do not need anyone to question you; this is why we believe that you came from God." ³¹ Jesus answered them, "Do you now believe? ³² Behold, the hour is coming, indeed it has come, when you will be scat-

¹ Some manuscripts *from the Father* ᵃ Ps. 35:19 or 69:4

tered, each to his own home, and will leave me alone. Yet I am not alone, for the Father is with me. ³³I have said these things to you, that in me you may have peace. In the world you will have tribulation. But take heart; I have overcome the world."

The High Priestly Prayer

17 When Jesus had spoken these words, he lifted up his eyes to heaven, and said, "Father, the hour has come; glorify your Son that the Son may glorify you, ²since you have given him authority over all flesh, to give eternal life to all whom you have given him. ³And this is eternal life, that they know you the only true God, and Jesus Christ whom you have sent. ⁴I glorified you on earth, having accomplished the work that you gave me to do. ⁵And now, Father, glorify me in your own presence with the glory that I had with you before the world existed.

⁶"I have manifested your name to the people whom you gave me out of the world. Yours they were, and you gave them to me, and they have kept your word. ⁷Now they know that everything that you have

given me is from you. ⁸For I have given them the words that you gave me, and they have received them and have come to know in truth that I came from you; and they have believed that you sent me. ⁹I am praying for them. I am not praying for the world but for those whom you have given me, for they are yours. ¹⁰All mine are yours, and yours are mine, and I am glorified in them. ¹¹And I am no longer in the world, but they are in the world, and I am coming to you. Holy Father, keep them in your name, which you have given me, that they may be one, even as we are one. ¹²While I was with them, I kept them in your name, which you have given me. I have guarded them, and not one of them has been lost except the son of destruction, that the Scripture might be fulfilled. ¹³But now I am coming to you, and these things I speak in the world, that they may have my joy fulfilled in themselves. ¹⁴I have given them your word, and the world has hated them because they are not of the world, just as I am not of the world. ¹⁵I do not ask that you take them out of the world, but that you keep them from

Know Yourself

verses to read
John 16:31-33

Ever feel like everything and everyone is against you? Is your life sometimes a battle? That's normal and even good. The natural state of things in a fallen world is not order and peace but mess and strife. Things naturally deteriorate—just like if you ignore your room, eventually the mess will overwhelm it. So don't be shocked when life gets hard, but determine whether you want to let the battle ruin you or improve you.

Your natural state is a mess too—sinful, not holy. Nobody is holy because they can't help it. They are holy because they stand and fight. They refuse to let the world win by making them into its likeness. Jesus made it clear: "In the world you will have tribulation" (John 16:33). When you feel like the world is against you, you need to decide whether you will just roll over and accept the attacks, or whether you will refuse to let them knock you down. When you choose holiness, you choose to say, "Hit me with your best shot. I have a King who has overcome, so I'm not afraid." Every time your flesh cries out in fear but your mind chooses to believe God and to take him at his word, you are winning the continual battle for holiness. So remember Jesus' words: "I have said these things to you, that in me you may have peace. In the world you will have tribulation. But take heart; I have overcome the world" (John 16:33).

the evil one.[1] [16]They are not of the world, just as I am not of the world. [17]Sanctify them[2] in the truth; your word is truth. [18]As you sent me into the world, so I have sent them into the world. [19]And for their sake I consecrate myself,[3] that they also may be sanctified[4] in truth.

[20]"I do not ask for these only, but also for those who will believe in me through their word, [21]that they may all be one, just as you, Father, are in me, and I in you, that they also may be in us, so that the world may believe that you have sent me. [22]The glory that you have given me I have given to them, that they may be one even as we are one, [23]I in them and you in me, that they may become perfectly one, so that the world may know that you sent me and loved them even as you loved me. [24]Father, I desire that they also, whom you have given me, may be with me where I am, to see my glory that you have given me because you loved me before the foundation of the world. [25]O righteous Father, even though the world does not know you, I know you, and these know that you have sent me. [26]I made known to them your name, and I will continue to make it known, that the love with which you have loved me may be in them, and I in them."

Betrayal and Arrest of Jesus

18 When Jesus had spoken these words, he went out with his disciples across the brook Kidron, where there was a garden, which he and his disciples entered. [2]Now Judas, who betrayed him, also knew the place, for Jesus often met there with his disciples. [3][a]So Judas, having procured a band of soldiers and some officers from the chief priests and the Pharisees, went there with lanterns and torches and weapons. [4]Then Jesus, knowing all that would happen to him, came forward and said to them, "Whom do you seek?" [5]They answered him, "Jesus of Nazareth." Jesus said to them, "I am he."[5] Judas, who betrayed him, was standing with them. [6]When Jesus[6] said to them, "I am he," they drew back and fell to the ground. [7]So he asked them again, "Whom do you seek?" And they said, "Jesus of Nazareth." [8]Jesus

answered, "I told you that I am he. So, if you seek me, let these men go." [9]This was to fulfill the word that he had spoken: "Of those whom you gave me I have lost not one." [10]Then Simon Peter, having a sword, drew it and struck the high priest's servant[7] and cut off his right ear. (The servant's name was Malchus.) [11]So Jesus said to Peter, "Put your sword into its sheath; shall I not drink the cup that the Father has given me?"

Ask Yourself . . .

ABOUT SUFFERING

- How am I suffering right now?
- What could God be trying to teach me through this?
- What do I fear about suffering?
- How can I react differently to suffering than I have in the past?
- In what way has God entered into the suffering of this world?

Jesus Faces Annas and Caiaphas

[12]So the band of soldiers and their captain and the officers of the Jews[8] arrested Jesus and bound him. [13]First they led him to Annas, for he was the father-in-law of Caiaphas, who was high priest that year. [14]It was Caiaphas who had advised the Jews that it would be expedient that one man should die for the people.

Peter Denies Jesus

[15]Simon Peter followed Jesus, and so did another disciple. Since that disciple was known to the high priest, he entered with Jesus into the courtyard of the high priest, [16][b]but Peter stood outside at the door. So the other disciple, who was known to the high priest, went out and spoke to the servant girl who kept watch at the door, and brought Peter in. [17]The servant girl at the

---

[1]Or from evil [2]Greek Set them apart (for holy service to God) [3]Or I sanctify myself; or I set myself apart (for holy service to God) [4]Greek may be set apart (for holy service to God) [5]Greek I am; also verses 6, 8 [6]Greek he [7]Greek bondservant; twice in this verse [8]Greek Ioudaioi probably refers here to Jewish religious leaders, and others under their influence, in that time; also verses 14, 31, 36, 38 [a]For 18:3-11 see parallels Matt. 26:47-56; Mark 14:43-50; Luke 22:47-53 [b]For 18:16-18 see parallels Matt. 26:69, 70; Mark 14:66-68; Luke 22:55-57

door said to Peter, "You also are not one of this man's disciples, are you?" He said, "I am not." [18] Now the servants[1] and officers had made a charcoal fire, because it was cold, and they were standing and warming themselves. Peter also was with them, standing and warming himself.

The High Priest Questions Jesus

[19] The high priest then questioned Jesus about his disciples and his teaching. [20] Jesus answered him, "I have spoken openly to the world. I have always taught in synagogues and in the temple, where all Jews come together. I have said nothing in secret. [21] Why do you ask me? Ask those who have heard me what I said to them; they know what I said." [22] When he had said these things, one of the officers standing by struck Jesus with his hand, saying, "Is that how you answer the high priest?" [23] Jesus answered him, "If what I said is wrong, bear witness about the wrong; but if what I said is right, why do you strike me?" [24] Annas then sent him bound to Caiaphas the high priest.

Peter Denies Jesus Again

[25] [a] Now Simon Peter was standing and warming himself. So they said to him, "You also are not one of his disciples, are you?" He denied it and said, "I am not." [26] One of the servants of the high priest, a relative of the man whose ear Peter had cut off, asked, "Did I not see you in the garden with him?" [27] Peter again denied it, and at once a rooster crowed.

Jesus Before Pilate

[28] Then they led Jesus from the house of Caiaphas to the governor's headquarters.[2] It was early morning. They themselves did not enter the governor's headquarters, so that they would not be defiled, but could eat the Passover. [29] [b] So Pilate went outside to them and said, "What accusation do you bring against this man?" [30] They answered him, "If this man were not doing evil, we would not have delivered him over to you." [31] Pilate said to them, "Take him yourselves and judge him by your own law." The Jews said to him, "It is not lawful for us to put anyone to death." [32] This was to fulfill the

[1] Greek bondservants; also verse 26 [2] Greek the praetorium [a] For 18:25-27 see parallels Matt. 26:71-75; Mark 14:69-72; Luke 22:58-62
[b] For 18:29-38 see parallels Matt. 27:11-14; Mark 15:1-5; Luke 23:1-3

Know True Happiness

verses to read
John 18:10-11

Peter was adamantly opposed to the idea that Jesus would have to suffer. He wanted Jesus to avoid it completely. But suffering can't be avoided; no matter how much you fight it, it's going to come. Everyone suffers in this world. For example, a lot of girls suffer insults and meanness from other girls. But what's important isn't the suffering but the result of that suffering. Will you let it destroy you, or will you let God use it for your good?

Like the athlete who strains her muscles to make them stronger, sometimes you have to suffer in areas where you are weak so that your strength will be complete. God uses your suffering to draw you to himself, to make you stronger, to purify you, and to produce endurance and character. When you can accept that, then suffering will be something you can not only handle but rise above. It won't have such agonizing power over you. You will have become stronger because of it.

Suffering has a purpose in the life of the God Girl. It is never in vain. So when you feel like fighting your suffering, or fighting the one who seems to be bringing it on you, put away your sword and follow Jesus instead. Remember that he suffered the cross so that our suffering will be limited to this world; we won't have to suffer eternally for our sin.

word that Jesus had spoken to show by what kind of death he was going to die.

My Kingdom Is Not of This World

³³ So Pilate entered his headquarters again and called Jesus and said to him, "Are you the King of the Jews?" ³⁴ Jesus answered, "Do you say this of your own accord, or did others say it to you about me?" ³⁵ Pilate answered, "Am I a Jew? Your own nation and the chief priests have delivered you over to me. What have you done?" ³⁶ Jesus answered, "My kingdom is not of this world. If my kingdom were of this world, my servants would have been fighting, that I might not be delivered over to the Jews. But my kingdom is not from the world." ³⁷ Then Pilate said to him, "So you are a king?" Jesus answered, "You say that I am a king. For this purpose I was born and for this purpose I have come into the world—to bear witness to the truth. Everyone who is of the truth listens to my voice." ³⁸ Pilate said to him, "What is truth?"

After he had said this, he went back outside to the Jews and told them, "I find no guilt in him. ³⁹ ᵃBut you have a custom that I should release one man for you at the Passover. So do you want me to release to you the King of the Jews?" ⁴⁰ They cried out again, "Not this man, but Barabbas!" Now Barabbas was a robber.¹

Jesus Delivered to Be Crucified

19 Then Pilate took Jesus and flogged him. ² And the soldiers twisted together a crown of thorns and put it on his head and arrayed him in a purple robe. ³ They came up to him, saying, "Hail, King of the Jews!" and struck him with their hands. ⁴ Pilate went out again and said to them, "See, I am bringing him out to you that you may know that I find no guilt in him." ⁵ So Jesus came out, wearing the crown of thorns and the purple robe. Pilate said to them, "Behold the man!" ⁶ When the chief priests and the officers saw him, they cried out, "Crucify him, crucify him!" Pilate said to them, "Take him yourselves and crucify him, for I find no guilt in him." ⁷ The Jews² answered him, "We have a law, and according to that law he ought to die because he has made himself the Son of God." ⁸ When

Pilate heard this statement, he was ever more afraid. ⁹ He entered his headquarters again and said to Jesus, "Where are you from?" But Jesus gave him no answer. ¹⁰ So Pilate said to him, "You will not speak to me? Do you not know that I have authority to release you and authority to crucify you?" ¹¹ Jesus answered him, "You would have no authority over me at all unless it had been given you from above. Therefore he who delivered me over to you has the greater sin."

A Prayer about... THE CROSS

Praise God for the gift of the Holy Spirit, who will teach me the secret of the cross of Christ! The Spirit strengthened Christ to offer himself to God on the cross. The cross gave Christ the right to receive the fullness of the Spirit from the Father and to pour it out on all flesh. The cross gives me the right to receive the Spirit. And the Spirit teaches me to love the cross and to live a life crucified with Christ.

O my Father, I thank you that you give the immediate, continual working of the Spirit in my heart, that the crucified Christ can be formed inside me and his life kept alive within me. Father, I beg you humbly, teach me and your people to know this work of the Spirit and to yield ourselves to him to take full possession of us, that the crucified Lord Jesus may be glorified in us.

Amen.

¹² From then on Pilate sought to release him, but the Jews cried out, "If you release this man, you are not Caesar's friend. Everyone who makes himself a king opposes Caesar." ¹³ So when Pilate heard these words, he brought Jesus out and sat down on the judgment seat at a place called The Stone Pavement, and in

---

¹ Or *an insurrectionist* ² Greek *Ioudaioi* probably refers here to Jewish religious leaders, and others under their influence, in that time; also verses 12, 14, 31, 38 ᵃ For 18:39, 40 see parallels Matt. 27:15-18, 20-23; Mark 15:6-14; Luke 23:18-23

Aramaic[1] Gabbatha. [14] Now it was the day of Preparation of the Passover. It was about the sixth hour.[2] He said to the Jews, "Behold your King!" [15] They cried out, "Away with him, away with him, crucify him!" Pilate said to them, "Shall I crucify your King?" The chief priests answered, "We have no king but Caesar." [16] So he delivered him over to them to be crucified.

The Crucifixion

So they took Jesus, [17] and he went out, bearing his own cross, to the place called The Place of a Skull, which in Aramaic is called Golgotha. [18] There they crucified him, and with him two others, one on either side, and Jesus between them. [19] Pilate also wrote an inscription and put it on the cross. It read, "Jesus of Nazareth, the King of the Jews." [20] Many of the Jews read this inscription, for the place where Jesus was crucified was near the city, and it was written in Aramaic, in Latin, and in Greek. [21] So the chief priests of the Jews said to Pilate, "Do not write, 'The King of the Jews,' but rather, 'This man said, I am King of the Jews.'" [22] Pilate answered, "What I have written I have written."

[23] When the soldiers had crucified Jesus, they took his garments and divided them into four parts, one part for each soldier; also his tunic.[3] But the tunic was seamless, woven in one piece from top to bottom, [24] so they said to one another, "Let us not tear it, but cast lots for it to see whose it shall be." This was to fulfill the Scripture which says,

> [a]"They divided my garments among
>   them,
>   and for my clothing they cast
>   lots."

So the soldiers did these things, [25] but standing by the cross of Jesus were his mother and his mother's sister, Mary the wife of Clopas, and Mary Magdalene. [26] When Jesus saw his mother and the disciple whom he loved standing nearby, he said to his mother, "Woman, behold, your son!" [27] Then he said to the disciple, "Behold, your mother!" And from that hour the disciple took her to his own home.

The Death of Jesus

[28] After this, Jesus, knowing that all was now finished, said (to fulfill the Scripture), "I thirst." [29] A jar full of sour wine stood there, so they put a sponge full of the sour wine on a hyssop branch and held it to his mouth. [30] When Jesus had received the sour wine, he said, "It is finished," and he bowed his head and gave up his spirit.

Jesus' Side Is Pierced

[31] Since it was the day of Preparation, and so that the bodies would not remain on the cross on the Sabbath (for that Sabbath was a high day), the Jews asked Pilate that their legs might be broken and that they might be taken away. [32] So the soldiers came and broke the legs of the first, and of the other who had been crucified with him. [33] But when they came to Jesus and saw that he was already dead, they did not break his legs. [34] But one of the soldiers pierced his side with a spear, and at once there came out blood and water. [35] He who saw it has borne witness— his testimony is true, and he knows that he is telling the truth— that you also may believe. [36] For these things took place that the Scripture might be fulfilled: [b]"Not one of his bones will be broken." [37] And again another Scripture says, [c]"They will look on him whom they have pierced."

Jesus Is Buried

[38] [d]After these things Joseph of Arimathea, who was a disciple of Jesus, but secretly for fear of the Jews, asked Pilate that he might take away the body of Jesus, and Pilate gave him permission. So he came and took away his body. [39] Nicodemus also, who earlier had come to Jesus[4] by night, came bringing a mixture of myrrh and aloes, about seventy-five pounds[5] in weight. [40] So they took the body of Jesus and bound it in linen cloths with the spices, as is the burial custom of the Jews. [41] Now in the place where he was crucified there was a garden, and in the garden a new tomb in which no one had yet been laid. [42] So because of the Jewish day of Preparation, since the tomb was close at hand, they laid Jesus there.

[1] Or *Hebrew*; also verses 17, 20 [2] That is, about noon [3] Greek *chiton*, a long garment worn under the cloak next to the skin [4] Greek *him* [5] Greek *one hundred litras*; a *litra* (or Roman pound) was equal to about 11 1/2 ounces or 327 grams [a] Ps. 22:18 [b] Ex. 12:46; Num. 9:12 [c] Zech. 12:10 [d] For 19:38-42 see parallels Matt. 27:57-61; Mark 15:42-47; Luke 23:50-56

The Resurrection

20 Now on the first day of the week Mary Magdalene came to the tomb early, while it was still dark, and saw that the stone had been taken away from the tomb. ² So she ran and went to Simon Peter and the other disciple, the one whom Jesus loved, and said to them, "They have taken the Lord out of the tomb, and we do not know where they have laid him." ³ So Peter went out with the other disciple, and they were going toward the tomb. ⁴ Both of them were running together, but the other disciple outran Peter and reached the tomb first. ⁵ And stooping to look in, he saw the linen cloths lying there, but he did not go in. ⁶ Then Simon Peter came, following him, and went into the tomb. He saw the linen cloths lying there, ⁷ and the face cloth, which had been on Jesus'¹ head, not lying with the linen cloths but folded up in a place by itself. ⁸ Then the other disciple, who had reached the tomb first, also went in, and he saw and believed; ⁹ for as yet they did not understand the Scripture, that he must rise from the dead. ¹⁰ Then the disciples went back to their homes.

Jesus Appears to Mary Magdalene

¹¹ But Mary stood weeping outside the tomb, and as she wept she stooped to look into the tomb. ¹² And she saw two angels in white, sitting where the body of Jesus had lain, one at the head and one at the feet. ¹³ They said to her, "Woman, why are you weeping?" She said to them, "They have taken away my Lord, and I do not know where they have laid him." ¹⁴ Having said this, she turned around and saw Jesus standing, but she did not know that it was Jesus. ¹⁵ Jesus said to her, "Woman, why are you weeping? Whom are you seeking?" Supposing him to be the gardener, she said to him, "Sir, if you have carried him away, tell me where you have laid him, and I will take him away." ¹⁶ Jesus said to her, "Mary." She turned and said to him in Aramaic,² "Rabboni!" (which means Teacher). ¹⁷ Jesus said to her, "Do not cling to me, for I have not yet ascended to the Father; but go to my brothers and say to them, 'I am ascending to my Father and your Father, to my God and your God.'" ¹⁸ Mary Magdalene went and announced to the disciples, "I have seen the Lord"—and that he had said these things to her.

Jesus Appears to the Disciples

¹⁹ On the evening of that day, the first day of the week, the doors being locked where the disciples were for fear of the Jews,³ Jesus came and stood among them and said to them, "Peace be with you." ²⁰ When he had said this, he showed them his hands and his side. Then the disciples were glad when they saw the Lord. ²¹ Jesus said to them again, "Peace be with you. As the Father has sent me, even so I am sending you." ²² And when he had said this, he breathed on them and said to them, "Receive the Holy Spirit. ²³ If you forgive the sins of any, they are forgiven them; if you withhold forgiveness from any, it is withheld."

Jesus and Thomas

²⁴ Now Thomas, one of the Twelve, called the Twin,⁴ was not with them when Jesus came. ²⁵ So the other disciples told him, "We have seen the Lord." But he said to them, "Unless I see in his hands the mark of the nails, and place my finger into the mark of the nails, and place my hand into his side, I will never believe."

²⁶ Eight days later, his disciples were inside again, and Thomas was with them. Although the doors were locked, Jesus came and stood among them and said, "Peace be with you." ²⁷ Then he said to Thomas, "Put your finger here, and see my hands; and put out your hand, and place it in my side. Do not disbelieve, but believe." ²⁸ Thomas answered him, "My Lord and my God!" ²⁹ Jesus said to him, "Have you believed because you have seen me? Blessed are those who have not seen and yet have believed."

The Purpose of This Book

³⁰ Now Jesus did many other signs in the presence of the disciples, which are not written in this book; ³¹ but these are written so that you may believe that Jesus is the Christ, the Son of God, and that by believing you may have life in his name.

Jesus Appears to Seven Disciples

21 After this Jesus revealed himself again to the disciples by the Sea of Tiberias, and he revealed himself in this

---

¹ Greek *his* ² Or *Hebrew* ³ Greek *Ioudaioi* probably refers here to Jewish religious leaders, and others under their influence, in that time ⁴ Greek *Didymus*

way. ² Simon Peter, Thomas (called the Twin), Nathanael of Cana in Galilee, the sons of Zebedee, and two others of his disciples were together. ³ Simon Peter said to them, "I am going fishing." They said to him, "We will go with you." They went out and got into the boat, but that night they caught nothing.

⁴ Just as day was breaking, Jesus stood on the shore; yet the disciples did not know that it was Jesus. ⁵ Jesus said to them, "Children, do you have any fish?" They answered him, "No." ⁶ He said to them, "Cast the net on the right side of the boat, and you will find some." So they cast it, and now they were not able to haul it in, because of the quantity of fish. ⁷ That disciple whom Jesus loved therefore said to Peter, "It is the Lord!" When Simon Peter heard that it was the Lord, he put on his outer garment, for he was stripped for work, and threw himself into the sea. ⁸ The other disciples came in the boat, dragging the net full of fish, for they were not far from the land, but about a hundred yards¹ off.

⁹ When they got out on land, they saw a charcoal fire in place, with fish laid out on it, and bread. ¹⁰ Jesus said to them, "Bring some of the fish that you have just caught." ¹¹ So Simon Peter went aboard and hauled the net ashore, full of large fish, 153 of them. And although there were so many, the net was not torn. ¹² Jesus said to them, "Come and have breakfast." Now none of the disciples dared ask him, "Who are you?" They knew it was the Lord. ¹³ Jesus came and took the bread and gave it to them, and so with the fish. ¹⁴ This was now the third time that Jesus was revealed to the disciples after he was raised from the dead.

Jesus and Peter

¹⁵ When they had finished breakfast, Jesus said to Simon Peter, "Simon, son of John, do you love me more than these?" He said to him, "Yes, Lord; you know that I love you." He said to him, "Feed my lambs." ¹⁶ He said to him a second time, "Simon, son of John, do you love me?" He said to him, "Yes, Lord; you know that I love you." He said to him, "Tend my sheep." ¹⁷ He said to him the third time, "Simon, son of John, do you love me?" Peter was grieved because he said to him the third time, "Do you love me?" and he said to him, "Lord, you know everything; you know that I love you." Jesus said to him, "Feed my sheep. ¹⁸ Truly, truly, I say to you, when you were young, you used to dress yourself and walk wherever you wanted, but when you are old, you will stretch out your hands, and another will dress you and carry you where you do not want to go." ¹⁹ (This he said to show by what kind of death he was to glorify God.) And after saying this he said to him, "Follow me."

Jesus and the Beloved Apostle

²⁰ Peter turned and saw the disciple whom Jesus loved following them, the one who also had leaned back against him during the supper and had said, "Lord, who is it that is going to betray you?" ²¹ When Peter saw him, he said to Jesus, "Lord, what about this man?" ²² Jesus said to him, "If it is my will that he remain until I come, what is that to you? You follow me!" ²³ So the saying spread abroad among the brothers² that this disciple was not to die; yet Jesus did not say to him that he was not to die, but, "If it is my will that he remain until I come, what is that to you?"

²⁴ This is the disciple who is bearing witness about these things, and who has written these things, and we know that his testimony is true.

²⁵ Now there are also many other things that Jesus did. Were every one of them to be written, I suppose that the world itself could not contain the books that would be written.

---

¹ Greek *two hundred cubits*; a *cubit* was about 18 inches or 45 centimeters   ² Or *brothers and sisters*

INTRODUCTION TO

Acts

Author: Luke, a Gentile doctor and the author of the Gospel of Luke

Time: Between A.D. 60 and 80

Place: Maybe Antioch, Ephesus, or Rome

Written to: Theophilus and other believers

The gist

Luke wanted to show how the church came into existence and grew, as God continued to be with his people through his Spirit after Jesus ascended to heaven. Acts shows us God's will that the church be made up of both Jews and Gentiles. You will notice an emphasis on the ministries of Paul and Peter.

Things to look for

• The importance of the Holy Spirit (more than forty references)

• The ministries of Paul and Peter

• How the early church took care of and supported each other

Know the Holy Spirit

> "You will receive power when the Holy Spirit has come upon you, and you will be my witnesses in Jerusalem and in all Judea and Samaria, and to the end of the earth."
>
> Acts 1:8

When Jesus was arrested, all the men who followed him ran off like scared little boys. They were not prepared for this sudden turn of events. A lot of them started to question their faith in Jesus. How could he die, if he really was the Son of God? They hid out and tried to figure out what to do next. But then something changed, and those scared boys suddenly became brave and fearless men. What happened? How did those fearful men turn into confident and powerful men in one moment? They saw Jesus; that's how. Before Jesus came back to life, these guys were scared and hiding, but once they saw the risen Jesus, they were convinced he was God, and from that point on nothing could stop them.

As a God Girl, you have to be convinced that Jesus is who he said he is. Nothing in you can be afraid of being associated with him, like Peter was. When things look bad, when God's Word seems to be failing, the God Girl doesn't turn tail and run; she stands strong and fearless because she has seen the risen King and has given him her full allegiance.

The book of Acts is the history of the first Christians. Though their lives were in danger from all sides, they pressed on to serve the one they were certain was, and is, and always will be the God of all.

As you read this book about the disciples' transition from life with Christ to life after the resurrection, take a look at Peter, the scared one who denied Christ three times (see Matt. 26:69–75). Now he's filled with the Holy Spirit and talking to everyone about Jesus, like a totally different guy. When Jesus becomes real to you and your life starts to change because of his presence in it through the Spirit, your bravery grows and you want to tell everyone about him. Also notice how the early believers loved and took care of each other and how nothing, not even the threat of death, could derail them from their mission to tell the world about Jesus.

Must-Know Terms and Verses

∽ *Pentecost* ∽

A Jewish festival and the day when the Holy Spirit came down on the believers and when thousands more came to faith in Christ (see Acts 2).

∽ *Sanhedrin* ∽

The judicial and administrative council of the Jewish faith, made up of the high priest, scribes, and elders. They were the ones who, just before Jesus' crucifixion, charged him with blasphemy.

And they were all filled with the Holy Spirit and began to speak in other tongues as the Spirit gave them utterance. *Acts 2:4*

"Repent and be baptized every one of you in the name of Jesus Christ for the forgiveness of your sins, and you will receive the gift of the Holy Spirit." *Acts 2:38*

And when they had prayed, the place in which they were gathered together was shaken, and they were all filled with the Holy Spirit and continued to speak the word of God with boldness. *Acts 4:31*

"Let it be known to you therefore, brothers, that through this man forgiveness of sins is proclaimed to you, and by him everyone who believes is freed from everything from which you could not be freed by the law of Moses." *Acts 13:38–39*

"Brothers, you know that in the early days God made a choice among you, that by my mouth the Gentiles should hear the word of the gospel and believe. And God, who knows the heart, bore witness to them, by giving them the Holy Spirit just as he did to us." *Acts 15:7–8*

"I do not account my life of any value nor as precious to myself, if only I may finish my course and the ministry that I received from the Lord Jesus, to testify to the gospel of the grace of God." *Acts 20:24*

The Acts

of the Apostles

The Promise of the Holy Spirit

1 In the first book, O Theophilus, I have dealt with all that Jesus began to do and teach, ²until the day when he was taken up, after he had given commands through the Holy Spirit to the apostles whom he had chosen. ³He presented himself alive to them after his suffering by many proofs, appearing to them during forty days and speaking about the kingdom of God.

⁴And while staying¹ with them he ordered them not to depart from Jerusalem, but to wait for the promise of the Father, which, he said, "you heard from me; ⁵for John baptized with water, but you will be baptized with² the Holy Spirit not many days from now."

The Ascension

⁶So when they had come together, they asked him, "Lord, will you at this time restore the kingdom to Israel?" ⁷He said to them, "It is not for you to know times or seasons that the Father has fixed by his own authority. ⁸But you will receive power when the Holy Spirit has come upon you, and you will be my witnesses in Jerusalem and in all Judea and Samaria, and to the end of the earth." ⁹And when he had said these things, as they were looking on, he was lifted up, and a cloud took him out of their sight. ¹⁰And while they were gazing into heaven as he went, behold, two men stood by them in white robes, ¹¹and said, "Men of Galilee, why do you stand looking into heaven? This Jesus, who was taken up from you into heaven, will come in the same way as you saw him go into heaven."

Matthias Chosen to Replace Judas

¹²Then they returned to Jerusalem from the mount called Olivet, which is near Jerusalem, a Sabbath day's journey away. ¹³And when they had entered, they went up to the upper room, where they were staying, Peter and John and James and Andrew, Philip and Thomas, Bartholomew and Matthew, James the son of Alphaeus and Simon the Zealot and Judas the son of James. ¹⁴All these with one accord were devoting themselves to prayer, together with the women and Mary the mother of Jesus, and his brothers.³

¹⁵In those days Peter stood up among the brothers (the company of persons was in all about 120) and said, ¹⁶"Brothers, the Scripture had to be fulfilled, which the Holy Spirit spoke beforehand by the mouth of David concerning Judas, who became a guide to those who arrested Jesus. ¹⁷For he was numbered among us and was allotted his share in this ministry." ¹⁸(Now this man acquired a field with the reward of his wickedness, and falling headlong⁴ he burst open in the middle and all his bowels gushed out. ¹⁹And it became known to all the inhabitants of Jerusalem, so that the field was called in their own language Akeldama, that is, Field of Blood.) ²⁰"For it is written in the Book of Psalms,

> ᵃ"'May his camp become desolate,
>   and let there be no one to dwell in
>   it';

and

> ᵇ"'Let another take his office.'

²¹So one of the men who have accompanied us during all the time that the Lord Jesus went in and out among us, ²²beginning from the baptism of John until the day when he was taken up from us—one of these men must become with us a witness to his resurrection." ²³And they put forward two, Joseph called Barsabbas, who was also called Justus, and Matthias.

[24] And they prayed and said, "You, Lord, who know the hearts of all, show which one of these two you have chosen [25] to take the place in this ministry and apostleship from which Judas turned aside to go to his own place." [26] And they cast lots for them, and the lot fell on Matthias, and he was numbered with the eleven apostles.

The Coming of the Holy Spirit

2 When the day of Pentecost arrived, they were all together in one place. [2] And suddenly there came from heaven a sound like a mighty rushing wind, and it filled the entire house where they were sitting. [3] And divided tongues as of fire appeared to them and rested[1] on each one of them. [4] And they were all filled with the Holy Spirit and began to speak in other tongues as the Spirit gave them utterance.

A Prayer for...

THE INDWELLING OF THE HOLY SPIRIT

O Lord of love, make a place for yourself in my heart. Empty my heart of every feeling, thought, emotion, desire, purpose, anxiety, and fear that might interfere with your love. Open my whole heart to let you in; don't let anything shut you out.

You alone can make my heart fit for you: clean it completely by your Spirit, so that it can completely love you; so that it can be completely filled with you; so that it can be completely penetrated, enlightened, and warmed by you; and so that you can live in it forever and it can love you with your own love in it forever.

Amen.

[5] Now there were dwelling in Jerusalem Jews, devout men from every nation under heaven. [6] And at this sound the multitude came together, and they were bewildered, because each one was hearing them speak in his own language. [7] And they were amazed and astonished, saying, "Are not all these who are speaking Galileans? [8] And how is it that we hear, each of us in his own native language? [9] Parthians and Medes and Elamites and residents of Mesopotamia, Judea and Cappadocia, Pontus and Asia, [10] Phrygia and Pamphylia, Egypt and the parts of Libya belonging to Cyrene, and visitors from Rome, [11] both Jews and proselytes, Cretans and Arabians—we hear them telling in our own tongues the mighty works of God." [12] And all were amazed and perplexed, saying to one another, "What does this mean?" [13] But others mocking said, "They are filled with new wine."

Peter's Sermon at Pentecost

[14] But Peter, standing with the eleven, lifted up his voice and addressed them: "Men of Judea and all who dwell in Jerusalem, let this be known to you, and give ear to my words. [15] For these people are not drunk, as you suppose, since it is only the third hour of the day.[2] [16] But this is what was uttered through the prophet Joel:

[17] [a] "'And in the last days it shall be, God declares,

that I will pour out my Spirit on all flesh,

and your sons and your daughters shall prophesy,

and your young men shall see visions,

and your old men shall dream dreams;

[18]   even on my male servants[3] and female servants

in those days I will pour out my Spirit, and they shall prophesy.

[19]   And I will show wonders in the heavens above

and signs on the earth below, blood, and fire, and vapor of smoke;

[20]   the sun shall be turned to darkness and the moon to blood,

before the day of the Lord comes, the great and magnificent day.

[21]   And it shall come to pass that everyone who calls upon the name of the Lord shall be saved.'

[22] "Men of Israel, hear these words: Jesus of Nazareth, a man attested to you by God

---

[1] Or And tongues as of fire appeared to them, distributed among them, and rested   [2] That is, 9 A.M.   [3] Greek bondservants; twice in this verse
[a] Joel 2:28-32

with mighty works and wonders and signs that God did through him in your midst, as you yourselves know— ²³this Jesus,¹ delivered up according to the definite plan and foreknowledge of God, you crucified and killed by the hands of lawless men. ²⁴God raised him up, loosing the pangs of death, because it was not possible for him to be held by it. ²⁵For David says concerning him,

ᵃ"'I saw the Lord always before me,
    for he is at my right hand that
        I may not be shaken;
²⁶ therefore my heart was glad, and my
        tongue rejoiced;
    my flesh also will dwell in hope.
²⁷ For you will not abandon my soul to
        Hades,
    or let your Holy One see corruption.
²⁸ You have made known to me the
        paths of life;
    you will make me full of gladness
        with your presence.'

²⁹"Brothers, I may say to you with confidence about the patriarch David that he both died and was buried, and his tomb is with us to this day. ³⁰Being therefore a prophet, and knowing that God had sworn with an oath to him that he would set one of his descendants on his throne, ³¹he foresaw and spoke about the resurrection of the Christ, that he was not abandoned to Hades, nor did his flesh see corruption. ³²This Jesus God raised up, and of that we all are witnesses. ³³Being therefore exalted at the right hand of God, and having received from the Father the promise of the Holy Spirit, he has poured out this that you yourselves are seeing and hearing. ³⁴For David did not ascend into the heavens, but he himself says,

ᵇ"'The Lord said to my Lord,
    "Sit at my right hand,
³⁵   until I make your enemies your
            footstool."'

³⁶Let all the house of Israel therefore know for certain that God has made him both Lord and Christ, this Jesus whom you crucified."

³⁷Now when they heard this they were cut to the heart, and said to Peter and the rest of the apostles, "Brothers, what shall we do?" ³⁸And Peter said to them, "Repent

and be baptized every one of you in the name of Jesus Christ for the forgiveness of your sins, and you will receive the gift of the Holy Spirit. ³⁹For the promise is for you and for your children and for all who are far off, everyone whom the Lord our God calls to himself." ⁴⁰And with many other words he bore witness and continued to exhort them, saying, "Save yourselves from this crooked generation." ⁴¹So those who received his word were baptized, and there were added that day about three thousand souls.

The Fellowship of the Believers

⁴²And they devoted themselves to the apostles' teaching and the fellowship, to the breaking of bread and the prayers. ⁴³And awe² came upon every soul, and many wonders and signs were being done through the apostles. ⁴⁴And all who believed were together and had all things in common. ⁴⁵And they were selling their possessions and belongings and distributing the proceeds to all, as any had need. ⁴⁶And day by day, attending the temple together and breaking bread in their homes, they received their food with glad and generous hearts, ⁴⁷praising God and having favor with all the people. And the Lord added to their number day by day those who were being saved.

The Lame Beggar Healed

3 Now Peter and John were going up to the temple at the hour of prayer, the ninth hour.³ ²And a man lame from birth was being carried, whom they laid daily at the gate of the temple that is called the Beautiful Gate to ask alms of those entering the temple. ³Seeing Peter and John about to go into the temple, he asked to receive alms. ⁴And Peter directed his gaze at him, as did John, and said, "Look at us." ⁵And he fixed his attention on them, expecting to receive something from them. ⁶But Peter said, "I have no silver and gold, but what I do have I give to you. In the name of Jesus Christ of Nazareth, rise up and walk!" ⁷And he took him by the right hand and raised him up, and immediately his feet and ankles were made strong. ⁸And leaping up he stood and began to walk, and entered the temple with them, walking and leaping and praising God. ⁹And all the people saw him walking and praising God,

---

¹Greek *this one* ²Or *fear* ³That is, 3 P.M. ᵃPs. 16:8-11 ᵇPs. 110:1

¹⁰and recognized him as the one who sat at the Beautiful Gate of the temple, asking for alms. And they were filled with wonder and amazement at what had happened to him.

Peter Speaks in Solomon's Portico

¹¹While he clung to Peter and John, all the people, utterly astounded, ran together to them in the portico called Solomon's. ¹²And when Peter saw it he addressed the people: "Men of Israel, why do you wonder at this, or why do you stare at us, as though by our own power or piety we have made him walk? ¹³The God of Abraham, the God of Isaac, and the God of Jacob, the God of our fathers, glorified his servant¹ Jesus, whom you delivered over and denied in the presence of Pilate, when he had decided to release him. ¹⁴But you denied the Holy and Righteous One, and asked for a murderer to be granted to you, ¹⁵and you killed the Author of life, whom God raised from the dead. To this we are witnesses. ¹⁶And his name—by faith in his name—has made this man strong whom you see and know, and the faith that is through Jesus² has given the man this perfect health in the presence of you all.

¹⁷"And now, brothers, I know that you acted in ignorance, as did also your rulers. ¹⁸But what God foretold by the mouth of all the prophets, that his Christ would suffer, he thus fulfilled. ¹⁹Repent therefore, and turn back, that your sins may be blotted out, ²⁰that times of refreshing may come from the presence of the Lord, and that he may send the Christ appointed for you, Jesus, ²¹whom heaven must receive until the time for restoring all the things about which God spoke by the mouth of his holy prophets long ago. ²²Moses said, 'The Lord God will raise up for you ᵃa prophet like me from your brothers. You shall listen to him in whatever he tells you. ²³And it shall be that every soul who does not listen to that prophet shall be destroyed from the people.' ²⁴And all the prophets who have spoken, from Samuel and those who came after him, also proclaimed these days. ²⁵You are the sons of the prophets and of the covenant that God made with your fathers, saying to Abraham, ᵇ'And in your offspring shall all the families of the earth be blessed.' ²⁶God, having raised up his servant, sent

him to you first, to bless you by turning every one of you from your wickedness."

Peter and John Before the Council

4 And as they were speaking to the people, the priests and the captain of the temple and the Sadducees came upon them, ²greatly annoyed because they were teaching the people and proclaiming in Jesus the resurrection from the dead. ³And they arrested them and put them in custody until the next day, for it was already evening. ⁴But many of those who had heard the word believed, and the number of the men came to about five thousand.

⁵On the next day their rulers and elders and scribes gathered together in Jerusalem, ⁶with Annas the high priest and Caiaphas and John and Alexander, and all who were of the high-priestly family. ⁷And when they had set them in the midst, they inquired, "By what power or by what name did you do this?" ⁸Then Peter, filled with the Holy Spirit, said to them, "Rulers of the people and elders, ⁹if we are being examined today concerning a good deed done to a crippled man, by what means this man has been healed, ¹⁰let it be known to all of you and to all the people of Israel that by the name of Jesus Christ of Nazareth, whom you crucified, whom God raised from the dead—by him this man is standing before you well. ¹¹This Jesus³ is the stone that was rejected by you, the builders, which has become the cornerstone.⁴ ¹²And there is salvation in no one else, for there is no other name under heaven given among men⁵ by which we must be saved."

¹³Now when they saw the boldness of Peter and John, and perceived that they were uneducated, common men, they were astonished. And they recognized that they had been with Jesus. ¹⁴But seeing the man who was healed standing beside them, they had nothing to say in opposition. ¹⁵But when they had commanded them to leave the council, they conferred with one another, ¹⁶saying, "What shall we do with these men? For that a notable sign has been performed through them is evident to all the inhabitants of Jerusalem, and we cannot deny it. ¹⁷But in order that it may spread no further among the people, let us warn them to speak no more to anyone

¹Or child; also verse 26 ²Greek him ³Greek This one ⁴Greek the head of the corner ⁵The Greek word anthropoi refers here to both men and women ᵃDeut. 18:15, 18, 19 ᵇGen. 22:18

in this name." ¹⁸So they called them and charged them not to speak or teach at all in the name of Jesus. ¹⁹But Peter and John answered them, "Whether it is right in the sight of God to listen to you rather than to God, you must judge, ²⁰for we cannot but speak of what we have seen and heard." ²¹And when they had further threatened them, they let them go, finding no way to punish them, because of the people, for all were praising God for what had happened. ²²For the man on whom this sign of healing was performed was more than forty years old.

The Believers Pray for Boldness

²³When they were released, they went to their friends and reported what the chief priests and the elders had said to them. ²⁴And when they heard it, they lifted their voices together to God and said, "Sovereign Lord, who made the heaven and the earth and the sea and everything in them, ²⁵who through the mouth of our father David, your servant,¹ said by the Holy Spirit,

ᵃ"'Why did the Gentiles rage,
    and the peoples plot in vain?
²⁶ The kings of the earth set themselves,
    and the rulers were gathered together,
    against the Lord and against his Anointed'²—

²⁷for truly in this city there were gathered together against your holy servant Jesus, whom you anointed, both Herod and Pontius Pilate, along with the Gentiles and the peoples of Israel, ²⁸to do whatever your hand and your plan had predestined to take place. ²⁹And now, Lord, look upon their threats and grant to your servants³ to continue to speak your word with all boldness, ³⁰while you stretch out your hand to heal, and signs and wonders are performed through the name of your holy servant Jesus." ³¹And when they had prayed, the place in which they were gathered together was shaken, and they were all filled with the Holy Spirit and continued to speak the word of God with boldness.

They Had Everything in Common

³²Now the full number of those who believed were of one heart and soul, and no one said that any of the things that belonged to him was his own, but they had everything in common. ³³And with great power the apostles were giving their testimony to the resurrection of the Lord Jesus, and great grace was upon them all. ³⁴There was not a needy person among them, for as many as were owners of lands or houses sold them and brought the proceeds of what was sold ³⁵and laid it at the apostles' feet, and it was distributed to each as any had need. ³⁶Thus Joseph, who was also called by the apostles Barnabas (which means son of encouragement), a Levite, a native of Cyprus, ³⁷sold a field that belonged to him and brought the money and laid it at the apostles' feet.

Ananias and Sapphira

5 But a man named Ananias, with his wife Sapphira, sold a piece of property, ²and with his wife's knowledge he kept back for himself some of the proceeds and brought only a part of it and laid it at the apostles' feet. ³But Peter said, "Ananias, why has Satan filled your heart to lie to the Holy Spirit and to keep back for yourself part of the proceeds of the land? ⁴While it remained unsold, did it not remain your own? And after it was sold, was it not at your disposal? Why is it that you have contrived this deed in your heart? You have not lied to man but to God." ⁵When Ananias heard these words, he fell down and breathed his last. And great fear came upon all who heard of it. ⁶The young men rose and wrapped him up and carried him out and buried him.

⁷After an interval of about three hours his wife came in, not knowing what had happened. ⁸And Peter said to her, "Tell me whether you⁴ sold the land for so much." And she said, "Yes, for so much." ⁹But Peter said to her, "How is it that you have agreed together to test the Spirit of the Lord? Behold, the feet of those who have buried your husband are at the door, and they will carry you out." ¹⁰Immediately she fell down at his feet and breathed her last. When the young men came in they found her dead, and they carried her out and buried her beside her husband. ¹¹And great fear came upon the whole church and upon all who heard of these things.

¹Or child; also verses 27, 30 ²Or Christ ³Greek bondservants ⁴The Greek for you is plural here ᵃPs. 2:1, 2

Many Signs and Wonders Done

¹² Now many signs and wonders were regularly done among the people by the hands of the apostles. And they were all together in Solomon's Portico. ¹³ None of the rest dared join them, but the people held them in high esteem. ¹⁴ And more than ever believers were added to the Lord, multitudes of both men and women, ¹⁵ so that they even carried out the sick into the streets and laid them on cots and mats, that as Peter came by at least his shadow might fall on some of them. ¹⁶ The people also gathered from the towns around Jerusalem, bringing the sick and those afflicted with unclean spirits, and they were all healed.

The Apostles Arrested and Freed

¹⁷ But the high priest rose up, and all who were with him (that is, the party of the Sadducees), and filled with jealousy ¹⁸ they arrested the apostles and put them in the public prison. ¹⁹ But during the night an angel of the Lord opened the prison doors and brought them out, and said, ²⁰ "Go and stand in the temple and speak to the people all the words of this Life." ²¹ And when they heard this, they entered the temple at daybreak and began to teach.

Now when the high priest came, and those who were with him, they called together the council, all the senate of the people of Israel, and sent to the prison to have them brought. ²² But when the officers came, they did not find them in the prison, so they returned and reported, ²³ "We found the prison securely locked and the guards standing at the doors, but when we opened them we found no one inside." ²⁴ Now when the captain of the temple and the chief priests heard these words, they were greatly perplexed about them, wondering what this would come to. ²⁵ And someone came and told them, "Look! The men whom you put in prison are standing in the temple and teaching the people." ²⁶ Then the captain with the officers went and brought them, but not by force, for they were afraid of being stoned by the people.

²⁷ And when they had brought them, they set them before the council. And the high priest questioned them, ²⁸ saying, "We strictly charged you not to teach in this name, yet here you have filled Jerusalem with your teaching, and you intend to bring this man's blood upon us." ²⁹ But Peter and the apostles answered, "We must obey God rather than men. ³⁰ The God of our fathers raised Jesus, whom you killed by hanging him on a tree. ³¹ God exalted him at his right hand as Leader and Savior, to give repentance to Israel and forgiveness of sins. ³² And we are witnesses to these things, and so is the Holy Spirit, whom God has given to those who obey him."

³³ When they heard this, they were enraged and wanted to kill them. ³⁴ But a Pharisee in the council named Gamaliel, a teacher of the law held in honor by all the people, stood up and gave orders to put the men outside for a little while. ³⁵ And he said to them, "Men of Israel, take care what you are about to do with these men. ³⁶ For before these days Theudas rose up, claiming to be somebody, and a number of men, about four hundred, joined him. He was killed, and all who followed him were dispersed and came to nothing. ³⁷ After him Judas the Galilean rose up in the days of the census and drew away some of the people after him. He too perished, and all who followed him were scattered. ³⁸ So in the present case I tell you, keep away from these men and let them alone, for if this plan or this undertaking is of man, it will fail; ³⁹ but if it is of God, you will not be able to overthrow them. You might even be found opposing God!" So they took his advice, ⁴⁰ and when they had called in the apostles, they beat them and charged them not to speak in the name of Jesus, and let them go. ⁴¹ Then they left the presence of the council, rejoicing that they were counted worthy to suffer dishonor for the name. ⁴² And every day, in the temple and from house to house, they did not cease teaching and preaching that the Christ is Jesus.

Seven Chosen to Serve

6 Now in these days when the disciples were increasing in number, a complaint by the Hellenists¹ arose against the Hebrews because their widows were being neglected in the daily distribution. ² And the twelve summoned the full number of the disciples and said, "It is not right that we should give up preaching the word of God to serve tables. ³ Therefore,

¹ That is, Greek-speaking Jews

brothers,[1] pick out from among you seven men of good repute, full of the Spirit and of wisdom, whom we will appoint to this duty. [4] But we will devote ourselves to prayer and to the ministry of the word." [5] And what they said pleased the whole gathering, and they chose Stephen, a man full of faith and of the Holy Spirit, and Philip, and Prochorus, and Nicanor, and Timon, and Parmenas, and Nicolaus, a proselyte of Antioch. [6] These they set before the apostles, and they prayed and laid their hands on them.

[7] And the word of God continued to increase, and the number of the disciples multiplied greatly in Jerusalem, and a great many of the priests became obedient to the faith.

Stephen Is Seized

[8] And Stephen, full of grace and power, was doing great wonders and signs among the people. [9] Then some of those who belonged to the synagogue of the Freedmen (as it was called), and of the Cyrenians, and of the Alexandrians, and of those from Cilicia and Asia, rose up and disputed with Stephen. [10] But they could not withstand the wisdom and the Spirit with which he was speaking. [11] Then they secretly instigated men who said, "We have heard him speak blasphemous words against Moses and God." [12] And they stirred up the people and the elders and the scribes, and they came upon him and seized him and brought him before the council, [13] and they set up false witnesses who said, "This man never ceases to speak words against this holy place and the law, [14] for we have heard him say that this Jesus of Nazareth will destroy this place and will change the customs that Moses delivered to us." [15] And gazing at him, all who sat in the council saw that his face was like the face of an angel.

Stephen's Speech

7 And the high priest said, "Are these things so?" [2] And Stephen said:

"Brothers and fathers, hear me. The God of glory appeared to our father Abraham

[1] Or brothers and sisters

verses to read
Acts 5:26–32

Know God

When given the choice between doing what you want and doing what your friends or even your enemies want, which do you choose? What if doing what God wants is going to cost you dearly? What if it means people won't like you, or worse yet, they will hate you or hurt you? How do you decide whom you're going to obey in those situations?

Your faith requires obedience. Going the other way and doing what people want instead of what God wants is sin. When the apostles were told to stop talking about Jesus or else, they didn't give a rip about the "or else" part. They just did what they were meant to do: proclaim the truth. The most precious thing in the universe to them was not saving their own skin but walking faithfully with the Lord, come what may. The source of that courage in their lives was the great rescue from their sins that Jesus had won for them, and the filling with the Spirit that Jesus sent to them.

Your life will be more meaningful and joyful as you train yourself to trust in the Lord by reflecting often on your own rescue from your sins, and the presence of the Spirit in your life. The main way to train yourself in this way is to read the Bible, which is God's great story of redemption. So dive in today and remember afresh God and his gracious redemption of your life.

when he was in Mesopotamia, before he lived in Haran, ³and said to him, ᵃ'Go out from your land and from your kindred and go into the land that I will show you.' ⁴Then he went out from the land of the Chaldeans and lived in Haran. And after his father died, God removed him from there into this land in which you are now living. ⁵Yet he gave him no inheritance in it, not even a foot's length, but promised to give it to him as a possession and to his offspring after him, though he had no child. ⁶And God spoke to this effect—that ᵇhis offspring would be sojourners in a land belonging to others, who would enslave them and afflict them four hundred years. ⁷'But I will judge the nation that they serve,' said God, 'and after that they shall come out and worship me in this place.' ⁸And he gave him the covenant of circumcision. And so Abraham became the father of Isaac, and circumcised him on the eighth day, and Isaac became the father of Jacob, and Jacob of the twelve patriarchs.

⁹"And the patriarchs, jealous of Joseph, sold him into Egypt; but God was with him ¹⁰and rescued him out of all his afflictions and gave him favor and wisdom before Pharaoh, king of Egypt, who made him ruler over Egypt and over all his household. ¹¹Now there came a famine throughout all Egypt and Canaan, and great affliction, and our fathers could find no food. ¹²But when Jacob heard that there was grain in Egypt, he sent out our fathers on their first visit. ¹³And on the second visit Joseph made himself known to his brothers, and Joseph's family became known to Pharaoh. ¹⁴And Joseph sent and summoned Jacob his father and all his kindred, seventy-five persons in all. ¹⁵And Jacob went down into Egypt, and he died, he and our fathers, ¹⁶and they were carried back to Shechem and laid in the tomb that Abraham had bought for a sum of silver from the sons of Hamor in Shechem.

¹⁷"But as the time of the promise drew near, which God had granted to Abraham, the people increased and multiplied in Egypt ¹⁸until there arose over Egypt another king who did not know Joseph. ¹⁹He dealt shrewdly with our race and forced our fathers to expose their infants, so that they would not be kept alive. ²⁰At this time Moses was born; and

he was beautiful in God's sight. And he was brought up for three months in his father's house, ²¹and when he was exposed, Pharaoh's daughter adopted him and brought him up as her own son. ²²And Moses was instructed in all the wisdom of the Egyptians, and he was mighty in his words and deeds.

²³"When he was forty years old, it came into his heart to visit his brothers, the children of Israel. ²⁴And seeing one of them being wronged, he defended the oppressed man and avenged him by striking down the Egyptian. ²⁵He supposed that his brothers would understand that God was giving them salvation by his hand, but they did not understand. ²⁶And on the following day he appeared to them as they were quarreling and tried to reconcile them, saying, 'Men, you are brothers. Why do you wrong each other?' ²⁷But the man who was wronging his neighbor thrust him aside, saying, 'Who made you a ruler and a judge over us? ²⁸Do you want to kill me as you killed the Egyptian yesterday?' ²⁹At this retort Moses fled and became an exile in the land of Midian, where he became the father of two sons.

³⁰"Now when forty years had passed, an angel appeared to him in the wilderness of Mount Sinai, in a flame of fire in a bush. ³¹When Moses saw it, he was amazed at the sight, and as he drew near to look, there came the voice of the Lord: ³²ᶜ'I am the God of your fathers, the God of Abraham and of Isaac and of Jacob.' And Moses trembled and did not dare to look. ³³Then the Lord said to him, 'Take off the sandals from your feet, for the place where you are standing is holy ground. ³⁴I have surely seen the affliction of my people who are in Egypt, and have heard their groaning, and I have come down to deliver them. And now come, I will send you to Egypt.'

³⁵"This Moses, whom they rejected, saying, 'Who made you a ruler and a judge?'—this man God sent as both ruler and redeemer by the hand of the angel who appeared to him in the bush. ³⁶This man led them out, performing wonders and signs in Egypt and at the Red Sea and in the wilderness for forty years. ³⁷This is the Moses who said to the Israelites, 'God will raise up for you ᵈa prophet like me from your brothers.' ³⁸This is the one who

ᵃGen. 12:1 ᵇGen. 15:13, 14 ᶜEx. 3:6 ᵈDeut. 18:15

was in the congregation in the wilderness with the angel who spoke to him at Mount Sinai, and with our fathers. He received living oracles to give to us. ³⁹ Our fathers refused to obey him, but thrust him aside, and in their hearts they turned to Egypt, ⁴⁰ saying to Aaron, ^a'Make for us gods who will go before us. As for this Moses who led us out from the land of Egypt, we do not know what has become of him.' ⁴¹ And they made a calf in those days, and offered a sacrifice to the idol and were rejoicing in the works of their hands. ⁴² But God turned away and gave them over to worship the host of heaven, as it is written in the book of the prophets:

^b"'Did you bring to me slain beasts and
	sacrifices,
		during the forty years in the wil-
		derness, O house of Israel?
⁴³	You took up the tent of Moloch
		and the star of your god Rephan,
		the images that you made to wor-
		ship;
	and I will send you into exile beyond
		Babylon.'

⁴⁴ "Our fathers had the tent of witness in the wilderness, just as he who spoke to Moses directed him to make it, according to the pattern that he had seen. ⁴⁵ Our fathers in turn brought it in with Joshua when they dispossessed the nations that God drove out before our fathers. So it was until the days of David, ⁴⁶ who found favor in the sight of God and asked to find a dwelling place for the God of Jacob.¹ ⁴⁷ But it was Solomon who built a house for him. ⁴⁸ Yet the Most High does not dwell in houses made by hands, as the prophet says,

⁴⁹ ^c"'Heaven is my throne,
		and the earth is my footstool.
	What kind of house will you build for
		me, says the Lord,
		or what is the place of my rest?
⁵⁰	Did not my hand make all these
		things?'

⁵¹ "You stiff-necked people, uncircumcised in heart and ears, you always resist the Holy Spirit. As your fathers did, so do you. ⁵² Which of the prophets did your fathers not persecute? And they killed those who announced beforehand the coming of the Righteous One, whom you have now betrayed and murdered, ⁵³ you who received the law as delivered by angels and did not keep it."

The Stoning of Stephen

⁵⁴ Now when they heard these things they were enraged, and they ground their teeth at him. ⁵⁵ But he, full of the Holy Spirit, gazed into heaven and saw the glory of God, and Jesus standing at the right hand of God. ⁵⁶ And he said, "Behold, I see the heavens opened, and the Son of Man standing at the right hand of God." ⁵⁷ But they cried out with a loud voice and stopped their ears and rushed together² at him. ⁵⁸ Then they cast him out of the city and stoned him. And the witnesses laid down their garments at the feet of a young man named Saul. ⁵⁹ And as they were stoning Stephen, he called out, "Lord Jesus, receive my spirit." ⁶⁰ And falling to his knees he cried out with a loud voice, "Lord, do not hold this sin against them." And when he had said this, he fell asleep.

Saul Ravages the Church

8 And Saul approved of his execution.
And there arose on that day a great persecution against the church in Jerusalem, and they were all scattered throughout the regions of Judea and Samaria, except the apostles. ² Devout men buried Stephen and made great lamentation over him. ³ But Saul was ravaging the church, and entering house after house, he dragged off men and women and committed them to prison.

Philip Proclaims Christ in Samaria

⁴ Now those who were scattered went about preaching the word. ⁵ Philip went down to the city³ of Samaria and proclaimed to them the Christ. ⁶ And the crowds with one accord paid attention to what was being said by Philip when they heard him and saw the signs that he did. ⁷ For unclean spirits, crying out with a loud voice, came out of many who had them, and many who were paralyzed or lame were healed. ⁸ So there was much joy in that city.

Simon the Magician Believes

⁹ But there was a man named Simon, who had previously practiced magic in the city

---

¹ Some manuscripts *for the house of Jacob* ² Or *rushed with one mind* ³ Some manuscripts *a city* ^a Ex. 32:1, 23 ^b Amos 5:25-27 ^c Isa. 66:1, 2

and amazed the people of Samaria, saying that he himself was somebody great. [10] They all paid attention to him, from the least to the greatest, saying, "This man is the power of God that is called Great." [11] And they paid attention to him because for a long time he had amazed them with his magic. [12] But when they believed Philip as he preached good news about the kingdom of God and the name of Jesus Christ, they were baptized, both men and women. [13] Even Simon himself believed, and after being baptized he continued with Philip. And seeing signs and great miracles[1] performed, he was amazed.

[14] Now when the apostles at Jerusalem heard that Samaria had received the word of God, they sent to them Peter and John, [15] who came down and prayed for them that they might receive the Holy Spirit, [16] for he had not yet fallen on any of them, but they had only been baptized in the name of the Lord Jesus. [17] Then they laid their hands on them and they received the Holy Spirit. [18] Now when Simon saw that the Spirit was given through the laying on of the apostles' hands, he offered them money, [19] saying, "Give me this power also, so that anyone on whom I lay my hands may receive the Holy Spirit." [20] But Peter said to him, "May your silver perish with you, because you thought you could obtain the gift of God with money! [21] You have neither part nor lot in this matter, for your heart is not right before God. [22] Repent, therefore, of this wickedness of yours, and pray to the Lord that, if possible, the intent of your heart may be forgiven you. [23] For I see that you are in the gall[2] of bitterness and in the bond of iniquity." [24] And Simon answered, "Pray for me to the Lord, that nothing of what you have said may come upon me."

[25] Now when they had testified and spoken the word of the Lord, they returned to Jerusalem, preaching the gospel to many villages of the Samaritans.

Philip and the Ethiopian Eunuch

[26] Now an angel of the Lord said to Philip, "Rise and go toward the south[3] to the road that goes down from Jerusalem to Gaza." This is a desert place. [27] And he rose and went. And there was an Ethiopian, a eunuch, a court official of Candace, queen of the Ethiopians, who was in charge of all her treasure. He had come to Jerusalem to worship [28] and was returning, seated in his chariot, and he was reading the prophet Isaiah. [29] And the Spirit said to Philip, "Go over and join this chariot." [30] So Philip ran to him and heard him reading Isaiah the prophet and asked, "Do you understand what you are reading?" [31] And he said, "How can I, unless someone guides me?" And he invited Philip to come up and sit with him. [32] Now the passage of the Scripture that he was reading was this:

[a]"Like a sheep he was led to the slaughter
　and like a lamb before its shearer
　　is silent,
　so he opens not his mouth.
[33]　In his humiliation justice was denied
　　him.
　Who can describe his generation?
　For his life is taken away from the
　　earth."

[34] And the eunuch said to Philip, "About whom, I ask you, does the prophet say this, about himself or about someone else?" [35] Then Philip opened his mouth, and beginning with this Scripture he told him the good news about Jesus. [36] And as they were going along the road they came to some water, and the eunuch said, "See, here is water! What prevents me from being baptized?"[4] [38] And he commanded the chariot to stop, and they both went down into the water, Philip and the eunuch, and he baptized him. [39] And when they came up out of the water, the Spirit of the Lord carried Philip away, and the eunuch saw him no more, and went on his way rejoicing. [40] But Philip found himself at Azotus, and as he passed through he preached the gospel to all the towns until he came to Caesarea.

The Conversion of Saul

9 But Saul, still breathing threats and murder against the disciples of the Lord, went to the high priest [2] and asked him for letters to the synagogues at Damascus, so that if he found any belonging to the Way, men or women, he might bring them bound to Jerusalem. [3] Now as he went on his way, he approached Damascus, and

---

[1] Greek works of power　[2] That is, a bitter fluid secreted by the liver; bile　[3] Or go at about noon　[4] Some manuscripts add all or most of verse 37: And Philip said, "If you believe with all your heart, you may." And he replied, "I believe that Jesus Christ is the Son of God." [a] Isa. 53:7, 8

suddenly a light from heaven shone around him. ⁴And falling to the ground he heard a voice saying to him, "Saul, Saul, why are you persecuting me?" ⁵And he said, "Who are you, Lord?" And he said, "I am Jesus, whom you are persecuting. ⁶But rise and enter the city, and you will be told what you are to do." ⁷The men who were traveling with him stood speechless, hearing the voice but seeing no one. ⁸Saul rose from the ground, and although his eyes were opened, he saw nothing. So they led him by the hand and brought him into Damascus. ⁹And for three days he was without sight, and neither ate nor drank.

¹⁰Now there was a disciple at Damascus named Ananias. The Lord said to him in a vision, "Ananias." And he said, "Here I am, Lord." ¹¹And the Lord said to him, "Rise and go to the street called Straight, and at the house of Judas look for a man of Tarsus named Saul, for behold, he is praying, ¹²and he has seen in a vision a man named Ananias come in and lay his hands on him so that he might regain his sight." ¹³But Ananias answered, "Lord, I have heard from many about this man, how much evil he has done to your saints at Jerusalem. ¹⁴And here he has authority from the chief priests to bind all who call on your name." ¹⁵But the Lord said to him, "Go, for he is a chosen instrument of mine to carry my name before the Gentiles and kings and the children of Israel. ¹⁶For I will show him how much he must suffer for the sake of my name." ¹⁷So Ananias departed and entered the house. And laying his hands on him he said, "Brother Saul, the Lord Jesus who appeared to you on the road by which you came has sent me so that you may regain your sight and be filled with the Holy Spirit." ¹⁸And immediately something like scales fell from his eyes, and he regained his sight. Then he rose and was baptized; ¹⁹and taking food, he was strengthened.

Saul Proclaims Jesus in Synagogues

For some days he was with the disciples at Damascus. ²⁰And immediately he proclaimed Jesus in the synagogues, saying, "He is the Son of God." ²¹And all who heard him were amazed and said, "Is not this the man who made havoc in Jerusalem of those who called upon this name? And has he not come here for this purpose, to bring them bound before the chief priests?" ²²But Saul increased all the more in strength, and confounded the Jews who lived in Damascus by proving that Jesus was the Christ.

Saul Escapes from Damascus

²³When many days had passed, the Jews¹ plotted to kill him, ²⁴but their plot became known to Saul. They were watching the gates day and night in order to kill him, ²⁵but his disciples took him by night and let him down through an opening in the wall,² lowering him in a basket.

Saul in Jerusalem

²⁶And when he had come to Jerusalem, he attempted to join the disciples. And they were all afraid of him, for they did not believe that he was a disciple. ²⁷But Barnabas took him and brought him to the apostles and declared to them how on the road he had seen the Lord, who spoke to him, and how at Damascus he had preached boldly in the name of Jesus. ²⁸So he went in and out among them at Jerusalem, preaching boldly in the name of the Lord. ²⁹And he spoke and disputed against the Hellenists.³ But they were seeking to kill him. ³⁰And when the brothers learned this, they brought him down to Caesarea and sent him off to Tarsus.

³¹So the church throughout all Judea and Galilee and Samaria had peace and was being built up. And walking in the fear of the Lord and in the comfort of the Holy Spirit, it multiplied.

The Healing of Aeneas

³²Now as Peter went here and there among them all, he came down also to the saints who lived at Lydda. ³³There he found a man named Aeneas, bedridden for eight years, who was paralyzed. ³⁴And Peter said to him, "Aeneas, Jesus Christ heals you; rise and make your bed." And immediately he rose. ³⁵And all the residents of Lydda and Sharon saw him, and they turned to the Lord.

Dorcas Restored to Life

³⁶Now there was in Joppa a disciple named Tabitha, which, translated, means

---

The Greek word *Ioudaioi* refers specifically here to Jewish religious leaders, and others under their influence, who opposed the Christian faith in that time ²Greek *through the wall* ³That is, Greek-speaking Jews

Tabitha

Read this God Girl story in Acts 9:36–42.

"Whoever would be great among you must be your servant, and whoever would be first among you must be slave of all. For even the Son of Man came not to be served but to serve, and to give his life as a ransom for many."

Mark 10:43-45

You won't be "ready to serve" sometime in the future. Your service starts today, the moment you learn of God's call on your life. Are you going to let your age disqualify you from serving your God? Of course not. Even a child can serve her parents in some ways.

Serving God means serving his people. Don't put off service till some magical time when you are "more qualified"; take the opportunities as they come up. No matter how demeaning, service is never in vain. If God has given you some unique gift, don't hide your talents and expect to get some great return. You've got to invest your talents in the lives of others. If your heart is compassionate toward those in need, serve them as if your life depended on it. Never refuse to take care of those in need because you aren't prepared. Where there is need, there needs to be workers.

Tabitha was a woman who gave her life to others. Her life meant so much to the people around her that when she died they were all there sobbing and missing her. They were talking about all she had done for them by giving them her clothes and her love.

Your life matters, just as Tabitha's did, no matter how much you know or don't know. Keep looking for more wisdom and more faith, but also keep serving others no matter how much knowledge you have or don't have or how together your life is right now. The situation is never going to be perfect to serve, but the perfect time is now. As Jesus served you in giving his life for you, you are now free to serve others.

Dorcas.[1] She was full of good works and acts of charity. **37** In those days she became ill and died, and when they had washed her, they laid her in an upper room. **38** Since Lydda was near Joppa, the disciples, hearing that Peter was there, sent two men to him, urging him, "Please come to us without delay." **39** So Peter rose and went with them. And when he arrived, they took him to the upper room. All the widows stood beside him weeping and showing tunics[2] and other garments that Dorcas made while she was with them. **40** But Peter put them all outside, and knelt down and prayed; and turning to the body he said, "Tabitha, arise." And she opened her eyes, and when she saw Peter she sat up. **41** And he gave her his hand and raised her up. Then calling the saints and widows, he presented her alive. **42** And it became known throughout all Joppa, and many believed in the Lord. **43** And he stayed in Joppa for many days with one Simon, a tanner.

Peter and Cornelius

10 At Caesarea there was a man named Cornelius, a centurion of what was known as the Italian Cohort, **2** a devout man who feared God with all his household, gave alms generously to the people, and prayed continually to God. **3** About the ninth hour of the day[3] he saw clearly in a vision an angel of God come in and say to him, "Cornelius." **4** And he stared at him in terror and said, "What is it, Lord?" And he said to him, "Your prayers and your alms have ascended as a memorial before God. **5** And now send men to Joppa and bring one Simon who is called Peter. **6** He is lodging with one Simon, a tanner, whose house is by the sea." **7** When the angel who spoke to him had departed, he called two of his servants and a devout soldier from among those who attended him, **8** and having related everything to them, he sent them to Joppa.

Peter's Vision

9 The next day, as they were on their journey and approaching the city, Peter went up on the housetop about the sixth hour[4] to pray. **10** And he became hungry and wanted something to eat, but while they were preparing it, he fell into a trance **11** and saw the heavens opened and something like a great sheet descending, being let down by its four corners upon the earth. **12** In it were all kinds of animals and reptiles and birds of the air. **13** And there came a voice to him: "Rise, Peter; kill and eat." **14** But Peter said, "By no means, Lord; for I have never eaten anything that is common or unclean." **15** And the voice came to him again a second time, "What God has made clean, do not call common." **16** This happened three times, and the thing was taken up at once to heaven.

17 Now while Peter was inwardly perplexed as to what the vision that he had seen might mean, behold, the men who were sent by Cornelius, having made inquiry for Simon's house, stood at the gate **18** and called out to ask whether Simon who was called Peter was lodging there. **19** And while Peter was pondering the vision, the Spirit said to him, "Behold, three men are looking for you. **20** Rise and go down and accompany them without hesitation,[5] for I have sent them." **21** And Peter went down to the men and said, "I am the one you are looking for. What is the reason for your coming?" **22** And they said, "Cornelius, a centurion, an upright and God-fearing man, who is well spoken of by the whole Jewish nation, was directed by a holy angel to send for you to come to his house and to hear what you have to say." **23** So he invited them in to be his guests.

The next day he rose and went away with them, and some of the brothers from Joppa accompanied him. **24** And on the following day they entered Caesarea. Cornelius was expecting them and had called together his relatives and close friends. **25** When Peter entered, Cornelius met him and fell down at his feet and worshiped him. **26** But Peter lifted him up, saying, "Stand up; I too am a man." **27** And as he talked with him, he went in and found many persons gathered. **28** And he said to them, "You yourselves know how unlawful it is for a Jew to associate with or to visit anyone of another nation, but God has shown me that I should not call any person common or unclean. **29** So when I was sent for, I came without objection. I ask then why you sent for me."

30 And Cornelius said, "Four days ago, about this hour, I was praying in my house

[1] The Aramaic name *Tabitha* and the Greek name *Dorcas* both mean *gazelle* [2] Greek *chiton*, a long garment worn under the cloak next to the skin [3] That is, 3 P.M. [4] That is, noon [5] Or *accompany them, making no distinction*

at the ninth hour,[1] and behold, a man stood before me in bright clothing [31] and said, 'Cornelius, your prayer has been heard and your alms have been remembered before God. [32] Send therefore to Joppa and ask for Simon who is called Peter. He is lodging in the house of Simon, a tanner, by the sea.' [33] So I sent for you at once, and you have been kind enough to come. Now therefore we are all here in the presence of God to hear all that you have been commanded by the Lord."

Gentiles Hear the Good News

[34] So Peter opened his mouth and said: "Truly I understand that God shows no partiality, [35] but in every nation anyone who fears him and does what is right is acceptable to him. [36] As for the word that he sent to Israel, preaching good news of peace through Jesus Christ (he is Lord of all), [37] you yourselves know what happened throughout all Judea, beginning from Galilee after the baptism that John proclaimed: [38] how God anointed Jesus of Nazareth with the Holy Spirit and with power. He went about doing good and healing all who were oppressed by the devil, for God was with him. [39] And we are witnesses of all that he did both in the country of the Jews and in Jerusalem. They put him to death by hanging him on a tree, [40] but God raised him on the third day and made him to appear, [41] not to all the people but to us who had been chosen by God as witnesses, who ate and drank with him after he rose from the dead. [42] And he commanded us to preach to the people and to testify that he is the one appointed by God to be judge of the living and the dead. [43] To him all the prophets bear witness that everyone who believes in him receives forgiveness of sins through his name."

The Holy Spirit Falls on the Gentiles

[44] While Peter was still saying these things, the Holy Spirit fell on all who heard the word. [45] And the believers from among the circumcised who had come with Peter were amazed, because the gift of the Holy Spirit was poured out even on the Gentiles. [46] For they were hearing them speaking in tongues and extolling God. Then Peter declared, [47] "Can any-

one withhold water for baptizing these people, who have received the Holy Spirit just as we have?" [48] And he commanded them to be baptized in the name of Jesus Christ. Then they asked him to remain for some days.

Peter Reports to the Church

11 Now the apostles and the brothers[2] who were throughout Judea heard that the Gentiles also had received the word of God. [2] So when Peter went up to Jerusalem, the circumcision party criticized him, saying, [3] "You went to uncircumcised men and ate with them." [4] But Peter began and explained it to them in order: [5] "I was in the city of Joppa praying and in a trance I saw a vision, something like a great sheet descending, being let down from heaven by its four corners and it came down to me. [6] Looking at it closely, I observed animals and beasts of prey and reptiles and birds of the air. [7] And I heard a voice saying to me, 'Rise, Peter; kill and eat.' [8] But I said, 'By no means, Lord; for nothing common or unclean has ever entered my mouth.' [9] But the voice answered a second time from heaven, 'What God has made clean, do not call common.' [10] This happened three times, and all was drawn up again into heaven. [11] And behold, at that very moment three men arrived at the house in which we were, sent to me from Caesarea. [12] And the Spirit told me to go with them, making no distinction. These six brothers also accompanied me, and we entered the man's house. [13] And he told us how he had seen the angel stand in his house and say, 'Send to Joppa and bring Simon who is called Peter; [14] he will declare to you a message by which you will be saved, you and all your household.' [15] As I began to speak, the Holy Spirit fell on them just as on us at the beginning. [16] And I remembered the word of the Lord, how he said, 'John baptized with water, but you will be baptized with the Holy Spirit.' [17] If then God gave the same gift to them as he gave to us when we believed in the Lord Jesus Christ, who was I that I could stand in God's way?" [18] When they heard these things they fell silent. And they glorified God, saying, "Then to the Gentiles also God has granted repentance that leads to life."

[1] That is, 3 P.M. [2] Or brothers and sisters [3] Or Jerusalem, those of the circumcision

The Church in Antioch

19 Now those who were scattered because of the persecution that arose over Stephen traveled as far as Phoenicia and Cyprus and Antioch, speaking the word to no one except Jews. **20** But there were some of them, men of Cyprus and Cyrene, who on coming to Antioch spoke to the Hellenists[1] also, preaching the Lord Jesus. **21** And the hand of the Lord was with them, and a great number who believed turned to the Lord. **22** The report of this came to the ears of the church in Jerusalem, and they sent Barnabas to Antioch. **23** When he came and saw the grace of God, he was glad, and he exhorted them all to remain faithful to the Lord with steadfast purpose, **24** for he was a good man, full of the Holy Spirit and of faith. And a great many people were added to the Lord. **25** So Barnabas went to Tarsus to look for Saul, **26** and when he had found him, he brought him to Antioch. For a whole year they met with the church and taught a great many people. And in Antioch the disciples were first called Christians.

27 Now in these days prophets came down from Jerusalem to Antioch. **28** And one of them named Agabus stood up and foretold by the Spirit that there would be a great famine over all the world (this took place in the days of Claudius). **29** So the disciples determined, every one according to his ability, to send relief to the brothers[2] living in Judea. **30** And they did so, sending it to the elders by the hand of Barnabas and Saul.

James Killed and Peter Imprisoned

12 About that time Herod the king laid violent hands on some who belonged to the church. **2** He killed James the brother of John with the sword, **3** and when he saw that it pleased the Jews, he proceeded to arrest Peter also. This was during the days of Unleavened Bread. **4** And when he had seized him, he put him in

[1] Or *Greeks* (that is, Greek-speaking non-Jews) [2] Or *brothers and sisters*

Know True Happiness

verses to read
Acts 12:1–11

Do you feel trapped by doubt? Are you living in isolation and fear of what other girls are thinking or saying about you? When you feel like the walls are closing in and everything and everyone is against you in these ways, you have landed in an imaginary prison of your own making. The walls feel as real as any prison walls ever could be. You are as paralyzed and as stuck as you would be if someone had really locked a door and thrown away the key. But the walls aren't real. Like a mime in a box, you struggle to free yourself from a nonexistent cell. As you moan about your inability to get out of this mess, you reinforce the walls, the bars, and the cold, hard floor where you restlessly sleep each night.

How tragic to sentence yourself to a prison that doesn't really exist. How crazy to believe all is lost and everyone is against you. Even if everyone around you *is* against you, is your God all you need to sustain you no matter what, or isn't he? He sent his Son for you—he's watching over the details, too.

For the child of God, there is freedom. The walls can hold you only as long as you keep your eyes on them. Once you stop considering your difficulties and start considering God's truth, you will find an open door to walk through. To be free, all you have to do is recognize that nothing matters except the call of God on your life, and that nothing happens to you unless God allows it. Let go of your need to fear the outside world and, by the grace of God, walk free, just as Peter walked out of his prison on the night the walls shook and set him free.

prison, delivering him over to four squads of soldiers to guard him, intending after the Passover to bring him out to the people. [5] So Peter was kept in prison, but earnest prayer for him was made to God by the church.

Peter Is Rescued

[6] Now when Herod was about to bring him out, on that very night, Peter was sleeping between two soldiers, bound with two chains, and sentries before the door were guarding the prison. [7] And behold, an angel of the Lord stood next to him, and a light shone in the cell. He struck Peter on the side and woke him, saying, "Get up quickly." And the chains fell off his hands. [8] And the angel said to him, "Dress yourself and put on your sandals." And he did so. And he said to him, "Wrap your cloak around you and follow me." [9] And he went out and followed him. He did not know that what was being done by the angel was real, but thought he was seeing a vision. [10] When they had passed the first and the second guard, they came to the iron gate leading into the city. It opened for them of its own accord, and they went out and went along one street, and immediately the angel left him. [11] When Peter came to himself, he said, "Now I am sure that the Lord has sent his angel and rescued me from the hand of Herod and from all that the Jewish people were expecting."

[12] When he realized this, he went to the house of Mary, the mother of John whose other name was Mark, where many were gathered together and were praying. [13] And when he knocked at the door of the gateway, a servant girl named Rhoda came to answer. [14] Recognizing Peter's voice, in her joy she did not open the gate but ran in and reported that Peter was standing at the gate. [15] They said to her, "You are out of your mind." But she kept insisting that it was so, and they kept saying, "It is his angel!" [16] But Peter continued knocking, and when they opened, they saw him and were amazed. [17] But motioning to them with his hand to be silent, he described to them how the Lord had brought him out of the prison. And he said, "Tell these things to James and to the brothers."[1] Then he departed and went to another place.

[18] Now when day came, there was no little disturbance among the soldiers over what had become of Peter. [19] And after Herod searched for him and did not find him, he examined the sentries and ordered that they should be put to death. Then he went down from Judea to Caesarea and spent time there.

The Death of Herod

[20] Now Herod was angry with the people of Tyre and Sidon, and they came to him with one accord, and having persuaded Blastus, the king's chamberlain,[2] they asked for peace, because their country depended on the king's country for food. [21] On an appointed day Herod put on his royal robes, took his seat upon the throne, and delivered an oration to them. [22] And the people were shouting, "The voice of a god, and not of a man!" [23] Immediately an angel of the Lord struck him down, because he did not give God the glory, and he was eaten by worms and breathed his last.

[24] But the word of God increased and multiplied.

[25] And Barnabas and Saul returned from[3] Jerusalem when they had completed their service, bringing with them John, whose other name was Mark.

Barnabas and Saul Sent Off

13 Now there were in the church at Antioch prophets and teachers, Barnabas, Simeon who was called Niger,[4] Lucius of Cyrene, Manaen a lifelong friend of Herod the tetrarch, and Saul. [2] While they were worshiping the Lord and fasting, the Holy Spirit said, "Set apart for me Barnabas and Saul for the work to which I have called them." [3] Then after fasting and praying they laid their hands on them and sent them off.

Barnabas and Saul on Cyprus

[4] So, being sent out by the Holy Spirit, they went down to Seleucia, and from there they sailed to Cyprus. [5] When they arrived at Salamis, they proclaimed the word of God in the synagogues of the Jews. And they had John to assist them. [6] When they had gone through the whole island as far as Paphos, they came upon a certain magician, a Jewish false prophet named Bar-Jesus. [7] He was with the proconsul,

---

[1] Or brothers and sisters [2] That is, trusted personal attendant [3] Some manuscripts to [4] Niger is a Latin word meaning black, or dark

Sergius Paulus, a man of intelligence, who summoned Barnabas and Saul and sought to hear the word of God. [8] But Elymas the magician (for that is the meaning of his name) opposed them, seeking to turn the proconsul away from the faith. [9] But Saul, who was also called Paul, filled with the Holy Spirit, looked intently at him [10] and said, "You son of the devil, you enemy of all righteousness, full of all deceit and villainy, will you not stop making crooked the straight paths of the Lord? [11] And now, behold, the hand of the Lord is upon you, and you will be blind and unable to see the sun for a time." Immediately mist and darkness fell upon him, and he went about seeking people to lead him by the hand. [12] Then the proconsul believed, when he saw what had occurred, for he was astonished at the teaching of the Lord.

Paul and Barnabas at Antioch in Pisidia

[13] Now Paul and his companions set sail from Paphos and came to Perga in Pamphylia. And John left them and returned to Jerusalem, [14] but they went on from Perga and came to Antioch in Pisidia. And on the Sabbath day they went into the synagogue and sat down. [15] After the reading from the Law and the Prophets, the rulers of the synagogue sent a message to them, saying, "Brothers, if you have any word of encouragement for the people, say it." [16] So Paul stood up, and motioning with his hand said:

"Men of Israel and you who fear God, listen. [17] The God of this people Israel chose our fathers and made the people great during their stay in the land of Egypt, and with uplifted arm he led them out of it. [18] And for about forty years he put up with[1] them in the wilderness. [19] And after destroying seven nations in the land of Canaan, he gave them their land as an inheritance. [20] All this took about 450 years. And after that he gave them judges until Samuel the prophet. [21] Then they asked for a king, and God gave them Saul the son of Kish, a man of the tribe of Benjamin, for forty years. [22] And when he had removed him, he raised up David to be their king, of whom he testified and said, [a]'I have found in David the son of Jesse [b]a man after my heart, who will do all my will.' [23] Of this man's offspring

God has brought to Israel a Savior, Jesus, as he promised. [24] Before his coming, John had proclaimed a baptism of repentance to all the people of Israel. [25] And as John was finishing his course, he said, 'What do you suppose that I am? I am not he. No, but behold, after me one is coming, the sandals of whose feet I am not worthy to untie.'

[26] "Brothers, sons of the family of Abraham, and those among you who fear God, to us has been sent the message of this salvation. [27] For those who live in Jerusalem and their rulers, because they did not recognize him nor understand the utterances of the prophets, which are read every Sabbath, fulfilled them by condemning him. [28] And though they found in him no guilt worthy of death, they asked Pilate to have him executed. [29] And when they had carried out all that was written of him, they took him down from the tree and laid him in a tomb. [30] But God raised him from the dead, [31] and for many days he appeared to those who had come up with him from Galilee to Jerusalem, who are now his witnesses to the people. [32] And we bring you the good news that what God promised to the fathers, [33] this he has fulfilled to us their children by raising Jesus, as also it is written in the second Psalm,

> [c]"'You are my Son,
>   today I have begotten you.'

[34] And as for the fact that he raised him from the dead, no more to return to corruption, he has spoken in this way,

> "'I will give you [d]the holy and sure
>   blessings of David.'

[35] Therefore he says also in another psalm,

> [e]"'You will not let your Holy One see corruption.'

[36] For David, after he had served the purpose of God in his own generation, fell asleep and was laid with his fathers and saw corruption, [37] but he whom God raised up did not see corruption. [38] Let it be known to you therefore, brothers, that through this man forgiveness of sins is proclaimed to you, [39] and by him everyone who believes is freed[2] from everything from which you could not be freed by the law of Moses.

[1] Some manuscripts *he carried* (compare Deuteronomy 1:31) [2] Greek *justified*; twice in this verse [a] Ps. 89:20 [b] 1 Sam. 13:14 [c] Ps. 2:7 [d] Isa. 55:3 [e] Ps. 16:10

40 Beware, therefore, lest what is said in the Prophets should come about:

41 a "'Look, you scoffers,
    be astounded and perish;
for I am doing a work in your days,
    a work that you will not believe,
        even if one tells it to you.'"

42 As they went out, the people begged that these things might be told them the next Sabbath. 43 And after the meeting of the synagogue broke up, many Jews and devout converts to Judaism followed Paul and Barnabas, who, as they spoke with them, urged them to continue in the grace of God.

44 The next Sabbath almost the whole city gathered to hear the word of the Lord. 45 But when the Jews saw the crowds, they were filled with jealousy and began to contradict what was spoken by Paul, reviling him. 46 And Paul and Barnabas spoke out boldly, saying, "It was necessary that the word of God be spoken first to you. Since you thrust it aside and judge yourselves unworthy of eternal life, behold, we are turning to the Gentiles. 47 For so the Lord has commanded us, saying,

b "'I have made you a light for the
        Gentiles,
    that you may bring salvation to the
        ends of the earth.'"

48 And when the Gentiles heard this, they began rejoicing and glorifying the word of the Lord, and as many as were appointed to eternal life believed. 49 And the word of the Lord was spreading throughout the whole region. 50 But the Jews[1] incited the devout women of high standing and the leading men of the city, stirred up persecution against Paul and Barnabas, and drove them out of their district. 51 But they shook off the dust from their feet against them and went to Iconium. 52 And the disciples were filled with joy and with the Holy Spirit.

Paul and Barnabas at Iconium

14 Now at Iconium they entered together into the Jewish synagogue and spoke in such a way that a great number of both Jews and Greeks believed. 2 But the unbelieving Jews stirred up the Gentiles and poisoned their minds against the brothers.[2] 3 So they remained for a long time, speaking boldly for the Lord, who bore witness to the word of his grace, granting signs and wonders to be done by their hands. 4 But the people of the city were divided; some sided with the Jews and some with the apostles. 5 When an attempt was made by both Gentiles and Jews, with their rulers, to mistreat them and to stone them, 6 they learned of it and fled to Lystra and Derbe, cities of Lycaonia, and to the surrounding country, 7 and there they continued to preach the gospel.

Paul and Barnabas at Lystra

8 Now at Lystra there was a man sitting who could not use his feet. He was crippled from birth and had never walked. 9 He listened to Paul speaking. And Paul, looking intently at him and seeing that he had faith to be made well,[3] 10 said in a loud voice, "Stand upright on your feet." And he sprang up and began walking. 11 And when the crowds saw what Paul had done, they lifted up their voices, saying in Lycaonian, "The gods have come down to us in the likeness of men!" 12 Barnabas they called Zeus, and Paul, Hermes, because he was the chief speaker. 13 And the priest of Zeus, whose temple was at the entrance to the city, brought oxen and garlands to the gates and wanted to offer sacrifice with the crowds. 14 But when the apostles Barnabas and Paul heard of it, they tore their garments and rushed out into the crowd, crying out, 15 "Men, why are you doing these things? We also are men, of like nature with you, and we bring you good news, that you should turn from these vain things to a living God, who made the heaven and the earth and the sea and all that is in them. 16 In past generations he allowed all the nations to walk in their own ways. 17 Yet he did not leave himself without witness, for he did good by giving you rains from heaven and fruitful seasons, satisfying your hearts with food and gladness." 18 Even with these words they scarcely restrained the people from offering sacrifice to them.

Paul Stoned at Lystra

19 But Jews came from Antioch and Iconium, and having persuaded the crowds,

---

[1] Greek *Ioudaioi* probably refers here to Jewish religious leaders, and others under their influence, in that time [2] Or *brothers and sisters* [3] Or *be saved* a Hab. 1:5 b Isa. 49:6

they stoned Paul and dragged him out of the city, supposing that he was dead. ²⁰But when the disciples gathered about him, he rose up and entered the city, and on the next day he went on with Barnabas to Derbe. ²¹When they had preached the gospel to that city and had made many disciples, they returned to Lystra and to Iconium and to Antioch, ²²strengthening the souls of the disciples, encouraging them to continue in the faith, and saying that through many tribulations we must enter the kingdom of God. ²³And when they had appointed elders for them in every church, with prayer and fasting they committed them to the Lord in whom they had believed.

Paul and Barnabas Return to Antioch in Syria

²⁴Then they passed through Pisidia and came to Pamphylia. ²⁵And when they had spoken the word in Perga, they went down to Attalia, ²⁶and from there they sailed to Antioch, where they had been commended to the grace of God for the work that they had fulfilled. ²⁷And when they arrived and gathered the church together, they declared all that God had done with them, and how he had opened a door of faith to the Gentiles. ²⁸And they remained no little time with the disciples.

The Jerusalem Council

15 But some men came down from Judea and were teaching the brothers, "Unless you are circumcised according to the custom of Moses, you cannot be saved." ²And after Paul and Barnabas had no small dissension and debate with them, Paul and Barnabas and some of the others were appointed to go up to Jerusalem to the apostles and the elders about this question. ³So, being sent on their way by the church, they passed through both Phoenicia and Samaria, describing in detail the conversion of the Gentiles, and brought great joy to all the brothers.¹ ⁴When they came to Jerusalem, they were welcomed by the church and the apostles and the elders, and they declared all that God had done with them. ⁵But some believers who belonged to the party of the Pharisees rose up and said, "It is necessary to circumcise them and to order them to keep the law of Moses."

⁶The apostles and the elders were gathered together to consider this matter. ⁷And after there had been much debate, Peter stood up and said to them, "Brothers, you know that in the early days God made a choice among you, that by my mouth the Gentiles should hear the word of the gospel and believe. ⁸And God, who knows the heart, bore witness to them, by giving them the Holy Spirit just as he did to us, ⁹and he made no distinction between us and them, having cleansed their hearts by faith. ¹⁰Now, therefore, why are you putting God to the test by placing a yoke on the neck of the disciples that neither our fathers nor we have been able to bear? ¹¹But we believe that we will be saved through the grace of the Lord Jesus, just as they will."

¹²And all the assembly fell silent, and they listened to Barnabas and Paul as they related what signs and wonders God had done through them among the Gentiles. ¹³After they finished speaking, James replied, "Brothers, listen to me. ¹⁴Simeon has related how God first visited the Gentiles, to take from them a people for his name. ¹⁵And with this the words of the prophets agree, just as it is written,

¹⁶ᵃ" 'After this I will return,
    and I will rebuild the tent of David
        that has fallen;
  I will rebuild its ruins,
    and I will restore it,
¹⁷   that the remnant² of mankind may
        seek the Lord,
  and all the Gentiles who are called
        by my name,
  says the Lord, who makes these
        things ¹⁸known from of old.'

¹⁹Therefore my judgment is that we should not trouble those of the Gentiles who turn to God, ²⁰but should write to them to abstain from the things polluted by idols, and from sexual immorality, and from what has been strangled, and from blood. ²¹For from ancient generations Moses has had in every city those who proclaim him, for he is read every Sabbath in the synagogues."

The Council's Letter to Gentile Believers

²²Then it seemed good to the apostles and the elders, with the whole church, to choose men from among them and send them to Antioch with Paul and Barnabas.

¹Or brothers and sisters; also verse 22 ²Or rest ᵃAmos 9:11, 12

They sent Judas called Barsabbas, and Silas, leading men among the brothers, [23] with the following letter: "The brothers, both the apostles and the elders, to the brothers[1] who are of the Gentiles in Antioch and Syria and Cilicia, greetings. [24] Since we have heard that some persons have gone out from us and troubled you[2] with words, unsettling your minds, although we gave them no instructions, [25] it has seemed good to us, having come to one accord, to choose men and send them to you with our beloved Barnabas and Paul, [26] men who have risked their lives for the name of our Lord Jesus Christ. [27] We have therefore sent Judas and Silas, who themselves will tell you the same things by word of mouth. [28] For it has seemed good to the Holy Spirit and to us to lay on you no greater burden than these requirements: [29] that you abstain from what has been sacrificed to idols, and from blood, and from what has been strangled, and from sexual immorality. If you keep yourselves from these, you will do well. Farewell."

[30] So when they were sent off, they went down to Antioch, and having gathered the congregation together, they delivered the letter. [31] And when they had read it, they rejoiced because of its encouragement. [32] And Judas and Silas, who were themselves prophets, encouraged the brothers with many words. [33] And after they had spent some time, they were sent off in peace by the brothers to those who had sent them.[3] [35] But Paul and Barnabas remained in Antioch, teaching and preaching the word of the Lord, with many others also.

Paul and Barnabas Separate

[36] And after some days Paul said to Barnabas, "Let us return and visit the brothers in every city where we proclaimed the word of the Lord, and see how they are." [37] Now Barnabas wanted to take with them John called Mark. [38] But Paul thought best not to take with them one who had withdrawn from them in Pamphylia and had not gone with them to the work. [39] And there arose a sharp disagreement, so that they separated from each other. Barnabas took Mark with him and sailed away to Cyprus, [40] but Paul chose Silas and

departed, having been commended by the brothers to the grace of the Lord. [41] And he went through Syria and Cilicia, strengthening the churches.

Timothy Joins Paul and Silas

16 Paul[4] came also to Derbe and to Lystra. A disciple was there, named Timothy, the son of a Jewish woman who was a believer, but his father was a Greek. [2] He was well spoken of by the brothers[5] at Lystra and Iconium. [3] Paul wanted Timothy to accompany him, and he took him and circumcised him because of the Jews who were in those places, for they all knew that his father was a Greek. [4] As they went on their way through the cities, they delivered to them for observance the decisions that had been reached by the apostles and elders who were in Jerusalem. [5] So the churches were strengthened in the faith, and they increased in numbers daily.

The Macedonian Call

[6] And they went through the region of Phrygia and Galatia, having been forbidden by the Holy Spirit to speak the word in Asia. [7] And when they had come up to Mysia, they attempted to go into Bithynia, but the Spirit of Jesus did not allow them. [8] So, passing by Mysia, they went down to Troas. [9] And a vision appeared to Paul in the night: a man of Macedonia was standing there, urging him and saying, "Come over to Macedonia and help us." [10] And when Paul[6] had seen the vision, immediately we sought to go on into Macedonia, concluding that God had called us to preach the gospel to them.

The Conversion of Lydia

[11] So, setting sail from Troas, we made a direct voyage to Samothrace, and the following day to Neapolis, [12] and from there to Philippi, which is a leading city of the[7] district of Macedonia and a Roman colony. We remained in this city some days. [13] And on the Sabbath day we went outside the gate to the riverside, where we supposed there was a place of prayer, and we sat down and spoke to the women who had come together. [14] One who heard us was a woman named Lydia, from the city of Thyatira, a seller of purple goods, who was

[1] Or brothers and sisters; also verses 32, 33, 36 [2] Some manuscripts some persons from us have troubled you [3] Some manuscripts insert verse 34: But it seemed good to Silas to remain there [4] Greek He [5] Or brothers and sisters; also verse 40 [6] Greek he [7] Or that

Lydia

Read this God Girl story in Acts 16:13–15, 40.

Contribute to the needs of the saints and seek to show hospitality.

Romans 12:13

Hospitality isn't just good etiquette; it's a command. It is faith in action because it takes the Word of God and makes it real in the lives of people in need. When you are hospitable, you put the needs of others above your own. Instead of worrying about what they will think of your messy life, you invite them in and love them, accept them, and give them rest. Your life doesn't have to be perfect in order to be hospitable. You don't have to prove that you've got it all together before you can help others get it together. The only thing hospitality needs is a willing and loving heart. The God Girl by her very nature will be hospitable because she knows how hospitable God, in Christ, has been to her! So she loves to reach out to others. You see this kind of reaching out and helping in the life of Lydia, who insisted on taking care of Paul and Silas by welcoming them into her home (see Acts 16:15).

Hospitality pulls others to you. As you make them comfortable, you give them the gift of acceptance. Hospitality is taking practical needs and finding a way to fill them. It's saying hi to strangers and making them feel at home. It's inviting someone you barely know over for dinner. It's finding out what people around you need and meeting those needs even though they've never met a need for you. Hospitality isn't about friends and loved ones but about strangers and the unlovable. It requires you to step outside of yourself and decide that even though you might get nothing out of it, you're going to serve others in the name of Jesus.

The most hospitable girls aren't those who have many friends, but those who don't think of anyone as a stranger. When your life is more about giving than about getting, then you have learned the secret of hospitality. As you look at the life of Lydia, see how she used the gifts God gave her to make the lives of those around her better by opening her home and her heart to them.

a worshiper of God. The Lord opened her heart to pay attention to what was said by Paul. [15] And after she was baptized, and her household as well, she urged us, saying, "If you have judged me to be faithful to the Lord, come to my house and stay." And she prevailed upon us.

Paul and Silas in Prison

[16] As we were going to the place of prayer, we were met by a slave girl who had a spirit of divination and brought her owners much gain by fortune-telling. [17] She followed Paul and us, crying out, "These men are servants[1] of the Most High God, who proclaim to you the way of salvation." [18] And this she kept doing for many days. Paul, having become greatly annoyed, turned and said to the spirit, "I command you in the name of Jesus Christ to come out of her." And it came out that very hour.

[19] But when her owners saw that their hope of gain was gone, they seized Paul and Silas and dragged them into the marketplace before the rulers. [20] And when they had brought them to the magistrates, they said, "These men are Jews, and they are disturbing our city. [21] They advocate customs that are not lawful for us as Romans to accept or practice." [22] The crowd joined in attacking them, and the magistrates tore the garments off them and gave orders to beat them with rods. [23] And when they had inflicted many blows upon them, they threw them into prison, ordering the jailer to keep them safely. [24] Having received this order, he put them into the inner prison and fastened their feet in the stocks.

The Philippian Jailer Converted

[25] About midnight Paul and Silas were praying and singing hymns to God, and the prisoners were listening to them, [26] and suddenly there was a great earthquake, so that the foundations of the prison were shaken. And immediately all the doors were opened, and everyone's bonds were unfastened. [27] When the jailer woke and saw that the prison doors were open, he drew his sword and was about to kill himself, supposing that the prisoners had escaped. [28] But Paul cried with a loud voice, "Do not harm yourself, for we are all here." [29] And the jailer[2] called for

lights and rushed in, and trembling with fear he fell down before Paul and Silas. [30] Then he brought them out and said, "Sirs, what must I do to be saved?" [31] And they said, "Believe in the Lord Jesus, and you will be saved, you and your household." [32] And they spoke the word of the Lord to him and to all who were in his house. [33] And he took them the same hour of the night and washed their wounds; and he was baptized at once, he and all his family. [34] Then he brought them up into his house and set food before them. And he rejoiced along with his entire household that he had believed in God.

[35] But when it was day, the magistrates sent the police, saying, "Let those men go." [36] And the jailer reported these words to Paul, saying, "The magistrates have sent to let you go. Therefore come out now and go in peace." [37] But Paul said to them, "They have beaten us publicly, uncondemned, men who are Roman citizens, and have thrown us into prison; and do they now throw us out secretly? No! Let them come themselves and take us out." [38] The police reported these words to the magistrates, and they were afraid when they heard that they were Roman citizens. [39] So they came and apologized to them. And they took them out and asked them to leave the city. [40] So they went out of the prison and visited Lydia. And when they had seen the brothers, they encouraged them and departed.

Paul and Silas in Thessalonica

17 Now when they had passed through Amphipolis and Apollonia, they came to Thessalonica, where there was a synagogue of the Jews. [2] And Paul went in, as was his custom, and on three Sabbath days he reasoned with them from the Scriptures, [3] explaining and proving that it was necessary for the Christ to suffer and to rise from the dead, and saying, "This Jesus, whom I proclaim to you, is the Christ." [4] And some of them were persuaded and joined Paul and Silas, as did a great many of the devout Greeks and not a few of the leading women. [5] But the Jews[3] were jealous, and taking some wicked men of the rabble, they formed a mob, set the city in an uproar, and attacked the house of Jason, seeking to bring them out

[1] Greek bondservants [2] Greek he [3] Greek Ioudaioi probably refers here to Jewish religious leaders, and others under their influence, in that time; also verse 13

to the crowd. [6] And when they could not find them, they dragged Jason and some of the brothers before the city authorities, shouting, "These men who have turned the world upside down have come here also, [7] and Jason has received them, and they are all acting against the decrees of Caesar, saying that there is another king, Jesus." [8] And the people and the city authorities were disturbed when they heard these things. [9] And when they had taken money as security from Jason and the rest, they let them go.

Paul and Silas in Berea

[10] The brothers[1] immediately sent Paul and Silas away by night to Berea, and when they arrived they went into the Jewish synagogue. [11] Now these Jews were more noble than those in Thessalonica; they received the word with all eagerness, examining the Scriptures daily to see if these things were so. [12] Many of them therefore believed, with not a few Greek women of high standing as well as men. [13] But when the Jews from Thessalonica learned that the word of God was proclaimed by Paul at Berea also, they came there too, agitating and stirring up the crowds. [14] Then the brothers immediately sent Paul off on his way to the sea, but Silas and Timothy remained there. [15] Those who conducted Paul brought him as far as Athens, and after receiving a command for Silas and Timothy to come to him as soon as possible, they departed.

Paul in Athens

[16] Now while Paul was waiting for them at Athens, his spirit was provoked within him as he saw that the city was full of idols. [17] So he reasoned in the synagogue with the Jews and the devout persons, and in the marketplace every day with those who happened to be there. [18] Some of the Epicurean and Stoic philosophers also conversed with him. And some said, "What does this babbler wish to say?" Others said, "He seems to be a preacher of foreign divinities"—because he was preaching Jesus and the resurrection. [19] And they took him and brought him to the Areopagus, saying, "May we know what this new teaching is that you are presenting? [20] For you bring some strange things to our ears. We wish

to know therefore what these things mean." [21] Now all the Athenians and the foreigners who lived there would spend their time in nothing except telling or hearing something new.

Paul Addresses the Areopagus

[22] So Paul, standing in the midst of the Areopagus, said: "Men of Athens, I perceive that in every way you are very religious. [23] For as I passed along and observed the objects of your worship, I found also an altar with this inscription, 'To the unknown god.' What therefore you worship as unknown, this I proclaim to you. [24] The God who made the world and everything in it, being Lord of heaven and earth, does not live in temples made by man,[2] [25] nor is he served by human hands, as though he needed anything, since he himself gives to all mankind life and breath and everything. [26] And he made from one man every nation of mankind to live on all the face of the earth, having determined allotted periods and the boundaries of their dwelling place, [27] that they should seek God, and perhaps feel their way toward him and find him. Yet he is actually not far from each one of us, [28] for

"'In him we live and move and have our being';[3]

as even some of your own poets have said,

"'For we are indeed his offspring.'[4]

[29] Being then God's offspring, we ought not to think that the divine being is like gold or silver or stone, an image formed by the art and imagination of man. [30] The times of ignorance God overlooked, but now he commands all people everywhere to repent, [31] because he has fixed a day on which he will judge the world in righteousness by a man whom he has appointed; and of this he has given assurance to all by raising him from the dead."

[32] Now when they heard of the resurrection of the dead, some mocked. But others said, "We will hear you again about this." [33] So Paul went out from their midst. [34] But some men joined him and believed, among whom also were Dionysius the Areopagite and a woman named Damaris and others with them.

---

[1] Or brothers and sisters; also verse 14 [2] Greek made by hands [3] Probably from Epimenides of Crete [4] From Aratus's poem "Phainomena"

Paul in Corinth

18 After this Paul[1] left Athens and went to Corinth. [2] And he found a Jew named Aquila, a native of Pontus, recently come from Italy with his wife Priscilla, because Claudius had commanded all the Jews to leave Rome. And he went to see them, [3] and because he was of the same trade he stayed with them and worked, for they were tentmakers by trade. [4] And he reasoned in the synagogue every Sabbath, and tried to persuade Jews and Greeks.

[5] When Silas and Timothy arrived from Macedonia, Paul was occupied with the word, testifying to the Jews that the Christ was Jesus. [6] And when they opposed and reviled him, he shook out his garments and said to them, "Your blood be on your own heads! I am innocent. From now on I will go to the Gentiles." [7] And he left there and went to the house of a man named Titius Justus, a worshiper of God. His house was next door to the synagogue. [8] Crispus, the ruler of the synagogue, believed in the Lord, together with his entire household. And many of the Corinthians hearing Paul believed and were baptized. [9] And the Lord said to Paul one night in a vision, "Do not be afraid, but go on speaking and do not be silent, [10] for I am with you, and no one will attack you to harm you, for I have many in this city who are my people." [11] And he stayed a year and six months, teaching the word of God among them.

[12] But when Gallio was proconsul of Achaia, the Jews[2] made a united attack on Paul and brought him before the tribunal, [13] saying, "This man is persuading people to worship God contrary to the law." [14] But when Paul was about to open his mouth, Gallio said to the Jews, "If it were a matter of wrongdoing or vicious crime, O Jews, I would have reason to accept your complaint. [15] But since it is a matter of questions about words and names and your own law, see to it yourselves. I refuse to be a judge of these things." [16] And he drove them from the tribunal. [17] And they all seized Sosthenes, the ruler of the synagogue, and beat him in front of the tribunal. But Gallio paid no attention to any of this.

Paul Returns to Antioch

[18] After this, Paul stayed many days longer and then took leave of the brothers[3] and set sail for Syria, and with him Priscilla and Aquila. At Cenchreae he had cut his hair, for he was under a vow. [19] And they came to Ephesus, and he left them there, but he himself went into the synagogue and reasoned with the Jews. [20] When they asked him to stay for a longer period, he declined. [21] But on taking leave of them he said, "I will return to you if God wills," and he set sail from Ephesus.

[22] When he had landed at Caesarea, he went up and greeted the church, and then went down to Antioch. [23] After spending some time there, he departed and went from one place to the next through the region of Galatia and Phrygia, strengthening all the disciples.

Apollos Speaks Boldly in Ephesus

[24] Now a Jew named Apollos, a native of Alexandria, came to Ephesus. He was an eloquent man, competent in the Scriptures. [25] He had been instructed in the way of the Lord. And being fervent in spirit,[4] he spoke and taught accurately the things concerning Jesus, though he knew only the baptism of John. [26] He began to speak boldly in the synagogue, but when Priscilla and Aquila heard him, they took him aside and explained to him the way of God more accurately. [27] And when he wished to cross to Achaia, the brothers encouraged him and wrote to the disciples to welcome him. When he arrived, he greatly helped those who through grace had believed, [28] for he powerfully refuted the Jews in public, showing by the Scriptures that the Christ was Jesus.

Paul in Ephesus

19 And it happened that while Apollos was at Corinth, Paul passed through the inland[5] country and came to Ephesus. There he found some disciples. [2] And he said to them, "Did you receive the Holy Spirit when you believed?" And they said, "No, we have not even heard that there is a Holy Spirit." [3] And he said, "Into what then were you baptized?" They said, "Into John's baptism." [4] And Paul said, "John baptized with the baptism of repentance,

---

[1] Greek *he* [2] Greek *Ioudaioi* probably refers here to Jewish religious leaders, and others under their influence, in that time; also verses 14 (twice), 28 [3] Or *brothers and sisters*; also verse 27 [4] Or *in the Spirit* [5] Greek *upper* (that is, highland)

Priscilla

Read this God Girl story in Acts 18:1-3, 18-19, 24-26; Romans 16:3-4; 1 Corinthians 16:19; and 2 Timothy 4:19.

> Preach the word; be ready in season and out of season; reprove, rebuke, and exhort, with complete patience and teaching.
>
> 2 Timothy 4:2

Spiritual mistakes can't just be overlooked. A lot of times you hear friends, family members, and even teachers speak spiritual lies, or you see sin in their lives—but instead of making a scene, you keep your mouth shut to keep the peace. While it's important to be quick to listen and slow to speak (see James 1:19), it's also important not to make a habit of ignoring sin just to keep everyone happy. If you fail to say anything just to be accepted or to be "nice," then your motives are selfish and not holy. Deciding when to talk about sin should be based not on how you feel but on how God feels about sin.

No one has God's approval; we all have turned away and failed God on numerous occasions (see Rom. 3:10-12). But you would not be a true friend if you allowed someone you knew to continue living a lie while believing or preaching that they were living the truth. Occasional sin is different from habitual sin or gross error. In the life of Priscilla we see a godly woman, a leader in the church, who instead of keeping the peace at all costs chose to confront a teacher about the mistakes he was making, with the hope of helping him become a better teacher (see Acts 18:24-26). But look how she went about it: she and Aquila, her husband, took the guy to their home, out of the public eye. They didn't rail at him in front of others. They didn't make a scene, but discreetly took him aside to show him what he was missing.

As a God Girl you too can and should love others enough to risk making them mad or hurting your relationship with them by helping them in matters of spiritual growth. When you do it in love and humility, your efforts will be appreciated. Trust God enough to follow the example of Priscilla, and you too will be helping God's people grow in truth.

telling the people to believe in the one who was to come after him, that is, Jesus." ⁵On hearing this, they were baptized in¹ the name of the Lord Jesus. ⁶And when Paul had laid his hands on them, the Holy Spirit came on them, and they began speaking in tongues and prophesying. ⁷There were about twelve men in all.

⁸And he entered the synagogue and for three months spoke boldly, reasoning and persuading them about the kingdom of God. ⁹But when some became stubborn and continued in unbelief, speaking evil of the Way before the congregation, he withdrew from them and took the disciples with him, reasoning daily in the hall of Tyrannus.² ¹⁰This continued for two years, so that all the residents of Asia heard the word of the Lord, both Jews and Greeks.

The Sons of Sceva

¹¹And God was doing extraordinary miracles by the hands of Paul, ¹²so that even handkerchiefs or aprons that had touched his skin were carried away to the sick, and their diseases left them and the evil spirits came out of them. ¹³Then some of the itinerant Jewish exorcists undertook to invoke the name of the Lord Jesus over those who had evil spirits, saying, "I adjure you by the Jesus whom Paul proclaims." ¹⁴Seven sons of a Jewish high priest named Sceva were doing this. ¹⁵But the evil spirit answered them, "Jesus I know, and Paul I recognize, but who are you?" ¹⁶And the man in whom was the evil spirit leaped on them, mastered all³ of them and overpowered them, so that they fled out of that house naked and wounded. ¹⁷And this became known to all the residents of Ephesus, both Jews and Greeks. And fear fell upon them all, and the name of the Lord Jesus was extolled. ¹⁸Also many of those who were now believers came, confessing and divulging their practices. ¹⁹And a number of those who had practiced magic arts brought their books together and burned them in the sight of all. And they counted the value of them and found it came to fifty thousand pieces of silver. ²⁰So the word of the Lord continued to increase and prevail mightily.

A Riot at Ephesus

²¹Now after these events Paul resolved in the Spirit to pass through Macedonia and Achaia and go to Jerusalem, saying "After I have been there, I must also see Rome." ²²And having sent into Macedonia two of his helpers, Timothy and Erastus, he himself stayed in Asia for a while.

²³About that time there arose no little disturbance concerning the Way. ²⁴For a man named Demetrius, a silversmith, who made silver shrines of Artemis, brought no little business to the craftsmen. ²⁵These he gathered together, with the workmen in similar trades, and said, "Men, you know that from this business we have our wealth. ²⁶And you see and hear that not only in Ephesus but in almost all of Asia this Paul has persuaded and turned away a great many people, saying that gods made with hands are not gods. ²⁷And there is danger not only that this trade of ours may come into disrepute but also that the temple of the great goddess Artemis may be counted as nothing, and that she may even be deposed from her magnificence, she whom all Asia and the world worship."

²⁸When they heard this they were enraged and were crying out, "Great is Artemis of the Ephesians!" ²⁹So the city was filled with the confusion, and they rushed together into the theater, dragging with them Gaius and Aristarchus, Macedonians who were Paul's companions in travel. ³⁰But when Paul wished to go in among the crowd, the disciples would not let him. ³¹And even some of the Asiarchs,⁴ who were friends of his, sent to him and were urging him not to venture into the theater. ³²Now some cried out one thing, some another, for the assembly was in confusion, and most of them did not know why they had come together. ³³Some of the crowd prompted Alexander, whom the Jews had put forward. And Alexander, motioning with his hand, wanted to make a defense to the crowd. ³⁴But when they recognized that he was a Jew, for about two hours they all cried out with one voice, "Great is Artemis of the Ephesians!"

³⁵And when the town clerk had quieted the crowd, he said, "Men of Ephesus, who is there who does not know that the city of the Ephesians is temple keeper of the

¹Or into ²Some manuscripts add from the fifth hour to the tenth (that is, from 11 A.M. to 4 P.M.) ³Or both ⁴That is, high-ranking officers of the province of Asia

great Artemis, and of the sacred stone that fell from the sky?[1] ³⁶ Seeing then that these things cannot be denied, you ought to be quiet and do nothing rash. ³⁷ For you have brought these men here who are neither sacrilegious nor blasphemers of our goddess. ³⁸ If therefore Demetrius and the craftsmen with him have a complaint against anyone, the courts are open, and there are proconsuls. Let them bring charges against one another. ³⁹ But if you seek anything further,[2] it shall be settled in the regular assembly. ⁴⁰ For we really are in danger of being charged with rioting today, since there is no cause that we can give to justify this commotion." ⁴¹ And when he had said these things, he dismissed the assembly.

Paul in Macedonia and Greece

20 After the uproar ceased, Paul sent for the disciples, and after encouraging them, he said farewell and departed for Macedonia. ² When he had gone through those regions and had given them much encouragement, he came to Greece. ³ There he spent three months, and when a plot was made against him by the Jews[3] as he was about to set sail for Syria, he decided to return through Macedonia. ⁴ Sopater the Berean, son of Pyrrhus, accompanied him; and of the Thessalonians, Aristarchus and Secundus; and Gaius of Derbe, and Timothy; and the Asians, Tychicus and Trophimus. ⁵ These went on ahead and were waiting for us at Troas, ⁶ but we sailed away from Philippi after the days of Unleavened Bread, and in five days we came to them at Troas, where we stayed for seven days.

Eutychus Raised from the Dead

⁷ On the first day of the week, when we were gathered together to break bread, Paul talked with them, intending to depart on the next day, and he prolonged his speech until midnight. ⁸ There were many lamps in the upper room where we were gathered. ⁹ And a young man named Eutychus, sitting at the window, sank into a deep sleep as Paul talked still longer. And being overcome by sleep, he fell down from the third story and was taken up dead. ¹⁰ But Paul went down and bent over him,

and taking him in his arms, said, "Do not be alarmed, for his life is in him." ¹¹ And when Paul had gone up and had broken bread and eaten, he conversed with them a long while, until daybreak, and so departed. ¹² And they took the youth away alive, and were not a little comforted.

¹³ But going ahead to the ship, we set sail for Assos, intending to take Paul aboard there, for so he had arranged, intending himself to go by land. ¹⁴ And when he met us at Assos, we took him on board and went to Mitylene. ¹⁵ And sailing from there we came the following day opposite Chios; the next day we touched at Samos; and[4] the day after that we went to Miletus. ¹⁶ For Paul had decided to sail past Ephesus, so that he might not have to spend time in Asia, for he was hastening to be at Jerusalem, if possible, on the day of Pentecost.

Paul Speaks to the Ephesian Elders

¹⁷ Now from Miletus he sent to Ephesus and called the elders of the church to come to him. ¹⁸ And when they came to him, he said to them:

"You yourselves know how I lived among you the whole time from the first day that I set foot in Asia, ¹⁹ serving the Lord with all humility and with tears and with trials that happened to me through the plots of the Jews; ²⁰ how I did not shrink from declaring to you anything that was profitable, and teaching you in public and from house to house, ²¹ testifying both to Jews and to Greeks of repentance toward God and of faith in our Lord Jesus Christ. ²² And now, behold, I am going to Jerusalem, constrained by[5] the Spirit, not knowing what will happen to me there, ²³ except that the Holy Spirit testifies to me in every city that imprisonment and afflictions await me. ²⁴ But I do not account my life of any value nor as precious to myself, if only I may finish my course and the ministry that I received from the Lord Jesus, to testify to the gospel of the grace of God. ²⁵ And now, behold, I know that none of you among whom I have gone about proclaiming the kingdom will see my face again. ²⁶ Therefore I testify to you this day that I am innocent of the blood of all, ²⁷ for I did

---

[1] The meaning of the Greek is uncertain [2] Some manuscripts *seek about other matters* [3] Greek *Ioudaioi* probably refers here to Jewish religious leaders, and others under their influence, in that time; also verse 19 [4] Some manuscripts add *after remaining at Trogyllium* [5] Or *bound in*

not shrink from declaring to you the whole counsel of God. ²⁸ Pay careful attention to yourselves and to all the flock, in which the Holy Spirit has made you overseers, to care for the church of God,[1] which he obtained with his own blood.[2] ²⁹ I know that after my departure fierce wolves will come in among you, not sparing the flock; ³⁰ and from among your own selves will arise men speaking twisted things, to draw away the disciples after them. ³¹ Therefore be alert, remembering that for three years I did not cease night or day to admonish every one with tears. ³² And now I commend you to God and to the word of his grace, which is able to build you up and to give you the inheritance among all those who are sanctified. ³³ I coveted no one's silver or gold or apparel. ³⁴ You yourselves know that these hands ministered to my necessities and to those who were with me. ³⁵ In all things I have shown you that

by working hard in this way we must help the weak and remember the words of the Lord Jesus, how he himself said, 'It is more blessed to give than to receive.'"

³⁶ And when he had said these things he knelt down and prayed with them all. ³⁷ And there was much weeping on the part of all; they embraced Paul and kissed him ³⁸ being sorrowful most of all because of the word he had spoken, that they would not see his face again. And they accompanied him to the ship.

Paul Goes to Jerusalem

21 And when we had parted from them and set sail, we came by a straight course to Cos, and the next day to Rhodes and from there to Patara.[3] ² And having found a ship crossing to Phoenicia, we went aboard and set sail. ³ When we had come in sight of Cyprus, leaving it on the left we sailed to Syria and landed at Tyre

[1] Some manuscripts *of the Lord* [2] Or *with the blood of his Own* [3] Some manuscripts add *and Myra*

Know Yourself

verses to read
Acts 20:17–24

When life starts spinning out of control, when you feel like you can't go on, and when nothing is going your way, there is something you can do: remember the bottom line. Review the facts—just the facts are all you need. Answer these questions:

1. Is God who he says he is?
2. Does he love you or not?
3. Is his will good or bad?
4. Does anything happen to you without his allowing it?
5. Does he truly work everything together for the good of the people who love him?
6. Do you want God's will or your own?

If you can honestly answer these questions, then you can get over any trauma in your life and get to the truth of the matter. After all, your feelings are just your simple interpretation of a situation, a lot of times without considering the facts of the matter. When you panic about life, you miss out on the bottom line—the truth about God and his role in your life. For a true believer, life is never spinning out of control and never near disaster. It is always built on the Rock and safe under his wings. When you allow your emotions to become your sacred truth, you lose all hope, and worry sets in. If you want to be free from fear and angst, you have to remember the facts. When you can look at your life through the reality of God's love for you in Christ, then you will find a whole new life full of peace and calm.

or there the ship was to unload its cargo. And having sought out the disciples, we tayed there for seven days. And through he Spirit they were telling Paul not to go n to Jerusalem. [5] When our days there vere ended, we departed and went on ur journey, and they all, with wives and hildren, accompanied us until we were utside the city. And kneeling down on the each, we prayed [6] and said farewell to one nother. Then we went on board the ship, nd they returned home.

[7] When we had finished the voyage rom Tyre, we arrived at Ptolemais, and ve greeted the brothers[1] and stayed with hem for one day. [8] On the next day we leparted and came to Caesarea, and we ntered the house of Philip the evangelist, vho was one of the seven, and stayed with im. [9] He had four unmarried daughters, vho prophesied. [10] While we were staying or many days, a prophet named Agabus ame down from Judea. [11] And coming o us, he took Paul's belt and bound his wn feet and hands and said, "Thus says he Holy Spirit, 'This is how the Jews[2] at erusalem will bind the man who owns his belt and deliver him into the hands of he Gentiles.'" [12] When we heard this, we nd the people there urged him not to go p to Jerusalem. [13] Then Paul answered, What are you doing, weeping and break-ng my heart? For I am ready not only to be mprisoned but even to die in Jerusalem for he name of the Lord Jesus." [14] And since e would not be persuaded, we ceased nd said, "Let the will of the Lord be done."

[15] After these days we got ready and went p to Jerusalem. [16] And some of the disci-ples from Caesarea went with us, bringing s to the house of Mnason of Cyprus, an early disciple, with whom we should lodge.

Paul Visits James

[17] When we had come to Jerusalem, the prothers received us gladly. [18] On the fol-owing day Paul went in with us to James, nd all the elders were present. [19] After greeting them, he related one by one he things that God had done among the Gentiles through his ministry. [20] And when hey heard it, they glorified God. And they said to him, "You see, brother, how many thousands there are among the Jews of those who have believed. They are all zeal-ous for the law, [21] and they have been told about you that you teach all the Jews who are among the Gentiles to forsake Moses, telling them not to circumcise their chil-dren or walk according to our customs. [22] What then is to be done? They will certainly hear that you have come. [23] Do therefore what we tell you. We have four men who are under a vow; [24] take these men and purify yourself along with them and pay their expenses, so that they may shave their heads. Thus all will know that there is nothing in what they have been told about you, but that you yourself also live in observance of the law. [25] But as for the Gentiles who have believed, we have sent a letter with our judgment that they should abstain from what has been sacri-ficed to idols, and from blood, and from what has been strangled,[3] and from sexual immorality." [26] Then Paul took the men, and the next day he purified himself along with them and went into the temple, giving notice when the days of purification would be fulfilled and the offering presented for each one of them.

Paul Arrested in the Temple

[27] When the seven days were almost completed, the Jews from Asia, seeing him in the temple, stirred up the whole crowd and laid hands on him, [28] crying out, "Men of Israel, help! This is the man who is teaching everyone everywhere against the people and the law and this place. Moreover, he even brought Greeks into the temple and has defiled this holy place." [29] For they had previously seen Trophimus the Ephesian with him in the city, and they supposed that Paul had brought him into the temple. [30] Then all the city was stirred up, and the people ran together. They seized Paul and dragged him out of the temple, and at once the gates were shut. [31] And as they were seeking to kill him, word came to the tribune of the cohort that all Jerusalem was in confusion. [32] He at once took soldiers and centurions and ran down to them. And when they saw the tribune and the soldiers, they stopped beating Paul. [33] Then the tribune came up and arrested him and ordered him to be bound with two chains. He inquired who

Or brothers and sisters; also verse 17 [2] Greek Ioudaioi probably refers here to Jewish religious leaders, and others under their influence, n that time [3] Some manuscripts omit and from what has been strangled he was and what he had done. ³⁴ Some in the crowd were shouting one thing, some another. And as he could not learn the facts because of the uproar, he ordered him to be brought into the barracks. ³⁵ And when he came to the steps, he was actually carried by the soldiers because of the violence of the crowd, ³⁶ for the mob of the people followed, crying out, "Away with him!"

Paul Speaks to the People

³⁷ As Paul was about to be brought into the barracks, he said to the tribune, "May I say something to you?" And he said, "Do you know Greek? ³⁸ Are you not the Egyptian, then, who recently stirred up a revolt and led the four thousand men of the Assassins out into the wilderness?" ³⁹ Paul replied, "I am a Jew, from Tarsus in Cilicia, a citizen of no obscure city. I beg you, permit me to speak to the people." ⁴⁰ And when he had given him permission, Paul, standing on the steps, motioned with his hand to the people. And when there was a great

hush, he addressed them in the Hebrew language,[1] saying:

22 "Brothers and fathers, hear the defense that I now make before you."

² And when they heard that he was addressing them in the Hebrew language, they became even more quiet. And he said:

³ "I am a Jew, born in Tarsus in Cilicia, but brought up in this city, educated at the feet of Gamaliel[3] according to the strict manner of the law of our fathers, being zealous for God as all of you are this day. ⁴ I persecuted this Way to the death, binding and delivering to prison both men and women, ⁵ as the high priest and the whole council of elders can bear me witness. From them I received letters to the brothers, and I journeyed toward Damascus to take those also who were there and bring them in bonds to Jerusalem to be punished.

⁶ "As I was on my way and drew near to Damascus, about noon a great light from heaven suddenly shone around me. ⁷ And I fell to the ground and heard a voice saying

[1] Or the Hebrew dialect (probably Aramaic) [2] Or the Hebrew dialect (probably Aramaic) [3] Or city at the feet of Gamaliel, educated

Know God

verses to read
Acts 22:1–21

There is nothing you can do that can't be forgiven except to deny that God is God. If you have made him Lord of your life, then you have forgiveness for all of your stuff. All of it! There is no dark corner, no seedy past, no horrible mistake that can't be wiped clean. If God could forgive Paul, who had persecuted Christians, and turn him into a holy man who wrote much of the New Testament, then surely your sin isn't too awful to be forgiven as well.

If you think your sin is too huge for the blood of Christ to cover, then you're saying that Christ died for nothing. But you know that isn't true. His death was sufficient to bring forgiveness to anyone who wants it, including you. You are not the most loathsome creature to ask for forgiveness. You are not a special case; you are a *human* case. And we are all the same: dirty, rotten sinners in need of salvation. Just agree with God that your sin was evil against him, then look to Christ, and every part of your past will be forgiven and cleansed. That means you don't have to hold on to it any longer. You don't have to worry about it, regret it, or wonder about it. It's gone—"as far as the east is from the west" (Ps. 103:12).

Once you accept God's forgiveness, you will be made new. Your life can be redeemed to change the world, just as Paul's was. By the powerful working of the Spirit, you can be freed from your old, empty way of life and set on a new path toward becoming a woman of God.

o me, 'Saul, Saul, why are you persecuting ne?' ⁸And I answered, 'Who are you, Lord?' ₁nd he said to me, 'I am Jesus of Nazareth, vhom you are persecuting.' ⁹Now those vho were with me saw the light but did ₁ot understand¹ the voice of the one who vas speaking to me. ¹⁰And I said, 'What ₃hall I do, Lord?' And the Lord said to me, Rise, and go into Damascus, and there you vill be told all that is appointed for you to ₃o.' ¹¹And since I could not see because of ₃he brightness of that light, I was led by ₃he hand by those who were with me, and ₃ame into Damascus.

¹²"And one Ananias, a devout man ₐccording to the law, well spoken of by all ₃he Jews who lived there, ¹³came to me, and ₃tanding by me said to me, 'Brother Saul, ₃eceive your sight.' And at that very hour ₃ received my sight and saw him. ¹⁴And he ₃aid, 'The God of our fathers appointed you ₃o know his will, to see the Righteous One ₐnd to hear a voice from his mouth; ¹⁵for ₃ou will be a witness for him to everyone of vhat you have seen and heard. ¹⁶And now vhy do you wait? Rise and be baptized and vash away your sins, calling on his name.'

¹⁷"When I had returned to Jerusalem ₐnd was praying in the temple, I fell into a ₃rance ¹⁸and saw him saying to me, 'Make ₃aste and get out of Jerusalem quickly, ₃ecause they will not accept your testi-₃ony about me.' ¹⁹And I said, 'Lord, they ₃hemselves know that in one synagogue ₐfter another I imprisoned and beat those vho believed in you. ²⁰And when the blood ₃f Stephen your witness was being shed, ₃ myself was standing by and approving ₐnd watching over the garments of those vho killed him.' ²¹And he said to me, 'Go, ₃or I will send you far away to the Gentiles.'"

₃aul and the Roman Tribune

²²Up to this word they listened to him. ₃hen they raised their voices and said, ₃Away with such a fellow from the earth! ₃or he should not be allowed to live." ²³And ₃s they were shouting and throwing off ₃heir cloaks and flinging dust into the air, ²⁴the tribune ordered him to be brought ₃nto the barracks, saying that he should ₃e examined by flogging, to find out why ₃hey were shouting against him like this. ²⁵But when they had stretched him out for ₃he whips,² Paul said to the centurion who

was standing by, "Is it lawful for you to flog a man who is a Roman citizen and uncondemned?" ²⁶When the centurion heard this, he went to the tribune and said to him, "What are you about to do? For this man is a Roman citizen." ²⁷So the tribune came and said to him, "Tell me, are you a Roman citizen?" And he said, "Yes." ²⁸The tribune answered, "I bought this citizenship for a large sum." Paul said, "But I am a citizen by birth." ²⁹So those who were about to examine him withdrew from him immediately, and the tribune also was afraid, for he realized that Paul was a Roman citizen and that he had bound him.

Paul Before the Council

³⁰But on the next day, desiring to know the real reason why he was being accused by the Jews, he unbound him and commanded the chief priests and all the council to meet, and he brought Paul down and set him before them.

23 And looking intently at the council, Paul said, "Brothers, I have lived my life before God in all good conscience up to this day." ²And the high priest Ananias commanded those who stood by him to strike him on the mouth. ³Then Paul said to him, "God is going to strike you, you whitewashed wall! Are you sitting to judge me according to the law, and yet contrary to the law you order me to be struck?" ⁴Those who stood by said, "Would you revile God's high priest?" ⁵And Paul said, "I did not know, brothers, that he was the high priest, for it is written, "'You shall not speak evil of a ruler of your people.'"

⁶Now when Paul perceived that one part were Sadducees and the other Pharisees, he cried out in the council, "Brothers, I am a Pharisee, a son of Pharisees. It is with respect to the hope and the resurrection of the dead that I am on trial." ⁷And when he had said this, a dissension arose between the Pharisees and the Sadducees, and the assembly was divided. ⁸For the Sadducees say that there is no resurrection, nor angel, nor spirit, but the Pharisees acknowledge them all. ⁹Then a great clamor arose, and some of the scribes of the Pharisees' party stood up and contended sharply, "We find nothing wrong in this man. What if a spirit or an angel spoke to him?" ¹⁰And when the dissension became violent, the tribune,

---

¹Or hear with understanding ²Or when they had tied him up with leather strips ᵃEx. 22:28

afraid that Paul would be torn to pieces by them, commanded the soldiers to go down and take him away from among them by force and bring him into the barracks.

[11] The following night the Lord stood by him and said, "Take courage, for as you have testified to the facts about me in Jerusalem, so you must testify also in Rome."

A Plot to Kill Paul

[12] When it was day, the Jews made a plot and bound themselves by an oath neither to eat nor drink till they had killed Paul. [13] There were more than forty who made this conspiracy. [14] They went to the chief priests and elders and said, "We have strictly bound ourselves by an oath to taste no food till we have killed Paul. [15] Now therefore you, along with the council, give notice to the tribune to bring him down to you, as though you were going to determine his case more exactly. And we are ready to kill him before he comes near."

[16] Now the son of Paul's sister heard of their ambush, so he went and entered the barracks and told Paul. [17] Paul called one of the centurions and said, "Take this young man to the tribune, for he has something to tell him." [18] So he took him and brought him to the tribune and said, "Paul the prisoner called me and asked me to bring this young man to you, as he has something to say to you." [19] The tribune took him by the hand, and going aside asked him privately, "What is it that you have to tell me?" [20] And he said, "The Jews have agreed to ask you to bring Paul down to the council tomorrow, as though they were going to inquire somewhat more closely about him. [21] But do not be persuaded by them, for more than forty of their men are lying in ambush for him, who have bound themselves by an oath neither to eat nor drink till they have killed him. And now they are ready, waiting for your consent." [22] So the tribune dismissed the young man, charging him, "Tell no one that you have informed me of these things."

Paul Sent to Felix the Governor

[23] Then he called two of the centurions and said, "Get ready two hundred soldiers, with seventy horsemen and two hundred spearmen to go as far as Caesarea at the third hour of the night.[1] [24] Also provide

mounts for Paul to ride and bring him safely to Felix the governor." [25] And he wrote a letter to this effect:

[26] "Claudius Lysias, to his Excellency the governor Felix, greetings. [27] This man was seized by the Jews and was about to be killed by them when I came upon them with the soldiers and rescued him, having learned that he was a Roman citizen. [28] And desiring to know the charge for which they were accusing him, I brought him down to their council. [29] I found that he was being accused about questions of their law, but charged with nothing deserving death or imprisonment. [30] And when it was disclosed to me that there would be a plot against the man, I sent him to you at once, ordering his accusers also to state before you what they have against him."

[31] So the soldiers, according to their instructions, took Paul and brought him by night to Antipatris. [32] And on the next day they returned to the barracks, letting the horsemen go on with him. [33] When they had come to Caesarea and delivered the letter to the governor, they presented Paul also before him. [34] On reading the letter, he asked what province he was from. And when he learned that he was from Cilicia, [35] he said, "I will give you a hearing when your accusers arrive." And he commanded him to be guarded in Herod's praetorium.

Paul Before Felix at Caesarea

24 And after five days the high priest Ananias came down with some elders and a spokesman, one Tertullus. They laid before the governor their case against Paul. [2] And when he had been summoned, Tertullus began to accuse him, saying:

"Since through you we enjoy much peace, and since by your foresight, most excellent Felix, reforms are being made for this nation, [3] in every way and everywhere we accept this with all gratitude. [4] But, to detain[2] you no further, I beg you in your kindness to hear us briefly. [5] For we have found this man a plague, one who stirs up riots among all the Jews throughout the world and is a ringleader of the sect of the Nazarenes. [6] He even tried to profane the temple, but we seized him.[3] [8] By examining him yourself you will be able to find

---

[1] That is, 9 P.M. [2] Or weary [3] Some manuscripts add and we would have judged him according to our law. [7] But the chief captain Lysias came and with great violence took him out of our hands, [8] commanding his accusers to come before you.

out from him about everything of which we accuse him."

⁹ The Jews also joined in the charge, affirming that all these things were so.

¹⁰ And when the governor had nodded to him to speak, Paul replied:

"Knowing that for many years you have been a judge over this nation, I cheerfully make my defense. ¹¹ You can verify that it is not more than twelve days since I went up to worship in Jerusalem, ¹² and they did not find me disputing with anyone or stirring up a crowd, either in the temple or in the synagogues or in the city. ¹³ Neither can they prove to you what they now bring up against me. ¹⁴ But this I confess to you, that according to the Way, which they call a sect, I worship the God of our fathers, believing everything laid down by the Law and written in the Prophets, ¹⁵ having a hope in God, which these men themselves accept, that there will be a resurrection of both the just and the unjust. ¹⁶ So I always take pains to have a clear conscience toward both God and man. ¹⁷ Now after several years I came to bring alms to my nation and to present offerings. ¹⁸ While I was doing this, they found me purified in the temple, without any crowd or tumult. But some Jews from Asia— ¹⁹ they ought to be here before you and to make an accusation, should they have anything against me. ²⁰ Or else let these men themselves say what wrongdoing they found when I stood before the council, ²¹ other than this one thing that I cried out while standing among them: 'It is with respect to the resurrection of the dead that I am on trial before you this day.'"

Paul Kept in Custody

²² But Felix, having a rather accurate knowledge of the Way, put them off, saying, "When Lysias the tribune comes down, I will decide your case." ²³ Then he gave orders to the centurion that he should be kept in custody but have some liberty, and that none of his friends should be prevented from attending to his needs.

²⁴ After some days Felix came with his wife Drusilla, who was Jewish, and he sent for Paul and heard him speak about faith in Christ Jesus. ²⁵ And as he reasoned about righteousness and self-control and the coming judgment, Felix was alarmed and said, "Go away for the present. When

I get an opportunity I will summon you." ²⁶ At the same time he hoped that money would be given him by Paul. So he sent for him often and conversed with him. ²⁷ When two years had elapsed, Felix was succeeded by Porcius Festus. And desiring to do the Jews a favor, Felix left Paul in prison.

Paul Appeals to Caesar

25 Now three days after Festus had arrived in the province, he went up to Jerusalem from Caesarea. ² And the chief priests and the principal men of the Jews laid out their case against Paul, and they urged him, ³ asking as a favor against Paul[1] that he summon him to Jerusalem— because they were planning an ambush to kill him on the way. ⁴ Festus replied that Paul was being kept at Caesarea and that he himself intended to go there shortly. ⁵ "So," said he, "let the men of authority among you go down with me, and if there is anything wrong about the man, let them bring charges against him."

⁶ After he stayed among them not more than eight or ten days, he went down to Caesarea. And the next day he took his seat on the tribunal and ordered Paul to be brought. ⁷ When he had arrived, the Jews who had come down from Jerusalem stood around him, bringing many and serious charges against him that they could not prove. ⁸ Paul argued in his defense, "Neither against the law of the Jews, nor against the temple, nor against Caesar have I committed any offense." ⁹ But Festus, wishing to do the Jews a favor, said to Paul, "Do you wish to go up to Jerusalem and there be tried on these charges before me?" ¹⁰ But Paul said, "I am standing before Caesar's tribunal, where I ought to be tried. To the Jews I have done no wrong, as you yourself know very well. ¹¹ If then I am a wrongdoer and have committed anything for which I deserve to die, I do not seek to escape death. But if there is nothing to their charges against me, no one can give me up to them. I appeal to Caesar." ¹² Then Festus, when he had conferred with his council, answered, "To Caesar you have appealed; to Caesar you shall go."

Paul Before Agrippa and Bernice

¹³ Now when some days had passed, Agrippa the king and Bernice arrived at

¹ Greek him

Caesarea and greeted Festus. [14] And as they stayed there many days, Festus laid Paul's case before the king, saying, "There is a man left prisoner by Felix, [15] and when I was at Jerusalem, the chief priests and the elders of the Jews laid out their case against him, asking for a sentence of condemnation against him. [16] I answered them that it was not the custom of the Romans to give up anyone before the accused met the accusers face to face and had opportunity to make his defense concerning the charge laid against him. [17] So when they came together here, I made no delay, but on the next day took my seat on the tribunal and ordered the man to be brought. [18] When the accusers stood up, they brought no charge in his case of such evils as I supposed. [19] Rather they had certain points of dispute with him about their own religion and about a certain Jesus, who was dead, but whom Paul asserted to be alive. [20] Being at a loss how to investigate these questions, I asked whether he wanted to go to Jerusalem and be tried there regarding them. [21] But when Paul had appealed to be kept in custody for the decision of the emperor, I ordered him to be held until I could send him to Caesar." [22] Then Agrippa said to Festus, "I would like to hear the man myself." "Tomorrow," said he, "you will hear him."

[23] So on the next day Agrippa and Bernice came with great pomp, and they entered the audience hall with the military tribunes and the prominent men of the city. Then, at the command of Festus, Paul was brought in. [24] And Festus said, "King Agrippa and all who are present with us, you see this man about whom the whole Jewish people petitioned me, both in Jerusalem and here, shouting that he ought not to live any longer. [25] But I found that he had done nothing deserving death. And as he himself appealed to the emperor, I decided to go ahead and send him. [26] But I have nothing definite to write to my lord about him. Therefore I have brought him before you all, and especially before you, King Agrippa, so that, after we have examined him, I may have something to write. [27] For it seems to me unreasonable, in sending a prisoner, not to indicate the charges against him."

Paul's Defense Before Agrippa

26 So Agrippa said to Paul, "You have permission to speak for yourself." Then Paul stretched out his hand and made his defense:

[2] "I consider myself fortunate that it is before you, King Agrippa, I am going to make my defense today against all the accusations of the Jews, [3] especially because you are familiar with all the customs and controversies of the Jews. Therefore I beg you to listen to me patiently.

[4] "My manner of life from my youth, spent from the beginning among my own nation and in Jerusalem, is known by all the Jews. [5] They have known for a long time, if they are willing to testify, that according to the strictest party of our religion I have lived as a Pharisee. [6] And now I stand here on trial because of my hope in the promise made by God to our fathers, [7] to which our twelve tribes hope to attain, as they earnestly worship night and day. And for this hope I am accused by Jews, O king! [8] Why is it thought incredible by any of you that God raises the dead?

[9] "I myself was convinced that I ought to do many things in opposing the name of Jesus of Nazareth. [10] And I did so in Jerusalem. I not only locked up many of the saints in prison after receiving authority from the chief priests, but when they were put to death I cast my vote against them. [11] And I punished them often in all the synagogues and tried to make them blaspheme, and in raging fury against them I persecuted them even to foreign cities.

Paul Tells of His Conversion

[12] "In this connection I journeyed to Damascus with the authority and commission of the chief priests. [13] At midday, O king, I saw on the way a light from heaven, brighter than the sun, that shone around me and those who journeyed with me. [14] And when we had all fallen to the ground, I heard a voice saying to me in the Hebrew language,[1] 'Saul, Saul, why are you persecuting me? It is hard for you to kick against the goads.' [15] And I said, 'Who are you, Lord?' And the Lord said, 'I am Jesus whom you are persecuting. [16] But rise and stand upon your feet, for I have appeared to you for this purpose, to appoint you as a servant and witness to the things in which

---

[1] Or *the Hebrew dialect* (probably Aramaic)

you have seen me and to those in which I will appear to you, **17** delivering you from your people and from the Gentiles—to whom I am sending you **18** to open their eyes, so that they may turn from darkness to light and from the power of Satan to God, that they may receive forgiveness of sins and a place among those who are sanctified by faith in me.'

19 "Therefore, O King Agrippa, I was not disobedient to the heavenly vision, **20** but declared first to those in Damascus, then in Jerusalem and throughout all the region of Judea, and also to the Gentiles, that they should repent and turn to God, performing deeds in keeping with their repentance. **21** For this reason the Jews seized me in the temple and tried to kill me. **22** To this day I have had the help that comes from God, and so I stand here testifying both to small and great, saying nothing but what the prophets and

Moses said would come to pass: **23** that the Christ must suffer and that, by being the first to rise from the dead, he would proclaim light both to our people and to the Gentiles."

24 And as he was saying these things in his defense, Festus said with a loud voice, "Paul, you are out of your mind; your great learning is driving you out of your mind." **25** But Paul said, "I am not out of my mind, most excellent Festus, but I am speaking true and rational words. **26** For the king knows about these things, and to him I speak boldly. For I am persuaded that none of these things has escaped his notice, for this has not been done in a corner. **27** King Agrippa, do you believe the prophets? I know that you believe." **28** And Agrippa said to Paul, "In a short time would you persuade me to be a Christian?"[1] **29** And Paul said, "Whether short or long, I would to God that not only you but also all who

[1] Or *In a short time you would persuade me to act like a Christian!*

Know How to Communicate

verses to read
Acts 26:9-23

What are you doing that proves your life has changed? When you were saved, you became a new person. But sometimes you still resort to your old ways of thinking, acting, talking, and even believing. But that won't do. You can't hang on to who you were. The old you with all of its selfish ways used to guide your life, but now you have been made new, so you are free to let go of your old nature and live out of your new nature.

As a God Girl you are growing, changing, and forever becoming the new and improved you. As you grow, you must continue to put to death the old and live out of who you now are (see Col. 3:5). Are you going to go back to your old ways, or will you keep moving toward a more holy way of life? To live like Christ, now that you are made new, is simply to be who you really are (see Gal. 2:20; Col. 3:1-3). Don't let the world tell you that compromise is okay because holiness is too hard. You are now free to act in accord with your new nature, not respond to your flaws by saying, "That's just who I am, so deal with it." No, that's not who you are; that's who you *were*. Now you are a new person—changing, growing, becoming a better girl and an amazing woman.

Look at the life of Paul. He was a violent person, persecuting the early followers of Christ (see Acts 26:11), but he changed when he was given a new nature in Christ. The same thing has happened to you. You can become more like Christ every day because of the great and lasting change that has taken place within you. And as you do, your reward will be good stuff like hope, joy, and peace.

hear me this day might become such as I am—except for these chains."

³⁰Then the king rose, and the governor and Bernice and those who were sitting with them. ³¹And when they had withdrawn, they said to one another, "This man is doing nothing to deserve death or imprisonment." ³²And Agrippa said to Festus, "This man could have been set free if he had not appealed to Caesar."

Paul Sails for Rome

27 And when it was decided that we should sail for Italy, they delivered Paul and some other prisoners to a centurion of the Augustan Cohort named Julius. ²And embarking in a ship of Adramyttium, which was about to sail to the ports along the coast of Asia, we put to sea, accompanied by Aristarchus, a Macedonian from Thessalonica. ³The next day we put in at Sidon. And Julius treated Paul kindly and gave him leave to go to his friends and be cared for. ⁴And putting out to sea from there we sailed under the lee of Cyprus, because the winds were against us. ⁵And when we had sailed across the open sea along the coast of Cilicia and Pamphylia, we came to Myra in Lycia. ⁶There the centurion found a ship of Alexandria sailing for Italy and put us on board. ⁷We sailed slowly for a number of days and arrived with difficulty off Cnidus, and as the wind did not allow us to go farther, we sailed under the lee of Crete off Salmone. ⁸Coasting along it with difficulty, we came to a place called Fair Havens, near which was the city of Lasea.

⁹Since much time had passed, and the voyage was now dangerous because even the Fast¹ was already over, Paul advised them, ¹⁰saying, "Sirs, I perceive that the voyage will be with injury and much loss, not only of the cargo and the ship, but also of our lives." ¹¹But the centurion paid more attention to the pilot and to the owner of the ship than to what Paul said. ¹²And because the harbor was not suitable to spend the winter in, the majority decided to put out to sea from there, on the chance that somehow they could reach Phoenix, a harbor of Crete, facing both southwest and northwest, and spend the winter there.

The Storm at Sea

¹³Now when the south wind blew gently, supposing that they had obtained their purpose, they weighed anchor and sailed along Crete, close to the shore. ¹⁴But soon a tempestuous wind, called the northeaster, struck down from the land. ¹⁵And when the ship was caught and could not face the wind, we gave way to it and were driven along. ¹⁶Running under the lee of a small island called Cauda,² we managed with difficulty to secure the ship's boat. ¹⁷After hoisting it up, they used supports to undergird the ship. Then, fearing that they would run aground on the Syrtis, they lowered the gear,³ and thus they were driven along. ¹⁸Since we were violently storm-tossed, they began the next day to jettison the cargo. ¹⁹And on the third day they threw the ship's tackle overboard with their own hands. ²⁰When neither sun nor stars appeared for many days, and no small tempest lay on us, all hope of our being saved was at last abandoned.

²¹Since they had been without food for a long time, Paul stood up among them and said, "Men, you should have listened to me and not have set sail from Crete and incurred this injury and loss. ²²Yet now I urge you to take heart, for there will be no loss of life among you, but only of the ship. ²³For this very night there stood before me an angel of the God to whom I belong and whom I worship, ²⁴and he said, 'Do not be afraid, Paul; you must stand before Caesar. And behold, God has granted you all those who sail with you.' ²⁵So take heart, men, for I have faith in God that it will be exactly as I have been told. ²⁶But we must run aground on some island."

²⁷When the fourteenth night had come, as we were being driven across the Adriatic Sea, about midnight the sailors suspected that they were nearing land. ²⁸So they took a sounding and found twenty fathoms.⁴ A little farther on they took a sounding again and found fifteen fathoms.⁵ ²⁹And fearing that we might run on the rocks, they let down four anchors from the stern and prayed for day to come. ³⁰And as the sailors were seeking to escape from the ship, and had lowered the ship's boat into the sea under pretense of laying out anchors from the bow, ³¹Paul said to the

¹That is, the Day of Atonement ²Some manuscripts *Clauda* ³That is, the sea-anchor (or possibly the mainsail) ⁴About 120 feet; a fathom (Greek *orguia*) was about 6 feet or 2 meters ⁵About 90 feet (see previous note)

centurion and the soldiers, "Unless these men stay in the ship, you cannot be saved." [32] Then the soldiers cut away the ropes of the ship's boat and let it go.

[33] As day was about to dawn, Paul urged them all to take some food, saying, "Today is the fourteenth day that you have continued in suspense and without food, having taken nothing. [34] Therefore I urge you to take some food. For it will give you strength,[1] for not a hair is to perish from the head of any of you." [35] And when he had said these things, he took bread, and giving thanks to God in the presence of all he broke it and began to eat. [36] Then they all were encouraged and ate some food themselves. [37] (We were in all 276[2] persons in the ship.) [38] And when they had eaten enough, they lightened the ship, throwing out the wheat into the sea.

The Shipwreck

[39] Now when it was day, they did not recognize the land, but they noticed a bay with a beach, on which they planned if possible to run the ship ashore. [40] So they cast off the anchors and left them in the sea, at the same time loosening the ropes that tied the rudders. Then hoisting the foresail to the wind they made for the beach. [41] But striking a reef,[3] they ran the vessel aground. The bow stuck and remained immovable, and the stern was being broken up by the surf. [42] The soldiers' plan was to kill the prisoners, lest any should swim away and escape. [43] But the centurion, wishing to save Paul, kept them from carrying out their plan. He ordered those who could swim to jump overboard first and make for the land, [44] and the rest on planks or on pieces of the ship. And so it was that all were brought safely to land.

Paul on Malta

28 After we were brought safely through, we then learned that the island was called Malta. [2] The native people[4] showed us unusual kindness, for they kindled a fire and welcomed us all, because it had begun to rain and was cold. [3] When Paul had gathered a bundle of sticks and put them on the fire, a viper came out because of the heat and fastened on his hand. [4] When

the native people saw the creature hanging from his hand, they said to one another, "No doubt this man is a murderer. Though he has escaped from the sea, Justice[5] has not allowed him to live." [5] He, however, shook off the creature into the fire and suffered no harm. [6] They were waiting for him to swell up or suddenly fall down dead. But when they had waited a long time and saw no misfortune come to him, they changed their minds and said that he was a god.

[7] Now in the neighborhood of that place were lands belonging to the chief man of the island, named Publius, who received us and entertained us hospitably for three days. [8] It happened that the father of Publius lay sick with fever and dysentery. And Paul visited him and prayed, and putting his hands on him healed him. [9] And when this had taken place, the rest of the people on the island who had diseases also came and were cured. [10] They also honored us greatly,[6] and when we were about to sail, they put on board whatever we needed.

Paul Arrives at Rome

[11] After three months we set sail in a ship that had wintered in the island, a ship of Alexandria, with the twin gods[7] as a figurehead. [12] Putting in at Syracuse, we stayed there for three days. [13] And from there we made a circuit and arrived at Rhegium. And after one day a south wind sprang up, and on the second day we came to Puteoli. [14] There we found brothers[8] and were invited to stay with them for seven days. And so we came to Rome. [15] And the brothers there, when they heard about us, came as far as the Forum of Appius and Three Taverns to meet us. On seeing them, Paul thanked God and took courage. [16] And when we came into Rome, Paul was allowed to stay by himself, with the soldier who guarded him.

Paul in Rome

[17] After three days he called together the local leaders of the Jews, and when they had gathered, he said to them, "Brothers, though I had done nothing against our people or the customs of our fathers, yet I was delivered as a prisoner from Jerusalem into the hands of the Romans. [18] When they had

---

[1] Or For it is for your deliverance [2] Some manuscripts seventy-six, or about seventy-six [3] Or sandbank, or crosscurrent; Greek place between two seas [4] Greek barbaroi (that is, non–Greek speakers); also verse 4 [5] Or justice [6] Greek honored us with many honors [7] That is, the Greek gods Castor and Pollux [8] Or brothers and sisters; also verses 15, 21

examined me, they wished to set me at liberty, because there was no reason for the death penalty in my case. [19] But because the Jews objected, I was compelled to appeal to Caesar—though I had no charge to bring against my nation. [20] For this reason, therefore, I have asked to see you and speak with you, since it is because of the hope of Israel that I am wearing this chain." [21] And they said to him, "We have received no letters from Judea about you, and none of the brothers coming here has reported or spoken any evil about you. [22] But we desire to hear from you what your views are, for with regard to this sect we know that everywhere it is spoken against."

[23] When they had appointed a day for him, they came to him at his lodging in greater numbers. From morning till evening he expounded to them, testifying to the kingdom of God and trying to convince them about Jesus both from the Law of Moses and from the Prophets. [24] And some were convinced by what he said, but others disbelieved. [25] And disagreeing among themselves, they departed after Paul had

made one statement: "The Holy Spirit was right in saying to your fathers through Isaiah the prophet:

[26] [a] "'Go to this people, and say,
"You will indeed hear but never understand,
and you will indeed see but never perceive."
[27]   For this people's heart has grown dull,
and with their ears they can barely hear,
and their eyes they have closed;
lest they should see with their eyes
and hear with their ears
and understand with their heart
and turn, and I would heal them.'

[28] Therefore let it be known to you that this salvation of God has been sent to the Gentiles; they will listen."[1]

[30] He lived there two whole years at his own expense,[2] and welcomed all who came to him, [31] proclaiming the kingdom of God and teaching about the Lord Jesus Christ with all boldness and without hindrance.

INTRODUCTION TO
Romans

Author: The apostle Paul

Time: Around A.D. 57

Place: Corinth, when Paul was on a missionary trip

Written to: The church in Rome

The gist

Romans is an essential book to read to figure out the meaning of life and the role of God in it all. Paul wants the Romans to know that they are saved by God's grace but are still called to be holy.

Things to look for

- The salvation message (see Romans 3)
- The answer to why you continue to mess up (see Romans 7)
- The relief offered to people who believe (see Rom. 8:1)
- The meaning and importance of the cross (see Rom. 1:18–11:36)

Know Salvation

For all have sinned and fall short of the glory of God, and are justified by his grace as a gift, through the redemption that is in Christ Jesus.

Romans 3:23–24

If you are in Jesus, then guilt no longer has any place in your life. When Jesus died on the cross, he took away your guilt. So guilty feelings are not telling you the truth. Conviction of sin? Now, that's from God. He makes you feel convicted, like a little red flag waving in your brain to tell you, "Something ain't right here." But conviction is totally different from guilt. God's Word is clear that, without God's grace, no one can gain his approval (see Rom. 3:10). That means that no one can get God's love by never messing up or sinning, so you're lying to yourself if you think that you are a special case who should be perfect and never mess up. The truth is that everyone has turned away and is rotten to the core; no one can do anything to deserve eternal life (see Rom. 3:10–12).

But in the book of Romans, Paul makes it clear that sin isn't the end. Through confession and repentance, and trusting Christ, the God Girl can be free from the guilt of anything she has done. When you confess that you were wrong and God was right and you promise to turn and go a new direction, you are no longer guilty—period, the end (see 1 John 1:9). Therefore, any guilt that you feel is just that: a feeling. And how many times have you *felt* something only to be proven wrong? Emotions can't always be trusted, but the Word of God can. You're believing a bold-faced lie if you think that you are still guilty once you've confessed your sin. Jesus came to set you free, not to keep you in guilt. His death and resurrection means that the one who has confessed and turned away from sin is no longer guilty.

So if there is an area in your life where you feel guilt instead of conviction, know that you are believing a lie. If you have accepted Jesus as the ransom for your guilt, you are not guilty! Read this amazing book of Romans and find out just what God has to say about your sin, your need for salvation, and your freedom from guilt.

Must-Know Terms and Verses

∽ *Justification* ∽

God's act of considering believers to be righteous, based not on our ability to fulfill the law but on our faith in Jesus. God accepts and treats all those who believe in Christ as righteous in the eyes of the law, or in other words, as having lived up to all its demands.

∽ *Law* ∽

The written will of God found in Scripture. This most often refers to the Mosaic Torah law of the Old Testament.

———————•❖•———————

By works of the law no human being will be justified in his sight, since through the law comes knowledge of sin. *Romans 3:20*

There is therefore now no condemnation for those who are in Christ Jesus. *Romans 8:1*

I consider that the sufferings of this present time are not worth comparing with the glory that is to be revealed to us. *Romans 8:18*

We know that for those who love God all things work together for good, for those who are called according to his purpose. *Romans 8:28*

If you confess with your mouth that Jesus is Lord and believe in your heart that God raised him from the dead, you will be saved. *Romans 10:9*

Do not be conformed to this world, but be transformed by the renewal of your mind. *Romans 12:2*

The Letter of Paul to the

Romans

Greeting

1 Paul, a servant[1] of Christ Jesus, called to be an apostle, set apart for the gospel of God, [2] which he promised beforehand through his prophets in the holy Scriptures, [3] concerning his Son, who was descended from David[2] according to the flesh [4] and was declared to be the Son of God in power according to the Spirit of holiness by his resurrection from the dead, Jesus Christ our Lord, [5] through whom we have received grace and apostleship to bring about the obedience of faith for the sake of his name among all the nations, [6] including you who are called to belong to Jesus Christ,

[7] To all those in Rome who are loved by God and called to be saints:

Grace to you and peace from God our Father and the Lord Jesus Christ.

Longing to Go to Rome

[8] First, I thank my God through Jesus Christ for all of you, because your faith is proclaimed in all the world. [9] For God is my witness, whom I serve with my spirit in the gospel of his Son, that without ceasing I mention you [10] always in my prayers, asking that somehow by God's will I may now at last succeed in coming to you. [11] For I long to see you, that I may impart to you some spiritual gift to strengthen you— [12] that is, that we may be mutually encouraged by each other's faith, both yours and mine. [13] I do not want you to be unaware, brothers,[3] that I have often intended to come to you (but thus far have been prevented), in order that I may reap some harvest among you as well as among the rest of the Gentiles. [14] I am under obligation both to Greeks and to barbarians,[4] both to the wise and to the foolish. [15] So I am eager to preach the gospel to you also who are in Rome.

The Righteous Shall Live by Faith

[16] For I am not ashamed of the gospel, for it is the power of God for salvation to everyone who believes, to the Jew first and also to the Greek. [17] For in it the righteousness of God is revealed from faith for faith,[5] [a] as it is written, "The righteous shall live by faith."[6]

> **Ask Yourself . . .**
>
> ABOUT HOW YOU LIVE
>
> - Do I live by faith or by feeling?
> - In what areas in my life do I lack faith?
> - Does my prayer life reflect my faith?
> - How could I change my prayer life in order to improve my faith?

God's Wrath on Unrighteousness

[18] For the wrath of God is revealed from heaven against all ungodliness and unrighteousness of men, who by their unrighteousness suppress the truth. [19] For what can be known about God is plain to them, because God has shown it to them. [20] For his invisible attributes, namely, his eternal power and divine nature, have been clearly perceived, ever since the creation of the world,[7] in the things that have been made. So they are without excuse. [21] For although they knew God, they did not honor him as

---

[1] Or *slave* (for the contextual rendering of the Greek word *doulos*, see About the ESV) [2] Or *who came from the offspring of David*
[3] Or *brothers and sisters.* The plural Greek word *adelphoi* (translated "brothers") refers to siblings in a family. In New Testament usage, depending on the context, *adelphoi* may refer either to men or to both men and women who are siblings (brothers and sisters) in God's family, the church [4] That is, non-Greeks [5] Or *beginning and ending in faith* [6] Or *The one who by faith is righteous shall live*
[7] Or *clearly perceived from the creation of the world* [a] Hab. 2:4

God or give thanks to him, but they became futile in their thinking, and their foolish hearts were darkened. [22] Claiming to be wise, they became fools, [23] and exchanged the glory of the immortal God for images resembling mortal man and birds and animals and creeping things.

[24] Therefore God gave them up in the lusts of their hearts to impurity, to the dishonoring of their bodies among themselves, [25] because they exchanged the truth about God for a lie and worshiped and served the creature rather than the Creator, who is blessed forever! Amen.

[26] For this reason God gave them up to dishonorable passions. For their women exchanged natural relations for those that are contrary to nature; [27] and the men likewise gave up natural relations with women and were consumed with passion for one another, men committing shameless acts with men and receiving in themselves the due penalty for their error.

[28] And since they did not see fit to acknowledge God, God gave them up to a debased mind to do what ought not to be done. [29] They were filled with all manner of unrighteousness, evil, covetousness, malice. They are full of envy, murder, strife, deceit, maliciousness. They are gossips, [30] slanderers, haters of God, insolent, haughty, boastful, inventors of evil, disobedient to parents, [31] foolish, faithless, heartless, ruthless. [32] Though they know God's righteous decree that those who practice such things deserve to die, they not only do them but give approval to those who practice them.

God's Righteous Judgment

2 Therefore you have no excuse, O man, every one of you who judges. For in passing judgment on another you condemn yourself, because you, the judge, practice the very same things. [2] We know that the judgment of God rightly falls on those who practice such things. [3] Do you suppose, O man—you who judge those who practice such things and yet do them yourself—that you will escape the judgment of God? [4] Or do you presume on the riches of his kindness and forbearance and patience, not knowing that God's kindness is meant to lead you to repentance? [5] But because of your hard and impenitent heart you are storing up wrath for yourself on the day

of wrath when God's righteous judgment will be revealed.

[6] He will render to each one according to his works: [7] to those who by patience in well-doing seek for glory and honor and immortality, he will give eternal life; [8] but for those who are self-seeking[1] and do not obey the truth, but obey unrighteousness, there will be wrath and fury. [9] There will be tribulation and distress for every human being who does evil, the Jew first and also the Greek, [10] but glory and honor and peace for everyone who does good, the Jew first and also the Greek. [11] For God shows no partiality.

God's Judgment and the Law

[12] For all who have sinned without the law will also perish without the law, and all who have sinned under the law will be judged by the law. [13] For it is not the hearers of the law who are righteous before God, but the doers of the law who will be justified. [14] For when Gentiles, who do not have the law, by nature do what the law requires, they are a law to themselves, even though they do not have the law. [15] They show that the work of the law is written on their hearts, while their conscience also bears witness, and their conflicting thoughts accuse or even excuse them [16] on that day when, according to my gospel, God judges the secrets of men by Christ Jesus.

[17] But if you call yourself a Jew and rely on the law and boast in God [18] and know his will and approve what is excellent, because you are instructed from the law; [19] and if you are sure that you yourself are a guide to the blind, a light to those who are in darkness, [20] an instructor of the foolish, a teacher of children, having in the law the embodiment of knowledge and truth— [21] you then who teach others, do you not teach yourself? While you preach against stealing, do you steal? [22] You who say that one must not commit adultery, do you commit adultery? You who abhor idols, do you rob temples? [23] You who boast in the law dishonor God by breaking the law. [24] For, [a] as it is written, "The name of God is blasphemed among the Gentiles because of you."

[25] For circumcision indeed is of value if you obey the law, but if you break the law, your circumcision becomes uncircumci-

---

[1] Or contentious   [a] Isa. 52:5

sion. **26** So, if a man who is uncircumcised keeps the precepts of the law, will not his uncircumcision be regarded[1] as circumcision? **27** Then he who is physically[2] uncircumcised but keeps the law will condemn you who have the written code[3] and circumcision but break the law. **28** For no one is a Jew who is merely one outwardly, nor is circumcision outward and physical. **29** But a Jew is one inwardly, and circumcision is a matter of the heart, by the Spirit, not by the letter. His praise is not from man but from God.

God's Righteousness Upheld

3 Then what advantage has the Jew? Or what is the value of circumcision? **2** Much in every way. To begin with, the Jews were entrusted with the oracles of God. **3** What if some were unfaithful? Does their faithlessness nullify the faithfulness of God? **4** By no means! Let God be true though every one were a liar, as it is written,

> [a]"That you may be justified in your words,
>   and prevail when you are judged."

5 But if our unrighteousness serves to show the righteousness of God, what shall we say? That God is unrighteous to inflict wrath on us? (I speak in a human way.) **6** By no means! For then how could God judge the world? **7** But if through my lie God's truth abounds to his glory, why am I still being condemned as a sinner? **8** And why not do evil that good may come?—as some people slanderously charge us with saying. Their condemnation is just.

No One Is Righteous

9 What then? Are we Jews[4] any better off?[5] No, not at all. For we have already charged that all, both Jews and Greeks, are under sin, **10** as it is written:

> [b]"None is righteous, no, not one;
> **11**   no one understands;
>   no one seeks for God.
> **12**   All have turned aside; together they
>   have become worthless;
>   no one does good,
>   not even one."
> **13** [c]"Their throat is an open grave;
>   they use their tongues to deceive."
> [d]"The venom of asps is under their lips."
> **14** [e]"Their mouth is full of curses and
>   bitterness."
> **15** [f]"Their feet are swift to shed blood;
> **16**   in their paths are ruin and misery,
> **17**   and the way of peace they have not
>   known."
> **18** [g]"There is no fear of God before their
>   eyes."

19 Now we know that whatever the law says it speaks to those who are under the law, so that every mouth may be stopped, and the whole world may be held accountable to God. **20** For by works of the law no human being[6] will be justified in his sight, since through the law comes knowledge of sin.

The Righteousness of God Through Faith

21 But now the righteousness of God has been manifested apart from the law, although the Law and the Prophets bear witness to it— **22** the righteousness of God through faith in Jesus Christ for all who believe. For there is no distinction: **23** for all have sinned and fall short of the glory of God, **24** and are justified by his grace as a gift, through the redemption that is in Christ Jesus, **25** whom God put forward as a propitiation by his blood, to be received by faith. This was to show God's righteousness, because in his divine forbearance he had passed over former sins. **26** It was to show his righteousness at the present time, so that he might be just and the justifier of the one who has faith in Jesus.

27 Then what becomes of our boasting? It is excluded. By what kind of law? By a law of works? No, but by the law of faith. **28** For we hold that one is justified by faith apart from works of the law. **29** Or is God the God of Jews only? Is he not the God of Gentiles also? Yes, of Gentiles also, **30** since God is one—who will justify the circumcised by faith and the uncircumcised through faith. **31** Do we then overthrow the law by this faith? By no means! On the contrary, we uphold the law.

Abraham Justified by Faith

4 What then shall we say was gained by[7] Abraham, our forefather according to the flesh? **2** For if Abraham was justified by works, he has something to boast

---

[1] Or counted [2] Or is by nature [3] Or the letter [4] Greek Are we [5] Or at any disadvantage? [6] Greek flesh [7] Some manuscripts say about
[a] Ps. 51:4 (Gk.). [b] Ps. 14:1-3; 53:1-3 [c] Ps. 5:9 [d] Ps. 140:3 [e] Ps. 10:7 (Gk.). [f] Prov. 1:16; 3:15-17; Isa. 59:7, 8 [g] Ps. 36:1

A Prayer for...
ACCEPTING FORGIVENESS

Eternal Father, I am absolutely amazed that you sent your Son to suffer in my place; that you gave your Spirit to teach, comfort, and guide; that you allowed the ministry of angels to protect me; and that all heaven serves the welfare of a nobody like me. I pray that your unseen servants will be vigilant in protecting me and happy when your grace grows in me. Don't let them rest until my conflict is over and I stand victorious on salvation's shore.

Please don't let my tendency to sin, my deadness to good, or my resistance to your Spirit's motions ever lead you to abandon me. May my sinfulness lead you to pity, not to wrath. And if the Enemy gets an advantage through my sinfulness, show everyone that heaven is stronger than hell, that those who are for me are greater than those who are against me. Rise up to help me under the blessing of the new covenant; keep me feeding in the pastures of your strengthening Word, searching Scripture to find you there.

If my selfishness leads to discipline, help me to take correction meekly, to bless your scolding hand, to understand the reason for the rebuke, and to respond quickly and do the first thing you ask. Let all your fatherly dealings make me a sharer of your holiness. Help me to sink lower on my knees every time I fall, and if I rise, may it be to loftier heights of devotion. May my every cross be sanctified, every loss be gain, every denial a spiritual advantage, every dark day a light of the Holy Spirit, and every night of trial a song.

Amen.

about, but not before God. [3]For what does the Scripture say? [a]"Abraham believed God, and it was counted to him as righteousness." [4]Now to the one who works, his wages are not counted as a gift but as his due. [5]And to the one who does not work but believes in[1] him who justifies the ungodly, his faith is counted as righteousness, [6]just as David also speaks of the blessing of the one to whom God counts righteousness apart from works:

[7] [b]"Blessed are those whose lawless
　　deeds are forgiven,
　　and whose sins are covered;
[8] 　blessed is the man against whom the
　　　　Lord will not count his sin."

[9]Is this blessing then only for the circumcised, or also for the uncircumcised? For we say that faith was counted to Abraham as righteousness. [10]How then was it counted to him? Was it before or after he had been circumcised? It was not after, but before he was circumcised. [11]He received the sign of circumcision as a seal of the righteousness that he had by faith while he was still uncircumcised. The purpose was to make him the father of all who believe without being circumcised, so that righteousness would be counted to them as well, [12]and to make him the father of the circumcised who are not merely circumcised but who also walk in the footsteps of the faith that our father Abraham had before he was circumcised.

The Promise Realized Through Faith

[13]For the promise to Abraham and his offspring that he would be heir of the world did not come through the law but through the righteousness of faith. [14]For if it is the adherents of the law who are to be the heirs, faith is null and the promise is void. [15]For the law brings wrath, but where there is no law there is no transgression.

[16]That is why it depends on faith, in order that the promise may rest on grace and be guaranteed to all his offspring—not only to the adherent of the law but also to the one who shares the faith of Abraham, who is the father of us all, [17]as it is written, [c]"I have made you the father of many nations"— in the presence of the God in whom he believed, who gives life to the dead and calls into existence the things that do not

---

[1]Or *but trusts*; compare verse 24　[a]Gen. 15:6 (Gk.)　[b]Ps. 32:1, 2　[c]Gen. 17:5

exist. [18] In hope he believed against hope, that he should become the father of many nations, as he had been told, [a] "So shall your offspring be." [19] He did not weaken in faith when he considered his own body, which was as good as dead (since he was about a hundred years old), or when he considered the barrenness[1] of Sarah's womb. [20] No unbelief made him waver concerning the promise of God, but he grew strong in his faith as he gave glory to God, [21] fully convinced that God was able to do what he had promised. [22] That is why his faith was 'counted to him as righteousness." [23] But the words "it was counted to him" were not written for his sake alone, [24] but for ours also. It will be counted to us who believe in him who raised from the dead Jesus our Lord, [25] who was delivered up for our trespasses and raised for our justification.

Peace with God Through Faith

5 Therefore, since we have been justified by faith, we[2] have peace with God through our Lord Jesus Christ. [2] Through him we have also obtained access by faith[3] into this grace in which we stand, and we[4] rejoice[5] in hope of the glory of God. [3] Not only that, but we rejoice in our sufferings, knowing that suffering produces endurance, [4] and endurance produces character, and character produces hope, [5] and hope does not put us to shame, because God's love has been poured into our hearts through the Holy Spirit who has been given to us.

[6] For while we were still weak, at the right time Christ died for the ungodly. [7] For one will scarcely die for a righteous person—though perhaps for a good person one would dare even to die— [8] but God shows his love for us in that while we were still sinners, Christ died for us. [9] Since, therefore, we have now been justified by his blood, much more shall we be saved by him from the wrath of God. [10] For if while we were enemies we were reconciled to God by the death of his Son, much more, now that we are reconciled, shall we be saved by his life. [11] More than that, we also rejoice in God through our Lord

[1] Greek deadness [2] Some manuscripts let us [3] Some manuscripts omit by faith [4] Or let us; also verse 3 [5] Or boast; also verses 3, 11
[a] Gen. 15:5

Know Yourself

verses to read
Romans 5:1–5

Are you a rescuer—forever helping people in need, saving them from trials and temptations? If you find that you aren't hearing from God or that you want more from your spiritual life than you are getting, then it might just be because you are trying to play God in the lives of your friends.

Suffering is a powerful tool in the hand of God. He uses it to shape people and to move them toward him. If you feel a need to stop the suffering of others and to give them advice that you have no right to be giving them, then you might be putting something between them and the voice of God. You can most certainly give advice to others, but it has to come from the knowledge and wisdom you have gained through discernment and constant prayer.

Always get back to God's Word. Are your friends suffering because they refuse to obey? Can God make something out of their suffering? What do they need to learn from this experience? Don't always think that your job is to help them get away from the trial. Sometimes the most important thing is for them to stay in it and to fall on their knees in complete surrender to the only one who can truly save them. Rather than trying to solve everyone else's problems, allow them to discover that they need God more than they need you.

Jesus Christ, through whom we have now received reconciliation.

Ask Yourself . . .

ABOUT FREEDOM

Do you want to be free from the chains that bind you? Then let's get to the bottom of the problem and see if the truth won't set you free. Ask yourself:

- What emotion controls me? Worry, fear, depression, bitterness, hatred?
- Is it fair to say that I am a slave to that emotion (see Rom. 6:16)?
- Have I tried to break free and been unable to do so?
- Do I really want to be set free?

The reality is that anything that controls you like a slave master is an idol (see Ex. 20:4–5; Matt; 6:24; Eph. 5:5–8; Col. 3:5; 1 John 5:21). What is the danger of idolatry, according to these verses?

If you are ready to get rid of your idols, look to Christ, adore him, rest in his outrageous mercy in the gospel. Continue to read and meditate on the Word of God, and the truth of it will break your chains.

Death in Adam, Life in Christ

¹²Therefore, just as sin came into the world through one man, and death through sin, and so death spread to all men¹ because all sinned— ¹³for sin indeed was in the world before the law was given, but sin is not counted where there is no law. ¹⁴Yet death reigned from Adam to Moses, even over those whose sinning was not like the transgression of Adam, who was a type of the one who was to come.

¹⁵But the free gift is not like the trespass. For if many died through one man's trespass, much more have the grace of God and the free gift by the grace of that one man Jesus Christ abounded for many. ¹⁶And the free gift is not like the result of that one man's sin. For the judgment following one trespass brought condemnation, but the free gift following many trespasses brought justification. ¹⁷For if, because of one man' trespass, death reigned through that one man, much more will those who receive the abundance of grace and the free gift of righteousness reign in life through the one man Jesus Christ.

¹⁸Therefore, as one trespass² led to condemnation for all men, so one act of righteousness³ leads to justification and life for all men. ¹⁹For as by the one man's disobedience the many were made sinners, so by the one man's obedience the many will be made righteous. ²⁰Now the law came in to increase the trespass, but where sin increased, grace abounded all the more, ²¹so that, as sin reigned in death, grace also might reign through righteousness leading to eternal life through Jesus Christ our Lord.

Dead to Sin, Alive to God

6 What shall we say then? Are we to continue in sin that grace may abound? ²By no means! How can we who died to sin still live in it? ³Do you not know that all of us who have been baptized into Christ Jesus were baptized into his death? ⁴We were buried therefore with him by baptism into death, in order that, just as Christ was raised from the dead by the glory of the Father, we too might walk in newness of life.

⁵For if we have been united with him in a death like his, we shall certainly be united with him in a resurrection like his. ⁶We know that our old self⁴ was crucified with him in order that the body of sin might be brought to nothing, so that we would no longer be enslaved to sin. ⁷For one who has died has been set free⁵ from sin. ⁸Now if we have died with Christ, we believe that we will also live with him. ⁹We know that Christ, being raised from the dead, will never die again; death no longer has dominion over him. ¹⁰For the death he died

¹The Greek word *anthropoi* refers here to both men and women; also twice in verse 18 ²Or *the trespass of one* ³Or *the act of righteousness of one* ⁴Greek *man* ⁵Greek *has been justified*

e died to sin, once for all, but the life he lives he lives to God. ¹¹So you also must consider yourselves dead to sin and alive to God in Christ Jesus.

¹²Let not sin therefore reign in your mortal body, to make you obey its passions. ¹³Do not present your members to sin as instruments for unrighteousness, but present yourselves to God as those who have been brought from death to life, and your members to God as instruments for righteousness. ¹⁴For sin will have no dominion over you, since you are not under law but under grace.

Slaves to Righteousness

¹⁵What then? Are we to sin because we are not under law but under grace? By no means! ¹⁶Do you not know that if you present yourselves to anyone as obedient slaves,¹ you are slaves of the one whom you obey, either of sin, which leads to death, or of obedience, which leads to righteousness? ¹⁷But thanks be to God,

that you who were once slaves of sin have become obedient from the heart to the standard of teaching to which you were committed, ¹⁸and, having been set free from sin, have become slaves of righteousness. ¹⁹I am speaking in human terms, because of your natural limitations. For just as you once presented your members as slaves to impurity and to lawlessness leading to more lawlessness, so now present your members as slaves to righteousness leading to sanctification.

²⁰For when you were slaves of sin, you were free in regard to righteousness. ²¹But what fruit were you getting at that time from the things of which you are now ashamed? For the end of those things is death. ²²But now that you have been set free from sin and have become slaves of God, the fruit you get leads to sanctification and its end, eternal life. ²³For the wages of sin is death, but the free gift of God is eternal life in Christ Jesus our Lord.

¹ For the contextual rendering of the Greek word *doulos*, see About the ESV (twice in this verse and verse 19; also once in verses 17, 20)

Know God

verses to read
Romans 6:8-18

You cannot serve two masters, but you *will* serve *one*. Whom do you serve? If you are a God Girl, then you are a servant of God, and not only that but his slave. A slave serves only the will of her master and nothing else. She is devoted to her master and her master's needs. An employee can serve two bosses, like having a day job with one boss and a night job with another. But as a God Girl you don't have that luxury. You can't obey your master sin and your master God—you must obey either one or the other. Who is your master? Finding the answer is easy: do you give in to the call of God only, or do you sometimes serve other gods, such as the god of comfort, popularity, sex, or food?

If you serve another god, then you are not yet a slave of Jesus Christ. Slavery to him annihilates slavery to sin. Want to be free from the bondage of sin in your life? Then give your life, your choices, and your days over to the Master. Think of yourself as dead to sin, and it will no longer be your master. As a God Girl, you don't have to be controlled by anything any longer. Your freedom is found in calling sin sin. Jesus' resurrection bought your freedom (see Rom. 6:8-11), and because of that you can have confidence that God is beside you, helping you to break free from any power that threatens to control you. Yes, we all have sinned and will continue to sin, but sin doesn't have to be your master anymore. Determine that you won't let your life be controlled by anything but God, because he has redeemed you and made you his own.

Released from the Law

7 Or do you not know, brothers[1]—for I am speaking to those who know the law—that the law is binding on a person only as long as he lives? [2] For a married woman is bound by law to her husband while he lives, but if her husband dies she is released from the law of marriage.[2] [3] Accordingly, she will be called an adulteress if she lives with another man while her husband is alive. But if her husband dies, she is free from that law, and if she marries another man she is not an adulteress.

[4] Likewise, my brothers, you also have died to the law through the body of Christ, so that you may belong to another, to him who has been raised from the dead, in order that we may bear fruit for God. [5] For while we were living in the flesh, our sinful passions, aroused by the law, were at work in our members to bear fruit for death. [6] But now we are released from the law, having died to that which held us captive, so that we serve in the new way of the Spirit and not in the old way of the written code.[3]

The Law and Sin

[7] What then shall we say? That the law is sin? By no means! Yet if it had not been for the law, I would not have known sin. For I would not have known what it is to covet if *a* the law had not said, "You shall not covet." [8] But sin, seizing an opportunity through the commandment, produced in me all kinds of covetousness. For apart from the law, sin lies dead. [9] I was once alive apart from the law, but when the commandment came, sin came alive and I died. [10] The very commandment that promised life proved to be death to me. [11] For sin, seizing an opportunity through the commandment, deceived me and through it killed me. [12] So the law is holy, and the commandment is holy and righteous and good.

[13] Did that which is good, then, bring death to me? By no means! It was sin, producing death in me through what is good, in order that sin might be shown to be sin, and through the commandment might become sinful beyond measure. [14] For we know that the law is spiritual, but I am of the flesh, sold under sin. [15] For I do not understand my own actions. For I do not do

[1] Or *brothers and sisters*; also verse 4 [2] Greek *law concerning the husband* [3] Greek *of the letter* *a* Ex. 20:17; Deut. 5:21

verses to read
Romans 7:14–25

Know Yourself

Has the truth set you free yet? Or is there something in your life that controls you—your emotions, your fear, your worry, and your happiness? The truth is that, until you are willing to listen to the truth, you will be a slave to the lies you believe. At some point in your life you gave in to yourself. You yielded to something you desperately wanted, and as a result you became a slave to that thing you wanted. When you are enslaved to your whims, it becomes very hard to see your chains, because after all, you willingly put them on, and you hold the key.

At the point when you gave in to your deep desire or lust for something, you became a slave to that thing. And even though you might hate it now, nothing you do to try to get rid of it will rescue you. You don't have the strength to free yourself, but there is hope, and it's found in knowing the truth. You have to honestly look at yourself and the Word of God and find out where you are believing a lie. So if there is something in your life that enslaves you and you want freedom from that thing, prayerfully read verses about that topic and ask the Lord to change you way down at the core of who you are. Think about what you believe about that thing, and then search the Word to find out if that is truth or a lie. Freedom requires truth, "and the truth will set you free" (John 8:32).

what I want, but I do the very thing I hate. [16] Now if I do what I do not want, I agree with the law, that it is good. [17] So now it is no longer I who do it, but sin that dwells within me. [18] For I know that nothing good dwells in me, that is, in my flesh. For I have the desire to do what is right, but not the ability to carry it out. [19] For I do not do the good I want, but the evil I do not want is what I keep on doing. [20] Now if I do what I do not want, it is no longer I who do it, but sin that dwells within me.

[21] So I find it to be a law that when I want to do right, evil lies close at hand. [22] For I delight in the law of God, in my inner being, [23] but I see in my members another law waging war against the law of my mind and making me captive to the law of sin that dwells in my members. [24] Wretched man that I am! Who will deliver me from this body of death? [25] Thanks be to God through Jesus Christ our Lord! So then, I myself serve the law of God with my mind, but with my flesh I serve the law of sin.

Life in the Spirit

8 There is therefore now no condemnation for those who are in Christ Jesus.[1] [2] For the law of the Spirit of life has set you[2] free in Christ Jesus from the law of sin and death. [3] For God has done what the law, weakened by the flesh, could not do. By sending his own Son in the likeness of sinful flesh and for sin,[3] he condemned sin in the flesh, [4] in order that the righteous requirement of the law might be fulfilled in us, who walk not according to the flesh but according to the Spirit. [5] For those who live according to the flesh set their minds on the things of the flesh, but those who live according to the Spirit set their minds on the things of the Spirit. [6] For to set the mind on the flesh is death, but to set the mind on the Spirit is life and peace. [7] For the mind that is set on the flesh is hostile to God, for it does not submit to God's law; indeed, it cannot. [8] Those who are in the flesh cannot please God.

[9] You, however, are not in the flesh but in the Spirit, if in fact the Spirit of God dwells in you. Anyone who does not have the Spirit of Christ does not belong to him. [10] But if Christ is in you, although the body is dead because of sin, the Spirit is life because of righteousness. [11] If the Spirit of him who raised Jesus from the dead dwells in you, he who raised Christ Jesus[4] from the dead will also give life to your mortal bodies through his Spirit who dwells in you.

Heirs with Christ

[12] So then, brothers,[5] we are debtors, not to the flesh, to live according to the flesh. [13] For if you live according to the flesh you will die, but if by the Spirit you put to death the deeds of the body, you will live. [14] For all who are led by the Spirit of God are sons[6] of God. [15] For you did not receive the spirit of slavery to fall back into fear, but you have received the Spirit of adoption as sons, by whom we cry, "Abba! Father!" [16] The Spirit himself bears witness with our spirit that we are children of God, [17] and if children, then heirs—heirs of God and fellow heirs with Christ, provided we suffer with him in order that we may also be glorified with him.

Future Glory

[18] For I consider that the sufferings of this present time are not worth comparing with the glory that is to be revealed to us. [19] For the creation waits with eager longing for the revealing of the sons of God. [20] For the creation was subjected to futility, not willingly, but because of him who subjected it, in hope [21] that the creation itself will be set free from its bondage to corruption and obtain the freedom of the glory of the children of God. [22] For we know that the whole creation has been groaning together in the pains of childbirth until now. [23] And not only the creation, but we ourselves, who have the firstfruits of the Spirit, groan inwardly as we wait eagerly for adoption as sons, the redemption of our bodies. [24] For in this hope we were saved. Now hope that is seen is not hope. For who hopes for what he sees? [25] But if we hope for what we do not see, we wait for it with patience.

[26] Likewise the Spirit helps us in our weakness. For we do not know what to pray for as we ought, but the Spirit himself intercedes for us with groanings too deep for words. [27] And he who searches hearts knows what is the mind of the Spirit, because[7] the Spirit intercedes for the saints according to the will of God. [28] And

---

[1] Some manuscripts add who walk not according to the flesh (but according to the Spirit) [2] Some manuscripts me [3] Or and as a sin offering [4] Some manuscripts lack Jesus [5] Or brothers and sisters; also verse 29 [6] See discussion on "sons" in About the ESV [7] Or that

we know that for those who love God all things work together for good,[1] for those who are called according to his purpose. [29] For those whom he foreknew he also predestined to be conformed to the image of his Son, in order that he might be the firstborn among many brothers. [30] And those whom he predestined he also called, and those whom he called he also justified, and those whom he justified he also glorified.

God's Everlasting Love

[31] What then shall we say to these things? If God is for us, who can be[2] against us? [32] He who did not spare his own Son but gave him up for us all, how will he not also with him graciously give us all things? [33] Who shall bring any charge against God's elect? It is God who justifies. [34] Who is to condemn? Christ Jesus is the one who died—more than that, who was raised—who is at the right hand of God, who indeed is interceding for us.[3] [35] Who shall separate us from the love of Christ? Shall tribulation, or distress, or persecution, or famine, or nakedness, or danger, or sword? [36] As it is written,

> [a]"For your sake we are being killed all
> the day long;
> we are regarded as sheep to be
> slaughtered."

[37] No, in all these things we are more than conquerors through him who loved us. [38] For I am sure that neither death nor life, nor angels nor rulers, nor things present nor things to come, nor powers, [39] nor height nor depth, nor anything else in all creation, will be able to separate us from the love of God in Christ Jesus our Lord.

God's Sovereign Choice

9 I am speaking the truth in Christ—I am not lying; my conscience bears me witness in the Holy Spirit— [2] that I have great sorrow and unceasing anguish in my heart. [3] For I could wish that I myself were

[1] Some manuscripts *God works all things together for good*, or *God works in all things for the good*   [2] Or *who is*   [3] Or *Is it Christ Jesus who died . . . for us?*   [a] Ps. 44:22

Know True Happiness

verses to read
Romans 8:28–39

Is a carefree life a holier life? Not necessarily. It's worth very little to have life just the way you want it. And on the other hand, it's sometimes worth a lot to have something in your life you wish *wasn't* there. Why? Well, because it's through trouble, distress, and danger that you get to know the power of God's love.

God doesn't promise to keep you from all trouble, but he promises to keep you close to him in the midst of it. He never promised the God Girl that her life would be free from suffering or testing. When trials come, you can trust the power of God to get you through. Some circumstances will come to you because of your own sinfulness or your own mistakes, and these have to be taken like discipline, with confession and repentance. But when things beyond your power plague you, you can't let them become your undoing. When there's something in your life you wish wasn't there, you can never let that separate you from the fact that, in Christ, God is with you.

Trouble, distress, demons, rulers, mean people, even violent death can't separate you from God's love. That means that, when you're faced with dangers, you can expect to find more of him. The more trials you overcome and cling to him through, the more your character grows along with your absolute confidence that he is who he says he is. So don't be sorry for the troubles in your life but let them be used for your good, not your destruction. Let them always draw you closer to him.

accursed and cut off from Christ for the sake of my brothers,[1] my kinsmen according to the flesh. [4] They are Israelites, and to them belong the adoption, the glory, the covenants, the giving of the law, the worship, and the promises. [5] To them belong the patriarchs, and from their race, according to the flesh, is the Christ, who is God over all, blessed forever. Amen.

[6] But it is not as though the word of God has failed. For not all who are descended from Israel belong to Israel, [7] and not all are children of Abraham because they are his offspring, but [a] "Through Isaac shall your offspring be named." [8] This means that it is not the children of the flesh who are the children of God, but the children of the promise are counted as offspring. [9] For this is what the promise said: [b] "About this time next year I will return, and Sarah shall have a son." [10] And not only so, but also when Rebekah had conceived children by one man, our forefather Isaac, [11] though they were not yet born and had done nothing either good or bad—in order that God's purpose of election might continue, not because of works but because of him who calls— [12] she was told, [c] "The older will serve the younger." [13] As it is written, [d] "Jacob I loved, but Esau I hated."

[14] What shall we say then? Is there injustice on God's part? By no means! [15] For he says to Moses, [e] "I will have mercy on whom I have mercy, and I will have compassion on whom I have compassion." [16] So then it depends not on human will or exertion,[2] but on God, who has mercy. [17] For the Scripture says to Pharaoh, [f] "For this very purpose I have raised you up, that I might show my power in you, and that my name might be proclaimed in all the earth." [18] So then he has mercy on whomever he wills, and he hardens whomever he wills.

[19] You will say to me then, "Why does he still find fault? For who can resist his will?" [20] But who are you, O man, to answer back to God? Will what is molded say to its molder, "Why have you made me like this?" [21] Has the potter no right over the clay, to make out of the same lump one vessel for honorable use and another for dishonorable use? [22] What if God, desiring to show his wrath and to make known his power, has endured with much patience

vessels of wrath prepared for destruction, [23] in order to make known the riches of his glory for vessels of mercy, which he has prepared beforehand for glory— [24] even us whom he has called, not from the Jews only but also from the Gentiles? [25] As indeed he says in Hosea,

> [g] "Those who were not my people I will
>   call 'my people,'
>   and her who was not beloved I will
>   call 'beloved.'"
> [26] [h] "And in the very place where it was
>   said to them, 'You are not my
>   people,'
>   there they will be called 'sons of
>   the living God.'"

[27] And Isaiah cries out concerning Israel: [i] "Though the number of the sons of Israel[3] be as the sand of the sea, only a remnant of them will be saved, [28] for the Lord will carry out his sentence upon the earth fully and without delay." [29] And as Isaiah predicted,

> [j] "If the Lord of hosts had not left us
>   offspring,
>   we would have been like Sodom
>   and become like Gomorrah."

Israel's Unbelief

[30] What shall we say, then? That Gentiles who did not pursue righteousness have attained it, that is, a righteousness that is by faith; [31] but that Israel who pursued a law that would lead to righteousness[4] did not succeed in reaching that law. [32] Why? Because they did not pursue it by faith, but as if it were based on works. They have stumbled over the stumbling stone, [33] as it is written,

> [k] "Behold, I am laying in Zion a stone
>   of stumbling, and a rock of
>   offense;
>   and whoever believes in him will
>   not be put to shame."

10 Brothers,[5] my heart's desire and prayer to God for them is that they may be saved. [2] For I bear them witness that they have a zeal for God, but not according to knowledge. [3] For, being ignorant of the righteousness of God, and seeking to establish their own, they did not

---

[1] Or brothers and sisters [2] Greek not of him who wills or runs [3] Or children of Israel [4] Greek a law of righteousness [5] Or Brothers and sisters
[a] Gen. 21:12 [b] Gen. 18:10, 14 [c] Gen. 25:23 [d] Mal. 1:2, 3 [e] Ex. 33:19 [f] Ex. 9:16 [g] Hos. 2:23 [h] Hos. 1:10 [i] Isa. 10:22, 23 [j] Isa. 1:9 [k] Isa. 28:16

submit to God's righteousness. [4] For Christ is the end of the law for righteousness to everyone who believes.[1]

The Message of Salvation to All

[5] For Moses writes about the righteousness that is based on the law, that the person who does the commandments shall live by them. [6] But the righteousness based on faith says, "Do not say in your heart, 'Who will ascend into heaven?'" (that is, to bring Christ down) [7] "or 'Who will descend into the abyss?'" (that is, to bring Christ up from the dead). [8] But what does it say? [a] "The word is near you, in your mouth and in your heart" (that is, the word of faith that we proclaim); [9] because, if you confess with your mouth that Jesus is Lord and believe in your heart that God raised him from the dead, you will be saved. [10] For with the heart one believes and is justified, and with the mouth one confesses and is saved. [11] For the Scripture says, "Everyone who believes in him will not be put to shame." [12] For there is no distinction between Jew and Greek; for the same Lord is Lord of all, bestowing his riches on all who call on him. [13] For [b] "everyone who calls on the name of the Lord will be saved."

[14] How then will they call on him in whom they have not believed? And how are they to believe in him of whom they have never heard?[2] And how are they to hear without someone preaching? [15] And how are they to preach unless they are sent? As it is written, [c] "How beautiful are the feet of those who preach the good news!" [16] But they have not all obeyed the

[1] Or end of the law, that everyone who believes may be justified [2] Or him whom they have never heard [a] Deut. 30:14 [b] Joel 2:32 [c] Isa. 52:7

Know God

verses to read
Romans 10:1–11

Salvation comes in an instant: "If you confess with your mouth that Jesus is Lord and believe in your heart that God raised him from the dead, you will be saved" (Rom. 10:9). When God opens your eyes to see your sin and the atonement provided in Christ, your life changes, and everything you do and think comes into focus in the light of God's Word. A lot of times you can look at your life and start to question your salvation. Was it real? Did I really mean it? The answer to that question isn't hard to find. When God saves you, he changes you. You are no longer the same. You are always changing, always getting better. Like a tree producing buckets of fruit, you will start to produce spiritual fruit. Things that were once difficult for you will become easier—not all of them, but a lot of them. And you'll find more and more evidence of God's work in your life.

When a girl makes Jesus her Lord, she makes him her master (see Rom. 6:16). That means that she takes her orders from him and not from anyone else. And this position as slave to Jesus is one that proves your salvation was not a passing fancy. It is not a seed planted in the rocky soil and choked out by the trials of life (see Matt. 13:18–23) but a real, life-saving salvation that can't be lost. The God Girl is certain of her salvation because *she wants what God wants*. She wants to know him more, to know his Word and to obey it, even though she has the occasional mess-up. Forgiveness is free for those who agree with God that they have sinned—for those who can accept the forgiveness that is there for all who believe. It's this forgiveness and your desire to get it right next time that should prove to *you* that you are saved. And it's your ever-increasing obedience that proves to *the world* and to *God* that you have truly made him Lord of your life (see John 15:14; 1 John 2:3–4; 5:3).

gospel. For Isaiah says, [a]"Lord, who has believed what he has heard from us?" [17]So faith comes from hearing, and hearing through the word of Christ.

[18]But I ask, have they not heard? Indeed they have, for

[b]"Their voice has gone out to all the earth,
and their words to the ends of the world."

[19]But I ask, did Israel not understand? First Moses says,

[c]"I will make you jealous of those who are not a nation;
with a foolish nation I will make you angry."

[20]Then Isaiah is so bold as to say,

[d]"I have been found by those who did not seek me;
I have shown myself to those who did not ask for me."

[21]But of Israel he says, [e]"All day long I have held out my hands to a disobedient and contrary people."

The Remnant of Israel

11 I ask, then, has God rejected his people? By no means! For I myself am an Israelite, a descendant of Abraham,[1] a member of the tribe of Benjamin. [2]God has not rejected his people whom he foreknew. Do you not know what the Scripture says of Elijah, how he appeals to God against Israel? [3][f]"Lord, they have killed your prophets, they have demolished your altars, and I alone am left, and they seek my life." [4]But what is God's reply to him? [g]"I have kept for myself seven thousand men who have not bowed the knee to Baal." [5]So too at the present time there is a remnant, chosen by grace. [6]But if it is by grace, it is no longer on the basis of works; otherwise grace would no longer be grace.

[7]What then? Israel failed to obtain what it was seeking. The elect obtained it, but the rest were hardened, [8]as it is written,

"God gave them a spirit of stupor,
eyes that would not see
and ears that would not hear,
down to this very day."

[9]And David says,

[h]"Let their table become a snare and a trap,
a stumbling block and a retribution for them;
[10]   let their eyes be darkened so that they cannot see,
and bend their backs forever."

Gentiles Grafted In

[11]So I ask, did they stumble in order that they might fall? By no means! Rather through their trespass salvation has come to the Gentiles, so as to make Israel jealous. [12]Now if their trespass means riches for the world, and if their failure means riches for the Gentiles, how much more will their full inclusion[2] mean!

[13]Now I am speaking to you Gentiles. Inasmuch then as I am an apostle to the Gentiles, I magnify my ministry [14]in order somehow to make my fellow Jews jealous, and thus save some of them. [15]For if their rejection means the reconciliation of the world, what will their acceptance mean but life from the dead? [16]If the dough offered as firstfruits is holy, so is the whole lump, and if the root is holy, so are the branches.

[17]But if some of the branches were broken off, and you, although a wild olive shoot, were grafted in among the others and now share in the nourishing root[3] of the olive tree, [18]do not be arrogant toward the branches. If you are, remember it is not you who support the root, but the root that supports you. [19]Then you will say, "Branches were broken off so that I might be grafted in." [20]That is true. They were broken off because of their unbelief, but you stand fast through faith. So do not become proud, but fear. [21]For if God did not spare the natural branches, neither will he spare you. [22]Note then the kindness and the severity of God: severity toward those who have fallen, but God's kindness to you, provided you continue in his kindness. Otherwise you too will be cut off. [23]And even they, if they do not continue in their unbelief, will be grafted in, for God has the power to graft them in again. [24]For if you were cut from what is by nature a wild olive tree, and grafted, contrary to nature, into a cultivated olive tree, how much more

[1]Or one of the offspring of Abraham [2]Greek their fullness [3]Greek root of richness; some manuscripts richness [a]Isa. 53:1 [b]Ps. 19:4 [c]Deut. 32:21 [d]Isa. 65:1 [e]Isa. 65:2 [f]1 Kgs. 19:10, 14 [g]1 Kgs. 19:18 [h]Ps. 69:22, 23

will these, the natural branches, be grafted back into their own olive tree.

The Mystery of Israel's Salvation

[25] Lest you be wise in your own sight, I do not want you to be unaware of this mystery, brothers:[1] a partial hardening has come upon Israel, until the fullness of the Gentiles has come in. [26] And in this way all Israel will be saved, as it is written,

> [a]"The Deliverer will come from Zion,
>   he will banish ungodliness from
>   Jacob";
> [27] "and this will be my covenant with
>   them
>   when I take away their sins."

[28] As regards the gospel, they are enemies for your sake. But as regards election, they are beloved for the sake of their forefathers. [29] For the gifts and the calling of God are irrevocable. [30] For just as you were at one time disobedient to God but now have received mercy because of their disobedi-ence, [31] so they too have now been disobedient in order that by the mercy shown to you they also may now[2] receive mercy. [32] For God has consigned all to disobedience, that he may have mercy on all.

[33] Oh, the depth of the riches and wisdom and knowledge of God! How unsearchable are his judgments and how inscrutable his ways!

[34] "For who has known the mind of the
            Lord,
        or who has been his counselor?"
[35] "Or who has given a gift to him
        that he might be repaid?"

[36] For from him and through him and to him are all things. To him be glory forever. Amen.

A Living Sacrifice

12 I appeal to you therefore, brothers,[3] by the mercies of God, to present your bodies as a living sacrifice, holy and acceptable to God, which is your spiritual worship.[4] [2] Do not be conformed to this

---

[1] Or brothers and sisters [2] Some manuscripts omit now [3] Or brothers and sisters [4] Or your rational service [a] Isa. 59:20, 21

Know God

verses to read
Romans 12:14-21

When you selfishly fight for your rights, you stab Jesus in the heart. When you demand that things go this way or that, you might not hurt anyone else, but you do persecute him and cause him to suffer because of your disbelief. You say you love the Lord and you even teach others about him, but your behavior says something different when you stand for anything other than Jesus Christ himself.

Remember, Jesus' call to you is humility. He says, "learn from me, for I am gentle and lowly in heart" (Matt. 11:29). He never demanded respect or stood up for his rights. Instead he "continued entrusting himself to him who judges justly" (1 Pet. 2:23). Don't demand more rights than the Son of God himself demanded! When you are mistreated, stand up for what's right, but don't take revenge. Let God take care of it (see Rom. 12:19). When someone else gets something better than you do, humbly say, "That's okay, I got much more than I deserve when Christ saved me." Trust God with everything and focus on the needs of other people instead of yourself.

When you live your life as Jesus did, you won't be concerned about being slighted, put upon, or ignored, because all your thoughts and hopes will be on him. That is true freedom and true faith. Don't let your thoughts of what you want or think you "deserve" overpower the life of Christ in you. Instead practice being one with him in meekness and humility.

world,[1] but be transformed by the renewal of your mind, that by testing you may discern what is the will of God, what is good and acceptable and perfect.[2]

Gifts of Grace

[3] For by the grace given to me I say to everyone among you not to think of himself more highly than he ought to think, but to think with sober judgment, each according to the measure of faith that God has assigned. [4] For as in one body we have many members,[3] and the members do not all have the same function, [5] so we, though many, are one body in Christ, and individually members one of another. [6] Having gifts that differ according to the grace given to us, let us use them: if prophecy, in proportion to our faith; [7] if service, in our serving; the one who teaches, in his teaching; [8] the one who exhorts, in his exhortation; the one who contributes, in generosity; the one who leads,[4] with zeal; the one who does acts of mercy, with cheerfulness.

Marks of the True Christian

[9] Let love be genuine. Abhor what is evil; hold fast to what is good. [10] Love one another with brotherly affection. Outdo one another in showing honor. [11] Do not be slothful in zeal, be fervent in spirit,[5] serve the Lord. [12] Rejoice in hope, be patient in tribulation, be constant in prayer. [13] Contribute to the needs of the saints and seek to show hospitality.

[14] Bless those who persecute you; bless and do not curse them. [15] Rejoice with those who rejoice, weep with those who weep. [16] Live in harmony with one another. Do not be haughty, but associate with the lowly.[6] Never be wise in your own sight. [17] Repay no one evil for evil, but give thought to do what is honorable in the sight of all. [18] If possible, so far as it depends on you, live peaceably with all. [19] Beloved, never avenge yourselves, but leave it[7] to the wrath of God, for it is written, [a]"Vengeance is mine, I will repay, says the Lord." [20] To the contrary, [b]"if your enemy is hungry, feed him; if he is thirsty, give him something to drink; for by so doing you will heap burning coals on his head." [21] Do not be overcome by evil, but overcome evil with good.

Submission to the Authorities

13 Let every person be subject to the governing authorities. For there is no authority except from God, and those that exist have been instituted by God. [2] Therefore whoever resists the authorities resists what God has appointed, and those who resist will incur judgment. [3] For rulers are not a terror to good conduct, but to bad. Would you have no fear of the one who is in authority? Then do what is good, and you will receive his approval, [4] for he is God's servant for your good. But if you do wrong, be afraid, for he does not bear the sword in vain. For he is the servant of God, an avenger who carries out God's wrath on the wrongdoer. [5] Therefore one must be in subjection, not only to avoid God's wrath but also for the sake of conscience. [6] For because of this you also pay taxes, for the authorities are ministers of God, attending to this very thing. [7] Pay to all what is owed to them: taxes to whom taxes are owed, revenue to whom revenue is owed, respect to whom respect is owed, honor to whom honor is owed.

Ask Yourself . . .

ABOUT AUTHORITY

Who's in charge of you? Is there anyone whom you have to submit to? Parents, boss, government? Ask yourself about authority:

- Do I have a problem with authority?

- Do I ever argue with people in authority over me?

- What do I think about people in authority?

- Do I submit well to God?

- Is submission something God wants from me?

- How can I practice obeying authority?

---

[1] Greek *age* [2] Or *what is the good and acceptable and perfect will of God* [3] Greek *parts*; also verse 5 [4] Or *gives aid* [5] Or *fervent in the Spirit* [6] Or *give yourselves to humble tasks* [7] Greek *give place* [a] Deut. 32:35 [b] Prov. 25:21, 22

Fulfilling the Law Through Love

[8] Owe no one anything, except to love each other, for the one who loves another has fulfilled the law. [9] For the commandments, [a] "You shall not commit adultery, You shall not murder, You shall not steal, You shall not covet," and any other commandment, are summed up in this word: [b] "You shall love your neighbor as yourself." [10] Love does no wrong to a neighbor; therefore love is the fulfilling of the law.

[11] Besides this you know the time, that the hour has come for you to wake from sleep. For salvation is nearer to us now than when we first believed. [12] The night is far gone; the day is at hand. So then let us cast off the works of darkness and put on the armor of light. [13] Let us walk properly as in the daytime, not in orgies and drunkenness, not in sexual immorality and sensuality, not in quarreling and jealousy. [14] But put on the Lord Jesus Christ, and make no provision for the flesh, to gratify its desires.

Do Not Pass Judgment on One Another

14 As for the one who is weak in faith, welcome him, but not to quarrel over opinions. [2] One person believes he may eat anything, while the weak person eats only vegetables. [3] Let not the one who eats despise the one who abstains, and let not the one who abstains pass judgment on the one who eats, for God has welcomed him. [4] Who are you to pass judgment on the servant of another? It is before his own master[1] that he stands or falls. And he will be upheld, for the Lord is able to make him stand.

[5] One person esteems one day as better than another, while another esteems all days alike. Each one should be fully convinced in his own mind. [6] The one who observes the day, observes it in honor of the Lord. The one who eats, eats in honor of the Lord, since he gives thanks to God, while the one who abstains, abstains in honor of the Lord and gives thanks to God.

[1] Or *lord* [a] Ex. 20:13-17; Deut. 5:17-21 [b] Lev. 19:18

Know God

verses to read
Romans 14:19–23

Are you ever unsure if what you're doing is good with God or not? Whenever you have doubts, you should stop immediately. Doubt signals trouble. It's a red flag in the life of a believer, a sign letting you know you've taken a detour. Don't go any farther on that wobbly bridge.

The best rule of thumb is, if in doubt, don't do it, because if you doubt and do it anyway, you are in danger of falling into sin. Take some time to search Scripture so that you can be more informed. Don't jump into things you doubt so quickly that you get used to accepting gray areas as okay areas for you to enter. Find out the truth. Be certain that what you do, how you act, and what you say are in line with what God wants from your life. Doubt is like a car gauge—it warns you when you're about to run into trouble. So read the manual and find out what the sign means and what you need to do next. If you have doubt after reading God's Word, or if someone has given you a reason to believe God is against what you are doing, then slow down and dig deeper.

If you can look at all of Scripture and see no command that would make what you want to do a sin, and if the action is in line with the kind of person that Scripture calls us to be, then doubt has no ground to stand on. So many times we worry about whether God wants us to do this or that when the Bible doesn't address the topic at all. If it fits with Scripture, then you can stop worrying about whether it's the right thing or not—and be confident in what you are doing.

7 For none of us lives to himself, and none of us dies to himself. **8** For if we live, we live to the Lord, and if we die, we die to the Lord. So then, whether we live or whether we die, we are the Lord's. **9** For to this end Christ died and lived again, that he might be Lord both of the dead and of the living. **10** Why do you pass judgment on your brother? Or you, why do you despise your brother? For we will all stand before the judgment seat of God; **11** for it is written,

> *a* "As I live, says the Lord, every knee
>   shall bow to me,
>   and every tongue shall confess¹ to
>   God."

12 So then each of us will give an account of himself to God.

Ask Yourself . . .

ABOUT MAKING DECISIONS

Here are seven things to ask yourself when you aren't sure what to do:

1. Am I in doubt about what I want to do (see Rom. 14:23)?

2. Is it consistent with Scripture, or does it go against it (see 2 Tim. 3:16)?

3. Will it honor Christ (see 1 Cor. 10:31)?

4. How might it affect someone who is spiritually weaker than I (see 1 Cor. 8:9)?

5. Is it pure, and will doing it leave me blameless (see Phil. 1:10)?

6. Will other believers approve (see Rom. 14:18–19)?

7. Will it build others up (see Rom. 15:1–2; 1 Thess. 5:11)?

Do Not Cause Another to Stumble

13 Therefore let us not pass judgment on one another any longer, but rather decide never to put a stumbling block or hindrance in the way of a brother. **14** I know and am persuaded in the Lord Jesus that nothing is unclean in itself, but it is unclean for anyone who thinks it unclean. **15** For if your brother is grieved by what you eat, you are no longer walking in love. By what you eat, do not destroy the one for whom Christ died. **16** So do not let what you regard as good be spoken of as evil. **17** For the kingdom of God is not a matter of eating and drinking but of righteousness and peace and joy in the Holy Spirit. **18** Whoever thus serves Christ is acceptable to God and approved by men. **19** So then let us pursue what makes for peace and for mutual upbuilding.

20 Do not, for the sake of food, destroy the work of God. Everything is indeed clean, but it is wrong for anyone to make another stumble by what he eats. **21** It is good not to eat meat or drink wine or do anything that causes your brother to stumble.² **22** The faith that you have, keep between yourself and God. Blessed is the one who has no reason to pass judgment on himself for what he approves. **23** But whoever has doubts is condemned if he eats, because the eating is not from faith. For whatever does not proceed from faith is sin.³

The Example of Christ

15 We who are strong have an obligation to bear with the failings of the weak, and not to please ourselves. **2** Let each of us please his neighbor for his good, to build him up. **3** For Christ did not please himself, but as it is written, *b* "The reproaches of those who reproached you fell on me." **4** For whatever was written in former days was written for our instruction, that through endurance and through the encouragement of the Scriptures we might have hope. **5** May the God of endurance and encouragement grant you to live in such harmony with one another, in accord with Christ Jesus, **6** that together you may with one voice glorify the God and Father of our Lord Jesus Christ. **7** Therefore welcome one another as Christ has welcomed you, for the glory of God.

Christ the Hope of Jews and Gentiles

8 For I tell you that Christ became a servant to the circumcised to show God's

---

¹ Or *shall give praise* ² Some manuscripts add *or be hindered or be weakened* ³ Some manuscripts insert here 16:25–27 *a* Isa. 45:23 *b* Ps. 69:9

truthfulness, in order to confirm the promises given to the patriarchs, [9] and in order that the Gentiles might glorify God for his mercy. As it is written,

[a]"Therefore I will praise you among the Gentiles,
　　and sing to your name."

[10] And again it is said,

[b]"Rejoice, O Gentiles, with his people."

[11] And again,

[c]"Praise the Lord, all you Gentiles,
　　and let all the peoples extol him."

[12] And again Isaiah says,

[d]"The root of Jesse will come,
　　even he who arises to rule the Gentiles;
　　in him will the Gentiles hope."

[13] May the God of hope fill you with all joy and peace in believing, so that by the power of the Holy Spirit you may abound in hope.

Paul the Minister to the Gentiles

[14] I myself am satisfied about you, my brothers,[1] that you yourselves are full of goodness, filled with all knowledge and able to instruct one another. [15] But on some points I have written to you very boldly by way of reminder, because of the grace given me by God [16] to be a minister of Christ Jesus to the Gentiles in the priestly service of the gospel of God, so that the offering of the Gentiles may be acceptable, sanctified by the Holy Spirit. [17] In Christ Jesus, then, I have reason to be proud of my work for God. [18] For I will not venture to speak of anything except what Christ has accomplished through me to bring the Gentiles to obedience—by word and deed, [19] by the power of signs and wonders, by the power of the Spirit of God—so that from Jerusalem and all the way around to Illyricum I have fulfilled the ministry of the gospel of Christ; [20] and thus I make it my ambition to preach the gospel, not where Christ has already been named, lest I build on someone else's foundation, [21] but as it is written,

[e]"Those who have never been told of him will see,
　　and those who have never heard will understand."

Paul's Plan to Visit Rome

[22] This is the reason why I have so often been hindered from coming to you. [23] But now, since I no longer have any room for work in these regions, and since I have longed for many years to come to you, [24] I hope to see you in passing as I go to Spain, and to be helped on my journey there by you, once I have enjoyed your company for a while. [25] At present, however, I am going to Jerusalem bringing aid to the saints. [26] For Macedonia and Achaia have been pleased to make some contribution for the poor among the saints at Jerusalem. [27] For they were pleased to do it, and indeed they owe it to them. For if the Gentiles have come to share in their spiritual blessings, they ought also to be of service to them in material blessings. [28] When therefore I have completed this and have delivered to them what has been collected,[2] I will leave for Spain by way of you. [29] I know that when I come to you I will come in the fullness of the blessing[3] of Christ.

[30] I appeal to you, brothers, by our Lord Jesus Christ and by the love of the Spirit, to strive together with me in your prayers to God on my behalf, [31] that I may be delivered from the unbelievers in Judea, and that my service for Jerusalem may be acceptable to the saints, [32] so that by God's will I may come to you with joy and be refreshed in your company. [33] May the God of peace be with you all. Amen.

Personal Greetings

16 I commend to you our sister Phoebe, a servant[4] of the church at Cenchreae, [2] that you may welcome her in the Lord in a way worthy of the saints, and help her in whatever she may need from you, for she has been a patron of many and of myself as well.

[3] Greet Prisca and Aquila, my fellow workers in Christ Jesus, [4] who risked their necks for my life, to whom not only I give thanks but all the churches of the Gentiles give thanks as well. [5] Greet also the church in their house. Greet my

---

[1] Or brothers and sisters; also verse 30 　[2] Greek sealed to them this fruit 　[3] Some manuscripts insert of the gospel 　[4] Or deaconess 　[a] 2 Sam. 22:50; Ps. 18:49 　[b] Deut. 32:43 　[c] Ps. 117:1 　[d] Isa. 11:10 　[e] Isa. 52:15

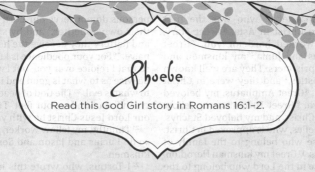

Phoebe

Read this God Girl story in Romans 16:1–2.

> And all who believed were together and had all things in common. And they were selling their possessions and belongings and distributing the proceeds to all, as any had need. And day by day, attending the temple together and breaking bread in their homes, they received their food with glad and generous hearts.
>
> *Acts 2:44–46*

As Christians, we are a family. We all have the same Father, the same Spirit, and the same goal: heaven. And as a family we all look out for each other, because it's the right thing to do. In fact, in the family of believers no one should ever be homeless, helpless, or hungry. Everything we have comes directly from the hand of God, so we can never call it our own. We're just stewards of his stuff, caring for God's gifts until the time that he asks us to move them on to someone else. In the early church, all the believers lived like this. They felt no need to hoard their possessions or even to hold on to them but sold all they had to give to those in need. What a wonderful family!

When you have something that you can't and won't give away, you have an idol in your life—something that stands between you and serving God. Things are meant to serve, not to be served, and holding on to them for dear life teaches your heart to serve the thing you fear losing. Cultivate your giving nature. Giving might not come naturally to you, but it should be one of the main ways others describe you as a God Girl. Giving draws people into your presence and shows them the hands and feet of God in their lives. Paul bragged about Phoebe, one of his colaborers, because of how much she cared for other believers.

Like Phoebe, the God Girl ought to lead her family of believers by learning the secret of both *accepting* their gifts when she has a need and also *giving* when she has extra to give. Bad times will come and go. You won't always be able to give and you won't always have to take, but both actions are necessary so that we all have a chance to be of service to each other. Your occasional need will let others practice the art of giving without pride but in humility and kindness. And when the time comes that you can give back, give back freely. You came into this world with nothing and you will leave the same way. Don't hoard what ultimately isn't even yours.

beloved Epaenetus, who was the first convert[1] to Christ in Asia. **6** Greet Mary, who has worked hard for you. **7** Greet Andronicus and Junia,[2] my kinsmen and my fellow prisoners. They are well known to the apostles,[3] and they were in Christ before me. **8** Greet Ampliatus, my beloved in the Lord. **9** Greet Urbanus, our fellow worker in Christ, and my beloved Stachys. **10** Greet Apelles, who is approved in Christ. Greet those who belong to the family of Aristobulus. **11** Greet my kinsman Herodion. Greet those in the Lord who belong to the family of Narcissus. **12** Greet those workers in the Lord, Tryphaena and Tryphosa. Greet the beloved Persis, who has worked hard in the Lord. **13** Greet Rufus, chosen in the Lord; also his mother, who has been a mother to me as well. **14** Greet Asyncritus, Phlegon, Hermes, Patrobas, Hermas, and the brothers[4] who are with them. **15** Greet Philologus, Julia, Nereus and his sister, and Olympas, and all the saints who are with them. **16** Greet one another with a holy kiss. All the churches of Christ greet you.

Final Instructions and Greetings

17 I appeal to you, brothers, to watch out for those who cause divisions and create obstacles contrary to the doctrine that you have been taught; avoid them. **18** For such persons do not serve our Lord Christ, but their own appetites,[5] and by smooth talk and flattery they deceive the hearts of the naive. **19** For your obedience is known to all, so that I rejoice over you, but I want you to be wise as to what is good and innocent as to what is evil. **20** The God of peace will soon crush Satan under your feet. The grace of our Lord Jesus Christ be with you.

21 Timothy, my fellow worker, greets you; so do Lucius and Jason and Sosipater, my kinsmen.

22 I Tertius, who wrote this letter, greet you in the Lord.

23 Gaius, who is host to me and to the whole church, greets you. Erastus, the city treasurer, and our brother Quartus, greet you.[6]

Doxology

25 Now to him who is able to strengthen you according to my gospel and the preaching of Jesus Christ, according to the revelation of the mystery that was kept secret for long ages **26** but has now been disclosed and through the prophetic writings has been made known to all nations, according to the command of the eternal God, to bring about the obedience of faith— **27** to the only wise God be glory forevermore through Jesus Christ! Amen.

---

[1] Greek *firstfruit* [2] Or *Junias* [3] Or *messengers* [4] Or *brothers and sisters*; also verse 17 [5] Greek *their own belly* [6] Some manuscripts insert verse 24: *The grace of our Lord Jesus Christ be with you all. Amen.*

INTRODUCTION TO

1 Corinthians

Author: The apostle Paul

Time: Sometime around A.D. 55

Place: Ephesus

Written to: The church in Corinth

The gist

The Corinthian church was a young church in a wild city, and because of that they had gotten kind of mixed up in the decadence of it all. They had forgotten the way of faith. Paul wrote this letter to help get them back on track.

Things to look for

- What the Bible has to say about love relationships (see 1 Corinthians 7)
- Teaching on worship (see 1 Corinthians 11)
- A description of your new body (1 Cor. 15:35–58)

Love Each Other Enough to Be Honest

> I am writing to you not to associate with anyone who bears the name of brother if he is guilty of sexual immorality or greed, or is an idolater, reviler, drunkard, or swindler—not even to eat with such a one.
>
> *1 Corinthians 5:11*

Tough love can look like anything but love. It's the kind of love that says no to a loved one's cries for someone to bail them out of a mess that only their repentance can get them out of. Tough love takes a stand, because it knows that a sin that continues to be adored and protected is a sin that will continue to bring much misery.

In his letter to the Corinthians, Paul warned the church in Corinth that they could no longer turn a blind eye to the sins of their brothers and sisters. That's because the one who accepts another in spite of their desire to continue living in sin commits a sin alongside them. And that is not love; it's codependency, and it encourages the sinner in his or her self-deception. This kind of false love is always selfish, because it's afraid to confront your friends about their sin out of fear of embarrassment or rejection. That false love puts fear before God and before the spiritual well-being of the other person. Being a God Girl means being fearless in the faith, unafraid to confront and distance yourself from believers who choose to live in sin without confessing it or attempting to repent.

While you should not be always on the offensive, attacking the sin of each and every human being you encounter, you should know that your closest friendships need a lot of honesty. And if you or your fellow God Girls are rejecting God's law by consciously choosing to live in some kind of sin, then, mindful of your own shortcomings and God's grace over them, you are called to let them know. You might even have to tell them you can't hang out with them anymore if they choose to keep on sinning instead of confessing. Heed the warning of 1 Corinthians, and don't let the approval of your friends' sinful habits become a conspiracy to sin.

Must-Know Verses

The word of the cross is folly to those who are perishing, but to us who are being saved it is the power of God. *1 Corinthians 1:18*

Do you not know that you are God's temple and that God's Spirit dwells in you? If anyone destroys God's temple, God will destroy him. For God's temple is holy, and you are that temple. *1 Corinthians 3:16–17*

I am writing to you not to associate with anyone who bears the name of brother if he is guilty of sexual immorality or greed, or is an idolater, reviler, drunkard, or swindler—not even to eat with such a one. *1 Corinthians 5:11*

Though I am free from all, I have made myself a servant to all, that I might win more of them. *1 Corinthians 9:19*

No temptation has overtaken you that is not common to man. God is faithful, and he will not let you be tempted beyond your ability, but with the temptation he will also provide the way of escape, that you may be able to endure it. *1 Corinthians 10:13*

Love is patient and kind; love does not envy or boast; it is not arrogant or rude. It does not insist on its own way; it is not irritable or resentful. *1 Corinthians 13:4–5*

The First Letter of Paul to the Corinthians

1 Corinthians

Greeting

1 Paul, called by the will of God to be an apostle of Christ Jesus, and our brother Sosthenes,

²To the church of God that is in Corinth, to those sanctified in Christ Jesus, called to be saints together with all those who in every place call upon the name of our Lord Jesus Christ, both their Lord and ours:

³Grace to you and peace from God our Father and the Lord Jesus Christ.

Thanksgiving

⁴I give thanks to my God always for you because of the grace of God that was given you in Christ Jesus, ⁵that in every way you were enriched in him in all speech and all knowledge— ⁶even as the testimony about Christ was confirmed among you— ⁷so that you are not lacking in any gift, as you wait for the revealing of our Lord Jesus Christ, ⁸who will sustain you to the end, guiltless in the day of our Lord Jesus Christ. ⁹God is faithful, by whom you were called into the fellowship of his Son, Jesus Christ our Lord.

Divisions in the Church

¹⁰I appeal to you, brothers,[1] by the name of our Lord Jesus Christ, that all of you agree, and that there be no divisions among you, but that you be united in the same mind and the same judgment. ¹¹For it has been reported to me by Chloe's people that there is quarreling among you, my brothers. ¹²What I mean is that each one of you says, "I follow Paul," or "I follow Apollos," or "I follow Cephas," or "I follow Christ." ¹³Is Christ divided? Was Paul crucified for you? Or were you baptized in the name of Paul? ¹⁴I thank God that I baptized none of you except Crispus and Gaius, ¹⁵so that no one may say that you were bap-

tized in my name. ¹⁶(I did baptize also the household of Stephanas. Beyond that, I do not know whether I baptized anyone else.) ¹⁷For Christ did not send me to baptize but to preach the gospel, and not with words of eloquent wisdom, lest the cross of Christ be emptied of its power.

Christ the Wisdom and Power of God

¹⁸For the word of the cross is folly to those who are perishing, but to us who are being saved it is the power of God. ¹⁹For it is written,

> ᵃ"I will destroy the wisdom of the wise,
>   and the discernment of the discerning I will thwart."

²⁰Where is the one who is wise? Where is the scribe? Where is the debater of this age? Has not God made foolish the wisdom of the world? ²¹For since, in the wisdom of God, the world did not know God through wisdom, it pleased God through the folly of what we preach[2] to save those who believe. ²²For Jews demand signs and Greeks seek wisdom, ²³but we preach Christ crucified, a stumbling block to Jews and folly to Gentiles, ²⁴but to those who are called, both Jews and Greeks, Christ the power of God and the wisdom of God. ²⁵For the foolishness of God is wiser than men, and the weakness of God is stronger than men.

²⁶For consider your calling, brothers: not many of you were wise according to worldly standards,[3] not many were powerful, not many were of noble birth. ²⁷But God chose what is foolish in the world to shame the wise; God chose what is weak in the world to shame the strong; ²⁸God chose what is low and despised in the world, even things that are not, to bring to nothing things that are, ²⁹so that no

---

[1] Or brothers and sisters. The plural Greek word adelphoi (translated "brothers") refers to siblings in a family. In New Testament usage, depending on the context, adelphoi may refer either to men or to both men and women who are siblings (brothers and sisters) in God's family, the church; also verses 11, 26 [2] Or the folly of preaching [3] Greek according to the flesh ᵃ Isa. 29:14

human being[1] might boast in the presence of God. **30** And because of him[2] you are in Christ Jesus, who became to us wisdom from God, righteousness and sanctification and redemption, **31** so that, as it is written, "Let the one who boasts, boast in the Lord."

Proclaiming Christ Crucified

2 And I, when I came to you, brothers,[3] did not come proclaiming to you the testimony[4] of God with lofty speech or wisdom. **2** For I decided to know nothing among you except Jesus Christ and him crucified. **3** And I was with you in weakness and in fear and much trembling, **4** and my speech and my message were not in plausible words of wisdom, but in demonstration of the Spirit and of power, **5** so that your faith might not rest in the wisdom of men[5] but in the power of God.

Wisdom from the Spirit

6 Yet among the mature we do impart wisdom, although it is not a wisdom of this age or of the rulers of this age, who are doomed to pass away. **7** But we impart a secret and hidden wisdom of God, which God decreed before the ages for our glory. **8** None of the rulers of this age understood this, for if they had, they would not have crucified the Lord of glory. **9** But, as it is written,

"What no eye has seen, nor ear heard,
    nor the heart of man imagined,
what God has prepared for those
    who love him"—

10 these things God has revealed to us through the Spirit. For the Spirit searches everything, even the depths of God. **11** For who knows a person's thoughts except the spirit of that person, which is in him? So

[1] Greek *no flesh* [2] Greek *And from him* [3] Or *brothers and sisters* [4] Some manuscripts *mystery* (or *secret*) [5] The Greek word *anthropoi* can refer to both men and women

Know God

verses to read
1 Corinthians 1:26–31

At the point when God gave you new birth and Jesus became the Lord of your life, everything changed. With that one decision came not only a change in your will but also a change in your very being. Now you are no longer your own but are filled with Christ himself in the person of the Holy Spirit. Scripture says that "you are in Christ Jesus" (1 Cor. 1:30). Being united to Christ is one of the great mysteries and wonders of our salvation. In a way, it means we are partners with him. Partners are two people who share in doing something together; they work together toward a common goal. This is a big deal, because it means that even when you feel like you can't do what's right, that's okay, because Jesus can. But this doesn't mean that we do our part and then he takes over. It means our whole lives are gifts of his grace, and every good thing we ever do is the fruit of God working through us. You may fail sometimes, you may mess up royally, but you have been made a partner with Christ, and so he will get you out of your mess if you are willing to let him. Look to him.

As a God Girl, you aren't just out there doing life on your own. You have been ransomed or bought away from sin, and that means sin no longer controls you—because you are one with Christ. You might forget that sometimes and give in to sin's commands, but it's not in charge of you any longer. Now you have the wisdom of Jesus on your side, and that means you can be free from sin and all its punishment. The more you read the Word of God, the more you understand God, but don't underestimate the wisdom that's already yours just because you've become one with Jesus and received his Holy Spirit into your life.

also no one comprehends the thoughts of God except the Spirit of God. [12] Now we have received not the spirit of the world, but the Spirit who is from God, that we might understand the things freely given us by God. [13] And we impart this in words not taught by human wisdom but taught by the Spirit, interpreting spiritual truths to those who are spiritual.[1]

[14] The natural person does not accept the things of the Spirit of God, for they are folly to him, and he is not able to understand them because they are spiritually discerned. [15] The spiritual person judges all things, but is himself to be judged by no one. [16][a] "For who has understood the mind of the Lord so as to instruct him?" But we have the mind of Christ.

Divisions in the Church

3 But I, brothers,[2] could not address you as spiritual people, but as people of the flesh, as infants in Christ. [2] I fed you with milk, not solid food, for you were not ready for it. And even now you are not yet ready, [3] for you are still of the flesh. For while there is jealousy and strife among you, are you not of the flesh and behaving only in a human way? [4] For when one says, "I follow Paul," and another, "I follow Apollos," are you not being merely human?

[5] What then is Apollos? What is Paul? Servants through whom you believed, as the Lord assigned to each. [6] I planted, Apollos watered, but God gave the growth. [7] So neither he who plants nor he who waters is anything, but only God who gives the growth. [8] He who plants and he who waters are one, and each will receive his wages according to his labor. [9] For we are God's fellow workers. You are God's field, God's building.

[10] According to the grace of God given to me, like a skilled master builder I laid a foundation, and someone else is building upon it. Let each one take care how he builds upon it. [11] For no one can lay a foundation other than that which is laid, which is Jesus Christ. [12] Now if anyone builds on the foundation with gold, silver, precious stones, wood, hay, straw— [13] each one's work will become manifest, for the Day will disclose it, because it will be revealed by fire, and the fire will test what sort of work each one has done. [14] If the work that anyone has built on the foundation survives, he will receive a reward. [15] If anyone's work is burned up, he will suffer loss, though he himself will be saved, but only as through fire.

[16] Do you not know that you[3] are God's temple and that God's Spirit dwells in you? [17] If anyone destroys God's temple, God will destroy him. For God's temple is holy, and you are that temple.

[18] Let no one deceive himself. If anyone among you thinks that he is wise in this age, let him become a fool that he may become wise. [19] For the wisdom of this world is folly with God. For it is written, [b] "He catches the wise in their craftiness," [20] and again, [c] "The Lord knows the thoughts of the wise, that they are futile." [21] So let no one boast in men. For all things are yours, [22] whether Paul or Apollos or Cephas or the world or life or death or the present or the future—all are yours, [23] and you are Christ's, and Christ is God's.

The Ministry of Apostles

4 This is how one should regard us, as servants of Christ and stewards of the mysteries of God. [2] Moreover, it is required of stewards that they be found faithful. [3] But with me it is a very small thing that I should be judged by you or by any human court. In fact, I do not even judge myself. [4] For I am not aware of anything against myself, but I am not thereby acquitted. It is the Lord who judges me. [5] Therefore do not pronounce judgment before the time, before the Lord comes, who will bring to light the things now hidden in darkness and will disclose the purposes of the heart. Then each one will receive his commendation from God.

[6] I have applied all these things to myself and Apollos for your benefit, brothers,[4] that you may learn by us not to go beyond what is written, that none of you may be puffed up in favor of one against another. [7] For who sees anything different in you? What do you have that you did not receive? If then you received it, why do you boast as if you did not receive it?

[8] Already you have all you want! Already you have become rich! Without us you have become kings! And would that you did

---

[1] Or interpreting spiritual truths in spiritual language, or comparing spiritual things with spiritual   [2] Or brothers and sisters   [3] The Greek for you is plural in verses 16 and 17   [4] Or brothers and sisters   [a] Isa. 40:13   [b] Job 5:13   [c] Ps. 94:11

reign, so that we might share the rule with you! [9] For I think that God has exhibited us apostles as last of all, like men sentenced to death, because we have become a spectacle to the world, to angels, and to men. [10] We are fools for Christ's sake, but you are wise in Christ. We are weak, but you are strong. You are held in honor, but we in disrepute. [11] To the present hour we hunger and thirst, we are poorly dressed and buffeted and homeless, [12] and we labor, working with our own hands. When reviled, we bless; when persecuted, we endure; [13] when slandered, we entreat. We have become, and are still, like the scum of the world, the refuse of all things.

[14] I do not write these things to make you ashamed, but to admonish you as my beloved children. [15] For though you have countless[1] guides in Christ, you do not have many fathers. For I became your father in Christ Jesus through the gospel. [16] I urge you, then, to be imitators of me. [17] That is why I sent[2] you Timothy, my beloved and faithful child in the Lord, to remind you of my ways in Christ,[3] as I teach them everywhere in every church. [18] Some are arrogant, as though I were not coming to you. [19] But I will come to you soon, if the Lord wills, and I will find out not the talk of these arrogant people but their power. [20] For the kingdom of God does not consist in talk but in power. [21] What do you wish? Shall I come to you with a rod, or with love in a spirit of gentleness?

Sexual Immorality Defiles the Church

5 It is actually reported that there is sexual immorality among you, and of a kind that is not tolerated even among pagans, for a man has his father's wife. [2] And you are arrogant! Ought you not rather to mourn? Let him who has done this be removed from among you.

[3] For though absent in body, I am present in spirit; and as if present, I have already pronounced judgment on the one who did such a thing. [4] When you are assembled in the name of the Lord Jesus and my spirit is present, with the power of our Lord Jesus, [5] you are to deliver this man to Satan for the destruction of the flesh, so that his spirit may be saved in the day of the Lord.[4]

[6] Your boasting is not good. Do you not know that a little leaven leavens the whole lump? [7] Cleanse out the old leaven that you may be a new lump, as you really are unleavened. For Christ, our Passover lamb, has been sacrificed. [8] Let us therefore celebrate the festival, not with the old leaven, the leaven of malice and evil, but with the unleavened bread of sincerity and truth.

A Prayer to...
SERVE HIM

O my King and Friend, I come to you to tell you that I love you. Even though I am totally unworthy, full of doubts and fears, with unsanctified thoughts and sinful motives, still I trust you and your redeeming love. You alone can make me worthy, and I come just as I am. I can find purity and peace only at your feet. I can see light only as I stand in the light of your face. And I thank you that you are willing and waiting to receive me and that you are ready to accept the love of my poor heart.

Take my hand in yours and lead me where you will. The way may be long and the shadows deep, but I can't be afraid when you are near. Let me serve you as a slave serves her master. And as your slave, let me lead people to you and fight in your battle for righteousness. My Lord, I am completely unworthy of such an honor. But when you call, I will come. All I am and all I have is yours. There is no place for me in this world except in your service. Only with you can I find strength and know the meaning of life. Fill me with joy as I live and toil to bring your kingdom.

Amen.

[9] I wrote to you in my letter not to associate with sexually immoral people— [10] not at all meaning the sexually immoral of this world, or the greedy and swindlers, or idolaters, since then you would need to go out of the world. [11] But now I am writing to you not to associate with anyone who

---

[1] Greek *you have ten thousand* [2] Or *am sending* [3] Some manuscripts add *Jesus* [4] Some manuscripts add *Jesus*

bears the name of brother if he is guilty of sexual immorality or greed, or is an idolater, reviler, drunkard, or swindler—not even to eat with such a one. [12] For what have I to do with judging outsiders? Is it not those inside the church[1] whom you are to judge? [13] God judges[2] those outside. "Purge the evil person from among you."

Lawsuits Against Believers

6 When one of you has a grievance against another, does he dare go to law before the unrighteous instead of the saints? [2] Or do you not know that the saints will judge the world? And if the world is to be judged by you, are you incompetent to try trivial cases? [3] Do you not know that we are to judge angels? How much more, then, matters pertaining to this life! [4] So if you have such cases, why do you lay them before those who have no standing in the church? [5] I say this to your shame. Can it be that there is no one among you wise enough to settle a dispute between the brothers, [6] but brother goes to law against brother, and that before unbelievers? [7] To have lawsuits at all with one another is already a defeat for you. Why not rather suffer wrong? Why not rather be defrauded? [8] But you yourselves wrong and defraud—even your own brothers![3]

[9] Or do you not know that the unrighteous[4] will not inherit the kingdom of God? Do not be deceived: neither the sexually immoral, nor idolaters, nor adulterers, nor men who practice homosexuality,[5] [10] nor thieves, nor the greedy, nor drunkards, nor revilers, nor swindlers will inherit the kingdom of God. [11] And such were some of you. But you were washed, you were sanctified, you were justified in the name of the Lord Jesus Christ and by the Spirit of our God.

Flee Sexual Immorality

[12] "All things are lawful for me," but not all things are helpful. "All things are lawful for me," but I will not be dominated by anything. [13] "Food is meant for the stomach and the stomach for food"—and God will destroy both one and the other. The body is not meant for sexual immorality, but for the Lord, and the Lord for the body. [14] And God raised the Lord and will also raise us up by his power. [15] Do you not know that your bodies are members of Christ? Shall I then take the members of Christ and make them members of a prostitute? Never! [16] Or do you not know that he who is joined[6] to a prostitute becomes one body with her? For, as it is written, [a]"The two will become one flesh." [17] But he who is joined to the Lord becomes one spirit with him. [18] Flee from sexual immorality. Every other sin[7] a person commits is outside the body, but the sexually immoral person sins against his own body. [19] Or do you not know that your body is a temple of the Holy Spirit within you, whom you have from God? You are not your own, [20] for you were bought with a price. So glorify God in your body.

Principles for Marriage

7 Now concerning the matters about which you wrote: "It is good for a man not to have sexual relations with a woman." [2] But because of the temptation to sexual immorality, each man should have his own wife and each woman her own husband. [3] The husband should give to his wife her conjugal rights, and likewise the wife to her husband. [4] For the wife does not have authority over her own body, but the husband does. Likewise the husband does not have authority over his own body, but the wife does. [5] Do not deprive one another, except perhaps by agreement for a limited time, that you may devote yourselves to prayer; but then come together again, so that Satan may not tempt you because of your lack of self-control.

[6] Now as a concession, not a command, I say this.[8] [7] I wish that all were as I myself am. But each has his own gift from God, one of one kind and one of another.

[8] To the unmarried and the widows I say that it is good for them to remain single as I am. [9] But if they cannot exercise self-control, they should marry. For it is better to marry than to burn with passion.

[10] To the married I give this charge (not I, but the Lord): the wife should not separate from her husband [11] (but if she does, she should remain unmarried or else be reconciled to her husband), and the husband should not divorce his wife.

---

[1] Greek *those inside* [2] *Or will judge* [3] Or *brothers and sisters* [4] Or *wrongdoers* [5] The two Greek terms translated by this phrase refer to the passive and active partners in consensual homosexual acts [6] Or *who holds fast* (compare Genesis 2:24 and Deuteronomy 10:20); also verse 17 [7] Or *Every sin* [8] Or *I say this:* [a] Gen. 2:24

¹²To the rest I say (I, not the Lord) that if any brother has a wife who is an unbeliever, and she consents to live with him, he should not divorce her. ¹³If any woman has a husband who is an unbeliever, and he consents to live with her, she should not divorce him. ¹⁴For the unbelieving husband is made holy because of his wife, and the unbelieving wife is made holy because of her husband. Otherwise your children would be unclean, but as it is, they are holy. ¹⁵But if the unbelieving partner separates, let it be so. In such cases the brother or sister is not enslaved. God has called you¹ to peace. ¹⁶For how do you know, wife, whether you will save your husband? Or how do you know, husband, whether you will save your wife?

Live as You Are Called

¹⁷Only let each person lead the life² that the Lord has assigned to him, and to which God has called him. This is my rule in all the churches. ¹⁸Was anyone at the time of his call already circumcised? Let him not seek to remove the marks of circumcision. Was anyone at the time of his call uncircumcised? Let him not seek circumcision. ¹⁹For neither circumcision counts for anything nor uncircumcision, but keeping the commandments of God. ²⁰Each one should remain in the condition in which he was called. ²¹Were you a bondservant³ when called? Do not be concerned about it. (But if you can gain your freedom, avail yourself of the opportunity.) ²²For he who was called in the Lord as a bondservant is a freedman of the Lord. Likewise he who was free when called is a bondservant of Christ. ²³You were bought with a price; do not become bondservants⁴ of men. ²⁴So, brothers,⁵ in whatever condition each was called, there let him remain with God.

The Unmarried and the Widowed

²⁵Now concerning⁶ the betrothed,⁷ I have no command from the Lord, but I give my judgment as one who by the Lord's mercy is trustworthy. ²⁶I think that in view of the present⁸ distress it is good for a person to remain as he is. ²⁷Are you bound to a wife? Do not seek to be free. Are you free from a wife? Do not seek a wife. ²⁸But if you do marry, you have not sinned, and if a betrothed woman⁹ marries, she has not sinned. Yet those who marry will have worldly troubles, and I would spare you that. ²⁹This is what I mean, brothers: the appointed time has grown very short. From now on, let those who have wives live as though they had none, ³⁰and those who mourn as though they were not mourning, and those who rejoice as though they were not rejoicing, and those who buy as though they had no goods, ³¹and those who deal with the world as though they had no dealings with it. For the present form of this world is passing away.

³²I want you to be free from anxieties. The unmarried man is anxious about the things of the Lord, how to please the Lord. ³³But the married man is anxious about worldly things, how to please his wife, ³⁴and his interests are divided. And the unmarried or betrothed woman is anxious about the things of the Lord, how to be holy in body and spirit. But the married woman is anxious about worldly things, how to please her husband. ³⁵I say this for your own benefit, not to lay any restraint upon you, but to promote good order and to secure your undivided devotion to the Lord.

³⁶If anyone thinks that he is not behaving properly toward his betrothed,¹⁰ if his¹¹ passions are strong, and it has to be, let him do as he wishes: let them marry—it is no sin. ³⁷But whoever is firmly established in his heart, being under no necessity but having his desire under control, and has determined this in his heart, to keep her as his betrothed, he will do well. ³⁸So then he who marries his betrothed does well, and he who refrains from marriage will do even better.

³⁹A wife is bound to her husband as long as he lives. But if her husband dies, she is free to be married to whom she wishes, only in the Lord. ⁴⁰Yet in my judgment she is happier if she remains as she is. And I think that I too have the Spirit of God.

Food Offered to Idols

8 Now concerning¹² food offered to idols: we know that "all of us possess knowledge." This "knowledge" puffs up, but love

---

¹Some manuscripts *us* ²Or *each person walk in the way* ³Or *slave*; also twice in verse 22 (for the contextual rendering of the Greek word *doulos*, see About the ESV) ⁴Or *slaves* (for the contextual rendering of the Greek word *doulos*, see About the ESV) ⁵Or *brothers and sisters*; also verse 29 ⁶The expression *Now concerning* introduces a reply to a question in the Corinthians' letter; see 7:1 ⁷Greek *virgins* ⁸Or *impending* ⁹Greek *virgin*; also verse 34 ¹⁰Greek *virgin*; also verses 37, 38 ¹¹Or *her* ¹²The expression *Now concerning* introduces a reply to a question in the Corinthians' letter; see 7:1

builds up. ²If anyone imagines that he knows something, he does not yet know as he ought to know. ³But if anyone loves God, he is known by God.¹

⁴Therefore, as to the eating of food offered to idols, we know that "an idol has no real existence," and that "there is no God but one." ⁵For although there may be so-called gods in heaven or on earth—as indeed there are many "gods" and many "lords"— ⁶yet for us there is one God, the Father, from whom are all things and for whom we exist, and one Lord, Jesus Christ, through whom are all things and through whom we exist.

⁷However, not all possess this knowledge. But some, through former association with idols, eat food as really offered to an idol, and their conscience, being weak, is defiled. ⁸Food will not commend us to God. We are no worse off if we do not eat, and no better off if we do. ⁹But take care that this right of yours does not somehow become a stumbling block to the weak. ¹⁰For if anyone sees you who have knowledge eating² in an idol's temple, will he not be encouraged,³ if his conscience is weak, to eat food offered to idols? ¹¹And so by your knowledge this weak person is destroyed, the brother for whom Christ died. ¹²Thus, sinning against your brothers⁴ and wounding their conscience when it is weak, you sin against Christ. ¹³Therefore, if food makes my brother stumble, I will never eat meat, lest I make my brother stumble.

Paul Surrenders His Rights

9 Am I not free? Am I not an apostle? Have I not seen Jesus our Lord? Are not you my workmanship in the Lord? ²If to others I am not an apostle, at least I am to you, for you are the seal of my apostleship in the Lord.

³This is my defense to those who would examine me. ⁴Do we not have the right to eat and drink? ⁵Do we not have the right to take along a believing wife,⁵ as do the other apostles and the brothers of the Lord and Cephas? ⁶Or is it only Barnabas and I who have no right to refrain from working for a living? ⁷Who serves as a soldier at his own expense? Who plants a vineyard without eating any of its fruit? Or who tends a flock without getting some of the milk?

⁸Do I say these things on human authority? Does not the Law say the same? ⁹For it is written in the Law of Moses, ᵃ"You shall not muzzle an ox when it treads out the grain." Is it for oxen that God is concerned? ¹⁰Does he not certainly speak for our sake? It was written for our sake, because the plowman should plow in hope and the thresher thresh in hope of sharing in the crop. ¹¹If we have sown spiritual things among you, is it too much if we reap material things from you? ¹²If others share this rightful claim on you, do not we even more?

Nevertheless, we have not made use of this right, but we endure anything rather than put an obstacle in the way of the gospel of Christ. ¹³Do you not know that those who are employed in the temple service get their food from the temple, and those who serve at the altar share in the sacrificial offerings? ¹⁴In the same way, the Lord commanded that those who proclaim the gospel should get their living by the gospel.

¹⁵But I have made no use of any of these rights, nor am I writing these things to secure any such provision. For I would rather die than have anyone deprive me of my ground for boasting. ¹⁶For if I preach the gospel, that gives me no ground for boasting. For necessity is laid upon me. Woe to me if I do not preach the gospel! ¹⁷For if I do this of my own will, I have a reward, but if not of my own will, I am still entrusted with a stewardship. ¹⁸What then is my reward? That in my preaching I may present the gospel free of charge, so as not to make full use of my right in the gospel.

¹⁹For though I am free from all, I have made myself a servant to all, that I might win more of them. ²⁰To the Jews I became as a Jew, in order to win Jews. To those under the law I became as one under the law (though not being myself under the law) that I might win those under the law. ²¹To those outside the law I became as one outside the law (not being outside the law of God but under the law of Christ) that I might win those outside the law. ²²To the weak I became weak, that I might win the weak. I have become all things to all people, that by all means I might save some. ²³I do it all for the sake of the gospel, that I may share with them in its blessings.

²⁴Do you not know that in a race all the runners run, but only one receives

¹Greek him ²Greek reclining at table ³Or fortified; Greek built up ⁴Or brothers and sisters ⁵Greek a sister as wife ᵃDeut. 25:4

the prize? So run that you may obtain it. [25] Every athlete exercises self-control in all things. They do it to receive a perishable wreath, but we an imperishable. [26] So I do not run aimlessly; I do not box as one beating the air. [27] But I discipline my body and keep it under control,[1] lest after preaching to others I myself should be disqualified.

Warning Against Idolatry

10 For I do not want you to be unaware, brothers,[2] that our fathers were all under the cloud, and all passed through the sea, [2] and all were baptized into Moses in the cloud and in the sea, [3] and all ate the same spiritual food, [4] and all drank the same spiritual drink. For they drank from the spiritual Rock that followed them, and the Rock was Christ. [5] Nevertheless, with most of them God was not pleased, for they were overthrown[3] in the wilderness.

[6] Now these things took place as examples for us, that we might not desire evil as they did. [7] Do not be idolaters as some of them were; as it is written, [a]"The people sat down to eat and drink and rose up to play." [8] We must not indulge in sexual immorality as some of them did, and twenty-three thousand fell in a single day. [9] We must not put Christ[4] to the test, as some of them did and were destroyed by serpents, [10] nor grumble, as some of them did and were destroyed by the Destroyer. [11] Now these things happened to them as an example, but they were written down for our instruction, on whom the end of the ages has come. [12] Therefore let anyone who thinks that he stands take heed lest he fall. [13] No temptation has overtaken you that is not common to man. God is faithful, and he will not let you be tempted beyond your ability, but with the temptation he will also provide the way of escape, that you may be able to endure it.

[14] Therefore, my beloved, flee from idolatry. [15] I speak as to sensible people; judge for yourselves what I say. [16] The cup of blessing that we bless, is it not a participation in the blood of Christ? The bread that we break, is it not a participation in the body of Christ? [17] Because there is one bread, we who are many are one body, for we all partake of the one bread. [18] Consider the people of Israel:[5] are not those who eat the sacrifices participants in the altar? [19] What do I imply then? That food offered to idols is anything, or that an idol is anything? [20] No, I imply that what pagans sacrifice they offer to demons and not to God. I do not want you to be participants with

[1] Greek *I pummel my body and make it a slave* [2] Or *brothers and sisters* [3] Or *were laid low* [4] Some manuscripts *the Lord* [5] Greek *Consider Israel according to the flesh* [a] Ex. 32:6

verses to read
1 Corinthians 10:1–4

No matter how lonely you feel or how bad things look, don't ever be deceived into thinking that God isn't there with you, waiting for you to turn to him and be comforted. He is called Provider, and that isn't just a part-time job. He always provides. Even when all seems to be lost, he is trustworthy.

When the Israelites wandered in the desert, they had no hope of finding food or drink, but God provided all they needed in the form of manna from heaven and water from rocks (see Ex. 16:4, 31; 17:6). The same God who gave them exactly what they needed is with you today. As a girl, you can easily let your emotions tell you that all is lost, but once you are saved, you are never again lost, even if you feel that way. You can't let your circumstances try to dictate the character of God. He is either God, ruler of all, or he isn't. When the going gets tough, take refuge in him and confess that he is still God and you can still trust him, even more now than ever.

demons. [21] You cannot drink the cup of the Lord and the cup of demons. You cannot partake of the table of the Lord and the table of demons. [22] Shall we provoke the Lord to jealousy? Are we stronger than he?

Do All to the Glory of God

[23] "All things are lawful," but not all things are helpful. "All things are lawful," but not all things build up. [24] Let no one seek his own good, but the good of his neighbor. [25] Eat whatever is sold in the meat market without raising any question on the ground of conscience. [26] For [a] "the earth is the Lord's, and the fullness thereof." [27] If one of the unbelievers invites you to dinner and you are disposed to go, eat whatever is set before you without raising any question on the ground of conscience. [28] But if someone says to you, "This has been offered in sacrifice," then do not eat it, for the sake of the one who informed you, and for the sake of conscience— [29] I do not mean your conscience, but his. For why should my liberty be determined by someone else's conscience? [30] If I partake with thankfulness, why am I denounced because of that for which I give thanks?

[31] So, whether you eat or drink, or whatever you do, do all to the glory of God. [32] Give no offense to Jews or to Greeks or to the church of God, [33] just as I try to please everyone in everything I do, not seeking my own advantage, but that of many, that they may be saved.

11 Be imitators of me, as I am of Christ.

Head Coverings

[2] Now I commend you because you remember me in everything and maintain the traditions even as I delivered them to you. [3] But I want you to understand that the head of every man is Christ, the head of a wife[1] is her husband, and the head of Christ is God. [4] Every man who prays or prophesies with his head covered dishonors his head, [5] but every wife[2] who prays or prophesies with her head uncovered dishonors her head, since it is the same as if her head were shaven. [6] For if a wife will not cover her head, then she should cut her hair short. But since it is disgraceful for a wife to cut

off her hair or shave her head, let her cover her head. [7] For a man ought not to cover his head, since he is the image and glory of God, but woman is the glory of man. [8] For man was not made from woman, but woman from man. [9] Neither was man created for woman, but woman for man. [10] That is why a wife ought to have a symbol of authority on her head, because of the angels.[3] [11] Nevertheless, in the Lord woman is not independent of man nor man of woman; [12] for as woman was made from man, so man is now born of woman. And all things are from God. [13] Judge for yourselves: is it proper for a wife to pray to God with her head uncovered? [14] Does not nature itself teach you that if a man wears long hair it is a disgrace for him, [15] but if a woman has long hair, it is her glory? For her hair is given to her for a covering. [16] If anyone is inclined to be contentious, we have no such practice, nor do the churches of God.

The Lord's Supper

[17] But in the following instructions I do not commend you, because when you come together it is not for the better but for the worse. [18] For, in the first place, when you come together as a church, I hear that there are divisions among you. And I believe it in part,[4] [19] for there must be factions among you in order that those who are genuine among you may be recognized. [20] When you come together, it is not the Lord's supper that you eat. [21] For in eating, each one goes ahead with his own meal. One goes hungry, another gets drunk. [22] What! Do you not have houses to eat and drink in? Or do you despise the church of God and humiliate those who have nothing? What shall I say to you? Shall I commend you in this? No, I will not.

[23] For I received from the Lord what I also delivered to you, that the Lord Jesus on the night when he was betrayed took bread, [24] and when he had given thanks, he broke it, and said, "This is my body which is for[5] you. Do this in remembrance of me."[6] [25] In the same way also he took the cup, after supper, saying, "This cup is the new covenant in my blood. Do this, as often as you drink it, in remembrance of me." [26] For as often as you eat this bread and drink the

[1] Greek *gunē*. This term may refer to a *woman* or a *wife*, depending on the context [2] In verses 5–13, the Greek word *gunē* is translated *wife* in verses that deal with wearing a veil, a sign of being married in first-century culture [3] Or *messengers*, that is, people sent to observe and report [4] Or *I believe a certain report* [5] Some manuscripts *broken for* [6] Or *as my memorial*; also verse 25 [a] Ps. 24:1

cup, you proclaim the Lord's death until he comes.

²⁷ Whoever, therefore, eats the bread or drinks the cup of the Lord in an unworthy manner will be guilty concerning the body and blood of the Lord. ²⁸ Let a person examine himself, then, and so eat of the bread and drink of the cup. ²⁹ For anyone who eats and drinks without discerning the body eats and drinks judgment on himself. ³⁰ That is why many of you are weak and ill, and some have died.¹ ³¹ But if we judged² ourselves truly, we would not be judged. ³² But when we are judged by the Lord, we are disciplined³ so that we may not be condemned along with the world.

³³ So then, my brothers,⁴ when you come together to eat, wait for⁵ one another— ³⁴ if anyone is hungry, let him eat at home—so that when you come together it will not be for judgment. About the other things I will give directions when I come.

Spiritual Gifts

12 Now concerning⁶ spiritual gifts,⁷ brothers,⁸ I do not want you to be uninformed. ² You know that when you were pagans you were led astray to mute idols, however you were led. ³ Therefore I want you to understand that no one speaking in the Spirit of God ever says "Jesus is accursed!" and no one can say "Jesus is Lord" except in the Holy Spirit.

⁴ Now there are varieties of gifts, but the same Spirit; ⁵ and there are varieties of service, but the same Lord; ⁶ and there are varieties of activities, but it is the same God who empowers them all in everyone. ⁷ To each is given the manifestation of the Spirit for the common good. ⁸ For to one is given through the Spirit the utterance of wisdom, and to another the utterance of knowledge according to the same Spirit, ⁹ to another faith by the same Spirit, to another gifts of healing by the one Spirit, ¹⁰ to another the working of miracles, to another prophecy, to another the ability to distinguish between spirits, to another various kinds of tongues, to another the interpretation of tongues. ¹¹ All these are empowered by one and the same Spirit, who apportions to each one individually as he wills.

One Body with Many Members

¹² For just as the body is one and has many members, and all the members of the body, though many, are one body, so it is with Christ. ¹³ For in one Spirit we were all baptized into one body—Jews or Greeks, slaves⁹ or free—and all were made to drink of one Spirit.

¹⁴ For the body does not consist of one member but of many. ¹⁵ If the foot should say, "Because I am not a hand, I do not belong to the body," that would not make it any less a part of the body. ¹⁶ And if the ear should say, "Because I am not an eye, I do not belong to the body," that would not make it any less a part of the body. ¹⁷ If the whole body were an eye, where would be the sense of hearing? If the whole body were an ear, where would be the sense of smell? ¹⁸ But as it is, God arranged the members in the body, each one of them, as he chose. ¹⁹ If all were a single member, where would the body be? ²⁰ As it is, there are many parts,¹⁰ yet one body.

²¹ The eye cannot say to the hand, "I have no need of you," nor again the head to the feet, "I have no need of you." ²² On the contrary, the parts of the body that seem to be weaker are indispensable, ²³ and on those parts of the body that we think less honorable we bestow the greater honor, and our unpresentable parts are treated with greater modesty, ²⁴ which our more presentable parts do not require. But God has so composed the body, giving greater honor to the part that lacked it, ²⁵ that there may be no division in the body, but that the members may have the same care for one another. ²⁶ If one member suffers, all suffer together; if one member is honored, all rejoice together.

²⁷ Now you are the body of Christ and individually members of it. ²⁸ And God has appointed in the church first apostles, second prophets, third teachers, then miracles, then gifts of healing, helping, administrating, and various kinds of tongues. ²⁹ Are all apostles? Are all prophets? Are all teachers? Do all work miracles? ³⁰ Do all possess gifts of healing? Do all speak with tongues? Do all interpret? ³¹ But earnestly desire the higher gifts.

---

¹ Greek *have fallen asleep* (as in 15:6, 20) ² Or *discerned* ³ Or *when we are judged we are being disciplined by the Lord* ⁴ Or *brothers and sisters* ⁵ Or *share with* ⁶ The expression *Now concerning* introduces a reply to a question in the Corinthians' letter; see 7:1 ⁷ Or *spiritual persons* ⁸ Or *brothers and sisters* ⁹ Or *servants*; Greek *bondservants* ¹⁰ Or *members*; also verse 22

And I will show you a still more excellent way.

The Way of Love

13 If I speak in the tongues of men and of angels, but have not love, I am a noisy gong or a clanging cymbal. ²And if I have prophetic powers, and understand all mysteries and all knowledge, and if I have all faith, so as to remove mountains, but have not love, I am nothing. ³If I give away all I have, and if I deliver up my body to be burned,[1] but have not love, I gain nothing.

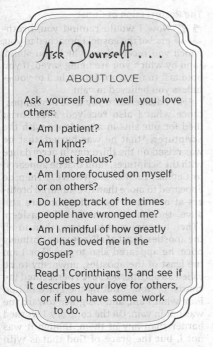

Ask Yourself . . .

ABOUT LOVE

Ask yourself how well you love others:

- Am I patient?
- Am I kind?
- Do I get jealous?
- Am I more focused on myself or on others?
- Do I keep track of the times people have wronged me?
- Am I mindful of how greatly God has loved me in the gospel?

Read 1 Corinthians 13 and see if it describes your love for others, or if you have some work to do.

⁴Love is patient and kind; love does not envy or boast; it is not arrogant ⁵or rude. It does not insist on its own way; it is not irritable or resentful;[2] ⁶it does not rejoice at wrongdoing, but rejoices with the truth. ⁷Love bears all things, believes all things, hopes all things, endures all things.

⁸Love never ends. As for prophecies, they will pass away; as for tongues, they will cease; as for knowledge, it will pass away. ⁹For we know in part and we prophesy in part, ¹⁰but when the perfect comes, the partial will pass away. ¹¹When I was a child, I spoke like a child, I thought like a child, I reasoned like a child. When I became a man, I gave up childish ways. ¹²For now we see in a mirror dimly, but then face to face. Now I know in part; then I shall know fully, even as I have been fully known.

¹³So now faith, hope, and love abide, these three; but the greatest of these is love.

Prophecy and Tongues

14 Pursue love, and earnestly desire the spiritual gifts, especially that you may prophesy. ²For one who speaks in a tongue speaks not to men but to God; for no one understands him, but he utters mysteries in the Spirit. ³On the other hand, the one who prophesies speaks to people for their upbuilding and encouragement and consolation. ⁴The one who speaks in a tongue builds up himself, but the one who prophesies builds up the church. ⁵Now I want you all to speak in tongues, but even more to prophesy. The one who prophesies is greater than the one who speaks in tongues, unless someone interprets, so that the church may be built up.

⁶Now, brothers,[3] if I come to you speaking in tongues, how will I benefit you unless I bring you some revelation or knowledge or prophecy or teaching? ⁷If even lifeless instruments, such as the flute or the harp, do not give distinct notes, how will anyone know what is played? ⁸And if the bugle gives an indistinct sound, who will get ready for battle? ⁹So with yourselves, if with your tongue you utter speech that is not intelligible, how will anyone know what is said? For you will be speaking into the air. ¹⁰There are doubtless many different languages in the world, and none is without meaning, ¹¹but if I do not know the meaning of the language, I will be a foreigner to the speaker and the speaker a foreigner to me. ¹²So with yourselves, since you are eager for manifestations of the Spirit, strive to excel in building up the church.

¹³Therefore, one who speaks in a tongue should pray that he may interpret. ¹⁴For if I pray in a tongue, my spirit prays but my mind is unfruitful. ¹⁵What am I to do? I will pray with my spirit, but I will pray with my mind also; I will sing praise with my spirit, but I will sing with my mind

[1] Some manuscripts *deliver up my body* [to death] *that I may boast* [2] Greek *irritable and does not count up wrongdoing* [3] Or *brothers and sisters*; also verses 20, 26, 39

also. [16] Otherwise, if you give thanks with your spirit, how can anyone in the position of an outsider[1] say "Amen" to your thanksgiving when he does not know what you are saying? [17] For you may be giving thanks well enough, but the other person is not being built up. [18] I thank God that I speak in tongues more than all of you. [19] Nevertheless, in church I would rather speak five words with my mind in order to instruct others, than ten thousand words in a tongue.

[20] Brothers, do not be children in your thinking. Be infants in evil, but in your thinking be mature. [21] In the Law it is written, [a]"By people of strange tongues and by the lips of foreigners will I speak to this people, and even then they will not listen to me, says the Lord." [22] Thus tongues are a sign not for believers but for unbelievers, while prophecy is a sign[2] not for unbelievers but for believers. [23] If, therefore, the whole church comes together and all speak in tongues, and outsiders or unbelievers enter, will they not say that you are out of your minds? [24] But if all prophesy, and an unbeliever or outsider enters, he is convicted by all, he is called to account by all, [25] the secrets of his heart are disclosed, and so, falling on his face, he will worship God and declare that God is really among you.

Orderly Worship

[26] What then, brothers? When you come together, each one has a hymn, a lesson, a revelation, a tongue, or an interpretation. Let all things be done for building up. [27] If any speak in a tongue, let there be only two or at most three, and each in turn, and let someone interpret. [28] But if there is no one to interpret, let each of them keep silent in church and speak to himself and to God. [29] Let two or three prophets speak, and let the others weigh what is said. [30] If a revelation is made to another sitting there, let the first be silent. [31] For you can all prophesy one by one, so that all may learn and all be encouraged, [32] and the spirits of prophets are subject to prophets. [33] For God is not a God of confusion but of peace.

As in all the churches of the saints, [34] the women should keep silent in the churches. For they are not permitted to speak, but should be in submission, as the Law also says. [35] If there is anything they desire to learn, let them ask their husbands at home. For it is shameful for a woman to speak in church.

[36] Or was it from you that the word of God came? Or are you the only ones it has reached? [37] If anyone thinks that he is a prophet, or spiritual, he should acknowledge that the things I am writing to you are a command of the Lord. [38] If anyone does not recognize this, he is not recognized. [39] So, my brothers, earnestly desire to prophesy, and do not forbid speaking in tongues. [40] But all things should be done decently and in order.

The Resurrection of Christ

15 Now I would remind you, brothers,[3] of the gospel I preached to you, which you received, in which you stand, [2] and by which you are being saved, if you hold fast to the word I preached to you—unless you believed in vain.

[3] For I delivered to you as of first importance what I also received: that Christ died for our sins in accordance with the Scriptures, [4] that he was buried, that he was raised on the third day in accordance with the Scriptures, [5] and that he appeared to Cephas, then to the twelve. [6] Then he appeared to more than five hundred brothers at one time, most of whom are still alive, though some have fallen asleep. [7] Then he appeared to James, then to all the apostles. [8] Last of all, as to one untimely born, he appeared also to me. [9] For I am the least of the apostles, unworthy to be called an apostle, because I persecuted the church of God. [10] But by the grace of God I am what I am, and his grace toward me was not in vain. On the contrary, I worked harder than any of them, though it was not I, but the grace of God that is with me. [11] Whether then it was I or they, so we preach and so you believed.

The Resurrection of the Dead

[12] Now if Christ is proclaimed as raised from the dead, how can some of you say that there is no resurrection of the dead? [13] But if there is no resurrection of the dead, then not even Christ has been raised. [14] And if Christ has not been raised, then our preaching is in vain and your faith is in vain. [15] We are even found to be misrepresenting God, because we testified about God that he

---

[1] Or of him that is without gifts [2] Greek lacks a sign [3] Or brothers and sisters; also verses 6, 31, 50, 58 [a] Isa. 28:11, 12

raised Christ, whom he did not raise if it is true that the dead are not raised. ¹⁶For if the dead are not raised, not even Christ has been raised. ¹⁷And if Christ has not been raised, your faith is futile and you are still in your sins. ¹⁸Then those also who have fallen asleep in Christ have perished. ¹⁹If in Christ we have hope[1] in this life only, we are of all people most to be pitied.

²⁰But in fact Christ has been raised from the dead, the firstfruits of those who have fallen asleep. ²¹For as by a man came death, by a man has come also the resurrection of the dead. ²²For as in Adam all die, so also in Christ shall all be made alive. ²³But each in his own order: Christ the firstfruits, then at his coming those who belong to Christ. ²⁴Then comes the end, when he delivers the kingdom to God the Father after destroying every rule and every authority and power. ²⁵For he must reign until he has put all his enemies under his feet. ²⁶The last enemy to be destroyed is death. ²⁷For [a]"God[2] has put all things in subjection under his feet." But when it says, "all things are put in subjection," it is plain that he is excepted who put all things in subjection under him. ²⁸When all things are subjected to him, then the Son himself will also be subjected to him who put all things in subjection under him, that God may be all in all.

²⁹Otherwise, what do people mean by being baptized on behalf of the dead? If the dead are not raised at all, why are people baptized on their behalf? ³⁰Why are we in danger every hour? ³¹I protest, brothers, by my pride in you, which I have in Christ Jesus our Lord, I die every day! ³²What do I gain if, humanly speaking, I fought with beasts at Ephesus? If the dead are not raised, [b]"Let us eat and drink, for tomorrow we die." ³³Do not be deceived: "Bad company ruins good morals."[3] ³⁴Wake up from your drunken stupor, as is right, and do not go on sinning. For some have no knowledge of God. I say this to your shame.

The Resurrection Body

³⁵But someone will ask, "How are the dead raised? With what kind of body do they come?" ³⁶You foolish person! What you sow does not come to life unless it dies. ³⁷And what you sow is not the body that is to be, but a bare kernel, perhaps of wheat or of some other grain. ³⁸But God gives it a body as he has chosen, and to each kind of seed its own body. ³⁹For not all flesh is the same, but there is one kind for humans, another for animals, another for birds, and another for fish. ⁴⁰There are heavenly bodies and earthly bodies, but the glory of the heavenly is of one kind, and the glory of the earthly is of another. ⁴¹There is one glory of the sun, and another glory of the moon, and another glory of the stars; for star differs from star in glory.

⁴²So is it with the resurrection of the dead. What is sown is perishable; what is raised is imperishable. ⁴³It is sown in dishonor; it is raised in glory. It is sown in weakness; it is raised in power. ⁴⁴It is sown a natural body; it is raised a spiritual body. If there is a natural body, there is also a spiritual body. ⁴⁵Thus it is written, "The first man Adam became a living being";[4] the last Adam became a life-giving spirit. ⁴⁶But it is not the spiritual that is first but the natural, and then the spiritual. ⁴⁷The first man was from the earth, a man of dust; the second man is from heaven. ⁴⁸As was the man of dust, so also are those who are of the dust, and as is the man of heaven, so also are those who are of heaven. ⁴⁹Just as we have borne the image of the man of dust, we shall[5] also bear the image of the man of heaven.

Mystery and Victory

⁵⁰I tell you this, brothers: flesh and blood cannot inherit the kingdom of God, nor does the perishable inherit the imperishable. ⁵¹Behold! I tell you a mystery. We shall not all sleep, but we shall all be changed, ⁵²in a moment, in the twinkling of an eye, at the last trumpet. For the trumpet will sound, and the dead will be raised imperishable, and we shall be changed. ⁵³For this perishable body must put on the imperishable, and this mortal body must put on immortality. ⁵⁴When the perishable puts on the imperishable, and the mortal puts on immortality, then shall come to pass the saying that is written:

[d]"Death is swallowed up in victory."
⁵⁵   "O death, where is your victory?
      O death, where is your sting?"

---

[1] Or we have hoped [2] Greek he [3] Probably from Menander's comedy Thais [4] Greek a living soul [5] Some manuscripts let us [a] Ps. 8:6 [b] Isa. 22:13 [c] Gen. 2:7 [d] Isa. 25:8

[56] The sting of death is sin, and the power of sin is the law. [57] But thanks be to God, who gives us the victory through our Lord Jesus Christ.

[58] Therefore, my beloved brothers, be steadfast, immovable, always abounding in the work of the Lord, knowing that in the Lord your labor is not in vain.

The Collection for the Saints

16 Now concerning[1] the collection for the saints: as I directed the churches of Galatia, so you also are to do. [2] On the first day of every week, each of you is to put something aside and store it up, as he may prosper, so that there will be no collecting when I come. [3] And when I arrive, I will send those whom you accredit by letter to carry your gift to Jerusalem. [4] If it seems advisable that I should go also, they will accompany me.

Plans for Travel

[5] I will visit you after passing through Macedonia, for I intend to pass through Macedonia, [6] and perhaps I will stay with you or even spend the winter, so that you may help me on my journey, wherever I go. [7] For I do not want to see you now just in passing. I hope to spend some time with you, if the Lord permits. [8] But I will stay in Ephesus until Pentecost, [9] for a wide door for effective work has opened to me, and there are many adversaries.

[10] When Timothy comes, see that you put him at ease among you, for he is doing the work of the Lord, as I am. [11] So let no one despise him. Help him on his way in peace, that he may return to me, for I am expecting him with the brothers.

Final Instructions

[12] Now concerning our brother Apollos, I strongly urged him to visit you with the other brothers, but it was not at all his will[2] to come now. He will come when he has opportunity.

[13] Be watchful, stand firm in the faith, act like men, be strong. [14] Let all that you do be done in love.

[15] Now I urge you, brothers[3]—you know that the household[4] of Stephanas were the first converts in Achaia, and that they have devoted themselves to the service of the saints— [16] be subject to such as these, and to every fellow worker and laborer. [17] I rejoice at the coming of Stephanas and Fortunatus and Achaicus, because they have made up for your absence, [18] for they refreshed my spirit as well as yours. Give recognition to such people.

Greetings

[19] The churches of Asia send you greetings. Aquila and Prisca, together with the church in their house, send you hearty greetings in the Lord. [20] All the brothers send you greetings. Greet one another with a holy kiss.

[21] I, Paul, write this greeting with my own hand. [22] If anyone has no love for the Lord, let him be accursed. Our Lord, come![5] [23] The grace of the Lord Jesus be with you. [24] My love be with you all in Christ Jesus. Amen.

---

[1] The expression *Now concerning* introduces a reply to a question in the Corinthians' letter; see 7:1; also verse 12 [2] Or *God's will for him* [3] Or *brothers and sisters*; also verse 20 [4] Greek *house* [5] Greek *Maranatha* (a transliteration of Aramaic)

INTRODUCTION TO
2 Corinthians

Author: The apostle Paul
Time: Probably around A.D. 56
Place: Macedonia
Written to: The church in Corinth

The gist

This is Paul's second letter to the Corinthians. In his earlier letter, he was kind of angry and frustrated with the young church for being so foolish. And it turns out that some people didn't like it and were accusing Paul of being a false teacher. Second Corinthians is Paul's attempt to restore his relationship with the church and reclaim his authority. Paul explains his trials, his hard work, and all that goes into his missionary work, but in the end it all comes from the power of Christ living in him. And so this book is about more than just the life of Paul; it's about the lives of all believers who struggle and suffer.

Things to look for

• The truth about relationships with nonbelievers (see 2 Cor. 6:14–18)

• How to face suffering (see 2 Cor. 1:9–11; 6:3–10; 7:8–11; 11:16–33; 12:7–10)

• Paul's relationship with the Corinthian church—what things he said to them and where he went during the writing of the two letters (see 2 Cor. 1:12–14, 19; 4:5; and for more insight see Acts 18:1–18; 20:1–2; 1 Cor. 1:10–17; 3:1–6, 10; 4:17–19; 5:9; 16:5–7, 10–12)

Be Restored

In Christ God was reconciling the world to himself, not counting their trespasses against them, and entrusting to us the message of reconciliation. Therefore, we are ambassadors for Christ, God making his appeal through us. We implore you on behalf of Christ, be reconciled to God.

2 Corinthians 5:19–20

God's goal for the lives of his children is restoration. He wants them to be reconciled, or restored, to himself and to one another. Restoration means moving away from being enemies and back to becoming friends again. Before you accepted Christ you were an enemy of God, but once you turned to him and confessed your need for him to forgive all the mess-ups of your past, you became his friend.

But reconciliation isn't just about you and God. If a friend or a family member is on your outs list because of something between you, he or she needs reconciliation as well. Anything else, and you are rejecting God's call to love your neighbor as yourself and even to love your enemies. Something terrible, even sinful, may have come between you, but forgiveness is required in the life of a believer (see Matt. 6:15; Mark 11:25; Luke 17:3).

Reconciliation is like pulling off a bandage: best done quickly! Don't wait to talk to someone who has something against you, but go to them as soon as you realize the problem. Work things out before it's too late. When a sister in the faith is mad at you or hurt by you, there's no time to waste; remembering God's kindness to you in the gospel, do your best, in humility, to talk to her and work things out. As a God Girl, you should know that whether you've been hurt, slandered, gossiped about, or judged, you are called to go to your sister or brother and do what you can to make things right. Sometimes that might mean apologizing when it's really the *other person* who should be apologizing. After all, what's more important, obedience to God or proving that you were right? A God Girl should never stand on her rights or try to prove herself at all costs—that's disobedience. When people stand on their rights, they create arguments and fights, and God isn't pleased. He wants his family members to be united and to love one another no matter what the differences. He wants reconciliation, both between him and his children and among all his children. Don't let the sin of pride get in the way of going to the believer who has something against you and working things out—according to God's Word, this process of reconciliation is more important even than worship (see Matt. 5:23–24).

Must-Know Verses

Blessed be the God and Father of our Lord Jesus Christ, the Father of mercies and God of all comfort, who comforts us in all our affliction, so that we may be able to comfort those who are in any affliction, with the comfort with which we ourselves are comforted by God. *2 Corinthians 1:3–4*

It is God who establishes us with you in Christ, and has anointed us, and who has also put his seal on us and given us his Spirit in our hearts as a guarantee. *2 Corinthians 1:21–22*

We look not to the things that are seen but to the things that are unseen. For the things that are seen are transient, but the things that are unseen are eternal. *2 Corinthians 4:18*

Do not be unequally yoked with unbelievers. For what partnership has righteousness with lawlessness? Or what fellowship has light with darkness? What accord has Christ with Belial? Or what portion does a believer share with an unbeliever? *2 Corinthians 6:14–15*

Whoever sows sparingly will also reap sparingly, and whoever sows bountifully will also reap bountifully. *2 Corinthians 9:6*

We destroy arguments and every lofty opinion raised against the knowledge of God, and take every thought captive to obey Christ. *2 Corinthians 10:5*

Satan disguises himself as an angel of light. So it is no surprise if his servants, also, disguise themselves as servants of righteousness. Their end will correspond to their deeds. *2 Corinthians 11:14–15*

Three times I pleaded with the Lord about this, that it should leave me. But he said to me, "My grace is sufficient for you, for my power is made perfect in weakness." Therefore I will boast all the more gladly of my weaknesses, so that the power of Christ may rest upon me. *2 Corinthians 12:8–9*

The Second Letter of Paul to the Corinthians

2 Corinthians

Greeting

1 Paul, an apostle of Christ Jesus by the will of God, and Timothy our brother,

To the church of God that is at Corinth, with all the saints who are in the whole of Achaia:

[2] Grace to you and peace from God our Father and the Lord Jesus Christ.

God of All Comfort

[3] Blessed be the God and Father of our Lord Jesus Christ, the Father of mercies and God of all comfort, [4] who comforts us in all our affliction, so that we may be able to comfort those who are in any affliction, with the comfort with which we ourselves are comforted by God. [5] For as we share abundantly in Christ's sufferings, so through Christ we share abundantly in comfort too.[1] [6] If we are afflicted, it is for your comfort and salvation; and if we are comforted, it is for your comfort, which you experience when you patiently endure the same sufferings that we suffer. [7] Our hope for you is unshaken, for we know that as you share in our sufferings, you will also share in our comfort.

[8] For we do not want you to be unaware, brothers,[2] of the affliction we experienced in Asia. For we were so utterly burdened beyond our strength that we despaired of life itself. [9] Indeed, we felt that we had received the sentence of death. But that was to make us rely not on ourselves but on God who raises the dead. [10] He delivered us from such a deadly peril, and he will deliver us. On him we have set our hope that he will deliver us again. [11] You also must help us by prayer, so that many will give thanks on our behalf for the blessing granted us through the prayers of many.

Paul's Change of Plans

[12] For our boast is this, the testimony of our conscience, that we behaved in the world with simplicity[3] and godly sincerity, not by earthly wisdom but by the grace of God, and supremely so toward you. [13] For we are not writing to you anything other than what you read and understand and I hope you will fully understand— [14] just as you did partially understand us—that on the day of our Lord Jesus you will boast of us as we will boast of you.

[15] Because I was sure of this, I wanted to come to you first, so that you might have a second experience of grace. [16] I wanted to visit you on my way to Macedonia, and to come back to you from Macedonia and have you send me on my way to Judea. [17] Was I vacillating when I wanted to do

---

[1] Or *For as the sufferings of Christ abound for us, so also our comfort abounds through Christ* [2] Or *brothers and sisters*. The plural Greek word *adelphoi* (translated "brothers") refers to siblings in a family. In New Testament usage, depending on the context, *adelphoi* may refer either to men or to both men and women who are siblings (brothers and sisters) in God's family, the church [3] Some manuscripts *holiness*

this? Do I make my plans according to the flesh, ready to say "Yes, yes" and "No, no" at the same time? ¹⁸ As surely as God is faithful, our word to you has not been Yes and No. ¹⁹ For the Son of God, Jesus Christ, whom we proclaimed among you, Silvanus and Timothy and I, was not Yes and No, but in him it is always Yes. ²⁰ For all the promises of God find their Yes in him. That is why it is through him that we utter our Amen to God for his glory. ²¹ And it is God who establishes us with you in Christ, and has anointed us, ²² and who has also put his seal on us and given us his Spirit in our hearts as a guarantee.[1]

²³ But I call God to witness against me— it was to spare you that I refrained from coming again to Corinth. ²⁴ Not that we lord it over your faith, but we work with you for your joy, for you stand firm in your faith.

2 For I made up my mind not to make another painful visit to you. ² For if I cause you pain, who is there to make me glad but the one whom I have pained? ³ And I wrote as I did, so that when I came I might not suffer pain from those who should have made me rejoice, for I felt sure of all of you, that my joy would be the joy of you all. ⁴ For I wrote to you out of much affliction and anguish of heart and with many tears, not to cause you pain but to let you know the abundant love that I have for you.

Forgive the Sinner

⁵ Now if anyone has caused pain, he has caused it not to me, but in some measure— not to put it too severely— to all of you. ⁶ For such a one, this punishment by the majority is enough, ⁷ so you should rather turn to forgive and comfort him, or he may be overwhelmed by excessive sorrow. ⁸ So I beg you to reaffirm your love for him. ⁹ For this is why I wrote, that I might test you and know whether you are obedient in everything. ¹⁰ Anyone whom you forgive, I also forgive. Indeed, what I have forgiven, if I have forgiven anything, has been for your sake in the presence of Christ, ¹¹ so that we would not be outwitted by Satan; for we are not ignorant of his designs.

Triumph in Christ

¹² When I came to Troas to preach the gospel of Christ, even though a door was opened for me in the Lord, ¹³ my spirit was not at rest because I did not find my brother Titus there. So I took leave of them and went on to Macedonia.

¹⁴ But thanks be to God, who in Christ always leads us in triumphal procession, and through us spreads the fragrance of the knowledge of him everywhere. ¹⁵ For we are the aroma of Christ to God among those who are being saved and among those who are perishing, ¹⁶ to one a fragrance from death to death, to the other a fragrance from life to life. Who is sufficient for these things? ¹⁷ For we are not, like so many, peddlers of God's word, but as men of sincerity, as commissioned by God, in the sight of God we speak in Christ.

Ministers of the New Covenant

3 Are we beginning to commend ourselves again? Or do we need, as some do, letters of recommendation to you, or from you? ² You yourselves are our letter of recommendation, written on our[2] hearts, to be known and read by all. ³ And you show that you are a letter from Christ delivered by us, written not with ink but with the Spirit of the living God, not on tablets of stone but on tablets of human hearts.[3]

⁴ Such is the confidence that we have through Christ toward God. ⁵ Not that we are sufficient in ourselves to claim anything as coming from us, but our sufficiency is from God, ⁶ who has made us sufficient to be ministers of a new covenant, not of the letter but of the Spirit. For the letter kills, but the Spirit gives life.

⁷ Now if the ministry of death, carved in letters on stone, came with such glory that the Israelites could not gaze at Moses' face because of its glory, which was being brought to an end, ⁸ will not the ministry of the Spirit have even more glory? ⁹ For if there was glory in the ministry of condemnation, the ministry of righteousness must far exceed it in glory. ¹⁰ Indeed, in this case, what once had glory has come to have no glory at all, because of the glory that surpasses it. ¹¹ For if what was being brought to an end came with glory, much more will what is permanent have glory.

¹² Since we have such a hope, we are very bold, ¹³ not like Moses, who would put a veil over his face so that the Israelites might not gaze at the outcome of what was being brought to an end. ¹⁴ But their minds were

¹ Or *down payment* ² Some manuscripts *your* ³ Greek *fleshly hearts*

hardened. For to this day, when they read the old covenant, that same veil remains unlifted, because only through Christ is it taken away. ¹⁵Yes, to this day whenever Moses is read a veil lies over their hearts. ¹⁶But when one[1] turns to the Lord, the veil is removed. ¹⁷Now the Lord[2] is the Spirit, and where the Spirit of the Lord is, there is freedom. ¹⁸And we all, with unveiled face, beholding the glory of the Lord,[3] are being transformed into the same image from one degree of glory to another. For this comes from the Lord who is the Spirit.

The Light of the Gospel

4 Therefore, having this ministry by the mercy of God,[4] we do not lose heart. ²But we have renounced disgraceful, underhanded ways. We refuse to practice[5] cunning or to tamper with God's word, but by the open statement of the truth we would commend ourselves to everyone's conscience in the sight of God. ³And even if our gospel is veiled, it is veiled to those who are perishing. ⁴In their case the god of this world has blinded the minds of the unbelievers, to keep them from seeing the light of the gospel of the glory of Christ, who is the image of God. ⁵For what we proclaim is not ourselves, but Jesus Christ as Lord, with ourselves as your servants[6] for Jesus' sake. ⁶For God, who said, "Let light shine out of darkness," has shone in our hearts to give the light of the knowledge of the glory of God in the face of Jesus Christ.

Treasure in Jars of Clay

⁷But we have this treasure in jars of clay, to show that the surpassing power belongs to God and not to us. ⁸We are afflicted in every way, but not crushed; perplexed, but not driven to despair; ⁹persecuted, but not forsaken; struck down, but not destroyed; ¹⁰always carrying in the body the death of Jesus, so that the life of Jesus may also be manifested in our bodies. ¹¹For we who live are always being given over to death for Jesus' sake, so that the life of Jesus also may be manifested in our mortal flesh. ¹²So death is at work in us, but life in you.

¹³Since we have the same spirit of faith according to what has been written,

[1] Greek he [2] Or this Lord [3] Or reflecting the glory of the Lord [4] Greek as we have received mercy [5] Greek to walk in [6] Greek bondservants

Know Love

verses to read
2 Corinthians 4:15–18

Your worst fear has come true, and now you are faced with the one thing you thought you could never handle. How do you stand when it seems just too hard to go on? What do you do when your life seems to be on the verge of extinction?

You've got to do the opposite of what your instinct says: don't fight, just surrender. Give up your will to God and stop fighting for your own way, your own survival. Sound illogical? Impossible? Well, it's neither. The place you are now, at the end of your rope, is just the place you are supposed to be. Nothing happens to you unless God allows it to happen. And if God allowed it, then you can be sure it is the very best thing that could have happened to you. But your heart can understand that only when you completely surrender to God. You can win the battle only when you submit to it.

Face your trial without fear and refuse to let it lead you to sin. Give your heart, soul, and mind to the one who loves you and will never leave you. Pain can make you stronger only if you don't fear it. So give it to God, trusting him no matter what, and then it will be used for your good. Stop asking "Why me?" and start saying, "Yes, God, your will be done, not mine. I am content to suffer if that is your will, knowing that all this is just temporary, but life with you is eternal."

^a"I believed, and so I spoke," we also believe, and so we also speak, ¹⁴knowing that he who raised the Lord Jesus will raise us also with Jesus and bring us with you into his presence. ¹⁵For it is all for your sake, so that as grace extends to more and more people it may increase thanksgiving, to the glory of God.

¹⁶So we do not lose heart. Though our outer self¹ is wasting away, our inner self is being renewed day by day. ¹⁷For this light momentary affliction is preparing for us an eternal weight of glory beyond all comparison, ¹⁸as we look not to the things that are seen but to the things that are unseen. For the things that are seen are transient, but the things that are unseen are eternal.

Our Heavenly Dwelling

5 For we know that if the tent that is our earthly home is destroyed, we have a building from God, a house not made with hands, eternal in the heavens. ²For in this

¹Greek *man* ²Some manuscripts *putting it off* ^aPs. 116:10

tent we groan, longing to put on our heavenly dwelling, ³if indeed by putting it on² we may not be found naked. ⁴For while we are still in this tent, we groan, being burdened—not that we would be unclothed, but that we would be further clothed, so that what is mortal may be swallowed up by life. ⁵He who has prepared us for this very thing is God, who has given us the Spirit as a guarantee.

⁶So we are always of good courage. We know that while we are at home in the body we are away from the Lord, ⁷for we walk by faith, not by sight. ⁸Yes, we are of good courage, and we would rather be away from the body and at home with the Lord. ⁹So whether we are at home or away, we make it our aim to please him. ¹⁰For we must all appear before the judgment seat of Christ, so that each one may receive what is due for what he has done in the body, whether good or evil.

Know God

verses to read
2 Corinthians 5:14–17

Do you want to identify with Christ? Do you want to be so much like him, so in step with him, that anything that isn't from him makes you sick and makes you run in the opposite direction? It's time for you to gladly submit your whole life to him. And that means you've got to tell Jesus either that you don't want sin to die in you or that you want to throw yourself on Christ and die to everything that isn't holy.

When you choose option number two, your whole life will change. The old self will begin to die away and the new self will take its place. When that happens, all the sickness brought on your life by the sin in it will start to lift. Your load will be lighter, and the power of sin in your life will start to be reversed. You can have freedom from the fear and pain in your life if you are only willing to find the sin in your life, admit it, and choose by grace to walk away from it because of what God has done in Christ to redeem you. It's a fairly simple process that requires a very difficult decision: to confront the sin that has become your friend and to make it your enemy. When you became a God Girl, you became a new creature, one who no longer lives for herself but for him. And this isn't as frightening as it sounds; in fact, it's freeing. When you become a new creature, the effects of your old sin may still remain, but your heart and mind will be set free to thank God for rescuing you from the path you were on. Let Jesus' life and death make a difference to your way of life, and you will find a way out of your sinful habits and choices.

The Ministry of Reconciliation

[11] Therefore, knowing the fear of the Lord, we persuade others. But what we are is known to God, and I hope it is known also to your conscience. [12] We are not commending ourselves to you again but giving you cause to boast about us, so that you may be able to answer those who boast about outward appearance and not about what is in the heart. [13] For if we are beside ourselves, it is for God; if we are in our right mind, it is for you. [14] For the love of Christ controls us, because we have concluded this: that one has died for all, therefore all have died; [15] and he died for all, that those who live might no longer live for themselves but for him who for their sake died and was raised.

[16] From now on, therefore, we regard no one according to the flesh. Even though we once regarded Christ according to the flesh, we regard him thus no longer. [17] Therefore, if anyone is in Christ, he is a new creation.[1] The old has passed away; behold, the new has come. [18] All this is from God, who through Christ reconciled us to himself and gave us the ministry of reconciliation; [19] that is, in Christ God was reconciling[2] the world to himself, not counting their trespasses against them, and entrusting to us the message of reconciliation. [20] Therefore, we are ambassadors for Christ, God making his appeal through us. We implore you on behalf of Christ, be reconciled to God. [21] For our sake he made him to be sin who knew no sin, so that in him we might become the righteousness of God.

6 Working together with him, then, we appeal to you not to receive the grace of God in vain. [2] For he says,

> [a]"In a favorable time I listened to you,
>   and in a day of salvation I have
>   helped you."

Behold, now is the favorable time; behold, now is the day of salvation. [3] We put no obstacle in anyone's way, so that no fault may be found with our ministry, [4] but as servants of God we commend ourselves in every way: by great endurance, in afflictions, hardships, calamities, [5] beatings, imprisonments, riots, labors, sleepless nights, hunger; [6] by purity, knowledge, patience, kindness, the Holy Spirit, genuine love; [7] by truthful speech, and the power of God; with the weapons of righteousness for the right hand and for the left; [8] through honor and dishonor, through slander and praise. We are treated as impostors, and yet are true; [9] as unknown, and yet well known; as dying, and behold, we live; as punished, and yet not killed; [10] as sorrowful, yet always rejoicing; as poor, yet making many rich; as having nothing, yet possessing everything.

[11] We have spoken freely to you,[3] Corinthians; our heart is wide open. [12] You are not restricted by us, but you are restricted in your own affections. [13] In return (I speak as to children) widen your hearts also.

The Temple of the Living God

[14] Do not be unequally yoked with unbelievers. For what partnership has righteousness with lawlessness? Or what fellowship has light with darkness? [15] What accord has Christ with Belial?[4] Or what portion does a believer share with an unbeliever? [16] What agreement has the temple of God with idols? For we are the temple of the living God; as God said,

> [b]"I will make my dwelling among them
>   and walk among them,
>   and I will be their God,
>   and they shall be my people.
> [17]   Therefore [c] go out from their midst,
>   and be separate from them, says
>   the Lord,
>   and touch no unclean thing;
>   then I will welcome you,
> [18]   and I will be a father to you,
>   and you shall be sons and daughters to me,
>   says the Lord Almighty."

7 Since we have these promises, beloved, let us cleanse ourselves from every defilement of body[5] and spirit, bringing holiness to completion in the fear of God.

Paul's Joy

[2] Make room in your hearts[6] for us. We have wronged no one, we have corrupted no one, we have taken advantage of no one. [3] I do not say this to condemn you, for I said before that you are in our hearts, to die together and to live together. [4] I am

---

[1] Or creature [2] Or God was in Christ, reconciling [3] Greek Our mouth is open to you [4] Greek Beliar [5] Greek flesh [6] Greek lacks in your hearts
[a] Isa. 49:8 [b] Lev. 26:12 [c] Isa. 52:11

acting with great boldness toward you; I have great pride in you; I am filled with comfort. In all our affliction, I am overflowing with joy.

⁵ For even when we came into Macedonia, our bodies had no rest, but we were afflicted at every turn—fighting without and fear within. ⁶ But God, who comforts the downcast, comforted us by the coming of Titus, ⁷ and not only by his coming but also by the comfort with which he was comforted by you, as he told us of your longing, your mourning, your zeal for me, so that I rejoiced still more. ⁸ For even if I made you grieve with my letter, I do not regret it—though I did regret it, for I see that that letter grieved you, though only for a while. ⁹ As it is, I rejoice, not because you were grieved, but because you were grieved into repenting. For you felt a godly grief, so that you suffered no loss through us.

¹⁰ For godly grief produces a repentance that leads to salvation without regret, whereas worldly grief produces death. ¹¹ For see what earnestness this godly grief has produced in you, but also what eagerness to clear yourselves, what indignation, what fear, what longing, what zeal, what punishment! At every point you have

¹ Or brothers and sisters

proved yourselves innocent in the matter. ¹² So although I wrote to you, it was not for the sake of the one who did the wrong, nor for the sake of the one who suffered the wrong, but in order that your earnestness for us might be revealed to you in the sight of God. ¹³ Therefore we are comforted.

And besides our own comfort, we rejoiced still more at the joy of Titus, because his spirit has been refreshed by you all. ¹⁴ For whatever boasts I made to him about you, I was not put to shame. But just as everything we said to you was true, so also our boasting before Titus has proved true. ¹⁵ And his affection for you is even greater, as he remembers the obedience of you all, how you received him with fear and trembling. ¹⁶ I rejoice, because I have complete confidence in you.

Encouragement to Give Generously

8 We want you to know, brothers,¹ about the grace of God that has been given among the churches of Macedonia, ² for in a severe test of affliction, their abundance of joy and their extreme poverty have overflowed in a wealth of generosity on their part. ³ For they gave according to their means, as I can testify, and beyond

Know Yourself

verse to read
2 Corinthians 7:1

You've prayed to be holy, but you keep sinning. Why? It's not a question of praying but of doing. Don't just ask God to take away your desire to sin and then go on living as normal. Start doing something about it. If there is something that won't seem to let up its choke hold on your life and is making you miserable, then the logical move is to give it up. Let go. Don't just beg God to do it—*you* have to do something too. God gives you the ability to get it done by his Spirit, and he gives you the power of his Word and his protection, but he doesn't do it for you as if you were a robot.

God never willed for anyone to sin. But he does want you to be holy. So why would you need to convince him of your need for holiness when that's been his goal from the beginning? The only one who *hasn't* been willing until now is you. God doesn't do this holiness stuff for you; he does it in you and with you. God has just been waiting for you to forsake the pleasures of sin for the far better pleasures of holiness. Until that happens, you'll take the easy road and keep the sin alive. So get up and get busy. The sooner you take action, the sooner you'll be free.

their means, of their own accord, [4]begging us earnestly for the favor[1] of taking part in the relief of the saints— [5]and this, not as we expected, but they gave themselves first to the Lord and then by the will of God to us. [6]Accordingly, we urged Titus that as he had started, so he should complete among you this act of grace. [7]But as you excel in everything—in faith, in speech, in knowledge, in all earnestness, and in our love for you[2]—see that you excel in this act of grace also.

[8]I say this not as a command, but to prove by the earnestness of others that your love also is genuine. [9]For you know the grace of our Lord Jesus Christ, that though he was rich, yet for your sake he became poor, so that you by his poverty might become rich. [10]And in this matter I give my judgment: this benefits you, who a year ago started not only to do this work but also to desire to do it. [11]So now finish doing it as well, so that your readiness in desiring it may be matched by your completing it out of what you have. [12]For if the readiness is there, it is acceptable according to what a person has, not according to what he does not have. [13]For I do not mean that others should be eased and you burdened, but that as a matter of fairness [14]your abundance at the present time should supply their need, so that their abundance may supply your need, that there may be fairness. [15]As it is written, [a]"Whoever gathered much had nothing left over, and whoever gathered little had no lack."

Commendation of Titus

[16]But thanks be to God, who put into the heart of Titus the same earnest care I have for you. [17]For he not only accepted our appeal, but being himself very earnest he is going[3] to you of his own accord. [18]With him we are sending[4] the brother who is famous among all the churches for his preaching of the gospel. [19]And not only that, but he has been appointed by the churches to travel with us as we carry out this act of grace that is being ministered by us, for the glory of the Lord himself and to show our good will. [20]We take this course so that no one should blame us about this generous gift that is being administered by us,

[21]for we aim at what is honorable not only in the Lord's sight but also in the sight of man. [22]And with them we are sending our brother whom we have often tested and found earnest in many matters, but who is now more earnest than ever because of his great confidence in you. [23]As for Titus, he is my partner and fellow worker for your benefit. And as for our brothers, they are messengers[5] of the churches, the glory of Christ. [24]So give proof before the churches of your love and of our boasting about you to these men.

The Collection for Christians in Jerusalem

9 Now it is superfluous for me to write to you about the ministry for the saints, [2]for I know your readiness, of which I boast about you to the people of Macedonia, saying that Achaia has been ready since last year. And your zeal has stirred up most of them. [3]But I am sending[6] the brothers so that our boasting about you may not prove empty in this matter, so that you may be ready, as I said you would be. [4]Otherwise, if some Macedonians come with me and find that you are not ready, we would be humiliated—to say nothing of you—for being so confident. [5]So I thought it necessary to urge the brothers to go on ahead to you and arrange in advance for the gift[7] you have promised, so that it may be ready as a willing gift, not as an exaction.[8]

The Cheerful Giver

[6]The point is this: whoever sows sparingly will also reap sparingly, and whoever sows bountifully[9] will also reap bountifully. [7]Each one must give as he has decided in his heart, not reluctantly or under compulsion, for God loves a cheerful giver. [8]And God is able to make all grace abound to you, so that having all sufficiency[10] in all things at all times, you may abound in every good work. [9]As it is written,

> [b]"He has distributed freely, he has given to the poor;
> his righteousness endures forever."

[10]He who supplies seed to the sower and bread for food will supply and multiply your seed for sowing and increase the harvest of your righteousness. [11]You will be

---

[1]The Greek word *charis* can mean *favor* or *grace* or *thanks*, depending on the context [2]Some manuscripts *in your love for us* [3]Or *he went* [4]Or *we sent*; also verse 22 [5]Greek *apostles* [6]Or *I have sent* [7]Greek *blessing*; twice in this verse [8]Or *a gift expecting something in return*; Greek *greed* [9]Greek *with blessings*; twice in this verse [10]Or *all contentment* [a]Ex. 16:18 [b]Ps. 112:9

enriched in every way to be generous in every way, which through us will produce thanksgiving to God. ¹² For the ministry of this service is not only supplying the needs of the saints but is also overflowing in many thanksgivings to God. ¹³ By their approval of this service, they¹ will glorify God because of your submission that comes from your confession of the gospel of Christ, and the generosity of your contribution for them and for all others, ¹⁴ while they long for you and pray for you, because of the surpassing grace of God upon you. ¹⁵ Thanks be to God for his inexpressible gift!

Paul Defends His Ministry

10 I, Paul, myself entreat you, by the meekness and gentleness of Christ—I who am humble when face to face with you, but bold toward you when I am away!— ² I beg of you that when I am present I may not have to show boldness with such confidence as I count on showing against some who suspect us of walk-

ing according to the flesh. ³ For though we walk in the flesh, we are not waging war according to the flesh. ⁴ For the weapons of our warfare are not of the flesh but have divine power to destroy strongholds. ⁵ We destroy arguments and every lofty opinion raised against the knowledge of God, and take every thought captive to obey Christ, ⁶ being ready to punish every disobedience, when your obedience is complete.

⁷ Look at what is before your eyes. If anyone is confident that he is Christ's, let him remind himself that just as he is Christ's, so also are we. ⁸ For even if I boast a little too much of our authority, which the Lord gave for building you up and not for destroying you, I will not be ashamed. ⁹ I do not want to appear to be frightening you with my letters. ¹⁰ For they say, "His letters are weighty and strong, but his bodily presence is weak, and his speech of no account." ¹¹ Let such a person understand that what we say by letter when absent, we do when present. ¹² Not that we dare to classify or compare ourselves with some of those who are

¹ Or you

verses to read
2 Corinthians 10:4–6

Are you spiritually confused? Is there something in your spiritual life that has you baffled, an area where you can't seem to hear from God or know what to do? The answer to your confusion might be, just do it. In reliance on the Spirit, remembering his great love for you, just do what God asks you to do in his Word. You will never get life all figured out or "find yourself" through all the soul-searching and crying you could ever do. But when you are confused about life, you've got to take every confusing thought captive (see 2 Cor. 10:5) and make it obedient to God's Word by doing what his Word says. In the Bible you will find the answer you need to your dilemma. The answer is for his will to be done, by you, right now. You have to do whatever it is that God is calling you to do right now. It might not make any sense to your mind, but when you start doing what you should be doing, then the confusion will lift.

Is he asking you to get over something or to turn the other cheek? It's got to be done, and now. Is he telling you to just trust him? Then do it. The first step in doing what God asks will be the first step toward clearing away any spiritual confusion that you may have. But don't let anyone tell you that all you need to do is "think through things," because when you are feeling any kind of spiritual pressure, the only thing you should do is to immediately do what God is asking, not worry over it. Just doing it brings immediate healing and hope.

commending themselves. But when they measure themselves by one another and compare themselves with one another, they are without understanding.

¹³ But we will not boast beyond limits, but will boast only with regard to the area of influence God assigned to us, to reach even to you. ¹⁴ For we are not overextending ourselves, as though we did not reach you. For we were the first to come all the way to you with the gospel of Christ. ¹⁵ We do not boast beyond limit in the labors of others. But our hope is that as your faith increases, our area of influence among you may be greatly enlarged, ¹⁶ so that we may preach the gospel in lands beyond you, without boasting of work already done in another's area of influence. ¹⁷ "Let the one who boasts, boast in the Lord." ¹⁸ For it is not the one who commends himself who is approved, but the one whom the Lord commends.

Paul and the False Apostles

11 I wish you would bear with me in a little foolishness. Do bear with me! ² For I feel a divine jealousy for you, since I betrothed you to one husband, to present you as a pure virgin to Christ. ³ But I am afraid that as the serpent deceived Eve by his cunning, your thoughts will be led astray from a sincere and pure devotion to Christ. ⁴ For if someone comes and proclaims another Jesus than the one we proclaimed, or if you receive a different spirit from the one you received, or if you accept a different gospel from the one you accepted, you put up with it readily enough. ⁵ Indeed, I consider that I am not in the least inferior to these super-apostles. ⁶ Even if I am unskilled in speaking, I am not so in knowledge; indeed, in every way we have made this plain to you in all things.

⁷ Or did I commit a sin in humbling myself so that you might be exalted, because I preached God's gospel to you free of charge? ⁸ I robbed other churches by accepting support from them in order to serve you. ⁹ And when I was with you and was in need, I did not burden anyone, for the brothers who came from Macedonia supplied my need. So I refrained and will refrain from burdening you in any way. ¹⁰ As the truth of Christ is in me, this boasting of mine will not be silenced in the regions of Achaia. ¹¹ And why? Because I do not love you? God knows I do!

A Prayer that...
I MAY SERVE YOU

Lord of immortality, before whom angels bow and archangels veil their faces, help me to serve you with reverence and godly fear. You who are Spirit and require truth in the inner parts, help me to worship you in spirit and in truth. You who are righteous, don't let me love sin in my heart, or allow myself to have a worldly temper, or to look for satisfaction in things that don't last.

I look forward to a time when earthly dreams and things will seem pointless to me and I won't care whether I have been rich or poor, successful or disappointed, admired or despised, but when it will be of eternal importance that I have mourned for sin, hungered and thirsted after righteousness, loved the Lord Jesus in sincerity, and gloried in his cross. May these objects take all my attention! Give me what I need, to make serving you my perfect freedom and perfect joy.

By your grace, get all sinful fear and shame out of my mind so that with firmness and courage I can confess the Redeemer before my friends, going forward with him, hearing his rebuke, being passionate about his knowledge, being filled with his wisdom, walking with his careful attention, asking counsel of him in all things, looking to Scripture for his orders, keeping my mind on his peace, and knowing that nothing can happen to me without his permission, appointment, and administration.

Amen.

¹² And what I am doing I will continue to do, in order to undermine the claim of those who would like to claim that in their boasted mission they work on the same terms as we do. ¹³ For such men are false apostles, deceitful workmen, disguising themselves as apostles of Christ. ¹⁴ And no

A Prayer for...
GIVING MYSELF

Father, I bring to you years stained with sin and failure. Your voice within me, too long muffled with false pleasures and empty dreams, has at last pierced me to the heart, and I am ashamed of all the evil I have done.

When I think of the mess of my life, I dread the look of your holiness, and yet I am driven to you by a longing which no fear can chill and no sin can wither. You are the virtue of my soul—I am in your Son, Jesus, and your Spirit lives inside me permanently. Strengthen me to live out of that union with Christ. I ask for no lessening of the pain that sin has brought me. Let my weakness be from you, for I know that then it shall be my strength.

Only stay with me, Lord of my conscience, Strengthener of my will, Fulfiller of my hopes, and I will fear no more. Give me the glory of an illumined mind so that from now on I can see myself as a servant to every person and count no sacrifice too grievous, no burden too heavy, if by it I can serve the humblest of your children—for this is what Jesus himself has done for me, and more. Don't let me sink in dismay before the greatness of my debt, but help me to muster all my strength and serve others with the joy of heaven.

Amen.

wonder, for even Satan disguises himself as an angel of light. **¹⁵**So it is no surprise if his servants, also, disguise themselves as servants of righteousness. Their end will correspond to their deeds.

Paul's Sufferings as an Apostle

¹⁶I repeat, let no one think me foolish. But even if you do, accept me as a fool, so that I too may boast a little. **¹⁷**What I am saying with this boastful confidence, I say not as

the Lord would¹ but as a fool. **¹⁸**Since many boast according to the flesh, I too will boast. **¹⁹**For you gladly bear with fools, being wise yourselves! **²⁰**For you bear it if someone makes slaves of you, or devours you, or takes advantage of you, or puts on airs, or strikes you in the face. **²¹**To my shame, I must say, we were too weak for that!

But whatever anyone else dares to boast of—I am speaking as a fool—I also dare to boast of that. **²²**Are they Hebrews? So am I. Are they Israelites? So am I. Are they offspring of Abraham? So am I. **²³**Are they servants of Christ? I am a better one—I am talking like a madman—with far greater labors, far more imprisonments, with countless beatings, and often near death. **²⁴**Five times I received at the hands of the Jews the forty lashes less one. **²⁵**Three times I was beaten with rods. Once I was stoned. Three times I was shipwrecked; a night and a day I was adrift at sea; **²⁶**on frequent journeys, in danger from rivers, danger from robbers, danger from my own people, danger from Gentiles, danger in the city, danger in the wilderness, danger at sea, danger from false brothers; **²⁷**in toil and hardship, through many a sleepless night, in hunger and thirst, often without food,² in cold and exposure. **²⁸**And, apart from other things, there is the daily pressure on me of my anxiety for all the churches. **²⁹**Who is weak, and I am not weak? Who is made to fall, and I am not indignant?

³⁰If I must boast, I will boast of the things that show my weakness. **³¹**The God and Father of the Lord Jesus, he who is blessed forever, knows that I am not lying. **³²**At Damascus, the governor under King Aretas was guarding the city of Damascus in order to seize me, **³³**but I was let down in a basket through a window in the wall and escaped his hands.

Paul's Visions and His Thorn

12 I must go on boasting. Though there is nothing to be gained by it, I will go on to visions and revelations of the Lord. **²**I know a man in Christ who fourteen years ago was caught up to the third heaven—whether in the body or out of the body I do not know, God knows. **³**And I know that this man was caught up into paradise—whether in the body or out of the body I do not know, God knows— **⁴**and

¹Greek *not according to the Lord* ²Or *often in fasting*

he heard things that cannot be told, which man may not utter. ⁵On behalf of this man I will boast, but on my own behalf I will not boast, except of my weaknesses— ⁶though if I should wish to boast, I would not be a fool, for I would be speaking the truth; but I refrain from it, so that no one may think more of me than he sees in me or hears from me. ⁷So to keep me from becoming conceited because of the surpassing greatness of the revelations,¹ a thorn was given me in the flesh, a messenger of Satan to harass me, to keep me from becoming conceited. ⁸Three times I pleaded with the Lord about this, that it should leave me. ⁹But he said to me, "My grace is sufficient for you, for my power is made perfect in weakness." Therefore I will boast all the more gladly of my weaknesses, so that the power of Christ may rest upon me. ¹⁰For the sake of Christ, then, I am content with weaknesses, insults, hardships, persecutions, and calamities. For when I am weak, then I am strong.

Concern for the Corinthian Church

¹¹I have been a fool! You forced me to it, for I ought to have been commended by you. For I was not at all inferior to these super-apostles, even though I am nothing. ¹²The signs of a true apostle were performed among you with utmost patience, with signs and wonders and mighty works. ¹³For in what were you less favored than the rest of the churches, except that I myself did not burden you? Forgive me this wrong!

¹⁴Here for the third time I am ready to come to you. And I will not be a burden, for I seek not what is yours but you. For children are not obligated to save up for their parents, but parents for their children. ¹⁵I will most gladly spend and be spent for your souls. If I love you more, am I to be loved less? ¹⁶But granting that I myself did not burden you, I was crafty, you say, and got the better of you by deceit. ¹⁷Did I take advantage of you through any of those whom I sent to you? ¹⁸I urged Titus to go, and sent the brother with him. Did Titus take advantage of you? Did we not act in the same spirit? Did we not take the same steps?

¹⁹Have you been thinking all along that we have been defending ourselves to you?

It is in the sight of God that we have been speaking in Christ, and all for your upbuilding, beloved. ²⁰For I fear that perhaps when I come I may find you not as I wish, and that you may find me not as you wish—that perhaps there may be quarreling, jealousy, anger, hostility, slander, gossip, conceit, and disorder. ²¹I fear that when I come again my God may humble me before you, and I may have to mourn over many of those who sinned earlier and have not repented of the impurity, sexual immorality, and sensuality that they have practiced.

Ask Yourself . . .

ABOUT TRIALS

When you have a trial in your life, ask yourself these questions:

- What does God want me to learn about myself from this?

- What does God want to teach me about himself through this?

- If so, then why is it happening again? Am I part of the cause of this trial?

- How can God use this for my good?

- How has Jesus himself experienced trials?

Final Warnings

13 This is the third time I am coming to you. Every charge must be established by the evidence of two or three witnesses. ²I warned those who sinned before and all the others, and I warn them now while absent, as I did when present on my second visit, that if I come again I will not spare them— ³since you seek proof that Christ is speaking in me. He is not weak in dealing with you, but is powerful among you. ⁴For he was crucified in weakness, but lives by the power of God. For we also are weak in him, but in dealing with you we will live with him by the power of God.

¹ Or hears from me, even because of the surpassing greatness of the revelations. So to keep me from becoming conceited

⁵Examine yourselves, to see whether you are in the faith. Test yourselves. Or do you not realize this about yourselves, that Jesus Christ is in you?—unless indeed you fail to meet the test! ⁶I hope you will find out that we have not failed the test. ⁷But we pray to God that you may not do wrong—not that we may appear to have met the test, but that you may do what is right, though we may seem to have failed. ⁸For we cannot do anything against the truth, but only for the truth. ⁹For we are glad when we are weak and you are strong. Your restoration is what we pray for. ¹⁰For this reason I write these things while I am away from you, that when I come I may not have to be severe in my use of the authority that the Lord has given me for building up and not for tearing down.

Final Greetings

¹¹Finally, brothers,[1] rejoice. Aim for restoration, comfort one another,[2] agree with one another, live in peace; and the God of love and peace will be with you. ¹²Greet one another with a holy kiss. ¹³All the saints greet you.

¹⁴The grace of the Lord Jesus Christ and the love of God and the fellowship of the Holy Spirit be with you all.

---

[1] Or brothers and sisters [2] Or listen to my appeal

INTRODUCTION TO
Galatians

Author: The apostle Paul

Time: Around A.D. 48–50

Place: Antioch of Syria

Written to: The churches in Galatia

The gist

Galatians is about the freedom that comes from the life of faith. Faith in Jesus Christ is the only way to be saved, but some of Paul's opponents were demanding all kinds of other things for salvation. Paul wants his readers to understand that Jesus sets us free so that we don't have to work to get his love, but that doesn't give us a free pass to sin. Definitely not! But both freedom and obedience exist in the life of faith. You are free from the need to do something to be saved, but you now *want* to obey—not to save your life but to show your love.

Things to look for

- Paul's story of salvation (see Galatians 1)
- The doctrine of justification by faith (see Galatians 3–4)
- How to live in the freedom that Christ gives you (see Galatians 5)
- Paul's description of a life lived with the Spirit (see Gal. 5:16, 18, 22–23, 25; 6:8)

Receive God's Approval

> If righteousness were through the law, then Christ died for no purpose.
>
> Galatians 2:21

No one gets right with God because of how good they are. You get right with God by trusting in the work of Christ, making him Lord of your life. When you say, "God can't forgive me; I've done something too awful," or "I'm just not good enough for God," you cheapen what Jesus did for you on the cross. You are saying that you are a particularly difficult case and Christ's death just wasn't enough for you because your sin needs more work, more effort on your part, for you to get right. But that is absurd. If more work needed to be done to save you, then Christ died for nothing, a pointless death.

You can be certain his death was anything but pointless. It was meant for a supreme purpose: to save sinners by taking on their sins. Not one sin sneaked by the cross uncovered; all the sins of his children are forgiven. And you are his child if you believe in him and make him Lord of your life. The God Girl can't allow her feelings to convince her that her salvation requires more than what Christ did on the cross.

Paul's letter to the Galatians is all about God's kindness and grace and how to receive it and live in light of it. Once you receive this gift from God out of love instead of obligation, then you start drawing closer to him. And it is love, leading to obedience, that proves to God, yourself, and everyone around you that you are truly a God Girl. But be certain of this: Christ's love and obedience are what saves you! What you do as a God Girl doesn't save you; it only demonstrates that you have allowed the Spirit to work in and through you. Don't count on what you do to save you, but know that it will prove you faithful. I encourage you to read through Galatians all in one sitting, and as you read it, soak in the freedom that comes from a life of faith in Christ.

Must-Know Terms and Verses

☙ *Fruit of the Spirit* ❧

Refers to nine character traits that are seen in the lives of believers, like a fruit of their faith, listed in Galatians 5:22–23. They are love, joy, peace, patience, kindness, goodness, faithfulness, gentleness, and self-control.

☙ *Gentiles* ❧

A general term meaning all people who are not Jewish.

For am I now seeking the approval of man, or of God? Or am I trying to please man? If I were still trying to please man, I would not be a servant of Christ. *Galatians 1:10*

If righteousness were through the law, then Christ died for no purpose. *Galatians 2:21*

Did you receive the Spirit by works of the law or by hearing with faith? Are you so foolish? Having begun by the Spirit, are you now being perfected by the flesh? *Galatians 3:2–3*

Does he who supplies the Spirit to you and works miracles among you do so by works of the law, or by hearing with faith—just as Abraham "believed God, and it was counted to him as righteousness"? *Galatians 3:5–6*

But the fruit of the Spirit is love, joy, peace, patience, kindness, goodness, faithfulness, gentleness, self-control. *Galatians 5:22–23*

The Letter of Paul to the
Galatians

Greeting

1 Paul, an apostle—not from men nor through man, but through Jesus Christ and God the Father, who raised him from the dead— ²and all the brothers[1] who are with me,

To the churches of Galatia:

³Grace to you and peace from God our Father and the Lord Jesus Christ, ⁴who gave himself for our sins to deliver us from the present evil age, according to the will of our God and Father, ⁵to whom be the glory forever and ever. Amen.

No Other Gospel

⁶I am astonished that you are so quickly deserting him who called you in the grace of Christ and are turning to a different gospel— ⁷not that there is another one, but there are some who trouble you and want to distort the gospel of Christ. ⁸But even if we or an angel from heaven should preach to you a gospel contrary to the one we preached to you, let him be accursed. ⁹As we have said before, so now I say again: If anyone is preaching to you a gospel contrary to the one you received, let him be accursed.

¹⁰For am I now seeking the approval of man, or of God? Or am I trying to please man? If I were still trying to please man, I would not be a servant[2] of Christ.

Paul Called by God

¹¹For I would have you know, brothers, that the gospel that was preached by me is not man's gospel.[3] ¹²For I did not receive it from any man, nor was I taught it, but I received it through a revelation of Jesus Christ. ¹³For you have heard of my former life in Judaism, how I persecuted the church of God violently and tried to destroy it. ¹⁴And I was advancing in Judaism beyond many of my own age among my people,

so extremely zealous was I for the traditions of my fathers. ¹⁵But when he who had set me apart before I was born,[4] and who called me by his grace, ¹⁶was pleased to reveal his Son to[5] me, in order that I might preach him among the Gentiles, I did not immediately consult with anyone;[6] ¹⁷nor did I go up to Jerusalem to those who were apostles before me, but I went away into Arabia, and returned again to Damascus.

Ask Yourself . . .

ABOUT GUYS

- When I got dressed today, whom was I trying to impress?

- Do I dress for guys or for God?

- What is more important to me, what a guy wants or what God wants?

- Whom do I think about more, guys or God?

- Whom would I rather spend most of my time with, a guy or God?

Today, every time you start wondering what a guy thinks of you, remind yourself that it's what God thinks that really matters.

¹⁸Then after three years I went up to Jerusalem to visit Cephas and remained with him fifteen days. ¹⁹But I saw none of the other apostles except James the Lord's

---

[1] Or brothers and sisters. The plural Greek word adelphoi (translated "brothers") refers to siblings in a family. In New Testament usage, depending on the context, adelphoi may refer either to men or to both men and women who are siblings (brothers and sisters) in God's family, the church; also verse 11 [2] Or slave; Greek bondservant [3] Greek not according to man [4] Greek set me apart from my mother's womb [5] Greek in [6] Greek with flesh and blood

brother. ²⁰(In what I am writing to you, before God, I do not lie!) ²¹Then I went into the regions of Syria and Cilicia. ²²And I was still unknown in person to the churches of Judea that are in Christ. ²³They only were hearing it said, "He who used to persecute us is now preaching the faith he once tried to destroy." ²⁴And they glorified God because of me.

Paul Accepted by the Apostles

2 Then after fourteen years I went up again to Jerusalem with Barnabas, taking Titus along with me. ²I went up because of a revelation and set before them (though privately before those who seemed influential) the gospel that I proclaim among the Gentiles, in order to make sure I was not running or had not run in vain. ³But even Titus, who was with me, was not forced to be circumcised, though he was a Greek. ⁴Yet because of false brothers secretly brought in—who slipped in to spy out our freedom that we have in Christ Jesus, so that they might bring us into slavery— ⁵to them we did not yield in submission even for a moment, so that the truth of the gospel might be preserved for you. ⁶And from those who seemed to be influential (what they were makes no difference to me; God shows no partiality)—those, I say, who seemed influential added nothing to me. ⁷On the contrary, when they saw that I had been entrusted with the gospel to the uncircumcised, just as Peter had been entrusted with the gospel to the circumcised ⁸(for he who worked through Peter for his apostolic ministry to the circumcised worked also through me for mine to the Gentiles), ⁹and when James and Cephas and John, who seemed to be pillars, perceived the grace that was given to me, they gave the right hand of fellowship to Barnabas and me, that we should go to the Gentiles and they to the circumcised. ¹⁰Only, they asked us to remember the poor, the very thing I was eager to do.

Paul Opposes Peter

¹¹But when Cephas came to Antioch, I opposed him to his face, because he stood condemned. ¹²For before certain men came from James, he was eating with the Gentiles; but when they came he drew back and separated himself, fearing the

¹Or fearing those of the circumcision

circumcision party.¹ ¹³And the rest of the Jews acted hypocritically along with him, so that even Barnabas was led astray by their hypocrisy. ¹⁴But when I saw that their conduct was not in step with the truth of the gospel, I said to Cephas before them all, "If you, though a Jew, live like a Gentile and not like a Jew, how can you force the Gentiles to live like Jews?"

Ask Yourself . . .

ABOUT YOUR SALVATION

Considering yourself of no value is just as wrong as considering yourself of too much value. Your value is found in the Spirit of the Christ who lives within you. To say, "I am worthless and cannot be redeemed, not even by the blood of Jesus" is to say Christ's death was worthless because you are just too bad to ever be saved, no matter what he did. But that is a bold-faced lie. No sin is unforgivable. Ask yourself:

- Have I acted as if Christ's death was pointless by believing that I have to do something beyond accepting what Christ did on the cross in order to be saved?

- Do I believe that I can't be forgiven?

- Is there something I can't seem to do that I believe is keeping me from salvation?

- What does God's Word say about salvation and how it's achieved?

- Are there any "works" that I believe I must do to keep my salvation? What does God's Word say about this?

Justified by Faith

¹⁵We ourselves are Jews by birth and not Gentile sinners; ¹⁶yet we know that a per-

son is not justified[1] by works of the law but through faith in Jesus Christ, so we also have believed in Christ Jesus, in order to be justified by faith in Christ and not by works of the law, because by works of the law no one will be justified.

[17] But if, in our endeavor to be justified in Christ, we too were found to be sinners, is Christ then a servant of sin? Certainly not! [18] For if I rebuild what I tore down, I prove myself to be a transgressor. [19] For through the law I died to the law, so that I might live to God. [20] I have been crucified with Christ. It is no longer I who live, but Christ who lives in me. And the life I now live in the flesh I live by faith in the Son of God, who loved me and gave himself for me. [21] I do not nullify the grace of God, for if righteousness[2] were through the law, then Christ died for no purpose.

By Faith, or by Works of the Law?

3 O foolish Galatians! Who has bewitched you? It was before your eyes that Jesus Christ was publicly portrayed as crucified. [2] Let me ask you only this: Did you receive the Spirit by works of the law or by hearing with faith? [3] Are you so foolish? Having begun by the Spirit, are you now being perfected by[3] the flesh? [4] Did you suffer[4] so many things in vain—if indeed it was in vain? [5] Does he who supplies the Spirit to you and works miracles among you do so by works of the law, or by hearing with faith— [6] just as [a]Abraham "believed God, and it was counted to him as righteousness"?

[7] Know then that it is those of faith who are the sons of Abraham. [8] And the Scripture, foreseeing that God would justify[5] the Gentiles by faith, preached the

[1] Or counted righteous (three times in verse 16); also verse 17 [2] Or justification [3] Or now ending with [4] Or experience [5] Or count righteous; also verses 11, 24 [a] Gen. 15:6

Know Yourself

verses to read
Galatians 3:1–5

The law is useless to save you. Before Christ came, people were expected to do exactly what the law said, but since no one could do that perfectly, sacrifices needed to be made. Their sins were too great and happened too often for them to be holy without some kind of sacrifice. Not much is different now: you were saved not because you were so perfect and holy but because Jesus was your sacrifice. When you entrusted yourself to that sacrifice, you were immediately saved. Nothing you did saved you except the empty hands of faith. And this is the foundation of your faith your whole life long.

When Jesus became your Lord he also gave you his Spirit, and that Spirit is what changes your life. A lot of times you mess up, you do what you don't want to do, and you feel terrible. You wonder how to fix it, how to make it right. And sometimes you feel powerless to change, and that is true: you *are* powerless, but the Spirit is not. Remember, it's through the Spirit that you were saved. And if he has the power to save you, he has the power to change you.

When you fail, don't hate yourself, don't fret, and don't give up. Just remember what you did when you were saved and do it again: turn to the Lord, confess your sin, and accept his forgiveness and cleansing. The ability to know the right thing to do and the strength to do it all come from the Holy Spirit who lives in you. Don't try to do it all by yourself. Call on him, beg him, and trust him to make you more like Christ every day. When you fail, get up, wipe yourself off, and keep moving forward. You can do all things through him (see Phil. 4:13). Trust him and receive his forgiveness.

gospel beforehand to Abraham, saying, *a*"In you shall all the nations be blessed." ⁹ So then, those who are of faith are blessed along with Abraham, the man of faith.

The Righteous Shall Live by Faith

¹⁰ For all who rely on works of the law are under a curse; for it is written, *b*"Cursed be everyone who does not abide by all things written in the Book of the Law, and do them." ¹¹ Now it is evident that no one is justified before God by the law, for *c*"The righteous shall live by faith."*¹* ¹² But the law is not of faith, rather *d*"The one who does them shall live by them." ¹³ Christ redeemed us from the curse of the law by becoming a curse for us—for it is written, *e*"Cursed is everyone who is hanged on a tree"— ¹⁴ so that in Christ Jesus the blessing of Abraham might come to the Gentiles, so that we might receive the promised Spirit*²* through faith.

The Law and the Promise

¹⁵ To give a human example, brothers:*³* even with a man-made covenant, no one annuls it or adds to it once it has been ratified. ¹⁶ Now the promises were made to Abraham and to his offspring. It does not say, "And to offsprings," referring to many, but referring to one, "And to your offspring," who is Christ. ¹⁷ This is what I mean: the law, which came 430 years afterward, does not annul a covenant previously ratified by God, so as to make the promise void. ¹⁸ For if the inheritance comes by the law, it no longer comes by promise; but God gave it to Abraham by a promise.

¹⁹ Why then the law? It was added because of transgressions, until the offspring should come to whom the promise had been made, and it was put in place through angels by an intermediary. ²⁰ Now an intermediary implies more than one, but God is one.

²¹ Is the law then contrary to the promises of God? Certainly not! For if a law had been given that could give life, then righteousness would indeed be by the law. ²² But the Scripture imprisoned everything under sin, so that the promise by faith in Jesus Christ might be given to those who believe.

²³ Now before faith came, we were held captive under the law, imprisoned until the coming faith would be revealed. ²⁴ So then, the law was our guardian until Christ came, in order that we might be justified by faith. ²⁵ But now that faith has come, we are no longer under a guardian, ²⁶ for in Christ Jesus you are all sons of God, through faith. ²⁷ For as many of you as were baptized into Christ have put on Christ. ²⁸ There is neither Jew nor Greek, there is neither slave*⁴* nor free, there is no male and female, for you are all one in Christ Jesus. ²⁹ And if you are Christ's, then you are Abraham's offspring, heirs according to promise.

Sons and Heirs

4 I mean that the heir, as long as he is a child, is no different from a slave,*⁵* though he is the owner of everything, ² but he is under guardians and managers until the date set by his father. ³ In the same way we also, when we were children, were enslaved to the elementary principles*⁶* of the world. ⁴ But when the fullness of time had come, God sent forth his Son, born of woman, born under the law, ⁵ to redeem those who were under the law, so that we might receive adoption as sons. ⁶ And because you are sons, God has sent the Spirit of his Son into our hearts, crying, "Abba! Father!" ⁷ So you are no longer a slave, but a son, and if a son, then an heir through God.

Paul's Concern for the Galatians

⁸ Formerly, when you did not know God, you were enslaved to those that by nature are not gods. ⁹ But now that you have come to know God, or rather to be known by God, how can you turn back again to the weak and worthless elementary principles of the world, whose slaves you want to be once more? ¹⁰ You observe days and months and seasons and years! ¹¹ I am afraid I may have labored over you in vain.

¹² Brothers,*⁷* I entreat you, become as I am, for I also have become as you are. You did me no wrong. ¹³ You know it was because of a bodily ailment that I preached the gospel to you at first, ¹⁴ and though my condition was a trial to you, you did not scorn or despise me, but received me as

---

¹ Or *The one who by faith is righteous will live* ² Greek *receive the promise of the Spirit* ³ Or *brothers and sisters* ⁴ Greek *bondservant* ⁵ Greek *bondservant; also verse 7* ⁶ Or *elemental spirits; also verse 9* ⁷ Or *Brothers and sisters; also verses 28, 31* *a* Gen. 12:3 *b* Deut. 27:26 *c* Hab. 2:4 *d* Lev. 18:5 *e* Deut. 21:23

an angel of God, as Christ Jesus. [15] What then has become of your blessedness? For I testify to you that, if possible, you would have gouged out your eyes and given them to me. [16] Have I then become your enemy by telling you the truth?[1] [17] They make much of you, but for no good purpose. They want to shut you out, that you may make much of them. [18] It is always good to be made much of for a good purpose, and not only when I am present with you, [19] my little children, for whom I am again in the anguish of childbirth until Christ is formed in you! [20] I wish I could be present with you now and change my tone, for I am perplexed about you.

Example of Hagar and Sarah

[21] Tell me, you who desire to be under the law, do you not listen to the law? [22] For it is written that Abraham had two sons, one by a slave woman and one by a free woman. [23] But the son of the slave was born according to the flesh, while the son of the free woman was born through promise. [24] Now this may be interpreted allegorically: these women are two covenants. One is from Mount Sinai, bearing children for slavery; she is Hagar. [25] Now Hagar is Mount Sinai in Arabia;[2] she corresponds to the present Jerusalem, for she is in slavery with her children. [26] But the Jerusalem above is free, and she is our mother. [27] For it is written,

> [a]"Rejoice, O barren one who does not bear;
> > break forth and cry aloud, you who are not in labor!
> For the children of the desolate one will be more
> > than those of the one who has a husband."

[28] Now you,[3] brothers, like Isaac, are children of promise. [29] But just as at that time he who was born according to the flesh persecuted him who was born according to the Spirit, so also it is now. [30] But what does the Scripture say? [b]"Cast out the slave woman and her son, for the son of the slave woman shall not inherit with the son of the free woman." [31] So, brothers, we are not children of the slave but of the free woman.

Christ Has Set Us Free

5 For freedom Christ has set us free; stand firm therefore, and do not submit again to a yoke of slavery.

[2] Look: I, Paul, say to you that if you accept circumcision, Christ will be of no advantage to you. [3] I testify again to every man who accepts circumcision that he is obligated to keep the whole law. [4] You are severed from Christ, you who would be justified[4] by the law; you have fallen away from grace. [5] For through the Spirit, by faith, we ourselves eagerly wait for the hope of righteousness. [6] For in Christ Jesus neither circumcision nor uncircumcision counts for anything, but only faith working through love.

[7] You were running well. Who hindered you from obeying the truth? [8] This persuasion is not from him who calls you. [9] A little leaven leavens the whole lump. [10] I have confidence in the Lord that you will take no other view, and the one who is troubling you will bear the penalty, whoever he is. [11] But if I, brothers,[5] still preach[6] circumcision, why am I still being persecuted? In that case the offense of the cross has been removed. [12] I wish those who unsettle you would emasculate themselves!

[13] For you were called to freedom, brothers. Only do not use your freedom as an opportunity for the flesh, but through love serve one another. [14] For the whole law is fulfilled in one word: [c]"You shall love your neighbor as yourself." [15] But if you bite and devour one another, watch out that you are not consumed by one another.

Keep in Step with the Spirit

[16] But I say, walk by the Spirit, and you will not gratify the desires of the flesh. [17] For the desires of the flesh are against the Spirit, and the desires of the Spirit are against the flesh, for these are opposed to each other, to keep you from doing the things you want to do. [18] But if you are led by the Spirit, you are not under the law. [19] Now the works of the flesh are evident: sexual immorality, impurity, sensuality, [20] idolatry, sorcery, enmity, strife, jealousy, fits of anger, rivalries, dissensions, divisions, [21] envy,[7] drunkenness, orgies, and things like these. I warn you, as I warned you before, that those who do such things

---

[1] Or by dealing truthfully with you [2] Some manuscripts For Sinai is a mountain in Arabia [3] Some manuscripts we [4] Or counted righteous [5] Or brothers and sisters; also verse 13 [6] Greek proclaim [7] Some manuscripts add murder [a] Isa. 54:1 [b] Gen. 21:10 [c] Lev. 19:18

will not inherit the kingdom of God. ²² But the fruit of the Spirit is love, joy, peace, patience, kindness, goodness, faithfulness, ²³ gentleness, self-control; against such things there is no law. ²⁴ And those who belong to Christ Jesus have crucified the flesh with its passions and desires.

Ask Yourself . . .

ABOUT WHAT YOU WANT

You want something. You really want it. No, you need it! But the more you ask, the farther away that thing seems. Could it be that God is doing something more important in your life right now? Could it be something that will change everything in you or around you, but you are so focused on this one little thing you want that you can't see anything else? Think about it for a minute. Could there be something bigger that God wants for you? To get the answers, read your Bible and see what God wants more of in your life. Galatians 5:22–23 is a good place to start.

²⁵ If we live by the Spirit, let us also keep in step with the Spirit. ²⁶ Let us not become conceited, provoking one another, envying one another.

Bear One Another's Burdens

6 Brothers,¹ if anyone is caught in any transgression, you who are spiritual should restore him in a spirit of gentleness. Keep watch on yourself, lest you too be tempted. ² Bear one another's burdens, and so fulfill the law of Christ. ³ For if anyone thinks he is something, when he is nothing, he deceives himself. ⁴ But let each one test his own work, and then his reason to boast will be in himself alone and not in his neighbor. ⁵ For each will have to bear his own load.

⁶ Let the one who is taught the word share all good things with the one who teaches. ⁷ Do not be deceived: God is not mocked, for whatever one sows, that will he also reap. ⁸ For the one who sows to his own flesh will from the flesh reap corruption, but the one who sows to the Spirit will from the Spirit reap eternal life. ⁹ And let us not grow weary of doing good, for in due season we will reap, if we do not give up. ¹⁰ So then, as we have opportunity, let us do good to everyone, and especially to those who are of the household of faith.

Final Warning and Benediction

¹¹ See with what large letters I am writing to you with my own hand. ¹² It is those who want to make a good showing in the flesh who would force you to be circumcised, and only in order that they may not be persecuted for the cross of Christ. ¹³ For even those who are circumcised do not themselves keep the law, but they desire to have you circumcised that they may boast in your flesh. ¹⁴ But far be it from me to boast except in the cross of our Lord Jesus Christ, by which² the world has been crucified to me, and I to the world. ¹⁵ For neither circumcision counts for anything, nor uncircumcision, but a new creation. ¹⁶ And as for all who walk by this rule, peace and mercy be upon them, and upon the Israel of God.

¹⁷ From now on let no one cause me trouble, for I bear on my body the marks of Jesus.

¹⁸ The grace of our Lord Jesus Christ be with your spirit, brothers. Amen.

---

¹ Or Brothers and sisters; also verse 18 ² Or through whom

INTRODUCTION TO

Author: The apostle Paul

Time: Around A.D. 60

Place: Most likely in Rome, while Paul was in prison

Written to: The church in Ephesus, as well as other churches in the area

The gist

You have been adopted—did you know that? Read the book of Ephesians and you'll see how God loved you so much that he made you his own. If you are feeling down about life and faith, read this book and get inspired.

Things to look for

- How much God loves you (see Eph. 2:4–10)

- What the "body" of believers means (see Ephesians 4–6)

- How to deal with your parents biblically (see Eph. 6:1–3)

- How to put on the full armor of God (see Eph. 6:10–18)

Imitate God

By grace you have been saved through faith. And this is not your own doing; it is the gift of God, not a result of works, so that no one may boast.

Ephesians 2:8–9

One of the great mysteries of faith is salvation—that a perfect God would not only accept imperfect you but take away all the stupid and sinful things you did in the past and make you his own child. The beauty of the book of Ephesians is this message that you haven't been saved by anything you've done but only by the blood of Christ given because of God's grace. Paul wants his readers to be encouraged in their faith. He wants them to find their strength in the sheer depth of God's love for them.

He also wants his readers to understand that God chose them to be holy and perfect. He didn't choose you to let you stay the way you were before you knew him but to make you better, more holy, more like Jesus. God not only does the hard work of saving you, he also works in you and with you to form you into the likeness of Jesus. He forgives you for everything you've ever done, but it doesn't end there. He has more plans for you—more work, yes, but also more good.

In this letter, Paul encourages holiness and oneness with Christ. And in that oneness you can find all you need in order to not only survive in this world but thrive. You have to remember, God Girl, that your life isn't a wrestling match with a human opponent, though those pesky humans might be your most obvious enemies. The real fight is against the Enemy of God and that enemy's dark forces. But have no fear: God provides everything you need to stand against the attacks. In this beautiful book you will find out how to put on the full armor of God, a spiritual armor that can protect you against all the "flaming darts of the evil one" (Eph. 6:16).

As a God Girl you are not adrift in this world, lost and lonely. You were saved for a special purpose: to know Christ, and in doing so to become more peaceful, faithful, confident, loving, and holy. Read the book of Ephesians and study all that God has given for you to find all the strength you need to overcome the evil in this world.

Must-Know Verses

In him we have redemption through his blood, the forgiveness of our trespasses, according to the riches of his grace. *Ephesians 1:7*

In him we have obtained an inheritance, having been predestined according to the purpose of him who works all things according to the counsel of his will, so that we who were the first to hope in Christ might be to the praise of his glory. *Ephesians 1:11–12*

But God, being rich in mercy, because of the great love with which he loved us, even when we were dead in our trespasses, made us alive together with Christ. *Ephesians 2:4–5*

For by grace you have been saved through faith. And this is not your own doing; it is the gift of God, not a result of works, so that no one may boast. *Ephesians 2:8–9*

Put on the new self, created after the likeness of God in true righteousness and holiness. *Ephesians 4:24*

Therefore be imitators of God, as beloved children. *Ephesians 5:1*

Wives, submit to your own husbands, as to the Lord. For the husband is the head of the wife even as Christ is the head of the church, his body, and is himself its Savior. Now as the church submits to Christ, so also wives should submit in everything to their husbands. *Ephesians 5:22–24*

Husbands, love your wives, as Christ loved the church and gave himself up for her, that he might sanctify her, having cleansed her by the washing of water with the word, so that he might present the church to himself in splendor, without spot or wrinkle or any such thing, that she might be holy and without blemish. *Ephesians 5:25–27*

Finally, be strong in the Lord and in the strength of his might. Put on the whole armor of God, that you may be able to stand against the schemes of the devil. *Ephesians 6:10–11*

The Letter of Paul to the

Ephesians

Greeting

1 Paul, an apostle of Christ Jesus by the will of God,

To the saints who are in Ephesus, and are faithful[1] in Christ Jesus:

2 Grace to you and peace from God our Father and the Lord Jesus Christ.

Spiritual Blessings in Christ

3 Blessed be the God and Father of our Lord Jesus Christ, who has blessed us in Christ with every spiritual blessing in the heavenly places, **4** even as he chose us in him before the foundation of the world, that we should be holy and blameless before him. In love **5** he predestined us[2] for adoption as sons through Jesus Christ, according to the purpose of his will, **6** to the praise of his glorious grace, with which he has blessed us in the Beloved. **7** In him we have redemption through his blood, the forgiveness of our trespasses, according to the riches of his grace, **8** which he lavished upon us, in all wisdom and insight **9** making known[3] to us the mystery of his will, according to his purpose, which he set forth in Christ **10** as a plan for the fullness of time, to unite all things in him, things in heaven and things on earth.

11 In him we have obtained an inheritance, having been predestined according to the purpose of him who works all things according to the counsel of his will, **12** so that we who were the first to hope in Christ might be to the praise of his glory. **13** In him you also, when you heard the word of truth, the gospel of your salvation, and believed in him, were sealed with the promised Holy Spirit, **14** who is the guarantee[4] of our inheritance until we acquire possession of it,[5] to the praise of his glory.

Thanksgiving and Prayer

15 For this reason, because I have heard of your faith in the Lord Jesus and your love[6] toward all the saints, **16** I do not cease to give thanks for you, remembering you in my prayers, **17** that the God of our Lord Jesus Christ, the Father of glory, may give you the Spirit of wisdom and of revelation in the knowledge of him, **18** having the eyes of your hearts enlightened, that you may know what is the hope to which he has called you, what are the riches of his glorious inheritance in the saints, **19** and what is the immeasurable greatness of his power toward us who believe, according to the working of his great might **20** that he worked in Christ when he raised him from the dead and seated him at his right hand in the heavenly places, **21** far above all rule and authority and power and dominion, and above every name that is named, not only in this age but also in the one to come. **22** And he put all things under his feet and gave him as head over all things to the church, **23** which is his body, the fullness of him who fills all in all.

By Grace Through Faith

2 And you were dead in the trespasses and sins **2** in which you once walked, following the course of this world, following the prince of the power of the air, the spirit that is now at work in the sons of disobedience— **3** among whom we all once lived in the passions of our flesh, carrying out the desires of the body[7] and the mind, and were by nature children of wrath, like the rest of mankind.[8] **4** But[9] God, being rich in mercy, because of the great love with which he loved us, **5** even when we were dead in our trespasses, made us alive together with Christ—by grace you have been saved— **6** and raised us up with him and seated us

---

[1] Some manuscripts *saints who are also faithful* (omitting *in Ephesus*) [2] Or *before him in love, having predestined us* [3] Or *he lavished upon us in all wisdom and insight, making known . . .* [4] Or *down payment* [5] Or *until God redeems his possession* [6] Some manuscripts omit *your love* [7] Greek *flesh* [8] Greek *like the rest* [9] Or *And*

with him in the heavenly places in Christ Jesus, [7] so that in the coming ages he might show the immeasurable riches of his grace in kindness toward us in Christ Jesus. [8] For by grace you have been saved through faith. And this is not your own doing; it is the gift of God, [9] not a result of works, so that no one may boast. [10] For we are his workmanship, created in Christ Jesus for good works, which God prepared beforehand, that we should walk in them.

One in Christ

[11] Therefore remember that at one time you Gentiles in the flesh, called "the uncircumcision" by what is called the circumcision, which is made in the flesh by hands— [12] remember that you were at that time separated from Christ, alienated from the commonwealth of Israel and strangers to the covenants of promise, having no hope and without God in the world. [13] But now in Christ Jesus you who once were far off have been brought near by the blood of Christ. [14] For he himself is our peace, who has made us both one and has broken down in his flesh the dividing

wall of hostility [15] by abolishing the law of commandments expressed in ordinances, that he might create in himself one new man in place of the two, so making peace, [16] and might reconcile us both to God in one body through the cross, thereby killing the hostility. [17] And he came and preached peace to you who were far off and peace to those who were near. [18] For through him we both have access in one Spirit to the Father. [19] So then you are no longer strangers and aliens,[1] but you are fellow citizens with the saints and members of the household of God, [20] built on the foundation of the apostles and prophets, Christ Jesus himself being the cornerstone, [21] in whom the whole structure, being joined together, grows into a holy temple in the Lord. [22] In him you also are being built together into a dwelling place for God by[2] the Spirit.

The Mystery of the Gospel Revealed

3 For this reason I, Paul, a prisoner for Christ Jesus on behalf of you Gentiles— [2] assuming that you have heard of the stewardship of God's grace that was given to me for you, [3] how the mystery was made

[1] Or sojourners [2] Or in

verses to read
Ephesians 1:7–12

Know Yourself

Beware of taking advantage of God's forgiveness. If you're about to do something wrong and you think, "Well, at least I know that God will forgive me," you've sorely misunderstood the gospel. Remember, the only reason you are forgiven is because of the horrific death that God's Son died on the cross. To take advantage of that as a free pass to sin is to trample on and ridicule his death. Never forget that the forgiveness that is so easy for you to take from God cost his Son sheer agony. Never forget the price at which you were bought.

God is good and kind. He loves you. He is there for you. But never, ever think that it is because of this love alone that he is able to forgive you. Your sin required something more: it required that a payment, or ransom, be given in return for your transgressions. God is not only loving, but also just. And because of Christ's blood and suffering, he can say, "Your sins are forgiven." This unfathomable gift of God—the persecution, torture, and death of his Son—is what gives you instant access to forgiveness. Never take God's forgiveness for granted, because it comes to you by the blood of his child. Christ hung on the cross so that you could have forgiveness. Remember that the next time you are about to take advantage of this amazing gift.

known to me by revelation, as I have written briefly. **4** When you read this, you can perceive my insight into the mystery of Christ, **5** which was not made known to the sons of men in other generations as it has now been revealed to his holy apostles and prophets by the Spirit. **6** This mystery is[1] that the Gentiles are fellow heirs, members of the same body, and partakers of the promise in Christ Jesus through the gospel.

7 Of this gospel I was made a minister according to the gift of God's grace, which was given me by the working of his power. **8** To me, though I am the very least of all the saints, this grace was given, to preach to the Gentiles the unsearchable riches of Christ, **9** and to bring to light for everyone what is the plan of the mystery hidden for ages in[2] God who created all things, **10** so

that through the church the manifold wisdom of God might now be made known to the rulers and authorities in the heavenly places. **11** This was according to the eternal purpose that he has realized in Christ Jesus our Lord, **12** in whom we have boldness and access with confidence through our faith in him. **13** So I ask you not to lose heart over what I am suffering for you, which is your glory.

Prayer for Spiritual Strength

14 For this reason I bow my knees before the Father, **15** from whom every family[3] in heaven and on earth is named, **16** that according to the riches of his glory he may grant you to be strengthened with power through his Spirit in your inner being, **17** so that Christ may dwell in your hearts

The words *This mystery is* are inferred from verse 4 2 Or *by* 3 Or *fatherhood*; the Greek word *patria* is closely related to the word for *father* in verse 14

Know Love

verses to read
Ephesians 3:14-21

A tree gets much of what it needs for life from its roots. And its roots grow in proportion to the soil they're in: in shallow ground, plants grow low and weak; in deep soil they grow tall and strong.

Where you sink your roots will determine how much you grow. Sink your roots in the shallow soil of the world, and your growth will be stunted. Because the world doesn't know love, it can't feed your soul or give it life in abundance. But a life buried in the soil of God's love will blossom and grow into an impressive and strong life, unshakeable in strong winds and able to protect anyone who comes under its impressive branches. Right now you are just a sapling, but one day you will be a mighty oak. Right now you are sinking your roots deeper and deeper, searching for rich soil, digging for water and nourishment from the love of God. The more you drink of this love, the more you ground yourself in it, and the more you offer it as shade to others, the deeper your roots will grow and the more unshakeable you will become.

The girl who has her life's roots sunk into the ground of God's love for her in the gospel is a girl who is determined to react to everyone she encounters with love. She refuses to allow anyone else's sin to become her sin. She doesn't consider bitterness, resentment, revenge, or retaliation to be an option, but instead she digs herself deeper into the meaning of love. She gives while others take. She smiles while others scowl. She forgives while others hate. After all, you scowled at and hated God, but he sent his Son to die for you; now you are free to love others the way God has loved you. You, God Girl, will grow strong and become an impressive young woman to those around you when you ground yourself in this love.

through faith—that you, being rooted and grounded in love, [18]may have strength to comprehend with all the saints what is the breadth and length and height and depth, [19]and to know the love of Christ that surpasses knowledge, that you may be filled with all the fullness of God.

[20]Now to him who is able to do far more abundantly than all that we ask or think, according to the power at work within us, [21]to him be glory in the church and in Christ Jesus throughout all generations, forever and ever. Amen.

Unity in the Body of Christ

4 I therefore, a prisoner for the Lord, urge you to walk in a manner worthy of the calling to which you have been called, [2]with all humility and gentleness, with patience, bearing with one another in love, [3]eager to maintain the unity of the Spirit in the bond of peace. [4]There is one body and one Spirit—just as you were called to the one hope that belongs to your call— [5]one Lord, one faith, one baptism, [6]one God and Father of all, who is over all and through all and in all. [7]But grace was given to each one of us according to the measure of Christ's gift. [8]Therefore it says,

[a]"When he ascended on high he led a
        host of captives,
    and he gave gifts to men."[1]

[9](In saying, "He ascended," what does it mean but that he had also descended into the lower regions, the earth?[2] [10]He who descended is the one who also ascended far above all the heavens, that he might fill all things.) [11]And he gave the apostles, the prophets, the evangelists, the shepherds[3] and teachers,[4] [12]to equip the saints for the work of ministry, for building up the body of Christ, [13]until we all attain to the unity of the faith and of the knowledge of the Son of God, to mature manhood,[5] to the measure of the stature of the fullness of Christ, [14]so that we may no longer be children, tossed to and fro by the waves and carried about by every wind of doctrine, by human cunning, by craftiness in deceitful schemes. [15]Rather, speaking the truth in love, we are to grow up in every way into him who is the head, into Christ, [16]from whom the whole body, joined and

held together by every joint with which it is equipped, when each part is working properly, makes the body grow so that it builds itself up in love.

Ask Yourself . . .

ABOUT PLEASING GOD

- Am I doing things that please God?

- What things am I doing that might not be pleasing him?

- Do I enjoy talking about other people's sin?

- What are some ways that I try to find out what God wants from me?

- What are ways that I try to please God when I don't need to, because of the gospel and what Jesus has done to please God *for* me?

The New Life

[17]Now this I say and testify in the Lord, that you must no longer walk as the Gentiles do, in the futility of their minds. [18]They are darkened in their understanding, alienated from the life of God because of the ignorance that is in them, due to their hardness of heart. [19]They have become callous and have given themselves up to sensuality, greedy to practice every kind of impurity. [20]But that is not the way you learned Christ!— [21]assuming that you have heard about him and were taught in him, as the truth is in Jesus, [22]to put off your old self,[6] which belongs to your former manner of life and is corrupt through deceitful desires, [23]and to be renewed in the spirit of your minds, [24]and to put on the new self, created after the likeness of God in true righteousness and holiness.

[25]Therefore, having put away falsehood, let each one of you speak the truth with his neighbor, for we are members one of

[1]The Greek word *anthropoi* can refer to both men and women [2]Or *the lower parts of the earth?* [3]Or *pastors* [4]Or *the shepherd-teachers*
[5]Greek *to a full-grown man* [6]Greek *man; also verse 24* [a]Ps. 68:18

another. ²⁶Be angry and do not sin; do not let the sun go down on your anger, ²⁷and give no opportunity to the devil. ²⁸Let the thief no longer steal, but rather let him labor, doing honest work with his own hands, so that he may have something to share with anyone in need. ²⁹Let no corrupting talk come out of your mouths, but only such as is good for building up, as fits the occasion, that it may give grace to those who hear. ³⁰And do not grieve the Holy Spirit of God, by whom you were sealed for the day of redemption. ³¹Let all bitterness and wrath and anger and clamor and slander be put away from you, along with all malice. ³²Be kind to one another, tenderhearted, forgiving one another, as God in Christ forgave you.

Walk in Love

5 Therefore be imitators of God, as beloved children. ²And walk in love, as Christ loved us and gave himself up for us, a fragrant offering and sacrifice to God.

³But sexual immorality and all impurity or covetousness must not even be named among you, as is proper among saints. ⁴Let there be no filthiness nor foolish talk nor crude joking, which are out of place, but instead let there be thanksgiving. ⁵For you may be sure of this, that everyone who is sexually immoral or impure, or who is covetous (that is, an idolater), has no inheritance in the kingdom of Christ and God. ⁶Let no one deceive you with empty words, for because of these things the wrath of God comes upon the sons of disobedience. ⁷Therefore do not become partners with them; ⁸for at one time you were darkness, but now you are light in the Lord. Walk as children of light ⁹(for the fruit of light is found in all that is good and right and true), ¹⁰and try to discern what is pleasing to the Lord. ¹¹Take no part in the unfruitful works of darkness, but instead expose them. ¹²For it is shameful even to speak of the things that they do in secret.

Know Yourself

verses to read
Ephesians 5:8–20

When your plans are interrupted, when your rest is stopped short, when your comfort is unattainable, how you react reveals your faith. When the unexpected happens and the unwelcome comes, what you do reflects your heart and your commitment to love the Lord and to serve him no matter what he asks. Obedience isn't proven on your good days or in the things you saw coming but in the dark nights and shocking situations. God's Word is for those moments as well as the easy ones.

You don't get a free pass to sin when life is just too hard. Sure, God offers forgiveness for all that the God Girl does, but the beauty of faith is that it unites you to Christ, fills you with the Spirit, and transforms self-trust into God-trust. When you commit to that kind of trust and obedience, you get perseverance, character, peace, and hope. Each time that you reject your dark and sinful nature and do the opposite of what your emotions are yelling at you to do, you get stronger, and doing the right thing the next time gets easier.

But obedience isn't all about duty; it's really about true love. It's something you do for the love of your life. And just as an added bonus, it brings true freedom from those painful emotions and the challenges of life! God's commandments are designed to make life better, not to make it more miserable. No matter how crazy or counterintuitive they might sound to the world, they really are for your benefit. When you trust him, you trust what he says—all of it. How much of God's Word do you trust with your life?

[13] But when anything is exposed by the light, it becomes visible, [14] for anything that becomes visible is light. Therefore it says,

"Awake, O sleeper,
 and arise from the dead,
 and Christ will shine on you."

[15] Look carefully then how you walk, not as unwise but as wise, [16] making the best use of the time, because the days are evil. [17] Therefore do not be foolish, but understand what the will of the Lord is. [18] And do not get drunk with wine, for that is debauchery, but be filled with the Spirit, [19] addressing one another in psalms and hymns and spiritual songs, singing and making melody to the Lord with your heart, [20] giving thanks always and for everything to God the Father in the name of our Lord Jesus Christ, [21] submitting to one another out of reverence for Christ.

Wives and Husbands

[22] Wives, submit to your own husbands, as to the Lord. [23] For the husband is the head of the wife even as Christ is the head of the church, his body, and is himself its Savior. [24] Now as the church submits to Christ, so also wives should submit in everything to their husbands.

[25] Husbands, love your wives, as Christ loved the church and gave himself up for her, [26] that he might sanctify her, having cleansed her by the washing of water with the word, [27] so that he might present the church to himself in splendor, without spot or wrinkle or any such thing, that she might be holy and without blemish.[1] [28] In the same way husbands should love

[1] Or holy and blameless

Know God

verses to read
Ephesians 6:10–20

How many times a week do you feel beaten down, attacked, worn out? How many times do you lose your strength and want to give up? And how many times a week do you put on the armor of God? If you want peace—if you want self-control, hope, and strength—then you've gotta put on the armor that God has laid out for you.

Every day when you get up, make it your first job to ask God to dress you up in the helmet of salvation, the breastplate of righteousness (God's approval), the belt of truth, and the shoes of the gospel of peace—and to put the shield of faith and the sword of the Spirit in your hands. As you imagine actually putting on each thing, remind yourself what each piece does for you. The helmet reminds you of your salvation and assurance of God's hand in your life. The breastplate of righteousness is there to cover you with the righteousness that comes not from your power but from Christ's. The belt of truth is there to remind you of everything that God has shown you and will show you. The shoes of the gospel of peace represent the power of the gospel in your life and your mission to share it with the people in your life. The shield of faith protects you from all the flaming arrows the Evil One shoots at you. And the sword of the Spirit, the Word of God, the Bible, is your most powerful weapon against the attacks of the Enemy. With it you can fight off attacks and pierce hearts with God's truth. You need to hold it tightly in your hand every day.

If you want to start experiencing the power and protection of God in your life, then pray through putting on the armor of God and remind yourself of the protection that is yours by grace!

their wives as their own bodies. He who loves his wife loves himself. [29] For no one ever hated his own flesh, but nourishes and cherishes it, just as Christ does the church, [30] because we are members of his body. [31] [a] "Therefore a man shall leave his father and mother and hold fast to his wife, and the two shall become one flesh." [32] This mystery is profound, and I am saying that it refers to Christ and the church. [33] However, let each one of you love his wife as himself, and let the wife see that she respects her husband.

Children and Parents

6 Children, obey your parents in the Lord, for this is right. [2] [b] "Honor your father and mother" (this is the first commandment with a promise), [3] "that it may go well with you and that you may live long in the land." [4] Fathers, do not provoke your children to anger, but bring them up in the discipline and instruction of the Lord.

Bondservants and Masters

[5] Bondservants,[1] obey your earthly masters[2] with fear and trembling, with a sincere heart, as you would Christ, [6] not by the way of eye-service, as people-pleasers, but as bondservants of Christ, doing the will of God from the heart, [7] rendering service with a good will as to the Lord and not to man, [8] knowing that whatever good anyone does, this he will receive back from the Lord, whether he is a bondservant[3] or is free. [9] Masters, do the same to them, and stop your threatening, knowing that he who is both their Master[4] and yours is in heaven, and that there is no partiality with him.

The Whole Armor of God

[10] Finally, be strong in the Lord and in the strength of his might. [11] Put on the whole armor of God, that you may be able to stand against the schemes of the devil. [12] For we do not wrestle against flesh and blood, but against the rulers, against the authorities, against the cosmic powers over this present darkness, against the spiritual forces of evil in the heavenly places. [13] Therefore take up the whole armor of God, that you may be able to withstand in the evil day, and having done all, to stand firm. [14] Stand therefore, having fastened on the belt of truth, and having put on the breastplate of righteousness, [15] and, as shoes for your feet, having put on the readiness given by the gospel of peace. [16] In all circumstances take up the shield of faith, with which you can extinguish all the flaming darts of the evil one; [17] and take the helmet of salvation, and the sword of the Spirit, which is the word of God, [18] praying at all times in the Spirit, with all prayer and supplication. To that end keep alert with all perseverance, making supplication for all the saints, [19] and also for me, that words may be given to me in opening my mouth boldly to proclaim the mystery of the gospel, [20] for which I am an ambassador in chains, that I may declare it boldly, as I ought to speak.

Final Greetings

[21] So that you also may know how I am and what I am doing, Tychicus the beloved brother and faithful minister in the Lord will tell you everything. [22] I have sent him to you for this very purpose, that you may know how we are, and that he may encourage your hearts.

[23] Peace be to the brothers,[5] and love with faith, from God the Father and the Lord Jesus Christ. [24] Grace be with all who love our Lord Jesus Christ with love incorruptible.

---

[1] Or slaves; also verse 6 (for the contextual rendering of the Greek word doulos, see About the ESV) [2] Or your masters according to the flesh [3] Or slave (for the contextual rendering of the Greek word doulos, see About the ESV) [4] Greek Lord [5] Or brothers and sisters
[a] Gen. 2:24 [b] Ex. 20:12

INTRODUCTION TO
Philippians

Author: The apostle Paul

Time: Most likely around
A.D. 60–62

Place: Probably in prison in
Rome, but may have
been Caesarea or
Ephesus

Written to: Believers in Philippi

The gist

The fact that Paul is writing
this letter from prison is just
one of the examples in this
letter of how you can be happy
(or joyful) no matter what
is happening around you.
Philippians teaches you that
how you feel about a situation
can change based on what you
spend time thinking about and
rejoicing in.

Things to look for

- Paul's description of the
  humility of Christ (see Phil.
  2:1–11)

- What we can learn about
  the secret to true happiness,
  or joy, by observing the life
  of Paul (see Phil. 1:4, 12–26;
  2:14; 3:1, 7–14; 4:4–13)

Be Joyful

> Rejoice in the Lord always; again I will say, rejoice.
>
> *Philippians 4:4*

Some say that happiness is based on circumstances, while
joy is based on focus. When your focus is your own happiness, most often you end up disappointed, but when your
focus is serving and pleasing God as your Father who loves
you, look out, 'cuz the happy train is coming 'round the
bend! In the middle of the most horrible trials you can be
happy, or rather joyful, when you know that God's hand is
on your life. Take the life of the apostle Paul. While locked
up in prison for preaching God's Word, Paul wrote this
letter to the Philippians. In it you will find out all about
the ability to find joy no matter what the circumstances.
The secret to being happy or joyful is not getting what you
want but being content with what you have, because in
Christ you have everything you could ever want. Paul has
learned that secret.

Paul wants his friends in Philippi to understand this
important and valuable truth: what you focus on will affect
how you feel. Focus on the negative and you'll feel bad, but
focus on the positive and you will feel much better. If you
let your mind wander into areas of negativity, fear, and
worry, then your faith will suffer. But if you refuse to worry
but instead trust God in everything, then your joy will be
unstoppable. Your faith, your future, and your feelings all
find their foundation in your thoughts. Consider what you
think about the most, and direct your thoughts upward.
Watch how the apostle Paul keeps not only his faith but also
his joy in the midst of his trials, and you will find an answer
for your own trials.

Must-Know Verses

I am sure of this, that he who began a good work in you will bring it to completion at the day of Jesus Christ. *Philippians 1:6*

For to me to live is Christ, and to die is gain. *Philippians 1:21*

It has been granted to you that for the sake of Christ you should not only believe in him but also suffer for his sake. *Philippians 1:29*

Do nothing from selfish ambition or conceit, but in humility count others more significant than yourselves. Let each of you look not only to his own interests, but also to the interests of others. *Philippians 2:3–4*

Have this mind among yourselves, which is yours in Christ Jesus, who, though he was in the form of God, did not count equality with God a thing to be grasped, but emptied himself, by taking the form of a servant, being born in the likeness of men. And being found in human form, he humbled himself by becoming obedient to the point of death, even death on a cross. *Philippians 2:5–8*

Finally, brothers, whatever is true, whatever is honorable, whatever is just, whatever is pure, whatever is lovely, whatever is commendable, if there is any excellence, if there is anything worthy of praise, think about these things. What you have learned and received and heard and seen in me—practice these things, and the God of peace will be with you. *Philippians 4:8–9*

The Letter of Paul to the

Philippians

Greeting

1 Paul and Timothy, servants[1] of Christ Jesus,

To all the saints in Christ Jesus who are at Philippi, with the overseers[2] and deacons:[3] [2] Grace to you and peace from God our Father and the Lord Jesus Christ.

Thanksgiving and Prayer

[3] I thank my God in all my remembrance of you, [4] always in every prayer of mine for you all making my prayer with joy, [5] because of your partnership in the gospel from the first day until now. [6] And I am sure of this, that he who began a good work in you will bring it to completion at the day of Jesus Christ. [7] It is right for me to feel this way about you all, because I hold you in my heart, for you are all partakers with me of grace,[4] both in my imprisonment and in the defense and confirmation of the gospel. [8] For God is my witness, how I yearn for you all with the affection of Christ Jesus. [9] And it is my prayer that your love may abound more and more, with knowledge and all discernment, [10] so that you may approve what is excellent, and so be pure and blameless for the day of Christ, [11] filled with the fruit of righteousness that comes through Jesus Christ, to the glory and praise of God.

The Advance of the Gospel

[12] I want you to know, brothers,[5] that what has happened to me has really served to advance the gospel, [13] so that it has become known throughout the whole imperial guard[6] and to all the rest that my imprisonment is for Christ. [14] And most of the brothers, having become confident in the Lord by my imprisonment, are much more bold to speak the word[7] without fear.

[15] Some indeed preach Christ from envy and rivalry, but others from good will. [16] The latter do it out of love, knowing that I am put here for the defense of the gospel. [17] The former proclaim Christ out of selfish ambition, not sincerely but thinking to afflict me in my imprisonment. [18] What then? Only that in every way, whether in pretense or in truth, Christ is proclaimed, and in that I rejoice.

To Live Is Christ

Yes, and I will rejoice, [19] for I know that through your prayers and the help of the Spirit of Jesus Christ this will turn out for my deliverance, [20] as it is my eager expectation and hope that I will not be at all ashamed, but that with full courage now as always Christ will be honored in my body, whether by life or by death. [21] For to me to live is Christ, and to die is gain. [22] If I am to live in the flesh, that means fruitful labor for me. Yet which I shall choose I cannot tell. [23] I am hard pressed between the two. My desire is to depart and be with Christ, for that is far better. [24] But to remain in the flesh is more necessary on your account. [25] Convinced of this, I know that I will remain and continue with you all, for your progress and joy in the faith, [26] so that in me you may have ample cause to glory in Christ Jesus, because of my coming to you again.

[27] Only let your manner of life be worthy[8] of the gospel of Christ, so that whether I come and see you or am absent, I may hear of you that you are standing firm in one spirit, with one mind striving side by side for the faith of the gospel, [28] and not frightened in anything by your opponents. This is a clear sign to them of their destruction, but of your salvation, and that from

---

[1] Or *slaves* (for the contextual rendering of the Greek word *doulos*, see About the ESV) [2] Or *bishops*; Greek *episkopoi* [3] Or *servants*, or *ministers*; Greek *diakonoi* [4] Or *you all have fellowship with me in grace* [5] Or *brothers and sisters*. The plural Greek word *adelphoi* (translated "brothers") refers to siblings in a family. In New Testament usage, depending on the context, *adelphoi* may refer either to men or to both men and women who are siblings (brothers and sisters) in God's family, the church; also verse 14 [6] Greek *in the whole praetorium* [7] Some manuscripts add *of God* [8] Greek *Only behave as citizens worthy*

God. ²⁹ For it has been granted to you that for the sake of Christ you should not only believe in him but also suffer for his sake, ³⁰ engaged in the same conflict that you saw I had and now hear that I still have.

Christ's Example of Humility

2 So if there is any encouragement in Christ, any comfort from love, any participation in the Spirit, any affection and sympathy, ² complete my joy by being of the same mind, having the same love, being in full accord and of one mind. ³ Do nothing from selfish ambition or conceit, but in humility count others more significant than yourselves. ⁴ Let each of you look not only to his own interests, but also to the interests of others. ⁵ Have this mind among yourselves, which is yours in Christ Jesus,¹ ⁶ who, though he was in the form of God, did not count equality with God a thing to be grasped, ⁷ but emptied himself, by taking the form of a servant,² being born in the likeness of men. ⁸ And being found in human form, he humbled himself by becoming obedient to the point of death, even death on a cross. ⁹ Therefore God has highly exalted him and bestowed on him the name that is above every name, ¹⁰ so that at the name of Jesus every knee should bow, in heaven and on earth and under the earth, ¹¹ and every tongue confess that Jesus Christ is Lord, to the glory of God the Father.

Lights in the World

¹² Therefore, my beloved, as you have always obeyed, so now, not only as in my presence but much more in my absence, work out your own salvation with fear and trembling, ¹³ for it is God who works in you, both to will and to work for his good pleasure.

¹⁴ Do all things without grumbling or disputing, ¹⁵ that you may be blameless and innocent, children of God without blemish in the midst of a crooked and twisted generation, among whom you shine as lights in the world, ¹⁶ holding fast to the word of life, so that in the day of Christ I may be proud that I did not run in vain or labor in vain. ¹⁷ Even if I am to be poured out as a drink offering upon the sacrificial offering of your faith, I am glad and rejoice with you

all. ¹⁸ Likewise you also should be glad and rejoice with me.

Ask Yourself . . .

ABOUT COMPLAINING

- What do I complain about the most, both out loud and to myself?
- Why do I complain?
- What do I think I deserve that I'm not getting?
- What makes me deserve it?
- Why could God not be giving me what I want?
- How do I feel when I'm complaining?
- How do I feel when other people complain?
- What makes complaining bad?

Timothy and Epaphroditus

¹⁹ I hope in the Lord Jesus to send Timothy to you soon, so that I too may be cheered by news of you. ²⁰ For I have no one like him, who will be genuinely concerned for your welfare. ²¹ For they all seek their own interests, not those of Jesus Christ. ²² But you know Timothy's³ proven worth, how as a son⁴ with a father he has served with me in the gospel. ²³ I hope therefore to send him just as soon as I see how it will go with me, ²⁴ and I trust in the Lord that shortly I myself will come also.

²⁵ I have thought it necessary to send to you Epaphroditus my brother and fellow worker and fellow soldier, and your messenger and minister to my need, ²⁶ for he has been longing for you all and has been distressed because you heard that he was ill. ²⁷ Indeed he was ill, near to death. But God had mercy on him, and not only on him but on me also, lest I should have sorrow upon sorrow. ²⁸ I am the more eager to send him, therefore, that you may rejoice at seeing him again, and that I may be less anxious.

¹ Or which was also in Christ Jesus ² Greek bondservant ³ Greek his ⁴ Greek child

[9]So receive him in the Lord with all joy, and honor such men, [30]for he nearly died for the work of Christ, risking his life to complete what was lacking in your service to me.

Righteousness Through Faith in Christ

3 Finally, my brothers,[1] rejoice in the Lord. To write the same things to you is no trouble to me and is safe for you.

[2]Look out for the dogs, look out for the evildoers, look out for those who mutilate the flesh. [3]For we are the circumcision, who worship by the Spirit of God[2] and glory in Christ Jesus and put no confidence in the flesh— [4]though I myself have reason for confidence in the flesh also. If anyone else thinks he has reason for confidence in the flesh, I have more: [5]circumcised on the eighth day, of the people of Israel, of the tribe of Benjamin, a Hebrew of Hebrews; as to the law, a Pharisee; [6]as to zeal, a per-

secutor of the church; as to righteousness under the law,[3] blameless. [7]But whatever gain I had, I counted as loss for the sake of Christ. [8]Indeed, I count everything as loss because of the surpassing worth of knowing Christ Jesus my Lord. For his sake I have suffered the loss of all things and count them as rubbish, in order that I may gain Christ [9]and be found in him, not having a righteousness of my own that comes from the law, but that which comes through faith in Christ, the righteousness from God that depends on faith— [10]that I may know him and the power of his resurrection, and may share his sufferings, becoming like him in his death, [11]that by any means possible I may attain the resurrection from the dead.

Straining Toward the Goal

[12]Not that I have already obtained this or am already perfect, but I press on to make

[1]Or brothers and sisters; also verses 13, 17 [2]Some manuscripts God in spirit [3]Greek in the law

Know Love

verses to read
Philippians 2:14–18

Don't complain—it's a sin. Familiar with it? When it comes to the weather, your clothes, friends, family, grades, work—how many times a day would you say that you sin by complaining? And while we're on the subject and you're getting all real with yourself, how does all this complaining make you feel? Better? Does it make people around you feel better about life? Just something to think about.

But wait, there's more. This little verse in Philippians (2:14) also says no arguing, making that a sin too. Ugh! Really? So when it comes to your friends, family, politicians, enemies, bosses—how many times a week would you say that you sin by arguing? And how does arguing work for you? Does it usually pan out the way you planned it, or does it make things worse? Does it make people happy with you, or more angry?

Complaining and arguing both promise to make things better, or at least to make you feel better, but the truth is that both not only make things worse but also lead you away from God, because sin separates you from God. The good news is, Jesus promises to set you free from your sin when you confess it and turn away from it. So here's your chance. If things aren't going so great and you want more of Jesus in your life, then say no to complaining and arguing. All the time. Every day. Always. Confess those times when you've messed up and complained or argued anyway, and then commit yourself to not doing it again—and I mean really commit yourself, not just say it.

When you start to make God's Word more important than talking, you become more holy and ultimately more happy. Just give it a try and see if it isn't so.

it my own, because Christ Jesus has made me his own. ¹³Brothers, I do not consider that I have made it my own. But one thing I do: forgetting what lies behind and straining forward to what lies ahead, ¹⁴I press on toward the goal for the prize of the upward call of God in Christ Jesus. ¹⁵Let those of us who are mature think this way, and if in anything you think otherwise, God will reveal that also to you. ¹⁶Only let us hold true to what we have attained.

¹⁷Brothers, join in imitating me, and keep your eyes on those who walk according to the example you have in us. ¹⁸For many, of whom I have often told you and now tell you even with tears, walk as enemies of the cross of Christ. ¹⁹Their end is destruction, their god is their belly, and they glory in their shame, with minds set on earthly things. ²⁰But our citizenship is in heaven, and from it we await a Savior, the Lord Jesus Christ, ²¹who will transform our lowly body to be like his glorious body, by the power that enables him even to subject all things to himself.

4 Therefore, my brothers,¹ whom I love and long for, my joy and crown, stand firm thus in the Lord, my beloved.

Exhortation, Encouragement, and Prayer

²I entreat Euodia and I entreat Syntyche to agree in the Lord. ³Yes, I ask you also, true companion,² help these women, who have labored side by side with me in the gospel together with Clement and the rest of my fellow workers, whose names are in the book of life.

⁴Rejoice in the Lord always; again I will say, rejoice. ⁵Let your reasonableness be known to everyone. The Lord is at hand; ⁶do not be anxious about anything, but in everything by prayer and supplication with thanksgiving let your requests be made known to God. ⁷And the peace of God, which surpasses all understanding, will guard your hearts and your minds in Christ Jesus.

⁸Finally, brothers, whatever is true, whatever is honorable, whatever is just, whatever is pure, whatever is lovely, whatever is commendable, if there is any excellence, if there is anything worthy of praise, think about these things. ⁹What you have learned and received and heard and seen

in me—practice these things, and the God of peace will be with you.

A Prayer for...
A QUIET HEART

Please, dear God, give me a peace that goes beyond anything I can imagine so that I can, even in the storms and troubles of this life, rest in you, knowing that all things are not only beneath your eyes but also under your care and governed by your will. Guard me by your love, so that with a quiet heart I can see through the storms of life, even the clouds and the thick darkness, always happy to know that the darkness and the light are both alike to you.

Guide, guard, and govern me even to the end, so that I won't miss out on eternity with you, through Jesus Christ our Lord.

Amen.

God's Provision

¹⁰I rejoiced in the Lord greatly that now at length you have revived your concern for me. You were indeed concerned for me, but you had no opportunity. ¹¹Not that I am speaking of being in need, for I have learned in whatever situation I am to be content. ¹²I know how to be brought low, and I know how to abound. In any and every circumstance, I have learned the secret of facing plenty and hunger, abundance and need. ¹³I can do all things through him who strengthens me.

¹⁴Yet it was kind of you to share³ my trouble. ¹⁵And you Philippians yourselves know that in the beginning of the gospel, when I left Macedonia, no church entered into partnership with me in giving and receiving, except you only. ¹⁶Even in Thessalonica you sent me help for my needs once and again. ¹⁷Not that I seek the gift, but I seek the fruit that increases to your credit.⁴ ¹⁸I have received full pay-

---

¹Or brothers and sisters; also verses 8, 21 ²Or loyal Syzygus; Greek true yokefellow ³Or have fellowship in ⁴Or I seek the profit that accrues to your account

ment, and more. I am well supplied, having received from Epaphroditus the gifts you sent, a fragrant offering, a sacrifice acceptable and pleasing to God. ¹⁹ And my God will supply every need of yours according to his riches in glory in Christ Jesus. ²⁰ To our God and Father be glory forever and ever. Amen.

Final Greetings

²¹ Greet every saint in Christ Jesus. The brothers who are with me greet you. ²² All the saints greet you, especially those of Caesar's household.

²³ The grace of the Lord Jesus Christ be with your spirit.

Know True Happiness

verses to read
Philippians 4:10–14

Is there something you are asking God for? A request that you have made with all your heart but haven't heard a peep out of heaven about? When you have passionately asked God to do something but you haven't seen him make a move toward doing it, you might think he's not listening. But that's not the case. Remember, he has a greater purpose in mind than any human.

The thing to remember is that the problem you're so concerned about isn't as important as your relationship with God. What you are asking might be getting in the way of your relationship with him, and he wants you to want him more than you want relief from your problem. In fact, he lets a lot of problems come your way so that you will come to him, trust him, and believe him. And when all you want is a way out of the mess, you can miss the very Rock in front of you that will protect you from the waves of the storm. He never promised that the crashing waters would stop—only that you would find peace in the midst of them. If stopping the stress is more important to you than finding God, chances are the stress will keep up until you get your priorities right.

So instead of begging him to do this or that, try telling him that no matter what the situation, no matter what the problem, you will still trust him, search for him, and rest in him. Stop making the problem bigger than God. When you truly trust him, even the biggest storm won't move you. And the more you trust, the more stable you will be whatever storms may come.

INTRODUCTION TO
Colossians

Author: The apostle Paul

Time: Around A.D. 60

Place: In prison in Rome

Written to: The Colossian church

The gist

Paul wanted the Colossians and all readers to understand their freedom in Christ and to stop falling for false teachings that say more stuff needs to be done before people can have access to God. In this little book he gives the confused Colossians a Christ-centered theology to help them understand pure faith.

Things to look for

- What God has done through Christ (see Col. 1:13–23)
- All the references to thankfulness (see Col. 1:3, 12; 2:7; 3:15–17; 4:2)

Keep Your Eyes on the Spiritual

> And you have been filled in him, who is the head of all rule and authority.
>
> Colossians 2:10

It's super easy to listen when the world talks, to see all the pretty things it has to offer, and to fall in love with them. It's so easy to make the world's way of thinking your own because, well, everyone is doing it. But the world's way of living is completely different than the life of faith. The world makes do with what it can figure out on its own because it puts no hope in the resurrection of Jesus. But the truth is, the God Girl needs only one hope and one salvation, and that is found in Jesus Christ, the full representation of God on earth.

In his letter to the Colossians, Paul confronts a church that has let the world's ideas become its own. Jewish traditions and un-Christian practices were taking precedence in the lives of the Colossians. They were putting their trust in the wrong things, jeopardizing their faith. Paul wants his readers to understand the nature of Jesus and their life with him. He doesn't want them to get off track with worldly thinking and silly traditions; he wants them to keep the main thing the main thing.

A lot of people would say that Jesus was just a prophet or a wise teacher, but that is a lie that leads to the destruction of faith. If Jesus was only a prophet, then he was a crazy prophet, because he claimed to be the Son of God. Paul was fighting the same battle against the world that we fight today. He spoke up so that our faith wouldn't get all watered down with the half-truths of this world. As a God Girl, you can't allow the world's thoughts on Jesus to be your own. You have to understand his divinity and your need for him. Many other ideas may come at you every day, but just like the early church, you've got to reject false teachings and hold on to the truth of who Jesus really is.

Paul's goal in teaching his readers is to make them mature Christians who won't be easily led astray and distracted by all that the world has to offer. As you read this book, remember that you are not so different from those early believers. You are just as inundated by the world's voices and visions of beauty. So keep your eyes focused not on the physical but on the spiritual. Look to the truth of God's Word, and look away from the lies of this world.

Must-Know Verses

He has delivered us from the domain of darkness and transferred us to the kingdom of his beloved Son, in whom we have redemption, the forgiveness of sins. *Colossians 1:13–14*

And you, who once were alienated and hostile in mind, doing evil deeds, he has now reconciled in his body of flesh by his death, in order to present you holy and blameless and above reproach before him. *Colossians 1:21–22*

I want you to know how great a struggle I have for you and for those at Laodicea and for all who have not seen me face to face, that their hearts may be encouraged, being knit together in love, to reach all the riches of full assurance of understanding and the knowledge of God's mystery, which is Christ, in whom are hidden all the treasures of wisdom and knowledge. *Colossians 2:1–3*

And you, who were dead in your trespasses and the uncircumcision of your flesh, God made alive together with him, having forgiven us all our trespasses. *Colossians 2:13*

If with Christ you died to the elemental spirits of the world, why, as if you were still alive in the world, do you submit to regulations—"Do not handle, Do not taste, Do not touch" (referring to things that all perish as they are used)—according to human precepts and teachings? *Colossians 2:20–22*

Set your minds on things that are above, not on things that are on earth. *Colossians 3:2*

But now you must put them all away: anger, wrath, malice, slander, and obscene talk from your mouth. *Colossians 3:8*

The Letter of Paul to the

Colossians

Greeting

Paul, an apostle of Christ Jesus by the will of God, and Timothy our brother, [2] To the saints and faithful brothers[1] in Christ at Colossae:

Grace to you and peace from God our Father.

Thanksgiving and Prayer

[3] We always thank God, the Father of our Lord Jesus Christ, when we pray for you, [4] since we heard of your faith in Christ Jesus and of the love that you have for all the saints, [5] because of the hope laid up for you in heaven. Of this you have heard before in the word of the truth, the gospel, [6] which has come to you, as indeed in the whole world it is bearing fruit and increasing—as it also does among you, since the day you heard it and understood the grace of God in truth, [7] just as you learned it from Epaphras our beloved fellow servant.[2] He is a faithful minister of Christ on your[3] behalf [8] and has made known to us your love in the Spirit.

[9] And so, from the day we heard, we have not ceased to pray for you, asking that you may be filled with the knowledge of his will in all spiritual wisdom and understanding, [10] so as to walk in a manner worthy of the Lord, fully pleasing to him, bearing fruit in every good work and increasing in the knowledge of God. [11] May you be strengthened with all power, according to his glorious might, for all endurance and patience with joy, [12] giving thanks[4] to the Father, who has qualified you[5] to share in the inheritance of the saints in light. [13] He has delivered us from the domain of darkness and transferred us to the kingdom of his beloved Son, [14] in whom we have redemption, the forgiveness of sins.

The Preeminence of Christ

[15] He is the image of the invisible God, the firstborn of all creation. [16] For by[6] him all things were created, in heaven and on earth, visible and invisible, whether thrones or dominions or rulers or authorities—all things were created through him and for him. [17] And he is before all things, and in him all things hold together. [18] And he is the head of the body, the church. He is the beginning, the firstborn from the dead, that in everything he might be preeminent. [19] For in him all the fullness of God was pleased to dwell, [20] and through him to reconcile to himself all things, whether on earth or in heaven, making peace by the blood of his cross.

[21] And you, who once were alienated and hostile in mind, doing evil deeds, [22] he has now reconciled in his body of flesh by his death, in order to present you holy and blameless and above reproach before him, [23] if indeed you continue in the faith, stable and steadfast, not shifting from the hope of the gospel that you heard, which has been proclaimed in all creation[7] under heaven, and of which I, Paul, became a minister.

Paul's Ministry to the Church

[24] Now I rejoice in my sufferings for your sake, and in my flesh I am filling up what is lacking in Christ's afflictions for the sake of his body, that is, the church, [25] of which I became a minister according to the stewardship from God that was given to me for you, to make the word of God fully known, [26] the mystery hidden for ages and generations but now revealed to his saints. [27] To them God chose to make known how great among the Gentiles are the riches of the glory of this mystery, which is Christ in you, the hope of glory. [28] Him we proclaim,

---

[1] Or brothers and sisters. The plural Greek word adelphoi (translated "brothers") refers to siblings in a family. In New Testament usage, depending on the context, adelphoi may refer either to men or to both men and women who are siblings (brothers and sisters) in God's family, the church [2] Greek fellow bondservant [3] Some manuscripts our [4] Or patience, with joy giving thanks [5] Some manuscripts us [6] That is, by means of; or in [7] Or to every creature

warning everyone and teaching everyone with all wisdom, that we may present everyone mature in Christ. [29] For this I toil, struggling with all his energy that he powerfully works within me.

2 For I want you to know how great a struggle I have for you and for those at Laodicea and for all who have not seen me face to face, [2] that their hearts may be encouraged, being knit together in love, to reach all the riches of full assurance of understanding and the knowledge of God's mystery, which is Christ, [3] in whom are hidden all the treasures of wisdom and knowledge. [4] I say this in order that no one may delude you with plausible arguments. [5] For though I am absent in body, yet I am with you in spirit, rejoicing to see your good order and the firmness of your faith in Christ.

Alive in Christ

[6] Therefore, as you received Christ Jesus the Lord, so walk in him, [7] rooted and built up in him and established in the faith, just as you were taught, abounding in thanksgiving.

[8] See to it that no one takes you captive by philosophy and empty deceit, accord-

ing to human tradition, according to the elemental spirits[1] of the world, and not according to Christ. [9] For in him the whole fullness of deity dwells bodily, [10] and you have been filled in him, who is the head of all rule and authority. [11] In him also you were circumcised with a circumcision made without hands, by putting off the body of the flesh, by the circumcision of Christ, [12] having been buried with him in baptism, in which you were also raised with him through faith in the powerful working of God, who raised him from the dead. [13] And you, who were dead in your trespasses and the uncircumcision of your flesh, God made alive together with him, having forgiven us all our trespasses, [14] by canceling the record of debt that stood against us with its legal demands. This he set aside, nailing it to the cross. [15] He disarmed the rulers and authorities[2] and put them to open shame, by triumphing over them in him.[3]

Let No One Disqualify You

[16] Therefore let no one pass judgment on you in questions of food and drink, or with regard to a festival or a new moon

---

[1] Or *elementary principles*; also verse 20   [2] Probably demonic rulers and authorities   [3] Or *in it* (that is, the cross)

verses to read
Colossians 2:9–10

When someone has authority over you, they have it for a reason. Whether it's a parent, a teacher, or a cop, no one is put into a position of authority without the approval of Christ himself. While obedience to people in power can seem impossible, when you think about it as obedience to the God who put them in charge, it gets easier. It might seem like a stretch, but by obeying the people in authority in your life, you prove God's authority over your life. And while many authority figures can be harsh and even cruel, that doesn't change the fact that God commands your obedience (see Eph. 6:5). No matter how crazy their demands on you, as long as they don't conflict with God's commands, you need to do what they want.

When being told what to do becomes almost unbearable, the God Girl has a way to freedom. She has to recognize how her actions relate to her faith in God. She must understand that her decision to obey authority will result in blessings, even if for a while she has to endure the hardship of doing what she's told without explanation. After a time this kind of response will pay off—if not in this present world, most certainly in the world to come.

or a Sabbath. [17] These are a shadow of the things to come, but the substance belongs to Christ. [18] Let no one disqualify you, insisting on asceticism and worship of angels, going on in detail about visions,[1] puffed up without reason by his sensuous mind, [19] and not holding fast to the Head, from whom the whole body, nourished and knit together through its joints and ligaments, grows with a growth that is from God.

[20] If with Christ you died to the elemental spirits of the world, why, as if you were still alive in the world, do you submit to regulations— [21] "Do not handle, Do not taste, Do not touch" [22] (referring to things that all perish as they are used)—according to human precepts and teachings? [23] These have indeed an appearance of wisdom in promoting self-made religion and asceticism and severity to the body, but they are of no value in stopping the indulgence of the flesh.

Put On the New Self

3 If then you have been raised with Christ, seek the things that are above, where Christ is, seated at the right hand of God. [2] Set your minds on things that are above, not on things that are on earth. [3] For you have died, and your life is hidden with Christ in God. [4] When Christ who is your[2] life appears, then you also will appear with him in glory.

[5] Put to death therefore what is earthly in you:[3] sexual immorality, impurity, passion, evil desire, and covetousness, which is idolatry. [6] On account of these the wrath of God is coming.[4] [7] In these you too once walked, when you were living in them. [8] But now you must put them all away: anger, wrath, malice, slander, and obscene talk from your mouth. [9] Do not lie to one another, seeing that you have put off the old self[5] with its practices [10] and have put on the new self, which is being renewed in knowledge after

[1] Or about the things he has seen   [2] Some manuscripts our   [3] Greek therefore your members that are on the earth   [4] Some manuscripts add upon the sons of disobedience   [5] Greek man; also as supplied in verse 10

verses to read
Colossians 3:1–11

When someone points out one of your weaknesses or bad character traits, have you ever said, "Well, that's just the way I am. I can't change it"? If something seems just too hard or even impossible to change, do you just accept it, live with it, and claim it as an inborn tendency? For example, you might say, "I worry, I'm a type A personality, so sue me," or "I'm prone to anger: it runs in my family."

The truth is that sin (or your weaknesses) will always be there nagging at you, pulling at your sleeve, begging you to listen, but that sin nature no longer defines you, because you are now God's child, indwelt by his Spirit. Do you really want to choose the call of sin's voice over God's? Well, that's what you do whenever you say, "That's just the way I am." That kind of giving in to your weaknesses is not only rebellion against God but also setting yourself up for failure. Do you want to be a victim of your weaknesses? Or, by God's power, a victor over them?

Don't let your sinful nature be an excuse for sin. We all have a sinful nature; that's why we need Jesus. You are not a particularly hard case, but you do need to do the hard work, by God's grace, of putting to death sin and living in accordance with your new nature. And you'll have to do this not just once but daily, even hourly.

Never be comfortable with the part of your nature that causes you to sin. And remember, sin is not your boss anymore. Maybe it used to be, but Jesus came to set you free from all that, so take him up on his generous gift and say no to your old self.

the image of its creator. [11] Here there is not Greek and Jew, circumcised and uncircumcised, barbarian, Scythian, slave,[1] free; but Christ is all, and in all.

[12] Put on then, as God's chosen ones, holy and beloved, compassionate hearts, kindness, humility, meekness, and patience, [13] bearing with one another and, if one has a complaint against another, forgiving each other; as the Lord has forgiven you, so you also must forgive. [14] And above all these put on love, which binds everything together in perfect harmony. [15] And let the peace of Christ rule in your hearts, to which indeed you were called in one body. And be thankful. [16] Let the word of Christ dwell in you richly, teaching and admonishing one another in all wisdom, singing psalms and hymns and spiritual songs, with thankfulness in your hearts to God. [17] And whatever you do, in word or deed, do everything in the name of the Lord Jesus, giving thanks to God the Father through him.

Rules for Christian Households

[18] Wives, submit to your husbands, as is fitting in the Lord. [19] Husbands, love your wives, and do not be harsh with them. [20] Children, obey your parents in everything, for this pleases the Lord. [21] Fathers, do not provoke your children, lest they become discouraged. [22] Bondservants,[2] obey in everything those who are your earthly masters,[3] not by way of eye-service,

[1] Greek bondservant [2] Or Slaves; also 4:1 (for the contextual rendering of the Greek word doulos, see About the ESV) [3] Or your masters according to the flesh

Know How to Communicate

verses to read
Colossians 3:18–4:1

Do you think that God speaks to other people besides you?

Do you think that God is in control?

If you said yes, then why do you argue when people in authority tell you to do something you don't want to do?

Scripture is clear that you are to obey the authority in your life. If you were in a court of law arguing a case and, when the opposition stood up to present their side, you stood up and started screaming, "That's not fair! He's wrong! He's wrong!" what do you think the judge would do? He would bang his gavel and say, "Order in the court!" And if you wouldn't shut up and respect the opposition, you would be held in contempt of court. So why would you stand in such contempt in God's court of your life? Why do you argue with your parents when God has put them in authority over you?

Living well under authority is just as much a command on your life as loving God and serving others. You can't cherry-pick God's commands, choosing only the ones that suit you. You have to obey God at every turn, and respectfully obeying the authority in your life is part of his commands.

Living under authority is also a chance to trust God. You have to believe that God can fix any situation, that he is always in control, and that he does talk to other people besides you. No matter how much you disagree with your parents, while you live in their house, you have to agree with God by respecting the authority he has given them. If you've struggled with this in the past, now's your chance to turn things around. Instead of fighting, pray and obey. Talk to God about the situation, trust him to bring about a good solution, and then move forward with obedience.

as people-pleasers, but with sincerity of heart, fearing the Lord. ²³Whatever you do, work heartily, as for the Lord and not for men, ²⁴knowing that from the Lord you will receive the inheritance as your reward. You are serving the Lord Christ. ²⁵For the wrongdoer will be paid back for the wrong he has done, and there is no partiality.

4 Masters, treat your bondservants justly and fairly, knowing that you also have a Master in heaven.

Further Instructions

²Continue steadfastly in prayer, being watchful in it with thanksgiving. ³At the same time, pray also for us, that God may open to us a door for the word, to declare the mystery of Christ, on account of which I am in prison— ⁴that I may make it clear, which is how I ought to speak.

Greek *fellow bondservant*; also verse 12

⁵Walk in wisdom toward outsiders, making the best use of the time. ⁶Let your speech always be gracious, seasoned with salt, so that you may know how you ought to answer each person.

Final Greetings

⁷Tychicus will tell you all about my activities. He is a beloved brother and faithful minister and fellow servant¹ in the Lord. ⁸I have sent him to you for this very purpose, that you may know how we are and that he may encourage your hearts, ⁹and with him Onesimus, our faithful and beloved brother, who is one of you. They will tell you of everything that has taken place here.

¹⁰Aristarchus my fellow prisoner greets you, and Mark the cousin of Barnabas (concerning whom you have received instructions— if he comes to you, welcome him),

Know How to Communicate

verses to read
Colossians 4:5–6

Wisdom is required when dealing with "outsiders"—those who are outside the Christian faith. You can't act the same with them as you do with believers. They don't understand your faith, they don't love God, and so they have to be treated differently.

Take friendship, for example. Best friends share their deepest thoughts and emotions with each other. They look to one another for advice and guidance, and they help each other make their way through life. But nonbelievers can't understand things of the Spirit, their advice isn't godly advice, and their thoughts aren't godly thoughts. And so the God Girl has to get smart about her nonbelieving friends. They'll never be best friends, because she can't share with them the way she shares with her sisters in the faith. Because her actions are based on her faith in God, she can't always expect to get good advice from someone who rejects her God. She can't dump her emotions or concerns on them; like it or not, she has to be the stronger one, the one they can turn to for guidance and hope. She represents God in their lives, so she has to represent him well.

"Walk in wisdom toward outsiders" (Col. 4:5), because how you act may either lead them to salvation or lead them to believe that your God is too weak to care for your emotional, spiritual, and even relational needs. You, God Girl, may be the only Christian influence your friends ever taste, so be wise in your relationship with them. Be strong, guide them, comfort them, and give them hope—but save the sharing of your needs for believers who are stronger than you and can lift you up in truth.

11 and Jesus who is called Justus. These are the only men of the circumcision among my fellow workers for the kingdom of God, and they have been a comfort to me. 12 Epaphras, who is one of you, a servant of Christ Jesus, greets you, always struggling on your behalf in his prayers, that you may stand mature and fully assured in all the will of God. 13 For I bear him witness that he has worked hard for you and for those in Laodicea and in Hierapolis. 14 Luke the beloved physician greets you,

as does Demas. 15 Give my greetings to the brothers[1] at Laodicea, and to Nympha and the church in her house. 16 And when this letter has been read among you, have it also read in the church of the Laodiceans, and see that you also read the letter from Laodicea. 17 And say to Archippus, "See that you fulfill the ministry that you have received in the Lord."

18 I, Paul, write this greeting with my own hand. Remember my chains. Grace be with you.

INTRODUCTION TO
1 & 2 Thessalonians

Author: The apostle Paul

Time: Early 50s A.D.

Place: Corinth

Written to: The church in Thessalonica

The gist

Thessalonica was the home of a very young church, and in his first letter to them Paul is teaching them the basics about faith and the gospel. They were also kind of confused about the second coming of Christ. So Paul sent his second letter to clear up a few things about that and to encourage them to keep the faith, even if they were being persecuted.

Things to look for

- Lots of references to the second coming of Christ

- Instructions on the way Christians should live (see 1 Thess. 4:1–12)

- What you can learn about prayer and what to pray for (see 2 Thess. 1:3, 11; 3:1–2, 16)

Live to Please God

> You yourselves are fully aware that the day of the Lord will come like a thief in the night.
>
> *1 Thessalonians 5:2*

When you are just a baby in your faith you need guidance—people to teach you, give you advice, protect you, and guide you in the way you should go. But not everyone has the luxury of having a family around them who knows God and can give wise counsel in the area of faith. Yet God doesn't leave you hanging. He gives you other sources for counsel and guidance, including his Word as well as letters, books, and writings from others who have gone before and who understand your questions and concerns. It's super important to listen to the wisdom of others who are older and wiser than you and who know God's Word better than you.

The believers in the town of Thessalonica were babies in the faith. They had been taught about Jesus by Paul, Silas, and Timothy, but because the Jews were jealous of how many people were being converted by Paul and his friends, they drove them out of town before the church could get all the teaching it needed. And so, after a brief checkup visit by Timothy, Paul felt the need to send the church some encouragement and teaching that would help them stay on track.

One of the key teachings in both books is the second coming of Christ. In the first book Paul teaches that Christ will come like a thief in the night. Apparently, after hearing this, many of the Thessalonians quit working and just sat around waiting for Christ's return. They took things a bit too far. And so in his second letter Paul clarifies that you can't just sit around waiting for Christ's return but must always be prepared.

When you are a new or young believer, you may have a hard time knowing who to listen to and what to believe. But there is hope for your faith found in the Bible. Just like you, other believers for centuries have looked to the Word of God for answers to their most urgent questions: What happens after you die? What will the second coming be like? All the answers you need are found in God's Word. You have questions, just like the early church did, and in these books Paul gives the answers.

Must-Know Terms and Verses

❧ *Day of the Lord* ❧

Refers to the second coming of Christ.

When you received the word of God, which you heard from us, you accepted it not as the word of men but as what it really is, the word of God, which is at work in you believers. *1 Thessalonians 2:13*

This is the will of God, your sanctification: that you abstain from sexual immorality. *1 Thessalonians 4:3*

You yourselves are fully aware that the day of the Lord will come like a thief in the night. *1 Thessalonians 5:2*

Since we belong to the day, let us be sober, having put on the breastplate of faith and love, and for a helmet the hope of salvation. For God has not destined us for wrath, but to obtain salvation through our Lord Jesus Christ. *1 Thessalonians 5:8–9*

We ought always to give thanks to God for you, brothers, as is right, because your faith is growing abundantly, and the love of every one of you for one another is increasing. *2 Thessalonians 1:3*

Indeed God considers it just to repay with affliction those who afflict you, and to grant relief to you who are afflicted as well as to us, when the Lord Jesus is revealed from heaven with his mighty angels in flaming fire, inflicting vengeance on those who do not know God and on those who do not obey the gospel of our Lord Jesus. *2 Thessalonians 1:6–8*

We always pray for you, that our God may make you worthy of his calling and may fulfill every resolve for good and every work of faith by his power. *2 Thessalonians 1:11*

Now we command you, brothers, in the name of our Lord Jesus Christ, that you keep away from any brother who is walking in idleness and not in accord with the tradition that you received from us. *2 Thessalonians 3:6*

1 Thessalonians

Greeting

1 Paul, Silvanus, and Timothy,
To the church of the Thessalonians in God the Father and the Lord Jesus Christ:
Grace to you and peace.

The Thessalonians' Faith and Example

² We give thanks to God always for all of you, constantly[1] mentioning you in our prayers, ³ remembering before our God and Father your work of faith and labor of love and steadfastness of hope in our Lord Jesus Christ. ⁴ For we know, brothers[2] loved by God, that he has chosen you, ⁵ because our gospel came to you not only in word, but also in power and in the Holy Spirit and with full conviction. You know what kind of men we proved to be among you for your sake. ⁶ And you became imitators of us and of the Lord, for you received the word in much affliction, with the joy of the Holy Spirit, ⁷ so that you became an example to all the believers in Macedonia and in Achaia. ⁸ For not only has the word of the Lord sounded forth from you in Macedonia and Achaia, but your faith in God has gone forth everywhere, so that we need not say anything. ⁹ For they themselves report concerning us the kind of reception we had among you, and how you turned to God from idols to serve the living and true God, ¹⁰ and to wait for his Son from heaven, whom he raised from the dead, Jesus who delivers us from the wrath to come.

Paul's Ministry to the Thessalonians

2 For you yourselves know, brothers,[3] that our coming to you was not in vain. ² But though we had already suffered and been shamefully treated at Philippi, as you know, we had boldness in our God to declare to you the gospel of God in the midst of much conflict. ³ For our appeal does not spring from error or impurity or any attempt to deceive, ⁴ but just as we have been approved by God to be entrusted with the gospel, so we speak, not to please man, but to please God who tests our hearts. ⁵ For we never came with words of flattery,[4] as you know, nor with a pretext for greed—God is witness. ⁶ Nor did we seek glory from people, whether from you or from others, though we could have made demands as apostles of Christ. ⁷ But we were gentle[5] among you, like a nursing mother taking care of her own children. ⁸ So, being affectionately desirous of you, we were ready to share with you not only the gospel of God but also our own selves, because you had become very dear to us.

Ask Yourself . . .

WHOM YOU IMITATE

To imitate means to follow as a pattern, model, or example. As a God Girl you are called to follow a certain model (see 1 Thess. 1:6). Which model do you follow? Ask yourself:

- Whom do I imitate the most?
- Whom do I want to be like someday?
- Is this a godly person to imitate?
- Do I imitate different people depending on whether I am happy or sad?
- How could I be more consistent?

---

[1] Or *without ceasing* [2] Or *brothers and sisters*. The plural Greek word *adelphoi* (translated "brothers") refers to siblings in a family. In New Testament usage, depending on the context, *adelphoi* may refer either to men or to both men and women who are siblings (brothers and sisters) in God's family, the church [3] Or *brothers and sisters*; also verses 9, 14, 17 [4] Or *with a flattering speech* [5] Some manuscripts *infants*

⁹For you remember, brothers, our labor and toil: we worked night and day, that we might not be a burden to any of you, while we proclaimed to you the gospel of God. ¹⁰You are witnesses, and God also, how holy and righteous and blameless was our conduct toward you believers. ¹¹For you know how, like a father with his children, ¹²we exhorted each one of you and encouraged you and charged you to walk in a manner worthy of God, who calls you into his own kingdom and glory.

¹³And we also thank God constantly¹ for this, that when you received the word of God, which you heard from us, you accepted it not as the word of men² but as what it really is, the word of God, which is at work in you believers. ¹⁴For you, brothers, became imitators of the churches of God in Christ Jesus that are in Judea. For you suffered the same things from your own countrymen as they did from the Jews,³ ¹⁵who killed both the Lord Jesus and the prophets, and drove us out, and displease God and oppose all mankind ¹⁶by hindering us from speaking to the Gentiles that they might be saved—so as always to fill up the measure of their sins. But wrath has come upon them at last!⁴

Paul's Longing to See Them Again

¹⁷But since we were torn away from you, brothers, for a short time, in person not in heart, we endeavored the more eagerly and with great desire to see you face to face, ¹⁸because we wanted to come to you—I, Paul, again and again— but Satan hindered us. ¹⁹For what is our hope or joy or crown of boasting before our Lord Jesus at his coming? Is it not you? ²⁰For you are our glory and joy.

3 Therefore when we could bear it no longer, we were willing to be left behind at Athens alone, ²and we sent Timothy, our brother and God's coworker⁵ in the gospel of Christ, to establish and exhort you in your faith, ³that no one be moved by these afflictions. For you your-

¹Or *without ceasing* ²The Greek word *anthropoi* can refer to both men and women ³The Greek word *Ioudaioi* can refer to Jewish religious leaders and others under their influence, who opposed the Christian faith in that time ⁴Or *completely*, or *forever* ⁵Some manuscripts *servant*

Know How to Communicate

verses to read
1 Thessalonians 2:7–12

How gentle are you when it comes to your faith? When you talk to other people about Jesus, are you kind and gentle or frustrated and angry? How you act with people whom you think just don't get it says a lot to those same people about who Jesus is. How you say it is just as important as what you say. And don't kid yourself: if you are judging someone but think you are being kind by telling them about their sin, they can sense your judgment, and it turns them off.

As a God Girl you are to judge right from wrong, to see sin, and to educate people on their wrongdoing, but you are not to judge them as if there is something peculiar about them that isn't the same for you. Remember, you're a sinner too, just in different ways. After all, you know God and still you sin against him! Someone who doesn't know God might not even realize they're doing something wrong. Witnessing to a nonbeliever can be an uncomfortable thing, and it can get even more uncomfortable when you don't show much kindness, compassion, or gentleness. If you have trouble talking to people about Jesus, then maybe it's because you want them to agree with you so badly that you forget that saving them is God's job, not yours. Your job is to love them and to show them how being a Christian transforms you as a person and makes you more compassionate and kind.

elves know that we are destined for this. For when we were with you, we kept telling you beforehand that we were to suffer affliction, just as it has come to pass, and just as you know. [5] For this reason, when I could bear it no longer, I sent to learn about your faith, for fear that somehow the tempter had tempted you and our labor would be in vain.

Timothy's Encouraging Report

[6] But now that Timothy has come to us from you, and has brought us the good news of your faith and love and reported that you always remember us kindly and long to see us, as we long to see you— [7] for this reason, brothers,[1] in all our distress and affliction we have been comforted about you through your faith. [8] For now we live, if you are standing fast in the Lord. [9] For what thanksgiving can we return to God for you, for all the joy that we feel for your sake before our God, [10] as we pray most earnestly night and day that we may see you face to face and supply what is lacking in your faith?

[11] Now may our God and Father himself, and our Lord Jesus, direct our way to you, [2] and may the Lord make you increase and abound in love for one another and for all, as we do for you, [13] so that he may establish your hearts blameless in holiness before our God and Father, at the coming of our Lord Jesus with all his saints.

A Life Pleasing to God

4 Finally, then, brothers,[2] we ask and urge you in the Lord Jesus, that as you received from us how you ought to walk and to please God, just as you are doing, that you do so more and more. [2] For you know what instructions we gave you through the Lord Jesus. [3] For this is the will of God, your sanctification:[3] that you abstain from sexual immorality; [4] that each one of you know how to control his own body[4] in holiness and honor, [5] not in the passion of lust like the Gentiles who do not know God; [6] that no one transgress and wrong his brother in this matter, because the Lord is an avenger in all these things, as we told you beforehand and solemnly warned you. [7] For God has not called us for impurity, but in holiness. [8] Therefore who-

ever disregards this, disregards not man but God, who gives his Holy Spirit to you.

[9] Now concerning brotherly love you have no need for anyone to write to you, for you yourselves have been taught by God to love one another, [10] for that indeed is what you are doing to all the brothers throughout Macedonia. But we urge you, brothers, to do this more and more, [11] and to aspire to live quietly, and to mind your own affairs, and to work with your hands, as we instructed you, [12] so that you may walk properly before outsiders and be dependent on no one.

The Coming of the Lord

[13] But we do not want you to be uninformed, brothers, about those who are asleep, that you may not grieve as others do who have no hope. [14] For since we believe that Jesus died and rose again, even so, through Jesus, God will bring with him those who have fallen asleep. [15] For this we declare to you by a word from the Lord,[5] that we who are alive, who are left until the coming of the Lord, will not precede those who have fallen asleep. [16] For the Lord himself will descend from heaven with a cry of command, with the voice of an archangel, and with the sound of the trumpet of God. And the dead in Christ will rise first. [17] Then we who are alive, who are left, will be caught up together with them in the clouds to meet the Lord in the air, and so we will always be with the Lord. [18] Therefore encourage one another with these words.

The Day of the Lord

5 Now concerning the times and the seasons, brothers,[6] you have no need to have anything written to you. [2] For you yourselves are fully aware that the day of the Lord will come like a thief in the night. [3] While people are saying, "There is peace and security," then sudden destruction will come upon them as labor pains come upon a pregnant woman, and they will not escape. [4] But you are not in darkness, brothers, for that day to surprise you like a thief. [5] For you are all children[7] of light, children of the day. We are not of the night or of the darkness. [6] So then let us not sleep, as others do, but let us keep awake

---

[1] Or brothers and sisters [2] Or brothers and sisters; also verses 10, 13 [3] Or your holiness [4] Or how to take a wife for himself; Greek how to possess his own vessel [5] Or by the word of the Lord [6] Or brothers and sisters; also verses 4, 12, 14, 25, 26, 27 [7] Or sons; twice in this verse

and be sober. 7 For those who sleep, sleep at night, and those who get drunk, are drunk at night. 8 But since we belong to the day, let us be sober, having put on the breastplate of faith and love, and for a helmet the hope of salvation. 9 For God has not destined us for wrath, but to obtain salvation through our Lord Jesus Christ, 10 who died for us so that whether we are awake or asleep we might live with him. 11 Therefore encourage one another and build one another up, just as you are doing.

Final Instructions and Benediction

12 We ask you, brothers, to respect those who labor among you and are over you in the Lord and admonish you, 13 and to esteem them very highly in love because of their work. Be at peace among yourselves. 14 And we urge you, brothers, admonish the idle,[1] encourage the fainthearted, help the weak, be patient with them all. 15 See

[1] Or disorderly, or undisciplined

that no one repays anyone evil for evil, but always seek to do good to one another and to everyone. 16 Rejoice always, 17 pray without ceasing, 18 give thanks in all circumstances; for this is the will of God in Christ Jesus for you. 19 Do not quench the Spirit. 20 Do not despise prophecies, 21 but test everything; hold fast what is good. 22 Abstain from every form of evil.

23 Now may the God of peace himself sanctify you completely, and may your whole spirit and soul and body be kept blameless at the coming of our Lord Jesus Christ. 24 He who calls you is faithful; he will surely do it.

25 Brothers, pray for us.

26 Greet all the brothers with a holy kiss.

27 I put you under oath before the Lord to have this letter read to all the brothers.

28 The grace of our Lord Jesus Christ be with you.

Know God

verses to read
1 Thessalonians 5:12-22

There is no such thing as an unanswered prayer. It's easy to believe that God is too busy or just not interested in what you want and need, especially when you pray and pray and never get what you ask for. But the truth is, he isn't ignoring you. He's heard every word and knows every need, and he has answered you—you just haven't heard his voice.

God never lets prayer go unanswered when it comes from the mouth of his children. The only prayer he ignores is the prayer of those who ignore him and don't truly love him (see Prov. 28:9; John 9:31). For the God Girl, that means you can be certain that all your prayers are being answered. It's not always the answer you wanted—sometimes God says no. And he might not show you the answer immediately—sometimes he says "wait"—but it will come. And when you are certain of that fact, you can rest in trust and not worry about every little thing.

God always answers in the best way—not just occasionally, but *always*. God knows what you need, and he will give you just that. And when he does, it will be the best thing at the best possible time. So don't give up praying for everything in your life. Never stop praying (see 1 Thess. 5:17). Remember that God hears every word you pray, and he will respond in just the right way at just the right time.

2 Thessalonians

Greeting

1 Paul, Silvanus, and Timothy,

To the church of the Thessalonians in God our Father and the Lord Jesus Christ:

²Grace to you and peace from God our Father and the Lord Jesus Christ.

Thanksgiving

³We ought always to give thanks to God for you, brothers,¹ as is right, because your faith is growing abundantly, and the love of every one of you for one another is increasing. ⁴Therefore we ourselves boast about you in the churches of God for your steadfastness and faith in all your persecutions and in the afflictions that you are enduring.

The Judgment at Christ's Coming

⁵This is evidence of the righteous judgment of God, that you may be considered worthy of the kingdom of God, for which you are also suffering— ⁶since indeed God considers it just to repay with affliction those who afflict you, ⁷and to grant relief to you who are afflicted as well as to us, when the Lord Jesus is revealed from heaven with his mighty angels ⁸in flaming fire, inflicting vengeance on those who do not know God and on those who do not obey the gospel of our Lord Jesus. ⁹They will suffer the punishment of eternal destruction, away from² the presence of the Lord and from the glory of his might, ¹⁰when he comes on that day to be glorified in his saints, and to be marveled at among all who have believed, because our testimony to you was believed. ¹¹To this end we always pray for you, that our God may make you worthy of his calling and may fulfill every resolve for good and every work of faith by his power, ¹²so that the name of our Lord Jesus may be glorified in you, and

you in him, according to the grace of our God and the Lord Jesus Christ.

The Man of Lawlessness

2 Now concerning the coming of our Lord Jesus Christ and our being gathered together to him, we ask you, brothers,³ ²not to be quickly shaken in mind or alarmed, either by a spirit or a spoken word, or a letter seeming to be from us, to the effect that the day of the Lord has come. ³Let no one deceive you in any way. For that day will not come, unless the rebellion comes first, and the man of lawlessness⁴ is revealed, the son of destruction,⁵ ⁴who opposes and exalts himself against every so-called god or object of worship, so that he takes his seat in the temple of God, proclaiming himself to be God. ⁵Do you not remember that when I was still with you I told you these things? ⁶And you know what is restraining him now so that he may be revealed in his time. ⁷For the mystery of lawlessness is already at work. Only he who now restrains it will do so until he is out of the way. ⁸And then the lawless one will be revealed, whom the Lord Jesus will kill with the breath of his mouth and bring to nothing by the appearance of his coming. ⁹The coming of the lawless one is by the activity of Satan with all power and false signs and wonders, ¹⁰and with all wicked deception for those who are perishing, because they refused to love the truth and so be saved. ¹¹Therefore God sends them a strong delusion, so that they may believe what is false, ¹²in order that all may be condemned who did not believe the truth but had pleasure in unrighteousness.

Stand Firm

¹³But we ought always to give thanks to God for you, brothers beloved by the Lord,

---

¹ Or *brothers and sisters*. The plural Greek word *adelphoi* (translated "brothers") refers to siblings in a family. In New Testament usage, depending on the context, *adelphoi* may refer either to men or to both men and women who are siblings (brothers and sisters) in God's family, the church ² Or *destruction that comes from* ³ Or *brothers and sisters*; also verses 13, 15 ⁴ Some manuscripts *sin* ⁵ Greek *the son of perdition* (a Hebrew idiom)

because God chose you as the firstfruits[1] to be saved, through sanctification by the Spirit and belief in the truth. [14] To this he called you through our gospel, so that you may obtain the glory of our Lord Jesus Christ. [15] So then, brothers, stand firm and hold to the traditions that you were taught by us, either by our spoken word or by our letter.

[16] Now may our Lord Jesus Christ himself, and God our Father, who loved us and gave us eternal comfort and good hope through grace, [17] comfort your hearts and establish them in every good work and word.

Pray for Us

3 Finally, brothers,[2] pray for us, that the word of the Lord may speed ahead and be honored,[3] as happened among you, [2] and that we may be delivered from wicked and evil men. For not all have faith. [3] But the Lord is faithful. He will establish you and guard you against the evil one.[4] [4] And we have confidence in the Lord about you, that you are doing and will do the thing that we command. [5] May the Lord direct your hearts to the love of God and to the steadfastness of Christ.

Warning Against Idleness

[6] Now we command you, brothers, in the name of our Lord Jesus Christ, that you keep away from any brother who is walking in idleness and not in accord with the tradition that you received from us. [7] For you yourselves know how you ought to imitate us, because we were not idle when we were with you, [8] nor did we eat anyone's bread without paying for it, but with toil and labor we worked night and day, tha

---

[1] Some manuscripts *chose you from the beginning* [2] Or *brothers and sisters;* also verses 6, 13 [3] Or *glorified* [4] Or *evil*

verse to read
2 Thessalonians 3:6

Frenemies: those girls whom you think are your friends, but some days you really have to wonder. Once they were nice but now they are fifty percent mean. When you have a friend who has changed and now much of her behavior is ungodly, what do you do?

God's Word has a prescription for you: if your friend is a believer and she has become mean, vengeful, a gossip, or a slanderer, or if she is abusing you or hating you, then it's time to break up. You can't let her sin become contagious. You can't take on her disobedience and make it your own.

The trouble with staying close to believers who desert God's truth is that it can lead you to sin. You sin when you hate her back, retaliate, want revenge, or start thinking negative thoughts or complaining.

The God Girl trusts God's Word and seeks to live in light of the gospel every day. A godly friend might mess up, she might make mistakes, she might even hurt you, but there is always redemption, always confession and reconciliation, because godly friends understand the redemption they themselves have received in Christ. But for some girls there is none of that because they are done with God's Word. It is no longer a part of their lives, and instead they live by their own emotions and desires. That kind of girl is not good for you.

So think about your frenemy: will confronting her work? Can there be reconciliation, or is it time to cut the strings that bind you to her? Don't be afraid to walk away if you have to. It doesn't make you a loser; it makes you a follower of Jesus. You are called to obey God's Word no matter what others think or say.

we might not be a burden to any of you. [9] It was not because we do not have that right, but to give you in ourselves an example to imitate. [10] For even when we were with you, we would give you this command: If anyone is not willing to work, let him not eat. [11] For we hear that some among you walk in idleness, not busy at work, but busybodies. [12] Now such persons we command and encourage in the Lord Jesus Christ to do their work quietly and to earn their own living.[1]

[13] As for you, brothers, do not grow weary in doing good. [14] If anyone does not obey what we say in this letter, take note of that person, and have nothing to do with him, that he may be ashamed. [15] Do not regard him as an enemy, but warn him as a brother.

Benediction

[16] Now may the Lord of peace himself give you peace at all times in every way. The Lord be with you all.

[17] I, Paul, write this greeting with my own hand. This is the sign of genuineness in every letter of mine; it is the way I write. [18] The grace of our Lord Jesus Christ be with you all.

---

[1] Greek *to eat their own bread*

INTRODUCTION TO
1&2 Timothy

Author: The apostle Paul

Time: About A.D. 62 and 67

Place: Macedonia for the first letter, and probably a Roman prison for the second

Written to: Timothy, a young pastor

The gist

Timothy was Paul's disciple and pastor of the church at Ephesus. In the first letter Paul sets Timothy up for success and teaches him how to be a godly leader and to serve the believers in his city. In the second letter, while Paul was waiting for the verdict of his trial, he gave Timothy some final instructions on leadership and the Christian life.

Things to look for

- The relationship between Paul and Timothy (see 1 Tim. 1:2; 3:14; 4:12–16; 5:23; 2 Tim. 1:2–6, 13–14; 2:1–2; for more background read Acts 16:3; 17:10–15; 19:22; 20:4–5; Rom. 16:21; 1 Cor. 4:17; Phil. 1:1; 2:19–23; Col. 1:1; Philem. 1)

- The Christian's call to courage (see 2 Tim. 1:8–12; 2:1–10; 3:10–13; 4:17–18)

- Paul's faith in times of suffering (see 2 Tim. 1:8, 16; 4:6–8)

Be an Example

> Let no one despise you for your youth, but set the believers an example in speech, in conduct, in love, in faith, in purity.
>
> *1 Timothy 4:12*

Many young believers have "spiritual parents"—those who aren't your flesh and blood but have raised you in your faith and taught you what you need to know in order to lead others into the same kind of faith. These spiritual moms and dads are really important and often can give us as much wisdom and hope as our earthly parents give us, if not more. The spiritual family is a valuable part of the life of a believer, as it has been for centuries. The apostle Paul could be considered the spiritual father of Timothy, whom he loved like a son (see 1 Tim. 1:2). And these two letters addressed to him are Paul's final lessons and inspiration meant to encourage and teach Timothy to carry the torch of Paul's ministry.

These letters were written near the end of Paul's life. He knew that Timothy was clearly gifted by God but that he was prone to being sick a lot and was a bit shy. Paul wanted to encourage Timothy and prepare him to continue his ministry in Ephesus after Paul was dead. Though Timothy was young, he had been very helpful in serving with Paul for years. Paul had learned to trust him and to love him. Now Paul would soon die at the hands of his persecutors, so he wanted to prepare his friend and leave him with the information he would need to keep the faith alive.

As a God Girl, you are not alone in this world. Others who are older and wiser have gone before you and are now leaving you direction and guidance as Paul did for Timothy. You should learn from the wise, seek their counsel, and learn from their experiences in the faith. Like Timothy, you may have a challenge ahead, but keep the faith, knowing that others who have gone before you can help. Seek them out, learn from them, and know that you are not alone.

Must-Know Terms and Verses

✑ *Deacon* ✑

A minister or lay leader in the church.

✑ *Overseer* ✑

An elder in the church.

The saying is trustworthy and deserving of full acceptance, that Christ Jesus came into the world to save sinners, of whom I am the foremost. *1 Timothy 1:15*

First of all, then, I urge that supplications, prayers, intercessions, and thanksgivings be made for all people, for kings and all who are in high positions, that we may lead a peaceful and quiet life, godly and dignified in every way. *1 Timothy 2:1–2*

He was manifested in the flesh,
    vindicated by the Spirit,
        seen by angels,
proclaimed among the nations,
    believed on in the world,
        taken up in glory. *1 Timothy 3:16*

Let no one despise you for your youth, but set the believers an example in speech, in conduct, in love, in faith, in purity. *1 Timothy 4:12*

God gave us a spirit not of fear but of power and love and self-control. *2 Timothy 1:7*

Share in suffering as a good soldier of Christ Jesus. No soldier gets entangled in civilian pursuits, since his aim is to please the one who enlisted him. An athlete is not crowned unless he competes according to the rules. *2 Timothy 2:3–5*

The First Letter of Paul to Timothy

1 Timothy

Greeting

1 Paul, an apostle of Christ Jesus by command of God our Savior and of Christ Jesus our hope,

[2] To Timothy, my true child in the faith:

Grace, mercy, and peace from God the Father and Christ Jesus our Lord.

Warning Against False Teachers

[3] As I urged you when I was going to Macedonia, remain at Ephesus so that you may charge certain persons not to teach any different doctrine, [4] nor to devote themselves to myths and endless genealogies, which promote speculations rather than the stewardship[1] from God that is by faith. [5] The aim of our charge is love that issues from a pure heart and a good conscience and a sincere faith. [6] Certain persons, by swerving from these, have wandered away into vain discussion, [7] desiring to be teachers of the law, without understanding either what they are saying or the things about which they make confident assertions.

[8] Now we know that the law is good, if one uses it lawfully, [9] understanding this, that the law is not laid down for the just but for the lawless and disobedient, for the ungodly and sinners, for the unholy and profane, for those who strike their fathers and mothers, for murderers, [10] the sexually immoral, men who practice homosexuality, enslavers,[2] liars, perjurers, and whatever else is contrary to sound[3] doctrine, [11] in accordance with the gospel of the glory of the blessed God with which I have been entrusted.

Christ Jesus Came to Save Sinners

[12] I thank him who has given me strength, Christ Jesus our Lord, because he judged me faithful, appointing me to his service, [13] though formerly I was a blasphemer, persecutor, and insolent opponent. But I received mercy because I had acted ignorantly in unbelief, [14] and the grace of our Lord overflowed for me with the faith and love that are in Christ Jesus. [15] The saying is trustworthy and deserving of full acceptance, that Christ Jesus came into the world to save sinners, of whom I am the foremost. [16] But I received mercy for this reason, that in me, as the foremost, Jesus Christ might display his perfect patience as an example to those who were to believe in him for eternal life. [17] To the King of the ages, immortal, invisible, the only God, be honor and glory forever and ever.[4] Amen.

Ask Yourself . . .

ABOUT FAITH

- What is faith?
- Where do I put my faith?
- On a scale of 1 to 10, how strong is my faith in God?
- How does my faith make me different from others?
- How does my faith affect my decisions?
- How is my faith changing me?
- Where do I lack faith?
- How can I get more faith?

[18] This charge I entrust to you, Timothy, my child, in accordance with the prophecies previously made about you, that by them you may wage the good warfare, [19] holding faith and a good conscience. By rejecting this, some have made shipwreck of their faith, [20] among whom are

---

[1] Or *good order* [2] That is, those who take someone captive in order to sell him into slavery [3] Or *healthy* [4] Greek *to the ages of ages*

Hymenaeus and Alexander, whom I have handed over to Satan that they may learn not to blaspheme.

Pray for All People

2 First of all, then, I urge that supplications, prayers, intercessions, and thanksgivings be made for all people, ²for kings and all who are in high positions, that we may lead a peaceful and quiet life, godly and dignified in every way. ³This is good, and it is pleasing in the sight of God our Savior, ⁴who desires all people to be saved and to come to the knowledge of the truth. ⁵For there is one God, and there is one mediator between God and men, the man¹ Christ Jesus, ⁶who gave himself as a ransom for all, which is the testimony given at the proper time. ⁷For this I was appointed a preacher and an apostle (I am telling the truth, I am not lying), a teacher of the Gentiles in faith and truth.

⁸I desire then that in every place the men should pray, lifting holy hands without anger or quarreling; ⁹likewise also that women should adorn themselves in respectable apparel, with modesty and self-control, not with braided hair and gold or pearls or costly attire, ¹⁰but with what is proper for women who profess godliness—with good works. ¹¹Let a woman learn quietly with all submissiveness. ¹²I do not permit a woman to teach or to exercise authority over a man; rather, she is to remain quiet. ¹³For Adam was formed first, then Eve; ¹⁴and Adam was not deceived, but the woman was deceived and became a transgressor. ¹⁵Yet she will be saved through childbearing—if they continue in faith and love and holiness, with self-control.

Qualifications for Overseers

3 The saying is trustworthy: If anyone aspires to the office of overseer, he desires a noble task. ²Therefore an overseer² must be above reproach, the husband of one wife,³ sober-minded, self-controlled, respectable, hospitable, able to teach, ³not a drunkard, not violent but gentle, not quarrelsome, not a lover of money. ⁴He must manage his own household well, with

¹ men and man render the same Greek word that is translated people in verses 1 and 4 ²Or bishop; Greek episkopos; a similar term occurs in verse 1 ³Or a man of one woman; also verse 12

verses to read
1 Timothy 2:1-3

Know God

God commands us to pray repeatedly for ourselves and for others. But a lot of times you might think that kind of prayer is something reserved for the mega-spiritual types. So you bow out because of your inability. But prayer isn't just for the super holy; it's required and possible for everyone, and it's how you overcome the world. Prayer moves the hand that moves the world. Why wouldn't you access his power in the challenges of this life? Why wouldn't you want more of him?

Prayer releases the power of God, especially when your prayer is for other people. It's called intercessory prayer, and it's just asking God to help, guide, and save others. If you trust God with your life, then your prayer can be focused on the needs of others instead of your own needs. That doesn't mean you don't ask for what you need, but the God Girl is no longer defined by selfishness. She doesn't hoard God's blessing for herself but thinks about others every single day.

When your prayer is purposefully focused outside of yourself and you are always thinking of the needs of others, your faith, your hope, and your happiness all increase. Your life begins to mean more as it becomes less about you and more about others. So practice intercessory prayer. It doesn't take any special gift, just a heart that wants to serve God and others.

all dignity keeping his children submissive, ⁵for if someone does not know how to manage his own household, how will he care for God's church? ⁶He must not be a recent convert, or he may become puffed up with conceit and fall into the condemnation of the devil. ⁷Moreover, he must be well thought of by outsiders, so that he may not fall into disgrace, into a snare of the devil.

Qualifications for Deacons

⁸Deacons likewise must be dignified, not double-tongued,¹ not addicted to much wine, not greedy for dishonest gain. ⁹They must hold the mystery of the faith with a clear conscience. ¹⁰And let them also be tested first; then let them serve as deacons if they prove themselves blameless. ¹¹Their wives likewise must² be dignified, not slanderers, but sober-minded, faithful in all things. ¹²Let deacons each be the husband of one wife, managing their children and their own households well. ¹³For those who serve well as deacons gain a good standing for themselves and also great confidence in the faith that is in Christ Jesus.

The Mystery of Godliness

¹⁴I hope to come to you soon, but I am writing these things to you so that, ¹⁵if I delay, you may know how one ought to behave in the household of God, which is the church of the living God, a pillar and buttress of the truth. ¹⁶Great indeed, we confess, is the mystery of godliness:

He³ was manifested in the flesh,
   vindicated⁴ by the Spirit,⁵
     seen by angels,
proclaimed among the nations,
   believed on in the world,
     taken up in glory.

Some Will Depart from the Faith

4 Now the Spirit expressly says that in later times some will depart from the faith by devoting themselves to deceitful spirits and teachings of demons, ²through the insincerity of liars whose consciences are seared, ³who forbid marriage and require abstinence from foods that God created to be received with thanksgiving

by those who believe and know the truth. ⁴For everything created by God is good, and nothing is to be rejected if it is received with thanksgiving, ⁵for it is made holy by the word of God and prayer.

A Good Servant of Christ Jesus

⁶If you put these things before the brothers,⁶ you will be a good servant of Christ Jesus, being trained in the words of the faith and of the good doctrine that you have followed. ⁷Have nothing to do with irreverent, silly myths. Rather train yourself for godliness; ⁸for while bodily training is of some value, godliness is of value in every way, as it holds promise for the present life and also for the life to come. ⁹The saying is trustworthy and deserving of full acceptance. ¹⁰For to this end we toil and strive,⁷ because we have our hope set on the living God, who is the Savior of all people, especially of those who believe.

¹¹Command and teach these things. ¹²Let no one despise you for your youth, but set the believers an example in speech, in conduct, in love, in faith, in purity. ¹³Until I come, devote yourself to the public reading of Scripture, to exhortation, to teaching. ¹⁴Do not neglect the gift you have, which was given you by prophecy when the council of elders laid their hands on you. ¹⁵Practice these things, immerse yourself in them,⁸ so that all may see your progress. ¹⁶Keep a close watch on yourself and on the teaching. Persist in this, for by so doing you will save both yourself and your hearers.

Instructions for the Church

5 Do not rebuke an older man but encourage him as you would a father, younger men as brothers, ²older women as mothers, younger women as sisters, in all purity.

³Honor widows who are truly widows. ⁴But if a widow has children or grandchildren, let them first learn to show godliness to their own household and to make some return to their parents, for this is pleasing in the sight of God. ⁵She who is truly a widow, left all alone, has set her hope on God and continues in supplications and prayers night and day, ⁶but she who is self-indulgent is dead even while she lives. ⁷Command these things as well, so

---

¹Or *devious in speech* ²Or *Wives, likewise, must*, or *Women, likewise, must* ³Greek *Who*; some manuscripts *God*; others *Which* ⁴Or *justified* ⁵Or *vindicated in spirit* ⁶Or *brothers and sisters*. The plural Greek word *adelphoi* (translated "brothers") refers to siblings in a family. In New Testament usage, depending on the context, *adelphoi* may refer either to men or to both men and women who are siblings (brothers and sisters) in God's family, the church ⁷Some manuscripts *and suffer reproach* ⁸Greek *be in them*

that they may be without reproach. ⁸But if anyone does not provide for his relatives, and especially for members of his household, he has denied the faith and is worse than an unbeliever.

⁹Let a widow be enrolled if she is not less than sixty years of age, having been the wife of one husband,¹ ¹⁰and having a reputation for good works: if she has brought up children, has shown hospitality, has washed the feet of the saints, has cared for the afflicted, and has devoted herself to every good work. ¹¹But refuse to enroll younger widows, for when their passions draw them away from Christ, they desire to marry ¹²and so incur condemnation for having abandoned their former faith. ¹³Besides that, they learn to be idlers, going about from house to house, and not only idlers, but also gossips and busybodies, saying what they should not. ¹⁴So I would have younger widows marry, bear children, manage their households, and give

the adversary no occasion for slander. ¹⁵For some have already strayed after Satan. ¹⁶If any believing woman has relatives who are widows, let her care for them. Let the church not be burdened, so that it may care for those who are truly widows.

¹⁷Let the elders who rule well be considered worthy of double honor, especially those who labor in preaching and teaching. ¹⁸For the Scripture says, ᵃ"You shall not muzzle an ox when it treads out the grain," and, "The laborer deserves his wages." ¹⁹Do not admit a charge against an elder except on the evidence of two or three witnesses. ²⁰As for those who persist in sin, rebuke them in the presence of all, so that the rest may stand in fear. ²¹In the presence of God and of Christ Jesus and of the elect angels I charge you to keep these rules without prejudging, doing nothing from partiality. ²²Do not be hasty in the laying on of hands, nor take part in the sins of others; keep yourself pure. ²³(No longer drink only

¹Or a woman of one man ᵃDeut. 25:4

Know How to Communicate

verses to read
1 Timothy 4:11–16

Do you ever feel like adults are looking down on you? Let it be because they don't know you, not because they do! Your actions, your words, and your love are the ways others know you truly are a God Girl. If they judge that you are bad based on some false idea of who you are, then be thankful that it is false. Would you rather they look down on you because of how you act, talk, or love instead? No, your life should be proof of your faith. People will know you are a believer by how you act, so act like one.

You can't let people look down on you because you act immature. Just being young can't be an excuse to misbehave. Joining the crowd and doing things just because everyone else is doing them makes you a follower, not an example. The God Girl is a leader of people and a follower of God, not the other way around. So follow his lead in everything. A lot of people might think you're not old enough to make a difference in this world, but remember that some of the people who made the most spiritual impact on the world in history were teenagers. Youth isn't an obstacle unless you choose to act your age. Enjoy your youth, but rise above the insanity of defying God just to fit in or have fun. Make sure people look favorably on you because, even though you are young, you already act in a godly and mature way. When you think about the fact that others are watching you and making decisions about who God is based on how you act, it's a sobering thought. Don't let them look down on you, but, looking to Christ, help them to look up to him too.

water, but use a little wine for the sake of your stomach and your frequent ailments.) ²⁴The sins of some people are conspicuous, going before them to judgment, but the sins of others appear later. ²⁵So also good works are conspicuous, and even those that are not cannot remain hidden.

6 Let all who are under a yoke as bond-servants¹ regard their own masters as worthy of all honor, so that the name of God and the teaching may not be reviled. ²Those who have believing masters must not be disrespectful on the ground that they are brothers; rather they must serve all the better since those who benefit by their good service are believers and beloved.

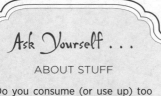

Ask Yourself . . .

ABOUT STUFF

Do you consume (or use up) too much? Ask yourself about your needs:

- Is there anything I consume that I don't need to consume?
- How much stuff is too much?
- What does my consumption of things say about my faith in God?
- What is the value of self-denial?
- In what areas could I look at cutting back today in order to give glory to God by my act of self-control?

False Teachers and True Contentment

Teach and urge these things. ³If anyone teaches a different doctrine and does not agree with the sound² words of our Lord Jesus Christ and the teaching that accords with godliness, ⁴he is puffed up with conceit and understands nothing. He has an unhealthy craving for controversy and for quarrels about words, which produce envy, dissension, slander, evil suspicions, ⁵and constant friction among people who are depraved in mind and deprived of the truth, imagining that godliness is a means of gain. ⁶But godliness with contentment is great gain, ⁷for we brought nothing into the world, and³ we cannot take anything out of the world. ⁸But if we have food and clothing, with these we will be content. ⁹But those who desire to be rich fall into temptation, into a snare, into many senseless and harmful desires that plunge people into ruin and destruction. ¹⁰For the love of money is a root of all kinds of evils. It is through this craving that some have wandered away from the faith and pierced themselves with many pangs.

Fight the Good Fight of Faith

¹¹But as for you, O man of God, flee these things. Pursue righteousness, godliness, faith, love, steadfastness, gentleness. ¹²Fight the good fight of the faith. Take hold of the eternal life to which you were called and about which you made the good confession in the presence of many witnesses. ¹³I charge you in the presence of God, who gives life to all things, and of Christ Jesus, who in his testimony before⁴ Pontius Pilate made the good confession, ¹⁴to keep the commandment unstained and free from reproach until the appearing of our Lord Jesus Christ, ¹⁵which he will display at the proper time—he who is the blessed and only Sovereign, the King of kings and Lord of lords, ¹⁶who alone has immortality, who dwells in unapproachable light, whom no one has ever seen or can see. To him be honor and eternal dominion. Amen.

¹⁷As for the rich in this present age, charge them not to be haughty, nor to set their hopes on the uncertainty of riches, but on God, who richly provides us with everything to enjoy. ¹⁸They are to do good, to be rich in good works, to be generous and ready to share, ¹⁹thus storing up treasure for themselves as a good foundation for the future, so that they may take hold of that which is truly life.

²⁰O Timothy, guard the deposit entrusted to you. Avoid the irreverent babble and contradictions of what is falsely called "knowledge," ²¹for by professing it some have swerved from the faith.

Grace be with you.⁵

¹Or *slaves* (for the contextual rendering of the Greek word *doulos*, see About the ESV) ²Or *healthy* ³Greek *for*; some manuscripts insert [it is] *certain* [that] ⁴Or *in the time of* ⁵The Greek for *you* is plural

The Second Letter of Paul to Timothy

2 Timothy

Greeting

1 Paul, an apostle of Christ Jesus by the will of God according to the promise of the life that is in Christ Jesus,

²To Timothy, my beloved child:

Grace, mercy, and peace from God the Father and Christ Jesus our Lord.

Guard the Deposit Entrusted to You

³I thank God whom I serve, as did my ancestors, with a clear conscience, as I remember you constantly in my prayers night and day. ⁴As I remember your tears, I long to see you, that I may be filled with joy. ⁵I am reminded of your sincere faith, a faith that dwelt first in your grandmother Lois and your mother Eunice and now, I am sure, dwells in you as well. ⁶For this reason I remind you to fan into flame the gift of God, which is in you through the laying on of my hands, ⁷for God gave us a spirit not of fear but of power and love and self-control.

⁸Therefore do not be ashamed of the testimony about our Lord, nor of me his prisoner, but share in suffering for the gospel by the power of God, ⁹who saved us and called us to¹ a holy calling, not because of our works but because of his own purpose and grace, which he gave us in Christ Jesus before the ages began,² ¹⁰and which now has been manifested through the appearing of our Savior Christ Jesus, who abolished death and brought life and immortality to light through the gospel, ¹¹for which I was appointed a preacher and apostle and teacher, ¹²which is why I suffer as I do. But I am not ashamed, for I know whom I have believed, and I am convinced that he is able to guard until that Day what has been entrusted to me.³ ¹³Follow the pattern of the sound⁴ words that you have heard from me, in the faith and love that are in Christ Jesus. ¹⁴By the Holy Spirit who

dwells within us, guard the good deposit entrusted to you.

¹⁵You are aware that all who are in Asia turned away from me, among whom are Phygelus and Hermogenes. ¹⁶May the Lord grant mercy to the household of Onesiphorus, for he often refreshed me and was not ashamed of my chains, ¹⁷but when he arrived in Rome he searched for me earnestly and found me— ¹⁸may the Lord grant him to find mercy from the Lord on that Day!—and you well know all the service he rendered at Ephesus.

A Good Soldier of Christ Jesus

2 You then, my child, be strengthened by the grace that is in Christ Jesus, ²and what you have heard from me in the presence of many witnesses entrust to faithful men⁵ who will be able to teach others also. ³Share in suffering as a good soldier of Christ Jesus. ⁴No soldier gets entangled in civilian pursuits, since his aim is to please the one who enlisted him. ⁵An athlete is not crowned unless he competes according to the rules. ⁶It is the hard-working farmer who ought to have the first share of the crops. ⁷Think over what I say, for the Lord will give you understanding in everything.

⁸Remember Jesus Christ, risen from the dead, the offspring of David, as preached in my gospel, ⁹for which I am suffering, bound with chains as a criminal. But the word of God is not bound! ¹⁰Therefore I endure everything for the sake of the elect, that they also may obtain the salvation that is in Christ Jesus with eternal glory. ¹¹The saying is trustworthy, for:

> If we have died with him, we will
>   also live with him;
> ¹²   if we endure, we will also reign with
>   him;

---

¹Or with ²Greek before times eternal ³Or what I have entrusted to him; Greek my deposit ⁴Or healthy ⁵The Greek word anthropoi can refer to both men and women, depending on the context

if we deny him, he also will deny us;

¹³ if we are faithless, he remains faithful—

for he cannot deny himself.

A Worker Approved by God

¹⁴ Remind them of these things, and charge them before God[1] not to quarrel about words, which does no good, but only ruins the hearers. ¹⁵ Do your best to present yourself to God as one approved,[2] a worker who has no need to be ashamed, rightly handling the word of truth. ¹⁶ But avoid irreverent babble, for it will lead people into more and more ungodliness, ¹⁷ and their talk will spread like gangrene. Among them are Hymenaeus and Philetus, ¹⁸ who have swerved from the truth, saying that the resurrection has already happened. They are upsetting the faith of some. ¹⁹ But God's firm foundation stands, bearing this seal: "The Lord knows those who are his," and, "Let everyone who names the name of the Lord depart from iniquity."

²⁰ Now in a great house there are not only vessels of gold and silver but also of wood and clay, some for honorable use, some for dishonorable. ²¹ Therefore, if anyone cleanses himself from what is dishonorable,[3] he will be a vessel for honorable use,

set apart as holy, useful to the master of the house, ready for every good work.

²² So flee youthful passions and pursue righteousness, faith, love, and peace, along with those who call on the Lord from a pure heart. ²³ Have nothing to do with foolish, ignorant controversies; you know that they breed quarrels. ²⁴ And the Lord's servant[4] must not be quarrelsome but kind to everyone, able to teach, patiently enduring evil, ²⁵ correcting his opponents with gentleness. God may perhaps grant them repentance leading to a knowledge of the truth, ²⁶ and they may come to their senses and escape from the snare of the devil, after being captured by him to do his will.

Godlessness in the Last Days

3 But understand this, that in the last days there will come times of difficulty. ² For people will be lovers of self, lovers of money, proud, arrogant, abusive, disobedient to their parents, ungrateful, unholy, ³ heartless, unappeasable, slanderous, without self-control, brutal, not loving good, ⁴ treacherous, reckless, swollen with conceit, lovers of pleasure rather than lovers of God, ⁵ having the appearance of godliness, but denying its power. Avoid such people. ⁶ For among them are those who creep into households and capture weak

[1] Some manuscripts *the Lord*   [2] That is, one approved after being tested   [3] Greek *from these things*   [4] Greek *bondservant*

Know Yourself

verses to read
2 Timothy 1:6–11

Before the world began, God planned to send Jesus Christ to die on the cross to save you from your sin, so that you could be his own. Your sin doesn't surprise God. He isn't shocked when you fail; he knew you would, just like he knew all of us would. Knowing all along that his Son would have to die for our mistakes and bad choices, he created the earth and all of humanity in order to show the glory of his grace.

Never underestimate how much God loves you. He loved you enough to bring you into this world even though he knew you would fail. He knew you would sin against him, but he also knew how much he was willing to pay for you. God's grace ought to be your inspiration, your hope. You are never a lost cause—never! Your sinfulness is nothing new. Millions before you have sinned just as badly, and worse, and have been forgiven. God didn't save you because you were perfectly holy—he saved you because *he* is holy.

women, burdened with sins and led astray by various passions, [7] always learning and never able to arrive at a knowledge of the truth. [8] Just as Jannes and Jambres opposed Moses, so these men also oppose the truth, men corrupted in mind and disqualified regarding the faith. [9] But they will not get very far, for their folly will be plain to all, as was that of those two men.

All Scripture Is Breathed Out by God

[10] You, however, have followed my teaching, my conduct, my aim in life, my faith, my patience, my love, my steadfastness, [11] my persecutions and sufferings that happened to me at Antioch, at Iconium, and at Lystra—which persecutions I endured; yet from them all the Lord rescued me. [12] Indeed, all who desire to live a godly life in Christ Jesus will be persecuted, [13] while evil people and impostors will go on from bad to worse, deceiving and being deceived. [14] But as for you, continue in what you have learned and have firmly believed, knowing from whom[1] you learned it [15] and how from childhood you have been acquainted with the sacred writings, which are able to make you wise for salvation through faith in Christ Jesus. [16] All Scripture is breathed out by God and profitable for teaching, for reproof, for correction, and for training in righteousness, [17] that the man of God[2] may be complete, equipped for every good work.

Preach the Word

4 I charge you in the presence of God and of Christ Jesus, who is to judge the living and the dead, and by his appearing and his kingdom: [2] preach the word; be ready in season and out of season; reprove, rebuke, and exhort, with complete patience and teaching. [3] For the time is coming when people will not endure sound[3] teaching,

---

[1] The Greek for *whom* is plural [2] That is, a messenger of God (the phrase echoes a common Old Testament expression) [3] Or *healthy*

Know God

verses to read
2 Timothy 3:10–17

God's Word: good for living or just good for your soul? You trust God and read his Word, but could he really expect you to live that way? To turn the other cheek when someone hits you? To love the people who hate you and hurt you? To die to self and say no to the things you really, really want? Surely God doesn't mean for you to live your life as if all of the Bible applies to your modern world. After all, you aren't a saint. Things are different now. Your situation is unique. The Bible is good to read and meditate on, but you've gotta live and you've gotta protect yourself. Right?

Yeah, some of the stuff he asks seems to go against every ounce of self-protection you have. And that is exactly why it has to be done. If his Word is to be considered true, it has to be considered true at every point. All of it is not only useful but essential for your life as a God Girl. You can't pick and choose which parts of your life you apply it to.

At any point that you are unwilling to make the Word of God a part of your everyday life, you have crossed over into Sinville. No matter how risky following his Word sounds, no matter how hard it may be, it's gotta be done. You can't just decide that certain commands don't apply to you; that's just an excuse to disobey. Forgiveness of sin is not for those who refuse to obey God's Word but for those who want to obey but don't always succeed at it. Learn what pleases the Lord and do it, and your life will be full of faith, hope, and love. When you mess up, fess up, and then thank him for his grace and his quick forgiveness in the gospel.

but having itching ears they will accumulate for themselves teachers to suit their own passions, [4] and will turn away from listening to the truth and wander off into myths. [5] As for you, always be sober-minded, endure suffering, do the work of an evangelist, fulfill your ministry.

[6] For I am already being poured out as a drink offering, and the time of my departure has come. [7] I have fought the good fight, I have finished the race, I have kept the faith. [8] Henceforth there is laid up for me the crown of righteousness, which the Lord, the righteous judge, will award to me on that Day, and not only to me but also to all who have loved his appearing.

Personal Instructions

[9] Do your best to come to me soon. [10] For Demas, in love with this present world, has deserted me and gone to Thessalonica.

Crescens has gone to Galatia,[1] Titus to Dalmatia. [11] Luke alone is with me. Get Mark and bring him with you, for he is very useful to me for ministry. [12] Tychicus I have sent to Ephesus. [13] When you come, bring the cloak that I left with Carpus at Troas, also the books, and above all the parchments. [14] Alexander the coppersmith did me great harm; the Lord will repay him according to his deeds. [15] Beware of him yourself, for he strongly opposed our message. [16] At my first defense no one came to stand by me, but all deserted me. May it not be charged against them! [17] But the Lord stood by me and strengthened me, so that through me the message might be fully proclaimed and all the Gentiles might hear it. So I was rescued from the lion's mouth. [18] The Lord will rescue me from every evil deed and bring me safely into his heavenly kingdom. To him be the glory forever and ever. Amen.

[1] Some manuscripts *Gaul*

Know True Happiness

verses to read
2 Timothy 4:1–4

Beware of wanting to hear only what makes you feel good. God's Word convicts, it rebukes, it calls you on your darkness. But it's easy to want teachers and preachers to say only things that inspire you and to talk only about God's kindness and forgiveness. Although these things are good, a steady diet of them will leave you spiritually sick. Your soul needs to be shaped to be fit, not flabby, and that means doing the hard work of looking in the mirror and seeing where your soul needs some truth, correction, and direction.

When the truth is applied to your dark parts, it hurts. The lights go on, and the brightness can hurt your eyes, but that's no reason to flip the switch back off. It's a spiritual illness to want only good news from God and not conviction of sin. When you are being taught, don't turn away from harsh news but embrace it. Though for a while you may feel pain, freedom is the ultimate result. Those who fear the initial sting of truth don't grow and never overcome the sin that controls them. But those who courageously accept what God's Word says about the sin in their lives, placing it under the cross, grow more and more into the likeness of Christ every day.

A true friend doesn't just tell you what you want to hear; she tells you the truth. Have too much of just what makes you feel good, and you will grow spiritually lazy. But you can never get too much of the truth. When you meet someone who is willing to tell you the hard truth, you have found a true friend. Embrace those who love God more than they love you and who aren't afraid to hurt you with the truth in order to help you.

Final Greetings

[19] Greet Prisca and Aquila, and the household of Onesiphorus. [20] Erastus remained at Corinth, and I left Trophimus, who was ill, at Miletus. [21] Do your best to come before winter. Eubulus sends greetings to you, as do Pudens and Linus and Claudia and all the brothers.[1]

[22] The Lord be with your spirit. Grace be with you.[2]

---

[1] Or *brothers and sisters*. The plural Greek word *adelphoi* (translated "brothers") refers to siblings in a family. In New Testament usage, depending on the context, *adelphoi* may refer either to men or to both men and women who are siblings (brothers and sisters) in God's family, the church [2] The Greek for *you* is plural

INTRODUCTION TO
Titus

Author: The apostle Paul

Time: Around A.D. 63–65

Place: Unknown, possibly Corinth

Written to: Titus, a pastor on the island of Crete

The gist

The letter to Titus is a key epistle that teaches about the roles of leaders in the church. Titus was Paul's right-hand man, so Paul wanted him to know all he could about leading the church after Paul was gone.

Things to look for

- Truth about grace (see Titus 2:11–14; 3:3–7)
- Instruction for how churches should deal with false teachers (see Titus 1:9–2:1; 2:7–8, 15; 3:9–11)
- The importance of doing good (see Titus 1:16; 2:7, 14; 3:1, 5, 8, 14)

Know Accurate Teaching

I want you to insist on these things, so that those who have believed in God may be careful to devote themselves to good works. These things are excellent and profitable for people.

Titus 3:8

At the time when Paul was traveling the world teaching about Jesus, the church was in its infancy and believers didn't know much about how to live like followers of Christ, but Paul was able to teach those who would continue leading the church after he was gone. Titus was one of those men. He had been a partner with Paul, helping him throughout his journeys, sending messages, teaching, traveling, and suffering for the gospel. Paul trusted him, and now toward the end of Paul's life he was leaving Titus to carry on. In his letters to Timothy, Paul stressed sound doctrine, but in this letter to Titus he stresses good works—not as something that can save you but as something that confirms that you have been saved (see Titus 2:14; 3:8, 14).

Titus was left in charge of the church in Crete, so this letter offers a lot of teaching on the roles of men and women and on how to deal with false teachers. As believers, we need to understand how God wants us to act. Salvation isn't just about getting to heaven; it's also about allowing Christ to live within you. When that happens, your life changes: you no longer want what the world wants but what God wants, and that affects your entire life. As a God Girl, you've got to know how God expects his children to live, to learn what pleases him, and then, as one who has been redeemed, you've got to do it. As you do, you will give evidence that your love for God and your salvation are real. Remember, God saved you not only *for* heaven but *from* sin. That means sin is no longer your master. Look now to God's Word so that you can serve him in strength and in hope. You may not have been left in charge of a church like Titus was, but you must know what God expects of the church. This will help you judge whether those who serve in the church you attend are guiding you on a path of righteousness or whether they're heading off into dangerous territory. As you read the book of Titus, know that every God Girl must study the Bible to be able to judge for herself the difference between accurate and false teaching.

Must-Know Verses

Train the young women to love their husbands and children, to be self-controlled, pure, working at home, kind, and submissive to their own husbands. *Titus 2:4–5*

Remind them to be submissive to rulers and authorities, to be obedient, to be ready for every good work, to speak evil of no one, to avoid quarreling, to be gentle, and to show perfect courtesy toward all people. *Titus 3:1–2*

He saved us, not because of works done by us in righteousness, but according to his own mercy, by the washing of regeneration and renewal of the Holy Spirit. *Titus 3:5*

The Letter of Paul to

Titus

Greeting

1 Paul, a servant[1] of God and an apostle of Jesus Christ, for the sake of the faith of God's elect and their knowledge of the truth, which accords with godliness, ²in hope of eternal life, which God, who never lies, promised before the ages began[2] ³and at the proper time manifested in his word through the preaching with which I have been entrusted by the command of God our Savior;

⁴To Titus, my true child in a common faith:

Grace and peace from God the Father and Christ Jesus our Savior.

Qualifications for Elders

⁵This is why I left you in Crete, so that you might put what remained into order, and appoint elders in every town as I directed you— ⁶if anyone is above reproach, the husband of one wife,[3] and his children are believers[4] and not open to the charge of debauchery or insubordination. ⁷For an overseer,[5] as God's steward, must be above reproach. He must not be arrogant or quick-tempered or a drunkard or violent or greedy for gain, ⁸but hospitable, a lover of good, self-controlled, upright, holy, and disciplined. ⁹He must hold firm to the trustworthy word as taught, so that he may be able to give instruction in sound[6] doctrine and also to rebuke those who contradict it.

¹⁰For there are many who are insubordinate, empty talkers and deceivers, especially those of the circumcision party.[7] ¹¹They must be silenced, since they are upsetting whole families by teaching for shameful gain what they ought not to teach. ¹²One of the Cretans,[8] a prophet of their own, said, "Cretans are always liars, evil beasts, lazy gluttons."[9] ¹³This testimony is true. Therefore rebuke them sharply, that they may be sound in the faith, ¹⁴not devoting themselves to Jewish myths and the commands of people who turn away from the truth. ¹⁵To the pure, all things are pure, but to the defiled and unbelieving, nothing is pure; but both their minds and their consciences are defiled. ¹⁶They profess to know God, but they deny him by their works. They are detestable, disobedient, unfit for any good work.

Teach Sound Doctrine

2 But as for you, teach what accords with sound[10] doctrine. ²Older men are to be sober-minded, dignified, self-controlled, sound in faith, in love, and in steadfastness. ³Older women likewise are to be reverent in behavior, not slanderers or slaves to much wine. They are to teach what is good, ⁴and so train the young women to love their husbands and children, ⁵to be self-controlled, pure, working at home, kind, and submissive to their own husbands, that the word of God may not be reviled. ⁶Likewise, urge the younger men to be self-controlled. ⁷Show yourself in all respects to be a model of good works, and in your teaching show integrity, dignity, ⁸and sound speech that cannot be condemned, so that an opponent may be put to shame, having nothing evil to say about us. ⁹Bondservants[11] are to be submissive to their own masters in everything; they are to be well-pleasing, not argumentative, ¹⁰not pilfering, but showing all good faith, so that in everything they may adorn the doctrine of God our Savior.

¹¹For the grace of God has appeared, bringing salvation for all people, ¹²training us to renounce ungodliness and worldly passions, and to live self-controlled, upright,

---

[1] Or *slave* (for the contextual rendering of the Greek word *doulos*, see About the ESV) [2] Greek *before times eternal* [3] Or *a man of one woman* [4] Or *are faithful* [5] Or *bishop*; Greek *episkopos* [6] Or *healthy*; also verse 13 [7] Or *especially those of the circumcision* [8] Greek *One of them* [9] Probably from Epimenides of Crete [10] Or *healthy*; also verses 2, 8 [11] Or *Slaves* (for the contextual rendering of the Greek word *doulos*, see About the ESV)

and godly lives in the present age, [13]waiting for our blessed hope, the appearing of the glory of our great God and Savior Jesus Christ, [14]who gave himself for us to redeem us from all lawlessness and to purify for himself a people for his own possession who are zealous for good works.

[15]Declare these things; exhort and rebuke with all authority. Let no one disregard you.

Be Ready for Every Good Work

3 Remind them to be submissive to rulers and authorities, to be obedient, to be ready for every good work, [2]to speak evil of no one, to avoid quarreling, to be gentle, and to show perfect courtesy toward all people. [3]For we ourselves were once foolish, disobedient, led astray, slaves to various passions and pleasures, passing our days in malice and envy, hated by others and hating one another. [4]But when the goodness and loving kindness of God our Savior appeared, [5]he saved us, not because of works done by us in righteousness, but according to his own mercy, by the washing of regeneration and renewal of the Holy Spirit, [6]whom he poured out on us richly through Jesus Christ our Savior, [7]so that being justified by his grace we might become heirs according to the hope of eternal life. [8]The saying is trustworthy, and I want you to insist on these things, so that those who have believed in God may be careful to devote themselves to good works. These things are excellent and profitable for people. [9]But avoid foolish controversies, genealogies, dissensions, and quarrels about the law, for they are unprofitable and worthless. [10]As for a person who stirs up division, after warning him once and then twice, have nothing more to do with him, [11]knowing that such a person is warped and sinful; he is self-condemned.

Final Instructions and Greetings

[12]When I send Artemas or Tychicus to you, do your best to come to me at Nicopolis, for I have decided to spend the winter there. [13]Do your best to speed Zenas the lawyer and Apollos on their way; see that they lack nothing. [14]And let our people

Know How to Communicate

verse to read
Titus 3:2

How you communicate says a lot about you. Most girls love to talk, no question, but how you talk says a lot. Is your speech kind, compassionate, generous, and loving? Or is it sarcastic, bitter, frustrated, or defiant? No matter who you are interacting with and no matter what they say, do, or command you to do, in your reaction you cannot sin. If what they say is unreasonable, vengeful, angry, or slanderous, your words cannot be. Their actions or sins are no excuse for you to sin in return.

Instead, your role is love and kindness. Your role is to speak gently and courteously to everyone. Kind speech demonstrates that you understand how kind God has been to you when you were defiant toward him. When others hear you, do you sound like a God Girl or a griping girl? Do you complain about those who have authority over you? Are you quarrelsome, or are you less concerned about being right than about being faithful?

Fighting is not a characteristic of a God Girl. Fighting is an irritating habit that usually just frustrates and angers those around you. And it is contrary to the fact that you have been saved totally by grace, even when you yourself were frustrating and angering God! If you want to live in light of the gospel and if you want fruitful relationships, then change your speech. Make it kinder, more gentle. When you do, you will prove your love for God and for the people he's put around you.

learn to devote themselves to good works, so as to help cases of urgent need, and not be unfruitful.

[15] All who are with me send greetings to you. Greet those who love us in the faith.

Grace be with you all.

INTRODUCTION TO

Author: The apostle Paul

Time: Around A.D. 60

Place: Probably a Roman prison

Written to: Philemon, Apphia, Archippus, and the church

The gist

Onesimus was a slave who had run away from his owner, Philemon, and had become friends with Paul. In this letter Paul is asking Philemon to forgive Onesimus and to accept him as a brother in Christ.

Things to look for

Paul's teaching on brotherly love (see Philem. 7, 9, 13, 20)

Forgive Others

> For this perhaps is why he was parted from you for a while, that you might have him back forever, no longer as a bondservant but more than a bondservant, as a beloved brother.
>
> *Philemon 15–16*

It's pretty easy to knock people who have hurt you or have stepped on your rights. And it can be just as easy to want to get even with them or find justice, but justice can't be looked at from a human perspective. A lot of times God's justice, true justice, looks like unfairness. The fact that both the girl who has been a faithful believer all her life and the girl who's led the most evil life imaginable can find salvation and full acceptance from the Father is baffling to the human mind. In our lives here on earth we have set up our own ideas of justice and what is right and wrong, but God often has a different idea. His ways are far better than your ways, his thoughts far better than your thoughts, so when things seem unfair and justice doesn't seem to be served, just remember that God's plan is always for your own good. How you react to the situations in life that demand justice, not how you feel about those situations, will determine your holiness.

In this small letter to Philemon we see Paul's plea to convince his fellow believer to accept back someone who has slighted him, his runaway slave—and not only to accept him back but to accept him as a brother, dearly loved. As you read this short book, consider how hard it would be for you to hear something similar to this in your own life. Consider who has offended you or sought to hurt you, and then consider what the proper response for a God Girl should be, as someone who has offended God but has been fully forgiven and restored.

❧ *Onesimus* ❧

A former slave of Philemon and helper of the apostle Paul. The name Onesimus means "useful."

I thank my God always when I remember you in my prayers. *Philemon 4*

I pray that the sharing of your faith may become effective for the full knowledge of every good thing that is in us for the sake of Christ. *Philemon 6*

For this perhaps is why he was parted from you for a while, that you might have him back forever, no longer as a bondservant but more than a bondservant, as a beloved brother. *Philemon 15–16*

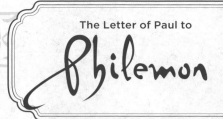

Philemon

Greeting

¹ Paul, a prisoner for Christ Jesus, and Timothy our brother,

To Philemon our beloved fellow worker ²and Apphia our sister and Archippus our fellow soldier, and the church in your house:

³ Grace to you and peace from God our Father and the Lord Jesus Christ.

Philemon's Love and Faith

⁴ I thank my God always when I remember you in my prayers, ⁵because I hear of your love and of the faith that you have toward the Lord Jesus and for all the saints, ⁶and I pray that the sharing of your faith may become effective for the full knowledge of every good thing that is in us for the sake of Christ.¹ ⁷For I have derived much joy and comfort from your love, my brother, because the hearts of the saints have been refreshed through you.

Paul's Plea for Onesimus

⁸ Accordingly, though I am bold enough in Christ to command you to do what is required, ⁹yet for love's sake I prefer to appeal to you—I, Paul, an old man and now a prisoner also for Christ Jesus— ¹⁰I appeal to you for my child, Onesimus,² whose father I became in my imprisonment. ¹¹(Formerly he was useless to you, but now he is indeed useful to you and to me.) ¹²I am sending him back to you, sending my very heart. ¹³I would have been glad to keep him with me, in order that he might serve me on your behalf during my imprisonment for the gospel, ¹⁴but I preferred to do nothing without your consent in order that your goodness might not be by compulsion but of your own accord. ¹⁵For this perhaps is why he was parted from you for a while, that you might have him back forever, ¹⁶no longer as a bondservant³ but more than a bondservant, as a beloved brother—especially to me, but how much more to you, both in the flesh and in the Lord.

¹⁷ So if you consider me your partner, receive him as you would receive me. ¹⁸If he has wronged you at all, or owes you anything, charge that to my account. ¹⁹I, Paul, write this with my own hand: I will repay it—to say nothing of your owing me even your own self. ²⁰Yes, brother, I want some benefit from you in the Lord. Refresh my heart in Christ.

²¹ Confident of your obedience, I write to you, knowing that you will do even more than I say. ²²At the same time, prepare a guest room for me, for I am hoping that through your prayers I will be graciously given to you.

Final Greetings

²³ Epaphras, my fellow prisoner in Christ Jesus, sends greetings to you, ²⁴and so do Mark, Aristarchus, Demas, and Luke, my fellow workers.

²⁵ The grace of the Lord Jesus Christ be with your spirit.

¹ Or for Christ's service ² Onesimus means useful (see verse 11) or beneficial (see verse 20) ³ Or slave; twice in this verse (for the contextual rendering of the Greek word doulos, see About the ESV)

INTRODUCTION TO
Hebrews

Author: Unknown
Time: Around A.D. 64
Place: Unknown
Written to: Probably Jewish Christians in Rome

The gist

Hebrews was written to help people who were starting to question their faith in the midst of persecution. Being used to the Jewish faith, they started to fall back into the old way of thinking that keeping the law and offering sacrifices was the way to be saved. Hebrews points to faith in Christ as the way to salvation.

Things to look for

- The truth about Christ's superiority to even the angels (see Heb. 1:4–7:28)
- Teaching on faith (see Hebrews 11–12)

Have Faith in the Blood

Therefore, brothers, since we have confidence to enter the holy places by the blood of Jesus, by the new and living way that he opened for us through the curtain, that is, through his flesh, and since we have a great priest over the house of God, let us draw near with a true heart in full assurance of faith, with our hearts sprinkled clean from an evil conscience and our bodies washed with pure water.

Hebrews 10:19–22

"I'm not good enough. I just can't do all this Christian stuff. I'm just not perfect." Sometimes it seems like there are so many rules, so much to do in order to be holy—how can you do it all? The answer is that you can't, but God can. For centuries the Jews tried to be good by doing what God commanded them to do, but they just couldn't be perfect. So God did something about it: he sent his Son to be the final sacrifice for all sin. Now, this side of the cross, the commandments still stand, but faith is the answer to your failure to perfectly obey God's Word. When you desire to follow and obey all the commands of God but fail, even daily, you can be sure that you are still accepted by God because of the sacrifice of his Son.

Your faith will grow in direct relationship to your access to God, and Christ is your all-access pass to the Father. Through the forgiveness of sin achieved by the blood of Christ, we all have access to the Father every minute of the day.

The book of Hebrews reminds those who want God's forgiveness and acceptance that it comes only through the supremacy of Christ and our faith in him as Savior. As you read through this book, look also for all the references to the Old Testament and how its prophecies were fulfilled in Christ.

Must-Know Terms and Verses

∞ *Melchizedek* ∞

The king and priest of Salem (probably Jerusalem), who foreshadowed the coming of the Messiah (see Gen. 14:17–20; Ps. 110:4; Hebrews 5–7).

In putting everything in subjection to him, he left nothing outside his control. *Hebrews 2:8*

Because he himself has suffered when tempted, he is able to help those who are being tempted. *Hebrews 2:18*

The word of God is living and active, sharper than any two-edged sword, piercing to the division of soul and of spirit, of joints and of marrow, and discerning the thoughts and intentions of the heart. *Hebrews 4:12*

It is a fearful thing to fall into the hands of the living God. *Hebrews 10:31*

Faith is the assurance of things hoped for, the conviction of things not seen. *Hebrews 11:1*

Do not neglect to show hospitality to strangers, for thereby some have entertained angels unawares. *Hebrews 13:2*

The Letter to the Hebrews

The Supremacy of God's Son

1 Long ago, at many times and in many ways, God spoke to our fathers by the prophets, ²but in these last days he has spoken to us by his Son, whom he appointed the heir of all things, through whom also he created the world. ³He is the radiance of the glory of God and the exact imprint of his nature, and he upholds the universe by the word of his power. After making purification for sins, he sat down at the right hand of the Majesty on high, ⁴having become as much superior to angels as the name he has inherited is more excellent than theirs.

⁵For to which of the angels did God ever say,

> ᵃ"You are my Son,
> today I have begotten you"?

Or again,

> ᵇ"I will be to him a father,
> and he shall be to me a son"?

⁶And again, when he brings the firstborn into the world, he says,

> ᶜ"Let all God's angels worship him."

⁷Of the angels he says,

> ᵈ"He makes his angels winds,
> and his ministers a flame of fire."

⁸But of the Son he says,

> ᵉ"Your throne, O God, is forever and
> ever,
> the scepter of uprightness is the
> scepter of your kingdom.
> ⁹ You have loved righteousness and
> hated wickedness;
> therefore God, your God, has
> anointed you
> with the oil of gladness beyond
> your companions."

¹⁰And,

> ᶠ"You, Lord, laid the foundation of the
> earth in the beginning,
> and the heavens are the work of
> your hands;
> ¹¹ they will perish, but you remain;
> they will all wear out like a gar-
> ment,
> ¹² like a robe you will roll them up,
> like a garment they will be
> changed.¹
> But you are the same,
> and your years will have no end."

¹³And to which of the angels has he ever said,

> ᵍ"Sit at my right hand
> until I make your enemies a foot-
> stool for your feet"?

¹⁴Are they not all ministering spirits sent out to serve for the sake of those who are to inherit salvation?

Warning Against Neglecting Salvation

2 Therefore we must pay much closer attention to what we have heard, lest we drift away from it. ²For since the message declared by angels proved to be reliable, and every transgression or disobedience received a just retribution, ³how shall we escape if we neglect such a great salvation? It was declared at first by the Lord, and it was attested to us by those who heard, ⁴while God also bore witness by signs and wonders and various miracles and by gifts of the Holy Spirit distributed according to his will.

The Founder of Salvation

⁵For it was not to angels that God subjected the world to come, of which we are speaking. ⁶It has been testified somewhere,

¹Some manuscripts omit *like a garment* ᵃPs. 2:7 ᵇ2 Sam. 7:14 ᶜDeut. 32:43 (Gk.) ᵈPs. 104:4 ᵉPs. 45:6, 7 ᶠPs. 102:25-27 ᵍPs. 110:1

^a"What is man, that you are mindful of
him,
    or the son of man, that you care for
    him?
7   You made him for a little while lower
    than the angels;
    you have crowned him with glory
    and honor,¹
8   putting everything in subjection
        under his feet."

Now in putting everything in subjection
to him, he left nothing outside his control.
At present, we do not yet see everything
in subjection to him. ⁹But we see him who
for a little while was made lower than
the angels, namely Jesus, crowned with
glory and honor because of the suffering
of death, so that by the grace of God he
might taste death for everyone.
¹⁰For it was fitting that he, for whom and
by whom all things exist, in bringing many
sons to glory, should make the founder of
their salvation perfect through suffering.
¹¹For he who sanctifies and those who are
sanctified all have one source.² That is why
he is not ashamed to call them brothers,³
¹²saying,

^b"I will tell of your name to my brothers;
    in the midst of the congregation
        I will sing your praise."

¹³And again,

    "I will put my trust in him."

And again,

^c"Behold, I and the children God has
    given me."

¹⁴Since therefore the children share
in flesh and blood, he himself likewise
partook of the same things, that through
death he might destroy the one who has
the power of death, that is, the devil,
¹⁵and deliver all those who through fear
of death were subject to lifelong slavery.
¹⁶For surely it is not angels that he helps,
but he helps the offspring of Abraham.
¹⁷Therefore he had to be made like his
brothers in every respect, so that he might
become a merciful and faithful high priest
in the service of God, to make propitiation

for the sins of the people. ¹⁸For because he
himself has suffered when tempted, he is
able to help those who are being tempted.

Ask Yourself . . .

ABOUT DYING

Hebrews 2:14-15 tells us that because Jesus died for our sins, we
don't need to be afraid of death.
Ask yourself:

• Am I afraid of dying?
• If so, why?
• What is my destiny after
  death?
• Do I trust God with my eternity?
• If not, why not?

Jesus Greater Than Moses

3 Therefore, holy brothers,⁴ you who
share in a heavenly calling, consider
Jesus, the apostle and high priest of our
confession, ²who was faithful to him who
appointed him, just as Moses also was
faithful in all God's⁵ house. ³For Jesus
has been counted worthy of more glory
than Moses—as much more glory as the
builder of a house has more honor than
the house itself. ⁴(For every house is built
by someone, but the builder of all things is
God.) ⁵Now Moses was faithful in all God's
house as a servant, to testify to the things
that were to be spoken later, ⁶but Christ is
faithful over God's house as a son. And we
are his house if indeed we hold fast our
confidence and our boasting in our hope.⁶

A Rest for the People of God

⁷Therefore, as the Holy Spirit says,

^d"Today, if you hear his voice,
8   do not harden your hearts as in the
    rebellion,
        on the day of testing in the wilder-
        ness,

---

¹Some manuscripts insert *and set him over the works of your hands* ²Greek *all are of one* ³Or *brothers and sisters*. The plural Greek word *adelphoi* (translated "brothers") refers to siblings in a family. In New Testament usage, depending on the context, *adelphoi* may refer either to men or to both men and women who are siblings (brothers and sisters) in God's family, the church; also verse 12 ⁴Or *brothers and sisters*; also verse 12 ⁵Greek *his*; also verses 5, 6 ⁶Some manuscripts insert *firm to the end* ^aPs. 8:4-6 ^bPs. 22:22 ^cIsa. 8:18 ^dPs. 95:7-11

9 where your fathers put me to the test
and saw my works for forty years.
10 Therefore I was provoked with that
generation,
and said, 'They always go astray in
their heart;
they have not known my ways.'
11 As I swore in my wrath,
'They shall not enter my rest.'"

12 Take care, brothers, lest there be in any of you an evil, unbelieving heart, leading you to fall away from the living God. 13 But exhort one another every day, as long as it is called "today," that none of you may be hardened by the deceitfulness of sin. 14 For we have come to share in Christ, if indeed we hold our original confidence firm to the end. 15 As it is said,

a"Today, if you hear his voice,
do not harden your hearts as in the
rebellion."

16 For who were those who heard and yet rebelled? Was it not all those who left Egypt led by Moses? 17 And with whom was he provoked for forty years? Was it not with those who sinned, whose bodies fell in the wilderness? 18 And to whom did he swear that they would not enter his rest, but to those who were disobedient? 19 So we see that they were unable to enter because of unbelief.

4 Therefore, while the promise of entering his rest still stands, let us fear lest any of you should seem to have failed to reach it. 2 For good news came to us just as to them, but the message they heard did not benefit them, because they were not united by faith with those who listened.[1] 3 For we who have believed enter that rest, as he has said,

b"As I swore in my wrath,
'They shall not enter my rest,'"

although his works were finished from the foundation of the world. 4 For he has somewhere spoken of the seventh day in this way: c"And God rested on the seventh day from all his works." 5 And again in this passage he said,

d"They shall not enter my rest."

6 Since therefore it remains for some to enter it, and those who formerly received the good news failed to enter because of disobedience, 7 again he appoints a certain day, "Today," saying through David so long afterward, in the words already quoted,

e"Today, if you hear his voice,
do not harden your hearts."

8 For if Joshua had given them rest, God[2] would not have spoken of another day later on. 9 So then, there remains a Sabbath rest for the people of God, 10 for whoever has entered God's rest has also rested from his works as God did from his.

11 Let us therefore strive to enter that rest, so that no one may fall by the same sort of disobedience. 12 For the word of God is living and active, sharper than any two-edged sword, piercing to the division of soul and of spirit, of joints and of marrow, and discerning the thoughts and intentions of the heart. 13 And no creature is hidden from his sight, but all are naked and exposed to the eyes of him to whom we must give account.

Jesus the Great High Priest

14 Since then we have a great high priest who has passed through the heavens, Jesus, the Son of God, let us hold fast our confession. 15 For we do not have a high priest who is unable to sympathize with our weaknesses, but one who in every respect has been tempted as we are, yet without sin. 16 Let us then with confidence draw near to the throne of grace, that we may receive mercy and find grace to help in time of need.

5 For every high priest chosen from among men is appointed to act on behalf of men in relation to God, to offer gifts and sacrifices for sins. 2 He can deal gently with the ignorant and wayward, since he himself is beset with weakness. 3 Because of this he is obligated to offer sacrifice for his own sins just as he does for those of the people. 4 And no one takes this honor for himself, but only when called by God, just as Aaron was.

5 So also Christ did not exalt himself to be made a high priest, but was appointed by him who said to him,

---

[1] Some manuscripts *it did not meet with faith in the hearers* [2] Greek *he* a Ps. 95:7, 8 b Ps. 95:11 c Gen. 2:2 d Ps. 95:11 e Ps. 95:7, 8

[a]"You are my Son,
today I have begotten you";

[6] as he says also in another place,

[b]"You are a priest forever,
after the order of Melchizedek."

[7] In the days of his flesh, Jesus[1] offered up prayers and supplications, with loud cries and tears, to him who was able to save him from death, and he was heard because of his reverence. [8] Although he was a son, he learned obedience through what he suffered. [9] And being made perfect, he became the source of eternal salvation to all who obey him, [10] being designated by God a high priest after the order of Melchizedek.

Warning Against Apostasy

[11] About this we have much to say, and it is hard to explain, since you have become dull of hearing. [12] For though by this time you ought to be teachers, you need someone to teach you again the basic principles of the oracles of God. You need milk, not solid food, [13] for everyone who lives on milk is unskilled in the word of righteousness, since he is a child. [14] But solid food is for the mature, for those who have their powers of discernment trained by constant practice to distinguish good from evil.

6 Therefore let us leave the elementary doctrine of Christ and go on to maturity, not laying again a foundation of repentance from dead works and of faith toward God, [2] and of instruction about washings,[2] the laying on of hands, the resurrection of the dead, and eternal judgment. [3] And this we will do if God permits. [4] For it is impossible, in the case of those who have once been enlightened, who have tasted the heavenly gift, and have shared in the Holy Spirit, [5] and have tasted the goodness of the word of God and the powers of the age to come, [6] and then have fallen away, to restore them again to repentance, since they are crucifying once again the Son of God to their own harm and holding him up to contempt. [7] For land that has drunk the rain that often falls on it, and produces a crop useful to those for whose sake it is cultivated, receives a blessing from God. [8] But if it bears thorns and thistles, it is worthless and near to being cursed, and its end is to be burned.

[1] Greek he [2] Or baptisms (that is, cleansing rites) [a] Ps. 2:7 [b] Ps. 110:4

verses to read
Hebrews 4:12–13

Depending on what you need, the Word of God can hurt or heal. The healing is obvious. When you are aching, fearful, or lonely, and you read about God's faithfulness and love and you are comforted, that's obvious, a no-brainer. But when it's time for a revelation in your life, when the old you is still lurking around and the new you needs to come out, God's Word can hurt. Its job is to divide soul and spirit, joints and marrow, and no other pain is so deep.

The beauty of the sting of God's Word is that it makes you desperate for God's help. Nothing else seems important, and you're finally willing to let go of the old you. Through this pain, truth sinks into your gut, moves deeper into you, and changes you.

If God's Word isn't "asking too much of you" or breaking your heart, then you're not letting God fully reveal himself to you. Don't run from the pain of revelation; receive it. Only when you're cut open and uncovered, laid bare before him, will you know without a doubt that you have been touched by the Word of God. So don't be afraid of what he'll ask of you, but look for it with hope and excitement, knowing that out of this painful process will come the glory of your soul.

[9] Though we speak in this way, yet in your case, beloved, we feel sure of better things—things that belong to salvation. [10] For God is not unjust so as to overlook your work and the love that you have shown for his name in serving the saints, as you still do. [11] And we desire each one of you to show the same earnestness to have the full assurance of hope until the end, [12] so that you may not be sluggish, but imitators of those who through faith and patience inherit the promises.

The Certainty of God's Promise

[13] For when God made a promise to Abraham, since he had no one greater by whom to swear, he swore by himself, [14] saying, [a] "Surely I will bless you and multiply you." [15] And thus Abraham,[1] having patiently waited, obtained the promise. [16] For people swear by something greater than themselves, and in all their disputes an oath is final for confirmation. [17] So when God desired to show more convincingly to the heirs of the promise the unchangeable character of his purpose, he guaranteed it with an oath, [18] so that by two unchangeable things, in which it is impossible for God to lie, we who have fled for refuge might have strong encouragement to hold fast to the hope set before us. [19] We have this as a sure and steadfast anchor of the soul, a hope that enters into the inner place behind the curtain, [20] where Jesus has gone as a forerunner on our behalf, having become a high priest forever after the order of Melchizedek.

The Priestly Order of Melchizedek

7 For this Melchizedek, king of Salem, priest of the Most High God, met Abraham returning from the slaughter of the kings and blessed him, [2] and to him Abraham apportioned a tenth part of everything. He is first, by translation of his name, king of righteousness, and then he is also king of Salem, that is, king of peace. [3] He is without father or mother or genealogy, having neither beginning of days nor end of life, but resembling the Son of God he continues a priest forever.

[4] See how great this man was to whom Abraham the patriarch gave a tenth of the spoils! [5] And those descendants of Levi who receive the priestly office have a commandment in the law to take tithes from the people, that is, from their brothers,[2] though these also are descended from Abraham. [6] But this man who does not have his descent from them received tithes from Abraham and blessed him who had the promises. [7] It is beyond dispute that the inferior is blessed by the superior. [8] In the one case tithes are received by mortal men, but in the other case, by one of whom it is testified that he lives. [9] One might even say that Levi himself, who receives tithes, paid tithes through Abraham, [10] for he was still in the loins of his ancestor when Melchizedek met him.

Jesus Compared to Melchizedek

[11] Now if perfection had been attainable through the Levitical priesthood (for under it the people received the law), what further need would there have been for another priest to arise after the order of Melchizedek, rather than one named after the order of Aaron? [12] For when there is a change in the priesthood, there is necessarily a change in the law as well. [13] For the one of whom these things are spoken belonged to another tribe, from which no one has ever served at the altar. [14] For it is evident that our Lord was descended from Judah, and in connection with that tribe Moses said nothing about priests.

[15] This becomes even more evident when another priest arises in the likeness of Melchizedek, [16] who has become a priest, not on the basis of a legal requirement concerning bodily descent, but by the power of an indestructible life. [17] For it is witnessed of him,

[b] "You are a priest forever,
    after the order of Melchizedek."

[18] For on the one hand, a former commandment is set aside because of its weakness and uselessness [19] (for the law made nothing perfect); but on the other hand, a better hope is introduced, through which we draw near to God.

[20] And it was not without an oath. For those who formerly became priests were made such without an oath, [21] but this one was made a priest with an oath by the one who said to him:

---

[1] Greek *he* [2] Or *brothers and sisters* [a] Gen. 22:17 [b] Ps. 110:4

[a]"The Lord has sworn
    and will not change his mind,
  'You are a priest forever.'"

22 This makes Jesus the guarantor of a better covenant.

23 The former priests were many in number, because they were prevented by death from continuing in office, **24** but he holds his priesthood permanently, because he continues forever. **25** Consequently, he is able to save to the uttermost[1] those who draw near to God through him, since he always lives to make intercession for them.

26 For it was indeed fitting that we should have such a high priest, holy, innocent, unstained, separated from sinners, and exalted above the heavens. **27** He has no need, like those high priests, to offer sacrifices daily, first for his own sins and then for those of the people, since he did this once for all when he offered up himself. **28** For the law appoints men in their weakness as high priests, but the word of the oath, which came later than the law, appoints a Son who has been made perfect forever.

Jesus, High Priest of a Better Covenant

8 Now the point in what we are saying is this: we have such a high priest, one who is seated at the right hand of the throne of the Majesty in heaven, **2** a minister in the holy places, in the true tent[2] that the Lord set up, not man. **3** For every high priest is appointed to offer gifts and sacrifices; thus it is necessary for this priest also to have something to offer. **4** Now if he were on earth, he would not be a priest at all, since there are priests who offer gifts according to the law. **5** They serve a copy and shadow of the heavenly things. For when Moses was about to erect the tent, he was instructed by God, saying, [b]"See that you make everything according to the pattern that was shown you on the mountain." **6** But as it is, Christ[3] has obtained a ministry that is as much more excellent than the old as the covenant he mediates is better, since it is enacted on better promises. **7** For if that first covenant had been faultless, there would have been no occasion to look for a second.

8 For he finds fault with them when he says:[4]

[c]"Behold, the days are coming, declares the Lord,
    when I will establish a new covenant with the house of Israel
    and with the house of Judah,
9 not like the covenant that I made
        with their fathers
    on the day when I took them by the
        hand to bring them out of the
        land of Egypt.
  For they did not continue in my covenant,
    and so I showed no concern for
        them, declares the Lord.
10 For this is the covenant that I will
        make with the house of Israel
    after those days, declares the Lord:
  I will put my laws into their minds,
    and write them on their hearts,
  and I will be their God,
    and they shall be my people.
11 And they shall not teach, each one
        his neighbor
    and each one his brother, saying,
        'Know the Lord,'
  for they shall all know me,
    from the least of them to the greatest.
12 For I will be merciful toward their
        iniquities,
    and I will remember their sins no
        more."

13 In speaking of a new covenant, he makes the first one obsolete. And what is becoming obsolete and growing old is ready to vanish away.

The Earthly Holy Place

9 Now even the first covenant had regulations for worship and an earthly place of holiness. **2** For a tent[5] was prepared, the first section, in which were the lampstand and the table and the bread of the Presence.[6] It is called the Holy Place. **3** Behind the second curtain was a second section[7] called the Most Holy Place, **4** having the golden altar of incense and the ark of the covenant covered on all sides with gold, in which was a golden urn holding the manna, and Aaron's staff that budded, and the tablets of the covenant. **5** Above it were the cherubim of glory overshadowing the mercy seat. Of these things we cannot now speak in detail.

---

[1] That is, completely; or at all times [2] Or tabernacle; also verse 5 [3] Greek he [4] Some manuscripts For finding fault with it he says to them
[5] Or tabernacle; also verses 11, 21 [6] Greek the presentation of the loaves [7] Greek tent; also verses 6, 8 [a] Ps. 110:4 [b] Ex. 25:40 [c] Jer. 31:31-34

⁶These preparations having thus been made, the priests go regularly into the first section, performing their ritual duties, ⁷but into the second only the high priest goes, and he but once a year, and not without taking blood, which he offers for himself and for the unintentional sins of the people. ⁸By this the Holy Spirit indicates that the way into the holy places is not yet opened as long as the first section is still standing ⁹(which is symbolic for the present age).¹ According to this arrangement, gifts and sacrifices are offered that cannot perfect the conscience of the worshiper, ¹⁰but deal only with food and drink and various washings, regulations for the body imposed until the time of reformation.

Redemption Through the Blood of Christ

¹¹But when Christ appeared as a high priest of the good things that have come,² then through the greater and more perfect tent (not made with hands, that is, not of this creation) ¹²he entered once for all into the holy places, not by means of the blood of goats and calves but by means of his own blood, thus securing an eternal redemption. ¹³For if the blood of goats and bulls, and the sprinkling of defiled persons with the ashes of a heifer, sanctify³ for the purification of the flesh, ¹⁴how much more will the blood of Christ, who through the eternal Spirit offered himself without blemish to God, purify our⁴ conscience from dead works to serve the living God.

¹⁵Therefore he is the mediator of a new covenant, so that those who are called may receive the promised eternal inheritance, since a death has occurred that redeems them from the transgressions committed under the first covenant.⁵ ¹⁶For where a will is involved, the death of the one who made it must be established. ¹⁷For a will takes effect only at death, since it is not in force as long as the one who made it is alive. ¹⁸Therefore not even the first covenant was inaugurated without blood. ¹⁹For when every commandment of the law had been declared by Moses to all the people, he took the blood of calves and goats, with water and scarlet wool and hyssop, and sprinkled both the book itself and all the people, ²⁰saying, ᵃ"This is the blood of the covenant that God commanded for you." ²¹And in the same way he sprinkled with the blood both the tent and all the vessels used in worship. ²²Indeed, under the law almost everything is purified with blood, and without the shedding of blood there is no forgiveness of sins.

²³Thus it was necessary for the copies of the heavenly things to be purified with these rites, but the heavenly things themselves with better sacrifices than these. ²⁴For Christ has entered, not into holy places made with hands, which are copies of the true things, but into heaven itself, now to appear in the presence of God on our behalf. ²⁵Nor was it to offer himself repeatedly, as the high priest enters the holy places every year with blood not his own, ²⁶for then he would have had to suffer repeatedly since the foundation of the world. But as it is, he has appeared once for all at the end of the ages to put away sin by the sacrifice of himself. ²⁷And just as it is appointed for man to die once, and after that comes judgment, ²⁸so Christ, having been offered once to bear the sins of many, will appear a second time, not to deal with sin but to save those who are eagerly waiting for him.

Christ's Sacrifice Once for All

10 For since the law has but a shadow of the good things to come instead of the true form of these realities, it can never, by the same sacrifices that are continually offered every year, make perfect those who draw near. ²Otherwise, would they not have ceased to be offered, since the worshipers, having once been cleansed, would no longer have any consciousness of sins? ³But in these sacrifices there is a reminder of sins every year. ⁴For it is impossible for the blood of bulls and goats to take away sins.

⁵Consequently, when Christ⁶ came into the world, he said,

ᵇ"Sacrifices and offerings you have not
    desired,
  but a body have you prepared for
    me;
⁶   in burnt offerings and sin offerings
    you have taken no pleasure.

---

¹Or which is symbolic for the age then present ²Some manuscripts good things to come ³Or For if the sprinkling of defiled persons with the blood of goats and bulls and with the ashes of a heifer sanctifies ⁴Some manuscripts your ⁵The Greek word means both covenant and will; also verses 16, 17 ⁶Greek he ᵃEx. 24:8 ᵇPs. 40:6-8

7 Then I said, 'Behold, I have come to
　　do your will, O God,
　　as it is written of me in the scroll
　　　of the book.'"

8 When he said above, "You have neither
desired nor taken pleasure in sacrifices
and offerings and burnt offerings and sin
offerings" (these are offered according to
the law), 9 then he added, "Behold, I have
come to do your will." He does away with
the first in order to establish the second.
10 And by that will we have been sanctified
through the offering of the body of Jesus
Christ once for all.

11 And every priest stands daily at his
service, offering repeatedly the same sacrifices, which can never take away sins.
12 But when Christ[1] had offered for all time
a single sacrifice for sins, he sat down at
the right hand of God, 13 waiting from that
time until his enemies should be made a
footstool for his feet. 14 For by a single offering he has perfected for all time those who
are being sanctified.

15 And the Holy Spirit also bears witness
to us; for after saying,

16 [a]"This is the covenant that I will make
　　with them
　　after those days, declares the
　　　Lord:

---

[1] Greek this one [2] Or brothers and sisters [a] Jer. 31:33 [b] Jer. 31:34

I will put my laws on their hearts,
　　and write them on their minds,"

17 then he adds,

[b]"I will remember their sins and their
　　lawless deeds no more."

18 Where there is forgiveness of these, there
is no longer any offering for sin.

The Full Assurance of Faith

19 Therefore, brothers,[2] since we have
confidence to enter the holy places by the
blood of Jesus, 20 by the new and living
way that he opened for us through the
curtain, that is, through his flesh, 21 and
since we have a great priest over the house
of God, 22 let us draw near with a true heart
in full assurance of faith, with our hearts
sprinkled clean from an evil conscience
and our bodies washed with pure water.
23 Let us hold fast the confession of our
hope without wavering, for he who promised is faithful. 24 And let us consider how
to stir up one another to love and good
works, 25 not neglecting to meet together,
as is the habit of some, but encouraging
one another, and all the more as you see
the Day drawing near.

26 For if we go on sinning deliberately
after receiving the knowledge of the truth,

Know Love

verses to read
Hebrews 10:8–10

The blood of Jesus makes you holy. Because he was willing to be the sacrifice
for your sin, you are no longer a lost sinner but have become a saint. But what
does that mean? Do you feel holy? Are you now sin-free? Doesn't holiness require perfection? It seems like the Bible contradicts itself when it says "none is
righteous, no, not one" (Rom. 3:10) and then in the next breath says that you
were "sanctified" by the sacrifice of Jesus (Heb. 10:10). How can you be both a
sinner and a saint?

The answer is this: Jesus' death and resurrection makes you righteous in the
eyes of God. It gives you access to the Father and justifies you. In this sense, you
are innocent before God, because Jesus took your punishment for you. But this
doesn't make your character holy. You still have sinful tendencies. You still fall and
get back up. Your character will become more holy as you confront the sin in your
life and kill it by the power of the Spirit, living out of your new nature.

there no longer remains a sacrifice for sins, ²⁷ but a fearful expectation of judgment, and a fury of fire that will consume the adversaries. ²⁸ Anyone who has set aside the law of Moses dies without mercy on the evidence of two or three witnesses. ²⁹ How much worse punishment, do you think, will be deserved by the one who has trampled underfoot the Son of God, and has profaned the blood of the covenant by which he was sanctified, and has outraged the Spirit of grace? ³⁰ For we know him who said, ᵃ"Vengeance is mine; I will repay." And again, ᵇ"The Lord will judge his people." ³¹ It is a fearful thing to fall into the hands of the living God.

³² But recall the former days when, after you were enlightened, you endured a hard struggle with sufferings, ³³ sometimes being publicly exposed to reproach and affliction, and sometimes being partners with those so treated. ³⁴ For you had compassion on those in prison, and you joyfully accepted the plundering of your property, since you knew that you yourselves had a better possession and an abiding one. ³⁵ Therefore do not throw away your confidence, which has a great reward. ³⁶ For you have need of endurance, so that when you have done the will of God you may receive what is promised. ³⁷ For,

> "Yet a little while,
>   and ᶜthe coming one will come and
>   will not delay;
> ³⁸ but my righteous one shall live by
>   faith,
>   and if he shrinks back,
> my soul has no pleasure in him."

³⁹ But we are not of those who shrink back and are destroyed, but of those who have faith and preserve their souls.

By Faith

11 Now faith is the assurance of things hoped for, the conviction of things not seen. ² For by it the people of old received their commendation. ³ By faith we understand that the universe was created by the word of God, so that what is seen was not made out of things that are visible.

⁴ By faith Abel offered to God a more acceptable sacrifice than Cain, through which he was commended as righteous, God commending him by accepting his gifts. And through his faith, though he died, he still speaks. ⁵ By faith Enoch was taken up so that he should not see death, and he was not found, because God had taken him. Now before he was taken he was commended as having pleased God. ⁶ And without faith it is impossible to please him, for whoever would draw near to God must believe that he exists and that he rewards those who seek him. ⁷ By faith Noah, being warned by God concerning events as yet unseen, in reverent fear constructed an ark for the saving of his household. By this he condemned the world and became an heir of the righteousness that comes by faith.

⁸ By faith Abraham obeyed when he was called to go out to a place that he was to receive as an inheritance. And he went out, not knowing where he was going. ⁹ By faith he went to live in the land of promise, as in a foreign land, living in tents with Isaac and Jacob, heirs with him of the same promise. ¹⁰ For he was looking forward to the city that has foundations, whose designer and builder is God. ¹¹ By faith Sarah herself received power to conceive, even when she was past the age, since she considered him faithful who had promised. ¹² Therefore from one man, and him as good as dead, were born descendants as many as the stars of heaven and as many as the innumerable grains of sand by the seashore.

¹³ These all died in faith, not having received the things promised, but having seen them and greeted them from afar, and having acknowledged that they were strangers and exiles on the earth. ¹⁴ For people who speak thus make it clear that they are seeking a homeland. ¹⁵ If they had been thinking of that land from which they had gone out, they would have had opportunity to return. ¹⁶ But as it is, they desire a better country, that is, a heavenly one. Therefore God is not ashamed to be called their God, for he has prepared for them a city.

¹⁷ By faith Abraham, when he was tested, offered up Isaac, and he who had received the promises was in the act of offering up his only son, ¹⁸ of whom it was said, ᵈ"Through Isaac shall your offspring be named." ¹⁹ He considered that God was able even to raise him from the dead, from which, figuratively speaking, he did receive

ᵃ Deut. 32:35 ᵇ Deut. 32:36 ᶜ Hab. 2:3, 4 ᵈ Gen. 21:12

him back. **20** By faith Isaac invoked future blessings on Jacob and Esau. **21** By faith Jacob, when dying, blessed each of the sons of Joseph, bowing in worship over the head of his staff. **22** By faith Joseph, at the end of his life, made mention of the exodus of the Israelites and gave directions concerning his bones.

23 By faith Moses, when he was born, was hidden for three months by his parents, because they saw that the child was beautiful, and they were not afraid of the king's edict. **24** By faith Moses, when he was grown up, refused to be called the son of Pharaoh's daughter, **25** choosing rather to be mistreated with the people of God than to enjoy the fleeting pleasures of sin. **26** He considered the reproach of Christ greater wealth than the treasures of Egypt, for he was looking to the reward. **27** By faith he left Egypt, not being afraid of the anger of the king, for he endured as seeing him

who is invisible. **28** By faith he kept the Passover and sprinkled the blood, so that the Destroyer of the firstborn might not touch them.

29 By faith the people crossed the Red Sea as on dry land, but the Egyptians, when they attempted to do the same, were drowned. **30** By faith the walls of Jericho fell down after they had been encircled for seven days. **31** By faith Rahab the prostitute did not perish with those who were disobedient, because she had given a friendly welcome to the spies.

32 And what more shall I say? For time would fail me to tell of Gideon, Barak, Samson, Jephthah, of David and Samuel and the prophets— **33** who through faith conquered kingdoms, enforced justice, obtained promises, stopped the mouths of lions, **34** quenched the power of fire, escaped the edge of the sword, were made strong out of weakness, became mighty in

Know Yourself

verses to read
Hebrews 11:1–2

Your life is filled with so many things that are a given and so many people who have everything planned out for you—your parents, your teachers, your friends. But what happens when you're faced with the unknown? When the future's not a given but a big old question mark? Do you freak?

Living with everything figured out is a piece of cake, but having no clue what's going to happen next leaves you with nothing but faith. Your future might be unknown, but your God is well known. Don't let an uncertain tomorrow erase what you know about God, and that is that he is in control of it all. No matter what you know or don't know, and no matter who attempts to intervene, he's still the ultimate authority in the life of the believer. You may be unsure of what's coming next in the journey of life, but big whoop—you *are* sure of God! And that means you can be sure of his protection and peace.

The evidence of the spiritual life in you is when your heart is okay living with the unknown, because the unknown is where faith lives. Without a few mysteries in life, your faith would be weak and useless, because it wouldn't be convinced of "things not seen." So don't freak when life seems all foggy and iffy, because those moments when you don't know what comes next are when your faith gets stronger and your belief gets a boost of encouragement. Without faith in Christ you would be like the nonbeliever, all worried about tomorrow and using all your energy to make sure there were never any unknowns. Be different! Accept the idea of uncertainty in your life, look to the one who is certain, and life will be a great adventure.

war, put foreign armies to flight. ³⁵Women received back their dead by resurrection. Some were tortured, refusing to accept release, so that they might rise again to a better life. ³⁶Others suffered mocking and flogging, and even chains and imprisonment. ³⁷They were stoned, they were sawn in two,¹ they were killed with the sword. They went about in skins of sheep and goats, destitute, afflicted, mistreated— ³⁸of whom the world was not worthy—wandering about in deserts and mountains, and in dens and caves of the earth.

³⁹And all these, though commended through their faith, did not receive what was promised, ⁴⁰since God had provided something better for us, that apart from us they should not be made perfect.

Jesus, Founder and Perfecter of Our Faith

12 Therefore, since we are surrounded by so great a cloud of witnesses, let us also lay aside every weight, and sin which clings so closely, and let us run with endurance the race that is set before us, looking to Jesus, the founder and perfecter of our faith, who for the joy that was set before him endured the cross, despising the shame, and is seated at the right hand of the throne of God.

Do Not Grow Weary

³Consider him who endured from sinners such hostility against himself, so that you may not grow weary or fainthearted. ⁴In your struggle against sin you have not yet resisted to the point of shedding your blood. ⁵And have you forgotten the exhortation that addresses you as sons?

ᵃ"My son, do not regard lightly the
    discipline of the Lord,
nor be weary when reproved by
    him.
⁶ For the Lord disciplines the one he
    loves,
and chastises every son whom he
    receives."

⁷It is for discipline that you have to endure. God is treating you as sons. For what son is there whom his father does not discipline? ⁸If you are left without discipline, in which all have participated, then you are illegitimate children and not sons. ⁹Besides this, we have had earthly fathers who disciplined us and we respected them. Shall we not much more be subject to the Father of spirits and live? ¹⁰For they disciplined us for a short time as it seemed best to them, but he disciplines us for our good, that we

Some manuscripts add *they were tempted* ᵃProv. 3:11, 12

Know True Happiness

verses to read
Hebrews 12:7-11

When you ask God for help with something that just won't go away and you see no change, maybe it's because you're looking in the wrong place. A lot of times the trouble in your life is something sent by God as discipline for your sin. As Hebrews 12:7-8 says, "It is for discipline that you have to endure. God is treating you as sons. For what son is there whom his father does not discipline? If you are left without discipline, in which all have participated, then you are illegitimate children and not sons." So be thankful for the trials in your life, especially when they are discipline pointing to a particular sin that you were previously oblivious to.

Don't ignore this stuff anymore. Hidden sins must be located and rooted out. But at the same time, take heart. If your progress in the faith is as slow as molasses, calm down and remember what is true in the gospel. If you are united to Christ, if you are trusting Christ to save you instead of trying to save yourself, be at peace. God will bring you through to the end. You will one day be restored to the glory you long for, the glory we all lost because of sin (see Rom. 3:23).

may share his holiness. **11** For the moment all discipline seems painful rather than pleasant, but later it yields the peaceful fruit of righteousness to those who have been trained by it.

12 Therefore lift your drooping hands and strengthen your weak knees, **13** and make straight paths for your feet, so that what is lame may not be put out of joint but rather be healed. **14** Strive for peace with everyone, and for the holiness without which no one will see the Lord. **15** See to it that no one fails to obtain the grace of God; that no "root of bitterness" springs up and causes trouble, and by it many become defiled; **16** that no one is sexually immoral or unholy like Esau, who sold his birthright for a single meal. **17** For you know that afterward, when he desired to inherit the blessing, he was rejected, for

¹ Or *church* ªEx. 19:12, 13

he found no chance to repent, though he sought it with tears.

A Kingdom That Cannot Be Shaken

18 For you have not come to what may be touched, a blazing fire and darkness and gloom and a tempest **19** and the sound of a trumpet and a voice whose words made the hearers beg that no further messages be spoken to them. **20** For they could not endure the order that was given, ª"If even a beast touches the mountain, it shall be stoned." **21** Indeed, so terrifying was the sight that Moses said, "I tremble with fear." **22** But you have come to Mount Zion and to the city of the living God, the heavenly Jerusalem, and to innumerable angels in festal gathering, **23** and to the assembly¹ of the firstborn who are enrolled in heaven, and to God, the judge of all, and to the spir

Know Love

verses to read
Hebrews 13:1–3

Strangers are strange. You don't know them, they don't know you, and who knows what they're like or what they'll say if you say hi or start talking to them? Eek! Yep, fear of the unknown can keep you from reaching out to others. You see their need but you fear their presence, so you walk away, and we all end up alone in the crowd. And you fail to do what God says is the greatest thing you could ever do: love others as yourself.

But guess what? Strangers are around you for a reason. And you'll never know that reason until you get your eyes off the ground and notice them—but don't just notice them; invite them into your life. How can you share the love of God with someone you're afraid to talk to, in light of the love God has shared with you? How can you help when you're afraid to reach out? You can't make friends with everyone, obviously, but you can take a risk and reach out to other girls who cross your path on a regular basis, like that girl who sits next to you on the bus but never looks at you, or that neighbor you see at the mailbox but never talk to. Remember, God reached out to you and made friends with you when you were his determined enemy.

If you want to be a bridge to God for a dying world, then you've gotta open yourself up and offer the same kindness and compassion to strangers that God has offered to you. This isn't just a good idea; it's a command: "Do not neglect to show hospitality to strangers" (Heb. 13:2). Be willing to trust God and to step out, even though you totally fear the person's response. This life is not about how they're going to respond but about how you respond to God's call to love. Be brave, God Girl, and you will most definitely be rewarded!

ts of the righteous made perfect, 24 and to esus, the mediator of a new covenant, and o the sprinkled blood that speaks a better vord than the blood of Abel.

25 See that you do not refuse him who is peaking. For if they did not escape when hey refused him who warned them on arth, much less will we escape if we reject im who warns from heaven. 26 At that time iis voice shook the earth, but now he has promised, a "Yet once more I will shake not only the earth but also the heavens." 27 This phrase, "Yet once more," indicates the emoval of things that are shaken—that s, things that have been made—in order hat the things that cannot be shaken may emain. 28 Therefore let us be grateful for eceiving a kingdom that cannot be shaken, nd thus let us offer to God acceptable worhip, with reverence and awe, 29 for our God s a consuming fire.

acrifices Pleasing to God

13 Let brotherly love continue. 2 Do not neglect to show hospitality to trangers, for thereby some have enterained angels unawares. 3 Remember those vho are in prison, as though in prison with hem, and those who are mistreated, since ou also are in the body. 4 Let marriage pe held in honor among all, and let the narriage bed be undefiled, for God will udge the sexually immoral and adulterous. Keep your life free from love of money, nd be content with what you have, for ie has said, b "I will never leave you nor orsake you." 6 So we can confidently say,

c "The Lord is my helper;
    I will not fear;
    what can man do to me?"

7 Remember your leaders, those who poke to you the word of God. Consider he outcome of their way of life, and imitate heir faith. 8 Jesus Christ is the same yesterlay and today and forever. 9 Do not be led iway by diverse and strange teachings, for t is good for the heart to be strengthened by grace, not by foods, which have not ben-

efited those devoted to them. 10 We have an altar from which those who serve the tent have no right to eat. 11 For the bodies of those animals whose blood is brought into the holy places by the high priest as a sacrifice for sin are burned outside the camp. 12 So Jesus also suffered outside the gate in order to sanctify the people through his own blood. 13 Therefore let us go to him outside the camp and bear the reproach he endured. 14 For here we have no lasting city, but we seek the city that is to come. 15 Through him then let us continually offer up a sacrifice of praise to God, that is, the fruit of lips that acknowledge his name. 16 Do not neglect to do good and to share what you have, for such sacrifices are pleasing to God.

17 Obey your leaders and submit to them, for they are keeping watch over your souls, as those who will have to give an account. Let them do this with joy and not with groaning, for that would be of no advantage to you.

18 Pray for us, for we are sure that we have a clear conscience, desiring to act honorably in all things. 19 I urge you the more earnestly to do this in order that I may be restored to you the sooner.

Benediction

20 Now may the God of peace who brought again from the dead our Lord Jesus, the great shepherd of the sheep, by the blood of the eternal covenant, 21 equip you with everything good that you may do his will, working in us[1] that which is pleasing in his sight, through Jesus Christ, to whom be glory forever and ever. Amen.

Final Greetings

22 I appeal to you, brothers,[2] bear with my word of exhortation, for I have written to you briefly. 23 You should know that our brother Timothy has been released, with whom I shall see you if he comes soon. 24 Greet all your leaders and all the saints. Those who come from Italy send you greetings. 25 Grace be with all of you.

Some manuscripts you [2] Or brothers and sisters [a] Hag. 2:6 [b] Josh. 1:5 [c] Ps. 118:6

Author: James, half brother of Jesus

Time: Possibly around A.D. 46, though some say later

Place: Unknown

Written to: Jewish Christians scattered all over the world

The gist

The main lesson found in James is about real faith. James teaches how faith proves itself through works. This is a very practical book for the Christian life, giving all kinds of essential training for making your way through life as a God Girl.

Things to look for

- The wisdom summarized in the section headings in this book

- Teaching about when you are tested (see James 1:2–15; 5:7–11)

- Advice about money (see James 1:9–11; 4:1–3; 5:1–6)

- Instruction about speaking wisely (see James 1:19–26; 3:1–12; 4:11–16)

Show Your Good Works

> You see that a person is justified by works and not by faith alone.
>
> James 2:24

Contrary to popular belief, Jesus wasn't half human and half divine; he was one hundred percent of both. He was equal to God but he "did not count equality with God a thing to be grasped" but as a human he "emptied himself, by taking the form of a servant" (Phil. 2:6–7). When you look at the life of Jesus and the commands of Scripture, you can't use your humanity as an excuse for not getting it right. Jesus never used his divinity to get through the hard parts of life. He didn't overcome temptation in the desert or come down from the cross by virtue of his divine nature. When human trials came his way, he survived them as a human in dependence on the Spirit so that you would have not only a sympathetic God but also a perfect example of holiness on earth, human style.

The good news for you is this: the life of Jesus proves that you can do it too as you depend on the Spirit. You *can* overcome temptation (see 1 Cor. 10:13); you *can* love God no matter what; you *can* resist the Devil—because if Jesus could do it, so can you, by the power of the Holy Spirit.

A recurring theme in James is that "faith apart from works is useless" (James 2:20). Now, this doesn't contradict the fact that your faith saved you, but it does contradict the idea that a dead kind of faith can save you. Nope. Believing is not all there is to it—if by "believing" all you mean is agreeing to certain truths with your head. As James puts it, "You believe that God is one; you do well. Even the demons believe—and shudder! Do you want to be shown, you foolish person, that faith apart from works is useless?" (James 2:19–20). Ouch! James is pretty adamant here that faith is what saves us, but only a certain kind of faith—true faith, living faith. As you read through James, look for all the ways that faith comes to life in a believer.

Must-Know Terms and Verses

∽ Works ∽

The things you do, your actions, those things that people can see. They are considered good works if they are done out of a motive to love and serve God, i.e., obedience. Bad works are things people do out of disobedience. You can know a person's faith by his or her works (see Matt. 5:16; 1 Cor. 3:14; Eph. 2:10; 5:11; 2 Tim. 2:21; 1 John 2:4–5).

Count it all joy, my brothers, when you meet trials of various kinds, for you know that the testing of your faith produces steadfastness. And let steadfastness have its full effect, that you may be perfect and complete, lacking in nothing. *James 1:2–4*

Each person is tempted when he is lured and enticed by his own desire. Then desire when it has conceived gives birth to sin, and sin when it is fully grown brings forth death. *James 1:14–15*

Let every person be quick to hear, slow to speak, slow to anger. *James 1:19*

You believe that God is one; you do well. Even the demons believe—and shudder! Do you want to be shown, you foolish person, that faith apart from works is useless? *James 2:19–20*

You do not have, because you do not ask. *James 4:2*

Therefore, confess your sins to one another and pray for one another, that you may be healed. *James 5:16*

The Letter of James

Greeting

1 James, a servant[1] of God and of the Lord Jesus Christ,

To the twelve tribes in the Dispersion:

Greetings.

Testing of Your Faith

[2] Count it all joy, my brothers,[2] when you meet trials of various kinds, [3] for you know that the testing of your faith produces steadfastness. [4] And let steadfastness have its full effect, that you may be perfect and complete, lacking in nothing.

[5] If any of you lacks wisdom, let him ask God, who gives generously to all without reproach, and it will be given him. [6] But let him ask in faith, with no doubting, for the one who doubts is like a wave of the sea that is driven and tossed by the wind. [7] For that person must not suppose that he will receive anything from the Lord; [8] he is a double-minded man, unstable in all his ways.

[9] Let the lowly brother boast in his exaltation, [10] and the rich in his humiliation, because like a flower of the grass[3] he will pass away. [11] For the sun rises with its scorching heat and withers the grass; its flower falls, and its beauty perishes. So also will the rich man fade away in the midst of his pursuits.

[12] Blessed is the man who remains steadfast under trial, for when he has stood the test he will receive the crown of life, which God has promised to those who love him. [13] Let no one say when he is tempted, "I am being tempted by God," for God cannot be tempted with evil, and he himself tempts no one. [14] But each person is tempted when he is lured and enticed by his own desire. [15] Then desire when it has conceived gives birth to sin, and sin when it is fully grown brings forth death.

Ask Yourself . . .

ABOUT HAPPINESS

Is happiness your goal? Who doesn't want to be happy? Happiness is a good thing. It's the opposite of sadness, and it draws people to you and proves that your faith is unshakeable. Ask yourself:

- Would I rather be happy or holy? Do I realize that the greatest happiness is in holiness?

- What kinds of sins have I committed in order to find happiness?

- Is "because it will make me happy" ever an excuse for sin?

- What does God have to say about happiness?

- What does he have to say about endurance and suffering?

- Why is happiness such an obsession?

---

[16] Do not be deceived, my beloved brothers. [17] Every good gift and every perfect gift is from above, coming down from the Father of lights with whom there is no variation or shadow due to change.[4] [18] Of his own will he brought us forth by the

---

[1] Or *slave* (for the contextual rendering of the Greek word *doulos*, see About the ESV) [2] Or *brothers and sisters*. The plural Greek word *adelphoi* (translated "brothers") refers to siblings in a family. In New Testament usage, depending on the context, *adelphoi* may refer either to men or to both men and women who are siblings (brothers and sisters) in God's family, the church; also verses 16, 19 [3] Or *a wild flower* [4] Some manuscripts *variation due to a shadow of turning*

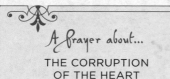

THE CORRUPTION OF THE HEART

O God, let your Spirit speak in me so that I can speak to you. I have no value except the value of Jesus in me. I am undeserving, but I look to your tender mercy. I am full of weaknesses, wants, and sin; you are full of grace.

I confess my sin—my all too frequent sin, my willful sin. All my powers of body and soul are messed up; a polluted river runs through my very nature. There are rooms of nasty images in my soul; I have gone from one repulsive room to another, walked in a no-man's-land of dangerous imaginations, pried into the secrets of my fallen nature.

I am completely ashamed that I am what I am in myself; I have no green shoot or fruit in me, but only thorns and thistles; I am a fading leaf that the wind drives away; I live bare and barren as a winter tree, unprofitable, fit to be cut down and burned. Lord, will you have mercy on me?

You have taken a good hit at my pride, at the false god of self, and I'm lying in pieces before you. But you have given me another Master and Lord, your Son, Jesus, and now my heart is turned toward holiness; my life speeds like a racehorse from its gate toward complete obedience to you. Help me in everything I do to put down my sin and make humble my pride. Save me from the love of the world and the pride of life, from everything that is natural to fallen man, and let Christ's nature be seen in me every day. Give me the grace to bear your will without resentment and to delight to be not only chiseled, carved, and broken apart but to be separated from the old rock where I have been embedded for so long. Lift me from the quarry to the upper air, where I can be built in Christ forever.

Amen.

word of truth, that we should be a kind of firstfruits of his creatures.

Hearing and Doing the Word

19 Know this, my beloved brothers: let every person be quick to hear, slow to speak, slow to anger; 20 for the anger of man does not produce the righteousness of God. 21 Therefore put away all filthiness and rampant wickedness and receive with meekness the implanted word, which is able to save your souls.

22 But be doers of the word, and not hearers only, deceiving yourselves. 23 For if anyone is a hearer of the word and not a doer, he is like a man who looks intently at his natural face in a mirror. 24 For he looks at himself and goes away and at once forgets what he was like. 25 But the one who looks into the perfect law, the law of liberty, and perseveres, being no hearer who forgets but a doer who acts, he will be blessed in his doing.

26 If anyone thinks he is religious and does not bridle his tongue but deceives his heart, this person's religion is worthless. 27 Religion that is pure and undefiled before God, the Father, is this: to visit orphans and widows in their affliction, and to keep oneself unstained from the world.

The Sin of Partiality

2 My brothers,[1] show no partiality as you hold the faith in our Lord Jesus Christ, the Lord of glory. 2 For if a man wearing a gold ring and fine clothing comes into your assembly, and a poor man in shabby clothing also comes in, 3 and if you pay attention to the one who wears the fine clothing and say, "You sit here in a good place," while you say to the poor man, "You stand over there," or, "Sit down at my feet," 4 have you not then made distinctions among yourselves and become judges with evil thoughts? 5 Listen, my beloved brothers, has not God chosen those who are poor in the world to be rich in faith and heirs of the kingdom, which he has promised to those who love him? 6 But you have dishonored the poor man. Are not the rich the ones who oppress you, and the ones who drag you into court? 7 Are they not the ones who blaspheme the honorable name by which you were called?

8 If you really fulfill the royal law according to the Scripture, [a]"You shall love your

[1] Or brothers and sisters; also verses 5, 14 [a] Lev. 19:18

neighbor as yourself," you are doing well. [9]But if you show partiality, you are committing sin and are convicted by the law as transgressors. [10]For whoever keeps the whole law but fails in one point has become accountable for all of it. [11]For he who said, [a]"Do not commit adultery," also said, [b]"Do not murder." If you do not commit adultery but do murder, you have become a transgressor of the law. [12]So speak and so act as those who are to be judged under the law of liberty. [13]For judgment is without mercy to one who has shown no mercy. Mercy triumphs over judgment.

Faith Without Works Is Dead

[14]What good is it, my brothers, if someone says he has faith but does not have works? Can that faith save him? [15]If a brother or sister is poorly clothed and lack-ing in daily food, [16]and one of you says to them, "Go in peace, be warmed and filled," without giving them the things needed for the body, what good[1] is that? [17]So also faith by itself, if it does not have works, is dead.

[18]But someone will say, "You have faith and I have works." Show me your faith apart from your works, and I will show you my faith by my works. [19]You believe that God is one; you do well. Even the demons believe—and shudder! [20]Do you want to be shown, you foolish person, that faith apart from works is useless? [21]Was not Abraham our father justified by works when he offered up his son Isaac on the altar? [22]You see that faith was active along with his works, and faith was completed by his works; [23]and the Scripture was fulfilled that says, [c]"Abraham believed God, and it was counted to him as righteousness"—

[1]Or benefit [a]Ex. 20:14 [b]Ex. 20:13 [c]Gen. 15:6

Know God

verses to read
James 2:12-13

How can the law set you free? Have you ever wondered about that? I mean, "law" sounds like something that holds you back. It's the great "don't touch that" or "I said no" of the spiritual world. If all you do is read the law but don't do what it says, that's exactly what it is: a bunch of dos and don't-dos. But a funny thing happens when, out of love for God, you actually do what the Word of God says to do and avoid what he says not to do: having already been set free by the gospel of grace, you are enabled to live as you were always meant to live.

See, you have all these things in your life that you have let control you without even realizing it, and all these things are actually sin, because letting them control you contradicts God's Word. Doing whatever you want, giving in to your passions, and just letting loose for a change might feel like freedom, but take a look at your heart. Does this thing that takes your eyes off God really give you the payoff it promises? Or does it eventually lead you to fear, depression, worry, loneliness, or anger?

If you look at God's Word and then decide that doing what it says just isn't worth the trouble, you miss out on your chance to be set free by grace from all that hurts you. Everything bad in your life is a result of sin. If you were to refuse to sin and choose rather to obey God's Word, you would find you have everything you've ever wanted. Freedom would be yours, because God's Word sets you free from the bondage of unmet needs, worry, and fear. It opens up your heart and your mind and sets you free from what your corrupt nature wants. So whatever you do, remember that you will be on the path of true joy as you follow Christ's instructions—as one who has become a child of God.

and he was called a friend of God. [24] You see that a person is justified by works and not by faith alone. [25] And in the same way was not also Rahab the prostitute justified by works when she received the messengers and sent them out by another way? [26] For as the body apart from the spirit is dead, so also faith apart from works is dead.

Taming the Tongue

3 Not many of you should become teachers, my brothers, for you know that we who teach will be judged with greater strictness. [2] For we all stumble in many ways. And if anyone does not stumble in what he says, he is a perfect man, able also to bridle his whole body. [3] If we put bits into the mouths of horses so that they obey us, we guide their whole bodies as well. [4] Look at the ships also: though they are so large and are driven by strong winds, they are guided by a very small rudder wherever the will of the pilot directs. [5] So also the tongue is a small member, yet it boasts of great things.

How great a forest is set ablaze by such a small fire! [6] And the tongue is a fire, a world of unrighteousness. The tongue is set among our members, staining the whole body, setting on fire the entire course of life,[1] and set on fire by hell.[2] [7] For every kind of beast and bird, of reptile and sea creature, can be tamed and has been tamed by mankind, [8] but no human being can tame the tongue. It is a restless evil, full of deadly poison. [9] With it we bless our Lord and Father, and with it we curse people who are made in the likeness of God. [10] From the same mouth come blessing and cursing. My brothers,[3] these things ought not to be so. [11] Does a spring pour forth from the same opening both fresh and salt water? [12] Can a fig tree, my brothers, bear olives, or a grapevine produce figs? Neither can a salt pond yield fresh water.

Wisdom from Above

[13] Who is wise and understanding among you? By his good conduct let him

---

[1] Or wheel of birth [2] Greek Gehenna [3] Or brothers and sisters; also verse 12

Know Yourself

verses to read
James 4:7–10

When you are in the middle of a dark spell, don't rush to get out. Don't clamor for guidance or for someone to help you. Just listen. What is God trying to teach you? If you look somewhere else, you'll only cover the voice of God with your complaints. Dark times are your time to listen, not to whine and complain. If you are willing to give up looking for a quick answer and are ready to wait for his response and his response alone, then you will find truth and hope. And at the end of your darkness you will find two things: happiness and humility.

Once you have truly heard God, you may feel like saying, "I'm such a dork! He's been talking this whole time and I haven't listened!" You will see your own sinfulness and be embarrassed by it. That's the humility part, and it will soften your heart and leave it ready for the seed of God's truth. Then you are ready to get the peace and hope that was promised you. Then your outlook will change from sadness to expectation, and your focus won't be on yourself anymore but on your powerful God. And what a better view that is!

Humility saves you from your emotional slavery. It brings you back to a correct assessment of who you are and who Christ is in your life. It's weird but true: when you truly let go of fighting for yourself and your rights, that's when you get all that you need. What do you think can lift you higher—your own effort, or the hand of God? God promises to lift you up!

show his works in the meekness of wisdom. **14** But if you have bitter jealousy and selfish ambition in your hearts, do not boast and be false to the truth. **15** This is not the wisdom that comes down from above, but is earthly, unspiritual, demonic. **16** For where jealousy and selfish ambition exist, there will be disorder and every vile practice. **17** But the wisdom from above is first pure, then peaceable, gentle, open to reason, full of mercy and good fruits, impartial and sincere. **18** And a harvest of righteousness is sown in peace by those who make peace.

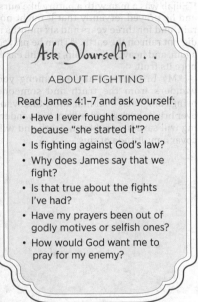

Ask Yourself . . .

ABOUT FIGHTING

Read James 4:1–7 and ask yourself:

- Have I ever fought someone because "she started it"?
- Is fighting against God's law?
- Why does James say that we fight?
- Is that true about the fights I've had?
- Have my prayers been out of godly motives or selfish ones?
- How would God want me to pray for my enemy?

Warning Against Worldliness

4 What causes quarrels and what causes fights among you? Is it not this, that your passions[1] are at war within you?[2] **2** You desire and do not have, so you murder. You covet and cannot obtain, so you fight and quarrel. You do not have, because you do not ask. **3** You ask and do not receive, because you ask wrongly, to spend it on your passions. **4** You adulterous people![3] Do you not know that friendship with the world is enmity with God? Therefore whoever wishes to be a friend of the world makes himself an enemy of God. **5** Or do you suppose it is to no purpose that the Scripture says, "He yearns jealously over the spirit that he has made to dwell in us"? **6** But he gives more grace. Therefore it says, [a] "God opposes the proud, but gives grace to the humble." **7** Submit yourselves therefore to God. Resist the devil, and he will flee from you. **8** Draw near to God, and he will draw near to you. Cleanse your hands, you sinners, and purify your hearts, you double-minded. **9** Be wretched and mourn and weep. Let your laughter be turned to mourning and your joy to gloom. **10** Humble yourselves before the Lord, and he will exalt you.

11 Do not speak evil against one another, brothers.[4] The one who speaks against a brother or judges his brother, speaks evil against the law and judges the law. But if you judge the law, you are not a doer of the law but a judge. **12** There is only one lawgiver and judge, he who is able to save and to destroy. But who are you to judge your neighbor?

Boasting About Tomorrow

13 Come now, you who say, "Today or tomorrow we will go into such and such a town and spend a year there and trade and make a profit"— **14** yet you do not know what tomorrow will bring. What is your life? For you are a mist that appears for a little time and then vanishes. **15** Instead you ought to say, "If the Lord wills, we will live and do this or that." **16** As it is, you boast in your arrogance. All such boasting is evil. **17** So whoever knows the right thing to do and fails to do it, for him it is sin.

Warning to the Rich

5 Come now, you rich, weep and howl for the miseries that are coming upon you. **2** Your riches have rotted and your garments are moth-eaten. **3** Your gold and silver have corroded, and their corrosion will be evidence against you and will eat your flesh like fire. You have laid up treasure in the last days. **4** Behold, the wages of the laborers who mowed your fields, which you kept back by fraud, are crying out against you, and the cries of the harvesters have reached the ears of the Lord of hosts. **5** You have lived on the earth in luxury and in self-indulgence. You have fattened your hearts in a day of slaughter.

---

1 Greek *pleasures*; also verse 3 **2** Greek *in your members* **3** Greek *You adulteresses!* **4** Or *brothers and sisters* **a** Prov. 3:34

⁶You have condemned and murdered the righteous person. He does not resist you.

Patience in Suffering

⁷Be patient, therefore, brothers,[1] until the coming of the Lord. See how the farmer waits for the precious fruit of the earth, being patient about it, until it receives the early and the late rains. ⁸You also, be patient. Establish your hearts, for the coming of the Lord is at hand. ⁹Do not grumble against one another, brothers, so that you may not be judged; behold, the Judge is standing at the door. ¹⁰As an example of suffering and patience, brothers, take the prophets who spoke in the name of the Lord. ¹¹Behold, we consider those blessed who remained steadfast. You have heard of the steadfastness of Job, and you have seen the purpose of the Lord, how the Lord is compassionate and merciful.

¹²But above all, my brothers, do not swear, either by heaven or by earth or by any other oath, but let your "yes" be yes and your "no" be no, so that you may not fall under condemnation.

The Prayer of Faith

¹³Is anyone among you suffering? Let him pray. Is anyone cheerful? Let him sing praise. ¹⁴Is anyone among you sick? Let him call for the elders of the church, and let them pray over him, anointing him with oil in the name of the Lord. ¹⁵And the prayer of faith will save the one who is sick, and the Lord will raise him up. And if he has committed sins, he will be forgiven. ¹⁶Therefore, confess your sins to one another and pray for one another, that you may be healed. The prayer of a righteous person has great power as it is working.[2] ¹⁷Elijah was a man with a nature like ours, and he prayed fervently that it might not rain, and for three years and six months it did not rain on the earth. ¹⁸Then he prayed again, and heaven gave rain, and the earth bore its fruit.

¹⁹My brothers, if anyone among you wanders from the truth and someone brings him back, ²⁰let him know that whoever brings back a sinner from his wandering will save his soul from death and will cover a multitude of sins.

---

[1] Or brothers and sisters; also verses 9, 10, 12, 19 [2] Or The effective prayer of a righteous person has great power

INTRODUCTION TO
1 Peter

Suffer with a Purpose

> For to this you have been called, because Christ also suffered for you, leaving you an example, so that you might follow in his steps. He committed no sin . . . ; when he suffered, he did not threaten, but continued entrusting himself to him who judges justly.
>
> *1 Peter 2:21–23*

Author: The apostle Peter

Time: Around A.D. 64

Place: Probably in Rome

Written to: Christians in Asia Minor

The gist

Christians in the early church had quickly found out that living for God wasn't always easy. Peter helped them to understand why suffering happens and how believers are to deal with it. In the end, God will judge everyone fairly, so trusting him to deal with the sins of other people is always the way of faith.

Things to look for

- How Jesus suffered in order to save you (see 1 Pet. 1:19; 2:21–24; 3:18–22)
- What to do when people are mean to you (see 1 Pet. 1:13–16, 22; and many others)

The apostle Peter knew about suffering at the hands of mean people, but he also knew where God was in the whole thing. So he wrote to tell people that suffering, though it hurts to no end, has a far greater purpose. Other people's sin is never an excuse for *our* sin. Quite the opposite: it is our chance to prove ourselves both to those watching us and to God.

Suffering might seem impossible to handle, but in the grand scheme of things it's only temporary. And when you live through it with faith that God will use it all for good, you learn more than you could ever learn in good times. Do not fear suffering, God Girl, but know that it is far better to suffer for doing good than for doing wrong (see 1 Pet. 3:17).

Peter also wants his readers to understand the difficult subject of submission. He goes so far as to say that, even if you don't like your authority figures, you are commanded to obey them. It's another way to show faith to those watching and to prove that doing what God commands is always the right choice, no matter how crazy it might seem. Revolt is never an option for the believer, because that only gets in the way of something called long-suffering, or patience—enduring the stuff mean people do without fighting back.

Think about the life of Christ: he suffered beyond belief on the day they hung him on that cross, yet he never fought back or resisted. He never argued his case but did the very thing he now asks us to do: endure hardship in faith, knowing that God can be trusted. Remember that suffering lasts only a while, and then comes the reward. And what a reward it will be! You have nothing to fear, because no one can harm your soul or take you away from the Father. Just trust him and obey his Word no matter what the world throws at you, and you will be sure to overcome.

Must-Know Terms and Verses

✥ *Born Again* ✥

To be born again is to undergo a spiritual renewal which makes you a new creature based on your belief in and acceptance of the life-giving death and resurrection of Jesus (see John 3:3, 7; 1 Pet. 1:23).

✥ *Cornerstone* ✥

The corner piece of a foundation; the place where two walls of a building meet. It aligns the whole building and helps keep it standing.

✥ *Good News* ✥

Refers to the message of the saving power of Christ. Another word for it is *gospel*.

✥ *Holy* ✥

A term used to express moral perfection and an essential part of God's nature. It also describes someone or something that is sanctified and set apart for divine service.

According to the foreknowledge of God the Father, in the sanctification of the Spirit, for obedience to Jesus Christ and for sprinkling with his blood: May grace and peace be multiplied to you. *1 Peter 1:2*

As obedient children, do not be conformed to the passions of your former ignorance, but as he who called you is holy, you also be holy in all your conduct, since it is written, "You shall be holy, for I am holy." *1 Peter 1:14–16*

Be subject for the Lord's sake to every human institution, whether it be to the emperor as supreme, or to governors as sent by him to punish those who do evil and to praise those who do good. *1 Peter 2:13–14*

Be sober-minded; be watchful. Your adversary the devil prowls around like a roaring lion, seeking someone to devour. *1 Peter 5:8*

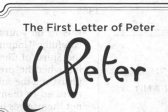

The First Letter of Peter

1 Peter

Greeting

1 Peter, an apostle of Jesus Christ,
To those who are elect exiles of the Dispersion in Pontus, Galatia, Cappadocia, Asia, and Bithynia, ²according to the foreknowledge of God the Father, in the sanctification of the Spirit, for obedience to Jesus Christ and for sprinkling with his blood:

May grace and peace be multiplied to you.

Born Again to a Living Hope

³Blessed be the God and Father of our Lord Jesus Christ! According to his great mercy, he has caused us to be born again to a living hope through the resurrection of Jesus Christ from the dead, ⁴to an inheritance that is imperishable, undefiled, and unfading, kept in heaven for you, ⁵who by God's power are being guarded through faith for a salvation ready to be revealed in the last time. ⁶In this you rejoice, though now for a little while, if necessary, you have been grieved by various trials, ⁷so that the tested genuineness of your faith—more precious than gold that perishes though it is tested by fire—may be found to result in praise and glory and honor at the revelation of Jesus Christ. ⁸Though you have not

Know How to Communicate

verse to read
1 Peter 1:2

God chose you. He chose you! Can you believe it? You didn't just show up at his doorstep, all wet and stinky; he chose you and made you his own. But why? What was his purpose for picking you? According to 1 Peter 1:2, it was for you to be holy (or sanctified). A lot of young people want a purpose in life. They want to know why they were created. But you don't have to search for the answer to that Q anymore, because it's right here, written in this book: you were chosen "in the sanctification of the Spirit, for obedience to Jesus Christ" (1 Pet. 1:2).

You were created to be holy. Wow, betcha didn't know that. How's it going? Feeling holy today? If you aren't, don't fear. You can achieve your purpose; in fact, you *will* achieve it. See, when God says you were meant to be holy, he isn't expecting the impossible. That would be cruel. That would be like asking a six-year-old to explain the Pythagorean theorem and then punishing her when she couldn't do it. Crazy! But God isn't crazy. He's got a plan, and he's part of it.

First Peter 1:2 tells you how you'll get it done: "in the sanctification of the Spirit." All you have to do is be willing to let his Spirit work with you, teach you, and guide you. And the way you start to do that is through the process of spiritual discipline—prayer, confession, repentance, study, and more prayer. Holiness can be yours, your life can be changed, as you recognize that by grace you have already been made holy. Trust God with your life and be willing to do whatever he says, no matter how hard it might sound. If you're ready for that, then ask him for the power to do it, and believe that he will help you.

A Prayer for...

CONSECRATION AND WORSHIP

My God, I feel like it is heaven to please you and to be what you want me to be. I want to be holy like you are holy, pure like Christ is pure, perfect like your Spirit is perfect! These are the best commands in your book, so should I break them? Do I have to break them? Am I in such a mess as long as I live here on this fallen earth?

I hate that I am such a sinner, that I grieve you so often. You who are infinite in goodness and grace! Even though I sin continually, you continually repeat your kindness to me.

At times I think I could handle any suffering; how can I dishonor this glorious God by not doing so? What can I do to glorify and worship this best of beings? I wish I could consecrate my soul and body to your service, without restraint, forever! I want to give myself up to you so I wouldn't ever be my own or have any will or affections that aren't perfectly conformed to your will and your love! But I cannot live and not sin.

May angels glorify you incessantly and, if possible, prostrate themselves lower before the blessed King of heaven! I join in with them in ceaseless praise, but when I have done all I can for eternity I won't be able to offer more than a small fraction of the respect and honor that the glorious God deserves. Give me a heart full of divine, heavenly love.

Amen.

was to be yours searched and inquired carefully, [11] inquiring what person or time the Spirit of Christ in them was indicating when he predicted the sufferings of Christ and the subsequent glories. [12] It was revealed to them that they were serving not themselves but you, in the things that have now been announced to you through those who preached the good news to you by the Holy Spirit sent from heaven, things into which angels long to look.

Called to Be Holy

[13] Therefore, preparing your minds for action,[1] and being sober-minded, set your hope fully on the grace that will be brought to you at the revelation of Jesus Christ. [14] As obedient children, do not be conformed to the passions of your former ignorance, [15] but as he who called you is holy, you also be holy in all your conduct, [16] since it is written, [a]"You shall be holy, for I am holy." [17] And if you call on him as Father who judges impartially according to each one's deeds, conduct yourselves with fear throughout the time of your exile, [18] knowing that you were ransomed from the futile ways inherited from your forefathers, not with perishable things such as silver or gold, [19] but with the precious blood of Christ, like that of a lamb without blemish or spot. [20] He was foreknown before the foundation of the world but was made manifest in the last times for the sake of you [21] who through him are believers in God, who raised him from the dead and gave him glory, so that your faith and hope are in God.

[22] Having purified your souls by your obedience to the truth for a sincere brotherly love, love one another earnestly from a pure heart, [23] since you have been born again, not of perishable seed but of imperishable, through the living and abiding word of God; [24] for

> [b]"All flesh is like grass
>   and all its glory like the flower of grass.
> The grass withers,
>   and the flower falls,
> [25] but the word of the Lord remains forever."

And this word is the good news that was preached to you.

seen him, you love him. Though you do not now see him, you believe in him and rejoice with joy that is inexpressible and filled with glory, [9] obtaining the outcome of your faith, the salvation of your souls.

[10] Concerning this salvation, the prophets who prophesied about the grace that

[1] Greek *girding up the loins of your mind* [a] Lev. 11:44 [b] Isa. 40:6, 8

A Living Stone and a Holy People

2 So put away all malice and all deceit and hypocrisy and envy and all slander. [2] Like newborn infants, long for the pure spiritual milk, that by it you may grow up into salvation— [3] if indeed you have tasted that the Lord is good.

[4] As you come to him, a living stone rejected by men but in the sight of God chosen and precious, [5] you yourselves like living stones are being built up as a spiritual house, to be a holy priesthood, to offer spiritual sacrifices acceptable to God through Jesus Christ. [6] For it stands in Scripture:

[a]"Behold, I am laying in Zion a stone,
a cornerstone chosen and precious,
and whoever believes in him will not
be put to shame."

[7] So the honor is for you who believe, but for those who do not believe,

[b]"The stone that the builders rejected
has become the cornerstone,"[1]

[8] and

[c]"A stone of stumbling,
and a rock of offense."

They stumble because they disobey the word, as they were destined to do.

[9] But you are a chosen race, a royal priesthood, a holy nation, a people for his own possession, that you may proclaim the excellencies of him who called you out of darkness into his marvelous light. [10] Once you were not a people, but now you are God's people; once you had not received mercy, but now you have received mercy.

[11] Beloved, I urge you as sojourners and exiles to abstain from the passions of the flesh, which wage war against your soul. [12] Keep your conduct among the Gentiles honorable, so that when they speak against you as evildoers, they may see your good deeds and glorify God on the day of visitation.

Submission to Authority

[13] Be subject for the Lord's sake to every human institution,[2] whether it be to the emperor[3] as supreme, [14] or to governors as sent by him to punish those who do evil

and to praise those who do good. [15] For this is the will of God, that by doing good you should put to silence the ignorance of foolish people. [16] Live as people who are free, not using your freedom as a cover-up for evil, but living as servants[4] of God. [17] Honor everyone. Love the brotherhood. Fear God. Honor the emperor.

Ask Yourself . . .

WHAT YOU WANT

The "passions of the flesh" (1 Pet. 2:11), those things you want that aren't what God wants, will draw you away from faith and toward fear, worry, stress, strife, jealousy, fighting. Ask yourself:

- What do I spend most of my time wishing I had?

- Are those things holy or worldly?

- What's more important to me: what the world says I need or what God says I need?

- What desires lead to all my bad emotions like fear, worry, stress, and jealousy?

- What does God want for me in those areas? (See the Quick Relief guide in the back of this Bible.)

- What verses can I memorize to remind myself to quit thinking about what I don't need?

---

[18] Servants, be subject to your masters with all respect, not only to the good and gentle but also to the unjust. [19] For this is a gracious thing, when, mindful of God, one endures sorrows while suffering unjustly. [20] For what credit is it if, when you sin and are beaten for it, you endure? But if when you do good and suffer for it you endure, this is a gracious thing in the sight of God.

---

[1] Greek *the head of the corner* [2] Or *every institution ordained for people* [3] Or *king*; also verse 17 [4] Greek *bondservants* [a] Isa. 28:16 [b] Ps. 118:22 [c] Isa. 8:14

²¹ For to this you have been called, because Christ also suffered for you, leaving you an example, so that you might follow in his steps. ²² He committed no sin, neither was deceit found in his mouth. ²³ When he was reviled, he did not revile in return; when he suffered, he did not threaten, but continued entrusting himself to him who judges justly. ²⁴ He himself bore our sins in his body on the tree, that we might die to sin and live to righteousness. By his wounds you have been healed. ²⁵ For you were straying like sheep, but have now returned to the Shepherd and Overseer of your souls.

Wives and Husbands

3 Likewise, wives, be subject to your own husbands, so that even if some do not obey the word, they may be won without a word by the conduct of their wives, ² when they see your respectful and pure conduct. ³ Do not let your adorning be external—the braiding of hair and the putting on of gold jewelry, or the clothing you wear— ⁴ but let your adorning be the hidden person of the heart with the imperishable beauty of a gentle and quiet spirit, which in God's sight is very precious. ⁵ For this is how the holy women who hoped in God used to adorn themselves, by submitting to their own husbands, ⁶ as Sarah obeyed Abraham, calling him lord. And you are her children, if you do good and do not fear anything that is frightening.

⁷ Likewise, husbands, live with your wives in an understanding way, showing honor to the woman as the weaker vessel, since they are heirs with you¹ of the grace of life, so that your prayers may not be hindered.

Suffering for Righteousness' Sake

⁸ Finally, all of you, have unity of mind, sympathy, brotherly love, a tender heart, and a humble mind. ⁹ Do not repay evil for evil or reviling for reviling, but on the

¹ Some manuscripts *since you are joint heirs*

verses to read
1 Peter 2:21-25

Forget about fighting fair—it's never holy to fight back. Period. End of story. It's never godly to argue in anger or resentment. Revenge is not for the God Girl. When it comes to your friends and enemies, you are free to trust God to judge the situation fairly and to work all things out for what he knows to be the best, not what *you* think is best. No matter how bad the mean, no matter how hard the test, the God Girl who wants to imitate Christ (see Eph. 5:1) doesn't retaliate, get even, or fight back.

The world tries to convince even strong believers that their battle is against flesh-and-blood people and that they have to fight back, when in fact the opposite is true. The battle isn't ours; it is the Father's. When people attack you, slander you, or cut you down, your natural reaction is to want revenge, but that is never an act of obedience. If Christ, whose very life was being beaten and drained from him, didn't find it necessary to retaliate or to fight back, then why would we who aren't facing anything nearly as gruesome think we have a fight on our hands?

The lesson of God's love is the lesson of dying to self. When your friends, family, or enemies attack, you are free to resist the urge to viciously fight back. You can trust the Word of God, choosing to live by it rather than to deny it and instead try to live by your own strength. Rejoice when others attack, because the testing of your faith develops endurance and maturity (see James 1:2-4). You can trust that these words are true and that God's power is sufficient.

contrary, bless, for to this you were called, that you may obtain a blessing. ¹⁰For

^a"Whoever desires to love life
    and see good days,
let him keep his tongue from evil
    and his lips from speaking deceit;
¹¹   let him turn away from evil and do
        good;
    let him seek peace and pursue it.
¹²   For the eyes of the Lord are on the
        righteous,
    and his ears are open to their prayer.
    But the face of the Lord is against
        those who do evil."

¹³Now who is there to harm you if you are zealous for what is good? ¹⁴But even if you should suffer for righteousness' sake, you will be blessed. Have no fear of them, nor be troubled, ¹⁵but in your hearts honor Christ the Lord as holy, always being prepared to make a defense to anyone who asks you for a reason for the hope that is in you; yet do it with gentleness and respect, ¹⁶having a good conscience, so that, when you are slandered, those who revile your good behavior in Christ may be put to shame. ¹⁷For it is better to suffer for doing good, if that should be God's will, than for doing evil.

¹⁸For Christ also suffered¹ once for sins, the righteous for the unrighteous, that he might bring us to God, being put to death in the flesh but made alive in the spirit, ¹⁹in which² he went and proclaimed³ to the spirits in prison, ²⁰because⁴ they formerly did not obey, when God's patience waited in the days of Noah, while the ark was being prepared, in which a few, that is, eight persons, were brought safely through water. ²¹Baptism, which corresponds to this, now saves you, not as a removal of dirt from the body but as an appeal to God for a good conscience, through the resurrection of Jesus Christ, ²²who has gone into heaven

---

¹ Some manuscripts *died* ² Or *the Spirit, in whom* ³ Or *preached* ⁴ Or *when* ᵃ Ps. 34:12-16

Know How to Communicate

verses to read
1 Peter 3:13-17

You probably have mean people in your life, people who hate you and want your destruction. Does that surprise you? Do you believe everyone should adore you? Why? Did you know that the world hated Christ too? It shouldn't shock you when people are mean or spiteful toward you, especially when it's for doing the right thing. It should give you faith in God's Word, because he promised that you, as his follower, would have trouble (see John 16:33).

Don't be afraid of those who want to harm you, and don't get upset. Their sin is their sin, and you can't make it yours. But what you can do is pray for them and love them. Obey God's commands, especially with those who hate you, and you will prove yourself faithful. What good is obedience in the easy parts of life? That proves nothing. But obedience in loving your enemies, in doing good to those who hate you, and in not fearing what others fear proves your faith and delivers you from all their evil.

There will always be mean people, but the God Girl can't allow their mean to become her mean. Rather, she has to act as Christ acted and refuse to retaliate or hit back. Don't get upset. Trust God and turn away from their sin and disobedience by refusing to join in with them. Obedience to God's Word demands love, and you must fearlessly offer it to others in the name of him who first offered it to save you. Your freedom and your faith are in your hands and no one else's. Suffer for doing good. Prove God's Word is trustworthy by doing what it says, and your faith will get stronger than you ever imagined.

and is at the right hand of God, with angels, authorities, and powers having been subjected to him.

Stewards of God's Grace

4 Since therefore Christ suffered in the flesh,[1] arm yourselves with the same way of thinking, for whoever has suffered in the flesh has ceased from sin, ²so as to live for the rest of the time in the flesh no longer for human passions but for the will of God. ³For the time that is past suffices for doing what the Gentiles want to do, living in sensuality, passions, drunkenness, orgies, drinking parties, and lawless idolatry. ⁴With respect to this they are surprised when you do not join them in the same flood of debauchery, and they malign you; ⁵but they will give account to him who is ready to judge the living and the dead. ⁶For this is why the gospel was preached even to those who are dead, that though judged in the flesh the way people are, they might live in the spirit the way God does.

⁷The end of all things is at hand; therefore be self-controlled and sober-minded for the sake of your prayers. ⁸Above all, keep loving one another earnestly, since love covers a multitude of sins. ⁹Show hospitality to one another without grumbling. ¹⁰As each has received a gift, use it to serve one another, as good stewards of God's varied grace: ¹¹whoever speaks, as one who speaks oracles of God; whoever serves, as one who serves by the strength that God supplies—in order that in everything God may be glorified through Jesus Christ. To him belong glory and dominion forever and ever. Amen.

Suffering as a Christian

¹²Beloved, do not be surprised at the fiery trial when it comes upon you to test you, as though something strange were happening to you. ¹³But rejoice insofar as you share Christ's sufferings, that you may also rejoice and be glad when his glory is revealed. ¹⁴If you are insulted for the name of Christ, you are blessed, because the Spirit of glory[2] and of God rests upon you. ¹⁵But let none of you suffer as a murderer or a thief or an evildoer or as a meddler. ¹⁶Yet if anyone suffers as a Christian, let him not be ashamed, but let him glorify God in that name. ¹⁷For it is time for judgment to begin at the household of God; and if it begins with us, what will be the

---

¹Some manuscripts add *for us*; some *for you*   ²Some manuscripts insert *and of power*

Know God

verses to read
1 Peter 5:7–11

As a believer you have to be aware of the fact that obsessing about the things of this world—success, money, clothes—will suck out of you anything that God put in you. The world is continually on the verge of breaking in on your soul and overwhelming it with worries about "not enough." Not enough money, food, friends, whatever. It never stops. And if you let yourself obsess about the things you lack, you lead yourself into dangerous waters. That's when your mind walks away from truth and dives into the lies of this world. The next step is drowning in them.

But Jesus offers you a lifeline. He says, "Don't worry about it. Obsess only over one thing, your relationship with me, and then everything else will fall into place." The world will say that's ridiculous. You have to worry about the necessities of life, don't you? But Jesus says, "No, you don't. I'll take care of all that stuff. Trust me. Just keep your mind on my abundance, and you will never lack anything."

Are your thoughts faltering? Have you let worry become your obsession? Turn away from it now and put your thoughts onto him who saves. You will not be disappointed.

outcome for those who do not obey the gospel of God? ¹⁸And

> "If the righteous is scarcely saved,
>   what will become of the ungodly
>   and the sinner?"¹

⁹Therefore let those who suffer according to God's will entrust their souls to a faithful Creator while doing good.

Shepherd the Flock of God

5 So I exhort the elders among you, as a fellow elder and a witness of the sufferings of Christ, as well as a partaker in the glory that is going to be revealed: ²shepherd the flock of God that is among you, exercising oversight,² not under compulsion, but willingly, as God would have you;³ not for shameful gain, but eagerly; ³not domineering over those in your charge, but being examples to the flock. ⁴And when the chief Shepherd appears, you will receive the unfading crown of glory. ⁵Likewise, you who are younger, be subject to the elders. Clothe yourselves, all of you, with humility toward one another, for "God opposes the proud but gives grace to the humble."

⁶Humble yourselves, therefore, under the mighty hand of God so that at the proper time he may exalt you, ⁷casting all your anxieties on him, because he cares for you. ⁸Be sober-minded; be watchful. Your adversary the devil prowls around like a roaring lion, seeking someone to devour. ⁹Resist him, firm in your faith, knowing that the same kinds of suffering are being experienced by your brotherhood throughout the world. ¹⁰And after you have suffered a little while, the God of all grace, who has called you to his eternal glory in Christ, will himself restore, confirm, strengthen, and establish you. ¹¹To him be the dominion forever and ever. Amen.

Final Greetings

¹²By Silvanus, a faithful brother as I regard him, I have written briefly to you, exhorting and declaring that this is the true grace of God. Stand firm in it. ¹³She who is at Babylon, who is likewise chosen, sends you greetings, and so does Mark, my son. ¹⁴Greet one another with the kiss of love.

Peace to all of you who are in Christ.

---

¹Greek *where will the ungodly and sinner appear?* ²Some manuscripts omit *exercising oversight* ³Some manuscripts omit *as God would have you*

INTRODUCTION TO
2 Peter

Author: The apostle Peter
Time: Around A.D. 65
Place: Probably Rome
Written to: All believers

The gist

This letter is a reminder to all believers not to fall for the distractions and temptations of false teachers but to stick to what we know to be true about God. Peter wants us to be prepared for the time when Jesus will come back. He wants us to avoid becoming slaves again to the things that used to control us, before our salvation.

Things to look for

- What a godly life looks like (see 2 Pet. 1:3–10; 3:10–18)
- How to recognize false teachers (see 2 Peter 2)
- Truth about the second coming of Christ (see 2 Peter 3)

Beware of False Teachers

> In their greed they will exploit you with false words.
>
> 2 Peter 2:3

Second Peter is an important letter. It reminds us that persecution from without is one thing, but danger from within is another. Persecution from nonbelievers isn't the only danger to the church. Sometimes the danger is people inside the church who take the truth and change it to fit their own ideas and experiences. That's why knowledge of the truth is so essential for all believers. Without it you can easily be led astray by people pretending to teach about true faith but really teaching a lie. As a God Girl, you can't simply accept what you are taught without considering how it aligns with God's Word.

Sometimes, teachers of God's Word allow the ideas of the world to seep into their way of thinking, and then over time they forget what is the world versus what is the Word. You are never too young to judge truth for yourself. The only excuse you might have for not doing so is that you don't know enough. But you can't let that stop you. The Word is available to everyone who is willing to look into it. Knowledge is a powerful thing, and it is essential for the life of faith. We can't let people draw us away with enticing arguments that appeal to our desire to be happy and comfortable. We need to bring everything back to the Word of God. Ask yourself, "Is what I'm hearing or thinking consistent with God's Word?" If not, then you must reject it.

As a God Girl, you can't let the world infiltrate your faith, even if it has infiltrated the lives of those who appear to know more than you. It's easy to let lies seep into your mind and become a part of your worldview (your beliefs about faith and living), but as the world starts to make its lies look like God's truth, your faith can become distorted. If you believe something to be true, check it against God's Word. You might be surprised how many "truths" you find out are complete and total lies. Don't let the world pull the wool over your eyes. Run it all by God and his Word before you believe a word of it. Be smart and, by grace, be a faithful God Girl!

Must-Know Terms and Verses

∽ *Day of the Lord* ∽

The second coming of Christ, as seen in 2 Peter 3:10.

∽ *False Teacher* ∽

Anyone who teaches something that is inconsistent with or contradictory to Scripture. False teachers can be those who teach about a false god or those who say they teach about or in the name of the true God but don't speak the truth. False teachers don't convict people of sin but offer them false hope in something other than God.

∽ *New Heavens and New Earth* ∽

Refers to a time when this earth will be destroyed and God will create a new one for all his children to live on for eternity (see Isa. 65:17; Matt. 24:35; 2 Pet. 3:13). It will happen right after the final judgment and will be so amazing that no one will remember the old earth (see Isa. 65:17).

Make every effort to supplement your faith with virtue, and virtue with knowledge, and knowledge with self-control, and self-control with steadfastness, and steadfastness with godliness, and godliness with brotherly affection, and brotherly affection with love. *2 Peter 1:5–7*

There will be false teachers among you, who will secretly bring in destructive heresies, even denying the Master who bought them, bringing upon themselves swift destruction. *2 Peter 2:1*

They promise them freedom, but they themselves are slaves of corruption. For whatever overcomes a person, to that he is enslaved. *2 Peter 2:19*

The Second Letter of Peter

2 Peter

Greeting

1 Simeon[1] Peter, a servant[2] and apostle of Jesus Christ,

To those who have obtained a faith of equal standing with ours by the righteousness of our God and Savior Jesus Christ:

[2] May grace and peace be multiplied to you in the knowledge of God and of Jesus our Lord.

Confirm Your Calling and Election

[3] His divine power has granted to us all things that pertain to life and godliness, through the knowledge of him who called us to[3] his own glory and excellence,[4] [4] by which he has granted to us his precious and very great promises, so that through them you may become partakers of the divine nature, having escaped from the corruption that is in the world because of sinful desire. [5] For this very reason, make every effort to supplement your faith with virtue,[5] and virtue with knowledge, [6] and knowledge with self-control, and self-control with steadfastness, and steadfastness with godliness, [7] and godliness with brotherly affection, and brotherly affection with love. [8] For if these qualities[6] are yours and are increasing, they keep you from being ineffective or unfruitful in the knowledge of our Lord Jesus Christ. [9] For whoever lacks these qualities is so nearsighted that he is blind, having forgotten that he was cleansed from his former sins. [10] Therefore, brothers,[7] be all the more diligent to confirm your calling and election, for if you practice these qualities you will never fall. [11] For in this way there will be richly provided for you an entrance into the eternal kingdom of our Lord and Savior Jesus Christ.

[12] Therefore I intend always to remind you of these qualities, though you know them and are established in the truth that you have. [13] I think it right, as long as I am in this body,[8] to stir you up by way of reminder, [14] since I know that the putting off of my body will be soon, as our Lord Jesus Christ made clear to me. [15] And I will make every effort so that after my departure you may be able at any time to recall these things.

Christ's Glory and the Prophetic Word

[16] For we did not follow cleverly devised myths when we made known to you the power and coming of our Lord Jesus Christ, but we were eyewitnesses of his majesty. [17] For when he received honor and glory from God the Father, and the voice was borne to him by the Majestic Glory, "This is my beloved Son,[9] with whom I am well pleased," [18] we ourselves heard this very voice borne from heaven, for we were with him on the holy mountain. [19] And we have the prophetic word more fully confirmed, to which you will do well to pay attention as to a lamp shining in a dark place, until the day dawns and the morning star rises in your hearts, [20] knowing this first of all, that no prophecy of Scripture comes from someone's own interpretation. [21] For no prophecy was ever produced by the will of man, but men spoke from God as they were carried along by the Holy Spirit.

False Prophets and Teachers

2 But false prophets also arose among the people, just as there will be false teachers among you, who will secretly bring in destructive heresies, even denying the Master who bought them, bringing upon themselves swift destruction. [2] And many

---

[1] Some manuscripts *Simeon* [2] Or *slave* (for the contextual rendering of the Greek word *doulos*, see About the ESV) [3] Or *by* [4] Or *virtue* [5] Or *excellence*; twice in this verse [6] Greek *these things*; also verses 9, 10, 12 [7] Or *brothers and sisters*. The plural Greek word *adelphoi* (translated "brothers") refers to siblings in a family. In New Testament usage, depending on the context, *adelphoi* may refer either to men or to both men and women who are siblings (brothers and sisters) in God's family, the church [8] Greek *tent*; also verse 14 [9] Or *my Son, my (or the) Beloved*

will follow their sensuality, and because of them the way of truth will be blasphemed. ³And in their greed they will exploit you with false words. Their condemnation from long ago is not idle, and their destruction is not asleep.

⁴For if God did not spare angels when they sinned, but cast them into hell¹ and committed them to chains² of gloomy darkness to be kept until the judgment; ⁵if he did not spare the ancient world, but preserved Noah, a herald of righteousness, with seven others, when he brought a flood upon the world of the ungodly; ⁶if by turning the cities of Sodom and Gomorrah to ashes he condemned them to extinction, making them an example of what is going to happen to the ungodly;³ ⁷and if he rescued righteous Lot, greatly distressed by the sensual conduct of the wicked ⁸(for as that righteous man lived among them day after day, he was tormenting his righteous soul over their lawless deeds that he saw and heard); ⁹then the Lord knows how to rescue the godly from trials,⁴ and to keep the unrighteous under punishment until the day of judgment, ¹⁰and especially those who indulge⁵ in the lust of defiling passion and despise authority.

Bold and willful, they do not tremble as they blaspheme the glorious ones, ¹¹whereas angels, though greater in might and power, do not pronounce a blasphemous judgment against them before the Lord. ¹²But these, like irrational animals, creatures of instinct, born to be caught and destroyed, blaspheming about matters of which they are ignorant, will also be destroyed in their destruction, ¹³suffering wrong as the wage for their wrongdo-

¹ Greek *Tartarus* ² Some manuscripts *pits* ³ Some manuscripts *an example to those who were to be ungodly* ⁴ Or *temptations* ⁵ Greek *who go after the flesh*

Know Yourself

verses to read
2 Peter 3:17–18

Everyone God touches changes. If your life isn't changing, then you haven't given it over to him. Once you meet face-to-face with the Creator of the universe, you are no longer the same. Each time you meet him you soften, you learn, you gain wisdom, self-control, and strength. Each day you grow and become more like Jesus Christ himself.

Is your life changing? Do you have encounters with God through his Word that shape you and rub off your rough edges? Staying the same should never be the goal of the God Girl. A lot of girls have no desire to grow and to mature, but the God Girl knows that change is a crucial part of spiritual growth. A plant that stops growing doesn't live, and no girl who has stopped growing is taking her life from the branch (see John 15:4; James 2:26). Growth, including even your daily perseverance in good times and bad, is a public and private reminder of your salvation.

Do you want to conquer life, to conquer your sin and weaknesses, to overcome challenges, and to gain the strength to do more than you've ever done before? When you want that, you have taken the first step to maturity. Accepting the status quo doesn't help anyone, but an irresistible thirst to go deeper proves not only your spiritual maturity but your emotional maturity as well.

Grow like a weed. Cling to the branch, accept its life-giving power, and grow as if your life depended on it, because it does. If God is changing you, then thank him, embrace the future and his hope, and let go of the old girl and welcome the new one—the new and improved you!

ing. They count it pleasure to revel in the daytime. They are blots and blemishes, reveling in their deceptions,[1] while they feast with you. [14] They have eyes full of adultery, insatiable for sin. They entice unsteady souls. They have hearts trained in greed. Accursed children! [15] Forsaking the right way, they have gone astray. They have followed the way of Balaam, the son of Beor, who loved gain from wrongdoing, [16] but was rebuked for his own transgression; a speechless donkey spoke with human voice and restrained the prophet's madness.

[17] These are waterless springs and mists driven by a storm. For them the gloom of utter darkness has been reserved. [18] For, speaking loud boasts of folly, they entice by sensual passions of the flesh those who are barely escaping from those who live in error. [19] They promise them freedom, but they themselves are slaves[2] of corruption. For whatever overcomes a person, to that he is enslaved. [20] For if, after they have escaped the defilements of the world through the knowledge of our Lord and Savior Jesus Christ, they are again entangled in them and overcome, the last state has become worse for them than the first. [21] For it would have been better for them never to have known the way of righteousness than after knowing it to turn back from the holy commandment delivered to them. [22] What the true proverb says has happened to them: "The dog returns to its own vomit, and the sow, after washing herself, returns to wallow in the mire."

The Day of the Lord Will Come

3 This is now the second letter that I am writing to you, beloved. In both of them I am stirring up your sincere mind by way of reminder, [2] that you should remember the predictions of the holy prophets and the commandment of the Lord and Savior through your apostles, [3] knowing this first of all, that scoffers will come in the last days with scoffing, following their own sinful desires. [4] They will say, "Where is the promise of his coming? For ever since the fathers fell asleep, all things are continuing as they were from the beginning of creation." [5] For they delib-

erately overlook this fact, that the heavens existed long ago, and the earth was formed out of water and through water by the word of God, [6] and that by means of these the world that then existed was deluged with water and perished. [7] But by the same word the heavens and earth that now exist are stored up for fire, being kept until the day of judgment and destruction of the ungodly.

[8] But do not overlook this one fact, beloved, that with the Lord one day is as a thousand years, and a thousand years as one day. [9] The Lord is not slow to fulfill his promise as some count slowness, but is patient toward you,[3] not wishing that any should perish, but that all should reach repentance. [10] But the day of the Lord will come like a thief, and then the heavens will pass away with a roar, and the heavenly bodies[4] will be burned up and dissolved, and the earth and the works that are done on it will be exposed.[5]

[11] Since all these things are thus to be dissolved, what sort of people ought you to be in lives of holiness and godliness, [12] waiting for and hastening the coming of the day of God, because of which the heavens will be set on fire and dissolved, and the heavenly bodies will melt as they burn! [13] But according to his promise we are waiting for new heavens and a new earth in which righteousness dwells.

Final Words

[14] Therefore, beloved, since you are waiting for these, be diligent to be found by him without spot or blemish, and at peace. [15] And count the patience of our Lord as salvation, just as our beloved brother Paul also wrote to you according to the wisdom given him, [16] as he does in all his letters when he speaks in them of these matters. There are some things in them that are hard to understand, which the ignorant and unstable twist to their own destruction, as they do the other Scriptures. [17] You therefore, beloved, knowing this beforehand, take care that you are not carried away with the error of lawless people and lose your own stability. [18] But grow in the grace and knowledge of our Lord and Savior Jesus Christ. To him be the glory both now and to the day of eternity. Amen.

[1] Some manuscripts *love feasts* [2] Greek *bondservants* [3] Some manuscripts *on your account* [4] Or *elements*; also verse 12 [5] Greek *found*; some manuscripts *will be burned up*

INTRODUCTION TO

1-3 John

Author: The apostle John

Time: Around A.D. 85 to 95

Place: Probably Ephesus

Written to: Believers, including a local church (2 John) and Gaius (3 John)

The gist

First John teaches about being obedient to God's Word, and about confession and forgiveness. In 2 John, he encourages his readers to love each other, but also reminds them of the truth about who Jesus was. The final letter, to Gaius (3 John), encouraged him to show hospitality to traveling believers, especially those sent by John himself.

Things to look for

- Important verses on obedience (see 1 John 1:6; 2:4–6, 9–11; and many others)
- Important verses on forgiveness (see 1 John 1:8–10; 3:21; 4:18)
- John's many uses of the word *truth*
- More instructions on dealing with false teachers (see 2 John 9–11)
- An example of problems in the church (see 3 John 9–10)

Admit Your Sin

> If we confess our sins, he is faithful and just to forgive us our sins and to cleanse us from all unrighteousness. If we say we have not sinned, we make him a liar, and his word is not in us.
>
> *1 John 1:9–10*

You cannot be saved if you say, "I've never sinned." If you really believed that, why would you even want to be saved? You don't need salvation if you've done nothing that would condemn you. But as a God Girl, you are aware of your own sin, and that's why you came to the cross, begging forgiveness because of what Christ did on your behalf. It's tempting to live by your own rules about what is right and what is wrong, because then you never get it wrong—after all, you made up the rules yourself! But that's not the life of faith. The life of faith continually takes God up on his offer of forgiveness.

First John makes some very strong statements about sin and obedience. It's a great place to look for inspiration to be obedient. It's a great reminder that what proves your love to God is not your words but your actions—doing what he asks. Anything else is rebellion, not love. But thank God that his love is greater than ours. And because of that, he never leaves us but is always there, waiting for the next time we come to him in humble confession.

As you read these books, highlight them, mark them up, and make them your own. Preach truth to yourself. See what God thinks and understand what the world thinks, then choose to obey God. First John can seem overwhelming, but don't forget that although perfection is your goal, you can't reach it this side of heaven. That doesn't make perfection a less important goal, but it does mean it's important not to condemn yourself when you don't attain it. And it's just as important to know that you have someone who speaks on your behalf to the Father, and his name is Jesus (see 1 John 2:1). What more could you ask for in this life!

Must-Know Terms and Verses

❧ *Antichrist* ❧

This can refer to a particular person who will come at the end of this age, doing the work of Satan while claiming to be God (also called the "man of sin" by Paul), but in 1 John 2:22 an antichrist is anyone who stands in opposition to Christ.

❧ *Heresy* ❧

Teaching anything other than biblical truth.

❧ *Purity* ❧

The quality of being free from any contamination, either morally or physically. It is the state of your heart when you are one hundred percent devoted to God.

❧ *Word of Life* ❧

Another name for Jesus, who is called "the Word" (John 1:1) and "the life" (John 14:6). Elsewhere, it may refer to the gospel of eternal life (see 1 John 1:1).

If we say we have fellowship with him while we walk in darkness, we lie and do not practice the truth. *1 John 1:6*

If we confess our sins, he is faithful and just to forgive us our sins and to cleanse us from all unrighteousness. If we say we have not sinned, we make him a liar, and his word is not in us. *1 John 1:9–10*

By this we know that we have come to know him, if we keep his commandments. Whoever says "I know him" but does not keep his commandments is a liar, and the truth is not in him. *1 John 2:3–4*

Everyone who goes on ahead and does not abide in the teaching of Christ, does not have God. Whoever abides in the teaching has both the Father and the Son. *2 John 9*

Do not imitate evil but imitate good. Whoever does good is from God; whoever does evil has not seen God. *3 John 11*

The Word of Life

1 That which was from the beginning, which we have heard, which we have seen with our eyes, which we looked upon and have touched with our hands, concerning the word of life— ²the life was made manifest, and we have seen it, and testify to it and proclaim to you the eternal life, which was with the Father and was made manifest to us— ³that which we have seen and heard we proclaim also to you, so that you too may have fellowship with us; and indeed our fellowship is with the Father and with his Son Jesus Christ. ⁴And we are writing these things so that our¹ joy may be complete.

Walking in the Light

⁵This is the message we have heard from him and proclaim to you, that God is light, and in him is no darkness at all. ⁶If we say we have fellowship with him while we walk in darkness, we lie and do not practice the truth. ⁷But if we walk in the light, as he is in the light, we have fellowship with one another, and the blood of Jesus his Son cleanses us from all sin. ⁸If we say we have no sin, we deceive ourselves, and the truth is not in us. ⁹If we confess our sins, he is faithful and just to forgive us our sins and to cleanse us from all unrighteousness. ¹⁰If we say we have not sinned, we make him a liar, and his word is not in us.

Christ Our Advocate

2 My little children, I am writing these things to you so that you may not sin. But if anyone does sin, we have an advocate with the Father, Jesus Christ the righteous. ²He is the propitiation for our sins, and not for ours only but also for the sins of the whole world. ³And by this we know that we have come to know him, if we keep his commandments. ⁴Whoever says "I know him" but does not keep his commandments

is a liar, and the truth is not in him, ⁵but whoever keeps his word, in him truly the love of God is perfected. By this we may know that we are in him: ⁶whoever says he abides in him ought to walk in the same way in which he walked.

The New Commandment

⁷Beloved, I am writing you no new commandment, but an old commandment that you had from the beginning. The old commandment is the word that you have heard. ⁸At the same time, it is a new commandment that I am writing to you, which is true in him and in you, because² the darkness is passing away and the true light is already shining. ⁹Whoever says he is in the light and hates his brother is still in darkness. ¹⁰Whoever loves his brother abides in the light, and in him³ there is no cause for stumbling. ¹¹But whoever hates his brother is in the darkness and walks in the darkness, and does not know where he is going, because the darkness has blinded his eyes.

¹²   I am writing to you, little children,
       because your sins are forgiven for
         his name's sake.
¹³   I am writing to you, fathers,
       because you know him who is
         from the beginning.
     I am writing to you, young men,
       because you have overcome the
         evil one.
     I write to you, children,
       because you know the Father.
¹⁴   I write to you, fathers,
       because you know him who is
         from the beginning.
     I write to you, young men,
       because you are strong,
     and the word of God abides in you,
     and you have overcome the evil
         one.

¹Some manuscripts *your* ²Or *that* ³Or *it*

Do Not Love the World

¹⁵ Do not love the world or the things in the world. If anyone loves the world, the love of the Father is not in him. ¹⁶ For all that is in the world—the desires of the flesh and the desires of the eyes and pride of life[1]—is not from the Father but is from the world. ¹⁷ And the world is passing away along with its desires, but whoever does the will of God abides forever.

Warning Concerning Antichrists

¹⁸ Children, it is the last hour, and as you have heard that antichrist is coming, so now many antichrists have come. Therefore we know that it is the last hour. ¹⁹ They went out from us, but they were not of us; for if they had been of us, they would have continued with us. But they went out, that it might become plain that they all are not of us. ²⁰ But you have been anointed by the Holy One, and you all have knowledge.[2] ²¹ I write to you, not because you do not know the truth, but because you know it, and because no lie is of the truth.

²² Who is the liar but he who denies that Jesus is the Christ? This is the antichrist, he who denies the Father and the Son. ²³ No one who denies the Son has the Father. Whoever confesses the Son has the Father also. ²⁴ Let what you heard from the beginning abide in you. If what you heard from the beginning abides in you, then you too will abide in the Son and in the Father. ²⁵ And this is the promise that he made to us[3]—eternal life.

²⁶ I write these things to you about those who are trying to deceive you. ²⁷ But the anointing that you received from him abides in you, and you have no need that anyone should teach you. But as his anointing teaches you about everything, and is true, and is no lie—just as it has taught you, abide in him.

Children of God

²⁸ And now, little children, abide in him, so that when he appears we may have confidence and not shrink from him in shame at his coming. ²⁹ If you know that he is

[1] Or pride in possessions [2] Some manuscripts you know everything [3] Some manuscripts you

Know God

verses to read
1 John 2:3-6

Is there some spiritual darkness in your life? Do you wish you could sense God's presence but he seems distant and inattentive to your pleas? Then check yourself. Are you waiting to do something that needs to be done? Is there something you are unwilling to do for fear that it isn't his will or you aren't strong enough? Doing what God wants you to do is the way you live in the presence of God (see John 15:10), and if you lack that presence, it may just be because of your unwillingness to do something you know you should be doing or to stop doing something you know you shouldn't be doing.

In the life of faith you are going to have good days and bad days, mountain peak days and dry old desert days. You can't let either one of them become your obsession. Don't worry and fret over how you feel; just trust him, knowing his great love for you. When you are a God Girl, your best example of how to live is how Jesus lived. Of course that doesn't mean walking on water and healing the blind, but it does mean having compassion, showing mercy, being kind, loving others, being humble, and caring. You could add a lot of things you see in the life of Jesus to your life today. But do you know right now what they are? If you want more of God, then learn more about Jesus. Learn how he walked, what he did, and how he loved, and you'll find yourself closer to God than you could ever have imagined.

righteous, you may be sure that everyone who practices righteousness has been born of him.

3 See what kind of love the Father has given to us, that we should be called children of God; and so we are. The reason why the world does not know us is that it did not know him. ²Beloved, we are God's children now, and what we will be has not yet appeared; but we know that when he appears¹ we shall be like him, because we shall see him as he is. ³And everyone who thus hopes in him purifies himself as he is pure.

⁴Everyone who makes a practice of sinning also practices lawlessness; sin is lawlessness. ⁵You know that he appeared in order to take away sins, and in him there is no sin. ⁶No one who abides in him keeps on sinning; no one who keeps on sinning has either seen him or known him. ⁷Little

children, let no one deceive you. Whoever practices righteousness is righteous, as he is righteous. ⁸Whoever makes a practice of sinning is of the devil, for the devil has been sinning from the beginning. The reason the Son of God appeared was to destroy the works of the devil. ⁹No one born of God makes a practice of sinning, for God's² seed abides in him, and he cannot keep on sinning because he has been born of God. ¹⁰By this it is evident who are the children of God, and who are the children of the devil: whoever does not practice righteousness is not of God, nor is the one who does not love his brother.

Love One Another

¹¹For this is the message that you have heard from the beginning, that we should love one another. ¹²We should not be like Cain, who was of the evil one and murdered

¹Or *when it appears* ²Greek *his*

verses to read
1 John 3:4–6

Face it: everyone sins. No exceptions. But Jesus came to set you free from sin, and that's exactly what he's done. The Bible says that no one goes on sinning if they know Jesus. "What?" you scream. "How is that possible? Does that mean I don't know Jesus, if I still sin?" No, it doesn't mean that, but it means once you turn your heart and will over to Jesus, something changes inside you.

Look at it like this: you are on a freeway, the freeway of faith, and you see an exit. It looks like it has all kinds of exciting attractions and services, so you get off. You weren't planning on exiting; you just lost control and, before you knew it, you were stopped at the light waiting to pull onto the city streets. But suddenly you realize this isn't a good place and you shouldn't be here—God told you not to exit here but you did it anyway—so you immediately get back onto the freeway. Phew! Sin noted and quickly confessed!

But let's suppose one day you take an exit again, and this time you not only get off but you also meander around the neighborhoods till finally you end up moving in. You don't get back on the freeway; you just stay where you don't belong. In this scenario you are continuing to sin, rather than sinning and then getting right back on the road to redemption.

Everyone sins. We all mess up—daily, in fact. That's why we need confession and repentance, or turning to God. But there is a difference between falling into temptation but confessing it when you realize it, and deciding that this sin is acceptable and you're going to keep living in it. So look for the signs and don't get off into dangerous territory. By the grace of God, stay on the route he wants you on.

his brother. And why did he murder him? Because his own deeds were evil and his brother's righteous. ¹³ Do not be surprised, brothers,[1] that the world hates you. ¹⁴ We know that we have passed out of death into life, because we love the brothers. Whoever does not love abides in death. ¹⁵ Everyone who hates his brother is a murderer, and you know that no murderer has eternal life abiding in him.

Ask Yourself . . .

ABOUT HATE

Read 1 John 3:14–15 and ask yourself:

- What do I hate?
- Whom do I hate?
- Why do I hate?
- What does God's Word say about hate?
- What did God do when I hated him? (see Rom. 5:8)

¹⁶ By this we know love, that he laid down his life for us, and we ought to lay down our lives for the brothers. ¹⁷ But if anyone has the world's goods and sees his brother in need, yet closes his heart against him, how does God's love abide in him? ¹⁸ Little children, let us not love in word or talk but in deed and in truth.

¹⁹ By this we shall know that we are of the truth and reassure our heart before him; ²⁰ for whenever our heart condemns us, God is greater than our heart, and he knows everything. ²¹ Beloved, if our heart does not condemn us, we have confidence before God; ²² and whatever we ask we receive from him, because we keep his commandments and do what pleases him. ²³ And this is his commandment, that we believe in the name of his Son Jesus Christ and love one another, just as he has commanded us. ²⁴ Whoever keeps his commandments abides in God,[2] and God[3] in

him. And by this we know that he abides in us, by the Spirit whom he has given us.

Test the Spirits

4 Beloved, do not believe every spirit, but test the spirits to see whether they are from God, for many false prophets have gone out into the world. ² By this you know the Spirit of God: every spirit that confesses that Jesus Christ has come in the flesh is from God, ³ and every spirit that does not confess Jesus is not from God. This is the spirit of the antichrist, which you heard was coming and now is in the world already. ⁴ Little children, you are from God and have overcome them, for he who is in you is greater than he who is in the world. ⁵ They are from the world; therefore they speak from the world, and the world listens to them. ⁶ We are from God. Whoever knows God listens to us; whoever is not from God does not listen to us. By this we know the Spirit of truth and the spirit of error.

God Is Love

⁷ Beloved, let us love one another, for love is from God, and whoever loves has been born of God and knows God. ⁸ Anyone who does not love does not know God, because God is love. ⁹ In this the love of God was made manifest among us, that God sent his only Son into the world, so that we might live through him. ¹⁰ In this is love, not that we have loved God but that he loved us and sent his Son to be the propitiation for our sins. ¹¹ Beloved, if God so loved us, we also ought to love one another. ¹² No one has ever seen God; if we love one another, God abides in us and his love is perfected in us.

¹³ By this we know that we abide in him and he in us, because he has given us of his Spirit. ¹⁴ And we have seen and testify that the Father has sent his Son to be the Savior of the world. ¹⁵ Whoever confesses that Jesus is the Son of God, God abides in him, and he in God. ¹⁶ So we have come to know and to believe the love that God has for us. God is love, and whoever abides in love abides in God, and God abides in him. ¹⁷ By this is love perfected with us, so that we may have confidence for the day of judgment, because as he is so also are we

---

[1] Or brothers and sisters. The plural Greek word adelphoi (translated "brothers") refers to siblings in a family. In New Testament usage, depending on the context, adelphoi may refer either to men or to both men and women who are siblings (brothers and sisters) in God's family, the church; also verses 14, 16 [2] Greek him [3] Greek he

in this world. [18] There is no fear in love, but perfect love casts out fear. For fear has to do with punishment, and whoever fears has not been perfected in love. [19] We love because he first loved us. [20] If anyone says, "I love God," and hates his brother, he is a liar; for he who does not love his brother whom he has seen cannot[1] love God whom he has not seen. [21] And this commandment we have from him: whoever loves God must also love his brother.

Overcoming the World

5 Everyone who believes that Jesus is the Christ has been born of God, and everyone who loves the Father loves whoever has been born of him. [2] By this we know that we love the children of God, when we love God and obey his commandments. [3] For this is the love of God, that we keep his commandments. And his commandments are not burdensome. [4] For everyone who has been born of God overcomes the world. And this is the victory that has over-

come the world—our faith. [5] Who is it that overcomes the world except the one who believes that Jesus is the Son of God?

Testimony Concerning the Son of God

[6] This is he who came by water and blood—Jesus Christ; not by the water only but by the water and the blood. And the Spirit is the one who testifies, because the Spirit is the truth. [7] For there are three that testify: [8] the Spirit and the water and the blood; and these three agree. [9] If we receive the testimony of men, the testimony of God is greater, for this is the testimony of God that he has borne concerning his Son. [10] Whoever believes in the Son of God has the testimony in himself. Whoever does not believe God has made him a liar, because he has not believed in the testimony that God has borne concerning his Son. [11] And this is the testimony, that God gave us eternal life, and this life is in his Son. [12] Whoever has the Son has life; whoever does not have the Son of God does not have life.

[1] Some manuscripts *how can he*

verses to read
1 John 5:1–5

Know God

If you love God, you will want to do what he says. But if you not only *don't want to do* what he says but *refuse to do* what he says and are okay with that, then according to his Word there is no sacrifice left for you (see Heb. 10:26). As a God Girl, you show your love to him by doing what he says. It sounds like a tall order. Obedience isn't normally presented as a part of the salvation story. Kindness, forgiveness, and restoration, yes, but obedience? That's too hard! But God's Word is clear: you must make him Lord of your life, and that means more than a verbal agreement that he is God. It's a willful choice, by the power of the Spirit, to trust him enough obey his Word (see Rom. 10:9; James 2:14–26; 1 John 2:3–4).

This doesn't mean you won't mess up or that God doesn't forgive you when you do—oh yes, he does: see 1 John 1:9! But it does mean that as a God Girl you will want to love him, and love obeys. Love doesn't want what God doesn't give; it doesn't turn away from truth; it doesn't make its own way; it stays faithful. It may fall down, it may be tempted or even distracted, but it never willfully disobeys. When love makes a mistake it corrects it; it doesn't hide from it.

As a God Girl, if you want the blessing of God's Spirit, then you will want to do what he says. And in order to do that, you have to know the gospel announced in his Word. Study it, memorize it, teach it. Make it part of the very fiber of your being. When you do, you will find that blessings abound.

That You May Know

[13] I write these things to you who believe in the name of the Son of God that you may know that you have eternal life. [14] And this is the confidence that we have toward him, that if we ask anything according to his will he hears us. [15] And if we know that he hears us in whatever we ask, we know that we have the requests that we have asked of him.

[16] If anyone sees his brother committing a sin not leading to death, he shall ask, and God[1] will give him life— to those who commit sins that do not lead to death. There is sin that leads to death; I do not say that one should pray for that. [17] All wrongdoing is sin, but there is sin that does not lead to death.

[18] We know that everyone who has been born of God does not keep on sinning, but he who was born of God protects him, and the evil one does not touch him.

[19] We know that we are from God, and the whole world lies in the power of the evil one.

[20] And we know that the Son of God has come and has given us understanding, so that we may know him who is true; and we are in him who is true, in his Son Jesus Christ. He is the true God and eternal life. [21] Little children, keep yourselves from idols.

---

[1] Greek he

The Second Letter of John

2 John

Greeting

¹The elder to the elect lady and her children, whom I love in truth, and not only I, but also all who know the truth, ²because of the truth that abides in us and will be with us forever:

³Grace, mercy, and peace will be with us, from God the Father and from Jesus Christ the Father's Son, in truth and love.

Walking in Truth and Love

⁴I rejoiced greatly to find some of your children walking in the truth, just as we were commanded by the Father. ⁵And now I ask you, dear lady— not as though I were writing you a new commandment, but the one we have had from the beginning— that we love one another. ⁶And this is love, that we walk according to his commandments; this is the commandment, just as you have heard from the beginning, so that you should walk in it. ⁷For many deceivers have gone out into the world, those who do not confess the coming of Jesus Christ in the flesh. Such a one is the deceiver and the antichrist. ⁸Watch yourselves, so that you may not lose what we[1] have worked for, but may win a full reward. ⁹Everyone who goes on ahead and does not abide in the teaching of Christ, does not have God. Whoever abides in the teaching has both the Father and the Son. ¹⁰If anyone comes to you and does not bring this teaching, do not receive him into your house or give him any greeting, ¹¹for whoever greets him takes part in his wicked works.

Ask Yourself . . .

ABOUT LOVE

- What does God's Word say about love?
- Are there people I am unwilling to love?
- In what ways do I not love God, according to 2 John 5–6?
- Do I live each day mindful of God's undeserved love for me?

Final Greetings

¹²Though I have much to write to you, I would rather not use paper and ink. Instead I hope to come to you and talk face to face, so that our joy may be complete.

¹³The children of your elect sister greet you.

---

[1] Some manuscripts *you*

The Third Letter of John

3 John

Greeting

¹ The elder to the beloved Gaius, whom I love in truth.

² Beloved, I pray that all may go well with you and that you may be in good health, as it goes well with your soul. ³ For I rejoiced greatly when the brothers[1] came and testified to your truth, as indeed you are walking in the truth. ⁴ I have no greater joy than to hear that my children are walking in the truth.

Support and Opposition

⁵ Beloved, it is a faithful thing you do in all your efforts for these brothers, strangers as they are, ⁶ who testified to your love before the church. You will do well to send them on their journey in a manner worthy of God. ⁷ For they have gone out for the sake of the name, accepting nothing from the Gentiles. ⁸ Therefore we ought to support people like these, that we may be fellow workers for the truth.

⁹ I have written something to the church, but Diotrephes, who likes to put himself first, does not acknowledge our authority. ¹⁰ So if I come, I will bring up what he is doing, talking wicked nonsense against us. And not content with that, he refuses to welcome the brothers, and also stops

[1] Or *brothers and sisters*. The plural Greek word *adelphoi* (translated "brothers") refers to siblings in a family. In New Testament usage, depending on the context, *adelphoi* may refer either to men or to both men and women who are siblings (brothers and sisters) in God's family, the church; also verses 5, 10

Know True Happiness

verse to read
3 John 11

"If she jumped off a cliff, would you?" Following the crowd can sometimes seem like the safest route. No one notices you. No one calls you out. No one judges you. But when the crowd is jumping off a cliff, how smart is diving to your destruction just to fit in?

The world doesn't know Jesus, so they think he's crazy. They create their own rules and values. They focus on what the eye can see and avoid what can't be seen. But as a God Girl you know there is more than the physical world. You are aware of the spiritual, that unseen world that surrounds you and fills you. Temporary happiness might be found in denying the existence of God and the commands of his law, but permanent happiness comes when you drop what the world believes and trust only what God says.

It's human nature to want to fit in, but when you act, look, and think like the rest of the world, you prove not your faith but your distrust. True God Girls follow not the world but the Savior, knowing his great love for them in the gospel. Going against the grain and doing what God wants you to do not only proves your faith but also increases it. Each time you risk disobeying the world by doing what is right, your faith grows.

those who want to and puts them out of the church.

¹¹Beloved, do not imitate evil but imitate good. Whoever does good is from God; whoever does evil has not seen God. ¹²Demetrius has received a good testimony from everyone, and from the truth itself. We also add our testimony, and you know that our testimony is true.

Final Greetings

¹³I had much to write to you, but I would rather not write with pen and ink. ¹⁴I hope to see you soon, and we will talk face to face.

¹⁵Peace be to you. The friends greet you. Greet the friends, each by name.

INTRODUCTION TO

Jude

Author: Jude, the brother of James

Time: Around A.D. 60–70

Place: Unknown

Written to: A local church

The gist

Jude wanted to encourage believers to beware of people in their midst who allowed and even encouraged sin. He also wanted to help believers to grow in their faith and to understand the purpose that God has for them.

Things to look for

- References to false believers—people who slip in and deceive a group of believers
- The ways Jude encourages readers to grow (see Jude 20–24)

Show Mercy

> Have mercy on those who doubt; save others by snatching them out of the fire; to others show mercy with fear, hating even the garment stained by the flesh.
>
> Jude 22–23

The book of Jude reminds us that just because someone claims to be a believer doesn't make it so. The best way to tell is from the fruit of their lives. Do they act like a believer? Do they teach things that are consistent with God's Word? It's easy to say you are a Christian but harder to prove it by how you act and what you say. When you find believers who fail to live out their faith, you need to help them understand that they have been living a lie, so that they do not continue to live in darkness.

As a God Girl you don't have to save the world, but you should look out for believers who might be mistakenly believing and even preaching a falsehood. You can't allow a fellow believer to be deceived just because you think that they aren't your responsibility. Your job is not to save them. God himself will do that. But perhaps you can remind them of a truth they may have forgotten or never known. You don't need to worry or become anxious over the sins of others; just share the truth and then trust God to work in their hearts and lives.

Must-Know Terms and Verses

☞ *The Judgment of the Great Day* ☜

The day when Jesus will return to judge the earth and all who are in it (see Jude 6; Rev. 20:7–15).

Certain people have crept in unnoticed who long ago were designated for this condemnation, ungodly people, who pervert the grace of our God into sensuality and deny our only Master and Lord, Jesus Christ. *Jude 4*

Yet in like manner these people also, relying on their dreams, defile the flesh, reject authority, and blaspheme the glorious ones. *Jude 8*

Have mercy on those who doubt; save others by snatching them out of the fire; to others show mercy with fear, hating even the garment stained by the flesh. *Jude 22–23*

The Letter of Jude

Greeting

¹ Jude, a servant¹ of Jesus Christ and brother of James,

To those who are called, beloved in God the Father and kept for² Jesus Christ:

² May mercy, peace, and love be multiplied to you.

Judgment on False Teachers

³ Beloved, although I was very eager to write to you about our common salvation, I found it necessary to write appealing to you to contend for the faith that was once for all delivered to the saints. ⁴ For certain people have crept in unnoticed who long ago were designated for this condemnation, ungodly people, who pervert the grace of our God into sensuality and deny our only Master and Lord, Jesus Christ.

⁵ Now I want to remind you, although you once fully knew it, that Jesus, who saved³ a people out of the land of Egypt, afterward destroyed those who did not believe. ⁶ And the angels who did not stay within their own position of authority, but left their proper dwelling, he has kept in eternal chains under gloomy darkness until the judgment of the great day— ⁷ just as Sodom and Gomorrah and the surrounding cities, which likewise indulged in sexual immorality and pursued unnatural desire,⁴ serve as an example by undergoing a punishment of eternal fire.

⁸ Yet in like manner these people also, relying on their dreams, defile the flesh, reject authority, and blaspheme the glorious ones. ⁹ But when the archangel Michael, contending with the devil, was disputing about the body of Moses, he did not presume to pronounce a blasphemous judgment, but said, "The Lord rebuke you." ¹⁰ But these people blaspheme all that they do not understand, and they are destroyed by all that they, like unreasoning animals, understand instinctively. ¹¹ Woe to them! For they walked in the way of Cain and abandoned themselves for the sake of gain to Balaam's error and perished in Korah's rebellion. ¹² These are hidden reefs⁵ at your love feasts, as they feast with you without fear, shepherds feeding themselves; waterless clouds, swept along by winds; fruitless trees in late autumn, twice dead, uprooted; ¹³ wild waves of the sea, casting up the foam of their own shame; wandering stars, for whom the gloom of utter darkness has been reserved forever.

¹⁴ It was also about these that Enoch, the seventh from Adam, prophesied, saying, "Behold, the Lord comes with ten thousands of his holy ones, ¹⁵ to execute judgment on all and to convict all the ungodly of all their deeds of ungodliness that they have committed in such an ungodly way, and of all the harsh things that ungodly sinners have spoken against him." ¹⁶ These are grumblers, malcontents, following their own sinful desires; they are loud-mouthed boasters, showing favoritism to gain advantage.

A Call to Persevere

¹⁷ But you must remember, beloved, the predictions of the apostles of our Lord Jesus Christ. ¹⁸ They⁶ said to you, "In the last time there will be scoffers, following their own ungodly passions." ¹⁹ It is these who cause divisions, worldly people, devoid of the Spirit. ²⁰ But you, beloved, building yourselves up in your most holy faith and praying in the Holy Spirit, ²¹ keep yourselves in the love of God, waiting for the mercy of our Lord Jesus Christ that leads to eternal life. ²² And have mercy on those who doubt; ²³ save others by snatching them out of the fire; to others show

---

¹ Or slave (for the contextual rendering of the Greek word doulos, see About the ESV) ² Or by ³ Some manuscripts although you fully knew it, that the Lord who once saved ⁴ Greek other flesh ⁵ Or are blemishes ⁶ Or Christ, because they

mercy with fear, hating even the garment[1] stained by the flesh.

Doxology

24 Now to him who is able to keep you from stumbling and to present you blameless before the presence of his glory with great joy, **25** to the only God, our Savior, through Jesus Christ our Lord, be glory, majesty, dominion, and authority, before all time and now and forever. Amen.

[1] Greek *chiton*, a long garment worn under the cloak next to the skin

---

verses to read
Jude 22–25

Mercy can't be afraid of getting dirty. When you reach out to help those who are hurting and have turned their backs on God, you can't be afraid of getting a little messy. Sure, you have to guard your heart against friendship with the world. You can't go around giving away your heart willy-nilly to those who hate God and haven't made him their Lord, but you can give them your hand. You can offer to help.

Mercy demonstrates a desire to show others the God who saves. How will they know if they haven't heard? How will they hear if you don't speak up? (See Romans 10:14–15.) Mercy requires your fearlessness. Mercy's target is misery—the misery of those who suffer because they don't know God or understand his love. Because of this darkness of their soul, they don't understand what they are doing; they don't know the depths of their sin. Forgive them, as you have been forgiven (see Eph. 4:32). Show them mercy, because they are in misery.

When people insult you, gossip about you, or otherwise prove their distance from the Father, as a God Girl you should have mercy on them, for their soul is in distress. You should find ways to serve, rather than to criticize. Your trademark reaction should always be showing mercy and compassion to those who are weaker than you. God "is able to keep you from stumbling and to present you blameless before the presence of his glory with great joy" (Jude 24), but you must put all your hope in him and turn all your thoughts onto him. Never focus so much on other people's misery that you take your eyes off of God. Obey *him*, love *them*, show them mercy and compassion, and pray for them, but never fear them and never turn your back on them in indifference or hate.

INTRODUCTION TO
Revelation

Author: Probably the apostle John, the son of Zebedee

Time: Around A.D. 95

Place: The island of Patmos

Written to: Seven churches in the province of Asia

The gist
Revelation was written to reveal the things that would happen before, during, and after the second coming of Jesus.

Things to look for
- Revelation about the second coming of Jesus (see Revelation 4–19)
- Description of the new heaven and the new earth (see Rev. 21:1–22:5)

Have No Fear

> It [the beast] was allowed to make war on the saints and to conquer them. And authority was given it over every tribe and people and language and nation.
>
> *Revelation 13:7*

Earth. Who's in charge? Satan. But he has control only insofar as God allows it. That's one of the reasons we have nothing to fear. The Enemy might plot against you, he might plan attacks, he might even succeed sometimes, but he doesn't win. The thing to remember is that no one has control or authority unless God allows them to have it. So when Satan wages war against God's holy people, it's because God allowed it (see Rev. 13:7). Why God allows the Enemy to do such things is a mystery, but it is one that we have to trust God in.

If God allows something to come to pass, he must have a good reason. The God Girl is fear-free and full of peace because of this. She knows who is in charge and who wins. She knows whose side she is on and the protection he offers. Even if God allows an apparently terrible thing to come into your life, don't fear, but trust that it is for your good. Rest in his wise, fatherly care for your life. When you willingly obey and refuse to accuse God of not living up to his promises, you will over time find yourself exactly where you need to be. And peace will be your constant companion.

As you read the book of Revelation, have no fear—all these things will and must come to pass for the good of God's people. Because of that you can rest assured that you, dear God Girl, can have peace as you consider the future. Allow this book to serve as a warning against becoming lukewarm and a chance to see who wins when all is said and done.

∞ *Crown of Life* ∞

Some believe this refers to eternal life, and others believe it is an actual crown that believers receive when they die and go to heaven. The kinds of crowns they get will depend on what they have done. Ultimately, however, all who receive these crowns will lay them down before God as they worship him (see Phil. 4:1; 2 Tim. 4:8; James 1:12; 1 Pet. 5:4; Rev. 2:10; 3:11; 4:4, 10).

So, because you are lukewarm, and neither hot nor cold, I will spit you out of my mouth. *Revelation 3:16*

Behold, I stand at the door and knock. If anyone hears my voice and opens the door, I will come in to him and eat with him, and he with me. *Revelation 3:20*

Day and night they never cease to say,

"Holy, holy, holy, is the Lord God Almighty,
who was and is and is to come!" *Revelation 4:8*

After this I looked, and behold, a great multitude that no one could number, from every nation, from all tribes and peoples and languages, standing before the throne and before the Lamb, clothed in white robes, with palm branches in their hands, and crying out with a loud voice, "Salvation belongs to our God who sits on the throne, and to the Lamb!" *Revelation 7:9–10*

The 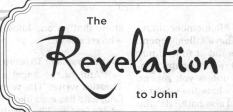 Revelation
to John

Prologue

1 The revelation of Jesus Christ, which God gave him to show to his servants[1] the things that must soon take place. He made it known by sending his angel to his servant[2] John, ²who bore witness to the word of God and to the testimony of Jesus Christ, even to all that he saw. ³Blessed is the one who reads aloud the words of this prophecy, and blessed are those who hear, and who keep what is written in it, for the time is near.

Greeting to the Seven Churches

⁴John to the seven churches that are in Asia:

Grace to you and peace from him who is and who was and who is to come, and from the seven spirits who are before his throne, ⁵and from Jesus Christ the faithful witness, the firstborn of the dead, and the ruler of kings on earth.

To him who loves us and has freed us from our sins by his blood ⁶and made us a kingdom, priests to his God and Father, to him be glory and dominion forever and ever. Amen. ⁷Behold, he is coming with the clouds, and every eye will see him, even those who pierced him, and all tribes of the earth will wail[3] on account of him. Even so. Amen.

⁸"I am the Alpha and the Omega," says the Lord God, "who is and who was and who is to come, the Almighty."

Vision of the Son of Man

⁹I, John, your brother and partner in the tribulation and the kingdom and the patient endurance that are in Jesus, was on the island called Patmos on account of the word of God and the testimony of Jesus. ¹⁰I was in the Spirit on the Lord's day, and I heard behind me a loud voice like a trumpet ¹¹saying, "Write what you see in a book and send it to the seven churches, to Ephesus and to Smyrna and to Pergamum and to Thyatira and to Sardis and to Philadelphia and to Laodicea."

¹²Then I turned to see the voice that was speaking to me, and on turning I saw seven golden lampstands, ¹³and in the midst of the lampstands one like a son of man, clothed with a long robe and with a golden sash around his chest. ¹⁴The hairs of his head were white, like white wool, like snow. His eyes were like a flame of fire, ¹⁵his feet were like burnished bronze, refined in a furnace, and his voice was like the roar of many waters. ¹⁶In his right hand he held seven stars, from his mouth came a sharp two-edged sword, and his face was like the sun shining in full strength.

¹⁷When I saw him, I fell at his feet as though dead. But he laid his right hand on me, saying, "Fear not, I am the first and the last, ¹⁸and the living one. I died, and behold I am alive forevermore, and I have the keys of Death and Hades. ¹⁹Write therefore the things that you have seen, those that are and those that are to take place after this. ²⁰As for the mystery of the seven stars that you saw in my right hand, and the seven golden lampstands, the seven stars are the angels of the seven churches, and the seven lampstands are the seven churches.

To the Church in Ephesus

2 "To the angel of the church in Ephesus write: 'The words of him who holds the seven stars in his right hand, who walks among the seven golden lampstands.

²"'I know your works, your toil and your patient endurance, and how you cannot bear with those who are evil, but have tested those who call themselves apostles and are not, and found them to be false. ³I know you are enduring patiently and bearing up for my name's sake, and you have not grown weary. ⁴But I have this against you, that you have abandoned the

---

¹Greek *bondservants* ²Greek *bondservant* ³Or *mourn*

love you had at first. ⁵Remember therefore from where you have fallen; repent, and do the works you did at first. If not, I will come to you and remove your lampstand from its place, unless you repent. ⁶Yet this you have: you hate the works of the Nicolaitans, which I also hate. ⁷He who has an ear, let him hear what the Spirit says to the churches. To the one who conquers I will grant to eat of the tree of life, which is in the paradise of God.'

To the Church in Smyrna

⁸"And to the angel of the church in Smyrna write: 'The words of the first and the last, who died and came to life.

⁹"'I know your tribulation and your poverty (but you are rich) and the slander¹ of those who say that they are Jews and are not, but are a synagogue of Satan. ¹⁰Do not fear what you are about to suffer. Behold, the devil is about to throw some of you into prison, that you may be tested, and for ten days you will have tribulation. Be faithful unto death, and I will give you the crown of life. ¹¹He who has an ear, let him hear what the Spirit says to the churches. The one who conquers will not be hurt by the second death.'

To the Church in Pergamum

¹²"And to the angel of the church in Pergamum write: 'The words of him who has the sharp two-edged sword.

¹³"'I know where you dwell, where Satan's throne is. Yet you hold fast my name, and you did not deny my faith² even in the days of Antipas my faithful witness, who was killed among you, where Satan dwells. ¹⁴But I have a few things against you: you have some there who hold the teaching of Balaam, who taught Balak to put a stumbling block before the sons of Israel, so that they might eat food sacrificed to idols and practice sexual immorality. ¹⁵So also you have some who hold the teaching of the Nicolaitans. ¹⁶Therefore repent. If not, I will come to you soon and war against them with the sword of my mouth. ¹⁷He who has an ear, let him hear what the Spirit says to the churches. To the one who conquers I will give some of the hidden manna, and I will give him a white stone, with a new name written on the stone that no one knows except the one who receives it.'

To the Church in Thyatira

¹⁸"And to the angel of the church in Thyatira write: 'The words of the Son of God, who has eyes like a flame of fire, and whose feet are like burnished bronze.

¹⁹"'I know your works, your love and faith and service and patient endurance, and that your latter works exceed the first. ²⁰But I have this against you, that you tolerate that woman Jezebel, who calls herself a prophetess and is teaching and seducing my servants³ to practice sexual immorality and to eat food sacrificed to idols. ²¹I gave her time to repent, but she refuses to repent of her sexual immorality. ²²Behold, I will throw her onto a sickbed, and those who commit adultery with her I will throw into great tribulation, unless they repent of her works, ²³and I will strike her children dead. And all the churches will know that I am he who searches mind and heart, and I will give to each of you according to your works. ²⁴But to the rest of you in Thyatira, who do not hold this teaching, who have not learned what some call the deep things of Satan, to you I say, I do not lay on you any other burden. ²⁵Only hold fast what you have until I come. ²⁶The one who conquers and who keeps my works until the end, to him I will give authority over the nations, ²⁷and he will rule them with a rod of iron, as when earthen pots are broken in pieces, even as I myself have received authority from my Father. ²⁸And I will give him the morning star. ²⁹He who has an ear, let him hear what the Spirit says to the churches.'

To the Church in Sardis

3 "And to the angel of the church in Sardis write: 'The words of him who has the seven spirits of God and the seven stars.

"'I know your works. You have the reputation of being alive, but you are dead. ²Wake up, and strengthen what remains and is about to die, for I have not found your works complete in the sight of my God. ³Remember, then, what you received and heard. Keep it, and repent. If you will not wake up, I will come like a thief, and you will not know at what hour I will come against you. ⁴Yet you have still a few names in Sardis, people who have not soiled their

¹Greek *blasphemy* ²Or *your faith in me* ³Greek *bondservants*

garments, and they will walk with me in white, for they are worthy. ⁵The one who conquers will be clothed thus in white garments, and I will never blot his name out of the book of life. I will confess his name before my Father and before his angels. ⁶He who has an ear, let him hear what the Spirit says to the churches.'

To the Church in Philadelphia

⁷"And to the angel of the church in Philadelphia write: 'The words of the holy one, the true one, who has the key of David, who opens and no one will shut, who shuts and no one opens.

⁸"'I know your works. Behold, I have set before you an open door, which no one is able to shut. I know that you have but little power, and yet you have kept my word and have not denied my name. ⁹Behold, I will make those of the synagogue of Satan who say that they are Jews and are not, but lie—behold, I will make them come and bow down before your feet, and they will learn that I have loved you. ¹⁰Because you have kept my word about patient endurance, I will keep you from the hour of trial that is coming on the whole world, to try those who dwell on the earth. ¹¹I am coming soon. Hold fast what you have, so that

no one may seize your crown. ¹²The one who conquers, I will make him a pillar in the temple of my God. Never shall he go out of it, and I will write on him the name of my God, and the name of the city of my God, the new Jerusalem, which comes down from my God out of heaven, and my own new name. ¹³He who has an ear, let him hear what the Spirit says to the churches.'

To the Church in Laodicea

¹⁴"And to the angel of the church in Laodicea write: 'The words of the Amen, the faithful and true witness, the beginning of God's creation.

¹⁵"'I know your works: you are neither cold nor hot. Would that you were either cold or hot! ¹⁶So, because you are lukewarm, and neither hot nor cold, I will spit you out of my mouth. ¹⁷For you say, I am rich, I have prospered, and I need nothing, not realizing that you are wretched, pitiable, poor, blind, and naked. ¹⁸I counsel you to buy from me gold refined by fire, so that you may be rich, and white garments so that you may clothe yourself and the shame of your nakedness may not be seen, and salve to anoint your eyes, so that you may see. ¹⁹Those whom I love, I reprove and discipline, so be zealous and repent. ²⁰Behold, I stand at the door

verses to read
Revelation 3:7-11

If you have only a little strength, use it for God's glory. When you are too weak to move and too tired to go on, all you have to do is trust him. Not sure what God wants you to do? Then receive what he says to you in his Word. Don't worry about hearing his voice right now. Don't fret over finding his will for your life today. All you need to know for today is found in the pages of the Bible. Truth is written there for the taking. With the little strength that you have, reach for truth.

It takes much less energy to take orders than to struggle and wrestle with indecision. A smart girl takes the resources she has and applies them to her life. As you move into adulthood, you will be met with all kinds of different choices that only you can make. When you were a child your parents made choices for you, but now it's up to you. And because of that you will be held responsible. You can't go blamin' your life on anyone else but yourself now. Are you willing to take God at his Word and do what he commands, or will you complain, disagree, and do it your own way? If you have only a little strength, pay attention to God's Word and don't deny his name.

and knock. If anyone hears my voice and opens the door, I will come in to him and eat with him, and he with me. ²¹ The one who conquers, I will grant him to sit with me on my throne, as I also conquered and sat down with my Father on his throne. ²² He who has an ear, let him hear what the Spirit says to the churches.' "

The Throne in Heaven

4 After this I looked, and behold, a door standing open in heaven! And the first voice, which I had heard speaking to me like a trumpet, said, "Come up here, and I will show you what must take place after this." ² At once I was in the Spirit, and behold, a throne stood in heaven, with one seated on the throne. ³ And he who sat there had the appearance of jasper and carnelian, and around the throne was a rainbow that had the appearance of an emerald. ⁴ Around the throne were twenty-four thrones, and seated on the thrones were twenty-four elders, clothed in white garments, with golden crowns on their heads. ⁵ From the throne came flashes of lightning, and rumblings[1] and peals of thunder, and before the throne were burning seven torches of fire, which are the seven spirits of God, ⁶ and before the throne there was as it were a sea of glass, like crystal.

And around the throne, on each side of the throne, are four living creatures, full of eyes in front and behind: ⁷ the first living creature like a lion, the second living creature like an ox, the third living creature with the face of a man, and the fourth living creature like an eagle in flight. ⁸ And the four living creatures, each of them with six wings, are full of eyes all around and within, and day and night they never cease to say,

"Holy, holy, holy, is the Lord God Almighty,
who was and is and is to come!"

⁹ And whenever the living creatures give glory and honor and thanks to him who is seated on the throne, who lives forever and ever, ¹⁰ the twenty-four elders fall down before him who is seated on the throne and worship him who lives forever and ever. They cast their crowns before the throne, saying,

¹¹ "Worthy are you, our Lord and God,
to receive glory and honor and power,
for you created all things,
and by your will they existed and were created."

The Scroll and the Lamb

5 Then I saw in the right hand of him who was seated on the throne a scroll written within and on the back, sealed with seven seals. ² And I saw a mighty angel proclaiming with a loud voice, "Who is worthy to open the scroll and break its seals?" ³ And no one in heaven or on earth or under the earth was able to open the scroll or to look into it, ⁴ and I began to weep loudly because no one was found worthy to open the scroll or to look into it. ⁵ And one of the elders said to me, "Weep no more; behold, the Lion of the tribe of Judah, the Root of David, has conquered, so that he can open the scroll and its seven seals."

⁶ And between the throne and the four living creatures and among the elders I saw a Lamb standing, as though it had been slain, with seven horns and with seven eyes, which are the seven spirits of God sent out into all the earth. ⁷ And he went and took the scroll from the right hand of him who was seated on the throne. ⁸ And when he had taken the scroll, the four living creatures and the twenty-four elders fell down before the Lamb, each holding a harp, and golden bowls full of incense, which are the prayers of the saints. ⁹ And they sang a new song, saying,

"Worthy are you to take the scroll
and to open its seals,
for you were slain, and by your blood you ransomed people for God
from every tribe and language and people and nation,
¹⁰ and you have made them a kingdom and priests to our God,
and they shall reign on the earth."

¹¹ Then I looked, and I heard around the throne and the living creatures and the elders the voice of many angels, numbering myriads of myriads and thousands of thousands, ¹² saying with a loud voice,

[1] Or voices, or sounds

"Worthy is the Lamb who was slain,
　to receive power and wealth and
　　wisdom and might
　and honor and glory and blessing!"

[13] And I heard every creature in heaven and on earth and under the earth and in the sea, and all that is in them, saying,

"To him who sits on the throne and to
　　the Lamb
　be blessing and honor and glory and
　　might forever and ever!"

[14] And the four living creatures said, "Amen!" and the elders fell down and worshiped.

The Seven Seals

6 Now I watched when the Lamb opened one of the seven seals, and I heard one of the four living creatures say with a voice like thunder, "Come!" [2] And I looked, and behold, a white horse! And its rider had a bow, and a crown was given to him, and he came out conquering, and to conquer.

[3] When he opened the second seal, I heard the second living creature say, "Come!" [4] And out came another horse, bright red. Its rider was permitted to take peace from the earth, so that people should slay one another, and he was given a great sword.

[5] When he opened the third seal, I heard the third living creature say, "Come!" And I looked, and behold, a black horse! And its rider had a pair of scales in his hand. [6] And I heard what seemed to be a voice in the midst of the four living creatures, saying, "A quart[1] of wheat for a denarius,[2] and three quarts of barley for a denarius, and do not harm the oil and wine!"

[7] When he opened the fourth seal, I heard the voice of the fourth living creature say, "Come!" [8] And I looked, and behold, a pale horse! And its rider's name was Death, and Hades followed him. And they were given authority over a fourth of the earth, to kill with sword and with famine and with pestilence and by wild beasts of the earth.

[9] When he opened the fifth seal, I saw under the altar the souls of those who had been slain for the word of God and for the witness they had borne. [10] They cried out with a loud voice, "O Sovereign Lord, holy and true, how long before you will judge

A Prayer for...
BEDTIME

Giver of all,

Another day is ending, and I take my place beneath my great Redeemer's cross, where healing streams continually flow, where balm is poured into every wound, where I wash each day in the all-cleansing blood, assured that you see no spots of sin in me at all. One day I will come home to you and will be in this world no more; help me to strengthen my heart and my mind, to enliven my step, to act as if each moment were my last, so that my life will be joy and my death glory.

I thank you for your earthly blessings—the refreshing air, the light of the sun, the food that gives me strength, the clothes that warm me, the home that shelters me, the sleep that gives me rest, the starry canopy of night, the summer breeze, the flowers' sweetness, the music of flowing streams, the happiness of family and friends. I thank you for things both animate and inanimate that give me comfort. My cup runs over. Help me not to be oblivious to these daily mercies. Your hand gives blessings; your power turns away evil. I thank you for the spiritual graces, the cheering presence of your Spirit, the strength of your restraining will, your power against enemy forces, and above all, the gospel of grace. Blessed be my sovereign Lord!

Amen.

and avenge our blood on those who dwell on the earth?" [11] Then they were each given a white robe and told to rest a little longer, until the number of their fellow servants[3] and their brothers[4] should be complete, who were to be killed as they themselves had been.

---

[1] Greek *choinix*, a dry measure equal to about a quart [2] A *denarius* was a day's wage for a laborer [3] Greek *fellow bondservants*
[4] Or *brothers and sisters*. The plural Greek word *adelphoi* (translated "brothers") refers to siblings in a family. In New Testament usage, depending on the context, *adelphoi* may refer either to men or to both men and women who are siblings (brothers and sisters) in God's family, the church

¹² When he opened the sixth seal, I looked, and behold, there was a great earthquake, and the sun became black as sackcloth, the full moon became like blood, ¹³ and the stars of the sky fell to the earth as the fig tree sheds its winter fruit when shaken by a gale. ¹⁴ The sky vanished like a scroll that is being rolled up, and every mountain and island was removed from its place. ¹⁵ Then the kings of the earth and the great ones and the generals and the rich and the powerful, and everyone, slave[1] and free, hid themselves in the caves and among the rocks of the mountains, ¹⁶ calling to the mountains and rocks, "Fall on us and hide us from the face of him who is seated on the throne, and from the wrath of the Lamb, ¹⁷ for the great day of their wrath has come, and who can stand?"

The 144,000 of Israel Sealed

7 After this I saw four angels standing at the four corners of the earth, holding back the four winds of the earth, that no wind might blow on earth or sea or against any tree. ² Then I saw another angel ascending from the rising of the sun, with the seal of the living God, and he called with a loud voice to the four angels who had been given power to harm earth and sea, ³ saying, "Do not harm the earth or the sea or the trees, until we have sealed the servants[2] of our God on their foreheads." ⁴ And I heard the number of the sealed, 144,000, sealed from every tribe of the sons of Israel:

⁵   12,000 from the tribe of Judah were
         sealed,
       12,000 from the tribe of Reuben,
       12,000 from the tribe of Gad,
⁶   12,000 from the tribe of Asher,
       12,000 from the tribe of Naphtali,
       12,000 from the tribe of Manasseh,
⁷   12,000 from the tribe of Simeon,
       12,000 from the tribe of Levi,
       12,000 from the tribe of Issachar,
⁸   12,000 from the tribe of Zebulun,
       12,000 from the tribe of Joseph,
       12,000 from the tribe of Benjamin
         were sealed.

A Great Multitude from Every Nation

⁹ After this I looked, and behold, a great multitude that no one could number, from every nation, from all tribes and peoples and languages, standing before the throne and before the Lamb, clothed in white robes, with palm branches in their hands, ¹⁰ and crying out with a loud voice, "Salvation belongs to our God who sits on the throne, and to the Lamb!" ¹¹ And all the angels were standing around the throne and around the elders and the four living creatures, and they fell on their faces before the throne and worshiped God, ¹² saying, "Amen! Blessing and glory and wisdom and thanksgiving and honor and power and might be to our God forever and ever! Amen."

¹³ Then one of the elders addressed me, saying, "Who are these, clothed in white robes, and from where have they come?" ¹⁴ I said to him, "Sir, you know." And he said to me, "These are the ones coming out of the great tribulation. They have washed their robes and made them white in the blood of the Lamb.

¹⁵   "Therefore they are before the throne
          of God,
        and serve him day and night in his
          temple;
        and he who sits on the throne will
          shelter them with his pres-
          ence.
¹⁶   They shall hunger no more, neither
          thirst anymore;
        the sun shall not strike them,
        nor any scorching heat.
¹⁷   For the Lamb in the midst of the
          throne will be their shepherd,
        and he will guide them to springs
          of living water,
        and God will wipe away every tear
          from their eyes."

The Seventh Seal and the Golden Censer

8 When the Lamb opened the seventh seal, there was silence in heaven for about half an hour. ² Then I saw the seven angels who stand before God, and seven trumpets were given to them. ³ And another angel came and stood at the altar with a golden censer, and he was given much incense to offer with the prayers of all the saints on the golden altar before the throne, ⁴ and the smoke of the incense, with the prayers of the saints, rose before God from the hand of the angel. ⁵ Then the angel

[1] Or *servant*; Greek *bondservant* [2] Greek *bondservants*

took the censer and filled it with fire from the altar and threw it on the earth, and there were peals of thunder, rumblings,[1] flashes of lightning, and an earthquake.

The Seven Trumpets

[6] Now the seven angels who had the seven trumpets prepared to blow them.

[7] The first angel blew his trumpet, and there followed hail and fire, mixed with blood, and these were thrown upon the earth. And a third of the earth was burned up, and a third of the trees were burned up, and all green grass was burned up.

[8] The second angel blew his trumpet, and something like a great mountain, burning with fire, was thrown into the sea, and a third of the sea became blood. [9] A third of the living creatures in the sea died, and a third of the ships were destroyed.

[10] The third angel blew his trumpet, and a great star fell from heaven, blazing like a torch, and it fell on a third of the rivers and on the springs of water. [11] The name of the star is Wormwood.[2] A third of the waters became wormwood, and many people died from the water, because it had been made bitter.

[12] The fourth angel blew his trumpet, and a third of the sun was struck, and a third of the moon, and a third of the stars, so that a third of their light might be darkened, and a third of the day might be kept from shining, and likewise a third of the night.

[13] Then I looked, and I heard an eagle crying with a loud voice as it flew directly overhead, "Woe, woe, woe to those who dwell on the earth, at the blasts of the other trumpets that the three angels are about to blow!"

9 And the fifth angel blew his trumpet, and I saw a star fallen from heaven to earth, and he was given the key to the shaft of the bottomless pit.[3] [2] He opened the shaft of the bottomless pit, and from the shaft rose smoke like the smoke of a great furnace, and the sun and the air were darkened with the smoke from the shaft. [3] Then from the smoke came locusts on the earth, and they were given power like the power of scorpions of the earth. [4] They were told not to harm the grass of the earth or any green plant or any tree, but only those people who do not have the seal of God on their foreheads. [5] They were allowed to torment them for five months, but not

---

[1] Or *voices*, or *sounds*   [2] *Wormwood* is the name of a plant and of the bitter-tasting extract derived from it   [3] Greek *the abyss*; also verses 2, 11

Know True Happiness

verses to read
Revelation 8:7–13

Worry might be your first response when things get tough. When everyone around you sees disaster coming and fears the worst, it's easy to jump on the worry train. But worry isn't meant to be a part of the life of a God Girl. Sure, things might look bleak. Trouble might be all around you, the earth may look like it's about to stop spinning, but no matter how bad things look, you can be sure of one thing: God has it all under control. Fear is no good, unless you're talking about the fear of God. He's the only one you need to fear. No one and nothing can take you away from him. So don't fear and don't worry when things seem tragic. Your life is in his hands, and even if the sky falls and the oceans all dry up, he won't let go.

When things get rough, don't let worry prove your lack of faith. Instead, prove how much you trust God by refusing to believe that he's not in control. Worry calls God a liar, but trust proves your faith in him. So don't fear the future, don't fear what God has ordained, don't fear what others fear. Your life is in his hands from beginning to end. He knows your destiny, he knows how the world will end, and he knows how to protect and care for you.

to kill them, and their torment was like the torment of a scorpion when it stings someone. ⁶And in those days people will seek death and will not find it. They will long to die, but death will flee from them.

⁷In appearance the locusts were like horses prepared for battle: on their heads were what looked like crowns of gold; their faces were like human faces, ⁸their hair like women's hair, and their teeth like lions' teeth; ⁹they had breastplates like breastplates of iron, and the noise of their wings was like the noise of many chariots with horses rushing into battle. ¹⁰They have tails and stings like scorpions, and their power to hurt people for five months is in their tails. ¹¹They have as king over them the angel of the bottomless pit. His name in Hebrew is Abaddon, and in Greek he is called Apollyon.¹

¹²The first woe has passed; behold, two woes are still to come.

¹³Then the sixth angel blew his trumpet, and I heard a voice from the four horns of the golden altar before God, ¹⁴saying to the sixth angel who had the trumpet, "Release the four angels who are bound at the great river Euphrates." ¹⁵So the four angels, who had been prepared for the hour, the day, the month, and the year, were released to kill a third of mankind. ¹⁶The number of mounted troops was twice ten thousand times ten thousand; I heard their number. ¹⁷And this is how I saw the horses in my vision and those who rode them: they wore breastplates the color of fire and of sapphire² and of sulfur, and the heads of the horses were like lions' heads, and fire and smoke and sulfur came out of their mouths. ¹⁸By these three plagues a third of mankind was killed, by the fire and smoke and sulfur coming out of their mouths. ¹⁹For the power of the horses is in their mouths and in their tails, for their tails are like serpents with heads, and by means of them they wound.

²⁰The rest of mankind, who were not killed by these plagues, did not repent of the works of their hands nor give up worshiping demons and idols of gold and silver and bronze and stone and wood, which cannot see or hear or walk, ²¹nor did they repent of their murders or their sorceries or their sexual immorality or their thefts.

The Angel and the Little Scroll

10 Then I saw another mighty angel coming down from heaven, wrapped in a cloud, with a rainbow over his head, and his face was like the sun, and his legs like pillars of fire. ²He had a little scroll open in his hand. And he set his right foot on the sea, and his left foot on the land, ³and called out with a loud voice, like a lion roaring. When he called out, the seven thunders sounded. ⁴And when the seven thunders had sounded, I was about to write, but I heard a voice from heaven saying, "Seal up what the seven thunders have said, and do not write it down." ⁵And the angel whom I saw standing on the sea and on the land raised his right hand to heaven ⁶and swore by him who lives forever and ever, who created heaven and what is in it, the earth and what is in it, and the sea and what is in it, that there would be no more delay, ⁷but that in the days of the trumpet call to be sounded by the seventh angel, the mystery of God would be fulfilled, just as he announced to his servants³ the prophets.

⁸Then the voice that I had heard from heaven spoke to me again, saying, "Go, take the scroll that is open in the hand of the angel who is standing on the sea and on the land." ⁹So I went to the angel and told him to give me the little scroll. And he said to me, "Take and eat it; it will make your stomach bitter, but in your mouth it will be sweet as honey." ¹⁰And I took the little scroll from the hand of the angel and ate it. It was sweet as honey in my mouth, but when I had eaten it my stomach was made bitter. ¹¹And I was told, "You must again prophesy about many peoples and nations and languages and kings."

The Two Witnesses

11 Then I was given a measuring rod like a staff, and I was told, "Rise and measure the temple of God and the altar and those who worship there, ²but do not measure the court outside the temple; leave that out, for it is given over to the nations, and they will trample the holy city for forty-two months. ³And I will grant authority to my two witnesses, and they will prophesy for 1,260 days, clothed in sackcloth."

⁴These are the two olive trees and the two lampstands that stand before the

Lord of the earth. ⁵And if anyone would harm them, fire pours from their mouth and consumes their foes. If anyone would harm them, this is how he is doomed to be killed. ⁶They have the power to shut the sky, that no rain may fall during the days of their prophesying, and they have power over the waters to turn them into blood and to strike the earth with every kind of plague, as often as they desire. ⁷And when they have finished their testimony, the beast that rises from the bottomless pit¹ will make war on them and conquer them and kill them, ⁸and their dead bodies will lie in the street of the great city that symbolically² is called Sodom and Egypt, where their Lord was crucified. ⁹For three and a half days some from the peoples and tribes and languages and nations will gaze at their dead bodies and refuse to let them be placed in a tomb, ¹⁰and those who dwell on the earth will rejoice over them and make merry and exchange presents, because these two prophets had been a torment to those who dwell on the earth. ¹¹But after the three and a half days a breath of life from God entered them, and they stood up on their feet, and great fear fell on those who saw them. ¹²Then they heard a loud voice from heaven saying to them, "Come up here!" And they went up to heaven in a cloud, and their enemies watched them. ¹³And at that hour there was a great earthquake, and a tenth of the city fell. Seven thousand people were killed in the earthquake, and the rest were terrified and gave glory to the God of heaven.

¹⁴The second woe has passed; behold, the third woe is soon to come.

The Seventh Trumpet

¹⁵Then the seventh angel blew his trumpet, and there were loud voices in heaven, saying, "The kingdom of the world has become the kingdom of our Lord and of his Christ, and he shall reign forever and ever." ¹⁶And the twenty-four elders who sit on their thrones before God fell on their faces and worshiped God, ¹⁷saying,

> "We give thanks to you, Lord God Almighty,
>   who is and who was,
>   for you have taken your great power and begun to reign.

¹⁸   The nations raged,
>   but your wrath came,
>   and the time for the dead to be judged,
> and for rewarding your servants,³ the prophets and saints,
>   and those who fear your name,
>   both small and great,
> and for destroying the destroyers of the earth."

¹⁹Then God's temple in heaven was opened, and the ark of his covenant was seen within his temple. There were flashes of lightning, rumblings,⁴ peals of thunder, an earthquake, and heavy hail.

The Woman and the Dragon

12 And a great sign appeared in heaven: a woman clothed with the sun, with the moon under her feet, and on her head a crown of twelve stars. ²She was pregnant and was crying out in birth pains and the agony of giving birth. ³And another sign appeared in heaven: behold, a great red dragon, with seven heads and ten horns, and on his heads seven diadems. ⁴His tail swept down a third of the stars of heaven and cast them to the earth. And the dragon stood before the woman who was about to give birth, so that when she bore her child he might devour it. ⁵She gave birth to a male child, one who is to rule all the nations with a rod of iron, but her child was caught up to God and to his throne, ⁶and the woman fled into the wilderness, where she has a place prepared by God, in which she is to be nourished for 1,260 days.

Satan Thrown Down to Earth

⁷Now war arose in heaven, Michael and his angels fighting against the dragon. And the dragon and his angels fought back, ⁸but he was defeated, and there was no longer any place for them in heaven. ⁹And the great dragon was thrown down, that ancient serpent, who is called the devil and Satan, the deceiver of the whole world— he was thrown down to the earth, and his angels were thrown down with him. ¹⁰And I heard a loud voice in heaven, saying, "Now the salvation and the power and the kingdom of our God and the authority of his Christ have come, for the accuser

---

¹Or *the abyss* ²Greek *spiritually* ³Greek *bondservants* ⁴Or *voices, or sounds*

of our brothers[1] has been thrown down, who accuses them day and night before our God. [11] And they have conquered him by the blood of the Lamb and by the word of their testimony, for they loved not their lives even unto death. [12] Therefore, rejoice, O heavens and you who dwell in them! But woe to you, O earth and sea, for the devil has come down to you in great wrath, because he knows that his time is short!"

[13] And when the dragon saw that he had been thrown down to the earth, he pursued the woman who had given birth to the male child. [14] But the woman was given the two wings of the great eagle so that she might fly from the serpent into the wilderness, to the place where she is to be nourished for a time, and times, and half a time. [15] The serpent poured water like a river out of his mouth after the woman, to sweep her away with a flood. [16] But the earth came to the help of the woman, and the earth opened its mouth and swallowed the river that the dragon had poured from his mouth. [17] Then the dragon became furious with the woman and went off to make war on the rest of her offspring, on those who keep the commandments of God and hold to the testimony of Jesus. And he stood[2] on the sand of the sea.

The First Beast

13 And I saw a beast rising out of the sea, with ten horns and seven heads, with ten diadems on its horns and blasphemous names on its heads. [2] And the beast that I saw was like a leopard; its feet were like a bear's, and its mouth was like a lion's mouth. And to it the dragon gave his power and his throne and great authority. [3] One of its heads seemed to have a mortal wound, but its mortal wound was healed, and the whole earth marveled as they followed the beast. [4] And they worshiped the dragon, for he had given his authority to the beast, and they worshiped the beast, saying, "Who is like the beast, and who can fight against it?"

[5] And the beast was given a mouth uttering haughty and blasphemous words, and it was allowed to exercise authority for forty-two months. [6] It opened its mouth to utter blasphemies against God, blaspheming his name and his dwelling,[3] that

is, those who dwell in heaven. [7] Also it was allowed to make war on the saints and to conquer them.[4] And authority was given it over every tribe and people and language and nation, [8] and all who dwell on earth will worship it, everyone whose name has not been written before the foundation of the world in the book of life of the Lamb who was slain. [9] If anyone has an ear, let him hear:

[10]   If anyone is to be taken captive,
            to captivity he goes;
        if anyone is to be slain with the
            sword,
        with the sword must he be slain.

Here is a call for the endurance and faith of the saints.

The Second Beast

[11] Then I saw another beast rising out of the earth. It had two horns like a lamb and it spoke like a dragon. [12] It exercises all the authority of the first beast in its presence,[5] and makes the earth and its inhabitants worship the first beast, whose mortal wound was healed. [13] It performs great signs, even making fire come down from heaven to earth in front of people, [14] and by the signs that it is allowed to work in the presence of[6] the beast it deceives those who dwell on earth, telling them to make an image for the beast that was wounded by the sword and yet lived. [15] And it was allowed to give breath to the image of the beast, so that the image of the beast might even speak and might cause those who would not worship the image of the beast to be slain. [16] Also it causes all, both small and great, both rich and poor, both free and slave,[7] to be marked on the right hand or the forehead, [17] so that no one can buy or sell unless he has the mark, that is, the name of the beast or the number of its name. [18] This calls for wisdom: let the one who has understanding calculate the number of the beast, for it is the number of a man, and his number is 666.[8]

The Lamb and the 144,000

14 Then I looked, and behold, on Mount Zion stood the Lamb, and with him 144,000 who had his name and his Father's name written on their foreheads. [2] And

---

[1] Or brothers and sisters [2] Some manuscripts And I stood, connecting the sentence with 13:1 [3] Or tabernacle [4] Some manuscripts omit this sentence [5] Or on its behalf [6] Or on behalf of [7] Greek bondservant [8] Some manuscripts 616

I heard a voice from heaven like the roar of many waters and like the sound of loud thunder. The voice I heard was like the sound of harpists playing on their harps, ³ and they were singing a new song before the throne and before the four living creatures and before the elders. No one could learn that song except the 144,000 who had been redeemed from the earth. ⁴ It is these who have not defiled themselves with women, for they are virgins. It is these who follow the Lamb wherever he goes. These have been redeemed from mankind as firstfruits for God and the Lamb, ⁵ and in their mouth no lie was found, for they are blameless.

The Messages of the Three Angels

⁶ Then I saw another angel flying directly overhead, with an eternal gospel to proclaim to those who dwell on earth, to every nation and tribe and language and people. ⁷ And he said with a loud voice, "Fear God and give him glory, because the hour of his judgment has come, and worship him who made heaven and earth, the sea and the springs of water."

⁸ Another angel, a second, followed, saying, "Fallen, fallen is Babylon the great, she who made all nations drink the wine of the passion¹ of her sexual immorality."

⁹ And another angel, a third, followed them, saying with a loud voice, "If anyone worships the beast and its image and receives a mark on his forehead or on his hand, ¹⁰ he also will drink the wine of God's wrath, poured full strength into the cup of his anger, and he will be tormented with fire and sulfur in the presence of the holy angels and in the presence of the Lamb. ¹¹ And the smoke of their torment goes up forever and ever, and they have no rest, day or night, these worshipers of the beast and its image, and whoever receives the mark of its name."

¹² Here is a call for the endurance of the saints, those who keep the commandments of God and their faith in Jesus.²

¹³ And I heard a voice from heaven saying, "Write this: Blessed are the dead who die in the Lord from now on." "Blessed indeed," says the Spirit, "that they may rest from their labors, for their deeds follow them!"

The Harvest of the Earth

¹⁴ Then I looked, and behold, a white cloud, and seated on the cloud one like a son of man, with a golden crown on his head, and a sharp sickle in his hand. ¹⁵ And another angel came out of the temple, calling with a loud voice to him who sat on the cloud, "Put in your sickle, and reap, for the hour to reap has come, for the harvest of the earth is fully ripe." ¹⁶ So he who sat on the cloud swung his sickle across the earth, and the earth was reaped.

¹⁷ Then another angel came out of the temple in heaven, and he too had a sharp sickle. ¹⁸ And another angel came out from the altar, the angel who has authority over the fire, and he called with a loud voice to the one who had the sharp sickle, "Put in your sickle and gather the clusters from the vine of the earth, for its grapes are ripe." ¹⁹ So the angel swung his sickle across the earth and gathered the grape harvest of the earth and threw it into the great winepress of the wrath of God. ²⁰ And the winepress was trodden outside the city, and blood flowed from the winepress, as high as a horse's bridle, for 1,600 stadia.³

The Seven Angels with Seven Plagues

15 Then I saw another sign in heaven, great and amazing, seven angels with seven plagues, which are the last, for with them the wrath of God is finished.

² And I saw what appeared to be a sea of glass mingled with fire—and also those who had conquered the beast and its image and the number of its name, standing beside the sea of glass with harps of God in their hands. ³ And they sing the song of Moses, the servant⁴ of God, and the song of the Lamb, saying,

"Great and amazing are your deeds,
  O Lord God the Almighty!
Just and true are your ways,
  O King of the nations!⁵
4 Who will not fear, O Lord,
  and glorify your name?
For you alone are holy.
  All nations will come
  and worship you,
for your righteous acts have been
  revealed."

¹ Or *wrath* ² Greek *and the faith of Jesus* ³ About 184 miles; a *stadion* was about 607 feet or 185 meters ⁴ Greek *bondservant* ⁵ Some manuscripts *the ages*

⁵After this I looked, and the sanctuary of the tent[1] of witness in heaven was opened, ⁶and out of the sanctuary came the seven angels with the seven plagues, clothed in pure, bright linen, with golden sashes around their chests. ⁷And one of the four living creatures gave to the seven angels seven golden bowls full of the wrath of God who lives forever and ever, ⁸and the sanctuary was filled with smoke from the glory of God and from his power, and no one could enter the sanctuary until the seven plagues of the seven angels were finished.

The Seven Bowls of God's Wrath

16 Then I heard a loud voice from the temple telling the seven angels, "Go and pour out on the earth the seven bowls of the wrath of God."

²So the first angel went and poured out his bowl on the earth, and harmful and painful sores came upon the people who bore the mark of the beast and worshiped its image.

³The second angel poured out his bowl into the sea, and it became like the blood of a corpse, and every living thing died that was in the sea.

⁴The third angel poured out his bowl into the rivers and the springs of water, and they became blood. ⁵And I heard the angel in charge of the waters[2] say,

"Just are you, O Holy One, who is and who was,
    for you brought these judgments.
⁶ For they have shed the blood of saints and prophets,
    and you have given them blood to drink.
  It is what they deserve!"

⁷And I heard the altar saying,

"Yes, Lord God the Almighty,
    true and just are your judgments!"

⁸The fourth angel poured out his bowl on the sun, and it was allowed to scorch people with fire. ⁹They were scorched by the fierce heat, and they cursed[3] the name of God who had power over these plagues. They did not repent and give him glory. ¹⁰The fifth angel poured out his bowl on the throne of the beast, and its kingdom was plunged into darkness. People gnawed their tongues in anguish ¹¹and cursed the God of heaven for their pain and sores. They did not repent of their deeds.

¹²The sixth angel poured out his bowl on the great river Euphrates, and its water was dried up, to prepare the way for the kings from the east. ¹³And I saw, coming out of the mouth of the dragon and out of the mouth of the beast and out of the mouth of the false prophet, three unclean spirits like frogs. ¹⁴For they are demonic spirits, performing signs, who go abroad to the kings of the whole world, to assemble them for battle on the great day of God the Almighty. ¹⁵("Behold, I am coming like a thief! Blessed is the one who stays awake, keeping his garments on, that he may not go about naked and be seen exposed!") ¹⁶And they assembled them at the place that in Hebrew is called Armageddon.

The Seventh Bowl

¹⁷The seventh angel poured out his bowl into the air, and a loud voice came out of the temple, from the throne, saying, "It is done!" ¹⁸And there were flashes of lightning, rumblings,[4] peals of thunder, and a great earthquake such as there had never been since man was on the earth, so great was that earthquake. ¹⁹The great city was split into three parts, and the cities of the nations fell, and God remembered Babylon the great, to make her drain the cup of the wine of the fury of his wrath. ²⁰And every island fled away, and no mountains were to be found. ²¹And great hailstones, about one hundred pounds[5] each, fell from heaven on people; and they cursed God for the plague of the hail, because the plague was so severe.

The Great Prostitute and the Beast

17 Then one of the seven angels who had the seven bowls came and said to me, "Come, I will show you the judgment of the great prostitute who is seated on many waters, ²with whom the kings of the earth have committed sexual immorality, and with the wine of whose sexual immorality the dwellers on earth have become drunk." ³And he carried me away in the Spirit into a wilderness, and I saw a woman sitting on a scarlet beast that was full of blasphemous names, and it had seven heads and ten horns. ⁴The woman was

---

[1]Or tabernacle [2]Greek angel of the waters [3]Greek blasphemed; also verses 11, 21 [4]Or voices, or sounds [5]Greek a talent in weight

arrayed in purple and scarlet, and adorned with gold and jewels and pearls, holding in her hand a golden cup full of abominations and the impurities of her sexual immorality. ⁵ And on her forehead was written a name of mystery: "Babylon the great, mother of prostitutes and of earth's abominations." ⁶ And I saw the woman, drunk with the blood of the saints, the blood of the martyrs of Jesus.¹

When I saw her, I marveled greatly. ⁷ But the angel said to me, "Why do you marvel? I will tell you the mystery of the woman, and of the beast with seven heads and ten horns that carries her. ⁸ The beast that you saw was, and is not, and is about to rise from the bottomless pit² and go to destruction. And the dwellers on earth whose names have not been written in the book of life from the foundation of the world will marvel to see the beast, because it was and is not and is to come. ⁹ This calls for a mind with wisdom: the seven heads are seven mountains on which the woman is seated; ¹⁰ they are also seven kings, five of whom have fallen, one is, the other has not yet come, and when he does come he must remain only a little while. ¹¹ As for the beast that was and is not, it is an eighth but it belongs to the seven, and it goes to destruction. ¹² And the ten horns that you saw are ten kings who have not yet received royal power, but they are to receive authority as kings for one hour, together with the beast. ¹³ These are of one mind, and they hand over their power and authority to the beast. ¹⁴ They will make war on the Lamb, and the Lamb will conquer them, for he is Lord of lords and King of kings, and those with him are called and chosen and faithful."

¹⁵ And the angel³ said to me, "The waters that you saw, where the prostitute is seated, are peoples and multitudes and nations and languages. ¹⁶ And the ten horns that you saw, they and the beast will hate the prostitute. They will make her desolate and naked, and devour her flesh and burn her up with fire, ¹⁷ for God has put it into their hearts to carry out his purpose by being of one mind and handing over their royal power to the beast, until the words of God are fulfilled. ¹⁸ And the woman that you saw is the great city that has dominion over the kings of the earth."

The Fall of Babylon

18 After this I saw another angel coming down from heaven, having great authority, and the earth was made bright with his glory. ² And he called out with a mighty voice,

"Fallen, fallen is Babylon the great!
> She has become a dwelling place
> > for demons,
> a haunt for every unclean spirit,
> > a haunt for every unclean bird,
> > a haunt for every unclean and
> > > detestable beast.
³ For all nations have drunk⁴
> > the wine of the passion of her
> > > sexual immorality,
> and the kings of the earth have committed immorality with her,
> and the merchants of the earth
> > have grown rich from the
> > power of her luxurious living."

⁴ Then I heard another voice from heaven saying,

"Come out of her, my people,
> lest you take part in her sins,
> lest you share in her plagues;
⁵ for her sins are heaped high as
> > heaven,
> and God has remembered her
> > iniquities.
⁶ Pay her back as she herself has paid
> > back others,
> and repay her double for her
> > deeds;
> > mix a double portion for her in the
> > > cup she mixed.
⁷ As she glorified herself and lived in
> > luxury,
> so give her a like measure of torment and mourning,
> since in her heart she says,
> 'I sit as a queen,
> I am no widow,
> > and mourning I shall never see.'
⁸ For this reason her plagues will
> > come in a single day,
> > death and mourning and famine,
> and she will be burned up with fire;
> > for mighty is the Lord God who has
> > > judged her."

⁹ And the kings of the earth, who committed sexual immorality and lived in luxury

---

¹ Greek *the witnesses to Jesus* ² Greek *the abyss* ³ Greek *he* ⁴ Some manuscripts *fallen by*

with her, will weep and wail over her when they see the smoke of her burning. [10]They will stand far off, in fear of her torment, and say,

> "Alas! Alas! You great city,
>   you mighty city, Babylon!
> For in a single hour your judgment
>   has come."

[11]And the merchants of the earth weep and mourn for her, since no one buys their cargo anymore, [12]cargo of gold, silver, jewels, pearls, fine linen, purple cloth, silk, scarlet cloth, all kinds of scented wood, all kinds of articles of ivory, all kinds of articles of costly wood, bronze, iron and marble, [13]cinnamon, spice, incense, myrrh, frankincense, wine, oil, fine flour, wheat, cattle and sheep, horses and chariots, and slaves, that is, human souls.[1]

[14]   "The fruit for which your soul longed
>   has gone from you,
>   and all your delicacies and your
>   splendors
>   are lost to you,
>   never to be found again!"

[15]The merchants of these wares, who gained wealth from her, will stand far off, in fear of her torment, weeping and mourning aloud,

[16]   "Alas, alas, for the great city
>   that was clothed in fine linen,
>   in purple and scarlet,
>   adorned with gold,
>   with jewels, and with pearls!
[17]   For in a single hour all this wealth
>   has been laid waste."

And all shipmasters and seafaring men, sailors and all whose trade is on the sea, stood far off [18]and cried out as they saw the smoke of her burning,

> "What city was like the great city?"

[19]And they threw dust on their heads as they wept and mourned, crying out,

> "Alas, alas, for the great city
>   where all who had ships at sea
>   grew rich by her wealth!
> For in a single hour she has been laid
>   waste.

[20]   Rejoice over her, O heaven,
>   and you saints and apostles and
>   prophets,
>   for God has given judgment for you
>   against her!"

[21]Then a mighty angel took up a stone like a great millstone and threw it into the sea, saying,

> "So will Babylon the great city be
>   thrown down with violence,
>   and will be found no more;
[22]   and the sound of harpists and musi-
>   cians, of flute players and
>   trumpeters,
>   will be heard in you no more,
>   and a craftsman of any craft
>   will be found in you no more,
>   and the sound of the mill
>   will be heard in you no more,
[23]   and the light of a lamp
>   will shine in you no more,
>   and the voice of bridegroom and
>   bride
>   will be heard in you no more,
>   for your merchants were the great
>   ones of the earth,
>   and all nations were deceived by
>   your sorcery.
[24]   And in her was found the blood of
>   prophets and of saints,
>   and of all who have been slain on
>   earth."

Rejoicing in Heaven

19 After this I heard what seemed to be the loud voice of a great multitude in heaven, crying out,

> "Hallelujah!
> Salvation and glory and power
>   belong to our God,
[2]   for his judgments are true and
>   just;
> for he has judged the great prostitute
>   who corrupted the earth with her
>   immorality,
> and has avenged on her the blood of
>   his servants."[2]

[3]Once more they cried out,

> "Hallelujah!
> The smoke from her goes up forever
>   and ever."

[1]Or and slaves, and human lives [2]Greek bondservants; also verse 5

⁴ And the twenty-four elders and the four living creatures fell down and worshiped God who was seated on the throne, saying, "Amen. Hallelujah!" ⁵ And from the throne came a voice saying,

> "Praise our God,
>   all you his servants,
> you who fear him,
>   small and great."

Ask Yourself . . .

ABOUT FAIRNESS

Have you ever said, "That's not fair"? When things don't seem fair, what do you do? Ask yourself these questions and find out the answer to the unfair parts of life:

- What in my life is unfair?

- Whose definition of fair am I using?

- Is God unfair, or is he true and just (see Rev. 19:2)?

- Can God work everything out for the good of those who love him (see Rom. 8:28)?

- How can what is unfair in my life be used for good?

The Marriage Supper of the Lamb

⁶ Then I heard what seemed to be the voice of a great multitude, like the roar of many waters and like the sound of mighty peals of thunder, crying out,

> "Hallelujah!
>   For the Lord our God
>   the Almighty reigns.
> ⁷   Let us rejoice and exult
>   and give him the glory,
>   for the marriage of the Lamb has
>   come,
>   and his Bride has made herself
>   ready;
> ⁸   it was granted her to clothe herself
>   with fine linen, bright and pure"—

for the fine linen is the righteous deeds of the saints.

⁹ And the angel said¹ to me, "Write this: Blessed are those who are invited to the marriage supper of the Lamb." And he said to me, "These are the true words of God." ¹⁰ Then I fell down at his feet to worship him, but he said to me, "You must not do that! I am a fellow servant² with you and your brothers who hold to the testimony of Jesus. Worship God." For the testimony of Jesus is the spirit of prophecy.

The Rider on a White Horse

¹¹ Then I saw heaven opened, and behold, a white horse! The one sitting on it is called Faithful and True, and in righteousness he judges and makes war. ¹² His eyes are like a flame of fire, and on his head are many diadems, and he has a name written that no one knows but himself. ¹³ He is clothed in a robe dipped in³ blood, and the name by which he is called is The Word of God. ¹⁴ And the armies of heaven, arrayed in fine linen, white and pure, were following him on white horses. ¹⁵ From his mouth comes a sharp sword with which to strike down the nations, and he will rule them with a rod of iron. He will tread the winepress of the fury of the wrath of God the Almighty. ¹⁶ On his robe and on his thigh he has a name written, King of kings and Lord of lords.

¹⁷ Then I saw an angel standing in the sun, and with a loud voice he called to all the birds that fly directly overhead, "Come, gather for the great supper of God, ¹⁸ to eat the flesh of kings, the flesh of captains, the flesh of mighty men, the flesh of horses and their riders, and the flesh of all men, both free and slave,⁴ both small and great." ¹⁹ And I saw the beast and the kings of the earth with their armies gathered to make war against him who was sitting on the horse and against his army. ²⁰ And the beast was captured, and with it the false prophet who in its presence⁵ had done the signs by which he deceived those who had received the mark of the beast and those who worshiped its image. These two were thrown alive into the lake of fire that burns with sulfur. ²¹ And the rest were slain by the sword that came from the mouth of him who was sitting on the horse, and all the birds were gorged with their flesh.

¹ Greek *he said* ² Greek *fellow bondservant* ³ Some manuscripts *sprinkled with* ⁴ Greek *bondservant* ⁵ Or *on its behalf*

The Thousand Years

20 Then I saw an angel coming down from heaven, holding in his hand the key to the bottomless pit[1] and a great chain. ²And he seized the dragon, that ancient serpent, who is the devil and Satan, and bound him for a thousand years, ³and threw him into the pit, and shut it and sealed it over him, so that he might not deceive the nations any longer, until the thousand years were ended. After that he must be released for a little while.

⁴Then I saw thrones, and seated on them were those to whom the authority to judge was committed. Also I saw the souls of those who had been beheaded for the testimony of Jesus and for the word of God, and those who had not worshiped the beast or its image and had not received its mark on their foreheads or their hands. They came to life and reigned with Christ for a thousand years. ⁵The rest of the dead did not come to life until the thousand years were ended. This is the first resurrection. ⁶Blessed and holy is the one who shares in the first resurrection! Over such the second death has no power, but they will be priests of God and of Christ, and they will reign with him for a thousand years.

The Defeat of Satan

⁷And when the thousand years are ended, Satan will be released from his prison ⁸and will come out to deceive the nations that are at the four corners of the earth, Gog and Magog, to gather them for battle; their number is like the sand of the sea. ⁹And they marched up over the broad plain of the earth and surrounded the camp of the saints and the beloved city, but fire came down from heaven[2] and consumed them, ¹⁰and the devil who had deceived them was thrown into the lake of fire and sulfur where the beast and the false prophet were, and they will be tormented day and night forever and ever.

Judgment Before the Great White Throne

¹¹Then I saw a great white throne and him who was seated on it. From his presence earth and sky fled away, and no place was found for them. ¹²And I saw the dead, great and small, standing before the throne, and books were opened. Then another book was opened, which is the book of life. And the dead were judged by what was written in the books, according to what they had done. ¹³And the sea gave up the dead who were in it, Death and Hades gave up the dead who were in them, and they were judged, each one of them, according to what they had done. ¹⁴Then Death and Hades were thrown into the lake of fire. This is the second death, the lake of fire. ¹⁵And if anyone's name was not found written in the book of life, he was thrown into the lake of fire.

The New Heaven and the New Earth

21 Then I saw a new heaven and a new earth, for the first heaven and the first earth had passed away, and the sea was no more. ²And I saw the holy city, new Jerusalem, coming down out of heaven from God, prepared as a bride adorned for her husband. ³And I heard a loud voice from the throne saying, "Behold, the dwelling place[3] of God is with man. He will dwell with them, and they will be his people,[4] and God himself will be with them as their God.[5] ⁴He will wipe away every tear from their eyes, and death shall be no more, neither shall there be mourning, nor crying, nor pain anymore, for the former things have passed away."

⁵And he who was seated on the throne said, "Behold, I am making all things new." Also he said, "Write this down, for these words are trustworthy and true." ⁶And he said to me, "It is done! I am the Alpha and the Omega, the beginning and the end. To the thirsty I will give from the spring of the water of life without payment. ⁷The one who conquers will have this heritage, and I will be his God and he will be my son. ⁸But as for the cowardly, the faithless, the detestable, as for murderers, the sexually immoral, sorcerers, idolaters, and all liars, their portion will be in the lake that burns with fire and sulfur, which is the second death."

The New Jerusalem

⁹Then came one of the seven angels who had the seven bowls full of the seven last plagues and spoke to me, saying, "Come, I will show you the Bride, the wife of the Lamb." ¹⁰And he carried me away in

---

[1] Greek *the abyss*; also verse 3 [2] Some manuscripts *from God, out of heaven*, or *out of heaven from God* [3] Or *tabernacle* [4] Some manuscripts *peoples* [5] Some manuscripts omit *as their God*

the Spirit to a great, high mountain, and showed me the holy city Jerusalem coming down out of heaven from God, [11]having the glory of God, its radiance like a most rare jewel, like a jasper, clear as crystal. [12]It had a great, high wall, with twelve gates, and at the gates twelve angels, and on the gates the names of the twelve tribes of the sons of Israel were inscribed— [13]on the east three gates, on the north three gates, on the south three gates, and on the west three gates. [14]And the wall of the city had twelve foundations, and on them were the twelve names of the twelve apostles of the Lamb.

[15]And the one who spoke with me had a measuring rod of gold to measure the city and its gates and walls. [16]The city lies foursquare, its length the same as its width. And he measured the city with his rod, 12,000 stadia.[1] Its length and width and height are equal. [17]He also measured its wall, 144 cubits[2] by human measurement, which is also an angel's measurement. [18]The wall was built of jasper, while the city was pure gold, like clear glass. [19]The foundations of the wall of the city were adorned with every kind of jewel. The first was jasper, the second sapphire, the third agate, the fourth emerald, [20]the fifth onyx, the sixth carnelian, the seventh chrysolite, the eighth beryl, the ninth topaz, the tenth chrysoprase, the eleventh jacinth, the twelfth amethyst. [21]And the twelve gates were twelve pearls, each of the gates made of a single pearl, and the street of the city was pure gold, like transparent glass.

[22]And I saw no temple in the city, for its temple is the Lord God the Almighty and the Lamb. [23]And the city has no need of sun or moon to shine on it, for the glory of God gives it light, and its lamp is the Lamb. [24]By its light will the nations walk, and the kings of the earth will bring their glory into it, [25]and its gates will never be shut by day—and there will be no night there. [26]They will bring into it the glory and the honor of the nations. [27]But nothing unclean will ever enter it, nor anyone who does what is detestable or false, but only those who are written in the Lamb's book of life.

The River of Life

22 Then the angel[3] showed me the river of the water of life, bright as crystal, flowing from the throne of God and of the Lamb [2]through the middle of the street of the city; also, on either side of the river, the tree of life[4] with its twelve kinds of fruit, yielding its fruit each month. The leaves of the tree were for the healing of the nations. [3]No longer will there be anything accursed, but the throne of God and of the Lamb will be in it, and his servants[5] will worship him. [4]They will see his face, and his name will be on their foreheads. [5]And night will be no more. They will need no light of lamp or sun, for the Lord God will be their light, and they will reign forever and ever.

Jesus Is Coming

[6]And he said to me, "These words are trustworthy and true. And the Lord, the God of the spirits of the prophets, has sent his angel to show his servants what must soon take place."

[7]"And behold, I am coming soon. Blessed is the one who keeps the words of the prophecy of this book."

[8]I, John, am the one who heard and saw these things. And when I heard and saw them, I fell down to worship at the feet of the angel who showed them to me, [9]but he said to me, "You must not do that! I am a fellow servant[6] with you and your brothers the prophets, and with those who keep the words of this book. Worship God."

[10]And he said to me, "Do not seal up the words of the prophecy of this book, for the time is near. [11]Let the evildoer still do evil, and the filthy still be filthy, and the righteous still do right, and the holy still be holy."

[12]"Behold, I am coming soon, bringing my recompense with me, to repay each one for what he has done. [13]I am the Alpha and the Omega, the first and the last, the beginning and the end."

[14]Blessed are those who wash their robes,[7] so that they may have the right to the tree of life and that they may enter the city by the gates. [15]Outside are the dogs and sorcerers and the sexually immoral and murderers and idolaters, and everyone who loves and practices falsehood.

---

[1] About 1,380 miles; a *stadion* was about 607 feet or 185 meters [2]A *cubit* was about 18 inches or 45 centimeters [3]Greek *he* [4]Or *the Lamb. In the midst of the street of the city, and on either side of the river, was the tree of life* [5]Greek *bondservants*; also verse 6 [6]Greek *fellow bondservant* [7]Some manuscripts *do his commandments*

¹⁶ "I, Jesus, have sent my angel to testify to you about these things for the churches. I am the root and the descendant of David, the bright morning star."

¹⁷ The Spirit and the Bride say, "Come." And let the one who hears say, "Come." And let the one who is thirsty come; let the one who desires take the water of life without price.

¹⁸ I warn everyone who hears the words of the prophecy of this book: if anyone

adds to them, God will add to him the plagues described in this book, ¹⁹ and if anyone takes away from the words of the book of this prophecy, God will take away his share in the tree of life and in the holy city, which are described in this book.

²⁰ He who testifies to these things says, "Surely I am coming soon." Amen. Come, Lord Jesus!

²¹ The grace of the Lord Jesus be with all.¹ Amen.

¹ Some manuscripts *all the saints*

verses to read
Revelation 22:18–19

Know God

Have you heard the voice of God? Has he told you to do something? To go somewhere? What will you do? These are the times when knowing God's Word is crucial, because if you are unfamiliar with his ways, with his voice, and with his truth, you can easily fall prey to imposters and to adding things to Scripture that aren't really there. God's Word says to test every spirit that you hear, because not every spirit that claims to be the Spirit (with a capital S) really is (see 1 John 4:1). Satan pretends to be God by dressing up as an "angel of light" (2 Cor. 11:14), so you can't be too quick to say "God told me" when there's a chance that the one who told you was only pretending to be someone he's not.

So how do you know who's talking? If what "God told you" contradicts God's Word, you can be sure that what you heard wasn't God's voice. How many times have you been sure God wanted you to do something or to have something, only to find out it wasn't going to happen? Do you blame God? Or do you stop and think that you might have been too quick to call the voice in your head the voice of God? Just because you hear something that sounds amazing and wonderful doesn't mean that it is God speaking to you. So resist the temptation to say, "God told me," because the only thing you can be sure God told you is what he has told his people in his written Word, the Bible.

God Girl Glossary

Aaron: Moses' brother, who served as his assistant in speaking for him (see Ex. 4:16) and was also the first high priest.

Abrahamic covenant: The covenant made between God and Abraham whereby God promises to give Abraham many descendants and to make them his people (see Gen. 12:1–3; 15:18; 22:15–18). The sign of this covenant is circumcision (Gen. 17:11–12).

AD: Abbreviation for *Anno Domini* ("in the year of our Lord"). Refers to the part of history following the birth of Jesus Christ. See also *BC*.

adultery: Sexual relations with someone other than the person you are married to.

amen: Greek form of a Hebrew word meaning "to confirm." When spoken at the end of a prayer, it means "let it be so."

Ammonites: The descendants of Ben Ammi, who was the son of Lot and his younger daughter (see Gen. 19:30–38). They refused to help the Israelites when they came out of Egypt (see Deut. 23:3–4).

angel: A supernatural messenger of God, often sent to carry out his will or to help human beings carry out his will.

anoint: To pour oil on someone, as in anointing a king as a symbol of his power (see Ex. 29:7; 1 Sam. 16:13; Luke 4:18). It can also be a spiritual anointing done by the presence of the Holy Spirit. "The Lord's Anointed" in Hebrew is Messiah.

antichrist: Can refer to a particular person who will come at the end of this age, doing the work of Satan and claiming to be God (also called the "man of lawlessness" by Paul), but in 1 John 2:22 an antichrist is anyone who stands in opposition to Christ.

apostate: Someone who claims to be a believer but has never truly been saved. Apostate people may be an active part of a church, but they deny the deity of Christ and teach things that are inconsistent with Scripture. See Jude 4, 7–10, 16 and 2 Peter 2:1–3, 10–12, 18.

apostle: Means "one who is sent" and refers to a person who is an official representative of another person. In the New Testament, it refers specifically to the those whom Jesus chose to represent him.

ark: "The ark of the covenant" or "the ark of the testimony" was the box-like container used to hold and to carry the two tablets of the covenant, the Ten Commandments.

atonement: The reconciliation of a person with God. Through his death and resurrection, Jesus Christ made atonement for the sins of believers.

BC: Abbreviation for "before Christ." Refers to the years before Jesus Christ was born. See also *AD*.

blasphemy: Talking bad about God, including cursing, hating, or lying about him. It can also include slandering or mocking people, angels, or demons (see Titus 3:2; Jude 1:8–10).

born again: To be born again is to undergo a spiritual renewal that makes you a new creature based on your belief in and acceptance of the life-giving death and resurrection of Jesus (see John 3:3, 7; 1 Pet. 1:23).

branch of righteousness or **a righteous branch for David:** A name referring to the Messiah who will come from the line of David (see Jer. 23:5–6).

burnt offering: An offering where the entire sacrificial animal was to be burned as an offering to the Lord. This was a permanent requirement on the Jews and was to take place day and night (see Lev. 6:9–23).

census: A counting of the people, usually to prepare for war or taxation.

church: From a Greek word meaning "assembly." The church includes everyone in the world who believes in Jesus Christ. It can also refer to a local gathering of believers.

cistern: An underground tank or chamber for storing water. Used as a holding cell for prisoners in Jeremiah 38:6.

city of David: The royal city that David captured and named Jerusalem (also known as Zion). It can also refer to the city of Bethlehem, where Jesus was born (see John 7:42).

conversion: The result of turning away from sin, accepting the truth of the gospel of Jesus Christ, and submitting to him.

cornerstone: The corner piece of a foundation; the place where two walls of a building meet. It aligns the whole building and helps keep it standing.

covenant: A formal agreement made between two people or groups of people where both parties have an obligation to fulfill in relation to each other.

coveting: See *greed*.

crown of life: Some believe this refers to eternal life and others believe it is an actual crown that believers receive when they die and go to heaven. The kinds of crowns they get will depend on what they have done. Ultimately, however, all who receive these crowns will lay them down before God as they worship him (see Phil. 4:1; 2 Tim. 4:8; James 1:12; 1 Pet. 5:4; Rev. 2:10; 3:11; 4:4).

Davidic covenant: The covenant that God made with David that his kingdom would continue for future generations (see 2 Sam. 7:12; 22:51). This covenant was considered unconditional and was fulfilled in the life of Christ (see Matt. 1:1; 2:4–6; Luke 1:30–33).

day of the Lord: A time in the future when God will judge everyone on earth, at which time God's enemies will be destroyed and his people will be exalted. The second coming of Christ, as seen in 2 Peter 3:10.

deacon: A minister or lay leader in a local church.

destroyer: The enemy that destroys Israel and/ or an agent of God used to deliver God's judgment (see Ex. 12:23; Isa. 49:17; Jer. 22:7).

disciple: Any person who submits to the teachings of another. In the New Testament, it refers to those who submitted themselves to the teaching of Jesus, especially those who traveled with him during his earthly ministry.

discipline: Correction or punishment for wrongdoing, or training in obedience and self-control.

Edomites: Edom was another name for Esau, the brother of Jacob, who gave up his inheritance for a bowl of soup. His descendants, the Edomites, refused to help the people of Judah when they were being attacked by the Babylonians (see Obadiah).

El: A Hebrew word meaning God.

elder: A leader in a local church who is responsible for the spiritual well-being of the church members.

Enemy, the: Refers to Satan, a spiritual being who is God's enemy and the enemy of our souls. He is also referred to as the Devil.

eternal death: The fate of those who are not saved.

eternal life: Refers to both the afterlife and the new life we live immediately when we are saved. Eternal life with God is the reward for everyone who is saved (see John 3:16; 5:24).

exile, the: Most often refers to the time when the people of Israel (Judah) were taken captive to Babylon in 586 BC. After Babylon was conquered by Persia, many of the people were allowed to return to their homeland in Judah. During and after the exile, they came to be known as Jews.

exodus, the: God's miraculous rescue of his people (the Israelites) from Egypt, after many years of oppression (see Exodus 1–19).

fall, the: Adam and Eve's disobedience of God by eating the fruit from the tree of the knowledge of good and evil. This resulted in their loss of innocence and favor with God, and it brought sin into the world (Genesis 2; Rom. 5:12–21; 1 Cor. 15:21–22).

fall asleep: This expression is often used as a metaphor for death, as in John 11:11.

false teacher: Anyone who teaches something that is inconsistent with or contradictory to Scripture. False teachers can be those who teach about a false god or those who say they teach about or in the name of the true God but don't speak the truth. False teachers don't convict people of sin but offer them false hope in something other than God.

fear of the Lord: Refers to the awe, respect, love, and reverence that we are to have for God. It is to fear his reaction or judgment more than anyone else's.

Feast of Harvest: A one-day festival to celebrate the end of the harvest, during which the Israelites offered two loaves of bread and ten animals. Also known as "the Feast of Weeks," "the Day of the First Fruits," or "the day of Pentecost."

feasts: Regularly scheduled community worship times for the people of Israel. Also called festivals.

fellowship offering: See *peace offering*.

flesh, the: In the Bible, this word often refers to our sinful human nature (Rom. 8:3).

fruit of the Spirit: Refers to nine character traits that are seen in the lives of believers, like a fruit of their faith, listed in Galatians 5:22–23. They are love, joy, peace, patience, kindness, goodness, faithfulness, gentleness, and self-control.

genealogy: A record of the descent of a family or group from their ancestors.

Gentiles: A general term meaning all people who are not Jewish.

Glory of Israel: Netsah Yisrael, also translated as "the Strength of Israel," is another name for the Lord (see 1 Sam. 15:29).

Good News: The message of the saving power of Christ. Another word for it is gospel.

gospel: The good news of Jesus Christ and the salvation he made possible by his crucifixion, burial, and resurrection. When the word begins with a capital letter (Gospel), it refers to each of the biblical accounts of Jesus' life on earth (Matthew, Mark, Luke, and John).

Grace: Unmerited favor. The free gift of salvation that God gives to believers because of their faith in Jesus Christ.

greed: An intense desire to have something, usually money but possibly anything you think you need more of including food, clothes, and so on. It is the ultimate idolatry, in which you worship yourself by giving yourself whatever you want. Also known as coveting.

heaven: Where God lives, and where believers live in his presence after death (1 Thess. 4:16–17).

hedonism: The belief that the only thing good in life is the pursuit of your own pleasure.

hell: A place of eternal torment for those who rebel against God and refuse to repent.

heresy: Teaching anything other than biblical truth. Its deception can destroy people's faith by giving them trust in a lie instead of the truth.

high places: Altars or places of worship set up to worship pagan gods.

holy: A term used to express moral perfection and an essential part of God's nature. It also describes someone or something that is sanctified and set apart for divine service.

Holy Spirit: One of the three persons of the Trinity. The Bible teaches that the Holy Spirit helps people see that they need to be saved, and then he helps them understand the Scriptures and live a Christian life. The Holy Spirit inspired the writers of Scripture, guiding them to record the exact words of God.

hospitality: Being friendly to fellow believers and strangers; inviting them to do things with you, serving them, and taking care of them.

house of Jacob: The family of the Israelites, starting with Jacob's twelve sons.

humility: A lack of pride in yourself or your ability to do things without God.

idolatry: Obsession with, attachment to, or worship of anything other than God.

Israel: A new name given to Jacob (Gen. 32:28). Later, the name applied to the nation formed by his descendants, who were God's chosen people. Then, when the nation divided, the name Israel applied to the ten northern tribes. (The two southern tribes became known as Judah.)

Jerusalem: The central city of Israel and capital of the southern kingdom of Judah. The name means "possession of peace."

Jew: A person belonging to one of the tribes of Israel. The term, derived from the word *Judah/Judean*, came into being around the time of the Babylonian exile (about 586 BC).

Judah: One of the twelve sons of Jacob, and the tribe made up of his descendants. After the division of Israel, it referred to the southern kingdom, made up of the tribes of Judah and Benjamin, whose capital was Jerusalem.

justification: God's act of considering believers to be righteous, based not on our ability to fulfill the law but on our faith in Jesus. God accepts and treats all those who believe in Christ as righteous in the eyes of the law, or in other words, as having lived up to all its demands.

kingdom of God or kingdom of heaven: At the present time, God's kingdom can be found in heaven and among his people (Matt. 6:9–10; Luke 17:20–21). After Christ returns, however, the kingdom of the world will become the kingdom of God (Rev. 11:15). Then all people will, either willingly or regretfully, acknowledge that he is King (Phil. 2:9–11).

koinonia: A Greek term that refers to spiritual relationships.

law: God's instructions to his people on how to live a life that honors and loves God.

legalism: Requirements that go beyond the commands of Scripture; or, the unbiblical belief that works are the means of becoming right with God.

Levites: Descendants of Levi who were set apart as religious workers. They were commanded to serve the name of the Lord forever (see Deut. 18:1–8).

light: Often used in Scripture to refer to Jesus (see John 1:9).

Lord of hosts: This name for God describes him as the leader and commander of all armies of the world, both spiritual and earthly.

mediator: One who intercedes between people to resolve a conflict or achieve a goal. Jesus is the Mediator between God and rebellious humanity (1 Tim. 2:5; compare Heb. 9:15; 12:24).

Melchizedek: The king and priest of Salem (probably Jerusalem) who foreshadowed the coming of the Messiah (see Gen. 14:17–20; Ps. 110:4; Hebrews 5–7).

mercy: Means not getting the punishment you really deserve. It is God's compassion for us even though we have offended him; he sees us in our misery and sin and loves us anyway.

mercy seat: The golden lid of the ark of the covenant, seen as the "place of propitiation" or the removal of God's wrath. It points forward to the saving gift of Christ.

Messiah: This term comes from a Hebrew word meaning "anointed one." It is the same as the Greek word *Christ*. Jesus is the Messiah sent from God (Matt. 16:16–17).

Minor Prophets: The books of Hosea through Malachi are referred to as the Minor Prophets. This refers to the length of the books, not the importance of the prophets.

miracle: A special act of God that goes beyond the laws of nature, thus demonstrating God's power.

Moabites: The descendants of Moab, who was the son of Lot and his older daughter (see Gen. 19:30–38). They refused to help the Israelites when they came out of Egypt (see Deut. 23:3–4).

Mosaic covenant: The covenant given to Moses on Mount Sinai, including the Ten Commandments. The sign of this covenant was to be the observance of the Sabbath (see Ex. 31:13). This is also called the Sinai covenant.

Most Holy Place: The part of the tabernacle and temple where the ark of the covenant was kept.

Nazirites: "Dedicated" or "consecrated" men or women who were set apart, sometimes before their birth, to be devoted to the service of God. They were not allowed to drink wine, cut their hair, or go near a dead body.

Nineveh: The capital of the pagan nation of Assyria. Considered to be one of the most evil cities of its time. Referred to in the books of Jonah, Nahum, 2 Kings 17–19, and 2 Chronicles 32–33.

Noahic covenant: God's covenant made with Noah whereby God promised never to flood the earth again (see Gen. 9:11–17).

offering: That which is sacrificed to God as an act of worship. It can be food, an animal, or money.

omnipotence: A word meaning that God is all-powerful.

omnipresence: A word meaning that God is present in all places at all times.

omniscience: A word meaning that God has complete knowledge and understanding of all things at all times.

overseer: An elder in the church.

parable: A story that uses everyday ideas and activities to teach a spiritual truth. Jesus often taught in parables (see, for instance, Matthew 13).

parousia: Greek word meaning "coming" or "presence," used to refer to the second coming of Christ as seen in 2 Peter 3:10.

Passover: Also known as "the Feast of Unleavened Bread" (see Ex. 12:17), this is an important Jewish festival in remembrance of the Lord passing over the homes of the Israelites when he killed the firstborn sons of the Egyptians. During the festival only unleavened bread (bread made without yeast) is allowed in the house.

peace offering: Also known as the fellowship offering, this offering was made to God, and then part of the offering was fed to the worshipers in attendance.

prayer: Communicating with God. It happens when someone who believes in him and trusts him (see John 4:24) pleads with him (see Ex. 32:11), pours out their heart to him (see 1 Sam. 1:15), calls to him (see 2 Chron. 32:20), unites with him (see Ps. 73:28), or kneels in front of him (see Eph. 3:14).

pride: Excessive self-esteem, the opposite of humility. Putting yourself on the throne over God. It is the foundation of all sin.

priest: In Old Testament Israel, the priests were mediators between God and the people. Their duties included receiving sacrifices from the people and overseeing the daily activities and maintenance of the tabernacle or temple. Jesus is now the High Priest for all who believe in him. This is explained in the book of Hebrews.

prophet or prophetess: A spokesperson for God. This person tells people the will of God for their lives. Sometimes, though not always, that might include information about the future.

proverb: A short general truth written in a way that is easy to remember and that is considered a popular saying.

providence: God's active involvement with and control of his creation. Belief in God's providence affirms that nothing happens by chance or fate, but everything is approved or disapproved by God for the good of his people. God has a purpose for all of human history.

psalms: Spiritual songs or poems used in worship.

purity: The quality of being free from any contamination, either morally or physically. It is the state of your heart when you are one hundred percent devoted to God.

ransom: A sum paid to set someone free from slavery or bondage, also known as redemption. Jesus paid the ransom for us by dying on the cross, which set us free from sin and the fear of death.

redemption: Payment of a price to get something back that was taken or lost. Refers to the price Jesus paid on the cross for your salvation.

repent: To turn away from sin and agree that God's commands are good. Repentance involves a change of your mind and your actions.

Sabbath: Saturday, the seventh day of the week, the Jewish day of worship and rest (Gen. 2:2–3; Ex. 31:13–17). Christians meet for worship on Sunday, the day of Christ's resurrection (Acts 20:7).

sacrifice: Giving back to God what God has given; a gift offered to God on the altar, either as a symbol of worship or as atonement for sin. Sacrifice often refers to an offering involving the shedding of blood.

salvation: Deliverance from the eternal consequences of sin. Jesus' death and resurrection purchased eternal salvation for believers (Rom. 1:16).

Samaria: The capital of the northern kingdom of Israel.

sanctification: The work of God's grace in our lives, which moves us closer to the image of God and make us more and more able to die to sin and live in righteousness.

Satan: A spiritual being whose name means "accuser." As the leader of all the demonic forces, he opposes God's rule and seeks to harm God's people and accuse them of wrongdoing. His power, however, is confined to the bounds that God has set for him, and one day he will be destroyed along with all his demons (Matt. 25:41; Rev. 20:10). See also *Enemy, the*.

savior: One who rescues another from destruction. Jesus is the Savior of all believers, rescuing them from sin and eternal punishment (Luke 2:11).

Scripture: The Bible, which is regarded by Christians as inspired by God. It is our trusted authority for all of life.

seer: Another word for prophet. Often refers to false prophets who were leading the people astray.

Selah: A musical term used in the book of Psalms. Its meaning is uncertain but may be "pause," "silence," "end," or even "louder."

sin: Anything you do that goes against the things God has commanded in the Bible. Sin is also referred to as disobedience.

Sodom and Gomorrah: Notorious cities of evil, destroyed by God because of their sinfulness (see Genesis 18–19; Isa. 1:9–10; 3:9; 13:19; Ezek. 16:49).

soul: Human beings have a visible part, the body, and an invisible part, the soul. Our bodies last only till death, but our souls will live forever, either in God's presence in heaven, or away from his presence in hell. The Bible tells us how to make heaven our eternal home.

sovereignty: This word describes God's supreme power and authority over all things (1 Tim. 6:15–16). He directs all things to carry out his good purposes for his people (Rom. 8:28–29).

spiritual gifts: Special abilities given by God to helping other believers stay strong in their faith (Romans 12; 1 Corinthians 12–14; Ephesians 4).

tabernacle: The tent where God dwelled on earth and communed with his people as Israel's divine king. Also referred to as the "tent of meeting" (Lev. 1:5). The temple in Jerusalem later replaced it.

temple: A place set aside as holy because of God's presence there. Solomon built the first temple of the Lord in Jerusalem, to replace the portable tabernacle. This temple was later destroyed by the Babylonians, rebuilt, and destroyed again by the Romans.

Trinity, the: This term refers to the three divine beings who make up the Godhead: God the Father, God the Son (who lived on earth as Jesus Christ), and God the Holy Spirit (see Matt. 28:19; Luke 1:35; 3:22; Gal. 4:6; 2 Thess. 2:13–14; Heb. 10:29).

unclean: Not fit for ceremonial worship, impure, unholy, dirty, foul, or morally unacceptable. The Old Testament teaches what God considers to be unclean and therefore not spiritually pure.

way, the: In the New Testament Jesus is called "the way," because he is our path to God.

wisdom: The ability to cope with life and to determine proper moral conduct in all situations.

witness: In the New Testament, refers especially to proclaiming the truth of the gospel (Acts 1:8).

Word: A term used in John to refer to Jesus.

word of Life: Another name for Jesus, who is called "the Word" (John 1:1) and "the life" (John 14:6). Elsewhere, it may refer to the gospel of eternal life (see 1 John 1:1).

works: The things you do, your actions, those things that people can see. They are considered good works if they are done out of a motive to love and serve God, i.e., obedience. Bad works are things people do out of disobedience. You can know a person's faith by his or her works (see Matt. 5:16; 1 Cor. 3:14; Eph. 2:10; 5:11; 2 Tim. 2:21; 1 John 2:4–5).

Yahweh: The English transliteration of the Hebrew letters *YHWH*. The Lord revealed this unique name for himself to Moses at the burning bush (Exodus 3). English Bibles usually render this name as "LORD," with small capital letters.

Zion: Can mean many things including fortress, citadel, the Temple Mount, God's holy mountain, the City of David, the City of God, the City of Jerusalem, the land of Judah, and the entire nation of Israel.

Spiritual Self-Check

Sometimes it's easy to ignore the sin in your life or to be just plain ignorant of it. But knowing what is sin and what isn't is a good place to start to make room for God in your life. Confession and repentance will quickly heal you of your sin and of the emotional, mental, and physical effects of your sin. Spotting your own sin is one of the best ways to make your life better, to gain self-control, and to find the power to redirect your path. So don't fear your sin, but rather look for it and then forsake it quickly. When you do, you'll find an amazing freedom. Spotting, confessing, and walking away from sin is a life-changing and empowering process. Don't let anyone tell you that you are a lost cause or that you can't change—you can, and all it takes is the courage to look into your life and agree with God about your own sin.

Following is a list of areas where sin can enter your life. Take a look at this list and then prayerfully consider your own life. Where is there sin and what do you need to do, according to God's Word, to walk away from it?

As you look over this list, circle the sins that you have in your life. After that, it's time to agree with God by confessing your sins and determining to turn away from them and never commit them again. Know that God will give you the strength to do this. He never commands anything that he won't help you to do. Freedom is just a confession away. Become aware of the areas where you've allowed sins in your life, study God's Word to fight their presence, and choose to give sin the boot! (Start your healing by checking out the Quick Relief section.)

Addiction
Adultery
Anger
Anorexia
Bad habits
Bitterness
Blasphemy
Bragging
Breaking your promises
Bulimia
Complaining
Coveting/Greed
Cutting
Denying Christ
Depression
Discontentment
Disobedience
Disobeying your parents
Doubt
Drunkenness
Envy
Fear
Giving Satan credit for what God has done

Gossip
Hate
Hypocrisy
Incest
Lack of mercy
Lack of self-control
Loving the world
Lying
Obsession
Occult practices (astrology, séances, witchcraft)
Perfectionism
Prayerlessness
Pride
Psychics/fortune-tellers
Resentment
Revenge
Self-hatred
Selfishness
Sex outside of marriage
Slander
Unthankfulness
Worry

Quick Relief

Where to Find Things in the Bible

ADDICTION.
See **IDOLATRY,
SELF-CONTROL**

ADULTERY
Exodus 20:14
Matthew 5:28
Matthew 19:7–9
1 Corinthians 6:9–10
2 Corinthians 12:21
Galatians 5:19
Hebrews 13:4

ANGER
Psalm 37:8
Proverbs 14:17
Proverbs 15:1
Proverbs 19:19
Proverbs 25:28
Matthew 5:22
2 Corinthians 12:20
Ephesians 4:26–27
Ephesians 4:31
Colossians 3:8
James 1:19–20

ANGELS
Genesis 19:1–22
Joshua 5:13–15
Job 38:4–7
Psalm 34:7
Psalm 91:9–13
Psalm 103:20
Daniel 9:20–23
Matthew 1:20–21
Matthew 4:11
Matthew 22:30
Matthew 24:31
Matthew 28:5–7
Luke 15:10
Luke 20:36
Acts 12:23
Hebrews 1:13–14
Jude 9

ANOREXIA. See
IDOLATRY

ASTROLOGY
Deuteronomy 4:19
Deuteronomy 17:2–4

Isaiah 47:12–14
Colossians 2:8

BAD HABITS.
See **SELF-CONTROL**

BIBLE STUDY
Psalm 19:8
Psalm 119:11
Psalm 119:97
Psalm 119:105
Psalm 119:130
Isaiah 55:11
Jeremiah 15:16
John 8:32
Acts 17:11
Ephesians 6:17
2 Timothy 2:15
2 Timothy 3:15–17
2 Timothy 4:2
Hebrews 4:12
James 1:21–25
1 Peter 2:2
2 Peter 1:21
Revelation 22:18–19

BITTERNESS
Proverbs 14:30
Proverbs 17:9
Ephesians 4:31
Hebrews 12:15
James 3:14

BLASPHEMY
Exodus 20:7
Leviticus 24:11–14
2 Chronicles 32:17
Psalm 73:9–11
Psalm 74:18
Isaiah 37:17
Isaiah 52:5
Romans 2:24
Titus 3:2
James 2:7
Jude 1:8–10

**BLASPHEMY
AGAINST THE HOLY
SPIRIT**
Matthew 12:31–32
Mark 3:28–29
Luke 12:10

BRAGGING. See
PRIDE

**BREAKING YOUR
PROMISES**
Proverbs 25:14
Ecclesiastes 5:4–5
Romans 1:30–31
1 Timothy 1:10

BULIMIA. See
IDOLATRY

COMMUNICATION
Psalm 141:3
Proverbs 6:16–17
Proverbs 10:19
Proverbs 15:28
Proverbs 16:32
Proverbs 18:13
Proverbs 21:23
Proverbs 25:11
Proverbs 26:4–5
Matthew 5:34–37
Matthew 12:34
Matthew 12:36
Ephesians 4:2–3
Ephesians 4:25
Ephesians 4:29–32
Colossians 4:6
James 3:2–10
James 4:11

COMPLAINING
Numbers 11:1
Lamentations 3:39
Luke 10:40
1 Corinthians 10:10
Philippians 2:14–15
Philippians 4:11–12
1 Thessalonians
    5:16–18
Hebrews 13:5
Jude 16

CONFESSION
Leviticus 5:5
Leviticus 16:20–22
Joshua 7:19
2 Samuel 24:10
Job 33:27–28
Psalm 25:11

Psalm 32:5
Psalm 38:18
Psalm 51:1–12
Proverbs 28:13
Jeremiah 3:13
Daniel 9:20–23
Hosea 5:15
Matthew 3:6
Mark 1:5
Luke 5:8
James 5:16
1 John 1:8–10
1 John 2:1

CONTENTMENT
Ecclesiastes 7:14
Philippians 4:8–9
Philippians 4:11–13
1 Timothy 6:6–8
Hebrews 13:5

COURAGE
Exodus 14:13–14
2 Chronicles 15:7
2 Chronicles 32:6–7
Psalm 112:7–8
Psalm 138:3
Isaiah 41:10
Isaiah 50:7
Isaiah 52:1
2 Corinthians 1:10
Ephesians 3:12
2 Timothy 1:7
Hebrews 13:6

COVETING. See
GREED

CUTTING. See also
TRUST
Leviticus 19:28
Deuteronomy 14:1
1 Corinthians 3:17
1 Corinthians 6:19
2 Corinthians 6:16
Ephesians 2:19–22

**DATING A
NONBELIEVER**
2 Corinthians 6:14

DEPRESSION. See also TRUST
Psalm 34:18
Proverbs 15:13-15
2 Corinthians 4:8-9
2 Corinthians 11:23-30
2 Corinthians 12:9-10
Philippians 4:8-9
Philippians 4:13
Hebrews 12:11
1 Peter 1:4-6
1 Peter 2:19

DIVORCE
Genesis 2:24
Matthew 5:32
Matthew 19:3-9
Mark 10:11-12
Luke 16:18
1 Corinthians 7:10-11

DISCONTENTMENT. See CONTENTMENT

DISOBEDIENCE. See OBEDIENCE

DISOBEYING YOUR PARENTS. See PARENTS

DOUBT. See TRUST

DRUNKENNESS
Proverbs 20:1
Isaiah 5:22
Luke 21:34-35
Romans 13:13
1 Corinthians 5:11
1 Corinthians 6:9-10
1 Thessalonians 5:6-8

DYING TO SELF
Matthew 10:38-39
Matthew 16:24
Matthew 20:16
Matthew 26:38-39
Mark 8:34
Luke 9:23
Luke 14:26-27
Romans 6:2-7
Romans 6:11
Romans 8:13
Romans 12:1
Romans 15:3
2 Corinthians 5:14-15
Galatians 6:14
Ephesians 4:22-24
Philippians 2:3-4
Philippians 3:8-11
Colossians 3:5
2 Timothy 2:19

ENVY
Proverbs 14:30
Proverbs 27:4
Romans 1:29
1 Corinthians 13:4
Galatians 5:19-21
1 Timothy 6:4
1 Peter 2:1-2

FAMILY. See also PARENTS
Psalm 133:1
Proverbs 6:16-19
1 Timothy 5:8

FEAR
Exodus 14:13-14
Deuteronomy 1:30-31
Deuteronomy 3:22
Deuteronomy 31:6-8
Joshua 1:9
Psalm 27:1
Psalm 56:3
Psalm 118:6
Proverbs 1:33
Proverbs 3:24
Proverbs 28:1
Proverbs 29:25
Isaiah 8:12
Isaiah 12:2
Isaiah 44:8
Isaiah 51:12
Isaiah 54:4
Jeremiah 1:8
Matthew 14:27
Luke 12:7
John 14:27
Romans 8:15

FEELINGS
Galatians 5:19-21
Galatians 5:22-23
Ephesians 4:31
Colossians 3:8-10
1 Peter 2:1

FIGHTING
Psalm 34:14
Matthew 5:9
Mark 9:50
Romans 12:18
Romans 14:19
2 Corinthians 13:11
Ephesians 4:2-3
Philippians 2:3-4
1 Thessalonians 5:13
2 Timothy 2:22
Hebrews 12:14
1 Peter 3:11

FORGIVENESS FROM GOD
Exodus 34:6
2 Chronicles 7:14

Nehemiah 9:17-18
Psalm 79:9
Psalm 86:15
Isaiah 55:6-7
Jeremiah 3:22
Jeremiah 33:8
Micah 7:18
Matthew 6:12
Matthew 6:14-15
Matthew 9:6
Matthew 18:21-35
Matthew 26:28
Mark 1:4
Mark 2:7-11
Mark 11:25
Luke 1:77
Luke 3:3
Luke 5:21-24
Luke 7:49
Luke 11:4
Luke 17:3
Luke 23:34
Luke 24:47
Acts 2:38
Acts 5:31
Acts 10:43
Acts 13:38
Acts 26:18
Ephesians 1:7
Ephesians 4:32
Colossians 1:14
Colossians 3:13
Titus 3:5
Hebrews 9:14
Hebrews 9:22
Hebrews 10:18-22
1 John 1:9

FORGIVING OTHERS
Matthew 5:23-24
Matthew 6:12
Matthew 6:14-15
Matthew 7:3-5
Matthew 18:21-35
Mark 11:25
Luke 17:3-4
John 20:23
2 Corinthians 2:7-10
Ephesians 4:32
Colossians 3:13

FORTUNE-TELLERS
Leviticus 20:6
Leviticus 20:27
Deuteronomy 18:10-14
2 Kings 23:24
Isaiah 2:6
Isaiah 8:19
Isaiah 44:25
Jeremiah 27:9-11
Zechariah 10:2
James 4:13-15

FRIENDS
Deuteronomy 13:6-8
Psalm 1:1
Psalm 119:63
Proverbs 13:20
Proverbs 17:17
Proverbs 18:24
Proverbs 27:6
Amos 3:3
Mark 9:50
1 Corinthians 15:33
James 4:4

FRUIT OF THE SPIRIT
John 15:1-8
Galatians 5:22-23
Galatians 5:25
Philippians 1:6
Philippians 1:11
2 Peter 1:5-8

GIVING
Deuteronomy 15:7-11
Ezra 2:68-69
Malachi 3:8
Matthew 5:42
Matthew 6:1-4
Matthew 19:21
Luke 3:11
Luke 12:33
Acts 2:44-45
Romans 12:6-8
Romans 12:13
2 Corinthians 8:3-5
2 Corinthians 8:11-14
2 Corinthians 9:6-7
2 Corinthians 9:12-13
Galatians 2:10
Galatians 6:10
1 Timothy 6:18
Hebrews 6:10
Hebrews 13:16

GOD'S WILL
Psalm 143:10
Isaiah 14:24
Isaiah 14:27
Isaiah 53:10
Jeremiah 29:11
Matthew 10:28-30
Matthew 26:39
Romans 12:2
1 Thessalonians 5:16-18

GOSSIP
Leviticus 19:16
Proverbs 11:13
Proverbs 16:28
Proverbs 20:19
Romans 1:29-31

2 Corinthians 12:20
1 Timothy 5:13

GRACE
Luke 18:13
Romans 4:5
Romans 4:8
Romans 5:1–2
Romans 5:5–6
Romans 8:8
Romans 8:1
Galatians 3:24
Ephesians 2:4–8
Colossians 2:13
Titus 3:4–7
Hebrews 9:14
Hebrews 10:19–20
1 Peter 2:24

GREED
Psalm 39:6
Proverbs 1:18–19
Habakkuk 2:9
Luke 12:13–21
Acts 5:1–10
1 Corinthians 6:9–10
Ephesians 5:5
Colossians 3:5
1 Timothy 6:9–11

HATE. See LOVE

HEALING
Isaiah 53:5
Matthew 10:1
Mark 16:17–18
John 11:4
Acts 3:16
2 Corinthians
    12:8–10
James 5:13–15

HEAVEN
Matthew 25:34
Mark 12:25–27
Luke 23:43
John 3:12–13
John 14:2–3
Romans 8:18–25
1 Corinthians 13:12
1 Corinthians
    15:35–37
1 Corinthians
    15:42–44
2 Corinthians 5:1–8
Philippians 3:20
1 Thessalonians
    4:16–17
2 Peter 3:13
Revelation 11:15
Revelation 21:1

HELL
Matthew 5:29–30
Matthew 8:12
Matthew 25:41–46

Romans 2:7–9
2 Thessalonians
    1:8–9
2 Peter 2:4
Revelation 14:11
Revelation 19:20
Revelation 20:10
Revelation 20:12–15

HOLY SPIRIT
Genesis 1:2
Genesis 6:3
Psalm 51:11
Psalm 139:7–12
Isaiah 32:14–15
Isaiah 61:1
Isaiah 63:10
Zechariah 12:10
Matthew 3:11
Mark 13:11
John 3:8
John 14:15–17
John 14:26
John 15:26
John 16:7–8
John 16:13–15
John 20:22
Acts 1:8
Acts 2:38
Acts 2:4
Acts 4:25
Acts 5:32
Acts 10:44
Acts 11:16
Romans 5:5
Romans 8:26
Romans 9:1
1 Corinthians 6:19
Ephesians 1:14
2 Peter 1:21
Jude 20

HOPE
Lamentations
    3:21–25
1 Corinthians 2:9
2 Corinthians 5:1–2
Ephesians 1:18

HOSPITALITY
Matthew 10:10
Matthew 10:42
Matthew 25:35
Romans 12:13
Titus 1:8
Hebrews 13:2
1 Peter 4:9

HUMILITY
Deuteronomy 8:2–3
Psalm 34:18
Proverbs 3:7
Proverbs 15:33
Proverbs 16:19
Proverbs 18:12

Proverbs 22:4
Proverbs 29:23
Isaiah 26:5
Isaiah 66:1–2
Micah 6:8
Matthew 5:3
Matthew 5:39
Matthew 18:4
Mark 10:31
Mark 10:43–45
Luke 14:11
Romans 15:2–3
Ephesians 4:2
Philippians 2:3–4
Philippians 2:7–8
Colossians 3:12
James 4:6
James 4:10
1 Peter 3:8

HUSBANDS
1 Corinthians 11:3
Ephesians 5:22–26
Ephesians 5:33
Colossians 3:18–19
1 Timothy 3:4–5
1 Timothy 5:8
1 Peter 3:7

HYPOCRISY
Isaiah 29:13
Isaiah 65:5
Ezekiel 33:31–32
Matthew 6:2
Matthew 6:5
Matthew 6:16
Matthew 15:1–9
Matthew 23:23–26
Luke 11:39
Luke 13:14–16
Luke 18:9–14
Luke 20:46–47

IDOLATRY
Exodus 20:2–5
Exodus 32:1–6
Exodus 32:31–34
Leviticus 19:4
Deuteronomy 5:6–9
Psalm 115:3–8
Jonah 2:8
Micah 5:13
Habakkuk 2:18
Matthew 6:24–25
Romans 6:16
1 Corinthians 6:9–10
1 John 5:21
2 Peter 2:19

INTERCESSION. See
also PRAYER
Genesis 17:18–23
Genesis 20:7, 17
Exodus 8:12–13,
    30–31

Exodus 9:33
Exodus 32:11–14,
    31–32
Numbers 12:13
Deuteronomy
    9:18–20
1 Samuel 12:23
1 Kings 8:46–54
1 Kings 17:2–23
Job 42:8–10
Psalm 122:6–7
Isaiah 62:6
Luke 23:34
Romans 15:30–32
Ephesians 6:18
1 Timothy 2:1–3
James 5:14–16
1 John 5:16

JEALOUSY
Proverbs 14:30
Proverbs 23:17
Proverbs 27:4
1 Corinthians 3:3
1 Corinthians 13:4
Galatians 5:19–21
Galatians 5:25–26
Romans 13:13
James 3:13–18

JOY
Psalm 30:11
Psalm 119:162
Ecclesiastes 2:26
Habakkuk 3:17–18
Romans 12:12
Romans 15:13
2 Corinthians 6:10
Galatians 5:22–23
Philippians 4:4
1 Thessalonians
    5:16–18
1 Peter 1:3–6

LOVE
Leviticus 19:17–18
Matthew 5:44–46
Luke 6:27–28
Luke 10:27
John 13:35
John 14:15
John 15:12
John 15:17
Romans 12:9–10
Romans 13:8–10
1 Corinthians 13:4–8
1 Corinthians 16:14
2 Corinthians
    5:14–21
Ephesians 2:4–7
Ephesians 5:1–2
Philippians 1:9–11
Philippians 2:3–4

1 Thessalonians
3:12–13
1 Thessalonians
4:9–12
1 Timothy 1:5
1 Peter 4:8
1 John 2:9–11
1 John 3:16–18
1 John 4:7–12
1 John 4:16
1 John 4:18–21
1 John 5:2–5
2 John 6

LOVING THE WORLD
Matthew 13:22
Mark 4:18–19
Luke 21:34–35
John 5:44
John 12:43
John 15:19
Romans 12:2
Colossians 3:2
Colossians 3:5
2 Timothy 2:3–5
James 2:1–4
James 4:4
James 5:5
1 Peter 2:11
1 Peter 4:3–4
1 John 2:15–17

LOVING YOUR ENEMIES
Matthew 5:39
Matthew 5:43–44
Matthew 5:46
Luke 6:27–29
Luke 6:32–34
Luke 6:35

LYING
Psalm 31:18
Psalm 58:3
Psalm 119:69
Psalm 119:128
Psalm 120:2
Proverbs 6:16–19
Proverbs 12:19
Proverbs 14:5
Proverbs 14:25
Proverbs 19:5
Proverbs 29:12
Jeremiah 9:3
Hosea 10:13
Romans 1:25
Ephesians 4:25

MARRIAGE
Genesis 2:18–24
Matthew 19:5–6
Romans 7:2–3
1 Corinthians 7:1–5
1 Corinthians
7:25–28

2 Corinthians 6:14
Ephesians 5:21–33
Hebrews 13:4

MERCY (FROM GOD TO PEOPLE)
Deuteronomy 5:10
1 Chronicles 16:34
Psalm 25:6
Psalm 51:1
Lamentations
3:21–23
Nehemiah 1:5
Ephesians 2:4
Titus 3:4–5
Hebrews 4:16
1 Peter 2:10

MERCY (SHOW TO OTHERS)
Proverbs 3:3
Proverbs 11:17
Proverbs 14:31
Zechariah 7:9
Matthew 5:7
Matthew 12:7
Matthew 23:23
2 Corinthians 2:6–8
James 2:13

OBEDIENCE
Exodus 15:26
Exodus 19:5
Exodus 23:20–22
Exodus 23:25
Deuteronomy
11:26–28
Deuteronomy 13:4
Deuteronomy 28
1 Samuel 12:14
1 Samuel 15:22
Proverbs 15:32
Proverbs 29:18
Isaiah 1:19
Jeremiah 7:23
Matthew 6:24
Matthew 7:21
Matthew 7:24–27
Matthew 12:30
Mark 3:35
Luke 6:46
Luke 11:28
Luke 12:47
John 8:31
John 9:31
John 14:15
John 14:21
John 15:10
John 15:14
Romans 6:16
Romans 6:19
Romans 10:3–11
Ephesians 5:10
2 Timothy 2:4

2 Timothy 2:15
2 Timothy 2:19
Titus 2:1
Titus 2:11–14
James 1:22–25
James 2:14–26
1 Peter 1:22
2 Peter 1:10
1 John 2:3–6
1 John 3:9–10
1 John 5:3–4
2 John 6

OBSESSION. See
IDOLATRY

OCCULT PRACTICES.
See **ASTROLOGY,
FORTUNE-TELLERS,
WITCHCRAFT**

PARENTS
Exodus 20:12
Exodus 21:17
Leviticus 19:3
Numbers 30:3–5
Proverbs 17:6
Romans 1:28–32
Ephesians 6:1

PERFECTIONISM.
See **PRIDE,
FORGIVENESS FROM
GOD, GRACE**

PRAYER. See also
INTERCESSION
Exodus 32:11
1 Samuel 1:10–18
2 Chronicles 32:20
Psalm 18:6
Psalm 66:18
Proverbs 28:9
Isaiah 62:6–7
Matthew 6:7–13
Matthew 18:19
Matthew 26:39
Luke 22:40
John 14:13–14
John 15:7
Acts 1:24–25
Romans 8:15
Romans 8:26–27
2 Corinthians 12:8–9
Galatians 4:6
Ephesians 3:14–20
Ephesians 6:18
1 Thessalonians 5:17
Hebrews 4:16
Hebrews 5:7
James 1:6–7
James 4:3
1 Peter 3:7
1 Peter 3:12
1 Peter 4:7
1 John 5:14–15

PREDESTINATION
John 6:37
John 6:44
John 6:65
John 15:16
John 17:2
John 17:9
John 17:20
Romans 9:11–13
Romans 9:16
Romans 9:17–18
Romans 11:6–8
1 Peter 5:10

PRIDE
Deuteronomy
8:11–18
2 Chronicles
26:16–21
Psalm 119:21
Proverbs 3:7
Proverbs 8:13
Proverbs 11:2
Proverbs 13:10
Proverbs 16:18
Proverbs 29:23
Ecclesiastes 7:8
Jeremiah 13:8–17
Daniel 4:30–32
Daniel 4:37
Hosea 13:4–6
Luke 18:9–14
Acts 12:21–23
Philippians 2:3
1 Peter 5:5–6

PROTECTION
Numbers 14:9
Ezra 8:21–23
Psalm 18:2
Psalm 91:4
Psalm 105:4
Proverbs 18:10
Song of Songs 2:4
Luke 21:36
Luke 22:40
John 17:11–12
2 Thessalonians 3:3
Hebrews 13:5–6
1 Peter 1:5

PSYCHICS. See
FORTUNE-TELLERS

PURITY
Psalm 18:20–22
Psalm 51:7
Psalm 51:10
Psalm 119:9
Proverbs 22:11
Matthew 5:8
Galatians 5:16
1 Timothy 1:5
2 Timothy 2:22
Titus 1:15

1 Peter 1:22
1 John 3:3

RECONCILIATION
Jeremiah 31:33
Hosea 2:14–23
Hosea 14
Matthew 5:23–24
Matthew 23:37
Romans 5:8–11
2 Corinthians
    5:18–20
Ephesians 2:11–19
Colossians 1:20–22
James 4:8

RESENTMENT
Leviticus 19:18
Proverbs 14:10
Proverbs 14:30
Proverbs 17:9
Isaiah 45:9
Romans 3:14
Ephesians 4:31
Hebrews 12:15
James 3:14

REST
Genesis 2:2–3
Exodus 20:10
Psalm 23:1–3
Isaiah 30:15
Isaiah 57:18–21
Jeremiah 6:16
Matthew 11:28–30
Mark 6:31–32
John 14:27
John 16:33
Romans 5:1
Romans 8:6
Hebrews 4:1–11
Revelation 14:13

REVENGE
Leviticus 19:18
Proverbs 20:22
Proverbs 24:17
Proverbs 24:29
Isaiah 53:7
Matthew 5:38–41
Luke 6:35
Romans 12:14
Romans 12:17
Romans 12:19
Hebrews 10:30
1 Peter 2:23
1 Peter 3:9

SALVATION
Isaiah 61:10
Matthew 13:18–23
John 3:3–18
John 5:24
John 6:40
John 6:44

John 6:47
John 6:53–54
Acts 2:38
Acts 4:12
Acts 16:31
Romans 3:23–26
Romans 8:38–39
Romans 10:9–10
Romans 10:13
Ephesians 2:4–6
Colossians 2:13
1 Timothy 1:15
Titus 3:5
Hebrews 10:20
1 Peter 1:8–9
1 John 5:11–12

SATAN
Genesis 3:1–6, 14–15
Job 2:1–6
Matthew 4:1–11
Luke 10:18
John 8:44
John 16:11
Ephesians 4:27
Ephesians 6:11
James 4:7
1 Peter 5:8
1 John 3:8
1 John 5:19

SCRIPTURE
Psalm 119:105
Psalm 119:160
John 17:17
2 Timothy 3:16
Hebrews 4:12
2 Peter 1:20–21
Revelation 22:18–19

SÉANCES. See
WITCHCRAFT

SELF-CONTROL
Psalm 39:1
Proverbs 25:28
Proverbs 29:11
Matthew 23:25
Romans 8:12–14
1 Corinthians
    9:24–27
2 Corinthians
    5:14–15
2 Corinthians 10:5
Galatians 5:17
Galatians 5:22–23
James 1:19–20
1 Peter 4:7
2 Peter 1:5–9

SELF-HATE. See
FORGIVENESS FROM
GOD, GRACE

SELFISHNESS. See
DYING TO SELF

SEX
Genesis 2:24
Acts 15:20
Acts 15:29
Romans 1:24
Romans 6:19
Romans 13:13
1 Corinthians 5:9
1 Corinthians 6:9–11
1 Corinthians 6:18
1 Corinthians 7:3–4
2 Corinthians 12:21
Galatians 5:19–21
Ephesians 5:3
Colossians 3:5
1 Thessalonians 4:3
Hebrews 13:4
1 John 3:9

SILENCE
Psalm 62:1
Psalm 62:5–6
Psalm 131:2
Proverbs 11:12
Proverbs 17:28
Ecclesiastes 3:7
Ecclesiastes 4:6
Isaiah 30:15
Isaiah 53:7
Lamentations
    3:25–28
Habakkuk 2:20
Zephaniah 1:7
Zechariah 2:13
Mark 6:31
Luke 6:12
James 1:19
1 Peter 3:4

SIN (DEFINITION OF)
Genesis 6:5
Psalm 14:1–3
Psalm 36:1–4
Matthew 15:10–11
Matthew 15:16–20
Mark 7:20–23
Romans 1:21–32
Romans 3:10–18
Romans 8:3–8
Romans 14:23
2 Corinthians 12:20
Galatians 5:19–21
James 4:17
1 John 3:4
1 John 5:17

SIN (FREEDOM FROM)
John 1:29
Romans 6:6–7
Romans 6:12–18
Romans 8:2
2 Corinthians 5:15
Galatians 1:4
Galatians 6:1
Ephesians 1:7
Hebrews 10:10
1 Peter 2:24
1 John 1:7
1 John 5:18–20

SIN (SEPARATING US FROM GOD)
Isaiah 59:2
Habakkuk 1:13
Matthew 7:23
Luke 13:27
Romans 3:23
Romans 8:7–8
Hebrews 10:26–29
Hebrews 12:14

SLANDER. See
LYING, LOVE

SPIRITUAL WARFARE
2 Kings 6:17
Isaiah 54:17
Mark 9:29
Romans 8:26
Romans 8:38–39
2 Corinthians 10:4–5
Ephesians 6:10–18
James 4:7
1 Peter 5:8–9
1 John 5:4–5

SUFFERING (PERSONAL)
Deuteronomy 26:6–7
Job 30:16
Psalm 25:18
Psalm 69:29
Psalm 88:1–9
Psalm 88:14–18
Psalm 94:12–14
Psalm 116:10
Psalm 119:71
Psalm 119:75
Ecclesiastes 4:1
Ecclesiastes 8:14
Lamentations 3:1–38
Romans 8:20–23
Romans 8:28
James 5:11

SUFFERING (FOR YOUR FAITH)
Matthew 16:24
John 12:24
Acts 5:41
Romans 5:3–5

Romans 8:17–18
2 Corinthians 4:17
2 Corinthians 6:7–10
Philippians 1:29
Philippians 3:10–11
Colossians 1:24
2 Thessalonians 1:5
2 Timothy 1:8
2 Timothy 2:3–6
2 Timothy 2:9–12
Hebrews 5:8
Hebrews 12:11
James 5:10–11
1 Peter 2:19–23
1 Peter 4:1–2
1 Peter 4:12–13
1 Peter 5:9–10

SUICIDE (REASONS TO LIVE)

Psalm 71:19–21
Psalm 119:50
Isaiah 40:11
Isaiah 40:28–31
Isaiah 43:18–19
Isaiah 44:22
Isaiah 61:1
Jeremiah 29:11
Jeremiah 31:13
Matthew 11:28–30
Mark 9:23
John 8:32
John 8:36
John 14:27
1 Corinthians 6:19–20
1 Corinthians 10:13
Galatians 2:20
Ephesians 2:4–6
Philippians 1:6
Colossians 1:13
Colossians 2:11–13
Titus 3:5

Hebrews 4:15
2 Peter 1:4
1 John 3:1
1 John 4:4
1 John 5:5

THANKFULNESS

Psalm 35:18
Psalm 50:14
Psalm 100:4
Psalm 106:1
Psalm 116:17
1 Corinthians 15:57
Ephesians 1:16
Ephesians 5:20
Philippians 1:3
Philippians 4:6
1 Thessalonians 1:2
1 Thessalonians 5:18
2 Thessalonians 2:13
1 Timothy 1:12
Hebrews 12:28

TRIALS

Psalm 23:1
Psalm 46:1–3
Psalm 65:5–7
Psalm 89:9
Psalm 91:2–7
Psalm 91:11–15
Isaiah 41:10
Matthew 6:25–34
Luke 12:7
Romans 8:28
Romans 8:31
James 1:2–4
1 Peter 1:6–7

TRUST

Psalm 22:4–5
Psalm 25:2–3
Psalm 31:14

Psalm 32:10
Psalm 33:21
Psalm 37:3–5
Psalm 52:8
Psalm 56:3–4
Psalm 84:12
Psalm 146:3
Proverbs 3:5
Proverbs 29:25
Jeremiah 17:7
Jeremiah 48:7
Ezekiel 33:13
2 Timothy 1:12

WITCHCRAFT

Deuteronomy 18:10–12
2 Chronicles 33:6
Isaiah 2:6
Micah 3:7
Revelation 21:8
Revelation 22:15

WIVES

Genesis 3:16
Proverbs 19:14
1 Corinthians 7:3–4
Ephesians 5:22–26
Ephesians 5:33
Colossians 3:18–19
1 Timothy 3:11
Titus 2:3–5
1 Peter 3:1
1 Peter 3:3–6

WORRY

Psalm 37:5–11
Proverbs 12:25
Matthew 6:25–34
Matthew 13:22
Luke 21:34–35
Philippians 4:6
1 Peter 5:7

Subject Index

Reading Plans

Use these Bible reading plans as a starting place to get to know your Bible and your God in a deeper way. Try starting with a short plan, like a 25- or 31-day plan, then progressing toward a 90-day or one-year plan. The important thing to remember is to spend time in God's Word every day. The Bible is the story of God and his people, and the hero of the story is Jesus.

25 God Girls in 25 Days

1. Eve: profile p. 5; Genesis 2:18–4:2; 4:25
2. Sarah: profile p. 15; Genesis 11:27–12:20; 16; 18:1–15; 21:1–13; 1 Peter 3:5–6
3. Rebekah: profile p. 28; Genesis 24:11–67; 25:19–28; 26:6–11; 26:34–27:46; Romans 9:9–12
4. Jochebed: profile p. 64; Exodus 2:1–10; 6:20; Numbers 26:59
5. Miriam: profile p. 156; Exodus 2:1–10; 15:20–21; Numbers 12:1–15; 20:1
6. Rahab: profile p. 228; Joshua 2; 6:15–25; Matthew 1:5; Hebrews 11:31; James 2:25
7. Deborah: profile p. 262; Judges 4:4–5:31
8. Ruth: profile p. 286; Ruth 1–4; Matthew 1:5
9. Hannah: profile p. 296; 1 Samuel 1:1–2:10, 18–21
10. Abigail: profile p. 320; 1 Samuel 25
11. Naaman's Servant Girl: profile p. 398; 2 Kings 5:1–4
12. Esther: profile p. 527; Esther 1–12
13. The Proverbs 31 Woman: profile p. 713; Proverbs 31:10–31
14. Rachel: profile p. 849; Genesis 29:1–33:20; 35:16–20; 46:19–22; Jeremiah 31:15; Matthew 2:18
15. Mary, Mother of Jesus: profile p. 1060; Matthew 1–2; Luke 1–2; John 2:1–12; 19:25–27; Acts 1:14
16. The Woman with Chronic Bleeding: profile p. 1070; Matthew 9:20–22; Mark 5:25–34; Luke 8:43–48
17. Elizabeth: profile p. 1128; Luke 1:5–25, 36–45, 57–63
18. Mary Magdalene: profile p. 1138; Matthew 27:55–56, 61; 28:1–10; Mark 15:40, 47; 16:1–11; Luke 8:1–3; 24:1–12; John 19:25; 20:1–2, 11–18
19. The Widow with Two Coins: profile p. 1158; Luke 21:1–4
20. The Woman at the Well: profile p. 1175; John 4:4–30
21. Martha: profile p. 1186; Luke 10:38–42, John 11:1–44; 12:1–2
22. Tabitha: profile p. 1214; Acts 9:36–42
23. Lydia: profile p. 1223; Acts 16:13–15, 40
24. Priscilla: profile p. 1227; Acts 18:1–3, 18–19, 24–26; Romans 16:3; 1 Corinthians 16:19; 2 Timothy 4:19
25. Phoebe: profile p. 1261; Romans 16:1–2

31 Days to Know God's Plan for Us

1. The Fall of Humanity: Genesis 3:1–19
2. A People Set Apart for God: Genesis 12:1–3; 28:10–15; 32:22–28
3. The Ten Commandments: Exodus 20:1–17
4. Sacrifices and the Law: Leviticus 5:14–19
5. Dealing with Sin Under the Law: Leviticus 20:7–27
6. Obedience from Love: Deuteronomy 6:1–9; 11:13–21
7. Humanity's Disobedience: Judges 2:10–19
8. The People Demand a King: 1 Samuel 8
9. Saul Fails and Is Rejected: 1 Samuel 15:17–23
10. Many Kings Fail to Heed God: Jeremiah 1–7
11. The Sins of the People Hurt God: Ezekiel 20:5–26
12. An Eternal King Promised: Jeremiah 23:1–6; Isaiah 9:6–7; Zechariah 9:9–10
13. The Promised Christ Is Born: Luke 2:1–20
14. The Word Became Flesh: John 1:1–18
15. Signs and Wonders of Jesus: Matthew 9:1–8; Luke 13:10–17
16. Jesus Fulfills the Law: Matthew 5:17–20; Romans 8:1–4
17. Jesus Teaches about Our New Life: John 3
18. Jesus Taken: John 18:1–11
19. Jesus' Death and Resurrection: Luke 23:44–24:12
20. Christ a Sacrifice for All: Hebrews 10:1–18; 11:1–3; 12:1–3
21. God's Righteous Wrath Explained: Romans 1:18–32
22. God's Judgment Explained: Romans 2:5–11
23. Saved by Grace Alone: Ephesians 2
24. Righteousness by Faith: Romans 3:9–26
25. Life through Christ: Romans 5:12–21
26. Life by the Spirit: Romans 8:1–17; Galatians 5:16–26
27. Living Sacrifices: Romans 12
28. Walking in the Light: 1 John 1–2
29. Living for God: 1 Peter 1–11
30. Love for One Another: 1 John 3:11–24
31. Promise of Eternity: 2 Corinthians 5:1–10; Revelation 21:1–4

31 Days to Know Jesus

1. Jesus Is Predicted: Isaiah 53
2. The Birth of Jesus: Matthew 1:18–25
3. John the Baptist Prepares the Way for Jesus: Matthew 3:1–4:11
4. Jesus' First Miracle (Water to Wine) and the Samaritan Woman: John 2:1–11; John 4:1–26
5. Jesus Is Rejected in His Own Hometown: Luke 4:14–30
6. Jesus Calls His Disciples: Luke 5:1–11; Matthew 9:9–13
7. The Sermon on the Mount: Luke 6:17–46
8. The Centurion, the Widow's Son, and a Sinful Woman: Matthew 8:1–13; Luke 7:11–17; 7:36–50
9. Jesus Encounters the Pharisees: Matthew 12:1–13; 22–45
10. Parables of the Sower, Weeds, and Seeds: Matthew 13:1–43
11. Jesus Calms the Storm and Walks on Water: Luke 8:22–25; Mark 6:45–56
12. Jesus Heals a Man, a Woman, and a Girl: Mark 5:1–43
13. Jesus Feeds the Five Thousand: John 6:1–14
14. Peter Knows Jesus Christ; the Transfiguration: Luke 9:18–27; Luke 17:1–8
15. Healing by Faith: Mark 9:14–32
16. More Teachings and Parables: Matthew 17:24–18:20
17. More Teachings and Parables: Matthew 18:21–19:15
18. The Rich Young Ruler: Mark 10:17–31
19. The Disciples Sent Out: Luke 10:1–24
20. The Great Commandment: Mark 12:28–44
21. The Parable of the Good Samaritan: Luke 10:25–37
22. The Lord's Prayer/Jesus Teaches Us How to Pray: Luke 11:1–13
23. Jesus Raises Lazarus from the Dead: John 11:1–44
24. The Triumphal Entry into Jerusalem: Matthew 21:1–27
25. The Last Supper: John 13:1–17; Matthew 26:17–35
26. The Love of Jesus for the Disciples: John 14–15
27. Jesus Arrested and Betrayed: Matthew 26:36–75
28. Jesus' Unfair Trial: John 18:19–19:16
29. Jesus' Crucifixion and Death: John 19:17–42
30. Jesus' Resurrection and Appearances: John 20–21
31. The Great Commission and the Ascension of Jesus: Matthew 28:16–20; Luke 24:50–53

90 Days through the New Testament

1. Matthew 1–4	46. 1 Corinthians 5–7
2. Matthew 5–7	47. 1 Corinthians 8–11
3. Matthew 8–10	48. 1 Corinthians 12–14
4. Matthew 11–13	49. 1 Corinthians 15–16
5. Matthew 14–16	50. 2 Corinthians 1–3
6. Matthew 17–19	51. 2 Corinthians 4–6
7. Matthew 20–22	52. 2 Corinthians 7–9
8. Matthew 23–25	53. 2 Corinthians 10–13
9. Matthew 26–28	54. Galatians 1–2
10. Mark 1–3	55. Galatians 3–4
11. Mark 4–6	56. Galatians 5–6
12. Mark 7–9	57. Ephesians 1–3
13. Mark 10–12	58. Ephesians 4–6
14. Mark 13–16	59. Philippians 1–2
15. Luke 1–3	60. Philippians 3–4
16. Luke 4–6	61. Colossians 1–2
17. Luke 7–9	62. Colossians 3–4
18. Luke 10–12	63. 1 Thessalonians 1–3
19. Luke 13–15	64. 1 Thessalonians 4–5
20. Luke 16–18	65. 2 Thessalonians 1–3
21. Luke 19–21	66. 1 Timothy 1–3
22. Luke 22–24	67. 1 Timothy 4–6
23. John 1–3	68. 2 Timothy 1–4
24. John 4–6	69. Titus 1–3
25. John 7–9	70. Philemon
26. John 10–12	71. Hebrews 1–2
27. John 13–16	72. Hebrews 3–4:13
28. John 17–18	73. Hebrews 4:14–7
29. John 19–21	74. Hebrews 8–10
30. Acts 1–3	75. Hebrews 11–13
31. Acts 4–6	76. James 1–3:12
32. Acts 7–9	77. James 3:13–5
33. Acts 10–12	78. 1 Peter 1–3:7
34. Acts 13–15	79. 1 Peter 3:8–5
35. Acts 16–18	80. 2 Peter 1–3
36. Acts 19–21:36	81. 1 John 1–3:10
37. Acts 21:37–25:22	82. 1 John 3:11–5:21
38. Acts 25:23–28:30	83. 2 John; 3 John; Jude
39. Romans 1–3	84. Revelation 1–3
40. Romans 4–6	85. Revelation 4–6
41. Romans 7–8	86. Revelation 7–9
42. Romans 9–11	87. Revelation 10–12
43. Romans 12–13	88. Revelation 13–15
44. Romans 14–16	89. Revelation 16–18
45. 1 Corinthians 1–4	90. Revelation 19–22

Through the Bible in One Year

1. Gen. 1:1–2:17; Matt. 1:1–25; Ps. 1:1–6
2. Gen. 2:18–4:16; Matt. 2:1–18; Ps. 2:1–12
3. Gen. 4:17–6:22; Matt. 2:19–3:17; Ps. 3:1–8
4. Gen. 7:1–9:17; Matt. 4:1–22; Prov. 1:1–7
5. Gen. 9:18–11:9; Matt. 4:23–5:20; Ps. 4:1–8
6. Gen. 11:10–13:18; Matt. 5:21–42; Ps. 5:1–12
7. Gen. 14–16; Matt. 5:43–6:24; Ps. 6
8. Gen. 17–18; Matt. 6:25–7:23; Prov. 1:8–19
9. Gen. 19–20; Matt. 7:24–8:22; Ps. 7:1–9
10. Gen. 21–23; Matt. 8:23–9:13; Ps. 7:10–17
11. Gen. 24; Matt. 9:14–38; Ps. 8:1–9
12. Gen. 25–26; Matt. 10:1–31; Prov. 1:20–33
13. Gen. 27–28; Matt. 10:32–11:15; Ps. 9:1–6
14. Gen. 29–30; Matt. 11:16–30; Ps. 9:7–12
15. Gen. 31; Matt. 12:1–21; Ps. 9:13–20
16. Gen. 32–33; Matt. 12:22–45; Prov. 2:1–11
17. Gen. 34–35; Matt. 12:46–13:17; Ps. 10:1–11
18. Gen. 36–37; Matt. 13:18–35; Ps. 10:12–18
19. Gen. 38–39; Matt. 13:36–58; Ps. 11:1–7
20. Gen. 40:1–41:40; Matt. 14:1–21; Prov. 2:12–22
21. Gen. 41:41–42:38; Matt. 14:22–15:9; Ps. 12:1–8
22. Gen. 43–44; Matt. 15:10–39; Ps. 13:1–6
23. Gen. 45–47:12; Matt. 16:1–20; Ps. 14:1–7
24. Gen. 47:13–48:22; Matt. 16:21–17:13; Prov. 3:1–10
25. Gen. 49–50; Matt. 17:14–18:9; Ps. 15:1–5
26. Job 1–3; Matt. 18:10–35; Ps. 16:1–11
27. Job 4–7; Matt. 19:1–15; Ps. 17:1–5
28. Job 8–10; Matt. 19:16–30; Prov. 3:11–20
29. Job 11–14; Matt. 20:1–19; Ps. 17:6–12
30. Job 15–18; Matt. 20:20–34; Ps. 17:13–15
31. Job 19–21; Matt. 21:1–17; Ps. 18:1–6
32. Job 22–24; Matt. 21:18–32; Prov. 3:21–35
33. Job 25–29; Matt. 21:33–22:14; Ps. 18:7–15
34. Job 30–32; Matt. 22:15–46; Ps. 18:16–24
35. Job 33–34; Matt. 23; Ps. 18:25–36
36. Job 35–37; Matt. 24:1–31; Prov. 4:1–9
37. Job 38:1–40:2; Matt. 24:32–25:13; Ps. 18:37–42
38. Job 40:3–42:17; Matt. 25:14–46; Ps. 18:43–50
39. Ex. 1–3; Matt. 26:1–30; Ps. 19:1–6
40. Ex. 4:1–6:13; Matt. 26:31–46; Prov. 4:10–19
41. Ex. 6:14–8:32; Matt. 26:47–68; Ps. 19:7–14
42. Ex. 9–10; Matt. 26:69–27:10; Ps. 20:1–9
43. Ex. 11–12; Matt. 27:11–44; Ps. 21:1–7
44. Ex. 13–14; Matt. 27:45–66; Prov. 4:20–27
45. Ex. 15–16; Matt. 28; Ps. 21:8–13
46. Ex. 17–18; Mark 1:1–28; Ps. 22:1–11
47. Ex. 19–20; Mark 1:29–2:17; Ps. 22:12–21
48. Ex. 21–22; Mark 2:18–3:30; Prov. 5:1–14
49. Ex. 23–24; Mark 3:31–4:29; Ps. 22:22–31
50. Ex. 25–26; Mark 4:30–5:20; Ps. 23:1–6
51. Ex. 27–28; Mark 5:21–6:6; Ps. 24:1–10
52. Ex. 29–30; Mark 6:6–29; Prov. 5:15–23
53. Ex. 31:1–33:6; Mark 6:30–56; Ps. 25:1–7
54. Ex. 33:7–34:35; Mark 7:1–30; Ps. 25:8–15
55. Ex. 35–36; Mark 7:31–8:13; Ps. 25:16–22
56. Ex. 37–38; Mark 8:14–9:1; Prov. 6:1–11
57. Ex. 39–40; Mark 9:2–32; Ps. 26:1–12
58. Lev. 1–3; Mark 9:33–10:12; Ps. 27:1–6
59. Lev. 4:1–5:14; Mark 10:13–31; Ps. 27:7–14
60. Lev. 5:14–7:10; Mark 10:32–52; Prov. 6:12–19
61. Lev. 7:11–8:36; Mark 11:1–25; Ps. 28
62. Lev. 9–10; Mark 11:27–12:12; Ps. 29
63. Lev. 11–12; Mark 12:13–27; Ps. 30:1–7
64. Lev. 13; Mark 12:28–44; Prov. 6:20–29
65. Lev. 14; Mark 13:1–31; Ps. 30:8–12
66. Lev. 15–16; Mark 13:32–14:16; Ps. 31:1–8
67. Lev. 17–18; Mark 14:17–42; Ps. 31:9–18
68. Lev. 19–20; Mark 14:43–72; Prov. 6:30–35
69. Lev. 21–22; Mark 15:1–32; Ps. 31:19–24
70. Lev. 23–24; Mark 15:33–47; Ps. 32
71. Lev. 25:1–26:13; Mark 16:1–20; Ps. 33:1–11
72. Lev. 26:14–27:34; Luke 1:1–25; Prov. 7:1–5
73. Num. 1:1–2:9; Luke 1:26–38; Ps. 33:12–22
74. Num. 2:10–3:51; Luke 1:39–56; Ps. 34:1–10
75. Num. 4:1–5:10; Luke 1:57–80; Ps. 34:11–22
76. Num. 5:11–6:27; Luke 2:1–20; Prov. 7:6–20
77. Num. 7:1–65; Luke 2:21–40; Ps. 35:1–10
78. Num. 7:66–9:14; Luke 2:41–52; Ps. 35:11–18
79. Num. 9:15–11:3; Luke 3:1–22; Ps. 35:19–28
80. Num. 11:4–13:25; Luke 3:23–4:13; Prov. 7:21–27
81. Num. 13:26–14:45; Luke 4:14–37; Ps. 36:1–12
82. Num. 15:1–16:35; Luke 4:38–5:16; Ps. 37:1–9
83. Num. 16:36–18:32; Luke 5:17–32; Ps. 37:10–20
84. Num. 19:1–21:3; Luke 5:33–6:11; Prov. 8:1–11
85. Num. 21:4–22:20; Luke 6:12–36; Ps. 37:21–31
86. Num. 22:21–23:26; Luke 6:37–7:10; Ps. 37:32–40
87. Num. 23:27–25:18; Luke 7:11–35; Ps. 38:1–11
88. Num. 26:1–27:11; Luke 7:36–50; Prov. 8:12–21
89. Num. 27:12–29:11; Luke 8:1–18; Ps. 38:12–22
90. Num. 29:12–31:24; Luke 8:19–39; Ps. 39:1–13
91. Num. 31:25–32:42; Luke 8:40–9:9; Ps. 40:1–8
92. Num. 33–34; Luke 9:10–27; Prov. 8:22–31
93. Num. 35:1–36:12; Luke 9:28–56; Ps. 40:9–17
94. Deut. 1:1–2:23; Luke 9:57–10:24; Ps. 41:1–6
95. Deut. 2:24–4:14; Luke 10:25–11:4; Ps. 41:7–13
96. Deut. 4:15–5:33; Luke 11:5–32; Prov. 8:32–36

178. 1 Kings 18:16–19:21; Acts 17:22–18:8; Ps. 78:17–31
179. 1 Kings 20–21; Acts 18:9–19:13; Ps. 78:32–39
180. 1 Kings 22:1–53; Acts 19:14–41; Prov. 15:31–16:7
181. 2 Kings 1–2; Acts 20:1–38; Ps. 78:40–55
182. 2 Kings 3:1–4:37; Acts 21:1–26; Ps. 78:56–72
183. 2 Kings 4:38–6:23; Acts 21:27–22:22; Ps. 79:1–13
184. 2 Kings 6:24–8:15; Acts 22:22–23:11; Prov. 16:8–17
185. 2 Kings 8:16–9:37; Acts 23:12–35; Ps. 80:1–7
186. 2 Kings 10–11; Acts 24; Ps. 80:8–19
187. 2 Kings 12:1–14:22; Acts 25:1–22; Ps. 81:1–7
188. 2 Kings 14:23–15:38; Acts 25:23–26:23; Prov. 16:18–27
189. 2 Kings 16–17; Acts 26:24–27:12; Ps. 81:8–16
190. 2 Kings 18:1–19:13; Acts 27:13–44; Ps. 82:1–8
191. 2 Kings 19:14–20:21; Acts 28:1–16; Ps. 83:1–18
192. 2 Kings 21–22; Acts 28:17–31; Prov. 16:28–17:4
193. 2 Kings 23:1–24:7; Rom. 1:1–17; Ps. 84:1–7
194. 2 Kings 24:8–25:30; Rom. 1:18–32; Ps. 84:8–12
195. Jonah 1–4; Rom. 2:1–16; Ps. 85:1–7
196. Amos 1–2; Rom. 2:17–3:8; Prov. 17:5–14
197. Amos 3–4; Rom. 3:9–31; Ps. 85:8–13
198. Amos 5; Rom. 4:1–15; Ps. 86:1–10
199. Amos 6–7; Rom. 4:16–5:11; Ps. 86:11–17
200. Amos 8–9; Rom. 5:12–21; Prov. 17:15–24
201. Hos. 1–2; Rom. 6:1–14; Ps. 87:1–7
202. Hos. 3–5; Rom. 6:15–7:6; Ps. 88:1–9
203. Hos. 6–7; Rom. 7:7–25; Ps. 88:10–19
204. Hos. 8–9; Rom. 8:1–17; Prov. 17:25–18:6
205. Hos. 10–11; Rom. 8:18–39; Ps. 89:1–8
206. Hos. 11–14; Rom. 9:1–21; Ps. 89:9–13
207. 1 Chron. 1:1–2:17; Rom. 9:22–10:4; Ps. 89:14–18
208. 1 Chron. 2:18–4:8; Rom. 10:5–11:10; Prov. 18:7–16
209. 1 Chron. 4:9–5:26; Rom. 11:11–32; Ps. 89:19–29
210. 1 Chron. 6; Rom. 11:33–12:21; Ps. 89:30–37
211. 1 Chron. 7–8; Rom. 13:1–14; Ps. 89:38–45
212. 1 Chron. 9:1–10:14; Rom. 14:1–18; Prov. 18:17–19:2
213. 1 Chron. 11:1–12:22; Rom. 14:19–15:13; Ps. 89:46–52
214. 1 Chron. 12:23–14:17; Rom. 15:14–33; Ps. 90:1–10
215. 1 Chron. 15:1–16:36; Rom. 16; Ps. 90:11–17
216. 1 Chron. 16:37–18:17; 1 Cor. 1:1–17; Prov. 19:3–12
217. 1 Chron. 19–21; 1 Cor. 1:18–2:5; Ps. 91:1–8
218. 1 Chron. 22–23; 1 Cor. 2:6–16; Ps. 91:9–16
219. 1 Chron. 24:1–26:19; 1 Cor. 3; Ps. 92:1–15

220. 1 Chron. 26:20–27:34; 1 Cor. 4; Prov. 19:13–22
221. 1 Chron. 28–29; 1 Cor. 5; Ps. 93:1–5
222. 2 Chron. 1:1–17; 1 Cor. 6; Ps. 94:1–11
223. Eccles. 1–3; 1 Cor. 7:1–16; Ps. 94:12–23
224. Eccles. 4–6; 1 Cor. 7:17–35; Prov. 19:23–20:4
225. Eccles. 7:1–9:12; 1 Cor. 7:36–8:13; Ps. 95:1–11
226. Eccles. 9:13–12:13; 1 Cor. 9:1–18; Ps. 96:1–13
227. 2 Chron. 2:1–5:1; 1 Cor. 9:19–10:13; Ps. 97:1–12
228. 2 Chron. 5:2–7:10; 1 Cor. 10:14–11:1; Prov. 20:5–14
229. 2 Chron. 7:11–9:31; 1 Cor. 11:2–34; Ps. 98:1–9
230. Song of Songs 1–4; 1 Cor. 12:1–26; Ps. 99:1–9
231. Song of Songs 5–8; 1 Cor. 12:27–13:13; Ps. 100:1–5
232. 2 Chron. 10–12; 1 Cor. 14:1–19; Prov. 20:15–24
233. 2 Chron. 13–15; 1 Cor. 14:20–40; Ps. 101:1–8
234. 2 Chron. 16:1–18:27; 1 Cor. 15:1–34; Ps. 102:1–11
235. 2 Chron. 18:28–20:37; 1 Cor. 15:35–49; Ps. 102:12–17
236. 2 Chron. 21–23; 1 Cor. 15:50–16:4; Prov. 20:25–21:4
237. 2 Chron. 24–25; 1 Cor. 16:5–24; Ps. 102:18–28
238. 2 Chron. 26–28; 2 Cor. 1:1–11; Ps. 103:1–12
239. 2 Chron. 29:1–31:1; 2 Cor. 1:12–22; Ps. 103:13–22
240. 2 Chron. 31:2–33:20; 2 Cor. 1:23–2:11; Prov. 21:5–16
241. 2 Chron. 33:21–35:19; 2 Cor. 2:12–3:6; Ps. 104:1–18
242. 2 Chron. 35:20–36:23; 2 Cor. 3:7–18; Ps. 104:19–30
243. Micah 1–4; 2 Cor. 4; Ps. 104:31–35
244. Micah 5–7; 2 Cor. 5:1–10; Prov. 21:17–26
245. Isa. 1–2; 2 Cor. 5:11–6:2; Ps. 105:1–11
246. Isa. 3:1–5:7; 2 Cor. 6:3–7:1; Ps. 105:12–22
247. Isa. 5:8–8:10; 2 Cor. 7:2–16; Ps. 105:23–36
248. Isa. 8:11–10:19; 2 Cor. 8:1–15; Prov. 21:27–22:6
249. Isa. 10:20–13:22; 2 Cor. 8:16–9:5; Ps. 105:37–45
250. Isa. 14–16; 2 Cor. 9:6–15; Ps. 106:1–15
251. Isa. 17–19; 2 Cor. 10; Ps. 106:16–31
252. Isa. 20–23; 2 Cor. 11:1–15; Prov. 22:7–16
253. Isa. 24–26; 2 Cor. 11:16–33; Ps. 106:32–39
254. Isa. 27–28; 2 Cor. 12:1–10; Ps. 106:40–48
255. Isa. 29:1–30:18; 2 Cor. 12:11–21; Ps. 107:1–9
256. Isa. 30:19–32:20; 2 Cor. 13; Prov. 22:17–27
257. Isa. 33–35; Gal. 1; Ps. 107:10–22
258. Isa. 36–37; Gal. 2:1–10; Ps. 107:23–32
259. Isa. 38–40; Gal. 2:11–3:9; Ps. 107:33–43

260. Isa. 41–42; Gal. 3:10–25; Prov. 22:28–23:9
261. Isa. 43:1–44:23; Gal. 3:26–4:20; Ps. 108:1–5
262. Isa. 44:24–46:13; Gal. 4:21–5:6; Ps. 108:6–13
263. Isa. 47–49:7; Gal. 5:7–26; Ps. 109:1–20
264. Isa. 49:8–51:16; Gal. 6; Prov. 23:10–18
265. Isa. 51:17–54:17; Eph. 1; Ps. 109:21–31
266. Isa. 55–57:13; Eph. 2; Ps. 110:1–7
267. Isa. 57:14–59:21; Eph. 3; Ps. 111:1–10
268. Isa. 60–62; Eph. 4:1–16; Prov. 23:19–28
269. Isa. 63:1–65:16; Eph. 4:17–5:7; Ps. 112:1–10
270. Isa. 65:17–66:24; Eph. 5:8–33; Ps. 113:1–9
271. Nah. 1–3; Eph. 6; Ps. 114:1–8
272. Zeph. 1–3; Phil. 1:1–26; Prov. 23:29–24:4
273. Jer. 1:1–2:30; Phil. 1:27–2:11; Ps. 115:1–11
274. Jer. 2:31–4:9; Phil. 2:12–30; Ps. 115:12–18
275. Jer. 4:10–5:31; Phil. 3; Ps. 116:1–11
276. Jer. 6:1–7:29; Phil. 4; Prov. 24:5–14
277. Jer. 7:30–9:16; Col. 1:1–23; Ps. 116:12–19
278. Jer. 9:17–11:17; Col. 1:24–2:5; Ps. 117:1–2
279. Jer. 11:18–13:27; Col. 2:6–23; Ps. 118:1–16
280. Jer. 14–15; Col. 3:1–4:1; Prov. 24:15–22
281. Jer. 16–17; Col. 4:2–18; Ps. 118:17–29
282. Jer. 18–20; 1 Thess. 1:1–2:16; Ps. 119:1–8
283. Jer. 21:1–23:8; 1 Thess. 2:17–3:13; Ps. 119:9–16
284. Jer. 23:9–25:14; 1 Thess. 4; Prov. 24:23–34
285. Jer. 25:15–26:24; 1 Thess. 5; Ps. 119:17–24
286. Jer. 27:1–29:23; 2 Thess. 1; Ps. 119:25–32
287. Jer. 29:24–31:14; 2 Thess. 2; Ps. 119:33–40
288. Jer. 31:15–32:25; 2 Thess. 3; Prov. 25:1–10
289. Jer. 32:26–34:22; 1 Tim. 1; Ps. 119:41–48
290. Jer. 35–37; 1 Tim. 2; Ps. 119:49–56
291. Jer. 38–40:6; 1 Tim. 3; Ps. 119:57–64
292. Jer. 40:7–42:22; 1 Tim. 4; Prov. 25:11–20
293. Jer. 43–45; 1 Tim. 5:1–6:2; Ps. 119:65–72
294. Jer. 46–47; 1 Tim. 6:3–21; Ps. 119:73–80
295. Jer. 48:1–49:6; 2 Tim. 1; Ps. 119:81–88
296. Jer. 49:7–50:10; 2 Tim. 2; Prov. 25:21–26:2
297. Jer. 50:11–51:14; 2 Tim. 3; Ps. 119:89–96
298. Jer. 51:15–64; 2 Tim. 4; Ps. 119:97–104
299. Jer. 52; Titus 1; Ps. 119:105–112
300. Hab. 1:1–3:19; Titus 2; Prov. 26:3–12
301. Lam. 1:1–2:6; Titus 3; Ps. 119:113–120
302. Lam. 2:7–3:39; Philem. 1; Ps. 119:121–128
303. Lam. 3:40–5:22; Heb. 1; Ps. 119:129–136
304. Obad. 1; Heb. 2; Prov. 26:13–22
305. Joel 1:1–2:17; Heb. 3; Ps. 119:137–144
306. Joel 2:18–3:21; Heb. 4:1–13; Ps. 119:145–152
307. Ezek. 1–3; Heb. 4:14–5:10; Ps. 119:153–160
308. Ezek. 4–6; Heb. 5:11–6:12; Prov. 26:23–27:4
309. Ezek. 7–9; Heb. 6:13–7:10; Ps. 119:161–168
310. Ezek. 10–12; Heb. 7:11–28; Ps. 119:169–176
311. Ezek. 13–15; Heb. 8; Ps. 120:1–7
312. Ezek. 16; Heb. 9:1–15; Prov. 27:5–14
313. Ezek. 17–18; Heb. 9:16–28; Ps. 121:1–8
314. Ezek. 19:1–20:44; Heb. 10:1–18; Ps. 122:1–9

315. Ezek. 20:45–22:22; Heb. 10:19–39; Ps. 123:1–4
316. Ezek. 22:23–23:49; Heb. 11:1–16; Prov. 27:15–22
317. Ezek. 24–25; Heb. 11:17–40; Ps. 124:1–8
318. Ezek. 26–27; Heb. 12:1–13; Ps. 125:1–5
319. Ezek. 28–29; Heb. 12:14–29; Ps. 126:1–6
320. Ezek. 30–31; Heb. 13; Prov. 27:23–28:6
321. Ezek. 32:1–33:20; James 1; Ps. 127:1–5
322. Ezek. 33:21–35:15; James 2; Ps. 128:1–6
323. Ezek. 36–37; James 3; Ps. 129:1–8
324. Ezek. 38–39; James 4; Prov. 28:7–17
325. Ezek. 40; James 5; Ps. 130:1–8
326. Ezek. 41–42; 1 Peter 1:1–2:3; Ps. 131:1–3
327. Ezek. 43–44; 1 Peter 2:4–45; Ps. 132:1–18
328. Ezek. 45–46; 1 Peter 3; Prov. 28:18–28
329. Ezek. 47–48; 1 Peter 4; Ps. 133:1–3
330. Dan. 1:1–2:23; 1 Peter 5; Ps. 134:1–3
331. Dan. 2:24–3:12; 2 Peter 1; Ps. 135:1–12
332. Dan. 3:13–4:18; 2 Peter 2; Prov. 29:1–9
333. Dan. 4:19–5:16; 2 Peter 3; Ps. 135:13–21
334. Dan. 5:17–6:28; 1 John 1–2; Ps. 136:1–12
335. Dan. 7:1–8:14; 1 John 2:12–27; Ps. 136:13–26
336. Dan. 8:15–9:19; 1 John 2:28–3:10; Prov. 29:10–18
337. Dan. 9:20–11:1; 1 John 3:11–4:6; Ps. 137:1–9
338. Dan. 11:2–35; 1 John 4:7–21; Ps. 138:1–8
339. Dan. 11:36–12:13; 1 John 5:1–21; Ps. 139:1–10
340. Hag. 1–2; 2 John 1:1–13; Prov. 29:19–27
341. Zech. 1–4; 3 John 1:1–14; Ps. 139:11–16
342. Zech. 5–8; Jude 1:1–25; Ps. 139:17–24
343. Zech. 9–11; Rev. 1; Ps. 140:1–5
344. Zech. 12–14; Rev. 2:1–17; Prov. 30:1–10
345. Esther 1:1–2:18; Rev. 2:18–3:6; Ps. 140:6–13
346. Esther 2:19–5:14; Rev. 3:7–22; Ps. 141:1–10
347. Esther 6–8; Rev. 4; Ps. 142:1–11
348. Esther 9–10; Rev. 5; Prov. 30:11–23
349. Mal. 1:1–2:16; Rev. 6; Ps. 143:1–12
350. Mal. 2:17–4:6; Rev. 7; Ps. 144:1–8
351. Ezra 1:1–2:67; Rev. 8:1–9:12; Ps. 144:9–15
352. Ezra 2:68–4:5; Rev. 9:13–10:11; Prov. 30:24–33
353. Ezra 4:6–5:17; Rev. 11; Ps. 145:1–7
354. Ezra 6:1–7:10; Rev. 12; Ps. 145:8–13
355. Ezra 7:11–8:14; Rev. 13; Ps. 145:13–21
356. Ezra 8:15–9:15; Rev. 14:1–13; Prov. 31:1–9
357. Ezra 10; Rev. 14:14–15:8; Ps. 146:1–10
358. Neh. 1–2; Rev. 16; Ps. 147:1–11
359. Neh. 3–4; Rev. 17; Ps. 147:12–20
360. Neh. 5:1–7:3; Rev. 18:1–17; Prov. 31:10–20
361. Neh. 7:4–8:18; Rev. 18:17–19:10; Ps. 148:1–6
362. Neh. 9:1–37; Rev. 19:11–21; Ps. 148:7–14
363. Neh. 9:38–11:21; Rev. 20; Ps. 149:1–9
364. Neh. 11:22–12:47; Rev. 21; Prov. 31:21–31
365. Neh. 13; Rev. 22; Ps. 150:1–56

English Standard Version

The Bible

"This Book [is] the most valuable thing that this world affords. Here is Wisdom; this is the royal Law; these are the lively Oracles of God." With these words the Moderator of the Church of Scotland hands a Bible to the new monarch in Britain's coronation service. These words echo the King James Bible translators, who wrote in 1611: "God's sacred Word . . . is that inestimable treasure that excelleth all the riches of the earth." This assessment of the Bible is the motivating force behind the publication of the English Standard Version.

Translation Legacy

The English Standard Version (ESV) stands in the classic mainstream of English Bible translations over the past half-millennium. The fountainhead of that stream was William Tyndale's New Testament of 1526; marking its course were the King James Version of 1611 (KJV), the English Revised Version of 1885 (RV), the American Standard Version of 1901 (ASV), and the Revised Standard Version of 1952 and 1971 (RSV). In that stream, faithfulness to the text and vigorous pursuit of accuracy were combined with simplicity, beauty, and dignity of expression. Our goal has been to carry forward this legacy for a new century.

To this end each word and phrase in the ESV has been carefully weighed against the original Hebrew, Aramaic, and Greek, to ensure the fullest accuracy and clarity and to avoid under-translating or overlooking any nuance of the original text. The words and phrases themselves grow out of the Tyndale–King James legacy, and most recently out of the RSV, with the 1971 RSV text providing the starting point for our work. Archaic language has been brought to current usage and significant corrections have been made in the translation of key texts. But throughout, our goal has been to retain the depth of meaning and enduring language that have made their indelible mark on the English-speaking world and have defined the life and doctrine of the church over the last four centuries.

Translation Philosophy

The ESV is an "essentially literal" translation that seeks as far as possible to capture the precise wording of the original text and the personal style of each Bible writer. As such, its emphasis is on "word-for-word" correspondence, at the same time taking into account differences of grammar, syntax, and idiom between current literary English and the original languages. Thus it seeks to be transparent to the original text, letting the reader see as directly as possible the structure and meaning of the original.

In contrast to the ESV, some Bible versions have followed a "thought-for-thought" rather than "word-for-word" translation philosophy, emphasizing "dynamic equivalence" rather than the "essentially literal" meaning of the original. A "thought-for-thought" translation is of necessity more inclined to reflect the interpretive opinions of the translator and the influences of contemporary culture.

Every translation is at many points a trade-off between literal precision and readability, between "formal equivalence" in expression and "functional equivalence" in communication, and the ESV is no exception. Within this framework we have sought to be "as literal as possible" while maintaining clarity of expression and literary excellence. Therefore, to the extent that plain English permits and the meaning in each case allows, we have sought to use the same English word for important recurring words in the original; and, as far as grammar and syntax allow, we have rendered Old Testament passages cited in the New in ways that show their correspondence. Thus in each of these areas, as well as throughout the Bible as a whole, we have sought to capture the echoes and overtones of meaning that are so abundantly present in the original texts.

As an essentially literal translation, then, the ESV seeks to carry over every possible nuance of meaning in the original words of Scripture into our own language. As such, the ESV is ideally suited for in-depth study of the Bible. Indeed, with its emphasis on literary excellence, the ESV is equally suited for public reading and preaching, for private reading and reflection, for both academic and devotional study, and for Scripture memorization.

Translation Principles and Style

The ESV also carries forward classic translation principles in its literary style. Accordingly it retains theological terminology—words such as grace, faith, justification, sanctification, redemption, regeneration, reconciliation, propitiation—because of their central importance for Christian doctrine and also because the underlying Greek words were already becoming key words and technical terms in New Testament times.

The ESV lets the stylistic variety of the biblical writers fully express itself—from the exalted prose that opens Genesis, to the flowing narratives of the historical books, to the rich metaphors and dramatic imagery of the poetic books, to the ringing rhetorical indictments in the prophetic books, to the smooth elegance of Luke, to the profound simplicities of John, and the closely reasoned logic of Paul.

In punctuating, paragraphing, dividing long sentences, and rendering connectives, the ESV follows the path that seems to make the ongoing flow of thought clearest in English. The biblical languages regularly connect sentences by frequent repetition of words such as "and," "but," and "for," in a way that goes beyond the conventions of literary English. Effective translation, however, requires that these links in the original be reproduced so that the flow of the argument will be transparent to the reader. We have therefore normally translated these connectives, though occasionally we have varied the rendering by using alternatives (such as "also," "however," "now," "so," "then," or "thus") when they better capture the sense in specific instances.

In the area of gender language, the goal of the ESV is to render literally what is in the original. For example, "anyone" replaces "any man" where there is no word corresponding to "man" in the original languages, and "people" rather than "men" is regularly used where the original languages refer to both men and women. But the words "man" and "men" are retained where a male meaning component is part of the original Greek or Hebrew. Likewise, the word "man" has been retained where the original text intends to convey a clear contrast between "God" on the one hand and "man" on the other hand, with "man" being used in the collective sense of the whole human race (see Luke 2:52). Similarly, the English word "brothers" (translating the Greek word *adelphoi*) is retained as an important familial form of address between fellow-Jews and fellow-Christians in the first century. A recurring note is included to indicate that the term "brothers" (*adelphoi*) was often used in Greek to refer to both men and women, and to indicate the specific instances in the text where this is the case. In addition, the English word "sons" (translating the Greek word *huioi*) is retained in specific instances because the underlying

Greek term usually includes a male meaning component and it was used as a legal term in the adoption and inheritance laws of first-century Rome. As used by the apostle Paul, this term refers to the status of all Christians, both men and women, who, having been adopted into God's family, now enjoy all the privileges, obligations, and inheritance rights of God's children.

The inclusive use of the generic "he" has also regularly been retained, because this is consistent with similar usage in the original languages and because an essentially literal translation would be impossible without it.

In each case the objective has been transparency to the original text, allowing the reader to understand the original on its own terms rather than on the terms of our present-day culture.

The Translation of Specialized Terms

In the translation of biblical terms referring to God, the ESV takes great care to convey the specific nuances of meaning of the original Hebrew and Greek terms. First, concerning terms that refer to God in the Old Testament: God, the Maker of heaven and earth, introduced himself to the people of Israel with a special personal name, the consonants for which are YHWH (see Exodus 3:14–15). Scholars call this the "Tetragrammaton," a Greek term referring to the four Hebrew letters YHWH. The exact pronunciation of YHWH is uncertain, because the Jewish people considered the personal name of God to be so holy that it should never be spoken aloud. Instead of reading the word YHWH, they would normally read the Hebrew word 'adonay ("Lord"), and the ancient translations into Greek, Syriac, and Aramaic also followed this practice. When the vowels of the word 'adonay are placed with the consonants of YHWH, this results in the familiar word Jehovah that was used in some earlier English Bible translations. As is common among English translations today, the ESV usually renders the personal name of God (YHWH) with the word LORD (printed in small capitals). An exception to this is when the Hebrew word 'adonay appears together with YHWH, in which case the two words are rendered together as "the Lord [in lower case] GOD [in small capitals]." In contrast to the personal name for God (YHWH), the more general name for God in Old Testament Hebrew is 'elohim and its related forms of 'el or 'eloah, all of which are normally translated "God" (in lower case letters). The use of these different ways to translate the Hebrew words for God is especially beneficial to the English reader, enabling the reader to see and understand the different ways that the personal name and the general name for God are both used to refer to the One True God of the Old Testament.

Second, in the New Testament, the Greek word Christos has been translated consistently as "Christ." Although the term originally meant "anointed," among Jews in New Testament times the term came to designate the Messiah, the great Savior that God had promised to raise up. In other New Testament contexts, however, especially among Gentiles, Christos ("Christ") was on its way to becoming a proper name. It is important, therefore, to keep the context in mind in understanding the various ways that Christos ("Christ") is used in the New Testament. At the same time, in accord with its "essentially literal" translation philosophy, the ESV has retained consistency and concordance in the translation of Christos ("Christ") throughout the New Testament.

Third, a particular difficulty is presented when words in biblical Hebrew and Greek refer to ancient practices and institutions that do not correspond directly to those in the modern world. Such is the case in the translation of 'ebed (Hebrew) and doulos (Greek), terms which are often rendered "slave." These terms, however, actually cover a range of relationships that require a range of renderings—either "slave," "bondservant," or "servant"—depending on the context. Further, the word "slave" currently carries associations with the often brutal and dehumanizing institution of slavery in nineteenth-century America. For this reason, the ESV translation of the words *'ebed* and *doulos* has been undertaken with particular attention to their meaning in each specific context. Thus in Old Testament times, one might enter slavery either voluntarily (e.g., to escape poverty or to pay off a debt) or involuntarily (e.g., by birth, by being captured in battle, or by judicial sentence). Protection for all in servitude in ancient Israel was provided by the Mosaic Law. In New Testament times, a *doulos* is often best described as a "bondservant"—that is, as someone bound to serve his master for a specific (usually lengthy) period of time, but also as someone who might nevertheless own property, achieve social advancement, and even be released or purchase his freedom. The ESV usage thus seeks to express the nuance of meaning in each context. Where absolute ownership by a master is in view (as in Romans 6), "slave" is used; where a more limited form of servitude is in view, "bondservant" is used (as in 1 Corinthians 7:21–24); where the context indicates a wide range of freedom (as in John 4:51), "servant" is preferred. Footnotes are generally provided to identify the Hebrew or Greek and the range of meaning that these terms may carry in each case.

Fourth, it is sometimes suggested that Bible translations should capitalize pronouns referring to deity. It has seemed best not to capitalize deity pronouns in the ESV, however, for the following reasons: first, there is nothing in the original Hebrew and Greek manuscripts that corresponds to such capitalization; second, the practice of capitalizing deity pronouns in English Bible translations is a recent innovation, which began only in the mid-twentieth century; and, third, such capitalization is absent from the KJV Bible and the whole stream of Bible translations that the ESV seeks to carry forward.

A fifth specialized term, the word "behold," usually has been retained as the most common translation for the Hebrew word *hinneh* and the Greek word *idou*. Both of these words mean something like "Pay careful attention to what follows! This is important!" Other than the word "behold," there is no single word in English that fits well in most contexts. Although "Look!" and "See!" and "Listen!" would be workable in some contexts, in many others these words lack sufficient weight and dignity. Given the principles of "essentially literal" translation, it is important not to leave *hinneh* and *idou* completely untranslated, and so to lose the intended emphasis in the original languages. The older and more formal word "behold" has usually been retained, therefore, as the best available option for conveying the original sense of meaning.

Textual Basis and Resources

The ESV is based on the Masoretic text of the Hebrew Bible as found in *Biblia Hebraica Stuttgartensia* (2nd ed., 1983), and on the Greek text in the 1993 editions of the *Greek New Testament* (4th corrected ed.), published by the United Bible Societies (UBS), and *Novum Testamentum Graece* (27th ed.), edited by Nestle and Aland. The currently renewed respect among Old Testament scholars for the Masoretic text is reflected in the ESV's attempt, wherever possible, to translate difficult Hebrew passages as they stand in the Masoretic text rather than resorting to emendations or to finding an alternative reading in the ancient versions. In exceptional, difficult cases, the Dead Sea Scrolls, the Septuagint, the Samaritan Pentateuch, the Syriac Peshitta, the Latin Vulgate, and other sources were consulted to shed possible light on the text, or, if necessary, to support a divergence from the Masoretic text. Similarly, in a few difficult cases in the New Testament, the ESV has followed a Greek text different from the text given preference in the UBS/Nestle-Aland 27th edition. Throughout, the translation team has benefited greatly from the massive textual resources that have become readily available recently, from new insights into biblical laws and culture, and from current advances in Hebrew and Greek lexicography and grammatical understanding.

Textual Footnotes

The footnotes that accompany the ESV text are an integral part of the ESV translation, informing the reader of textual variations and difficulties and showing how these have been resolved by the ESV translation team. In addition to this, the footnotes indicate significant alternative readings and occasionally provide an explanation for technical terms or for a difficult reading in the text.

Publishing Team

The ESV publishing team includes more than a hundred people. The fourteen-member Translation Oversight Committee has benefited from the work of more than fifty biblical experts serving as Translation Review Scholars and from the comments of the more than fifty members of the Advisory Council, all of which has been carried out under the auspices of the Crossway Board of Directors. This hundred-plus-member team shares a common commitment to the truth of God's Word and to historic Christian orthodoxy and is international in scope, including leaders in many denominations.

To God's Honor and Praise

We know that no Bible translation is perfect or final; but we also know that God uses imperfect and inadequate things to his honor and praise. So to our triune God and to his people we offer what we have done, with our prayers that it may prove useful, with gratitude for much help given, and with ongoing wonder that our God should ever have entrusted to us so momentous a task.

> *Soli Deo Gloria!*—To God alone be the glory!
> *The Translation Oversight Committee**

*A complete list of the Translation Oversight Committee, the Translation Review Scholars, and the Advisory Council, is available upon request from Crossway.

Contributors

Devotionals and Supplemental Content
Hayley DiMarco
Hungry Planet

www.GodGirl.com
www.HungryPlanet.net

Cover Design
Erik Maldre

Interior Design
Abigail Heidorn